DICTIONARY OF AMERICAN BIOGRAPHY

AMERICAN
COUNCIL
* OF *
LEARNED
SOCIETIES
*

DICTIONARY
OF AMERICAN BIOGRAPHY

PUBLISHED UNDER THE AUSPICES OF
THE AMERICAN COUNCIL OF LEARNED SOCIETIES

The American Council of Learned Societies, organized in 1919 for the purpose of advancing the study of the humanities and of the humanistic aspects of the social sciences, is a nonprofit federation comprising forty-six national scholarly groups. The Council represents the humanities in the United States in the International Union of Academies, provides fellowships and grants-in-aid, supports research-and-planning conferences and symposia, and sponsors special projects and scholarly publications.

MEMBER ORGANIZATIONS
AMERICAN PHILOSOPHICAL SOCIETY, 1743
AMERICAN ACADEMY OF ARTS AND SCIENCES, 1780
AMERICAN ANTIQUARIAN SOCIETY, 1812
AMERICAN ORIENTAL SOCIETY, 1842
AMERICAN NUMISMATIC SOCIETY, 1858
AMERICAN PHILOLOGICAL ASSOCIATION, 1869
ARCHAEOLOGICAL INSTITUTE OF AMERICA, 1879
SOCIETY OF BIBLICAL LITERATURE, 1880
MODERN LANGUAGE ASSOCIATION OF AMERICA, 1883
AMERICAN HISTORICAL ASSOCIATION, 1884
AMERICAN ECONOMIC ASSOCIATION, 1885
AMERICAN FOLKLORE SOCIETY, 1888
AMERICAN DIALECT SOCIETY, 1889
AMERICAN PSYCHOLOGICAL ASSOCIATION, 1892
ASSOCIATION OF AMERICAN LAW SCHOOLS, 1900
AMERICAN PHILOSOPHICAL ASSOCIATION, 1901
AMERICAN ANTHROPOLOGICAL ASSOCIATION, 1902
AMERICAN POLITICAL SCIENCE ASSOCIATION, 1903
BIBLIOGRAPHICAL SOCIETY OF AMERICA, 1904
ASSOCIATION OF AMERICAN GEOGRAPHERS, 1904
HISPANIC SOCIETY OF AMERICA, 1904
AMERICAN SOCIOLOGICAL ASSOCIATION, 1905
AMERICAN SOCIETY OF INTERNATIONAL LAW, 1906
ORGANIZATION OF AMERICAN HISTORIANS, 1907
AMERICAN ACADEMY OF RELIGION, 1909
COLLEGE ART ASSOCIATION OF AMERICA, 1912
HISTORY OF SCIENCE SOCIETY, 1924
LINGUISTIC SOCIETY OF AMERICA, 1924
MEDIEVAL ACADEMY OF AMERICA, 1925
AMERICAN MUSICOLOGICAL SOCIETY, 1934
SOCIETY OF ARCHITECTURAL HISTORIANS, 1940
ECONOMIC HISTORY ASSOCIATION, 1940
ASSOCIATION FOR ASIAN STUDIES, 1941
AMERICAN SOCIETY FOR AESTHETICS, 1942
AMERICAN ASSOCIATION FOR THE ADVANCEMENT OF SLAVIC STUDIES, 1948
METAPHYSICAL SOCIETY OF AMERICA, 1950
AMERICAN STUDIES ASSOCIATION, 1950
RENAISSANCE SOCIETY OF AMERICA, 1954
SOCIETY FOR ETHNOMUSICOLOGY, 1955
AMERICAN SOCIETY FOR LEGAL HISTORY, 1956
AMERICAN SOCIETY FOR THEATRE RESEARCH, 1956
SOCIETY FOR THE HISTORY OF TECHNOLOGY, 1958
AMERICAN COMPARATIVE LITERATURE ASSOCIATION, 1960
MIDDLE EAST STUDIES ASSOCIATION, 1966
AMERICAN SOCIETY FOR EIGHTEENTH-CENTURY STUDIES, 1969
ASSOCIATION FOR JEWISH STUDIES, 1969

DICTIONARY
OF
American Biography

Comprehensive Index

COMPLETE THROUGH SUPPLEMENT EIGHT

Charles Scribner's Sons *New York*

The preparation of the original twenty volumes of the Dictionary was made possible by the public-spirited action of the New York Times Company and its president, the late Adolph S. Ochs, in furnishing a large subvention. The preparation and publication of the index have been supported by the sale of those volumes and the eight Supplements. Entire responsibility for the contents of the Dictionary and its Supplements rests with the American Council of Learned Societies.

Library of Congress Cataloging-in-Publication Data

Dictionary of American biography.
Comprehensive index: complete through supplement eight.
    1. Dictionary of American Biography—Indexes.
    2. United States—Biography.
E176.D563   Index 3   920'.073—dc20   89-28910
ISBN 0-684-19114-8 (Index)

Printed in the United States of America

INTRODUCTION

The *Dictionary of American Biography* was published originally in twenty volumes between 1928 and 1936. Eight supplementary volumes were added between 1944 and 1988. In 1946, the twenty base volumes were reissued in ten double volumes. In the current format, Volume 1 (Abbe-Brazer) contains Volumes I and II of the original edition, but these are now denominated "Part 1" and "Part 2" of the Volume. Volumes 2 through 10 are arranged similarly, the Second Part in each instance representing a volume of the original series, with the original pagination maintained.

This index references the ten-volume edition and Supplements 1–8. Owners of the base set in twenty volumes may consult the following table for easy transposition from volume references in this index.

CURRENT, 10-VOLUME EDITION OF A–Z BASE SET	ORIGINAL, 20-VOLUME EDITION OF A–Z BASE SET
Volume 1, Part 1	Volume I
Volume 1, Part 2	Volume II
Volume 2, Part 1	Volume III
Volume 2, Part 2	Volume IV
Volume 3, Part 1	Volume V
Volume 3, Part 2	Volume VI
Volume 4, Part 1	Volume VII
Volume 4, Part 2	Volume VIII
Volume 5, Part 1	Volume IX
Volume 5, Part 2	Volume X
Volume 6, Part 1	Volume XI
Volume 6, Part 2	Volume XII
Volume 7, Part 1	Volume XIII
Volume 7, Part 2	Volume XIV
Volume 8, Part 1	Volume XV
Volume 8, Part 2	Volume XVI
Volume 9, Part 1	Volume XVII
Volume 9, Part 2	Volume XVIII
Volume 10, Part 1	Volume XIX
Volume 10, Part 2	Volume XX

For example: You wish to locate Benjamin Franklin. Turning to *Franklin, Benjamin* in the "Subjects of Biographies" division of the Index, you find

Franklin, Benjamin, Jan. 17, 1706–Apr. 17, 1790
(Vol. 3, Part 2–585)

By reference to the table above, Volume 3, Part 2 is seen to be Volume VI of the twenty-volume edition. There, on page 585, you will find your reference.

MAIN DIVISIONS OF THE INDEX VOLUME

1. *Subjects:* Alphabetical list of the persons about whom articles have been written, with the dates of birth and death and the volume, part, and page of the article.

2. *Contributors:* The names of all contributors arranged alphabetically, followed by the names of the persons whose biographies they wrote.

3. *Birthplaces:* The name of each state or foreign country in which the subject of an article was born, followed by lists of those persons born within that state or country.

4. *Schools and Colleges:* The educational institutions attended by the subjects of the biographies, followed in each case by an alphabetical list of those persons in the *Dictionary* who attended the institution.

5. *Occupations:* The persons in the *Dictionary* grouped according to occupation, using in most instances the occupation or occupations given at the beginning of the article.

6. *Topics:* An index of all the topics of importance discussed substantively in the *Dictionary*. Certain specific topics have been collected in groups, for example, homesteads and plantations, ships, nicknames, etc.

HOW TO USE THE INDEX

1. To find the name of the subject of an article included in the *Dictionary*, the reader should turn to the first main division (pp. 1–224) to find out if the name is in the *Dictionary*.

2. To find the name of the contributor of a particular article in the A-Z base volumes, the reader should first find the initials at the end of the article and then refer to the list of contributors at the beginning of the particular volume. In the supplements, the full name of each contributor is given at the end of each article.

3. To find the names of other articles by the same contributor, the reader should consult the second main division of the Index (pp. 225–331).

4. To find the name of a state or foreign country in which one of the subjects was born, the reader should consult the particular article.

5. To find what subjects were born in any state or country, the reader should refer to the third main division of the Index (pp. 333–419).

6. To find the school or college attended by the subjects of the biographies, the reader should refer to the specific articles.

7. To find all the names of subjects who have attended any school or college, the reader should refer to the fourth main division of the Index (pp. 421–506). In a number of instances the person attended one or more institutions. In all cases the name of the subject is given under the name of the institution from which he received a degree. In many instances the name will also be found under the name of the institution with which he was closely associated for a period of time.

8. To find the occupation or occupations of any subject of a biography, the reader should refer to the beginning of the particular biography.

9. To find all the names of subjects who practiced a particular occupation, the reader should refer to the fifth main division of the Index (pp. 507 665).

THE PUBLISHERS

CONTENTS

SUBJECTS OF BIOGRAPHIES

Aandahl, Fred George, Apr. 9, 1897–Apr. 7, 1966.
Supp. 8–1
Abbe, Cleveland, Dec. 3, 1838–Oct. 28, 1916.
Vol. 1, Pt. 1–1
Abbett, Leon, Oct. 8, 1836–Dec. 4, 1894.
Vol. 1, Pt. 1–2
Abbey, Edwin Austin, Apr. 1, 1852–Aug. 1, 1911.
Vol. 1, Pt. 1–3
Abbey, Henry, July 11, 1842–June 7, 1911.
Vol. 1, Pt. 1–8
Abbey, Henry Eugene, June 27, 1846–Oct. 17, 1896.
Vol. 1, Pt. 1–8
Abbot, Benjamin, Sept. 17, 1762–Oct. 25, 1849.
Vol. 1, Pt. 1–9
Abbot, Ezra, Apr. 28, 1819–Mar. 21, 1884.
Vol. 1, Pt. 1–10
Abbot, Francis Ellingwood, Nov. 6, 1836–Oct. 23, 1903.
Vol. 1, Pt. 1–11
Abbot, Gorham Dummer, Sept. 3, 1807–Aug. 3, 1874.
Vol. 1, Pt. 1–12
Abbot, Henry Larcom, Aug. 13, 1831–Oct. 1, 1927.
Vol. 1, Pt. 1–13
Abbot, Joel, Jan. 18, 1793–Dec. 14, 1855.
Vol. 1, Pt. 1–14
Abbot, Willis John, Mar. 16, 1863–May 19, 1934.
Supp. 1–1
Abbott, Austin, Dec. 18, 1831–Apr. 19, 1896.
Vol. 1, Pt. 1–15
Abbott, Benjamin, 1732–Aug. 14, 1796.
Vol. 1, Pt. 1–16
Abbott, Benjamin Vaughan, June 4, 1830–Feb. 17, 1890.
Vol. 1, Pt. 1–16
Abbott, Charles Conrad, June 4, 1843–July 27, 1919.
Vol. 1, Pt. 1–17
Abbott, Edith, Sept. 26, 1876–July 28, 1957.
Supp. 6–1
Abbott, Edward, July 15, 1841–Apr. 5, 1908.
Vol. 1, Pt. 1–18
Abbott, Eleanor Hallowell, Sept. 22, 1872–June 2, 1958.
Supp. 6–2
Abbott, Emma, Dec. 9, 1850–Jan. 5, 1891.
Vol. 1, Pt. 1–18
Abbott, Frank, Sept. 5, 1836–Apr. 20, 1897.
Vol. 1, Pt. 1–19
Abbott, Frank Frost, Mar. 27, 1860–July 23, 1924.
Vol. 1, Pt. 1–20
Abbott, Grace, Nov. 17, 1878–June 19, 1939.
Supp. 2–1
Abbott, Horace, July 29, 1806–Aug. 8, 1887.
Vol. 1, Pt. 1–21
Abbott, Jacob, Nov. 14, 1803–Oct. 31, 1879.
Vol. 1, Pt. 1–21
Abbott, John Stevens Cabot, Sept. 18, 1805–June 17, 1877.
Vol. 1, Pt. 1–22
Abbott, Joseph Carter, July 15, 1825–Oct. 8, 1881.
Vol. 1, Pt. 1–23
Abbott, Lyman, Dec. 18, 1835–Oct. 22, 1922.
Vol. 1, Pt. 1–24
Abbott, Robert Sengstacke, Nov. 28, 1868–Feb. 29, 1940.
Supp. 2–2
Abbott, Samuel Warren, June 12, 1837–Oct. 22, 1904.
Vol. 1, Pt. 1–25
Abbott, William Hawkins, Oct. 27, 1819–Jan. 8, 1901.
Vol. 1, Pt. 1–26
Abeel, David, June 12, 1804–Sept. 4, 1846.
Vol. 1, Pt. 1–26
Abel, John Jacob, May 19, 1857–May 26, 1938.
Supp. 2–4
Abel-Henderson, Annie Heloise, Feb. 18, 1873–Mar. 14, 1947. Supp. 4–1
Abell, Arunah Shepherdson, Aug. 10, 1806–Apr. 19, 1888.
Vol. 1, Pt. 1–27

Abercromby, James, 1706–Apr. 23, 1781.
Vol. 1, Pt. 1–28
Abernethy, George, Oct. 7, 1807–May 2, 1877.
Vol. 1, Pt. 1–29
Abert, John James, Sept. 17, 1788–Jan. 27, 1863.
Supp. 1–2
Aborn, Milton, May 18, 1864–Nov. 12, 1933.
Supp. 1–3
Abrams, Albert, Dec. 8, 1863–Jan. 13, 1924.
Vol. 1, Pt. 1–30
Abt, Isaac Arthur, Dec. 18, 1867–Nov. 22, 1955.
Supp. 5–1
Accau (Accault) Michel. [See Aco, Michel, fl. 1680–1702.]
Acheson, Edward Goodrich, Mar. 9, 1856–July 6, 1931.
Supp. 1–4
Acker, Charles Ernest, Mar. 19, 1868–Oct. 18, 1920.
Vol. 1, Pt. 1–31
Aco, Michel, fl. 1680–1702.
Vol. 1, Pt. 1–31
Acosta, Bertram Blanchard ("Bert"), Jan. 1, 1895–Sept. 1, 1954. Supp. 5–2
Acrelius, Israel, Dec. 4, 1714–Apr. 25, 1800.
Vol. 1, Pt. 1–32
Adair, James, c. 1709–c. 1783.
Vol. 1, Pt. 1–33
Adair, John, Jan. 9, 1757–May 19, 1840.
Vol. 1, Pt. 1–34
Adamic, Louis, Mar. 23, 1899–Sept. 4, 1951.
Supp. 5–3
Adams, Abigail, Nov. 11, 1744–Oct. 28, 1818.
Vol. 1, Pt. 1–35
Adams, Abijah, c. 1754–May 18, 1816.
Vol. 1, Pt. 1–35
Adams, Alva, May 14, 1850–Nov. 1, 1922.
Vol. 1, Pt. 1–36
Adams, Alvin, June 16, 1804–Sept. 1, 1877.
Vol. 1, Pt. 1–37
Adams, Andrew, Dec. 11, 1736–Nov. 27, 1797.
Vol. 1, Pt. 1–37
Adams, Andy, May 3, 1859–Sept. 26, 1935.
Supp. 1–5
Adams, Annette Abbott, Mar. 12, 1877–Oct. 26, 1956.
Supp. 6–3
Adams, Brooks, June 24, 1848–Feb. 13, 1927.
Vol. 1, Pt. 1–38
Adams, Charles, Dec. 19, 1845?–Aug. 19, 1895.
Vol. 1, Pt. 1–39
Adams, Charles Baker, Jan. 11, 1814–Jan. 18, 1853.
Vol. 1, Pt. 1–39
Adams, Charles Follen, Apr. 21, 1842–Mar. 8, 1918.
Vol. 1, Pt. 1–40
Adams, Charles Francis, Aug. 2, 1866–June 11, 1954.
Supp. 5–5
Adams, Charles Francis, Aug. 18, 1807–Nov. 21, 1886.
Vol. 1, Pt. 1–40
Adams, Charles Francis, May 27, 1835–Mar. 20, 1915.
Vol. 1, Pt. 1–48
Adams, Charles Kendall, Jan. 24, 1835–July 26, 1902.
Vol. 1, Pt. 1–52
Adams, Charles R., Feb. 9, 1834–July 4, 1900.
Vol. 1, Pt. 1–54
Adams, Cyrus Cornelius, Jan. 7, 1849–May 4, 1928.
Supp. 1–6
Adams, Daniel, Sept. 29, 1773–June 8, 1864.
Vol. 1, Pt. 1–54
Adams, Daniel Weissiger, 1820–June 13, 1872.
Vol. 1, Pt. 1–55
Adams, Dudley W., Nov. 30, 1831–Feb. 13, 1897.
Vol. 1, Pt. 1–56
Adams, Ebenezer, Oct. 22, 1765–Aug. 15, 1841.
Vol. 1, Pt. 1–56
Adams, Edward Dean, Apr. 9, 1846–May 20, 1931.
Supp. 1–7

Adams, Edwin, Feb. 3, 1834–Oct. 28, 1877.
    Vol. 1, Pt. 1–57
Adams, Eliphalet, Mar. 26, 1677–Oct. 4, 1753.
    Vol. 1, Pt. 1–58
Adams, Ephraim Douglass, Dec. 18, 1865–Sept. 1, 1930.
    Supp. 1–8
Adams, Franklin Pierce, Nov. 15, 1881–Mar. 23, 1960.
    Supp. 6–4
Adams, Frank Ramsay, July 7, 1883–Oct. 8, 1963.
    Supp. 7–1
Adams, Frederick Upham, Dec. 10, 1859–Aug. 28, 1921.
    Vol. 1, Pt. 1–58
Adams, George Burton, June 3, 1851–May 26, 1925.
    Vol. 1, Pt. 1–59
Adams, Hannah, Oct. 2, 1755–Dec. 15, 1831.
    Vol. 1, Pt. 1–60
Adams, Henry Brooks, Feb. 16, 1838–Mar. 27, 1918.
    Vol. 1, Pt. 1–61
Adams, Henry Carter, Dec. 31, 1851–Aug. 11, 1921.
    Vol. 1, Pt. 1–67
Adams, Henry Cullen, Nov. 28, 1850–July 9, 1906.
    Vol. 1, Pt. 1–69
Adams, Herbert Baxter, Apr. 16, 1850–July 30, 1901.
    Vol. 1, Pt. 1–69
Adams, Herbert Samuel, Jan. 28, 1858–May 21, 1945.
    Supp. 3–1
Adams, Isaac, Aug. 16, 1802–July 19, 1883.
    Vol. 1, Pt. 1–71
Adams, James Hopkins, Mar. 15, 1812–July 13, 1861.
    Vol. 1, Pt. 1–71
Adams, James Truslow, Oct. 18, 1878–May 18, 1949.
    Supp. 4–2
Adams, Jasper, Aug. 27, 1793–Oct. 25, 1841.
    Vol. 1, Pt. 1–72
Adams, John, July 1, 1825–Nov. 30, 1864.
    Vol. 1, Pt. 1–82
Adams, John, Oct. 19, 1735–July 4, 1826.
    Vol. 1, Pt. 1–72
Adams, John, Sept. 18, 1772–Apr. 24, 1863.
    Vol. 1, Pt. 1–82
Adams, John Coleman, Oct. 25, 1849–June 22, 1922.
    Vol. 1, Pt. 1–83
Adams, John Quincy, July 11, 1767–Feb. 23, 1848.
    Vol. 1, Pt. 1–84
Adams, Joseph Alexander, 1803–Sept. 11, 1880.
    Vol. 1, Pt. 1–93
Adams, Joseph Quincy, Mar. 23, 1881–Nov. 10, 1946.
    Supp. 4–4
Adams, Maude, Nov. 11, 1872–July 17, 1953.
    Supp. 5–7
Adams, Nehemiah, Feb. 19, 1806–Oct 6, 1878.
    Vol. 1, Pt. 1–93
Adams, Randolph Greenfield, Nov. 7, 1892–Jan. 4, 1951.
    Supp. 5–8
Adams, Robert, Feb. 26, 1846–June 1, 1906.
    Vol. 1, Pt. 1–94
Adams, Samuel, Sept. 27, 1722–Oct. 2, 1803.
    Vol. 1, Pt. 1–95
Adams, Samuel Hopkins, Jan. 26, 1871–Nov. 15, 1958.
    Supp. 6–6
Adams, Thomas Sewall, Dec. 29, 1873–Feb. 8, 1933.
    Supp. 1–9
Adams, Walter Sydney, Dec. 20, 1876–May 11, 1956.
    Supp. 6–7
Adams, William, Jan. 25, 1807–Aug. 31, 1880.
    Vol. 1, Pt. 1–101
Adams, William Lysander, Feb. 5, 1821–Apr. 26, 1906.
    Vol. 1, Pt. 1–102
Adams, William Taylor, July 30, 1822–Mar. 27, 1897.
    Vol. 1, Pt. 1–102
Adams, William Wirt, Mar. 22, 1819–May 1, 1888.
    Vol. 1, Pt. 1–103
Addams, Jane, Sept. 6, 1860–May 21, 1935.
    Supp. 1–10
Addicks, John Edward O'Sullivan, Nov. 21, 1841–Aug. 7, 1919. Vol. 1, Pt. 1–104
Ade, George, Feb. 9, 1866–May 16, 1944.
    Supp. 3–2
Adee, Alvey Augustus, Nov. 27, 1842–July 5, 1924.
    Vol. 1, Pt. 1–105
Adgate, Andrew, d. 1793.
    Vol. 1, Pt. 1–107

Adie, David Craig, Sept. 3, 1888–Feb. 23, 1943.
    Supp. 3–4
Adkins, Homer Burton, Jan. 16, 1892–Aug. 10, 1949.
    Supp. 4–5
Adler, Cyrus, Sept. 13, 1863–Apr. 7, 1940.
    Supp. 2–5
Adler, Elmer, July 22, 1884–Jan. 11, 1962.
    Supp. 7–2
Adler, Felix, Aug. 13, 1851–Apr. 24, 1933.
    Supp. 1–13
Adler, Felix, June 17, 1897–Feb. 1, 1960.
    Supp. 6–8
Adler, George J., 1821–Aug. 24, 1868.
    Vol. 1, Pt. 1–107
Adler, Polly, Apr. 16, 1900–June 9, 1962.
    Supp. 7–3
Adler, Samuel, Dec. 3, 1809–June 9, 1891.
    Vol. 1, Pt. 1–108
Adler, Sara, 1858–Apr. 28, 1953.
    Supp. 5–10
Adlum, John, Apr. 29, 1759–Mar. 1, 1836.
    Vol. 1, Pt. 1–109
Adrain, Robert, Sept. 30, 1775–Aug. 10, 1843.
    Vol. 1, Pt. 1–109
Adrian, Gilbert, Mar. 3, 1903–Sept. 13, 1959.
    Supp. 6–9
Affleck, Thomas, July 13, 1812–Dec. 30, 1868.
    Vol. 1, Pt. 1–110
Agassiz, Alexander, Dec. 17, 1835–Mar. 27, 1910.
    Vol. 1, Pt. 1–111
Agassiz, Elizabeth Cabot Cary, Dec. 5, 1822–June 27, 1907.
    Vol. 1, Pt. 1–114
Agassiz, Jean Louis Rodolphe, May 28, 1807–Dec. 14, 1873.
    Vol. 1, Pt. 1–114
Agate, Alfred T., Feb. 14, 1812–Jan. 5, 1846.
    Vol. 1, Pt. 1–122
Agate, Frederick Styles, Jan. 29, 1803–May 1, 1844.
    Vol. 1, Pt. 1–123
Agee, James Rufus, Nov. 27, 1909–May 16, 1955.
    Supp. 5–11
Aggrey, James Emman Kwegyir, Oct. 18, 1875–July 30, 1927.
    Supp. 1–14
Agnew, Cornelius Rea, Aug. 8, 1830–Apr. 18, 1888.
    Vol. 1, Pt. 1–123
Agnew, David Hayes, Nov. 24, 1818–Mar. 22, 1892.
    Vol. 1, Pt. 1–124
Agnew, Eliza, Feb. 2, 1807–June 14, 1883.
    Vol. 1, Pt. 1–125
Agnus, Felix, May 5, 1839–Oct. 31, 1925.
    Vol. 1, Pt. 1–125
Agramonte Y Simoni, Aristides, June 3, 1868–Aug. 17, 1931.
    Supp. 1–14
Aiken, Charles Augustus, Oct. 20, 1827–Jan. 14, 1892.
    Vol. 1, Pt. 1–126
Aiken, David Wyatt, Mar. 17, 1828–Apr. 6, 1887.
    Vol. 1, Pt. 1–127
Aiken, George L., Dec. 19, 1830–Apr. 27, 1876.
    Vol. 1, Pt. 1–127
Aiken, William, Jan. 28, 1806–Sept. 6, 1887.
    Vol. 1, Pt. 1–128
Aikens, Andrew Jackson, Oct. 31, 1830–Jan. 22, 1909.
    Vol. 1, Pt. 1–129
Aime, Valcour, 1798–Dec. 31, 1867.
    Vol. 1, Pt. 1–130
Ainslie, Hew, Apr. 5, 1792–Mar. 11, 1878.
    Vol. 1, Pt. 1–130
Ainslie, Peter, Jun 3, 1867–Feb. 23, 1934.
    Supp. 1–15
Ainsworth, Frederick Crayton, Sept. 11, 1852–June 5, 1934.
    Supp. 1–16
Aitken, Robert, 1734–July 15, 1802.
    Vol. 1, Pt. 1–131
Aitken, Robert Grant, Dec. 31, 1864–Oct. 29, 1951.
    Supp. 5–13
Akeley, Carl Ethan, May 19, 1864–Nov. 17, 1926.
    Vol. 1, Pt. 1–132
Akeley, Mary Leonore, Jan. 29, 1878–July 19, 1966.
    Supp. 8–2
Akerman, Amos Tappan, Feb. 23, 1821–Dec. 21, 1880.
    Vol. 1, Pt. 1–133
Akers, Benjamin Paul, July 10, 1825–May 21, 1861.
    Vol. 1, Pt. 1–134

Ames, Edward Raymond, May 20, 1806–Apr. 25, 1879.
   Vol. 1, Pt. 1–242
Ames, Edward Scribner, Apr. 21, 1870–June 29, 1958.
   Supp. 6–13
Ames, Ezra, May 5, 1768–Feb. 23, 1836.
   Vol. 1, Pt. 1–243
Ames, Fisher, Apr. 9, 1758–July 4, 1808.
   Vol. 1, Pt. 1–244
Ames, Frederick Lothrop, June 8, 1835–Sept. 13, 1893
Ames, Herman Vandenburg, Aug. 7, 1865–Feb. 7, 1935.
   Supp. 1–28
Ames, James Barr, June 22, 1846–Jan. 8, 1910.
   Vol. 1, Pt. 1–247
Ames, James Tyler, May 13, 1810–Feb. 16, 1883.
   Vol. 1, Pt. 1–248
Ames, Joseph Alexander, 1816–Oct. 30, 1872. 1–249
Ames, Joseph Sweetman, July 3, 1864–June 24, 1943.
   Supp. 3–11
Ames, Mary Clemmer. [See Clemmer, Mary, 1831–1884.]
Ames, Nathaniel, July 22, 1708–July 11, 1764.
   Vol. 1, Pt. 1–250
Ames, Nathan Peabody, Sept. 1, 1803–Apr. 3, 1847.
   Vol. 1, Pt. 1–249
Ames, Oakes, Jan. 10, 1804–May 8, 1873.
   Vol. 1, Pt. 1–251
Ames, Oakes, Sept. 26, 1874–Apr. 28, 1950.
   Supp. 4–16
Ames, Oliver, Apr. 11, 1779–Sept. 11, 1863.
   Vol. 1, Pt. 1–253
Ames, Oliver, Nov. 5, 1807–Mar. 9, 1877.
   Vol. 1, Pt. 1–253
Ames, Oliver, Feb. 4, 1831–Oct. 22, 1895.
   Vol. 1, Pt. 1–254
Ames, Samuel, Sept. 6, 1806–Dec. 20, 1865.
   Vol. 1, Pt. 1–256
Ames, Winthrop, Nov. 25, 1870–Nov. 3, 1937.
   Supp. 2–10
Amherst, Jeffery, Jan. 29, 1717–Aug. 3, 1797.
   Vol. 1, Pt. 1–256
Amidon, Charles Fremont, Aug. 17, 1856–Dec. 26, 1937.
   Supp. 2–11
Ammann, Othmar Hermann, Mar. 26, 1879–Sept. 22, 1965.
   Supp. 7–11
Ammen, Daniel, May 16, 1819–July 11, 1898.
   Vol. 1, Pt. 1–258
Ammen, Jacob, Jan. 7, 1807–Feb. 6, 1894,.
   Vol. 1, Pt. 1–259
Ammons, Elias Milton, July 28, 1860–May 20, 1925.
   Vol. 1, Pt. 1–259
Amory, Thomas, May 1682–June 20, 1728.
   Vol. 1, Pt. 1–260
Anagnos, Michael, Nov. 7, 1837–June 29, 1906.
   Vol. 1, Pt. 1–261
Anderson, Alexander, Apr. 21, 1775–Jan. 17, 1870.
   Vol. 1, Pt. 1–262
Anderson, Benjamin McAlester, May 1, 1886–Jan. 19, 1949.
   Supp. 4–17
Anderson, David Lawrence, Feb. 4, 1850–Feb. 16, 1911.
   Vol. 1, Pt. 1–262
Anderson, Edwin Hatfield, Sept. 27, 1861–Apr. 29, 1947.
   Supp. 4–18
Anderson, Elizabeth Milbank, Dec. 20, 1850–Feb. 22, 1921.
   Vol. 1, Pt. 1–263
Anderson, Galusha, Mar. 7, 1832–July 20, 1918.
   Vol. 1, Pt. 1–264
Anderson, George Thomas, Mar. 3, 1824–Apr. 4, 1901.
   Vol. 1, Pt. 1–265
Anderson, Henry Tompkins, Jan. 27, 1812–Sept. 19, 1872.
   Vol. 1, Pt. 1–265
Anderson, James Patton, Feb. 12, 1822–Sept. 1, 1872.
   Vol. 1, Pt. 1–266
Anderson, John Alexander, June 26, 1834–May 18, 1892.
   Vol. 1, Pt. 1–267
Anderson, Joseph, Nov. 5, 1757–Apr. 17, 1837.
   Vol. 1, Pt. 1–267
Anderson, Joseph Reid, Feb. 6, 1813–Sept. 7, 1892.
   Vol. 1, Pt. 1–268
Anderson, Martin Brewer, Feb. 12, 1815–Feb. 22, 1890.
   Vol. 1, Pt. 1–269
Anderson, Mary, July 28, 1859–May 29, 1940.
   Supp. 2–12
Anderson, Mary, Aug. 27, 1872–Jan. 29, 1964.
   Supp. 7–12

Anderson, Maxwell, Dec. 15, 1888–Feb. 28, 1959.
   Supp. 6–14
Anderson, Paul Y., Aug. 29, 1893–Dec. 6, 1938.
   Supp. 2–13
Anderson, Richard Clough, Jan. 12, 1750–Oct. 16, 1826.
   Vol. 1, Pt. 1–270
Anderson, Richard Clough, Aug. 4, 1788–July 24, 1826.
   Vol. 1, Pt. 1–271
Anderson, Richard Heron, Oct. 7, 1821–June 26, 1879.
   Vol. 1, Pt. 1–271
Anderson, Robert, June 14, 1805–Oct. 26, 1871.
   Vol. 1, Pt. 1–274
Anderson, Sherwood, Sept. 13, 1876–Mar. 8, 1941.
   Supp. 3–12
Anderson, Victor Vance, Dec. 26, 1879–July 26, 1960.
   Supp. 6–16
Anderson, William, Dec. 1762–Dec. 1829.
   Vol. 1, Pt. 1–275
André, Louis, May 28, 1631 or 1623–Sept. 19, 1715.
   Vol. 1, Pt. 1–276
Andreis, Andrew James Felix Bartholomew de, Dec. 12, 1778
   –Oct. 15, 1820. Vol. 1, Pt. 1–276
Andrew, Abram Piatt, Feb. 12, 1873–June 3, 1936.
   Supp. 2–15
Andrew, James Osgood, May 3, 1794–Mar. 2, 1871.
   Vol. 1, Pt. 1–277
Andrew, John Albion, May 31, 1818–Oct. 30, 1867.
   Vol. 1, Pt. 1–279
Andrew, Samuel, Jan. 29, 1656–Jan. 24, 1738.
   Vol. 1, Pt. 1–281
Andrews, Alexander Boyd, July 23, 1841–Apr. 17, 1915.
   Vol. 1, Pt. 1–282
Andrews, Bert, June 2, 1901–Aug. 21, 1953.
   Supp. 5–18
Andrews, Charles, May 27, 1827–Oct. 22, 1918.
   Vol. 1, Pt. 1–282
Andrews, Charles Bartlett, Nov. 4, 1836–Sept. 12, 1902.
   Vol. 1, Pt. 1–283
Andrews, Charles McLean, Feb. 22, 1863–Sept. 9, 1943.
   Supp. 3–15
Andrews, Chauncey Hummason, Dec. 2, 1823–Dec. 25,
   1893. Vol. 1, Pt. 1–283
Andrews, Christopher Columbus, Oct. 27, 1829–Sept. 21,
   1922. Vol. 1, Pt. 1–284
Andrews, Edward Gayer, Aug. 7, 1825–Dec. 31, 1907.
   Vol. 1, Pt. 1–285
Andrews, Elisha Benjamin, Jan. 10, 1844–Oct. 30, 1917.
   Vol. 1, Pt. 1–286
Andrews, Frank Maxwell, Feb. 3, 1884–May 3, 1943.
   Supp. 3–16
Andrews, Garnett, May 15, 1837–May 6, 1903.
   Vol. 1, Pt. 1–291
Andrews, George Leonard, Aug. 31, 1828–Apr. 4, 1899.
   Vol. 1, Pt. 1–291
Andrews, George Pierce, Sept. 29, 1835–May 24, 1902.
   Vol. 1, Pt. 1–292
Andrews, Israel DeWolf, d. Feb. 17, 1871.
   Supp. 1–29
Andrews, Israel Ward, Jan. 3, 1815–Apr. 18, 1888.
   Vol. 1, Pt. 1–293
Andrews, John, Apr. 4, 1746–Mar. 29, 1813.
   Vol. 1, Pt. 1–293
Andrews, John Bertram, Aug. 2, 1880–Jan. 4, 1943.
   Supp. 3–18
Andrews, Joseph, c. 1805–May 7, 1873.
   Vol. 1, Pt. 1–294
Andrews, Lorin, Apr. 1, 1819–Sept. 18, 1861.
   Vol. 1, Pt. 1–295
Andrews, Lorrin, Apr. 29, 1795–Sept. 29, 1868.
   Vol. 1, Pt. 1–295
Andrews, Roy Chapman, Jan. 26, 1884–Mar. 11, 1960.
   Supp. 6–17
Andrews, Samuel James, July 31, 1817–Oct. 11, 1906.
   Vol. 1, Pt. 1–296
Andrews, Sherlock James, Nov. 17, 1801–Feb. 11, 1880.
   Vol. 1, Pt. 1–297
Andrews, Sidney, Oct. 7, 1835–Apr. 10, 1880.
   Vol. 1, Pt. 1–297
Andrews, Stephen Pearl, Mar. 22, 1812–May 21, 1886.
   Vol. 1, Pt. 1–298
Andrews, William Loring, Sept. 9, 1837–Mar. 19, 1920.
   Vol. 1, Pt. 1–299

Atwater, Wilbur Olin, May 3, 1844–Sept. 22, 1907.
    Vol. 1, Pt. 1–417
Atwood, Charles B., May 18, 1849–Dec. 19, 1895.
    Vol. 1, Pt. 1–418
Atwood, David, Dec. 15, 1815–Dec. 11, 1889.
    Vol. 1, Pt. 1–419
Atwood, Lewis John, Apr. 8, 1827–Feb. 23, 1909.
    Vol. 1, Pt. 1–419
Atwood, Wallace Walter, Oct. 1, 1872–July 24, 1949.
    Supp. 4–31
Atzerodt, George A., c. 1832–1865. [See Booth, John Wilkes.]
Auchmuty, Richard Tylden, July 15, 1831–July 18, 1893.
    Vol. 1, Pt. 1–420
Auchmuty, Robert, d. 1750.
    Vol. 1, Pt. 1–421
Auchmuty, Robert, d. November 1788.
    Vol. 1, Pt. 1–421
Auchmuty, Samuel, Jan. 26, 1722–Mar. 4, 1777.
    Vol. 1, Pt. 1–422
Audsley, George Ashdown, Sept. 6, 1838–June 21, 1925.
    Vol. 1, Pt. 1–422
Audubon, John James, Apr. 26, 1785–Jan. 27, 1851.
    Vol. 1, Pt. 1–423
Auer, John, Mar. 30, 1875–Apr. 30, 1948.
    Supp. 4–34
Augur, Christopher Columbus, July 10, 1821–Jan. 16, 1898.
    Vol. 1, Pt. 1–427
Augur, Hezekiah, Feb. 21, 1791–Jan. 10, 1858.
    Vol. 1, Pt. 1–428
Augustus, John, 1785–June 21, 1859.
    Vol. 1, Pt. 1–429
Austell, Alfred, Jan. 14, 1814–Dec. 7, 1881.
    Vol. 1, Pt. 1–429
Austen, (Elizabeth) Alice, Mar. 17, 1866–June 9, 1952.
    Supp. 5–24
Austen, Peter Townsend, Sept. 10, 1852–Dec. 30, 1907.
    Vol. 1, Pt. 1–430
Austin, Benjamin, Nov. 18, 1752–May 4, 1820.
    Vol. 1, Pt. 1–431
Austin, David, Mar. 19, 1759–Feb. 5, 1831.
    Vol. 1, Pt. 1–432
Austin, Henry, Dec. 4, 1804–Dec. 17, 1891.
    Vol. 1, Pt. 1–432
Austin, James Trecothick, Jan. 10, 1784–May 8, 1870.
    Vol. 1, Pt. 1–433
Austin, Jane Goodwin, Feb. 25, 1831–Mar. 30, 1894.
    Vol. 1, Pt. 1–434
Austin, Jonathan Loring, Jan. 2, 1748–May 10, 1826.
    Vol. 1, Pt. 1–435
Austin, Mary, Sept. 9, 1868–Aug. 13, 1934.
    Supp. 1–34
Austin, Moses, Oct. 4, 1761–June 10, 1821.
    Vol. 1, Pt. 1–435
Austin, Samuel, Oct. 7, 1760–Dec. 4, 1830.
    Vol. 1, Pt. 1–436
Austin, Stephen Fuller, Nov. 3, 1793–Dec. 27, 1836.
    Vol. 1, Pt. 1–437
Austin, Warren Robinson, Nov. 12, 1877–Dec. 25, 1962.
    Supp. 7–22
Austin, William, Mar. 2, 1778–June 27, 1841.
    Vol. 1, Pt. 1–440
Averell, William Woods, Nov. 5, 1832–Feb. 3, 1900.
    Vol. 1, Pt. 1–441
Avery, Benjamin Parke, Nov. 11, 1828–Nov. 8, 1875.
    Vol. 1, Pt. 1–443
Avery, Isaac Wheeler, May 2, 1837–Sept. 8, 1897.
    Vol. 1, Pt. 1–444
Avery, John, Sept. 18, 1837–Sept. 1, 1887.
    Vol. 1, Pt. 1–444
Avery, Milton Clark, Mar. 7, 1893–Jan. 3, 1965.
    Supp. 7–24
Avery, Oswald Theodore, Oct. 21, 1877–Feb. 20, 1955.
    Supp. 5–25
Avery, Samuel Putnam, Mar. 17, 1822–Aug. 11, 1904.
    Vol. 1, Pt. 1–445
Avery, Sewell Lee, Nov. 4, 1874–Oct. 31, 1960.
    Supp. 6–27
Avery, William Waigstill, May 25, 1816–July 3, 1864.
    Vol. 1, Pt. 1–445
Awl, William Maclay, May 24, 1799–Nov. 19, 1876.
    Vol. 1, Pt. 1–446

Axtell, Samuel Beach, Oct. 14, 1819–Aug. 6 or 7, 1891.
    Vol. 1, Pt. 1–446
Ayala, Juan Manuel de, fl. 1775.
    Vol. 1, Pt. 1–447
Aycock, Charles Brantley, Nov. 1, 1859–Apr. 4, 1912.
    Vol. 1, Pt. 1–447
Aydelotte, Frank, Oct. 16, 1880–Dec. 17, 1956.
    Supp. 6–29
Ayer, Edward Everett, Nov. 16, 1841–May 3, 1927.
    Vol. 1, Pt. 1–448
Ayer, Francis Wayland, Feb. 4, 1848–Mar. 5, 1923.
    Vol. 1, Pt. 1–449
Ayer, James Cook, May 5, 1818–July 3, 1878.
    Vol. 1, Pt. 1–450
Ayllon, Lucas Vasquez de, c. 1475–Oct. 18, 1526.
    Vol. 1, Pt. 1–451
Aylwin, John Cushing, c. 1780–Jan. 28, 1813.
    Vol. 1, Pt. 1–452
Ayres, Anne, Jan. 3, 1816–Feb. 9, 1896.
    Vol. 1, Pt. 1–452
Ayres, Brown, May 25, 1856–Jan. 28, 1919.
    Vol. 1, Pt. 1–453
Ayres, Leonard Porter, Sept. 15, 1879–Oct. 29, 1946.
    Supp. 4–35
Ayres, Romeyn Beck, Dec. 20, 1825–Dec. 4, 1888.
    Vol. 1, Pt. 1–453
Ayres, William Augustus, Apr. 19, 1867–Feb. 17, 1952.
    Supp. 5–26
Azarias, Brother, June 29, 1847–Aug. 20, 1893.
    Vol. 1, Pt. 1–454

Baade, Wilhelm Heinrich Walter, Mar. 24, 1893–June 25, 1960. Supp. 6–30
Babbitt, Benjamin Talbot, 1809–Oct. 20, 1889.
    Vol. 1, Pt. 1–455
Babbitt, Irving, Aug. 2, 1865–July 15, 1933.
    Supp. 1–36
Babbitt, Isaac, July 26, 1799–May 26, 1862.
    Vol. 1, Pt. 1–456
Babcock, George Herman, June 17, 1832–Dec. 16, 1893.
    Vol. 1, Pt. 1–456
Babcock, Howard Edward, Feb. 23, 1889–July 12, 1950.
    Supp. 4–36
Babcock, James Francis, Feb. 23, 1844–July 19, 1897.
    Vol. 1, Pt. 1–457
Babcock, James Woods, Aug. 11, 1856–Mar. 3, 1922.
    Vol. 1, Pt. 1–458
Babcock, Joseph Weeks, Mar. 6, 1850–Apr. 27, 1909.
    Vol. 1, Pt. 1–458
Babcock, Maltbie Davenport, Aug. 3, 1858–May 18, 1901.
    Vol. 1, Pt. 1–459
Babcock, Orville E., Dec. 25, 1835–June 2, 1884.
    Vol. 1, Pt. 1–460
Babcock, Stephen Moulton, Oct. 22, 1843–July 2, 1931.
    Supp. 1–37
Babcock, Washington Irving, Sept. 26, 1858–Aug. 7, 1917.
    Vol. 1, Pt. 1–461
Babson, Roger Ward, July 6, 1875–Mar. 5, 1967.
    Supp. 8–18
Baccaloni, Salvatore, Apr. 14, 1900–Dec. 31, 1969.
    Supp. 8–19
Bache, Alexander Dallas, July 19, 1806–Feb. 17, 1867.
    Vol. 1, Pt. 1–461
Bache, Benjamin Franklin, Aug. 12, 1769–Sept. 10, 1798.
    Vol. 1, Pt. 1–462
Bache, Franklin, Oct. 25, 1792–Mar. 19, 1864.
    Vol. 1, Pt. 1–463
Bache, Jules Semon, Nov. 9, 1861–Mar. 24, 1944.
    Supp. 3–24
Bache, Richard, 1737–July 29, 1811. 1–464
Bache, Theophylact, Jan. 17, 1734/35–Oct. 30, 1807.
    Vol. 1, Pt. 1–464
Bachelder, John, Mar. 7, 1817–July 1, 1906.
    Vol. 1, Pt. 1–465
Bacheller, Irving, Sept. 26, 1859–Feb. 24, 1950.
    Supp. 4–38
Bacher, Otto Henry, Mar. 31, 1856–Aug. 16, 1909.
    Vol. 1, Pt. 1–465
Bachman, John, Feb. 4, 1790–Feb. 24, 1874.
    Vol. 1, Pt. 1–466
Bachmann, Werner Emmanuel, Nov. 13, 1901–Mar. 22, 1951. Supp. 5–28

Bachrach, Louis Fabian, July 16, 1881–July 24, 1963.
  Supp. 7–25
Backus, Azel, Oct. 13, 1765–Dec. 9, 1817.
  Vol. 1, Pt. 1–467
Backus, Isaac, Jan. 9, 1724–Nov. 20, 1806.
  Vol. 1, Pt. 1–468
Backus, Truman Jay, Feb. 11, 1842–Mar. 25, 1908.
  Vol. 1, Pt. 1–472
Bacon, Alice Mabel, Feb. 6, 1858–May 1, 1918.
  Vol. 1, Pt. 1–473
Bacon, Augustus Octavius, Oct. 20, 1839–Feb. 14, 1914.
  Vol. 1, Pt. 1–473
Bacon, Benjamin Wisner, Jan. 15, 1860–Feb. 1, 1932.
  Supp. 1–38
Bacon, David, Sept. 4, 1771–Aug. 27, 1817. 1–474
Bacon, Delia Salter, Feb. 2, 1811–Sept. 2, 1859.
  Vol. 1, Pt. 1–475
Bacon, Edward Payson, May 16, 1834–Feb. 16, 1916.
  Vol. 1, Pt. 1–476
Bacon, Edwin Munroe, Oct. 20, 1844–Feb. 24, 1916.
  Vol. 1, Pt. 1–476
Bacon, Frank, Jan. 16, 1864–Nov. 19, 1922. 1–477
Bacon, Henry, Nov. 28, 1866–Feb. 16, 1924.
  Vol. 1, Pt. 1–477
Bacon, John, Apr. 9, 1738–Oct. 25, 1820.
  Vol. 1, Pt. 1–478
Bacon, Leonard, May 26, 1887–Jan. 1, 1954.
  Supp. 5–29
Bacon, Leonard, Feb. 19, 1802–Dec. 24, 1881. 1–479
Bacon, Leonard Woolsey, Jan. 1, 1830–May 12, 1907.
  Vol. 1, Pt. 1–481
Bacon, Nathaniel, Jan. 2, 1647–Oct. 1676.
  Vol. 1, Pt. 1–482
Bacon, Robert, July 5, 1860–May 29, 1919.
  Vol. 1, Pt. 1–483
Bacon, Thomas, c. 1700–May 24, 1768.
  Vol. 1, Pt. 1–484
Badè, William Frederic, Jan. 22, 1871–Mar. 4, 1936.
  Supp. 2–16
Badeau, Adam, Dec. 29, 1831–Mar. 19, 1895.
  Vol. 1, Pt. 1–485
Badger, Charles Johnston, Aug. 6, 1853–Sept. 7, 1932.
  Supp. 1–39
Badger, George Edmund, Apr. 17, 1795–May 11, 1866.
  Vol. 1, Pt. 1–485
Badger, Joseph, Mar. 14, 1708–1765.
  Vol. 1, Pt. 1–486
Badger, Joseph, Feb. 28, 1757–Apr. 5, 1846.
  Vol. 1, Pt. 1–487
Badger, Oscar Charles, Aug. 12, 1823–June 20, 1899.
  Vol. 1, Pt. 1–488
Badin, Stephen Theodore, July 17, 1768–Apr. 19, 1853.
  Vol. 1, Pt. 1–488
Baekeland, Leo Hendrik, Nov. 14, 1863–Feb. 23, 1944.
  Supp. 3–25
Baer, George Frederick, Sept. 26, 1842–Apr. 26, 1914.
  Vol. 1, Pt. 1–489
Baer, William Stevenson, Nov. 25, 1872–Apr. 7, 1931.
  Supp. 1–40
Baermann, Carl, July 9, 1839–Jan. 17, 1913.
  Vol. 1, Pt. 1–491
Baetjer, Frederick Henry, Aug. 7, 1874–July 17, 1933.
  Supp. 1–41
Bagby, Arthur Pendleton, 1794–Sept. 21, 1858.
  Vol. 1, Pt. 1–491
Bagby, George William, Aug. 13, 1828–Nov. 29, 1883.
  Vol. 1, Pt. 1–492
Bagley, William Chandler, Mar. 15, 1874–July 1, 1946.
  Supp. 4–39
Bailey, Ann, 1742–Nov. 22, 1825.
  Vol. 1, Pt. 1–493
Bailey, Anna Warner, Oct. 1758–Jan. 10, 1851.
  Vol. 1, Pt. 1–493
Bailey, Ebenezer, June 25, 1795–Aug. 5, 1839.
  Vol. 1, Pt. 1–494
Bailey, Florence Augusta Merriam, Aug. 8, 1863–Sept. 22, 1948. Supp. 4–41
Bailey, Francis, c. 1735–1815.
  Vol. 1, Pt. 1 494
Bailey, Frank Harvey, June 29, 1851–Apr. 9, 1921.
  Vol. 1, Pt. 1–495
Bailey, Gamaliel, Dec. 3, 1807–June 5, 1859.
  Vol. 1, Pt. 1–496

Bailey, (Irene) Temple, 188?–July 6, 1953.
  Supp. 5–33
Bailey, Jacob, 1731–Mar. 22, 1818.
  Vol. 1, Pt. 1–497
Bailey, Jacob Whitman, Apr. 29, 1811–Feb. 27, 1857.
  Vol. 1, Pt. 1–498
Bailey, James Anthony, 1847–Apr. 11, 1906.
  Vol. 1, Pt. 1–498
Bailey, James Montgomery, Sept. 25, 1841–Mar. 4, 1894.
  Vol. 1, Pt. 1–499
Bailey, Joseph, May 6, 1825–Mar. 21, 1867.
  Vol. 1, Pt. 1–500
Bailey, Joseph Weldon, Oct. 6, 1863–Apr. 13, 1929
  Supp. 1–42
Bailey, Josiah William, Sept. 14, 1873–Dec. 15, 1946.
  Supp. 4–42
Bailey, Liberty Hyde, Mar. 15, 1858–Dec. 25, 1954.
  Supp. 5–30
Bailey, Lydia R., Feb. 1, 1779–Feb. 21, 1869.
  Vol. 1, Pt. 1–500
Bailey, Mildred, Feb. 27, 1907–Dec. 12, 1951.
  Supp. 5–32
Bailey, Rufus William, Apr. 13, 1793–Apr. 25, 1863.
  Vol. 1, Pt. 1–501
Bailey, Solon Irving, Dec. 29, 1854–June 5, 1931.
  Supp. 1–43
Bailey, Theodorus, Apr. 12, 1805–Feb. 10, 1877.
  Vol. 1, Pt. 1–501
Bailly, Joseph Alexis, Jan. 21, 1825–June 15, 1883.
  Vol. 1, Pt. 1–502
Bain, George Luke Scobie, May 5, 1836–Oct. 22, 1891.
  Vol. 1, Pt. 1–503
Bainbridge, William, May 7, 1774–July 27, 1833.
  Vol. 1, Pt. 1–504
Baird, Absalom, Aug. 20, 1824–June 14, 1905.
  Vol. 1, Pt. 1–507
Baird, Charles Washington, Aug. 28, 1828–Feb. 10, 1887.
  Vol. 1, Pt. 1–508
Baird, Henry Carey, Sept. 10, 1825–Dec. 30, 1912.
  Vol. 1, Pt. 1–509
Baird, Henry Martyn, Jan. 17, 1832–Nov. 11, 1906.
  Vol. 1, Pt. 1–510
Baird, Matthew, 1817–May 19, 1877.
  Vol. 1, Pt. 1–511
Baird, Robert, Oct. 6, 1798–Mar. 15, 1863.
  Vol. 1, Pt. 1–511
Baird, Samuel John, Sept. 17, 1817–Apr. 10, 1893.
  Vol. 1, Pt. 1–512
Baird, Spencer Fullerton, Feb. 3, 1823–Aug. 19, 1888.
  Vol. 1, Pt. 1–513
Baker, Benjamin A., Apr. 4, 1818–Sept. 6, 1890.
  Vol. 1, Pt. 1–515
Baker, Benjamin Franklin, July 10, 1811–Mar. 11, 1889.
  Vol. 1, Pt. 1–516
Baker, Carl Lotus, Sept. 7, 1873–Apr. 10, 1945.
  Supp. 3–46
Baker, Daniel, Aug. 17, 1791–Dec. 10, 1857.
  Vol. 1, Pt. 1–517
Baker, Dorothy Dodds, Apr. 21, 1907–June 17, 1968.
  Supp. 8–20
Baker, Edward Dickinson, Feb. 24, 1811–Oct. 22, 1861.
  Vol. 1, Pt. 1–517
Baker, Frank, Aug. 22, 1841–Sept. 30, 1918.
  Vol. 1, Pt. 1–519
Baker, George Augustus, Mar. 1821–Apr. 2, 1880.
  Vol. 1, Pt. 1–519
Baker, George Fisher, Mar. 27, 1840–May 2, 1931.
  Supp. 1–44
Baker, George Pierce, Apr. 4, 1866–Jan. 6, 1935.
  Supp. 1–45
Baker, Harvey Humphrey, Apr. 11, 1869–Apr. 10, 1915.
  Vol. 1, Pt. 1–520
Baker, Hugh Potter, Jan. 20, 1878–May 24, 1950.
  Supp. 4–43
Baker, James, Dec. 19, 1818–May 15, 1898.
  Vol. 1, Pt. 1–520
Baker, James Heaton, May 6, 1829–May 25, 1913.
  Vol. 1, Pt. 1–521
Baker, James Hutchins, Oct. 13, 1848–Sept. 10, 1925.
  Vol. 1, Pt. 1–522
Baker, Jehu, Nov. 4, 1822–Mar. 1, 1903.
  Supp. 1–46

Baker, John Franklin, Mar. 13, 1886–June 28, 1963.
Supp. 7–27
Baker, La Fayette Curry, Oct. 13, 1826–July 3, 1868.
Vol. 1, Pt. 1–523
Baker, Laurence Simmons, May 15, 1830–Apr. 10, 1907.
Vol. 1, Pt. 1–523
Baker, Lorenzo Dow, Mar. 15, 1840–June 21, 1908.
Vol. 1, Pt. 1–524
Baker, Marcus, Sept. 23, 1849–Dec. 12, 1903.
Vol. 1, Pt. 1–525
Baker, Newton Diehl, Dec. 3, 1871–Dec. 25, 1937.
Supp. 2–17
Baker, Oliver Edwin, Sept. 10, 1883–Dec. 2, 1949.
Supp. 4–44
Baker, Osmon Cleander, July 30, 1812–Dec. 20, 1871.
Vol. 1, Pt. 1–525
Baker, Peter Carpenter, Mar. 22, 1822–May 19, 1889.
Vol. 1, Pt. 1–525
Baker, Ray Stannard, Apr. 17, 1870–July 12, 1946.
Supp. 4–46
Baker, Remember, June 1737–Aug. 1775.
Vol. 1, Pt. 1–526
Baker, Sara Josephine, Nov. 15, 1873–Feb. 21, 1945.
Supp. 3–27
Baker, Walter Ransom Gail, Nov. 30, 1892–Oct. 30, 1960.
Supp. 6–32
Baker, William Mumford, June 5, 1825–Aug. 20, 1883.
Vol. 1, Pt. 1–527
Balbach, Edward, July 4, 1839–Dec. 30, 1910.
Vol. 1, Pt. 1–527
Balch, Emily Greene, Jan. 8, 1867–Jan. 9, 1961.
Supp. 7–28
Balch, George Beall, Jan. 3, 1821–Apr. 16, 1908.
Vol. 1, Pt. 1–528
Balch, Thomas Willing, June 13, 1866–June 7, 1927.
Vol. 1, Pt. 1–529
Baldwin, Abraham, Nov. 22, 1754–Mar. 4, 1807.
Vol. 1, Pt. 1–530
Baldwin, Edward Robinson, Sept. 8, 1864–May 6, 1947.
Supp. 4–48
Baldwin, Elihu Whittlesey, Dec. 25, 1789–Oct. 15, 1840.
Vol. 1, Pt. 1–532
Baldwin, Evelyn Briggs, July 22, 1862–Oct. 25, 1933.
Supp. 1–47
Baldwin, Frank Stephen, Apr. 10, 1838–Apr. 8, 1925.
Vol. 1, Pt. 1–533
Baldwin, Henry, Jan. 14, 1780–Apr. 21, 1844.
Vol. 1, Pt. 1–533
Baldwin, Henry Perrine, Aug. 29, 1842–July 8, 1911.
Supp. 1–48
Baldwin, Henry Porter, Feb. 22, 1814–Dec. 31, 1892.
Vol. 1, Pt. 1–534
Baldwin, James Mark, Jan. 12, 1861–Nov. 8, 1934.
Supp. 1–49
Baldwin, John, Oct. 13, 1799–Dec. 28, 1884.
Vol. 1, Pt. 1–535
Baldwin, John Brown, Jan. 11, 1820–Sept. 30, 1873.
Vol. 1, Pt. 1–536
Baldwin, John Denison, Sept. 28, 1809–July 8, 1883.
Vol. 1, Pt. 1–537
Baldwin, Joseph, Oct. 31, 1827–Jan. 13, 1899.
Vol. 1, Pt. 1–537
Baldwin, Joseph Glover, Jan. 1815–Sept. 30, 1864.
Vol. 1, Pt. 1–538
Baldwin, Loammi, Jan. 21, 1744–Oct. 20, 1807.
Vol. 1, Pt. 1–539
Baldwin, Loammi, May 16, 1780–June 30, 1838.
Vol. 1, Pt. 1–540
Baldwin, Matthias William, Nov. 10, 1795–Sept. 7, 1866.
Vol. 1, Pt. 1–541
Baldwin, Roger Sherman, Jan. 4, 1793–Feb. 19, 1863.
Vol. 1, Pt. 1–542
Baldwin, Simeon, Dec. 14, 1761–May 26, 1851.
Vol. 1, Pt. 1–543
Baldwin, Simeon Eben, Feb. 5, 1840–Jan. 30, 1927.
Vol. 1, Pt. 1–544
Baldwin, Theron, July 21, 1801–Apr. 10, 1870.
Vol. 1, Pt. 1–547
Baldwin, William, Mar. 29, 1779–Aug. 31, 1819.
Vol. 1, Pt. 1–547
Baldwin, William Henry, Feb. 5, 1863–Jan. 3, 1905.
Vol. 1, Pt. 1–548

Balestier, Charles Wolcott, Dec. 13, 1861–Dec. 6, 1891.
Vol. 1, Pt. 1–549
Ball, Albert, May 7, 1835–Feb. 7, 1927.
Vol. 1, Pt. 1–550
Ball, Ephraim, Aug. 12, 1812–Jan. 1, 1872.
Vol. 1, Pt. 1–551
Ball, Frank Clayton, Nov. 24, 1857–Mar. 19, 1943.
Supp. 3–29
Ball, George Alexander, Nov. 5, 1862–Oct. 22, 1955.
Supp. 5–34
Ball, Thomas, June 3, 1819–Dec. 11, 1911.
Vol. 1, Pt. 1–552
Ballantine, Arthur Atwood, Aug. 3, 1883–Oct. 10, 1960.
Supp. 6–33
Ballard, Bland Williams, Oct. 16, 1759–Sept. 5, 1853.
Vol. 1, Pt. 1–554
Ballinger, Richard Achilles, July 9, 1858–June 6, 1922.
Vol. 1, Pt. 1–555
Ballou, Adin, Apr. 23, 1803–Aug. 5, 1890.
Vol. 1, Pt. 1–556
Ballou, Hosea, Apr. 30, 1771–June 7, 1852.
Vol. 1, Pt. 1–557
Ballou, Hosea, Oct. 18, 1796–May 27, 1861.
Vol. 1, Pt. 1–559
Ballou, Maturin Murray, Apr. 14, 1820–Mar. 27, 1895.
Vol. 1, Pt. 1–560
Baltimore, Charles Calvert, Third Lord. [See Calvert, Charles, 1637–1715.]
Baltimore, George Calvert, First Lord. [See Calvert, George, c. 1580–1632.]
Bamberger, Louis, May 15, 1855–Mar. 11, 1944.
Supp. 3–30
Bancroft, Aaron, Nov. 10, 1755–Aug. 19, 1839.
Vol. 1, Pt. 1–560
Bancroft, Cecil Franklin Patch, Nov. 25, 1839–Oct. 4, 1901.
Vol. 1, Pt. 1–561
Bancroft, Edgar Addison, Nov. 20, 1857–July 28, 1925.
Vol. 1, Pt. 1–562
Bancroft, Edward, Jan. 9, 1744–Sept. 8, 1821.
Vol. 1, Pt. 1–563
Bancroft, Frederic, Oct. 30, 1860–Feb. 22, 1945.
Supp. 3–31
Bancroft, George, Oct. 3, 1800–Jan. 17, 1891.
Vol. 1, Pt. 1–564
Bancroft, Hubert Howe, May 5, 1832–Mar. 2, 1918.
Vol. 1, Pt. 1–570
Bancroft, Wilder Dwight, Oct. 1, 1867–Feb. 7, 1953.
Supp. 5–35
Bandelier, Adolph Francis Alphonse, Aug. 6, 1840–Mar. 18, 1914. Vol. 1, Pt. 1–571
Bangs, Francis Nehemiah, Feb. 23, 1828–Nov. 30, 1885.
Vol. 1, Pt. 1–572
Bangs, Frank C., Oct. 13, 1833–June 12, 1908.
Vol. 1, Pt. 1–573
Bangs, John Kendrick, May 27, 1862–Jan. 21, 1922.
Vol. 1, Pt. 1–573
Bangs, Nathan, May 2, 1778–May 3, 1862.
Vol. 1, Pt. 1–574
Banister, John, 1650–May 1692.
Vol. 1, Pt. 1–575
Banister, John, Dec. 26, 1734–Sept. 30, 1788.
Vol. 1, Pt. 1–576
Banister, Zilpah Polly Grant, May 30, 1794–Dec. 3, 1874.
Vol. 1, Pt. 1–576
Bankhead, John Hollis, Sept. 13, 1842–Mar. 1, 1920.
Vol. 1, Pt. 1–577
Bankhead, John Hollis, July 8, 1872–June 12, 1946.
Supp. 4–49
Bankhead, Tallulah, Jan. 31, 1902–Dec. 12, 1968.
Supp. 8–21
Bankhead, William Brockman, Apr. 12, 1874–Sept. 15, 1940.
Supp. 2–19
Banks, Charles Edward, July 6, 1854–Oct. 21, 1931.
Supp. 1–50
Banks, Nathaniel Prentiss, Jan. 30, 1816–Sept. 1, 1894.
Vol. 1, Pt. 1–577
Banner, Peter, fl. 1794–1828.
Vol. 1, Pt. 1–580
Bannister, Nathaniel Harrington, Jan. 13, 1813–Nov. 2, 1847. Vol. 1, Pt. 1–581
Banvard, John, Nov. 15, 1815–May 16, 1891.
Vol. 1, Pt. 1–582

Barringer, Rufus, Dec. 2, 1821–Feb. 3, 1895.
    Vol. 1, Pt. 1–649
Barron, Clarence Walker, July 2, 1855–Oct. 2, 1928.
    Supp. 1–52
Barron, James, 1769–Apr. 21, 1851.
    Vol. 1, Pt. 1–649
Barron, Samuel, Nov. 28, 1809–Feb. 26, 1888.
    Vol. 1, Pt. 1–650
Barrow, Edward Grant, May 10, 1868–Dec. 15, 1953.
    Supp. 5–40
Barrow, Washington, Oct. 5, 1817–Oct. 19, 1866.
    Vol. 1, Pt. 1–651
Barrows, Alice Prentice, Nov. 15, 1877–Oct. 2, 1954.
    Supp. 5–41
Barrows, David Prescott, June 27, 1873–Sept. 5, 1954.
    Supp. 5–42
Barrows, John Henry, July 11, 1847–June 3, 1902.
    Vol. 1, Pt. 1–651
Barrows, Samuel June, May 26, 1845–Apr. 21, 1909.
    Vol. 1, Pt. 1–652
Barry, John, 1745–Sept. 13, 1803.
    Vol. 1, Pt. 1–654
Barry, John Stewart, Jan. 29, 1802–Jan. 14, 1870.
    Vol. 1, Pt. 1–654
Barry, Patrick, May 24, 1816–June 23, 1890.
    Vol. 1, Pt. 1–655
Barry, Philip James Quinn, June 18, 1896–Dec. 3, 1949.
    Supp. 4–54
Barry, William Taylor Sullivan, Dec. 10, 1821–Jan. 29, 1868.
    Vol. 1, Pt. 1–658
Barry, William Farquhar, Aug. 18, 1818–July 18, 1879.
    Vol. 1, Pt. 1–655
Barry, William Taylor, Feb. 5, 1785–Aug. 30, 1835.
    Vol. 1, Pt. 1–656
Barrymore, Ethel, Aug. 15, 1879–June 18, 1959.
    Supp. 6–38
Barrymore, Georgiana Emma Drew, 1856–July 2, 1893.
    Vol. 1, Pt. 1–659
Barrymore, John, Feb. 15, 1882–May 29, 1942.
    Supp. 3–34
Barrymore, Lionel, Apr. 28, 1878–Nov. 15, 1954.
    Supp. 5–44
Barrymore, Maurice, 1847–Mar. 26, 1905.
    Vol. 1, Pt. 1–659
Barsotti, Charles, Jan. 4, 1850–Mar. 30, 1927.
    Vol. 1, Pt. 2–1
Barstow, William Augustus, Sept. 13, 1813–Dec. 13, 1865.
    Vol. 1, Pt. 2–1
Barth, Carl Georg Lange, Feb. 28, 1860–Oct. 28, 1939.
    Supp. 2–26
Barthelmess, Richard, May 9, 1895–Aug. 17, 1963.
    Supp. 7–32
Bartholdt, Richard, Nov. 2, 1855–Mar. 19, 1932.
    Supp. 1–53
Bartholomew, Edward Sheffield, July 8, 1822–May 1858.
    Vol. 1, Pt. 2–2
Bartholow, Roberts, Nov. 28, 1831–May 10, 1904.
    Vol. 1, Pt. 2–2
Bartlet, William, Jan. 31, 1748 N.S.–Feb. 8, 1841.
    Vol. 1, Pt. 2–3
Bartlett, Edward Lewis ("Bob"), Apr. 20, 1904–Dec. 11, 1968. Supp. 8–25
Bartlett, Elisha, Oct. 6, 1804–July 19, 1855.
    Vol. 1, Pt. 2–3
Bartlett, Francis Alonzo, Nov. 13, 1882–Nov. 21, 1963.
    Supp. 7–32
Bartlett, Homer Newton, Dec. 28, 1845–Apr. 3, 1920.
    Vol. 1, Pt. 2–5
Bartlett, Ichabod, July 24, 1786–Oct. 19, 1853.
    Vol. 1, Pt. 2–5
Bartlett, John, June 14, 1820–Dec. 3, 1905.
    Vol. 1, Pt. 2–6
Bartlett, John Russell, Oct. 23, 1805–May 28, 1886.
    Vol. 1, Pt. 2–7
Bartlett, John Sherren, 1790–Aug. 23, 1863.
    Vol. 1, Pt. 2–8
Bartlett, Joseph, June 10, 1762–Oct. 20, 1827.
    Vol. 1, Pt. 2–8
Bartlett, Josiah, Nov. 21, 1729–May 19, 1795.
    Vol. 1, Pt. 2–9
Bartlett, Paul Wayland, Jan. 24, 1865–Sept. 20, 1925.
    Vol. 1, Pt. 2–11

Bartlett, Samuel Colcord, Nov. 25, 1817–Nov. 16, 1898.
    Vol. 1, Pt. 2–15
Bartlett, William Holmes Chambers, Sept. 4, 1804–Feb. 11, 1893. Supp. 1–54
Bartley, Mordecai, Dec. 16, 1783–Oct. 10, 1870.
    Vol. 1, Pt. 2–16
Bartol, Cyrus Augustus, Apr. 30, 1813–Dec. 16, 1900.
    Vol. 1, Pt. 2–17
Barton, Benjamin Smith, Feb. 10, 1766–Dec. 19, 1815.
    Vol. 1, Pt. 2–17
Barton, Bruce Fairchild, Aug. 5, 1886–July 5, 1967.
    Supp. 8–26
Barton, Clara, Dec. 25, 1821–Apr. 12, 1912.
    Vol. 1, Pt. 2–18
Barton, David, Dec. 14, 1783–Sept. 28, 1837.
    Supp. 1–55
Barton, George Aaron, Nov. 12, 1859–June 28, 1942.
    Supp. 3–36
Barton, James Edward, Nov. 1, 1890–Feb. 19, 1962.
    Supp. 7–33
Barton, James Levi, Sept. 23, 1855–July 21, 1936.
    Supp. 2–27
Barton, John Rhea, Apr. 1794–Jan. 1, 1871.
    Vol. 1, Pt. 2–21
Barton, Robert Thomas, Nov. 24, 1842–Jan. 17, 1917.
    Vol. 1, Pt. 2–22
Barton, Seth Maxwell, Sept. 8, 1829–Apr. 11, 1900.
    Vol. 1, Pt. 2–23
Barton, Thomas Pennant, 1803–Apr. 5, 1869.
    Vol. 1, Pt. 2–23
Barton, William Paul Crillon, Nov. 17, 1786–Feb. 29, 1856.
    Vol. 1, Pt. 2–25
Barton, William, May 26, 1748–Oct. 22, 1831.
    Vol. 1, Pt. 2–24
Barton, William Eleazar, June 28, 1861–Dec. 7, 1930.
    Supp. 1–56
Bartram, John, Mar. 23, 1699–Sept. 22, 1777.
    Vol. 1, Pt. 2–26
Bartram, William, Feb. 9, 1739–July 22, 1823.
    Vol. 1, Pt. 2–28
Baruch, Bernard Mannes, Aug. 19, 1870–June 20, 1965.
    Supp. 7–34
Baruch, Simon, July 29, 1840–June 3, 1921.
    Vol. 1, Pt. 2–29
Barus, Carl, Feb. 19, 1856–Sept. 20, 1935.
    Supp. 1–57
Barzynski, Vincent, Sept. 20, 1838–May 2, 1899.
    Vol. 1, Pt. 2–30
Bascom, Florence, July 14, 1862–June 18, 1945.
    Supp. 3–37
Bascom, Henry Bidleman, May 27, 1796–Sept. 8, 1850.
    Vol. 1, Pt. 2–30
Bascom, John, May 1, 1827–Oct. 2, 1911.
    Vol. 1, Pt. 2–32
Bashford, Coles, Jan. 24, 1816–Apr. 25, 1878.
    Vol. 1, Pt. 2–33
Bashford, James Whitford, May 29, 1849–Mar. 18, 1919.
    Vol. 1, Pt. 2–33
Baskerville, Charles, June 18, 1870–Jan. 28, 1922.
    Vol. 1, Pt. 2–34
Bass, Edward, Nov. 23, 1726–Sept. 10, 1803.
    Vol. 1, Pt. 2–34
Bass, Sam, July 21, 1851–July 21, 1878.
    Vol. 1, Pt. 2–35
Bass, William Capers, Jan. 13, 1831–Nov. 15, 1894.
    Vol. 1, Pt. 2–36
Basse, Jeremiah, d. 1725.
    Vol. 1, Pt. 2–36
Bassett, Edward Murray, Feb. 7, 1863–Oct. 27, 1948.
    Supp. 4–55
Bassett, James, Jan. 31, 1834–Mar. 10, 1906.
    Vol. 1, Pt. 2–37
Bassett, John Spencer, Sept. 10, 1867–Jan. 27, 1928.
    Vol. 1, Pt. 2–38
Bassett, Richard, Apr. 2, 1745–Sept. 15, 1815.
    Vol. 1, Pt. 2–39
Bassett, William Hastings, Mar. 7, 1868–July 21, 1934.
    Supp. 1–58
Basso, (Joseph) Hamilton, Sept. 5, 1904–May 13, 1964.
    Supp. 7–37
Batchelder, John Putnam, Aug. 6, 1784–Apr. 8, 1868.
    Vol. 1, Pt. 2–40

Bean, Tarleton Hoffman, Oct. 8, 1846–Dec. 28, 1916.
  Vol. 1, Pt. 2–92
Beard, Charles Austin, Nov. 27, 1874–Sept. 1, 1948.
  Supp. 4–61
Beard, Daniel Carter, June 21, 1850–June 11, 1941.
  Supp. 3–44
Beard, George Miller, May 8, 1839–Jan. 23, 1883.
  Vol. 1, Pt. 2–92
Beard, James Carter, June 6, 1837–Nov. 15, 1913.
  Vol. 1, Pt. 2–93
Beard, James Henry, May 20, 1812–Apr. 4, 1893.
  Vol. 1, Pt. 2–94
Beard, Mary, Nov. 14, 1876–Dec. 4, 1946.
  Supp. 4–64
Beard, Mary Ritter, Aug. 5, 1876–Aug. 14, 1958.
  Supp. 6–40
Beard, Richard, Nov. 27, 1799–Dec. 2, 1880.
  Vol. 1, Pt. 2–94
Beard, Thomas Francis, Feb. 6, 1842–Sept. 28, 1905.
  Vol. 1, Pt. 2–95
Beard, William Holbrook, Apr. 13, 1824–Feb. 20, 1900.
  Vol. 1, Pt. 2–95
Beardshear, William Miller, Nov. 7, 1850–Aug. 5, 1902.
  Vol. 1, Pt. 2–96
Beardsley, Eben Edwards, Jan. 8, 1808–Dec. 21, 1891.
  Vol. 1, Pt. 2–96
Beardsley, Samuel, Feb. 6, 1790–May 6, 1860.
  Vol. 1, Pt. 2–97
Beary, Donald Bradford, Dec. 4, 1888–Mar. 7, 1966.
  Supp. 8–29
Beasley, Frederick, 1777–Nov. 1, 1845.
  Vol. 1, Pt. 2–98
Beasley, Mercer, Mar. 27, 1815–Feb. 19, 1897.
  Vol. 1, Pt. 2–98
Beattie, Francis Robert, Mar. 31, 1848–Sept. 3, 1906.
  Vol. 1, Pt. 2–99
Beatty, Adam, May 10, 1777–June 9, 1858.
  Vol. 1, Pt. 2–99
Beatty, Charles Clinton, c. 1715–Aug. 13, 1772.
  Vol. 1, Pt. 2–109
Beatty, Clyde Raymond, June 10, 1903–July 19, 1965.
  Supp. 7–41
Beatty, John, Dec. 19, 1749–Apr. 30, 1826.
  Vol. 1, Pt. 2–100
Beatty, John, Dec. 16, 1828–Dec. 21, 1914.
  Vol. 1, Pt. 2–101
Beatty, Willard Walcott, Sept. 17, 1891–Sept. 29, 1961.
  Supp. 7–42
Beatty, William Henry, Feb. 18, 1838–Aug. 4, 1914.
  Vol. 1, Pt. 2–102
Beaty, Amos Leonidas, Sept. 1, 1870–Apr. 29, 1939.
  Supp. 2–29
Beauchamp, William, Apr. 26, 1772–Oct. 7, 1824.
  Vol. 1, Pt. 2–102
Beauchamp, William Martin, Mar. 25, 1830–Dec. 13, 1925.
  Vol. 1, Pt. 2–103
Beaumont, John Colt, Aug. 27, 1821–Aug. 2, 1882.
  Vol. 1, Pt. 2–104
Beaumont, William, Nov. 21, 1785–Apr. 25, 1853.
  Vol. 1, Pt. 2–104
Beaupré, Arthur Matthias, July 29, 1853–Sept. 13, 1919.
  Vol. 1, Pt. 2–110
Beauregard, Pierre Gustave Toutant, May 28, 1818–Feb. 20, 1893. Vol. 1, Pt. 2–111
Beaux, Cecilia, May 1, 1855–Sept. 17, 1942.
  Supp. 3–45
Beaver, James Addams, Oct. 21, 1837–Jan. 31, 1914.
  Vol. 1, Pt. 2–112
Beavers, Louise, Mar. 8, 1902–Oct. 26, 1962.
  Supp. 7–43
Bechet, Sidney, May 14, 1897–May 14, 1959.
  Supp. 6–42
Beck, Carl, Apr. 4, 1856–June 9, 1911.
  Vol. 1, Pt. 2–113
Beck, Charles, Aug. 19, 1798–Mar. 19, 1866.
  Vol. 1, Pt. 2–113
Beck, James Montgomery, July 9, 1861–Apr. 12, 1936.
  Supp. 2–30
Beck, Johann Heinrich, Sept. 12, 1856–May 25, 1924.
  Vol. 1, Pt. 2–114
Beck, John Brodhead, Sept. 18, 1794–Apr. 9, 1851.
  Vol. 1, Pt. 2–115

Beck, Lewis Caleb, Oct. 4, 1798–Apr. 20, 1853.
  Vol. 1, Pt. 2–116
Beck, Martin, July 30, 1867–Nov. 16, 1940.
  Supp. 2–32
Beck, Theodric Romeyn, Aug. 11, 1791–Nov. 19, 1855.
  Vol. 1, Pt. 2–116
Becker, George Ferdinand, Jan. 5, 1847–Apr. 20, 1919.
  Vol. 1, Pt. 2–117
Becket, Frederick Mark, Jan. 11, 1875–Dec. 1, 1942.
  Supp. 3–48
Becknell, William, c. 1790–c. 1832.
  Vol. 1, Pt. 2–119
Beckwith, Clarence Augustine, July 21, 1849–Apr. 2, 1931.
  Supp. 1–64
Beckwith, James Carroll, Sept. 23, 1852–Oct. 24, 1917.
  Vol. 1, Pt. 2–120
Beckwourth, James P., Apr. 26, 1798–c. 1867.
  Vol. 1, Pt. 2–122
Bedaux, Charles Eugene, Oct. 11, 1886–Feb. 18, 1944.
  Supp. 3–49
Bedford, Gunning, Apr. 7, 1742–September 1797.
  Vol. 1, Pt. 2–122
Bedford, Gunning, 1747–Mar. 30, 1812.
  Vol. 1, Pt. 2–123
Bedinger, George Michael, Dec. 10, 1756–Dec. 8, 1843.
  Vol. 1, Pt. 2–124
Bee, Barnard Elliott, February or March 1824–July 22, 1861.
  Vol. 1, Pt. 2–124
Bee, Hamilton Prioleau, July 22, 1822–Oct. 2, 1897.
  Vol. 1, Pt. 2–125
Beebe, (Charles) William, July 29, 1877–June 4, 1962.
  Supp. 7–45
Beecher, Catharine Esther, Sept. 6, 1800–May 12, 1878.
  Vol. 1, Pt. 2–125
Beecher, Charles, Oct. 7, 1815–Apr. 21, 1900.
  Vol. 1, Pt. 2–126
Beecher, Charles Emerson, Oct. 9, 1856–Feb. 14, 1904.
  Vol. 1, Pt. 2–127
Beecher, Edward, Aug. 27, 1803–July 28, 1895.
  Vol. 1, Pt. 2–128
Beecher, Henry Ward, June 24, 1813–Mar. 8, 1887.
  Vol. 1, Pt. 2–129
Beecher, Lyman, Oct. 12, 1775–Jan. 10, 1863.
  Vol. 1, Pt. 2–135
Beecher, Thomas Kinnicut, Feb. 10, 1824–Mar. 14, 1900.
  Vol. 1, Pt. 2–136
Beer, George Louis, July 26, 1872–Mar. 15, 1920.
  Vol. 1, Pt. 2–137
Beer, Thomas, Nov. 22, 1889–Apr. 18, 1940.
  Supp. 2–33
Beer, William, May 1, 1849–Feb. 1, 1927.
  Vol. 1, Pt. 2–138
Beers, Clifford Whittingham, Mar. 30, 1876–July 9, 1943.
  Supp. 3–50
Beers, Ethel Lynn, Jan. 13, 1827–Oct. 11, 1879.
  Vol. 1, Pt. 2–139
Beers, Henry Augustin, Jan. 2, 1847–Sept. 7, 1926.
  Vol. 1, Pt. 2–139
Beery, Wallace Fitzgerald, Apr. 1, 1885–Apr. 15, 1949.
  Supp. 4–66
Beeson, Charles Henry, Oct. 2, 1870–Dec. 26, 1949.
  Supp. 4–67
Begley, Edward James ("Ed"), Mar. 25, 1901–Apr. 28, 1970.
  Supp. 8–31
Behan, William James, Sept. 25, 1840–May 4, 1928.
  Vol. 1, Pt. 2–140
Behn, Sosthenes, Jan. 30, 1882–June 6, 1957.
  Supp. 6–43
Behrend, Bernard Arthur, May 9, 1875–Mar. 25, 1932.
  Supp. 1–65
Behrends, Adolphus Julius Frederick, Dec. 18, 1839–May 22, 1900. Vol. 1, Pt. 2–141
Behrendt, Walter Curt, Dec. 16, 1884–Apr. 26, 1945.
  Supp. 3–52
Behrens, Henry, Dec. 10, 1815–Oct. 17, 1895.
  Vol. 1, Pt. 2–141
Beissel, Johann Conrad, April 1690–July 6, 1768.
  Vol. 1, Pt. 2–142
Belasco, David, July 25, 1853–May 14, 1931.
  Supp. 1–66
Belcher, Jonathan, Jan. 8, 1681/2–Aug. 31, 1757.
  Vol. 1, Pt. 2–143

Belcourt, George Antoine, Apr. 22, 1803–May 31, 1874.
Vol. 1, Pt. 2–145
Belden, Josiah, May 4, 1815–Apr. 23, 1892.
Vol. 1, Pt. 2–145
Belknap, George Eugene, Jan. 22, 1832–Apr. 7, 1903.
Vol. 1, Pt. 2–146
Belknap, Jeremy, June 4, 1744–June 20, 1798.
Vol. 1, Pt. 2–147
Belknap, William Worth, Sept. 22, 1829–Oct. 13, 1890.
Vol. 1, Pt. 2–147
Bell, Alexander Graham, Mar. 3, 1847–Aug. 2, 1922.
Vol. 1, Pt. 2–148
Bell, Alexander Melville, Mar. 1, 1819–Aug. 7, 1905.
Vol. 1, Pt. 2–152
Bell, Bernard Iddings, Oct. 13, 1886–Sept. 5, 1958.
Supp. 6–15
Bell, Charles Henry, Nov. 18, 1823–Nov. 11, 1893.
Vol. 1, Pt. 2–153
Bell, Clark, Mar. 12, 1832–Feb. 22, 1918.
Vol. 1, Pt. 2–153
Bell, De Benneville ("Bert"), Feb. 25, 1894–Oct. 11, 1959.
Supp. 6–47
Bell, Eric Temple, Feb. 7, 1883–Dec. 21, 1960.
Supp. 6–48
Bell, Frederic Somers, Mar. 19, 1859–Mar. 13, 1938.
Supp. 2–34
Bell, Henry Haywood, Apr. 13, 1808–Jan. 11, 1868.
Vol. 1, Pt. 2–154
Bell, Isaac, Nov. 6, 1846–Jan. 20, 1889.
Vol. 1, Pt. 2–155
Bell, Jacob, Dec. 17, 1792–July 21, 1852.
Vol. 1, Pt. 2–155
Bell, James Ford, Aug. 16, 1879–May 7, 1961.
Supp. 7–46
Bell, James Franklin, Jan. 9, 1856–Jan. 8, 1919.
Supp. 1–67
Bell, James Madison, Apr. 3, 1826–1902.
Vol. 1, Pt. 2–156
Bell, James Stroud, June 30, 1847–Apr. 5, 1915.
Vol. 1, Pt. 2–156
Bell, John, Feb. 15, 1797–Sept. 10, 1869.
Vol. 1, Pt. 2–157
Bell, Lawrence Dale, Apr. 5, 1894–Oct. 20, 1956.
Supp. 6–49
Bell, Louis, Dec. 5, 1864–June 14, 1923.
Vol. 1, Pt. 2–159
Bell, Luther Vose, Dec. 20, 1806–Feb. 11, 1862.
Vol. 1, Pt. 2–160
Bell, Peter Hansborough, Mar. 11, 1808–Mar. 8, 1898.
Vol. 1, Pt. 2–160
Bell, Robert, c. 1732–Sept. 23, 1784.
Vol. 1, Pt. 2–161
Bell, Samuel, Feb. 8, 1770–Dec. 23, 1850.
Vol. 1, Pt. 2–162
Bellamy, Edward, Mar. 26, 1850–May 22, 1898.
Vol. 1, Pt. 2–163
Bellamy, Elizabeth Whitfield Croom, Apr. 17, 1837–Apr. 13, 1900. Vol. 1, Pt. 2–164
Bellamy, Joseph, Feb. 20, 1719–Mar. 6, 1790.
Vol. 1, Pt. 2–165
Bellanca, Dorothy Jacobs, Aug. 10, 1894–Aug. 16, 1946.
Supp. 4–69
Bellanca, Giuseppe Mario, Mar. 19, 1886–Dec. 26, 1960.
Supp. 6–51
Bellew, Frank Henry Temple, Apr. 18, 1828–June 29, 1888.
Vol. 1, Pt. 2–165
Bellingham, Richard, c. 1592–Dec. 7, 1672.
Vol. 1, Pt. 2–166
Bellomont, Earl of. [See Coote, Richard, 1636–1701.]
Bellows, Albert Fitch, Nov. 29, 1829–Nov. 24, 1883.
Vol. 1, Pt. 2–167
Bellows, George Wesley, Aug. 12, 1882–Jan. 8, 1925.
Vol. 1, Pt. 2–167
Bellows, Henry Whitney, June 11, 1814–Jan. 30, 1882.
Vol. 1, Pt. 2–169
Belmont, Alva Ertskin Smith Vanderbilt, Jan. 17, 1853–Jan. 26, 1933. Supp. 1–68
Belmont, August, Dec. 2, 1816–Nov. 24, 1890.
Vol. 1, Pt. 2–169
Belo, Alfred Horatio, May 27, 1839–Apr. 19, 1901.
Vol. 1, Pt. 2–170
Beman, Nathan Sidney Smith, Nov. 26, 1785–Aug. 6, 1871.
Vol. 1, Pt. 2–171

Bemelmans, Ludwig, Apr. 27, 1898–Oct. 1, 1962.
Supp. 7–47
Bement, Caleb N., 1790–Dec. 22, 1868.
Vol. 1, Pt. 2–172
Bement, Clarence Sweet, Apr. 11, 1843–Jan. 27, 1923.
Vol. 1, Pt. 2–173
Bemis, George, Oct. 13, 1816–Jan. 5, 1878.
Vol. 1, Pt. 2–173
Bemis, Harold Edward, June 3, 1883–Apr. 4, 1931.
Supp. 1–69
Benavides, Alonzo de, fl. 1600–1664.
Vol. 1, Pt. 2–174
Benbridge, Henry, May 20, 1774–February 1812.
Vol. 1, Pt. 2–175
Benchley, Robert Charles, Sept. 15, 1889–Nov. 21, 1945.
Supp. 3–53
Bender, Charles Albert ("Chief"), May 5, 1883–May 22, 1954. Supp. 5–47
Bender, George Harrison, Sept. 29, 1896–June 17 or 18, 1961. Supp. 7–49
Bendix, Vincent, Aug. 12, 1881–Mar. 27, 1945.
Supp. 3–54
Benedict, David, Oct. 10, 1779–Dec. 5, 1874.
Vol. 1, Pt. 2–176
Benedict, Erastus Cornelius, Mar. 19, 1800–Oct. 22, 1880.
Vol. 1, Pt. 2–176
Benedict, Ruth Fulton, June 5, 1887–Sept. 17, 1948.
Supp. 4–70
Benedict, Stanley Rossiter, Mar. 17, 1884–Dec. 21, 1936.
Supp. 2–35
Benét, Stephen Vincent, July 22, 1898–Mar. 13, 1943.
Supp. 3–56
Benét, William Rose, Feb. 2, 1886–May 4, 1950.
Supp. 4–73
Benezet, Anthony, Jan. 31, 1713–May 3, 1784.
Vol. 1, Pt. 2–177
Benham, Henry Washington, Apr. 8, 1813–June 1, 1884.
Vol. 1, Pt. 2–178
Benjamin, Asher, June 15, 1773–July 26, 1845.
Vol. 1, Pt. 2–179
Benjamin, George Hillard, Dec. 25, 1852–Nov. 10, 1927.
Vol. 1, Pt. 2–180
Benjamin, Judah Philip, Aug. 6, 1811–May 6, 1884.
Vol. 1, Pt. 2–181
Benjamin, Nathan, Dec. 14, 1811–Jan. 27, 1855.
Vol. 1, Pt. 2–186
Benjamin, Park, Aug. 14, 1809–Sept. 12, 1864.
Vol. 1, Pt. 2–187
Benjamin, Park, May 11, 1849–Aug. 21, 1922.
Vol. 1, Pt. 2–188
Benjamin, Samuel Greene Wheeler, Feb. 13, 1837–July 19, 1914. Vol. 1, Pt. 2–189
Benner, Philip, May 19, 1762–July 27, 1832.
Vol. 1, Pt. 2–189
Bennet, Sanford Fillmore, June 21, 1836–June 11, 1898.
Vol. 1, Pt. 2–190
Bennett, Caleb Prew, Nov. 11, 1758–May 9, 1836.
Vol. 1, Pt. 2–190
Bennett, Charles Edwin, Apr. 6, 1858–May 2, 1921.
Vol. 1, Pt. 2–191
Bennett, Constance Campbell, Oct. 22, 1904–July 25, 1965.
Supp. 7–50
Bennett, de Robigne Mortimer, Dec. 23, 1818–Dec. 6, 1882.
Vol. 1, Pt. 2–192
Bennett, Edmund Hatch, Apr. 6, 1824–Jan. 2, 1898.
Vol. 1, Pt. 2–193
Bennett, Emerson, Mar. 16, 1822–May 11, 1905.
Vol. 1, Pt. 2–193
Bennett, Floyd, Oct. 25, 1890–Apr. 25, 1928.
Vol. 1, Pt. 2–194
Bennett, Henry Garland, Dec. 14, 1886–Dec. 22, 1951.
Supp. 5–48
Bennett, Hugh Hammond, Apr. 15, 1881–July 7, 1960.
Supp. 6–52
Bennett, James Gordon, 1795–June 1, 1872.
Vol. 1, Pt. 2–195
Bennett, James Gordon, May 10, 1841–May 14, 1918.
Vol. 1, Pt. 2–199
Bennett, Nathaniel, June 27, 1818–Apr. 20, 1886.
Vol. 1, Pt. 2–202
Bennett, Richard, May 21, 1870–Oct. 22, 1944.
Supp. 3–58

Benning, Henry Lewis, Apr. 2, 1814–July 10, 1875.
    Vol. 1, Pt. 2–202
Bensley, Robert Russell, Nov. 13, 1867–June 11, 1956.
    Supp. 6–53
Benson, Egbert, June 21, 1746–Aug. 24, 1833.
    Vol. 1, Pt. 2–204
Benson, Eugene, Nov. 1, 1839–Feb. 28, 1908.
    Vol. 1, Pt. 2–204
Benson, Frank Weston, Mar. 24, 1862–Nov. 14, 1951.
    Supp. 5–49
Benson, Oscar Herman, July 8, 1875–Aug. 15, 1951.
    Supp. 5–50
Benson, William Shepherd, Sept. 25, 1855–May 20, 1932.
    Supp. 1–70
Bent, Charles, Nov. 11, 1799–Jan. 19, 1847.
    Vol. 1, Pt. 2–205
Bent, Josiah, Apr. 26, 1771–Apr. 26, 1836.
    Vol. 1, Pt. 2–205
Bent, Silas, Oct. 10, 1820–Aug. 26, 1887.
    Vol. 1, Pt. 2–206
Bent, Silas, May 9, 1882–July 30, 1945.
    Supp. 3–59
Bent, William, May 23, 1809–May 19, 1869.
    Vol. 1, Pt. 2–206
Bentley, Arthur Fisher, Oct. 16, 1870–May 21, 1957.
    Supp. 6–54
Bentley, Elizabeth Terrill, Jan. 1, 1908–Dec. 3, 1963.
    Supp. 7–51
Bentley, William, June 22, 1759–Dec. 29, 1819.
    Vol. 1, Pt. 2–207
Bentley, Wilson Alwyn, Feb. 9, 1865–Dec. 23, 1931.
    Supp. 1–71
Benton, Allen Richardson, Oct. 1, 1822–Jan. 1, 1914.
    Vol. 1, Pt. 2–208
Benton, James Gilchrist, Sept. 15, 1820–Aug. 23, 1881.
    Vol. 1, Pt. 2–208
Benton, Joel, May 29, 1832–Sept. 15, 1911.
    Vol. 1, Pt. 2–209
Benton, Josiah Henry, Aug. 4, 1843–Feb. 6, 1917.
    Vol. 1, Pt. 2–210
Benton, Thomas Hart, Mar. 14, 1782–Apr. 10, 1858.
    Vol. 1, Pt. 2–210
Benton, Thomas Hart, Sept. 5, 1816–Apr. 10, 1879.
    Vol. 1, Pt. 2–213
Berenson, Bernard, June 26, 1865–Oct. 6, 1959.
    Supp. 6–55
Berenson, Senda, Mar. 19, 1868–Feb. 16, 1954.
    Supp. 5–51
Berg, Gertrude Edelstein, Oct. 3, 1899–Sept. 14, 1966.
    Supp. 8–32
Berg, Joseph Frederic, June 3, 1812–July 20, 1871.
    Vol. 1, Pt. 2–213
Berger, Daniel, Feb. 14, 1832–Sept. 12, 1920.
    Vol. 1, Pt. 2–214
Berger, Meyer, Sept. 1, 1898–Feb. 8, 1959.
    Supp. 6–57
Berger, Victor Louis, Feb. 28, 1860–Aug. 7, 1929.
    Supp. 1–72
Bergh, Christian, Apr. 30, 1763–June 24, 1843.
    Vol. 1, Pt. 2–214
Bergh, Henry, Aug. 29, 1811–Mar. 12, 1888.
    Vol. 1, Pt. 2–215
Bergmann, Carl, Apr. 11, 1821–Aug. 10, 1876.
    Vol. 1, Pt. 2–216
Bergmann, Max, Feb. 12, 1886–Nov. 7, 1944.
    Supp. 3–60
Berkeley, John, d. Mar. 22, 1622.
    Vol. 1, Pt. 2–217
Berkeley, Norborne. [See Botetourt, Norborne Berkeley, Baron de, c. 1718–1770.]
Berkeley, Sir William, 1606–July 9, 1677.
    Vol. 1, Pt. 2–217
Berkenmeyer, Wilhelm Christoph, 1686–1751.
    Vol. 1, Pt. 2–218
Berkman, Alexander, Nov. 21, 1870–June 28, 1936.
    Supp. 2–36
Berkowitz, Henry, Mar. 18, 1857–Feb. 7, 1924.
    Vol. 1, Pt. 2–219
Berliner, Emile, May 20, 1851–Aug. 3, 1929.
    Supp. 1–75
Bermudez, Edouard Edmond, Jan. 19, 1832–Aug. 22, 1892.
    Vol. 1, Pt. 2–220

Bernard, Bayle. [See Bernard, William Bayle, 1807–1875.]
Bernard, Sir Francis, July ?, 1712–June 16, 1779.
    Vol. 1, Pt. 2–221
Bernard, John, 1756–Nov. 29, 1828.
    Vol. 1, Pt. 2–222
Bernard, Simon, Apr. 22, 1779–Nov. 5, 1839.
    Vol. 1, Pt. 2–223
Bernard, William Bayle, Nov. 27, 1807–Aug. 5, 1875.
    Vol. 1, Pt. 2–223
Bernays, Augustus Charles, Oct. 13, 1854–May 22, 1907.
    Vol. 1, Pt. 2–224
Bernet, John Joseph, Feb. 9, 1868–July 5, 1935.
    Supp. 1–76
Bernstein, Aline, Dec. 22, 1882–Sept. 7, 1955.
    Supp. 5–52
Bernstein, Herman, Sept. 21, 1876–Aug. 31, 1935.
    Supp. 1–77
Berrien, John Macpherson, Aug. 23, 1781–Jan. 1, 1856.
    Vol. 1, Pt. 2–225
Berry, Edward Wilber, Feb. 10, 1875–Sept. 20, 1945.
    Supp. 3–61
Berry, George Leonard, Sept. 12, 1882–Dec. 4, 1948.
    Supp. 4–74
Berry, Hiram Gregory, Aug. 27, 1824–May 3, 1863.
    Vol. 1, Pt. 2–226
Berry, James Henderson, May 15, 1841–Jan. 30, 1913.
    Vol. 1, Pt. 2–226
Berry, Martha McChesney, Oct. 7, 1866–Feb. 27, 1942.
    Supp. 3–62
Berry, Nathaniel Springer, Sept. 1, 1796–Apr. 27, 1894.
    Vol. 1, Pt. 2–227
Berryman, Clifford Kennedy, Apr. 2, 1869–Dec. 11, 1949.
    Supp. 4–75
Bertram, John, Feb. 11, 1796–Mar. 22, 1882.
    Vol. 1, Pt. 2–228
Berwind, Edward Julius, June 17, 1848–Aug. 18, 1936.
    Supp. 2–37
Besse, Arthur Lyman, Apr. 13, 1887–Nov. 24, 1951.
    Supp. 5–54
Bessey, Charles Edwin, May 21, 1845–Feb. 25, 1915.
    Vol. 1, Pt. 2–229
Bestor, Arthur Eugene, May 19, 1879–Feb. 3, 1944.
    Supp. 3–64
Bethune, George Washington, Mar. 18, 1805–Apr. 28, 1862.
    Vol. 1, Pt. 2–229
Bethune, Mary McLeod, July 10, 1875–May 18, 1955.
    Supp. 5–55
Bettendorf, William Peter, July 1, 1857–June 3, 1910.
    Vol. 1, Pt. 2–230
Bettman, Alfred, Aug. 26, 1873–Jan. 21, 1945.
    Supp. 3–65
Betts, Samuel Rossiter, June 8, 1786–Nov. 3, 1868.
    Vol. 1, Pt. 2–231
Bevan, Arthur Dean, Aug. 9, 1861–June 10, 1943.
    Supp. 3–67
Beveridge, Albert Jeremiah, Oct. 6, 1862–Apr. 27, 1927.
    Vol. 1, Pt. 2–231
Beverley, Robert, c. 1673–1722.
    Vol. 1, Pt. 2–233
Bevier, Isabel, Nov. 14, 1860–Mar. 17, 1942.
    Supp. 3–67
Bewley, Anthony, May 22, 1804–Sept. 13, 1860.
    Vol. 1, Pt. 2–233
Biard, Pierre, c. 1567–Nov. 17, 1622.
    Vol. 1, Pt. 2–234
Bibb, George Mortimer, Oct. 30, 1776–Apr. 14, 1859.
    Vol. 1, Pt. 2–235
Bibb, William Wyatt, Oct. 2, 1781–July 10, 1820.
    Vol. 1, Pt. 2–235
Bickel, Luke Washington, Sept. 21, 1866–May 11, 1917.
    Vol. 1, Pt. 2–236
Bickerdyke, Mary Ann Ball, July 19, 1817–Nov. 8, 1901.
    Vol. 1, Pt. 2–237
Bickett, Thomas Walter, Feb. 28, 1869–Dec. 28, 1921.
    Vol. 1, Pt. 2–238
Bickmore, Albert Smith, Mar. 1, 1839–Aug. 12, 1914.
    Vol. 1, Pt. 2–238
Bidaga. [See Son of Many Beads, 1866–1954.]
Biddle, Anthony Joseph Drexel, Jr., Dec. 17, 1896–Nov. 13, 1961. Supp. 7–52
Biddle, Clement, May 10, 1740–July 14, 1814.
    Vol. 1, Pt. 2–239

Biddle, Francis Beverley, May 9, 1886–Oct. 4, 1968.
Supp. 8–34
Biddle, Horace P., Mar. 24, 1811–May 13, 1900.
Vol. 1, Pt. 2–240
Biddle, James, Feb. 18, 1783–Oct. 1, 1848.
Vol. 1, Pt. 2–240
Biddle, Nicholas, Sept. 10, 1750–Mar. 7, 1778.
Vol. 1, Pt. 2–241
Biddle, Nicholas, Jan. 8, 1786–Feb. 27, 1844.
Vol. 1, Pt. 2–243
Bidlack, Benjamin Alden, Sept. 8, 1804–Feb. 6, 1849.
Vol. 1, Pt. 2–245
Bidwell, Barnabas, Aug. 23, 1763–July 27, 1833.
Vol. 1, Pt. 2–246
Bidwell, John, Aug. 5, 1819–Apr. 4, 1900.
Vol. 1, Pt. 2–247
Bidwell, Marshall Spring, Feb. 16, 1799–Oct. 24, 1872.
Vol. 1, Pt. 2–248
Bidwell, Walter Hilliard, June 21, 1798–Sept. 11, 1881.
Vol. 1, Pt. 2–249
Bien, Julius, Sept. 27, 1826–Dec. 21, 1909.
Vol. 1, Pt. 2–249
Bienville, Jean Baptiste Le Moyne, Sieur de, Feb. 23, 1680–
Mar. 7, 1768. Vol. 1, Pt. 2–250
Bierce, Ambrose Gwinett, June 24, 1842–1914?.
Vol. 1, Pt. 2–252
Bierstadt, Albert, Jan. 7, 1830–Feb. 18, 1902.
Vol. 1, Pt. 2–253
Biffle, Leslie L, Oct. 9, 1889–Apr. 6, 1966.
Supp. 8–35
Bigelow, Erastus Brigham, Apr. 2, 1814–Dec. 6, 1879.
Vol. 1, Pt. 2–254
Bigelow, Frank Hagar, Aug. 28, 1851–Mar. 2, 1924.
Vol. 1, Pt. 2–255
Bigelow, Harry Augustus, Sept. 22, 1874–Jan. 8, 1950.
Supp. 4–77
Bigelow, Henry Bryant, Oct. 3, 1879–Dec. 11, 1967.
Supp. 8–37
Bigelow, Henry Jacob, Mar. 11, 1818–Oct. 30, 1890.
Vol. 1, Pt. 2–256
Bigelow, Jacob, Feb. 27, 1786–Jan. 10, 1879.
Vol. 1, Pt. 2–257
Bigelow, John, Nov. 25, 1817–Dec. 19, 1911.
Vol. 1, Pt. 2–258
Bigelow, Melville Madison, Aug. 2, 1846–May 4, 1921.
Vol. 1, Pt. 2–260
Bigelow, William Sturgis, Apr. 4, 1850–Oct. 6, 1926.
Vol. 1, Pt. 2–261
Biggers, Earl Derr, Aug. 26, 1884–Apr. 5, 1933.
Supp. 1–79
Biggs, Asa, Feb. 4, 1811–Mar. 6, 1878.
Vol. 1, Pt. 2–262
Biggs, Hermann Michael, Sept. 29, 1859–June 28, 1923.
Vol. 1, Pt. 2–262
Bigler, John, Jan. 8, 1805–Nov. 29, 1871.
Vol. 1, Pt. 2–263
Bigler, William, Jan. 1, 1814–Aug. 9, 1880.
Vol. 1, Pt. 2–264
Bilbo, Theodore Gilmore, Oct. 13, 1877–Aug. 21, 1947.
Supp. 4–78
Billikopf, Jacob, June 1, 1883–Dec. 31, 1950.
Supp. 4–79
Billings, Asa White Kenney, Feb. 8, 1876–Nov. 3, 1949.
Supp. 4–80
Billings, Charles Ethan, Dec. 5, 1835–June 5, 1920.
Vol. 1, Pt. 2–264
Billings, Frank, Apr. 2, 1854–Sept. 20, 1932.
Supp. 1–80
Billings, Frederick, Sept. 27, 1823–Sept. 30, 1890.
Vol. 1, Pt. 2–265
Billings, John Shaw, Apr. 12, 1838–Mar. 11, 1913.
Vol. 1, Pt. 2–266
Billings, Josh. [See Shaw, Henry Wheeler, 1818–1885.]
Billings, William, Oct. 7, 1746–Sept. 26, 1800.
Vol. 1, Pt. 2–269
Billingsley, John Sherman, Mar. 10, 1900–Oct. 4, 1966.
Supp. 8–38
Billy the Kid, Nov. 23, 1859–July 15, 1881.
Vol. 1, Pt. 2–271
Bimeler, Joseph Michael, c. 1778–Aug. 27, 1853.
Vol. 1, Pt. 2–271
Binford, Jessie Florence, Jan. 20, 1876–July 9, 1966.
Supp. 8–39

Binga, Jesse, Apr. 10, 1865–June 13, 1950.
Supp. 4–82
Bingay, Malcolm Wallace, Dec. 16, 1884–Aug. 21, 1953.
Supp. 5–57
Bingham, Amelia, Mar. 20, 1869–Sept. 1, 1927.
Vol. 1, Pt. 2–272
Bingham, Anne Willing, Aug. 1, 1764–May 11, 1801.
Vol. 1, Pt. 2–273
Bingham, Caleb, Apr. 15, 1757–Apr. 6, 1817.
Vol. 1, Pt. 2–273
Bingham, George Caleb, Mar. 20, 1811–July 7, 1879.
Vol. 1, Pt. 2–274
Bingham, Harry, Mar. 30, 1821–Sept. 12, 1900.
Vol. 1, Pt. 2–275
Bingham, Hiram, Oct. 30, 1789–Nov. 11, 1869.
Vol. 1, Pt. 2–276
Bingham, Hiram, Aug. 16, 1831–Oct. 25, 1908.
Vol. 1, Pt. 2–276
Bingham, Hiram, Nov. 19, 1875–June 6, 1956.
Supp. 6–58
Bingham, John Armor, Jan. 21, 1815–Mar. 19, 1900.
Vol. 1, Pt. 2–277
Bingham, Robert Worth, Nov. 8, 1871–Dec. 18, 1937.
Supp. 2–38
Bingham, Walter Van Dyke, Oct. 20, 1880–July 7, 1952.
Supp. 5–58
Bingham, William, Apr. 8, 1752–Feb. 6, 1804.
Vol. 1, Pt. 2–278
Bingham, William, July 7, 1835–Feb. 18, 1873.
Vol. 1, Pt. 2–279
Binkley, Robert Cedric, Dec. 10, 1897–Apr. 11, 1940.
Supp. 2–40
Binkley, Wilfred Ellsworth, July 29, 1883–Dec. 8, 1965.
Supp. 7–53
Binney, Amos, Oct. 18, 1803–Feb. 18, 1847.
Vol. 1, Pt. 2–279
Binney, Horace, Jan. 4, 1780–Aug. 12, 1875.
Vol. 1, Pt. 2–280
Binns, John, Dec. 22, 1772–June 16, 1860.
Vol. 1, Pt. 2–282
Binns, John Alexander, c. 1761–1813.
Vol. 1, Pt. 2–283
Birch, Reginald Bathurst, May 2, 1856–June 17, 1943.
Supp. 3–69
Birch, Thomas, July 26, 1779–Jan. 14, 1851.
Vol. 1, Pt. 2–283
Birch, William Russell, Apr. 9, 1755–Aug. 7, 1834.
Vol. 1, Pt. 2–284
Birchall, Frederick Thomas, 1868–Mar. 7, 1955.
Supp. 5–60
Bird, Arthur, July 23, 1856–Dec. 22, 1923.
Vol. 1, Pt. 2–285
Bird, Frederic Mayer, June 28, 1838–Apr. 2, 1908.
Vol. 1, Pt. 2–285
Bird, Robert Montgomery, Feb. 5, 1806–Jan. 23, 1854.
Vol. 1, Pt. 2–286
Birdseye, Clarence, Dec. 9, 1886–Oct. 7, 1956.
Supp. 6–60
Bird Woman. [See Sacagawea, c. 1787–1812.]
Birge, Edward Asahel, Sept. 7, 1851–June 9, 1950.
Supp. 4–84
Birge, Henry Warner, Aug. 25, 1825–June 1, 1888.
Vol. 1, Pt. 2–288
Birkbeck, Morris, Jan. 23, 1764–June 4, 1825.
Vol. 1, Pt. 2–289
Birkhoff, George David, Mar. 21, 1884–Nov. 12, 1944.
Supp. 3–70
Birney, David Bell, May 29, 1825–Oct. 18, 1864.
Vol. 1, Pt. 2–290
Birney, James, June 7, 1817–May 8, 1888.
Vol. 1, Pt. 2–291
Birney, James Gillespie, Feb. 4, 1792–Nov. 25, 1857.
Vol. 1, Pt. 2–291
Birney, William, May 28, 1819–Aug. 14, 1907.
Vol. 1, Pt. 2–294
Bishop, Abraham, Feb. 5, 1763–Apr. 28, 1844.
Vol. 1, Pt. 2–294
Bishop, Charles Reed, Jan. 25, 1822–June 7, 1915.
Supp. 1–82
Bishop, Joel Prentiss, Mar. 10, 1814–Nov. 4, 1901.
Vol. 1, Pt. 2–295
Bishop, John Peale, May 21, 1892–Apr. 4, 1944.
Supp. 3–71

Bishop, Nathan, Aug. 12, 1808–Aug. 7, 1880.
    Vol. 1, Pt. 2–296
Bishop, Robert Hamilton, July 26, 1777–Apr. 29, 1855.
    Supp. 1–83
Bishop, Robert Roberts, Mar. 30, 1834–Oct. 7, 1909.
    Vol. 1, Pt. 2–297
Bishop, Seth Scott, Feb. 7, 1852–Sept. 6, 1923.
    Vol. 1, Pt. 2–298
Bishop, William Darius, Sept. 14, 1827–Feb. 4, 1904.
    Vol. 1, Pt. 2–298
Bispham, David Scull, Jan. 5, 1857–Oct. 2, 1921.
    Vol. 1, Pt. 2–299
Bissell, Edwin Cone, Mar. 2, 1832–Apr. 10, 1894.
    Vol. 1, Pt. 2–300
Bissell, George Edwin, Feb. 16, 1839–Aug. 30, 1920.
    Vol. 1, Pt. 2–300
Bissell, George Henry, Nov. 8, 1821–Nov. 19, 1884.
    Vol. 1, Pt. 2–301
Bissell, William Henry, Apr. 25, 1811–Mar. 18, 1860.
    Vol. 1, Pt. 2–302
Bissell, Wilson Shannon, Dec. 31, 1847–Oct 6, 1903.
    Vol. 1, Pt. 2–302
Bitter, Karl Theodore Francis, Dec. 6, 1867–Apr. 10, 1915.
    Vol. 1, Pt. 2–303
Bitzer, George William, Apr. 21, 1872–Apr. 29, 1944.
    Supp. 3–73
Bixby, Horace Ezra, May 8, 1826–Aug. 1, 1912.
    Vol. 1, Pt. 2–305
Bixby, James Thompson, July 30, 1843–Dec. 26, 1921.
    Vol. 1, Pt. 2–306
Bjerregaard, Carl Henrik Andreas, May 24, 1845–Jan. 28,
    1922. Vol. 1, Pt. 2–307
Black, Eugene Robert, Jan. 7, 1873–Dec. 19, 1934.
    Supp. 1–84
Black, Frank Sweet, Mar. 8, 1853–Mar. 22, 1913.
    Vol. 1, Pt. 2–308
Black, Greene Vardiman, Aug. 3, 1836–Aug. 31, 1915.
    Vol. 1, Pt. 2–308
Black, James, Sept. 23, 1823–Dec. 16, 1893.
    Vol. 1, Pt. 2–310
Black, Jeremiah Sullivan, Jan. 10, 1810–Aug. 19, 1883.
    Vol. 1, Pt. 2–310
Black, John Charles, Jan. 27, 1839–Aug. 17, 1915.
    Vol. 1, Pt. 2–313
Black, William Murray, Dec. 8, 1855–Sept. 24, 1933.
    Supp. 1–85
Blackburn, Gideon, Aug. 27, 1772–Aug. 23, 1838.
    Vol. 1, Pt. 2–314
Blackburn, Joseph, fl. 1753–63.
    Vol. 1, Pt. 2–315
Blackburn, Joseph Clay Styles, Oct. 1, 1838–Sept. 12, 1918.
    Vol. 1, Pt. 2–316
Blackburn, Luke Pryor, June 16, 1816–Sept. 14, 1887.
    Vol. 1, Pt. 2–317
Blackburn, William Maxwell, Dec. 30, 1828–Dec. 29, 1898.
    Vol. 1, Pt. 2–317
Blackfan, Kenneth Daniel, Sept. 9, 1883–Nov. 29, 1941.
    Supp. 3–74
Blackford, Charles Minor, Oct. 17, 1833–Mar. 10, 1903.
    Vol. 1, Pt. 2–318
Black Hawk, 1767–Oct. 3, 1838.
    Vol. 1, Pt. 2–313
Blackmur, Richard Palmer, Jan. 21, 1904–Feb. 2, 1965.
    Supp. 7–54
Blackstone, Harry, Sept. 27, 1885–Nov. 16, 1965.
    Supp. 7–56
Blackstone, William, 1595–May 26? o.s., 1675.
    Vol. 1, Pt. 2–319
Blackton, James Stuart, Jan. 5, 1875–Aug. 13, 1941.
    Supp. 3–75
Blackwell, Alice Stone, Sept. 14, 1857–Mar. 15, 1950.
    Supp. 4–85
Blackwell, Antoinette Louisa Brown, May 20, 1825–Nov. 5,
    1921. Vol. 1, Pt. 2–319
Blackwell, Elizabeth, Feb. 3, 1821–May 31, 1910.
    Vol. 1, Pt. 2–320
Blackwell, Henry Brown, May 4, 1825–Sept. 7, 1909.
    Vol. 1, Pt. 2–321
Blackwell, Lucy Stone. [See Stone, Lucy, 1818–1893.]
Bladen, William, Feb. 27, 1673–August 1718.
    Vol. 1, Pt. 2–321
Blaikie, William, May 24, 1843–Dec. 6, 1904.
    Vol. 1, Pt. 2–322

Blaine, Anita (Eugenie) McCormick, July 4, 1866–Feb. 12,
    1954. Supp. 5–60
Blaine, James Gillespie, Jan. 31, 1830–Jan. 27, 1893.
    Vol. 1, Pt. 2–322
Blaine, John James, May 4, 1875–Apr. 16, 1934.
    Supp. 1–86
Blair, Austin, Feb. 8, 1818–Aug. 6, 1894.
    Vol. 1, Pt. 2–329
Blair, Emily Newell, Jan. 9, 1877–Aug. 3, 1951.
    Supp. 5–61
Blair, Francis Preston, Apr. 12, 1791–Oct. 18, 1876.
    Vol. 1, Pt. 2–330
Blair, Francis Preston, Feb. 19, 1821–July 9, 1875.
    Vol. 1, Pt. 2–332
Blair, Henry William, Dec. 6, 1834–Mar. 14, 1920.
    Vol. 1, Pt. 2–334
Blair, James, 1655–Apr. 18, 1743.
    Vol. 1, Pt. 2–335
Blair, John, 1687–1771.
    Vol. 1, Pt. 2–337
Blair, John, 1732–Aug. 31, 1800.
    Vol. 1, Pt. 2–337
Blair, John Insley, Aug. 22, 1802–Dec. 2, 1899.
    Vol. 1, Pt. 2–338
Blair, Montgomery, May 10, 1813–July 27, 1883.
    Vol. 1, Pt. 2–339
Blair, Samuel, June 14, 1712–July 5, 1751.
    Vol. 1, Pt. 2–340
Blair, William Richards, Nov. 7, 1874–Sept. 2, 1962.
    Supp. 7–58
Blake, Eli Whitney, Jan. 27, 1795–Aug. 18, 1886.
    Vol. 1, Pt. 2–341
Blake, Francis, Dec. 25, 1850–Jan. 19, 1913.
    Vol. 1, Pt. 2–342
Blake, Francis Gilman, Feb. 22, 1887–Feb. 1, 1952.
    Supp. 5–63
Blake, Homer Crane, Feb. 1, 1822–Jan. 21, 1880.
    Vol. 1, Pt. 2–342
Blake, John Lauris, Dec. 21, 1788–July 6, 1857.
    Vol. 1, Pt. 2–343
Blake, Lillie Devereux, Aug. 12, 1835–Dec. 30, 1913.
    Vol. 1, Pt. 2–343
Blake, Lyman Reed, Aug. 24, 1835–Oct. 5, 1883.
    Vol. 1, Pt. 2–344
Blake, Mary Elizabeth McGrath, Sept. 1, 1840–Feb. 26, 1907.
    Vol. 1, Pt. 2–345
Blake, William Phipps, June 21, 1825–May 22, 1910.
    Vol. 1, Pt. 2–345
Blake, William Rufus, 1805–Apr. 22, 1863.
    Vol. 1, Pt. 2–346
Blakeley, George Henry, Apr. 19, 1865–Dec. 25, 1942.
    Supp. 3–77
Blakelock, Ralph Albert, Oct. 15, 1847–Aug. 9, 1919.
    Vol. 1, Pt. 2–347
Blakely, Johnston, October 1781–October 1814.
    Vol. 1, Pt. 2–348
Blakeslee, Erastus, Sept. 2, 1838–July 12, 1908.
    Vol. 1, Pt. 2–348
Blakeslee, Howard Walter, Mar. 21, 1880–May 2, 1952.
    Supp. 5–64
Blalock, Alfred, Apr. 5, 1899–Sept. 15, 1964.
    Supp. 7–59
Blalock, Nelson Gales, Feb. 17, 1836–Mar. 14, 1913.
    Vol. 1, Pt. 2–349
Blanc, Antoine, Oct. 11, 1792–June 20, 1860.
    Vol. 1, Pt. 2–350
Blanchard, Jonathan, Jan. 19, 1811–May 14, 1892.
    Vol. 1, Pt. 2–350
Blanchard, Newton Crain, Jan. 29, 1849–June 22, 1922.
    Vol. 1, Pt. 2–351
Blanchard, Thomas, June 24, 1788–Apr. 16, 1864.
    Vol. 1, Pt. 2–351
Blanchet, Francois Norbert, Sept. 3, 1795–June 18, 1883.
    Vol. 1, Pt. 2–352
Bland, Richard, May 6, 1710–Oct. 26, 1776.
    Vol. 1, Pt. 2–354
Bland, Richard Parks, Aug. 19, 1835–June 15, 1899.
    Vol. 1, Pt. 2–355
Bland, Theodorick, Mar. 21, 1742–June 1, 1790.
    Vol. 1, Pt. 2–356
Bland, Thomas, Oct. 4, 1809–Aug. 20, 1885.
    Vol. 1, Pt. 2–357

Blandy, William Henry Purnell, June 28, 1890–Jan. 12, 1954.
   Supp. 5–65
Blankenburg, Rudolph, Feb. 16, 1843–Apr. 12, 1918.
   Vol. 1, Pt. 2–357
Blasdel, Henry Goode, Jan. 20, 1825–July 26, 1900.
   Vol. 1, Pt. 2–358
Blashfield, Edwin Howland, Dec. 15, 1848–Oct. 12, 1936.
   Supp. 2–41
Blatch, Harriot Eaton Stanton, Jan. 20, 1856–Nov. 20, 1940.
   Supp. 2–43
Blatchford, Richard Milford, Apr. 23, 1798–Sept. 4, 1875.
   Vol. 1, Pt. 2–359
Blatchford, Samuel, Mar. 9, 1820–July 7, 1893.
   Vol. 1, Pt. 2–359
Blaustein, David, May 5, 1866–Aug. 26, 1912.
   Vol. 1, Pt. 2–360
Blavatsky, Helena Petrovna Hahn, July 30, 1831–May 8, 1891.
   Vol. 1, Pt. 2–361
Blease, Coleman Livingston, Oct. 8, 1868–Jan. 19, 1942.
   Supp. 3–77
Bleckley, Logan Edwin, July 3, 1827–Mar. 6, 1907.
   Vol. 1, Pt. 2–363
Bledsoe, Albert Taylor, Nov. 9, 1809–Dec. 8, 1877.
   Vol. 1, Pt. 2–364
Bleecker, Ann Eliza, October 1752–Nov. 23, 1783.
   Vol. 1, Pt. 2–365
Blenk, James Hubert, July 28, 1856–Apr. 20, 1917.
   Vol. 1, Pt. 2–366
Blennerhassett, Harman, Oct. 8, 1765–Feb. 2, 1831.
   Vol. 1, Pt. 2–367
Bleyer, Willard Grosvenor, Aug. 27, 1873–Oct. 31, 1935.
   Supp. 1–87
Blichfeldt, Hans Frederik, Jan. 9, 1873–Nov. 16, 1945.
   Supp. 3–79
Blinn, Holbrook, Jan. 23, 1872–June 24, 1928.
   Vol. 1, Pt. 2–368
Bliss, Aaron Thomas, May 22, 1837–Sept. 16, 1906.
   Vol. 1, Pt. 2–368
Bliss, Cornelius Newton, Jan. 26, 1833–Oct. 9, 1911.
   Vol. 1, Pt. 2–369
Bliss, Cornelius Newton, Apr. 13, 1874–Apr. 5, 1949.
   Supp. 4–87
Bliss, Daniel, Aug. 17, 1823–July 27, 1916.
   Vol. 1, Pt. 2–369
Bliss, Edwin Elisha, Apr. 12, 1817–Dec. 20, 1892.
   Vol. 1, Pt. 2–370
Bliss, Edwin Munsell, Sept. 12, 1848–Aug. 6, 1919.
   Vol. 1, Pt. 2–371
Bliss, Eliphalet Williams, Apr. 12, 1836–July 21, 1903.
   Vol. 1, Pt. 2–371
Bliss, Frederick Jones, Jan. 22, 1859–June 3, 1937.
   Supp. 2–44
Bliss, George, Apr. 21, 1816–Feb. 2, 1896.
   Vol. 1, Pt. 2–372
Bliss, George, May 3, 1830–Sept. 2, 1897.
   Vol. 1, Pt. 2–373
Bliss, Gilbert Ames, May 9, 1876–May 8, 1951.
   Supp. 5–67
Bliss, Howard Sweetser, Dec. 6, 1860–May 2, 1920.
   Vol. 1, Pt. 2–374
Bliss, Jonathan, Oct. 1, 1742–Oct. 1, 1822.
   Vol. 1, Pt. 2–374
Bliss, Philemon, July 28, 1813–Aug. 24, 1889.
   Vol. 1, Pt. 2–375
Bliss, Philip Paul, July 9, 1838–Dec. 29, 1876.
   Vol. 1, Pt. 2–376
Bliss, Porter Cornelius, Dec. 28, 1838–Feb. 2, 1885.
   Vol. 1, Pt. 2–376
Bliss, Robert Woods, Aug. 5, 1875–Apr. 19, 1962.
   Supp. 7–60
Bliss, Tasker Howard, Dec. 31, 1853–Nov. 9, 1930.
   Supp. 1–88
Bliss, William Dwight Porter, Aug. 20, 1856–Oct. 8, 1926.
   Vol. 1, Pt. 2–377
Blitz, Antonio, June 21, 1810–Jan. 28, 1877.
   Vol. 1, Pt. 2–378
Blitzstein, Marc, Mar. 2, 1905–Jan. 22, 1964.
   Supp. 7–60
Bloch, Claude Charles, July 12, 1878–Oct. 6, 1967.
   Supp. 8–41
Bloch, Ernest, July 24, 1880–July 15, 1959.
   Supp. 6–62

Block, Adriaen, fl. 1610–1624.
   Vol. 1, Pt. 2–378
Block, Paul, Nov. 2, 1877–June 22, 1941.
   Supp. 3–80
Blodget, Lorin, May 25, 1823–Mar. 24, 1901.
   Vol. 1, Pt. 2–379
Blodget, Samuel, Apr. 1, 1724–Sept. 1, 1807.
   Vol. 1, Pt. 2–379
Blodget, Samuel, Aug. 28, 1757–Apr. 11, 1814.
   Vol. 1, Pt. 2–380
Blodgett, Benjamin Colman, Mar. 12, 1838–Sept. 22, 1925.
   Vol. 1, Pt. 2–381
Blodgett, Henry Williams, July 21, 1821–Feb. 9, 1905.
   Vol. 1, Pt. 2–382
Blodgett, John Wood, July 16, 1860–Nov. 11, 1951.
   Supp. 5–68
Bloede, Gertrude, Aug. 10, 1845–Aug. 14, 1905.
   Vol. 1, Pt. 2–383
Blood, Benjamin Paul, Nov. 21, 1832–Jan. 15, 1919.
   Vol. 1, Pt. 2–383
Bloodgood, Joseph Colt, Nov. 1, 1867–Oct. 22, 1935.
   Supp. 1–90
Bloodworth, Timothy, 1736–Aug. 24, 1814.
   Vol. 1, Pt. 2–384
Bloom, Sol, Mar. 9, 1870–Mar. 7, 1949.
   Supp. 4–87
Bloomer, Amelia Jenks, May 27, 1818–Dec. 30, 1894.
   Vol. 1, Pt. 2–385
Bloomfield, Joseph, Oct. 18, 1753–Oct. 3, 1823.
   Vol. 1, Pt. 2–385
Bloomfield, Leonard, Apr. 1, 1887–Apr. 18, 1949.
   Supp. 4–89
Bloomfield, Maurice, Feb. 23, 1855–June 13, 1928.
   Vol. 1, Pt. 2–386
Bloomfield, Meyer, Feb. 11, 1878–Mar. 12, 1938.
   Supp. 2–45
Bloomfield–Zeisler, Fannie. [See Zeisler, Fannie Bloomfield, 1863–1927.]
Bloomgarden, Solomon, March 1870–Jan. 10, 1927.
   Vol. 1, Pt. 2–388
Bloor, Ella Reeve, July 8, 1862–Aug. 10, 1951.
   Supp. 5–69
Blount, James Henderson, Sept. 12, 1837–Mar. 8, 1903.
   Vol. 1, Pt. 2–388
Blount, Thomas, May 10, 1759–Feb. 7, 1812.
   Vol. 1, Pt. 2–389
Blount, William, Mar. 26, 1749–Mar. 21, 1800.
   Vol. 1, Pt. 2–390
Blount, Willie, Apr. 18, 1768–Sept. 10, 1835.
   Vol. 1, Pt. 2–391
Blow, Henry Taylor, July 15, 1817–Sept. 11, 1875.
   Vol. 1, Pt. 2–391
Blow, Susan Elizabeth, June 7, 1843–Mar. 26, 1916.
   Vol. 1, Pt. 2–392
Blowers, Sampson Salter, Mar. 10, 1742–Oct. 25, 1842.
   Vol. 1, Pt. 2–393
Bloxham, William Dunnington, July 9, 1835–Mar. 15, 1911.
   Vol. 1, Pt. 2–394
Blue, Gerald Montgomery ("Monte"), Jan. 11, 1887[?]–Feb. 18, 1963. Supp. 7–62
Blue, Victor, Dec. 6, 1865–Jan. 22, 1928.
   Vol. 1, Pt. 2–395
Bluemner, Oscar Florians, June 21, 1867–Jan. 12, 1938.
   Supp. 2–46
Blum, Robert Frederick, July 9, 1857–June 8, 1903.
   Vol. 1, Pt. 2–395
Blunt, Edmund March, June 20, 1770–Jan. 4, 1862.
   Vol. 1, Pt. 2–397
Blunt, George William, Mar. 11, 1802–Apr. 19. 1878.
   Vol. 1, Pt. 2–398
Blunt, James Gillpatrick, July 21, 1826–July 25, 1881.
   Vol. 1, Pt. 2–399
Blythe, Herbert. [See Barrymore, Maurice, 1847–1905.]
Boardman, Mabel Thorp, Oct. 12, 1860–Mar. 17, 1946.
   Supp. 4–91
Boardman, Thomas Danforth, Jan. 21, 1784–Sept. 10, 1873.
   Vol. 1, Pt. 2–400
Boas, Emil Leopold, Nov. 15, 1854–May 3, 1912.
   Vol. 1, Pt. 2–400
Boas, Franz July 9, 1858–Dec. 21, 1942.
   Supp. 3–81
Bôcher, Maxime, Aug. 28, 1867–Sept. 12, 1918.
   Vol. 1, Pt. 2–401

Bocock, Thomas Stanley, May 18, 1815–Aug. 5, 1891.
  Vol. 1, Pt. 2–402
Bodanzky, Artur, Dec. 16, 1877–Nov. 23, 1939.
  Supp. 2–47
Bode, Boyd Henry, Oct. 4, 1873–Mar. 29, 1953.
  Supp. 5–71
Bodenheim, Maxwell, May 26, 1892–Feb. 7, 1954.
  Supp. 5–72
Boehler, Peter, Dec. 31, 1712–Apr. 27, 1775.
  Vol. 1, Pt. 2–402
Boehm, Henry, June 8, 1775–Dec. 28, 1875.
  Vol. 1, Pt. 2–403
Boehm, John Philip, 1683–Apr. 29, 1749.
  Vol. 1, Pt. 2–404
Boehm, Martin, Nov. 30, 1725–Mar. 23, 1812.
  Vol. 1, Pt. 2–404
Boeing, William Edward, Oct. 1, 1881–Sept. 28, 1956.
  Supp. 6–63
Boelen, Jacob, c. 1654–1729.
  Vol. 1, Pt. 2–406
Bogan, Louise Marie, Aug. 11, 1897–Feb. 4, 1970.
  Supp. 8–42
Bogardus, Everardus, 1607–Sept. 27, 1647.
  Vol. 1, Pt. 2–406
Bogardus, James, Mar. 14, 1800–Apr. 13, 1874.
  Vol. 1, Pt. 2–407
Bogart, Humphrey DeForest, Dec. 25, 1899–Jan. 14, 1957.
  Supp. 6–64
Bogart, John, Feb. 8, 1836–Apr. 25, 1920.
  Vol. 1, Pt. 2–408
Boggs, Charles Stuart, Jan. 28, 1811–Apr. 22, 1888.
  Vol. 1, Pt. 2–408
Boggs, Lillburn W., Dec. 14, 1792–Mar. 14, 1860.
  Vol. 1, Pt. 2–409
Bogue, Virgil Gay, July 20, 1846–Oct. 14, 1916.
  Vol. 1, Pt. 2–410
Bogy, Lewis Vital, Apr. 9, 1813–Sept. 20, 1877.
  Vol. 1, Pt. 2–410
Bohm, Max, Jan. 21, 1861–Sept. 19, 1923.
  Vol. 1, Pt. 2–411
Bohune, Lawrence, d. Mar. 19, 1621.
  Vol. 1, Pt. 2–412
Boies, Henry Martyn, Aug. 18, 1837–Dec. 12, 1903.
  Vol. 1, Pt. 2–412
Boies, Horace, Dec. 7, 1827–Apr. 4, 1923.
  Vol. 1, Pt. 2–413
Boise, Reuben Patrick, June 9, 1819–Apr. 10, 1907.
  Vol. 1, Pt. 2–414
Boisen, Anton Theophilus, Oct. 29, 1876–Oct. 1, 1965.
  Supp. 7–63
Boissevain, Inez Milholland, Aug. 6, 1886–Nov. 25, 1916.
  Vol. 1, Pt. 2–415
Bok, Edward William, Oct. 9, 1863–Jan. 9, 1930.
  Supp. 1–91
Boker, George Henry, Oct. 6, 1823–Jan. 2, 1890.
  Vol. 1, Pt. 2–415
Boldt, George C., Apr. 25, 1851–Dec. 5, 1916.
  Vol. 1, Pt. 2–418
Boll, Jacob, May 29, 1828–Sept. 29, 1880.
  Vol. 1, Pt. 2–419
Boller, Alfred Pancoast, Feb. 23, 1840–Dec. 9, 1912.
  Vol. 1, Pt. 2–420
Bolles, Frank, Oct. 31, 1856–Jan. 10, 1894.
  Vol. 1, Pt. 2–421
Bollman, Justus Erich, 1769–Dec. 9, 1821.
  Vol. 1, Pt. 2–421
Bollman, William, c. 1710–c. 1776.
  Vol. 1, Pt. 2–420
Bolm, Adolph Rudolphovitch, Sept. 25, 1884–Apr. 16, 1951.
  Supp. 5–74
Bolton, Henry Carrington, Jan. 28, 1843–Nov. 19, 1903.
  Vol. 1, Pt. 2–422
Bolton, Herbert Eugene, July 20, 1870–Jan. 30, 1953.
  Supp. 5–76
Bolton, Sarah Knowles, Sept. 15, 1841–Feb. 21, 1916.
  Vol. 1, Pt. 2–423
Bolton, Sarah Tittle Barrett, Dec. 18, 1814–Aug. 4, 1893.
  Vol. 1, Pt. 2–424
Boltwood, Bertram Borden, July 27, 1870–Aug. 15, 1927.
  Vol. 1, Pt. 2–424
Boltzius, Johann Martin, Dec. 15, 1703–Nov. 19, 1765.
  Vol. 1, Pt. 2–425

Bolza, Oskar, May 12, 1857–July 5, 1942.
  Supp. 3–86
Bomberger, John Henry Augustus, Jan. 13, 1817–Aug. 19, 1890. Vol. 1, Pt. 2–426
Bomford, George, 1782–Mar. 25, 1848.
  Vol. 1, Pt. 2–427
Bonaparte, Charles Joseph, June 9, 1851–June 28, 1921.
  Vol. 1, Pt. 2–427
Bonaparte, Elizabeth Patterson, Feb. 6, 1785–Apr. 4, 1879.
  Vol. 1, Pt. 2–428
Bonaparte, Jerome Napoleon, Nov. 5, 1830–Sept. 3, 1893.
  Vol. 1, Pt. 2–429
Bonard, Louis, 1809–Feb. 21, 1871.
  Vol. 1, Pt. 2–429
Bond, Carrie Jacobs, Aug. 11, 1862–Dec. 28, 1946.
  Supp. 4–93
Bond, Elizabeth Powell, Jan. 25, 1841–Mar. 29, 1926.
  Vol. 1, Pt. 2–430
Bond, George Phillips, May 20, 1825–Feb. 17, 1865.
  Vol. 1, Pt. 2–430
Bond, Hugh Lennox, Dec. 16, 1828–Oct. 24, 1893.
  Vol. 1, Pt. 2–431
Bond, Shadrach, c. 1773–Apr. 13, 1832.
  Vol. 1, Pt. 2–432
Bond, Thomas, 1712–Mar. 26, 1784.
  Vol. 1, Pt. 2–433
Bond, William Cranch, Sept. 9, 1789–Jan. 29, 1859.
  Vol. 1, Pt. 2–434
Boner, John Henry, Jan. 31, 1845–Mar. 6, 1903.
  Vol. 1, Pt. 2–435
Bonfils, Frederick Gilmer, Dec. 31, 1860–Feb. 2, 1933.
  Supp. 1–93
Bonham, Milledge Luke, Dec. 25, 1813–Aug. 27, 1890.
  Vol. 1, Pt. 2–436
Bonner, John, c. 1643–Jan. 30, 1725/6.
  Vol. 1, Pt. 2–436
Bonner, Robert, Apr. 28, 1824–July 6, 1899.
  Vol. 1, Pt. 2–437
Bonneville, Benjamin Louis Eulalie de, Apr. 14, 1796–June 12, 1878. Vol. 1, Pt. 2–438
Bonney, Charles Carroll, Sept. 4, 1831–Aug. 23, 1903.
  Vol. 1, Pt. 2–439
Bonney, William H., 1859–1881. [See Billy the Kid, 1859]-1881.]
Bonsal, Stephen, Mar. 29, 1865–June 8, 1951.
  Supp. 5–78
Bonstelle, Jessie, 1872–Oct. 14, 1932.
  Supp. 1–96
Bonwill, William Gibson Arlington, Oct. 4, 1833–Sept. 24, 1899. Vol. 1, Pt. 2–440
Bonzano, Adolphus, Dec. 5, 1830–May 5, 1913.
  Vol. 1, Pt. 2–441
Boole, Ella Alexander, July 26, 1858–Mar. 13, 1952.
  Supp. 5–79
Boone, Daniel, Nov. 2, N.S., 1734–Sept. 26, 1820.
  Vol. 1, Pt. 2–441
Boorman, James, 1783–Jan. 24, 1866.
  Vol. 1, Pt. 2–443
Booth, Agnes, Oct. 4, 1846–Jan. 2, 1910.
  Vol. 1, Pt. 2–444
Booth, Albert James, Jr. ("Albie"), Feb. 1, 1908–Mar. 1, 1959. Supp. 6–66
Booth, Ballington, July 28, 1857–Oct. 5, 1940.
  Supp. 2–48
Booth, Edwin Thomas, Nov. 13, 1833–June 7, 1893.
  Vol. 1, Pt. 2–444
Booth, Evangeline Cory, Dec. 25, 1865–July 17, 1950.
  Supp. 4–95
Booth, James Curtis, July 28, 1810–Mar. 21, 1888.
  Vol. 1, Pt. 2–446
Booth, John Wilkes, 1838–Apr. 26, 1865.
  Vol. 1, Pt. 2–448
Booth, Junius Brutus, May 1, 1796–Nov. 30, 1852.
  Vol. 1, Pt. 2–452
Booth, Mary Louise, Apr. 19, 1831–Mar. 5, 1889.
  Vol. 1, Pt. 2–454
Booth, Newton, Dec. 30, 1825–July 14, 1892.
  Vol. 1, Pt. 2–455
Booth-Tucker, Emma Moss, Jan. 8, 1860–Oct. 28, 1903.
  Vol. 1, Pt. 2–456
Boott, Kirk, Oct. 20, 1790–Apr. 11, 1837.
  Vol. 1, Pt. 2–456

Borah, William Edgar, June 29, 1865–Jan. 19, 1940.
  Supp. 2–49
Borchard, Edwin Montefiore, Oct. 17, 1884–July 22, 1951.
  Supp. 5–81
Borden, Gail, Nov. 9, 1801–Jan. 11, 1874.
  Vol. 1, Pt. 2–457
Borden, Lizzie Andrew, July 19, 1860–June 1, 1927.
  Supp. 1–97
Borden, Richard, Apr. 12, 1795–Feb. 25, 1874.
  Vol. 1, Pt. 2–458
Borden, Simeon, Jan. 29, 1798–Oct. 28, 1856.
  Vol. 1, Pt. 2–459
Bordley, John Beale, Feb. 11, 1727–Jan. 26, 1804.
  Vol. 1, Pt. 2–460
Boré, Jean Étienne, Dec. 27, 1741–Feb. 2, 1820.
  Vol. 1, Pt. 2–461
Boreman, Arthur Ingram, July 24, 1823–Apr. 19, 1896.
  Vol. 1, Pt. 2–461
Borg, George William, Oct. 24, 1887–Feb. 21, 1960.
  Supp. 6–67
Borglum, John Gutzon de la Mothe, Mar. 25, 1867–Mar. 6, 1941. Supp. 3–87
Borglum, Solon Hannibal, Dec. 22, 1868–Jan. 31, 1922.
  Vol. 1, Pt. 2–462
Bori, Lucrezia, Dec. 24, 1887–May 14, 1960.
  Supp. 6–68
Borie, Adolphe, Jan. 5, 1877–May 14, 1934.
  Supp. 1–97
Borie, Adolph Edward, Nov. 25, 1809–Feb. 5, 1880.
  Vol. 1, Pt. 2–464
Boring, Edwin Garrigues, Oct. 23, 1886–July 1, 1968.
  Supp. 8–43
Boring, William Alciphron, Sept. 9, 1859–May 5, 1937.
  Supp. 2–53
Borland, Solon, Sept. 21, 1808–Jan. 1 or 31, 1864.
  Vol. 1, Pt. 2–464
Borzage, Frank, Apr. 23, 1893–June 19, 1962.
  Supp. 7–65
Boss, Lewis, Oct. 26, 1846–Oct. 5, 1912.
  Vol. 1, Pt. 2–465
Boston, Charles Anderson, Aug. 31, 1863–Mar. 8, 1935.
  Supp. 1–98
Bostwick, Arthur Elmore, Mar. 8, 1860–Feb. 13, 1942.
  Supp. 3–90
Bosworth, Edward Increase, Jan. 10, 1861–July 1, 1927.
  Vol. 1, Pt. 2–466
Bosworth, Francke Huntington, Jan. 25, 1843–Oct. 17, 1925.
  Vol. 1, Pt. 2–466
Boteler, Alexander Robinson, May 16, 1815–May 8, 1892.
  Vol. 1, Pt. 2–467
Botetourt, Norborne Berkeley, Baron de, c. 1718–Oct. 15, 1770. Vol. 1, Pt. 2–468
Botsford, George Willis, May 9, 1862–Dec. 13, 1917.
  Vol. 1, Pt. 2–468
Botta, Anne Charlotte Lynch, Nov. 11, 1815–Mar. 23, 1891.
  Vol. 1, Pt. 2–469
Botta, Vincenzo, Nov. 11, 1818–Oct. 5, 1894.
  Vol. 1, Pt. 2–470
Bottineau, Pierre, c. 1817–July 26, 1895.
  Vol. 1, Pt. 2–470
Bottome, Margaret McDonald, Dec. 29, 1827–Nov. 4, 1906.
  Vol. 1, Pt. 2–471
Botts, Charles Tyler, 1809–1884.
  Vol. 1, Pt. 2–472
Botts, John Minor, Sept. 16, 1802–Jan. 7, 1869.
  Vol. 1, Pt. 2–472
Bouché, René Robert, Sept. 20, 1905–July 3, 1963.
  Supp. 7–66
Boucher, Horace Edward, Apr. 24, 1873–Apr. 27, 1935.
  Supp. 1–99
Boucher, Jonathan, Mar. 12, 1737/8–Apr. 27, 1804.
  Vol. 1, Pt. 2–473
Boucicault, Dion, Dec. 26, 1820–Sept. 18, 1890.
  Vol. 1, Pt. 2–475
Bouck, William C., Jan. 7, 1786–Apr. 19, 1859.
  Vol. 1, Pt. 2–476
Boudin, Louis Boudinoff, Feb. 15, 1874–May 29, 1952.
  Supp. 5–82
Boudinot, Elias, May 2, 1740–Oct. 24, 1821.
  Vol. 1, Pt. 2–477
Boudinot, Elias, c. 1803–June 22, 1839.
  Vol. 1, Pt. 2–478

Boudinot, Elias Cornelius, Aug. 1, 1835–Sept. 27, 1890.
  Vol. 1, Pt. 2–479
Bouligny, Dominique, c. 1771–Mar. 5, 1833.
  Vol. 1, Pt. 2–479
Bounetheau, Henry Brintnell, Dec. 14, 1797–Jan. 31, 1877.
  Vol. 1, Pt. 2–479
Bouquet, Henry, 1719–Sept. 2, 1765.
  Vol. 1, Pt. 2–480
Bouquillon, Thomas Joseph, May 16, 1840–Nov. 5, 1902.
  Vol. 1, Pt. 2–481
Bourgmont, Étienne Venyard, Sieur de, c. 1680–c. 1730.
  Vol. 1, Pt. 2–482
Bourke, John Gregory, June 23, 1846–June 8, 1896.
  Vol. 1, Pt. 2–483
Bourne, Benjamin, Dec. 9, 1755–Sept. 17, 1808.
  Vol. 1, Pt. 2–483
Bourne, Edward Gaylord, June 24, 1860–Feb. 24, 1908.
  Vol. 1, Pt. 2–484
Bourne, George, June 13, 1780–Nov. 20, 1845.
  Vol. 1, Pt. 2–485
Bourne, Jonathan, Feb. 23, 1855–Sept. 1, 1940.
  Supp. 2–54
Bourne, Nehemiah, c. 1611–1691.
  Vol. 1, Pt. 2–485
Bourne, Randolph Silliman, May 30, 1886–Dec. 22, 1918.
  Vol. 1, Pt. 2–486
Boutell, Henry Sherman, Mar. 14, 1856–Mar. 11, 1926.
  Vol. 1, Pt. 2–486
Boutelle, Charles Addison, Feb. 9, 1839–May 21, 1901.
  Vol. 1, Pt. 2–487
Bouton, John Bell, Mar. 15, 1830–Nov. 18, 1902.
  Vol. 1, Pt. 2–488
Bouton, Nathaniel, June 29, 1799–June 6, 1878.
  Vol. 1, Pt. 2–488
Boutwell, George Sewall, Jan. 28, 1818–Feb. 27, 1905.
  Vol. 1, Pt. 2–489
Bouvet, Marie Marguerite, Feb. 14, 1865–May 27, 1915.
  Vol. 1, Pt. 2–490
Bouvier, John, 1787–Nov. 18, 1851.
  Vol. 1, Pt. 2–490
Bovard, Oliver Kirby, May 27, 1872–Nov. 3, 1945.
  Supp. 3–91
Bovie, William T., Sept. 11, 1882–Jan. 1, 1958.
  Supp. 6–69
Bow, Clara Gordon, July 29, 1905–Sept. 26, 1965.
  Supp. 7–67
Bowden, John, Jan. 7, 1751–July 31, 1817.
  Vol. 1, Pt. 2–491
Bowditch, Charles Pickering, Sept. 30, 1842–June 1, 1921.
  Vol. 1, Pt. 2–492
Bowditch, Henry Ingersoll, Aug. 9, 1808–Jan. 14, 1892.
  Vol. 1, Pt. 2–492
Bowditch, Henry Pickering, Apr. 4, 1840–Mar. 13, 1911.
  Vol. 1, Pt. 2–494
Bowditch, Nathaniel, Mar. 26, 1773–Mar. 17, 1838.
  Vol. 1, Pt. 2–496
Bowdoin, James, Aug. 7, 1726–Nov. 6, 1790.
  Vol. 1, Pt. 2–498
Bowdoin, James, Sept. 22, 1752–Oct. 11, 1811.
  Vol. 1, Pt. 2–501
Bowen, Abel, Dec. 3, 1790–Mar. 11, 1850.
  Vol. 1, Pt. 2–502
Bowen, Francis, Sept. 8, 1811–Jan. 21, 1890.
  Vol. 1, Pt. 2–503
Bowen, George, Apr. 30, 1816–Feb. 5, 1888.
  Vol. 1, Pt. 2–504
Bowen, Henry Chandler, Sept. 11, 1813–Feb. 24, 1896.
  Vol. 1, Pt. 2–505
Bowen, Herbert Wolcott, Feb. 29, 1856–May 29, 1927.
  Vol. 1, Pt. 2–505
Bowen, Louise De Koven, Feb. 26, 1859–Nov. 9, 1953.
  Supp. 5–84
Bowen, Norman Levi, June 21, 1887–Sept. 11, 1956.
  Supp. 6–70
Bowen, Thomas Meade, Oct. 26, 1835–Dec. 30, 1906.
  Vol. 1, Pt. 2–506
Bowers, Claude Gernade, Nov. 20, 1878–Jan. 21, 1958.
  Supp. 6–72
Bowers, Elizabeth Crocker, Mar. 12, 1830–Nov. 6, 1895.
  Vol. 1, Pt. 2–507
Bowers, Lloyd Wheaton, Mar. 9, 1859–Sept. 9, 1910.
  Vol. 1, Pt. 2–508

Bowers, Theodore Shelton, Oct. 10, 1832–Mar. 6, 1866.
    Vol. 1, Pt. 2–508
Bowes, Edward J., June 14, 1874–June 13, 1946.
    Supp. 4–96
Bowie, James, 1799–Mar. 6, 1836.
    Vol. 1, Pt. 2–509
Bowie, Oden, Nov. 10, 1826–Dec. 4, 1894.
    Vol. 1, Pt. 2–510
Bowie, Richard Johns, June 23, 1807–Mar. 12, 1881.
    Vol. 1, Pt. 2–511
Bowie, Robert, March 1750–Jan. 8, 1818.
    Vol. 1, Pt. 2–511
Bowie, William, May 6, 1872–Aug. 28, 1940.
    Supp. 2–55
Bowker, Richard Rogers, Sept. 4, 1848–Nov. 12, 1933.
    Supp. 1–100
Bowler, Metcalf, 1726–Sept. 24, 1789.
    Vol. 1, Pt. 2–512
Bowles, Samuel, June 8, 1797–Sept. 8, 1851.
    Vol. 1, Pt. 2–513
Bowles, Samuel, Feb. 9, 1826–Jan. 16, 1878.
    Vol. 1, Pt. 2–514
Bowles, Samuel, Oct. 15, 1851–Mar. 14, 1915.
    Vol. 1, Pt. 2–518
Bowles, William Augustus, Oct. 22, 1763–Dec. 23, 1805.
    Vol. 1, Pt. 2–519
Bowman, Isaiah, Dec. 26, 1878–Jan. 6, 1950.
    Supp. 4–98
Bowman, John Bryan, Oct. 16, 1824–Sept. 29, 1891.
    Vol. 1, Pt. 2–520
Bowman, Thomas, July 15, 1817–Mar. 3, 1914.
    Vol. 1, Pt. 2–521
Bowne, Borden Parker, Jan. 14, 1847–Apr. 1, 1910.
    Vol. 1, Pt. 2–522
Bowne, John, c. Mar. 1, 1627/28–Oct. 10, 1695.
    Vol. 1, Pt. 2–523
Boyce, James Petigru, Jan. 11, 1827–Dec. 28, 1888.
    Vol. 1, Pt. 2–523
Boyd, Belle, May 9, 1843–June 11, 1900.
    Vol. 1, Pt. 2–524
Boyd, David French, Oct. 5, 1834–May 27, 1899.
    Vol. 1, Pt. 2–525
Boyd, Harriet Ann. [See Hawes, Harriet Ann Boyd, 1871–1945.]
Boyd, James, July 2, 1888–Feb. 25, 1944.
    Supp. 3–92
Boyd, John Parker, Dec. 21, 1764–Oct. 4, 1830.
    Vol. 1, Pt. 2–526
Boyd, Lynn, Nov. 22, 1800–Dec. 17, 1859.
    Vol. 1, Pt. 2–527
Boyd, Richard Henry, Mar. 15, 1843–Aug. 23, 1922.
    Vol. 1, Pt. 2–528
Boyd, Thomas Alexander, July 3, 1898–Jan. 27, 1935.
    Supp. 1–102
Boyd, Thomas Duckett, Jan. 20, 1854–Nov. 2, 1932.
    Supp. 1–103
Boyd, William Kenneth, Jan. 10, 1879–Jan. 19, 1938.
    Supp. 2–56
Boyden, Roland William, Oct. 18, 1863–Oct. 25, 1931.
    Supp. 1–104
Boyden, Seth, Nov. 17, 1788–Mar. 31, 1870.
    Vol. 1, Pt. 2–528
Boyden, Uriah Atherton, Feb. 17, 1804–Oct. 17, 1879.
    Vol. 1, Pt. 2–529
Boyé, Martin Hans, Dec. 6, 1812–Mar. 5, 1909.
    Vol. 1, Pt. 2–530
Boyesen, Hjalmar Hjorth, Sept. 23, 1849–Oct. 4, 1895.
    Vol. 1, Pt. 2–530
Boyle, Jeremiah Tilford, May 22, 1818–July 28, 1871.
    Vol. 1, Pt. 2–532
Boyle, John, Oct. 28, 1774–Jan. 28, 1835.
    Vol. 1, Pt. 2–532
Boyle, John J., Jan. 12, 1851–Feb. 10, 1917.
    Vol. 1, Pt. 2–533
Boyle, Michael J., June 11, 1879–May 17, 1958.
    Supp. 6–73
Boyle, Thomas, June 29, 1776?–Oct. 12, 1825?.
    Vol. 1, Pt. 2–534
Boylston, Zabdiel, Mar. 9, 1679–Mar. 1, 1766.
    Vol. 1, Pt. 2–535
Boynton, Charles Brandon, June 12, 1806–Apr. 27, 1883.
    Vol. 1, Pt. 2–536

Boynton, Edward Carlisle, Feb. 1, 1824–May 13, 1893.
    Vol. 1, Pt. 2–537
Bozeman, John M., 1835–Apr. 20, 1867.
    Vol. 1, Pt. 2–537
Bozeman, Nathan, Mar. 25, 1825–Dec. 16, 1905.
    Vol. 1, Pt. 2–539
Bozman, John Leeds, Aug. 25, 1757–Apr. 20, 1823.
    Vol. 1, Pt. 2–539
Brace, Charles Loring, June 19, 1826–Aug. 11, 1890.
    Vol. 1, Pt. 2–539
Brace, Charles Loring, June 2, 1855–May 24, 1938.
    Supp. 2–57
Brace, Dewitt Bristol, Jan. 5, 1859–Oct. 2, 1905.
    Vol. 1, Pt. 2–540
Brace, Donald Clifford, Dec. 27, 1881–Sept. 20, 1955.
    Supp. 5–85
Brace, John Pierce, Feb. 10, 1793–Oct. 18, 1872.
    Vol. 1, Pt. 2–541
Brachvogel, Udo, Sept. 26, 1835–Jan. 30, 1913.
    Vol. 1, Pt. 2–541
Brackenridge, Henry Marie, May 11, 1786–Jan. 18, 1871.
    Vol. 1, Pt. 2–543
Brackenridge, Hugh Henry, 1748–June 25, 1816.
    Vol. 1, Pt. 2–544
Brackenridge, William D., June 10, 1810–Feb. 3, 1893.
    Vol. 1, Pt. 2–545
Brackett, Anna Callender, May 21, 1836–Mar. 9, 1911.
    Vol. 1, Pt. 2–546
Brackett, Charles William, Nov. 26, 1892–Mar. 9, 1969.
    Supp. 8–45
Brackett, Edward Augustus, Oct. 1, 1818–Mar. 15, 1908.
    Vol. 1, Pt. 2–547
Brackett, Jeffrey Richardson, Oct. 20, 1860–Dec. 4, 1949.
    Supp. 4–100
Bradbury, James Ware, June 10, 1802–Jan. 6, 1901.
    Vol. 1, Pt. 2–547
Bradbury, Theophilus, Nov. 13, 1739–Sept. 6, 1803.
    Vol. 1, Pt. 2–548
Bradbury, William Batchelder, Oct. 6, 1816–Jan. 7, 1868.
    Vol. 1, Pt. 2–549
Braddock, Edward, 1695–July 13, 1755.
    Vol. 1, Pt. 2–550
Bradford, Alden, Nov. 19, 1765–Oct. 26, 1843.
    Vol. 1, Pt. 2–551
Bradford, Alexander Warfield, Feb. 23, 1815–Nov. 5, 1867.
    Vol. 1, Pt. 2–551
Bradford, Amory Howe, Apr. 14, 1846–Feb. 18, 1911.
    Vol. 1, Pt. 2–552
Bradford, Andrew, 1686–Nov. 24, 1742.
    Vol. 1, Pt. 2–552
Bradford, Augustus Williamson, Jan. 9, 1806–Mar. 1, 1881.
    Vol. 1, Pt. 2–553
Bradford, Edward Green, July 17, 1819–Jan. 16, 1884.
    Vol. 1, Pt. 2–555
Bradford, Edward Hickling, June 9, 1848–May 7, 1926.
    Vol. 1, Pt. 2–555
Bradford, Gamaliel, Jan. 15, 1831–Aug. 20, 1911.
    Vol. 1, Pt. 2–556
Bradford, Gamaliel, Oct. 9, 1863–Apr. 11, 1932.
    Supp. 1–105
Bradford, John, June 6, 1749–Mar. 20, 1830.
    Vol. 1, Pt. 2–557
Bradford, Joseph, Oct. 24, 1843–Apr. 13, 1886.
    Vol. 1, Pt. 2–558
Bradford, Roark Whitney Wickliffe, Aug. 21, 1896–Nov. 13, 1948. Supp. 4–101
Bradford, Thomas, May 4, 1745–May 7, 1838.
    Vol. 1, Pt. 2–558
Bradford, William, 1589/90–May 9/19, 1657.
    Vol. 1, Pt. 2–559
Bradford, William, May 20, 1663–May 23, 1752.
    Vol. 1, Pt. 2–563
Bradford, William, Jan. 19, 1721/22–Sept. 25, 1791.
    Vol. 1, Pt. 2–564
Bradford, William, Sept. 14, 1755–Aug. 23, 1795.
    Vol. 1, Pt. 2–566
Bradford, William, Apr. 30, 1823–Apr. 25, 1892.
    Vol. 1, Pt. 2–566
Bradish, Luther, Sept. 15, 1783–Aug. 30, 1863.
    Vol. 1, Pt. 2–567
Bradley, Charles Henry, Feb. 13, 1860–Jan. 30, 1922.
    Vol. 1, Pt. 2–568

Bradley, Charles William, June 27, 1807–Mar. 8, 1865.
    Vol. 1, Pt. 2–568
Bradley, Denis Mary, Feb. 25, 1846–Dec. 13, 1903.
    Vol. 1, Pt. 2–569
Bradley, Frank Howe, Sept. 20, 1838–Mar. 27, 1879.
    Vol. 1, Pt. 2–570
Bradley, Frederick Worthen, Feb. 21, 1863–July 6, 1933.
    Supp. 1–107
Bradley, John Edwin, Aug. 8, 1839–Oct. 7, 1912.
    Vol. 1, Pt. 2–570
Bradley, Joseph P., Mar. 14, 1813–Jan. 22, 1892.
    Vol. 1, Pt. 2–571
Bradley, Lydia Moss, July 81, 1816–Jan. 16, 1908.
    Vol. 1, Pt. 2–573
Bradley, Milton, Nov. 8, 1836–May 30, 1911.
    Vol. 1, Pt. 2–574
Bradley, Stephen Row, Feb. 20, 1754–Dec. 9, 1830.
    Vol 1, Pt. 2–575
Bradley, William Czar, Mar. 23, 1782–Mar. 3, 1867.
    Vol. 1, Pt. 2–576
Bradley, William O'Connell, Mar. 18, 1847–May 23, 1914.
    Vol. 1, Pt. 2–576
Bradstreet, Anne, c. 1612–Sept. 16, 1672.
    Vol. 1, Pt. 2–577
Bradstreet, John, c. 1711–Sept. 25, 1774.
    Vol. 1, Pt. 2–578
Bradstreet, Simon, March 1603–March 1697.
    Vol. 1, Pt. 2–579
Bradwell, James Bolesworth, Apr. 16, 1828–Nov. 29, 1907.
    Vol. 1, Pt. 2–580
Bradwell, Myra, Feb. 12, 1831–Feb. 14, 1894.
    Vol. 1, Pt. 2–581
Brady, Alice, Nov. 2, 1892–Oct. 28, 1939.
    Supp. 2–58
Brady, Anthony Nicholas, Aug. 22, 1843–July 22, 1913.
    Vol. 1, Pt. 2–581
Brady, Cyrus Townsend, Dec. 20, 1861–Jan. 24, 1920.
    Vol. 1, Pt. 2–582
Brady, James Topham, Apr. 9, 1815–Feb. 9, 1869.
    Vol. 1, Pt. 2–583
Brady, John Green, May 25, 1848–Dec. 17, 1918.
    Supp. 1–108
Brady, Mathew B., c. 1823–Jan. 15, 1896.
    Vol. 1, Pt. 2–584
Brady, Mildred Alice Edie, June 3, 1906–July 27, 1965.
    Supp. 7–68
Brady, William Aloysius, June 19, 1863–Jan. 6, 1950.
    Supp. 4–103
Bragdon, Claude Fayette, Aug. 1, 1866–Sept. 17, 1946.
    Supp. 4–105
Bragg, Braxton, Mar. 22, 1817–Sept. 27, 1876.
    Vol. 1, Pt. 2–585
Bragg, Edward Stuyvesant, Feb. 20, 1827–June 20, 1912.
    Vol. 1, Pt. 2–587
Bragg, Thomas, Nov. 9, 1810–Jan. 21, 1872.
    Vol. 1, Pt. 2–588
Brainard, Daniel, May 15, 1812–Oct. 10, 1866.
    Vol. 1, Pt. 2–589
Brainard, John Gardiner Calkins, Oct. 21, 1796–Sept. 26, 1828. Vol. 1, Pt. 2–590
Brainerd, David, Apr. 20, 1718–Oct. 9, 1747.
    Vol. 1, Pt. 2–591
Brainerd, Erastus, Feb. 25, 1855–Dec. 25, 1922.
    Vol. 1, Pt. 2–592
Brainerd, Ezra, Dec. 17, 1844–Dec. 8, 1924.
    Vol. 1, Pt. 2–593
Brainerd, John, Feb. 28, 1720–Mar. 18, 1781.
    Vol. 1, Pt. 2–593
Brainerd, Lawrence, Mar. 16, 1794–May 9, 1870.
    Vol. 1, Pt. 2–594
Brainerd, Thomas, June 17, 1804–Aug. 21, 1866.
    Vol. 1, Pt. 2–594
Bramlette, Thomas E., Jan. 3, 1817–Jan. 12, 1875.
    Vol. 1, Pt. 2–595
Branch, John, Nov. 4, 1782–Jan. 4, 1863.
    Vol. 1, Pt. 2–596
Branch, Lawrence O'Bryan, Nov. 28, 1820–Sept. 17, 1862.
    Vol. 1, Pt. 2–597
Brand, Max. [See Faust, Frederick Schiller, 1892–1944.]
Brandegee, Frank Bosworth, July 8, 1864–Oct. 14, 1924.
    Vol. 1, Pt. 2–598
Brandegee, Townshend Stith, Feb. 16, 1843–Apr. 7, 1925.
    Vol. 1, Pt. 2–599

Brandeis, Louis Dembitz, Nov. 13, 1856–Oct. 5, 1941.
    Supp. 3–93
Brandon, Gerard Chittocque, Sept. 15, 1788–Mar. 28, 1850.
    Vol. 1, Pt. 2–600
Braniff, Thomas Elmer, Dec. 6, 1883–Jan. 10, 1954.
    Supp. 5–85
Brann, William Cowper, Jan. 4, 1855–Apr. 2, 1898.
    Supp. 1–108
Brannan, John Milton, July 1, 1819–Dec. 16, 1892.
    Vol. 1, Pt. 2–600
Brannan, Samuel, Mar. 2, 1819–May 5, 1889.
    Vol. 1, Pt. 2–601
Branner, John Casper, July 4, 1850–Mar. 1, 1922.
    Vol. 1, Pt. 2–602
Brannon, Henry, Nov. 26, 1837–Nov. 24, 1914.
    Vol. 1, Pt. 2–603
Brant, Joseph, 1742–Nov. 24, 1807.
    Vol. 1, Pt. 2–604
Brantley, Theodore, Feb. 12, 1851–Sept. 16, 1922,.
    Vol. 1, Pt. 2–605
Brashear, John Alfred, Nov. 24, 1840–Apr. 8, 1920.
    Vol. 1, Pt. 2–605
Braslau, Sophie, Aug. 16, 1892–Dec. 22, 1935.
    Supp. 1–109
Brattle, Thomas, June 20, 1658–May 18, 1713.
    Vol. 1, Pt. 2–606
Brattle, William, Nov. 22, 1662–Feb. 15, 1716/17.
    Vol. 1, Pt. 2–607
Bratton, John, Mar. 7, 1831–Jan. 12, 1898.
    Vol. 1, Pt. 2–608
Brawley, William Hiram, May 13, 1841–Nov. 15, 1916.
    Vol. 1, Pt. 2–609
Braxton, Carter, Sept. 10, 1736–Oct. 10, 1797.
    Vol. 1, Pt. 2–609
Bray, Thomas, 1656–Feb. 15, 1729/30.
    Vol. 1, Pt. 2–610
Brayman, Mason, May 23, 1813–Feb. 27, 1895.
    Vol. 1, Pt. 2–611
Brayton, Charles Ray, Aug. 16, 1840–Sept. 23, 1910.
    Vol. 1, Pt. 2–612
Brazer, John, Sept. 21, 1789–Feb. 25, 1846.
    Vol. 1, Pt. 2–612
Brearly, David, June 11, 1745–Aug. 16, 1790.
    Vol. 2, Pt. 1–1
Breasted, James Henry, Aug. 27, 1865–Dec. 2, 1935.
    Supp. 1–110
Breaux, Joseph Arsenne, Feb. 18, 1838–July 23, 1926.
    Vol. 2, Pt. 1–2
Breck, George William, Sept. 1, 1863–Nov. 22, 1920.
    Vol. 2, Pt. 1–2
Breck, James Lloyd, June 27, 1818–Mar. 30, 1876.
    Vol. 2, Pt. 1–3
Breck, Samuel, July 17, 1771–Aug. 31, 1862.
    Vol. 2, Pt. 1–4
Breckenridge, James, Mar. 7, 1763–May 13, 1833.
    Vol. 2, Pt. 1–5
Breckenridge, Sophonisba Preston, Apr. 1, 1866–July 30, 1948. Supp. 4–106
Breckinridge, Aida de Acosta, July 28, 1884–May 27, 1962.
    Supp. 7–69
Breckinridge, Desha, Aug. 5, 1867–Feb. 18, 1935.
    Supp. 1–113
Breckinridge, Henry Skillman, May 25, 1886–May 2, 1960.
    Supp. 6–75
Breckinridge, John, Dec. 2, 1760–Dec. 14, 1806.
    Vol. 2, Pt. 1–6
Breckinridge, John, July 4, 1797–Aug. 4, 1841.
    Vol. 2, Pt. 1–6
Breckinridge, John Cabell, Jan. 15, 1821–May 17, 1875.
    Vol. 2, Pt. 1–7
Breckinridge, Robert Jefferson, Mar. 8, 1800–Nov. 27, 1871.
    Vol. 2, Pt. 1–10
Breckinridge, William Campbell Preston, Aug. 28, 1837–Nov. 19, 1904. Vol. 2, Pt. 1–11
Breed, Ebenezer, May 12, 1766–Dec. 23, 1839.
    Vol. 2, Pt. 1–12
Breen, Joseph Ignatius, Oct. 14, 1890–Dec. 7, 1965.
    Supp. 7–70
Breen, Patrick, d. Dec. 21, 1868.
    Vol. 2, Pt. 1–13
Breese, Kidder Randolph, Apr. 14, 1831–Sept. 13, 1881,.
    Vol. 2, Pt. 1–13

Breese, Sidney, July 15, 1800–June 27, 1878.
    Vol. 2, Pt. 1–14
Brennan, Alfred Laurens, Feb. 14, 1853–June 14, 1921.
    Vol. 2, Pt. 1–16
Brennan, Francis James, May 7, 1894–July 2, 1968.
    Supp. 8–46
Brennemann, Joseph, Sept. 25, 1872–July 2, 1944.
    Supp. 3–100
Brenner, Victor David, June 12, 1871–Apr. 5, 1924.
    Vol. 2, Pt. 1–17
Brenon, Herbert, Jan. 13, 1880–June 21, 1958.
    Supp. 6–76
Brent, Charles Henry, Apr. 9, 1862–Mar. 27, 1929.
    Supp. 1–115
Brent, Margaret, 1600–1670/71.
    Vol. 2, Pt. 1–18
Brentano, Lorenz, Nov. 4, 1813–Sept. 17, 1891.
    Vol. 2, Pt. 1–19
Brereton, John. [See Brierton, John, fl. 1572–1619.]
Brereton, Lewis Hyde, June 21, 1890–July 19, 1967.
    Supp. 8–47
Brett, George Platt, Dec. 8, 1858–Sept. 19, 1936.
    Supp. 2–59
Brett, William Howard, July 1, 1846–Aug. 24, 1918.
    Vol. 2, Pt. 1–20
Brevoort, James Renwick, July 20, 1832–Dec. 15, 1918.
    Vol. 2, Pt. 1–21
Brewer, Charles, Mar. 27, 1804–Oct. 11, 1885.
    Vol. 2, Pt. 1–21
Brewer, David Josiah, June 20, 1837–Mar. 28, 1910.
    Vol. 2, Pt. 1–22
Brewer, Mark Spencer, Oct. 22, 1837–Mar. 18, 1901.
    Vol. 2, Pt. 1–24
Brewer, Thomas Mayo, Nov. 21, 1814–Jan. 23, 1880.
    Vol. 2, Pt. 1–24
Brewer, William Henry, Sept. 14, 1828–Nov. 2, 1910.
    Vol. 2, Pt. 1–25
Brewster, Benjamin Harris, Oct. 13, 1816–Apr. 4, 1888.
    Vol. 2, Pt. 1–26
Brewster, Frederick Carroll, May 15, 1825–Dec. 30, 1898.
    Vol. 2, Pt. 1–27
Brewster, James, Aug. 6, 1788–Nov. 22, 1866.
    Vol. 2, Pt. 1–27
Brewster, Osmyn, Aug. 2, 1797–July 15, 1889.
    Vol. 2, Pt. 1–28
Brewster, Ralph Owen, Feb. 22, 1888–Dec. 25, 1961.
    Supp. 7–72
Brewster, William, 1567–Apr. 10, 1644.
    Vol. 2, Pt. 1–29
Brewster, William, July 5, 1851–July 11, 1919.
    Vol. 2, Pt. 1–30
Brice, Calvin Stewart, Sept. 17, 1845–Dec. 15, 1898.
    Vol. 2, Pt. 1–31
Brice, Fanny, Oct. 29, 1891–May 29, 1951.
    Supp. 5–87
Brickell, Henry Herschel, Sept. 13, 1889–May 29, 1952.
    Supp. 5–88
Brickell, Robert Coman, Apr. 4, 1824–Nov. 20, 1900.
    Vol. 2, Pt. 1–32
Bridger, James, Mar. 17, 1804–July 17, 1881.
    Vol. 2, Pt. 1–33
Bridgers, Robert Rufus, Nov. 28, 1819–Dec. 10, 1888.
    Vol. 2, Pt. 1–33
Bridges, Calvin Blackman, Jan. 11, 1889–Dec. 27, 1938.
    Supp. 2–60
Bridges, (Henry) Styles, Sept. 9, 1898–Nov. 26, 1961.
    Supp. 7–73
Bridges, Robert, d. 1656.
    Vol. 2, Pt. 1–34
Bridges, Robert, Mar. 5, 1806–Feb. 20, 1882.
    Vol. 2, Pt. 1–35
Bridges, Thomas Jefferson Davis ("Tommy"), Dec. 28, 1906
    –Apr. 19, 1968. Supp. 8–49
Bridgman, Elijah Coleman, Apr. 22, 1801–Nov. 2, 1861.
    Vol. 2, Pt. 1–36
Bridgman, Frederic Arthur, Nov. 10, 1847–Jan. 13, 1927.
    Vol. 2, Pt. 1–36
Bridgman, Herbert Lawrence, May 30, 1844–Sept. 24, 1924.
    Vol. 2, Pt. 1–37
Bridgman, Laura Dewey, Dec. 21, 1829–May 24, 1889.
    Vol. 2, Pt. 1–38
Bridgman, Percy Williams, Apr. 21, 1882–Aug. 20, 1961.
    Supp. 7–74

Brierton, John, fl. 1572–1619.
    Vol. 2, Pt. 1–39
Briggs, Charles Augustus, Jan. 15, 1841–June 8, 1913.
    Vol. 2, Pt. 1–40
Briggs, Charles Frederick, Dec. 30, 1804–June 20, 1877.
    Vol. 2, Pt. 1–41
Briggs, Clare A., Aug. 5, 1875–Jan. 3, 1930.
    Supp. 1–117
Briggs, George Nixon, Apr. 12, 1796–Sept. 12, 1861.
    Vol. 2, Pt. 1–41
Briggs, LeBaron Russell, Dec. 11, 1855–Apr. 24, 1934.
    Supp. 1–118
Briggs, Lloyd Vernon, Aug. 13, 1863–Feb. 28, 1941.
    Supp. 3–101
Briggs, Lyman James, May 7, 1874–Mar. 25, 1963.
    Supp. 7–76
Brigham, Albert Perry, June 12, 1855–Mar. 31, 1932.
    Supp. 1–119
Brigham, Amariah, Dec. 26, 1798–Sept. 8, 1849.
    Vol. 2, Pt. 1–42
Brigham, Joseph Henry, Dec. 12, 1838–June 29, 1904.
    Vol. 2, Pt. 1–43
Brigham, Mary Ann, Dec. 6, 1829–June 29, 1889.
    Vol. 2, Pt. 1–44
Bright, Edward, Oct. 6, 1808–May 17, 1894.
    Vol. 2, Pt. 1–44
Bright, James Wilson, Oct. 2, 1852–Nov. 29, 1926.
    Vol. 2, Pt. 1–45
Bright, Jesse David, Dec. 18, 1812–May 20, 1875.
    Vol. 2, Pt. 1–45
Bright Eyes, 1854–May 26, 1903.
    Vol. 2, Pt. 1–46
Brightly, Frederick Charles, Aug. 26, 1812–Jan. 24, 1888.
    Vol. 2, Pt. 1–47
Brightman, Edgar Sheffield, Sept. 20, 1884–Feb. 25, 1953.
    Supp. 5–90
Brill, Abraham Arden, Oct. 12, 1874–Mar. 2, 1948.
    Supp. 4–107
Brill, Nathan Edwin, Jan. 13, 1859–Dec. 13, 1925.
    Vol. 2, Pt. 1–47
Brincklé, William Draper, Feb. 9, 1798–Dec. 16, 1862.
    Vol. 2, Pt. 1–48
Brinkerhoff, Jacob, Aug. 31, 1810–July 19, 1880.
    Vol. 2, Pt. 1–49
Brinkerhoff, Roeliff, June 28, 1828–June 4, 1911.
    Vol. 2, Pt. 1–49
Brinkley, John Richard, July 8, 1885–May 26, 1942.
    Supp. 3–103
Brinton, Clarence Crane, Feb. 2, 1898–Sept. 7, 1968.
    Supp. 8–50
Brinton, Daniel Garrison, May 13, 1837–July 31, 1899.
    Vol. 2, Pt. 1–50
Brinton, John Hill, May 21, 1832–Mar. 18, 1907.
    Vol. 2, Pt. 1–51
Brisbane, Albert, Aug. 22, 1809–May 1, 1890.
    Vol. 2, Pt. 1–52
Brisbane, Arthur, Dec. 12, 1864–Dec. 25, 1936.
    Supp. 2–62
Bristed, Charles Astor, Oct. 6, 1820–Jan. 14, 1874.
    Vol. 2, Pt. 1–53
Bristed, John, Oct. 17, 1778–Feb. 23, 1855.
    Vol. 2, Pt. 1–54
Bristol, John Bunyan, Mar. 14, 1826–Aug. 31, 1909.
    Vol. 2, Pt. 1–54
Bristol, Mark Lambert, Apr. 17, 1868–May 13, 1939.
    Supp. 2–65
Bristol, William Henry, July 5, 1859–June 18, 1930.
    Supp. 1–120
Bristow, Benjamin Helm, June 20, 1832–June 22, 1896.
    Vol. 2, Pt. 1–55
Bristow, George Frederick, Dec. 19, 1825–Dec. 13, 1898.
    Vol. 2, Pt. 1–56
Bristow, Joseph Little, July 22, 1861–July 14, 1944.
    Supp. 3–105
Britton, Nathaniel Lord, Jan. 15, 1859–June 25, 1934.
    Supp. 1–121
Broadhead, Garland Carr, Oct. 30, 1827–Dec. 12, 1912.
    Vol. 2, Pt. 1–57
Broadhead, James Overton, May 29, 1819–Aug. 7, 1898.
    Vol. 2, Pt. 1–58
Broadus, John Albert, Jan. 24, 1827–Mar. 16, 1895.
    Vol. 2, Pt. 1–59

Brown, George, Apr. 17, 1787–Aug. 26, 1859.
    Vol. 2, Pt. 1–116
Brown, George, Oct. 11, 1823–May 6, 1892.
    Vol. 2, Pt. 1–117
Brown, George Pliny, Nov. 10, 1836–Feb. 1, 1910.
    Vol. 2, Pt. 1–118
Brown, George William, Oct. 13, 1812–Sept. 5, 1890.
    Vol. 2, Pt. 1–118
Brown, Gertrude Foster, July 29, 1867–Mar. 1, 1956.
    Supp. 6–79
Brown, Goold, Mar. 7, 1791–Mar. 31, 1857.
    Vol. 2, Pt. 1–119
Brown, Henry Billings, Mar. 2, 1836–Sept. 4, 1913.
    Vol. 2, Pt. 1–120
Brown, Henry Cordis, Nov. 18, 1820–Mar. 6, 1906.
    Vol. 2, Pt. 1–121
Brown, Henry Kirke, Feb. 24, 1814–July 10, 1886.
    Vol. 2, Pt. 1–121
Brown, Isaac Van Arsdale, Nov. 4, 1784–Apr. 19, 1861.
    Vol. 2, Pt. 1–124
Brown, Jacob Jennings, May 9, 1775–Feb. 24, 1828.
    Vol. 2, Pt. 1–124
Brown, James, Sept. 11, 1766–Apr. 7, 1835.
    Vol. 2, Pt. 1–126
Brown, James, Feb. 4, 1791–Nov. 1, 1877.
    Vol. 2, Pt. 1–126
Brown, James, May 19, 1800–Mar. 10, 1855.
    Vol. 2, Pt. 1–127
Brown, James Salisbury, Dec. 23, 1802–Dec. 29, 1879.
    Vol. 2, Pt. 1–127
Brown, John, Jan. 27, 1736–Sept. 20, 1803.
    Vol. 2, Pt. 1–128
Brown, John, Oct. 19, 1744–Oct. 19, 1780.
    Vol. 2, Pt. 1–129
Brown, John, Sept. 12, 1757–Aug. 28, 1837.
    Vol. 2, Pt. 1–130
Brown, John, May 9, 1800–Dec. 2, 1859.
    Vol. 2, Pt. 1–131
Brown, John A., May 21, 1788–Dec. 31, 1872.
    Vol. 2, Pt. 1–134
Brown, John Appleton, July 12, 1844–Jan. 18, 1902.
    Vol. 2, Pt. 1–135
Brown, John Calvin, Jan. 6, 1827–Aug. 17, 1889.
    Vol. 2, Pt. 1–135
Brown, John Carter, Aug. 28, 1797–June 10, 1874.
    Vol. 2, Pt. 1–136
Brown, John George, Nov. 11, 1831–Feb. 8, 1913.
    Vol. 2, Pt. 1–137
Brown, John Mason, Jr., July 3, 1900–Mar. 16, 1969.
    Supp. 8–53
Brown, John Mifflin, Sept. 8, 1817–Mar. 16, 1893.
    Vol. 2, Pt. 1–138
Brown, John Newton, June 29, 1803–May 14, 1868.
    Vol. 2, Pt. 1–139
Brown, John Porter, Aug. 17, 1814–Apr. 28, 1872.
    Vol. 2, Pt. 1–139
Brown, John Young, June 28, 1835–Jan. 11, 1904.
    Vol. 2, Pt. 1–140
Brown, Joseph, Dec. 3/14, 1733–Dec. 3, 1785.
    Vol. 2, Pt. 1–141
Brown, Joseph Emerson, Apr. 15, 1821–Nov. 30, 1894.
    Vol. 2, Pt. 1–141
Brown, Joseph Rogers, Jan. 26, 1810–July 23, 1876.
    Vol. 2, Pt. 1–143
Brown, Lawrason, Sept. 29, 1871–Dec. 26, 1937.
    Supp. 2–70
Brown, Margaret Wise, May 23, 1910–Nov. 13, 1952.
    Supp. 5–92
Brown, Mather, Oct. 7, 1761–May 25, 1831.
    Vol. 2, Pt. 1–144
Brown, Morris, Feb. 12, 1770–May 9, 1849.
    Vol. 2, Pt. 1–145
Brown, Moses, Sept. 12/23, 1738–Sept. 7, 1836.
    Vol. 2, Pt. 1–146
Brown, Moses, Oct. 2, 1742–Feb. 9, 1827.
    Vol. 2, Pt. 1–147
Brown, Neill Smith, Apr. 18, 1810–Jan. 30, 1886.
    Vol. 2, Pt. 1–147
Brown, Nicholas, July 28, 1729 o.s.–May 29, 1791.
    Vol. 2, Pt. 1–148
Brown, Nicholas, Apr. 4, 1769–Sept. 27, 1841.
    Vol. 2, Pt. 1–149

Brown, Obadiah, July 15, 1771–Oct. 15, 1822.
    Vol. 2, Pt. 1–150
Brown, Olympia, Jan. 5, 1835–Oct. 23, 1926.
    Vol. 2, Pt. 1–151
Brown, Percy, Nov. 24, 1875–Oct. 8, 1950.
    Supp. 4–111
Brown, Phoebe Hinsdale, May 1, 1783–Aug. 10, 1861.
    Vol. 2, Pt. 1–151
Brown, Ralph Hall, Jan. 12, 1898–Feb. 23, 1948.
    Supp. 4–112
Brown, Samuel, Jan. 30, 1769–Jan. 12, 1830.
    Vol. 2, Pt. 1–152
Brown, Samuel Gilman, Jan. 4, 1813–Nov. 4, 1885.
    Vol. 2, Pt. 1–153
Brown, Samuel Robbins, June 16, 1810–June 20, 1880.
    Vol. 2, Pt. 1–153
Brown, Simon, Nov. 29, 1802–Feb. 26, 1873.
    Vol. 2, Pt. 1–154
Brown, Solyman, Nov. 17, 1790–Feb. 13, 1876.
    Vol. 2, Pt. 1–155
Brown, Sylvanus, May 24, 1747 o.s.–July 30, 1824.
    Vol. 2, Pt. 1–156
Brown, Walter Folger, May 31, 1869–Jan. 26, 1961.
    Supp. 7–85
Brown, William, 1752–Jan. 11, 1792.
    Vol. 2, Pt. 1–157
Brown, William Adams, Dec. 29, 1865–Dec. 15, 1943.
    Supp. 3–110
Brown, William Carlos, July 29, 1853–Dec. 6, 1924.
    Vol. 2, Pt. 1–157
Brown, William Garrott, Apr. 24, 1868–Oct. 19, 1913.
    Vol. 2, Pt. 1–158
Brown, William Henry, Feb. 29, 1836–June 25, 1910.
    Vol. 2, Pt. 1–159
Brown, William Hill, 1765–Sept. 2, 1793.
    Supp. 1–125
Brown, William Hughey, Jan. 15, 1815–Oct. 12, 1875.
    Vol. 2, Pt. 1–160
Brown, William Wells, c. 1816–Nov. 6, 1884.
    Vol. 2, Pt. 1–161
Browne, Benjamin Frederick, July 14, 1793–Nov. 23, 1873.
    Vol. 2, Pt. 1–161
Browne, Charles Albert, Aug. 12, 1870–Feb. 3, 1947.
    Supp. 4–113
Browne, Charles Farrar, Apr. 26, 1834–Mar. 6, 1867.
    Vol. 2, Pt. 1–162
Browne, Daniel Jay, b. Dec. 4, 1804.
    Vol. 2, Pt. 1–164
Browne, Francis Fisher, Dec. 1, 1843–May 11, 1913.
    Vol. 2, Pt. 1–165
Browne, Herbert Wheildon Cotton, Nov. 22, 1860–Apr. 29, 1946. Supp. 4–115
Browne, Irving, Sept. 14, 1835–Feb. 6, 1899.
    Vol. 2, Pt. 1–165
Browne, John, d. Apr. 10, 1662.
    Vol. 2, Pt. 1–166
Browne, John Ross, Feb. 11, 1821–Dec. 8, 1875.
    Vol. 2, Pt. 1–167
Browne, Junius Henri, Oct. 14, 1833–Apr. 2, 1902.
    Vol. 2, Pt. 1–168
Browne, Thomas, d. Aug. 3, 1825.
    Vol. 2, Pt. 1–168
Browne, William, Mar. 5, 1737–Feb. 13, 1802.
    Vol. 2, Pt. 1–169
Browne, William Hand, Dec. 31, 1828–Dec. 13, 1912.
    Vol. 2, Pt. 1–170
Brownell, Henry Howard, Feb. 6, 1820–Oct. 31, 1872.
    Vol. 2, Pt. 1–171
Brownell, Thomas Church, Oct. 19, 1779–Jan. 13, 1865.
    Vol. 2, Pt. 1–171
Brownell, William Crary, Aug. 30, 1851–July 22, 1928.
    Vol. 2, Pt. 1–172
Browning, John Moses, Jan. 21, 1855–Nov. 26, 1926.
    Vol. 2, Pt. 1–174
Browning, Orville Hickman, Feb. 10, 1806–Aug. 10, 1881.
    Vol. 2, Pt. 1–175
Browning, Tod, July 12, 1880–Oct. 6, 1962.
    Supp. 7–86
Brownlee, James Forbis, July 29, 1891–Oct. 12, 1960.
    Supp. 6–80
Brownlee, William Craig, 1784–Feb. 10, 1860.
    Vol. 2, Pt. 1–176

Brownlow, William Gannaway, Aug. 29, 1805–Apr. 29, 1877.
  Vol. 2, Pt. 1–177
Brownson, Orestes Augustus, Sept. 16, 1803–Apr. 17, 1876.
  Vol. 2, Pt. 1–178
Brownson, Willard Herbert, July 8, 1845–Mar. 16, 1935.
  Supp. 1–126
Bruce, Andrew Alexander, Apr. 15, 1866–Dec. 6, 1934.
  Supp. 1–128
Bruce, Archibald, Feb. 1777–Feb. 22, 1818.
  Vol. 2, Pt. 1–179
Bruce, Blanche K., Mar. 1, 1841–Mar. 17, 1898.
  Vol. 2, Pt. 1–180
Bruce, Edward Bright, Apr. 13, 1879–Jan. 26, 1943.
  Supp. 3–111
Bruce, George, June 26, 1781–July 5, 1866
  Vol. 2, Pt. 1–181
Bruce, Lenny, Oct. 13, 1925–Aug. 3, 1966.
  Supp. 8–55
Bruce, Philip Alexander, Mar. 7, 1856–Aug. 16, 1933.
  Supp. 1–129
Bruce, Robert, Feb. 20, 1778–June 14, 1846.
  Vol. 2, Pt. 1–181
Bruce, William Cabell, Mar. 12, 1860–May 9, 1946.
  Supp. 4–116
Brucker, Wilber Marion, June 23, 1894–Oct. 28, 1968.
  Supp. 8–56
Brühl, Gustav, May 31, 1826–Feb. 16, 1903.
  Vol. 2, Pt. 1–182
Brulé, Étienne, c. 1592–1632.
  Vol. 2, Pt. 1–183
Brumby, Richard Trapier, Aug. 4, 1804–Oct. 6, 1875.
  Vol. 2, Pt. 1–184
Brumidi, Constantino, July 26, 1805–Feb. 19, 1880.
  Vol. 2, Pt. 1–184
Brunner, Arnold William, Sept. 25, 1857–Feb. 12, 1925.
  Vol. 2, Pt. 1–185
Brunswick, Ruth Mack, Feb. 17, 1897–Jan. 24, 1946.
  Supp. 4–117
Brunton, David William, June 11, 1849–Dec. 20, 1927.
  Vol. 2, Pt. 1–186
Brush, Charles Francis, Mar. 17, 1849–June 15, 1929.
  Supp. 1–129
Brush, Edward Nathaniel, Apr. 23, 1852–Jan. 10, 1933.
  Supp. 1–130
Brush, George de Forest, Sept. 28, 1855–Apr. 24, 1941.
  Supp. 3–112
Brush, George Jarvis, Dec. 15, 1831–Feb. 6, 1912.
  Vol. 2, Pt. 1–187
Bruté de Rémur, Simon William Gabriel, Mar. 20, 1779–June 26, 1839. Vol. 2, Pt. 1–188
Bryan, Charles Wayland, Feb. 10, 1867–Mar. 4, 1945.
  Supp. 3–114
Bryan, George, Aug. 11, 1731–Jan. 27, 1791.
  Vol. 2, Pt. 1–189
Bryan, John Stewart, Oct. 23, 1871–Oct. 16, 1944.
  Supp. 3–115
Bryan, Kirk, July 22, 1888–Aug. 22, 1950.
  Supp. 4–118
Bryan, Mary Edwards, May 17, 1842–June 15, 1913.
  Vol. 2, Pt. 1–190
Bryan, Thomas Barbour, Dec. 22, 1828–Jan. 25, 1906.
  Vol. 2, Pt. 1–190
Bryan, William Jennings, Mar. 19, 1860–July 26, 1925.
  Vol. 2, Pt. 1–191
Bryant, Gridley, Aug. 26, 1789–June 13, 1867.
  Vol. 2, Pt. 1–197
Bryant, John Howard, July 22, 1807–Jan. 14, 1902.
  Vol. 2, Pt. 1–198
Bryant, Joseph Decatur, Mar. 12, 1845–Apr. 7, 1914.
  Vol. 2, Pt. 1–199
Bryant, Louise Frances Stevens, Sept. 19, 1885–Aug. 29, 1959. Supp. 6–80
Bryant, Ralph Clement, Jan. 22, 1877–Feb. 1, 1939.
  Supp. 2–72
Bryant, William Cullen, Nov. 3, 1794–June 12, 1878.
  Vol. 2, Pt. 1–200
Bryce, Lloyd Stephens, Sept. 20, 1851–Apr. 2, 1917.
  Vol. 2, Pt. 1–205
Bryson, Lyman Lloyd, July 12, 1888–Nov. 24, 1959.
  Supp. 6–82
Buchanan, Franklin, Sept. 17, 1800–May 11, 1874.
  Vol. 2, Pt. 1–206

Buchanan, James, Apr. 23, 1791–June 1, 1868.
  Vol. 2, Pt. 1–207
Buchanan, John, 1772–Nov. 6, 1844.
  Vol. 2, Pt. 1–214
Buchanan, Joseph, Aug. 24, 1785–Sept. 29, 1829.
  Vol. 2, Pt. 1–215
Buchanan, Joseph Ray, Dec. 6, 1851–Sept. 13, 1924.
  Vol. 2, Pt. 1–215
Buchanan, Joseph Rodes, Dec. 11, 1814–Dec. 26, 1899.
  Vol. 2, Pt. 1–216
Buchanan, Robert Christie, Mar. 1, 1811–Nov. 29, 1878.
  Vol. 2, Pt. 1–217
Buchanan, Scott Milross, Mar. 17, 1895–Mar. 25, 1968.
  Supp. 8–58
Buchanan, Thomas, Dec. 21, 1711–Nov. 10, 1815.
  Vol. 2, Pt. 1–218
Buchanan, William Insco, Sept. 10, 1852–Oct. 16, 1909.
  Vol. 2, Pt. 1–219
Bucher, John Conrad, June 10, 1730–Aug. 15, 1780.
  Vol. 2, Pt. 1–220
Buchman, Frank Nathan Daniel, June 4, 1878–Aug. 7, 1961.
  Supp. 7–88
Buchtel, John Richards, Jan. 18, 1820–May 23, 1892.
  Vol. 2, Pt. 1–221
Buck, Albert Henry, Oct. 20, 1842–Nov. 16, 1922.
  Vol. 2, Pt. 1–221
Buck, Daniel, Nov. 9, 1753–Aug. 16, 1816.
  Vol. 2, Pt. 1–222
Buck, Dudley, Mar. 10, 1839–Oct. 6, 1909.
  Vol. 2, Pt. 1–222
Buck, Franklyn Howard, Mar. 17, 1884–Mar. 25, 1950.
  Supp. 4–119
Buck, Gurdon, May 4, 1807–Mar. 6, 1877.
  Vol. 2, Pt. 1–223
Buck, Leffert Lefferts, Feb. 5, 1837–July 17, 1909.
  Vol. 2, Pt. 1–224
Buck, Philo Melvin, May 15, 1846–Sept. 8, 1924.
  Vol. 2, Pt. 1–225
Buckalew, Charles Rollin, Dec. 28, 1821–May 19, 1899.
  Vol. 2, Pt. 1–225
Buckhout, Isaac Craig, Nov. 7, 1830–Sept. 27, 1874.
  Vol. 2, Pt. 1–226
Buckingham, Joseph Tinker, Dec. 21, 1779–Apr. 11, 1861.
  Vol. 2, Pt. 1–227
Buckingham, William Alfred, May 28, 1804–Feb. 5, 1875.
  Vol. 2, Pt. 1–228
Buckland, Cyrus, Aug. 10, 1799–Feb. 26, 1891.
  Vol. 2, Pt. 1–229
Buckland, Ralph Pomeroy, Jan. 20, 1812–May 27, 1892.
  Vol. 2, Pt. 1–230
Buckler, Thomas Hepburn, Jan. 4, 1812–Apr. 20, 1901.
  Vol. 2, Pt. 1–230
Buckley, James Monroe, Dec. 16, 1836–Feb. 8, 1920.
  Vol. 2, Pt. 1–231
Buckley, Oliver Ellsworth, Aug. 8, 1887–Dec. 14, 1959.
  Supp. 6–84
Buckley, Samuel Botsford, May 9, 1809–Feb. 18, 1883.
  Vol. 2, Pt. 1–232
Buckminster, Joseph Stevens, May 26, 1784–June 9, 1812.
  Vol. 2, Pt. 1–233
Bucknell, William, Apr. 1, 1811–Mar. 5, 1890.
  Vol. 2, Pt. 1–234
Buckner, Emory Roy, Aug. 7, 1877–Mar. 11, 1941.
  Supp. 3–116
Buckner, Simon Bolivar, Apr. 1, 1823–Jan. 8, 1914.
  Vol. 2, Pt. 1–234
Buckner, Simon Bolivar, July 18, 1886–June 18, 1945.
  Supp. 3–117
Budd, Edward Gowen, Dec. 28, 1870–Nov. 30, 1946.
  Supp. 4–120
Budd, Joseph Lancaster, July 3, 1835–Dec. 20, 1904.
  Vol. 2, Pt. 1–236
Budd, Ralph, Aug. 20, 1879–Feb. 2, 1962.
  Supp. 7–89
Buehler, Huber Gray, Dec. 3, 1864–June 20, 1924.
  Vol. 2, Pt. 1–237
Buel, Jesse, Jan. 4, 1778–Oct. 6, 1839.
  Vol. 2, Pt. 1–238
Buell, Abel, Feb. 1, 1741/42–Mar. 10, 1822.
  Vol. 2, Pt. 1–239
Buell, Don Carlos, Mar. 23, 1818–Nov. 19, 1898.
  Vol. 2, Pt. 1–240

Burnett, Charles Henry, May 28, 1842–Jan. 30, 1902.
Vol. 2, Pt. 1–296
Burnett, Frances Eliza Hodgson, Nov. 24, 1849–Oct. 29, 1924. Vol. 2, Pt. 1–297
Burnett, Henry Lawrence, Dec. 26, 1838–Jan. 4, 1916.
Vol. 2, Pt. 1–298
Burnett, Joseph, Nov. 11, 1820–Aug. 11, 1894.
Vol. 2, Pt. 1–299
Burnett, Peter Hardeman, Nov. 15, 1807–May 17, 1895.
Vol. 2, Pt. 1–300
Burnett, Swan Moses, Mar. 16, 1847–Jan. 18, 1906.
Vol. 2, Pt. 1–301
Burnham, Clara Louise Root, May 26, 1854–June 20, 1927.
Vol. 2, Pt. 1–301
Burnham, Daniel Hudson, Sept. 4, 1846–June 1, 1912.
Vol. 2, Pt. 1–302
Burnham, Frederick Russell, May 11, 1861–Sept. 1, 1947.
Supp. 4–126
Burnham, Sherburne Wesley, Dec. 12, 1838–Mar. 11, 1921.
Vol. 2, Pt. 1–307
Burnham, William Henry, Dec. 3, 1855–June 25, 1941.
Supp. 3–119
Burns, Anthony, May 31, 1834–July 27, 1862.
Vol. 2, Pt. 1–308
Burns, Bob, Aug. 2, 1890–Feb. 2, 1956.
Supp. 6–88
Burns, Otway, 1775?–Oct. 25, 1850.
Vol. 2, Pt. 1–308
Burns, William John, Oct. 19, 1861–Apr. 14, 1932.
Supp. 1–134
Burnside, Ambrose Everett, May 23, 1824–Sept. 13, 1881,.
Vol. 2, Pt. 1–309
Burr, Aaron, Feb. 6, 1756–Sept. 14, 1836.
Vol. 2, Pt. 1–314
Burr, Aaron, Jan. 4, 1715/16–Sept. 24, 1757.
Vol. 2, Pt. 1–313
Burr, Alfred Edmund, Mar. 27, 1815–Jan. 8, 1900.
Vol. 2, Pt. 1–321
Burr, Enoch Fitch, Oct. 21, 1818–May 8, 1907.
Vol. 2, Pt. 1–321
Burr, George Lincoln, Jan. 30, 1857–June 27, 1938.
Supp. 2–75
Burr, Theodosia, June 21, 1783–Jan. 1813.
Vol. 2, Pt. 1–322
Burr, William Hubert, July 14, 1851–Dec. 13, 1934.
Supp. 1–135
Burrage, Henry Sweetser, Jan. 7, 1837–Mar. 9, 1926.
Vol. 2, Pt. 1–323
Burrage, Walter Lincoln, Oct. 26, 1860–Jan. 26, 1935.
Supp. 1–136
Burrall, William Porter, Sept. 18, 1806–Mar. 3, 1874.
Vol. 2, Pt. 1–324
Burrell, David James, Aug. 1, 1844–Dec. 5, 1926.
Vol. 2, Pt. 1–324
Burrill, Alexander Mansfield, June 19, 1807–Feb. 7, 1869.
Vol. 2, Pt. 1–325
Burrill, James, Apr. 25, 1772–Dec. 25, 1820.
Vol. 2, Pt. 1–325
Burrill, Thomas Jonathan, Apr. 25, 1839–Apr. 14, 1916.
Vol. 2, Pt. 1–326
Burrington, George, c. 1680–Feb. 1759.
Vol. 2, Pt. 1–327
Burritt, Elihu, Dec. 8, 1810–Mar. 6, 1879.
Vol. 2, Pt. 1–328
Burroughs, Bryson, Sept. 8, 1869–Nov. 16, 1934.
Supp. 1–137
Burroughs, Edgar Rice, Sept. 1, 1875–Mar. 19, 1950.
Supp. 4–128
Burroughs, John, Apr. 3, 1837–Mar. 29, 1921.
Vol. 2, Pt. 1–330
Burroughs, John Curtis, Dec. 2, 1817–Apr. 21, 1892.
Vol. 2, Pt. 1–334
Burroughs, William Seward, Jan. 28, 1855–Sept. 15, 1898.
Supp. 1–138
Burrow, Trigant, Sept. 7, 1875–May 24, 1950.
Supp. 4–130
Burrowes, Edward Thomas, July 25, 1852–Mar. 10, 1918.
Vol. 2, Pt. 1–334
Burrowes, Thomas Henry, Nov. 16, 1805–Feb. 25, 1871.
Vol. 2, Pt. 1–335
Burrows, Julius Caesar, Jan. 9, 1837–Nov. 16, 1915.
Vol. 2, Pt. 1–336

Burrows, William, Oct. 6, 1785–Sept. 5, 1813.
Vol. 2, Pt. 1–337
Burson, William Worth, Sept. 22, 1832–Apr. 10, 1913.
Vol. 2, Pt. 1–337
Burt, John, Apr. 18, 1814–Aug. 16, 1886.
Vol. 2, Pt. 1–338
Burt, Mary Elizabeth, June 11, 1850–Oct. 17, 1918.
Vol. 2, Pt. 1–339
Burt, William Austin, June 13, 1792–Aug. 18, 1858.
Vol. 2, Pt. 1–339
Burton, Asa, Aug. 25, 1752–May 1, 1836.
Vol. 2, Pt. 1–340
Burton, Clarence Monroe, Nov. 18, 1853–Oct. 23, 1932.
Supp. 1–139
Burton, Ernest De Witt, Feb. 4, 1856–May 26, 1925.
Vol. 2, Pt. 1–341
Burton, Frederick Russell, Feb. 23, 1861–Sept. 30, 1909.
Vol. 2, Pt. 1–342
Burton, Harold Hitz, June 22, 1888–Oct. 28, 1964.
Supp. 7–95
Burton, Hutchins Gordon, c. 1774–Apr. 21, 1836.
Vol. 2, Pt. 1–34
Burton, Marion Le Roy, Aug. 30, 1874–Feb. 18, 1925.
Vol. 2, Pt. 1–343
Burton, Nathaniel Judson, Dec. 17, 1824–Oct. 13, 1887.
Vol. 2, Pt. 1–344
Burton, Richard Eugene, Mar. 14, 1861–Apr. 8, 1940.
Supp. 2–76
Burton, Theodore Elijah, Dec. 20, 1851–Oct. 28, 1929.
Supp. 1–141
Burton, Warren, Nov. 23, 1800–June 6, 1866.
Vol. 2, Pt. 1–344
Burton, William, Oct. 16, 1789–Aug. 5, 1866.
Vol. 2, Pt. 1–345
Burton, William Evans, Sept. 24, 1804–Feb. 10, 1860.
Vol. 2, Pt. 1–346
Busch, Adolphus, July 10, 1839–Oct. 10, 1913.
Supp. 1–141
Bush, George, June 12, 1796–Sept. 19, 1859.
Vol. 2, Pt. 1–347
Bush, Lincoln, Dec. 14, 1860–Dec. 10, 1940.
Supp. 2–77
Bush-Brown, Henry Kirke, Apr. 21, 1857–Mar. 1, 1935.
Supp. 1–143
Bushman, Francis Xavier, Jan. 10, 1883–Aug. 23, 1966.
Supp. 8–65
Bushnell, Asa Smith, Sept. 16, 1834–Jan. 15, 1904.
Vol. 2, Pt. 1–347
Bushnell, David, c. 1742–1824.
Vol. 2, Pt. 1–348
Bushnell, George Ensign, Sept. 10, 1853–July 19, 1924.
Vol. 2, Pt. 1–349
Bushnell, Horace, Apr. 14, 1802–Feb. 17, 1876.
Vol. 2, Pt. 1–350
Bussey, Cyrus, Oct. 5, 1833–Mar. 2, 1915.
Vol. 2, Pt. 1–354
Butler, Andrew Pickens, Nov. 18, 1796–May 25, 1857.
Vol. 2, Pt. 1–355
Butler, Benjamin Franklin, Dec. 14, 1795–Nov. 8, 1858.
Vol. 2, Pt. 1–356
Butler, Benjamin Franklin, Nov. 5, 1818–Jan. 11, 1893.
Vol. 2, Pt. 1–357
Butler, Burridge Davenal, Feb. 5, 1868–Mar. 30, 1948.
Supp. 4–131
Butler, Charles, Jan. 15, 1802–Dec. 13, 1897.
Vol. 2, Pt. 1–359
Butler, Ezra, Sept. 24, 1763–July 12, 1838.
Vol. 2, Pt. 1–360
Butler, Howard Crosby, Mar. 7, 1872–Aug. 13?, 1922.
Vol. 2, Pt. 1–361
Butler, John, 1728–May 1796.
Vol. 2, Pt. 1–361
Butler, John Wesley, Oct. 13, 1851–Mar. 17, 1918.
Vol. 2, Pt. 1–362
Butler, Marion, May 20, 1863–June 3, 1938.
Supp. 2–78
Butler, Matthew Calbraith, Mar. 8, 1836–Apr. 14, 1909.
Vol. 2, Pt. 1–363
Butler, Nicholas Murray, Apr. 2, 1862–Dec. 7, 1947.
Supp. 4–133
Butler, Pierce, July 11, 1744–Feb. 15, 1822.
Vol. 2, Pt. 1–364

Butler, Pierce, Mar. 17, 1866–Nov. 16, 1939.
    Supp. 2–79
Butler, Pierce Mason, Apr. 11, 1798–Aug. 20, 1847.
    Vol. 2, Pt. 1–365
Butler, Richard, Apr. 1, 1743–Nov. 4, 1791.
    Vol. 2, Pt. 1–366
Butler, Simeon, Mar. 25, 1770?–Nov. 7, 1847.
    Vol. 2, Pt. 1–366
Butler, Smedley Darlington, July 30, 1881–June 21, 1940.
    Supp. 2–80
Butler, Thomas Belden, Aug. 22, 1806–June 8, 1873.
    Vol. 2, Pt. 1–367
Butler, Walter N., d. Oct. 30, 1781.
    Vol. 2, Pt. 1–367
Butler, William, Dec. 17, 1759–Sept. 23, 1821.
    Vol. 2, Pt. 1–368
Butler, William, Jan. 30, 1818–Aug. 18, 1899.
    Vol. 2, Pt. 1–369
Butler, William Allen, Feb. 20, 1825–Sept. 9, 1902.
    Vol. 2, Pt. 1–369
Butler, William Orlando, Apr. 19, 1791–Aug. 6, 1880.
    Vol. 2, Pt. 1–371
Butler, Zebulon, Jan. 23, 1731–July 28, 1795.
    Vol. 2, Pt. 1–372
Butterfield, Daniel, Oct. 31, 1831–July 17, 1901.
    Vol. 2, Pt. 1–372
Butterfield, John, Nov. 18, 1801–Nov. 14, 1869.
    Vol. 2, Pt. 1–374
Butterfield, Kenyon Leech, June 11, 1868–Nov. 26, 1935.
    Supp. 1–144
Butterick, Ebenezer, May 29, 1826–Mar. 31, 1903.
    Vol. 2, Pt. 1–375
Butterworth, Benjamin, Oct. 22, 1837–Jan. 16, 1898.
    Vol. 2, Pt. 1–376
Butterworth, Hezekiah, Dec. 22, 1839–Sept. 5, 1905.
    Vol. 2, Pt. 1–376
Buttrick, Wallace, Oct. 23, 1853–May 27, 1926.
    Vol. 2, Pt. 1–377
Butts, Isaac, Jan. 11, 1816–Nov. 20, 1874.
    Vol. 2, Pt. 1–378
Buttz, Henry Anson, Apr. 18, 1835–Oct. 6, 1920.
    Vol. 2, Pt. 1–379
Byerly, William Elwood, Dec. 13, 1849–Dec. 20, 1935.
    Supp. 1–145
Byford, William Heath, Mar. 20, 1817–May 21, 1890.
    Vol. 2, Pt. 1–379
Byington, Cyrus, Mar. 11, 1793–Dec. 31, 1868.
    Vol. 2, Pt. 1–380
Byles, Mather, Mar. 15, 1706/7–July 5, 1788.
    Vol. 2, Pt. 1–381
Bynum, William Preston, June 16, 1820–Dec. 30, 1909.
    Vol. 2, Pt. 1–382
Byoir, Carl Robert, June 24, 1888–Feb. 3, 1957.
    Supp. 6–89
Byrd, Harry Flood, June 10, 1887–Oct. 20, 1966.
    Supp. 8–67
Byrd, Richard Evelyn, Oct. 25, 1888–Mar. 11, 1957.
    Supp. 6–91
Byrd, William, 1652–Dec. 4. 1704.
    Vol. 2, Pt. 1–382
Byrd, William, Mar. 28, 1674–Aug. 26, 1744.
    Vol. 2, Pt. 1–383
Byrne, Andrew, Dec. 5, 1802–June 10, 1862.
    Vol. 2, Pt. 1–384
Byrne, Donn. [See Donn-Byrne, Brian Oswald, 1889– 1928.]
Byrne, John, Oct. 13, 1825–Oct. 1, 1902.
    Vol. 2, Pt. 1–385
Byrnes, Thomas F., 1842–May 7, 1910.
    Vol. 2, Pt. 1–386
Byrns, Joseph Wellington, July 20, 1869–June 4, 1936.
    Supp. 2–82

Cabell, James Branch, Apr. 14, 1879–May 5, 1958.
    Supp. 6–94
Cabell, James Lawrence, Aug. 26, 1813–Aug. 13, 1889.
    Vol. 2, Pt. 1–386
Cabell, Joseph Carrington, Dec. 28, 1778–Feb. 5, 1856.
    Vol. 2, Pt. 1–387
Cabell, Nathaniel Francis, July 23, 1807–Sept. 1, 1891.
    Vol. 2, Pt. 1–388
Cabell, Samuel Jordan, Dec. 15, 1756–Aug. 4, 1818.
    Vol. 2, Pt. 1–388

Cabell, William, Mar. 13, 1729/30–Mar. 23, 1798.
    Vol. 2, Pt. 1–389
Cabell, William H., Dec. 16, 1772–Jan. 12, 1853.
    Vol. 2, Pt. 1–390
Cabell, William Lewis, Jan. 1, 1827–Feb. 22, 1911.
    Vol. 2, Pt. 1–390
Cabet, Étienne, Jan. 1, 1788–Nov. 8, 1856.
    Vol. 2, Pt. 1–391
Cable, Frank Taylor, June 19, 1863–May 21, 1945.
    Supp. 3–120
Cable, George Washington, Oct. 12, 1844–Jan. 31, 1925.
    Vol. 2, Pt. 1–392
Cabot, Arthur Tracy, Jan. 25, 1852–Nov. 4, 1912.
    Vol. 2, Pt. 1–393
Cabot, Edward Clarke, Apr. 17, 1818–Jan. 5, 1901.
    Vol. 2, Pt. 1–394
Cabot, George, Jan. 16, 1752–Apr. 18, 1823.
    Vol. 2, Pt. 1–395
Cabot, Godfrey Lowell, Feb. 26, 1861–Nov. 2, 1962.
    Supp. 7–97
Cabot, Hugh, Aug. 11, 1872–Aug. 14, 1945.
    Supp. 3–121
Cabot, Richard Clarke, May 21, 1868–May 7, 1939.
    Supp. 2–83
Cabrillo, Juan Rodriguez, d. Jan. 3, 1543.
    Vol. 2, Pt. 1–396
Cabrini, Francis Xavier, July 15, 1850–Dec. 22, 1917.
    Supp. 1–146
Cadillac, Antoine de la Mothe Sieur, c. 1656–Oct. 18, 1730.
    Vol. 2, Pt. 1–397
Cadman, Charles Wakefield, Dec. 24, 1881–Dec. 30, 1946.
    Supp. 4–138
Cadman, Samuel Parkes, Dec. 18, 1864–July 12, 1936.
    Supp. 2–85
Cadwalader, John, Jan. 1742–Feb. 10, 1786.
    Vol. 2, Pt. 1–398
Cadwalader, John, Apr. 1, 1805–Jan. 26, 1879.
    Vol. 2, Pt. 1–398
Cadwalader, Lambert, 1743–Sept. 13, 1823.
    Vol. 2, Pt. 1–399
Cadwalader, Thomas, 1707/8–Nov. 14, 1799.
    Vol. 2, Pt. 1–400
Cady, Daniel, Apr. 29, 1773–Oct. 31, 1859.
    Vol. 2, Pt. 1–401
Cady, Sarah Louise Ensign, Sept. 13, 1829–Nov. 8, 1912.
    Vol. 2, Pt. 1–402
Caffery, Donelson, Sept. 10, 1835–Dec. 30, 1906.
    Vol. 2, Pt. 1–402
Caffin, Charles Henry, June 4, 1854–Jan. 14, 1918.
    Vol. 2, Pt. 1–403
Cahan, Abraham, July 7, 1860–Aug. 31, 1951.
    Supp. 5–95
Cahill, Holger, Jan. 13, 1887–July 8, 1960.
    Supp. 6–95
Cahn, Edmond Nathaniel, Jan. 17, 1906–Aug. 9, 1964.
    Supp. 7–99
Cain, Richard Harvey, Apr. 12, 1825–Jan. 18, 1887.
    Vol. 2, Pt. 1–403
Cain, William, May 14, 1847–Dec. 7, 1930.
    Supp. 1–148
Caines, George, 1771–July 10, 1825.
    Vol. 2, Pt. 1–404
Cajori, Florian, Feb. 28, 1859–Aug. 14, 1930.
    Supp. 1–148
Calder, Alexander Stirling, Jan. 11, 1870–Jan. 7, 1945.
    Supp. 3–123
Caldwell, Alexander, Mar. 1, 1830–May 19, 1917.
    Vol. 2, Pt. 1–405
Caldwell, Charles, May 14, 1772–July 9, 1853.
    Vol. 2, Pt. 1–406
Caldwell, Charles Henry Bromedge, June 11, 1823–Nov. 30, 1877. Vol. 2, Pt. 1–406
Caldwell, David, Mar. 22, 1725–Aug. 25, 1824.
    Vol. 2, Pt. 1–407
Caldwell, Eugene Wilson, Dec. 3, 1870–June 20, 1918.
    Vol. 2, Pt. 1–407
Caldwell, Henry Clay, Sept. 4, 1832–Feb. 15, 1915.
    Vol. 2, Pt. 1–408
Caldwell, James, Apr. 1734–Nov. 24, 1781.
    Vol. 2, Pt. 1–408
Caldwell, Joseph, Apr. 21, 1773–Jan. 27, 1835.
    Vol. 2, Pt. 1–409

Caldwell, Otis William, Dec. 18, 1869–July 5, 1947.
Supp. 4–139
Calef, Robert, 1648–Apr. 13, 1719.
Vol. 2, Pt. 1–410
Calhoun, John, Oct. 14, 1806–Oct. 13, 1859.
Vol. 2, Pt. 1–410
Calhoun, John Caldwell, Mar. 18, 1782–Mar. 31, 1850.
Vol. 2, Pt. 1–411
Calhoun, Patrick, Mar. 21, 1856–June 16, 1943.
Supp. 3–125
Calhoun, William Barron, Dec. 29, 1795–Nov. 8, 1865.
Vol. 2, Pt. 1–419
Calhoun, William James, Oct. 5, 1848–Sept. 10, 1916.
Vol. 2, Pt. 1–420
California, Joe, May 8, 1829–Oct. 29, 1876.
Vol. 2, Pt. 1–421
Calkins, Earnest Elmo, Mar. 25, 1868–Oct. 4, 1964.
Supp. 7–100
Calkins, Gary Nathan, Jan. 18, 1869–Jan. 4, 1943.
Supp. 3–126
Calkins, Mary Whiton, Mar. 30, 1863–Feb. 26, 1930.
Supp. 1–149
Calkins, Norman Allison, Sept. 9, 1822–Dec. 22, 1895.
Vol. 2, Pt. 1–421
Calkins, Phineas Wolcott, June 10, 1831–Dec. 31, 1924.
Vol. 2, Pt. 1–422
Calkins, Wolcott. [See Calkins, Phineas Wolcott, 1831–1924.]
Call, Richard Keith, 1791–Sept. 14, 1862.
Vol. 2, Pt. 1–422
Callahan, Patrick Henry, Oct. 15, 1865–Feb. 4, 1940.
Supp. 2–86
Callaway, Morgan, Nov. 3, 1862–Apr. 3, 1936.
Supp. 2–88
Callaway, Samuel Rodger, Dec. 24, 1850–June 1, 1904.
Vol. 2, Pt. 1–423
Callender, Guy Stevens, Nov. 9, 1865–Aug. 8, 1915.
Vol. 2, Pt. 1–424
Callender, James Thomson, 1758–July 17, 1803.
Vol. 2, Pt. 1–425
Callender, John, 1706–Jan. 26, 1748.
Vol. 2, Pt. 1–426
Callimachos, Panos Demetrios, Dec. 4, 1879–Oct. 13, 1963.
Supp. 7–102
Calverley, Charles, Nov. 1, 1833–Feb. 25, 1914.
Vol. 2, Pt. 1–426
Calvert, Charles, Aug. 27, 1637–Feb. 21, 1715.
Vol. 2, Pt. 1–427
Calvert, Charles Benedict, Aug. 23, 1808–May 12, 1864.
Vol. 2, Pt. 1–427
Calvert, George, c. 1580–Apr. 15, 1632.
Vol. 2, Pt. 1–428
Calvert, George Henry, June 2, 1803–May 24, 1889.
Vol. 2, Pt. 1–429
Calvert, Leonard, 1606–June 9, 1647.
Vol. 2, Pt. 1–430
Calverton, Victor Francis, June 25, 1900–Nov. 20, 1940.
Supp. 2–89
Calvin, Samuel, Feb. 2, 1840–Apr. 17, 1911.
Vol. 2, Pt. 1–431
Cambreleng, Churchill Caldom, 1786–Apr. 30, 1862.
Vol. 2, Pt. 1–432
Camden, Johnson Newlon, Mar. 6, 1828–Apr. 25, 1908.
Vol. 2, Pt. 1–433
Cameron, Andrew Carr, Sept. 28, 1834–May 28, 1890.
Vol. 2, Pt. 1–433
Cameron, Archibald, c. 1771–Dec. 4, 1836.
Vol. 2, Pt. 1–434
Cameron, James Donald, May 14, 1833–Aug. 30, 1918.
Vol. 2, Pt. 1–435
Cameron, Robert Alexander, Feb. 22, 1828–Mar. 15, 1894.
Vol. 2, Pt. 1–436
Cameron, Simon, Mar. 8, 1799–June 26, 1889.
Vol. 2, Pt. 1–437
Cameron, William Evelyn, Nov. 29, 1842–Jan. 25, 1927.
Vol. 2, Pt. 1–439
Camm, John, 1718–1778.
Vol. 2, Pt. 1–440
Cammerhoff, John Christopher Frederick, July 28, 1721–Apr. 28, 1751. Vol. 2, Pt. 1–441
Camp, David Nelson, Oct. 13, 1820–Oct. 19, 1916.
Vol. 2, Pt. 1–441

Camp, Hiram, Apr. 9, 1811–July 8, 1893.
Vol. 2, Pt. 1–442
Camp, John Lafayette, Feb. 20, 1828–July 16, 1891.
Vol. 2, Pt. 1–443
Camp, John Lafayette, Sept. 23, 1855–Aug. 10, 1918,.
Vol. 2, Pt. 1–443
Camp, Walter Chauncey, Apr. 7, 1859–Mar. 14, 1925.
Vol. 2, Pt. 1–444
Campanius, John, Aug. 15, 1601–Sept. 17, 1683.
Vol. 2, Pt. 1–445
Campau, Joseph, Feb. 25, 1769–July 23, 1863.
Vol. 2, Pt. 1–446
Campbell, Alexander, Sept. 12, 1778–Mar. 4, 1866.
Vol. 2, Pt. 1–446
Campbell, Allen, Oct. 11, 1815–Mar. 18, 1894.
Vol. 2, Pt. 1–448
Campbell, Andrew, June 14, 1821–Apr. 13, 1890.
Vol. 2, Pt. 1–449
Campbell, Bartley, Aug. 12, 1843–July 30, 1888.
Vol. 2, Pt. 1–450
Campbell, Charles, May 1, 1807–July 11, 1876.
Vol. 2, Pt. 1–451
Campbell, Charles Macfie, Sept. 8, 1876–Aug. 7, 1943.
Supp. 3–127
Campbell, Douglas Houghton, Dec. 16, 1859–Feb. 24, 1953.
Supp. 5–97
Campbell, Francis Joseph, Oct. 9, 1832–June 30, 1914.
Vol. 2, Pt. 1–451
Campbell, George Washington, Feb. 8, 1769–Feb. 17, 1848.
Vol. 2, Pt. 1–452
Campbell, George Washington, Jan. 12, 1817–July 15, 1898.
Vol. 2, Pt. 1–452
Campbell, Henry Fraser, Feb. 10, 1824–Dec. 15, 1891.
Vol. 2, Pt. 1–453
Campbell, James, Sept. 1, 1812–Jan. 27, 1893.
Vol. 2, Pt. 1–454
Campbell, James Hepburn, Feb. 8, 1820–Apr. 12, 1895.
Vol. 2, Pt. 1–455
Campbell, James Valentine, Feb. 25, 1823–Mar. 26, 1890.
Vol. 2, Pt. 1–455
Campbell, John. [See Loudoun, John Campbell, Fourth Earl of, 1705–1782.]
Campbell, John, 1653–Mar. 4, 1727/28.
Vol. 2, Pt. 1–456
Campbell, John Archibald, June 24, 1811–Mar. 12, 1889.
Vol. 2, Pt. 1–456
Campbell, John Wilson, Feb. 23, 1782–Sept. 24, 1833.
Vol. 2, Pt. 1–459
Campbell, Josiah A. Patterson, Mar. 2, 1830–Jan. 10, 1917.
Vol. 2, Pt. 1–460
Campbell, Lewis Davis, Aug. 9, 1811–Nov. 26, 1882.
Vol. 2, Pt. 1–461
Campbell, Marius Robinson, Sept. 30, 1858–Dec. 7, 1940.
Supp. 2–90
Campbell, Prince Lucien, Oct. 6, 1861–Aug. 14, 1925.
Vol. 2, Pt. 1–462
Campbell, Robert, Mar. 1804–Oct. 16, 1879.
Vol. 2, Pt. 1–462
Campbell, Thomas, Feb. 1, 1763–Jan. 4, 1854.
Vol. 2, Pt. 1–463
Campbell, Thomas Joseph, Apr. 29, 1848–Dec. 14, 1925.
Vol. 2, Pt. 1–463
Campbell, Lord William, d. Sept. 5, 1778.
Vol. 2, Pt. 1–464
Campbell, William, 1745–Aug. 22, 1781.
Vol. 2, Pt. 1–465
Campbell, William, June 24, 1876–Dec. 16, 1936.
Supp. 2–91
Campbell, William Bowen, Feb. 1, 1807–Aug. 19, 1867.
Vol. 2, Pt. 1–466
Campbell, William Edward March, Sept. 18, 1893–May 15, 1954. Supp. 5–99
Campbell, William Henry, Sept. 14, 1808–Dec. 7, 1890.
Vol. 2, Pt. 1–466
Campbell, William W., June 10, 1806–Sept. 7, 1881.
Vol. 2, Pt. 1–467
Campbell, William Wallace, Apr. 11, 1862–June 14, 1938.
Supp. 2–91
Canaga, Alfred Bruce, Nov. 2, 1850–Dec. 24, 1906.
Vol. 2, Pt. 1–468
Canby, Edward Richard Sprigg, Aug. 1817–Apr. 11, 1873.
Vol. 2, Pt. 1–468

Canby, Henry Seidel, Sept. 6, 1878–Apr. 5, 1961.
  Supp. 7–103
Candee, Leverett, June 1, 1795–Nov. 27, 1863.
  Vol. 2, Pt. 1–469
Candler, Allen Daniel, Nov. 4, 1834–Oct. 26, 1910.
  Vol. 2, Pt. 1–470
Candler, Asa Griggs, Dec. 30, 1851–Mar. 12, 1929.
  Vol. 2, Pt. 1–470
Candler, Warren Akin, Aug. 23, 1857–Sept. 25, 1941.
  Supp. 3–128
Canfield, James Hulme, Mar. 18, 1847–Mar. 29, 1909.
  Vol. 2, Pt. 1–472
Canfield, Richard A., June 17, 1855–Dec. 11, 1914.
  Vol. 2, Pt. 1–472
Cannon, Annie Jump, Dec. 11, 1863–Apr. 13, 1941.
  Supp. 3–130
Cannon, Charles James, Nov. 4, 1800–Nov. 9, 1860.
  Vol. 2, Pt. 1–473
Cannon, Clarence, Apr. 11, 1879–May 12, 1964.
  Supp. 7–104
Cannon, George Quayle, Jan. 11, 1827–Apr. 12, 1901.
  Vol. 2, Pt. 1–474
Cannon, Harriet Starr, May 7, 1823–Apr. 5, 1896.
  Vol. 2, Pt. 1–475
Cannon, Ida Maud, June 29, 1877–July 8, 1960.
  Supp. 6–97
Cannon, James, Nov. 13, 1864–Sept. 6, 1944.
  Supp. 3–131
Cannon, James Graham, July 26, 1858–July 5, 1916.
  Vol. 2, Pt. 1–475
Cannon, Joseph Gurney, May 7, 1836–Nov. 12, 1926.
  Vol. 2, Pt. 1–476
Cannon, Newton, May 22, 1781–Sept. 16, 1841.
  Vol. 2, Pt. 1–477
Cannon, Walter Bradford, Oct. 19, 1871–Oct. 1, 1945.
  Supp. 3–133
Cannon, William, Mar. 15, 1809–Mar. 1, 1865.
  Vol. 2, Pt. 1–478
Canonchet, d. Apr. 1676.
  Vol. 2, Pt. 1–479
Canonge, Louis Placide, June 29, 1822–Jan. 22, 1893.
  Vol. 2, Pt. 1–479
Canonicus, c. 1565–1647.
  Vol. 2, Pt. 1–480
Cantor, Eddie, Jan. 31, 1892–Oct. 10, 1964.
  Supp. 7–105
Cantril, Albert Hadley, June 16, 1906–May 28, 1969.
  Supp. 8–69
Capen, Elmer Hewitt, Apr. 5, 1838–Mar. 22, 1905.
  Vol. 2, Pt. 1–481
Capen, Nahum, Apr. 1, 1804–Jan. 8, 1886.
  Vol. 2, Pt. 1–481
Capen, Samuel Billings, Dec. 12, 1842–Jan. 29, 1914.
  Vol. 2, Pt. 1–482
Capen, Samuel Paul, Mar. 21, 1878–June 22, 1956.
  Supp. 6–98
Capers, Ellison, Oct. 14, 1837–Apr. 22, 1908.
  Vol. 2, Pt. 1–483
Capers, William, Jan. 26, 1790–Jan. 29, 1855.
  Vol. 2, Pt. 1–483
Capone, Alphonse, Jan. 17, 1899–Jan. 25, 1947.
  Supp. 4–140
Capper, Arthur, July 14, 1865–Dec. 19, 1951.
  Supp. 5–100
Capps, Edward, Dec. 21, 1866–Aug. 21, 1950.
  Supp. 4–142
Capps, Washington Lee, Jan. 31, 1864–May 31, 1935.
  Supp. 1–150
Capron, Horace, Aug. 31, 1804–Feb. 22, 1885.
  Vol. 2, Pt. 1–484
Captain Jack, 1837?–Oct. 3, 1873.
  Vol. 2, Pt. 1–485
Caraway, Hattie Ophelia Wyatt, Feb. 1, 1878–Dec. 21, 1950.
  Supp. 4–144
Caraway, Thaddeus Horatius, Oct. 17, 1871–Nov. 6, 1931.
  Supp. 1–151
Carbutt, John, Dec. 2, 1832–July 26, 1905.
  Vol. 2, Pt. 1–485
Cárdenas, Garcia López de, fl. 1540.
  Vol. 2, Pt. 1–486
Cardozo, Benjamin Nathan, May 24, 1870–July 9, 1938.
  Supp. 2–93

Cardozo, Jacob Newton, June 17, 1786–Aug. 30, 1873.
  Vol. 2, Pt. 1–486
Carey, Henry Charles, Dec. 15, 1793–Oct. 13, 1879.
  Vol. 2, Pt. 1–487
Carey, Joseph Maull, Jan. 19, 1845–Feb. 5, 1924.
  Vol. 2, Pt. 1–487
Carey, Mathew, Jan. 28, 1760–Sept. 16, 1839.
  Vol. 2, Pt. 1–489
Carleton, Henry, c. 1785–Mar. 28, 1863.
  Vol. 2, Pt. 1–491
Carleton, Henry Guy, June 21, 1856–Dec. 10, 1910.
  Vol. 2, Pt. 1–492
Carleton, Will, Oct. 21, 1845–Dec. 18, 1912.
  Vol. 2, Pt. 1–492
Carlile, John Snyder, Dec. 16, 1817–Oct. 24, 1878.
  Vol. 2, Pt. 1–493
Carlisle, Floyd Leslie, Mar. 5, 1881–Nov. 9, 1942.
  Supp. 3–137
Carlisle, James Mandeville, May 22, 1814–May 19, 1877.
  Vol. 2, Pt. 1–494
Carlisle, John Griffin, Sept. 5, 1835–July 31, 1910.
  Vol. 2, Pt. 1–494
Carll, John Franklin, May 7, 1828–Mar. 13, 1904.
  Vol. 2, Pt. 1–496
Carlson, Anton Julius, Jan. 29, 1875–Sept. 2, 1956.
  Supp. 6–99
Carlson, Chester Floyd, Feb. 8, 1906–Sept. 19, 1968.
  Supp. 8–70
Carlson, Evans Fordyce, Feb. 26, 1896–May 27, 1947.
  Supp. 4–145
Carmack, Edward Ward, Nov. 5, 1858–Nov. 9, 1908.
  Vol. 2, Pt. 1–496
Carmichael, Oliver Cromwell, Oct. 3, 1891–Sept. 25, 1966.
  Supp. 8–72
Carmichael, William, d. Feb. 9, 1795.
  Vol. 2, Pt. 1–497
Carnahan, James, Nov. 15, 1775–Mar. 3, 1859.
  Vol. 2, Pt. 1–498
Carnap, Rudolf, May 18, 1891–Sept. 14, 1970.
  Supp. 8–74
Carnegie, Andrew, Nov. 25, 1835–Aug. 11, 1919.
  Vol. 2, Pt. 1–499
Carnegie, Dale, Nov. 24, 1888–Nov. 1, 1955.
  Supp. 5–101
Carnegie, Hattie, Mar. 14, 1886–Feb. 22, 1956.
  Supp. 6–100
Carnegie, Mary Crowninshield Endicott Chamberlain, Mar. 15, 1864–May 17, 1957. Supp. 6–101
Carney, Thomas, Aug. 20, 1824–July 28, 1888.
  Vol. 2, Pt. 1–506
Carnochan, John Murray, July 4, 1817–Oct. 28, 1887.
  Vol. 2, Pt. 1–506
Carondelet, Francisco Luis Hector, Baron de, c. 1748–Aug. 10, 1807. Vol. 2, Pt. 1–507
Carothers, Wallace Hume, Apr. 27, 1896–Apr. 29, 1937.
  Supp. 2–96
Carpenter, Cyrus Clay, Nov. 24, 1829–May 29, 1898.
  Vol. 2, Pt. 1–508
Carpenter, Edmund Janes, Oct. 16, 1845–Feb. 21, 1924.
  Vol. 2, Pt. 1–509
Carpenter, Francis Bicknell, Aug. 6, 1830–May 23, 1900.
  Vol. 2, Pt. 1–510
Carpenter, Frank George, May 8, 1855–June 18, 1924.
  Vol. 2, Pt. 1–510
Carpenter, Franklin Reuben, Nov. 5, 1848–Apr. 1, 1910.
  Vol. 2, Pt. 1–511
Carpenter, George Rice, Oct. 25, 1863–Apr. 8, 1909.
  Vol. 2, Pt. 1–511
Carpenter, John Alden, Feb. 28, 1876–Apr. 26, 1951.
  Supp. 5–103
Carpenter, Matthew Hale, Dec. 22, 1824–Feb. 24, 1881.
  Vol. 2, Pt. 1–512
Carpenter, Stephen Cullen, died c. 1820.
  Vol. 2, Pt. 1–513
Carpenter, Stephen Haskins, Aug. 7, 1831–Dec. 7, 1878.
  Vol. 2, Pt. 1–513
Carr, Benjamin, 1769–May 24, 1831.
  Vol. 2, Pt. 1–514
Carr, Charlotte Elizabeth, May 3, 1890–July 12, 1956.
  Supp. 6–102
Carr, Dabney, Apr. 27, 1773–Jan. 8, 1837.
  Vol. 2, Pt. 1–515

Carr, Dabney Smith, Mar. 5, 1802–Mar. 24, 1854.
  Vol. 2, Pt. 1–515
Carr, Elias, Feb. 25, 1839–July 22, 1900.
  Vol. 2, Pt. 1–516
Carr, Eugene Asa, Mar. 20, 1830–Dec. 2, 1910.
  Vol. 2, Pt. 1–516
Carr, Joseph Bradford, Aug. 16, 1828–Feb. 24, 1895.
  Vol. 2, Pt. 1–517
Carr, Matthew. [See Carr, Thomas Matthew, 1750–1820.]
Carr, Thomas Matthew, 1750–Sept. 29, 1820.
  Vol. 2, Pt. 1–518
Carr, Wilbur John, Oct. 31, 1870–June 26, 1942.
  Supp. 3–138
Carrel, Alexis, June 28, 1873–Nov. 5, 1944.
  Supp. 3–139
Carrère, John Merven, Nov. 9, 1858–Mar. 1, 1911.
  Vol. 2, Pt. 1–518
Carrick, Samuel, July 17, 1760–Aug. 17, 1809.
  Vol. 2, Pt. 1–520
Carrier, Willis Haviland, Nov. 26, 1876–Oct. 7, 1950.
  Supp. 4–148
Carrington, Elaine Stern, June 14, 1891–May 4, 1958.
  Supp. 6–103
Carrington, Henry Beebee, Mar. 2, 1824–Oct. 26, 1912.
  Vol. 2, Pt. 1–520
Carrington, Paul, Mar. 16, 1733–June 23, 1818.
  Vol. 2, Pt. 1–522
Carroll, Charles, Sept. 19, 1737–Nov. 14, 1832.
  Vol. 2, Pt. 1–522
Carroll, Daniel, July 22, 1730–May 7, 1796.
  Vol. 2, Pt. 1–523
Carroll, Earl, Sept. 16, 1893–June 17, 1948.
  Supp. 4–149
Carroll, Howard, Sept. 17, 1854–Dec. 30, 1916.
  Vol. 2, Pt. 1–524
Carroll, James, June 5, 1854–Sept. 16, 1907.
  Vol. 2, Pt. 1–525
Carroll, John, Jan. 8, 1735–Dec. 3, 1815.
  Vol. 2, Pt. 1–526
Carroll, John Lee, Sept. 30, 1830–Feb. 27, 1911.
  Vol. 2, Pt. 1–528
Carroll, William, Mar. 3, 1788–Mar. 22, 1844.
  Vol. 2, Pt. 1–529
Carroll Samuel Sprigg, Sept. 21, 1832–Jan. 28, 1893.
  Vol. 2, Pt. 1–528
Carrora, Joseph. [See Dundee, Johnny, 1893–1965.]
Carruth, Fred Hayden, Oct. 31, 1862–Jan. 3, 1932.
  Supp. 1–152
Carryl, Guy Wetmore, Mar. 4, 1873–Apr. 1, 1904.
  Vol. 2, Pt. 1–530
Carson, Christopher, Dec. 24, 1809–May 23, 1868.
  Vol. 2, Pt. 1–530
Carson, Hampton Lawrence, Feb. 21, 1852–July 18, 1929.
  Supp. 1–153
Carson, Jack, Oct. 27, 1910–Jan. 2, 1963.
  Supp. 7–107
Carson, John Renshaw, June 28, 1886–Oct. 31, 1940.
  Supp. 2–97
Carson, Joseph, Apr. 19, 1808–Dec. 30, 1876.
  Vol. 2, Pt. 1–532
Carson, Rachel Louise, May 27, 1907–Apr. 14, 1964.
  Supp. 7–108
Carson, Simeon Lewis, Jan. 16, 1882–Sept. 8, 1954.
  Supp. 5–104
Carter, Boake, Sept. 28, 1898–Nov. 16, 1944.
  Supp. 3–142
Carter, Caroline Louise Dudley, June 10, 1862–Nov. 13, 1937. Supp. 2–98
Carter, Elias, May 30, 1781–Mar. 23, 1864.
  Vol. 2, Pt. 1–533
Carter, Franklin, Sept. 30, 1837–Nov. 22, 1919.
  Vol. 2, Pt. 1–533
Carter, Henry Alpheus Peirce, Aug. 7, 1837–Nov. 1, 1891.
  Vol. 2, Pt. 1–534
Carter, Henry Rose, Aug. 25, 1852–Sept. 14, 1925.
  Vol. 2, Pt. 1–535
Carter, James Coolidge, Oct. 14, 1827–Feb. 14, 1905.
  Vol. 2, Pt. 1–536
Carter, James Gordon, Sept. 7, 1795–July 21, 1849.
  Vol. 2, Pt. 1–538
Carter, Jesse Benedict, June 16, 1872–July 20, 1917.
  Vol. 2, Pt. 1–539

Carter, John, 1737–1781.
  Vol. 2, Pt. 1–539
Carter, John, July 21, 1745–Aug. 19, 1814.
  Vol. 2, Pt. 1–540
Carter, Landon, Jan. 29, 1760–June 5, 1800.
  Vol. 2, Pt. 1–541
Carter, Mrs. Leslie. [See Carter, Caroline Louise Dudley, 1862–1937.]
Carter, Robert, 1663–Aug. 4, 1732.
  Vol. 2, Pt. 1–541
Carter, Robert, Feb. 5, 1819–Feb. 15, 1879.
  Vol. 2, Pt. 1–542
Carter, Samuel Powhatan, Aug. 6, 1819–May 26, 1891.
  Vol. 2, Pt. 1–543
Carter, Thomas Henry, Oct. 30, 1854–Sept. 17, 1911.
  Vol. 2, Pt. 1–544
Carter, William Samuel, Aug. 11, 1859–Mar. 15, 1923.
  Vol. 2, Pt. 1–545
Carteret, Philip, 1639–1682.
  Vol. 2, Pt. 1–546
Cartwright, Peter, Sept. 1, 1785–Sept. 25, 1872.
  Vol. 2, Pt. 1–546
Carty, John Joseph, Apr. 14, 1861–Dec. 27, 1932.
  Supp. 1–155
Carus, Paul, July 18, 1852–Feb. 11, 1919.
  Vol. 2, Pt. 1–548
Caruso, Enrico, Feb. 25, 1873–Aug. 2, 1921.
  Vol. 2, Pt. 1–549
Caruthers, William Alexander, c. 1800–Aug. 29, 1846.
  Vol. 2, Pt. 1–551
Carvalho, Solomon Solis, Jan. 16, 1856–Apr. 12, 1942.
  Supp. 3–143
Carver, George Washington, c. 1861–Jan. 5, 1943.
  Supp. 3–145
Carver, John, c. 1576–Apr. 5, 1621.
  Vol. 2, Pt. 1–551
Carver, Jonathan, Apr. 13, 1710–Jan. 31, 1780.
  Vol. 2, Pt. 1–552
Cary, Alice, Apr. 26, 1820–Feb. 12, 1871.
  Vol. 2, Pt. 1–552
Cary, Annie Louise, Oct. 22, 1842–Apr. 3, 1921.
  Vol. 2, Pt. 1–553
Cary, Archibald, 1721–1787.
  Vol. 2, Pt. 1–554
Cary, Edward, June 5, 1840–May 23, 1917.
  Vol. 2, Pt. 1–554
Cary, Elisabeth Luther, May 18, 1867–July 13, 1936.
  Supp. 2–99
Cary, Lott, 1780?–Nov. 10, 1828.
  Vol. 2, Pt. 1–555
Cary, Phoebe, Sept. 4, 1824–July 31, 1871.
  Vol. 2, Pt. 1–555
Casanowicz, Immanuel Moses, July 25, 1853–Sept. 26, 1927.
  Vol. 2, Pt. 1–556
Case, Francis Higbee, Dec. 9, 1896–June 22, 1962.
  Supp. 7–110
Case, Jerome Increase, Dec. 11, 1818–Dec. 22, 1891.
  Vol. 2, Pt. 1–556
Case, Leonard, July 29, 1786–Dec. 7, 1864.
  Vol. 2, Pt. 1–557
Case, Leonard, June 27, 1820–Jan. 6, 1880.
  Vol. 2, Pt. 1–558
Case, Shirley Jackson, Sept. 28, 1872–Dec. 5, 1947.
  Supp. 4–151
Case, William Scoville, June 27, 1863–Feb. 28, 1921.
  Vol. 2, Pt. 1–558
Casey, Joseph, Dec. 17, 1814–Feb. 10, 1879.
  Vol. 2, Pt. 1–559
Casey, Silas, July 12, 1807–Jan. 22, 1882.
  Vol. 2, Pt. 1–560
Casey, Thomas Lincoln, May 10, 1831–Mar. 25, 1896.
  Supp. 1–156
Cash, Wilbur Joseph, May 2, 1900–July 1, 1941.
  Supp. 3–147
Casilear, John William, June 25, 1811–Aug. 17, 1893.
  Vol. 2, Pt. 1–560
Cass, George Washington, Mar. 12, 1810–Mar. 21, 1888.
  Vol. 2, Pt. 1–561
Cass, Lewis, Oct. 9, 1782–June 17, 1866.
  Vol. 2, Pt. 1–562
Cassatt, Alexander Johnston, Dec. 8, 1839–Dec. 28, 1906.
  Vol. 2, Pt. 1–564

Cassatt, Mary, May 22, 1845–June 14, 1926.
Vol. 2, Pt. 1–567
Cassidy, Marshall Whiting, Feb. 21, 1892–Oct. 23, 1968.
Supp. 8–75
Cassidy, William, Aug. 12, 1815–Jan. 23, 1873.
Vol. 2, Pt. 1–568
Cassin, John, Sept. 6, 1813–Jan. 10, 1869.
Vol. 2, Pt. 1–568
Cassoday, John Bolivar, July 7, 1830–Dec. 30, 1907.
Supp. 1–157
Castle, Irene Foote, Apr. 7, 1893–Jan. 25, 1969.
Supp. 8–76
Castle, Vernon Blythe, May 2, 1887–Feb. 15, 1918.
Vol. 2, Pt. 1–569
Castle, William Richards, Jr., June 19, 1878–Oct. 13, 1963.
Supp. 7–112
Caswell, Alexis, Jan. 29, 1799–Jan. 8, 1877.
Vol. 2, Pt. 1–570
Caswell, Richard, Aug. 3, 1729–Nov. 1789.
Vol. 2, Pt. 1–571
Cataldo, Joseph Maria, Mar. 17, 1837–Apr. 9, 1928.
Supp. 1–158
Catchings, Waddill, Sept. 6, 1879–Dec. 31, 1967.
Supp. 8–78
Catesby, Mark, c. 1679–Dec. 23, 1749.
Vol. 2, Pt. 1–571
Cathcart, James Leander, June 1, 1767–Oct. 6, 1843.
Vol. 2, Pt. 1–572
Cathcart, William, Nov. 8, 1826–July 8, 1908.
Vol. 2, Pt. 1–573
Cather, Willa, Dec. 7, 1873–Apr. 24, 1947.
Supp. 4–153
Catherwood, Mary Hartwell, Dec. 16, 1847–Dec. 26, 1902.
Vol. 2, Pt. 1–573
Catlett, Sidney, Jan. 17, 1910–Mar. 25, 1951.
Supp. 5–105
Catlin, George, July 26, 1796–Dec. 23, 1872.
Vol. 2, Pt. 1–574
Caton, John Dean, Mar. 19, 1812–July 30, 1895.
Vol. 2, Pt. 1–575
Catron, John, c. 1786–May 30, 1865.
Vol. 2, Pt. 1–576
Catt, Carrie Clinton Lane Chapman, Jan. 9, 1859–Mar. 9, 1947. Supp. 4–155
Cattell, Alexander Gilmore, Feb. 12, 1816–Apr. 8, 1894.
Vol. 2, Pt. 1–577
Cattell, James McKeen, May 25, 1860–Jan. 20, 1944.
Supp. 3–148
Cattell, William Cassaday, Aug. 30, 1827–Feb. 11, 1898.
Vol. 2, Pt. 1–578
Cawein, Madison Julius, Mar. 23, 1865–Dec. 8, 1914.
Vol. 2, Pt. 1–578
Cayton, Horace Roscoe, Apr. 12, 1903–Jan. 22, 1970.
Supp. 8–79
Cayvan, Georgia, 1858–Nov. 19, 1906.
Vol. 2, Pt. 1–580
Cazenove, Théophile, Oct. 13, 1740–Mar. 6, 1811.
Vol. 2, Pt. 1–580
Celestin, Oscar "Papa," Jan. 1, 1884–Dec. 15, 1954.
Supp. 5–106
Céloron de Blainville, Pierre Joseph de, Dec. 29, 1693–Apr. 12, 1759. Vol. 2, Pt. 1–581
Cermak, Anton Joseph, May 9, 1873–Mar. 6, 1933.
Supp. 1–159
Cerré, Jean Gabriel, Aug. 12, 1734–Apr. 4, 1805.
Vol. 2, Pt. 1–582
Cesare, Oscar Edward, Oct. 7, 1883–July 24, 1948.
Supp. 4–159
Cesnola, Luigi Palma di, June 29, 1832–Nov. 20, 1904.
Vol. 2, Pt. 1–583
Chace, Elizabeth Buffum, Dec. 9, 1806–Dec. 12, 1899.
Vol. 2, Pt. 1–584
Chadbourne, Paul Ansel, Oct. 21, 1823–Feb. 23, 1883.
Vol. 2, Pt. 1–585
Chadwick, French Ensor, Feb. 29, 1844–Jan. 27, 1919.
Vol. 2, Pt. 1–586
Chadwick, George Whitefield, Nov. 13, 1854–Apr. 4, 1931.
Supp. 1–160
Chadwick, Henry, Oct. 5, 1824–Apr. 20, 1908.
Vol. 2, Pt. 1–587
Chadwick, James Read, Nov. 2, 1844–Sept. 23, 1905.
Vol. 2, Pt. 1–588

Chadwick, John White, Oct. 19, 1840–Dec. 11, 1904.
Vol. 2, Pt. 1–588
Chafee, Zechariah, Jr., Dec. 7, 1885–Feb. 8, 1957.
Supp. 6–104
Chaffee, Adna Romanza, Apr. 14, 1842–Nov. 1, 1914.
Vol. 2, Pt. 1–589
Chaffee, Adna Romanza, Sept. 23, 1884–Aug. 22, 1941.
Supp. 3–151
Chaffee, Jerome Bonaparte, Apr. 17, 1825–Mar. 9, 1886.
Vol. 2, Pt. 1–590
Chaffee, Roger Bruce, Feb. 15, 1935–Jan. 27, 1967.
Supp. 8–81
Chafin, Eugene Wilder, Nov. 1, 1852–Nov. 30, 1920.
Vol. 2, Pt. 1–590
Chaillé-Long, Charles, July 2, 1842–Mar. 24, 1917.
Vol. 2, Pt. 1–591
Chalkley, Thomas, May 3, 1675–Nov. 4, 1741.
Vol. 2, Pt. 1–592
Chalmers, James Ronald, Jan. 11, 1831–Apr. 9, 1898.
Vol. 2, Pt. 1–593
Chalmers, William James, July 10, 1852–Dec. 10, 1938.
Supp. 2–100
Chamberlain, Alexander Francis, Jan. 12, 1865–Apr. 8, 1914.
Vol. 2, Pt. 1–594
Chamberlain, Charles Joseph, Feb. 23, 1863–Jan. 5, 1943.
Supp. 3–153
Chamberlain, Daniel Henry, June 23, 1835–Apr. 13, 1907.
Vol. 2, Pt. 1–595
Chamberlain, George Earle, Jan. 1, 1854–July 9, 1928.
Vol. 2, Pt. 1–595
Chamberlain, Henry Richardson, Aug. 25, 1859–Feb. 15, 1911. Vol. 2, Pt. 1–596
Chamberlain, Jacob, Apr. 13, 1835–Mar. 2, 1908.
Vol. 2, Pt. 1–597
Chamberlain, Joseph Perkins, Oct. 1, 1873–May 21, 1951.
Supp. 5–107
Chamberlain, Joshua Lawrence, Sept. 8, 1828–Feb. 24, 1914.
Vol. 2, Pt. 1–597
Chamberlain, Mellen, June 4, 1821–June 25, 1900.
Vol. 2, Pt. 1–598
Chamberlain, Nathan Henry, Dec. 28, 1828?–Apr. 1, 1901.
Vol. 2, Pt. 1–599
Chamberlain, William Isaac, Feb. 11, 1837–June 30, 1920.
Vol. 2, Pt. 1–600
Chamberlin, Edward Hastings, May 18, 1899–July 16, 1967.
Supp. 8–82
Chamberlin, Thomas Chrowder, Sept. 25, 1843–Nov. 15, 1928. Vol. 2, Pt. 1–600
Chambers, Charles Julius. [See Chambers, James Julius, 1850–1920.]
Chambers, Ezekiel Forman, Feb. 28, 1788–Jan. 30, 1867.
Vol. 2, Pt. 1–602
Chambers, George, Feb. 24, 1786–Mar. 25, 1866.
Vol. 2, Pt. 1–602
Chambers, James Julius, Nov. 21, 1850–Feb. 12, 1920.
Vol. 2, Pt. 1–603
Chambers, John, Oct. 6, 1780–Sept. 21, 1852.
Vol. 2, Pt. 1–603
Chambers, Julius. [See Chambers, James Julius, 1850–1920.]
Chambers, Robert William, May 26, 1865–Dec. 16, 1933.
Supp. 1–162
Chambers, Talbott Wilson, Feb. 25, 1819–Feb. 3, 1896.
Vol. 2, Pt. 1–604
Chambers, Whittaker, Apr. 1, 1901–July 9, 1961.
Supp. 7–113
Champlain, Samuel de, c. 1567–Dec. 25, 1635.
Vol. 2, Pt. 1–605
Champlin, John Denison, Jan. 29, 1834–Jan. 8, 1915,.
Vol. 2, Pt. 1–607
Champlin, John Wayne, Feb. 7, 1831–July 24, 1901.
Vol. 2, Pt. 1–608
Champlin, Stephen, Nov. 17, 1789–Feb. 20, 1870.
Vol. 2, Pt. 1–609
Champney, Benjamin, Nov. 17, 1817–Dec. 11, 1907,.
Vol. 2, Pt. 1–609
Champney, James Wells, July 16, 1843–May 1, 1903.
Vol. 2, Pt. 1–610
Chanche, John Mary Joseph, Oct. 4, 1795–July 22, 1852.
Vol. 2, Pt. 1–610
Chandler, Charles Frederick, Dec. 6, 1836–Aug. 25, 1925.
Vol. 2, Pt. 1–611
Chandler, Elizabeth Margaret, Dec. 24, 1807–Nov. 2, 1834.
Vol. 2, Pt. 1–613

Chandler, Harry, May 17, 1864–Sept. 23, 1944.
  Supp. 3–154
Chandler, John, Feb. 1, 1762–Sept. 25, 1841.
  Vol. 2, Pt. 1–613
Chandler, John Scudder, Apr. 12, 1849–June 19, 1934.
  Supp. 1–163
Chandler, Joseph Ripley, Aug. 25, 1792–July 10, 1880.
  Vol. 2, Pt. 1–614
Chandler, Julian Alvin Carroll, Oct. 29, 1872–May 31, 1934.
  Supp. 1–164
Chandler, Peleg Whitman, Apr. 12, 1816–May 28, 1889.
  Vol. 2, Pt. 1–615
Chandler, Raymond Thornton, July 23, 1888–Mar. 26, 1959.
  Supp. 6–166
Chandler, Seth Carlo, Sept. 17, 1846–Dec. 31, 1913.
  Vol. 2, Pt. 1–615
Chandler, Thomas Bradbury, Apr. 26, 1726–June 17, 1790.
  Vol. 2, Pt. 1–616
Chandler, William Eaton, Dec. 28, 1835–Nov. 30, 1917.
  Vol. 2, Pt. 1–616
Chandler, Zachariah, Dec. 10, 1813–Nov. 1, 1879.
  Vol. 2, Pt. 1–618
Chaney, Lon, Apr. 1, 1883–Aug. 26, 1930.
  Supp. 1–165
Chanfrau, Francis S., Feb. 22, 1824–Oct. 2, 1884.
  Vol. 2, Pt. 2–1
Chanfrau, Henrietta Baker, 1837–Sept. 21, 1909.
  Vol. 2, Pt. 2–2
Chang and Eng, May 1811–Jan. 17, 1874.
  Vol. 2, Pt. 2–2
Channing, Edward, June 15, 1856–Jan. 7, 1931.
  Supp. 1–166
Channing, Edward Tyrrell, Dec. 12, 1790–Feb. 8, 1856.
  Vol. 2, Pt. 2–3
Channing, Walter, Apr. 15, 1786–July 27, 1876.
  Vol. 2, Pt. 2–3
Channing, William Ellery, Apr. 7, 1780–Oct. 2, 1842.
  Vol. 2, Pt. 2–4
Channing, William Ellery, Nov. 29, 1818–Dec. 23, 1901.
  Vol. 2, Pt. 2–7
Channing, William Francis, Feb. 22, 1820–Mar. 19, 1901.
  Vol. 2, Pt. 2–8
Channing, William Henry, May 25, 1810–Dec. 23, 1884.
  Vol. 2, Pt. 2–9
Chanute, Octave, Feb. 18, 1832–Nov. 23, 1910.
  Vol. 2, Pt. 2–10
Chapelle, Dickey, Mar. 14, 1918–Nov. 4, 1965.
  Supp. 7–115
Chapelle, Placide Louis, Aug. 28, 1842–Aug. 9, 1905.
  Vol. 2, Pt. 2–11
Chapin, Aaron Lucius, Feb. 6, 1817–July 22, 1892.
  Vol. 2, Pt. 2–12
Chapin, Alonzo Bowen, Mar. 10, 1808–July 9, 1858.
  Vol. 2, Pt. 2–13
Chapin, Calvin, July 22, 1763–Mar. 16, 1851.
  Vol. 2, Pt. 2–13
Chapin, Charles Value, Jan. 17, 1856–Jan. 31, 1941.
  Supp. 3–157
Chapin, Chester William, Dec. 16, 1798–June 10, 1883.
  Vol. 2, Pt. 2–14
Chapin, Edwin Hubbell, Dec. 29, 1814–Dec. 26, 1880.
  Vol. 2, Pt. 2–15
Chapin, Henry Dwight, Feb. 4, 1857–June 27, 1942.
  Supp. 3–159
Chapin, James Paul, July 9, 1889–Apr. 5, 1964.
  Supp. 7–116
Chapin, Roy Dikeman, Feb. 23, 1880–Feb. 16, 1936.
  Supp. 2–101
Chaplin, Jeremiah, Jan. 2, 1776–May 7, 1841.
  Vol. 2, Pt. 2–15
Chaplin, Ralph Hosea, Aug. 30, 1887–Mar. 23, 1961.
  Supp. 7–118
Chapman, Alvan Wentworth, Sept. 28, 1809–Apr. 6, 1899.
  Vol. 2, Pt. 2–16
Chapman, Frank Michler, June 12, 1864–Nov. 15, 1945.
  Supp. 3–161
Chapman, Henry Cadwalader, Aug. 17, 1845–Sept. 7, 1909.
  Vol. 2, Pt. 2–17
Chapman, John, c. 1775–Mar. 11, 1847.
  Vol. 2, Pt. 2–17
Chapman, John Gadsby, Dec. 8, 1808–Nov. 28, 1889.
  Vol. 2, Pt. 2–18

Chapman, John Jay, Mar. 2, 1862–Nov. 4, 1933.
  Supp. 1–168
Chapman, John Wilbur, June 17, 1859–Dec. 25, 1918.
  Vol. 2, Pt. 2–19
Chapman, Maria Weston, July 25, 1806–July 12, 1885.
  Vol. 2, Pt. 2–19
Chapman, Nathaniel, May 28, 1780–July 1, 1853.
  Vol. 2, Pt. 2–19
Chapman, Reuben, July 15, 1802–May 17, 1882.
  Vol. 2, Pt. 2–20
Chapman, Victor Emmanuel, Apr. 17, 1890–June 23, 1916.
  Vol. 2, Pt. 2–21
Chappell, Absalom Harris, Dec. 18, 1801–Dec. 11, 1878.
  Vol. 2, Pt. 2–21
Charles, William, 1776–Aug. 29, 1820.
  Vol. 2, Pt. 2–22
Charless, Joseph, July 16, 1772–July 28, 1834.
  Vol. 2, Pt. 2–23
Charlevoix, Pierre Francois Xavier de, Oct. 24, 1682–Feb. 1, 1761. Vol. 2, Pt. 2–23
Charlton, Thomas Usher Pulaski, Nov. 1779–Dec. 14, 1835.
  Vol. 2, Pt. 2–24
Chase, Edna Woolman, Mar. 14, 1877–Mar. 20, 1957.
  Supp. 6–107
Chase, George, Dec. 29, 1849–Jan. 8, 1924.
  Vol. 2, Pt. 2–25
Chase, Harry Woodburn, Apr. 11, 1883–Apr. 20, 1955.
  Supp. 5–108
Chase, Irah, Oct. 5, 1793–Nov. 1, 1864.
  Vol. 2, Pt. 2–25
Chase, (Mary) Agnes Merrill, Apr. 20, 1869–Sept. 24, 1963.
  Supp. 7–119
Chase, Philander, Dec. 14, 1775–Sept. 20, 1852.
  Vol. 2, Pt. 2–26
Chase, Pliny Earle, Aug. 18, 1820–Dec. 17, 1886.
  Vol. 2, Pt. 2–27
Chase, Salmon Portland, Jan. 13, 1808–May 7, 1873.
  Vol. 2, Pt. 2–27
Chase, Samuel, Apr. 17, 1741–June 19, 1811.
  Vol. 2, Pt. 2–34
Chase, Thomas, June 16, 1827–Oct. 5, 1892.
  Vol. 2, Pt. 2–37
Chase, William Merritt, Nov. 1, 1849–Oct. 25, 1916.
  Vol. 2, Pt. 2–38
Chatard, Francis Silas, Dec. 13, 1834–Sept. 7, 1918.
  Vol. 2, Pt. 2–39
Chatterton, Ruth, Dec. 24, 1893–Nov. 24, 1961.
  Supp. 7–120
Chaumonot, Pierre Joseph Marie, Mar. 9, 1611–Feb. 21, 1693. Vol. 2, Pt. 2–40
Chauncey, Isaac, Feb. 20, 1772–Jan. 27, 1840.
  Vol. 2, Pt. 2–40
Chauncy, Charles, 1592–Feb. 19, 1671/2.
  Vol. 2, Pt. 2–41
Chauncy, Charles, Jan. 1, 1705–Feb. 10, 1787.
  Vol. 2, Pt. 2–42
Chauvenet, William, May 24, 1820–Dec. 13, 1870.
  Vol. 2, Pt. 2–43
Chavez, Dennis, Apr. 8, 1888–Nov. 18, 1962.
  Supp. 7–121
Chavis, John, c. 1763–1838.
  Vol. 2, Pt. 2–44
Cheatham, Benjamin Franklin, Oct. 20, 1820–Sept. 4, 1886.
  Vol. 2, Pt. 2–45
Checkley, John, 1680–Feb. 15, 1754.
  Vol. 2, Pt. 2–46
Cheesman, Forman, Dec. 11, 1763–Oct. 10, 1821.
  Vol. 2, Pt. 2–46
Cheetham, James, 1772–Sept. 19, 1810.
  Vol. 2, Pt. 2–47
Cheever, Ezekiel, Jan. 25, 1614/15–Aug. 21, 1708.
  Vol. 2, Pt. 2–47
Cheever, George Barrell, Apr. 17, 1807–Oct. 1, 1890.
  Vol. 2, Pt. 2–48
Cheever, Henry Theodore, Feb. 6, 1814–Feb. 13, 1897.
  Vol. 2, Pt. 2–49
Cheney, Benjamin Pierce, Aug. 12, 1815–July 23, 1895.
  Vol. 2, Pt. 2–50
Cheney, Charles Edward, Feb. 12, 1836–Nov. 15, 1916.
  Vol. 2, Pt. 2–51
Cheney, Ednah Dow Littlehale, June 27, 1824–Nov. 19, 1904.
  Vol. 2, Pt. 2–51

Cheney, John, Oct. 20, 1801–Aug. 20, 1885.
    Vol. 2, Pt. 2–52
Cheney, John Vance, Dec. 29, 1848–May 1, 1922.
    Vol. 2, Pt. 2–53
Cheney, Oren Burbank, Dec. 10, 1816–Dec. 22, 1903.
    Vol. 2, Pt. 2–53
Cheney, Person Colby, Feb. 25, 1828–June 19, 1901.
    Vol. 2, Pt. 2–54
Cheney, Seth Wells, Nov. 26, 1810–Sept. 10, 1856.
    Vol. 2, Pt. 2–55
Cheney, Ward, Feb. 23, 1813–Mar. 22, 1876.
    Vol. 2, Pt. 2–56
Chennault, Claire Lee, Sept. 6, 1893–July 27, 1958.
    Supp. 6–108
Cherrington, Ernest Hurst, Nov. 24, 1877–Mar. 13, 1950.
    Supp. 4–160
Chesebrough, Caroline, Mar. 30, 1825–Feb. 16, 1873.
    Vol. 2, Pt. 2–56
Cheshire, Joseph Blount, Mar. 27, 1850–Dec. 27, 1932.
    Supp. 1–169
Chesnut, James, Jan. 18, 1815–Feb. 1, 1885.
    Vol. 2, Pt. 2–57
Chessman, Caryl Whittier, May 27, 1921–May 2, 1960.
    Supp. 6–110
Chester, Colby Mitchell, Feb. 29, 1844–May 4, 1932.
    Supp. 1–170
Chester, Colby Mitchell, July 23, 1877–Sept. 26, 1965.
    Supp. 7–122
Chester, George Randolph, 1869–Feb. 26, 1924.
    Vol. 2, Pt. 2–58
Chester, Joseph Lemuel, Apr. 30, 1821–May 26, 1882.
    Vol. 2, Pt. 2–58
Chetlain, Augustus Louis, Dec. 26, 1824–Mar. 15, 1914.
    Vol. 2, Pt. 2–60
Chever, James W., Apr. 20, 1791–May 2, 1857.
    Vol. 2, Pt. 2–60
Cheverus, John Louis Ann Magdalen Lefebre de, Jan. 28,
    1768–July 19, 1836. Vol. 2, Pt. 2–61
Cheves, Langdon, Sept. 17, 1776–June 26, 1857.
    Vol. 2, Pt. 2–62
Chew, Benjamin, Nov. 29, 1722–Jan. 20, 1810.
    Vol. 2, Pt. 2–64
Cheyney, Edward Potts, Jan. 17, 1861–Feb. 1, 1947.
    Supp. 4–162
Chickering, Jonas, Apr. 5, 1798–Dec. 8, 1853.
    Vol. 2, Pt. 2–65
Chiera, Edward, Aug. 5, 1885–June 20, 1933.
    Supp. 1–171
Child, Charles Manning, Feb. 2, 1869–Dec. 19, 1954.
    Supp. 5–109
Child, David Lee, July 8, 1794–Sept. 18, 1874.
    Vol. 2, Pt. 2–65
Child, Francis James, Feb. 1, 1825–Sept. 11, 1896.
    Vol. 2, Pt. 2–66
Child, Frank Samuel, Mar. 20, 1854–May 4, 1922.
    Vol. 2, Pt. 2–67
Child, Lydia Maria Francis, Feb. 11, 1802–Oct. 20, 1880.
    Vol. 2, Pt. 2–67
Child, Richard Washburn, Aug. 5, 1881–Jan. 31, 1935.
    Supp. 1–172
Child, Robert, c. 1613–1654.
    Supp. 1–174
Childe, John, Aug. 30, 1802–Feb. 2, 1858.
    Vol. 2, Pt. 2–69
Childs, Cephas Grier, Sept. 8, 1793–July 7, 1871.
    Vol. 2, Pt. 2–69
Childs, George William, May 12, 1829–Feb. 3, 1894.
    Vol. 2, Pt. 2–70
Childs, Thomas, 1796–Oct. 8, 1853.
    Vol. 2, Pt. 2–71
Chilton, William Paris, Aug. 10, 1810–Jan. 20, 1871.
    Vol. 2, Pt. 2–71
Chini, Eusebio Francisco. [See Kino, Eusebio Francisco,
    1645–1711.]
Chipman, Daniel, Oct. 22, 1765–Apr. 23, 1850.
    Vol. 2, Pt. 2–72
Chipman, Nathaniel, Nov. 15, 1752–Feb. 15, 1843.
    Vol. 2, Pt. 2–73
Chipman, Ward, July 30, 1754–Feb. 9, 1824.
    Vol. 2, Pt. 2–74
Chisholm, Hugh Joseph, May 2, 1847–July 8, 1912.
    Vol. 2, Pt. 2–74

Chisolm, Alexander Robert, Nov. 19, 1834–Mar. 10, 1910.
    Vol. 2, Pt. 2–75
Chisolm, John Julian, Apr. 16, 1830–Nov. 2, 1903.
    Vol. 2, Pt. 2–76
Chisum, John Simpson, Aug. 15, 1824–Dec. 23, 1884.
    Vol. 2, Pt. 2–77
Chittenden, Hiram Martin, Oct. 25, 1858–Oct. 9, 1917.
    Vol. 2, Pt. 2–77
Chittenden, Martin, Mar. 12, 1763–Sept. 5, 1840.
    Vol. 2, Pt. 2–78
Chittenden, Russell Henry, Feb. 18, 1856–Dec. 26, 1943.
    Supp. 3–162
Chittenden, Simeon Baldwin, Mar. 29, 1814–Apr. 14, 1889.
    Vol. 2, Pt. 2–79
Chittenden, Thomas, Jan. 6, 1730–Aug. 25, 1797.
    Vol. 2, Pt. 2–80
Chivers, Thomas Holley, Oct. 18, 1809–Dec. 18, 1858.
    Vol. 2, Pt. 2–81
Choate, Anne Hyde Clarke, Oct. 27, 1886–May 17, 1967.
    Supp. 8–83
Choate, Joseph Hodges, Jan. 24, 1832–May 14, 1917.
    Vol. 2, Pt. 2–83
Choate, Rufus, Oct. 1, 1799–July 13, 1859.
    Vol. 2, Pt. 2–86
Chopin, Kate O'Flaherty, Feb. 8, 1851–Aug. 22, 1904.
    Vol. 2, Pt. 2–90
Chorpenning, George, June 1, 1820–Apr. 3, 1894.
    Vol. 2, Pt. 2–91
Chotzinoff, Samuel, July 4, 1889–Feb. 9, 1964.
    Supp. 7–123
Chouart, Medart, [See Grosseilliers, Medart Chouart, Sieur
    des, 1621?–1698?.]
Chouteau, Auguste, [See Chouteau, René Auguste, 1750–
    1829.]
Chouteau, Auguste Pierre, May 9, 1786–Dec. 25, 1838.
    Vol. 2, Pt. 2–92
Chouteau, Jean Pierre, Oct. 10, 1758–July 10, 1849.
    Vol. 2, Pt. 2–93
Chouteau, Pierre, Jan. 19, 1789–Sept. 6, 1865.
    Vol. 2, Pt. 2–93
Chouteau, Pierre. [See Chouteau, Jean Pierre, 1758–1849.]
Chouteau, René Auguste, Sept. 1749–Feb. 24, 1829.
    Vol. 2, Pt. 2–94
Chovet, Abraham, May 25, 1704–Mar. 24, 1790.
    Vol. 2, Pt. 2–95
Christian, Henry Asbury, Feb. 17, 1876–Aug. 24, 1951.
    Supp. 5–111
Christian, William, c. 1743–Apr. 9, 1786.
    Vol. 2, Pt. 2–96
Christiancy, Isaac Peckham, Mar. 12, 1812–Sept. 8, 1890.
    Vol. 2, Pt. 2–96
Christie, John Walter, May 6, 1865–Jan. 11, 1944.
    Supp. 3–165
Christy, David, b. 1802.
    Vol. 2, Pt. 2–97
Christy, Edwin P., 1815–May 21, 1862.
    Vol. 2, Pt. 2–98
Christy, Howard Chandler, Jan. 10, 1873–Mar. 4, 1952.
    Supp. 5–112
Chrysler, Walter Percy, Apr. 2, 1875–Aug. 18, 1940.
    Supp. 2–103
Church, Alonzo, Apr. 9, 1793–May 18, 1862.
    Vol. 2, Pt. 2–98
Church, Benjamin, 1639–Jan. 17, 1718.
    Vol. 2, Pt. 2–99
Church, Benjamin, Aug. 24, 1734–1776.
    Vol. 2, Pt. 2–100
Church, Frederick Edwin, May 4, 1826–Apr. 7, 1900.
    Vol. 2, Pt. 2–101
Church, Frederick Stuart, Dec. 1, 1842–Feb. 18, 1924,.
    Vol. 2, Pt. 2–101
Church, George Earl, Dec. 7, 1835–Jan. 5, 1910.
    Vol. 2, Pt. 2–102
Church, Irving Porter, July 22, 1851–May 8, 1931.
    Supp. 1–175
Church, John Adams, Apr. 5, 1843–Feb. 12, 1917.
    Vol. 2, Pt. 2–103
Church, Pharcellus, Sept. 11, 1801–June 5, 1886.
    Vol. 2, Pt. 2–104
Church, William Conant, Aug. 11, 1836–May 23, 1917.
    Vol. 2, Pt. 2–104
Churchill, Thomas James, Mar. 10, 1824–Mar. 10, 1905.
    Vol. 2, Pt. 2–105

Churchill, William, Oct. 5, 1859–June 9, 1920.
    Vol. 2, Pt. 2–106
Churchill, Winston, Nov. 10, 1871–March 12, 1947.
    Supp. 4–163
Churchman, William Henry, Nov. 23, 1818–May 18, 1882.
    Vol. 2, Pt. 2–106
Cicotte, Edward Victor, June 19, 1884–May 5, 1969.
    Supp. 8–85
Cilley, Joseph, 1734–Aug. 25, 1799.
    Vol. 2, Pt. 2–107
Cist, Charles, Aug. 15, 1738–Dec. 1, 1805.
    Vol. 2, Pt. 2–108
Cist, Charles, Apr. 24, 1792–Sept. 5, 1868.
    Vol. 2, Pt. 2–108
Cist, Henry Martyn, Feb. 20, 1839–Dec. 17, 1902.
    Vol. 2, Pt. 2–109
Cist, Jacob, Mar. 13, 1782–Dec. 30, 1825.
    Vol. 2, Pt. 2–109
Claflin, Horace Brigham, Dec. 18, 1811–Nov. 14, 1885.
    Vol. 2, Pt. 2–110
Claflin, John, July 24, 1850–June 11, 1938.
    Supp. 2–104
Claflin, Tennessee, 1845–1923. [See Woodhull, Victoria, 1838–1927.]
Claflin, William, Mar. 6, 1818–Jan. 5, 1905.
    Vol. 2, Pt. 2–110
Clagett, Wyseman, August 1721–Dec. 4, 1784.
    Vol. 2, Pt. 2–111
Claghorn, George, July 6, 1748–Feb. 3, 1824.
    Vol. 2, Pt. 2–112
Claiborne, John Francis Hamtramck, Apr. 24, 1807–May 17, 1884. Vol. 2, Pt. 2–112
Claiborne, Nathaniel Herbert, Nov. 14, 1777–Aug. 15, 1859.
    Vol. 2, Pt. 2–113
Claiborne, William, c. 1587–c. 1677.
    Vol. 2, Pt. 2–114
Claiborne, William Charles Coles, 1775–Nov. 23, 1817.
    Vol. 2, Pt. 2–115
Clap, Thomas, June 26, 1703–Jan. 7, 1767.
    Vol. 2, Pt. 2–116
Clapp, Asa, Mar. 15, 1762–Apr. 17, 1848.
    Vol. 2, Pt. 2–117
Clapp, Charles Horace, June 5, 1883–May 9, 1935.
    Supp. 1–175
Clapp, George Alfred. [See Dockstader, Lew, 1856–1924.]
Clapp, William Warland, Apr. 11, 1826–Dec. 8, 1891.
    Vol. 2, Pt. 2–118
Clapper, Raymond Lewis, May 30, 1892–Feb. 1, 1944.
    Supp. 3–166
Clark, Abraham, Feb. 15, 1726–Sept. 15, 1794.
    Vol. 2, Pt. 2–118
Clark, Alvan, Mar. 8, 1804–Aug. 19, 1887.
    Vol. 2, Pt. 2–119
Clark, Alvan Graham, July 10, 1832–June 9, 1897.
    Vol. 2, Pt. 2–120
Clark, Arthur Hamilton, Dec. 27, 1841–July 5, 1922.
    Vol. 2, Pt. 2–120
Clark, Bennett Champ, Jan. 8, 1890–July 13, 1954.
    Supp. 5–113
Clark, Bobby, June 16, 1888–Feb. 12, 1960.
    Supp. 6–112
Clark, Champ, Mar. 7, 1850–Mar. 2, 1921.
    Vol. 2, Pt. 2–121
Clark, Charles, 1810–Dec. 18, 1877.
    Vol. 2, Pt. 2–122
Clark, Charles Edgar, Aug. 10, 1843–Oct. 2, 1922.
    Vol. 2, Pt. 2–122
Clark, Charles Heber, July 11, 1847–Aug. 10, 1915.
    Vol. 2, Pt. 2–123
Clark, Charles Hopkins, Apr. 1, 1848–Sept. 5, 1926.
    Vol. 2, Pt. 2–124
Clark, Daniel, 1766–Aug. 16, 1813.
    Vol. 2, Pt. 2–125
Clark, Daniel, Oct. 24, 1809–Jan. 2, 1891.
    Vol. 2, Pt. 2–125
Clark, Felton Grandison, Oct. 13, 1903–July 5, 1970.
    Supp. 8–86
Clark, Francis Edward, Sept. 12, 1851–May 26, 1927.
    Vol. 2, Pt. 2–126
Clark, George Rogers, Nov. 19, 1752–Feb. 13, 1818.
    Vol. 2, Pt. 2–127
Clark, George Whitefield, Feb. 15, 1831–Nov. 10, 1911.
    Vol. 2, Pt. 2–130

Clark, Greenleaf, Aug. 23, 1835–Dec. 4, 1904.
    Vol. 2, Pt. 2–131
Clark, Grenville, Nov. 5, 1882–Jan. 13, 1967.
    Supp. 8–87
Clark, Henry James, June 22, 1826–July 1, 1873.
    Vol. 2, Pt. 2–131
Clark, Horace Francis, Nov. 29, 1815–June 19, 1873.
    Vol. 2, Pt. 2–132
Clark, James, Jan. 16, 1779–Sept. 27, 1839.
    Vol. 2, Pt. 2–133
Clark, John, Feb. 28, 1766–Oct. 12, 1832.
    Vol. 2, Pt. 2–134
Clark, John Bates, Jan. 26, 1847–Mar. 21, 1938.
    Supp. 2–105
Clark, John Maurice, Nov. 30, 1884–June 27, 1963.
    Supp. 7–124
Clark, Jonas, Dec. 14, 1730 o.s.–Nov. 15, 1805.
    Vol. 2, Pt. 2–195
Clark, Jonas Gilman, Feb. 1, 1815–May 23, 1900.
    Vol. 2, Pt. 2–135
Clark, Joseph Sylvester, Dec. 19, 1800–Aug. 17, 1861.
    Vol. 2, Pt. 2–136
Clark, Joshua Reuben, Jr., Sept. 1, 1871–Oct. 6, 1961.
    Supp. 7–125
Clark, Lewis Gaylord, Oct. 5, 1808–Nov. 3, 1873,.
    Vol. 2, Pt. 2–137
Clark, Myron Holley, Oct. 23, 1806–Aug. 23, 1892.
    Vol. 2, Pt. 2–138
Clark, Sheldon, Jan. 31, 1785–Apr. 10, 1840.
    Vol. 2, Pt. 2–138
Clark, Thomas March, July 4, 1812–Sept. 7, 1903.
    Vol. 2, Pt. 2–199
Clark, Walter, Aug. 19, 1846–May 19, 1924.
    Vol. 2, Pt. 2–140
Clark, Walter Leighton, Jan. 9, 1859–Dec. 18, 1935.
    Supp. 1–176
Clark, William, Aug. 1, 1770–Sept. 1, 1838.
    Vol. 2, Pt. 2–141
Clark, William Andrews, Jan. 8, 1839–Mar. 2, 1925.
    Vol. 2, Pt. 2–144
Clark, William Bullock, Dec. 15, 1860–July 27, 1917.
    Vol. 2, Pt. 2–146
Clark, William Smith, July 31, 1826–Mar. 9, 1886.
    Vol. 2, Pt. 2–146
Clark, William Thomas, June 29, 1831–Oct. 12, 1905.
    Vol. 2, Pt. 2–147
Clark, Willis Gaylord, Oct. 5, 1808–June 12, 1841.
    Vol. 2, Pt. 2–148
Clarke, Sir Caspar Purdon, Dec. 21, 1846–Mar. 29, 1911.
    Vol. 2, Pt. 2–149
Clarke, Elijah, 1733–Jan. 15, 1799.
    Vol. 2, Pt. 2–150
Clarke, Francis Devereux, Jan. 31, 1849–Sept. 7, 1913.
    Vol. 2, Pt. 2–150
Clarke, Frank Wigglesworth, Mar. 19, 1847–May 23, 1931.
    Supp. 1–177
Clarke, George, 1676–Jan. 12, 1760.
    Vol. 2, Pt. 2–151
Clarke, Helen Archibald, Nov. 13, 1860–Feb. 8, 1926.
    Vol. 2, Pt. 2–152
Clarke, James Freeman, Apr. 4, 1810–June 8, 1888.
    Vol. 2, Pt. 2–153
Clarke, James Paul, Aug. 18, 1854–Oct. 1, 1916.
    Vol. 2, Pt. 2–154
Clarke, John, Oct. 8, 1609–Apr. 28, 1676.
    Vol. 2, Pt. 2–154
Clarke, John Hessin, Sept. 18, 1857–Mar. 22, 1945.
    Supp. 3–167
Clarke, John Mason, Apr. 15, 1857–May 29, 1925.
    Vol. 2, Pt. 2–156
Clarke, John Sleeper, Sept. 3, 1833–Sept. 24, 1899.
    Vol. 2, Pt. 2–156
Clarke, Jonas. [See Clark, Jonas, 1730–1805.]
Clarke, Joseph Ignatius Constantine, July 31, 1846–Feb. 27, 1925. Vol. 2, Pt. 2–157
Clarke, McDonald, June 18, 1798–Mar. 5, 1842.
    Vol. 2, Pt. 2–158
Clarke, Mary Bayard Devereux, May 13, 1827–Mar. 30, 1886.
    Vol. 2, Pt. 2–158
Clarke, Mary Francis, Mar. 2, 1803–Dec. 4, 1887.
    Vol. 2, Pt. 2–159
Clarke, Rebecca Sophia, Feb. 22, 1833–Aug. 16, 1906.
    Vol. 2, Pt. 2–160

Clarke, Richard, May 1, 1711–Feb. 27, 1795.
  Vol. 2, Pt. 2–161
Clarke, Robert, May 1, 1829–Aug. 26, 1899.
  Vol. 2, Pt. 2–162
Clarke, Thomas Benedict, Dec. 11, 1848–Jan. 18, 1931.
  Supp. 1–178
Clarke, Thomas Shields, Apr. 25, 1860–Nov. 15, 1920.
  Vol. 2, Pt. 2–162
Clarke, Walter, c. 1638–May 23, 1714.
  Vol. 2, Pt. 2–163
Clarke, William Newton, Dec. 2, 1841–Jan. 14, 1912.
  Vol. 2, Pt. 2–164
Clarkson, Coker Fifield, Jan. 21, 1811–May 7, 1890.
  Vol. 2, Pt. 2–164
Clarkson, John Gibson, July 1, 1861–Feb. 4, 1909.
  Vol. 2, Pt. 2–165
Clarkson, Matthew, Oct. 17, 1758–Apr. 25, 1825.
  Vol. 2, Pt. 2–166
Clausen, Claus Lauritz, Nov. 3, 1820–Feb. 20, 1892.
  Vol. 2, Pt. 2–166
Claxton, Kate, 1848–May 5, 1924.
  Vol. 2, Pt. 2–167
Clay, Albert Tobias, Dec. 4, 1866–Sept. 14, 1925.
  Vol. 2, Pt. 2–168
Clay, Cassius Marcellus, Oct. 19, 1810–July 22, 1903.
  Vol. 2, Pt. 2–169
Clay, Clement Claiborne, Dec. 13, 1816–Jan. 3, 1882.
  Vol. 2, Pt. 2–170
Clay, Clement Comer, Dec. 17, 1789–Sept. 7, 1866.
  Vol. 2, Pt. 2–171
Clay, Edward Williams, Apr. 19, 1799–Dec. 31, 1857.
  Vol. 2, Pt. 2–172
Clay, Green, Aug. 14, 1757–Oct. 31, 1826.
  Vol. 2, Pt. 2–172
Clay, Henry, Apr. 12, 1777–June 29, 1852.
  Vol. 2, Pt. 2–173
Clay, Joseph, Oct. 16, 1741–Nov. 15, 1804.
  Vol. 2, Pt. 2–179
Clay, Joseph, Aug. 16, 1764–Jan. 11, 1811.
  Vol. 2, Pt. 2–180
Clay, Matthew, Mar. 25, 1754–May 27, 1815.
  Vol. 2, Pt. 2–181
Claypole, Edward Waller, June 1, 1835–Aug. 17, 1901.
  Vol. 2, Pt. 2–181
Clayton, Augustin Smith, Nov. 27, 1783–June 21, 1839.
  Vol. 2, Pt. 2–182
Clayton, Henry De Lamar, Feb. 10, 1857–Dec. 21, 1929.
  Supp. 1–179
Clayton, John, c. 1685–Dec. 15, 1773.
  Vol. 2, Pt. 2–184
Clayton, John Middleton, July 24, 1796–Nov. 9, 1856.
  Vol. 2, Pt. 2–185
Clayton, Joshua, Dec. 20, 1744–Aug. 11, 1798.
  Vol. 2, Pt. 2–186
Clayton, Powell, Aug. 7, 1833–Aug. 25, 1914.
  Vol. 2, Pt. 2–187
Clayton, Thomas, July 1777–Aug. 21, 1854.
  Vol. 2, Pt. 2–188
Clayton, William Lockhart, Feb. 7, 1880–Feb. 8, 1966.
  Supp. 8–88
Cleaveland, Moses, Jan. 29, 1754–Nov. 16, 1806.
  Vol. 2, Pt. 2–188
Cleaveland, Parker, Jan. 15, 1780–Oct. 15, 1858.
  Vol. 2, Pt. 2–189
Cleburne, Patrick Ronayne Mar. 17, 1828–Nov. 30, 1864.
  Vol. 2, Pt. 2–190
Cleghorn, Sarah Norcliffe, Feb. 4, 1876–Apr. 4, 1959.
  Supp. 6–113
Clemens, Jeremiah, Dec. 28, 1814–May 21, 1865.
  Vol. 2, Pt. 2–191
Clemens, Samuel Langhorne, Nov. 30, 1835–Apr. 21, 1910.
  Vol. 2, Pt. 2–192
Clement, Edward Henry, Apr. 19, 1843–Feb. 7, 1920.
  Vol. 2, Pt. 2–198
Clement, Frank Goad, June 2, 1920–Nov. 4, 1969.
  Supp. 8–90
Clement, Martin Withington, Dec. 5, 1881–Aug. 30, 1966.
  Supp. 8–92
Clement, Rufus Early, June 26, 1900–Nov. 7, 1967.
  Supp. 8–94
Clements, Frederic Edward, Sept. 16, 1874–July 26, 1945.
  Supp. 3–168

Clements, Judson Claudius, Feb. 12, 1846–June 18, 1917.
  Vol. 2, Pt. 2–199
Clements, William Lawrence, Apr. 1, 1861–Nov. 6, 1934.
  Supp. 1–179
Clemmer, Mary, May 6, 1839–Aug. 18, 1884.
  Vol. 2, Pt. 2–199
Clemson, Thomas Green, July 1, 1807–Apr. 6, 1888.
  Vol. 2, Pt. 2–200
Clerc, Laurent, Dec. 26, 1785–July 18, 1869.
  Vol. 2, Pt. 2–201
Cleveland, Aaron, Oct. 29, 1715–Aug. 11, 1757.
  Vol. 2, Pt. 2–202
Cleveland, Benjamin, May 26, 1738–Oct. 1806.
  Vol. 2, Pt. 2–202
Cleveland, Chauncey Fitch, Feb. 16, 1799–June 6, 1887.
  Vol. 2, Pt. 2–203
Cleveland, Grover. [See Cleveland Stephen Grover, 1837–1908.]
Cleveland, Horace William Shaler, Dec. 16, 1814–Dec. 5, 1900. Vol. 2, Pt. 2–203
Cleveland, Richard Jeffry, Dec. 19, 1773–Nov. 23, 1860.
  Vol. 2, Pt. 2–204
Cleveland, Stephen Grover, Mar. 18, 1837–June 24, 1908.
  Vol. 2, Pt. 2–205
Clevenger, Shobal Vail, Oct. 22, 1812–Sept. 1843.
  Vol. 2, Pt. 2–212
Clevenger, Shobal Vail, Mar. 24, 1843–Mar. 24, 1920.
  Vol. 2, Pt. 2–213
Clewell, John Henry, Sept. 19, 1855–Feb. 20, 1922.
  Vol. 2, Pt. 2–214
Clews, Henry, Aug. 14, 1834–Jan. 31, 1923.
  Vol. 2, Pt. 2–215
Clifford, John Henry, Jan. 16, 1809–Jan. 2, 1876.
  Vol. 2, Pt. 2–215
Clifford, Nathan, Aug. 18, 1803–July 25, 1881.
  Vol. 2, Pt. 2–216
Cliffton, William, 1772–Dec. 1799.
  Vol. 2, Pt. 2–218
Clift, Edward Montgomery, Oct. 17, 1920–July 23, 1966.
  Supp. 8–95
Clifton, Josephine, 1813–Nov. 21, 1847.
  Vol. 2, Pt. 2–219
Clinch, Charles Powell, Oct. 20, 1797–Dec. 16, 1880.
  Vol. 2, Pt. 2–219
Cline, Genevieve Rose, July 2, 1879–Oct. 25, 1959.
  Supp. 6–114
Clingman, Thomas Lanier, July 27, 1812–Nov. 3, 1897.
  Vol. 2, Pt. 2–220
Clinton, De Witt, Mar. 2, 1769–Feb. 11, 1828.
  Vol. 2, Pt. 2–221
Clinton, George, c. 1686–July 10, 1761.
  Vol. 2, Pt. 2–225
Clinton, George, July 26, 1739–Apr. 20, 1812.
  Vol. 2, Pt. 2–226
Clinton, George Wylie, Mar. 28, 1859–May 12, 1921.
  Vol. 2, Pt. 2–228
Clinton, James, Aug. 9, 1733–Dec. 22, 1812.
  Vol. 2, Pt. 2–229
Clopton, David, Sept. 29, 1820–Feb. 5, 1892.
  Vol. 2, Pt. 2–230
Clopton, John, Feb. 7, 1756–Sept. 11, 1816.
  Vol. 2, Pt. 2–230
Closson, William Baxter, Oct. 13, 1848–May 31, 1926.
  Vol. 2, Pt. 2–231
Clothier, William Jackson, Sept. 27, 1881–Sept. 4, 1962.
  Supp. 7–127
Cloud, Henry Roe, December 28, 1886–Feb. 9, 1950.
  Supp. 4–165
Cloud, Noah Bartlett, Jan. 26, 1809–Nov. 5, 1875.
  Vol. 2, Pt. 2–231
Clough, John Everett, July 16, 1836–Nov. 24, 1910.
  Vol. 2, Pt. 2–232
Clough, William Pitt, Mar. 20, 1845–Aug. 17, 1916.
  Vol. 2, Pt. 2–233
Cluett, Sanford Lockwood, June 6, 1874–May 18, 1968.
  Supp. 8–97
Clyman, James, Feb. 1, 1792–Dec. 27, 1881.
  Vol. 2, Pt. 2–234
Clymer, George, Mar. 16, 1739–Jan. 24, 1813.
  Vol. 2, Pt. 2–234
Clymer, George E., 1754–Aug. 27, 1834.
  Vol. 2, Pt. 2–235

Coker, David Robert, Nov. 20, 1870–Nov. 28, 1938.
Supp. 2–110
Coker, James Lide, Jan. 3, 1837–June 25, 1918.
Vol. 2, Pt. 2–280
Colburn, Dana Pond, Sept. 29, 1823–Dec. 15, 1859.
Vol. 2, Pt. 2–281
Colburn, Irving Wightman, May 16, 1861–Sept. 4, 1917.
Vol. 2, Pt. 2–282
Colburn, Warren, Mar. 1, 1793–Sept. 13, 1833.
Vol. 2, Pt. 2–282
Colburn, Zerah, Sept. 1, 1804–Mar. 2, 1839.
Vol. 2, Pt. 2–283
Colby, Bainbridge, Dec. 22, 1869–Apr. 11, 1950.
Supp. 4–170
Colby, Frank Moore, Feb. 10, 1865–Mar. 3, 1925.
Vol. 2, Pt. 2–284
Colby, Gardner, Sept. 3, 1810–Apr. 2, 1879.
Vol. 2, Pt. 2–284
Colby, Luther, Oct. 12, 1814–Oct. 7, 1894.
Vol. 2, Pt. 2–285
Colcord, Lincoln Ross, Aug. 14, 1883–Nov. 16, 1947.
Supp. 4–171
Colden, Cadwallader, Feb. 7, 1688 N.S.–Sept. 28, 1776.
Vol. 2, Pt. 2–286
Colden, Cadwallader David, Apr. 4, 1769–Feb. 7, 1834.
Vol. 2, Pt. 2–287
Colden, Jane, Mar. 27, 1724–Mar. 10, 1766.
Vol. 2, Pt. 2–288
Cole, Chester Cicero, June 4, 1824–Oct. 4, 1913.
Vol. 2, Pt. 2–289
Cole, Frank Nelson, Sept. 20, 1861–May 26, 1926.
Vol. 2, Pt. 2–290
Cole, George Watson, Sept. 6, 1850–Oct. 10, 1939.
Supp. 2–111
Cole, Joseph Foxcroft, Nov. 9, 1837–May 2, 1892.
Vol. 2, Pt. 2–290
Cole, Nat ("King"), Mar. 17, 1919–Feb. 15, 1965.
Supp. 7–131
Cole, Thomas, Feb. 1, 1801–Feb. 11, 1848.
Vol. 2, Pt. 2–291
Cole, Timothy, Apr. 6, 1852–May 17, 1931.
Supp. 1–185
Coleman, Charles Caryl, Apr. 25, 1840–Dec. 4, 1928.
Vol. 2, Pt. 2–292
Coleman, Leighton, May 3, 1837–Dec. 14, 1907.
Vol. 2, Pt. 2–293
Coleman, Lyman, June 14, 1796–Mar. 16, 1882.
Vol. 2, Pt. 2–293
Coleman, William, Feb. 14, 1766–July 14, 1829.
Vol. 2, Pt. 2–294
Coleman, William Tell, Feb. 29, 1824–Nov. 22, 1893.
Vol. 2, Pt. 2–295
Coles, Edward, Dec. 15, 1786–July 7, 1868.
Vol. 2, Pt. 2–296
Colfax, Schuyler, Mar. 23, 1823–Jan. 13, 1885.
Vol. 2, Pt. 2–297
Colgate, James Boorman, Mar. 4, 1818–Feb. 7, 1904.
Vol. 2, Pt. 2–298
Colgate, William, Jan. 25, 1783–Mar. 25, 1857.
Vol. 2, Pt. 2–299
Collamer, Jacob, Jan. 8, 1791–Nov. 9, 1865.
Vol. 2, Pt. 2–300
Collens, Thomas Wharton, June 23, 1812–Nov 3, 1879.
Vol. 2, Pt. 2–300
Colles, Christopher, 1738–Oct. 4, 1816.
Vol. 2, Pt. 2–301
Collier, Barron Gift, Mar. 23, 1873–Mar. 13, 1939.
Supp. 2–112
Collier, Constance, Jan. 22, 1878–Apr. 25, 1955.
Supp. 5–123
Collier, Henry Walkins, Jan. 17, 1801–Aug. 28, 1855.
Vol. 2, Pt. 2–302
Collier, Hiram Price, May 25, 1860–Nov. 3, 1913.
Vol. 2, Pt. 2–303
Collier, John, May 4, 1884–May 8, 1968.
Supp. 8–98
Collier, Peter, Aug. 17, 1835–June 29, 1896.
Vol. 2, Pt. 2–304
Collier, Peter Fenelon, Dec. 12, 1849–Apr. 24, 1909.
Vol. 2, Pt. 2–304
Collier, Price. [See Collier, Hiram Price, 1860–1913.]
Collins, Edward Knight, Aug. 5, 1802–Jan. 22, 1878.
Vol. 2, Pt. 2–305

Collins, Edward Trowbridge, May 2, 1887–Mar. 25, 1951.
Supp. 5–124
Collins, Frank Shipley, Feb. 6, 1848–May 25, 1920.
Vol. 2, Pt. 2–306
Collins, Guy N., Aug. 9, 1872–Aug. 14, 1938.
Supp. 2–113
Collins, John, Nov. 1, 1717–Mar. 4, 1795.
Vol. 2, Pt. 2–307
Collins, John Anderson, fl. 1810–1879.
Vol. 2, Pt. 2–307
Collins, Napoleon, Mar. 4, 1814–Aug. 9, 1875.
Vol. 2, Pt. 2–308
Collins, Patrick Andrew, Mar. 12, 1844–Sept. 14, 1905.
Vol. 2, Pt. 2–309
Collyer, Robert, Dec. 8, 1823–Nov. 30, 1912.
Vol. 2, Pt. 2–310
Colman, Benjamin, Oct. 19, 1673–Aug. 29, 1747.
Vol. 2, Pt. 2–311
Colman, Henry, Sept. 12, 1785–Aug. 17, 1849.
Vol. 2, Pt. 2–312
Colman, John, Jan. 3, 1670–c. 1753.
Vol. 2, Pt. 2–312
Colman, Lucy Newhall, July 26, 1817–Jan. 18, 1906.
Vol. 2, Pt. 2–313
Colman, Norman Jay, May 16, 1827–Nov. 3, 1911.
Vol. 2, Pt. 2–314
Colman, Ronald Charles, Feb. 9, 1891–May 19, 1958.
Supp. 6–119
Colman, Samuel, Mar. 4, 1832–Mar. 26, 1920.
Vol. 2, Pt. 2–314
Colpitts, Edwin Henry, Jan. 9, 1872–Mar. 6, 1949.
Supp. 4–173
Colquitt, Alfred Holt, Apr. 20, 1824–Mar. 26, 1894.
Vol. 2, Pt. 2–315
Colquitt, Walter Terry, Dec. 27, 1799–May 7, 1855.
Vol. 2, Pt. 2–316
Colston, Raleigh Edward, Oct. 31, 1825–July 29, 1896.
Vol. 2, Pt. 2–317
Colt, LeBaron Bradford, June 25, 1846–Aug. 18, 1924.
Vol. 2, Pt. 2–317
Colt, Samuel, July 19, 1814–Jan. 10, 1862.
Vol. 2, Pt. 2–318
Colter, John, c. 1775–November 1813.
Vol. 2, Pt. 2–319
Colton, Calvin, Sept. 14, 1789–Mar. 13, 1857.
Vol. 2, Pt. 2–320
Colton, Elizabeth Avery, Dec. 30, 1872–Aug. 26, 1924.
Vol. 2, Pt. 2–321
Colton, Gardner Quincy, Feb. 7, 1814–Aug. 9, 1898.
Vol. 2, Pt. 2–321
Colton, George Radcliffe, Apr. 10, 1865–Apr. 6, 1916.
Vol. 2, Pt. 2–322
Colton, Walter, May 9, 1797–Jan. 22, 1851.
Vol. 2, Pt. 2–323
Coltrane, John William, Sept. 23, 1926–July 17, 1967.
Supp. 8–99
Colver, Nathaniel, May 10, 1794–Sept. 25, 1870.
Vol. 2, Pt. 2–324
Colver, William Byron, Sept. 26, 1870–May 28, 1926.
Vol. 2, Pt. 2–325
Colvin, Stephen Sheldon, Mar. 29, 1869–July 15, 1923.
Vol. 2, Pt. 2–325
Colvocoresses, George Musalas, Oct. 22, 1816–June 3, 1872.
Vol. 2, Pt. 2–326
Colwell, Stephen, Mar. 25, 1800–Jan. 15, 1871.
Vol. 2, Pt. 2–327
Coman, Charlotte Buell, 1833–Nov. 11, 1924.
Vol. 2, Pt. 2–327
Combs, Leslie, Nov. 29, 1793–Aug. 22, 1881.
Vol. 2, Pt. 2–328
Combs, Moses Newell, 1753–Apr. 12, 1834.
Vol. 2, Pt. 2–328
Comer, Braxton Bragg, Nov. 7, 1848–Aug. 15, 1927.
Vol. 2, Pt. 2–329
Comfort, Will Levington, Jan. 17, 1878–Nov. 2, 1932.
Supp. 1–186
Comiskey, Grace Elizabeth Reidy, May 15, 1893–Dec. 10, 1956. Supp. 6–120
Commons, John Rogers, Oct. 13, 1862–May 11, 1945.
Supp. 3–176
Compton, Arthur Holly, Sept. 10, 1892–Mar. 15, 1962.
Supp. 7–132

Compton, Karl Taylor, Sept. 14, 1887–June 22, 1954.
Supp. 5–125
Comstock, Anthony, Mar. 7, 1844–Sept. 21, 1915.
Vol. 2, Pt. 2–330
Comstock, Elizabeth L., Oct. 30, 1815–Aug. 3, 1891.
Vol. 2, Pt. 2–331
Comstock, George Cary, Feb. 12, 1855–May 11, 1934.
Supp. 1–186
Comstock, George Franklin, Aug. 24, 1811–Sept. 27, 1892.
Vol. 2, Pt. 2–332
Comstock, Henry Tompkins Paige, 1820–Sept. 27, 1870.
Vol. 2, Pt. 2–333
Comstock, John Henry, Feb. 24, 1849–Mar. 20, 1931.
Supp. 1–187
Conant, Alban Jasper, Sept. 24, 1821–Feb. 8, 1915.
Vol. 2, Pt. 2–333
Conant, Charles Arthur, July 2, 1861–July 5, 1915.
Vol. 2, Pt. 2–334
Conant, Hannah O'Brien Chaplin, Sept. 5, 1809–Feb. 18, 1865. Vol. 2, Pt. 2–335
Conant, Hezekiah, July 28, 1827–Jan. 22, 1902.
Vol. 2, Pt. 2–335
Conant, Roger, c. 1592–Nov. 19, 1679.
Vol. 2, Pt. 2–336
Conant, Thomas Jefferson, Dec. 13, 1802–Apr. 30, 1891.
Vol. 2, Pt. 2–337
Conaty, Thomas James, Aug. 1, 1847–Sept. 18, 1915.
Vol. 2, Pt. 2–337
Conboy, Martin, Aug. 28, 1878–Mar. 5, 1944.
Supp. 3–180
Conboy, Sara Agnes McLaughlin, Apr. 3, 1870–Jan. 7, 1928.
Vol. 2, Pt. 2–338
Condit, John, July 8, 1755–May 4, 1834.
Vol. 2, Pt. 2–338
Condon, Thomas, Mar. 3, 1822–Feb. 11, 1907.
Vol. 2, Pt. 2–339
Cone, Claribel, Nov. 14, 1864–Sept. 20, 1929.
Supp. 4–174
Cone, Etta, Nov. 30, 1870–Aug. 31, 1949.
Supp. 4–174
Cone, Hutchinson Ingham, Apr. 26, 1871–Feb. 12, 1941.
Supp. 3–181
Cone, Moses Herman, June 29, 1857–Dec. 8, 1908.
Vol. 2, Pt. 2–340
Cone, Orello, Nov. 16, 1835–June 23, 1905.
Vol. 2, Pt. 2–341
Cone, Russell Glenn, Mar. 22, 1896–Jan. 21, 1961.
Supp. 7–135
Cone, Spencer Houghton, Apr. 30, 1785–Aug. 28, 1855.
Vol. 2, Pt. 2–342
Coney, Jabez, Oct. 21, 1804–Jan. 23, 1872.
Vol. 2, Pt. 2–342
Coney, John, Jan. 5, 1655–Aug. 20, 1722.
Vol. 2, Pt. 2–343
Congdon, Charles Taber, Apr. 7, 1821–Jan. 18, 1891.
Vol. 2, Pt. 2–343
Conger, Edwin Hurd, Mar. 7, 1843–May 18, 1907.
Vol. 2, Pt. 2–344
Conklin, Edwin Grant, Nov. 24, 1863–Nov. 21, 1952.
Supp. 5–127
Conklin, Jennie Maria Drinkwater. [See Drinkwater, Jennie Maria, 1841–1900.]
Conkling, Alfred, Oct. 12, 1789–Feb. 5, 1874.
Vol. 2, Pt. 2–345
Conkling, Roscoe, Oct. 30, 1829–Apr. 18, 1888.
Vol. 2, Pt. 2–346
Connally, Thomas Terry ("Tom"), Aug. 19, 1877–Oct. 28, 1963. Supp. 7–136
Connelly, Cornelia, Jan. 15, 1809–Apr. 18, 1879.
Vol. 2, Pt. 2–347
Connelly, Henry, 1800–July 1866.
Vol. 2, Pt. 2–348
Connelly, Pierce Francis, b. Mar. 29, 1841.
Vol. 2, Pt. 2–348
Conner, Charlotte Mary Sanford Barnes. [See Barnes, Charlotte Mary Sanford, 1818–1863.]
Conner, David, 1792–Mar. 20, 1856.
Vol. 2, Pt. 2–349
Conner, James, Sept. 1, 1829–June 26, 1883.
Vol. 2, Pt. 2–350
Conney, John. [See Coney, John, 1655–1722.]
Connick, Charles Jay, Sept. 27, 1875–Dec. 28, 1945.
Supp. 3–183

Connolly, John, c. 1743–Jan. 30, 1813.
Supp. 1–188
Connolly, John, 1750–Feb. 6, 1825.
Vol. 2, Pt. 2–351
Connolly, Maureen Catherine, Sept. 17, 1934–June 21, 1969.
Supp. 8–101
Connolly, Thomas H., Dec. 31, 1870–Apr. 28, 1961.
Supp. 7–139
Connor, Henry Groves, July 3, 1852–Nov. 23, 1924.
Vol. 2, Pt. 2–352
Connor, Patrick Edward, Mar. 17, 1820–Dec. 17, 1891.
Vol. 2, Pt. 2–352
Connor, Robert Digges Wimberly, Sept. 26, 1878–Feb. 25, 1950. Supp. 4–175
Conover, Harry Sayles, Aug. 29, 1911–July 21, 1965.
Supp. 7–140
Conover, Obadiah Milton, Oct. 8, 1825–Apr. 29, 1884.
Vol. 2, Pt. 2–353
Conrad, Charles Magill, Dec. 24, 1804–Feb. 11, 1878.
Vol. 2, Pt. 2–354
Conrad, Frank, May 4, 1874–Dec. 11, 1941.
Supp. 3–184
Conrad, Holmes, Jan. 31, 1840–Sept. 4, 1916.
Vol. 2, Pt. 2–354
Conrad, Robert Taylor, June 10, 1810–June 27, 1858.
Vol. 2, Pt. 2–355
Conried, Heinrich, Sept. 13, 1855–Apr. 27, 1909.
Vol. 2, Pt. 2–356
Considérant, Victor Prosper, Oct. 12, 1808–Dec. 27, 1893.
Vol. 2, Pt. 2–357
Converse, Charles Crozat, Oct. 7, 1832–Oct. 18, 1918.
Vol. 2, Pt. 2–358
Converse, Edmund Cogswell, Nov. 7, 1849–Apr. 4, 1921.
Vol. 2, Pt. 2–359
Converse, Frederick Shepherd, Jan. 5, 1871–June 8, 1940.
Supp. 2–114
Converse, James Booth, Apr. 8, 1844–Oct. 31, 1914.
Vol. 2, Pt. 2–360
Converse, John Heman, Dec. 2, 1840–May 31, 1910.
Vol. 2, Pt. 2–360
Conway, Elias Nelson, May 17, 1812–Feb. 28, 1892.
Vol. 2, Pt. 2–361
Conway, Frederick Bartlett, Feb. 10, 1819–Sept. 7, 1874.
Vol. 2, Pt. 2–362
Conway, James Sevier, Dec. 9, 1798–Mar. 3, 1855.
Vol. 2, Pt. 2–363
Conway, Martin Franklin, Nov. 19, 1827–Feb. 15, 1882.
Vol. 2, Pt. 2–363
Conway, Moncure Daniel, Mar. 17, 1832–Nov. 15, 1907.
Vol. 2, Pt. 2–364
Conway, Thomas, Feb. 27, 1735–c. 1800.
Vol. 2, Pt. 2–365
Conwell, Henry, c. 1745–Apr. 22, 1842.
Vol. 2, Pt. 2–366
Conwell, Russell Herman, Feb. 15, 1843–Dec. 6, 1925.
Vol. 2, Pt. 2–367
Conyngham, Gustavus, c. 1744–Nov. 27, 1819.
Vol. 2, Pt. 2–368
Coode, John, d. 1709.
Vol. 2, Pt. 2–369
Cook, Albert Stanburrough, Mar. 6, 1853–Sept. 1, 1927.
Vol. 2, Pt. 2–370
Cook, Clarence Chatham, Sept. 8, 1828–June 2, 1900.
Vol. 2, Pt. 2–371
Cook, Flavius Josephus, Jan. 26, 1838–June 24, 1901.
Vol. 2, Pt. 2–371
Cook, Frederick Albert, June 10, 1865–Aug. 5, 1940.
Supp. 2–115
Cook, George Cram, Oct. 7, 1873–Jan. 14, 1924.
Vol. 2, Pt. 2–372
Cook, George Hammell, Jan. 5, 1818–Sept. 22, 1889.
Vol. 2, Pt. 2–373
Cook, Isaac, July 4, 1810–June 23, 1886.
Vol. 2, Pt. 2–374
Cook, James Merrill, Nov. 19, 1807–Apr. 12, 1868.
Vol. 2, Pt. 2–375
Cook, John Williston, Apr. 20, 1844–July 16, 1922.
Vol. 2, Pt. 2–375
Cook, Joseph. [See Cook, Flavius Josephus, 1838–1901.]
Cook, Martha Elizabeth Duncan Walker, July 23, 1806–Sept. 15, 1874. Vol. 2, Pt. 2–376
Cook, Philip, July 30, 1817–May 20, 1894.
Vol. 2, Pt. 2–377

Cook, Robert Johnson, Mar. 21, 1849–Dec. 3, 1922.
  Vol. 2, Pt. 2–377
Cook, Russell S., Mar. 6, 1811–Sept. 4, 1864.
  Vol. 2, Pt. 2–378
Cook, Tennessee Celeste Claflin, Lady, 1845–1923. [See
  Woodhull, Victoria, 1838–1927.]
Cook, Walter, July 23, 1846–Mar. 25, 1916.
  Vol. 2, Pt. 2–379
Cook, Walter Wheeler, June 4, 1873–Nov. 7, 1943.
  Supp. 3–185
Cook, Will Marion, Jan. 27, 1869–July 19, 1944.
  Supp. 3–187
Cook, Zebedee, Jan. 11, 1786–Jan. 24, 1858.
  Vol. 2, Pt. 2–380
Cooke, Ebenezer, c. 1670–c. 1732.
  Supp. 1–189
Cooke, Elisha, Sept. 16, 1637–Oct. 31, 1715.
  Vol. 2, Pt. 2–380
Cooke, Elisha, Dec. 20, 1678–Aug. 24, 1737.
  Vol. 2, Pt. 2–381
Cooke, George Willis, Apr. 23, 1848–Apr. 30, 1923.
  Vol. 2, Pt. 2–382
Cooke, Henry David, Nov. 23, 1825–Feb. 24, 1881.
  Vol. 2, Pt. 2–382
Cooke, Jay, Aug. 10, 1821–Feb. 16, 1905.
  Vol. 2, Pt. 2–383
Cooke, John Esten, Mar. 2, 1783–Oct. 19, 1853.
  Vol. 2, Pt. 2–384
Cooke, John Esten, Nov. 3, 1830–Sept. 27, 1886.
  Vol. 2, Pt. 2–385
Cooke, John Rogers, 1788–Dec. 15, 1854.
  Vol. 2, Pt. 2–386
Cooke, Josiah Parsons, Oct. 12, 1827–Sept. 3, 1894.
  Vol. 2, Pt. 2–387
Cooke, Morris Llewellyn, May, 11, 1872–Mar. 5, 1960.
  Supp. 6–121
Cooke, Philip Pendleton, Oct. 26, 1816–Jan. 20, 1850.
  Vol. 2, Pt. 2–388
Cooke, Philip St. George, June 13, 1809–Mar. 20, 1895.
  Vol. 2, Pt. 2–389
Cooke, Robert Anderson, Aug. 17, 1880–May 7, 1960.
  Supp. 6–123
Cooke, Rose Terry, Feb. 17, 1827–July 18, 1892.
  Vol. 2, Pt. 2–390
Cooke, Samuel, Dec. 19, 1898–May 22, 1965.
  Supp. 7–141
Coolbrith, Ina Donna, Mar. 10, 1842–Feb. 29, 1928.
  Vol. 2, Pt. 2–390
Cooley, Edwin Gilbert, Mar. 12, 1857–Sept. 28, 1923.
  Supp. 1–190
Cooley, Lyman Edgar, Dec. 5, 1850–Feb. 3, 1917.
  Vol. 2, Pt. 2–391
Cooley, Mortimer Elwyn, Mar. 28, 1855–Aug. 25, 1944.
  Supp. 3–188
Cooley, Thomas Benton, June 23, 1871–Oct. 13, 1945.
  Supp. 3–189
Cooley, Thomas McIntyre, Jan. 6, 1824–Sept. 12, 1898.
  Vol. 2, Pt. 2–392
Coolidge, Archibald Cary, Mar. 6, 1866–Jan. 14, 1928.
  Vol. 2, Pt. 2–393
Coolidge, Calvin, July 4, 1872–Jan. 5, 1933.
  Supp. 1–191
Coolidge, Charles Allerton, Nov. 30, 1858–Apr. 1, 1936.
  Supp. 2–117
Coolidge, Elizabeth Penn Sprague, Oct. 30, 1864–Nov. 4,
  1953. Supp. 5–128
Coolidge, Julian Lowell, Sept. 28, 1873–Mar. 5, 1954.
  Supp. 5–129
Coolidge, Thomas Jefferson, Aug. 26, 1831–Nov. 17, 1920.
  Vol. 2, Pt. 2–395
Coolidge, Thomas Jefferson, Sept. 17, 1893–Aug. 6, 1959.
  Supp. 6–124
Coomaraswamy, Ananda Kentish, Aug. 22, 1877–Sept. 9,
  1947. Supp. 4–176
Coombe, Thomas, Oct. 21, 1747–Aug. 15, 1822.
  Vol. 2, Pt. 2–395
Coontz, Robert Edward, June 11, 1864–Jan. 26, 1935.
  Supp. 1–199
Cooper, Edward, Oct. 26, 1824–Feb. 25, 1905.
  Vol. 2, Pt. 2–396
Cooper, Elias Samuel, Nov. 25, 1820–Oct. 13, 1862.
  Vol. 2, Pt. 2–397

Cooper, Ezekiel, Feb. 22, 1763–Feb. 21, 1847.
  Vol. 2, Pt. 2–397
Cooper, Gary, May 7, 1901–May 13, 1961.
  Supp. 7–142
Cooper, Henry Ernest, Aug. 28, 1857–May 14, 1929.
  Vol. 2, Pt. 2–398
Cooper, Hugh Lincoln, Apr. 28, 1865–June 24, 1937.
  Supp. 2–118
Cooper, Jacob, Dec. 7, 1830–Jan. 31, 1904.
  Vol. 2, Pt. 2–399
Cooper, James, May 8, 1810–Mar. 28, 1863.
  Vol. 2, Pt. 2–400
Cooper, James Fenimore, Sept. 15, 1789–Sept. 14, 1851.
  Vol. 2, Pt. 2–400
Cooper, James Graham, June 19, 1830–July 19, 1902.
  Vol. 2, Pt. 2–406
Cooper, John Montgomery, Oct. 28, 1881–May 22, 1949.
  Supp. 4–178
Cooper, Joseph Alexander, Nov. 25, 1823–May 20, 1910.
  Vol. 2, Pt. 2–407
Cooper, Kent, Mar. 22, 1880–Jan. 31, 1965.
  Supp. 7–144
Cooper, (Leon) Jere, July 20, 1893–Dec. 18, 1957.
  Supp. 6–125
Cooper, Mark Anthony, Apr. 20, 1800–Mar. 17, 1885.
  Vol. 2, Pt. 2–407
Cooper, Myles, Feb. 1737–May 20, 1785.
  Vol. 2, Pt. 2–408
Cooper, Oswald Bruce, Apr. 13, 1879–Dec. 17, 1940.
  Supp. 2–119
Cooper, Peter, Feb. 12, 1791–Apr. 4, 1883.
  Vol. 2, Pt. 2–409
Cooper, Samuel, Mar. 28, 1725–Dec. 23, 1783.
  Vol. 2, Pt. 2–410
Cooper, Samuel, June 12, 1798–Dec. 3, 1876.
  Vol. 2, Pt. 2–411
Cooper, Sarah Brown Ingersoll, Dec. 12, 1836–Dec. 11,
  1896. Vol. 2, Pt. 2–412
Cooper, Susan Fenimore, Apr. 17, 1813–Dec. 31, 1894.
  Vol. 2, Pt. 2–412
Cooper, Theodore, Jan. 13, 1839–Aug. 24, 1919.
  Vol. 2, Pt. 2–413
Cooper, Thomas, Oct. 22, 1759–May 11, 1839.
  Vol. 2, Pt. 2–414
Cooper, Thomas Abthorpe, Dec. 16, 1776–Apr. 21, 1849.
  Vol. 2, Pt. 2–416
Cooper, William, Dec. 2, 1754–Dec. 22, 1809.
  Vol. 2, Pt. 2–417
Cooper, William John, Nov. 24, 1882–Sept. 19, 1935.
  Supp. 1–199
Cooper-Poucher, Matilda S., Feb. 2, 1839–Apr. 5, 1900.
  Vol. 2, Pt. 2–418
Coote, Richard, 1636–Mar. 5, 1701.
  Vol. 2, Pt. 2–418
Cope, Arthur Clay, June 27, 1909–June 4, 1966.
  Supp. 8–102
Cope, Caleb, July 18, 1797–May 12, 1888.
  Vol. 2, Pt. 2–420
Cope, Edward Drinker, July 28, 1840–Apr. 12, 1897.
  Vol. 2, Pt. 2–420
Cope, Thomas Pym, Aug. 26, 1768–Nov. 22, 1854.
  Vol. 2, Pt. 2–421
Cope, Walter, Oct. 20, 1860–Nov. 1, 1902.
  Vol. 2, Pt. 2–422
Copeland, Charles Townsend, Apr. 27, 1860–July 24, 1952.
  Supp. 5–131
Copeland, Charles W., 1815–Feb. 5, 1895.
  Vol. 2, Pt. 2–423
Copeland, Royal Samuel, Nov. 7, 1868–June 17, 1938.
  Supp. 2–120
Copley, Ira Clifton, Oct. 25, 1864–Nov. 2, 1947.
  Supp. 4–180
Copley, John Singleton, 1738–Sept. 9, 1815.
  Vol. 2, Pt. 2–423
Copley, Lionel, d. Sept. 9, 1693,.
  Vol. 2, Pt. 2–430
Copley, Thomas, 1595–c. 1652.
  Vol. 2, Pt. 2–430
Coppée, Henry, Oct. 13, 1821–Mar. 21, 1895.
  Vol. 2, Pt. 2–431
Coppens, Charles, May 24, 1835–Dec. 14, 1920.
  Vol. 2, Pt. 2–432

Cox, Henry Hamilton, *c.* 1769–*c.* 1821.
  Vol. 2, Pt. 2–475
Cox, Jacob Dolson, Oct. 27, 1828–Aug. 8, 1900.
  Vol. 2, Pt. 2–476
Cox, James Middleton, Mar. 31, 1870–July 15, 1957.
  Supp. 6–128
Cox, Kenyon, Oct. 27, 1856–Mar. 17, 1919.
  Vol. 2, Pt. 2–478
Cox, Lemuel, 1736–Feb. 18, 1806.
  Vol. 2, Pt. 2–479
Cox, Palmer, Apr. 28, 1840–July 24, 1924.
  Vol. 2, Pt. 2–480
Cox, Rowland, July 9, 1842–May 13, 1900.
  Vol. 2, Pt. 2–480
Cox, Samuel Hanson, Aug. 25, 1793–Oct. 2, 1880.
  Vol. 2, Pt. 2–481
Cox, Samuel Sullivan, Sept. 30, 1824–Sept. 10, 1889.
  Vol. 2, Pt. 2–482
Cox, William Ruffin, Mar. 11, 1832–Dec. 26, 1919.
  Vol. 2, Pt. 2–483
Coxe, Arthur Cleveland, May 10, 1818–July 20, 1896.
  Vol. 2, Pt. 2–484
Coxe, Daniel, August 1673–Apr. 25, 1739.
  Vol. 2, Pt. 2–484
Coxe, Eckley Brinton, June 4, 1839–May 13, 1895.
  Vol. 2, Pt. 2–485
Coxe, John Redman, Sept. 16, 1773–Mar. 22, 1864.
  Vol. 2, Pt. 2–486
Coxe, Richard Smith, January 1792–Apr. 28, 1865.
  Vol. 2, Pt. 2–487
Coxe, Tench, May 22, 1755–July 16, 1824.
  Vol. 2, Pt. 2–488
Coxe, William, May 3, 1762–Feb. 25, 1831.
  Vol. 2, Pt. 2–489
Coxetter, Louis Mitchell, Dec. 10, 1818–July 10, 1873.
  Vol. 2, Pt. 2–490
Coxey, Jacob Sechler, Apr. 16, 1854–May 18, 1951.
  Supp. 5–139
Coyle, Grace Longwell, Mar. 22, 1892–Mar. 8, 1962.
  Supp. 7–151
Cozzens, Frederick Swartwout, Mar. 11, 1818–Dec. 23, 1869.
  Vol. 2, Pt. 2–490
Crabtree, Lotta, Nov. 7, 1847–Sept. 25, 1924.
  Vol. 2, Pt. 2–491
Craddock, Charles Egbert. [See Murfree, Mary Noailles, 1850–1922.]
Crafts, James Mason, Mar. 8, 1839–June 20, 1917.
  Vol. 2, Pt. 2–492
Crafts, William, Jan. 24, 1787–Sept. 23, 1826.
  Vol. 2, Pt. 2–493
Craig, Austin, July 14, 1824–Aug. 27, 1881.
  Vol. 2, Pt. 2–494
Craig, Daniel H., *c.* 1814–Jan. 5, 1895.
  Vol. 2, Pt. 2–495
Craig, Malin, Aug. 5, 1875–July 25, 1945.
  Supp. 3–193
Craig, Thomas, Dec. 20, 1855–May 8, 1900.
  Vol. 2, Pt. 2–496
Craig, Winchell McKendree, Apr. 27, 1892–Feb. 12, 1960.
  Supp. 6–130
Craighead, Edwin Boone, Mar. 3, 1861–Oct. 22, 1920.
  Vol. 2, Pt. 2–496
Craigie, Andrew, June 7, 1743–Sept. 19, 1819.
  Vol. 2, Pt. 2–497
Craik, James, 1730–Feb. 6, 1814.
  Vol. 2, Pt. 2–498
Cram, Ralph Adams, Dec. 16, 1863–Sept. 22, 1942.
  Supp. 3–194
Cramer, Michael John, Feb. 6, 1835–Jan. 23, 1898.
  Vol. 2, Pt. 2–499
Cramp, Charles Henry, May 9, 1828–June 6, 1913.
  Vol. 2, Pt. 2–499
Cramp, William, Sept. 22, 1807–July 6, 1879.
  Vol. 2, Pt. 2–500
Cranch, Christopher Pearse, Mar. 8, 1813–Jan. 20, 1892.
  Vol. 2, Pt. 2–501
Cranch, William, July 17, 1769–Sept. 1, 1855.
  Vol. 2, Pt. 2–502
Crandall, Charles Henry, June 19, 1858–Mar. 23, 1923.
  Vol. 2, Pt. 2–503
Crandall, Prudence, Sept. 3, 1803–Jan. 28, 1889.
  Vol. 2, Pt. 2–503

Crane, Anne Moncure, Jan. 7, 1838–Dec. 10, 1872.
  Vol. 2, Pt. 2–504
Crane, Charles Richard, Aug. 7, 1858–Feb. 15, 1939.
  Supp. 2–128
Crane, Frank, May 12, 1861–Nov. 5, 1928.
  Vol. 2, Pt. 2–504
Crane, Frederick Evan, Mar. 2, 1869–Nov. 21, 1947.
  Supp. 4–190
Crane, Harold Hart, July 21, 1899–Apr. 27, 1932.
  Supp. 1–206
Crane, John, Dec. 7, 1744–Aug. 21, 1805.
  Vol. 2, Pt. 2–505
Crane, Jonathan Townley, June 18, 1819–Feb. 16, 1880.
  Vol. 2, Pt. 2–506
Crane, Stephen, Nov. 1, 1871–June 5, 1900.
  Vol. 2, Pt. 2–506
Crane, Thomas Frederick, July 12, 1844–Dec. 9, 1927.
  Vol. 2, Pt. 2–508
Crane, William Henry, Apr. 30, 1845–Mar. 7, 1928.
  Vol. 2, Pt. 2–509
Crane, William Montgomery, Feb. 1, 1784–Mar. 18, 1846.
  Vol. 2, Pt. 2–510
Crane, Winthrop Murray, Apr. 23, 1853–Oct. 2, 1920.
  Vol. 2, Pt. 2–510
Cranston, Earl, June 27, 1840–Aug. 18, 1932.
  Supp. 1–208
Cranston, John, 1625–Mar. 12, 1680.
  Vol. 2, Pt. 2–511
Cranston, Samuel, August 1659–Apr. 26, 1727.
  Vol. 2, Pt. 2–512
Crapsey, Adelaide, Sept. 9, 1878–Oct. 8, 1914.
  Vol. 2, Pt. 2–513
Crapsey, Algernon Sidney, June 28, 1847–Dec. 31, 1927.
  Vol. 2, Pt. 2–513
Crary, Isaac Edwin, Oct. 2, 1804–May 8, 1854.
  Vol. 2, Pt. 2–514
Cratty, Mabel, June 30, 1868–Feb. 27, 1928.
  Vol. 2, Pt. 2–515
Cravath, Erastus Milo, July 1, 1833–Sept. 4, 1900.
  Vol. 2, Pt. 2–516
Cravath, Paul Drennan, July 14, 1861–July 1, 1940.
  Supp. 2–130
Craven, Braxton, Aug. 22, 1822–Nov. 7, 1882.
  Vol. 2, Pt. 2–516
Craven, Frank, Aug. 24, 1875[?]–Sept. 1, 1945.
  Supp. 3–197
Craven, John Joseph, Sept. 8, 1822–Feb. 14, 1893.
  Vol. 2, Pt. 2–517
Craven, Thomas Tingey, Dec. 20, 1808–Aug. 23, 1887.
  Vol. 2, Pt. 2–517
Craven, Tunis Augustus MacDonough, Jan. 11, 1813–Aug. 5, 1864. Vol. 2, Pt. 2–518
Crawford, Francis Marion, Aug. 2, 1854–Apr. 9, 1909.
  Vol. 2, Pt. 2–519
Crawford, George Walker, Dec. 22, 1798–July 22, 1872.
  Vol. 2, Pt. 2–520
Crawford, James Pyle Wickersham, Feb. 19, 1882–Sept. 22, 1939. Supp. 2–131
Crawford, John, May 3, 1746–May 9, 1813.
  Vol. 2, Pt. 2–521
Crawford, John Martin, Oct. 18, 1845–Aug. 11, 1916.
  Vol. 2, Pt. 2–522
Crawford, John Wallace (Captain Jack), Mar. 4, 1847–Feb. 28, 1917. Vol. 2, Pt. 2–522
Crawford, Martin Jenkins, Mar. 17, 1820–July 23, 1883.
  Vol. 2, Pt. 2–523
Crawford, Samuel Earl, Apr. 18, 1880–June 15, 1968.
  Supp. 8–105
Crawford, Samuel Johnson, Apr. 15, 1835–Oct. 21, 1913.
  Vol. 2, Pt. 2–523
Crawford, Thomas, Mar. 22, 1813?–Oct. 10, 1857.
  Vol. 2, Pt. 2–524
Crawford, William, 1732–June 11, 1782.
  Vol. 2, Pt. 2–527
Crawford, William Harris, Feb. 24, 1772–Sept. 15, 1834.
  Vol. 2, Pt. 2–527
Crazy Horse, *c.* 1849–Sept. 5, 1877.
  Vol. 2, Pt. 2–530
Creamer, David, Nov. 20, 1812–Apr. 8, 1887.
  Vol. 2, Pt. 2–531
Creath, Jacob, Feb. 22, 1777–Mar. 13, 1854.
  Vol. 2, Pt. 2–531

Creath, Jacob, Jan. 17, 1799–Jan. 8, 1886.
    Vol. 2, Pt. 2–532
Creel, George, Dec. 1, 1876–Oct. 2, 1953.
    Supp. 5–141
Creelman, James, Nov. 12, 1859–Feb. 12, 1915.
    Vol. 2, Pt. 2–533
Creesy, Josiah Perkins, Mar. 23, 1814–June 5, 1871.
    Vol. 2, Pt. 2–533
Creighton, Edward, Aug. 31, 1820–Nov. 5, 1874.
    Vol. 2, Pt. 2–534
Creighton, James Edwin, Apr. 8, 1861–Oct. 8, 1924.
    Vol. 2, Pt. 2–535
Creighton, John Andrew, Oct. 15, 1831–Feb. 7, 1907.
    Vol. 2, Pt. 2–535
Creighton, William, Oct. 29, 1778–Oct. 1, 1851.
    Vol. 2, Pt. 2–536
Crerar, John, Mar. 8, 1827–Oct. 19, 1889.
    Vol. 2, Pt. 2–537
Cresap, Michael, June 29, 1742–Oct. 18, 1775.
    Vol. 2, Pt. 2–538
Cresap, Thomas, c. 1702–c. 1790.
    Vol. 2, Pt. 2–538
Crespi, Juan, 1721–Jan. 1, 1782.
    Vol. 2, Pt. 2–539
Cresson, Elliott, Mar. 2, 1796–Feb. 20, 1854.
    Vol. 2, Pt. 2–540
Cresson, Ezra Townsend, June 18, 1838–Apr. 19, 1926.
    Vol. 2, Pt. 2–540
Creswell, John Angel James, Nov. 18, 1828–Dec. 23, 1891.
    Vol. 2, Pt. 2–541
Cret, Paul Philippe, Oct. 23, 1876–Sept. 8, 1945.
    Supp. 3–199
Crétin, Joseph, Dec. 19, 1799–Feb. 22, 1857.
    Vol. 2, Pt. 2–542
Crèvecoeur, J. Hector St. John. [See Crèvecoeur, Michel-Guillaume, Jean de, 1735–1813.]
Crèvecoeur, Michel-Guillaume Jean de, Jan. 31, 1735–Nov. 12, 1813. Vol. 2, Pt. 2–542
Crile, George Washington, Nov. 11, 1864–Jan. 7, 1943.
    Supp. 3–200
Crimmins, John Daniel, May 18, 1844–Nov. 9, 1917.
    Vol. 2, Pt. 2–544
Crisp, Charles Frederick, Jan. 29, 1845–Oct. 23, 1896.
    Vol. 2, Pt. 2–544
Crissinger, Daniel Richard, Dec. 10, 1860–July 12, 1942.
    Supp. 3–203
Crittenden, George Bibb, Mar. 20, 1812–Nov. 27, 1880.
    Vol. 2, Pt. 2–545
Crittenden, John Jordan, Sept. 10, 1787–July 26, 1863.
    Vol. 2, Pt. 2–546
Crittenden, Thomas Leonidas, May 15, 1819–Oct. 23, 1893.
    Vol. 2, Pt. 2–549
Crittenden, Thomas Theodore, Jan. 1, 1832–May 29, 1909.
    Vol. 2, Pt. 2–550
Crittenton, Charles Nelson, Feb. 20, 1833–Nov. 16, 1909.
    Vol. 2, Pt. 2–550
Crocker, Alvah, Oct. 14, 1801–Dec. 26, 1874.
    Vol. 2, Pt. 2–551
Crocker, Charles, Sept. 16, 1822–Aug. 14, 1888.
    Vol. 2, Pt. 2–552
Crocker, Francis Bacon, July 4, 1861–July 9, 1921.
    Vol. 2, Pt. 2–553
Crocker, Hannah Mather, June 27, 1752–July 11, 1829.
    Vol. 2, Pt. 2–553
Crocker, Uriel, Sept. 13, 1796–July 19, 1887.
    Vol. 2, Pt. 2–554
Crocker, William, Jan. 27, 1874–Feb. 11, 1950.
    Supp. 4–191
Crockett, David, Aug. 17, 1786–Mar. 6, 1836.
    Vol. 2, Pt. 2–555
Croghan, George, d. Aug. 31, 1782.
    Vol. 2, Pt. 2–556
Croghan, George, Nov. 15, 1791–Jan. 8, 1849.
    Vol. 2, Pt. 2–557
Croix, Teodoro De, June 30, 1730–1792.
    Vol. 2, Pt. 2–557
Croker, Richard, Nov. 23, 1841–Apr. 29, 1922.
    Vol. 2, Pt. 2–558
Croly, David Goodman, Nov. 3, 1829–Apr. 29, 1889.
    Vol. 2, Pt. 2–560
Croly, Herbert David, Jan. 23, 1869–May 17, 1930.
    Supp. 1–209

Croly, Jane Cunningham, Dec. 19, 1829–Dec. 23, 1901.
    Vol. 2, Pt. 2–560
Crompton, George, Mar. 23, 1829–Dec. 29, 1886.
    Vol. 2, Pt. 2–561
Crompton, William, Sept. 10, 1806–May 1, 1891.
    Vol. 2, Pt. 2–561
Cromwell, Dean Bartlett, Sept. 20, 1879–Aug. 3, 1962.
    Supp. 7–152
Cromwell, Gladys Louise Husted, Nov. 28, 1885–Jan. 24, 1919. Vol. 2, Pt. 2–562
Cromwell, William Nelson, Jan. 17, 1854–July 19, 1948.
    Supp. 4–192
Crook, George, Sept. 23, 1829–Mar. 21, 1890.
    Vol. 2, Pt. 2–563
Crooks, George Richard, Feb. 3, 1822–Feb. 20, 1897.
    Vol. 2, Pt. 2–564
Crooks, Ramsay, Jan. 2, 1787–June 6, 1859.
    Vol. 2, Pt. 2–565
Cropsey, Jaspar Francis, Feb. 18, 1823–June 22, 1900.
    Vol. 2, Pt. 2–565
Crosby, Ernest Howard, Nov. 4, 1856–Jan. 3, 1907.
    Vol. 2, Pt. 2–566
Crosby, Fanny, Mar. 24, 1820–Feb. 12, 1915,.
    Vol. 2, Pt. 2–567
Crosby, Howard, Feb. 27, 1826–Mar. 29, 1891.
    Vol. 2, Pt. 2–567
Crosby, John Schuyler, Sept. 19, 1839–Aug. 8, 1914.
    Vol. 2, Pt. 2–568
Crosby, Peirce, Jan. 16, 1824–June 15, 1899.
    Vol. 2, Pt. 2–569
Crosby, Percy Lee, Dec. 8, 1891–Dec. 8, 1964.
    Supp. 7–153
Crosby, William Otis, Jan. 14, 1850–Dec. 31, 1925.
    Vol. 2, Pt. 2–569
Crosley, Powel, Jr., Sept. 18, 1886–Mar. 28, 1961.
    Supp. 7–154
Cross, Arthur Lyon, Nov. 14, 1873–June 21, 1940.
    Supp. 2–132
Cross, Charles Whitman, Sept. 1, 1854–Apr. 20, 1949.
    Supp. 4–194
Cross, Edward, Nov. 11, 1798–Apr. 6, 1887.
    Vol. 2, Pt. 2–570
Cross, Samuel Hazzard, July 1, 1891–Oct. 14, 1946.
    Supp. 4–195
Cross, Wilbur Lucius, Apr. 10, 1862–Oct. 5, 1948.
    Supp. 4–196
Crosser, Robert, June 7, 1874–June 3, 1957.
    Supp. 6–131
Crosswaith, Frank Rudolph, July 16, 1892–June 17, 1965.
    Supp. 7–155
Croswell, Edwin, May 29, 1797–June 13, 1871.
    Vol. 2, Pt. 2–571
Croswell, Harry, June 16, 1778–Mar. 13, 1858.
    Vol. 2, Pt. 2–571
Crothers, Rachel, Dec. 12, 1878–July 5, 1958.
    Supp. 6–133
Crothers, Samuel McChord, June 7, 1857–Nov. 9, 1927.
    Vol. 2, Pt. 2–572
Crounse, Lorenzo, Jan. 27, 1834–May 13, 1909.
    Vol. 2, Pt. 2–573
Crouse, Russel McKinley, Feb. 20, 1893–Apr. 3, 1966.
    Supp. 8–107
Crouter, Albert Louis Edgerton, Sept. 15, 1846–June 26, 1925. Vol. 2, Pt. 2–574
Crowder, Enoch Herbert, Apr. 11, 1859–May 7, 1932.
    Supp. 1–210
Crowe, Francis Trenholm, Oct. 12, 1882–Feb. 26, 1946.
    Supp. 4–198
Crowell, Luther Childs, Sept. 7, 1840–Sept. 16, 1903.
    Vol. 2, Pt. 2–575
Crowne, John, 1640–April 1712.
    Vol. 2, Pt. 2–576
Crowne, William, c. 1617–1683.
    Vol. 2, Pt. 2–576
Crowninshield, Benjamin Williams, Dec. 27, 1772–Feb. 3, 1851. Vol. 2, Pt. 2–577
Crowninshield, Francis Welch, June 24, 1872–Dec. 28, 1947.
    Supp. 4–199
Crowninshield, Frederic, Nov. 27, 1845–Sept. 13, 1918.
    Vol. 2, Pt. 2–578
Crowninshield, George, May 27, 1766–Nov. 26, 1817.
    Vol. 2, Pt. 2–578

Crowninshield, Jacob, May 31, 1770–Apr. 15, 1808.
    Vol. 2, Pt. 2–579
Croy, Homer, Mar. 11, 1883–May 24, 1965.
    Supp. 7–156
Crozer, John Price, Jan. 13, 1793–Mar. 11, 1866.
    Vol. 2, Pt. 2–579
Crozet, Claude, Jan. 1, 1790–Jan. 29, 1864.
    Vol. 2, Pt. 2–580
Crozier, William, Feb. 19, 1855–Nov. 10, 1942.
    Supp. 3–204
Cruger, Henry, Nov. 22, 1739–Apr. 24, 1827.
    Vol. 2, Pt. 2–581
Cruger, John, July 18, 1710–Dec. 27, 1791.
    Vol. 2, Pt. 2–582
Crumbine, Samuel Jay, Sept. 17, 1862–July 12, 1954.
    Supp. 5–143
Crump, Edward Hull, Oct. 2, 1874–Oct. 16, 1954.
    Supp. 5–144
Crump, William Wood, Nov. 25, 1819–Feb. 27, 1897.
    Vol. 2, Pt. 2–582
Crunden, Frederick Morgan, Sept. 1, 1847–Oct. 28, 1911.
    Vol. 2, Pt. 2–583
Cubberley, Ellwood Patterson, June 6, 1868–Sept. 14, 1941.
    Supp. 3–205
Cubero, Pedro Rodriguez, 1645–1704.
    Vol. 2, Pt. 2–584
Cudahy, Edward Aloysius, Jr., Aug. 22, 1885–Jan. 8, 1966.
    Supp. 8–109
Cudahy, Michael, Dec. 7, 1841–Nov. 27, 1910.
    Vol. 2, Pt. 2–584
Cuffe, Paul, Jan. 17, 1759–Sept. 9, 1817.
    Vol. 2, Pt. 2–585
Culberson, Charles Allen, June 10, 1855–March 19, 1925.
    Vol. 2, Pt. 2–585
Culberson, David Browning, Sept. 29, 1830–May 7, 1900.
    Vol. 2, Pt. 2–586
Culbertson, Ely, July 22, 1891–Dec. 27, 1955.
    Supp. 5–145
Culbertson, Josephine Murphy, 1899–Mar. 23, 1956.
    Supp. 6–134
Cullen, Countée Porter, May 30, 1903–Jan. 9, 1946.
    Supp. 4–200
Cullen, Hugh Roy, July 3, 1881–July 4, 1957.
    Supp. 6–135
Cullen, Thomas Stephen, Nov. 20, 1868–Mar. 4, 1953.
    Supp. 5–146
Cullinan, Joseph Stephen, Dec. 31, 1860–Mar. 11, 1937.
    Supp. 2–133
Cullis, Charles, Mar. 7, 1833–June 18, 1892.
    Vol. 2, Pt. 2–587
Cullom, Shelby Moore, Nov. 22, 1829–Jan. 28, 1914.
    Vol. 2, Pt. 2–588
Cullum, George Washington, Feb. 25, 1809–Feb. 28, 1892.
    Vol. 2, Pt. 2–589
Culpeper, Thomas Lord, 1635–Jan. 27, 1689.
    Vol. 2, Pt. 2–590
Cuming, Sir Alexander, c. 1690–Aug. 1775.
    Vol. 2, Pt. 2–591
Cuming, Fortescue, Feb. 26, 1762–1828.
    Vol. 2, Pt. 2–592
Cumming, Alfred, Sept. 4, 1802–Oct. 9, 1873.
    Vol. 2, Pt. 2–592
Cummings, Amos Jay, May 15, 1841–May 2, 1902.
    Vol. 2, Pt. 2–593
Cummings, Charles Amos, June 26, 1833–Aug. 11, 1905.
    Vol. 2, Pt. 2–594
Cummings, Edward, Apr. 20, 1861–Nov. 2, 1926.
    Vol. 2, Pt. 2–594
Cummings, E. E., Oct. 14, 1894–Sept. 3, 1962.
    Supp. 7–157
Cummings, Homer Stillé, Apr. 30, 1870–Sept. 10, 1956.
    Supp. 6–136
Cummings, John, Feb. 12, 1785–June 8, 1867.
    Vol. 2, Pt. 2–595
Cummings, Joseph, Mar. 3, 1817–May 7, 1890.
    Vol. 2, Pt. 2–596
Cummings, Thomas Seir, Aug. 26, 1804–Sept. 24, 1894.
    Vol. 2, Pt. 2–596
Cummings, Walter Joseph, June 24, 1879–Aug. 20, 1967.
    Supp. 8–111
Cummins, Albert Baird, Feb. 15, 1850–July 30, 1926.
    Vol. 2, Pt. 2–597

Cummins, George David, Dec. 11, 1822–June 26, 1876.
    Vol. 2, Pt. 2–599
Cummins, Maria Susanna, Apr. 9, 1827–Oct. 1, 1866.
    Vol. 2, Pt. 2–600
Cunliffe-Owen, Philip Frederick, Jan. 30, 1855–June 30, 1926. Vol. 2, Pt. 2–600
Cunningham, Ann Pamela, Aug. 15, 1816–May 1, 1875.
    Vol. 2, Pt. 2–601
Cunningham, Kate (Richards) O'Hare. [See O'Hare, Kate Richards Cunningham, 1877–1948.]
Cuppia, Jerome Chester, Sept. 29, 1890–Sept. 20, 1966.
    Supp. 8–112
Cupples, Samuel, Sept. 13, 1831–Jan. 6, 1912.
    Vol. 2, Pt. 2–602
Cuppy, William Jacob (Will), Aug. 23, 1884–Sept. 19, 1949.
    Supp. 4–201
Curley, James Michael, Nov. 20, 1874–Nov. 12, 1958.
    Supp. 6–138
Curme, George Oliver, Jan. 14, 1860–Apr. 29, 1948.
    Supp. 4–203
Curran, John Joseph, June 20, 1859–Nov. 7, 1936.
    Supp. 2–134
Curran, Thomas Jerome, Nov. 28, 1898–July 29, 1958.
    Supp. 6–141
Currier, Charles Warren, Mar. 22, 1857–Sept. 23, 1918.
    Vol. 2, Pt. 2–602
Currier, Moody, Apr. 22, 1806–Aug. 23, 1898.
    Vol. 2, Pt. 2–603
Currier, Nathaniel, Mar. 27, 1813–Nov. 20, 1888.
    Vol. 2, Pt. 2–604
Curry, George Law, July 2, 1820–July 28, 1878.
    Vol. 2, Pt. 2–604
Curry, Jabez Lamar Monroe, June 5, 1825–Feb. 12, 1903.
    Vol. 2, Pt. 2–605
Curry, John Steuart, Nov. 14, 1897–Aug. 29, 1946.
    Supp. 4–204
Curtin, Andrew Gregg, Apr. 23, 1815?–Oct. 7, 1894.
    Vol. 2, Pt. 2–606
Curtin, Jeremiah, Sept. 6, 1840?–Dec. 14, 1906.
    Vol. 2, Pt. 2–608
Curtis, Alfred Allen, July 4, 1831–July 11, 1908.
    Vol. 2, Pt. 2–608
Curtis, Benjamin Robbins, Nov. 4, 1809–Sept. 15, 1874.
    Vol. 2, Pt. 2–609
Curtis, Charles, Jan. 25, 1860–Feb. 8, 1936.
    Supp. 2–136
Curtis, Charles Pelham, May 8, 1891–Dec. 23, 1959.
    Supp. 6–142
Curtis, Cyrus Hermann Kotzschmar, June 18, 1850–June 7, 1933. Supp. 1–212
Curtis, Edward Lewis, Oct. 13, 1853–Aug. 26, 1911.
    Vol. 2, Pt. 2–611
Curtis, Edward Sheriff, Feb. 19, 1868–Oct. 19, 1952.
    Supp. 5–148
Curtis, Edwin Upton, Mar. 26, 1861–Mar. 28, 1922.
    Vol. 2, Pt. 2–612
Curtis, George, Feb. 23, 1796–Jan. 9, 1856.
    Vol. 2, Pt. 2–612
Curtis, George Ticknor, Nov. 28, 1812–Mar. 28, 1894.
    Vol. 2, Pt. 2–613
Curtis, George William, Feb. 24, 1824–Aug. 31, 1892.
    Vol. 2, Pt. 2–614
Curtis, Heber Doust, June 27, 1872–Jan. 9, 1942.
    Supp. 3–207
Curtis, John Green, Oct. 29, 1844–Sept. 20, 1913.
    Vol. 2, Pt. 2–616
Curtis, Moses Ashley, May 11, 1808–Apr. 10, 1872.
    Vol. 2, Pt. 2–617
Curtis, Newton Martin, May 21, 1835–Jan. 8, 1910.
    Vol. 2, Pt. 2–618
Curtis, Olin Alfred, Dec. 10, 1850–Jan. 8, 1918.
    Vol. 2, Pt. 2–619
Curtis, Samuel Ryan, Feb. 3, 1805–Dec. 26, 1866.
    Vol. 2, Pt. 2–619
Curtis, William Eleroy, Nov. 5, 1850–Oct. 5, 1911.
    Vol. 2, Pt. 2–620
Curtiss, Glenn Hammond, May 21, 1878–July 23, 1930.
    Supp. 1–213
Curtiss, Samuel Ives, Feb. 5, 1844–Sept. 22, 1904.
    Vol. 2, Pt. 2–621
Curtiz, Michael, Dec. 24, 1888–Apr. 11, 1962.
    Supp. 7–159

Curwen, Samuel, Dec. 17, 1715–Apr. 9, 1802.
  Vol. 2, Pt. 2–622
Curwood, James Oliver, June 12, 1878–Aug. 13, 1927.
  Vol. 2, Pt. 2–622
Cushing, Caleb, Jan. 17, 1800–Jan. 2, 1879.
  Vol. 2, Pt. 2–623
Cushing, Frank Hamilton, July 22, 1857–Apr. 10, 1900.
  Vol. 2, Pt. 2–630
Cushing, Harvey Williams, Apr. 9, 1869–Oct. 7, 1939.
  Supp. 2–137
Cushing, John Perkins, Apr. 22, 1787–Apr. 12, 1862.
  Vol. 2, Pt. 2–630
Cushing, Josiah Nelson, May 4, 1840–May 17, 1905.
  Vol. 2, Pt. 2–631
Cushing, Luther Stearns, June 22, 1803–June 22, 1856.
  Vol. 2, Pt. 2–632
Cushing, Richard James, Aug. 24, 1895–Nov. 2, 1970.
  Supp. 8–114
Cushing, Thomas, Mar. 24, 1725–Feb. 28, 1788.
  Vol. 2, Pt. 2–632
Cushing, William, Mar. 1, 1732–Sept. 13, 1810.
  Vol. 2, Pt. 2–633
Cushing, William Barker, Nov. 4, 1842–Dec. 17, 1874.
  Vol. 2, Pt. 2–635
Cushman, Charlotte Saunders, July 23, 1816–Feb 17, 1876.
  Vol. 3, Pt. 1–1
Cushman, George Hewitt, June 5, 1814–Aug. 3, 1876.
  Vol. 3, Pt. 1–3
Cushman, Joseph Augustine, Jan. 31, 1881–Apr. 16, 1949.
  Supp. 4–205
Cushman, Joshua, Apr. 11, 1761–Jan. 27, 1834.
  Vol. 3, Pt. 1–3
Cushman, Pauline, June 10, 1835–Dec. 2, 1893.
  Vol. 3, Pt. 1–4
Cushman, Robert, c. 1579–1625.
  Vol. 3, Pt. 1–5
Cushman, Susan Webb, Mar. 17, 1822–May 10, 1859.
  Vol. 3, Pt. 1–5
Cushman, Vera Charlotte Scott, Sept. 19, 1876–Feb. 1, 1946.
  Supp. 4–207
Cushny, Arthur Robertson, Mar. 6, 1866–Feb. 25, 1926.
  Vol. 3, Pt. 1–6
Custer, George Armstrong, Dec. 5, 1839–June 25, 1876.
  Vol. 3, Pt. 1–7
Custis, George Washington Parke, Apr. 30, 1781–Oct. 10, 1857.
  Vol. 3, Pt. 1–9
Cutbush, James, 1788–Dec. 15, 1823.
  Vol. 3, Pt. 1–10
Cutler, Carroll, Jan. 31, 1829–Jan. 24, 1894.
  Vol. 3, Pt. 1–10
Cutler, Elliott Carr, July 30, 1888–Aug. 16, 1947.
  Supp. 4–208
Cutler, James Goold, Apr. 24, 1848–Apr. 21, 1927.
  Vol. 3, Pt. 1–11
Cutler, Lizzie Petit, 1831–Jan. 16, 1902.
  Vol. 3, Pt. 1–12
Cutler, Manasseh, May 13, 1742–July 28, 1823.
  Vol. 3, Pt. 1–12
Cutler, Timothy, May 31, 1684–Aug. 17, 1765.
  Vol. 3, Pt. 1–14
Cutter, Charles Ammi, Mar. 14, 1837–Sept. 6, 1903.
  Vol. 3, Pt. 1–15
Cutter, Ephraim, Sept. 1, 1832–Apr. 25, 1917.
  Vol. 3, Pt. 1–16
Cutter, George Washington, 1801–Dec. 25, 1865.
  Vol. 3, Pt. 1–17
Cutting, Bronson Murray, June 23, 1883–May 6, 1935.
  Supp. 1–215
Cutting, James Ambrose, 1814–Aug. 6, 1867.
  Vol. 3, Pt. 1–17
Cutting, Robert Fulton, June 24, 1852–Sept. 21, 1934.
  Supp. 1–216
Cuyler, Theodore, Sept. 14, 1819–Apr. 5, 1876.
  Vol. 3, Pt. 1–18
Cuyler, Theodore Ledyard, Jan. 10, 1822–Feb. 26, 1909.
  Vol. 3, Pt. 1–18

Dablon, Claude, Jan. 21, 1619 or February 1618–May 3 or Sept. 20, 1697. Vol. 3, Pt. 1–19
Dabney, Charles William, June 19, 1855–June 15, 1945.
  Supp. 3–208
Dabney, Richard, 1787–Nov. 25, 1825.
  Vol. 3, Pt. 1–20

Dabney, Robert Lewis, Mar. 5, 1820–Jan. 3, 1898.
  Vol. 3, Pt. 1–20
Dabney, Thomas Smith Gregory, Jan. 4, 1798–Feb. 28, 1885.
  Vol. 3, Pt. 1–21
Dabney, Virginius, Feb. 15, 1835–June 2, 1894.
  Vol. 3, Pt. 1–22
Daboll, Nathan, Apr. 24, 1750–Mar. 9, 1818.
  Vol. 3, Pt. 1–23
Dabrowski, Joseph, Jan. 19, 1842–Feb. 15, 1903.
  Vol. 3, Pt. 1–23
Da Costa, Jacob Mendez, Feb. 7, 1833–Sept. 11, 1900.
  Vol. 3, Pt. 1–24
Da Costa, John Chalmers, Nov. 15, 1863–May 16, 1933.
  Supp. 1–217
Daeger, Albert Thomas, Mar. 5, 1872–Dec. 2, 1932.
  Supp. 1–218
Daft, Leo, Nov. 13, 1843–Mar. 28, 1922.
  Vol. 3, Pt. 1–25
Dagg, John Leadley, Feb. 13, 1794–June 11, 1884.
  Vol. 3, Pt. 1–26
Daggett, David, Dec. 31, 1764–Apr. 12, 1851.
  Vol. 3, Pt. 1–26
Daggett, Ellsworth, May 24, 1845–Jan. 5, 1923.
  Vol. 3, Pt. 1–27
Daggett, Naphtali, Sept. 8, 1727–Nov. 25, 1780.
  Vol. 3, Pt. 1–28
Dahl, Theodor Halvorson, Apr. 2, 1845–Jan. 18, 1923.
  Vol. 3, Pt. 1–28
Dahlgren, John Adolphus Bernard, Nov. 13, 1809–July 12, 1870. Vol. 3, Pt. 1–29
Dahlgren, Sarah Madeleine Vinton, July 13, 1825–May 28, 1898. Vol. 3, Pt. 1–31
Dakin, Henry Drysdale, Mar. 12, 1880–Feb. 10, 1952.
  Supp. 5–149
Dakin, James Harrison, Aug. 24, 1806–May 10, 1852.
  Supp. 1–219
Dalcho, Frederick, 1770–Nov. 24, 1836.
  Vol. 3, Pt. 1–32
Dale, Chester, May 3, 1883–Dec. 16, 1962.
  Supp. 7–161
Dale, Maud Murray Thompson, June 25, 1875–Aug. 5, 1953.
  Supp. 5–150
Dale, Richard, Nov. 6, 1756–Feb. 26, 1826.
  Vol. 3, Pt. 1–32
Dale, Samuel, 1772–May 24, 1841.
  Vol. 3, Pt. 1–33
Dale, Sir Thomas, d. Aug. 9, 1619.
  Vol. 3, Pt. 1–34
Dall, Caroline Wells Healey, June 22, 1822–Dec. 17, 1912.
  Vol. 3, Pt. 1–35
Dall, William Healey, Aug. 21, 1845–Mar. 27, 1927.
  Vol. 3, Pt. 1–35
Dallas, Alexander James, June 21, 1759–Jan. 16, 1817.
  Vol. 3, Pt. 1–36
Dallas, George Mifflin, July 10, 1792–Dec. 31, 1864.
  Vol. 3, Pt. 1–38
Dallin, Cyrus Edwin, Nov. 22, 1861–Nov. 14, 1944.
  Supp. 3–210
D'Aloes, Claude Jean. [See Allouez, Claude Jean, 1622–1689.]
Dalton, John Call, Feb. 2, 1825–Feb. 12, 1889.
  Vol. 3, Pt. 1–40
Dalton, Robert, 1867–Oct. 5, 1892.
  Vol. 3, Pt. 1–40
Daly, Arnold. [See Daly, Peter Christopher Arnold, 1875–1927.]
Daly, Augustin. [See Daly, John Augustin, 1838–1899.]
Daly, Charles Patrick, Oct. 31, 1816–Sept. 19, 1899.
  Vol. 3, Pt. 1–41
Daly, John Augustin, July 20, 1838–June 7, 1899.
  Vol. 3, Pt. 1–42
Daly, Marcus, Dec. 5, 1841–Nov. 12, 1900.
  Vol. 3, Pt. 1–45
Daly, Peter Christopher Arnold, Oct. 22, 1875–Jan. 13, 1927.
  Vol. 3, Pt. 1–46
Daly, Reginald Aldworth, May 19, 1871–Sept. 19, 1957.
  Supp. 6–143
Dalzell, John, Apr. 19, 1845–Oct. 2, 1927.
  Vol. 3, Pt. 1–47
Dalzell, Robert M., 1793–Jan. 19, 1873.
  Vol. 3, Pt. 1–48
Damon, Ralph Shepard, July 6, 1897–Jan. 4, 1956.
  Supp. 6–145

Damrosch, Frank Heino, June 22, 1859–Oct. 22, 1937.
    Supp. 2–140
Damrosch, Leopold, Oct. 22, 1832–Feb. 15, 1885.
    Vol. 3, Pt. 1–48
Damrosch, Walter Johannes, Jan. 30, 1862–Dec. 22, 1950.
    Supp. 4–210
Dana, Charles Anderson, Aug. 8, 1819–Oct. 17, 1897.
    Vol. 3, Pt. 1–49
Dana, Charles Loomis, Mar. 25, 1852–Dec. 12, 1935.
    Supp. 1–220
Dana, Edward Salisbury, Nov. 16, 1849–June 16, 1935.
    Supp. 1–221
Dana, Francis, June 13, 1743–Apr. 25, 1811.
    Vol. 3, Pt. 1–52
Dana, James, 1735–Aug. 18, 1812.
    Vol. 3, Pt. 1–54
Dana, James Dwight, Feb. 12, 1813–Apr. 14, 1895.
    Vol. 3, Pt. 1–55
Dana, James Freeman, Sept. 23, 1793–Apr. 14, 1827.
    Vol. 3, Pt. 1–56
Dana, John Cotton, Aug. 19, 1856–July 21, 1929.
    Vol. 3, Pt. 1–56
Dana, Napoleon Jackson Tecumseh, Apr. 15, 1822–July 15, 1905. Vol. 3, Pt. 1–58
Dana, Richard, June 26, 1700–May 17, 1772.
    Vol. 3, Pt. 1–58
Dana, Richard Henry, Nov. 15, 1787–Feb. 2, 1879.
    Vol. 3, Pt. 1–59
Dana, Richard Henry, Aug. 1, 1815–Jan. 6, 1882.
    Vol. 3, Pt. 1–60
Dana, Samuel Luther, July 11, 1795–Mar. 11, 1868.
    Vol. 3, Pt. 1–61
Dana, Samuel Whittelsey, Feb. 13, 1760–July 21, 1830.
    Vol. 3, Pt. 1–61
Dancel, Christian, Feb. 14, 1847–Oct. 13, 1898.
    Vol. 3, Pt. 1–62
Dandridge, Dorothy Jean, Nov. 9, 1922–Sept. 8, 1965.
    Supp. 7–162
Dandy, Walter Edward, Apr. 6, 1886–Apr. 19, 1946.
    Supp. 4–213
Dane, Nathan, Dec. 29, 1752–Feb. 15, 1835.
    Vol. 3, Pt. 1–63
Danenhower, John Wilson, Sept. 30, 1849–Apr. 20, 1887.
    Vol. 3, Pt. 1–64
Danforth, Charles, Aug. 30, 1797–Mar. 22, 1876.
    Vol. 3, Pt. 1–65
Danforth, Moseley Isaac, Dec. 11, 1800–Jan. 19, 1862.
    Vol. 3, Pt. 1–66
Danforth, Thomas, November 1623–Nov. 5, 1699.
    Vol. 3, Pt. 1–66
Danforth, Thomas, May 22, 1703–c. 1786.
    Vol. 3, Pt. 1–67
Daniel, John Moncure, Oct. 24, 1825–Mar. 30, 1865.
    Vol. 3, Pt. 1–67
Daniel, John Warwick, Sept. 5, 1842–June 29, 1910.
    Vol. 3, Pt. 1–68
Daniel, Peter Vivian, Apr. 24, 1784–May 31, 1860.
    Vol. 3, Pt. 1–69
Daniels, Frank Albert, Aug. 15, 1856–Jan. 12, 1935.
    Supp. 1–222
Daniels, Fred Harris, June 16, 1853–Aug. 30, 1913.
    Vol. 3, Pt. 1–69
Daniels, Josephus, May 18, 1862–Jan. 15, 1948.
    Supp. 4–215
Daniels, Winthrop More, Sept. 30, 1867–Jan. 2, 1944.
    Supp. 3–211
Dannreuther, Gustav, July 21, 1853–Dec. 19, 1923.
    Vol. 3, Pt. 1–70
Da Ponte, Lorenzo, Mar. 10, 1749–Aug. 17, 1838.
    Vol. 3, Pt. 1–71
Darby, John, Sept. 27, 1804–Sept. 1, 1877.
    Vol. 3, Pt. 1–72
Darby, William, Aug. 14, 1775–Oct. 9, 1854.
    Vol. 3, Pt. 1–73
Dare, Virginia, b. Aug. 18, 1587.
    Vol. 3, Pt. 1–73
Dargan, Edmund Strother, Apr. 15, 1805–Nov. 24, 1879.
    Vol. 3, Pt. 1–74
Dargan, Edwin Preston, Sept. 7, 1879–Dec. 13, 1940.
    Supp. 2–141
Darke, William, May 6, 1736–Nov. 26, 1801.
    Vol. 3, Pt. 1–74

Darley, Felix Octavius Carr, June 23, 1822–Mar. 27, 1888.
    Vol. 3, Pt. 1–75
Darling, Flora Adams, July 25, 1840–Jan. 6, 1910.
    Vol. 3, Pt. 1–76
Darling, Henry, Dec. 27, 1823–Apr. 20, 1891.
    Vol. 3, Pt. 1–77
Darling, Jay Norwood ("Ding"), Oct. 21, 1876–Feb. 12, 1962. Supp. 7–163
Darling, Samuel Taylor, Apr. 6, 1872–May 20, 1925.
    Vol. 3, Pt. 1–77
Darlington, William, Apr. 28, 1782–Apr. 23, 1863.
    Vol. 3, Pt. 1–78
Darrow, Clarence Seward, Apr. 18, 1857–Mar. 13, 1938.
    Supp. 2–141
Dart, Henry Paluché, Feb. 5, 1858–Sept. 27, 1934.
    Supp. 1–223
Darton, Nelson Horatio, Dec. 17, 1865–Feb. 28, 1948.
    Supp. 4–218
Darwell, Jane, Oct. 15, 1880–Aug. 14, 1967.
    Supp. 8–116
Daugherty, Harry Micajah, Jan. 26, 1860–Oct. 12, 1941.
    Supp. 3–214
Daveis, Charles Stewart, May 10, 1788–Mar. 29, 1865.
    Vol. 3, Pt. 1–79
Daveiss, Joseph Hamilton, Mar. 4, 1774–Nov. 8, 1811.
    Vol. 3, Pt. 1–80
Davenport, Charles Benedict, June 1, 1866–Feb. 8, 1944.
    Supp. 3–214
Davenport, Edward Loomis, Nov. 15, 1815–Sept. 1, 1877.
    Vol. 3, Pt. 1–80
Davenport, Eugene, June 20, 1856–Mar. 31, 1941.
    Supp. 3–216
Davenport, Fanny Lily Gypsy, Apr. 10, 1850–Sept. 26, 1898.
    Vol. 3, Pt. 1–82
Davenport, George, 1783–July 4, 1845.
    Vol. 3, Pt. 1–82
Davenport, Herbert Joseph, Aug. 10, 1861–June 16, 1931.
    Supp. 1–224
Davenport, Homer Calvin, Mar. 8, 1867–May 2, 1912.
    Vol. 3, Pt. 1–83
Davenport, Ira Erastus, Sept. 17, 1839–July 8, 1911.
    Vol. 3, Pt. 1–84
Davenport, James, 1716–1757.
    Vol. 3, Pt. 1–84
Davenport, John, 1597–Mar. 1669/70.
    Vol. 3, Pt. 1–85
Davenport, Russell Wheeler, July 12, 1899–Apr. 19, 1954.
    Supp. 5–152
Davenport, Thomas, July 9, 1802–July 6, 1851.
    Vol. 3, Pt. 1–87
Davenport, William H., 1841–1877. [See Davenport, Ira Erastus, 1839–1911.]
Davey, John, June 6, 1846–Nov. 8, 1923.
    Vol. 3, Pt. 1–88
D'Avezac, Auguste Geneviève Valentin, May 1780–Feb. 15, 1851. Vol. 3, Pt. 1–89
David, John Baptist Mary, June 4, 1761–July 12, 1841.
    Vol. 3, Pt. 1–89
Davidge, John Beale, 1768–Aug. 23, 1829.
    Vol. 3, Pt. 1–91
Davidge, William Pleater, Apr. 17, 1814–Aug. 7, 1888.
    Vol. 3, Pt. 1–91
Davidson, George, May 9, 1825–Dec. 2, 1911.
    Vol. 3, Pt. 1–92
Davidson, Israel, May 27, 1870–June 27, 1939.
    Supp. 2–144
Davidson, James Wood, Mar. 9, 1829–c. June 15, 1905.
    Vol. 3, Pt. 1–93
Davidson, Jo, Mar. 30, 1883–Jan. 2, 1952.
    Supp. 5–153
Davidson, John Wynn, Aug. 18, 1823–June 26, 1881.
    Vol. 3, Pt. 1–93
Davidson, Lucretia Maria, Sept. 27, 1808–Aug. 27, 1825.
    Vol. 3, Pt. 1–94
Davidson, Margaret Miller, Mar. 26, 1823–Nov. 25, 1838.
    Vol. 3, Pt. 1–94
Davidson, Robert, 1750–Dec. 13, 1812.
    Vol. 3, Pt. 1–95
Davidson, Thomas, Oct. 25, 1840–Sept. 14, 1900.
    Vol. 3, Pt. 1–95
Davidson, William Lee, 1746–Feb. 1, 1781.
    Vol. 3, Pt. 1–97

Davie, William Richardson, June 20, 1756–Nov. 29, 1820.
Vol. 3, Pt. 1–98
Davies, Arthur Bowen, Sept. 26, 1862–Oct. 24, 1928.
Vol. 3, Pt. 1–99
Davies, Henry Eugene, July 2, 1836–Sept. 6, 1894.
Vol. 3, Pt. 1–101
Davies, John Vipond, Oct. 13, 1862–Oct. 4, 1939.
Supp. 2–145
Davies, Joseph Edward, Nov. 29, 1876–May 9, 1958.
Supp. 6–146
Davies, Marion Cecilia, Jan. 3, 1897–Sept. 22, 1961.
Supp. 7–165
Davies, Samuel, Nov. 3, 1723–Feb. 4, 1761.
Vol. 3, Pt. 1–102
Daviess, Joseph Hamilton. [See Daveiss, Joseph Hamilton, 1774–1811.]
Daviess, Maria Thompson, Nov. 25, 1872–Sept. 3, 1924.
Vol. 3, Pt. 1–103
Davis, Alexander Jackson, July 24, 1803–Jan. 14, 1892.
Vol. 3, Pt. 1–103
Davis, Andrew Jackson, Aug. 11, 1826–Jan. 13, 1910.
Vol. 3, Pt. 1–105
Davis, Andrew McFarland, Dec. 30, 1833–Mar. 29, 1920.
Vol. 3, Pt. 1–105
Davis, Arthur Powell, Feb. 9, 1861–Aug. 7, 1933.
Supp. 1–224
Davis, Arthur Vining, May 30, 1867–Nov. 17, 1962.
Supp. 7–166
Davis, Benjamin Oliver, Sr., July 1, 1877–Nov. 26, 1970.
Supp. 8–118
Davis, Charles Harold, Jan. 7, 1856–Aug. 5, 1933.
Supp. 1–226
Davis, Charles Henry, Jan. 16, 1807–Feb. 18, 1877.
Vol. 3, Pt. 1–106
Davis, Charles Henry, Aug. 28, 1845–Dec. 27, 1921.
Vol. 3, Pt. 1–107
Davis, Charles Henry Stanley, Mar. 2, 1840–Nov. 7, 1917.
Vol. 3, Pt. 1–108
Davis, Cushman Kellogg, June 16, 1838–Nov. 27, 1900.
Vol. 3, Pt. 1–109
Davis, David, Mar. 9, 1815–June 26, 1886.
Vol. 3, Pt. 1–110
Davis, Dwight Filley, July 5, 1879–Nov. 28, 1945.
Supp. 3–217
Davis, Edmund Jackson, Oct. 2, 1827–Feb. 7, 1883.
Vol. 3, Pt. 1–112
Davis, Edwin Hamilton, Jan. 22, 1811–May 15, 1888.
Vol. 3, Pt. 1–113
Davis, Elmer Holmes, Jan. 13, 1890–May 18, 1958.
Supp. 6–148
Davis, Ernest R. ("Ernie"), Dec. 14, 1939–May 18, 1963.
Supp. 7–167
Davis, Francis Breese, Jr., Sept. 16, 1883–Dec. 22, 1962.
Supp. 7–169
Davis, Garret, Sept. 10, 1801–Sept. 22, 1872.
Vol. 3, Pt. 1–113
Davis, George, Mar. 1, 1820–Feb. 23, 1896.
Vol. 3, Pt. 1–114
Davis, George Breckenridge, Feb. 13, 1847–Dec. 15, 1914.
Vol. 3, Pt. 1–115
Davis, George Whitefield, July 26, 1839–July 12, 1918.
Vol. 3, Pt. 1–115
Davis, Harvey Nathaniel, June 6, 1881–Dec. 3, 1952.
Supp. 5–154
Davis, Henry, Sept. 15, 1771–Mar. 8, 1852.
Vol. 3, Pt. 1–116
Davis, Henry Gassaway, Nov. 16, 1823–Mar. 11, 1916.
Vol. 3, Pt. 1–117
Davis, Henry Gassett, Nov. 4, 1807–Nov. 18, 1896.
Vol. 3, Pt. 1–118
Davis, Henry Winter, Aug. 16, 1817–Dec. 30, 1865.
Vol. 3, Pt. 1–119
Davis, Horace, Mar. 16, 1831–July 12, 1916.
Vol. 3, Pt. 1–121
Davis, James John, Oct. 27, 1873–Nov. 22, 1947.
Supp. 4–219
Davis, Jeff, May 6, 1862–Jan. 3, 1913.
Vol. 3, Pt. 1–122
Davis, Jefferson, June 3, 1808–Dec. 6, 1889.
Vol. 3, Pt. 1–123
Davis, Jefferson Columbus, Mar. 2, 1828–Nov. 30, 1879.
Vol. 3, Pt. 1–131

Davis, Jerome Dean, Jan. 17, 1838–Nov. 4, 1910.
Vol. 3, Pt. 1–131
Davis, John, Jan. 25, 1761–Jan. 14, 1847.
Vol. 3, Pt. 1–132
Davis, John, c. 1780–c. 1838.
Vol. 3, Pt. 1–133
Davis, John, Jan. 13, 1787–Apr. 19, 1854.
Vol. 3, Pt. 1–133
Davis, John Chandler Bancroft, Dec. 29, 1822–Dec. 27, 1907.
Vol. 3, Pt. 1–134
Davis, John Lee, Sept. 3, 1825–Mar. 12, 1889.
Vol. 3, Pt. 1–136
Davis, John Staige, Jan. 15, 1872–Dec. 23, 1946.
Supp. 4–220
Davis, John Wesley, Apr. 16, 1799–Aug. 22, 1859.
Vol. 3, Pt. 1–136
Davis, John William, Apr. 13, 1873–Mar. 24, 1955).
Supp. 5–155
Davis, Joseph Robert, Jan. 12, 1825–Sept. 15, 1896.
Vol. 3, Pt. 1–137
Davis, Katharine Bement, Jan. 15, 1860–Dec. 10, 1935.
Supp. 1–227
Davis, Mary Evelyn Moore, Apr. 12, 1852–Jan. 1, 1909.
Vol. 3, Pt. 1–137
Davis, Matthew Livingston, Oct. 28, 1773–June 21, 1850.
Vol. 3, Pt. 1–138
Davis, Nathan Smith, Jan. 9, 1817–June 16, 1904.
Vol. 3, Pt. 1–139
Davis, Noah, Sept. 10, 1818–Mar. 20, 1902.
Vol. 3, Pt. 1–140
Davis, Noah Knowles, May 15, 1830–May 3, 1910.
Vol. 3, Pt. 1–140
Davis, Norman Hezekiah, Aug. 9, 1878–July 2, 1944.
Supp. 3–218
Davis, Oscar King, Jan. 13, 1866–June 3, 1932.
Supp. 1–228
Davis, Owen Gould, Jan. 28, 1874–Oct. 14, 1956.
Supp. 6–149
Davis, Paulina Kellogg Wright, Aug. 7, 1813–Aug. 24, 1876.
Vol. 3, Pt. 1–141
Davis, Pauline Morton Sabin, 1887–Dec. 27, 1955).
Supp. 5–156
Davis, Phineas, 1800–Sept. 27, 1835.
Vol. 3, Pt. 1–142
Davis, Raymond Cazallis, June 23, 1836–June 10, 1919.
Vol. 3, Pt. 1–142
Davis, Rebecca Blaine Harding, June 24, 1831–Sept. 29, 1910. Vol. 3, Pt. 1–143
Davis, Reuben, Jan. 18, 1813–Oct. 14, 1890.
Vol. 3, Pt. 1–144
Davis, Richard Harding, Apr. 18, 1864–Apr. 11, 1916.
Vol. 3, Pt. 1–144
Davis, Stuart, Dec. 7, 1894–June 24, 1964.
Supp. 7–170
Davis, Varina Anne Jefferson, June 27, 1864–Sept. 18, 1898.
Vol. 3, Pt. 1–145
Davis, Varina Howell, May 7, 1826–Oct. 16, 1906.
Vol. 3, Pt. 1–146
Davis, Watson, Apr. 29, 1896–June 27, 1967.
Supp. 8–119
Davis, William Augustine, Sept. 21, 1809–Jan. 15, 1875.
Vol. 3, Pt. 1–146
Davis, William Hammatt, Aug. 29, 1879–Aug. 13, 1964.
Supp. 7–171
Davis, William Morris, Feb. 12, 1850–Feb. 5, 1934.
Supp. 1–229
Davis, William Thomas, Mar. 3, 1822–Dec. 3, 1907.
Vol. 3, Pt. 1–147
Davis, Winnie. [See Davis, Varina Anne Jefferson, 1864–1898.]
Davison, George Willets, Mar. 25, 1872–June 16, 1953.
Supp. 5–157
Davison, Gregory Caldwell, Aug. 12, 1871–May 7, 1935.
Supp. 1–231
Davison, Henry Pomeroy, June 13, 1867–May 6, 1922.
Vol. 3, Pt. 1–148
Davisson, Clinton Joseph, Oct. 22, 1881–Feb. 1, 1958.
Supp. 6–150
Dawes, Charles Gates, Aug. 27, 1865–Apr. 23, 1951.
Supp. 5–159
Dawes, Henry Laurens, Oct. 30, 1816–Feb. 5, 1903.
Vol. 3, Pt. 1–149

Dawes, Rufus Cutler, July 30, 1867–Jan. 8, 1940.
    Supp. 2–146
Dawes, William, Apr. 6, 1745–Feb. 25, 1799.
    Vol. 3, Pt. 1–150
Dawkins, Henry, fl. 1753–1780.
    Vol. 3, Pt. 1–150
Dawley, Almena, 1890–Dec. 12, 1956.
    Supp. 6–152
Dawson, Francis Warrington, May 17, 1840–Mar. 12, 1889.
    Vol. 3, Pt. 1–151
Dawson, Henry Barton, June 8, 1821–May 23, 1889.
    Vol. 3, Pt. 1–152
Dawson, John, 1762–Mar. 30, 1814.
    Vol. 3, Pt. 1–152
Dawson, Thomas Cleland, July 30, 1865–May 1, 1912.
    Vol. 3, Pt. 1–153
Dawson, William Crosby, Jan. 4, 1798–May 5, 1856.
    Vol. 3, Pt. 1–154
Dawson, William Levi, Apr. 26, 1886–Nov. 9, 1970.
    Supp. 8–120
Day, Arthur Louis, Oct. 30, 1869–Mar. 2, 1960.
    Supp. 6–152
Day, Benjamin Henry, Apr. 10, 1810–Dec. 21, 1889.
    Vol. 3, Pt. 1–155
Day, Clarence Shepard, Nov. 18, 1874–Dec. 28, 1935.
    Supp. 1–232
Day, David Alexander, Feb. 17, 1851–Dec. 17, 1897.
    Vol. 3, Pt. 1–156
Day, David Talbot, Sept. 10, 1859–Apr. 15, 1925.
    Vol. 3, Pt. 1–156
Day, Edmund Ezra, Dec. 7, 1883–Mar. 23, 1951.
    Supp. 5–160
Day, Frank Miles, Apr. 5, 1861–June 15, 1918.
    Vol. 3, Pt. 1–157
Day, George Parmly, Sept. 4, 1876–Oct. 24, 1959.
    Supp. 6–154
Day, Henry Noble, Aug. 4, 1808–Jan. 12, 1890.
    Vol. 3, Pt. 1–158
Day, Holman Francis, Nov. 6, 1865–Feb. 19, 1935.
    Supp. 1–234
Day, Horace H., July 10, 1813–Aug. 23, 1878.
    Vol. 3, Pt. 1–159
Day, James Gamble, June 28, 1832–May 1, 1898.
    Vol. 3, Pt. 1–159
Day, James Roscoe, Oct. 17, 1845–Mar. 13, 1923.
    Vol. 3, Pt. 1–160
Day, Jeremiah, Aug. 3, 1773–Aug. 22, 1867.
    Vol. 3, Pt. 1–161
Day, Luther, July 9, 1813–Mar. 8, 1885.
    Vol. 3, Pt. 1–162
Day, Stephen, c. 1594–Dec. 22, 1668.
    Vol. 3, Pt. 1–163
Day, William Rufus, Apr. 17, 1849–July 9, 1923.
    Vol. 3, Pt. 1–163
Dayton, Elias, May 1, 1737–Oct. 22, 1807.
    Vol. 3, Pt. 1–165
Dayton, Jonathan, Oct. 16, 1760–Oct. 9, 1824.
    Vol. 3, Pt. 1–166
Dayton, William Lewis, Feb. 17, 1807–Dec. 1, 1864.
    Vol. 3, Pt. 1–166
Deady, Matthew Paul, May 12, 1824–Mar. 24, 1893.
    Vol. 3, Pt. 1–167
Dealey, George Bannerman, Sept. 18, 1859–Feb. 26, 1946.
    Supp. 4–221
Dean, Amos, Jan. 16, 1803–Jan. 26, 1868.
    Vol. 3, Pt. 1–168
Dean, Bashford, Oct. 28, 1867–Dec. 6, 1928.
    Vol. 3, Pt. 1–169
Dean, Gordon Evans, Dec. 28, 1905–Aug. 15, 1958.
    Supp. 6–155
Dean, James Byron, Feb. 8, 1931–Sept. 30, 1955.
    Supp. 5–162
Dean, Julia, July 22, 1830–Mar. 6, 1868.
    Vol. 3, Pt. 1–170
Dean, "Man Mountain." [See Leavitt, Frank Simmons.]
Dean, Sidney, Nov. 16, 1818–Oct. 29, 1901.
    Vol. 3, Pt. 1–171
Dean, William Henry, Jr., July 6, 1910–Jan. 9, 1952.
    Supp. 5–163
Deane, Charles, Nov. 10, 1813–Nov. 13, 1889.
    Vol. 3, Pt. 1–171
Deane, Samuel, July 10, 1733–Nov. 12, 1814.
    Vol. 3, Pt. 1–172

Deane, Silas, Dec. 24, 1737–Sept. 23, 1789.
    Vol. 3, Pt. 1–173
De Angelis, Thomas Jefferson, Nov. 30, 1859–Mar. 20, 1933.
    Supp. 1–234
Dearborn, Henry, Feb. 23, 1751–June 6, 1829.
    Vol. 3, Pt. 1–174
Dearborn, Henry Alexander Scammwell, Mar. 3, 1783–July 29, 1851. Vol. 3, Pt. 1–176
Dearing, John Lincoln, Dec. 10, 1858–Dec. 20, 1916.
    Vol. 3, Pt. 1–176
Dearth, Henry Golden, Apr. 22, 1864–Mar. 27, 1918.
    Vol. 3, Pt. 1–177
Deas, Zachariah Cantey, Oct. 25, 1819–Mar. 6, 1882.
    Vol. 3, Pt. 1–178
Deaver, John Blair, July 25, 1855–Sept. 25, 1931.
    Supp. 1–235
De Bardeleben, Henry Fairchild, July 22, 1840–Dec. 6, 1910.
    Vol. 3, Pt. 1–179
De Barenne, Joannes Gregorius Dusser. [See Dusser de Barenne, Joannes Gregorius, 1885–1940.]
De Berdt, Dennys, c. 1694–Apr. 11, 1770.
    Vol. 3, Pt. 1–180
De Bow, James Dunwoody Brownson, July 10, 1820–Feb. 27, 1867. Vol. 3, Pt. 1–130
De Brahm, William Gerard, 1717–c. 1799.
    Vol. 3, Pt. 1–182
Debs, Eugene Victor, Nov. 5, 1855–Oct. 20, 1926.
    Vol. 3, Pt. 1–183
Debye, Peter Joseph William, Mar. 24, 1884–Nov. 2, 1966.
    Supp. 8–121
De Camp, Joseph Rodefer, Nov. 5, 1858–Feb. 11, 1923.
    Vol. 3, Pt. 1–185
Decatur, Stephen, 1752–Nov. 14, 1808.
    Vol. 3, Pt. 1–186
Decatur, Stephen, Jan. 5, 1779–Mar. 22, 1820.
    Vol. 3, Pt. 1–187
De Coppet, Edward J., May 28, 1855–Apr. 30, 1916.
    Vol. 3, Pt. 1–190
De Costa, Benjamin Franklin, July 10, 1831–Nov. 4, 1904.
    Vol. 3, Pt. 1–190
De Cuevas, Marquis, May 26, 1885–Feb. 22, 1961.
    Supp. 7–173
Deemer, Horace Emerson, Sept. 24, 1858–Feb. 26, 1917.
    Vol. 3, Pt. 1–191
Deems, Charles Force, Dec. 4, 1820–Nov. 18, 1893.
    Vol. 3, Pt. 1–192
Deere, John, Feb. 7, 1804–May 17, 1886.
    Vol. 3, Pt. 1–193
"Deerfoot," 1828–Jan. 18, 1897.
    Vol. 3, Pt. 1–194
Deering, Nathaniel, June 25, 1791–Mar. 25, 1881.
    Vol. 3, Pt. 1–194
Deering, William, Apr. 25, 1826–Dec. 9, 1913.
    Vol. 3, Pt. 1–195
De Fontaine, Felix Gregory, 1834–Dec. 11, 1896.
    Vol. 3, Pt. 1–196
De Forest, Alfred Victor, Apr. 7, 1888–Apr. 5, 1945.
    Supp. 3–219
De Forest, David Curtis, Jan. 10, 1774–Feb. 22, 1825.
    Vol. 3, Pt. 1–196
De Forest, Erastus Lyman, June 27, 1834–June 6, 1888.
    Vol. 3, Pt. 1–197
De Forest, John Kinne Hyde, June 25, 1844–May 8, 1911.
    Vol. 3, Pt. 1–198
De Forest, John William, May 31, 1826–July 17, 1906.
    Vol. 3, Pt. 1–199
De Forest, Lee, Aug. 26, 1873–June 30, 1961.
    Supp. 7–174
De Forest, Robert Weeks, Apr. 25, 1848–May 6, 1931.
    Supp. 1–236
De Graffenried, Christopher. [See Graffenried, Christopher Baron de, 1661–1743.]
De Haas, Jacob. [See Haas, Jacob Judah Aaron de, 1872–1937.]
De Haas, John Philip, c. 1735–June 3, 1786.
    Vol. 3, Pt. 1–199
De Haven, Edwin Jesse, May 7, 1816–May 1, 1865.
    Vol. 3, Pt. 1–200
Deindörfer, Johannes, July 28, 1828–May 14, 1907.
    Vol. 3, Pt. 1–201
Deitzler, George Washington, Nov. 30, 1826–Apr. 10, 1884.
    Vol. 3, Pt. 1–201

De Rose, Peter, Mar. 10, 1900–Apr. 23, 1953.
    Supp. 5–167
De Rosset, Moses John, July 4, 1838–May 1, 1881.
    Vol. 3, Pt. 1–253
De Saussure, Henry William, Aug. 16, 1763–Mar. 29, 1839.
    Vol. 3, Pt. 1–253
De Schweinitz, Edmund Alexander. [See Schweinitz, Edmund Alexander de, 1825–1887.
De Schweinitz, George Edmund. [See Schweintz, George Edmund de, 1858–1938.]
Desha, Joseph, Dec. 9, 1768–Oct. 12, 1842.
    Vol. 3, Pt. 1–254
De Smet, Pierre-Jean, Jan. 30, 1801–May 23, 1873.
    Vol. 3, Pt. 1–255
De Soto, Hernando, c. 1500–May 21, 1542.
    Vol. 3, Pt. 1–256
De Sylva, George Gard "Buddy", Jan. 27, 1896–July 11, 1950. Supp. 4–225
Detmold, Christian Edward, Feb. 2, 1810–July 2, 1887.
    Vol. 3, Pt. 1–258
De Trobriand, Régis Denis De Keredern, June 4, 1816–July 15, 1897. Vol. 3, Pt. 1–258
Dett, Robert Nathaniel, Oct. 11, 1882–Oct. 2, 1943.
    Supp. 3–224
Deutsch, Gotthard, Jan. 31, 1859–Oct. 14, 1921.
    Vol. 3, Pt. 1–259
Devaney, John Patrick, June 30, 1883–Sept. 21, 1941.
    Supp. 3–226
De Vargas Zapata Y Lujan Ponce De Leon, Diego, c. 1650–Apr. 4, 1704. Vol. 3, Pt. 1–260
Devens, Charles, Apr. 4, 1820–Jan. 7, 1891.
    Vol. 3, Pt. 1–260
De Vere, Maximilian Schele. [See Schele, Maxmilian De Vere, 1820–1898.]
Devereux, John Henry, Apr. 5, 1832–Mar. 17, 1886.
    Vol. 3, Pt. 1–262
Devin, Thomas Casimer, Dec. 10, 1822–Apr. 4, 1878.
    Vol. 3, Pt. 1–263
Devine, Edward Thomas, May 6, 1867–Feb. 27, 1948.
    Supp. 4–226
De Vinne, Theodore Low, Dec. 25, 1828–Feb. 16, 1914.
    Vol. 3, Pt. 1–263
DeVoto, Bernard Augustine, Jan. 11, 1897–Nov. 13, 1955.
    Supp. 5–168
Devoy, John, Sept. 3, 1842–Sept. 29, 1928.
    Vol. 3, Pt. 1–264
De Vries, David Pietersen, fl. 1618–1655.
    Vol. 3, Pt. 1–265
Dew, Thomas Roderick, Dec. 5, 1802–Aug. 6, 1846.
    Vol. 3, Pt. 1–266
Dewees, William Potts, May 5, 1768–May 20, 1841.
    Vol. 3, Pt. 1–267
Dewey, Chester, Oct. 25, 1784–Dec. 15, 1867.
    Vol. 3, Pt. 1–267
Dewey, George, Dec. 26, 1837–Jan. 16, 1917.
    Vol. 3, Pt. 1–268
Dewey, John, Oct. 20, 1859–June 1, 1952.
    Supp. 5–169
Dewey, Melvil, Dec. 10, 1851–Dec. 26, 1931.
    Supp. 1–241
Dewey, Orville, Mar. 28, 1794–Mar. 21, 1882.
    Vol. 3, Pt. 1–272
Dewey, Richard Smith, Dec. 6, 1845–Aug. 4, 1933.
    Supp. 1–243
Dewing, Francis, fl. 1716–1722.
    Vol. 3, Pt. 1–272
Dewing, Maria Richards Oakey, Oct. 27, 1845–Dec. 13, 1927.
    Vol. 3, Pt. 1–273
Dewing, Thomas Wilmer, May 4, 1851–Nov. 5, 1938.
    Supp. 2–149
De Witt, Simeon, Dec. 25, 1756–Dec. 3, 1834.
    Vol. 3, Pt. 1–274
De Wolf, James, Mar. 18, 1764–Dec. 21, 1837.
    Vol. 3, Pt. 1–275
De Wolfe, Elsie, Dec. 20, 1865–July 12, 1950.
    Supp. 4–228
Dexter, Franklin, Nov. 5, 1793–Aug. 14, 1857.
    Vol. 3, Pt. 1–275
Dexter, Franklin Bowditch, Sept. 11, 1842–Aug. 13, 1920.
    Vol. 3, Pt. 1–276
Dexter, Henry, Oct. 11, 1806–June 23, 1876.
    Vol. 3, Pt. 1–277

Dexter, Henry, Mar. 14, 1813–July 11, 1910.
    Vol. 3, Pt. 1–278
Dexter, Henry Martyn, Aug. 13, 1821–Nov. 13, 1890.
    Vol. 3, Pt. 1–279
Dexter, Samuel, Mar. 16, 1726–June 10, 1810.
    Vol. 3, Pt. 1–280
Dexter, Samuel, May 14, 1761–May 4, 1816.
    Vol. 3, Pt. 1–280
Dexter, Timothy, Jan. 22, 1747–Oct. 23, 1806.
    Vol. 3, Pt. 1–281
Dexter, Wirt, Oct. 25, 1832–May 17, 1890.
    Vol. 3, Pt. 1–282
De Young, Michel Harry, Sept. 30, 1849–Feb. 15, 1925.
    Vol. 3, Pt. 1–283
D'Harnoncourt, René, May 17, 1901–Aug. 13, 1968.
    Supp. 8–125
Diat, Louis Felix, May 5, 1885–Aug. 29, 1957.
    Supp. 6–164
Diaz, Abby Morton, 1821–Apr. 1, 1904.
    Vol. 3, Pt. 1–284
Dibble, Roy Floyd, Mar. 12, 1887–Dec. 3, 1929.
    Vol. 3, Pt. 1–285
Dibrell, George Gibbs, Apr. 12, 1822–May 6, 1888.
    Vol. 3, Pt. 1–286
Dick, Elisha Cullen, Mar. 15, 1762–Sept. 22, 1825.
    Vol. 3, Pt. 1–286
Dick, Robert Paine, Oct. 5, 1823–Sept. 12, 1898.
    Vol. 3, Pt. 1–287
Dickerson, Edward Nicoll, Feb. 11, 1824–Dec. 12, 1889.
    Vol. 3, Pt. 1–288
Dickerson, Mahlon, Apr. 17, 1770–Oct. 5, 1853.
    Vol. 3, Pt. 1–289
Dickerson, Philemon, June 26, 1788–Dec. 10, 1862.
    Vol. 3, Pt. 1–290
Dickey, Theophilus Lyle, Oct. 2, 1811–July 22, 1885.
    Vol. 3, Pt. 1–290
Dickie, George William, July 17, 1844–Aug. 17, 1918.
    Vol. 3, Pt. 1–291
Dickins, John, c. Aug. 24, 1747–Sept. 27, 1798.
    Vol. 3, Pt. 1–292
Dickinson, Anna Elizabeth, Oct. 28, 1842–Oct. 22, 1932.
    Supp. 1–244
Dickinson, Anson, Apr. 19, 1779–Mar. 9, 1852.
    Vol. 3, Pt. 1–293
Dickinson, Charles Monroe, Nov. 15, 1842–July 3, 1924.
    Vol. 3, Pt. 1–294
Dickinson, Daniel Stevens, Sept. 11, 1800–Apr. 12, 1866.
    Vol. 3, Pt. 1–294
Dickinson, Donald McDonald, Jan. 17, 1846–Oct. 15, 1917.
    Vol. 3, Pt. 1–295
Dickinson, Edwin De Witt, May 19, 1887–Mar. 26, 1961.
    Supp. 7–181
Dickinson, Emily Elizabeth, Dec. 10, 1830–May 15, 1886.
    Vol. 3, Pt. 1–297
Dickinson, Jacob McGavock, Jan. 30, 1851–Dec. 13, 1928.
    Vol. 3, Pt. 1–298
Dickinson, John, Nov. 8, 1732–Feb. 14, 1808.
    Vol. 3, Pt. 1–299
Dickinson, John, Feb. 24, 1894–Apr. 9, 1952.
    Supp. 5–173
Dickinson, John Woodbridge, Oct. 12, 1825–Feb. 16, 1901.
    Vol. 3, Pt. 1–301
Dickinson, Jonathan, Apr. 22, 1688–Oct. 7, 1747.
    Vol. 3, Pt. 1–301
Dickinson, Philemon, Apr. 5, 1739–Feb. 4, 1809.
    Vol. 3, Pt. 1–302
Dickinson, Preston, Sept. 9, 1889–Nov. 30, 1930.
    Supp. 1–245
Dickinson, Robert Latou, Feb. 21, 1861–Nov. 29, 1950.
    Supp. 4–230
Dickman, Joseph Theodore, Oct. 6, 1857–Oct. 23, 1927.
    Vol. 3, Pt. 1–303
Dickson, David, July 6, 1809–Feb. 18, 1885.
    Vol. 3, Pt. 1–304
Dickson, Earle Ensign, Oct. 10, 1892–Sept. 21, 1961.
    Supp. 7–182
Dickson, Leonard Eugene, Jan. 22, 1874–Jan. 17, 1954.
    Supp. 5–174
Dickson, Robert, c. 1765–June 20, 1823.
    Vol. 3, Pt. 1–305
Dickson, Samuel Henry, Sept. 20, 1798–Mar. 31, 1872.
    Vol. 3, Pt. 1–305

Dickson, Thomas, Mar. 26, 1824–July 31, 1884.
    Vol. 3, Pt. 1–306
Didier, Eugene Lemoine, Dec. 22, 1838–Sept. 8, 1913.
    Vol. 3, Pt. 1–307
Dielman, Frederick, Dec. 25, 1847–Aug. 25, 1935.
    Supp. 1–246
Dietrichson, Johannes Wilhelm Christian, Apr. 4, or Aug. 23,
    1815–Nov. 14, 1883. Vol. 3, Pt. 1–307
Dietz, Peter Ernest, July 10, 1878–Oct. 11, 1947.
    Supp. 4–232
Digges, Dudley, June 9, 1880–Oct. 24, 1947.
    Supp. 4–233
Dike, Samuel Warren, Feb. 13, 1839–Dec. 3, 1913.
    Vol. 3, Pt. 1–308
Dill, James Brooks, July 25, 1854–Dec. 2, 1910.
    Vol. 3, Pt. 1–329
Dillard, James Hardy, Oct. 24, 1856–Aug. 2, 1940.
    Supp. 2–150
Dille, John Flint, Apr. 27, 1884–Sept. 10, 1957.
    Supp. 6–165
Diller, Burgoyne, Jan. 13, 1906–Jan. 30, 1965.
    Supp. 7–183
Diller, Joseph Silas, Aug. 27, 1850–Nov. 13, 1928.
    Supp. 1–247
Dillinger, John, June 28, 1902–July 22, 1934.
    Supp. 1–248
Dillingham, Charles Bancroft, May 30, 1868–Aug. 30, 1934.
    Supp. 1–249
Dillingham, Walter Francis, Apr. 5, 1875–Oct. 22, 1963.
    Supp. 7–184
Dillingham, William Paul, Dec. 12, 1843–July 12, 1923.
    Vol. 3, Pt. 1–310
Dillon, John Forrest, Dec. 25, 1831–May 6, 1914.
    Vol. 3, Pt. 1–311
Dillon, Sidney, May 7, 1812–June 9, 1892.
    Vol. 3, Pt. 1–312
Diman, Jeremiah Lewis, May 1, 1831–Feb. 3, 1881.
    Vol. 3, Pt. 1–312
Dimitry, Alexander, Feb. 7, 1805–Jan. 30, 1883.
    Vol. 3, Pt. 1–313
Dimitry, Charles Patton, July 31, 1837–Nov. 10, 1910.
    Vol. 3, Pt. 1–314
Dingley, Nelson, Feb. 15, 1832–Jan. 13, 1899.
    Vol. 3, Pt. 1–314
Dingman, Mary Agnes, Apr. 9, 1864–Mar. 21, 1961.
    Supp. 7–185
Dinsmoor, Robert, Oct. 7, 1757–Mar. 16, 1836.
    Vol. 3, Pt. 1–315
Dinwiddie, Albert Bledsoe, Apr. 3, 1871–Nov. 21, 1935.
    Supp. 1–250
Dinwiddie, Courtenay, Oct. 9, 1882–Sept. 13, 1943.
    Supp. 3–227
Dinwiddie, Edwin Courtland, Sept. 29, 1867–May 5, 1935.
    Supp. 1–251
Dinwiddie, Robert, 1693–July 27, 1770.
    Vol. 3, Pt. 1–316
Dirksen, Everett McKinley, Jan. 4, 1896–Sept. 7, 1969.
    Supp. 8–127
Disbrow, William Stephen, Mar. 18, 1861–Dec. 26, 1922.
    Vol. 3, Pt. 1–317
Disney, Walter Elias ("Walt"), Dec. 5, 1901–Dec. 15, 1966.
    Supp. 8–129
Disston, Henry, May 23, 1819–Mar. 16, 1878.
    Vol. 3, Pt. 1–318
Disturnell, John, Oct. 6, 1801–Oct. 1, 1877.
    Vol. 3, Pt. 1–319
Ditmars, Raymond Lee, June 20, 1876–May 12, 1942.
    Supp. 3–228
Ditrichstein, Leo, Jan. 6, 1865–June 28, 1928.
    Vol. 3, Pt. 1–319
Ditson, George Leighton, Aug. 5, 1812–Jan. 29, 1895.
    Vol. 3, Pt. 1–320
Ditson, Oliver, Oct. 20, 1811–Dec. 21, 1888.
    Vol. 3, Pt. 1–321
Dittemore, John Valentine, Sept. 20, 1876–May 10, 1937.
    Supp. 2–151
Diven, Alexander Samuel, Feb. 10, 1809–June 11, 1896.
    Vol. 3, Pt. 1–322
Divine, Father, (c. 1878/1880–Sept. 10, 1965.
    Supp. 7–186
Dix, Dorothea Lynde, Apr. 4, 1802–July 17, 1887.
    Vol. 3, Pt. 1–323

Dix, Dorothy. [See Gilmer, Elizabeth Meriwether.]
Dix, John Adams, July 24, 1798–Apr. 21, 1879.
    Vol. 3, Pt. 1–325
Dix, John Homer, Sept. 30, 1811–Aug. 25, 1884.
    Vol. 3, Pt. 1–327
Dix, Morgan, Nov. 1, 1827–Apr. 29, 1908.
    Vol. 3, Pt. 1–327
Dixon, James, Aug. 5, 1814–Mar. 27, 1873.
    Vol. 3, Pt. 1–328
Dixon, Joseph, Jan. 18, 1799–June 15, 1869.
    Vol. 3, Pt. 1–329
Dixon, Luther Swift, June 17, 1825–Dec. 6, 1891.
    Vol. 3, Pt. 1–330
Dixon, Roland Burrage, Nov. 6, 1875–Dec. 19, 1934.
    Supp. 1–252
Dixon, Thomas, Jan. 11, 1864–Apr. 3, 1946.
    Supp. 4–234
Dixon, William, Sept. 25, 1850–Mar. 9, 1913.
    Vol. 3, Pt. 1–331
Dixwell, John, c. 1607–Mar. 18, 1688/9.
    Vol. 3, Pt. 1–331
Doak, Samuel, August 1749–Dec. 12, 1830.
    Vol. 3, Pt. 1–332
Doane, George Washington, May 27, 1799–Apr. 27, 1859.
    Vol. 3, Pt. 1–333
Doane, Thomas, Sept. 20, 1821–Oct. 22, 1897.
    Vol. 3, Pt. 1–334
Doane, William Croswell, Mar. 2, 1832–May 17, 1913.
    Vol. 3, Pt. 1–334
Dobbin, James Cochran, Jan. 17, 1814–Aug. 4, 1857.
    Vol. 3, Pt. 1–335
Dobbs, Arthur, Apr. 2, 1689–Mar. 28, 1765.
    Vol. 3, Pt. 1–336
Dobie, Gilmour, Jan. 31, 1878–Dec. 23, 1948.
    Supp. 4–236
Dobie, J(ames) Frank, Sept. 26, 1888–Sept. 18, 1964.
    Supp. 7–188
Dock, Christopher, c. 1698–1771.
    Vol. 3, Pt. 1–337
Dock, Lavinia Lloyd, Feb. 26, 1858–Apr. 17, 1956.
    Supp. 6–166
Dockstader, Lew, Aug. 7, 1856–Oct. 26, 1924.
    Vol. 3, Pt. 1–338
Dod, Albert Baldwin, Mar. 24, 1805–Nov. 19, 1845.
    Vol. 3, Pt. 1–338
Dod, Daniel, Sept. 8, 1778–May 9, 1823.
    Vol. 3, Pt. 1–339
Dod, Thaddeus, Mar. 7, 1740 o.s.–May 20, 1793.
    Vol. 3, Pt. 1–340
Dodd, Bella Visono, Oct. 1904–Apr. 29, 1969.
    Supp. 8–132
Dodd, Frank Howard, Apr. 12, 1844–Jan. 10, 1916.
    Vol. 3, Pt. 1–340
Dodd, Lee Wilson, July 11, 1879–May 16, 1933.
    Supp. 1–253
Dodd, Monroe Elmon, Sept. 8, 1878–Aug. 6, 1952.
    Supp. 5–175
Dodd, Samuel Calvin Tate, Feb. 20, 1836–Jan. 30, 1907.
    Vol. 3, Pt. 1–341
Dodd, William Edward, Oct. 21, 1869–Feb. 9, 1940.
    Supp. 2–152
Doddridge, Joseph, Oct. 14, 1769–Nov. 9, 1826.
    Vol. 3, Pt. 1–342
Doddridge, Philip, May 17, 1773–Nov. 19, 1832.
    Vol. 3, Pt. 1–343
Dodge, Augustus Caesar, Jan. 2, 1812–Nov. 20, 1883.
    Vol. 3, Pt. 1–344
Dodge, David Low, June 14, 1774–Apr. 23, 1852.
    Vol. 3, Pt. 1–344
Dodge, Ebenezer, Apr. 21, 1819–Jan. 5, 1890.
    Vol. 3, Pt. 1–345
Dodge, Grace Hoadley, May 21, 1856–Dec. 27, 1914.
    Vol. 3, Pt. 1–346
Dodge, Grenville Mellen, Apr. 12, 1831–Jan. 3, 1916.
    Vol. 3, Pt. 1–347
Dodge, Henry, Oct. 12, 1782–June 19, 1867.
    Vol. 3, Pt. 1–348
Dodge, Henry Chee, 1860–Jan. 7, 1947.
    Supp. 4–237
Dodge, Jacob Richards, Sept. 28, 1823–Oct. 1, 1902.
    Vol. 3, Pt. 1–310
Dodge, Joseph Morrell, Nov. 18, 1890–Dec. 2, 1964.
    Supp. 7–189

Dodge, Mary Abigail, Mar. 31, 1833–Aug. 17, 1896.
Vol. 3, Pt. 1–350
Dodge, Mary Elizabeth Mapes, Jan. 26, 1831–Aug. 21, 1905.
Vol. 3, Pt. 1–351
Dodge, Raymond, Feb. 20, 1871–Apr. 8, 1942.
Supp. 3–229
Dodge, Theodore Ayrault, May 28, 1842–Oct. 25, 1909.
Vol. 3, Pt. 1–351
Dodge, William De Leftwich, Mar. 9, 1867–Mar. 25, 1935.
Supp. 1–254
Dodge, William Earl, Sept. 4, 1805–Feb. 9, 1883.
Vol. 3, Pt. 1–352
Dods, John Bovee, 1795–Mar. 21, 1872.
Vol. 3, Pt. 1–353
Doe, Charles, Apr. 11, 1830–Mar. 9, 1896.
Vol. 3, Pt. 1–354
Doheny, Edward Laurence, Aug. 10, 1856–Sept. 8, 1935.
Supp. 1–254
Doherty, Henry Latham, May 15, 1870–Dec. 26, 1939.
Supp. 2–154
Dolan, Thomas, Oct. 27, 1834–June 12, 1914.
Vol. 3, Pt. 1–355
Dold, Jacob, June 25, 1825–Oct. 25, 1909.
Vol. 3, Pt. 1–356
Dole, Charles Fletcher, May 17, 1845–Nov. 27, 1927.
Vol. 3, Pt. 1–357
Dole, James Drummond, Sept. 27, 1877–May 14, 1958.
Supp. 6–168
Dole, Nathan Haskell, Aug. 31, 1852–May 9, 1935.
Supp. 1–255
Dole, Sanford Ballard, Apr. 23, 1844–June 9, 1926.
Vol. 3, Pt. 1–358
D'Olier, Franklin, Apr. 28, 1877–Dec. 10, 1953.
Supp. 5–177
Dollar, Robert, Mar. 20, 1844–May 16, 1932.
Supp. 1–256
Dolliver, Jonathan Prentiss, Feb. 6, 1858–Oct. 15, 1910.
Vol. 3, Pt. 1–359
Dolph, Joseph Norton, Oct. 19, 1835–Mar. 10, 1897.
Vol. 3, Pt. 1–360
Dombrowski, Joseph. [See Dabrowski, Joseph, 1842–1903.]
Dominguez, Francisco Atanasio. [See Escalante, Silvestre Velez de, c. 1776.]
Donahoe, Patrick, Mar. 17, 1811–Mar. 18, 1901.
Vol. 3, Pt. 1–361
Donahue, Peter, Jan. 11, 1822–Nov. 26, 1885.
Vol. 3, Pt. 1–362
Donaldson, Henry Herbert, May 12, 1857–Jan. 23, 1938.
Supp. 2–156
Donaldson, Jesse Monroe, Aug. 17, 1885–Mar. 25, 1970.
Supp. 8–133
Donck, Adriaen Van Der. [See Van der Donck, Adrian, 1620–1655.]
Donelson, Andrew Jackson, Aug. 25, 1799–June 26, 1871.
Vol. 3, Pt. 1–363
Dongan, Thomas, 1634–Dec. 14, 1715.
Vol. 3, Pt. 1–364
Doniphan, Alexander William, July 9, 1808–Aug. 8, 1887.
Vol. 3, Pt. 1–365
Donlevy, Harriet Farley. [See Farley, Harriet, 1817–1907.]
Donn-Byrne, Brian Oswald, Nov. 20, 1889–June 18, 1928.
Vol. 3, Pt. 1–366
Donnell, James C., Apr. 20, 1854–Jan. 10, 1927.
Vol. 3, Pt. 1–366
Donnell, Robert, April 1784–May 24, 1855.
Vol. 3, Pt. 1–367
Donnelly, Charles Francis, Oct. 14, 1836–Jan. 31, 1909.
Vol. 3, Pt. 1–368
Donnelly, Eleanor Cecilia, Sept. 6, 1838–Apr. 30, 1917.
Vol. 3, Pt. 1–369
Donnelly, Ignatius, Nov. 3, 1831–Jan. 1, 1901.
Vol. 3, Pt. 1–369
Donoghue, John, 1853–July 1, 1903.
Vol. 3, Pt. 1–371
Donovan, James Britt, Feb. 29, 1916–Jan. 19, 1970.
Supp. 8–134
Donovan, John Joseph, Sept. 8, 1858–Jan. 9, 1937.
Supp. 2–157
Donovan, William Joseph, Jan. 1, 1883–Feb. 8, 1959.
Supp. 6–169
D'Ooge, Martin Luther, July 17, 1839–Sept. 12, 1915.
Vol. 3, Pt. 1–372

Dooley, Thomas Anthony, III, Jan. 17, 1927–Jan. 18, 1961.
Supp. 7–190
Doolittle, Amos, May 18, 1754–Jan. 30, 1832.
Vol. 3, Pt. 1–372
Doolittle, Charles Leander, Nov. 12, 1843–Mar. 3, 1919.
Vol. 3, Pt. 1–373
Doolittle, Eric, July 26, 1869–Sept. 21, 1920.
Vol. 3, Pt. 1–374
Doolittle, James Rood, Jan. 3, 1815–July 27, 1897.
Vol. 3, Pt. 1–374
Doran, George Henry, Dec. 19, 1869–Jan. 7, 1956.
Supp. 6–171
Dorchester, Daniel, Mar. 11, 1827–Mar. 13, 1907.
Vol. 3, Pt. 1–375
Doremus, Robert Ogden, Jan. 11, 1824–Mar. 22, 1906.
Vol. 3, Pt. 1–376
Doremus, Sarah Platt Haines, Aug. 3, 1802–Jan. 29, 1877.
Vol. 3, Pt. 1–377
Dorgan, Thomas Aloysius, Apr. 29, 1877–May 2, 1929.
Vol. 3, Pt. 1–378
Dorion, Marie, c. 1791–Sept. 3, 1850.
Vol. 3, Pt. 1–379
Dorn, Harold Fred, July 30, 1906–May 9, 1963.
Supp. 7–191
Dornin, Thomas Aloysius, May 1, 1800–Apr. 22, 1874.
Vol. 3, Pt. 1–380
Dorr, Julia Caroline Ripley, Feb. 13, 1825–Jan. 18, 1913.
Vol. 3, Pt. 1–381
Dorr, Thomas Wilson, Nov. 5, 1805–Dec. 27, 1854.
Vol. 3, Pt. 1–381
Dorrell, William, Mar. 15, 1752–Aug. 28, 1846.
Vol. 3, Pt. 1–382
Dorsch, Eduard, Jan. 10, 1822–Jan. 10, 1887.
Vol. 3, Pt. 1–383
Dorset, Marion, Dec. 14, 1872–July 14, 1935.
Supp. 1–258
Dorsey, Anna Hanson McKenney, Dec. 12, 1815–Dec. 25, 1896. Vol. 3, Pt. 1–384
Dorsey, George Amos, Feb. 6, 1868–Mar. 29, 1931.
Supp. 1–258
Dorsey, James Owen, Oct. 31, 1848–Feb. 4, 1895.
Vol. 3, Pt. 1–384
Dorsey, John Syng, Dec. 23, 1783–Nov. 12, 1818.
Vol. 3, Pt. 1–385
Dorsey, Sarah Anne Ellis, Feb. 16, 1829–July 4, 1879.
Vol. 3, Pt. 1–386
Dorsey, Stephen Wallace, Feb. 28, 1842–Mar. 20, 1916.
Vol. 3, Pt. 1–387
Dorsey, Thomas Francis ("Tommy"), Nov. 19, 1905–Nov. 26, 1956. Supp. 6–172
Dorsheimer, William Edward, Feb. 5, 1832–Mar. 26, 1888.
Vol. 3, Pt. 1–387
Dos Passos, John Randolph, July 31, 1844–Jan. 27, 1917.
Vol. 3, Pt. 1–388
Dos Passos, John Roderigo, Jan. 14, 1896–Sept. 28, 1970.
Supp. 8–135
Doty, Elihu, Sept. 20, 1809–Nov. 30, 1864.
Vol. 3, Pt. 1–389
Doty, James Duane, Nov. 5, 1799–June 13, 1865.
Vol. 3, Pt. 1–390
Doubleday, Abner, June 26, 1819–Jan. 26, 1893.
Vol. 3, Pt. 1–391
Doubleday, Frank Nelson, Jan. 8, 1862–Jan. 30, 1934.
Supp. 1–259
Doubleday, Nelson, June 16, 1889–Jan. 11, 1949.
Supp. 4–239
Doubleday, Neltje de Graff, Oct. 23, 1865–Feb. 21, 1918.
Vol. 3, Pt. 1–392
Dougherty, Dennis Joseph, Aug. 16, 1865–May 31, 1951.
Supp. 5–178
Dougherty, Raymond Philip, Aug. 5, 1877–July 13, 1933.
Supp. 1–260
Doughton, Robert Lee, Nov. 7, 1863–Oct. 2, 1954.
Supp. 5–180
Doughty, Thomas, July 19, 1793–July 22, 1856.
Vol. 3, Pt. 1–392
Doughty, William Henry, Feb. 5, 1836–Mar. 27, 1905.
Vol. 3, Pt. 1–393
Douglas, Amanda Minnie, July 14, 1831–July 18, 1916.
Vol. 3, Pt. 1–394
Douglas, Benjamin, Apr. 3, 1816–June 26, 1894.
Vol. 3, Pt. 1–394

Douglas, Henry Kyd, Sept. 29, 1838–Dec. 18, 1903.
  Vol. 3, Pt. 1–395
Douglas, James, Nov. 4, 1837–June 25 1918.
  Vol. 3, Pt. 1–396
Douglas, Lloyd Cassel, Aug. 27, 1877–Feb. 13, 1951.
  Supp. 5–181
Douglas, Stephen Arnold, Apr. 23, 1813–June 3, 1861.
  Vol. 3, Pt. 1–397
Douglas, William, Jan. 27, 1742/3–May 28, 1777.
  Vol. 3, Pt. 1–403
Douglas, William Lewis, Aug. 22, 1845–Sept. 17, 1924.
  Vol. 3, Pt. 1–404
Douglass, Andrew Ellicott, July 5, 1867–Mar. 20, 1962.
  Supp. 7–193
Douglass, David Bates, Mar. 21, 1790–Oct. 21, 1849.
  Vol. 3, Pt. 1–405
Douglass, Frederick, February 1817?–Feb. 20, 1895.
  Vol. 3, Pt. 1–406
Douglass, William, c. 1691–Oct. 21, 1752.
  Vol. 3, Pt. 1–407
Doull, James Angus, Sept. 8, 1889–Apr. 6, 1963.
  Supp. 7–194
Dove, Arthur Garfield, Aug. 2, 1880–Nov. 23, 1946.
  Supp. 4–240
Dove, David James, c. 1696–April 1769.
  Vol. 3, Pt. 1–408
Dow, Alex, Apr. 12, 1862–Mar. 22, 1942.
  Supp. 3–230
Dow, Henry, 1634–May 6, 1707.
  Vol. 3, Pt. 1–409
Dow, Herbert Henry, Feb. 26, 1866–Oct. 15, 1930.
  Supp. 1–261
Dow, Lorenzo, Oct. 16, 1777–Feb. 2, 1834.
  Vol. 3, Pt. 1–410
Dow, Lorenzo, July 10, 1825–Oct. 12, 1899.
  Vol. 3, Pt. 1–410
Dow, Neal, Mar. 20, 1804–Oct. 2, 1897.
  Vol. 3, Pt. 1–411
Dowell, Greensville, Sept. 1, 1822–June 9, 1881.
  Vol. 3, Pt. 1–412
Dowie, John Alexander, May 25, 1847–Mar. 9, 1907.
  Vol. 3, Pt. 1–413
Dowling, Austin, Apr. 6, 1868–Nov. 29, 1930.
  Supp. 1–262
Dowling, Noel Thomas, Aug. 14, 1885–Feb. 11, 1969.
  Supp. 8–138
Downer, Eliphalet, Apr. 4, 1744–Apr. 3, 1806.
  Vol. 3, Pt. 1–414
Downer, Samuel, Mar. 8, 1807–Sept. 20, 1881.
  Vol. 3, Pt. 1–415
Downes, John, Dec. 23, 1784–Aug. 11, 1854.
  Vol. 3, Pt. 1–415
Downes (Edwin) Olin, Jan. 27, 1886–Aug. 22, 1955.
  Supp. 5–183
Downey, John, c. 1765–July 21, 1826.
  Vol. 3, Pt. 1–416
Downey, June Etta, July 13, 1875–Oct. 11, 1932.
  Supp. 1–263
Downey, Sheridan, Mar. 9, 1884–Oct. 25, 1961.
  Supp. 7–195
Downing, Andrew Jackson, Oct. 30, 1815–July 28, 1852.
  Vol. 3, Pt. 1–417
Downing, Charles, July 9, 1802–Jan. 18, 1885.
  Vol. 3, Pt. 1–418
Downing, George, August 1623–July 1684.
  Vol. 3, Pt. 1–419
Dowse, Thomas, Dec. 28, 1772–Nov. 4, 1856.
  Vol. 3, Pt. 1–419
Doyle, Alexander, Jan. 28, 1857–Dec. 21, 1922.
  Vol. 3, Pt. 1–420
Doyle, Alexander Patrick, Feb. 28, 1857–Aug. 9, 1912.
  Vol. 3, Pt. 1–421
Doyle, John Thomas, Nov. 26, 1819–Dec. 23, 1906.
  Vol. 3, Pt. 1–421
Doyle, Sarah Elizabeth, Mar. 23, 1830–Dec. 21, 1922.
  Vol. 3, Pt. 1–423
Drake, Alexander Wilson, 1843–Feb. 4, 1916.
  Vol. 3, Pt. 1–423
Drake, Benjamin, 1795–Apr. 1, 1841.
  Vol. 3, Pt. 1–424
Drake, Charles Daniel, Apr. 11, 1811–Apr. 1, 1892.
  Vol. 3, Pt. 1–425

Drake, Daniel, Oct. 20, 1785–Nov. 6, 1852.
  Vol. 3, Pt. 1–426
Drake, Edwin Laurentine, Mar. 29, 1819–Nov. 8, 1880.
  Vol. 3, Pt. 1–427
Drake, Frances Ann Denny, Nov. 6, 1797–Sept. 1, 1875.
  Vol. 3, Pt. 1–428
Drake, Francis Marion, Dec. 30, 1830–Nov. 20, 1903.
  Vol. 3, Pt. 1–429
Drake, Francis Samuel, Feb. 22, 1828–Feb. 22, 1885.
  Vol. 3, Pt. 1–430
Drake, John Burroughs, Jan. 17, 1826–Nov. 12, 1895.
  Vol. 3, Pt. 1–430
Drake, Joseph Rodman, Aug. 7, 1795–Sept. 21, 1820.
  Vol. 3, Pt. 1–431
Drake, Samuel, Nov. 15, 1768–Oct. 16, 1854.
  Vol. 3, Pt. 1–432
Drake, Samuel Adams, Dec. 19, 1833–Dec. 4, 1905.
  Vol. 3, Pt. 1–432
Drake, Samuel Gardner, Oct. 11, 1798–June 14, 1875.
  Vol. 3, Pt. 1–433
Draper, Andrew Sloan, June 21, 1848–Apr. 27, 1913.
  Vol. 3, Pt. 1–434
Draper, Dorothy, Nov. 22, 1889–Mar. 10, 1969.
  Supp. 8–140
Draper, Eben Sumner, June 17, 1858–Apr. 9, 1914.
  Vol. 3, Pt. 1–435
Draper, Henry, Mar. 7, 1837–Nov. 20, 1882.
  Vol. 3, Pt. 1–435
Draper, Ira, Dec. 24, 1764–Jan. 22, 1848.
  Vol. 3, Pt. 1–437
Draper, John, Oct. 29, 1702–Nov. 29, 1762.
  Vol. 3, Pt. 1–437
Draper, John William, May 5, 1811–Jan. 4, 1882.
  Vol. 3, Pt. 1–438
Draper, Lyman Copeland, Sept. 4, 1815–Aug. 26, 1891.
  Vol. 3, Pt. 1–441
Draper, Margaret Green, fl. 1750–1807.
  Vol. 3, Pt. 1–442
Draper, Richard, Feb. 24, 1726/7–June 5, 1774.
  Vol. 3, Pt. 1–443
Draper, Ruth, Dec. 2, 1884–Dec. 30, 1956.
  Supp. 6–173
Draper, William Franklin, Apr. 9, 1842–Jan. 28, 1910.
  Vol. 3, Pt. 1–443
Drayton, John, June 22, 1766–Nov. 27, 1822.
  Vol. 3, Pt. 1–444
Drayton, Percival, Aug. 25, 1812–Aug. 4, 1865.
  Vol. 3, Pt. 1–445
Drayton, Thomas Fenwick, Aug. 24, 1808–Feb. 18, 1891.
  Vol. 3, Pt. 1–446
Drayton, William, Mar. 21, 1732–May 18, 1790.
  Vol. 3, Pt. 1–447
Drayton, William, Dec. 30, 1776–May 24, 1846.
  Vol. 3, Pt. 1–448
Drayton, William Henry, September 1742–Sept. 3, 1779.
  Vol. 3, Pt. 1–448
Dreier, Katherine Sophie, 1877–Mar. 29, 1952.
  Supp. 5–184
Dreier, Margaret. [See Robins, Margaret Dreier.]
Dreier, Mary Elisabeth, Sept. 26, 1875–Aug. 15, 1963.
  Supp. 7–196
Dreiser, Theodore, Aug. 27, 1871–Dec. 28, 1945.
  Supp. 3–232
Dresel, Otto, c. 1826–July 26, 1890.
  Vol. 3, Pt. 1–449
Dressen, Charles Walter, Sept. 20, 1898–Aug. 10, 1966.
  Supp. 8–141
Dresser, Louise Kerlin, Oct. 5, 1882–Apr. 24, 1965.
  Supp. 7–197
Dressler, Marie, Nov. 9, 1871–July 28, 1934.
  Supp. 1–264
Drew, Charles Richard, June 3, 1904–Apr. 1, 1950.
  Supp. 4–242
Drew, Daniel, July 29, 1797–Sept. 18, 1879.
  Vol. 3, Pt. 1–450
Drew, Georgiana Emma. [See Barrymore, Georgiana Emma Drew, 1856–1893.]
Drew, John, Nov. 13, 1853–July 9, 1927.
  Vol. 3, Pt. 1–452
Drew, John, Sept. 3, 1827–May 21, 1862.
  Vol. 3, Pt. 1–451
Drew, Louisa Lane, Jan. 10, 1820–Aug. 31, 1897.
  Vol. 3, Pt. 1–454

Drexel, Anthony Joseph, Sept. 13, 1826–June 30, 1893.
    Vol. 3, Pt. 1–455
Drexel, Francis Martin, Apr. 7, 1792–June 5, 1863.
    Vol. 3, Pt. 1–456
Drexel, Joseph William, Jan. 24, 1833–Mar. 25, 1888.
    Vol. 3, Pt. 1–457
Drexel, Katharine Mary, Nov. 26, 1858–Mar. 3, 1955.
    Supp. 5–185
Dreyfus, Max, Apr. 1, 1874–May 12, 1964.
    Supp. 7–198
Drinker, Catharine Ann. [See Janvier, Catharine Ann, 1841–1922.]
Drinker, Cecil Kent, Mar. 17, 1887–Apr. 14, 1956.
    Supp. 6–174
Drinkwater, Jennie Maria, Apr. 12, 1841–Apr. 28, 1900.
    Vol. 3, Pt. 1–457
Dripps, Isaac L., April 14, 1810–Dec. 28, 1892.
    Vol. 3, Pt. 1–458
Drisler, Henry, Dec. 27, 1818–Nov. 30, 1897.
    Vol. 3, Pt. 1–458
Dromgoole, William Allen, Oct. 25, 1860–Sept. 1, 1934.
    Supp. 1–265
Dropsie, Moses Aaron, Mar. 9, 1821–July 8, 1905.
    Vol. 3, Pt. 1–459
Drown, Thomas Messinger, Mar. 19, 1842–Nov. 16, 1904.
    Vol. 3, Pt. 1–460
Druillettes, Gabriel, Sept. 29, 1610–Apr. 8, 1681.
    Vol. 3, Pt. 1–462
Drum, Hugh Aloysius, Sept. 19, 1879–Oct. 3, 1951.
    Supp. 5–186
Drumgoole, John Christopher, Aug. 15, 1816–Mar. 28, 1888.
    Vol. 3, Pt. 1–462
Drury, John Benjamin, Aug. 15, 1838–Mar. 21, 1909.
    Vol. 3, Pt. 1–463
Dryden, John Fairfield, Aug. 7, 1839–Nov. 24, 1911.
    Vol. 3, Pt. 1–463
Dryfoos, Orvil E., Nov. 8, 1912–May 25, 1963.
    Supp. 7–199
Duane, Alexander, Sept. 1, 1858–June 10, 1926.
    Vol. 3, Pt. 1–464
Duane, James, Feb. 6, 1733–Feb. 1, 1797.
    Vol. 3, Pt. 1–465
Duane, James Chatham, June 30, 1824–Nov. 8, 1897.
    Vol. 3, Pt. 1–466
Duane, William, May 17, 1760–Nov. 24, 1835.
    Vol. 3, Pt. 1–467
Duane, William, Feb. 17, 1872–Mar. 7, 1935.
    Supp. 1–266
Duane, William John, May 9, 1780–Sept. 26, 1865.
    Vol. 3, Pt. 1–468
Dubbs, Joseph Henry, Oct. 5, 1838–Apr. 1, 1910.
    Vol. 3, Pt. 1–469
Dubois, Augustus Jay, Apr. 25, 1849–Oct. 19, 1915.
    Vol. 3, Pt. 1–470
Dubois, John, Aug. 24, 1764–Dec. 20, 1842.
    Vol. 3, Pt. 1–470
Du Bois, William Edward Burghardt, Feb. 23, 1868–Aug. 27, 1963. Supp. 7–200
Du Bois, William Ewing, Dec. 15, 1810–July 14, 1881.
    Vol. 3, Pt. 1–472
Du Bose, William Porcher, Apr. 11, 1836–Aug. 18, 1918.
    Vol. 3, Pt. 1–472
Du Bourg, Louis Guillaume Valentin, Feb. 13, 1766–Dec. 12, 1833. Vol. 3, Pt. 1–473
Dubuque, Julien, Jan. 10, 1762–Mar. 24, 1810.
    Vol. 3, Pt. 1–475
Du Chaillu, Paul Belloni, July 31, 1835–Apr. 30, 1903.
    Vol. 3, Pt. 1–475
Duché, Jacob, Jan. 31, 1737/38–Jan. 3, 1798.
    Vol. 3, Pt. 1–476
Duchesne, Rose Philippine, Aug. 29, 1769–Nov. 18, 1852.
    Vol. 3, Pt. 1–477
Duchin, Edward Frank ("Eddy"), Apr. 1, 1909–Feb. 9, 1951.
    Supp. 5–187
Dudley, Benjamin Winslow, Apr. 12, 1785–Jan. 20, 1870.
    Vol. 3, Pt. 1–478
Dudley, Charles Benjamin, July 14, 1842–Dec. 21, 1909.
    Vol. 3, Pt. 1–479
Dudley, Charles Edward, May 23, 1780–Jan. 23, 1841.
    Vol. 3, Pt. 1–480
Dudley, Edward Bishop, Dec. 15, 1789–Oct. 30, 1855.
    Vol. 3, Pt. 1–480

Dudley, Joseph, Sept. 23, 1647–Apr. 2, 1720.
    Vol. 3, Pt. 1–481
Dudley, Paul, Sept. 3, 1675–Jan. 25, 1751.
    Vol. 3, Pt. 1–483
Dudley, Thomas, 1576–July 31, 1653.
    Vol. 3, Pt. 1–484
Dudley, William Russel, Mar. 1, 1849–June 4, 1911.
    Vol. 3, Pt. 1–485
Duer, John, Oct. 7, 1782–Aug. 8, 1858.
    Vol. 3, Pt. 1–485
Duer, William, Mar. 18, 1747–May 7, 1799.
    Vol. 3, Pt. 1–486
Duer, William Alexander, Sept. 8, 1780–May 30, 1858.
    Vol. 3, Pt. 1–488
Duff, James Henderson, Jan. 21, 1883–Dec. 20, 1969.
    Supp. 8–143
Duff, Mary Ann Dyke, 1794–Sept. 5, 1857.
    Vol. 3, Pt. 1–488
Duffield, George, Oct. 7, 1732–Feb. 2, 1790.
    Vol. 3, Pt. 1–489
Duffield, George, July 4, 1794–June 26, 1868.
    Vol. 3, Pt. 1–490
Duffield, Samuel Augustus Willoughby, Sept. 24, 1843–May 12, 1887. Vol. 3, Pt. 1–491
Duffy, Edmund, Mar. 1, 1899–Sept. 13, 1962.
    Supp. 7–205
Duffy, Francis Patrick, May 2, 1871–June 26, 1932.
    Supp. 1–267
Duffy, Hugh, Nov. 26, 1866–Oct. 19, 1954.
    Supp. 5–188
Dufour, John James, c. 1763–Feb. 9, 1827.
    Vol. 3, Pt. 1–491
Duganne, Augustine Joseph Hickey, 1823–Oct. 20, 1884.
    Vol. 3, Pt. 1–492
Dugdale, Richard Louis, 1841–July 23, 1883.
    Vol. 3, Pt. 1–493
Duggar, Benjamin Minge, Sept. 1, 1872–Sept. 10, 1956.
    Supp. 6–175
Dugué, Charles Oscar, May 1, 1821–Aug. 29, 1872.
    Vol. 3, Pt. 1–493
Duhring, Louis Adolphus, Dec. 23, 1845–May 8, 1913.
    Vol. 3, Pt. 1–494
Duke, Basil Wilson, May 28, 1838–Sept. 16, 1916.
    Vol. 3, Pt. 1–495
Duke, Benjamin Newton, Apr. 27, 1855–Jan. 8, 1929.
    Vol. 3, Pt. 1–496
Duke, James Buchanan, Dec. 23, 1856–Oct. 10, 1925.
    Vol. 3, Pt. 1–497
Duke, Vernon, Oct. 10, 1903–Jan. 16, 1969.
    Supp. 8–144
Dulany, Daniel, 1685–Dec. 5, 1753.
    Vol. 3, Pt. 1–498
Dulany, Daniel, June 28, 1722–Mar. 17, 1797.
    Vol. 3, Pt. 1–499
Dulles, Allen Welsh, Apr. 7, 1893–Jan. 29, 1969.
    Supp. 8–146
Dulles, John Foster, Feb. 25, 1888–May 24, 1959.
    Supp. 6–177
Duluth, Daniel Greysolon, Sieur, 1636–Feb. 25, 1710.
    Vol. 3, Pt. 1–500
Dumaine, Frederic Christopher, Mar. 6, 1866–May 27, 1951.
    Supp. 5–190
Dummer, Jeremiah, Sept. 14, 1645–May 25, 1718.
    Vol. 3, Pt. 1–501
Dummer, Jeremiah, c. 1679–May 19, 1739.
    Vol. 3, Pt. 1–502
Dumont, Allen Balcom, Jan. 29, 1901–Nov. 15, 1965.
    Supp. 7–206
Dumont, Margaret, Oct. 20, 1889–Mar. 6, 1965.
    Supp. 7–207
Dun, Robert Graham, Aug. 7, 1826–Nov. 10, 1900.
    Vol. 3, Pt. 1–503
Dunbar, Charles Franklin, July 28, 1830–Jan. 29, 1900.
    Vol. 3, Pt. 1–503
Dunbar, (Helen) Flanders, May 14, 1902–Aug. 21, 1959.
    Supp. 6–180
Dunbar, Moses, June 14, 1746–Mar. 19, 1777.
    Vol. 3, Pt. 1–504
Dunbar, Paul Laurence, June 27, 1872–Feb. 9, 1906.
    Vol. 3, Pt. 1–505
Dunbar, Robert, Dec. 13, 1812–Sept. 18, 1890.
    Vol. 3, Pt. 1–506

Dunbar, William, 1749–October 1810.
Vol. 3, Pt. 1–507
Duncan, Isadora, May 27, 1878–Sept. 14, 1927.
Vol. 3, Pt. 1–508
Duncan, James, May 5, 1857–Sept. 14, 1928.
Supp. 1–269
Duncan, James, May 5, 1857–Sept. 14, 1928.
Vol. 3, Pt. 1–510
Duncan, Joseph, Feb. 22, 1794–Jan. 15, 1844.
Vol. 3, Pt. 1–510
Duncan, Robert Kennedy, Nov. 1, 1868–Feb. 18, 1914.
Vol. 3, Pt. 1–511
Dundee, Johnny, Nov. 22, 1893–Apr. 22, 1965.
Supp. 7–209
Dunglison, Robley, Jan. 4, 1708–April 1, 1869.
Vol. 3, Pt. 1–512
Dunham, Henry Morton, July 27, 1853–May 4, 1929.
Vol. 3, Pt. 1–513
Duniway, Abigail Jane Scott, Oct. 22, 1834–Oct. 11, 1915.
Vol. 3, Pt. 1–513
Dunlap, John, 1747–Nov. 27, 1812.
Vol. 3, Pt. 1–514
Dunlap, Robert Pinckney, Aug. 17, 1794–Oct. 20, 1859.
Vol. 3, Pt. 1–515
Dunlap, William, Feb. 19, 1766–Sept. 28, 1839.
Vol. 3, Pt. 1–516
Dunlop, James, 1795–April 9, 1856.
Vol. 3, Pt. 1–518
Dunmore, John Murray, Earl of, 1732–Mar. 5, 1809.
Vol. 3, Pt. 1–519
Dunn, Charles, Dec. 28, 1799–Apr. 7, 1872.
Vol. 3, Pt. 1–520
Dunn, William McKee, Dec. 12, 1814–July 24, 1887.
Vol. 3, Pt. 1–521
Dunn, Williamson, Dec. 25, 1781–Nov. 11, 1854.
Vol. 3, Pt. 1–522
Dunne, Finley Peter, July 10, 1867–Apr. 24, 1936.
Supp. 2–158
Dunning, Albert Elijah, Jan. 5, 1844–Nov. 14, 1923.
Vol. 3, Pt. 1–522
Dunning, William Archibald, May 12, 1857–Aug. 25, 1922.
Vol. 3, Pt. 1–523
Dunster, Henry, 1609–Feb. 27, 1658/59?.
Vol. 3, Pt. 1–524
Dunwoody, William Hood, Mar. 14, 1841–Feb. 8, 1914.
Vol. 3, Pt. 1–524
Du Ponceau, Pierre Étienne, June 3, 1760–April 1, 1844.
Vol. 3, Pt. 1–525
Du Pont, Alfred Irénée, May 12. 1864–Apr. 29, 1935.
Supp. 1–270
Du Pont, Eleuthère Irénée, June 24, 1771–Oct. 31, 1834.
Vol. 3, Pt. 1–526
Du Pont, Francis Irénée, Dec. 3, 1873–Mar. 16, 1942.
Supp. 3–238
Du Pont, Henry, Aug. 8, 1812–Aug. 8, 1889.
Vol. 3, Pt. 1–528
Du Pont, Henry Algernon, July 30, 1838–Dec. 31, 1926.
Vol. 3, Pt. 1–528
Du Pont, Irénée, Dec. 21, 1876–Dec. 19, 1963.
Supp. 7–209
Du Pont, Lammot, Oct. 12, 1880–July 24, 1954.
Supp. 5–191
Du Pont, Pierre Samuel, Jan. 15, 1870–Apr. 5, 1954.
Supp. 5–192
Du Pont, Samuel Francis, Sept. 27, 1803–June 23, 1865.
Vol. 3, Pt. 1–529
Du Pont, Thomas Coleman, Dec. 11, 1863–Nov. 11, 1930.
Supp. 1–271
Du Pont, Victor Marie, Oct. 1, 1767–Jan. 30, 1827.
Vol. 3, Pt. 1–533
Dupratz, Antoine Simon Le Page, fl. 1718–1758.
Vol. 3, Pt. 1–534
Dupuy, Eliza Ann, 1814–Jan. 15, 1881.
Vol. 3, Pt. 1–534
Durand, Asher Brown, Aug. 21, 1796–Sept. 17, 1886.
Vol. 3, Pt. 1–535
Durand, Cyrus, Feb. 27, 1787–Sept. 18, 1868.
Vol. 3, Pt. 1–538
Durand, Élie Magloire, Jan. 25, 1794–Aug. 14, 1873.
Vol. 3, Pt. 1–538
Durand, William Frederick, Mar. 5, 1859–Aug. 9, 1958.
Supp. 6–181

Durant, Charles Ferson, Sept. 19, 1805–March 2, 1873.
Vol. 3, Pt. 1–540
Durant, Henry, June 18, 1802–Jan. 22, 1875.
Vol. 3, Pt. 1–540
Durant, Henry Fowle, Feb. 20, 1822–Oct. 3, 1881.
Vol. 3, Pt. 1–541
Durant, Thomas Clark, Feb. 6, 1820–Oct. 5, 1885.
Vol. 3, Pt. 1–542
Durant, Thomas Jefferson, Aug. 8, 1817–Feb. 3, 1882.
Vol. 3, Pt. 1–543
Durant, William Crapo, Dec. 8, 1861–Mar. 18, 1947.
Supp. 4–243
Duranty, Walter, May 25, 1884–Oct. 3, 1957.
Supp. 6–183
Durbin, John Price, Oct. 10, 1800–Oct. 19, 1876.
Vol. 3, Pt. 1–544
Durell, Edward Henry, July 14, 1810–March 29, 1887.
Vol. 3, Pt. 1–545
Durfee, Job, Sept. 20, 1790–July 26, 1847.
Vol. 3, Pt. 1–546
Durfee, Thomas, Feb. 6, 1826–June 6, 1901.
Vol. 3, Pt. 1–546
Durfee, William Franklin, Nov. 15, 1833–Nov. 14, 1899.
Vol. 3, Pt. 1–547
Durfee, Zoheth Sherman, April 22, 1831–June 8, 1880.
Vol. 3, Pt. 1–548
Durham, Caleb Wheeler, Feb. 6, 1848–March 28, 1910.
Vol. 3, Pt. 1–549
Durivage, Francis Alexander, 1814–Feb. 1, 1881.
Vol. 3, Pt. 1–549
Durkee, John, Dec. 11, 1728–May 29, 1782.
Vol. 3, Pt. 1–550
Durkin, Martin Patrick, Mar. 18, 1894–Nov. 13, 1955.
Supp. 5–194
Durrett, Reuben Thomas, Jan. 22, 1824–Sept. 16, 1913.
Vol. 3, Pt. 1–550
Durrie, Daniel Steele, Jan. 2, 1819–Aug. 31, 1892.
Vol. 3, Pt. 1–551
Durstine, Roy Sarles, Dec. 13, 1886–Nov. 28, 1962.
Supp. 7–211
Duryea, Charles Edgar, Dec. 15, 1861–Sept. 28, 1938.
Supp. 2–160
Duryea, Hermanes Barkulo, Dec. 13, 1863–Jan. 25, 1916.
Vol. 3, Pt. 1–552
Duryea, James Frank, Oct. 8, 1869–Feb. 15, 1967.
Supp. 8–148
Duryée, Abram, April 29, 1815–Sept. 27, 1890.
Vol. 3, Pt. 1–553
Du Simitière, Pierre Eugène, c. 1736–Oct. 1784.
Vol. 3, Pt. 1–553
Dusser de Barenne, Joannes Gregorius, June 6, 1885–June 9, 1940. Supp. 2–161
Dustin, Hannah, b. Dec. 23, 1657.
Vol. 3, Pt. 1–554
Dutton, Clarence Edward, May 15, 1841–Jan. 4, 1912.
Vol. 3, Pt. 1–555
Dutton, Henry, Feb. 12, 1796–Apr. 12, 1869.
Vol. 3, Pt. 1–555
Dutton, Samuel Train, Oct. 16, 1849–Mar. 28, 1919.
Vol. 3, Pt. 1–556
Duval, William Pope, 1784–Mar. 19, 1854.
Vol. 3, Pt. 1–557
Duvall, Gabriel, Dec. 6, 1752–Mar. 6, 1844.
Supp. 1–272
Duveneck, Frank, Oct. 9, 1848–Jan. 3, 1919.
Vol. 3, Pt. 1–558
Duyckinck, Evert Augustus, Nov. 23, 1816–Aug. 13, 1878.
Vol. 3, Pt. 1–561
Duyckinck, George Long, Oct. 17, 1823–Mar. 30, 1863.
Vol. 3, Pt. 1–562
Dwenger, Joseph, Sept. 7, 1837–Jan. 22, 1893.
Vol. 3, Pt. 1–562
Dwiggins, William Addison, June 19, 1880–Dec. 25, 1956.
Supp. 6–185
Dwight, Arthur Smith, Mar. 18, 1864–Apr. 1, 1946.
Supp. 4–245
Dwight, Benjamin Woodbridge, Apr. 5, 1816–Sept. 18, 1889.
Vol. 3, Pt. 1–563
Dwight, Edmund, Nov. 28, 1780–Apr. 1, 1849.
Vol. 3, Pt. 1–563
Dwight, Francis, Mar. 14, 1808–Dec. 15, 1845.
Vol. 3, Pt. 1–564

Dwight, Harrison Gray Otis, Nov. 22, 1803–Jan. 25, 1862.
    Vol. 3, Pt. 1–565
Dwight, Henry Otis, June 3, 1843–June 20, 1917.
    Vol. 3, Pt. 1–566
Dwight, John Sullivan, May 13, 1813–Sept. 5, 1893.
    Vol. 3, Pt. 1–567
Dwight, Nathaniel, Jan. 31, 1770–June 11, 1831.
    Vol. 3, Pt. 1–568
Dwight, Sereno Edwards, May 18, 1786–Nov. 30, 1850.
    Vol. 3, Pt. 1–569
Dwight, Theodore, Mar. 3, 1796–Oct. 16, 1866.
    Vol. 3, Pt. 1–570
Dwight, Theodore. Dec. 15, 1764–June 12, 1846.
    Vol. 3, Pt. 1–569
Dwight, Theodore William, July 18, 1822–June 29, 1892.
    Vol. 3, Pt. 1–571
Dwight, Thomas, Oct. 13, 1843–Sept. 9, 1911.
    Vol. 3, Pt. 1–573
Dwight, Timothy, May 14, 1752–Jan. 11, 1817.
    Vol. 3, Pt. 1–573
Dwight, Timothy, Nov. 16, 1828–May 26, 1916.
    Vol. 3, Pt. 1–577
Dwight, William, July 14, 1831–Apr. 21, 1888.
    Vol. 3, Pt. 1–578
Dworshak, Henry Clarence, Aug. 29, 1894–July 23, 1962.
    Supp. 7–212
Dyar, Harrison Gray, Feb. 14, 1866–Jan. 21, 1929.
    Vol. 3, Pt. 1–578
Dye, William McEntyre, Feb. 1831–Nov. 13, 1899.
    Vol. 3, Pt. 1–579
Dyer, Alexander Brydie, Jan. 10, 1815–May 20, 1874.
    Vol. 3, Pt. 1–580
Dyer, Eliphalet, Sept. 14, 1721–May 13, 1807.
    Vol. 3, Pt. 1–581
Dyer, Isadore, Nov. 2, 1865–Oct. 12, 1920.
    Vol. 3, Pt. 1–582
Dyer, Louis, Sept. 30, 1851–July 20, 1908.
    Vol. 3, Pt. 1–582
Dyer, Mary, d. June 1, 1660.
    Vol. 3, Pt. 1–584
Dyer, Nehemiah Mayo, Feb. 19, 1839–Jan. 27, 1910.
    Vol. 3, Pt. 1–584
Dykstra, Clarence Addison, Feb. 25, 1883–May 6, 1950.
    Supp. 4–246
Dylander, John, c. 1709–Nov. 2, 1741.
    Vol. 3, Pt. 1–585
Dymond, John, May 3, 1836–Mar. 5, 1922.
    Vol. 3, Pt. 1–585
Dyott, Thomas W., 1771–Jan. 17, 1861.
    Vol. 3, Pt. 1–586

Eads, James Buchanan, May 23, 1820–Mar. 8, 1887.
    Vol. 3, Pt. 1–587
Eagels, Jeanne, June 26, 1894(1890?)–Oct. 3, 1929.
    Vol. 3, Pt. 1–589
Eakins, Thomas, July 25, 1844–June 25, 1916.
    Vol. 3, Pt. 1–590
Eames, Charles, Mar. 20, 1812–Mar. 16, 1867.
    Vol. 3, Pt. 1–592
Eames, Wilberforce, Oct. 12, 1855–Dec. 6, 1937.
    Supp. 2–162
Earhart, Amelia Mary, July 24, 1897–July 2[?], 1937.
    Supp. 2–163
Earle, Alice Morse, Apr. 27, 1853–Feb. 16, 1911.
    Vol. 3, Pt. 1–593
Earle, Edward Mead, May 20, 1894–June 24, 1954.
    Supp. 5–195
Earle, James, May 1, 1761–Aug. 18, 1796.
    Vol. 3, Pt. 1–594
Earle, Mortimer Lamson, Oct. 14, 1864–Sept. 26, 1905.
    Vol. 3, Pt. 1–594
Earle, Pliny, Dec. 17, 1762–Nov. 29, 1832.
    Vol. 3, Pt. 1–595
Earle, Pliny (son of Pliny), Dec. 31, 1809–May 17, 1892.
    Vol. 3, Pt. 1–595
Earle, Ralph, May 11, 1751–Aug. 16, 1801.
    Vol. 3, Pt. 1–596
Earle, Ralph, May 3, 1874–Feb. 13, 1939.
    Supp. 2–165
Earle, Thomas, Apr. 21, 1796–July 14, 1849.
    Vol. 3, Pt. 1–597
Early, John, Jan. 1, 1786–Nov. 5, 1873.
    Vol. 3, Pt. 1–597

Early, Jubal Anderson, Nov. 3, 1816–Mar. 2, 1894.
    Vol. 3, Pt. 1–598
Early, Peter, June 20, 1773–Aug. 15, 1817.
    Vol. 3, Pt. 1–599
Early, Stephen Tyree, Aug. 27, 1889–Aug. 11, 1951.
    Supp. 5–196
Easley, Ralph Montgomery, Feb. 25, 1856–Sept. 7, 1939.
    Supp. 2–166
East, Edward Murray, Oct. 4, 1879–Nov. 9, 1938.
    Supp. 2–167
Eastman, Arthur MacArthur, June 8, 1810–Sept. 3, 1877.
    Vol. 3, Pt. 1–600
Eastman, Charles Gamage, June 1, 1816–Sept. 16, 1860.
    Vol. 3, Pt. 1–600
Eastman, Enoch Worthen, Apr. 15, 1810–Jan. 9, 1885.
    Vol. 3, Pt. 1–601
Eastman, George, July 12, 1854–Mar. 14, 1932.
    Supp. 1–274
Eastman, Harvey Gridley, Oct. 16, 1832–July 13, 1878.
    Vol. 3, Pt. 1–602
Eastman, John Robie, July 29, 1836–Sept. 26, 1913.
    Vol. 3, Pt. 1–602
Eastman, Joseph Bartlett, June 26, 1882–Mar. 15, 1944.
    Supp. 3–240
Eastman, Max Forrester, Jan. 4, 1883–Mar. 25, 1969.
    Supp. 8–149
Eastman, Timothy Corser, May 30, 1821–Oct. 11, 1893.
    Vol. 3, Pt. 1–603
Eastman, William Reed, Oct. 19, 1835–Mar. 25, 1925.
    Vol. 3, Pt. 1–604
Easton, John, c. 1625–Dec. 12, 1705.
    Vol. 3, Pt. 1–604
Easton, Nicholas, 1593–Aug. 15, 1675.
    Vol. 3, Pt. 1–605
Eaton, Amos, May 17, 1776–May 10, 1842.
    Vol. 3, Pt. 1–605
Eaton, Benjamin Harrison, Dec. 15, 1833–Oct. 29, 1904.
    Vol. 3, Pt. 1–606
Eaton, Charles Aubrey, Mar. 29, 1868–Jan. 23, 1953.
    Supp. 5–197
Eaton, Daniel Cady, Sept. 12, 1834–June 29, 1895.
    Vol. 3, Pt. 1–606
Eaton, Dorman Bridgman, June 27, 1823–Dec. 23, 1899.
    Vol. 3, Pt. 1–607
Eaton, Homer, Nov. 16, 1834–Feb. 9, 1913.
    Vol. 3, Pt. 1–608
Eaton, John, Dec. 5, 1829–Feb. 9, 1906.
    Vol. 3, Pt. 1–608
Eaton, John Henry, June 18, 1790–Nov. 17, 1856.
    Vol. 3, Pt. 1–609
Eaton, Joseph Oriel, Feb 8, 1829–Feb. 7, 1875.
    Vol. 3, Pt. 1–610
Eaton, Margaret L. O'Neill. [See O'Neill, Margaret L., 1796–
    1879.]
Eaton, Nathaniel, c. 1609–1674.
    Vol. 3, Pt. 1–611
Eaton, Samuel, 1596?–Jan. 9, 1665.
    Vol. 3, Pt. 1–611
Eaton, Theophilus, 1590–Jan. 7, 1658.
    Vol. 3, Pt. 1–612
Eaton, William, Feb. 23, 1764–June 1, 1811.
    Vol. 3, Pt. 1–613
Eaton, Wyatt, May 6, 1849–June 7, 1896.
    Vol. 3, Pt. 1–613
Eberle, Edward Walter, Aug. 17, 1864–July 6, 1929.
    Vol. 3, Pt. 1–614
Eberle, John, Dec. 10, 1787–Feb. 2, 1838.
    Vol. 3, Pt. 1–615
Echols, John, Mar. 20, 1823–May 24, 1896.
    Vol. 3, Pt. 2–1
Eckart, William Roberts, June 17, 1841–Dec. 8, 1914.
    Vol. 3, Pt. 2–2
Eckels, James Herron, Nov. 22, 1858–Apr. 14, 1907.
    Vol. 3, Pt. 2–2
Eckert, Thomas Thompson, Apr. 23, 1825–Oct. 20, 1910.
    Vol. 3, Pt. 2–3
Eckford, Henry, Mar. 12, 1775–Nov. 12, 1832.
    Vol. 3, Pt. 2–4
Eckstein, John, c. 1750–c. 1817.
    Vol. 3, Pt. 2–5
Eckstorm, Fannie Hardy, June 18, 1865–Dec. 31, 1946.
    Supp. 4–248

Emerson, Haven, Oct. 19, 1874–May 21, 1957.
  Supp. 6–192
Emerson, James Ezekiel, Nov. 2, 1823–Feb. 17, 1900.
  Vol. 3, Pt. 2–129
Emerson, Joseph, Oct. 13, 1777–May 14, 1833.
  Vol. 3, Pt. 2–129
Emerson, Mary Moody, Aug. 25, 1774–May 1, 1863.
  Vol. 3, Pt. 2–130
Emerson, Oliver Farrar, May 24, 1860–Mar. 13, 1927.
  Vol. 3, Pt. 2–131
Emerson, Ralph, May 8, 1831–Aug. 19, 1914.
  Vol. 3, Pt. 2–131
Emerson, Ralph Waldo, May 25, 1803–Apr. 27, 1882
  Vol. 3, Pt. 2–132
Emerson, Rollins Adams, May 5, 1873–Dec. 8, 1947.
  Supp. 4–252
Emerson, William, May 6, 1769–May 12, 1811.
  Vol. 3, Pt. 2–141
Emerton, Ephraim, Feb. 18, 1851–Mar. 3, 1935.
  Supp. 1–285
Emerton, James Henry, Mar. 31, 1847–Dec. 5, 1930.
  Supp. 1–286
Emery, Albert Hamilton, June 21, 1834–Dec. 2, 1926.
  Vol. 3, Pt. 2–142
Emery, Charles Edward, Mar. 29, 1838–June 1, 1898.
  Vol. 3, Pt. 2–142
Emery, Henry Crosby, Dec. 21, 1872–Feb. 6, 1924.
  Vol. 3, Pt. 2–143
Emery, Lucilius Alonzo, July 27, 1840–Aug. 26, 1920.
  Vol. 3, Pt. 2–144
Emery, Stephen Albert, Oct. 4, 1841–Apr. 15, 1891.
  Vol. 3, Pt. 2–145
Emmet, Thomas Addis, Apr. 24, 1764–Nov. 14, 1827.
  Vol. 3, Pt. 2–145
Emmet, Thomas Addis, May 29, 1828–Mar. 1, 1919.
  Vol. 3, Pt. 2–147
Emmet, William Le Roy, July 10, 1859–Sept. 26, 1941.
  Supp. 3–251
Emmett, Burton, Nov. 11, 1871–May 6, 1935.
  Supp. 1–287
Emmett, Daniel Decatur, Oct. 29, 1815–June 28, 1904.
  Vol. 3, Pt. 2–148
Emmons, Ebenezer, May 16, 1799–Oct. 1, 1863.
  Vol. 3, Pt. 2–149
Emmons, George Foster, Aug. 23, 1811–July 23, 1884.
  Vol. 3, Pt. 2–149
Emmons, Nathanael, Apr. 20, 1745 o.s.–Sept. 23, 1840.
  Vol. 3, Pt. 2–150
Emmons, Samuel Franklin, Mar. 29, 1841–Mar. 28, 1911.
  Vol. 3, Pt. 2–151
Emory, John, Apr. 11, 1789–Dec. 16, 1835.
  Vol. 3, Pt. 2–152
Emory, William Hemsley, Sept. 7, 1811–Dec. 1, 1887.
  Vol. 3, Pt. 2–153
Emott, James, Mar. 14, 1771–Apr. 7, 1850.
  Vol. 3, Pt. 2–154
Emott, James, Apr. 23, 1823–Sept. 11, 1884.
  Vol. 3, Pt. 2–154
Endecott, John, c. 1589–Mar. 15, 1665.
  Vol. 3, Pt. 2–155
Endicott, Charles Moses, Dec. 6, 1793–Dec. 14, 1863.
  Vol. 3, Pt. 2–157
Endicott, John. [See Endecott, John, c. 1589–1665.]
Endicott, Mordecai Thomas, Nov. 26, 1844–Mar. 5, 1926.
  Vol. 3, Pt. 2–157
Endicott, William Crowninshield, Nov. 19, 1826–May 6,
  1900. Vol. 3, Pt. 2–158
Enelow, Hyman Gerson, Oct. 26, 1877–Feb. 5, 1934.
  Supp. 1–288
Engel, Carl, July 21, 1883–May 6, 1944.
  Supp. 3–252
Engelhardt, Zephyrin, Nov. 13, 1851–Apr. 27, 1934.
  Supp. 1–289
Engelmann, George, Feb. 2, 1809–Feb. 4, 1884.
  Vol. 3, Pt. 2–159
Engelmann, George Julius, July 2, 1847–Nov. 16, 1903.
  Vol. 3, Pt. 2–160
England, John, Sept. 23, 1786–Apr. 11, 1842.
  Vol. 3, Pt. 2–161
Engle, Clair William Walter, Sept. 21, 1911–July 30, 1964.
  Supp. 7–224
Englis, John, Nov. 27, 1808–Oct. 25, 1888.
  Vol. 3, Pt. 2–163

English, Elbert Hartwell, Mar. 6, 1816–Sept. 1, 1884.
  Vol. 3, Pt. 2–164
English, George Bethune, Mar. 7, 1787–Sept. 20, 1828.
  Vol. 3, Pt. 2–165
English, James Edward, Mar. 13, 1812–Mar. 2, 1890.
  Vol. 3, Pt. 2–165
English, Thomas Dunn, June 29, 1819–Apr. 1, 1902.
  Vol. 3, Pt. 2–166
English, William Hayden, Aug. 27, 1822–Feb. 7, 1896.
  Vol. 3, Pt. 2–167
Enneking, John Joseph, Oct. 4, 1841–Nov. 17, 1916.
  Vol. 3, Pt. 2–168
Eno, William Phelps, June 3, 1858–Dec. 3, 1945.
  Supp. 3–253
Ensley, Enoch, Nov. 8, 1836–Nov. 18, 1891.
  Vol. 3, Pt. 2–169
Entwistle, James, July 8, 1837–Mar. 23, 1910.
  Vol. 3, Pt. 2–170
Eppes, John Wayles, Apr. 7, 1773–Sept. 15, 1823.
  Vol. 3, Pt. 2–170
Epstein, Abraham, Apr. 20, 1892–May 2, 1942.
  Supp. 3–254
Epstein, Jacob, Nov. 10, 1880–Aug. 19, 1959.
  Supp. 6–193
Epstein, Philip G., Aug. 22, 1909–Feb. 7, 1952.
  Supp. 5–209
Erdman, Charles Rosenbury, July 20, 1866–May 9, 1960.
  Supp. 6–195
Ericsson, John, July 31, 1803–Mar. 8, 1889.
  Vol. 3, Pt. 2–171
Erlanger, Abraham Lincoln, May 4, 1860–Mar. 7, 1930.
  Vol. 3, Pt. 2–176
Erlanger, Joseph, Jan. 5, 1874–Dec. 5, 1965.
  Supp. 7–225
Ernst, Harold Clarence, July 31, 1856–Sept. 7, 1922.
  Vol. 3, Pt. 2–177
Ernst, Oswald Herbert, June 27, 1842–Mar. 21, 1926.
  Vol. 3, Pt. 2–178
Errett, Isaac, Jan. 2, 1820–Dec. 19, 1888.
  Vol. 3, Pt. 2–179
Errol, Leon, July 3, 1881–Oct. 12, 1951.
  Supp. 5–210
Erskine, John, Sept. 13, 1813–Jan. 27, 1895.
  Vol. 3, Pt. 2–180
Erskine, John, Oct. 5, 1879–June 2, 1951.
  Supp. 5–211
Erskine, Robert, Sept. 7, 1735–Oct. 2, 1780.
  Vol. 3, Pt. 2–180
Erving, George William, July 15, 1769–July 22, 1850.
  Vol. 3, Pt. 2–181
Esbjörn, Lars Paul, Oct. 16, 1808–July 2, 1870.
  Vol. 3, Pt. 2–182
Escalante, Silvestre Velez De, fl. 1768–1779.
  Vol. 3, Pt. 2–183
Esch, John Jacob, Mar. 20, 1861–Apr. 27, 1941.
  Supp. 3–256
Esher, John Jacob, Dec. 11, 1823–Apr. 16, 1901.
  Vol. 3, Pt. 2–184
Espejo, Antonio De, fl. 1581–1583.
  Vol. 3, Pt. 2–184
Espy, James Pollard, May 9, 1785–Jan. 24, 1860.
  Vol. 3, Pt. 2–185
Estabrook, Joseph, Dec. 7, 1793–May 18, 1855.
  Vol. 3, Pt. 2–186
Estaugh, Elizabeth Haddon, c. 1680–Mar. 30, 1762.
  Vol. 3, Pt. 2–186
Esterbrook, Richard, Feb. 21, 1813–Oct. 11, 1895.
  Vol. 3, Pt. 2–187
Esterly, George, Oct. 17, 1809–June 7, 1893.
  Vol. 3, Pt. 2–188
Estes, Dana, Mar. 4, 1840–June 16, 1909.
  Vol. 3, Pt. 2–188
Estey, Jacob, Sept. 30, 1814–Apr. 15, 1890.
  Vol. 3, Pt. 2–189
Ettwein, John, June 29, 1721–Jan. 2, 1802.
  Vol. 3, Pt. 2–190
Eustis, Dorothy Leib Harrison Wood, May 30, 1886–Sept. 8,
  1946. Supp. 4–253
Eustis, George, Oct. 20, 1796–Dec. 22, 1858.
  Vol. 3, Pt. 2–191
Eustis, George, Sept. 29, 1828–Mar. 15, 1872.
  Vol. 3, Pt. 2–191

Eustis, Henry Lawrence, Feb. 1, 1819–Jan. 11, 1885.
  Vol. 3, Pt. 2–192
Eustis, James Biddle, Aug. 21, 1834–Sept. 9, 1899.
  Vol. 3, Pt. 2–193
Eustis, William, June 10, 1753–Feb. 6, 1825.
  Vol. 3, Pt. 2–193
Evans, Anthony Walton Whyte, Oct. 31, 1817–Nov. 28, 1886.
  Vol. 3, Pt. 2–195
Evans, Augusta Jane, May 8, 1835–May 9, 1909.
  Vol. 3, Pt. 2–195
Evans, Charles, Nov. 13, 1850–Feb. 8, 1935.
  Supp. 1–290
Evans, Clement Anselm, Feb. 25, 1833–July 2, 1911.
  Vol. 3, Pt. 2–196
Evans, Edward Payson, Dec. 8, 1831–Mar. 6, 1917.
  Vol. 3, Pt. 2–197
Evans, Evan, 1671–1721.
  Vol. 3, Pt. 2–198
Evans, Frederick William, June 9, 1808–Mar. 6, 1893.
  Vol. 3, Pt. 2–198
Evans, George, Jan. 12, 1797–Apr. 6, 1867.
  Vol. 3, Pt. 2–199
Evans, George Alfred, Oct. 1, 1850–July 14, 1925.
  Vol. 3, Pt. 2–200
Evans, George Henry, Mar. 25, 1805–Feb. 2, 1856.
  Vol. 3, Pt. 2–201
Evans, Henry Clay, June 18, 1843–Dec. 12, 1921.
  Vol. 3, Pt. 2–202
Evans, Hugh Davey, Apr. 26, 1792–July 16, 1868.
  Vol. 3, Pt. 2–203
Evans, John, fl. 1703–1731.
  Vol. 3, Pt. 2–204
Evans, John, Mar. 9, 1814–July 3, 1897.
  Vol. 3, Pt. 2–204
Evans, Lawrence Boyd, Feb. 3, 1870–Oct. 30, 1928.
  Vol. 3, Pt. 2–205
Evans, Lewis, c. 1700–June 12, 1756.
  Vol. 3, Pt. 2–206
Evans, Nathan George, Feb. 6, 1824–Nov. 30, 1868.
  Vol. 3, Pt. 2–207
Evans, Nathaniel, June 8, 1742–Oct. 29, 1767.
  Vol. 3, Pt. 2–208
Evans, Oliver, 1755–Apr. 15, 1819.
  Vol. 3, Pt. 2–208
Evans, Robley Dunglison, Aug. 18, 1846–Jan. 3, 1912.
  Vol. 3, Pt. 2–210
Evans, Thomas, Feb. 23, 1798–May 25, 1868.
  Vol. 3, Pt. 2–210
Evans, Thomas Wiltberger, Dec. 23, 1823–Nov. 14, 1897.
  Vol. 3, Pt. 2–211
Evans, Walter, Sept. 18, 1842–Dec. 30, 1923.
  Vol. 3, Pt. 2–212
Evans, Warren Felt, Dec. 23, 1817–Sept. 4, 1889.
  Vol. 3, Pt. 2–213
Evans, William Thomas, Nov. 13, 1843–Nov. 25, 1918.
  Vol. 3, Pt. 2–214
Evarts, Jeremiah, Feb. 3, 1781–May 10, 1831.
  Vol. 3, Pt. 2–215
Evarts, William Maxwell, Feb. 6, 1818–Feb. 28, 1901.
  Vol. 3, Pt. 2–215
Eve, Joseph, May 24, 1760–Nov. 14, 1835.
  Vol. 3, Pt. 2–218
Eve, Paul Fitzsimons, June 27, 1806–Nov. 3, 1877.
  Vol. 3, Pt. 2–219
Everendon, Walter, d. 1725.
  Vol. 3, Pt. 2–220
Everett, Alexander Hill, Mar. 19, 1790–June 29, 1847.
  Vol. 3, Pt. 2–220
Everett, Charles Carroll, June 19, 1829–Oct. 16, 1900.
  Vol. 3, Pt. 2–221
Everett, David, Mar. 29, 1770–Dec. 21, 1813.
  Vol. 3, Pt. 2–222
Everett, Edward, Apr. 11, 1794–Jan. 15, 1865.
  Vol. 3, Pt. 2–223
Everett, Robert, Jan. 2, 1791–Feb. 25, 1875.
  Vol. 3, Pt. 2–226
Everleigh, Ada, Feb. 15, 1876–Jan. 3, 1960.
  Supp. 4–255
Everleigh, Minna, July 5, 1878–Sept. 16, 1948.
  Supp. 4–255
Evermann, Barton Warren, Oct. 24, 1853–Sept. 27, 1932.
  Supp. 1–291

Evers, Medgar Wiley, July 2, 1925–June 12, 1963.
  Supp. 7–227
Ewbank, Thomas, Mar. 11, 1792–Sept. 16, 1870.
  Vol. 3, Pt. 2–227
Ewell, Benjamin Stoddert, June 10, 1810–June 19, 1894. Armistead Churchill Gordon, Jr.). Vol. 3, Pt. 2–228
Ewell, James, Feb. 16, 1773–Nov. 2, 1832.
  Vol. 3, Pt. 2–229
Ewell, Richard Stoddert, Feb. 8, 1817–Jan. 25, 1872.
  Vol. 3, Pt. 2–229
Ewell, Thomas, May 22, 1785–May 1, 1826.
  Vol. 3, Pt. 2–230
Ewer, Ferdinand Cartwright, May 22, 1826–Oct. 10, 1883.
  Vol. 3, Pt. 2–231
Ewing, Charles, June 8, 1780–Aug. 5, 1832.
  Vol. 3, Pt. 2–232
Ewing, Finis, July 10, 1773–July 4, 1841.
  Vol. 3, Pt. 2–233
Ewing, Hugh Boyle, Oct. 31, 1826–June 30, 1905.
  Vol. 3, Pt. 2–234
Ewing, James, Aug. 3, 1736–Mar. 1, 1806.
  Vol. 3, Pt. 2–234
Ewing, James, Dec. 25, 1866–May 16, 1943.
  Supp. 3–257
Ewing, James Caruthers Rhea, June 23, 1854–Aug. 20, 1925.
  Vol. 3, Pt. 2–235
Ewing, John, July 22, 1732–Sept. 8, 1802.
  Vol. 3, Pt. 2–236
Ewing, Thomas, Dec. 28, 1789–Oct. 26, 1871.
  Vol. 3, Pt. 2–237
Ewing, Thomas, Aug. 7, 1829–Jan. 21, 1896.
  Vol. 3, Pt. 2–238
Eytinge, Rose, Nov. 21, 1835–Dec. 20, 1911. (Mary Bronson Hartt). Vol. 3, Pt. 2–239
Ezekiel, Moses Jacob, Oct. 28, 1844–Mar. 27, 1917.
  Vol. 3, Pt. 2–240

Faber, John Eberhard, Dec. 6, 1822–Mar. 2, 1879.
  Vol. 3, Pt. 2–241
Faccioli, Giuseppe, Apr. 7, 1877–Jan. 13, 1934.
  Supp. 1–292
Fackler, David Parks, Apr. 4, 1841–Oct. 30, 1924.
  Vol. 3, Pt. 2–242
Faesch, John Jacob, 1729–May 26, 1799.
  Vol. 3, Pt. 2–243
Fagan, James Fleming, Mar. 1, 1828–Sept. 1, 1893.
  Vol. 3, Pt. 2–243
Fagan, Mark Matthew, Sept. 29, 1869–July 16, 1955.
  Supp. 5–212
Fages, Pedro, fl. 1767–1796.
  Vol. 3, Pt. 2–244
Faget, Jean Charles, June 26, 1818–Dec. 7, 1884.
  Vol. 3, Pt. 2–244
Fahnestock, Harris Charles, Feb. 27, 1835–June 4, 1914.
  Vol. 3, Pt. 2–245
Fair, James Graham, Dec. 3, 1831–Dec. 28, 1894.
  Vol. 3, Pt. 2–246
Fairbank, Calvin, Nov. 3, 1816–Oct. 12, 1898.
  Vol. 3, Pt. 2–247
Fairbanks, Charles Warren, May 11, 1852–June 4, 1918.
  Vol. 3, Pt. 2–248
Fairbanks, Douglas, May 23, 1883–Dec. 12, 1939.
  Supp. 2–172
Fairbanks, Erastus, Oct. 28, 1792–Nov. 20, 1864.
  Vol. 3, Pt. 2–249
Fairbanks, Henry, May 6, 1830–July 7, 1918.
  Vol. 3, Pt. 2–250
Fairbanks, Thaddeus, Jan. 17, 1796–Apr. 12, 1886.
  Vol. 3, Pt. 2–250
Fairburn, William Armstrong, Oct. 12, 1876–Oct. 1, 1947.
  Supp. 4–256
Fairchild, Blair, June 23, 1877–Apr. 23, 1933.
  Supp. 1–293
Fairchild, Charles Stebbins, Apr. 30, 1842–Nov. 24, 1924.
  Vol. 3, Pt. 2–251
Fairchild, David Grandison, Apr. 7, 1869–Aug. 6, 1954.
  Supp. 5–213
Fairchild, Fred Rogers, Aug. 5, 1877–Apr. 13, 1966.
  Supp. 8–165
Fairchild, George Thompson, Oct. 6, 1838–Mar. 16, 1901.
  Vol. 3, Pt. 2–252
Fairchild, James Harris, Nov. 25, 1817–Mar. 19, 1902.
  Vol. 3, Pt. 2–253

Fairchild, Lucius, Dec. 27, 1831–May 23, 1896.
  Vol. 3, Pt. 2–253
Fairchild, Mary Salome Cutler, June 21, 1855–Dec. 20, 1921.
  Vol. 3, Pt. 2–254
Fairchild, Muir Stephen, Sept. 2, 1894–Mar. 17, 1950.
  Supp. 4–258
Fairfax, Beatrice. [See Manning, Marie.]
Fairfax, Donald McNeill, Mar. 10, 1821–Jan. 10, 1894.
  Vol. 3, Pt. 2–255
Fairfax, Thomas, Oct. 22, 1693–Dec. 9, 1781.
  Vol. 3, Pt. 2–255
Fairfield, Edmund Burke, Aug. 7, 1821–Nov. 17, 1904.
  Vol. 3, Pt. 2–257
Fairfield, John, Jan. 30, 1797–Dec. 24, 1847.
  Vol. 3, Pt. 2–257
Fairfield, Sumner Lincoln, June 25, 1803–Mar. 6, 1844.
  Vol. 3, Pt. 2–258
Fairlamb, James Remington, Jan. 23, 1838–Apr. 16, 1908.
  Vol. 3, Pt. 2–259
Fairless, Benjamin F., May 3, 1890–Jan. 1, 1962.
  Supp. 7–228
Fairlie, John Archibald, Oct. 30, 1872–Jan. 23, 1947.
  Supp. 4–259
Falckner, Daniel, Nov. 25, 1666–c. 1741.
  Vol. 3, Pt. 2–259
Falckner, Justus, Nov. 22, 1672–1723.
  Vol. 3, Pt. 2–260
Falk, Maurice, Dec. 15, 1866–Mar. 18, 1946.
  Supp. 4–261
Falk, Otto Herbert, June 18, 1865–May 21, 1940.
  Supp. 2–173
Falkner, Roland Post, Apr. 14, 1866–Nov. 27, 1940.
  Supp. 2–174
Fall, Albert Bacon, Nov. 26, 1861–Nov. 30, 1944.
  Supp. 3–258
Fall, Bernard B., Nov. 11, 1926–Feb. 21, 1967.
  Supp. 8–167
Fallows, Samuel, Dec. 13, 1835–Sept. 5, 1922.
  Vol. 3, Pt. 2–261
Faneuil, Peter, June 20, 1700–Mar. 3, 1743.
  Vol. 3, Pt. 2–262
Fannin, James Walker, c. Jan. 1, 1804–Mar. 27, 1836.
  Vol. 3, Pt. 2–263
Fanning, Alexander Campbell Wilder, 1788–Aug. 18, 1846.
  Vol. 3, Pt. 2–264
Fanning, David, c. 1755–Mar. 14, 1825.
  Vol. 3, Pt. 2–264
Fanning, Edmund, Apr. 24, 1739–Feb. 28, 1818.
  Vol. 3, Pt. 2–266
Fanning, Edmund, July 16, 1769–Apr. 23, 1841.
  Vol. 3, Pt. 2–265
Fanning, John Thomas, Dec. 31, 1837–Feb. 6, 1911.
  Vol. 3, Pt. 2–267
Fanning, Nathaniel, May 31, 1755–Sept. 30, 1805.
  Vol. 3, Pt. 2–267
Fanning, Tolbert, May 10, 1810–May 3, 1874.
  Vol. 3, Pt. 2–268
Farabee, William Curtis, Feb. 2, 1865–June 24, 1925.
  Vol. 3, Pt. 2–269
Faran, James John, Dec. 29, 1808–Dec. 12, 1892.
  Vol. 3, Pt. 2–270
Fargo, William George, May 20, 1818–Aug. 3, 1881.
  Vol. 3, Pt. 2–271
Faribault, Jean Baptiste, Oct. 29, 1775–Aug. 20, 1860.
  Vol. 3, Pt. 2–272
Farish, William Stamps, Feb. 23, 1881–Nov. 29, 1942.
  Supp. 3–260
Farley, Harriet, Feb. 18, 1817–Nov. 12, 1907.
  Vol. 3, Pt. 2–272
Farley, John Murphy, Apr. 20, 1842–Sept. 17, 1918.
  Vol. 3, Pt. 2–273
Farlow, William Gilson, Dec. 17, 1844–June 3, 1919.
  Vol. 3, Pt. 2–274
Farman, Elbert Eli, Apr. 23, 1831–Dec. 30, 1911.
  Vol. 3, Pt. 2–275
Farmer, Fannie Merritt, Mar. 23, 1857–Jan. 15, 1915.
  Vol. 3, Pt. 2–276
Farmer, Ferdinand, Oct. 13, 1720–Aug. 17, 1786.
  Vol. 3, Pt. 2–276
Farmer, Hannah Tobey Shapleigh, Mar. 20, 1823–June 27, 1891. Vol. 3, Pt. 2–277
Farmer, John, June 12, 1789–Aug. 13, 1838.
  Vol. 3, Pt. 2–278

Farmer, John, Feb. 9, 1798–Mar. 24, 1859.
  Vol. 3, Pt. 2–278
Farmer, Moses Gerrish, Feb. 9, 1820–May 25, 1893.
  Vol. 3, Pt. 2–279
Farnam, Henry, Nov. 9, 1803–Oct. 4, 1883.
  Vol. 3, Pt. 2–281
Farnam, Henry Walcott, Nov. 6, 1853–Sept. 5, 1933.
  Supp. 1–293
Farnham, Eliza Woodson Burhans, Nov. 17, 1815–Dec. 15, 1864. Vol. 3, Pt. 2–282
Farnham, Russel, 1784–Oct. 23, 1832.
  Vol. 3, Pt. 1–282
Farnham, Thomas Jefferson, 1804–Sept. 13, 1848.
  Vol. 3, Pt. 2–283
Farnsworth, Elon John, July 30, 1837–July 3, 1863.
  Vol. 3, Pt. 2–284
Farnsworth, John Franklin, Mar. 27, 1820–July 14, 1897.
  Vol. 3, Pt. 2–284
Farnum, Dustin Lancy, May 27, 1874–July 3, 1929.
  Vol. 3, Pt. 2–285
Farnum, Franklyn, June 5, 1878[?]–July 4, 1961.
  Supp. 7–229
Farquhar, Percival, Oct. 19, 1864–Aug. 4, 1953.
  Supp. 5–214
Farragut, David Glasgow, July 5, 1801–Aug. 14, 1870.
  Vol. 3, Pt. 2–286
Farragut, George, Sept. 29, 1755–June 4, 1817.
  Vol. 3, Pt. 2–291
Farrand, Beatrix Cadwalader Jones, June 19, 1872–Feb. 7, 1959. Supp. 6–196
Farrand, Livingston, June 14, 1867–Nov. 8, 1939.
  Supp. 2–176
Farrand, Max, Mar. 29, 1869–June 17, 1945.
  Supp. 3–261
Farrar, Edgar Howard, June 20, 1849–Jan. 6, 1922.
  Vol. 3, Pt. 2–291
Farrar, Geraldine, Feb. 28, 1882–Mar. 11, 1967.
  Supp. 8–168
Farrar, John, July 1, 1779–May 8, 1853.
  Vol. 3, Pt. 2–292
Farrar, Timothy, Mar. 17, 1788–Oct. 27, 1874.
  Vol. 3, Pt. 2–293
Farrell, James Augustine, Feb. 15, 1862–Mar. 28, 1943.
  Supp. 3–262
Farrer, Henry, Mar. 23, 1843–Feb. 24, 1903.
  Vol. 3, Pt. 2–293
Farrington, Joseph Rider, Oct. 15, 1897–June 19, 1954.
  Supp. 5–216
Farrington, Wallace Rider, May 3, 1871–Oct. 6, 1933.
  Supp. 1–295
Farson, Negley, May 14, 1890–Dec. 12, 1960.
  Supp. 6–197
Farwell, Arthur, Apr. 23, 1872–Jan. 20, 1952.
  Supp. 5–217
Farwell, Charles Benjamin, July 1, 1823–Sept. 23, 1903.
  Vol. 3, Pt. 2–294
Farwell, John Villiers, July 29, 1825–Aug. 20, 1908.
  Vol. 3, Pt. 2–295
Fassett, Cornelia Adèle Strong, Nov. 9, 1831–Jan. 4, 1898.
  Vol. 3, Pt. 2–296
Fassett, Jacob Sloat, Nov. 13, 1853–Apr. 21, 1924.
  Vol. 3, Pt. 2–296
Father Divine. [See Divine, Father.]
Faulk, Andrew Jackson, Nov. 26, 1814–Sept. 4, 1898.
  Vol. 3, Pt. 2–297
Faulkner, Charles James, July 6, 1806–Nov. 1, 1884.
  Vol. 3, Pt. 2–298
Faulkner, Charles James, Sept. 21, 1847–Jan. 13, 1929.
  Vol. 3, Pt. 2–299
Faulkner (Falkner), William Cuthbert, Sept. 25, 1897–July 6, 1962. Supp. 7–230
Faunce, William Herbert Perry, Jan. 15, 1859–Jan. 31, 1930.
  Vol. 3, Pt. 2–299
Fauquier, Francis, 1704?–Mar. 3, 1768.
  Vol. 3, Pt. 2–301
Fauset, Jessie Redmon, Apr. 27, 1882[?]–Apr. 30, 1961.
  Supp. 7–236
Faust, Frederick Schiller, May 29, 1892–May 12, 1944.
  Supp. 3–264
Faversham, William Alfred, Feb. 12, 1868–Apr. 7, 1940.
  Supp. 2–178
Favill, Henry Baird, Aug. 14, 1860–Feb. 20, 1916.
  Vol. 3, Pt. 2–301

Fawcett, Edgar, May 26, 1847–May 2, 1904.
  Vol. 3, Pt. 2–302
Fay, Edward Allen, Nov. 22, 1843–July 14, 1923.
  Vol. 3, Pt. 2–303
Fay, Edwin Whitfield, Jan. 1, 1865–Feb. 17, 1920.
  Vol. 3, Pt. 2–304
Fay, Francis Anthony ("Frank"), Nov. 17, 1897–Sept. 25, 1961. Supp. 7–237
Fay, Jonas, Jan. 28, 1737 n.s.–Mar. 6, 1818.
  Vol. 3, Pt. 2–304
Fay, Sidney Bradshaw, Apr. 13, 1876–Aug. 29, 1967.
  Supp. 8–168
Fay, Theodore Sedgwick, Feb. 10, 1807–Nov. 24, 1898.
  Vol. 3, Pt. 2–305
Fayerweather, Daniel Burton, Mar. 12, 1822–Nov. 15, 1890.
  Vol. 3, Pt. 2–306
Fayssoux, Peter, 1745–Feb. 1, 1795.
  Vol. 3, Pt. 2–307
Fazenda, Louise Marie, June 17, 1896–Apr. 17, 1962.
  Supp. 7–238
Fearing, Kenneth Flexner, July 28, 1902–June 26, 1961.
  Supp. 7–239
Fearn, John Walker, Jan. 13, 1832–Apr. 7, 1809.
  Vol. 3, Pt. 2–307
Featherston, Winfield Scott, Aug. 8, 1819–May 28, 1891.
  Vol. 3, Pt. 2–308
Febiger, Christian, 1746–Sept. 20, 1796.
  Vol. 3, Pt. 2–309
Fechter, Charles Albert, Oct. 23, 1824–Aug. 5, 1879.
  Vol. 3, Pt. 2–309
Fee, John Gregg, Sept. 9, 1816–Jan. 11, 1901.
  Vol. 3, Pt. 2–310
Feehan, Patrick Augustine, Aug. 28, 1829–July 12, 1902.
  Vol. 3, Pt. 2–311
Feininger, Lyonel (Charles Léonell Adrian), July 17, 1871–Jan. 13, 1956. Supp. 6–198
Fejos, Paul, Jan. 24, 1897–Apr. 23, 1963.
  Supp. 7–240
Feke, Robert, c. 1705–c. 1750.
  Vol. 3, Pt. 2–312
Felch, Alpheus, Sept. 28, 1804–June 13, 1896.
  Vol. 3, Pt. 2–313
Fell, John, Feb. 5, 1721–May 15, 1798.
  Vol. 3, Pt. 2–314
Fels, Joseph, Dec. 16, 1854–Feb. 22, 1914.
  Vol. 3, Pt. 2–314
Fels, Samuel Simeon, Feb. 16, 1860–June 23, 1950.
  Supp. 4–262
Felsenthal, Bernhard, Jan. 2, 1822–Jan. 12, 1908.
  Vol. 3, Pt. 2–315
Felt, Joseph Barlow, Dec. 22, 1789–Sept. 8, 1869.
  Vol. 3, Pt. 2–316
Felton, Cornelius Conway, Nov. 6, 1807–Feb. 26, 1862.
  Vol. 3, Pt. 2–317
Felton, Rebecca Latimer, June 10, 1835–Jan. 24, 1930.
  Vol. 3, Pt. 2–318
Felton, Samuel Morse, July 17, 1809–Jan. 24, 1889.
  Vol. 3, Pt. 2–318
Felton, William Harrell, June 19, 1823–Sept. 24, 1909.
  Vol. 3, Pt. 2–319
Fendall, Josias, c. 1620–c. 1687.
  Vol. 3, Pt. 2–320
Fenger, Christian, Nov. 3, 1840–Mar. 7, 1902.
  Vol. 3, Pt. 2–320
Fenichel, Otto, Dec. 2, 1897–Jan. 22, 1946.
  Supp. 4–263
Fenn, William Wallace, Feb. 12, 1862–Mar. 6, 1932.
  Supp. 1–296
Fennell, James, Dec. 11, 1766–June 13, 1816.
  Vol. 3, Pt. 2–321
Fenneman, Nevin Melancthon, Dec. 26, 1865–July 4, 1945.
  Supp. 3–265
Fenner, Arthur, Dec. 10, 1745–Oct. 15, 1805.
  Vol. 3, Pt. 2–322
Fenner, Burt Leslie, Sept. 1, 1869–Jan. 24, 1926.
  Vol. 3, Pt. 2–323
Fenner, Charles Erasmus, Feb. 14, 1834–Oct. 24, 1911.
  Vol. 3, Pt. 2–323
Fenner, James, Jan. 22, 1771–Apr. 17, 1846.
  Vol. 3, Pt. 2–324
Fenno, John, Aug. 12, 1751 o.s.–Sept. 14, 1798.
  Vol. 3, Pt. 2–325

Fenollosa, Ernest Francisco, Feb. 18, 1853–Sept. 21, 1908.
  Vol. 3, Pt. 2–325
Fenton, Reuben Eaton, July 4, 1819–Aug. 25, 1885.
  Vol. 3, Pt. 2–326
Fenwick, Benedict Joseph, Sept. 3, 1782–Aug. 11, 1846.
  Vol. 3, Pt. 2–327
Fenwick, Edward Dominic, Aug. 19, 1768–Sept. 26, 1832.
  Vol. 3, Pt. 2–328
Fenwick, George, 1603–Mar. 15, 1656/7.
  Vol. 3, Pt. 2–329
Fenwick, John, 1618–Dec. 1683.
  Vol. 3, Pt. 2–330
Fenwicke, John. [See Fenwick, John, 1618–1683.]
Ferber, Edna Jessica, Aug. 15, 1885–Apr. 16, 1968.
  Supp. 8–170
Ferguson, Alexander Hugh, Feb. 27, 1853–Oct. 20, 1911.
  Vol. 3, Pt. 2–331
Ferguson, Elizabeth Graeme, Feb. 3, 1737–Feb. 23, 1801.
  Vol. 3, Pt. 2–331
Ferguson, James Edward, Aug. 31, 1871–Sept. 21, 1944.
  Supp. 3–266
Ferguson, John Calvin, Mar. 1, 1866–Aug. 3, 1945.
  Supp. 3–267
Ferguson, Miriam Amanda Wallace, June 13, 1875–June 25, 1961. Supp. 7–241
Ferguson, Samuel, Nov. 18, 1874–Feb. 10, 1950.
  Supp. 4–264
Ferguson, Thomas Barker, Aug. 8, 1841–Aug. 11, 1922.
  Vol. 3, Pt. 2–332
Ferguson, William Porter Frisbee, Dec. 13, 1861–June 23, 1929. Vol. 3, Pt. 2–334
Ferguson, William Jason, June 8, 1844–May 4, 1930.
  Vol. 3, Pt. 2–333
Fermi, Enrico, Sept. 29, 1901–Nov. 28,1954.
  Supp. 5–219
Fernald, Charles Henry, Mar. 16, 1838–Feb. 22, 1921.
  Vol. 3, Pt. 2–334
Fernald, James Champlin, Aug. 18, 1838–Nov. 10, 1918.
  Vol. 3, Pt. 2–335
Fernald, Merritt Lyndon, Oct. 5, 1873–Sept. 22, 1950.
  Supp. 4–266
Fernow, Bernhard Eduard, Jan. 7, 1851–Feb. 6, 1923.
  Vol. 3, Pt. 2–336
Fernow, Berthold, Nov. 28, 1837–Mar. 3, 1908.
  Vol. 3, Pt. 2–337
Ferree, Clarence Errol, Mar. 11, 1877–July 26, 1942.
  Supp. 3–269
Ferrel, William, Jan. 29, 1817–Sept. 18, 1891.
  Vol. 3, Pt. 2–338
Ferrero, Edward, Jan. 18, 1831–Dec. 11, 1899.
  Vol. 3, Pt. 2–338
Ferris, George Washington Gale, Feb. 14, 1859–Nov. 22, 1896. Vol. 3, Pt. 2–339
Ferris, Isaac, Oct. 9, 1798–June 16, 1873.
  Vol. 3, Pt. 2–340
Ferris, Jean Léon Gérôme, Aug. 8, 1863–Mar. 18, 1930.
  Vol. 3, Pt. 2–340
Ferris, Woodbridge Nathan, Jan. 6, 1853–Mar. 23, 1928.
  Vol. 3, Pt. 2–341
Ferry, Elisha Peyre, Aug. 9, 1825–Oct. 14, 1895.
  Vol. 3, Pt. 2–342
Ferry, Orris Sanford, Aug. 15, 1823–Nov. 21, 1875.
  Vol. 3, Pt. 2–342
Ferry, Thomas White, June 1, 1827–Oct. 14, 1896.
  Vol. 3, Pt. 2–343
Fersen, Hans Axel, Count Von, Sept. 4, 1755–June 20, 1810.
  Vol. 3, Pt. 2–344
Fess, Simeon Davidson, Dec. 11, 1861–Dec. 23, 1936.
  Supp. 2–180
Fessenden, Francis, Mar. 18, 1839–Jan. 2, 1906.
  Vol. 3, Pt. 2–345
Fessenden, James Deering, Sept. 28, 1833–Nov. 18, 1882.
  Vol. 3, Pt. 2–345
Fessenden, Reginald Aubrey, Oct. 6, 1866–July 22, 1932.
  Supp. 1–296
Fessenden, Samuel, July 16, 1784–Mar. 19, 1869.
  Vol. 3, Pt. 2–346
Fessenden, Thomas Green, Apr. 22, 1771–Nov. 11, 1837.
  Vol. 3, Pt. 2–347
Fessenden, William Pitt, Oct. 16, 1806–Sept. 8, 1869.
  Vol. 3, Pt. 2–348
Fetter, Frank Albert, Mar. 8, 1863–Mar. 21, 1949.
  Supp. 4–267

Foote, Arthur William, Mar. 5, 1853–Apr. 8, 1937.
Supp. 2–197
Foote, Henry Stuart, Feb. 28, 1804–May 20, 1880.
Vol. 3, Pt. 2–500
Foote, John Ambrose, June 9, 1874–Apr. 12, 1931.
Supp. 1–309
Foote, Lucius Harwood, Apr. 10, 1826–June 4, 1913.
Vol. 3, Pt. 2–501
Foote, Samuel Augustus. [See Foot, Samuel Augustus, 1780
–1846.]
Foote, William Henry, Dec. 20, 1794–Nov. 22, 1869.
Supp. 1–310
Foraker, Joseph Benson, July 5, 1846–May 10, 1917.
Vol. 3, Pt. 2–502
Forbes, Edwin, 1839–Mar. 6, 1895.
Vol. 3, Pt. 2–504
Forbes, Esther, June 28, 1891–Aug. 12, 1967.
Supp. 8–180
Forbes, John, 1710–Mar. 11, 1759.
Vol. 3, Pt. 2–504
Forbes, John, d. Sept. 17, 1783.
Vol. 3, Pt. 2–505
Forbes, John, 1769–May 13, 1823.
Vol. 3, Pt. 2–506
Forbes, John Murray, Aug. 13, 1771–June 14, 1831.
Vol. 3, Pt. 2–506
Forbes, John Murray, Feb. 23, 1813–Oct. 12, 1898.
Vol. 3, Pt. 2–507
Forbes, Robert Bennet, Sept. 18, 1804–Nov. 23, 1889.
Vol. 3, Pt. 2–508
Forbes, Stephen Alfred, May 29, 1844–Mar. 13, 1930.
Vol. 3, Pt. 2–509
Forbes, William Cameron, May 21, 1870–Dec. 24, 1959.
Supp. 6–210
Forbush, Edward Howe, Apr. 24, 1858–Mar. 8, 1929.
Vol. 3, Pt. 2–510
Force, Juliana Rieser, Dec. 25, 1876–Aug. 28, 1948.
Supp. 4–289
Force, Manning Ferguson, Dec. 17, 1824–May 8, 1899.
Vol. 3, Pt. 2–511
Force, Peter, Nov. 26, 1790–Jan. 23, 1868.
Vol. 3, Pt. 2–512
Ford, Daniel Sharp, Apr. 5, 1822–Dec. 24, 1899.
Vol. 3, Pt. 2–513
Ford, Edsel Bryant, Nov. 6, 1893–May 26, 1943.
Supp. 3–283
Ford, George Burdett, June 24, 1879–Aug. 13, 1930.
Supp. 1–311
Ford, Gordon Lester, Dec. 16, 1823–Nov. 14, 1891.
Vol. 3, Pt. 2–514
Ford, Guy Stanton, May 9, 1873–Dec. 29, 1962.
Supp. 7–252
Ford, Hannibal Choate, May 8, 1877–Mar. 13, 1955.
Supp. 5–228
Ford, Henry, July 30, 1863–Apr. 7, 1947.
Supp. 4–291
Ford, Henry Jones, Aug. 25, 1851–Aug. 29, 1925.
Vol. 3, Pt. 2–515
Ford, Jacob, Feb. 10, 1738–Jan 11, 1777.
Vol. 3, Pt. 2–516
Ford, John Baptiste, Nov. 17, 1811–May 1, 1903.
Vol. 3, Pt. 2–516
Ford, John Thomson, Apr. 16, 1829–Mar. 14, 1894.
Vol. 3, Pt. 2–517
Ford, Patrick, Apr. 12, 1835–Sept. 23, 1913.
Vol. 3, Pt. 2–518
Ford, Paul Leicester, Mar. 23, 1865–May 8, 1902.
Vol. 3, Pt. 2–518
Ford, Thomas, Dec. 5, 1800–Nov. 3, 1850.
Vol. 3, Pt. 2–520
Ford, Worthington Chauncey, Feb. 16, 1858–Mar. 7, 1941.
Supp. 3–285
Fordney, Joseph Warren, Nov. 5, 1853–Jan. 8, 1932.
Supp. 1–312
Fordyce, John Addison, Feb. 16, 1858–June 4, 1925.
Vol. 3, Pt. 2–521
Forepaugh, Adam, 1831–Jan. 22, 1890.
Vol. 3, Pt. 2–522
Forester, Cecil Scott, Aug. 27, 1899–Apr. 2, 1966.
Supp. 8–181
Forester, Frank. [See Herbert, Henry William, 1807–1858.]
Foresti, Eleutario Felice, 1793–Sept. 14, 1858.
Vol. 3, Pt. 2–522

Forgan, James Berwick, Apr. 11, 1852–Oct. 28, 1924.
Vol. 3, Pt. 2–523
Forman, David, Nov. 3, 1745–Sept. 12, 1797.
Vol. 3, Pt. 2–524
Forman, Joshua, Sept. 6, 1777–Aug. 4, 1848.
Vol. 3, Pt. 2–525
Forman, Justus Miles, Nov. 1, 1875–May 7, 1915.
Vol. 3, Pt. 2–526
Forney, John Wien, Sept. 30, 1817–Dec. 9, 1881.
Vol. 3, Pt. 2–526
Forney, Matthias Nace, Mar. 28, 1835–Jan. 14, 1908.
Vol. 3, Pt. 2–527
Forney, William Henry, Nov. 9, 1823–Jan. 16, 1894.
Vol. 3, Pt. 2–528
Forrest, Edwin, Mar. 9, 1806–Dec. 12, 1872.
Vol. 3, Pt. 2–529
Forrest, French, Oct. 4, 1796–Nov. 22, 1866.
Vol. 3, Pt. 2–531
Forrest, Nathan Bedford, July 13, 1821–Oct. 29, 1877.
Vol. 3, Pt. 2–532
Forrestal, James Vincent, Feb. 15, 1892–May 22, 1949.
Supp. 4–304
Forsyth, John, Oct. 22, 1780–Oct. 21, 1841.
Vol. 3, Pt. 2–533
Forsyth, John, Dec. 31, 1810–Oct. 17, 1886.
Vol. 3, Pt. 2–535
Forsyth, Thomas, Dec. 5, 1771–Oct. 29, 1833.
Vol. 3, Pt. 2–536
Forten, James, Sept. 2, 1766–Mar. 4, 1842.
Vol. 3, Pt. 2–536
Fortescue, Charles LeGeyt, Nov. 7, 1876–Dec. 4, 1936.
Supp. 2–198
Fortier, Alcée, June 5, 1856–Feb. 14, 1914.
Vol. 3, Pt. 2–537
Forward, Walter, Jan. 24, 1786–Nov. 24, 1852.
Vol. 3, Pt. 2–537
Forwood, William Henry, Sept. 7, 1838–May 12, 1915.
Vol. 3, Pt. 2–538
Fosdick, Charles Austin, Sept. 16, 1842–Aug. 22, 1915.
Vol. 3, Pt. 2–539
Fosdick, Harry Emerson, May 24, 1878–Oct. 5, 1969.
Supp. 8–182
Fosdick, William Whiteman, Jan. 28, 1825–Mar. 8, 1862.
Vol. 3, Pt. 2–540
Foshag, William Frederick, Mar. 17, 1894–May 21, 1956.
Supp. 6–212
Foss, Cyrus David, Jan. 17, 1834–Jan. 29, 1910.
Vol. 3, Pt. 2–540
Foss, Sam Walter, June 19, 1858–Feb. 26, 1911.
Vol. 3, Pt. 2–541
Foster, Abiel, Aug. 8, 1735–Feb. 6, 1806.
Vol. 3, Pt. 2–542
Foster, Abigail Kelley, Jan. 15, 1810–Jan. 14, 1887.
Vol. 3, Pt. 2–542
Foster, Benjamin, July 31, 1852–Jan. 28, 1926.
Vol. 3, Pt. 2–543
Foster, Charles, Apr. 12, 1828–Jan. 9, 1904.
Vol. 3, Pt. 2–544
Foster, Charles James, Nov. 24, 1820–Sept. 12, 1883.
Vol. 3, Pt. 2–545
Foster, David Skaats, Jan. 23, 1852–June 23, 1920.
Vol. 3, Pt. 2–545
Foster, Ephraim Hubbard, Sept. 17, 1794–Sept. 6, 1854.
Vol. 3, Pt. 2–546
Foster, Frank Hugh, June 18, 1851–Oct. 20, 1935.
Supp. 1–313
Foster, Frank Pierce, Nov. 26, 1841–Aug. 13, 1911.
Vol. 3, Pt. 2–546
Foster, George Burman, Apr. 2, 1858–Dec. 22, 1918.
Vol. 3, Pt. 2–547
Foster, Hannah Webster, 1759–Apr. 17, 1840.
Vol. 3, Pt. 2–548
Foster, John, 1648–Sept. 9, 1681.
Vol. 3, Pt. 2–549
Foster, John Gray, May 27, 1823–Sept. 2, 1874.
Vol. 3, Pt. 2–549
Foster, John Pierrepont Codrington, Mar. 2, 1847–Apr. 1,
1910. Vol. 3, Pt. 2–550
Foster, John Watson, Mar. 2, 1836–Nov. 15, 1917.
Vol. 3, Pt. 2–551
Foster, Judith Ellen Horton, Nov. 3, 1840–Aug. 11, 1910.
Vol. 3, Pt. 2–552

Foster, Lafayette Sabine, Nov. 22, 1806–Sept. 19, 1880.
Vol. 3, Pt. 2–553
Foster, Murphy James, Jan. 12, 1849–June 12, 1921.
Vol. 3, Pt. 2–554
Foster, Randolph Sinks, Feb. 22, 1820–May 1, 1903.
Vol. 3, Pt. 2–554
Foster, Robert Sanford, Jan. 27, 1834–Mar. 3, 1903.
Vol. 3, Pt. 2–555
Foster, Roger Sherman Baldwin, Apr. 21, 1857–Feb. 22, 1924. Vol. 3, Pt. 2–556
Foster, Stephen Collins, July 4, 1826–Jan. 13, 1864.
Vol. 3, Pt. 2–557
Foster, Stephen Symonds, Nov. 17, 1809–Sept. 8, 1881.
Vol. 3, Pt. 2–558
Foster, Theodore, Apr. 29, 1752–Jan. 13, 1828.
Vol. 3, Pt. 2–558
Foster, Thomas Jefferson, Jan. 1, 1843–Oct. 14, 1936.
Supp. 2–199
Foster, William Trufant, Jan. 18, 1879–Oct. 8, 1950.
Supp. 4–306
Foster, William Z., Feb. 25, 1881–Sept. 1, 1961.
Supp. 7–254
Foulk, George Clayton, Oct. 30, 1856–Aug. 6, 1893.
Vol. 3, Pt. 2–559
Foulke, William Dudley, Nov. 20, 1848–May 30, 1935.
Supp. 1–314
Foulois, Benjamin Delahauf, Dec. 9, 1879–Apr. 25, 1967.
Supp. 8–184
Fowke, Gerard, June 25, 1855–Mar. 5, 1933.
Supp. 1–315
Fowle, Daniel, October 1715–June 8, 1787.
Vol. 3, Pt. 2–560
Fowle, William Bentley, Oct. 17, 1795–Feb. 6, 1865.
Vol. 3, Pt. 2–561
Fowler, Charles Henry, Aug. 11, 1837–Mar. 20, 1908.
Vol. 3, Pt. 2–562
Fowler, Frank, July 12, 1852–Aug. 18, 1910.
Vol. 3, Pt. 2–562
Fowler, Gene, Mar. 8, 1890–July 2, 1960.
Supp. 6–213
Fowler, George Ryerson, Dec. 25, 1848–Feb. 6, 1906.
Vol. 3, Pt. 2–563
Fowler, Joseph Smith, Aug. 31, 1820–Apr. 1, 1902.
Vol. 3, Pt. 2–564
Fowler, Orin, July 29, 1791–Sept. 3, 1852.
Vol. 3, Pt. 2–565
Fowler, Orson Squire, Oct. 11, 1809–Aug. 18, 1887.
Vol. 3, Pt. 2–565
Fowler, Russell Story, May 1, 1874–Jan. 5, 1959.
Supp. 6–214
Fox, Charles Kemble, Aug. 15, 1833–Jan. 17, 1875.
Vol. 3, Pt. 2–566
Fox, Dixon Ryan, Dec. 7, 1887–Jan. 30, 1945.
Supp. 3–286
Fox, Fontaine Talbot, Jr., June 4, 1884–Aug. 9, 1964.
Supp. 7–257
Fox, George Washington Lafayette, July 3, 1825–Oct. 24, 1877. Vol. 3, Pt. 2–567
Fox, Gilbert, 1776–1807?.
Vol. 3, Pt. 2–567
Fox, Gustavus Vasa, June 13, 1821–Oct. 29, 1883.
Vol. 3, Pt. 2–568
Fox, Harry, Sept. 29, 1826–Sept. 4, 1883.
Vol. 3, Pt. 2–569
Fox, John William, Dec. 16, 1863–July 8, 1919.
Vol. 3, Pt. 2–570
Fox, Margaret, Oct. 7, 1833–Mar. 8, 1893.
Vol. 3, Pt. 2–570
Fox, Richard Kyle, Aug. 12, 1846–Nov. 14, 1922.
Vol. 3, Pt. 2–571
Fox, William, Jan. 1, 1879–May 8, 1952.
Supp. 5–229
Fox, Williams Carlton, May 20, 1855–Jan. 20, 1924.
Vol. 3, Pt. 2–572
Foxall, Henry, May 24, 1758–Dec. 11, 1823.
Vol. 3, Pt. 2–573
Foxx, James Emory, Oct. 22, 1907–July 21, 1967.
Supp. 8–186
Foy, Eddie, Mar. 9, 1856–Feb. 16, 1928.
Vol. 3, Pt. 2–573
Fraina, Louis C. [See Corey, Lewis.]
Fraley, Frederick, May 28, 1804–Sept. 23, 1901.
Vol. 3, Pt. 2–574

Frame, Alice Seymour Browne, Oct. 29, 1878–Aug. 16, 1941.
Supp. 3–287
Franchère, Gabriel, Nov. 3, 1786–Apr. 12, 1863.
Vol. 3, Pt. 2–575
Francis, Charles Spencer, June 17, 1853–Dec. 1, 1911.
Vol. 3, Pt. 2–576
Francis, Charles Stephen, Jan. 9, 1805–Dec. 1, 1887.
Vol. 3, Pt. 2–576
Francis, David Rowland, Oct. 1, 1850–Jan. 15, 1927.
Vol. 3, Pt. 2–577
Francis, James Bicheno, May 18, 1815–Sept. 18, 1892.
Vol. 3, Pt. 2–578
Francis, John Brown, May 31, 1791–Aug. 9, 1864.
Vol. 3, Pt. 2–579
Francis, John Morgan, Mar. 6, 1823–June 18, 1897.
Vol. 3, Pt. 2–580
Francis, John Wakefield, Nov. 17, 1789–Feb. 8, 1861.
Vol. 3, Pt. 2–581
Francis, Joseph, Mar. 12, 1801–May 10, 1893.
Vol. 3, Pt. 2–582
Francis, Kay, Jan. 13, 1905–Aug. 26, 1968.
Supp. 8–187
Francis, Paul James, Jan. 16, 1863–Feb. 8, 1940.
Supp. 2–201
Francis, Samuel Ward, Dec. 26, 1835–Mar. 25, 1886.
Vol. 3, Pt. 2–583
Francis, Tench, d. Aug. 16, 1758.
Vol. 3, Pt. 2–583
Francis Convers, Nov. 9, 1795–Apr. 7, 1863.
Vol. 3, Pt. 2–577
Franck, James, Aug. 26, 1882–May 21, 1964.
Supp. 7–258
Francke, Kuno, Sept. 27, 1855–June 25, 1930.
Vol. 3, Pt. 2–584
Frank, Glenn, Oct. 1, 1887–Sept. 15, 1940.
Supp. 2–202
Frank, Jerome, Sept. 10, 1889–Jan. 13, 1957.
Supp. 6–215
Frank, Lawrence Kelso, Dec. 6, 1890–Sept. 23, 1968.
Supp. 8–188
Frank, Philipp G., Mar. 20, 1884–July 21, 1966.
Supp. 8–189
Frank, Tenney, May 19, 1876–Apr. 3, 1939.
Supp. 2–203
Frank, Waldo David, Aug. 25, 1889–Jan. 9, 1967.
Supp. 8–191
Frankfurter, Alfred Moritz, Oct. 4, 1906–May 12, 1965.
Supp. 7–259
Frankfurter, Felix, Nov. 15, 1882–Feb. 22, 1965.
Supp. 7–260
Frankland, Lady Agnes Surriage, 1726–Apr. 23, 1783.
Vol. 3, Pt. 2–585
Franklin, Benjamin, Jan. 17, 1706–Apr. 17, 1790.
Vol. 3, Pt. 2–585
Franklin, Benjamin, Feb. 1, 1812–Oct. 22, 1878.
Vol. 3, Pt. 2–598
Franklin, Edward Curtis, Mar. 1, 1862–Feb. 13, 1937.
Supp. 2–205
Franklin, Fabian, Jan. 18, 1853–Jan. 9, 1939.
Supp. 2–206
Franklin, James, Feb. 4, 1696/7–February 1735.
Vol. 3, Pt. 2–599
Franklin, Jesse, Mar. 24, 1760–Aug. 31, 1823.
Vol. 3, Pt. 2–600
Franklin, Philip Albright Small, Feb. 1, 1871–Aug. 14, 1939.
Supp. 2–207
Franklin, William, 1731–Nov. 16, 1813.
Vol. 3, Pt. 2–600
Franklin, William Buel, Feb. 27, 1823–Mar. 8, 1903.
Vol. 3, Pt. 2–601
Franz, Shepherd Ivory, May 27, 1874–Oct. 14, 1933.
Supp. 1–316
Frary, Francis Cowles, July 9, 1884–Feb. 4, 1970.
Supp. 8–193
Frasch, Herman, Dec. 25, 1851?–May 1, 1914.
Vol. 3, Pt. 2–602
Fraser, Charles, Aug. 20, 1782–Oct. 5, 1860.
Vol. 3, Pt. 2–603
Fraser, James Earle, Nov. 4, 1876–Oct. 11, 1953.
Supp. 5–231
Fraser, Leon, Nov. 27, 1889–Apr. 8, 1945.
Supp. 3–289

Fraunces, Samuel, *c.* 1722–Oct. 10, 1795.
  Vol. 4, Pt. 1–1
Frayne, Hugh, Nov. 8. 1869–July 13, 1934.
  Supp. 1–317
Frazee, John, July 18, 1790–Feb. 24, 1852.
  Vol. 4, Pt. 1–1
Frazer, John Fries, July 8, 1812–Oct. 12, 1872.
  Vol. 4, Pt. 1–3
Frazer, Oliver, Feb. 4, 1808–Feb. 9, 1864.
  Vol. 4, Pt. 1–3
Frazer, Persifor, Aug. 9, 1736–Apr. 24, 1792.
  Vol. 4, Pt. 1–4
Frazer, Persifor, July 24, 1844–Apr. 9, 1909.
  Vol. 4, Pt. 1–4
Frazier, Charles Harrison, Apr. 19, 1870–July 26, 1936.
  Supp. 2–208
Frazier, Edward Franklin, Sept. 24, 1894–May 17, 1962.
  Supp. 7–265
Frazier, Lynn Joseph, Dec. 21, 1874–Jan. 11, 1947.
  Supp. 4–308
Frear, William, Mar. 24, 1860–Jan. 7, 1922.
  Vol. 4, Pt. 1–5
Freas, Thomas Bruce, Nov. 2, 1868–Mar. 15, 1928.
  Vol. 4, Pt. 1–6
Frederic, Harold, Aug. 19, 1856–Oct. 19, 1898.
  Vol. 4, Pt. 1–7
Freed, Alan J., Dec. 15, 1921–Jan. 20, 1965.
  Supp. 7–266
Freedman, Andrew, Sept. 1, 1860–Dec. 4, 1915.
  Vol. 4, Pt. 1–8
Freeman, Allen Weir, Jan. 7, 1881–July 3, 1954.
  Supp. 5–232
Freeman, Bernardus, d. 1741.
  Vol. 4, Pt. 1–8
Freeman, Douglas Southall, May 16, 1886–June 13, 1953.
  Supp. 5–233
Freeman, Frederick Kemper, June 15, 1841–Sept. 9, 1928.
  Vol. 4, Pt. 1–9
Freeman, James, Apr. 22, 1759–Nov. 14, 1835.
  Vol. 4, Pt. 1–10
Freeman, James Edwards, 1808–Nov. 21, 1884.
  Vol. 4, Pt. 1–11
Freeman, John Ripley, July 27, 1855–Oct. 6, 1932.
  Supp. 1–318
Freeman, Joseph, Oct. 7, 1897–Aug. 9, 1965.
  Supp. 7–268
Freeman, Mary Eleanor Wilkins, Oct. 31, 1852–Mar. 13, 1930. Vol. 4, Pt. 1–11
Freeman, Nathaniel, Mar. 28, 1741–Sept. 20, 1827.
  Vol. 4, Pt. 1–12
Freeman, Thomas, d. Nov. 8, 1821.
  Vol. 4, Pt. 1–13
Freer, Charles Lang, Feb. 25, 1856–Sept. 25, 1919.
  Vol. 4, Pt. 1–14
Frelinghuysen, Frederick Theodore, Aug. 4, 1817–May 20, 1885. Vol. 4, Pt. 1–15
Frelinghuysen, Frederick, Apr. 13, 1753–Apr. 13, 1804.
  Vol. 4, Pt. 1–15
Frelinghuysen, Theodore, Mar. 28, 1787–Apr. 12, 1862.
  Vol. 4, Pt. 1–16
Frelinghuysen, Theodorus Jacobus, 1691–*c.* 1748.
  Vol. 4, Pt. 1–17
Frémont, Jessie Benton, May 31, 1824–Dec. 27, 1902.
  Vol. 4, Pt. 1–18
Frémont, John Charles, Jan. 21, 1813–July 13, 1890.
  Vol. 4, Pt. 1–19
French, Aaron, Mar. 23, 1823–Mar. 24, 1902.
  Vol. 4, Pt. 1–23
French, Alice, Mar. 18, 1850–Jan. 9, 1934.
  Supp. 1–320
French, Daniel Chester, Apr. 20, 1850–Oct. 7, 1931.
  Supp. 1–320
French, Edwin Davis, Jan. 19, 1851–Dec. 8, 1906.
  Vol. 4, Pt. 1–24
French, Lucy Virginia Smith, Mar. 16, 1825–Mar. 31, 1881.
  Vol. 4, Pt. 1–25
French, Paul Comly, Mar. 19, 1903–June 3, 1960.
  Supp. 6–217
French, William Merchant Richardson, Oct. 1, 1843–June 3, 1914. Vol. 4, Pt. 1–26
French, William Henry, Jan. 13, 1815–May 20, 1881.
  Vol. 4, Pt. 1–25

Freneau, Philip Morin, Jan. 2, 1752–Dec. 19, 1832.
  Vol. 4, Pt. 1–27
Freund, Ernst, Jan. 30, 1864–Oct. 20, 1932.
  Supp. 1–323
Frey, John Philip, Feb. 24, 1871–Nov. 29, 1957.
  Supp. 6–218
Frey, Joseph Samuel Christian Frederick, Sept. 21, 1771–June 5, 1850. Vol. 4, Pt. 1–28
Frick, Henry Clay, Dec. 19, 1849–Dec. 2, 1919.
  Vol. 4, Pt. 1–29
Friday, *c.* 1822–May 13, 1881.
  Vol. 4, Pt. 1–31
Friedenwald, Aaron, Dec. 20, 1836–Aug. 26, 1902.
  Vol. 4, Pt. 1–31
Friedlaender, Israel, Sept. 8, 1876–July 5, 1920.
  Vol. 4, Pt. 1–31
Friedlaender, Walter Ferdinand, Mar. 10, 1873–Sept. 6, 1966. Supp. 8–194
Friedman, William Frederick, Sept. 24, 1891–Nov. 2, 1969.
  Supp. 8–195
Fries, Francis, Oct. 17, 1812–Aug. 1, 1863.
  Vol. 4, Pt. 1–33
Fries, John *c.* 1750–February 1818.
  Vol. 4, Pt. 1–34
Frieseke, Frederick Carl, Apr. 7, 1874–Aug. 24, 1939.
  Supp. 2–209
Frieze, Henry Simmons, Sept. 15, 1817–Dec. 7, 1889.
  Vol. 4, Pt. 1–34
Frisbie, Levi, Sept. 15, 1783–July 9, 1822.
  Vol. 4, Pt. 1–35
Frissell, Hollis Burke, July 14, 1851–Aug. 5, 1917.
  Vol. 4, Pt. 1–36
Fritschel, Conrad Sigmund, Dec. 2, 1833–Apr. 26, 1900.
  Vol. 4, Pt. 1–37
Fritschel, Gottfried Leonhard Wilhelm, Dec. 19, 1836–July 13, 1889. Vol. 4, Pt. 1–37
Fritz, John, Aug. 21, 1822–Feb. 13, 1913.
  Vol. 4, Pt. 1–38
Frizell, Joseph Palmer, Mar. 13, 1832–May 4, 1910.
  Vol. 4, Pt. 1–39
Frohman, Charles, June 17, 1860–May 7, 1915.
  Vol. 4, Pt. 1–40
Frohman, Daniel, Aug. 22, 1851–Dec. 26, 1940.
  Supp. 2–210
Fromm-Reichmann, Frieda, Oct. 23, 1889–Apr. 28, 1957.
  Supp. 6–219
Frost, Arthur Burdett, Jan. 17, 1851–June 22, 1928.
  Vol. 4, Pt. 1–41
Frost, Edwin Brant, July 14, 1866–May 14, 1935.
  Supp. 1–324
Frost, Holloway Halstead, Apr. 11, 1889–Jan. 26, 1935.
  Supp. 1–325
Frost, Robert Lee, Mar. 26, 1874–Jan. 29, 1963.
  Supp. 7–270
Frost, Wade Hampton, Mar. 3, 1880–Apr. 30, 1938.
  Supp. 2–211
Frothingham, Arthur Lincoln, June 21, 1859–July 28, 1923.
  Vol. 4, Pt. 1–42
Frothingham, Nathaniel Langdon, July 23, 1793–Apr. 4, 1870. Vol. 4, Pt. 1–43
Frothingham, Octavius Brooks, Nov. 26, 1822–Nov. 27, 1895. Vol. 4, Pt. 1–44
Frothingham, Paul Revere, July 6, 1864–Nov. 27, 1926.
  Vol. 4, Pt. 1–44
Frothingham, Richard, Jan. 31, 1812–Jan. 29, 1880.
  Vol. 4, Pt. 1–45
Fry, Birkett Davenport, June 24, 1822–Jan. 21, 1891.
  Vol. 4, Pt. 1–46
Fry, James Barnet, Feb. 22, 1827–July 11, 1894.
  Vol. 4, Pt. 1–47
Fry, Joshua, *c.* 1700–May 31, 1754.
  Vol. 4, Pt. 1–48
Fry, Richard, fl. 1731–1741.
  Vol. 4, Pt. 1–49
Fry, William Henry, Aug. 10, 1815–Dec. 21, 1864.
  Vol. 4, Pt. 1–49
Frye, Joseph, Mar. 8/19, 1711/12–July 25, 1794.
  Vol. 4, Pt. 1–50
Frye, William John ("Jack"), Mar. 18, 1904–Feb. 3, 1959.
  Supp. 6–220
Frye, William Pierce, Sept. 2, 1831–Aug. 8, 1911.
  Vol. 4, Pt. 1–51

Fryer, Douglas Henry, Nov. 7, 1891–Dec. 24, 1960.
Supp. 6–222
Fuertes, Estevan Antonio, May 10, 1838–Jan. 16, 1903.
Vol. 4, Pt. 1–52
Fuertes, Louis Agassiz, Feb. 7, 1874–Aug. 22, 1927.
Vol. 4, Pt. 1–53
Fullam, Frank L., Jan. 6, 1870–July 31, 1951.
Supp. 5–235
Fuller, Andrew S., Aug. 3, 1828–May 4, 1896.
Vol. 4, Pt. 1–53
Fuller, George, Jan. 17, 1822–Mar. 21, 1884.
Vol. 4, Pt. 1–54
Fuller, George Warren, Dec. 21, 1868–June 15, 1934.
Supp. 1–325
Fuller, Henry Blake, Jan. 9, 1857–July 28, 1929.
Vol. 4, Pt. 1–56
Fuller, Hiram, Sept. 6, 1814–Nov. 19, 1880.
Vol. 4, Pt. 1–57
Fuller, John Wallace, July 28, 1827–Mar. 12, 1891
Vol. 4, Pt. 1–58
Fuller, Joseph Vincent, Sept. 27, 1890–Apr. 1, 1932.
Supp. 1–327
Fuller, Levi Knight, Feb. 24, 1841–Oct. 10, 1896.
Vol. 4, Pt. 1–59
Fuller, Loie, Jan. 15, 1862–Jan. 1, 1928.
Vol. 4, Pt. 1–59
Fuller, Margaret. [See Fuller, Sarah Margaret, 1810–1850.]
Fuller, Melville Weston, Feb. 11, 1833–July 4, 1910.
Vol. 4, Pt. 1–60
Fuller, Richard, Apr. 22, 1804–Oct. 20, 1876.
Vol. 4, Pt. 1–62
Fuller, Robert Mason, Oct. 27, 1845–Dec. 28, 1919.
Vol. 4, Pt. 1–63
Fuller, Sarah Margaret, May 23, 1810–July 19, 1850.
Vol. 4, Pt. 1–63
Fuller, Thomas Charles, Feb. 27, 1832–Oct. 20, 1901.
Vol. 4, Pt. 1–66
Fullerton, George Stuart, Aug. 18, 1859–Mar. 23, 1925.
Vol. 4, Pt. 1–66
Fulton, John Farquhar, Nov. 1, 1899–May 29, 1960.
Supp. 6–222
Fulton, Justin Dewey, Mar. 1, 1828–Apr. 16, 1901.
Vol. 4, Pt. 1–68
Fulton, Robert, Nov. 14, 1765–Feb. 24, 1815.
Vol. 4, Pt. 1–68
Fulton, Robert Burwell, Apr. 8, 1849–May 29, 1919.
Vol. 4, Pt. 1–72
Funk, Casimir, Feb. 23, 1884–Nov. 20, 1967.
Supp. 8–197
Funk, Isaac Kauffman, Sept. 10, 1839–Apr. 4, 1912.
Vol. 4, Pt. 1–72
Funk, Wilfred John, Mar. 20, 1883–June 1, 1965.
Supp. 7–274
Funston, Frederick, Nov. 9, 1865–Feb. 19, 1917.
Vol. 4, Pt. 1–73
Furlow, Floyd Charles, Apr. 9, 1877–Apr. 26, 1923.
Vol. 4, Pt. 1–75
Furman, James Clement, Dec. 5, 1809–Mar. 3, 1891.
Vol. 4, Pt. 1–75
Furman, Richard, Oct. 9, 1755–Aug. 25, 1825.
Vol. 4, Pt. 1–76
Furnas, Robert Wilkinson, May 5, 1824–June 1, 1905.
Vol. 4, Pt. 1–77
Furness, Horace Howard, Nov. 2, 1833–Aug. 13, 1912.
Vol. 4, Pt. 1–78
Furness, Horace Howard, Jan. 24, 1865–Apr. 15, 1930.
Vol. 4, Pt. 1–79
Furness, William Henry, Apr. 20, 1802–Jan. 30, 1896.
Vol. 4, Pt. 1–80
Furst, Clyde Bowman, Aug. 29, 1873–Mar. 6, 1931.
Supp. 1–327
Furuseth, Andrew, Mar. 12, 1854–Jan. 22, 1938.
Supp. 2–212
Fussell, Bartholomew, Jan. 9, 1794–Feb. 15, 1871.
Vol. 4, Pt. 1–80

Gabb, William More, Jan. 20, 1839–May 30, 1878.
Vol. 4, Pt. 1–81
Gable, (William) Clark, Feb. 1, 1901–Nov. 10, 1960.
Supp. 6–224
Gabrilowitsch, Ossip, Feb. 7, 1878–Sept. 14, 1936.
Supp. 2–213

Gadsden, Christopher, Feb. 16, 1724–Aug. 28, 1805.
Vol. 4, Pt. 1–82
Gadsden, James, May 15, 1788–Dec. 26, 1858.
Vol. 4, Pt. 1–83
Gaffney, Margaret. [See Haughery, Margaret Gaffney, c. 1814–1882.]
Gág, Wanda (Hazel), Mar. 11, 1893–June 27, 1946.
Supp. 4–309
Gage, Frances Dana Barker, Oct. 12, 1808–Nov. 10, 1884.
Vol. 4, Pt. 1–84
Gage, Lyman Judson, June 28, 1836–Jan. 26, 1927.
Vol. 4, Pt. 1–85
Gage, Matilda Joslyn, Mar. 24, 1826–Mar. 18, 1898.
Vol. 4, Pt. 1–86
Gage, Thomas, 1721–Apr. 2, 1787.
Vol. 4, Pt. 1–87
Gaillard, David Du Bose, Sept. 4, 1859–Dec. 5, 1913.
Vol. 4, Pt. 1–88
Gaillard, Edwin Samuel, Jan. 16, 1827–Feb. 2, 1885.
Vol. 4, Pt. 1–90
Gaillard, John, Sept. 5, 1765–Feb. 26, 1826.
Vol. 4, Pt. 1–90
Gaillardet, Théodore Frédéric, Apr. 7, 1808–Aug. 13, 1882.
Vol. 4, Pt. 1–91
Gailor, Thomas Frank, Sept. 17, 1856–Oct. 3, 1935.
Supp. 1–329
Gaine, Hugh, 1726/27–Apr. 25, 1807.
Vol. 4, Pt. 1–91
Gaines, Edmund Pendleton, Mar. 20, 1777–June 6, 1849.
Vol. 4, Pt. 1–92
Gaines, George Strother, c. 1784–Jan. 21, 1873.
Vol. 4, Pt. 1–93
Gaines, John Pollard, Sept. 22, 1795–Dec. 9, 1857.
Vol. 4, Pt. 1–94
Gaines, Reuben Reid, Oct. 30, 1836–Oct. 13, 1914.
Vol. 4, Pt. 1–95
Gaines, Wesley John, Oct. 4, 1840–Jan. 12, 1912.
Vol. 4, Pt. 1–96
Gaither, Horace Rowan, Jr., Nov. 23, 1909–Apr. 7, 1961.
Supp. 7–275
Galberry, Thomas, 1833–Oct. 10, 1878.
Vol. 4, Pt. 1–97
Galbreath, Charles Burleigh, Feb. 25, 1858–Feb. 23, 1934.
Supp. 1–329
Gale, Benjamin, Dec. 14, 1715–May 6, 1790.
Vol. 4, Pt. 1–97
Gale, Elbridge, Dec. 25, 1824–Nov. 7, 1907.
Vol. 4, Pt. 1–98
Gale, George Washington, Dec. 3, 1789–Sept. 13, 1861.
Vol. 4, Pt. 1–99
Gale, Henry Gordon, Sept. 12, 1874–Nov. 16, 1942.
Supp. 3–290
Gale, Zona, Aug. 26, 1874–Dec. 27, 1938.
Supp. 2–215
Gales, Joseph, Feb. 4, 1761–Aug. 24, 1841.
Vol. 4, Pt. 1–99
Gales, Joseph, Apr. 10, 1786–July 21, 1860.
Vol. 4, Pt. 1–100
Gall, c. 1840–Dec. 5, 1894.
Vol. 4, Pt. 1–101
Gallagher,, May 27, 1881–July 31, 1952.
Supp. 5–235
Gallagher, Hugh Patrick, Mar. 26, 1815–Mar. 10, 1882.
Vol. 4, Pt. 1–102
Gallagher, William Davis, Aug. 21, 1808–June 27, 1894.
Vol. 4, Pt. 1–102
Gallatin, Abraham Alfonse Albert, Jan. 29, 1761–Aug. 12, 1849. Vol. 4, Pt. 1–103
Gallaudet, Edward Miner, Feb. 5, 1837–Sept. 26, 1917.
Vol. 4, Pt. 1–110
Gallaudet, Thomas, June 3, 1822–Aug. 27, 1902.
Vol. 4, Pt. 1–110
Gallaudet, Thomas Hopkins, Dec. 10, 1787–Sept. 10, 1851.
Vol. 4, Pt. 1–111
Galli-Curci, Amelita, Nov. 18, 1882–Nov. 26, 1963.
Supp. 7–277
Gallier, James, July 24, 1798–May 16, 1868.
Supp. 1–330
Gallinger, Jacob Harold, Mar. 28, 1837–Aug. 17, 1918.
Vol. 4, Pt. 1–112
Gallitzin, Demetrius Augustine, Dec. 22, 1770–May 6, 1840.
Vol. 4, Pt. 1–113

Galloway, Beverly Thomas, Oct. 16, 1863–June 13, 1938.
  Supp. 2–217
Galloway, Charles Betts, Sept. 1, 1849–May 12, 1909.
  Vol. 4, Pt. 1–115
Galloway, Joseph, c. 1731–Aug. 29, 1803.
  Vol. 4, Pt. 1–116
Galloway, Samuel, Mar. 22, 1811–Apr. 5, 1872.
  Vol. 4, Pt. 1–117
Gallup, Joseph Adams, Mar. 30, 1769–Oct. 12, 1849.
  Vol. 4, Pt. 1–118
Gally, Merritt, Aug. 15, 1838–Mar. 7, 1916.
  Vol. 4, Pt. 1–118
Galpin, Charles Josiah, Mar. 16, 1864–June 1, 1947.
  Supp. 4–311
Gálvez, Bernardo de, July 23, 1746–Nov. 30, 1786.
  Vol. 4, Pt. 1–119
Gamble, Hamilton Rowan, Nov. 29, 1798–Jan. 31, 1864.
  Vol. 4, Pt. 1–120
Gambrell, James Bruton, Aug. 21, 1841–June 10, 1921.
  Vol. 4, Pt. 1–121
Gammon, Elijah Hedding, Dec. 23, 1819–July 3, 1891.
  Vol. 4, Pt. 1–122
Gamow, George, Mar. 4, 1904–Aug. 20, 1968.
  Supp. 8–198
Gannett, Ezra Stiles, May 4, 1801–Aug. 26, 1871.
  Vol. 4, Pt. 1–122
Gannett, Frank Ernest, Sept. 15, 1876–Dec. 3, 1957.
  Supp. 6–226
Gannett, Henry, Aug. 24, 1846–Nov. 5, 1914.
  Vol. 4, Pt. 1–123
Gannett, William Channing, Mar. 13, 1840–Dec. 15, 1923.
  Vol. 4, Pt. 1–124
Gano, John, July 22, 1727–Aug. 10, 1804.
  Vol. 4, Pt. 1–125
Gano, Stephen, Dec. 25, 1762–Aug. 18, 1828.
  Vol. 4, Pt. 1–126
Gansevoort, Leonard, July, 1751–Aug. 26, 1810.
  Vol. 4, Pt. 1–126
Gansevoort, Peter, July, 1749–July 2, 1812.
  Vol. 4, Pt. 1–127
Ganso, Emil, Apr. 14, 1895–Apr. 18, 1941.
  Supp. 3–291
Ganss, Henry George, Feb. 22, 1855–Dec. 25, 1912.
  Vol. 4, Pt. 1–128
Gantt, Henry Laurence, May 20, 1861–Nov. 23, 1919.
  Vol. 4, Pt. 1–129
Garakonthie, Daniel, c. 1600–1676.
  Vol. 4, Pt. 1–130
Garcelon, Alonzo, May 6, 1813–Dec. 8, 1906.
  Vol. 4, Pt. 1–131
Garcés, Francisco Tomás Hermenegildo, Apr. 12, 1738–July
  18, 1781. Vol. 4, Pt. 1–132
Garden, Alexander, c. 1730–Apr. 15, 1791.
  Vol. 4, Pt. 1–132
Garden, Alexander, Dec. 4, 1757–Feb. 24, 1829.
  Vol. 4, Pt. 1–133
Garden, Mary, Feb. 20, 1874–Jan. 3, 1967.
  Supp. 8–200
Gardener, Helen Hamilton, Jan. 21, 1853–July 26, 1925.
  Vol. 4, Pt. 1–134
Gardiner, Sir Christopher, fl. 1630–1632.
  Vol. 4, Pt. 1–135
Gardiner, Harry Norman, Nov. 6, 1855–Dec. 29, 1927.
  Supp. 1–331
Gardiner, James Terry, May 6, 1842–Sept. 10, 1912.
  Vol. 4, Pt. 1–136
Gardiner, John Sylvester John, June, 1765–July 29, 1830.
  Vol. 4, Pt. 1–137
Gardiner, John, Dec. 4, 1737–Oct. 15, 1793.
  Vol. 4, Pt. 1–136
Gardiner, Lion, 1599–1663.
  Vol. 4, Pt. 1–138
Gardiner, Robert Hallowell, Feb. 10, 1782–Mar. 22, 1864.
  Vol. 4, Pt. 1–139
Gardiner, Silvester, June 29, 1708–Aug. 8, 1786.
  Vol. 4, Pt. 1–139
Gardner, Caleb, Jan. 24, 1739–Dec. 24, 1806.
  Vol. 4, Pt. 1–140
Gardner, Charles Kitchel, June 24, 1787–Nov. 1, 1869.
  Vol. 4, Pt. 1–141
Gardner, Erle Stanley, July 17, 1889–Mar. 11, 1970.
  Supp. 8–202

Gardner, Gilson, Mar. 16, 1869–Aug. 16, 1935.
  Supp. 1–333
Gardner, Helen, Mar. 17, 1878–June 4, 1946.
  Supp. 4–312
Gardner, Henry Joseph, June 14, 1818–July 21, 1892.
  Vol. 4, Pt. 1–142
Gardner, Isabella Stewart, Apr. 14, 1840–July 17, 1924.
  Vol. 4, Pt. 1–142
Gardner, John Lane, Aug. 1, 1793–Feb. 19, 1869.
  Vol. 4, Pt. 1–144
Gardner, Leroy Upson, Dec. 9, 1888–Oct. 24, 1946.
  Supp. 4–313
Gardner, Oliver Maxwell, Mar. 22, 1882–Feb. 6, 1947.
  Supp. 4–315
Garey, Thomas Andrew, July 7, 1830–Aug. 20, 1909.
  Vol. 4, Pt. 1–144
Garfield, Harry Augustus, Oct. 11, 1863–Dec. 12, 1942.
  Supp. 3–292
Garfield, James Abram, Nov. 19, 1831–Sept. 19, 1881.
  Vol. 4, Pt. 1–145
Garfield, James Rudolph, Oct. 17, 1865–Mar. 24, 1950.
  Supp. 4–316
Garfield, John, Mar. 4, 1913–May 19, 1952.
  Supp. 5–237
Garis, Howard Roger, Apr. 25, 1873–Nov. 5, 1962.
  Supp. 7–278
Garland, Augustus Hill, June 11, 1832–Jan. 26, 1899.
  Vol. 4, Pt. 1–150
Garland, Hamlin, Sept. 14, 1860–Mar. 4, 1940.
  Supp. 2–218
Garland, Judy, June 10, 1922–June 22, 1969.
  Supp. 8–203
Garland, Landon Cabell, Mar. 21, 1810–Feb. 12, 1895.
  Vol. 4, Pt. 1–151
Garlick, Theodatus, Mar. 30, 1805–Dec. 9, 1884.
  Vol. 4, Pt. 1–152
Garman, Charles Edward, Dec. 18, 1850–Feb. 9, 1907.
  Vol. 4, Pt. 1–153
Garman, Samuel, June 5, 1843–Sept. 30, 1927.
  Vol. 4, Pt. 1–154
Garner, James Wilford, Nov. 22, 1871–Dec. 9, 1938.
  Supp. 2–220
Garner, John Nance, Nov. 22, 1868–Nov. 7, 1967.
  Supp. 8–205
Garnet, Henry Highland, 1815–Feb. 13, 1882.
  Vol. 4, Pt. 1–154
Garnett, Alexander Yelverton Peyton, Sept. 19, 1819–July
  11, 1888. Vol. 4, Pt. 1–155
Garnett, James Mercer, June 8, 1770–Apr. 23, 1843.
  Vol. 4, Pt. 1–156
Garnett, James Mercer, Apr. 24, 1840–Feb. 18, 1916.
  Vol. 4, Pt. 1–157
Garnett, Muscoe Russell Hunter, July 25, 1821–Feb. 14,
  1864. Vol. 4, Pt. 1–158
Garnett, Robert Selden, Dec. 16, 1819–July 13, 1861.
  Vol. 4, Pt. 1–158
Garrard, James, Jan. 14, 1749–Jan. 19, 1822.
  Vol. 4, Pt. 1–159
Garrard, Kenner, c. Sept. 1, 1828–May 15, 1879.
  Vol. 4, Pt. 1–16
Garreau, Armand, Sept. 13, 1817–Mar. 28, 1865.
  Vol. 4, Pt. 1–160
Garret, William Robertson, Apr. 12, 1839–Feb. 12, 1904.
  Vol. 4, Pt. 1–165
Garretson, Austin Bruce, Sept. 14, 1856–Feb. 27, 1931.
  Supp. 1–333
Garretson, James Edmund, Oct. 18, 1828–Oct. 26, 1895.
  Vol. 4, Pt. 1–161
Garrett, Edmund Henry, Oct. 19, 1853–Apr. 2, 1929.
  Vol. 4, Pt. 1–162
Garrett, Finis James, Aug. 26, 1875–May 25, 1956.
  Supp. 6–227
Garrett, John Work, July 31, 1820–Sept. 26, 1884.
  Vol. 4, Pt. 1–163
Garrett, Robert, May 2, 1783–Feb. 4, 1857.
  Vol. 4, Pt. 1–164
Garrett, Thomas, Aug. 21, 1789–Jan. 25, 1871.
  Vol. 4, Pt. 1–164
Garrettson, Freeborn, Aug. 15, 1752–Sept. 26, 1827.
  Vol. 4, Pt. 1–166
Garrigan, Philip Joseph, Sept. 8, 1840–Oct. 14, 1919.
  Vol. 4, Pt. 1–167

Garrison, Cornelius Kingsland, Mar. 1, 1809–May 1, 1885.
Vol. 4, Pt. 1–167
Garrison, Fielding Hudson, Nov. 5, 1870–Apr. 18, 1935.
Supp. 1–334
Garrison, Lindley Miller, Nov. 28, 1864–Oct. 19, 1932.
Supp. 1–335
Garrison, William Re Tallack, June 18, 1834–July 1, 1882.
Vol. 4, Pt. 1–172
Garrison, William Lloyd, Dec. 10, 1805–May 24, 1879.
Vol. 4, Pt. 1–168
Garry, Spokane, 1811–Jan. 13, 1892.
Vol. 4, Pt. 1–173
Gartrell, Lucius Jeremiah, Jan. 7, 1821–Apr. 7, 1891.
Vol. 4, Pt. 1–173
Garvey, Marcus Moziah, Aug. 17, 1887–June 10, 1940.
Supp. 2–221
Garvin, Lucius Fayette Clark, Nov. 13, 1841–Oct. 2, 1922.
Vol. 4, Pt. 1–174
Gary, Elbert Henry, Oct. 8, 1846–Aug. 15, 1927.
Vol. 4, Pt. 1–175
Gary, James Albert, Oct. 22, 1833–Oct. 31, 1920.
Vol. 4, Pt. 1–176
Gary, Martin Witherspoon, Mar. 25, 1831–Apr. 9, 1881.
Vol. 4, Pt. 1–177
Gaskill, Harvey Freeman, Jan. 19, 1845–Apr. 1, 1889.
Vol. 4, Pt. 1–177
Gass, Patrick, June 12, 1771–Apr. 30, 1870.
Vol. 4, Pt. 1–178
Gasser, Herbert Spencer, July 5, 1888–May 11, 1963.
Supp. 7–279
Gasson, Thomas Ignatius, Sept. 23, 1859–Feb. 27, 1930.
Vol. 4, Pt. 1–179
Gaston, Herbert Earle, Aug. 20, 1881–Dec. 7, 1956.
Supp. 6–228
Gaston, James McFadden, Dec. 27, 1824–Nov. 15, 1903.
Vol. 4, Pt. 1–179
Gaston, William, Oct. 3, 1820–Jan. 19, 1894.
Vol. 4, Pt. 1–181
Gaston, William, Sept. 19, 1778–Jan. 23, 1844.
Vol. 4, Pt. 1–180
Gates, Caleb Frank, Oct. 18, 1857–Apr. 9, 1946.
Supp. 4–318
Gates, Frederick Taylor, July 2, 1853–Feb. 6, 1929.
Vol. 4, Pt. 1–182
Gates, George Augustus, Jan. 24, 1851–Nov. 20, 1912.
Vol. 4, Pt. 1–183
Gates, Horatio, c. 1728/29–Apr. 10, 1806.
Vol. 4, Pt. 1–184
Gates, John Warne, May 8, 1855–Aug. 9, 1911.
Vol. 4, Pt. 1–188
Gates, Sir Thomas, d. 1621.
Vol. 4, Pt. 1–190
Gates, Thomas Sovereign, Mar. 21, 1873–Apr. 8, 1948.
Supp. 4–320
Gatling, Richard Jordan, Sept. 12, 1818–Feb. 26, 1903.
Vol. 4, Pt. 1–191
Gatschet, Albert Samuel, Oct. 3, 1832–Mar. 16, 1907.
Vol. 4, Pt. 1–192
Gatti-Casazza, Giulio, Feb. 3, 1869–Sept. 2, 1940.
Supp. 2–222
Gaul, William Gilbert, Mar. 31, 1855–Dec. 21, 1919.
Vol. 4, Pt. 1–193
Gauss, Christian Frederick, Feb. 2, 1878–Nov. 1, 1951.
Supp. 5–238
Gauss, Clarence Edward, Jan. 12, 1887–Apr. 8, 1960.
Supp. 6–229
Gaut, John McReynolds, Oct. 1, 1841–Dec. 19, 1918.
Vol. 4, Pt. 1–193
Gauvreau, Emile Henry, Feb. 4, 1891–Oct. 15, 1956.
Supp. 6–231
Gavin, Frank Stanton Burns, Oct. 31, 1890–Mar. 20, 1938.
Supp. 2–223
Gaxton, William, Dec. 2, 1893–Feb. 2, 1963.
Supp. 7–281
Gay, Ebenezer, Aug. 15, 1696–Mar. 18, 1787.
Vol. 4, Pt. 1–194
Gay, Edwin Francis, Oct. 27, 1867–Feb. 8, 1946.
Supp. 4–321
Gay, Frederick Parker, July 22, 1874–July 14, 1939.
Supp. 2–224
Gay, Sydney Howard, May 22, 1814–June 25, 1888.
Vol. 4, Pt. 1–195

Gay, Winckworth Allan, Aug. 18, 1821–Feb. 23, 1910.
Vol. 4, Pt. 1–195
Gayarré, Charles Étienne Arthur, Jan. 9, 1805–Feb. 11, 1895.
Vol. 4, Pt. 1–196
Gayle, John, Sept. 11, 1792–July 21, 1859.
Vol. 4, Pt. 1–197
Gayler, Charles, Apr. 1, 1820–May 28, 1892.
Vol. 4, Pt. 1–198
Gayley, James, Oct. 11, 1855–Feb. 25, 1920.
Vol. 4, Pt. 1–198
Gaylord, Willis, 1792–Mar. 27, 1844.
Vol. 4, Pt. 1–199
Gaynor, William Jay, Feb. 23, 1849–Sept. 10, 1913.
Vol. 4, Pt. 1–200
Gayoso de Lemos, Manuel, c. 1752–July 18, 1799.
Vol. 4, Pt. 1–20
Gear, John Henry, Apr. 7, 1825–July 14, 1900.
Vol. 4, Pt. 1–202
Geary, John White, Dec. 30, 1819–Feb. 8, 1873.
Vol. 4, Pt. 1–203
Geddes, James, July 22, 1763–Aug. 19, 1838.
Vol. 4, Pt. 1–204
Geddes, James Loraine, Mar. 19, 1827–Feb. 21, 1887.
Vol. 4, Pt. 1–205
Geddes, Norman Bel, Apr. 27, 1893–May 8, 1958.
Supp. 6–232
Geers, Edward Franklin, Jan. 25, 1851–Sept. 3, 1924.
Vol. 4, Pt. 1–206
Gehrig, Henry Louis, June 19, 1903–June 2, 1941.
Supp. 3–294
Geiger, Roy Stanley, Jan. 25, 1885–Jan. 23, 1947.
Supp. 4–322
Gellatly, John, 1853–Nov. 8, 1931.
Supp. 1–337
Gemünder, August Martin Ludwig, Mar. 22, 1814–Sept. 7, 1895. Vol. 4, Pt. 1–207
Gemünder, George, Apr. 13, 1816–Jan. 15, 1899. [See Gemünder, August M. L.]
Genet, Edmond Charles, Jan. 8, 1763–July 15, 1834.
Vol. 4, Pt. 1–207
Genin, John Nicholas, Oct. 19, 1819–Apr. 30, 1878.
Vol. 4, Pt. 1–209
Genovese, Vito, Nov. 31[?], 1897–Feb. 14, 1969.
Supp. 8–207
Genth, Frederick Augustus, May 17, 1820–Feb. 2, 1893.
Vol. 4, Pt. 1–209
Genthe, Arnold, Jan. 8, 1869, Aug. 9, 1942.
Supp. 3–295
Genung, John Franklin, Jan. 27, 1850–Oct. 1, 1919.
Vol. 4, Pt. 1–210
George, Gladys, Sept. 13, 1904–Dec. 8, 1954.
Supp. 5–240
George, Grace, Dec. 25, 1879–May 19, 1961.
Supp. 7–282
George, Henry, Nov. 3, 1862–Nov. 14, 1916.
Vol. 4, Pt. 1–215
George, Henry, Sept. 2, 1839–Oct. 29, 1897.
Vol. 4, Pt. 1–211
George, James Zachariah, Oct. 20, 1826–Aug. 14, 1897.
Vol. 4, Pt. 1–216
George, Walter Franklin, Jan. 29, 1878–Aug. 4, 1957.
Supp. 6–234
George, William Reuben, June 4, 1866–Apr. 25, 1936.
Supp. 2–226
Gerard, James Watson, 1794–Feb. 7, 1874.
Vol. 4, Pt. 1–217
Gerard, James Watson, Aug. 25, 1867–Sept. 6, 1951.
Supp. 5–241
Gerber, (Daniel) Frank, Jan. 12, 1873–Oct. 7, 1952.
Supp. 5–242
Gerber, Daniel (Frank), May 6, 1898–Mar. 16, 1974.
Supp. 5–242
Gerhard, William Wood, July 23, 1809–Apr. 28, 1872.
Vol. 4, Pt. 1–218
Gerhart, Emanuel Vogel, June 13, 1817–May 6, 1904.
Vol. 4, Pt. 1–219
Gericke, Wilhelm, Apr. 18, 1845–Oct. 27, 1925.
Vol. 4, Pt. 1–219
Gernsback, Hugo, Aug. 16, 1884–Aug. 19, 1967.
Supp. 8–209
Geronimo, June 1829–Feb. 17, 1909.
Vol. 4, Pt. 1–220

Gerrish, Frederic Henry, Mar. 21, 1845–Sept. 8, 1920.
    Vol. 4, Pt. 1–221
Gerry, Elbridge, July 17, 1744–Nov. 23, 1814.
    Vol. 4, Pt. 1–222
Gerry, Elbridge Thomas, Dec. 25, 1837–Feb. 18, 1927.
    Vol. 4, Pt. 1–227
Gershwin, George, Sept. 26, 1898–July 11, 1937.
    Supp. 2–227
Gerster, Arpad Geyza Charles, Dec. 22, 1848–Mar. 11, 1923.
    Vol. 4, Pt. 1–228
Gerstle, Lewis, Dec. 17, 1824–Nov. 19, 1902.
    Vol. 4, Pt. 1–229
Gesell, Arnold Lucius, June 21, 1880–May 29, 1961.
    Supp. 7–283
Gest, Morris, Jan. 17, 1881–May 16, 1942.
    Supp. 3–296
Getty, George Washington, Oct. 2, 1819–Oct. 1, 1901.
    Vol. 4, Pt. 1–230
Geyer, Henry Sheffie, Dec. 9, 1790–Mar. 5, 1859.
    Vol. 4, Pt. 1–231
Ghent, William James, Apr. 29, 1866–July 10, 1942.
    Supp. 3–297
Gherardi, Bancroft, Nov. 10, 1832–Dec. 10, 1903.
    Vol. 4, Pt. 1–232
Gherardi, Bancroft, Apr. 6, 1873–Aug. 14, 1941.
    Supp. 3–298
Gholson, Samuel Jameson, May 19, 1808–Oct. 16, 1883.
    Vol. 4, Pt. 1–232
Gholson, Thomas Saunders, Dec. 9, 1808–Dec. 12, 1868.
    Vol. 4, Pt. 1–233
Gholson, William Yates, Dec. 25, 1807–Sept. 21, 1870.
    Vol. 4, Pt. 1–234
Giannini, Amadeo Peter, May 6, 1870–June 3, 1949.
    Supp. 4–324
Gibault, Pierre, Apr. 1737–1804.
    Vol. 4, Pt. 1–234
Gibbes, Robert Wilson, July 8, 1809–Oct. 15, 1866.
    Vol. 4, Pt. 1–235
Gibbes, William Hasell, Mar. 16, 1754–Feb. 13, 1834.
    Vol. 4, Pt. 1–236
Gibbon, John, Apr. 20, 1827–Feb. 6, 1896.
    Vol. 4, Pt. 1–236
Gibbons, Abigail Hopper, Dec. 7, 1801–Jan. 16, 1893.
    Vol. 4, Pt. 1–237
Gibbons, Floyd, July 16, 1887–Sept. 24, 1939.
    Supp. 2–230
Gibbons, Herbert Adams, Apr. 9, 1880–Aug. 7, 1934.
    Supp. 1–337
Gibbons, James, July 23, 1834–Mar. 24, 1921.
    Vol. 4, Pt. 1–238
Gibbons, James Sloan, July 1, 1810–Oct. 17, 1892.
    Vol. 4, Pt. 1–242
Gibbons, Thomas, Dec. 15, 1757–May 16, 1826.
    Vol. 4, Pt. 1–242
Gibbons, William, Apr. 8, 1726–Sept. 27, 1800.
    Vol. 4, Pt. 1–243
Gibbons, William, Aug. 10, 1781–July 25, 1845.
    Vol. 4, Pt. 1–244
Gibbs, Arthur Hamilton, Mar. 9, 1888–May 24, 1964.
    Supp. 7–285
Gibbs, George, Jan. 7, 1776–Aug. 5, 1833.
    Vol. 4, Pt. 1–244
Gibbs, George, July 17, 1815–Apr. 9, 1873.
    Vol. 4, Pt. 1–245
Gibbs, George, Apr. 19, 1861–May 19, 1940.
    Supp. 2–231
Gibbs, James Ethan Allen, Aug. 1, 1829–Nov. 25, 1902.
    Vol. 4, Pt. 1–246
Gibbs, Josiah Willard, Apr. 30, 1790–Mar. 25, 1861.
    Vol. 4, Pt. 1–247
Gibbs, Josiah Willard, Feb. 11, 1839–Apr. 28, 1903.
    Vol. 4, Pt. 1–248
Gibbs, Oliver Wolcott, Feb. 21, 1822–Dec. 9, 1908.
    Vol. 4, Pt. 1–251
Gibbs, (Oliver) Wolcott, Mar. 15, 1902–Aug. 16, 1958.
    Supp. 6–236
Gibbs, Wolcott. [See Gibbs, Oliver Wolcott, 1822–1908.]
Gibson, Charles Dana, Sept. 14, 1867–Dec. 23, 1944.
    Supp. 3–300
Gibson, Edmund Richard ("Hoot"), Aug. 6, 1892–Aug. 23, 1962. Supp. 7–286
Gibson, George, Oct. 1747–Dec. 14, 1791.
    Vol. 4, Pt. 1–252

Gibson, John, May 23, 1740–Apr. 16, 1822.
    Vol. 4, Pt. 1–253
Gibson, John Bannister, Nov. 8, 1780–May 3, 1853.
    Vol. 4, Pt. 1–254
Gibson, Joshua, Dec. 21, 1911–Jan. 20, 1947.
    Supp. 4–327
Gibson, Paris, July 1, 1830–Dec. 16, 1920.
    Vol. 4, Pt. 1–256
Gibson, Randall Lee, Sept. 10, 1832–Dec. 15, 1892.
    Vol. 4, Pt. 1–256
Gibson, Walter Murray, 1823–Jan. 21, 1888.
    Vol. 4, Pt. 1–257
Gibson, William, Mar. 14, 1788–Mar. 2, 1868.
    Vol. 4, Pt. 1–258
Gibson, William Hamilton, Oct. 5, 1850–July 16, 1896.
    Vol. 4, Pt. 1–259
Giddings, Franklin Henry, Mar. 23, 1885–June 11, 1931.
    Supp. 1–339
Giddings, Joshua Reed, Oct. 6, 1795–May 27, 1864.
    Vol. 4, Pt. 1–260
Gideon, Peter Miller, Feb. 9, 1820–Oct. 27, 1899.
    Vol. 4, Pt. 1–261
Gidley, James Williams, Jan. 7, 1866–Sept. 26, 1931.
    Supp. 1–340
Giesler-Anneke, Mathilde Franziska, Apr. 3, 1817–Nov. 25, 1884. Vol. 4, Pt. 1–262
Gifford, Robert Swain, Dec. 23, 1840–Jan. 15, 1905.
    Vol. 4, Pt. 1–263
Gifford, Sanford Robinson, July 10, 1823–Aug. 29, 1880.
    Vol. 4, Pt. 1–264
Gifford, Sanford Robinson, Jan. 8, 1892–Feb. 25, 1944.
    Supp. 3–301
Gifford, Walter Sherman, Jan. 10, 1885–May 7, 1966.
    Supp. 8–210
Gihon, Albert Leary, Sept. 28, 1833–Nov. 17, 1901.
    Vol. 4, Pt. 1–265
Gilbert, Alfred Carlton, Feb. 15, 1884–Jan. 24, 1961.
    Supp. 7–287
Gilbert, Anne Hartley, Oct. 21, 1821–Dec. 2, 1904.
    Vol. 4, Pt. 1–266
Gilbert, Cass, Nov. 24, 1859–May 17, 1934.
    Supp. 1–341
Gilbert, Charles Henry, Dec. 5, 1859–Apr. 20, 1928.
    Vol. 4, Pt. 1–267
Gilbert, Eliphalet Wheeler, Dec. 19, 1793–July 31, 1853.
    Vol. 4, Pt. 1–267
Gilbert, Grove Karl, May 6, 1843–May 1, 1918.
    Vol. 4, Pt. 1–268
Gilbert, Henry Franklin Belknap, Sept. 26, 1868–May 19, 1928. Vol. 4, Pt. 1–269
Gilbert, John, July 10, 1897–Jan. 9, 1936.
    Supp. 2–232
Gilbert, John Gibbs, Feb. 27, 1810–June 17, 1889.
    Vol. 4, Pt. 1–270
Gilbert, Linda, May 13, 1847–Oct. 24, 1895.
    Vol. 4, Pt. 1–271
Gilbert, Rufus Henry, Jan. 26, 1832–July 10, 1885.
    Vol. 4, Pt. 1–271
Gilbert, Seymour Parker, Oct. 13, 1892–Feb. 23, 1938.
    Supp. 2–234
Gilbert, William Lewis, Dec. 30, 1806–June 29, 1890.
    Vol. 4, Pt. 1–272
Gilchrist, Robert, Aug. 21, 1825–July 6, 1888.
    Vol. 4, Pt. 1–273
Gilchrist, William Wallace, Jan. 8, 1846–Dec. 20, 1916.
    Vol. 4, Pt. 1–274
Gilder, Jeannette Leonard, Oct. 3, 1849–Jan. 17, 1916.
    Vol. 4, Pt. 1–274
Gilder, Richard Watson, Feb. 8, 1844–Nov. 18, 1909.
    Vol. 4, Pt. 1–275
Gilder, William Henry, Aug. 16, 1838–Feb. 5, 1900.
    Vol. 4, Pt. 1–278
Gildersleeve, Basil Lanneau, Oct. 23, 1831–Jan. 9, 1924.
    Vol. 4, Pt. 1–278
Gildersleeve, Virginia Crocheron, Oct. 3, 1877–July 7, 1965.
    Supp. 7–288
Giles, Chauncey, May 11, 1813–Nov. 6, 1893.
    Vol. 4, Pt. 1–282
Giles, William Branch, Aug. 12, 1762–Dec. 4, 1830.
    Vol. 4, Pt. 1–283
Gill, John, May 17, 1732–Aug. 25, 1785.
    Vol. 4, Pt. 1–284

Gill, Laura Drake, Aug. 24, 1860–Feb. 3, 1926.
Vol. 4, Pt. 1–284
Gill, Theodore Nicholas, Mar. 21, 1837–Sept. 25, 1914.
Vol. 4, Pt. 1–285
Gillam, Bernhard, Apr. 28, 1856–Jan. 19, 1896.
Vol. 4, Pt. 1–286
Gillem, Alvan Cullem, July 29, 1830–Dec. 2, 1875.
Vol. 4, Pt. 1–287
Gillespie, Eliza Maria. [See Angela, Mother, 1824–1887.]
Gillespie, Mabel, Mar. 4, 1867–Sept. 24, 1923.
Vol. 4, Pt. 1–288
Gillespie, William Mitchell, 1816–Jan. 1, 1868.
Vol. 4, Pt. 1–288
Gillet, Ransom Hooker, Jan. 27, 1800–Oct. 24, 1876.
Vol. 4, Pt. 1–289
Gillett, Ezra Hall, July 15, 1823–Sept. 2, 1875.
Vol. 4, Pt. 1–290
Gillett, Frederick Huntington, Oct. 16, 1851–July 31, 1935.
Supp. 1–343
Gillett, Horace Wadsworth, Dec. 12, 1883–Mar. 2, 1950.
Supp. 4–328
Gillette, Francis, Dec. 14, 1807–Sept. 30, 1879.
Vol. 4, Pt. 1–290
Gillette, King Camp, Jan. 5, 1855–July 9, 1932.
Supp. 1–345
Gillette, William Hooker, July 24, 1853–Apr. 29, 1937.
Supp. 2–235
Gilliam, David Tod, Apr. 3, 1844–Oct. 2, 1923.
Vol. 4, Pt. 1–291
Gillis, James Martin, Nov. 12, 1876–Mar. 14, 1957.
Supp. 6–237
Gilliss, James Melville, Sept. 6, 1811–Feb. 9, 1865.
Vol. 4, Pt. 1–292
Gilliss, Walter, May 17, 1855–Sept. 24, 1925.
Vol. 4, Pt. 1–293
Gillman, Henry, Nov. 16, 1833–July 30, 1915.
Vol. 4, Pt. 1–294
Gillmore, Quincy Adams, Feb. 28, 1825–Apr. 7, 1888.
Vol. 4, Pt. 1–295
Gillon, Alexander, Aug. 13, 1741–Oct. 6, 1794.
Vol. 4, Pt. 1–296
Gilman, Arthur, June 22, 1837–Dec. 27, 1909.
Vol. 4, Pt. 1–297
Gilman, Arthur Delevan, Nov. 5, 1821–July 11, 1882.
Vol. 4, Pt. 1–297
Gilman, Caroline Howard, Oct. 8, 1794–Sept. 15, 1888.
Vol. 4, Pt. 1–298
Gilman, Charlotte Perkins Stetson, July 3, 1860–Aug. 17, 1935. Supp. 1–346
Gilman, Daniel Coit, July 6, 1831–Oct. 13, 1908.
Vol. 4, Pt. 1–299
Gilman, John Taylor, Dec. 19, 1753–Aug. 31, 1828.
Vol. 4, Pt. 1–303
Gilman, Lawrence, July 5, 1878–Sept. 8, 1939.
Supp. 2–237
Gilman, Nicholas, Aug. 3, 1755–May 2, 1814.
Vol. 4, Pt. 1–304
Gilman, Samuel, Feb. 16, 1791–Feb. 9, 1858.
Vol. 4, Pt. 1–305
Gilmer, Elizabeth Meriwether ("Dorothy Dix"), Nov. 18, 1870–Dec. 16, 1951. Supp. 5–243
Gilmer, Francis Walker, Oct. 9, 1790–Feb. 25, 1826.
Vol. 4, Pt. 1–306
Gilmer, George Rockingham, Apr. 11, 1790–Nov. 16, 1859.
Vol. 4, Pt. 1–306
Gilmer, John Adams, Nov. 4, 1805–May 14, 1868.
Vol. 4, Pt. 1–307
Gilmer, Thomas Walker, Apr. 6, 1802–Feb. 28, 1844.
Vol. 4, Pt. 1–308
Gilmor, Harry, Jan. 24, 1838–Mar. 4, 1883.
Vol. 4, Pt. 1–309
Gilmore, James Roberts, Sept. 10, 1822–Nov. 16, 1903.
Vol. 4, Pt. 1–309
Gilmore, Joseph Albree, June 10, 1811–Apr. 17, 1867.
Vol. 4, Pt. 1–311
Gilmore, Joseph Henry, Apr. 29, 1834–July 23, 1918.
Vol. 4, Pt. 1–311
Gilmore, Patrick Sarsfield, Dec. 25, 1829–Sept. 24, 1892.
Vol. 4, Pt. 1–312
Gilmour, Richard, Sept. 28, 1824–Apr. 13, 1891.
Vol. 4, Pt. 1–313
Gilpin, Charles Sidney, Nov. 20, 1878–May 6, 1930.
Vol. 4, Pt. 1–314

Gilpin, Edward Woodward, July 13, 1803–Apr. 29, 1876.
Vol. 4, Pt. 1–314
Gilpin, Henry Dilworth, Apr. 14, 1801–Jan. 29, 1860.
Vol. 4, Pt. 1–315
Gilpin, William, Oct. 4, 1813–Jan. 20, 1894.
Vol. 4, Pt. 1–316
Gimbel, Bernard Feustman, Apr. 10, 1885–Sept. 29, 1966.
Supp. 8–212
Ginn, Edwin, Feb. 14, 1838–Jan. 21, 1914.
Vol. 4, Pt. 1–317
Ginter, Lewis, Apr. 4, 1824–Oct. 2, 1897.
Vol. 4, Pt. 1–317
Giovannitti, Arturo, Jan. 7, 1884–Dec. 31, 1959.
Supp. 6–238
Girard, Charles Frédéric, Mar. 9, 1822–Jan. 29, 1895.
Vol. 4, Pt. 1–319
Girard, Stephen, May 20, 1750–Dec. 26, 1831.
Vol. 4, Pt. 1–319
Girardeau, John Lafayette, Nov. 14, 1825–June 23, 1898.
Vol. 4, Pt. 1–322
Girdler, Tom Mercer, May 19, 1877–Feb. 4, 1965.
Supp. 7–289
Girsch, Frederick, Mar. 31, 1821–Dec. 18, 1895.
Vol. 4, Pt. 1–322
Girty, Simon, 1741–Feb. 18, 1818.
Vol. 4, Pt. 1–323
Gish, Dorothy, Mar. 11, 1898–June 4, 1968.
Supp. 8–213
Gist, Christopher, c. 1706–1759.
Vol. 4, Pt. 1–323
Gist, Mordecai, Feb. 22, 1742/43–Aug. 2, 1792.
Vol. 4, Pt. 1–324
Gist, William Henry, Aug. 22, 1807–Sept. 30, 1874.
Vol. 4, Pt. 1–325
Gitlow, Benjamin, Dec. 22, 1891–July 19, 1965.
Supp. 7–290
Glackens, William James, Mar. 13, 1870–May 22, 1938.
Supp. 2–238
Gladden, Wahington, Feb. 11, 1836–July 2, 1918.
Vol. 4, Pt. 1–325
Gladwin, Henry, Nov. 19, 1729–June 22, 1791.
Vol. 4, Pt. 1–327
Glasgow, Ellen Anderson Gholson, Apr. 22, 1873–Nov. 21, 1945. Supp. 3–302
Glaspell, Susan Keating, July 1, 1876–July 27, 1948.
Supp. 4–329
Glass, Carter, Jan. 4, 1858–May 28, 1946.
Supp. 4–330
Glass, Franklin Potts, June 7, 1858–Jan. 10, 1934.
Supp. 1–346
Glass, Hugh, fl. 1823–1833.
Vol. 4, Pt. 1–327
Glass, Montague Marsden, July 23, 1877–Feb. 3, 1934.
Supp. 1–347
Glassford, Pelham Davis, Aug. 8, 1883–Aug. 9, 1959.
Supp. 6–239
Gleason, Frederic Grant, Dec. 18, 1848–Dec. 6, 1903.
Vol. 4, Pt. 1–328
Gleason, Kate, Nov. 25, 1865–Jan. 9, 1933.
Supp. 1–348
Gleaves, Albert, Jan. 1, 1858–Jan. 6, 1937.
Supp. 2–239
Glenn, Hugh, Jan. 7, 1788–May 28, 1833.
Vol. 4, Pt. 1–329
Glenn, John Mark, Oct. 28, 1858–Apr. 20, 1950.
Supp. 4–332
Glennon, John Joseph, June 14, 1862–Mar. 9, 1946.
Supp. 4–334
Glidden, Charles Jasper, Aug. 29, 1857–Sept. 11, 1927.
Vol. 4, Pt. 1–329
Glidden, Joseph Farwell, Jan. 18, 1813–Oct. 9, 1906.
Vol. 4, Pt. 1–330
Glover, John, Nov. 5, 1732–Jan. 30, 1797.
Vol. 4, Pt. 1–331
Glover, Samuel Taylor, Mar. 9, 1813–Jan. 22, 1884.
Vol. 4, Pt. 1–332
Glover, Townend, Feb. 20, 1813–Sept. 7, 1883.
Vol. 4, Pt. 1–333
Gluck, Alma, May 11, 1884–Oct. 27, 1938.
Supp. 2–240
Glynn, James, June 28, 1801–May 13, 1871.
Vol. 4, Pt. 1–334

Glynn, Martin Henry, Sept. 27, 1871–Dec. 14, 1924.
Vol. 4, Pt. 1–334
Gmeiner, John, Dec. 5, 1847–Nov. 11, 1913.
Vol. 4, Pt. 1–335
Gobrecht, Christian, Dec. 23, 1785–July 23, 1844.
Vol. 4, Pt. 1–336
Godbe, William Samuel, June 26, 1833–Aug. 1, 1902.
Vol. 4, Pt. 1–337
Goddard, Calvin Hooker, Oct. 30, 1891–Feb. 22, 1955.
Supp. 5–244
Goddard, Calvin Luther, Jan. 22, 1822–Mar. 29, 1895.
Vol. 4, Pt. 1–338
Goddard, Henry Herbert, Aug. 14, 1866–June 19, 1957.
Supp. 6–240
Goddard, John, Jan. 20, 1723/4–July 1785.
Vol. 4, Pt. 1–338
Goddard, Luther Marcellus, Oct. 27, 1840–May 20, 1917.
Vol. 4, Pt. 1–339
Goddard, Morrill, Oct. 7, 1865–July 1, 1937.
Supp. 2–241
Goddard, Paul Beck, Jan. 26, 1811–July 3, 1866.
Vol. 4, Pt. 1–340
Goddard, Pliny Earle, Nov. 24, 1869–July 12, 1928.
Vol. 4, Pt. 1–340
Goddard, Robert Hutchings, Oct. 5, 1882–Aug. 10, 1945.
Supp. 3–305
Goddard, William, 1740–Dec. 23, 1817.
Vol. 4, Pt. 1–341
Goddu, Louis, Oct. 1, 1837–June 18, 1919.
Vol. 4, Pt. 1–342
Godefroy, Maximilian, fl. 1806–1824.
Vol. 4, Pt. 1–343
Godey, Louis Antoine, June 6, 1804–Nov. 29, 1878.
Vol. 4, Pt. 1–343
Godfrey, Benjamin, Dec. 4, 1794–Apr. 13, 1862.
Vol. 4, Pt. 1–344
Godfrey, Thomas, 1704–Dec. 1749.
Vol. 4, Pt. 1–345
Godfrey, Thomas, Dec. 4, 1736–Aug. 3, 1763.
Vol. 4, Pt. 1–346
Godkin, Edwin Lawrence, Oct. 2, 1831–May 21, 1902.
Vol. 4, Pt. 1–347
Godman, John Davidson, Dec. 20, 1794–Apr. 17, 1830.
Vol. 4, Pt. 1–350
Godowsky, Leopold, Feb. 13, 1870–Nov. 21, 1938.
Supp. 2–243
Godwin, Parke, Feb. 25, 1816–Jan. 7, 1904.
Vol. 4, Pt. 1–351
Goebel, William, Jan. 4, 1856–Feb. 3, 1900.
Vol. 4, Pt. 1–352
Goerz, David, June 2, 1849–May 7, 1914.
Vol. 4, Pt. 1–353
Goessmann, Charles Anthony, June 13, 1827–Sept. 1, 1910.
Vol. 4, Pt. 1–354
Goethals, George Washington, June 29, 1858–Jan. 21, 1928.
Vol. 4, Pt. 1–355
Goetschius, John Henry, Mar. 8, 1718–Nov. 14, 1774.
Vol. 4, Pt. 1–357
Goetschius, Percy, Aug. 30, 1853–Oct. 29, 1943.
Supp. 3–308
Goetz, George. [See Calverton, Victor Francis, 1900–1940.]
Goetz, George Washington, Feb. 17, 1856–Jan. 15, 1897.
Vol. 4, Pt. 1–358
Goff, Emmet Stull, Sept. 3, 1852–June 6, 1902.
Vol. 4, Pt. 1–359
Goff, John William, Jan. 1, 1848–Nov. 9, 1924.
Vol. 4, Pt. 1–359
Goffe, William, d. 1679?.
Vol. 4, Pt. 1–360
Goforth, William, 1766–May 12, 1817.
Vol. 4, Pt. 1–361
Going, Jonathan, Mar. 7, 1786–Nov. 9, 1844.
Vol. 4, Pt. 1–362
Gold, Michael, Apr. 12, 1893–May 14, 1967.
Supp. 8–215
Goldbeck, Robert, Apr. 19, 1839–May 16, 1908.
Vol. 4, Pt. 1–362
Goldberg, Reuben Lucius ("Rube"), July 4, 1883–Dec. 7, 1970. Supp. 8–217
Goldberger, Joseph, July 16, 1874–Jan. 17, 1929.
Vol. 4, Pt. 1–363
Golden, John, June 27, 1874–June 17, 1955.
Supp. 5–245

Goldenweiser, Alexander Alexandrovich, Jan. 29, 1880–July 6, 1940. Supp. 2–244
Goldenweiser, Emanuel Alexander, July 31, 1883–Mar. 31, 1953. Supp. 5–247
Golder, Frank Alfred, Aug. 11, 1877–Jan. 7, 1929.
Vol. 4, Pt. 1–364
Goldfine, Bernard, c. Oct. 1889–Sept. 21, 1967.
Supp. 8–218
Goldin, Horace, Dec. 17, 1873–Aug. 22, 1939.
Supp. 2–245
Goldman, Edwin Franko, Jan. 1, 1878–Feb. 21, 1956.
Supp. 6–241
Goldman, Emma, June 27, 1869–May 14, 1940.
Supp. 2–246
Goldman, Mayer C., Sept. 2, 1874–Nov. 24, 1939.
Supp. 2–248
Goldmark, Henry, June 15, 1857–Jan. 15, 1941.
Supp. 3–310
Goldmark, Rubin, Aug. 15, 1872–Mar. 6, 1936.
Supp. 2–249
Goldsborough, Charles, July 15, 1765–Dec. 13, 1834.
Vol. 4, Pt. 1–365
Goldsborough, Louis Malesherbes, Feb. 18, 1805–Feb. 20, 1877. Vol. 4, Pt. 1–365
Goldsborough, Robert, Dec. 3, 1733–Dec. 22, 1788. (W. C. Mallalieu). Vol. 4, Pt. 1–366
Goldsborough, Thomas Alan, Sept. 16, 1877–June 16, 1951.
Supp. 5–248
Goldschmidt, Jakob, Dec. 31, 1882–Sept. 23, 1955.
Supp. 5–249
Goldsmith, Middleton, Aug. 5, 1818–Nov. 26, 1887.
Vol. 4, Pt. 1–367
Goldstein, Max Aaron, Apr. 19, 1870–July 27, 1941.
Supp. 3–311
Goldthwaite, George, Dec. 10, 1809–Mar. 16, 1879.
Vol. 4, Pt. 1–368
Goldthwaite, Henry Barnes, Apr. 10, 1802–Oct. 19, 1847.
Vol. 4, Pt. 1–369
Goldwater, Sigismund Schulz, Feb. 7, 1873–Oct. 22, 1942.
Supp. 3–312
Gomberg, Moses, Feb. 8, 1866–Feb. 12, 1947.
Supp. 4–335
Gompers, Samuel, Jan. 27, 1850–Dec. 13, 1924.
Vol. 4, Pt. 1–369
Gonzales, Ambrose Elliott, May 29, 1857–July 11, 1926.
Vol. 4, Pt. 1–373
Gooch, Sir William, Oct. 21, 1681–Dec. 17, 1751.
Vol. 4, Pt. 1–373
Good, Adolphus Clemens, Dec. 19, 1856–Dec. 13, 1894.
Vol. 4, Pt. 1–375
Good, James Isaac, Dec. 31, 1850–Jan. 22, 1924.
Vol. 4, Pt. 1–375
Good, Jeremiah Haak, Nov. 22, 1822–Jan. 25, 1888.
Vol. 4, Pt. 1–376
Good, John, Dec. 20, 1841–Mar. 23, 1908.
Vol. 4, Pt. 1–377
Goodale, George Lincoln, Aug. 3, 1839–Apr. 12, 1923.
Vol. 4, Pt. 1–378
Goodale, Stephen Lincoln, Aug. 14, 1815–Nov. 5, 1897.
Vol. 4, Pt. 1–379
Goodall, Harvey L., May 28, 1836–Mar. 28, 1900.
Vol. 4, Pt. 1–379
Goodall, Thomas, Sept. 1, 1823–May 10, 1910.
Vol. 4, Pt. 1–380
Goode, George Brown, Feb. 13, 1851–Sept. 6, 1896.
Vol. 4, Pt. 1–381
Goode, John, May 27, 1829–July 14, 1909.
Vol. 4, Pt. 1–382
Goode, John Paul, Nov. 21, 1862–Aug. 5, 1932.
Supp. 1–349
Goodell, Henry Hill, May 20, 1839–Apr. 23, 1905.
Vol. 4, Pt. 1–383
Goodell, William, Feb. 14, 1792–Feb. 18, 1867.
Vol. 4, Pt. 1–383
Goodell, William, Oct. 25, 1792–Feb. 14, 1878.
Vol. 4, Pt. 1–384
Goodenow, John Milton, 1782–July, 1838.
Vol. 4, Pt. 1–385
Goodhue, Benjamin, Sept. 20, 1748–July 28, 1814.
Vol. 4, Pt. 1–386
Goodhue, Bertram Grosvenor, Apr. 28, 1869–Apr. 23, 1924.
Vol. 4, Pt. 1–386

Goodhue, James Madison, Mar. 31, 1810–Aug. 27, 1852.
    Vol. 4, Pt. 1–389
Goodloe, Daniel Reaves, May 28, 1814–Jan. 18, 1902.
    Vol. 4, Pt. 1–390
Goodloe, William Cassius, June 27, 1841–Nov. 10, 1889.
    Vol. 4, Pt. 1–391
Goodman, Charles, 1796–Feb. 11, 1835.
    Vol. 4, Pt. 1–392
Goodman, Kenneth Sawyer, Sep. 19, 1883–Nov. 29, 1918.
    Vol. 4, Pt. 1–392
Goodman, Louis Earl, Jan. 2, 1892–Sept. 15, 1961.
    Supp. 7–292
Goodnight, Charles, Mar. 5, 1836–Dec. 12, 1929.
    Vol. 4, Pt. 1–393
Goodnough, Xanthus Henry, Oct. 23, 1860–Aug. 10, 1935.
    Supp. 1–350
Goodnow, Frank Johnson, Jan. 18, 1859–Nov. 15, 1939.
    Supp. 2–250
Goodnow, Isaac Tichenor, Jan. 17, 1814–Mar. 20, 1894.
    Vol. 4, Pt. 1–394
Goodrich, Alfred John, May 8, 1847–Apr. 25, 1920.
    Vol. 4, Pt. 1–395
Goodrich, Annie Warburton, Feb. 6, 1866–Dec. 31, 1954.
    Supp. 5–251
Goodrich, Benjamin Franklin, Nov. 4, 1841–Aug. 3, 1888.
    Vol. 4, Pt. 1–396
Goodrich, Charles Augustus, Aug. 19, 1790–June 4, 1862.
    Vol. 4, Pt. 1–397
Goodrich, Chauncey, Oct. 20, 1759–Aug. 18, 1815.
    Vol. 4, Pt. 1–397
Goodrich, Chauncey, Sept. 10, 1798–Sept. 11, 1858.
    Vol. 4, Pt. 1–398
Goodrich, Chauncey, June 4, 1836–Sept. 28, 1925.
    Vol. 4, Pt. 1–399
Goodrich, Chauncey Allen, Oct. 23, 1790–Feb. 25, 1860.
    Vol. 4, Pt. 1–399
Goodrich, Elizur, Oct. 26, 1734–Nov. 22, 1797.
    Vol. 4, Pt. 1–400
Goodrich, Elizur, Mar. 24, 1761–Nov. 1, 1849.
    Vol. 4, Pt. 1–401
Goodrich, Frank Boott, Dec. 14, 1826–Mar. 15, 1894.
    Vol. 4, Pt. 1–401
Goodrich, Samuel Griswold, Aug. 19, 1793–May 9, 1860.
    Vol. 4, Pt. 1–402
Goodrich, Sarah. [See Goodridge, Sarah, 1788–1853.]
Goodrich, William Marcellus, July 21, 1777–Sept. 15, 1833.
    Vol. 4, Pt. 1–403
Goodridge, Sarah, Feb. 5, 1788–Dec. 28, 1853.
    Vol. 4, Pt. 1–404
Goodridge, William Marcellus. [See Goodrich, William Marcellus, 1777–1833.]
Goodsell, Daniel Ayres, Nov. 5, 1840–Dec. 5, 1909.
    Vol. 4, Pt. 1–405
Goodspeed, Thomas Wakefield, Sept. 4, 1842–Dec. 16, 1927. Vol. 4, Pt. 1–405
Goodwin, Daniel Raynes, Apr. 12, 1811–Mar. 15, 1890.
    Vol. 4, Pt. 1–406
Goodwin, Elijah, Jan. 16, 1807–Sept. 4, 1879.
    Vol. 4, Pt. 1–407
Goodwin, Hannibal Williston, Apr. 30, 1822–Dec. 31, 1900.
    Vol. 4, Pt. 1–408
Goodwin, Ichabod, Oct. 8, 1794–July 4, 1882.
    Vol. 4, Pt. 1–408
Goodwin, John Noble, Oct. 18, 1824–Apr. 29, 1887.
    Vol. 4, Pt. 1–409
Goodwin, Nathaniel Carll, July 25, 1857–Jan. 31, 1919.
    Vol. 4, Pt. 1–410
Goodwin, William Watson, May 9, 1831–June 15, 1912.
    Vol. 4, Pt. 1–411
Goodyear, Anson Conger, June 20, 1877–Apr. 23, 1964.
    Supp. 7–293
Goodyear, Charles, Dec. 29, 1800–July 1, 1860.
    Vol. 4, Pt. 1–413
Goodyear, Charles, Jan. 1, 1833–May 22, 1896.
    Vol. 4, Pt. 1–415
Goodyear, William Henry, Apr. 21, 1846–Feb. 19, 1923.
    Vol. 4, Pt. 1–416
Gookin, Daniel, 1612–Mar. 19, 1686/7.
    Vol. 4, Pt. 1–417
Goold, William A., Nov. 5, 1830–Dec. 19, 1912.
    Vol. 4, Pt. 1–418
Gorcey, Leo, June 3, 1917–June 2, 1969.
    Supp. 8–220

Gordin, Jacob, May 1, 1853–June 11, 1909.
    Vol. 4, Pt. 1–418
Gordon, Andrew, Sept. 17, 1828–Aug. 13, 1887.
    Vol. 4, Pt. 1–419
Gordon, George Angier, Jan. 2, 1853–Oct. 25, 1929.
    Vol. 4, Pt. 1–419
Gordon, George Byron, Aug. 4, 1870–Jan. 30, 1927.
    Vol. 4, Pt. 1–421
Gordon, George Henry, July 19, 1823–Aug. 30, 1886.
    Vol. 4, Pt. 1–421
Gordon, George Phineas, Apr. 21, 1810–Jan. 27, 1878.
    Vol. 4, Pt. 1–422
Gordon, George Washington, Oct. 5, 1836–Aug. 9, 1911.
    Vol. 4, Pt. 1–423
Gordon, James, Dec. 6, 1833–Nov. 28, 1912.
    Vol. 4, Pt. 1–423
Gordon, John Brown, Feb. 6, 1832–Jan. 9, 1904.
    Vol. 4, Pt. 1–424
Gordon, Laura De Force, Aug. 17, 1838–Apr. 6, 1907.
    Vol. 4, Pt. 1–425
Gordon, Waxey. [See Wexler, Irving.]
Gordon, William, 1728–Oct. 19, 1807.
    Vol. 4, Pt. 1–426
Gordon, William Fitzhugh, Jan. 13, 1787–Aug. 28, 1858.
    Vol. 4, Pt. 1–426
Gordon, William Washington, Jan. 17, 1796–Mar. 20, 1842.
    Vol. 4, Pt. 1–427
Gordy, John Pancoast, Dec. 21, 1851–Dec. 31, 1908.
    Vol. 4, Pt. 1–428
Gore, Thomas Pryor, Dec. 10, 1870–Mar. 16, 1949.
    Supp. 4–337
Gorgas, Josiah, July 1, 1818–May 15, 1883.
    Vol. 4, Pt. 1–428
Gorgas, William Crawford, Oct. 3, 1854–July 3, 1920.
    Vol. 4, Pt. 1–430
Gorham, Jabez, Feb. 18, 1792–Mar. 24, 1869.
    Vol. 4, Pt. 1–432
Gorham, John, Feb. 24, 1783–Mar. 27, 1829.
    Vol. 4, Pt. 1–433
Gorham, Nathaniel, May 1738–June 11, 1796.
    Vol. 4, Pt. 1–433
Gorky, Arshile, 1904 or 1905–July 1, 1948.
    Supp. 4–339
Gorman, Arthur Pue, Mar. 11, 1839–June 4, 1906.
    Vol. 4, Pt. 1–434
Gorman, Willis Arnold, Jan. 12, 1816–May 20, 1876.
    Vol. 4, Pt. 1–435
Gorrell, Edgar Staley, Feb. 3, 1891–Mar. 5, 1945.
    Supp. 3–313
Gorrie, John, Oct. 3, 1803–June 16, 1855.
    Vol. 4, Pt. 1–436
Gorringe, Henry Honeychurch, Aug. 11, 1841–July 6, 1885.
    Vol. 4, Pt. 1–437
Gortner, Ross Aiken, Mar. 20, 1885–Sept. 30, 1942.
    Supp. 3–314
Gorton, Samuel, c. 1592–1677.
    Vol. 4, Pt. 1–438
Gosnold, Bartholomew, fl. 1572–1607.
    Vol. 4, Pt. 1–439
Goss, Albert Simon, Oct. 14, 1882–Oct. 25, 1950.
    Supp. 4–340
Goss, James Walker, Dec. 29, 1812–Nov. 26, 1870.
    Vol. 4, Pt. 1–440
Gossett, Benjamin Brown, Aug. 18, 1884–Nov. 13, 1951.
    Supp. 5–252
Gostelowe, Jonathan, 1744–Feb. 3, 1795.
    Vol. 4, Pt. 1–440
Gotshall, William Charles, May 9, 1870–Aug. 20, 1935.
    Supp. 1–351
Gottheil, Gustav, May 28, 1827–Apr. 15, 1903.
    Vol. 4, Pt. 1–441
Gottheil, Richard James Horatio, Oct. 13, 1862–May 22, 1936. Supp. 2–251
Gottschalk, Louis Moreau, May 8, 1829–Dec. 18, 1869.
    Vol. 4, Pt. 1–441
Goucher, John Franklin, June 7, 1845–July 19, 1922.
    Vol. 4, Pt. 1–442
Goudy, Frederic William, Mar. 8, 1865–May 11, 1947.
    Supp. 4–341
Goudy, William Charles, May 15, 1824–Apr. 27, 1893.
    Vol. 4, Pt. 1–443
Gouge, William M., Nov. 10, 1796–July 14, 1863.
    Vol. 4, Pt. 1–444

Gough, John Bartholomew, Aug. 22, 1817–Feb. 18, 1886.
    Vol. 4, Pt. 1–445
Gould, Augustus Addison, Apr. 23, 1805–Sept. 15, 1866.
    Vol. 4, Pt. 1–446
Gould, Benjamin Apthorp, June 15, 1787–Oct. 24, 1859.
    Vol. 4, Pt. 1–447
Gould, Benjamin Apthorp, Sept. 27, 1824–Nov. 26, 1896.
    Vol. 4, Pt. 1–447
Gould, Edward Sherman, May 11, 1805–Feb. 21, 1885.
    Vol. 4, Pt. 1–449
Gould, Elgin Ralston Lovell, Aug. 15, 1860–Aug. 18, 1915.
    Vol. 4, Pt. 1–449
Gould, George Jay, Feb. 6, 1864–May 16, 1923.
    Vol. 4, Pt. 1–450
Gould, George Milbry, Nov. 8, 1848–Aug. 8, 1922.
    Vol. 4, Pt. 1–451
Gould, Hannah Flagg, Sept. 3, 1789–Sept. 5, 1865.
    Vol. 4, Pt. 1–452
Gould, James, Dec. 5, 1770–May 11, 1838.
    Vol. 4, Pt. 1–453
Gould, Jay, May 27, 1836–Dec. 2, 1892.
    Vol. 4, Pt. 1–454
Gould, Nathaniel Duren, Nov. 26, 1781–May 28, 1864.
    Vol. 4, Pt. 1–455
Gould, Robert Simonton, Dec. 16, 1826–June 30, 1904.
    Vol. 4, Pt. 1–455
Gould, Thomas Ridgeway, Nov. 5, 1818–Nov. 26, 1881.
    Vol. 4, Pt. 1–456
Goulding, Francis Robert, Sept. 28, 1810–Aug. 22, 1881.
    Vol. 4, Pt. 1–457
Goupil, René, c. 1607–Sept. 29, 1642.
    Vol. 4, Pt. 1–458
Govan, Daniel Chevilette, July 4, 1829–Mar. 12, 1911.
    Vol. 4, Pt. 1–458
Gove, Aaron Estellus, Sept. 26, 1839–Aug. 1, 1919.
    Vol. 4, Pt. 1–459
Gowans, William, Mar. 29, 1803–Nov. 27, 1870.
    Vol. 4, Pt. 1–459
Gowen, Franklin Benjamin, Feb. 9, 1836–Dec. 14, 1889.
    Vol. 4, Pt. 1–460
Grabau, Amadeus William, Jan. 9, 1870–Mar. 20, 1946.
    Supp. 4–343
Grabau, Johannes Andreas August, Mar. 18, 1804–June 2,
    1879. Vol. 4, Pt. 1–461
Gräbner, August Lawrence, July 10, 1849–Dec. 7, 1904.
    Vol. 4, Pt. 1–462
Grace, Eugene Gifford, Aug. 27, 1876–July 25, 1960.
    Supp. 6–243
Grace, William Russell, May 10, 1832–Mar. 21, 1904.
    Vol. 4, Pt. 1–463
Gracie, Archibald, Dec. 1, 1832–Dec. 2, 1864.
    Vol. 4, Pt. 1–463
Gradle, Henry, Aug. 17, 1855–Apr. 4, 1911.
    Vol. 4, Pt. 1–464
Grady, Henry Francis, Feb. 12, 1882–Sept. 14, 1957.
    Supp. 6–244
Grady, Henry Woodfin, May 24, 1850–Dec. 23, 1889.
    Vol. 4, Pt. 1–465
Graebner, August Lawrence. [See Gräbner, August Law-
    rence, 1849–1904.]
Graessl, Lawrence, Aug. 18, 1753–c. Oct. 12, 1793.
    Vol. 4, Pt. 1–466
Graff, Everett Dwight, Aug. 7, 1885–Mar. 11, 1964.
    Supp. 7–294
Graff, Frederic, May 23, 1817–Mar. 30, 1890.
    Vol. 4, Pt. 1–466
Graff, Frederick, Aug. 27, 1774–Apr. 13, 1847.
    Vol. 4, Pt. 1–467
Graffenried, Christopher, Baron de, 1661–1743.
    Vol. 4, Pt. 1–468
Grafly, Charles, Dec. 3, 1862–May 5, 1929.
    Vol. 4, Pt. 1–468
Grafton, Charles Chapman, Apr. 12, 1830–Aug. 30, 1912.
    Vol. 4, Pt. 1–470
Graham, Charles Kinnaird, June 3, 1824–Apr. 15, 1889.
    Vol. 4, Pt. 1–471
Graham, David, Feb. 8, 1808–May 27, 1852.
    Vol. 4, Pt. 1–471
Graham, Edward Kidder, Oct. 11, 1876–Oct. 26, 1918.
    Vol. 4, Pt. 1–472
Graham, Ernest Robert, Aug. 22, 1866–Nov. 22, 1936.
    Supp. 2–252

Graham, Evarts Ambrose, Mar. 19, 1883–Mar. 4, 1957.
    Supp. 6–245
Graham, George Rex, Jan. 18, 1813–July 13, 1894.
    Vol. 4, Pt. 1–473
Graham, Isabella Marshall, July 29, 1742–July 27, 1814.
    Vol. 4, Pt. 1–474
Graham, James, d. Jan. 1700/01.
    Vol. 4, Pt. 1–475
Graham, James Duncan, Apr. 4, 1799–Dec. 28, 1865.
    Vol. 4, Pt. 1–476
Graham, John, c. 1718–Nov. 1795.
    Vol. 4, Pt. 1–476
Graham, John, 1774–Aug. 6, 1820.
    Vol. 4, Pt. 1–477
Graham, John Andrew, June 10, 1764–Aug. 29, 1841.
    Vol. 4, Pt. 1–478
Graham, Joseph, Oct. 13, 1759–Nov. 12, 1836.
    Vol. 4, Pt. 1–479
Graham, Philip Leslie, July 18, 1915–Aug. 3, 1963.
    Supp. 7–295
Graham, Sylvester, July 5, 1794–Sept. 11, 1851.
    Vol. 4, Pt. 1–479
Graham, William Alexander, Sept. 5, 1804–Aug. 11, 1875.
    Vol. 4, Pt. 1–480
Graham, William Montrose, Sept. 28, 1834–Jan. 16, 1916.
    Vol. 4, Pt. 1–481
Grainger, George Percy, July 8, 1882–Feb. 20, 1961.
    Supp. 7–297
Grandgent, Charles Hall, Nov. 14, 1862–Sept. 11, 1939.
    Supp. 2–254
Granger, Alfred Hoyt, May 31, 1867–Dec. 3, 1939.
    Supp. 2–255
Granger, Francis, Dec. 1, 1792–Aug. 28, 1868.
    Vol. 4, Pt. 1–482
Granger, Gideon, July 19, 1767–Dec. 31, 1822.
    Vol. 4, Pt. 1–483
Granger, Gordon, Nov. 6, 1822–Jan. 10, 1876.
    Vol. 4, Pt. 1–484
Granger, Walter, Nov. 7, 1872–Sept. 6, 1941.
    Supp. 3–316
Grant, Albert Weston, Apr. 14, 1856–Sept. 30, 1930.
    Vol. 4, Pt. 1–485
Grant, Asahel, Aug. 17, 1807–Apr. 24, 1844.
    Vol. 4, Pt. 1–485
Grant, Claudius Buchanan, Oct. 25, 1835–Feb. 28, 1921.
    Vol. 4, Pt. 1–486
Grant, Frederick Dent, May 30, 1850–Apr. 11, 1912.
    Vol. 4, Pt. 1–487
Grant, George Barnard, Dec. 21, 1849–Aug. 16, 1917.
    Vol. 4, Pt. 1–487
Grant, Harry Johnston, Sept. 15, 1881–July 12, 1963.
    Supp. 7–298
Grant, James Benton, Jan. 2, 1848–Nov. 1, 1911.
    Vol. 4, Pt. 1–488
Grant, John Thomas, Dec. 13, 1813–Jan. 18, 1887.
    Vol. 4, Pt. 1–489
Grant, Lewis Addison, Jan. 17, 1829–Mar. 20, 1918.
    Vol. 4, Pt. 1–490
Grant, Madison, Nov. 19, 1865–May 30, 1937.
    Supp. 2–256
Grant, Percy Stickney, May 13, 1860–Feb. 13, 1927.
    Vol. 4, Pt. 1–490
Grant, Robert, Jan. 24, 1852–May 19, 1940.
    Supp. 2–257
Grant, Ulysses Simpson, Apr. 27, 1822–July 23, 1885.
    Vol. 4, Pt. 1–492
Grant, Zilpah Polly. [See Banister, Zilpah Polly Grant, 1794–
    1874.]
Grass, John, 1837–May 10, 1918.
    Vol. 4, Pt. 1–501
Grasselli Caesar Augustin, Nov. 7, 1850–July 28, 1927.
    Vol. 4, Pt. 1–502
Grasty, Charles Henry, Mar. 3, 1863–Jan. 19, 1924.
    Vol. 4, Pt. 1–503
Gratiot, Charles, 1752–Apr. 20, 1817.
    Vol. 4, Pt. 1–503
Gratz, Barnard, 1738–Apr. 20, 1801.
    Vol. 4, Pt. 1–504
Gratz, Michael, 1740–Sept. 8, 1811.
    Vol. 4, Pt. 1–504
Gratz, Rebecca, Mar. 4, 1781–Aug. 29, 1869.
    Vol. 4, Pt. 1–505

Grau, Maurice, 1849–Mar. 14, 1907.
    Vol. 4, Pt. 1–506
Graupner, Johann Christian Gottlieb, Oct. 6, 1767–Apr. 16,
    1836. Vol. 4, Pt. 1–506
Gravenor, John. [See Altham, John, 1589–1640.]
Graves, Alvin Cushman, Nov. 4, 1909–July 29, 1965.
    Supp. 7–299
Graves, David Bibb, Apr. 1, 1873–Mar. 14, 1942.
    Supp. 3–317
Graves, Frederick Rogers, Oct. 24, 1858–May 17, 1940.
    Supp. 2–258
Graves, James Robinson, Apr. 10, 1820–June 26, 1893.
    Vol. 4, Pt. 1–507
Graves, John Temple, Nov. 9, 1856–Aug. 8, 1925.
    Vol. 4, Pt. 1–508
Graves, Rosewell Hobart, May 29, 1833–June 3, 1912.
    Vol. 4, Pt. 1–509
Graves, William Phillips, Jan. 29, 1870–Jan. 25, 1933.
    Supp. 1–352
Graves, William Sidney, Mar. 27, 1865–Feb. 27, 1940.
    Supp. 2–259
Graves, Zuinglius Calvin, Apr. 15, 1816–May 18, 1902.
    Vol. 4, Pt. 1–510
Gravier, Jacques, May 17, 1651–Apr. 23, 1708.
    Vol. 4, Pt. 1–510
Gray, Asa, Nov. 18, 1810–Jan. 30, 1888.
    Vol. 4, Pt. 1–511
Gray, Carl Raymond, Sept. 28, 1867–May 9, 1939.
    Supp. 2–260
Gray, Elisha, Aug. 2, 1835–Jan. 21, 1901.
    Vol. 4, Pt. 1–514
Gray, Francis Calley, Sept. 19, 1790–Dec. 29, 1856.
    Vol. 4, Pt. 1–514
Gray, George, May 4, 1840–Aug. 7, 1925.
    Vol. 4, Pt. 1–515
Gray, George Alexander, Sept. 28, 1851–Feb. 8, 1912.
    Vol. 4, Pt. 1–516
Gray, Gilda, Oct. 24, 1899–Dec. 22, 1959.
    Supp. 6–247
Gray, Glen ("Spike"), June 7, 1900–Aug. 23, 1963.
    Supp. 7–300
Gray, Harold Lincoln, Jan. 20, 1894–May 9, 1968.
    Supp. 8–221
Gray, Henry Peters, June 23, 1819–Nov. 12, 1877.
    Vol. 4, Pt. 1–517
Gray, Horace, Mar. 24, 1828–Sept. 15, 1902.
    Vol. 4, Pt. 1–518
Gray, Isaac Pusey, Oct. 18, 1828–Feb. 14, 1895.
    Vol. 4, Pt. 1–519
Gray, John Chipman, July 14, 1839–Feb. 25, 1915.
    Vol. 4, Pt. 1–520
Gray, John Purdue, Aug. 6, 1825–Nov. 29, 1886.
    Vol. 4, Pt. 1–521
Gray, Joseph W., Aug. 5, 1813–May 26, 1862.
    Vol. 4, Pt. 1–522
Gray, Robert, May 10, 1755–1806.
    Vol. 4, Pt. 1–522
Gray, William, June 27, 1750, o.s.–Nov. 3, 1825.
    Vol. 4, Pt. 1–523
Gray, William Scott, Jr., June 5, 1885–Sept. 8, 1960.
    Supp. 6–248
Graydon, Alexander, Apr. 10, 1752–May 2, 1818.
    Vol. 4, Pt. 1–524
Grayson, William, 1736?–Mar. 12, 1790.
    Vol. 4, Pt. 1–525
Greathouse, Clarence Ridgeby, c. 1845–Oct. 21, 1899.
    Vol. 4, Pt. 1–526
Greaton, John, Mar. 10, 1741–Dec. 16, 1783.
    Vol. 4, Pt. 1–526
Greaton, Joseph, Feb. 12, 1679–Aug. 19, 1753.
    Vol. 4, Pt. 1–527
Greeley, Horace, Feb. 3, 1811–Nov. 29, 1872.
    Vol. 4, Pt. 1–528
Greely, Adolphus Washington, Mar. 27, 1844–Oct. 20, 1935.
    Supp. 1–352
Green, Alexander Little Page, June 26, 1806–July 15, 1874.
    Vol. 4, Pt. 1–534
Green, Andrew Haswell, Oct. 6, 1820–Nov. 13, 1903.
    Vol. 4, Pt. 1–535
Green, Anna Katharine. [See Rohlfs, Anna Katharine Green,
    1846–1935.]
Green, Asa, Feb. 11, 1789–c. 1837.
    Vol. 4, Pt. 1–536

Green, Ashbel, July 6, 1762–May 19, 1848.
    Vol. 4, Pt. 1–536
Green, Bartholomew, Oct. 12, 1666–Dec. 28, 1732.
    Vol. 4, Pt. 1–537
Green, Benjamin Edwards, Feb. 5, 1822–May 12, 1907.
    Vol. 4, Pt. 1–538
Green, Beriah, Mar. 24, 1795–May 4, 1874.
    Vol. 4, Pt. 1–539
Green, Duff, Aug. 15, 1791–June 10, 1875.
    Vol. 4, Pt. 1–540
Green, Frances Harriet Whipple, Sept. 1805–June 10, 1878.
    Vol. 4, Pt. 1–542
Green, Francis, Aug. 21, 1742 o.s.–Apr. 21, 1809.
    Vol. 4, Pt. 1–542
Green, Francis Mathews, Feb. 23, 1835–Dec. 19, 1902.
    Vol. 4, Pt. 1–543
Green, Gabriel Marcus, Oct. 19, 1891–Jan. 24, 1919.
    Vol. 4, Pt. 1–544
Green, Henrietta Howland Robinson, Nov. 21, 1834–July 3,
    1916. Vol. 4, Pt. 1–545
Green, Henry Woodhull, Sept. 20, 1804–Dec. 19, 1876.
    Vol. 4, Pt. 1–546
Green, Horace, Dec. 24, 1802–Nov. 29, 1866.
    Vol. 4, Pt. 1–547
Green, Jacob, Feb. 2, 1722–May 24, 1790.
    Vol. 4, Pt. 1–548
Green, Jacob, July 26, 1790–Feb. 1, 1841.
    Vol. 4, Pt. 1–548
Green, James Stephens, Feb. 28, 1817–Jan. 19, 1870.
    Vol. 4, Pt. 1–549
Green, John, Apr. 2, 1835–Dec. 7, 1913.
    Vol. 4, Pt. 1–550
Green, John Cleve, Apr. 4, 1800–Apr. 29, 1875.
    Vol. 4, Pt. 1–551
Green, Jonas, 1712–Apr. 11, 1767.
    Vol. 4, Pt. 1–552
Green, Joseph, 1706–Dec. 11, 1780.
    Vol. 4, Pt. 1–553
Green, Lewis Warner, Jan. 28, 1806–May 26, 1863.
    Vol. 4, Pt. 1–553
Green, Nathan, 1787?–1825.
    Vol. 4, Pt. 1–554
Green, Norvin, Apr. 17, 1818–Feb. 12, 1893.
    Vol. 4, Pt. 1–555
Green, Samuel, 1615–Jan. 1, 1701/02.
    Vol. 4, Pt. 1–555
Green, Samuel Abbott, Mar. 16, 1830–Dec. 5, 1918.
    Vol. 4, Pt. 1–556
Green, Samuel Bowdlear, Sept. 15, 1859–July 11, 1910.
    Vol. 4, Pt. 1–556
Green, Samuel Swett, Feb. 20, 1837–Dec. 8, 1918.
    Vol. 4, Pt. 1–557
Green, Seth, Mar. 19, 1817–Aug. 20, 1888.
    Vol. 4, Pt. 1–558
Green, Theodore Francis, Oct. 2, 1867–May 19, 1966.
    Supp. 8–222
Green, Thomas, Aug. 25, 1735–May, 1812.
    Vol. 4, Pt. 1–558
Green, William, Nov. 10, 1806–July 29, 1880.
    Vol. 4, Pt. 1–559
Green, William, Mar. 3, 1870–Nov. 21, 1952.
    Supp. 5–253
Green, William Henry, Jan. 27, 1825–Feb. 10, 1900.
    Vol. 4, Pt. 1–560
Green, William Joseph, Jr., Mar. 5, 1910–Dec. 21, 1963.
    Supp. 7–301
Greenbaum, Edward Samuel, Apr. 13, 1890–June 12, 1970.
    Supp. 8–224
Greene, Albert Gorton, Feb. 10, 1802–Jan. 3, 1868.
    Vol. 4, Pt. 1–561
Greene, Belle Da Costa, Dec. 13, 1883–May 10, 1950.
    Supp. 4–344
Greene, Charles Ezra, Feb. 12, 1842–Oct. 16, 1903.
    Vol. 4, Pt. 1–562
Greene, Charles Sumner, Oct. 12, 1868–June 11, 1957.
    Supp. 5–255
Greene, Christopher, May 12, 1737–May 14, 1781.
    Vol. 4, Pt. 1–563
Greene, Daniel Crosby, Feb. 11, 1843–Sept. 15, 1913.
    Vol. 4, Pt. 1–563
Greene, Edward Lee, Aug. 20, 1843–Nov. 10, 1915.
    Vol. 4, Pt. 1–564

Greene, Frances Harriet Whipple. [See Green, Frances Harriet Whipple, 1805–1878.

Greene, Francis Vinton, June 27, 1850–May 15, 1921.
Vol. 4, Pt. 1–565

Greene, George Sears, May 6, 1801–Jan. 28, 1899.
Vol. 4, Pt. 1–566

Greene, George Sears, Nov. 26, 1837–Dec. 23, 1922.
Vol. 4, Pt. 1–567

Greene, George Washington, Apr. 8, 1811–Feb. 2, 1883.
Vol. 4, Pt. 1–568

Greene, Henry Mather, Jan. 23, 1870–Oct. 2, 1954.
Supp. 5–255

Greene, Jerome Davis, Oct. 12, 1874–Mar. 29, 1959.
Supp. 6–249

Greene, Nathanael, July 27/Aug. 7, 1742–June 19, 1786.
Vol. 4, Pt. 1–569

Greene, Nathaniel, May 20, 1797–Nov. 29, 1877.
Vol. 4, Pt. 1–573

Greene, Roger Sherman, May 29, 1881–Mar. 27, 1947.
Supp. 4–346

Greene, Samuel Dana, Feb. 11, 1840–Dec. 11, 1884.
Vol. 4, Pt. 1–573

Greene, Samuel Stillman, May 3, 1810–Jan. 24, 1883.
Vol. 4, Pt. 1–574

Greene, William, Mar. 16, 1695/96–Feb. 1758.
Vol. 4, Pt. 1–575

Greene, William, Aug. 16, 1731–Nov. 29, 1809.
Vol. 4, Pt. 1–576

Greene, William Cornell, 1851–Aug. 5, 1911.
Vol. 4, Pt. 1–577

Greener, Richard Theodore, Jan. 30, 1844–May 2, 1922.
Vol. 4, Pt. 1–578

Greenhalge, Frederic Thomas, July 19, 1842–Mar. 5, 1896.
Vol. 4, Pt. 1–579

Greenhow, Robert, b. 1800–Mar. 27, 1854.
Vol. 4, Pt. 1–580

Greenlaw, Edwin Almiron, Apr. 6, 1874–Sept. 10, 1931.
Supp. 1–355

Greenleaf, Benjamin, Sept. 25, 1786–Oct. 29, 1864.
Vol. 4, Pt. 1–581

Greenleaf, Halbert Stevens, Apr. 12, 1827–Aug. 25, 1906.
Vol. 4, Pt. 1–581

Greenleaf, Moses, Oct. 17, 1777–Mar. 20, 1834.
Vol. 4, Pt. 1–582

Greenleaf, Simon, Dec. 5, 1783–Oct. 6, 1853.
Vol. 4, Pt. 1–583

Greenleaf, Thomas, 1755–Sept. 14, 1798.
Vol. 4, Pt. 1–584

Greenough, Henry, Oct. 5, 1807–Oct. 31, 1883.
Vol. 4, Pt. 1–585

Greenough, Horatio, Sept. 6, 1805–Dec. 18, 1852.
Vol. 4, Pt. 1–586

Greenough, James Bradstreet, May 4, 1833–Oct. 11, 1901.
Vol. 4, Pt. 1–588

Greenough, Richard Saltonstall, Apr. 27, 1819–Apr. 23, 1904. Vol. 4, Pt. 1–589

Greenslet, Ferris, June 30, 1875–Nov. 19, 1959.
Supp. 6–250

Greenstreet, Sydney Hughes, Dec. 27, 1879–Jan. 18, 1954.
Supp. 5–257

Greenup, Christopher, c. 1750–Apr. 27, 1818.
Vol. 4, Pt. 1–589

Greenwald, Emanuel, Jan. 13, 1811–Dec. 21, 1885.
Vol. 4, Pt. 1–590

Greenway, John Campbell, July 6, 1872–Jan. 19, 1926.
Supp. 1–357

Greenwood, Grace. [See Lippincott, Sarah Jane Clarke, 1823–1904.]

Greenwood, Isaac, May 11, 1702–Oct. 12, 1745.
Vol. 4, Pt. 1–591

Greenwood, John, May 17, 1760–Nov. 16, 1819.
Vol. 4, Pt. 1–592

Greenwood, Miles, Mar. 19, 1807–Nov. 5, 1885.
Vol. 4, Pt. 1–592

Greer, David Hummell, Mar. 20, 1844–May 19, 1919.
Vol. 4, Pt. 1–593

Greer, James Augustin, Feb. 28, 1833–June 17, 1904.
Vol. 4, Pt. 1–594

Gregg, Alan, July 11, 1890–June 19, 1957.
Supp. 6–252

Gregg, Andrew, June 10, 1755–May 20, 1835.
Vol. 4, Pt. 1–595

Gregg, David McMurtrie Apr. 10, 1833–Aug. 7, 1916.
Vol. 4, Pt. 1–596

Gregg, John, Sept. 28, 1828–Oct. 7, 1864.
Vol. 4, Pt. 1–597

Gregg, John Andrew, Feb. 18, 1877–Feb. 17, 1953.
Supp. 5–258

Gregg, John Robert, June 17, 1867–Feb. 23, 1948.
Supp. 4–347

Gregg, Josiah, July 19, 1806–Feb. 25, 1850.
Vol. 4, Pt. 1–597

Gregg, Maxcy, 1814–Dec. 14, 1862.
Vol. 4, Pt. 1–598

Gregg, William, Feb. 2, 1800–Sept. 13, 1867.
Vol. 4, Pt. 1–599

Gregg, Willis Ray, Jan. 4, 1880–Sept. 14, 1938.
Supp. 2–261

Gregory, Caspar René, Nov. 6, 1846–Apr. 9, 1917.
Vol. 4, Pt. 1–601

Gregory, Charles Noble, Aug. 27, 1851–July 10, 1932.
Supp. 1–358

Gregory, Clifford Verne, Oct. 20, 1883–Nov. 18, 1941.
Supp. 3–318

Gregory, Daniel Seelye, Aug. 21, 1832–Apr. 14, 1915.
Vol. 4, Pt. 1–602

Gregory, Eliot, Oct. 13, 1854?–June 1, 1915.
Vol. 4, Pt. 1–602

Gregory, John Milton, July 6, 1822–Oct. 19, 1898.
Vol. 4, Pt. 1–603

Gregory, Menas Sarkas Boulgourjian, July 14, 1872–Nov. 2, 1941. Supp. 3–319

Gregory, Samuel, Apr. 19, 1813–Mar. 23, 1872.
Vol. 4, Pt. 1–604

Gregory, Stephen Strong, Nov. 16, 1849–Oct. 24, 1920.
Vol. 4, Pt. 1–605

Gregory, Thomas Barger, Oct. 15, 1860–July 11, 1951.
Supp. 5–259

Gregory, Thomas Watt, Nov. 6, 1861–Feb. 26, 1933.
Supp. 1–358

Greist, John Milton, May 9, 1850–Feb. 23, 1906.
Vol. 4, Pt. 1–605

Grellet, Stephen, Nov. 2, 1773–Nov. 16, 1855.
Vol. 4, Pt. 1–606

Gresham, Walter Quintin, Mar. 17, 1832–May 28, 1895.
Vol. 4, Pt. 1–607

Grew, Joseph Clark, May 27, 1880–May 25, 1965.
Supp. 7–302

Grew, Theophilus, d. 1759.
Vol. 4, Pt. 1–609

Grey, Zane, Jan. 31, 1872–Oct. 23, 1939.
Supp. 2–262

Gridley, Charles Vernon, Nov. 24, 1844–June 5, 1898.
Vol. 4, Pt. 1–610

Gridley, Jeremiah, Mar. 10, 1701/02–Sept. 10, 1767.
Vol. 4, Pt. 1–611

Gridley, Richard, Jan. 3, 1710/11–June 21, 1796.
Vol. 4, Pt. 1–611

Grier, Robert Cooper, Mar. 5, 1794–Sept. 25, 1870.
Vol. 4, Pt. 1–612

Grierson, Benjamin Henry, July 8, 1826–Sept. 1, 1911.
Vol. 4, Pt. 1–613

Grierson, Francis, Sept. 18, 1848–May 29, 1927.
Vol. 4, Pt. 1–614

Grieve, Miller, Jan. 11, 1801–c. 1878.
Vol. 4, Pt. 1–615

Griffes, Charles Tomlinson, Sept. 17, 1884–Apr. 8, 1920.
Vol. 4, Pt. 1–616

Griffin, Appleton Prentiss Clark, July 24, 1852–Apr. 16, 1926. Vol. 4, Pt. 1–617

Griffin, Charles, Dec. 18, 1825–Sept. 15, 1867.
Vol. 4, Pt. 1–617

Griffin, Cyrus, July 16, 1748–Dec. 14, 1810.
Vol. 4, Pt. 1–618

Griffin, Edward Dorr, Jan. 6, 1770–Nov. 8, 1837.
Vol. 4, Pt. 1–619

Griffin, Eugene, Oct. 13, 1855–Apr. 11, 1907.
Vol. 4, Pt. 1–620

Griffin, Martin Ignatius Joseph, Oct. 23, 1842–Nov. 10, 1911.
Supp. 1–360

Griffin, Robert Stanislaus, Sept. 27, 1857–Feb. 21, 1933.
Supp. 1–361

Griffin, Simon Goodell, Aug. 9, 1824–Jan. 14, 1902.
Vol. 4, Pt. 1–621

Griffin, Solomon Bulkley, Aug. 13, 1852–Dec. 11, 1925.
Vol. 4, Pt. 1–622
Griffing, Josephine Sophie White, Dec. 18, 1814–Feb. 18, 1872. Vol. 4, Pt. 1–622
Griffis, William Elliot, Sept. 17, 1843–Feb. 5, 1928.
Vol. 4, Pt. 1–623
Griffith, Benjamin, Oct. 16, 1688–c. Oct. 5, 1768.
Vol. 4, Pt. 1–624
Griffith, Clark Calvin, Nov. 20, 1869–Oct. 27, 1955.
Supp. 5–260
Griffith, David Wark, Jan. 22, 1875–July 23, 1948.
Supp. 4–348
Griffith, Goldsborough Sappington, Nov. 4, 1814–Feb. 24, 1904. Vol. 4, Pt. 1–624
Griffith, William, 1766–June 7, 1826.
Vol. 4, Pt. 1–625
Griffiths, John Willis, Oct. 6, 1809?–Mar. 30, 1882.
Vol. 4, Pt. 1–626
Griggs, Everett Gallup, Dec. 27, 1868–Mar. 6, 1938.
Supp. 2–263
Griggs, John William, July 10, 1849–Nov. 28, 1927.
Vol. 4, Pt. 1–627
Grigsby, Hugh Blair, Nov. 22, 1806–Apr. 28, 1881.
Vol. 4, Pt. 1–628
Grim, David, Aug. 25, 1737–Mar. 26, 1826.
Vol. 4, Pt. 1–629
Grimes, Absalom Carlisle, Aug. 22, 1834–Mar. 27, 1911.
Vol. 4, Pt. 1–629
Grimes, James Stanley, May 10, 1807–Sept. 27, 1903.
Vol. 4, Pt. 1–630
Grimes, James Wilson, Oct. 20, 1816–Feb. 7, 1872.
Vol. 4, Pt. 1–631
Grimké, John Faucheraud, Dec. 16, 1752–Aug. 9, 1819.
Vol. 4, Pt. 1–633
Grimké, Sarah Moore, Nov. 26, 1792–Dec. 23, 1873.
Vol. 4, Pt. 1–634
Grimké, Thomas Smith, Sept. 26, 1786–Oct. 12, 1834.
Vol. 4, Pt. 1–635
Grimké Angelina Emily, 1805–1879. [See Grimké, Sarah Moore, 1792–1873.]
Grimké Archibald Henry, Aug. 17, 1849–Feb. 25, 1930.
Vol. 4, Pt. 1–632
Grinnell, Frederick, Aug. 14, 1836–Oct. 21, 1905.
Vol. 4, Pt. 2–1
Grinnell, George Bird, Sept. 20, 1849–Apr. 11, 1938.
Supp. 2–264
Grinnell, Henry, Feb. 13, 1799–June 30, 1874.
Vol. 4, Pt. 2–2
Grinnell, Henry Walton, Nov. 19, 1843–Sept. 2, 1920.
Vol. 4, Pt. 2–2
Grinnell, Joseph, Nov. 17, 1788–Feb. 7, 1885.
Vol. 4, Pt. 2–3
Grinnell, Josiah Bushnell, Dec. 22, 1821–Mar. 31, 1891.
Vol. 4, Pt. 2–4
Grinnell, Moses Hicks, Mar. 3, 1803–Nov. 24, 1877.
Vol. 4, Pt. 2–5
Griscom, Clement Acton, Mar. 15, 1841–Nov. 10, 1912.
Vol. 4, Pt. 2–6
Griscom, John, Sept. 27, 1774–Feb. 26, 1852.
Vol. 4, Pt. 2–7
Griscom, Lloyd Carpenter, Nov. 4, 1872–Feb. 8, 1959.
Supp. 6–253
Griscom, Ludlow, June 17, 1890–May 28, 1959.
Supp. 6–254
Grissom Virgil Ivan ("Gus"), Apr. 3, 1926–Jan. 27, 1967.
Supp. 8–225
Griswold, Alexander Viets, Apr. 22, 1766–Feb. 15, 1843.
Vol. 4, Pt. 2–7
Griswold, Alfred Whitney, Oct. 27, 1906–Apr. 19, 1963.
Supp. 7–303
Griswold, John Augustus, Nov. 11, 1818–Oct. 31, 1872.
Vol. 4, Pt. 2–8
Griswold, Matthew, Mar. 25, 1714–Apr. 28, 1799.
Vol. 4, Pt. 2–9
Griswold, Roger, May 21, 1762–Oct. 25, 1812.
Vol. 4, Pt. 2–10
Griswold, Rufus Wilmot, Feb. 15, 1815–Aug. 27, 1857.
Vol. 4, Pt. 2–10
Griswold, Stanley, Nov. 14, 1763–Aug. 21, 1815.
Vol. 4, Pt. 2–11
Griswold, William McCrillis, Oct. 9, 1853–Aug. 3, 1899.
Vol. 4, Pt. 2–13

Groesbeck, William Slocum, July 24, 1815–July 7, 1897.
Vol. 4, Pt. 2–13
Gronlund, Laurence, July 13, 1846–Oct. 15, 1899.
Vol. 4, Pt. 2–14
Gropius, Walter Adolf Georg, May 18, 1883–July 5, 1969.
Supp. 8–226
Gros, John Daniel, 1738–May 25, 1812.
Vol. 4, Pt. 2–15
Grose, William, Dec. 16, 1812–July 30, 1900.
Vol. 4, Pt. 2–16
Groseilliers, Médart Chouart, Sieur de, fl. 1625–1684.
Vol. 4, Pt. 2–17
Gross, Charles, Feb. 10, 1857–Dec. 3, 1909.
Vol. 4, Pt. 2–18
Gross, Milt, Mar. 4, 1895–Nov. 28, 1953.
Supp. 5–261
Gross, Samuel David, July 8, 1805–May 6, 1884.
Vol. 4, Pt. 2–18
Gross, Samuel Weissell, Feb. 4, 1837–Apr. 16, 1889.
Vol. 4, Pt. 2–20
Grosscup, Peter Stenger, Feb. 15, 1852–Oct. 1, 1921.
Vol. 4, Pt. 2–21
Grosset, Alexander, Jan. 17, 1870–Oct. 27, 1934.
Supp. 1–361
Grossmann, Georg Martin, Oct. 18, 1823–Aug. 24, 1897.
Vol. 4, Pt. 2–22
Grossmann, Louis, Feb. 24, 1863–Sept. 21, 1926.
Vol. 4, Pt. 2–23
Grosvenor, Charles Henry, Sept. 20, 1833–Oct. 30, 1917.
Vol. 4, Pt. 2–24
Grosvenor, Edwin Prescott, Oct. 25, 1875–Feb. 28, 1930.
Vol. 4, Pt. 2–24
Grosvenor, Gilbert Hovey, Oct. 28, 1875–Feb. 4, 1966.
Supp. 8–227
Grosvenor, John. [See Altham, John, 1589–1640.]
Grosvenor, William Mason, Apr. 24, 1835–July 20, 1900.
Vol. 4, Pt. 2–26
Grosz, George, July 26, 1893–July 6, 1959.
Supp. 6–256
Grote, Augustus Radcliffe, Feb. 7, 1841–Sep. 12, 1903.
Vol. 4, Pt. 2–27
Grouard, Frank, Sept. 20, 1850–Aug. 15, 1905.
Vol. 4, Pt. 2–27
Grover, Cuvier, July 29, 1828–June 6, 1885.
Vol. 4, Pt. 2–28
Grover, La Fayette, Nov. 29, 1823–May 10, 1911.
Vol. 4, Pt. 2–29
Groves, Leslie Richard, Jr., Aug. 17, 1896–July 13, 1970.
Supp. 8–229
Grow, Galusha Aaron, Aug. 31, 1822–Mar. 31, 1907.
Vol. 4, Pt. 2–30
Grube, Bernhard Adam, June 24, 1715–Mar. 20, 1808.
Vol. 4, Pt. 2–31
Gruening, Emil, Oct. 2, 1842–May 30, 1914.
Vol. 4, Pt. 2–32
Grund, Francis Joseph, 1798–Sept. 29, 1863.
Supp. 1–362
Grundy, Felix, Sept. 11, 1777–Dec. 19, 1840.
Vol. 4, Pt. 2–32
Grundy, Joseph Ridgway, Jan. 13, 1863–Mar. 3, 1961.
Supp. 7–304
Gue, Benjamin T., Dec. 25, 1828–June 1, 1904.
Vol. 4, Pt. 2–33
Guèrin, Anne-Thérèse, Oct. 2, 1798–May 14, 1856.
Vol. 4, Pt. 2–34
Guernsey, Egbert, July 8, 1823–Sept. 19, 1903.
Vol. 4, Pt. 2–35
Guess, George. [See Sequoyah, 1770–1843.]
Guest, Edgar Albert, Aug. 20, 1881–Aug. 5, 1959.
Supp. 6–258
Guffey, James McClurg, Jan. 19, 1839–Mar. 20, 1930.
Vol. 4, Pt. 2–35
Guffey, Joseph F., Dec. 29, 1870–Mar. 6, 1959.
Supp. 6–259
Guggenheim, Daniel, July 9, 1856–Sept. 28, 1930.
Vol. 4, Pt. 2–36
Guggenheim, Meyer, Feb. 1, 1828–Mar. 15, 1905.
Vol. 4, Pt. 2–38
Guggenheim, Simon, Dec. 30, 1867–Nov. 2, 1941.
Supp. 3–321
Guggenheim, Solomon Robert, Feb. 2, 1861–Nov. 3, 1949.
Supp. 4–351

Guignas, Louis Ignace. [See Guignas, Michel, 1681–1752.]
Guignas, Michel, Jan. 22, 1681–Feb. 6, 1752.
   Vol. 4, Pt. 2–40
Guild, Curtis, Feb. 2, 1860–Apr. 6, 1915.
   Vol. 4, Pt. 2–41
Guild, Curtis, Jan. 13, 1827–Mar. 12, 1911.
   Vol. 4, Pt. 2–40
Guild, La Fayette, Nov. 23, 1825–July 4, 1870.
   Supp. 1–364
Guild, Reuben Aldridge, May 4, 1822–May 13, 1899.
   Vol. 4, Pt. 2–42
Guilday, Peter Keenan, Mar. 25, 1884–July 31, 1947.
   Supp. 4–352
Guilford, Nathan, July 19, 1786–Dec. 18, 1854.
   Vol. 4, Pt. 2–43
Guiney, Louise Imogen, Jan. 7, 1861–Nov. 2, 1920.
   Vol. 4, Pt. 2–43
Guinzburg, Harold Kleinert, Dec. 13, 1899–Oct. 18, 1961.
   Supp. 7–306
Guiteras, Juan, Jan. 4, 1852–Oct. 28, 1925.
   Vol. 4, Pt. 2–44
Gulick, John Thomas, Mar. 13, 1832–Apr. 14, 1923.
   Vol. 4, Pt. 2–45
Gulick, Luther Halsey, June 10, 1828–Apr. 8, 1891.
   Vol. 4, Pt. 2–46
Gulick, Luther Halsey, Dec. 4, 1865–Aug. 13, 1918.
   Vol. 4, Pt. 2–47
Gulick, Sidney Lewis, Apr. 10, 1860–Dec. 20, 1945.
   Supp. 3–322
Gummere, Francis Barton, Mar. 6, 1855–May 30, 1919.
   Vol. 4, Pt. 2–48
Gummere, John, 1784–May 31, 1845.
   Vol. 4, Pt. 2–49
Gummere, Samuel James, Apr. 28, 1811–Oct. 23, 1874.
   Vol. 4, Pt. 2–49
Gummere, Samuel René, Feb. 19, 1849–May 28, 1920.
   Vol. 4, Pt. 2–50
Gummere, William Stryker, June 24, 1850–Jan. 26, 1933.
   Supp. 1–365
Gunn, Frederick William, Oct. 4, 1816–Aug. 16, 1881.
   Vol. 4, Pt. 2–50
Gunn, James Newton, 1867–Nov. 26, 1927.
   Vol. 4, Pt. 2–51
Gunn, Ross, May 12, 1897–Oct. 15, 1966.
   Supp. 8–231
Gunn, Selskar Michael, May 25, 1883–Aug. 2, 1944.
   Supp. 3–323
Gunnison, Foster, June 9, 1896–Oct. 19, 1961.
   Supp. 7–307
Gunnison, John Williams, Nov. 11, 1812–Oct. 26, 1853.
   Vol. 4, Pt. 2–52
Gunsaulus, Frank Wakeley, Jan. 1, 1856–Mar. 17, 1921.
   Vol. 4, Pt. 2–52
Gunter, Archibald Clavering, Oct. 25, 1847–Feb. 24, 1907.
   Vol. 4, Pt. 2–54
Gunther, Charles Frederick, Mar. 6, 1837–Feb. 10, 1920.
   Vol. 4, Pt. 2–54
Gunther, John, Aug. 30, 1901–May 29, 1970.
   Supp. 8–232
Gunton, George, Sept. 8, 1845–Sept. 11, 1919.
   Vol. 4, Pt. 2–55
Gurley, Ralph Randolph, May 26, 1797–July 30, 1872.
   Vol. 4, Pt. 2–56
Gurney, Ephraim Whitman, Feb. 18, 1829–Sept. 12, 1886.
   Vol. 4, Pt. 2–57
Gurowski, Adam, Sept. 10, 1805–May 4, 1866.
   Supp. 1–366
Guthe, Karl Eugen, Mar. 5, 1866–Sept. 10, 1915.
   Vol. 4, Pt. 2–58
Gutherz, Carl, Jan. 28, 1844–Feb. 7, 1907.
   Vol. 4, Pt. 2–58
Guthrie, Alfred, Apr. 1, 1805–Aug. 17, 1882.
   Vol. 4, Pt. 2–59
Guthrie, Edwin Ray, Jr., Jan. 9, 1886–Apr. 23, 1959.
   Supp. 6–261
Guthrie, George Wilkins, Sept. 5, 1848–Mar. 8, 1917.
   Vol. 4, Pt. 2–60
Guthrie, James, Dec. 5, 1792–Mar. 13, 1869.
   Vol. 4, Pt. 2–60
Guthrie, Samuel, 1782–Oct. 19, 1848.
   Vol. 4, Pt. 2–62
Guthrie, William Dameron, Feb. 3, 1859–Dec. 8, 1935.
   Supp. 1–367

Guthrie, Woody, July 14, 1912–Oct. 3, 1967.
   Supp. 8–234
Guy, Seymour Joseph, Jan. 16, 1824–Dec. 10, 1910.
   Vol. 4, Pt. 2–62
Guyot, Arnold Henry, Sept. 28, 1807–Feb. 8, 1884.
   Vol. 4, Pt. 2–63
Guzik, Jack, 1886/1888–Feb. 21, 1956.
   Supp. 6–263
Gwin, William McKendree, Oct. 9, 1805–Sept. 3, 1885.
   Vol. 4, Pt. 2–64
Gwinnett, Button, c. 1735–May 16, 1777.
   Vol. 4, Pt. 2–65

Haan, William George, Oct. 4, 1863–Oct. 26, 1924.
   Vol. 4, Pt. 2–66
Haarstick, Henry Christian, July 26, 1836–Jan. 26, 1919.
   Vol. 4, Pt. 2–67
Haas, Francis Joseph, Mar. 18, 1889–Aug. 29, 1953.
   Supp. 5–263
Haas, Jacob Judah Aaron de, Aug. 13, 1872–Mar. 21, 1937.
   Supp. 2–265
Habberton, John, Feb. 24, 1842–Feb. 24, 1921.
   Vol. 4, Pt. 2–67
Habersham, Alexander Wylly, Mar. 24, 1826–Mar. 26, 1883.
   Vol. 4, Pt. 2–68
Habersham, James, January 1712 o.s.–Aug. 28, 1775.
   Vol. 4, Pt. 2–68
Habersham, Joseph, July 28, 1751–Nov. 17, 1815.
   Vol. 4, Pt. 2–70
Hack, George, c. 1623–c. 1665.
   Vol. 4, Pt. 2–70
Hackett, Francis, Jan. 21, 1883–Apr. 24, 1962.
   Supp. 7–309
Hackett, Frank Warren, Apr. 11, 1841–Aug. 10, 1926.
   Vol. 4, Pt. 2–71
Hackett, Horatio Balch, Dec. 27, 1808–Nov. 2, 1875.
   Vol. 4, Pt. 2–72
Hackett, James Henry, Mar. 15, 1800–Dec. 28, 1871.
   Vol. 4, Pt. 2–72
Hackett, James Keteltas, Sept. 6, 1869–Nov. 8, 1926.
   Vol. 4, Pt. 2–74
Hackley, Charles Henry, Jan. 3, 1837–Feb. 10, 1905.
   Vol. 4, Pt. 2–75
Hadas, Moses, June 25, 1900–Aug. 17, 1966.
   Supp. 8–235
Haddock, Charles Brickett, June 20, 1796–Jan. 15, 1861.
   Vol. 4, Pt. 2–76
Haddon, Elizabeth. [See Estaugh, Elizabeth Haddon, c. 1680
   –1762.]
Hadfield, George, c. 1764–Feb. 5, 1826.
   Vol. 4, Pt. 2–76
Hadley, Arthur Twining, Apr. 23, 1856–Mar. 6, 1930.
   Vol. 4, Pt. 2–77
Hadley, Henry Kimball, Dec. 20, 1871–Sept. 6, 1937.
   Supp. 2–267
Hadley, Herbert Spencer, Feb. 20, 1872–Dec. 1, 1927.
   Vol. 4, Pt. 2–80
Hadley, James, Mar. 30, 1821–Nov. 14, 1872.
   Vol. 4, Pt. 2–81
Ha-Ga-Sa-Do-Ni. [See Deerfoot, 1828–1897.]
Hagedorn, Hermann Ludwig Gebhard, July 18, 1882–July
   27, 1964. Supp. 7–310
Hagen, Hermann August, May 30, 1817–Nov. 9, 1893.
   Vol. 4, Pt. 2–82
Hagen, Walter Charles, Dec. 21, 1892–Oct. 5, 1969.
   Supp. 8–237
Hager, John Sharpenstein, Mar. 12, 1818–Mar. 19, 1890.
   Vol. 4, Pt. 2–82
Haggerty, Melvin Everett, Jan. 17, 1875–Oct. 6, 1937.
   Supp. 2–268
Haggin, James Ben Ali, Dec. 9, 1827–Sept. 12, 1914.
   Vol. 4, Pt. 2–83
Hagner, Peter, Oct. 1, 1772–July 16, 1850.
   Vol. 4, Pt. 2–84
Hagood, Johnson, Feb. 21, 1829–Jan. 4, 1898.
   Vol. 4, Pt. 2–85
Hague, Arnold, Dec. 3, 1840–May 14, 1917.
   Vol. 4, Pt. 2–85
Hague, Frank, Jan. 17, 1876–Jan. 1, 1956.
   Supp. 6–265
Hague, James Duncan, Feb. 24, 1836–Aug. 3, 1908.
   Vol. 4, Pt. 2–87

Hague, Robert Lincoln, Mar. 2, 1880–Mar. 8, 1939.
 Supp. 2–269
Hahn, Georg Michael Decker, Nov. 24, 1830–Mar. 15, 1886.
 Vol. 4, Pt. 2–87
Haid, Leo, July 15, 1849–July 24, 1924.
 Vol. 4, Pt. 2–88
Haight, Charles Coolidge, Mar. 17, 1841–Feb. 8, 1917.
 Vol. 4, Pt. 2–89
Haight, Henry Huntly, May 20, 1825–Sept. 2, 1878.
 Vol. 4, Pt. 2–90
Hailmann, William Nicholas, Oct. 20, 1836–May 13, 1920.
 Vol. 4, Pt. 2–90
Haines, Charles Glidden, Jan. 24, 1792–July 3, 1825.
 Vol. 4, Pt. 2–91
Haines, Daniel, Jan. 6, 1801–Jan. 26, 1877.
 Vol. 4, Pt. 2–92
Haines, Lynn, Apr. 12, 1876–Oct. 9, 1929.
 Vol. 4, Pt. 2–93
Haish, Jacob, Mar. 9, 1826–Feb. 19, 1926.
 Vol. 4, Pt. 2–93
Haldeman, Samuel Steman, Aug. 12, 1812–Sept. 10, 1880.
 Vol. 4, Pt. 2–94
Haldeman-Julius, Emanuel, July 30, 1889–July 31, 1951.
 Supp. 5–264
Halderman, John A., Apr. 15, 1833–Sept. 21, 1908.
 Vol. 4, Pt. 2–95
Hale, Benjamin, Nov. 23, 1797–July 15, 1863.
 Vol. 4, Pt. 2–96
Hale, Charles, June 7, 1831–Mar. 1, 1882.
 Vol. 4, Pt. 2–96
Hale, Charles Reuben, Mar. 14, 1837–Dec. 25, 1900.
 Vol. 4, Pt. 2–97
Hale, David, Apr. 25, 1791–Jan. 20, 1849.
 Vol. 4, Pt. 2–98
Hale, Edward Everett, Apr. 3, 1822–June 10, 1909.
 Vol. 4, Pt. 2–99
Hale, Edward Joseph, Dec. 25, 1839–Feb. 15, 1922.
 Vol. 4, Pt. 2–100
Hale, Edwin Moses, Feb. 2, 1829–Jan. 15, 1899.
 Vol. 4, Pt. 2–101
Hale, Enoch, Jan. 19, 1790–Nov. 12, 1848.
 Vol. 4, Pt. 2–102
Hale, Eugene, June 9, 1836–Oct. 27, 1918.
 Vol. 4, Pt. 2–102
Hale, Frederick, Oct. 7, 1874–Sept. 28, 1963.
 Supp. 7–312
Hale, George Ellery, June 29, 1868–Feb. 21, 1938.
 Supp. 2–270
Hale, Horatio Emmons, May 3, 1817–Dec. 28, 1896.
 Vol. 4, Pt. 2–104
Hale, John Parker, Mar. 31, 1806–Nov. 19, 1873.
 Vol. 4, Pt. 2–105
Hale, Louise Closser, Oct. 13, 1872–July 26, 1933.
 Supp. 1–368
Hale, Lucretia Peabody, Sept. 2, 1820–June 12, 1900.
 Vol. 4, Pt. 2–107
Hale, Nathan, Aug. 16, 1784–Feb. 8, 1863.
 Vol. 4, Pt. 2–109
Hale, Nathan, June 6, 1755–Sept. 22, 1776.
 Vol. 4, Pt. 2–107
Hale, Philip, Mar. 5, 1854–Nov. 13, 1934.
 Supp. 1–369
Hale, Philip Leslie, May 21, 1865–Feb. 2, 1931.
 Vol. 4, Pt. 2–110
Hale, Robert Safford, Sept. 24, 1822–Dec. 14, 1881.
 Vol. 4, Pt. 2–110
Hale, Sarah Josepha Buell, Oct. 24, 1788–Apr. 30, 1879.
 Vol. 4, Pt. 2–111
Hale, William Bayard, Apr. 6, 1869–Apr. 10, 1924.
 Vol. 4, Pt. 2–112
Hale, William Gardner, Feb. 9, 1849–June 23, 1928.
 Vol. 4, Pt. 2–113
Hall, Abraham Oakey, July 26, 1826–Oct. 7, 1898.
 Vol. 4, Pt. 2–114
Hall, Arethusa, Oct. 13, 1802–May 24, 1891.
 Vol. 4, Pt. 2–116
Hall, Arthur Crawshay Alliston, Apr. 12, 1847–Feb. 26, 1930.
 Vol. 4, Pt. 2–116
Hall, Asaph, Oct. 15, 1829–Nov. 22, 1907.
 Vol. 4, Pt. 2–117
Hall, Baynard Rush, Jan. 28, 1798–Jan. 23, 1863.
 Vol. 4, Pt. 2–118

Hall, Bolton, Aug. 5, 1854–Dec. 10, 1938.
 Supp. 2–271
Hall, Charles Cuthbert, Sept. 3, 1852–Mar. 25, 1908.
 Vol. 4, Pt. 2–119
Hall, Charles Francis, 1821–Nov. 8, 1871.
 Vol. 4, Pt. 2–120
Hall, Charles Henry, Nov. 7, 1820–Sept. 12, 1895.
 Vol. 4, Pt. 2–121
Hall, Charles Martin, Dec. 6, 1863–Dec. 27, 1914.
 Vol. 4, Pt. 2–122
Hall, David, 1714–Dec. 24, 1772.
 Vol. 4, Pt. 2–123
Hall, Dominick Augustin, c. 1765–Dec. 19, 1820.
 Vol. 4, Pt. 2–123
Hall, Edwin Herbert, Nov. 7, 1855–Nov. 20, 1938.
 Supp. 2–275
Hall, Fitzedward, Mar. 21, 1825–Feb. 1, 1901.
 Vol. 4, Pt. 2–124
Hall, Florence Marion Howe, Aug. 25, 1845–Apr. 10, 1922.
 Vol. 4, Pt. 2–126
Hall, George Henry, Sept. 21, 1825–Feb. 17, 1913.
 Vol. 4, Pt. 2–126
Hall, Granville Stanley, Feb. 1, 1844–Apr. 24, 1924.
 Vol. 4, Pt. 2–127
Hall, Hazel, Feb. 7, 1886–May 11, 1924.
 Vol. 4, Pt. 2–130
Hall, Henry Bryan, Mar. 11, 1808–Apr. 25, 1884.
 Vol. 4, Pt. 2–131
Hall, Hiland, July 20, 1795–Dec. 18, 1885.
 Vol. 4, Pt. 2–131
Hall, Isaac Hollister, Dec. 12, 1837–July 2, 1896.
 Vol. 4, Pt. 2–132
Hall, James, Aug. 22, 1744–July 25, 1826.
 Vol. 4, Pt. 2–133
Hall, James, Aug. 19, 1793–July 5, 1868.
 Vol. 4, Pt. 2–134
Hall, James, Sept. 12, 1811–Aug. 7, 1898.
 Vol. 4, Pt. 2–135
Hall, James Norman, Apr. 22, 1887–July 6, 1951.
 Supp. 5–266
Hall, John, July 31, 1829–Sept. 17, 1898.
 Vol. 4, Pt. 2–137
Hall, John Elihu, Dec. 27, 1783–June 12, 1829.
 Vol. 4, Pt. 2–138
Hall, Juanita Armethea, Nov. 6, 1901–Feb. 28, 1968.
 Supp. 8–238
Hall, Luther Egbert, Aug. 30, 1869–Nov. 6, 1921.
 Vol. 4, Pt. 2–139
Hall, Lyman, Apr. 12, 1724–Oct. 19, 1790.
 Vol. 4, Pt. 2–139
Hall, Nathan Kelsey, Mar. 28, 1810–Mar. 2, 1874.
 Vol. 4, Pt. 2–140
Hall, Samuel, Nov. 2, 1740–Oct. 30, 1807.
 Vol. 4, Pt. 2–141
Hall, Samuel, Apr. 23, 1800–Nov. 13, 1870.
 Vol. 4, Pt. 2–142
Hall, Samuel Read, Oct. 27, 1795–June 24, 1877.
 Vol. 4, Pt. 2–142
Hall, Sarah Ewing, Oct. 30, 1761–Apr. 8, 1830.
 Vol. 4, Pt. 2–143
Hall, Sherman, Apr. 30, 1800–Sept. 1, 1879.
 Vol. 4, Pt. 2–144
Hall, Thomas, Feb. 4, 1834–Nov. 19, 1911.
 Vol. 4, Pt. 2–144
Hall, Thomas Seavey, Apr. 1, 1827–Dec. 1, 1880.
 Vol. 4, Pt. 2–145
Hall, Willard, Dec. 24, 1780–May 10, 1875.
 Vol. 4, Pt. 2–146
Hall, Willard Preble, May 9, 1820–Nov. 3, 1882.
 Vol. 4, Pt. 2–146
Hall, William Whitty, Oct. 15, 1810–May 10, 1876.
 Vol. 4, Pt. 2–147
Hallam, Lewis, c. 1740–Nov. 1, 1808.
 Vol. 4, Pt. 2–148
Halleck, Fitz-Greene, July 8, 1790–Nov. 19, 1867.
 Vol. 4, Pt. 2–149
Halleck, Henry Wager, Jan. 16, 1815–Jan. 9, 1872.
 Vol. 4, Pt. 2–150
Hallet, Étienne Sulpice, fl. 1789–1796.
 Vol. 4, Pt. 2–152
Hallet, Stephen. [See Hallet, Étienne Sulpice, fl. 1789–1796.]
Hallett, Benjamin, Jan. 18, 1760–Dec. 31, 1849.
 Vol. 4, Pt. 2–154

Hallett, Benjamin Franklin, Dec. 2, 1797–Sept. 30, 1862.
  Vol. 4, Pt. 2–154
Hallett, Moses, July 16, 1834–Apr. 25, 1913.
  Vol. 4, Pt. 2–155
Hallidie, Andrew Smith, Mar. 16, 1836–Apr. 24, 1900.
  Vol. 4, Pt. 2–156
Hallock, Charles, Mar. 13, 1834–Dec. 2, 1917.
  Vol. 4, Pt. 2–156
Hallock, Gerard, Mar. 18, 1800–Jan. 4, 1866.
  Vol. 4, Pt. 2–157
Hallock, William Allen, June 2, 1794–Oct. 2, 1880.
  Vol. 4, Pt. 2–158
Hallowell, Benjamin, Aug. 17, 1799–Sept. 7, 1877.
  Vol. 4, Pt. 2–159
Hallowell, Richard Price, Dec. 16, 1835–Jan. 5, 1904.
  Vol. 4, Pt. 2–160
Halpert, Edith Gregor, Apr. 25, 1900–Oct. 6, 1970.
  Supp. 8–239
Halpine, Charles Graham, Nov. 20, 1829–Aug. 3, 1868.
  Vol. 4, Pt. 2–160
Halsey, Frederick Arthur, July 12, 1856–Oct. 20, 1935.
  Supp. 1–370
Halsey, John, Mar. 1, 1670–1716.
  Vol. 4, Pt. 2–161
Halsey, Thomas Lloyd, c. 1776–Feb. 2, 1855.
  Vol. 4, Pt. 2–162
Halsey, William Frederick, Jr., Oct. 30, 1882–Aug. 16, 1959.
  Supp. 6–266
Halstead, Murat, Sept. 2, 1829–July 2, 1908.
  Vol. 4, Pt. 2–163
Halsted, George Bruce, Nov. 25, 1853–Mar. 16, 1922.
  Vol. 4, Pt. 2–163
Halsted, William Stewart, Sept. 23, 1852–Sept. 7, 1922.
  Vol. 4, Pt. 2–164
Hambidge, Jay, Jan. 13, 1867–June 20, 1924.
  Vol. 4, Pt. 2–165
Hambleton, Thomas Edward, May 17, 1829–Sept. 21, 1906.
  Vol. 4, Pt. 2–167
Hamblin, Joseph Eldridge, Jan. 13, 1828–July 3, 1870.
  Vol. 4, Pt. 2–167
Hamblin, Thomas Sowerby, May 14, 1800–Jan. 8, 1853.
  Vol. 4, Pt. 2–168
Hamer, Thomas Lyon, July 1800–Dec. 2, 1846.
  Vol. 4, Pt. 2–169
Hamilton, Alexander, Jan. 11, 1757–July 12, 1804.
  Vol. 4, Pt. 2–171
Hamilton, Alexander, 1712–May 11, 1756.
  Vol. 4, Pt. 2–170
Hamilton, Alice, Feb. 27, 1869–Sept. 22, 1970.
  Supp. 8–241
Hamilton, Allan McLane, Oct. 6, 1848–Nov. 23, 1919.
  Vol. 4, Pt. 2–179
Hamilton, Andrew, d. Apr. 26, 1703.
  Vol. 4, Pt. 2–180
Hamilton, Andrew, d. Aug. 4, 1741.
  Vol. 4, Pt. 2–181
Hamilton, Andrew Jackson, Jan. 28, 1815–Apr. 11, 1875.
  Vol. 4, Pt. 2–182
Hamilton, Charles Smith, Nov. 16, 1822–Apr. 17, 1891.
  Vol. 4, Pt. 2–183
Hamilton, Clayton, Nov. 14, 1881–Sept. 17, 1946.
  Supp. 4–354
Hamilton, Edith, Aug. 12, 1867–May 31, 1963.
  Supp. 7–313
Hamilton, Edward John, Nov. 29, 1834–Nov. 21, 1918.
  Vol. 4, Pt. 2–184
Hamilton, Frank Hastings, Sept. 10, 1813–Aug. 11, 1886.
  Vol. 4, Pt. 2–185
Hamilton, Gail. [See Dodge, Mary Abigail, 1833–1896.]
Hamilton, James, c. 1710–Aug. 14, 1783.
  Vol. 4, Pt. 2–186
Hamilton, James, May 8, 1786–Nov. 15, 1857.
  Vol. 4, Pt. 2–187
Hamilton, James Alexander, Apr. 14, 1788–Sept. 24, 1878.
  Vol. 4, Pt. 2–188
Hamilton, John William, Mar. 18, 1845–July 24, 1934.
  Supp. 1–371
Hamilton, Maxwell McGaughey, Dec. 20, 1896–Nov. 12, 1957. Supp. 6–269
Hamilton, Paul, Oct. 16, 1762–June 30, 1816.
  Vol. 4, Pt. 2–189
Hamilton, Peter, Nov. 7, 1817–Nov. 22, 1888.
  Vol. 4, Pt. 2–190

Hamilton, Schuyler, July 25, 1822–Mar. 18, 1903.
  Vol. 4, Pt. 2–191
Hamilton, Walton Hale, Oct. 30, 1881–Oct. 27, 1958.
  Supp. 6–271
Hamilton, William Thomas, Dec. 6, 1822–May 24, 1908.
  Vol. 4, Pt. 2–192
Hamilton, William Thomas, Sept. 8, 1820–Oct. 26, 1888.
  Vol. 4, Pt. 2–191
Hamlin, Alfred Dwight Foster, Sept. 5, 1855–Mar. 21, 1926.
  Vol. 4, Pt. 2–193
Hamlin, Charles, Sept. 13, 1837–May 15, 1911.
  Vol. 4, Pt. 2–194
Hamlin, Charles Sumner, Aug. 30, 1861–Apr. 24, 1938.
  Supp. 2–273
Hamlin, Cyrus, Jan. 5, 1811–Aug. 8, 1900.
  Vol. 4, Pt. 2–195
Hamlin, Emmons, Nov. 16, 1821–Apr. 8, 1885.
  Vol. 4, Pt. 2–196
Hamlin, Hannibal, Aug. 27, 1809–July 4, 1891.
  Vol. 4, Pt. 2–196
Hamlin, Talbot Faulkner, June 16, 1889–Oct. 7, 1956.
  Supp. 6–272
Hamlin, William, Oct. 15, 1772–Nov. 22, 1869.
  Vol. 4, Pt. 2–198
Hamline, Leonidas Lent, May 10, 1797–Mar. 23, 1865.
  Vol. 4, Pt. 2–198
Hammer, William Joseph, Feb. 26, 1858–Mar. 24, 1934.
  Supp. 1–373
Hammerstein, Oscar, c. 1847–Aug. 1, 1919.
  Vol. 4, Pt. 2–199
Hammerstein, Oscar, II, July 12, 1895–Aug. 23, 1960.
  Supp. 6–273
Hammett, Henry Pinckney, Dec. 31, 1822–May 8, 1891.
  Vol. 4, Pt. 2–200
Hammett, Samuel Adams, Feb. 4, 1816–Dec. 24, 1865.
  Vol. 4, Pt. 2–201
Hammett, Samuel Dashiell, May 27, 1894–Jan. 10, 1961.
  Supp. 7–314
Hammon, Jupiter, c. 1720–c. 1800.
  Vol. 4, Pt. 2–201
Hammond, Bray, Nov. 20, 1886–July 20, 1968.
  Supp. 8–242
Hammond, Charles, Sept. 19, 1779–Apr. 3, 1840.
  Vol. 4, Pt. 2–202
Hammond, Edward Payson, Sept. 1, 1831–Aug. 14, 1910.
  Vol. 4, Pt. 2–203
Hammond, Edwin, May 20, 1801–Dec. 31, 1870.
  Vol. 4, Pt. 2–203
Hammond, George Henry, May 5, 1838–Dec. 29, 1886.
  Vol. 4, Pt. 2–204
Hammond, Jabez Delano, Aug. 2, 1778–Aug. 18, 1885.
  Vol. 4, Pt. 2–205
Hammond, James Bartlett, Apr. 23, 1839–Jan. 27, 1913.
  Vol. 4, Pt. 2–206
Hammond, James Henry, Nov. 15, 1807–Nov. 13, 1864.
  Vol. 4, Pt. 2–207
Hammond, John Hays, Mar. 31, 1855–June 8, 1936.
  Supp. 2–275
Hammond, Nathaniel Job, Dec. 26, 1833–Apr. 20, 1899.
  Vol. 4, Pt. 2–208
Hammond, Percy Hunter, Mar. 7, 1873–Apr. 25, 1936.
  Supp. 2–277
Hammond, Samuel, Sept. 21, 1757–Sept. 11, 1842.
  Vol. 4, Pt. 2–209
Hammond, William Alexander, Aug. 28, 1828–Jan. 5, 1900.
  Vol. 4, Pt. 2–210
Hammond, William Gardiner, May 3, 1829–Apr. 12, 1894.
  Vol. 4, Pt. 2–211
Hampden, Walter, June 30, 1879–June 11, 1955.
  Supp. 5–267
Hampton, Wade, 1751 or 1752–Feb. 4, 1835.
  Vol. 4, Pt. 2–212
Hampton, Wade, Mar. 28, 1818–Apr. 11, 1902.
  Vol. 4, Pt. 2–213
Hamtranck, John Francis, Apr. 19, 1798–Apr. 21, 1858.
  Vol. 4, Pt. 2–215
Hanaford, Phoebe Ann Coffin, May 6, 1829–June 2, 1921.
  Vol. 4, Pt. 2–216
Hanby, Benjamin Russel, July 22, 1833–Mar. 16, 1867.
  Vol. 4, Pt. 2–217
Hanchett, Henry Granger, Aug. 29, 1853–Aug. 19, 1918.
  Vol. 4, Pt. 2–217

Hancock, John, Jan. 12, 1736/7–Oct. 8, 1793.
    Vol. 4, Pt. 2–218
Hancock, John, Oct. 24, 1824–July 19, 1893.
    Vol. 4, Pt. 2–220
Hancock, Thomas, July 13, 1703–Aug. 1, 1764.
    Vol. 4, Pt. 2–220
Hancock, Winfield Scott, Feb. 14, 1824–Feb. 9, 1886.
    Vol. 4, Pt. 2–221
Hand, Augustus Noble, July 26, 1869–Oct. 28, 1954.
    Supp. 5–269
Hand, Daniel, July 16, 1801–Dec. 17, 1891.
    Vol. 4, Pt. 2–222
Hand, Edward, Dec. 31, 1744–Sept. 3, 1802.
    Vol. 4, Pt. 2–223
Hand, Learned, Jan. 27, 1872–Aug. 18, 1961.
    Supp. 7–315
Handerson, Henry Ebenezer, Mar. 21, 1837–Apr. 23, 1918.
    Vol. 4, Pt. 2–224
Handy, Alexander Hamilton, Dec. 25, 1809–Sept. 12, 1883.
    Vol. 4, Pt. 2–225
Handy, William Christopher, Nov. 16, 1873–Mar. 28, 1958.
    Supp. 6–274
Hanna, Edward Joseph, July 21, 1860–July 10, 1944.
    Supp. 3–325
Hanna, Marcus Alonzo, Sept. 24, 1837–Feb. 15, 1904.
    Vol. 4, Pt. 2–225
Hannagan, Stephen Jerome, Apr. 4, 1899–Feb. 5, 1953.
    Supp. 5–270
Hannegan, Edward Allen, June 25, 1807–Feb. 25, 1859.
    Vol. 4, Pt. 2–228
Hannegan, Robert Emmet, June 30, 1903–Oct. 6, 1949.
    Supp. 4–355
Hansberry, Lorraine Vivian, May 19, 1930–Jan. 12, 1965.
    Supp. 7–318
Hansen, George, Apr. 15, 1863–Mar. 31, 1908.
    Vol. 4, Pt. 2–229
Hansen, Marcus Lee, Dec. 8, 1892–May 11, 1938.
    Supp. 2–278
Hansen, Niels Ebbesen, Jan. 4, 1866–Oct. 5, 1950.
    Supp. 4–357
Hansen, William Webster, May 27, 1909–May 23, 1949.
    Supp. 4–357
Hanson, Alexander Contee, Oct. 22, 1749–Jan. 16, 1806.
    Vol. 4, Pt. 2–230
Hanson, Alexander Contee, Feb. 27, 1786–Apr. 23, 1819.
    Vol. 4, Pt. 2–231
Hanson, James Christian Meinich, Mar. 13, 1864–Nov. 8, 1943. Supp. 3–326
Hanson, John, Apr. 13, 1721–Nov. 22, 1783.
    Vol. 4, Pt. 2–231
Hanson, Ole, Jan. 6, 1874–July 6, 1940.
    Supp. 2–279
Hanson, Roger Weightman, Aug. 27, 1827–Jan. 4, 1863.
    Vol. 4, Pt. 2–232
Hanus, Paul Henry, Mar. 14, 1855–Dec. 14, 1941.
    Supp. 3–327
Hapgood, Hutchins, May 21, 1869–Nov. 18, 1944.
    Supp. 3–329
Hapgood, Isabel Florence, Nov. 21, 1850–June 26, 1928.
    Vol. 4, Pt. 2–233
Hapgood, Norman, Mar. 28, 1868–Apr. 29, 1937.
    Supp. 2–280
Happer, Andrew Patton, Oct. 20, 1818–Oct. 27, 1894.
    Vol. 4, Pt. 2–234
Haraden, Jonathan, Nov. 11, 1744–Nov. 23, 1803.
    Vol. 4, Pt. 2–234
Harahan, James Theodore, Jan. 12, 1841–Jan. 22, 1912.
    Vol. 4, Pt. 2–235
Harahan, William Johnson, Dec. 22, 1867–Dec. 14, 1937.
    Supp. 2–282
Haraszthy De Mokcsa, Agoston, c. 1812–July 6, 1869.
    Vol. 4, Pt. 2–236
Harbaugh, Henry, Oct. 28, 1817–Dec. 28, 1867.
    Vol. 4, Pt. 2–237
Harben, William Nathaniel, July 5, 1858–Aug. 7, 1919.
    Vol. 4, Pt. 2–238
Harbord, James Guthrie, Mar. 21, 1866–Aug. 20, 1947.
    Supp. 4–359
Harby, Isaac, Nov. 9, 1788–Dec. 14, 1828.
    Vol. 4, Pt. 2–239
Harcourt, Alfred, Jan. 31, 1881–June 21, 1954.
    Supp. 5–271

Hard, William, Sept. 15, 1878–Jan. 30, 1962.
    Supp. 7–320
Hardee, William Joseph, Oct. 12, 1815–Nov. 6, 1873.
    Vol. 4, Pt. 2–239
Hardenbergh, Henry Janeway, Feb. 6, 1847–Mar. 13, 1918.
    Vol. 4, Pt. 2–240
Hardenbergh, Jacob Rutsen, 1736–Nov. 2, 1790.
    Vol. 4, Pt. 2–241
Hardey, Mother Mary Aloysia, Dec. 8, 1809–June 17, 1886.
    Vol. 4, Pt. 2–242
Hardie, James Allen, May 5, 1823–Dec. 14, 1876.
    Vol. 4, Pt. 2–242
Hardin, Ben, Feb. 29, 1784–Sept. 24, 1852.
    Vol. 4, Pt. 2–243
Hardin, Charles Henry, July 15, 1820–July 29, 1892.
    Vol. 4, Pt. 2–244
Hardin, John, Oct. 1, 1753–May 1792.
    Vol. 4, Pt. 2–245
Hardin, John J., Jan. 6, 1810–Feb. 23, 1847.
    Vol. 4, Pt. 2–246
Hardin, Martin D., June 21, 1780–Oct. 8, 1823.
    Vol. 4, Pt. 2–246
Harding, Abner Clark, Feb. 10, 1807–July 19, 1874.
    Vol. 4, Pt. 2–247
Harding, Chester, Sept. 1, 1792–Apr. 1, 1866.
    Vol. 4, Pt. 2–248
Harding, George, Oct. 26, 1827–Nov. 17, 1902.
    Vol. 4, Pt. 2–249
Harding, Jesper, Nov. 5, 1799–Aug. 21, 1865.
    Vol. 4, Pt. 2–250
Harding, Robert, Oct. 6, 1701–Sept. 1, 1772.
    Vol. 4, Pt. 2–250
Harding, Seth, Apr. 17, 1734–Nov. 20, 1814,.
    Vol. 4, Pt. 2–251
Harding, Warren Gamaliel, Nov. 2, 1865–Aug. 2, 1923.
    Vol. 4, Pt. 2–252
Harding, William Procter Gould, May 5, 1864–Apr. 7, 1930.
    Vol. 4, Pt. 2–257
Harding, William White, Nov. 1, 1830–May 15, 1889.
    Vol. 4, Pt. 2–259
Hardwick, Thomas William, Dec. 9, 1872–Jan. 31, 1944.
    Supp. 3–330
Hardwicke, Cedric Webster, Feb. 19, 1893–Aug. 6, 1964.
    Supp. 7–321
Hardy, Arthur Sherburne, Aug. 13, 1847–Mar. 13, 1930.
    Vol. 4, Pt. 2–259
Hardy, Oliver Norvell, Jan. 18, 1892–Aug. 7, 1957.
    Supp. 6–276
Hardy, Samuel, c. 1758–Oct. 17, 1785.
    Vol. 4, Pt. 2–260
Hardy, William Harris, Feb. 12, 1837–Feb. 18, 1917.
    Vol. 4, Pt. 2–261
Hare, George Emlen, Sept. 4, 1808–Feb. 15, 1892.
    Vol. 4, Pt. 2–261
Hare, James H., Oct. 3, 1856–June 24, 1946.
    Supp. 4–360
Hare, John Innes Clark, Oct. 17, 1816–Dec. 29, 1905.
    Vol. 4, Pt. 2–262
Hare, Robert, Jan. 17, 1781–May 15, 1858.
    Vol. 4, Pt. 2–263
Hare, William Hobart, May 17, 1838–Oct. 23, 1909.
    Vol. 4, Pt. 2–264
Hargrove, Robert Kennon, Sept. 17, 1829–Aug. 3, 1905.
    Vol. 4, Pt. 2–265
Haring, Clarence, Feb. 9, 1885–Sept. 4, 1960.
    Supp. 6–277
Harkins, William Draper, Dec. 28, 1873–Mar. 7, 1951.
    Supp. 5–273
Harkness, Albert, Oct. 6, 1822–May 27, 1907.
    Vol. 4, Pt. 2–265
Harkness, Edward Stephen, Jan. 22, 1874–Jan. 29, 1940.
    Supp. 2–283
Harkness, William, Dec. 17, 1837–Feb. 28, 1903.
    Vol. 4, Pt. 2–266
Harlan, James, June 22, 1800–Feb. 18, 1863.
    Vol. 4, Pt. 2–267
Harlan, James, Aug. 26, 1820–Oct. 5, 1899.
    Vol. 4, Pt. 2–268
Harlan, John Marshall, June 1, 1833–Oct. 14, 1911.
    Vol. 4, Pt. 2–269
Harlan, Josiah, June 12, 1799–October 1871.
    Vol. 4, Pt. 2–272

Harlan, Richard, Sept. 19, 1796–Sept. 30, 1843.
　　Vol. 4, Pt. 2–273
Harland, Henry, Mar. 1, 1861–Dec. 20, 1905.
　　Vol. 4, Pt. 2–274
Harland, Marion. [See Terhune, Mary Virginia, 1830–1922.]
Harland, Thomas, 1735–Mar. 31, 1807.
　　Vol. 4, Pt. 2–275
Harlow, Jean, Mar. 3, 1911–June 7, 1937.
　　Supp. 2–285
Harlow, Ralph Volney, May 4, 1884–Oct. 3, 1956.
　　Supp. 6–278
Harmar, Josiah, Nov. 10, 1753–Aug. 20, 1813.
　　Vol. 4, Pt. 2–275
Harmon, Daniel Williams, Feb. 19, 1778–Mar. 26, 1845.
　　Vol. 4, Pt. 2–276
Harmon, Judson, Feb. 3, 1846–Feb. 22, 1927.
　　Vol. 4, Pt. 2–276
Harnden, William Frederick, Aug. 23, 1812–Jan. 14, 1845.
　　Vol. 4, Pt. 2–278
Harnett, Cornelius, Apr. 20, 1723?–Apr. 28, 1781.
　　Vol. 4, Pt. 2–279
Harney, Benjamin Robertson, Mar. 6, 1871–Mar. 1, 1938.
　　Supp. 2–286
Harney, William Selby, Aug. 22, 1800–May 9, 1889.
　　Vol. 4, Pt. 2–280
Harper, Fletcher, Jan. 31, 1806–May 29, 1877.
　　Vol. 4, Pt. 2–281
Harper, Ida Husted, Feb. 18, 1851–Mar. 14, 1931.
　　Vol. 4, Pt. 2–281
Harper, James, Apr. 13, 1795–Mar. 27, 1869.
　　Vol. 4, Pt. 2–282
Harper, John, 1797–1875. [See Harper, James, 1795–1869.]
Harper, John Lyell, Sept. 21, 1873–Nov. 28, 1924.
　　Vol. 4, Pt. 2–283
Harper, Joseph Wesley, 1801–1870. [See Harper, James, 1795–1869.]
Harper, Robert Francis, Oct. 18, 1864–Aug. 5, 1914.
　　Vol. 4, Pt. 2–284
Harper, Robert Goodloe, January 1765–Jan. 14, 1825.
　　Vol. 4, Pt. 2–285
Harper, William, Jan. 17, 1790–Oct. 10, 1847.
　　Vol. 4, Pt. 2–286
Harper, William Rainey, July 24, 1856–Jan. 10, 1906.
　　Vol. 4, Pt. 2–287
Harpster, John Henry, Apr. 27, 1844–Feb. 1, 1911.
　　Vol. 4, Pt. 2–292
Harpur, Robert, Jan. 25, 1731?–Apr. 15, 1825.
　　Vol. 4, Pt. 2–293
Harrah, Charles Jefferson, Jan. 1, 1817–Feb. 18, 1890.
　　Vol. 4, Pt. 2–294
Harrell, John, Oct. 21, 1806–Dec. 8, 1876.
　　Vol. 4, Pt. 2–294
Harrigan, Edward, Oct. 26, 1845–June 6, 1911.
　　Vol. 4, Pt. 2–295
Harriman, Edward Henry, Feb. 20, 1848–Sept. 9, 1909.
　　Vol. 4, Pt. 2–296
Harriman, Florence Jaffray Hurst, July 21, 1870–Aug. 30, 1967. Supp. 8–243
Harriman, Walter, Apr. 8, 1817–July 25, 1884.
　　Vol. 4, Pt. 2–300
Harrington, Charles, July 29, 1856–Sept. 11, 1908.
　　Vol. 4, Pt. 2–301
Harrington, John Lyle, Dec. 7, 1868–May 20, 1942.
　　Supp. 3–331
Harrington, Mark Walrod, Aug. 18, 1848–Oct. 9, 1926.
　　Vol. 4, Pt. 2–301
Harrington, Samuel Maxwell, Feb. 5, 1803–Nov. 28, 1865.
　　Vol. 4, Pt. 2–302
Harrington, Thomas Francis, June 10, 1866–Jan. 19, 1919.
　　Vol. 4, Pt. 2–303
Harris, Benjamin, fl. 1673–1716.
　　Vol. 4, Pt. 2–303
Harris, Caleb Fiske, Mar. 9, 1818–Oct. 2, 1881.
　　Vol. 4, Pt. 2–305
Harris, Chapin Aaron, May 6, 1806–Sept. 29, 1860.
　　Vol. 4, Pt. 2–305
Harris, Charles Kassell, May 1, 1865–Dec. 22, 1930.
　　Vol. 4, Pt. 2–306
Harris, Daniel Lester, Feb. 6, 1818–July 11, 1879.
　　Vol. 4, Pt. 2–307
Harris, Elisha, Mar. 5, 1824–Jan. 31, 1884.
　　Vol. 4, Pt. 2–307

Harris, George Washington, Mar. 20, 1814–Dec. 11, 1869.
　　Vol. 4, Pt. 2–309
Harris, George, Apr. 1, 1844–Mar. 1, 1922.
　　Vol. 4, Pt. 2–308
Harris, Ira, May 31, 1802–Dec. 2, 1875.
　　Vol. 4, Pt. 2–310
Harris, Isham Green, Feb. 10, 1818–July 8, 1897.
　　Vol. 4, Pt. 2–310
Harris, James Arthur, Sept. 29, 1880–Apr. 24, 1930.
　　Vol. 4, Pt. 2–311
Harris, Joel Chandler, Dec. 9, 1848–July 3, 1908.
　　Vol. 4, Pt. 2–312
Harris, John, 1726–July 29, 1791.
　　Vol. 4, Pt. 2–314
Harris, John Woods, 1810–Apr. 1, 1887.
　　Vol. 4, Pt. 2–314
Harris, Joseph, June 29, 1828–Nov. 18, 1892.
　　Vol. 4, Pt. 2–315
Harris, Julian La Rose, June 21, 1874–Feb. 9, 1963.
　　Supp. 7–323
Harris, Maurice Henry, Nov. 9, 1859–June 23, 1930.
　　Vol. 4, Pt. 2–316
Harris, Merriman Colbert, July 9, 1846–May 8, 1921.
　　Vol. 4, Pt. 2–316
Harris, Miriam Coles, July 7, 1834–Jan. 23, 1925.
　　Vol. 4, Pt. 2–317
Harris, Nathaniel Harrison, Aug. 22, 1834–Aug. 23, 1900.
　　Vol. 4, Pt. 2–318
Harris, Paul Percy, Apr. 19, 1868–Jan. 27, 1947.
　　Supp. 4–361
Harris, Rollin Arthur, Apr. 18, 1863–Jan. 20, 1918.
　　Vol. 4, Pt. 2–318
Harris, Sam Henry, Feb. 3, 1872–July 3, 1941.
　　Supp. 3–332
Harris, Samuel, June 14, 1814–June 25, 1899.
　　Vol. 4, Pt. 2–319
Harris, Thaddeus Mason, July 7, 1768–Apr. 3, 1842.
　　Vol. 4, Pt. 2–320
Harris, Thaddeus William, Nov. 12, 1795–Jan. 16, 1856.
　　Vol. 4, Pt. 2–321
Harris, Thomas Lake, May 15, 1823–Mar. 23, 1906.
　　Vol. 4, Pt. 2–322
Harris, Townsend, Oct. 3, 1804–Feb. 25, 1878.
　　Vol. 4, Pt. 2–324
Harris, Wiley Pope, Nov. 9, 1818–Dec. 3, 1891.
　　Vol. 4, Pt. 2–325
Harris, William, Apr. 29, 1765–Oct. 18, 1829.
　　Vol. 4, Pt. 2–325
Harris, William Alexander, Oct. 29, 1841–Dec. 20, 1909.
　　Vol. 4, Pt. 2–326
Harris, William Littleton, July 6, 1807–Nov. 26, 1868.
　　Vol. 4, Pt. 2–327
Harris, William Logan, Nov. 14, 1817–Sept. 2, 1887.
　　Vol. 4, Pt. 2–327
Harris, William Torrey, Sept. 10, 1835–Nov. 5, 1909.
　　Vol. 4, Pt. 2–328
Harrison, Alexander. [See Harrison, Thomas Alexander, 1853–1930.]
Harrison, Benjamin, 1726?–Apr. 24, 1791.
　　Vol. 4, Pt. 2–330
Harrison, Benjamin, Aug. 20, 1833–Mar. 13, 1901.
　　Vol. 4, Pt. 2–331
Harrison, Birge. [See Harrison, Lovell Birge, 1854–1929.]
Harrison, Byron Patton, Aug. 29, 1881–June 22, 1941.
　　Supp. 3–334
Harrison, Carter Henry, Feb. 15, 1825–Oct. 28, 1893.
　　Vol. 4, Pt. 2–335
Harrison, Carter Henry, Jr., Apr. 23, 1860–Dec. 25, 1953.
　　Supp. 5–274
Harrison, Charles Custis, May 3, 1844–Feb. 12, 1929.
　　Vol. 4, Pt. 2–336
Harrison, Constance Cary, Apr. 25, 1843–Nov. 21, 1920.
　　Vol. 4, Pt. 2–337
Harrison, Elizabeth, Sept. 1, 1849–Oct. 31, 1927.
　　Vol. 4, Pt. 2–338
Harrison, Fairfax, Mar. 13, 1869–Feb. 2, 1938.
　　Supp. 2–286
Harrison, Francis Burton, Dec. 18, 1873–Nov. 21, 1957.
　　Supp. 6–279
Harrison, Gabriel, Mar. 25, 1818–Dec. 15, 1902.
　　Vol. 4, Pt. 2–339
Harrison, George Paul, Mar. 19, 1841–July 17, 1922.
　　Vol. 4, Pt. 2–340

Harrison, Gessner, June 26, 1807–Apr. 7, 1862.
Vol. 4, Pt. 2–340
Harrison, Henry Baldwin, Sept. 11, 1821–Oct. 29, 1901.
Vol. 4, Pt. 2–341
Harrison, Henry Sydnor, Feb. 12, 1880–July 14, 1930.
Vol. 4, Pt. 2–342
Harrison, James, Oct. 10, 1803–Aug. 3, 1870.
Vol. 4, Pt. 2–343
Harrison, James Albert, Aug. 21, 1848–Jan. 31, 1911.
Vol. 4, Pt. 2–343
Harrison, John, Dec. 17, 1773–July 19, 1833.
Vol. 4, Pt. 2–344
Harrison, Joseph, Sept. 20, 1810–Mar. 27, 1874.
Vol. 4, Pt. 2–345
Harrison, Lovell Birge, Oct. 28, 1854–May 11, 1929.
Vol. 4, Pt. 2–346
Harrison, Pat. [See Harrison, Byron Patton.]
Harrison, Peter, June 14, 1716–Apr. 30, 1775.
Vol. 4, Pt. 2–347
Harrison, Richard Berry, Sept. 28, 1864–Mar. 14, 1935.
Supp. 1–374
Harrison, Ross Granville, Jan. 13, 1870–Sept. 30, 1959.
Supp. 6–281
Harrison, Thomas Alexander, Jan. 17, 1853–Oct. 13, 1930.
Vol. 4, Pt. 2–347
Harrison, William Henry, Feb. 9, 1773–Apr. 4, 1841.
Vol. 4, Pt. 2–348
Harrison, William Pope, Sept. 3, 1830–Feb. 7, 1895.
Vol. 4, Pt. 2–352
Harrisse, Henry, Mar. 24, 1829–May 13, 1910.
Supp. 1–374
Harrod, Benjamin Morgan, Feb. 19, 1837–Sept. 7, 1912.
Vol. 4, Pt. 2–353
Harrod, James, 1742–July 1793.
Vol. 4, Pt. 2–353
Harshberger, John William, Jan. 1, 1869–Apr. 27, 1929.
Vol. 4, Pt. 2–354
Harshe, Robert Bartholow, May 26, 1879–Jan. 11, 1938.
Supp. 2–287
Hart, Abraham, Dec. 15, 1810–July 23, 1885.
Vol. 4, Pt. 2–355
Hart, Albert Bushnell, July 1, 1854–June 16, 1943.
Supp. 3–335
Hart, Charles Henry, Feb. 4, 1847–July 29, 1918.
Vol. 4, Pt. 2–355
Hart, Edmund Hall, Dec. 26, 1839–Apr. 22, 1898.
Vol. 4, Pt. 2–356
Hart, Edward, Nov. 18, 1854–June 6, 1931.
Supp. 1–376
Hart, Edwin Bret, Dec. 25, 1874–Mar. 12, 1953.
Supp. 5–275
Hart, George Overbury, May 10, 1868–Sept. 9, 1933.
Supp. 1–376
Hart, Hastings Hornell, Dec. 14, 1851–May 9, 1932.
Supp. 1–377
Hart, James MacDougal, May 10, 1828–Oct. 24, 1901.
Vol. 4, Pt. 2–356
Hart, James Morgan, Nov. 2, 1839–Apr. 18, 1916.
Vol. 4, Pt. 2–357
Hart, Joel Tanner, Feb. 10, 1810–Mar. 2, 1877.
Vol. 4, Pt. 2–358
Hart, John, 1711?–May 11, 1779.
Vol. 4, Pt. 2–359
Hart, John Seely, Jan. 28, 1810–Mar. 26, 1877.
Vol. 4, Pt. 2–359
Hart, Lorenz Milton, May 2, 1895–Nov. 22, 1943.
Supp. 3–338
Hart, Moss, Oct. 24, 1904–Dec. 20, 1961.
Supp. 7–324
Hart, Samuel, June 4, 1845–Feb. 25, 1917.
Vol. 4, Pt. 2–360
Hart, Virgil Chittenden, Jan. 2, 1840–Feb. 24, 1904.
Vol. 4, Pt. 2–361
Hart, William, Mar. 31, 1823–June 17, 1894.
Vol. 4, Pt. 2–361
Hart, William Surrey, Dec. 6, 1862[?]–June 23, 1946.
Supp. 4–362
Harte, Francis Brett, Aug. 25, 1836–May 5, 1902.
Vol. 4, Pt. 2–362
Hartford, George Huntington, Sept. 5, 1833–Aug. 29, 1917.
Supp. 5–276
Hartford, George Ludlum, Nov. 7, 1864–Sept. 23, 1957.
Supp. 5–276

Hartford, John Augustine, Feb. 10, 1872–Sept. 20, 1951.
Supp. 5–276
Hartley, Frank, June 10, 1856–June 19, 1913.
Vol. 4, Pt. 2–365
Hartley, Fred Allen, Jr., Feb. 22, 1903–May 11, 1969.
Supp. 8–245
Hartley, Jonathan Scott, Sept. 23, 1845–Dec. 6, 1912.
Vol. 4, Pt. 2–365
Hartley, Marsden, Jan. 4, 1877–Sept. 2, 1943.
Supp. 3–339
Hartley, Thomas, Sept. 7, 1748–Dec. 21, 1800.
Vol. 4, Pt. 2–366
Hartmann, Carl Sadakichi, Nov. 8, 1867[?]–Nov. 21, 1944.
Supp. 3–341
Hartness, James, Sept. 3, 1861–Feb. 2, 1934.
Supp. 1–378
Hartranft, Chester David, Oct. 15, 1839–Dec. 30, 1914
Vol. 4, Pt. 2–367
Hartranft, John Frederick, Dec. 16, 1830–Oct. 17, 1889.
Vol. 4, Pt. 2–368
Hartshorne, Henry, Mar. 16, 1823–Feb. 10, 1897.
Vol. 4, Pt. 2–368
Hartsuff, George Lucas, May 28, 1830–May 16, 1874.
Vol. 4, Pt. 2–369
Hartwig, Johann Christoph, Jan. 6, 1714–July 17, 1796.
Vol. 4, Pt. 2–370
Hartzell, Joseph Crane, June 1, 1842–Sept. 6, 1928.
Vol. 4, Pt. 2–370
Harvard, John, November 1607–Sept. 14, 1638.
Vol. 4, Pt. 2–371
Harvey, "Coin." [See Harvey, William Hope, 1851–1936.]
Harvey, George Brinton McClellan, Feb. 16, 1864–Aug. 20,
1928. Vol. 4, Pt. 2–372
Harvey, Hayward Augustus, Jan. 17, 1824–Aug. 28, 1893.
Vol. 4, Pt. 2–373
Harvey, Louis Powell, July 22, 1820–Apr. 19, 1862.
Vol. 4, Pt. 2–374
Harvey, Sir John, d. 1646.
Supp. 1–379
Harvey, William Hope, Aug. 16, 1851–Feb. 11, 1936.
Supp. 2–288
Harvie, John, 1742–Feb. 6, 1807.
Vol. 4, Pt. 2–375
Hasbrouck, Abraham Bruyn, Nov. 29, 1791–Feb. 23, 1879.
Vol. 4, Pt. 2–375
Hasbrouck, Lydia Sayer, Dec. 20, 1827–Aug. 24, 1910.
Vol. 4, Pt. 2–376
Hascall, Milo Smith, Aug. 5, 1829–Aug. 30, 1904.
Vol. 4, Pt. 2–377
Haseltine, James Henry, Nov. 2, 1833–Nov. 9, 1907.
Vol. 4, Pt. 2–377
Haselton, Seneca, Feb. 26, 1848–July 21, 1921.
Vol. 4, Pt. 2–378
Hasenclever, Peter, Nov. 24, 1716–June 13, 1793.
Vol. 4, Pt. 2–379
Haskell, Charles Nathaniel, Mar. 13, 1860–July 5, 1933.
Supp. 1–380
Haskell, Dudley Chase, Mar. 23, 1842–Dec. 16, 1883.
Vol. 4, Pt. 2–380
Haskell, Ella Louise Knowles, July 31, 1860–Jan. 27, 1911.
Vol. 4, Pt. 2–380
Haskell, Ernest, July 30, 1876–Nov. 2, 1925.
Vol. 4, Pt. 2–381
Haskell, Henry Jospeh, Mar. 8, 1874–Aug. 20, 1952.
Supp. 5–278
Hasket, Elias, Apr. 25, 1670–Mar. 9, 1739?.
Vol. 4, Pt. 2–382
Haskins, Charles Homer, Dec. 21, 1870–May 14, 1937.
Supp. 2–289
Hassam, Frederick Childe, Oct. 17, 1859–Aug. 27, 1935.
Supp. 1–381
Hassard, John Rose Greene, Sept. 4, 1836–Apr. 18, 1888.
Vol. 4, Pt. 2–382
Hassaurek, Friedrich, Oct. 8, 1831–Oct. 3, 1885.
Vol. 4, Pt. 2–383
Hasselquist, Tuve Nilsson, Mar. 2, 1816–Feb. 4, 1891.
Vol. 4, Pt. 2–384
Hassler, Ferdinand Rudolph, Oct. 7, 1770–Nov. 20, 1843.
Vol. 4, Pt. 2–385
Hastings, Charles Sheldon, Nov. 27, 1848–Jan. 31, 1932.
Supp. 1–383
Hastings, Daniel Oren, Mar. 5, 1874–May 9, 1966.
Supp. 8–246

Hastings, Samuel Dexter, July 24, 1816–Mar. 26, 1903.
  Vol. 4, Pt. 2–386
Hastings, Serranus Clinton, Nov. 22, 1814–Feb. 18, 1893.
  Vol. 4, Pt. 2–387
Hastings, Thomas, Oct. 15, 1784–May 15, 1872.
  Vol. 4, Pt. 2–387
Hastings, Thomas, Mar. 11, 1860–Oct. 22, 1929.
  Vol. 4, Pt. 2–388
Hastings, William Wirt, Dec. 31, 1866–Apr. 8, 1938.
  Supp. 2–291
Haswell, Anthony, Apr. 6, 1756–May 22, 1816.
  Vol. 4, Pt. 2–390
Haswell, Charles Haynes, May 22, 1809–May 12, 1907.
  Vol. 4, Pt. 2–391
Hatch, Carl A., Nov. 27, 1889–Sept. 15, 1963.
  Supp. 7–326
Hatch, Edward, Dec. 23, 1832–Apr. 11, 1889.
  Vol. 4, Pt. 2–392
Hatch, John Porter, Jan. 9, 1822–Apr. 12, 1901.
  Vol. 4, Pt. 2–392
Hatch, Rufus, Jun. 24, 1832–Feb. 23, 1893.
  Vol. 4, Pt. 2–393
Hatch, William Henry, Sept. 11, 1833–Dec. 23, 1896.
  Vol. 4, Pt. 2–394
Hatcher, Orie Latham, Dec. 10, 1868–Apr. 1, 1946.
  Supp. 4–364
Hatcher, Robert Anthony, Feb. 6, 1868–Apr. 1, 1944.
  Supp. 3–342
Hatcher, William Eldridge, July 25, 1834–Aug. 24, 1912.
  Vol. 4, Pt. 2–395
Hatfield, Edwin Francis, Jan. 9, 1807–Sept. 22, 1883.
  Vol. 4, Pt. 2–395
Hathorne, William, c. 1607–1681.
  Vol. 4, Pt. 2–396
Hatlo, Jimmy, Sept. 1, 1898–Dec. 1, 1963.
  Supp. 7–327
Hatton, Frank, Apr. 28, 1846–Apr. 30, 1894.
  Vol. 4, Pt. 2–397
Haugen, Gilbert Nelson, Apr. 21, 1859–July 18, 1933.
  Supp. 1–384
Haugen, Nils Pederson, Mar. 9, 1849–Apr. 23, 1931.
  Supp. 1–385
Haughery, Margaret Gaffney, c. 1814–Feb. 9, 1882.
  Vol. 4, Pt. 2–398
Haughton, Percy Duncan, July 11, 1876–Oct. 27, 1924.
  Vol. 4, Pt. 2–398
Hauk, Minnie, Nov. 16, 1852?–Feb. 6, 1929.
  Vol. 4, Pt. 2–399
Haupt, Alma Cecelia, Mar. 19, 1893–Mar. 15, 1956.
  Supp. 6–283
Haupt, Herman, Mar. 26, 1817–Dec. 14, 1905.
  Vol. 4, Pt. 2–400
Haupt, Paul, Nov. 25, 1858–Dec. 15, 1926.
  Vol. 4, Pt. 2–401
Hauser, Samuel Thomas, Jan. 10, 1833–Nov. 10, 1914.
  Vol. 4, Pt. 2–402
Havell, Robert, Nov. 25, 1793–Nov. 11, 1878.
  Vol. 4, Pt. 2–403
Havemeyer, Henry Osborne, Oct. 18, 1847–Dec. 4, 1907.
  Vol. 4, Pt. 2–404
Havemeyer, William Frederick, Feb. 12, 1804–Nov. 30, 1874.
  Vol. 4, Pt. 2–405
Haven, Alice B. [See Haven, Emily Bradley Neal, 1827–
  1863.]
Haven, Emily Bradley Neal, Sept. 13, 1827–Aug. 23, 1863.
  Vol. 4, Pt. 2–406
Haven, Gilbert, Sept. 19, 1821–Jan. 3, 1880.
  Vol. 4, Pt. 2–407
Haven, Henry Philemon, Feb. 11, 1815–Apr. 30, 1876.
  Vol. 4, Pt. 2–408
Haven, Joseph, Jan. 4, 1816–May 23, 1874.
  Vol. 4, Pt. 2–409
Haven Erastus Otis, Nov. 1, 1820–Aug. 2, 1881.
  Vol. 4, Pt. 2–406
Havens, James Smith, May 28, 1859–Feb. 27, 1927.
  Vol. 4, Pt. 2–410
Haverly, Christopher, June 30, 1837–Sept. 28, 1901.
  Vol. 4, Pt. 2–410
Haverly, Jack H. [See Haverly, Christopher, 1837–1901.]
Haviland, Clarence Floyd, Aug. 15, 1875–Jan. 1, 1930.
  Vol. 4, Pt. 2–411
Haviland, John, Dec. 15, 1792–Mar. 28, 1852.
  Vol. 4, Pt. 2–412

Hawes, Charles Boardman, Jan. 24, 1889–July 15, 1923.
  Vol. 4, Pt. 2–413
Hawes, Harriet Ann Boyd, Oct. 11, 1871–Mar. 31, 1945.
  Supp. 3–343
Hawkins, Benjamin, Aug. 15, 1754–June 6, 1818.
  Vol. 4, Pt. 2–413
Hawkins, Dexter Arnold, June 24, 1825–July 24, 1886.
  Vol. 4, Pt. 2–414
Hawkins, Rush Christopher, Sept. 14, 1831–Oct. 25, 1920.
  Vol. 4, Pt. 2–415
Hawks, Francis Lister, June 10, 1798–Sept. 27, 1866.
  Vol. 4, Pt. 2–416
Hawks, John, 1731–Feb. 16, 1790.
  Vol. 4, Pt. 2–417
Hawley, Gideon, Nov. 5, 1727–Oct. 3, 1807.
  Vol. 4, Pt. 2–418
Hawley, Gideon, Sept. 26, 1785–July 17, 1870.
  Vol. 4, Pt. 2–418
Hawley, James Henry, Jan. 17, 1847–Aug. 3, 1929.
  Vol. 4, Pt. 2–419
Hawley, Joseph, Oct. 8, 1723–Mar. 10, 1788.
  Vol. 4, Pt. 2–420
Hawley, Joseph Roswell, Oct. 31, 1826–Mar. 18, 1905.
  Vol. 4, Pt. 2–421
Hawley, Paul Ramsey, Jan. 31, 1891–Nov. 24, 1965.
  Supp. 7–328
Hawley, Willis Chatman, May 5, 1864–July 24, 1941.
  Supp. 3–345
Haworth, Joseph, Apr. 7, 1855?–Aug. 28, 1903.
  Vol. 4, Pt. 2–422
Hawthorne, Charles Webster, Jan. 8, 1872–Nov. 29, 1930.
  Vol. 4, Pt. 2–423
Hawthorne, Julian, June 22, 1846–July 14, 1934.
  Supp. 1–386
Hawthorne, Nathaniel, July 4, 1804–May 18 or 19, 1864.
  Vol. 4, Pt. 2–424
Hawthorne, Rose. [See Alphonsa, Mother, 1851–1926.]
Hay, Charles Augustus, Feb. 11, 1821–June 26, 1893.
  Vol. 4, Pt. 2–429
Hay, George, Dec. 15, 1765–Sept. 21, 1830.
  Vol. 4, Pt. 2–429
Hay, John Milton, Oct. 8, 1838–July 1, 1905.
  Vol. 4, Pt. 2–430
Hay, Mary Garrett, Aug. 29, 1857–Aug. 29, 1928.
  Vol. 4, Pt. 2–436
Hay, Oliver Perry, May 22, 1846–Nov. 2, 1930.
  Vol. 4, Pt. 2–436
Hayden, Amos Sutton, Sept. 17, 1813–Sept. 10, 1880.
  Vol. 4, Pt. 2–437
Hayden, Charles, July 9, 1870–Jan. 8, 1937.
  Supp. 2–292
Hayden, Charles Henry, Aug. 4, 1856–Aug. 4, 1901.
  Vol. 4, Pt. 2–438
Hayden, Edward Everett, Apr. 14, 1858–Nov. 17, 1932.
  Supp. 1–387
Hayden, Ferdinand Vandiveer, Sept. 7, 1829–Dec. 22, 1887.
  Vol. 4, Pt. 2–438
Hayden, Hiram Washington, Feb. 10, 1820–July 18, 1904.
  Vol. 4, Pt. 2–440
Hayden, Horace H., Oct. 13, 1769–Jan. 26, 1844.
  Vol. 4, Pt. 2–440
Hayden, Joseph Shepard, July 31, 1802–Feb. 17, 1877.
  Vol. 4, Pt. 2–442
Hayden, William, June 30, 1799–Apr. 7, 1863.
  Vol. 4, Pt. 2–442
Hayes, Augustus Allen, Feb. 28, 1806–June 21, 1882.
  Vol. 4, Pt. 2–443
Hayes, Carlton Joseph Huntley, May 16, 1882–Sept. 3, 1964.
  Supp. 7–329
Hayes, Charles Willard, Oct. 8, 1858–Feb. 8, 1916.
  Vol. 4, Pt. 2–444
Hayes, Edward Carey, Feb. 10, 1868–Aug. 7, 1928.
  Supp. 1–388
Hayes, Gabby, May 7, 1885–Feb. 9, 1969.
  Supp. 8–248
Hayes, Isaac Israel, Mar. 5, 1832–Dec. 17, 1881.
  Vol. 4, Pt. 2–445
Hayes, John Lord, Apr. 13, 1812–Apr. 18, 1887.
  Vol. 4, Pt. 2–446
Hayes, John William, Dec. 26, 1854–Nov. 25, 1942.
  Supp. 3–345
Hayes, Max Sebastian, May 25, 1866–Oct. 11, 1945.
  Supp. 3–346

Hayes, Patrick Joseph, Nov. 20, 1867–Sept. 4, 1938.
  Supp. 2–293
Hayes, Rutherford Birchard, Oct. 4, 1822–Jan. 17, 1893.
  Vol. 4, Pt. 2–446
Hayes, William Henry, 1829–March 1877.
  Vol. 4, Pt. 2–451
Hayford, John Fillmore, May 19, 1868–Mar. 10, 1925.
  Vol. 4, Pt. 2–452
Haygood, Atticus Green, Nov. 19, 1839–Jan. 19, 1896.
  Vol. 4, Pt. 2–452
Haygood, Laura Askew, Oct. 14, 1845–Apr. 29, 1900.
  Vol. 4, Pt. 2–453
Hayne, Isaac, Sept. 23, 1745–Aug. 4, 1781.
  Vol. 4, Pt. 2–454
Hayne, Paul Hamilton, Jan. 1, 1830–July 6, 1886.
  Vol. 4, Pt. 2–455
Hayne, Robert Young, Nov. 10, 1791–Sept. 24, 1839.
  Vol. 4, Pt. 2–456
Haynes, George Edmund, May 11, 1880–Jan. 8, 1960.
  Supp. 6–284
Haynes, John, 1594?–Jan. 1653/54.
  Vol. 4, Pt. 2–459
Haynes, John Henry, June 27, 1849–June 29, 1910.
  Vol. 4, Pt. 2–460
Haynes, Williams, July 29, 1886–Nov. 16, 1970.
  Supp. 8–249
Hays, Alexander, July 8, 1819–May 5, 1864.
  Vol. 4, Pt. 2–460
Hays, Arthur Garfield, Dec. 12, 1881–Dec. 14, 1954.
  Supp. 5–279
Hays, Harry Thompson, Apr. 14, 1820–Aug. 21, 1876.
  Vol. 4, Pt. 2–461
Hays, Isaac, July 5, 1796–Apr. 13, 1879.
  Vol. 4, Pt. 2–462
Hays, John Coffee, Jan. 28, 1817–Apr. 28, 1883.
  Vol. 4, Pt. 2–463
Hays, Will H., Nov. 5, 1879–Mar. 7, 1954.
  Supp. 5–280
Hays, William Jacob, Aug. 8, 1830–Mar. 13, 1875.
  Vol. 4, Pt. 2–463
Hays, William Shakespeare, July 19, 1837–July 23, 1907.
  Vol. 4, Pt. 2–464
Hayward, George, Mar. 9, 1791–Oct. 7, 1863.
  Vol. 4, Pt. 2–464
Hayward, Nathaniel Manley, Jan. 19, 1808–July 18, 1865.
  Vol. 4, Pt. 2–465
Haywood, Allan Shaw, Oct. 9, 1888–Feb. 21, 1953.
  Supp. 5–282
Haywood, John, Mar. 16, 1762–Dec. 22, 1826.
  Vol. 4, Pt. 2–466
Haywood, William Dudley, Feb. 4, 1869–May 18, 1928.
  Vol. 4, Pt. 2–467
Hazard, Augustus George, Apr. 28, 1802–May 7, 1868.
  Vol. 4, Pt. 2–469
Hazard, Jonathan J., b. 1744?–d. after 1824.
  Vol. 4, Pt. 2–470
Hazard, Rowland Gibson, Oct. 9, 1801–June 24, 1888.
  Vol. 4, Pt. 2–471
Hazard, Samuel, May 26, 1784–May 22, 1870.
  Vol. 4, Pt. 2–472
Hazard, Thomas, Sept. 15, 1720–Aug. 26, 1798.
  Vol. 4, Pt. 2–472
Hazard, Thomas Robinson, Jan. 3, 1797–Mar. 26, 1886.
  Vol. 4, Pt. 2–473
Hazard Ebenezer, Jan. 15, 1744–June 13, 1817.
  Vol. 4, Pt. 2–469
Hazelius, Ernest Lewis, Sept. 6, 1777–Feb. 20, 1853.
  Vol. 4, Pt. 2–474
Hazeltine, Mayo Williamson, Apr. 24, 1841–Sept. 14, 1909.
  Vol. 4, Pt. 2–475
Hazelton, George Cochrane, Jan. 20, 1868–June 24, 1921.
  Vol. 4, Pt. 2–475
Hazelwood, John, c. 1726–Mar. 1, 1800.
  Vol. 4, Pt. 2–476
Hazen, Allen, Aug. 28, 1869–July 26, 1930.
  Supp. 1–389
Hazen, Henry Allen, Jan. 12, 1849–Jan. 23, 1900.
  Vol. 4, Pt. 2–477
Hazen, Moses, June 1, 1733–Feb. 3, 1803.
  Vol. 4, Pt. 2–477
Hazen, William Babcock, Sept. 27, 1830–Jan. 16, 1887.
  Vol. 4, Pt. 2–478

Headley, Joel Tyler, Dec. 30, 1813–Jan. 16, 1897.
  Vol. 4, Pt. 2–479
Headley, Phineas Camp, June 24, 1819–Jan. 5, 1903.
  Vol. 4, Pt. 2–480
Healy, George Peter Alexander, July 15, 1813–June 24, 1894.
  Vol. 4, Pt. 2–480
Heap, Samuel Davies, Oct. 8, 1781–Oct. 2, 1853.
  Vol. 4, Pt. 2–481
Heard, Augustine, Mar. 30, 1785–Sept. 14, 1868.
  Vol. 4, Pt. 2–482
Heard, Dwight Bancroft, May 1, 1869–Mar. 14, 1929.
  Vol. 4, Pt. 2–483
Heard, Franklin Fiske, Jan. 17, 1825–Sept. 29, 1889.
  Vol. 4, Pt. 2–483
Hearn, Lafcadio, June 27, 1850–Sept. 26, 1904.
  Vol. 4, Pt. 2–484
Hearst, George, Sept. 3, 1820–Feb. 28, 1891.
  Vol. 4, Pt. 2–487
Hearst, Phoebe Apperson, Dec. 3, 1842–Apr. 13, 1919.
  Vol. 4, Pt. 2–488
Hearst, William Randolph, Apr. 20, 1863–Aug. 14, 1951.
  Supp. 5–283
Heath, James Ewell, July 8, 1792–June 28, 1862.
  Vol. 4, Pt. 2–489
Heath, Perry Sanford, Aug. 31, 1857–Mar. 30, 1927.
  Vol. 4, Pt. 2–489
Heath, Thomas Kurton. [See McIntyre, James, 1857–1937.]
Heath, Thomas Kurton, Aug. 11, 1853–Aug. 18, 1938.
  Supp. 2–412
Heath, William, Mar. 2, 1737–Jan. 24, 1814.
  Vol. 4, Pt. 2–490
Heathcote, Caleb, Mar. 6, 1665/66–Mar. 1, 1720/21.
  Vol. 4, Pt. 2–491
Heaton, John Langdon, Jan. 29, 1860–Feb. 21, 1935.
  Supp. 1–390
Hébert, Louis, Mar. 13, 1820–Jan. 7, 1901.
  Vol. 4, Pt. 2–492
Hébert, Paul Octave, Dec. 12, 1818–Aug. 29, 1880.
  Vol. 4, Pt. 2–492
Hecht, Ben, Feb. 28, 1894–Apr. 18, 1964.
  Supp. 7–331
Hecht, Selig, Feb. 8, 1892–Sept. 18, 1947.
  Supp. 4–366
Heck, Barbara, 1734–Aug. 17, 1804.
  Vol. 4, Pt. 2–493
Hecker, Friedrich Karl Franz, Sept. 28, 1811–Mar. 24, 1881.
  Vol. 4, Pt. 2–493
Hecker, Isaac Thomas, Dec. 18, 1819–Dec. 22, 1888.
  Vol. 4, Pt. 2–495
Heckewelder, John Gottlieb Ernestus, Mar. 12, 1743–Jan. 31, 1823. Vol. 4, Pt. 2–495
Heckscher, August, Aug. 26, 1848–Apr. 26, 1941.
  Supp. 3–348
Hector, Francisco Luis. [See Carondelet, Francisco Luis Hector, Baron de, c. 1748–1807.]
Hedding, Elijah, June 7, 1780–Apr. 9, 1852.
  Vol. 4, Pt. 2–497
Hedge, Frederic Henry, Dec. 12, 1805–Aug. 21, 1890.
  Vol. 4, Pt. 2–498
Hedge, Levi, Apr. 19, 1766–Jan. 3, 1844.
  Vol. 4, Pt. 2–499
Heenan, John Carmel, May 2, 1835–Oct. 25, 1873.
  Vol. 4, Pt. 2–499
Heffelfinger, William Walter "Pudge", Dec. 20, 1867–Apr. 2, 1954. Supp. 5–288
Heflin, James Thomas, Apr. 9, 1869–Apr. 22, 1951.
  Supp. 5–290
Hegeman, John Rogers, Apr. 18, 1844–Apr. 6, 1919.
  Vol. 4, Pt. 2–500
Heilmann, Harry, Aug. 3, 1894–July 9, 1951.
  Supp. 5–291
Heilprin, Angelo, Mar. 31, 1853–July 17, 1907.
  Vol. 4, Pt. 2–501
Heilprin, Michael, 1823–May 10, 1888.
  Vol. 4, Pt. 2–502
Heineman, Daniel Webster ("Dannie"), Nov. 23, 1872–Jan. 31, 1962. Supp. 7–332
Heinemann, Ernst, Feb. 19, 1848–May 11, 1912.
  Vol. 4, Pt. 2–503
Heinrich, Antony Philip, Mar. 11, 1781–May 3, 1861.
  Vol. 4, Pt. 2–504
Heinrich, Max, June 14, 1853–Aug. 9, 1916.
  Vol. 4, Pt. 2–505

Heintzelman, Samuel Peter, Sept. 30, 1805–May 1, 1880.
    Vol. 4, Pt. 2–505
Heintzelman, Stuart, Nov. 19, 1876–July 6, 1935.
    Supp. 1–391
Heinz, Henry John, Oct. 11, 1844–May 14, 1919.
    Vol. 4, Pt. 2–506
Heinze, Frederick Augustus, Dec. 5, 1869–Nov. 4, 1914.
    Vol. 4, Pt. 2–507
Heinzen, Karl Peter, Feb. 22, 1809–Nov. 12, 1880.
    Vol. 4, Pt. 2–508
Heiss, Michael, Apr. 12, 1818–Mar. 26, 1890.
    Vol. 4, Pt. 2–509
Helbron, Peter, 1739–Apr. 24, 1816.
    Vol. 4, Pt. 2–510
Helburn, Theresa, Jan. 12, 1887–Aug. 18, 1959.
    Supp. 6–285
Held, John, Jr., Jan. 10, 1889–Mar. 2, 1958.
    Supp. 6–287
Helffenstein, John Albert Conrad, Feb. 16, 1748–May 17,
    1790. Vol. 4, Pt. 2–511
Heller, Maximilian, Jan. 31, 1860–Mar. 30, 1929.
    Vol. 4, Pt. 2–511
Heller, Robert. [See Palmer, William Henry, 1828–1878.]
Helm, Charles John, June 21, 1817–February 1868.
    Vol. 4, Pt. 2–512
Helm, John Larue, July 4, 1802–Sept. 8, 1867.
    Vol. 4, Pt. 2–513
Helmer, Bessie Bradwell, Oct. 20, 1858–Jan. 10, 1927.
    Vol. 4, Pt. 2–514
Helmpraecht, Joseph, Jan. 14, 1820–Dec. 15, 1884.
    Vol. 4, Pt. 2–515
Helmuth, Justus Henry Christian, May 16, 1745–Feb. 5,
    1825. Vol. 4, Pt. 2–515
Helmuth, William Tod, Oct. 30, 1833–May 15, 1902.
    Vol. 4, Pt. 2–516
Helper, Hinton Rowan, Dec. 27, 1829–Mar. 8, 1909.
    Vol. 4, Pt. 2–517
Hemenway, Mary Porter Tileston, Dec. 20, 1820–Mar. 6,
    1894. Vol. 4, Pt. 2–518
Hemingway, Ernest Miller, July 21, 1899–July 2, 1961.
    Supp. 7–333
Hemmeter, John Conrad, Apr. 26, 1863–Feb. 25, 1931.
    Vol. 4, Pt. 2–519
Hempel, Charles Julius, Sept. 5, 1811–Sept. 24, 1879.
    Vol. 4, Pt. 2–520
Hemphill, John, Dec. 18, 1803–Jan. 4, 1862.
    Vol. 4, Pt. 2–520
Hemphill, Joseph, Jan. 7, 1770–May 29, 1842.
    Vol. 4, Pt. 2–521
Hempl, George, June 6, 1859–Aug. 14, 1921.
    Vol. 4, Pt. 2–521
Hench, Philip Showalter, Feb. 28, 1896–Mar. 30, 1965.
    Supp. 7–340
Henchman, Daniel, Jan. 21, 1689–Feb. 25, 1761.
    Supp. 1–392
Henck, John Benjamin, Oct. 20, 1815–Jan. 3, 1903.
    Vol. 4, Pt. 2–522
Hendel, John William, Nov. 20, 1740–Sept. 29, 1798.
    Vol. 4, Pt. 2–523
Henderson, Archibald, Aug. 7, 1768–Oct. 21, 1822.
    Vol. 4, Pt. 2–523
Henderson, Charles Richmond, Dec. 17, 1848–Mar. 29,
    1915. Vol. 4, Pt. 2–524
Henderson, Daniel McIntyre, July 10, 1851–Sept. 8, 1906.
    Vol. 4, Pt. 2–525
Henderson, David Bremner, Mar. 14, 1840–Feb. 25, 1906.
    Vol. 4, Pt. 2–525
Henderson, Fletcher Hamilton, Dec. 18, 1897–Dec. 29, 1952.
    Supp. 5–292
Henderson, James Pinckney, Mar. 31, 1808–June 4, 1858.
    Vol. 4, Pt. 2–526
Henderson, John, Feb. 28, 1795–Sept. 16, 1857.
    Vol. 4, Pt. 2–527
Henderson, John Brooks, Nov. 16, 1826–Apr. 12, 1913.
    Vol. 4, Pt. 2–527
Henderson, Lawrence Joseph, June 3, 1878–Feb. 10, 1942.
    Supp. 3–349
Henderson, Leonard, Oct. 6, 1772–Aug. 13, 1833.
    Vol. 4, Pt. 2–529
Henderson, Paul, Mar. 13, 1884–Dec. 19, 1951.
    Supp. 5–294
Henderson, Peter, June 9, 1822–Jan. 17, 1890.
    Vol. 4, Pt. 2–530

Henderson, Ray, Dec. 1, 1896–Dec. 31, 1970.
    Supp. 8–250
Henderson, Richard, Apr. 20, 1735–Jan. 30, 1785.
    Vol. 4, Pt. 2–530
Henderson, Thomas, Aug. 15, 1743–Dec. 15, 1824.
    Vol. 4, Pt. 2–532
Henderson, William James, Dec. 4, 1855–June 5, 1937.
    Supp. 2–295
Henderson, Yandell, Apr. 23, 1873–Feb. 18, 1944.
    Supp. 3–352
Hendrick, c. 1680–Sept. 8, 1755.
    Vol. 4, Pt. 2–532
Hendrick, Burton Jesse, Dec. 8, 1870–Mar. 23, 1949.
    Supp. 4–367
Hendrick, Ellwood, Dec. 19, 1861–Oct. 29, 1930.
    Vol. 4, Pt. 2–533
Hendricks, Thomas Andrews, Sept. 7, 1819–Nov. 25, 1885.
    Vol. 4, Pt. 2–534
Hendricks, William, Nov. 12, 1782–May 16, 1850.
    Vol. 4, Pt. 2–535
Hendrix, Eugene Russell, May 17, 1847–Nov. 11, 1927.
    Vol. 4, Pt. 2–536
Hendrix, Jimi, Nov. 27, 1942–Sept. 18, 1970.
    Supp. 8–252
Hendrix, Joseph Clifford, May 25, 1853–Nov. 9, 1904.
    Vol. 4, Pt. 2–536
Heney, Francis Joseph, Mar. 17, 1859–Oct. 31, 1937.
    Supp. 2–296
Henie, Sonja, Apr. 8, 1912–Oct. 12, 1969.
    Supp. 8–253
Hening, William Waller, 1767/8–Apr. 1, 1828.
    Vol. 4, Pt. 2–537
Henkel, Paul, Dec. 15, 1754–Nov. 27, 1825.
    Vol. 4, Pt. 2–538
Henley, Robert, Jan. 5, 1783–Oct. 6, 1828.
    Vol. 4, Pt. 2–539
Hennepin, Louis, Apr. 7, 1640–1701 or later.
    Vol. 4, Pt. 2–540
Hennessy, John, Aug. 20, 1825–Mar. 4, 1900.
    Vol. 4, Pt. 2–541
Hennessy, William John, July 11, 1839–Dec. 26, 1917.
    Vol. 4, Pt. 2–541
Henni, John Martin, June 15, 1805–Sept. 7, 1881.
    Vol. 4, Pt. 2–542
Henningsen, Charles Frederick, Feb. 21, 1815–June 14,
    1877. Vol. 4, Pt. 2–543
Henny, David Christiaan, Nov. 15, 1860–July 14, 1935.
    Supp. 1–393
Henri, Robert, June 25, 1865–July 12, 1929.
    Vol. 4, Pt. 2–544
Henrici, Arthur Trautwein, Mar. 31, 1889–Apr. 23, 1943.
    Supp. 3–354
Henrotin, Charles, Apr. 15, 1843–July 25, 1914.
    Vol. 4, Pt. 2–545
Henrotin, Fernand, Sept. 28, 1847–Dec. 9, 1906.
    Vol. 4, Pt. 2–545
Henry, Alexander, Aug. 1739–Apr. 4, 1824.
    Supp. 1–393
Henry, Alice, Mar. 21, 1857–Feb. 14, 1943.
    Supp. 3–355
Henry, Andrew, c. 1775–June 10, 1833.
    Vol. 4, Pt. 2–546
Henry, Caleb Sprague, Aug. 2, 1804–Mar. 9, 1884.
    Vol. 4, Pt. 2–547
Henry, Edward Lamson, Jan. 12, 1841–May 9, 1919.
    Vol. 4, Pt. 2–547
Henry, John, 1746–October 1794.
    Vol. 4, Pt. 2–548
Henry, John, November 1750–Dec. 16, 1798.
    Vol. 4, Pt. 2–549
Henry, John, fl. 1807–1820.
    Vol. 4, Pt. 2–549
Henry, Joseph, Dec. 17, 1797–May 13, 1878.
    Vol. 4, Pt. 2–550
Henry, Morris Henry, July 26, 1835–May 19, 1895.
    Vol. 4, Pt. 2–553
Henry, O. [See Porter, William Sydney, 1862–1910.]
Henry, Patrick, May 29, 1736–June 6, 1799.
    Vol. 4, Pt. 2–554
Henry, Robert, Dec. 6, 1792–Feb. 6, 1856.
    Vol. 4, Pt. 2–559
Henry, William, May 19, 1729–Dec. 15, 1786.
    Vol. 4, Pt. 2–560

Henry, William Arnon, June 16, 1850–Nov. 24, 1932.
Supp. 1–394
Henry, William Wirt, Feb. 14, 1831–Dec. 5, 1900.
Vol. 4, Pt. 2–561
Henshall, James Alexander, Feb. 29, 1836–Apr. 4, 1925.
Vol. 4, Pt. 2–562
Henshaw, David, Apr. 2, 1791–Nov. 11, 1852.
Vol. 4, Pt. 2–562
Henshaw, Henry Wetherbee, Mar. 3, 1850–Aug. 1, 1930.
Vol. 4, Pt. 2–564
Henson, Josiah, June 15, 1789–May 5, 1883.
Vol. 4, Pt. 2–564
Henson, Matthew Alexander, Aug. 8, 1866–Mar. 9, 1955.
Supp. 5–295
Hentz, Caroline Lee Whiting, June 1, 1800–Feb. 11, 1856.
Vol. 4, Pt. 2–565
Hepburn, Alonzo Barton, July 24, 1846–Jan. 25, 1922.
Vol. 4, Pt. 2–566
Hepburn, James Curtis, Mar. 19, 1815 Sept. 21, 1911.
Vol. 4, Pt. 2–567
Hepburn, Katharine Houghton, Feb. 2, 1878–Mar. 17, 1951.
Supp. 5–296
Hepburn, William Peters, Nov. 4, 1833–Feb. 7, 1916.
Vol. 4, Pt. 2–568
Hepworth, George Hughes, Feb. 4, 1833–June 7, 1902.
Vol. 4, Pt. 2–569
Herbermann, Charles George, Dec. 8, 1840–Aug. 24, 1916.
Vol. 4, Pt. 2–570
Herbert, Frederick Hugh, May 29, 1897–May 17, 1958.
Supp. 6–288
Herbert, Henry William, Apr. 7, 1807–May 17, 1858.
Vol. 4, Pt. 2–570
Herbert, Hilary Abner, Mar. 12, 1834–Mar. 6, 1919.
Vol. 4, Pt. 2–572
Herbert, Victor, Feb. 1, 1859–May 26, 1924.
Vol. 4, Pt. 2–573
Herbst, Josephine Frey, Mar. 5, 1892–Jan. 28, 1969.
Supp. 8–255
Herdic, Peter, Dec. 14, 1824–Mar. 2, 1888.
Vol. 4, Pt. 2–574
Herford, Oliver Brooke, Dec. 1, 1863–July 5, 1935.
Supp. 1–395
Hergesheimer, Joseph, Feb. 15, 1880–Apr. 25, 1954.
Supp. 5–297
Hering, Carl, Mar. 29, 1860–May 10, 1926.
Vol. 4, Pt. 2–574
Hering, Constantine, Jan. 1, 1800–July 23, 1880.
Vol. 4, Pt. 2–575
Hering, Rudolph, Feb. 26, 1847–May 30, 1923.
Vol. 4, Pt. 2–576
Herkimer, Nicholas, 1728–Aug. 16, 1777.
Vol. 4, Pt. 2–577
Herman, Lebrecht Frederick, Oct. 2, 1761–Jan. 30, 1848.
Vol. 4, Pt. 2–578
Herndon, William Henry, Dec. 25, 1818–Mar. 18, 1891.
Vol. 4, Pt. 2–579
Herndon, William Lewis, Oct. 25, 1813–Sept. 12, 1857.
Vol. 4, Pt. 2–579
Herne, Chrystal Katharine, June 17, 1882–Sept. 19, 1950.
Supp. 4–368
Herne, James A., Feb. 1, 1839–June 2, 1901.
Vol. 4, Pt. 2–580
Herold, David E. [See Booth, John Wilkes, 1838–1865.]
Heron, Matilda Agnes, Dec. 1, 1830–Mar. 7, 1877.
Vol. 4, Pt. 2–582
Heron, William, 1742–Jan. 8, 1819.
Vol. 4, Pt. 2–583
Herr, Herbert Thacker, Mar. 19, 1876–Dec. 19, 1933.
Supp. 1–396
Herr, John, Sept. 18, 1781–May 3, 1850.
Vol. 4, Pt. 2–584
Herreshoff, James Brown, Mar. 18, 1834–Dec. 5, 1930.
Vol. 4, Pt. 2–584
Herreshoff, John Brown, Apr. 24, 1841–July 20, 1915.
Vol. 4, Pt. 2–585
Herreshoff, Nathanael Greene, Mar. 18, 1848–June 2, 1938.
Supp. 2–298
Herrick, Edward Claudius, Feb. 24, 1811–June 11, 1862.
Vol. 4, Pt. 2–586
Herrick, Myron Timothy, Oct. 9, 1854–Mar. 31, 1929.
Vol. 4, Pt. 2–587
Herrick, Robert Welch, Apr. 26, 1868–Dec. 23, 1938.
Supp. 2–299

Herrick, Sophia McIlvaine Bledsoe, Mar. 26, 1837–Oct. 9, 1919. Vol. 4, Pt. 2–589
Herriman, George Joseph, Aug. 22, 1880–Apr. 25, 1944.
Supp. 3–356
Herring, Augustus Moore, Aug. 3, 1867–July 17, 1926.
Vol. 4, Pt. 2–590
Herring, James, Jan. 12, 1794–Oct. 8, 1867.
Vol. 4, Pt. 2–590
Herring, Silas Clark, 1803–June 23, 1881.
Vol. 4, Pt. 2–591
Herrman, Augustine, c. 1605–1686.
Vol. 4, Pt. 2–592
Herrmann, Alexander, Feb. 10, 1844–Dec. 17, 1896.
Vol. 4, Pt. 2–593
Herron, Francis Jay, Feb. 17, 1837–Jan. 8, 1902.
Vol. 4, Pt. 2–593
Herron, George Davis, Jan. 21, 1862–Oct. 9, 1925.
Vol. 4, Pt. 2–594
Herschel, Clemens, Mar. 23, 1842–Mar. 1, 1930.
Vol. 4, Pt. 2–595
Hersey, Evelyn Weeks, Dec. 9, 1897–Nov. 3, 1963.
Supp. 7–341
Hershey, Milton Snavely, Sept. 13, 1857–Oct. 13, 1945.
Supp. 3–357
Herter, Christian, Jan. 8, 1840–Nov. 2, 1883.
Vol. 4, Pt. 2–596
Herter, Christian Archibald, Sept. 3, 1865–Dec. 5, 1910.
Vol. 4, Pt. 2–597
Herter, Christian Archibald, Mar. 28, 1895–Dec. 30, 1966.
Supp. 8–256
Herty, Charles Holmes, Dec. 4, 1867–July 27, 1938.
Supp. 2–300
Hertz, Alfred, July 15, 1872–Apr. 17, 1942.
Supp. 3–359
Hertz, John Daniel, Apr. 10, 1879–Oct. 8, 1961.
Supp. 7–342
Hess, Alfred Fabian, Oct. 19, 1875–Dec. 5, 1933.
Supp. 1–397
Hess, Victor Franz, June 24, 1883–Dec. 17, 1964.
Supp. 7–343
Hesselius, Gustavus, 1682–May 25, 1755.
Vol. 4, Pt. 2–598
Hesselius, John, 1728–Apr. 9, 1778.
Vol. 4, Pt. 2–598
Hessoun, Joseph, Aug. 8, 1830–July 4, 1906.
Vol. 4, Pt. 2–599
Heth, Henry, Dec. 16, 1825–Sept. 27, 1899.
Vol. 4, Pt. 2–600
Hewat, Alexander, c. 1745–c. 1829.
Vol. 4, Pt. 2–601
Hewes, Joseph, Jan. 23, 1730–Nov. 10, 1779.
Vol. 4, Pt. 2–601
Hewes, Robert, 1751–July 1830.
Vol. 4, Pt. 2–602
Hewett, Waterman Thomas, Jan. 10, 1846–Sept. 13, 1921.
Vol. 4, Pt. 2–603
Hewit, Augustine Francis, Nov. 27, 1820–July 3, 1897.
Vol. 4, Pt. 2–604
Hewit, Nathaniel Augustus. [See Hewit, Augustine Francis, 1820–1897.]
Hewitt, Abram Stevens, July 31, 1822–Jan. 18, 1903.
Vol. 4, Pt. 2–604
Hewitt, James, June 4, 1770–1827.
Vol. 4, Pt. 2–606
Hewitt, John Hill, July 11, 1801–Oct. 7, 1890.
Vol. 4, Pt. 2–606
Hewitt, Peter Cooper, May 5, 1861–Aug. 25, 1921.
Vol. 4, Pt. 2–607
Heydt, Hans Jöst. [See Hite, Jost, d. 1760.]
Heye, George Gustav, Sept. 16, 1874–Jan. 20, 1957.
Supp. 6–289
Heyer, John Christian Frederick, July 10, 1793–Nov. 7, 1873.
Vol. 4, Pt. 2–608
Heyward, DuBose, Aug. 31, 1885–June 16, 1940.
Supp. 2–302
Heyward, Thomas, July 28, 1746–Mar. 6, 1809.
Vol. 4, Pt. 2–609
Heywood, Ezra Hervey, Sept. 29, 1829–May 22, 1893.
Vol. 4, Pt. 2–609
Heywood, Levi, Dec. 10, 1800–July 21, 1882.
Vol. 4, Pt. 2–611
Hiacoomes, c. 1610–1690.
Vol. 4, Pt. 2–611

Hindman, Thomas Carmichael, Jan. 28, 1828–Sept. 28, 1868. Vol. 5, Pt. 1–61
Hindman, William, Apr. 1, 1743–Jan. 19, 1822.
  Vol. 5, Pt. 1–62
Hinds, Asher Crosby, Feb. 6, 1863–May 1, 1919.
  Vol. 5, Pt. 1–62
Hindus, Maurice Gerschon, Feb. 27, 1891–July 8, 1969.
  Supp. 8–260
Hine, Charles De Lano, Mar. 15, 1867–Feb. 13, 1927.
  Vol. 5, Pt. 1–63
Hine, Lewis Wickes, Sept. 26, 1874–Nov. 3, 1940.
  Supp. 2–305
Hines, Duncan, Mar. 26, 1880–Mar. 15, 1959.
  Supp. 6–291
Hines, Frank Thomas, Apr. 11, 1879–Apr. 3, 1960.
  Supp. 6–293
Hines, James J., Dec. 18, 1876–Mar. 26, 1957.
  Supp. 6 294
Hines, John Leonard ("Birdie"), May 21, 1868–Oct. 13, 1968. Supp. 8–261
Hines, Walker Downer, Feb. 2, 1870–Jan. 14, 1934.
  Supp. 1–406
Hinkle, Beatrice Moses, Oct. 10, 1874–Feb. 28, 1953.
  Supp. 5–301
Hinman, Elisha, Mar. 9, 1734–Aug. 29, 1805.
  Vol. 5, Pt. 1–64
Hinman, George Wheeler, Nov. 19, 1864–Mar. 31, 1927.
  Vol. 5, Pt. 1–65
Hinman, Joel, Jan. 27, 1802–Feb. 21, 1870.
  Vol. 5, Pt. 1–65
Hinsdale, Burke Aaron, Mar. 31, 1837–Nov. 29, 1900.
  Vol. 5, Pt. 1–66
Hinshaw, David Schull, Nov. 4, 1882–Nov. 5, 1953.
  Supp. 5–303
Hires, Charles Elmer, Aug. 19, 1851–July 31, 1937.
  Supp. 2–306
Hirsch, Emil Gustav, May 22, 1851–Jan. 7, 1923.
  Vol. 5, Pt. 1–67
Hirsch, Isaac Seth, Dec. 3, 1880–Mar. 24, 1942.
  Supp. 3–360
Hirsch, Maximilian Justice, July 30, 1880–Apr. 3, 1969.
  Supp. 8–263
Hirschbein, Peretz, Nov. 7, 1880–Aug. 16, 1948.
  Supp. 4–377
Hirschensohn, Chaim, Aug. 31, 1857–Sept. 15, 1935.
  Supp. 1–407
Hirst, Barton Cooke, July 20, 1861–Sept. 2, 1935.
  Supp. 1–408
Hirst, Henry Beck, Aug. 23, 1817–Mar. 30, 1874.
  Vol. 5, Pt. 1–68
Hirth, William Andrew, Mar. 28, 1875–Oct. 24, 1940.
  Supp. 2–307
Hiscock, Frank Harris, Apr. 16, 1856–July 2, 1946.
  Supp. 4–379
Hise, Elijah, July 4, 1801–May 8, 1867.
  Vol. 5, Pt. 1–69
Hitchcock, Charles Henry, Aug. 23, 1836–Nov. 5, 1910.
  Vol. 5, Pt. 1–69
Hitchcock, Edward, May 23, 1828–Feb. 15, 1911.
  Vol. 5, Pt. 1–71
Hitchcock, Edward, May 24, 1793–Feb. 27, 1864.
  Vol. 5, Pt. 1–70
Hitchcock, Enos, Mar. 7, 1744–Feb. 26, 1803.
  Vol. 5, Pt. 1–72
Hitchcock, Ethan Allen, May 18, 1798–Aug. 5, 1870.
  Vol. 5, Pt. 1–73
Hitchcock, Ethan Allen, Sept. 19, 1835–Apr. 9, 1909.
  Vol. 5, Pt. 1–74
Hitchcock, Frank. [See Murdoch, Frank Hitchcock, d. 1872.]
Hitchcock, Frank Harris, Oct. 5, 1867–Aug. 5, 1935.
  Supp. 1–409
Hitchcock, Gilbert Monell, Sept. 18, 1859–Feb. 3, 1934.
  Supp. 1–410
Hitchcock, Henry, July 3, 1829–Mar. 18, 1902.
  Vol. 5, Pt. 1–75
Hitchcock, James Ripley Wellman, July 3, 1857–May 4, 1918.
  Vol. 5, Pt. 1–76
Hitchcock, Peter, Oct. 19, 1781–Mar. 4, 1853.
  Vol. 5, Pt. 1–77
Hitchcock, Phineas Warrener, Nov. 30, 1831–July 10, 1881.
  Vol. 5, Pt. 1–78
Hitchcock, Raymond, Oct. 22, 1865–Nov. 25, 1929.
  Vol. 5, Pt. 1–78

Hitchcock, Ripley. [See Hitchcock, James Ripley Wellman, 1857–1918.]
Hitchcock, Roswell Dwight, Aug. 15, 1817–June 16, 1887.
  Vol. 5, Pt. 1–79
Hitchcock, Thomas, Feb. 11, 1900–Apr. 19, 1944.
  Supp. 3–360
Hite, Jost, d. 1760.
  Vol. 5, Pt. 1–80
Hitt, Robert Roberts, Jan. 16, 1834–Sept. 20, 1906.
  Vol. 5, Pt. 1–80
Hittell, John Shertzer, Dec. 25, 1825–Mar. 8, 1901.
  Vol. 5, Pt. 1–81
Hittell, Theodore Henry, Apr. 5, 1830–Feb. 23, 1917.
  Vol. 5, Pt. 1–82
Hoadley, David, Apr. 29, 1774–July 1839.
  Vol. 5, Pt. 1–82
Hoadley, John Chipman, Dec. 10, 1818–Oct. 21, 1886.
  Vol. 5, Pt. 1–83
Hoadly, George, July 31, 1826–Aug. 26, 1902.
  Vol. 5, Pt. 1–84
Hoag, Joseph, Apr. 22, 1762–Nov. 21, 1846.
  Vol. 5, Pt. 1–85
Hoagland, Charles Lee, June 6, 1907–Aug. 2, 1946.
  Supp. 4–380
Hoagland, Dennis Robert, Apr. 2, 1884–Sept. 5, 1949.
  Supp. 4–381
Hoan, Daniel Webster, Mar. 12, 1881–June 11, 1961.
  Supp. 7–348
Hoar, Ebenezer Rockwood, Feb. 21, 1816–Jan. 31, 1895.
  Vol. 5, Pt. 1–86
Hoar, George Frisbie, Aug. 29, 1826–Sept. 30, 1904.
  Vol. 5, Pt. 1–87
Hoar, Leonard, c. 1630–Nov. 28, 1675.
  Vol. 5, Pt. 1–88
Hoar, Samuel, May 18, 1778–Nov. 2, 1856.
  Vol. 5, Pt. 1–89
Hoard, William Dempster, Oct. 10, 1836–Nov. 22, 1918.
  Vol. 5, Pt. 1–90
Hoban, James, c. 1762–Dec. 8, 1831.
  Vol. 5, Pt. 1–91
Hobart, Alice Nourse Tisdale, Jan. 28, 1882–Mar. 14, 1967.
  Supp. 8–264
Hobart, Garret Augustus, June 3, 1844–Nov. 21, 1899.
  Vol. 5, Pt. 1–92
Hobart, John Henry, Sept. 14, 1775–Sept. 12, 1830.
  Vol. 5, Pt. 1–93
Hobart, John Sloss, May 6, 1738–Feb. 4, 1805.
  Vol. 5, Pt. 1–94
Hobbs, Alfred Charles, Oct. 7, 1812–Nov. 5, 1891.
  Vol. 5, Pt. 1–95
Hobby, William Pettus, Mar. 26, 1878–June 7, 1964.
  Supp. 7–349
Hobson, Edward Henry, July 11, 1825–Sept. 14, 1901.
  Vol. 5, Pt. 1–96
Hobson, Richmond Pearson, Aug. 17, 1870–Mar. 16, 1937.
  Supp. 2–308
Hoch, August, Apr. 20, 1868–Sept. 23, 1919.
  Vol. 5, Pt. 1–97
Hocking, William Ernest, Aug. 10, 1873–June 12, 1966.
  Supp. 8–265
Hodes, Henry Irving, Mar. 19, 1899–Feb. 14, 1962.
  Supp. 7–350
Hodge, Archibald Alexander, July 18, 1823–Nov. 11, 1886.
  Vol. 5, Pt. 1–97
Hodge, Charles, Dec. 27, 1797–June 19, 1878.
  Vol. 5, Pt. 1–98
Hodge, Hugh Lenox, June 27, 1796–Feb. 26, 1873.
  Vol. 5, Pt. 1–99
Hodge, John Reed, June 12, 1893–Nov. 12, 1963.
  Supp. 7–351
Hodge, William Thomas, Nov. 1, 1874–Jan. 30, 1932.
  Supp. 1–411
Hodgen, John Thompson, Jan. 29, 1826–Apr. 28, 1882.
  Vol. 5, Pt. 1–100
Hodges, Courtney Hicks, Jan. 5, 1887–Jan. 16, 1966.
  Supp. 8–266
Hodges, George, Oct. 6, 1856–May 27, 1919.
  Vol. 5, Pt. 1–100
Hodges, Harry Foote, Feb. 25, 1860–Sept. 24, 1929.
  Vol. 5, Pt. 1–101
Hodgkinson, Francis, June 16, 1867–Nov. 4, 1949.
  Supp. 4–383

Hodgkinson, John, c. 1767–Sept. 12, 1805.
    Vol. 5, Pt. 1–102
Hodgson, William Brown, Sept. 1, 1801–June 26, 1871.
    Supp. 1–412
Hodson, William, Apt. 25, 1891–Jan. 15, 1943.
    Supp. 3–361
Hodur, Francis, Apr. 2, 1866–Feb. 16, 1953.
    Supp. 5–304
Hoe, Richard March, Sept. 12, 1812–June 7, 1886.
    Vol. 5, Pt. 1–104
Hoe, Robert, Oct. 29, 1784–Jan. 4, 1833.
    Vol. 5, Pt. 1–105
Hoe, Robert, Mar. 10, 1839–Sept. 22, 1909.
    Vol. 5, Pt. 1–105
Hoecken, Christian, Feb. 28, 1808–June 19, 1851.
    Vol. 5, Pt. 1–106
Hoen, August, Dec. 28, 1817–Sept. 20, 1886.
    Vol. 5, Pt. 1–107
Hoenecke, Gustav Adolf Felix Theodor, Feb. 25, 1835–Jan.
    3, 1908. Vol. 5, Pt. 1–108
Hoerr, Normand Louis, May 3, 1902–Dec. 14, 1958.
    Supp. 6–295
Hoey, Clyde Roark, Dec. 11, 1877–May 12, 1954.
    Supp. 5–306
Hoff, John Van Rensselaer, Apr. 11, 1848–Jan. 14, 1920.
    Vol. 5, Pt. 1–109
Hoffman, Charles Fenno, Feb. 7, 1806–June 7, 1884.
    Vol. 5, Pt. 1–110
Hoffman, Clare Eugene, Sept. 10, 1875–Nov. 3, 1967.
    Supp. 8–268
Hoffman, David, Dec. 24, 1784–Nov. 11, 1854.
    Vol. 5, Pt. 1–111
Hoffman, David Murray, Sept. 29, 1791–May 7, 1878.
    Vol. 2, Pt. 2–112
Hoffman, Eugene Augustus, Mar. 21, 1829–June 17, 1902.
    Vol. 5, Pt. 1–112
Hoffman, Frederick Ludwig, May 2, 1865–Feb. 23, 1946.
    Supp. 4–384
Hoffman, John Thompson, Jan. 10, 1828–Mar. 24, 1888.
    Vol. 5, Pt. 1–113
Hoffman, Josiah Ogden, Apr. 14, 1766–Jan. 24, 1837.
    Vol. 5, Pt. 1–114
Hoffman, Ogden, May 3, 1793–May 1, 1856.
    Vol. 5, Pt. 1–115
Hoffman, Richard, Mar. 24, 1831–Aug. 17, 1909.
    Vol. 5, Pt. 1–117
Hoffman, Wickham, Apr. 2, 1821–May 21, 1900.
    Vol. 5, Pt. 1–117
Hoffmann, Francis Arnold, June 5, 1822–Jan. 23, 1903.
    Vol. 5, Pt. 1–118
Hofman, Heinrich Oscar, Aug. 13, 1852–Apr 28, 1924.
    Vol. 5, Pt. 1–119
Hofmann, Hans, Mar. 21, 1880–Feb. 17, 1966.
    Supp. 8–270
Hofmann, Josef Casimir, Jan. 20, 1876–Feb. 16, 1957.
    Supp. 6–297
Hofstadter, Richard, Aug. 6, 1916–Oct. 24, 1970.
    Supp. 8–271
Hogan, John, Jan. 2, 1805–Feb. 5, 1892.
    Vol. 5, Pt. 1–119
Hogan, John Vincent Lawless, Feb. 14, 1890–Dec. 29, 1960.
    Supp. 6–298
Hoge, Moses, Feb. 15, 1752–July 5, 1820.
    Vol. 5, Pt. 1–120
Hoge, Moses Drury, Sept. 17, 1819–Jan. 6, 1899.
    Vol. 5, Pt. 1–121
Hogg, George, June 22, 1784–Dec. 5, 1849.
    Vol. 5, Pt. 1–122
Hogg, James Stephen, Mar. 24, 1851–Mar. 3, 1906.
    Vol. 5, Pt. 1–122
Hogue, Wilson Thomas, Mar. 6, 1852–Feb. 13, 1920.
    Vol. 5, Pt. 1–123
Hogun, James, d. Jan. 4, 1781.
    Vol. 5, Pt. 1–123
Hohfeld, Wesley Newcomb, Aug. 8, 1879–Oct. 21, 1918.
    Vol. 5, Pt. 1–124
Hoisington, Henry Richard, Aug. 23, 1801–May 16, 1858.
    Vol. 5, Pt. 1–125
Hoke, Robert Frederick, May 27, 1837–July 3, 1912.
    Vol. 5, Pt. 1–126
Hokinson, Helen Elna, June 29, 1893–Nov. 1, 1949.
    Supp. 4–385

Holabird, William, Sept. 11, 1854–July 19, 1923.
    Vol. 5, Pt. 1–127
Holbrook, Alfred, Feb. 17, 1816–Apr. 16, 1909.
    Vol. 5, Pt. 1–128
Holbrook, Frederick, Feb. 15, 1813–Apr. 28, 1909.
    Vol. 5, Pt. 1–128
Holbrook, John Edwards, Dec. 30, 1794–Sept. 8, 1871.
    Vol. 5, Pt. 1–129
Holbrook, Josiah, 1788–June 17, 1854.
    Vol. 5, Pt. 1–130
Holbrook, Stewart Hall, Aug. 22, 1893–Sept. 3, 1964.
    Supp. 7–353
Holcomb, Amasa, June 18, 1787–Feb. 27, 1875.
    Vol. 5, Pt. 1–131
Holcomb, Silas Alexander, Aug. 25, 1858–Apr. 25, 1920.
    Vol. 5, Pt. 1–132
Holcombe, Chester, Oct. 16, 1844–Apr. 25, 1912.
    Vol. 5, Pt. 1–132
Holcombe, Henry, Sept. 22, 1762–May 22, 1824.
    Vol. 5, Pt. 1–133
Holcombe, James Philemon, Sept. 20, 1820–Aug. 22, 1873.
    Vol. 5, Pt. 1–134
Holcombe, William Henry, May 29, 1825–Nov. 28, 1893.
    Vol. 5, Pt. 1–135
Holden, Edward Singleton, Nov. 5, 1846–Mar. 16, 1914.
    Vol. 5, Pt. 1–136
Holden, Hale, Aug. 11, 1869–Sept. 23, 1940.
    Supp. 2–309
Holden, Liberty Emery, June 20, 1833–Aug. 26, 1913.
    Vol. 5, Pt. 1–137
Holden, Oliver, Sept. 18, 1765–Sept. 4, 1844.
    Vol. 5, Pt. 1–138
Holden, William Woods, Nov. 24, 1818–Mar. 1, 1892.
    Vol. 5, Pt. 1–138
Holder, Charles Frederick, Aug. 5, 1851–Oct. 10, 1915.
    Vol. 5, Pt. 1–140
Holder, Joseph Bassett, Oct. 26, 1824–Feb. 27, 1888.
    Vol. 5, Pt. 1–140
Holdrege, George Ward, Mar. 26, 1847–Sept. 14, 1926.
    Supp. 1–413
Holiday, Billie, Apr. 7, 1915–July 17, 1959.
    Supp. 6–299
Holladay, Ben, October 1819–July 8, 1887.
    Vol. 5, Pt. 1–141
Holland, Clifford Milburn, Mar. 13, 1883–Oct. 27, 1924.
    Vol. 5, Pt. 1–142
Holland, Edmund Milton, Sept. 7, 1848–Nov. 24, 1913.
    Vol. 5, Pt. 1–143
Holland, Edwin Clifford, c. 1794–Sept. 11, 1824.
    Vol. 5, Pt. 1–143
Holland, George, Dec. 6, 1791–Dec. 20, 1870.
    Vol. 5, Pt. 1–144
Holland, John Philip, Feb. 29, 1840–Aug. 12, 1914.
    Vol. 5, Pt. 1–144
Holland, Joseph Jefferson, Dec. 20, 1860–Sept. 25, 1926.
    Vol. 5, Pt. 1–146
Holland, Josiah Gilbert, July 24, 1819–Oct 12, 1881.
    Vol. 5, Pt. 1–146
Holland, William Jacob, Aug. 16, 1848–Dec. 13, 1932.
    Supp. 1–414
Hollander, Jacob Harry, July 23, 1871–July 9, 1940.
    Supp. 2–310
Hollerith, Herman, Feb. 29, 1860–Nov. 17, 1929.
    Supp. 1–415
Holley, Alexander Lyman, July 20, 1832–Jan. 29, 1882.
    Vol. 5, Pt. 1–148
Holley, Horace, Feb. 13, 1781–July 31, 1827.
    Vol. 5, Pt. 1–149
Holley, Marietta, July 16, 1836–Mar. 1, 1926.
    Vol. 5, Pt. 1–150
Holley, Myron, Apr. 29, 1779–Mar. 4, 1841.
    Vol. 5, Pt. 1–150
Hollick, Charles Arthur, Feb. 6, 1857–Mar. 11, 1933.
    Supp. 1–416
Holliday, Cyrus Kurtz, Apr. 3, 1826–Mar. 29, 1900.
    Vol. 5, Pt. 1–151
Holliday, Judy, June 21, 1921–June 7, 1965.
    Supp. 7–354
Hollingworth, Leta Stetter, May 25, 1886–Nov. 27, 1939.
    Supp. 2–312
Hollins, George Nichols, Sept. 20, 1799–Jan. 18, 1878.
    Vol. 5, Pt. 1–152

Hollis, Ira Nelson, Mar. 7, 1856–Aug. 14, 1930.
    Vol. 5, Pt. 1–152
Hollister, Gideon Hiram, Dec. 14, 1817–Mar. 24, 1881.
    Vol. 5, Pt. 1–153
Holloway, John, c. 1666–Dec. 14, 1734.
    Vol. 5, Pt. 1–154
Holloway, Joseph Flavius, Jan. 18, 1825–Sept. 1, 1896.
    Vol. 5, Pt. 1–155
Holls, Frederick William. [See Holls, George Frederick William, 1857–1903.]
Holls, George Frederick William, July 1, 1857–July 23, 1903.
    Vol. 5, Pt. 1–155
Holly, Charles Hardin ("Buddy"), Sept. 7, 1936–Feb. 3, 1959. Supp. 6–300
Holly, James Theodore, Oct. 3, 1829–Mar. 13, 1911.
    Vol. 5, Pt. 1–156
Hollyer, Samuel, Feb. 24, 1826–Dec. 29, 1919.
    Vol. 5, Pt. 1–157
Holman, Jesse Lynch, Oct. 24, 1784–Mar. 28, 1842.
    Vol. 5, Pt. 1–158
Holman, William Steele, Sept. 6, 1822–Apr. 22, 1897.
    Vol. 5, Pt. 1–158
Holme, Thomas, 1624–1695.
    Vol. 5, Pt. 1–159
Holmes, Abiel, Dec. 24, 1763–June 4, 1837.
    Vol. 5, Pt. 1–160
Holmes, Bayard Taylor, July 29, 1852–Apr. 3, 1924.
    Vol. 5, Pt. 1–161
Holmes, Daniel Henry, July 16, 1851–Dec. 15, 1908.
    Vol. 5, Pt. 1–161
Holmes, David, Mar. 10, 1770–Aug. 20, 1832.
    Vol. 5, Pt. 1–162
Holmes, Elias Burton, Jan. 8, 1870–July 22, 1958.
    Supp. 6–302
Holmes, Ezekiel, Aug. 24, 1801–Feb. 9, 1865.
    Vol. 5, Pt. 1–163
Holmes, George Frederick, Aug. 2, 1820–Nov. 4, 1897.
    Vol. 5, Pt. 1–164
Holmes, Isaac Edward, Apr. 6, 1796–Feb. 24, 1867.
    Vol. 5, Pt. 1–165
Holmes, Israel, Dec. 19, 1800–July 15, 1874.
    Vol. 5, Pt. 1–165
Holmes, John, Mar. 28, 1773–July 7, 1843.
    Vol. 5, Pt. 1–166
Holmes, John Haynes, Nov. 29, 1879–Apr. 3, 1964.
    Supp. 7–355
Holmes, Joseph Austin, Nov. 23, 1859–July 12, 1915.
    Vol. 5, Pt. 1–167
Holmes, Julius Cecil, Apr. 24, 1899–July 14, 1968.
    Supp. 8–274
Holmes, Mary Jane Hawes, Apr. 5, 1825–Oct. 6, 1907.
    Vol. 5, Pt. 1–168
Holmes, Nathaniel, Jan. 2, 1815–Feb. 26, 1901.
    Vol. 5, Pt. 1–168
Holmes, Oliver Wendell, Aug. 29, 1809–Oct. 7, 1894.
    Vol. 5, Pt. 1–169
Holmes, Oliver Wendell, Mar. 8, 1841–Mar. 6, 1935.
    Supp. 1–417
Holmes, Theophilus Hunter, Nov. 13, 1804–June 21, 1880.
    Vol. 5, Pt. 1–176
Holmes, William Henry, Dec. 1, 1846–Apr. 20, 1933.
    Supp. 1–427
Holsey, Lucius Henry, c. 1842–Aug. 3, 1920.
    Vol. 5, Pt. 1–176
Holst, Hermann Eduard von, June 19, 1841–Jan. 20, 1904.
    Vol. 5, Pt. 1–177
Holt, Arthur Erastus, Nov. 23, 1876–Jan. 13, 1942.
    Supp. 3–362
Holt, Edwin Bissell, Aug. 21, 1873–Jan. 25, 1946.
    Supp. 4–387
Holt, Edwin Michael, Jan. 14, 1807–May 15, 1884.
    Vol. 5, Pt. 1–179
Holt, Hamilton Bowen, Aug. 19, 1872–Apr. 26, 1951.
    Supp. 5–307
Holt, Henry, Jan. 3, 1840–Feb. 13, 1926.
    Vol. 5, Pt. 1–179
Holt, John, 1721–Jan. 30, 1784.
    Vol. 5, Pt. 1–180
Holt, Joseph, Jan. 6, 1807–Aug. 1, 1894.
    Vol. 5, Pt. 1–181
Holt, Luther Emmett, Mar. 4, 1855–Jan. 14, 1924.
    Vol. 5, Pt. 1–183

Holt, William Franklin, Jan. 18, 1864–Nov. 22, 1951.
    Supp. 5–309
Holt, Winifred, Nov. 17, 1870–June 14, 1945.
    Supp. 3–364
Holten, Samuel, June 9, 1738–Jan. 2, 1816.
    Vol. 5, Pt. 1–184
Holyoke, Edward Augustus, Aug. 1, 1728–Mar. 31, 1829.
    Vol. 5, Pt. 1–185
Holyoke, Samuel, Oct. 15, 1762–Feb. 21, 1820.
    Vol. 5, Pt. 1–186
Homer, Louise Dilworth Beatty, Apr. 30, 1871–May 6, 1947.
    Supp. 4–388
Homer, Winslow, Feb. 24, 1836–Sept. 29, 1910.
    Vol. 5, Pt. 1–186
Homes, Henry Augustus, Mar. 10, 1812–Nov. 3, 1887.
    Vol. 5, Pt. 1–191
Hone, Philip, Oct. 25, 1780–May 5, 1851.
    Vol. 5, Pt. 1–192
Hontan, Louis-Armand De Lom D'Arce, Baron de la. [See Lahontan, Louis Armand de Lom d'Arce, 1666–c. 1713.]
Hood, James Walker, May 30, 1831–Oct. 30, 1918.
    Vol. 5, Pt. 1–192
Hood, John Bell, June 1, 1831–Aug. 30, 1879.
    Vol. 5, Pt. 1–193
Hood, Raymond Mathewson, Mar. 29, 1881–Aug. 14, 1934.
    Supp. 1–428
Hood, Washington, Feb. 2, 1808–July 17, 1840.
    Vol. 5, Pt. 1–194
Hooker, Donald Russell, Sept. 7, 1876–Aug. 1, 1946.
    Supp. 4–390
Hooker, Elon Huntington, Nov. 23, 1869–May 10, 1938.
    Supp. 2–313
Hooker, Isabella Beecher, Feb. 22, 1822–Jan. 25, 1907.
    Vol. 5, Pt. 1–195
Hooker, Joseph, Nov. 13, 1814–Oct. 31, 1879.
    Vol. 5, Pt. 1–196
Hooker, Philip, Oct. 28, 1766–Jan. 31, 1836.
    Vol. 5, Pt. 1–198
Hooker, Samuel Cox, Apr. 19, 1864–Oct. 12, 1935.
    Supp. 1–431
Hooker, Thomas, 1586(?)–July 7, 1647.
    Vol. 5, Pt. 1–199
Hooker, William, fl. 1804–1846.
    Vol. 5, Pt. 1–200
Hooker, Worthington, Mar. 3, 1806–Nov. 6, 1867.
    Vol. 5, Pt. 1–201
Hooper, Claude Ernest, May 31, 1898–Dec. 15, 1954.
    Supp. 5–310
Hooper, Jessie Annette Jack, Nov. 8, 1865–May 8, 1935.
    Supp. 1–432
Hooper, Johnson Jones, June 9, 1815–June 7, 1862.
    Vol. 5, Pt. 1–202
Hooper, Lucy Hamilton, Jan. 20, 1835–Aug. 31, 1893.
    Vol. 5, Pt. 1–202
Hooper, Samuel, Feb. 3, 1808–Feb. 14, 1875.
    Vol. 5, Pt. 1–203
Hooper, William, June 17, 1742–Oct. 14, 1790.
    Vol. 5, Pt. 1–204
Hooton, Earnest Albert, Nov. 20, 1887–May 3, 1954.
    Supp. 5–312
Hoover, Charles Franklin, Aug. 2, 1865–June 15, 1927.
    Vol. 5, Pt. 1–205
Hoover, Herbert Clark, Aug. 10, 1874–Oct. 20, 1964.
    Supp. 7–357
Hoover, Herbert Clark, Jr., Aug. 4, 1903–July 9, 1969.
    Supp. 8–275
Hoover, Herbert William, Oct. 30, 1877–Sept. 16, 1954.
    Supp. 5–313
Hoover, James Matthews, Aug. 26, 1872–Feb. 11, 1935.
    Supp. 1–433
Hope, Clifford Ragsdale, June 9, 1893–May 16, 1970.
    Supp. 8–277
Hope, James Barron, Mar. 23, 1829–Sept. 15, 1887.
    Vol. 5, Pt. 1–205
Hope, John, June 2, 1868–Feb. 20, 1936.
    Supp. 2–314
Hopkins, Arthur Francis, Oct. 18, 1794–Nov. 10, 1865.
    Vol. 5, Pt. 1–206
Hopkins, Cyril George, July 22, 1866–Oct. 6, 1919.
    Vol. 5, Pt. 1–207
Hopkins, Edward, 1600–March 1657.
    Vol. 5, Pt. 1–207

Hopkins, Edward Augustus, Nov. 29, 1822–June 10, 1891.
Vol. 5, Pt. 1–208
Hopkins, Edward Washburn, Sept. 8, 1857–July 16, 1932.
Supp. 1–433
Hopkins, Esek, Apr. 26, 1718–Feb. 26, 1802.
Vol. 5, Pt. 1–209
Hopkins, Harry Lloyd, Aug. 17, 1890–Jan. 29, 1946.
Supp. 4–391
Hopkins, Isaac Stiles, June 20, 1841–Feb. 3, 1914.
Vol. 5, Pt. 1–210
Hopkins, James Campbell, Apr. 27, 1819–Sept. 3, 1877.
Vol. 5, Pt. 1–211
Hopkins, John Burroughs, Aug. 25, 1742–Dec. 5, 1796.
Vol. 5, Pt. 1–211
Hopkins, John Henry, Jan. 30, 1792–Jan. 9, 1868.
Vol. 5, Pt. 1–212
Hopkins, Johns, May 19, 1795–Dec. 24, 1873.
Vol. 5, Pt. 1–213
Hopkins, Juliet Ann Opie, May 7, 1818–Mar. 9, 1890.
Vol. 5, Pt. 1–214
Hopkins, Lemuel, June 19, 1750–Apr. 14, 1801.
Vol. 5, Pt. 1–215
Hopkins, Mark, Feb. 4, 1802–June 17, 1887.
Vol. 5, Pt. 1–215
Hopkins, Samuel, Sept. 17, 1721–Dec. 20, 1803.
Vol. 5, Pt. 1–217
Hopkins, Samuel, Apr. 9, 1753–Sept. 16, 1819.
Vol. 5, Pt. 1–218
Hopkins, Stephen, Mar. 7, 1707–July 13, 1785.
Vol. 5, Pt. 1–219
Hopkinson, Francis, Oct. 2, 1737–May 9, 1791.
Vol. 5, Pt. 1–220
Hopkinson, Joseph, Nov. 12, 1770–Jan. 15, 1842.
Vol. 5, Pt. 1–223
Hoppe, William Frederick ("Willie"), Oct. 11, 1887–Feb. 1, 1959. Supp. 6–303
Hopper, DeWolf, Mar. 30, 1858–Sept. 23, 1935.
Supp. 1–434
Hopper, Edna Wallace, Jan. 17, 1864[?]–Dec. 14, 1959.
Supp. 6–305
Hopper, Edward, July 22, 1882–May 15, 1967.
Supp. 8–278
Hopper, Hedda, May 2, 1885–Feb. 1, 1966.
Supp. 8–281
Hopper, Isaac Tatem, Dec. 3, 1771–May 7, 1852.
Vol. 5, Pt. 1–224
Hoppin, Augustus, July 13, 1828–Apr. 1, 1896.
Vol. 5, Pt. 1–225
Hoppin, James Mason, Jan. 17, 1820–Nov. 15, 1906.
Vol. 5, Pt. 1–225
Hoppin, Joseph Clark, May 23, 1870–Jan. 30, 1925.
Vol. 5, Pt. 1–226
Hoppin, William Warner, Sept. 1, 1807–Apr. 19, 1890.
Vol. 5, Pt. 1–227
Hopson, Howard Colwell, May 8, 1882–Dec. 22, 1949.
Supp. 4–394
Hopwood, Avery, May 28, 1882–July 1, 1928.
Vol. 5, Pt. 1–228
Horlick, William, Feb. 23, 1846–Sept. 25, 1936.
Supp. 2–316
Hormel, George Albert, Dec. 4, 1860–June 5, 1946.
Supp. 4–395
Hormel, Jay Catherwood, Sept. 11, 1892–Aug. 30, 1954.
Supp. 5–314
Horn, Edward Traill, June 10, 1850–Mar. 4, 1915.
Vol. 5, Pt. 1–228
Horn, George Henry, Apr. 7, 1840–Nov. 24, 1897.
Vol. 5, Pt. 1–229
Horn, Tom, Nov. 21, 1860–Nov. 20, 1903.
Vol. 5, Pt. 1–230
Hornaday, William Temple, Dec. 1, 1854–Mar. 6, 1937.
Supp. 2–316
Hornblower, Joseph Coerten, May 6, 1777–June 11, 1864.
Vol. 5, Pt. 1–230
Hornblower, Josiah, Feb. 23, 1729 N.S.–Jan. 21, 1809.
Vol. 5, Pt. 1–231
Hornblower, William Butler, May 13, 1851–June 16, 1914.
Vol. 5, Pt. 1–232
Horner, Henry, Nov. 30, 1878–Oct. 6, 1940.
Supp. 2–318
Horner, William Edmonds, June 3, 1793–Mar. 13, 1853.
Vol. 5, Pt. 1–233

Horney, Karen Danielssen, Sept. 16, 1885–Dec. 4, 1952.
Supp. 5–315
Hornsby, Rogers, Apr. 27, 1896–Jan. 5, 1963.
Supp. 7–364
Horr, George Edwin, Jan. 19, 1856–Jan. 22, 1927.
Vol. 5, Pt. 1–234
Horrocks, James, c. 1734–Mar. 20, 1772.
Vol. 5, Pt. 1–235
Horsfield, Thomas, May 12, 1773–July 24, 1859.
Vol. 5, Pt. 1–236
Horsford, Eben Norton, July 27, 1818–Jan. 1, 1893.
Vol. 5, Pt. 1–236
Horsmanden, Daniel, June 4, 1694–Sept. 23, 1778.
Vol. 5, Pt. 1–237
Horst, Louis, Jan. 12, 1884–Jan. 23, 1964.
Supp. 7–366
Horton, Edward Everett, Jr., Mar. 18, 1886–Sept. 29, 1970.
Supp. 8–283
Horton, Samuel Dana, Jan. 16, 1844–Feb. 23, 1895.
Vol. 5, Pt. 1–238
Horton, Valentine Baxter, Jan. 29, 1802–Jan. 14, 1888.
Vol. 5, Pt. 1–238
Hosack, Alexander Eddy, Apr. 6, 1805–Mar. 2, 1871.
Vol. 5, Pt. 1–239
Hosack, David, Aug. 31, 1769–Dec. 22, 1835.
Vol. 5, Pt. 1–239
Hoshour, Samuel Klinefelter, Dec. 9, 1803–Nov. 29, 1883.
Vol. 5, Pt. 1–240
Hosmer, Frederick Lucian, Oct. 16, 1840–June 7, 1929.
Vol. 5, Pt. 1–241
Hosmer, Harriet Goodhue, Oct. 9, 1830–Feb. 21, 1908.
Vol. 5, Pt. 1–242
Hosmer, Hezekiah Lord, Dec. 10, 1814–Oct. 31, 1893.
Vol. 5, Pt. 1–243
Hosmer, James Kendall, Jan. 29, 1834–May 11, 1927.
Vol. 5, Pt. 1–244
Hosmer, Titus, 1737–Aug. 4, 1780.
Vol. 5, Pt. 1–245
Hosmer, William Howe Cuyler, May 25, 1814–May 23, 1877.
Vol. 5, Pt. 1–245
Hotchkiss, Benjamin Berkeley, Oct. 1, 1826–Feb. 14, 1885.
Vol. 5, Pt. 1–246
Hotchkiss, Horace Leslie, Mar. 27, 1842–May 10, 1929.
Vol. 5, Pt. 1–247
Hotz, Ferdinand Carl, July 12, 1843–Mar. 21, 1909.
Vol. 5, Pt. 1–247
Houdini, Harry, Apr. 6, 1874–Oct. 31, 1926.
Vol. 5, Pt. 1–248
Houdry, Eugene Jules, Apr. 18, 1892–July 18, 1962.
Supp. 7–367
Hough, Charles Merrill, May 18, 1858–Apr. 22, 1927.
Vol. 5, Pt. 1–249
Hough, Emerson, June 28, 1857–Apr. 30, 1923.
Vol. 5, Pt. 1–250
Hough, Franklin Benjamin, July 22, 1822–June 11, 1885.
Vol. 5, Pt. 1–250
Hough, George Washington, Oct. 24, 1836–Jan. 1, 1909.
Vol. 5, Pt. 1–252
Hough, Theodore, June 19, 1865–Nov. 30, 1924.
Vol. 5, Pt. 1–252
Hough, Walter, Apr. 23, 1859–Sept. 20, 1935.
Supp. 1–435
Hough, Warwick, Jan. 26, 1836–Oct. 28, 1915.
Vol. 5, Pt. 1–253
Houghton, Alanson Bigelow, Oct. 10, 1863–Sept. 16, 1941.
Supp. 3–365
Houghton, Douglass, Sept. 21, 1809–Oct. 13, 1845.
Vol. 5, Pt. 1–254
Houghton, George Hendric, Feb. 1, 1820–Nov. 17, 1897.
Vol. 5, Pt. 1–255
Houghton, Henry Oscar, Apr. 30, 1823–Aug. 25, 1895.
Vol. 5, Pt. 1–255
Houk, Leonidas Campbell, June 8, 1836–May 25, 1891.
Vol. 5, Pt. 1–256
Hourwich, Isaac Aaronovich, Apr. 26, 1860–July 9, 1924.
Vol. 5, Pt. 1–257
House, Edward Howard, Sept. 5, 1836–Dec. 17, 1901.
Vol. 5, Pt. 1–257
House, Edward Mandell, July 26, 1858–Mar. 28, 1938.
Supp. 2–319
House, Henry Alonzo, Apr. 23, 1840–Dec. 18, 1930.
Vol. 5, Pt. 1–258

House, Royal Earl, Sept. 9, 1814–Feb. 25, 1895.
    Vol. 5, Pt. 1–259
House, Samuel Reynolds, Oct. 16, 1817–Aug. 13, 1899.
    Vol. 5, Pt. 1–260
Houston, Charles Hamilton, Sept. 3, 1895–Apr. 22, 1950.
    Supp. 4–396
Houston, David Franklin, Feb. 17, 1866–Sept. 2, 1940.
    Supp. 2–321
Houston, Edwin James, July 9, 1847–Mar. 1, 1914.
    Vol. 5, Pt. 1–261
Houston, George Smith, Jan. 17, 1811–Dec. 31, 1879.
    Vol. 5, Pt. 1–261
Houston, Henry Howard, Oct. 3, 1820–June 21, 1895.
    Vol. 5, Pt. 1–262
Houston, Samuel, Mar. 2, 1793–July 26, 1863.
    Vol. 5, Pt. 1–263
Houston, William Churchill, c. 1746–Aug. 12, 1788.
    Vol. 5, Pt. 1–267
Houstoun, John, Aug. 31, 1744–July 20, 1796.
    Vol. 5, Pt. 1–268
Hove, Elling, Mar. 25, 1863–Dec. 17, 1927.
    Vol. 5, Pt. 1–268
Hovenden, Thomas, Dec. 23, 1840–Aug. 14, 1895.
    Vol. 5, Pt. 1–269
Hovey, Alvah, Mar. 5, 1820–Sept. 6, 1903.
    Vol. 5, Pt. 1–270
Hovey, Alvin Peterson, Sept. 6, 1821–Nov. 23, 1891.
    Vol. 5, Pt. 1–270
Hovey, Charles Edward, Apr. 26, 1827–Nov. 17, 1897.
    Vol. 5, Pt. 1–271
Hovey, Charles Mason, Oct. 26, 1810–Sept. 2, 1887.
    Vol. 5, Pt. 1–272
Hovey, Otis Ellis, Apr. 9, 1864–Apr. 15, 1941.
    Supp. 3–366
Hovey, Richard, May 4, 1864–Feb. 24, 1900.
    Vol. 5, Pt. 1–273
Hovgaard, William, Nov. 28, 1857–Jan. 5, 1950.
    Supp. 4–398
Howard, Ada Lydia, Dec. 19, 1829–Mar. 3, 1907.
    Vol. 5, Pt. 1–274
Howard, Benjamin, 1760–Sept. 18, 1814.
    Vol. 5, Pt. 1–274
Howard, Benjamin Chew, Nov. 5, 1791–Mar. 6, 1872.
    Vol. 5, Pt. 1–275
Howard, Blanche Willis, July 21, 1847–Oct. 7, 1898.
    Vol. 5, Pt. 1–275
Howard, Bronson Crocker, Oct. 7, 1842–Aug. 4, 1908.
    Vol. 5, Pt. 1–276
Howard, Charles Perry, Sept. 14, 1879–July 21, 1938.
    Supp. 2–322
Howard, Edgar, Sept. 16, 1858–July 19, 1951.
    Supp. 5–318
Howard, George Elliott, Oct. 1, 1849–June 9, 1928.
    Vol. 5, Pt. 1–277
Howard, Henry, July 5, 1868–Aug. 26, 1951.
    Supp. 5–319
Howard, Jacob Merritt, July 10, 1805–Apr. 2, 1871.
    Vol. 5, Pt. 1–278
Howard, John Eager, June 4, 1752–Oct. 12, 1827.
    Vol. 5, Pt. 1–279
Howard, Joseph Kinsey, Feb. 28, 1906–Aug. 25, 1951.
    Supp. 5–320
Howard, Leland Ossian, June 11, 1857–May 1, 1950.
    Supp. 4–399
Howard, Leslie, Apr. 3, 1893–June 1, 1943.
    Supp. 3–367
Howard, Oliver Otis, Nov. 8, 1830–Oct. 26, 1909.
    Vol. 5, Pt. 1–279
Howard, Roy Wilson, Jan. 1, 1883–Nov. 20, 1964.
    Supp. 7–369
Howard, Sidney Coe, June 26, 1891–Aug. 23, 1939.
    Supp. 2–324
Howard, Timothy Edward, Jan. 27, 1837–July 9, 1916.
    Vol. 5, Pt. 1–281
Howard, Volney Erskine, Oct. 22, 1809–May 14, 1889.
    Vol. 5, Pt. 1–282
Howard, William Alanson, Apr. 8, 1813–Apr. 10, 1880.
    Vol. 5, Pt. 1–282
Howard, William Travis, Jan. 12, 1821–July 31, 1907.
    Supp. 1–436
Howard, Willie, Apr. 13, 1886–Jan. 12, 1949.
    Supp. 4–400

Howe, Albion Parris, Mar. 25, 1818–Jan. 25, 1897.
    Vol. 5, Pt. 1–283
Howe, Andrew Jackson, Apr. 14, 1825–Jan. 16, 1892.
    Vol. 5, Pt. 1–283
Howe, Edgar Watson, May 3, 1853–Oct. 3, 1937.
    Supp. 2–325
Howe, Elias, July 9, 1819–Oct. 3, 1867.
    Vol. 5, Pt. 1–284
Howe, Frederic Clemson, Nov. 21, 1867–Aug. 3, 1940.
    Supp. 2–326
Howe, Frederick Webster, Aug. 28, 1822–Apr. 25, 1891.
    Vol. 5, Pt. 1–286
Howe, George, Nov. 6, 1802–Apr. 15, 1883.
    Vol. 5, Pt. 1–286
Howe, George Augustus, c. 1724–July 6, 1758.
    Vol. 5, Pt. 1–287
Howe, Henry, Oct. 11, 1816–Oct. 14, 1893.
    Vol. 5, Pt. 1–288
Howe, Henry Marion, Mar. 2, 1848–May 14, 1922.
    Vol. 5, Pt. 1–289
Howe, Herbert Alonzo, Nov. 22, 1858–Nov. 2, 1926.
    Vol. 5, Pt. 1–289
Howe, John Ireland, July 20, 1793–Sept. 10, 1876.
    Vol. 5, Pt. 1–290
Howe, Julia Ward, May 27, 1819–Oct. 17, 1910.
    Vol. 5, Pt. 1–291
Howe, Louis McHenry, Jan. 14, 1871–Apr. 18, 1936.
    Supp. 2–328
Howe, Lucien, Sept. 18, 1848–Dec. 27, 1928.
    Vol. 5, Pt. 1–293
Howe, Mark Anthony DeWolfe, Apr. 5, 1808–July 31, 1895.
    Vol. 5, Pt. 1–293
Howe, Mark Antony De Wolfe, Aug. 23, 1864–Dec. 6, 1960.
    Supp. 6–306
Howe, Mark De Wolfe, May 22, 1906–Feb. 28, 1967.
    Supp. 8–284
Howe, Percy Rogers, Sept. 20, 1864–Feb. 28, 1950.
    Supp. 4–401
Howe, Robert, 1732–Dec. 14, 1786.
    Vol. 5, Pt. 1–294
Howe, Samuel, June 20, 1785–Jan. 20, 1828.
    Vol. 5, Pt. 1–295
Howe, Samuel Gridley, Nov. 10, 1801–Jan. 9, 1876.
    Vol. 5, Pt. 1–296
Howe, Timothy Otis, Feb. 24, 1816–Mar. 25, 1883.
    Vol. 5, Pt. 1–297
Howe, William, May 12, 1803–Sept. 19, 1852.
    Vol. 5, Pt. 1–298
Howe, William F., July 7, 1828–Sept. 1, 1902.
    Vol. 5, Pt. 1–299
Howe, William Henry, Nov. 22, 1846–Mar. 16, 1929.
    Vol. 5, Pt. 1–299
Howe, William Wirt, Nov. 24, 1833–Mar. 17, 1909.
    Vol. 5, Pt. 1–300
Howell, Albert Summers, Apr. 17, 1879–Jan. 3, 1951.
    Supp. 5–321
Howell, Clark, Sept. 21, 1863–Nov. 14, 1936.
    Supp. 2–329
Howell, David, Jan. 1, 1747–July 30, 1824.
    Vol. 5, Pt. 1–301
Howell, Evan Park, Dec. 10, 1839–Aug. 6, 1905.
    Vol. 5, Pt. 1–301
Howell, James Bruen, July 4, 1816–June 17, 1880.
    Vol. 5, Pt. 1–302
Howell, John Adams, Mar. 16, 1840–Jan. 10, 1918.
    Vol. 5, Pt. 1–303
Howell, Richard, Oct. 25, 1754–Apr. 28, 1802.
    Vol. 5, Pt. 1–304
Howell, Robert Boyté Crawford, Mar. 10, 1801–Apr. 5, 1868.
    Vol. 5, Pt. 1–304
Howell, Thomas Jefferson, Oct. 9, 1842–Dec. 3, 1912.
    Vol. 5, Pt. 1–305
Howell, William Henry, Feb. 20, 1860–Feb. 6, 1945.
    Supp. 3–369
Howells, William Dean, Mar. 1, 1837–May 11, 1920.
    Vol. 5, Pt. 1–306
Howey, Walter Crawford, Jan. 16, 1882–Mar. 21, 1954.
    Supp. 5–323
Howison, George Holmes, Nov. 29, 1834–Dec. 31, 1916.
    Vol. 5, Pt. 1–311
Howland, Alfred Cornelius, Feb. 12, 1838–Mar. 17, 1909.
    Vol. 5, Pt. 1–311

Howland, Emily, Nov. 20, 1827–June 29, 1929.
  Vol. 5, Pt. 1–312
Howland, Gardiner Greene, Sept. 4, 1787–Nov. 9, 1851.
  Vol. 5, Pt. 1–312
Howland, John, Feb. 3, 1873–June 20, 1926.
  Vol. 5, Pt. 1–313
Howley, Richard, 1740–1784.
  Vol. 5, Pt. 1–314
Howry, Charles Bowen, May 14, 1844–July 20, 1928.
  Vol. 5, Pt. 1–315
Howze, Robert Lee, Aug. 22, 1864–Sept. 19, 1926.
  Vol. 5, Pt. 1–315
Hoxie, Robert Franklin, Apr. 29, 1868–June 22, 1916.
  Vol. 5, Pt. 1–316
Hoxie, Vinnie Ream, Sept. 25, 1847–Nov. 20, 1914.
  Vol. 5, Pt. 1–317
Hoxie, William Dixie, July 1, 1866–Jan. 12, 1925.
  Vol. 5, Pt. 1–318
Hoyme, Gjermund, Oct. 8, 1847–June 9, 1902.
  Vol. 5, Pt. 1–319
Hoyt, Albert Harrison, Dec. 6, 1826–June 10, 1915.
  Vol. 5, Pt. 1–319
Hoyt, Charles Hale, July 26, 1860–Nov. 20, 1900.
  Vol. 5, Pt. 1–320
Hoyt, Henry Martyn, June 8, 1830–Dec. 1, 1892.
  Vol. 5, Pt. 1–321
Hoyt, John Sherman, July 29, 1869–Mar. 30, 1954.
  Supp. 5–324
Hoyt, John Wesley, Oct. 13, 1831–May 23, 1912.
  Vol. 5, Pt. 1–321
Hrdlicka, Ales, Mar. 29, 1869–Sept. 5, 1943.
  Supp. 3–371
Hubbard, Bernard Rosecrans, Nov. 24, 1888–May 28, 1962.
  Supp. 7–370
Hubbard, David, c. 1792–Jan. 20, 1874.
  Vol. 5, Pt. 1–322
Hubbard, Elbert, June 19, 1856–May 7, 1915.
  Vol. 5, Pt. 1–323
Hubbard, Frank McKinney, Sept. 1, 1868–Dec. 26, 1930.
  Vol. 5, Pt. 1–324
Hubbard, Gardiner Greene, Aug. 25, 1822–Dec. 11, 1897.
  Vol. 5, Pt. 1–324
Hubbard, Gurdon Saltonstall, Aug. 22, 1802–Sept. 14, 1886.
  Vol. 5, Pt. 1–326
Hubbard, Henry Griswold, Oct. 8, 1814–July 29, 1891.
  Vol. 5, Pt. 1–327
Hubbard, Henry Guernsey, May 6, 1850–Jan. 18, 1899.
  Vol. 5, Pt. 1–327
Hubbard, John, Mar. 22, 1794–Feb. 6, 1869.
  Vol. 5, Pt. 1–328
Hubbard, Joseph Stillman, Sept. 7, 1823–Aug. 16, 1863.
  Vol. 5, Pt. 1–329
Hubbard, Kin. [See Hubbard, Frank McKinney, 1868–1930.]
Hubbard, Lucius Frederick, Jan. 26, 1836–Feb. 5, 1913.
  Vol. 5, Pt. 1–330
Hubbard, Richard Bennett, Nov. 1, 1832–July 12, 1901.
  Vol. 5, Pt. 1–331
Hubbard, Richard William, Oct. 15, 1816–Dec. 21, 1888.
  Vol. 5, Pt. 1–331
Hubbard, Thomas Hamlin, Dec. 20, 1838–May 19, 1915.
  Vol. 5, Pt. 1–332
Hubbard, William, c. 1621–Sept. 14, 1704.
  Vol. 5, Pt. 1–333
Hubbard, Wynant Davis, Aug. 28, 1900–Dec. 9, 1961.
  Supp. 7–371
Hubbell, John Lorenzo, Nov. 27, 1853–Nov. 12, 1930.
  Supp. 1–437
Hubble, Edwin, Nov. 20, 1899–Sept. 28–1953.
  Supp. 5–325
Hubbs, Rebecca, Dec. 3, 1772–Sept. 29, 1852.
  Vol. 5, Pt. 1–334
Huber, Gotthelf Carl, Aug. 30, 1865–Dec. 26, 1934.
  Supp. 1–438
Hubert, Conrad, 1855–Mar. 14, 1928.
  Vol. 5, Pt. 1–334
Hubner, Charles William, Jan. 16, 1835–Jan. 3, 1929.
  Vol. 5, Pt. 1–335
Hudde, Andries, 1608–Nov. 4, 1663.
  Vol. 5, Pt. 1–335
Hudson, Charles, Nov. 14, 1795–May 4, 1881.
  Vol. 5, Pt. 1–336
Hudson, Claude Silbert, Jan. 26, 1881–Dec. 27, 1952.
  Supp. 5–327

Hudson, Daniel Eldred, Dec. 18, 1849–Jan. 12, 1934.
  Supp. 1–440
Hudson, Edward, October 1772–Jan. 3, 1833.
  Vol. 5, Pt. 1–337
Hudson, Frederic, Apr. 25, 1819–Oct. 21, 1875.
  Supp. 1–441
Hudson, Henry, d. after June 23, 1611.
  Vol. 5, Pt. 1–338
Hudson, Henry Norman, Jan. 28, 1814–Jan. 16, 1886.
  Vol. 5, Pt. 1–340
Hudson, Manley Ottmer, May 19, 1886–Apr. 13, 1960.
  Supp. 6–307
Hudson, Mary Clemmer Ames. [See Clemmer, Mary, 1839–1884.]
Hudson, Thomson Jay, Feb. 22, 1834–May 26, 1903.
  Vol. 5, Pt. 1–341
Hudson, William Smith, Mar. 13, 1810–July 20, 1881.
  Vol. 5, Pt. 1–342
Huebner, Solomon Stephen, Mar. 6, 1882–July 17, 1964.
  Supp. 7–373
Huebsch, Benjamin W., Mar. 21, 1876–Aug. 7, 1964.
  Supp. 7–373
Huger, Benjamin, Nov. 22, 1805–Dec. 7, 1877.
  Vol. 5, Pt. 1–343
Huger, Daniel Elliott, June 28, 1779–Aug. 21, 1854.
  Vol. 5, Pt. 1–343
Huger, Francis Kinloch, Sept. 17, 1773–Feb. 14, 1855.
  Vol. 5, Pt. 1–344
Huger, Isaac, Mar. 19, 1742/43–Oct. 17, 1797.
  Vol. 5, Pt. 1–344
Huger, John, June 5, 1744–Jan. 22, 1804.
  Vol. 5, Pt. 1–345
Huggins, Miller James, Apr. 19, 1879–Sept. 25, 1929.
  Vol. 5, Pt. 1–345
Hughes, Charles Evans, Apr. 11, 1862–Aug. 27, 1948.
  Supp. 4–403
Hughes, Charles Frederick, Oct. 14, 1866–May 28, 1934.
  Supp. 1–441
Hughes, Christopher, 1786–Sept. 18, 1849.
  Vol. 5, Pt. 1–346
Hughes, David Edward, May 16, 1831–Jan. 22, 1900.
  Vol. 5, Pt. 1–347
Hughes, Dudley Mays, Oct. 10, 1848–Jan. 20, 1927.
  Vol. 5, Pt. 1–348
Hughes, Edwin Holt, Dec. 7, 1866–Feb. 12, 1950.
  Supp. 4–408
Hughes, George Wurtz, Sept. 30, 1806–Dec. 3, 1870.
  Vol. 5, Pt. 1–348
Hughes, Hector James, Oct. 23, 1871–Mar. 1, 1930.
  Vol. 5, Pt. 1–349
Hughes, Henry, d. Oct. 3, 1862.
  Vol. 5, Pt. 1–350
Hughes, Howard Robard, Sept. 9, 1869–Jan. 14, 1924.
  Vol. 5, Pt. 1–351
Hughes, James, Nov. 24, 1823–Oct. 21, 1873.
  Vol. 5, Pt. 1–351
Hughes, James Langston, Feb. 1, 1902–May 22, 1967.
  Supp. 8–285
Hughes, John Joseph, June 24, 1797–Jan. 3, 1864.
  Vol. 5, Pt. 1–352
Hughes, Price, d. 1715.
  Vol. 5, Pt. 1–355
Hughes, Robert Ball, Jan. 19, 1806–Mar. 5, 1868.
  Vol. 5, Pt. 1–356
Hughes, Robert William, Jan. 16, 1821–Dec. 10, 1901.
  Vol. 5, Pt. 1–357
Hughes, Rupert, Jan. 31, 1872–Sept. 9, 1956.
  Supp. 6–308
Huidekoper, Frederic, Apr. 7, 1817–May 16, 1892.
  Vol. 5, Pt. 1–358
Huidekoper, Harm Jan, Apr. 3, 1776–May 22, 1854.
  Vol. 5, Pt. 1–359
Hulbert, Archer Butler, Jan. 26, 1873–Dec. 24, 1933.
  Supp. 1–442
Hulbert, Edwin James, Apr. 30, 1829–Oct. 20, 1910.
  Vol. 5, Pt. 1–360
Hull, Clark Leonard, May 24, 1884–May 10, 1952.
  Supp. 5–328
Hull, Cordell, Oct. 2, 1871–July 23, 1955.
  Supp. 5–331
Hull, Isaac, Mar. 9, 1773–Feb. 13, 1843.
  Vol. 5, Pt. 1–360

Hull, John, Dec. 18, 1624–Oct. 1, 1683.
Vol. 5, Pt. 1–362
Hull, Josephine, Jan. 3, 1886[?]–Mar. 12, 1957.
Supp. 6–310
Hull, William, June 24, 1753–Nov. 29, 1825.
Vol. 5, Pt. 1–363
Hullihen, Simon P., Dec. 10, 1810–Mar. 27, 1857.
Vol. 5, Pt. 1–364
Humbert, Jean Joseph Amable, Nov. 25, 1755–Jan. 2, 1823.
Vol. 5, Pt. 1–365
Hume, Edgar Erskine, Dec. 26, 1889–Jan. 24, 1952.
Supp. 5–335
Hume, Robert Allen, Mar. 18, 1847–June 24, 1929.
Vol. 5, Pt. 1–365
Hume, William, Nov. 19, 1830–June 25, 1902.
Vol. 5, Pt. 1–366
Humes, Thomas William, Apr. 22, 1815–Jan. 16, 1892.
Vol. 5, Pt. 1–367
Humiston, William Henry, Apr. 27, 1869–Dec. 5, 1923.
Vol. 5, Pt. 1–367
Hummel, Abraham Henry, July 27, 1850–Jan. 22, 1926.
Vol. 5, Pt. 1–368
Humphrey, Doris, Oct. 17, 1895–Dec. 29, 1958.
Supp. 6–312
Humphrey, George Magoffin, Mar. 8, 1890–Jan. 20, 1970.
Supp. 8–289
Humphrey, Heman, Mar. 26, 1779–Apr. 3, 1861.
Vol. 5, Pt. 1–369
Humphreys, Alexander Crombie, Mar. 30, 1851–Aug. 14, 1927. Vol. 5, Pt. 1–370
Humphreys, Andrew Atkinson, Nov. 2, 1810–Dec. 27, 1883.
Vol. 5, Pt. 1–371
Humphreys, Benjamin Grubb, Aug. 24 or 26, 1808–Dec. 20, 1882. Vol. 5, Pt. 1–372
Humphreys, David, July 10, 1752–Feb. 21, 1818.
Vol. 5, Pt. 1–373
Humphreys, James, Jan. 15, 1748–Feb. 2, 1810.
Vol. 5, Pt. 1–375
Humphreys, Joshua, June 17, 1751–Jan. 12, 1838.
Vol. 5, Pt. 1–376
Humphreys, Milton Wylie, Sept. 15, 1844–Nov. 20, 1928.
Vol. 5, Pt. 1–377
Humphreys, West Hughes, Aug. 26, 1806–Oct. 16, 1882.
Vol. 5, Pt. 1–378
Humphreys, Wiliam Jackson, Feb. 3, 1862–Nov. 10, 1949.
Supp. 4–409
Humphries, George Rolfe, Nov. 20, 1894–Apr. 22, 1969.
Supp. 8–290
Huneker, James Gibbons, Jan. 31, 1860–Feb. 9, 1921.
Vol. 5, Pt. 1–379
Hunnewell, Horatio Hollis, July 27, 1810–Mar. 20, 1902.
Vol. 5, Pt. 1–380
Hunnewell, James, Feb. 10, 1794–May 2, 1869.
Vol. 5, Pt. 1–381
Hunt, Alfred Ephraim, Mar. 31, 1855–Apr. 26, 1899.
Vol. 5, Pt. 1–381
Hunt, Benjamin Weeks, May 18, 1847–June 26, 1934.
Supp. 1–443
Hunt, Carleton, Jan. 1, 1836–Aug. 14, 1921.
Vol. 5, Pt. 1–382
Hunt, Charles Wallace, Oct. 13, 1841–Mar. 27, 1911.
Vol. 5, Pt. 1–383
Hunt, Freeman, Mar. 21, 1804–Mar. 2, 1858.
Vol. 5, Pt. 1–384
Hunt, Gaillard, Sept. 8, 1862–Mar. 20, 1924.
Vol. 5, Pt. 1–385
Hunt, George Wylie Paul, Nov. 1, 1859–Dec. 24, 1934.
Supp. 1–444
Hunt, Harriot Kezia, Nov. 9, 1805–Jan. 2, 1875.
Vol. 5, Pt. 1–385
Hunt, Henry Jackson, Sept. 14, 1819–Feb. 11, 1889.
Vol. 5, Pt. 1–386
Hunt, Isaac, c. 1742–1809.
Vol. 5, Pt. 1–387
Hunt, Lester Callaway, July 8, 1892–June 19, 1954.
Supp. 5–336
Hunt, Mary Hannah Hanchett, June 4, 1830–Apr. 24, 1906.
Vol. 5, Pt. 1–388
Hunt, Nathan, Oct. 26, 1758–Aug. 8, 1853.
Vol. 5, Pt. 1–389
Hunt, Reid, Apr. 20, 1870–Mar. 10, 1948.
Supp. 4–410

Hunt, Richard Morris, Oct. 31, 1827–July 31, 1895.
Vol. 5, Pt. 1–389
Hunt, Robert, c. 1568–1608.
Vol. 5, Pt. 1–391
Hunt, Robert Woolston, Dec. 9, 1838–July 11, 1923.
Vol. 5, Pt. 1–392
Hunt, Theodore Whitefield, Feb. 19, 1844–Apr. 12, 1930.
Vol. 5, Pt. 1–393
Hunt, Thomas Sterry, Sept. 5, 1826–Feb. 12, 1892.
Vol. 5, Pt. 1–393
Hunt, Ward, June 14, 1810–Mar. 24, 1886.
Vol. 5, Pt. 1–394
Hunt, Washington, Aug. 5, 1811–Feb. 2, 1867.
Vol. 5, Pt. 1–395
Hunt, William Gibbes, Feb. 21, 1791–Aug. 13, 1833.
Vol. 5, Pt. 1–396
Hunt, William Henry, June 12, 1823–Feb. 27, 1884.
Vol. 5, Pt. 1–396
Hunt, William Morris, Mar. 31, 1824–Sept. 8, 1879.
Vol. 5, Pt. 1–397
Hunt, Wilson Price, 1782?–April 1842.
Vol. 5, Pt. 1–398
Hunter, Andrew, 1751–Feb. 24, 1823.
Vol. 5, Pt. 1–399
Hunter, Croil, Feb. 18, 1893–July 21, 1970.
Supp. 8–291
Hunter, David, July 21, 1802–Feb. 2, 1886.
Vol. 5, Pt. 1–400
Hunter, Robert, d. March 1734.
Vol. 5, Pt. 1–401
Hunter, Robert, Apr. 10, 1874–May 15, 1942.
Supp. 3–372
Hunter, Robert Mercer Taliaferro, Apr. 21, 1809–July 18, 1887. Vol. 5, Pt. 1–403
Hunter, Thomas, Oct. 19, 1831–Oct. 14, 1915.
Vol. 5, Pt. 1–405
Hunter, Walter David, Dec. 14, 1875–Oct. 13, 1925.
Vol. 5, Pt. 1–406
Hunter, Whiteside Godfrey, Dec. 25, 1841–Nov. 2, 1917.
Vol. 5, Pt. 1–406
Hunter, William, Nov. 26, 1774–Dec. 3, 1849.
Vol. 5, Pt. 1–407
Hunter, William C., 1812–June 25, 1891.
Vol. 5, Pt. 1–408
Huntington, Collis Potter, Oct. 22, 1821–Aug. 13, 1900.
Vol. 5, Pt. 1–408
Huntington, Daniel, Oct. 14, 1816–Apr. 18, 1906.
Vol. 5, Pt. 1–412
Huntington, Edward Vermilye, Apr. 26, 1874–Nov. 25, 1952.
Supp. 5–338
Huntington, Elisha, Apr. 9, 1796–Dec. 13, 1865.
Vol. 5, Pt. 1–413
Huntington, Ellsworth, Sept. 16, 1876–Oct. 17, 1947.
Supp. 4–412
Huntington, Frederic Dan, May 28, 1819–July 11, 1904.
Vol. 5, Pt. 1–413
Huntington, Henry Edwards, Feb. 27, 1850–May 23, 1927.
Vol. 5, Pt. 1–414
Huntington, Jabez, Aug. 7, 1719–Oct. 5, 1786.
Vol. 5, Pt. 1–416
Huntington, Jedediah Vincent, Jan. 20, 1815–Mar. 10, 1862.
Vol. 5, Pt. 1–417
Huntington, Jedediah, Aug. 4, 1743–Sept. 25, 1818.
Vol. 5, Pt. 1–416
Huntington, Margaret Jane Evans, Jan. 9, 1842–Mar. 17, 1926. Vol. 5, Pt. 1–418
Huntington, Samuel, July 3, 1731–Jan. 5, 1796.
Vol. 5, Pt. 1–418
Huntington, Samuel, Oct. 4, 1765–June 8, 1817.
Vol. 5, Pt. 1–419
Huntington, William Edwards, July 30, 1844–Dec. 6, 1930.
Vol. 5, Pt. 1–420
Huntington, William Reed, Sept. 20, 1838–July 26, 1909.
Vol. 5, Pt. 1–420
Hunton, Eppa, Sept. 22, 1822–Oct. 11, 1908.
Vol. 5, Pt. 1–421
Hunton, George Kenneth, Mar. 24, 1888–Nov. 11, 1967.
Supp. 8–293
Hunton, William Lee, Feb. 16, 1864–Oct. 12, 1930.
Vol. 5, Pt. 1–422
Hupp, Louis Gorham, Nov. 13, 1872–Dec. 10, 1961.
Supp. 7–375

Hurd, John Codman, Nov. 11, 1816–June 25, 1892.
    Vol. 5, Pt. 1–423
Hurd, Nathaniel, Feb. 13, 1730–Dec. 17, 1777.
    Vol. 5, Pt. 1–423
Hurlbert, William Henry, July 3, 1827–Sept. 4, 1895.
    Vol. 5, Pt. 1–424
Hurlbut, Jesse Lyman, Feb. 15, 1843–Aug. 2, 1930.
    Vol. 5, Pt. 1–424
Hurlbut, Stephen Augustus, Nov. 29, 1815–Mar. 27, 1882.
    Vol. 5, Pt. 1–425
Hurley, Edward Nash, July 31, 1864–Nov. 14, 1933.
    Supp. 1–446
Hurley, Joseph Patrick, Jan. 21, 1894–Oct. 30, 1967.
    Supp. 8–294
Hurley, Patrick Jay, Jan. 8, 1883–July 30, 1963.
    Supp. 7–376
Hurst, Fannie, Oct. 19, 1889–Feb. 23, 1968.
    Supp. 8–296
Hurst, John Fletcher, Aug. 17, 1834–May 4, 1903.
    Vol. 5, Pt. 1–426
Hurston, Zora Neale, Jan. 3, 1901[?]–Jan. 28, 1960.
    Supp. 6–313
Husbands, Hermon, Oct. 3, 1724–1795.
    Vol. 2, Pt. 2–427
Huse, Caleb, Feb. 11, 1831–Mar. 11, 1905.
    Vol. 5, Pt. 1–428
Husing, Edward Britt ("Ted"), Nov. 27, 1901–Aug. 10, 1962.
    Supp. 7–377
Husk, Charles Ellsworth, Dec. 19, 1872–Mar. 20, 1916.
    Vol. 5, Pt. 1–429
Husmann, George, Nov. 4, 1827–Nov. 5, 1902.
    Vol. 5, Pt. 1–430
Hussey, Curtis Grubb, Aug. 11, 1802–Apr. 25, 1893.
    Vol. 5, Pt. 1–430
Hussey, Obed, 1792–Aug. 4, 1860.
    Vol. 5, Pt. 1–431
Hussey, William Joseph, Aug. 10, 1862–Oct. 28, 1926.
    Vol. 5, Pt. 1–432
Husting, Paul Oscar, Apr. 25, 1866–Oct. 21, 1917.
    Vol. 5, Pt. 1–433
Huston, Charles, July 23, 1822–Jan. 5, 1897.
    Vol. 5, Pt. 1–433
Huston, Walter, Apr. 6, 1884–Apr. 7, 1950.
    Supp. 4–414
Hutcheson, William Levi, Feb. 7, 1874–Oct. 20, 1953.
    Supp. 5–339
Hutchins, Harry Burns, Apr. 8, 1847–Jan. 25, 1930.
    Vol. 5, Pt. 1–434
Hutchins, Thomas, 1730–Apr. 28, 1789.
    Vol. 5, Pt. 1–435
Hutchinson, Anne, 1591–1643.
    Vol. 5, Pt. 1–436
Hutchinson, Benjamin Peters, July 24, 1829–Mar. 16, 1899.
    Vol. 5, Pt. 1–437
Hutchinson, Charles Lawrence, Mar. 7, 1854–Oct. 7, 1924.
    Vol. 5, Pt. 1–438
Hutchinson, James, Jan. 29, 1752–Sept. 5, 1793.
    Vol. 5, Pt. 1–438
Hutchinson, Paul, Aug. 10, 1890–Apr. 15, 1956.
    Supp. 6–315
Hutchinson, Thomas, Sept. 9, 1711–June 3, 1780.
    Vol. 5, Pt. 1–439
Hutchinson, Woods, Jan. 3, 1862–Apr. 26, 1930.
    Vol. 5, Pt. 1–443
Hutson, Richard, July 9, 1748–Apr. 12, 1795.
    Vol. 5, Pt. 1–443
Hutton, Edward Francis, Sept. 7, 1875–July 11, 1962.
    Supp. 7–379
Hutton, Frederick Remsen, May 28, 1853–May 14, 1918.
    Vol. 5, Pt. 1–444
Hutton, Laurence, Aug. 8, 1843–June 10, 1904.
    Vol. 5, Pt. 1–445
Hutton, Levi William, Oct. 22, 1860–Nov. 3, 1928.
    Vol. 5, Pt. 1–445
Huxley, Aldous Leonard, July 26, 1894–Nov. 22, 1963.
    Supp. 7–380
Hyatt, Alpheus, Apr. 5, 1838–Jan. 15, 1902.
    Vol. 5, Pt. 1–446
Hyatt, John Wesley, Nov. 28, 1837–May 10, 1920.
    Vol. 5, Pt. 1–447
Hyde, Arthur Mastick, July 12, 1877–Oct. 17, 1947.
    Supp. 4–415

Hyde, Charles Cheney, May 22, 1873–Feb. 13, 1952.
    Supp. 5–340
Hyde, Edward, c. 1650–Sept. 8, 1712.
    Vol. 5, Pt. 1–449
Hyde, Edward. [See Cornbury, Edward Hyde, Viscount, 1661–1723.]
Hyde, Helen, Apr. 6, 1868–May 13, 1919.
    Vol. 5, Pt. 1–449
Hyde, Henry Baldwin, Feb. 15, 1834–May 2, 1899.
    Vol. 5, Pt. 1–450
Hyde, James Nevins, June 21, 1840–Sept. 6, 1910.
    Vol. 5, Pt. 1–451
Hyde, William DeWitt, Sept. 23, 1858–June 29, 1917.
    Vol. 5, Pt. 1–452
Hyer, Robert Stewart, Oct. 18, 1860–May 29, 1929.
    Vol. 5, Pt. 1–453
Hylan, John Francis, Apr. 20, 1868–Jan. 12, 1936.
    Supp. 2–330
Hyrne, Edmund Massingberd, Jan. 14, 1748–Dec. 1783.
    Vol. 5, Pt. 1–454
Hyslop, James Hervey, Aug. 18, 1854–June 17, 1920.
    Vol. 5, Pt. 1–454
Hyvernat, Henri, June 30, 1858–May 29, 1941.
    Supp. 3–374

Iberville, Pierre Le Moyne Sieur d', July 1661–July 9, 1706.
    Vol. 5, Pt. 1–455
Ickes, Harold Le Clair, Mar. 15, 1874–Feb. 3, 1952.
    Supp. 5–341
Iddings, Joseph Paxon, Jan. 21, 1857–Sept. 8, 1920.
    Vol. 5, Pt. 1–457
Ide, Henry Clay, Sept. 18, 1844–June 13, 1921.
    Vol. 5, Pt. 1–458
Ide, John Jay, June 26, 1892–Jan. 12, 1962.
    Supp. 7–381
Iglesias, Santiago, Feb. 22, 1872–Dec. 5, 1939.
    Supp. 2–331
Ik Marvel. [See Mitchell, Donald Grant, 1822–1908.]
Illington, Margaret, July 23, 1879–Mar. 11, 1934.
    Supp. 1–447
Ilpendam, Jan Jansen Van. [See Van Ilpendam, Jan Jansen, c. 1595–1647.]
Imber, Naphtali Herz, Dec. 27, 1856–Oct. 8, 1909.
    Vol. 5, Pt. 1–459
Imbert, Antoine, d. c. 1835.
    Vol. 5, Pt. 1–460
Imboden, John Daniel, Feb. 16, 1823–Aug. 15, 1895.
    Vol. 5, Pt. 1–460
Imlay, Gilbert, c. 1754–Nov. 20, 1828?.
    Vol. 5, Pt. 1–461
Ingalls, John James, Dec. 29, 1833–Aug. 16, 1900.
    Vol. 5, Pt. 1–462
Ingalls, Marilla Baker, Nov. 25, 1828–Dec. 17, 1902.
    Vol. 5, Pt. 1–463
Ingalls, Melville Ezra, Sept. 6, 1842–July 11, 1914.
    Vol. 5, Pt. 1–464
Ingals, Ephraim Fletcher, Sept. 29, 1848–Apr. 30, 1918.
    Vol. 5, Pt. 1–464
Ingersoll, Charles Jared, Oct. 3, 1782–May 14, 1862.
    Vol. 5, Pt. 1–465
Ingersoll, Edward, Apr. 2, 1817–Feb. 19, 1893.
    Vol. 5, Pt. 1–467
Ingersoll, Jared, 1722–Aug. 25, 1781.
    Vol. 5, Pt. 1–467
Ingersoll, Jared, Oct. 27, 1749–Oct. 31, 1822.
    Vol. 5, Pt. 1–468
Ingersoll, Robert Green, Aug. 11, 1833–July 21, 1899.
    Vol. 5, Pt. 1–469
Ingersoll, Robert Hawley, Dec. 26, 1859–Sept. 4, 1928.
    Vol. 5, Pt. 1–470
Ingersoll, Royal Rodney, Dec. 4, 1847–Apr. 21, 1931.
    Vol. 5, Pt. 1–471
Ingersoll, Simon, Mar. 3, 1818–July 24, 1894.
    Vol. 5, Pt. 1–472
Ingham, Charles Cromwell, 1796–Dec. 10, 1863.
    Vol. 5, Pt. 1–473
Ingham, Samuel Delucenna, Sept. 16, 1779–June 5, 1860.
    Vol. 5, Pt. 1–473
Ingle, Richard, 1609–c. 1653.
    Vol. 5, Pt. 1–474
Inglis, Alexander James, Nov. 24, 1879–Apr. 12, 1924.
    Vol. 5, Pt. 1–475

Inglis, Charles, 1734–Feb. 24, 1816.
    Vol. 5, Pt. 1–476
Ingraham, Duncan Nathaniel, Dec. 6, 1802–Oct. 16, 1891.
    Vol. 5, Pt. 1–476
Ingraham, Edward Duffield, Feb. 12, 1793–Nov. 5, 1854.
    Vol. 5, Pt. 1–477
Ingraham, Joseph, 1762–1800.
    Vol. 5, Pt. 1–478
Ingraham, Joseph Holt, Jan. 25 or 26, 1809–Dec. 18, 1860.
    Vol. 5, Pt. 1–479
Ingraham, Prentiss, Dec. 22, 1843–Aug. 16, 1904.
    Vol. 5, Pt. 1–480
Ingram, Jonas Howard, Oct. 15, 1886–Sept. 10, 1952.
    Supp. 5–344
Inman, George, Dec. 3, 1755–c. February 1789.
    Vol. 5, Pt. 1–480
Inman, Henry, July 30, 1837–Nov. 13, 1899.
    Vol. 5, Pt. 1–482
Inman, Henry, Oct. 28, 1801–Jan. 17, 1846.
    Vol. 5, Pt. 1–481
Inman, John, 1805 Mar. 30, 1850.
    Vol. 5, Pt. 1–483
Inman, John Hamilton, Oct. 6, 1844–Nov. 5, 1896.
    Vol. 5, Pt. 1–484
Inman, Samuel Martin, Feb. 19, 1843–Jan. 12, 1915.
    Vol. 5, Pt. 1–485
Innes, Harry, Jan. 4, 1752 o.s.–Sept. 20, 1816.
    Vol. 5, Pt. 1–485
Innes, James, 1754–Aug. 2, 1798.
    Vol. 5, Pt. 1–486
Inness, George, May 1, 1825–Aug. 3, 1894.
    Vol. 5, Pt. 1–487
Innokentii, Aug. 26, 1797–Mar. 31, 1879.
    Vol. 5, Pt. 1–498
Inshtatheamba. [See Bright Eyes, 1854–1903.]
Inskip, John Swanel, Aug. 10, 1816–Mar. 7, 1884.
    Vol. 5, Pt. 1–490
Insull, Samuel, Nov. 11, 1859–July 16, 1938.
    Supp. 2–333
Ïoasaf, Jan. 22/Feb. 4, 1761–November 1799.
    Vol. 5, Pt. 1–491
Ioor, William, fl. 1780–1830.
    Vol. 5, Pt. 1–491
Iredell, James, Oct. 5, 1751–Oct. 20, 1799.
    Vol. 5, Pt. 1–492
Ireland, John, Jan. 1, 1827–Mar. 15, 1896.
    Vol. 5, Pt. 1–493
Ireland, John, Sept. 11, 1838–Sept. 25, 1918.
    Vol. 5, Pt. 1–494
Ireland, Joseph Norton, Apr. 24, 1817–Dec. 29, 1898.
    Vol. 5, Pt. 1–497
Irene, Sister, May 12, 1823–Aug. 14, 1896.
    Vol. 5, Pt. 1–498
Ironside, Henry Allan, Oct. 14, 1876–Jan. 15, 1951.
    Supp. 5–345
Irvine, James, Aug. 4, 1735–Apr. 28, 1819.
    Vol. 5, Pt. 1–499
Irvine, William, Nov. 3, 1741–July 29, 1804.
    Vol. 5, Pt. 1–500
Irvine, William Mann, Oct. 13, 1865–June 11, 1928.
    Vol. 5, Pt. 1–501
Irving, John Beaufain, Nov. 26, 1825–Apr. 20, 1877.
    Vol. 5, Pt. 1–501
Irving, John Duer, Aug. 18, 1874–July 20, 1918.
    Vol. 5, Pt. 1–502
Irving, John Treat, Dec. 2, 1812–Feb. 27, 1906.
    Vol. 5, Pt. 1–503
Irving, Peter, Oct. 30, 1771–June 27, 1838.
    Vol. 5, Pt. 1–503
Irving, Pierre Munro, 1803–1876.
    Vol. 5, Pt. 1–504
Irving, Roland Duer, Apr. 29, 1847–May 27, 1888.
    Vol. 5, Pt. 1–505
Irving, Washington, Apr. 3, 1783–Nov. 28, 1859.
    Vol. 5, Pt. 1–505
Irving, William, Aug. 15, 1766–Nov. 9, 1821.
    Vol. 5, Pt. 1–511
Irwin, Elisabeth Antoinette, Aug. 29, 1880–Oct. 16, 1942.
    Supp. 3–375
Irwin, George Le Roy, Apr. 26, 1868–Feb. 19, 1931.
    Vol. 5, Pt. 1–512
Irwin, May, June 27, 1862–Oct. 22, 1938.
    Supp. 2–335

Irwin, Robert Benjamin, June 2, 1883–Dec. 12, 1951.
    Supp. 5–347
Irwin, William Henry, Sept. 14, 1873–Feb. 24, 1948.
    Supp. 4–417
Isaacs, Abram Samuel, Aug. 30, 1851–Dec. 22, 1920.
    Vol. 5, Pt. 1–513
Isaacs, Samuel Myer, Jan. 4, 1804–May 19, 1878.
    Vol. 5, Pt. 1–513
Isbrandtsen, Hans Jeppesen, Sept. 7, 1891–May 13, 1953.
    Supp. 5–348
Isham, Ralph Heyward, July 2, 1890–June 13, 1955.
    Supp. 5–349
Isham, Samuel, May 12, 1855–June 12, 1914.
    Vol. 5, Pt. 1–514
Isherwood, Benjamin Franklin, Oct. 6, 1822–June 19, 1915.
    Vol. 5, Pt. 1–515
Isom, Mary Frances, Feb. 27, 1865–Apr. 15, 1920.
    Vol. 5, Pt. 1–516
Iverson, Alfred, Dec. 3, 1798–Mar. 4, 1873.
    Vol. 5, Pt. 1–517
Ives, Charles Edward, Oct. 20, 1874–May 19, 1954.
    Supp. 5–351
Ives, Chauncey Bradley, Dec. 14, 1810–Aug. 2, 1894.
    Vol. 5, Pt. 1–518
Ives, Eli, Feb. 7, 1778–Oct. 8, 1861.
    Vol. 5, Pt. 1–518
Ives, Frederic Eugene, Feb. 17, 1856–May 27, 1937.
    Supp. 2–337
Ives, Halsey Cooley, Oct. 27, 1847–May 5, 1911.
    Vol. 5, Pt. 1–519
Ives, Irving McNeil, Jan. 24, 1896–Feb. 24, 1962.
    Supp. 7–382
Ives, James Merritt, Mar. 5, 1824–Jan. 3, 1895.
    Vol. 5, Pt. 1–520
Ives, Joseph Christmas, 1828–Nov. 12, 1868.
    Vol. 5, Pt. 1–520
Ives, Levi Silliman, Sept. 16, 1797–Oct. 13, 1867.
    Vol. 5, Pt. 1–521
Ivins, Anthony Woodward, Sept. 16, 1852–Sept. 23, 1934.
    Supp. 1–448
Ivins, William Mills, Apr. 22, 1851–July 23, 1915.
    Vol. 5, Pt. 1–522
Izard, George, Oct. 21, 1776–Nov. 22, 1828.
    Vol. 5, Pt. 1–523
Izard, Ralph, Jan. 23, 1741/2–May 30, 1804.
    Vol. 5, Pt. 1–524

Jack, Captain. [See Captain Jack, 1837?–1873.]
Jackling, Daniel Cowan, Aug. 14, 1869–Mar. 13, 1956.
    Supp. 6–316
Jackman, Wilbur Samuel, Jan. 12, 1855–Jan. 28, 1907.
    Vol. 5, Pt. 1–525
Jackson, Abraham Reeves, June 17, 1827–Nov. 12, 1892.
    Vol. 5, Pt. 1–525
Jackson, Abraham Valentine Williams, Feb. 9, 1862–Aug. 8, 1937. Supp. 2–338
Jackson, Andrew, Mar. 15, 1767–June 8, 1845.
    Vol. 5, Pt. 1–526
Jackson, Charles, May 31, 1775–Dec. 13, 1855.
    Vol. 5, Pt. 1–534
Jackson, Charles Douglas, Mar. 16, 1902–Sept. 18, 1964.
    Supp. 7–383
Jackson, Charles Reginald, Apr. 6, 1903–Sept. 21, 1968.
    Supp. 8–297
Jackson, Charles Samuel, Sept. 15, 1860–Dec. 27, 1924.
    Vol. 5, Pt. 1–535
Jackson, Charles Thomas, June 21, 1805–Aug. 28, 1880.
    Vol. 5, Pt. 1–536
Jackson, Chevalier, Nov. 4, 1865–Aug. 16, 1958.
    Supp. 6–317
Jackson, Claiborne Fox, Apr. 4, 1806–Dec. 6, 1862.
    Vol. 5, Pt. 1–538
Jackson, Clarence Martin, Apr. 12, 1875–Jan. 17, 1947.
    Supp. 4–419
Jackson, David, 1747?–Sept. 17, 1801.
    Vol. 5, Pt. 1–538
Jackson, Dugald Caleb, Feb. 13, 1865–July 1, 1951.
    Supp. 5–354
Jackson, Dunham, July 24, 1888–Nov. 6, 1946.
    Supp. 4–420
Jackson, Edward, Mar. 30, 1856–Oct. 29, 1942.
    Supp. 3–377

Janney, Russell Dixon, Apr. 14, 1885–July 14, 1963.
Supp. 7–389
Janney, Samuel McPherson, Jan. 11, 1801–Apr. 30, 1880.
Vol. 5, Pt. 1–611
Jansen, Reinier, d. Mar. 6, 1706 N.S.
Vol. 5, Pt. 1–611
Jansky, Karl Guthe, Oct. 22, 1905–Feb. 14, 1950.
Supp. 4–422
Janson, Kristofer Nagel, May 5, 1841–Nov. 17, 1917.
Vol. 5, Pt. 1–612
Janssens, Francis, Oct. 17, 1843–June 10, 1897.
Vol. 5, Pt. 1–613
Janvier, Catharine Ann, May 1, 1841–July 19, 1922.
Vol. 5, Pt. 1–613
Janvier, Margaret Thomson, February 1844–February 1913.
Vol. 5, Pt. 1–614
Janvier, Thomas Allibone, July 16, 1849–June 18, 1913.
Vol. 5, Pt. 1–615
Jaquess, James Frazier, Nov. 18, 1819–June 17, 1898.
Vol. 5, Pt. 1–615
Jardine, William Marion, Jan. 16, 1879–Jan. 17, 1955.
Supp. 5–364
Jarratt, Devereux, Jan. 17, 1733–Jan. 29, 1801.
Vol. 5, Pt. 1–616
Jarrell, Randall, May 6, 1914–Oct. 14, 1965.
Supp. 7–390
Jarves, Deming, 1790–Apr. 15, 1869.
Vol. 5, Pt. 1–617
Jarves, James Jackson, Aug. 20, 1818–June 28, 1888.
Vol. 5, Pt. 1–618
Jarvis, Abraham, May 5, 1739 O.S.–May 3, 1813.
Vol. 5, Pt. 1–620
Jarvis, Charles H., Dec. 20, 1837–Feb. 25, 1895.
Vol. 5, Pt. 1–621
Jarvis, Edward, Jan. 9, 1803–Oct. 31, 1884.
Vol. 5, Pt. 1–621
Jarvis, John Wesley, 1781–Jan. 14, 1839.
Vol. 5, Pt. 1–622
Jarvis, Thomas Jordan, Jan. 18, 1836–June 17, 1915.
Vol. 5, Pt. 1–623
Jarvis, William, Feb. 2, 1770–Oct. 21, 1859.
Vol. 5, Pt. 1–624
Jarvis, William Chapman, May 13, 1855–July 30, 1895.
Vol. 5, Pt. 1–625
Jasper, William, c. 1750–Oct. 9, 1779.
Vol. 5, Pt. 2–1
Jastrow, Joseph, Jan. 30, 1863–Jan. 8, 1944.
Supp. 3–383
Jastrow, Marcus, June 5, 1829–Oct. 13, 1903.
Vol. 5, Pt. 2–1
Jastrow, Morris, Aug. 13, 1861–June 22, 1921.
Vol. 5, Pt. 2–3
Jay, Allen, Oct. 11, 1831–May 8, 1910.
Vol. 5, Pt. 2–3
Jay, Sir James, Oct. 27, 1732–Oct. 12 or 20, 1815.
Vol. 5, Pt. 2–4
Jay, John, Dec. 12, 1745–May 17, 1829.
Vol. 5, Pt. 2–5
Jay, John, June 23, 1817–May 5, 1894.
Vol. 5, Pt. 2–10
Jay, Peter Augustus, Jan. 24, 1776–Feb. 20, 1843.
Vol. 5, Pt. 2–11
Jay, William, June 16, 1789–Oct. 14, 1858.
Vol. 5, Pt. 2–11
Jayne, Horace Fort, Mar. 17, 1859–July 8, 1913.
Vol. 5, Pt. 2–12
Jeanes, Anna, T., Apr. 7, 1822–Sept. 24, 1907.
Vol. 5, Pt. 2–13
Jeffers, John Robinson, Jan. 10, 1887–Jan. 20, 1962.
Supp. 7–391
Jeffers, William Martin, Jan. 2, 1876–Mar. 6, 1953.
Supp. 5–365
Jeffers, William Nicholson, Oct. 16, 1824–July 23, 1883.
Vol. 5, Pt. 2–14
Jefferson, Charles Edward, Aug. 29, 1860–Sept. 12, 1937.
Supp. 2–344
Jefferson, Joseph, 1774–Aug. 4, 1832.
Vol. 5, Pt. 2–14
Jefferson, Joseph, Feb. 20, 1829–Apr. 23, 1905.
Vol. 5, Pt. 2–15
Jefferson, Mark Sylvester William, Mar. 1, 1863–Aug. 8, 1949. Supp. 4–423

Jefferson, Thomas, Apr. 2/13, 1743–July 4, 1826.
Vol. 5, Pt. 2–17
Jeffery, Edward Turner, Apr. 6, 1843–Sept. 24, 1927.
Vol. 5, Pt. 2–35
Jeffrey, Edward Charles, May 21, 1866–Apr. 19, 1952.
Supp. 5–366
Jeffrey, Joseph Andrew, Jan. 17, 1836–Aug. 27, 1928.
Vol. 5, Pt. 2–36
Jeffrey, Rosa Griffith Vertner Johnson, 1828–Oct. 6, 1894.
Vol. 5, Pt. 2–37
Jeffries, Benjamin Joy, Mar. 26, 1833–Nov. 21, 1915.
Vol. 5, Pt. 2–37
Jeffries, James Jackson, Apr. 15, 1875–Mar. 3, 1953.
Supp. 5–368
Jeffries, John, Feb. 5, 1744/5–Sept. 16, 1819.
Vol. 5, Pt. 2–38
Jelliffe, Smith Ely, Oct. 27, 1866–Sept. 25, 1945.
Supp. 3–384
Jemison, Alice Mae Lee, Oct. 9, 1901–Mar. 6, 1964.
Supp. 7–392
Jemison, Mary, 1743–Sept. 19, 1833.
Vol. 5, Pt. 2–39
Jenckes, Joseph, 1632–Jan. 4, 1717.
Vol. 5, Pt. 2–40
Jenckes, Joseph, 1656–June 15, 1740.
Vol. 5, Pt. 2–40
Jenckes, Joseph. [See Jenks, Joseph, 1602–1683.]
Jenckes, Thomas Allen, Nov. 2, 1818–Nov. 4, 1875.
Vol. 5, Pt. 2–41
Jenifer, Daniel of St. Thomas, 1723–Nov. 16, 1790.
Vol. 5, Pt. 2–42
Jenkins, Albert Gallatin, Nov. 10, 1830–May 21, 1864.
Vol. 5, Pt. 2–43
Jenkins, Charles Jones, Jan. 6, 1805–June 14, 1883.
Vol. 5, Pt. 2–44
Jenkins, Edward Hopkins, May 31, 1850–Nov. 6, 1931.
Vol. 5, Pt. 2–44
Jenkins, Howard Malcolm, Mar. 30, 1842–Oct. 11, 1902.
Vol. 5, Pt. 2–45
Jenkins, James Graham, July 18, 1834–Aug. 6, 1921.
Vol. 5, Pt. 2–46
Jenkins, John, Feb. 15, 1728–November 1785.
Vol. 5, Pt. 2–47
Jenkins, John, Nov. 27, 1751 O.S.–Mar. 19, 1827.
Vol. 5, Pt. 2–47
Jenkins, John Stilwell, Feb. 15, 1818–Sept. 20, 1852.
Vol. 5, Pt. 2–48
Jenkins, Micah, Dec. 1, 1835–May 6, 1864.
Vol. 5, Pt. 2–49
Jenkins, Nathaniel, June 7, 1812–May 20, 1872.
Vol. 5, Pt. 2–49
Jenkins, Thornton Alexander, Dec. 11, 1811–Aug. 9, 1893.
Vol. 5, Pt. 2–50
Jenks, George Charles, Apr. 13, 1850–Sept. 12, 1929.
Vol. 5, Pt. 2–51
Jenks, Jeremiah Whipple, Sept. 2, 1856–Aug. 24, 1929.
Vol. 5, Pt. 2–52
Jenks, Joseph, 1602–March 1683 N.S.
Vol. 5, Pt. 2–53
Jenks, Tudor Storrs, May 7, 1857–Feb. 11, 1922.
Vol. 5, Pt. 2–53
Jenks, William, Nov. 25, 1778–Nov. 13, 1866.
Vol. 5, Pt. 2–54
Jenney, William Le Baron, Sept. 25, 1832–June 15, 1907.
Vol. 5, Pt. 2–55
Jennings, Hennen. [See Jennings, James Hennen, 1854–1920.]
Jennings, Herbert Spencer, Apr. 8, 1868–Apr. 14, 1947.
Supp. 4–424
Jennings, James Hennen, May 6, 1854–Mar. 5, 1920.
Vol. 5, Pt. 2–55
Jennings, John, c. 1738–Jan. 14, 1802.
Vol. 5, Pt. 2–56
Jennings, Jonathan, 1784–July 26, 1834.
Vol. 5, Pt. 2–57
Jensen, Benton Franklin ("Ben"), Dec. 16, 1892–Feb. 5, 1970. Supp. 8–299
Jensen, Jens, Sept. 13, 1860–Oct. 1, 1951.
Supp. 5–369
Jensen, Peter Laurits, May 16, 1886–Oct. 25, 1961.
Supp. 7–394
Jepson, Willis Linn, Aug. 19, 1867–Nov. 7, 1946.
Supp. 4–428

Jerome, Chauncey, June 10, 1793–Apr. 20, 1868.
    Vol. 5, Pt. 2–58
Jerome, William Travers, Apr. 18, 1859–Feb. 13, 1934.
    Supp. 1–450
Jervis, John Bloomfield, Dec. 14, 1795–Jan. 12, 1885.
    Vol. 5, Pt. 2–59
Jesse, Richard Henry, Mar. 1, 1853–Jan. 22, 1921.
    Vol. 5, Pt. 2–60
Jessup, Henry Harris, Apr. 19, 1832–Apr. 28, 1910.
    Vol. 5, Pt. 2–61
Jessup, Walter Albert, Aug. 12, 1877–July 5, 1944.
    Supp. 3–386
Jesup, Morris Ketchum, June 21, 1830–Jan. 22, 1908.
    Vol. 5, Pt. 2–61
Jesup, Thomas Sidney, Dec. 16, 1788–June 10, 1860.
    Vol. 5, Pt. 2–62
Jeter, Jeremiah Bell, July 18, 1802–Feb. 18, 1880.
    Vol. 5, Pt. 2–63
Jewell, Harvey, May 26, 1820–Dec. 8, 1881.
    Vol. 5, Pt. 2–64
Jewell, Marshall, Oct. 20, 1825–Feb. 10, 1883.
    Vol. 5, Pt. 2–65
Jewett, Charles Coffin, Aug. 12, 1816–Jan. 9, 1868.
    Vol. 5, Pt. 2–65
Jewett, Clarence Frederick, Sept. 1, 1852–May 3, 1909.
    Vol. 5, Pt. 2–66
Jewett, David, June 17, 1772–July 26, 1842.
    Vol. 5, Pt. 2–67
Jewett, Frank Baldwin, Sept. 5, 1879–Nov. 18, 1949.
    Supp. 4–429
Jewett, Hugh Judge, July 1, 1817–Mar. 6, 1898.
    Vol. 5, Pt. 2–68
Jewett, John Punchard, Aug. 16, 1814–May 14, 1884.
    Vol. 5, Pt. 2–69
Jewett, Milo Parker, Apr. 27, 1808–June 9, 1882.
    Vol. 5, Pt. 2–69
Jewett, Sarah Orne, Sept. 3, 1849–June 24, 1909.
    Vol. 5, Pt. 2–70
Jewett, William, Jan. 14, 1792–Mar. 24, 1874.
    Vol. 5, Pt. 2–72
Jewett, William Cornell, Feb. 19, 1823–Oct. 27, 1893.
    Vol. 5, Pt. 2–73
Jocelyn, Nathaniel, Jan. 31, 1796–Jan. 13, 1881.
    Vol. 5, Pt. 2–73
Jogues, Isaac, Jan. 10, 1607–Oct. 18, 1646.
    Vol. 5, Pt. 2–74
Johns, Clayton, Nov. 24, 1857–Mar. 5, 1932.
    Supp. 1–451
Johns, John, July 10, 1796–Apr. 4, 1876.
    Vol. 5, Pt. 2–75
Johns, Kensey, June 14, 1759–Dec. 20, 1848.
    Vol. 5, Pt. 2–76
Johns, Kensey, Dec. 10, 1791–Mar. 28, 1857.
    Vol. 5, Pt. 2–76
Johnsen, Erik Kristian, Sept. 20, 1863–Jan. 21, 1923.
    Vol. 5, Pt. 2–77
Johnson. [See also Johnston.]
Johnson, Albert, Mar. 5, 1869–Jan. 17, 1957.
    Supp. 6–319
Johnson, Alexander, Jan. 2, 1847–May 17, 1941.
    Supp. 3–388
Johnson, Alexander Bryan, May 29, 1786–Sept. 9, 1867.
    Vol. 5, Pt. 2–78
Johnson, Alexander Smith, July 30, 1817–Jan. 26, 1878.
    Vol. 5, Pt. 2–79
Johnson, Allen, Jan. 29, 1870–Jan. 18, 1931.
    Vol. 5, Pt. 2–79
Johnson, Andrew, Dec. 29, 1808–July 31, 1875.
    Vol. 5, Pt. 2–81
Johnson, Benjamin Pierce, Nov. 30, 1793–Apr. 12, 1869.
    Vol. 5, Pt. 2–90
Johnson, Bradley Tyler, Sept. 29, 1829–Oct. 5, 1903.
    Vol. 5, Pt. 2–90
Johnson, Bushrod Rust, Oct. 7, 1817–Sept. 12, 1880.
    Vol. 5, Pt. 2–91
Johnson, Byron Bancroft, Jan. 6, 1864–Mar. 28, 1931.
    Vol. 5, Pt. 2–92
Johnson, Cave, Jan. 11, 1793–Nov. 23, 1866.
    Vol. 5, Pt. 2–93
Johnson, Chapman, Mar. 12, 1779–July 12, 1849.
    Vol. 5, Pt. 2–93
Johnson, Charles Spurgeon, July 24, 1893–Oct. 27, 1956.
    Supp. 6–321

Johnson, David Bancroft, Jan. 10, 1856–Dec. 26, 1928.
    Vol. 5, Pt. 2–94
Johnson, Douglas Wilson, Nov. 30, 1878–Feb. 24, 1944.
    Supp. 3–389
Johnson, Eastman. [See Johnson, Jonathan Eastman, 1824–1906.]
Johnson, Edward, September 1598–Apr. 23, 1672.
    Vol. 5, Pt. 2–95
Johnson, Edward, Apr. 16, 1816–Mar. 2, 1873.
    Vol. 5, Pt. 2–95
Johnson, Edward, Aug. 22, 1878–Apr. 20, 1959.
    Supp. 6–322
Johnson, Edward Austin, Nov. 23, 1860–July 24, 1944.
    Supp. 3–390
Johnson, Edwin Carl, Jan. 1, 1884–May 30, 1970.
    Supp. 8–300
Johnson, Edwin Ferry, May 23, 1803–Apr. 12, 1872.
    Vol. 5, Pt. 2–96
Johnson, Eldridge Reeves, Feb. 6, 1867–Nov. 14, 1945.
    Supp. 3–391
Johnson, Elias Henry, Oct. 15, 1841–Mar. 10, 1906.
    Vol. 5, Pt. 2–97
Johnson, Elijah, c. 1780–Mar. 23, 1849.
    Vol. 5, Pt. 2–97
Johnson, Ellen Cheney, Dec. 20, 1829–June 28, 1899.
    Vol. 5, Pt. 2–98
Johnson, Franklin, Nov. 2, 1836–Oct. 9, 1916.
    Vol. 5, Pt. 2–99
Johnson, George, Feb. 22, 1889–June 5, 1944.
    Supp. 3–393
Johnson, George Francis, Oct. 14, 1857–Nov. 28, 1948.
    Supp. 4–431
Johnson, Guy, c. 1740–Mar. 5, 1788.
    Vol. 5, Pt. 2–100
Johnson, Harold Ogden ("Chic") [See Olsen, John Sigvard ("Ole") and Johnson, Harold.]
Johnson, Harold Ogden ("Chic"), Mar. 5, 1891–Feb. 26, 1962. Supp. 7–588
Johnson, Helen Louise Kendrick, Jan. 4, 1844–Jan. 3, 1917.
    Vol. 5, Pt. 2–100
Johnson, Henry, June 25, 1855–Feb. 7, 1918.
    Vol. 5, Pt. 2–101
Johnson, Herschel Vespasian, Sept. 18, 1812–Aug. 16, 1880.
    Vol. 5, Pt. 2–102
Johnson, Hiram Warren, Sept. 2, 1866–Aug. 6, 1945.
    Supp. 3–393
Johnson, Hugh Samuel, Aug. 5, 1882–Apr. 15, 1942.
    Supp. 3–398
Johnson, Jack, Mar. 31, 1878–June 10, 1946.
    Supp. 4–432
Johnson, James, Jan. 1, 1774–Aug. 13, 1826.
    Vol. 5, Pt. 2–103
Johnson, James Weldon, June 17, 1871–June 26, 1938.
    Supp. 2–345
Johnson, Sir John, Nov. 5, 1742–Jan. 4, 1830.
    Vol. 5, Pt. 2–103
Johnson, John Albert, July 28, 1861–Sept. 21, 1909.
    Vol. 5, Pt. 2–104
Johnson, John Butler, June 11, 1850–June 23, 1902.
    Vol. 5, Pt. 2–105
Johnson, John Graver, Apr. 4, 1841–Apr. 14, 1917.
    Vol. 5, Pt. 2–106
Johnson, Jonathan Eastman, July 29, 1824–Apr. 5, 1906.
    Vol. 5, Pt. 2–107
Johnson, Joseph, June 15, 1776–Oct. 6, 1862.
    Vol. 5, Pt. 2–108
Johnson, Joseph French, Aug. 24, 1853–Jan. 22, 1925.
    Vol. 5, Pt. 2–109
Johnson, Levi, Apr. 25, 1786–Dec. 19, 1871.
    Vol. 5, Pt. 2–109
Johnson, Louis Arthur, Jan. 10, 1891–Apr. 24, 1966.
    Supp. 8–302
Johnson, Magnus, Sept. 19, 1871–Sept. 13, 1936.
    Supp. 2–347
Johnson, Marmaduke, d. Dec. 25, 1674.
    Vol. 5, Pt. 2–110
Johnson, Sir Nathaniel, c. 1645–1713.
    Vol. 5, Pt. 2–111
Johnson, Oliver, Dec. 27, 1809–Dec. 10, 1889.
    Vol. 5, Pt. 2–112
Johnson, Osa, Mar. 14, 1894–Jan. 7, 1953.
    Supp. 5–370

Johnson, Owen McMahon, Aug. 27, 1878–Jan. 27, 1952.
  Supp. 5–371
Johnson, Reverdy, May 21, 1796–Feb. 10, 1876.
  Vol. 5, Pt. 2–112
Johnson, Richard Mentor, 1780–Nov. 19, 1850.
  Vol. 5, Pt. 2–114
Johnson, Richard W., Feb. 7, 1827–Apr. 21, 1897.
  Vol. 5, Pt. 2–116
Johnson, Robert, c. 1676–May 3, 1735.
  Vol. 5, Pt. 2–116
Johnson, Robert Underwood, Jan. 12, 1853–Oct. 14, 1937.
  Supp. 2–348
Johnson, Robert Ward, July 22, 1814–July 26, 1879.
  Vol. 5, Pt. 2–117
Johnson, Samuel, Oct. 14, 1696–Jan. 6, 1772.
  Vol. 5, Pt. 2–118
Johnson, Samuel, Oct. 10, 1822–Feb. 19, 1882.
  Vol. 5, Pt. 2–119
Johnson, Samuel William, July 3, 1830–July 21, 1909.
  Vol. 5, Pt. 2–120
Johnson, Seth Whitmore, May 3, 1811–Feb. 13, 1907.
  Vol. 5, Pt. 2–121
Johnson, Thomas, Nov. 4, 1732–Oct. 26, 1819.
  Vol. 5, Pt. 2–121
Johnson, Tom Loftin, July 18, 1854–Apr. 10, 1911.
  Vol. 5, Pt. 2–122
Johnson, Treat Baldwin, Mar. 29, 1875–July 28, 1947.
  Supp. 4–434
Johnson, Virginia Wales, Dec. 28, 1849–Jan. 16, 1916.
  Vol. 5, Pt. 2–124
Johnson, Walter Perry, Nov. 6, 1887–Dec. 10, 1946.
  Supp. 4–435
Johnson, Wendell Andrew Leroy, Apr. 16, 1906–Aug. 29,
  1965. Supp. 7–395
Johnson, Sir William, 1715–July 11, 1774.
  Vol. 5, Pt. 2–124
Johnson, William, Dec. 17, 1769–June 25, 1848.
  Vol. 5, Pt. 2–128
Johnson, William, Dec. 27, 1771–Aug. 4, 1834.
  Vol. 5, Pt. 2–128
Johnson, William Bullein, June 13, 1782–Oct. 2, 1862.
  Vol. 5, Pt. 2–129
Johnson, William Ransom, 1782–Feb. 10, 1849.
  Vol. 5, Pt. 2–130
Johnson, William Samuel, Oct. 7, 1727–Nov. 14, 1819.
  Vol. 5, Pt. 2–131
Johnson, William Woolsey, June 23, 1841–May 14, 1927.
  Vol. 5, Pt. 2–134
Johnson, Willis Fletcher, Oct. 7, 1857–Mar. 28, 1931.
  Vol. 5, Pt. 2–134
Johnston, Albert Sidney, Feb. 2, 1803–Apr. 6, 1862.
  Vol. 5, Pt. 2–135
Johnston, Alexander, Apr. 29, 1849–July 20, 1889.
  Vol. 5, Pt. 2–136
Johnston, Annie Fellows, May 15, 1863–Oct. 5, 1931.
  Vol. 5, Pt. 2–137
Johnston, Augustus, c. 1730–c. 1790.
  Vol. 5, Pt. 2–138
Johnston, David Claypoole, March 1799–Nov. 8, 1865.
  Vol. 5, Pt. 2–139
Johnston, Eric Allen, Dec. 21, 1896–Aug. 22, 1963.
  Supp. 7–396
Johnston, Frances Benjamin, Jan. 15, 1864–May 16, 1952.
  Supp. 5–373
Johnston, Gabriel, 1699–July 17, 1752.
  Vol. 5, Pt. 2–140
Johnston, George Ben, July 25, 1853–Dec. 20, 1916.
  Vol. 5, Pt. 2–140
Johnston, Henrietta, d. March 1728/9.
  Vol. 5, Pt. 2–141
Johnston, Henry Phelps, Apr. 19, 1842–Feb. 28, 1923.
  Vol. 5, Pt. 2–142
Johnston, John, Apr. 11, 1791–Nov. 24, 1880.
  Vol. 5, Pt. 2–142
Johnston, John, Oct. 13, 1881–Sept. 12, 1950.
  Supp. 4–437
Johnston, John Taylor, Apr. 8, 1820–Mar. 24, 1893.
  Vol. 5, Pt. 2–143
Johnston, Joseph Eggleston, Feb. 3, 1807–Mar. 21, 1891.
  Vol. 5, Pt. 2–144
Johnston, Joseph Forney, Mar. 23, 1843–Aug. 8, 1913.
  Vol. 5, Pt. 2–146

Johnston, Josiah Stoddard, Nov. 24, 1784–May 19, 1833.
  Vol. 5, Pt. 2–147
Johnston, Mary, Nov. 21, 1870–May 9, 1936.
  Supp. 2–349
Johnston, Olin DeWitt Talmadge, Nov. 18, 1896–Apr. 18,
  1965. Supp. 7–398
Johnston, Peter, Jan. 6, 1763–Dec. 8, 1831.
  Vol. 5, Pt. 2–147
Johnston, Richard Malcolm, Mar. 8, 1822–Sept. 23, 1898.
  Vol. 5, Pt. 2–148
Johnston, Robert Matteson, Apr. 11, 1867–Jan. 28, 1920.
  Vol. 5, Pt. 2–149
Johnston, Samuel, Dec. 15, 1733–Aug. 17, 1816.
  Vol. 5, Pt. 2–150
Johnston, Samuel, Feb. 9, 1835–Apr. 15, 1911.
  Vol. 5, Pt. 2–151
Johnston, Thomas, c. 1708–May 8, 1767.
  Vol. 5, Pt. 2–152
Johnston, William Andrew, Jan. 26, 1871–Feb. 16, 1929.
  Vol. 5, Pt. 2–152
Johnston, William Hartshorne, Oct. 19, 1861–Feb. 20, 1933.
  Supp. 1–452
Johnston, William Hugh, Dec. 30, 1874–Mar. 26, 1937.
  Supp. 2–350
Johnston, William Preston, Jan. 5, 1831–July 16, 1899.
  Vol. 5, Pt. 2–153
Johnston, Zachariah, 1742–January 1800.
  Vol. 5, Pt. 2–154
Johnstone, Edward Ransom, Dec. 27, 1870–Dec. 29, 1946.
  Supp. 4–438
Johnstone, Job, June 7, 1793–Apr. 8, 1862.
  Vol. 5, Pt. 2–155
Joline, Adrian Hoffman, June 30, 1850–Oct. 15, 1912.
  Vol. 5, Pt. 2–155
Jolliet, Louis, September 1645–1700.
  Vol. 5, Pt. 2–156
Jolson, Al, May 26, 1886–Oct. 23, 1950.
  Supp. 4–439
Jones, Abner, Apr. 28, 1772–May 29, 1841.
  Vol. 5, Pt. 2–157
Jones, Alexander, c. 1802–Aug. 22, 1863.
  Vol. 5, Pt. 2–158
Jones, Alfred, Apr. 7, 1819–Apr. 28, 1900.
  Vol. 5, Pt. 2–158
Jones, Allen, Dec. 24, 1739–Nov. 14, 1807.
  Vol. 5, Pt. 2–159
Jones, Amanda Theodosia, Oct. 19, 1835–Mar. 31, 1914.
  Vol. 5, Pt. 2–160
Jones, Anson, Jan. 20, 1798–Jan. 9, 1858.
  Vol. 5, Pt. 2–161
Jones, Benjamin Allyn, Dec. 31, 1882–June 13, 1961.
  Supp. 7–399
Jones, Benjamin Franklin, Aug. 8, 1824–May 19, 1903.
  Vol. 5, Pt. 2–162
Jones, Calvin, Apr. 2, 1775–Sept. 20, 1846.
  Vol. 5, Pt. 2–163
Jones, Catesby A. P. Roger, Apr. 15, 1821–June 20, 1877.
  Vol. 5, Pt. 2–164
Jones, Charles Colcock, Oct. 28, 1831–July 19, 1893.
  Vol. 5, Pt. 2–165
Jones, David, May 12, 1736–Feb. 5, 1820.
  Vol. 5, Pt. 2–165
Jones, David Rumph, Apr. 5, 1825–Jan. 15, 1863.
  Vol. 5, Pt. 2–166
Jones, Ernest Lester, Apr. 14, 1876–Apr. 9, 1929.
  Vol. 5, Pt. 2–167
Jones, Evan William, 1852–Dec. 30, 1908.
  Vol. 5, Pt. 2–168
Jones, Frank, Sept. 15, 1832–Oct. 2, 1902.
  Vol. 5, Pt. 2–168
Jones, Gabriel, May 17, 1724–Oct 6, 1806.
  Vol. 5, Pt. 2–169
Jones, George, July 30, 1800–Jan. 22, 1870.
  Vol. 5, Pt. 2–170
Jones, George, Aug. 16, 1811–Aug. 12, 1891.
  Vol. 5, Pt. 2–171
Jones, George Heber, Aug. 14, 1867–May 11, 1919.
  Vol. 5, Pt. 2–171
Jones, George Wallace, Apr. 12, 1804–July 22, 1896.
  Vol. 5, Pt. 2–172
Jones, Harry Clary, Nov. 11, 1865–Apr. 9, 1916.
  Vol. 5, Pt. 2–173

Jones, Herschel Vespasian, Aug. 30, 1861–May 24, 1928.
  Vol. 5, Pt. 2–174
Jones, Hilary Pollard, Nov. 14, 1863–Jan. 1, 1938.
  Supp. 2–351
Jones, Hugh, c. 1670–Sept. 8, 1760.
  Vol. 5, Pt. 2–175
Jones, Hugh Bolton, Oct. 20, 1848–Sept. 24, 1927.
  Vol. 5, Pt. 2–175
Jones, Jacob, March 1768–Aug. 3, 1850.
  Vol. 5, Pt. 2–176
Jones, James Chamberlayne, June 7, 1809–Oct. 29, 1859.
  Vol. 5, Pt. 2–177
Jones, James Kimbrough, Sept. 29, 1829–June 1, 1908.
  Vol. 5, Pt. 2–177
Jones, Jehu Glancy, Oct. 7, 1811–Mar. 24, 1878.
  Vol. 5, Pt. 2–178
Jones, Jenkin Lloyd, Nov. 14, 1843–Sept. 12, 1918.
  Vol. 5, Pt. 2–179
Jones, Jesse Holman, Apr. 5, 1874–June 1, 1956.
  Supp. 6–324
Jones, Joel, Oct. 25, 1795–Feb. 3, 1860.
  Vol. 5, Pt. 2–180
Jones, John, 1729–June 23, 1791.
  Vol. 5, Pt. 2–181
Jones, John B., Dec. 22, 1834–July 19, 1881.
  Vol. 5, Pt. 2–182
Jones, John Beauchamp, Mar. 6, 1810–Feb. 4, 1866.
  Vol. 5, Pt. 2–182
Jones, John Paul, July 6, 1747–July 18, 1792.
  Vol. 5, Pt. 2–183
Jones, John Percival, Jan. 27, 1829–Nov. 27, 1912.
  Vol. 5, Pt. 2–188
Jones, John Peter, Sept. 4, 1847–Oct. 3, 1916.
  Vol. 5, Pt. 2–189
Jones, John Price, Aug. 12, 1877–Dec. 23, 1964.
  Supp. 7–401
Jones, John Taylor, July 16, 1802–Sept. 13, 1851.
  Vol. 5, Pt. 2–190
Jones, John William, Sept. 25, 1836–Mar. 17, 1909.
  Vol. 5, Pt. 2–190
Jones, John Winston, Nov. 22, 1791–Jan. 29, 1848.
  Vol. 5, Pt. 2–191
Jones, Joseph, 1727–Oct. 26, 1805.
  Vol. 5, Pt. 2–192
Jones, Joseph, Sept. 6, 1833–Feb. 17, 1896.
  Vol. 5, Pt. 2–193
Jones, Joseph Stevens, Sept. 28, 1809–Dec. 29, 1877.
  Vol. 5, Pt. 2–193
Jones, Leonard Augustus, Jan. 13, 1832–Dec. 9, 1909.
  Vol. 5, Pt. 2–194
Jones, Lewis Ralph, Dec. 5, 1864–Apr. 1, 1945.
  Supp. 3–400
Jones, Lindley Armstrong ("Spike"), Dec. 14, 1911–May 1,
  1965. Supp. 7–403
Jones, Lynds, Jan. 5, 1865–Feb. 11, 1951.
  Supp. 5–373
Jones, Mary Harris, May 1, 1830–Nov. 30, 1930.
  Vol. 5, Pt. 2–195
Jones, Noble Wymberley, c. 1724–Jan. 9, 1805.
  Vol. 5, Pt. 2–196
Jones, Richard Foster, July 7, 1886–Sept. 12, 1965.
  Supp. 7–402
Jones, Robert Edmond, Dec. 12, 1887–Nov. 26, 1954.
  Supp. 5–375
Jones, Robert Reynolds ("Bob"), Oct. 30, 1883–Jan. 16,
  1968. Supp. 8–303
Jones, Rufus Matthew, Jan. 25, 1863–June 16, 1948.
  Supp. 4–441
Jones, Samuel, July 26, 1734–Nov. 25, 1819.
  Vol. 5, Pt. 2–197
Jones, Samuel, May 26, 1770–Aug. 9, 1853.
  Vol. 5, Pt. 2–198
Jones, Samuel Milton, Aug. 8, 1846–July 12, 1904.
  Supp. 1–453
Jones, Samuel Porter, Oct. 16, 1847–Oct. 15, 1906.
  Vol. 5, Pt. 2–199
Jones, Sybil, Feb. 28, 1808–Dec. 4, 1873.
  Vol. 5, Pt. 2–199
Jones, Thomas, Apr. 30, 1731–July 25, 1792.
  Vol. 5, Pt. 2–200
Jones, Thomas Ap Catesby, Apr. 24, 1790–May 30, 1858.
  Vol. 5, Pt. 2–201

Jones, Thomas Goode, Nov. 26, 1844–Apr. 28, 1914.
  Vol. 5, Pt. 2–202
Jones, Thomas P., 1774–Mar. 11, 1848.
  Vol. 5, Pt. 2–202
Jones, Walter, Oct. 7, 1776–Oct. 14, 1861.
  Vol. 5, Pt. 2–203
Jones, Wesley Livsey, Oct. 9, 1863–Nov. 19, 1932.
  Supp. 1–454
Jones, William, Oct. 8, 1753–Apr. 9, 1822.
  Vol. 5, Pt. 2–204
Jones, William, 1760–Sept. 6, 1831.
  Vol. 5, Pt. 2–205
Jones, William, Mar. 28, 1871–Mar. 29, 1909.
  Vol. 5, Pt. 2–205
Jones, William Alfred, June 26, 1817–May 6, 1900.
  Vol. 5, Pt. 2–206
Jones, William Palmer, Oct. 17, 1819–Sept. 25, 1897.
  Vol. 5, Pt. 2–207
Jones, William Patterson, Apr. 23, 1831–Aug. 3, 1886.
  Vol. 5, Pt. 2–207
Jones, William Richard, Feb. 23, 1839–Sept. 28, 1889.
  Vol. 5, Pt. 2–208
Jones, Willie, c. 1741–June 18, 1801.
  Vol. 5, Pt. 2–210
Joplin, Janis Lyn, Jan. 19, 1943–Oct. 4, 1970.
  Supp. 8–305
Jordan, David Starr, Jan. 19, 1851–Sept. 19, 1931.
  Vol. 5, Pt. 2–211
Jordan, Eben Dyer, Nov. 7, 1857–Aug. 1, 1916.
  Vol. 5, Pt. 2–214
Jordan, Edwin Oakes, July 28, 1866–Sept. 2, 1936.
  Supp. 2–352
Jordan, John Woolf, Sept. 14, 1840–June 11, 1921.
  Vol. 5, Pt. 2–215
Jordan, Kate, Dec. 23, 1862–June 20, 1926.
  Vol. 5, Pt. 2–215
Jordan, Thomas, Sept. 30, 1819–Nov. 27, 1895.
  Vol. 5, Pt. 2–216
Jordan, Virgil Justin, June 3, 1892–Apr. 28, 1965.
  Supp. 7–404
Jordan, William George, Mar. 6, 1864–Apr. 20, 1928.
  Vol. 5, Pt. 2–217
Joseffy, Rafael, July 3, 1852–June 25, 1915.
  Vol. 5, Pt. 2–217
Joseph, c. 1840–Sept. 21, 1904.
  Vol. 5, Pt. 2–218
Josselyn, John, fl. 1638–1675.
  Vol. 5, Pt. 2–219
Joubert de la Muraille, James Hector Marie Nicholas, Sept.
  6, 1777–Nov. 5, 1843. Vol. 5, Pt. 2–220
Jouett, James Edward, Feb. 7, 1826–Sept. 30, 1902.
  Vol. 5, Pt. 2–221
Jouett, John, Dec. 7, 1754–Mar. 1, 1822.
  Vol. 5, Pt. 2–221
Jouett, Matthew Harris, Apr. 22, 1787–Aug. 10, 1827.
  Vol. 5, Pt. 2–222
Joutel, Henri, c. 1645–after 1723.
  Vol. 5, Pt. 2–223
Joy, Agnes Eliza. [See Salm Salm, Agnes Eliza Joy, Princess,
  1840–1912.]
Joy, Charles Turner, Feb. 17, 1895–June 6, 1956.
  Supp. 6–326
Joy, Henry Bourne, Nov. 23, 1864–Nov. 6, 1936.
  Supp. 2–354
Joy, James Frederick, Dec. 2, 1810–Sept. 24, 1896.
  Vol. 5, Pt. 2–224
Joy, Thomas, c. 1610–Oct. 21, 1678.
  Vol. 5, Pt. 2–225
Joyce, Isaac Wilson, Oct. 11, 1836–July 28, 1905.
  Vol. 5, Pt. 2–226
Joynes, Edward Southey, Mar. 2, 1834–June 18, 1917.
  Vol. 5, Pt. 2–226
Judah, Samuel, July 10, 1798–Apr. 24, 1869.
  Vol. 5, Pt. 2–227
Judah, Samuel Benjamin Helbert, c. 1799–July 21, 1876.
  Vol. 5, Pt. 2–228
Judah, Theodore Dehone, Mar. 4, 1826–Nov. 2, 1863.
  Vol. 5, Pt. 2–229
Juday, Chancey, May 5, 1871–Mar. 29, 1944.
  Supp. 3–401
Judd, Charles Hubbard, Feb. 20, 1873–July 18, 1946.
  Supp. 4–443

Keeler, James Edward, Sept. 10, 1857–Aug. 12, 1900.
    Vol. 5, Pt. 2–278
Keeler, Ralph Olmstead, Aug. 29, 1840–Dec. 17, 1873.
    Vol. 5, Pt. 2–279
Keeley, Leslie E., 1832–Feb. 21, 1900.
    Vol. 5, Pt. 2–280
Keely, John Ernst Worrell, Sept. 3, 1827–Nov. 18, 1898.
    Vol. 5, Pt. 2–280
Keen, Morris Longstreth, May 24, 1820–Nov. 2, 1883.
    Vol. 5, Pt. 2–281
Keen, William Williams, Jan. 19, 1837–June 7, 1932.
    Supp. 1–459
Keenan, James Francis, Apr. 8, 1858–Feb. 24, 1929.
    Vol. 5, Pt. 2–282
Keene, James Robert, 1838–Jan. 3, 1913.
    Vol. 5, Pt. 2–283
Keene, Laura, c. 1826–Nov. 4, 1873.
    Vol. 5, Pt. 2–283
Keene, Thomas Wallace, Oct. 26, 1840–June 1, 1898.
    Vol. 5, Pt. 2–284
Keener, William Albert, Mar. 10, 1856–Apr. 22, 1913.
    Vol. 5, Pt. 2–285
Keep, Henry, June 22, 1818–July 30, 1869.
    Vol. 5, Pt. 2–286
Keep, Robert Porter, Apr. 26, 1844–June 3, 1904.
    Vol. 5, Pt. 2–286
Kefauver, (Carey) Estes, July 26, 1903–Aug. 10, 1963.
    Supp. 7–415
Kefauver, Grayson Neikirk, Aug. 31, 1900–Jan. 4, 1946.
    Supp. 4–449
Kehew, Mary Morton Kimball, Sept. 8, 1859–Feb. 13, 1918.
    Vol. 5, Pt. 2–287
Keifer, Joseph Warren, Jan. 30, 1836–Apr. 22, 1932.
    Supp. 1–460
Keimer, Samuel, Feb. 11, 1688–c. 1739.
    Vol. 5, Pt. 2–288
Keith, Arthur, Sept. 30, 1864–Feb. 7, 1944.
    Supp. 3–407
Keith, Benjamin Franklin, Jan. 26, 1846–Mar. 26, 1914.
    Vol. 5, Pt. 2–289
Keith, George, c. 1638–Mar. 27, 1716.
    Vol. 5, Pt. 2–289
Keith, James, Sept. 7, 1839–Jan. 2, 1918.
    Vol. 5, Pt. 2–290
Keith, Minor Cooper, Jan. 19, 1848–June 14, 1929.
    Vol. 5, Pt. 2–291
Keith, Sir William, 1680–Nov. 18, 1749.
    Vol. 5, Pt. 2–292
Keith, William, Nov. 21, 1839–Apr. 13, 1911.
    Vol. 5, Pt. 2–293
Keitt, Lawrence Massillon, Oct. 4, 1824–June 2, 1864.
    Vol. 5, Pt. 2–294
Kelland, Clarence Budington, July 11, 1881–Feb. 18, 1964.
    Supp. 7–416
Keller, Arthur Ignatius, July 4, 1867–Dec. 2, 1924.
    Vol. 5, Pt. 2–294
Keller, Helen Adams, June 27, 1880–June 1, 1968.
    Supp. 8–316
Keller, Kaufman Thuma, Nov. 27, 1885–Jan. 21, 1966.
    Supp. 8–318
Keller, Mathias, Mar. 20, 1813–Oct. 12, 1875.
    Vol. 5, Pt. 2–295
Kellerman, Karl Frederic, Dec. 9, 1879–Aug. 30, 1934.
    Supp. 1–461
Kellett, William Wallace, Dec. 20,1891–July 22, 1951.
    Supp. 3–377
Kelley, Alfred, Nov. 7, 1789–Dec. 2, 1859.
    Vol. 5, Pt. 2–296
Kelley, Edgar Stillman, Apr. 14, 1857–Nov. 12, 1944.
    Supp. 3–408
Kelley, Edith Summers, Apr. 28, 1884–June 9, 1956.
    Supp. 6–328
Kelley, Florence, Sept. 12, 1859–Feb. 17, 1932.
    Supp. 1–462
Kelley, Hall Jackson, Feb. 24, 1790–Jan. 20, 1874.
    Vol. 5, Pt. 2–297
Kelley, James Douglas Jerrold, Dec. 25, 1847–Apr. 30, 1922.
    Vol. 5, Pt. 2–298
Kelley, Oliver Hudson, Jan. 7, 1826–Jan. 20, 1913.
    Vol. 5, Pt. 2–298
Kelley, William Darrah, Apr. 12, 1814–Jan. 9, 1890.
    Vol. 5, Pt. 2–299

Kellogg, Albert, Dec. 6, 1813–Mar. 31, 1887.
    Vol. 5, Pt. 2–300
Kellogg, Clara Louise, July 12, 1842–May 13, 1916.
    Vol. 5, Pt. 2–301
Kellogg, Edward, Oct. 18, 1790–Apr. 29, 1858.
    Vol. 5, Pt. 2–302
Kellogg, Elijah, May 20, 1813–Mar. 17, 1901.
    Vol. 5, Pt. 2–302
Kellogg, Frank Billings, Dec. 22, 1856–Dec. 21, 1937.
    Supp. 2–355
Kellogg, John Harvey, Feb. 26, 1852–Dec. 14, 1943.
    Supp. 3–409
Kellogg, Martin, Mar. 15, 1828–Aug. 26, 1903.
    Vol. 5, Pt. 2–303
Kellogg, Paul Underwood, Sept. 30, 1879–Nov. 1, 1958.
    Supp. 6–329
Kellogg, Samuel Henry, Sept. 6, 1839–May 3, 1899.
    Vol. 5, Pt. 2–304
Kellogg, William Pitt, Dec. 8, 1830–Aug. 10, 1918.
    Vol. 5, Pt. 2–305
Kellogg, Will Keith, Apr. 7, 1860–Oct. 6, 1951.
    Supp. 5–378
Kellor, Frances (Alice), Oct. 20, 1873–Jan. 4, 1952.
    Supp. 5–380
Kelly, Aloysius Oliver Joseph, June 13, 1870–Feb. 23, 1911.
    Vol. 5, Pt. 2–306
Kelly, Edmond, Mar. 28, 1851–Oct. 4, 1909.
    Vol. 5, Pt. 2–307
Kelly, Edward Joseph, May 1, 1876–Oct. 20, 1950.
    Supp. 4–450
Kelly, Eugene, Nov. 25, 1808–Dec. 19, 1894.
    Vol. 5, Pt. 2–307
Kelly, Howard Atwood, Feb. 20, 1858–Jan. 12, 1943.
    Supp. 3–411
Kelly, John, Apr. 20, 1822–June 1, 1886.
    Vol. 5, Pt. 2–308
Kelly, John Brendan, Oct. 4, 1889–June 20, 1960.
    Supp. 6–330
Kelly, Luther Sage, July 27, 1849–Dec. 17, 1928.
    Vol. 5, Pt. 2–309
Kelly, Machine Gun (George Kelly Barnes, Jr.), July 17, 1895
    –July 17, 1954. Supp. 5–381
Kelly, Michael J., Dec. 31, 1857–Nov. 8, 1894.
    Vol. 5, Pt. 2–309
Kelly, Myra, Aug. 26, 1875–Mar. 30, 1910.
    Vol. 5, Pt. 2–310
Kelly, William, Aug. 21, 1811–Feb. 11, 1888.
    Vol. 5, Pt. 2–311
Kelpius, Johann, 1673–1708.
    Vol. 5, Pt. 2–312
Kelser, Raymond Alexander, Dec. 2, 1892–Apr. 16, 1952.
    Supp. 5–382
Kelsey, Francis Willey, May 23, 1858–May 14, 1927.
    Vol. 5, Pt. 2–313
Kelsey, Rayner Wickersham, Jan. 29, 1879–Oct. 29, 1934.
    Supp. 1–463
Kelton, John Cunningham, June 24, 1828–July 15, 1893.
    Vol. 5, Pt. 2–314
Kemble, Frances Anne, Nov. 27, 1809–Jan. 15, 1893.
    Vol. 5, Pt. 2–315
Kemble, Gouverneur, Jan. 25, 1786–Sept. 16, 1875.
    Vol. 5, Pt. 2–316
Kemeys, Edward, Jan. 31, 1843–May 11, 1907.
    Vol. 5, Pt. 2–317
Kemmerer, Edwin Walter, June 29, 1875–Dec. 16, 1945.
    Supp. 3–413
Kemp, James, May 20, 1764–Oct. 28, 1827.
    Vol. 5, Pt. 2–318
Kemp, James Furman, Aug. 14, 1859–Nov. 17, 1926.
    Vol. 5, Pt. 2–319
Kemp, John, Apr. 10, 1763–Nov. 15, 1812.
    Vol. 5, Pt. 2–319
Kemp, Robert H., June 6, 1820–May 15, 1897.
    Vol. 5, Pt. 2–320
Kemper, Jackson, Dec. 24, 1789–May 24, 1870.
    Vol. 5, Pt. 2–321
Kemper, James Lawson, June 11, 1823–Apr. 7, 1895.
    Vol. 5, Pt. 2–322
Kemper, Reuben, d. Jan. 28, 1827.
    Vol. 5, Pt. 2–323
Kempff, Louis, Oct. 11, 1841–July 29, 1920.
    Vol. 5, Pt. 2–323

Kempster, Walter, May 25, 1841–Aug. 22, 1918.
    Vol. 5, Pt. 2–324
Kendall, Amos, Aug. 16, 1789–Nov. 12, 1869.
    Vol. 5, Pt. 2–325
Kendall, George Wilkins, Aug. 22, 1809–Oct. 21, 1867.
    Vol. 5, Pt. 2–327
Kendrick, Asahel Clark, Dec. 7, 1809–Oct. 21, 1895.
    Vol. 5, Pt. 2–328
Kendrick, John, c. 1740–Dec. 12, 1794.
    Vol. 5, Pt. 2–329
Kendrick, John Benjamin, Sept. 6, 1857–Nov. 3, 1933.
    Supp. 1–464
Kenedy, Patrick John, Sept. 4, 1843–Jan. 4, 1906.
    Vol. 5, Pt. 2–329
Kenna, John Edward, Apr. 10, 1848–Jan. 11, 1893.
    Vol. 5, Pt. 2–330
Kennan, George, Feb. 16, 1845–May 10, 1924.
    Vol. 5, Pt. 2–331
Kennedy, Archibald, 1685–June 14, 1763.
    Vol. 5, Pt. 2–332
Kennedy, John Doby, Jan. 5, 1840–Apr. 14, 1896.
    Vol. 5, Pt. 2–332
Kennedy, John Fitzgerald, May 29, 1917–Nov. 22, 1963.
    Supp. 7–418
Kennedy, John Pendleton, Oct. 25, 1795–Aug. 18, 1870.
    Vol. 5, Pt. 2–333
Kennedy, John Stewart, Jan. 4, 1830–Oct. 31, 1909.
    Vol. 5, Pt. 2–334
Kennedy, Joseph Camp Griffith, Apr. 1, 1813–July 13, 1887.
    Vol. 5, Pt. 2–335
Kennedy, Joseph Patrick, Sept. 6, 1888–Nov. 18, 1969.
    Supp. 8–320
Kennedy, Robert Foster, Feb. 7, 1884–Jan. 7, 1952.
    Supp. 5–383
Kennedy, Robert Francis, Nov. 20, 1925–June 6, 1968.
    Supp. 8–321
Kennedy, Robert Patterson, Jan. 23, 1840–May 6, 1918.
    Vol. 5, Pt. 2–336
Kennedy, William Sloane, Sept. 26, 1850–Aug. 4, 1929.
    Vol. 5, Pt. 2–336
Kennelly, Arthur Edwin, Dec. 17, 1861–June 18, 1939.
    Supp. 2–357
Kenner, Duncan Farrar, Feb. 11, 1813–July 3, 1887.
    Vol. 5, Pt. 2–337
Kenney, Mary. [See O'Sullivan, Mary Kenney.]
Kennicott, Robert, Nov. 13, 1835–May 13, 1866.
    Vol. 5, Pt. 2–338
Kenrick, Francis Patrick, Dec. 3, 1796–July 8, 1863.
    Vol. 5, Pt. 2–339
Kenrick, Peter Richard, Aug. 17, 1806–Mar. 4, 1896.
    Vol. 5, Pt. 2–340
Kenrick, William, Dec. 24, 1789–Feb. 14, 1872.
    Vol. 5, Pt. 2–341
Kensett, John Frederick, Mar. 22, 1816–Dec. 14, 1872.
    Vol. 5, Pt. 2–342
Kent, Arthur Atwater, Dec. 3, 1873–Mar. 4, 1949.
    Supp. 4–451
Kent, Charles Foster, Aug. 13, 1867–May 2, 1925.
    Vol. 5, Pt. 2–343
Kent, Edward, Jan. 8, 1802–May 19, 1877.
    Vol. 5, Pt. 2–343
Kent, James, July 31, 1763–Dec. 12, 1847.
    Vol. 5, Pt. 2–344
Kent, Joseph, Jan. 14, 1779–Nov. 24, 1837.
    Vol. 5, Pt. 2–347
Kent, William, Mar. 5, 1851–Sept. 18, 1918.
    Vol. 5, Pt. 2–348
Kenton, Simon, Apr. 3, 1755–Apr. 29, 1836.
    Vol. 5, Pt. 2–349
Kenyon, Josephine Hemenway, May 10, 1880–Jan. 10, 1965.
    Supp. 7–427
Kenyon, William Squire, June 10, 1869–Sept. 9, 1933.
    Supp. 1–465
Keokuk, fl. 1790–1848.
    Vol. 5, Pt. 2–350
Kephart, Ezekiel Boring, Nov. 6, 1834–Jan. 24, 1906.
    Vol. 5, Pt. 2–350
Kephart, Isaiah Lafayette, Dec. 10, 1832–Oct. 28, 1908.
    Vol. 5, Pt. 2–351
Kephart, John William, Nov. 12, 1872–Aug. 6, 1944.
    Supp. 3–414
Keppel, Frederick, Mar. 22, 1845–Mar. 7, 1912.
    Vol. 5, Pt. 2–351

Keppel, Frederick Paul, July 2, 1875–Feb. 8, 1943.
    Supp. 3–415
Keppler, Joseph, Feb. 1, 1838–Feb. 19, 1894.
    Vol. 5, Pt. 2–352
Kerby, William Joseph, Feb. 20, 1870–July 27, 1936.
    Supp. 2–359
Kerens, Richard C., Nov. 12, 1842–Sept. 4, 1916.
    Vol. 5, Pt. 2–353
Kerfoot, John Barrett, Mar. 1, 1816–July 10, 1881.
    Vol. 5, Pt. 2–354
Kerlin, Isaac Newton, May 27, 1834–Oct. 25, 1893.
    Vol. 5, Pt. 2–354
Kern, Jerome David, Jan. 27, 1885–Nov. 11, 1945.
    Supp. 3–417
Kern, John Worth, Dec. 20, 1849–Aug. 17, 1917.
    Vol. 5, Pt. 2–355
Kernan, Francis, Jan. 14, 1816–Sept. 7, 1892.
    Vol. 5, Pt. 2–356
Kerney, James, Apr. 29, 1873–Apr. 8, 1934.
    Supp. 1–466
Kerouac, Jack, Mar. 12, 1922–Oct. 21, 1969.
    Supp. 8–325
Kerr, John Glasgow, Nov. 30, 1824–Aug. 10, 1901.
    Vol. 5, Pt. 2–357
Kerr, Robert Samuel, Sept. 11, 1896–Jan. 1, 1963.
    Supp. 7–428
Kerr, Sophie, Aug. 23, 1880–Feb. 6, 1965.
    Supp. 7–429
Kerr, Walter Craig, Nov. 8, 1858–May 8, 1910.
    Vol. 5, Pt. 2–357
Kerr, Washington Caruthers, May 24, 1827–Aug. 9, 1885.
    Vol. 5, Pt. 2–358
Kershaw, Joseph Brevard, Jan. 5, 1822–Apr. 13, 1894.
    Vol. 5, Pt. 2–359
Kester, Paul, Nov. 2, 1870–June 20, 1933.
    Supp. 1–467
Kester, Vaughan, Sept. 12, 1869–July 4, 1911.
    Vol. 5, Pt. 2–360
Kettell, Samuel, Aug. 5, 1800–Dec. 3, 1855.
    Vol. 5, Pt. 2–360
Kettering, Charles Franklin, Aug. 29, 1876–Nov. 25, 1958.
    Supp. 6–332
Key, David McKendree, Jan. 27, 1824–Feb. 3, 1900.
    Vol. 5, Pt. 2–361
Key, Francis Scott, Aug. 1, 1779–Jan. 11, 1843.
    Vol. 5, Pt. 2–362
Key, Philip Barton, Apr. 12, 1757–July 28, 1815.
    Vol. 5, Pt. 2–363
Key, Valdimer Orlando, Jr., Mar. 13, 1908–Oct. 4, 1963.
    Supp. 7–430
Keyes, Edward Lawrence, Aug. 28, 1843–Jan. 24, 1924.
    Vol. 5, Pt. 2–364
Keyes, Elisha Williams, Jan. 23, 1828–Nov. 29, 1910.
    Vol. 5, Pt. 2–365
Keyes, Erasmus Darwin, May 29, 1810–Oct. 14, 1895.
    Vol. 5, Pt. 2–365
Keyes, Frances Parkinson, July 21, 1885–July 3, 1970.
    Supp. 8–327
Keys, Clement Melville, Apr. 7, 1876–Jan. 12, 1952.
    Supp. 5–384
Keyt, Alonzo Thrasher, Jan. 10, 1827–Nov. 9, 1885.
    Vol. 5, Pt. 2–366
Kharasch, Morris Selig, Aug. 24, 1895–Oct. 9, 1957.
    Supp. 6–333
Kiam, Omar, 1894–Mar. 28, 1954.
    Supp. 5–385
Kicking Bird, d. May 3, 1875.
    Vol. 5, Pt. 2–367
Kidd, William, c. 1645–May 23, 1701.
    Vol. 5, Pt. 2–367
Kidder, Alfred Vincent, Oct. 29, 1885–June 11, 1963.
    Supp. 7–431
Kidder, Daniel Parish, Oct. 18, 1815–July 29, 1891.
    Vol. 5, Pt. 2–369
Kidder, Frederic, Apr. 16, 1804–Dec. 19, 1885.
    Vol. 5, Pt. 2–370
Kieft, Willem, Sept. 1597–Sept. 27, 1647.
    Vol. 5, Pt. 2–370
Kientpoos. [See Captain Jack, 1837?–1873.]
Kier, Samuel M., 1813–Oct. 6, 1874.
    Vol. 5, Pt. 2–371
Kilbourne, James, Oct. 19, 1770–Apr. 9, 1850.
    Vol. 5, Pt. 2–372

Kilby, Christopher, May 25, 1705–Oct. [?], 1771.
Supp. 1–467
Kildahl, Johan Nathan, Jan. 4, 1857–Sept. 25, 1920.
Vol. 5, Pt. 2–373
Kilgallen, Dorothy Mae, July 3, 1913–Nov. 8, 1965.
Supp. 7–433
Kilgore, Harley Martin, Jan. 11, 1893–Feb. 28, 1956.
Supp. 6–335
Kilmer, Alfred Joyce, Dec. 6, 1886–July 30, 1918.
Vol. 5, Pt. 2–373
Kilpatrick, Hugh Judson, Jan. 14, 1836–Dec. 2, 1881.
Vol. 5, Pt. 2–374
Kilpatrick, John Reed, June 15, 1889–May 7, 1960.
Supp. 6–336
Kilpatrick, William Heard, Nov. 20, 1871–Feb. 13, 1965.
Supp. 7–434
Kilty, William, 1757–Oct. 10, 1821.
Vol. 5, Pt. 2–375
Kimball, Dan Able, Mar. 1, 1896–July 30, 1970.
Supp. 8–329
Kimball, Dexter Simpson, Oct. 21, 1865–Nov. 1, 1952.
Supp. 5–386
Kimball, Gilman, Dec. 8, 1804–July 27, 1892.
Vol. 5, Pt. 2–376
Kimball, Heber Chase, June 14, 1801–June 22, 1868.
Vol. 5, Pt. 2–377
Kimball, Nathan, Nov. 22, 1823?–Jan. 21, 1898.
Vol. 5, Pt. 2–378
Kimball, Richard Burleigh, Oct. 11, 1816–Dec. 28, 1892.
Vol. 5, Pt. 2–378
Kimball, (Sidney) Fiske, Dec. 8, 1888–Aug. 14, 1955.
Supp. 5–387
Kimball, Sumner Increase, Sept. 2, 1834–June 21, 1923.
Vol. 5, Pt. 2–379
Kimball, William Wirt, Jan 9, 1848–Jan. 26, 1930.
Vol. 5, Pt. 2–380
Kimmel, Husband Edward, Feb. 26, 1882–May 14, 1968.
Supp. 8–330
King, Albert Freeman Africanus, Jan. 18, 1841–Dec. 13, 1914. Vol. 5, Pt. 2–381
King, Alexander, Nov. 13, 1900–Nov. 17, 1965.
Supp. 7–436
King, Austin Augustus, Sept. 21, 1802–Apr. 22, 1870.
Vol. 5, Pt. 2–382
King, Basil. [See King, William Benjamin Basil, 1859–1928.]
King, Carol Weiss, Aug. 24, 1895–Jan. 22, 1952.
Supp. 5–389
King, Charles, Mar. 16, 1789–Sept. 27, 1867.
Vol. 5, Pt. 2–382
King, Charles William, c. 1809–Sept. 27, 1845.
Vol. 5, Pt. 2–383
King, Clarence, Jan. 6, 1842–Dec. 24, 1901.
Vol. 5, Pt. 2–384
King, Dan, Jan. 27, 1791–Nov. 13, 1864.
Vol. 5, Pt. 2–386
King, Edward Leonard, Dec. 5, 1873–Dec. 27, 1933.
Supp. 1–468
King, Edward Skinner, May 31, 1861–Sept. 10, 1931.
Vol. 5, Pt. 2–387
King, Edward Smith, Sept. 8, 1848–Mar. 27, 1896.
Vol. 5, Pt. 2–387
King, Ernest Joseph, Nov. 23, 1878–June 25, 1956.
Supp. 6–338
King, Franklin Hiram, June 8, 1848–Aug. 4, 1911.
Vol. 5, Pt. 2–388
King, Grace Elizabeth, Nov. 29, 1851–Jan. 14, 1932.
Vol. 5, Pt. 2–389
King, Henry, May 11, 1842–Mar. 15, 1915.
Vol. 5, Pt. 2–390
King, Henry Churchill, Sept. 18, 1858–Feb. 27, 1934.
Supp. 1–469
King, Henry Melville, Sept. 3, 1838–June 16, 1919.
Vol. 5, Pt. 2–391
King, Horatio, June 21, 1811–May 20, 1897.
Vol. 5, Pt. 2–391
King, James Gore, May 8, 1791–Oct. 3, 1853.
Vol. 5, Pt. 2–392
King, John, Jan. 1, 1813–June 19, 1893.
Vol. 5, Pt. 2–393
King, John Alsop, Jan. 3, 1788–July 7, 1867.
Vol. 5, Pt. 2–394
King, John Pendleton, Apr. 3, 1799–Mar. 19, 1888.
Vol. 5, Pt. 2–395

King, Jonas, July 29, 1792–May 22, 1869.
Vol. 5, Pt. 2–395
King, Martin Luther, Jr., Jan. 15, 1929–Apr. 4, 1968.
Supp. 8–332
King, Preston, Oct. 14, 1806–Nov. 13, 1865.
Vol. 5, Pt. 2–396
King, Richard, July 10, 1825–Apr. 14, 1885.
Vol. 5, Pt. 2–397
King, Rufus, Mar. 24, 1755–Apr. 29, 1827.
Vol. 5, Pt. 2–398
King, Rufus, Jan. 26, 1814–Oct. 13, 1876.
Vol. 5, Pt. 2–400
King, Samuel, Jan. 24, 1748–Dec. 30, 1819.
Vol. 5, Pt. 2–401
King, Samuel Archer, Apr. 9, 1828–Nov. 3, 1914.
Vol. 5, Pt. 2–401
King, Samuel Ward, May 23, 1786–Jan. 21, 1851.
Vol. 5, Pt. 2–402
King, Stanley, May 11, 1883–Apr. 28, 1951.
Supp. 5–390
King, Thomas Butler, Aug. 27, 1800–May 10, 1864.
Vol. 5, Pt. 2–403
King, Thomas Starr, Dec. 17, 1824–Mar. 4, 1864.
Vol. 5, Pt. 2–403
King, William, Feb. 9, 1768–June 17, 1852.
Vol. 5, Pt. 2–405
King, William Benjamin Basil, Feb. 26, 1859–June 22, 1928.
Vol. 5, Pt. 2–406
King, William Rufus Devane, Apr. 7, 1786–Apr. 18, 1853.
Vol. 5, Pt. 2–406
King of William, James, Jan. 28, 1822–May 20, 1856.
Vol. 5, Pt. 2–407
Kingsbury, Albert, Dec. 23, 1862–July 28, 1943.
Supp. 3–418
Kingsbury, John, May 26, 1801–Dec. 21, 1874.
Vol. 5, Pt. 2–408
Kingsford, Thomas, Sept. 29, 1799–Nov. 28, 1869.
Vol. 5, Pt. 2–409
Kingsley, Calvin, Sept. 8, 1812–Apr. 6, 1870.
Vol. 5, Pt. 2–410
Kingsley, Darwin Pearl, May 5, 1857–Oct. 6, 1932.
Supp. 1–470
Kingsley, Elbridge, Sept. 17, 1842–Aug. 28, 1918.
Vol. 5, Pt. 2–411
Kingsley, Elizabeth Seelman, Oct. 9, 1871–June 7, 1957.
Supp. 6–341
Kingsley, James Luce, Aug. 28, 1778–Aug. 31, 1852.
Vol. 5, Pt. 2–411
Kingsley, Norman William, Oct. 26, 1829–Feb. 20, 1913.
Vol. 5, Pt. 2–412
Kinkead, Edgar Benton, Mar. 14, 1863–Apr. 9, 1930.
Vol. 5, Pt. 2–413
Kinloch, Cleland, 1760–Sept. 12, 1823.
Vol. 5, Pt. 2–414
Kinloch, Robert Alexander, Feb. 20, 1826–Dec. 23, 1891.
Vol. 5, Pt. 2–414
Kinne, La Vega George, Nov. 5, 1846–Mar. 16, 1906.
Vol. 5, Pt. 2–415
Kinnersley, Ebenezer, Nov. 30, 1711–July 4, 1778.
Vol. 5, Pt. 2–416
Kinney, Elizabeth Clementine Dodge Stedman, Dec. 18, 1810–Nov. 19, 1889. Vol. 5, Pt. 2–417
Kinney, William Burnet, Sept. 4, 1799–Oct. 21, 1880.
Vol. 5, Pt. 2–417
Kinnicutt, Leonard Parker, May 22, 1854–Feb. 6, 1911.
Vol. 5, Pt. 2–418
Kino, Eusebio Francisco, c. 1645–Mar. 15, 1711.
Vol. 5, Pt. 2–419
Kinsella, Thomas, Dec. 31, 1832–Feb. 11, 1884.
Vol. 5, Pt. 2–420
Kinsey, Alfred Charles, June 23, 1894–Aug. 25, 1956.
Supp. 6–342
Kinsey, John, 1693–May 11, 1750– o.s.
Vol. 5, Pt. 2–421
Kintpuash. [See Captain Jack, 1837?–1873.]
Kinzie, John, Dec. 3, 1763–Jan. 6, 1828.
Vol. 5, Pt. 2–422
Kip, William Ingraham, Oct. 3, 1811–Apr. 7, 1893.
Vol. 5, Pt. 2–422
Kiphuth, Robert John Herman, Nov. 17, 1890–Jan. 7, 1967.
Supp. 8–336
Kiplinger, Willard Monroe, Jan. 8, 1891–Aug. 6, 1967.
Supp. 8–337

Kirby, Ephraim, Feb. 23, 1757–Oct. 20, 1804.
Vol. 5, Pt. 2–423
Kirby, George Hughes, Feb. 9, 1875–Aug. 11, 1935.
Supp. 1–471
Kirby, J. Hudson, Apr. 3, 1819–1848.
Vol. 5, Pt. 2–424
Kirby, Rollin, Sept. 4, 1875–May 9, 1952.
Supp. 5–391
Kirby-Smith, Edmund, May 16, 1824–Mar. 28, 1893.
Vol. 5, Pt. 2–424
Kirchhoff, Charles William Henry, Mar. 28, 1853–July 22, 1916. Vol. 5, Pt. 2–426
Kirchmayer, John, c. 1860–Nov. 29, 1930.
Vol. 5, Pt. 2–426
Kirchwey, George Washington, July 9, 1855–Mar. 3, 1942.
Supp. 3–420
Kirk, Alan Goodrich, Oct. 30, 1888–Oct. 15, 1963.
Supp. 7–437
Kirk, Edward Norris, Aug. 14, 1802–Mar. 27, 1874.
Vol. 5, Pt. 2–427
Kirk, John Foster, Mar. 22, 1824–Sept. 21, 1904.
Vol. 5, Pt. 2–428
Kirk, Norman Thomas, Jan. 3, 1888–Aug. 13, 1960.
Supp. 6–344
Kirkbride, Thomas Story, July 31, 1809–Dec. 16, 1883.
Vol. 5, Pt. 2–429
Kirkland, Caroline Matilda Stansbury, Jan. 12, 1801–Apr. 6, 1864. Vol. 5, Pt. 2–430
Kirkland, James Hampton, Sept. 9, 1859–Aug. 5, 1939.
Supp. 2–360
Kirkland, John Thornton, Aug. 17, 1770–Apr. 26, 1840.
Vol. 5, Pt. 2–431
Kirkland, Joseph, Jan. 7, 1830–Apr. 29, 1894.
Vol. 5, Pt. 2–431
Kirkland, Samuel, Nov. 20, 1741–Feb. 28, 1808.
Vol. 5, Pt. 2–432
Kirkman, Marshall Monroe, July 10, 1842–Apr. 18, 1921.
Vol. 5, Pt. 2–434
Kirkpatrick, Andrew, Feb. 17, 1756–Jan. 6, 1831.
Vol. 5, Pt. 2–435
Kirkwood, Daniel, Sept. 27, 1814–June 11, 1895.
Vol. 5, Pt. 2–436
Kirkwood, John Gamble, May 30, 1907–Aug. 9, 1959.
Supp. 6–345
Kirkwood, Samuel Jordan, Dec. 20, 1813–Sept. 1, 1894.
Vol. 5, Pt. 2–436
Kirlin, Joseph Louis Jerome, Mar. 20, 1868–Nov. 26, 1926.
Vol. 5, Pt. 2–437
Kirstein, Louis Edward, July 9, 1867–Dec. 10, 1942.
Supp. 3–421
Kirtland, Jared Potter, Nov. 10, 1793–Dec. 10, 1877.
Vol. 5, Pt. 2–438
Kiss, Max, Nov. 9, 1882–June 22, 1967.
Supp. 8–338
Kitchin, Claude, Mar. 24, 1869–May 31, 1923.
Vol. 5, Pt. 2–439
Kitchin, William Walton, Oct. 9, 1866–Nov. 9, 1924.
Vol. 5, Pt. 2–440
Kittredge, George Lyman, Feb. 28, 1860–July 23, 1941.
Supp. 3–422
Kittson, Norman Wolfred, Mar. 5, 1814–May 10, 1888.
Vol. 5, Pt. 2–441
Klauder, Charles Zeller, Feb. 9, 1872–Oct. 30, 1938.
Supp. 2–362
Klaw, Marc, May 29, 1858–June 14, 1936.
Supp. 2–363
Klein, August Clarence, Apr. 1, 1887–Feb. 3, 1948.
Supp. 4–453
Klein, Bruno Oscar, June 6, 1858–June 22, 1911.
Vol. 5, Pt. 2–442
Klein, Charles, Jan. 7, 1867–May 7, 1915.
Vol. 5, Pt. 2–442
Klein, Charles Herbert ("Chuck"), Oct. 7, 1904–Mar. 28, 1956. Supp. 6–346
Klein, Joseph Frederic, Oct. 10, 1849–Feb. 11, 1918.
Vol. 5, Pt. 2–443
Klem, William J. (Bill), Feb. 22, 1874–Sept. 16, 1951.
Supp. 5–393
Kline, Franz Josef, May 23, 1910–Mary 13, 1962.
Supp. 7–438
Kline, George, c. 1757–Nov. 12, 1820.
Vol. 5, Pt. 2–444

Klingelsmith, Margaret Center, Nov. 27, 1859–Jan. 19, 1931.
Vol. 5, Pt. 2–444
Klippart, John Hancock, July 26, 1823–Oct. 24, 1878.
Vol. 5, Pt. 2–445
Klipstein, Louis Frederick, Jan. 2, 1813–Aug. 20, 1878.
Vol. 5, Pt. 2–446
Klopsch, Louis, Mar. 26, 1852–Mar. 7, 1910.
Vol. 5, Pt. 2–447
Knab, Frederick, Sept. 22, 1865–Nov. 2, 1918.
Vol. 5, Pt. 2–448
Knabe, Valentine Wilhelm Ludwig, June 3, 1803–May 21, 1864. Vol. 5, Pt. 2–448
Knapp, Bradford, Dec. 24, 1870–June 11, 1938.
Supp. 2–361
Knapp, George, Sept. 25, 1814–Sept. 18, 1883.
Vol. 5, Pt. 2–448
Knapp, Herman, Mar. 17, 1832–Apr. 30, 1911.
Vol. 5, Pt. 2–449
Knapp, Joseph Palmer, May 14, 1864–Jan. 30, 1951.
Supp. 5–394
Knapp, Martin Augustine, Nov. 6, 1843–Feb. 10, 1923.
Vol. 5, Pt. 2–450
Knapp, Philip Coombs, June 3, 1858–Feb. 23, 1920.
Vol. 5, Pt. 2–451
Knapp, Samuel Lorenzo, Jan. 19, 1783–July 8, 1838.
Vol. 3, Pt. 1–452
Knapp, Seaman Asahel, Dec. 16, 1833–Apr. 1, 1911.
Vol. 5, Pt. 2–452
Knapp, William Ireland, Mar. 10, 1835–Dec. 6, 1908.
Vol. 5, Pt. 2–453
Knappen, Theodore Temple, Nov. 21, 1900–Mar. 20, 1951.
Supp. 5–395
Knauth, Oswald Whitman, June 3, 1887–July 13, 1962.
Supp. 7–440
Kneass, Samuel Honeyman, Nov. 5, 1806–Feb. 15, 1858.
Vol. 5, Pt. 2–454
Kneass, Strickland, July 29, 1821–Jan. 14, 1884.
Vol. 5, Pt. 2–455
Kneass, William, Sept. 25, 1780–Aug. 27, 1840.
Vol. 5, Pt. 2–456
Kneeland, Abner, Apr. 7, 1774–Aug. 27, 1844.
Vol. 5, Pt. 2–457
Kneeland, Samuel, Jan. 31, 1697–Dec. 14, 1769.
Vol. 5, Pt. 2–458
Kneeland, Samuel, Aug. 1, 1821–Sept. 27, 1888.
Vol. 5, Pt. 2–459
Kneeland, Stillman Foster, May 17, 1845–Aug. 30, 1926.
Vol. 5, Pt. 2–459
Kneisel, Franz, Jan. 26, 1865–Mar. 26, 1926.
Vol. 5, Pt. 2–460
Knickerbocker, Herman, July 27, 1779–Jan. 30, 1855.
Vol. 5, Pt. 2–461
Knight, Austin Melvin, Dec. 16, 1854–Feb 26, 1927.
Vol. 5, Pt. 2–462
Knight, Daniel Ridgway, Mar. 15, 1840–Mar. 9, 1924.
Vol. 5, Pt. 2–463
Knight, Edward Collings, Dec. 8, 1813–July 21, 1892.
Vol. 5, Pt. 2–463
Knight, Edward Henry, June 1, 1824–Jan. 22, 1883.
Vol. 5, Pt. 2–464
Knight, Frederick Irving, May 18, 1841–Feb. 20, 1909.
Vol. 5, Pt. 2–465
Knight, Goodwin Jess ("Goodie"), Dec. 9, 1896–May 22, 1970. Supp. 8–339
Knight, Henry Cogswell, Jan. 29, 1789–Jan. 10, 1835.
Vol. 5, Pt. 2–466
Knight, Jonathan, Nov. 22, 1787–Nov. 22, 1858.
Vol. 5, Pt. 2–467
Knight, Jonathan, Sept. 4, 1789–Aug. 25, 1864.
Vol. 5, Pt. 2–467
Knight, Lucian Lamar, Feb. 9, 1868–Nov. 19, 1933.
Supp. 1–471
Knight, Ridgway. [See Knight, Daniel Ridgway, 1839–1924.]
Knight, Sarah Kemble, Apr. 19, 1666–Sept. 25, 1727.
Vol. 5, Pt. 2–468
Knopf, Blanche Wolf, July 30, 1893–June 4, 1966.
Supp. 8–341
Knott, Aloysius Leo, May 12, 1829–Apr. 18, 1918.
Vol. 5, Pt. 2–469
Knott, James Proctor, Aug. 29, 1830–June 18, 1911.
Vol. 5, Pt. 2–470
Knowles, Lucius James, July 2, 1819–Feb. 25, 1884.
Vol. 5, Pt. 2–470

Knowlton, Charles, May 10, 1800–Feb. 20, 1850.
   Vol. 5, Pt. 2–471
Knowlton, Frank Hall, Sept. 2, 1860–Nov. 22, 1926.
   Vol. 5, Pt. 2–472
Knowlton, Marcus Perrin, Feb. 3, 1839–May 7, 1918.
   Vol. 5, Pt. 2–473
Knowlton, Thomas, Nov. 1740–Sept. 16, 1776.
   Vol. 5, Pt. 2–474
Knox, Dudley Wright, June 21, 1877–June 11, 1960.
   Supp. 6–348
Knox, Frank, Jan. 1, 1874–Apr. 28, 1944.
   Supp. 3–424
Knox, George William, Aug. 11, 1853–Apr. 25, 1912.
   Vol. 5, Pt. 2–475
Knox, Henry, July 25, 1750–Oct. 25, 1806.
   Vol. 5, Pt. 2–475
Knox, John Jay, Mar. 19, 1828–Feb. 9, 1892.
   Vol. 5, Pt. 2–477
Knox, Philander Chase, May 6, 1853–Oct. 12, 1921.
   Vol. 5, Pt. 2–478
Knox, Rose Markward, Nov. 18, 1857–Sept. 27, 1950.
   Supp. 4–454
Knox, Samuel, 1756–Aug. 31, 1832.
   Vol. 5, Pt. 2–480
Knox, Thomas Wallace, June 26, 1835–Jan. 6, 1896.
   Vol. 5, Pt. 2–481
Knudsen, William S., Mar. 25, 1879–Apr. 27, 1948.
   Supp. 4–456
Knutson, Harold, Oct. 20, 1880–Aug. 21, 1953.
   Supp. 5–396
Kobbé, Gustav, Mar. 4, 1857–July 27, 1918.
   Vol. 5, Pt. 2–482
Kober, George Martin, Mar. 28, 1850–Apr. 24, 1931.
   Vol. 5, Pt. 2–483
Koch, Fred Conrad, May 16, 1876–Jan. 26, 1948.
   Supp. 4–459
Koch, Frederick Henry, Sept. 12, 1877–Aug. 16, 1944.
   Supp. 3–426
Koch, Vivienne, 1911–Nov. 29, 1961.
   Supp. 7–441
Kocherthal, Josua von, 1669–Dec. 27, 1719.
   Vol. 5, Pt. 2–484
Koehler, Robert, Nov. 28, 1850–Apr. 23, 1917.
   Vol. 5, Pt. 2–484
Koehler, Sylvester Rosa, Feb. 11, 1837–Sept. 15, 1900.
   Vol. 5, Pt. 2–485
Koemmenich, Louis, Oct. 4, 1866–Aug. 14, 1922.
   Vol. 5, Pt. 2–486
Koenig, George Augustus, May 12, 1844–Jan. 14, 1913.
   Vol. 5, Pt. 2–486
Koenigsberg, Moses, Apr. 16, 1878–Sept. 21, 1945.
   Supp. 3–427
Koerner, Gustave Philip. [See Korner, Gustav Philipp, 1809–1896.]
Koffka, Kurt, Mar. 18, 1886–Nov. 22, 1941.
   Supp. 3–428
Kofoid, Charles Atwood, Oct. 11, 1865–May 30, 1947.
   Supp. 4–461
Kohlberg, Alfred, Jan. 27, 1887–Apr. 7, 1960.
   Supp. 6–349
Kohler, Elmer Peter, Nov. 6, 1865–May 24, 1938.
   Supp. 2–365
Kohler, Kaufmann, May 10, 1843–Jan. 28, 1926.
   Vol. 5, Pt. 2–487
Kohler, Max James, May 22, 1871–July 24, 1934.
   Supp. 1–472
Kohler, Walter Jodok, Mar. 3, 1875–Apr. 21, 1940.
   Supp. 2–366
Köhler, Wolfgang, Jan. 21, 1887–June 11, 1967.
   Supp. 8–343
Kohlmann, Anthony, July 13, 1771–Apr. 10, 1836.
   Vol. 5, Pt. 2–488
Kohlsaat, Herman Henry, Mar. 22, 1853–Oct. 17, 1924.
   Vol. 5, Pt. 2–489
Kohut, Alexander, Apr. 22, 1842–May 25, 1894.
   Vol. 5, Pt. 2–490
Kohut, George Alexander, Feb. 11, 1874–Dec. 31, 1933.
   Supp. 1–473
Kolb, Dielman, Nov. 10, 1691–Dec. 28, 1756.
   Vol. 5, Pt. 2–491
Kolb, Reuben Francis, Apr. 15, 1839–Mar. 23, 1918.
   Vol. 5, Pt. 2–492

Kolle, Frederick Strange, Nov. 22, 1872–May 10, 1929.
   Vol. 5, Pt. 2–492
Koller, Carl, Dec. 3, 1857–Mar. 21, 1944.
   Supp. 3–430
Kollock, Shepard, Sept. 1750–July 28, 1839.
   Vol. 5, Pt. 2–493
Koopman, Augustus, Jan. 2, 1869–Jan. 31, 1914.
   Vol. 5, Pt. 2–494
Kooweskowe. [See Ross, John, c. 1790–1866.]
Koren, John, Mar. 3, 1861–Nov. 9, 1923.
   Vol. 5, Pt. 2–494
Koren, Ulrik Vilhelm, Dec. 22, 1826–Dec. 20, 1910.
   Vol. 5, Pt. 2–495
Körner, Gustav Philipp, Nov. 20, 1809–Apr. 9, 1896.
   Vol. 5, Pt. 2–496
Korngold, Erich Wolfgang, May 29, 1897–Nov. 29, 1957.
   Supp. 6–351
Kosciuszko, Tadeusz Andrzej Bonawentura, Feb. 12, 1746–Oct. 15, 1817. Vol. 5, Pt. 2–497
Koussevitzky, Serge Alexandrovich, July 26, 1874–June 4, 1951. Supp. 5–397
Kovacs, Ernie, Jan. 23, 1919–Jan. 13, 1962.
   Supp. 7–442
Koyl, Charles Herschel, Aug. 14, 1855–Dec. 18, 1931.
   Vol. 5, Pt. 2–498
Kracauer, Siegfried, Feb. 8, 1889–Nov. 26, 1966.
   Supp. 8–346
Kraemer, Henry, July 22, 1868–Sept. 9, 1924.
   Vol. 5, Pt. 2–499
Kraft, James Lewis, Nov. 11, 1874–Feb. 16, 1953.
   Supp. 5–399
Krantz, Philip. [See Rombro, Jacob, 1858–1922.]
Krapp, George Philip, Sept. 1, 1872–Apr. 21, 1934.
   Supp. 1–474
Kraus, John, Feb. 2, 1815–Mar. 4, 1896.
   Vol. 5, Pt. 2–499
Kraus-Boelté, Maria, Nov. 8, 1836–Nov. 1, 1918.
   Vol. 5, Pt. 2–500
Krause, Allen Kramer, Feb. 13, 1881–May 12, 1941.
   Supp. 3–431
Krauskopf, Joseph, Jan. 21, 1858–June 12, 1923.
   Vol. 5, Pt. 2–500
Krauth, Charles Philip, May 7, 1797–May 30, 1867.
   Vol. 5, Pt. 2–501
Krauth, Charles Porterfield, Mar. 17, 1823–Jan. 2, 1883.
   Vol. 5, Pt. 2–502
Krehbiel, Christian, Oct. 18, 1832–Apr. 30, 1909.
   Vol. 5, Pt. 2–503
Krehbiel, Henry Edward, Mar. 10, 1854–Mar. 20, 1923.
   Vol. 5, Pt. 2–504
Kreisler, Fritz, Feb. 2, 1875–Jan. 29, 1962.
   Supp. 7–443
Kremers, Edward, Feb. 23, 1865–July 9, 1941.
   Supp. 3–432
Kresge, Sebastian Spering, July 31, 1867–Oct. 18, 1966.
   Supp. 8–347
Kress, Samuel Henry, July 23, 1863–Sept. 22, 1955.
   Supp. 5–400
Kreymborg, Alfred Francis, Dec. 10, 1883–Aug. 14, 1966.
   Supp. 8–349
Krez, Konrad, Apr. 27, 1828–Mar. 9, 1897.
   Vol. 5, Pt. 2–505
Krimmel, John Lewis, 1789–July 15, 1821.
   Vol. 5, Pt. 2–506
Kroeber, Alfred Louis, June 11, 1876–Oct. 5, 1960.
   Supp. 6–352
Kroeger, Adolph Ernst, Dec. 28, 1837–Mar. 8, 1882.
   Vol. 5, Pt. 2–507
Kroeger, Ernest Richard, Aug. 10, 1862–Apr. 7, 1934.
   Supp. 1–475
Kroger, Bernhard Henry, Jan. 24, 1860–July 21, 1938.
   Supp. 2–367
Krol, Bastiaen Jansen, 1595–1674.
   Vol. 5, Pt. 2–508
Krueger, Walter, Jan. 26, 1881–Aug. 20, 1967.
   Supp. 8–351
Kruell, Gustav, Oct. 31, 1843–Jan. 2, 1907.
   Vol. 5, Pt. 2–508
Kruesi, John, May 15, 1843–Feb. 22, 1899.
   Vol. 5, Pt. 2–509
Krug, Julius Albert, Nov. 23, 1907–Mar. 26, 1970.
   Supp. 8–352

Krüsi, Hermann. [See Krüsi, Johann Heinrich Hermann, 1817–1903.]
Krüsi, Johann Heinrich Hermann, June 24, 1817–Jan. 28, 1903. Vol. 5, Pt. 2–509
Krutch, Joseph Wood, Nov. 25, 1893–May 22, 1970. Supp. 8–353
Kugelman, Frederick Benjamin. [See Kaye, Frederick Benjamin, 1892–1930.]
Kuhn, Adam, Nov. 17, 1741–July 5, 1817. Vol. 5, Pt. 2–510
Kuhn, Joseph Ernst, June 14, 1864–Nov. 12, 1935. Supp. 1–476
Kuhn, Walt, Oct. 27, 1877–July 13, 1949. Supp. 4–462
Kumler, Henry, Jan. 3, 1775–Jan. 8, 1854. Vol. 5, Pt. 2–511
Kuniyoshi, Yasuo, Sept. 1, 1893–May 14, 1953. Supp. 5–402
Kunz, George Frederick, Sept. 29, 1856–June 29, 1932. Supp. 1–476
Kunze, John Christopher, Aug. 5, 1744–July 24, 1807. Vol. 5, Pt. 2–512
Kunze, Richard Ernest, Apr. 7, 1838–Feb. 7, 1919. Vol. 5, Pt. 2–513
Kurtz, Benjamin, Feb. 28, 1795–Dec. 29, 1865. Vol. 5, Pt. 2–514
Kuskov, Ivan Aleksandrovich, 1765–October 1823. Vol. 5, Pt. 2–514
Kuykendall, Ralph Simpson, Apr. 12, 1885–May 9, 1963. Supp. 7–445
Kyle, David Braden, Oct. 11, 1863–Oct. 23, 1916. Vol. 5, Pt. 2–515
Kyle, James Henderson, Feb. 24, 1854–July 1, 1901. Vol. 5, Pt. 2–515
Kyne, Peter Bernard, Oct. 12, 1880–Nov. 25, 1957. Supp. 6–353
Kynett, Alpha Jefferson, Aug. 12, 1829–Feb. 23, 1899. Vol. 5, Pt. 2–516

La Barge, Joseph, Oct. 1, 1815–Apr. 3, 1899. Vol. 5, Pt. 2–517
La Borde, Maximilian, June 5, 1804–Nov. 6, 1873. Vol. 5, Pt. 2–518
Lacey, John, Feb. 4, 1755–Feb. 17, 1814. Vol. 5, Pt. 2–519
Lacey, John Fletcher, May 30, 1841–Sept. 29, 1913. Vol. 5, Pt. 2–519
Lachaise, Gaston, Mar. 19, 1882–Oct. 18, 1935. Supp. 1–477
Lackaye, Wilton, Sept. 30, 1862–Aug. 22, 1932. Supp. 1–479
Laclede, Pierre, c. 1724–June 20, 1778. Vol. 5, Pt. 2–520
Lacock, Abner, July 9, 1770–Apr. 12, 1837. Vol. 5, Pt. 2–521
Lacy, Drury, Oct. 5, 1758–Dec. 6, 1815. Vol. 5, Pt. 2–522
Lacy, Ernest, Sept. 19, 1863–June 17, 1916. Vol. 5, Pt. 2–522
Ladd, Alan Walbridge, Sept. 3, 1913–Jan. 29, 1964. Supp. 7–446
Ladd, Carl Edwin, Feb. 25, 1888–July 23, 1943. Supp. 3–433
Ladd, Catherine, Oct. 28, 1808–Jan. 30, 1899. Vol. 5, Pt. 2–524
Ladd, Edwin Fremont, Dec. 13, 1859–June 22, 1925. Vol. 5, Pt. 2–524
Ladd, George Trumbull, Jan. 19, 1842–Aug. 8, 1921. Vol. 5, Pt. 2–525
Ladd, Joseph Brown, July 7, 1764–Nov. 2, 1786. Vol. 5, Pt. 2–526
Ladd, Kate Macy, Apr. 6, 1863–Aug. 27, 1945. Supp. 3–434
Ladd, William, May 10, 1778–Apr. 9, 1841. Vol. 5, Pt. 2–527
Ladd, William Sargent, Oct. 10, 1826–Jan. 6, 1893. Vol. 5, Pt. 2–528
Ladd-Franklin, Christine, Dec. 1, 1847–Mar. 5, 1930. Vol. 5, Pt. 2–528
Laemmle, Carl, Jan. 17, 1867–Sept. 24, 1939. Supp. 2–368
La Farge, Christopher Grant, Jan. 5, 1862–Oct. 11, 1938. Supp. 2–369

La Farge, Christopher Grant, Dec. 10, 1897–Jan. 5, 1956. Supp. 6–355
La Farge, Grant. [See La Farge, Christopher Grant, 1862–1938.]
La Farge, John, Mar. 31, 1835–Nov. 14, 1910. Vol. 5, Pt. 2–530
LaFarge, John, Feb. 13, 1880–Nov. 24, 1963. Supp. 7–447
La Farge, Oliver Hazard Perry, Dec. 19, 1901–Aug. 2, 1963. Supp. 7–448
Lafayette, Marie Joseph Paul Yves Roch Gilbert du Motier, Marquis de, Sept 6, 1757–May 20, 1834. Vol. 5, Pt. 2–535
Lafever, Minard, Aug. 10, 1798–Sept. 26, 1854. Supp. 1–479
Laffan, William Mackay, Jan. 22, 1848–Nov. 19, 1909. Vol. 5, Pt. 2–539
Laffite, Jean, fl. 1809–1821. Vol. 5, Pt. 2–540
Lafitte, Jean. [See Laffite, Jean, fl. 1809–1821.]
La Flesche, Susette. [See Bright Eyes, 1854–1903.]
La Follette, Philip Fox, May 8, 1897–Aug. 18, 1965. Supp. 7–450
La Follette, Robert Marion, June 14, 1855–June 18, 1925. Vol. 5, Pt. 2–541
La Follette, Robert Marion, Jr., Feb. 6, 1895–Feb. 24, 1953. Supp. 5–403
Lafon, Thomy, Dec. 28, 1810–Dec. 22, 1893. Vol. 5, Pt. 2–546
La Guardia, Fiorello Henry, Dec. 11, 1882–Sept. 20, 1947. Supp. 4–464
Laguna, Theodore de Leo de, July 22, 1876–Sept. 22, 1930. Vol. 5, Pt. 2–547
Lahey, Frank Howard, June 1, 1880–June 27, 1953. Supp. 5–404
Lahontan, Louis-Armand de Lom d'Arce Baron de, June 9, 1666–c. 1713. Vol. 5, Pt. 2–548
Lahr, Bert, Aug. 13, 1895–Dec. 4, 1967. Supp. 8–354
Laimbeer, Nathalie Schenck, Dec. 4, 1882–Oct. 25, 1929. Vol. 5, Pt. 2–549
Lait, Jacquin Leonard (Jack), Mar. 13, 1883–Apr. 1, 1954. Supp. 5–406
Lajoie, Napoleon ("Larry"), Sept. 5, 1875–Feb. 7, 1959. Supp. 6–356
Lake, Kirsopp, Apr. 7, 1872–Nov. 10, 1946. Supp. 4–467
Lake, Simon, Sept. 4, 1866–June 23, 1945. Supp. 3–435
Lalor, Alice. [See Teresa, Mother, 1766–1846.]
Lamar, Gazaway Bugg, Oct. 2, 1798–Oct. 5, 1874. Vol. 5, Pt. 2–549
Lamar, Joseph Rucker, Oct. 14, 1857–Jan. 2, 1916. Vol. 5, Pt. 2–550
Lamar, Lucius Quintus Cincinnatus, Sept. 17, 1825–Jan. 23, 1893. Vol. 5, Pt. 2–551
Lamar, Mirabeau Buonaparte, Aug. 16, 1798–Dec. 19, 1859. Vol. 5, Pt. 2–553
Lamb, Arthur Becket, Feb. 25, 1880–May 15, 1952. Supp. 5–406
Lamb, Isaac Wixom, Jan. 8, 1840–July 14, 1906. Vol. 5, Pt. 2–554
Lamb, John, Jan. 1, 1735–May 31, 1800. Vol. 5, Pt. 2–555
Lamb, Martha Joanna Reade Nash, Aug. 13, 1829–Jan. 2, 1893. Vol. 5, Pt. 2–556
Lamb, William Frederick, Nov. 21, 1883–Sept. 8, 1952. Supp. 5–408
Lambdin, James Reid, May 10, 1807–Jan. 31, 1889. Vol. 5, Pt. 2–557
Lambeau, Earl Louis ("Curly"), Apr. 9, 1898–June 1, 1965. Supp. 7–451
Lambert, Louis Aloisius, Apr. 13, 1835–Sept. 25, 1910. Vol. 5, Pt. 2–557
Lamberton, Benjamin Peffer, Feb. 25, 1844–June 9, 1912. Vol. 5, Pt. 2–558
Lambing, Andrew Arnold, Feb. 1, 1842–Dec. 24, 1918. Vol. 5, Pt. 2–559
Lambuth, James William, Mar. 2, 1830–Apr. 28, 1892. Vol. 5, Pt. 2–560
Lambuth, Walter Russell, Nov. 10, 1854–Sept. 26, 1921. Vol. 5, Pt. 2–560

Lardner, Ringgold Wilmer, Mar. 6, 1885–Sept. 25, 1933.
Supp. 1–482
Larkin, John, Feb. 2, 1801–Dec. 11, 1858.
Vol. 5, Pt. 2–616
Larkin, Thomas Oliver, Sept. 16, 1802–Oct. 27, 1858.
Vol. 5, Pt. 2–617
Larned, Joseph Gay Eaton, Apr. 29, 1819–June 3, 1870.
Vol. 6, Pt. 1–1
Larned, Josephus Nelson, May 11, 1836–Aug. 15, 1913.
Vol. 6, Pt. 1–2
Larned, William Augustus, Dec. 30, 1872–Dec. 16, 1926.
Vol. 6, Pt. 1–2
LaRoche, René, Sept. 23, 1795–Dec. 9, 1872.
Vol. 6, Pt. 1–3
La Ronde, Louis Denis, Sieur de, 1675–March 1741.
Vol. 6, Pt. 1–4
Larpenteur, Charles, May 8, 1807–Nov. 15, 1872.
Vol. 6, Pt. 1–4
Larrabee, Charles Hathaway, Nov. 9, 1820–Jan. 20, 1883.
Vol. 6, Pt. 1–5
Larrabee, William, Jan. 20, 1832–Nov. 16, 1912.
Vol. 6, Pt. 1–6
Larrabee, William Clark, Dec. 23, 1802–May 5, 1859.
Vol. 6, Pt. 1–7
Larrazolo, Octaviano Ambrosio, Dec. 7, 1859–Apr. 7, 1930.
Vol. 6, Pt. 1–7
Larrínaga, Tulio, Jan. 15, 1847–Apr. 28, 1917.
Vol. 6, Pt. 1–8
Larsen, Peter Laurentius, Aug. 10, 1833–Mar. 1, 1915.
Vol. 6, Pt. 1–9
Larson, Laurence Marcellus, Sept. 23, 1868–Mar. 9, 1938.
Supp. 2–371
La Salle, Robert Cavelier, Sieur de, November 1643–Mar. 19, 1687. Vol. 6, Pt. 1–10
Lasater, Edward Cunningham, Nov. 5, 1860–Mar. 20, 1930.
Vol. 6, Pt. 1–12
Lashley, Karl Spencer, June 7, 1890–Aug. 7, 1958.
Supp. 6–367
Lasker, Albert Davis, May 1, 1880–May 30, 1952.
Supp. 5–410
Lasky, Jesse Louis, Sept. 13, 1880–Jan. 13, 1958.
Supp. 6–368
Lasser, Jacob Kay, Oct. 7, 1896–May 11, 1954.
Supp. 5–412
Latané, John Holladay, Apr. 1, 1869–Jan. 1, 1932.
Supp. 1–483
Latham, Milton Slocum, May 23, 1827–Mar. 4, 1882.
Vol. 6, Pt. 1–13
Lathbury, Mary Artemisia, Aug. 10, 1841–Oct. 20, 1913.
Vol. 6, Pt. 1–13
Lathrop, Francis Augustus, June 22, 1849–Oct. 18, 1909.
Vol. 6, Pt. 1–14
Lathrop, George Parsons, Aug. 25, 1851–Apr. 19, 1898.
Vol. 6, Pt. 1–15
Lathrop, John, Jan. 13, 1772–Jan. 30, 1820.
Vol. 6, Pt. 1–16
Lathrop, John Hiram, Jan. 22, 1799–Aug. 2, 1866.
Vol. 6, Pt. 1–16
Lathrop, Julia Clifford, June 29, 1858–Apr. 15, 1932.
Supp. 1–484
Lathrop, Rose Hawthorne. [See Alphonsa, Mother, 1851–1926.]
Latil, Alexandre, Oct. 6, 1816–March 1851.
Vol. 6, Pt. 1–17
Latimer, Mary Elizabeth Wormeley, July 26, 1822–Jan. 4, 1904. Vol. 6, Pt. 1–18
Latimer, Wendell Mitchell, Apr. 22, 1893–July 6, 1955.
Supp. 5–413
La Tour, Le Blond de, d. Oct. 14, 1723.
Vol. 6, Pt. 1–19
Latourette, Kenneth Scott, Aug. 9, 1884–Dec. 26, 1968.
Supp. 8–359
Latrobe, Benjamin Henry, May 1, 1764–Sept. 3, 1820.
Vol. 6, Pt. 1–20
Latrobe, Benjamin Henry, Dec. 19, 1806–Oct. 19, 1878.
Vol. 6, Pt. 1–25
Latrobe, Charles Hazlehurst, Dec. 25, 1834–Sept. 19, 1902.
Vol. 6, Pt. 1–26
Latrobe, John Hazlehurst Boneval, May 4, 1803–Sept. 11, 1891. Vol. 6, Pt. 1–27
Latta, Alexander Bonner, June 11, 1821–Apr. 28, 1865.
Vol. 6, Pt. 1–28

Lattimore, William, Feb. 9, 1774–Apr. 3, 1843.
Vol. 6, Pt. 1–29
Laudonnière, René Goulaine de, fl. 1562–1582.
Vol. 6, Pt. 1–30
Laufer, Berthold, Oct. 11, 1874–Sept. 13, 1934.
Supp. 1–486
Laughlin, Harry Hamilton, Mar. 11, 1880–Jan. 6, 1943.
Supp. 3–445
Laughlin, James Laurence, Apr. 2, 1850–Nov. 28, 1933.
Supp. 1–487
Laughton, Charles, July 1, 1899–Dec. 15, 1962.
Supp. 7–460
Launitz, Robert Eberhard Schmidt Von Der, Nov. 4, 1806–Dec. 13, 1870. Vol. 6, Pt. 1–31
Laurance, John, 1750–Nov. 11, 1810.
Vol. 6, Pt. 1–31
Laurel, Stan, June 16, 1890–Feb. 23, 1965.
Supp. 7–462
Laurens, Henry, Mar. 6, 1724–Dec. 8, 1792.
Vol. 6, Pt. 1–32
Laurens, John, Oct. 28, 1754–Aug. 27, 1782.
Vol. 6, Pt. 1–35
Laurie, James, May 9, 1811–Mar. 16, 1875.
Vol. 6, Pt. 1–36
La Vérendrye, Pierre Gaultier De Varennes, Sieur de, Nov. 17, 1685–Dec. 6, 1749. Vol. 6, Pt. 1–37
Law, Andrew, March 1748/49–July 13, 1821.
Vol. 6, Pt. 1–38
Law, Evander McIvor, Aug. 7, 1836–Oct. 31, 1920.
Vol. 6, Pt. 1–38
Law, George, Oct. 25, 1806–Nov. 18, 1881.
Vol. 6, Pt. 1–39
Law, John, Oct. 28, 1796–Oct. 7, 1873.
Vol. 6, Pt. 1–40
Law, Jonathan, Aug. 6, 1674–Nov. 6, 1750.
Vol. 6, Pt. 1–41
Law, Richard, Mar. 7, 1733–Jan. 26, 1806.
Vol. 6, Pt. 1–41
Law, Sallie Chapman Gordon, Aug. 27, 1805–June 28, 1894.
Vol. 6, Pt. 1–42
Lawes, Lewis Edward, Sept. 13, 1883–Apr. 23, 1947.
Supp. 4–471
Lawley, George Frederick, Dec. 8, 1848–Mar. 20, 1928.
Vol. 6, Pt. 1–43
Lawrance, Charles Lanier, Sept. 30, 1882–June 24, 1950.
Supp. 4–473
Lawrance, John. [See Laurance, John, 1750–1810.]
Lawrance, Marion. [See Lawrance, Uriah Marion, 1850–1924.]
Lawrance, Uriah Marion, Oct. 2, 1850–May 1, 1924.
Vol. 6, Pt. 1–43
Lawrence, Abbott, Dec. 16, 1792–Aug. 18, 1855.
Vol. 6, Pt. 1–44
Lawrence, Amos, Apr. 22, 1786–Dec. 31, 1852.
Vol. 6, Pt. 1–46
Lawrence, Amos Adams, July 31, 1814–Aug. 22, 1886.
Vol. 6, Pt. 1–47
Lawrence, David Leo, June 18, 1889–Nov. 21, 1966.
Supp. 8–360
Lawrence, Ernest Orlando, Aug. 8, 1901–Aug. 27, 1958.
Supp. 6–369
Lawrence, George Newbold, Oct. 20, 1806–Jan. 17, 1895.
Vol. 6, Pt. 1–49
Lawrence, Gertrude, July 4, 1898–Sept. 6, 1952.
Supp. 5–414
Lawrence, James, Oct. 1, 1781–June 4, 1813.
Vol. 6, Pt. 1–49
Lawrence, Richard Smith, Nov. 22, 1817–Mar. 10, 1892.
Vol. 6, Pt. 1–51
Lawrence, William, Sept. 7, 1783–Oct. 14, 1848.
Vol. 6, Pt. 1–51
Lawrence, William, June 26, 1819–May 8, 1899.
Vol. 6, Pt. 1–52
Lawrence, William, May 30, 1850–Nov. 6, 1941.
Supp. 3–446
Lawrence, William Beach, Oct. 23, 1800–Mar. 26, 1881.
Vol. 6, Pt. 1–53
Lawrie, Alexander, Feb. 25, 1828–Feb. 15, 1917.
Vol. 6, Pt. 1–54
Laws, Samuel Spahr, Mar. 23, 1824–Jan. 9, 1921.
Vol. 6, Pt. 1–54
Lawson, Alexander, Dec. 19, 1773–Aug. 22, 1846.
Vol. 6, Pt. 1–56

Lee, Luther, Nov. 30, 1800–Dec. 13, 1889.
    Vol. 6, Pt. 1–115
Lee, Porter Raymond, Dec. 21, 1879–Mar. 8, 1939.
    Supp. 2–376
Lee, Richard, d. 1664.
    Vol. 6, Pt. 1–116
Lee, Richard Bland, Jan. 20, 1761–Mar. 12, 1827.
    Vol. 6, Pt. 1–117
Lee, Richard Henry, Jan. 20, 1732–June 19, 1794.
    Vol. 6, Pt. 1–117
Lee, Robert Edward, Jan. 19, 1807–Oct. 12, 1870.
    Vol. 6, Pt. 1–120
Lee, Samuel Phillips, Feb. 13, 1812–June 5, 1897.
    Vol. 6, Pt. 1–129
Lee, Stephen Dill, Sept. 22, 1833–May 28, 1908.
    Vol. 6, Pt. 1–130
Lee, Thomas, Dec. 1, 1769–Oct. 24, 1839.
    Vol. 6, Pt. 1–131
Lee, Thomas Sim, Oct. 29, 1745–Nov. 9, 1819.
    Vol. 6, Pt. 1–132
Lee, William, Aug. 31, 1739–June 27, 1795.
    Vol. 6, Pt. 1–132
Lee, William Granville, Nov. 29, 1859–Nov. 2, 1929.
    Vol. 6, Pt. 1–133
Lee, William Henry Fitzhugh, May 31, 1837–Oct. 15, 1891.
    Vol. 6, Pt. 1–134
Lee, William Little, Feb. 8, 1821–May 28, 1857.
    Vol. 6, Pt. 1–135
Lee, Willis Augustus, May 11, 1888–Aug. 25, 1945.
    Supp. 3–450
Leedom, Boyd Stewart, Sept. 28, 1906–Aug. 11, 1969.
    Supp. 8–365
Leeds, Daniel, 1652–Sept. 28, 1720.
    Vol. 6, Pt. 1–135
Leeds, John, May 18, 1705–March 1790.
    Vol. 6, Pt. 1–136
Lees, Ann. [See Lee, Ann, 1736–1784.]
Leeser, Isaac, Dec. 12, 1806–Feb. 1, 1868.
    Vol. 6, Pt. 1–137
Leete, William, c. 1613–Apr. 16, 1683.
    Vol. 6, Pt. 1–138
Lefevere, Peter Paul, Apr. 30, 1804–Mar. 4, 1869.
    Vol. 6, Pt. 1–138
Leffel, James, Apr. 19, 1806–June 11, 1866.
    Vol. 6, Pt. 1–139
Lefferts, George Morewood, Feb. 24, 1846–Sept. 21, 1920.
    Vol. 6, Pt. 1–140
Lefferts, Marshall, Jan. 15, 1821–July 3, 1876.
    Vol. 6, Pt. 1–140
Leffingwell, Russell Cornell, Sept. 10, 1878–Oct. 2, 1960.
    Supp. 6–376
Leffler, Isaac, Nov. 25, 1788–Mar. 8, 1866.
    Vol. 6, Pt. 1–141
Leffler, Shepherd, Apr. 24, 1811–Sept. 7, 1879.
    Vol. 6, Pt. 1–142
Leffmann, Henry, Sept. 9, 1847–Dec. 25, 1930.
    Vol. 6, Pt. 1–142
Leflore, Greenwood, June 3, 1800–Aug. 31, 1865.
    Vol. 6, Pt. 1–143
Legaré, Hugh Swinton, Jan. 2, 1797–June 20, 1843.
    Vol. 6, Pt. 1–144
LeGendre, Charles William, Aug. 26, 1830–Sept. 1, 1899.
    Vol. 6, Pt. 1–145
Legge, Alexander, July 13, 1866–Dec. 3, 1933.
    Supp. 1–490
Leggett, Mortimer Dormer, Apr. 19, 1821–Jan. 6, 1896.
    Vol. 6, Pt. 1–146
Leggett, William, Apr. 30, 1801–May 29, 1839.
    Vol. 6, Pt. 1–147
Legler, Henry Eduard, June 22, 1861–Sept. 13, 1917.
    Vol. 6, Pt. 1–148
Lehman, Adele Lewisohn, May 17, 1882–Aug. 11, 1965.
    Supp. 7–465
Lehman, Arthur, June 1, 1873–May 16, 1936.
    Supp. 2–376
Lehman, Herbert Henry, Mar. 28, 1878–Dec. 5, 1963.
    Supp. 7–466
Lehman, Irving, Jan. 28, 1876–Sept. 22, 1945.
    Supp. 3–451
Lehman, Robert, Sept. 29, 1891–Aug. 9, 1969.
    Supp. 8–367
Lehmann, Frederick William, Feb. 28, 1853–Sept. 12, 1931.
    Vol. 6, Pt. 1–149

Leib, Michael, Jan. 8, 1760–Dec. 28, 1822.
    Vol. 6, Pt. 1–149
Leiber, Fritz, Jan. 31, 1882–Oct. 14, 1949.
    Supp. 4–477
Leidy, Joseph, Sept. 9, 1823–Apr. 29, 1891.
    Vol. 6, Pt. 1–150
Leigh, Benjamin Watkins, June 18, 1781–Feb. 2, 1849.
    Vol. 6, Pt. 1–152
Leigh, Vivien, Nov. 5, 1913–July 7, 1967.
    Supp. 8–368
Leigh, William Robinson, Sept. 23, 1866–Mar. 11, 1955.
    Supp. 5–420
Leighton, William, fl. 1825–1868.
    Vol. 6, Pt. 1–153
Leiper, Thomas, Dec. 15, 1745–July 6, 1825.
    Vol. 6, Pt. 1–154
Leipzig, Nate, May 13, 1873–Oct. 13, 1939.
    Supp. 2–377
Leipziger, Henry Marcus, Dec. 29, 1854–Dec. 1, 1917.
    Vol. 6, Pt. 1–154
Leiserson, William Morris, Apr. 15, 1883–Feb. 12, 1957.
    Supp. 6–378
Leishman, John G. A., Mar. 28, 1857–Mar. 27, 1924. (Asher Isaacs). Vol. 6, Pt. 1–155
Leisler, Jacob, 1640–May 16, 1691.
    Vol. 6, Pt. 1–156
Leiter, Joseph, Dec. 4, 1868–Apr. 11, 1932.
    Supp. 1–491
Leiter, Levi Zeigler, Nov. 2, 1834–June 9, 1904.
    Vol. 6, Pt. 1–157
Le Jau, Francis, 1665–Sept. 15, 1717.
    Vol. 6, Pt. 1–158
Lejeune, John Archer, Jan. 10, 1867–Nov. 20, 1942.
    Supp. 3–452
Leland, Charles Godfrey, Aug. 15, 1824–Mar. 20, 1903.
    Vol. 6, Pt. 1–158
Leland, George Adams, Sept. 7, 1850–Mar. 17, 1924.
    Vol. 6, Pt. 1–160
Leland, John, May 14, 1754–Jan. 14, 1841.
    Vol. 6, Pt. 1–160
Leland, Waldo Gifford, July 17, 1879–Oct. 19, 1966.
    Supp. 8–369
Lemke, Peter Henry, July 27, 1796–Nov. 29, 1882.
    Vol. 6, Pt. 1–161
Lemke, William Frederick, Aug. 13, 1878–May 30, 1950.
    Supp. 4–479
Lemmon, John Gill, Jan. 2, 1832–Nov. 24, 1908.
    Vol. 6, Pt. 1–162
LeMoyne, Francis Julius, Sept. 4, 1798–Oct. 14, 1879.
    Vol. 6, Pt. 1–163
Le Moyne, Jean Baptiste. [See Bienville, Jean Baptiste Le Moyne, Sieur de, 1680–1768.]
Le Moyne, Pierre. [See Iberville, Pierre Le Moyne, Sieur d', 1661–1706.]
Le Moyne, William J., Apr. 29, 1831–Nov. 6, 1905.
    Vol. 6, Pt. 1–164
Leney, William Satchwell, Jan. 16, 1769–Nov. 26, 1831.
    Vol. 6, Pt. 1–165
L'Enfant, Pierre Charles, Aug. 2, 1754–June 14, 1825.
    Vol. 6, Pt. 1–165
Lenker, John Nicholas, Nov. 28, 1858–May 16, 1929.
    Vol. 6, Pt. 1–169
Lennon, John Brown, Oct. 12, 1850–Jan. 17, 1923.
    Vol. 6, Pt. 1–170
Lennox, Charlotte Ramsay, 1720–Jan. 4, 1804.
    Vol. 6, Pt. 1–171
Lenox, James, Aug. 19, 1800–Feb. 17, 1880.
    Vol. 6, Pt. 1–172
Lenroot, Irvine Luther, Jan. 31, 1869–Jan. 26, 1949.
    Supp. 4–481
Lenthall, John, Sept. 16, 1807–Apr. 11, 1882.
    Vol. 6, Pt. 1–173
Lenz, Sidney Samuel, July 12, 1873–Apr. 12, 1960.
    Supp. 6–379
Leonard, Charles Lester, Dec. 29, 1861–Sept. 22, 1913.
    Vol. 6, Pt. 1–173
Leonard, Daniel, May 18, 1740–June 27, 1829.
    Vol. 6, Pt. 1–174
Leonard, George, Nov. 23, 1742–Apr. 1, 1826.
    Vol. 6, Pt. 1–175
Leonard, Harry Ward, Feb. 8, 1861–Feb. 18, 1915.
    Vol. 6, Pt. 1–176

Lewis, Sinclair. [See Lewis, Harry Sinclair.]
Lewis, Tayler, Mar. 27, 1802–May 11, 1877.
  Vol. 6, Pt. 1–224
Lewis, Wilfred, Oct. 16, 1854–Dec. 19, 1929.
  Supp. 1–492
Lewis, William, Feb. 2, 1751 o.s.–Aug. 16, 1819.
  Vol. 6, Pt. 1–225
Lewis, William Berkeley, 1784–Nov. 12, 1866.
  Vol. 6, Pt. 1–226
Lewis, William David, Sept. 22, 1792–Apr. 1, 1881.
  Vol. 6, Pt. 1–226
Lewis, William Draper, Apr. 27, 1867–Sept. 2, 1949.
  Supp. 4–490
Lewis, William Gaston, Sept. 3, 1835–Jan. 7, 1901.
  Vol. 6, Pt. 1–227
Lewis, William Henry, Nov. 28, 1868–Jan. 1, 1949.
  Supp. 4–492
Lewis, Winslow, May 11, 1770–May 19, 1850.
  Vol. 6, Pt. 1–228
Lewisohn, Adolph, May 27, 1849–Aug. 17, 1938.
  Supp. 2–383
Lewisohn, Ludwig, May 30, 1882–Dec. 31, 1955.
  Supp. 5–424
Lewisohn, Sam Adolph, Mar. 21, 1884–Mar. 13, 1951.
  Supp. 5–426
Lexow, Clarence, Sept. 16, 1852–Dec. 30, 1910.
  Vol. 6, Pt. 1–229
Ley, Willy, Oct. 2, 1906–June 24, 1969.
  Supp. 8–379
Leyendecker, Joseph Christian, Mar. 23, 1874–July 25, 1951.
  Supp. 5–428
Leyner, John George, Aug. 26, 1860–Aug. 5, 1920.
  Vol. 6, Pt. 1–229
Leypoldt, Frederick, Nov. 17, 1835–Mar. 31, 1884.
  Vol. 6, Pt. 1–230
L'Halle, Constantin de, d. June 6, 1706.
  Vol. 6, Pt. 1–231
L'Halle, Nicolas Benoit Constantin de. [See L'Halle, Constantin de, d. 1706.]
Lhévinne, Josef, Dec. 14, 1874–Dec. 2, 1944.
  Supp. 3–458
L'Hommedieu, Ezra, Aug. 30, 1734–Sept. 27, 1811.
  Vol. 6, Pt. 1–232
Libbey, Edward Drummond, Apr. 17, 1854–Nov. 13, 1925.
  Vol. 6, Pt. 1–233
Libby, Orin Grant, June 9, 1864–Mar. 29, 1952.
  Supp. 5–429
Libman, Emanuel, Aug. 22, 1972–June 28, 1946.
  Supp. 4–494
Lick, James, Aug. 21, 1796–Oct. 1, 1876.
  Vol. 6, Pt. 1–234
Lie, Jonas, Apr. 29, 1880–Jan. 10, 1940.
  Supp. 2–384
Lieb, John William, Feb. 12, 1860–Nov. 1, 1929.
  Vol. 6, Pt. 1–234
Lieber, Francis, Mar. 18, 1800–Oct. 2, 1872.
  Vol. 6, Pt. 1–236
Liebling, Abbott Joseph, Oct. 18, 1904–Dec. 28, 1963.
  Supp. 7–472
Liebling, Emil, Apr. 12, 1851–Jan. 20, 1914.
  Vol. 6, Pt. 1–238
Liebling, Estelle, Apr. 21, 1880–Sept. 25, 1970.
  Supp. 8–380
Liebman, Joshua Loth, Apr. 7, 1907–June 9, 1948.
  Supp. 4–495
Lienau, Detlef, Feb. 17, 1818–Aug. 29, 1887.
  Supp. 1–493
Liggett, Hunter, Mar. 21, 1857–Dec. 30, 1935.
  Supp. 1–494
Liggett, Louis Kroh, Apr. 4, 1875–June 5, 1946.
  Supp. 4–496
Liggett, Walter William, Feb. 14, 1886–Dec. 9, 1935.
  Supp. 1–495
Lightburn, Joseph Andrew Jackson, Sept. 21, 1824–May 17, 1901. Vol. 6, Pt. 1–239
Ligon, Thomas Watkins, May 1, 1810–Jan. 12, 1881.
  Vol. 6, Pt. 1–239
Lile, William Minor, Mar. 28, 1859–Dec. 13, 1935.
  Supp. 1–497
Lilienthal, Max, Oct. 16, 1815–Apr. 5, 1882.
  Vol. 6, Pt. 1–240
Lillie, Frank Rattray, June 27, 1870–Nov. 5, 1947.
  Supp. 4–497

Lillie, Gordon William, Feb. 14, 1860–Feb. 3, 1942.
  Supp. 3–459
Lilly, Josiah Kirby, Nov. 18, 1861–Feb. 8, 1948.
  Supp. 4–499
Lincecum, Gideon, Apr. 22, 1793–Nov. 28, 1874.
  Vol. 6, Pt. 1–241
Lincoln, Abraham, Feb. 12, 1809–Apr. 15, 1865.
  Vol. 6, Pt. 1–242
Lincoln, Benjamin, Jan. 24, 1733–May 9, 1810.
  Vol. 6, Pt. 1–259
Lincoln, Enoch, Dec. 28, 1788–Oct. 8, 1829.
  Vol. 6, Pt. 1–261
Lincoln, John Larkin, Feb. 23, 1817–Oct. 17, 1891.
  Vol. 6, Pt. 1–262
Lincoln, Joseph Crosby, Feb. 13, 1870–Mar. 10, 1944.
  Supp. 3–460
Lincoln, Levi, May 15, 1749–Apr. 14, 1820.
  Vol. 6, Pt 1–262
Lincoln, Levi, Oct. 25, 1782–May 29, 1868.
  Vol. 6, Pt. 1–264
Lincoln, Mary Johnson Bailey, July 8, 1844–Dec. 2, 1921.
  Vol. 6, Pt. 1–265
Lincoln, Mary Todd, Dec. 13, 1818–July 16, 1882.
  Vol. 6, Pt. 1–265
Lincoln, Robert Todd, Aug. 1, 1843–July 26, 1926.
  Vol. 6, Pt. 1–266
Lincoln, Rufus Pratt, Apr. 27, 1840–Nov. 27, 1900.
  Vol. 6, Pt. 1–267
Lind, John, Mar. 25, 1854–Sept. 18, 1930.
  Vol. 5, Pt. 1–268
Lindabury, Richard Vliet, Oct. 13, 1850–July 15, 1925.
  Vol. 6, Pt. 1–269
Lindberg, Conrad Emil, June 9, 1852–Aug. 2, 1930.
  Vol. 6, Pt. 1–270
Lindbergh, Charles Augustus, Jan. 20, 1859–May 24, 1924.
  Vol. 6, Pt. 1–271
Linde, Christian, Feb. 19, 1817–Nov. 24, 1887.
  Vol. 6, Pt. 1–271
Lindeman, Eduard Christian, May 9, 1885–Apr. 13, 1953.
  Supp. 5–430
Lindenkohl, Adolph, Mar. 6, 1833–June 22, 1904.
  Vol. 6, Pt. 1–272
Lindenthal, Gustav, May 21, 1850–July 31, 1935.
  Supp. 1–498
Linderman, Henry Richard, Dec. 26, 1825–Jan. 27, 1879.
  Vol. 6, Pt. 1–273
Lindgren, Waldemar, Feb. 14, 1860–Nov. 3, 1939.
  Supp. 2–385
Lindheimer, Ferdinand Jacob, May 21, 1801–Dec. 2, 1879.
  Vol. 6, Pt. 1–273
Lindley, Curtis Holbrook, Dec. 14, 1850–Nov. 20, 1920.
  Vol. 6, Pt. 1–274
Lindley, Daniel, Aug. 24, 1801–Sept. 3, 1880.
  Supp. 1–499
Lindley, Jacob, June 13, 1774–Jan. 29, 1857.
  Vol. 6, Pt. 1–275
Lindsay, Howard, Mar. 29, 1889–Feb. 11, 1968.
  Supp. 8–382
Lindsay, Nicholas Vachel, Nov. 10, 1879–Dec. 5, 1931.
  Vol. 6, Pt. 1–276
Lindsay, Vachel. [See Lindsay, Nicholas Vachel, 1879–1931.]
Lindsay, William, Sept. 4, 1835–Oct. 15, 1909.
  Vol. 6, Pt. 1–277
Lindsey, Benjamin Barr, Nov. 25, 1869–Mar. 26, 1943.
  Supp. 3–461
Lindsey, William, Aug. 12, 1858–Nov. 25, 1922.
  Vol. 6, Pt. 1–278
Lindsley, John Berrien, Oct. 24, 1822–Dec. 7, 1897.
  Vol. 6, Pt. 1–278
Lindsley, Philip, Dec. 21, 1786–May 25, 1855.
  Vol. 6, Pt. 1–279
Lingelbach, Anna Lane, Oct. 10, 1873–July 14, 1954.
  Supp. 5–432
Lining, John, 1708–Sept. 21, 1760.
  Vol. 6, Pt. 1–280
Link, Henry Charles, Aug. 27, 1889–Jan. 9, 1952.
  Supp. 5–433
Linn, John Blair, Mar. 14, 1777–Aug. 30, 1804.
  Vol. 6, Pt. 1–281
Linn, Lewis Fields, Nov. 5, 1795–Oct. 3, 1843.
  Vol. 6, Pt. 1–282
Linn, William Alexander, Sept. 4, 1846–Feb. 23, 1917.
  Vol. 6, Pt. 1–283

Lintner, Joseph Albert, Feb. 8, 1822–May 5, 1898.
Vol. 6, Pt. 1–283
Linton, Ralph, Feb. 27, 1893–Dec. 24, 1953.
Supp. 5–434
Linton, William James, Dec. 7, 1812–Dec. 29, 1897.
Vol. 6, Pt. 1–284
Lipman, Jacob Goodale, Nov. 18, 1874–Apr. 19, 1939.
Supp. 2–387
Lippard, George, Apr. 10, 1822–Feb. 9, 1854.
Vol. 6, Pt. 1–285
Lippincott, James Starr, Apr. 12, 1819–Mar. 17, 1885.
Vol. 6, Pt. 1–286
Lippincott, Joshua Ballinger, Mar. 18, 1813–Jan. 5, 1886.
Vol. 6, Pt. 1–287
Lippincott, Sara Jane Clarke, Sept. 23, 1823–Apr. 20, 1904.
Vol. 6, Pt. 1–288
Lippitt, Henry, Oct. 9, 1818–June 5, 1891.
Vol. 6, Pt. 1–289
Lipscomb, Abner Smith, Feb. 10, 1789–Dec. 8, 1856.
Vol. 6, Pt. 1–289
Lipscomb, Andrew Adgate, Sept. 16, 1816–Nov. 23, 1890.
Vol. 6, Pt. 1–290
Lisa, Manuel, Sept. 8, 1772–Aug. 12, 1820.
Vol. 6, Pt. 1–291
List, Georg Friedrich, Aug. 6, 1789–Nov. 30, 1846.
Vol. 6, Pt. 1–291
Listemann, Bernhard, Aug. 28, 1841–Feb. 11, 1917.
Vol. 6, Pt. 1–293
Litchfield, Electus Backus, Feb. 15, 1813–May 12, 1889.
Vol. 6, Pt. 1–294
Litchfield, Paul Weeks, July 26, 1875–Mar. 18, 1959.
Supp. 6–380
Littauer, Lucius Nathan, Jan. 20, 1859–Mar. 2, 1944.
Supp. 3–463
Littell, Eliakim, Jan. 2, 1797–May 17, 1870.
Vol. 6, Pt. 1–295
Littell, Squier, Dec. 9, 1803–July 4, 1886.
Vol. 6, Pt. 1–295
Littell, William, 1768–Sept. 26, 1824.
Vol. 6, Pt. 1–296
Little, Arthur Dehon, Dec. 15, 1863–Aug. 1, 1935.
Supp. 1–500
Little, Charles Coffin, July 25, 1799–Aug. 9, 1869.
Vol. 6, Pt. 1–297
Little, Charles Joseph, Sept. 21, 1840–Mar. 11, 1911.
Vol. 6, Pt. 1–298
Little, Charles Sherman, Feb. 12, 1869–June 6, 1936.
Supp. 2–388
Little, George, Apr. 15, 1754–July 22, 1809.
Vol. 6, Pt. 1–298
Little, William Lawson, Jr., June 23, 1910–Feb. 1, 1968.
Supp. 8–383
Little Crow V, c. 1803–July 3, 1863.
Vol. 6, Pt. 1–299
Littledale, Clara Savage, Jan. 31, 1891–Jan. 9, 1956.
Supp. 6–382
Littlefield, George Washington, June 21, 1842–Nov. 10, 1920. Vol. 6, Pt. 1–300
Littlejohn, Abram Newkirk, Dec. 13, 1824–Aug. 3, 1901.
Vol. 6, Pt. 1–301
Littlepage, Lewis, Dec. 19, 1762–July 19, 1802.
Vol. 6, Pt. 1–302
Littleton, Martin Wiley, Jan. 12, 1872–Dec. 19, 1934.
Supp. 1–501
Little Turtle, c. 1752–July 14, 1812.
Vol. 6, Pt. 1–300
Liveright, Horace Brisbin, Dec. 10, 1886–Sept. 24, 1933.
Supp. 1–502
Livermore, Abiel Abbot, Oct. 30, 1811–Nov. 28, 1892.
Vol. 6, Pt. 1–303
Livermore, Arthur, July 29, 1766–July 1, 1853.
Vol. 6, Pt. 1–304
Livermore, Edward St. Loe, Apr. 5, 1762–Sept. 15, 1832.
Vol. 6, Pt. 1–304
Livermore, George, July 10, 1809–Aug. 30, 1865.
Vol. 6, Pt. 1–305
Livermore, Mary Ashton Rice, Dec. 19, 1820–May 23, 1905.
Vol. 6, Pt. 1–306
Livermore, Samuel, May 25, 1732–May 18, 1803.
Vol. 6, Pt. 1–307
Livermore, Samuel, Aug. 26, 1786–July 11, 1833.
Vol. 6, Pt. 1–308

Livingston, Burton Edward, Feb. 9, 1875–Feb. 8, 1948.
Supp. 4–500
Livingston, Edward, May 28, 1764–May 23, 1836.
Vol. 6, Pt. 1–309
Livingston, Henry Brockholst, Nov. 25, 1757–Mar. 18, 1823.
Vol. 6, Pt. 1–312
Livingston, James, Mar. 27, 1747–Nov. 29, 1832.
Vol. 6, Pt. 1–313
Livingston, John Henry, May 30, 1746–Jan. 20, 1825.
Vol. 6, Pt. 1–314
Livingston, John William, May 22, 1804–Sept. 10, 1885.
Vol. 6, Pt. 1–315
Livingston, Peter Van Brugh, October 1710–Dec. 28, 1792.
Vol. 6, Pt. 1–315
Livingston, Philip, Jan. 15, 1716–June 12, 1778.
Vol. 6, Pt. 1–316
Livingston, Robert, Dec. 13, 1654–Oct. 1, 1728.
Vol. 6, Pt. 1–318
Livingston, Robert R., August 1718–Dec. 9, 1775.
Vol. 6, Pt. 1–319
Livingston, Robert R., Nov. 27, 1746–Feb. 26, 1813.
Vol. 6, Pt. 1–320
Livingston, William, November 1723–July 25, 1790.
Vol. 6, Pt. 1–325
Livingstone, Belle, Jan. 20, 1875[?]–Feb. 7, 1957.
Supp. 6–383
Livingstone, William, Jan. 21, 1844–Oct. 17, 1925.
Vol. 6, Pt. 1–327
Llewellyn, Karl Nickerson, May 22, 1893–Feb. 13, 1962.
Supp. 7–474
Lloyd, Alfred Henry, Jan. 3, 1864–May 11, 1927.
Vol. 6, Pt. 1–328
Lloyd, David, c. 1656–Apr. 6, 1731 o.s.
Vol. 6, Pt. 1–329
Lloyd, Edward, Nov. 15, 1744–July 8, 1796.
Vol. 6, Pt. 1–330
Lloyd, Edward, July 22, 1779–June 2, 1834.
Vol. 6, Pt. 1–331
Lloyd, Henry Demarest, May 1, 1847–Sept. 28, 1903.
Vol. 6, Pt. 1–331
Lloyd, James, Mar. 24, 1728–Mar. 14, 1810.
Vol. 6, Pt. 1–333
Lloyd, John Uri, Apr. 19, 1849–Apr. 9, 1936.
Supp. 2–389
Lloyd, Marshall Burns, Mar. 10, 1858–Aug. 10, 1927.
Vol. 6, Pt. 1–333
Lloyd, Thomas, Apr. 17, 1640 o.s.–Sept. 10, 1694 o.s.
Vol. 6, Pt. 1–334
Lochman, John George, Dec. 2, 1773–July 10, 1826.
Vol. 6, Pt. 1–335
Locke, Alain Leroy, Sept. 13, 1886–June 9, 1954.
Supp. 5–436
Locke, Bessie, Aug. 7, 1865–Apr. 9, 1952.
Supp. 5–437
Locke, David Ross, Sept. 20, 1833–Feb. 15, 1888.
Vol. 6, Pt. 1–336
Locke, John, Feb. 19, 1792–July 10, 1856.
Vol. 6, Pt. 1–337
Locke, Matthew, 1730–Sept. 7, 1801.
Vol. 6, Pt. 1–338
Locke, Richard Adams, Sept. 22, 1800–Feb. 16, 1871.
Vol. 6, Pt. 1–338
Lockhart, Charles, Aug. 2, 1818–Jan. 26, 1905.
Vol. 6, Pt. 1–339
Lockheed, Allan Haines, Jan. 20, 1889–May 26, 1969.
Supp. 8–384
Lockheed, Malcolm, 1887[?]–Aug. 13, 1958.
Supp. 6–385
Lockrey, Sarah Hunt, Apr. 21, 1863–Nov. 8, 1929.
Vol. 6, Pt. 1–340
Lockwood, Belva Ann Bennett, Oct. 24, 1830–May 19, 1917.
Vol. 6, Pt. 1–341
Lockwood, James Booth, Oct. 9, 1852–Apr. 9, 1884.
Vol. 6, Pt. 1–341
Lockwood, Ralph Ingersoll, July 8, 1798–Apr. 12, 1858(?).
Vol. 6, Pt. 1–342
Lockwood, Robert Wilton, Sept. 12, 1861–Mar. 20, 1914.
Vol. 6, Pt. 1–343
Lockwood, Samuel Drake, Aug. 2, 1789–Apr. 23, 1874.
Vol. 6, Pt. 1–344
Lockwood, Wilton [See Lockwood, Robert Wilton, 1861–1914.]

Locy, William Albert, Sept. 14, 1857–Oct. 9, 1924.
Vol. 6, Pt. 1–345
Lodge, George Cabot, Oct. 10, 1873–Aug. 21, 1909.
Vol. 6, Pt. 1–345
Lodge, Henry Cabot, May 12, 1850–Nov. 9, 1924.
Vol. 6, Pt. 1–346
Lodge, John Ellerton, Aug. 1, 1876–Dec. 29, 1942.
Supp. 3–464
Loeb, Jacques, Apr. 7, 1859–Feb. 11, 1924.
Vol. 6, Pt. 1–349
Loeb, James, Aug. 6, 1867–May 29, 1933.
Supp. 1–503
Loeb, Leo, Sept. 21, 1869–Dec. 28, 1959.
Supp. 6–385
Loeb, Louis, Nov. 7, 1866–July 12, 1909.
Vol. 6, Pt. 1–352
Loeb, Morris, May 23, 1863–Oct. 8, 1912.
Vol. 6, Pt. 1–353
Loeb, Sophie Irene Simon, July 4, 1876–Jan. 18, 1929.
Vol. 6, Pt. 1–354
Loeffler, Charles Martin, Jan. 30, 1861–May 19, 1935.
Supp. 1–504
Loesser, Frank, June 29, 1910–July 28, 1969.
Supp. 8–385
Loew, Marcus, May 7, 1870–Sept. 5, 1927.
Vol. 6, Pt. 1–355
Loewenthal, Isidor, c. 1827–Apr. 27, 1864.
Vol. 6, Pt. 1–356
Loewi, Otto, June 3, 1873–Dec. 25, 1961.
Supp. 7–475
Logan, Benjamin, c. 1743–Dec. 11, 1802.
Vol. 6, Pt. 1–356
Logan, Cornelius Ambrose, Aug. 24, 1832–Jan. 30, 1899.
Vol. 6, Pt. 1–357
Logan, Cornelius Ambrosius, May 4, 1806–Feb. 22, 1853.
Vol. 6, Pt. 1–358
Logan, Deborah Norris, Oct. 19, 1761–Feb. 2, 1839.
Vol. 6, Pt. 1–359
Logan, George, Sept. 9, 1753–Apr. 9, 1821.
Vol. 6, Pt. 1–359
Logan, James, Oct. 20, 1674–Oct. 31, 1751.
Vol. 6, Pt. 1–360
Logan, James, c. 1725–1780.
Vol. 6, Pt. 1–362
Logan, James Harvey, Dec. 8, 1841–July 16, 1928.
Vol. 6, Pt. 1–363
Logan, John Alexander, Feb. 9, 1826–Dec. 26, 1886.
Vol. 6, Pt. 1–363
Logan, Olive, Apr. 22, 1839–Apr. 27, 1909.
Vol. 6, Pt. 1–365
Logan, Stephen Trigg, Feb. 24, 1800–July 17, 1880.
Vol. 6, Pt. 1–365
Logan, Thomas Muldrup, July 31, 1808–Feb. 13, 1876.
Vol. 6, Pt. 1–366
Logan, Thomas Muldrup, Nov. 3, 1840–Aug. 11, 1914.
Vol. 6, Pt. 1–367
Loguen, Jermain Wesley, c. 1813–Sept. 30, 1872.
Vol. 6, Pt. 1–368
Lomax, John Avery, Sept. 23, 1867–Jan. 26, 1948.
Supp. 4–501
Lomax, John Tayloe, Jan. 19, 1781–Oct. 1, 1862.
Vol. 6, Pt. 1–369
Lomax, Louis Emanuel, Aug. 16, 1922–July 30, 1970.
Supp. 8–387
Lomax, Lunsford Lindsay, Nov. 4, 1835–May 28, 1913.
Vol. 6, Pt. 1–369
Lombard, Carole, Oct. 6, 1908–Jan. 16, 1942.
Supp. 3–465
Lombard, Warren Plimpton, May 29, 1855–July 13, 1939.
Supp. 2–390
Lombardi, Vincent Thomas, June 11, 1913–Sept. 3, 1970.
Supp. 8–389
London, Jack, Jan. 12, 1876–Nov. 22, 1916.
Vol. 6, Pt. 1–370
London, Meyer, Dec. 29, 1871–June 6, 1926.
Vol. 6, Pt. 1–372
Lonesome Charley. [See Reynolds, Charles Alexander, c. 1842–1876.]
Long, Armistead Lindsay, Sept. 3, 1825–Apr. 29, 1891.
Vol. 6, Pt. 1–374
Long, Breckinridge, May 16, 1881–Sept. 26, 1958.
Supp. 6–387

Long, Charles Chaillé. [See Chaillé-Long, Charles, 1842–1917.]
Long, Crawford Williamson, Nov. 1, 1815–June 16, 1878.
Vol. 6, Pt. 1–374
Long, Earl Kemp, Aug. 26, 1895–Sept. 5, 1960.
Supp. 6–390
Long, Huey Pierce, Aug. 30, 1893–Sept. 10, 1935.
Supp. 1–506
Long, James, c. 1793–Apr. 8, 1822.
Vol. 6, Pt. 1–376
Long, John Davis, Oct. 27, 1838–Aug. 28, 1915.
Vol. 6, Pt. 1–377
Long, John Harper, Dec. 26, 1856–June 14, 1918.
Vol. 6, Pt. 1–378
Long, John Luther, Jan. 1, 1861–Oct. 31, 1927.
Vol. 6, Pt. 1–379
Long, Joseph Ragland, Dec. 15, 1870–Mar. 15, 1932.
Supp. 1–508
Long, Perrin Hamilton, Apr. 7, 1899–Dec. 17, 1965.
Supp. 7–477
Long, Stephen Harriman, Dec. 30, 1784–Sept. 4, 1864.
Vol. 6, Pt. 1–380
Longacre, James Barton, Aug. 11, 1794–Jan. 1, 1869.
Vol. 6, Pt. 1–380
Longcope, Warfield, Theobald, Mar. 29, 1877–Apr. 25, 1953. Supp. 5–438
Longfellow, Ernest Wadsworth, Nov. 23, 1845–Nov. 24, 1921. Vol. 6, Pt. 1–381
Longfellow, Henry Wadsworth, Feb. 27, 1807–Mar. 24, 1882.
Vol. 6, Pt. 1–382
Longfellow, Samuel, June 18, 1819–Oct. 3, 1892.
Vol. 6, Pt. 1–387
Longfellow, Stephen, Mar. 23, 1776–Aug. 3, 1849.
Vol. 6, Pt. 1–388
Longfellow, William Pitt Preble, Oct. 25, 1836–Aug. 3, 1913.
Vol. 6, Pt. 1–388
Longley, Alcander, Mar. 31, 1832–Apr. 17, 1918.
Vol. 6, Pt. 1–389
Longstreet, Augustus Baldwin, Sept. 22, 1790–July 9, 1870.
Vol. 6, Pt. 1–390
Longstreet, James, Jan. 8, 1821–Jan. 2, 1904.
Vol. 6, Pt. 1–391
Longstreet, William, Oct. 6, 1759–Sept. 1, 1814.
Vol. 6, Pt. 1–393
Longworth, Nicholas, Jan. 16, 1782–Feb. 10, 1863.
Vol. 6, Pt. 1–393
Longworth, Nicholas, Nov. 5, 1869–Apr. 9, 1931.
Vol. 6, Pt. 1–394
Longyear, John Munroe, Apr. 15, 1850–May 28, 1922.
Vol. 6, Pt. 1–395
Loomis, Arphaxed, Apr. 9, 1798–Sept. 15, 1885.
Vol. 6, Pt. 1–396
Loomis, Charles Battell, Sept. 16, 1861–Sept. 23, 1911.
Vol. 6, Pt. 1–397
Loomis, Dwight, July 27, 1821–Sept. 17, 1903.
Vol. 6, Pt. 1–397
Loomis, Elias, Aug. 7, 1811–Aug. 15, 1889.
Vol. 6, Pt. 1–398
Loomis, Elmer Howard, May 24, 1861–Jan. 22, 1931.
Vol. 6, Pt. 1–399
Loomis, Mahlon, July 21, 1826–Oct. 13, 1886.
Vol. 6, Pt. 1–399
Loop, Henry Augustus, Sept. 9, 1831–Oct. 20, 1895.
Vol. 6, Pt. 1–400
Loos, Charles Louis, Dec. 23, 1823–Feb. 27, 1912.
Vol. 6, Pt. 1–401
Lopez, Aaron, 1731–May 28, 1782.
Vol. 6, Pt. 1–402
Loras, Jean Mathias Pierre, Aug. 30, 1792–Feb. 19, 1858.
Vol. 6, Pt. 1–403
Lord, Asa Dearborn, June 17, 1816–Mar. 7, 1875.
Vol. 6, Pt. 1–403
Lord, Chester Sanders, Mar. 18, 1850–Aug. 1, 1933.
Supp. 1–509
Lord, Daniel, Sept. 23, 1795–Mar. 4, 1868.
Vol. 6, Pt. 1–404
Lord, David Nevins, Mar. 4, 1792–July 14, 1880.
Vol. 6, Pt. 1–405
Lord, Eleazar, Sept. 9, 1788–June 3, 1871.
Vol. 6, Pt. 1–405
Lord, Henry Curwen, Apr. 17, 1866–Sept. 15, 1925.
Vol. 6, Pt. 1–406

Lord, Herbert Mayhew, Dec. 6, 1859–June 2, 1930.
Vol. 6, Pt. 1–407
Lord, Jeremy. [See Redman, Benjamin Ray.]
Lord, John, Dec. 27, 1810–Dec. 15, 1894.
Vol. 6, Pt. 1–408
Lord, Nathan, Nov. 28, 1792–Sept. 9, 1870.
Vol. 6, Pt. 1–409
Lord, Otis Phillips, July 11, 1812–Mar. 13, 1884.
Vol. 6, Pt. 1–409
Lord, Pauline, Aug. 8, 1890–Oct. 11, 1950.
Supp. 4–503
Lord, William Paine, July 1, 1839–Feb. 17, 1911.
Vol. 6, Pt. 1–410
Lord, William Wilberforce, Oct. 28, 1819–Apr. 22, 1907.
Vol. 6, Pt. 1–410
Loree, Leonor Fresnel, Apr. 23, 1858–Sept. 6, 1940.
Supp. 2–391
Lorillard, Pierre, Oct. 13, 1833–July 7, 1901.
Vol. 6, Pt. 1–411
Lorimer, George Claude, June 4, 1838–Sept. 7, 1904.
Vol. 6, Pt. 1–412
Lorimer, George Horace, Oct. 6, 1867–Oct. 22, 1937.
Supp. 2–393
Lorimer, William, Apr. 27, 1861–Sept. 13, 1934.
Supp. 1–511
Lorimier, Pierre Louis, March 1748–June 26, 1812.
Vol. 6, Pt. 1–413
Loring, Charles Harding, Dec. 26, 1828–Feb. 5, 1907.
Vol. 6, Pt. 1–413
Loring, Charles Morgridge, Nov. 13, 1832–Mar. 18, 1922.
Vol. 6, Pt. 1–414
Loring, Edward Greely, Sept. 28, 1837–Apr. 23, 1888.
Vol. 6, Pt. 1–415
Loring, Ellis Gray, Apr. 14, 1803–May 24, 1858.
Vol. 6, Pt. 1–416
Loring, Frederick Wadsworth, Dec. 12, 1848–Nov. 5, 1871.
Vol. 6, Pt. 1–417
Loring, George Bailey, Nov. 8, 1817–Sept. 14, 1891.
Vol. 6, Pt. 1–417
Loring, Joshua, Aug. 3, 1716–October 1781.
Vol. 6, Pt. 1–418
Loring, Joshua, Nov. 1, 1744–August 1789.
Vol. 6, Pt. 1–419
Loring, William Wing, Dec. 4, 1818–Dec. 30, 1886.
Vol. 6, Pt. 1–420
Lorre, Peter, June 26, 1904–Mar. 23, 1964.
Supp. 7–478
Loskiel, George Henry, Nov. 7, 1740–Feb. 23, 1814.
Vol. 6, Pt. 1–421
Lossing, Benson John, Feb. 12, 1813–June 3, 1891.
Vol. 6, Pt. 1–421
Lothrop, Alice Louise Higgins, May 28, 1870–Sept. 2, 1920.
Vol. 6, Pt. 1–422
Lothrop, Amy. [See Warner, Anna Bartlett, 1820–1915.]
Lothrop, Daniel, Aug. 11, 1831–Mar. 18, 1892.
Vol. 6, Pt. 1–423
Lothrop, George Van Ness, Aug. 8, 1817–July 12, 1897.
Vol. 6, Pt. 1–424
Lothrop, Harriett Mulford Stone, June 22, 1844–Aug. 2, 1924. Vol. 6, Pt. 1–424
Lothropp, John, 1584–Nov. 8, 1653.
Vol. 6, Pt. 1–425
Lotka, Alfred James, Mar. 2, 1880–Dec. 5, 1949.
Supp. 4–505
Lotta. [See Crabtree, Charlotte, 1847–1924.]
Loucks, Henry Langford, May 24, 1846–Dec. 29, 1928.
Vol. 6, Pt. 1–426
Loudon, Samuel, c. 1727–Feb. 24, 1813.
Vol. 6, Pt. 1–427
Loudoun, John Campbell, Fourth Earl of, May 5, 1705–Apr. 27, 1782. Vol. 6, Pt. 1–428
Loughridge, Robert McGill, Dec. 24, 1809–July 8, 1900.
Vol. 6, Pt. 1–428
Louis, Morris, Nov. 28, 1912–Sept. 7, 1962.
Supp. 7–479
Lounsbury, Thomas Raynesford, Jan. 1, 1838–Apr. 9, 1915.
Vol. 6, Pt. 1–429
Love, Alfred Henry, Sept. 7, 1830–June 29, 1913.
Vol. 6, Pt. 1–431
Love, Emanuel King, July 27, 1850–Apr. 24, 1900.
Vol. 6, Pt. 1–432
Love, Robertus Donnell, Jan. 6, 1867–May 7, 1930.
Vol. 6, Pt. 1–432

Lovejoy, Arthur Oncken, Oct. 10, 1873–Dec. 30, 1962.
Supp. 7–480
Lovejoy, Asa Lawrence, Mar. 14, 1808–Sept. 10, 1882.
Vol. 6, Pt. 1–433
Lovejoy, Elijah Parish, Nov. 9, 1802–Nov. 7, 1837.
Vol. 6, Pt. 1–434
Lovejoy, Owen, Jan. 6, 1811–Mar. 25, 1864.
Vol. 6, Pt. 1–435
Lovejoy, Owen Reed, Sept. 9, 1866–June 29, 1961.
Supp. 7–483
Lovelace, Francis, c. 1621–1675.
Vol. 6, Pt. 1–436
Loveland, William Austin Hamilton, May 30, 1826–Dec. 17, 1894. Vol. 6, Pt. 1–437
Lovell, James, Oct. 31, 1737–July 14, 1814.
Vol. 6, Pt. 1–438
Lovell, John, Apr. 1, 1710–1778.
Vol. 6, Pt. 1–439
Lovell, John Epy, Apr. 23, 1795–May 3, 1892.
Vol. 6, Pt. 1–440
Lovell, Joseph, Dec. 22, 1788–Oct. 17, 1836.
Vol. 6, Pt. 1–440
Lovell, Mansfield, Oct. 20, 1822–June 1, 1884.
Vol. 6, Pt. 1–441
Loveman, Amy, May 16, 1881–Dec. 11, 1955.
Supp. 5–439
Lovering, Joseph, Dec. 25, 1813–Jan. 18, 1892.
Vol. 6, Pt. 1–442
Lovett, Robert Morss, Dec. 25, 1870–Feb. 8, 1956.
Supp. 6–391
Lovett, Robert Scott, June 22, 1860–June 19, 1932.
Supp. 1–513
Lovett, Robert Williamson, Nov. 18, 1859–July 2, 1924.
Vol. 6, Pt. 1–443
Lovewell, John, Oct. 14, 1691–May 8, 1725.
Vol. 6, Pt. 1–444
Low, Abiel Abbot, Feb. 7, 1811–Jan. 7, 1893.
Vol. 6, Pt. 1–444
Low, Frederick Ferdinand, June 30, 1828–July 21, 1894.
Vol. 6, Pt. 1–445
Low, Isaac, Apr. 13, 1735–July 25, 1791.
Vol. 6, Pt. 1–446
Low, John Gardner, Jan. 10, 1835–Nov. 10, 1907.
Vol. 6, Pt. 1–447
Low, Juliette Gordon, Oct. 31, 1860–Jan. 17, 1927.
Vol. 6, Pt. 1–447
Low, Nicholas, Mar. 30, 1739–Nov. 15, 1826.
Vol. 6, Pt. 1–448
Low, Seth, Jan. 18, 1850–Sept. 17, 1916.
Vol. 6, Pt. 1–449
Low, Will Hicok, May 31, 1853–Nov. 27, 1932.
Supp. 1–513
Lowden, Frank Orren, Jan. 26, 1861–Mar. 20, 1943.
Supp. 3–467
Lowe, Charles, Nov. 18, 1828–June 20, 1874.
Vol. 6, Pt. 1–450
Lowe, Ralph Phillips, Nov. 27, 1805–Dec. 22, 1883.
Vol. 6, Pt. 1–451
Lowe, Thaddeus Sobieski Coulincourt, Aug. 20, 1832–Jan. 16, 1913. Vol. 6, Pt. 1–452
Lowell, Abbott Lawrence, Dec. 13, 1856–Jan. 6, 1943.
Supp. 3–468
Lowell, Amy, Feb. 9, 1874–May 12, 1925.
Vol. 6, Pt. 1–453
Lowell, Edward Jackson, Oct. 18, 1845–May 11, 1894.
Vol. 6, Pt. 1–455
Lowell, Francis Cabot, Apr. 7, 1775–Aug. 10, 1817.
Vol. 6, Pt. 1–456
Lowell, Guy, Aug. 6, 1870–Feb. 4, 1927.
Vol. 6, Pt. 1–457
Lowell, James Russell, Feb. 22, 1819–Aug. 12, 1891.
Vol. 6, Pt. 1–458
Lowell, John, June 17, 1743–May 6, 1802.
Vol. 6, Pt. 1–464
Lowell, John, Oct. 6, 1769–Mar. 12, 1840.
Vol. 6, Pt. 1–465
Lowell, John, May 11, 1799–Mar. 4, 1836.
Vol. 6, Pt. 1–466
Lowell, John, Oct. 18, 1824–May 14, 1897.
Vol. 6, Pt. 1–466
Lowell, Josephine Shaw, Dec. 16, 1843–Oct. 12, 1905.
Vol. 6, Pt. 1–467

Lowell, Percival, Mar. 13, 1855–Nov. 12, 1916.
Vol. 6, Pt. 1–468
Lowell, Robert Traill Spence, Oct. 8, 1816–Sept. 12, 1891.
Vol. 6, Pt. 1–470
Lower, William Edgar, May 6, 1867–June 17, 1948.
Supp. 4–507
Lowery, Woodbury, Feb. 17, 1853–Apr. 11, 1906.
Vol. 6, Pt. 1–470
Lowes, John Livingston, Dec. 20, 1867–Aug. 15, 1945.
Supp. 3–474
Lowie, Robert Harry, June 12, 1883–Sept. 21, 1957.
Supp. 6–392
Lowndes, Lloyd, Feb. 21, 1845–Jan. 8, 1905.
Vol. 6, Pt. 1–471
Lowndes, Rawlins, January 1721–Aug. 24, 1800.
Vol. 6, Pt. 1–472
Lowndes, William, Feb. 11, 1782–Oct. 27, 1822.
Vol. 6, Pt. 1–473
Lowrey, Mark Perrin, Dec. 30, 1828–Feb. 27, 1885.
Vol. 6, Pt. 1–474
Lowrie, James Walter, Sept. 16, 1856–Jan. 26, 1930.
Vol. 6, Pt. 1–475
Lowrie, Walter, Dec. 10, 1784–Dec. 14, 1868.
Vol. 6, Pt. 1–476
Lowry, Hiram Harrison, May 29, 1843–Jan. 13, 1924.
Vol. 6, Pt. 1–476
Lowry, Robert, Mar. 10, 1830–Jan. 19, 1910.
Vol. 6, Pt. 1–477
Lowry, Thomas, Feb. 27, 1843–Feb. 4, 1909.
Vol. 6, Pt. 1–477
Loy, Matthias, Mar. 17, 1828–Jan. 26, 1915.
Vol. 6, Pt. 1–478
Loyd, Samuel, Jan. 31, 1841–Apr. 10, 1911.
Vol. 6, Pt. 1–479
Lozier, Clemence Sophia Harned, Dec. 11, 1813–Apr. 26, 1888. Vol. 6, Pt. 1–480
Lubbock, Francis Richard, Oct. 16, 1815–June 22, 1905.
Vol. 6, Pt. 1–480
Lubin, David, June 10, 1849–Jan. 1, 1919.
Vol. 6, Pt. 1–481
Lubitsch, Ernst, Jan. 29, 1892–Nov. 30, 1947.
Supp. 4–508
Lucas, Anthony Francis, Sept. 9, 1855–Sept. 2, 1921.
Vol. 6, Pt. 1–482
Lucas, Daniel Bedinger, Mar. 16, 1836–July 28, 1909.
Vol. 6, Pt. 1–483
Lucas, Eliza. [See Pinckney, Eliza Lucas, 1722–1793.]
Lucas, Frederic Augustus, Mar. 25, 1852–Feb. 9, 1929.
Vol. 6, Pt. 1–484
Lucas, James H., Nov. 12, 1800–Nov. 9, 1873.
Vol. 6, Pt. 1–484
Lucas, John Baptiste Charles, Aug. 14, 1758–Aug. 29, 1842.
Vol. 6, Pt. 1–485
Lucas, Jonathan, 1754–Apr. 1, 1821.
Vol. 6, Pt. 1–486
Lucas, Jonathan, 1775–Dec. 29, 1832.
Vol. 6, Pt. 1–487
Lucas, Robert, Apr. 1, 1781–Feb. 7, 1853.
Vol. 6, Pt. 1–487
Lucas, Scott Wike, Feb. 19, 1892–Feb. 22, 1968.
Supp. 8–391
Luce, Henry Robinson, Apr. 3, 1898–Feb. 28, 1967.
Supp. 8–392
Luce, Henry Winters, Sept. 24, 1868–Dec. 8, 1941.
Supp. 3–476
Luce, Stephen Bleecker, Mar. 25, 1827–July 28, 1917.
Vol. 6, Pt. 1–488
Luchese, Thomas, 1899[?]–July 13, 1967.
Supp. 8–396
Luciano, Charles ("Lucky"), Nov. 11, 1897[?]–Jan. 26, 1962.
Supp. 7–484
Luckenbach, J(ohn) Lewis, Nov. 19, 1883–July 4, 1951.
Supp. 5–440
Ludeling, John Theodore, Jan. 27, 1827–Jan. 21, 1891.
Vol. 6, Pt. 1–489
Ludlow, Daniel, Aug. 2, 1750–Sept. 26, 1814.
Vol. 6, Pt. 1–490
Ludlow, Fitz Hugh, Sept. 11, 1836–Sept. 12, 1870.
Vol. 6, Pt. 1–491
Ludlow, Gabriel George, Apr. 16, 1736–Feb. 12, 1808.
Vol. 6, Pt. 1–491
Ludlow, George Duncan, 1734–Nov. 13, 1808.
Vol. 6, Pt. 1–492

Ludlow, Noah Miller, July 3, 1795–Jan. 9, 1886.
Vol. 6, Pt. 1–493
Ludlow, Roger, fl. 1590–1664.
Vol. 6, Pt. 1–493
Ludlow, Thomas William, June 14, 1795–July 17, 1878.
Vol. 6, Pt. 1–494
Ludlow, William, Nov. 27, 1843–Aug. 30, 1901.
Vol. 6, Pt. 1–495
Ludlowe, Roger. [See Ludlow, Roger, fl. 1590–1664.]
Ludwell, Philip, fl. 1660–1704.
Vol. 6, Pt. 1–496
Ludwick, Christopher, Oct. 17, 1720–June 17, 1801.
Vol. 6, Pt. 1–497
Luelling, Henderson, Apr. 23, 1809–Dec. 28, 1878.
Vol. 6, Pt. 1–498
Lufbery, Raoul Gervais Victor, Mar. 21, 1885–May 19, 1918.
Vol. 6, Pt. 1–499
Lugosi, Bela, Oct. 30, 1882–Aug. 16, 1956.
Supp. 6–394
Luhan, Mabel Dodge, Feb. 26, 1879–Aug. 13, 1962.
Supp. 7–485
Lukeman, Henry Augustus, Jan. 28, 1871–Apr. 3, 1935.
Supp. 1–515
Lukens, Rebecca Webb Pennock, Jan. 6, 1794–Dec. 10, 1854.
Vol. 6, Pt. 1–499
Luks, George Benjamin, Aug. 13, 1867–Oct. 29, 1933.
Supp. 1–516
Lull, Edward Phelps, Feb. 20, 1836–Mar. 5, 1887.
Vol. 6, Pt. 1–500
Lumbrozo, Jacob, fl. 1656–1665.
Vol. 6, Pt. 1–501
Lummis, Charles Fletcher, Mar. 1, 1859–Nov. 25, 1928.
Vol. 6, Pt. 1–501
Lumpkin, Joseph Henry, Dec. 23, 1799–June 4, 1867.
Vol. 6, Pt. 1–502
Lumpkin, Wilson, Jan. 14, 1783–Dec. 28, 1870.
Vol. 6, Pt. 1–503
Luna y Arellano, Tristan de, fl. 1530–1561.
Vol. 6, Pt. 1–504
Lunceford, James Melvin ("Jimmie"), June 6, 1902–July 12, 1947. Supp. 4–509
Lundeberg, Harry, Mar. 25, 1901–Jan. 28, 1957.
Supp. 6–396
Lundeen, Ernest, Aug. 4, 1878–Aug. 31, 1940.
Supp. 2–394
Lundie, John, Dec. 14, 1857–Feb. 9, 1931.
Vol. 6, Pt. 1–505
Lundin, Carl Axel Robert, Jan. 13, 1851–Nov. 28, 1915.
Vol. 6, Pt. 1–505
Lundy, Benjamin, Jan. 4, 1789–Aug. 22, 1839.
Vol. 6, Pt. 1–506
Lunn, George Richard, June 23, 1873–Nov. 27, 1948.
Supp. 4–511
Lunt, George, Dec. 31, 1803–May 16, 1885.
Vol. 6, Pt. 1–507
Lunt, Orrington, Dec. 24, 1815–Apr. 5, 1897.
Vol. 6, Pt. 1–508
Lurton, Horace Harmon, Feb. 26, 1844–July 12, 1914.
Vol. 6, Pt. 1–509
Lusk, Graham, Feb. 15, 1866–July 18, 1932.
Supp. 1–517
Lusk, William Thompson, May 23, 1838–June 12, 1897.
Vol. 6, Pt. 1–510
Luther, Seth, fl. 1817–1846.
Vol. 6, Pt. 1–511
Lutkin, Peter Christian, Mar. 27, 1858–Dec. 27, 1931.
Vol. 6, Pt. 1–511
Lutz, Frank Eugene, Sept. 15, 1879–Nov. 27, 1943.
Supp. 3–477
Lyall, James, Sept. 13, 1836–Aug. 23, 1901.
Vol. 6, Pt. 1–512
Lybrand, William Mitchell, Aug. 14, 1867–Nov. 19, 1960.
Supp. 6–397
Lydenberg, Harry Miller, Nov. 18, 1874–Apr. 16, 1960.
Supp. 6–398
Lydston, George Frank, Mar. 3, 1857–Mar. 14, 1923.
Vol. 6, Pt. 1–513
Lyman, Albert Josiah, Dec. 24, 1845–Aug. 22, 1915.
Vol. 6, Pt. 1–514
Lyman, Benjamin Smith, Dec. 11, 1835–Aug. 30, 1920.
Vol. 6, Pt. 1–514
Lyman, Chester Smith, Jan. 13, 1814–Jan. 29, 1890.
Vol. 6, Pt. 1–515

Lyman, Eugene William, Apr. 4, 1872–Mar. 15, 1948.
Supp. 4–512
Lyman, Joseph Bardwell, Oct. 6, 1829–Jan. 28, 1872.
Vol. 6, Pt. 1–516
Lyman, Phineas, 1715–Sept. 10, 1774.
Vol. 6, Pt. 1–517
Lyman, Theodore, Feb. 20, 1792–July 18, 1849.
Vol. 6, Pt. 1–518
Lyman, Theodore, Aug. 23, 1833–Sept. 9, 1897.
Vol. 6, Pt. 1–519
Lyman, Theodore, Nov. 23, 1874–Oct. 11, 1954.
Supp. 5–441
Lynch, Anna Charlotte. [See Botta, Anna Charlotte Lynch, 1815–1891.]
Lynch, Charles, 1736–Oct. 29, 1796.
Vol. 6, Pt. 1–519
Lynch, James Daniel, Jan. 6, 1836–July 19, 1903.
Vol. 6, Pt. 1–520
Lynch, James Mathew, Jan. 11, 1867–July 16, 1930.
Vol. 6, Pt. 1–521
Lynch, John Roy, Sept. 10, 1847–Nov. 2, 1939.
Supp. 2–395
Lynch, Patrick Neeson, Mar. 10, 1817–Feb. 26, 1882.
Vol. 6, Pt. 1–521
Lynch, Robert Clyde, Sept. 8, 1880–May 12, 1931.
Vol. 6, Pt. 1–522
Lynch, Thomas, 1727–December 1776.
Vol. 6, Pt. 1–523
Lynch, Thomas, Aug. 5, 1749–1779.
Vol. 6, Pt. 1–523
Lynch, William Francis, Apr. 1, 1801–Oct. 17, 1865.
Vol. 6, Pt. 1–524
Lynd, Robert Staughton, Sept. 26, 1892–Nov. 1, 1970.
Supp. 8–398
Lynde, Benjamin, Oct. 5, 1700–Oct. 5, 1781.
Vol. 6, Pt. 1–525
Lynde, Francis, Nov. 12, 1856–May 16, 1930.
Vol. 6, Pt. 1–526
Lynds, Elam, 1784–Jan. 8, 1855.
Vol. 6, Pt. 1–527
Lyon, Caleb, Dec. 8, 1821–Sept 7, 1875.
Vol. 6, Pt. 1–527
Lyon, David Gordon, May 24, 1852–Dec. 4, 1935.
Supp. 1–518
Lyon, David Willard, May 13, 1870–Mar. 16, 1949.
Supp. 4–514
Lyon, Francis Strother, Feb. 25, 1800–Dec. 31, 1882.
Vol. 6, Pt. 1–528
Lyon, Harris Merton, Dec. 22, 1883–June 2, 1916.
Vol. 6, Pt. 1–529
Lyon, James, July 1, 1735–Oct. 12, 1794.
Vol. 6, Pt. 1–530
Lyon, James Benjamin, Apr. 21, 1821–Apr. 16, 1909.
Vol. 6, Pt. 1–530
Lyon, Mary, Feb. 28, 1797–Mar. 5, 1849.
Vol. 6, Pt. 1–531
Lyon, Matthew, July 14, 1750–Aug. 1, 1822.
Vol. 6, Pt. 1–532
Lyon, Nathaniel, July 14, 1818–Aug. 10, 1861.
Vol. 6, Pt. 1–534
Lyon, Theodatus Timothy, Jan. 23, 1813–Feb. 6, 1900.
Vol. 6, Pt. 1–535
Lyon, William Penn, Oct. 28, 1822–Apr. 4, 1913.
Vol. 6, Pt. 1–536
Lyons, Peter, 1734/35–July 30, 1809.
Vol. 6, Pt. 1–536
Lyster, Henry Francis Le Hunte, Nov. 8, 1837–Oct. 3, 1894.
Vol. 6, Pt. 1–537
Lytle, William Haines, Nov. 2, 1826–Sept. 20, 1863.
Vol. 6, Pt. 1–538
Lyttelton, William Henry, Dec. 24, 1724–Sept. 14, 1808.
Vol. 6, Pt. 1–538

Maas, Anthony J., Aug. 23, 1858–Feb. 20, 1927.
Vol. 6, Pt. 1–539
Mabery, Charles Frederic, Jan. 13, 1850–June 26, 1927.
Vol. 6, Pt. 1–540
Mabie, Hamilton Wright, Dec. 13, 1845–Dec. 31, 1916.
Vol. 6, Pt. 1–540
McAdams, Clark, Jan. 29, 1874–Nov. 29, 1935.
Supp. 1–519
McAdie, Alexander George, Aug. 4, 1863–Nov. 1, 1943.
Supp. 3–478

McAdoo, William Gibbs, Oct. 31, 1863–Feb. 1, 1941.
Supp. 3–479
McAfee, John Armstrong, Dec. 12, 1831–June 12, 1890.
Vol. 6, Pt. 1–541
McAfee, Robert Breckinridge, Feb. 18, 1784–Mar. 12, 1849.
Vol. 6, Pt. 1–542
Macalester, Charles, Apr. 5, 1765–Aug. 29, 1832.
Vol. 6, Pt. 1–543
Macalester, Charles, Feb. 17, 1798–Dec. 9, 1873.
Vol. 6, Pt. 1–543
McAlexander, Ulysses Grant, Aug. 30, 1864–Sept. 18, 1936.
Supp. 2–396
MacAlister, James, Apr. 26, 1840–Dec. 11, 1913.
Vol. 6, Pt. 1–544
McAllister, Charles Albert, May 29, 1867–Jan. 6, 1932.
Vol. 6, Pt. 1–545
McAllister, Hall, Feb. 9, 1826–Dec. 1, 1888.
Vol. 6, Pt. 1–545
McAllister, Matthew Hall, Nov. 26, 1800–Dec. 19, 1865.
Vol. 6, Pt. 1–546
McAllister, Samuel Ward, December 1827–Jan. 31, 1895.
Vol. 6, Pt. 1–547
McAlpine, William Jarvis, Apr. 30, 1812–Feb. 16, 1890.
Vol. 6, Pt. 1–548
McAnally, David Rice, Feb. 17, 1810–July 11, 1895.
Vol. 6, Pt. 1–549
McAndrew, William, Aug. 20, 1863–June 27, 1937.
Supp. 2–398
MacArthur, Arthur, June 2, 1845–Sept. 5, 1912.
Supp. 1–521
MacArthur, Charles Gordon, Nov. 5, 1895–Apr. 21, 1956.
Supp. 6–400
MacArthur, Douglas, Jan. 26, 1880–Apr. 5, 1964.
Supp. 7–487
McArthur, Duncan, Jan. 14, 1772–Apr. 28, 1839.
Vol. 6, Pt. 1–549
McArthur, John, May 13, 1823–Jan. 8, 1890.
Vol. 6, Pt. 1–550
McArthur, John, Nov. 17, 1826–May 15, 1906.
Vol. 6, Pt. 1–551
MacArthur, Robert Stuart, July 31, 1841–Feb. 23, 1923.
Vol. 6, Pt. 1–552
McArthur, William Pope, Apr. 2, 1814–Dec. 23, 1850.
Vol. 6, Pt. 1–552
Macauley, Edward Yorke. [See McCauley, Edward Yorke, 1827–1894.]
McAuley, Jeremiah, c. 1839–Sept. 18, 1884.
Vol. 6, Pt. 1–553
McAuley, Thomas, Apr. 21, 1778–May 11, 1862.
Vol. 6, Pt. 1–554
McBain, Howard Lee, July 20, 1880–May 7, 1936.
Supp. 2–399
McBride, F(rancis) Scott, July 29, 1872–Apr. 23, 1955.
Supp. 5–442
McBride, Henry, July 25, 1867–Mar. 31, 1962.
Supp. 7–493
McBryde, John McLaren, Jan. 1, 1841–Mar. 20, 1923.
Vol. 6, Pt. 1–554
McBurney, Charles, Feb. 17, 1845–Nov. 7, 1913.
Vol. 6, Pt. 1–555
McBurney, Robert Ross, Mar. 31, 1837–Dec. 27, 1898.
Vol. 6, Pt. 1–556
McCabe, Charles Cardwell, Oct. 11, 1836–Dec. 19, 1906.
Vol. 6, Pt. 1–557
McCabe, John Collins, Nov. 12, 1810–Feb. 26, 1875.
Vol. 6, Pt. 1–558
McCabe, William Gordon, Aug. 4, 1841–June 1, 1920.
Vol. 6, Pt. 1–558
McCaffrey, John, Sept. 6, 1806–Sept. 26, 1881.
Vol. 6, Pt. 1–559
McCaine, Alexander, c. 1768–June 1, 1856.
Vol. 6, Pt. 1–560
McCaleb, Theodore Howard, Feb. 10, 1810–Apr. 29, 1864.
Vol. 6, Pt. 1–560
McCall, Edward Rutledge, Aug. 6, 1790–July 31, 1853.
Vol. 6, Pt. 1–561
McCall, John Augustine, Mar. 2, 1849–Feb. 18, 1906.
Vol. 6, Pt. 1–562
McCall, Samuel Walker, Feb. 28, 1851–Nov. 4, 1923.
Vol. 6, Pt. 1–562
McCalla, Bowman Hendry, June 19, 1844–May 6, 1910.
Vol. 6, Pt. 1–564

McCalla, William Latta, Nov. 25, 1788–Oct. 12, 1859.
Vol. 6, Pt. 1–564
McCallum, Daniel Craig, Jan. 21, 1815–Dec. 27, 1878.
Vol. 6, Pt. 1–565
MacCallum, William George, Apr. 18, 1874–Feb. 3, 1944.
Supp. 3–482
MacCameron, Robert, Jan. 14, 1866–Dec. 29, 1912.
Vol. 6, Pt. 1–566
McCann, Alfred Watterson, Jan. 9, 1879–Jan. 19, 1931.
Vol. 6, Pt. 1–567
McCann, William Penn, May 4, 1830–Jan. 15, 1906.
Vol. 6, Pt. 1–567
McCardell, Claire, May 24, 1905–Mar. 22, 1958.
Supp. 6–401
McCarran, Patrick Anthony, Aug. 8, 1876–Sept. 28, 1954.
Supp. 5–443
McCarren, Patrick Henry, June 18, 1847–Oct. 23, 1909.
Vol. 6, Pt. 1–568
McCarroll, James, Aug. 3, 1814–Apr. 10, 1892.
Vol. 6, Pt. 1–569
McCartee, Divie Bethune, Jan. 13, 1820–July 17, 1900.
Vol. 6, Pt. 1–569
McCarthy, Charles, June 29, 1873–Mar. 26, 1921.
Vol. 6, Pt. 1–570
McCarthy, Charles Louis (Clem), Sept. 9, 1882–June 4, 1962.
Supp. 7–494
McCarthy, Daniel Joseph, June 22, 1874–Oct. 9, 1958.
Supp. 6–402
McCarthy, Joseph Raymond, Nov. 14, 1908–May 2, 1957.
Supp. 6–404
McCartney, Washington, Aug. 24, 1812–July 15, 1856.
Vol. 6, Pt. 1–571
McCauley, Charles Stewart, Feb. 3, 1793–May 21, 1869.
Vol. 6, Pt. 1–572
MacCauley, Clay, May 8, 1843–Nov. 15, 1925.
Vol. 6, Pt. 1–572
McCauley, Edward Yorke, Nov. 2, 1827–Sept. 14, 1894.
Vol. 6, Pt. 1–573
McCauley, Mary Ludwig Hays, Oct. 13, 1754–Jan. 22, 1832.
Vol. 6, Pt. 1–574
McCausland, John, Sept. 13, 1836–Jan. 22, 1927.
Vol. 6, Pt. 1–575
McCaw, James Brown, July 12, 1823–Aug. 13, 1906.
Vol. 6, Pt. 1–575
McCawley, Charles Grymes, Jan. 29, 1827–Oct. 13, 1891.
Vol. 6, Pt. 1–576
McCawley, Charles Laurie, Aug. 24, 1865–Apr. 29, 1935.
Supp. 1–522
McCay, Charles Francis, Mar. 8, 1810–Mar. 13, 1889.
Vol. 6, Pt. 1–577
McCay, Henry Kent, Jan. 8, 1820–July 30, 1886.
Vol. 6, Pt. 1–578
McClain, Emlin, Nov. 26, 1851–May 25, 1915.
Vol. 6, Pt. 1–578
McClatchy, Charles Kenny, Nov. 1, 1858–Apr. 27, 1936.
Supp. 2–400
McClellan, George, Dec. 23, 1796–May 9, 1847.
Vol. 6, Pt. 1–579
McClellan, George, Oct. 29, 1849–Mar. 29, 1913.
Vol. 6, Pt. 1–580
McClellan, George Brinton, Dec. 3, 1826–Oct. 29, 1885.
Vol. 6, Pt. 1–581
McClellan, George Brinton, Nov. 23, 1865–Nov. 30, 1940.
Supp. 2–401
McClellan, Henry Brainerd, Oct. 17, 1840–Oct. 1, 1904.
Vol. 6, Pt. 1–585
McClellan, Robert, 1770–Nov. 22, 1815.
Vol. 6, Pt. 1–586
McClelland, Robert, Aug. 1, 1807–Aug. 30, 1880.
Vol. 6, Pt. 1–586
McClenahan, Howard, Oct. 19, 1872–Dec. 17, 1935.
Supp. 1–522
McClernand, John Alexander, May 30, 1812–Sept. 20, 1900.
Vol. 6, Pt. 1–587
McClintic, Guthrie, Aug. 6, 1893–Oct. 29, 1961.
Supp. 7–495
McClintock, Emory, Sept. 19, 1840–July 10, 1916.
Vol. 6, Pt. 1–588
McClintock, James Harvey, Feb. 23, 1864–May 10, 1934.
Supp. 1–523
M'Clintock, John, Oct. 27, 1814–Mar. 4, 1870.
Vol. 6, Pt. 1–589

McClintock, Oliver, Oct. 20, 1839–Oct 10, 1922.
Vol. 6, Pt. 1–590
McCloskey, John, Mar. 10, 1810–Oct. 10, 1885.
Vol. 6, Pt. 1–591
McCloskey, William George, Nov. 10, 1823–Sept. 17, 1909.
Vol. 6, Pt. 1–592
McClung, Clarence Erwin, Apr. 5, 1870–Jan. 17, 1946.
Supp. 4–515
McClure, Alexander Kelly, Jan. 9, 1828–June 6, 1909.
Vol. 6, Pt. 1–593
McClure, Alexander Wilson, May 8, 1808–September 1865.
Vol. 6, Pt. 1–594
McClure, George, c. 1770–Aug. 16, 1851.
Vol. 6, Pt. 1–594
McClure, Robert Alexis, Mar. 4, 1897–Jan. 1, 1957.
Supp. 6–406
McClure, Samuel Sidney, Feb. 17, 1857–Mar. 21, 1949.
Supp. 4–516
McClurg, Alexander Caldwell, Sept. 9, 1832–Apr. 15, 1901.
Vol. 6, Pt. 1–595
McClurg, James, c. 1746–July 9, 1823.
Vol. 6, Pt. 1–596
McClurg, Joseph Washington, Feb. 22, 1818–Dec. 2, 1900.
Vol. 6, Pt. 1–597
McComas, Louis Emory, Oct. 28, 1846–Nov. 10, 1907.
Vol. 6, Pt. 1–598
McComb, John, Oct. 17, 1763–May 25, 1853.
Vol. 6, Pt. 1–599
McConnel, John Ludlum, Nov. 11, 1826–Jan. 17, 1862.
Vol. 6, Pt. 1–600
McConnell, Francis John, Aug. 18, 1871–Aug. 18, 1953.
Supp. 5–445
McConnell, Ira Welch, Oct. 17, 1871–Jan. 7, 1933.
Supp. 1–524
McCook, Alexander McDowell, April 22, 1831–June 12, 1903. Vol. 6, Pt. 1–600
McCook, Anson George, Oct. 10, 1835–Dec. 30, 1917.
Vol. 6, Pt. 1–601
McCook, Edward Moody, June 15, 1833–Sept. 9, 1909.
Vol. 6, Pt. 1–602
McCook, Henry Christopher, July 3, 1837–Oct. 31, 1911.
Vol. 6, Pt. 1–603
McCook, John James, Feb. 2, 1843–Jan. 9, 1927.
Vol. 6, Pt. 1–603
McCord, David James, January 1797–May 12, 1855.
Vol. 6, Pt. 1–604
McCord, James Bennett, Apr. 5, 1870–Oct. 5, 1950.
Supp. 4–519
McCord, Louisa Susanna Cheves, Dec. 3, 1810–Nov. 23, 1879. Vol. 6, Pt. 1–605
McCormack, John Francis, June 14, 1884–Sept. 16, 1945.
Supp. 3–483
McCormack, Joseph Nathaniel, Nov. 9, 1847–May 4, 1922.
Vol. 6, Pt. 1–606
McCormick, Anne Elizabeth O'Hare, May 16, 1882–May 29, 1954. Supp. 5–446
McCormick, Cyrus Hall, Feb. 15, 1809–May 13, 1884.
Vol. 6, Pt. 1–607
McCormick, Cyrus Hall, May 16, 1859–June 2, 1936.
Supp. 2–402
McCormick, Joseph Medill, May 16, 1877–Feb. 25, 1925.
Vol. 6, Pt. 1–609
McCormick, Leander James, Feb. 8, 1819–Feb. 20, 1900.
Vol. 6, Pt. 1–610
McCormick, Lynde Dupuy, Aug. 12, 1895–Aug. 16, 1956.
Supp. 6–407
McCormick, Medill. [See McCormick, Joseph Medill, 1877–1925.]
McCormick, Richard Cunningham, May 23, 1832–June 2, 1901. Vol. 6, Pt. 1–610
McCormick, Robert Sanderson, July 26, 1849–Apr. 16, 1919.
Vol. 6, Pt. 1–612
McCormick, Robert, June 8, 1780–July 4, 1846.
Vol. 6, Pt. 1–611
McCormick, Robert Rutherford, July 30, 1880–Apr. 1, 1955.
Supp. 5–448
McCormick, Ruth Hanna. [See Simms, Ruth Hanna McCormick.]
McCormick, Samuel Black, May 6, 1858–Apr. 18, 1928.
Vol. 6, Pt. 1–613
McCormick, Stephen, Aug. 26, 1784–Aug. 28, 1875.
Vol. 6, Pt. 1–614

McCosh, Andrew James, Mar. 15, 1858–Dec. 2, 1908.
    Vol. 6, Pt. 1–614
McCosh, James, Apr. 1, 1811–Nov. 16, 1894.
    Vol. 6, Pt. 1–615
McCoy, Eljiah, Mar. 27, 1843–Oct. 10, 1929.
    Vol. 6, Pt. 1–617
McCoy, Isaac, June 13, 1784–June 21, 1846.
    Vol. 6, Pt. 1–617
McCoy, Joseph Geating, Dec. 21, 1837–Oct. 19, 1915.
    Vol. 6, Pt. 1–618
MacCracken, Henry Mitchell, Sept. 28, 1840–Dec. 24, 1918.
    Vol. 6, Pt. 1–619
McCracken, Joan, Dec. 31, 1922–Nov. 1, 1961.
    Supp. 7–496
McCrady, Edward, Apr. 8, 1833–Nov. 1, 1903.
    Vol. 6, Pt. 2–1
McCrae, Thomas, Dec. 16, 1870–June 30, 1935.
    Supp. 1–525
McCrary, George Washington, Aug. 29, 1835–June 23, 1890.
    Vol. 6, Pt. 2–2
McCreary, James Bennett, July 8, 1838–Oct. 8, 1918.
    Vol. 6, Pt. 2–3
McCreery, Charles, June 13, 1785–Aug. 27, 1826.
    Vol. 6, Pt. 2–3
McCreery, James Work, July 13, 1849–Feb. 20, 1923.
    Vol. 6, Pt. 2–4
McCullagh, Joseph Burbridge, Nov. 1842–Dec. 31, 1896.
    Vol. 6, Pt. 2–5
McCullers, Carson, Feb. 19, 1917–Sept. 29, 1967.
    Supp. 8–399
McCulloch, Ben, Nov. 11, 1811–Mar. 7, 1862.
    Vol. 6, Pt. 2–5
McCulloch, Hugh, Dec. 7, 1808–May 24, 1895.
    Vol. 6, Pt. 2–6
McCulloch, Oscar Carleton, July 2, 1843–Dec. 10, 1891.
    Vol. 6, Pt. 2–8
McCullough, Ernest, May 22, 1867–Oct. 1, 1931.
    Vol. 6, Pt. 2–8
McCullough, John, Nov. 14, 1832–Nov. 8, 1885.
    Vol. 6, Pt. 2–9
McCullough, John Griffith, Sept. 16, 1835–May 29, 1915.
    Vol. 6, Pt. 2–10
McCumber, Porter James, Feb. 3, 1858–May 18, 1933.
    Supp. 1–525
MacCurdy, George Grant, Apr. 17, 1863–Nov. 15, 1947.
    Supp. 4–520
McCurdy, Richard Aldrich, Jan. 29, 1835–Mar. 6, 1916.
    Vol. 6, Pt. 2–11
McCutcheon, George Barr, July 26, 1866–Oct. 23, 1928.
    Vol. 6, Pt. 2–12
McDaniel, Hattie, June 10, 1898–Oct. 26, 1952.
    Supp. 5–451
McDaniel, Henry Dickerson, Sept. 4, 1836–July 25, 1926.
    Vol. 6, Pt. 2–13
McDill, James Wilson, Mar. 4, 1834–Feb. 28, 1894.
    Vol. 6, Pt. 2–14
MacDonald, Betty, Mar. 26, 1908–Feb. 7, 1958.
    Supp. 6–408
Macdonald, Charles Blair, Nov. 14, 1856–Apr. 21, 1939.
    Supp. 2–404
McDonald, Charles James, July 9, 1793–Dec. 16, 1860.
    Vol. 6, Pt. 2–15
McDonald, James Grover, Nov. 29, 1886–Sept. 26, 1964.
    Supp. 7–497
MacDonald, James Wilson Alexander, Aug. 25, 1824–Aug.
    14, 1908. Vol. 6, Pt. 2–16
MacDonald, Jeanette Anna, June 18, 1907–Jan. 14, 1965.
    Supp. 7–499
McDonald, John Bartholomew, Nov. 7, 1844–Mar. 17, 1911.
    Vol. 6, Pt. 2–16
McDonald, Joseph Ewing, Aug. 29, 1819–June 21, 1891.
    Vol. 6, Pt. 2–17
MacDonald, Ranald, Feb. 3, 1824–Aug. 26, 1894.
    Vol. 6, Pt. 2–18
McDonogh, John, Dec. 29, 1779–Oct. 26, 1850.
    Vol. 6, Pt. 2–19
MacDonough, Thomas, Dec. 31, 1783–Nov. 10, 1825.
    Vol. 6, Pt. 2–19
McDougal, David Stockton, Sept. 27, 1809–Aug. 7, 1882.
    Vol. 6, Pt. 2–21
McDougall, Alexander, July or August 1732–June 9, 1786.
    Vol. 6, Pt. 2–21

McDougall, Alexander, Mar. 16, 1845–May 23, 1923.
    Vol. 6, Pt. 2–22
McDougall, Frances Harriet. [See Green, Frances Harriet
    Whipple, 1805–1878.]
McDougall, William, June 22, 1871–Nov. 28, 1938.
    Supp. 2–405
McDowell, Charles, c. 1743–Mar. 31, 1815.
    Vol. 6, Pt. 2–23
MacDowell, Edward Alexander, Dec. 18, 1861–Jan. 23, 1908.
    Vol. 6, Pt. 2–24
McDowell, Ephraim, Nov. 11, 1771–June 25, 1830.
    Vol. 6, Pt. 2–27
McDowell, Irvin, Oct. 15, 1818–May 4, 1885.
    Vol. 6, Pt. 2–29
McDowell, James, Oct. 13, 1795–Aug. 24, 1851.
    Vol. 6, Pt. 2–30
McDowell, John, Feb. 11, 1751–Dec. 22, 1820.
    Vol. 6, Pt. 2–31
McDowell, John, Sept. 10, 1780–Feb. 13, 1863.
    Vol. 6, Pt. 2–32
McDowell, Joseph, Feb. 15, 1756–Aug. 11, 1801.
    Vol. 6, Pt. 2–33
MacDowell, Katherine Sherwood Bonner, Feb. 26, 1849–July
    22, 1883. Vol. 6, Pt. 2–33
McDowell, Mary Eliza, Nov. 30, 1854–Oct. 14, 1936.
    Supp. 2–407
McDowell, William Fraser, Feb. 4, 1858–Apr. 26, 1937.
    Supp. 2–409
McDuffie, George, Aug. 10, 1790–Mar. 11, 1851.
    Vol. 6, Pt. 2–34
McElrath, Thomas, May 1, 1807–June 6, 1888.
    Vol. 6, Pt. 2–36
McElroy, John, May 14, 1782–Sept. 12, 1877.
    Vol. 6, Pt. 2–36
McElroy, John, Aug. 25, 1846–Oct. 12, 1929.
    Vol. 6, Pt. 2–37
McElroy, Robert McNutt, Dec. 28, 1872–Jan. 16, 1959.
    Supp. 6–409
McElwaine, William Howe, Feb. 11, 1867–Jan. 10, 1908.
    Vol. 6, Pt. 2–38
McEnery, Samuel Douglas, May 28, 1837–June 28, 1910.
    Vol. 6, Pt. 2–39
McEntee, James Joseph, Sept. 9, 1884–Oct. 13, 1957.
    Supp. 6–411
McEntee, Jervis, July 14, 1828–Jan. 27, 1891.
    Vol. 6, Pt. 2–39
Macfadden, Bernarr, Aug. 16, 1868–Oct. 12, 1955.
    Supp. 5–452
McFadden, Louis Thomas, July 25, 1876–Oct. 1, 1936.
    Supp. 2–410
McFarland, George Bradley, Dec. 1, 1886–May 3, 1942.
    Supp. 3–485
McFarland, John Horace, Sept. 24, 1859–Oct. 2, 1948.
    Supp. 4–521
McFarland, John Thomas, Jan. 2, 1851–Dec. 22, 1913.
    Vol. 6, Pt. 2–40
McFarland, Samuel Gamble, Dec. 11, 1830–Apr. 25, 1897.
    Vol. 6, Pt. 2–41
McFarland, Thomas Bard, Apr. 19, 1828–Sept. 16, 1908.
    Vol. 6, Pt. 2–42
Macfarlane, Charles William, Nov. 5, 1850–May 15, 1931.
    Vol. 6, Pt. 2–42
Macfarlane, Robert, Apr. 23, 1815–Dec. 20, 1883.
    Vol. 6, Pt. 2–43
McFaul, James Augustine, June 6, 1850–June 16, 1917.
    Vol. 6, Pt. 2–44
McFee, William, June 15, 1881–July 2, 1966.
    Supp. 8–402
McFerrin, John Berry, June 15, 1807–May 10, 1887.
    Vol. 6, Pt. 2–44
MacGahan, Januarius Aloysius, June 12, 1844–June 9, 1878.
    Vol. 6, Pt. 2–45
McGarrah, Gates White, July 20, 1863–Nov. 5, 1940.
    Supp. 2–410
McGarvey, John William, Mar. 1, 1829–Oct. 6, 1911.
    Vol. 6, Pt. 2–46
McGee, William John, Apr. 17, 1853–Sept. 4, 1912.
    Vol. 6, Pt. 2–47
McGeehan, William O'Connell, Nov. 22, 1879–Nov. 29,
    1933. Supp. 1–526
McGhee, Charles McClung, Jan. 23, 1828–May 5, 1907.
    Vol. 6, Pt. 2–48

McGiffert, Arthur Cushman, Mar. 4, 1851–Feb. 25, 1933.
  Supp. 1–527
McGiffin, Philo Norton, Dec. 13, 1860–Feb. 11, 1897.
  Vol. 6, Pt. 2–48
McGill, John, Nov. 4, 1809–Jan. 14, 1872.
  Vol. 6, Pt. 2–49
McGill, Ralph Emerson, Feb. 5, 1898–Feb. 3, 1969.
  Supp. 8–403
McGillivray, Alexander, c. 1759–Feb. 17, 1793.
  Vol. 6, Pt. 2–50
McGilvary, Daniel, May 16, 1828–Aug. 22, 1911.
  Vol. 6, Pt. 2–51
McGivney, Michael Joseph, Aug. 12, 1852–Aug. 14, 1890.
  Vol. 6, Pt. 2–52
McGlothlin, William Joseph, Nov. 29, 1867–May 28, 1933.
  Supp. 1–529
McGlynn, Edward, Sept. 27, 1837–Jan. 7, 1900.
  Vol. 6, Pt. 2–53
McGovern, John, Feb. 18, 1850–Dec. 17, 1917.
  Vol. 6, Pt. 2–54
McGowan, Samuel, Oct. 9, 1819–Aug. 9, 1897.
  Vol. 6, Pt. 2–55
McGranery, James Patrick, July 8, 1895–Dec. 23, 1962.
  Supp. 7–500
McGrath, James, June 26, 1835–Jan. 12, 1898.
  Vol. 6, Pt. 2–55
McGrath, James Howard, Nov. 28, 1903–Sept. 2, 1966.
  Supp. 8–405
McGrath, Matthew J., Dec. 20, 1876–Jan. 29, 1941.
  Supp. 3–486
McGraw, James Herbert, Dec. 17, 1860–Feb. 21, 1948.
  Supp. 4–523
McGraw, John Harte, Oct. 4, 1850–June 23, 1910.
  Vol. 6, Pt. 2–55
McGraw, John Joseph, Apr. 7, 1873–Feb. 25, 1934.
  Supp. 1–529
McGready, James, c. 1758–February 1817.
  Vol. 6, Pt. 2–56
McGroarty, Susan. [See Julia, Sister, 1827–1901.]
McGuffey, William Holmes, Sept. 23, 1800–May 4, 1873.
  Vol. 6, Pt. 2–57
McGuire, Charles Bonaventure, Dec. 16, 1768–July 17, 1833.
  Vol. 6, Pt. 2–58
McGuire, Hunter Holmes, Oct. 11, 1835–Sept. 19, 1900.
  Vol. 6, Pt. 2–59
McGuire, Joseph Deakins, Nov. 26, 1842–Sept. 6, 1916.
  Vol. 6, Pt. 2–60
McHale, Kathryn, July 22, 1889–Oct. 8, 1956.
  Supp. 6–412
Machebeuf, Joseph Projectus, Aug. 11, 1812–July 10, 1889.
  Vol. 6, Pt. 2–61
Machen, John Gresham, July 28, 1881–Jan. 1, 1937.
  Supp. 2–411
McHenry, James, Nov. 16, 1753–May 3, 1816.
  Vol. 6, Pt. 2–62
McHenry, James, Dec. 20, 1785–July 21, 1845.
  Vol. 6, Pt. 2–63
McHugh, Rose John, July 11, 1881–Dec. 12, 1952.
  Supp. 5–454
McIlvaine, Charles Pettit, Jan. 18, 1799–Mar. 13, 1873.
  Vol. 6, Pt. 2–64
McIlwaine, Richard, May 28, 1834–Aug. 10, 1913.
  Vol. 6, Pt. 2–65
McIntire, Ross, Aug. 11, 1889–Dec. 8, 1959.
  Supp. 6–413
McIntire, Samuel, January 1757–Feb. 6, 1811.
  Vol. 6, Pt. 2–65
Macintosh, Douglas Clyde, Feb. 18, 1877–July 6, 1948.
  Supp. 4–524
McIntosh, John Baillie, June 6, 1829–June 29, 1888.
  Vol. 6, Pt. 2–69
McIntosh, Lachlan, Mar. 17, 1725–Feb. 20, 1806.
  Vol. 6, Pt. 2–69
McIntosh, William, c. 1775–May 1, 1825.
  Vol. 6, Pt. 2–70
McIntyre, Alfred Robert, Aug. 22, 1886–Nov. 28, 1948.
  Supp. 4–526
McIntyre, James, Aug. 8, 1857–Aug. 18, 1937.
  Supp. 2–412
McIntyre, Oscar Odd, Feb. 18, 1884–Feb. 14, 1938.
  Supp. 2–414
McIver, Charles Duncan, Sept. 27, 1860–Sept. 17, 1906.
  Vol. 6, Pt. 2–71

MacIver, Robert Morrison, Apr. 17, 1882–June 15, 1970.
  Supp. 8–406
Mack, Connie, Dec. 22, 1862–Feb. 8, 1956.
  Supp. 6–414
Mack, Julian William, July 19, 1866–Sept. 5, 1943.
  Supp. 3–487
Mackay, Clarence Hungerford, Apr. 17, 1874–Nov. 12, 1938.
  Supp. 2–415
McKay, Claude, Sept. 15, 1889–May 22, 1948.
  Supp. 4–527
McKay, David Oman, Sept. 8, 1873–Jan. 18, 1970.
  Supp. 8–408
McKay, Donald, Sept. 4, 1810–Sept. 20, 1880.
  Vol. 6, Pt. 2–72
McKay, Gordon, May 4, 1821–Oct. 19, 1903.
  Vol. 6, Pt. 2–73
Mackay, James, 1759?–Mar. 16, 1822.
  Vol. 6, Pt. 2–74
McKay, (James) Douglas, June 24, 1893–July 22, 1959.
  Supp. 6–416
McKay, James Iver, July 17, 1792–Sept. 14, 1853.
  Vol. 6, Pt. 2–75
Mackay, John William, Nov. 28, 1831–July 20, 1902.
  Vol. 6, Pt. 2–75
MacKaye, James Morrison Steele, June 6, 1842–Feb. 25, 1894. Vol. 6, Pt. 2–76
MacKaye, Percy Wallace, Mar. 16, 1875–Aug. 31, 1956.
  Supp. 6–417
MacKaye, Steele. [See MacKaye, James Morrison Steele, 1842–1894.]
McKean, James William, Mar. 10, 1860–Feb. 9, 1949.
  Supp. 4–529
McKean, Joseph Borden, July 28, 1764–Sept. 3, 1826.
  Vol. 6, Pt. 2–77
McKean, Samuel, Apr. 7, 1787–Dec. 14, 1841.
  Vol. 6, Pt. 2–78
McKean, Thomas, Mar. 19, 1734–June 24, 1817.
  Vol. 6, Pt. 2–79
McKean, William Wister, Sept. 19, 1800–Apr. 22, 1865.
  Vol. 6, Pt. 2–81
McKechnie, William Boyd, Aug. 7, 1886–Oct. 29, 1965.
  Supp. 7–501
McKee, John, 1771–Aug. 12, 1832.
  Vol. 6, Pt. 2–82
McKeen, Joseph, Oct. 15, 1757–July 15, 1807.
  Vol. 6, Pt. 2–83
McKellar, Kenneth Douglas, Jan. 29, 1869–Oct. 25, 1957.
  Supp. 6–418
Mackellar, Patrick, 1717–Oct. 22, 1778.
  Vol. 6, Pt. 2–83
MacKellar, Thomas, Aug. 12, 1812–Dec. 29, 1899.
  Vol. 6, Pt. 2–84
McKelway, St. Clair, Mar. 15, 1845–July 16, 1915.
  Vol. 6, Pt. 2–85
McKendree, William, July 6, 1757–Mar. 5, 1835.
  Vol. 6, Pt. 2–85
McKenna, Charles Hyacinth, May 8, 1835–Feb. 21, 1917.
  Vol. 6, Pt. 2–87
McKenna, Joseph, Aug. 10, 1843–Nov. 21, 1926.
  Vol. 6, Pt. 2–87
McKennan, Thomas McKean Thompson, Mar. 31, 1794–July 9, 1852. Vol. 6, Pt. 2–88
McKenney, Thomas Loraine, Mar. 21, 1785–Feb. 20, 1859.
  Vol. 6, Pt. 2–89
McKenzie, Alexander, Dec. 14, 1830–Aug. 6, 1914.
  Vol. 6, Pt. 2–90
Mackenzie, Alexander Slidell, Apr. 6, 1803–Sept. 13, 1848.
  Vol. 6, Pt. 2–90
Mackenzie, Donald, June 15, 1783–Jan. 20, 1851.
  Vol. 6, Pt. 2–91
Mackenzie, George Henry, Nov. 24, 1837–Apr. 14, 1891.
  Vol. 6, Pt. 2–92
Mackenzie, James Cameron, Aug. 15, 1852–May 10, 1931.
  Vol. 6, Pt. 2–93
Mackenzie, John Noland, Oct. 20, 1853–May 21, 1925.
  Vol. 6, Pt. 2–93
Mackenzie, Kenneth, Apr. 15, 1797–Apr. 26, 1861.
  Vol. 6, Pt. 2–94
Mackenzie, Murdo, Apr. 24, 1850–May 30, 1939.
  Supp. 2–416
Mackenzie, Ranald Slidell, July 27, 1840–Jan. 19, 1889.
  Vol. 6, Pt. 2–95

Mackenzie, Robert Shelton, June 22, 1809–Nov. 21, 1881.
     Vol. 6, Pt. 2–96
McKenzie, Robert Tait, May 26, 1867–Apr. 28, 1938.
     Supp. 2–417
Mackenzie, William, July 30, 1758–July 23, 1828.
     Vol. 6, Pt. 2–97
Mackey, Albert Gallatin, Mar. 12, 1807–June 20, 1881.
     Vol. 6, Pt. 2–98
McKim, Charles Follen, Aug. 24, 1847–Sept. 14, 1909.
     Vol. 6, Pt. 2–99
McKim, Isaac, July 21, 1775–Apr. 1, 1838.
     Vol. 6, Pt. 2–102
McKim, James Miller, Nov. 14, 1810–June 13, 1874.
     Vol. 6, Pt. 2–103
McKinley, Albert Edward, Sept. 11, 1870–Feb. 26, 1936.
     Supp. 2–418
McKinley, Carlyle, Nov. 22, 1847–Aug. 24, 1904.
     Vol. 6, Pt. 2–104
McKinley, John, May 1, 1780–July 19, 1852.
     Vol. 6, Pt. 2–104
McKinley, William, Jan. 29, 1843–Sept. 14, 1901.
     Vol. 6, Pt. 2–105
McKinley, William Brown, Sept. 5, 1856–Dec. 7, 1926.
     Supp. 1–530
McKinly, John, Feb. 24, 1721–Aug. 31, 1796.
     Vol. 6, Pt. 2–109
McKinstry, Alexander, Mar. 7, 1822–Oct. 9, 1879.
     Vol. 6, Pt. 2–110
McKinstry, Elisha Williams, Apr. 11, 1825–Nov. 1, 1901.
     Vol. 6, Pt. 2–110
McKnight, Robert, c. 1789–March 1846.
     Vol. 6, Pt. 2–111
Mackubin, Florence, May 19, 1861–Feb. 2, 1918.
     Vol. 6, Pt. 2–112
McLaglen, Victor, Dec. 11, 1886–Nov. 6, 1959.
     Supp. 6–420
McLane, Allan, Aug. 8, 1746–May 22, 1829.
     Vol. 6, Pt. 2–112
McLane, Louis, May 28, 1786–Oct. 7, 1857.
     Vol. 6, Pt. 2–113
McLane, Robert Milligan, June 23, 1815–Apr. 16, 1898.
     Vol. 6, Pt. 2–115
McLaren, John, Dec. 20, 1846–Jan. 12, 1943.
     Supp. 3–490
McLaren, William Edward, Dec. 13, 1831–Feb. 19, 1905.
     Vol. 6, Pt. 2–116
McLaughlin, Andrew Cunningham, Feb. 14, 1861–Sept. 24,
     1947. Supp. 4–530
McLaughlin, Hugh, Apr. 2, 1826?–Dec. 7, 1904.
     Vol. 6, Pt. 2–117
McLaughlin, James, Feb. 12, 1842–July 28, 1923.
     Vol. 6, Pt. 2–117
McLaurin, Anselm Joseph, Mar. 26, 1848–Dec. 22, 1909.
     Vol. 6, Pt. 2–118
Maclaurin, Richard Cockburn, June 5, 1870–Jan. 15, 1920.
     Vol. 6, Pt. 2–119
McLaws, Lafayette, Jan. 15, 1821–July 24, 1897.
     Vol. 6, Pt. 2–120
Maclay, Edgar Stanton, Apr. 18, 1863–Nov. 2, 1919.
     Vol. 6, Pt. 2–121
Maclay, Robert Samuel, Feb. 7, 1824–Aug. 18, 1907.
     Vol. 6, Pt. 2–121
Maclay, Samuel, June 17, 1741–Oct. 5, 1811.
     Vol. 6, Pt. 2–122
Maclay, William, July 27, 1734–Apr. 16, 1804.
     Vol. 6, Pt. 2–123
Maclay, William Brown, Mar. 20, 1812–Feb. 19, 1882.
     Vol. 6, Pt. 2–124
McLean, Angus Wilton, Apr. 20, 1870–June 21, 1935.
     Supp. 1–532
McLean, Archibald, Sept. 6, 1849–Dec. 15, 1920.
     Vol. 6, Pt. 2–125
McLean, Edward Beale, Jan. 31, 1886–July 27, 1941.
     Supp. 3–491
MacLean, George Edwin, Aug. 31, 1850–May 3, 1938.
     Supp. 2–419
Maclean, John, Mar. 1, 1771–Feb. 17, 1814.
     Vol. 6, Pt. 2–126
McLean, John, Mar. 11, 1785–Apr. 4, 1861.
     Vol. 6, Pt. 2–127
Maclean, John, Mar. 3, 1800–Aug. 10, 1886.
     Vol. 6, Pt. 2–128

McLean, Walter, July 30, 1855–Mar. 20, 1930.
     Vol. 6, Pt. 2–129
McLean, William Lippard, May 4, 1852–July 30, 1931.
     Vol. 6, Pt. 2–130
McLellan, Isaac, May 21, 1806–Aug. 20, 1899.
     Vol. 6, Pt. 2–130
McLeod, Alexander, June 12, 1774–Feb. 17, 1833.
     Vol. 6, Pt. 2–131
McLeod, Hugh, Aug. 1, 1814–Jan. 2, 1862.
     Vol. 6, Pt. 2–132
McLeod, Martin, Aug. 30, 1813–Nov. 20, 1860.
     Vol. 6, Pt. 2–133
McLevy, Jasper, Mar. 27, 1878–Nov. 19, 1962.
     Supp. 7–502
McLoughlin, John, Oct. 19, 1784–Sept. 3, 1857.
     Vol. 6, Pt. 2–134
McLoughlin, Maurice Evans, Jan. 7, 1890–Dec. 10, 1957.
     Supp. 6–421
Maclure, William, Oct. 27, 1763–Mar. 23, 1840.
     Vol. 6, Pt. 2–135
McMahon, Bernard, d. Sept. 18, 1816.
     Vol. 6, Pt. 2–137
McMahon, Brien, Oct. 6, 1903–July 28, 1952.
     Supp. 5–455
McMahon, John Van Lear, Oct. 18, 1800–June 15, 1871.
     Vol. 6, Pt. 2–137
McManes, James, Apr. 13, 1822–Nov. 23, 1899.
     Vol. 6, Pt. 2–138
McManus, George, Jan. 23, 1884[?]–Oct. 22, 1954.
     Supp. 5–456
McMaster, Guy Humphreys, Jan. 31, 1829–Sept. 13, 1887.
     Vol. 6, Pt. 2–139
McMaster, James Alphonsus, Apr. 1, 1820–Dec. 29, 1886.
     Vol. 6, Pt. 2–140
McMaster, John Bach, June 29, 1852–May 24, 1932.
     Vol. 6, Pt. 2–140
McMath, Robert Emmet, Apr. 28, 1833–May 31, 1918.
     Vol. 6, Pt. 2–142
McMichael, Morton, Oct. 20, 1807–Jan. 6, 1879.
     Vol. 6, Pt. 2–142
McMillan, James, May 12, 1838–Aug. 10, 1902.
     Vol. 6, Pt. 2–143
McMillan, James Winning, Apr. 28, 1825–Mar. 9, 1903.
     Vol. 6, Pt. 2–145
McMillin, Alvin Nugent ("Bo"), Jan. 12, 1895–Mar. 31, 1952.
     Supp. 5–457
McMillin, Benton, Sept. 11, 1845–Jan. 8, 1933.
     Supp. 1–533
McMinn, Joseph, June 22, 1758–Nov. 17, 1824.
     Vol. 6, Pt. 2–145
MacMonnies, Frederick William, Sept. 28, 1863–Mar. 22,
     1937. Supp. 2–420
McMurrich, James Playfair, Oct. 16, 1859–Feb. 9, 1939.
     Supp. 2–422
McMurry, Frank Morton, July 2, 1862–Aug. 1, 1936.
     Supp. 2–423
McMurtrie, Douglas Crawford, July 20, 1888–Sept. 29, 1944.
     Supp. 3–492
McMurtrie, William, Mar. 10, 1851–May 24, 1913.
     Vol. 6, Pt. 2–146
McNair, Alexander, May 5, 1775–Mar. 18, 1826.
     Vol. 6, Pt. 2–147
McNair, Frederick Vallette, Jan. 13, 1839–Nov. 28, 1900.
     Vol. 6, Pt. 2–148
McNair, Fred Walter, Dec. 3, 1862–June 30, 1924.
     Vol. 6, Pt. 2–148
MacNair, Harley Farnsworth, July 22, 1891–June 22, 1947.
     Supp. 4–532
McNair, Lesley James, May 25, 1883–July 25, 1944.
     Supp. 3–493
McNamee, Graham, July 10, 1888–May 9, 1942.
     Supp. 3–495
McNary, Charles Linza, June 12, 1874–Feb. 25, 1944.
     Supp. 3–496
Macnaughtan, Myra Kelly. [See Kelly, Myra, 1875–1910.]
MacNeil, Hermon Atkins, Feb. 27, 1866–Oct. 4, 1947.
     Supp. 4–533
McNeill, Daniel, Apr. 5, 1748–1833.
     Vol. 6, Pt. 2–149
McNeill, George Edwin, Aug. 4, 1837–May 19, 1906.
     Vol. 6, Pt. 2–150
McNeill, Hector, Oct. 10, 1728–Dec. 25, 1785.
     Vol. 6, Pt. 2–151

McNeill, John Hanson, June 12, 1815–Nov. 10, 1864.
Vol. 6, Pt. 2–151
McNeill, William Gibbs, Oct. 3, 1801–Feb. 16, 1853.
Vol. 6, Pt. 2–152
MacNeven, William James, Mar. 21, 1763–July 12, 1841.
Vol. 6, Pt. 2–153
McNicholas, John Timothy, Dec. 15, 1877–Apr. 22, 1950.
Supp. 4–534
MacNider, Hanford, Oct. 2, 1889–Feb. 17, 1968.
Supp. 8–409
McNulty, Frank Joseph, Aug. 10, 1872–May 26, 1926.
Vol. 6, Pt. 2–154
McNulty, John Augustine, Nov. 1, 1895–July 29, 1956.
Supp. 6–422
McNutt, Alexander, c. 1725–c. 1811.
Vol. 6, Pt. 2–155
McNutt, Paul Vories, July 19, 1891–Mar. 24, 1955.
Supp. 5–459
Macomb, Alexander, Apr. 3, 1782–June 25, 1841.
Vol. 6, Pt. 2–155
Macomber, Mary Lizzie, Aug. 21, 1861–Feb. 4, 1916.
Vol. 6, Pt. 2–157
Macon, Nathaniel, Dec. 17, 1758–June 29, 1837.
Vol. 6, Pt. 2–157
McPherson, Aimee Semple, Oct. 9, 1890–Sept. 27, 1944.
Supp. 3–497
McPherson, Edward, July 31, 1830–Dec. 14, 1895.
Vol. 6, Pt. 2–159
McPherson, James Birdseye, Nov. 14, 1828–July 22, 1864.
Vol. 6, Pt. 2–160
McPherson, Logan Grant, Aug. 11, 1863–Mar. 23, 1925.
Vol. 6, Pt. 2–161
McPherson, Smith, Feb. 14, 1848–Jan. 17, 1915.
Vol. 6, Pt. 2–162
McQuaid, Bernard John, Dec. 15, 1823–Jan. 18, 1909.
Vol. 6, Pt. 2–163
McQuillen, John Hugh, Feb. 12, 1826–Mar. 3, 1879.
Vol. 6, Pt. 2–164
McRae, Duncan Kirkland, Aug. 16, 1820–Feb. 12, 1888.
Vol. 6, Pt. 2–164
Macrae, John, Aug. 25, 1866–Feb. 18, 1944.
Supp. 3–499
McRae, Milton Alexander, June 13, 1858–Oct. 11, 1930.
Vol. 6, Pt. 2–165
McRae, Thomas Chipman, Dec. 21, 1851–June 2, 1929.
Vol. 6, Pt. 2–166
McReynolds, James Clark, Feb. 3, 1862–Aug. 24, 1946.
Supp. 4–536
McReynolds, Samuel Davis, Apr. 16, 1872–July 11, 1939.
Supp. 2–424
MacSparran, James, Sept. 10, 1693–Dec. 1, 1757.
Vol. 6, Pt. 2–167
McTammany, John, June 26, 1845–Mar. 26, 1915.
Vol. 6, Pt. 2–168
McTyeire, Holland Nimmons, July 28, 1824–Feb. 15, 1889.
Vol. 6, Pt. 2–169
Macune, Charles William, May 20, 1851–Nov. 3, 1940.
Supp. 2–425
MacVeagh, Charles, June 6, 1860–Dec. 4, 1931.
Supp. 1–534
MacVeagh, Franklin, Nov. 22, 1837–July 6, 1934.
Supp. 1–535
MacVeagh, Isaac Wayne, Apr. 19, 1833–Jan. 11, 1917.
Vol. 6, Pt. 2–170
McVey, Frank Lerond, Nov. 10, 1869–Jan. 4, 1953.
Supp. 5–461
MacVicar, Malcolm, Sept. 30, 1829–May 18, 1904.
Vol. 6, Pt. 2–171
McVickar, John, Aug. 10, 1787–Oct. 29, 1868.
Vol. 6, Pt. 2–172
McVickar, William Neilson, Oct. 19, 1843–June 28, 1910.
Vol. 6, Pt. 2–173
McVicker, James Hubert, Feb. 14, 1822–Mar. 7, 1896.
Vol. 6, Pt. 2–174
MacWhorter, Alexander, July 15, 1734 o.s.–July 20, 1807.
Vol. 6, Pt. 2–175
Macy, Jesse, June 21, 1842–Nov. 3, 1919.
Vol. 6, Pt. 2–176
Macy, John Albert, Apr. 10, 1877–Aug. 26, 1932.
Vol. 6, Pt. 2–177
Macy, Josiah, Feb. 25, 1785–May 15, 1872.
Vol. 6, Pt. 2–178

Macy, Valentine Everit, Mar. 23, 1871–Mar. 21, 1930.
Vol. 6, Pt. 2–179
Madden, John Edward, Dec. 28, 1856–Nov. 3, 1929.
Vol. 6, Pt. 2–180
Madden, Martin Barnaby, Mar. 20, 1855–Apr. 27, 1928.
Vol. 6, Pt. 2–180
Madden, Owen Victor ("Owney"), June 1892–Apr1 24, 1965.
Supp. 7–504
Madigan, Laverne, Sept. 13, 1912–Aug. 21, 1962.
Supp. 7–505
Madison, Dolly Payne, May 20, 1768–July 12, 1849.
Vol. 6, Pt. 2–181
Madison, James, Aug. 27, 1749–Mar. 6, 1812.
Vol. 6, Pt. 2–182
Madison, James, Mar. 5/16, 1750/51–June 28, 1836.
Vol. 6, Pt. 2–184
Maeder, Clara Fisher. [See Fisher, Clara, 1811–1898.]
Macs, Camillus Paul, Mar. 13, 1846–May 11, 1915.
Vol. 6, Pt. 2–193
Maffitt, David, d. May 1, 1838.
Vol. 6, Pt. 2–194
Maffitt, John Newland, Feb. 22, 1819–May 15, 1886.
Vol. 6, Pt. 2–195
Magee, Christoher Lyman, Apr. 14, 1848–Mar. 8, 1901.
Vol. 6, Pt. 2–196
Magie, William Jay, Dec. 9, 1832–Jan. 15, 1917.
Vol. 6, Pt. 2–197
Magill, Edward Hicks, Sept. 24, 1825–Dec. 10, 1907.
Vol. 6, Pt. 2–198
Maginnis, Charles Donagh, Jan. 7, 1867–Feb. 16, 1955.
Supp. 5–462
Maginnis, Martin, Oct. 27, 1841–Mar. 27, 1919.
Vol. 6, Pt. 2–199
Magnes, Judah Leon, July 5, 1877–Oct. 27, 1948.
Supp. 4–538
Magoffin, Beriah, Apr. 18, 1815–Feb. 28, 1885.
Vol. 6, Pt. 2–199
Magoffin, James Wiley, 1799–Sept. 27, 1868.
Vol. 6, Pt. 2–200
Magonigle, Harold Van Buren, Oct. 17, 1867–Aug. 29, 1935.
Supp. 1–536
Magoon, Charles Edward, Dec. 5, 1861–Jan. 14, 1920.
Vol. 6, Pt. 2–201
Magoun, George Frederic, Mar. 29, 1821–Jan. 30, 1896.
Vol. 6, Pt. 2–202
Magrath, Andrew Gordon, Feb. 8, 1813–Apr. 9, 1893.
Vol. 6, Pt. 2–203
Magruder, George Lloyd, Nov. 1, 1848–Jan. 28, 1914.
Vol. 6, Pt. 2–204
Magruder, John Bankhead, Aug. 15, 1810–Feb. 18, 1871.
Vol. 6, Pt. 2–204
Magruder, Julia, Sept. 14, 1854–June 9, 1907.
Vol. 6, Pt. 2–206
Maguire, Charles Bonaventure. [See McGuire, Charles
Bonaventure, 1768–1833.]
Mahan, Alfred Thayer, Sept. 27, 1840–Dec. 1, 1914.
Vol. 6, Pt. 2–206
Mahan, Asa, Nov. 9, 1799–Apr. 4, 1889.
Vol. 6, Pt. 2–208
Mahan, Dennis Hart, Apr. 2, 1802–Sept. 16, 1871.
Vol. 6, Pt. 2–209
Mahan, Milo, May 24, 1819–Sept. 3, 1870.
Vol. 6, Pt. 2–210
Mahler, Herbert, Nov. 6, 1890–Aug. 17, 1961.
Supp. 7–506
Mahone, William, Dec. 1, 1826–Oct. 8, 1895.
Vol. 6, Pt. 2–211
Mahoney, John Friend, Aug. 1, 1889–Feb. 23, 1957.
Supp. 6–423
Maier, Walter Arthur, Oct. 4, 1893–Jan. 11, 1950.
Supp. 4–540
Mailly, William, Nov. 22, 1871–Sept. 4, 1912.
Vol. 6, Pt. 2–212
Main, Charles Thomas, Feb. 16, 1856–Mar. 6, 1943.
Supp. 3–500
Main, John Hanson Thomas, Apr. 2, 1859–Apr. 1, 1931.
Supp. 1–537
Maisch, John Michael, Jan. 30, 1831–Sept. 10, 1893.
Vol. 6, Pt. 2–213
Major, Charles, July 25, 1856–Feb. 13, 1913.
Vol. 6, Pt. 2–214
Majors, Alexander, Oct. 4, 1814–Jan. 12, 1900.
Vol. 6, Pt. 2–214

Ma-Ka-Tai-Me-She-Kia-Kiak. [See Black Hawk, 1767–1838.]
Makemie, Francis, c. 1658–1708.
    Vol. 6, Pt. 2–215
Malbone, Edward Greene, August 1777–May 7, 1807.
    Vol. 6, Pt. 2–216
Malcolm, Daniel, Nov. 29, 1725–Oct. 23, 1769.
    Vol. 6, Pt. 2–218
Malcolm, James Peller, August 1767–Apr. 5, 1815.
    Vol. 6, Pt. 2–219
Malcolm X, May 19, 1925–Feb. 21, 1965.
    Supp. 7–507
Malcom, Daniel. [See Malcolm, Daniel, 1725–1769.]
Malcom, Howard, Jan. 19, 1799–Mar. 25, 1879.
    Vol. 6, Pt. 2–220
Malcom, James Peller. [See Malcolm, James Peller, 1767–1815.]
Malin, Patrick Murphy, May 8, 1903–Dec. 13, 1964.
    Supp. 7–510
Mall, Franklin Paine, Sept. 28, 1862–Nov. 17, 1917.
    Vol. 6, Pt. 2–220
Mallary, Rollin Carolas, May 27, 1784–Apr. 15, 1831.
    Vol. 6, Pt. 2–221
Mallery, Garrick, Apr. 23, 1831–Oct. 24, 1894.
    Vol. 6, Pt. 2–222
Mallet, John William, Oct. 10, 1832–Nov. 7, 1912.
    Vol. 6, Pt. 2–223
Mallinckrodt, Edward, Jan. 21, 1845–Feb. 1, 1928.
    Vol. 6, Pt. 2–224
Mallinckrodt, Edward, Jr., Nov. 17, 1878–Jan. 19, 1967.
    Supp. 8–411
Mallory, Anna Margrethe ("Molla") Bjurstedt, 1892–Nov. 22, 1959. Supp. 6–424
Mallory, Clifford Day, May 26, 1881–Apr. 7, 1941.
    Supp. 3–501
Mallory, Frank Burr, Nov. 12, 1862–Sept. 27, 1941.
    Supp. 3–502
Mallory, Stephen Russell, c. 1813–Nov. 9, 1873.
    Vol. 6, Pt. 2–224
Malone, Dudley Field, June 3, 1882–Oct. 5, 1950.
    Supp. 4–541
Malone, Sylvester, May 8, 1821–Dec. 29, 1899.
    Vol. 6, Pt. 2–226
Malone, Walter, Feb. 10, 1866–May 18, 1915.
    Vol. 6, Pt. 2–227
Maloney, Martin, Dec. 11, 1847–May 8, 1929.
    Vol. 6, Pt. 2–227
Malter, Henry, Mar. 23, 1864–Apr. 4, 1925.
    Vol. 6, Pt. 2–228
Manatt, James Irving, Feb. 17, 1845–Feb. 13, 1915.
    Vol. 6, Pt. 2–229
Manderson, Charles Frederick, Feb. 9, 1837–Sept. 28, 1911.
    Vol. 6, Pt. 2–230
Maney, George Earl, Aug. 24, 1826–Feb. 9, 1901.
    Vol. 6, Pt. 2–231
Mangin, Joseph Francois, fl. 1794–1818.
    Vol. 6, Pt. 2–231
Mangum, Willie Person, May 10, 1792–Sept. 7, 1861.
    Vol. 6, Pt. 2–232
Manigault, Arthur Middleton, Oct. 26, 1824–Aug. 16, 1886.
    Vol. 6, Pt. 2–233
Manigault, Gabriel, Apr. 21, 1704–June 5, 1781.
    Vol. 6, Pt. 2–234
Manigault, Peter, Oct. 10, 1731–Nov. 12, 1773.
    Vol. 6, Pt. 2–234
Manigault, Pierre, d. December 1729.
    Vol. 6, Pt. 2–235
Mankiewicz, Herman Jacob, Nov. 4, 1897–Mar. 5, 1953.
    Supp. 5–463
Manley, John, c. 1734–Feb. 12, 1793.
    Vol. 6, Pt. 2–236
Manley, Joseph Homan, Oct. 13, 1842–Feb. 7, 1905.
    Vol. 6, Pt. 2–236
Manly, Basil, Jan. 29, 1798–Dec. 21, 1868.
    Vol. 6, Pt. 2–237
Manly, Basil, Dec. 19, 1825–Jan. 31, 1892.
    Vol. 6, Pt. 2–238
Manly, Basil Maxwell, Mar. 14, 1886–May 11, 1950.
    Supp. 4–543
Manly, Charles Matthews, Apr. 24, 1876–Oct. 15, 1927.
    Vol. 6, Pt. 2–239
Manly, John Matthews, Sept. 2, 1865–Apr. 2, 1940.
    Supp. 2–427

Mann, Ambrose Dudley, Apr. 26, 1801–November 1889.
    Vol. 6, Pt. 2–239
Mann, Horace, May 4, 1796–Aug. 2, 1859.
    Vol. 6, Pt. 2–240
Mann, James, July 22, 1759–Nov. 7, 1832.
    Vol. 6, Pt. 2–243
Mann, James Robert, Oct. 20, 1856–Nov. 30, 1922.
    Vol. 6, Pt. 2–244
Mann, Louis, Apr. 20, 1865–Feb. 15, 1931.
    Vol. 6, Pt. 2–244
Mann, Mary Tyler Peabody, Nov. 16, 1806–Feb. 11, 1887.
    Vol. 6, Pt. 2–245
Mann, Newton, Jan. 16, 1836–July 25, 1926.
    Vol. 6, Pt. 2–246
Mann, William Julius, May 29, 1819–June 20, 1892.
    Vol. 6, Pt. 2–247
Manners, John Hartley, Aug. 10, 1870–Dec. 19, 1928.
    Vol. 6, Pt. 2–248
Mannes, Clara Damrosch, Dec. 12, 1869–Mar. 16, 1948.
    Supp. 4–544
Mannes, David, Feb. 16, 1866–Apr. 25, 1959.
    Supp. 6–426
Mannes, Leopold Damrosch, Dec. 26, 1899–Aug. 11, 1964.
    Supp. 7–511
Manning, Daniel, May 16, 1831–Dec. 24, 1887.
    Vol. 6, Pt. 2–248
Manning, James, Oct. 22, 1738–July 29, 1791.
    Vol. 6, Pt. 2–249
Manning, Marie, Jan. 22, 1873[?]–Nov. 28, 1945.
    Supp. 3–503
Manning, Richard Irvine, May 1, 1789–May 1, 1836.
    Vol. 6, Pt. 2–251
Manning, Richard Irvine, Aug. 15, 1859–Sept. 11, 1931.
    Vol. 6, Pt. 2–251
Manning, Robert, July 18, 1784–Oct. 10, 1842.
    Vol. 6, Pt. 2–252
Manning, Thomas Courtland, Sept. 14, 1825–Oct. 11, 1887.
    Vol. 6, Pt. 2–253
Manning, Vannoy Hartrog, Dec. 15, 1861–July 13, 1932.
    Vol. 6, Pt. 2–253
Manning, William Thomas, May 12, 1866–Nov. 18, 1949.
    Supp. 4–546
Mansell, William Albert, Mar. 30, 1864–Mar. 4, 1913.
    Vol. 6, Pt. 2–254
Mansfield, Edward Deering, Aug. 17, 1801–Oct. 27, 1880.
    Vol. 6, Pt. 2–255
Mansfield, Jared, May 23, 1759–Feb. 3, 1830.
    Vol. 6, Pt. 2–256
Mansfield, Jayne, Apr. 19, 1933–June 29, 1967.
    Supp. 8–412
Mansfield, Joseph King Fenno, Dec. 22, 1803–Sept. 18, 1862.
    Vol. 6, Pt. 2–257
Mansfield, Richard, Oct. 1, 1723–Apr. 12, 1820.
    Vol. 6, Pt. 2–258
Mansfield, Richard, May 24, 1854–Aug. 30, 1907.
    Vol. 6, Pt. 2–258
Manship, Paul Howard, Dec. 24, 1885–Jan. 31, 1966.
    Supp. 8–413
Manson, Otis Frederick, Oct. 10, 1822–Jan. 25, 1888.
    Vol. 6, Pt. 2–261
Mantell, Robert Bruce, Feb. 7, 1854–June 27, 1928.
    Vol. 6, Pt. 2–262
Mantle, (Robert) Burns, Dec. 23, 1873–Feb. 9, 1948.
    Supp. 4–548
Manville, Thomas Franklyn ("Tommy"), Jr., Apr. 9, 1894–Oct. 8, 1967. Supp. 8–415
Mapes, Charles Victor, July 4, 1836–Jan. 23, 1916.
    Vol. 6, Pt. 2–263
Mapes, James Jay, May 29, 1806–Jan. 10, 1866.
    Vol. 6, Pt. 2–264
Mappa, Adam Gerard, Nov. 25, 1754–Apr. 15, 1828.
    Vol. 6, Pt. 2–265
Maranville, Walter James Vincent ("Rabbit"), Nov. 11, 1891–Jan. 5, 1954. Supp. 5–465
Marble, Albert Prescott, May 21, 1836–Mar. 25, 1906.
    Vol. 6, Pt. 2–265
Marble, Danforth, Apr. 27, 1810–May 13, 1849.
    Vol. 6, Pt. 2–266
Marble, Manton Malone, Nov. 15, 1835–July 24, 1917.
    Vol. 6, Pt. 2–267
Marburg, Theodore, July 10, 1862–Mar. 3, 1946.
    Supp. 4–550

Marbury, Elisabeth, June 19, 1856–Jan. 22, 1933.
  Supp. 1–538
Marbut, Curtis Fletcher, July 19, 1863–Aug. 25, 1935.
  Supp. 1–539
Marcantonio, Vito Anthony, Dec. 10, 1902–Aug. 9, 1954.
  Supp. 5–466
March, Alden, Sept. 20, 1795–June 17, 1869.
  Vol. 6, Pt. 2–268
March, Francis Andrew, Oct. 25, 1825–Sept. 9, 1911.
  Vol. 6, Pt. 2–268
March, Francis Andrew, Mar. 2, 1863–Feb. 28, 1928.
  Vol. 6, Pt. 2–270
March, Peyton Conway, Dec. 27, 1864–Apr. 13, 1955.
  Supp. 5–467
March, William Edward. [See Campbell, William March.]
Marchand, John Bonnett, Aug. 27, 1808–Apr. 13, 1875.
  Vol. 6, Pt. 2–270
Marchant, Henry, April 1741–Aug. 30, 1796.
  Vol. 6, Pt. 2–271
Marciano, Rocky, Sept. 1, 1923–Aug. 31, 1969.
  Supp. 8–417
Marcosson, Isaac Frederick, Sept. 13, 1876–Mar. 14, 1961.
  Supp. 7–512
Marcou, Jules, Apr. 20, 1824–Apr. 17, 1898.
  Vol. 6, Pt. 2–272
Marcus, Bernard Kent, 1890[?]–July 16, 1954.
  Supp. 5–469
Marcy, Henry Orlando, June 23, 1837–Jan. 1, 1924.
  Vol. 6, Pt. 2–273
Marcy, Randolph Barnes, Apr. 9, 1812–Nov. 22, 1887.
  Vol. 6, Pt. 2–273
Marcy, William Learned, Dec. 12, 1786–July 4, 1857.
  Vol. 6, Pt. 2–274
Marden, Charles Carroll, Dec. 21, 1867–May 11, 1932.
  Vol. 6, Pt. 2–277
Marden, Orison Swett, 1850–Mar. 10, 1924.
  Vol. 6, Pt. 2–278
Maréchal, Ambrose, Aug. 28, 1764–Jan. 29, 1828.
  Vol. 6, Pt. 2–279
Marest, Pierre Gabriel, Oct. 14, 1662–Sept. 15, 1714.
  Vol. 6, Pt. 2–280
Maretzek, Max, June 28, 1821–May 14, 1897.
  Vol. 6, Pt. 2–281
Margolis, Max Leopold, Oct. 15, 1866–Apr. 2, 1932.
  Vol. 6, Pt. 2–281
Marigny, Bernard, Oct. 28, 1785–Feb. 3, 1868.
  Vol. 6, Pt. 2–282
Marin, John (Cheri), Dec. 23, 1870–Oct. 1, 1951.
  Supp. 5–470
Marion, Francis, c. 1732–Feb. 26, 1795.
  Vol. 6, Pt. 2–283
Markham, Charles Henry, May 22, 1861–Nov. 24, 1930.
  Vol. 6, Pt. 2–284
Markham, Edwin, Apr. 23, 1852–Mar. 7, 1940.
  Supp. 2–428
Markham, William, c. 1635–June 12, 1704 o.s.
  Vol. 6, Pt. 2–285
Markoe, Abraham, July 2, 1727–Aug. 28, 1806.
  Vol. 6, Pt. 2–286
Markoe, Peter, c. 1752–Jan. 30, 1792.
  Vol. 6, Pt. 2–287
Marks, Amasa Abraham, Apr. 3, 1825–July 19, 1905.
  Vol. 6, Pt. 2–288
Marks, Elias, Dec. 2, 1790–June 22, 1886.
  Vol. 6, Pt. 2–289
Marland, Ernest Whitworth, May 8, 1874–Oct. 3, 1941.
  Supp. 3–504
Marlatt, Abby Lillian, Mar. 7, 1869–June 23, 1943.
  Supp. 3–506
Marling, Alfred Erskine, Oct. 5, 1858–May 29, 1935.
  Supp. 1–540
Marling, John Leake, Dec. 22, 1825–Oct. 16, 1856.
  Vol. 6, Pt. 2–289
Marlowe, Julia, Aug. 17, 1866–Nov. 12, 1950.
  Supp. 4–551
Marmaduke, John Sappington, Mar. 14, 1833–Dec. 28, 1887.
  Vol. 6, Pt. 2–290
Marquand, Allan, Dec. 10, 1853–Sept. 24, 1924.
  Vol. 6, Pt. 2–291
Marquand, Henry Gurdon, Apr. 11, 1819–Feb. 26, 1902.
  Vol. 6, Pt. 2–292
Marquand, John Phillips, Nov. 10, 1893–July 16, 1960.
  Supp. 6–427

Marquett, Turner Mastin, July 9, 1829–Dec. 22, 1894.
  Vol. 6, Pt. 2–293
Marquette, Jacques, June 1, 1637–May 18, 1675.
  Vol. 6, Pt. 2–294
Marquis, Albert Nelson, Jan. 10, 1855–Dec. 21, 1943.
  Supp. 3–507
Marquis, Donald Robert Perry, July 29, 1878–Dec. 29, 1937.
  Supp. 2–430
Marquis, John Abner, Dec. 27, 1861–July 5, 1931.
  Vol. 6, Pt. 2–295
Marquis De Cuevas. [See De Cuevas, Marquis.]
Marriott, Williams McKim, Mar. 5, 1885–Nov. 11, 1936.
  Supp. 2–432
Marsh, Charles Wesley, Mar. 22, 1834–Nov. 9, 1918.
  Vol. 6, Pt. 2–296
Marsh, Frank Burr, Mar. 4, 1880–May 31, 1940.
  Supp. 2–433
Marsh, George Perkins, Mar. 15, 1801–July 23, 1882.
  Vol. 6, Pt. 2–297
Marsh, Grant Prince, May 11, 1834–Jan. 2, 1916.
  Vol. 6, Pt. 2–298
Marsh, James, July 19, 1794–July 3, 1842.
  Vol. 6, Pt. 2–299
Marsh, John, Apr. 2, 1788–Aug. 4, 1868.
  Vol. 6, Pt. 2–300
Marsh, John, June 5, 1799–Sept. 24, 1856.
  Vol. 6, Pt. 2–301
Marsh, Othniel Charles, Oct. 29, 1831–Mar. 18, 1899.
  Vol. 6, Pt. 2–302
Marsh, Reginald, Mar. 14, 1898–July 3, 1954.
  Supp. 5–472
Marsh, Sylvester, Sept. 30, 1803–Dec. 30, 1884.
  Vol. 6, Pt. 2–303
Marsh, William Wallace, Apr. 15, 1836–May 2, 1918.
  Vol. 6, Pt. 2–304
Marshall, Benjamin, 1782–Dec. 2, 1858.
  Vol. 6, Pt. 2–304
Marshall, Charles Henry, Apr. 8, 1792–Sept. 23, 1865.
  Vol. 6, Pt. 2–305
Marshall, Christopher, Nov. 6, 1709–May 4, 1797.
  Vol. 6, Pt. 2–306
Marshall, Clara, c. 1848–Mar. 13, 1931.
  Vol. 6, Pt. 2–307
Marshall, Daniel, 1706–Nov. 2, 1784.
  Vol. 6, Pt. 2–308
Marshall, Frank James, Aug. 10, 1877–Nov. 9, 1944.
  Supp. 3–508
Marshall, George Catlett, Jr., Dec. 31, 1880–Oct. 16, 1959.
  Supp. 6–428
Marshall, Henry Rutgers, July 22, 1852–May 3, 1927.
  Vol. 6, Pt. 2–308
Marshall, Humphrey, 1760–June 26, 1841.
  Vol. 6, Pt. 2–309
Marshall, Humphrey, Jan. 13, 1812–Mar. 28, 1872.
  Vol. 6, Pt. 2–310
Marshall, Humphry, Oct. 10, 1722 o.s.–Nov. 5, 1801.
  Vol. 6, Pt. 2–311
Marshall, James Fowle Baldwin, Aug. 8, 1818–May 6, 1891.
  Vol. 6, Pt. 2–312
Marshall, James Markham, Mar. 12, 1764–Apr. 26, 1848.
  Vol. 6, Pt. 2–313
Marshall, James Wilson, Oct. 8, 1810–Aug. 10, 1885.
  Vol. 6, Pt. 2–314
Marshall, John, Sept. 24, 1755–July 6, 1835.
  Vol. 6, Pt. 2–315
Marshall, Louis, Oct. 7, 1773–April 1866.
  Vol. 6, Pt. 2–325
Marshall, Louis, Dec. 14, 1856–Sept. 11, 1929.
  Vol. 6, Pt. 2–326
Marshall, Thomas, Apr. 2, 1730–June 22, 1802.
  Vol. 6, Pt. 2–328
Marshall, Thomas Alexander, Jan. 15, 1794–Apr. 17, 1871.
  Vol. 6, Pt. 2–329
Marshall, Thomas Riley, Mar. 14, 1854–June 1, 1925.
  Vol. 6, Pt. 2–330
Marshall, William Edgar, June 30, 1837–Aug. 29, 1906.
  Vol. 6, Pt. 2–331
Marshall, William Louis, June 11, 1846–July 2, 1920.
  Vol. 6, Pt. 2–332
Marshall, William Rainey, Oct. 17, 1825–Jan. 8, 1896.
  Vol. 6, Pt. 2–333
Martel, Charles, Mar. 5, 1860–May 15, 1945.
  Supp. 3–509

Martin, Alexander, 1740–Nov. 2, 1807.
Vol. 6, Pt. 2–333
Martin, Anne Henrietta, Sept. 30, 1875–April 15, 1951.
Supp. 5–473
Martin, Artemas, Aug. 3, 1835–Nov. 7, 1918.
Vol. 6, Pt. 2–334
Martin, Edward Sandford, Jan. 2, 1856–June 13, 1939.
Supp. 2–434
Martin, Elizabeth Price, Dec. 14, 1864–Apr. 5, 1932.
Supp. 1–541
Martin, Everett Dean, July 5, 1880–May 10, 1941.
Supp. 3–511
Martin, Francois-Xavier, Mar. 17, 1762–Dec. 10, 1846.
Vol. 6, Pt. 2–335
Martin, Franklin Henry, July 13, 1857–Mar. 7, 1935.
Supp. 1–542
Martin, Frederick Townsend, Dec. 6, 1849–Mar. 8, 1914.
Vol. 6, Pt. 2–336
Martin, Glenn Luther ("Cy"), Jan. 17, 1886–Dec. 4, 1955.
Supp. 5–475
Martin, Henry Austin, July 23, 1824–Dec. 7, 1884.
Vol. 6, Pt. 2–337
Martin, Henry Newell, July 1, 1848–Oct. 27, 1896.
Vol. 6, Pt. 2–337
Martin, Homer Dodge, Oct. 28, 1836–Feb. 12, 1897.
Vol. 6, Pt. 2–338
Martin, James Green, Feb. 14, 1819–Oct. 4, 1878.
Vol. 6, Pt. 2–340
Martin, John Alexander, Mar. 10, 1839–Oct. 2, 1889.
Vol. 6, Pt. 2–341
Martin, John Hill, Jan. 13, 1823–Apr. 7, 1906.
Vol. 6, Pt. 2–342
Martin, Johnny Leonard Roosevelt ("Pepper"), Feb. 29,
1904–Mar. 5, 1965. Supp. 7–513
Martin, Joseph William, Jr., Nov. 3, 1884–Mar. 7, 1968.
Supp. 8–420
Martin, Josiah, 1737–1786.
Vol. 6, Pt. 2–343
Martin, Luther, c. 1748–July 10, 1826.
Vol. 6, Pt. 2–343
Martin, Thomas Commerford, July 22, 1856–May 17, 1924.
Vol. 6, Pt. 2–345
Martin, Thomas Staples, July 29, 1847–Nov. 12, 1919.
Vol. 6, Pt. 2–346
Martin, Victoria Claflin Woodhull. [See Woodhull, Victoria
Claflin, 1838–1927.]
Martin, Warren Homer, Aug. 15, 1901–Jan. 22, 1968.
Supp. 8–418
Martin, William Alexander Parsons, Apr. 10, 1827–Dec. 17,
1916. Vol. 6, Pt. 2–347
Martin, William Thompson, Mar. 25, 1823–Mar. 16, 1910.
Vol. 6, Pt. 2–348
Martindale, John Henry, Mar. 20, 1815–Dec. 13, 1881.
Vol. 6, Pt. 2–349
Martinelli, Giovanni, Oct. 22, 1885–Feb. 2, 1969.
Supp. 8–422
Martiny, Philip, May 19, 1858–June 25, 1927.
Vol. 6, Pt. 2–350
Marty, Martin, Jan. 12, 1834–Sept. 19, 1896.
Vol. 6, Pt. 2–352
Martyn, Sarah Towne Smith, Aug. 15, 1805–Nov. 22, 1879.
Vol. 6, Pt. 2–352
Marvel, Ik. [See Mitchell, Donald Grant, 1822–1908.]
Marvin, Charles Frederick, Oct. 7, 1858–June 5, 1943.
Supp. 3–511
Marvin, Dudley, May 29, 1786–June 25, 1852.
Vol. 6, Pt. 2–353
Marvin, Enoch Mather, June 12, 1823–Nov. 26, 1877.
Vol. 6, Pt. 2–354
Marwedel, Emma Jacobina Christiana, Feb. 27, 1818–Nov.
17, 1893. Vol. 6, Pt. 2–354
Marx, Adolf Arthur ("Harpo"), Nov. 23, 1893–Sept. 28,
1964. Supp. 7–514
Marx, Leonard ("Chico"), Mar. 22, 1891–Oct. 11, 1961.
Supp. 7–514
Marzo, Eduardo, Nov. 29, 1852–June 7, 1929.
Vol. 6, Pt. 2–356
Maschke, Heinrich, Oct. 24, 1853–Mar. 1, 1908.
Vol. 6, Pt. 2–356
Masliansky, Zvi Hirsch, May 16, 1856–Jan. 11, 1943.
Supp. 3–512
Maslow, Abraham H., Apr. 1, 1908–June 8, 1970.
Supp. 8–423

Mason, Arthur John, June 1, 1857–June 28, 1933.
Supp. 1–543
Mason, Charles, Oct. 24, 1804–Feb. 25, 1882.
Vol. 6, Pt. 2–357
Mason, Claibourne Rice, Nov. 28, 1800–Jan. 12, 1885.
Vol. 6, Pt. 2–358
Mason, Daniel Gregory, Nov. 20, 1873–Dec. 4, 1953.
Supp. 5–476
Mason, Francis, Apr. 2, 1799–Mar. 3, 1874.
Vol. 6, Pt. 2–358
Mason, Frank Stuart, Oct. 21, 1883–Oct. 25, 1929.
Vol. 6, Pt. 2–359
Mason, George, c. 1629–c. 1686.
Vol. 6, Pt. 2–360
Mason, George, 1725–Oct. 7, 1792.
Vol. 6, Pt. 2–361
Mason, Henry, Oct. 10, 1831–May 15, 1890.
Vol. 6, Pt. 2–364
Mason, James Murray, Nov. 3, 1798–Apr. 28, 1871.
Vol. 6, Pt. 2–364
Mason, Jeremiah, Apr. 27, 1768–Oct. 14, 1848.
Vol. 6, Pt. 2–365
Mason, John, c. 1600–Jan. 30, 1672.
Vol. 6, Pt. 2–367
Mason, John, Oct. 28, 1858–Jan. 12, 1919.
Vol. 6, Pt. 2–367
Mason, John Mitchell, Mar. 19, 1770–Dec. 26, 1829.
Vol. 6, Pt. 2–368
Mason, John Young, Apr. 18, 1799–Oct. 3, 1859.
Vol. 6, Pt. 2–369
Mason, Jonathan, Sept. 12, 1756–Nov. 1, 1831.
Vol. 6, Pt. 2–370
Mason, Lowell, Jan. 8, 1792–Aug. 11, 1872.
Vol. 6, Pt. 2–371
Mason, Lucy Randolph, July 26, 1882–May 6, 1959.
Supp. 6–433
Mason, Luther Whiting, Apr. 3, 1828–July 14, 1896.
Vol. 6, Pt. 2–372
Mason, Max, Oct. 26, 1877–Mar. 23, 1961.
Supp. 7–516
Mason, Otis Tufton, Apr. 10, 1838–Nov. 5, 1908.
Vol. 6, Pt. 2–372
Mason, Richard Barnes, Jan. 16, 1797–July 25, 1850.
Vol. 6, Pt. 2–373
Mason, Samuel, c. 1750–July 1803.
Vol. 6, Pt. 2–374
Mason, Stevens Thomson, Dec. 29, 1760–May 10, 1803.
Vol. 6, Pt. 2–374
Mason, Stevens Thomson, Oct. 27, 1811–Jan. 4, 1843.
Vol. 6, Pt. 2–375
Mason, Thomson, 1733–Feb. 26, 1785.
Vol. 6, Pt. 2–376
Mason, Walt, May 4, 1862–June 22, 1939.
Supp. 2–435
Mason, William, Sept. 2, 1808–May 21, 1883.
Vol. 6, Pt. 2–377
Mason, William, Jan. 24, 1829–July 14, 1908.
Vol. 6, Pt. 2–378
Mason, William Ernest, July 7, 1850–June 16, 1921.
Vol. 6, Pt. 2–379
Masquerier, Lewis, b. Mar. 14, 1802.
Vol. 6, Pt. 2–379
Massassoit, d. 1661.
Vol. 6, Pt. 2–380
Massey, George Betton, Nov. 15, 1856–Mar. 29, 1927.
Vol. 6, Pt. 2–381
Massey, John Edward, Apr. 2, 1819–Apr. 24, 1901.
Vol. 6, Pt. 2–382
Masson, Thomas Lansing, July 21, 1866–June 18, 1934.
Supp. 1–544
Mast, Phineas Price, Jan. 3, 1825–Nov. 20, 1898.
Vol. 6, Pt. 2–382
Masters, Edgar Lee, Aug. 23, 1869–Mar. 5, 1950.
Supp. 4–554
Masterson, William Barclay, Nov. 24, 1853–Oct. 25, 1921.
Vol. 6, Pt. 2–383
Mastin, Claudius Henry, June 4, 1826–Oct. 3, 1898.
Vol. 6, Pt. 2–384
Masury, John Wesley, Jan. 1, 1820–May 14, 1895.
Vol. 6, Pt. 2–384
Matas, Rudolph, Sept. 12, 1860–Sept. 23, 1957.
Supp. 6–434

Mateer, Calvin Wilson, Jan. 9, 1836–Sept. 28, 1908.
Vol. 6, Pt. 2–385
Mather, Cotton, Feb. 12, 1662/63–Feb. 13, 1727/28.
Vol. 6, Pt. 2–386
Mather, Frank Jewett, Jr., July 6, 1868–Nov. 11, 1953.
Supp. 5–478
Mather, Fred, Aug. 2, 1833–Feb. 14, 1900.
Vol. 6, Pt. 2–389
Mather, Increase, June 21, 1639–Aug. 23, 1723.
Vol. 6, Pt. 2–390
Mather, Richard, 1596–Apr. 22, 1669.
Vol. 6, Pt. 2–394
Mather, Samuel, Oct. 30, 1706–June 27, 1785.
Vol. 6, Pt. 2–395
Mather, Samuel, July 13, 1851–Oct. 18, 1931.
Vol. 6, Pt. 2–396
Mather, Samuel Holmes, Mar. 20, 1813–Jan. 14, 1894.
Vol. 6, Pt. 2–397
Mather, Samuel Livingston, July 1, 1817 Oct. 8, 1890.
Vol. 6, Pt. 2–398
Mather, Stephen Tyng, July 4, 1867–Jan. 22, 1930.
Vol. 6, Pt. 2–398
Mather, William Williams, May 24, 1804–Feb. 26, 1859.
Vol. 6, Pt. 2–399
Mather, Winifred Holt. [See Holt, Winifred.]
Matheson, William John, Sept. 15, 1856–May 15, 1930.
Vol. 6, Pt. 2–400
Mathews, Albert, Sept. 8, 1820–Sept. 9, 1903.
Vol. 6, Pt. 2–401
Mathews, Cornelius, Oct. 28, 1817–Mar. 25, 1889.
Vol. 6, Pt. 2–402
Mathews, George, Aug. 30, 1739–Aug. 30, 1812.
Vol. 6, Pt. 2–403
Mathews, Henry Mason, Mar. 29, 1834–Apr. 28, 1884.
Vol. 6, Pt. 2–404
Mathews, John, 1744–Oct. 26, 1802.
Vol. 6, Pt. 2–404
Mathews, John Alexander, May 20, 1872–Jan. 11, 1935.
Supp. 1–545
Mathews, Samuel, c. 1600–January 1660.
Vol. 6, Pt. 2–405
Mathews, Shailer, May 26, 1863–Oct. 23, 1941.
Supp. 3–514
Mathews, William Smythe Babcock, May 8, 1837–Apr. 1, 1912. Vol. 6, Pt. 2–407
Mathews, William, July 28, 1818–Feb. 14, 1909.
Vol. 6, Pt. 2–406
Mathewson, Christopher, Aug. 12, 1880–Oct. 7, 1925.
Vol. 6, Pt. 2–407
Mathewson, Edward Payson, Oct. 16, 1864–July 13, 1948.
Supp. 4–556
Matignon, Francis Anthony, Nov. 10, 1753–Sept. 19, 1818.
Vol. 6, Pt. 2–408
Matlack, Timothy, d. Apr. 14, 1829.
Vol. 6, Pt. 2–409
Matteson, Joel Aldrich, Aug. 2, 1808–Jan. 31, 1873.
Vol. 6, Pt. 2–410
Matteson, Tompkins Harrison, May 9, 1813–Feb. 2, 1884.
Vol. 6, Pt. 2–411
Matthes, François Émile, Mar. 16, 1874–June 21, 1948.
Supp. 4–557
Matthes, Gerard Hendrik, Mar. 16, 1874–Apr. 8, 1959.
Supp. 6–435
Matthew, William Diller, Feb. 19, 1871–Sept. 24, 1930.
Vol. 6, Pt. 2–411
Matthews, Brander. [See Matthews, James Brander, 1852–1929.]
Matthews, Claude, Dec. 14, 1845–Aug. 28, 1898.
Vol. 6, Pt. 2–412
Matthews, Francis Patrick, Mar. 15, 1887–Oct. 18, 1952.
Supp. 5–479
Matthews, Franklin, May 14, 1858–Nov. 26, 1917.
Vol. 6, Pt. 2–413
Matthews, James Brander, Feb. 21, 1852–Mar. 31, 1929.
Vol. 6, Pt. 2–414
Matthews, John, 1808–Jan. 12, 1870.
Vol. 6, Pt. 2–416
Matthews, Joseph Brown, June 28, 1894–July 16, 1966.
Supp. 8–424
Matthews, Joseph Merritt, June 9, 1874–Oct. 11, 1931.
Vol. 6, Pt. 2–417
Matthews, Nathan, Mar. 28, 1854–Dec. 11, 1927.
Vol. 6, Pt. 2–417

Matthews, Stanley, July 21, 1824–Mar. 22, 1889.
Vol. 6, Pt. 2–418
Matthews, Washington, July 17, 1843–Apr. 29, 1905.
Vol. 6, Pt. 2–420
Matthews, William, Mar. 29, 1822–Apr. 15, 1896.
Vol. 6, Pt. 2–420
Matthiessen, Francis Otto, Feb. 19, 1902–Apr. 1, 1950.
Supp. 4–559
Matthiessen, Frederick William, Mar. 5, 1835–Feb. 11, 1918.
Vol. 6, Pt. 2–421
Mattice, Asa Martines, Aug. 1, 1853–Apr. 19, 1925.
Vol. 6, Pt. 2–422
Mattingly, Garrett, May 6, 1900–Dec. 18, 1962.
Supp. 7–517
Mattison, Hiram, Feb. 8, 1811–Nov. 24, 1868.
Vol. 6, Pt. 2–423
Mattocks, John, Mar. 4, 1777–Aug. 14, 1847.
Vol. 6, Pt. 2–423
Mattoon, Stephen, May 5, 1816–Aug. 15, 1889.
Vol. 6, Pt. 2–424
Mattson, Hans, Dec. 23, 1832–Mar. 5, 1893.
Vol. 6, Pt. 2–425
Matzeliger, Jan Ernst, 1852–1889.
Vol. 6, Pt. 2–426
Mauran, John Lawrence, Nov. 19, 1866–Sept. 23, 1933.
Supp. 1–546
Maurer, James Hudson, Apr. 15, 1864–Mar. 16, 1944.
Supp. 3–516
Maurin, Peter Aristide, May 9, 1877–May 15, 1949.
Supp. 4–561
Maury, Dabney Herndon, May 21, 1822–Jan. 11, 1900.
Vol. 6, Pt. 2–427
Maury, Francis Fontaine, Aug. 9, 1840–June 4, 1879.
Vol. 6, Pt. 2–428
Maury, Matthew Fontaine, Jan. 14, 1806–Feb. 1, 1873.
Vol. 6, Pt. 2–428
Maus, Marion Perry, Aug. 25, 1850–Feb. 9, 1930.
Vol. 6, Pt. 2–431
Maverick, (Fontaine) Maury, Oct. 23, 1895–June 7, 1954.
Supp. 5–480
Maverick, Peter, Oct. 22, 1780–June 7, 1831.
Vol. 6, Pt. 2–432
Maverick, Samuel, c. 1602–c. 1676.
Vol. 6, Pt. 2–432
Maxcy, Jonathan, Sept. 2, 1768–June 4, 1820.
Vol. 6, Pt. 2–433
Maxcy, Virgil, May 5, 1785–Feb. 28, 1844.
Vol. 6, Pt. 2–434
Maxey, Samuel Bell, Mar. 30, 1825–Aug. 16, 1895.
Vol. 6, Pt. 2–435
Maxim, Hiram Percy, Sept. 2, 1869–Feb. 17, 1936.
Supp. 2–436
Maxim, Hiram Stevens, Feb. 5, 1840–Nov. 24, 1916.
Vol. 6, Pt. 2–436
Maxim, Hudson, Feb. 3, 1853–May 6, 1927.
Vol. 6, Pt. 2–437
Maxwell, Augustus Emmett, Sept. 21, 1820–May 5, 1903.
Vol. 6, Pt. 2–438
Maxwell, David Hervey, Sept. 17, 1786–May 24, 1854.
Vol. 6, Pt. 2–439
Maxwell, Elsa, May 24, 1883–Nov. 1, 1963.
Supp. 7–518
Maxwell, George Hebard, June 3, 1860–Dec. 1, 1946.
Supp. 4–563
Maxwell, George Troup, Aug. 6, 1827–Sept. 2, 1897.
Vol. 6, Pt. 2–440
Maxwell, Hugh, 1787–Mar. 31, 1873.
Vol. 6, Pt. 2–441
Maxwell, Lucien Bonaparte, Sept. 14, 1818–July 25, 1875.
Vol. 6, Pt. 2–441
Maxwell, Samuel, May 20, 1825–Feb. 11, 1901.
Vol. 6, Pt. 2–442
Maxwell, William, c. 1733–Nov. 4, 1796.
Vol. 6, Pt. 2–443
Maxwell, William, c. 1755–1809.
Vol. 6, Pt. 2–444
Maxwell, William, Feb. 27, 1784–Jan. 10, 1857,
Vol. 6, Pt. 2–444
Maxwell, William Henry, Mar. 5, 1852–May 3, 1920.
Vol. 6, Pt. 2–445
May, Andrew Jackson, June 24, 1875–Sept. 6, 1959.
Supp. 6–436

May, Edward Harrison, 1824–May 17, 1887.
  Vol. 6, Pt. 2–446
May, Morton Jay, July 13, 1881–May 17, 1968.
  Supp. 8–427
May, Samuel Joseph, Sept. 12, 1797–July 1, 1871.
  Vol. 6, Pt. 2–447
May, Sophie. [See Clarke, Rebecca Sophia, 1833–1906.]
Maybank, Burnet Rhett, Mar. 7, 1899–Sept. 1, 1954.
  Supp. 5–481
Maybeck, Bernard Ralph, Feb. 7, 1862–Oct. 3, 1957.
  Supp. 6–438
Mayer, Alfred Goldsborough. [See Mayor, Alfred Goldsborough, 1868–1922.]
Mayer, Alfred Marshall, Nov. 13, 1836–July 13, 1897.
  Vol. 6, Pt. 2–448
Mayer, Brantz, Sept. 27, 1809–Feb. 23, 1879.
  Vol. 6, Pt. 2–449
Mayer, Constant, Oct. 3, 1829–May 12, 1911.
  Vol. 6, Pt. 2–449
Mayer, Emil, May 23, 1854–Oct. 20, 1931.
  Vol. 6, Pt. 2–450
Mayer, Lewis, Mar. 26, 1783–Aug. 25, 1849.
  Vol. 6, Pt. 2–451
Mayer, Louis Burt, 1885[?]–Oct. 29, 1957.
  Supp. 6–439
Mayer, Oscar Gottfried, Mar. 10, 1888–Mar. 5, 1965.
  Supp. 7–519
Mayer, Philip Frederick, Apr. 1, 1781–Apr. 16, 1858.
  Vol. 6, Pt. 2–452
Mayes, Edward, Dec. 15, 1846–Aug. 9, 1917.
  Vol. 6, Pt. 2–452
Mayes, Joel Bryan, Oct. 2, 1833–Dec. 14, 1891.
  Vol. 6, Pt. 2–453
Mayhew, Experience, Feb. 5, 1673 N.S.–Nov. 29, 1758.
  Vol. 6, Pt. 2–453
Mayhew, Jonathan, Oct. 8, 1720–July 9, 1766.
  Vol. 6, Pt. 2–454
Mayhew, Thomas, 1593–Mar. 25, 1682.
  Vol. 6, Pt. 2–455
Mayhew, Thomas, c. 1621–1657.
  Vol. 6, Pt. 2–456
Maynard, Charles Johnson, May 6, 1845–Oct. 15, 1929.
  Vol. 6, Pt. 2–457
Maynard, Edward, Apr. 26, 1813–May 4, 1891.
  Vol. 6, Pt. 2–457
Maynard, George William, June 12, 1839–Feb. 12, 1913.
  Vol. 6, Pt. 2–458
Maynard, George Willoughby, Mar. 5, 1843–Apr. 5, 1923.
  Vol. 6, Pt. 2–459
Maynard, Horace, Aug. 30, 1814–May 3, 1882.
  Vol. 6, Pt. 2–460
Mayo, Amory Dwight, Jan. 31, 1823–Apr. 8, 1907.
  Vol. 6, Pt. 2–461
Mayo, Charles Horace, July 19, 1865–May 26, 1939.
  Supp. 2–438
Mayo, Frank, Apr. 18, 1839–June 8, 1896.
  Vol. 6, Pt. 2–462
Mayo, George Elton, Dec. 26, 1880–Sept. 1, 1949.
  Supp. 4–564
Mayo, Henry Thomas, Dec. 8, 1856–Feb. 23, 1937.
  Supp. 2–437
Mayo, Mary Anne Bryant, May 24, 1845–Apr. 21, 1903.
  Vol. 6, Pt. 2–462
Mayo, Sarah Carter Edgarton, Mar. 17, 1819–July 9, 1848.
  Vol. 6, Pt. 2–463
Mayo, William, c. 1684–1744.
  Vol. 6, Pt. 2–464
Mayo, William James, June 29, 1861–July 28, 1939.
  Supp. 2–438
Mayo, William Kennon, May 29, 1829–Apr. 9, 1900.
  Vol. 6, Pt. 2–464
Mayo, William Starbuck, Apr. 15, 1811–Nov. 22, 1895.
  Vol. 6, Pt. 2–465
Mayo, William Worrell, May 31, 1819–Mar. 6, 1911.
  Vol. 6, Pt. 2–466
Mayor, Alfred Goldsborough, Apr. 16, 1868–June 24, 1922.
  Vol. 6, Pt. 2–468
Mayo-Smith, Richmond, Feb. 9, 1854–Nov. 11, 1901.
  Vol. 6, Pt. 2–467
Maytag, Frederick Louis, July 14, 1857–Mar. 26, 1937.
  Supp. 2–441
Mazureau, Étienne, 1777–May 25, 1849.
  Vol. 6, Pt. 2–469

Mazzei, Philip, Dec. 25, 1730–Mar. 19, 1816.
  Vol. 6, Pt. 2–469
Mazzuchelli, Samuel Charles, Nov. 4, 1806–Feb. 23, 1864.
  Vol. 6, Pt. 2–470
Mead, Charles Marsh, Jan. 28, 1836–Feb. 15, 1911.
  Vol. 6, Pt. 2–471
Mead, Edwin Doak, Sept. 29, 1849–Aug. 17, 1937.
  Supp. 2–442
Mead, Elwood, Jan. 16, 1858–Jan. 26, 1936.
  Supp. 2–443
Mead, George Herbert, Feb. 27, 1863–Apr. 26, 1931.
  Supp. 1–547
Mead, James Michael, Dec. 27, 1885–Mar. 15, 1964.
  Supp. 7–521
Mead, Larkin Goldsmith, Jan. 3, 1835–Oct. 15, 1910.
  Vol. 6, Pt. 2–472
Mead, William Rutherford, Aug. 20, 1846–June 20, 1928.
  Vol. 6, Pt. 2–473
Meade, George, Feb. 27, 1741–Nov. 9, 1808.
  Vol. 6, Pt. 2–473
Meade, George Gordon, Dec. 31, 1815–Nov. 6, 1872.
  Vol. 6, Pt. 2–474
Meade, Richard Kidder, July 14, 1746–Feb. 9, 1805.
  Vol. 6, Pt. 2–476
Meade, Richard Worsam, June 23, 1778–June 25, 1828.
  Vol. 6, Pt. 2–477
Meade, Richard Worsam, Mar. 21, 1807–Apr. 16, 1870.
  Vol. 6, Pt. 2–478
Meade, Richard Worsam, Oct. 9, 1837–May 4, 1897.
  Vol. 6, Pt. 2–478
Meade, Robert Leamy, Dec. 26, 1841–Feb. 11, 1910.
  Vol. 6, Pt. 2–479
Meade, William, Nov. 11, 1789–Mar. 14, 1862.
  Vol. 6, Pt. 2–480
Meagher, Thomas Francis, Aug. 23, 1823–July 1, 1867.
  Vol. 6, Pt. 2–481
Means, Gaston Bullock, July 11, 1879–Dec. 12, 1938.
  Supp. 2–444
Meany, Edmond Stephen, Dec. 28, 1862–Apr. 22, 1935.
  Supp. 1–548
Mearns, Edgar Alexander, Sept. 11, 1856–Nov. 1, 1916.
  Vol. 6, Pt. 2–482
Mears, David Otis, Feb. 22, 1842–Apr. 29, 1915.
  Vol. 6, Pt. 2–483
Mears, Helen Farnsworth, Dec. 21, 1876–Feb. 17, 1916.
  Vol. 6, Pt. 2–483
Mears, John William, Aug. 10, 1825–Nov. 10, 1881.
  Vol. 6, Pt. 2–484
Mears, Otto, May 3, 1840–June 24, 1931.
  Vol. 6, Pt. 2–485
Mease, James, Aug. 11, 1771–May 14, 1846.
  Vol. 6, Pt. 2–486
Meason, Isaac, 1742–Jan. 23, 1818.
  Vol. 6, Pt. 2–487
Mechem, Floyd Russell, May 9, 1858–Dec. 11, 1928.
  Vol. 6, Pt. 2–487
Mecom, Benjamin, b. Dec. 29, 1732.
  Vol. 6, Pt. 2–488
Medary, Milton Bennett, Feb. 6, 1874–Aug. 7, 1929.
  Vol. 6, Pt. 2–489
Medary, Samuel, Feb. 25, 1801–Nov. 7, 1864.
  Vol. 6, Pt. 2–490
Medill, Joseph, Apr. 6, 1823–Mar. 16, 1899.
  Vol. 6, Pt. 2–491
Meehan, Thomas, Mar. 21, 1826–Nov. 19, 1901.
  Vol. 6, Pt. 2–492
Meek, Alexander Beaufort, July 17, 1814–Nov. 1, 1865.
  Vol. 6, Pt. 2–493
Meek, Fielding Bradford, Dec. 10, 1817–Dec. 21, 1876.
  Vol. 6, Pt. 2–493
Meek, Joseph L., 1810–June 20, 1875.
  Vol. 6, Pt. 2–494
Meeker, Ezra, Dec. 29, 1830–Dec. 3, 1928.
  Vol. 6, Pt. 2–495
Meeker, Jotham, Nov. 8, 1804–Jan. 12, 1855.
  Vol. 6, Pt. 2–496
Meeker, Moses, June 17, 1790–July 7, 1865.
  Vol. 6, Pt. 2–496
Meeker, Nathan Cook, July 12, 1817–Sept. 29, 1879.
  Vol. 6, Pt. 2–497
Meerschaert, Théophile, Aug. 24, 1847–Feb. 21, 1924.
  Vol. 6, Pt. 2–498

Mees, Arthur, Feb. 13, 1850–Apr. 26, 1923.
    Vol. 6, Pt. 2–499
Mees, Charles Edward Kenneth, May 26, 1882–Aug. 15, 1960. Supp. 6–441
Megapolensis, Johannes, 1603–1670.
    Vol. 6, Pt. 2–499
Megrue, Roi Cooper, June 12, 1883–Feb. 27, 1927.
    Vol. 6, Pt. 2–500
Meière, Marie Hildreth, Sept. 3, 1892–May 2, 1961.
    Supp. 7–522
Meiggs, Henry, July 7, 1811–Sept. 29, 1877.
    Vol. 6, Pt. 2–501
Meigs, Arthur Vincent, Nov. 1, 1850–Jan. 1, 1912.
    Vol. 6, Pt. 2–502
Meigs, Charles Delucena, Feb. 19, 1792–June 22, 1869.
    Vol. 6, Pt. 2–503
Meigs, James Aitken, July 31, 1829–Nov. 9, 1879.
    Vol. 6, Pt. 2–504
Meigs, John, Aug. 31, 1852–Nov. 6, 1911.
    Vol. 6, Pt. 2–504
Meigs, John Forsyth, Oct. 3, 1818–Dec. 16, 1882.
    Vol. 6, Pt. 2–505
Meigs, Josiah, Aug. 21, 1757–Sept. 4, 1822.
    Vol. 6, Pt. 2–506
Meigs, Montgomery Cunningham, May 3, 1816–Jan. 2, 1892.
    Vol. 6, Pt. 2–507
Meigs, Return Jonathan, Dec. 17, 1740–Jan. 28, 1823.
    Vol. 6, Pt. 2–508
Meigs, Return Jonathan, Nov. 17, 1764–Mar. 29, 1824.
    Vol. 6, Pt. 2–509
Meigs, Return Jonathan, Apr. 14, 1801–Oct. 19, 1891.
    Vol. 6, Pt. 2–510
Meigs, William Montgomery, Aug. 12, 1852–Dec. 30, 1929.
    Vol. 6, Pt. 2–511
Meiklejohn, Alexander, Feb. 3, 1872–Dec. 16, 1964.
    Supp. 7–523
Meinzer, Oscar Edward, Nov. 28, 1876–June 14, 1948.
    Supp. 4–567
Melcher, Frederic Gershom, Apr. 12, 1879–Mar. 9, 1963.
    Supp. 7–524
Melchers, Gari, Aug. 11, 1860–Nov. 30, 1932.
    Vol. 6, Pt. 2–512
Melish, John, June 13, 1771–Dec. 30, 1822.
    Vol. 6, Pt. 2–513
Mell, Patrick Hues, July 19, 1814–Jan. 26, 1888.
    Vol. 6, Pt. 2–514
Mell, Patrick Hues, May 24, 1850–Oct. 12, 1918.
    Vol. 6, Pt. 2–515
Mellen, Charles Sanger, Aug. 16, 1851–Nov. 17, 1927.
    Vol. 6, Pt. 2–515
Mellen, Grenville, June 19, 1799–Sept. 5, 1841.
    Vol. 6, Pt. 2–516
Mellen, Prentiss, Oct. 11, 1764–Dec. 31, 1840.
    Vol. 6, Pt. 2–517
Mellette, Arthur Calvin, June 23, 1842–May 25, 1896.
    Vol. 6, Pt. 2–518
Mellon, Andrew William, Mar. 24, 1855–Aug. 26, 1937.
    Supp. 2–446
Mellon, William Larimer, June 1, 1868–Oct. 8, 1949.
    Supp. 4–568
Melsheimer, Friedrich Valentin, Sept. 25, 1749–June 30, 1814. Vol. 6, Pt. 2–518
Melton, James, Jan. 2, 1904–Apr. 21, 1961.
    Supp. 7–525
Meltzer, Samuel James, Mar. 22, 1851–Nov. 7, 1920.
    Vol. 6, Pt. 2–519
Melville, David, Mar. 21, 1773–Sept. 3, 1856.
    Vol. 6, Pt. 2–520
Melville, George Wallace, Jan. 10, 1841–Mar. 17, 1912.
    Vol. 6, Pt. 2–521
Melville, Herman, Aug. 1, 1819–Sept. 28, 1891.
    Vol. 6, Pt. 2–522
Membré, Zenobius, 1645–1687?.
    Vol. 6, Pt. 2–526
Memminger, Christopher Gustavus, Jan. 9, 1803–Mar. 7, 1888. Vol. 6, Pt. 2–527
Menard, Michel Branamour, Dec. 5, 1805–Sept. 2, 1856.
    Vol. 6, Pt. 2–528
Menard, Pierre, Oct. 7, 1766–June 13, 1844.
    Vol. 6, Pt. 2–529
Ménard, René, Sept. 7, 1605–Aug. 1661.
    Vol. 6, Pt. 2–530

Mencken, Henry Louis, Sept. 12, 1880–Jan. 29, 1956.
    Supp. 6–443
Mendel, Lafayette Benedict, Feb. 5, 1872–Dec. 9, 1935.
    Supp. 1–549
Mendelsohn, Erich (or Eric), Mar. 21, 1887–Sept. 15, 1953.
    Supp. 5–482
Mendelsohn, Samuel, Mar. 3, 1895–Feb. 3, 1966.
    Supp. 8–428
Mendenhall, Charles Elwood, Aug. 1, 1872–Aug. 18, 1935.
    Supp. 1–550
Mendenhall, Thomas Corwin, Oct. 4, 1841–Mar. 22, 1924.
    Vol. 6, Pt. 2–530
Mendes, Frederic De Sola, July 8, 1850–Oct. 26, 1927.
    Vol. 6, Pt. 2–532
Mendes, Henry Pereira, Apr. 13, 1852–Oct. 20, 1937.
    Supp. 2–452
Meneely, Andrew, May 19, 1802–Oct. 14, 1851.
    Vol. 6, Pt. 2–532
Menéndez De Avilés, Pedro, Feb. 15, 1519–Sept. 17, 1574.
    Vol. 6, Pt. 2–533
Menetrey, Joseph, Nov. 28, 1812–Apr. 27, 1891.
    Vol. 6, Pt. 2–534
Menewa, fl. 1814–1835.
    Vol. 6, Pt. 2–535
Mengarini, Gregory, July 21, 1811–Sept. 23, 1886.
    Vol. 6, Pt. 2–535
Menjou, Adolphe Jean, Feb. 18, 1890–Oct. 29, 1963.
    Supp. 7–526
Menken, Adah Isaacs, June 15, 1835?–Aug. 10, 1868.
    Vol. 6, Pt. 2–536
Menninger, Charles Frederick, July 11, 1862–Nov. 28, 1953.
    Supp. 5–483
Menninger, William Claire, Oct. 15, 1899–Sept. 6, 1966.
    Supp. 8–428
Menocal, Aniceto Garcia, Sept. 1, 1836–July 20, 1908.
    Vol. 6, Pt. 2–537
Menoher, Charles Thomas, Mar. 20, 1862–Aug. 11, 1930.
    Vol. 6, Pt. 2–538
Mercer, Charles Fenton, June 16, 1778–May 4, 1858.
    Vol. 6, Pt. 2–539
Mercer, Henry Chapman, June 24, 1856–Mar. 9, 1930.
    Vol. 6, Pt. 2–539
Mercer, Hugh, c. 1725–Jan. 12, 1777.
    Vol. 6, Pt. 2–541
Mercer, James, Feb. 26, 1736–Oct. 31, 1793.
    Vol. 6, Pt. 2–542
Mercer, Jesse, Dec. 16, 1769–Sept. 6, 1841.
    Vol. 6, Pt. 2–542
Mercer, John Francis, May 17, 1759–Aug. 30, 1821.
    Vol. 6, Pt. 2–543
Mercer, Lewis Pyle, June 27, 1847–July 6, 1906.
    Vol. 6, Pt. 2–544
Mercer, Margaret, July 1, 1791–Sept. 17, 1846.
    Vol. 6, Pt. 2–545
Mercier, Charles Alfred, June 3, 1816–May 12, 1894.
    Vol. 6, Pt. 2–546
Merck, George Wilhelm, Mar. 29, 1894–Nov. 9, 1957.
    Supp. 6–447
Mercur, Ulysses, Aug. 12, 1818–June 6, 1887.
    Vol. 6, Pt. 2–547
Meredith, Edna C. Elliott, Apr. 25, 1879–Jan. 1, 1961.
    Supp. 7–527
Meredith, Edwin Thomas, Dec. 23, 1876–June 17, 1928.
    Vol. 6, Pt. 2–547
Meredith, Samuel, 1741–Feb. 10, 1817.
    Vol. 6, Pt. 2–548
Meredith, William Morris, June 8, 1799–Aug. 17, 1873.
    Vol. 6, Pt. 2–548
Mergenthaler, Ottmar, May 11, 1854–Oct. 28, 1899.
    Vol. 6, Pt. 2–549
Mergler, Marie Josepha, May 18, 1851–May 17, 1901.
    Vol. 6, Pt. 2–550
Merriam, Augustus Chapman, May 30, 1843–Jan. 19, 1895.
    Vol. 6, Pt. 2–551
Merriam, Charles, Nov. 31, 1806–July 9, 1887.
    Vol. 6, Pt. 2–552
Merriam, Charles Edward, Jr., Nov. 15, 1874–Jan. 8, 1953.
    Supp. 5–484
Merriam, Clinton Hart, Dec. 5, 1855–Mar. 19, 1942.
    Supp. 3–517
Merriam, Henry Clay, Nov. 13, 1837–Nov. 18, 1912.
    Vol. 6, Pt. 2–553

Merriam, John Campbell, Oct. 20, 1869–Oct. 30, 1945.
Supp. 3-519
Merriam, William Rush, July 26, 1849–Feb. 18, 1931.
Vol. 6, Pt. 2-554
Merrick, Edwin Thomas, July 9, 1808–Jan. 12, 1897.
Vol. 6, Pt. 2-555
Merrick, Frederick, Jan. 29, 1810–Mar. 5, 1894.
Vol. 6, Pt. 2-555
Merrick, Pliny, Aug. 2, 1794–Jan. 31, 1867.
Vol. 6, Pt. 2-556
Merrick, Samuel Vaughan, May 4, 1801–Aug. 18, 1870.
Vol. 6, Pt. 2-557
Merrill, Charles Edward, Oct. 19, 1885–Oct. 6, 1956.
Supp. 6-448
Merrill, Daniel, Mar. 18, 1765–June 3, 1833.
Vol. 6, Pt. 2-558
Merrill, Elmer Drew, Oct. 15, 1876–Feb. 25, 1956.
Supp. 6-449
Merrill, Elmer Truesdell, Jan. 1, 1860–Apr. 19, 1936.
Supp. 2-453
Merrill, Frank Dow, Dec. 4, 1903–Dec. 11, 1955.
Supp. 5-486
Merrill, George Edmands, Dec. 19, 1846–June 11. 1908.
Vol. 6, Pt. 2-559
Merrill, George Perkins, May 31, 1854–Aug. 15, 1929.
Vol. 6, Pt. 2-559
Merrill, Gretchen Van Zandt, Nov. 2, 1925–Apr. 15, 1965.
Supp. 7-528
Merrill, James Cushing, Mar. 26, 1853–Oct. 27, 1902.
Vol. 6, Pt. 2-560
Merrill, James Griswold, Aug. 20, 1840–Dec. 22, 1920.
Vol. 6, Pt. 2-561
Merrill, Joshua, Oct. 6, 1820–Jan. 15, 1904.
Vol. 6, Pt. 2-562
Merrill, Samuel, Oct. 29, 1792–Aug. 24, 1855.
Vol. 6, Pt. 2-563
Merrill, Selah, May 2, 1837–Jan. 22, 1909.
Vol. 6, Pt. 2-564
Merrill, Stephen Mason, Sept. 16, 1825–Nov. 12, 1905.
Vol. 6, Pt. 2-565
Merrill, Stuart Fitzrandolph, Aug. 1, 1863–Dec. 1, 1915.
Vol. 6, Pt. 2-566
Merrill, William Bradford, Feb. 27, 1861–Nov. 26, 1928.
Vol. 6, Pt. 2-568
Merrill, William Emery, Oct. 11, 1837–Dec. 14, 1891.
Vol. 6, Pt. 2-568
Merrimon, Augustus Summerfield, Sept. 15, 1830–Nov. 14, 1892. Vol. 6, Pt. 2-569
Merritt, Anna Lea, Sept. 13, 1844–Apr. 7, 1930.
Vol. 6, Pt. 2-570
Merritt, Israel John, Aug. 23, 1829–Dec. 13, 1911.
Vol. 6, Pt. 2-571
Merritt, Leonidas, Feb. 20, 1844–May 9, 1926.
Vol. 6, Pt. 2-571
Merritt, Wesley, June 16, 1834–Dec. 3, 1910.
Vol. 6, Pt. 2-572
Merry, Ann Brunton, May 30, 1769–June 28, 1808.
Vol. 6, Pt. 2-574
Merry, William Lawrence, Dec. 27, 1842–Dec. 14, 1911.
Vol. 6, Pt. 2-574
Merton, Thomas, Jan. 31, 1915–Dec. 10, 1968.
Supp. 8-430
Mervine, William, Mar. 14, 1791–Sept. 15, 1868.
Vol. 6, Pt. 2-575
Merz, Karl, Sept. 19, 1836–Jan. 30, 1890.
Vol. 6, Pt. 2-576
Meserve, Frederick Hill, Nov. 1, 1865–June 25, 1962.
Supp. 7-529
Meserve, Nathaniel, c. 1705–June 28, 1758.
Vol. 6, Pt. 2-577
Messer, Asa, May 31, 1769–Oct. 11, 1836.
Vol. 6, Pt. 2-578
Messersmith, George Strausser, Oct. 3, 1883–Jan. 29, 1960.
Supp. 6-450
Messler, Thomas Doremus, May 9, 1833–Aug. 11, 1893.
Vol. 6, Pt. 2-578
Messmer, Sebastian Gebhard, Aug. 29, 1847–Aug. 4, 1930.
Vol. 6, Pt. 2-579
Mestrovic, Ivan, Aug. 15, 1883–Jan. 16, 1962.
Supp. 7-530
Metalious, Grace, Sept. 8, 1924–Feb. 25, 1964.
Supp. 7-531

Metcalf, Henry Harrison, Apr. 7, 1841–Feb. 5, 1932.
Vol. 6, Pt. 2-580
Metcalf, Joel Hastings, Jan. 4, 1866–Feb. 21, 1925.
Vol. 6, Pt. 2-581
Metcalf, Theron, Oct. 16, 1784–Nov. 13, 1875.
Vol. 6, Pt. 2-582
Metcalf, Willard Leroy, July 1, 1858–Mar. 9, 1925.
Vol. 6, Pt. 2-582
Metcalf, William, Sept. 3, 1838–Dec. 5, 1909.
Vol. 6, Pt. 2-583
Metcalfe, Samuel Lytler, Sept. 21, 1798–July 17, 1856.
Vol. 6, Pt. 2-584
Metcalfe, Thomas, Mar. 20, 1780–Aug. 18, 1855.
Vol. 6, Pt. 2-584
Mettauer, John Peter, 1787–Nov. 22, 1875.
Vol. 6, Pt. 2-585
Metz, Christian, Dec. 30, 1794–July 27, 1867.
Vol. 6, Pt. 2-586
Meyer, Adolf, Sept. 13, 1866–Mar. 17, 1950.
Supp. 4-569
Meyer, Agnes Elizabeth Ernst, Jan. 2, 1887–Sept. 1, 1970.
Supp. 8-432
Meyer, Albert Gregory, Mar. 9, 1903–Apr. 9, 1965.
Supp. 7-532
Meyer, Annie Nathan, Feb. 19, 1867–Sept. 23, 1951.
Supp. 5-487
Meyer, Eugene Isaac, Oct. 31, 1875–July 17, 1959.
Supp. 6-452
Meyer, George von Lengerke, June 24, 1858–Mar. 9, 1918.
Vol. 6, Pt. 2-587
Meyer, Henry Coddington, Apr. 14, 1844–Mar. 27, 1935.
Supp. 1-552
Meyer, Martin Abraham, Jan. 15, 1879–June 27, 1923.
Vol. 6, Pt. 2-588
Meyerhof, Otto, Apr. 12, 1884–Oct. 6, 1951.
Supp. 5-488
Mezes, Sidney Edward, Sept. 23, 1863–Sept. 10, 1931.
Vol. 6, Pt. 2-588
Miantonomo, d. 1643.
Vol. 6, Pt. 2-589
Mich, Daniel Danforth, Jan. 8, 1905–Nov. 22, 1965.
Supp. 7-535
Michael, Arthur, Aug. 7, 1853–Feb. 8, 1942.
Supp. 3-520
Michaelis, Leonor, Jan. 16, 1875–Oct. 8, 1949.
Supp. 4-572
Michaëlius, Jonas, b. 1584.
Vol. 6, Pt. 2-590
Michaux, André, Mar. 7, 1746–Nov. 1802.
Vol. 6, Pt. 2-591
Michaux, François André, Aug. 16, 1770–Oct. 23, 1855.
Vol. 6, Pt. 2-592
Michaux, Lightfoot Solomon, 1885[?]–Oct. 20, 1968.
Supp. 8-434
Micheaux, Oscar, Jan. 2[?], 1884–Mar. 26, 1951.
Supp. 5-490
Michel, Virgil George, June 26, 1890–Nov. 26, 1938.
Supp. 2-454
Michel, William Middleton, Jan. 22, 1822–June 4, 1894.
Vol. 6, Pt. 2-593
Michelson, Albert Abraham, Dec. 19, 1852–May 9, 1931.
Vol. 6, Pt. 2-593
Michelson, Charles, Apr. 18, 1868–Jan. 8, 1948.
Supp. 4-574
Michener, Ezra, Nov. 24, 1794–June 24, 1887.
Vol. 6, Pt. 2-596
Michie, Peter Smith, Mar. 24, 1839–Feb. 16, 1901.
Vol. 6, Pt. 2-597
Michikinikwa. [See Little Turtle, c. 1752–1812.]
Michler, Nathaniel, Sept. 13, 1827–July 17, 1881.
Supp. 1-552
Middleton, Arthur, 1681–Sept. 7, 1737.
Vol. 6, Pt. 2-598
Middleton, Arthur, June 26, 1742–Jan. 1, 1787.
Vol. 6, Pt. 2-599
Middleton, Henry, 1717–June 13, 1784.
Vol. 6, Pt. 2-600
Middleton, Henry, Sept. 28, 1770–June 14, 1846.
Vol. 6, Pt. 2-600
Middleton, John Izard, Aug. 13, 1785–Oct. 5, 1849.
Vol. 6, Pt. 2-601
Middleton, Nathaniel Russell, Apr. 1, 1810–Sept. 6, 1890.
Vol. 6, Pt. 2-602

Mills, Cyrus Taggart, May 4, 1819–Apr. 20, 1884.
    Vol. 7, Pt. 1–5
Mills, Darius Ogden, Sept. 5, 1825–Jan. 4, 1910.
    Vol. 7, Pt. 1–6
Mills, Elijah Hunt, Dec. 1, 1776–May 5, 1829.
    Vol. 7, Pt. 1–7
Mills, Enos Abijah, Apr. 22, 1870–Sept. 21, 1922.
    Supp. 1–554
Mills, Hiram Francis, Nov. 1, 1836–Oct. 4, 1921.
    Vol. 7, Pt. 1–8
Mills, Lawrence Heyworth, 1837–Jan. 29, 1918.
    Vol. 7, Pt. 1–9
Mills, Ogden Livingston, Aug. 23, 1884–Oct. 11, 1937.
    Supp. 2–459
Mills, Robert, Aug. 12, 1781–Mar. 3, 1855.
    Vol. 7, Pt. 1–9
Mills, Robert, Mar. 9, 1809–Apr. 13, 1888.
    Vol. 7, Pt. 1–13
Mills, Roger Quarles, Mar. 30, 1832–Sept. 2, 1911.
    Vol. 7, Pt. 1–14
Mills, Samuel John, Apr. 21, 1783–June 16, 1818.
    Vol. 7, Pt. 1–15
Mills, Susan Lincoln Tolman, Nov. 18, 1826–Dec. 12, 1912.
    Vol. 7, Pt. 1–16
Millspaugh, Charles Frederick, June 20, 1854–Sept. 15, 1923. Vol. 7, Pt. 1–17
Milner, John Turner, Sept. 29, 1826–Aug. 18, 1898.
    Vol. 7, Pt. 1–19
Milner, Moses Embree. [See California Joe, 1829–1876.]
Milner, Thomas Picton. [See Picton, Thomas, 1822–1891.]
Milroy, Robert Huston, June 11, 1816–Mar. 29, 1890.
    Vol. 7, Pt. 1–20
Milton, George Fort, Nov. 19, 1894–Nov. 12, 1955.
    Supp. 5–497
Milton, John, Apr. 20, 1807–Apr. 1, 1865.
    Vol. 7, Pt. 1–21
Miner, Alonzo Ames, Aug. 17, 1814–June 14, 1895.
    Vol. 7, Pt. 1–21
Miner, Charles, Feb. 1, 1780–Oct. 26, 1865.
    Vol. 7, Pt. 1–22
Miner, Myrtilla, Mar. 4, 1815–Dec. 17, 1864.
    Vol. 7, Pt. 1–23
Ming, John Joseph, Sept. 20, 1838–June 17, 1910.
    Vol. 7, Pt. 1–24
Minnigerode, Lucy, Feb. 8, 1871–Mar. 24, 1935.
    Supp. 1–555
Minor, Benjamin Blake, Oct. 21, 1818–Aug. 1 1905.
    Vol. 7, Pt. 1–25
Minor, John Barbee, June 2, 1813–July 29, 1895.
    Vol. 7, Pt. 1–26
Minor, Lucian, Apr. 24, 1802–July 8, 1858.
    Vol. 7, Pt. 1–27
Minor, Raleigh Colston, Jan. 24, 1869–June 14, 1923.
    Vol. 7, Pt. 1–27
Minor, Robert, July 15, 1884–Nov. 26, 1952.
    Supp. 5–498
Minor, Robert Crannell, Apr. 30, 1839–Aug. 3 1904.
    Vol. 7, Pt. 1–28
Minor, Virginia Louisa, Mar. 27, 1824–Aug. 14, 1894.
    Vol. 7, Pt. 1–29
Minot, Charles Sedgwick, Dec. 23, 1852–Nov. 19, 1914.
    Vol. 7, Pt. 1–30
Minot, George Richards, Dec. 2, 1885–Feb. 25, 1950.
    Supp. 4–580
Minot, George Richards, Dec. 22, 1758–Jan. 2, 1802.
    Vol. 7, Pt. 1–31
Minto, Walter, Dec. 5, 1753–Oct. 21, 1796.
    Vol. 7, Pt. 1–32
Minton, Sherman, Oct. 20, 1890–Apr. 9, 1965.
    Supp. 7–540
Minturn, Robert Bowne, Nov. 16, 1805–Jan. 9, 1866.
    Vol. 7, Pt. 1–32
Minty, Robert Horatio George, Dec. 4, 1831–Aug. 24, 1906.
    Vol. 7, Pt. 1–33
Minuit, Peter, 1580–1638.
    Vol. 7, Pt. 1–33
Miranda, Carmen, Feb. 9, 1909–Aug. 5, 1955.
    Supp. 5–500
Miró, Esteban Rodriguez, 1744–1795.
    Vol. 7, Pt. 1–35
Mitchel, John, Nov. 3, 1815–Mar. 20, 1875.
    Vol. 7, Pt. 1–35

Mitchel, John Purroy, July 19, 1879–July 6, 1918.
    Vol. 7, Pt. 1–37
Mitchel, Ormsby MacKnight July 28, 1809–Oct. 30, 1862.
    Vol. 7, Pt. 1–38
Mitchell, Albert Graeme, Feb. 21, 1889–June 1, 1941.
    Supp. 3–525
Mitchell, Alexander, Oct. 18, 1817–Apr. 19, 1887.
    Vol. 7, Pt. 1–39
Mitchell, David Brydie, Oct. 22, 1766–Apr. 22, 1837.
    Vol. 7, Pt. 1–40
Mitchell, David Dawson, July 31, 1806–May 23, 1861.
    Vol. 7, Pt. 1–41
Mitchell, Donald Grant, Apr. 12, 1822–Dec. 15, 1908.
    Vol. 7, Pt. 1–41
Mitchell, Edward Cushing, Sept. 20, 1829–Feb. 27, 1900.
    Vol. 7, Pt. 1–42
Mitchell, Edward Page, Mar. 24, 1852–Jan. 22, 1927.
    Vol. 7, Pt. 1–43
Mitchell, Edwin Knox, Dec. 23, 1853–Oct. 5, 1934.
    Supp. 1–556
Mitchell, Elisha, Aug. 19, 1793–June 27, 1857.
    Vol. 7, Pt. 1–45
Mitchell, George Edward, Mar. 3, 1781–June 28, 1832.
    Vol. 7, Pt. 1–46
Mitchell, Henry, Sept. 16, 1830–Dec. 1, 1902.
    Vol. 7, Pt. 1–47
Mitchell, Hinckley Gilbert Thomas, Feb. 22, 1846–May 19, 1920. Vol. 7, Pt. 1–47
Mitchell, Isaac, c. 1759–Nov. 26, 1812.
    Vol. 7, Pt. 1–48
Mitchell, James Paul, Nov. 12, 1900–Oct. 19, 1964.
    Supp. 7–542
Mitchell, James Tyndale, Nov. 9, 1834–July 4, 1915.
    Vol. 7, Pt. 1–49
Mitchell, John, d. 1768.
    Vol. 7, Pt. 1–50
Mitchell, John, Feb. 4, 1870–Sept. 9, 1919.
    Vol. 7, Pt. 1–51
Mitchell, John Ames, Jan. 17, 1845–June 29, 1918.
    Vol. 7, Pt. 1–52
Mitchell, John Hipple, June 22, 1835–Dec. 8, 1905.
    Vol. 7, Pt. 1–53
Mitchell, John Kearsley, May 12, 1793–Apr. 4, 1858.
    Vol. 7, Pt. 1–54
Mitchell, Jonathan, 1624–July 9, 1668.
    Vol. 7, Pt. 1–55
Mitchell, Langdon Elwyn, Feb. 17, 1862–Oct. 21, 1935.
    Supp. 1–557
Mitchell, Lucy Myers Wright, Mar. 20, 1845–Mar. 10, 1888.
    Vol. 7, Pt. 1–56
Mitchell, Lucy Sprague, July 2, 1878–Oct. 15, 1967.
    Supp. 8–442
Mitchell, Margaret Julia, June 14, 1837–Mar. 22, 1918.
    Vol. 7, Pt. 1–56
Mitchell, Margaret Munnerlyn, Nov. 8, 1900–Aug. 16, 1949.
    Supp. 4–583
Mitchell, Maria, Aug. 1, 1818–June 28, 1889.
    Vol. 7, Pt. 1–57
Mitchell, Nahum, Feb. 12, 1769–Aug. 1, 1853.
    Vol. 7, Pt. 1–58
Mitchell, Nathaniel, 1753–Feb. 21, 1814.
    Vol. 7, Pt. 1–59
Mitchell, Robert Byington, Apr. 4, 1823–Jan. 26, 1882.
    Vol. 7, Pt. 1–60
Mitchell, Samuel Augustus, Mar. 20, 1792–Dec. 18, 1868.
    Vol. 7, Pt. 1–61
Mitchell, Sidney Zollicoffer, Mar. 17, 1862–Feb. 17, 1944.
    Supp. 3–526
Mitchell, Silas Weir, Feb. 15, 1829–Jan. 4, 1914.
    Vol. 7, Pt. 1–62
Mitchell, Stephen Mix, Dec. 9, 1743–Sept. 30, 1835.
    Vol. 7, Pt. 1–65
Mitchell, Thomas Duché, 1791–May 13, 1865.
    Vol. 7, Pt. 1–66
Mitchell, Thomas Gregory, July 11, 1892–Dec. 17, 1962.
    Supp. 7–544
Mitchell, Wesley Clair, Aug. 5, 1874–Oct. 29, 1948.
    Supp. 4–584
Mitchell, William, Dec. 20, 1791–Apr. 1, 1869.
    Vol. 7, Pt. 1–66
Mitchell, William, 1798–May 11, 1856.
    Vol. 7, Pt. 1–67

Mitchell, William, Feb. 24, 1801–Oct. 6, 1886.
Vol. 7, Pt. 1–68
Mitchell, William, Nov. 19, 1832–Aug. 21, 1900.
Vol. 7, Pt. 1–68
Mitchell, William, Dec. 29, 1879–Feb. 19, 1936.
Supp. 2–460
Mitchell, William DeWitt, Sept. 9, 1874–Aug. 24, 1955.
Supp. 5–501
Mitchill, Samuel Latham, Aug. 20, 1764–Sept. 7, 1831.
Vol. 7, Pt. 1–69
Mitropoulos, Dimitri, Mar. 1, 1896–Nov. 2, 1960.
Supp. 6–456
Mitscher, Marc Andrew, Jan. 20, 1887–Feb. 3, 1947.
Supp. 4–588
Mitten, Thomas Eugene, Mar. 31, 1864–Oct. 1, 1929.
Vol. 7, Pt. 1–71
Mix, Tom, Jan. 6, 1880–Oct. 12, 1940.
Supp. 2–462
Mixter, Samuel Jason, May 10, 1855–Jan. 19, 1926.
Vol. 7, Pt. 1–72
Mizner, Addison, 1872–Feb. 5, 1933.
Supp. 1–558
Modjeska, Helena, Oct. 12, 1840–Apr. 8, 1909.
Vol. 7, Pt. 1–73
Modjeski, Ralph, Jan. 27, 1861–June 26, 1940.
Supp. 2–463
Moeller, Henry, Dec. 11, 1849–Jan. 5, 1925.
Vol. 7, Pt. 1–74
Moffat, David Halliday, July 22, 1839–Mar. 18, 1911.
Vol. 7, Pt. 1–75
Moffat, James Clement, May 30, 1811–June 7, 1890.
Vol. 7, Pt. 1–75
Moffat, Jay Pierrepont, July 18, 1896–Jan. 24, 1943.
Supp. 3–528
Moffatt, James, July 4, 1870–June 27, 1944.
Supp. 3–529
Moffett, Cleveland Langston, Apr. 27, 1863–Oct. 14, 1926.
Vol. 7, Pt. 1–76
Moffett, William Adger, Oct. 31, 1869–Apr. 4, 1933.
Supp. 1–560
Moholy-Nagy, László, July 20, 1895–Nov. 24, 1946.
Supp. 4–590
Mohr, Charles Theodore, Dec. 28, 1824–July 17, 1901.
Vol. 7, Pt. 1–77
Möise, Penina, Apr. 23, 1797–Sept. 13, 1880.
Vol. 7, Pt. 1–78
Moisseiff, Leon Solomon, Nov. 10, 1872–Sept. 3, 1943.
Supp. 3–530
Moldehnke, Edward Frederick, Aug. 10, 1836–June 25, 1904.
Vol. 7, Pt. 1–78
Moldenke, Richard George Gottlob, Nov. 1, 1864–Nov. 17, 1930. Vol. 7, Pt. 1–79
Mollenhauer, Emil, Aug. 4, 1855–Dec. 10, 1927.
Vol. 7, Pt. 1–80
Möllhausen, Heinrich Baldwin, Jan. 27, 1825–May 28, 1905.
Vol. 7, Pt. 1–80
Molyneux, Robert, July 24, 1738–Dec. 9, 1808.
Vol. 7, Pt. 1–81
Mombert, Jacob Isidor, Nov. 6, 1829–Oct. 7, 1913.
Vol. 7, Pt. 1–82
Monckton, Robert, June 24, 1726–May 21, 1782.
Vol. 7, Pt. 1–83
Moncure, Richard Cassius Lee, Dec. 11, 1805–Aug. 24, 1882.
Vol. 7, Pt. 1–84
Mondell, Frank Wheeler, Nov. 6, 1860–Aug. 6, 1939.
Supp. 2–464
Monette, John Wesley, Apr. 5, 1803–Mar. 1, 1851.
Vol. 7, Pt. 1–85
Money, Hernando De Soto, Aug. 26, 1839–Sept. 18, 1912.
Vol. 7, Pt. 1–85
Monis, Judah, Feb. 4, 1683–Apr. 25, 1764.
Vol. 7, Pt. 1–86
Monroe, Harriet, Dec. 23, 1860–Sept. 26, 1936.
Supp. 2–466
Monroe, James, Apr. 28, 1758–July 4, 1831.
Vol. 7, Pt. 1–87
Monroe, Marilyn, June 1, 1926–Aug. 5, 1962.
Supp. 7–545
Monroe, Paul, June 7, 1869–Dec. 6, 1947.
Supp. 4–591
Monsky, Henry, Feb. 4, 1890–May 2, 1947.
Supp. 4–593

Montague, Andrew Jackson, Oct. 3, 1862–Jan. 24, 1937.
Supp. 2–467
Montague, Gilbert Holland, May 27, 1880–Feb. 4, 1961.
Supp. 7–547
Montague, Henry James, Jan. 20, 1843–Aug. 11, 1878.
Vol. 7, Pt. 1–93
Montague, William Pepperell, Nov. 11, 1873–Aug. 1, 1953.
Supp. 5–503
Montefiore, Joshua, Aug. 7, 1762–June 26, 1843.
Vol. 7, Pt. 1–93
Monteux, Pierre Benjamin, Apr. 4, 1875–July 1, 1964.
Supp. 7–548
Montgomery, David Henry, Apr. 7, 1837–May 28, 1928.
Vol. 7, Pt. 1–94
Montgomery, Edmund Duncan, Mar. 19, 1835–Apr. 17, 1911. Vol. 7, Pt. 1–95
Montgomery, George Washington, 1804–June 5, 1841.
Vol. 7, Pt. 1–96
Montgomery, James, Dec. 22, 1814–Dec. 6, 1871.
Vol. 7, Pt. 1–97
Montgomery, James Alan, June 13, 1866–Feb. 6, 1949.
Supp. 4–594
Montgomery, John Berrien, Nov. 17, 1794–Mar. 25, 1873.
Vol. 7, Pt. 1–97
Montgomery, Richard, Dec. 2, 1738–Dec. 31, 1775.
Vol. 7, Pt. 1–98
Montgomery, Thomas Harrison, Mar. 5, 1873–Mar. 19, 1912. Vol. 7, Pt. 1–99
Montgomery, William Bell, Aug. 21, 1829–Sept. 25, 1904.
Vol. 7, Pt. 1–100
Montrésor, James Gabriel, Nov. 19, 1702–Jan. 6, 1776.
Vol. 7, Pt. 1–100
Montrésor, John, Apr. 6, 1736–June 26, 1799.
Vol. 7, Pt. 1–101
Mood, Francis Asbury, June 23, 1830–Nov. 12, 1884.
Vol. 7, Pt. 1–102
Moody, (Arthur Edson) Blair, Feb. 13, 1902–July 20, 1954.
Supp. 5–504
Moody, Dwight Lyman, Feb. 5, 1837–Dec. 22, 1899.
Vol. 7, Pt. 1–103
Moody, James, 1744–Apr. 6, 1809.
Vol. 7, Pt. 1–106
Moody, John, May 2, 1868–Feb. 16, 1958.
Supp. 6–457
Moody, Paul, May 21, 1779–July 8, 1831.
Vol. 7, Pt. 1–106
Moody, William Henry, Dec. 23, 1853–July 2, 1917.
Vol. 7, Pt. 1–107
Moody, William Vaughan, July 8, 1869–Oct. 17, 1910.
Vol. 7, Pt. 1–108
Moon, Parker Thomas, June 5, 1892–June 11, 1936.
Supp. 2–468
Mooney, James, Feb. 10, 1861–Dec. 22, 1921.
Vol. 7, Pt. 1–110
Mooney, Thomas Joseph, Dec. 8, 1882–Mar. 6, 1942.
Supp. 3–531
Mooney, William, 1756–Nov. 27, 1831.
Vol. 7, Pt. 1–111
Moore, Addison Webster, July 30, 1866–Aug. 25, 1930.
Vol. 7, Pt. 1–111
Moore, Alfred, May 21, 1755–Oct. 15, 1810.
Vol. 7, Pt. 1–112
Moore, Andrew, 1752–May 24, 1821.
Vol. 7, Pt. 1–113
Moore, Anne Carroll, July 12, 1871–Jan. 20, 1961.
Supp. 7–550
Moore, Annie Aubertine Woodward, Sept. 27, 1841–Sept. 22, 1929. Vol. 7, Pt. 1–114
Moore, (Austin) Merrill, Sept. 11, 1903–Sept. 20, 1957.
Supp. 6–461
Moore, Bartholomew Figures, Jan. 29, 1801–Nov. 27, 1878.
Vol. 7, Pt. 1–114
Moore, Benjamin, Oct. 5, 1748–Feb. 27, 1816.
Vol. 7, Pt. 1–115
Moore, Charles, Oct. 20, 1855–Sept. 25, 1942.
Supp. 3–533
Moore, Charles Herbert, Apr 10, 1840–Feb. 15, 1930.
Vol. 7, Pt. 1–116
Moore, Clarence Lemuel Elisha, May 12, 1876–Dec. 5, 1931.
Vol. 7, Pt. 1–117
Moore, Clement Clarke, July 15, 1779–July 10, 1863.
Vol. 7, Pt. 1–118

Moore, Clifford Herschel, Mar. 11, 1866–Aug. 31, 1931.
　Vol. 7, Pt. 1–119
Moore, Edward Mott, July 15, 1814–Mar. 3, 1902.
　Vol. 7, Pt. 1–119
Moore, Edwin Ward, June 1810–Oct. 5, 1865.
　Vol. 7, Pt. 1–120
Moore, Eliakim Hastings, Jan. 26, 1862–Dec. 30, 1932.
　Supp. 1–561
Moore, Ely, July 4, 1798–Jan. 27, 1860.
　Vol. 7, Pt. 1–121
Moore, Frank, Dec. 17, 1828–Aug. 10, 1904.
　Vol. 7, Pt. 1–122
Moore, Frederick Randolph, June 16, 1857–Mar. 1, 1943.
　Supp. 3–534
Moore, Gabriel, 1785?–June 9, 1845?.
　Vol. 7, Pt. 1–122
Moore, George Fleming, July 17, 1822–Aug. 30, 1883.
　Vol. 7, Pt. 1–123
Moore, George Foot, Oct. 15, 1851–May 16, 1931.
　Vol. 7, Pt. 1–124
Moore, George Henry, Apr. 20, 1823–May 5, 1892.
　Vol. 7, Pt. 1–125
Moore, Grace, Dec. 5, 1901–Jan. 26, 1947.
　Supp. 4–596
Moore, Sir Henry, Feb. 7, 1713–Sept. 11, 1769.
　Vol. 7, Pt. 1–126
Moore, Henry Ludwell, Nov. 21, 1869–Apr. 28, 1958.
　Supp. 6–458
Moore, Jacob Bailey, Oct. 31, 1797–Sept. 1, 1853.
　Vol. 7, Pt. 1–127
Moore, James, d. 1706.
　Vol. 7, Pt. 1–127
Moore, James, 1737–April 1777.
　Vol. 7, Pt. 1–128
Moore, James, 1764–June 22, 1814.
　Vol. 7, Pt. 1–129
Moore, James Edward, Mar. 2, 1852–Nov. 2, 1918.
　Vol. 7, Pt. 1–129
Moore, John, c. 1659–Dec. 2, 1732.
　Vol. 7, Pt. 1–130
Moore, John, June 24, 1834–July 30, 1901.
　Vol. 7, Pt. 1–131
Moore, John Bassett, Dec. 3, 1860–Nov. 12, 1947.
　Supp. 4–597
Moore, John Trotwood, Aug. 26, 1858–May 10, 1929.
　Vol. 7, Pt. 1–132
Moore, John Weeks, Apr. 11, 1807–Mar. 23, 1889.
　Vol. 7, Pt. 1–133
Moore, Joseph Earle, July 9, 1892–Dec. 6, 1957.
　Supp. 6–460
Moore, Joseph Haines, Sept. 7, 1878–Mar. 15, 1949.
　Supp. 4–600
Moore, Maurice, 1735–1777.
　Vol. 7, Pt. 1–133
Moore, Nathaniel Fish, Dec. 25, 1782–Apr. 27, 1872.
　Vol. 7, Pt. 1–134
Moore, Nicholas. [See More, Nicholas, d. 1689.]
Moore, Philip North, July 8, 1849–Jan. 19, 1930.
　Vol. 7, Pt. 1–135
Moore, Richard Bishop, May 6, 1871–Jan. 20, 1931.
　Vol. 7, Pt. 1–136
Moore, Richard Channing, Aug. 21, 1762–Nov. 11, 1841.
　Vol. 7, Pt. 1–136
Moore, Samuel Preston, 1813–May 31, 1889.
　Vol. 7, Pt. 1–137
Moore, Thomas Overton, Apr. 10, 1804–June 25, 1876.
　Vol. 7, Pt. 1–138
Moore, Thomas Patrick, 1796?–July 21, 1853.
　Vol. 7, Pt. 1–139
Moore, Veranus Alva, Apr. 13, 1859–Feb. 11, 1931.
　Vol. 7, Pt. 1–140
Moore, Victor Frederick, Feb. 24, 1876–July 23, 1962.
　Supp. 7–551
Moore, William, May 6, 1699–May 30, 1783.
　Vol. 7, Pt. 1–141
Moore, William, c. 1735–July 24, 1793.
　Vol. 7, Pt. 1–142
Moore, William Henry, Oct. 25, 1848–Jan. 11, 1923.
　Vol. 7, Pt. 1–142
Moore, William Thomas, Aug. 27, 1832–Sept. 7, 1926.
　Vol. 7, Pt. 1–145
Moore, Zephaniah Swift, Nov. 20, 1770–June 30, 1823.
　Vol. 7, Pt. 1–146

Moorehead, William Gallogly, Mar. 19, 1836–Mar. 1, 1914.
　Vol. 7, Pt. 1–147
Moorhead, James Kennedy, Sept. 7, 1806–Mar. 6, 1884.
　Vol. 7, Pt. 1–147
Moosmüller, Oswald William, Feb. 26, 1832–Jan. 10, 1901.
　Vol. 7, Pt. 1–148
Morais, Sabato, Apr. 13, 1823–Nov. 11, 1897.
　Vol. 7, Pt. 1–149
Moran, Benjamin, Aug. 1, 1820–June 20, 1886.
　Vol. 7, Pt. 1–150
Moran, Daniel Edward, Apr. 12, 1864–July 3, 1937.
　Supp. 2–469
Moran, Edward, Aug. 19, 1829–June 9, 1901.
　Vol. 7, Pt. 1–151
Moran, Eugene Francis, Mar. 24, 1872–Apr. 13, 1961.
　Supp. 7–552
Moran, Peter, Mar. 4, 1841–Nov. 9, 1914.
　Vol. 7, Pt. 1–152
Moran, Thomas, Jan. 12, 1837–Aug. 26, 1926.
　Vol. 7, Pt. 1–152
Morawetz, Victor, Apr. 3, 1859–May 18, 1938.
　Supp. 2–470
Mordecai, Alfred, Jan. 3, 1804–Oct. 23, 1887.
　Vol. 7, Pt. 1–153
Mordecai, Moses Cohen, Feb. 19, 1804–Dec. 30, 1888.
　Vol. 7, Pt. 1–154
More, Nicholas, d. 1689.
　Vol. 7, Pt. 1–155
More, Paul Elmer, Dec. 12, 1864–Mar. 9, 1937.
　Supp. 2–471
Moreau de Saint-Méry, Médéric-Louis-Élie, Jan. 13, 1750–
　Jan 28, 1819. Vol. 7, Pt. 1–156
Moreau-Lislet, Louis Casimir Elisabeth, 1767–Dec. 3, 1832.
　Vol. 7, Pt. 1–157
Morehead, Charles Slaughter, July 7, 1802–Dec. 21, 1868.
　Vol. 7, Pt. 1–157
Morehead, James Turner, May 24, 1797–Dec. 28, 1854.
　Vol. 7, Pt. 1–158
Morehead, John Motley, Nov. 3, 1870–Jan. 7, 1965.
　Supp. 7–553
Morehead, John Motley, July 4, 1796–Aug. 27, 1866.
　Vol. 7, Pt. 1–159
Morehouse, Henry Lyman, Oct. 2, 1834–May 5, 1917.
　Vol. 7, Pt. 1–159
Morehouse, Ward, Nov. 24, 1899–Dec. 8, 1966.
　Supp. 8–443
Morell, George Webb, Jan. 8, 1815–Feb. 11, 1883.
　Vol. 7, Pt. 1–160
Morey, Samuel, Oct. 23, 1762–Apr. 17, 1843.
　Vol. 7, Pt. 1–161
Morfit, Campbell, Nov. 19, 1820–Dec. 8, 1897.
　Vol. 7, Pt. 1–162
Morford, Henry, Mar. 10, 1823–Aug. 4, 1881.
　Vol. 7, Pt. 1–162
Morgan, Abel, 1673–Dec. 16, 1722.
　Vol. 7, Pt. 1–163
Morgan, Anne, July 25, 1873–Jan. 29, 1952.
　Supp. 5–505
Morgan, Charles, Apr. 21, 1795–May 8, 1878.
　Vol. 7, Pt. 1–164
Morgan, Charles Hill, Jan. 8, 1831–Jan. 10, 1911.
　Vol. 7, Pt. 1–165
Morgan, Daniel, 1736–July 6, 1802.
　Vol. 7, Pt. 1–166
Morgan, Edwin Barber, May 2, 1806–Oct. 13, 1881.
　Vol. 7, Pt. 1–167
Morgan, Edwin Denison, Feb. 8, 1811–Feb. 14, 1883.
　Vol. 7, Pt. 1–168
Morgan, Edwin Vernon, Feb. 22, 1865–Apr. 16, 1934.
　Supp. 1–563
Morgan, George Washington, Sept. 20, 1820–July 26, 1893.
　Vol. 7, Pt. 1–170
Morgan, George, Feb. 14, 1743–Mar. 10, 1810.
　Vol. 7, Pt. 1–169
Morgan, Helen, Aug. 2, 1900–Oct. 8, 1941.
　Supp. 3–535
Morgan, James Dada, Aug. 1, 1810–Sept. 12, 1896.
　Vol. 7, Pt. 1–171
Morgan, James Morris, Mar. 10, 1845–Apr. 21, 1928.
　Vol. 7, Pt. 1–172
Morgan, John, June 10, 1735–Oct. 15, 1789.
　Vol. 7, Pt. 1–172

Morgan, John Harcourt Alexander, Aug. 31, 1867–Aug. 25, 1950. Supp. 4–601

Morgan, John Hunt, June 1, 1825–Sept. 4, 1864.
  Vol. 7, Pt. 1–174

Morgan, John Pierpont, Apr. 17, 1837–Mar. 31, 1913.
  Vol. 7, Pt. 1–175

Morgan, John Pierpont, Sept. 7, 1867–Mar. 13, 1943.
  Supp. 3–537

Morgan, John Tyler, June 20, 1824–June 11, 1907.
  Vol. 7, Pt. 1–180

Morgan, Julia, Jan. 26, 1872–Feb. 2, 1957.
  Supp. 6–462

Morgan, Junius Spencer, Apr. 14, 1813–Apr. 8, 1890.
  Vol. 7, Pt. 1–181

Morgan, Justin, 1747–Mar. 22, 1798.
  Vol. 7, Pt. 1–182

Morgan, Lewis Henry, Nov. 21, 1818–Dec. 17, 1881.
  Vol. 7, Pt. 1–183

Morgan, Matthew Somerville, Apr. 27, 1839–June 2, 1890.
  Vol. 7, Pt. 1–185

Morgan, Morris Hicky, Feb. 8, 1859–Mar. 16, 1910.
  Vol. 7, Pt. 1–186

Morgan, Philip Hicky, Nov. 9, 1825–Aug. 12, 1900.
  Vol. 7, Pt. 1–187

Morgan, Thomas Hunt, Sept. 25, 1866–Dec. 4, 1945.
  Supp. 3–538

Morgan, Thomas Jefferson, Aug. 17, 1839–July 13, 1902.
  Vol. 7, Pt. 1–187

Morgan, William, Aug. 7, 1774?–1826?.
  Vol. 7, Pt. 1–188

Morgenthau, Henry, Apr. 26, 1856–Nov. 25, 1946.
  Supp. 4–602

Morgenthau, Henry, Jr., May 11, 1891–Feb. 6, 1967.
  Supp. 8–445

Moriarity, Patrick Eugene, July 4, 1804–July 10, 1875.
  Vol. 7, Pt. 1–189

Morini, Austin John, Mar. 4, 1826–July 29, 1909.
  Vol. 7, Pt. 1–190

Morison, George Shattuck, Dec. 19, 1842–July 1, 1903.
  Vol. 7, Pt. 1–191

Morley, Christopher Darlington, May 5, 1890–Mar. 28, 1957.
  Supp. 6–464

Morley, Edward Williams, Jan. 29, 1838–Feb. 24, 1923.
  Vol. 7, Pt. 1–192

Morley, Frank, Sept. 9, 1860–Oct. 17, 1937.
  Supp. 2–473

Morley, Margaret Warner, Feb. 17, 1858–Dec. 12, 1923.
  Vol. 7, Pt. 1–193

Morley, Sylvanus Griswold, June 7, 1883–Sept. 2, 1948.
  Supp. 4–605

Morphy, Paul Charles, June 22, 1837–July 10, 1884.
  Vol. 7, Pt. 1–193

Morrell, Benjamin, July 5, 1795–1839.
  Vol. 7, Pt. 1–195

Morril, David Lawrence, June 10, 1772–Jan. 28, 1849.
  Vol. 7, Pt. 1–195

Morrill, Anson Peaslee, June 10, 1803–July 4, 1887.
  Vol. 6, Pt. 2–196

Morrill, Edmund Needham, Feb. 12, 1834–Mar. 14, 1909.
  Vol. 7, Pt. 1–197

Morrill, Justin Smith, Apr. 14, 1810–Dec. 28, 1898.
  Vol. 7, Pt. 1–198

Morrill, Lot Myrick, May 3, 1812–Jan. 10, 1883.
  Vol. 7, Pt. 1–199

Morris, Anthony, Aug. 23, 1654–Oct. 23, 1721.
  Vol. 7, Pt. 1–200

Morris, Anthony, Feb. 10, 1766–Nov. 3, 1860.
  Vol. 7, Pt. 1–201

Morris, Cadwalader, Apr. 19, 1741 o.s.–Jan. 25, 1795.
  Vol. 7, Pt. 1–201

Morris, Caspar, May 2, 1805–Mar. 17, 1884.
  Vol. 7, Pt. 1–202

Morris, Charles, July 26, 1784–Jan. 27, 1856.
  Vol. 7, Pt. 1–202

Morris, Clara, Mar. 17, 1848–Nov. 20, 1925.
  Vol. 7, Pt. 1–203

Morris, Edmund, Aug. 28, 1804–May 4, 1874.
  Vol. 7, Pt. 1–204

Morris, Edward Dafydd, Oct. 31, 1825–Nov. 21, 1915.
  Vol. 7, Pt. 1–205

Morris, Edward Joy, July 16, 1815–Dec. 31, 1881.
  Vol. 7, Pt. 1–206

Morris, Elizabeth, c. 1753–Apr. 17, 1826.
  Vol. 7, Pt. 1–206

Morris, George Pope, Oct. 10, 1802–July 6, 1864.
  Vol. 7, Pt. 1–207

Morris, George Sylvester, Nov. 15, 1840–Mar. 23, 1889.
  Vol. 7, Pt. 1–208

Morris, Gouverneur, Jan. 31, 1752–Nov. 6, 1816.
  Vol. 7, Pt. 1–209

Morris, John Gottlieb, Nov. 14, 1803–Oct. 10, 1895.
  Vol. 7, Pt. 1–212

Morris, Lewis, Oct. 15, 1671–May 21, 1746.
  Vol. 7, Pt. 1–213

Morris, Lewis, Apr. 8, 1726–Jan. 22, 1798.
  Vol. 7, Pt. 1–214

Morris, Lewis Richard, Nov. 2, 1760–Dec. 29, 1825.
  Vol. 7, Pt. 1–215

Morris, Luzon Burritt, Apr. 16, 1827–Aug. 22, 1895
  Vol. 7, Pt. 1–216

Morris, Mary Philipse, 1730–1825. [See Morris, Roger, 1727 –1794.]

Morris, Nelson, Jan. 21, 1838–Aug. 27, 1907.
  Vol. 7, Pt. 1–217

Morris, Mrs. Owen. [See Morris, Elizabeth, c. 1753–1826.]

Morris, Richard, Aug. 15, 1730–Apr. 11, 1810.
  Vol. 7, Pt. 1–218

Morris, Richard Valentine, Mar. 8, 1768–May 13, 1815.
  Vol. 7, Pt. 1–219

Morris, Robert, Jan. 31, 1734–May 8, 1806.
  Vol. 7, Pt. 1–219

Morris, Robert, c. 1745–June 2, 1815.
  Vol. 7, Pt. 1–223

Morris, Robert, Aug. 31, 1818–July 31, 1888.
  Vol. 7, Pt. 1–224

Morris, Robert Hunter, c. 1700–Jan. 27, 1764.
  Vol. 7, Pt. 1–225

Morris, Roger, Jan. 28, 1727–Sept. 13, 1794.
  Vol. 7, Pt. 1–226

Morris, Thomas, Jan. 3, 1776–Dec. 7, 1844.
  Vol. 7, Pt. 1–226

Morris, Thomas Armstrong, Dec. 26, 1811–Mar. 22, 1904.
  Vol. 7, Pt. 1–227

Morris, William Hopkins, Apr. 22, 1827–Aug. 26, 1900.
  Vol. 7, Pt. 1–228

Morrison, Delesseps Story, Jan. 18, 1912–May 22, 1964.
  Supp. 7–555

Morrison, Frank, Nov. 23, 1859–Mar. 12, 1949.
  Supp. 4–606

Morrison, John Irwin, July 25, 1806–July 17, 1882.
  Vol. 7, Pt. 1–229

Morrison, Nathan Jackson, Nov. 25, 1828–Apr. 12, 1907.
  Vol. 7, Pt. 1–230

Morrison, William McCutchan, Nov. 10, 1867–Mar. 14, 1918. Vol. 7, Pt. 1–231

Morrison, William Ralls, Sept. 14, 1824?–Sept. 29, 1909.
  Vol. 7, Pt. 1–232

Morrison, William, Mar. 14, 1763–Apr. 19, 1837.
  Vol. 7, Pt. 1–230

Morrissey, John, Feb. 12, 1831–May 1, 1878.
  Vol. 7, Pt. 1–233

Morrow, Dwight Whitney, Jan. 11, 1873–Oct. 5, 1931.
  Vol. 7, Pt. 1–234

Morrow, Edwin Porch, Nov. 30, 1877–June 15, 1935.
  Supp. 1–564

Morrow, Jeremiah, Oct. 6, 1771–Mar. 22, 1852.
  Vol. 7, Pt. 1–235

Morrow, Prince Albert, Dec. 19, 1846–Mar. 17, 1913.
  Vol. 7, Pt. 1–236

Morrow, Thomas Vaughan, Apr. 14, 1804–July 16, 1850.
  Vol. 7, Pt. 1–237

Morrow, William W., July 15, 1843–July 24, 1929.
  Vol. 7, Pt. 1–238

Morse, Anson Daniel, Aug. 13, 1846–Mar. 13, 1916.
  Vol. 7, Pt. 1–239

Morse, Charles Wyman, Oct. 21, 1856–Jan. 12, 1933.
  Vol. 7, Pt. 1–239

Morse, Edward Sylvester, June 18, 1838–Dec. 20, 1925.
  Vol. 7, Pt. 1–242

Morse, Freeman Harlow, Feb. 18, 1807–Feb. 6, 1891.
  Vol. 7, Pt. 1–243

Morse, Harmon Northrop, Oct. 15, 1848–Sept. 8, 1920.
  Vol. 7, Pt. 1–243

Morse, Henry Dutton, Apr. 20, 1826–Jan. 2, 1888.
  Vol. 7, Pt. 1–244

Morse, Jedidiah, Aug. 23, 1761–June 9, 1826.
  Vol. 7, Pt. 1–245
Morse, John Lovett, Apr. 21, 1865–Apr. 3, 1940.
  Supp. 2–474
Morse, John Torrey, Jan. 9, 1840–Mar. 27, 1937.
  Supp. 2–475
Morse, Samuel Finley Breese, Apr. 27, 1791–Apr. 2, 1872.
  Vol. 7, Pt. 1–247
Morse, Sidney Edwards, Feb. 7, 1794–Dec. 23, 1871.
  Vol. 7, Pt. 1–251
Mortimer, Mary, Dec. 2, 1816–July 14, 1877.
  Vol. 7, Pt. 1–252
Morton, Charles, c. 1627–Apr. 11, 1698.
  Vol. 7, Pt. 1–253
Morton, Charles Gould, Jan. 15, 1861–July 18, 1933.
  Supp. 1–564
Morton, Charles Walter, Feb. 10, 1899–Sept. 23, 1967.
  Supp. 8–447
Morton, Ferdinand Joseph ("Jelly Roll"), Sept. 20, 1885[?]–
  July 10, 1941. Supp. 3–541
Morton, Ferdinand Quintin, Sept. 9, 1881–Nov. 8, 1949.
  Supp. 4–607
Morton, George, 1585–June 1624.
  Vol. 7, Pt. 1–254
Morton, Henry, Dec. 11, 1836–May 9, 1902.
  Vol. 7, Pt. 1–254
Morton, James St. Clair, Sept. 24, 1829–June 17, 1864.
  Vol. 7, Pt. 1–255
Morton, Jelly Roll. [See Morton, Ferdinand Joseph.]
Morton, John, c. 1724–April 1777.
  Vol. 7, Pt. 1–256
Morton, Julius Sterling, Apr. 22, 1832–Apr. 27, 1902.
  Vol. 7, Pt. 1–257
Morton, Levi Parsons, May 16, 1824–May 16, 1920.
  Vol. 7, Pt. 1–258
Morton, Marcus, Feb. 19, 1784–Feb. 6, 1864.
  Vol. 7, Pt. 1–259
Morton, Marcus, Apr. 8, 1819–Feb. 10, 1891.
  Vol. 7, Pt. 1–260
Morton, Nathaniel, 1613–June 29, 1685 o.s.
  Vol. 7, Pt. 1–261
Morton, Oliver Perry, Aug. 4, 1823–Nov. 1, 1877.
  Vol. 7, Pt. 1–262
Morton, Paul, May 22, 1857–Jan. 19, 1911.
  Vol. 7, Pt. 1–264
Morton, Robert Russa, Aug. 26, 1867–May 31, 1940.
  Supp. 2–476
Morton, Samuel George, Jan. 26, 1799–May 15, 1851.
  Vol. 7, Pt. 1–265
Morton, Sarah Wentworth Apthorp, 1759–May 14, 1846.
  Vol. 7, Pt. 1–266
Morton, Thomas, fl. 1622–1647.
  Vol. 7, Pt. 1–267
Morton, William Thomas Green, Aug. 9, 1819–July 15, 1868.
  Vol. 7, Pt. 1–268
Morton, William James, July 3, 1845–Mar. 26, 1920.
  Vol. 7, Pt. 1–267
Morwitz, Edward, June 11, 1815–Dec. 13, 1893.
  Vol. 7, Pt. 1–271
Mosby, John Singleton, Dec. 6, 1833–May 30, 1916.
  Vol. 7, Pt. 1–272
Moscoso De Alvarado Luis de, fl. 1530–1543.
  Vol. 7, Pt. 1–273
Moseley, Edward Augustus, Mar. 23, 1846–Apr. 18, 1911.
  Vol. 7, Pt. 1–274
Moser, Christopher Otto, May 29, 1885–July 11, 1935.
  Supp. 1–565
Moses, Anna Mary Robertson ("Grandma"), Sept. 7, 1860–
  Dec. 13, 1961. Supp. 7–556
Moses, Bernard, Aug. 27, 1846–Mar. 4, 1930.
  Vol. 7, Pt. 1–274
Moses, Franklin J., 1838–Dec. 11, 1906.
  Vol. 7, Pt. 1–275
Moses, George Higgins, Feb. 9, 1869–Dec. 20, 1944.
  Supp. 3–542
Moses, Montrose Jonas, Sept. 2, 1878–Mar. 29, 1934.
  Supp. 1–566
Mosessohn, David Nehemiah, Jan. 1, 1883–Dec. 16, 1930.
  Vol. 7, Pt. 1–276
Mosher, Eliza Maria, Oct. 2, 1846–Oct. 16, 1928.
  Vol. 7, Pt. 1–277
Mosher, Thomas Bird, Sept. 11, 1852–Aug. 31, 1923.
  Vol. 7, Pt. 1–278

Moskowitz, Belle Lindner Israels, Oct. 5, 1877–Jan. 2, 1933.
  Supp. 1–567
Mosler, Henry, June 6, 1841–Apr. 21, 1920.
  Vol. 7, Pt. 1–279
Moss, Frank, Mar. 16, 1860–June 5, 1920.
  Vol. 7, Pt. 1–279
Moss, John Calvin, Jan. 5, 1838–Apr. 8, 1892.
  Vol. 7, Pt. 1–280
Moss, Lemuel, Dec. 27, 1829–July 12, 1904.
  Vol. 7, Pt. 1–281
Moss, Sanford Alexander, Aug. 23, 1872–Nov. 10, 1946.
  Supp. 4–608
Most, Johann Joseph, Feb. 5, 1846–Mar. 17, 1906.
  Vol. 7, Pt. 1–282
Motley, John Lothrop, Apr. 15, 1814–May 29, 1877.
  Vol. 7, Pt. 1–282
Motley, Willard Francis, July 14, 1909–Mar. 4, 1965.
  Supp. 7–557
Mott, Frank Luther, Apr. 4, 1886–Oct. 23, 1964.
  Supp. 7–559
Mott, Gershom, Apr. 7, 1822–Nov. 29, 1884.
  Vol. 7, Pt. 1–287
Mott, James, June 20, 1788–Jan. 26, 1868.
  Vol. 7, Pt. 1–288
Mott, John R., May 25, 1865–Jan. 31, 1955.
  Supp. 5–506
Mott, Lucretia Coffin, Jan. 3, 1793–Nov. 11, 1880.
  Vol. 7, Pt. 1–288
Mott, Valentine, Aug. 20, 1785–Apr. 26, 1865.
  Vol. 7, Pt. 1–290
Moulton, Ellen Louise Chandler, Apr. 10, 1835–Aug. 10,
  1908. Vol. 7, Pt. 1–291
Moulton, Forest Ray, Apr. 29, 1872–Dec. 7, 1952.
  Supp. 5–508
Moulton, Richard Green, May 5, 1849–Aug. 15, 1924.
  Vol. 7, Pt. 1–291
Moultrie, John, Jan. 18, 1729–Mar. 19, 1798.
  Vol. 7, Pt. 1–292
Moultrie, William, Nov. 23/Dec. 4, 1730–Sept. 27, 1805.
  Vol. 7, Pt. 1–293
Mount, William Sidney, Nov. 26, 1807–Nov. 19, 1868.
  Vol. 7, Pt. 1–294
Mourt, George. [See Morton, George, 1585–1624.]
Mouton, Alexander, Nov. 19, 1804–Feb. 12, 1885.
  Vol. 7, Pt. 1–295
Mowatt, Anna Cora Ogden, Mar. 5, 1819–July 21, 1870.
  Vol. 7, Pt. 1–295
Mowbray, George Mordey, May 5, 1814–June 21, 1891.
  Vol. 7, Pt. 1–297
Mowbray, Henry Siddons, Aug. 5, 1858–Jan. 13, 1928.
  Vol. 7, Pt. 1–298
Mower, Joseph Anthony, Aug. 22, 1827–Jan. 6, 1870.
  Vol. 7, Pt. 1–299
Mowry, William Augustus, Aug. 13, 1829–May 22, 1917.
  Vol. 7, Pt. 1–300
Moxham, Arthur James, Sept. 19, 1854–May 16, 1931.
  Vol. 7, Pt. 1–301
Moxom, Philip Stafford, Aug. 10, 1848–Aug. 13, 1923.
  Vol. 7, Pt. 1–301
Moylan, Stephen, 1737–Apr. 13, 1811.
  Vol. 7, Pt. 1–302
Mozier, Joseph, Aug. 22, 1812–Oct. 3, 1870.
  Vol. 7, Pt. 1–303
Mudd, Samuel A. [See Booth, John Wilkes, 1838–1865.]
Mudge, Enoch, June 28, 1776–Apr. 2, 1850.
  Vol. 7, Pt. 1–304
Mudge, James, Apr. 5, 1844–May 7, 1918.
  Vol. 7, Pt. 1–305
Muhlenberg, Frederick Augustus, Aug. 25, 1818–Mar. 21,
  1901. Vol. 7, Pt. 1–306
Muhlenberg, Frederick Augustus Conrad, Jan. 1, 1750–June
  4, 1801. Vol. 7, Pt. 1–307
Muhlenberg, Gotthilf Henry Ernest, Nov. 17, 1753–May 23,
  1815. Vol. 7, Pt. 1–308
Mühlenberg, Henry Augustus Philip, May 13, 1782–Aug. 11,
  1844. Vol. 7, Pt. 1–309
Muhlenberg, Henry Melchior, Sept. 6, 1711–Oct. 7, 1787.
  Vol. 7, Pt. 1–310
Muhlenberg, John Peter Gabriel, Oct. 1, 1746–Oct. 1, 1807.
  Vol. 7, Pt. 1–311
Mühlenberg, William Augustus, Sept. 16, 1796–Apr. 8, 1877.
  Vol. 7, Pt. 1–313

Muir, Charles Henry, July 18, 1860–Dec. 8, 1933.
   Supp. 1–568
Muir, John, Apr. 21, 1838–Dec. 24, 1914.
   Vol. 7, Pt. 1–314
Muldoon, William, May 25, 1852–June 3, 1933.
   Supp. 1–569
Mulford, Clarence Edward, Feb. 3, 1883–May 10, 1956.
   Supp. 6–466
Mulford, Elisha, Nov. 19, 1833–Dec. 9, 1885.
   Vol. 7, Pt. 1–316
Mulford, Prentice, Apr. 5, 1834–c. May 27, 1891.
   Vol. 7, Pt. 1–317
Mulholland, St. Clair Augustin, Apr. 1, 1839–Feb. 17, 1910.
   Vol. 7, Pt. 1–318
Mulholland, William, Sept. 11, 1855–July 22, 1935.
   Supp. 1–569
Mullan, John, July 31, 1830–Dec. 28, 1909.
   Vol. 7, Pt. 1–319
Mullany, James Robert Madison, Oct. 26, 1818–Sept. 17, 1887. Vol. 7, Pt. 1–320
Mullany, Patrick Francis. [See Azarias, Brother, 1847–1893.]
Müller, Hermann Joseph, Dec. 21, 1890–Apr. 5, 1967.
   Supp. 8–448
Muller, Wilhelm Max, May 15, 1862–July 12, 1919.
   Vol. 7, Pt. 1–320
Mulligan, Charles J., Sept. 28, 1866–Mar. 25, 1916.
   Vol. 7, Pt. 1–321
Mulliken, Samuel Parsons, Dec. 19, 1864–Oct. 24, 1934.
   Supp. 1–570
Mullins, Edgar Young, Jan. 5, 1860–Nov. 23, 1928.
   Vol. 7, Pt. 1–322
Mulry, Thomas Maurice, Feb. 13, 1855–Mar. 10, 1916.
   Vol. 7, Pt. 1–323
Mumford, James Gregory, Dec. 2, 1863–Oct. 18, 1914.
   Vol. 7, Pt. 1–324
Munch, Charles, Sept. 26, 1891–Nov. 6, 1968.
   Supp. 8–450
Mundé, Paul Fortunatus, Sept. 7, 1846–Feb. 7, 1902.
   Vol. 7, Pt. 1–325
Mundelein, George William, July 2, 1872–Oct. 2, 1939.
   Supp. 2–477
Munford, Robert, d. 1784.
   Vol. 7, Pt. 1–325
Munford, William, Aug. 15, 1775–June 21, 1825.
   Vol. 7, Pt. 1–326
Munger, Robert Sylvester, July 24, 1854–Apr. 20, 1923.
   Vol. 7, Pt. 1–327
Munger, Theodore Thornton, Mar. 5, 1830–Jan. 11, 1910.
   Vol. 7, Pt. 1–327
Muni, Paul, Sept. 22, 1895–Aug. 25, 1967.
   Supp. 8–452
Munn, Orson Desaix, June 11, 1824–Feb. 28, 1907.
   Vol. 7, Pt. 1–328
Muñoz-Rivera, Luis, July 17, 1859–Nov. 15, 1916.
   Vol. 7, Pt. 1–329
Munro, Dana Carleton, June 7, 1866–Jan. 13, 1933.
   Vol. 7, Pt. 1–330
Munro, George, Nov. 12, 1825–Apr. 23, 1896.
   Vol. 7, Pt. 1–331
Munro, Henry, 1730–May 30, 1801.
   Vol. 7, Pt. 1–332
Munro, William Bennett, Jan. 5, 1875–Sept. 4, 1957.
   Supp. 6–467
Munroe, Charles Edward, May 24, 1849–Dec. 7, 1938.
   Supp. 2–479
Munsell, Joel, Apr. 14, 1808–Jan. 15, 1880.
   Vol. 7, Pt. 1–333
Munsey, Frank Andrew, Aug. 21, 1854–Dec. 22, 1925.
   Vol. 7, Pt. 1–334
Munson, Thomas Volney, Sept. 26, 1843–Jan. 21, 1913.
   Vol. 7, Pt. 1–335
Munson, Walter David, Feb. 18, 1843–Apr. 24, 1908.
   Vol. 7, Pt. 1–336
Münsterberg, Hugo, June 1, 1863–Dec. 16, 1916.
   Vol. 7, Pt. 1–337
Murat, Achille, Jan. 21, 1801–Apr. 15, 1847.
   Vol. 7, Pt. 1–339
Murchison, Clinton Williams, Oct. 17, 1895–June 20, 1969.
   Supp. 8–454
Murdoch, Frank Hitchcock, Mar. 11, 1843–Nov. 13, 1872.
   Vol. 7, Pt. 1–340
Murdock, James, Feb. 16, 1776–Aug. 10, 1856.
   Vol. 7, Pt. 1–342

Murdock, James Edward, Jan. 25, 1811–May 19, 1893.
   Vol. 7, Pt. 1–341
Murdock, Joseph Ballard, Feb. 13, 1851–Mar. 20, 1931.
   Vol. 7, Pt. 1–342
Murdock, Victor, Mar. 18, 1871–July 8, 1945.
   Supp. 3–544
Murel, John A. [See Murrell, John A., fl. 1804–1844.]
Murfee, James Thomas, Sept. 13, 1833–Apr. 23. 1912.
   Vol. 7, Pt. 1–343
Murfree, Mary Noailles, Jan. 24, 1850–July 31, 1922.
   Vol. 7, Pt. 1–344
Murietta (Murieta), Joaquin. [See Murrieta, Joaquin, c. 1832–1853.]
Murphey, Archibald De Bow, 1777?–Feb. 1, 1832.
   Vol. 7, Pt. 1–345
Murphy, Charles Francis, June 20, 1858–Apr. 25, 1924.
   Vol. 7, Pt. 1–346
Murphy, Dominic Ignatius, May 31, 1847–Apr. 13, 1930.
   Vol. 7, Pt. 1–347
Murphy, Edgar Gardner, Aug. 31, 1869–June 23, 1913.
   Vol. 7, Pt. 1–348
Murphy, Francis, Apr. 24, 1836–June 30, 1907.
   Vol. 7, Pt. 1–349
Murphy, Frank, Apr. 13, 1890–July 19, 1949.
   Supp. 4–610
Murphy, Franklin, Jan. 3, 1846–Feb. 24, 1920.
   Vol. 7, Pt. 1–350
Murphy, Frederick E., Dec. 5, 1872–Feb. 14, 1940.
   Supp. 2–480
Murphy, Gerald Clery, Mar. 25, 1888–Oct. 17, 1964.
   Supp. 7–560
Murphy, Henry Cruse, July 5, 1810–Dec. 1, 1882.
   Vol. 7, Pt. 1–350
Murphy, Isaac, Oct. 16, 1802–Sept. 8, 1882.
   Vol. 7, Pt. 1–352
Murphy, James Bumgardner, Aug. 4, 1884–Aug. 24, 1950.
   Supp. 4–615
Murphy, John, Mar. 12, 1812–May 27, 1880.
   Vol. 7, Pt. 1–352
Murphy, John Benjamin, Dec. 21, 1857–Aug. 11, 1916.
   Vol. 7, Pt. 1–353
Murphy, John Francis, Dec. 11, 1853–Jan. 30, 1921.
   Vol. 7, Pt. 1–354
Murphy, John W., Jan. 20, 1828–Sept. 27, 1874.
   Vol. 7, Pt. 1–355
Murphy, Michael Charles, Feb. 28, 1861–June 4, 1913.
   Vol. 7, Pt. 1–355
Murphy, William Sumter, 1796?–July 13, 1844.
   Vol. 7, Pt. 1–356
Murphy, William Walton, Apr. 3, 1816–June 8, 1886.
   Vol. 7, Pt. 1–357
Murray, Alexander, July 12, 1754 or 1755–Oct. 6, 1821.
   Vol. 7, Pt. 1–357
Murray, David, Oct. 15, 1830–Mar. 6, 1905.
   Vol. 7, Pt. 1–358
Murray, James Edward, May 3, 1876–Mar. 23, 1961.
   Supp. 7–561
Murray, James Ormsbee, Nov. 27, 1827–Mar. 27, 1899.
   Vol. 7, Pt. 1–359
Murray, John, 1737–Oct. 11, 1808.
   Vol. 7, Pt. 1–359
Murray, John, Dec. 10, 1741–Sept. 3, 1815.
   Vol. 7, Pt. 1–360
Murray, John Gardner, Aug. 31, 1857–Oct. 3, 1929.
   Vol. 7, Pt. 1–362
Murray, Joseph, c. 1694–Apr. 28, 1757.
   Vol. 7, Pt. 1–363
Murray, Judith Sargent Stevens, May 1, 1751–July 6, 1820.
   Vol. 7, Pt. 1–364
Murray, Lindley, June 7, 1745–Jan. 16, 1826.
   Vol. 7, Pt. 1–365
Murray, Louise Shipman Welles, Jan. 2, 1854–Apr. 22, 1931.
   Vol. 7, Pt. 1–366
Murray, Mae, May 10, 1889–Mar. 23, 1965.
   Supp. 7–563
Murray, Philip, May 25, 1886–Nov. 9, 1952.
   Supp. 5–509
Murray, Robert, 1721–July 22, 1786
   Vol. 7, Pt. 1–367
Murray, Thomas Edward, Oct. 21, 1860–July 21, 1929.
   Vol. 7, Pt. 1–367
Murray, Thomas Edward, June 20, 1891–May 26, 1961.
   Supp. 7–564

Murray, William Henry David, Nov. 21, 1869–Oct. 15, 1956.
Supp. 6–468
Murray, William Vans, Feb. 9, 1760–Dec. 11, 1803.
Vol. 7, Pt. 1–368
Murrell, John A., fl. 1804–1844.
Vol. 7, Pt. 1–369
Murrieta, Joaquin, c. 1832–July 25, 1853.
Vol. 7, Pt. 1–370
Murrow, Edward (Egbert) Roscoe, Apr. 25, 1908–Apr. 27, 1965. Supp. 7–565
Murrow, Joseph Samuel, June 7, 1835–Sept. 8, 1929.
Vol. 7, Pt. 1–370
Musica, Philip Mariano Fausto, May 12, 1884–Dec. 16, 1938.
Supp. 2–480
Musin, Ovide, Sept. 22, 1854–Nov. 24, 1929.
Vol. 7, Pt. 1–371
Musmanno, Michael Angelo, Apr. 7, 1897–Oct. 12, 1968.
Supp. 8–455
Mussey, Ellen Spencer, May 13, 1850–Apr. 21, 1936.
Supp. 2–482
Mussey, Reuben Dimond, June 23, 1780–June 21, 1866.
Vol. 7, Pt. 1–372
Muste, Abraham Johannes, Jan. 8, 1885–Feb. 11, 1967.
Supp. 8–457
Muybridge, Eadweard, Apr. 9, 1830–May 8, 1904.
Vol. 7, Pt. 1–373
Muzzey, David Saville, Oct. 9, 1870–Apr. 14, 1965.
Supp. 7–567
Myer, Albert James, Sept. 20, 1829–Aug. 24, 1880.
Vol. 7, Pt. 1–374
Myers, Abraham Charles, May ?, 1811–June 20, 1889.
Vol. 7, Pt. 1–375
Myers, Gustavus, Mar. 20, 1872–Dec. 7, 1942.
Supp. 3–545
Myers, Jerome, Mar. 20, 1867–June 19, 1940.
Supp. 2–483
Myerson, Abraham, Nov. 23, 1881–Sept. 3, 1948.
Supp. 4–617
Myles, John, c. 1621–Feb. 3, 1683.
Vol. 7, Pt. 1–376
Myrick, Herbert, Aug. 20, 1860–July 6, 1927.
Vol. 7, Pt. 1–376

Nack, James M., Jan. 4, 1809–Sept. 23, 1879.
Vol. 7, Pt. 1–377
Nadal, Ehrman Syme, Feb. 13, 1843–July 26, 1922.
Vol. 7, Pt. 1–378
Nadelman, Elie, Feb. 20, 1882–Dec. 28, 1946.
Supp. 4–618
Nagel, Conrad, Mar. 16, 1897–Feb. 24, 1970.
Supp. 8–459
Nairne, Thomas, d. April 1715.
Vol. 7, Pt. 1–379
Naismith, James, Nov. 6, 1861–Nov. 28, 1939.
Supp. 2–484
Nancrède, Charles Beylard Guérard de, Dec. 30, 1847–Apr. 12, 1921. Vol. 7, Pt. 1–379
Nancrède, Paul Joseph Guérard de, Mar. 16, 1761–Dec. 15, 1841. Vol. 7, Pt. 1–380
Nanuntenoo. [See Canonchet, d. 1676.]
Napton, William Barclay, Mar. 23, 1808–Jan. 8, 1883.
Vol. 7, Pt. 1–381
Narváez, Panfilo de, c. 1478–1528.
Vol. 7, Pt. 1–382
Nasby, Petroleum V. [See Locke, David Ross, 1833–1888.]
Nash, Abner, c. 1740–Dec. 2, 1786.
Vol. 7, Pt. 1–383
Nash, Arthur, June 26, 1870–Oct. 30, 1927.
Vol. 7, Pt. 1–384
Nash, Charles Sumner, Feb. 18, 1856–Nov. 22, 1926.
Vol. 7, Pt. 1–385
Nash, Charles Williams, Jan. 28, 1864–June 6, 1948.
Supp. 4–620
Nash, Daniel, May 28, 1763–June 4, 1836.
Vol. 7, Pt. 1–386
Nash, Francis, c. 1742–Oct. 7, 1777.
Vol. 7, Pt. 1–386
Nash, Frederick, Feb. 19, 1781–Dec. 4, 1858.
Vol. 7, Pt. 1–387
Nash, Henry Sylvester, Dec. 23, 1854–Nov. 6, 1912.
Vol. 7, Pt. 1–388
Nash, John Henry, Mar. 12, 1871–May 24, 1947.
Supp. 4–621

Nash, Simeon, Sept. 21, 1804–Jan. 18, 1879.
Vol. 7, Pt. 1–388
Nason, Elias, Apr. 21, 1811–June 17, 1887.
Vol. 7, Pt. 1–389
Nason, Henry Bradford, June 22, 1831–Jan. 18, 1895.
Vol. 7, Pt. 1–390
Nassau, Robert Hamill, Oct. 11, 1835–May 6, 1921.
Vol. 7, Pt. 1–390
Nast, Condé Montrose, Mar. 26, 1873–Sept. 19, 1942.
Supp. 3–546
Nast, Thomas, Sept. 27, 1840–Dec. 7, 1902.
Vol. 7, Pt. 1–391
Nast, William, June 15, 1807–May 16, 1899.
Vol. 7, Pt. 1–393
Nathan, George Jean, Feb. 14, 1882–Apr. 8, 1958.
Supp. 6–470
Nathan, Maud, Oct. 20, 1862–Dec. 15, 1946.
Supp. 4–622
Nation, Carry Amelia Moore, Nov. 25, 1846–June 9, 1911.
Vol. 7, Pt. 1–394
Navarre, Pierre, Mar. 28, 1790?–Mar. 20, 1874.
Vol. 7, Pt. 1–395
Nazimova, Alla, June 4, 1878–July 13, 1945.
Supp. 3–547
Neagle, John, Nov. 4, 1796–Sept. 17, 1865.
Vol. 7, Pt. 1–396
Neal, Alice Bradley. [See Haven, Emily Bradley, 1827–1863.]
Neal, David Dalhoff, Oct. 20, 1838–May 2, 1915.
Vol. 7, Pt. 1–397
Neal, John, Aug. 25, 1793–June 20, 1876.
Vol. 7, Pt. 1–398
Neal, Joseph Clay, Feb. 3, 1807–July 17, 1847.
Vol. 7, Pt. 1–399
Neal, Josephine Bicknell, Oct. 10, 1880–Mar. 19, 1955.
Supp. 5–511
Neale, Leonard, Oct. 15, 1746–June 18, 1817.
Vol. 7, Pt. 1–400
Needham, James, d. September 1673.
Vol. 7, Pt. 1–401
Neef, Francis Joseph Nicholas, Dec. 6, 1770–Apr. 6, 1854.
Vol. 7, Pt. 1–402
Neely, Matthew Mansfield, Nov. 9, 1874–Jan. 18, 1958.
Supp. 6–472
Neely, Thomas Benjamin, June 12, 1841–Sept. 4, 1925.
Vol. 7, Pt. 1–402
Nef, John Ulric, June 14, 1862–Aug. 13, 1915.
Vol. 7, Pt. 1–403
Negley, James Scott, Dec. 22, 1826–Aug. 7, 1901.
Vol. 7, Pt. 1–404
Nehrling, Henry, May 9, 1853–Nov. 22, 1929.
Vol. 7, Pt. 1–405
Neidhard, Charles, Apr. 19, 1809–Apr. 17, 1895.
Vol. 7, Pt. 1–406
Neighbors, Robert Simpson, Nov. 3, 1815–Sept. 14, 1859.
Vol. 7, Pt. 1–407
Neill, Edward Duffield, Aug. 9, 1823–Sept. 26, 1893.
Vol. 7, Pt. 1–408
Neill, John, July 9, 1819–Feb. 11, 1880.
Vol. 7, Pt. 1–409
Neill, Thomas Hewson, Apr. 9, 1826–Mar. 12, 1885.
Vol. 7, Pt. 1–409
Neill, William, d. Aug. 8, 1860.
Vol. 7, Pt. 1–410
Neilson, John, Mar. 11, 1745–Mar. 3, 1833.
Vol. 7, Pt. 1–411
Neilson, William Allan, Mar. 28, 1869–Feb. 13, 1946.
Supp. 4–624
Neilson, William George, Aug. 12, 1842–Dec. 29, 1906.
Vol. 7, Pt. 1–412
Nell, William Cooper, Dec. 20, 1816–May 25, 1874.
Vol. 7, Pt. 1–412
Nelson, Charles Alexander, Apr. 14, 1839–Jan. 13, 1933.
Vol. 7, Pt. 1–413
Nelson, David, Sept. 24, 1793–Oct. 17, 1844.
Vol. 7, Pt. 1–414
Nelson, Donald Marr, Nov. 17, 1888–Sept. 29, 1959.
Supp. 6–473
Nelson, Edward William, May 8, 1855–May 19, 1934.
Supp. 1–571
Nelson, Henry Loomis, Jan. 5, 1846–Feb. 29, 1908.
Vol. 7, Pt. 1–415
Nelson, Hugh, Sept. 30, 1768–Mar. 18, 1836.
Vol. 7, Pt. 1–416

Nelson, John, 1654–Nov. 15, 1734.
    Vol. 7, Pt. 1–417
Nelson, Julius, Mar. 6, 1858–Feb. 15, 1916.
    Vol. 7, Pt. 1–418
Nelson, Knute, Feb. 2, 1843–Apr. 28, 1923.
    Vol. 7, Pt. 1–418
Nelson, Marjorie Maxine, Dec. 24, 1909–Nov. 28, 1962.
    Supp. 7–568
Nelson, Nels Christian, Apr. 9, 1875–March 5, 1964.
    Supp. 7–569
Nelson, Nelson Olsen, Sept. 11, 1844–Oct. 5, 1922.
    Vol. 7, Pt. 1–419
Nelson, Rensselaer Russell, May 12, 1826–Oct. 15, 1904.
    Vol. 7, Pt. 1–420
Nelson, Reuben, Dec. 16, 1818–Feb. 20, 1879.
    Vol. 7, Pt. 1–421
Nelson, Roger, 1759–June 7, 1815.
    Vol. 7, Pt. 1–421
Nelson, Samuel, Nov. 10, 1792–Dec. 13, 1873.
    Vol. 7, Pt. 1–422
Nelson, Thomas, Dec. 26, 1738–Jan. 4, 1789.
    Vol. 7, Pt. 1–424
Nelson, Thomas Henry, c. 1823–Mar. 14, 1896.
    Vol. 7, Pt. 1–424
Nelson, William, 1711–Nov. 19, 1772.
    Vol. 7, Pt. 1–425
Nelson, William, Sept. 27, 1824–Sept. 29, 1862.
    Vol. 7, Pt. 1–426
Nelson, William, Feb. 10, 1847–Aug. 10, 1914.
    Vol. 7, Pt. 1–427
Nelson, William Rockhill, Mar. 7, 1841–Apr. 13, 1915.
    Vol. 7, Pt. 1–427
Nerinckx, Charles, Oct. 2, 1761–Aug. 12, 1824.
    Vol. 7, Pt. 1–428
Nesbit, Evelyn Florence, Dec. 25, 1884–Jan. 17, 1967.
    Supp. 8–460
Nesbitt, John Maxwell, c. 1730–Jan. 22, 1802.
    Vol. 7, Pt. 1–429
Nesmith, James Willis, July 23, 1820–June 17, 1885.
    Vol. 7, Pt. 1–430
Nesmith, John, Aug. 3, 1793–Oct. 15, 1869.
    Vol. 7, Pt. 1–431
Nessler, Karl Ludwig, May 2, 1872–Jan. 22, 1951.
    Supp. 5–512
Nestle, Charles. [See Nessler, Karl Ludwig.]
Nestor, Agnes, June 24, 1880–Dec. 28, 1948.
    Supp. 4–625
Nettleton, Alvred Bayard, Nov. 14, 1838–Aug. 10, 1911.
    Vol. 7, Pt. 1–431
Nettleton, Asahel, Apr. 21, 1783–May 16, 1844.
    Vol. 7, Pt. 1–432
Nettleton, Edwin S., Oct. 22, 1831–Apr. 22, 1901.
    Vol. 7, Pt. 1–433
Neuberger, Richard Lewis, Dec. 26, 1912–Mar. 9, 1960.
    Supp. 6–474
Neuendorff, Adolph Heinrich Anton Magnus, June 13, 1843
    –Dec. 4, 1897. Vol. 7, Pt. 1–434
Neumann, Franz Leopold, May 23, 1900–Sept. 2, 1954.
    Supp. 5–513
Neumann, John Nepomucene, Mar. 28, 1811–Jan. 5, 1860.
    Vol. 7, Pt. 1–435
Neumann, John Von. [See Von Neumann, John.]
Neumark, David, Aug. 3, 1866–Dec. 15, 1924.
    Vol. 7, Pt. 1–436
Neutra, Richard Joseph, Apr. 8, 1892–Apr. 15, 1970.
    Supp. 8–462
Nevada, Emma, Feb. 7, 1859–June 20, 1940.
    Supp. 2–485
Neville, John, July 26, 1731–July 29, 1803.
    Vol. 7, Pt. 1–437
Neville, Wendell Cushing, May 12, 1870–July 8, 1930.
    Vol. 7, Pt. 1–438
Nevin, Alfred, Mar. 14, 1816–Sept. 2, 1890.
    Vol. 7, Pt. 1–438
Nevin, Edwin Henry, May 9, 1814–June 2, 1889.
    Vol. 7, Pt. 1–439
Nevin, Ethelbert Woodbridge, Nov. 25, 1862–Feb. 17, 1901.
    Vol. 7, Pt. 1–440
Nevin, George Balch, Mar. 15, 1859–Apr. 17, 1933.
    Vol. 7, Pt. 1–441
Nevin, John Williamson, Feb. 20, 1803–June 6, 1886.
    Vol. 7, Pt. 1–442

Nevin, Robert Peebles, July 31, 1820–June 28, 1908.
    Vol. 7, Pt. 1–443
Nevius, John Livingston, Mar. 4, 1829–Oct. 19, 1893.
    Vol. 7, Pt. 1–444
New, Harry Stewart, Dec. 31, 1858–May 9, 1937.
    Supp. 2–486
Newberry, John Stoughton, Nov. 18, 1826–Jan. 2, 1887.
    Vol. 7, Pt. 1–444
Newberry, John Strong, Dec. 22, 1822–Dec. 7, 1892.
    Vol. 7, Pt. 1–445
Newberry, Oliver, Nov. 17, 1789–July 30, 1860.
    Vol. 7, Pt. 1–446
Newberry, Truman Handy, Nov. 5, 1864–Oct. 3, 1945.
    Supp. 3–549
Newberry, Walter Loomis, Sept. 18, 1804–Nov. 6, 1868.
    Vol. 7, Pt. 1–447
Newbold, William Romaine, Nov. 20, 1865–Sept. 26, 1926.
    Vol. 7, Pt. 1–448
Newbrough, John Ballou, June 5, 1828–Apr. 22, 1891.
    Vol. 7, Pt. 1 449
Newcomb, Charles Leonard, Aug. 7, 1854–Mar. 13, 1930.
    Vol. 7, Pt. 1–449
Newcomb, Harvey, Sept. 2, 1803–Aug. 30, 1863.
    Vol. 7, Pt. 1–450
Newcomb, Josephine Louise LeMonnier, Oct. 31, 1816–Apr.
    7, 1901. Vol. 7, Pt. 1–451
Newcomb, Simon, Mar. 12, 1835–July 11, 1909.
    Vol. 7, Pt. 1–452
Newcomer, Christian, Jan 21, 1749 o.s.–Mar. 12, 1830.
    Vol. 7, Pt. 1–455
Newel, Stanford, June 7, 1839–Apr. 6, 1907.
    Vol. 7, Pt. 1–456
Newell, Edward Theodore, Jan. 15, 1886–Feb. 18, 1941.
    Supp. 3–551
Newell, Frederick Haynes, Mar. 5, 1862–July 5, 1932.
    Vol. 7, Pt. 1–456
Newell, Peter Sheaf Hersey, Mar. 5, 1862–Jan. 15, 1924.
    Vol. 7, Pt. 1–457
Newell, Robert, Mar. 30, 1807–November 1869.
    Vol. 7, Pt. 1–458
Newell, Robert Henry, Dec. 13, 1836–July 1901.
    Vol. 7, Pt. 1–458
Newell, William Augustus, Sept. 5, 1817–Aug. 8, 1901.
    Vol. 7, Pt. 1–459
Newell, William Wells, Jan. 24, 1839–Jan. 21, 1907.
    Vol. 7, Pt. 1–460
Newhouse, Samuel, Oct. 14, 1853–Sept. 22, 1930.
    Vol. 7, Pt. 1–461
Newlands, Francis Griffith, Aug. 28, 1848–Dec. 24, 1917.
    Vol. 7, Pt. 1–462
Newlon, Jesse Homer, July 16, 1882–Sept. 1, 1941.
    Supp. 3–552
Newman, Albert Henry, Aug. 25, 1852–June 4, 1933.
    Supp. 1–572
Newman, Alfred, Mar. 17, 1900–Feb. 17, 1970.
    Supp. 8–464
Newman, Barnett, Jan. 29, 1905–July 4, 1970.
    Supp. 8–466
Newman, Henry, Nov. 20, 1670–June 26, 1743.
    Vol. 7, Pt. 1–463
Newman, Henry Roderick, c. 1843–1918.
    Vol. 7, Pt. 1–464
Newman, John Philip, Sept. 1, 1826–July 5, 1899.
    Vol. 7, Pt. 1–464
Newman, Robert Loftin, Nov. 10, 1827–Mar. 31, 1912.
    Vol. 7, Pt. 1–465
Newman, Samuel Phillips, June 6, 1797–Feb. 10, 1842.
    Vol. 7, Pt. 1–466
Newman, William H., Sept. 6, 1847–Aug. 10, 1918.
    Supp. 1–573
Newman, William Truslow, June 23, 1843–Feb. 14, 1920.
    Vol. 7, Pt. 1–467
Newport, Christopher, d. August 1617.
    Vol. 7, Pt. 1–467
Newsam, Albert, May 20, 1809–Nov. 20, 1864.
    Vol. 7, Pt. 1–469
Newsom, Herschel David, May 1, 1905–July 2, 1970.
    Supp. 8–468
Newton, Henry Jotham, Feb. 9, 1823–Dec. 23, 1895.
    Vol. 7, Pt. 1–469
Newton, Hubert Anson, Mar. 19, 1830–Aug. 12, 1896.
    Vol. 7, Pt. 1–470

Newton, Isaac, Jan. 10, 1794–Nov. 23, 1858.
    Vol. 7, Pt. 1–471
Newton, Isaac, Mar. 31, 1800–June 19, 1867.
    Vol. 7, Pt. 1–472
Newton, John, Aug. 24, 1823–May 1, 1895.
    Vol. 7, Pt. 1–473
Newton, Joseph Fort, July 21, 1876–Jan. 24, 1950.
    Supp. 4–627
Newton, Richard, July 26, 1812–May 25, 1887.
    Vol. 7, Pt. 1–474
Newton, Richard Heber, Oct. 31, 1840–Dec. 19, 1914.
    Vol. 7, Pt. 1–474
Newton, Robert Safford, Dec. 12, 1818–oct. 9, 1881.
    Vol. 7, Pt. 1–475
Newton, Thomas, June 10, 1660–May 28, 1721.
    Vol. 7, Pt. 1–476
Newton, Thomas, Nov. 21, 1768–1847.
    Vol. 7, Pt. 1–477
Newton, William Wilberforce, Nov. 4, 1843–June 25, 1914.
    Vol. 7, Pt. 1–478
Ney, Elisabet, Jan. 26, 1833–June 29, 1907.
    Vol. 7, Pt. 1–478
Neyland, Robert Reese, Jr., Feb. 17, 1892–Mar. 28, 1962.
    Supp. 7–571
Ng Poon Chew, Apr. 28, 1866–Mar. 13, 1931.
    Vol. 7, Pt. 1–479
Niblack, Albert Parker, July 25, 1859–Aug. 20, 1929.
    Vol. 7, Pt. 1–480
Niblack, William Ellis, May 19, 1822–May 7, 1893.
    Vol. 7, Pt. 1–481
Niblo, William, 1789–Aug. 21, 1878.
    Vol. 7, Pt. 1–482
Nicholas, George, 1754?–June 1799.
    Vol. 7, Pt. 1–482
Nicholas, John, 1756?–Dec. 31, 1819.
    Vol. 7, Pt. 1–483
Nicholas, Philip Norborne, 1775?–Aug. 18, 1849.
    Vol. 7, Pt. 1–484
Nicholas, Robert Carter, Jan. 28, 1728–Sept. 8, 1780.
    Vol. 7, Pt. 1–485
Nicholas, Wilson Cary, Jan. 31, 1761–Oct. 10, 1820.
    Vol. 7, Pt. 1–486
Nicholls, Francis Redding Tillou, Aug. 20, 1834–Jan 4, 1912.
    Vol. 7, Pt. 1–487
Nicholls, Rhoda Holmes, Mar. 28, 1854–Sept. 7, 1930.
    Vol. 7, Pt. 1–488
Nichols, Charles Henry, Oct. 19, 1820–Dec. 16, 1889.
    Vol. 7, Pt. 1–489
Nichols, Charles Lemuel, May 29, 1851–Feb. 19, 1929.
    Vol. 7, Pt. 1–490
Nichols, Clarina Irene Howard, Jan. 25, 1810–Jan. 11, 1885.
    Vol. 7, Pt. 1–490
Nichols, Dudley, Apr. 6, 1895–Jan. 5, 1960.
    Supp. 6–475
Nichols, Edward Leamington, Sept. 14, 1854–Nov. 10, 1937.
    Supp. 2–487
Nichols, Ernest Fox, June 1, 1869–Apr. 29, 1924.
    Vol. 7, Pt. 1–491
Nichols, George Ward, June 21, 1831–Sept. 15, 1885.
    Vol. 7, Pt. 1–494
Nichols, James Robinson, July 18, 1819–Jan. 2, 1888.
    Vol. 7, Pt. 1–494
Nichols, Mary Sargeant Neal Gove, Aug. 10, 1810–May 30, 1884. Vol. 7, Pt. 1–495
Nichols, Ruth Rowland, Feb. 23, 1901–Sept. 25, 1960.
    Supp. 6–477
Nichols, Thomas Low, 1815–1901.
    Vol. 7, Pt. 1–496
Nichols, William Ford, June 9, 1849–June 5, 1924.
    Vol. 7, Pt. 1–497
Nicholson, Alfred Osborne Pope, Aug. 31, 1808–Mar. 23, 1876. Vol. 7, Pt. 1–498
Nicholson, Eliza Jane Poitevent Holbrook, Mar. 11, 1849–Feb. 15, 1896. Vol. 7, Pt. 1–499
Nicholson, Francis, Nov. 12, 1655–Mar. 5, 1728.
    Vol. 7, Pt. 1–499
Nicholson, James, c. 1736–Sept. 2, 1804.
    Vol. 7, Pt. 1–502
Nicholson, James Bartram, Jan. 28, 1820–Mar. 4, 1901.
    Vol. 7, Pt. 1–503
Nicholson, James William Augustus, Mar. 10, 1821–Oct. 28, 1887. Vol. 7, Pt. 1–503

Nicholson, John, d. Dec. 5, 1800.
    Vol. 7, Pt. 1–504
Nicholson, Joseph Hopper, May 15, 1770–Mar. 4, 1817.
    Vol. 7, Pt. 1–505
Nicholson, Meredith, Dec. 9, 1866–Dec. 21, 1947.
    Supp. 4–629
Nicholson, Samuel, 1743–Dec. 29, 1811.
    Vol. 7, Pt. 1–506
Nicholson, Samuel Danford, Feb. 22, 1859–Mar. 24, 1923.
    Vol. 7, Pt. 1–507
Nicholson, Seth Barnes, Nov. 12, 1891–July 2, 1963.
    Supp. 7–572
Nicholson, Timothy, Nov. 2, 1828–Sept. 15, 1924.
    Vol. 7, Pt. 1–507
Nicholson, William Thomas, Mar. 22, 1834–Oct. 17, 1893.
    Vol. 7, Pt. 1–509
Nicholson, William Jones, Jan. 16, 1856–Dec. 20, 1931.
    Vol. 7, Pt. 1–508
Nicola, Lewis, 1717–Aug. 9, 1807.
    Vol. 7, Pt. 1–509
Nicolay, John George, Feb. 26, 1832–Sept. 26, 1901.
    Vol. 7, Pt. 1–510
Nicolet, Jean, 1598–Nov. 1, 1642.
    Vol. 7, Pt. 1–511
Nicoll. [See also Nicolls.]
Nicoll, De Lancey, June 24, 1854–Mar. 31, 1931.
    Vol. 7, Pt. 1–512
Nicoll, James Craig, Nov. 22, 1847–July 25, 1918.
    Vol. 7, Pt. 1–513
Nicollet, Joseph Nicolas, July 24, 1786–Sept. 11, 1843.
    Vol. 7, Pt. 1–514
Nicolls, Matthias, Mar. 29, 1626–Dec. 22, 1687?.
    Vol. 7, Pt. 1–514
Nicolls, Richard, 1624–May 28, 1672.
    Vol. 7, Pt. 1–515
Nicolls, William, 1657–May 1723.
    Vol. 7, Pt. 1–516
Niebuhr, Helmut Richard, Sept. 3, 1894–July 5, 1962.
    Supp. 7–573
Niedringhaus, Frederick Gottlieb, Oct. 21, 1837–Nov. 25, 1922. Vol. 7, Pt. 1–517
Niehaus, Charles Henry, Jan. 24, 1855–June 19, 1935.
    Supp. 1–574
Nielsen, Alice, June 7, 1870[?]–Mar. 8, 1943.
    Supp. 3–553
Nieman, Lucius William, Dec. 13, 1857–Oct. 1, 1935.
    Supp. 1–576
Niemeyer, John Henry, June 25, 1839–Dec. 7, 1932.
    Vol. 7, Pt. 1–518
Nies, James Buchanan, Nov. 22, 1856–June 18, 1922.
    Vol. 7, Pt. 1–519
Nies, Konrad, Oct. 17, 1861–Aug. 10, 1921.
    Vol. 7, Pt. 1–519
Nieuwland, Julius Arthur, Feb. 14, 1878–June 11, 1936.
    Supp. 2–488
Niles, David K., Nov. 23, 1892–Sept. 28, 1952.
    Supp. 5–514
Niles, Hezekiah, Oct. 10, 1777–Apr. 2, 1839.
    Vol. 7, Pt. 1–521
Niles, John Milton, Aug. 20, 1787–May 31, 1856.
    Vol. 7, Pt. 1–522
Niles, Nathaniel, Apr. 3, 1741–Oct. 31, 1828.
    Vol. 7, Pt. 1–523
Niles, Nathaniel, Dec. 27, 1791–Nov. 16, 1869.
    Vol. 7, Pt. 1–524
Niles, Samuel, May 1, 1674–May 1, 1762.
    Vol. 7, Pt. 1–524
Nimitz, Chester William, Feb. 24, 1885–Feb. 20, 1966.
    Supp. 8–469
Nipher, Francis Eugene, Dec. 10, 1847–Oct. 6, 1926.
    Vol. 7, Pt. 1–525
Nisbet, Charles Jan. 21, 1736–Jan. 18, 1804.
    Vol. 7, Pt. 1–526
Nisbet, Eugenius Aristides, Dec. 7, 1803–Mar. 18, 1871.
    Vol. 7, Pt. 1–527
Nitchie, Edward Bartlett, Nov. 18, 1876–Oct. 5, 1917.
    Vol. 7, Pt. 1–528
Nitschmann, David, Dec. 27, 1696–Oct. 8, 1772.
    Vol. 7, Pt. 1–529
Nixon, John, Mar. 1, 1727–Mar. 24, 1815.
    Vol. 7, Pt. 1–530
Nixon, John, 1733–Dec. 31, 1808.
    Vol. 7, Pt. 1–530

Nixon, John Thompson, Aug. 31, 1820–Sept. 28, 1889.
Vol. 7, Pt. 1–531
Nixon, William Penn, Mar. 19, 1833–Feb. 20, 1912.
Vol. 7, Pt. 1–532
Niza, Marcos de, d. Mar. 25, 1558.
Vol. 7, Pt. 1–533
Nizza, Marcos de. [See Niza, Marcos de, d. 1558.]
Noah, Mordecai Manuel, July 19, 1785–Mar. 22, 1851.
Vol. 7, Pt. 1–534
Noailles, Louis Marie, Vicomte de, Apr. 17, 1756–Jan. 5,
1804. Vol. 7, Pt. 1–535
Nobili, John, Apr. 8, 1812–Mar. 1, 1856.
Vol. 7, Pt. 1–536
Noble, Alfred, Aug. 7, 1844–Apr. 19, 1914.
Vol. 7, Pt. 1–536
Noble, Frederick Alphonso, Mar. 17, 1832–Dec. 31, 1917.
Vol. 7, Pt. 1–537
Noble, Gladwyn Kingsley, Sept. 20, 1894–Dec. 9, 1940.
Supp. 2 489
Noble, James, Dec. 16, 1783–Feb. 26, 1831.
Vol. 7, Pt. 1–538
Noble, John Willock, Oct. 26, 1831–Mar. 22, 1912.
Vol. 7, Pt. 1–539
Noble, Samuel, Nov. 22, 1834–Aug. 14, 1888.
Vol. 7, Pt. 1–540
Nock, Albert Jay, Oct. 13, 1870–Aug. 19, 1945.
Supp. 3–554
Noeggerath, Emil Oscar Jacob Bruno, Oct. 5, 1827–May 3,
1895. Vol. 7, Pt. 1–541
Noguchi, Hideyo, Nov. 24, 1876–May 21, 1928.
Vol. 7, Pt. 1–542
Nolan, Philip, c. 1771–Mar. 21, 1801.
Vol. 7, Pt. 1–543
Nolen, John, June 14, 1869–Feb. 18, 1937.
Supp. 2–490
Noll, John Francis, Jan. 25, 1875–July 31, 1956.
Supp. 6–478
Noonan, James Patrick, Dec. 15, 1878–Dec. 4, 1929.
Vol. 7, Pt. 1–544
Norbeck, Peter, Aug. 27, 1870–Dec. 20, 1936.
Supp. 2–491
Norcross, Orlando Whitney, Oct. 25, 1839–Feb. 27, 1920.
Vol. 7, Pt. 1–545
Nordberg, Bruno Victor, Apr. 11, 1857–Oct. 30, 1924.
Vol. 7, Pt. 1–546
Norden, Carl Lukas, Apr. 23, 1880–June 15, 1965.
Supp. 7–576
Nordheimer, Isaac, 1809–Nov. 3, 1842.
Vol. 7, Pt. 1–547
Nordhoff, Charles, Aug. 31, 1830–July 14, 1901.
Vol. 7, Pt. 1–548
Nordhoff, Charles Bernard, Feb. 1, 1887–Apr. 10, 1947.
Supp. 5–266
Nordica, Lillian, May 12, 1859–May 10, 1914.
Vol. 7, Pt. 1–548
Norelius, Eric, Oct. 26, 1833–Mar. 15, 1916.
Vol. 7, Pt. 1–549
Norman, John, c. 1748–June 8, 1817.
Vol. 7, Pt. 1–550
Norris, Benjamin Franklin, Mar. 5, 1870–Oct. 25, 1902.
Vol. 7, Pt. 1–551
Norris, Charles Gilman Smith, Apr. 23, 1881–July 25, 1945.
Supp. 3–555
Norris, Edward, d. Dec. 23, 1659.
Vol. 7, Pt. 1–552
Norris, Frank. [See Norris, Benjamin Franklin, 1870–1902.]
Norris, George Washington, Nov. 6, 1808–Mar. 4, 1875.
Vol. 7, Pt. 1–553
Norris, George William, July 11, 1861–Sept. 2, 1944.
Supp. 3–557
Norris, Isaac, July 26, 1671–June 4, 1735.
Vol. 7, Pt. 1–553
Norris, Isaac, Oct. 23, 1701–July 13, 1766.
Vol. 7, Pt. 1–554
Norris, James Flack, Jan. 20, 1871–Aug. 4, 1940.
Supp. 2–492
Norris, John Franklyn, Sept. 18, 1877–Aug. 20, 1952.
Supp. 5–516
Norris, Kathleen Thompson, July 16, 1880–Jan. 18, 1966.
Supp. 8–471
Norris, Mary Harriott, Mar. 16, 1848–Sept. 14, 1919.
Vol. 7, Pt. 1–555

Norris, William, July 2, 1802–Jan. 5, 1867.
Vol. 7, Pt. 1–555
Norris, William Fisher, Jan. 6, 1839–Nov. 18, 1901.
Vol. 7, Pt. 1–556
Norsworthy, Naomi, Sept. 29, 1877–Dec. 25, 1916.
Vol. 7, Pt. 1–557
North, Edward, Mar. 9, 1820–Sept. 13, 1903.
Vol. 7, Pt. 1–558
North, Elisha, Jan. 8, 1771–Dec. 29, 1843.
Vol. 7, Pt. 1–559
North, Frank Joshua, Mar. 10, 1840–Mar. 14, 1885.
Vol. 7, Pt. 1–559
North, Frank Mason, Dec. 3, 1850–Dec. 17, 1935.
Supp. 1–577
North, Simeon, Sept. 7, 1802–Feb. 9, 1884.
Vol. 7, Pt. 1–561
North, Simon Newton Dexter, Nov. 29, 1848–Aug. 3, 1924.
Vol. 7, Pt. 1–562
North, William, 1755–Jan. 3, 1836.
Vol. 7, Pt. 1–563
Northen, William Jonathan, July 9, 1835–Mar. 25, 1913.
Vol. 7, Pt. 1–564
Northend, Charles, Apr. 2, 1814–Aug. 7, 1895.
Vol. 7, Pt. 1–564
Northrop, Birdsey Grant, July 18, 1817–Apr. 27, 1898.
Vol. 7, Pt. 1–565
Northrop, Cyrus, Sept. 30, 1834–Apr. 3, 1922.
Vol. 7, Pt. 1–566
Northrop, Lucius Bellinger, Sept. 8, 1811–Feb. 9, 1894.
Vol. 7, Pt. 1–567
North Simeon, July 13, 1765–Aug. 25 1852.
Vol. 7, Pt. 1–561
Norton, Alice Peloubet. [See Norton, Mary Alice Peloubet,
1860–1928.]
Norton, Andrews, Dec. 31, 1786–Sept. 18, 1853.
Vol. 7, Pt. 1–568
Norton, Charles Eliot, Nov. 16, 1827–Oct. 21, 1908.
Vol. 7, Pt. 1–569
Norton, Charles Hotchkiss, Nov. 23, 1851–Oct. 27, 1942.
Supp. 3–561
Norton, Elijah Hise, Nov. 21, 1821–Aug. 5, 1914.
Vol. 7, Pt. 1–572
Norton, John, May 6, 1606–Apr. 5, 1663.
Vol. 7, Pt. 1–572
Norton, John Nicholas, 1820–Jan. 18, 1881.
Vol. 7, Pt. 1–574
Norton, John Pitkin, July 19, 1822–Sept. 5, 1852.
Vol. 7, Pt. 1–574
Norton, Mary Alice Peloubet, Feb. 25, 1860–Feb. 23, 1928.
Vol. 7, Pt. 1–575
Norton, Mary Teresa Hopkins, Mar. 7, 1875–Aug. 2, 1959.
Supp. 6–479
Norton, William Edward, June 28, 1843–Feb. 28, 1916.
Vol. 7, Pt. 1–576
Norton, William Warder, Sept. 17, 1891–Nov. 7, 1945.
Supp. 3–563
Norwood, Robert Winkworth, Mar. 27, 1874–Sept. 28, 1932.
Vol. 7, Pt. 1–577
Noss, Theodore Bland, May 10, 1852–Feb. 28, 1909.
Vol. 7, Pt. 1–578
Notestein, Wallace, Dec. 16, 1878–Feb. 2, 1969.
Supp. 8–472
Nott, Abraham, Feb. 5, 1768–Jun 19, 1830.
Vol. 7, Pt. 1–578
Nott, Charles Cooper, Sept. 16, 1827–Mar. 6, 1916.
Vol. 7, Pt. 1–579
Nott, Eliphalet, Jun 25, 1773–Jan. 29, 1866.
Vol. 7, Pt. 1–580
Nott, Henry Junius, Nov. 4, 1797–Oct. 9, 1837.
Vol. 7, Pt. 1–581
Nott, Josiah Clark, Mar. 31, 1804–Mar. 31, 1873.
Vol. 7, Pt. 1–582
Nott, Samuel, Jan. 23, 1754–May 26, 1852.
Vol. 7, Pt. 1–583
Notz, Frederick William Augustus, Feb. 2, 1841–Dec. 16,
1921. Vol. 7, Pt. 1–583
Novarro, Ramon, Feb. 6, 1899–Oct. 31, 1968.
Supp. 8–473
Novy, Frederick George, Dec. 9, 1864–Aug. 8, 1957.
Supp. 6–481
Noyan, Gilles-Augustin Payen de, 1697–Feb. 26, 1751.
Vol. 7, Pt. 1–584

Oemler, Arminius, Sept. 12, 1827–Aug. 8, 1897.
    Vol. 7, Pt. 1–629
Oertel, Johannes Adam Simon, Nov 3, 1823–Dec. 9, 1909.
    Vol. 7, Pt. 1–630
O'Fallon, Benjamin, Sept. 20, 1793–Dec. 17, 1842.
    Vol. 7, Pt. 1–631
O'Fallon, James, Mar. 11, 1749–1794?.
    Vol. 7, Pt. 1–632
O'Fallon, John, Nov. 17, 1791–Dec. 17, 1865.
    Vol. 7, Pt. 1–632
O'Ferrall, Charles Triplett, Oct. 21, 1840–Sept. 22, 1905.
    Vol. 7, Pt. 1–633
Offley, David, d. Oct. 4, 1838.
    Vol. 7, Pt. 1–634
Oftedal, Sven, Mar. 22, 1844–Mar. 30, 1911.
    Vol. 7, Pt. 1–635
Ogburn, William Fielding, June 29, 1886–Apr. 27, 1959.
    Supp. 6–482
Ogden, Aaron, Dec. 3, 1756–Apr. 19, 1839.
    Vol. 7, Pt. 1–636
Ogden, David, 1707–1798.
    Vol. 7, Pt. 1–637
Ogden, David Bayard, Oct. 31, 1775–July 16, 1849.
    Vol. 7, Pt. 1–638
Ogden, Francis Barber, Mar. 3, 1783–July 4, 1857.
    Vol. 7, Pt. 1–639
Ogden, Herbert Gouverneur, Apr. 4, 1846–Feb. 25, 1906.
    Vol. 7, Pt. 1–640
Ogden, Peter Skene, 1794–September 1854.
    Vol. 7, Pt. 1–640
Ogden, Robert Curtis, June 20, 1836–Aug. 6, 1913.
    Vol. 7, Pt. 1–641
Ogden, Rollo, Jan. 19, 1856–Feb. 22, 1937.
    Supp. 2–498
Ogden, Samuel, Dec. 9, 1746–Dec. 1, 1810.
    Vol. 7, Pt. 1–642
Ogden, Thomas Ludlow, Dec. 12, 1773–Dec. 17, 1844.
    Vol. 7, Pt. 1–643
Ogden, Uzal, 1744–Nov. 4, 1822.
    Vol. 7, Pt. 1–643
Ogden, William Butler, June 15, 1805–Aug. 3, 1877.
    Vol. 7, Pt. 1–644
Ogg, Frederic Austin, Feb. 8, 1878–Oct. 23, 1951.
    Supp. 5–521
Ogilvie, James, d. Sept. 18, 1820.
    Vol. 7, Pt. 1–645
Ogilvie, John, 1724–Nov. 26, 1774.
    Vol. 7, Pt. 1–646
Ogle, Samuel, c. 1702–May 3, 1752.
    Vol. 7, Pt. 1–647
Oglesby, Richard James, July 25, 1824–Apr. 24, 1899.
    Vol. 7, Pt. 1–648
Oglethorpe, James Edward, Dec. 22, 1696–June 30, 1785.
    Vol. 7, Pt. 2–1
O'Gorman, Thomas, May 1, 1843–Sept. 18, 1921.
    Vol. 7, Pt. 2–3
O'Hara, James, 1752–Dec. 16, 1819.
    Vol. 7, Pt. 2–3
O'Hara, John Henry, Jan. 31, 1905–Apr. 11, 1970.
    Supp. 8–480
O'Hara, Theodore, Feb. 11, 1820–June 6, 1867.
    Vol. 7, Pt. 2–4
O'Hare, Kate (Richards) Cunningham, Mar. 26, 1877–Jan. 10, 1948. Supp. 4–635
O'Higgins, Harvey Jerrold, Nov. 14, 1876–Feb. 28, 1929.
    Vol. 7, Pt. 2–5
Ohlmacher, Albert Philip, Aug. 19, 1865–Nov. 9, 1916.
    Vol. 7, Pt. 2–6
O'Kelly, James, c. 1735–Oct. 16, 1826.
    Vol. 7, Pt. 2–7
Okey, John Waterman, Jan. 3, 1827–July 25, 1885.
    Vol. 7, Pt. 2–8
O'Laughlin, Michael. [See Booth, John Wilkes, c. 1838–Sept. 23, 1867.]
Olcott, Chancellor John. [See Olcott, Chauncey, 1860–1932.]
Olcott, Chauncey, July 21, 1860–Mar. 18, 1932.
    Vol. 7, Pt. 2–8
Olcott, Eben Erskine, Mar. 11, 1854–June 5, 1929.
    Vol. 7, Pt. 2–9
Olcott, Henry Steel, Aug. 2, 1832–Feb. 17, 1907.
    Vol. 7, Pt. 2–10

Olden, Charles Smith, Feb. 19, 1799–Apr. 7, 1876.
    Vol. 7, Pt. 2–11
Older, Fremont, Aug. 30, 1856–Mar. 3, 1935.
    Supp. 1–580
Oldfather, William Abbott, Oct. 23, 1880–May 27, 1945.
    Supp. 3–571
Oldfield, ("Barney") Berna Eli, Jan. 29, 1878–Oct. 4, 1946.
    Supp. 4–636
Oldham, John, c. 1600–July 1636.
    Vol. 7, Pt. 2–12
Oldham, William Fitzjames, Dec. 15, 1854–Mar. 27, 1937.
    Supp. 2–499
Oldham, Williamson Simpson, June 19, 1813–May 8, 1868.
    Vol. 7, Pt. 2–12
Olds, Irving Sands, Jan. 22, 1887–Mar. 4, 1963.
    Supp. 7–586
Olds, Leland, Dec. 31, 1890–Aug. 3, 1960.
    Supp. 6–483
Olds, Ransom Eli, June 3, 1864–Aug. 26, 1950.
    Supp. 4–637
Olds, Robert Edwin, Oct. 22, 1875–Nov. 24, 1932.
    Supp. 1–582
Oldschool, Oliver. [See Sargent, Nathan, 1794–1875.]
O'Leary, Daniel, June 29, 1846[?]–May 29, 1933.
    Supp. 1–583
Olin, Stephen, Mar. 2, 1797–Aug. 16, 1851.
    Vol. 7, Pt. 2–13
Oliphant, Herman, Aug. 31, 1884–Jan. 11, 1939.
    Supp. 2–500
Oliver, Andrew, Mar. 28, 1706–Mar. 3, 1774.
    Vol. 7, Pt. 2–14
Oliver, Andrew, Nov. 13, 1731–Dec. 6, 1799.
    Vol. 7, Pt. 2–15
Oliver, Charles Augustus, Dec. 14, 1853–Apr. 8, 1911.
    Vol. 7, Pt. 2–16
Oliver, Fitch Edward, Nov. 25, 1819–Dec. 8, 1892.
    Vol. 7, Pt. 2–17
Oliver, George Tener, Jan. 26, 1848–Jan. 22, 1919.
    Vol. 7, Pt. 2–18
Oliver, Henry Kemble, Nov. 24, 1800–Aug. 12, 1885.
    Vol. 7, Pt. 2–18
Oliver, Henry William, Feb. 25, 1840–Feb. 8, 1904
Oliver, James, Aug. 28, 1823–Mar. 2, 1908.
    Vol. 7, Pt. 2–20
Oliver, Joseph, c. 1885–Apr. 8, 1938.
    Supp. 2–501
Oliver, "King." [See Oliver, Joseph, c. 1885–1938.]
Oliver, Paul Ambrose, July 18, 1830–May 17, 1912.
    Vol. 7, Pt. 2–21
Oliver, Peter, Mar. 26, 1713–October 1791.
    Vol. 7, Pt. 2–22
Olmstead, Albert Ten Eyck, Mar. 23, 1880–Apr. 11, 1945.
    Supp. 3–572
Olmstead, Gideon. [See Olmsted, Gideon, 1749–1845.]
Olmsted, Denison, June 18, 1791–May 13, 1859.
    Vol. 7, Pt. 2–23
Olmsted, Frederick Law, July 24, 1870–Dec. 25, 1957.
    Supp. 6–485
Olmsted, Frederick Law, Apr. 26, 1822–Aug. 28, 1903.
    Vol. 7, Pt. 2–24
Olmsted, Gideon, Feb. 12, 1749–Feb. 8, 1845.
    Vol. 7, Pt. 2–28
Olmsted, John Charles, Sept. 14, 1852–Feb. 24, 1920.
    Vol. 7, Pt. 2–29
Olmsted, Marlin Edgar, May 21, 1847–July 19, 1913.
    Vol. 7, Pt. 2–30
Olney, Jesse, Oct. 12, 1798–July 30, 1872.
    Vol. 7, Pt. 2–31
Olney, Richard, Sept. 15, 1835–Apr. 8, 1917.
    Vol. 7, Pt. 2–32
Olsen, John Sigvard ("Ole"), Nov. 6, 1892–Jan. 26, 1963.
    Supp. 7–588
Olson, Floyd Bjerstjerne, Nov. 13, 1891–Aug. 22, 1936.
    Supp. 2–502
Olyphant, David Washington Cincinnatus, Mar. 7, 1789–June 10, 1851. Vol. 7, Pt. 2–34
Olyphant, Robert Morrison, Sept. 9, 1824–May 3, 1918.
    Vol. 7, Pt. 2–34
O'Mahoney, Joseph Christopher, Nov. 5, 1884–Dec. 1, 1962.
    Supp. 7–589
O'Mahony, John, 1816–Feb. 6, 1877.
    Vol. 7, Pt. 2–35

O'Malley, Frank Ward, Nov. 30, 1875–Oct. 19, 1932.
Vol. 7, Pt. 2–36
Oñate, Juan de, c. 1549–c. 1624.
Vol. 7, Pt. 2–37
Onderdonk, Benjamin Tredwell, July 15, 1791–Apr. 30, 1861. Vol. 7, Pt. 2–38
Onderdonk, Henry, June 11, 1804–June 22, 1886.
Vol. 7, Pt. 2–39
Onderdonk, Henry Ustick, Mar. 16, 1789–Dec. 6, 1858.
Vol. 7, Pt. 2–40
O'Neal, Edward Asbury, Sept. 20, 1818–Nov. 7, 1890.
Vol. 7, Pt. 2–41
O'Neal, Edward Asbury, III, Oct. 26, 1875–Feb. 26, 1958.
Supp. 6–487
O'Neale, Margaret, 1796–Nov. 8, 1879.
Vol. 7, Pt. 2–41
O'Neall, John Belton, Apr. 10, 1793–Dec. 27, 1863.
Vol. 7, Pt. 2–42
O'Neill, Eugene, Oct. 16, 1888–Nov. 27, 1953.
Supp. 5–522
O'Neill, James, Nov. 15, 1849–Aug. 10, 1920.
Vol. 7, Pt. 2–43
O'Neill, John, Mar. 8, 1834–Jan. 7, 1878.
Vol. 7, Pt. 2–44
O'Neill, Margaret L. [See O'Neale, Margaret, 1796–1879.]
O'Neill, Rose Cecil, June 25, 1874–Apr. 6, 1944.
Supp. 3–573
Opdyke, George, Dec. 7, 1805–June 12, 1880.
Vol. 7, Pt. 2–45
Oppenheim, James, May 24, 1882–Aug. 4, 1932.
Vol. 7, Pt. 2–46
Oppenheimer, Julius Robert, Apr. 22, 1904–Feb. 18, 1967.
Supp. 8–482
Opper, Frederick Burr, Jan. 2, 1857–Aug. 27, 1937.
Supp. 2–504
Optic, Oliver. [See Adams, William Taylor, 1822–1897.]
Orcutt, Hiram, Feb. 3, 1815–Apr. 17, 1899.
Vol. 7, Pt. 2–47
Ord, Edward Otho Cresap, Oct. 18, 1818–July 22, 1883.
Vol. 7, Pt. 2–48
Ord, George, Mar. 4, 1781–Jan. 24, 1866.
Vol. 7, Pt. 2–49
Ordronaux, John, Aug. 3, 1830–Jan. 20, 1908.
Vol. 7, Pt. 2–50
Ordway, John, c. 1775–c. 1817.
Vol. 7, Pt. 2–51
O'Reilly, Alexander, 1722–Mar. 23, 1794.
Vol. 7, Pt. 2–51
O'Reilly, Henry, Feb. 6, 1806–Aug. 17, 1886.
Vol. 7, Pt. 2–52
O'Reilly, John Boyle, June 28, 1844–Aug. 10, 1890.
Vol. 7, Pt. 2–53
O'Reilly, Robert Maitland, Jan. 14, 1845–Nov. 3, 1912.
Vol. 7, Pt. 2–54
O'Rielly, Henry. [See O'Reilly, Henry, 1806–1886.]
Ormsby, Waterman Lilly, 1809–Nov. 1, 1883.
Vol. 7, Pt. 2–55
Orne, John, Apr. 29, 1834–Nov. 29, 1911.
Vol. 7, Pt. 2–55
Orr, Alexander Ector, Mar. 2, 1831–June 3, 1914.
Vol. 7, Pt. 2–56
Orr, Gustavus John, Aug. 9, 1819–Dec. 11, 1887.
Vol. 7, Pt. 2–57
Orr, Hugh, Jan. 2, 1715–Dec. 6, 1798.
Vol. 7, Pt. 2–57
Orr, James Lawrence, May 12, 1822–May 5, 1873.
Vol. 7, Pt. 2–59
Orr, Jehu Amaziah, Apr. 10, 1828–Mar. 9, 1921.
Vol. 7, Pt. 2–60
Orry-Kelly, Dec. 31, 1897–Feb. 26, 1964.
Supp. 7–591
Orth, Godlove Stein, Apr. 22, 1817–Dec. 16, 1882.
Vol. 6, Pt. 2–60
Orthwein, Charles F., Jan. 28, 1839–Dec. 28, 1898.
Vol. 7, Pt. 2–61
Orton, Edward Francis Baxter, Mar. 9, 1829–Oct. 16, 1899.
Vol. 7, Pt. 2–62
Orton, Harlow South, Nov. 23, 1817–July 4, 1895.
Vol. 7, Pt. 2–63
Orton, Helen Fuller, Nov. 1, 1872–Feb. 16, 1955.
Supp. 5–526
Orton, James, Apr. 21, 1830–Sept. 25, 1877.
Vol. 7, Pt. 2–64

Orton, William, June 14, 1826–Apr. 22, 1878.
Vol. 7, Pt. 2–65
Ortynsky, Stephen Soter, Jan. 29, 1866–Mar. 24, 1916.
Vol. 7, Pt. 2–66
Osborn, Charles, Aug. 21, 1775–Dec. 29, 1850.
Vol. 7, Pt. 2–66
Osborn, Chase Salmon, Jan. 22, 1860–Apr. 11, 1949.
Supp. 4–639
Osborn, Henry Fairfield, Jan. 15, 1887–Sept. 16, 1969.
Supp. 8–485
Osborn, Henry Fairfield, Aug. 8, 1857–Nov. 6, 1935.
Supp. 1–584
Osborn, Henry Stafford, Aug. 17, 1823–Feb. 2, 1894.
Vol. 7, Pt. 2–67
Osborn, Laughton, c. 1809–Dec. 13, 1878.
Vol. 7, Pt. 2–68
Osborn, Norris Galpin, Apr. 17, 1858–May 6, 1932.
Vol. 7, Pt. 2–69
Osborn, Selleck, c. 1782–c. October 1826.
Vol. 7, Pt. 2–69
Osborn, Thomas Andrew, Oct. 26, 1836–Feb. 4, 1898.
Vol. 7, Pt. 2–70
Osborn, Thomas Ogden, Aug. 11, 1832–Mar. 27, 1904.
Vol. 7, Pt. 2–71
Osborn, William Henry, Dec. 21, 1820–Mar. 2, 1894.
Vol. 7, Pt. 2–72
Osborne, James Walker, Jan. 5, 1859–Sept. 7, 1919.
Vol. 7, Pt. 2–73
Osborne, Thomas Burr, Aug. 5, 1859–Jan. 29, 1929.
Vol. 7, Pt. 2–74
Osborne, Thomas Mott, Sept. 23, 1859–Oct. 20, 1926.
Vol. 7, Pt. 2–75
Osceola, c. 1800–Jan. 30, 1838.
Vol. 7, Pt. 2–76
Osgood, Frances Sargent Locke, June 18, 1811–May 12, 1850. Vol. 7, Pt. 2–77
Osgood, George Laurie, Apr. 3, 1844–Dec. 12, 1922.
Vol. 7, Pt. 2–78
Osgood, Herbert Levi, Apr. 9, 1855–Sept. 11, 1918.
Vol. 7, Pt. 2–78
Osgood, Howard, Jan. 4, 1831–Nov. 28, 1911.
Vol. 7, Pt. 2–79
Osgood, Jacob, Mar. 16, 1777–Nov. 29, 1844.
Vol. 7, Pt. 2–80
Osgood, Samuel, Feb. 3, 1747/48–Aug. 12, 1813.
Vol. 7, Pt. 2–81
Osgood, William Fogg, Mar. 10, 1864–July 22, 1943.
Supp. 3–574
O'Shaughnessy, Michael Maurice, May 28, 1864–Oct. 12, 1934. Supp. 1–587
O'Shaughnessy, Nelson Jarvis Waterbury, Feb. 12, 1876–July 25, 1932. Supp. 1–589
O'Shea, Michael Vincent, Sept. 17, 1866–Jan. 14, 1932.
Vol. 7, Pt. 2–82
Osler, William, July 12, 1849–Dec. 29, 1919.
Vol. 7, Pt. 2–83
Ossoli, Margaret Fuller. [See Fuller, Sarah Margaret, 1810–1850.]
Ostenaco. [See Outacity, fl. 1756–1777.]
Osten Sacken, Carl Robert Romanovich Von Der, Aug 21, 1828–May 20, 1906. Vol. 7, Pt. 2–87
Osterhaus, Peter Joseph, Jan. 4, 1823–Jan. 2, 1917.
Vol. 7, Pt. 2–88
Osterhout, Winthrop John Vanleuven, Aug. 2, 1871–Apr. 9, 1964. Supp. 7–592
Ostromislensky, Iwan Iwanowich, Sept. 8, 1880–Jan. 16, 1939. Supp. 7–505
O'Sullivan, John Louis, November 1813–Feb. 24, 1895.
Vol. 7, Pt. 2–89
O'Sullivan, Mary Kenney, Jan. 8, 1864–Jan. 18, 1943.
Supp. 3–575
Oswald, Lee Harvey, Oct. 18, 1939–Nov. 24, 1963.
Supp. 7–593
Otacite, [See Outacity, fl. 1756–1777.]
Otermín, Antonio de, fl. 1678–1683.
Vol. 7, Pt. 2–89
Otey, James Hervey, Jan. 27, 1800–Apr. 23, 1863.
Vol. 7, Pt. 2–90
Otis, Arthur Sinton, July 28, 1886–Jan. 1, 1964.
Supp. 7–594
Otis, Bass, July 17, 1784–Nov. 3, 1861.
Vol. 7, Pt. 2–91

Otis, Charles Eugene, May 11, 1846–Nov. 8, 1917.
  Vol. 7, Pt. 2–92
Otis, Charles Rollin, Apr. 29, 1835–May 24, 1927.
  Vol. 7, Pt. 2–93
Otis, Elisha Graves, Aug. 3, 1811–Apr. 8, 1861.
  Vol. 7, Pt. 2–93
Otis, Elwell Stephen, Mar. 25, 1838–Oct. 21, 1909.
  Vol. 7, Pt. 2–94
Otis, Fessenden Nott, Mar. 6, 1825–May 24, 1900.
  Vol. 7, Pt. 2–95
Otis, George Alexander, Nov. 12, 1830–Feb. 23, 1881.
  Vol. 7, Pt. 2–96
Otis, Harrison Gray, Oct. 8, 1765–Oct. 28, 1848.
  Vol. 7, Pt. 2–98
Otis, Harrison Gray, Feb. 10, 1837–July 30, 1917.
  Vol. 7, Pt. 2–100
Otis, James, Feb. 5, 1725–May 23, 1783.
  Vol. 7, Pt. 2–101
Ott, Isaac, Nov. 30, 1847–Jan. 1, 1916
  Vol. 7, Pt. 2–105
Ott, Melvin Thomas ("Mel"), Mar. 2, 1909–Nov. 21, 1958.
  Supp. 6–488
Ottassite. [See Outacity, fl. 1756–1777.]
Ottendorfer, Anna Behr Uhl, Feb. 13, 1815–Apr. 1, 1884.
  Vol. 7, Pt. 2–106
Ottendorfer, Oswald, Feb. 26, 1826–Dec. 15, 1900.
  Vol. 7, Pt. 2–107
Otterbein, Philip William, June 3, 1726–Nov. 17, 1813.
  Vol. 7, Pt. 2–107
Ottley, Roi, Aug. 2, 1906–Oct. 1, 1960.
  Supp. 6–489
Otto, Bodo, 1711–June 12, 1787.
  Vol. 7, Pt. 2–108
Otto, John Conrad, Mar. 15, 1774–June 26, 1844.
  Vol. 7, Pt. 2–109
Otto, William Tod, Jan. 19, 1816–Nov. 7, 1905.
  Vol. 7, Pt. 2–110
Ouconnastote. [See Oconostota, d. 1785.]
Ouimet, Francis Desales, May 8, 1893–Sept. 2, 1967.
  Supp. 8–486
Ouray, c. 1833–Aug. 24, 1880.
  Vol. 7, Pt. 2–110
Oursler, (Charles) Fulton, Jan. 22, 1893–May 24, 1952.
  Supp. 5–527
Outacity, fl. 1756–1777.
  Vol. 7, Pt. 2–111
Outcault, Richard Felton, Jan. 14, 1863–Sept. 25, 1928.
  Vol. 7, Pt. 2–112
Outerbridge, Alexander Ewing, July 31, 1850–Jan. 15, 1928.
  Vol. 7, Pt. 2–112
Outerbridge, Eugenius Harvey, Mar. 8, 1860–Nov. 10, 1932.
  Supp. 1–589
Overman, Frederick, c. 1803–Jan. 7, 1852.
  Vol. 7, Pt. 2–113
Overman, Lee Slater, Jan. 3, 1854–Dec. 12, 1930.
  Vol. 7, Pt. 2–114
Overstreet, Harry Allen, Oct. 25, 1875–Aug. 17, 1970.
  Supp. 8–487
Overton, John, Apr. 9, 1766–Apr. 12, 1833.
  Vol. 7, Pt. 2–115
Owen, David Dale, June 24, 1807–Nov. 13, 1860.
  Vol. 7, Pt. 2–116
Owen, Edward Thomas, Mar. 4, 1850–Nov. 9, 1931.
  Vol. 7, Pt. 2–117
Owen, Griffith, c. 1647–Aug. 19, 1717.
  Vol. 7, Pt. 2–118
Owen, Robert Dale, Nov. 9, 1801–June 24, 1877.
  Vol. 7, Pt. 2–118
Owen, Robert Latham, Feb. 2, 1856–July 19, 1947.
  Supp. 4–640
Owen, Stephen Joseph, Apr. 21, 1898–May 17, 1964.
  Supp. 7–595
Owen, Thomas McAdory, Dec. 15, 1866–Mar. 25, 1920.
  Supp. 1–590
Owen, William Florence, 1844–May 4, 1906.
  Vol. 7, Pt. 2–120
Owens, John Edmond, Apr. 2, 1823–Dec. 7, 1886.
  Vol. 7, Pt. 2–121
Owens, Michael Joseph, Jan. 1, 1859–Dec. 27, 1923.
  Vol. 7, Pt. 2–122
Owre, Alfred, Dec. 16, 1870–Jan. 2, 1935.
  Supp. 1–591

Owsley, Frank Lawrence, Jan. 20, 1890–Oct. 21, 1956.
  Supp. 6–491
Owsley, William, 1782–Dec. 9, 1862.
  Vol. 7, Pt. 2–122
Oxnam, Garfield Bromley, Aug. 14, 1891–Mar. 12, 1963.
  Supp. 7–596

Paca, William, Oct. 31, 1740–Oct. 13, 1799.
  Vol. 7, Pt. 2–123
Pace, Edward Aloysius, July 3, 1861–Apr. 26, 1938.
  Supp. 2–506
Pacheco, Romualdo, Oct. 31, 1831–Jan. 23, 1899.
  Vol. 7, Pt. 2–124
Pack, Charles Lathrop, May 7, 1857–June 14, 1937.
  Supp. 2–507
Packard, Alpheus Spring, Dec. 23, 1798–July 13, 1884.
  Vol. 7, Pt. 2–125
Packard, Alpheus Spring, Feb. 19, 1839–Feb. 14, 1905.
  Vol. 7, Pt. 2–126
Packard, Frederick Adolphus, Sept. 26, 1794–Nov. 11, 1867.
  Vol. 7, Pt. 2–127
Packard, James Ward, Nov. 5, 1863–Mar. 20, 1928.
  Vol. 7, Pt. 2–128
Packard, John Hooker, Aug. 15, 1832–May 21, 1907.
  Vol. 7, Pt. 2–129
Packard, Joseph, Dec. 23, 1812–May 3, 1902.
  Vol. 7, Pt. 2–130
Packard, Silas Sadler, Apr. 28, 1826–Oct. 27, 1898.
  Vol. 7, Pt. 2–130
Packer, Asa, Dec. 29, 1805–May 17, 1879.
  Vol. 7, Pt. 2–131
Packer, William Fisher, Apr. 2, 1807–Sept. 27, 1870.
  Vol. 7, Pt. 2–132
Paddock, Algernon Sidney, Nov. 9, 1830–Oct. 17, 1897.
  Vol. 7, Pt. 2–133
Paddock, Benjamin Henry, Feb. 29, 1828–Mar. 9, 1891.
  Vol. 7, Pt. 2–133
Paddock, John Adams, Jan. 19, 1825–Mar. 4, 1894.
  Vol. 7, Pt. 2–134
Padilla, Juan De c. 1500–c. 1544.
  Vol. 7, Pt. 2–135
Page, Charles Grafton, Jan. 25, 1812–May 5, 1868.
  Vol. 7, Pt. 2–135
Page, David Perkins, July 4, 1810–Jan. 1, 1848.
  Vol. 7, Pt. 2–136
Page, John, Apr. 17, 1743 o.s.–Oct. 11, 1808.
  Vol. 7, Pt. 2–137
Page, Leigh, Oct. 13, 1884–Sept. 14, 1952.
  Supp. 5–528
Page, Mann, 1691–Jan. 24, 1730.
  Vol. 7, Pt. 2–138
Page, Oran Thaddeus ("Lips"), Jan. 27, 1908–Nov. 5, 1954.
  Supp. 5–529
Page, Richard Lucian, Dec. 20, 1807–Aug. 9, 1901.
  Vol. 7, Pt. 2–139
Page, Thomas Jefferson, Jan. 4, 1808–Oct. 26, 1899.
  Vol. 7, Pt. 2–140
Page, Thomas Nelson, Apr. 23, 1853–Nov. 1, 1922.
  Vol. 7, Pt. 2–141
Page, Thomas Walker, Dec. 4, 1866–Jan. 13, 1937.
  Supp. 2–508
Page, Walter Hines, Aug. 15, 1855–Dec. 21, 1918.
  Vol. 7, Pt. 2–142
Page, William, January 1811–Sept. 30, 1885.
  Vol. 7, Pt. 2–144
Paine, Albert Bigelow, July 10, 1861–Apr. 9, 1937.
  Supp. 2–509
Paine, Byron, Oct. 10, 1827–Jan. 13, 1871.
  Vol. 7, Pt. 2–145
Paine, Charles, Apr. 15, 1799–July 6, 1853.
  Vol. 7, Pt. 2–146
Paine, Charles Jackson, Aug. 26, 1833–Aug. 12, 1916.
  Vol. 7, Pt. 2–147
Paine, Elijah, Jan. 21, 1757–Apr. 28, 1842.
  Vol. 7, Pt. 2–148
Paine, Halbert Eleazer, Feb. 4, 1826–Apr. 14, 1905.
  Vol. 7, Pt. 2–148
Paine, Henry Warren, Aug. 30, 1810–Dec. 26, 1893.
  Vol. 7, Pt. 2–149
Paine, John Alsop, Jan. 14, 1840–July 24, 1912.
  Vol. 7, Pt. 2–150
Paine, John Knowles, Jan. 9, 1839–Apr. 25, 1906.
  Vol. 7, Pt. 2–151

Pastor, Antonio, May 28, 1837–Aug. 26, 1908.
 Vol. 7, Pt. 2–290
Pastorius, Francis Daniel, Sept. 26, 1651–c. Jan. 1, 1720.
 Vol. 7, Pt. 2–290
Pasvolsky, Leo, Apr. 22, 1893–May 5, 1953.
 Supp. 5–537
Patch, Alexander McCarrell, Nov. 23, 1889–Nov. 21, 1945.
 Supp. 3–582
Patch, Sam, c. 1807–Nov. 13, 1829.
 Vol. 7, Pt. 2–291
Pate, Maurice, Oct. 14, 1894–Jan. 19, 1965.
 Supp. 7–599
Paterson, John, 1744–July 19, 1808.
 Vol. 7, Pt. 2–292
Paterson, William, Dec. 24, 1745–Sept. 9, 1806.
 Vol. 7, Pt. 2–293
Patillo, Henry, 1726–1801.
 Vol. 7, Pt. 2–295
Paton, Lewis Bayles, June 27, 1864–Jan. 24, 1932.
 Vol. 7, Pt. 2–295
Patri, Angelo, Nov. 27, 1876–Sept. 13, 1965.
 Supp. 7–600
Patrick, Edwin Hill ("Ted"), Sept. 3, 1901–Mar. 11, 1964.
 Supp. 7–601
Patrick, Hugh Talbot, May 11, 1860–Jan. 5, 1939.
 Supp. 2–515
Patrick, Marsena Rudolph, Mar. 11, 1811–July 27, 1888.
 Vol. 7, Pt. 2–296
Patrick, Mary Mills, Mar. 10, 1850–Feb. 25, 1940.
 Supp. 2–516
Patrick, Mason Mathews, Dec. 13, 1863–Jan. 29, 1942.
 Supp. 3–584
Patten, Gilbert, Oct. 25, 1866–Jan. 16, 1945.
 Supp. 3–585
Patten, James A., May 8, 1852–Dec. 8, 1928.
 Vol. 7, Pt. 2–297
Patten, Simon Nelson, May 1, 1852–July 24, 1922.
 Vol. 7, Pt. 2–298
Patten, William, Mar. 15, 1861–Oct. 27, 1932.
 Vol. 7, Pt. 2–300
Patterson, Alicia, Oct. 15, 1906–July 2, 1963.
 Supp. 7–603
Patterson, Daniel Todd, Mar. 6, 1786–Aug. 25, 1839.
 Vol. 7, Pt. 2–301
Patterson, Eleanor Medill, Nov. 7, 1881–July 24, 1948.
 Supp. 4–643
Patterson, James Kennedy, Mar. 26, 1833–Aug. 15, 1922.
 Vol. 7, Pt. 2–302
Patterson, James Willis, July 2, 1823–May 4, 1893.
 Vol. 7, Pt. 2–303
Patterson, John Henry, Dec. 13, 1844–May 7, 1922.
 Vol. 7, Pt. 2–304
Patterson, Joseph Medill, Jan. 6, 1879–May 25, 1946.
 Supp. 4–645
Patterson, Morris, Oct. 26, 1809–Oct. 23, 1878.
 Vol. 7, Pt. 2–305
Patterson, Richard Cunningham, Jr., Jan. 31, 1886–Sept. 30, 1966. Supp. 8–494
Patterson, Robert, May 30, 1743–July 22, 1824.
 Vol. 7, Pt. 2–305
Patterson, Robert, Jan. 12, 1792–Aug. 7, 1881.
 Vol. 7, Pt. 2–306
Patterson, Robert Mayne, July 17, 1832–Apr. 5, 1911.
 Vol. 7, Pt. 2–307
Patterson, Robert Porter, Feb. 12, 1891–Jan. 22, 1952.
 Supp. 5–538
Patterson, Rufus Lenoir, June 11, 1872–Apr. 11, 1943.
 Supp. 3–587
Patterson, Thomas MacDonald, Nov. 4, 1839–July 23, 1916.
 Vol. 7, Pt. 2–308
Patterson, Thomas Harman, May 10, 1820–Apr. 9, 1889.
 Vol. 7, Pt. 2–307
Patterson, William, Nov. 1, 1752–July 7, 1835.
 Vol. 7, Pt. 2–309
Pattie, James Ohio, 1804–1850?.
 Vol. 7, Pt. 2–310
Pattison, Granville Sharp, c. 1791–Nov. 12, 1851.
 Vol. 7, Pt. 2–311
Pattison, James William, July 14, 1844–May 29, 1915.
 Vol. 7, Pt. 2–311
Pattison, John M., June 13, 1847–June 18, 1906.
 Vol. 7, Pt. 2–312

Pattison, Robert Emory, Dec. 8, 1850–Aug. 1, 1904.
 Vol. 7, Pt. 2–313
Pattison, Thomas, Feb. 8, 1822–Dec. 17, 1891.
 Vol. 7, Pt. 2–314
Patton, Francis Landey, Jan. 22, 1843–Nov. 25, 1932.
 Vol. 7, Pt. 2–315
Patton, George Smith, Nov. 11, 1885–Dec. 21, 1945.
 Supp. 3–588
Patton, John Mercer, Aug. 10, 1797–Oct. 29, 1858.
 Vol. 7, Pt. 2–316
Patton, William, Aug. 23, 1798–Sept. 9, 1879.
 Vol. 7, Pt. 2–317
Pauger, Adrien de, d. June 9, 1726.
 Vol. 7, Pt. 2–318
Paul, Elliot Harold, Feb. 13, 1891–Apr. 7, 1958.
 Supp. 6–497
Paul, Father. [See Francis, Paul James, 1863–1940.]
Paul, Henry Martyn, June 25, 1851–Mar. 15, 1931.
 Vol. 7, Pt. 2–319
Paul, John. [See Webb, Charles Henry, 1834–1905.]
Paul, Josephine Bay, Aug. 10, 1900–Aug. 6, 1962.
 Supp. 7–604
Paulding, Hiram, Dec. 11, 1797–Oct. 20, 1878.
 Vol. 7, Pt. 2–320
Paulding, James Kirke, Aug. 22, 1778–Apr. 6, 1860.
 Vol. 7, Pt. 2–321
Pavy, Octave, June 22, 1844–June 6, 1884.
 Vol. 7, Pt. 2–323
Pawnee Bill. [See Lillie, Gordon William.]
Payne, Bruce Ryburn, Feb. 18, 1874–Apr. 21, 1937.
 Supp. 2–517
Payne, Christopher Harrison, Sept. 7, 1848–Dec. 4, 1925.
 Vol. 7, Pt. 2–323
Payne, Daniel Alexander, Feb. 24, 1811–Nov. 29, 1893.
 Vol. 7, Pt. 2–324
Payne, Henry B., Nov. 30, 1810–Sept. 9, 1896.
 Vol. 7, Pt. 2–325
Payne, Henry Clay, Nov. 23, 1843–Oct. 4, 1904.
 Vol. 7, Pt. 2–326
Payne, John Barton, Jan. 26, 1855–Jan. 24, 1935.
 Supp. 1–594
Payne, John Howard, June 9, 1791–Apr. 9, 1852.
 Vol. 7, Pt. 2–327
Payne, Lewis Thornton Powell, 1845–1865. [See Booth, John Wilkes.]
Payne, Oliver Hazard, July 21, 1839–June 27, 1917.
 Vol. 7, Pt. 2–329
Payne, Sereno Elisha, June 26, 1843–Dec. 10, 1914.
 Vol. 7, Pt. 2–330
Payne, William Harold, May 12, 1836–June 18, 1907.
 Vol. 7, Pt. 2–331
Payne, William Morton, Feb. 14, 1858–July 11, 1919.
 Vol. 7, Pt. 2–332
Payson, Edward, July 25, 1783–Oct. 22, 1827.
 Vol. 7, Pt. 2–333
Payson, Seth, Sept. 30, 1758–Feb. 26, 1820.
 Vol. 7, Pt. 2–334
Peabody, Andrew Preston, Mar. 19, 1811–Mar. 10, 1893.
 Vol. 7, Pt. 2–334
Peabody, Cecil Hobart, Aug. 9, 1855–May 4, 1934.
 Supp. 1–595
Peabody, Elizabeth Palmer, May 16, 1804–Jan. 3, 1894.
 Vol. 7, Pt. 2–335
Peabody, Endicott, May 30, 1857–Nov. 17, 1944.
 Supp. 3–591
Peabody, Francis Greenwood, Dec. 4, 1847–Dec. 28, 1936.
 Supp. 2–518
Peabody, George, Feb. 18, 1795–Nov. 4, 1869.
 Vol. 7, Pt. 2–336
Peabody, George Foster, July 27, 1852–Mar. 4, 1938.
 Supp. 2–520
Peabody, Joseph, Dec. 12, 1757–Jan. 5, 1844.
 Vol. 7, Pt. 2–338
Peabody, Josephine Preston, May 30, 1874–Dec. 4, 1922.
 Vol. 7, Pt. 2–339
Peabody, Lucy Whitehead, Mar. 2, 1861–Feb. 26, 1949.
 Supp. 4–646
Peabody, Nathaniel, Mar. 1, 1741–June 27, 1823.
 Vol. 7, Pt. 2–340
Peabody, Oliver William Bourn, July 9, 1799–July 5, 1848.
 Vol. 7, Pt. 2–340
Peabody, Robert Swain, Feb. 22, 1845–Sept. 23, 1917.
 Vol. 7, Pt. 2–341

Peabody, Selim Hobart, Aug. 20, 1829–May 26, 1903.
Vol. 7, Pt. 2–342
Peabody, William Bourn Oliver, July 9, 1799–May 28, 1847.
Vol. 7, Pt. 2–343
Peale, Anna Claypoole, Mar. 6, 1791–Dec. 25, 1878.
Vol. 7, Pt. 2–344
Peale, Charles Willson, Apr. 15, 1741–Feb. 22, 1827.
Vol. 7, Pt. 2–344
Peale, James, 1749–May 24, 1831.
Vol. 7, Pt. 2–347
Peale, Raphael, Feb. 17, 1774–Mar. 4, 1825.
Vol. 7, Pt. 2–348
Peale, Rembrandt, Feb. 22, 1778–Oct. 3, 1860.
Vol. 7, Pt. 2–348
Peale, Sarah Miriam, May 9, 1800–Feb. 4, 1885.
Vol. 7, Pt. 2–350
Peale, Titian Ramsay, Nov. 17, 1799–Mar. 13, 1885.
Vol. 7, Pt. 2–351
Pearce, Charles Sprague, Oct. 19, 1851–May 18, 1914.
Vol. 7, Pt. 2–352
Pearce, James Alfred, Dec. 14, 1805–Dec. 20, 1862.
Vol. 7, Pt. 2–352
Pearce, Richard, June 29, 1837–May 18, 1927.
Vol. 7, Pt. 2–353
Pearce, Richard Mills, Mar. 3, 1874–Feb. 16, 1930.
Vol. 7, Pt. 2–354
Pearce, Stephen Austen, Nov. 7, 1836–Apr. 8, 1900.
Vol. 7, Pt. 2–355
Pearl, Raymond, June 3, 1879–Nov. 17, 1940.
Supp. 2–521
Pearse, John Barnard Sweet, Apr. 19, 1842–Aug. 24, 1914.
Vol. 7, Pt. 2–356
Pearson, Drew, Dec. 13, 1897–Sept. 1, 1969.
Supp. 8–496
Pearson, Edmund Lester, Feb. 11, 1880–Aug. 8, 1937.
Supp. 2–522
Pearson, Edward Jones, Oct. 4, 1863–Dec. 7, 1928.
Vol. 7, Pt. 2–357
Pearson, Eliphalet, June 11, 1752–Sept. 12, 1826.
Vol. 7, Pt. 2–358
Pearson, Fred Stark, July 3, 1861–May 7, 1915.
Vol. 7, Pt. 2–358
Pearson, Leonard, Aug. 17, 1868–Sept. 20, 1909.
Vol. 7, Pt. 2–359
Pearson, Raymond Allen, Apr. 9, 1873–Feb. 13, 1939.
Supp. 2–523
Pearson, Richmond Mumford, June 28, 1805–Jan. 5, 1878.
Vol. 7, Pt. 2–360
Pearson, Thomas Gilbert, Nov. 10, 1873–Sept. 3, 1943.
Supp. 3–592
Pearsons, Daniel Kimball Apr. 14, 1820–Apr. 27, 1912.
Vol. 7, Pt. 2–361
Peary, Josephine Diebitsch, May 22, 1863–Dec. 19, 1955.
Supp. 5–539
Peary, Robert Edwin, May 6, 1856–Feb. 20, 1920.
Vol. 7, Pt. 2–362
Pease, Alfred Humphreys, May 6, 1838–July 13, 1882.
Vol. 7, Pt. 2–367
Pease, Calvin, Sept. 9, 1776–Sept. 17, 1839.
Vol. 7, Pt. 2–368
Pease, Elisha Marshall, Jan. 3, 1812–Aug. 26, 1883.
Vol. 7, Pt. 2–368
Pease, Joseph Ives, Aug. 9, 1809–July 2, 1883.
Vol. 7, Pt. 2–369
Peaslee, Edmund Randolph, Jan. 22, 1814–Jan. 21, 1878.
Vol. 7, Pt. 2–370
Peattie, Donald Culross, June 21, 1898–Nov. 16, 1964.
Supp. 7–605
Peavey, Frank Hutchinson, Jan. 18, 1850–Dec. 30, 1901.
Vol. 7, Pt. 2–371
Peay, Austin, June 1, 1876–Oct. 2, 1927.
Vol. 7, Pt. 2–371
Peck, Charles Horton, Mar. 30, 1833–July 11, 1917.
Vol. 7, Pt. 2–372
Peck, Charles Howard, June 18, 1870–Mar. 28, 1927.
Vol. 7, Pt. 2–373
Peck, George, Aug. 8, 1797–May 20, 1876.
Vol. 7, Pt. 2–374
Peck, George Record, May 15, 1843–Feb. 22, 1923.
Vol. 7, Pt. 2–375
Peck, George Washington, Dec. 4, 1817–June 6, 1859.
Vol. 7, Pt. 2–375

Peck, George Wilbur, Sept. 28, 1840–Apr. 16, 1916.
Vol. 7, Pt. 2–376
Peck, Harry Thurston, Nov. 24, 1856–Mar. 23, 1914.
Vol. 7, Pt. 2–377
Peck, James Hawkins, c. 1790–Apr. 29, 1836.
Vol. 7, Pt. 2–379
Peck, Jesse Truesdell, Apr. 4, 1811–May 17, 1883.
Vol. 7, Pt. 2–379
Peck, John James, Jan. 4, 1821–Apr. 21, 1878.
Vol. 7, Pt. 2–380
Peck, John Mason, Oct. 31, 1789–Mar. 14, 1858.
Vol. 7, Pt. 2–381
Peck, Lillie, Dec. 28, 1888–Feb. 21, 1957.
Supp. 6–499
Peck, Thomas Ephraim, Jan. 29, 1822–Oct. 2, 1893.
Vol. 7, Pt. 2–382
Peck, Tracy, May 24, 1838–Nov. 24, 1921.
Vol. 7, Pt. 2–382
Peck, William Dandridge, May 8, 1763–Oct. 3, 1822.
Vol. 7, Pt. 2–383
Peckham, George Williams, Mar. 23, 1845–Jan. 10, 1914.
Vol. 7, Pt. 2–384
Peckham, Rufus Wheeler, Nov. 8, 1838–Oct. 24, 1909.
Vol. 7, Pt. 2–385
Peckham, Stephen Farnum, Mar. 26, 1839–July 11, 1918.
Vol. 7, Pt. 2–386
Peckham, Wheeler Hazard, Jan. 1, 1833–Sept. 27, 1905.
Vol. 7, Pt. 2–387
Pedder, James, July 29, 1775–Aug. 27, 1859.
Vol. 7, Pt. 2–387
Peek, Frank William, Aug. 20, 1881–July 26, 1933.
Vol. 7, Pt. 2–388
Peek, George Nelson, Nov. 19, 1873–Dec. 17, 1943.
Supp. 3–593
Peers, Benjamin Orrs, Apr. 20, 1800–Aug. 20, 1842.
Vol. 7, Pt. 2–389
Peerson, Cleng, 1783–Dec. 16, 1865.
Vol. 7, Pt. 2–390
Peet, Harvey Prindle, Nov. 19, 1794–Jan. 1, 1873.
Vol. 7, Pt. 2–390
Peet, Isaac Lewis, Dec. 4, 1824–Dec. 27, 1898.
Vol. 7, Pt. 2–391
Peet, Stephen Denison, Dec. 2, 1831–May 24, 1914.
Vol. 7, Pt. 2–392
Peffer, William Alfred, Sept. 10, 1831–Oct. 6, 1912.
Vol. 7, Pt. 2–393
Pegler, Westbrook, Aug. 2, 1894–June 24, 1969.
Supp. 8–497
Pegram, George Braxton, Oct. 24, 1876–Aug. 12, 1958.
Supp. 6–500
Peirce, Benjamin, Apr. 4, 1809–Oct. 6, 1880.
Vol. 7, Pt. 2–393
Peirce, Benjamin Osgood, Feb. 11, 1854–Jan. 14, 1914.
Vol. 7, Pt. 2–397
Peirce, Bradford Kinney, Feb. 3, 1819–Apr. 19, 1889.
Vol. 7, Pt. 2–398
Peirce, Charles Sanders, Sept. 10, 1839–Apr. 19, 1914.
Vol. 7, Pt. 2–398
Peirce, Cyrus, Aug. 15, 1790–Apr. 5, 1860.
Vol. 7, Pt. 2–403
Peirce, Henry Augustus, Dec. 15, 1808–July 29, 1885.
Vol. 7, Pt. 2–404
Peirce, James Mills, May 1, 1834–Mar. 21, 1906.
Vol. 7, Pt. 2–405
Peirce, William, c. 1590–1641.
Vol. 7, Pt. 2–406
Peixotto, Benjamin Franklin, Nov. 13, 1834–Sept. 18, 1890.
Vol. 7, Pt. 2–406
Pelham, Henry, Feb. 14, 1748/49–1806.
Vol. 7, Pt. 2–407
Pelham, John, Sept. 14, 1838–Mar. 17, 1863.
Vol. 7, Pt. 2–408
Pelham, Peter, c. 1695–December 1751.
Vol. 7, Pt. 2–409
Pelham, Robert A., Jan. 4, 1859–June 12, 1943.
Supp. 3–595
Pellew, Henry Edward, Apr. 26, 1828–Feb. 4, 1923.
Vol. 7, Pt. 2–409
Peloubet, Francis Nathan, Dec. 2, 1931–Mar. 27, 1920.
Vol. 7, Pt. 2–410
Pelz, Paul Johannes, Nov. 18, 1841–Mar. 30, 1918.
Vol. 7, Pt. 2–411

Perley, Ira, Nov. 9, 1799–Feb. 26, 1874.
Vol. 7, Pt. 2–478
Perlman, Philip Benjamin, Mar. 5, 1890–July 31, 1960.
Supp. 6–502
Perlman, Selig, Dec. 9, 1888–Aug. 14, 1959.
Supp. 6–503
Perrin, Bernadotte, Sept. 15, 1847–Aug. 31, 1920.
Vol. 7, Pt. 2–478
Perrine, Charles Dillon, July 28, 1867–June 21, 1951.
Supp. 5–540
Perrine, Frederic Auten Combs, Aug. 25, 1862–Oct. 21, 1908. Vol. 7, Pt. 2–479
Perrine Henry Apr. 5, 1797–Aug. 7, 1840.
Vol. 7, Pt. 2–480
Perrot, Nicolas, 1644–c. 1718.
Vol. 7, Pt. 2–481
Perry, Antoinette, June 27, 1888–June 28, 1946.
Supp. 4–652
Perry, Arthur Latham, Feb. 27, 1830–July 9, 1905.
Vol. 7, Pt. 2–482
Perry, Benjamin Franklin, Nov. 20, 1805–Dec. 3, 1886.
Vol. 7, Pt. 2–483
Perry, Bliss, Nov. 25, 1860–Feb. 13, 1954.
Supp. 5–541
Perry, Christopher Raymond, Dec 4, 1761–June 1, 1818.
Vol. 7, Pt. 2–484
Perry, Clarence Arthur, Mar. 4, 1872–Sept. 5, 1944.
Supp. 3–600
Perry, Edward Aylesworth, Mar. 15, 1831–Oct. 15, 1889.
Vol. 7, Pt. 2–484
Perry, Edward Baxter, Feb. 14, 1855–June 13, 1924.
Vol. 7, Pt. 2–485
Perry, Enoch Wood, July 31, 1831–Dec. 14, 1915.
Vol. 7, Pt. 2–485
Perry, Matthew Calbraith, Apr. 10, 1794–Mar. 4, 1858.
Vol. 7, Pt. 2–486
Perry, Nora, 1831–May 13, 1896.
Vol. 7, Pt. 2–489
Perry, Oliver Hazard, Aug. 20, 1785–Aug. 23, 1819.
Vol. 7, Pt. 2–490
Perry, Pettis, Jan. 4, 1897–July 24, 1965.
Supp. 7–611
Perry, Ralph Barton, July 3, 1876–Jan. 22, 1957.
Supp. 6–504
Perry, Rufus Lewis, Mar. 11, 1834–June 18, 1895.
Vol. 7, Pt. 2–492
Perry, Stuart, Nov. 2, 1814–Feb. 9, 1890.
Vol. 7, Pt. 2–492
Perry, Thomas Sergeant, Jan. 23, 1845–May 7, 1928.
Vol. 7, Pt. 2–493
Perry, Walter Scott, Dec. 26, 1855–Aug. 22, 1934.
Supp. 1–596
Perry, William, Dec. 20, 1788–Jan. 11, 1887.
Vol. 7, Pt. 2–494
Perry, William Flake, 1823–Dec. 18, 1901.
Vol. 7, Pt. 2–494
Perry, William Stevens, Jan. 22, 1832–May 13, 1898.
Vol. 7, Pt. 2–495
Pershing, John Joseph, Sept. 13, 1860–July 15, 1948.
Supp. 4–653
Person, Thomas, Jan. 19, 1733–Nov. 16, 1800.
Vol. 7, Pt. 2–496
Persons, Warren Milton, Mar. 12, 1878–Oct. 11, 1937.
Supp. 2–529
Peter, Hugh, 1598–Oct. 16, 1660.
Vol. 7, Pt. 2–496
Peter, John Frederick, May 19, 1746–July 19, 1813.
Vol. 7, Pt. 2–498
Peter, Robert, Jan. 21, 1805–Apr. 26, 1894.
Vol. 7, Pt. 2–499
Peter, Sarah Worthington King, May 10, 1800–Feb. 6, 1877.
Vol. 7, Pt. 2–500
Peterkin, George William, Mar. 21, 1841–Sept. 22, 1916.
Vol. 7, Pt. 2–501
Peterkin, Julia Mood, Oct. 31, 1880–Aug. 10, 1961.
Supp. 7–612
Peters, Absalom, Sept. 19, 1793–May 18, 1869.
Vol. 7, Pt. 2–502
Peters, Christian Henry Frederick, Sept. 19, 1813–July 19, 1890. Vol. 7, Pt. 2–502
Peters, Edward Dyer, June 1, 1849–Feb. 17, 1917.
Vol. 7, Pt. 2–504

Peters, John Andrew, Oct. 9, 1822–Apr. 2, 1904.
Vol. 7, Pt. 2–504
Peters, John Charles, July 6, 1819–Oct. 21, 1893.
Vol. 7, Pt. 2–505
Peters, John Punnett, Dec. 16, 1852–Nov. 10, 1921.
Vol. 7, Pt. 2–506
Peters, Madison Clinton, Nov. 6, 1859–Oct. 12, 1918.
Vol. 7, Pt. 2–507
Peters, Phillis Wheatley. [See Wheatley, Phillis, c. 1754–1784.]
Peters, Richard, c. 1704–July 10, 1776.
Vol. 7, Pt. 2–508
Peters, Richard, June 22, 1744–Aug. 22, 1828.
Vol. 7, Pt. 2–509
Peters, Richard, Nov. 10, 1810–Feb. 6, 1889.
Vol. 7, Pt. 2–510
Peters, Samuel Andrew, Nov. 20, 1735–Apr. 19, 1826.
Vol. 7, Pt. 2–511
Peters, William Cumming, Mar. 10, 1805–Apr. 20, 1866.
Vol. 7, Pt. 2–512
Peterson, Charles Jacobs, July 20, 1819–Mar. 4, 1887.
Vol. 7, Pt. 2–512
Peterson, Henry, Dec. 7, 1818–Oct. 10, 1891.
Vol. 7, Pt. 2–513
Petigru, James Louis, May 10, 1789–Mar. 9, 1863.
Vol. 7, Pt. 2–514
Petri, Angelo, Sept. 5, 1883–Oct. 4, 1961.
Supp. 7–613
Pettigrew, Charles, Mar. 20, 1743–Apr. 7, 1807.
Vol. 7, Pt. 2–515
Pettigrew, James Johnston, July 4, 1828–July 17, 1863.
Vol. 7, Pt. 2–516
Pettigrew, Richard Franklin, July 23, 1848–Oct. 5, 1926.
Vol. 7, Pt. 2–516
Pettit, Charles, 1736–Sept. 3, 1806.
Vol. 7, Pt. 2–517
Pettit, Thomas McKean, Dec. 26, 1797–May 30, 1853.
Vol. 7, Pt. 2–518
Pettus, Edmund Winston, July 6, 1821–July 27, 1907.
Vol. 7, Pt. 2–519
Pew, Joseph Newton, Jr., Nov. 12, 1886–Apr. 9, 1963.
Supp. 7–615
Peyton, John Lewis, Sept. 15, 1824–May 21, 1896.
Vol. 7, Pt. 2–520
Pfahler, George Edward, Jan. 29, 1874–Jan. 29, 1957.
Supp. 6–505
Pfister, Alfred, Sept. 3, 1880–Apr. 3, 1964.
Supp. 7–616
Pfund, August Herman, Dec. 28, 1879–Jan. 4, 1949.
Supp. 4–658
Phelan, David Samuel, July 16, 1841–Sept. 21, 1915.
Vol. 7, Pt. 2–520
Phelan, James, Apr. 23, 1824–Dec. 23, 1892.
Vol. 7, Pt. 2–521
Phelan, James, Dec. 7, 1856–Jan. 30, 1891.
Vol. 7, Pt. 2–522
Phelan, James Duval, Apr. 20, 1861–Aug. 7, 1930.
Vol. 7, Pt. 2–523
Phelps, Almira Hart Lincoln, July 15, 1793–July 15, 1884.
Vol. 7, Pt. 2–524
Phelps, Anson Greene, Mar. 24, 1781–Nov. 30, 1853.
Vol. 7, Pt. 2–525
Phelps, Austin, Jan. 7, 1820–Oct. 13, 1890.
Vol. 7, Pt. 2–526
Phelps, Charles Edward, May 1, 1833–Dec. 27, 1908.
Vol. 7, Pt. 2–527
Phelps, Edward John, July 11, 1822–Mar. 9, 1900.
Vol. 7, Pt. 2–528
Phelps, Elizabeth Stuart, 1815–1852, and Phelps, Elizabeth Stuart, 1844–1911. [See Ward, Elizabeth Stuart Phelps, 1844–1911.]
Phelps, Guy Rowland, Apr. 1, 1802–Mar. 18, 1869.
Vol. 7, Pt. 2–529
Phelps, John Smith, Dec. 22, 1814–Nov. 20, 1886.
Vol. 7, Pt. 2–530
Phelps, Oliver, Oct. 21, 1749–Feb. 21, 1809.
Vol. 7, Pt. 2–530
Phelps, Thomas Stowell, Nov. 2, 1822–Jan. 10, 1901.
Vol. 7, Pt. 2–531
Phelps, William Franklin, Feb. 15, 1822–Aug. 15, 1907.
Vol. 7, Pt. 2–532
Phelps, William Lyon, Jan. 2, 1865–Aug. 21, 1943.
Supp. 3–601

Phelps, William Walter, Aug. 24, 1839–June 17, 1894.
    Vol. 7, Pt. 2–533
Philip, d. Aug. 12, 1676.
    Vol. 7, Pt. 2–534
Philip, John Woodward, Aug. 26, 1840–June 30, 1900.
    Vol. 7, Pt. 2–534
Philipp, Emanuel Lorenz, Mar. 25, 1861–June 15, 1925.
    Vol. 7, Pt. 2–535
Philips, John Finis, Dec. 31, 1834–Mar. 13, 1919.
    Vol. 7, Pt. 2–536
Philips, Martin Wilson, June 17, 1806–Feb. 26, 1889.
    Vol. 7, Pt. 2–537
Philipse, Frederick, Nov. 6, 1626–1702.
    Vol. 7, Pt. 2–538
Philipson, David, Aug. 9, 1862–June 29, 1949.
    Supp. 4–659
Phillips, David Graham, Oct. 31, 1867–Jan. 24, 1911.
    Vol. 7, Pt. 2–538
Phillips, Francis Clifford, Apr. 2, 1850–Feb. 16, 1920.
    Vol. 7, Pt. 2–539
Phillips, Frank, Nov. 28, 1873–Aug. 23, 1950.
    Supp. 4–660
Phillips, George, 1593–July 1, 1644.
    Vol. 7, Pt. 2–540
Phillips, Harry Irving, Nov. 26, 1889–Mar. 15, 1965.
    Supp. 7–617
Phillips, Henry, Sept. 6, 1838–June 6, 1895.
    Vol. 7, Pt. 2–541
Phillips, John, Dec. 27, 1719–Apr. 21, 1795.
    Vol. 7, Pt. 2–542
Phillips, John Sanburn, July 2, 1861–Feb. 28, 1949.
    Supp. 4–661
Phillips, Lena Madesin, Oct. 15, 1881–May 22, 1955.
    Supp. 5–542
Phillips, Philip, Aug. 13, 1834–June 25, 1895.
    Vol. 7, Pt. 2–542
Phillips, Samuel, Feb. 5, 1752–Feb. 10, 1802.
    Vol. 7, Pt. 2–543
Phillips, Thomas Wharton, Feb. 23, 1835–July 21, 1912.
    Vol. 7, Pt. 2–544
Phillips, Ulrich Bonnell, Nov. 4, 1877–Jan. 21, 1934.
    Supp. 1–597
Phillips, Walter Polk, June 14, 1846–Jan. 31, 1920.
    Vol. 7, Pt. 2–545
Phillips, Wendell, Nov. 29, 1811–Feb. 2, 1884.
    Vol. 7, Pt. 2–546
Phillips, Willard, Dec. 19, 1784–Sept. 9, 1873.
    Vol. 7, Pt. 2–547
Phillips, William, Mar. 30, 1750 o.s.–May 26, 1827.
    Vol. 7, Pt. 2–548
Phillips, William, May 30, 1878–Feb. 23, 1968.
    Supp. 8–500
Phillips, William Addison, Jan. 14, 1824–Nov. 30, 1893.
    Vol. 7, Pt. 2–548
Phinizy, Ferdinand, Jan. 20, 1819–Oct. 20, 1889.
    Vol. 7, Pt. 2–549
Phipps, Henry, Sept. 27, 1839–Sept. 22, 1930.
    Vol. 7, Pt. 2–550
Phipps, Lawrence Cowle, Aug. 30, 1862–Mar. 1, 1958.
    Supp. 6–506
Phips Sir William, Feb. 2, 1650/51–Feb. 18, 1694/95.
    Vol. 7, Pt. 2–551
Phisterer, Frederick, Oct. 11, 1836–July 13, 1909.
    Vol. 7, Pt. 2–552
Phoenix, John. [See Derby, George Horatio, 1823–1861.]
Phyfe, Duncan, 1768–Aug. 16, 1854.
    Vol. 7, Pt. 2–553
Physick, Philip Syng, July 7, 1768–Dec. 15, 1837.
    Vol. 7, Pt. 2–554
Piatt, Donn, June 29, 1819–Nov. 12, 1891.
    Vol. 7, Pt. 2–555
Piatt, John James, Mar. 1, 1835–Feb. 16, 1917.
    Vol. 7, Pt. 2–556
Piatt, Sarah Morgan Bryan, Aug. 11, 1836–Dec. 22, 1919.
    Vol. 7, Pt. 2–557
Piccard, Jean Felix, Jan. 28, 1884–Jan. 28, 1963.
    Supp. 7–618
Pick, Lewis Andrew, Nov. 18, 1890–Dec. 2, 1956.
    Supp. 6–507
Pickard, Samuel Thomas, Mar. 1, 1828–Feb. 12, 1915.
    Vol. 7, Pt. 2–558
Pickens, Andrew, Sept. 19, 1739–Aug. 11, 1817.
    Vol. 7, Pt. 2–558

Pickens, Francis Wilkinson, Apr. 7, 1805–Jan. 25, 1869.
    Vol. 7, Pt. 2–559
Pickens, Israel, Jan. 30, 1780–Apr. 23, 1827.
    Vol. 7, Pt. 2–561
Pickens, William, Jan. 15, 1881–Apr. 6, 1954.
    Supp. 5–543
Pickering, Charles, Nov. 10, 1805–Mar. 17, 1878.
    Vol. 7, Pt. 2–562
Pickering, Edward Charles, July 19, 1846–Feb. 3, 1919.
    Vol. 7, Pt. 2–562
Pickering, John, c. 1738–Apr. 11, 1805.
    Vol. 7, Pt. 2–563
Pickering, John, Feb. 7, 1777–May 5, 1846.
    Vol. 7, Pt. 2–564
Pickering, Timothy, July 17, 1745–Jan. 29, 1829.
    Vol. 7, Pt. 2–565
Picket, Albert, Apr. 15, 1771–Aug. 3, 1850.
    Vol. 7, Pt. 2–568
Pickett, Albert James, Aug. 13, 1810–Oct. 28, 1858.
    Vol. 7, Pt. 2–569
Pickett, George Edward, Jan. 25, 1825–July 30, 1875.
    Vol. 7, Pt. 2–570
Pickett, James Chamberlayne, Feb. 6, 1793–July 10, 1872.
    Vol. 7, Pt. 2–571
Picknell, William Lamb, Oct. 23, 1853–Aug. 8, 1897.
    Vol. 7, Pt. 2–572
Picton, Thomas, May 16, 1822–Feb. 20, 1891.
    Vol. 7, Pt. 2–572
Pidgin, Charles Felton, Nov. 11, 1844–June 3, 1923.
    Vol. 7, Pt. 2–573
Pieper, Franz August Otto, June 27, 1852–June 3, 1931.
    Vol. 7, Pt. 2–574
Pierce, Benjamin, Dec. 25, 1757–Apr. 1, 1839.
    Vol. 7, Pt. 2–575
Pierce, Edward Lillie, Mar. 29, 1829–Sept. 5, 1897.
    Vol. 7, Pt. 2–575
Pierce, Franklin, Nov. 23, 1804–Oct. 8, 1869.
    Vol. 7, Pt. 2–576
Pierce, George Foster, Feb. 3, 1811–Sept. 3, 1884.
    Vol. 7, Pt. 2–580
Pierce, Gilbert Ashville, Jan. 11, 1839–Feb. 15, 1901.
    Vol. 7, Pt. 2–581
Pierce, Henry Lillie, Aug. 23, 1825–Dec. 17, 1896.
    Vol. 7, Pt. 2–582
Pierce, John Davis, Feb. 18, 1797–Apr. 5, 1882.
    Vol. 7, Pt. 2–583
Pierce, William Leigh, c. 1740–Dec. 10, 1789.
    Vol. 7, Pt. 2–583
Pierpont, Francis Harrison, Jan. 25, 1814–Mar. 24, 1899.
    Vol. 7, Pt. 2–584
Pierpont, James, Jan. 4, 1659/60–Nov. 22, 1714.
    Vol. 7, Pt. 2–585
Pierpont, John, Apr. 6, 1785–Aug. 27, 1866.
    Vol. 7, Pt. 2–586
Pierrepont, Edwards, Mar. 4, 1817–Mar. 6, 1892.
    Vol. 7, Pt. 2–587
Pierson, Abraham, 1609–Aug. 9, 1678.
    Vol. 7, Pt. 2–587
Pierson, Abraham, c. 1645–Mar. 5, 1707.
    Vol. 7, Pt. 2–588
Pierson, Arthur Tappan, Mar. 6, 1837–June 3, 1911.
    Vol. 7, Pt. 2–589
Pierson, Hamilton Wilcox, Sept. 22, 1817–Sept. 7, 1888.
    Vol. 7, Pt. 2–591
Pierz, Franz, Nov. 20, 1785–Jan. 22, 1880.
    Vol. 7, Pt. 2–591
Piez, Charles, Sept. 24, 1866–Oct. 2, 1933.
    Supp. 1–598
Piggot, Robert, May 20, 1795–July 23, 1887.
    Vol. 7, Pt. 2–592
Piggott, James, c. 1739–Feb. 20, 1799.
    Vol. 7, Pt. 2–592
Pike, Albert, Dec. 29, 1809–Apr. 2, 1891.
    Vol. 7, Pt. 2–593
Pike, James Shepherd, Sept. 8, 1811–Nov. 29, 1882.
    Vol. 7, Pt. 2–595
Pike, Mary Hayden Green, Nov. 30, 1824–Jan. 15, 1908.
    Vol. 7, Pt. 2–597
Pike, Nicolas, Oct. 6, 1743–Dec. 9, 1819.
    Vol. 7, Pt. 2–597
Pike, Robert, c. 1616–Dec. 12, 1708.
    Vol. 7, Pt. 2–598

Pike, Zebulon Montgomery, Jan. 5, 1779–Apr. 27, 1813.
    Vol. 7, Pt. 2–599
Pilat, Ignaz Anton, June 27, 1820–Sept. 17, 1870.
    Vol. 7, Pt. 2–600
Pilcher, Joshua, Mar. 15, 1790–June 5, 1843.
    Vol. 7, Pt. 2–601
Pilcher, Lewis Stephen, July 28, 1845–Dec. 24, 1934.
    Supp. 1–599
Pilcher, Paul Monroe, Apr. 11, 1876–Jan. 4, 1917.
    Vol. 7, Pt. 2–601
Pilkington, James, Jan. 4, 1851–Apr. 25, 1929.
    Vol. 7, Pt. 2–602
Pilling, James Constantine, Nov. 16, 1846–July 26, 1895.
    Vol. 7, Pt. 2–603
Pillow, Gideon Johnson, June 8, 1806–Oct. 8, 1878.
    Vol. 7, Pt. 2–603
Pillsbury, Charles Alfred, Dec. 3, 1842–Sept. 17, 1899.
    Vol. 7, Pt. 2–604
Pillsbury, Harry Nelson, Dec. 5, 1872–June 17, 1906.
    Vol. 7, Pt. 2–606
Pillsbury, John Elliott, Dec. 15, 1846–Dec. 30, 1919.
    Vol. 7, Pt. 2–606
Pillsbury, John Sargent, July 29, 1828–Oct. 18, 1901.
    Vol. 7, Pt. 2–607
Pillsbury, Parker, Sept. 22, 1809–July 7, 1898.
    Vol. 7, Pt. 2–608
Pilmore, Joseph, Oct. 31, 1739–July 24, 1825.
    Vol. 7, Pt. 2–609
Pilsbury, Amos, Feb. 8, 1805–July 14, 1873.
    Vol. 7, Pt. 2–610
Pinchback, Pinckney Benton Stewart, May 10, 1837–Dec. 21, 1921. Vol. 7, Pt. 2–611
Pinchot, Amos Richards Eno, Dec. 6, 1873–Feb. 18, 1944.
    Supp. 3–603
Pinchot, Cornelia Elizabeth Bryce, Aug. 26, 1881–Sept. 9, 1960. Supp. 6–509
Pinchot, Gifford, Aug. 11, 1865–Oct. 4, 1946.
    Supp. 4–663
Pinckney, Charles Cotesworth, Feb. 25, 1746–Aug. 16, 1825.
    Vol. 7, Pt. 2–614
Pinckney, Charles, Oct. 26, 1757–Oct. 29, 1824.
    Vol. 7, Pt. 2–611
Pinckney, Elizabeth Lucas, c. 1722–May 26, 1793.
    Vol. 7, Pt. 2–616
Pinckney, Henry Laurens, Sept. 24, 1794–Feb. 3, 1863.
    Vol. 7, Pt. 2–617
Pinckney, Thomas, Oct. 23, 1750–Nov. 2, 1828.
    Vol. 7, Pt. 2–617
Pincus, Gregory Goodwin ("Goody"), Apr. 9, 1903–Aug. 22, 1967. Supp. 8–502
Pine, Robert Edge, 1730–Nov. 19, 1788.
    Vol. 7, Pt. 2–620
Piñero Jiménez, JesÚs Toribio, Apr. 16, 1897–Nov. 19, 1952. Supp. 5–545
Pingree, Hazen Stuart, Aug. 30, 1840–June 18, 1901.
    Vol. 7, Pt. 2–621
Pinkerton, Allan, Aug. 25, 1819–July 1, 1884.
    Vol. 7, Pt. 2–622
Pinkerton, Lewis Letig, Jan. 28, 1812–Jan. 28, 1875.
    Vol. 7, Pt. 2–623
Pinkham, Lydia Estes, Feb. 9, 1819–May 17, 1883.
    Vol. 7, Pt. 2–624
Pinkney, Edward Coote, Oct. 1, 1802–Apr. 11, 1828.
    Vol. 7, Pt. 2–625
Pinkney, Ninian, June 7, 1811–Dec. 15, 1877.
    Vol. 7, Pt. 2–625
Pinkney, William, Mar. 17, 1764–Feb. 25, 1822.
    Vol. 7, Pt. 2–626
Pinney, Norman, Oct. 21, 1804–Oct. 1, 1862.
    Vol. 7, Pt. 2–629
Pino, José. [See Son of Many Beads.]
Pintard, John, May 18, 1759–June 21, 1844.
    Vol. 7, Pt. 2–629
Pintard, Lewis, Oct. 1, 1732–Mar. 25, 1818.
    Vol. 7, Pt. 2–630
Pinto, Isaac, June 12, 1720–Jan. 17, 1791.
    Vol. 7, Pt. 2–631
Pinza, Ezio, May 18, 1892–May 9, 1957.
    Supp. 6–510
Piper, Charles Vancouver, June 16, 1867–Feb. 11, 1926.
    Vol. 7, Pt. 2–632
Piper, William Thomas, Jan. 8, 1881–Jan. 15, 1970.
    Supp. 8–503

Pippin, Horace, Feb. 22, 1888–July 6, 1946.
    Supp. 4–666
Pirsson, Louis Valentine, Nov. 3, 1860–Dec. 8, 1919.
    Vol. 6, Pt. 2–633
Pise, Charles Constantine, Nov. 22, 1801–May 26, 1866.
    Vol. 7, Pt. 2–634
Pitcairn, John, 1722–June 1775.
    Vol. 7, Pt. 2–635
Pitcairn, John, Jan. 10, 1841–July 22, 1916.
    Vol. 7, Pt. 2–635
Pitcher, Molly. [See McCauley, Mary Ludwig Hays, 1754–1832.]
Pitcher, Zina, Apr. 12, 1797–Apr. 5, 1872.
    Vol. 7, Pt. 2–636
Pitchlynn, Peter Perkins, Jan. 30, 1806–Jan. 17, 1881.
    Vol. 7, Pt. 2–637
Pitkin, Frederick Walker, Aug. 31, 1837–Dec. 18, 1886.
    Vol. 7, Pt. 2–638
Pitkin, Timothy, Jan. 21, 1766–Dec. 18, 1847.
    Vol. 7, Pt. 2–639
Pitkin, Walter Boughton, Feb. 6, 1878–Jan. 25, 1953.
    Supp. 5–546
Pitkin, William, 1635–Dec. 15, 1694.
    Vol. 7, Pt. 2–639
Pitkin, William, Apr. 30, 1694–Oct. 1, 1769.
    Vol. 7, Pt. 2–640
Pitkin, William, 1725–Dec. 12, 1789.
    Vol. 7, Pt. 2–641
Pitman, Benn, July 24, 1822–Dec. 28, 1910.
    Vol. 7, Pt. 2–641
Pitney, Mahlon, Feb. 5, 1858–Dec. 9, 1924.
    Vol. 7, Pt. 2–642
Pittman, Key, Sept. 19, 1872–Nov. 10, 1940.
    Supp. 2–530
Pittock, Henry Lewis, Mar. 1, 1836–Jan. 28, 1919.
    Vol. 7, Pt. 2–643
Pitts, Hiram Avery, c. 1800–Sept. 19, 1860.
    Vol. 7, Pt. 2–644
Pitts, Zasu, Jan. 3, 1898–June 7, 1963.
    Supp. 7–620
Placide, Henry, Sept. 8, 1799–Jan. 23, 1870.
    Vol. 7, Pt. 2–644
Plaisted, Harris Merrill, Nov. 2, 1828–Jan. 31, 1898.
    Vol. 7, Pt. 2–645
Plant, Henry Bradley, Oct. 27, 1819–June 23, 1899.
    Vol. 7, Pt. 2–646
Plater, George, Nov. 8, 1735–Feb. 10, 1792.
    Vol. 7, Pt. 2–647
Plath, Sylvia, Oct. 27, 1932–Feb. 11, 1963.
    Supp. 7–621
Platner, Samuel Ball, Dec. 4, 1863–Aug. 20, 1921.
    Vol. 7, Pt. 2–648
Platt, Charles Adams, Oct. 16, 1861–Sept. 12, 1933.
    Vol. 8, Pt. 1–1
Platt, Orville Hitchcock, July 19, 1827–Apr. 21, 1905.
    Vol. 8, Pt. 1–2
Platt, Thomas Collier, July 15, 1833–Mar. 6, 1910.
    Vol. 8, Pt. 1–4
Pleasants, James, Oct. 24, 1769–Nov. 9, 1836.
    Vol. 8, Pt. 1–6
Pleasants, John Hampden, Jan. 4, 1797–Feb. 27, 1846.
    Vol. 8, Pt. 1–7
Pleasonton, Alfred, June 7, 1824–Feb. 17, 1897.
    Vol. 8, Pt. 1–8
Plimpton, George Arthur, July 13, 1855–July 1, 1936.
    Supp. 2–532
Plotz, Harry, Apr. 17, 1890–Jan. 6, 1947.
    Supp. 4–667
Plowman, George Taylor, Oct. 19, 1869–Mar. 26, 1932.
    Vol. 8, Pt. 1–9
Plumb, Glenn Edward, Sept. 30, 1866–Aug. 1, 1922.
    Vol. 8, Pt. 1–9
Plumb, Preston B., Oct. 12, 1837–Dec. 20, 1891.
    Vol. 8, Pt. 1–10
Plumbe, John, July 1809–July 1857.
    Vol. 8, Pt. 1–11
Plumer, William, June 25, 1759–Dec. 22, 1850.
    Vol. 8, Pt. 1–12
Plumer, William Swan, July 26, 1802–Oct. 22, 1880.
    Vol. 8, Pt. 1–13
Plumley, Frank, Dec. 17, 1844–Apr. 30, 1924.
    Vol. 8, Pt. 1–14

Plummer, Henry, d. Jan. 10, 1864.
    Vol. 8, Pt. 1–15
Plummer, Henry Stanley, Mar. 3, 1874–Dec. 31, 1936.
    Supp. 2–533
Plummer, Jonathan, July 13, 1761–Sept. 13, 1819.
    Vol. 8, Pt. 1–16
Plummer, Mary Wright, Mar. 8, 1856–Sept. 21, 1916.
    Vol. 8, Pt. 1–17
Plunkett, Charles Peshall, Feb. 15. 1864–Mar. 24, 1931.
    Vol. 8, Pt. 1–17
Pocahontas, c. 1595–March 1617.
    Vol. 8, Pt. 1–18
Poe, Edgar Allan, Jan. 19, 1809–Oct. 7, 1849.
    Vol. 8, Pt. 1–19
Poe, Orlando Metcalfe, Mar. 7, 1832–Oct. 2, 1895.
    Vol. 8, Pt. 1–28
Poindexter, George, 1779–Sept. 5, 1853.
    Vol. 8, Pt. 1–29
Poindexter, Miles, Apr. 22, 1868–Sept. 21, 1946.
    Supp. 4–669
Poinsett, Joel Roberts, Mar. 2, 1779–Dec. 12, 1851.
    Vol. 8, Pt. 1–30
Polak, John Osborn, Mar. 12, 1870–June 29, 1931.
    Vol. 8, Pt. 1–32
Poland, Luke Potter, Nov. 1, 1815–July 2, 1887.
    Vol. 8, Pt. 1–33
Poling, Daniel Alfred, Nov. 30, 1884–Feb. 7, 1968.
    Supp. 8–505
Polk, Frank Lyon, Sept. 13, 1871–Feb. 7, 1943.
    Supp. 3–605
Polk, James Knox, Nov. 2, 1795–June 15, 1849.
    Vol. 8, Pt. 1–34
Polk, Leonidas, Apr. 10, 1806–June 14, 1864.
    Vol. 8, Pt. 1–39
Polk, Leonidas Lafayette, Apr. 24, 1837–June 11, 1892.
    Vol. 8, Pt. 1–40
Polk, Lucius Eugene, July 10, 1833–Dec. 1, 1892.
    Vol. 8, Pt. 1–41
Polk, Thomas, c. 1732–Jan. 26, 1794.
    Vol. 8, Pt. 1–42
Polk, Trusten, May 29, 1811–Apr. 16, 1876.
    Vol. 8, Pt. 1–43
Polk, William, July 9, 1758–Jan. 14, 1834.
    Vol. 8, Pt. 1–43
Polk, William Mecklenburg, Aug. 15, 1844–June 23, 1918.
    Vol. 8, Pt. 1–44
Polk, Willis Jefferson, Oct. 3, 1867–Sept. 10, 1924.
    Vol. 8, Pt. 1–45
Pollak, Gustav, May 4, 1849–Nov. 1, 1919.
    Vol. 8, Pt. 1–46
Pollak, Walter Heilprin, June 4, 1887–Oct. 2, 1940.
    Supp. 2–534
Pollard, Edward Alfred, Feb. 27, 1831–Dec. 16, 1872.
    Vol. 8, Pt. 1–47
Pollard, Joseph Percival, Jan. 29, 1869–Dec. 17, 1911.
    Vol. 8, Pt. 1–48
Pollock, Channing, Mar. 4, 1880–Aug. 17, 1946.
    Supp. 4–670
Pollock, James, Sept. 11, 1810–Apr. 19, 1890.
    Vol. 8, Pt. 1–49
Pollock, Oliver, c. 1737–Dec. 17, 1823.
    Vol. 8, Pt. 1–50
Pollock, (Paul), Jackson, Jan. 28, 1912–Aug. 11, 1956.
    Supp. 6–511
Polock, Moses, May 14, 1817–Aug. 16, 1903.
    Vol. 8, Pt. 1–51
Pomerene, Atlee, Dec. 6, 1863–Nov. 12, 1937.
    Supp. 2–535
Pomeroy, John Norton, Apr. 12, 1828–Feb. 15, 1885.
    Vol. 8, Pt. 1–52
Pomeroy, Marcus Mills, Dec. 25, 1833–May 30, 1896.
    Vol. 8, Pt. 1–53
Pomeroy, Samuel Clarke, Jan. 3, 1816–Aug. 27, 1891.
    Vol. 8, Pt. 1–54
Pomeroy, Seth, May 20, 1706–Feb. 19, 1777.
    Vol. 8, Pt. 1–55
Ponce de León, Juan, c. 1460–1521.
    Vol. 8, Pt. 1–56
Pond, Allen Bartlit, Nov. 21, 1858–Mar. 17, 1929.
    Vol. 8, Pt. 1–57
Pond, Enoch, July 29, 1791–Jan. 21, 1882.
    Vol. 8, Pt. 1–58

Pond, Frederick Eugene, Apr. 8, 1856–Nov. 1, 1925.
    Vol. 8, Pt. 1–58
Pond, George Edward, Mar. 11, 1837–Sept. 22, 1899.
    Vol. 8, Pt. 1–59
Pond, Irving Kane, May 1, 1857–Sept. 29, 1939.
    Supp. 2–536
Pond, James Burton, June 11, 1838–June 21, 1903.
    Vol. 8, Pt. 1–60
Pond, Peter, Jan. 18, 1740–1807.
    Vol. 8, Pt. 1–61
Pond, Samuel William, Apr. 10, 1808–Dec. 12, 1891.
    Vol. 8, Pt. 1–61
Pontiac, d. 1769.
    Vol. 8, Pt. 1–62
Pool, Joe Richard, Feb. 18, 1911–July 14, 1968.
    Supp. 8–506
Pool, John, June 16, 1826–Aug. 16, 1884.
    Vol. 8, Pt. 1–64
Pool, Maria Louise, Aug. 20, 1841–May 19, 1898.
    Vol. 8, Pt. 1–65
Poole, Ernest Cook, Jan. 23, 1880–Jan. 10, 1950.
    Supp. 4–671
Poole, Fitch, June 13, 1803–Aug. 19, 1873.
    Vol. 8, Pt. 1–65
Poole, William Frederick, Dec. 24, 1821–Mar. 1, 1894.
    Vol. 8, Pt. 1–66
Poor, Charles Henry, June 9, 1808–Nov. 5, 1882.
    Vol. 8, Pt. 1–67
Poor, Daniel, June 27, 1789–Feb. 3, 1855.
    Vol. 8, Pt. 1–68
Poor, Enoch, June 21, 1736–Sept. 8, 1780.
    Vol. 8, Pt. 1–69
Poor, Henry Varnum, Dec. 8, 1812–Jan. 4, 1905.
    Vol. 8, Pt. 1–70
Poor, John, July 8, 1752–Dec. 5, 1829.
    Vol. 8, Pt. 1–71
Poor, John Alfred, Jan. 8, 1808–Sept. 5, 1871.
    Vol. 8, Pt. 1–71
Poore, Benjamin Perley, Nov. 2, 1820–May 29, 1887.
    Vol. 8, Pt. 1–73
Pope, Albert Augustus, May 20, 1843–Aug. 10, 1909.
    Vol. 8, Pt. 1–74
Pope, Franklin Leonard, Dec. 2, 1840–Oct. 13, 1895.
    Vol. 8, Pt. 1–75
Pope, James Pinckney, Mar. 31, 1884–Jan. 23, 1966.
    Supp. 8–507
Pope, John, Mar. 16, 1822–Sept. 23, 1892.
    Vol. 8, Pt. 1–76
Pope, John Russell, Apr. 24, 1874–Aug. 27, 1937.
    Supp. 2–538
Pope, Nathaniel, Jan. 5, 1784–Jan. 22, 1850.
    Vol. 8, Pt. 1–77
Popham, George, d. Feb. 5, 1608.
    Vol. 8, Pt. 1–78
Porcher, Francis Peyre, Dec. 14, 1825–Nov. 19, 1895.
    Vol. 8, Pt. 1–79
Pormort, Philemon, c. 1595–c. 1656.
    Vol. 8, Pt. 1–80
Porter, Albert Gallatin, Apr. 20, 1824–May 3, 1897.
    Vol. 8, Pt. 1–80
Porter, Alexander, June 24, 1785–Jan. 13, 1844.
    Vol. 8, Pt. 1–81
Porter, Andrew, Sept. 24, 1743–Nov. 16, 1813.
    Vol. 8, Pt. 1–82
Porter, Arthur Kingsley, Feb. 6, 1883–July 8, 1933.
    Supp. 1–601
Porter, Benjamin Curtis, Aug. 29, 1845–Apr. 2, 1908.
    Vol. 8, Pt. 1–83
Porter, Cole, June 9, 1891–Oct. 15, 1964.
    Supp. 7–622
Porter, David, Feb. 1, 1780–Mar. 3, 1843.
    Vol. 8, Pt. 1–83
Porter, David Dixon, June 8, 1813–Feb. 13, 1891.
    Vol. 8, Pt. 1–85
Porter, David Rittenhouse, Oct. 31, 1788–Aug. 6, 1867.
    Vol. 8, Pt. 1–89
Porter, Ebenezer, Oct. 5, 1772–April 8, 1834.
    Vol. 8, Pt. 1–89
Porter, Edwin Stanton, Apr. 21, 1870–Apr. 30, 1941.
    Supp. 3–606
Porter, Fitz-John, Aug. 31, 1822–May 21, 1901.
    Vol. 8, Pt. 1–90

Porter, Gene Stratton, Aug. 17, 1863–Dec. 6, 1924.
Supp. 1–601
Porter, Holbrook Fitz-John, Feb. 28, 1858–Jan. 25, 1933.
Vol. 8, Pt. 1–91
Porter, Horace, Apr. 15, 1837–May 29, 1921.
Vol. 8, Pt. 1–92
Porter, James Davis, Dec. 17, 1828–May 18, 1912.
Vol. 8, Pt. 1–93
Porter, James Madison, Jan. 6, 1793–Nov. 11, 1862.
Vol. 8, Pt. 1–94
Porter, Jermain Gildersleeve, Jan. 8, 1852–Apr. 14, 1933.
Vol. 8, Pt. 1–95
Porter, John Addison, Mar. 15, 1822–Aug. 25, 1866.
Vol. 8, Pt. 1–96
Porter, John Luke, Sept. 19, 1813–Dec. 14, 1893.
Vol. 8, Pt. 1–97
Porter, Noah, Dec. 14, 1811–Mar. 4, 1892.
Vol. 8, Pt. 1–97
Porter, Peter Buell, Aug. 14, 1773–Mar. 20, 1844.
Vol. 8, Pt. 1–99
Porter, Robert Percival, June 30, 1852–Feb. 28, 1917.
Vol. 8, Pt. 1–100
Porter, Rufus, May 1, 1792–Aug. 13, 1884.
Vol. 8, Pt. 1–101
Porter, Russell Williams, Dec. 13, 1871–Feb. 22, 1949.
Supp. 4–674
Porter, Samuel, Jan. 12, 1810–Sept. 3, 1901.
Vol. 8, Pt. 1–102
Porter, Sarah, Aug. 16, 1813–Feb. 17, 1900.
Vol. 8, Pt. 1–103
Porter, Stephen Geyer, May 18, 1869–June 27, 1930.
Vol. 8, Pt. 1–103
Porter, Thomas Conrad, Jan. 22, 1822–Apr. 27, 1901.
Vol. 8, Pt. 1–104
Porter, William Sydney, Sept. 11, 1862–June 5, 1910.
Vol. 8, Pt. 1–105
Porter, William Townsend, Sept. 24, 1862–Feb. 16, 1949.
Supp. 4–675
Porter, William Trotter, Dec. 24, 1809–July 19, 1858.
Vol. 8, Pt. 1–107
Portier, Michael, Sept. 7, 1795–May 14, 1859.
Vol. 8, Pt. 1–108
Portolá, Gaspar de, fl. 1734–1784.
Vol. 8, Pt. 1–109
Pory, John, 1572–September 1635.
Vol. 8, Pt. 1–110
Posey, Alexander Lawrence, Aug. 3, 1873–May 27, 1908.
Vol. 8, Pt. 1–111
Posey, Thomas, July 9, 1750–Mar. 19, 1818.
Vol. 8, Pt. 1–111
Post, Augustus, Dec. 8, 1873–Oct. 4, 1952.
Supp. 5–547
Post, Charles William, Oct. 26, 1854–May 9, 1914.
Vol. 8, Pt. 1–112
Post, Christian Frederick, c. 1710–May 1, 1785.
Vol. 8, Pt. 1–113
Post, Emily Price, Oct. 3, 1873–Sept. 25, 1960.
Supp. 6–514
Post, George Adams, Sept. 1, 1854–Oct. 31, 1925.
Vol. 8, Pt. 1–114
Post, George Browne, Dec. 15, 1837–Nov. 28, 1913.
Vol. 8, Pt. 1–115
Post, George Edward, Dec. 17, 1838–Sept. 29, 1909.
Vol. 8, Pt. 1–116
Post, Isaac, Feb. 26, 1798–May 9, 1872.
Vol. 8, Pt. 1–117
Post, Louis Freeland, Nov. 15, 1849–Jan. 10, 1928.
Vol. 8, Pt. 2–118
Post, Melville Davisson, Apr. 19, 1871–June 23, 1930.
Vol. 8, Pt. 1–119
Post, Truman Marcellus, June 3, 1810–Dec. 31, 1886.
Vol. 8, Pt. 1–120
Post, Wiley, Nov. 22, 1899–Aug. 15, 1935.
Supp. 1–603
Post, Wright, Feb. 19, 1766–June 14, 1828.
Vol. 8, Pt. 1–121
Postl, Carl. [See Sealsfield, Charles, 1793–1864.]
Poston, Charles Debrill, Apr. 20, 1825–June 24, 1902.
Vol. 8, Pt. 1–121
Potamian, Brother, Sept. 29, 1847–Jan. 20, 1917.
Vol. 8, Pt. 1–122
Pott, Francis Lister Hawks, Feb. 22, 1864–Mar. 7, 1949.
Supp. 4–677

Pott, John, ?–c. 1642.
Vol. 8, Pt. 1–123
Potter, Alonzo, July 6, 1800–July 4, 1865.
Vol. 8, Pt. 1–124
Potter, Charles Francis, Oct. 28, 1885–Oct. 4, 1962.
Supp. 7–623
Potter, Edward Clark, Nov. 26, 1857–June 21, 1923.
Vol. 8, Pt. 1–125
Potter, Eliphalet Nott, Sept. 20, 1836–Feb. 6, 1901.
Vol. 8, Pt. 1–126
Potter, Elisha Reynolds, June 20, 1811–Apr. 10, 1882.
Vol. 8, Pt. 1–126
Potter, Ellen Culver, Aug. 5, 1871–Feb. 9, 1958.
Supp. 6–515
Potter, Henry Codman, May 25, 1835–July 21, 1908.
Vol. 8, Pt. 1–127
Potter, Horatio, Feb. 9, 1802–Jan. 2, 1887.
Vol. 8, Pt. 1–129
Potter, James, 1729–November 1789.
Vol. 8, Pt. 1–129
Potter, Louis McClellan, Nov. 14, 1873–Aug. 29, 1912.
Vol. 8, Pt. 1–130
Potter, Nathaniel, 1770–Jan. 2, 1843.
Vol. 8, Pt. 1–131
Potter, Paul Meredith, June 3, 1853–Mar. 7, 1921.
Vol. 8, Pt. 1–132
Potter, Platt, Apr. 6, 1800–Aug. 11, 1891.
Vol. 8, Pt. 1–132
Potter, Robert, c. 1800–Mar. 2, 1842.
Vol. 8, Pt. 1–133
Potter, Robert Brown, July 16, 1829–Feb. 19, 1887.
Vol. 8, Pt. 1–134
Potter, William Bancroft, Feb. 19, 1863–Jan. 15, 1934.
Supp. 1–604
Potter, William James, Feb. 1, 1829–Dec. 21, 1893.
Vol. 8, Pt. 1–135
Potts, Benjamin Franklin, Jan. 29, 1836–June 17, 1887.
Vol. 8, Pt. 1–135
Potts, Charles Sower, Jan. 30, 1864–Feb. 16, 1930.
Vol. 8, Pt. 1–136
Potts, Jonathan, Apr. 11, 1745–October 1781.
Vol. 8, Pt. 1–137
Potts, Richard, July 19, 1753–Nov. 25, 1808.
Vol. 8, Pt. 1–138
Pou, Edward William, Sept. 9, 1863–Apr. 1, 1934.
Supp. 1–605
Poulson, Niels, Feb. 27, 1843–May 3, 1911.
Vol. 8, Pt. 1–138
Poulson, Zachariah, Sept. 5, 1761–July 31, 1844.
Vol. 8, Pt. 1–139
Pound, Cuthbert Winfred, June 20, 1864–Feb. 3, 1935.
Supp. 1–606
Pound, (Nathan) Roscoe, Oct. 27, 1890–July 1, 1964.
Supp. 7–624
Pound, Thomas, c. 1650–1703.
Vol. 8, Pt. 1–140
Pourtalès, Louis François de, Mar. 4, 1823–July 18, 1880.
Vol. 8, Pt. 1–141
Powderly, Terence Vincent, Jan. 22, 1849–June 24, 1924.
Vol. 8, Pt. 1–142
Powdermaker, Hortense, Dec. 24, 1896–June 15, 1970.
Supp. 8–509
Powel, John Hare, Apr. 22, 1786–June 14, 1856.
Vol. 8, Pt. 1–143
Powell. [See Osceola, c. 1800–1838.]
Powell, Adam Clayton, Sr., May 5, 1865–June 12, 1953.
Supp. 5–547
Powell, Alma Webster, Nov. 20, 1874–Mar. 11, 1930.
Vol. 8, Pt. 1–144
Powell, Edward Payson, May 9, 1833–May 14, 1915.
Vol. 8, Pt. 1–144
Powell, George Harold, Feb. 8, 1872–Feb. 18, 1922.
Vol. 8, Pt. 1–145
Powell, John Benjamin, Apr. 18, 1886–Feb. 28, 1947.
Supp. 4–678
Powell, John Wesley, Mar. 24, 1834–Sept. 23, 1902.
Vol. 8, Pt. 1–146
Powell, Lucien Whiting, Dec. 13, 1846–Sept. 27, 1930.
Vol. 8, Pt. 1–149
Powell, Maud, Aug. 22, 1868–Jan. 8, 1920.
Vol. 8, Pt. 1–149
Powell, Richard Ewing ("Dick"), Nov. 14, 1904–Jan. 2, 1963.
Supp. 7–628

Powell, Snelling, 1758–Apr. 8, 1821.
	Vol. 8, Pt. 1–150
Powell, Thomas, Sept. 3, 1809–Jan. 14, 1887.
	Vol. 8, Pt. 1–151
Powell, Thomas Reed, Apr. 29, 1880–Aug. 16, 1955.
	Supp. 5–549
Powell, William Bramwell, Dec. 22, 1836–Feb. 6, 1904.
	Vol. 8, Pt. 1–152
Powell, William Byrd, Jan. 8, 1799–May 13, 1866.
	Vol. 8, Pt. 1–152
Powell, William Henry, Feb. 14, 1823–Oct. 6, 1879.
	Vol. 8, Pt. 1–153
Powell Lazarus Whitehead, Oct. 6, 1812–July 3, 1867.
	Vol. 8, Pt. 1–148
Power, Frederick Belding, Mar. 4, 1853–Mar. 26, 1927.
	Vol. 8, Pt. 1–154
Power, Frederick Dunglison, Jan. 23, 1851–June 14, 1911.
	Vol. 8, Pt. 1–155
Power, Frederick Tyrone, May 2, 1869–Dec. 30, 1931.
	Vol. 8, Pt. 1–156
Power, John, June 19, 1792–Apr. 14, 1849.
	Vol. 8, Pt. 1–156
Power, Tyrone, May 5, 1914–Nov. 15, 1958.
	Supp. 6–516
Power, Tyrone. [See Power, Frederick Tyrone, 1869–1931.]
Powers, Daniel William, June 14, 1818–Dec. 11, 1897.
	Vol. 8, Pt. 1–157
Powers, Hiram, July 29, 1805–June 27, 1873.
	Vol. 8, Pt. 1–158
Powhatan, d. 1618.
	Vol. 8, Pt. 1–160
Pownall, Thomas, 1722–Feb. 25, 1805.
	Vol. 8, Pt. 1–161
Poydras, Julien de Lalande, Apr. 3, 1746–June 23, 1824.
	Vol. 8, Pt. 1–163
Poznanski, Gustavus, 1804–Jan. 7, 1879.
	Vol. 8, Pt. 1–164
Prall, David Wight, Oct. 5, 1886–Oct. 21, 1940.
	Supp. 2–540
Prang, Louis, Mar. 12, 1824–June 14, 1909.
	Vol. 8, Pt. 1–165
Prang, Mary Amelia Dana Hicks, Oct. 7, 1836–Nov. 7, 1927.
	Vol. 8, Pt. 1–166
Pratt, Bela Lyon, Dec. 11, 1867–May 18, 1917.
	Vol. 8, Pt. 1–166
Pratt, Charles, Oct. 2, 1830–May 4, 1891.
	Vol. 8, Pt. 1–168
Pratt, Daniel, July 20, 1799–May 13, 1873.
	Vol. 8, Pt. 1–170
Pratt, Daniel, Apr. 11, 1809–June 20, 1887.
	Vol. 8, Pt. 1–170
Pratt, Eliza Anna Farman, Nov. 1, 1837–May 22, 1907.
	Vol. 8, Pt. 1–171
Pratt, Enoch, Sept. 10, 1808–Sept. 17, 1896.
	Vol. 8, Pt. 1–171
Pratt, Francis Ashbury, Feb. 15, 1827–Feb. 10, 1902.
	Vol. 8, Pt. 1–172
Pratt, James Bissett, June 22, 1875–Jan. 15, 1944.
	Supp. 3–608
Pratt, John, Apr. 14, 1831–c. 1900.
	Vol. 8, Pt. 1–173
Pratt, Matthew, Sept. 23, 1734–Jan. 9, 1805.
	Vol. 8, Pt. 1–174
Pratt, Orson, Sept. 19, 1811–Oct. 3, 1881.
	Supp. 1–607
Pratt, Parley Parker, Apr. 12, 1807–May 13, 1857.
	Vol. 8, Pt. 1–175
Pratt, Richard Henry, Dec. 6, 1840–Mar. 15, 1924.
	Vol. 8, Pt. 1–175
Pratt, Sereno Stansbury, Mar. 12, 1858–Sept. 14, 1915.
	Vol. 8, Pt. 1–176
Pratt, Silas Gamaliel, Aug. 4, 1846–Oct. 30, 1916.
	Vol. 8, Pt. 1–177
Pratt, Thomas George, Feb. 18, 1804–Nov. 9, 1869.
	Vol. 8, Pt. 1–178
Pratt, Thomas Willis, July 4, 1812–July 10, 1875.
	Vol. 8, Pt. 1–179
Pratt, Waldo Selden, Nov. 10, 1857–July 29, 1939.
	Supp. 2–541
Pratt, William Veazie, Feb. 28, 1869–Nov. 25, 1957.
	Supp. 6–518
Pratt, Zadock, Oct. 30, 1790–Apr. 6, 1871.
	Vol. 8, Pt. 1–179

Pratte, Bernard, June 11, 1771–Apr. 1, 1836.
	Vol. 8, Pt. 1–180
Pray, Isaac Clark, May 15, 1813–Nov. 28, 1869.
	Vol. 8, Pt. 1–181
Preber Christian. [See Priber, Christian, fl. 1734–1744.]
Preble, Edward, Aug. 15, 1761–Aug. 25, 1807.
	Vol. 8, Pt. 1–182
Preble, George Henry, Feb. 25, 1816–Mar. 1, 1885.
	Vol. 8, Pt. 1–183
Preble, William Pitt, Nov. 27, 1783–Oct. 11, 1857.
	Vol. 8, Pt. 1–184
Preetorius, Emil, Mar. 15, 1827–Nov. 19, 1905.
	Vol. 8, Pt. 1–185
Prendergast, Maurice Brazil, Oct. 27, 1861–Feb. 1, 1924.
	Vol. 8, Pt. 1–186
Prentice, George Dennison, Dec. 18, 1802–Jan. 22, 1870.
	Vol. 8, Pt. 1–186
Prentice, Samuel Oscar, Aug. 8, 1850–Nov. 2, 1924.
	Vol. 8, Pt. 1–187
Prentis, Henning Webb, Jr., July 11, 1884–Oct. 29, 1959.
	Supp. 6–519
Prentiss, Benjamin Mayberry, Nov. 23, 1819–Feb. 8, 1901.
	Vol. 8, Pt. 1–188
Prentiss, Elizabeth Payson, Oct. 26, 1818–Aug. 13, 1878.
	Vol. 8, Pt. 1–188
Prentiss, George Lewis, May 12, 1816–Mar. 18, 1903.
	Vol. 8, Pt. 1–189
Prentiss, Samuel, Mar. 31, 1782–Jan. 15, 1857.
	Vol. 8, Pt. 1–190
Prentiss, Seargent Smith, Sept. 30, 1808–July 1, 1850.
	Vol. 8, Pt. 1–191
Presbrey, Eugene Wiley, Mar. 13, 1853–Sept. 9, 1931.
	Vol. 8, Pt. 1–192
Prescott, Albert Benjamin, Dec. 12, 1832–Feb. 25, 1905.
	Vol. 8, Pt. 1–192
Prescott, George Bartlett, Sept. 16, 1830–Jan. 18, 1894.
	Vol. 8, Pt. 1–193
Prescott, Oliver, Apr. 27, 1731–Nov. 17, 1804.
	Vol. 8, Pt. 1–194
Prescott, Samuel, Aug. 19, 1751–c. 1777.
	Vol. 8, Pt. 1–195
Prescott, Samuel Cate, Apr. 5, 1872–Mar. 20, 1962.
	Supp. 7–629
Prescott, William, Feb. 20, 1726–Oct. 13, 1795.
	Vol. 8, Pt. 1–195
Prescott, William Hickling, May 14, 1796–Jan. 28, 1859.
	Vol. 8, Pt. 1–196
Presser, Theodore, July 3, 1848–Oct. 28, 1925.
	Vol. 8, Pt. 1–200
Pressman, Lee, July 1, 1906–Nov. 19, 1969.
	Supp. 8–510
Preston, Ann, Dec. 1, 1813–Apr. 18, 1872.
	Vol. 8, Pt. 1–201
Preston, Harriet Waters, Aug. 6, 1836–May 14, 1911.
	Vol. 8, Pt. 1–202
Preston, John Smith, Apr. 20, 1809–May 1, 1881.
	Vol. 8, Pt. 1–202
Preston, Jonas, Jan. 25, 1764–Apr. 4, 1836.
	Vol. 8, Pt. 1–203
Preston, Margaret Junkin, May 19, 1820–Mar. 28, 1897.
	Vol. 8, Pt. 1–204
Preston, Thomas Scott, July 23, 1824–Nov. 4, 1891.
	Vol. 8, Pt. 1–205
Preston, William, Oct. 16, 1816–Sept. 21, 1887.
	Vol. 8, Pt. 1–205
Preston, William Ballard, Nov. 29, 1805–Nov. 16, 1862.
	Vol. 8, Pt. 1–206
Preston, William Campbell, Dec. 27, 1794–May 22, 1860.
	Vol. 8, Pt. 1–207
Preus, Christian Keyser, Oct. 13, 1852–May 28, 1921.
	Vol. 8, Pt. 1–208
Prevost, François Maire, c. 1764–May 18, 1842.
	Vol. 8, Pt. 1–209
Priber, Christian, fl. 1734–1744.
	Vol. 8, Pt. 1–210
Price, Bruce, Dec. 12, 1845–May 29, 1903.
	Vol. 8, Pt. 1–210
Price, Eli Kirk, July 20, 1797–Nov. 15, 1884.
	Vol. 8, Pt. 1–211
Price, Eli Kirk, May 10, 1860–Jan. 24, 1933.
	Supp. 1–608
Price, George Edward McCready, Aug. 26, 1870–Jan. 24,
	1963. Supp. 7–631

Ralph, Julian, May 27, 1853–Jan. 20, 1903.
Vol. 8, Pt. 1–332
Ralston, Samuel Moffett, Dec. 1, 1857–Oct. 14, 1925.
Vol. 8, Pt. 1–333
Ralston, William Chapman, June 12, 1826–Aug. 27, 1875.
Vol. 8, Pt. 1–333
Ramage, John, c. 1748–Oct. 24, 1802.
Vol. 8, Pt. 1–334
Rambaut, Mary Lucinda Bonney, June 8, 1816–July 24, 1900.
Vol. 8, Pt. 1–335
Ramée, Joseph Jacques, Apr. 18, 1764–May 18, 1842.
Vol. 8, Pt. 1–336
Ramsay, Alexander, 1754?–Nov. 24, 1891
Vol. 8, Pt. 1–337
Ramsay, David, Apr. 2, 1749–May 8, 1815.
Vol. 8, Pt. 1–338
Ramsay, Erskine, Sept. 24, 1864–Aug. 17, 1953.
Supp. 5–556
Ramsay, Francis Munroe, Apr. 5, 1835–July 19, 1914.
Vol. 8, Pt. 1–339
Ramsay, George Douglas, Feb. 21, 1802–May 23, 1882.
Vol. 8, Pt. 1–340
Ramsay, Nathaniel, May 1, 1741–Oct. 24, 1817.
Vol. 8, Pt. 1–340
Ramseur, Stephen Dodson, May 31, 1837–Oct. 20, 1864.
Vol. 8, Pt. 1–341
Ramsey, Alexander, Sept. 8, 1815–Apr. 22, 1903.
Vol. 8, Pt. 1–341
Ramsey, James Gettys McGready, March 25, 1797–Apr. 11,
1884. Vol. 8, Pt. 1–342
Rand, Addison Crittenden, Sept. 17, 1841–Mar. 9, 1900.
Vol. 8, Pt. 1–343
Rand, Benjamin, July 17, 1856–Nov. 9, 1934.
Supp. 1–619
Rand, Edward Kennard, Dec. 20, 1871–Oct. 28, 1945.
Supp. 3–617
Rand, Edward Sprague, June 23, 1782–Oct. 22, 1863.
Vol. 8, Pt. 1–344
Rand, James Henry, May 29, 1859–Sept. 15, 1944.
Supp. 3–618
Randall, Alexander Williams, Oct. 31, 1819–July 26, 1872.
Vol. 8, Pt. 1–344
Randall, Benjamin, Feb. 7, 1749–Oct. 22, 1808.
Vol. 8, Pt. 1–345
Randall, Burton Alexander, Sept. 21, 1858–Jan. 4, 1932.
Vol. 8, Pt. 1–346
Randall, Clarence Belden, Mar. 5, 1891–Aug. 4, 1967.
Supp. 8–517
Randall, Henry Stephens, May 3, 1811–Aug. 14, 1876.
Vol. 8, Pt. 1–347
Randall, James Garfield, June 24, 1881–Feb. 20, 1953.
Supp. 5–556
Randall, James Ryder, Jan. 1, 1839–Jan. 14, 1908.
Vol. 8, Pt. 1–348
Randall, Robert Richard, c. 1750–June 1801.
Vol. 8, Pt. 1–348
Randall, Samuel, Feb. 10, 1778–Mar. 5, 1864.
Vol. 8, Pt. 1–349
Randall, Samuel Jackson, Oct. 10, 1828–Apr. 13, 1890.
Vol. 8, Pt. 1–350
Randall, Samuel Sidwell, May 27, 1809–June 3, 1881.
Vol. 8, Pt. 1–351
Randall, Wyatt William, Jan. 10, 1867–July 22, 1930.
Vol. 8, Pt. 1–352
Randolph, Alfred Magill, Aug. 31, 1836–Apr. 6, 1918.
Vol. 8, Pt. 1–352
Randolph, Edmund, Aug. 10, 1753–Sept. 12, 1813.
Vol. 8, Pt. 1–353
Randolph, Edmund, June 9, 1819–Sept. 8, 1861.
Vol. 8, Pt. 1–355
Randolph, Edward, c. July 9, 1632–April 1703.
Vol. 8, Pt. 1–356
Randolph, Epes, Aug. 16, 1856–Aug. 22, 1921.
Vol. 8, Pt. 1–357
Randolph, George Wythe, Mar. 10, 1818–Apr. 3, 1867.
Vol. 8, Pt. 1–358
Randolph, Isham, Mar. 25, 1848–Aug. 2, 1920.
Vol. 8, Pt. 1–359
Randolph, Jacob, Nov. 25, 1796–Feb. 29, 1848.
Vol. 8, Pt. 1–360
Randolph, Sir John, c. 1693–March 2, 1736/37.
Vol. 8, Pt. 1–361

Randolph, John, 1727–or 1728–Jan. 31, 1784.
Vol. 8, Pt. 1–362
Randolph, John, June 2, 1773–May 24, 1833.
Vol. 8, Pt. 1–363
Randolph, Peyton, c. 1721–Oct. 22, 1775.
Vol. 8, Pt. 1–367
Randolph, Sarah Nicholas, Oct. 12, 1839–Apr. 25, 1892.
Vol. 8, Pt. 1–368
Randolph, Theodore Fitz, June 24, 1826–Nov. 7, 1883.
Vol. 8, Pt. 1–369
Randolph, Thomas Jefferson, Sept. 11, 1792–Oct. 7, 1875.
Vol. 8, Pt. 1–369
Randolph, Thomas Mann, Oct. 1, 1768–June 20, 1828.
Vol. 8, Pt. 1–370
Randolph, William, c. 1651–Apr. 11, 1711.
Vol. 8, Pt. 1–371
Raney, George Pettus, Oct. 11, 1845–Jan. 8, 1911.
Vol. 8, Pt. 1–372
Ranger, Henry Ward, Jan. 29, 1858–Nov. 7, 1916.
Vol. 8, Pt. 1–373
Rankin, Jeremiah Eames, Jan. 2, 1828–Nov. 28, 1904.
Vol. 8, Pt. 1–374
Rankin, John Elliott, Mar. 29, 1882–Nov. 26, 1960.
Supp. 6–525
Rankin, McKee, Feb. 6, 1844–Apr. 17, 1914.
Vol. 8, Pt. 1–374
Rankine, William Birch, Jan. 4, 1858–Sept. 30, 1905.
Vol. 8, Pt. 1–375
Ranney, Ambrose Loomis, June 10, 1848–Dec. 1, 1905.
Vol. 8, Pt. 1–376
Ranney, Rufus Percival, Oct. 30, 1813–Dec. 6, 1891.
Vol. 8, Pt. 1–376
Ranney, William Tylee, May 9, 1813–Nov. 18, 1857.
Vol. 8, Pt. 1–377
Ransohoff, Joseph, May 26, 1853–Mar. 10, 1921.
Vol. 8, Pt. 1–378
Ransom, Matt Whitaker, Oct. 8, 1826–Oct. 8, 1904.
Vol. 8, Pt. 1–379
Ransom, Thomas Edward Greenfield, Nov. 29, 1834–Oct.
29, 1864. Vol. 8, Pt. 1–379
Ransome, Frederick Leslie, Dec. 2, 1868–Oct. 6, 1935.
Supp. 1–620
Ranson, Stephen Walter, Aug. 28, 1880–Aug. 30, 1942.
Supp. 3–619
Rantoul, Robert, Nov. 23, 1778–Oct. 24, 1858.
Vol. 8, Pt. 1–380
Rantoul, Robert, Aug. 13, 1805–Aug. 7, 1852.
Vol. 8, Pt. 1–381
Rapaport, David, Sept. 30, 1911–Dec. 14, 1960.
Supp. 6–526
Raphall, Morris Jacob, Oct. 3, 1798–June 23, 1868.
Vol. 8, Pt. 1–382
Rapp, George, Nov. 1, 1757–Aug. 7, 1847.
Vol. 8, Pt. 1–383
Rapp, Wilhelm, July 14, 1828–Mar. 1, 1907.
Vol. 8, Pt. 1–384
Rarey, John Solomon, Dec. 6, 1827–Oct. 4, 1866.
Vol. 8, Pt. 1–385
Raskob, John Jakob, Mar. 19, 1879–Oct. 15, 1950.
Supp. 4–681
Rasle, Sébastien. [See Râle, Sébastien, d. 1724.]
Rathbone, Basil, June 13, 1892–July 21, 1967.
Supp. 8–518
Rathbone, Justus Henry, Oct. 29, 1839–Dec. 9, 1889.
Vol. 8, Pt. 1–385
Rathbun, Richard, Jan. 25, 1852–July 16, 1918.
Vol. 8, Pt. 1–386
Rattermann, Heinrich Armin, Oct. 14, 1832–Jan. 6, 1923.
Vol. 8, Pt. 1–387
Rau, Charles, 1826–July 25, 1887.
Vol. 8, Pt. 1–388
Rauch, Frederick Augustus, July 27, 1806–Mar. 2, 1841.
Vol. 8, Pt. 1–389
Rauch, John Henry, Sept. 4, 1828–Mar. 24, 1894.
Vol. 8, Pt. 1–390
Raue, Charles Gottlieb, May 11, 1820–Aug. 21, 1896.
Vol. 8, Pt. 1–390
Raulston, John Tate, Sept. 22, 1868–July 11, 1956.
Supp. 6–528
Raum, Green Berry, Dec. 3, 1829–Dec. 18, 1909.
Vol. 8, Pt. 1–391
Rauschenbusch, Walter, Oct. 4, 1861–July 25, 1918.
Vol. 8, Pt. 1–392

Rautenstrauch, Walter, Sept. 7, 1880–Jan. 3, 1951.
    Supp. 5–558
Ravalli, Antonio, May 16, 1811–Oct. 2, 1884.
    Vol. 8, Pt. 1–393
Ravenel, Edmund, Dec. 8, 1797–July 27, 1871.
    Vol. 8, Pt. 1–394
Ravenel, Harriott Horry Rutledge, Aug. 12, 1832–July 2,
    1912. Vol. 8, Pt. 1–395
Ravenel, Henry William, May 19, 1814–July 17, 1887.
    Vol. 8, Pt. 1–396
Ravenel, Mazyck Porcher, June 16, 1861–Jan. 14, 1946.
    Supp. 4–683
Ravenel, St. Julien, Dec. 19, 1819–Mar. 17, 1882.
    Vol. 8, Pt. 1–397
Ravenscroft, John Stark, May 17, 1772–Mar. 5, 1830.
    Vol. 8, Pt. 1–397
Ravoux, Augustin, Jan. 11, 1815–Jan. 17, 1906.
    Vol. 8, Pt. 1–398
Rawle, Francis, c. 1662–Mar. 5, 1726/27.
    Vol. 8, Pt. 1–399
Rawle, Francis, Aug. 7, 1846–Jan. 28, 1930.
    Vol. 8, Pt. 1–400
Rawle, William, Apr. 28, 1759–Apr. 12, 1836.
    Vol. 8, Pt. 1–400
Rawle, William Henry, Aug. 31, 1823–Apr. 19, 1889.
    Vol. 8, Pt. 1–401
Rawlings, Marjorie Kinnan, Aug. 8, 1896–Dec. 14, 1953.
    Supp. 5–559
Rawlins, John Aaron, Feb. 13, 1831–Sept. 6, 1869.
    Vol. 8, Pt. 1–402
Rawlinson, Frank Joseph, Jan. 9, 1871–Aug. 14, 1937.
    Supp. 2–548
Ray, Charles Bennett, Dec. 25, 1807–Aug. 15, 1886.
    Vol. 8, Pt. 1–403
Ray, Isaac, Jan. 16, 1807–Mar. 31, 1881.
    Vol. 8, Pt. 1–404
Rayburn, Samuel Taliaferro ("Sam"), Jan. 6, 1882–Nov. 16,
    1961. Supp. 7–634
Raymond, Alexander Gillespie, Oct. 2, 1909–Sept. 6, 1956.
    Supp. 6–529
Raymond, Benjamin Wright, Oct. 23, 1801–Apr. 5, 1883.
    Vol. 8, Pt. 1–405
Raymond, Charles Walker, Jan. 14, 1842–May 3, 1913.
    Vol. 8, Pt. 1–406
Raymond, Daniel, 1786–1849?.
    Vol. 8, Pt. 1–406
Raymond, George Lansing, Sept. 3, 1839–July 11, 1929.
    Vol. 8, Pt. 1–407
Raymond, Harry Howard, Dec. 16, 1864–Dec. 27, 1935.
    Supp. 1–621
Raymond, Henry Jarvis, Jan. 24, 1820–June 18, 1869.
    Vol. 8, Pt. 1–408
Raymond, John Howard, Mar. 7, 1814–Aug. 14, 1878.
    Vol. 8, Pt. 1–412
Raymond, John T., Apr. 5, 1836–Apr. 10, 1887.
    Vol. 8, Pt. 1–413
Raymond, Miner, Aug. 29, 1811–Nov. 25, 1897.
    Vol. 8, Pt. 1–413
Raymond, Rossiter Worthington, Apr. 27, 1840–Dec. 31,
    1918. Vol. 8, Pt. 1–414
Rayner, Isidor, Apr. 11, 1850–Nov. 25, 1912.
    Vol. 8, Pt. 1–415
Rayner, Kenneth, c. 1810–Mar. 5, 1884.
    Vol. 8, Pt. 1–416
Rea, Samuel, Sept. 21, 1855–Mar. 24, 1929.
    Vol. 8, Pt. 1–417
Reach, Alfred James, May 25, 1840–Jan. 14, 1928.
    Vol. 8, Pt. 1–418
Read, Charles, c. 1713–Dec. 27, 1774.
    Vol. 8, Pt. 1–419
Read, Charles William, May 12, 1840–Jan. 25, 1890.
    Vol. 8, Pt. 1–420
Read, Conyers, Apr. 25, 1881–Dec. 23, 1959.
    Supp. 6–531
Read, Daniel, Nov. 16, 1757–Dec. 4, 1836.
    Vol. 8, Pt. 1–420
Read, Daniel, June 24, 1805–Oct. 3, 1878.
    Vol. 8, Pt. 1–421
Read, George, Sept. 18, 1733–Sept. 21, 1798.
    Vol. 8, Pt. 1–422
Read, George Campbell, 1787–Aug. 22, 1862.
    Vol. 8, Pt. 1–424

Read, George Windle, Nov. 19, 1860–Nov. 6, 1934.
    Supp. 1–622
Read, Jacob, 1752–July 16, 1816.
    Vol. 8, Pt. 1–425
Read, John, Jan. 29, 1679/80–Feb. 7, 1749.
    Vol. 8, Pt. 1–425
Read, John, July 17, 1769–July 13, 1854.
    Vol. 8, Pt. 1–427
Read, John Meredith, July 21, 1797–Nov. 29, 1874.
    Vol. 8, Pt. 1–427
Read, John Meredith, Feb. 21, 1837–Dec. 27, 1896.
    Vol. 8, Pt. 1–428
Read, Nathan, July 2, 1759–Jan. 20, 1849.
    Vol. 8, Pt. 1–429
Read, Opie Pope, Dec. 22, 1852–Nov. 2, 1939.
    Supp. 2–549
Read, Thomas, 1740?–Oct. 26, 1788.
    Vol. 8, Pt. 1–430
Read, Thomas Buchanan, Mar. 12, 1822–May 11, 1872.
    Vol. 8, Pt. 1–431
Reade, Edwin Godwin, Nov. 13, 1812–Oct. 18, 1894.
    Vol. 8, Pt. 1–432
Reagan, John Henninger, Oct. 8, 1818–Mar. 6, 1905.
    Vol. 8, Pt. 1–432
Realf, Richard, June 14, 1834–Oct. 28, 1878.
    Vol. 8, Pt. 1–434
Ream, Norman Bruce, Nov. 5, 1844–Feb. 9, 1915.
    Vol. 8, Pt. 1–435
Record, Samuel James, Mar. 10, 1881–Feb. 3, 1945.
    Supp. 3–620
Rector, Henry Massey, May 1, 1816–Aug. 12, 1899.
    Vol. 8, Pt. 1–436
Red Cloud, 1822–Dec. 10, 1909.
    Vol. 8, Pt. 1–437
Red Eagle. [See Weatherford, William, 1765–1824.]
Redfield, Amasa Angell, May 19, 1837–Oct. 19, 1902.
    Vol. 8, Pt. 1–439
Redfield, Isaac Fletcher, Apr. 10, 1804–Mar. 23, 1876.
    Vol. 8, Pt. 1–439
Redfield, Justus Starr, Jan. 2, 1810–Mar. 24, 1888.
    Vol. 8, Pt. 1–440
Redfield, Robert, Dec. 4, 1897–Oct. 16, 1958.
    Supp. 6–532
Redfield, William C., Mar. 26, 1789–Feb. 12, 1857.
    Vol. 8, Pt. 1–441
Redfield, William Cox, June 18, 1858–June 13, 1932.
    Vol. 8, Pt. 1–441
Red Jacket, c. 1758–Jan. 20, 1830.
    Vol. 8, Pt. 1–437
Redman, Ben Ray, Feb. 21, 1896–Aug. 1, 1961.
    Supp. 7–637
Redman, John, Feb. 27, 1722–Mar. 19, 1808.
    Vol. 8, Pt. 1–443
Redpath, James, 1833–Feb. 10, 1891.
    Vol. 8, Pt. 1–443
Red Wing, c. 1750–c. 1825.
    Vol. 8, Pt. 1–438
Redwood, Abraham, Apr. 15, 1709–Mar. 8, 1788.
    Vol. 8, Pt. 1–444
Reece, Brazilla Carroll, Dec. 22, 1889–Mar. 19, 1961.
    Supp. 7–638
Reed, Daniel Alden, Sept. 15, 1875–Feb. 19, 1959.
    Supp. 6–534
Reed, David, Feb. 6, 1790–June 7, 1870.
    Vol. 8, Pt. 1–445
Reed, David Aiken, Dec. 21, 1880–Feb. 10, 1953.
    Supp. 5–560
Reed, Earl Howell, July 5, 1863–July 9, 1931.
    Vol. 8, Pt. 1–446
Reed, Elizabeth Armstrong, May 16, 1842–June 16, 1915.
    Vol. 8, Pt. 1–446
Reed, Henry Hope, July 11, 1808–Sept. 27, 1854.
    Vol. 8, Pt. 1–447
Reed, James, Jan. 8, 1722 o.s.–Feb. 13, 1807.
    Vol. 8, Pt. 1–448
Reed, James, Dec. 8, 1834–May 21, 1921.
    Vol. 8, Pt. 1–448
Reed, James Alexander, Nov. 9, 1861–Sept. 8, 1944.
    Supp. 3–621
Reed, James Hay, Sept. 10, 1853–June 17, 1927.
    Vol. 8, Pt. 1–449
Reed, John, Jan. 6, 1757–May 28, 1845.
    Vol. 8, Pt. 1–450

Richardson, Anna Euretta, Sept. 5, 1883–Feb. 3, 1931.
  Vol. 8, Pt. 1–563
Richardson, Charles Williamson, Aug. 22, 1861–Aug. 25,
  1929. Vol. 8, Pt. 1–564
Richardson, Charles Francis, May 29, 1851–Oct. 8, 1913.
  Vol. 8, Pt. 1–564
Richardson, Edmund, June 28, 1818–Jan. 11, 1886.
  Vol. 8, Pt. 1–565
Richardson, Henry Hobson, Sept. 29, 1838–Apr. 27, 1886.
  Vol. 8, Pt. 1–566
Richardson, Israel Bush, Dec. 26, 1815–Nov. 3, 1862.
  Vol. 8, Pt. 1–570
Richardson, James Daniel, Mar. 10, 1843–July 24, 1914.
  Vol. 8, Pt. 1–570
Richardson, Joseph, Sept. 17, 1711–Dec. 3, 1784.
  Vol. 8, Pt. 1–571
Richardson, Maurice Howe, Dec. 31, 1851–July 30, 1912.
  Vol. 8, Pt. 1–572
Richardson, Robert, Sept. 25, 1806–Oct. 22, 1876.
  Vol. 8, Pt. 1–572
Richardson, Rufus Byam, Apr. 18, 1845–Mar. 10, 1914.
  Vol. 8, Pt. 1–574
Richardson, Sid Williams, Apr. 25, 1891–Sept. 30, 1959.
  Supp. 6–539
Richardson, Tobias Gibson, Jan. 3, 1827–May 26, 1892.
  Vol. 8, Pt. 1–575
Richardson, Wilds Preston, Mar. 20, 1861–May 20, 1929.
  Vol. 8, Pt. 1–576
Richardson, Willard, June 24, 1802–July 26, 1875.
  Vol. 8, Pt. 1–576
Richardson, William Adams, Nov. 2, 1821–Oct. 19, 1896.
  Vol. 8, Pt. 1–577
Richardson, William Lambert, Sept. 6, 1842–Oct. 20, 1932.
  Vol. 8, Pt. 1–578
Richardson, William Merchant, Jan. 4, 1774–Mar. 23, 1838.
  Vol. 8, Pt. 1–579
Richberg, Donald Randall, July 10, 1881–Nov. 27, 1960.
  Supp. 6–541
Richings, Peter, May 19, 1798–Jan. 18, 1871.
  Vol. 8, Pt. 1–580
Richmond, Charles Wallace, Dec. 31, 1868–May 19, 1932.
  Vol. 8, Pt. 1–581
Richmond, Dean, Mar. 31, 1804–Aug. 27, 1866.
  Vol. 8, Pt. 1–582
Richmond, John Lambert, Apr. 5, 1785–Oct. 12, 1855.
  Vol. 8, Pt. 1–583
Richmond, John Wilkes, Sept. 25, 1775–Mar. 4, 1857.
  Vol. 8, Pt. 1–583
Richmond, Mary Ellen, Aug. 5, 1861–Sept. 12, 1928.
  Vol. 8, Pt. 1–584
Richter, Conrad Michael, Oct. 13, 1890–Oct. 30, 1968.
  Supp. 8–532
Richtmyer, Floyd Karker, Oct. 12, 1881–Nov. 7, 1939.
  Supp. 2–556
Rickard, George Lewis, Jan. 2, 1871–Jan. 6, 1929.
  Vol. 8, Pt. 1–585
Rickert, Martha Edith, July 11, 1871–May 23, 1938.
  Supp. 2–557
Ricketson, Daniel, July 30, 1813–July 16, 1898.
  Vol. 8, Pt. 1–586
Ricketts, Claude Vernon, Feb. 23, 1906–July 6, 1964.
  Supp. 7–644
Ricketts, Howard Taylor, Feb. 9, 1871–May 3, 1910.
  Supp. 1–628
Ricketts, James Brewerton, June 21, 1817–Sept. 22, 1887.
  Vol. 8, Pt. 1–587
Ricketts, Palmer Chamberlaine, Jan. 17, 1856–Dec. 10, 1934.
  Supp. 1–629
Rickey, Wesley Branch, Dec. 20, 1881–Dec. 9, 1965.
  Supp. 7–645
Ricord, Frederick William, Oct. 7, 1819–Aug. 12, 1897.
  Vol. 8, Pt. 1–587
Ricord, Philippe, Dec. 10, 1800–Oct. 22, 1889.
  Vol. 8, Pt. 1–588
Riddell, John Leonard, Feb. 20, 1807–Oct. 7, 1865.
  Vol. 8, Pt. 1–589
Ridder, Herman, Mar. 5, 1851–Nov. 1, 1915.
  Vol. 8, Pt. 1–590
Riddle, Albert Gallatin, May 28, 1816–May 16, 1902.
  Vol. 8, Pt. 1–591
Riddle, George Peabody, Sept. 22, 1851–Nov. 26, 1910.
  Vol. 8, Pt. 1–591

Riddle, Matthew Brown, Oct. 17, 1836–Aug. 30, 1916.
  Vol. 8, Pt. 1–592
Riddle, Samuel Doyle, July 1, 1861–Jan. 8, 1951.
  Supp. 5–568
Rideing, William Henry, Feb. 17, 1853–Aug. 22, 1918.
  Vol. 8, Pt. 1–593
Rideout, Henry Milner, Apr. 25, 1877–Sept. 17, 1927.
  Vol. 8, Pt. 1–594
Ridgaway, Henry Bascom, Sept. 7, 1830–Mar. 30, 1895.
  Vol. 8, Pt. 1–594
Ridge, Major, c. 1771–June 22, 1839.
  Vol. 8, Pt. 1–595
Ridgely, Charles Goodwin, July 2, 1784–Feb. 4, 1848.
  Vol. 8, Pt. 1–595
Ridgely, Daniel Bowly, Aug. 1, 1813–May 5, 1868.
  Vol. 8, Pt. 1–596
Ridgely, Nicholas, Sept. 30, 1762–Apr. 1, 1830.
  Vol. 8, Pt. 1–597
Ridgway, Robert, July 2, 1850–Mar. 25, 1929.
  Vol. 8, Pt. 1–598
Ridgway, Robert, Oct. 19, 1862–Dec. 19, 1938.
  Supp. 2–558
Ridpath, John Clark, Apr. 26, 1840–July 31, 1900.
  Vol. 8, Pt. 1–599
Rieger, Johann Georg Joseph Anton, Apr. 23, 1811–Aug. 20,
  1869. Vol. 8, Pt. 1–599
Riegger, Wallingford, Apr. 29, 1885–Apr. 2, 1961.
  Supp. 7–647
Rigdon, Sidney, Feb. 19, 1793–July 14, 1876.
  Vol. 8, Pt. 1–600
Rigge, William Francis, Sept. 9, 1857–Mar. 31 1927.
  Vol. 8, Pt. 1–601
Riggs, Elias, Nov. 19, 1810–Jan. 17, 1901.
  Vol. 8, Pt. 1–602
Riggs, George Washington, July 4, 1813–Aug. 24, 1881.
  Vol. 8, Pt. 1–603
Riggs, John Mankey, Oct. 25, 1810–Nov. 11, 1885.
  Vol. 8, Pt. 1–604
Riggs, Stephen Return, Mar. 23, 1812–Aug. 24, 1883.
  Vol. 8, Pt. 1–605
Riggs, William Henry, Mar. 22, 1837–Aug. 31, 1924.
  Vol. 8, Pt. 1–606
Riis, Jacob August, May 3, 1849–May 26, 1914.
  Vol. 8, Pt. 1–606
Riis, Mary Phillips, Apr. 29, 1877–Aug. 4, 1967.
  Supp. 8–534
Riley, Benjamin Franklin, July 16, 1849–Dec. 14, 1925.
  Vol. 8, Pt. 1–608
Riley, Bennet, Nov. 27, 1787–June 9, 1853.
  Vol. 8, Pt. 1–608
Riley, Charles Valentine, Sept. 18, 1843–Sept. 14, 1895.
  Vol. 8, Pt. 1–609
Riley, Isaac Woodbridge, May 20, 1869–Sept. 2, 1933.
  Vol. 8, Pt. 1–610
Riley, James Whitcomb, Oct. 7, 1849–July 22, 1916.
  Vol. 8, Pt. 1–611
Riley, William Bell, Mar. 22, 1861–Dec. 5, 1947.
  Supp. 4–691
Rimmer, William, Feb. 20, 1816–Aug. 20, 1879.
  Vol. 8, Pt. 1–613
Rindge, Frederick Hastings, Dec. 21, 1857–Aug. 29, 1905.
  Vol. 8, Pt. 1–614
Rinehart, Mary Roberts, Aug. 12, 1876–Sept. 22, 1958.
  Supp. 6–542
Rinehart, Stanley Marshall, Jr., Aug. 18, 1897–Apr. 26, 1969.
  Supp. 8–535
Rinehart, William Henry, Sept. 13, 1825–Oct. 28, 1874.
  Vol. 8, Pt. 1–615
Ringgold, Cadwalader, Aug. 20, 1802–Apr. 29, 1867.
  Vol. 8, Pt. 1–617
Ringling, Charles, Dec. 2, 1863–Dec. 3, 1926.
  Vol. 8, Pt. 1–618
Riordan, Patrick William, Aug. 27, 1841–Dec. 27, 1914.
  Vol. 8, Pt. 1–619
Ripley, Edward Hastings, Nov. 11, 1839–Sept. 14, 1915.
  Vol. 8, Pt. 1–619
Ripley, Edward Payson, Oct. 30, 1845–Feb. 4, 1920.
  Vol. 8, Pt. 1–620
Ripley, Eleazar Wheelock, Apr. 15, 1782–Mar. 2, 1839.
  Vol. 8, Pt. 1–621
Ripley, Ezra, May 1, 1751–Sept. 21, 1841.
  Vol. 8, Pt. 1–622

Ripley, George, Oct. 3, 1802–July 4, 1880.
　Vol. 8, Pt. 1–623
Ripley, James Wolfe, Dec. 10, 1794–Mar. 15, 1870.
　Vol. 8, Pt. 1–625
Ripley, Robert LeRoy, Dec. 26, 1893–May 27, 1949.
　Supp. 4–692
Ripley, Roswell Sabine, Mar. 14, 1823–Mar. 29, 1887.
　Vol. 8, Pt. 1–625
Ripley, William Zebina, Oct. 13, 1867–Aug. 16, 1941.
　Supp. 3–632
Rising, Johan Classon, 1617–April 1672.
　Vol. 8, Pt. 1–626
Rister, Carl Coke, June 30, 1889–Apr. 16, 1955.
　Supp. 5–569
Ritchey, George Willis, Dec. 31, 1864–Nov. 4, 1945.
　Supp. 3–633
Ritchie, Albert Cabell, Aug. 29, 1876–Feb. 24, 1936.
　Supp. 2–559
Ritchie, Alexander Hay, Jan. 14, 1822–Sept. 19, 1895.
　Vol. 8, Pt. 1–627
Ritchie, Anna Cora. [See Mowatt, Anna Cora Ogden, 1819–
　1870.]
Ritchie, Thomas, Nov. 5, 1778–July 3, 1854.
　Vol. 8, Pt. 1–628
Ritner, Joseph, Mar. 25, 1780–Oct. 16, 1869.
　Vol. 8, Pt. 1–629
Rittenhouse, David, Apr. 8, 1732–June 26, 1796.
　Vol. 8, Pt. 1–630
Rittenhouse, Jessie Belle, Dec. 8, 1869–Sept. 28, 1948.
　Supp. 4–693
Rittenhouse, William, 1644–Feb. 17, 1708.
　Vol. 8, Pt. 1–632
Ritter, Frédéric Louis, June 22, 1834–July 6, 1891.
　Vol. 8, Pt. 1–632
Ritter, Joseph Elmer, July 20, 1892–June 10, 1967.
　Supp. 8–536
Ritter, William Emerson, Nov. 19, 1856–Jan. 10, 1944.
　Supp. 3–635
Rivera, Luis Jose Munoz. [See Munoz-Rivera, Luis Jose,
　1859–1916.]
Rivers, Lucius Mendel, Sept. 28, 1905–Dec. 28, 1970.
　Supp. 8–538
Rivers, Thomas Milton, Sept. 3, 1888–May 12, 1962.
　Supp. 7–648
Rivers, William James, July 17, 1822–June 22, 1909.
　Vol. 8, Pt. 1–633
Rives, George Lockhart, May 1, 1849–Aug. 18, 1917.
　Vol. 8, Pt. 1–634
Rives, Hallie Erminie, May 2, 1876–Aug. 16, 1956.
　Supp. 6–544
Rives, John Cook, May 24, 1795–Apr. 10, 1864.
　Vol. 8, Pt. 1–635
Rives, William Cabell, May 4, 1793–Apr. 25, 1868.
　Vol. 8, Pt. 1–635
Rivington, James, 1724–July 4, 1802.
　Vol. 8, Pt. 1–637
Rix, Julian Walbridge, Dec. 30, 1850–Nov. 24, 1903.
　Vol. 8, Pt. 1–638
Roach, John, Dec. 25, 1813–Jan. 10, 1887.
　Vol. 8, Pt. 1–639
Roane, Archibald, 1759–Jan. 4, 1819.
　Vol. 8, Pt. 1–640
Roane, John Selden, Jan. 8, 1817–Apr. 8, 1867.
　Vol. 8, Pt. 1–641
Roane, Spencer, Apr. 4, 1762–Sept. 4, 1822.
　Vol. 8, Pt. 1–642
Roark, Ruric Nevel, May 19, 1859–Apr. 14, 1909.
　Vol. 8, Pt. 1–643
Robb, James, Apr. 2, 1814–July 30, 1881.
　Vol. 8, Pt. 1–644
Robb, William Lispenard, May 9, 1861–Jan. 26, 1933.
　Supp. 1–630
Robbins, Chandler, Feb. 14, 1810–Sept. 11, 1882.
　Vol. 8, Pt. 1–644
Robbins, Thomas, Aug. 11, 1777–Sept. 13, 1856.
　Vol. 8, Pt. 1–645
Roberdeau, Daniel, 1727–Jan. 5, 1795.
　Vol. 8, Pt. 1–646
Roberdeau, Isaac, Sept. 11, 1763–Jan. 15, 1829.
　Vol. 8, Pt. 1–647
Robert, Christopher Rhinelander, Mar. 23, 1802–Oct. 27,
　1878. Vol. 8, Pt. 2–1

Robert, Henry Martyn, May 2, 1837–May 11, 1923.
　Supp. 1–631
Roberts, Benjamin Stone, Nov. 18, 1810–Jan. 29, 1875.
　Vol. 8, Pt. 2–2
Roberts, Benjamin Titus, July 25, 1823–Feb. 27, 1893.
　Vol. 8, Pt. 2–2
Roberts, Brigham Henry, Mar. 13, 1857–Sept. 27, 1933.
　Vol. 8, Pt. 2–3
Roberts, Edmund, June 29, 1784–June 12, 1836.
　Vol. 8, Pt. 2–4
Roberts, Elizabeth Wentworth, June 10, 1871–Mar. 12, 1927.
　Vol. 8, Pt. 2–5
Roberts, Elizabeth Madox, Oct. 30, 1881–Mar. 13, 1941.
　Supp. 3–636
Roberts, Ellis Henry, Sept. 30, 1827–Jan. 8, 1918.
　Vol. 8, Pt. 2–6
Roberts, George Brooke, Jan. 15, 1833–Jan. 30, 1897.
　Vol. 8, Pt. 2–6
Roberts, Howard, Apr. 9, 1843–Apr. 18, 1900.
　Vol. 8, Pt. 2–7
Roberts, Issachar Jacob, Feb. 17, 1802–Dec. 28, 1871.
　Vol. 8, Pt. 2–8
Roberts, Job, Mar. 23, 1756–Aug. 20, 1851.
　Vol. 8, Pt. 2–8
Roberts, Jonathan, Aug. 16, 1771–July 21, 1854.
　Vol. 8, Pt. 2–9
Roberts, Joseph Jenkins, Mar. 15, 1809–Feb. 24, 1876.
　Vol. 8, Pt. 2–10
Roberts, Kenneth Lewis, Dec. 8, 1885–July 21, 1957.
　Supp. 6–545
Roberts, Marshall Owen, Mar. 22, 1814–Sept. 11, 1880.
　Vol. 8, Pt. 2–11
Roberts, Nathan S., July 28, 1776–Nov. 24, 1852.
　Vol. 8, Pt. 2–12
Roberts, Oran Milo, July 1815–May 19, 1898.
　Vol. 8, Pt. 2–13
Roberts, Owen Josephus, May 2, 1875–May 17, 1955.
　Supp. 5–571
Roberts, Robert Richford, Aug. 2, 1778–Mar. 26, 1843.
　Vol. 8, Pt. 2–14
Roberts, Solomon White, Aug. 3, 1811–Mar. 22, 1882.
　Vol. 8, Pt. 2–15
Roberts, Theodore, Oct. 8, 1861–Dec. 14, 1928.
　Vol. 8, Pt. 2–16
Roberts, William Charles, Sept. 23, 1832–Nov. 27, 1903.
　Vol. 8, Pt. 2–17
Roberts, William Milnor, Feb. 12, 1810–July 14, 1881.
　Vol. 8, Pt. 2–18
Roberts, William Randall, Feb. 6, 1830–Aug. 9, 1897.
　Vol. 8, Pt. 2–19
Robertson, Alice Mary, Jan. 2, 1854–July 1, 1931.
　Vol. 8, Pt. 2–20
Robertson, Archibald, May 8, 1765–Dec. 6, 1835.
　Vol. 8, Pt. 2–21
Robertson, Ashley Herman, Dec. 14, 1867–July 13, 1930.
　Vol. 8, Pt. 2–22
Robertson, George, Nov. 18, 1790–May 16, 1874.
　Vol. 8, Pt. 2–22
Robertson, James, b. 1740.
　Vol. 8, Pt. 2–23
Robertson, James, June 28, 1742–Sept. 1, 1814.
　Vol. 8, Pt. 2–24
Robertson, James Alexander, Aug. 19, 1873–Mar. 20, 1939.
　Supp. 2–560
Robertson, Jerome Bonaparte, Mar. 14, 1815–Jan. 7, 1891.
　Vol. 8, Pt. 2–25
Robertson, John, Apr. 13, 1787–July 5, 1873.
　Vol. 8, Pt. 2–26
Robertson, Morgan Andrew, Sept. 30, 1861–Mar. 24, 1915.
　Vol. 8, Pt. 2–27
Robertson, Thomas Bolling, Feb. 27, 1779–Oct. 5, 1828.
　Vol. 8, Pt. 2–28
Robertson, William Henry, Oct. 10, 1823–Dec. 6, 1898.
　Vol. 8, Pt. 2–28
Robertson, William Joseph, Dec. 30, 1817–May 27, 1898.
　Vol. 8, Pt. 2–29
Robertson, William Schenck, Jan. 11, 1820–June 26, 1881.
　Vol. 8, Pt. 2–30
Robertson, William Spence, Oct. 7, 1872–Oct. 24, 1955.
　Supp. 5–577
Robertson, Wyndham, Jan. 26, 1803–Feb. 11, 1888.
　Vol. 8, Pt. 2–30

Roberts William Henry, Jan. 31, 1844–June 26, 1920.
Vol. 8, Pt. 2–17
Robeson, George Maxwell, Mar. 16, 1829–Sept. 27, 1897.
Vol. 8, Pt. 2–31
Robidou, Antoine, Sept. 24, 1794–Aug. 29, 1860.
Vol. 8, Pt. 2–32
Robins, Henry Ephraim, Sept. 30, 1827–Apr. 23, 1917.
Vol. 8, Pt. 2–32
Robins, Margaret Dreier, Sept. 6, 1868–Feb. 21, 1945.
Supp. 3–638
Robins, Raymond, Sept. 17, 1873–Sept. 26, 1954.
Supp. 5–578
Robinson, Albert Alonzo, Oct. 21, 1844–Nov. 7, 1918.
Vol. 8, Pt. 2–33
Robinson, Benjamin Lincoln, Nov. 8, 1864–July 27, 1935.
Supp. 1–631
Robinson, Beverley, Jan. 11, 1722 O.S.–Apr. 9, 1792.
Vol. 8, Pt. 2–34
Robinson, Bill (Bojangles), May 25, 1878–Nov. 25, 1949.
Supp. 4–695
Robinson, Boardman, Sept. 6, 1876–Sept. 5, 1952.
Supp. 5–580
Robinson, Charles, July 21, 1818–Aug. 17, 1894.
Vol. 8, Pt. 2–34
Robinson, Charles Mulford, Apr. 30, 1869–Dec. 30, 1917.
Vol. 8, Pt. 2–36
Robinson, Charles Seymour, Mar. 31, 1829–Feb. 1, 1899.
Vol. 8, Pt. 2–37
Robinson, Christopher, May 15, 1806–Oct. 3, 1889.
Vol. 8, Pt. 2–38
Robinson, Claude Everett, Mar. 22, 1900–Aug. 7, 1961.
Supp. 7–649
Robinson, Conway, Sept. 15, 1805–Jan. 30, 1884.
Vol. 8, Pt. 2–39
Robinson, Edward, Apr. 10, 1794–Jan. 27, 1863.
Vol. 8, Pt. 2–39
Robinson, Edward, Nov. 1, 1858–Apr. 18, 1931.
Vol. 8, Pt. 2–40
Robinson, Edward Mott, Jan. 8, 1800–June 14, 1865.
Vol. 8, Pt. 2–41
Robinson, Edward Stevens, Apr. 18, 1893–Feb. 27, 1937.
Supp. 2–561
Robinson, Edward Van Dyke, Dec. 20, 1867–Dec. 10, 1915.
Vol. 8, Pt. 2–42
Robinson, Edwin Arlington, Dec. 22, 1869–Apr. 6, 1935.
Supp. 1–632
Robinson, Ezekiel Gilman, Mar. 23, 1815–June 13, 1894.
Vol. 8, Pt. 2–43
Robinson, Frederick Byron, Apr. 11, 1855–Mar. 23, 1910.
Vol. 8, Pt. 2–44
Robinson, George Canby, Nov. 4, 1878–Aug. 31, 1960.
Supp. 6–546
Robinson, Harriet Jane Hanson, Feb. 8, 1825–Dec. 22, 1911.
Vol. 8, Pt. 2–44
Robinson, Henry Cornelius, Aug. 28, 1832–Feb. 14, 1900.
Vol. 8, Pt. 2–45
Robinson, Henry Morton, Sept. 7, 1898–Jan. 13, 1961.
Supp. 7–650
Robinson, James Harvey, June 29, 1863–Feb. 16, 1936.
Supp. 2–562
Robinson, John, Feb. 3, 1704–May 11, 1766.
Vol. 8, Pt. 2–46
Robinson, John Cleveland, Apr. 10, 1817–Feb. 18, 1897.
Vol. 8, Pt. 2–46
Robinson, John Mitchell, Dec. 6, 1827–Jan. 14, 1896.
Vol. 8, Pt. 2–47
Robinson, Joseph Taylor, Aug. 26, 1872–July 14, 1937.
Supp. 2–566
Robinson, Moncure, Feb. 2, 1802–Nov. 10, 1891.
Vol. 8, Pt. 2–48
Robinson, Moses, Mar. 26, 1742–May 26, 1813.
Vol. 8, Pt. 2–49
Robinson, Rowland Evans, May 14, 1833–Oct. 15, 1900.
Vol. 8, Pt. 2–50
Robinson, Ruby Doris Smith, Apr. 25, 1942–Oct. 7, 1967.
Supp. 8–539
Robinson, Solon, Oct. 21, 1803–Nov. 3, 1880.
Vol. 8, Pt. 2–50
Robinson, Stillman Williams, Mar. 6, 1838–Oct. 31, 1910.
Vol. 8, Pt. 2–52
Robinson, Stuart, Nov. 14, 1814–Oct. 5, 1881.
Vol. 8, Pt. 2–53

Robinson, Theodore, June 3, 1852–Apr. 2, 1896.
Vol. 8, Pt. 2–54
Robinson, Therese Albertine Louise Von Jakob, Jan. 26, 1797–Apr. 13, 1870. Vol. 8, Pt. 2–55
Robinson, William, Nov. 22, 1840–Jan. 2, 1921.
Vol. 8, Pt. 2–56
Robinson, William Callyhan, July 26, 1834–Nov. 6, 1911.
Vol. 8, Pt. 2–56
Robinson, William Erigena, May 6, 1814–Jan. 23, 1892.
Vol. 8, Pt. 2–57
Robinson, William Stevens, Dec. 7, 1818–Mar. 11, 1876.
Vol. 8, Pt. 2–58
Robinson-Smith, Gertrude, July 13, 1881–Oct. 22, 1963.
Supp. 7–651
Robot, Isidore, July 18, 1837–Feb. 15, 1887.
Vol. 8, Pt. 2–59
Robson, May, Apr. 19, 1858–Oct. 20, 1942.
Supp. 3–639
Robson, Stuart, Mar. 4, 1836–Apr. 29, 1903.
Vol. 8, Pt. 2–59
Rochambeau, Jean Baptiste Donatien De Vimeur, Comte [de, July 1, 1725–May 10, 1807. Vol. 8, Pt. 2–60
Roche, Arthur Somers, Apr. 27, 1883–Feb. 17, 1935.
Supp. 1–634
Roche, James Jeffrey, May 31, 1847–Apr. 3, 1908.
Vol. 8, Pt. 2–63
Rochester, Nathaniel, Feb. 21, 1752–May 17, 1831.
Vol. 8, Pt. 2–63
Rock, John, Aug. 19, 1836–Aug. 9, 1904.
Vol. 8, Pt. 2–64
Rockefeller, Abby Greene Aldrich, Oct. 26, 1874–Apr. 5, 1948. Supp. 4–696
Rockefeller, John Davison, July 8, 1839–May 23, 1937.
Supp. 2–568
Rockefeller, John Davison, Jr., Jan. 29, 1874–May 11, 1960.
Supp. 6–547
Rockefeller, William, May 31, 1841–June 24, 1922.
Vol. 8, Pt. 2–65
Rockhill, William Woodville, April 1854–Dec. 8, 1914.
Vol. 8, Pt. 2–66
Rockne, Knute Kenneth, Mar. 4, 1888–Mar. 31, 1931.
Vol. 8, Pt. 2–67
Rockwell, Alphonso David, May 18, 1840–Apr. 12, 1933.
Vol. 8, Pt. 2–68
Rockwell, George Lincoln, Mar. 9, 1918–Aug. 25, 1967.
Supp. 8–540
Rockwell, Kiffin Yates, Sept. 20, 1892–Sept. 23, 1916.
Vol. 8, Pt. 2–69
Roddey, Philip Dale, 1820–August 1897.
Vol. 8, Pt. 2–70
Rodenbough, Theophilus Francis, Nov. 5, 1838–Dec. 19, 1912. Vol. 8, Pt. 2–71
Rodes, Robert Emmett, Mar. 29, 1829–Sept. 19, 1864.
Vol. 8, Pt. 2–71
Rodgers, Christopher Raymond Perry, Nov. 14, 1819–Jan. 8, 1892. Vol. 8, Pt. 2–72
Rodgers, George Washington, Feb. 22, 1787–May 21, 1832.
Vol. 8, Pt. 2–73
Rodgers, George Washington, Oct. 30, 1822–Aug. 17, 1863.
Vol. 8, Pt. 2–74
Rodgers, John, Aug. 5, 1727–May 7, 1811.
Vol. 8, Pt. 2–74
Rodgers, John, 1773–Aug. 1, 1838.
Vol. 8, Pt. 2–75
Rodgers, John, Aug. 8, 1812–May 5, 1882.
Vol. 8, Pt. 2–77
Rodgers, John, Jan. 15, 1881–Aug. 27, 1926.
Vol. 8, Pt. 2–79
Rodman, Issac Peace, Aug. 18, 1822–Sept. 30, 1862.
Vol. 8, Pt. 2–79
Rodman, Thomas Jackson, July 30, 1815–June 7, 1871.
Vol. 8, Pt. 2–80
Rodney, Caesar, Oct. 7, 1728–June 26, 1784.
Vol. 8, Pt. 2–81
Rodney, Caesar Augustus, Jan. 4, 1772–June 10, 1824.
Vol. 8, Pt. 2–82
Rodney, Thomas, June 4, 1744–Jan. 2, 1811.
Vol. 8, Pt. 2–83
Rodzinski, Artur, Jan. 2, 1892–Nov. 27, 1958.
Supp. 6–549
Roe, Edward Payson, Mar. 7, 1838–July 19, 1888.
Vol. 8, Pt. 2–84

Roe, Francis Asbury, Oct. 4, 1823–Dec. 28, 1901.
  Vol. 8, Pt. 2–85
Roe, Gilbert Ernstein, Feb. 7, 1865–Dec. 22, 1929.
  Vol. 8, Pt. 2–86
Roebling, John Augustus, June 12, 1806–July 22, 1869.
  Vol. 8, Pt. 2–86
Roebling, Washington Augustus, May 26, 1837–July 21, 1926. Vol. 8, Pt. 2–89
Roeding, George Christian, Feb. 4, 1868–July 23, 1928.
  Vol. 8, Pt. 2–90
Roemer, Karl Ferdinand, Jan. 5, 1818–Dec. 14, 1891.
  Vol. 8, Pt. 2–91
Roethke, Theodore Huebner, May 25, 1908–Aug. 1, 1963.
  Supp. 7–652
Rogers, Clara Kathleen Barnett, Jan. 14, 1844–Mar. 8, 1931.
  Vol. 8, Pt. 2–92
Rogers, Edith Nourse, Mar. 19, 1881–Sept. 10, 1960.
  Supp. 6–551
Rogers, Edward Staniford, June 28, 1826–Mar. 29, 1899.
  Vol. 8, Pt. 2–92
Rogers, Harriet Burbank, Apr. 12, 1834–Dec. 12, 1919.
  Vol. 8, Pt. 2–93
Rogers, Henry Darwin, Aug. 1, 1808–May 29, 1866.
  Vol. 8, Pt. 2–94
Rogers, Henry Huttleston, Jan. 29, 1840–May 19, 1909.
  Vol. 8, Pt. 2–95
Rogers, Henry J., Mar. 10, 1811–Aug. 20, 1879.
  Vol. 8, Pt. 2–96
Rogers, Henry Wade, Oct. 10, 1853–Aug. 16, 1926.
  Vol. 8, Pt. 2–97
Rogers, Isaiah, Aug. 17, 1800–Apr. 13, 1869.
  Vol. 8, Pt. 2–98
Rogers, James Blythe, Feb. 11, 1802–June 15, 1852.
  Vol. 8, Pt. 2–99
Rogers, James Gamble, Mar. 3, 1867–Oct. 1, 1947.
  Supp. 4–697
Rogers, James Harris, July 13, 1856–Dec. 12, 1929.
  Vol. 8, Pt. 2–100
Rogers, James Harvey, Sept. 25, 1886–Aug. 13, 1939.
  Supp. 2–576
Rogers, John, Dec. 1, 1648–Oct. 17, 1721.
  Vol. 8, Pt. 2–101
Rogers, John, Oct. 30, 1829–July 26, 1904.
  Vol. 8, Pt. 2–102
Rogers, John Almanza Rowley, Nov. 12, 1828–July 22, 1906.
  Vol. 8, Pt. 2–103
Rogers, John Ignatius, May 27, 1843–Mar. 13, 1910.
  Vol. 8, Pt. 2–104
Rogers, John Rankin, Sept. 4, 1838–Dec. 26, 1901.
  Vol. 8, Pt. 2–104
Rogers, John Raphael, Dec. 11, 1856–Feb. 18, 1934.
  Vol. 8, Pt. 2–105
Rogers, Mary Josephine, Oct. 27, 1882–Oct. 9, 1955.
  Supp. 5–581
Rogers, Moses, c. 1779–Oct. 15, 1821.
  Vol. 8, Pt. 2–106
Rogers, Randolph, July 6, 1825–Jan. 15, 1892.
  Vol. 8, Pt. 2–107
Rogers, Robert, Nov. 7, 1731 o.s.–May 18, 1795.
  Vol. 8, Pt. 2–108
Rogers, Robert Empie, Mar. 29, 1813–Sept. 6, 1884.
  Vol. 7, Pt. 2–109
Rogers, Robert William, Feb. 14, 1864–Dec. 12, 1930.
  Vol. 8, Pt. 2–110
Rogers, Stephen, January 1826–May 23, 1878.
  Vol. 8, Pt. 2–111
Rogers, Thomas, Mar. 16, 1792–Apr. 19, 1856.
  Vol. 8, Pt. 2–112
Rogers, Will, Nov. 4, 1879–Aug. 15, 1935.
  Supp. 1–635
Rogers, William Crowninshield, July 26, 1823–July 2, 1888.
  Vol. 8, Pt. 2–115
Rogers, William Allen, May 23, 1854–Oct. 20, 1931.
  Vol. 8, Pt. 2–113
Rogers, William Augustus, Nov. 13, 1832–Mar. 1, 1898.
  Vol. 8, Pt. 2–114
Rogers, William Barton, Dec. 7, 1804–May 30, 1882.
  Vol. 8, Pt. 2–115
Rohde, Ruth Bryan Owen, Oct. 2, 1885–July 27, 1954.
  Supp. 5–582
Rohé, George Henry, Jan. 26, 1851–Feb. 6, 1899.
  Vol. 8, Pt. 2–116

Roheim, Geza, Sept. 12, 1891–June 7, 1953.
  Supp. 5–583
Rohlfs, Anna Katharine Green, Nov. 11, 1846–Apr. 11, 1935.
  Supp. 1–637
Rolette, Jean Joseph, Sept. 23, 1781–Dec. 1, 1842.
  Vol. 8, Pt. 2–117
Rolfe, John, 1585–1622.
  Vol. 8, Pt. 2–117
Rolfe, Robert Abial ("Red"), Oct. 17, 1908–July 8, 1969.
  Supp. 8–541
Rolfe, William James, Dec. 10, 1827–July 7, 1910.
  Vol. 8, Pt. 2–118
Rollins, Alice Marland Wellington, June 12, 1847–Dec. 5, 1897. Vol. 8, Pt. 2–119
Rollins, Edward Henry, Oct. 3, 1824–July 31, 1889.
  Vol. 8, Pt. 2–120
Rollins, Frank West, Feb. 24, 1860–Oct. 27, 1915.
  Vol. 8, Pt. 2–120
Rollins, James Sidney, Apr. 19, 1812–Jan. 9, 1888.
  Vol. 8, Pt. 2–121
Rollinson, William, Apr. 15, 1762–Sept. 21, 1842.
  Vol. 8, Pt. 2–122
Rolph, James, Aug. 23, 1869–June 2, 1934.
  Supp. 1–638
Rolshoven, Julius, Oct. 28, 1858–Dec. 7, 1930.
  Vol. 8, Pt. 2–123
Rölvaag, Ole Edvart, Apr. 22, 1876–Nov. 5, 1931.
  Vol. 8, Pt. 2–124
Roman, André Bienvenu, Mar. 5, 1795–Jan. 28, 1866.
  Vol. 8, Pt. 2–125
Romans, Bernard, c. 1720–c. 1784.
  Vol. 8, Pt. 2–126
Romayne, Nicholas, September 1756–July 21, 1817.
  Vol. 8, Pt. 2–127
Rombauer, Irma Louise, Oct. 30, 1877–Oct. 14, 1962.
  Supp. 7–656
Romberg, Sigmund, July 29, 1887–Nov. 9, 1951.
  Supp. 5–584
Rombro, Jacob Oct. 10, 1858–Nov. 28, 1922.
  Vol. 8, Pt. 2–128
Romeike, Henry, Nov. 19, 1855–June 3, 1903.
  Vol. 8, Pt. 2–129
Rommel, Edwin Americus ("Eddie"), Sept. 13, 1897–Aug. 26, 1970. Supp. 8–543
Rondthaler, Edward, July 24, 1842–Jan. 31, 1931.
  Vol. 8, Pt. 2–130
Rood, Ogden Nicholas, Feb. 3, 1831–Nov. 12, 1902.
  Vol. 8, Pt. 2–131
Rooney, Pat, July 4, 1880–Sept. 9, 1962.
  Supp. 7–657
Roosa, Daniel Bennett St. John, Apr. 4, 1838–Mar. 8, 1908.
  Vol. 8, Pt. 2–132
Roosevelt, (Anna) Eleanor, Oct. 11, 1884–Nov. 7, 1962.
  Supp. 7–658
Roosevelt, Franklin Delano, Jan. 30, 1882–Apr. 12, 1945.
  Supp. 3–641
Roosevelt, Hilborne Lewis, Dec. 21, 1849–Dec. 30, 1886.
  Vol. 8, Pt. 2–133
Roosevelt, Kermit, Oct. 10, 1889–June 4, 1943.
  Supp. 3–667
Roosevelt, Nicholas J., Dec. 27, 1767–July 30, 1854.
  Vol. 8, Pt. 2–133
Roosevelt, Robert Barnwell, Aug. 7, 1829–June 14, 1906.
  Vol. 8, Pt. 2–134
Roosevelt, Theodore, Oct. 27, 1858–Jan. 6, 1919.
  Vol. 8, Pt. 2–135
Roosevelt, Theodore, Sept. 13, 1887–July 12, 1944.
  Supp. 3–668
Root, Amos Ives, Dec. 9, 1839–Apr. 30, 1923.
  Vol. 8, Pt. 2–144
Root, Elihu, Feb. 15, 1845–Feb. 7, 1937.
  Supp. 2–577
Root, Elisha King, May 10, 1808–Aug. 31, 1865.
  Vol. 8, Pt. 2–144
Root, Erastus, Mar. 16, 1773–Dec. 24, 1846.
  Vol. 8, Pt. 2–145
Root, Frank Albert, July 3, 1837–June 20, 1926.
  Vol. 8, Pt. 2–146
Root, Frederic Woodman, June 13, 1846–Nov. 8, 1916.
  Vol. 8, Pt. 2–146
Root, George Frederick, Aug. 30, 1820–Aug. 6, 1895.
  Vol. 8, Pt. 2–147

Root, Jesse, Dec. 28, 1736 o.s.–Mar. 29, 1822.
    Vol. 8, Pt. 2–148
Root, John Wellborn, Jan. 10, 1850–Jan. 15, 1891.
    Vol. 8, Pt. 2–149
Root, Joseph Pomeroy, Apr. 23, 1826–July 20, 1885.
    Vol. 8, Pt. 2–150
Roper, Daniel Calhoun, Apr. 1, 1867–Apr. 11, 1943.
    Supp. 3–669
Ropes, James Hardy, Sept. 3, 1866–Jan. 7, 1933.
    Vol. 8, Pt. 2–151
Ropes, John Codman, Apr. 28, 1836–Oct. 28, 1899.
    Vol. 8, Pt. 2–152
Ropes, Joseph, Dec. 15, 1770–Sept. 29, 1850.
    Vol. 8, Pt. 2–152
Rorer, David, May 12, 1806–July 7, 1884.
    Vol. 8, Pt. 2–153
Rorimer, James Joseph, Sept. 7, 1905–May 11, 1966.
    Supp. 8–544
Rosa, Edward Bennett, Oct. 4, 1861–May 17, 1921.
    Vol. 8, Pt. 2–154
Rosati, Joseph, Jan. 12, 1789–Sept. 25, 1843.
    Vol. 8, Pt. 2–155
Rose, Aquila, c. 1695–1723.
    Vol. 8, Pt. 2–156
Rose, Billy, Sept. 6, 1899–Feb. 10, 1966.
    Supp. 8–545
Rose, Chauncey, Dec. 24, 1794–Aug. 13, 1877.
    Vol. 8, Pt. 2–156
Rose, Edward, fl. 1811–1834.
    Vol. 8, Pt. 2–157
Rose, Ernestine Louise Siismondi Potowski, Jan. 13, 1810–
    Aug. 4, 1892. Vol. 8, Pt. 2–158
Rose, John Carter, Apr. 27, 1861–Mar. 26, 1927.
    Vol. 8, Pt. 2–159
Rose, Joseph Nelson, Jan. 11, 1862–May 4, 1928.
    Vol. 8, Pt. 2–159
Rose, Mary Davies Swartz, Oct. 31, 1874–Feb. 1, 1941.
    Supp. 3–670
Rose, Uriah Milton, Mar. 5, 1834–Aug. 12, 1913.
    Vol. 8, Pt. 2–161
Rose, Walter Malins, Nov. 25, 1872–Feb. 12, 1908.
    Vol. 8, Pt. 2–161
Rose, Wickliffe, Nov. 19, 1862–Sept. 5, 1931.
    Supp. 1–639
Rosecrans, Sylvester Horton, Feb. 5, 1827–Oct. 21, 1878.
    Vol. 8, Pt. 2–162
Rosecrans, William Starke, Sept. 6, 1819–Mar. 11, 1898.
    Vol. 8, Pt. 2–163
Roselins, Christian, Aug. 10, 1803–Sept. 5, 1873.
    Vol. 8, Pt. 2–164
Rosen, Joseph A., Feb. 15, 1878–Apr. 2, 1949.
    Supp. 4–698
Rosenau, Milton Joseph, Jan. 1, 1869–Apr. 9, 1946.
    Supp. 4–700
Rosenbach, Abraham Simon Wolf, July 22, 1876–July 1,
    1952. Supp. 5–586
Rosenbach, Philip Hyman, Sept. 29, 1863–Mar. 5, 1953.
    Supp. 5–586
Rosenberg, Abraham Hayyim, Oct. 17, 1838–Aug. 5, 1925.
    Vol. 8, Pt. 2–165
Rosenberg, Ethel, Sept. 28, 1915–June 19, 1953.
    Supp. 5–588
Rosenberg, Henry, June 22, 1824–May 12, 1893.
    Vol. 8, Pt. 2–166
Rosenberg, Julius, May 12, 1918–June 19, 1953.
    Supp. 5–588
Rosenberg, Paul, Dec. 29, 1881–June 30, 1959.
    Supp. 6–552
Rosenblatt, Bernard Abraham, June 15, 1886–Oct. 14, 1969.
    Supp. 8–548
Rosenblatt, Joseph, May 9, 1882–June 19, 1933.
    Vol. 8, Pt. 2–167
Rosenfeld, Morris, Dec. 28, 1862–June 22, 1923.
    Vol. 8, Pt. 2–167
Rosenfeld, Paul Leopold, May 4, 1890–July 21, 1946.
    Supp. 4–702
Rosenthal, Herman, Oct. 6, 1843–Jan. 27, 1917.
    Vol. 8, Pt. 2–168
Rosenthal, Toby Edward, Mar. 15, 1848–Dec. 23, 1917.
    Vol. 8, Pt. 2–170
Rosenthal Max, Nov. 23, 1833–Aug. 8, 1918.
    Vol. 8, Pt. 2–169

Rosenwald, Julius, Aug. 12, 1862–Jan. 6, 1932.
    Vol. 8, Pt. 2–170
Rosewater, Edward, Jan. 28, 1841–Aug. 30, 1906.
    Vol. 8, Pt. 2–171
Rosewater, Victor, Feb. 13, 1871–July 12, 1940.
    Supp. 2–582
Ross, Abel Hastings, Apr. 28, 1831–May 13, 1893.
    Vol. 8, Pt. 2–172
Ross, Alexander, May 9, 1783–Oct. 23, 1856.
    Vol. 8, Pt. 2–173
Ross, Alexander Coffman, May 31, 1812–Feb. 26, 1883.
    Vol. 8, Pt. 2–174
Ross, Araminta. [See Tubman, Harriet, c. 1821–1913.]
Ross, Betsy, Jan. 1, 1752–Jan. 30, 1836.
    Vol. 8, Pt. 2–174
Ross, Charles Griffith, Nov. 9, 1885–Dec. 5, 1950.
    Supp. 4–703
Ross, Denman Waldo, Jan. 10, 1853–Sept. 12, 1935.
    Supp. 1–640
Ross, Edmund Gibson, Dec. 7, 1826–May 8, 1907.
    Vol. 8, Pt. 2–175
Ross, Edward Alsworth, Dec. 12, 1866–July 22, 1951.
    Supp. 5–591
Ross, Erskine Mayo, June 30, 1845–Dec. 10, 1928.
    Vol. 8, Pt. 2–176
Ross, George, May 10, 1730–July 14, 1779.
    Vol. 8, Pt. 2–177
Ross, Harold Wallace, Nov. 6, 1892–Dec. 6, 1951.
    Supp. 5–593
Ross, James, July 12, 1762–Nov. 27, 1847.
    Vol. 8, Pt. 2–178
Ross, James Delmage McKenzie, Nov. 9, 1872–Mar. 14,
    1939. Supp. 2–583
Ross, John, Oct. 3, 1790–Aug. 1, 1866.
    Vol. 8, Pt. 2–178
Ross, Lawrence Sullivan, Sept. 27, 1838–Jan. 3, 1898.
    Vol. 8, Pt. 2–179
Ross, Martin, Nov. 27, 1762–1827.
    Vol. 8, Pt. 2–180
Rossen, Robert, Mar. 16, 1908–Feb. 18, 1966.
    Supp. 8–550
Rosser, Thomas Lafayette, Oct. 15, 1836–Mar. 29, 1910.
    Vol. 8, Pt. 2–181
Rossiter, Clinton Lawrence, III, Sept. 18, 1917–July 10, 1970.
    Supp. 8–551
Rossiter, Thomas Prichard, Sept. 29, 1818–May 17, 1871.
    Vol. 8, Pt. 2–182
Rossiter, William Sidney, Sept. 9, 1861–Jan. 23, 1929.
    Vol. 8, Pt. 2–182
Rostovtzeff, Michael Ivanovitch, Nov. 10, 1870–Oct. 20,
    1952. Supp. 5–594
Rotch, Abbott Lawrence, Jan. 6, 1861–Apr. 7, 1912.
    Vol. 8, Pt. 2–183
Rotch, Arthur, May 13, 1850–Aug. 15, 1894.
    Vol. 8, Pt. 2–184
Rotch, Thomas Morgan, Dec. 9, 1849–Mar. 9, 1914.
    Vol. 8, Pt. 2–185
Rotch, William, Dec. 4, 1734 o.s.–May 16, 1828.
    Vol. 8, Pt. 2–186
Rothafel, Samuel Lionel, July 9, 1881–Jan. 13, 1936.
    Supp. 2–584
Rothermel, Peter Frederick, July 8, 1817–Aug. 15, 1895.
    Vol. 8, Pt. 2–187
Rothko, Mark, Sept. 25, 1903–Feb. 25, 1970.
    Supp. 8–552
Rothrock, Joseph Trimble, Apr. 9, 1839–June 2, 1922.
    Vol. 8, Pt. 2–188
Rothwell, Richard Pennefather, May 1, 1836–Apr. 17, 1901.
    Vol. 8, Pt. 2–189
Roulstone, George, Oct. 8, 1767–1804.
    Vol. 8, Pt. 2–190
Round, William Marshall Fitts, Mar. 26, 1845–Jan. 2, 1906.
    Vol. 8, Pt. 2–190
Rouquette, Adrien Emmanuel, Feb. 13, 1813–July 15, 1887.
    Vol. 8, Pt. 2–191
Rouquette, François Dominique, Jan. 2, 1810–May 1890.
    Vol. 8, Pt. 2–192
Rourke, Constance Mayfield, Nov. 14, 1885–Mar. 23, 1941.
    Supp. 3–672
Rous, Francis Peyton, Oct. 5, 1879–Feb. 16, 1970.
    Supp. 8–555
Rousseau, Harry Harwood, Apr. 19, 1870–July 24, 1930.
    Vol. 8, Pt. 2–193

Rousseau, Lovell Harrison, Aug. 4, 1818–Jan. 7, 1869.
    Vol. 8, Pt. 2–194
Rovenstine, Emery Andrew, July 20, 1895–Nov. 9, 1960.
    Supp. 6–553
Rowan, John, July 12, 1773–July 13, 1843.
    Vol. 8, Pt. 2–195
Rowan, Stephen Clegg, Dec. 25, 1808–Mar. 31, 1890.
    Vol. 8, Pt. 2–196
Rowe, Leo Stanton, Sept. 17, 1871–Dec. 5, 1946.
    Supp. 4–705
Rowe, Lynwood Thomas, Jan. 11, 1912–Jan. 8, 1961.
    Supp. 7–662
Roweli, George Presbury, July 4, 1838–Aug. 28, 1908.
    Vol. 8, Pt. 2–197
Rowell, Chester Harvey, Nov. 1, 1867–Apr. 12, 1948.
    Supp. 4–706
Rowland, Henry Augustus, Nov. 27, 1848–Apr. 16. 1901.
    Vol. 8, Pt. 2–198
Rowland, Henry Cottrell, May 12, 1874–June 6, 1933.
    Vol. 8, Pt. 2–199
Rowland, Thomas Fitch, Mar. 15, 1831–Dec. 13, 1907.
    Vol. 8, Pt. 2–200
Rowlands, William, Oct. 10, 1807–Oct. 27, 1866.
    Vol. 8, Pt. 2–201
Rowlandson, Mary White, c. 1635–c. 1678.
    Vol. 8, Pt. 2–201
Rowse, Samuel Worcester, Jan. 29, 1822–May 24, 1901.
    Vol. 8, Pt. 2–202
Rowson, Susanna Haswell, c. 1762–Mar. 2, 1824.
    Vol. 8, Pt. 2–203
"Roxy." [See Rothafel, Samuel Lionel, 1881–1936.]
Royall, Anne Newport, June 11, 1769–Oct. 1, 1854.
    Vol. 8, Pt. 2–204
Royce, Josiah, Nov. 20, 1855–Sept. 14, 1916.
    Vol. 8, Pt. 2–205
Royce, Ralph, June 28, 1890–Aug. 7, 1965.
    Supp. 7–663
Roye, Edward James, Feb. 3, 1815–Feb. 12, 1872.
    Vol. 8, Pt. 2–212
Royster, James Finch, June 26, 1880–Mar. 21, 1930.
    Vol. 8, Pt. 2–212
Ruark, Robert Chester, Dec. 29, 1915–July 1, 1965.
    Supp. 7–665
Rubin, Isidor Clinton, Jan. 8, 1883–July 10, 1958.
    Supp. 6–554
Rubinow, Isaac Max, Apr. 19, 1875–Sept. 1, 1936.
    Supp. 2–585
Rubinstein, Helena, Dec. 25, 1870–Apr. 1, 1965.
    Supp. 7–666
Rublee, George, July 7, 1868–Apr. 26, 1957.
    Supp. 6–556
Rublee, Horace, Aug. 19, 1829–Oct. 19, 1896.
    Vol. 8, Pt. 2–213
Ruby, Jack L., Mar. 25, 1911–Jan. 3, 1967.
    Supp. 8–557
Rucker, George ("Nap"), Sept. 30, 1884–Dec. 19, 1970.
    Supp. 8–558
Ruckstull, Frederick Wellington, May 22, 1853–May 26, 1942. Supp. 3–673
Rudge, William Edwin, Nov. 23, 1876–June 12, 1931.
    Vol. 8, Pt. 2–214
Ruditsky, Barney, Jan. 3, 1898–Oct. 18, 1962.
    Supp. 7–667
Rudkin, Margaret Fogarty, Sept. 14, 1897–June 1, 1967.
    Supp. 8–559
Ruef, Abraham, Sept. 2, 1864–Feb. 29, 1936.
    Supp. 2–587
Ruffin, Edmund, Jan. 5, 1794–June 18, 1865.
    Vol. 8, Pt. 2–214
Ruffin, Thomas, Nov. 17, 1787–Jan. 15, 1870.
    Vol. 8, Pt. 2–216
Ruffner, Henry, Jan. 16, 1790–Dec. 17, 1861.
    Vol. 8, Pt. 2–217
Ruffner, William Henry, Feb. 11, 1824–Nov. 24, 1908.
    Vol. 8, Pt. 2–218
Ruger, Thomas Howard, Apr. 2, 1833–June 3, 1907.
    Vol. 8, Pt. 2–219
Rugg, Arthur Prentice, Aug. 20, 1862–June 12, 1938.
    Supp. 2–588
Rugg, Harold Ordway, Jan. 17, 1886–May 17, 1960.
    Supp. 6–557
Ruggles, Samuel Bulkley, Apr. 11, 1800–Aug. 28, 1881.
    Vol. 8, Pt. 2–220

Ruggles, Timothy, Oct. 20, 1711–Aug. 4, 1795.
    Vol. 8, Pt. 2–221
Ruhl, Arthur Brown, Oct. 1, 1876–June 7, 1935.
    Supp. 1–642
Ruhräh, John, Sept. 26, 1872–Mar. 10, 1935.
    Supp. 1–643
Rumford, Benjamin Thompson, Count. [See Thompson, Benjamin, 1753–1814.]
Ruml, Beardsley, Nov. 5, 1894–Apr. 18, 1960.
    Supp. 6–558
Rummel, Joseph Francis, Oct. 14, 1876–Nov. 8, 1964.
    Supp. 7–668
Rumsey, Charles Cary, Aug. 29, 1879–Sept. 21, 1922.
    Vol. 8, Pt. 2–222
Rumsey, James, March 1743–Dec. 20, 1792.
    Vol. 8, Pt. 2–223
Rumsey, Mary Harriman, Nov. 17, 1881–Dec. 18, 1934.
    Supp. 1–644
Rumsey, William, Oct. 18, 1841–Jan. 16, 1903.
    Vol. 8, Pt. 2–223
Runcie, Constance Faunt Le Roy, Jan. 15, 1836–May 17, 1911. Vol. 8, Pt. 2–224
Runkle, John Daniel, Oct. 11, 1822–July 8, 1902.
    Vol. 8, Pt. 2–225
Runyon, Damon, Oct. 3, 1880–Dec. 10, 1946.
    Supp. 4–708
Rupp, Israel Daniel, July 10, 1803–May 31, 1878.
    Vol. 8, Pt. 2–225
Rupp, William, Apr. 17, 1839–Apr. 3, 1904.
    Vol. 8, Pt. 2–226
Ruppert, Jacob, Aug. 5, 1867–Jan. 13, 1939.
    Supp. 2–589
Rusby, Henry Hurd, Apr. 26, 1855–Nov. 18, 1940.
    Supp. 2–590
Rush, Benjamin, Dec. 24, 1745 o.s.–Apr. 19, 1813.
    Vol. 8, Pt. 2–227
Rush, James, Mar. 15, 1786–May 26, 1869.
    Vol. 8, Pt. 2–231
Rush, Richard, Aug. 29, 1780–July 30, 1859.
    Vol. 8, Pt. 2–231
Rush, William, July 4, 1756–Jan. 17, 1833.
    Vol. 8, Pt. 2–234
Rusk, Jeremiah McClain, June 17, 1830–Nov. 21, 1893.
    Vol. 8, Pt. 2–235
Rusk, Thomas Jefferson, Dec. 5, 1803–July 29, 1857.
    Vol. 8, Pt. 2–236
Russ, John Dennison, Sept. 1, 1801–Mar. 1, 1881.
    Vol. 8, Pt. 2–237
Russell, Annie, Jan. 12, 1864–Jan. 16, 1936.
    Supp. 2–592
Russell, Benjamin, Sept. 13, 1761–Jan. 4, 1845.
    Vol. 8, Pt. 2–238
Russell, Charles Edward, Sept. 25, 1860–Apr. 23, 1941.
    Supp. 3–674
Russell, Charles Ellsworth ("Pee Wee"), Mar. 27, 1906–Feb. 15, 1969. Supp. 8–561
Russell, Charles Taze, Feb. 16, 1852–Oct. 31, 1916.
    Vol. 8, Pt. 2–240
Russell, Charles Wells, Mar. 16, 1856–Apr. 5, 1927.
    Vol. 8, Pt. 2–241
Russell, David Allen, Dec. 10, 1820–Sept. 19, 1864.
    Vol. 8, Pt. 2–241
Russell, Henry Norris, Oct. 25, 1877–Feb. 18, 1957.
    Supp. 6–560
Russell, Irwin, June 3, 1853–Dec. 23, 1879.
    Vol. 8, Pt. 2–242
Russell, Israel Cook, Dec. 10, 1852–May 1, 1906.
    Vol. 8, Pt. 2–243
Russell, James Earl, July 1, 1864–Nov. 4, 1945).
    Supp. 3–676
Russell, James Solomon, Dec. 20, 1857–Mar. 28, 1935.
    Supp. 1–645
Russell, John Henry, July 4, 1827–Apr. 1, 1897.
    Vol. 8, Pt. 2–244
Russell, Jonathan, Feb. 27, 1771–Feb. 17, 1832.
    Vol. 8, Pt. 2–245
Russell, Joseph, Oct. 8, 1719 o.s.–Oct. 16, 1804.
    Vol. 8, Pt. 2–245
Russell, Lillian, Dec. 4, 1861–June 6, 1922.
    Vol. 8, Pt. 2–246
Russell, Mother Mary Baptist, Apr. 18, 1829–Aug. 6, 1898.
    Vol. 8, Pt. 2–247

Salmon, Lucy Maynard, July 27, 1853–Feb. 14, 1927.
    Vol. 8, Pt. 2–312
Salmon, Thomas William, Jan. 6, 1876–Aug. 13, 1927.
    Vol. 8, Pt. 2–313
Salm-Salm, Agnes Elisabeth Winona Leclercq Joy, Princess,
    Dec. 25, 1840–Dec. 21, 1912. Vol. 8, Pt. 2–310
Salomon, Haym, c. 1740–Jan. 6, 1785.
    Vol. 8, Pt. 2–313
Salter, William, Nov. 17, 1821–Aug. 15, 1910.
    Vol. 8, Pt. 2–314
Salter, William Mackintire, Jan. 30, 1853–July 18, 1931.
    Vol. 8, Pt. 2–315
Saltonstall, Dudley, Sept. 8, 1738–1796.
    Vol. 8, Pt. 2–316
Saltonstall, Gordon, Mar. 27, 1666 o.s.–Sept. 20, 1724 o.s.
    Vol. 8, Pt. 2–317
Saltonstall, Richard, c. 1610–Apr. 29, 1694.
    Vol. 8, Pt. 2–318
Saltus, Edgar Evertson, Oct. 8, 1855–July 31, 1921.
    Vol. 8, Pt. 2–319
Samaroff, Olga, Aug. 8, 1882–May 17, 1948.
    Supp. 4–717
Sampson, Martin Wright, Sept. 7, 1866–Aug. 22, 1930.
    Vol. 8, Pt. 2–320
Sampson, William, January 1764–Dec. 28, 1836.
    Vol. 8, Pt. 2–321
Sampson, William Thomas, Feb. 9, 1840–May 6, 1902.
    Vol. 8, Pt. 2–321
Samuels, Edward Augustus, July 4, 1836–May 27, 1908.
    Vol. 8, Pt. 2–323
Samuels, Samuel, Mar. 14, 1823–May 18, 1908.
    Vol. 8, Pt. 2–324
Sanborn, Edwin David, May 14, 1808–Dec. 29, 1885.
    Vol. 8, Pt. 2–325
Sanborn, Franklin Benjamin, Dec. 15, 1831–Feb. 24, 1917.
    Vol. 8, Pt. 2–326
Sanborn, Katherine Abbott, July 11, 1839–July 9, 1917.
    Vol. 8, Pt. 2–327
Sanborn, Walter Henry, Oct. 19, 1845–May 10, 1928.
    Vol. 8, Pt. 2–328
Sandburg, Carl August, Jan. 6, 1878–July 22, 1967.
    Supp. 8–562
Sande, Earl, Nov. 13, 1898–Aug. 20, 1968.
    Supp. 8–565
Sandeman, Robert, Apr. 29, 1718–Apr. 2, 1771.
    Vol. 8, Pt. 2–329
Sanders, Billington McCarter, Dec. 2, 1789–Mar. 12, 1854.
    Vol. 8, Pt. 2–329
Sanders, Charles Walton, Mar. 24, 1805–July 5, 1889.
    Vol. 8, Pt. 2–330
Sanders, Daniel Clarke, May 3, 1768–Oct. 18, 1850.
    Vol. 8, Pt. 2–331
Sanders, Daniel Jackson, Feb. 15, 1847–Mar. 6, 1907.
    Vol. 8, Pt. 2–332
Sanders, Elizabeth Elkins, Aug. 12, 1762–Feb. 19, 1851.
    Vol. 8, Pt. 2–332
Sanders, Frank Knight, June 5, 1861–Feb. 20, 1933.
    Vol. 8, Pt. 2–333
Sanders, George Nicholas, Feb. 27, 1812–Aug. 12, 1873.
    Vol. 8, Pt. 2–334
Sanders, James Harvey, Oct. 9, 1832–Dec. 22, 1899.
    Vol. 8, Pt. 2–335
Sanders, Thomas, Aug. 18, 1839–Aug. 7, 1911.
    Vol. 8, Pt. 2–336
Sanders, Wilbur Fisk, May 2, 1834–July 7, 1905.
    Vol. 8, Pt. 2–336
Sanderson, Ezra Dwight, Sept. 25, 1878–Sept. 27, 1944.
    Supp. 3–683
Sanderson, John, 1783–Apr. 5, 1844.
    Vol. 8, Pt. 2–337
Sanderson, Robert, 1608–Oct. 7, 1693.
    Vol. 8, Pt. 2–338
Sanderson, Sibyl, Dec. 7, 1865–May 16, 1903.
    Vol. 8, Pt. 2–338
Sandham, Henry, May 24, 1842–June 21, 1910.
    Vol. 8, Pt. 2–339
Sandler, Jacob Koppel, Aug. 6, 1856–Feb. 23, 1931.
    Vol. 8, Pt. 2–340
Sandoz, Mari, May 11, 1896–Mar. 10, 1966.
    Supp. 8–566
Sands, Benjamin Franklin, Feb. 11, 1812–June 30, 1883.
    Vol. 8, Pt. 2–341

Sands, Comfort, Feb. 26, 1748–Sept. 22, 1834.
    Vol. 8, Pt. 2–341
Sands, David, Oct. 4, 1745–June 4, 1818.
    Vol. 8, Pt. 2–342
Sands, Joshua Ratoon, May 13, 1795–Oct. 2, 1883.
    Vol. 8, Pt. 2–343
Sands, Robert Charles, May 11, 1799–Dec. 16, 1832.
    Vol. 8, Pt. 2–344
Sandys, George, Mar. 2, 1577/78–Mar. 4, 1643/44.
    Vol. 8, Pt. 2–344
Sanford, Edmund Clark, Nov. 10, 1859–Nov. 22, 1924.
    Vol. 8, Pt. 2–346
Sanford, Edward Terry, July 23, 1865–Mar. 8, 1930.
    Vol. 8, Pt. 2–347
Sanford, Elias Benjamin, June 6, 1843–July 3, 1932.
    Vol. 8, Pt. 2–347
Sanford, Henry Shelton, June 15, 1823–May 21, 1891.
    Vol. 8, Pt. 2–348
Sanford, Nathan, Nov. 5, 1777–Oct. 17, 1838.
    Vol. 8, Pt. 2–349
Sanger, Charles Robert, Aug. 31, 1860–Feb. 25, 1912.
    Vol. 8, Pt. 2–350
Sanger, George Partridge, Nov. 27, 1819–July 3, 1890.
    Vol. 8, Pt. 2–350
Sanger, Margaret Higgins, Sept. 14, 1879–Sept. 6, 1966.
    Supp. 8–567
Sangster, Margaret Elizabeth Munson, Feb. 22, 1838–June 4,
    1912. Vol. 8, Pt. 2–351
Sankey, Ira David, Aug. 28, 1840–Aug. 13, 1908.
    Vol. 8, Pt. 2–352
Santayana, George, Dec. 16, 1863–Sept. 26, 1952.
    Supp. 5–601
Sapir, Edward, Jan. 26, 1884–Feb. 4, 1939.
    Supp. 2–593
Sappington, John, May 15, 1776–Sept. 7, 1856.
    Vol. 8, Pt. 2–353
Sardi, Melchiorre Pio Vencenzo ("Vincent"), Dec. 23, 1885–
    Nov. 19, 1969. Supp. 8–570
Sarg, Tony, Apr. 24, 1880–Mar. 7, 1942.
    Supp. 3–684
Sargent, Aaron Augustus, Oct. 28, 1827–Aug. 14, 1887.
    Vol. 8, Pt. 2–353
Sargent, Charles Sprague, Apr. 24, 1841–Mar. 22, 1927.
    Vol. 8, Pt. 2–354
Sargent, Dudley Allen, Sept. 28, 1849–July 21, 1924.
    Vol. 8, Pt. 2–355
Sargent, Epes, Sept. 27, 1813–Dec. 30, 1880.
    Vol. 8, Pt. 2–356
Sargent, Fitzwilliam, Jan. 17, 1820–Apr. 25, 1889.
    Vol. 8, Pt. 2–357
Sargent, Frank Pierce, Nov. 18, 1854–Sept. 4, 1908.
    Vol. 8, Pt. 2–358
Sargent, Frederick, Nov. 11, 1859–July 26, 1919.
    Vol. 8, Pt. 2–359
Sargent, George Henry, May 5, 1867–Jan. 14, 1931.
    Vol. 8, Pt. 2–359
Sargent, Henry, c. November, 1770–Feb. 21, 1845.
    Vol. 8, Pt. 2–360
Sargent, Henry Winthrop, Nov. 26, 1810–Nov. 11, 1882.
    Vol. 8, Pt. 2–361
Sargent, James, Dec. 5, 1824–Jan. 12, 1910.
    Vol. 8, Pt. 2–361
Sargent, John Osborne, Sept. 20, 1811–Dec. 28, 1891.
    Vol. 8, Pt. 2–362
Sargent, John Singer, Jan. 12, 1856–Apr. 15, 1925.
    Vol. 8, Pt. 2–363
Sargent, Lucius Manlius, June 25, 1786–June 2, 1867.
    Vol. 8, Pt. 2–367
Sargent, Nathan, May 5, 1794–Feb. 2, 1875.
    Vol. 8, Pt. 2–368
Sargent, Winthrop, May 1, 1753–Jan. 3, 1820.
    Vol. 8, Pt. 2–368
Sargent, Winthrop, Sept. 23, 1825–May 18, 1870.
    Vol. 8, Pt. 2–369
Sarpy, Peter A., Nov. 3, 1805–Jan. 4, 1865.
    Vol. 8, Pt. 2–370
Sartain, Emily, Mar. 17, 1841–June 18, 1927.
    Vol. 8, Pt. 2–370
Sartain, John, Oct. 24, 1808–Oct. 25, 1897.
    Vol. 8, Pt. 2–371
Sartain, Samuel, Oct. 8, 1830–Dec. 20, 1906.
    Vol. 8, Pt. 2–372

Sartain, William, Nov. 21, 1843–Oct. 25, 1924.
   Vol. 8, Pt. 2–373
Sarton, George Alfred Léon, Aug. 31, 1884–Mar. 22, 1956.
   Supp. 6–564
Sartwell, Henry Parker, Apr. 18, 1792–Nov. 15, 1867.
   Vol. 8, Pt. 2–374
Saslavsky, Alexander, Feb. 8, 1876–Aug. 2, 1924.
   Vol. 8, Pt. 2–374
Sassacus, c. 1560–June 1637.
   Vol. 8, Pt. 2–375
Satterlee, Henry Yates, Jan. 11, 1843–Feb. 22, 1908.
   Vol. 8, Pt. 2–375
Satterlee, Richard Sherwood, Dec. 6, 1798–Nov. 10, 1880.
   Vol. 8, Pt. 2–376
Sauganash, c. 1780–Sept. 28, 1841.
   Vol. 8, Pt. 2–376
Saugrain De Vigni, Antoine François, Feb. 17, 1763–c. May
   19, 1820. Vol. 8, Pt. 2–377
Saulsbury, Eli, Dec. 29, 1817–Mar. 22, 1893.
   Vol. 8, Pt. 2–378
Saulsbury, Gove, May 29, 1815–July 31, 1881.
   Vol. 8, Pt. 2–378
Saulsbury, Willard, June 2, 1820–Apr. 6, 1892.
   Vol. 8, Pt. 2–379
Saulsbury, Willard, Apr. 17, 1861–Feb. 20, 1927.
   Vol. 8, Pt. 2–380
Saunders, Alvin, July 12, 1817–Nov. 1, 1899.
   Vol. 8, Pt. 2–380
Saunders, Clarence, Dec. 1881–Oct. 14, 1953.
   Supp. 5–603
Saunders, Frederick, Aug. 14, 1807–Dec. 12, 1902.
   Vol. 8, Pt. 2–381
Saunders, Prince, d. Feb. 1839.
   Vol. 8, Pt. 2–382
Saunders, Romulus Mitchell, Mar. 3, 1791–Apr. 21, 1867.
   Vol. 8, Pt. 2–382
Saunders, William, Dec 7, 1822–Sept. 11, 1900.
   Vol. 8, Pt. 2–383
Saunders, William Laurence, July 30, 1835–Apr. 2, 1891.
   Vol. 8, Pt. 2–384
Saunders, William Lawrence, Nov. 1, 1856–June 25, 1931.
   Vol. 8, Pt. 2–385
Saur, Christopher. [See Sower, Christopher.]
Sauveur, Albert, June 21, 1863–Jan. 26, 1939.
   Supp. 2–594
Savage, Edward, Nov. 26, 1761–July 6, 1817.
   Vol. 8, Pt. 2–386
Savage, Henry Wilson, Mar. 21, 1859–Nov. 29, 1927.
   Vol. 8, Pt. 2–386
Savage, James, July 13, 1784–Mar. 8, 1873.
   Vol. 8, Pt. 2–387
Savage, John, Dec. 13, 1828–Oct. 9, 1888.
   Vol. 8, Pt. 2–388
Savage, John Lucian ("Jack"), Dec. 25, 1879–Dec. 28, 1967.
   Supp. 8–572
Savage, Minot Judson, June 10, 1841–May 22, 1918.
   Vol. 8, Pt. 2–389
Savage, Philip Henry, Feb. 11, 1868–June 4, 1899.
   Vol. 8, Pt. 2–390
Savage, Thomas Staughton, June 7, 1804–Dec. 29, 1880.
   Vol. 8, Pt. 2–391
Savery, William, 1721–May 1787.
   Vol. 8, Pt. 2–392
Savery, William, Sept. 14, 1750 o.s.–June 19, 1804.
   Vol. 8, Pt. 2–392
Saville, Marshall Howard, June 24, 1867–May 7, 1935.
   Supp. 1–647
Sawyer, Leicester Ambrose, July 28, 1807–Dec. 29, 1898.
   Vol. 8, Pt. 2–393
Sawyer, Lemuel, 1777–Jan. 9, 1852.
   Vol. 8, Pt. 2–394
Sawyer, Lorenzo, May 23, 1820–Sept. 7, 1891.
   Vol. 8, Pt. 2–395
Sawyer, Philetus, Sept. 22, 1816–Mar. 29, 1900.
   Vol. 8, Pt. 2–396
Sawyer, Sylvanus, Apr. 15, 1822–Oct. 13, 1895.
   Vol. 8, Pt. 2–397
Sawyer, Thomas Jefferson, Jan. 9, 1804–July 24, 1899.
   Vol. 8, Pt. 2–397
Sawyer, Walter Howard, May 21, 1867–Dec. 21, 1923.
   Vol. 8, Pt. 2–398
Sawyer, Wilbur Augustus, Aug. 7, 1879–Nov. 12, 1951.
   Supp. 5–604

Saxe, John Godfrey, June 2, 1816–Mar. 31, 1887.
   Vol. 8, Pt. 2–399
Saxton, Eugene Francis, Aug. 11, 1884–June 26, 1943.
   Supp. 3–685
Saxton, Joseph, Mar. 22, 1799–Oct. 26, 1873.
   Vol. 8, Pt. 2–400
Say, Benjamin, Aug. 28, 1755–Apr. 23, 1813.
   Vol. 8, Pt. 2–400
Say, Thomas, June 27, 1787–Oct. 10, 1834.
   Vol. 8, Pt. 2–401
Sayles, John, Mar. 9, 1825–May 22, 1897.
   Vol. 8, Pt. 2–402
Sayre, Lewis Albert, Feb. 29, 1820–Sept. 21, 1900.
   Vol. 8, Pt. 2–403
Sayre, Reginald Hall, Oct. 18, 1859–May 29, 1929.
   Vol. 8, Pt. 2–404
Sayre, Robert Heysham, Oct. 13, 1824–Jan. 5, 1907.
   Vol. 8, Pt. 2–405
Sayre, Stephen, June 12, 1736–Sept. 27, 1818.
   Vol. 8, Pt. 2–406
Scammell, Alexander, Mar. 27, 1747–Oct. 6, 1781.
   Vol. 8, Pt. 2–406
Scammon, Jonathan Young, July 27, 1812–Mar. 17, 1890.
   Vol. 8, Pt. 2–407
Scanlan, Lawrence, Sept. 29, 1843–May 10, 1915.
   Vol. 8, Pt. 2–408
Scarborough, Dorothy, Jan. 27, 1878–Nov. 7, 1935.
   Supp. 1–648
Scarborough, Lee Rutland, July 4, 1870–Apr. 10, 1945.
   Supp. 3–686
Scarborough, William Saunders, Feb. 16, 1852?–Sept. 9,
   1926. Vol. 8, Pt. 2–409
Scarbrough, William, Feb. 18, 1776–June 11, 1838.
   Vol. 8, Pt. 2–410
Scattergood, Thomas, Jan. ? 23, 1748–Apr. 24, 1814.
   Vol. 8, Pt. 2–410
Schadle, Jacob Evans, June 23, 1849–May 29, 1908.
   Vol. 8, Pt. 2–411
Schaeberle, John Martin, Jan. 10, 1853–Sept. 19, 1924.
   Vol. 8, Pt. 2–412
Schaeffer, Charles Frederick, Sept. 3, 1807–Nov. 23, 1879.
   Vol. 8, Pt. 2–412
Schaeffer, Charles William, May 5, 1813–Mar. 15, 1896.
   Vol. 8, Pt. 2–413
Schaeffer, David Frederick, July 22, 1787–May 5, 1837.
   Vol. 8, Pt. 2–414
Schaeffer, Frederick Christian, Nov. 12, 1792–Mar. 26, 1831.
   Vol. 8, Pt. 2–415
Schaeffer, Frederick David, Nov. 15, 1760–Jan. 27, 1836.
   Vol. 8, Pt. 2–415
Schaeffer, Nathan Christ, Feb. 3, 1849–Mar. 15, 1919.
   Vol. 8, Pt. 2–416
Schaff, Philip, Jan. 1, 1819–Oct. 20, 1893.
   Vol. 8, Pt. 2–417
Schalk, Raymond William ("Cracker"), Aug. 12, 1892–May
   19, 1970. Supp. 8–573
Schall, Thomas David, June 4, 1877–Dec. 22, 1935.
   Supp. 1–649
Schamberg, Jay Frank, Nov. 6, 1870–Mar. 30, 1934.
   Vol. 8, Pt. 2–418
Scharf, John Thomas, May 1, 1843–Feb. 28, 1898.
   Vol. 8, Pt. 2–419
Schauffler, Henry Albert, Sept. 4, 1837–Feb. 15, 1905.
   Vol. 8, Pt. 2–420
Schauffler, William Gottlieb, Aug. 22, 1798–Jan. 26, 1883.
   Vol. 8, Pt. 2–420
Schechter, Solomon, Dec. 7, 1850–Nov. 15, 1915.
   Vol. 8, Pt. 2–421
Scheel, Fritz, Nov. 7, 1852–Mar. 13, 1907.
   Vol. 8, Pt. 2–423
Schele De Vere, Maximilian, Nov. 1, 1820–May 12, 1898.
   Vol. 8, Pt. 2–423
Schell, Augustus, Aug. 1, 1812–Mar. 27, 1884.
   Vol. 8, Pt. 2–424
Schelling, Ernest Henry, July 26, 1876–Dec. 8, 1939.
   Supp. 2–595
Schelling, Felix Emanuel, Sept. 3, 1858–Dec. 15, 1945.
   Supp. 3–688
Schem, Alexander Jacob, Mar. 16, 1826–May 21, 1881.
   Vol. 8, Pt. 2–425
Schenck, Ferdinand Schureman, Aug. 6, 1845–Apr. 6, 1925.
   Vol. 8, Pt. 2–426

Schuyler, Robert Livingston, Feb. 26, 1883–Aug. 15, 1966.
  Supp. 8–579
Schwab, Charles Michael, Feb. 18, 1862–Sept. 18, 1939.
  Supp. 2–601
Schwab, John Christopher, Apr. 1, 1865–Jan. 12, 1916.
  Vol. 8, Pt. 2–480
Schwartz, Delmore David, Dec. 8, 1913–July 11, 1966.
  Supp. 8–581
Schwartz, Maurice, June 15, 1889–May 10, 1960.
  Supp. 6–566
Schwarz, Engene Amandus, Apr. 21, 1844–Oct. 15, 1928.
  Vol. 8, Pt. 2–480
Schwatka, Frederick, Sept. 29, 1849–Nov. 2, 1892.
  Vol. 8, Pt. 2–481
Schweinitz, Edmund Alexander de, Mar. 20, 1825–Dec. 18,
  1887. Vol. 8, Pt. 2–482
Schweinitz, Emil Alexander de, Jan. 18, 1866–Feb. 15, 1904.
  Vol. 8, Pt. 2–483
Schweinitz, George Edmund de, Oct. 26, 1858–Aug. 22,
  1938. Supp. 2–603
Schweinitz, Lewis David von, Feb. 13, 1780–Feb. 8, 1834.
  Vol. 8, Pt. 2–483
Schwellenbach, Lewis Baxter, Sept. 20, 1894–June 10, 1948.
  Supp. 4–723
Schwidetzky, Oscar Otto Rudolf, Dec. 31, 1874–Oct. 11,
  1963. Supp. 7–678
Schwimmer, Rosika, Sept. 11, 1877–Aug. 3, 1948.
  Supp. 4–724
Scidmore, Eliza Ruhamah, Oct. 14, 1856–Nov. 3, 1928.
  Vol. 8, Pt. 2–484
Scollard, Clinton, Sept. 18, 1860–Nov. 19, 1932.
  Vol. 8, Pt. 2–485
Scopes, John Thomas, Aug. 3, 1900–Oct. 21, 1970.
  Supp. 8–582
Scott, Allen Cecil, Aug. 16, 1882–May 1, 1964.
  Supp. 7–679
Scott, Austin, Aug. 10, 1848–Aug. 15, 1922.
  Vol. 8, Pt. 2–486
Scott, Charles, c. 1739–Oct. 22, 1813.
  Vol. 8, Pt. 2–487
Scott, Colin Alexander, Feb. 11, 1861–Apr. 5, 1925.
  Vol. 8, Pt. 2–487
Scott, Dred, c. 1795–Sept. 17, 1858.
  Vol. 8, Pt. 2–488
Scott, Emmett Jay, Feb. 13, 1873–Dec. 12, 1957.
  Supp. 6–567
Scott, Fred Newton, Aug. 20, 1860–May 29, 1931.
  Vol. 8, Pt. 2–489
Scott, Gustavus, 1753–Dec. 25, 1800.
  Vol. 8, Pt. 2–490
Scott, Harvey Whitefield, Feb. 1, 1838–Aug. 7, 1910.
  Vol. 8, Pt. 2–491
Scott, Hugh Lenox, Sept. 22, 1853–Apr. 30, 1934.
  Supp. 1–651
Scott, Irving Murray, Dec. 25, 1837–Apr. 28, 1903.
  Vol. 8, Pt. 2–491
Scott, James Brown, June 3, 1866–June 25, 1943.
  Supp. 3–699
Scott, James Wilmot, June 26, 1849–Apr. 14, 1895.
  Vol. 8, Pt. 2–492
Scott, Job, Oct. 18, 1751–Nov. 22, 1793.
  Vol. 8, Pt. 2–493
Scott, John, c. 1630–1696.
  Vol. 8, Pt. 2–494
Scott, John Adams, Sept. 15, 1867–Oct. 27, 1947.
  Supp. 4–728
Scott, John Morin, c. 1730–Sept. 14, 1784.
  Vol. 8, Pt. 2–495
Scott, John Prindle, Aug. 16, 1877–Dec. 2, 1952.
  Vol. 8, Pt. 2–496
Scott, Leroy, May 11, 1875–July 21, 1929.
  Vol. 8, Pt. 2–496
Scott, Orange, Feb. 13, 1800–July 31, 1847.
  Vol. 8, Pt. 2–497
Scott, Robert Kingston, July 8, 1826–Aug. 12, 1900.
  Vol. 8, Pt. 2–498
Scott, Samuel Parsons, July 8, 1846–May 30, 1929.
  Vol. 8, Pt. 2–499
Scott, Thomas Alexander, Dec. 28, 1823–May 21, 1881.
  Vol. 8, Pt. 2–500
Scott, Thomas Fielding, Mar. 12, 1807–July 14, 1867.
  Vol. 8, Pt. 2–501

Scott, Walter, Oct. 31, 1796–Apr. 23, 1861.
  Vol. 8, Pt. 2–502
Scott, Walter Dill, May 1, 1869–Sept. 23, 1955.
  Supp. 5–611
Scott, Walter Edward, 1870[?]–Jan. 5, 1954.
  Supp. 5–613
Scott, William, June 7, 1804–May 18, 1862.
  Vol. 8, Pt. 2–503
Scott, William Anderson, Jan. 31, 1813–Jan. 14, 1885.
  Vol. 8, Pt. 2–503
Scott, William Berryman, Feb. 12, 1858–Mar. 29, 1947.
  Supp. 4–729
Scott, W(illiam) Kerr, Apr. 17, 1896–Apr. 16, 1958.
  Supp. 6–568
Scott, William Lawrence, July 2, 1828–Sept. 19, 1891.
  Vol. 8, Pt. 2–504
Scott, Winfield, June 13, 1786–May 29, 1866.
  Vol. 8, Pt. 2–505
Scovel, Henry Sylvester, July 29, 1869–Feb. 11, 1905.
  Vol. 8, Pt. 2–511
Scovel, Sylvester. [See Scovel, Henry Sylvester, 1869–1905.]
Scovell, Melville Amasa, Feb. 26, 1855–Aug. 15, 1912.
  Vol. 8, Pt. 2–512
Scoville, Joseph Alfred, Jan. 30, 1815–June 25, 1864.
  Vol. 8, Pt. 2–513
Scranton, George Whitfield, May 23, 1811–Mar. 24, 1861.
  Vol. 8, Pt. 2–513
Screws, William Wallace, Feb. 25, 1839–Aug. 7, 1913.
  Vol. 8, Pt. 2–514
Scribner, Charles, Feb. 21, 1821–Aug. 26, 1871.
  Vol. 8, Pt. 2–515
Scribner, Charles, Oct. 18, 1854–Apr. 19, 1930.
  Vol. 8, Pt. 2–516
Scribner, Charles, Jan. 26, 1890–Feb. 11, 1952.
  Supp. 5–614
Scripps, Edward Wyllis, June 18, 1854–Mar. 12, 1926.
  Vol. 8, Pt. 2–517
Scripps, Ellen Browning, Oct. 18, 1836–Aug. 3, 1932.
  Vol. 8, Pt. 2–518
Scripps, James Edmund, Mar. 19, 1835–May 29, 1906.
  Vol. 8, Pt. 2–519
Scripps, Robert Paine, Oct. 27, 1895–Mar. 2, 1938.
  Supp. 2–605
Scripps, William Edmund, May 6, 1882–June 12, 1952.
  Supp. 5–615
Scruggs, William Lindsay, Sept. 14, 1836–July 18, 1912.
  Vol. 8, Pt. 2–520
Scrymser, James Alexander, July 18, 1839–Apr. 21, 1918.
  Vol. 8, Pt. 2–521
Scudder, Horace Elisha, Oct. 16, 1838–Jan. 11, 1902.
  Vol. 8, Pt. 2–522
Scudder, John, Sept 3, 1793–Jan. 13, 1855.
  Vol. 8, Pt. 2–523
Scudder, John Milton, Sept. 8, 1829–Feb. 17, 1894.
  Vol. 8, Pt. 2–524
Scudder, (Julia) Vida Dutton, Dec. 15, 1861–Oct. 9, 1954.
  Supp. 5–616
Scudder, Nathaniel, May 10?, 1733–Oct. 16, 1781.
  Vol. 8, Pt. 2–524
Scudder, Samuel Hubbard, Apr. 13, 1837–May 17, 1911.
  Vol. 8, Pt. 2–525
Scull, John, 1765–Feb. 8, 1828.
  Vol. 8, Pt. 2–526
Scullin, John, Aug. 17, 1836–May 28, 1920.
  Vol. 8, Pt. 2–527
Seabury, George John, Nov. 10, 1844–Feb. 13, 1909.
  Vol. 8, Pt. 2–527
Seabury, Samuel, Nov. 30, 1729–Feb. 25, 1796.
  Vol. 8, Pt. 2–528
Seabury, Samuel, June 9, 1801–Oct. 10, 1872.
  Vol. 8, Pt. 2–530
Seabury, Samuel, Feb. 22, 1873–May 7, 1958.
  Supp. 6–569
Seager, Henry Rogers, July 21, 1870–Aug. 23, 1930.
  Vol. 8, Pt. 2–531
Seagrave, Gordon Stifler, Mar. 18, 1897–Mar. 28, 1965.
  Supp. 7–679
Sealsfield, Charles, Mar. 3, 1793–May 26, 1864.
  Vol. 8, Pt. 2–532
Seaman, Elizabeth Cochrane, May 5, 1867–Jan. 27, 1922.
  Vol. 8, Pt. 2–533
Searing, Laura Catherine Redden, Feb. 9, 1840–Aug. 10,
  1923. Vol. 8, Pt. 2–534

Searle, Arthur, Oct. 21, 1837–Oct. 23, 1920.
   Vol. 8, Pt. 2–534
Searle, James, 1733–Aug. 7, 1797.
   Vol. 8, Pt. 2–535
Searle, John Preston, Sept. 12, 1854–July 26, 1922.
   Vol. 8, Pt. 2–536
Sears, Barnas, Nov. 19, 1802–July 6, 1880.
   Vol. 8, Pt. 2–537
Sears, Edmund Hamilton, Apr. 6, 1810–Jan. 16, 1876.
   Vol. 8, Pt. 2–538
Sears, Isaac, c. July 1, 1730–Oct. 28, 1786.
   Vol. 8, Pt. 2–539
Sears, Richard Dudley, Oct. 26, 1861–Apr. 8, 1943.
   Supp. 3–701
Sears, Richard Warren, Dec. 7, 1863–Sept. 28, 1914.
   Vol. 8, Pt. 2–540
Sears, Robert, June 28, 1810–Feb. 17, 1892.
   Vol. 8, Pt. 2–541
Seashore, Carl Emil, Jan. 28, 1866–Oct. 16, 1949.
   Supp. 4–730
Seaton, William Winston, Jan. 11, 1785–June 16, 1866.
   Vol. 8, Pt. 2–541
Seattle, c. 1786–June 7, 1866.
   Vol. 8, Pt. 2–542
Seawell, Molly Elliot, Oct. 23, 1860–Nov. 15, 1916.
   Vol. 8, Pt. 2–543
Sebastian, Benjamin, c. 1745–March 1834.
   Vol. 8, Pt. 2–543
Seccomb, John, Apr. 25, 1708–Oct. 27, 1792.
   Vol. 8, Pt. 2–544
Seddon, James Alexander, July 13, 1815–Aug. 19, 1880.
   Vol. 8, Pt. 2–545
Sedella, Antoine. [See Antoine, Père, 1748–1829.]
Sedgwick, Anne Douglas, Mar. 28, 1873–July 19, 1935.
   Supp. 1–652
Sedgwick, Arthur George, Oct. 6, 1844–July 14, 1915.
   Vol. 8, Pt. 2–546
Sedgwick, Catharine Maria, Dec. 28, 1789–July 31, 1867.
   Vol. 8, Pt. 2–547
Sedgwick, Ellery, Feb. 27, 1872–Apr. 21, 1960.
   Supp. 6–571
Sedgwick, John, Sept. 13, 1813–May 9, 1864.
   Vol. 8, Pt. 2–548
Sedgwick, Robert, c. 1613–May 24, 1656.
   Vol. 8, Pt. 2–549
Sedgwick, Theodore, May 9, 1746–Jan. 24, 1813.
   Vol. 8, Pt. 2–549
Sedgwick, Theodore, December 1780–Nov. 7, 1839.
   Vol. 8, Pt. 2–551
Sedgwick, Theodore, Jan. 27, 1811–Dec. 8, 1859.
   Vol. 8, Pt. 2–551
Sedgwick, William Thompson, Dec. 29, 1855–Jan. 21, 1921.
   Vol. 8, Pt. 2–552
Sedley, William Henry. [See Smith, William Henry, 1806–1872.]
See, Horace, July 17, 1835–Dec. 14, 1909.
   Vol. 8, Pt. 2–553
Seed, Miles Ainscough, Feb. 24, 1843–Dec. 4, 1913.
   Vol. 8, Pt. 2–554
Seeger, Alan, June 22, 1888–July 4, 1916.
   Vol. 8, Pt. 2–555
Seelye, Julius Hawley, Sept. 14, 1824–May 12, 1895.
   Vol. 8, Pt. 2–555
Seelye, Laurenus Clark, Sept. 20, 1837–Oct. 12, 1924.
   Vol. 8, Pt. 2–557
Seevers, William Henry, Apr. 8, 1822–Mar. 24, 1895.
   Vol. 8, Pt. 2–558
Seghers, Charles Jean, Dec. 26, 1839–Nov. 28, 1886.
   Vol. 8, Pt. 2–558
Seguin, Edouard, Jan. 20, 1812–Oct. 28, 1880.
   Vol. 8, Pt. 2–559
Seguin, Edward Constant, 1843–Feb. 19, 1898.
   Vol. 8, Pt. 2–560
Seiberling, Frank Augustus, Oct. 6, 1859–Aug. 11, 1955.
   Supp. 5–617
Seibold, Louis, Oct. 10, 1863–May 10, 1945.
   Supp. 3–702
Seidel, George Lukas Emil, Dec. 13, 1864–June 24, 1947.
   Supp. 4–732
Seidensticker, Oswald, May 3, 1825–Jan. 10, 1894.
   Vol. 8, Pt. 2–561
Seidl, Anton, May 7, 1850–Mar. 28, 1898.
   Vol. 8, Pt. 2–561

Seiler, Carl, Apr. 14, 1849–Oct. 11, 1905.
   Vol. 8, Pt. 2–562
Seip, Theodore Lorenzo, June 25, 1842–Nov. 28, 1903.
   Vol. 8, Pt. 2–563
Seiss, Joseph Augustus, Mar. 18, 1823–Jun 20, 1904.
   Vol. 8, Pt. 2–563
Seitz, Don Carlos, Oct. 4, 1862–Dec. 4, 1935.
   Supp. 1–653
Seixas, Gershom Mendes, Jan. 15, 1746–July 2, 1816.
   Vol. 8, Pt. 2–564
Séjour, Victor, June 2, 1817–Sept. 21, 1874.
   Vol. 8, Pt. 2–565
Selby, William, 1739?–December 1798.
   Vol. 8, Pt. 2–566
Selden, George Baldwin, Sept. 14, 1846–Jan. 17, 1922.
   Vol. 8, Pt. 2–567
Seldes, Gilbert Vivian, Jan. 3, 1893–Sept. 29, 1970.
   Supp. 8–584
Selfridge, Thomas Oliver, Feb. 6, 1836–Feb. 4, 1924.
   Vol. 8, Pt. 2–568
Selig, William Nicholas, Mar. 14, 1864–July 15, 1948.
   Supp. 4–734
Seligman, Arthur, June 14, 1871–Sept. 25, 1933.
   Vol. 8, Pt. 2–569
Seligman, Edwin Robert Anderson, Apr. 25, 1861–July 18, 1939. Supp. 2–606
Seligman, Isaac Newton, July 10, 1855–Sept. 30, 1917.
   Vol. 8, Pt. 2–570
Seligman, Jesse, Aug. 11, 1827–Apr. 23, 1894.
   Vol. 8, Pt. 2–571
Seligman, Joseph, Nov. 22, 1819–Apr. 25, 1880.
   Vol. 8, Pt. 2–571
Selijns, Henricus, 1636–1701.
   Vol. 8, Pt. 2–572
Selikovitsch, Goetzel, May 23, 1863–Nov. 27, 1926.
   Vol. 8, Pt. 2–573
Sellers, Coleman, Jan. 28, 1827–Dec. 28, 1907.
   Vol. 8, Pt. 2–574
Sellers, Isaiah, c. 1802–Mar. 6, 1864.
   Vol. 8, Pt. 2–575
Sellers, Matthew Bacon, Mar. 29, 1869–Apr. 5, 1932.
   Vol. 8, Pt. 2–576
Sellers, William, Sept. 19, 1824–Jan. 24, 1905.
   Vol. 8, Pt. 2–576
Sellstedt, Lars Gustaf, Apr. 30, 1819–June 4, 1911.
   Vol. 8, Pt. 2–577
Selyns, Henricus. [See Selijns, Henricus, 1636–1701.]
Selznick, David O., May 10, 1902–June 22, 1965.
   Supp. 7–681
Sembrich, Marcella, Feb. 15, 1858–jan. 11, 1935.
   Supp. 1–654
Semmes, Alexander Jenkins, Dec. 17, 1828–Sept. 20, 1898.
   Vol. 8, Pt. 2–578
Semmes, Raphael, Sept. 27, 1809–Aug. 30, 1877.
   Vol. 8, Pt. 2–579
Semmes, Thomas Jenkins, Dec. 16, 1824–June 23, 1899.
   Vol. 8, Pt. 2–582
Semple, Ellen Churchill, Jan. 8, 1863–May 8, 1932.
   Vol. 8, Pt. 2–583
Seney, George Ingraham, May 12, 1826–Apr. 7, 1893.
   Vol. 8, Pt. 2–583
Senn, Nicholas, Oct. 31, 1844–Jan. 2, 1908.
   Vol. 8, Pt. 2–584
Sennett, George Burritt, July 28, 1840–Mar. 18, 1900.
   Vol. 8, Pt. 2–585
Sennett, Mack, Jan. 17, 1880–Nov. 5, 1960.
   Supp. 6–572
Sequoyah, 1770?–August 1843.
   Vol. 8, Pt. 2–586
Sergeant, Henry Clark, Nov. 2, 1834–Jan. 30, 1907.
   Vol. 8, Pt. 2–586
Sergeant, John, 1710–July 27, 1749.
   Vol. 8, Pt. 2–587
Sergeant, John, Dec. 5, 1779–Nov. 23, 1852.
   Vol. 8, Pt. 2–588
Sergeant, Jonathan Dickinson, 1746–Oct. 8, 1793.
   Vol. 8, Pt. 2–589
Sergeant, Thomas, Jan. 14, 1782–May 5, 1860.
   Vol. 8, Pt. 2–590
Serra, Junípero, Nov. 24, 1713–Aug. 28, 1784.
   Vol. 8, Pt. 2–591
Serrell, Edward Wellman, Nov. 5, 1826–Apr. 25, 1906.
   Vol. 8, Pt. 2–592

Service, Robert William, Jan. 16, 1874–Sept. 11, 1958.
Supp. 6–574
Servoss, Thomas Lowery, Oct. 14, 1786–Nov. 30, 1866.
Vol. 8, Pt. 2–593
Sessions, Henry Howard, June 21, 1847–Mar. 14, 1915.
Vol. 8, Pt. 2–593
Sestini, Benedict, Mar. 20, 1816–Jan. 17, 1890.
Vol. 8, Pt. 2–594
Setchell, William Albert, Apr. 15, 1864–Apr. 5, 1943.
Supp. 3–703
Seth, James, May 6, 1860–July 24, 1924.
Vol. 8, Pt. 2–595
Seton, Elizabeth Ann Bayley, Aug. 28, 1774–Jan. 4, 1821.
Vol. 8, Pt. 2–596
Seton, Ernest Thompson, Aug. 14, 1860–Oct. 23, 1946.
Supp. 4–735
Seton, Grace Gallatin Thompson, Jan. 28, 1872–Mar. 19,
1959. Supp. 6–575
Seton, Robert, Aug. 28, 1839–Mar. 22, 1927.
Vol. 8, Pt. 2–597
Seton, William, Jan. 28, 1835–Mar. 15, 1905.
Vol. 8, Pt. 2–598
Settle, Thomas, Jan. 23, 1831–Dec. 1, 1888.
Vol. 8, Pt. 2–598
Severance, Caroline Maria Seymour, Jan. 12. 1820–Nov. 10,
1914. Vol. 8, Pt. 2–599
Severance, Frank Hayward, Nov. 28, 1856–Jan. 26, 1931.
Vol. 8, Pt. 2–600
Severance, Louis Henry, Aug. 1, 1838–June 25, 1913.
Vol. 8, Pt. 2–601
Sevier, Ambrose Hundley, Nov. 4, 1801–Dec. 31, 1848.
Vol. 8, Pt. 2–601
Sevier, John, Sept. 23, 1745–Sept. 24, 1815.
Vol. 8, Pt. 2–602
Sewall, Arthur, Nov. 25, 1835–Sept. 5, 1900.
Vol. 8, Pt. 2–605
Sewall, Frank, Sept. 24, 1837–Dec. 7, 1915.
Vol. 8, Pt. 2–606
Sewall, Harold Marsh, Jan. 3, 1860–Oct. 28, 1924.
Vol. 8, Pt. 2–606
Sewall, Jonathan, Aug. 17, 1728–Sept. 26, 1796.
Vol. 8, Pt. 2–607
Sewall, Jonathan Mitchell, 1748–Mar. 29, 1808.
Vol. 8, Pt. 2–608
Sewall, Joseph Addison, Apr. 20, 1830–Jan. 17, 1917.
Vol. 8, Pt. 2–609
Sewall, May Eliza Wright, May 27, 1844–July 22, 1920.
Vol. 8, Pt. 2–610
Sewall, Samuel, Mar. 28, 1652–Jan. 1, 1730.
Vol. 8, Pt. 2–610
Sewall, Stephen, Apr. 4, 1734–July 23, 1804.
Vol. 8, Pt. 2–612
Seward, Frederick William, July 8, 1830–Apr. 25, 1915.
Vol. 8, Pt. 2–612
Seward, George Frederick, Nov. 8, 1840–Nov. 28, 1910.
Vol. 8, Pt. 2–613
Seward, Theodore Frelinghuysen, Jan. 25, 1835–Aug. 30,
1902. Vol. 8, Pt. 2–614
Seward, William Henry, May 16, 1801–Oct. 10, 1872.
Vol. 8, Pt. 2–615
Sewell, William Joyce, Dec. 6, 1835–Dec. 27, 1901.
Vol. 9, Pt. 1–1
Seybert, Adam, May 16, 1773–May 2, 1825.
Vol. 9, Pt. 1–2
Seybert, Henry, Dec. 23, 1801–Mar. 3, 1883.
Vol. 9, Pt. 1–3
Seybert, John, July 7, 1791–Jan. 4, 1860.
Vol. 9, Pt. 1–3
Seyffarth, Gustavus, July 13, 1796–Nov. 17, 1885.
Vol. 9, Pt. 1–4
Seymour, Charles, Jan. 1, 1885–Aug. 11, 1963.
Supp. 7–682
Seymour, George Franklin, Jan. 5, 1829–Dec. 8, 1906.
Vol. 9, Pt. 1–5
Seymour, Horatio, May 31, 1810–Feb. 12, 1886.
Vol. 9, Pt. 1–6
Seymour, Horatio Winslow, 1854–Dec. 17, 1920.
Vol. 9, Pt. 1–9
Seymour, Thomas Day, Apr. 1, 1848–Dec. 31, 1907.
Vol. 9, Pt. 1–10
Seymour, Thomas Hart, Sept. 29, 1807–Sept. 3, 1868.
Vol. 9, Pt. 1–11

Seymour, Truman, Sept. 24, 1824–Oct. 30, 1891.
Vol. 9, Pt. 1–12
Seymour, William, Dec. 19, 1855–Oct. 2, 1933.
Vol. 9, Pt. 1–13
Shabonee, c. 1775–July 1859.
Vol. 9, Pt. 1–13
Shafer, Helen Almira, Sept. 23, 1839–Jan. 20, 1894.
Vol. 9, Pt. 1–14
Shafroth, John Franklin, June 9, 1854–Feb. 20, 1922.
Vol. 9, Pt. 1–14
Shafter, William Rufus, Oct. 16, 1835–Nov. 12, 1906.
Vol. 9, Pt. 1–15
Shahan, Thomas Joseph, Sept. 11, 1857–Mar. 9, 1932.
Vol. 9, Pt. 1–16
Shahn, Benjamin ("Ben"), Sept. 12, 1898–Mar. 14, 1969.
Supp. 8–586
Shaikewitz, Nahum Meir. [See Schomer, Nahum Meir, 1849
–1905.]
Shakallamy. [See Shikellamy, d. 1748.]
Shaler, Nathaniel Southgate, Feb. 20, 1841–Apr. 10, 1906.
Vol. 9, Pt. 1–17
Shaler, William, c. 1773–Mar. 29, 1833.
Vol. 9, Pt. 1–19
Shannon, Fred Albert, Feb. 12, 1893–Feb. 4, 1963.
Supp. 7–684
Shannon, Wilson, Feb. 24, 1802–Aug. 30, 1877.
Vol. 9, Pt. 1–20
Sharkey, William Lewis, July 12, 1798–Mar. 30, 1873.
Vol. 9, Pt. 1–21
Sharp, Dallas Lore, Dec. 13, 1870–Nov. 29, 1929.
Vol. 9, Pt. 1–22
Sharp, Daniel, Dec. 25, 1783–June 23, 1853.
Vol. 9, Pt. 1–23
Sharp, John, Nov. 9, 1820–Dec. 23, 1891.
Vol. 9, Pt. 1–23
Sharp, Katharine Lucinda, May 25, 1865–June 1, 1914.
Vol. 9, Pt. 1–24
Sharp, William Graves, Mar. 14, 1859–Nov. 17, 1922.
Vol. 9, Pt. 1–25
Sharpe, Horatio, Nov. 15, 1718–Nov. 9, 1790.
Vol. 9, Pt. 1–25
Sharples, James, c. 1751–Feb. 26, 1811.
Vol. 9, Pt. 1–26
Sharpless, Isaac, Dec. 16, 1848–Jan. 16, 1920.
Vol. 9, Pt. 1–27
Sharswood, George, July 7, 1810–May 28, 1883.
Vol. 9, Pt. 1–28
Shattuck, Aaron Draper, Mar. 9, 1832–July 30, 1928.
Vol. 9, Pt. 1–29
Shattuck, Frederick Cheever, Nov. 1, 1847–Jan. 11, 1929.
Vol. 9, Pt. 1–30
Shattuck, George Brune, Aug. 18, 1844–Mar. 12, 1923.
Vol. 9, Pt. 1–31
Shattuck, George Cheyne, July 17, 1783–Mar. 18, 1854.
Vol. 9, Pt. 1–31
Shattuck, George Cheyne, July 22, 1813–Mar. 22, 1893.
Vol. 9, Pt. 1–32
Shattuck, Lemuel, Oct. 15, 1793–Jan. 17, 1859.
Vol. 9, Pt. 1–33
Shaubena. [See Shabonee, c. 1775–1859.]
Shauck, John Allen, Mar. 26, 1841–Jan. 3, 1918.
Vol. 9, Pt. 1–34
Shaughnessy, Clark Daniel, Mar. 6, 1892–May 15, 1970.
Supp. 8–587
Shaw, Albert, July 23, 1857–June 25, 1947.
Supp. 4–738
Shaw, Anna Howard, Feb. 14, 1847–July 2, 1919.
Vol. 9, Pt. 1–35
Shaw, Edward Richard, Jan. 13, 1850–Feb. 11, 1903.
Vol. 9, Pt. 1–37
Shaw, Elijah, Dec. 19, 1793–May 5, 1851.
Vol. 9, Pt. 1–37
Shaw, Henry, July 24, 1800–Aug. 25, 1889.
Vol. 9, Pt. 1–38
Shaw, Henry Wheeler, Apr. 21, 1818–Oct. 14, 1885.
Vol. 9, Pt. 1–39
Shaw, Howard Van Doren, May 7, 1869–May 6, 1926.
Vol. 9, Pt. 1–40
Shaw, John, 1773–Sept. 17, 1823.
Vol. 9, Pt. 1–41
Shaw, John, May 4, 1778–Jan. 10, 1809.
Vol. 9, Pt. 1–41

Shaw, Lemuel, Jan. 9, 1781–Mar. 30, 1861.
    Vol. 9, Pt. 1–42
Shaw, Leslie Mortier, Nov. 2, 1848–Mar. 28, 1932.
    Vol. 9, Pt. 1–43
Shaw, Mary, Jan. 25, 1854–May 18, 1929.
    Vol. 9, Pt. 1–44
Shaw, Nathaniel, Dec. 5, 1735–Apr. 15, 1782.
    Vol. 9, Pt. 1–45
Shaw, Oliver, Mar. 13, 1779–Dec. 31, 1848.
    Vol. 9, Pt. 1–46
Shaw, Pauline Agassiz, Feb. 6, 1841–Feb. 10, 1917.
    Vol. 9, Pt. 1–46
Shaw, Samuel, Oct. 2, 1754–May 30, 1794.
    Vol. 9, Pt. 1–47
Shaw, Thomas, May 5, 1838–Jan. 19, 1901.
    Vol. 9, Pt. 1–48
Shaw, (Warren) Wilbur, Oct. 31, 1902–Oct. 30, 1954.
    Supp. 5–618
Shaw, William Smith, Aug. 12, 1778–Apr. 25, 1826.
    Vol. 9, Pt. 1–49
Shays, Daniel, c. 1747–Sept. 29, 1825.
    Vol. 9, Pt. 1–49
Shea, John Dawson Gilmary, July 22, 1824–Feb. 22, 1892.
    Vol. 9, Pt. 1–50
Shean, Albert, May 12, 1868–Aug. 12, 1949.
    Supp. 4–739
Shear, Theodore Leslie, Aug. 11, 1880–July 3, 1945.
    Supp. 3–704
Shearman, Thomas Gaskell, Nov. 25, 1834–Sept. 29, 1900.
    Vol. 9, Pt. 1–52
Shecut, John Linnaeus Edward Whitridge, Dec. 4, 1770–June
    1, 1836. Vol. 9, Pt. 1–53
Shedd, Fred Fuller, Feb. 9, 1871–Apr. 2, 1937.
    Supp. 2–609
Shedd, Joel Herbert, May 31, 1834–Nov. 27, 1915.
    Vol. 9, Pt. 1–53
Shedd, John Graves, July 20, 1850–Oct. 22, 1926.
    Vol. 9, Pt. 1–54
Shedd, William Greenough Thayer, June 21, 1820–Nov. 17,
    1894. Vol. 9, Pt. 1–56
Shedd, William Ambrose, Jan. 24, 1865–Aug. 7, 1918.
    Vol. 9, Pt. 1–55
Sheedy, Dennis, Sept. 26, 1846–Oct. 16, 1923.
    Vol. 9, Pt. 1–57
Sheeler, Charles R., Jr., July 16, 1883–May 7, 1965.
    Supp. 7–685
Sheffield, Devello Zelotes, Aug. 13, 1841–July 1, 1913.
    Vol. 9, Pt. 1–57
Sheffield, Joseph Earl, June 19, 1793–Feb. 16, 1882.
    Vol. 9, Pt. 1–58
Sheil, Bernard James, Feb. 18, 1886–Sept. 13, 1969.
    Supp. 8–588
Shelby, Evan, 1719–Dec. 4, 1794.
    Vol. 9, Pt. 1–59
Shelby, Isaac, Dec. 11, 1750–July 18, 1826.
    Vol. 9, Pt. 1–60
Shelby, Joseph Orville, Dec. 12, 1830–Feb. 13, 1897.
    Vol. 9, Pt. 1–62
Sheldon, Charles Monroe, Feb. 26, 1857–Feb. 24, 1946.
    Supp. 4–740
Sheldon, Edward Austin, Oct. 4, 1823–Aug. 26, 1897.
    Vol. 9, Pt. 1–63
Sheldon, Edward Stevens, Nov. 21, 1851–Oct. 16, 1925.
    Vol. 9, Pt. 1–64
Sheldon, Henry Newton, June 28, 1843–Jan. 14, 1926.
    Vol. 9, Pt. 1–65
Sheldon, Mary Downing. [See Barnes, Mary Downing
    Sheldon, 1850–1898.]
Sheldon, Walter Lorenzo, Sept. 5, 1858–June 5, 1907.
    Vol. 9, Pt. 1–66
Sheldon, William Evarts, Oct. 22, 1832–Apr. 16, 1900.
    Vol. 9, Pt. 1–66
Shelekhov, Grigorii Ivanovich, 1747–July 31, 1795.
    Vol. 9, Pt. 1–67
Shellabarger, Samuel, May 18, 1888–Mar. 21, 1954.
    Supp. 5–619
Shelton, Albert Leroy, June 9, 1875–Feb. 17, 1922.
    Vol. 9, Pt. 1–68
Shelton, Edward Mason, Aug. 7, 1846–May 9, 1928.
    Vol. 9, Pt. 1–69
Shelton, Frederick William, May 20, 1815–June 20, 1881.
    Vol. 9, Pt. 1–70

Shepard, Charles Upham, June 29, 1804–May 1, 1886.
    Vol. 9, Pt. 1–71
Shepard, Edward Morse, July 23, 1850–July 28, 1911.
    Vol. 9, Pt. 1–72
Shepard, Fred Douglas, Sept. 11, 1855–Dec. 18, 1915.
    Vol. 9, Pt. 1–73
Shepard, James Edward, Nov. 3, 1875–Oct. 6, 1947.
    Supp. 4–742
Shepard, James Henry, Apr. 14, 1850–Feb. 21, 1918.
    Vol. 9, Pt. 1–73
Shepard, Jesse. [See Grierson, Francis, 1848–1927.]
Shepard, Seth, Apr. 23, 1847–Dec. 3, 1917.
    Vol. 9, Pt. 1–74
Shepard, Thomas, Nov. 5, 1605–Aug. 25, 1649.
    Vol. 9, Pt. 1–75
Shepard, William, Dec. 1, 1737–Nov. 16, 1817.
    Vol. 9, Pt. 1–76
Shepherd, Alexander Robey, Jan. 31, 1835–Sept. 12, 1902.
    Vol. 9, Pt. 1–77
Shepherd, William Robert, June 12, 1871–June 7, 1934.
    Supp. 1–655
Shepley, Ether, Nov. 2, 1789–Jan. 15, 1877.
    Vol. 9, Pt. 1–78
Shepley, George Foster, Jan. 1, 1819–July 20, 1878.
    Vol. 9, Pt. 1–78
Sheppard, John Morris, May 28, 1875–Apr. 9, 1941.
    Supp. 3–706
Sheppard, Samuel Edward, July 29, 1882–Sept. 29, 1948.
    Supp. 4–743
Sheridan, Philip Henry, Mar. 6, 1831–Aug. 5, 1888.
    Vol. 9, Pt. 1–79
Sherman, Forrest Percival, Oct. 30, 1896–July 22, 1951.
    Supp. 5–620
Sherman, Frank Dempster, May 6, 1860–Sept. 19, 1916.
    Vol. 9, Pt. 1–81
Sherman, Frederick Carl, May 27, 1888–July 27, 1957.
    Supp. 6–576
Sherman, Henry Clapp, Oct. 16, 1875–Oct. 7, 1955.
    Supp. 5–622
Sherman, James Schoolcraft, Oct. 24, 1855–Oct. 30, 1912.
    Vol. 9, Pt. 1–82
Sherman, John, Dec. 26, 1613–Aug. 8, 1685.
    Vol. 9, Pt. 1–83
Sherman, John, May 10, 1823–Oct. 22, 1900.
    Vol. 9, Pt. 1–84
Sherman, Roger, Apr. 19, 1721 o.s.–July 23, 1793.
    Vol. 9, Pt. 1–88
Sherman, Stuart Pratt, Oct. 1, 1881–Aug. 21, 1926.
    Vol. 9, Pt. 1–91
Sherman, Thomas West, Mar. 26, 1813–Mar. 16, 1879.
    Vol. 9, Pt. 1–92
Sherman, William Tecumseh, Feb. 8, 1820–Feb. 14, 1891.
    Vol. 9, Pt. 1–93
Sherry, Louis, 1856–June 9, 1926.
    Vol. 9, Pt. 1–97
Sherwin, Thomas, Mar. 26, 1799–July 23, 1869.
    Vol. 9, Pt. 1–98
Sherwood, Adiel, Oct. 3, 1791–Aug. 18, 1879.
    Vol. 9, Pt. 1–99
Sherwood, Isaac Ruth, Aug. 13, 1835–Oct. 15, 1925.
    Vol. 9, Pt. 1–100
Sherwood, Katharine Margaret Brownlee, Sept. 24, 1841–
    Feb. 15, 1914. Vol. 9, Pt. 1–100
Sherwood, Mary Elizabeth Wilson, Oct. 27, 1826–Sept. 12,
    1903. Vol. 9, Pt. 1–101
Sherwood, Robert Emmet, Apr. 4, 1896–Nov. 14, 1955.
    Supp. 5–623
Sherwood, Thomas Adiel, June 2, 1834–Nov. 11, 1918.
    Vol. 9, Pt. 1–102
Sherwood, William Hall, Jan. 31, 1854–Jan. 7, 1911.
    Vol. 9, Pt. 1–103
Shick Calamys. [See Shikellamy, d. 1748.]
Shields, Charles Woodruff, Apr. 4, 1825–Aug. 26, 1904.
    Vol. 9, Pt. 1–104
Shields, George Howell, June 19, 1842–Apr. 27, 1924.
    Vol. 9, Pt. 1–105
Shields, George Oliver, Aug. 26, 1846–Nov. 11, 1925.
    Vol. 9, Pt. 1–106
Shields, James, May 12, 1806–June 1, 1879.
    Vol. 9, Pt. 1–106
Shields, John Knight, Aug. 15, 1858–Sept. 30, 1934.
    Supp. 1–656

Shields, Thomas Edward, May 9, 1862–Feb. 15, 1921.
Vol. 9, Pt. 1–107
Shikellamy, d. Dec. 6, 1748.
Vol. 9, Pt. 1–109
Shillaber, Benjamin Penhallow, July 12, 1814–Nov. 25, 1890.
Vol. 9, Pt. 1–109
Shinn, Asa, May 3, 1781–Feb. 11, 1853.
Vol. 9, Pt. 1–110
Shinn, Everett, Nov. 6, 1876–May 1, 1953.
Supp. 5–624
Shipherd, John Jay, Mar. 28, 1802–Sept. 16, 1844.
Vol. 9, Pt. 1–111
Shipley, Ruth Bielaski, 1885–Nov. 3, 1966.
Supp. 8–589
Shipman, Andrew Jackson, Oct. 15, 1857–Oct. 17, 1915.
Vol. 9, Pt. 1–112
Shipp, Albert Micajah, June 15, 1819–June 27, 1887.
Vol. 9, Pt. 1–113
Shipp, Scott, Aug. 2, 1839–Dec. 4, 1917.
Vol. 9, Pt. 1–114
Shippen, Edward, 1639–Oct. 2, 1712.
Vol. 9, Pt. 1–115
Shippen, Edward, Feb. 16/26, 1728/29–Apr. 15, 1806.
Vol. 9, Pt. 1–116
Shippen, William, Oct. 21, 1736–July 11, 1808.
Vol. 9, Pt. 1–117
Shipstead, Henrik, Jan. 8, 1881–June 26, 1960.
Supp. 6–577
Shiras, George, Jan. 26, 1832–Aug. 2, 1924.
Vol. 9, Pt. 1–118
Shiras, Oliver Perry, Oct. 22, 1833–Jan. 7, 1916.
Vol. 9, Pt. 1–118
Shirlaw, Walter, Aug. 6, 1838–Dec. 26, 1909.
Vol. 9, Pt. 1–119
Shirley, William, Dec. 2, 1694–Mar. 24, 1771.
Vol. 9, Pt. 1–120
Shobonier. [See Shabonee, c. 1775–1859.]
Sholes, Christopher Latham, Feb. 14, 1819–Feb. 17, 1890.
Vol. 9, Pt. 1–122
Shonts, Theodore Perry, May 5, 1856–Sept. 21, 1919.
Vol. 9, Pt. 1–123
Shook, Alfred Montgomery, July 16, 1845–Mar. 18, 1923.
Vol. 9, Pt. 1–124
Shorey, Paul, Aug. 3, 1857–Apr. 24, 1934.
Vol. 9, Pt. 1–125
Short, Charles, May 28, 1821–Dec. 24, 1886.
Vol. 9, Pt. 1–126
Short, Charles Wilkins, Oct. 6, 1794–Mar. 7, 1863.
Vol. 9, Pt. 1–127
Short, Joseph Hudson, Jr., Feb. 11, 1904–Sept. 18, 1952.
Supp. 5–626
Short, Sidney Howe, Oct. 8, 1858–Oct. 21, 1902.
Vol. 9, Pt. 1–128
Short, Walter Campbell, Mar. 30, 1880–Sept. 3, 1949.
Supp. 4–744
Short, William, Sept. 30, 1759–Dec. 5, 1849.
Vol. 9, Pt. 1–128
Shorter, John Gill, Apr. 23, 1818–May 29, 1872.
Vol. 9, Pt. 1–129
Shotwell, James Thomson, Aug. 6, 1874–July 15, 1965.
Supp. 7–687
Shoup, Francis Asbury, Mar. 22, 1834–Sept. 4, 1896.
Vol. 9, Pt. 1–130
Shoup, George Laird, June 15, 1836–Dec. 21, 1904.
Vol. 9, Pt. 1–131
Shouse, Jouett, Dec. 10, 1879–June 2, 1968.
Supp. 8–591
Showerman, Grant, Jan. 9, 1870–Nov. 13, 1935.
Supp. 1–657
Shrady, George Frederick, Jan. 14, 1837–Nov. 30, 1907.
Vol. 9, Pt. 1–132
Shrady, Henry Merwin, Oct. 24, 1871–Apr. 12, 1922.
Vol. 9, Pt. 1–132
Shreve, Henry Miller, Oct. 21, 1785–Mar. 6, 1851.
Vol. 9, Pt. 1–133
Shreve, Thomas Hopkins, Dec. 17, 1808–Dec. 22, 1853.
Vol. 9, Pt. 1–134
Shubert, Lee, Mar. 15, 1873[?]–Dec. 25, 1953.
Supp. 5–626
Shubrick, John Templer, Sept. 12, 1788–July 1815.
Vol. 9, Pt. 1–135
Shubrick, William Branford, Oct. 31, 1790–May 27, 1874.
Vol. 9, Pt. 1–136

Shuck, Jehu Lewis, Sept. 4, 1812–Aug. 20, 1863.
Vol. 9, Pt. 1–137
Shuey, Edwin Longstreet, Jan. 3, 1857–Sept. 27, 1924.
Vol. 9, Pt. 1–138
Shuey, William John, Feb. 9, 1827–Feb. 21, 1920.
Vol. 9, Pt. 1–138
Shufeldt, Robert Wilson, Feb. 21, 1822–Nov. 7, 1895.
Vol. 9, Pt. 1–139
Shull, George Harrison, Apr. 15, 1874–Sept. 28, 1954.
Supp. 5–628
Shulze, John Andrew, July 19, 1775–Nov. 18, 1852.
Vol. 9, Pt. 1–140
Shunk, Francis Rawn, Aug. 7, 1788–July 30, 1848.
Vol. 9, Pt. 1–141
Shurtleff, Nathaniel Bradstreet, June 29, 1810–Oct. 17, 1874.
Vol. 9, Pt. 1–141
Shurtleff, Roswell Morse, June 14, 1838–Jan. 6, 1915.
Vol. 9, Pt. 1–142
Shuster, W(illiam) Morgan, Feb. 23, 1877–May 26, 1960.
Supp. 6–579
Shute, Samuel, Jan. 12, 1662–Apr. 15, 1742.
Vol. 9, Pt. 1–143
Siamese Twins. [See Chang and Eng, 1811–1874.]
Sibert, William Luther, Oct. 12, 1860–Oct. 16, 1935.
Supp. 1–658
Sibley, George Champlain, Apr. 1, 1782–Jan. 31, 1863.
Vol. 9, Pt. 1–144
Sibley, Henry Hastings, Feb. 20, 1811–Feb. 18, 1891.
Vol. 9, Pt. 1–144
Sibley, Hiram, Feb. 6, 1807–July 12, 1888.
Vol. 9, Pt. 1–145
Sibley, John, May 19, 1757–Apr. 8, 1837.
Vol. 9, Pt. 1–146
Sibley, John Langdon, Dec. 29, 1804–Dec. 9, 1885.
Vol. 9, Pt. 1–147
Sibley, Joseph Crocker, Feb. 18 1850–May 19, 1926.
Vol. 9, Pt. 1–148
Sicalamous. [See Shikellamy, d. 1748.]
Sicard, Montgomery, Sept. 30, 1836–Sept. 14, 1900.
Vol. 9, Pt. 1–148
Sickels, Frederick Ellsworth, Sept 20, 1819–Mar. 8, 1895.
Vol. 9, Pt. 1–149
Sickles, Daniel Edgar, Oct. 20, 1825–May 3, 1914.
Vol. 9, Pt. 1–150
Sidell, William Henry, Aug. 21, 1810–July 1, 1873.
Vol. 9, Pt. 1–151
Sidis, Boris, Oct. 12, 1867–Oct. 24, 1923.
Vol. 9, Pt. 1–152
Sidney, Margaret. [See Lothrop, Harriett Mulford Stone, 1844–1924.]
Sieber, Al, Feb. 29, 1844–Feb. 19, 1907.
Supp. 1–659
Sigel, Franz, Nov. 18, 1824–Aug. 21, 1902.
Vol. 9, Pt. 1–153
Sigerist, Henry Ernest, Apr. 7, 1891–Mar. 17, 1957.
Supp. 6–580
Sigman, Morris, May 15, 1881–July 20, 1931.
Vol. 9, Pt. 1–154
Sigourney, Lydia Howard Huntley, Sept. 1, 1791–June 10, 1865. Vol. 9, Pt. 1–155
Sigsbee, Charles Dwight, Jan. 16, 1845–July 19, 1923.
Vol. 9, Pt. 1–156
Sikes, William Wirt, Nov. 23, 1836–Aug. 18, 1883.
Vol. 9, Pt. 1–157
Silcox, Ferdinand Augustus, Dec. 25, 1882–Dec. 20, 1939.
Supp. 2–610
Sill, Anna Peck, Aug. 9, 1816–June 18, 1889.
Vol. 9, Pt. 1–157
Sill, Edward Rowland, Apr. 29, 1841–Feb. 27, 1887.
Vol. 9, Pt. 1–158
Silliman, Benjamin, Aug. 8, 1779–Nov. 24, 1864.
Vol. 9, Pt. 1–160
Silliman, Benjamin, Dec. 4, 1816–Jan. 14, 1885.
Vol. 9, Pt. 1–163
Sills, Milton, Jan. 12, 1882–Sept. 15, 1930.
Vol. 9, Pt. 1–164
Siloti, Alexander Ilyitch, Oct. 10, 1863–Dec. 8, 1945.
Supp. 3–707
Silsbee, Nathaniel, Jan. 14, 1773–July 14, 1850.
Vol. 9, Pt. 1–165
Silver, Abba Hillel, Jan. 28, 1893–Nov. 28, 1963.
Supp. 7–688

Silver, Gray, Feb. 17, 1871–July 28, 1935.
　Supp. 1–660
Silver, Thomas, June 17, 1813–Apr. 12, 1888.
　Vol. 9, Pt. 1–165
Silverman, Joseph, Aug. 25, 1860–July 26, 1930.
　Vol. 9, Pt. 1–166
Silverman, Sime, May 18, 1873–Sept. 22, 1933.
　Vol. 9, Pt. 1–167
Silvers, Louis, Sept. 6, 1889–Mar. 26, 1954.
　Supp. 5–629
Simkhovitch, Mary Melinda Kingsbury, Sept. 8, 1867–Nov.
　15, 1951. Supp. 5–630
Simmons, Edward, Oct. 27, 1852–Nov. 17, 1931.
　Vol. 9, Pt. 1–168
Simmons, Franklin, Jan. 11, 1839–Dec. 6, 1913.
　Vol. 9, Pt. 1–169
Simmons, Furnifold McLendel, Jan. 20, 1854–Apr. 30, 1940.
　Supp. 2–611
Simmons, George Henry, Jan. 2, 1852–Sept. 1, 1937.
　Supp. 2–612
Simmons, James Stevens, June 7, 1890–July 31, 1954.
　Supp. 5–631
Simmons, Roscoe Conkling Murray, June 20, 1878–Apr. 27,
　1951. Supp. 5–632
Simmons, Thomas Jefferson, June 25, 1837–Sept. 12, 1905.
　Vol. 9, Pt. 1–169
Simmons, William Joseph, May 6, 1880–May 18, 1945.
　Supp. 3–708
Simmons (Szymanski), Aloysius Harry, May 22, 1903–May
　26, 1956. Supp. 6–581
Simms, Ruth Hanna McCormick, Mar. 27, 1880–Dec. 31,
　1944. Supp. 3–710
Simms, William Elliott, Jan. 2, 1822–June 25, 1898.
　Vol. 9, Pt. 1–170
Simms, William Gilmore, Apr. 17, 1806–June 11, 1870.
　Vol. 9, Pt. 1–171
Simon, Richard Leo, Mar. 6, 1899–July 29, 1960.
　Supp. 6–582
Simonds, Frank Herbert, Apr. 5, 1878–Jan. 23, 1936.
　Supp. 2–613
Simons, Algie Martin, Oct. 9, 1870–Mar. 11, 1950.
　Supp. 4–745
Simons, Henry Calvert, Oct. 9, 1899–June 19, 1946.
　Supp. 4–747
Simonton, Charles Henry, July 11, 1829–Apr. 25, 1904.
　Vol. 9, Pt. 1–174
Simonton, James William, Jan. 30, 1823–Nov. 2, 1882.
　Vol. 9, Pt. 1–175
Simpson, Albert Benjamin, Dec. 15, 1843–Oct. 29, 1919.
　Vol. 9, Pt. 1–176
Simpson, Charles Torrey, June 3, 1846–Dec. 17, 1932.
　Supp. 1–661
Simpson, Edmund Shaw, 1784–July 31, 1848.
　Vol. 9, Pt. 1–177
Simpson, Edward, Mar. 3, 1824–Dec. 1, 1888.
　Vol. 9, Pt. 1–178
Simpson, James Hervey, Mar. 9, 1813–Mar. 2, 1883.
　Vol. 9, Pt. 1–179
Simpson, Jerry, Mar. 31, 1842–Oct. 23, 1905.
　Vol. 9, Pt. 1–179
Simpson, John Andrew, July 4, 1871–Mar. 15, 1934.
　Vol. 9, Pt. 1–180
Simpson, Matthew, June 21, 1811–June 18, 1884.
　Vol. 9, Pt. 1–181
Simpson, Michael Hodge, Nov. 15, 1809–Dec. 21, 1884.
　Vol. 9, Pt. 1–182
Simpson, Stephen, July 24, 1789–Aug. 17, 1854.
　Vol. 9, Pt. 1–183
Simpson, William Dunlap, Oct. 27, 1823–Dec. 26. 1890.
　Vol. 9, Pt. 1–184
Simpson, William Kelly, Apr. 10, 1855–Feb. 6, 1914.
　Vol. 9, Pt. 1–185
Sims, Charles N., May 18, 1835–Mar. 27, 1908.
　Vol. 9, Pt. 1–185
Sims, James Marion, Jan. 25, 1813–Nov. 13, 1883.
　Vol. 9, Pt. 1–186
Sims, William Sowden, Oct. 15, 1858–Sept. 28, 1936.
　Supp. 2–614
Sims, Winfield Scott, Apr. 6, 1844–Jan. 7, 1918.
　Vol. 9, Pt. 1–188
Sinclair, Harry Ford, July 6, 1876–Nov. 10, 1956.
　Supp. 6–584

Sinclair, Upton Beall, Jr., Sept. 20, 1878–Nov. 25, 1968.
　Supp. 8–593
Singer, Isaac Merrit, Oct. 27, 1811–July 23, 1875.
　Vol. 9, Pt. 1–188
Singer, Israel Joshua, Nov. 30, 1893–Feb. 10, 1944.
　Supp. 3–711
Singerly, William Miskey, Dec. 27, 1832–Feb. 27, 1898.
　Vol. 9, Pt. 1–189
Singleton, Esther, Nov. 4, 1865–July 2, 1930.
　Vol. 9, Pt. 1–190
Singleton, James Washington, Nov. 23, 1811–Apr. 4, 1892.
　Vol. 9, Pt. 1–191
Sinnott, Edmund Ware, Feb. 5, 1888–Jan. 6, 1968.
　Supp. 8–595
Siringo, Charles A., Feb. 7, 1855–Oct. 19, 1928.
　Vol. 9, Pt. 1–191
Sitting Bull, 1834?–Dec. 15, 1890.
　Vol. 9, Pt. 1–192
Sizer, Nelson, May 27, 1812–Oct. 18, 1897.
　Vol. 9, Pt. 1–193
Skaniadariio, c. 1735–Aug. 10, 1815.
　Vol. 9, Pt. 1–194
Skenandoa, 1706?–Mar. 11, 1816.
　Vol. 9, Pt. 1–194
Skene, Alexander Johnston Chalmers, June 17, 1837–July 4,
　1900. Vol. 9, Pt. 1–194
Skidmore, Louis, Apr. 8, 1897–Sept. 27, 1962.
　Supp. 7–690
Skillern, Ross Hall, Nov. 13, 1875–Sept. 20, 1930.
　Vol. 9, Pt. 1–195
Skinner, Aaron Nichols, Aug. 10, 1845–Aug. 14, 1918.
　Vol. 9, Pt. 1–196
Skinner, Alanson Buck, Sept. 7, 1886–Aug. 17, 1925.
　Vol. 9, Pt. 1–197
Skinner, Charles Rufus, Aug. 4, 1844–June 30, 1928.
　Vol. 9, Pt. 1–197
Skinner, Halcyon, Mar. 6, 1824–Nov. 28, 1900.
　Vol. 9, Pt. 1–198
Skinner, Harry, May 25, 1855–May 19, 1929.
　Vol. 9, Pt. 1–199
Skinner, John Stuart, Feb. 22, 1788–Mar. 21, 1851.
　Vol. 9, Pt. 1–199
Skinner, Otis, June 28, 1858–Jan. 4, 1942.
　Supp. 3–713
Skinner, Thomas Harvey, Mar. 7, 1791–Feb. 1, 1871.
　Vol. 9, Pt. 1–201
Skinner, William, Nov. 14, 1824–Feb. 28, 1902.
　Vol. 9, Pt. 1–202
Skouras, George Panagiotes, Apr. 23, 1896–Mar. 16, 1964.
　Supp. 7–691
Slade, Joseph Alfred, c. 1824–Mar. 10, 1864.
　Vol. 9, Pt. 1–202
Slade, William, May 9, 1786–Jan. 16, 1859.
　Vol. 9, Pt. 1–203
Slafter, Edmund Farwell, May 30, 1816–Sept. 22, 1906.
　Vol. 9, Pt. 1–204
Slater, John Fox, Mar. 4, 1815–May 7, 1884.
　Vol. 9, Pt. 1–205
Slater, Samuel, June 9, 1768–Apr. 21, 1835.
　Vol. 9, Pt. 1–205
Slattery, Charles Lewis, Dec. 9, 1867–Mar. 12, 1930.
　Vol. 9, Pt. 1–206
Slaughter, Philip, Oct. 26, 1808–June 12, 1890.
　Vol. 9, Pt. 1–207
Sleeper, Jacob, Nov. 21, 1802–Mar. 31, 1889.
　Vol. 9, Pt. 1–208
Slemp, Campbell Bascom, Sept. 4, 1870–Aug. 7, 1943.
　Supp. 3–714
Slicer, Thomas Roberts, Apr. 16, 1847–May 29, 1916. xvii–
　209
Slichter, Sumner Huber, Jan. 8, 1892–Sept. 27, 1959.
　Supp. 6–585
Slidell, John, 1793–July 29, 1871.
　Vol. 9, Pt. 1–209
Slipher, Vesto Melvin, Nov. 11, 1875–Nov. 8, 1969.
　Supp. 8–597
Sloan, Alfred Pritchard, Jr., May 23, 1875–Feb. 17, 1966.
　Supp. 8–598
Sloan, George Arthur, May 30, 1893–May 20, 1955.
　Supp. 5–633
Sloan, Harold Paul, Dec. 12, 1881–May 22, 1961.
　Supp. 7–693

Smith, Frank Leslie, Nov. 24, 1867–Aug. 30, 1950.
  Supp. 4–751
Smith, Fred Burton, Dec. 24, 1865–Sept. 4, 1936.
  Supp. 2–617
Smith, George, Feb. 10, 1806–Oct. 7, 1899.
  Vol. 9, Pt. 1–267
Smith, George Albert, Apr. 4, 1870–Apr. 4, 1951.
  Supp. 5–639
Smith, George Henry, Oct. 20, 1873–Jan. 9, 1931.
  Vol. 9, Pt. 1–268
Smith, George Otis, Feb. 22, 1871–Jan. 10, 1944.
  Supp. 3–724
Smith, Gerald Birney, May 3, 1868–Apr. 3, 1929.
  Vol. 9, Pt. 1–269
Smith, Gerrit, Mar. 6, 1797–Dec. 28, 1874.
  Vol. 9, Pt. 1–270
Smith, Giles Alexander, Sept. 29, 1829–Nov. 5, 1876.
  Vol. 9, Pt. 1–271
Smith, Gustavus Woodson, March 1822–June 24, 1896.
  Vol. 9, Pt. 1–272
Smith, Hamilton, July 5, 1840–July 4, 1900.
  Vol. 9, Pt. 1–273
Smith, Hannah Whitall, Feb. 7, 1832–May 1, 1911.
  Vol. 9, Pt. 1–274
Smith, Harold Babbitt, May 23, 1869–Feb. 9, 1932.
  Vol. 9, Pt. 1–275
Smith, Harold Dewey, June 6, 1898–Jan. 23, 1947.
  Supp. 4–753
Smith, Harry Bache, Dec. 28, 1860–Jan. 1, 1936.
  Supp. 2–618
Smith, Harry James, May 24, 1880–Mar. 16, 1918.
  Vol. 9, Pt. 1–276
Smith, Henry Augustus Middleton, Apr. 30, 1853–Nov. 23,
  1924. Vol. 9, Pt. 1–276
Smith, Henry Boynton, Nov. 21, 1815–Feb. 7, 1877.
  Vol. 9, Pt. 1–277
Smith, Henry Justin, June 19, 1875–Feb. 9, 1936.
  Supp. 2–619
Smith, Henry Louis, July 30, 1859–Feb. 27, 1951.
  Supp. 5–641
Smith, Henry Preserved, Oct. 23, 1847–Feb. 26, 1927.
  Vol. 9, Pt. 1–278
Smith, Hezekiah, Apr. 21, 1737–Jan. 24, 1805.
  Vol. 9, Pt. 1–279
Smith, Hiram, Feb. 19, 1817–May 15, 1890.
  Vol. 9, Pt. 1–280
Smith, Hoke, Sept. 2, 1855–Nov. 27, 1931.
  Vol. 9, Pt. 1–280
Smith, Holland McTyeire, Apr. 20, 1882–Jan. 12, 1967.
  Supp. 8–602
Smith, Homer William, Jan. 2, 1895–Mar. 25, 1962.
  Supp. 7–699
Smith, Horace, Oct. 28, 1808–Jan. 15, 1893.
  Vol. 9, Pt. 1–282
Smith, Horatio Elwin, May 8, 1886–Sept. 9, 1946.
  Supp. 4–754
Smith, Horton, May 22, 1908–Oct. 15, 1963.
  Supp. 7–700
Smith, Israel, Apr. 6, 1759–Dec. 2, 1810.
  Vol. 9, Pt. 1–283
Smith, James, c. 1719–July 11, 1806.
  Vol. 9, Pt. 1–283
Smith, James, c. 1737–c. 1814.
  Vol. 9, Pt. 1–284
Smith, James, June 12, 1851–Apr. 1, 1927.
  Vol. 9, Pt. 1–285
Smith, James Allen, May 5, 1860–Jan. 30, 1924.
  Vol. 9, Pt. 1–286
Smith, James Francis, Jan. 28, 1859–June 29, 1928.
  Vol. 9, Pt. 1–287
Smith, James McCune, Apr. 18, 1813–Nov. 17, 1865.
  Vol. 9, Pt. 1–288
Smith, James Perrin, Nov. 27, 1864–Jan. 1, 1931.
  Vol. 9, Pt. 1–289
Smith, Jedediah Strong, June 24, 1798–May 27, 1831.
  Vol. 9, Pt. 1–290
Smith, Jeremiah, Nov. 29, 1759–Sept. 21, 1842.
  Vol. 9, Pt. 1–291
Smith, Jeremiah, July 14, 1837–Sept. 3, 1921.
  Vol. 9, Pt. 1–292
Smith, Jeremiah, Jan. 14, 1870–Mar. 12, 1935.
  Supp. 1–662

Smith, Job Lewis, Oct. 15, 1827–June 9, 1897.
  Vol. 9, Pt. 1–293
Smith, Joel West, Sept. 17, 1837–May 9, 1924.
  Vol. 9, Pt. 1–294
Smith, John, 1579/80–June 21, 1631.
  Vol. 9, Pt. 1–294
Smith, John, c. 1735–c. 1824.
  Vol. 9, Pt. 1–296
Smith, John Augustine, Aug. 29, 1782–Feb. 9, 1865.
  Vol. 9, Pt. 1–297
Smith, John Bernhard, Nov. 21, 1858–Mar. 12, 1912.
  Vol. 9, Pt. 1–298
Smith, John Blair, June 12, 1756–Aug. 22, 1799.
  Vol. 9, Pt. 1–299
Smith, John Cotton, Feb. 12, 1765–Dec. 7, 1845.
  Vol. 9, Pt. 1–300
Smith, John Cotton, Aug. 4, 1826–Jan. 9, 1882.
  Vol. 9, Pt. 1–300
Smith, John Eugene, Aug. 3, 1816–Jan. 29, 1897.
  Vol. 9, Pt. 1–301
Smith, John Gregory, July 22, 1818–Nov. 6, 1891.
  Vol. 9, Pt. 1–302
Smith, John Jay, June 16, 1798–Sept. 23, 1881.
  Vol. 9, Pt. 1–303
Smith, John Lawrence, Dec. 17, 1818–Oct. 12, 1883.
  Vol. 9, Pt. 1–304
Smith, John Merlin Powis, Dec. 28, 1866–Sept. 26, 1932.
  Vol. 9, Pt. 1–305
Smith, John Rowson, May 11, 1810–Mar. 21, 1864.
  Vol. 9, Pt. 1–306
Smith, John Rubens, Jan. 23, 1775–Aug. 21, 1849.
  Vol. 9, Pt. 1–307
Smith, Jonas Waldo, Mar. 9, 1861–Oct. 14, 1933.
  Vol. 9, Pt. 1–307
Smith, Jonathan Bayard, Feb. 21, 1742–June 16, 1812.
  Vol. 9, Pt. 1–308
Smith, Joseph, Mar. 30. 1790–Jan. 17, 1877.
  Vol. 9, Pt. 1–309
Smith, Joseph, Dec. 23, 1805–June 27, 1844.
  Vol. 9, Pt. 1–310
Smith, Joseph, Nov. 6, 1832–Dec. 10, 1914.
  Vol. 9, Pt. 1–312
Smith, Joseph Fielding, Nov. 13, 1838–Nov. 19, 1918.
  Vol. 9, Pt. 1–313
Smith, Judson, June 28, 1837–June 29, 1906.
  Vol. 9, Pt. 1–314
Smith, Julia Evelina, 1792–1886. [See Smith, Abby Hadas-
  sah, 1797–1878.]
Smith, Junius, Oct. 2, 1780–Jan. 22, 1853.
  Vol. 9, Pt. 1–315
Smith, Justin Harvey, Jan. 13, 1857–Mar. 21, 1930.
  Vol. 9, Pt. 1–316
Smith, Lillian Eugenia, Dec. 12, 1897–Sept. 28, 1966.
  Supp. 8–604
Smith, Lloyd Logan Pearsall, Oct. 18, 1865–Mar. 2, 1946.
  Supp. 4–755
Smith, Lloyd Pearsall, Feb. 6, 1822–July 2, 1886.
  Vol. 9, Pt. 1–317
Smith, Lucy Harth, Jan. 24, 1888–Sept. 20, 1955.
  Supp. 5–641
Smith, Marcus. Jan. 7, 1829–Aug. 11, 1874.
  Vol. 9, Pt. 1–318
Smith, Margaret Bayard, Feb. 20, 1778–June 7, 1844.
  Vol. 9, Pt. 1–318
Smith, Martin Luther, Sept. 9, 1819–July 29, 1866.
  Vol. 9, Pt. 1–319
Smith, Melancton, May 7, 1744–July 29, 1798.
  Vol. 9, Pt. 1–319
Smith, Melancton, May 24, 1810–July 19, 1893.
  Vol. 9, Pt. 1–320
Smith, Meriwether, 1730–Jan. 24, 1794.
  Vol. 9, Pt. 1–321
Smith, Milton Hannibal, Sept. 12, 1836–Feb. 22, 1921.
  Vol. 9, Pt. 1–322
Smith, Morgan Lewis, Mar. 8, 1821–Dec. 28, 1874.
  Vol. 9, Pt. 1–323
Smith, Nathan, Sept. 30, 1762–Jan. 26, 1829.
  Vol. 9, Pt. 1–324
Smith, Nathan, Jan. 8, 1770–Dec. 6, 1835.
  Vol. 9, Pt. 1–327
Smith, Nathaniel, Jan. 6, 1762–Mar. 9, 1822.
  Vol. 9, Pt. 1–329

Smith, Nathan Ryno, May 21, 1797–July 3, 1877.
    Vol. 9, Pt. 1–327
Smith, Oliver, Jan. 20, 1766–Dec. 22, 1845.
    Vol. 9, Pt. 1–329
Smith, Oliver Hampton, Oct. 23, 1794–Mar. 19, 1859.
    Vol. 9, Pt. 1–330
Smith, Ormond Gerald, Aug. 30, 1860–Apr. 17, 1933.
    Supp. 1–664
Smith, Persifor Frazer, Nov. 16, 1798–May 17, 1858.
    Vol. 9, Pt. 1–331
Smith, Peter, Nov. 15, 1768–Apr. 14, 1837.
    Vol. 9, Pt. 1–332
Smith, Preserved, July 22, 1880–May 15, 1911.
    Supp. 3–725
Smith, Richard, Mar. 22, 1735–Sept. 17, 1803.
    Vol. 9, Pt. 1–332
Smith, Richard Penn, Mar. 13, 1799–Aug. 12, 1854.
    Vol. 9, Pt. 1–333
Smith, Richard Somers, Oct. 30, 1813–Jan. 23, 1877.
    Vol. 9, Pt. 1–334
Smith, Robert, c. 1722–Feb. 11, 1777.
    Vol. 9, Pt. 1–335
Smith, Robert, Aug. 14, 1732–o.s. Oct. 28, 1801.
    Vol. 9, Pt. 1–336
Smith, Robert, Nov. 3, 1757–Nov. 26, 1842.
    Vol. 9, Pt. 1–337
Smith, Robert Alexander C., Feb. 22, 1857–July 27, 1933.
    Vol. 9, Pt. 1–338
Smith, Robert Barnwell. [See Rhett, Robert Barnwell, 1800–1876.]
Smith, Robert Hardy, Mar. 21, 1813–Mar. 13, 1878.
    Vol. 9, Pt. 1–339
Smith, Robert Sidney, Feb. 13, 1877–Oct. 20, 1935.
    Supp. 1–665
Smith, Roswell, Mar. 30, 1829–Apr. 19, 1892.
    Vol. 9, Pt. 1–339
Smith, Russell, Apr. 26, 1812–Nov. 8, 1896.
    Vol. 9, Pt. 1–340
Smith, Samuel, July 27, 1752–Apr. 22, 1839.
    Vol. 9, Pt. 1–341
Smith, Samuel Francis, Oct. 21, 1808–Nov. 16, 1895.
    Vol. 9, Pt. 1–342
Smith, Samuel Harrison, 1772–Nov. 1, 1845.
    Vol. 9, Pt. 1–343
Smith, Samuel Stanhope, Mar. 16, 1750–Aug. 21, 1819.
    Vol. 9, Pt. 1–344
Smith, Seba, Sept. 14, 1792–July 28, 1868.
    Vol. 9, Pt. 1–345
Smith, Solomon Franklin, Apr. 20, 1801–Feb. 14, 1869.
    Vol. 9, Pt. 1–346
Smith, Sophia, Aug. 27, 1796–June 12, 1870.
    Vol. 9, Pt. 1–347
Smith, Stephen, Feb. 19, 1823–Aug. 26, 1922.
    Vol. 9, Pt. 1–348
Smith, Theobald, July 31, 1859–Dec. 10, 1934.
    Supp. 1–665
Smith, Theodate Louise, Apr. 9, 1859–Feb. 16, 1914.
    Vol. 9, Pt. 1–349
Smith, Thomas Adams, Aug. 12, 1781–June 25, 1844.
    Supp. 1–667
Smith, Thomas Vernor, Apr. 26, 1890–May 24, 1964.
    Supp. 7–701
Smith, Truman, Nov. 27, 1791–May 3, 1884.
    Vol. 9, Pt. 1–350
Smith, Uriah, May 2, 1832–Mar. 6, 1903.
    Vol. 9, Pt. 1–350
Smith, Walter Bedell, Oct. 5, 1895–Aug. 9, 1961.
    Supp. 7–702
Smith, Walter Inglewood, July 10, 1862–Jan. 27, 1922.
    Vol. 9, Pt. 1–351
Smith, William, Oct. 8, 1697–Nov. 22, 1769.
    Vol. 9, Pt. 1–352
Smith, William, Sept. 7, 1727–May 14, 1803.
    Vol. 9, Pt. 1–353
Smith, William, June 25, 1728–Dec. 3, 1793.
    Vol. 9, Pt. 1–357
Smith, William, c. 1754–Apr. 6, 1821.
    Vol. 9, Pt. 1–358
Smith, William, c. 1762–June 26, 1840.
    Vol. 9, Pt. 1–359
Smith, William, Sept. 6, 1797–May 18, 1887.
    Vol. 9, Pt. 1–361

Smith, William Andrew, Nov. 29, 1802–Mar. 1, 1870.
    Vol. 9, Pt. 1–361
Smith, William Farrar, Feb. 17, 1824–Feb. 28, 1903.
    Vol. 9, Pt. 1–362
Smith, William Henry, Dec. 4, 1806–Jan. 17, 1872.
    Vol. 9, Pt. 1–363
Smith, William Henry, Dec. 1, 1833–July 27, 1896.
    Vol. 9, Pt. 1–364
Smith, William Loughton, c. 1758–Dec. 19, 1812.
    Vol. 9, Pt. 1–365
Smith, William Nathan Harrell, Sept. 24, 1812–Nov. 14, 1889. Vol. 9, Pt. 1–366
Smith, William Russell, Mar. 27, 1815–Feb. 26, 1896.
    Vol. 9, Pt. 1–366
Smith, William Sooy, July 22, 1830–Mar. 4, 1916.
    Vol. 9, Pt. 1–367
Smith, William Stephens, Nov. 8, 1755–June 10, 1816.
    Vol. 9, Pt. 1–368
Smith, William Waugh, Mar. 12, 1845–Nov. 29, 1912.
    Vol. 9, Pt. 1–369
Smith, Winchell, Apr. 5, 1871–June 10, 1933.
    Vol. 9, Pt. 1–370
Smith, Xanthus Russell, Feb. 26, 1839–Dec. 2, 1929.
    Vol. 9, Pt. 1–371
Smith James Youngs, Sept 15, 1809–Mar. 26, 1876.
    Vol. 9, Pt. 1–289
Smohalla, c. 1815–1907.
    Vol. 9, Pt. 1–371
Smoot, Reed Owen, Jan. 10, 1862–Feb. 9, 1941.
    Supp. 3–726
Smyth, Albert Henry, June 18, 1863–May 4, 1907.
    Vol. 9, Pt. 1–372
Smyth, Alexander, 1765–Apr. 17, 1830.
    Vol. 9, Pt. 1–373
Smyth, Egbert Coffin, Aug. 24, 1829–Apr. 12, 1904.
    Vol. 9, Pt. 1–374
Smyth, Herbert Weir, Aug. 8, 1857–July 16, 1937.
    Supp. 2–620
Smyth, John Henry, July 14, 1844–Sept. 5, 1908.
    Vol. 9, Pt. 1–375
Smyth, Julian Kennedy, Aug. 8, 1856–Apr. 4, 1921.
    Vol. 9, Pt. 1–376
Smyth, Newman, June 25, 1843–Jan. 6, 1925.
    Vol. 9, Pt. 1–376
Smyth, Thomas, June 14, 1808–Aug. 20, 1873.
    Vol. 9, Pt. 1–377
Smyth, William, Feb. 2, 1797–Apr. 4, 1868.
    Vol. 9, Pt. 1–378
Snead, Thomas Lowndes, Jan. 10, 1828–Oct. 17, 1890.
    Vol. 9, Pt. 1–379
Snell, Bertrand Hollis, Dec. 9, 1870–Feb. 2, 1958.
    Supp. 6–587
Snelling, Henry Hunt, Nov. 8, 1817–June 24, 1897.
    Vol. 9, Pt. 1–379
Snelling, Josiah, 1782–Aug. 20, 1828.
    Vol. 9, Pt. 1–380
Snelling, William Joseph, Dec. 26, 1804–Dec. 24, 1848.
    Vol. 9, Pt. 1–381
Snethen, Nicholas, Nov. 15, 1769–May 30, 1845.
    Vol. 9, Pt. 1–382
Snider, Denton Jaques, Jan. 9, 1841–Nov. 25, 1925.
    Vol. 9, Pt. 1–383
Snow, Carmel White, Aug. 21, 1887–May 7, 1961.
    Supp. 7–704
Snow, Eliza Roxey, Jan. 21, 1804–Dec. 5, 1887.
    Vol. 9, Pt. 1–384
Snow, Francis Huntington, June 29, 1840–Sept. 20, 1908.
    Vol. 9, Pt. 1–385
Snow, Jessie Baker, May 26, 1868–June 16, 1947.
    Supp. 4–756
Snow, Lorenza, Apr. 3, 1814–Oct. 10, 1901.
    Vol. 9, Pt. 1–386
Snow, William Freeman, July 13, 1874–June 12, 1950.
    Supp. 4–758
Snowden, James Ross, Dec. 9, 1809–Mar. 21, 1878.
    Vol. 9, Pt. 1–387
Snowden, Thomas, Aug. 12, 1857–Jan. 27, 1930.
    Vol. 9, Pt. 1–387
Snyder, Edwin Reagan, Sept. 2, 1872–Jan. 13, 1925.
    Vol. 9, Pt. 1–388
Snyder, Howard McCrum, Feb. 7, 1881–Sept. 22, 1970.
    Supp. 8–608

Snyder, John Francis, Mar. 22, 1830–Apr. 30, 1921.
    Vol. 9, Pt. 1–389
Snyder, Simon, Nov. 5, 1759–Nov. 9, 1819.
    Vol. 9, Pt. 1–389
Sobolewski, J. Friedrich Eduard, Oct. 1, 1808–May 17, 1872.
    Vol. 9, Pt. 1–390
Sokolsky, George Ephraim, Sept. 5, 1893–Dec. 12, 1962.
    Supp. 7–705
Soldan, Frank Louis, Oct. 20, 1842–Mar. 27, 1908.
    Vol. 9, Pt. 1–391
Soley, James Russell, Oct. 1, 1850–Sept. 11, 1911.
    Vol. 9, Pt. 1–392
Solger, Reinhold, July 17, 1817–Jan. 11, 1866.
    Vol. 9, Pt. 1–392
Solis-Cohen, Jacob Da Silva. [See Cohen, Jacob Da Silva Solis, 1838–1927.]
Solomons, Adolphus Simeon, Oct. 26, 1826–Mar. 18, 1910.
    Vol. 9, Pt. 1–393
Somers, Richard, Sept. 15, 1778–Sept. 4, 1804.
    Vol. 9, Pt. 1–394
Somervell, Brehon Burke, May 9, 1892–Feb. 13, 1955.
    Supp. 5–642
Sonneck, Oscar George Theodore, Oct. 6, 1873–Oct. 30, 1928. Vol. 9, Pt. 1–395
Sonnichsen, Albert, May 5, 1878–Aug. 15, 1931.
    Vol. 9, Pt. 1–396
Son of Many Beads, c. 1866–July 30, 1954.
    Supp. 5–644
Sooysmith, Charles, July 20, 1856–June 1, 1916.
    Vol. 9, Pt. 1–397
Sophocles, Evangelinus Apostolides, c. 1805–Dec. 17, 1883.
    Vol. 9, Pt. 1–397
Sorensen, Charles, Sept. 27, 1881–Aug. 13, 1968.
    Supp. 8–609
Sorge, Friedrich Adolph, Nov. 9, 1828–Oct. 26, 1906.
    Vol. 9, Pt. 1–398
Sorin, Edward Frederick, Feb. 6, 1814–Oct. 31, 1893.
    Vol. 9, Pt. 1–399
Sothern, Edward Askew, Apr. 1, 1826–Jan. 20, 1881.
    Vol. 9, Pt. 1–400
Sothern, Edward Hugh, Dec. 6, 1859–Oct. 28, 1933.
    Vol. 9, Pt. 1–401
Soto, Hernando De. [See De Soto, Hernando, c. 1500–1542.]
Souchon, Edmond, Dec. 1, 1841–Aug. 5, 1924.
    Vol. 9, Pt. 1–402
Soulé, George, May 14, 1834–Jan. 26, 1926.
    Vol. 9, Pt. 1–403
Soule, Joshua, Aug. 1, 1781–Mar. 6, 1867.
    Vol. 9, Pt. 1–404
Soulé, Pierre, Aug. 31, 1801–Mar. 26, 1870.
    Vol. 9, Pt. 1–405
Sousa, John Philip, Nov. 6, 1854–Mar. 6, 1932.
    Vol. 9, Pt. 1–407
Southack, Cyprian, Mar. 25, 1662–Mar. 27, 1745.
    Vol. 9, Pt. 1–408
Southall, James Cocke, Apr. 2, 1828–Sept. 13, 1897.
    Vol. 9, Pt. 1–409
Southard, Elmer Ernest, July 28, 1876–Feb. 8, 1920.
    Vol. 9, Pt. 1–410
Southard, Lucien H., Feb. 4, 1827–Jan. 10, 1881.
    Vol. 9, Pt. 1–411
Southard, Samuel Lewis, June 9, 1787–June 26, 1842.
    Vol. 9, Pt. 1–411
Southern, Julia Marlowe. [See Marlowe, Julia.]
Southgate, Horatio, July 5, 1812–Apr. 12, 1894.
    Supp. 1–668
Southmayd, Charles Ferdinand, Nov. 27, 1824–July 11, 1911.
    Vol. 9, Pt. 1–412
Southwick, Solomon, Dec. 25, 1773–Nov. 18, 1839.
    Vol. 9, Pt. 1–413
Southworth, Emma Dorothy Eliza Nevitte, Dec. 26, 1819–June 30, 1899. Vol. 9, Pt. 1–414
Sower, Christopher, 1693–Sept. 25, 1758.
    Vol. 9, Pt. 1–415
Sower, Christopher, September 1721–Aug. 26, 1784.
    Vol. 9, Pt. 1–416
Sower, Christopher, Jan. 27, 1754–July 3, 1799.
    Vol. 9, Pt. 1–417
Spaeth, Adolph, Oct. 29, 1839–June 25, 1910.
    Vol. 9, Pt. 1–418
Spaeth, John Duncan, Sept. 27, 1868–July 26, 1954.
    Supp. 5–645

Spaeth, Sigmund, Apr. 10, 1885–Nov. 11, 1965.
    Supp. 7–706
Spahr, Charles Barzillai, July 20, 1860–Aug. 30, 1904.
    Vol. 9, Pt. 1–418
Spaight, Richard Dobbs, Mar. 25, 1758–Sept. 6, 1802.
    Vol. 9, Pt. 1–419
Spalding, Albert, Aug. 15, 1888–May 26, 1953.
    Supp. 5–646
Spalding, Albert Goodwill, Sept. 2, 1850–Sept. 9, 1915.
    Vol. 9, Pt. 1–420
Spalding, Catherine, Dec. 23, 1793–Mar. 20, 1858.
    Vol. 9, Pt. 1–421
Spalding, Franklin Spencer, Mar. 13, 1865–Sept. 25, 1914.
    Vol. 9, Pt. 1–422
Spalding, John Lancaster, June 2, 1840–Aug. 25, 1916.
    Vol. 9, Pt. 1–422
Spalding, Lyman, June 5, 1775–Oct. 21, 1821.
    Vol. 9, Pt. 1–423
Spalding, Martin John, May 23, 1810–Feb. 7, 1872.
    Vol. 9, Pt. 1–424
Spalding, Thomas, Mar. 26, 1774–Jan. 4, 1851.
    Vol. 9, Pt. 1–426
Spalding, Volney Morgan, Jan. 29, 1849–Nov. 12, 1918.
    Vol. 9, Pt. 1–427
Spangenberg, Augustus Gottlieb, July 15, 1704–Sept. 18, 1792. Vol. 9, Pt. 1–428
Spangler, Edward. [See Booth, John Wilkes, 1838–1865.]
Spangler, Henry Wilson, Jan. 18, 1858–Mar. 17, 1912.
    Vol. 9, Pt. 1–429
Spargo, John, Jan. 31, 1876–Aug. 17, 1966.
    Supp. 8–610
Sparks, Edwin Erle, July 16, 1860–June 15, 1924.
    Vol. 9, Pt. 1–430
Sparks, Jared, May 10, 1789–Mar. 14, 1866.
    Vol. 9, Pt. 1–430
Sparks, William Andrew Jackson, Nov. 19, 1828–May 7, 1904. Vol. 9, Pt. 1–434
Sparrow, William, Mar. 12, 1801–Jan. 17, 1874.
    Vol. 9, Pt. 1–435
Spaulding, Charles Clinton, Aug. 1, 1874–Aug. 1, 1952.
    Supp. 5–647
Spaulding, Edward Gleason, Aug. 6, 1873–Jan. 31, 1940.
    Supp. 2–621
Spaulding, Elbridge Gerry, Feb. 24, 1809–May 5, 1897.
    Vol. 9, Pt. 1–436
Spaulding, Levi, Aug. 22, 1791–June 18, 1873.
    Vol. 9, Pt. 1–437
Spaulding, Oliver Lyman, Aug. 2, 1833–July 30, 1922.
    Vol. 9, Pt. 1–438
Speaker, Tris E., Apr. 4, 1888–Dec. 8, 1958.
    Supp. 6–588
Speaks, Oley, June 28, 1874–Aug. 27, 1948.
    Supp. 4–759
Spear, Charles, May 1, 1801–Apr. 13, 1863.
    Vol. 9, Pt. 1–438
Spear, William Thomas, June 3, 1834–Dec. 8, 1913.
    Vol. 9, Pt. 1–439
Speck, Frank Gouldsmith, Nov. 8, 1881–Feb. 6, 1950.
    Supp. 4–761
Speed, James, Mar. 11, 1812–June 25, 1887.
    Vol. 9, Pt. 1–440
Speer, Emma Bailey, May 15, 1872–Apr. 25, 1961.
    Supp. 7–707
Speer, Emory, Sept. 3, 1848–Dec. 13, 1918.
    Vol. 9, Pt. 1–441
Speer, Robert Elliott, Sept. 10, 1867–Nov. 23, 1947.
    Supp. 4–763
Speer, William, Apr. 24, 1822–Feb. 15, 1904.
    Vol. 9, Pt. 1–442
Speir, Samuel Fleet, Apr. 9, 1838–Dec. 19, 1895.
    Vol. 9, Pt. 1–443
Speiser, Ephraim Avigdor, Jan. 24, 1902–June 15, 1965.
    Supp. 7–709
Spellman, Francis Joseph, May 4, 1889–Dec. 2, 1967.
    Supp. 8–612
Spence, Brent, Dec. 24, 1874–Sept. 18, 1967.
    Supp. 8–615
Spencer, Ambrose, Dec. 13, 1765–Mar. 13, 1848.
    Vol. 9, Pt. 1–443
Spencer, Anna Garlin, Apr. 17, 1851–Feb. 12, 1931.
    Vol. 9, Pt. 1–445
Spencer, Christopher Miner, June 20, 1833–Jan. 14, 1922.
    Vol. 9, Pt. 1–446

Spencer, Cornelia Phillips, Mar. 20, 1825–Mar. 11, 1908.
Vol. 9, Pt. 1–447
Spencer, Elihu, Feb. 12, 1721–Dec. 27, 1784.
Vol. 9, Pt. 1–447
Spencer, Jesse Ames, June 17, 1816–Sept. 2, 1898.
Vol. 9, Pt. 1–448
Spencer, John Canfield, Jan. 8, 1788–May 17, 1855.
Vol. 9, Pt. 1–449
Spencer, Joseph, Oct. 3, 1714–Jan. 13, 1789.
Vol. 9, Pt. 1–450
Spencer, Pitman Clemens, July 28, 1793–Jan. 15, 1860.
Vol. 9, Pt. 1–451
Spencer, Platt Rogers, Nov. 7, 1800–May 16, 1864.
Vol. 9, Pt. 1–451
Spencer, Robert, Dec. 1, 1879–July 10, 1931.
Vol. 9, Pt. 1–452
Spencer, Samuel, Mar. 2, 1847–Nov. 29, 1906.
Vol. 9, Pt. 1–453
Sperry, Elmer Ambrose, Oct. 12, 1860–June 16, 1930.
Vol. 9, Pt. 1–454
Sperry, Nehemiah Day, July 10, 1827–Nov. 13, 1911.
Vol. 9, Pt. 1–456
Sperry, Willard Learoyd, Apr. 5, 1882–May 15, 1954.
Supp. 5–648
Speyer, James Joseph, July 22, 1861–Oct. 31, 1941.
Supp. 3–728
Spicker, Max, Aug. 16, 1858–Oct. 15, 1912.
Vol. 9, Pt. 1–456
Spier, Leslie, Dec. 13, 1893–Dec. 3, 1961.
Supp. 7–710
Spiering, Theodore, Sept. 5, 1871–Aug. 11, 1925.
Vol. 9, Pt. 1–457
Spillman, William Jasper, Oct. 23, 1863–July 11, 1931.
Vol. 9, Pt. 1–458
Spilsbury, Edmund Gybbon, Dec. 7, 1845–May 28, 1920.
Vol. 9, Pt. 1–459
Spingarn, Joel Elias, May 17, 1875–July 26, 1939.
Supp. 2–622
Spink, John George Taylor, Nov. 6, 1888–Dec. 7, 1962.
Supp. 7–711
Spinner, Francis Elias, Jan. 21, 1802–Dec. 31, 1890.
Vol. 9, Pt. 1–460
Spitzka, Edward Anthony, June 17, 1876–Sept. 4, 1922.
Vol. 9, Pt. 1–461
Spitzka, Edward Charles, Nov. 10, 1852–Jan. 13, 1914.
Vol. 9, Pt. 1–461
Spivak, Charles David, Dec. 25, 1861–Oct. 16, 1927.
Vol. 9, Pt. 1–462
Spofford, Ainsworth Rand, Sept. 12, 1825–Aug. 11, 1908.
Vol. 9, Pt. 1–463
Spofford, Harriet Elizabeth Prescott, Apr. 3, 1835–Aug. 14, 1921. Vol. 9, Pt. 1–464
Spooner, John Coit, Jan. 6, 1843–June 11, 1919.
Vol. 9, Pt. 1–465
Spooner, Lysander, Jan. 19, 1808–May 14, 1887.
Vol. 9, Pt. 1–466
Spooner, Shearjashub, Dec 3, 1809–Mar. 14, 1859.
Vol. 9, Pt. 1–467
Spotswood, Alexander, 1676–June 7, 1740.
Vol. 9, Pt. 1–467
Spotted Tail, c. 1833–Aug. 5, 1881.
Vol. 9, Pt. 1–469
Sprague, Achsa W., c. 1828–July 6, 1862.
Vol. 9, Pt. 1–469
Sprague, Charles, Oct. 26, 1791–Jan. 22, 1875.
Vol. 9, Pt. 1–470
Sprague, Charles Arthur, Nov. 12, 1887–Mar. 13, 1969.
Supp. 8–616
Sprague, Charles Ezra, Oct. 9, 1842–Mar. 21, 1912.
Vol. 9, Pt. 1–471
Sprague, Frank Julian, July 25, 1857–Oct. 25, 1934.
Supp. 1–669
Sprague, Homer Baxter, Oct. 19, 1829–Mar. 23, 1918.
Vol. 9, Pt. 1–472
Sprague, Kate Chase, Aug. 13, 1840–July 31, 1899.
Vol. 9, Pt. 1–473
Sprague, Oliver Mitchell Wentworth, Apr. 22, 1873–May 24, 1953. Supp. 5–650
Sprague, Peleg, Apr. 27, 1793–Oct. 13, 1880.
Vol. 9, Pt. 1–473
Sprague, William, June 5, 1773–Mar. 28, 1836.
Vol. 9, Pt. 1–474

Sprague, William, Sept. 12, 1830–Sept. 11, 1915.
Vol. 9, Pt. 1–475
Sprague, William Buell, Oct. 16, 1795–May 7, 1876.
Vol. 9, Pt. 1–476
Sprecher, Samuel, Dec. 28, 1810–Jan. 10, 1906.
Vol. 9, Pt. 1–477
Spreckels, Claus, July 9, 1828–Dec. 26, 1908.
Vol. 9, Pt. 1–478
Spreckels, John Diedrich, Aug. 16, 1853–June 7, 1926.
Vol. 9, Pt. 1–479
Spreckels, Rudolph, Jan. 1, 1872–Oct. 4, 1958.
Supp. 6–599
Spring, Gardiner, Feb. 24, 1785–Aug. 18, 1873.
Vol. 9, Pt. 1–479
Spring, Leverett Wilson, Jan. 5, 1840–Dec. 23, 1917.
Vol. 9, Pt. 1–480
Spring, Samuel, Feb. 27, 1746 o.s.–Mar. 4, 1819.
Vol. 9, Pt. 1–481
Springer, Charles, Dec. 19, 1857–Feb. 12, 1932.
Supp. 1–670
Springer, Frank, June 17, 1848–Sept. 22, 1927.
Vol. 9, Pt. 1–482
Springer, Reuben Runyan, Nov. 16, 1800–Dec. 11, 1884.
Vol. 9, Pt. 1–482
Springer, William McKendree, May 30, 1836–Dec. 4, 1903.
Vol. 9, Pt. 1–483
Sproul, William Cameron, Sept. 16, 1870–Mar. 21, 1928.
Vol. 9, Pt. 1–484
Sproule, William, Nov. 25, 1858–Jan. 1, 1935.
Supp. 1–671
Sproull, Thomas, Sept. 15, 1803–Mar. 21, 1892.
Vol. 9, Pt. 1–485
Spruance, Raymond Ames, July 3, 1886–Dec. 13, 1969.
Supp. 8–618
Sprunt, James, June 9, 1846–July 9, 1924.
Vol. 9, Pt. 1–486
Spurr, Josiah Edward, Oct. 1, 1870–Jan. 12, 1950.
Supp. 4–764
Squanto, d. 1622.
Vol. 9, Pt. 1–487
Squibb, Edward Robinson, July 4, 1819–Oct. 25, 1900.
Vol. 9, Pt. 1–487
Squier, Ephraim George, June 17, 1821–Apr. 17, 1888.
Vol. 9, Pt. 1–488
Squier, George Owen, Mar. 21, 1865–Mar. 24, 1934.
Vol. 9, Pt. 1–489
Squiers, Herbert Goldsmith, Apr. 20, 1859–Oct. 20, 1911.
Vol. 9, Pt. 1–490
Squire, Watson Carvosso, May 18, 1838–June 7, 1926.
Vol. 9, Pt. 1–491
Stacy, Walter Parker, Dec. 26, 1884–Sept. 13, 1951.
Supp. 5–651
Stager, Anson, Apr. 20, 1825–Mar. 26, 1885.
Vol. 9, Pt. 1–492
Stagg, Amos Alonzo, Aug. 16, 1862–Mar. 17, 1965.
Supp. 7–712
Stahel, Julius, Nov. 5, 1825–Dec. 4, 1912.
Vol. 9, Pt. 1–493
Stahlman, Edward Bushrod, Sept. 2, 1843–Aug. 12, 1930.
Vol. 9, Pt. 1–493
Stahr, John Summers, Dec. 2, 1841–Dec. 21, 1915.
Vol. 9, Pt. 1–494
Staley, Cady, Dec. 12, 1840–June 27, 1928.
Vol. 9, Pt. 1–495
Stallings, Laurence Tucker, Nov. 24, 1894–Feb. 28, 1968.
Supp. 8–621
Stallo, Johann Bernhard, Mar. 16, 1823–Jan. 6, 1900.
Vol. 9, Pt. 1–496
Stanard, Mary Mann Page Newton, Aug. 15, 1865–June 5, 1929. Vol. 9, Pt. 1–497
Stanard, William Glover, Oct. 2, 1858–May 6, 1933.
Vol. 9, Pt. 1–497
Stanbery, Henry, Feb. 20, 1803–June 26, 1881.
Vol. 9, Pt. 1–498
Stanchfield, John Barry, Mar. 30, 1855–June 25, 1921.
Vol. 9, Pt. 1–499
Standerren, Ann Lees [See Lee, Ann, 1736–1784.]
Standish, Burt L. [See Patten, Gilbert.]
Standish, Myles, c. 1584–Oct. 3, 1656.
Vol. 9, Pt. 1–500
Standley, William Harrison, Dec. 18, 1872–Oct. 25, 1963.
Supp. 7–713

Stanford, John, Oct. 20, 1754–Jan. 14, 1834.
    Vol. 9, Pt. 1–500
Stanford, Leland, Mar. 9, 1824–June 21, 1895.
    Vol. 9, Pt. 1–501
Stang, William, Apr. 21, 1854–Feb. 2, 1907.
    Vol. 9, Pt. 1–506
Stanley, Albert Augustus, May 25, 1851–May 19, 1932.
    Vol. 9, Pt. 1–506
Stanley, Ann Lee. [See Lee, Ann, 1736–1784.]
Stanley, Augustus Owsley, May 21, 1867–Aug. 12, 1958.
    Supp. 6–591
Stanley, David Sloane, June 1, 1828–Mar. 13, 1902.
    Vol. 9, Pt. 1–507
Stanley, Francis Edgar, June 1, 1849–July 31, 1918.
    Vol. 9, Pt. 1–508
Stanley, Harold, Oct. 2, 1885–May 14, 1963.
    Supp. 7–714
Stanley, Henry Morton, 1841–May 10, 1904.
    Vol. 9, Pt. 1–509
Stanley, John Mix, Jan. 17, 1814–Apr. 10, 1872.
    Vol. 9, Pt. 1–513
Stanley, Robert Crooks, Aug. 1, 1876–Feb. 12, 1951.
    Supp. 5–652
Stanley, William, Nov. 22, 1858–May 14, 1916.
    Vol. 9, Pt. 1–514
Stanly, Edward, July 13, 1810–July 12, 1872.
    Vol. 9, Pt. 1–515
Stansbury, Howard, Feb. 8, 1806–Apr. 17, 1863.
    Vol. 9, Pt. 1–516
Stansbury, Joseph, Jan. 9, 1742 o.s.?–Nov. 9, 1809.
    Vol. 8, Pt. 2–516
Stanton, Edwin McMasters, Dec. 19, 1814–Dec. 24, 1869.
    Vol. 9, Pt. 1–517
Stanton, Elizabeth Cady, Nov. 12, 1815–Oct. 26, 1902.
    Vol. 9, Pt. 1–521
Stanton, Frank Lebby, Feb 22, 1857–Jan. 7, 1927.
    Vol. 9, Pt. 1–523
Stanton, Frederick Perry, Dec. 22, 1814–June 4, 1894.
    Vol. 9, Pt. 1–523
Stanton, Henry Brewster, June 27, 1805–Jan. 14, 1887.
    Vol. 9, Pt. 1–524
Stanton, Richard Henry, Sept. 9, 1812–Mar. 20, 1891.
    Vol. 9, Pt. 1–525
Stanwood, Edward, Sept. 16, 1841–Oct. 11, 1923.
    Vol. 9, Pt. 1–526
Staples, Waller Redd, Feb. 24, 1826–Aug. 20, 1897.
    Vol. 9, Pt. 1–527
Staples, William Read, Oct. 10, 1798–Oct. 19, 1868.
    Vol. 9, Pt. 1–528
Starbuck, Edwin Diller, Feb. 20, 1866–Nov. 19, 1947.
    Supp. 4–766
Starin, John Henry, Aug. 27, 1825–Mar. 22, 1909.
    Vol. 9, Pt. 1–529
Stark, Edward Josef, Apr. 29, 1858–Apr. 22, 1918.
    Vol. 9, Pt. 1–530
Stark, John, Aug. 28, 1728–May 8, 1822.
    Vol. 9, Pt. 1–530
Stark, Louis, May 1, 1888–May 17, 1954.
    Supp. 5–653
Starks, Edwin Chapin, Jan. 25, 1867–Dec. 30, 1932.
    Supp. 1–672
Starr, Eliza Allen, Aug. 29, 1824–Sept. 7, 1901.
    Vol. 9, Pt. 1–531
Starr, Frederick, Sept. 2, 1858–Aug. 14, 1933.
    Vol. 9, Pt. 1–532
Starr, Louis, Apr. 25, 1849–Sept. 12, 1925.
    Vol. 9, Pt. 1–533
Starr, Merritt, Feb. 27, 1856–Aug. 2, 1931.
    Vol. 9, Pt. 1–534
Starr, Moses Allen, May 16, 1854–Sept. 4, 1932.
    Vol. 9, Pt. 1–534
Starrett, Laroy S., Apr. 25, 1836–Apr. 23, 1922.
    Vol. 9, Pt. 1–535
Starrett, Paul, Nov. 25, 1866–July 5, 1957.
    Supp. 6–592
Starrett, William Aiken, June 14, 1877–Mar. 26, 1932.
    Vol. 9, Pt. 1–536
Statler, Ellsworth Milton, Oct. 26, 1863–Apr. 16, 1928.
    Vol. 9, Pt. 1–537
Stauffer, David McNeely, Mar. 24, 1845–Feb. 5, 1913.
    Vol. 9, Pt. 1–538
Staughton, William, Jan. 4, 1770–Dec. 12, 1829.
    Vol. 9, Pt. 1–539

Stayton, John William, Dec. 24, 1830–July 5, 1894.
    Vol. 9, Pt. 1–540
Steagall, Henry Bascom, May 19, 1873–Nov. 22, 1943.
    Supp. 3–729
Stearns, Abel, Feb. 9, 1798–Aug. 23, 1871.
    Vol. 9, Pt. 1–540
Stearns, Asahel, June 17, 1774–Feb. 5, 1839.
    Vol. 9, Pt. 1–541
Stearns, Eben Sperry, Dec. 23, 1819–Apr. 11, 1887.
    Vol. 9, Pt. 1–542
Stearns, Frank Ballou, Nov. 6, 1878–July 5, 1955.
    Supp. 5–654
Stearns, Frank Waterman, Nov. 8, 1856–Mar. 6, 1939.
    Supp. 2–623
Stearns, Frederic Pike, Nov. 11, 1851–Dec. 1, 1919.
    Vol. 9, Pt. 1–542
Stearns, George Luther, Jan. 8, 1809–Apr. 9, 1867.
    Vol. 9, Pt. 1–543
Stearns, Harold Edmund, May 7, 1891–Aug. 13, 1943.
    Supp. 3–730
Stearns, Henry Putnam, Apr. 18, 1828–May 27, 1905.
    Vol. 9, Pt. 1–544
Stearns, Irving Ariel, Sept. 12, 1845–Oct. 5, 1920.
    Vol. 9, Pt. 1–545
Stearns, John Newton, May 24, 1829–Apr. 21, 1895.
    Vol. 9, Pt. 1–546
Stearns, Oliver, June 3, 1807–July 18, 1885.
    Vol. 9, Pt. 1–546
Stearns, Robert Edwards Carter, Feb. 1, 1827–July 27, 1909.
    Vol. 9, Pt. 1–547
Stearns, Shubal, Jan. 28, 1706–Nov. 20, 1771.
    Vol. 9, Pt. 1–548
Stearns, William Augustus, Mar. 17, 1805–June 8, 1876.
    Vol. 9, Pt. 1–549
Stebbins, Horatio, Aug. 8, 1821–Apr. 8, 1902.
    Vol. 9, Pt. 1–549
Stebbins, Rufus Phineas, Mar. 3, 1810–Aug. 13, 1885.
    Vol. 9, Pt. 1–550
Steck, George, July 19, 1829–Mar. 31, 1897.
    Vol. 9, Pt. 1–551
Stedman, Edmund Clarence, Oct. 8, 1833–Jan. 18, 1908.
    Vol. 9, Pt. 1–552
Steedman, Charles, Sept. 20, 1811–Nov. 13, 1890.
    Vol. 9, Pt. 1–553
Steedman, James Blair, July 29, 1817–Oct. 18, 1883.
    Vol. 9, Pt. 1–554
Steele, Daniel, Oct. 5, 1824–Sept. 2, 1914.
    Vol. 9, Pt. 1–555
Steele, Frederick, Jan. 14, 1819–Jan. 12, 1868.
    Vol. 9, Pt. 1–555
Steele, Joel Dorman, May 14, 1836–May 25, 1886.
    Vol. 9, Pt. 1–556
Steele, John, Nov. 16, 1764–Aug. 14, 1815.
    Vol. 9, Pt. 1–557
Steele, Wilbur Daniel, Mar. 17, 1886–May 26, 1970.
    Supp. 8–622
Steendam, Jacob, 1616–c. 1672.
    Vol. 9, Pt. 1–557
Steenwijck, Cornelis Van. [See Steenwyck, Cornelis, d. 1684.]
Steenwyck, Cornelis, d. 1684.
    Vol. 9, Pt. 1–558
Steers, George, July 20, 1820–Sept. 25, 1856.
    Vol. 9, Pt. 1–559
Stefansson, Vilhjalmur, Nov. 3, 1879–Aug. 26, 1962.
    Supp. 7–715
Steffens, Lincoln, Apr. 6, 1886–Aug. 9, 1936.
    Supp. 2–624
Stehle, Aurelius Aloysius, Apr. 30, 1877–Feb. 12, 1930.
    Vol. 9, Pt. 1–560
Stein, Evaleen, Oct. 12, 1863–Dec. 11, 1923.
    Vol. 9, Pt. 1–561
Stein, Gertrude, Feb. 3, 1874–July 27, 1946.
    Supp. 4–767
Stein, Leo Daniel, May 11, 1872–July 29, 1947.
    Supp. 4–770
Steinbeck, John Ernst, Jr., Feb. 27, 1902–Dec. 20, 1968.
    Supp. 8–624
Steiner, Bernard Christian, Aug. 13, 1867–Jan. 12, 1926.
    Vol. 9, Pt. 1–561
Steiner, Lewis Henry, May 4, 1827–Feb. 18, 1892.
    Vol. 9, Pt. 1–562

Steinert, Morris, Mar. 9, 1831–Jan. 21, 1912.
 Vol. 9, Pt. 1–563
Steinhardt, Laurence Adolph, Oct. 6, 1892–Mar. 28, 1950.
 Supp. 4–771
Steinitz, William, May 17, 1836–Aug. 12, 1900.
 Vol. 9, Pt. 1–564
Steinman, David Barnard, June 11, 1886–Aug. 21, 1960.
 Supp. 6–593
Steinmetz, Charles Proteus, Apr. 9, 1865–Oct. 26, 1923.
 Vol. 9, Pt. 1–565
Steinmeyer, Ferdinand. [See Farmer, Father, 1720–1786.]
Steinway, Christian Friedrich Theodore, Nov. 6, 1825–Mar.
 26, 1889. Vol. 9, Pt. 1–566
Steinway, Henry Engelhard, Feb. 15, 1797–Feb. 7, 1871.
 Vol. 9, Pt. 1–567
Steinway, William, Mar. 5, 1835–Nov. 30, 1896.
 Vol. 9, Pt. 1–568
Stejneger, Leonhard Hess, Oct. 30, 1851–Feb. 28, 1943.
 Supp. 3–732
Stella, Joseph, June 13, 1877–Nov. 5, 1946.
 Supp. 4–773
Stelzle, Charles, June 4, 1869–Feb. 27, 1941.
 Supp. 3–733
Stengel, Alfred, Nov. 3, 1868–Apr. 10, 1939.
 Supp. 2–628
Stephens, Alexander Hamilton, Feb. 11, 1812–Mar. 4, 1883.
 Vol. 9, Pt. 1–569
Stephens, Alice Barber, July 1, 1858–July 13, 1932.
 Vol. 9, Pt. 1–575
Stephens, Ann Sophia, 1813–Aug. 20, 1886.
 Vol. 9, Pt. 1–576
Stephens, Charles Asbury, Oct. 21, 1844–Sept. 22, 1931.
 Vol. 9, Pt. 1–577
Stephens, Edwin William, Jan. 21, 1849–May 22, 1931.
 Vol. 9, Pt. 1–577
Stephens, Henry Morse, Oct. 3, 1857–Apr. 16, 1919.
 Vol. 9, Pt. 1–578
Stephens, John Lloyd, Nov. 28, 1805–Oct. 12, 1852.
 Vol. 9, Pt. 1–579
Stephens, Linton, July 1, 1823–July 14, 1872.
 Vol. 9, Pt. 1–580
Stephens, Uriah Smith, Aug. 3, 1821–Feb. 13, 1882.
 Vol. 9, Pt. 1–581
Stephenson, Benjamin Franklin, Oct. 3, 1823–Aug. 30, 1871.
 Vol. 9, Pt. 1–582
Stephenson, Carl, Aug. 10, 1886–Oct. 3, 1954.
 Supp. 5–655
Stephenson, Isaac, June 18, 1829–Mar. 15, 1918.
 Vol. 9, Pt. 1–582
Stephenson, John, July 4, 1809–July 31, 1893.
 Vol. 9, Pt. 1–583
Stephenson, Nathaniel Wright, July 10, 1867–Jan. 17, 1935.
 Supp. 1–673
Sterett, Andrew, Jan. 27, 1778–Jan. 9, 1807.
 Vol. 9, Pt. 1–584
Sterki, Victor, Sept. 27, 1846–Jan. 25, 1933.
 Vol. 9, Pt. 1–585
Sterling, George, Dec. 1, 1869–Nov. 17, 1926.
 Vol. 9, Pt. 1–585
Sterling, James, 1701?–Nov. 10, 1763.
 Vol. 9, Pt. 1–586
Sterling, John Whalen, July 17, 1816–Mar. 9, 1885.
 Vol. 9, Pt. 1–587
Sterling, John William, May 12, 1844–July 5, 1918.
 Vol. 9, Pt. 1–588
Sterling, Ross Shaw, Feb. 11, 1875–Mar. 25, 1949.
 Supp. 4–775
Stern, Joseph William, Jan. 11, 1870–Mar. 31, 1934.
 Vol. 9, Pt. 1–589
Stern, Kurt Guenter, Sept. 19, 1904–Feb. 3, 1956.
 Supp. 6–595
Stern, Otto, Feb. 17, 1888–Aug. 17, 1969.
 Supp. 8–627
Sternberg, Constantin Ivanovich, Edler von, July 9, 1852–
 Mar. 31, 1924. Vol. 9, Pt. 1–590
Sternberg, George Miller, June 8, 1838–Nov. 3, 1915.
 Vol. 9, Pt. 1–590
Sterne, Maurice, July 13, 1878–July 23, 1957.
 Supp. 6–596
Sterne, Simon, July 23, 1839–Sept. 22, 1901.
 Vol. 9, Pt. 1–592
Sterne, Stuart. [See Bloede Gertrude, 1845–1905.]

Sterrett, James Macbride, Jan. 13, 1847–May 31, 1923.
 Vol. 9, Pt. 1–593
Sterrett, John Robert Sitlington, Mar. 4, 1851–June 15, 1914.
 Vol. 9, Pt. 1–594
Stetefeldt, Carl August, Sept. 28, 1838–Mar. 17, 1896.
 Vol. 9, Pt. 1–595
Stetson, Augusta Emma Simmons, c. 1842–Oct. 12, 1928.
 Vol. 9, Pt. 1–595
Stetson, Charles Augustus, Apr. 1, 1810–Mar. 28, 1888.
 Vol. 9, Pt. 1–596
Stetson, Charles Walter, Mar. 25, 1858–July 20, 1911.
 Vol. 9, Pt. 1–597
Stetson, Francis Lynde, Apr. 23, 1846–Dec. 5, 1920.
 Vol. 9, Pt. 1–598
Stetson, Henry Crosby, Oct. 10, 1900–Dec. 3, 1955.
 Supp. 5–656
Stetson, John Batterson, May 5, 1830–Feb. 18, 1906.
 Vol. 9, Pt. 1–599
Stetson, William Wallace, June 17, 1849–July 1, 1910.
 Vol. 9, Pt. 1–599
Stettinius, Edward Reilly, Oct. 22, 1900–Oct. 31, 1949.
 Supp. 4–776
Stettinius, Edward Riley, Feb. 15, 1865–Sept. 3, 1925.
 Vol. 9, Pt. 1–600
Steuben, Friedrich Wilhelm Ludolf Gerhard Augustin, Bar-
 on von, Sept. 17, 1730–Nov. 28, 1794. Vol. 9, Pt. 1–601
Steuben, John, Oct. 31, 1906–May 9, 1957.
 Supp. 6–597
Steuer, Max David, Sept. 6, 1870[?]–Aug. 21, 1940.
 Supp. 2–629
Stevens, Abel, Jan. 17, 1815–Sept. 11, 1897.
 Vol. 9, Pt. 1–604
Stevens, Alexander Hodgdon, Sept. 4, 1789–Mar. 30, 1869.
 Vol. 9, Pt. 1–605
Stevens, Ashton, Aug. 11, 1872–July 11, 1951.
 Supp. 5–657
Stevens, Benjamin Franklin, Feb. 19, 1833–Mar. 5, 1902.
 Vol. 9, Pt. 1–606
Stevens, Clement Hoffman, Aug. 21, 1821–July 25, 1864.
 Vol. 9, Pt. 1–607
Stevens, Doris, Oct. 26, 1892–Mar. 22, 1963.
 Supp. 7–717
Stevens, Edwin Augustus, July 28, 1795–Aug. 7, 1868.
 Vol. 9, Pt. 1–608
Stevens, Emily, Feb. 27, 1882–Jan. 2, 1928.
 Vol. 9, Pt. 1–609
Stevens, Frank Mozley, Aug. 10, 1880–Jan. 3, 1965.
 Supp. 7–718
Stevens, George Washington, Jan. 16, 1866–Oct. 29, 1926.
 Vol. 9, Pt. 1–610
Stevens, George Barker, July 13, 1854–June 22, 1906.
 Vol. 9, Pt. 1–610
Stevens, Harry Mozley, June 14, 1855–May 3, 1934.
 Supp. 7–718
Stevens, Henry, Aug. 24, 1819–Feb. 28, 1886.
 Vol. 9, Pt. 1–611
Stevens, Hiram Fairchild, Sept. 11, 1852–Mar. 9, 1904.
 Vol. 9, Pt. 1–612
Stevens, Isaac Ingalls, Mar. 25, 1818–Sept. 1, 1862.
 Vol. 9, Pt. 1–612
Stevens, John, 1749–Mar. 6, 1838.
 Vol. 9, Pt. 1–614
Stevens, John Austin, Jan. 22, 1795–Oct. 19, 1874.
 Vol. 9, Pt. 1–616
Stevens, John Austin, Jan. 21, 1827–June 16, 1910.
 Vol. 9, Pt. 1–617
Stevens, John Frank, Apr. 25, 1853–June 2, 1943.
 Supp. 3–735
Stevens, John Harrington, June 13, 1820–May 28, 1900.
 Vol. 9, Pt. 1–617
Stevens, John Leavitt, Aug. 1, 1820–Feb. 8, 1895.
 Vol. 9, Pt. 1–618
Stevens, Robert Livingston, Oct. 18, 1787–Apr. 20, 1856.
 Vol. 9, Pt. 1–619
Stevens, Thaddeus, Apr. 4, 1792–Aug. 11, 1868.
 Vol. 9, Pt. 1–620
Stevens, Thomas Holdup, Feb. 22, 1795–Jan. 21, 1841.
 Vol. 9, Pt. 1–625
Stevens, Thomas Holdup, May 27, 1819–May 15, 1896.
 Vol. 9, Pt. 1–626
Stevens, Wallace, Oct. 2, 1879–Aug. 2, 1955.
 Supp. 5–658

Stevens, Walter Husted, Aug. 24, 1827–Nov. 12, 1867.
  Vol. 9, Pt. 1–627
Stevens, William Arnold, Feb. 5, 1839–Jan. 2, 1910.
  Vol. 9, Pt. 1–627
Stevens, William Bacon, July 13, 1815–June 11, 1887.
  Vol. 9, Pt. 1–628
Stevenson, Adlai Ewing, Oct. 23, 1835–June 14, 1914.
  Vol. 9, Pt. 1–629
Stevenson, Adlai Ewing, II, Feb. 5, 1900–July 14, 1965.
  Supp. 7–719
Stevenson, Andrew, Jan. 21, 1784–Jan. 25, 1857.
  Vol. 9, Pt. 1–630
Stevenson, Carter Littlepage, Sept. 21. 1817–Aug. 15, 1888.
  Vol. 9, Pt. 1–631
Stevenson, James, Dec. 24, 1840–July 25, 1888.
  Vol. 9, Pt. 1–631
Stevenson, John James, Oct. 10, 1841–Aug. 10, 1924.
  Vol. 9, Pt. 1–632
Stevenson, John White, May 4, 1812–Aug. 10, 1886.
  Vol. 9, Pt. 1–633
Stevenson, Matilda Coxe Evans, c. 1850–June 24, 1915.
  Vol. 9, Pt. 1–634
Stevenson, Sara Yorke, Feb. 19, 1847–Nov. 14, 1921.
  Vol. 9, Pt. 1–635
Steward, Ira, May 10, 1831–Mar. 13, 1883.
  Vol. 9, Pt. 2–1
Stewardson, John, Mar. 21, 1858–Jan. 6, 1896.
  Vol. 9, Pt. 2–2
Stewart, Alexander Peter, Oct. 2, 1821–Aug. 30, 1908.
  Vol. 9, Pt. 2–3
Stewart, Alexander Turney, Oct. 12, 1803–Apr. 10, 1876.
  Vol. 9, Pt. 2–3
Stewart, Alvan, Sept. 1, 1790–May 1, 1849.
  Vol. 9, Pt. 2–5
Stewart, Andrew, June 11, 1791–July 16, 1872.
  Vol. 9, Pt. 2–6
Stewart, Charles, July 28, 1778–Nov. 6, 1869.
  Vol. 9, Pt. 2–6
Stewart, Edwin, May 5, 1837–Feb. 28, 1933.
  Vol. 9, Pt. 2–7
Stewart, Eliza Daniel, Apr. 25, 1816–Aug. 6, 1908.
  Vol. 9, Pt. 2–8
Stewart, George Neil, Apr. 18, 1860–May 28, 1930.
  Vol. 9, Pt. 2–9
Stewart, Humphrey John, May 22, 1854–Dec. 28, 1932.
  Vol. 9, Pt. 2–10
Stewart, John Aikman, Aug. 26, 1822–Dec. 17, 1926.
  Vol. 9, Pt. 2–10
Stewart, John George, June 2, 1890–May 24, 1970.
  Supp. 8–629
Stewart, Philo Penfield, July 6, 1798–Dec. 13, 1868.
  Vol. 9, Pt. 2–11
Stewart, Robert Marcellus, Mar. 12, 1815–Sept. 21, 1871.
  Vol. 9, Pt. 2–13
Stewart, Robert, Jan. 31, 1839–Oct. 23, 1915.
  Vol. 9, Pt. 2–12
Stewart, Walter Winne, May 24, 1885–Mar. 6, 1958.
  Supp. 6–598
Stewart, William Rhinelander, Dec. 3, 1852–Sept. 4, 1929.
  Vol. 9, Pt. 2–15
Stewart, William Morris, Aug. 9, 1827–Apr. 23, 1909.
  Vol. 9, Pt. 2–13
Stickney, Alpheus Beede, June 27, 1840–Aug. 9, 1916.
  Vol. 9, Pt. 2–15
Stiegel, Henry William, May 13, 1729–Jan. 10, 1785.
  Vol. 9, Pt. 2–16
Stieglitz, Alfred, Jan. 1, 1864–July 13, 1946.
  Supp. 4–778
Stieglitz, Julius, May 26, 1867–Jan. 10, 1937.
  Supp. 2–630
Stigler, William Grady, July 7, 1891–Aug. 21, 1952.
  Supp. 5–661
Stiles, Charles Wardell, May 15, 1867–Jan. 24, 1941.
  Supp. 3–737
Stiles, Ezra, Nov. 29, 1727 o.s.–May 12, 1795.
  Vol. 9, Pt. 2–18
Stiles, Henry Reed, Mar. 10, 1832–Jan. 7, 1909.
  Vol. 9, Pt. 2–21
Still, Andrew Taylor, Aug. 6, 1828–Dec. 12, 1917.
  Vol. 9, Pt. 2–21
Still, William, Oct. 7, 1821–July 14, 1902.
  Vol. 9, Pt. 2–22

Stillé, Alfred, Oct. 30, 1813–Sept. 24, 1900.
  Vol. 9, Pt. 2–23
Stillé, Charles Janeway, Sept. 23, 1819–Aug. 11, 1899.
  Vol. 9, Pt. 2–24
Stillman, James, June 9, 1850–Mar. 15, 1918.
  Vol. 9, Pt. 2–25
Stillman, Samuel, Feb. 27, 1737 o.s.–Mar. 12, 1807.
  Vol. 9, Pt. 1–26
Stillman, Thomas Bliss, May 24, 1852–Aug. 10, 1915.
  Vol. 9, Pt. 2–27
Stillman, Thomas Edgar, Mar. 23, 1837–Sept. 4, 1906.
  Vol. 9, Pt. 2–28
Stillman, William James, June 1, 1828–July 6, 1901.
  Vol. 9, Pt. 2–29
Stilwell, Joseph Warren, Mar. 19, 1883–Oct. 12, 1946.
  Supp. 4–781
Stilwell, Silas Moore, June 6, 1800–May 16, 1881.
  Vol. 9, Pt. 2–30
Stilwell, Simpson Everett, Aug. 25, 1849–Feb. 17, 1903.
  Vol. 9, Pt. 2–31
Stimpson, William, Feb. 14, 1832–May 26, 1872.
  Vol. 9, Pt. 2–31
Stimson, Alexander Lovett, Dec. 14, 1816–Jan. 2, 1906.
  Vol. 9, Pt. 2–32
Stimson, Frederic Jesup, July 20, 1855–Nov. 19, 1943.
  Supp. 3–739
Stimson, Henry Lewis, Sept. 21, 1867–Oct. 20, 1950.
  Supp. 4–784
Stimson, Julia Catherine, May 26, 1881–Sept. 29, 1948.
  Supp. 4–788
Stimson, Lewis Atterbury, Aug. 24, 1844–Sept. 17, 1917.
  Vol. 9, Pt. 2–33
Stine, Charles Milton Altland, Oct. 18, 1882–May 28, 1954.
  Supp. 5–662
Stiness, John Henry, Aug. 9, 1840–Sept. 6, 1913.
  Vol. 9, Pt. 2–34
Stirling, Lord William. [See Alexander, William, 1726–
  1783.]
Stith, William, 1707–Sept. 19, 1755.
  Vol. 9, Pt. 2–34
Stitt, Edward Rhodes, July 22, 1867–Nov. 13, 1948.
  Supp. 4–790
Stobo, Robert, 1727–c. 1772.
  Vol. 9, Pt. 2–35
Stock, Frederick August, Nov. 11, 1872–Oct. 20, 1942.
  Supp. 3–740
Stockard, Charles Rupert, Feb. 27, 1879–Apr. 7, 1939.
  Supp. 2–631
Stockbridge, Henry, Sept. 18, 1856–Mar. 22, 1924.
  Vol. 9, Pt. 2–36
Stockbridge, Henry Smith, Aug. 31, 1822–Mar. 11, 1895.
  Vol. 9, Pt. 2–37
Stockbridge, Horace Edward, May 19, 1857–Oct. 30, 1930.
  Vol. 9, Pt. 2–37
Stockbridge, Levi, Mar. 13, 1820–May 2, 1904.
  Vol. 9, Pt. 2–38
Stockdale, Thomas Ringland, Mar. 28, 1828–Jan. 8, 1899.
  Vol. 9, Pt. 2–39
Stöckhardt, Karl Georg, Feb. 17, 1842–Jan. 9, 1913.
  Vol. 9, Pt. 2–40
Stockton, Charles G., Aug. 27, 1853–Jan. 5, 1931.
  Vol. 9, Pt. 2–41
Stockton, Charles Herbert, Oct. 13, 1845–May 31, 1924.
  Vol. 9, Pt. 2–41
Stockton, Frank Richard, Apr. 5, 1834–Apr. 20, 1902.
  Vol. 9, Pt. 2–42
Stockton, John Potter, Aug. 2, 1826–Jan. 22, 1900.
  Vol. 9, Pt. 2–44
Stockton, Richard, Apr. 17, 1764–Mar. 7, 1828.
  Vol. 9, Pt. 2–47
Stockton, Richard, Oct. 1, 1730–Feb. 28, 1781.
  Vol. 9, Pt. 2–45
Stockton, Robert Field, Aug. 20, 1795–Oct. 7, 1866.
  Vol. 9, Pt. 2–48
Stockton, Thomas Hewlings, June 4, 1808–Oct. 9, 1868.
  Vol. 9, Pt. 2–49
Stockwell, John Nelson, Apr. 10, 1832–May 18, 1920.
  Vol. 9, Pt. 2–50
Stoddard, Amos, Oct. 26, 1762–May 11, 1813.
  Vol. 9, Pt. 2–51
Stoddard, Charles Warren, Aug. 7, 1843–Apr. 23, 1909.
  Vol. 9, Pt. 2–52

Stoddard, David Tappan, Dec. 2, 1818–Jan. 22, 1857.
  Vol. 9, Pt. 2–52
Stoddard, Elizabeth Drew Barstow, May 6, 1823–Aug. 1,
  1902. Vol. 9, Pt. 2–53
Stoddard, John Fair, July 20, 1825–Aug. 6, 1873.
  Vol. 9, Pt. 2–54
Stoddard, John Lawson, Apr. 24, 1850–June 5, 1931.
  Vol. 9, Pt. 2–55
Stoddard, John Tappan, Oct. 20, 1852–Dec. 9, 1919.
  Vol. 9, Pt. 2–56
Stoddard, Joshua C., Aug. 26, 1814–Apr. 3, 1902.
  Vol. 9, Pt. 2–56
Stoddard, Richard Henry July 2 1825 May 12, 1903.
  Vol. 9, Pt. 2–57
Stoddard, Solomon, September 1643–Feb. 11, 1728/29.
  Vol. 9, Pt. 2–59
Stoddard, Theodore Lothrop, June 29, 1883–May 1, 1950.
  Supp. 4–791
Stoddard, William Osborn, Sept. 24, 1835–Aug. 29, 1925.
  Vol. 9, Pt. 2–60
Stoddart, James Henry, Oct. 13, 1827–Dec. 9, 1907.
  Vol. 9, Pt. 2–61
Stoddart, Joseph Marshall, Aug. 10, 1845–Feb. 25, 1921.
  Vol. 9, Pt. 2–62
Stoddert, Benjamin, 1751–Dec. 17, 1813.
  Vol. 9, Pt. 2–62
Stoeckel, Carl, Dec. 7, 1858–Nov. 1, 1925.
  Vol. 9, Pt. 2–64
Stoek, Harry Harkness, Jan. 16, 1866–Mar. 1, 1923.
  Vol. 9, Pt. 2–64
Stoessel, Albert Frederic, Oct. 11, 1894–May 12, 1943.
  Supp. 3–742
Stoever, Martin Luther, Feb. 17, 1820–July 22, 1870.
  Vol. 9, Pt. 2–65
Stokes, Anson Phelps, Feb. 22, 1838–June 28, 1913.
  Vol. 9, Pt. 2–66
Stokes, Anson Phelps, Apr. 13, 1874–Aug. 13, 1958.
  Supp. 6–599
Stokes, Caroline Phelps, 1854–1909. [See Stokes, Olivia
  Egleston Phelps, 1847–1927.]
Stokes, Frederick Abbot, Nov. 4, 1857–Nov. 15, 1939.
  Supp. 2–633
Stokes, Isaac Newton Phelps, Apr. 11, 1867–Dec. 18, 1944.
  Supp. 3–743
Stokes, Maurice, June 17, 1933–Apr. 6, 1970.
  Supp. 8–631
Stokes, Montfort, Mar. 12, 1762–Nov. 4, 1842.
  Vol. 9, Pt. 2–67
Stokes, Olivia Egleston Phelps, Jan. 11, 1847–Dec. 14,
  1927. Vol. 9, Pt. 2–68
Stokes, Rose Harriet Pastor, July 18, 1879–June 20, 1933.
  Vol. 9, Pt. 2–68
Stokes, Thomas Lunsford, Jr., Nov. 1, 1898–May 14, 1958.
  Supp. 6–601
Stokes, William Earl Dodge, May 22, 1852–May 19, 1926.
  Vol. 9, Pt. 2–69
Stolberg, Benjamin, Nov. 30, 1891–Jan. 21, 1951.
  Supp. 5–663
Stone, Abraham, Oct. 30, 1890–July 3, 1959.
  Supp. 6–602
Stone, Amasa, Apr. 27, 1818–May 11, 1883.
  Vol. 9, Pt. 2–70
Stone, Barton Warren, Dec. 24, 1772–Nov. 9, 1844.
  Vol. 9, Pt. 2–71
Stone, Charles Augustus, Jan. 16, 1867–Feb. 25, 1941.
  Supp. 3–744
Stone, Charles Pomeroy, Sept. 30, 1824–Jan. 24, 1887.
  Vol. 9, Pt. 2–72
Stone, David, Feb. 17, 1770–Oct. 7, 1818.
  Vol. 9, Pt. 2–72
Stone, David Marvin, Dec. 23, 1817–Apr. 2, 1895.
  Vol. 9, Pt. 2–73
Stone, Ellen Maria, July 24, 1846–Dec. 13, 1927.
  Vol. 9, Pt. 2–74
Stone, George Washington, Oct. 24, 1811–Mar. 11, 1894.
  Vol. 9, Pt. 2–74
Stone, Harlan Fiske, Oct. 11, 1872–Apr. 22, 1946.
  Supp. 4–799
Stone, Horatio, Dec. 25, 1808–Aug. 25, 1875.
  Vol. 9, Pt. 2–75
Stone, James Kent, Nov. 10, 1840–Oct. 14, 1921.
  Vol. 9, Pt. 2–76

Stone, John Augustus, Dec. 15, 1800–May 29, 1834.
  Vol. 9, Pt. 2–77
Stone, John Marshall, Apr. 30, 1830–Mar. 26, 1900.
  Vol. 9, Pt. 2–78
Stone, John Seely, Oct. 7, 1795–Jan. 13, 1882.
  Vol. 9, Pt. 2–79
Stone, John Stone, Sept. 24, 1869–May 20, 1943.
  Supp. 3–747
Stone, John Wesley, July 18, 1838–Mar. 24, 1922.
  Vol. 9, Pt. 2–79
Stone, Lucy, Aug. 13, 1818–Oct. 18, 1893.
  Vol. 9, Pt. 2–80
Stone, Melville Elijah, Aug. 22, 1848–Feb. 15, 1929.
  Vol. 9, Pt. 2–81
Stone, Ormond, Jan. 11, 1847–Jan. 17, 1933.
  Supp. 1–674
Stone, Richard French, Apr. 1, 1844–Oct. 3, 1913.
  Vol. 9, Pt. 2–83
Stone, Samuel, July 1602–July 20, 1663.
  Vol. 9, Pt. 2–83
Stone, Thomas, 1743–Oct. 5, 1787.
  Vol. 9, Pt. 2–84
Stone, Warren, Feb. 3, 1808–Dec. 6, 1872.
  Vol. 9, Pt. 2–85
Stone, Warren Sanford, Feb. 1, 1860–June 12, 1925.
  Vol. 9, Pt. 2–86
Stone, Wilbur Fisk, Dec. 28, 1833–Dec. 27, 1920.
  Vol. 9, Pt. 2–86
Stone, William, c. 1603–c. 1660.
  Vol. 9, Pt. 2–87
Stone, William Joel, May 7, 1848–Apr. 14, 1918.
  Vol. 9, Pt. 2–88
Stone, William Leete, Apr. 20, 1792–Aug. 15, 1844.
  Vol. 9, Pt. 2–89
Stone, William Leete, Apr. 4, 1835–June 11, 1908.
  Vol. 9, Pt. 2–90
Stone, William Oliver, Sept. 26, 1830–Sept. 15, 1875.
  Vol. 9, Pt. 2–91
Stone, Witmer, Sept. 22, 1866–May 23, 1939.
  Supp. 2–633
Stoneman, George, Aug. 8, 1822–Sept. 5, 1894.
  Vol. 9, Pt. 2–92
Stong, Phil(lip Duffield), Jan. 27, 1899–Apr. 26, 1957.
  Supp. 6–603
Storer, Bellamy, Aug. 28, 1847–Nov. 12, 1922.
  Vol. 9, Pt. 2–93
Storer, David Humphreys, Mar. 26, 1804–Sept. 10, 1891.
  Vol. 9, Pt. 2–93
Storer, Francis Humphreys, Mar. 27, 1832–July 30, 1914.
  Vol. 9, Pt. 2–94
Storer, Horatio Robinson, Feb. 27, 1830–Sept. 18, 1922.
  Vol. 9, Pt. 2–95
Storey, Moorfield, Mar. 19, 1845–Oct. 24, 1929.
  Vol. 9, Pt. 2–96
Storey, Wilbur Fisk, Dec. 19, 1819–Oct. 27, 1884.
  Vol. 9, Pt. 2–97
Storrow, Charles Storer, Mar. 25, 1809–Apr. 30, 1904.
  Vol. 9, Pt. 2–98
Storrow, James Jackson. July 29, 1837–Apr. 15, 1897.
  Vol. 9, Pt. 2–99
Storrs, Richard Salter, Feb. 6, 1787–Aug. 11, 1873.
  Vol. 9, Pt. 2–100
Storrs, Richard Salter, Aug. 21, 1821–June 5, 1900.
  Vol. 9, Pt. 2–101
Story, Isaac, Aug. 7, 1774–July 19, 1803.
  Vol. 9, Pt. 2–102
Story, Joseph, Sept. 18, 1779–Sept. 10, 1845.
  Vol. 9, Pt. 2–102
Story, Julian Russell, Sept. 8, 1857–Feb. 23, 1919.
  Vol. 9, Pt. 2–108
Story, William Edward, Apr. 29, 1850–Apr. 10, 1930.
  Vol. 9, Pt. 2–109
Story, William Wetmore, Feb. 12, 1819–Oct. 7, 1895.
  Vol. 9, Pt. 2–109
Stotesbury, Edward Townsend, Feb. 26, 1849–May 16, 1938.
  Supp. 2–634
Stott, Henry Gordon, May 13, 1866–Jan. 15, 1917.
  Vol. 9, Pt. 2–111
Stouffer, Samuel Andrew, June 6, 1900–Aug. 24, 1960.
  Supp. 6–604
Stoughton, Edwin Wallace, May 1, 1818–Jan. 7, 1882.
  Vol. 9, Pt. 2–112

Stoughton, William, Sept. 30, 1631–July 7, 1701.
    Vol. 9, Pt. 2–113
Stovall, Pleasant Alexander, July 10, 1857–May 14, 1935.
    Supp. 1–675
Stow, Baron, June 16. 1801–Dec. 27, 1869.
    Vol. 9, Pt. 2–114
Stowe, Calvin Ellis, Apr. 26, 1802–Aug. 22, 1886.
    Vol. 9, Pt. 2–115
Stowe, Harriet Elizabeth Beecher, June 14, 1811–July 1,
    1896. Vol. 9, Pt. 2–115
Strachey, William, fl. 1606–1618.
    Vol. 9, Pt. 2–120
Straight, Willard Dickerman, Jan. 31, 1880–Dec. 1, 1918.
    Vol. 9, Pt. 2–121
Strain, Isaac G., Mar. 4, 1821–May 14, 1857.
    Vol. 9, Pt. 2–122
Stranahan, James Samuel Thomas, Apr. 25, 1808–Sept. 3,
    1898. Vol. 9, Pt. 2–122
Strang, James Jesse, Mar. 21, 1813–July 9, 1856.
    Vol. 9, Pt. 2–123
Strange, Michael, Oct. 1, 1890–Nov. 5, 1950.
    Supp. 4–797
Stratemeyer, Edward, Oct. 4, 1862–May 10, 1930.
    Vol. 9, Pt. 2–125
Stratemeyer, George Edward, Nov. 24, 1890–Aug. 9, 1969.
    Supp. 8–632
Straton, John Roach, Apr. 6, 1875–Oct. 29, 1929.
    Vol. 9, Pt. 2–125
Stratton, Charles Sherwood, Jan. 4, 1838–July 15, 1883.
    Vol. 9, Pt. 2–126
Stratton, Samuel Wesley, July 18, 1861–Oct. 18, 1931.
    Vol. 9, Pt. 2–127
Stratton-Porter, Gene. [See Porter, Gene Stratton, 1863–
    1924.]
Straus, Isidor, Feb. 6, 1845–Apr. 15, 1912.
    Vol. 9, Pt. 2–128
Straus, Jesse Isidor, June 25, 1872–Oct. 4, 1936.
    Supp. 2–635
Straus, Nathan, Jan. 31, 1848–Jan. 11, 1931.
    Vol. 9, Pt. 2–129
Straus, Oscar Solomon, Dec. 23, 1850–May 3, 1926.
    Vol. 9, Pt. 2–130
Straus, Percy Selden, June 27, 1876–Apr. 6, 1944.
    Supp. 3–748
Straus, Roger W(illiams), Dec. 14, 1891–July 28, 1957.
    Supp. 6–606
Straus, Simon William, Dec. 23, 1866–Sept. 7, 1930.
    Vol. 9, Pt. 2–132
Strauss, Joseph Baermann, Jan. 9, 1870–May 16, 1938.
    Supp. 2–636
Strawbridge, Robert, d. August 1781.
    Vol. 9, Pt. 2–132
Strawn, Jacob, May 30, 1800–Aug. 23, 1865.
    Vol. 9, Pt. 2–133
Strawn, Silas Hardy, Dec. 15, 1866–Feb. 4, 1946.
    Supp. 4–799
Street, Alfred Billings, Dec. 18, 1811–June 2, 1881.
    Vol. 9, Pt. 2–134
Street, Augustus Russell, Nov. 5, 1791–June 12, 1866.
    Vol. 9, Pt. 2–135
Street, Joseph Montfort, Dec. 18, 1782–May 5, 1840.
    Vol. 9, Pt. 2–136
Streeter, George Linius, Jan. 12, 1873–July 27, 1948.
    Supp. 4–800
Stribling, Thomas Sigismund, Mar. 4, 1881–July 8, 1965.
    Supp. 7–724
Strickland, William, c. 1787–Apr. 6, 1854.
    Vol. 9, Pt. 2–137
Stringfellow, Franklin, June 18, 1840–June 8, 1913.
    Vol. 9, Pt. 2–138
Stringham, Silas Horton, Nov. 7, 1797–Feb. 7, 1876.
    Vol. 9, Pt. 2–139
Stringham, Washington Irving, Dec. 10, 1847–Oct. 5, 1909.
    Vol. 9, Pt. 2–140
Stritch, Samuel Alphonsus, Aug. 17, 1887–May 27, 1958.
    Supp. 6–607
Strobel, Charles Louis, Oct. 6, 1852–Apr. 4, 1936.
    Supp. 2–638
Strobel, Edward Henry, Dec. 7, 1855–Jan. 15, 1908.
    Vol. 9, Pt. 2–140
Stroheim, Erich Von. [See Von Stroheim, Erich.]
Stromme, Peer Olsen, Sept. 15, 1856–Sept. 15, 1921.
    Vol. 9, Pt. 2–141

Strong, Anna Louise, Nov. 24, 1885–Mar. 29, 1970.
    Supp. 8–634
Strong, Augustus Hopkins, Aug. 3, 1836–Nov. 29, 1921.
    Vol. 9, Pt. 2–142
Strong, Benjamin, Dec. 22, 1872–Oct. 16, 1928.
    Vol. 9, Pt. 2–143
Strong, Caleb, Jan. 9, 1745–Nov. 7, 1819.
    Vol. 9, Pt. 2–144
Strong, Charles Augustus, Nov. 28, 1862–Jan. 23, 1940.
    Supp. 2–638
Strong, Charles Lyman, Aug. 15, 1826–Feb. 9, 1883.
    Vol. 9, Pt. 2–146
Strong, Harriet Williams Russell, July 23, 1844–Sept. 16,
    1926. Vol. 9, Pt. 2–147
Strong, James, Aug. 14, 1822–Aug. 7, 1894.
    Vol. 9, Pt. 2–147
Strong, James Hooker, Apr. 26, 1814–Nov. 28, 1882.
    Vol. 9, Pt. 2–148
Strong, James Woodward, Sept. 29, 1833–Feb. 24, 1913.
    Vol. 9, Pt. 2–149
Strong, Josiah, Jan. 19, 1847–Apr. 28, 1916.
    Vol. 9, Pt. 2–150
Strong, Moses McCure, May 20, 1810–July 20, 1894.
    Vol. 9, Pt. 2–151
Strong, Richard Pearson, Mar. 18, 1872–July 4, 1948.
    Supp. 4–802
Strong, Theodore, July 26, 1790–Feb. 1, 1869.
    Vol. 9, Pt. 2–152
Strong, Walter Ansel, Aug. 13, 1883–May 10, 1931.
    Vol. 9, Pt. 2–152
Strong, William, May 6, 1808–Aug. 19, 1895.
    Vol. 9, Pt. 2–153
Strong, William Barstow, May 16, 1837–Aug. 3, 1914.
    Vol. 9, Pt. 2–154
Strong, William Lafayette, Mar. 22, 1827–Nov. 2, 1900.
    Vol. 9, Pt. 2–155
Strother, David Hunter, Sept. 26, 1816–Mar. 8, 1888.
    Vol. 9, Pt. 2–156
Strubberg, Friedrich Armand, Mar. 18, 1806–Apr. 3, 1889.
    Vol. 9, Pt. 2–157
Strudwick, Edmund Charles Fox, Mar. 25, 1802–Nov. 30,
    1879. Vol. 9, Pt. 2–158
Strunsky, Simeon, July 23, 1879–Feb. 5, 1948.
    Supp. 4–803
Struve, Gustav, Oct. 11, 1805–Aug. 21, 1870.
    Vol. 9, Pt. 2–158
Struve, Otto, Aug. 12, 1897–Apr. 6, 1963.
    Supp. 7–726
Stryker, Lloyd Paul, June 5, 1885–June 21, 1955.
    Supp. 5–664
Stryker, Melancthon Woolsey, Jan. 7, 1851–Dec. 6, 1929.
    Vol. 9, Pt. 2–159
Stuart, Alexander Hugh Holmes, Apr. 2, 1807–Feb. 13,
    1891. Vol. 9, Pt. 2–160
Stuart, Archibald, Mar. 19, 1757–July 11, 1832.
    Vol. 9, Pt. 2–161
Stuart, Charles Macaulay, Aug. 20, 1853–Jan. 26, 1932.
    Vol. 9, Pt. 2–163
Stuart, Charles, 1783–1865.
    Vol. 9, Pt. 2–162
Stuart, Charles Beebe, June 4, 1814–Jan. 4, 1881.
    Vol. 9, Pt. 2–163
Stuart, Elbridge Amos, Sept. 10, 1856–Jan. 14, 1944.
    Supp. 3–749
Stuart, Francis Lee, Dec. 3, 1866–Jan. 15, 1935.
    Supp. 1–676
Stuart, Gilbert, Dec. 3, 1755–July 9, 1828.
    Vol. 9, Pt. 2–164
Stuart, Granville, Aug. 27, 1834–Oct. 2, 1918.
    Vol. 9, Pt. 2–168
Stuart, Henry Robson. [See Robson, Stuart, 1836–1903.]
Stuart, Isaac William, June 13, 1809–Oct. 2, 1861.
    Vol. 9, Pt. 2–169
Stuart, James Ewell Brown, Feb. 6, 1833–May 12, 1864.
    Vol. 9, Pt. 2–170
Stuart, John, c. 1700–Mar. 25, 1779.
    Vol. 9, Pt. 2–172
Stuart, John Leighton, June 24, 1876–Sept. 19, 1962.
    Supp. 7–727
Stuart, John Todd, Nov. 10, 1807–Nov. 28, 1885.
    Vol. 9, Pt. 2–173
Stuart, Moses, Mar. 26, 1780–Jan. 4, 1852.
    Vol. 9, Pt. 2–174

Stuart, Robert, Feb. 19, 1785–Oct. 29, 1848.
Vol. 9, Pt. 2–175
Stuart, Robert Leighton, July 21, 1806–Dec. 12, 1882.
Vol. 9, Pt. 2–176
Stuart, Ruth McEnery, May 21, 1849–May 6, 1917.
Vol. 9, Pt. 2–177
Stub, Hans Gerhard, Feb. 23, 1849–Aug. 1, 1931.
Vol. 9, Pt. 2–178
Stubbs, Walter Roscoe, Nov. 7, 1858–Mar. 25, 1929.
Supp. 1–677
Stuck, Hudson, Nov. 11, 1863–Oct. 10, 1920.
Vol. 9, Pt. 2–178
Stuckenberg, John Henry Wilbrandt, Jan. 0, 1835–May 28, 1903. Vol. 9, Pt. 2–179
Studebaker, Clement, Mar. 12, 1831–Nov. 27, 1901.
Vol. 9, Pt. 2–180
Stuhldreher, Harry A., Oct. 14, 1901–Jan. 26, 1965.
Supp. 7–728
Sturges, Preston, Aug. 29, 1898–Aug. 6, 1959.
Supp. 6–608
Sturgis, Russell, Oct. 16, 1836–Feb. 11, 1909.
Vol. 9, Pt. 2–181
Sturgis, Samuel Davis, June 11, 1822–Sept. 28, 1889.
Vol. 9, Pt. 2–182
Sturgis, William, Feb. 25, 1782–Oct. 21, 1863.
Vol. 9, Pt. 2–183
Sturtevant, Benjamin Franklin, Jan. 18, 1833–Apr. 17, 1890.
Vol. 9, Pt. 2–184
Sturtevant, Edward Lewis, Jan. 23, 1842–July 30, 1898.
Vol. 9, Pt. 2–185
Sturtevant, Julian Monson, July 26, 1805–Feb. 11, 1886.
Vol. 9, Pt. 2–186
Stutz, Harry Clayton, Sept. 12, 1876–June 25, 1930.
Vol. 9, Pt. 2–186
Stuyvesant, Petrus, 1592–February 1672.
Vol. 9, Pt. 2–187
Sublette, William Lewis, 1799?–July 23, 1845.
Vol. 9, Pt. 2–189
Sullavan, Margaret, May 16, 1909–Jan. 1, 1960.
Supp. 6–610
Sullivan, George, Aug. 29, 1771–June 14, 1838.
Vol. 9, Pt. 2–189
Sullivan, Harry Stack, Psychiatrist.
Supp. 4–805
Sullivan, James, Apr. 22, 1744–Dec. 10, 1808.
Vol. 9, Pt. 2–190
Sullivan, James Edward, Nov. 18, 1860–Sept. 16, 1914.
Vol. 9, Pt. 2–191
Sullivan, James William, Mar. 9, 1848–Sept. 27, 1938.
Supp. 2–640
Sullivan, John, Feb. 17, 1740–Jan. 23, 1795.
Vol. 9, Pt. 2–192
Sullivan, John Florence. [See Allen, Fred.]
Sullivan, John Lawrence, Oct. 15, 1858–Feb. 2, 1918.
Vol. 9, Pt. 2–193
Sullivan, Louis Henri, Sept. 3, 1856–Apr. 14, 1924.
Vol. 9, Pt. 2–194
Sullivan, Louis Robert, May 21, 1892–Apr. 23, 1925.
Vol. 9, Pt. 2–197
Sullivan, Mark, Sept. 10, 1874–Aug. 13, 1952.
Supp. 5–666
Sullivan, Timothy Daniel, July 23, 1862–Aug. 31, 1913.
Vol. 9, Pt. 2–198
Sullivan, William, November 1774–Sept. 3, 1839.
Vol. 9, Pt. 2–199
Sullivan, William Henry, Aug. 9, 1864–Jan. 26, 1929.
Vol. 9, Pt. 2–200
Sullivant, William Starling, Jan. 15, 1803–Apr. 30, 1873.
Vol. 9, Pt. 2–201
Sully, Daniel John, Mar. 9, 1861–Sept. 19, 1930.
Vol. 9, Pt. 2–201
Sully, Thomas, 1783–Nov. 5, 1872.
Vol. 9, Pt. 2–202
Sulzberger, Arthur Hays, Sept. 12, 1891–Dec. 11, 1968.
Supp. 8–636
Sulzberger, Cyrus Lindauer, July 11, 1858–Apr. 30, 1932.
Vol. 9, Pt. 2–205
Sulzberger, Mayer, June 22, 1843–Apr. 20, 1923.
Vol. 9, Pt. 2–205
Sulzer, William, Mar. 18, 1863–Nov. 6, 1941.
Supp. 3–751
Summerall, Charles Pelot, Mar. 4, 1867–May 14, 1955.
Supp. 5–668

Summers, Edith. [See Kelley, Edith Summers.]
Summers, George William, Mar. 4, 1804–Sept. 19, 1868.
Vol. 9, Pt. 2–206
Summers, Thomas Osmond, Oct. 11, 1812–May 6, 1882.
Vol. 9, Pt. 2–207
Sumner, Charles, Jan. 6, 1811–Mar. 11, 1874.
Vol. 9, Pt. 2–208
Sumner, Edwin Vose, Jan. 30, 1797–Mar. 21, 1863.
Vol. 9, Pt. 2–214
Sumner, Francis Bertody, Aug. 1, 1874–Sept. 6, 1945.
Supp. 3–752
Sumner, Increase, Nov. 27, 1746–June 7, 1799.
Vol. 9, Pt. 2–215
Sumner, James Batcheller, Nov. 19, 1887–Aug. 12, 1955.
Supp. 5–669
Sumner, Jethro, c. 1733–March 1785.
Vol. 9, Pt. 2–216
Sumner, Walter Taylor, Dec. 5, 1873–Sept. 4, 1935.
Supp. 1–678
Sumner, William Graham, Oct. 30, 1840–Apr. 12, 1910.
Vol. 9, Pt. 2–217
Sumners, Hatton, William, May 30, 1875–Apr. 19, 1962.
Supp. 7–730
Sumter, Thomas, Aug. 14, 1734–June 1, 1832.
Vol. 9, Pt. 2–219
Sunday, William Ashley, Nov. 18, 1862–Nov. 6, 1935.
Supp. 1–679
Sunderland, Eliza Jane Read, Apr. 19, 1839–Mar. 3, 1910.
Vol. 9, Pt. 2–221
Sunderland, La Roy, Apr. 22, 1804–May 15, 1885.
Vol. 9, Pt. 2–222
Surratt, John H., b. 1844. [See Booth, John Wilkes, 1838–1865.]
Surratt, Mary E., 1820–1865. [See Booth, John Wilkes, 1838–1865.]
Sutherland, Edwin Hardin, Aug. 13, 1883–Oct. 11, 1950.
Supp. 4–808
Sutherland, George, Mar. 25, 1862–July 18, 1942.
Supp. 3–753
Sutherland, Joel Barlow, Feb. 26, 1792–Nov. 15, 1861.
Vol. 9, Pt. 2–222
Sutherland, Richard Kerens, Nov. 27, 1893–June 25, 1966.
Supp. 8–637
Sutro, Adolph Heinrich Joseph, Apr. 29, 1830–Aug. 8, 1898.
Vol. 9, Pt. 2–223
Sutter, John Augustus, February 1803–June 18, 1880.
Vol. 9, Pt. 2–224
Sutton, William Seneca, Aug. 12, 1860–Nov. 26, 1928.
Vol. 9, Pt. 2–225
Suzzallo, Henry, Aug. 22, 1875–Sept. 25, 1933.
Vol. 9, Pt. 2–226
Sverdrup, Georg, Dec. 16, 1848–May 3, 1907.
Vol. 9, Pt. 2–229
Swain, Clara A., July 18, 1834–Dec. 25, 1910.
Vol. 9, Pt. 2–229
Swain, David Lowry, Jan. 4, 1801–Aug. 27, 1868.
Vol. 9, Pt. 2–230
Swain, George Fillmore, Mar. 2, 1857–July 1, 1931.
Supp. 1–680
Swain, James Barrett, July 30, 1820–May 27, 1895.
Vol. 9, Pt. 2–231
Swallow, George Clinton, Nov. 17, 1817–Apr. 20, 1899.
Vol. 9, Pt. 2–232
Swallow, Silas Comfort, Mar. 5, 1839–Aug. 13, 1930.
Vol. 9, Pt. 2–233
Swan, James, 1754–July 31, 1830.
Vol. 9, Pt. 2–234
Swan, Joseph Rockwell, Dec. 28, 1802–Dec. 18, 1884.
Vol. 9, Pt. 2–234
Swan, Timothy, July 23, 1758–July 23, 1842.
Vol. 9, Pt. 2–235
Swank, James Moore, July 12, 1832–June 21, 1914.
Vol. 9, Pt. 2–236
Swann, Thomas, c. 1806–July 24, 1883.
Vol. 9, Pt. 2–237
Swanson, Claude Augustus, Mar. 31, 1862–July 7, 1939.
Supp. 2–641
Swanton, John Reed, Feb. 19, 1873–May 2, 1958.
Supp. 6–611
Swartwout, Samuel, Nov. 17, 1783–Nov. 21, 1856.
Vol. 9, Pt. 2–238
Swasey, Ambrose, Dec. 19, 1846–June 15, 1937.
Supp. 2–642

Swayne, Noah Haynes, Dec. 7, 1804–June 8, 1884.
    Vol. 9, Pt. 2–239
Swayne, Wager, Nov. 10, 1834–Dec. 18, 1902.
    Vol. 9, Pt. 2–240
Sweeney, Martin Leonard, Apr. 15, 1885–May 1, 1960.
    Supp. 6–613
Sweeny, Peter Barr, Oct. 9, 1825–Aug. 30, 1911.
    Vol. 9, Pt. 2–241
Sweeny, Thomas William, Dec. 25, 1820–Apr. 10, 1892.
    Vol. 9, Pt. 2–242
Sweet, John Edson, Oct. 21, 1832–May 8, 1916.
    Vol. 9, Pt. 2–243
Swenson, David Ferdinand, Oct. 29, 1876–Feb. 11, 1940.
    Supp. 2–643
Swensson, Carl Aaron, June 25, 1857–Feb. 16, 1904.
    Vol. 9, Pt. 2–243
Swett, John, July 31, 1830–Aug. 22, 1913.
    Vol. 9, Pt. 2–244
Swift, Gustavus Franklin, June 24, 1839–Mar. 29, 1903.
    Vol. 9, Pt. 2–245
Swift, John Franklin, Feb. 28, 1829–Mar. 10, 1891.
    Vol. 9, Pt. 2–246
Swift, Joseph Gardner, Dec. 31, 1783–July 23, 1865.
    Vol. 9, Pt. 2–247
Swift, Lewis, Feb. 29, 1820–Jan. 4, 1913.
    Vol. 9, Pt. 2–247
Swift, Linton Bishop, July 15, 1888–Apr. 11, 1946.
    Supp. 4–810
Swift, Louis Franklin, Sept. 27, 1861–May 12, 1937.
    Supp. 2–644
Swift, Lucius Burrie, July 31, 1844–July 3, 1929.
    Vol. 9, Pt. 2–248
Swift, William Henry, Nov. 6, 1800–Apr. 7, 1879.
    Vol. 9, Pt. 2–249
Swift, Zephaniah, Feb. 27, 1759–Sept. 27, 1823.
    Vol. 9, Pt. 2–250
Swing, David, Aug. 23, 1830–Oct. 3, 1894.
    Vol. 9, Pt. 2–251
Swing, Raymond Edwards (Gram), Mar. 25, 1887–Dec. 22, 1968. Supp. 8–639
Swinton, John, Dec. 12, 1829–Dec. 15, 1901.
    Vol. 9, Pt. 2–252
Swinton, William, Apr. 23, 1833–Oct. 24, 1892.
    Vol. 9, Pt. 2–252
Swisshelm, Jane Grey Cannon, Dec. 6, 1815–July 22, 1884.
    Vol. 9, Pt. 2–253
Switzler, William Franklin, Mar. 16, 1819–May 24, 1906.
    Vol. 9, Pt. 2–254
Swope, Gerard, Dec. 1, 1872–Nov. 20, 1957.
    Supp. 6–614
Swope, Herbert Bayard, Jan. 5, 1882–June 20, 1958.
    Supp. 6–615
Sydenstricker, Edgar, July 15, 1881–Mar. 19, 1936.
    Supp. 2–645
Sydnor, Charles Sackett, July 21, 1898–Mar. 2, 1954.
    Supp. 5–671
Sykes, George, Oct. 9, 1822–Feb. 8, 1880.
    Vol. 9, Pt. 2–255
Sylvester, Frederick Oakes, Oct. 8, 1869–Mar. 2, 1915.
    Vol. 9, Pt. 2–255
Sylvester, James Joseph, Sept. 3, 1814–Mar. 15, 1897.
    Vol. 9, Pt. 2–256
Sylvis, William H., Nov. 26, 1828–July 27, 1869.
    Vol. 9, Pt. 2–257
Symmes, John Cleves, July 21, 1742–Feb. 26, 1814.
    Vol. 9, Pt. 2–258
Symons, George Gardner, 1865–Jan. 12, 1930.
    Vol. 9, Pt. 2–259
Symons, Thomas William, Feb. 7, 1849–Nov. 23, 1920.
    Vol. 9, Pt. 2–260
Syms, Benjamin, 1591?–1642.
    Vol. 9, Pt. 2–260
Syng, Philip, Sept. 29, 1703–May 8, 1789.
    Vol. 9, Pt. 2–261
Szell, George, June 7, 1897–July 30, 1970.
    Supp. 8–641
Szilard, Leo, Feb. 11, 1898–May 30, 1964.
    Supp. 7–731
Szold, Benjamin, Nov. 15, 1829–July 31, 1902.
    Vol. 9, Pt. 2–262
Szold, Henrietta, Dec. 21, 1860–Feb. 13, 1945.
    Supp. 3–756

Szyk, Arthur, June 3, 1894–Sept. 13, 1951.
    Supp. 5–672

Tabb, John Banister, Mar. 22, 1845–Nov. 19, 1909.
    Vol. 9, Pt. 2–262
Taber, John, May 5, 1880–Nov. 22, 1965.
    Supp. 7–733
Tabor, Horace Austin Warner, Nov. 26, 1830–Apr. 10, 1899.
    Vol. 9, Pt. 2–263
Taft, Alphonso, Nov. 5, 1810–May 21, 1891.
    Vol. 9, Pt. 2–264
Taft, Charles Phelps, Dec. 21, 1843–Dec. 31, 1929.
    Vol. 9, Pt. 2–265
Taft, Henry Waters, May 27, 1859–Aug. 11, 1945.
    Supp. 3–758
Taft, Lorado Zadoc, Apr. 29, 1860–Oct. 30, 1936.
    Supp. 2–647
Taft, Robert Alphonso, Sept. 8, 1889–July 31, 1953.
    Supp. 5–673
Taft, William Howard, Sept. 15, 1857–Mar. 8, 1930.
    Vol. 9, Pt. 2–266
Taggard, Genevieve, Nov. 28, 1894–Nov. 8, 1948.
    Supp. 4–811
Taggart, Thomas, Nov. 17, 1856–Mar. 6, 1929.
    Vol. 9, Pt. 2–272
Tagliabue, Giuseppe, Aug. 10, 1812–May 7, 1878.
    Vol. 9, Pt. 2–273
Tait, Arthur Fitzwilliam, Aug. 5, 1819–Apr. 28, 1905.
    Vol. 9, Pt. 2–273
Tait, Charles, Feb. 1, 1768–Oct. 7, 1835.
    Vol. 9, Pt. 2–274
Takamine, Jokichi, Nov. 3, 1854–July 22, 1922.
    Vol. 9, Pt. 2–275
Talbot, Arthur Newell, Oct. 21, 1857–Apr. 3, 1942.
    Supp. 3–759
Talbot, Emily Fairbanks, Feb. 22, 1834–Oct. 29, 1900.
    Vol. 9, Pt. 2–276
Talbot, Ethelbert, Oct. 9, 1848–Feb. 27, 1928.
    Vol. 9, Pt. 2–276
Talbot, Francis Xavier, Jan. 25, 1889–Dec. 3, 1953.
    Supp. 5–677
Talbot, Henry Paul, May 15, 1864–June 18, 1927.
    Vol. 9, Pt. 2–277
Talbot, Israel Tisdale, Oct. 29, 1829–July 2, 1899.
    Vol. 9, Pt. 2–278
Talbot, John, 1645–Nov. 29, 1727.
    Vol. 9, Pt. 2–278
Talbot, Silas, Jan. 11, 1751–June 30, 1813.
    Vol. 9, Pt. 2–280
Talbott, Harold Elstner, Mar. 31, 1888–Mar. 2, 1957.
    Supp. 6–617
Talcott, Andrew, Apr. 20, 1797–Apr. 22, 1883.
    Vol. 9, Pt. 2–281
Talcott, Eliza, May 23, 1836–Nov. 1, 1911.
    Vol. 9, Pt. 2–281
Talcott, Joseph, November 1669–Nov. 11, 1741.
    Vol. 9, Pt. 2–282
Taliaferro, Lawrence, Feb. 28, 1794–Jan. 22, 1871.
    Vol. 9, Pt. 2–283
Taliaferro, William Booth, Dec. 28, 1822–Feb. 27, 1898.
    Vol. 9, Pt. 2–283
Tallmadge, Benjamin, Feb. 25, 1754–Mar. 7, 1835.
    Vol. 9, Pt. 2–284
Tallmadge, James, Jan. 28, 1778–Sept. 29, 1853.
    Vol. 9, Pt. 2–285
Talmadge, Eugene, Sept. 23, 1884–Dec. 21, 1946.
    Supp. 4–812
Talmadge, Norma, May 2, 1897–Dec. 24, 1957.
    Supp. 6–618
Talmage, James Edward, Sept. 21, 1862–July 27, 1933.
    Vol. 9, Pt. 2–286
Talmage, John Van Nest, Aug. 18, 1819–Aug. 19, 1892.
    Vol. 9, Pt. 2–286
Talmage, Thomas DeWitt, Jan. 7, 1832–Apr. 12, 1902.
    Vol. 9, Pt. 2–287
Talvj. [See Robinson, Therese Albertine Louise Von Jakob, 1797–1870.]
Tamarkin, Jacob David, July 11, 1888–Nov. 18, 1945.
    Supp. 3–760
Tamarón, Pedro, d. Dec. 21, 1768.
    Vol. 9, Pt. 2–288
Tamiris, Helen, Apr. 23, 1903–Aug. 4, 1966.
    Supp. 8–642

Taylor, Robert Love, July 31, 1850–Mar. 31, 1912.
    Vol. 9, Pt. 2–341
Taylor, Robert Tunstall, Jan. 16, 1867–Feb. 21, 1929.
    Vol. 9, Pt. 2–343
Taylor, Samuel Harvey, Oct. 3, 1807–Jan. 29, 1871.
    Vol. 9, Pt. 2–343
Taylor, Stevenson, Feb. 12, 1848–May 19, 1926.
    Vol. 9, Pt. 2–344
Taylor, William, May 2, 1821–May 18, 1902.
    Vol. 9, Pt. 2–345
Taylor, William Chittenden, Mar. 3, 1886–Nov. 2, 1958.
    Supp. 6–623
Taylor, William Ladd, Dec. 10, 1854–Dec. 26, 1926.
    Vol. 9, Pt. 2–346
Taylor, William Mackergo, Oct. 23, 1829–Feb. 8, 1895.
    Vol. 9, Pt. 2–347
Taylor, William Rogers, Nov. 7, 1811–Apr. 14, 1889.
    Vol. 9, Pt. 2–347
Taylor, William Vigneron, Apr. 11, 1780–Feb. 11, 1858.
    Vol. 9, Pt. 2–348
Taylor, Zachary, Nov. 24, 1784–July 9, 1850.
    Vol. 9, Pt. 2–349
Tazewell, Henry, Nov. 27, 1753–Jan. 24, 1799.
    Vol. 9, Pt. 2–354
Tazewell, Littleton Waller, Dec. 17, 1774–May 6, 1860.
    Vol. 9, Pt. 2–355
Tchelitchew, Pavel, Sept. 21, 1898–July 31, 1957.
    Supp. 6–624
Teagarden, Weldon Leo ("Jack"), Aug. 20, 1905–Jan. 15,
    1964. Supp. 7–735
Teall, Francis Augustus, Aug. 16, 1822–Nov. 16, 1894.
    Vol. 9, Pt. 2–357
Teasdale, Sara, Aug. 8, 1884–Jan. 29, 1933.
    Vol. 9, Pt. 2–357
Tecumseh, Mar. 1768?–Oct. 5, 1813.
    Vol. 9, Pt. 2–358
Tedyuskung, c. 1700–Apr. 19, 1763.
    Vol. 9, Pt. 2–360
Teeple, John Edgar, Jan. 4, 1874–Mar. 23, 1931.
    Supp. 1–682
Teggart, Frederick John, May 9, 1870–Oct. 12, 1946.
    Supp. 4–823
Telfair, Edward, c. 1735–Sept. 19, 1807.
    Vol. 9, Pt. 2–361
Teller, Henry Moore, May 23, 1830–Feb. 23, 1914.
    Vol. 9, Pt. 2–362
Temple, Oliver Perry, Jan. 27, 1820–Nov. 2, 1907.
    Vol. 9, Pt. 2–363
Temple, William Grenville, Mar. 23, 1824–June 28, 1894.
    Vol. 9, Pt. 2–364
Templeton, Alec Andrew, July 4, 1910–Mar. 28, 1963.
    Supp. 7–737
Ten Broeck, Abraham, May 13, 1734–Jan. 19, 1810.
    Vol. 9, Pt. 2–365
Ten Broeck, Richard, May 1812–Aug. 1, 1892.
    Vol. 9, Pt. 2–365
Tené-Angpóte. [See Kicking Bird, d. May 3, 1875.]
Tennent, Gilbert, Feb. 5, 1703–July 23, 1764.
    Vol. 9, Pt. 2–366
Tennent, John, c. 1700–c. 1760.
    Vol. 9, Pt. 2–369
Tennent, William, 1673–May 6, 1745.
    Vol. 9, Pt. 2–369
Tennent, William, June 3, 1705–Mar. 8, 1777.
    Vol. 9, Pt. 2–370
Tenney, Charles Daniel, June 29, 1857–Mar. 14, 1930.
    Vol. 9, Pt. 2–371
Tenney, Edward Payson, Sept. 29, 1835–July 24, 1916.
    Vol. 9, Pt. 2–373
Tenney, Tabitha Gilman, Apr. 7, 1762–May 2, 1837.
    Vol. 9, Pt. 2–373
Tenney, William Jewett, 1811–Sept. 20, 1883.
    Vol. 9, Pt. 2–374
Tenskwatawa, Mar. 1768?–1834?.
    Vol. 9, Pt. 2–375
Teresa, Mother, c. 1766–Sept. 9, 1846.
    Vol. 9, Pt. 2–376
Terhune, Albert Payson, Dec. 21, 1872–Feb. 18, 1942.
    Supp. 3–766
Terhune, Mary Virginia Hawes, Dec. 21, 1830–June 3, 1922.
    Vol. 9, Pt. 2–376
Terman, Lewis Madison, Jan. 15, 1877–Dec. 21, 1956.
    Supp. 6–626

Terrell, Edwin Holland, Nov. 21, 1848–July 1, 1910.
    Vol. 9, Pt. 2–377
Terrell, Mary Eliza Church, Sept. 23, 1863–July 24, 1954.
    Supp. 5–679
Terry, Alfred Howe, Nov. 10, 1827–Dec. 16, 1890.
    Vol. 9, Pt. 2–378
Terry, David Smith, Mar. 8, 1823–Aug. 14, 1889.
    Vol. 9, Pt. 2–379
Terry, Eli, Apr. 13, 1772–Feb. 26, 1852.
    Vol. 9, Pt. 2–380
Terry, Marshall Orlando, June 21, 1848–Oct. 11, 1933.
    Vol. 9, Pt. 2–381
Terry, Milton Spenser, Feb. 22, 1840–July 13, 1914.
    Vol. 9, Pt. 2–382
Tesla, Nikola, July 9, 1856–Jan. 7, 1943.
    Supp. 3–767
Testut, Charles, c. 1818–July 1, 1892.
    Vol. 9, Pt. 2–383
Teusler, Rudolf Bolling, Feb. 25, 1876–Aug. 10, 1934.
    Vol. 9, Pt. 2–383
Tevis, Lloyd, Mar. 20, 1824–July 24, 1899.
    Vol. 9, Pt. 2–384
Thacher, Edwin, Oct. 12, 1839–Sept. 21, 1920.
    Vol. 9, Pt. 2–385
Thacher, George, Apr. 12, 1754–Apr. 6, 1824.
    Vol. 9, Pt. 2–386
Thacher, James, Feb. 14, 1754–May 23, 1844.
    Vol. 9, Pt. 2–387
Thacher, John Boyd, Sept. 11, 1847–Feb. 25, 1909.
    Vol. 9, Pt. 2–388
Thacher, Peter, July 18, 1651–Dec. 17, 1727.
    Vol. 9, Pt. 2–389
Thacher, Peter, Mar. 21, 1752–Dec. 16, 1802.
    Vol. 9, Pt. 2–390
Thacher, Samuel Cooper, Dec. 14, 1785–Jan. 2, 1818.
    Vol. 9, Pt. 2–391
Thacher, Thomas Anthony Jan. 11, 1815–Apr. 7, 1886.
    Vol. 9, Pt. 2–392
Thacher, Thomas Day, Sept. 10, 1881–Nov. 12, 1950.
    Supp. 4–825
Thalberg, Irving Grant, May 30, 1899–Sept. 14, 1936.
    Supp. 2–656
Thanet, Octave. [See French, Alice, 1850–1934.]
Thatcher, Benjamin Bussey, Oct. 8, 1809–July 14, 1840.
    Vol. 9, Pt. 2–393
Thatcher, George. [See Thacher, George, 1754–1824.]
Thatcher, Henry Knox, May 26, 1806–Apr. 5, 1880.
    Vol. 9, Pt. 2–393
Thatcher, Mahlon Daniel, Dec. 6, 1839–Feb. 22, 1916.
    Vol. 9, Pt. 2–394
Thatcher, Roscoe Wilfred, Oct. 5, 1872–Dec. 6, 1933.
    Vol. 9, Pt. 2–395
Thaw, Harry Kendall, Feb. 1, 1871–Feb. 22, 1947.
    Supp. 4–826
Thaw, William, Oct. 12, 1818–Aug. 17, 1889.
    Vol. 9, Pt. 2–396
Thaxter, Celia Laighton, June 29, 1835–Aug. 26, 1894.
    Vol. 9, Pt. 2–397
Thaxter, Roland, Aug. 28, 1858–Apr. 22, 1932.
    Vol. 9, Pt. 2–398
Thayer, Abbott Handerson, Aug. 12, 1849–May 29, 1921.
    Vol. 9, Pt. 2–399
Thayer, Alexander Wheelock, Oct. 22, 1817–July 15, 1897.
    Vol. 9, Pt. 2–401
Thayer, Amos Madden, Oct. 10, 1841–Apr. 24, 1905.
    Vol. 9, Pt. 2–402
Thayer, Eli, June 11, 1819–Apr. 15, 1899.
    Vol. 9, Pt. 2–402
Thayer, Ezra Ripley, Feb. 21, 1866–Sept. 14, 1915.
    Vol. 9, Pt. 2–403
Thayer, Gideon French, Sept. 21, 1793–Mar. 27, 1864.
    Vol. 9, Pt. 2–404
Thayer, James Bradley, Jan. 15, 1831–Feb. 14, 1902.
    Vol. 9, Pt. 2–405
Thayer, John, May 15, 1758–Feb. 17, 1815.
    Vol. 9, Pt. 2–406
Thayer, John Milton, Jan. 24, 1820–Mar. 19, 1906.
    Vol. 9, Pt. 2–407
Thayer, Joseph Henry, Nov. 7, 1828–Nov. 26, 1901.
    Vol. 9, Pt. 2–408
Thayer, Nathaniel, Sept. 11, 1808–Mar. 7, 1883.
    Vol. 9, Pt. 2–409

Thayer, Sylvanus, June 9, 1785–Sept. 7, 1872.
Vol. 9, Pt. 2–410
Thayer, Thomas Baldwin, Sept. 10, 1812–Feb. 12, 1886.
Vol. 9, Pt. 2–411
Thayer, Tiffany Ellsworth, Mar. 1, 1902–Aug. 23, 1959.
Supp. 6–627
Thayer, Whitney Eugene, Dec. 11, 1838–June 27, 1889.
Vol. 9, Pt. 2–411
Thayer, William Makepeace, Feb. 23, 1820–Apr. 7, 1898.
Vol. 9, Pt. 2–412
Thayer, William Roscoe, Jan. 16, 1859–Sept. 7, 1923.
Vol. 9, Pt. 2–413
Thayer, William Sydney, June 23, 1864–Dec. 10, 1932.
Vol. 9, Pt. 2–414
Thébaud, Augustus J., Nov. 20, 1807–Dec. 17, 1885.
Vol. 9, Pt. 2–415
Theobald, Robert Alfred, Jan. 25, 1884–May 13, 1957.
Supp. 6–628
Theobald, Samuel, Nov. 12, 1846–Dec. 20, 1930.
Vol. 9, Pt. 2–416
Theus, Jeremiah, c. 1719–May 18, 1774.
Vol. 9, Pt. 2–416
Thierry, Camille, Oct. 1814–Apr. 1875.
Vol. 9, Pt. 2–417
Thilly, Frank, Aug. 18, 1865–Dec. 28, 1934.
Supp. 1–682
Thoburn, Isabella, Mar. 29, 1840–Sept. 1, 1901.
Vol. 9, Pt. 2–418
Thoburn, James Mills, Mar. 7, 1836–Nov. 28, 1922.
Vol. 9, Pt. 2–418
Thomas, Allen, Dec. 14, 1830–Dec. 3, 1907.
Vol. 9, Pt. 2–420
Thomas, Amos Russell, Oct. 3, 1826–Oct. 31, 1895.
Vol. 9, Pt. 2–420
Thomas, Augustus, Jan. 8, 1857–Aug. 12, 1934.
Vol. 9, Pt. 2–421
Thomas, Calvin, Oct. 28, 1854–Nov. 4, 1919.
Vol. 9, Pt. 2–422
Thomas, Charles Spalding, Dec. 6, 1849–June 24, 1934.
Vol. 9, Pt. 2–423
Thomas, Christian Friedrich Theodore, Oct. 11, 1835–Jan. 4, 1905. Vol. 9, Pt. 2–424
Thomas, Cyrus, July 27, 1825–June 26, 1910.
Vol. 9, Pt. 2–426
Thomas, David, June 11, 1762–Nov. 27, 1831.
Vol. 9, Pt. 2–426
Thomas, David, Nov. 3, 1794–June 20, 1882.
Vol. 9, Pt. 2–427
Thomas, Edith Matilda, Aug. 12, 1854–Sept. 13, 1925.
Vol. 9, Pt. 2–428
Thomas, Elbert Duncan, June 17, 1883–Feb. 11, 1953.
Supp. 5–680
Thomas, Francis, Feb. 3, 1799–Jan. 22, 1876.
Vol. 9, Pt. 2–429
Thomas, Frederick William, Oct. 25, 1806–Aug. 27, 1866.
Vol. 9, Pt. 2–430
Thomas, George, c. 1695–Dec. 31, 1774.
Vol. 9, Pt. 2–431
Thomas, George Allison, 1911–Oct. 18, 1968.
Supp. 8–647
Thomas, George Clifford, Oct. 28, 1839–Apr. 21, 1909.
Vol. 9, Pt. 2–431
Thomas, George Henry, July 31, 1816–Mar. 28, 1870.
Vol. 9, Pt. 2–432
Thomas, Isaiah, Jan. 19, 1749 o.s.–Apr. 4, 1831.
Vol. 9, Pt. 2–435
Thomas, Jesse Burgess, 1777–May 3, 1853.
Vol. 9, Pt. 2–436
Thomas, Jesse Burgess, July 29, 1832–June 6, 1915.
Vol. 9, Pt. 2–437
Thomas, John, Nov. 9, 1724–June 2, 1776.
Vol. 9, Pt. 2–438
Thomas, John Charles, Sept. 6, 1891–Dec. 13, 1960.
Supp. 6–630
Thomas, John Jacobs, Jan. 8, 1810–Feb. 22, 1895.
Vol. 9, Pt. 2–439
Thomas, John Parnell, Jan. 16, 1895–Nov. 19, 1970.
Supp. 8–648
Thomas, (John William) Elmer, Sept. 8, 1876–Sept. 19, 1965.
Supp. 7–738
Thomas, John Wilson, Aug. 24, 1830–Feb. 12, 1906.
Vol. 9, Pt. 2–440

Thomas, Joseph, Sept. 23, 1811–Dec. 24, 1891.
Vol. 9, Pt. 2–440
Thomas, Lorenzo, Oct. 1804–Mar. 2, 1875.
Vol. 9, Pt. 2–441
Thomas, Martha Carey, Jan. 2, 1857–Dec. 2, 1935.
Supp. 1–684
Thomas, Norman Mattoon, Nov. 20, 1884–Dec. 19, 1968.
Supp. 8–649
Thomas, Philip Evan, Nov. 11, 1776–Sept. 1, 1861.
Vol. 9, Pt. 2–442
Thomas, Philip Francis, Sept. 12, 1810–Oct. 2, 1890.
Vol. 9, Pt. 2–443
Thomas, Richard Henry, Jan. 26, 1854–Oct. 3, 1904.
Vol. 9, Pt. 2–443
Thomas, Robert Bailey, Apr. 24, 1766–May 19, 1846.
Vol. 9, Pt. 2–444
Thomas, Roland Jay, June 9, 1900–Apr. 18, 1967.
Supp. 8–651
Thomas, Seth, Aug. 19, 1785–Jan. 29, 1859.
Vol. 9, Pt. 2–445
Thomas, Theodore. [See Thomas, Christian Friedrich Theodore, 1835–1905.]
Thomas, Theodore Gaillard, Nov. 21, 1831–Feb. 28, 1903.
Vol. 9, Pt. 2–446
Thomas, William Isaac, Aug. 13, 1863–Dec. 6, 1947.
Supp. 4–827
Thomas, William Widgery, Aug. 26, 1839–Apr. 25, 1927.
Vol. 9, Pt. 2–447
Thomes, William Henry, May 5, 1824–Mar. 6, 1895.
Vol. 9, Pt. 2–447
Thompson, Alfred Wordsworth, May 26, 1840–Aug. 28, 1896. Vol. 9, Pt. 2–448
Thompson, Arthur Webster, May 8, 1875–Nov. 9, 1930.
Vol. 9, Pt. 2–449
Thompson, Benjamin, July 14, 1642–Apr. 10?, 1714.
Vol. 9, Pt. 2–584
Thompson, Benjamin, Mar. 26, 1753–Aug. 21, 1814.
Vol. 9, Pt. 2–449
Thompson, Cephas Giovanni, Aug. 3, 1809–Jan. 5, 1888.
Vol. 9, Pt. 2–452
Thompson, Charles Oliver, Sept. 25, 1836–Mar. 17, 1885.
Vol. 9, Pt. 2–453
Thompson, Daniel Pierce, Oct. 1, 1795–June 6, 1868.
Vol. 9, Pt. 2–454
Thompson, David, Apr. 30, 1770–Feb. 10, 1857.
Vol. 9, Pt. 2–455
Thompson, David P., Nov. 8, 1834–Dec. 13, 1901.
Vol. 9, Pt. 2–455
Thompson, Denman, Oct. 15, 1833–Apr. 14, 1911.
Vol. 9, Pt. 2–456
Thompson, Dorothy, July 9, 1893–Jan. 30, 1961.
Supp. 7–739
Thompson, Edward Herbert, Sept. 28, 1856–May 11, 1935.
Supp. 1–685
Thompson, Egbert, June 6, 1822–Jan. 5, 1881.
Vol. 9, Pt. 2–457
Thompson, Hugh Miller, June 5, 1830–Nov. 18, 1902.
Vol. 9, Pt. 2–458
Thompson, Hugh Smith, Jan. 24, 1836–Nov. 20, 1904.
Vol. 9, Pt. 2–458
Thompson, Jacob, May 15, 1810–Mar. 24, 1885.
Vol. 9, Pt. 2–459
Thompson, James Maurice, Sept. 9, 1844–Feb. 15, 1901.
Vol. 9, Pt. 2–460
Thompson, Jeremiah, Dec. 9, 1784–Nov. 10, 1835.
Vol. 9, Pt. 2–461
Thompson, Jerome B., Jan. 30, 1814–May 1, 1886.
Vol. 9, Pt. 2–462
Thompson, John. [See Thomson, John, 1776–1799.]
Thompson, John, Nov. 2, 1802–Apr. 19, 1891.
Vol. 9, Pt. 2–462
Thompson, John Bodine, Oct. 14, 1830–Sept. 4, 1907.
Vol. 9, Pt. 2–463
Thompson, John Reuben, Oct. 23, 1823–Apr. 30, 1873.
Vol. 9, Pt. 2–464
Thompson, Joseph Parrish, Aug. 7, 1819–Sept. 20, 1879.
Vol. 9, Pt. 2–464
Thompson, Josiah Van Kirk, Feb. 15, 1854–Sept. 27, 1933.
Vol. 9, Pt. 2–465
Thompson, Launt, Feb. 8, 1833–Sept. 26, 1894.
Vol. 9, Pt. 2–466
Thompson, Malvina Cynthia, Jan. 9, 1893–Apr. 12, 1953.
Supp. 5–682

Thompson, Martin E., *c.* 1786–July 24, 1877.
    Vol. 9, Pt. 2–467
Thompson, Maurice. [See Thompson, James Maurice, 1844
    –1901.]
Thompson, Oscar Lee, Oct. 10, 1887–July 3, 1945.
    Supp. 3–770
Thompson, Richard Wigginton, June 9, 1809–Feb. 9, 1900.
    Vol. 9, Pt. 2–468
Thompson, Robert Ellis, Apr. 5, 1844–Oct. 19, 1924.
    Vol. 9, Pt. 2–469
Thompson, Robert Means, Mar. 2, 1849–Sept. 5, 1930.
    Supp. 1–687
Thompson, Samuel Rankin, Apr. 17, 1833–Oct. 28, 1896.
    Vol. 9, Pt. 2–470
Thompson, Seymour Dwight, Sept. 18, 1842–Aug. 11, 1904.
    Vol. 9, Pt. 2–471
Thompson, Slason, Jan. 5, 1849–Dec. 22, 1935.
    Supp. 1–688
Thompson, Smith, Jan. 17, 1768–Dec. 18, 1843.
    Vol. 9, Pt. 2–471
Thompson, Thomas Larkin, May 31, 1838–Feb. 1, 1898.
    Vol. 9, Pt. 2–473
Thompson, Waddy, Sept. 8, 1798–Nov. 23, 1868.
    Vol. 9, Pt. 2–473
Thompson, Wiley, Sept. 23, 1781–Dec. 28, 1835.
    Vol. 9, Pt. 2–474
Thompson, Will Lamartine, Nov. 7, 1847–Sept. 20, 1909.
    Vol. 9, Pt. 2–475
Thompson, William, 1736–Sept. 3, 1781.
    Vol. 9, Pt. 2–476
Thompson, William Boyce, May 13, 1869–June 27, 1930.
    Vol. 9, Pt. 2–476
Thompson, William Gilman, Dec. 25, 1856–Oct. 27, 1927.
    Vol. 9, Pt. 2–477
Thompson, William Hale, May 14, 1867–Mar. 19, 1944.
    Supp. 3–771
Thompson, William Oxley, Nov. 5, 1855–Dec. 9, 1933.
    Vol. 9, Pt. 2–478
Thompson, William Tappan, Aug. 31, 1812–Mar. 24, 1882.
    Vol. 9, Pt. 2–479
Thompson, Zadock, May 23, 1796–Jan. 19, 1856.
    Vol. 9, Pt. 2–480
Thomson, Charles, Nov. 29, 1729–Aug. 16, 1824.
    Vol. 9, Pt. 2–481
Thomson, Edward, Oct. 12, 1810–Mar. 22, 1870.
    Vol. 9, Pt. 2–482
Thomson, Edward William, Feb. 12, 1849–Mar. 5, 1924.
    Vol. 9, Pt. 2–483
Thomson, Elihu, Mar. 29, 1853–Mar. 13, 1937.
    Supp. 2–657
Thomson, Frank, July 5, 1841–June 5, 1899.
    Vol. 9, Pt. 2–483
Thomson, John, Nov. 3, 1776–Jan. 25, 1799.
    Vol. 9, Pt. 2–484
Thomson, John, Oct. 25, 1853–June 1, 1926.
    Vol. 9, Pt. 2–485
Thomson, John Edgar, Feb. 10, 1808–May 27, 1874.
    Vol. 9, Pt. 2–486
Thomson, Mortimer Neal, Sept. 2, 1831–June 25, 1875.
    Vol. 9, Pt. 2–487
Thomson, Samuel, Feb. 9, 1769–Oct. 4, 1843.
    Vol. 9, Pt. 2–488
Thomson, William, Jan. 16, 1727–Nov. 2, 1796.
    Vol. 9, Pt. 2–489
Thomson, William McClure, Dec. 31, 1806–Apr. 8, 1894.
    Vol. 9, Pt. 2–490
Thorburn, Grant, Feb. 18, 1773–Jan. 21, 1863.
    Vol. 9, Pt. 2–490
Thoreau, Henry David, July 12, 1817–May 6, 1862.
    Vol. 9, Pt. 2–491
Thorek, Max, Mar. 10, 1880–Jan. 25, 1960.
    Supp. 6–631
Thorndike, Ashley Horace, Dec. 26, 1871–Apr. 17, 1933.
    Vol. 9, Pt. 2–497
Thorndike, Edward Lee, Aug. 31, 1874–Aug. 9, 1949.
    Supp. 4–831
Thorndike, Israel, Apr. 30, 1755–May 8, 1832.
    Vol. 9, Pt. 2–498
Thorndike, Lynn, July 24, 1882–Dec. 28, 1965.
    Supp. 7–741
Thorne, Charles Robert, *c.* 1814–Dec. 13, 1893.
    Vol. 9, Pt. 2–499

Thorne, Charles Robert, 1840–Feb. 10, 1883.
    Vol. 9, Pt. 2–500
Thornton, Henry Worth, Nov. 6, 1871–Mar. 14, 1933.
    Vol. 9, Pt. 2–501
Thornton, Jessy Quinn, Aug. 24, 1810–Feb. 5, 1888.
    Vol. 9, Pt. 2–502
Thornton, John Wingate, Aug. 12, 1818–June 6, 1878.
    Vol. 9, Pt. 2–503
Thornton, Matthew, *c.* 1714–June 24, 1803.
    Vol. 9, Pt. 2–503
Thornton, William, May 20, 1759–Mar. 28, 1828.
    Vol. 9, Pt. 2–504
Thornwell, James Henley, Dec. 9, 1812–Aug. 1, 1862.
    Vol. 9, Pt. 2–507
Thorp, John, 1784–Nov. 15, 1848.
    Vol. 9, Pt. 2–508
Thorpe, James Francis, May 28, 1888–Mar. 28, 1953.
    Supp. 5–683
Thorpe, Rose Alnora Hartwick, July 18, 1850–July 19, 1939.
    Supp. 2–659
Thorpe, Thomas Bangs, Mar. 1, 1815–Sept. 20, 1878.
    Vol. 9, Pt. 2–509
Thrasher, John Sidney, 1817–Nov. 10, 1879.
    Vol. 9, Pt. 2–509
Throop, Enos Thompson, Aug. 21, 1784–Nov. 1, 1874.
    Vol. 9, Pt. 2–510
Throop, Montgomery Hunt, Jan. 26, 1827–Sept. 11, 1892.
    Vol. 9, Pt. 2–511
Thulstrup, Bror Thure, Apr. 5, 1848–June 9, 1930.
    Vol. 9, Pt. 2–512
Thumb, Tom. [See Stratton, Charles Sherwood, 1838–
    1883.]
Thurber, Charles, Jan. 2, 1803–Nov. 7, 1886.
    Vol. 9, Pt. 2–513
Thurber, Christopher Carson, May 19, 1880–May 31, 1930.
    Vol. 9, Pt. 2–513
Thurber, George, Sept. 2, 1821–Apr. 2, 1890.
    Vol. 9, Pt. 2–514
Thurber, James Grover, Dec. 8, 1894–Nov. 2, 1961.
    Supp. 7–742
Thurber, Jeannette Meyer, Jan. 29, 1850–Jan. 2, 1946.
    Supp. 4–834
Thurman, Allen Granberry, Nov. 13, 1813–Dec. 12, 1895.
    Vol. 9, Pt. 2–515
Thursby, Emma Cecilia, Feb. 21, 1845–July 4, 1931.
    Vol. 9, Pt. 2–516
Thurston, Howard, July 20, 1869–Apr. 13, 1936.
    Supp. 2–660
Thurston, Lorrin Andrews, July 31, 1858–May 11, 1931.
    Vol. 9, Pt. 2–517
Thurston, Robert Henry, Oct. 25, 1839–Oct. 25, 1903.
    Vol. 9, Pt. 2–518
Thurston, Robert Lawton, Dec. 13, 1800–Jan. 13, 1874.
    Vol. 9, Pt. 2–520
Thurstone, Louis Leon, May 29, 1887–Sept. 29, 1955.
    Supp. 5–684
Thwaites, Reuben Gold, May 15, 1853–Oct. 22, 1913.
    Vol. 9, Pt. 2–521
Thwing, Charles Franklin, Nov. 9, 1853–Aug. 29, 1937.
    Supp. 2–663
Thye, Edward John, Apr. 26, 1896–Aug. 28, 1969.
    Supp. 8–653
Tibbett, Lawrence Mervil, Nov. 16, 1896–July 15, 1960.
    Supp. 6–632
Tibbles, Susette La Flesche. [See Bright Eyes, 1854–1903.]
Tibbles, Thomas Henry, May 22, 1838–May 14, 1928.
    Vol. 9, Pt. 2–522
Tichenor, Isaac, Feb. 8, 1754–Dec. 11, 1838.
    Vol. 9, Pt. 2–523
Tichenor, Isaac Taylor, Nov. 11, 1825–Dec. 2, 1902.
    Vol. 9, Pt. 2–523
Ticknor, Elisha, Mar. 25, 1757–June 22, 1821.
    Vol. 9, Pt. 2–524
Ticknor, Francis Orray, Nov. 13, 1822–Dec. 18, 1874.
    Vol. 9, Pt. 2–525
Ticknor, George, Aug. 1, 1791–Jan. 26, 1871.
    Vol. 9, Pt. 2–525
Ticknor, William Davis, Aug. 6, 1810–Apr. 10, 1864.
    Vol. 9, Pt. 2–528
Tidball, John Caldwell, Jan. 25, 1825–May 15, 1906.
    Vol. 9, Pt. 2–529
Tiebout, Cornelius, *c.* 1773–*c.* 1830.
    Vol. 9, Pt. 2–530

Tiedeman, Christopher Gustavus, July 16, 1857–Aug. 25, 1903. Vol. 9, Pt. 2–531
Tiernan, Frances Christine Fisher, July 5, 1846–Mar. 24, 1920. Vol. 9, Pt. 2–531
Tierney, Richard Henry, Sept. 2, 1870–Feb. 10, 1928. Vol. 9, Pt. 2–532
Tiffany, Charles Lewis, Feb. 15, 1812–Feb. 18, 1902. Vol. 9, Pt. 2–533
Tiffany, Katrina Brandes Ely, Mar. 25, 1875–Mar. 11, 1927. Vol. 9, Pt. 2–533
Tiffany, Louis Comfort, Feb. 18, 1848–Jan. 17, 1933. Vol. 9, Pt. 2–534
Tiffany, Louis McLane, Oct. 10, 1844–Oct. 23, 1916. Vol. 9, Pt. 2–535
Tiffin, Edward, June 19, 1766–Aug. 9, 1829. Vol. 9, Pt. 2–535
Tigert, John James, Nov. 25, 1856–Nov. 21, 1906. Vol. 9, Pt. 2–536
Tigert, John James, IV, Feb. 11, 1882–Jan. 21, 1965. Supp. 7–744
Tikamthi. [See Tecumseh, 1768?–1813.]
Tilden, Samuel Jones, Feb. 9, 1814–Aug. 4, 1886. Vol. 9, Pt. 2–537
Tilden, William Tatem ("Big Bill"), Feb. 10, 1893–June 5, 1953. Supp. 5–686
Tileston, Thomas, Aug. 13, 1793–Feb. 29, 1864. Vol. 9, Pt. 2–541
Tilghman, Edward, Feb. 11, 1750/51–Nov. 1, 1815. Vol. 9, Pt. 2–542
Tilghman, Matthew, Feb. 17, 1718–May 4, 1790. Vol. 9, Pt. 2–543
Tilghman, Richard Albert, May 24, 1824–Mar. 24, 1899. Vol. 9, Pt. 2–544
Tilghman, Tench, Dec. 25, 1744–Apr. 18, 1786. Vol. 9, Pt. 2–545
Tilghman, William, Aug. 12, 1756–Apr. 29, 1827. Vol. 9, Pt. 2–545
Tilghman, William Matthew, July 4, 1854–Nov. 1, 1924. Vol. 9, Pt. 2–546
Tillich, Paul, Aug. 20, 1886–Oct. 22, 1965. Supp. 7–745
Tillman, Benjamin Ryan, Aug. 11, 1847–July 3, 1918. Vol. 9, Pt. 2–547
Tilney, Frederick, June 4, 1875–Aug. 7, 1938. Supp. 2–664
Tilson, John Quillin, Apr. 5, 1866–Aug. 14, 1958. Supp. 6–633
Tilton, Edward Lippincott, Oct. 19, 1861–Jan. 5, 1933. Vol. 9, Pt. 2–549
Tilton, James, June 1, 1745–May 14, 1822. Vol. 9, Pt. 2–550
Tilton, John Rollin, June 8, 1828–Mar. 22, 1888. Vol. 9, Pt. 2–551
Tilton, Theodore, Oct. 2, 1835–May 25, 1907. Vol. 9, Pt. 2–551
Tilyou, George Cornelius, Feb. 3, 1862–Nov. 30, 1914. Vol. 9, Pt. 2–553
Tilzer, Harry Von, July 8, 1872–Jan. 10, 1946. Supp. 4–835
Timberlake, Gideon, Mar. 6, 1876–Mar. 1, 1951. Supp. 5–688
Timberlake, Henry, 1730–Sept. 30, 1765. Vol. 9, Pt. 2–553
Timby, Theodore Ruggles, Apr. 5, 1822–Nov. 9, 1909. Vol. 9, Pt. 2–554
Timken, Henry, Aug. 16, 1831–Mar. 16, 1909. Vol. 9, Pt. 2–555
Timm, Henry Christian, July 11, 1811–Sept. 5, 1892. Vol. 9, Pt. 2–555
Timme, Walter, Feb. 24, 1874–Feb. 12, 1956. Supp. 6–634
Timon, John, Feb. 12, 1797–Apr. 16, 1867. Vol. 9, Pt. 2–556
Timothy, Lewis, d. December 1738. Vol. 9, Pt. 2–557
Timrod, Henry, Dec. 8, 1828–Oct. 6, 1867. Vol. 9, Pt. 2–558
Tincker, Mary Agnes, July 18, 1831–Nov. 27, 1907. Vol. 9, Pt. 2–560
Tingey, Thomas, Sept. 11, 1750–Feb. 23, 1829. Vol. 9, Pt. 2–560
Tingley, Katherine Augusta Westcott, July 6, 1847–July 11, 1929. Vol. 9, Pt. 2–561

Tinkham, George Holden, Oct. 20, 1870–Aug. 28, 1956. Supp. 6–635
Tipton, John, Aug. 15, 1730–Aug. 1813. Vol. 9, Pt. 2–562
Tipton, John, Aug. 14, 1786–Apr. 5, 1839. Vol. 9, Pt. 2–563
Tisquantum. [See Squanto, d. 1622.]
Titchener, Edward Bradford, Jan. 11, 1867–Aug. 3, 1927. Vol. 9, Pt. 2–564
Titcomb, John Wheelock, Feb. 24, 1860–Jan. 26, 1932. Vol. 9, Pt. 2–565
Tittle, Ernest Fremont, Oct. 21, 1885–Aug. 3, 1949. Supp. 4–836
Tobani, Theodore Moses, May 2, 1855–Dec. 12, 1933. Vol. 9, Pt. 2–566
Tobey, Charles William, July 22, 1880–July 24, 1953. Supp. 5–689
Tobey, Edward Silas, Apr. 5, 1813–Mar. 29, 1891. Vol. 9, Pt. 2–567
Tobias, Channing Heggie, Feb. 1, 1882–Nov. 5, 1961. Supp. 7–748
Tobin, Daniel Joseph, Apr. 3, 1875–Nov. 14, 1955. Supp. 5–690
Tobin, Maurice Joseph, May 22, 1901–July 19, 1953. Supp. 5–691
Tod, David, Feb. 21, 1805–Nov. 13, 1868. Vol. 9, Pt. 2–567
Tod, George, Dec. 11, 1773–Apr. 11, 1841. Vol. 9, Pt. 2–568
Tod, John, Nov. 1779–Mar. 27, 1830. Vol. 9, Pt. 2–569
Todd, Charles Stewart, Jan. 22, 1791–May 17, 1871. Vol. 9, Pt. 2–569
Todd, Eli, July 22, 1769–Nov. 17, 1833. Vol. 9, Pt. 2–570
Todd, Henry Alfred, Mar. 13, 1854–Jan. 3, 1925. Vol. 9, Pt. 2–571
Todd, John, Oct. 9, 1800–Aug. 24, 1873. Vol. 9, Pt. 2–572
Todd, Mabel Loomis, Nov. 10, 1856–Oct. 14, 1932. Vol. 9, Pt. 2–573
Todd, Mike, June 22, 1909–Mar. 22, 1958. Supp. 6–637
Todd, Sereno Edwards, June 3, 1820–Dec. 26, 1898. Vol. 9, Pt. 2–574
Todd, Thomas, Jan. 23, 1765–Feb. 7, 1826. Vol. 9, Pt. 2–574
Todd, Thomas Wingate, Jan. 15, 1885–Dec. 28, 1938. Supp. 2–665
Todd, Walter Edmond Clyde, Sept. 6, 1874–June 25, 1969. Supp. 8–654
Toklas, Alice Babette, Apr. 30, 1877–Mar. 7, 1967. Supp. 8–655
Toland, Hugh Huger, Apr. 16, 1806–Feb. 27, 1880. Vol. 9, Pt. 2–575
Tolley, Howard Ross, Sept. 30, 1889–Sept. 18, 1958. Supp. 6–638
Tolman, Edward Chace, Apr. 14, 1886–Nov. 19, 1959. Supp. 6–639
Tolman, Herbert Cushing, Nov. 4, 1865–Nov. 24, 1923. Vol. 9, Pt. 2–576
Tolman, Richard Chace, Mar. 4, 1881–Sept. 5, 1948. Supp. 4–837
Tome, Jacob, Aug. 13, 1810–Mar. 16, 1898. Vol. 9, Pt. 2–577
Tomkins, Floyd Williams, Feb. 7, 1850–Mar. 24, 1932. Vol. 9, Pt. 2–578
Tomlin, Bradley Walker, Aug. 19, 1899–May 11, 1953. Supp. 5–692
Tomlins, William Lawrence, Feb. 4, 1844–Sept. 26, 1930. Vol. 9, Pt. 2–578
Tomlinson, Everett Titsworth, May 23, 1859–Oct. 30, 1931. Vol. 9, Pt. 2–579
Tomochichi, 1650?–Oct. 5, 1739. Vol. 9, Pt. 2–580
Tompkins, Arnold, Sept. 10, 1849–Aug. 12, 1905. Vol. 9, Pt. 2–580
Tompkins, Daniel Augustus, Oct. 12, 1851–Oct. 18, 1914. Vol. 9, Pt. 2–581
Tompkins, Daniel D., June 21, 1774–June 11, 1825. Vol. 9, Pt. 2–583
Tompkins, Sally Louisa, Nov. 9, 1833–July 25, 1916. Vol. 9, Pt. 2–584

Tondorf, Francis Anthony, July 17, 1870–Nov. 29, 1929.
    Vol. 9, Pt. 2–585
Tone, Stanislas Pascal Franchot, Feb. 27, 1905–Sept. 18,
    1968. Supp. 8–657
Toner, Joseph Meredith, Apr. 30, 1825–July 30, 1896.
    Vol. 9, Pt. 2–586
Tonty, Henry de, 1650–1704.
    Vol. 9, Pt. 2–587
Toole, Edwin Warren, Mar. 24, 1839–May 17, 1905.
    Vol. 9, Pt. 2–588
Toole, Joseph Kemp, May 12, 1851–Mar. 11, 1929.
    Vol. 9, Pt. 2–589
Toombs, Robert Augustus, July 2, 1810–Dec. 15, 1885.
    Vol. 9, Pt. 2–590
Topliff, Samuel, Apr. 25, 1789–Dec. 11, 1864.
    Vol. 9, Pt. 2–592
Torbert, Alfred Thomas Archimedes, July 1, 1833–Aug. 29,
    1880. Vol. 9, Pt. 2–593
Torrence, Frederick Ridgely, Nov. 27, 1874–Dec. 25, 1950.
    Supp. 4–840
Torrence, Joseph Thatcher, Mar. 15, 1843–Oct. 31, 1896.
    Vol. 9, Pt. 2–594
Torrey, Bradford, Oct. 9, 1843–Oct. 7, 1912.
    Vol. 9, Pt. 2–594
Torrey, Charles Cutler, Dec. 20, 1863–Nov. 12, 1956.
    Supp. 6–641
Torrey, Charles Turner, Nov. 21, 1813–May 9, 1846.
    Vol. 9, Pt. 2–595
Torrey, John, Aug. 15, 1796–Mar. 10, 1873.
    Vol. 9, Pt. 2–596
Toscanini, Arturo, Mar. 25, 1867–Jan. 16, 1957.
    Supp. 6–642
Totten, George Muirson, May 28, 1809–May 17, 1884.
    Vol. 9, Pt. 2–598
Totten, Joseph Gilbert, Aug. 23, 1788–Apr. 22, 1864.
    Vol. 9, Pt. 2–598
Tou, Erik Hansen, Oct. 11, 1857–Nov. 14, 1917.
    Vol. 9, Pt. 2–599
Toucey, Isaac, Nov. 15, 1792–July 30, 1869.
    Vol. 9, Pt. 2–600
Toulmin, Harry Theophilus, Mar. 4, 1838–Nov. 12, 1916.
    Vol. 9, Pt. 2–602
Toulmin, Harry, Apr. 7, 1766–Nov. 11, 1823.
    Vol. 9, Pt. 2–601
Toumey, James William, Apr. 17, 1865–May 6, 1932.
    Vol. 9, Pt. 2–603
Tourgée, Albion Winegar, May 2, 1838–May 21, 1905.
    Vol. 9, Pt. 2–603
Tourjée, Eben, June 1, 1834–Apr. 12, 1891.
    Vol. 9, Pt. 2–605
Tousard, Anne Louis de, Mar. 12, 1749–May 8, 1817.
    Vol. 9, Pt. 2–605
Tousey, Sinclair, July 18, 1815–June 16, 1887.
    Vol. 9, Pt. 2–606
Tower, Charlemagne, Apr. 17, 1848–Feb. 24, 1923.
    Vol. 9, Pt. 2–607
Tower, Zealous Bates, Jan. 12, 1819–Mar. 20, 1900.
    Vol. 9, Pt. 2–608
Towers, John Henry, Jan. 30, 1885–Apr. 30, 1955.
    Supp. 5–694
Towle, George Makepeace, Aug. 27, 1841–Aug. 9, 1893.
    Vol. 9, Pt. 2–609
Towler, John, June 20, 1811–Apr. 2, 1889.
    Vol. 9, Pt. 2–609
Town, Ithiel, Oct. 3, 1784–June 13, 1844.
    Vol. 9, Pt. 2–610
Towne, Benjamin, d. July 8, 1793.
    Vol. 9, Pt. 2–611
Towne, Charles Arnette, Nov. 21, 1858–Oct. 22, 1928.
    Vol. 9, Pt. 2–612
Towne, Charles Hanson, Feb. 2, 1877–Feb. 28, 1949.
    Supp. 4–841
Towne, Henry Robinson, Aug. 28, 1844–Oct. 15, 1924.
    Vol. 9, Pt. 2–613
Towne, John Henry, Feb. 20, 1818–Apr. 6, 1875.
    Vol. 9, Pt. 2–614
Townley, Arthur Charles, Dec. 30, 1880–Nov. 7, 1959.
    Supp. 6–644
Towns, George Washington Bonaparte, May 4, 1801–July
    15, 1854. Vol. 9, Pt. 2–615
Townsend, Edward Davis, Aug. 22, 1817–May 10, 1893.
    Vol. 9, Pt. 2–615

Townsend, Francis Everett, Jan. 13, 1867–Sept. 1, 1960.
    Supp. 6–645
Townsend, George Alfred, Jan. 30, 1841–Apr. 15, 1914.
    Vol. 9, Pt. 2–616
Townsend, John Kirk, Aug. 10, 1809–Feb. 6, 1851.
    Vol. 9, Pt. 2–617
Townsend, Luther Tracy, Sept. 27, 1838–Aug. 2, 1922.
    Vol. 9, Pt. 2–618
Townsend, Mary Ashley, Sept. 24, 1832–June 7, 1901.
    Vol. 9, Pt. 2–619
Townsend, Mira Sharpless, Sept. 26, 1798–Nov. 20, 1859.
    Vol. 9, Pt. 2–619
Townsend, Robert, Oct. 21, 1819–Aug. 15, 1866.
    Vol. 9, Pt. 2–620
Townsend, Virginia Frances, 1836–Aug. 11, 1920.
    Vol. 9, Pt. 2–621
Townsend, Willard Saxby, Jr., Dec. 4, 1895–Feb. 3, 1957.
    Supp. 6–647
Toy, Crawford Howell, Mar. 23, 1836–May 12, 1919.
    Vol. 9, Pt. 2–621
Tracy, Benjamin Franklin, Apr. 26, 1830–Aug. 6, 1915.
    Vol. 9, Pt. 2–622
Tracy, Joseph, Nov. 3, 1793–Mar. 24, 1874.
    Vol. 9, Pt. 2–623
Tracy, Nathaniel, Aug. 11, 1751–Sept. 20, 1796.
    Vol. 9, Pt. 2–624
Tracy, Spencer Bonaventure, Apr. 5, 1900–June 10, 1967.
    Supp. 8–658
Tracy, Uriah, Feb. 2, 1755–July 19, 1807.
    Vol. 9, Pt. 2–624
Traetta Filippo. [See Trajetta, Philip, c. 1776–1854.]
Train, Arthur Cheney, Sept. 6, 1875–Dec. 22, 1945.
    Supp. 3–773
Train, Enoch, May 2, 1801–Sept. 8, 1868.
    Vol. 9, Pt. 2–625
Train, George Francis, May. 24, 1829–Jan. 19, 1904.
    Vol. 9, Pt. 2–626
Trajetta, Philip, c. 1776–Jan. 9, 1854.
    Vol. 9, Pt. 2–627
Trask, James Dowling, Aug. 21, 1890–May 24, 1942.
    Supp. 3–774
Traubel, Horace L., Dec. 19, 1858–Sept. 8, 1919.
    Vol. 9, Pt. 2–627
Trautwine, John Cresson, Mar. 30, 1810–Sept. 14, 1883.
    Vol. 9, Pt. 2–628
Travers, Jerome Dunstan, May 19, 1887–Mar. 30, 1951.
    Supp. 5–695
Travis, Walter John, Jan. 10, 1862–July 31, 1927.
    Vol. 9, Pt. 2–629
Travis, William Barret, Aug. 9, 1809–Mar. 6, 1836.
    Vol. 9, Pt. 2–630
Traylor, Melvin Alvah, Oct. 21, 1878–Feb. 14, 1934.
    Vol. 9, Pt. 2–631
Treadwell, Daniel, Oct. 10, 1791–Feb. 27, 1872.
    Vol. 9, Pt. 2–631
Treat, Robert, 1622?–July 12, 1710.
    Vol. 9, Pt. 2–633
Treat, Samuel, Dec. 17, 1815–Aug. 31, 1902.
    Vol. 9, Pt. 2–634
Treat, Samuel Hubbel, June 21, 1811–Mar. 27, 1887.
    Vol. 9, Pt. 2–634
Tree, Lambert, Nov. 29, 1832–Oct. 9, 1910.
    Vol. 9, Pt. 2–635
Trelease, William, Feb. 22, 1857–Jan. 1, 1945.
    Supp. 3–775
Tremain, Henry Edwin, Nov. 14, 1840–Dec. 9, 1910.
    Vol. 9, Pt. 2–636
Tremaine, Henry Barnes, July 20, 1866–May 13, 1932.
    Vol. 9, Pt. 2–636
Trenchard, Stephen Decatur, July 10, 1818–Nov. 15, 1883.
    Vol. 9, Pt. 2–637
Trenholm, George Alfred, Feb. 25, 1807–Dec. 9, 1876.
    Supp. 1–689
Trent, William, Feb. 13, 1715–1787?.
    Vol. 9, Pt. 2–638
Trent, William Peterfield, Nov. 10, 1862–Dec. 6, 1939.
    Supp. 2–666
Tresca, Carlo, Mar. 9, 1879–Jan 11, 1943.
    Supp. 3–776
Trescot, William Henry, Nov. 10, 1822–May 4, 1898.
    Vol. 9, Pt. 2–639
Trevellick, Richard F., May 1830–Feb. 15, 1895.
    Vol. 9, Pt. 2–640

Tupper, Henry Allen, Feb. 29, 1828–Mar. 27, 1902.
    Vol. 10, Pt. 1–53
Turell, Jane, Feb. 25, 1708–Mar. 26, 1735.
    Vol. 10, Pt. 1–54
Turkevich, Leonid Ieronimovich. [See Leonty, Metropolitan.]
Turnbull, Andrew, c. 1718–Mar. 13, 1792.
    Vol. 10, Pt. 1–54
Turnbull, Robert James, January 1775–June 15, 1833.
    Vol. 10, Pt. 1–55
Turnbull, William, 1800–Dec. 9, 1857.
    Vol. 10, Pt. 1–57
Turner, Asa, June 11, 1799–Dec. 13, 1885.
    Vol. 10, Pt. 1–57
Turner, Charles Yardley, Nov. 25, 1850–Dec. 31, 1918.
    Vol. 10, Pt. 1–59
Turner, Daniel, 1794–Feb. 4, 1850.
    Vol. 10, Pt. 1–59
Turner, Edward, Nov. 25, 1778–May 23, 1860.
    Vol. 10, Pt. 1–60
Turner, Edward Raymond, May 28, 1881–Dec. 31, 1929.
    Vol. 10, Pt. 1–61
Turner, Fennell Parrish, Feb. 25, 1867–Feb. 10, 1932.
    Vol. 10, Pt. 1–61
Turner, Frederick Jackson, Nov. 14, 1861–Mar. 14, 1932.
    Vol. 10, Pt. 1–62
Turner, George, Feb. 25, 1850–Jan. 26, 1932.
    Vol. 10, Pt. 1–64
Turner, George Kibbe, Mar. 23, 1869–Feb. 15, 1952.
    Supp. 5–698
Turner, Henry McNeal, Feb. 1, 1834–May 8, 1915.
    Vol. 10, Pt. 1–65
Turner, James Milton, May 16, 1840–Nov. 1, 1915.
    Vol. 10, Pt. 1–66
Turner, John Wesley, July 19, 1833–Apr. 8, 1899.
    Vol. 10, Pt. 1–67
Turner, Jonathan Baldwin, Dec. 7, 1805–Jan. 10, 1899.
    Vol. 10, Pt. 1–68
Turner, Josiah, Dec. 27, 1821–Oct. 26, 1901.
    Vol. 10, Pt. 1–68
Turner, Nat, Oct. 2, 1800–Nov. 11, 1831.
    Vol. 10, Pt. 1–69
Turner, Richmond Kelly, May 27, 1885–Feb. 12, 1961.
    Supp. 7–749
Turner, Ross Sterling, June 29, 1847–Feb. 12, 1915.
    Vol. 10, Pt. 1–70
Turner, Samuel Hulbeart, Jan. 23, 1790–Dec. 21, 1861.
    Vol. 10, Pt. 1–71
Turner, Walter Victor, Apr. 3, 1866–Jan. 9, 1919.
    Vol. 10, Pt. 1–71
Turner, William, Apr. 8, 1871–July 10, 1936.
    Supp. 2–671
Turney, Peter, Sept. 22, 1827–Oct. 19, 1903.
    Vol. 10, Pt. 1–72
Turpin, Ben, Sept. 19, 1869[?]–July 1, 1940.
    Supp. 2–672
Tuthill, William Burnet, Feb. 11, 1855–Aug. 25, 1929.
    Vol. 10, Pt. 1–73
Tuttle, Charles Wesley, Nov. 1, 1829–July 17, 1881.
    Vol. 10, Pt. 1–74
Tuttle, Daniel Sylvester, Jan. 26, 1837–Apr. 17, 1923.
    Vol. 10, Pt. 1–75
Tuttle, Herbert, Nov. 29, 1846–June 21, 1894.
    Vol. 10, Pt. 1–75
Tutwiler, Henry, Nov. 16, 1807–Sept. 22, 1884.
    Vol. 10, Pt. 1–76
Tutwiler, Julia Strudwick, Aug. 15, 1841–Mar. 24, 1916.
    Vol. 10, Pt. 1–77
Twachtman, John Henry, Aug. 4, 1853–Aug. 8, 1902.
    Vol. 10, Pt. 1–78
Twain, Mark. [See Clemens, Samuel Langhorne, 1835–1910.]
Tweed, Harrison, Oct. 18, 1885–June 16, 1969.
    Supp. 8–662
Tweed, William Marcy, Apr. 3, 1823–Apr. 12, 1878.
    Vol. 10, Pt. 1–79
Twichell, Joseph Hopkins, May 27, 1838–Dec. 20, 1918.
    Vol. 7, Pt. 2–82
Twiggs, David Emanuel, 1790–July 15, 1862.
    Vol. 10, Pt. 1–83
Twining, Alexander Catlin, July 5, 1801–Nov. 22, 1884.
    Vol. 10, Pt. 1–83

Twitchell, Amos, Apr. 11, 1781–May 26, 1850.
    Vol. 10, Pt. 1–84
Tydings, Millard Evelyn, Apr. 6, 1890–Feb. 9, 1961.
    Supp. 7–750
Tyler, Bennet, July 10, 1783–May 14, 1858.
    Vol. 10, Pt. 1–85
Tyler, Charles Mellen, Jan. 8, 1832–May 15, 1918.
    Vol. 10, Pt. 1–86
Tyler, Daniel, Jan. 7, 1799–Nov. 30, 1882.
    Vol. 10, Pt. 1–86
Tyler, George Crouse, Apr. 13, 1867–Mar. 13, 1946.
    Supp. 4–842
Tyler, John, Feb. 28, 1747–Jan. 6, 1813.
    Vol. 10, Pt. 1–87
Tyler, John, Mar. 29, 1790–Jan. 18, 1862.
    Vol. 10, Pt. 1–88
Tyler, Lyon Gardiner, Aug. 1853–Feb. 12, 1935.
    Supp. 1–691
Tyler, Moses Coit, Aug. 2, 1835–Dec. 28, 1900.
    Vol. 10, Pt. 1–92
Tyler, Ransom Hubert, Nov. 18, 1815–Nov. 21, 1881.
    Vol. 10, Pt. 1–93
Tyler, Robert, Sept. 9, 1816–Dec. 3, 1877.
    Vol. 10, Pt. 1–94
Tyler, Robert Ogden, Dec. 22, 1831–Dec. 1, 1874.
    Vol. 10, Pt. 1–94
Tyler, Royall, July 18, 1757–Aug. 26, 1826.
    Vol. 10, Pt. 1–95
Tyler, Royall, May 4, 1884–Mar. 2, 1953.
    Supp. 5–699
Tyler, Samuel, Oct. 22, 1809–Dec. 15, 1877.
    Vol. 10, Pt. 1–97
Tyler, William, June 5, 1806–June 18, 1849.
    Vol. 10, Pt. 1–98
Tyler, William Seymour, Sept. 2, 1810–Nov. 19, 1897.
    Vol. 10, Pt. 1–99
Tyndale, Hector, Mar. 24, 1821–Mar. 19, 1880.
    Vol. 10, Pt. 1–100
Tyng, Edward, 1683–Sept. 8, 1755.
    Vol. 10, Pt. 1–100
Tyng, Stephen Higginson, Mar. 1, 1800–Sept. 3, 1885.
    Vol. 10, Pt. 1–101
Tyson, George Emory, Dec. 15, 1829–Oct. 18, 1906.
    Vol. 10, Pt. 1–102
Tyson, James, Oct. 26, 1841–Feb. 21, 1919.
    Vol. 10, Pt. 1–103
Tyson, Job Roberts, Feb. 8, 1803–June 27, 1858.
    Vol. 10, Pt. 1–103
Tyson, Lawrence Davis, July 4, 1861–Aug. 24, 1929.
    Vol. 10, Pt. 1–104
Tyson, Stuart Lawrence, Nov. 12, 1873–Sept. 16, 1932.
    Vol. 10, Pt. 1–105
Tytus, John Butler, Dec. 6, 1875–June 2, 1944.
    Supp. 3–781

Udden, Johan August, Mar. 19, 1859–Jan. 5, 1932.
    Vol. 10, Pt. 1–106
Uhler, Philip Reese, June 3, 1835–Oct. 21, 1913.
    Vol. 10, Pt. 1–106
Ulloa, Antonio de, Jan. 12, 1716–July 5, 1795.
    Vol. 10, Pt. 1–107
Ulrich, Edward Oscar, Feb. 1, 1857–Feb. 22, 1944.
    Supp. 3–782
Unangst, Erias, Aug. 8, 1824–Oct. 12, 1903.
    Vol. 10, Pt. 1–108
Uncas, c. 1588–c. 1683.
    Vol. 10, Pt. 1–108
Underhill, Frank Pell, Dec. 21, 1877–June 28, 1932.
    Vol. 10, Pt. 1–109
Underhill, John, c. 1597–Sept. 21, 1672.
    Vol. 10, Pt. 1–110
Underwood, Benjamin Franklin, July 6, 1839–Nov. 10, 1914.
    Vol. 10, Pt. 1–111
Underwood, Francis Henry, Jan. 12, 1825–Aug. 7, 1894.
    Vol. 10, Pt. 1–112
Underwood, Frederick Douglas, Feb. 1, 1849–Feb. 18, 1942.
    Supp. 3–783
Underwood, Horace Grant, July 19, 1859–Oct. 12, 1916.
    Vol. 10, Pt. 1–113
Underwood, John Curtiss, Mar. 14, 1809–Dec. 7, 1873.
    Vol. 10, Pt. 1–113
Underwood, John Thomas, Apr. 12, 1857–July 2, 1937.
    Supp. 2–673

Underwood, Joseph Rogers, Oct. 24, 1791–Aug. 23, 1876.
Vol. 10, Pt. 1–114
Underwood, Loring, Feb. 15, 1874–Jan. 13, 1930.
Vol. 10, Pt. 1–115
Underwood, Lucien Marcus, Oct. 26, 1853–Nov. 16, 1907.
Vol. 10, Pt. 1–116
Underwood, Oscar Wilder, May 6, 1862–Jan. 25, 1929.
Vol. 10, Pt. 1–117
Untermyer, Samuel, June 6, 1858–Mar. 16, 1940.
Supp. 2–674
Upchurch, John Jordan, Mar. 26, 1820–Jan. 18, 1887.
Vol. 10, Pt. 1–119
Updegraff, David Brainard, Aug. 23, 1830–May 23, 1894.
Vol. 10, Pt. 1–188
Updike, Daniel, c. 1693–May 15, 1757.
Vol. 10, Pt. 1–120
Updike, Daniel Berkeley, Feb. 24, 1860–Dec. 29, 1941.
Supp. 3–784
Upham, Charles Wentworth, May 4, 1802–June 15, 1875.
Vol. 10, Pt. 1–121
Upham, Samuel Foster, May 19, 1834–Oct. 5, 1904.
Vol. 10, Pt. 1–122
Upham, Thomas Cogswell, Jan. 30, 1799–Apr. 2, 1872.
Vol. 10, Pt. 1–123
Upham, Warren, Mar. 8, 1850–Jan. 29, 1934.
Vol. 10, Pt. 1–124
Upjohn, Richard, Jan. 22, 1802–Aug. 17, 1878.
Vol. 10, Pt. 1–125
Upjohn, Richard Michell, Mar. 7, 1828–Mar. 3, 1903.
Vol. 10, Pt. 1–126
Upshaw, William David, Oct. 15, 1866–Nov. 21, 1952.
Supp. 5–701
Upshur, Abel Parker, June 17, 1791–Feb. 28, 1844.
Vol. 10, Pt. 1–127
Upshur, John Henry, Dec. 5, 1823–May 30, 1917.
Vol. 10, Pt. 1–128
Upton, Emory, Aug. 27, 1839–Mar. 15, 1881.
Vol. 10, Pt. 1–128
Upton, George Bruce, Oct. 11, 1804–July 1, 1874.
Vol. 10, Pt. 1–130
Upton, George Putnam, Oct. 25, 1834–May 19, 1919.
Vol. 10, Pt. 1–131
Upton, Winslow, Oct. 12, 1853–Jan. 8, 1914.
Vol. 10, Pt. 1–132
Urban, Joseph, May 26, 1872–July 10, 1933.
Vol. 10, Pt. 1–132
U'Ren, William Simon, Jan. 10, 1859–Mar. 8, 1949.
Supp. 4–844
Urso, Camilla, June 13, 1842–Jan. 20, 1902.
Vol. 10, Pt. 1–134
Usher, John Palmer, Jan. 9, 1816–Apr. 13, 1889.
Vol. 10, Pt. 1–134
Usher, Nathaniel Reilly, Apr. 7, 1855–Jan. 9, 1931.
Vol. 10, Pt. 1–135
Utley, George Burwell, Dec. 3, 1876–Oct. 4, 1946.
Supp. 4–845

Vaca, Alvar Núñez Cabeza de. [See Núñez Cabeza de, Vaca, Alvar, c. 1490–c. 1557.]
Vail, Aaron, Oct. 24, 1796–Nov. 4, 1878.
Vol. 10, Pt. 1–136
Vail, Alfred, Sept. 25, 1807–Jan. 18, 1859.
Vol. 10, Pt. 1–136
Vail, Robert William Glenroie, Mar. 26, 1890–June 21, 1966.
Supp. 8–663
Vail, Stephen Montfort, Jan. 15, 1816–Nov. 26, 1880.
Vol. 10, Pt. 1–137
Vail, Theodore Newton, July 16, 1845–Apr. 16, 1920.
Vol. 10, Pt. 1–138
Vaillant, George Clapp, Apr. 5, 1901–May 13, 1945.
Supp. 3–786
Valentine, David Thomas, Sept. 15, 1801–Feb. 25, 1869.
Vol. 10, Pt. 1–140
Valentine, Edward Virginius, Nov. 12, 1838–Oct. 19, 1930.
Vol. 10, Pt. 1–140
Valentine, Milton, Jan. 1, 1825–Feb. 7, 1906.
Vol. 10, Pt. 1–141
Valentine, Robert Grosvenor, Nov. 29, 1872–Nov. 14, 1916.
Vol. 10, Pt. 1–142
Vallandigham, Clement Laird, July 29, 1820–June 17, 1871.
Vol. 10, Pt. 1–143
Vallejo, Mariano Guadalupe, July 7, 1808–Jan. 18, 1890.
Vol. 10, Pt. 1–145

Vallentine, Benjamin Bennaton, Sept. 7, 1843–Mar. 30, 1926. Vol. 10, Pt. 1–146
Valliant, Leroy Branch, June 14, 1838–Mar. 3, 1913.
Vol. 10, Pt. 1–147
Van Allen, Frank, Jan. 10, 1860–Aug. 28, 1923.
Vol. 10, Pt. 1–148
Van Alstyne, Fanny Crosby. [See Crosby, Fanny, 1820–1915.]
Van Amringe, John Howard, Apr. 3, 1835–Sept. 10, 1915.
Vol. 10, Pt. 1–148
Van Anda, Carr Vattel, Dec. 2, 1864–Jan. 28, 1945.
Supp. 3–787
Van Beuren, Johannes, c. 1680–July 27, 1755.
Vol. 10, Pt. 1–149
Van Brunt, Henry, Sept. 5, 1832–Apr. 8, 1903.
Vol. 10, Pt. 1–150
Van Buren, John, Feb. 10, 1810–Oct. 13, 1866.
Vol. 10, Pt. 1–151
Van Buren, Martin, Dec. 5, 1782–July 24, 1862.
Vol. 10, Pt. 1–152
Van Buren, William Holme, Apr. 4, 1819–Mar. 25, 1883.
Vol. 10, Pt. 1–157
Vance, Ap Morgan, May 24, 1854–Dec. 9, 1915.
Vol. 10, Pt. 1–157
Vance, Arthur Charles ("Dazzy"), Mar. 4, 1891–Feb. 16, 1961. Supp. 7–751
Vance, Harold Sines, Aug. 22, 1890–Aug. 31, 1959.
Supp. 6–649
Vance, Louis Joseph, Sept. 19, 1879–Dec. 16, 1933.
Supp. 1–691
Vance, Zebulon Baird, May 13, 1830–Apr. 14, 1894.
Vol. 10, Pt. 1–158
Van Cortlandt, Oloff Stevenszen, 1600–Apr. 5, 1684.
Vol. 10, Pt. 1–161
Van Cortlandt, Philip, Aug. 21, 1749–Nov. 5, 1831.
Vol. 10, Pt. 1–162
Van Cortlandt, Pierre, Jan. 10, 1721–May 1, 1814.
Vol. 10, Pt. 1–163
Van Cortlandt, Stephanus, May 7, 1643–Nov. 25, 1700.
Vol. 10, Pt. 1–164
Van Curler, Arent, 1620–July 1667.
Vol. 10, Pt. 1–165
Van Dam, Rip, c. 1660–June 10, 1749.
Vol. 10, Pt. 1–166
Van de Graaff, Robert Jemison, Dec. 20, 1901–Jan. 16, 1967.
Supp. 8–665
Van Deman, Esther Boise, Oct. 1, 1862–May 3, 1937.
Supp. 2–676
Vandenberg, Arthur Hendrick, Mar. 22, 1884–Apr. 18, 1951.
Supp. 5–702
Vandenberg, Hoyt Sanford, Jan. 24, 1899–Apr. 2, 1954.
Supp. 5–705
Vandenhoff, George, 1813–June 16, 1885.
Vol. 10, Pt. 1–167
Van Depoele, Charles Joseph, Apr. 27, 1846–Mar. 18, 1892.
Vol. 10, Pt. 1–168
Vanderbilt, Arthur T., July 7, 1888–June 16, 1957.
Supp. 6–650
Vanderbilt, Cornelius, May 27, 1794–Jan. 4, 1877.
Vol. 10, Pt. 1–169
Vanderbilt, Cornelius, Nov. 27, 1843–Sept. 12, 1899.
Vol. 10, Pt. 1–173
Vanderbilt, George Washington, Nov. 14, 1862–Mar. 6, 1914. Vol. 10, Pt. 1–174
Vanderbilt, Gloria Morgan, Aug. 23, 1904–Feb. 13, 1965.
Supp. 7–752
Vanderbilt, Grace Graham Wilson, Sept. 3, 1870–Jan. 7, 1953. Supp. 5–707
Vanderbilt, William Kissam, Dec. 12, 1849–July 22, 1920.
Vol. 10, Pt. 1–176
Vanderbilt, William Henry, May 8, 1821–Dec. 8, 1885.
Vol. 10, Pt. 1–175
Vanderburgh, William Henry, c. 1798–Oct. 14, 1832.
Vol. 10, Pt. 1–177
Van Der Donck, Adriaen, May 7, 1620–c. 1655.
Vol. 10, Pt. 1–178
Vandergrift, Jacob Jay, Apr. 10, 1827–Dec. 26, 1899.
Vol. 10, Pt. 1–179
Vandergrift, Margaret. [See Janvier, Margaret Thomson, 1844–1913.]
Van Der Kemp, Francis Adrian, May 4, 1752–Sept. 7, 1829.
Vol. 10, Pt. 1–179

Vanderlip, Frank Arthur, Nov. 17, 1864–June 29, 1937.
Supp. 2–677
Vanderlyn, John, Oct. 15, 1775–Sept. 23, 1852.
Vol. 10, Pt. 1–180
Van Der Stucken, Frank Valentin, Oct. 15, 1858–Aug. 16, 1929. Vol. 10, Pt. 1–181
Vander Veer, Albert, July 10, 1841–Dec. 19, 1929.
Vol. 10, Pt. 1–182
Vander Wee, John Baptist, Feb. 20, 1824–Feb. 24, 1900.
Vol. 10, Pt. 1–183
Van Devanter, Willis, Apr. 17, 1859–Feb. 8, 1941.
Supp. 3–788
Van de Velde, James Oliver, Apr. 3, 1795–Nov. 13, 1855.
Vol. 10, Pt. 1–184
Van de Warker, Edward Ely, Nov. 27, 1841–Sept. 5, 1910.
Vol. 10, Pt. 1–184
Van Dine, S. S. [See Wright, Willard Huntington, 1888–1939.]
Van Doren, Carl Clinton, Sept. 10, 1884–July 18, 1950.
Supp. 4–846
Van Doren, Irita Bradford, Mar. 16, 1891–Dec. 18, 1966.
Supp. 8–666
Van Dorn, Earl, Sept. 17, 1820–May 8, 1863.
Vol. 10, Pt. 1–185
Van Druten, John William, June 1, 1901–Dec. 19, 1957.
Supp. 6–652
Van Dyck, Cornelius Van Alen, Aug. 13, 1818–Nov. 13, 1895.
Vol. 10, Pt. 1–186
Van Dyke, Henry, Nov. 10, 1852–Apr. 10, 1933.
Vol. 10, Pt. 1–186
Van Dyke, John Charles, Apr. 21, 1856–Dec. 5, 1932.
Vol. 10, Pt. 1–188
Van Dyke, John Wesley, Dec. 27, 1849–Sept. 13, 1939.
Supp. 2–679
Van Dyke, Nicholas, Sept. 25, 1738–Feb. 19, 1789.
Vol. 10, Pt. 1–189
Van Dyke, Nicholas, Dec. 20, 1770–May 21, 1826.
Vol. 10, Pt. 1–190
Van Dyke, Paul, Mar. 25, 1859–Aug. 30, 1933.
Vol. 10, Pt. 1–191
Vane, Sir Henry, 1613–June 14, 1662.
Vol. 10, Pt. 1–191
Van Fleet, Walter, June 18, 1857–Jan. 26, 1922.
Vol. 10, Pt. 1–193
Van Hise, Charles Richard, May 29, 1857–Nov. 19, 1918.
Vol. 10, Pt. 1–194
Van Hook, Weller, May 16, 1862–July 1, 1933.
Vol. 10, Pt. 1–195
Van Horn, Robert Thompson, May 19, 1824–Jan. 3, 1916.
Vol. 10, Pt. 1–196
Van Horne, William Cornelius, Feb. 3, 1843–Sept. 11, 1915.
Vol. 10, Pt. 1–197
Van Ilpendam, Jan Jansen, c. 1595–1647.
Vol. 10, Pt. 1–199
Van Lennep, Henry John, Mar. 18, 1815–Jan. 11, 1889.
Vol. 10, Pt. 1–199
Van Lennep, William Bird, Dec. 5, 1853–Jan. 9, 1919.
Vol. 10, Pt. 1–200
Van Loon, Hendrik Willem, Jan. 14, 1882–Mar. 11, 1944.
Supp. 3–789
Van Meter, John Blackford, Sept. 6, 1842–Apr. 8, 1930.
Vol. 10, Pt. 1–201
Van Name, Addison, Nov. 15, 1835–Sept. 29, 1922.
Vol. 10, Pt. 1–201
Van Ness, William Peter, c. 1778–Sept. 6, 1826.
Vol. 10, Pt. 1–202
Van Nest, Abraham Rynier, Feb. 16, 1823–June 1, 1892.
Vol. 10, Pt. 1–203
Van Nostrand, David, Dec. 5, 1811–June 14, 1886.
Vol. 10, Pt. 1–203
Van Osdel, John Mills, July 31, 1811–Dec. 21, 1891.
Vol. 10, Pt. 1–204
Van Quickenborne, Charles Felix, Jan. 21, 1788–Aug. 17, 1837. Vol. 10, Pt. 1–205
Van Raalte, Albertus Christiaan, Oct. 17, 1811–Nov. 7, 1876.
Vol. 10, Pt. 1–206
Van Rensselaer, Mariana Griswold, Feb. 25, 1851–Jan. 20, 1934. Vol. 10, Pt. 1–207
Van Rensselaer, Nicholas, c. Sept. 25, 1636–1678.
Vol. 10, Pt. 1–209
Van Rensselaer, Cortlandt, May 26, 1808–July 25, 1860.
Vol. 10, Pt. 1–207

Van Rensselaer, Martha, June 21, 1864–May 26, 1932.
Vol. 10, Pt. 1–208
Van Rensselaer, Solomon, Aug. 6, 1774–Apr. 23, 1852.
Vol. 10, Pt. 1–210
Van Rensselaer, Stephen, Nov. 1, 1764–Jan. 26, 1839.
Vol. 10, Pt. 1–211
Van Santvoord, George, Dec. 8, 1819–Mar. 6, 1863.
Vol. 10, Pt. 1–212
Van Schaack, Henry Cruger, Apr. 2, 1802–Dec. 16, 1887.
Vol. 10, Pt. 1–213
Van Schaack, Peter, March 1747–Sept. 17, 1832.
Vol. 10, Pt. 1–213
Van Schaick, Goose, Sept. 5, 1736–July 4, 1789.
Vol. 10, Pt. 1–214
Van Slyke, Lucius Lincoln, Jan. 6, 1859–Sept. 30, 1931.
Vol. 10, Pt. 1–215
Van Sweringen, Mantis James, July 8, 1881–Dec. 12, 1935.
Supp. 1–692
Van Twiller, Wouter, c. 1580–c. 1656.
Vol. 10, Pt. 1–216
Van Tyne, Claude Halstead, Oct. 16, 1869–Mar. 21, 1930.
Vol. 10, Pt. 1–217
Vanuxem, Lardner, July 23, 1792–Jan. 25, 1848.
Vol. 10, Pt. 1–218
Van Vechten, Abraham, Dec. 5, 1762–Jan. 6, 1837.
Vol. 10, Pt. 1–218
Van Vechten, Carl, June 17, 1880–Dec. 21, 1964.
Supp. 7–753
Van Vleck, Edward Burr, June 7, 1863–June 2, 1943.
Supp. 3–791
Van Winkle, Peter Godwin, Sept. 7, 1808–Apr. 15, 1872.
Vol. 10, Pt. 1–219
Van Wyck, Charles Henry, May 10, 1824–Oct. 24, 1895.
Vol. 10, Pt. 1–220
Vanzetti, Bartolomeo, 1888–1927. [See Sacco, Nicola, 1891–1927.]
Vardaman, James Kimble, July 26, 1861–June 25, 1930.
Vol. 10, Pt. 1–221
Vardill, John, 1749–Jan. 16, 1811.
Vol. 10, Pt. 1–222
Vare, William Scott, Dec. 24, 1867–Aug. 7, 1934.
Vol. 10, Pt. 1–223
Varela Y Morales, Félix Francisco José María de la Concepción, Nov. 20, 1788–Feb. 18, 1853. Vol. 10, Pt. 1–224
Varèse, Edgard, Dec. 22, 1883–Nov. 6, 1965.
Supp. 7–755
Varick, James, fl. 1796–1828.
Vol. 10, Pt. 1–225
Varick, Richard, Mar. 25, 1753–July 30, 1831.
Vol. 10, Pt. 1–226
Varnum, James Mitchell, Dec. 17, 1748–Jan. 10, 1789.
Vol. 10, Pt. 1–227
Varnum, Joseph Bradley, Jan. 29, 1750/51–Sept. 11, 1821.
Vol. 10, Pt. 1–228
Vasey, George, Feb. 28, 1822–Mar. 4, 1893.
Vol. 10, Pt. 1–229
Vasiliev, Alexander Alexandrovich, Oct. 5, 1867–May 30, 1953. Supp. 5–708
Vassall, John, 1625–July ?, 1688.
Vol. 10, Pt. 1–230
Vassar, Matthew, Apr. 29, 1792–June 23, 1868.
Vol. 10, Pt. 1–230
Vattemare, Nicolas Marie Alexandre, Nov. 8, 1796–Apr. 7, 1864. Vol. 10, Pt. 1–231
Vauclain, Samuel Matthews, May 18, 1856–Feb. 4, 1940.
Supp. 2–680
Vaudreuil-Cavagnal, Pierre de Rigaud, Marquis de, 1704–Aug. 4, 1778. Vol. 10, Pt. 1–232
Vaughan, Benjamin, Apr. 30, 1751–Dec. 8, 1835.
Vol. 10, Pt. 1–233
Vaughan, Charles, June 30, 1759–May 15, 1839.
Vol. 10, Pt. 1–235
Vaughan, Daniel, c. 1818–Apr. 6, 1879.
Vol. 10, Pt. 1–235
Vaughan, Thomas Wayland, Sept. 20, 1870–Jan. 16, 1952.
Supp. 5–709
Vaughan, Victor Clarence, Oct. 27, 1851–Nov. 21, 1929.
Vol. 10, Pt. 1–236
Vaux, Calvert, Dec. 20, 1824–Nov. 19, 1895.
Vol. 10, Pt. 1–237
Vaux, Richard, Dec. 19, 1816–Mar. 22, 1895.
Vol. 10, Pt. 1–238

Vonnoh, Robert William, Sept. 17, 1858–Dec. 28, 1933.
    Vol. 10, Pt. 1–289
Von Ruck, Karl, July 10, 1849–Nov. 5, 1922.
    Vol. 10, Pt. 1–290
Von Sternberg, Josef, May 29, 1894–Dec. 22, 1969.
    Supp. 8–671
Von Stroheim, Erich, Sept. 22, 1885–May 12, 1957.
    Supp. 6–656
Von Teuffel, Blanche Willis Howard. [See Howard, Blanche
    Willis, 1847–1898.]
Von Wiegand, Karl Henry, Sept. 11, 1874–June 7, 1961.
    Supp. 7–758
Voorhees, Daniel Wolsey, Sept. 26, 1827–Apr. 10, 1897.
    Vol. 10, Pt. 1–291
Voorhees, Edward Burnett, June 22, 1856–June 6, 1911.
    Vol. 10, Pt. 1–291
Voorhees, Philip Falkerson, 1792–Feb. 23, 1862.
    Vol. 10, Pt. 1–292
Voorsanger, Jacob, Nov. 13, 1852–Apr. 27, 1908.
    Vol. 10, Pt. 1–293
Vopicka, Charles Joseph, Nov. 3, 1857–Sept. 3, 1935.
    Supp. 1–694
Voris, John Ralph, June 6, 1880–Jan. 12, 1968.
    Supp. 8–673
Vorse, Mary Heaton, Oct. 9, 1874–June 14, 1966.
    Supp. 8–674
Vose, George Leonard, Apr. 19, 1831–Mar. 30, 1910.
    Vol. 10, Pt. 1–294
Vought, Chance Milton, Feb. 26, 1890–July 25, 1930.
    Vol. 10, Pt. 1–294
Vroom, Peter Dumont, Dec. 12, 1791–Nov. 18, 1873.
    Vol. 10, Pt. 1–295

Wabasha, c. 1773–c. 1855.
    Vol. 10, Pt. 1–296
Wachsmuth, Charles, Sept. 13, 1829–Feb. 7, 1896.
    Vol. 10, Pt. 1–297
Wacker, Charles Henry, Aug. 29, 1856–Oct. 31, 1929.
    Vol. 10, Pt. 1–298
Waddel, James, July 1739–Sept. 17, 1805.
    Vol. 10, Pt. 1–298
Waddel, John Newton, Apr. 2, 1812–Jan. 9, 1895.
    Vol. 10, Pt. 1–299
Waddel, Moses, July 29, 1770–July 21, 1840.
    Vol. 10, Pt. 1–300
Waddell, Alfred Moore, Sept. 16, 1834–Mar. 17, 1912.
    Vol. 10, Pt. 1–300
Waddell, Hugh, 1734?–Apr. 9, 1773.
    Vol. 10, Pt. 1–301
Waddell, James Iredell, July 13, 1824–Mar. 15, 1886.
    Vol. 10, Pt. 1–302
Waddell, John Alexander Low, Jan. 15, 1854–Mar. 3, 1938.
    Supp. 2–685
Wade, Benjamin Franklin, Oct. 27, 1800–Mar. 2, 1878.
    Vol. 10, Pt. 1–303
Wade, Decius Spear, Jan. 23, 1835–Aug. 3, 1905.
    Vol. 10, Pt. 1–305
Wade, Jeptha Homer, Aug. 11, 1811–Aug. 9, 1890.
    Vol. 10, Pt. 1–306
Wade, Jeptha Homer, Oct. 15, 1857–Mar. 6, 1926.
    Supp. 1–695
Wade, Martin Joseph, Oct. 20, 1861–Apr. 16, 1931.
    Vol. 10, Pt. 1–307
Wadsworth, Eliot, Sept. 10, 1876–May 29, 1959.
    Supp. 6–659
Wadsworth, James, Apr. 20, 1768–June 7, 1844.
    Vol. 10, Pt. 1–307
Wadsworth, James Samuel, Oct. 30, 1807–May 8, 1864.
    Vol. 10, Pt. 1–308
Wadsworth, James Wolcott, Jr., Aug. 12, 1877–June 21,
    1952. Supp. 5–715
Wadsworth, Jeremiah, July 12, 1743–Apr. 30, 1804.
    Vol. 10, Pt. 1–309
Wadsworth, Peleg, May 6, 1748–Nov. 12, 1829.
    Vol. 10, Pt. 1–310
Waesche, Russell Randolph, Jan 6, 1886–Oct. 17, 1946.
    Supp. 4–853
Wagener, John Andreas, July 23, 1816–Aug. 28, 1876.
    Supp. 1–696
Waggaman, Mary Teresa McKee, Sept. 21, 1846–July 30,
    1931. Vol. 10, Pt. 1–311
Wagner, Clinton, Oct. 28, 1837–Nov. 25, 1914.
    Vol. 10, Pt. 1–311

Wagner, John Peter, Feb. 24, 1874–Dec. 5, 1955.
    Supp. 5–716
Wagner, Robert Ferdinand, June 8, 1877–May 4, 1953.
    Supp. 5–717
Wagner, Webster, Oct. 2, 1817–Jan. 13, 1882.
    Vol. 10, Pt. 1–312
Wagner, William, Jan. 15, 1796–Jan. 17, 1885.
    Vol. 10, Pt. 1–313
Wahl, William Henry, Dec. 14, 1848–Mar. 23, 1909.
    Vol. 10, Pt. 1–314
Waidner, Charles William, Mar. 6, 1873–Mar. 10, 1922.
    Vol. 10, Pt. 1–315
Wailes, Benjamin Leonard Covington, Aug. 1, 1797–Nov.
    16, 1862. Vol. 10, Pt. 1–315
Wainwright, Jonathan Mayhew, Feb. 24, 1792–Sept. 21,
    1854. Vol. 10, Pt. 1–316
Wainwright, Jonathan Mayhew, July 21, 1821–Jan. 1, 1863.
    Vol. 10, Pt. 1–317
Wainwright, Jonathan Mayhew, Aug. 23, 1883–Sept. 2, 1953.
    Supp. 5–719
Wainwright, Richard, Jan. 5, 1817–Aug. 10, 1862.
    Vol. 10, Pt. 1–318
Wainwright, Richard, Dec. 17, 1849–Mar. 6, 1926.
    Vol. 10, Pt. 1–319
Wait, Samuel, Dec. 19, 1789–July 28, 1867.
    Vol. 10, Pt. 1–320
Wait, William, Feb. 2, 1821–Dec. 29, 1880.
    Vol. 10, Pt. 1–320
Wait, William Bell, Mar. 25, 1839–Oct. 25, 1916.
    Vol. 10, Pt. 1–321
Waite, Henry Matson, May 15, 1869–Sept. 1, 1944.
    Supp. 3–795
Waite, Morrison Remick, Nov. 29, 1816–Mar. 23, 1888.
    Vol. 10, Pt. 1–322
Wakeley, Joseph Burton, Feb. 18, 1809–Apr. 27, 1875.
    Vol. 10, Pt. 1–325
Walcot, Charles Melton, c. 1816–May 15, 1868.
    Vol. 10, Pt. 1–326
Walcot, Charles Melton, July 1, 1840–Jan. 1, 1921.
    Vol. 10, Pt. 1–326
Walcott, Charles Doolittle, Mar. 31, 1850–Feb. 9, 1927.
    Vol. 10, Pt. 1–327
Walcott, Henry Pickering, Dec. 23, 1838–Nov. 11, 1932.
    Vol. 10, Pt. 1–329
Wald, Lillian D., Mar. 10, 1867–Sept. 1, 1940.
    Supp. 2–687
Walden, Jacob Treadwell, Apr. 25, 1830–May 21, 1918.
    Vol. 10, Pt. 1–330
Walden, John Morgan, Feb. 11, 1831–Jan. 21, 1914.
    Vol. 10, Pt. 1–330
Walderne, Richard, c. 1615–June 1689.
    Vol. 10, Pt. 1–331
Waldo, David, Apr. 30, 1802–May 20, 1878.
    Vol. 10, Pt. 1–332
Waldo, Samuel, 1695–May 23, 1759.
    Vol. 10, Pt. 1–333
Waldo, Samuel Lovett, Apr. 6, 1783–Feb. 16, 1861.
    Vol. 10, Pt. 1–333
Waldo, Samuel Putnam, Mar. 12, 1779–Feb. 23, 1826.
    Vol. 10, Pt. 1–334
Waldron, Richard. [See Walderne, Richard, 1615–1689.]
Wales, James Albert, Aug. 30, 1852–Dec. 6, 1886.
    Vol. 10, Pt. 1–335
Wales, Leonard Eugene, Nov. 26, 1823–Feb. 8, 1897.
    Vol. 10, Pt. 1–336
Walgreen, Charles Rudolph, Oct. 9, 1873–Dec. 11, 1939.
    Supp. 2–688
Walke, Henry, Dec. 24, 1808–Mar. 8, 1896.
    Vol. 10, Pt. 1–336
Walker, Alexander, Oct. 13, 1818–Jan. 24, 1893.
    Vol. 10, Pt. 1–337
Walker, Amasa, May 4, 1799–Oct. 29, 1875.
    Vol. 10, Pt. 1–338
Walker, Asa, Nov. 13, 1845–Mar. 7, 1916.
    Vol. 10, Pt. 1–339
Walker, Madame C. J. [See Walker, Sarah Breedlove, 1865–
    1919.]
Walker, David, Sept. 28, 1785–June 28, 1830.
    Vol. 10, Pt. 1–340
Walker, David, Feb. 19, 1806–Sept. 30, 1879.
    Vol. 10, Pt. 1–340
Walker, David Shelby, May 2, 1815–July 20, 1891.
    Vol. 10, Pt. 1–341

Walker, Francis Amasa, July 2, 1840–Jan. 5, 1897.
  Vol. 10, Pt. 1–342
Walker, Frank Comerford, May 30, 1886–Sept. 13, 1959.
  Supp. 6–660
Walker, Gilbert Carlton, Aug. 1, 1832–May 11, 1885.
  Vol. 10, Pt. 1–344
Walker, Henry Oliver, May 14, 1843–Jan. 14, 1929.
  Vol. 10, Pt. 1–345
Walker, James, Aug. 16, 1794–Dec. 23, 1874.
  Vol. 10, Pt. 1–346
Walker, James Barr, July 29, 1805–Mar. 6, 1887.
  Vol. 10, Pt. 1–347
Walker, James John, June 19, 1881–Nov. 18, 1946.
  Supp. 4–854
Walker, John Brisben, Sept. 10, 1847–July 7, 1931.
  Vol. 10, Pt. 1–347
Walker, John Grimes, Mar. 20, 1835–Sept. 15, 1907.
  Vol. 10, Pt. 1–348
Walker, Jonathan Hoge, July 20, 1754–Jan. 1824.
  Vol. 10, Pt. 1–349
Walker, Joseph Reddeford, Dec. 13, 1798–Oct. 27, 1876.
  Vol. 10, Pt. 1–350
Walker, Leroy Pope, Feb. 7, 1817–Aug. 22, 1884.
  Vol. 10, Pt. 1–351
Walker, Mary Edwards, Nov. 26, 1832–Feb. 21, 1919.
  Vol. 10, Pt. 1–352
Walker, Pinkney Houston, June 18, 1815–Feb. 7, 1885.
  Vol. 10, Pt. 1–352
Walker, Reuben Lindsay, May 29, 1827–June 7, 1890.
  Vol. 10, Pt. 1–353
Walker, Robert Franklin, Nov. 29, 1850–Nov. 19, 1930.
  Vol. 10, Pt. 1–354
Walker, Robert John, July 19, 1801–Nov. 11, 1869.
  Vol. 10, Pt. 1–355
Walker, Sarah Breedlove, Dec. 23, 1867–May 25, 1919.
  Vol. 10, Pt. 1–358
Walker, Sears Cook, Mar. 23, 1805–Jan. 30, 1853.
  Vol. 10, Pt. 1–359
Walker, Stuart Armstrong, Mar. 4, 1880–Mar. 13, 1941.
  Supp. 3–796
Walker, Thomas, Jan. 25, 1715–Nov. 9, 1794.
  Vol. 10, Pt. 1–360
Walker, Thomas Barlow, Feb. 1, 1840–July 28, 1928.
  Vol. 10, Pt. 1–361
Walker, Timothy, July 27, 1705–Sept. 1, 1782.
  Vol. 10, Pt. 1–362
Walker, Timothy, Dec. 1, 1802–Jan. 15, 1856.
  Vol. 10, Pt. 1–363
Walker, Walton Harris, Dec. 3, 1889–Dec. 23, 1950.
  Supp. 4–856
Walker, William, May 8, 1824–Sept. 12, 1860.
  Vol. 10, Pt. 1–363
Walker, William Henry Talbot, Nov. 26, 1816–July 22, 1864.
  Vol. 10, Pt. 1–365
Walker, William Johnson, Mar. 15, 1790–Apr. 2, 1865.
  Vol. 10, Pt. 1–366
Walker, Williston, July 1, 1860–Mar. 9, 1922.
  Vol. 10, Pt. 1–366
Wallace, Charles William, Feb. 6, 1865–Aug. 7, 1932.
  Vol. 10, Pt. 1–367
Wallace, David, Apr. 24, 1799–Sept. 4, 1859.
  Vol. 10, Pt. 1–368
Wallace, Henry, Mar. 19, 1836–Feb. 22, 1916.
  Vol. 10, Pt. 1–369
Wallace, Henry Agard, Oct. 7, 1888–Nov. 18, 1965.
  Supp. 7–759
Wallace, Henry Cantwell, May 11, 1866–Oct. 25, 1924.
  Vol. 10, Pt. 1–370
Wallace, Horace Binney, Feb. 26, 1817–Dec. 16, 1852.
  Vol. 10, Pt. 1–370
Wallace, Hugh Campbell, Feb. 10, 1863–Jan. 1, 1931.
  Vol. 10, Pt. 1–371
Wallace, John Findley, Sept. 10, 1852–July 3, 1921.
  Vol. 10, Pt. 1–372
Wallace, John Hankins, Aug. 16, 1822–May 2, 1903.
  Vol. 10, Pt. 1–373
Wallace, John William, Feb. 17, 1815–Jan. 12, 1884.
  Vol. 10, Pt. 1–374
Wallace, Lewis, Apr. 10, 1827–Feb. 15, 1905.
  Vol. 10, Pt. 1–375
Wallace, Lurleen Burns, Sept. 19, 1926–May 7, 1968.
  Supp. 8–676

Wallace, William, Mar. 16, 1825–May 20, 1904.
  Vol. 10, Pt. 1–376
Wallace, William Alexander Anderson, Apr. 3, 1817–Jan. 7, 1899. Vol. 10, Pt. 1–377
Wallace, William James, Apr. 14, 1837–Mar. 11, 1917.
  Vol. 10, Pt. 1–378
Wallace, William Ross, 1819–May 5, 1881.
  Vol. 10, Pt. 1–378
Wallack, Henry John, 1790–Aug. 30, 1870.
  Vol. 10, Pt. 1–379
Wallack, James William, c. 1795–Dec. 25, 1864.
  Vol. 10, Pt. 1–380
Wallack, James William, Feb. 24, 1818–May 24, 1873.
  Vol. 10, Pt. 1–381
Wallack, John Lester. [See Wallack, Lester, 1820–1888.]
Wallack, Lester, Jan. 1, 1820–Sept. 6, 1888.
  Vol. 10, Pt. 1–382
Waller, Emma, c. 1820–Feb. 28, 1899.
  Vol. 10, Pt. 1–383
Waller, Fats. [See Waller, Thomas Wright.]
Waller, Frederic, Mar. 10, 1886–May 18, 1954.
  Supp. 5–721
Waller, John Lightfoot, Nov. 23, 1809–Oct. 10, 1854.
  Vol. 10, Pt. 1–383
Waller, Thomas Macdonald, c. 1840–Jan. 25, 1924.
  Vol. 10, Pt. 1–384
Waller, Thomas Wright, May 21, 1904–Dec. 15, 1943.
  Supp. 3–797
Waller, Willard Walter, July 30, 1899–July 26, 1945.
  Supp. 3–799
Wallgren, Mon[rad] C[harles], Apr. 17, 1891–Sept. 18, 1961.
  Supp. 7–763
Walling, William English, Mar. 14, 1877–Sept. 12, 1936.
  Supp. 2–689
Wallis, Severn Teackle, Sept. 8, 1816–Apr. 11, 1894.
  Vol. 10, Pt. 1–385
Waln, Nicholas, Sept. 19, 1742–Sept. 29, 1813.
  Vol. 10, Pt. 1–386
Waln, Robert, Feb. 22, 1765–Jan. 24, 1836.
  Vol. 10, Pt. 1–387
Waln, Robert, Oct. 20, 1794–July 4, 1825.
  Vol. 10, Pt. 1–387
Walsh, Benjamin Dann, Sept. 21, 1808–Nov. 18, 1869.
  Vol. 10, Pt. 1–388
Walsh, Blanche, Jan. 4, 1873–Oct. 31, 1915.
  Vol. 10, Pt. 1–389
Walsh, David Ignatius, Nov. 11, 1872–June 11, 1947.
  Supp. 4–857
Walsh, Edmund Aloysius, Oct. 10, 1885–Oct. 31, 1956.
  Supp. 6–661
Walsh, Edward Augustine, May 14, 1881–May 26, 1959.
  Supp. 6–662
Walsh, Francis Patrick, July 20, 1864–May 2, 1939.
  Supp. 2–690
Walsh, Henry Collins, Nov. 23, 1863–Apr. 29, 1927.
  Vol. 10, Pt. 1–390
Walsh, James Anthony, Feb. 24, 1867–Apr. 14, 1936.
  Supp. 2–691
Walsh, Michael, c. 1815–Mar. 17, 1859.
  Vol. 10, Pt. 1–390
Walsh, Robert, Aug. 30, 1784–Feb. 7, 1859.
  Vol. 10, Pt. 1–391
Walsh, Thomas, Oct. 14, 1871–Oct. 29, 1928.
  Vol. 10, Pt. 1–392
Walsh, Thomas James, June 12, 1859–Mar. 2, 1933.
  Vol. 10, Pt. 1–393
Walsh, Thomas Joseph, Dec. 6, 1873–June 6, 1952.
  Supp. 5–722
Walter, Albert G., June 21, 1811–Oct. 14, 1876.
  Vol. 10, Pt. 1–395
Walter, Bruno, Sept. 15, 1876–Feb. 17, 1962.
  Supp. 7–764
Walter, Eugene, Nov. 27, 1874–Sept. 26, 1941.
  Supp. 3–800
Walter, Francis Eugene, May 26, 1894–May 31, 1963.
  Supp. 7–766
Walter, Thomas, c. 1740–Jan. 17, 1789.
  Vol. 10, Pt. 1–396
Walter, Thomas, Dec. 13, 1696–Jan. 10, 1725.
  Vol. 10, Pt. 1–395
Walter, Thomas Ustick, Sept. 4, 1804–Oct. 30 1887.
  Vol. 10, Pt. 1–397

Walters, Alexander, Aug. 1, 1858–Feb. 2, 1917.
Vol. 10, Pt. 1–398
Walters, Henry, Sept. 26, 1848–Nov. 30, 1931.
Vol. 10, Pt. 1–399
Walters, William Thompson, May 23, 1820–Nov. 22, 1894.
Vol. 10, Pt. 1–400
Walthall, Edward Cary, Apr. 4, 1831–Apr. 21, 1898.
Vol. 10, Pt. 1–401
Walthall, Henry Brazeal, Mar. 16, 1878–June 17, 1936.
Supp. 2–693
Walther, Carl Ferdinand Wilhelm, Oct. 25, 1811–May 7, 1887. Vol. 10, Pt. 1–402
Walton, George, 1741–Feb. 2, 1804.
Vol. 10, Pt. 1–403
Walton, Lester Aglar, Apr. 20, 1882–Oct. 16, 1965.
Supp. 7–767
Walworth, Clarence Augustus, May 30, 1820–Sept. 19, 1900.
Vol. 10, Pt. 1–405
Walworth, Jeannette Ritchie Hadermann, Feb. 22, 1837–Feb. 4, 1918. Vol. 10, Pt. 1–406
Walworth, Reuben Hyde, Oct. 26, 1788–Nov. 28, 1867.
Vol. 10, Pt. 1–406
Wambaugh, Sarah, Mar. 6, 1882–Nov. 12, 1955.
Supp. 5–723
Wanamaker, John, July 11, 1838–Dec. 12, 1922.
Vol. 10, Pt. 1–407
Wanamaker, Lewis Rodman, Feb. 13, 1863–Mar. 9, 1928.
Vol. 10, Pt. 1–409
Wanamaker, Reuben Melville, Aug. 2, 1866–June 18, 1924.
Vol. 10, Pt. 1–410
Waner, Paul Glee, Apr. 16, 1903–Aug. 29, 1965.
Supp. 7–768
Wanger, Walter, July 11, 1894–Nov. 18, 1968.
Supp. 8–677
Wanless, William James, May 1, 1865–Mar. 3, 1933.
Vol. 10, Pt. 1–411
Wanton, Joseph, Aug. 15, 1705–July 19, 1780.
Vol. 10, Pt. 1–412
Warbasse, James Peter, Nov. 22, 1866–Feb. 22, 1957.
Supp. 6–663
Warburg, Felix Moritz, Jan. 14, 1871–Oct. 20, 1937.
Supp. 2–694
Warburg, James Paul, Aug. 18, 1896–June 3, 1969.
Supp. 8–679
Warburg, Paul Moritz, Aug. 10, 1868–Jan. 24, 1932.
Vol. 10, Pt. 1–412
Ward, Aaron Montgomery, Feb. 17, 1843–Dec. 7, 1913.
Vol. 10, Pt. 1–414
Ward, Arch Burdette, Dec. 27, 1896–July 9, 1955.
Supp. 5–724
Ward, Artemas, Nov. 26, 1727–Oct. 28, 1800.
Vol. 10, Pt. 1–415
Ward, Artemus. [See Browne, Charles Farrar, 1834–1867.]
Ward, Charles Alfred, Oct. 12, 1883–Jan. 12, 1951.
Supp. 5–725
Ward, Charles Henshaw, Nov. 5, 1872–Oct. 9, 1935.
Supp. 1–697
Ward, Cyrenus Osborne, Oct. 28, 1831–Mar. 19, 1902.
Vol. 10, Pt. 1–416
Ward, Elizabeth Stuart Phelps, Aug. 31, 1844–Jan. 28, 1911.
Vol. 10, Pt. 1–417
Ward, Frederick Townsend, Nov. 29, 1831–Sept. 21, 1862.
Vol. 10, Pt. 1–419
Ward, Genevieve, Mar. 27, 1838–Aug. 18, 1922.
Vol. 10, Pt. 1–420
Ward, George Gray, Dec. 30, 1844–June 15, 1922.
Vol. 10, Pt. 1–421
Ward, Harry Frederick, Oct. 15, 1873–Dec. 9, 1966.
Supp. 8–680
Ward, Henry Augustus, Mar. 9, 1834–July 4, 1906.
Vol. 10, Pt. 1–421
Ward, Henry Baldwin, Mar. 4, 1865–Nov. 30, 1945.
Supp. 3–802
Ward, Henry Dana, Jan. 13, 1797–Feb. 29, 1884.
Vol. 10, Pt. 1–422
Ward, Herbert Dickinson, June 30, 1861–June 18, 1932.
Vol. 10, Pt. 1–423
Ward, James Edward, Feb. 25, 1836–July 23, 1894.
Vol. 10, Pt. 1–424
Ward, James Harmon, Sept. 25, 1806–June 27, 1861.
Vol. 10, Pt. 1–425
Ward, James Warner, June 5, 1816–June 28, 1897.
Vol. 10, Pt. 1–426

Ward, John Elliott, Oct. 2, 1814–Nov. 29, 1902.
Vol. 10, Pt. 1–426
Ward, John Quincy Adams, June 29, 1830–May 1, 1910.
Vol. 10, Pt. 1–427
Ward, Joseph, May 5, 1838–Dec. 11, 1889.
Vol. 10, Pt. 1–429
Ward, Lester Frank, June 18, 1841–Apr. 18, 1913.
Vol. 10, Pt. 1–430
Ward, Lydia Arms Avery Coonley, Jan. 31, 1845–Feb. 26, 1924. Vol. 10, Pt. 1–432
Ward, Marcus Lawrence, Nov. 9, 1812–Apr. 25, 1884.
Vol. 10, Pt. 1–432
Ward, Montgomery. [See Ward, Aaron Montgomery, 1843–1913.]
Ward, Nancy, fl. 1776–1781.
Vol. 10, Pt. 1–433
Ward, Nathaniel, c. 1578–October 1652.
Vol. 10, Pt. 1–433
Ward, Richard, Apr. 15, 1689–Aug. 21, 1763.
Vol. 10, Pt. 1–434
Ward, Richard Halsted, June 17, 1837–Oct. 28, 1917.
Vol. 10, Pt. 1–435
Ward, Robert De Courcy, Nov. 29, 1867–Nov. 12, 1931.
Vol. 10, Pt. 1–436
Ward, Samuel, May 27, 1725–Mar. 26, 1776.
Vol. 10, Pt. 1–437
Ward, Samuel, Nov. 17, 1756–Aug. 16, 1832.
Vol. 10, Pt. 1–437
Ward, Samuel, May 1, 1786–Nov. 27, 1839.
Vol. 10, Pt. 1–438
Ward, Samuel, Jan. 25, 1814–May 19, 1884.
Vol. 10, Pt. 1–439
Ward, Samuel Ringgold, Oct. 17, 1817–1866?.
Vol. 10, Pt. 1–440
Ward, Thomas, June 8, 1807–Apr. 13, 1873.
Vol. 10, Pt. 1–440
Ward, Thomas Wren, Nov. 20, 1786–Mar. 4, 1858.
Vol. 10, Pt. 1–441
Ward, William Hayes, June 25, 1835–Aug. 28, 1916.
Vol. 10, Pt. 1–442
Warde, Frederick Barkham, Feb. 23, 1851–Feb. 7, 1935.
Supp. 1–698
Warden, David Bailie, 1772–Oct. 9, 1845.
Vol. 10, Pt. 1–443
Warden, Robert Bruce, Jan. 18, 1824–Dec. 3, 1888.
Vol. 10, Pt. 1–444
Warder, John Aston, Jan. 19, 1812–July 14, 1883.
Vol. 10, Pt. 1–444
Wardman, Ervin, Dec. 25, 1865–Jan. 13, 1923.
Vol. 10, Pt. 1–445
Ware, Ashur, Feb. 10, 1782–Sept. 10, 1873.
Vol. 10, Pt. 1–446
Ware, Edmund Asa, Dec. 22, 1837–Sept. 25, 1885.
Vol. 10, Pt. 1–446
Ware, Henry, Apr. 1, 1764–July 12, 1845.
Vol. 10, Pt. 1–447
Ware, Henry, Apr. 21, 1794–Sept. 22, 1843.
Vol. 10, Pt. 1–448
Ware, John, Dec. 19, 1795–Apr. 29, 1864.
Vol. 10, Pt. 1–449
Ware, John Fothergill Waterhouse, Aug. 31, 1818–Feb. 26, 1881. Vol. 10, Pt. 1–450
Ware, Nathaniel A., d. 1854.
Vol. 10, Pt. 1–451
Ware, William, Aug. 3, 1797–Feb. 19, 1852.
Vol. 10, Pt. 1–451
Ware, William Robert, May 27, 1832–June 9, 1915.
Vol. 10, Pt. 1–452
Warfield, Benjamin Breckinridge, Nov. 5, 1851–Feb. 16, 1921. Vol. 10, Pt. 1–453
Warfield, Catherine Ann Ware, June 6, 1816–May 21, 1877.
Vol. 10, Pt. 1–454
Warfield, David, Nov. 28, 1866–June 27, 1951.
Supp. 5–726
Warfield, Solomon Davies, Sept. 4, 1859–Oct. 24, 1927.
Vol. 10, Pt. 1–455
Waring, George Edwin, July 4, 1833–Oct. 29, 1898.
Vol. 10, Pt. 1–456
Waring, Julius Waties, July 27, 1880–Jan. 11, 1968.
Supp. 8–682
Warman, Cy, June 22, 1855–Apr. 7, 1914.
Vol. 10, Pt. 1–457

Warmoth, Henry Clay, May 9, 1842–Sept. 30, 1931.
Vol. 10, Pt. 1–457
Warner, Adoniram Judson, Jan. 13, 1834–Aug. 12, 1910.
Vol. 10, Pt. 1–459
Warner, Amos Griswold, Dec. 21, 1861–Jan. 17, 1900.
Vol. 10, Pt. 1–460
Warner, Anna Bartlett, Aug. 31, 1827–Jan. 22, 1915.
Vol. 10, Pt. 1–461
Warner, Anne Richmond, Oct. 14, 1869–Feb. 1, 1913.
Vol. 10, Pt. 1–461
Warner, Charles Dudley, Sept. 12, 1829–Oct. 20, 1900.
Vol. 10, Pt. 1–462
Warner, Edward Pearson, Nov. 9, 1894–July 12, 1958.
Supp. 6–665
Warner, Fred Maltby, July 21, 1865–Apr. 17, 1923.
Vol. 10, Pt. 1–463
Warner, Glenn Scobey ("Pop"), Apr. 5, 1871–Sept. 7, 1954.
Supp. 5–727
Warner, Harry Morris, Dec. 12, 1881–July 25, 1958.
Supp. 6–667
Warner, Hiram, Oct. 29, 1802–June 30, 1881.
Vol. 10, Pt. 1–464
Warner, James Cartwright, Aug. 20, 1830–July 21, 1895.
Vol. 10, Pt. 1–465
Warner, Jonathan Trumbull, Nov. 20, 1807–Apr. 22, 1895.
Vol. 10, Pt. 1–466
Warner, Juan José. [See Warner, Jonathan Trumbull, 1807–1895.]
Warner, Langdon, Aug. 1, 1881–June 9, 1955.
Supp. 5–729
Warner, Olin Levi, Apr. 9, 1844–Aug. 14, 1896.
Vol. 10, Pt. 1–467
Warner, Seth, May 6, 1743 o.s.–Dec. 26, 1784.
Vol. 10, Pt. 1–468
Warner, Susan Bogert, July 11, 1819–Mar. 17, 1885.
Vol. 10, Pt. 1–469
Warner, William, June 11, 1840–Oct. 4, 1916.
Vol. 10, Pt. 1–469
Warner, William Lloyd, Oct. 26, 1898–May 23, 1970.
Supp. 8–683
Warner, Worcester Reed, May 16, 1846–June 25, 1929.
Vol. 10, Pt. 1–470
Warren, Charles, Mar. 9, 1868–Aug. 16, 1954.
Supp. 5–730
Warren, Cyrus Moors, Jan. 15, 1824–Aug. 13, 1891.
Vol. 10, Pt. 1–471
Warren, Francis Emroy, June 20, 1844–Nov. 24, 1929.
Vol. 10, Pt. 1–472
Warren, George Frederick, Feb. 16, 1874–May 24, 1938.
Supp. 2–695
Warren, Gouverneur Kemble, Jan. 8, 1830–Aug. 8, 1882,.
Vol. 10, Pt. 1–473
Warren, Henry Clarke, Nov. 18, 1854–Jan. 3, 1899.
Vol. 10, Pt. 1–474
Warren, Henry Ellis, May 21, 1872–Sept. 21, 1957.
Supp. 6–668
Warren, Henry White, Jan. 4, 1831–July 22, 1912.
Vol. 10, Pt. 1–475
Warren, Herbert Langford, Mar. 29, 1857–June 27, 1917.
Supp. 1–698
Warren, Howard Crosby, June 12, 1867–Jan. 4, 1934.
Vol. 10, Pt. 1–476
Warren, Israel Perkins, Apr. 8, 1814–Oct. 9, 1892.
Vol. 10, Pt. 1–477
Warren, James, Sept. 28, 1726–Nov. 28, 1808.
Vol. 10, Pt. 1–478
Warren, John, July 27, 1753–Apr. 4, 1815.
Vol. 10, Pt. 1–479
Warren, John Collins, Aug. 1, 1778–May 4, 1856.
Vol. 10, Pt. 1–480
Warren, John Collins, May 4, 1842–Nov. 3, 1927.
Vol. 10, Pt. 1–481
Warren, Joseph, June 11, 1741–June 17, 1775.
Vol. 10, Pt. 1–482
Warren, Josiah, c. 1798–Apr. 14, 1874.
Vol. 10, Pt. 1–483
Warren, Leonard, Apr. 21, 1911–Mar. 4, 1960.
Supp. 6–669
Warren, Mercy Otis, Sept. 14, 1728–o.s. Oct. 19, 1814.
Vol. 10, Pt. 1–484
Warren, Minton, Jan. 29, 1850–Nov. 26, 1907.
Vol. 10, Pt. 1–485

Warren, Sir Peter, Mar. 10, 1703–July 29, 1752.
Vol. 10, Pt. 1–485
Warren, Richard Henry, Sept. 17, 1859–Dec. 3, 1933.
Vol. 10, Pt. 1–487
Warren, Russell, Aug. 5, 1783–Nov. 16, 1860.
Vol. 10, Pt. 1–487
Warren, Samuel Prowse, Feb. 18, 1841–Oct. 7, 1915.
Vol. 10, Pt. 1–488
Warren, William, May 10, 1767–Oct. 19, 1832.
Vol. 10, Pt. 1–489
Warren, William, Nov. 17, 1812–Sept. 21, 1888.
Vol. 10, Pt. 1–489
Warren, William Fairfield, Mar. 13, 1833–Dec. 6, 1929.
Vol. 10, Pt. 1–490
Warrington, Albert Powell, Aug. 27, 1886–June 16, 1939.
Supp. 2–697
Warrington, Lewis, Nov. 3, 1782–Oct. 12, 1851.
Vol. 10, Pt. 1–492
Warthin, Aldred Scott, Oct. 21, 1866–May 23, 1931.
Vol. 10, Pt. 1–493
Washakie, c. 1804–Feb. 15, 1900.
Vol. 10, Pt. 1–494
Washburn, Albert Henry, Apr. 11, 1866–Apr. 2, 1930.
Vol. 10, Pt. 1–494
Washburn, Cadwallader Colden, Apr. 22, 1818–May 14, 1882. Vol. 10, Pt. 1–495
Washburn, Charles Grenfill, Jan. 28, 1857–May 25, 1928.
Vol. 10, Pt. 1–497
Washburn, Edward Abiel, Apr. 16, 1819–Feb. 2, 1881.
Vol. 10, Pt. 1–498
Washburn, Edward Wight, May 10, 1881–Feb. 6, 1934.
Vol. 10, Pt. 1–498
Washburn, Elihu Benjamin. [See Washburne, Elihu Benjamin.]
Washburn, Emory, Feb. 14, 1800–Mar. 18, 1877.
Vol. 10, Pt. 1–499
Washburn, George, Mar. 1, 1833–Feb. 15, 1915.
Vol. 10, Pt. 1–500
Washburn, Ichabod, Aug. 11, 1798–Dec. 30, 1868.
Vol. 10, Pt. 1–501
Washburn, Israel, June 6, 1813–May 12, 1883.
Vol. 10, Pt. 1–502
Washburn, Margaret Floy, July 25, 1871–Oct. 29, 1939.
Supp. 2–698
Washburn, Nathan, Apr. 22, 1818–Sept. 13, 1903.
Vol. 10, Pt. 1–503
Washburn, William Drew, Jan. 14, 1831–July 29, 1912.
Vol. 10, Pt. 1–504
Washburne, Elihu Benjamin, Sept. 23, 1816–Oct. 23, 1887.
Vol. 10, Pt. 1–504
Washington, Booker Taliaferro, Apr. 5, 1856–Nov. 14, 1915.
Vol. 10, Pt. 1–506
Washington, Bushrod, June 5, 1762–Nov. 26, 1829.
Vol. 10, Pt. 1–508
Washington, Dinah, Aug. 1924–Dec. 14, 1963.
Supp. 7–769
Washington, George, Feb. 11/22, 1732–Dec. 14, 1799.
Vol. 10, Pt. 1–509
Washington, Henry Stephens, Jan. 15, 1867–Jan. 7, 1934.
Vol. 10, Pt. 1–527
Washington, John Macrae, October 1797–Dec. 24, 1853.
Vol. 10, Pt. 1–528
Waterhouse, Benjamin, Mar. 4, 1754–Oct. 2, 1846.
Vol. 10, Pt. 1–529
Waterhouse, Frank, Aug. 8, 1867–Mar. 20, 1930.
Vol. 10, Pt. 1–532
Waterhouse, Sylvester, Sept. 15, 1830–Feb. 12, 1902.
Vol. 10, Pt. 1–533
Waterman, Alan Tower, June 4, 1892–Dec. 1, 1967.
Supp. 8–685
Waterman, Lewis Edson, Nov. 20, 1837–May 1, 1901.
Vol. 10, Pt. 1–533
Waterman, Robert H., Mar. 4, 1808–Aug. 9, 1884.
Vol. 10, Pt. 1–534
Waterman, Thomas Whitney, June 28, 1821–Dec. 7, 1898.
Vol. 10, Pt. 1–535
Waters, Daniel, June 20, 1731–Mar. 26, 1816.
Vol. 10, Pt. 1–536
Waters, William Everett, Dec. 20, 1856–Aug. 3, 1924.
Vol. 10, Pt. 1–537
Watie, Stand, Dec. 12, 1806–Sept. 9, 1871.
Vol. 10, Pt. 1–537

Watkins, George Claiborne, Nov. 25, 1815–Dec. 7, 1872.
    Vol. 10, Pt. 1–538
Watkins, John Elfreth, May 17, 1852–Aug. 11, 1903.
    Vol. 10, Pt. 1–539
Watson, Andrew, Feb. 15, 1834–Dec. 9, 1916.
    Vol. 10, Pt. 1–539
Watson, Charles Roger, July 17, 1873–Jan. 10, 1948.
    Supp. 4–859
Watson, David Thompson, Jan. 2, 1844–Feb. 24, 1916.
    Vol. 10, Pt. 1–540
Watson, Elkanah, Jan. 22, 1758–Dec. 5, 1842.
    Vol. 10, Pt. 1–541
Watson, Henry Clay, 1831–June 24, 1867.
    Vol. 10, Pt. 1–542
Watson, Henry Cood, Nov. 4, 1818–Dec. 2, 1875.
    Vol. 10, Pt. 1–543
Watson, James Craig, Jan. 28, 1838–Nov. 22, 1880.
    Vol. 10, Pt. 1–543
Watson, James Eli, Nov. 2, 1864–July 29, 1948.
    Supp. 4–861
Watson, James Madison, Feb. 8, 1827–Sept. 29, 1900.
    Vol. 10, Pt. 1–544
Watson, John Broadus, Jan. 9, 1878–Sept. 25, 1958.
    Supp. 6–670
Watson, John Crittenden, Aug. 24, 1842–Dec. 14, 1923.
    Vol. 10, Pt. 1–545
Watson, John Fanning, June 13, 1779–Dec. 23, 1860.
    Vol. 10, Pt. 1–546
Watson, John William Clark, Feb. 27, 1808–Sept. 24, 1890.
    Vol. 10, Pt. 1–547
Watson, Sereno, Dec. 1, 1826–Mar. 9, 1892.
    Vol. 10, Pt. 1–547
Watson, Thomas Augustus, Jan. 18, 1854–Dec. 13, 1934.
    Vol. 10, Pt. 1–548
Watson, Thomas Edward, Sept. 5, 1856–Sept. 26, 1922.
    Vol. 10, Pt. 1–549
Watson, Thomas John, Feb. 17, 1874–June 19, 1956.
    Supp. 6–673
Watson, William, Jan. 19, 1834–Sept. 30, 1915.
    Vol. 10, Pt. 1–551
Watterson, Harvey Magee, Nov. 23, 1811–Oct. 1, 1891.
    Vol. 10, Pt. 1–551
Watterson, Henry, Feb. 16, 1840–Dec. 22, 1921.
    Vol. 10, Pt. 1–552
Watterston, George, Oct. 23, 1783–Feb. 4, 1854.
    Vol. 10, Pt. 1–555
Watts, Frederick, May 9, 1801–Aug. 17, 1889.
    Vol. 10, Pt. 1–556
Watts, Thomas Hill, Jan. 3, 1819–Sept. 16, 1892.
    Vol. 10, Pt. 1–557
Wattson, Lewis Thomas. [See Francis, Paul James, 1863–1940.]
Waugh, Beverly, Oct. 25, 1789–Feb. 9, 1858.
    Vol. 10, Pt. 1–558
Waugh, Frederick Judd, Sept. 13, 1861–Sept. 10, 1940.
    Supp. 2–699
Waxman, Franz, Dec. 24, 1906–Feb. 24, 1967.
    Supp. 8–688
Wayland, Francis, Mar. 11, 1796–Sept. 30, 1865.
    Vol. 10, Pt. 1–558
Wayland, Francis, Aug. 23, 1826–Jan. 9, 1904.
    Vol. 10, Pt. 1–560
Waymack, William Wesley, Oct. 18, 1888–Nov. 5, 1960.
    Supp. 6–676
Wayman, Alexander Walker, September 1821–Nov. 30, 1895. Vol. 10, Pt. 1–561
Waymouth, George, fl. 1601–1612.
    Vol. 10, Pt. 1–562
Wayne, Anthony, Jan. 1, 1745–Dec. 15, 1796.
    Vol. 10, Pt. 1–563
Wayne, Arthur Trezevant, Jan. 1, 1863–May 5, 1930.
    Vol. 10, Pt. 1–565
Wayne, James Moore, c. 1790–July 5, 1867.
    Vol. 10, Pt. 1–565
Weare, Meshech, Jan. 16, 1713–Jan. 14, 1786.
    Vol. 10, Pt. 1–566
Weatherford, William, c. 1780–Mar. 9, 1824.
    Vol. 10, Pt. 1–567
Weaver, Aaron Ward, July 1, 1832–Oct. 2, 1919.
    Vol. 10, Pt. 1–568
Weaver, James Baird, June 12, 1833–Feb. 6, 1912.
    Vol. 10, Pt. 1–568

Weaver, Philip, b. 1791.
    Vol. 10, Pt. 1–570
Weaver, William Dixon, Aug. 30, 1857–Nov. 2, 1919.
    Vol. 10, Pt. 1–570
Webb, Alexander Stewart, Feb. 15, 1835–Feb. 12, 1911.
    Vol. 10, Pt. 1–571
Webb, Charles Henry, Jan. 24, 1834–May 24, 1905.
    Vol. 10, Pt. 1–572
Webb, Clifton, Nov. 19, 1893–Oct. 13, 1966.
    Supp. 8–690
Webb, Daniel, c. 1700–Nov. 11, 1773.
    Vol. 10, Pt. 1–573
Webb, George James, June 24, 1803–Oct. 7, 1887.
    Vol. 10, Pt. 1–574
Webb, Harry Howard, Aug. 15, 1853–June 2, 1939.
    Supp. 2–700
Webb, James Watson, Feb. 8, 1802–June 7, 1884.
    Vol. 10, Pt. 1–574
Webb, John Burkitt, Nov. 22, 1841–Feb. 17, 1912.
    Vol. 10, Pt. 1–575
Webb, Thomas, c. 1724–Dec. 10, 1796.
    Vol. 10, Pt. 1–576
Webb, Thomas Smith, Oct. 30, 1771–July 6, 1819.
    Vol. 10, Pt. 1–577
Webb, Walter Prescott, Apr. 3, 1888–Mar. 8, 1963.
    Supp. 7–770
Webb, William Henry, June 19, 1816–Oct. 30, 1899.
    Vol. 10, Pt. 1–578
Webb, William Robert, Nov. 11, 1842–Dec. 19, 1926.
    Vol. 10, Pt. 1–579
Webber, Charles Wilkins, May 29, 1819–April 1856.
    Vol. 10, Pt. 1–580
Webber, Herbert John, Dec. 27, 1865–Jan. 18, 1946.
    Supp. 4–862
Weber, Albert, July 8, 1828–June 25, 1879.
    Vol. 10, Pt. 1–581
Weber, Gustav Carl Erich, May 26, 1828–Mar. 21, 1912.
    Vol. 10, Pt. 1–581
Weber, Henry Adam, July 12, 1845–June 14, 1912.
    Vol. 10, Pt. 1–582
Weber, Joseph Morris, Aug. 11, 1867–May 10, 1942.
    Supp. 3–803
Weber, Max, Apr. 18, 1881–Oct. 4, 1961.
    Supp. 7–772
Webster, Alice Jane Chandler, July 24, 1876–June 11, 1916.
    Vol. 10, Pt. 1–583
Webster, Arthur Gordon, Nov. 28, 1863–May 15, 1923.
    Vol. 10, Pt. 1–584
Webster, Daniel, Jan. 18, 1782–Oct. 24, 1852.
    Vol. 10, Pt. 1–585
Webster, Edwin Sibley, Aug. 26, 1867–May 10, 1950.
    Supp. 3–744
Webster, Edwin Sibley. [See Stone, Charles Augustus.]
Webster, Harold Tucker, Sept. 21, 1885–Sept. 22, 1952.
    Supp. 5–731
Webster, Jean. [See Webster, Alice Jane Chandler, 1876–1916.]
Webster, John White, May 20, 1793–Aug. 30, 1850.
    Vol. 10, Pt. 1–592
Webster, Joseph Dana, Aug. 25, 1811–Mar. 12, 1876.
    Vol. 10, Pt. 1–593
Webster, Noah, Oct. 16, 1758–May 28, 1843.
    Vol. 10, Pt. 1–594
Webster, Pelatiah, Nov. 24, 1726–Sept. 2, 1795.
    Vol. 10, Pt. 1–597
Webster-Powell, Alma. [See Powell, Alma Webster, 1874–1930.]
Weddell, Alexander Wilbourne, Apr. 6, 1876–Jan. 1, 1948.
    Supp. 4–863
Weed, Lewis Hill, Nov. 15, 1886–Dec. 21, 1952.
    Supp. 5–733
Weed, Thurlow, Nov. 15, 1797–Nov. 22, 1882.
    Vol. 10, Pt. 1–598
Weeden, William Babcock, Sept. 1, 1834–Mar. 28, 1912.
    Vol. 10, Pt. 1–600
Weeks, Edwin Lord, 1849–Nov. 17, 1903.
    Vol. 10, Pt. 1–601
Weeks, John Elmer, Aug. 9, 1853–Feb. 2, 1949.
    Supp. 4–864
Weeks, John Wingate, Apr. 11, 1860–July 12, 1926.
    Vol. 10, Pt. 1–601
Weeks, Joseph Dame, Dec. 3, 1840–Dec. 26, 1896.
    Vol. 10, Pt. 1–602

Weeks, Stephen Beauregard, Feb. 2, 1865–May 3, 1918.
    Vol. 10, Pt. 1–603
Weems, Mason Locke, Oct. 11, 1759–May 23, 1825.
    Vol. 10, Pt. 1–604
Weems, Ted, Sept. 26, 1901–May 6, 1963.
    Supp. 7–774
Wegmann, Edward, Nov. 27, 1850–Jan. 3, 1935.
    Supp. 1–699
Wehle, Louis Brandeis, Sept. 13, 1880–Feb. 13, 1959.
    Supp. 6–677
Weidenmann, Jacob, Aug. 22, 1829–Feb. 6, 1893.
    Vol. 10, Pt. 1–605
Weidenreich, Franz, June 7, 1873–July 11, 1948.
    Supp. 4–866
Weidig, Adolf, Nov. 28, 1867 Sept. 23, 1931.
    Vol. 10, Pt. 1–606
Weidner, Revere Franklin, Nov. 22, 1851–Jan. 6, 1915.
    Vol. 10, Pt. 1–606
Weigel, Gustave, Jan. 15, 1906–Jan. 3, 1964.
    Supp. 7–775
Weightman, William, Sept. 30, 1813–Aug. 25, 1904.
    Vol. 10, Pt. 1–607
Weil, Richard, Oct. 15, 1876–Nov. 19, 1917.
    Vol. 10, Pt. 1–608
Weill, Kurt, Mar. 2, 1900–Apr. 3, 1950.
    Supp. 4–867
Weir, Ernest Tener, Aug. 1, 1875–June 26, 1957.
    Supp. 6–678
Weir, John Ferguson, Aug. 28, 1841–Apr. 8, 1926.
    Vol. 10, Pt. 1–608
Weir, Julian Alden, Aug. 30, 1852–Dec. 8, 1919.
    Vol. 10, Pt. 1–609
Weir, Robert Fulton, Feb. 16, 1838–Apr. 6, 1927.
    Vol. 10, Pt. 1–611
Weir, Robert Walter, June 18, 1803–May 1, 1889
Weisenburg, Theodore Herman, Apr. 10, 1876–Aug. 3,
    1934. Vol. 10, Pt. 1–613
Weiser, Johann Conrad, Nov. 2, 1696–July 13, 1760.
    Vol. 10, Pt. 1–614
Weiss, Ehrich. [See Houdini, Harry, 1874–1926.]
Weiss, John, June 28, 1818–Mar. 9, 1879.
    Vol. 10, Pt. 1–615
Weiss, Soma, Jan. 27, 1899–Jan. 31, 1942.
    Supp. 3–805
Weitzel, Godfrey, Nov. 1, 1835–Mar. 19, 1884.
    Vol. 10, Pt. 1–616
Welby, Amelia Ball Coppuck, Feb. 3, 1819–May 3, 1852.
    Vol. 10, Pt. 1–617
Welch, Adonijah Strong, Apr. 12, 1821–Mar. 14, 1889.
    Vol. 10, Pt. 1–617
Welch, Ashbel, Dec. 4, 1809–Sept. 25, 1882.
    Vol. 10, Pt. 1–618
Welch, Charles Clark, June 14, 1830–Feb. 1, 1908.
    Vol. 10, Pt. 1–619
Welch, John, Oct. 28, 1805–Aug. 5, 1891.
    Vol. 10, Pt. 1–620
Welch, Joseph Nye, Oct. 22, 1890–Oct. 6, 1960.
    Supp. 6–679
Welch, Philip Henry, Mar. 1, 1849–Feb. 24, 1889.
    Vol. 10, Pt. 1–620
Welch, William Henry, Apr. 8, 1850–Apr. 30, 1934.
    Vol. 10, Pt. 1–621
Welch, William Wickham, Dec. 10, 1818–July 30, 1892.
    Vol. 10, Pt. 1–624
Weld, Arthur Cyril Gordon, Mar. 4, 1862–Oct. 11, 1914.
    Vol. 10, Pt. 1–625
Weld, Theodore Dwight, Nov. 23, 1803–Feb. 3, 1895.
    Vol. 10, Pt. 1–625
Weld, Thomas, 1595–Mar. 23, 1660/61.
    Vol. 10, Pt. 1–627
Welker, Herman, Dec. 11, 1906–Oct. 30, 1957.
    Supp. 6–681
Weller, John B., Feb. 22, 1812–Aug. 17, 1875.
    Vol. 10, Pt. 1–628
Welles, (Benjamin) Sumner, Oct. 14, 1892–Sept. 24, 1961.
    Supp. 7–776
Welles, Gideon, July 1, 1802–Feb. 11, 1878.
    Vol. 10, Pt. 1–629
Welles, Noah, Sept. 25, 1718–Dec. 31, 1776,
    Vol. 10, Pt. 1–632
Welles, Roger, Dec. 7, 1862–Apr. 26, 1932.
    Vol. 10, Pt. 1–632

Welling, James Clarke, July 14, 1825–Sept. 4, 1894.
    Vol. 10, Pt. 1–633
Welling, Richard Ward Greene, Aug. 27, 1858–Dec. 17,
    1946. Supp. 4–869
Wellington, Arthur Mellen, Dec. 20, 1847–May 16, 1895.
    Vol. 10, Pt. 1–634
Wellman, Samuel Thomas, Feb. 5, 1847–July 11, 1919.
    Vol. 10, Pt. 1–635
Wellman, Walter, Nov. 3, 1858–Jan. 31, 1934.
    Vol. 10, Pt. 1–635
Wellons, William Brock, Nov. 9, 1821–Feb. 16, 1877.
    Vol. 10, Pt. 1–636
Wells, David Ames, June 17, 1828–Nov. 5, 1898.
    Vol. 10, Pt. 1–637
Wells, Erastus, Dec. 2, 1823–Oct. 2, 1893.
    Vol. 10, Pt. 1–638
Wells, Harriet Sheldon, 1873–Feb. 8, 1961.
    Supp. 7–778
Wells, Harry Gideon, July 21, 1875–Apr. 26, 1943.
    Supp. 3–806
Wells, Henry, Dec. 12, 1805–Dec. 10, 1878.
    Vol. 10, Pt. 1–639
Wells, Horace, Jan. 21, 1815–Jan. 24, 1848.
    Vol. 10, Pt. 1–640
Wells, James Madison, Jan. 8, 1808–Feb. 28, 1899.
    Vol. 10, Pt. 1–641
Wells, John, c. 1770–Sept. 7, 1823.
    Vol. 10, Pt. 1–642
Wells, Robert William, Nov. 29, 1795–Sept. 22, 1864.
    Vol. 10, Pt. 1–643
Wells, Samuel Roberts, Apr. 4, 1820–Apr. 13, 1875.
    Vol. 10, Pt. 1–643
Wells, William Charles, May 24, 1757–Sept. 18, 1817.
    Vol. 10, Pt. 1–644
Wells, William Harvey, Feb. 27, 1812–Jan. 21, 1885.
    Vol. 10, Pt. 1–645
Wells, William Vincent, Jan. 2, 1826–June 1, 1876.
    Vol. 10, Pt. 1–646
Welsh, John, Nov. 9, 1805–Apr. 10, 1886.
    Vol. 10, Pt. 1–647
Wemyss, Francis Courtney, May 13, 1797–Jan. 5, 1859.
    Vol. 10, Pt. 1–647
Wende, Ernest, July 23, 1853–Feb. 11, 1910.
    Vol. 10, Pt. 1–648
Wende, Grover William, Apr. 6, 1867–Feb. 9, 1926.
    Vol. 10, Pt. 1–649
Wendell, Barrett, Aug. 23, 1855–Feb. 8, 1921.
    Vol. 10, Pt. 1–649
Wendte, Charles William, June 11, 1844–Sept. 9, 1931.
    Vol. 10, Pt. 1–651
Wenley, Robert Mark, July 19, 1861–Mar. 29, 1929.
    Vol. 10, Pt. 1–652
Wenner, George Unangst, May 17, 1844–Nov. 1, 1934.
    Vol. 10, Pt. 1–653
Wentworth, Benning, July 24, 1696–Oct. 14, 1770.
    Vol. 10, Pt. 1–653
Wentworth, Cecile de, d. Aug. 28, 1933.
    Vol. 10, Pt. 1–654
Wentworth, George Albert, July 31, 1835–May 24, 1906.
    Vol. 10, Pt. 1–655
Wentworth, John, Aug. 20, 1737 N. s.–Apr. 8, 1820.
    Vol. 10, Pt. 1–656
Wentworth, John, Mar. 5, 1815–Oct. 16, 1888.
    Vol. 10, Pt. 1–657
Wentworth, Paul, d. December 1793.
    Vol. 10, Pt. 1–659
Werden, Reed, Feb. 28, 1818–July 11, 1886.
    Vol. 10, Pt. 2–1
Wergeland, Agnes Mathilde, May 8, 1857–Mar. 6, 1914.
    Vol. 10, Pt. 2–1
Wernwag, Lewis, Dec. 4, 1769–Aug. 12, 1843.
    Vol. 10, Pt. 2–2
Wertenbaker, Charles Christian, Feb. 11, 1901–Jan. 8, 1955.
    Supp. 5–734
Wertenbaker, Thomas Jefferson, Feb. 6, 1879–Apr. 22, 1966.
    Supp. 8–691
Wertheimer, Max, Apr. 15, 1880–Oct. 12, 1943.
    Supp. 3–808
Westbrook, Frank Fairchild, July 12, 1868–Oct. 20, 1918.
    Vol. 10, Pt. 2–3
Wesselhoeft, Conrad, Mar. 23, 1834–Dec. 17, 1904.
    Vol. 10, Pt. 2–4

Wesselhoeft, Walter, 1838–1920. [See Wesselhoeft, Conrad, 1834–1904.]
Wesson, Daniel Baird, May 18, 1825–Aug. 4, 1906.
    Vol. 10, Pt. 2–4
West, Allen Brown, June 19, 1886–Sept. 18, 1936.
    Supp. 2–701
West, Andrew Fleming, May 17, 1853–Dec. 27, 1943.
    Supp. 3–809
West, Benjamin, March 1730–Aug. 26, 1813.
    Vol. 10, Pt. 2–5
West, Benjamin, Oct. 10, 1728–Mar. 11, 1820.
    Vol. 10, Pt. 2–6
West, Francis, Oct. 28, 1586–1634.
    Vol. 10, Pt. 2–9
West, George, Feb. 17, 1823–Sept. 20, 1901.
    Vol. 10, Pt. 2–10
West, Henry Sergeant, Jan. 21, 1827–Apr. 1, 1876.
    Vol. 10, Pt. 2–10
West, James Edward, May 16, 1876–May 15, 1948.
    Supp. 4–871
West, Joseph, d. 1692?.
    Vol. 10, Pt. 2–11
West, Oswald, May 20, 1873–Aug. 22, 1960.
    Supp. 6–682
West, Roy Owen, Oct. 27, 1868–Nov. 29, 1958.
    Supp. 6–683
West, Samuel, Mar. 3, 1730 o.s.–Sept. 24, 1807.
    Vol. 10, Pt. 2–12
West, William Edward, Dec. 10, 1788–Nov. 2, 1857.
    Vol. 10, Pt. 2–12
Westcott, Edward Noyes, Sept. 27, 1846–Mar. 31, 1898.
    Vol. 10, Pt. 2–13
Westcott, Thompson, June 5, 1820–May 8, 1888.
    Vol. 10, Pt. 2–14
Westergaard, Harald Malcolm, Oct. 9, 1888–June 22, 1950.
    Supp. 4–873
Westermann, William Linn, Sept. 15, 1873–Oct. 4, 1954.
    Supp. 5–735
Western, Lucille, Jan. 8, 1843–Jan. 11, 1877.
    Vol. 10, Pt. 2–14
Westervelt, Jacob Aaron, Jan. 20, 1800–Feb. 21, 1879.
    Vol. 10, Pt. 2–15
Westinghouse, George, Oct. 6, 1846–Mar. 12, 1914.
    Vol. 10, Pt. 2–16
Westley, Helen, Mar. 28, 1875–Dec. 12, 1942.
    Supp. 3–811
Weston, Edward, May 9, 1850–Aug. 20, 1936.
    Supp. 2–702
Weston, Edward Henry, Mar. 24, 1886–Jan. 1, 1958.
    Supp. 6–684
Weston, Edward Payson, Mar. 15, 1839–May 12, 1929.
    Vol. 10, Pt. 2–18
Weston, Nathan Austin, Apr. 5, 1868–Nov. 29, 1933.
    Vol. 10, Pt. 2–19
Weston, Thomas, c. 1575–c. 1644.
    Vol. 10, Pt. 2–20
Weston, William, c. 1752–Aug. 29, 1833.
    Vol. 10, Pt. 2–21
Wetherill, Charles Mayer, Nov. 4, 1825–Mar. 5, 1871.
    Vol. 10, Pt. 2–22
Wetherill, Samuel, Apr. 12, 1736–Sept. 24, 1816.
    Vol. 10, Pt. 2–23
Wetherill, Samuel, May 27, 1821–June 24, 1890.
    Vol. 10, Pt. 2–23
Wetzel, Lewis, 1764–1808?.
    Vol. 10, Pt. 2–24
Wexler, Irving ("Waxey Gordon"), 1888–June 24, 1952.
    Supp. 5–736
Weyerhaeuser, Frederick Edward, Nov. 4, 1872–Oct. 18, 1945. Supp. 3–812
Weyl, Hermann, Nov. 9, 1885–Dec. 1955.
    Supp. 5–737
Weymouth, Frank Elwin, June 2, 1874–July 22, 1941.
    Supp. 3–813
Whalen, Grover Aloysius, June 2, 1886–Apr. 20, 1962.
    Supp. 7–779
Whalley, Edward, d. 1674 or 1675.
    Vol. 10, Pt. 2–25
Wharton, Anne Hollingsworth, Dec. 15, 1845–July 29, 1928.
    Vol. 10, Pt. 2–25
Wharton, Charles Henry, May 25, 1748 o.s.– July 23, 1833.
    Vol. 10, Pt. 2–26

Wharton, Edith Newbold Jones, Jan. 24, 1862–Aug. 11, 1937.
    Supp. 2–703
Wharton, Francis, Mar. 7, 1820–Feb. 21, 1889.
    Vol. 10, Pt. 2–27
Wharton, Greene Lawrence, July 17, 1847–Nov. 4, 1906.
    Vol. 10, Pt. 2–28
Wharton, Joseph, Mar. 3, 1826–Jan. 11, 1909.
    Vol. 10, Pt. 2–29
Wharton, Richard, d. May 14, 1689.
    Vol. 10, Pt. 2–30
Wharton, Robert, Jan. 12, 1757–Mar. 7, 1834.
    Vol. 10, Pt. 2–31
Wharton, Samuel, May 3, 1732–1800.
    Vol. 10, Pt. 2–32
Wharton, Thomas, 1735–May 22, 1778.
    Vol. 10, Pt. 2–33
Wharton, Thomas Isaac, May 17, 1791–Apr. 7, 1856.
    Vol. 10, Pt. 2–34
Wharton, William H., 1802–Mar. 14, 1839.
    Vol. 10, Pt. 2–35
Whatcoat, Richard, Feb. 23, 1736–July 5, 1806.
    Vol. 10, Pt. 2–36
Wheatley, Phillis, c. 1753–Dec. 5, 1784.
    Vol. 10, Pt. 2–36
Wheatley, William, Dec. 5, 1816–Nov. 3, 1876.
    Vol. 10, Pt. 2–37
Wheaton, Frank, May 8, 1833–June 18, 1903.
    Vol. 10, Pt. 2–38
Wheaton, Henry, Nov. 27, 1785–Mar. 11, 1848.
    Vol. 10, Pt. 2–39
Wheaton, Nathaniel Sheldon, Aug. 20, 1792–Mar. 18, 1862.
    Vol. 10, Pt. 2–42
Whedon, Daniel Denison, Mar. 20, 1808–June 8, 1885.
    Vol. 10, Pt. 2–43
Wheeler, Andrew Carpenter, June 4, 1835–Mar. 10, 1903.
    Vol. 10, Pt. 2–44
Wheeler, Arthur Leslie, Aug. 12, 1872–May 22, 1932.
    Supp. 1–700
Wheeler, Benjamin Ide, July 15, 1854–May 2, 1927.
    Vol. 10, Pt. 2–44
Wheeler, Everett Pepperrell, Mar. 10, 1840–Feb. 8, 1925.
    Vol. 10, Pt. 2–46
Wheeler, George Montague, Oct. 9, 1842–May 3, 1905.
    Vol. 10, Pt. 2–47
Wheeler, (George) Post, Aug. 6, 1869–Dec. 23, 1956.
    Supp. 6–686
Wheeler, George Wakeman, Dec. 1, 1860–July 27, 1932.
    Vol. 10, Pt. 2–48
Wheeler, James Rignall, Feb. 15, 1859–Feb. 9, 1918.
    Vol. 10, Pt. 2–49
Wheeler, John Hill, Aug. 2, 1806–Dec. 7, 1882.
    Vol. 10, Pt. 2–50
Wheeler, John Martin, Nov. 10, 1879–Aug. 22, 1938.
    Supp. 2–706
Wheeler, Joseph, Sept. 10, 1836–Jan. 25, 1906.
    Vol. 10, Pt. 2–50
Wheeler, Nathaniel, Sept. 7, 1820–Dec. 31, 1893.
    Vol. 10, Pt. 2–52
Wheeler, Royall Tyler, 1810–April 1864.
    Vol. 10, Pt. 2–53
Wheeler, Schuyler Skaats, May 17, 1860–Apr. 20, 1923.
    Vol. 10, Pt. 2–53
Wheeler, Wayne Bidwell, Nov. 10, 1869–Sept. 5, 1927.
    Vol. 10, Pt. 2–54
Wheeler, William, Dec. 6, 1851–July 1, 1932.
    Vol. 10, Pt. 2–55
Wheeler, William Adolphus, Nov. 14, 1833–Oct. 28, 1874.
    Vol. 10, Pt. 2–56
Wheeler, William Almon, June 30, 1819–June 4, 1887.
    Vol. 10, Pt. 2–57
Wheeler, William Morton, Mar. 19, 1865–Apr. 19, 1937.
    Supp. 2–707
Wheelock, Eleazar, Apr. 22, 1711–Apr. 24, 1779.
    Vol. 10, Pt. 2–58
Wheelock, John, Jan. 28, 1754–Apr. 4, 1817.
    Vol. 10, Pt. 2–59
Wheelock, Joseph Albert, Feb. 8, 1831–May 9, 1906.
    Vol. 10, Pt. 2–60
Wheelock, Lucy, Feb. 1, 1857–Oct. 2, 1946.
    Supp. 4–874
Wheelwright, Edmund March, Sept. 14, 1854–Aug. 14, 1912.
    Vol. 10, Pt. 2–61

Wheelwright, John, c. 1592–Nov. 15, 1679.
 Vol. 10, Pt. 2–62
Wheelwright, Mary Cabot, Oct. 2, 1878–July 19, 1958.
 Supp. 6–687
Wheelwright, William, Mar. 16, 1798–Sept. 26, 1873.
 Vol. 10, Pt. 2–63
Wheery, Elwood Morris, Mar. 26, 1843–Oct. 5, 1927.
 Vol. 10, Pt. 2–65
Whelpley, Henry Milton, May 24, 1861–June 26, 1926.
 Vol. 10, Pt. 2–64
Wherry, Kenneth Spicer, Feb. 28, 1892–Nov. 29, 1951.
 Supp. 5–738
Whetzel, Herbert Hice, Sept. 5, 1877–Nov. 30, 1944.
 Supp. 3–814
Whipple, Abraham, Sept. 26, 1733–May 27, 1819.
 Vol. 10, Pt. 2–66
Whipple, Amiel Weeks, 1816–May 7, 1863.
 Vol. 10, Pt. 2–66
Whipple, Edwin Percy, Mar. 8, 1819–June 16, 1886.
 Vol. 10, Pt. 2–67
Whipple, Frances Harriet. [See Green, Frances Harriet
 Whipple, 1805–1878.]
Whipple, Henry Benjamin, Feb. 15, 1822–Sept. 16, 1901.
 Vol. 10, Pt. 2–68
Whipple, Sherman Leland, Mar. 4, 1862–Oct. 20, 1930.
 Vol. 10, Pt. 2–69
Whipple, Squire, Sept. 16, 1804–Mar. 15, 1888.
 Vol. 10, Pt. 2–70
Whipple, William, Jan. 14, 1730–Nov. 10, 1785.
 Vol. 10, Pt. 2–71
Whistler, George Washington, May 19, 1800–Apr. 7, 1849.
 Vol. 10, Pt. 2–72
Whistler, James Abbott McNeill, July 10, 1834–July 17, 1903.
 Vol. 10, Pt. 2–73
Whitaker, Alexander, 1585–March 1616/17.
 Vol. 10, Pt. 2–79
Whitaker, Charles Harris, May 19, 1872–Aug. 10, 1938.
 Supp. 2–708
Whitaker, Daniel Kimball, Apr. 13, 1801–Mar. 24, 1881.
 Vol. 10, Pt. 2–80
Whitaker, Nathaniel, November 1730–Jan. 26, 1795.
 Vol. 10, Pt. 2–81
Whitcher, Frances Miriam Berry, Nov. 1, 1814–Jan. 4, 1852.
 Vol. 10, Pt. 2–82
Whitcomb, James, Dec. 1, 1795–Oct. 4, 1852.
 Vol. 10, Pt. 2–82
Whitcomb, Seldon Lincoln, July 19, 1866–Apr. 22, 1930.
 Vol. 10, Pt. 2–83
White, Albert Smith, Oct. 24, 1803–Sept. 4, 1864.
 Vol. 10, Pt. 2–84
White, Alexander, c. 1738–Oct. 9, 1804.
 Vol. 10, Pt. 2–85
White, Alexander, Mar. 30, 1814–Mar. 18, 1872.
 Vol. 10, Pt. 2–85
White, Alfred Tredway, May 28, 1846–Jan. 29, 1921.
 Vol. 10, Pt. 2–86
White, Alma Bridwell, June 16, 1862–June 26, 1946.
 Supp. 4–875
White, Andrew, 1579–Dec. 27, 1656.
 Vol. 10, Pt. 2–87
White, Andrew Dickson, Nov. 7, 1832–Nov. 4, 1918.
 Vol. 10, Pt. 2–88
White, Benjamin Franklin, Feb. 3, 1873–May 20, 1958.
 Supp. 6–688
White, Canvass, Sept. 8, 1790–Dec. 18, 1834.
 Vol. 10, Pt. 2–93
White, Charles Abiathar, Jan. 26, 1826–June 29, 1910.
 Vol. 10, Pt. 2–93
White, Charles Ignatius, Feb. 1, 1807–Apr. 1, 1878.
 Vol. 10, Pt. 2–94
White, Clarence Cameron, Aug. 10, 1880–June 30, 1960.
 Supp. 6–689
White, David, July 1, 1862–Feb. 7, 1935.
 Supp. 1–701
White, Edward Douglass, Mar. 1795–Apr. 18, 1847.
 Vol. 10, Pt. 2–95
White, Edward Douglass, Nov. 3, 1845–May 19, 1921.
 Vol. 10, Pt. 2–96
White, Edward Higgins, II, Nov. 14, 1930–Jan. 27, 1967.
 Supp. 8–693
White, Ellen Gould Harmon, Nov. 26, 1827–July 16, 1915.
 Vol. 10, Pt. 2–98

White, Emerson Elbridge, Jan. 10, 1829–Oct. 21, 1902.
 Vol. 10, Pt. 2–99
White, George, Mar. 12, 1802–Apr. 30, 1887.
 Vol. 10, Pt. 2–99
White, George, 1890–Oct. 11, 1968.
 Supp. 8–694
White, George Leonard, Sept. 20, 1838–Nov. 8, 1895.
 Vol. 10, Pt. 2–100
White, Henry, Mar. 28, 1732–Dec. 23, 1786.
 Vol. 10, Pt. 2–101
White, Henry, Mar. 29, 1850–July 15, 1927.
 Vol. 10, Pt. 2–102
White, Henry Clay, Dec. 30, 1848–Dec. 1, 1927.
 Vol. 10, Pt. 2–103
White, Horace, Aug. 10, 1834–Sept. 16, 1916.
 Vol. 10, Pt. 2–104
White, Hugh Lawson, Oct. 30, 1773–Apr. 10, 1840.
 Vol. 10, Pt. 2–105
White, Israel Charles, Nov. 1, 1848–Nov. 25, 1927.
 Vol. 10, Pt. 2–107
White, James, 1747–Aug. 14, 1821.
 Vol. 10, Pt. 2–108
White, James Clarke, July 7, 1833–Jan. 5, 1916.
 Vol. 10, Pt. 2–108
White, James William, Nov. 2, 1850–Apr. 24, 1916.
 Vol. 10, Pt. 2–109
White, John, fl. 1585–1593.
 Vol. 10, Pt. 2–110
White, John Blake, Sept. 2, 1781–c. Aug. 24, 1859.
 Vol. 10, Pt. 2–111
White, John De Haven, Aug. 19, 1815–Dec. 25, 1895.
 Vol. 10, Pt. 2–112
White, John Williams, Mar. 5, 1849–May 9, 1917.
 Vol. 10, Pt. 2–112
White, Joseph Malachy, Oct. 14, 1891–Feb. 28, 1959.
 Supp. 6–691
White, Josh, Feb. 11, 1915–Sept. 5, 1969.
 Supp. 8–695
White, Leonard Dupee, Jan. 17, 1891–Feb. 23, 1958.
 Supp. 6–692
White, Pearl, Mar. 4, 1889–Aug. 4, 1938.
 Supp. 2–710
White, Richard Grant, May 23, 1821–Apr. 8, 1885.
 Vol. 10, Pt. 2–113
White, Samuel, Dec. 1770–Nov. 4, 1809.
 Vol. 10, Pt. 2–114
White, Samuel Stockton, June 19, 1822–Dec. 30, 1879.
 Vol. 10, Pt. 2–115
White, Stanford, Nov. 9, 1853–June 25, 1906.
 Vol. 10, Pt. 2–116
White, Stephen Mallory, Jan. 19, 1853–Feb. 21, 1901.
 Vol. 10, Pt. 2–118
White, Stephen Van Culen, Aug. 1, 1831–Jan. 18, 1913.
 Vol. 10, Pt. 2–119
White, Stewart Edward, Mar. 12, 1873–Sept. 18, 1946.
 Supp. 4–877
White, Thomas Willis, Mar. 28, 1788–Jan. 19, 1843.
 Vol. 10, Pt. 2–120
White, Walter Francis, July 1, 1893–Mar. 21, 1955.
 Supp. 5–740
White, William, Apr. 4, 1748 N.S.–July 17, 1836.
 Vol. 10, Pt. 2–121
White, William Alanson, Jan. 24, 1870–Mar. 7, 1937.
 Supp. 2–711
White, William Allen, Feb. 10, 1868–Jan. 29, 1944.
 Supp. 3–815
White, William Nathaniel, Nov. 28, 1819–July 14, 1867.
 Vol. 10, Pt. 2–122
White Eyes, d. 1778.
 Vol. 10, Pt. 2–123
Whitefield, George, Dec. 16, 1714 O.S.– Sept. 30, 1770.
 Vol. 10, Pt. 2–124
Whitehead, Alfred North, Feb. 15, 1861–Dec. 30, 1947.
 Supp. 4–878
Whitehead, Wilbur Cherrier, May 22, 1866–June 27, 1931.
 Vol. 10, Pt. 2–129
Whitehead, William Adee, Feb. 19, 1810–Aug. 8, 1884.
 Vol. 10, Pt. 2–130
Whitehill, Clarence Eugene, Nov. 5, 1871–Dec. 18, 1932.
 Vol. 10, Pt. 2–131
Whitehill, Robert, July 21, 1738–Apr. 7, 1813.
 Vol. 10, Pt. 2–131

Williams, Edwin, Sept. 25, 1797–Oct. 21, 1854.
    Vol. 10, Pt. 2–254
Williams, Eleazar, c. 1789–Aug. 28, 1858.
    Vol. 10, Pt. 2–255
Williams, Elisha, Aug. 24, 1694–July 24, 1755.
    Vol. 10, Pt. 2–256
Williams, Elisha, Aug. 29, 1773–June 29, 1833.
    Vol. 10, Pt. 2–257
Williams, Elkanah, Dec. 19, 1822–Oct. 5, 1888.
    Vol. 10, Pt. 2–258
Williams, Ephraim, Mar. 7, 1714 N.S.–Sept. 8, 1755.
    Vol. 10, Pt. 2–259
Williams, Fannie Barrier, Feb. 12, 1855–Mar. 4, 1944.
    Supp. 3–827
Williams, Francis Henry, Apr. 15, 1852–June 22, 1936.
    Supp. 2–717
Williams, Frank Martin, Apr. 11, 1873–Feb. 20, 1930.
    Vol. 10, Pt. 2–260
Williams, Frederick Wells, Oct. 31, 1857–Jan. 22, 1928.
    Vol. 10, Pt. 2–260
Williams, Gaar Campbell, Dec. 12, 1880–June 15, 1935.
    Supp. 1–707
Williams, Gardner Fred, Mar. 14, 1842–Aug. 22, 1922.
    Vol. 10, Pt. 2–261
Williams, George Huntington, Jan. 28, 1856–July 12, 1894.
    Vol. 10, Pt. 2–263
Williams, George Henry, Mar. 26, 1820–Apr. 4, 1910.
    Vol. 10, Pt. 2–262
Williams, George Washington, Oct. 16, 1849–Aug. 4, 1891.
    Vol. 10, Pt. 2–263
Williams, Harrison Charles, Mar. 16, 1873–Nov. 10, 1953.
    Supp. 5–749
Williams, Henry Shaler, Mar. 6, 1847–July 31, 1918.
    Vol. 10, Pt. 2–264
Williams, Henry Willard, Dec. 11, 1821–June 13, 1895.
    Vol. 10, Pt. 2–265
Williams, (Hiram) Hank, Sept. 17, 1923–Jan. 1, 1953.
    Supp. 5–748
Williams, Israel, Nov. 30, 1709–Jan. 10, 1788.
    Vol. 10, Pt. 2–266
Williams, James, July 1, 1796–Apr. 10, 1869.
    Vol. 10, Pt. 2–267
Williams, James Douglas, Jan. 16, 1808–Nov. 20, 1880.
    Vol. 10, Pt. 2–267
Williams, Jesse Lynch, May 6, 1807–Oct. 9, 1886.
    Vol. 10, Pt. 2–268
Williams, Jesse Lynch, Aug. 17, 1871–Sept. 14, 1929.
    Vol. 10, Pt. 2–269
Williams, John, Dec. 10, 1664–June 12, 1729.
    Vol. 10, Pt. 2–270
Williams, John, Apr. 28, 1761–Oct. 12, 1818.
    Vol. 10, Pt. 2–270
Williams, John, Jan. 29, 1778–Aug. 10, 1837.
    Vol. 10, Pt. 2–271
Williams, John, Aug. 30, 1817–Feb. 7, 1899.
    Vol. 10, Pt. 2–272
Williams, John Elias, June 11, 1871–Mar. 24, 1927.
    Vol. 10, Pt. 2–274
Williams, John Elias, Oct. 28, 1853–Jan. 2, 1919.
    Vol. 10, Pt. 2–273
Williams, John Fletcher, Sept. 25, 1834–Apr. 28, 1895.
    Vol. 10, Pt. 2–275
Williams, John Foster, Oct. 12, 1743–June 24, 1814.
    Vol. 10, Pt. 2–276
Williams, John Joseph, Apr. 27, 1822–Aug. 30, 1907.
    Vol. 10, Pt. 2–276
Williams, John Sharp, July 30, 1854–Sept. 27, 1932.
    Vol. 10, Pt. 2–277
Williams, John Skelton, July 6, 1865–Nov. 4, 1926.
    Vol. 10, Pt. 2–279
Williams, John Whitridge, Jan. 26, 1866–Oct. 21, 1931.
    Vol. 10, Pt. 2–280
Williams, Jonathan, May 26, 1750–May 16, 1815.
    Vol. 10, Pt. 2–280
Williams, Linsly Rudd, Jan. 28, 1875–Jan. 8, 1934.
    Vol. 10, Pt. 2–282
Williams, Marshall Jay, Feb. 22, 1837–July 7, 1902.
    Vol. 10, Pt. 2–283
Williams, Nathaniel, Aug. 25, 1675–Jan. 10, 1737/38.
    Vol. 10, Pt. 2–283
Williams, Otho Holland, March 1749–July 15, 1794.
    Vol. 10, Pt. 2–284

Williams, Reuel, June 2, 1783–July 25, 1862.
    Vol. 10, Pt. 2–285
Williams, Robert, c. 1745–Sept. 26, 1775.
    Vol. 10, Pt. 2–286
Williams, Roger, c. 1603–1682/83.
    Vol. 10, Pt. 2–286
Williams, Samuel May, Oct. 4, 1795–Sept. 13, 1858.
    Vol. 10, Pt. 2–289
Williams, Samuel Wells, Sept. 22, 1812–Feb. 16, 1884.
    Vol. 10, Pt. 2–290
Williams, Stephen West, Mar. 27, 1790–July 6, 1855.
    Vol. 10, Pt. 2–291
Williams, Talcott, July 20, 1849–Jan. 24, 1928.
    Vol. 10, Pt. 2–291
Williams, Thomas Scott, June 26, 1777–Dec. 15, 1861.
    Vol. 10, Pt. 2–292
Williams, Walter, July 2, 1864–July 29, 1935.
    Supp. 1–708
Williams, William, Apr. 8, 1731–Aug. 2, 1811.
    Vol. 10, Pt. 2–293
Williams, William, Oct. 12, 1787–June 10, 1850.
    Vol. 10, Pt. 2–294
Williams, William Carlos, Sept. 17, 1883–Mar. 4, 1963.
    Supp. 7–788
Williams, William R., Oct. 14, 1804–Apr. 1, 1885.
    Vol. 10, Pt. 2–295
Williams, William Sherley, d. March 1849.
    Vol. 10, Pt. 2–296
Williamson, Andrew, c. 1730–Mar. 21, 1786.
    Vol. 10, Pt. 2–296
Williamson, Charles, July 12, 1757–Sept. 4, 1808.
    Vol. 10, Pt. 2–297
Williamson, Hugh, Dec. 5, 1735–May 22, 1819.
    Vol. 10, Pt. 2–298
Williamson, Isaac Halsted, Sept. 27 1767–July 10, 1844.
    Vol. 10, Pt. 2–300
Williamson, William Durkee, July 31, 1779–May 27, 1846.
    Vol. 10, Pt. 2–301
Willie, Asa Hoxie, Oct. 11, 1829–Mar. 16, 1899.
    Vol. 10, Pt. 2–302
Willing, Thomas, Dec. 19, 1731 O.S.–Jan. 19, 1821.
    Vol. 10, Pt. 2–302
Willingham, Robert Josiah, May 15, 1854–Dec. 20, 1914.
    Vol. 10, Pt. 2–304
Willis, Albert Shelby, Jan. 22, 1843–Jan. 6, 1897.
    Vol. 10, Pt. 2–304
Willis, Bailey, May 31, 1857–Feb. 19, 1949.
    Supp. 4–896
Willis, Henry Parker, Aug. 14, 1874–July 18, 1937.
    Supp. 2–718
Willis, Nathaniel, June 6, 1780–May 26, 1870.
    Vol. 10, Pt. 2–305
Willis, Nathaniel Parker, Jan. 20, 1806–Jan. 20, 1867.
    Vol. 10, Pt. 2–306
Willis, Olympia Brown. [See Brown, Olympia, 1835–1926.]
Willis, William, Aug. 31, 1794–Feb. 17, 1870.
    Vol. 10, Pt. 2–309
Williston, Samuel, June 17, 1795–July 18, 1874.
    Vol. 10, Pt. 2–309
Williston, Samuel, Sept. 24, 1861–Feb. 18, 1963.
    Supp. 7–791
Williston, Samuel Wendell, July 10, 1852–Aug. 30, 1918.
    Vol. 10, Pt. 2–310
Williston, Seth, Apr. 4, 1770–Mar. 2, 1851.
    Vol. 10, Pt. 2–311
Willkie, Wendell Lewis, Feb. 18, 1892–Oct. 8, 1944.
    Supp. 3–828
Willoughby, Westel Woodbury, July 20, 1867–Mar. 26, 1945.
    Supp. 3–830
Wills, Childe Harold, June 1, 1878–Dec. 30, 1940.
    Supp. 2–720
Wills, Harry, May 15, 1889[?]–Dec. 21, 1958.
    Supp. 6–699
Willson, Augustus Everett, Oct. 13, 1846–Aug. 24, 1931.
    Vol. 10, Pt. 2–312
Willys, John North, Oct. 25, 1873–Aug. 26, 1935.
    Supp. 1–709
Wilmarth, Lemuel Everett, Mar. 11, 1835–July 27, 1918.
    Vol. 10, Pt. 2–312
Wilmer, James Jones, Jan. 15, 1749/50–Apr. 14, 1814.
    Vol. 10, Pt. 2–313
Wilmer, Joseph Père Bell, Feb. 11, 1812–Dec. 2, 1878.
    Vol. 10, Pt. 2–314

Wilmer, Richard Hooker, Mar. 15, 1816–June 14, 1900.
   Vol. 10, Pt. 2–315
Wilmer, William Holland, Oct. 29, 1782–July 24, 1827.
   Vol. 10, Pt. 2–315
Wilmer, William Holland, Aug. 26, 1863–Mar. 12, 1936.
   Supp. 2–721
Wilmot, David, Jan. 20, 1814–Mar. 16, 1868.
   Vol. 10, Pt. 2–317
Wilson, Alexander, July 6, 1766–Aug. 23, 1813.
   Vol. 10, Pt. 2–317
Wilson, Allen Benjamin, Oct. 18, 1824–Apr. 29, 1888.
   Vol. 10, Pt. 2–319
Wilson, Augusta Jane Evans. [See Evans, Augusta Jane, 1835
   –1909.]
Wilson, Bird, Jan. 8, 1777–Apr. 14, 1859.
   Vol. 10, Pt. 2–320
Wilson, Charles Erwin, July 18, 1890–Sept. 26, 1961.
   Supp. 7–793
Wilson, Clarence Truc, Apr. 24, 1872–Feb. 16, 1939.
   Supp. 2–722
Wilson, Edith Bolling, Oct. 15, 1872–Dec. 28, 1961.
   Supp. 7–795
Wilson, Edmund Beecher, Oct. 19, 1856–Mar. 3, 1939.
   Supp. 2–724
Wilson, Ernest Henry, Feb. 15, 1876–Oct. 15, 1930.
   Vol. 10, Pt. 2–321
Wilson, Francis, Feb. 7, 1854–Oct. 7, 1935.
   Supp. 1–710
Wilson, George Francis, Dec. 7, 1818–Jan. 19, 1883.
   Vol. 10, Pt. 2–322
Wilson, George Grafton, Mar. 29, 1863–Apr. 30, 1951.
   Supp. 5–751
Wilson, Halsey William, May 12, 1868–Mar. 1, 1954.
   Supp. 5–752
Wilson, Harry Leon, May 1, 1867–June 28, 1939.
   Supp. 2–725
Wilson, Henry, Feb. 16, 1812–Nov. 22, 1875.
   Vol. 10, Pt. 2–322
Wilson, Henry Lane, Nov. 3, 1857–Dec. 22, 1932.
   Vol. 10, Pt. 2–325
Wilson, Henry Parke Custis, Mar. 5, 1827–Dec. 27, 1897.
   Vol. 10, Pt. 2–326
Wilson, Hugh Robert, Jan. 29, 1885–Dec. 29, 1946.
   Supp. 4–897
Wilson, James, Sept. 14, 1742–Aug. 21, 1798.
   Vol. 10, Pt. 2–326
Wilson, James, Aug. 16, 1836–Aug. 26, 1920.
   Vol. 10, Pt. 2–330
Wilson, James Falconer, Oct. 19, 1828–Apr. 22 1895.
   Vol. 10, Pt. 2–331
Wilson, J(ames) Finley, Aug. 28, 1881–Feb. 19, 1952.
   Supp. 5–754
Wilson, James Grant, Apr. 28, 1832–Feb. 1, 1914.
   Vol. 10, Pt. 2–333
Wilson, James Harrison, Sept. 2, 1837–Feb. 23, 1925.
   Vol. 10, Pt. 2–334
Wilson, James Southall, Nov. 12, 1880–June 26, 1963.
   Supp. 7–796
Wilson, John, c. 1591–Aug. 7, 1667.
   Vol. 10, Pt. 2–336
Wilson, John Fleming, Feb. 22, 1877–Mar. 5, 1922.
   Vol. 10, Pt. 2–337
Wilson, John Leighton, Mar. 25, 1809–July 13, 1886.
   Vol. 10, Pt. 2–337
Wilson, John Lockwood, Aug. 7, 1850–Nov. 6, 1912.
   Vol. 10, Pt. 2–338
Wilson, Joseph Miller, June 20, 1838–Nov. 24, 1902.
   Vol. 10, Pt. 2–339
Wilson, Joshua Lacy, Sept. 22, 1774–Aug. 14, 1846.
   Vol. 10, Pt. 2–340
Wilson, Louis Blanchard, Dec. 22, 1866–Oct. 5, 1943.
   Supp. 3–831
Wilson, Mortimer, Aug. 6, 1876–Jan. 27, 1932.
   Vol. 10, Pt. 2–341
Wilson, Peter, Nov. 23, 1746–Aug. 1, 1825.
   Vol. 10, Pt. 2–341
Wilson, Robert Burns, Oct. 30, 1850–Mar. 31, 1916.
   Vol. 10, Pt. 2–342
Wilson, Samuel, Sept. 13, 1766–July 31, 1854.
   Vol. 10, Pt. 2–343
Wilson, Samuel Graham, Feb. 11, 1858–July 2, 1916.
   Vol. 10, Pt. 2–343

Wilson, Samuel Mountford, c. 1823–June 4, 1892.
   Vol. 10, Pt. 2–344
Wilson, Samuel Ramsay, June 4, 1818–Mar. 3, 1886.
   Vol. 10, Pt. 2–345
Wilson, Samuel Thomas, 1761–May 23, 1824.
   Vol. 10, Pt. 2–346
Wilson, Theodore Delavan, May 11, 1840–June 29, 1896.
   Vol. 10, Pt. 2–346
Wilson, Thomas Woodrow. [See Wilson, Woodrow, 1856–
   1924.]
Wilson, Warren Hugh, May 1, 1867–Mar. 2, 1937.
   Supp. 2–726
Wilson, William, Apr. 27, 1794–Apr. 29, 1857.
   Vol. 10, Pt. 2–347
Wilson, William, Dec. 25, 1801–Aug. 25, 1860.
   Vol. 10, Pt. 2–348
Wilson, William Bauchop, Apr. 2, 1862–May 25, 1934.
   Vol. 10, Pt. 2–348
Wilson, William Dexter, Feb. 28, 1816–July 30, 1900.
   Vol. 10, Pt. 2–349
Wilson, William Hasell, Nov. 5, 1811–Aug. 17, 1902.
   Vol. 10, Pt. 2–350
Wilson, William Lyne, May 3, 1843–Oct. 17, 1900.
   Vol. 10, Pt. 2–351
Wilson, Woodrow, Dec. 28, 1856–Feb. 3, 1924.
   Vol. 10, Pt. 2–352
Wiltz, Louis Alfred, Oct. 22, 1843–Oct. 16, 1881.
   Vol. 10, Pt. 2–368
Wimar, Carl, Feb. 19, 1828–Nov. 28, 1862.
   Vol. 10, Pt. 2–369
Wimmer, Boniface, Jan. 14, 1809–Dec. 8, 1887.
   Vol. 10, Pt. 2–370
Winans, Ross, Oct. 17, 1796–Apr. 11, 1877.
   Vol. 10, Pt. 2–371
Winans, Thomas De Kay, Dec. 6, 1820–June 10, 1878.
   Vol. 10, Pt. 2–372
Winans, William, Nov. 3, 1788–Aug. 31, 1857.
   Vol. 10, Pt. 2–373
Winant, John Gilbert, Feb. 23, 1889–Nov. 3, 1947.
   Supp. 4–899
Winchell, Alexander, Dec. 31, 1824–Feb. 19, 1891.
   Vol. 10, Pt. 2–373
Winchell, Horace Vaughn, Nov. 1, 1865–July 28, 1923.
   Vol. 10, Pt. 2–374
Winchell, Newton Horace, Dec. 17, 1839–May 2, 1914.
   Vol. 10, Pt. 2–375
Winchester, Caleb Thomas, Jan. 18, 1847–Mar. 24, 1920.
   Vol. 10, Pt. 2–376
Winchester, Elhanan, Sept. 30, 1751–Apr. 18, 1797.
   Vol. 10, Pt. 2–377
Winchester, James, Feb. 6, 1752–July 26, 1826.
   Vol. 10, Pt. 2–378
Winchester, Oliver Fisher, Nov. 30, 1810–Dec. 11, 1880.
   Vol. 10, Pt. 2–379
Winchevsky, Morris, Aug. 9, 1856–Mar. 18, 1932.
   Vol. 10, Pt. 2–379
Winder, John Henry, Feb. 21, 1800–Feb. 8, 1865.
   Vol. 10, Pt. 2–380
Winder, Levin, Sept. 4, 1757–July 1, 1819.
   Vol. 10, Pt. 2–381
Winder, William Henry, Feb. 18, 1775–May 24, 1824.
   Vol. 10, Pt. 2–382
Windom, William, May 10, 1827–Jan. 29, 1891.
   Vol. 10, Pt. 2–383
Winebrenner, John, Mar. 25, 1797–Sept. 12, 1860.
   Vol. 10, Pt. 2–384
Wines, Enoch Cobb, Feb. 17, 1806–Dec. 10, 1879.
   Vol. 10, Pt. 2–385
Wines, Frederick Howard, Apr. 9, 1838–Jan. 31, 1912.
   Vol. 10, Pt. 2–386
Wing, Joseph Elwyn, Sept. 14, 1861–Sept. 10, 1915.
   Vol. 10, Pt. 2–386
Wingate, Paine, May 14, 1739–Mar. 7, 1838.
   Vol. 10, Pt. 2–387
Wingfield, Edward Maria, fl. 1586–1613.
   Vol. 10, Pt. 2–388
Winkler, Edwin Theodore, Nov. 13, 1823–Nov. 10, 1883.
   Vol. 10, Pt. 2–389
Winlock, Herbert Eustis, Feb. 1, 1884–Jan. 26, 1950.
   Supp. 4–901
Winlock, Joseph, Feb. 6, 1826–June 11, 1875.
   Vol. 10, Pt. 2–389

Winn, Richard, 1750–Dec. 19, 1818.
    Vol. 10, Pt. 2–390
Winnemucca, Sarah, c. 1844–Oct. 16, 1891.
    Vol. 10, Pt. 2–391
Winship, Albert Edward, Feb. 24, 1845–Feb. 17, 1933.
    Vol. 10, Pt. 2–391
Winship, Blanton, Nov. 23, 1869–Oct. 9, 1947.
    Supp. 4–902
Winship, George Parker, July 29, 1871–June 22, 1952.
    Supp. 5–755
Winslow, Cameron McRae, July 29, 1854–Jan. 2, 1932.
    Vol. 10, Pt. 2–392
Winslow, Charles-Edward Amory, Feb. 4, 1877–Jan. 8, 1957.
    Supp. 6–701
Winslow, Edward, Oct. 18, 1595–May 8, 1655.
    Vol. 10, Pt. 2–393
Winslow, Edward, Nov. 1, 1669–Dec. 1, 1753.
    Vol. 10, Pt. 2–394
Winslow, Edward Francis, Sept. 28, 1837–Oct. 22, 1914.
    Vol. 10, Pt. 2–395
Winslow, Hubbard, Oct. 30, 1799–Aug. 13, 1864.
    Vol. 10, Pt. 2–396
Winslow, John, May 10, 1703–Apr. 17, 1774.
    Vol. 10, Pt. 2–396
Winslow, John Ancrum, Nov. 19, 1811–Sept. 29, 1873.
    Vol. 10, Pt. 2–397
Winslow, John Bradley, Oct. 4, 1851–July 13, 1920.
    Vol. 10, Pt. 2–398
Winslow, John Flack, Nov. 10, 1810–Mar. 10, 1892.
    Vol. 10, Pt. 2–399
Winslow, Josiah, c. 1629–Dec. 18, 1680.
    Vol. 10, Pt. 2–400
Winslow, Miron, Dec. 11, 1789–Oct. 22, 1864.
    Vol. 10, Pt. 2–401
Winslow, Sidney Wilmot, Sept. 20, 1854–June 18, 1917.
    Vol. 10, Pt. 2–401
Winslow, William Copley, Jan. 13, 1840–Feb. 2, 1925.
    Vol. 10, Pt. 2–402
Winsor, Justin, Jan. 2, 1831–Oct. 22, 1897.
    Vol. 10, Pt. 2–403
Winston, John Anthony, Sept. 4, 1812–Dec. 21, 1871.
    Vol. 10, Pt. 2–404
Winston, Joseph, June 17, 1746–Apr. 21, 1815.
    Vol. 10, Pt. 2–405
Winter, William, July 15, 1836–June 30, 1917.
    Vol. 10, Pt. 2–405
Winthrop, Fitz-John. [See Winthrop, John, 1638–1707.]
Winthrop, James, Mar. 28, 1752–Sept. 26, 1821.
    Vol. 10, Pt. 2–407
Winthrop, John, Jan. 12, 1587/88 o.s.–Mar. 26, 1649.
    Vol. 10, Pt. 2–408
Winthrop, John, Feb. 12, 1605/06 o.s.–Apr. 5, 1676.
    Vol. 10, Pt. 2–411
Winthrop, John, Mar. 14, 1638–Nov. 27, 1707.
    Vol. 10, Pt. 2–413
Winthrop, John, Dec. 19, 1714–May 3, 1779.
    Vol. 10, Pt. 2–414
Winthrop, Robert Charles, May 12, 1809–Nov. 16, 1894.
    Vol. 10, Pt. 2–416
Winthrop, Theodore, Sept. 28, 1828–June 10, 1861.
    Vol. 10, Pt. 2–417
Winton, Alexander, June 20, 1860–June 21, 1932.
    Vol. 10, Pt. 2–417
Wirt, William, Nov. 8, 1772–Feb. 18, 1834.
    Vol. 10, Pt. 2–418
Wirt, William Albert, Jan. 21. 1874–Mar. 11, 1938.
    Supp. 2–727
Wise, Aaron, May 2, 1844–Mar. 30, 1896.
    Vol. 10, Pt. 2–421
Wise, Daniel, Jan. 10, 1813–Dec. 19, 1898.
    Vol. 10, Pt. 2–422
Wise, Henry Alexander, Dec. 3, 1806–Sept. 12, 1876.
    Vol. 10, Pt. 2–423
Wise, Henry Augustus, May 24, 1819–Apr. 2, 1869.
    Vol. 10, Pt. 2–425
Wise, Isaac Mayer, Mar. 29, 1819–Mar. 26, 1900.
    Vol. 10, Pt. 2–426
Wise, John, August 1652–Apr. 8, 1725.
    Vol. 10, Pt. 2–427
Wise, John, Feb. 24, 1808–Sept. 29, 1879.
    Vol. 10, Pt. 2–428
Wise, John Sergeant, Dec. 27, 1846–May 12, 1913.
    Vol. 10, Pt. 2–429

Wise, Stephen Samuel, Mar. 17, 1874–Apr. 19, 1949.
    Supp. 4–903
Wise, Thomas Alfred, Mar. 23, 1865–Mar. 21, 1928.
    Vol. 10, Pt. 2–430
Wislizenus, Frederick Adolph, May 21, 1810–Sept. 22, 1889.
    Vol. 10, Pt. 2–430
Wislocki, George Bernays, Mar. 25, 1892–Oct. 22, 1956.
    Supp. 6–703
Wisner, Henry, 1720–Mar. 4, 1790.
    Vol. 10, Pt. 2–431
Wissler, Clark, Sept. 18, 1870–Aug. 25, 1947.
    Supp. 4–906
Wistar, Caspar, Feb. 3, 1696–Mar. 21, 1752.
    Vol. 10, Pt. 2–432
Wistar, Caspar, Sept. 13, 1761–Jan. 22, 1818.
    Vol. 10, Pt. 2–433
Wister, Owen, July 14, 1860–July 21, 1938.
    Supp. 2–728
Wister, Sarah, July 20, 1761–Apr. 21, 1804.
    Vol. 10, Pt. 2–434
Withers, Frederick Clarke, Feb. 4, 1828–Jan. 7, 1901.
    Vol. 10, Pt. 2–435
Witherspoon, Alexander Maclaren, Oct. 31, 1894–Mar. 4, 1964. Supp. 7–797
Witherspoon, Herbert, July 21, 1873–May 10, 1935.
    Supp. 1–711
Witherspoon, John, Feb. 5, 1723–Nov. 15, 1794.
    Vol. 10, Pt. 2–436
Witherspoon, John Alexander, Sept. 13, 1864–Apr. 26, 1929.
    Vol. 10, Pt. 2–438
Witmark, Isidore, June 15, 1869–Apr. 9, 1941.
    Supp. 3–833
Witte, Edwin Emil, Jan. 4, 1887–May 20, 1960.
    Supp. 6–705
Witthaus, Rudolph August, Aug. 30, 1846–Dec. 19, 1915.
    Vol. 10, Pt. 2–439
Woerner, John Gabriel, Apr. 28, 1826–Jan. 20, 1900.
    Vol. 10, Pt. 2–439
Wofford, William Tatum, June 28, 1823–May 22, 1884.
    Vol. 10, Pt. 2–440
Wolcott, Edward Oliver, Mar. 26, 1848–Mar. 1, 1905.
    Vol. 10, Pt. 2–441
Wolcott, Oliver, Nov. 20, 1726–Dec. 1, 1797.
    Vol. 10, Pt. 2–442
Wolcott, Oliver, Jan. 11, 1760–June 1, 1833.
    Vol. 10, Pt. 2–443
Wolcott, Roger, Jan. 4, 1679–May 17, 1767.
    Vol. 10, Pt. 2–445
Wolf, George, Aug. 12, 1777–Mar. 11, 1840.
    Vol. 10, Pt. 2–446
Wolf, Henry, Aug. 3, 1852–Mar. 18, 1916.
    Vol. 10, Pt. 2–447
Wolf, Innocent William, Apr. 13, 1843–Oct. 14, 1922.
    Vol. 10, Pt. 2–448
Wolf, Simon, Oct. 28, 1836–June 4, 1923.
    Vol. 10, Pt. 2–448
Wolfe, Catharine Lorillard, Mar. 1828–Apr. 4, 1887.
    Vol. 10, Pt. 2–449
Wolfe, Harry Kirke, Nov. 10, 1858–July 30, 1918.
    Vol. 10, Pt. 2–450
Wolfe, John David, July 24, 1792–May 17, 1872.
    Vol. 10, Pt. 2–451
Wolfe, Thomas Clayton, Oct. 3, 1900–Sept. 15, 1938.
    Supp. 2–730
Wolff, Kurt August Paul, Mar. 3, 1887–Oct. 21, 1963.
    Supp. 7–798
Wolfskill, William, Mar. 20, 1798–Oct. 3, 1866.
    Vol. 10, Pt. 2–451
Wolfsohn, Carl, Dec. 14, 1834–July 30, 1907.
    Vol. 10, Pt. 2–452
Wolfson, Erwin Service, Mar. 27, 1902–June 26, 1962.
    Supp. 7–799
Wolheim, Louis Robert, Mar. 28, 1881–Feb. 18, 1931.
    Supp. 1–712
Woll, Matthew, Jan. 25, 1880–June 1, 1956.
    Supp. 6–706
Wolle, John Frederick, Apr. 4, 1863–Jan. 12, 1933.
    Vol. 10, Pt. 2–453
Wolman, Leo, Feb. 24, 1890–Oct. 2, 1961.
    Supp. 7–800
Wong, Anna May, Jan. 3, 1907–Feb. 3, 1961.
    Supp. 7–801

Wood, Abraham, fl. 1638–1680.
  Vol. 10, Pt. 2–454
Wood, Casey Albert, Nov. 21, 1856–Jan. 26, 1942.
  Supp. 3–834
Wood, Charles Erskine Scott, Feb. 20, 1852–Jan. 22, 1944.
  Supp. 3–836
Wood, Craig Ralph, c. 1901–May 7, 1968.
  Supp. 8–702
Wood, David Duffie, Mar. 2, 1838–Mar. 27, 1910.
  Vol. 10, Pt. 2–454
Wood, Edith Elmer, Sept. 24, 1871–Apr. 29, 1945.
  Supp. 3–837
Wood, Edward Stickney, Apr. 28, 1846–July 11, 1905.
  Vol. 10, Pt. 2–455
Wood, Fernando, June 14, 1812–Feb. 14, 1881.
  Vol. 10, Pt. 2–456
Wood, Frederick Hill, Jan. 2, 1877–Dec. 28, 1943.
  Supp. 3–839
Wood, George, Jan. 1789–Mar. 17, 1860.
  Vol. 10, Pt. 2–457
Wood, George Bacon, Mar. 12, 1797–Mar. 30, 1879.
  Vol. 10, Pt. 2–458
Wood, Grant, Feb. 13, 1892–Feb. 12, 1942.
  Supp. 3–840
Wood, Henry Alexander Wise, Mar. 1, 1866–Apr. 9, 1939.
  Supp. 2–733
Wood, Horatio Charles, Jan. 13, 1841–Jan. 3, 1920.
  Vol. 10, Pt. 2–459
Wood, James, July 12, 1799–Apr. 7, 1867.
  Vol. 10, Pt. 2–460
Wood, James, Nov. 12, 1839–Dec. 19, 1925.
  Vol. 10, Pt. 2–460
Wood, James Frederick, Apr. 27, 1813–June 20, 1883.
  Vol. 10, Pt. 2–461
Wood, James J., Mar. 25, 1856–Apr. 19, 1928.
  Vol. 10, Pt. 2–462
Wood, James Rushmore, Sept. 14, 1813–May 4, 1882.
  Vol. 10, Pt. 2–463
Wood, Jethro, Mar. 16, 1774–Sept. 18, 1834.
  Vol. 10, Pt. 2–464
Wood, John, c. 1775–May 15, 1822.
  Vol. 10, Pt. 2–464
Wood, John Stephens, Feb. 8, 1885–Sept. 12, 1968.
  Supp. 8–703
Wood, John Taylor, Aug. 13, 1830–July 19, 1904.
  Vol. 10, Pt. 2–465
Wood, Joseph, c. 1778–c. 1832.
  Vol. 10, Pt. 2–466
Wood, Leonard, Oct. 9, 1860–Aug. 7, 1927.
  Vol. 10, Pt. 2–467
Wood, Mary Elizabeth, Aug. 22, 1861–May 1, 1931.
  Vol. 10, Pt. 2–46
Wood, Reuben, c. 1792–Oct. 1, 1864.
  Vol. 10, Pt. 2–470
Wood, Robert Elkington, June 13, 1879–Nov. 6, 1969.
  Supp. 8–704
Wood, Samuel, July 17, 1760–May 5, 1844.
  Vol. 10, Pt. 2–471
Wood, Sarah Sayward Barrell Keating, Oct. 1, 1759–Jan. 6,
  1855. Vol. 10, Pt. 2–472
Wood, Thomas, Aug. 22, 1813–Nov. 21, 1880.
  Vol. 10, Pt. 2–473
Wood, Thomas Bond, Mar. 17, 1844–Dec. 18, 1922.
  Vol. 10, Pt. 2–473
Wood, Thomas John, Sept. 25, 1823–Feb. 25, 1906.
  Vol. 10, Pt. 2–474
Wood, Walter Abbott, Oct. 23, 1815–Jan. 15, 1892.
  Vol. 10, Pt. 2–475
Wood, William, fl. 1629–1635.
  Vol. 10, Pt. 2–476
Wood, William Burke, May 26, 1779–Sept. 23, 1861.
  Vol. 10, Pt. 2–476
Wood, William Robert, Jan. 5, 1861–Mar. 7, 1933.
  Vol. 10, Pt. 2–478
Woodberry, George Edward, May 12, 1855–Jan. 2, 1930.
  Vol. 10, Pt. 2–478
Woodbridge, Frederick James Eugene, Mar. 26, 1867–June
  1, 1940. Supp. 2–734
Woodbridge, John, 1613–Mar. 17, 1695.
  Vol. 10, Pt. 2–481
Woodbridge, Samuel Merrill, Apr. 5, 1819–June 24, 1905.
  Vol. 10, Pt. 2–482

Woodbridge, William Channing, Dec. 18, 1794–Nov. 9,
  1845. Vol. 10, Pt. 2–484
Woodbridge, William, Aug. 20, 1780–Oct. 20, 1861.
  Vol. 10, Pt. 2–483
Woodbury, Charles Jeptha Hill, May 4, 1851–Mar. 20, 1916.
  Vol. 10, Pt. 2–485
Woodbury, Daniel Phineas, Dec. 16, 1812–Aug. 15, 1864.
  Vol. 10, Pt. 2–485
Woodbury, Helen Laura Sumner, Mar. 12, 1876–Mar. 10,
  1933. Vol. 10, Pt. 2–486
Woodbury, Isaac Baker, Oct. 23, 1819–Oct. 26, 1858.
  Vol. 10, Pt. 2–487
Woodbury, Levi, Dec. 22, 1789–Sept. 4, 1851.
  Vol. 10, Pt. 2–488
Woodford, Stewart Lyndon, Sept. 3, 1835–Feb. 14, 1913.
  Vol. 10, Pt. 2–489
Woodford, William, Oct. 6, 1734–Nov. 13, 1780.
  Vol. 10, Pt. 2–490
Woodhouse, James, Nov. 17, 1770–June 4, 1809.
  Vol. 10, Pt. 2–491
Woodhull, Alfred Alexander, Apr. 13, 1837–Oct. 18, 1921.
  Vol. 10, Pt. 2–492
Woodhull, Nathaniel, Dec. 30, 1722–Sept. 20, 1776.
  Vol. 10, Pt. 2–492
Woodhull, Victoria Claflin, Sept. 23, 1838–June 10, 1927.
  Vol. 10, Pt. 2–493
Woodin, William Hartman, May 27, 1868–May 3, 1934.
  Vol. 10, Pt. 2–494
Woodring, Harry Hines, May 31, 1887–Sept. 9, 1967.
  Supp. 8–705
Woodrow, James, May 30, 1828–Jan. 17, 1907.
  Vol. 10, Pt. 2–495
Woodruff, Charles Edward, Oct. 2, 1860–June 13, 1915.
  Vol. 10, Pt. 2–496
Woodruff, Lorande Loss, July 14, 1879–June 23, 1947.
  Supp. 4–909
Woodruff, Theodore Tuttle, Apr. 8, 1811–May 2, 1892.
  Vol. 10, Pt. 2–497
Woodruff, Timothy Lester, Aug. 4, 1858–Oct. 12, 1913.
  Vol. 10, Pt. 2–498
Woodruff, Wilford, Mar. 1, 1807–Sept. 2, 1898.
  Vol. 10, Pt. 2–498
Woodruff, William Edward, Dec. 24, 1795–June 19, 1885.
  Vol. 10, Pt. 2–500
Woods, Alva, Aug. 13, 1794–Sept. 6, 1887.
  Vol. 10, Pt. 2–500
Woods, Charles Robert, Feb. 19, 1827–Feb. 26, 1885.
  Vol. 10, Pt. 2–501
Woods, James Haughton, Nov. 27, 1864–Jan. 14, 1935.
  Supp. 1–713
Woods, Leonard, June 19, 1774–Aug. 24, 1854.
  Vol. 10, Pt. 2–502
Woods, Leonard, Nov. 24, 1807–Dec. 24, 1878.
  Vol. 10, Pt. 2–502
Woods, Robert Archey, Dec. 9, 1865–Feb. 18, 1925.
  Vol. 10, Pt. 2–503
Woods, William Allen, May 16, 1837–June 29, 1901.
  Vol. 10, Pt. 2–504
Woods, William Burnham, Aug. 3, 1824–May 14, 1887.
  Vol. 10, Pt. 2–505
Woodson, Carter Godwin, Dec. 19, 1875–Apr. 3, 1950.
  Supp. 4–910
Woodward, Augustus Brevoort, 1774–June 12, 1827.
  Vol. 10, Pt. 2–506
Woodward, Calvin Milton, Aug. 25, 1837–Jan. 12, 1914.
  Vol. 10, Pt. 2–507
Woodward, Henry, c. 1646–c. 1686.
  Vol. 8, Pt. 1–508
Woodward, Joseph Janvier, Oct. 30, 1833–Aug. 17, 1884.
  Vol. 10, Pt. 2–509
Woodward, Robert Simpson, July 21, 1849–June 29, 1924.
  Vol. 10, Pt. 2–510
Woodward, Samuel Bayard, Jan. 10, 1787–Jan. 3, 1850.
  Vol. 10, Pt. 2–511
Woodward, William, Apr. 7, 1876–Sept. 26, 1953.
  Supp. 5–756
Woodworth, Jay Backus, Jan. 2, 1865–Aug. 4 1925.
  Vol. 10, Pt. 2–511
Woodworth, Samuel, Jan. 13, 1784–Dec. 9, 1842.
  Vol. 10, Pt. 2–512
Wool, Jolin Ellis, Feb. 29, 1784–Nov. 10, 1869.
  Vol. 10, Pt. 2–513

Woolf, Benjamin Edward, Feb. 16, 1836–Feb. 7, 1901.
    Vol. 10, Pt. 2–514
Woollcott, Alexander Humphreys, Jan. 19, 1887–Jan. 23,
    1943. Supp. 3–842
Woolley, Celia Parker, June 14, 1848–Mar. 9, 1918.
    Vol. 10, Pt. 2–515
Woolley, Edgar Montillion ("Monty"), Aug. 17, 1888–May 6,
    1963. Supp. 7–802
Woolley, John Granville, Feb. 15, 1850–Aug. 13, 1922.
    Vol. 10, Pt. 2–515
Woolley, Mary Emma, July 13, 1863–Sept. 5, 1947.
    Supp. 4–912
Woolman, Collett Everman, Oct. 8, 1889–Sept. 11, 1966.
    Supp. 8–707
Woolman, John, Oct. 19, 1720–Oct. 7, 1772.
    Vol. 10, Pt. 2–516
Woolsey, John Munro, Jan. 3, 1877–May 4, 1945.
    Supp. 3–843
Woolsey, Melancthon Taylor, June 5, 1780–May 19, 1838.
    Vol. 10, Pt. 2–517
Woolsey, Sarah Chauncy, Jan. 29, 1835–Apr. 9, 1905.
    Vol. 10, Pt. 2–518
Woolsey, Theodore Salisbury, Oct. 22, 1852–Apr. 24, 1929.
    Vol. 10, Pt. 2–520
Woolsey, Theodore Dwight, Oct. 31, 1801–July 1, 1889.
    Vol. 10, Pt. 2–519
Woolson, Abba Louisa Goold, Apr. 30, 1838–Feb. 6, 1921.
    Vol. 10, Pt. 2–521
Woolson, Constance Fenimore, March 1840–Jan. 24, 1894.
    Vol. 10, Pt. 2–522
Woolworth, Frank Winfield, Apr. 13, 1852–Aug. 8, 1919.
    Vol. 10, Pt. 2–523
Wooster, Charles Whiting, 1780–1848.
    Vol. 10, Pt. 2–524
Wooster, David, Mar. 2, 1711–May 2, 1777.
    Vol. 10, Pt. 2–524
Wootassite. [See Outacity, fl. 1756–1777.]
Wootton, Richens Lacy, May 6, 1816–Aug. 21, 1893.
    Vol. 10, Pt. 2–525
Worcester, Edwin Dean, Nov. 19, 1828–June 13, 1904.
    Vol. 10, Pt. 2–526
Worcester, Elwood, May 16, 1862–July 19, 1940.
    Supp. 2–735
Worcester, Joseph Emerson, Aug. 24, 1784–Oct. 27, 1865.
    Vol. 10, Pt. 2–526
Worcester, Noah, Nov. 25, 1758–Oct. 31, 1837.
    Vol. 10, Pt. 2–528
Worcester, Samuel, Nov. 1, 1770–June 7, 1821.
    Vol. 10, Pt. 2–529
Worcester, Samuel Austin, Jan. 19, 1798–Apr. 20, 1859.
    Vol. 10, Pt. 2–530
Worden, John Lorimer, Mar. 12, 1818–Oct. 18, 1897.
    Vol. 10, Pt. 2–531
Work, Henry Clay, Oct. 1, 1832–June 8, 1884.
    Vol. 10, Pt. 2–531
Work, Hubert, July 3, 1860–Dec. 14, 1942.
    Supp. 3–845
Work, Milton Cooper, Sept. 15, 1864–June 27, 1934.
    Vol. 10, Pt. 2–532
Workman, Fanny Bullock, Jan. 8, 1859–Jan. 22, 1925.
    Vol. 10, Pt. 2–533
Wormeley, Katharine Prescott, Jan. 14, 1830–Aug. 4, 1908.
    Vol. 10, Pt. 2–534
Wormeley, Mary Elizabeth. [See Latimer, Mary Elizabeth
    Wormeley, 1822–1904.]
Wormley, James, Jan. 16, 1819–Oct. 18, 1884.
    Vol. 10, Pt. 2–534
Wormley, Theodore George, Apr. 1, 1826–Jan. 3, 1897.
    Vol. 10, Pt. 2–535
Worth, Jonathan, Nov. 18, 1802–Sept. 5, 1869.
    Vol. 10, Pt. 2–536
Worth, William Jenkins, Mar. 1, 1794–May 7, 1849.
    Vol. 10, Pt. 2–536
Worthen, Amos Henry, Oct. 31, 1813–May 6, 1888.
    Vol. 10, Pt. 2–537
Worthen, William Ezra, Mar. 14, 1819–Apr. 2, 1897.
    Vol. 10, Pt. 2–538
Worthington, Henry Rossiter, Dec. 17, 1817–Dec. 17, 1880.
    Vol. 10, Pt. 2–539
Worthington, John, Nov. 24, 1719–Apr. 25, 1800.
    Vol. 10, Pt. 2–539
Worthington, Thomas, July 16, 1773–June 20, 1827.
    Vol. 10, Pt. 2–540

Wovoka, c. 1856–October 1932.
    Vol. 10, Pt. 2–541
Woytinsky, Wladimir Savelievich, Nov. 12, 1885–June 11,
    1960. Supp. 6–708
Wragg, William, 1714–Sept. 2, 1777.
    Vol. 10, Pt. 2–541
Wrather, William Embry, Jan. 20, 1883–Nov. 28, 1963.
    Supp. 7–803
Wraxall, Peter, d. July 10, 1759.
    Vol. 10, Pt. 2–542
Wright, Benjamin, Oct. 10, 1770–Aug. 24, 1842.
    Vol. 10, Pt. 2–543
Wright, Carroll Davidson, July 25, 1840–Feb. 20, 1909.
    Vol. 10, Pt. 2–544
Wright, Charles, Oct. 29, 1811–Aug. 11, 1885.
    Vol. 10, Pt. 2–545
Wright, Charles Barstow, Jan. 8, 1822–Mar. 24, 1898.
    Vol. 10, Pt. 2–546
Wright, Chauncey, Sept. 20, 1830–Sept. 12, 1875.
    Vol. 10, Pt. 2–547
Wright, Elizur, Feb. 12, 1804–Nov. 21, 1885.
    Vol. 10, Pt. 2–548
Wright, Fielding Lewis, May 16, 1895–May 4, 1956.
    Supp. 6–710
Wright, Frances, Sept. 6, 1795–Dec. 13, 1852.
    Vol. 10, Pt. 2–549
Wright, Frank Lloyd, June 8, 1867–Apr. 9, 1959.
    Supp. 6–711
Wright, George, Jan. 28, 1847–Aug. 21, 1937.
    Supp. 2–737
Wright, George Frederick, Jan. 22, 1838–Apr. 20, 1921.
    Vol. 10, Pt. 2–550
Wright, George Grover, Mar. 24, 1820–Jan. 11, 1896.
    Vol. 10, Pt. 2–551
Wright, Hamilton Kemp, Aug. 2, 1867–Jan. 9, 1917.
    Vol. 10, Pt. 2–552
Wright, Harold Bell, May 4, 1872–May 24, 1944.
    Supp. 3–846
Wright, Hendrick Bradley, Apr. 24, 1808–Sept. 2, 1881.
    Vol. 10, Pt. 2–553
Wright, Henry, Jan. 10, 1835–Oct. 3, 1895.
    Vol. 10, Pt. 2–554
Wright, Henry, July 2, 1878–July 9, 1936.
    Supp. 2–737
Wright, Horatio Gouverneur, Mar. 6, 1820–July 2, 1899.
    Vol. 10, Pt. 2–554
Wright, James Lendrew, Apr. 6, 1816–Aug. 3, 1893.
    Vol. 10, Pt. 2–555
Wright, John Henry, Feb. 4, 1852–Nov. 25, 1908.
    Vol. 10, Pt. 2–556
Wright, John Stephen, July 16, 1815–Sept. 26, 1874.
    Vol. 10, Pt. 2–557
Wright, Jonathan Jasper, Feb. 11, 1840–Feb. 18, 1885.
    Vol. 10, Pt. 2–558
Wright, Joseph Jefferson Burr, Apr. 27, 1801–May 14, 1878.
    Vol. 10, Pt. 2–560
Wright, Joseph, July 16, 1756–1793.
    Vol. 10, Pt. 2–559
Wright, Joseph Albert, Apr. 17, 1810–May 11, 1867.
    Vol. 10, Pt. 2–559
Wright, Luke Edward, Aug. 29, 1846–Nov. 17, 1922.
    Vol. 10, Pt. 2–561
Wright, Marcus Joseph, June 5, 1831–Dec. 27, 1922.
    Vol. 10, Pt. 2–561
Wright, Orville, Aug. 19, 1871–Jan. 30, 1948.
    Supp. 4–913
Wright, Patience Lovell, 1725–Mar. 23, 1786.
    Vol. 10, Pt. 2–562
Wright, Philip Green, Oct. 3, 1861–Sept. 4, 1934.
    Vol. 10, Pt. 2–563
Wright, Richard Nathaniel, Sept. 4, 1908–Nov. 28, 1960.
    Supp. 6–715
Wright, Richard Robert, May 16, 1853–July 2, 1947.
    Supp. 4–915
Wright, Robert, Nov. 20, 1752–Sept. 7, 1826.
    Vol. 10, Pt. 2–564
Wright, Robert William, Feb. 22, 1816–Jan. 9, 1885.
    Vol. 10, Pt. 2–565
Wright, Silas, May 24, 1795–Aug. 27, 1847.
    Vol. 10, Pt. 2–565
Wright, Theodore Lyman, Sept. 13, 1858–Oct. 4, 1926.
    Vol. 10, Pt. 2–567

CONTRIBUTORS WITH SUBJECTS

The names in capitals are the contributors—the names listed below are the subjects of their contributions.

Easton, John
Easton, Nicholas
Eaton, Nathaniel
Eaton, Samuel
Eaton, Theophilus
Eliot, John
Ellis, George Edward
Endecott, John
Everendon, Walter
Faneuil, Peter
Fanning, David
Fanning, Edmund, 1739–1818
Fiske, John, 1842–1901
Frothingham, Richard
Gage, Thomas
Gardiner, Sir Christopher
Gardiner, Lion
Gookin, Daniel
Gorham, Nathaniel
Gorton, Samuel
Green, Francis
Gridley, Jeremiah
Hancock, John, 1736–1793
Hibbins, Ann
Higginson, Francis
Higginson, John
Higginson, Stephen
Hooker, Thomas
Hopkins, Edward
Hutchinson, Anne
Johnson, Samuel
Leverett, John, 1616–1679
Lincoln, Benjamin
Lowell, John, 1743–1802
Massasoit
Maverick, Samuel
Miantonomo
Montgomery, Richard
Morton, Thomas
Norton, John
Oldham, John
Oliver, Andrew
Oliver, Peter
Palfrey, John Gorham
Parkman, Francis
Pepperell, Sir William
Popham, George
Putnam, Israel
Quincy, Josiah
Randolph, Edward
Sewall, Samuel
Shays, Daniel
Shirley, William
Shute, Samuel
Smith, John, 1579–1631
Sullivan, James
Uncas
Vane, Sir Henry
Warren, Joseph
Wheelwright, John
Winsor, Justin
Winthrop, John, 1587–1649
Winthrop, John, 1605–1676
Wise, John
ADAMS, RANDOLPH GREENFIELD
Arnold, Benedict
Clements, William Lawrence
Clinton, James
Conway, Thomas
Gates, Horatio
Gladwin, Henry
Greene, Nathanael
Harrisse, Henry

Lee, Charles, 1731–1782
Pontiac
Sullivan, John
ADAMS, RAYMOND WILLIAM
Hecker, Isaac Thomas
Hedge, Frederic Henry
Hewit, Augustine Francis
Lathrop, George Parsons
Peabody, Elizabeth Palmer
Ripley, George
Thoreau, Henry David
ADAMS, WALTER S.
Hale, George Ellery
Moody, (Arthur Edson) Blair
ADDISON, DANIEL DULANY
Hobart, John Henry
Huntington, William Reed
Mulford, Elisha
Nash, Henry Sylvester
Perry, William Stevens
ADKINS, NELSON F.
Davis, Oscar King
Inman, John
Irving, John Treat
Lardner, Ringgold Wilmer
McMaster, Guy Humphreys
Morford, Henry
Morris, George Pope
Picton, Thomas
Pond, George Edward
Porter, William Trotter
Ruhl, Arthur Brown
Sands, Robert Charles
Scollard, Clinton
Scoville, Joseph Alfred
Seton, William
Sikes, William Wirt
Sprague, Charles
Stillman, William James
Tuckerman, Henry Theodore
Woodworth, Samuel
ADLER, CYRUS
Dropsie, Moses Aaron
Jacobs, Joseph, 1854–1916
Lesser, Isaac
Malter, Henry
Margalis, Max Leopold
Morais, Sabato
Schechter, Solomon
Schiff, Jacob Henry
Sulzberger, Mayer
AGAR, HERBERT
Bingham, Robert Worth
AGARD, W. R.
Showerman, Grant
AGGER, EUGENE E.
Gilbert, Seymour Parker
Vanderlip, Frank Arthur
AHLSTROM, SYDNEY E.
Peabody, Francis Greenwood
AITKEN, HUGH G. J.
Crozier, William
AKERS, CHARLES W.
McMillin Alvin Nugent ("Bo")
AKIN, WILLIAM E.
Rautenstrauch, Walter
ALBERTSON, DEAN
Wickard, Claude Raymond
ALBION, ROBERT G.
Barker, Josiah
Bayard, William
Bell, Jacob
Bertram, John

Boyle, Thomas
Buchanan, Thomas
Chever, James W.
Cobb, Elijah
Collins, Edward Knight
Creesy, Josiah Perkins
Crowninshield, George
Earle, Ralph
Fanning, Edmund
Fanning, Nathaniel
Fish, Preserved
Forbes, Robert Bennet
Gardner, Caleb
Gibbons, Thomas
Grace, William Russell
Green, John Cleve
Green, Nathan
Griffiths, John Willis
Hall, Samuel, 1800–1870
Howland, Gardiner Greene
Jumel, Stephen
Knight, Edward Collings
Laurens, Henry
Law, George
McAllister, Charles Albert
Marshall, Charles Henry
Merry, William Lawrence
Minturn, Robert Bowne
Morgan, Charles
Munson, Walter David
Ogden, Aaron
Ogden, David Bayard
Olden, Charles Smith
Outerbridge, Eugenius Harvey
Palmer, Nathaniel Brown
Peabody, Joseph
Pintard, John
Pintard, Lewis
Price, Rodman McCamley
Quintard, George William
Roberts, Marshall Owen
Samuels, Samuel
Sands, Comfort
Scarbrough, William
Scudder, Nathaniel
Servoss, Thomas Lowery
Sewall, Arthur
Sewall, Harold Marsh
Sewell, William Joyce
Slocum, Joshua
Smith, Junius
Smith, Richard
Smith, Robert Alexander C.
Southard, Samuel Lewis
Starin, John Henry
Stephens, John Lloyd
Tileston, Thomas
Train, Enoch
Vaughan, Charles
Vernon, William
Ward, James Edward
Webb, William Henry
Westervelt, Jacob Aaron
Wheelwright, William
Williamson, Isaac Halsted
ALBRIGHT, WILLIAM F.
Bliss, Frederick Jones
Merrill, Selah
Paine, John Alsop
Robinson, Edward, 1794–1863
Smith, Eli
Stuart, Moses

ALDEN, CARROLL STORRS
  Bailey, Theodorus
  Dewey, George
  Graham, James Duncan
  Kearny, Lawrence
  Lamberton, Benjamin Peffer
  McCalla, Bowman Hendry
  McGiffin, Philo Norton
  Niblack, Albert Parker
  Perkins, George Hamilton
  Roe, Francis Asbury
ALDEN, EDMUND KIMBALL
  Alden, Ichabod
  Alden, John
  Alexander, William
  Anderson, George Thomas
  Angell, Israel
  Antes, Henry
  Archer, James J.
  Armistead, George
  Armstrong, John
  Arnold, Jonathan
  Asboth, Alexander Sandor
  Ashe, John
  Ashe, John Baptista
  Ashmead, Isaac
  Attucks, Crispus
  Auchmuty, Robert, d. 1750
  Auchmuty, Robert, d. 1788
  Auchmuty, Samuel
  Avery, Isaac Wheeler
  Bache, Benjamin Franklin
  Bache, Richard
  Bache, Theophylact
  Bailey, Ann
  Bailey, Anna Warner
  Bailey, James Anthony
  Bancroft, Edward
  Banister, John, 1734–1788
  Barber, Francis
  Barclay, Thomas
  Barnum, Henry A.
  Barnwell, John
  Barton, William
  Bassett, Richard
  Batcheller, George Sherman
  Bates, John Coalter
  Baxter, Henry
  Baylor, George
  Beall, John Yates
  Beatty, John, 1749–1826
  Bedford, Gunning, 1742–1797
  Bedford, Gunning, 1747–1812
  Berry, Hiram Gregory
  Boyd, John Parker
  Brearly, David
  Brooke, Francis Taliaferro
  Browne, Thomas
  Buford, Abraham, 1749–1833
  Cadwalader, John, 1742–1786
  Cadwalader, Lambert
  Caldwell, David
  Caldwell, James
  Campbell, William, 1745–1781
  Caswell, Richard
  Cilley, Joseph
  Clarke, Elijah
  Cobb, David
  Crawford, William
  Ewing, James
  Frazer, Persifor, 1736–1792
  Gansevoort, Peter
  Harmar, Josiah

  Hayne, Isaac
  Hazen, Moses
  Herkimer, Nicholas
  Howard, John Eager
  Ledyard, William
  Parker, John
  Parker, Josiah
  Pierce, William Leigh
  Ramsay, Nathaniel
ALDRICH, MICHELE L.
  Berry, Edward Wilber
  Darton, Nelson Horatio
  Foshag, William Frederick
  Stetson, Henry Crosby
ALDRICH, RICHARD
  Paine, John Knowles
ALEX, WILLIAM
  Olmsted, Frederick Law
ALEXANDER, CHARLES C.
  Foxx, James Emory
  Simmons, William Joseph
  Warner, Glenn Scobey ("Pop")
ALFORD, L. P.
  Gantt, Henry Laurence
ALGER, JOHN LINCOLN
  Greene, Samuel Stillman
  Leach, Daniel Dyer
  Mowry, William Augustus
ALLARD, DEAN C.
  Joy, Charles Turner
ALLEMANN, ALBERT
  Beck, Carl
  Bozeman, Nathan
  Caldwell, Eugene Wilson
ALLEN, ARTHUR A.
  Fuertes, Louis Agassiz
ALLEN, EDWARD ELLIS
  Anagnos, Michael
  Campbell, Francis Joseph
  Churchman, William Henry
  Fisher, John Dix
  Howe, Samuel Gridley
  Smith, Joel West
ALLEN, FORREST C.
  Naismith, James
ALLEN, FREEMAN H.
  Merrill, George Edmands
ALLEN, GARDNER W.
  Haraden, Jonathan
  Hinman, Elisha
  Hopkins, John Burroughs
  Hull, Isaac
  McNeill, Daniel
  McNeill, Hector
  Maffitt, David
  Preble, Edward
  Ridgely, Charles Goodwin
  Ropes, Joseph
  Saltonstall, Dudley
ALLEN, GARLAND E.
  Hart, Edwin Bret
ALLEN, HERVEY
  Poe, Edgar Allan
ALLEN, HORACE NEWTON
  Appenzeller, Henry Gerhard
  Harris, Merriman Colbert
  Underwood, Horace Grant
ALLEN, HOWARD W.
  Poindexter, Miles
ALLEN, MARY BERNARD
  Holt, Joseph

ALLEY, ROBERT S.
  Gorcey, Leo
ALLING, ARTHUR N.
  Thomson, Samuel
ALLINSON, FRANCIS G.
  Gildersleeve, Basil Lanneau
  Harkness, Albert
  Lincoln, John Larkin
ALLISON, WILLIAM HENRY
  Backus, Isaac
  Burrage, Henry Sweetser
  Cathcart, William
  Chase, Irah
  Church, Pharcellus
  Clarke, John
  Clarke, William Newton
  Dodge, Ebenezer
  Edwards, Morgan
  Furman, Richard
  Gano, John
  Gano, Stephen
  Going, Jonathan
  Griffith, Benjamin
  Hackett, Horatio Balch
  Horr, George Edwin
  Hovey, Alvah
  Jeter, Jeremiah Bell
  Johnson, Elias Henry
  Judson, Adoniram
  Judson, Ann Hasseltine
  Judson, Edward
  Judson, Sarah Hall Boardman
  King, Henry Melville
  Kneeland, Abner
  Loguen, Jeremain Wesley
  Love, Emanuel King
  Pendleton, James Madison
  Randall, Benjamin
  Rhees, Morgan John
  Rice, Luther
  Smith, Hezekiah
  Smith, Samuel Francis
  Staughton, William
  Stearns, Shubal
  Stevens, William Arnold
  Stillman, Samuel
  Stow, Baron
  Strong, Augustus Hopkins
ALLPORT, GORDON W.
  Holt, Edwin Bissell
ALMACK, JOHN C.
  Swett, John
ALPERN, SARA
  Meyer, Agnes Elizabeth Ernst
ALTER, DINSMORE
  Alter, David
AMACHER, PETER
  Coghill, George Ellett
AMBERSON, J. BURNS
  Miller, James Alexander
AMBLER, CHARLES HENRY
  Atkinson, George Wesley
  Boreman, Arthur Ingram
  Hunter, Robert Mercer
    Taliaferro
AMEND, KATHARINE H.
  Blitz, Antonio
  Boelen, Jacob
  Collins, John Anderson
  Coney, John
  Cooke, Henry David
  Cummings, Amos Jay
  Cushman, Pauline

Davenport, Ira Erastus
Edwards, John, c. 1671–1746
Forepaugh, Adam
Fox, Margaret
Gilbert, Anne Hartley
Gilbert, John Gibbs
Griffing, Josephine Sophie
  White
Hamlin, William
Harland, Thomas
Hart, James MacDougal
Hart, William
Henry, Edward Lamson
Herrmann, Alexander
Houdini, Harry
Howland, Alfred Cornelius
Hull, John
Hurd, Nathaniel
Palmer, William Henry
AMES, JOSEPH SWEETMAN
  Alexander, John Henry
  Rowland, Henry Augustus
AMES, WILLIAM E.
  Gilmer, Elizabeth Meriwether
    ("Dorothy Dix")
  Post, Emily Price
  Revell, Nellie MacAleney
  Sokolsky,
AMES, WINSLOW
  Lachaise, Gaston
AMOROSO, E. C.
  Wislocki, George Bernays
AMSTERDAM, GUSTAV G.
  Wharton, Thomas Isaac
ANDERSON, BENJAMIN M., JR.
  Hepburn, Alonzo Barton
ANDERSON, BERN
  Bristol, Mark Lambert
ANDERSON, DAVID D.
  Bromfield, Louis
  Cohen, Octavus Roy
  Gardner, Erle Stanley
  Hillyer, Robert Silliman
  Morley, Christopher Darlington
  O'Connor, Mary Flannery
  Paul, Elliot Harold
  Rinehart, Mary Roberts
  White, Josh
ANDERSON, DICE R.
  Randolph, Edmund, 1753–1813
ANDERSON, FRANK MALOY
  Kendall, Amos
ANDERSON, GEORGE M.
  Volck, Adalbert John
ANDERSON, GEORGE POMEROY
  Young, Thomas
ANDERSON, HAROLD M.
  Mitchell, Edward Page
ANDERSON, J. DOUGLAS
  Geers, Edward Franklin
  Johnson, William Ransom
ANDERSON, LEWIS FLINT
  Hailmann, William Nicholas
  Holbrook, Alfred
  Lewis, Samuel
  Lindley, Jacob
  Lord, Asa Dearborn
ANDERSON, NEAL L.
  Murphy, Edgar Gardner
ANDERSON, OSCAR E.
  Carrier, Willis Haviland

ANDERSON, OSCAR E., JR.
  Goddard, Robert Hutchings
ANDERSON, PETER J.
  Byrd, Richard Evelyn
  Smith, Edward Hanson
ANDERSON, RUSSELL H.
  Strawn, Jacob
  Studebaker, Clement
  Todd, Sereno Edwards
  Warder, John Aston
  Wing, Joseph Elwyn
  Wood, Jethro
  Wright, John Stephen
ANDREWS, CLARENCE
  Robinson, Henry Morton
ANDREWS, CLARENCE A.
  Stong, Phil(lip Duffield)
ANDREWS, JAMES PARKHILL
  Case, William Scoville
ANDREWS, J. D.
  Ferree, Clarence Errol
ANDREWS, WAYNE
  Aldrich, Chester Holmes
  Mackay, Clarence Hungerford
  Saarinen, Gottlieb Eliel
  Trumbauer, Horace
ANGELL, PATRICIA VAUGHN
  Morgan, Julia
ANGER, CHARLES L.
  Summerall, Charles Pelot
ANGLE, PAUL M.
  Horner, Henry
  Lewis, Lloyd Downs
  Thompson, William Hale
ANKER, ROY M.
  Fosdick, Harry Emerson
ANNAN, GERTRUDE L.
  Polak, John Osborn
  Purple, Samuel Smith
  Roosa, Daniel Bennett St. John
  Shrady, George Frederick
  Skene, Alexander Johnston
    Chalmers
  Smith, Stephen
  Stevens, Alexander Hodgdon
  Thomas, Theodore Gaillard
  Thompson, William Gilman
  Vander Veer, Albert
  Van de Warker, Edward Ely
  Wilcox, Reynold Webb
  Witthaus, Rudolph August
  Wyeth, John Allan
ANNUNZIATA, FRANK
  Bell, Bernard Iddings
  Brace, Donald Clifford
ANTHONY, KATHARINE
  Fuller, Sarah Margaret
  Stowe, Harriet Elizabeth
    Beecher
  Willard, Frances Elizabeth
  Wright, Frances
APPLETON, MARGUERITE
  Partridge, Richard
  Ward, Richard
  Ward, Samuel, 1725–1776
  Ward, Samuel, 1756–1832
  Wilbur, Samuel
APPLETON, WILLIAM M.
  Janis, Elsie
APPLETON, WILLIAM W.
  Adams, Maude
  Clark, Bobby
  Flynn, Errol Leslie

Gray, Gilda
Hardy, Oliver Norvell
Lawrence, Gertrude
Talmadge, Norma
ARBAUGH, GEORGE B.
  Smith, Joseph
ARCHER, JOHN
  Rudge, William Edwin
ARCHER, JOHN CLARK
  Abeel, David
  Agnew, Eliza
  Ainslie, Peter
  Allen, David Oliver
  Allen, Young John
  Anderson, David Lawrence
  Andrews, Lorrin
  Ashmore, William
  Bassett, James
  Bingham, Hiram, 1789–1869
  Bingham, Hiram, 1831–1908
  Bliss, Daniel
  Bliss, Edwin Elisha
  Bliss, Edwin Munsell
  Bliss, Howard Sweetser
  Butler, William, 1818–1899
  Chandler, John Scudder
  Clough, John Everett
  Coan, Titus
  Cushing, Josiah Nelson
  De Forest, John Kinne Hyde
  Dwight, Harrison Gray Otis
  Dwight, Henry Otis
  Ewing, James Caruthers Rhea
  Fletcher, James Cooley
  Heyer, John Christian Frederick
  Hume, Robert Allen
  Jessup, Henry Harris
  Jones, John Peter
  Kellogg, Samuel Henry
  Loewenthal, Isidor
  McLeen, Archibold
  Mansell, William Albert
  Mason, Francis
  Mudge, James
  Schauffler, William Gottlieb
  Spaulding, Levi
  Stewart, Robert
  Van Allen, Frank
  West, Henry Sergeant
  Wharton, Greene Lawrence
  Wheery, Elwood Morris
  Winslow, Miron
ARCHIBALD, RAYMOND CLARE
  Armstead, George B.
  Bowditch, Nathaniel
  Byerly, William Elwood
  Cajori, Florian
  Clark, Charles Hopkins
  Peirce, Benjamin
  Peirce, Benjamin Osgood
  Peirce, James Mills
  Story, William Edward
  Strong, Theodore
  Upton, Winslow
  West, Benjamin
AREY, LESLIE B.
  Ranson, Stephen Walter
ARMOUR, ROBERT
  Lindsay, Howard
ARMOUR, ROBERT A.
  Miller, Gilbert Heron
  Nagel, Conrad

ARMSTEAD, GEORGE B.
  Clark, Charles Hopkins
ARMSTRONG, EDWARD C.
  Elliott, Aaron Marshall
  Marden, Charles Carroll
ARMSTRONG, FLORENCE A.
  Younger, Maud
ARNASON, H. HARVARD
  Calder, Alexander Stirling
ARNAUD, LEOPOLD
  Boring, William Alciphron
ARNON, DANIEL I.
  Hoagland, Dennis Robert
ARNOULD, RICHARD J.
  Hormel, George Albert
ARRINGTON, LEONARD J.
  Jackling, Daniel Cowan
  McKay, David Oman
  Smith, George Albert
ARROWOOD, CHARLES F.
  Mercer, Charles Fenton
  Palmer, Benjamin Morgan
ARVIN, NEWTON
  Sill, Edward Rowland
ASHBURN, FRANK D.
  Peabody, Endicott
ASHBURN, PERCY M.
  Dick, Elisha Cullen
  Gihon, Albert Leary
  Hoff, John Van Rensselaer
  Kober, George Martin
  Lawson, Thomas
  Lovell, Joseph
  McCaw, James Brown
  McDowell, Ephraim
  McGuire, Hunter Holmes
  Mann, James
  Mitchell, Thomas Duché
  Moore, Samuel Preston
  Otis, George Alexander
  Peck, Charles Howard
  Potts, Jonathan
  Rauch, John Henry
ASHBY, CLIFFORD
  Nazimova, Alla
ASHDOWN, AVERY A.
  Norris, James Flack
ASHHURST, ASTLEY P.C.
  Neill, John
  Norris, George Washington
  Packard, John Hooker
ASHLEY, CLIFFORD W.
  Macy, Joseph
  Morrell, Benjamin
ASHLEY, FREDERICK WILLIAM
  Brough, John
  Cutter, Charles Ammi
  Green, Samuel Swett
  Griffin, Appleton Prentiss Clark
  Griswold, William McCrillis
  Lowery, Woodbury
  Nichols, Charles Lemuel
  Watterson, George
ATHERTON, LEWIS E.
  Maytag, Frederick Louis
ATKINSON, BROOKS
  Mantle, (Robert) Burns
ATWATER, HELEN W.
  Richardson, Anna Euretta
ATWATER, KATHARINE L.
  Richards, Thomas Addison

ATWELL, CHARLES B.
  Locy, William Albert
ATWOOD, ALBERT W.
  Morgan, John Pierpont
  Morgan, Junius Spencer
ATWOOD, JOHN MURRAY
  Cone, Orello
AUB, JOSEPH C.
  Edsall, David Linn
AUBREY, EDWIN EWART
  Smith, Gerald Birney
AULT, WARREN O.
  Newton, Thomas, 1660–1721
AUSTIN, JAMES B.
  Johnston, John
AUSTIN, MARY L.
  Calkins, Gary Nathan
AUSTRIAN, ROBERT
  Long, Perrin Hamilton
AVINOFF, A.
  Holland, William Jacob
AXFORD, C. B.
  Hayden, Charles
AYER, JOSEPH CULLEN
  Kemp, James
  Kerfoot, John Barrett
  Lay, Henry Champlin
  Lee, Alfred
  Newton, Richard
  Newton, Richard Heber
  Newton, William Wilberforce
  Pilmore, Joseph
  Potter, Alonzo
  Potter, Eliphalet Nott
  Potter, Henry Codman,
  Potter, Horatio
  White, William
AYRES, SAMUEL GARDINER
  Hurlbut, Jesse Lyman
  Peck, Jesse Truesdell
  Peirce, Bradford Kinney

BABCOCK, HAROLD D.
  St. John, Charles Edward
BABCOCK, KENDRIC C.
  Gregory, John Milton
BACH, C. A.
  Bailey, Joseph
  Baird, Absalom
  Barnes, James
  Barry, William Farquhar
  Grant, Ulysses Simpson
BACHRACK, STANLEY D.
  Kohlberg, Alfred
BACK, E. A.
  Emerton, James Henry
BACON, BENJAMIN WISNER
  Abbot, Ezra
  Bissell, Edwin Cone
  Bouton, Nathaniel
  Burr, Enoch Fitch
  Curtis, Edward Lewis
  Edwards, Jonathan, 1745–1801
  Emmons, Nathanael
  Fisher, George Park
  Hall, Isaac Hollister
BACON, ELIZABETH M.
  Pemberton, Israel
  Pemberton, James
  Pemberton, John
  Penington, Edward, 1667–1701
  Penington, Edward, 1726–1796

BACON, HAROLD M.
  Blichfeldt, Hans Frederik
BACON, JOSEPHINE DASKAM
  Wiggin, Kate Douglas
BACON, THEODORE D.
  Abbott, Edward
  Albright, Jacob
  Bellamy, Joseph
  Bradford, Amory Howe
  Chadwick, John White
  Chapin, Alonzo Bowen
  Cook, Flavius Josephus
BADE, WILLIAM F.
  Muir, John
BAEHR, GEORGE
  Sachs, Bernard
BAGBY, WESLEY M.
  Rublee, George
BAILEY, EDWARD M.
  Norton, John Pitkin
BAILEY, JOY JULIAN
  Jennings, Jonathan
BAILEY, MABEL DRISCOLL
  Anderson, Maxwell
BAINTON, ROLAND H.
  McGiffert, Arthur Cushman
  Mitchell, Jonathan
  Mombert, Jacob Isidor
  Murdock, James
  Walker, Williston
BAIRD, BIL
  Sarg, Tony
BAKELESS, JOHN
  Bellamy, Edward
  Littell, Eliakim
  Mabie, Hamilton Wright
  Pratt, Richard Henry
  Putnam, George Haven
  Putnam, George Palmer
  Spahr, Charles Barzillai
BAKER, CARLOS H.
  Hemingway, Ernest Miller
  Very, Jones
  Very, Lydia Louisa Ann
BAKER, CHRISTINA H.
  Dix, Dorothea Lynde
  Gilman, Arthur
  Peabody, Josephine Preston
BAKER, FRANK COLLINS
  Gould, Augustus Addison
  Kennicott, Robert
  Sterki, Victor
  Stimpson, William
  Tryon, George Washington
BAKER, HORACE B.
  Green, Jacob
  Harshberger, John William
  Meigs, James Aitkin
  Michaux, André
  Michaux, François André
  Montgomery, Thomas Harrison
  Parry, John Stubbs
  Parvin, Theophilus
BAKER, JOHN H.
  Cortissoz, Royal
  Kuhn, Walt
  Miller, Kenneth Hayes
  Sloan, John French
BAKER, NEWTON B.
  Johnson, Tom Loftin
BAKER, PAUL R.
  Barnes, Albert Coombs

BAKER, RAY PALMER
  Babcock, Washington Irving
  Beman, Nathan Sidney Smith
  Buck, Leffert Lefferts
  Francis, Charles Spencer
  Francis, John Morgan
  Gardiner, James Terry
  Geddes, James
  Graff, Frederick
  Greene, George Sears,
    1837–1922
  Griffin, Eugene
  Griswold, John Augustus
  Guthrie, Alfred
  Menocal, Aniceto Garcia
  Mills, Hiram Francis
  Murphy, John W.
  Nason, Henry Bradford
  Ricketts, Palmer Chamberlaine
BAKER-CROTHERS, HAYES
  Archdale, John
  Bozman, John Leeds
  Bull, William, 1683–1755
  Bull, William, 1710–1791
  Campbell, Lord William
  Johnson, Sir Nathaniel
  Johnson, Robert
  Lowndes, Rawlins
  Lyttelton, William Henry
  Middleton, Arthur
  Moore, James, d. 1706
  West, Joseph
  Yeamans, Sir John
BAKEWELL, CHARLES MONTAGUE
  Alden, Timothy
  Davidson, Thomas
  Gardiner, Harry Norman
BALABKINS, NICHOLAS W.
  Babson, Roger Ward
BALCH, MARSTON
  Wheatley, William
  Wood, William Burke
BALDWIN, CHARLES S.
  Price, Thomas Randolph
BALDWIN, LELAND D.
  Wetzel, Lewis
  Ziegler, David
BALL, GORDON
  Kerouac, Jack
BALL, WILLIAM W.
  Manning, Richard Irvine
BALLAGH, JAMES CURTIS
  Bradford, William, 1755–1795
  Campbell, Charles
  Chavis, John
  Chew, Benjamin
  Clymer, George
BALLIET, THOMAS M.
  Shaw, Edward Richard
BAMBERGER, WERNER
  Isbrandtsen, Hans Jeppesen
  Luckenbach, J(ohn) Lewis
BANNER, LOIS W.
  Helburn, Theresa
BANNISTER, ROBERT C.
  Odum, Howard Washington
BANNISTER, ROBERT C., JR.
  Baker, Ray Stannard
BANNISTER, TURPIN C.
  Mauran, John Lawrence
  Mizner, Addison

BANNON, JOHN FRANCIS
  Bolton, Herbert Eugene
BARBA, PRESTON A.
  Sealsfield, Charles
  Strubberg, Friedrich Armand
BARBEAU, ARTHUR E.
  Davis, Benjamin Oliver, Sr.
BARBOUR, HENRY G.
  Underhill, Franklin Pell
BARCLAY, ALBERT H.
  Cook, Robert Johnson
  Courtney, Charles Edward
BARCLAY, SHEPARD
  Whitehead, Wilbur Cherrier
  Work, Milton Cooper
BARCLAY, THOMAS S.
  Adams, Ephraim Douglass
  Blow, Henry Taylor
  Bogy, Lewis Vital
  Drake, Charles Daniel
  Folk, Joseph Wingate
  Gamble, Hamilton Rowan
  Hardin, Charles Henry
  Hatch, William Henry
  Hitchcock, Ethan Allen,
    1835–1909
  King, Austin Augustus
  Linn, Lewis Fields
  Lucas, James H.
  McBain, Howard Lee
  McNeill, John Hanson
  Noble, John Willock
  Philips, John Finis
  Preetorius, Emil
  Price, Thomas Lawson
  Ralston, William Chapman
  Rollins, James Sidney
  Rolph, James
  Scott, Dred
  Scott, William
  Sherwood, Thomas Adiel
  Shields, George Howell
BARCLAY, WADE CRAWFORD
  Oldham, William Fitzjames
BARDEEN, CHARLES RUSSELL
  Baxley, Henry Willis
  Baynham, William
BARGER, A. CLIFFORD
  Porter, William Townsend
BARKER, EUGENE CAMPBELL
  Archer, Branch Tanner
  Austin, Moses
  Austin, Stephen Fuller
BARKER, LEWELLYS F.
  McCrae, Thomas
  Noguchi, Hideyo
  Osler, William
  Thayer, William Sydney
BARKER, VIRGIL
  Bluemner, Oscar Florians
  Frieseke, Frederick Carl
  Lawson, Ernest
  Tucker, Allen
BARNARD, ELLSWORTH
  Willkie, Wendell Lewis
BARNARD, HARRY
  Couzens, James
  Mack, Julian William
BARNARD, JOHN
  Vincent, George Edgar
BARNES, GILBERT H.
  Lee, Luther
  Lovejoy, Elijah Parish

  Lovejoy, Owen
  Nelson, David
  Stewart, Alvan
  Stockton, Thomas Hewlings
  Stuart, Charles
  Sutherland, La Roy
  Torrey, Charles Turner
  Weld, Theodore Dwight
  Wright, Elizur
BARNES, HOWARD
  Eagels, Jeanne
BARNES, JAMES
  Thulstrup, Bror Thure
BARNES, VIOLA FLORENCE
  Andros, Sir Edmund
  Bradstreet, Simon
  Glover, John
  Greaton, John
  Greene, Christopher
  Hawley, Gideon, 1727–1807
  Hubbard, William
  Phips, Sir William
  Wharton, Richard
BARNETT, CLARIBEL RUTH
  Affleck, Thomas
  Browne, Daniel Jay
  Butterfield, Kenyon Leech
  Capron, Horace
  Dodge, Jacob Richards
  Dufour, John James
  Ellsworth, Henry Leavitt
  Flint, Charles Louis
  Gaylord, Willis
  Goodall, Harvey L.
  Johnson, Benjamin Pierce
  Johnston, John
  Klippart, John Hancock
  Knapp, Samuel Asabel
  Le Duc, William Gates
  Mayo, Mary Anne Bryant
  Newton, Isaac, 1800–1867
  Oemler, Arminius
  Pedder, James
  Philips, Martin Wilson
  Powell, George Harold
  Stockbridge, Horace Edward
  Tucker, Luther
  Vick, James
  Watts, Frederick
  Wiley, David
BARNHART, JOHN DONALD
  Willey, Waitman Thomas
BARNHART, JOHN H.
  Rydberg, Per Axel
  Torrey, John
BARNOUW, ADRIAAN J.
  Megapolensis, Johannes
  Michaelius, Jonas
  Minuit, Peter
  Selijns, Henricus
  Steendam, Jacob
BARON, SALO W.
  Bernstein, Herman
BARRETT, HARRY MCWHIRTER
  Baker, James Hutchins
  Gove, Aaron Estellus
BARRON, DONALD H.
  Donaldson, Henry Herbert
BARROWS, ANNA
  Lincoln, Mary Johnson Bailey
BARROWS, DAVID P.
  Pacheco, Romualdo

BARROWS, HAROLD K.
  Fitzgerald, Desmond
  Henny, David Christiaan
  Kay, Edgar Boyd
  Koyl, Charles Herschel
  Lundie, John
  McNeill, William Gibbs
  Sawyer, Walter Howard
  Schuyler, James Dix
  Shedd, Joel Herbert
  Smith, Jonas Waldo
  Stearns, Frederic Pike
  Storrow, Charles Storer
  Vose, George Leonard
  Wheeler, William
  Whistler, George Washington
  Wiley, Andrew Jackson
  Worthen, William Ezra
BARTEE, WAYNE C.
  Hartley, Fred Allen, Jr.
BARTHOLD, ALLEN J.
  Nancrède, Paul Joseph Guérard
    de
BARTLETT, CLARENCE
  Hale, Edwin Moses
  Hempel, Charles Julius
  Hering, Constantine
  Holcombe, William Henry
  Jackson, Mercy Ruggles Bisbe
  Janney, Oliver Edward
  Neidhard, Charles
  Peters, John Charles
  Pulte, Joseph Hippolyt
  Raue, Charles Gottlieb
  Small, Alvan Edmond
  Talbot, Israel Tisdale
  Thomas, Amos Russell
  Van Lennep, William Bird
BARTLETT, HOWARD R.
  Penhallow, Samuel
BARTLETT, J. HENRY
  Evans, Thomas
BARTLEY, NUMAN V.
  Cox, Edward Eugene
BARTON, GEORGE A.
  Clay, Albert Tobias
  Gordon, George Byron
  Harper, Robert Francis
  Haupt, Paul
  Haynes, John Henry
  Hilprecht, Herman Volrath
  Jastrow, Morris
  Müller, Wilhelm Max
  Peters, John Punnett
  Rogers. Robert William
  Ward, William Hayes
BARTSCH, PAUL
  Holmes, William Henry
  Simpson, Charles Torrey
BASS, LAWRENCE W.
  Levene, Phoebus Aaron
    Theodore
BASS, ROBERT DUNCAN
  McCord, Louisa Susanna
    Cheves
  McKinley, Carlyle
  Moïse, Penina
BASSETT, JOHN SPENCER
  Adams, Herbert Baxter
  Bryan, William Jennings
BASSETT, T. D. SEYMOUR
  Fisher, Dorothea Frances
    Canfield

Peattie, Donald Culross
BASTERT, RUSSELL H.
  Barrett, John
BASTIN, EDSON S.
  Penrose, Richard Alexander
    Fullerton
BATEMAN, ALAN M.
  Pirsson, Louis Valentine
BATES, ERNEST SUTHERLAND
  Albee, Ernest
  Alcott, Amos Bronson
  Alden, Henry Mills
  Alger, Horatio
  Allyn, Robert
  Alsop, George
  Ament, William Scott
  Andrews, John
  Andrews, Stephen Pearl
  Apes, William
  Bacon, Delia Salter
  Baldwin, Matthias William
  Bascom, John
  Bates, Walter
  Beasley, Frederick
  Beers, Ethel Lynn
  Blackwell, Antoinette Louisa
    Brown
  Blavatsky, Helena Petrovna
    Hahn
  Bleecker, Ann Eliza
  Blood, Benjamin Paul
  Bolton, Sarah Knowles
  Booth, Edwin Thomas
  Booth, John Wilkes
  Booth, Junius Brutus
  Bourne, Randolph Silliman
  Bowen, Francis
  Brace, Charles Loring
  Brokmeyer, Henry C.
  Brownell, William Crary
  Brownson, Orestes Augustus
  Buchanan, Joseph Rodes
  Cammerhoff, John Christopher
  Cartwright, Peter
  Carus, Paul
  Caruso, Enrico
  Considérant, Victor Prosper
  Crosby, Ernest Howard
  Dowie, John Alexander
  Duncan, Isadora
  Foster, George Burman
  Fowler, Orson Squire
  Frederic, Harold
  Gayarré, Charles Étienne
    Arthur
  Grierson, Francis
  Grimes, James Stanley
  Harris, William Torrey
  Hedge, Levi
  Hickok, Laurens Perseus
  Hitchcock, Ethan Allen,
    1798–1870
  Howison, George Holmes
  Judge, William Quan
  Lindsay, Nicholas Vachel
  Lloyd, Alfred Henry
  Miller, Cincinnatus Hiner
  Olcott, Henry Steel
  Quimby, Phineas Parkhurst
  Reed, John, 1887–1920
  Riley, Isaac Woodbridge
  Russell, Charles Taze
  Sherman, Stuart Pratt

Smith, Charles Sprague
Smith, Harry James
Snider, Denton Jaques
Stedman, Edmund Clarence
Stetson, Augusta Emma
  Simmons
Tingley, Katherine Augusta
  Westcott
Underwood, Benjamin Franklin
Wenley, Robert Mark
Wiggins, James Henry
Wilder, Alexander
Wilkinson, Jemima
Wilson, William Dexter
Wright, Chauncey
BATES, FRANCES
  Newell, Peter Sheaf Hersey
BATTLE, GEORGE GORDON
  Osborne, James Walker
BATTLE, WILLIAM JAMES
  Fay, Edwin Whitfield
BAUER, G. PHILIP
  Mason, John, c. 1600–1672
  Sassacus
  Walderne, Richard
  Warren, James
  Warren, Mercy Otis
BAUER, LOUIS AGRICOLA
  Bache, Alexander Dallas
BAUER, THOMAS J.
  Walsh, James Anthony
BAUGH, ALBERT C.
  Mackenzie, Robert Shelton
  McMichael, Morton
  Markoe, Peter
BAUGHIN, WILLIAM A.
  Dykstra, Clarence Addison
BAUGHMAN, JAMES L.
  Cooper, Gary
  Kovacs, Ernie
  Luce, Henry Robinson
BAUGHMAN, JAMES P.
  Mallory, Clifford Day
BAUR, JOHN I. H.
  Grosz, George
BAUR, WILLIAM L.
  Rieger, Johann Georg Joseph
    Anton
BAXANDALL, LEE
  Corey, Lewis
BAXTER, ANNETTE K.
  Woolley, Mary Emma
BAXTER, GREGORY P.
  Richards, Theodore William
BAXTER, WILLIAM T.
  Henchman, Daniel
  Kilby, Christopher
BAYNE-JONES, STANHOPE
  Jordan, Edwin Oakes
  Zinsser, Hans
BAYOR, RONALD H.
  Crump, Edward Hull
BEACH, ARTHUR GRANDVILLE
  Andrews, Israel Ward
BEADLE, GEORGE W.
  Morgan, Thomas Hunt
BEALE, HOWARD K.
  Kavanagh, Edward
  Welles, Gideon
BEAN, JOHN W.
  Lombard, Warren Plimpton

BEAN, MALCOLM
  Stephenson, Carl
BEAN, WALTON
  Ruef, Abraham
  Spreckels, Rudolph
BEAN, WILLIAM G.
  Lee, George Washington Custis
  Letcher, John
  McCausland, John
  Mason, John Young
  O'Ferrall, Charles Triplett
  Peyton, John Lewis
  Shipp, Scott
  Smith, Francis Henney
  Tucker, Henry St. George,
    1853–1932
  Tucker, John Randolph,
    1823–1897
  Upshur, Abel Parker
BEARD, MARY R.
  Maclay, William
BEARDSLEY, WILLIAM A.
  Bass, Edward
  Beardsley, Eben Edwards
  Bowden, John
  Brownell, Thomas Church
  Burgess, Alexander
  Burgess, George
  Doolittle, Amos
BEATTY, WILLIAM K.
  Bovie, William T.
  Drinker, Cecil Kent
BEATY, JOHN O.
  Cooke, John Esten
BEAVER, DONALD deB.
  De Forest, Lee
BEAVER, R. PIERCE
  Cort, Edwin Charles
  McKean, James William
  Peabody, Lucy Whitehead
  Reed, Mary
BECK, ROBERT W.
  Ross, James Delmage McKenzie
BECKER, CARL LOTUS
  Adams, Samuel
  Franklin, Benjamin, 1706–1790
  Hutchinson, Thomas
BECKER, CARL M.
  Falk, Maurice
  Tytus, John Butler
  Verity, George Matthew
BECKER, DOROTHY G.
  Morgan, Anne
BECKER, STANLEY L.
  Schmidt, Carl Louis August
BECKER, STEPHEN
  Field, Marshall, III
BECKHART, BENJAMIN HAGGOTT
  Anderson, Benjamin McAlester
  Fraser, Leon
  Willis, Henry Parker
BEDDIE, JAMES S.
  Smith, Jeremiah
BEDE, JEAN-ALBERT
  Smith, Horatio Elwin
BEEZLEY, WILLIAM H.
  O'Doul, Francis Joseph
    ("Lefty")
  Rucker, George ("Nap")
BEHRINGER, CLARA M.
  Cowl, Jane
  Robson, May

BELDEN, CHARLES F. D.
  Benton, Josiah Henry
  Chamberlain, Mellen
BELL, DANIEL
  Vladeck, Baruch Charney
BELLINGER, ALFRED L.
  Newell, Edward Theodore
BELLOWS, ROBERT P.
  Peabody, Robert Swain
BELLUSH, BERNARD
  Winant, John Gilbert
BEMIS, SAMUEL FLAGG
  Fuller, Joseph Vincent
  Jay, John
BENDER, HAROLD H.
  Green, William Henry
  Whitney, William Dwight
BENDER, W. J.
  Morton, Charles
BENDIXEN, ALFRED
  Forbes, Esther
  Vorse, Mary Heaton
BENEDICT, H.Y.
  Sutton, William Seneca
BENJAMIN, MARCUS
  Dall, William Healey
  Rathbun, Richard
  Rhees, William Jones
  Seabury, George John
BENNETT, DAVID H.
  Langer, William
  Townsend, Francis Everett
BENNETT, EDWARD
  Grew, Joseph Clark
BENNETT, ORVAL
  Niedringhaus, Frederick
    Gottlieb
  Orthwein, Charles F.
BENNETT, WELLS
  Blodget, Samuel
BENSON, ADOLPH B.
  Henningsen, Charles Frederick
  Morton, John
  Poulson, Niels
  Reeves, Arthur Middleton
BENSON, C. C.
  Johnston, Albert Sidney
  Ord, Edward Otho Cresap
  Osterhaus, Peter Joseph
  Parke, John Grubb
  Pemberton, John Clifford
  Phisterer, Frederick
  Pickett, George Edward
  Pleasonton, Alfred
  Potter, Robert Brown
  Reynolds, John Fulton
  Schriver, Edmund
  Shelby, Joseph Orville
BENSON, JACKSON J.
  Steinbeck, John Ernst, Jr.
BENSON, JANE A.
  Breckinridge, Aida de Acosta
  Dingman, Mary Agnes
  Williams, Harrison Charles
BENTINCK-SMITH, WILLIAM
  Greene, Jerome Davis
BENTON, ELBERT JAY
  Barber, Ohio Columbus
  Brinkerhoff, Jacob
  Brinkerhoff, Roeliff
  Brown, Alexander Ephraim
  Burke, Stevenson
  Burton, Theodore Elijah

Case, Leonard, 1786–1864
Case, Leonard, 1820–1880
Cleaveland, Moses
Cowles, Edwin
Delano, Columbus
Devereux, John Henry
Eells, Dan Parmelee
Giddings, Joshua Reed
Grasselli, Caesar Augustin
Hinman, George Wheeler
Hinsdale, Burke Aaron
Holden, Liberty Emery
Johnson, Levi
Johnston, Seth Whitmore
Kelley, Alfred
Mather, Samuel
Mather, Samuel Holmes
Mather, Samuel Livingston
Ranney, Rufus Percival
Severance, Louis Henry
Stone, Amasa
Wade, Jeptha Homer
BERDAHL, CLARENCE
  Garner, James Wilford
BERDAN, JOHN M.
  Beers, Henry Augustin
BERGER, JEANNETTE L.
  Young, John Russell
BERGMAN, J. PETER
  Arnold, Edward
BERKELEY, FRANCIS L., JR.
  Smith, Thomas Adams
BERMAN, HYMAN
  Price, George Moses
BERNER, ROBERT L.
  Bemelmans, Ludwig
  Cooke, Samuel
  Ferber, Edna Jessica
  Kresge, Sebastian Spering
  May, Morton Jay
  Mayer, Oscar Gottfried
  Sandoz, Mari
BERNSTEIN, ALISON
  Madigan, Laverne
BERNSTEIN, DAVID
  Crawford, Samuel Earl
  Dressen, Charles Walter
  McKechnie, William Boyd
  Schalk, Raymond William
    ("Cracker")
BERRY, EDWARD W.
  White, David
BERRY, S. STILLMAN
  Stearns, Robert Edwards Carter
BERRYMAN, JACK W.
  Hoppe, William Frederick
    ("Willie")
  Jones, Benjamin Allyn
  McCarthy, Charles Louis
    (Clem)
  Mallory, Anna Margrethe
    ("Molla") Bjurstedt
  Travers, Jerome Dunstan
BERTOCCI, PETER A.
  Brightman, Edgar Sheffield
BETTEN, FRANCIS S.
  Behrens, Henry
BETTS, JOHN R.
  Hitchcock, Thomas
  McGrath, Matthew J.
BETTS, THOMAS JEFFRIES
  Wheeler, Joseph
  Wood, Leonard

BEWER, JULIUS AUGUST
  Smith, Henry Preserved
BEYER, RICHARD L.
  Hunter, Robert
BEYERCHEN, ALAN
  Franck, James
BEZILLA, MICHAEL
  Clement, Martin Withington
BEZOU, HENRY C.
  Rummel, Joseph Francis
BICKEL, ALEXANDER M.
  Van Devanter, Willis
BIDDLE, GEORGE
  Borie, Adolphe
BIDWELL, PERCY W.
  Callender, Guy Stevens
  Emery, Henry Crosby
  Holls, George Frederick
    William
  Hourwich, Isaac Aaronovich
  Jenks, Jeremiah Whipple
  Leach, Shepherd
  Lee, Henry, 1782–1867
  Longley, Alcander
  Luther, Seth
  McFadden, Louis Thomas
  McPherson, Logan Grant
  Masquerier, Lewis
  Maxwell, Hugh
  Moore, Ely
  Moss, Frank
  Nordhoff, Charles
  North, Simon Newton Dexter
  Noyes, John Humphrey
  Parsons, Frank
  Pitkin, Timothy
  Plant, Henry Bradley
  Porter, Robert Percival
  Stilwell, Silas Moore
  Wilkeson, Samuel
BIEBER, RALPH PAUL
  Bain, George Luke Scobie
  Brannan, Samuel
BIEDER, ROBERT E.
  Cohen, Felix Solomon
BIERLEY, PAUL E.
  Pryor, Arthur W.
BIGELOW, BRUCE M.
  Lopez, Aaron
BIGELOW, GORDON E.
  Rawlings, Marjorie Kinnan
BILLARD, F. C.
  Kimball, Sumner Increase
BILLINGTON, MONROE
  Barrows, Alice Prentice
  Gore, Thomas Pryor
  Smith, Lucy Harth
BILSTEIN, ROGER E.
  Buckley, Oliver Ellsworth
  Howard, Henry
  Schroeder, Rudolph William
  Warner, Edward Pearson
BING, FRANKLIN C.
  Lining, John
BINGHAM, EUGENE C.
  Hart, Edward
BINGHAM, WOODBRIDGE
  Williams, Edward Thomas
BINING, ARTHUR C.
  McKinley, Albert Edward
BINKLEY, WILLIAM C.
  Porter, James Davis
  Stahlman, Edward Bushrod

Taylor, Alfred Alexander
Taylor, Robert Love
Thomas, John Wilson
Turney, Peter
BIRCH, FRANCIS
  Daly, Reginald Aldworth
BIRNBAUM, GEORGE PHILIP
  Arliss, George
  Cohan, George Michael
  Errol, Leon
  Greenstreet, Sydney Hughes
  Lord, Pauline
  Skinner, Otis
  Youmans, Vincent Millie
BIRR, KENDALL
  Emmet, William Le Roy
  Gherardi, Bancroft
  Hill, Ernest Rowland
  Kent, Arthur Atwater
BLACK, J. WILLIAM
  Potter, Platt
BLACKBURN, GLEN A.
  Tipton, John
BLACKMAR, FRANK WILSON
  Anderson, John Alexander
  Anthony, George Tobey
BLACKMER, ALAN ROGERS
  Morrill, Justin Smith
  Quincy, Edmund
  Quincy, Josiah Phillips
BLACKORBY, EDWARD C.
  Burdick, Usher Lloyd
  Lemke, William Frederick
BLACKWELL, ROBERT EMORY
  Smith, William Andrew
BLAKE, JOHN B.
  Snow, William Freeman
BLAKE, MARION E.
  Van Deman, Esther Boise
BLAKESLEE, GEORGE H.
  Dennis, Alfred Lewis Pinneo
BLANCHARD, ARTHUR A.
  Mulliken, Samuel Parsons
  Talbot, Henry Paul
BLANCHARD, EDITH R.
  Garvin, Lucius Fayette Clark
  Harris, Caleb Fiske
  Hopkins, Esek
  Hoppin, William Warner
  Howell, David
  Hunter, William
  Jenckes, Joseph, 1632–1717
  Jenckes, Joseph, 1656–1740
  Jenks, Joseph
  Lippitt, Henry
  Potter, Elisha Reynolds
  Redwood, Abraham
  Smith, James Youngs
  Sprague, William, 1830–1915
  Stiness, John Henry
  Updike, Daniel
BLANTON, WYNDHAM B.
  Smith, John Augustine
  Tennent, John
BLANTZ, THOMAS E.
  Dooley, Thomas Anthony, III
  Glennon, John Joseph
  Haas, Francis Joseph
  Stritch, Samuel Alphonsus
BLASHFIELD, EDWIN HOWLAND
  Alexander, John White

BLAUT, JULIA
  Rothko, Mark
BLEGEN, THEODORE C.
  Andrews, Christopher
  Columbus
  Baker, James Heaton
  Bottineau, Pierre
  Flandrau, Charles Eugene
  Haugen, Nils Pederson
  McLeod, Martin
  Peerson, Cleng
  Reierson, Johan Reinert
  Rynning, Ole
  Schall, Thomas David
  Williams, John Fletcher
BLESH, RUDI
  Harney, Benjamin Robertson
BLESSING, ARTHUR R.
  Cochrane, Henry Clay
  Dyer, Nehemiah Mayo
  Evans, Robley Dunglison
  Gridley, Charles Vernon
  Hamblin, Joseph Eldridge
  Herndon, William Lewis
  Hichborn, Philip
  Loring, Charles Harding
  Luce, Stephen Bleecker
BLEYER, WILLIARD GROSVENOR
  Hale, David
  Hallock, Charles
  Hallock, Gerard
  Peck, George Wilbur
  Ralph, Julian
  Rublee, Horace
  Scripps, Edward Wyllis
  Scripps, James Edmund
  Smith, William Henry,
    1833–1896
  Storey, Wilbur Fisk
  Tousey, Sinclair
BLISS, GILBERT A.
  Moore, Eliakim Hastings
BLISS, JOHN ALDEN
  Doherty, Henry Latham
  Mitchell, Sidney Zollicoffer
BLIVEN, BRUCE
  Straight, Willard Dickerman
BLODGET, LOUISE PEARSON
  Linderman, Henry Richard
  Park, James
  Pitcairn, John
  Russell, Lillian
  Spencer, Samuel
  Walsh, Thomas James
BLODGETT, GEOFFREY
  Churchill, Winston
  Hughes, Charles Evans
  Moses, George Higgins
  Tarbell, Ida Minerva
BLOOM, LANSING B.
  Larrazolo, Octaviano Ambrosio
  Peralta, Pedro de
  Rhodes, Eugene Manlove
  Seligman, Arthur
  Springer, Charles
BLOOMFIELD, MAXWELL H.
  Day, George Parmly
  Doran, George Henry
  Golden, John
  Guinzburg, Harold Kleinert
  Knapp, Joseph Palmer
  Odell, George Clinton
  Densmore

Scribner, Charles
Simon, Richard Leo
BLOTNER, JOSEPH
Faulkner (Falkner), William
Cuthbert
BLUE, GEORGE VERNE
Robinson, Christopher
Root, Joseph Pomeroy
Scruggs, William Lindsay
BLUM, JOHN MORTON
Burleson, Albert Sidney
Morgenthau, Henry, Jr.
Tumulty, Joseph Patrick
BLUMENSON, MARTIN
Patton, George Smith
Walker, Walton Harris
BLUMER, G. ALDER
Beard, George Miller
Beck, John Brodhead
Gallup, Joseph Adams
Holyoke, Edward Augustus
King, Dan
Ordronaux, John
Parsons, Usher
Ray, Isaac
BLUMER, GEORGE
Barton, Benjamin Smith
Beck, Theodric Romeyn
Bell, Luther Vose
Brill, Nathan Edwin
Brown, William
Byrne, John
Cohen, Jacob da Silva Solis
Edebohls, George Michael
Emmet, Thomas Addis,
1828–1919
BOARDMAN, ROGER S.
Altman, Benjamin
Bailey, Gamaliel
Bailey, James Montgomery
Baldwin, John Denison
Ballou, Adin
Barnard, Charles Francis
Buffum, Arnold
Chace, Elizabeth Buffum
Colman, Lucy Newhall
Cox, Hannah Peirce
BOAS, R. P.
Huntington, Edward Vermilye
BOATFIELD, HELEN C.
Child, Robert
Fletcher, Benjamin
Hare, Robert
Hazen, Moses
Nolan, Philip
Noyan, Gilles-Augustin Payen
de
Noyan, Pierre-Jacques Payen de
Radisson, Pierre Esprit
Stuart, Francis Lee
Walsh, Michael
Weed, Thurlow
BOCHNER, SALOMON
Bateman, Harry
Weyl, Hermann
BODAYLA, STEPHEN D.
Bliss, Robert Woods
Brooks, Overton
Brown, Clarence James
Cochrane, Gordon Stanley
("Mickey")
Cummings, Walter Joseph
Davis, Francis Breese, Jr.

Downey, Sheridan
Ford, Hannibal Choate
Goddard, Calvin Hooker
Hupp, Louis Gorham
Hutton, Edward Francis
Lasser, Jacob Kay
Lehman, Robert
Mead, James Michael
Murchison, Clinton Williams
Robinson, Claude Everett
Speaker, Tris E.
Stanley, Harold
Warburg, James Paul
Ward, Charles Alfred
BODDINGTON, ERNEST F.
Corcoran, James Andrew
Egan, Michael
Farmer, Ferdinand
BODE, CARL
Thorpe, Rose Alnora Hartwick
BODIAN, DAVID
Hoerr, Normand Louis
BOGART, ERNEST LUDLOW
Harahan, James Theodore
Harding, Abner Clark
Jewett, Hugh Judge
Joy, James Frederick
Matteson, Joel Aldrich
Oakes, Thomas Fletcher
Ogden, William Butler
Payne, Henry Clay
Perkins, Charles Elliott
Plumb, Glenn Edward
Stickney, Alpheus Beede
Traylor, Melvin Alvah
BOGUE, ALLAN G.
Gregory, Clifford Verne
BOHJALIAN, ANDREW
Barton, Bruce Fairchild
BOLANDER, LOUIS H.
Corbin, Henry Clark
Heintzelman, Stuart
McCawley, Charles Laurie
Morton, Charles Gould
Muir, Charles Henry
Read, George Windle
Reynolds, William
Rhind, Alexander Colden
Robertson, Ashley Herman
Russell, John Henry
Schenck, James Findlay
Schroeder, Seaton
Selfridge, Thomas Oliver
Sigsbee, Charles Dwight
Snowden, Thomas
Steedman, Charles
Strain, Isaac G.
Stringham, Silas Horton
Strong, James Hooker
Townsend, Robert
Trenchard, Stephen Decatur
Usher, Nathaniel Reilly
Voorhees, Philip Falkerson
Walker, Asa
Ward, James Harmon
Weaver, Aaron Ward
Welles, Roger
Wickes, Lambert
Wyman, Robert Harris
BOLT, JOSEPH S.
Nadelman, Elie

BOLT, JOSEPH SULLIVAN
Flannagan, John Bernard
BOLTON, CHARLES K.
Howe, Mark Anthony De Wolfe
Jewett, Clarence Frederick
Montgomery, David Henry
Poole, Fitch
Rindge, Frederick Hastings
Shaw, William Smith
Shurtleff, Nathaniel Bradstreet
Thornton, John Wingate
Tudor, William
Whipple, Edwin Percy
Whitmore, William Henry
Widener, Harry Elkins
Winthrop, Robert Charles
Young, Alexander
BOLTON, ETHEL STANWOOD
Topliff, Samuel
Tuckerman, Joseph
BOLTON, HERBERT EUGENE
Cabrillo, Juan Rodriguez
Cárdenas, García López de
Coronada, Francisco Vázquez
Crespi, Juan
De Mézières Y Chigny,
Athanase
Kino, Eusebio Francisco
Palóu, Francisco
BOLTON, LAETITIA TODD
Dickinson, Anson
BOLTON, THEODORE
Alexander, Francis
Ames, Ezra
Ames, Joseph Alexander
Armstrong, David Maitland
Baker, George Augustus
Beard, James Carter
Beard, James Henry
Beard, William Holbrook
Bellows, George Wesley
Bounetheau, Henry Brintnell
BOLWELL, ROBERT W.
King, Edward Smith
Lawson, James
Lennox, Charlotte Ramsay
MacDowell, Katherine
Sherwood Bonner
McGovern, John
Magruder, Julia
Parker, Jane Marsh
Pike, Mary Hayden Green
Prentiss, Elizabeth Payson
Reid, Thomas Mayne
Searing, Laura Catherine
Redden
Shreve, Thomas Hopkins
Smith, Elizabeth Oakes Prince
Southworth, Emma Dorothy
Eliza Nevitte
Stratemeyer, Edward
BOND, BEVERLEY W. JR.
Andrews, Sherlock James
Burnet, Jacob
Putnam, Rufus
Symmes, John Cleves
BOND, EARLE D.
Kirkbride, Thomas Story
BOND, W. H.
Jackson, William Alexander
BONHAM, MILLEDGE LOUIS
Brant, Joseph
Cambreleng, Churchill Caldom

Conkling, Alfred
Dickinson, Daniel Stevens
Dorsheimer, William Edward
Duryée, Abram
Dwight, William
Morgan, George Washington
Morgan, James Morris
BONSAL, STEPHEN
Bowen, Herbert Wolcott
Calhoun, William James
BOOKER, JOHN MANNING
Greenlaw, Edwin Almiron
BORCHARD, EDWIN M.
Penfield, William Lawrence
BORING, WILLIAM A.
Hamlin, Alfred Dwight Foster
BORIS, EILEEN C.
Scudder, (Julia) Vida Dutton
BORNEMANN, ALFRED
Laughlin, James Laurence
BOROME, JOSEPH A.
Bostwick, Arthur Elmore
Utley, George Burwell
BOSHA, FRANCIS J.
Chatterton, Ruth
Hardwicke, Cedric Webster
BOSTON, LEONARD NAPOLEON
Maury, Francis Fontaine
BOSTWICK, ARTHUR E.
Ives, Halsey Cooley
BOSWELL, WILLIAM E.
Moore, Grace
Samaroff, Olga
BOTEIN, STEPHEN
Crane, Frederick Evan
Cromwell, William Nelson
Hiscock, Frank Harris
Lewis, William Draper
Wigmore, John Henry
BOURNE, HENRY E.
Putnam, Ruth
Tuttle, Herbert
BOUTON, ARCHIBALD LEWIS
Cannon, Charles James
Clinch, Charles Powell
Cook, Martha Elizabeth Duncan
  Walker
Coombe, Thomas
Cozzens, Frederick Swartwout
Drake, Joseph Rodman
Janvier, Catharine Ann
Janvier, Thomas Allibone
Kimball, Richard Burleigh
McLellan, Isaac
Mayo, William Starbuck
BOWDEN, WITT
Boies, Henry Martyn
Borie, Adolph Edward
Buckalew, Charles Rollin
Dickson, Thomas
Disston, Henry
Dolan, Thomas
Drexel, Anthony Joseph
Drexel, Francis Martin
Drexel, Joseph William
Hartranft, John Frederick
Hays, Alexander
Hopkinson, Joseph
Hoyt, Henry Martyn
Ingersoll, Charles Jared
Ingersoll, Jared, 1749–1822
Lewis, Lawrence

McKennan, Thomas McKean
  Thompson
Mercur, Ulysses
Mitchell, James Tyndale
Ward, Cyrenus Osborne
Wilson, William Bauchop
BOWERMAN, GEORGE F.
Noyes, Crosby Stuart
BOWERMAN, SARAH G.
Banister, Zilpah Polly Grant
Banvard, John
Banvard, Joseph
Barrett, Kate Waller
Bartlett, John
Bloede, Gertrude
Bouvet, Marie Marguerite
Bristed, Charles Astor
Bristed, John
Brockett, Linus Pierpont
Brooks, Elbridge Streeter
Brooks, James Gordon
Brown, Charlotte Emerson
Bulfinch, Thomas
Burleigh, William Henry
Burnham, Clara Louise Root
Burt, Mary Elizabeth
Carpenter, Frank George
Chandler, Elizabeth Margaret
Cheney, Ednah Dow Littlehale
Chesebrough, Caroline
Clarke, Rebecca Sophia
Clemmer, Mary
Cooke, Rose Terry
Cornwallis, Kinaban
Cratty, Mabel
Cummins, Maria Susanna
Cutter, George Washington
Dahlgren, Sarah Madeline
  Vinton
Darling, Flora Adams
Dodge, Grace Hoadley
Dodge, Mary Elizabeth Mapes
Elder, Susan Blanchard
Ellet, Elizabeth Fries Lummis
Finley, Martha Farquharson
Foster, Hannah Webster
French, Lucy Virginia Smith
Gardener, Helen Hamilton
Habberton, John
Hale, Lucretia Peabody
Hall, Florence Marion Howe
Harris, Miriam Coles
Harrison, Constance Cary
Holmes, Mary Jane Hawes
Howard, Blanche Willis
Janvier, Margaret Thomson
Jenks, Tudor Storrs
Johnson, Helen Louise
  Kendrick
Johnson, Virginia Wales
Jordan, Kate
Judson, Emily Chubbuck
Kelly, Myra
Lathbury, Mary Artemisia
Latimer, Mary Elizabeth
  Wormeley
Leslie, Eliza
Lewis, Estelle Anna Blanche
  Robinson
Lippincott, Sara Jane Clarke
McCutcheon, George Barr
Milburn, William Henry

Miller, Emily Clarke
  Huntington
Miller, Harriet Mann
Miner, Myrtilla
Morley, Margaret Warner
Moulton, Ellen Louise Chandler
Norris, Mary Harriott
Norton, Mary Alice Peloubet
Parton, Sara Payson Willis
Perry, Nora
Piatt, John James
Piatt, Sara Morgan Bryan
Powell, William Bramwell
Pratt, Eliza Anna Farman
Preston, Harriet Waters
Prud'homme, John Francis
  Eugene
Richards, Zalmon
Rollins, Alice Marland
  Wellington
Sangster, Margaret Elizabeth
  Munson
Seawell, Molly Elliot
Sherwood, Mary Elizabeth
  Wilson
Tiernan, Frances Christine
  Fisher
Wilkins, William
Wormley, Katharine Prescott
BOWERS, CLAUDE G.
Coleman, William
Duane, William
BOWIE, THEODORE
Warner, Langdon
BOWIE, WALTER RUSSELL
Meigs, John
Norwood, Robert Winkworth
BOWLERS, CLAUDE G.
Coleman, William
Duane, William
BOWMAN, F. E.
McLellan, Isaac
BOYD, CATHERINE E.
Taylor, Henry Osborn
BOYD, CHARLES N.
Archer, Frederic
Bergmann, Carl
Blodgett, Benjamin Colman
Bristow, George Frederick
BOYD, JULIAN P.
Maclay, Samuel
Murray, Louise Shipman Welles
Oliver, Paul Ambrose
Palmer, Henry Wilbur
Sergeant, John, 1779–1852
Sergeant, Jonathan Dickinson
Sergeant, Thomas
Sherman, Roger
Smith, Melancton, 1744–1798
Spencer, Ambrose
Stone, William Leete
Wilson, James
Wright, Hendrick Bradley
BOYD, LYLE G.
Richards, Laura Elizabeth Howe
Smith, David Eugene
BOYD, WILLIAM KENNETH
Alexander, Abraham
Bassett, John Spencer
Burke, Thomas, c. 1747–1783
Clingman, Thomas Lanier
Craven, Braxton
Ellis, John Willis

Graffenried, Christopher
Lawson, John
Morehead, John Motley
Murphey, Archibald De Bow
Overman, Lee Slater
BOYDEN, E. A.
Jackson, Clarence Martin
BOYDEN, WILLIAM L.
Mackey, Albert Gallatin
Morris, Robert, 1818–1888
BOYER, BLANCHE B.
Beeson, Charles Henry
BOYER, PAUL S.
Buck, Franklyn Howard
Crowninshield, Francis Welch
D'Olier, Franklin
Doubleday, Nelson
Harris, Paul Percy
Hines, Duncan
Holmes, Elias Burton
McGraw, James Herbert
McIntyre, Alfred Robert
Macrae, John
Oldfield, ("Barney") Berna Eli
Sheldon, Charles Monroe
Thaw, Harry Kendall
Towne, Charles Hanson
Woolsey, John Munro
BOYLAN, JAMES
Annenberg, Moses Louis
Dealey, George Bannerman
Gauvreau, Emile Henry
Gunther, John
Hearst, William Randolph
Kaempffert, Waldemar
Bernhard
Koenigsberg, Moses
Lait, Jacquin Leonard (Jack)
Manly, Basil Maxwell
Michelson, Charles
Rice, (Henry) Grantland
Seibold, Louis
Thompson, Dorothy
BOYNTON, PERCY H.
Fuller, Henry Blake
Howard, Bronson Crocker
Hubbard, Elbert
Hutton, Laurence
BRACKETT, JEFFREY R.
Cummings, Edward
Hemenway, Mary Porter
Tileston
Johnson, Ellen Cheney
BRADEN, CHARLES S.
Dittemore, John Valentine
Warrington, Albert Powell
BRADLEY, EDWARD SCULLEY
Ireland, Joseph Norton
BRADLEY, MICHAEL R.
Little, William Lawson, Jr.
Meserve, Frederick Hill
Newsom, Herschel David
BRADLEY, WILLIAM JOSEPH
Mercer, Jesse
BRADNER, LEICESTER
Brooke, Charles Frederick
Tucker
BRADWAY, JOHN S.
Goldman, Mayer C.
BRANDERIS, HERMAN
Joubert de la Muraille, James
Hector Marie Nicholas

BRANDES, JOSEPH
Hoover, Herbert Clark
Hoover, Herbert William
BRANDT, ALLAN M.
Doull, James Angus
Gasser, Herbert Spencer
Kenyon, Josephine Hemenway
BRANDT, LILIAN
Anderson, Elizabeth Milbank
Baker, Harvey Humphrey
BRASCH, FREDERICK EDWARD
Alexander, Stephen
Winthrop, John
BRAUER, JERALD C.
Case, Shirley Jackson
BRAUER, KINLEY J.
Wilson, George Grafton
BRAUN, WILLIAM A.
Thomas, Calvin
BRAVERMAN, SAUL
Hofmann, Josef Casimir
Kreisler, Fritz
BRAWLEY, BENJAMIN
Bell, James Madison
Cary, Lott
Cuffe, Paul
Delany, Martin Robinson
Dunbar, Paul Laurence
Forten, James
Hammon, Jupiter
Henson, Josiah
Holly, James Theodore
Holsey, Lucius Henry
Hood, James Walker
BREBNER, J. BARTLET
Hansen, Marcus Lee
Vetch, Samuel
BRECK, EDWARD
Abbot, Joel
Allen, William Henry
Aylwin, John Cushing
Badger, Oscar Charles
Bainbridge, William
Barker, Albert Smith
Barney, Joshua
Barron, James
Barry, John
Belknap, George Eugene
Bell, Henry Haywood
Biddle, James
Biddle, Nicholas
Blake, Homer Crane
Blakely, Johnston
Boggs, Charles Stuart
Breck, Samuel
Breese, Kidder Randolp
Bullard, William Hannum
Grubb
Burrows, William
Caldwell, Charles Henry
Bromedge
Clark, Charles Edgar
Cushing, William Barker
BRECKENRIDGE, ELIZABETH
Palmer, John McAuley
BRECKINRIDGE, SOPHONISBA P.
Kelley, Florence
BREESKIN, ADELYN D.
Avery, Milton Clark
BREEZLEY, WILLIAM H.
Crosley, Powel, Jr.

BREMNER, ROBERT H.
Abbott, Edith
BRETT, AGNES B.
Ingham, Charles Cromwell
Irving, John Beaufain
Jewett, William
BRETZ, J. HARLEN
Taylor, Frank Bursley
BREWER, HELENE MAXWELL
Pinchot, Amos Richards Eno
BRIAND, PAUL L., JR.
Hall, James Norman
Nordhoff, Charles Bernard
BRIDENBAUGH, CARL
Thatcher, Benjamin Bussey
Tucker, Nathaniel Beverley,
1784–1851
Weiser, Johann Conrad
BRIDENBAUGH, JESSICA HILL
Royall, Anne Newport
Sedgwick, Theodore,
1780–1839
Tenney, Tabitha Gilman
Woolson, Abba Louisa Goold
BRIDGES, ROBERT
Burlingame, Edward Livermore
Williams, Jesse Lynch,
1871–1929
BRIDGEWATER, WILLIAM
Laffite, Jean
Little Turtle
McLeod, Hugh
Navarre, Pierre
You, Dominique
BRIDGMAN, HOWARD ALLEN
Abbot, Lyman
BRIDGMAN, P. W.
Duane, William
Hall, Edwin Herbert
BRIEGER, GERT H.
Kelser, Raymond Alexander
Lewis, Dean De Witt
BRIGGS, GEORGE W.
Buck, Philo Melvin
BRIGGS, JOHN E.
Conger, Edwin Hurd
Hurd, John Codman
Koussevitzky, Serge
Alexandrovich
McPherson, Smith
Rorer, David
Seevers, William Henry
Shiras, Oliver Perry
Smith, Walter Inglewood
Wade, Martin Joseph
Wright, George Grover
BRIGGS, LYMAN J.
Burgess, George Kimball
McNair, Fred Walter
BRIGHAM, ALBERT PERRY
Baker, Marcus
BRIGHAM, CLARENCE SAUNDERS
Arthur, William
Barnard, John
Bartlett, John Russell
Evans, Charles
BRIGHAM, HERBERT O.
Bourne, Benjamin
BRILL, A. A.
Kirby, George Hughes
BRINBAUM, GEORGE P.
George, Gladys

BROWN, STERLING A.
 Johnson, James Weldon
 Whitman, Albery Allson
BROWN, TRUESDELL S.
 Westermann, William Linn
BROWN, WILLIAM ADAMS
 Hall, Charles Cuthbert
 Hitchcock, Roswell Dwight
BROWNE, C. A.
 Johnson, Samuel William
 Smith, Edgar Fahs
 Stillman, Thomas Bliss
 Storer, Francis Humphreys
 Thatcher, Roscoe Wilfred
 Warren, Cyrus Moors
 Weber, Henry Adam
 Weichmann, Ferdinand
  Gerhard
 Wetherill, Charles Mayer
 White, Henry Clay
 Wiley, Harvey Washington
 Wurtz, Henry
BROWNE, CHARLES A.
 Clarke, Frank Wigglesworth
 Hooker, Samuel Cox
BROWNE, HENRY J.
 Curran, John Joseph
 Hayes, Patrick Joseph
BROWNE, RICHARD G.
 Fifer, Joseph Wilson
BROWNE, WALDO R.
 Ward, Lydia Arms Avery
  Coonley
BROWNSON, CARLETON L.
 Mezes, Sidney Edward
BRUBACHER, ABRAM R.
 Hawley, Gideon, 1785–1870
BRUBACHER, JOHN S.
 Brackett, Anna Callender
 Bulkley, John Williams
 Calkins, Norman Allison
 Cooper-Poucher, Matilda S.
 Lovell, John Epy
 MacVicar, Malcolm
 Marble, Albert Prescott
 Maxwell, William Henry
BRUCCOLI, MATTHEW J.
 O'Hara, John Henry
BRUCE, KATHLEEN
 Berkeley, John
 Cabell, William
 Cary, Archibald
 Mallory, Stephen Russell
BRUCE, PHILIP ALEXANDER
 Argall, Sir Samuel
 Bacon, Nathaniel
 Berkeley, Sir William
 Botetourt, Norborne Berkeley,
  Baron de
 Upton, Emory
 Wilson, James Harrison
BRUCE, ROBERT V.
 Billings, Asa White Kenney
 Hodgkinson, Francis
 Klein, August Clarence
 Mackenzie, Ranald Slidell
 Moss, Sanford Alexander
 North, Frank Joshua
 Richards, Robert Hallowell
 Terry, Alfred Howe
 Upton, Emory
 Wilson, James Harrison

BRUNNER, EDMUND DeS.
 Wilson, Warren Hugh
BRUNO, FRANK J.
 Eliot, William Greenleaf
BRYAN, GEORGE SANDS
 Batterson, James Goodwin
 Bishop, William Darius
 Boardman, Thomas Danford
 Brandegee, Frank Bosworth
 Brewster, James
 Buckingham, William Alfred
 Butler, Thomas Belden
BRYAN, PAUL E.
 Pardee, Don Albert
BRYANT, LYNWOOD
 Kettering, Charles Franklin
BRYDON, G. MacLAREN
 Madison, James
 Meade, William
 Pendleton, William Nelson
 Penick, Charles Clifton
 Peterkin, George William
 Slaughter, Philip
 Whitaker, Alexander
 Wilmer, Richard Hooker
 Wilmer, William Holland
BUCCO, MARTIN
 Steele, Wilbur Daniel
BUCHANAN, A. RUSSELL
 Nelson, Donald Marr
 Patterson, Robert Porter
BUCHANAN, JOHN
 Bache, Jules Semon
BUCK, ELIZABETH HAWTHORN
 Connolly, John
BUCK, OSCAR MacMILLAN
 Bowen, George
 Butler, John Wesley
 Hoisington, Henry Richard
 Strong, James
 Taylor, William
 Thoburn, Isabella
 Thoburn, James Mills
 Wood, Thomas Bond
BUCK, PAUL H.
 Hallett, Benjamin Franklin
 Holten, Samuel
 Hooper, Samuel
 Long, John Davis
 Lowell, John, 1799–1836
 Lyman, Theodore, 1792–1849
 Meyer, George von Lengerke
BUCK, SOLON JUSTUS
 Alvord, Clarence Walworth
 Folwell, William Watts
 Goodhue, James Madison
 Green, Samuel Bowdlear
 Hosmer, James Kendall
 Hubbard, Lucius Frederick
 Johnson, John Albert
 Kelley, Oliver Hudson
 Neill, Edward Duffield
 Nelson, Knute
 Nelson, Rensselaer Russell
 Ramsey, Alexander
 Rice, Edmund
 Rice, Henry Mower
 Scott, William Lawrence
 Scull, John
 Sibley, Henry Hastings
 Sibley, Joseph Crocker
 Stewart, Andrew
 Thaw, William

 Wilkins, William
BUCKHAM, JOHN W.
 Nash, Charles Sumner
BUDD, RALPH
 Gray, Carl Raymond
BUDER, STANLEY
 Bassett, Edward Murray
 Wood, Edith Elmer
BUENKER, JOHN D.
 Fitzgerald, John Francis
BUFFINGTON, ARTHUR H.
 Willard, Simon
BUHITE, RUSSELL D.
 Griswold, Alfred Whitney
 Hurley, Patrick Jay
BULLARD, F. LAURISTON
 Greene, Nathaniel
 Kendall, George Wilkins
 MacGahan, Januarius Aloysius
 O'Reilly, John Boyle
 Rice, Charles Allen Thorndike
 Taylor, Charles Henry
BULLARD, FRED M.
 Jaggar, Thomas Augustus, Jr.
BULMAN, RAYMOND F.
 Tillich, Paul
BUNI, ANDREW
 Dixon, Thomas
 Wright, Richard Robert
BURD, RACHEL
 Bartlett, Francis Alonzo
BURGESS, GEORGE K.
 Rosa, Edward Bennett
BURKLEO, SANDRA F. VAN
 Hays, Arthur Garfield
BURLINGAME, C. C.
 Stearns, Henry Putnam
 Todd, Eli
 Woodward, Samuel Bayard
BURLINGAME, ROGER
 Berliner, Emile
 Edison, Thomas Alva
 Fessenden, Reginald Aubrey
BURNER, DAVID
 Smith, Alfred Emanuel
BURNET, DUNCAN
 Burnet, William, 1730–1791
BURNET, ROBERTA B.
 Eaton, William
 Lear, Tobias
BURNETT, CHARLES T.
 Hyde, William DeWitt
BURNETT, EDMUND C.
 Hardy, Samuel
 Harrison, Benjamin, 1726–1791
 Harvie, John
 Langworthy, Edward
 Lee, Arthur
 Lee, Richard Henry
 Lee, William
 L'Hommedieu, Ezra
 Lovell, James
 Osgood, Samuel
 Smith, Meriwether
 Thomson, Charles
BURNHAM, ALAN
 Flagg, Ernest
 Pope, John Russell
BURNHAM, GUY H.
 Blunt, Edmund March
 Blunt, George William
 Chaillé-Long, Charles
 Danenhower, John Wilson

DeLong, George Washington
DeWitt, Simeon
Du Chaillu, Paul Belloni
Erskine, Robert
Evans, Lewis
Farmer, John, 1798–1859
BURNHAM, JOHN C.
  Brill, Abraham Arden
  Burrow, Trigant
  Jelliffe, Smith Ely
  Oberndorf, Clarence Paul
  Watson, John Broadus
BURNHAM, WILLIAM H.
  Smith, Theodate Louise
BURNS, JAMES ALOYSIUS
  Angela, Mother
BURR, CHARLES W.
  Mitchell, John Kearsley
  Mitchell, Silas Weir
BURR, GEORGE LINCOLN
  White, Andrew Dickson
BURRAGE, WALTER LINCOLN
  Agnew, Cornelius Rea
  Agnew, David Hayes
  Archer, John
  Awl, William Maclay
  Bard, John
  Bard, Samuel
  Bartlett, Elisha
  Loring, Edward Greely
  Reid, William Wharry
BURRETT, CLAUDE A.
  Helmuth, William Tod
  Wesselhoeft, Conrad
BURROWS, MILLAR
  Schmidt, Nathaniel
BURSTYN, HAROLD L.
  Wrather, William Embry
BURT, C. PAULINE
  Stoddard, John Tappan
BURTON, DAVID H.
  Binkley, Wilfred Ellsworth
  Harlow, Ralph Volney
  Muzzey, David Saville
  Pringle, Henry Fowles
BURTON, ROBERT E.
  Neuberger, Richard Lewis
BUSH, DOUGLAS
  Lowes, John Livingston
BUSH, RONNIE BETH
  Thorek, Max
BUSSEY, GERTRUDE C.
  Calkins, Mary Whiton
BUSTER, ALAN
  Browning, Tod
  Hayes, Gabby
  Mansfield, Jayne
  Wanger, Walter
BUTLER, CHARLES HENRY
  Bancroft, Edgar Addison
BUTLER, PIERCE
  Bermudez, Edouard Edmond
  Breaux, Joseph Arsenne
BUTLER, WILLIAM MILL
  McTammany, John
  O'Reilly, Henry
  Rathbone, Justus Henry
BUTTERFIELD, L. H.
  Ford, Worthington Chauncey
BYERS, JANET LYNN
  Edmondson, William
  Lamb, William Frederick

BYRNE, FRANK L.
  Flanagan, Edward Joseph

CADBURY, HENRY J.
  Penn, John
  Penn, Richard
  Penn, Thomas
  Thayer, Joseph Henry
CAFFEY, FRANCIS GORDON
  Brown, William Garrott
CAHILL, CHARLES T.
  Breed, Ebenezer
CAIN, LOUIS P.
  Tolley, Howard Ross
CAIRNS, HUNTINGTON
  Hornblower, William Butler
  Howry, Charles Bowen
  Ivins, William Mills
  Lockwood, Ralph Ingersoll
  Moseley, Edward Augustus
  Nicholson, Joseph Hopper
  Phelps, Charles Edward
  Potts, Richard
  Rayner, Isidor
  Robinson, John Mitchell
  Rose, John Carter
  Whyte, William Pinkney
CAIRNS, WILLIAM B.
  Benjamin, Park, 1809–1864
  Buckingham, Joseph Tinker
  Conway, Moncure Daniel
  Field, Eugene
  Gilder, Jeannette Leonard
  Gilder, Richard Watson
  Godwin, Parke
  Goodrich, Samuel Griswold
  Holland, Josiah Gilbert
  Sargent, Epes
CALDER, ISABEL M.
  Chipman, Ward
  De La Warr, Thomas West,
    Baron
  Dixwell, John
  Dow, Henry
  Fenwick, George
  Gates, Sir Thomas
  Goffe, William
  Haynes, John
  Jenkins, John Stilwell
  Lane, Sir Ralph
  Lechford, Thomas
  Lothropp, John
  MacSparran, James
  Mansfield, Richard
  Peter, Hugh
  Peters, Samuel Andrew
  Trumbull, James Hammond
  Whalley, Edward
CALDER, WILLIAM M., III
  Capps, Edward
  Hadas, Moses
  Jaeger, Werner Wilhelm
CALDWELL, ORESTES HAMPTON
  Westinghouse, George
CALDWELL, ROBERT G.
  Clark, William Thomas
  Fannin, James Walker
  Flanagan, Webster
  Gaines, Reuben Reid
  Gould, Robert Simonton
  Hamilton, Andrew Jackson
  Hancock, John, 1824–1893
  Hogg, James Stephen

Houston, Samuel
Jones, Anson
King, Richard
Lamar, Mirabeau Buonaparte
Lane, Walter Page
McCulloch, Ben
Maxey, Samuel Bell
Mills, Roger Quarles
Rice, William Marsh
CALHOUN, CHARLES W.
  McElroy, Robert McNutt
CALINGER, RONALD
  Bliss, Gilbert Ames
  Dickson, Leonard Eugene
CALKINS, EARNEST ELMO
  Nitchie, Edward Bartlett
CALKINS, FRANK C.
  Diller, Joseph Silas
CALLAHAN, JAMES MORTON
  Bulloch, James Dunwody
  Camden, Johnson Newlon
  Davis, Henry Gassaway
  Elkins, Stephen Benton
  Faulkner, Charles James,
    1847–1929
  Fleming, Aretas Brooks
  Holcombe, James Philemon
  Lightburn, Joseph Andrew
    Jackson
  Summers, George William
CALLEN, ALFRED COPELAND
  Stoek, Harry Harkness
CALVERT, MONTE A.
  Cooley, Mortimer Elwyn
  Kimball, Dexter Simpson
CAMPBELL, CHRISTIANA McFADYEN
  Alexander, Will Winton
CAMPBELL, KILLIS
  Lynch, James Daniel
CAMPBELL, LAWRENCE
  Davidson, Jo
  Dreier, Katherine Sophie
  Fisher, Henry Conroy ("Bud")
  Kuniyoshi, Yasuo
  Robinson, Boardman
CAMPBELL, LEON
  Bailey, Solon Irving
  Rogers, William Augustus
CANBY, HENRY SEIDEL
  Dodd, Lee Wilson
  Thoreau, Henry David
CANBY, ROBERT C.
  Arents, Albert
  Church, John Adams
  Daggett, Ellsworth
  Eilers, Frederic Anton
  Goetz, George Washington
  Hill, Nathaniel Peter
  Hofman, Heinrich Oscar
  Howe, Henry Marion
  Hunt, Robert Woolston
  Raht, August Wilhelm
CANTOR, LOUIS
  Whitfield, Owen
CAPPON, LESTER J.
  Ginter, Lewis
  Milner, John Turner
  Noble, Samuel
  Shook, Alfred Montgomery
  Tyler, Daniel
  Warner James Cartwright

CARBONE, PETER F., JR.
Rugg, Harold Ordway
CARDOSO, JACK J.
Gray, William Scott, Jr.
Kalmus, Herbert Thomas
Kalmus, Natalie Mabelle Dunfee
Pickens, William
Royce, Ralph
Zook, George Frederick
CARDWELL, KENNETH H.
Draper, Dorothy
Gropius, Walter Adolf Georg
Maybeck, Bernard Ralph
Skidmore, Louis
CAREY, CHARLES F.
Benton, James Gilchrist
Browning, John Moses
Dahlgren, John Adolphus
Bernard
Davidson, John Wynn
Dent, Frederick Tracy
Dyer, Alexander Brydie
Edwards, Oliver
Elliott, Washington Lafayette
Ellsworth, Elmer Ephraim
Emory, William Hemsley
Lewis, Isaac Newton
Sims, Winfield Scott
CAREY, GARY
Lombard, Carole
CARLETON, WILLIAM G.
Fletcher, Duncan Upshaw
CARLHIAN, JEAN PAUL
Coolidge, Charles Allerton
CARLIN, PHILIP H.
Perin, Charles Page
CARLSON, AVERY L.
Williams, Samuel May
CARLSON, ELOF AXEL
Muller, Hermann Joseph
CARLTON, FRANK T.
Duncan, James
CARMAN, HARRY J.
Bouck, William C.
Coker, David Robert
Colles, Christopher
De Forest, Robert Weeks
Finley, John Huston
Hall, Abraham Oakey
Hamilton, James Alexander
Higgins, Frank Wayland
Hill, David Bennett
Hunt, Washington
McCook, Anson George
Maclay, William Brown
Manning, Daniel
Morgan, Edwin Denison
CARMAN, J. ERNEST
Prosser, Charles Smith
CARMICHAEL, O. C.
Pritchett, Henry Smith
CARNES, MARK C.
Groves, Leslie Richard, Jr.
CAROSSO, VINCENT P.
Giannini, Amadeo Peter
Lamont, Thomas William
Whitney, George
Wiggin, Albert Henry
CARPENTER, F. M.
Wheeler, William Morton
CARPENTER, FREDERIC IVES
Reed, Elizabeth Armstrong

CARPENTER, WILLIAM S.
Livingston, Edward
Magie, William Jay
Murray, William Vans
Parker, James
Parker, John Cortlandt
Paterson, William
CARR, IRVING J.
Squier, George Owen
CARR, WILLIAM G.
Kefauver, Grayson Neikirk
CARROLL, JOHN B.
Whorf, Benjamin Lee
CARROLL, JOHN M.
Bartlett, Edward Lewis ("Bob")
Donaldson, Jesse Monroe
Donovan, James Britt
Eisler, Gerhart
Ruby, Jack L.
Young, Owen D.
CARROLL, PATRICK J.
Zahn, John Augustine
CARSON, GERALD
Billingsley, John Sherman
Birdseye, Clarence
Brinkley, John Richard
Byoir, Carl Robert
Calkins, Earnest Elmo
Crumbine, Samuel Jay
Kellogg, Will Keith
Kiss, Max
Littledale, Clara Savage
Manville, Thomas Franklyn
("Tommy"), Jr.
Pew, Joseph Newton, Jr.
CARSON, WILLIAM GLASGOW
BRUCE
Dean, Julia
Drake, Frances Ann Denny
Drake, Samuel
Smith, Marcus
Smith, Solomon Franklin
CARSON, WILLIAM W.
Ridpath, John Clark
CARSTENSEN, VERNON
Horlick, William
Jessup, Walter Albert
CARTER, CLARENCE EDWIN
Allen, William
Ashley, James Mitchell
Bartley, Mordecai
CARTER, EVERETT
Garland, Hamlin
Grey, Zane
CARTER, PAUL A.
Adams, Samuel Hopkins
McConnell, Francis John
Potter, Charles Francis
Thurber, James Grover
CARTWRIGHT, RICHARD S.
Elliott, Walter Hackett Robert
CARVER, W. O.
McGlothlin, William Joseph
CASADA, JAMES A.
Eklund, Carl Robert
Hubbard, Wynant Davis
Jacobs, Hirsch
Shaughnessy, Clark Daniel
CASAMAJOR, LOUIS
Tilney, Frederick
CASE, ARTHUR E.
Kaye, Frederick Benjamin
Lewis, Charlton Thomas

Lewis, Enoch
CASE, ERMINE COWLES
Williston, Samuel Wendell
CASKEY, MARIE
Booth, Evangeline Cory
Burroughs, Edgar Rice
Herriman, George Joseph
Rourke, Constance Mayfield
White, Alma Bridwell
CASSEDY, JAMES H.
Chapin, Charles Value
Hoffman, Frederick Ludwig
Stiles, Charles Wardell
CASTLE, W. B.
Minot, George Richards
CASWELL, JOHN E.
Ellsworth, Lincoln
Peary, Josephine Diebitsch
CATCHINGS, BENJAMIN
Colby, Gardner
Corson, Robert Rodgers
Crozer, John Price
Cupples, Samuel
CATE, JAMES LEA
Arnold, Henry Harley
Mitchell, William
CATTERALL, LOUISE FONTAINE
Mettauer, John Peter
Spencer, Pitman Clemens
CAUTHEN, IRBY B., JR.
Wilson, James Southall
CAUTHEN, KENNETH
Macintosh, Douglas Clyde
CAVERT, SAMUEL McCREA
Brown, William Adams
Sanford, Elias Benjamin
CAWLEY, F. STANTON
Schofield, William Henry
CHADWICK, CHARLES W.
Juengling, Frederick
CHADWICK, GEORGE I.
Ganss, Henry George
CHAFEE, ZECHARIAH, JR.
Heard, Franklin Fiske
Heywood, Ezra Hervey
Hilliard, Francis
Holmes, Nathaniel
Lowell, John, 1824–1897
Manatt, James Irving
Parsons, Theophilus
Pollak, Walter Heilprin
Schofield, Henry
Sedgwick, Theodore,
1746–1813
Shaw, Lemuel
Smith, Jeremiah, 1837–1921
Sumner, Increase
Washburn, Emory
CHAFFIN, NORA C.
Few, William Preston
CHALMERS, W. ELLISON
Cameron, Andrew Carr
Gronlund, Laurence
CHAMBERLAIN, CHARLES J.
Coulter, John Merle
Millspaugh, Charles Frederick
CHAMBERLAIN, HOPE S.
Battle, Kemp Plummer
Battle, William Horn
Spencer, Cornelia Phillips
CHAMBERLAIN, JOSEPH EDGAR
Stephens, Charles Asbury

CHAMBERLAIN, JOSEPH S.
Goessmann, Charles Anthony
CHAMBERS, CLARKE A.
Elliott, John Lovejoy
Hodson, William
Kellogg, Paul Underwood
Lindeman, Eduard Christian
CHAMBERS, JOHN WHITECLAY, II
Andrews, Roy Chapman
McCarran, Patrick Anthony
Norton, Mary Teresa Hopkins
Pick, Lewis Andrew
CHAMBERS, WILL GRANT
McCormick, Samuel Black
CHAMBLISS, HARDEE
Austen, Peter Townsend
Babcock, James Francis
Barker, George Frederick
CHANDLER, ALFRED D., JR.
Cortelyou, George Bruce
Du Pont, Pierre Samuel
Raskob, John Jakob
Sloan, Alfred Pritchard, Jr.
CHANDLER, CHARLES LYON
Halsey, Thomas Lloyd
Jewett, David
Wooster, Charles Whiting
CHAPELLE, HOWARD I.
Herreshoff, Nathanael Greene
CHAPMAN, CHARLES E.
Moses, Bernard
CHAPMAN, HENRY S.
Ford, Daniel Sharp
Stanwood, Edward
Thomson, Edward William
Torrey, Bradford
CHAPMAN, J. VIRGIL
Roark, Ruric Nevel
CHASE, FRANK H.
Balestier, Charles Wolcott
Barton, Thomas Pennant
Benton, Joel
CHASE, GEORGE H.
Hoppin, Joseph Clark
CHASE, GILBERT
Cadman, Charles Wakefield
Carpenter, John Alden
Farwell, Arthur
Weill, Kurt
CHASE, LEW ALLEN
Hulbert, Edwin James
CHASE, STANLEY P.
Abbott, Jacob
Abbott, John Stevens Cabot
CHASE, WAYLAND J.
Beecher, Catharine Esther
Bingham, Caleb
Brooks, Charles
Colburn, Warren
Darby, John
Dickinson, John Woodbridge
O'Shea, Michael Vincent
Salisbury, Albert
Sterling, John Whalen
CHAVKIN, ALLAN
Menjou, Adolphe Jean
CHERNY, ROBERT W.
Howard, Edgar
CHESSMAN, G. WALLACE
Roosevelt, Kermit
CHESTERMAN, E. E.
Wright, William

CHEYNEY, EDWARD P.
Motley, John Lothrop
Munro, Dana Carleton
CHILDS, ARNEY R.
Elliott, Stephen
Gibbes, Robert Wilson
Gibbes, William Hasell
Michel, William Middleton
Porcher, Francis Peyre
Ravenel, Henry William
Ravenel, St. Julien
Shecut, John Linnaeus Edward
Whitridge
CHILDS, JAMES B.
Martel, Charles
CHILTON, ALEXANDER W.
Hamilton, Schuyler
Hardie, James Allen
Hartsuff, George Lucas
Hascall, Milo Smith
Hatch, John Porter
CHINOY, HELEN KRICH
Craven, Frank
MacKaye, Percy Wallace
CHITTENDEN, RUSSELL HENRY
Brewer, William Henry
Curtis, John Green
Dalton, John Call
Dunglison, Robley
Hough, Theodore
Lusk, Graham
Martin, Henry Newell
Meltzer, Samuel James
Mendel, Lafayette Benedict
CHITWOOD, O. P.
Mathews, Henry Mason
Van Winkle, Peter Godwin
CHORLEY, E. CLOWES
Burleson, Hugh Latimer
Gailor, Thomas Frank
Thompson, Hugh Miller
Tyng, Stephen Higginson
CHRISTENSON, CORNELIA V.
Kinsey, Alfred Charles
CHRISTIAN, HENRY A.
Folin, Otto Knut Olof
CHRISTIE, FRANCIS ALBERT
Abbot, Francis Ellingwood
Ballon, Hosea, 1771–1852
Ballon, Hosea, 1796–1861
Bancroft, Aaron
Bixby, James Thompson
Edwards, Jonathan, 1703–1758
Huidekoper, Frederic
Huidekoper, Harm Jan
Jackson, Samuel Macauley
Livermore, Abiel Abbot
Longfellow, Samuel
Lowe, Charles
Murray, John, 1741–1815
Parker, Theodore
Stearns, Oliver
Stebbins, Rufus Phineas
CHRISTIE, JEAN
Cooke, Morris Llewellyn
CHRISTOPHER, PAUL
Bachrach, Louis Fabian
CHRISTY, ARTHUR E.
Sherman, Frank Dempster
CHURCH, ROBERT L.
Stimson, Frederic Jesup

CHURCH, SAMUEL HARDEN
Scott, Thomas Alexander
CHURCHILL, ALLEN L.
Belmont, August
Bliss, Cornelius Newton
Butterick, Ebenezer
CHYET, STANLEY F.
Szold, Henrietta
CIKOVSKY, NICOLAI, JR.
Beaux, Cecilia
CLAGETT, MARSHALL
Thorndike, Lynn
CLAPESATTLE, HELEN
Mayo, Charles Horace
Mayo, William James
CLAPP, MARGARET
Pendleton, Ellen Fitz
CLARK, BARRETT H.
Hazelton, George Cochrane
CLARK, CHARLES E.
Prentice, Samuel Oscar
Rogers, Henry Wade
Wayland, Francis, 1826–1904
Wheeler, George Wakeman
Williams, Thomas Scott
CLARK, DORA MAE
Boehler, Peter
Boehm, Martin
Egle, William Henry
Evans, Evan
Evans, John, fl. 1703–1731
Ewing, John
Jacobson, John Christian
Jungman, John George
Kolb, Dielman
CLARK, ELIOT
Hassam, Frederick Childe
Robinson, Theodore
Twachtman, John Henry
Waugh, Frederick Judd
Weir, Julian Alden
Wyant, Alexander Helwig
CLARK, ELIOT C.
Lie, Jonas
CLARK, GEORGE H.
Loomis, Mahlon
CLARK, HARRY HAYDEN
More, Paul Elmer
CLARK, HUBERT LYMAN
Allen, Timothy Field
Field, Herbert Haviland
Garman, Samuel
Girard, Charles Frederic
Holbrook, John Edwards
Hyatt, Alpheus
Marcou, Jules
Pourtalès, Louis François De
Samuels, Edward Augustus
Wyman, Jeffries
CLARK, JANE
Heron, William
Parsons, Samuel Holden
Robinson, Beverley
Stansbury, Joseph
CLARK, NORMAN H.
Willebrandt, Mabel Walker
CLARK, ROBERT C.
Curry, George Law
Deady, Matthew Paul
Dolph, Joseph Norton
Duniway, Abigail Jane Scott
Hume, William
Jackson, Charles Samuel

COE, SAMUEL GWYNN
Carmichael, William
COE, WESLEY R.
Verrill, Addison Emery
COFFEE, RUDOLPH I.
Meyer, Martin Abraham
COFFEY, HOBART
Stone, John Wesley
Wilkins, Ross
COFFIN, HENRY SLOANE
Hall, John
COFFIN, ROBERT P. TRISTRAM
Nack, James M.
Paine, Robert Treat
COFFMAN, EDWARD M.
Harbord, James Guthrie
March, Peyton Conway
COGLEY, JOHN
Gillis, James Martin
COHEN, LIBBY OKUN
Singer, Israel Joshua
COHEN, SOL
Irwin, Elisabeth Antoinette
COHEN, WARREN I.
Greene, Roger Sherman
COLBERT, THOMAS BURNELL
Barton, James Edward
Fay, Francis Anthony ("Frank")
COLBY, ELBRIDGE
Winthrop, Theodore
COLBY, JAMES FAIRBANKS
Atherton, Joshua
Bartlett, Josiah
Poland, Luke Potter
COLBY, WILLIAM E.
Lindley, Curtis Holbrook
COLE, ARTHUR C.
Hanna, Marcus Alonzo
Harmon, Judson
Keifer, Joseph Warren
Webster, Daniel
COLE, CHARLES WILLIAM
Reid, Thomas Mayne
COLE, ESTHER
Cabet, Étienne
Swift, Gustavus Franklin
COLE, FANNIE L. GWINNER
Adams, Charles R.
Apthorp, William Foster
Baermann, Carl
Baker, Benjamin Franklin
Billings, William
Emmett, Daniel Decatur
Fillmore, John Comfort
Finck, Henry Theophilus
Fry, William Henry
Goldbeck, Robert
Goodrich, Alfred John
Gottschalk, Louis Moreau
Graupner, Johann Christian
Gottlieb
Griffes, Charles Tomlinson
Jarvis, Charles H.
Joseffy, Rafael
Klein, Bruno Oscar
Kneisel, Franz
Krehbiel, Henry Edward
Liebling, Emil
Mees, Arthur
Merz, Karl
Mollenhauer, Emil
Pearce, Stephen Austen
Pease, Alfred Humphreys

Perabo, Johann Ernst
Perry, Edward Baxter
Pratt, Silas Gamaliel
Rice, Fenelon Bird
Root, Frederic Woodman
Scheve, Edward Benjamin
Sherwood, William Hall
Spiering, Theodore
Wolfsohn, Carl
COLE, FAY-COOPER
Dorsey, George Amos
Starr, Frederick
COLE, ROSSETTER GLEASON
Buck, Dudley
Lutkin, Peter Christian
Nevin, Ethelbert Woodbridge
Stanley, Albert Augustus
Upton, George Putnam
Weidig, Adolf
Zeisler, Fannie Bloomfield
COLE, WAYNE S.
Shipstead, Henrik
COLEGROVE, KENNETH WALLACE
Bond, Shadrach
Breese, Sidney
COLEMAN, CHRISTOPHER B.
Foulke, William Dudley
Law, John
McCulloch, Oscar Carleton
Merrill, Samuel
Morris, Thomas Armstrong
Whitcomb, James
Williams, Charles Richard
Williams, James Douglas
COLEMAN, MARY C.
Rogers, Mary Josephine
COLEMAN, MELVIN E.
Stone, Melville Elijah
COLEMAN, NORMAN F.
Reed, Simeon Gannett
COLEMAN, R. V.
Ludlow, Roger
COLESTOCK, HENRY T.
Malcom, Howard
COLETTA, PAOLO E.
Bryan, Charles Wayland
Raulston, John Tate
Rohde, Ruth Bryan Owen
COLGROVE, KENNETH WALLACE
Breese, Sidney
COLL, BLANCHE D.
Brackett, Jeffrey Richardson
Glenn, John Mark
Hersey, Evelyn Weeks
COLLIER, THEODORE
Lawrence, William Beach
Wayland, Francis, 1796–1865
COLLINGWOOD, G. HARRIS
Silcox, Ferdinand Augustus
COLLINS, EDWARD H.
Mills, Ogden Livingston
COLLINS, GUY N.
Rock, John
Roeding, George Christian
COLLINS, JOHN W.
Marshall, Frank James
COLLINS, PATRICK W.
Weigel, Gustave
COLMAN, EDNA MARY
Brent, Margaret
COLMAN, GOULD P.
Ladd, Carl Edwin

COMMAGER, HENRY STEELE
McLaughlin, Andrew
Cunningham
COMMONS, JOHN R.
Gompers, Samuel
Kellogg, Edward
Lennon, John Brown
McNeill, George Edwin
Mitchell, John, 1870–1919
COMPTON, W. D.
Chaffee, Roger Bruce
Grissom Virgil Ivan ("Gus")
White, Edward Higgins, II
CONANT, KENNETH J.
Warren, Herbert Langford
CONDIT, CARL W.
Graham, Ernest Robert
Moisseiff, Leon Solomon
Parker, Theodore Bissell
Perkins, Dwight Heald
Pond, Irving Kane
Purdy, Corydon Tyler
Rogers, James Gamble
Waite, Henry Matson
CONE, JR., THOMAS E.
Cooley, Thomas Benton
CONGER, GEORGE P.
Swenson, David Ferdinand
CONN, STETSON
McNair, Lesley James
Short, Walter Campbell
CONNELLEY, WILLIAM E.
Hickok, James Butler
CONNICK, CHARLES JAY
Willit, William
CONNOR, R. D. W.
Gaston, William
Hall, James, 1744–1826
Harnett, Cornelius
Hogun, James
Hyde, Edward
Vance, Zebulon Baird
CONNORS, RICHARD J.
Hague, Frank
CONRAD, HENRY C.
Bennett, Caleb Prew
CONSTANCE, LINCOLN
Jepson, Willis Linn
CONVERSE, FLORENCE
Bates, Katharine Lee
Palmer, Alice Elvira Freeman
Shafer, Helen Almira
CONWELL, RALPH E.
Kendrick, John Benjamin
COOKE, JACOB E.
Bancroft, Frederic
COOLIDGE, CHARLES A.
Perkins, Thomas Nelson
COOLIDGE, MARY ROBERTS
Warner, Amos Griswold
COOPER, G. ARTHUR
Ulrich, Edward Oscar
COOPER, LANE
Bartram, William
Cook, Albert Stanburrough
COOPER, WILLIAM J., JR.
Percy, William Alexander
CORBETT, JOHN
Campbell, Thomas Joseph
Goupil, René
CORNELL, GRETA A.
Wentworth, Cecile de

CORNELL, THOMAS DAVID
Van de Graaff, Robert Jemison
CORNER, GEORGE V.
Landsteiner, Karl
CORNER, GEORGE W.
Auer, John
Carrel, Alexis
Cullen, Thomas Stephen
Flexner, Simon
Hoagland, Charles Lee
Hooker, Donald Russell
Howell, William Henry
Hume, Edgar Erskine
Kelly, Howard Atwood
Loeb, Leo
Murphy, James Bumgardner
Pepper, William, III
Rivers, Thomas Milton
Sabin, Florence Rena
Stockard, Charles Rupert
Streeter, George Linius
Weed, Lewis Hill
CORNWELL, ELMER E., JR.
Key, Valdimer Orlando, Jr.
CORTISSOZ, ROYAL
Isham, Samuel
La Farge, John
Melchers, Gari
Saint-Gaudens, Augustus
Scribner, Charles, 1821–1871
Scribner, Charles, 1854–1930
Whistler, James Abbott McNeill
CORWIN, EDWARD S.
Bradley, Joseph P.
Chase, Samuel
Field, Stephen Johnson
Ford, Henry Jones
Marshall, John
CORY, DANIEL M.
Strong, Charles Augustus
COSTA, ALBERT B.
Bachmann, Werner Emmanuel
Ellis, Carleton
Johnson, Treat Baldwin
Michael, Arthur
Noyes, William Albert
Sherman, Henry Clapp
Stine, Charles Milton Altland
COTNER, ROBERT C.
Murray, William Henry David
COTNER, ROBERT CRAWFORD
Macune, Charles William
COTTERILL, R. S.
Beattie, Francis Robert
Biddle, Clement
Blackburn, Joseph Clay Styles
Boyle, Jeremiah Tilford
Bullitt, Alexander Scott
Clark, James
Combs, Leslie
Cooper, Joseph Alexander
Covode, John
Durrett, Reuben Thomas
Evans, Walter
Filson, John
Garrard, James
Goebel, William
Goodloe, William Cassius
Green, Norvin
Guthrie, James
Hamtranck, John Francis
Harlan, James, 1800–1863
Hay, George

Henderson, Leonard
Henderson, Richard
Letcher, Robert Perkins
Lewis, Joseph Horace
Littell, William
Logan, Benjamin
Maxwell, Augustus Emmett
Mills, Benjamin
Milton, John
Moore, Thomas Patrick
Morrow, Edwin Porch
Pasco, Samuel
Perry, Edward Aylesworth
Raney, George Pettus
Walker, David Shelby
Watterson, Harvey Magee
Wickliffe, Charles Anderson
Willson, Augustus Everett
Woods, Alva
Yulee, David Levy
COTTMAN, GEORGE S.
Maxwell, David Hervey
Milroy, Robert Huston
Parke, Benjamin
Perkins, Samuel Elliott
Posey, Thomas
COTTON, ROBERT C.
Jesup, Thomas Sidney
Parsons, Lewis Baldwin
Patterson, Robert
Prentiss, Benjamin Mayberry
COULTER, ELLIS MERTON
Adair, John
Anderson, Richard Clough,
1750–1826
Anderson, Richard Clough,
1788–1826
Barry, William Taylor
Bedinger, George Michael
Bibb, George Mortimer
Blackburn, Luke Pryor
Boyd, Lynn
Boyle, John
Bradley, William O'Connell
Bramlette, Thomas E.
Breckinridge, John
Breckinridge, John Cabell
Breckinridge, Robert Jefferson
Breckinridge, William Campbell
Preston
Brown, John
Brown, John Young
Buckner, Simon Bolivar
Butler, William Orlando
Carlisle, John Griffin
Church, Alonzo
Clay, Cassius Marcellus
Clay, Green
Clay, Henry
Cofer, Martin Hardin
Crittenden, George Bibb
Crittenden, John Jordan
Crittenden, Thomas Leonidas
Davis, Garrett
Desha, Joseph
Edwards, John, 1748–1837
Greenup, Christopher
Hardin, Ben
Hardin, Martin D.
Harrod, James
Hopkins, Samuel, 1753–1819
Howard, Benjamin
Jacob, Richard Taylor

Jones, Noble Wymberley
King, John Pendleton
King, Thomas Butler
Magoffin, Beriah
Marshall, Humphrey,
1760–1841
Marshall, Humphrey,
1812–1872
Marshall, James Markham
Marshall, Louis
Marshall, Thomas Alexander
Mell, Patrick Hues, 1814–1888
Orr, Gustavus John
Peters, Richard
Phinizy, Ferdinand
Powell, Lazarus Whitehead
Preston, William
Procter, John Robert
Robertson, George
Rousseau, Lovell Harrison
Rowan, John
Simmons, Thomas Jefferson
Simms, William Elliott
Speed, James
Stevens, William Bacon
Stevenson, John White
Telfair, Edward
Underwood, Joseph Rogers
White, George
White, William Nathaniel
COULTER, E. MERTON
Hunt, Benjamin Weeks
Knight, Lucian Lamar
Phillips, Ulrich Bonnell
COULTER, STANLEY
Bailey, Jacob Whitman
COUPER, WALTER J.
Lloyd, Henry Demarest
COURSAULT, JESSE H.
Jesse, Richard Henry
Lathrop, John Hiram
Laws, Samuel Spahr
Read, Daniel, 1805–1878
Soldan, Frank Louis
COURT, W. H. B.
Catesby, Mark
COVERT, WILLIAM C.
Speer, William
COWAN, RUTH SCHWARTZ
McClung, Clarence Erwin
COWDREY, MARY BARTLETT
Dewing, Thomas Wilmer
COWIE, ALEXANDER
Trumbull, John, 1750–1831
COX, ISAAC JOSLIN
Blennerhassett, Harman
Bollman, Justus Erich
Burr, Aaron
Claiborne, William Charles
Coles
Clark, Daniel, 1776–1813
Daveiss, Joseph Hamilton
Kemper, Reuben
Mathews, George
Sebastian, Benjamin
Smith, John, 1735–1824
Swartwout, Samuel
Toulmin, Harry
Wilkinson, James
Williamson, Charles
COX, JOHN, JR.
Bowne, John
Wood, Samuel

Cox, Theodore S.
Lomax, John Tavloe
Minor, John Barbee
Minor, Raleigh Colston
Moncure, Richard Cassius Lee
Munford, William
Parker, Marsena Rudolph
Parker, Richard Elliot
Patrick, Marsena Rudolph
Patton, John Mercer
Wickham, John
Wythe, George
Coy, Owen C.
Marshall, James Wilson
Crabb, A. L.
Priestley, James
Craig, Frank A.
Flick, Lawrence Francis
Cram, Marshall P.
Cleaveland, Parker
Crane, Esther
Shaw, Pauline Agassiz
Syms, Benjamin
Crane, Katharine Elizabeth
Hopkins, Edward Augustus
Kamaikan
Kicking Bird
Leschi
Livingston, James
McKee, John
Mathews, John
Menewa
Middleton, Arthur
Morgan, William
Oconostota
Osceola
Outacity
Palmer, Joel
Pushmataha
Reed, James, 1722–1807
Ridge, Major
Riggs, George Washington
Scammell, Alexander
Seattle
Shabonee
Shepard, William
Shikellamy
Skenandoa
Spencer, Joseph
Sprague, Kate Chase
Sprague, William, 1830–1915
Street, Joseph Montfort
Tecumseh
Tedyuskung
Tenskwatawa
Thompson, John Bodine
Tomochichi
Tucker, Nathaniel Beverley,
    1820–1890
Vassall, John
Ward, Nancy
Weatherford, William
Wovoka
Crane, Verner W.
Bray, Thomas
Coram, Thomas
Cross, Arthur Lyon
Cuming, Sir Alexander
Hughes, Price
McCrady, Edward
Marchant, Henry
Nairne, Thomas
Priber, Christian

Purry, Jean Pierre
Woodward, Henry
Cranefield, Paul F.
Cohn, Alfred Einstein
Cratty, Robert Irvin
Pammel, Louis Hermann
Craven, Avery
Dodd, William Edward
Craven, Avery O.
Aime, Valcour
Binns, John Alexander
Doré, Jean Étienne
Botts, Charles Tyler
Brigham, Joseph Henry
Garnett, James Mercer
Ruffin, Edmund
Taylor, John
Craven, Wayne
Dallin, Cyrus Edwin
MacNeil, Hermon Atkins
Ruckstull, Frederick Wellington
Craven, Wesley Frank
West, Francis
White, John, 1585–1593
Wingfield, Edward Maria
Wyatt, Sir Francis
Yeardley, Sir George
Cravens, Hamilton
Prescott, Samuel Cate
Waterman, Alan Tower
Yerkes, Robert Mearns
Crawford, Nelson Antrim
Ainslie, Hew
Atkinson, Wilmer
Buel, Jesse
Fuller, Andrew S.
Crawford, Richard
Romberg, Sigmund
Creer, Leland Hargrave
Dern, George Henry
Cremin, Lawrence A.
Dewey, John
McMurry, Frank Morton
Thorndike, Edward Lee
Cressey, Donald R.
Sutherland, Edwin Hardin
Cresson, Margaret French
MacMonnies, Frederick William
Crew, Henry
Bell, Louis
Cripps, Thomas R
McDaniel, Hattie
Moore, Frederick Randolph
Robinson, Bill (Bojangles)
Crittenden, Charles C.
McLean, Angus Wilton
Crockett, Walter Hill
Bradley, Stephen Row
Brainerd, Lawrence
Buck, Daniel
Butler, Ezra
Haselton, Seneca
Holbrook, Frederick
Crofton, Barbara McCarthy
Conover, Harry Sayles
Petri, Angelo
Croneis, Carey
Worthen, Amos Henry
Cronon, E. David
Daniels, Josephus
Garvey, Marcus Moziah

Crooks, James B.
Bruce, William Cabell
Crosbie, Laurence Murray
Abbot, Benjamin
Crosby, Douglas R.
Eisenhart, Luther Pfahler
Crosby, Elizabeth
Huber, Gotthelf Carl
Cross, Arthur Lyon
Van Tyne, Claude Halstead
Cross, Hardy
Lindenthal, Gustav
Swain, George Fillmore
Cross, Jennifer
Saunders, Clarence
Cross, Robert D.
Cushing, Richard James
Schlesinger, Arthur Meier
Smith, Courtney Craig
Cross, Whitman
Washington, Henry Stephens
Crothers, Samuel M.
Channing, William Ellery
Crowl, Philip A.
Forrestal, James Vincent
Crownfield, Frederic R.
Mercer, Lewis Pyle
Reed, James, 1834–1921
Sewall, Frank
Crowther, Bosley
Allen, Kelcey
Jones, Robert Edmond
Laemmle, Carl
Mayer, Louis Burt
Thalberg, Irving Grant
Crowther, Simeon J.
Holt, William Franklin
Kraft, James Lewis
Moore, Henry Ludwell
Crunden, Robert M.
Nock, Albert Jay
Cruse, Harold W.
Lee, Canada
Cuddihy, Paul R.
Vizetelly, Frank Horace
Cuff, Robert D.
Baruch, Bernard Mannes
Cummins, George B.
Arthur, Joseph Charles
Cunliffe, Marcus
Freeman, Douglas Southall
Cunningham, C. C.
Tarbell, Edmund Charles
Cunningham, Frank R.
Gold, Michael
Odets, Clifford
Cunningham, G. Watts
Thilly, Frank
Cunningham, Susan J.
Higgins, Marguerite
Cunningham, William James
Baldwin, William Henry
Brown, William Carlos
Callaway, Samuel Rodger
Hill, James Jerome
Lovett, Robert Scott
Newman, William H.
Sproule, William
Thornton, Henry Worth
Van Horne, William Cornelius
Curlee, Abigail
Mills, Robert, 1809–1888

CURRAN, GRACE WICKHAM
Wilmarth, Lemuel Everett
CURRENT, RICHARD N.
Underwood, John Thomas
CURTI, MERLE E.
Brattle, William
Brazer, John
Buchanan, Joseph
Burritt, Elihu
Grimké, Angelina Emily
Grimké, Sarah Moore
Grimké, Thomas Smith
Ladd, William
Love, Alfred Henry
Rantoul, Robert, 1778–1858
Rantoul, Robert, 1805–1852
Sanders, George Nicholas
Trueblood, Benjamin Franklin
CURTIS, EDWARD E.
Cornell, Ezekiel
Crane, John
Durkee, John
Learned, Ebenezer
Lynde, Benjamin
Meade, Richard Kidder
Mercer, Hugh
Nixon, John, 1727–1815
North, William
Oliver, Andrew
Paterson, John
Pitcairn, John
Poor, Enoch
Prescott, Oliver
Prescott, William
Shaw, Samuel
Smith, William Stephens
Stark, John
Thomas, John
Thompson, William
Trumbull, Jonathan, 1740–1809
Trumbull, Joseph
Wadsworth, Jeremiah
Wadsworth, Peleg
Ward, Artemas
Warner, Seth
Williams, Otho Holland
Williams, William, 1731–1811
Woodford, William
CURTISS, THOMAS QUINN
Von Stroheim, Erich
CUSHMAN, ROBERT E.
Brewer, David Josiah
Dill, James Brooks
Dillon, John Forrest
Dodd, Samuel Calvin Tate
Harlan, John Marshall
Hunt, Ward
Lansing, John
Lindabury, Richard Vliet
Livingston, Henry Brockholst
Nelson, Samuel
Nott, Charles Cooper
Noyes, Walter Chadwick
Pound, Cuthbert Winfred
Thompson, Smith
Throop, Montgomery Hunt
CUTLER, CARL C.
Rogers, William Crowninshield
Waterman, Robert H.
CUTLER, DOROTHY P.
Farabee, William Curtis

CUTTER, R. AMMI
Field, Fred Tarbell

DABNEY, CHARLES WILLIAM
McBryde, John McLaren
Vawtor, Charles Erastus
Venable, Charles Scott
DABNEY, VIRGINIUS
Chandler, Julian Alvin Carroll
Martin, Thomas Staples
Underwood, Oscar Wilder
DA BOLL, RAYMOND FRANKLIN
Cooper, Oswald Bruce
DA COSTA, J. CHALMERS
Gross, Samuel David
Gross, Samuel Weissell
DAGGETT, STUART
Hine, Charles De Lano
Huntington, Collis Potter
Judah, Theodore Dehone
Markham, Charles Henry
Ripley, Edward Payson
Stanford, Leland
Strong, William Barstow
DAHER, MICHAEL
Connolly, Thomas H.
DAHL, GEORGE
Kent, Charles Foster
DAIGLE, LENNET J.
Redman, Ben Ray
DAIN, NORMAN
Beers, Clifford Whittingham
DAIN, PHYLLIS
Lydenberg, Harry Miller
Wilson, Halsey William
DAINS, FRANK BURNETT
Long, John Harper
DALE, EDWARD E.
Haskell, Charles Nathaniel
McCoy, Isaac
Mayes, Joel Bryan
Pitchlynn, Peter Perkins
Posey, Alexander Lawrence
Robertson, Alice Mary
Robertson, William Schenck
Ross, John
Watie, Stand
Worcester, Samuel Austin
DALE, HARRISON CLIFFORD
Ashley, William Henry
Becknell, William
Beckwourth, James P.
Bozeman, John M.
Bridger, James
Hawley, James Henry
Hutton, Levi William
Long, Stephen Harriman
DALEY, ARTHUR J.
Sullivan, James Edward
DALFIUME, RICHARD M.
Crosswaith, Frank Rudolph
DALRYMPLE, CANDICE
Norden, Carl Lukas
DALY, LLOYD W.
Oldfather, William Abbott
DALY, REGINALD ALDWORTH
Woodworth, Jay Backus
DAMON, S. FOSTER
Chivers, Thomas Holley
DAMON, THERON J.
Cole, George Watson

DANCE, HELEN OAKLEY
Bailey, Mildred
Holiday, Billie
DANCE, STANLEY
Bechet, Sidney
Catlett, Sidney
Henderson, Fletcher Hamilton
Lunceford, James Melvin
("Jimmie")
Page, Oran Thaddeus ("Lips")
DANDY, WALTER E.
Bloodgood, Joseph Colt
DANIEL, MARJORIE
Zubly, John Joachim
DANIELS, DAVID I.
Culbertson, Josephine Murphy
Lenz, Sidney Samuel
DANIELS, ROGER
Glassford, Pelham Davis
Ickes, Harold Le Clair
Kennedy, Joseph Patrick
Lehman, Herbert Henry
Sherwood, Robert Emmet
DANIELS, WINTHROP M.
Prouty, Charles Azro
DANZIG, ALLISON
Tilden, William Tatem ("Big
Bill")
DARGAN, MARION
Drayton, William Henry
DARLING, ARTHUR BURR
Appleton, Nathan
Appleton, Samuel
Henshaw, David
Newlands, Francis Griffith
DARNELL, REGNA
MacCurdy, George Grant
Spier, Leslie
DAUGHRITY, KENNETH L.
Willis, Nathaniel
Willis, Nathaniel Parker
DAVENPORT, CHARLES B.
Mall, Franklin Paine
Mayor, Alfred Goldsborough
DAVIDSON, ABRAHAM A.
Reinhardt, Ad
Shahn, Benjamin ("Ben")
DAVIDSON, CHALMERS G.
Fayssoux, Peter
Gaston, James McFadden
Irvine, William
DAVIDSON, DONALD
Malone, Walter
Marling, John Leake
Moore, John Trotwood
DAVIDSON, MARSHALL B.
Taylor, Francis Henry
DAVIES, CLARENCE E.
Main, Charles Thomas
DAVIES, WALLACE EVAN
Bara, Theda
White, Pearl
DAVIS, ALLEN
Simkhovitch, Mary Melinda
Kingsbury
DAVIS, ALLEN F.
Bowen, Louise De Koven
Breckenridge, Sophonisba
Preston
DAVIS, ARTHUR KYLE JR.
Smith, Charles Alphonso

DAVIS, ARTHUR POWELL
  Newell, Frederick Haynes
DAVIS, AUDREY B.
  Osterhout, Winthrop John
    Vanleuven
  Schwidetzky, Oscar Otto Rudolf
DAVIS, CHARLES B.
  Peck, James Hawkins
DAVIS, ELMER
  Jones, George
  Raymond, Henry Jarvis
DAVIS, HENRY C.
  Marks, Elias
DAVIS, JEROME
  Gough, John Bartholomew
DAVIS, KENNETH S.
  Post, Augustus
DAVIS, MARJORY HENDRICKS
  Chase, Pliny Earle
DAVIS, TENNEY L.
  Thompson, Benjamin
  Watson, William
DAVIS, WILLIAM W.
  Haskell, Dudley Chase
DAVISON, ELIZABETH THOMPSON
  Bowie, Oden
  Bowie, Richard Johns
  Bowie, Robert
  Bradford, Augustus Williamson
DAVOL, RALPH
  Boylies, Francis
  Leonard, Daniel
  Paine, Robert Treat
DAWES, CHESTER L.
  Kennelly, Arthur Edwin
DAWES, NORMAN H.
  Saltonstall, Richard
DAWSON, GILES E.
  Adams, Joseph Quincy
DAWSON, JOSEPH MARTIN
  Newman, Albert Henry
DAWSON, NELSON L.
  Sweeney, Martin Leonard
DAY, CLIVE
  Farnam, Henry
  Schwab, John Christopher
  Sheffield, Joseph Earl
DAY, RICHARD E.
  Hasenclever, Peter
  Jamison, David
  McElrath, Thomas
  Macfarlane, Robert
  Munsell, Joel
  Murray, John, 1737–1808
  Murray, Robert
  Ogden, Samuel
  Onderdonk, Henry
  Philipse, Frederick
  Pratt, Zadock
  Schuyler, Peter
  Steenwyck, Cornelis
  Van Curler, Arent
  Van Dam, Rip
  Van der Kemp, Francis Adrian
  Van Rensselaer, Nicholas
  Viele, Aernout Cornelissen
DAY, ROY
  Fleming, William Maybury
  Ford, John Thomson
  Fox, Charles Kemble
  Fox, George Washington
    Lafayette

DEALEY, JAMES QUAYLE
  Ward, Lester Frank
DEAN, VERA MICHELES
  Simonds, Frank Herbert
DEARBORN, NED H.
  Kraus-Boelté, Maria
  Krauss, John
  Krüsi, Johann Heinrich
    Hermann
DEARDORFF, NEVA R.
  Cabot, Richard Clarke
  Lee, Joseph
  Rubinow, Isaac Max
DEARING, MARY R.
  Boardman, Mabel Thorp
DEBO, ANGIE
  Hastings, William Wirt
DE BRUHL, MARSHALL
  Carson, Rachel Louise
  Hatlo, Jimmy
  Johnson, Edward
  Metalious, Grace
DEFORD, RONALD K.
  Bryan, Kirk
DE GREGORIO, VINCENT J.
  Glackens, William James
DEGREGORIO, WILLIAM A.
  Biffle, Leslie L
  Brucker, Wilber Marion
  Duffy, Edmund
  Perez, Leander Henry
DEKAY, CHARLES
  Bierstadt, Albert
  Blakelock, Ralph Albert
DE KIEWIET, C. W.
  Rhees, Rush
DELAPLAINE, EDWARD S.
  Johnson, Thomas
  Martin, Luther
DELAVAN, D. BRYSON
  Leland, George Adams
  Mackenzie, John Noland
  Simpson, William Kelly
  Wagner, Clinton
DELL, FLOYD
  Cook, George Cram
DE LONG, IRWIN H.
  Dubbs, Joseph Henry
DEMAREST, WILLIAM H. S.
  Livingston, John Henry
  Milledoler, Philip
  Riddle, Matthew Brown
  Schenck, Ferdinand Schureman
  Scott, Austin
  Searle, John Preston
  Van Nest, Abraham Rynier
  Woodbridge, Samuel Merrill
DENNES, WILLIAM R.
  Prall, David Wight
DENNETT, TYLER
  Burlingame, Anson
  Harris, Townsend
DENNIS, ALFRED L. P.
  Hay, John Milton
DENNIS, EVERETTE E.
  Berryman, Clifford Kennedy
  Dille, John Flint
  Fisher, Hammond Edward
  Fox, Fontaine Talbot, Jr.
  Gross, Milt
  Raymond, Alexander Gillespie

DENTAN, ROBERT C.
  Barton, George Aaron
DE PORTE, JOSEPH V.
  Wilbur, Cressy Livingston
DERISH, JUDITH
  Brenon, Herbert
DERLETH, AUGUST
  Gale, Zona
DESCHAMPS, CHRISTIANE L.
  Adler, Polly
DETLEFSEN, ELLEN GAY
  Neal, Josephine Bicknell
  Pfahler, George Edward
  Stone, Abraham
DE TURK, ERNEST E.
  Hopkins, Cyril George
DEUTSCH, BABETTE
  Oppenheim, James
DEUTSCH, HERMAN J.
  Atwood, David
  Carpenter, Matthew Hale
  Jones, Wesley Livsey
  Lander, Edward
  Leary, John
  Meany, Edmond Stephen
  Rogers, John Rankin
  Squire, Watson Carvosso
DE VENCENTES, PHILIP
  Bowes, Edward J.
  Burnham, Frederick Russell
  Gregg, John Robert
  Morton, Ferdinand Quintin
  Whitney, Alexander Fell
DEVINE, MICHAEL J.
  Bundy, Harvey Hollister
DEVORKIN, DAVID H.
  Adams, Walter Sydney
  Russell, Henry Norris
  Struve, Otto
DE VOTO, BERNARD
  Smith, Joseph, 1805–1844
  Young, Brigham
DEWEY, DAVIS R.
  Colman, John
  Conant, Charles Arthur
  Davis, Andrew McFarland
  Del Mar, Alexander
  Dunbar, Charles Franklin
  Gouge, William M.
  Gunton, George
DEWEY, EDWARD H.
  Prince, Thomas
  Shepard, Thomas
  Sherman, John, 1613–1685
  Talbot, John
  Thacher, Peter, 1651–1727
  Thacher, Peter, 1752–1802
  Thacher, Samuel Cooper
  Walker, Timothy, 1705–1782
  Ward, Nathaniel
  West, Samuel
  Whitefield, Henry
  Wigglesworth, Edward,
    1693–1765
  Wigglesworth, Edward,
    1732–1794
DEWEY, FRED H.
  Baldwin, Matthias William
DEWULF, BERNARD G.
  Burnham, William Henry
DIAMOND, LOUIS K.
  Blackfan, Kenneth Daniel

Nolan, Philip
Putnam, Arthur
Radisson, Pierre Esprit
Shaler, Nathaniel Southgate
DODD, LEE WILSON
  Miller, Henry
DODD, WILIAM E.
  Davis, Henry Winter
  Henry, Patrick
  Stringfellow, Franklin
DODGE, CHARLES WRIGHT
  Dewey, Chester
  Sartwell, Henry Parker
DODGE, ERNEST S.
  Benson, Frank Weston
DODGE, MARY DANFORTH
  Danforth, Moseley Isaac
DODGE, RICHARD E.
  Brigham, Albert Perry
DODGE, ROBERT G.
  Rugg, Arthur Prentice
DODSON, LEONIDAS
  Mayo, William
  Spotswood, Alexander
DOENECKE, JUSTUS D.
  Borchard, Edwin Montefiore
  Knutson, Harold
DOETSCH, RAYMOND N.
  Henrici, Arthur Trautwein
DOLAN, JOHN J.
  Guthrie, William Dameron
  Pinkney, William
  Tyler, Samuel
  Zane, Charles Schuster
DOLMETSCH, CARL R.
  Nathan, George Jean
DONALD, DAVID HERBERT
  Randall, James Garfield
DONALDSON, SCOTT
  Tarkington, Booth
  Torrence, Frederick Ridgely
DONDORE, DOROTHY ANN
  Catherwood, Mary Hartwell
  Chopin, Kate O'Flaherty
  Flint, Timothy
  Howe, Henry
  Ingraham, Joseph Holt
  Ingraham, Prentiss
  Kirkland, Caroline Matilda
    Stansbury
  Kirkland, Joseph
  McConnel, John Ludlum
  McKenney, Thomas Loraine
DONNAN, ELIZABETH
  Capen, Samuel Billings
  Durant, Henry Fowle
  Elder, William
  Emerson, Joseph
  Fry, Richard
  Harnden, William Frederick
  Howard, Ada Lydia
  Hunnewell, Horatio Hollis
  Livermore, Mary Ashton Rice
  Lowell, Josephine Shaw
  Raguet, Condy
  Sabine, Lorenzo
  Sewall, Jonathan
  Sullivan, William
  Walker, Amasa
  Webster, Pelatiah
DONNELLY, HAROLD I.
  Packard, Frederick Adolphus

DONOVAN, ROBERT J.
  Johnson, Louis Arthur
DORFMAN, JOSEPH
  Mitchell, Wesley Clair
  Seligman, Edwin Robert
    Anderson
DORN, HAROLD
  Davis, Harvey Nathaniel
DORN, JACOB H.
  Holt, Arthur Erastus
DORSETT, LYLE W.
  Pendergast, Thomas Joseph
DORSON, RICHARD M.
  Read, Opie Pope
  Swanton, John Reed
DOTY, WILLIAM KAVANAUGH
  Henley, Robert
  Hollins, George Nichols
  Holmes, Daniel Henry
DOUGLAS, DOROTHY W.
  Steward, Ira
DOW, MARGARET ELDER
  Kane, Elisha Kent
DOWLING, JOHN E.
  Parker, George Howard
DOWNER, ALAN S.
  Ames, Winthrop
  Beck, Martin
  Faversham, William Alfred
  Howard, Sidney Coe
  Irwin, May
DOWNES, EDWARD O. D.
  Aldrich, Richard
  Henderson, William James
DOWNES, RANDOLPH C.
  St. Clair, Arthur
  Slocum, Frances
  Tupper, Benjamin
  Wayne, Anthony
  White Eyes
  Zane, Ebenezer
DOWNES, WILLIAM HOWE
  Bridgman, Frederic Arthur
  De Camp, Josejh Rodefer
  Doughty, Thomas
  Durand, Asher Brown
  Duveneck, Frank
  Eakins, Thomas
  Fuller, George
  Garrett, Edmund Henry
  Gaul, William Gilbert
  Gay, Winckworth Allan
  Gifford, Robert Swain
  Gifford, Sanford Robinson
  Gray, Henry Peters
  Guy, Seymour Joseph
  Hale, Philip Leslie
  Harrison, Lovell Birge
  Harrison, Thomas Alexander
  Hayden, Charles Henry
  Hays, William Jacob
  Hennessy, William John
  Henri, Robert
  Homer, Winslow
  Hoppin, Augustus
  Howe, William Henry
  Hunt, William Morris
  Inman, Henry, 1801–1846
  Inness, George
  Jarvis, John Wesley
  Johnson, Jonathan Eastman
  Johnston, Henrietta
  Jones, Hugh Bolton

Kensett, John Frederick
Lathrop, Francis Augustus
Le Clear, Thomas
Leslie, Charles Robert
Leutze, Emanuel
Lewis, Edmund Darch
Loeb, Louis
Loop, Henry Augustus
McEntee, Jervis
Macomber, Mary Lizzie
Matteson, Tompkins Harrison
May, Edward Harrison
Mayer, Constant
Maynard, George Willoughby
Merritt, Anna Lea
Metcalf, Willard Leroy
Mignot, Louis Remy
Miller, Charles Henry
Minor, Robert Crannell
Moran, Edward
Moran, Peter
Moran, Thomas
Mosler, Henry
Mowbray, Henry Siddons
Murphy, John Francis
Neagle, John
Neal, David Dalhoff
Newman, Henry Roderick
Newman, Robert Loftin
Nicoll, James Craig
Norton, William Edward
Oertel, Johannes Adam Simon
Page, William
Palmer, Walter Launt
Pearce, Charles Sprague
Picknell, William Lamb
Porter, Benjamin Curtis
Powell, William Henry
Prendergast, Maurice Brazil
Quidor, John
Ranney, William Tylee
Reid, Robert
Reinhart, Benjamin Franklin
Reinhart, Charles Stanley
Reuterdahl, Henry
Ritchie, Alexander Hay
Rosenthal, Toby Edward
Rossiter, Thomas Prichard
Ryder, Albert Pinkham
Sandham, Henry
Sargent, John Singer
Shirlaw, Walter
Shurtleff, Roswell Morse
Smedley, William Thomas
Smillie, George Henry
Smillie, James
Smillie, James David
Stone, William Oliver
Symons, George Gardner
Tait, Arthur Fitzwilliam
Thompson, Alfred Wordsworth
Tilton, John Rollin
Vanderlyn, John
Vedder, Elihu
Vinton, Frederic Porter
Waldo, Samuel Lovett
Walker, Henry Oliver
Weeks, Edwin Lord
West, William Edward
Wiggins, Carleton
Wylie, Robert
Zogbaum, Rufus Fairchild

Dows, Olin
  Bruce, Edward Bright
Doyle, Henry Grattan
  Winship, Albert Edward
Dozer, Donald Marquand
  Brickell, Henry Herschel
  Myles, John
Drinker, Sophie H.
  Mussey, Ellen Spencer
Driver, Carl S.
  Robertson, James, 1742–1814
  Smith, Daniel
  White, James
  Williams, John, 1778–1837
  Wright, Marcus Joseph
Droze, Wilmon H.
  Crowe, Francis Trenholm
Drumm, Stella M.
  Cerré, Jean Gabriel
  Chouteau, Pierre
  Crunden, Frederick Morgan
  Doniphan, Alexander William
  Glenn, Hugh
  Hall, Willard Preble
  Harrison, James
  Hogan, John
  Lange, Louis
  Lorimier, Pierre Louis
  McCoy, Joseph Geating
  Mackay, James
  Mackenzie, Donald
  Mackenzie, Kenneth
  McKnight, Robert
  Majors, Alexander
  Mitchell, David Dawson
  Pilcher, Joshua
  Pratte, Bernard
  Provost, Etienne
  St. Ange De Bellerive, Louis
  St. Vrain, Ceran DeHault de
    Lassus de
  Saugrain de Vigni, Antoine
    François
  Sublette, William Lewis
  Truteau, Jean Baptiste
  Vigo, Joseph Maria Francesco
  Waldo, David
Drury, Augustus Waldo
  Berger, Daniel
Dubofsky, Melvyn
  Bellanca, Dorothy Jacobs
  Chaplin, Ralph Hosea
  Hunter, Robert
  Lewis, John Llewellyn
  Mahler, Herbert
  O'Hare, Kate (Richards)
    Cunningham
Du Bois, W. E. Burghardt
  De Wolf, James
  Douglass, Frederick
  Johnson, Elijah
  Roberts, Joseph Jenkins
  Roye, Edward James
  Russwurm, John Brown
DuBridge, Lee A.
  Millikan, Robert Andrews
Dudden, Arthur Power
  Fels, Samuel Simeon
Duddy, Edward A.
  Farwell, John Villiers
  Field, Marshall
  Forgan, James Berwick
  Henrotin, Charles

Hutchinson, Benjamin Peters
Hutchinson, Charles Lawrence
Lawson, Victor Freemont
Leiter, Levi Zeigler
Patten, James A.
Raymond, Benjamin Wright
Ream, Norman Bruce
Ryerson, Martin Antoine
Schuttler, Peter
Sears, Richard Warren
Shedd, John Graves
Torrence, Joseph Thatcher
Ward, Aaron Montgomery
Duffey, Bernard
  Monroe, Harriet
Duffy, John
  Emerson, Haven
  Goldwater, Sigismund Schulz
  Matas, Rudolph
Dugan, Raymond Smith
  Barnard, Edward Emerson
  Bond, George Phillips
  Bond, William Cranch
  Boss, Lewis
  Brooks, William Robert
  Burnham, Sherburne Wesley
  Chandler, Seth Carlo
  Clark, Alvan
  Clark, Alvan Graham
  Davidson, George
  Doolittle, Charles Leander
  Doolittle, Eric
  Draper, Henry
  Eastman, John Robie
  Fleming, Williamina Paton
    Stevens
  Flint, Albert Stowell
  Gillis, James Melville
  Gould, Benjamin Apthorp
  Hall, Asaph
  Harkness, William
  Holden, Edward Singleton
  Hough, George Washington
  Hubbard, Joseph Stillman
  Hussey, William Joseph
  Keeler, James Edward
  Kirkwood, Daniel
  Leavenworth, Francis Preserved
  Leavitt, Henrietta Swan
  Lord, Henry Curwen
  Lowell, Percival
  Metcalf, Joel Hastings
  Parkhurst, John Adelbert
  Peters, Christian Henry
    Frederick
  Rees, John Krom
  Rutherfurd, Lewis Morris
  Young, Charles Augustus
Duke, Escal F.
  Sheppard, John Morris
Du Mez, Andrew G.
  Jacobs, Joseph, 1859–1929
  Kraemer, Henry
  Parrish, Edward
  Proctor, William
  Smith, Daniel B.
  Spalding, Lyman
  Squibb, Edward Robinson
  Weightman, William
Dumke, Glenn S.
  Widney, Joseph Pomeroy

Dumond, Dwight L.
  Yancey, William Lowndes
Dunbar, B. A.
  Shepard, James Henry
Dunbar, Louise B.
  Nicola, Lewis
Dunham, Dorothy Knight
  Roche, Arthur Somers
Dunham, Dows
  Reisner, George Andrew
Dunham, Harold H.
  Sparks, William Andrew
    Jackson
Duniway, Clyde Augustus
  Adams, Alva
  Baker, Edward Dickinson
  Strong, James Woodward
Dunn, Joseph
  Currier, Charles Warren
Dunn, Waldo H.
  Mitchell, Donald Grant
Dunning, William B.
  Brophy, Truman William
  Flagg, Josiah Foster
  Hudson, Edward
Dunnington, John H.
  Weeks, John Elmer
Durand, William Frederick
  Allen, Jeremiah Mervin
  Copeland, Charles W.
  Dickie, George William
  Eckart, William Roberts
  Ericsson, John
  Thurston, Robert Henry
  Timby, Theodore Ruggles
Durel, Lionel C.
  Canonge, Louis Placide
  Deléry, François Charles
  Dugué, Charles Oscar
  Dupratz, Antoine Simon Le
    Page
  Garreau, Armand
  Humbert, Jean Joseph Amable
  Mercier, Charles Alfred
  Moreau-Lislet, Louis Casimir
    Elisabeth
Dutcher, George Matthew
  Stephens, Henry Morse
Dutton, George B.
  Nelson, Henry Loomis
Dwight, Harrison Griswold
  Adee, Alvey Augustus
  Ellicott, Andrew
  James, George Wharton
  Whitlock, Brand
Dwyer, Donald Harris
  Atterbury, Grosvenor
Dyer, Frank L.
  Martin, Thomas Commerford
Dyer, Walter A.
  Phyfe, Duncan
  Stiegel, Henry William
Dykes, Jr., De Witt S.
  Bethune, Mary McLeod
Dykstra, Robert R.
  Scott, Walter Edward

Earl, Polly Anne
  Dennison, Henry Sturgis
Earle, A. Scott
  Crile, George Washington

EARLE, ROSAMONDE HOPKINS
 Payne, William Harold
 Pierce, John Davis
EASTERBY, J. H.
 Adams, James Hopkins
 Aiken, David Wyatt
 Aiken, William
 Allston, Robert Francis Withers
 Alston, Joseph
 Bratton, John
 Brumby, Richard Trapier
 Chestnut, James
 Conner, James
 De Saussure, Henry William
 Drayton, John
 Drayton, Thomas Fenwick
 Drayton, William, 1732–1790
 Drayton, William, 1776–1846
 Hampton, Wade, 1751–1835
 Hampton, Wade, 1818–1902
 Pinckney, Charles
 Pinckney, Henry Laurens
 Pringle, John Julius
 Stephenson, Nathaniel Wright
EASTMAN, EDWARD R.
 Harris, Joseph
EASTMAN, LINDA ANNE
 Brett, William Howard
 Galbreath, Charles Burleigh
EATON, ARTHUR WENTWORTH
 HAMILTON
 Winslow, William Copley
EATON, EDWARD DWIGHT
 Chapin, Aaron Lucius
 Fairchild, James Harris
 Hallock, William Allen
 Hammond, Edward Payson
 Hand, Daniel
 Hillis, Newell Dwight
 Hopkins, John Henry
 McKenzie, Alexander
 Mahan, Asa
 Mead, Charles Marsh
 Mears, David Otis
 Morris, Edward Dafydd
 Morrison, Nathan Jackson
 Noble, Frederick Alphonso
 Pearsons, Daniel Kimball
 Post, Truman Marcellus
 Rankin, Jeremiah Eames
 Robinson, Charles Seymour
 Smith, Judson
 Stewart, Philo Penfield
 Stowe, Calvin Ellis
 Warren, Israel Perkins
 Wright, Theodore Lyman
EATON, LEONARD K.
 Jensen, Jens
EATON, WALTER PRICHARD
 Baker, George Pierce
 Belasco, David
 Booth, Agnes
 Boucicault, Dion
 Brougham, John
 Burk, John Daly
 Burton, William Evans
 Clifton, Josephine
 Coghlan, Rose
 Conway, Frederick Bartlett
 Cushman, Charlotte Saunders
 Cushman, Susan Webb
 Daly, Peter Christopher Arnold
 Daniels, Frank Albert

Drew, John, 1827–1862
Drew, John, 1853–1927
Drew, Louisa Lane
Fiske, Minnie Maddern
Forrest, Edwin
Goodwin, Nathaniel Carll
Hackett, James Henry
Hackett, James Keteltas
Herne, James A.
Hopper, DeWolf
Janauschek, Franziska
 Magdalena Romance
Jefferson, Joseph, 1774–1832
Jefferson, Joseph, 1829–1905
Keene, Thomas Wallace
Kemble, Frances Anne
Long, John Luther
MacKaye, James Morrison
 Steele
Mansfield, Richard
Modjeska, Helena
Moody, William Vaughn
Olcott, Chauncey
Power, Frederick Tyrone
Rehan, Ada
Silverman, Sime
Smith, Winchell
Sothern, Edward Askew
Sothern, Edward Hugh
Stevens, Emily
Stoddart, James Henry
Thomas, Augustus
Thompson, Denman
Thorne, Charles Robert,
 1814–1893
Thorne, Charles Robert,
 1840–1883
Urban, Joseph
Vandenhoff, George
Walcot, Charles Melton, c.
 1816–1868
Walcot, Charles Melton,
 1840–1921
Ward, Genevieve
Wemyss, Francis Courtney
Williams, Barney
Williams, Bert
Wilson, Francis
Winter, William
Wise, Thomas Alfred
Ziegfeld, Florenz
ECKENRODE, H. J.
 Lee, Francis Lightfoot
 Lee, Henry, 1756–1818
 Lee, Richard Bland
EDEL, LEON
 Wharton, Edith Newbold Jones
EDELMAN, EDWARD
 Hancock, Thomas
EDGELL, GEORGE H.
 Lowell, Guy
EDGERTON, FRANKLIN
 Hodgson, William Brown
 Hopkins, Edward Washburn
EDGERTON, MILTON T.
 Davis, John Staige
EDGETT, EDWIN FRANCIS
 Bacon, Frank
 Ballou, Maturin Murray
 Barrett, Lawrence
 Bernard, William Bayle
 Bonstelle, Jessie
 Burgess, Neil

Burke, Charles St. Thomas
Cayvan, Georgia
Chaney, Lon
Christy, Edwin P.
Claxton, Kate
Dana, Richard Henry,
 1787–1879
Dana, Richard Henry,
 1815–1882
De Angelis, Thomas Jefferson
Deering, Nathaniel
De Mille, Henry Churchill
Ditrichstein, Leo
Dressler, Marie
Durivage, Francis Alexander
Edes, Benjamin
Edeson, Robert
Estes, Dana
Field, Mary Katherine Keemle
Hale, Louise Closser
Hale, Nathan
Hale, Philip
Harrison, Richard Berry
Hitchcock, Raymond
Hodge, William Thomas
Hudson, Charles
Illington, Margaret
James, Louis
Jones, Joseph Stevens
Kester, Paul
Kirby, J. Hudson
Klein, Charles
Lackaye, Wilton
Le Moyne, William J.
Lewis, Arthur
Liveright, Horace Brisbin
Logan, Cornelius Ambrosius
Logan, Olive
McCullough, John
Manners, John Hartley
Mantell, Robert Bruce
Mason, John, 1858–1919
Megrue, Roi Cooper
Mitchell, William, 1798–1856
Montague, Henry James
O'Neill, James
Osborn, Laughton
Owen, William Florence
Owens, John Edmond
Parker, Henry Taylor
Placide, Henry
Potter, Paul Meredith
Powell, Snelling
Powell, Thomas
Pray, Isaac Clark
Presbrey, Eugene Wiley
Proctor, Joseph
Rankin, McKee
Raymond, John T.
Richings, Peter
Riddle, George Peabody
Roberts, Theodore
Robson, Stuart
Russell, Sol Smith
Sargent, George Henry
Seymour, William
Shaw, Mary
Sills, Milton
Smith, William Henry,
 1806–1872
Vezin, Hermann
Vincent, Mary Ann
Waller, Emma

Warde, Frederick Barkham
Warren, William, 1767–1832
Warren, William, 1812–1888
Western, Lucille
Wolheim, Louis Robert
EDMINSTER, LYNN R.
Page, Thomas Walker
EDMONDS, ANTHONY O.
Jacobs, Michael Strauss
EDMONDS, JOHN H.
Bonner, John
Burgis, William
EDSALL, JOHN T.
Cohn, Edwin Joseph
Henderson, Lawrence Joseph
EDSON, HOWARD A.
Pritchard, Frederick John
EDWARD, BROTHER
Azarias, Brother
EDWARDS, ANNE
Leigh, Vivien
EDWARDS, EVERETT E.
Periam, Jonathan
Reid, James L.
Scovell, Melville Amasa
Silver, Gray
Spillman, William Jasper
Sturtevant, Edward Lewis
True, Alfred Charles
EDWARDS, G. FRANKLIN
Frazier, Edward Franklin
EDWARDS, GRANVILLE D.
Moore, William Thomas
EDWARDS, HERBERT J.
Herne, Chrystal Katharine
EGAN, MARTIN
Morrow, Dwight Whitney
EGGERT, GERALD
Gimbel, Bernard Feustman
EGGERT, GERALD G.
Cabot, Godfrey Lowell
Fairless, Benjamin F.
Girdler, Tom Mercer
Randall, Clarence Belden
EGGLESTON, JOSEPH D.
Foote, William Henry
Hoge, Moses
Hoge, Moses Drury
Lacy, Drury
McIlwaine, Richard
Maxwell, William
EGLI, CLARA
Southack, Cyprian
EHRENZWEIG, ALBERT A.
Radin, Max
EHRLICH, EVELYN
Bennett, Constance Campbell
EISELEN, FREDERICK C.
Raymond, Miner
Ridgaway, Henry Bascom
EISENHART, KATHARINE S.
Marquand, Henry Gurdon
EISENHART, LUTHER P.
Minto, Walter
EISENSTADT, A. S.
Adams, James Truslow
EKBLAW, W. ELMER
Greely, Adolphus Washington
ELIOT, ALEXANDER
Frankfurter, Alfred Moritz
McBride, Henry

ELIOT, MARTHA M.
Abbott, Grace
ELIOT, SAMUEL ATKINS
Armstrong, Samuel Chapman
Bartol, Cyrus Augustus
Batchelor, George
Bellows, Henry Whitney
ELKUS, ABRAM I.
Straus, Oscar Solomon
ELLIOTT, EDWARD C.
Purdue, John
ELLIOTT, THOMPSON C.
Ogden, Peter Skene
Thompson, David
ELLIOTT, WILLIAM G.
Griffith, William
Haines, Charles Glidden
Haines, Lynn
Hanson, Alexander Contee, 1749–1806
Hayes, John Lord
Howard, Benjamin Chew
ELLIS, ELIZABETH BRECKENRIDGE
Oglesby, Richard James
Pope, Nathaniel
Springer, William McKendree
Thomas, Jesse Burgess
ELLIS, ELMER
Teller, Henry Moore
Williams, Walter
ELLIS, JOHN TRACY
Guilday, Peter Keenan
ELLIS, L. ETHAN
Judd, Norman Buel
Kellogg, Frank Billings
Madden, Martin Barnaby
Mann, James Robert
Mason, William Ernest
Rutgers, Henry
Trumbull, Lyman
Washburne, Elihu Benjamin
ELLIS, MILTON
Brown, William Hill
Day, Holman Francis
Fessenden, Thomas Green
Mellen, Grenville
Morton, Sarah Wentworth Apthorp
Murray, Judith Sargent Stevens
Neal, John
Rowson, Susanna Haswell
Smith, Elihu Hubbard
Wood, Sarah Sayward Barrell Keating
ELLIS, WILLIAM E.
Hess, Victor Franz
Szilard, Leo
ELSON, ARTHUR
Carr, Benjamin
Coerne, Louis Adolphe
Converse, Charles Crozat
Edwards, Julian
Eichberg, Julius
Emery, Stephen Albert
ELZAS, BARNETT A.
Mordecai, Moses Cohen
Pinto, Isaac
Poznanski, Gustavus
ELZY, MARTIN I.
Verrill, Alpheus Hyatt
EMERSON, HORTON W., JR.
Baker, John Franklin
Sande, Earl

Stagg, Amos Alonzo
EMERSON, KENDALL
Coolidge, Archibald Cary
Crothers, Samuel McChord
Emerton, Ephraim
Felton, Cornelius Conway
Frothingham, Paul Revere
Gross, Charles
Gurney, Ephraim Whitman
Thayer, William Roscoe
Williams, Linsly Rudd
EMERTON, EPHRAIM
Coolidge, Archibald Cary
Crothers, Samuel McChord
Felton, Cornelius Conway
Frothingham, Paul Revere
Gross, Charles
Gurney, Ephraim Whitman
Thayer, William Roscoe
EMERY, EDWIN
Noyes, Frank Brett
Reid, Ogden Mills
Van Anda, Carr Vattel
EMERY, WILLIAM M.
Banks, Charles Edward
Putnam, Eben
Ricketson, Daniel
Robinson, Edward Mott
Rotch, William
Sturgis, William
Warren, Russell
Williams, Catharine Read Arnold
EMMONS, WILLIAM HARVEY
Upham, Warren
ENGEL, CARL
Schirmer, Gustav
Schirmer, Rudolph Edward
Sonneck, Oscar George Theodore
ENGEL, WILLIAM J.
Lower, William Edgar
ENGLISH, JOHN P.
Macdonald, Charles Blair
ENNIS, J. HAROLD
Dallas, Alexander James
ENSIGN, FOREST CHESTER
Benton, Thomas Hart
EPSTEIN, DENA J.
Stock, Frederick August
ERDMAN, CHARLES R., JR.
Abbett, Leon
Blair, John Insley
Dickerson, Mahlon
Dryden, John Fairfield
Field, Richard Stockton
Frelinghuysen, Frederick
Frelinghuysen, Theodore
Kinney, William Burnet
Robeson, George Maxwell
ERICKSON, ERLING A.
Morgan, John Pierpont
ERMARTH, MARGARET SITTLER
Tipton, John
ERSKINE, JOHN
MacDowell, Edward Alexander
ERSKINE, MARJORY
Duchesne, Rose Philippine
ESAREY, LOGAN
Benton, Allen Richardson
Bright, Jesse David

ESPENSCHIED, LLOYD
Carson, John Renshaw
ESTES, J. A.
Locke, David Ross
ETTENBERG, EUGENE M.
Dwiggins, William Addison
ETTINGER, AMOS A.
Oglethorpe, James Edward
Soulé, Pierre
EUGENIA, SISTER
Guérin, Ann-Thérèse
EURICH, ALVIN C.
Coffman, Lotus Delta
EVANS, AUSTIN P.
Burr, George Lincoln
EVANS, DANIEL
Fenn, William Wallace
Park, Edwards Amasa
Porter, Ebenezer
EVANS, G. HEBERTON, JR.
Barnett, George Ernest
EVANS, HOWARD, E.
Howard, Leland Ossian
EVANS, JAMES F.
Butler, Burridge Davenal
EVANS, JOHN NORRIS
Noyes, Henry Drury
EVANS, LAWRENCE BOYD
Bacon, John
Briggs, George Nixon
EVANS, PAUL D.
Cazenove, Théophile
Ellicott, Joseph
Everett, Robert
Harpur, Robert
Ludlow, Thomas William
Mappa, Adam Gerard
Mitchell, Stephen Mix
Morris, Luzon Burritt
Morrison, William McCutchan
Niles, Nathaniel, 1741–1828
Olney, Jesse
Paine, Charles
Paine, Elijah
Painter, Gamaliel
Palmer, William Adams
Phelps, Oliver
Prentiss, Samuel
Pringle, Cyrus Guernsey
Rowlands, William
Sanders, Daniel Clarke
Slade, William
Slafter, Edmund Farwell
Smith, John Gregory
EVERETT, WALTER G.
Seth, James
EVERMANN, BARTON WARREN
Jordan, David Starr
EVJENS, JOHN O.
Johnsen, Erik Kristian
Oftedal, Sven
Preus, Christian Keyser
Richard, James William
Schmauk, Theodore Emanuel
Schmidt, Friedrich August
Schodde, George Henry
Seyffarth, Gustavus
Stromme, Peer Olsen
Stub, Hans Gerhard
Stuckenberg, John Henry
Wilbrandt
Sverdrup, Georg
Tou, Erik Hansen

Weidner, Revere Franklin
EWAN, JOSEPH
McLaren, John
Trelease, William
EWEN, DAVID
Baccaloni, Salvatore
Bloch, Ernest
Bori, Lucrezia
De Rose, Peter
De Sylva, George Gard
"Buddy"
Farrar, Geraldine
Gatti-Casazza, Giulio
Gershwin, George
Hammerstein, Oscar, II
Kahn, Gustav Gerson
Martinelli, Giovanni
Melton, James
Pinza, Ezio
Riegger, Wallingford
Schnabel, Artur
Schoenberg, Arnold
Tibbett, Lawrence Mervil
Toscanini, Arturo
EWING, GEORGE HENRY
Lorimer, George Claude
EZELL, JOHN S.
Beaty, Amos Leonidas
Berry, Martha McChesney
Cullinan, Joseph Stephen
Marland, Ernest Whitworth
Phillips, Frank
Truett, George Washington

FABRE, MICHEL
Wright, Richard Nathaniel
FAGLEY, FREDERICK L.
Cadman, Samuel Parkes
FAILING, PATRICIA
Arno, Peter
Epstein, Jacob
Halpert, Edith Gregor
Lewisohn, Sam Adolph
Marsh, Reginald
Moses, Anna Mary Robertson
("Grandma")
Newman, Barnett
Tomlin, Bradley Walker
Zorach, William
FAILING, PATRICIA STIPE
Stein, Leo Daniel
FAIRCHILD, FRED R.
Adams, Thomas Sewall
FAIRCHILD, HENRY PRATT
Holt, Henry
Richmond, Mary Ellen
FAIRCHILD, HERMAN L.
Perkins, George Henry
FAIRMAN, CHARLES
Butler, Pierce
Jackson, Charles
Knowlton, Marcus Perrin
Lord, Otis Phillips
Loring, Ellis Gray
McCullough, John Griffith
Merrick, Pliny
Metcalf, Theron
Miller, Samuel Freeman
Montefiore, Joshua
Parker, Joel
Parsons, Theophilus
Phillips, Willard
Pierce, Edward Lillie

Richardson, William Adams
Ruggles, Timothy
FALCONER, JOHN I.
Root, Amos Ives
FALK, STANLEY L.
Wilbur, Curtis Dwight
FANGER, DONALD
Cross, Samuel Hazzard
FARIS, ELLSWORTH
Small, Albion Woodbury
FARIS, PAUL PATTON
McAfee, John Armstrong
McLeod, Alexander
Mason, John Mitchell
Miller, James Russell
Miller, Samuel
Neill, William
Nevin, Alfred
Nevin, Edwin Henry
Parker, Joel
Patterson, Robert Mayne
Patton, William
Pentecost, George Frederick
Peters, Madison Clinton
Roberts, William Charles
Scott, William Anderson
Shedd, William Greenough
Thayer
Simpson, Albert Benjamin
Skinner, Thomas Harvey
FARISH, HUNTER D.
Tait, Charles
FARMER, HALLIE
Clayton, Henry De Lamar
Fry, Birkett Davenport
Hamilton, Peter
Herbert, Hilary Abner
Hilliard, Henry Washington
Hopkins, Arthur Francis
Hopkins, Juliet Ann Opie
Houston, George Smith
Lane, James Henry
Lyon, Francis Strother
McKinstry, Alexander
Oates, William Calvin
O'Neal, Edward Asbury
Owen, Thomas McAdory
Parsons, Lewis Eliphalet
Perry, William Flake
Pickett, Albert James
Screws, William Wallace
Shorter, John Gill
Smith, Robert Hardy
Smith, William Russell
Stone, George Washington
Tutwiler, Henry
Tutwiler, Julia Strudwick
Watts, Thomas Hill
Winston, John Anthony
FARNHAM, WILLARD
Tatlock, John Strong Perry
FARNUM, GRACE C.
Swanson, Claude Augustus
FARR, ALBERT M.
Hoffman, Eugene Augustus
FARR, FINIS
Johnson, Jack
FARRAR, CLARENCE B.
Dewey, Richard Smith
FAULK, ODIE B.
Croy, Homer
Mulford, Clarence Edward

FAULKNER, ETHEL WEBB
Dwight, Benjamin Woodbridge
Dwight, Nathaniel
Dwight, Sereno Edwards
Parker, Richard Green
Smith, Sophia
Steele, Joel Dorman
Stoddard, John Fair
FAULKNER, HAROLD UNDERWOOD
Abbott, Horace
Alger, Cyrus
Ames, James Tyler
Ames, Nathan Peabody
Babbitt, Benjamin Talbot
Bates, Joshua
Benner, Philip
Bent, Josiah
Bliss, Eliphalet Williams
Borden, Richard
Bradley, Milton
Bridges, Robert, d. 1656
Brooker, Charles Frederick
Brown, Ebenezer
Burrowes, Edward Thomas
Butler, Simeon
Candee, Leverett
Chapin, Chester William
Cheney, Ward
Chickering, Jonas
Chisholm, Hugh Joseph
Cobb, Jonathan Holmes
Combs, Moses Newell
Coney, Jabez
Crocker, Alvah
Cummings, John
Dennison, Aaron Lufkin
Douglas, Benjamin
Downer, Samuel
Draper, Eben Sumner
Draper, William Franklin
Dwight, Edmund
Eastman, Arthur MacArthur
Fordney, Joseph Warren
Gary, Elbert Henry
Gilbert, William Lewis
Jackson, Patrick Tracy
James, Charles Tillinghast
Lowell, Francis Cabot
Mackay, John William
Merriam, Charles
Merrill, Joshua
Perry, William
Phelps, Anson Greene
Phelps, Guy Rowland
Pope, Albert Augustus
Sperry, Nehemiah Day
Ward, George Gray
FAULKNER, JOHN ALFRED
Atkinson, John
Baker, Osmon Cleander
Bashford, James Whitford
FAULKNER, WILLIAM H.
Harrison, James Albert
FAUSOLD, MARTIN L.
Gannett, Frank Ernest
Wadsworth, James Wolcott, Jr.
FAUST, ALBERT BERNHARDT
Bartholdt, Richard
Brachvogel, Udo
Brentano, Lorenz
Brühl, Gustav
Dorsch, Eduard
Grund, Francis Joseph

Hart, James Morgan
Hecker, Friedrich Karl Franz
Heinzen, Karl Peter
Hewett, Waterman Thomas
Hilgard, Theodor Erasmus
Learned, Marion Dexter
Rapp, Wilhelm
Rattermann, Heinrich Armin
FAWCETT, ELLEN DOUGLASS
Cunningham, Ann Pamela
FAWCETT, JAMES WALDO
Scott, Thomas Fielding
Slattery, Charles Lewis
FAXON, HARRIET
Robinson, Edward, 1858–1931
FEE, WALTER R.
Stockton, Richard
FEINBERG, GERALD
Einstein, Albert
FEINSTEIN, ESTELLE F.
Bingham, Hiram
FELEKY, CHARLES
Haraszthy de Mokcsa, Agoston
Xántus, János
FELLNER, FELIX
Schnerr, Leander
Stehle, Aurelius Aloysius
Wimmer, Boniface
Wolf, Innocent William
FELLOWS, GEORGE EMORY
Cannon, George Quayle
FELTUS, GEORGE HAWS
House, Samuel Reynolds
Jones, John Taylor
McFarland, Samuel Gamble
McGilvary, Daniel
Matton, Stephen
FENN, WILLIAM PURVIANCE
Fee, John Gregg
FENN, WILLIAM W.
Chauncy, Charles, 1592–1671/2
Chauncy, Charles, 1705–1787
Clarke, James Freeman
Gordon, George Angier
Hodges, George
Hopkins, Mark
FENTON, NORMAN
Southard, Elmer Ernest
FERGUSON, EUGENE S.
Kingsbury, Albert
FERGUSON, WALLACE K.
Smith, Preserved
FERLING, JOHN E.
Ward, Arch Burdette
FERM, ROBERT L.
McPherson, Aimee Semple
FERM, VERGILIUS
Krauth, Charles Porterfield
Schmucker, Samuel Simon
FERN, ALAN M.
Ganso, Emil
FERRELL, ROBERT H.
Carr, Wilbur John
Clark, Joshua Reuben, Jr.
Eisenhower, Dwight David
Hull, Cordell
Levinson, Salmon Oliver
FERRELL, SARAH
Bolm, Adolph Rudolphovitch
FERRIS, WILLIAM R.
Lomax, John Avery

FERRIS, WILLIAM R., JR.
Ledbetter, Huddie
("Leadbelly")
FERRY, W. HAWKINS
Kahn, Albert
FERTIG, WALTER L.
Nicholson, Meredith
FETTER, FRANK W.
Kemmerer, Edwin Walter
FIEBEGER, GUSTAVE JOSEPH
Anderson, James Patton
Anderson, Richard Heron
Barnard, John Gross
Burnside, Ambrose Everett
Crook, George
Duane, James Chatham
Humphreys, Andrew Atkinson
Mahan, Dennis Hart
Mansfield, Joseph King Fenno
Marshall, William Louis
Merrill, William Emery
Michie, Peter Smith
Talcott, Andrew
Thayer, Sylvanus
Tower, Zealous Bates
Trimble, Isaac Ridgeway
Turnbull, William
Turner, John Wesley
FIEDLER, LESLIE A.
Leonard, William Ellery
FIELD, JAMES A., JR.
Mitscher, Marc Andrew
Sims, William Sowden
FIELDING, MANTLE
Anderson, Alexander
Sully, Thomas
West, Benjamin, 1728–1820
FIESER, LOUIS F.
Kohler, Elmer Peter
FILLER, LOUIS
Bennett, Hugh Hammond
Boole, Ella Alexander
Clark, Grenville
Coulter, Ernest Kent
Dunne, Finley Peter
Filene, Edward Albert
Flandrau, Charles Macomb
Hall, Bolton
Hapgood, Hutchins
Hapgood, Norman
Kellor, Frances (Alice)
Lovett, Robert Morss
Markham, Edwin
Myers, Gustavus
Pinchot, Cornelia Elizabeth
Bryce
Rittenhouse, Jessie Belle
Spaeth, John Duncan
Steffens, Lincoln
Van Loon, Hendrik Willem
FINCH, JAMES KIP
Bates, Onward
Burr, William Hubert
Cooper, Hugh Lincoln
Davies, John Vipond
Fletcher, Robert
Mead, Elwood
Modjeski, Ralph
Moran, Daniel Edward
Parsons, William Barclay
Ridgway, Robert
Symons, Thomas William
Thacher, Edwin

Thompson, Charles Oliver
Totten, George Muirson
Waddell, John Alexander Low
Whipple, Squire
White, Canvass
Wright, Benjamin
FINDLING, JOHN E.
  Allen, George Venable
  Bullitt, William Christian
  Castle, William Richards, Jr.
  Clayton, William Lockhart
FINE, SIDNEY
  Murphy, Frank
FINGER, CHARLES J.
  Reedy, William Marion
  Woodruff, William Edward
FINNEY, BYRON A.
  Davis, Raymond Cazallis
FIRKINS, OSCAR W.
  Howells, William Dean
  Northrop, Cyrus
FIROR, WARFIELD M.
  Reid, Mont Rogers
FISCHER, LE ROY H.
  Gurowski, Adam
FISH, CARL RUSSELL
  Blaine, James Gillespie
  Buchanan, James
  Butler, Benjamin Franklin,
    1818–1893
  Curtis, George Ticknor
FISH, PETER GRAHAM
  Parker, John Johnston
FISHBEIN, MORRIS
  Blalock, Nelson Gales
  DeLee, Joseph Bolivar
  Simmons, George Henry
FISHER, GALEN R.
  Chessman, Caryl Whittier
FISHER, G. CLYDE
  Akeley, Carl Ethan
FISHER, H. H.
  Golder, Frank Alfred
FISHER, JAMES
  Koenig, George Augustus
FISHER, WALTER
  Dett, Robert Nathaniel
FISK, DANIEL M.
  Harlan, Richard
  Morton, Samuel George
FISKE, HERBERT H.
  Warden, David Bailie
FITCH, EDWARD
  Mears, John William
  North, Edward
  North, Simeon, 1802–1884
FITCH, JAMES M.
  Whitaker, Charles Harris
FITCH, JOHN A.
  Lee, Porter Raymond
FITE, GILBERT C.
  Murphy, Frederick E.
  Norbeck, Peter
  Peek, George Nelson
FITTRO, MARY ELIZABETH
  Leeds, John
  Paca, William
  Stone, Thomas
  Stone, William
FITZPATRICK, EDWARD A.
  Katzer, Frederic Xavier

FITZPATRICK, JOHN
  Greenwood, John
  Jackson, William, 1759–1828
  Tilghman, Tench
  Varick, Richard
  Washington, George
  Waxman, Franz
FITZPATRICK, PAUL J.
  Falkner, Roland Post
FITZSIMONS, NEAL
  Hovey, Otis Ellis
  Stevens, John Frank
FLACK, J. KIRKPATRICK
  Kaltenborn, Hans Von
  Patrick, Edwin Hill ("Ted")
FLAHERTY, DAVID HARRIS
  Train, Arthur Cheney
FLANNERY-HERZFELD, REGINA
  Cooper, John Montgomery
FLEMING, DONALD
  Cannon, Walter Bradford
FLEMING, WALTER LYNWOOD
  Barrow, Washington
  Bate, William Brimage
  Baxter, John
  Brown, John Calvin
  Brown, Neill Smith
  Carmack, Edward Ward
  Catron, John
FLETCHER, ROBERT S.
  Shipherd, John Jay
FLEXNER, SIMON
  Councilman, William Thomas
  Rose, Wickliffe
FLICK, ALEXANDER CLARENCE
  Barnard, Daniel Dewey
  Beardsley, Samuel
  Betts, Samuel Rossiter
  Black, Frank Swett
  Fernow, Berthold
  Stone, William Leete
  Tilden, Samuel Jones
FLIPPIN, PERCY SCOTT
  Culpeper, Thomas Lord
  Ellis, Henry
  Fauquier, Francis
  Gooch, Sir William
  Hewat, Alexander
  Heyward, Thomas
  Hyrne, Edmund Massingberd
  Johnson, Herschel Vespasian
FLITCROFT, JOHN E.
  Gilchrist, Robert
  Hobart, Garret Augustus
  Murphy, Franklin
  Rix, Julian Walbridge
  Thompson, Daniel Pierce
FLOM, GEORGE T.
  Eielsen, Elling
  Janson, Kristofer Nagel
FLOWER, DEAN
  Arlen, Michael
  Arvin, Newton
  Atherton, Gertrude Franklin
    (Horn)
  Bacon, Leonard
  Cabell, James Branch
  Coffin, Robert Peter Tristram
  La Farge, Christopher Grant
  McNulty, John Augustine
  Parker, Dorothy Rothschild
  Stribling, Thomas Sigismund

FLYNN, GEORGE Q.
  Niles, David K.
  Walker, Frank Comerford
FLYNN, JOHN T.
  Rockefeller, William
FOERSTER, NORMAN
  Babbitt, Irving
  Burroughs, John
FOGARTY, GERALD P., S.J.
  Spellman, Francis Joseph
FOIIL, PAUL J.
  Padilla, Juan de
FOLLIARD, EDWARD T.
  McLean, Edward Beale
FOLMSBEE, STANLEY J.
  Byrns, Joseph Wellington
FOLSOM, JOSEPH FULFORD
  Young, David
FOOTE, ARTHUR
  Schmidt, Arthur Paul
FOOTE, FRANKLIN M.
  Lewis, Francis Park
FOOTE, HARRY W.
  Silliman, Benjamin, 1816–1885
FOOTE, HENRY WILDER
  Norton, Andrews
  Phillips, George
FORBES, ALLYN B.
  Newman, Henry
FORD, AMELIA C.
  Mortimer, Mary
  Waldo, Samuel
FORD, JEREMIAH D. M.
  Hills, Elijah Clarence
  Lang, Henry Roseman
  Sheldon, Edward Stevens
  Ticknor, George
FORD, WORTHINGTON CHAUNCEY
  Adams, Brooks
  Adams, Charles Francis,
    1807–1886
  Adams, Charles Francis,
    1835–1915
  Adams, John
  Adams, John Quincy
FORSYTH, KING LOGAN
  Quesnay, Alexandre-Marie
FORTSON, BLANTON
  Benning, Henry Lewis
  Bleckley, Logan Edwin
  Campbell, John Archibald
  Charlton, Thomas Usher
    Pulaski
  Clay, Joseph, 1741–1804
  Cobb, Andrew Jackson
  Erskine, John
  Jackson, James, 1819–1887
  Lamar, Joseph Rucker
  Lumpkin, Joseph Henry
  Warner, Hiram
FOSBROKE, HUGHELL E. W.
  Moore, Clement Clarke
  Turner, Samuel Hulbeart
FOSTER, WILLIAM
  Maclean, John
FOWKES, FREDERICK M.
  Harkins, William Draper
FOWLER, HAROLD L.
  Bryan, John Stewart
FOWLER, HAROLD NORTH
  Abbott, Frank Frost
  Allen, Frederic De Forest
  Allen, William Francis

Anthon, Charles
Beck, Charles
Bennett, Charles Edwin
Bingham, William
Botsford, George Willis
Burnam, John Miller
Carter, Jesse Benedict
Chase, Thomas
Dennison, Walter
Mitchell, Lucy Myers Wright
Platner, Samuel Ball
FOWLER, HENRY THATCHER
Sanders, Frank Knight
FOX, DANIEL M.
Ayres, Leonard Porter
Bliss, Cornelius Newton
Embree, Edwin Rogers
Leathers, Waller Smith
Rockefeller, Abby Greene
Aldrich
Sawyer, Wilbur Augustus
Strong, Richard Pearson
FOX, DIXON RYAN
Clinton, DeWitt
Hammond, Jabez Delano
Heathcote, Caleb
Osgood, Herbert Levi
FOX, EARLY LEE
Bocock, Thomas Stanley
Boteler, Alexander Robinson
Clay, Matthew
Clopton, John
Dawson, John
FOX, GEORGE HENRY
Jackson, George Thomas
FOX, JOHN DAVID
Chambers, Whittaker
FOX, LOUIS H.
Farnum, Dustin Lancy
Lander, Jean Margaret
Davenport
Lewis, James
Ludlow, Noah Miller
FOX, L. WEBSTER
Burnett, Swan Moses
Littell, Squier
Norris, William Fisher
Oliver, Charles Augustus
FOX, WILLIAM LLOYD
Dandy, Walter Edward
Elsberg, Charles Albert
FOYE, WILBUR G.
Rice, William North
FRAME, JAMES EVERETT
Vincent, Marvin Richardson
FRANCIS, JOHN, JR.
Verbeck, William
FRANCKE, KUNO
Follen, Charles
FRANK, BENIS M.
Higgins, Andrew Jackson
FRANK, ELIZABETH
Bogan, Louise Marie
FRANKEL, CHARLES
Edman, Irwin
FRANKENSTEIN, ALFRED V.
Hartley, Marsden
Hertz, Alfred
FRANKFURTER, FELIX
Cardozo, Benjamin Nathan
Holmes, Oliver Wendell
Valentine, Robert Grosvenor

FRANKLIN, FABIAN
Heilprin, Michael
FRANKLIN, JOHN HOPE
Lynch, John Roy
FRANKLIN, PHILIP
Moore, Clarence Lemuel Elisha
FRANKLIN, WILLIAM M.
Welles, (Benjamin) Sumner
FRANTZ, JOE B.
Richardson, Sid Williams
FRASER, RUSSELL
Blackmur, Richard Palmer
FRAZER, JOSEPH C. W.
Morse, Harmon Northrop
FRAZIER, E. FRANKLIN
Miller, Kelly
FREDERICK, JOHN H.
Burrall, William Porter
Cass, George Washington
Clark, Horace Francis
Crocker, Charles
Dillon, Sidney
Eastman, Timothy Corser
Eckert, Thomas Thompson
Elkins, William Lukens
Fitler, Edwin Henry
Florence, Thomas Birch
Fraley, Frederick
Griscom, Clement Acton
Guthrie, George Wilkins
Habersham, Alexander Wylly
Harding, Jesper
Harding, William White
Harrah, Charles Jefferson
Harrison, John
Harrison, Joseph
Haupt, Herman
Hillegas, Michael
Houston, Henry Howard
Humphreys, Joshua
Huston, Charles
Hutchinson, James
Ingham, Samuel Delucenna
Johnson, John Graver
Jones, Jehu Glancy
Jones, Joel
Jones, Thomas P.
Jones, William
Kane, John Kintzing
Kane, Thomas Leiper
Keating, William Hypolitus
Keep, Henry
Knight, Jonathan
Leiper, Thomas
Lewis, William
Lippincott, Joshua Ballinger
Lukens, Rebecca Webb
Pennock
Macalester, Charles, 1765–1832
Macalester, Charles, 1798–1873
Martin, John Hill
Meade, George
Meade, Richard Worsam
Meredith, Samuel
Merrick, Samuel Vaughan
Miner, Charles
Mitten, Thomas Eugene
Morris, Anthony, 1766–1860
Morris, Cadwalader
Moxham, Arthur James
Nesbitt, John Maxwell
Nixon, John, 1733–1808
Packer, William Fisher

Parrish, Charles
Patterson, Morris
Pattison, Robert Emory
Pollock, James
Porter, David Rittenhouse
Post, George Adams
Preston, Jonas
Rea, Samuel
Read, John, 1769–1854
Roach, John
Roberts, George Brooke
Roberts, Solomon White
Sayre, Robert Heysham
Scranton, George Whitfield
FREDERIKSON, EDNA TUTT
St. John, John Pierce
FREEDLEY, GEORGE
Anderson, Mary
FREEDMAN, DAVID NOEL
Montgomery, James Alan
FREEDMAN, ESTELLE B.
Blair, Emily Newell
Phillips, Lena Madesin
FREEHAFER, EDWARD G.
Anderson, Edwin Hatfield
FREEMAN, DOUGLAS SOUTHALL
Alexander, Edward Porter
Allen, Henry Watkins
Hill, Ambrose Powell
Hood, John Bell
Jackson, Thomas Jonathan
Lee, Fitzhugh
Lee, Robert Edward
Longstreet, James
Stuart, James Ewell Brown
FREEMAN, JOSHUA B.
Quill, Michael Joseph
FREEMAN-WITTHOFT, BONITA
Lomax, Louis Emanuel
FREIDEL, FRANK
Howe, Louis McHenry
Roosevelt, Franklin Delano
FRENCH, JOHN C.
Beadle, Erastus Flavel
Chambers, Robert William
Comfort, Will Levington
Harrison, Henry Sydnor
Hewitt, John Hill
Kennedy, William Sloane
Lynde, Francis
Mathews, William
Mifflin, Lloyd
Miles, George Henry
Norris, Benjamin Franklin
Parke, John
Phillips, Henry
Pinkney, Edward Coote
Preston, Margaret Junkin
Prime, Benjamin Youngs
Randall, James Ryder
Reese, Lizette Woodworth
Requier, Augustus Julian
Scarborough, Dorothy
Sedgwick, Anne Douglas
Thomas, Frederick William
Visscher, William Lightfoot
FRENCH, ROBERT D.
Cochran, Alexander Smith
Hadley, Arthur Twining
Jocelyn, Nathaniel
Lounsbury, Thomas Raynesford

FREUND, PAUL A.
  Brandeis, Louis Dembitz
  Frankfurter, Felix
  Powell, Thomas Reed
FRIDLINGTON, ROBERT J.
  Bamberger, Louis
  Ladd, Kate Macy
FRIED, RICHARD M.
  Millikin, Eugene Donald
  Welch, Joseph Nye
FRIEDENWALD, HARRY
  Reuling, George
FRIEDMAN, B. H.
  Kline, Franz Josef
  Pollock, (Paul), Jackson
FRIEDMANN, HERBERT
  Nelson, Edward William
  Ober, Frederick Albion
  Richmond, Charles Wallace
  Sennett, George Burritt
FRIERSON, J. NELSON
  Johnstone, Job
FRIERSON, WILLIAM LITTLE
  Andrews, Garnett
  Brown, John Calvin
  Brown, Neill Smith
  Carmack, Edward Ward
  Catron, John
  Jackson, Howell Edmunds
  Key, David McKendree
  Lurton, Horace Harmon
FRIESS, HORACE L.
  Adler, Felix
FRIGUGLIETTI, JAMES
  Brinton, Clarence Crane
  Notestein, Wallace
FRIIS, HERMAN R.
  Abert, John James
  Davis, William Morris
FRIO, DANIEL
  Rowe, Lynwood Thomas
FROST, RICHARD H.
  Mooney, Thomas Joseph
FRUTON, JOSEPH S.
  Bergmann, Max
  Meyerhof, Otto
FRYKMAN, GEORGE A.
  Howard, Joseph Kinsey
  Johnson, Albert
  Wallgren, Mon[rad] C[harles]
FUCHS, RALPH F.
  Cook, Walter Wheeler
  Rutledge, Wiley Blount
FUESS, CLAUDE MOORE
  Adams, John
  Bacon, Edwin Munroe
  Bancroft, Cecil Franklin Patch
  Bartlet, William
  Bishop, Robert Roberts
  Bradley, Charles Henry
  Brown, Moses, 1738–1836
  Brown, Moses, 1742–1827
  Brown, Obadiah
  Carter, Franklin
  Carter, Robert, 1819–1879
  Choate, Rufus
  Clifford, John Henry
  Cushing, Caleb
  Cushing, John Perkins
  Cushing, Luther Stearns
  Cutler, Manasseh
  Davis, John, 1787–1854
  Davis, John Chandler Bancroft

Dawes, Henry Laurens
Devens, Charles
Dexter, Timothy
Douglas, William Lewis
Earle, Alice Morse
Edwards, Bela Bates
Edwards, Justin
Eliot, Samuel Atkins
Endicott, Charles Moses
Endicott, William
  Crowninshield
Eustis, Henry Lawrence
Eustis, William
Fields, Annie Adams
Fields, James Thomas
Fox, Gustavus Vasa
Gardner, Henry Joseph
Garrison, William Lloyd
Gaston, William
Ginn, Edwin
Gray, William
Greenhalge, Frederic Thomas
Guild, Curtis, 1827–1911
Guild, Curtis, 1860–1915
Houghton, Henry Oscar
Keep, Robert Porter
King, Rufus
Knox, Henry
Mallary, Rollin Carolas
Mason, Jeremiah
Mattocks, John
Morrill, Justin Smith
Morton, Marcus, 1819–1891
Pearson, Eliphalet
Phillips, John
Phillips, Samuel
Phillips, Wendell
Phillips, William
Stearns, Frank Waterman
FULLER, GEORGE W.
  Dennis, Graham Barclay
  McGraw, John Harte
  Turner, George
  Waterhouse, Frank
  Wilson, John Lockwood
FULLER, JOSEPH V.
  Fish, Hamilton
  Fish, Nicholas
  MacVeagh, Isaac Wayne
  Olney, Richard
  Penfield, Frederic Courtland
  Phelps, William Walter
  Porter, Horace
  Pruyn, Robert Hewson
  Read, John Meredith,
    1837–1896
FULLER, RAYMOND GARFIELD
  Angell, George Thorndike
  Auchmuty, Richard Tylden
FULLERTON, KEMPER
  Bosworth, Edward Increase
  Wright, George Frederick
FULTON, JOHN F.
  Alden, Ebenezer
  Allen, Nathan
  Appleton, Nathaniel Walker
  Beach, Wooster
  Bean, Tarleton Hoffman
  Bigelow, Henry Jacob
  Bigelow, Jacob
  Bigelow, William Sturgis
  Bishop, Seth Scott
  Blackwell, Elizabeth

Bosworth, Francke Huntington
Bowditch, Henry Ingersoll
Boylston, Zabdiel
Brown, Frederic Tilden
Bryant, Joseph Decatur
Buck, Albert Henry
Buck, Gurdon
Buckler, Thomas Hepburn
Bull, William Tillinghast
Bushnell, George Ensign
Cabot, Arthur Tracy
Capen, Nahum
Colton, Gardner Quincy
Cushing, Harvey Williams
Cushny, Arthur Robertson
Darling, Samuel Taylor
Davis, Henry Gassett
Delafield, Edward
Delafield, Francis
Douglass, William
Duane, Alexander
Dusser de Barenne, Joannes
  Gregorius
Dwight, Thomas
Fitz, Reginald Heber
Foster, John Pierrepont
  Codrington
Gale, Benjamin
Gardiner, Silvester
Gerhard, William Wood
Green, Horace
Harrington, Charles
Hayward, George
Horsfield, Thomas
Jackson, Charles Thomas
Jackson, James, 1777–1867
Knapp, Philip Coombs
Kneeland, Samuel
Langford, Nathaniel Pitt
Long, Crawford Williamson
Martin, Henry Austin
Morton, William Thomas Green
Parker, Willard
Pearce, Richard Mills
Post, Wright
Priestley, Joseph
Wells, Horace
FUNK, ELMER H.
  Keating, John Marie
FURFEY, PAUL HANLY
  Regan, Agnes Gertrude
  Teresa, Mother
FURLONG, PATRICK J.
  Hodes, Henry Irving
  Jones, John Price
  Keller, Kaufman Thuma
FURLONG, PHILIP J.
  Kohlmann, Anthony
FURMAN, FRANKLIN DE R.
  Mayer, Alfred Marshall
  Morton, Henry
FURNESS, CAROLINE E.
  Mitchell, Maria
  Whitney, Mary Watson
FURNESS, CLIFTON JOSEPH
  Gilbert, Henry Franklin
  Belknap
FUTRELL, ROBERT FRANK
  Fairchild, Muir Stephen
  Gorrell, Edgar Staley

GABARD, WILLIAM M.
  Hardwick, Thomas William
GABRIEL, RALPH HENRY
  Cross, Wilbur Lucius
  Dana, Samuel Whittlesey
  Gardiner, Robert Hallowell
  Hale, Benjamin
  Hawley, Joseph Roswell
  Holmes, Ezekiel
  Loring, George Bailey
  Lubin, David
  Lyman, Joseph Bardwell
GAFFEY, JAMES P.
  Hanna, Edward Joseph
GAGEY, EDMOND M.
  Bennett, Richard
  Westley, Helen
GAINES, FRANCIS PENDLETON
  Barnwell, Robert Woodward
  Butler, Andrew Pickens
  Butler, Matthew Calbraith
  Butler, Pierce Mason
  Capers, Ellison
  Chamberlain, Daniel Henry
  Coker, James Lide
  Hagood, Johnson
  Hill, Daniel Harvey
  Holmes, Isaac Edward
GALBREATH, CHARLES BURLEIGH
  Carrington, Henry Beebee
  Maxwell, William
  Ross, Alexander Coffman
GALE, ESSON M.
  Rockhill, William Woodville
  Tenney, Charles Daniel
GALLAGHER, KATHARINE JEANNE
  Chase, Philander
  De Koven, James
  Hamilton, William Thomas,
    1820–1888
  Hanson, Alexander Contee,
    1786–1819
  Kemper, Jackson
GALLAHER, RUTH A.
  Curtis, Samuel Ryan
GALLINGER, HERBERT P.
  Moore, Zephaniah Swift
GALLOWAY, EILENE MARIE
  Hegeman, John Rogers
  Proctor, Lucien Brock
  Rambaut, Mary Lucinda
    Bonney
GALLUP, CLARENCE M.
  Benedict, David
GALPIN, W. FREEMAN
  Miller, Warner
  Smith, Peter
GALVIN, JOHN T.
  Green, William Joseph, Jr.
  Lawrence, David Leo
  Tinkham, George Holden
GAMBRELL, HERBERT P.
  Ellet, Charles
  Hyer, Robert Stewart
  Menard, Michel Branamour
  Yoakum, Henderson
GANFIELD, DOROTHY
  Husting, Paul Oscar
GANNON, DAVID
  Francis, Paul James
GANOE, WILLIAM A.
  Halleck, Henry Wager
  Hooker, Joseph

Mason, Richard Barnes
Meade, George Gordon
Scott, Winfield
Totten, Joseph Gilbert
Twiggs, David Emanuel
Warren, Gouverneur Kemble
Washington, John Macrae
Wool, John Ellis
Worth, William Jenkins
GARBER, PAUL N.
  Lane, John
  Olin, Stephen
  Paine, Robert
  Pierce, George Foster
  Soule, Joshua
  Waugh, Beverly
  Whatcoat, Richard
  Wiley, Ephraim Emerson
  Williams, Robert
  Winans, William
GARBY, LEE
  Mapes, Charles Victor
  Mapes, James Jay
  Piper, Charles Vancouver
  Voorhees, Edward Burnett
GARDNER, ALBERT TEN EYCK
  Barnard, George Grey
GARDNER, LLOYD C.
  Dulles, John Foster
GARDNER, W. U.
  Allen, Edgar
GARLICH, RICHARD CECIL, JR.
  Mazzei, Philip
GARRAGHAN, GILBERT J.
  Cataldo, Joseph Maria
  O'Fallon, John
GARRATT, GEORGE A.
  Bryant, Ralph Clement
  Record, Samuel James
GARRATY, JOHN A.
  Mondell, Frank Wheeler
  Woytinsky, Wladimir
    Savelievich
GARRETT, C. G. B.
  Bensley, Robert Russell
  Carlson, Anton Julius
  Novy, Frederick George
  Steinman, David Barnard
  Warren, Henry Ellis
  Wiener, Norbert
GARRETT, CHARLES
  Thacher, Thomas Day
GARRETT, SHIRLEY STONE
  Ferguson, John Calvin
  Frame, Alice Seymour Browne
  Lyon, David Willard
  Pott, Francis Lister Hawks
GARRETT, WENDELL D.
  Nutting, Wallace
  Sack, Israel
GARRISON, CURTIS W.
  Brown, George William
  Calvert, Charles Benedict
  Carroll, Daniel
  Chambers, Ezekiel Forman
  Clayton, Joshua
  Clayton, Thomas
  Gist, Mordecai
  Hall, Willard
  Hambleton, Thomas Edward
  Handy, Alexander Hamilton
  Harrington, Samuel Maxwell
  Hughes, George Wurtz

Johns, Kensey, 1759–1848
Johns, Kensey, 1791–1857
McDonogh, John
McLane, Allan
Mitchell, Nathaniel
Morgan, John Tyler
Stoddert, Benjamin
Swain, James Barrett
Tome, Jacob
Wyeth, John
GARRISON, FIELDING H.
  Bowditch, Henry Pickering
  Handerson, Henry Ebenezer
GARRISON, F. LYNWOOD
  Neilson, William George
  Outerbridge, Alexander Ewing
  Trautwine, John Cresson
  Vanuxem, Lardner
  Wahl, William Henry
GARRISON, HAZEL SHIELDS
  Semple, Ellen Churchill
  Taylor, Richard Cowling
GARRISON, WINIFRED ERNEST
  Richardson, Robert
  Scott, Walter
GARSOIAN, NINA G.
  Vasiliev, Alexander
    Alexandrovich
GASTON, EDWIN W., JR.
  Richter, Conrad Michael
GATES, PAUL W.
  Buley, Roscoe Carlyle
  Farrand, Livingston
  Shannon, Fred Albert
  Warren, George Frederick
GATES, SYLVESTER
  Sacco, Nicola
GATEWOOD, WILLARD B., JR.
  Harrison, Francis Burton
  Ironside, Henry Allan
  Upshaw, William David
GAULD, CHARLES A.
  Farquhar, Percival
GAUSTAD, EDWIN S.
  Stokes, Anson Phelps
GAVIN, DONALD P.
  Schrembs, Joseph
GAYLORD, WINFIELD R.
  Sargent, Frank Pierce
  Sorge, Friedrich Adolph
GEBHARD, DAVID
  Schindler, Rudolph Michael
GEHRENBECK, RICHARD K.
  Davisson, Clinton Joseph
  Frank, Philipp G.
  Millikan, Clark Blanchard
  Rademacher, Hans
  Stern, Otto
GEILING, E. M. K.
  Abel, John Jacob
GEISER, KARL FREDERICK
  Brice, Calvin Stewart
GEISER, SAMUEL W.
  Boll, Jacob
  Lincecum, Gideon
  Lindheimer, Ferdinand Jacob
  Mohr, Charles Theodore
  Montgomery, Edmund Duncan
  Munson, Thomas Volney
  Ney, Elisabet
  Wright, Charles

GEIST, CHRISTOPHER D.
  O'Brien, Willis Harold
GELB, BARBARA
  O'Neill, Eugene
GELFAND, LAWRENCE E.
  Polk, Frank Lyon
GENTILE, RICHARD H.
  Clement, Frank Goad
  Herter, Christian Archibald
  Shipley, Ruth Bielaski
GENZMER, GEORGE H.
  Acrelius, Israel
  Adler, George J.
  Agnus, Felix
  Alden, Raymond Macdonald
  Ayer, Francis Wayland
  Barr, Charles
  Bateman, Newton
  Baugher, Henry Louis
  Benjamin, Samuel Greene
    Wheeler
  Bennett, de Robigne Mortimer
  Bennett, Floyd
  Berkenmeyer, Wilhelm
    Christoph
  Bewley, Anthony
  Bimeler, Joseph Michael
  Bingham, Amelia
  Bingham, George Caleb
  Bird, Frederic Mayer
  Birkbeck, Morris
  Bixby, Horace Ezra
  Blake, John Lauris
  Blinn, Holbrook
  Boehm, John Philip
  Bolles, Frank
  Boltzius, Johann Martin
  Bonaparte, Elizabeth Patterson
  Bourne, Nehemiah
  Boynton, Charles Brandon
  Bradford, Gamaliel
  Brady, Cyrus Townsend
  Brattle, Thomas
  Brown, Goold
  Browne, Benjamin Frederick
  Bryant, John Howard
  Bryce, Lloyd Stephens
  Bucher, John Conrad
  Buford, Napoleon Bonaparte
  Bunce, Oliver Bell
  Burleigh, George Shepard
  Cabell, James Lawrence
  Campanius, John
  Campbell, William Henry
  Capers, William
  Carpenter, Francis Bicknell
  Carryl, Guy Wetmore
  Chambers, Talbot Wilson
  Chang and Eng
  Channing, William Ellery,
    1818–1901
  Child, Francis James
  Clark, Charles Heber
  Clarke, Helen Archibald
  Clarke, Joseph Ignatius
    Constantine
  Clarke, Mary Francis
  Cleveland, Aaron
  Cleveland, Richard Jeffry
  Cobb, Sylvanus
  Cobbett, William
  Codman, John
  Coggeshall, George

Coit, Henry Augustus
Coit, Henry Leber
Coit, Thomas Winthrop
Colby, Frank Moore
Condon, Thomas
Converse, Edmund Cogswell
Converse, James Booth
Coppens, Charles
Copway, George
Crafts, William
Crane, Frank
Crane, Jonathan Townley
Crapsey, Algernon Sidney
Creamer, David
Crosby, Fanny
Crowninshield, Benjamin
  Williams
Crowninshield, Jacob
Cutler, Carroll
Dall, Caroline Wells Healey
Dana, John Cotton
Davidson, Lucretia Maria
Davidson, Margaret Miller
Davidson, Robert
Davis, Matthew Livingston
Day, Henry Noble
Day, James Roscoe
Deindörfer, Johannes
Demme, Charles Rudolph
Derby, Elias Hasket, 1766–1826
Derby, Elias Hasket, 1803–1880
Disbrow, William Stephen
Doane, George Washington
Dockstader, Lew
Dod, Albert Baldwin
Dole, Charles Fletcher
Downing, George
Drury, John Benjamin
Duganne, Augustine Joseph
  Hickey
Durand Elie Magloire
Duryea, Hermanes Barkulo
Dwight, Francis
Dwight, Theodore, 1796–1866
Dylander, John
Eastman, Charles Gamage
Eastman, Harvey Gridley
Eddy, Daniel Clarke
Eliot, Samuel
Elliot, James
Embury, Emma Catherine
Emerson, Edward Waldo
Emerson, Mary Moody
Emerson, Oliver Farrar
Evans, Edward Payson
Fairbank, Calvin
Falckner, Daniel
Falckner, Justus
Fay, Theodore Sedgwick
Fechter, Charles Albert
Fernald, James Champlin
Ferris, Isaac
Finotti, Joseph Maria
Fitz, Henry
Fleischmann, Charles Louis
Fletcher, Horace
Flower, George
Flower, Richard
Flügel, Ewald
Folger, Henry Clay
Folger, Peter
Forsyth, John, 1810–1886
Fosdick, Charles Austin

Fox, Richard Kyle
Francke, Kuno
Frankland, Lady Agnes Surriage
Franklin, James
Freedman, Andrew
Freeman, Bernardus
Frelinghuysen, Theodorus
  Jacobus
Frey, Joseph Samuel Christian
  Frederick
Frisbie, Levi
Fritschel, Conrad Sigmund
Fritschel, Gottfried Leonhard
  Wilhelm
Frothingham, Nathaniel
  Langdon
Frothingham, Octavius Brooks
Fuller, Hiram
Furness, Horace Howard,
  1833–1912
Furness, Horace Howard,
  1865–1930
Fussell, Bartholomew
Gayler, Charles
Gerhart, Emanuel Vogel
Gibbons, James Sloan
Gibbons, William
Giesler-Anneke, Mathilde
  Franziska
Gillespie, William Mitchell
Godfrey, Benjamin
Goetschius, John Henry
Good, James Isaac
Good, Jeremiah Haak
Goodall, Thomas
Goodrich, Charles Augustus
Goodrich, Chauncey
Goodwin, John Noble
Gould, Benjamin Apthorp
Gould, Hannah Flagg
Grabau Johannes Andreas
  August
Gräbner, August Lawrence
Graham, George Rex
Gray, Asa
Greene, Albert Gorton
Greenwald, Emanuel
Griffin, Edward Dorr
Griffin, Solomon Bulkley
Griswold, Rufus Wilmot
Gros, John Daniel
Grossmann, Georg Martin
Grube, Bernhard Adam
Guild, Reuben Aldridge
Guiney, Louise Imogen
Gummere, Francis Barton
Gummere, John
Gummere, Samuel James
Gunter, Archibald Clavering
Hammett, Samuel Adams
Harbaugh, Henry
Harby, Isaac
Hardy, Arthur Sherburne
Harpster, John Henry
Harris, Joel Chandler
Hartwig, Johann Christoph
Hay, Charles Augustus
Hazelius, Ernest Lewis
Helffenstein, John Albert
  Conrad
Helmuth, Justus Henry
  Christian
Hendel, John William

Henkel, Paul
Hentz, Caroline Lee Whiting
Herman, Lebrecht Frederick
Herr, John
Hillard, George Stillman
Holland, Edwin Clifford
Horn, Edward Traill
Hosmer, William Howe Cuyler
Hubbs, Rebecca
Hummel, Abraham Henry
Jacobs, Michael
Jacoby, Ludwig Sigmund
Jones, Sybil
Judson, Edward Zane Carroll
Keimer, Samuel
Kelpius, Johann
Kettell, Samuel
Klipstein, Louis Frederick
Knapp, Samuel Lorenzo
Kocherthal, Josua von
Kollack, Shepard
Krauth, Charles Philip
Krez, Konrad
Kroeger, Adolf Ernst
Kunze, John Christopher
Kurtz, Benjamin
Latrobe, Charles Hazlehurst
Leighton, William
Leland, Charles Godfrey
Leonard, Levi Washburn
Lewis, Alfred Henry
Lochman, John George
Loy, Matthias
Lyon, Harris Merton
Mann, Mary Tyler Peabody
Mann, William Julius
Mason, Stevens Thomson
Maxim, Hiram Stevens
Mayer, Lewis
Mayer, Philip Frederick
Mayo, Frank
Melsheimer, Friedrich Valentin
Miller, George
Miller, John Peter
Moldehnke, Edward Frederick
Morris, John Gottlieb
Morse, Henry Dutton
Morse, Samuel Finley Breese
Muhlenberg, Frederick
   Augustus
Muhlenberg, Frederick
   Augustus Conrad
Mühlenberg, Gotthilf Henry
   Ernest
Muhlenberg, Henry Augustus
   Philip
Mühlenberg, Henry Melchior
Muhlenberg, John Peter Gabriel
Muhlenberg, William Augustus
Murdock, Frank Hitchcock
Murray, Lindley
Notz, Frederick William
   Augustus
Oakley, Annie
O'Brien, Frederick
O'Connor, William Douglas
O'Hara, Theodore
Otterbein, Philip William
Parrington, Vernon Louis
Parton, James
Passavant, William Alfred
Pastorius, Francis Daniel
Patch, Sam

Peabody, Oliver William Bourn
Peabody, William Bourn Oliver
Peck, Harry Thurston
Pickering, John
Pierpont, John
Pilkington, James
Pinkham, Lydia Estes
Plumbe, John
Plummer, Henry
Pond, Frederick Eugene
Pratt, Daniel
Printz, Johan Björnsson
Quick, John Herbert
Rafinesque, Constantine Samuel
Rapp, George
Read, Thomas Buchanan
Reed, Henry Hope
Reed, Myrtle
Reed, Sampson
Rice, Dan
Richardson, Albert Deane
Richardson, Charles Francis
Ricord, Frederick William
Rising, Johan Classon
Robinson, Rowland Evans
Roe, Edward Payson
Rolfe, William James
Rose, Aquila
Ross, Betsy
Roulstone, George
Rupp, Israel Daniel
Sachse, Julius Friedrich
Sadtler, John Philip Benjamin
Sanborn, Franklin Benjamin
Saxe, John Godfrey
Schaeffer, Charles Frederick
Schaeffer, Charles William
Schaeffer, David Frederick
Schaeffer, Frederick Christian
Schaeffer, Frederick David
Schmucker, Beale Melanchthon
Schmucker, John George
Schöpf, Johann David
Seidensticker, Oswald
Seip, Theodore Lorenzo
Seiss, Joseph Augustus
Seybert, John
Shaw, Henry Wheeler
Shaw, John, 1778–1809
Short, Charles
Smith, Benjamin Eli
Smith, Byron Caldwell
Sower, Christopher, 1693–1758
Sower, Christopher, 1721–1784
Spaeth, Adolph
Spencer, Platt Rogers
Stöckhardt, Karl Georg
Stoever, Martin Luther
Stokes, Caroline Phelps
Stokes, Olivia Egleston Phelps
Stratton, Charles Sherwood
Tanneberger, David
Teall, Francis Augustus
Tenney, William Jewett
Thompson, Joseph Parrish
Traubel, Horace L.
Trowbridge, John Townsend
Victor, Frances Fuller
Victor, Orville James
Walther, Carl Ferdinand
   Wilhelm
Weiss, John
White, Richard Grant

Wilkes, George
Williams, Ephraim
Winebrenner, John
Zinzendorf, Nicolaus Ludwig
GENZMER, MARGARET WADSWORTH
   Graham Sylvester
   McCann, Alfred Watterson
GEORGINI, SUSAN J.
   Friedlaender, Walter Ferdinand
GERBER, WILLIAM
   O'Brien, Thomas James
   O'Shaughnessy, Nelson Jarvis
   Waterbury
GERIG, JOHN LAWRENCE
   Todd, Henry Alfred
GEROULD, JAMES THAYER
   Vinton, Frederic
GEROULD, JOHN H.
   Patten, William
GERRY, MARGARITA S.
   Howe, Julia Ward
GERSON, VIRGINIA
   Fitch, William Clyde
GESELL, BEATRICE CHANDLER
   Blow, Susan Elizabeth
   Harrison, Elizabeth
GETTLEMAN, MARVIN E.
   Stokes, Isaac Newton Phelps
GHENT, W.J.
   Adair, James
   Addicks, John Edward
   O'Sullivan
   Allerton, Samuel Waters
   Ambler, James Markham
   Marshall
   Armour, Philip Danforth
   Armstrong, George Buchanan
   Astor, John Jacob, 1763–1848
   Astor, John Jacob, 1822–1890
   Astor, John Jacob, 1864–1912
   Astor, William Backhouse
   Astor, William Waldorf
   Atkinson, Henry
   Atwater, Caleb
   Avery, Benjamin Parke
   Ayer, Edward Everett
   Baer, George Frederick
   Baird, Matthew
   Baker, James
   Baldwin, John
   Ballard, Bland Williams
   Bard, William
   Barker, Jacob
   Barker, Wharton
   Barlow, John Whitney
   Barnum, Zenus
   Bass, Sam
   Bates, Barnabas
   Beale, Edward Fitzgerald
   Belden, Josiah
   Bell, James Stroud
   Bent, Charles
   Bent, William
   Bidwell, John
   Billy the Kid
   Bliss, William Dwight Porter
   Boas, Emil Leopold
   Bonneville, Benjamin Louis
   Eulalie de
   Boone, Daniel
   Bowie, James
   Brady, Mathew B.
   Breen, Patrick

Bridgman, Herbert Lawrence
Bright Eyes
Broderick, David Colbreth
Buchanan, Joseph Ray
Burden, Henry
Burgess, Edward
Burnett, Henry Lawrence
Burnett, Peter Hardeman
Californa Joe
Cameron, Robert Alexander
Campbell, Robert
Carson, Christopher
Carter, William Samuel
Chisum, John Simpson
Chittenden, Hiram Martin
Chouteau, Auguste Pierre
Chouteau, Jean Pierre
Chouteau, René Auguste
Clyman, James
Cody, William Frederick
Coleman, William Tell
Colgate, James Boorman
Colgate, William
Colter, John
Connelly, Henry
Connor, Patrick Edward
Crawford, John Wallace
   (Captain Jack)
Crazy Horse
Crockett, David
Crooks, Ramsay
Cumming, Alfred
Custer, George Armstrong
Dalton, Robert
Debs, Eugene Victor
De Leon, Daniel
Dixon, William
Dorion, Marie
Farnham, Russel
Fitzpatrick, Thomas
Fonda, John H.
Friday
Gall
Geronimo
Girty, Simon
Gist, Christopher
Glass, Hugh
Grass, John
Gratiot, Charles
Gregg, Josiah
Grouard, Frank
Gunnison, John Williams
Harmon, Daniel Williams
Haywood, William Dudley
Henry, Andrew
Horn, Tom
Hunt, Wilson Price
Inman, Henry, 1837–1899
James, Jesse Woodson
James, Thomas
Joseph
Kearney, Stephen Watts
Kenton, Simon
La Barge, Joseph
Laclede, Pierre
Langworthy, James Lyon
Laramie, Jacques
Larpenteur, Charles
Leavenworth, Henry
Ledyard, John
Lee, Jason
Leonard, Zenas
Little Crow V

Lynch, James Mathew
McClellan, Robert
McLaughlin, James
Marsh, Grant Prince
Mason, Samuel
Masterson, William Barclay
Maus, Marion Perry
Maxwell, Lucien Bonaparte
Meek, Joseph L.
Meeker, Ezra
Menard, Pierre
Morrison, William
Murrieta, Joaquin
Newell, Robert
Ouray
Parsons, Albert Richard
Pattie, James Ohio
Pryor, Nathaniel
Quanah
Red Cloud
Red Wing
Reynolds, Charles Alexander
Richardson, Wilds Preston
Robidou, Antoine
Ross, Alexander
Russell, Osborne
Russell, William Henry
Russell, William Hepburn
Sacagawea
Sauganash
Sequoyah
Sibley, George Champlain
Sitting Bull
Slade, Joseph Alfred
Spotted Tail
Stansbury, Howard
Stearns, Abel
Stilwell, Simpson Everett
Stokes, Montford
Stone, Warren Sanford
Stuart, Granville
Stuart, Robert
Swinton, John
Tammany
Thornton, Jessy Quinn
Tibbles, Thomas Henry
Tilghman, William Matthew
Truman, Benjamin Cummings
Wabasha
Walker, Joseph Reddeford
Warner, Jonathan Trumbull
Warren, Josiah
Washakie
Williams, William Sherley
Winemucca, Sarah
Wislizenus, Frederick Adolph
Wolfskill, William
Wootton, Richens Lacy
Young, Ewing
Younger, Thomas Coleman
Yount, George Concepción
GIESE, WILLIAM FREDERIC
   Owen, Edward Thomas
GIFFEN, M. B.
   Sanford, Henry Shelton
GIFFORD, ALICE J.
   Beard, Mary
GIGLIO, JAMES N.
   Brown, Walter Folger
   Daugherty, Harry Micajah
   Edison, Charles
   Rich, Robert
   Taber, John

GILBERT, DANIEL R.
   Cheyney, Edward Potts
   Davis, Ernest R. ("Ernie")
   Lombardi, Vincent Thomas
   Marciano, Rocky
   Neyland, Robert Reese, Jr.
GILCREEST, EDGAR L.
   Toland, Hugh Huger
GILES, HOWARD E.
   Hambridge, Jay
GILL, BRENDAN
   Ross, Harold Wallace
GILL, MERTON M.
   Rapaport, David
GILL, TOM
   Pack, Charles Lathrop
GILLIAM, J. F.
   Rostovtzeff, Michael Ivanovitch
GILMORE, C. W.
   Gidley, James Williams
GILMORE, MYRON P.
   Berenson, Bernard
GINGER, RAY
   Darrow, Clarence Seward
GINGERICH, OWEN
   Baade, Wilhelm Heinrich
      Walter
GIPSON, LAWRENCE H.
   Clewell, John Henry
   Coppée, Henry
   Ettwein, John
   Fisher, Sydney George,
      1856–1927
   Ingersoll, Jared, 1722–1781
   Packer, Asa
   Schweinitz, Edmund Alexander
      de
GLASRUD, BRUCE A.
   Dean, William Henry, Jr.
GLASS, H. BENTLEY
   Shull, George Harrison
GLASSER, OTTO
   Williams, Francis Henry
GLEASON, H. A.
   Britton, Nathaniel Lord
   Hollick, Charles Arthur
GLEASON, PHILIP
   Noll, John Francis
GLENN, LEONIDAS CHALMERS
   Troost, Gerard
GLUECK, NELSON
   Fisher, Clarence Stanley
GOBLE, GEORGE W.
   Grier, Robert Cooper
   Hohfeld, Wesley Newcomb
   Todd, Thomas
   Treat, Samuel Hubbel
   Trimble, Robert
   Walker, Pinkney Houston
   Washington, Bushrod
   Wilson, William, 1794–1857
   Woods, William Allen
   Zeisler, Sigmund
GODDARD, HAROLD C.
   Emerson, William
GODWIN, BLAKE-MORE
   Libbey, Edward Drummond
   Stevens, George Washington
GOEBEL, DOROTHY BURNE
   Harrison, William Henry
GOEBEL, JULIUS
   Körner, Gustav Philipp

GOEN, C. C.
Hughes, Edwin Holt
Newton, Joseph Fort
Scarborough, Lee Rutland
GOLD, HARRY
Hatcher, Robert Anthony
GOLDER, FRANK A.
Baranov, Alexander Andreevich
GOLDMAN, EDWARD A.
Henshaw, Henry Wetherbee
GOLDMAN, RICHARD FRANKO
Damrosch, Frank Heino
Goldmark, Rubin
GOLDSTEIN, MALCOLM
Beery, Wallace Fitzgerald
Blackton, James Stuart
Epstein, Philip G.
Garfield, John
Kaufman, George S.
Rossen, Robert
GOLENBOCK, PETER J.
Bender, Charles Albert
("Chief")
Walsh, Edward Augustine
GOLER, GEORGE W.
Moore, Edward Mott
GOMERY, DOUGLAS
Warner, Harry Morris
GOMES, PETER J.
Sperry, Willard Learoyd
GOOD, CARTER V.
McAndrew, William
Wirt, William Albert
GOOD, HARRY GEHMAN
Picket, Albert
Youmans, Edward Livingston
Youmans, William Jay
GOODLOE, ROBERT W.
Harrell, John
McAnally, David Rice
McFerrin, John Berry
Marvin, Enoch Mather
GOODMAN, WALTER
Rankin, John Elliott
GOODSELL, FRED FIELD
Barton, James Levi
GOODSTEIN, JUDITH R.
Tolman, Richard Chace
GOODWIN, CARDINAL
Browne, John Ross
Mills, Cyrus Taggart
Mills, Susan Lincoln Tolman
GOODWIN, G. F.
Del Ruth, Roy
Dumont, Margaret
Horton, Edward Everett, Jr.
Matthews, Joseph Brown
Taylor, Robert
Tracy, Spencer Bonaventure
GOODWIN, WILLARD E.
Young, Hugh Hampton
GOODYKOONTZ, COLIN B.
Ammons, Elias Milton
Bowen, Thomas Meade
Brown, Henry Cordis
Costigan, Edward Prentiss
Hulbert, Archer Butler
O'Donnell, Thomas Jefferson
Patterson, Thomas MacDonald
Pitkin, Frederick Walker
Sewall, Joseph Addison
Willard, James Field

GOOSSEN, E. C.
Davis, Stuart
GORDON, ARMISTEAD CHURCHILL, JR.
Banister, John
Cabell, Joseph Carrington
Cameron, William Evelyn
Claiborne, Nathaniel Herbert
Cocke, John Hartwell
Cocke, Philip St. George
Dabney, Richard
Dabney, Thomas Smith Gregory
Doddridge, Joseph
Ewell, Benjamin Stoddert
Ewell, Richard Stoddert
Fleming, William
Garnett, James Mercer
Garnett, Muscoe Russell Hunter
Garnett, Robert Selden
Gholson, Thomas Saunders
Gholson, William Yates
Gilmer, Thomas Walker
Goode, John
Graham, John
Green, James Stephens
Griffin, Cyrus
Grigsby, Hugh Blair
Hardin, John
Hayne, Paul Hamilton
Heath, James Ewell
Hening, William Waller
Innes, James
Jackson, John George
Janney, Samuel McPherson
Johnston, Peter
Jones, Hugh
Jones, John Beauchamps
Jones, John William
Jones, John Winston
Jones, Joseph
Jouett, John
Keith, James
Law, Sallie Chapman Gordon
McCabe, John Collins
McCabe, William Gordon
Mathews, Samuel
Munford, Robert
Percy, George
Pory, John
Pott, John
Robertson, John
Sandys, George
Schele De Vere, Maximilian
Southall, James Cocke
Stanard, Mary Mann Page Newton
Stanard, William Glover
Stith, William
Strachey, William
Ticknor, Francis Orray
Timrod, Henry
Tompkins, Sally Louisa
GORDON, RITA WERNER
De Priest, Oscar Stanton
GOREN, ARTHUR A.
Magnes, Judah Leon
GORTNER, ROSS AIKEN
Harris, James Arthur
GOTWALS, VERNON
De Luca, Giuseppe
Speaks, Oley

Yon, Pietro Alessandro
GOUGH, ROBERT
Bell, James Ford
GOULD, HARRIS PERLEY
Campbell, George Washington, 1817–1898
Coxe, William
Gale, Elbridge
Garey, Thomas Andrew
Kendrick, William
GOULD, KENNETH M.
McClintock, Oliver
Murphy, Francis
Nation, Carry Amelia Moore
Noss, Theodore Bland
Oliver, Henry William
Porter, Stephen Geyer
GOULD, LEWIS L.
Breckinridge, Henry Skillman
Connally, Thomas Terry ("Tom")
Lanham, Frederick Garland ("Fritz")
McNutt, Paul Vories
Pool, Joe Richard
Stanley, Augustus Owsley
Sumners, Hatton, William
GOULD, OLIVIA H.
Wilder, Laura Ingalls
GOULD, STEPHEN JAY
Cushman, Joseph Augustine
GOWANS, ALAN
Maginnis, Charles Donagh
GOWEN, HERBERT H.
Shelton, Edward Mason
GRACY, DAVID B., II
Bennett, Henry Garland
GRAD, FRANK P.
Chamberlain, Joseph Perkins
GRAEBNER, ALAN
Maier, Walter Arthur
GRAEBNER, NORMAN A.
George, Walter Franklin
GRAEBNER, WILLIAM
Coyle, Grace Longwell
Kilpatrick, William Heard
Rice, John Andrew
Spargo, John
GRAF, LEROY P.
McReynolds, Samuel Davis
GRAFF, HENRY F.
Cobb, Tyrus Raymond ("Ty")
Gehrig, Henry Louis
Hornsby, Rogers
Ott, Melvin Thomas ("Mel")
Ruppert, Jacob
Wagner, John Peter
Zimmerman, Henry ("Heinie")
GRAFLY, DOROTHY
Knight, Daniel Ridgway
Krimmel, John Lewis
Lambdin, James Reid
Miller, Leslie William
Rehn, Frank Knox Morton
Roberts, Howard
Rothermel, Peter Frederick
Sartain, Emily
Sartain, John
Sartain, Samuel
Sartain, William
Schussele, Christian
Sharples, James
Smith, Russell

Smith, Xanthus Russell
Spencer, Robert
Stephens, Alice Barber
Taylor, Frank Walter
Wood, Joseph
Wright, Joseph
GRAHAM, ALICE ARCHER
Prentiss, Elizabeth Payson
GRAHAM, FRANK
Rickard, George Lewis
GRAHAM, GLADYS
Bingham, Anne Willing
Crapsey, Adelaide
Dodge, Mary Abigail
Doubleday, Neltje De Graff
Douglas, Amanda Minnie
Dupuy, Eliza Ann
Jeffrey, Rosa Griffith Vertner
Johnson
Kinney, Elizabeth Clementine
Dodge Stedman
Lazarus, Emma
GRAHAM, HUGH DAVIS
Wright, Fielding Lewis
GRAHAM, JOHN A.
Morley, Sylvanus Griswold
GRAHAM, OTIS L., JR.
McAdoo, William Gibbs
Russell, Charles Edward
GRAHAM, PATRICIA ALBJERG
Caldwell, Otis William
GRAHAM, THEODORA R.
Williams, William Carlos
GRAHAM, WILLIAM CREIGHTON
Smith, John Merlin Powis
GRAM, LEWIS M.
Greene, Charles Ezra
GRANCSAY, STEPHEN V.
Riggs, William Henry
GRANGER, WALTER
Lucas, Frederic Augustus
Matthew, William Diller
Ward, Henry Augustus
GRANNISS, RUTH SHEPARD
Gilliss, Walter
Matthews, William
GRANT, E. ALLISON
Payne, John Howard
GRANT, FRANCIS C.
Frazier, Charles Harrison
GRANT, H. ROGER
Seiberling, Frank Augustus
Stearns, Frank Ballou
GRANT, WALTER S.
Anderson, Joseph Reid
Armstrong, Frank C.
Ashby, Turner
Benham, Henry Washington
GRANTHAM, DEWEY W.
Bilbo, Theodore Gilmore
Lea, Luke
Owen, Robert Latham
GRANTHAM, G. E.
Nichols, Edward Leamington
GRAS, N. S. B.
Baker, George Fisher
Flint, Charles Ranlett
GRATON, L. C.
Ransome, Frederick Leslie
GRAVES, CHARLES
Alger, William Rounseville
Allen, Joseph Henry
Ames, Charles Gordon

Peabody, Andrew Preston
Potter, William James
Powell, Edward Payson
Sears, Edmund Hamilton
Thayer, Thomas Baldwin
Whittemore, Thomas
GRAVES, HENRY SOLON
Fernow, Bernhard Edward
Hough, Franklin Benjamin
Toumey, James William
GRAY, JAMES
Burton, Richard Eugene
GRAY, LOUIS HERBERT
Bradley, Charles William
Brown, John Porter
Mills, Lawrence Heyworth
Nies, James Buchanan
GRAY, RALPH D.
Ball, George Alexander
GRAY, VIRGINIA
Richardson, Tobias Gibson
Riddell, John Leonard
GRAY, VIRGINIA GEARHART
Haarstick, Henry Christian
Hall, Luther Egbert
Souchon, Edmond
Stone, Warren
GRAYBAR, LLOYD J.
Blandy, William Henry Purnell
Eichelberger, Robert Lawrence
Kimball, Dan Able
Millis, Walter
Nimitz, Chester William
Shaw, Albert
Snyder, Howard McCrum
Talbott, Harold Elstner
Turner, Richmond Kelly
GREBSTEIN, SHELDON NORMAN
Lewis, Harry Sinclair
GREELEY, W. B.
Donovan, John Joseph
Griggs, Everett Gallup
GREELY, A. W.
Hall, Charles Francis
Hayes, Isaac Israel
Lockwood, James Booth
GREELY, JOHN N.
Merritt, Wesley
Mordecai, Alfred
Myer, Albert James
GREEN, EDWIN L.
Middleton, John Izard
Nott, Henry Junius
Rivers, William James
GREEN, FLETCHER M.
Fleming, Walter Lynwood
Green, Benjamin Edwards
Green, Duff
Reed, John, 1757–1845
Spalding, Thomas
Stephens, Linton
Thompson, Wiley
Towns, George Washington
Bonaparte
Troup, George Michael
Walton, George
Wofford, William Tatum
Young, Pierce Manning Butler
GREENE, EVARTS B.
James, Edmund Janes
Johnson, William Samuel

GREENE, JEROME DAVIS
Buttrick, Wallace
GREENE, LARRY A.
Malcolm X
GREENLEAF, WILLIAM
Budd, Edward Gowen
Fisher, Frederic John
Ford, Henry
Knudsen, William S.
Newberry, Truman Handy
Norton, Charles Hotchkiss
Selig, William Nicholas
GREENOUGH, CHESTER N.
Wendell, Barrett
GREENSLET, FERRIS
Lodge, George Cabot
GREENSTEIN, JESSE L.
Jansky, Karl Guthe
GREENWALD, DOROTHY
Scott, Fred Newton
Tarbox, Increase Niles
GREEP, ROY O.
Howe, Percy Rogers
GREEVER, GARLAND
Cheney, John Vance
GREGORIE, ANNE KING
Hill, William
Howe, George
Kinlock, Cleland
LaBorde, Maximilian
Ladd, Catherine
Lee, Thomas
Lucas, Jonathan, 1754–1821
Lucas, Jonathan, 1775–1832
Pickens, Andrew
Pinckney, Elizabeth Lucas
Ravenel, Edmund
Ravenel, Harriott Horry
Rutledge
Read, Jacob
Smith, Henry Augustus
Middleton
Smith, William Loughton
Sumter, Thomas
Thomson, William
Vesey, Denmark, c. 1767–1822
Wayne, Arthur Trezevant
Williamson, Andrew
Wilson, John Leighton
Winn, Richard
GREGORY, WILLIAM B.
Harrod, Benjamin Morgan
Hébert, Louis
GREINER, DONALD J.
Frost, Robert Lee
GRENIER, JUDSON A.
Chandler, Harry
GRICE, WARREN
Akerman, Amos Tappan
Bacon, Augustus Octavius
GRIEVES, BERENICE ELAINE
Southworth, Emma Dorothy
Eliza Nevitte
GRIFFITH, ERNEST S.
Matthews, Nathan
Parker, Isaac
Pierce, Henry Lillie
GRIFFITH, IVOR
Remington, Joseph Price
GRIFFITH, RICHARD
Gilbert, John
Mix, Tom

GRIFFITH, ROBERT
  McCarthy, Joseph Raymond
GRIGG, E. R. N.
  Coutard, Henri
GRILL, FREDERICK
  Schneider, Albert
GRIMES, ALAN P.
  Ogg, Frederic Austin
  Rossiter, Clinton Lawrence, III
  Smith, Thomas Vernor
GRINNELL, FRANK W.
  Sheldon, Henry Newton
  Sprague, Peleg
  Stearns, Asahel
GRINNELL, JOSEPH
  Cooper, James Graham
GRINSTEAD, WREN JONES
  Colton, Elizabeth Avery
GRINSTEIN, HYMAN B.
  Revel, Bernard
GROAT, GEORGE GORHAM
  Arthur, Peter M.
GROSVENOR, GILBERT
  Bell, Alexander Melville
GRUBAR, FRANCIS S.
  Archipenko, Alexander
GRUENING, ERNEST
  Macy, John Albert
GRUENING, MARTHA
  Stokes, Rose Harriet Pastor
  Walker, David, 1785–1830
  Walker, Sarah Breedlove
  Ware, Edmund Asa
  White, George Leonard
GRUENSTEIN, S. E.
  Eddy, Clarence
GRUSD, EDWARD E.
  Monsky, Henry
GUE, GURNEY C.
  Hildreth, Samuel Clay
  Morgan, Justin
  Rarey, John Solomon
  Ten Broeck, Richard
GUEST, IVOR
  Fokine, Michel
GUILDAY, PETER
  Bayley, James Rosevelt
GULICK, CHARLES BURTON
  Dyer, Louis
  Goodwin, William Watson
  Greenough, James Bradstreet
  Leach, Abby
  Moore, Clifford Herschel
  Sophocles, Evangelinus
    Apostolides
  White, John Williams
  Wright, John Henry
GUMMERE, AMELIA MOTT
  Benezet, Anthony
GUMMERE, RICHARD M.
  Parrish, Anne
GUNN, SIDNEY
  Johnston, Thomas
  Joy, Thomas
  Kneeland, Samuel
  Knight, Sarah Kemble
  Lapham, William Berry
  Leavitt, Mary Greenleaf
    Clement
  Lee, Eliza Buckminster
  Lee, Hannah Farnham Sawyer
  Lewis, Winslow
  Lindsey, William

Little, Charles Coffin
Lothrop, Daniel
Paine, Charles Jackson
Peck, George Washington
Perkins, Thomas Handasyd
Pidgin, Charles Felton
Prang, Louis
Prang, Mary Amelia Dana Hicks
Rand, Edward Sprague
Russell, Joseph
Sargent, John Osborne
Sargent, Lucius Manlius
Savage, James
Sharp, Dallas Lore
Silsbee, Nathaniel
Simpson, Michael Hodge
Storey, Moorfield
Thayer, Nathaniel
Thorndike, Israel
Tobey, Edward Silas
Towle, George Makepeace
Train, George Francis
Upton, George Bruce
Ward, Samuel, 1814–1884
Winslow, Sidney Wilmot
Wyman, Seth
GUNTHER, GERALD
  Hand, Learned
GUTMAN, JUDITH MARA
  Austen, (Elizabeth) Alice
  Johnston, Frances Benjamin
GUY, JAMES SAMUEL
  Jones, Harry Clary
  Pendleton, Edmund Monroe
GUZDA, HENRY P.
  Mitchell, James Paul

HAAS, ROBERT BARTLETT
  Eilshemius, Louis Michel
  Gorky, Arshile
HABEL, SUE
  Adler, Felix
  Burns, Bob
HACHTEN, WILLIAM A.
  Grant, Harry Johnston
HACKETT, BYRNE
  Andrews, William Loring
HACKETT, CHARLES W.
  Croix, Teodoro de
  Escalante, Silvestre Velez De
  Niza, Marcos de
  Oñate, Juan de
  Otermin, Antonio de
  Peñalosa, Briceño Diego
    Dioniso de
  Tamarón, Pedrol
  Villagrá, Gasper Pérez de
HADDON, RAWSON W.
  Davis, Charles Harold
  Low, Will Hicok
HADLOCK, RICHARD B.
  Waller, Thomas Wright
HAEHN, OLIVIA A.
  Bacheller, Irving
  Brown, Margaret Wise
  White, Stewart Edward
HAFEN, LeROY R.
  Adams, Andy
  Adams, Charles
  Butterfield, John
  Chorpenning, George
  Holladay, Ben
  Holliday, Cyrus Kurtz

McCreery, James Work
Mears, Otto
Nicholson, Samuel Danford
Pike, Zebulon Montgomery
Shafroth, John Franklin
Sheedy, Dennis
Stone, Wilbur Fisk
Tabor, Horace Austin Warner
Welch, Charles Clark
HAGAN, HORACE H.
  Terry, David Smith
HAIGHT, GORDON S.
  Sigourney, Lydia Howard
    Huntley
  Witherspoon, Alexander
    Maclaren
HAIL, WILLIAM J.
  Burgevine, Henry Andrea
  McCartee, Divie Bethune
  Ward, Frederick Townsend
HAINES, SAMUEL F.
  Plummer, Henry Stanley
HALE, EDWARD E.
  Lewis, Tayler
HALE, NANCY
  Hinkle, Beatrice Moses
HALE, ROBERT
  Appleton, John, 1804–1891
  Appleton, John, 1815–1864
HALEY, J. EVETTS
  Goodnight, Charles
  Lasater, Edward Cunningham
  Littlefield, George Washington
  Siringo, Charles A.
HALL, CLIFTON L.
  Payne, Bruce Ryburn
HALL, COURTNEY R.
  Seybert, Adam
  Seybert, Henry
HALL, DAVID D.
  Appleton, William Sumner
HALL, EDWIN H.
  Lovering, Joseph
  Sabine, Wallace Clement Ware
  Trowbridge, John
HALL, JOHN PHILIP
  Furuseth, Andrew
HALL, LAURENCE P.
  Gibbs, Oliver Wolcott
HALL, PERCIVAL
  Clarke, Francis Devereux
  Clerc, Laurent
  Crouter, Albert Louis Edgerton
  Fay, Edward Allen
  Gallaudet, Edward Miner
  Gallaudet, Thomas
  Gallaudet, Thomas Hopkins
  Peet, Harvey Prindle
  Peet, Isaac Lewis
  Porter, Samuel
HALL, THOMAS B.
  Sappington, John
HALLER, MARK H.
  Capone, Alphonse
  Guzik, Jack
  Laughlin, Harry Hamilton
HALLION, RICHARD P.
  Pangborn, Clyde Edward
HAM, MARY C.
  Biard, Pierre
HAM, ROBERT EDMOND
  Abbott, John Stevens Cabot

HAMBY, ALONZO L.
Barkley, Alben William
Dirksen, Everett McKinley
McGranery, James Patrick
Rayburn, Samuel Taliaferro
("Sam")
HAMER, MARGUERITE BARTLETT
McGhee, Charles McClung
McMinn, Joseph
Phelan, James
Rhea, John
HAMER, PHILIP M.
Beard, Richard
Bell, John
Blount, William
Blount, Willie
Campbell, George Washington,
1769–1848
Campbell, William Bowen
Cannon, Newton
Carrick, Samuel
Carroll, William
Cocke, William
Cravath, Erastus Milo
Embree, Elihu
Fitzpatrick, Morgan Cassius
Foster, Ephraim Hubbard
Garrett, William Robertson
Gillem, Alvan Cullem
Humes, Thomas William
Maynard, Horace
Meigs, Return Jonathan
Nicholson, Alfred Osborne
Pope
Peay, Austin
Pillow, Gideon Johnson
Ramsey, James Gettys
McGready
HAMILTON, EARL J.
Gay, Edwin Francis
HAMILTON, EDWARD P.
Frizell, Joseph Palmer
HAMILTON, GEORGE L.
Crane, Thomas Frederick
HAMILTON, HOLMAN
Bowers, Claude Gernade
HAMILTON, J.G. DE ROULHAC
Ashe, Thomas Samuel
Badger, George Edmund
Barringer, Daniel Moreau
Bickett, Thomas Walter
Connor, Henry Groves
Dick, Robert Paine
Dobbin, James Cochran
Dobbs, Arthur
Dunning, William Archibald
Edwards, Weldon Nathaniel
Elmore, Franklin Harper
Fowler, Joseph Smith
Franklin, Jesse
Fuller, Thomas Charles
Gaines, Edmund Pendleton
Gilmer, John Adams
Goodloe, Daniel Reaves
Graham, Joseph
Hale, Edward Joseph
Hamilton, James, 1786–1857
Hammond, James Henry
Harper, Robert Goodloe
Harper, William
Hawks, Francis Lister
Helper, Hinton Rowan
Henderson, James Pinckney

Henderson, John Brooks
Hewes, Joseph
Holden, William Woods
Hooper, William
Howard, Oliver Otis
Howe, Robert
Husbands, Hermon
Iredell, James
Jarvis, Thomas Jordan
Johnson, Joseph
Johnson, William
Johnston, Samuel
Jones, Willie
Kirby-Smith, Edmund
Kitchin, Claude
Legaré, Hugh Swinton
McDuffie, George
McKay, James Iver
Macon, Nathaniel
Mangum, Willie Person
Martin, François-Xavier
Merrimon, Augustus
Summerfield
Moore, Bartholomew Figures
Pearson, Richmond Mumford
Penn, John
Perry, Benjamin Franklin
Person, Thomas
Petigru, James Louis
Pinckney, Charles Cotesworth
Pinckney, Thomas
Polk, William
Pollard, Edward Alfred
Pool, John
Preston, John Smith
Preston, William Campbell
Pritchard, Jeter Connelly
Quintard, Charles Todd
Ransom, Matt Whitaker
Rayner, Kenneth
Reade, Edwin Godwin
Reid, David Settle
Revels, Hiram Rhoades
Ripley, Roswell Sabine
Ross, Edmund Gibson
Ruffin, Thomas
Saunders, Romulus Mitchell
Saunders, William Laurence
Settle, Thomas
Skinner, Harry
Smith, Robert, 1732 o.s.–1801
Smith, William, c. 1762–1840
Smith, William Nathan Harrell
Spaight, Richard Dobbs
Sprunt, James
Stanly, Edward
Steele, John
Stone, David
Swain, David Lowry
Tourgée, Albion Winegar
Turnbull, Robert James
Turner, Josiah
Turner, Nat
Walker, Leroy Pope
Wheeler, John Hill
Williamson, Hugh
Worth, Jonathan
Wragg, William
HAMILTON, PETER JOSEPH
Bankhead, John Hollis
HAMILTON, VIRGINIA V.
Heflin, James Thomas

HAMILTON, WALTON H.
Hoxie, Robert Franklin
HAMLIN, TALBOT F.
Albro, Lewis Colt
Atwood, Charles B.
Audsley, George Ashdown
Banner, Peter
Barber, Donn
Benjamin, Asher
Brunner, Arnold William
Cabot, Edward Clarke
Carrère, John Merven
Carter, Elias
Cope, Walter
Dakin, James Harrison
Davis, Alexander Jackson
Day, Frank Miles
Fenner, Burt Leslie
Gallier, James
Gilman, Arthur Delevan
Greenough, Henry
Haight, Charles Coolidge
Hardenbergh, Henry Janeway
Hastings, Thomas
Hood, Raymond Mathewson
Lafever, Minard
Lienau, Detlef
McComb, John
Magonigle, Harold Van Buren
Mangin, Joseph François
Marshall, Henry Rutgers
Parris, Alexander
Pelz, Paul Johannes
Post, George Browne
Price, Bruce
Ramée, Joseph Jacques
Renwick, James, 1818–1895
Richardson, Henry Hobson
Rogers, Isaiah
Root, John Wellborn
Rotch, Arthur
Starrett, William Aiken
Stewardson, John
Sturgis, Russell
Thompson, Martin E.
Tilton, Edward Lippincott
Tuthill, William Burnet
Upjohn, Richard
Upjohn, Richard Michell
Van Brunt, Henry
Van Rensselaer, Mariana
Griswold
Ware, William Robert
Wheelwright, Edmund March
Willard, Solomon
Withers, Frederick Clarke
Young, Ammi Burnham
HAMMERSMITH, JACK L.
Borzage, Frank
HAMMOND, J.W.
Ryan, Walter D'Arcy
HAMMOND, WILLIAM A.
Laguna, Theodore de Leo de
Moore, Addison Webster
Sackett, Henry Woodward
HAMOR, WILLIAM A.
Duncan, Robert Kennedy
HAND, IRVING F.
Gregg, Willis Ray
HANDLIN, OSCAR
Morse, John Torrey

HANDY, ROBERT T.
Jefferson, Charles Edward
Stelzle, Charles
Wilson, Clarence True
HANEY, JOHN LOUIS
Armstrong, Paul
Barnard, Charles
Brown, David Paul
Coates, Florence Earle
Conrad, Robert Taylor
HANKE, LEWIS
Rowlandson, Mary White
HANLEY, MILES L.
Wheeler, William Adolphus
Worcester, Joseph Emerson
HANNA, ALFRED J.
Trenholm, George Alfred
HANSCOM, ELIZABETH DEERING
Freeman, Mary Eleanor Wilkins
Larcom, Lucy
Pool, Maria Louise
Sanborn, Katherine Abbott
Ward, Elizabeth Stuart Phelps
Yale, Caroline Ardelia
HANSON, HOWARD
Goetschius, Percy
HANSON, JOSEPH MILLS
Rosser, Thomas Lafayette
Stevens, Clement Hoffman
Taliaferro, William Booth
Vanderburgh, William Henry
Whiting, William Henry Chase
Wilcox, Cadmus Marcellus
Wood, Thomas John
Wright, Horatio Gouverneur
HARBAGE, ALFRED
Schelling, Felix Emanuel
HARBAUGH, WILIAM H.
Davis, John William
HARBESON, JOHN F.
Klauder, Charles Zeller
HARDING, GEORGE L.
Zamorano, Agustin Juan
Vicente
HARDY, EDWARD ROCHIE, JR.
Rainsford, William Stephen
Seabury, Samuel, 1801–1872
Seymour, George Franklin
Southgate, Horatio
Talbot, Ethelbert
Walden, Jacob Treadwell
Wilson, Bird
HARDY, E. R.
Coffin, Henry Sloane
Gavin, Frank Stanton Burns
Manning, William Thomas
HARDY, STEPHEN
Owen, Stephen Joseph
HARE, LLOYD C.M.
Mayhew, Thomas
Wainwright, Jonathan Mayhew,
1792–1854
HARKNESS, R. E. E.
Vedder, Henry Clay
HARLAN, ROBERT D.
Nash, John Henry
HARLEY, L. GIBB
Longyear, John Munroe
HARLOW, ALVIN E.
Alden, Cynthia May Westover
HARLOW, ALVIN F.
Adams, Edward Dean
Atterbury, William Wallace

Belmont, Alva Ertskin Smith
Vanderbilt
Borden, Lizzie Andrew
Brann, William Cowper
Burns, William John
Collier, Barron Gift
Corbett, James John
Corey, William Ellis
Crane, William Henry
Cutting, Robert Fulton
Dillinger, John
Dillingham, Charles Bancroft
Doheny, Edward Laurence
Dollar, Robert
Du Pont, Thomas Coleman
Flegenheimer, Arthur
Foy, Eddie
George, William Reuben
Heath, Thomas Kurton
Hires, Charles Elmer
Hitchcock, James Ripley
Wellman
Hopwood, Avery
Hough, Emerson
Hurlbert, William Henry
Jerome, William Travers
Johnston, William Andrew
Kahn, Otto Herman
Keenan, James Francis
Kingsley, Darwin Pearl
Kroger, Bernhard Henry
Kunz, George Frederick
Lawson, Thomas William
Lee, Ivy Ledbetter
Leiter, Joseph
Littleton, Martin Wiley
McGeehan, William O'Connell
McGraw, John Joseph
McIntyre, James
Mann, Louis
Marbury, Elisabeth
Marling, Alfred Erskine
Maxim, Hiram Percy
Mercer, Henry Chapman
Moffett, Cleveland Langston
Morawetz, Victor
Muldoon, William
Myrick, Herbert
O'Leary, Daniel
Post, Wiley
Price, Theodore Hazeltine
Price, William Thompson
Quantrill, William Clarke
Redpath, James
Reick, William Charles
Rice, Calvin Winsor
Ringling, Charles
Rogers, Henry Huttleston
Romeike, Henry
Rumsey, Mary Harriman
Ryan, John Dennis
Sage, Russell
Saunders, Frederick
Savage, Henry Wilson
Sherry, Louis
Sonnichsen, Albert
Statler, Ellsworth Milton
Stetson, Charles Augustus
Stewart, Alexander Turney
Stewart, John Aikman
Stewart, William Rhinelander
Stimson, Alexander Lovett
Stokes, William Earl Dodge

Stone, David Marvin
Straus, Jesse Isidor
Straus, Simon William
Strong, William Lafayette
Sullivan, Timothy Daniel
Sully, Daniel John
Sweeny, Peter Barr
Talmage, Thomas De Witt
Tevis, Lloyd
Thorburn, Grant
Tiffany, Charles Lewis
Tiffany, Louis Comfort
Tilyou, George Cornelius
Tripp, Guy Eastman
Tweed, William Marcy
Vanderbilt, Cornelius,
1794–1877
Vanderbilt, Cornelius,
1843–1899
Vanderbilt, George Washington
Vanderbilt, William Henry
Vanderbilt, William Kissam
Van Nostrand, David
Van Sweringen, Mantis James
Vibbard, Chauncey
Viele, Egbert Ludovicus
Wallack, Henry John
Wallack, James William, c.
1795–1864
Wallack, James William,
1818–1873
Wallack, Lester
Walsh, Blanche
Whitney, Caspar
Whitney, Harry Payne
Willard, Josiah Flint
Wood, Henry Alexander Wise
Woodhull, Victoria Claflin
Woolworth, Frank Winfield
Wrigley, William
Young, George
Ziegler, William
HARLOW, RALPH V.
Dana, Francis
Deane, Silas
Elliot, Jonathan
Force, Peter
Hathorne, William
Heath, William
Smith, Gerrit
HARPER, GEORGE M.
Maclean, John
Murray, James Ormsbee
HARPER, GEORGE MCLEAN
Patton, Francis Landey
Shields, Charles Woodruff
HARPER, IDA HUSTED
Shaw, Anna Howard
HARPER, LAWRENCE A.
Gillette, King Camp
HARRADON, H. D.
Bauer, Louis Agricola
HARRELL, ISAAC S.
Andrews, Sidney
HARRINGTON, KEVIN
Mies Van Der Rohe, Ludwig
HARRIS, BRICE
Westcott, Edward Noyes
HARRIS, CHARLES M.
Mitchell, Margaret Munnerlyn
Williams, Ben Ames

HARRIS, GILBERT DENNISON
  Williams, Henry Shaler
HARRIS, MICHAEL R.
  Flexner, Abraham
HARRIS, REBECCA S.
  Lamoureux, Andrew Jackson
HARRIS, ROBERT L., JR.
  Robinson, Ruby Doris Smith
HARRIS, THOMAS LE GRAND
  Caldwell, Alexander
  Carney, Thomas
  Conway, Martin Franklin
  Crawford, Samuel Johnson
  Deitzler, George Washington
  Usher, John Palmer
HARRIS, WILLIAM H.
  Townsend, Willard Saxby, Jr.
HARRISON, FAIRFAX
  Beverley, Robert
  Fairfax, Thomas
HARRISON, JOHN M.
  Blakeslee, Howard Walter
HARRISON, RICHARD A.
  Choate, Anne Hyde Clarke
  Harriman, Florence Jaffray
    Hurst
  Miller, David Hunter
HARROW, BENJAMIN
  Atwater, Wilbur Olin
  Baruch, Simon
  Baskerville, Charles
  Biggs, Hermann Michael
HARROWER, MOLLY
  Koffka, Kurt
HARSHBERGER, JOHN W.
  Meehan, Thomas
HART, ALBERT BUSHNELL
  Oakes, George Washington
    Ochs
HART, EDWARD
  Bolton, Henry Carrington
  McMurtrie, William
HART, EDWIN B.
  Babcock, Stephen Moulton
HART, FANCHON
  Rusby, Henry Hurd
HART, FREEMAN H.
  Johnston, Zachariah
  Jones, Gabriel
  McClurg, James
  Mason, Thomson
  Moore, Andrew
  Stuart, Archibald
  White, Alexander
HART, JOHN E.
  Crouse, Russel McKinley
  Dell, Floyd James
  Kreymborg, Alfred Francis
  McFee, William
  O'Connor, Edwin Greene
  Toklas, Alice Babette
HARTLEY, E. NEAL
  Schwab, Charles Michael
HARTT, MARY BRONSON
  Dean, Bashford
  Eytinge, Rose
  Fisher, Clara
  Florence, William Jermyn
  Foster, Benjamin
  Gill, Laura Drake
  Gillespie, Mabel
  Goodyear, William Henry
  Hall, Arethusa

Hall, Henry Bryan
Hapgood, Isabel Florence
Harrison, Gabriel
Havell, Robert
Haworth, Joseph
Heinemann, Ernst
Herter, Christian
Hill, John
Holder, Joseph Bassett
Holland, Edmund Milton
Holland, George
Holland, Joseph Jefferson
Hollyer, Samuel
Hunt, Mary Hannah Hanchett
Jacobi, Mary Corinna Putnam
Kehew, Mary Morton Kimball
Keller, Arthur Ignatius
Keppel, Frederick
Lawrie, Alexander
Leney, William Satchwell
Loeb, Sophie Irene Simon
Lothrop, Alice Louise Higgins
Marshall, William Edgar
Mitchell, Margaret Julia
Terhune, Mary Virginia Hawes
HARTWELL, JOHN AUGUSTUS
  Weir, Robert Fulton
HARVEY, A. McGEHEE
  Blalock, Alfred
  Longcope, Warfield, Theobald
  Robinson, George Canby
HARVEY, GEORGE C.
  Gould, George Milbry
  Haldeman, Samuel Steman
  Hart, Charles Henry
HARVEY, SAMUEL C.
  Da Costa, John Chalmers
  Judd, Edward Starr
HARWOOD, MARGARET
  Mitchell, William, 1791–1869
  Searle, Arthur
  Winlock, Joseph
HASKELL, DANIEL C.
  McDougall, Alexander
  Moore, Sir Henry
  Morgan, Daniel
HAST, ADELE
  Briggs, Lyman James
  Cooke, Robert Anderson
  Fejos, Paul
  Kidder, Alfred Vincent
  Nelson, Nels Christian
HASTINGS, GEORGE E.
  Duché, Jacob
  Ferguson, Elizabeth Graeme
  Hopkinson, Francis
HATCH, LOUIS C.
  Allen, Elisha Hunt
  Bates, James
  Boutelle, Charles Addison
  Bradbury, James Ware
  Coburn, Abner
HATCHER, WILLIAM H.
  Willoughby, Westel Woodbury
HAUGEN, EINAR R.
  Rölvaag, Ole Edvart
HAUPTMAN, LAURENCE M.
  Beatty, Willard Walcott
  Jemison, Alice Mae Lee
  Thomas, George Allison
HAUPTMAN, ROBERT
  McCullers, Carson

HAUSER, PHILIP M.
  Ogburn, William Fielding
HAVENS, GEORGE R.
  Armstrong, Edward Cooke
HAVENS, W. W., JR.
  Pegram, George Braxton
HAVIG, ALAN R.
  Carrington, Elaine Stern
  Denny, George Vernon, Jr.
  Hooper, Claude Ernest
  Husing, Edward Britt ("Ted")
HAWKINS, HUGH
  Ames, Joseph Sweetman
  Butler, Nicholas Murray
  Lowell, Abbott Lawrence
HAWLEY, ELLIS W.
  Arnold, Thurman Wesley
  Swope, Gerard
HAWLEY, FRANCES B.
  Cesnola, Luigi Palma di
  Clarke, Sir Caspar Purdon
  Cook, Clarence Chatham
  Vincent, Frank
HAWORTH, PAUL L.
  Davis, John Wesley
  Dunn, William McKee
  Dunn, Williamson
  English, William Hayden
  Judah, Samuel
  Julian, George Washington
  Kern, John Worth
  Kimball, Nathan
  Lane, Henry Smith
  Lanier, James Franklin Doughty
HAY, CHARLES C., III
  Barnes, Julius Howland
  Reynolds, Richard Samuel, Sr.
  Reynolds, William Neal
  Thomas, John Parnell
  Thomas, (John William) Elmer
HAY, MELBA PORTER
  Andrus, Ethel Percy
  Brewster, Ralph Owen
  Dole, James Drummond
  Hale, Frederick
  Hamilton, Alice
  Hoffman, Clare Eugene
  Pope, James Pinckney
  Wiley, Alexander
HAY, THOMAS ROBSON
  Beatty, John
HAYCRAFT, ROBERT
  Arensberg, Walter Conrad
  Lancaster, Henry Carrington
HAYES, CARLTON J. H.
  Moon, Parker Thomas
HAYES, DOREMUS A.
  Little, Charles Joseph
  Lunt, Orrington
  Terry, Milton Spenser
HAYES, JOHN D.
  Gleaves, Albert
  Reeves, Joseph Mason
  Taussig, Joseph Knefler
HAYES, ROBERT C.
  Livingston, Robert R.,
    1718–1775
  Livingston, Robert R.,
    1746–1813
HAYLOR, ADA P.
  Morehead, John Motley

HAYNES, FRED E.
  Clarkson, Coker Fifield
  Cole, Chester Cicero
  Cummins, Albert Baird
  Dawson, Thomas Cleland
  Deemer, Horace Emerson
  Ellis, Seth Hockett
  Evans, George Henry
  Larrabee, William
  Lewelling, Lorenzo Dow
  Perkins, George Douglas
  Pettigrew, Richard Franklin
  Price, Hiram
HAYNES, GEORGE HENRY
  Ashmun, George
  Banks, Nathaniel Prentiss
  Crane, Winthrop Murray
  Gillett, Frederick Huntington
  Hoar, Ebenezer Rockwood
  Hoar, George Frisbie
  Hoar, Samuel
  Sumner, Charles
  Thompson, Edward Herbert
  Washburn, Charles Grenfill
  Wilson, Henry
HAYNES, RICHARD F.
  Matthews, Francis Patrick
  Tucker, Henry St. George
HAYWOOD, MARSHALL DELANCEY
  Atkinson, Thomas
  Burrington, George
  Eden, Charles
  Ludwell, Philip
HAZLITT, HENRY
  Pollak, Gustav
HEALY, DAVID F.
  Griscom, Lloyd Carpenter
HEALY, JOHN DAVID
  Brophy, Thomas D'Arcy
  Dickinson, Edwin De Witt
  Goodman, Louis Earl
HEBARD, GRACE RAYMOND
  Carey, Joseph Maull
  Wergeland, Agnes Mathilde
HECK, EARL L.W.
  Hack, George
  Hawks, John
  Hayes, William Henry
  Herrman, Augustine
  Hunt, William Gibbes
  Johnston, Gabriel
  Palmer, Joseph
  Peirce, William
  Pound, Thomas
  Sedgwick, Theodore,
    1811–1859
  Van der Donck, Adriaen
HECK-RABI, LOUISE
  Templeton, Alec Andrew
HEDGES, JAMES B.
  Villard, Henry
  Weeden, William Babcock
HEEFNER, DANIEL
  Irvine, William Mann
HEFELBOWER, SAMUEL G.
  Sprecher, Samuel
  Unangst, Erias
  Wenner, George Unangst
HEFTON, JOHN M.
  Murray, Mae
HEIDER, GRACE M.
  Lewin, Kurt
  Wertheimer, Max

HEIDNER, SAMUEL J.
  Page, Richard Lucian
  Pender, William Dorsey
  Ramsay, George Douglas
  Ramseur, Stephen Dodson
  Reynolds, Joseph Jones
  Richardson, Israel Bush
  Ricketts, James Brewerton
  Riley, Bennett
  Ripley, James Wolfe
  Russell, David Allen
  St. John, Isaac Munroe
  Sidell, William Henry
  Sigel, Franz
  Smith, Charles Henry,
    1827–1902
  Smith, John Eugene
  Stahel, Julius
HEILBRONER, ROBERT L.
  Morgenthau, Henry
HEILBRONNER, HANS
  Rosen, Joseph A.
HEILMAN, ELIZABETH WILTBANK
  Scidmore, Eliza Ruhamah
  Shields, George Oliver
  Stuck, Hudson
  Workman, Fanny Bullock
HEILMAN, ROBERT B.
  Roethke, Theodore Huebner
HEIM, KEITH M.
  Ammann, Othmar Hermann
HEINL, ROBERT DEBS, JR.
  Lejeune, John Archer
HELLMAN, GEOFFREY T.
  Guggenheim, Solomon Robert
  Lehman, Arthur
  Lewisohn, Adolph
HELLMAN, GEORGE S.
  Curtis, George William
  Spingarn, Joel Elias
HELLWEG, J.F.
  Skinner, Aaron Nichols
HENCH, ATCHESON L.
  Eggleston, George Cary
  Johnson, Chapman
HENDERSON, EDWARD P.
  Cross, Charles Whitman
HENDERSON, RICHARD B.
  Maverick, (Fontaine) Maury
HENDERSON, VIRGINIA
  Goodrich, Annie Warburton
HENDERSON, WILLIAM J.
  Huneker, James Gibbons
HENDRICK, BURTON JESSE
  Carnegie, Andrew
HENDRICK, ELLWOOD
  Chandler, Charles Frederick
  Draper, John William
  Freas, Thomas Bruce
HENDRICKSON, G.L.
  Hale, William Gardner
  Warren, Minton
HENDRICKSON, KENNETH E., JR.
  Lunn, George Richard
HENLEY, R. R.
  Dorset, Marion
HENLINE, H.H.
  Perrine, Frederic Auten Combs
HENMON, VIVIAN ALLEN CHARLES
  Carpenter, Stephen Haskins
  Conover, Obadiah Milton

HENNESEY, JAMES, S.J.
  Talbot, Francis Xavier
HENRY, BRUCE
  Collier, Constance
HENSON, PAMELA M.
  Akeley, Mary Leonore
  Chase, (Mary) Agnes Merrill
  Dorn, Harold Fred
HERBEN, STEPHEN J.
  Kynett, Alpha Jefferson
  Nelson, Reuben
HERBERT P. GALLINGER
  Moore, Zephaniah Swift
HEROLD, AMOS L.
  Paulding, James Kirke
HERON, DAVID W.
  Chester, Colby Mitchell
  Patterson, Richard
    Cunningham, Jr.
HERON, DAVID WINSTON
  Gilbert, Alfred Carlton
  Langlie, Arthur Bernard
HERRICK, GLENN W.
  Comstock, John Henry
HERRICK, ROBERT
  Tarbell, Frank Bigelow
HERRING, GEORGE C.
  Fall, Bernard B.
HERRIOT, FRANK I.
  Drake, Francis Marion
HERRNSTEIN, R. J.
  Lashley, Karl Spencer
HERRON, STELLA
  Blanc, Antoine
  Blenk, James Hubert
  Janssens, Francis
HERSEY, FRANK WILSON CHENEY
  Malcolm, Daniel
  Prescott, Samuel
HERSEY, JOHN
  Wertenbaker, Charles Christian
HERTY, CHARLES H.
  Venable, Francis Preston
HERTZBERG, ARTHUR
  Haas, Jacob Judah Aaron de
  Masliansky, Zvi Hirsch
  Wise, Stephen Samuel
HERVEY, JOHN L.
  Madden, John Edward
  Sloan, James Forman
  Wallace, John Hankins
HESS, GARY R.
  Hamilton, Maxwell McGaughey
HESSEN, ROBERT
  Grace, Eugene Gifford
  Rand, James Henry
HEWES, EDWIN B.
  Higginson, Nathaniel
HEWES, JAMES E., JR.
  Somervell, Brehon Burke
HEWLETT, RICHARD G.
  Dean, Gordon Evans
  Murray, Thomas Edward
HEXTER, MAURICE B.
  Warburg, Felix Moritz
HEY, KENNETH R.
  Skouras, George Panagiotes
HIBBARD, RUFUS P.
  Miles, Manly
HIBBEN, JOHN GRIER
  McCosh, James

HICKERSON, JOHN D.
  Moffat, Jay Pierrepont
HICKMAN, EMILY
  Fargo, William George
  Wells, Henry
HICKMAN, RUSSELL
  Block, Adriaen
HICKS, FREDERICK CHARLES
  Boston, Charles Anderson
  Carter, James Coolidge
  Choate, Joseph Hodges
  Coudert, Frederic René
  Emmet, Thomas Addis,
    1764–1827
  Evarts, William Maxwell
  Field, David Dudley, 1805–1894
  Gummere, William Stryker
  Hutchins, Thomas
  Kent, James
  Kirby, Ephraim
  O'Conor, Charles
  Wheaton, Henry
HICKS, GRANVILLE
  Boyd, Thomas Alexander
  Glass, Montague Marsden
  Gregory, Eliot
  Ladd, Joseph Brown
  Meneely, Andrew
  Nadal, Ehrman Syme
  Phillips, David Graham
  Rohlfs, Anna Katharine Green
  Saltus, Edgar Evertson
  Scott, Leroy
  Vance, Louis Joseph
  Warner, Anna Bartlett
  Warner, Susan Bogert
  Wilcox, Ella Wheeler
HICKS, JOHN DONALD
  Allen, William Vincent
  Barrett, Charles Simon
  Billings, Frederick
  Blaine, John James
  Creighton, John Andrew
  Crounse, Lorenzo
  Donnelly, Ignatius
  Fairbanks, Charles Warren
  Frank, Glenn
  Furnas, Robert Wilkinson
  Hitchcock, Phineas Warrener
  Holcomb, Silas Alexander
  McDonald, Joseph Ewing
  Manderson, Charles Frederick
  Marquett, Turner Mastin
  Marshall, Thomas Riley
  Matthews, Claude
  Maxwell, Samuel
  Morton, Julius Sterling
  Morton, Oliver Perry
  New, Harry Stewart
  Paddock, Algernon Sidney
  Polk, Leonidas Lafayette
  Rosewater, Edward
  Stevenson, Adlai Ewing
  Washburn, Cadwallader Colden
  Weaver, James Baird
HIDY, MURIEL E.
  Claflin, John
HIDY, RALPH WILLARD
  Van Dyke, John Wesley
  Ward, Thomas Wren
  Weyerhaeuser, Frederick
    Edward

HIGGINS, ROGER WOLCOTT
  Plummer, Jonathan
HIGGS, ROBERT J.
  Hagen, Walter Charles
HIGHAM, CHARLES
  DeMille, Cecil Blount
HIGHAM, ROBIN
  Bell, Lawrence Dale
  Lockheed, Malcolm
  Martin, Glenn Luther ("Cy")
  Scott, Allen Cecil
HIGHTOWER, RAYMOND L.
  Wilson, Joshua Lacy
  Wilson, Samuel Ramsay
HILDEBRAND, JOEL H.
  Latimer, Wendell Mitchell
HILGARD, ERNEST R.
  Robinson, Edward Stevens
  Tolman, Edward Chace
HILL, CHARLES E.
  Erving, George William
  Foster, John Watson
HILL, DAVID JAYNE
  Herrick, Myron Timothy
HILL, FRANK ERNEST
  Duryea, Charles Edgar
  Firestone, Harvey Samuel
  Ford, Edsel Bryant
  Wills, Childe Harold
HILL, HAMLIN
  Faust, Frederick Shiller
HILL, HELEN
  Mason, George
HILL, JIM DAN
  Waddell, James Iredell
  Wilkinson, John
  Winslow, John Ancrum
HILL, LEWIS WEBB
  Morse, John Lovett
HILLE, EINAR
  Tamarkin, Jacob David
HILLER, E. T.
  Hayes, Edward Carey
HIMES, NORMAN E.
  Knowlton, Charles
HINES, THOMAS S.
  Neutra, Richard Joseph
HINKE, WILLIAM J.
  Schlatter, Michael
HINMAN, EDGAR L.
  Wolfe, Harry Kirke
HINTON, EDWARD M.
  Grimké, Archibald Henry
  McAllister, Samuel Ward
  McCarroll, James
  McHenry, James
  Marden, Orison Swett
  Martin, Frederick Townsend
  Mathews, Albert
  Matthews, Franklin
HIRSCH, ARTHUR H.
  Le Jau, Francis
HIRSCH, FOSTER
  Hopper, Edna Wallace
HIRSCH, MARK D.
  Copeland, Royal Samuel
  O'Brien, Morgan Joseph
HIRSCHLAND, ELLEN B.
  Cone, Claribel
  Cone, Etta
  Dale, Chester
  Dale, Maud Murray Thompson

HIRSH, FREDERICK R., JR.
  Richtmyer, Floyd Karker
HISE, FRANK L.
  Abbott, Frank
  Allen, John
  Black, Greene Vardiman
  Bonwill, William Gibson
    Arlington
HITCHINGS, SINCLAIR
  Wyeth, Newell Convers
HOBBS, JOSEPH P.
  Hodges, Courtney Hicks
  Smith, Walter Bedell
HOBBS, WILLIAM H.
  Russell, Israel Cook
HOCKETT, CHARLES F.
  Bloomfield, Leonard
HOCKETT, HOMER CAREY
  Buckland, Ralph Pomeroy
  Bushnell, Asa Smith
  Corwin, Thomas
  Cox, Jacob Dolson
  Cox, Samuel Sullivan
  Day, William Rufus
  Dennison, William
  Foster, Charles
  Hamer, Thomas Lyon
  Hickenlooper, Andrew
  Hitchcock, Peter
  Hoadly, George
HOCKING, WILLIAM ERNEST
  Palmer, George Herbert
HODDER, FRANK H.
  Eldridge, Shalor Winchell
HODGE, FREDERICK W.
  Hough, Walter
  Morgan, Lewis Henry
HODGES, JAMES A.
  Berry, George Leonard
  Haywood, Allan Shaw
HODGES, PAUL C.
  Brown, Percy
  Hirsch, Isaac Seth
HOFF, SYLVIA G.
  Fromm-Reichmann, Frieda
HOFFMAN, M.M.
  Crétin, Joseph
  Hennessy, John
  Loras, Jean Mathias Pierre
  Mazzuchelli, Samuel Charles
HOFFMAN, RAND
  Holly, Charles Hardin
    ("Buddy")
HOFMANN, GEORGE F.
  Christie, John Walter
HOHNER, ROBERT A.
  Cannon, James
  Cherrington, Ernest Hurst
  LaFarge, John
HOLCOMBE, ARTHUR N.
  Lawrence, Abbott
  Lawrence, Amos
  Lawrence, Amos Adams
  Lawrence, William, 1783–1848
HOLDEN, RAYMOND
  MacCameron, Robert
  Mitchell, John Ames
  Morgan, Matthew Somerville
HOLLANDER, STANLEY C.
  Hartford, George Huntington
  Hartford, George Ludlum
  Hartford, John Augustine

HOLLEY, I. B., JR.
Hines, John Leonard ("Birdie")
Palmer, John McAuley
HOLLI, MELVIN G.
Cobo, Albert Eugene
HOLLIS, DANIEL WALKER
Blease, Coleman Livingston
Smith, Ellison DuRant
HOLLON, W. EUGENE
Rister, Carl Coke
HOLLY, MICHAEL ANN
Panofsky, Erwin
HOLMAN, C. HUGH
Glasgow, Ellen Anderson
Gholson
HOLMES, EUGENE C.
Locke, Alain Leroy
HOLMES, HARRY N.
Hall, Charles Martin
HOLMES, JOHN HAYNES
Grant, Percy Stickney
Haven, Joseph
Janes, Lewis George
Levermore, Charles Herbert
Lowell, Robert Traill Spence
Lyman, Albert Josiah
Moxom, Philip Stafford
Parkhurst, Charles Henry
Riis, Jacob August
Spencer, Anna Garlin
Straton, John Roach
Strong, Josiah
Tyson, Stuart Lawrence
Villard, Helen Frances Garrison
HOLMES, OLIVER W.
Keith, Minor Cooper
Litchfield, Electus Backus
McCarren, Patrick Henry
Maxwell, George Hebard
Meiggs, Henry
Munro, George
Murphy, Henry Cruse
Murrell, John A.
Newton, Henry Jotham
Newton, Isaac, 1794–1858
Orr, Alexander Ector
Payne, Oliver Hazard
Pinkerton, Allan
Revell, Fleming Hewitt
Richmond, Dean
Rogers, Moses
Schell, Augustus
HOLT, IVAN LEE
Palmore, William Beverly
HOLT, JEAN MACKINNON
Breck, George William
Brevoort, James Renwick
Davenport, Homer Calvin
Dearth, Henry Golden
Dewing, Maria Richards Oakey
Earle, James
Eaton, Joseph Oriel
Eaton, Wyatt
Edmonds, Francis William
Eichholtz, Jacob
Elliott, Charles Loring
Elliott, John
Enneking, John Joseph
Farrer, Henry
Fassett, Cornelia Adèle Strong
Fisher, Alvan
Flagg, George Whiting
Flagg, Jared Bradley

HOLT, LUCIUS H.
Goodrich, Frank Boott
Hoffman, Charles Fenno
Hoffman, John Thompson
Hoffman, Wickham
Kelly, John
Kernan, Francis
Kinsella, Thomas
Knickerbocker, Herman
HOLT, W. STULL
Scharf, John Thomas
HOLTER, MARY FRANCES
Yerkes, Charles Tyson
HOMER, WILLIAM I.
Stieglitz, Alfred
HONEYMAN, A. VAN DOREN
Maxwell, William
Neilson, John
Nelson, William, 1847–1914
Newell, William Augustus
Odell, Jonathan
Ogden, David
Vroom, Peter Dumont
Ward, Marcus Lawrence
Whitehead, William Adee
HONIG, JOEL
Livingstone, Belle
HOOGENBOOM, ARI
Bloom, Sol
Cudahy, Edward Aloysius, Jr.
Ellmaker, (Emmett) Lee
Gibbs, (Oliver) Wolcott
Littauer, Lucius Nathan
Reed, David Aiken
Volstead, Andrew John
HOOGENBOOM, OLIVE
Arden, Elizabeth
Castle, Irene Foote
Chase, Edna Woolman
Garden, Mary
Hopper, Hedda
Kilgallen, Dorothy Mae
Luhan, Mabel Dodge
Norris, Kathleen Thompson
Rose, Billy
Vanderbilt, Gloria Morgan
HOOKER, HELENE MAXWELL
Heney, Francis Joseph
HOOKER, HENRY D.
Husmann, George
Longworth, Nicholas,
1782–1863
HOOKER, MARJORIE
Keith, Arthur
HOOKER, ROLAND MATHER
Talcott, Joseph
Trumbull, Benjamin
Winthrop, John
Wyllys, George
HOOVER, DWIGHT W.
Matthes, Gerard Hendrik
Micheaux, Oscar
HOOVER, HARVEY D.
Hunton, William Lee
HOPE, ARTHUR J.
Hudson, Daniel Eldred
HOPF, RITA HILBORN
Barth, Carl Georg Lange
HOPKINS, ALBERT A.
Adams, Isaac
Beach, Alfred Ely
Blanchard, Thomas

HOPKINS, B. SMITH
Parr, Samuel Wilson
HOPKINS, C. HOWARD
Mott, John R.
Smith, Fred Burton
HOPKINS, E. WASHBURN
Hall, Fitzedward
HOPKINS, L. THOMAS
Newlon, Jesse Homer
HORACK, FRANK E.
Kinne, La Vega George
Kirkwood, Samuel Jordan
HORGAN, PAUL
Saxton, Eugene Francis
HORGAN, STEPHEN HENRY
Levy, Louis Edward
Moss, John Calvin
HORMELL, ORREN C.
Kent, Edward
HORNBLOW, ARTHUR
Adams, Edwin
Aldrich, Louis
Aldridge, Ira Frederick
Arden, Edwin Hunter
Pendleton
Blake, William Rufus
Bowers, Elizabeth Crocker
Chanfrau, Francis S.
Chanfrau, Henrietta Baker
HORNER, HARLAN H.
Randall, Samuel Sidwell
Rice, Victor Moreau
HORTON, WALTER M.
King, Henry Churchill
HOSAY, PHILIP M.
Graves, David Bibb
Sanderson, Ezra Dwight
HOSKINS, HALFORD LANCASTER
Tufts, Charles
HOUGH, HENRY BEETLE
Lincoln, Joseph Crosby
HOUGH, WALTER
Barber, Edwin Atlee
Bourke, John Gregory
Brower, Jacob Vradenberg
Byington, Cyrus
Casanowicz, Immanuel Moses
Churchill, William
Curtin, Jeremiah
Cushing, Frank Hamilton
Davis, Edwin Hamilton
Dorsey, James Owen
Emerson, Ellen Russell
Fewkes, Jesse Walter
Gatschet, Albert Samuel
Goddard, Pliny Earle
Hale, Horatio Emmons
Jones, William
McGee, William John
McGuire, Joseph Deakins
Mallery, Garrick
Mason, Ottis Tufton
Matthews, Washington
Mooney, James
Pilling, James Constantine
Rau, Charles
Schoolcraft, Henry Rowe
Skinner, Alanson Buck
Smith, Erminnie Adelle Platt
Stevenson, James
Stevenson, Matilda Coxe Evans
Thomas, Cyrus

HOUNSHELL, DAVID A.
  Gunnison, Foster
HOUSE, ALBERT V., JR.
  Randall, Samuel Jackson
HOWARD, HARVEY J.
  Green, John
HOWARD, JAMES L.
  Harding, Seth
HOWARD, JOHN TASKER
  Braslau, Sophie
  Chadwick, George Whitefield
  Fairchild, Blair
  Hadley, Henry Kimball
  Johns, Clayton
  Kroeger, Ernest Richard
  Loeffler, Charles Martin
  Nevin, George Balch
  Oberhoffer, Emil Johann
  Oehmler, Leo Carl Martin
  Parsons, Albert Ross
  Peters, William Cumming
  Pratt, Waldo Selden
  Root, George Frederick
  Runcie, Constance Faunt Le
    Roy
  Sanderson, Sibyl
  Saslavsky, Alexander
  Scheel, Fritz
  Schindler, Kurt
  Schradieck, Henry
  Seidl, Anton
  Selby, William
  Sembrich, Marcella
  Seward, Theodore
    Frelinghuysen
  Shaw, Oliver
  Sousa, John Philip
  Southard, Lucien H.
  Spicker, Max
  Steck, George
  Steinway, Christian Friedrich
    Theodore
  Steinway, Henry Engelhard
  Steinway, William
  Stern, Joseph William
  Sternberg, Constantin
    Ivanovich, Edler von
  Stewart, Humphrey John
  Stoeckel, Carl
  Tapper, Bertha Feiring
  Taylor, Raynor
  Thayer, Alexander Wheelock
  Thayer, Whitney Eugene
  Thomas, Christian Friedrich
    Theodore
  Thursby, Emma Cecilia
  Timm, Henry Christian
  Tobani, Theodore Moses
  Trajetta, Philip
  Tremaine, Henry Barnes
  Tuckey, William
  Urso, Camilla
  Van der Stucken, Frank
    Valentin
  Verbrugghen, Henri
  Vogrich, Max Wilhelm Karl
  Warren, Richard Henry
  Watson, Henry Cood
  Webb, George James
  Webb, Thomas Smith
  Weber, Albert
  Weld, Arthur Cyril Gordon
  Whitehill, Clarence Eugene

  Whiting, George Elbridge
  Whitney, Myron William
  Wight, Frederick Coit
  Wilson, Mortimer
  Witherspoon, Herbert
  Wood, David Duffle
  Woodbury, Isaac Baker
  Work, Henry Clay
  Zerrahn, Carl
HOWARD, LELAND OSSIAN
  Ashmead, William Harris
  Coquillett, Daniel William
  Cresson, Ezra Townsend
  Dyar, Harrison Gray
  Edwards, William Henry
  Fernald, Charles Henry
  Fitch, Asa
  Forbes, Stephen Alfred
  Glover, Townend
  Grote, Augustus Radcliffe
  Hagen, Hermann August
  Harris, Thaddeus William
  Horn, George Henry
  Hubbard, Henry Guernsey
  Hunter, Walter David
  Knab, Frederick
  LeConte, John Lawrence
  Lintner, Joseph Albert
  McCook, Henry Christopher
  Osten Sacken, Carl Robert
    Romanovich, Von Der
  Packard, Alpheus Spring
  Peck, William Dandridge
  Peckham, George Williams
  Riley, Charles Valentine
  Say, Thomas
  Schwarz, Eugene Amandus
  Scudder, Samuel Hubbard
  Smith, John Bernhard
  Snow, Francis Huntington
  Uhler, Philip Reese
  Walsh, Benjamin Dann
HOWARD, SAMUEL F., JR.
  Untermyer, Samuel
HOWAY, F.W.
  Gray, Robert
  Ingraham, Joseph
  Kendrick, John
HOWE, HARRISON E.
  Dow, Herbert Henry
  Slosson, Edwin Emery
  Teeple, John Edgar
HOWE, M.A. DEWOLFE
  Bancroft, George
  Bradford, Gamaliel
  Chapman, John Jay
  Hale, Edward Everett
  Higginson, Thomas Wentworth
  Holmes, Abiel
  Holmes, Oliver Wendell
  Lowell, James Russell
  Rideing, William Henry
  Scudder, Horace Elisha
HOWE, WALTER
  Quelch, John
HOWE, WILL D.
  Doubleday, Frank Nelson
  Riley, James Whitcomb
HOWER, RALPH M.
  Straus, Percy Selden
HOWLAND, HAROLD
  Booth, Mary Louise
  Bowen, Henry Chandler

  Briggs, Charles Frederick
  Brooks, Erastus
  Brooks, Noah
  Browne, Junius Henri
  Bundy, Jonas Mills
  Burchard, Samuel Dickinson
HOWLETT, CHARLES F.
  Connolly, Maureen Catherine
  Lapchick, Joseph Bohomiel
  Stokes, Maurice
  Warter, Paul Olee
HOXIE, ELIZABETH F.
  Brady, William Aloysius
  Pollock, Channing
HUBBARD, CLIFFORD CHESLEY
  Ellery, William
HUBBARD, G. EVANS
  Nicholson, John
HUBBARD, JOSEPH B.
  Persons, Warren Milton
HUBBARD, THEODORA KIMBALL
  Cleveland, Horace William
    Shaler
  Eliot, Charles
  Olmsted, Frederick Law
  Olmsted, John Charles
HUBBELL, HARRY M.
  Kingsley, James Luce
  Perrin, Bernadotte
HUBBS, CARL L.
  Sumner, Francis Bertody
HUDSON, JAMES J.
  Andrews, Frank Maxwell
  Patrick, Mason Mathews
HUDSON, WINTHROP S.
  Barbour, Clarence Augustus
HUGHES, ELIZABETH S.
  Gossett, Benjamin Brown
HUGHES, THOMAS PARKE
  Bendix, Vincent
  Cottrell, Frederick Gardner
  Jewett, Frank Baldwin
  Lewis, George William
  Stone, Charles Augustus
  Webster, Edwin Sibley
HUGHES, WILLIAM
  Bankhead, Tallulah
  Begley, Edward James ("Ed")
  Burke, Billie
  Clift, Edward Montgomery
  Keaton, Joseph Francis
    ("Buster"), V
  Laurel, Stan
  Muni, Paul
  Novarro, Ramon
  Pitts, Zasu
HUHNER, LEON
  Kohler, Max James
HULBERT, ARCHER B.
  Tenney, Edward Payson
HULBERT, J. R.
  Manly, John Matthews
  Rickert, Martha Edith
HULL, CHARLES H.
  Cornell, Alonzo B.
HULL, HANNAH CLOTHIER
  Bond, Elizabeth Powell
HULL, WILLIAM I.
  Magill, Edward Hicks
HUME, EDWARD ERSKINE
  Bullitt, Henry Massie
  Caldwell, Charles
  Campbell, Henry Fraser

Chisolm, John Julian
Davidge, John Beale
De Rosset, Moses John
Dickson, Samuel Henry
Doughty, William Henry
Dowell, Greensville
Dudley, Benjamin Winslow
Dyer, Isadore
Eberle, John
HUMMEL, ARTHUR W.
Hunter, William C.
Ng Poon Chew
HUMPHREY, EDWARD FRANK
Bulkeley, Morgan Gardner
Camp, Hiram
Colton, Calvin
HUMPHREYS, R. A.
Robertson, William Spence
HUMPHREYS, WILLIAM JACKSON
Abbe, Cleveland
Bentley, Wilson Alwyn
Bigelow, Frank Hagar
Blodget, Lorin
Coffin, James Henry
Espy, James Pollard
Ferrel, William
Harrington, Mark Walrod
Hazen, Henry Allen
Redfield, William C.
Ward, Robert De Courcy
HUNGARLAND, ROBERT L.
Dillingham, Walter Francis
Parkinson, Thomas Ignatius
HUNGERFORD, EDWARD BUELL
Sizer, Nelson
Thompson, Arthur Webster
Wells, Samuel Roberts
HUNT, J. RAMSAY
Starr, Moses Allen
HUNTER, ADELAIDE MEADOR
McKenzie, Robert Tait
HUNTER, LOUIS C.
Howe, Samuel
Mills, Elijah Hunt
HUNTER, THOMAS MARSHALL
Foster, Thomas Jefferson
HUNTER, W. C.
McCumber, Porter James
HUREWITZ, J. C.
Speiser, Ephraim Avigdor
HURLEY, ALFRED F.
Vandenberg, Hoyt Sanford
HUTCHINSON, WILLIAM T.
Lowden, Frank Orren
McArthur, John, 1826–1906
McClernand, John Alexander
HUTCHISON, WILLIAM R.
Lyman, Eugene William
HUTHMACHER, J. JOSEPH
Walsh, David Ignatius
HYDE, CHARLES GILMAN
Fuller, George Warren
HYDE, FRANCIS EDWIN
Perham, Josiah
HYDE, GRANT M.
Bleyer, Willard Grosvenor
HYMA, ALBERT
Campbell, James Valentine
Christiancy, Isaac Peckham
Crary, Isaac Edwin
Felch, Alpheus
Ferry, Thomas White
Kieft, Willem

Lothrop, George Van Ness
Palmer, Thomas Witherell
Van Cortlandt, Oloff
Stevenszen
Van Raalte, Albertus Christiaan
Van Twiller, Wouler
HYMAN, HERBERT H.
Stouffer, Samuel Andrew

IBBOTSON, JOSEPH D.
Kirkland, Samuel
IHDE, AARON J.
Adkins, Homer Burton
Baekeland, Leo Hendrik
Bancroft, Wilder Dwight
Chittenden, Russell Henry
Cluett, Sanford Lockwood
Elvehjem, Conrad Arnold
Gomberg, Moses
Gortner, Ross Aiken
Haynes, Williams
Hudson, Claude Silbert
Kirkwood, John Gamble
Koch, Fred Conrad
Schoenheimer, Rudolf
Stern, Kurt Guenter
IMMERMAN, RICHARD H.
Dulles, Allen Welsh
INGALLS, DANIEL H. H.
Lanman, Charles Rockwell
INGERSOLL, L. R.
Mendenhall, Charles Elwood
INGLIS, WILLIAM O.
Sullivan, John Lawrence
INGRAHAM, MARK H.
Birge, Edward Asahel
INGRAM, AUGUSTUS E.
Halderman, John A.
Le Gendre, Charles William
McCormick, Robert Sanderson
Magoffin, James Wiley
Maney, George Earl
Morris, Edward Joy
Murphy, Dominic Ignatius
IRELAND, JOHN, 1827–1896
Long, James
IRWIN, RAY W.
Morris, Richard Valentine
O'Brien, Richard
Shaw, John, 1773–1823
Somers, Richard
Spencer, John Canfield
Sterett, Andrew
Stewart, Charles
Tallmadge, Benjamin
Tallmadge, James
Throop, Enos Thompson
Trippe, John
Tyndale, Hector
Underwood, John Curtiss
Valentine, David Thomas
ISAACS, ASHER
Donnell, James C.
Ford, John Baptiste
French, Aaron
Guffey, James McClurg
Heinz, Henry John
Hogg, George
Horton, Valentine Baxter
Jones, Benjamin Franklin
Jones, William Richard
Leishman, John G.A.
Lockhart, Charles

Lyon, James Benjamin
Metcalf, William
Moorhead, James Kennedy
Mowbray, George Mordey
Nevin, Robert Peebles
O'Hara, James
Oliver, George Tener
Reed, James Hay
Rees, James
Vandergrift, Jacob Jay
ISAACS, EDITH J.R.
Bloomgarden, Solomon
Gordin, Jacob
Niblo, William
Palmer, Albert Marshman
Pastor, Antonio
ISAACS, LEWIS M.
Conried, Heinrich
ISRAEL, FRED L.
Long, Breckinridge
ISRAEL, JERRY
Davis, Dwight Filley
IVES, SAMUEL A.
Plimpton, George Arthur

JACK, JOHN G.
Sargent, Charles Sprague
Wilson, Ernest Henry
JACK, OLIVE M.
Jewell, Harvey
JACK, THEODORE HENLEY
Bagby, Arthur Pendleton
Candler, Asa Griggs
Clay, Clement Claiborne
Clay, Clement Comer
Clemens, Jeremiah
Jackson, Henry Rootes
Johnston, Joseph Forney
Jones, Thomas Goode
Lewis, Dixon Hall
JACKSON, A.V. WILLIAMS
Bloomfield, Maurice
JACKSON, DANIEL D.
Hendrick, Ellwood
JACKSON, DUGALD C.
Behrend, Bernard Arthur
JACKSON, GEORGE STUYVESANT
Lowell, John, 1769–1840
JACKSON, JOSEPH
Archer, Samuel
Bailey, Lydia R.
Carbutt, John
Charles, William
Childs, Cephas Grier
Childs, George William
Clay, Edward Williams
Currier, Nathaniel
Cushman, George Hewett
Dawkins, Henry
Drake, Alexander Wilson
Dunlap, John
Du Simitière, Pierre Eugène
Eckstein, John
Edwin, David
Ehninger, John Whetten
Fitzgerald, Thomas
Folwell, Samuel
Fox, Gilbert
Girsch, Frederick
Gobrecht, Christian
Goddard, Paul Beck
Godfrey, Thomas, 1704–1749
Goodman, Charles

Gostelowe, Jonathan
Hall, David
Hall, Sarah Ewing
Hart, Abraham
Heilprin, Angelo
Hill, Richard
Humphreys, James
Ives, James Merritt
Jackson, David
Jansen, Reinier
Jenkins, John, 1728–1785
Jenkins, John, 1751–1827
Jennings, John
Johnston, David Claypoole
Jordan, John Woolf
Kearney, Francis
Kneass, Samuel Honeyman
Kneass, Strickland
Kneass, William
Lawson, Alexander
Leaming, Thomas
Leavitt, Dudley
Leeds, Daniel
Lewis, Wilfred
Lippard, George
Longacre, James Barton
Ludwick, Christopher
MacKellar, Thomas
Malcolm, James Peller
Markoe, Abraham
Mease, James
Melish, John
Miles, Edward
Miller, John Henry
Morwitz, Edward
Newsam, Albert
Nicholson, James Bartram
Otis, Bass
Pease, Joseph Ives
Pendleton, John B.
Piggot, Robert
Rosenthal, Max
Savery, William, 1721–1787
Smith, John Jay
Smith, Lloyd Pearsall
Snowden, James Ross
Stoddart, Joseph Marshall
Tanner, Benjamin
Tiebout, Cornelius
Wagner, William
Watson, John Fanning
Westcott, Thompson
Wetherill, Samuel
Wharton, Robert
JACKSON, KENNETH T.
Flynn, Edward Joseph
JACKSON, LUTHER P., JR.
Ottley, Roi
JACKSON, RICHARD
Goldman, Edwin Franko
JACKSON, RUSSELL LEIGH
Jackson, Hall
Tracy, Nathaniel
JACOBS, TRAVIS BEAL
Steinhardt, Laurence Adolph
JACOBS, WILBUR R.
Farrand, Max
JACOBSEN, EDNA L.
Southwick, Solomon
Ten Broeck, Abraham
Vesey, William
West, George
Wisner, Henry

Woodhull, Nathaniel
Young, John
JACOBSON, ARTHUR C.
Kearsley, John
JAFFE, IRMA B.
Stella, Joseph
JAMES, ALFRED P.
Negley, James Scott
Olmsted, Marlin Edgar
JAMES, D. CLAYTON
Friedman, William Frederick
MacArthur, Douglas
Sutherland, Richard Kerens
Whitney, Courtney
JAMES, EDWARD T.
Coxey, Jacob Sechler
Hayes, John William
U'Ren, William Simon
JAMES, JAMES ALTON
Bissell, William Henry
Black, John Charles
Clark, George Rogers
Gibault, Pierre
Pollock, Oliver
JAMES, M. C.
Green, Seth
Henshall, James Alexander
Mather, Fred
Titcomb, John Wheelock
JAMESON, J. FRANKLIN
Hunt, Gaillard
Johnson, Allen
JANOWITZ, MORRIS
Thomas, William Isaac
JARVIS, ERIC
Boring, Edwin Garrigues
Evers, Medgar Wiley
Malin, Patrick Murphy
JAY, MARTIN
Neumann, Franz Leopold
JEBSEN, HARRY, JR.
Cromwell, Dean Bartlett
Vance, Arthur Charles
    ("Dazzy")
JEFFERSON, PAUL
Reid, Ira De Augustine
JELLIFFE, SMITH ELY
Dana, Charles Loomis
Morton, William James
JELLINEK, GEORGE
Nevada, Emma
JENKINS, CHARLES F.
Matlack, Timothy
JENKINS, EDWARD HOPKINS
Adams, Dudley W.
Adlum, John
Armsby, Henry Prentiss
Arnold, Lauren Briggs
Budd, Joseph Lancaster
Chamberlain, William Isaac
Coburn, Foster Dwight
Collier, Peter
Colman, Henry
Deane, Samuel
Dickson, David
Eliot, Jared
Emerson, George Barrell
Fairchild, George Thompson
JENKINS, REESE V.
Mees, Charles Edward Kenneth
Watson, Thomas John

JENKINS, WALTER S.
Beach, Amy Marcy Cheney
JENKS, WILLIAM L.
Woodward, Augustus Brevoort
JENNINGS, WALTER LOUIS
Hill, Henry Barker
Kinnicutt, Leonard Parker
JENSEN, GORDON M.
Easley, Ralph Montgomery
JENSEN, PAUL M.
Nichols, Dudley
JENSON, CAROL ELIZABETH
Adams, Annette Abbott
JEPSON, WILLIS L.
Greene, Edward Lee
Hansen, George
Holder, Charles Frederick
Howell, Thomas Jefferson
Kellogg, Albert
Knowlton, Frank Hall
Kuhn, Adam
Kunze, Richard Ernest
Lemmon, John Gill
Parry, Charles Christopher
Wickson, Edward James
JERVEY, THEODORE D.
Trott, Nicholas
JESSUP, MARY E.
Bush, Lincoln
Eddy, Harrison Prescott
Strauss, Joseph Baermann
JESSUP, PHILIP C.
Root, Elihu
JESSUP, WALTER E.
Hill, Louis Clarence
JEWELL, EDWARD ALDEN
Raymond, George Lansing
JEWELL, WILLIAM M.
Brush, George de Forest
Gardner, Helen
JEWETT, FRANK B.
Carty, John Joseph
JOERG, W. L. G.
Adams, Cyrus Cornelius
Bien, Julius
Hoen, August
Tanner, Henry Schenck
JOHANNINGMEIER, ERWIN V.
Bagley, William Chandler
JOHANNINGMEIER, E. V.
Day, Edmund Ezra
JOHANSEN, DOROTHY O.
Foster, William Trufant
JOHNSON, ALLEN
Adams, Henry Brooks
Asbury, Francis
Boucher, Jonathan
Brown, John, 1800–1859
Bryan, William Jennings
Claghorn, George
Cooper, Myles
Douglas, Stephen Arnold
Eddy, Mary Morse Baker
Evans, Warren Felt
JOHNSON, ALLEN S.
Hoover, Charles Franklin
JOHNSON, ALONZO
Belo, Alfred Horatio
JOHNSON, ALVIN
Clark, John Bates
JOHNSON, ARTHUR M.
Mellon, William Larimer

JOHNSON, CECIL
  Lowrey, Mark Perrin
  Lowry, Robert
JOHNSON, CECIL M.
  Durfee, Zoheth Sherman
JOHNSON, CLAUDIUS O.
  Harrison, Carter Henry
JOHNSON, DIANE
  Duggar, Benjamin Minge
JOHNSON, EDGAR A. J.
  Amory, Thomas
  Cook, Elisha
  Cushing, Thomas
JOHNSON, EDGAR HUTCHINSON
  Bumstead, Horace
  Candler, Allen Daniel
  Haygood, Atticus Green
  Hopkins, Isaac Stiles
JOHNSON, EDWIN LEE
  Tolman, Herbert Cushing
JOHNSON, GUY B.
  Gonzales, Ambrose Elliott
JOHNSON, H. EARLE
  Fisher, William Arms
  Homer, Louise Dilworth Beatty
  Mason, Daniel Gregory
JOHNSON, HENRY
  De Costa, Benjamin Franklin
  Dutton, Samuel Train
JOHNSON, JAMES P.
  Oswald, Lee Harvey
JOHNSON, JOHN R.
  Carothers, Wallace Hume
JOHNSON, JOSEPH E.
  Taylor, George
JOHNSON, PETER LEO
  Heiss, Michael
  Henni, John Martin
JOHNSON, ROGER T.
  La Follette, Robert Marion, Jr.
JOHNSON, T. CARY, JR.
  Millington, John
  Robertson, William Joseph
  Robinson, Conway
  Smith, John Blair
  Smith, John Lawrence
  Waddel, James
JOHNSON, THOMAS H.
  Taylor, Edward
JOHNSON, WALTER
  Stettinius, Edward Reilly
  Stevenson, Adlai Ewing, II
JOHNSTON, J. WESLEY
  Ames, Edward Raymond
  Andrews, Edward Gayer
JONES, D. F.
  East, Edward Murray
JONES, H. G.
  Connor, Robert Digges
    Wimberly
JONES, HORACE LEONARD
  Sterrett, John Robert Sitlington
JONES, HOWARD MUMFORD
  Murat, Achille
  Royster, James Finch
  Tyler, Moses Coit
JONES, JAMES H.
  Gregg, Alan
JONES, LAWRENCE N.
  Powell, Adam Clayton, Sr.
JONES, PETER D'A.
  Coit, Stanton
  Gerber, (Daniel) Frank

Gerber, Daniel (Frank)
JONES, PHILLIP S.
  Jackson, Dunham
  Miller, George Abram
JONES, ROBERT L.
  Sedgwick, Robert
JONES, RUFUS M.
  Coffin, Charles Fisher
  Comstock, Elizabeth L.
  Gibbons, Abigail Hopper
  Hicks, Elias
  Hoag, Joseph
  Hopper, Isaac Tatem
  Hunt, Nathan
  Jay, Allen
  Keith, George
  Kelsey, Rayner Wickersham
  Owen, Griffith
  Sands, David
  Scattergood, Thomas
  Smith, Hannah Whitall
  Thomas, Richard Henry
  Updegraff, David Brainard
  Waln, Nicholas
  Wilbur, John
  Wood, James, 1839–1925
JONES, THEODORE F.
  Brown, Elmer Ellsworth
  Mathews, Cornelius
JONES, WILLARD LEONARD
  Jacobs, William Plumer
JONES, WILLIAM
  Cranston, John
  Van Beuren, Johannes
  Van Buren, William Holme
JORDAN, DANIEL P.
  Stacy, Walter Parker
JORDAN, DAVID STARR
  Agassiz, Jean Louis Rodolphe
  Baird, Spencer Fullerton
  Gilbert, Charles Henry
  Gill, Theodore Nicholas
  Goode, George Brown
  Lesueur, Charles Alexandre
JORDAN, H. DONALDSON
  Helm, Charles John
  Huse, Caleb
  Murphy, William Sumter
  Thayer, Eli
  Voorhees, Daniel Wolsey
  Walker, Robert John
JORDAN, JESSIE KNIGHT
  Agassiz, Jean Louis Rodolphe
  Baird, Spencer Fullerton
JORDAN, PHILIP D.
  Salter, William
  Salter, William Mackintire
  Winslow, Edward Francis
  Wylie, Andrew
JORDAN, WHITMAN H.
  Goodale, Stephen Lincoln
JOSEPHSON, HAROLD
  Gitlow, Benjamin
  Shotwell, James Thomson
JOY, JAMES R.
  Cranston, Earl
  Fowler, Charles Henry
  Hamilton, John William
  Hartzell, Joseph Crane
  Haven, Erastus Otis
  Haven, Gilbert
  Kidder, Daniel Parish
  McFarland, John Thomas

Mattison, Hiram
Merrick, Frederick
Merrill, Stephen Mason
Mudge, Enoch
Neely, Thomas Benjamin
Newman, John Philip
Salm-Salm, Agnes Elisabeth
  Winona Leclercq Joy,
  Princess
Vincent, John Heyl
JUDD, CHARLES H.
  Colvin, Stephen Sheldon
  Jackman, Wilbur Samuel
  Parker, Francis Wayland
  Parker, Samuel Chester
  Young, Ella Flagg
JUDSON, SHELDON
  Johnson, Douglas Wilson
JUNGEBLUT, CLAUS W.
  Gay, Frederick Parker

KAESE, HAROLD
  Sears, Richard Dudley
  Wright, George
KAHN, JEFFREY A.
  Ewing, James
  Libman, Emanuel
  MacCallum, William George
KAHN, LOTHAR
  Feuchtwanger, Lion
KAHRL, GEORGE MORROW
  Stobo, Robert
KALK, DANIEL S.
  Fairchild, David Grandison
  Merrill, Elmer Drew
KAMMETT, LAWRENCE
  Will, Allen Sinclair
KANE, HOPE FRANCES
  Arnold, Samuel Greene
  Bowler, Metcalf
  Richmond, John Wilkes
KARL, BARRY D.
  Merriam, Charles Edward, Jr.
KARPINSKI, LOUIS C.
  Loyd, Samuel
  Mackenzie, George Henry
  Morphy, Paul Charles
  Pike, Nicolas
  Pillsbury, Harry Nelson
  Steinitz, William
KASTEN, MARIE A.
  Bacon, Alice Mabel
  Beard, Thomas Francis
  Beatty, Charles Clinton
  Beauchamp, William
  Bennet, Sanford Fillmore
  Blake, Lillie Devereux
  Bloomer, Amelia Jenks
  Boissevain, Inez Milholland
  Bond, Hugh Lennox
  Booth-Tucker, Emma Moss
  Bottome, Margaret McDonald
  Bourne, George
  Boyd, Belle
  Bradford, Edward Green
  Bradley, Lydia Moss
  Bridgman, Laura Dewey
  Brigham, Mary Ann
  Bromfield, John
  Brown, George, 1823–1892
  Brown, Isaac Van Arsdale
  Bucknell, William
  Burnett, Joseph

Burns, Anthony
Burroughs, John Curtis
Capen, Elmer Hewitt
Chaplin, Jeremiah
Chapman, Maria Weston
Cheney, Oren Burbank
Church, William Conant
Coffin, Levi
Coffin, Lorenzo S.
Crosby, Howard
KATZ, IRVING
Dodge, Joseph Morrell
Wolfson, Erwin Service
KATZMAN, DAVID M.
Binga, Jesse
Hutcheson, William Levi
Pelham, Robert A.
KAUFMAN, PAUL
Knox, Thomas Wallace
Lea, Homer
Poore, Benjamin Perley
Scovel, Henry Sylvester
Simonton, James William
KAUFMANN, EDGAR, JR.
Wright, Frank Lloyd
KAY, DELBERT
Nordberg, Bruno Victor
KAZIN, ALFRED
Van Doren, Carl Clinton
KEATS, SHEILA
Stoessel, Albert Frederic
KEBLER, LYMAN F.
Beck, Lewis Caleb
Craigie, Andrew
KEEP, ROBERT PORTER
Porter, Sarah
KEHL, GEORGE L.
Campbell, William
KELLAR, HERBERT ANTHONY
Atkins, Jearum
Bement, Caleb N.
Downing, Andrew Jackson
Downing, Charles
McCormick, Cyrus Hall
McCormick, Leander James
McCormick, Robert
McCormick, Stephen
Robinson, Solon
Skinner, John Stuart
Wilder, Marshall Pinckney
Wood, Walter Abbott
KELLAR, LUCILE O'CONNOR
McCormick, Cyrus Hall
KELLER, ALBERT G.
Day, Clarence Shepard
KELLER, DEANE
Fisher, Harrison
KELLER, FRANKLIN J.
Bloomfield, Meyer
KELLER, MORTON
Beck, James Montgomery
Richberg, Donald Randall
KELLEY, DONALD R.
Mattingly, Garrett
KELLOCK, KATHARINE AMEND
Revere, Paul
Richardson, Joseph
Sanderson, Robert
Syng, Philip
Vernon, Samuel
Winslow, Edward

KELLOGG, LOUISE PHELPS
Alemany, José Sadoc
Altham, John
André, Louis
Badin, Stephen Theodore
Bapst, John
Baraga, Frederic
Bienville, Jean Baptiste Le
Moyne, Sieur de
Bourgmont, Étienne Venyard,
Sieur de
Brodhead, Daniel
Brulé, Etienne
Cadillac, Antoine de la Mothe,
Sieur
Carver, Jonathan
Céleron, de Blainville, Pierre
Joseph de
Champlain, Samuel de
Charlevoix, Pierre François
Xavier de
Chaumonot, Pierre Joseph
Marie
Clark, William
Cornstalk
Dablon, Claude
De Langlade, Charles Michel
Druillettes, Gabriel
Duluth, Daniel Greysolon, Sieur
Dunmore, John Murray
Faribault, Jean Baptiste
Fish, Carl Russell
Forsyth, Thomas
Garakonthie, Daniel
Gass, Patrick
Gravier, Jacques
Guignas, Michel
Hennepin, Louis
Henry, Alexander
Hooper, Jessie Annette Jack
Iberville, Pierre Le Moyne,
Sieur d'
Jogues, Isaac
Jolliet, Louis
Joutel, Henri
Juneau, Solomon Laurent
Kinzie, John
Lahontan, Louis-Armand de
Lom d'Arce, Baron de
Lapham, Increase Allen
La Ronde, Louis Denis, Sieur
de
La Salle, Robert Cavelier, Sieur
de
Laudonnière, René Goulaine de
La Vérendrye, Pierre Gaultier
De Varennes, Sieur de
Legler, Henry Eduard
Léry, Joseph Gaspard
Chaussegros de
Le Sueur, Pierre
Lewis, Meriwether
L'Halle, Constantin de
Marest, Pierre Gabriel
Marquette, Jacques
Membré, Zenobius
Ménard, René
Monette, John Wesley
Nicolet, Jean
Nicollet, Joseph Nicolas
Ordway, John
Perrot, Nicolas
Pond, Peter

Râle, Sébastien
Ribaut, Jean
Rolette, Jean Joseph
Saenderl, Simon
St. Denis (Denys), Louis
Juchereau de
St. Lusson, Simon François
Daumont, Sieur de
Thwaites, Reuben Gold
Tonty, Henry de
Vaudreuil-Cavagnal, Pierre du
Rigaud, Marquis de
Verwyst, Chrysostom Adrian
Vincennes, François Marie
Bissot, Sieur de
Vincennes, Jean Baptiste Bissot,
Sieur de
Williams, Eleazar
KELLOGG, REMINGTON
Savage, Thomas Staughton
KELLOGG, VERNON LYMAN
Burbank, Luther
KELLY, ALFRED H.
Jackson, Robert Houghwout
KELLY, HOWARD A.
Burrage, Walter Lincoln
Howard, William Travis
Sims, James Marion
Williams, John Whitridge
Wilson, Henry Parke Custis
KELSEY, HARRY
Abel-Henderson, Annie Heloise
KELSEY, RAYNER W.
Chalkley, Thomas
Cox, Henry Hamilton
Eddy, Thomas
Hallowell, Richard Price
Larkin, Thomas Oliver
Mifflin, Warner
Morris, Anthony, 1654–1721
Penn, William
Savery, William, 1750–1804
Scott, Job
Sharpless, Isaac
KEMMERER, DONALD L.
Andrew, Abram Piatt
Crissinger, Daniel Richard
Hamlin, Charles Sumner
Noyes, Alexander Dana
Reynolds, George McClelland
KEMP, WILLIAM WEBB
Burk, Frederic Lister
Cooper, Sarah Brown Ingersoll
Lange, Alexis Frederick
Le Conte, John
KEMPTON, J. H.
Collins, Guy N
KENDALL, ISOLINE RODD
Beer, William
KENDALL, LANE C.
Franklin, Philip Albright Small
Hague, Robert Lincoln
KENDLE, BURTON
Campbell, William Edward
March
KENDRICK, ALEXANDER
Murrow, Edward (Egbert)
Roscoe
Swing, Raymond Edwards
(Gram)
KENDRICK, BENJAMIN B.
McIver, Charles Duncan

KENDRICK, M. SLADE
  Davenport, Herbert Joseph
KENNEDY, ALBERT JOSEPH
  Addams, Jane
  Woods, Robert Archey
KENNEDY, DAVID M.
  Dickinson, Robert Latou
  Sanger, Margaret Higgins
  Sullivan, Mark
KENNEDY, RICHARD S.
  Wolfe, Thomas Clayton
KENNEDY, SUSAN ESTABROOK
  Anderson, Mary
  Dodd, Bella Visono
  Dreier, Mary Elisabeth
  Goldenweiser, Emanuel
    Alexander
  Marcus, Bernard Kent
  Maybank, Burnet Rhett
  Wadsworth, Eliot
KENNELLY, KAREN, C.S.J.
  Brown, Charlotte Hawkins
KENNELLY, KAREN M.
  Mitchell, Lucy Sprague
  Voris, John Ralph
KENNY, ROBERT W.
  Ralph, James
KENT, FRANK RICHARDSON
  Brown, Alexander, 1764–1834
  Brown, George, 1787–1859
  Brown, James, 1791–1877
  Brown, John A.
KENT, G. C.
  Whetzel, Herbert Hice
KENT, ROLAND G.
  Newbold, William Romaine
KENYON, BERNICE
  Gluck, Alma
KEOGH, ANDREW
  Van Name, Addison
KEPLEY, DAVID R.
  Reynolds, Robert Rice
KEPPEL, FREDERICK P.
  Suzzallo, Henry
KERBY, WILLIAM JOSEPH
  Alphonsa, Mother
  Anthony, Sister
  Bouquillon, Thomas Joseph
  Conaty, Thomas James
  Keane, John Joseph
KERN, JOHN D.
  Woolson, Constance Fenimore
KERN, LOUIS J.
  Jackson, Shirley Hardie
  Kelland, Clarence Budington
KERNAN, WARWICK J.
  Roberts, Ellis Henry
KERWIN, JEROME G.
  Walgreen, Charles Rudolph
KETRING, RUTH ANNA
  Osborn, Charles
KEY, JACK D.
  Craig, Winchell McKendree
KEY, J. B.
  Bankhead, John Hollis
  Steagall, Henry Bascom
KEY, PIERRE VAN RENSSELAER
  Cary, Annie Louise
KEYES, CHARLES R.
  Wachsmuth, Charles
KEYES, EDWARD L.
  Otis, Fessenden Nott

KEYS, ALICE M.
  Colden, Cadwallader
KIDDER, ALFRED VINCENT
  Bandelier, Adolph Francis
    Alphonse
KIERAN, JOHN
  Huggins, Miller James
  Johnson, Byron Bancroft
  Mathewson, Christopher
  Morrissey, John
  Rockne, Knute Kenneth
  Spalding, Albert Goodwill
  Travis, Walter John
  Weston, Edward Payson
  Wright, Henry
KIERSTEAD, CAROLINE HEMINWAY
  Scott, William Berryman
KIGER, JOSEPH C.
  French, Paul Comly
  Keppel, Frederick Paul
  Smith, Henry Louis
KILLEFFER, D. H.
  Herty, Charles Holmes
  Landis, Walter Savage
KILPATRICK, CARROLL
  Bankhead, William Brockman
KIMBALL, FISKE
  Bulfinch, Charles
  Godefroy, Maximilian
  Goodhue, Bertram Grosvenor
  Hadfield, George
  Hallet, Étienne Sulpice
  Harrison, Peter
  Haviland, John
  Hoban, James
  Latrobe, Benjamin Henry,
    1764–1820
  L'Enfant, Pierre Charles
  McIntire, Samuel
  Mills, Robert, 1781–1855
  Thornton, William
KIMBALL, MARIE GOEBEL
  Short, William
KIMBALL, WARREN F.
  Jones, Jesse Holman
KINDILIEN, CARLIN T.
  Fite, Warner
  Pitkin, Walter Boughton
  Runyon, Damon
KING, ALMA DEXTA
  Oldham, Williamson Simpson
KING, EDWARD S.
  Pickering, Edward Charles
KING, JAMES GORE
  Parmentier, Andrew
KING, JAMES GORE, JR.
  Mayhew, Thomas
  Strong, Caleb
KING, JOHN O.
  Gregory, Thomas Barger
KING, PHILIP B.
  Willis, Bailey
KING, ROY T.
  Wells, Robert William
KING, WILLIAM BRUCE
  Corcoran, William Wilson
KINLEY, DAVID
  Weston, Nathan Austin
KIRBY, RICHARD S.
  Cain, William
  Weston, William

KIRK, GRAYSON L.
  Reinsch, Paul Samuel
KIRK, RICHARD R.
  King, Grace Elizabeth
  Stuart, Ruth McEnery
KIRKENDALL, RICHARD S.
  Baker, Oliver Edwin
  Cannon, Clarence
  Klem, William J. (Bill)
  McMahon, Brien
  Pressman, Lee
KIRKLAND, EDWARD CHASE
  Daniels, Winthrop More
  Gilmore, James Roberts
  Jaquess, James Frazier
  Jewett, William Cornell
  King, Samuel Ward
  Willis, William
KIRSCH, FELIX M.
  Antoine, Père
KIRSHNER, RALPH
  Asbury, Herbert
  Blackstone, Harry
  Fitzsimmons, James Edward
    ("Sunny Jim")
  George, Grace
  Hirsch, Maximilian Justice
  Kiphuth, Robert John Herman
  Ouimet, Francis Desales
  Sloane, Isabel Cleves Dodge
  Stuart, John Leighton
KIRWAN, ALBERT D.
  Harrison, Byron Patton
KISH, DOROTHY
  Francis, Kay
  Tanguay, Eva
KLEENE, GUSTAV A.
  McCook, John James
KLEIN, LOUIS A.
  Pearson, Leonard
KLEIN, MAURY
  Calhoun, Patrick
KLEINFIELD, H. L.
  Barrymore, John
  Barrymore, Lionel
  Huston, Walter
  Marlowe, Julia
  Woollcott, Alexander
    Humphreys
KLEMIN, ALEXANDER
  Chanute, Octave
  Vought, Chance Milton
  Wellman, Walter
  Wise, John
  Wright, Wilbur
KLINE, ALLEN MARSHALL
  Dillingham, William Paul
  Fairbanks, Erastus
  Fuller, Levi Knight
  Hall, Hiland
  Hammond, Edwin
KLINE, JOHN R.
  Patterson, Robert
KLINGBERG, FRANK J.
  Tappan, Arthur
  Tappan, Lewis
KNAPP, CHARLES M.
  James, Ollie Murray
KNAPP, JOSEPH G.
  Babcock, Howard Edward
KNAUSS, JAMES O.
  Duval, William Pope
  Hackley, Charles Henry

Howard, Jacob Merritt
Howard, William Alanson
Sower, Christopher, 1754–1799
KNIGHT, ARTHUR
    Fairbanks, Douglas
    Turpin, Ben
KNIGHT, EDGAR WALLACE
    Aycock, Charles Brantley
    Caldwell, Joseph
    Wiley, Calvin Henderson
KNIGHT, GRANT C.
    Bowman, John Bryan
    Cawein, Madison Julius
    Loos, Charles Louis
    Patterson, James Kennedy
    Peers, Benjamin Orrs
    Prentice, George Dennison
    Warfield, Catherine Ann Ware
    Wilson, Robert Burns
KNIGHT, OLIVER
    Block, Paul
    Copley, Ira Clifton
KNITTLE, RHEA MANSFIELD
    Danforth, Thomas, 1703–1788
    Dyott, Thomas W.
    Hewes, Robert
    Jarves, Deming
    Wistar, Caspar
KNOEFEL, PETER K.
    Barbour, Henry Gray
KNOTT, H. W. HOWARD
    Abbott, Austin
    Abbott, Benjamin Vaughan
    Aldrich, Edgar
    Allen, Charles
    Allen, John James
    Ames, Samuel
    Andrews, Charles
    Andrews, George Pierce
    Angel, Benjamin Franklin
    Angell, Joseph Kinnicutt
    Anthon, John
    Arrington, Alfred W.
    Baldwin, John Brown
    Bangs, Francis Nehemiah
    Barbour, Oliver Lorenzo
    Barlow, Samuel Latham Mitchill
    Barradall, Edward
    Barton, Robert Thomas
    Bates, Daniel Moore
    Bates, George Handy
    Beach, William Augustus
    Beall, Samuel Wootton
    Beaman, Charles Cotesworth
    Beaupré, Arthur Matthias
    Bell, Clark
    Bemis, George
    Benedict, Erastus Cornelius
    Benjamin, Judah Philip
    Bennett, Edmund Hatch
    Bennett, Nathaniel
    Bidwell, Marshall Spring
    Bigelow, Melville Madison
    Bingham, Harry
    Binney, Horace
    Bishop, Joel Prentiss
    Blackford, Charles Minor
    Blatchford, Richard Milford
    Bliss, George
    Bliss, Jonathan
    Blowers, Sampson Salter
    Bonney, Charles Carroll
    Bradbury, Theophilus

Bradford, Alexander Warfield
Bradwell, James Bolesworth
Bradwell, Myra
Brady, James Topham
Brannon, Henry
Brewster, Frederick Carroll
Brightly, Frederick Charles
Brown, Addison
Brown, Henry Billings
Browne, Irving
Burdick, Francis Marion
Burke, Thomas, 1849–1925
Burrill, Alexander Mansfield
Butterworth, Benjamin
Bynum, William Preston
Cadwalader, John, 1805–1879
Cady, Daniel
Caines, George
Caldwell, Henry Clay
Carlisle, James Mandeville
Casey, Joseph
Caton, John Dean
Chambers, George
Champlin, John Wayne
Chandler, Peleg Whitman
Chase, George
Chilton, William Paris
Chipman, Daniel
Chisolm, Alexander Robert
Clagett, Wyseman
Clark, Greenleaf
Clopton, David
Clough, William Pitt
Comstock, George Franklin
Conrad, Holmes
Cooke, John Rogers
Cowley, Charles
Cox, Rowland
Coxe, Richard Smith
Cranch, William
Cross, Edward
Crump, William Wood
Curtis, Edwin Upton
Cuyler, Theodore
Daly, Charles Patrick
Dana, Richard
Dane, Nathan
Daniel, Peter Vivian
Dargan, Edmund Strother
Daveis, Charles Stewart
D'avezac, Auguste Geneviève
    Valentin
Davis, George Breckenridge
Davis, John, 1761–1847
Davis, Noah, 1818–1902
Davis, William Thomas
Day, James Gamble
Day, Luther
Dean, Amos
Dearborn, Henry Alexander
    Scammell
Delmas, Delphin Michael
Deming, Henry Champion
Denver, James William
Dexter, Franklin
Dexter, Samuel, 1761–1816
Dexter, Wirt
Dickerson, Edward Nicoll
Dickerson, Philemon
Dickey, Theophilus Lyle
Diven, Alexander Samuel
Dixon, Luther Swift
Doddridge, Philip

Doe, Charles
Donnelly, Charles Francis
Dos Passos, John Randolph
Douglas, Henry Kyd
Doyle, John Thomas
Duane, William John
Dudley, Paul
Duer, John
Duer, William
Dunlop, James
DuPonceau, Pierre Étienne
Durant, Thomas Jefferson
Durell, Edward Henry
Durfee, Job
Durfee, Thomas
Dutton, Henry
Dwight, Theodore William
Dyer, Eliphalet
Earle, Thomas
Edmonds, John Worth
Edwards, Charles
Elliott, Benjamin
Ellis, George Washington
Ellsworth, Henry William
Emery, Lucilius Alonzo
Emott, James, 1771–1850
Emott, James, 1823–1884
Evarts, Jeremiah
Ewing, Charles
Farrar, Edgar Howard
Farrar, Timothy
Fenner, Charles Erasmus
Field, Maunsell Bradhurst
Field, Walbridge Abner
Fitzhugh, William
Flagg, Azariah Cutting
Flanders, Henry
Fletcher, Calvin
Fletcher, Richard
Fletcher, William Asa
Folger, Walter
Ford, Gordon Lester
Foster, Roger Sherman Baldwin
Francis, Tench
Gardiner, John
Garrison, Cornelius Kingsland
Garrison, William Re Tallack
Gerard, James Watson
Gerry, Elbridge Thomas
Gibson, John Bannister
Gilpin, Edward Woodward
Glover, Samuel Taylor
Goddard, Luther Marcellus
Goff, John William
Goudy, William Charles
Gould, James
Graham, David
Graham, John Andrew
Gray, Francis Calley
Gray, George
Gray, John Chipman
Green, Andrew Haswell
Green, Henry Woodhull
Green, William
Greenleaf, Simon
Gregory, Stephen Strong
Grinnell, Henry
Grinnell, Joseph
Grinnell, Moses Hicks
Howe, William F.
KNOWLES, MORRIS
    Herschel, Clemens
    Hill, Frank Alpine

Holbrook, Josiah
Knowlton, Daniel C.
KNUDSON, ALBERT C.
Townsend, Luther Tracy
KOCH, G. ADOLF
Palmer, Elihu
KOELSCH, WILLIAM A.
Atwood, Wallace Walter
Brown, Ralph Hall
Fenneman, Nevin Melancthon
KOENIG, HARRY C.
Mundelein, George William
KOGAN, HERMAN
Kelly, Edward Joseph
Smith, Henry Justin
KOHLER, MAX J.
Marshall, Louis
Peixotto, Benjamin Franklin
Seligman, Isaac Newton
Seligman, Jesse
Seligman, Joseph
KOLB, HAROLD H., JR.
Ade, George
KOLB, JR., HAROLD H.
Patten, Gilbert
KOLMER, JOHN A.
Schamberg, Jay Frank
KOOPMAN, HARRY LYMAN
Faunce, William Herbert Perry
Foss, Sam Walter
Langdon, Courtney
KOPF, EDWIN W.
Fackler, David Parks
Harris, Elisha
McCay, Charles Francis
KOPPERL, SHELDON J.
Dakin, Henry Drysdale
KORHONEN, CYNTHIA S.
Burton, Harold Hitz
KORMAN, GERD
Commons, John Rogers
KORNWOLF, JAMES D.
Elmslie, George Grant
KOUDELKA, JANET B.
Freeman, Allen Weir
KOVARIK, ALOIS F.
Boltwood, Bertram Borden
Hastings, Charles Sheldon
Mansfield, Jared
Olmsted, Denison
Pupin, Michael Idvorsky
KRAEMER, CASPAR JOHN, JR.
Waters, William Everett
KRAMER, PAUL J.
Livingston, Burton Edward
KRAUT, ALAN M.
Hines, James J.
Shaw, (Warren) Wilbur
KRAYER, OTTO
Hunt, Reid
KREHBIEL, C. E.
Goerz, David
KREMPEL, DANIEL S.
Colman, Ronald Charles
Langner, Lawrence
Laughton, Charles
Rains, Claude
KREUTER, GRETCHEN VON LOEWE
Simons, Algie Martin
KREUTER, KENT
Mitchell, William DeWitt

KREY, A. C.
Haggerty, Melvin Everett
KROCK, ARTHUR
Watterson, Henry
KROEBER, ALFRED L.
Dixon, Roland Burrage
KROGMAN, W. M.
Todd, Thomas Wingate
KROHN, ERNST C.
Reinagle, Alexander
Sobolewski, J. Friedrich Edward
Warren, Samuel Prowse
Zach, Max Wilhelm
Ziehn, Bernard
KROOSS, HERMAN E.
Berwind, Edward Julius
McGarrah, Gates White
Speyer, James Joseph
KROUT, JOHN A.
Fox, Dixon Ryan
Livingston, Peter Van Brugh
Livingston, Philip
Livingston, Robert
Livingston, William, 1723–1790
Morris, Lewis, 1671–1746
Morris, Lewis, 1726–1798
Morris, Richard
Morris, Robert, 1745–1815
Morris, Robert Hunter
Raines, John
Schuyler, George Washington
Schuyler, Margarita
Schuyler, Philip John
Van Cortlandt, Philip
Van Cortlandt, Pierre
Van Cortlandt, Stephanus
KRUEGER, LEONARD B.
Mitchell, Alexander
Smith, George
KRUM, GRACIE BRAINERD
Gillman, Henry
KRUMBHAAR, E. B.
Otto, John Conrad
KRUSEN, WILMER
Leffmann, Henry
KUBLER, ERNEST A.
Reisinger, Hugo
Robinson, Therese Albertine
    Louise Von Jakob
KUEHL, OLGA LLANO
Siloti, Alexander Ilyitch
KUEHL, WARREN F.
Atkinson, Henry Avery
Holt, Hamilton Bowen
Hyde, Charles Cheney
McDonald, James Grover
Marburg, Theodore
Scott, James Brown
Wambaugh, Sarah
KUHLMANN, CHARLES B.
Pillsbury, Charles Alfred
KUMMER, GEORGE
O'Neill, Rose Cecil
KUNKEL, BEVERLEY WAUGH
Porter, Thomas Conrad
KURLAND, GERALD
Duffy, Hugh
Kilpatrick, John Reed
Kingsley, Elizabeth Seelman
Lajoie, Napoleon ("Larry")
Richards, Vincent

KUYKENDALL, RALPH S.
Baldwin, Henry Perrine
Bishop, Charles Reed
Cooper, Henry Ernest
Dole, Sanford Ballard
Farrington, Wallace Rider
Judd, Gerrit Parmele
Kalanianaole, Jonah Kuhio
Restarick, Henry Bond
Richards, William
Thurston, Lorrin Andrews
Willis, Albert Shelby

LABAREE, LEONARD W.
Andrews, Charles McLean
Clinton, George
Douglas, William, 1742–1777
Fitch, Thomas
Law, Jonathan
Nicholson, Francis
Nicolls, Matthias
Nicolls, Richard
Nicolls, William
Pownall, Thomas
Saltonstall, Gurdon
Treat, Robert
Trumbull, Jonathan, 1710–1785
Tryon, William
LACH, DONALD F.
MacNair, Harley Farnsworth
LACHER, J. H. A.
Hoffmann, Francis Arnold
LADD, HARRY S.
Vaughan, Thomas Wayland
LADD, WILLIAM PALMER
Hart, Samuel
Leaming, Jeremiah
Smith, William, 1754–1821
LA FOLLETTE, ROBERT
Swan, James
LA FOLLETTE, SUANNE
Hibben, Paxton Pattison
LA FORTE, ROBERT SHERMAN
Bristow, Joseph Little
LAGEMANN, ELLEN CONDLIFFE
Bryson, Lyman Lloyd
LAHUE, KALTON C.
Sennett, Mack
LAING, GORDON J.
Shorey, Paul
LAMB, ARTHUR B.
Sanger, Charles Robert
LAMBERT, WALTER D.
Bowie, William
LAMONT, CORLISS
Flynn, Elizabeth Gurley
LAMPL, PAUL
Higgins, Daniel Paul
LAND, ROBERT H.
Fitzpatrick, John Clement
LAND, ROBERT HUNT
Tyler, Lyon Gardiner
LAND, WILLIAM G.
Hill, Thomas, 1818–1891
Robbins, Thomas
Robinson, Henry Cornelius
Root, Jesse
Seymour, Thomas Hart
Waller, Thomas MacDonald
LANDAU, SARAH BRADFORD
Delano, William Adams

LANDMAN, J. H.
  Stoughton, Edwin Wallace
LANDON, FRED
  Lay, Benjamin
  Lundy, Benjamin
  Realf, Richard
  Ward, Samuel Ringgold
LANE, ANN J.
  Beard, Mary Ritter
LANE, ELBERT C.
  Mitchell, Edwin Knox
  Paton, Lewis Bayles
LANE, ERNEST PRESTON
  Wilczynski, Ernest Julius
LANE, WILLIAM C.
  Cogswell, Joseph Green
  Folsom, Charles
  Jewett, Charles Coffin
LANE, WINTHROP D.
  Round, William Marshall Fitts
LANG, JOHN W.
  Field, Charles William
  Morell, George Webb
  Morton, James St. Clair
  North, Simeon, 1765–1852
LANGDON, WILLIAM CHAUNCY
  Bell, Alexander Graham
  Hubbard, Gardiner Greene
  Orton, William
  Sanders, Thomas
  Smith, Chauncey
  Storrow, James Jackson
  Vail, Theodore Newton
  Watson, Thomas Augustus
  Woodbury, Charles Jeptha Hill
LANGFELD, HERBERT S.
  Baldwin, James Mark
  Hamilton, Edward John
  McDougall, William
  Münsterberg, Hugo
  Sidis, Boris
  Warren, Howard Crosby
LANGSDORF, ALEXANDER S.
  Nipher, Francis Eugene
LANZA, CONRAD H.
  Barlow, Francis Channing
  Beaver, James Addams
  Bragg, Braxton
  Buell, Don Carlos
  Heintzelman, Samuel Peter
  Hunt, Henry Jackson
  Hunter, David
  Johnston, Joseph Eggleston
  Jones, David Rumph
  Morgan, John Hunt
  Mosby, John Singleton
  Sickles, Daniel Edgar
  Smith, William Farrar
  Stanley, David Sloane
  Sykes, George
  Taylor, Harry
  Townsend, Edward Davis
  Tyler, Robert Ogden
  Wheaton, Frank
  Woods, Charles Robert
LARKIN, FREDERICK V.
  Halsey, Frederick Arthur
  Haswell, Charles Haynes
  Herr, Herbert Thacker
  Porter, Holbrook Fitz-John
  Spangler, Henry Wilson
  Wetherill, Samuel, 1821–1890

LARROWE, C. PATRIC
  King, Carol Weiss
LARSEN, CHARLES E.
  Lindsey, Benjamin Barr
  Pegler, Westbrook
LARSON, CEDRIC A.
  Marquis, Albert Nelson
LARSON, HENRIETTA M.
  Farish, William Stamps
  Gallagher,
LARSON, OLAF F.
  Galpin, Charles Josiah
LARSON, T. A.
  Hunt, Lester Callaway
LA SALA, LINDA
  Holliday, Judy
LASH, JOSEPH P.
  Roosevelt, (Anna) Eleanor
LATANE, JOHN H.
  Lathrop, Barnes F.
  Schouler, James
LATHROP, BARNES F.
  Hoover, James Matthews
  Ireland, John, 1827–1896
  Long, James
LATOURETTE, KENNETH S.
  Beach, Harlan Page
  Graves, Rosewell Hobart
  Happer, Andrew Patton
  Hart, Virgil Chittenden
  Holcombe, Chester
  Hoover, James Matthews
  Kerr, John Glascow
  Laufer, Berthold
  Lowry, Hiram Harrison
  Martin, William Alexander
    Parsons
  Mateer, Calvin Wilson
  Olyphant, David Washington
    Cincinnatus
  Parker, Alvin Pierson
  Parker, Peter
  Pye, Watts Orson
  Schereschewsky, Samuel Isaac
    Joseph
  Sheffield, Devello Zelotes
  Shelton, Albert Leroy
  Shuck, Jehu Lewis
  Smith, Arthur Henderson
  Stoddard, David Tappan
  Stone, Ellen Maria
  Talmage, John Van Nest
  Teusler Rudolf Bolling
  Turner, Fennell Parrish
  Verbeck, Guido Herman
    Fridolin
  Watson, Andrew
  Williams, Channing Moore
  Williams, Frederick Wells
  Williams, Samuel Wells
  Yates, Matthew Tyson
  Yung, Wing
LAW, ROBERT ADGER
  Callaway, Morgan
LaWALL, CHARLES H.
  Chapman, Nathaniel
  Maisch, John Michael
LAWRENCE, A. A.
  Walker, William Johnson
LAWRENCE, BARBARA
  Allen, Glover Morrill

LAWRENCE, WILLIAM
  Stone, John Seely
LAWSON, MICHAEL L.
  Artzybasheff, Boris
  Parrish, Maxfield
LAWTON, GEORGE
  Post, Isaac
LAYTON, EDWIN
  Bedaux, Charles Eugene
  Harrington, John Lyle
LEAB, DANIEL J.
  Boudin, Louis Boudinoff
  Kracauer, Siegfried
  Lasky, Jesse Louis
  Von Sternberg, Josef
LEACOCK, STEPHEN
  Browne, Charles Farrar
  Newell, Robert Henry
  Nye, Edgar Wilson
LEAKE, CHAUNCEY D.
  Miller, William Snow
LEARNED, H. BARRETT
  Marcy, William Learned
LEARY, JOHN J., JR.
  Conboy, Sara Agnes
    McLaughlin
LEARY, WILLIAM M.
  Arnold, Leslie Philip
  Foulois, Benjamin Delahauf
  Ide, John Jay
  Krueger, Walter
  MacNider, Hanford
  Wright, Theodore Paul
LEARY, WILLIAM M., JR.
  Bellanca, Giuseppe Mario
LEDOUX, LOUIS V.
  Robinson, Edwin Arlington
LeDuc, THOMAS
  Aydelotte, Frank
  King, Stanley
  Meiklejohn, Alexander
  Todd, Walter Edmond Clyde
LeDuc, THOMAS, II
  Andrews, Israel DeWolf
LEE, ALGERNON
  London, Meyer
LEE, AMY
  Jones, Lindley Armstrong
    ("Spike")
  Weems, Ted
LEE, EDWIN A.
  Snyder, Edwin Reagan
LEE, JAMES MELVIN
  Barsotti, Charles
  Bonner, Robert
  Bradford, Andrew
  Bradford, John
  Bradford, Joseph
  Bradford, Thomas
  Carroll, Howard
  Chamberlain, Henry
    Richardson
  Charless, Joseph
  Clark, Willis Gaylord
  Cobb, Frank Irving
  Cockerill, John Albert
  Congdon, Charles Taber
  Cooper, William
  Creelman, James
  Cunliffe-Owen, Philip Frederick
  Curtis, William Eleroy
  De Young, Michel Harry
  Grasty, Charles Henry

LEE, R. ALTON
  Schwellenbach, Lewis Baxter
  Wherry, Kenneth Spicer
LEE, RENSSELAER W.
  Mather, Frank Jewett, Jr.
LEFFERT, HENRY
  Hovey, Richard
  Russell, Irwin
LEFLER, HUGH T.
  Kelley, William Darrah
  Pou, Edward William
LEHMANN, PHYLLIS WILLIAMS
  Hawes, Harriet Ann Boyd
LEICESTER, HENRY M.
  Browne, Charles Albert
LEIGHTON, RICHARD M.
  Chennault, Claire Lee
  Hodge, John Reed
  Zacharias, Ellis Mark
LEIGHTON, RICHARD N.
  Stratemeyer, George Edward
LEINBACH, PAUL S.
  Beissel, Johann Conrad
LEISY, ERNEST E.
  Johnston, Mary
  Krehbiel, Christian
LEITCH, ALEXANDER
  Burr, Aaron, 1716–1757
LELAND, WALDO G.
  Vignaud, Henry
LELAND, WALDO GIFFORD
  Jameson, John Franklin
LEMMON, SARAH MCCULLOH
  Talmadge, Eugene
LEMON, HARVEY B.
  Michelson, Albert Abraham
LEMONS, J. STANLEY
  Brown, Gertrude Foster
  Park, Maud Wood
  Stevens, Doris
LENNIG, ARTHUR
  Lorre, Peter
  Lugosi, Bela
LEONARD, IDA REID
  Poston, Charles Debrill
LEONARD, NEIL
  Morton, Ferdinand Joseph
    ("Jelly Roll")
LEONARD, THOMAS C.
  Creel, George
  Duranty, Walter
  Farson, Negley
  Flynn, John Thomas
  McGill, Ralph Emerson
  Wagner, Robert Ferdinand
LEONARD, WILLIAM ELLERY
  Leonard, Sterling Andrus
LEONARD, WILLIAM R.
  Jarvis, Edward
  Kennedy, Joseph Camp
  Mayo-Smith, Richmond
LEOPOLD, W. F.
  Curme, George Oliver
LEPPARD, H. M.
  Goode, John Paul
LERNER, EDNA ALBERS
  Alexander, Franz Gabriel
  Berger, Victor Louis
  Frank, Lawrence Kelso
  Hillquit, Morris
  Lynd, Robert Staughton
  Reik, Theodor
  Roheim, Geza

LERNER, MAX
  Gates, John Warne
  Greene, William Cornell
  Guggenheim, Daniel
  Guggenheim, Meyer
  Hamilton, Walton Hale
  Moore, William Henry
  Morse, Charles Wyman
  Ryan, Thomas Fortune
  Swope, Herbert Bayard
  Veblen, Thorstein Bunde
  Yerkes, Charles Tyson
LESLIE, JOHN KENNETH
  Crawford, James Pyle
    Wickersham
LESLIE, J. PAUL
  Long, Earl Kemp
  Morrison, Delesseps Story
LESSER, ALLEN F.
  Menken, Adah Isaacs
LESSER, SOL
  McLaglen, Victor
LESSER, STEPHEN O.
  Costello, Lou
LESSING, LAWRENCE
  Armstrong, Edwin Howard
LESTER, H. H.
  Sauveur, Albert
LESTER, ROBIN D.
  Yost, Fielding Harris
LEUCHTENBURG, WILLIAM E.
  Borah, William Edgar
  Johnson, Hugh Samuel
  McReynolds, James Clark
LEVENSON, J. C.
  Dreiser, Theodore
LEVIN, GAIL
  Hopper, Edward
LEVINE, STUART
  Cloud, Henry Roe
LEVSTIK, FRANK R.
  Barthelmess, Richard
  Schuster, Max Lincoln
  Vedder, Edward Bright
LEVY, EUGENE
  Cook, Will Marion
LEVY, MILTON
  Michaelis, Leonor
LEWENSTEIN, BRUCE V.
  Davis, Watson
LEWINSON, EDWIN R.
  Johnson, Edward Austin
LEWIS, CHARLES LEE
  Balch, George Beall
  Brooke, John Mercer
  Buchanan, Franklin
  Cheever, Henry Theodore
  Colton, Walter
  Dromgoole, William Allen
  Jones, Catesby Ap Roger
  Jones, George
  Jones, Thomas Ap Catesby
  Murfree, Mary Noailles
  Porter, John Luke
  Queen, Walter W.
  Ramsay, Francis Munroe
  Rideout, Henry Milner
  Ridgely, Daniel Bowly
  Robert, Henry Martyn
  Robertson, Morgan Andrew
  Rowan, Stephen Clegg
  Wilson, John Fleming

LEWIS, DAVID L.
  Hershey, Milton Snavely
LEWIS, EDWARD S.
  Tobias, Channing Heggie
LEWIS, FRANK GRANT
  Dagg, John Leadley
LEWIS, FREDERIC THOMAS
  Minot, Charles Sedgwick
LEWIS, GEORGE M.
  Fordyce, John Addison
  Morrow, Prince Albert
  Palmer, Alonzo Benjamin
  Pilcher, Paul Monroe
  Ranney, Ambrose Loomis
  Wende, Ernest
  Wende, Grover William
LEWIS, H. G.
  Schultz, Henry
LEWIS, JOHN V.
  Coffey, James Vincent
  Hastings, Serranus Clinton
LEWIS, W. DAVID
  Hunter, Croil
  Jensen, Peter Laurits
  Kirchwey, George Washington
  Lawes, Lewis Edward
  Taylor, William Chittenden
LEWIS, WILLIAM S.
  Garry, Spokane
  MacDonald, Ranald
LEWIS, WINSTON B.
  Leahy, William Daniel
LEWIS, W. LEE
  Nef, John Ulric
LEYDENBERG, HARRY MILLER
  Plummer, Mary Wright
LEYS, WAYNE A. R.
  Tufts, James Hayden
LIBBEY, JAMES K.
  Fletcher, Henry Prather
LIBBY, ORIN G.
  Belcourt, George Antoine
  Pierce, Gilbert Ashville
LICH, GLEN E.
  Dobie, J(ames) Frank
  O'Daniel, Wilbert Lee
    ("Pappy")
  Peterkin, Julia Mood
LICHLITER, WILLIAM F.
  Gibson, Charles Dana
LICHTENSTEIN, NELSON
  Davis, William Hammatt
  Leiserson, William Morris
  Stolberg, Benjamin
LICHTENWANGER, WILLIAM
  Gabrilowitsch, Ossip
  Godowsky, Leopold
  McCormack, John Francis
  Schelling, Ernest Henry
  Whiting, Arthur Battelle
LIEBERT, HERMAN W.
  Isham, Ralph Heyward
LIEN, ARNOLD J.
  Hammond, William Gardiner
  Jameson, John Alexander
  Judson, Frederick Newton
  Keener, William Albert
  Minor, Virginia Louisa
LIKNESS, CRAIG S.
  Duke, Vernon
  Rooney, Pat

LILLIE, FRANK RATTRAY
  Whitman, Charles Otis
LINCOLN, CHARLES H.
  Adams, Robert
  Allen, Andrew
  Allen, William, 1704–1780
  Anderson, William
  Bailey, Francis
  Bayard, James Ash(e)ton,
    1767–1815
  Bayard, James Asheton,
    1799–1880
  Bayard, John Bubenheim
  Bayard, Richard Henry
  Bingham, William
LINDLEY, HARLOW
  Kennedy, Robert Patterson
  Kilbourne, James
  Riddle, Albert Gallatin
LINDSAY, R. B.
  Barus, Carl
LINEHAN, PAUL H.
  Herbermann, Charles George
LINFORTH, IVAN MORTIMER
  Wheeler, Benjamin Ide
LINGELBACH, ANNA LANE
  Jenkins, Howard Malcolm
  Klingelsmith, Margaret Center
  Lockrey, Sarah Hunt
  Logan, Deborah Norris
  Logan, George
  Martin, Elizabeth Price
  Oberholtzer, Sara Louisa
    Vickers
  Penniman, James Hosmer
  Pepper, George Seckel
  Poulson, Zachariah
  Price, Eli Kirk
  Proud, Robert
  Sanderson, John
  Smyth, Albert Henry
  Stevenson, Sara Yorke
  Stillé, Charles Janeway
  Townsend, Mira Sharpless
  Wallace, David
  Wallace, Lewis
  Wharton, Anne Hollingsworth
  Wister, Sarah
LINGELBACH, WILLIAM E.
  Ames, Herman Vandenburg
  Carson, Hampton Lawrence
  Girard, Stephen
  Jarvis, William
  McMaster, John Bach
LINGLE, WALTER LEE
  Plumer, William Swan
  Reed, Richard Clark
  Rice, David
  Rice, Nathan Lewis
  Smyth, Thomas
  Waddel, John Newton
LINGLEY, CHARLES RAMSDELL
  Babcock, Orville E.
  Badeau, Adam
  Belknap, William Worth
  Dingley, Nelson
  Frye, William Pierce
LINK, A. S.
  Houston, David Franklin
LINK, EUGENE P.
  Putnam, Helen Cordelia

LIPPMAN, MONROE
  Klaw, Marc
LIPSEY, ROGER
  Coomaraswamy, Ananda
    Kentish
LITTELL, JOHN STOCKTON, II
  Roberts, Issachar Jacob
LITTLEHALES, GEORGE W.
  Green, Francis Mathews
  Hilgard, Julius Erasmus
  Jones, Ernest Lester
  Trowbridge, William Petit
  Walker, Sears Cook
LIVINGSTON, ARTHUR
  Coltrane, John William
LIVINGSTON, ARTHUR P.
  Bruce, Lenny
  Russell, Charles Ellsworth
    ("Pee Wee")
LIVINGSTON, ARTHUR PAUL
  Cole, Nat ("King")
LLOYD, CRAIG
  Hinshaw, David Schull
LLOYD, JOHN URI
  Howe, Andrew Jackson
LLOYD, TREVOR
  Cook, Frederick Albert
LOBDELL, GEORGE H., JR.
  Knox, Frank
LOBINGIER, CHARLES SUMNER
  Hosmer, Hezekiah Lord
  Ingraham, Edward Duffield
  Jay, Peter Angustus
  Paine, Henry Warren
  Peckham, Rufus Wheeler
  Peckham, Wheeler Hazard
  Penrose, Charles Bingham
  Pitney, Mahlon
  Pomeroy, John Norton
  Price, Eli Kirk
  Quitman, John Anthony
  Rawle, Francis (1846–1930)
  Rawle, William
  Rawle, William Henry
  Redfield, Amasa Angell
  Redfield, Isaac Fletcher
  Richardson, James Daniel
  Richardson, William Merchant
  Robinson, William Callyhan
  Rose, Walter Malins
  Russell, Charles Wells
  Sanborn, Walter Henry
  Sanford, Edward Terry
  Sanger, George Partridge
  Saulsbury, Eli
  Saulsbury, Gove
  Saulsbury, Willard, 1820–1892
  Saulsbury, Willard, 1861–1927
  Scott, Samuel Parsons
  Sloan, Richard Elihu
  Trude, Alfred Samuel
  Wales, Leonard Eugene
  Watson, David Thompson
LOCKE, L. LELAND
  Baldwin, Frank Stephen
  Grant, George Barnard
LOCKMILLER, DAVID A.
  Crowder, Enoch Herbert
LOCKWOOD, FRANK C.
  Greenway, John Campbell
  Hubbell, John Lorenzo
  McClintock, James Harvey
  Sieber, Al

LOEB, ROBERT F.
  Palmer, Walter Walker
LOETSCHER, FREDERICK WILLIAM
  Alexander, Archibald
  Alexander, Joseph Addison
  Alexander, Samuel Davies
LOETSCHER, LEFFERTS A.
  Machen, John Gresham
  Speer, Robert Elliott
LOGAN, ANDY
  Whitman, Charles Seymour
LOGAN, RAYFORD W.
  Drew, Charles Richard
  Hope, John
  Houston, Charles Hamilton
  Woodson, Carter Godwin
LOHR, LENOX R.
  Dawes, Rufus Cutler
LOMASK, MILTON
  Guggenheim, Simon
LOMBARD, GEORGE F. F.
  Mayo, George Elton
LOMBARD, MILDRED E.
  Peters, John Andrew
  Sayre, Stephen
  Searle, James
  Wentworth, Paul
  White, Henry
  Williams, Jonathan
LONDON, HARVEY
  Martin, Everett Dean
LONDON, HERBERT I.
  Duchin, Edward Frank
    ("Eddy")
  Tilzer, Harry Von
LONG, C. N. H.
  Henderson, Yandell
LONG, ESMOND R.
  Baldwin, Edward Robinson
  Brown, Lawrason
  Gardner, Leroy Upson
  Krause, Allen Kramer
LONG, FRANCIS TAYLOR
  Johnston, Richard Malcolm
LONGCOPE, WARFIELD T.
  Baetjer, Frederick Henry
  Smith, Nathan, 1762–1829
  Smith, Nathan Ryno
LONGWELL, CHESTER R.
  Dana, Edward Salisbury
LONN, ELLA
  Ames, Adelbert
  Darke, William
  Garrett, John Work
  Garrett, Robert
  Garrett, Thomas
  Griffith, Goldsborough
    Sappington
  Hicks, Thomas Holliday
  Kellogg, William Pitt
  Latrobe, John Hazlehurst
    Boneval
  Lee, Thomas Sim
  Ligon, Thomas Watkins
  Lloyd, Edward, 1744–1796
  Lloyd, Edward, 1779–1834
  Lowndes, Lloyd
  Nelson, Roger
  Nicholls, Francis Redding
    Tillou
  Pearce, James Alfred
  Pinchback, Pinckney Benton
  Plater, George

McCARTHY, RAYMOND G.
Cooke, Elisha
McCAUGHEY, ROBERT A.
Gildersleeve, Virginia
Crocheron
Meyer, Annie Nathan
McCAUL, ROBERT L.
Judd, Charles Hubbard
McCAUSLAND, ELIZABETH
Cary, Elisabeth Luther
Myers, Jerome
McCLEAN, ALBERT F.
Fields, Lewis Maurice
McCLURE, CLARENCE H.
Fletcher, Thomas Clement
McCLURE, N. E.
Linn, John Blair
Neal, Joseph Clay
McCLUSKEY, NEIL G.
Johnson, George
MacCOLL, MARY
Webster, Alice Jane Chandler
McCOLLESTER, LEE SULLIVAN
Adams, John Coleman
Amherst, Jeffery
McCOLLUM, E. V.
Hess, Alfred Fabian
McCONNELL, J. W.
Weisenburg, Theodore Herman
McCORD, DAVID
Copeland, Charles Townsend
McCORMAC, EUGENE I.
McLane, Louis
Polk, James Knox
McCORMICK, SAMUEL BLACK
Bruce, Robert
McCORMICK, THOMAS DENTON
Baker, La Fayette Curry
Bingham, John Armor
Blount, Thomas
Buchanan, John
Bulloch, Archibald
Burrowes, Thomas Henry
Cameron, Archibald
Christian, William
De Haas, John Philip
Faulk, Andrew Jackson
Fenno, John
Frazer, John Fries
Frazer, Persifor
Fries, John
Gibson, George
Gibson, John
Goss, James Walker
McCOY, DONALD R.
Dawes, Charles Gates
Garner, John Nance
Hoover, Herbert Clark, Jr.
Kefauver, (Carey) Estes
O'Mahoney, Joseph Christopher
Reece, Brazilla Carroll
Scopes, John Thomas
Wallace, Lurleen Burns
Wood, John Stephens
McCOY, GARNETT
Smith, David Roland
McCOY, SONDRA VAN METER
Hope, Clifford Ragsdale
MacCRACKEN, HENRY N
Jewett, Milo Parker
Raymond, John Howard
Taylor, James Monroe
Vassar, Matthew

McCRACKEN, ROBERT T.
Von Moschzisker, Robert
McCRAE, THOMAS
Da Costa, Jacob Mendez
Dewees, William Potts
Dorsey, John Syng
Gibson, William
Hartshorne, Henry
Hays, Isaac
Hodge, Hugh Lenox
McClellan, George, 1796-1847
McClellan, George, 1849-1913
Pepper, William
Physick, Philip Syng
Smith, Albert Holmes
McCRAW, THOMAS K.
McKellar, Kenneth Douglas
Morgan, John Harcourt
Alexander
Olds, Leland
McCREA, NELSON GLENN
Merriam, Augustus Chapman
Wilson, Peter
McCREA, ROSWELL CHENEY
Atkinson, Edward
Bergh, Henry
McCUE, WILLIAM T.
Rice, Alice Caldwell Hegan
McCUTCHEON, ROGER P.
Dinwiddie, Albert Bledsoe
Hunt, Carleton
Nicholson, Eliza Jane Poitevent
Holbrook
Pinney, Norman
Poydras, Julien De Lalande
Soulé, George
Townsend, Mary Ashley
Walker, Alexander
Walworth, Jeannette Ritchie
Hadermann
McDANIEL, ARTHUR S.
Hale, Robert Safford
Johnson, Alexander Smith
Jones, Samuel
Loomis, Arphaxed
Lord, Daniel
McDANIEL, W. B., 2D
Landis, Henry Robert Murray
Schweinitz, George Edmund de
McDONAGH, DON
Draper, Ruth
Humphrey, Doris
McDONALD, ARCHIE P.
Hobby, William Pettus
McDONALD, FORREST
Carlisle, Floyd Leslie
Couch, Harvey Crowley
Insull, Samuel
Sloan, Matthew Scott
McDONALD, GERALD D.
Harlow, Jean
McDONALD, PHILIP B.
Argall, Philip
Balbach, Edward
Bayles, James Copper
Billings, Charles Ethan
Boyden, Uriah Atherton
Brunton, David William
Coxe, Eckley Brinton
Day, David Talbot
Douglas, James
Field, Cyrus West
Frick, Henry Clay

Fritz, John
Holmes, Joseph Austin
Humphreys, Alexander
Crombie
Hyatt, John Wesley
Janin, Louis
Jennings, James Hennen
Kirchhoff, Charles William
Raymond, Charles Walker
Raymond, Rossiter
Worthington
Rothwell, Richard Pennefather
Winchell, Horace Vaughn
MacDONALD, WILLIAM L.
Bigelow, John
Birney, James
Birney, James Gillespie
Birney, William
Brayton, Charles Ray
Cannon, Joseph Gurney
Chamberlain, Joshua Lawrence
Chandler, Zachariah
Clark, Champ
Colfax, Schuyler
Whittemore, Thomas
MACDOUGALL, DIANNE NEWELL
Snow, Jessie Baker
McDOUGALL, RICHARD
Beach, Sylvia Woodbridge
McDOWELL, FREDERICK P. W.
Roberts, Elizabeth Madox
McDOWELL, GEORGE TREMAINE
Boner, John Henry
MACE, RUTH LOWENS
Nolen, John
MACE, WILLIAM HARRISON
Bardeen, Charles William
MACELWANE, JAMES B.
Odenbach, Frederick Louis
MACFARLAND, FRANK M.
Starks, Edwin Chapin
McFARLAND, JOSEPH
Meigs, Arthur Vincent
Meigs, Charles Delucena
Meigs, John Forsyth
Pancoast, Joseph
Pancoast, Seth
Stillé, Alfred
White, James William
Wood, George Bacon
Wood, Horatio Charles
Wormley, Theodore George
Young, John Richardson
McFARLAND, KEITH D.
Woodring, Harry Hines
McFARLAND, MARVIN W.
Wright, Orville
McFARLAND, WALTER MARTIN
Babcock, George Herman
Bailey, Frank Harvey
Canaga, Alfred Bruce
Hoxie, William Dixie
Kafer, John Christian
Mattice, Asa Martines
Taylor, Stevenson
Wilcox, Stephen
McGIFFERT, ARTHUR CUSHMAN
Briggs, Charles Augustus
Brown, Francis, 1849-1916
McGILL, RALPH
Howell, Clark

McGLANNAN, ALEXIUS
  Tiffany, Louis McLane
McGLOTHLIN, W. J.
  Johnson, William Bullein
  Manly, Basil
  Marshal, Daniel
  Mullins, Edgar Young
  Murrow, Joseph Samuel
  Riley, Benjamin Franklin
  Sanders, Billington McCarter
  Sherwood, Adiel
  Tucker, Henry Holcombe
McGOLDRICK, JOSEPH D.
  Hylan, John Francis
McGRANE, REGINALD C.
  Christy, David
  Cist, Charles, 1738–1805
  Cist, Charles, 1792–1868
  Clarke, Robert
  Cox, George Barnsdale
  Edgerton, Alfred Peck
  Elder, William Henry
  Ellis, John Washington
  Ewing, Hugh Boyle
  Ewing, Thomas, 1789–1871
  Ewing, Thomas, 1829–1896
  Faran, James John
  Findlay, James
  Foraker, Joseph Benson
  Force, Manning Ferguson
  Gage, Lyman Judson
  Galloway, Samuel
  Greenwood, Miles
  Guilford, Nathan
  Gunther, Charles Frederick
  Hammond, Charles
  Hovey, Charles Edward
  Ingalls, Melville Ezra
  Langston, John Mercer
  Lawrence, William, 1819–1899
  Leaming, Jacob Spicer
  Leavitt, Humphrey Howe
  Lytle, William Haines
  McLean, John
  Pattison, John M.
  Pendleton, George Hunt
  Schneider, Herman
  Springer, Reuben Runyan
  Thurman, Allen Granberry
  Warden, Robert Bruce
  Zimmerman, Eugene
McGREGOR, MALCOLM F.
  West, Allen Brown
MACINTOSH, DOUGLAS CLYDE
  Beckwith, Clarence Augustine
MACK, WARREN B.
  Landreth, David
  Lippincott, James Starr
  Powel, John Hare
McKAY, ERNEST A.
  Cohn, Alfred A.
  Cohn, Harry
  Fox, William
  Garland, Judy
  MacDonald, Jeanette Anna
  Morehouse, Ward
  Nichols, Ruth Rowland
  Rathbone, Basil
  Sturges, Preston
  Tucker, Sophie
McKAY, SETH SHEPARD
  Camp, John Lafayette,
    1828–1891

Camp, John Lafayette,
  1855–1918
Davis, Edmund Jackson
Gary, Martin Witherspoon
Gregg, Maxcy
Reagan, John Henninger
Ross, Lawrence Sullivan
Rusk, Thomas Jefferson
Shepard, Seth
MACKAY-SMITH, ALEXANDER
  Woodward, William
McKEE, OLIVER, JR.
  Fisher, Walter Lowrie
  Garrison, Lindley Miller
  Lane, Franklin Knight
  Longworth, Nicholas,
    1869–1931
  Payne, John Barton
  Wood, William Robert
  Woodin, William Hartman
McKELVEY, BLAKE
  Bausch, Edward
  Eastman, George
  Gleason, Kate
  Spear, Charles
  Wines, Enoch Cobb
  Wines, Frederick Howard
McKELVEY, JEAN TREPP
  Davis, Katharine Bement
McKENNA, MARIAN C.
  May, Andrew Jackson
McKENZIE, KENNETH
  Parsons, Thomas William
McKENZIE, R. TAIT
  Murphy, Michael Charles
McKERNS, JOSEPH P.
  Brokenshire, Norman Ernest
  Freed, Alan J.
McKINNEY, GORDON B.
  Jeffries, James Jackson
  Simmons (Szymanski), Aloysius
    Harry
McKINSTRY, H. E.
  Lindgren, Waldemar
McLAUGHLIN, ANDREW C.
  Cooley, Thomas McIntyre
  Judson, Harry Pratt
McLAUGHLIN, CHARLES CAPEN
  Moore, Charles
McLEAN, ALBERT F.
  Bogart, Humphrey DeForest
  Bragdon, Claude Fayette
  Curry, John Steuart
  Dean, James Byron
  Howard, Willie
  Monroe, Marilyn
  Shean, Albert
  Strange, Michael
  Weber, Joseph Morris
McLEAN, ALBERT F., JR.
  Carroll, Earl
  Jolson, Al
  Taylor, Charles Alonzo
  Wood, Grant
MACLEAR, ANNE BUSH
  Cochrane, John
  Curtis, Newton Martin
  Hunter, Thomas
MACMAHON, ARTHUR W.
  Goodnow, Frank Johnson
McMAHON, EDWARD
  Smith, James Allen

McMILLAN, DOUGLAS J.
  Baker, Dorothy Dodds
  Ruark, Robert Chester
McMURRAY, DONALD L.
  Cattell, William Cassaday
  Eaton, John
  McCartney, Washington
  Pardee, Ario
  Porter, James Madison
McMURTRIE, DOUGLAS C.
  Meeker, Jotham
  Timothy, Lewis
MacNAIR, HARLEY FARNSWORTH
  King, Charles William
McNALLY, MICHAEL J.
  Hurley, Joseph Patrick
McNAMARA, KATHERINE
  Pilat, Ignaz Anton
  Robinson, Charles Mulford
  Sargent, Henry Winthrop
  Underwood, Loring
  Vaux, Calvert
  Vitale, Ferruccio
  Weidenmann, Jacob
McNAMARA, WILLIAM
  Sorin, Edward Frederick
McNAUGHER, JOHN
  Moorehead, William Gallogly
McNEILL, T. F.
  Poe, Orlando Metcalfe
  Quinby, Isaac Ferdinand
  Ransom, Thomas Edward
    Greenfield
  Ripley, Edward Hastings
  Rodes, Robert Emmett
  Seymour, Truman
  Sherman, Thomas West
  Smith, Charles Ferguson
  Smith, Giles Alexander
  Smith, Morgan Lewis
  Smith, Persifor Frazer
  Tidball, John Caldwell
  Torbert, Alfred Thomas
    Archimedes
MACNIE, JOHN P.
  Wheeler, John Martin
McPHEETERS, W. E.
  King, Rufus
McPHERSON, JOHN HANSON
    THOMAS
  Ashmun, Jehudi
  Atkinson, William Yates
  Blount, James Henderson
  Clark, John
  Gilmer, George Rockingham
  Milledge, John
  Mitchell, David Brydie
  Newman, William Truslow
  Nisbet, Eugenius Aristides
  Northen, William Jonathan
  Speer, Emory
McWILLIAMS, CAREY
  Sterling, George
MADARAS, LAWRENCE H.
  Roosevelt, Theodore
MADDEN, EVA ANNE
  Elliott, Sarah Barnwell
MADDOX, JERALD C.
  Genthe, Arnold
MADDOX, ROBERT FRANKLIN
  Kilgore, Harley Martin

MADDOX, ROBERT JAMES
  Slemp, Campbell Bascom
MADISON, CHARLES A.
  Harcourt, Alfred
MADISON, JAMES H.
  Whiteside, Arthur Dare
MAGEE, JAMES D.
  Johnson, Alexander Bryan
  Johnson, Joseph French
MAGEE, M. D'ARCY
  Magruder, George Lloyd
MAGIE, WILLIAM FRANCIS
  Fine, Henry Burchard
  Henry, Joseph
  Loomis, Elmer Howard
MAGILL, ROSWELL
  Cravath, Paul Drennan
MAHAN, BRUCE E.
  Carpenter, Cyrus Clay
  Chambers, John
  Davenport, George
  Dubuque, Julien
  Eastman, Enoch Worthen
  Leffler, Isaac
  Leffler, Shepard
MAHONEY, JOSEPH F.
  Walsh, Edmund Aloysius
  Walsh, Thomas Joseph
MAKINSON, RANDELL L.
  Greene, Charles Sumner
  Greene, Henry Mather
MALAND, CHARLES J.
  Brackett, Charles William
  Curtiz, Michael
  Johnston, Eric Allen
MALIN, JAMES C.
  Curtis, Charles
  Lease, Mary Elizabeth Clyens
  Logan, Cornelius Ambrose
  Martin, John Alexander
  Morrill, Edmund Needham
  Phillips, William Addison
  Root, Frank Albert
  Stubbs, Walter Roscoe
MALLALIEU, W. C.
  Gary, James Albert
  Goldsborough, Charles
  Goldsborough, Louis
    Malesherbes
  Goldsborough, Robert
  Grimké, John Faucheraud
  Hunter, Whiteside Godfrey
  Johnson, Bradley Tyler
  Kent, Joseph
  Key, Philip Barton
  Lindsay, William
  McAfee, Robert Breckinridge
  McCreary, James Bennett
  Metcalfe, Thomas
  Morehead, Charles Slaughter
  Morehead, James Turner
  Owsley, William
MALLISON, A. G.
  Gregory, Thomas Watt
MALLOCH, ARCHIBALD C.
  Church, Benjamin
  Craik, James
MALONE, DUMAS
  Alderman, Edwin Anderson
  Baldwin, Abraham
  Barbour, James
  Barbour, Philip Pendelton
  Callender, James Thomson

Cooper, Thomas
Drayton, John
Drayton, William, 1732–1790
Drayton, William, 1776–1846
Fulton, Robert Burwell
Giles, William Branch
Gilmer, Francis Walker
Henry, William Wirt
Humphreys, Benjamin Grubb
Jefferson, Thomas
Madison, Dolly Payne
Randolph, John, 1773–1833
Rhodes, James Ford
MALONE, KEMP
  March, Francis Andrew,
    1825–1911
  March, Francis Andrew,
    1863–1928
  Webster, Noah
MANCHESTER, MARY E.
  Adams, Andrew
  Andrews, Charles Bartlett
  Baldwin, Roger Sherman
  Baldwin, Simeon
MANDEL, BERNARD
  Hayes, Max Sebastian
MANDELBAUM, DAVID G.
  Sapir, Edward
MANGIONE, JERRE
  Cahill, Holger
MANN, ARTHUR T.
  La Guardia, Fiorello Henry
  Mead, Edwin Doak
  Moore, James Edward
  Walker, James John
MANN, HELEN JO SCOTT
  De Young, Michel Harry
  Freeman, Frederick Kemper
  Sprague, Charles Ezra
MANN, LOUIS LEOPOLD
  Adler, Samuel
  Asher, Joseph Mayor
  Hirsch, Emil Gustav
  Rosenwald, Julius
MANN, ROBERT S.
  Lee, James Melvin
MANN, RUTH J.
  Funk, Casimir
  Hench, Philip Showalter
MANNING, HELEN TAFT
  Rhoades, James E.
  Taylor, Joseph Wright
  Thomas, Martha Carey
MANROSS, WILLIAM W.
  Schroeder, John Frederick
MANVILLE, RICHARD H.
  Merriam, Clinton Hart
MARCOSSON, ISAAC F.
  Frohman, Charles
MARCUSON, ISAAC E.
  Grossman, Louis
MARGOLIS, JOHN D.
  Eliot, T(homas) S(tearns)
  Krutch, Joseph Wood
MARGULIES, HERBERT F.
  Lenroot, Irvine Luther
MARKHAM, JESSE WILLIAM
  Fetter, Frank Albert
MARKS, HENRY SEYMOUR
  Kearns, Jack
  Maranville, Walter James
    Vincent ("Rabbit")

MARKS, LIONEL S.
  Hollis, Ira Nelson
MARMARELLI, RONALD S.
  Covici, Pascal ("Pat")
  Funk, Wilfred John
  Hard, William
  High, Stanley Hoflund
  Sulzberger, Arthur Hays
MARMER, HARRY A.
  Bent, Silas
  Limbeck, William
  Harris, Rollin Arthur
  Hassler, Ferdinand Rudolph
  Hayford, John Fillmore
  Lindenkohl, Adolph
  Martin, Artemas
  Maury, Matthew Fontaine
  Mendenhall, Thomas Corwin
  Mitchell, Henry
  Pavy, Octave
  Peary, Robert Edwin
  Schott, Charles Anthony
MARRARO, HOWARD R.
  Foresti, Eleutario Felice
MARSDEN, BRIAN G.
  Moulton, Forest Ray
  Perrine, Charles Dillon
MARSHALL, GEORGE
  Williams, John Elias
  Yoakum, Benjamin Franklin
MARSHALL, JAMES TRIMBLE, JR.
  Brown, John Appleton
  Brown, John George
  Bunce, William Gedney
MARSHALL, S. L. A.
  McAlexander, Ulysses Grant
MARSHALL, THOMAS M.
  Bates, Edward
  Bates, Frederick
MARSHALL, WILLIAM B.
  Lea, Isaac
MARSZALEK, JOHN F.
  Michaux, Lightfoot Solomon
  Perkins, Marion
  Wilson, J(ames) Finley
MARTENS, FREDERICK HERMAN
  Abbott, Emma
  Bispham, David Scull
  Damrosch, Leopold
  Dannreuther, Gustav
  Davis, John, c. 1780–1825
  De Coppet, Edward J.
  De Koven, Henry Louis
    Reginald
  Dresel, Otto
  Estey, Jacob
  Fairlamb, James Remington
  Fischer, Emil Friedrich August
  Fletcher, Alice Cunningham
  Gemünder, August Martin
    Ludwig
  Gericke, Wilhelm
  Gilchrist, William Wallace
  Gilmore, Patrick Sarsfield
  Gleason, Frederic Grant
  Hamlin, Emmons
  Hammerstein, Oscar
  Hanchett, Henry Granger
  Harris, Charles Kassell
  Hauk, Minnie
  Heinrich, Max
  Herbert, Victor
  Hewitt, James

Hill, Ureli Corelli
Hoffman, Richard
Humiston, William Henry
Kellogg, Clara Louise
Knabe, Valentine Wilhelm
Kobbé, Gustav
Koemmenich, Louis
Maretzek, Max
Marzo, Eduardo
Mason, Henry
Mason, Lowell
Mason, Luther Whiting
Mason, William
Mathews, William Smythe Babcock
Moore, Annie Aubertine Woodward
Moore, John Weeks
Musin, Ovide
Neuendorff, Adolph Heinrich Anton Magnus
Nordica, Lillian
Nunó, Jamie
Osgood, George Laurie
Phillips, Philip
Powell, Alma Webster
Powell, Maud
Presser, Theodore
Ritter, Frédéric Louis
Rogers, Clara Kathleen Barnett
Roosevelt, Hilborne Lewis
Rybner, Martin Cornelius
MARTIN, ALBERT R.
Munroe, Charles Edward
MARTIN, ALBRO
Cowen, Joshua Lionel
Damon, Ralph Shepard
Frye, William John ("Jack")
Gifford, Walter Sherman
Moody, John
Moran, Eugene Francis
Rockefeller, John Davison, Jr.
Starrett, Paul
MARTIN, ASA EARL
Dinwiddie, Edwin Courtland
Findley, William
Fitzsimmons, or Fitzsimins, Thomas
Forward, Walter
Shulze, John Andrew
Shunk, Francis Rawn
Sparks, Edwin Erle
Swallow, Silas Comfort
Wolf, George
MARTIN, BERNARD
Philipson, David
MARTIN, GEOFFREY
Bowman, Isaiah
MARTIN, GEOFFREY I.
Jefferson, Mark Sylvester William
MARTIN, GEOFFREY J.
Huntington, Ellsworth
MARTIN, JAMES J.
Berkman, Alexander
Goldman, Emma
Tucker, Benjamin Ricketson
MARTIN, KAREN
Tarr, Ralph Stockman
MARTIN, LAWRENCE
Mitchell, John, d. 1768

MARX, PAUL B.
Michel, Virgil George
MASON, ALPHEUS THOMAS
Corwin, Edward Samuel
Haines, Daniel
Hornblower, Joseph Coerten
Roberts, Owen Josephus
Stone, Harlan Fiske
MASON, CHRISTINE GIBBONS
Masters, Edgar Lee
MASON, DANIEL GREGORY
Savage, Philip Henry
MASON, EDWARD S.
Taussig, Frank William
MASON, LESTER B.
Verplanck, Gulian Crommelin
MASSON, THOMAS L.
Bangs, John Kendrick
MATAS, RUDOLPH
Prevost, François Marie
Richardson, Tobias Gibson
Riddell, John Leonard
MATES, JULIAN
Harris, Sam Henry
MATHER, ANNE D.
McCormick, Anne Elizabeth O'Hare
MATHER, FRANK JEWETT, JR.
Abbey, Edwin Austin
Davies, Arthur Bowen
Marquand, Allan
Martin, Homer Dodge
Tryon, Dwight William
Van Dyke, John Charles
MATHEWS, ALBERT P.
Drake, Benjamin
Drake, Daniel
Elwell, John Johnson
Gaillard, Edwin Samuel
Garlick, Theodatus
Goforth, William
Goldsmith, Middleton
Hildreth, Samuel Prescott
Jackson, John Davies
Keyt, Alonzo Thrasher
King, John
Rachford, Benjamin Knox
Ransohoff, Joseph
MATHEWS, SHAILER
Barrows, John Henry
Miller, Lewis
Moulton, Richard Green
MATHEWS, THOMAS G.
Winship, Blanton
MATTESON, DAVID M.
Adams, Abijah
Brown, Jameson, 1800–1855
Campbell, John
Draper, John
Fitch, Samuel
Fleming, John, 1764–1800
Gill, John
Green, Bartholomew
Green, Samuel
Johnson, Marmaduke
MATTHEWS, BRANDER
Bunner, Henry Cuyler
MATTHEWS, FRED H.
Park, Robert Ezra
MATTHIESSEN, FRANCIS O.
Crane, Harold Hart
Jewett, Sarah Orne

MAURY, JEAN WEST
Sprague, Kate Chase
MAXCY, KENNETH F.
Frost, Wade Hampton
MAXCY, SPENCER J.
Baziotes, William
Louis, Morris
MAXON, WILLIAM R.
Eaton, Daniel Cady
Peck, Charles Horton
Perrine, Henry
Pursh, Fredrick
Rose, Joseph Nelson
Safford, William Edwin
Spalding, Volney Morgan
Sullivant, William Starling
Tuckerman, Edward
Underwood, Lucien Marcus
Vasey, George
Walter, Thomas
MAXWELL, ROBERT S.
Esch, John Jacob
La Follette, Philip Fox
MAY, JOSEPH
Bender, George Harrison
Lucas, Scott Wike
MAYALL, MARGARET W.
Cannon, Annie Jump
MAYER, ANDRE
Lahey, Frank Howard
MAYER, EMIL
Asch, Morris Joseph
Gruening, Emil
MAYER, GEORGE H.
Lundeen, Ernest
Olson, Floyd Bjerstjerne
MAYER, GEORGE LOUIS
Liebling, Estelle
MAYER, MARTIN
Buckner, Emory Roy
MAYHEW, THEODORE L.
Astor, William Vincent
Kelley, Edith Summers
Whalen, Grover Aloysius
MAYO, BERNARD
Dunlap, Robert Pinckney
Hamlin, Charles
Hubbard, John
King, Horatio
MAYO, LAURENCE SHAW
Belknap, Jeremy
Dexter, Samuel, 1726–1810
Dowse, Thomas
Farmer, John, 1789–1838
Felt, Joseph Barlow
Goodhue, Benjamin
Hoyt, Albert Harrison
Langdon, Samuel
Langdon, Woodbury
Lathrop, John
Livermore, George
Lossing, Benson John
Lovell, John
Lowell, Edward Jackson
Lunt, George
Mason, Jonathan
MAYOCK, THOMAS J.
Mason, Arthur John
Moser, Christopher Otto
MAZUZAN, GEORGE T.
Austin, Warren Robinson
Bridges, (Henry) Styles

MAZZARO, JEROME
  Jarrell, Randall
  Ley, Willy
MEADE, JULIAN R.
  Whitaker, Daniel Kimball
MEADE, ROBERT DOUTHAT
  Jenkins, Albert Gallatin
  Jenkins, Micah
  Lee, William Henry Fitzhugh
  Logan, Thomas Muldrup,
    1840–1914
  Long, Armistead Lindsay
  McClellan, Henry Brainerd
  Magruder, John Bankhead
  Martin, James Green
  Maury, Dabney Herndon
  Northrop, Lucius Bellinger
  Pelham, John
  Polk, Leonidas
  Polk, Lucius Eugene
  Randolph, Alfred Magill
  Randolph, George Wythe
  Ravenscroft, John Stark
  Seddon, James Alexander
  Shoup, Francis Asbury
  Walker, Reuben Lindsay
  Walker, William Henry Talbot
  Winder, John Henry
  Wise, Henry Alexander
  Wise, Henry Augustus
  Wise, John Sergeant
MEANS, STEWART
  Allen, Alexander Viets Griswold
MEANY, EDMOND S.
  Ferry, Elisha Peyre
MECHLIN, LEILA
  Brackett, Edward Augustus
  Bradford, William, 1823–1892
  Bristol, John Bunyan
  Brooks, Richard Edwin
  Burroughs, Bryson
  Bush-Brown, Henry Kirke
  Dielman, Frederick
  Evans, William Thomas
  Ffoulke, Charles Mather
  Freer, Charles Lang
  French, William Merchant
    Richardson
  Lukeman, Henry Augustus
  Niehaus, Charles Henry
  Paris, Walter
  Pattison, James William
  Pine, Robert Edge
  Powell, Lucien Whiting
  White, John Blake
  Whittridge, Worthington
  Wolf, Henry
MEDINA, HAROLD R.
  Steuer, Max David
MEEKS, CARROLL L. V.
  Ford, George Burdett
  Granger, Alfred Hoyt
MEENES, MAX
  Jastrow, Joseph
MEGARGEE, RICHARD
  Moore, John Bassett
MEIN, WILLIAM WALLACE
  Webb, Harry Howard
MEINE, FRANKLIN J.
  Harris, George Washington,
    1814–1869
  Pomeroy, Marcus Mills
  Shillaber, Benjamin Penhallow

  Thomson, Mortimer Neal
  Thorpe, Thomas Bangs
MELAND, BERNARD E.
  Mathews, Shailer
MELCHER, FREDERIC G.
  Brett, George Platt
MENDEL, LAFAYETTE B.
  Osborne, Thomas Burr
MENDELL, CLARENCE W.
  Hadley, James
  Peck, Tracy
  Seymour, Thomas Day
  Thacher, Thomas Anthony
  Wheeler, Arthur Leslie
MENDENHALL, JOHN C.
  Waln, Robert, 1794–1825
MENEELY, A. HOWARD
  Cameron, James Donald
  Cameron, Simon
  Harvey, George Brinton
    McClellan
  Kerney, James
  Page, Walter Hines
  Redfield, William Cox
  Smith, James, 1851–1927
  Stanbery, Henry
  Stanton, Edwin McMasters
  Thomas Lorenzo
  Wade, Benjamin Franklin
MENNEL, ROBERT M.
  Flexner, Bernard
  Swift, Linton Bishop
MENSH, MARK
  Fischer, Louis
MENZEL, DONALD H.
  Campbell, William Wallace
  Howe, Herbert Alonzo
  Lewis, Exum Percival
  Schaeberle, John Martin
MEREDITH, ALBERT B.
  Northrop, Birdsey Grant
MERENESS, NEWTON D.
  Calvert, Charles
  Calvert, George
  Calvert, Leonard
  Claiborne, William
  Coode, John
  Copley, Lionel
  Copley, Thomas
  Dulany, Daniel, 1685–1753
  Dulany, Daniel, 1722–1797
  Eddis, William
  Eden, Robert
  Fendall, Josias
  Hanson, John
  Henry, John, 1750–1798
  Hindman, William
  McMahon, John Van Lear
  Ogle, Samuel
  Scott, Gustavus
  Smallwood, William
  Smith, Caleb Blood
  Smith, Oliver Hampton
  Tilghman, Matthew
  Vinton, Samuel Finley
  White, Albert Smith
  Winder, Levin
  Wright, Joseph Albert
  Wright, Robert
MERGEN, BERNARD
  Piper, William Thomas

MERINO, BARBARA B.
  Lybrand, William Mitchell
MERIWETHER, ROBERT LEE
  Burke, AEdanus
  Butler, Pierce
  Butler, William, 1759–1821
  Gadsden, Christopher
  Gaillard, John
  Garden, Alexander, 1757–1829
  Hutson, Richard
  Jamison, David Flavel
  Keitt, Lawrence Massillon
  McCord, David James
  Marion, Francis
  Moultrie, William
  Ramsay, David
  Rutledge, Edward
  Rutledge, John
MERRIAM, CHARLES E.
  Burgess, John William
  Freund, Ernst
MERRIAM, JOHN CAMPBELL
  Chamberlin, Thomas Chrowder
MERRILL, GEORGE PERKINS
  Ashburner, Charles Albert
  Barrell, Joseph
  Becker, George Ferdinand
  Beecher, Charles Emerson
  Blake, William Phipps
  Bradley, Frank Howe
  Branner, John Casper
  Broadhead, Garland Carr
  Brooks, Alfred Hulse
  Brooks, Thomas Benton
  Brush, George Jarvis
  Calvin, Samuel
  Clark, William Bullock
  Clarke, John Mason
  Claypole, Edward Waller
  Cook, George Hammell
  Cope, Edward Drinker
  Crosby, William Otis
  Dana, James Dwight
  Dutton, Clarence Edward
  Eaton, Amos
  Emmons, Ebenezer
  Emmons, Samuel Franklin
  Gilbert, Grove Karl
  Hague, Arnold
  Hague, James Duncan
  Hall, James, 1811–1898
  Hayden, Ferdinand Vandiveer
  Hayes, Charles Willard
  Hilgard, Eugene Woldemar
  Hitchcock, Charles Henry
  Hitchcock, Edward, 1793–1864
  Houghton, Douglass
  Iddings, Joseph Paxon
  Irving, Roland Duer
  Jackson, Charles Thomas
  Kemp, James Furman
  Kerr, Washington Caruthers
  King, Clarence
  LeConte, Joseph
  Leidy, Joseph
  Lesley, Peter
  Lesquereux, Leo
  Maclure, William
  Marsh, Othniel Charles
  Mather, William Williams
  Meek, Fielding Bradford
  Newberry, John Strong
  Orton, Edward Francis Baxter

Owen, David Dale
Powell, John Wesley
Pumpelly, Raphael
Rogers, Henry Darwin
Rogers, William Barton
Safford, James Merrill
Salisbury, Rollin D.
Shaler, Nathaniel Southgate
Smith, Eugene Allen
Springer, Frank
Stevenson, John James
Swallow, George Clinton
Van Hise, Charles Richard
Walcott, Charles Doolittle
White, Israel Charles
Whitney, Josiah Dwight
Williams, George Huntington
Winchell, Alexander
Winchell, Newton Horace
MERRILL, MARION
Becket, Frederick Mark
MERRILL, MILTON R.
Smoot, Reed Owen
MERRIMAN, ROGER B.
Bigelow, Erastus Brigham
Prescott, William Hickling
MERRITT, ERNEST
Anthony, William Arnold
MERRITT, RAYMOND HARLAND
Blakeley, George Henry
Howell, Albert Summers
Talbot, Arthur Newell
MERYMAN, RICHARD S.
Mankiewicz, Herman Jacob
MESERVE, WALTER J.
Anglin, Margaret Mary
MESICK, JANE LOUISE
Butterworth, Hezekiah
MESSBARGER, PAUL R.
Repplier, Agnes
MESSER, HELAINE
Goodyear, Anson Conger
METCALF, FRANK J.
Holden, Oliver
Holyoke, Samuel
Jackson, George K.
Keller, Mathias
Kemp, Robert H.
Law, Andrew
Oatman, Johnson
Oliver, Henry Kemble
Palmer, Horatio Richmond
Palmer, Ray
Read, Daniel, 1757–1836
Scott, John Prindle
Swan, Timothy
Thompson, Will Lamartine
Willard, Samuel
METCALF, JOHN CALVIN
Cooke, Philip Pendleton
METZGER, BRUCE M.
Lake, Kirsopp
MEYER, ADOLF
Brush, Edward Nathaniel
Phipps, Henry
MEYER, DONALD
Carnegie, Dale
Fillmore, Charles
Oursler, (Charles) Fulton
MEYER, HERMAN H. B.
Flint, Weston
Lanman, Charles
Sabin, Joseph

MEYER, LEO J.
Platt, Orville Hitchcock
MEYLAN, GEORGE L.
Gulick, Luther Halsey,
1865–1918
Sargent, Dudley Allen
MEZZACAPPA, ANTONIO L.
Grandgent, Charles Hall
MICHELSON, TRUMAN
Brinton, Daniel Garrison
MIDDLEKAUFF, ROBERT
Miller, Perry Gilbert Eddy
MIDDLETON, CHARLES R.
Armour, Thomas Dickson
("Tommy")
Merrill, Gretchen Van Zandt
Smith, Horton
Wood, Craig Ralph
MILES, EDWIN A.
Carson, Jack
Fazenda, Louise Marie
Schenck, Nicholas Michael
Yates, Herbert John
MILES, WYNDHAM D.
Lamb, Arthur Becket
MILLER, DARLIS A.
Dworshak, Henry Clarence
Ferguson, Miriam Amanda
Wallace
Johnson, Edwin Carl
MILLER, DOUGLASS W.
Craig, Daniel H.
Dexter, Henry 1813–1910
Dickinson, Charles Monroe
Fiske, Stephen Ryder
Gallagher, William Davis
Gray, Joseph W.
MILLER, FRED D.
Just, Ernest Everett
MILLER, GENEVIEVE
Sigerist, Henry Ernest
MILLER, GERRIT S.
Mearns, Edgar Alexander
MILLER, HAROLD P.
Hawthorne, Julian
MILLER, JAMES R.
Hamilton, Clayton
Tyler, George Crouse
MILLER, JANE A.
Mallinckrodt, Edward, Jr.
MILLER, JERRY L.
Meredith, Edna C. Elliott
Putnam, Nina Wilcox
MILLER, JOHN PERRY
Fisher, Irving
MILLER, JOHN VEIL, JR.
Johnson, Eldridge Reeves
MILLER, J. RONALD
Eaton, Charles Aubrey
MILLER, LILLIAN B.
Whitney, Gertrude Vanderbilt
MILLER, LINDA PATTERSON
Burchfield, Charles Ephraim
Manship, Paul Howard
Murphy, Gerald Clery
MILLER, PERRY
Nurse, Rebecca
Walker, James
MILLER, PHILIP LIESON
Galli-Curci, Amelita
White, Joseph Malachy

MILLER, RANDALL M.
Smith, Lillian Eugenia
MILLER, RAYMOND C.
Dow, Alex
Harris, William Alexander
Ingalls, John James
Peffer, William Alfred
Pingree, Hazen Stuart
Simpson, Jerry
MILLER, ROBERT MOATS
Fisher, Frederick Bohn
Tittle, Ernest Fremont
MILLER, T. GRIER
Stengel, Alfred
MILLER, WILLIAM D.
Maurin, Peter Aristide
MILLER, WILLIAM SNOW
Godman, John Davidson
Horner, William Edmonds
Kempster, Walter
MILLER, WILLIAM THOMAS
Beals, Ralph Albert
MILLETT, ALLAN R.
Bullard, Robert Lee
Ely, Hanson Edward
MILLICAN, C. BOWIE
Van Depoele, Charles Joseph
MILLIGAN, FLORENCE
Osborn, William Henry
MILLIKEN, WILLIAM M.
Dickinson, Preston
MIMS, EDWIN
Ayres, Brown
Bledsoe, Albert Taylor
Kirkland, James Hampton
Lanier, Sidney
MIMS, EDWIN, JR.
Erlanger, Abraham Lincoln
Gansevoort, Leonard
Grau, Maurice
Hawkins, Dexter Arnold
Hill, Frederick Trevor
Holley, Marietta
McVicker, James Hubert
Marble, Danforth
Murdoch, James Edward
MINDIL, CLINTON
Clark, Lewis Gaylord
Coates, George Henry
MINER, LOUIE M.
Deming, Philander
MINNICH, HARVEY C.
McGuffey, William Holmes
Osborn, Henry Stafford
Tappan, Eli Todd
Thompson, William Oxley
White, Emerson Elbridge
MITCHELL, BROADUS
Alvey, Richard Henry
Archer, Stevenson
Baird, Henry Carey
Basso, (Joseph) Hamilton
Cardozo, Jacob Newton
Carey, Henry Charles
Carey, Mathew
Catchings, Waddill
Clark, John Maurice
Colwell, Stephen
Cone, Moses Herman
Coxe, Tench
Dawson, Francis Warrington
De Bow, James Dunwoody
Brownson

Dew, Thomas Roderick
Dugdale, Richard Louis
Duke, Benjamin Newton
Duke, James Buchanan
Du Pont, Eleuthère Irénée
Du Pont, Henry
Du Pont, Henry Algernon
Du Pont, Victor Marie
Fitzhugh, George
Fries, Francis
George, Henry, 1839–1897
George, Henry, 1862–1916
Gray, George Alexander
Gregg, William
Hammett, Henry Pinckney
Hammond, Bray
Hollander, Jacob Harry
Holt, Edwin Michael
Hopkins, Johns
Hughes, Henry
Jordan, Virgil Justin
Niles, Hezekiah
Nugent, John Frost
Owen, Robert Dale
Pasvolsky, Leo
Patten, Simon Nelson
Patterson, William
Perry, Arthur Latham
Post, Louis Freeland
Pratt, Enoch
Rae, John
Raymond, Daniel
Robinson, Edward Van Dyke
Ruml, Beardsley
Schoenhof, Jacob
Simpson, Stephen
Spooner, Lysander
Thomas, Philip Evan
Thompson, Robert Ellis
Tompkins, Daniel Augustus
Tucker, George
Vethake, Henry
Walters, Henry
Walters, William Thompson
Ware, Nathaniel A.
Warfield, Solomon Davies
Wells, David Ames
Wildman, Murray Shipley
Wolman, Leo
Wright, Carroll Davidson
MITCHELL, CATHERINE PALMER
Frazer, Oliver
Freeman, James Edwards
French, Edwin Davis
Frost, Arthur Burdett
Gibson, William Hamilton
Gillam, Bernhard
Gilpin, Charles Sidney
Goodridge, Sarah
Gutherz, Carl
Keppler, Joseph
MITCHELL, FRANKLIN D.
Hyde, Arthur Mastick
MITCHELL, LARRY R.
Waller, Willard Walter
MITCHELL, MARY HEWITT
Brace, John Pierce
Cady, Sarah Louise Ensign
MITCHELL, ROBERT J.
Zellerbach, James David
MITCHELL, SAMUEL CHILES
Curry, Jabez Lamar Monroe
Gilman, Daniel Coit

Hatcher, William Eldridge
Henry, Robert
Holmes, George Frederick
Maxcy, Jonathan
Puryear, Bennet
MITCHELL, STEWART
Minot, George Richards
Mitchell, Nahum
Russell, Jonathan
Russell, William Eustis
Seymour, Horatio
MITCHELL, WALTER, JR.
Rowell, George Presbury
MITCHELL, WILMOT B.
Kellogg, Elijah
Newman, Samuel Phillips
Pickard, Samuel Thomas
MITGANG, HERBERT
Seabury, Samuel
MITMAN, CARL W.
Abbott, William Hawkins
Allen, Horatio
Arnold, Aza
Babbitt, Isaac
Ball, Albert
Beach, Frederick Converse
Benjamin, George Hillard
Blake, Eli Whitney
Blake, Francis
Bogardus, James
Borden, Gail
Borden, Simeon
Brown, Fayette
Brown, James Salisbury
Brown, Joseph Emerson
Buckland, Cyrus
Bullock, William A.
Burson, William Worth
Burt, John
Burt, William Austin
Bushnell, David
Campbell, Andrew
Case, Jerome Increase
Channing, William Francis
Cist, Jacob
Clymer, George E.
Colburn, Irving Wightman
Colt, Samuel
Conant, Hezekiah
Corliss, George Henry
Cottrell, Calvert Byron
Craven, John Joseph
Crowell, Luther Childs
Cutler, James Goold
Cutting, James Ambrose
Daft, Leo
Dalzell, Robert M.
Dancel, Christian
Danforth, Charles
Daniels, Fred Harris
Davenport, Thomas
Davis, Phineas
Davis, William Augustine
Deere, John
Deering, William
Delany, Patrick Bernard
Detmold, Christian Edward
Dixon, Joseph
Dod, Daniel
Dow, Lorenzo, 1825–1899
Drake, Edwin Laurentine
Dripps, Isaac L.
Dunbar, Robert

Dunwoody, William Hood
Durand, Cyrus
Durham, Caleb Wheeler
Eads, James Buchanan
Earle, Pliny
Edgar, Charles
Edwards, Talmadge
Edwards, William
Eickemeyer, Rudolf
Emerson, James Ezekiel
Emerson, Ralph
Emery, Albert Hamilton
Esterbrook, Richard
Esterly, George
Evans, Oliver
Ewbank, Thomas
Fairbanks, Henry
Fairbanks, Thaddeus
Farmer, Hannah Tobey
  Shapleigh
Farmer, Moses Gerrish
Field, Stephen Dudley
Fitch, John
Flad, Henry
Forney, Matthias Nace
Francis, James Bicheno
Francis, Joseph
Fulton, Robert
Furlow, Floyd Charles
Gally, Merritt
Gaskill, Harvey Freeman
Gatling, Richard Jordan
Gayley, James
Gibbs, James Ethan Allen
Gilbert, Rufus Henry
Glidden, Joseph Farwell
Goddard, Calvin Luther
Goddu, Louis
Good, John
Goodrich, Benjamin Franklin
Goodwin, Hannibal Williston
Goodyear, Charles, 1800–1860
Goodyear, Charles, 1833–1896
Gordon, George Phineas
Gorrie, John
Gray, Elisha
Greist, John Milton
Grinnell, Frederick
Gunn, James Newton
Haish, Jacob
Hall, Thomas
Hall, Thomas Seavey
Hallidie, Andrew Smith
Hammond, James Bartlett
Harvey, Hayward Augustus
Hayden, Joseph Shepard
Hayward, Nathaniel Manley
Henry, William
Herdic, Peter
Herreshoff, James Brown
Heywood, Levi
Hoe, Richard March
Hoe, Robert, 1784–1833
Hoe, Robert, 1839–1909
Holland, John Philip
Holley, Alexander Lyman
Hotchkiss, Benjamin Berkeley
House, Henry Alonzo
House, Royal Earl
Howe, Elias
Howe, Frederick Webster
Howe, John Ireland
Howe, William

Howell, John Adams
Hubbard, Henry Griswold
Hubert, Conrad
Hudson, William Smith
Hughes, David Edward
Hughes, Howard Robard
Hussey, Obed
Ingersoll, Simon
Janney, Eli Hamilton
Jeffrey, Joseph Andrew
Jenkins, Nathaniel
Jenney, William Le Baron
Jerome, Chauncey
Johnston, Samuel
Jones, Amanda Theodosia
Keen, Morris Longstreth
Kent, William
Kier, Samuel M.
Kingsford, Thomas
Knight, Edward Henry
Kruesi, John
Lamb, Isaac Wixom
Lamme, Benjamin Garver
Lampson, Sir Curtis Miranda
Langley, John Williams
Lanston, Tolbert
Larned, Joseph Gay Eaton
Latta, Alexander Bonner
Lawrence, Richard Smith
Lay, John Louis
Leavitt, Erasmus Darwin
Leavitt, Frank McDowell
Leffel, James
Leggett, Mortimer Dormer
Levy, Max
Leyner, John George
Lieb, John William
Lloyd, Marshall Burns
Locke, John
Longstreet, William
Lucas, Anthony Francis
Lyall, James
Lyman, Benjamin Smith
McCoy, Elijah
McDougall, Alexander
McKay, Gordon
Marks, Amasa Abraham
Marsh, Charles Wesley
Marsh, Sylvester
Marsh, William Wallace
Mason, William
Mast, Phineas Price
Masury, John Wesley
Matthews, John
Matzeliger, Jan Ernst
Maxim, Hudson
Maynard, Edward
Melville, David
Mergenthaler, Ottmar
Merritt, Israel John
Miller, Ezra
Moody, Paul
Morey, Samuel
Morgan, Charles Hill
Munger, Robert Sylvester
Munn, Orson Desaix
Murray, Thomas Edward
Muybridge, Eadweard
Newcomb, Charles Leonard
Nicholson, William Thomas
Norris, William
Noyes, La Verne
Ogden, Francis Barber

Oliver, James
Orr, Hugh
Otis, Charles Rollin
Otis, Elisha Graves
Packard, James Ward
Page, Charles Grafton
Painter, William
Parrott, Robert Parker
Peek, Frank William
Perkins, Jacob
Perry, Stuart
Pitts, Hiram Avery
Pope, Franklin Leonard
Porter, Rufus
Pratt, Francis Ashbury
Pratt, John
Prescott, George Bartlett
Priest, Edward Dwight
Pullman, George Mortimer
Read, Nathan
Reese, Abram
Reese, Isaac
Reese, Jacob
Remington, Eliphalet
Remington, Philo
Renwick, Edward Sabine
Renwick, Henry Brevoort
Reynolds, Edwin
Reynolds, Samuel Godfrey
Rice, Richard Henry
Roberts, William Milnor
Robinson, Stillman Williams
Robinson, William
Rogers, Henry J.
Rogers, James Harris
Rogers, John Raphael
Rogers, Thomas
Roosevelt, Nicholas J.
Root, Elisha King
Rowland, Thomas Fitch
Rumsey, James
Sargent, James
Saunders, William Lawrence
Sawyer, Sylvanus
Saxton, Joseph
Schieren, Charles Adolph
Schneller, George Otto
Scott, Irving Murray
See, Horace
Seed, Miles Ainscough
Selden, George Baldwin
Sellers, Coleman
Sellers, William
Sergeant, Henry Clark
Sessions, Henry Howard
Shaw, Thomas
Sholes, Christopher Latham
Short, Sidney Howe
Sickels, Frederick Ellsworth
Silver, Thomas
Singer, Isaac Merrit
Skinner, Halcyon
Slater, Samuel
Slocum, Samuel
Smith, Horace
Spencer, Christopher Miner
Sperry, Elmer Ambrose
Sprague, William, 1773–1836
Stager, Anson
Stanley, Francis Edgar
Stanley, William
Starrett, Laroy S.
Steinmetz, Charles Proteus

Stephenson, John
Stevens, Edwin Augustus
Stevens, John
Stevens, Robert Livingston
Stoddard, Joshua C.
Sturtevant, Benjamin Franklin
Stutz, Harry Clayton
Sweet, John Edson
Tagliabue, Giuseppe
Taylor, Frederick Winslow
Terry, Eli
Thomas, Seth
Thomson, John
Thorp, John
Thurber, Charles
Thurston, Robert Lawton
Timken, Henry
Towne, Henry Robinson
Treadwell, Daniel
Turner, Walter Victor
Twining, Alexander Catlin
Vail, Alfred
Wagner, Webster
Wallace, William
Warner, Worcester Reed
Washburn, Ichabod
Washburn, Nathan
Waterman, Lewis Edson
Watkins, John Elfreth
Weaver, William Dixon
Webb, John Burkitt
Welch, Ashbel
Wellman, Samuel Thomas
Wesson, Daniel Baird
Wheeler, Nathaniel
Whitney, Asa
Whitney, Eli
Whittemore, Amos
Wilkinson, David
Wilkinson, Jeremiah
Willard, Simon
Wilson, Allen Benjamin
Wilson, George Francis
Winchester, Oliver Fisher
Winslow, John Flack
Winton, Alexander
Wood, James J.
Woodruff, Theodore Tuttle
Worthington, Henry Rossiter
Wyman, Horace
Yale, Linus
MIZENER, ARTHUR
     Fitzgerald, Francis Scott Key
MOEHLMAN, CONRAD HENRY
     MacArthur, Robert Stuart
     Morehouse, Henry Lyman
     Morgan, Thomas Jefferson
     Moss, Lemuel
     Osgood, Howard
     Robins, Henry Ephraim
MOFFETT, E. V.
     Hill, James
     Livermore, Arthur
     Livermore, Edward St. Loe
     Livermore, Samuel, 1732–1803
     Morril, David Lawrence
MOHLER, JOHN FREDERICK
     Himes, Charles Francis
MOHLER, JOHN R.
     Moore, Veranus Alva
MOLEY, RAYMOND
     Murphy, Charles Francis

MONAGHAN, FRANK
Bierce, Ambrose Gwinett
Bohm, Max
Burns, Otway
Clinton, George
Coffin, Sir Isaac
Coke, Thomas
Coxe, Daniel
Crowne, John
Crowne, William
Devoy, John
Dewing, Francis
Donn-Byrne, Brian Oswald
Dove, David James
Evans, Thomas Wiltberger
Field, David Dudley, 1781–1867
Field, Henry Martyn
Field, Thomas Warren
Fox, Harry
Foxall, Henry
Gaillardet, Théodore Frédéric
Gay, Sydney Howard
Gibbs, George, 1815–1873
Gilder, William Henry
Gordon, George Henry
Gordon, William
Goucher, John Franklin
Graydon, Alexander
Greene, George Washington
Grover, Cuvier
Hagner, Peter
Hall, Samuel Read
Halpine, Charles Graham
Halsey, John
Halstead, Murat
Hanaford, Phoebe Ann Coffin
Harris, Benjamin
Hart, John Seely
Hastings, Samuel Dexter
Haven, Henry Philemon
Haverly, Christopher
Hazeltine, Mayo Williamson
Headley, Joel Tyler
Holley, Myron
Hollister, Gideon Hiram
Hunt, Isaac
Huntington, Jabez
Huntington, Jedediah
Ingle, Richard
Jackson, James Caleb
Kalb, Johann
Kapp, Friedrich
Kidd, William
Kirk, John Foster
Kosciuszko, Tadeusz Andrezej
  Bonaventura
Lafayette, Marie Joseph Paul
  Yves Roch Gilbert du Motier
  Marquis de
Littlepage, Lewis
Mitchel, John
Moylan, Stephen
O'Brien, Fitz-James
Pollard, Joseph Percival
Pulaski, Casimir
Robinson, William Erigena
Rochambeau, Jean Baptiste
  Donatien De Vimeur, Comte
  de
Sargent, Winthrop, 1825–1870
Savage, John
Schwatka, Frederick
Seaman, Elizabeth Cochrane

Shepherd, William Robert
Spooner, Shearjashub
Stearns, John Newton
Tuckerman, Bayard
Ward, Charles Henshaw
Watson, Elkanah
Wikoff, Henry
Wood, Abraham
MONROE, HARRIET
Teasdale, Sara
Trowbridge, Augustus
MONTGOMERY, THOMAS L.
Edmonds, John
MONTGOMERY, WALTER A.
Harrison, Gessner
MOOD, FULMER
Brierton, John
Fiske, John, 1744–1797
Freeman, Nathaniel
Gosnold, Bartholomew
Inman, George
Jewett, John Punchard
Josselyn, John
May, Samuel Joseph
Mayhew, Jonathan
Mood, Francis Asbury
MOODY, HERBERT R.
Doremus, Robert Ogden
MOODY, RICHARD
Walker, Stuart Armstrong
MOODY, ROBERT E.
Allan, John
Chandler, John
Claflin, William
Clapp, Asa
Cushman, Joshua
Dawson, Henry Barton
Frye, Joseph
Greenleaf, Moses
Hall, Samuel, 1740–1807
Holmes, John
Huntington, William Edwards
Jackson, William, 1783–1855
Jewell, Marshall
Kidder, Frederic
King, William
Longfellow, Stephen
Manley, Joseph Homan
Mellen, Prentiss
Morrill, Anson Peaslee
Morrill, Lot Myrick
Morse, Freeman Harlow
Parris, Albion Keith
Plaisted Harris Merrill
Preble, William Pitt
Putnam, William LeBaron
Rice, Alexander Hamilton
Rich, Isaac
Shepley, Ether
Shepley, George Foster
Sleeper, Jacob
Thacher, George
Ware, Ashur
Warren, William Fairfield
Whitman, Ezekiel
Williamson, William Durkee
MOONEY, HUGHSON
Hart, Lorenz Milton
Kern, Jerome David
Morgan, Helen
Witmark, Isidore

MOORE, ALBERT B.
Chapman, Reuben
Comer, Braxton Bragg
Deas, Zachariah Cantey
Fitzpatrick, Benjamin
Forney, William Henry
Gaines, George Strother
Gayle, John
Goldthwaite, George
Goldthwaite, Henry Barnes
Goold, William A.
Gracie, Archibald
Hubbard, David
Kolb, Reuben Francis
McKinley, John
Meek, Alexander Beaufort
Murfee, James Thomas
MOORE, AUSTIN L.
Noyes, William Curtis
Oakley, Thomas Jackson
Ogden, Thomas Ludlow
Radcliff, Jacob
MOORE, C. EARL
Stotesbury, Edward Townsend
MOORE, CHARLES
Baldwin, Henry Porter
Blair, Austin
Bliss, Aaron Thomas
Brewer, Mark Spencer
Burnham, Daniel Hudson
Burrows, Julius Caesar
French, Daniel Chester
McKim, Charles Follen
McKim, James Miller
McMillan, James
Mead, William Rutherford
Medary, Milton Bennett
Millet, Francis Davis
Norton, Charles Eliot
Platt, Charles Adams
Richardson, Charles Williamson
Shrady, Henry Merwin
White, Stanford
MOORE, DEBORAH DASH
Rosenblatt, Bernard Abraham
MOORE, EDWARD CALDWELL
Harris, George
Ropes, James Hardy
MOORE, GEORGE T.
Engelmann, George
Shaw, Henry
MOORE, JACK B.
Bodenheim, Maxwell
Cayton, Horace Roscoe
Viereck, George Sylvester
MOORE, JAMES G.
Goff, Emmet Stull
MOORE, JOHN ROBERT
Bailey, Josiah William
MOORE, LOUISE M.
Smith, Elizabeth Oakes Prince
MOORE, MARY ATWELL
Carpenter, Stephen Cullen
Cheetham, James
Croswell, Harry
MOORE, ROSS H.
Lattimore, William
MOORE, STEPHEN C.
Bishop, John Peale
MOORE, WILLIAM HOWARD
Barrett, Frank Aloysius
Engle, Clair William Walter
Leedom, Boyd Stewart

MOOREHEAD, WARREN KING
  Peet, Stephen Denison
  Snyder, John Francis
MORA, GEORGE
  Horney, Karen Danielssen
  Zilboorg, Gregory
MORAIS, HERBERT M.
  Leland, John
MORAN, HUGH A.
  Klopsch, Louis
  Lord, Eleazar
MORAN, KEVIN J.
  Young, Stark
MORAN, THOMAS F.
  Biddle, Horace P.
MORBY, EDWIN S.
  Schevill, Rudolph
MORDELL, ALBERT
  Whittier, John Greenleaf
MORGAN, ALFRED L.
  Grundy, Joseph Ridgway
  Lewis, Ed ("Strangler")
  Luchese, Thomas
  Pepper, George Wharton
  Walter, Francis Eugene
MORGAN, ANNE HODGES
  Kerr, Robert Samuel
MORGAN, JOHN HILL
  Ramage, John
  Stuart, Gilbert
MORGAN, THEODORE H.
  Smith, Harold Babbitt
MORIARTY, G. ANDREWS, JR.
  Hasket, Elias
MORISON, ELTING E.
  Baker, Newton Diehl
  Disney, Walter Elias ("Walt")
  Fiske, Bradley Allen
  Hobson, Richmond Pearson
  Jones, Hilary Pollard
  Stimson, Henry Lewis
MORISON, SAMUEL ELIOT
  Ames, Fisher
  Austin, Benjamin
  Austin, Jonathan Loring
  Bradford, William, 1589–1657
  Brooks, John
  Brooks, Peter Chardon
  Cabot, George
  Clark, Arthur Hamilton
  Day, Stephen
  Gerry, Elbridge
  Hart, Albert Bushnell
  Harvard, John
  Hoar, Leonard
  Johnson, Edward
  Kirkland, John Thornton
  Leverett, John, 1662–1724
  McKay, Donald
  Oakes, Urian
  Otis, Harrison Gray
  Otis, James
  Parker, Thomas
  Pynchon, William
  Quincy, Josiah, 1772–1864
  Sparks, Jared
  Squanto
  Wilkinson, Theodore Stark
MORLAN, ROBERT L.
  Townley, Arthur Charles
MORRIS, HARRISON S.
  Ferris, Jean Léon Gérôme

MORRIS, JAMES POLK
  Rovenstine, Emery Andrew
  Seagrave, Gordon Stifler
  Timberlake, Gideon
  Timme, Walter
MORRIS, RICHARD B.
  Campbell, William W.
  Cockran, William Bourke
  Colden, Cadwallader David
  Cramer, Michael John
  Fassett, Jacob Sloat
  Fenton, Reuben Eaton
  Floyd, William
  Folger, Charles James
  Gaynor, William Jay
  Glynn, Martin Henry
  Hoffman, David Murray
  Hoffman, Josiah Ogden
  Hoffman, Ogden
  Low, Abiel Abbot
  Low, Isaac
  Low, Nicholas
  Low, Seth
  Mitchel, John Purroy
  Murray, Joseph
  Read, John, 1679/80–1749
  Reed, Joseph
  Scott, John Morin
  Smith, William, 1697–1769
  Smith, William, 1728–1793
  Stockton, Richard
  Trowbridge, Edmund
  Van Santvoord, George
  Van Vechten, Abraham
  Walworth, Reuben Hyde
  Wells, John
  Williams, Elisha, 1773–1833
  Zenger, John Peter
MORRIS, RICHARD KNOWLES
  Cable, Frank Taylor
  Lake, Simon
MORRIS, WILLIAM ALFRED
  Bancroft, Hubert Howe
MORRISON, FRANK B.
  Henry, William Arnon
MORRISON, JOSEPH L.
  Cash, Wilbur Joseph
MORSE, JARVIS M.
  Dixon, James
  Edwards, Henry Waggaman
  Ellsworth, William Wolcott
  English, James Edward
  Foot, Samuel Augustus
  Foster, Lafayette Sabine
  Green, Thomas
  Loomis, Dwight
  Niles, John Milton
  Toucey, Isaac
  Wanton, Joseph
MORSE, JOSIAH
  Ogilvie, James
MORSE, SAMUEL FRENCH
  Stevens, Wallace
MORSE, SIDNEY G.
  Stoughton, William
MORTON, LOUIS
  Buckner, Simon Bolivar
  Earle, Edward Mead
  Wainwright, Jonathan Mayhew
MORTON, RICHARD L.
  Barbour, John Strode, Jr.
  Bayly, Thomas Henry
  Braxton, Carter

  Cabell, Nathaniel Francis
  Cabell, Samuel Jordan
  Cabell, William H.
  Cabell, William Lewis
  Camm, John
  Carr, Dabney
  Carrington, Paul
  Fry, Joshua
  Holloway, John
  Horrocks, James
  Johns, John
  Lee, Richard
  Lewis, Andrew
  Lewis, Fielding
  Mercer, James
MOSES, MONTROSE J.
  Bangs, Frank C.
  Barnabee, Henry Clay
  Barrett, George Horton
  Barrymore, Georgiana Emma
    Drew
  Barrymore, Maurice
  Bateman, Kate Josephine
MOSS, ALFRED
  Clement, Rufus Early
MOTT, FRANK LUTHER
  Hudson, Frederic
  Perkins, James Handasyd
  Peterson, Charles Jacobs
  Peterson, Henry
  Walker, John Brisben
  Young, Lafayette
MOTT, PETER
  Cummings, E. E.
MOULTON, HAROLD G.
  Brookings, Robert Somers
MOUNTCASTLE, HARRY W.
  Stockwell, John Nelson
MOWER, EDMUND C.
  Phelps, Edward John
  Robinson, Moses
MOWRY, GEORGE E.
  Johnson, Hiram Warren
  Wickersham, George
    Woodward
MOYER, ALBERT E.
  Bridgman, Percy Williams
MUCCIGROSSO, ROBERT
  Welling, Richard Ward Greene
MUGLESTON, WILLIAM F.
  Harris, Julian La Rose
  Hindus, Maurice Gerschon
  Pearson, Drew
  Smith, Albert Merriman
MUGRIDGE, DONALD H.
  Newport, Christopher
MULDER, RONALD A.
  Crosser, Robert
  Scott, W(illiam) Kerr
  Stigler, William Grady
  Thompson, Malvina Cynthia
MULDER, WILLIAM
  Thomas, Elbert Duncan
MULHOLLAND, JAMES A.
  De Forest, Alfred Victor
  Gillett, Horace Wadsworth
MULHOLLAND, JOHN
  Goldin, Horace
  Leipzig, Nate
  Thurston, Howard
MULL, GEORGE FULMER
  Apple, Thomas Gilmore
  Bausman, Benjamin

Bomberger, John Henry
  Augustus
Rauch, Frederic Augustus
Rupp, William
MULLIGAN, WILLIAM H., JR.
Bushman, Francis Xavier
Gibson, Edmund Richard
  ("Hoot")
Marx, Adolf Arthur ("Harpo")
Marx, Leonard ("Chico")
MUMFORD, LEWIS
Behrendt, Walter Curt
Wright, Henry
MUNRO, DANA C.
Lea, Henry Charles
MUNRO, WILLIAM BENNETT
Eaton, Dorman Bridgman
Jenckes, Thomas Allen
Lodge, Henry Cabot
MUNROE, CHARLES E.
Dudley, Charles Benjamin
MURCHISON, CARL
Sanford, Edmund Clark
MURDOCK, EUGENE C.
Rolfe, Robert Abial ("Red")
MURDOCK, KENNETH BALLARD
Byles, Mather
Green, Joseph
Hildreth, Richard
Mather, Cotton
Mather, Increase
Mather, Richard
Mather, Samuel
Wigglesworth, Michael
Wilson, John
Wood, William
MURNAGHAN, F. D.
Morley, Frank
MURPHY, EARL FINBAR
Kephart, John William
MURPHY, LAWRENCE R.
Watson, Charles Roger
MURPHY, PAUL L.
Devaney, John Patrick
MURPHY, ROBERT CUSHMAN
Stone, Witmer
MURRAY, CHARLES
Bemis, Harold Edward
MURRAY, J. FLORENCE
Searing, Laura Catherine
  Redden
MURRAY, ROBERT K.
Hanson, Ole
Palmer, Alexander Mitchell
MURRELL, WILLIAM
Briggs, Clare A.
Demuth, Charles
Opper, Frederick Burr
Smith, Robert Sidney
Zimmerman, Eugene
MURRIN, JOHN M.
Wertenbaker, Thomas Jefferson
MUSSER, PAUL H.
Barker, James Nelson
MUSSEY, H. R.
Barrows, Samuel June
MUZZEY, DAVID SAVILLE
Butler, Benjamin Franklin,
  1795–1858
Butler, Charles
Butler, William Allen
Gallatin, Abraham Alfonse
  Albert

Morris, Gouverneur
MYCUE, DAVID JOHN
Moore, Anne Carroll
Vail, Robert William Glenroie
MYERS, GEORGE B.
Du Bose, William Porcher
MYERS, GEORGE S.
Eigenmann, Carl H.

NACHLAS, I. WILLIAM
Taylor, Robert Tunstall
NADWORNY, MILTON J.
Alford, Leon Pratt
NAGEL, ERNEST
Cohen, Morris Raphael
Lewis, Clarence Irving
NASH, EDWIN G.
Akers, Benjamin Paul
Amateis, Louis
Augur, Hezekiah
Bailly, Joseph Alexis
Ball, Thomas
Bartholomew, Edward Sheffield
Bissell, George Edwin
Calverley, Charles
Clarke, Thomas Shields
Clevenger, Shobal Vail
Cogdell, John Stevens
Connelly, Pierce Francis
Donaghue, John
NASH, FRANK
Brooks, George Washington
Graham, William Alexander
NASH, GERALD D.
Andrews, John Bertram
Epstein, Abraham
Sinclair, Harry Ford
NASH, RAY
Goudy, Frederic William
NASH, RODERICK
Leopold, (Rand) Aldo
McFarland, John Horace
NATHANS, ELIZABETH S.
Hatcher, Orie Latham
NAVIN, THOMAS R.
Straus, Roger W(illiams)
NAYLOR, NATALIE A.
Monroe, Paul
NEAL, DONN C.
Donovan, William Joseph
Munro, William Bennett
Reed, Daniel Alden
NEAL, NEVIN E.
Robinson, Joseph Taylor
NEAL, STEVE
Bingay, Malcolm Wallace
Byrd, Harry Flood
Cordon, Guy
Goldfine, Bernard
Ives, Irving McNeil
Martin, Joseph William, Jr.
Sprague, Charles Arthur
Van Doren, Irita Bradford
West, Oswald
NEFF, FRANK HOWARD
Staley, Cady
NEIDLE, CECYLE S.
Lehman, Adele Lewisohn
NEILSON, WILLIAM ALLAN
Seelye, Laurenus Clark
Thorndike, Ashley Horace

NELLI, HUMBERT S.
Giovannitti, Arturo
NELSON, ALLAN
Crosby, Percy Lee
Eddy, Nelson
Luciano, Charles ("Lucky")
Madden, Owen Victor
  ("Owney")
Profaci, Joseph
Wolff, Kurt August Paul
NELSON, CLARK W.
Wilson, Louis Blanchard
NELSON, CLIFFORD M.
Wieland, George Reber
NELSON, ELIZABETH R.
Beavers, Louise
Dresser, Louise Kerlin
Farnum, Franklyn
Gish, Dorothy
Johnson, Harold Ogden
  ("Chic")
Joplin, Janis Lyn
Kane, Helen
Olsen, John Sigvard ("Ole")
NELSON, JOHN HERBERT
Allen, James Lane
Baldwin, Joseph Glover
Page, Thomas Nelson
Thompson, William Tappan
NELSON, LOWRY
Ivins, Anthony Woodward
Roberts, Brigham Henry
Talmage, James Edward
NELSON, THOMAS K.
Packard, Joseph
NELSON, WALDO E.
Mitchell, Albert Graeme
NETTLES, H. EDWARD
Geyer, Henry Sheffie
Jackson, Claiborne Fox
Kerens, Richard C.
Lyon, Nathaniel
McClurg, Joseph Washington
McNair, Alexander
Marmaduke, John Sappington
Miller, John
Napton, William Barclay
Norton, Elijah Hise
Phelps, John Smith
Polk, Trusten
Price, Sterling
Stewart, Robert Marcellus
Stone, William Joel
Sweeny, Thomas William
Van Horn, Robert Thompson
Vest, George Graham
Warner, William
NEU, IRENE D.
Lilly, Josiah Kirby
Stuart, Elbridge Amos
NEUMAN, ABRAHAM A.
Adler, Cyrus
NEVINS, ALLAN
Ames, Oakes
Arthur, Timothy Shay
Bennett, James Gordon,
  1795–1872
Bennett, James Gordon,
  1841–1918
Bowles, Samuel, 1797–1851
Bowles, Samuel, 1826–1878
Bowles, Samuel, 1851–1915
Bristow, Benjamin Helm

Brooks, James
Bryant, William Cullen
Coolidge, Calvin
Cornell, Ezra
Dana, Charles Anderson
Dix, John Adams
Drew, Daniel
Fisk, James, 1834–1872
Ford, Paul Leicester
Franklin, Fabian
Frémont, John Charles
Gould, Jay
Greeley, Horace
Hamilton, Alexander,
  1757–1804
Harding, Warren Gamaliel
Hayes, Rutherford Birchard
Hone, Philip
Johnson, Willis Fletcher
Leupp, Francis Ellington
Mellon, Andrew William
Nast, Thomas
Ogden, Rollo
Payne, Sereno Elisha
Platt, Thomas Collier
Reid, Whitelaw
rémont, John Charles
Rockefeller, John Davison
Stevens, Thaddeus
Strunsky, Simeon
Tilton, Theodore
White, Henry, 1850–1927
Wilson, William Lyne
NEVIUS, BLAKE
  Herrick, Robert Welch
NEWELL, FRANK W.
  Jackson, Edward
NEWELL, LYMAN C.
  Booth, James Curtis
  Cooke, Josiah Parsons
  Dana, James Freeman
  Dana, Samuel Luther
  Genth, Frederick Augustus
  Gorham, John
  Guthrie, Samuel
  Hayes, Augustus Allen
  Horsford, Eben Norton
  Hunt, Thomas Sterry
  James, Charles
  Loeb, Morris
  Mabery, Charles Frederic
  Metcalfe, Samuel Lytler
  Mitchill, Samuel Latham
  Moore, Richard Bishop
  Morfit, Campbell
  Nichols, James Robinson
  Peckham, Stephen Farnum
  Phillips, Francis Clifford
  Porter, John Addison
  Power, Frederick Belding
  Prescott, Albert Benjamin
  Randall, Wyatt William
  Rogers, Robert Empie
NEWHALL, BEAUMONT
  Hine, Lewis Wickes
  Jackson, William Henry
NEWLIN, CLAUDE M.
  Brackenridge, Henry Marie
  Brackenridge, Hugh Henry
NEWMAN, LOUIS I.
  Gottheil, Richard James
    Horatio

NEWMAN, ROGER K.
  Cahn, Edmond Nathaniel
  Tweed, Harrison
NEWMAN, RONALD B.
  Benchley, Robert Charles
NEWMARK, NATHAN M.
  Westergaard, Harald Malcolm
NEWSOME, A. R.
  Henderson, Archibald
  Jones, Allen
  Locke, Matthew
  Martin, Alexander
  Martin, Josiah
  Moore, Alfred
  Moore, James, 1737–1777
  Moore, Maurice
  Nash, Abner
  Nash, Francis
  Nash, Frederick
  Polk, Thomas
  Sawyer, Lemuel
  Sumner, Jethro
  Taylor, John Louis
  Waddell, Alfred Moore
  Waddell, Hugh
  Weeks, Stephen Beauregard
NEWTON, WESLEY PHILLIPS
  Acosta, Bertram Blanchard
    ("Bert")
  Henderson, Paul
  Woolman, Collett Everman
NEYMAN, CLINTON ANDREW
  Shreve, Thomas Hopkins
NICHOLS, CHARLES L.
  Fowle, Daniel
NICHOLS, FRANKLIN T.
  Stone, Samuel
NICHOLS, FREDERICK D.
  Kimball, (Sidney) Fiske
NICHOLS, JEANNETTE P.
  Allison, William Boyd
  Dalzell, John
  Dolliver, Jonathan Prentiss
  Harvey, William Hope
  Meigs, William Montgomery
  Pittman, Key
  Ritner, Joseph
  Roberts, Jonathan
  Sherman, John, 1823–1900
  Thomas, George Clifford
  Walker, Francis Amasa
NICHOLS, ROBERT H.
  Cooper, Jacob
  Curtis, Olin Alfred
  Darling, Henry
  Davis, Henry
  Dennis, James Shepard
  Donnell, Robert
  Ewing, Finis
  Green, Ashbel
  Green, Jacob
  Hatfield, Edwin Francis
  Hodge, Archibald Alexander
  Hodge, Charles
  Lane, Horace M.
  Lansing, Gulian
  Lindsley, John Berrien
  Lindsley, Philip
  Loughridge, Robert McGill
  Marquis, John Abner
  Moffat, James Clement
  Morgan, Edwin Barber
  Nassau, Robert Hamill

Prime, Samuel Irenaeus
Roberts, William Henry
Smith, Henry Boynton
Spring, Gardiner
Sproull, Thomas
Stryker, Melancthon Woolsey
Taylor, Archibald Alexander
  Edward
Thomson, William McClure
Walker, James Barr
Warfield, Benjamin
  Breckinridge
Williston, Seth
Wood, James, 1799–1867
Yeomans, John William
Young, Samuel Hall
NICHOLS, ROY F.
  Bigler, William
  Black, Jeremiah Sullivan
  Cambell, James
  Dallas, George Mifflin
  Forney, John Wien
  Geary, John White
  Gilpin, Henry Dilworth
  Grow, Galusha Aaron
  King, William Rufus Devane
  McClelland, Robert
  Meredith, William Morris
  Oberholtzer, Ellis Paxson
  Pierce, Benjamin
  Pierce, Franklin
  Reed, William Bradford
  Sutherland, Joel Barlow
  Tyson, Job Roberts
  Welsh, John
  Wilmot, David
NICOLSON, MARJORIE
  Neilson, William Allan
NIEMCZYK, CAROLINE
  Reid, Helen Miles Rogers
NIEMEYER, GLENN A.
  Olds, Ransom Eli
NIEMTZOW, ANNETTE
  Dawley, Almena
  Hepburn, Katharine Houghton
  Whitney, Charlotte Anita
NISBET, ROBERT
  Teggart, Frederick John
NISSENBAUM, STEPHEN
  Bond, Carrie Jacobs
NIXON, HERMAN C.
  Gaut, John McReynolds
  Robb, James
  Robertson, Thomas Bolling
  Roselius, Christian
  Sage, Bernard Janin
  Tulane, Paul
  Villeré, Jacques Philippe
  White, Edward Douglas
  Wiltz, Louis Alfred
NOBLE, A. B.
  Beardshear, William Miller
  Welch, Adonijah Strong
NOBLE, CHARLES
  Bacon, David
  Bacon, Leonard Woolsey
  Bangs, Nathan
  Barnes, Albert
  Bartlett, Samuel Colcord
  Bates, Arlo
  Baxter, William
  Behrends, Adolphus Julius

NOBLE, FREDERICK PERRY
  Whitworth, George Frederic
NOBLE, HAROLD J.
  Dye, William McEntyre
  Foulk, George Clayton
  Greathouse, Clarence Ridgeby
  Heard, Augustine
  Jones, George Heber
NOLAN, HUGH J.
  Dougherty, Dennis Joseph
NOLAN, J. BENNETT
  Otto, Bodo
NOLAND, LOWELL E.
  Juday, Chancey
NOLAND, STEPHEN
  Hubbard, Frank McKinney
NOLL, JOHN F.
  Dwenger, Joseph
NOLLEN, JOHN SCHOLTE
  Edgren, August Hjalmar
  Gates, George Augustus
  Magoun, George Frederic
  Scholte, Hendrik Peter
NORFLEET, FILLMORE
  Saint-Mémin, Charles Balthazar
NORRIS, JOE L.
  Niblack, William Ellis
  Noble, James
  Orth, Godlove Stein
  Otto, William Tod
NORRIS, WALTER B.
  Dornin, Thomas Aloysius
  Downer, Eliphalet
  Ellery, Frank
  Endicott, Mordecai Thomas
  Entwistle, James
  Jouett, James Edward
  Kempff, Louis
  Knight, Austin Melvin
  Lee, Samuel Phillips
  Lenthall, John
  Livingston, John William
  McCann, William Penn
  McCauley, Edward Yorke
  McDougal, David Stockton
  McKean, William Wister
  Palmer, James Shedden
  Pillsbury, John Elliott
NORTON, ELLIOT
  Geddes, Norman Bel
NORTON, NANCY P.
  Knox, Rose Markward
  Litchfield, Paul Weeks
NOTZ, WILLIAM
  List, Georg Friedrich
NOYES, ALEXANDER D.
  Harding, William Procter Gould
  McCulloch, Hugh
  Mills, Darius Ogden
  Tappen, Frederick Dobbs
  Warburg, Paul Moritz
NOYES, CLARA E.
  Delano, Jane Arminda
NOYES, HERMON M.
  Niles, Samuel
NOYES, W. A.
  Remsen, Ira
  Smith, Alexander
NUGENT, W T K.
  Murdock, Victor
NUMBERS, RONALD L.
  Price, George Edward
    McCready

NUTE, GRACE LEE
  Dickson, Robert
  Hall, Sherman
  Pierz, Franz
  Pond, Samuel William
  Ravoux, Augustin
  Riggs, Stephen Return
  Taliaferro, Lawrence
  Whipple, Henry Benjamin
NUTTER, E. J. M.
  Brook, James Lloyd
NUTTING, WALLACE
  Goddard, John

OATES, STEPHEN B.
  King, Martin Luther, Jr.
OBERHOLTZER, ELLIS P.
  Cooke, Jay
  Harrison, Charles Custis
  Morris, Robert, 1734–1806
O'BRIEN, DAVID J.
  Dietz, Peter Ernest
  O'Connell, William Henry
O'BRIEN, FRANK M.
  Beach, Moses Sperry
  Beach, Moses Yale
  Day, Benjamin Henry
  Laffan, William Mackay
  Locke, Richard Adams
  O'Malley, Frank Ward
O'CONNOR, RAYMOND G.
  Cone, Hutchinson Ingham
O'DANIEL, V. F.
  Connolly, John
ODELL, GEORGE C. D.
  Matthews, James Brander
OESPER, RALPH E.
  Midgley, Thomas
OESTREICH, THOMAS
  Haid, Leo
OFFNER, ARNOLD A.
  Wilson, Hugh Robert
OGDEN, CHARLES J.
  Jackson, Abraham Valentine
    Williams
OGDEN, HENRY N.
  Fuertes, Estevan Antonio
OGDEN, ROLLO
  Godkin, Edwin Lawrence
OGILBY, REMSEN B.
  Brent, Charles Henry
O'GRADY, JOHN
  Burke, John Joseph
OHL, JOHN KENNEDY
  Drum, Hugh Aloysius
  Eddy, Manton Sprague
  Hines, Frank Thomas
  O'Callahan, Joseph Timothy
  Rudkin, Margaret Fogarty
  Theobald, Robert Alfred
OLBY, ROBERT
  Avery, Oswald Theodore
  Campbell, Douglas Houghton
  Jeffrey, Edward Charles
OLCH, PETER D.
  Elman, Robert
  Graham, Evarts Ambrose
OLIN, REUEL K.
  McCracken, Joan
OLIN, SPENCER C., JR.
  Rowell, Chester Harvey

OLIPHANT, HERMAN
  Mechem, Floyd Russell
OLIVER, JOHN CHADWICK
  Mussey, Reuben Dimond
OLIVER, JOHN RATHBONE
  Crawford, John
  Jackson, Samuel
  James, Thomas Chalkley
  Jameson, Horatio Gates
  Kerlin, Isaac Newton
OLIVER, JOHN W.
  Black, James
  Brown, William Hughey
  Vauclain, Samuel Matthews
OLIVIER, CHARLES P.
  Stone, Ormond
OLMSTED, A. J.
  Snelling, Henry Hunt
OLNEY, LOUIS A.
  Matthews, Joseph Merritt
OLSON, FREDERICK I.
  Hoan, Daniel Webster
  Seidel, George Lukas Emil
  Ward, Harry Frederick
OLSON, JAMES C.
  Rosewater, Victor
OLSON, KENNETH E.
  Shedd, Fred Fuller
O'NEILL, WILLIAM L.
  Eastman, Max Forrester
  Thomas, Norman Mattoon
ONIGMAN, MARC
  Stuhldreher, Harry A.
ORROK, GEORGE A.
  Hammer, William Joseph
  Sargent, Frederick
OSBORN, HENRY FAIRFIELD
  Allen, Joel Asaph
  Butler, Howard Crosby
  Grant, Madison
  Grinnell, George Bird
  Hornaday, William Temple
OSBORN, NORRIS GALPIN
  Bromley, Isaac Hill
  Camp, Walter Chauncey
OSBORNE, JAMES HARVEY
  Baldwin, Elihu Whittlesey
OSGOOD, ROBERT B.
  Bradford, Edward Hickling
  Lovett, Robert Williamson
  Sayre, Lewis Albert
  Sayre, Reginald Hall
  Taylor, Charles Fayette
OSTERHOUT, WINTHROP J. V.
  Loeb, Jacques
OSTRANDER, GILMAN M.
  McBride, F(rancis) Scott
O'SULLIVAN, VINCENT
  Merrill, Stuart Fitz Randolph
OVERHOLSER, WINFRED
  White, William Alanson
OVERTON, RICHARD C.
  Budd, Ralph
  Holden, Hale
OWEN, DAVID EDWARD
  Ferry, Orris Sanford
  Gillette, Francis
OWEN, MARIE BANKHEAD
  Bibb, William Wyatt
  Brickell, Robert Coman
OWSLEY, FRANK LAWRENCE
  Anderson, Joseph
  Brown, Aaron Venable

Harney, William Selby
Harris, Isham Green
Helm, John Larue
Houk, Leonidas Campbell
Mann, Ambrose Dudley
Mason, James Murray
Williams, James
OXNAM, G. BROMLEY
McDowell, William Fraser

PACH, WALTER
Healy, George Peter Alexander
Hicks, John, 1823–1890
Hovenden, Thomas
PACHTER, MARC
De Wolfe, Elsie
Smith, Lloyd Logan Pearsall
Stearns, Harold Edmund
PACKARD, FRANCIS RANDOLPH
Allen, Harrison
Ashhurst, John
Atkinson, William Biddle
Bartholow, Roberts
Bond, Thomas
Bridges, Robert, 1806–1882
Burnett, Charles Henry
Cadwalader, Thomas
Carson, Joseph
Chapman, Henry Cadwalader
Chovet, Abraham
Coakley, Cornelius Godfrey
Coxe, John Redman
Keen, William Williams
Knight, Frederick Irving
Kyle, David Braden
Mayer, Emil
Parrish, Joseph
Pascalis-Ouvrière, Felix
Randall, Burton Alexander
Sajous, Charles Euchariste De
  Médicis
Sargent, Fitzwilliam
Say, Benjamin
Seiler, Carl
Shippen, William
Skillern, Ross Hall
Tyson, James
Wistar, Caspar
PACKARD, HYLAND
Hackett, Francis
PACKARD, LAURENCE B.
Perkins, James Breck
PAGE, LEIGH
Bumstead, Henry Andrews
Nichols, Ernest Fox
PAHLOW, EDWIN WILLIAM
Brodhead, John Romeyn
PAINTER, PATRICIA
Brady, Mildred Alice Edie
PAINTER, PATRICIA SCOLLARD
Chapelle, Dickey
Nesbit, Evelyn Florence
PALLISTER, JOHN C.
Lutz, Frank Eugene
PALMER, CATHERINE W.
Ferguson, William Jason
Forbes, Edwin
Foster, Stephen Collins
Fowler, Frank
PALMER, FREDERICK
Bliss, Tasker Howard

PALMER, HENRY R.
Colt, Le Baron Bradford
PALMER, JOHN MCAULEY
Steuben, Friedrich Wilhelm
  Ludolf Gerhard Augustin,
  Baron von
PALMER, MILDRED B.
Earle, Ralph
Godbe, William Samuel
Hill, Robert Andrews
Kimball, Heber Chase
Pratt, Parley Parker
Smiley, Albert Keith
PALMER, THEODORE SHERMAN
Buckley, Samuel Botsford
PALTSITS, VICTOR HUGO
Allibone, Samuel Austin
Bradford, William, 1663–1752
Bradford, William,
  1721/22–1791
Duyckinck, Evert Augustus
Duyckinck, George Long
Fleet, Thomas
Foster, John
Gaine, Hugh
Goddard, William
Green, Jonas
Greenleaf, Thomas
Holt, John
Hudson, Henry
Lovelace, Francis
Mecom, Benjamin
Parker, James
Rivington, James
Robertson, James, b. 1740
Stuyvesant, Petrus
PANCOAST, HENRY K.
Leonard, Charles Lester
PAPADEMETRIOU, PETER C.
Saarinen, Eero
PAPENFUSS, GEORGE F.
Setchell, William Albert
PARADISE, SCOTT H.
Fowle, William Bentley
Gardiner, John Sylvester John
Gilman, Caroline Howard
Gilman, Samuel
Morton, Marcus, 1784–1864
Peabody, George
Taylor, Samuel Harvey
PARCEL, JOHN I.
Flather, John Joseph
McAlpine, William Jarvis
McDonald, John Bartholomew
Morison, George Shattuck
Okerson, John Augustus
Pratt, Thomas Willis
Smith, Charles Shaler
Smith, William Sooy
Sooysmith, Charles
PARE, GEORGE W.
Lefevere, Peter Paul
PARET, J. PARMLY
Larned, William Augustus
PARGELLIS, STANLEY M.
Abercromby, James
Bouquet, Henry
Braddock, Edward
Bradstreet, John
Forbes, John, 1710–1759
Howe, George Augustus,
  Viscount
Leisler, Jacob

Loudoun, John Campbell, Earl
  of
Lyman, Phineas
Mackellar, Patrick
Meserve, Nathaniel
Monckton, Robert
Montrésor, James Gabriel
Montrésor, John
Morris, Roger
Reynolds, John, 1713–1788
Rogers, Robert
Shaw, Nathaniel
Webb, Daniel
Winslow, John
Wolcott, Oliver, 1726–1797
Wolcott, Roger
Wooster, David
Yale, Elihu
PARISH, JOHN C.
Dodge, Augustus Caesar
Dodge, Henry
Lucas, Robert
Lummis, Charles Fletcher
O'Fallon, James
PARK, EDWARDS A.
Holt, Luther Emmett
Howland, John
PARK, FRANCES FENTON
Lockwood, Belva Ann Bennett
PARK, JULIAN
Putnam, James Osborne
PARK, STEPHEN A.
Liggett, Hunter
PARK, THOMAS
Pearl, Raymond
PARKER, ARTHUR C.
Skaniadariio
PARKER, CHARLES W.
Nixon, John Thompson
Pennington, William Sandford
Rellstab, John
PARKER, FRANKLIN
Blaine, Anita (Eugenie)
  McCormick
Chase, Harry Woodburn
Locke, Bessie
PARKER, GAIL THAIN
Blackwell, Alice Stone
PARKER, JAMES REID
Hokinson, Helen Elna
PARKER, WILLIAM BELMONT
Aldrich, Thomas Bailey
Andrew, John Albion
Anthony, Henry Bowen
Cooper, Edward
Cooper, Peter
Curtin, Andrew Gregg
Hewitt, Abram Stevens
Hewitt, Peter Cooper
PARKES, HENRY B.
Harris, Thaddeus Mason
Marsh, James
Merrill, Daniel
Mills, Samuel John
Nason, Elias
Norris, Edward
Osgood, Jacob
Rogers, John, 1648–1721
Seccomb, John
Stoddard, Solomon
PARKMAN, FRANCIS
Menéndez, De Avilés, Pedro

PARKS, EDD WINFIELD
Stearns, Eben Sperry
Webb, William Robert
Winchester, James
Zollicoffer, Felix Kirk
PARKS, GARY
De Cuevas, Marquis
PARMELEE, JULIUS H.
Bernet, John Joseph
Fink, Albert
Hines, Walker Downer
Messler, Thomas Doremus
Poor, Henry Varnum
Poor, John Alfred
PARMENTER, CLARENCE E.
Dargan, Edwin Preston
PARMET, HERBERT S.
McKay, (James) Douglas
PAROT, JOSEPH J.
Hodur, Francis
PARRY, ELLWOOD C., III
Leyendecker, Joseph Christian
Sheeler, Charles R., Jr.
Weston, Edward Henry
PARRY, JOHN JAY
Morgan, Abel
Pugh, Ellis
PARSHLEY, HOWARD M.
Wilder, Harris Hawthorne
PARSONS, EDWARD L.
Kip, William Ingraham
Nichols, William Ford
PARSONS, GEOFFREY
Hammond, Percy Hunter
PASCHALL, CLARENCE
Schilling, Hugo Karl
PASCHALL, JOHN
Cohen, John Sanford
PASSER, HAROLD C.
Thomson, Elihu
Weston, Edward
PATERSON, THOMAS G.
Gauss, Clarence Edward
PATTEE, FRED LEWIS
Atherton, George Washington
Burnett, Francis Eliza Hodgson
Cable, George Washington
Crawford, Francis Marion
Davis, Rebecca Blaine Harding
Davis, Richard Harding
Freneau, Philip Morin
Pugh, Evan
PATTEN, WILLIAM
Wales, James Albert
Yohn, Frederick Coffay
PATTERSON, GEORGE W.
Guthe, Karl Eugen
PATTERSON, JAMES T.
Taft, Robert Alphonso
PATTERSON, MERRILL R.
Fairfield, Sumner Lincoln
PATTERSON, S. HOWARD
Macfarlane, Charles William
PATTON, JAMES W.
Jasper, William
Magrath, Andrew Gordon
Manigault, Arthur Middleton
Nott, Abraham
O'Neall, John Belton
Williams, David Rogerson
PATTON, W. KENNETH
Stitt, Edward Rhodes

PAUL, JOHN R.
Trask, James Dowling
PAUL, RODMAN W.
Fleming, Arthur Henry
PAULING, LINUS
Lewis, Gilbert Newton
Noyes, Arthur Amos
PAULLIN, CHARLES OSCAR
Baldwin, Evelyn Briggs
Benson, William Shepherd
Black, William Murray
Boucher, Horace Edward
Brownson, Willard Herbert
Brush, Charles Francis
Burroughs, William Seward
Capps, Washington Lee
Caraway, Thaddeus Horatius
Carter, John, 1737-1781
Carter, Landon
Carter, Robert
Carter, Samuel Powhatan
Chadwick, French Ensor
Chauncey, Isaac
Conyngham, Gustavus
Craven, Thomas Tingey
Craven, Tunis Augustus
MacDonough
Curtiss, Glenn Hammond
Cutting, Bronson Murray
Dale, Richard
Davison, Gregory Caldwell
De Haven, Edwin Jesse
Dellenbaugh, Frederick Samuel
Downes, John
Drayton, Percival
Duncan, James
Du Pont, Samuel Francis
Edwards, Clarence Ransom
Elliott, Jesse Duncan
Emerson, Benjamin Kendall
Emmons, George Foster
Farragut, David Glasgow
Farragut, George
Frost, Holloway Halstead
Gherardi, Bancroft
Greene, Samuel Dana
Greer, James Augustin
Hurley, Edward Nash
Jones, John Paul
Kuhn, Joseph Ernst
Landais, Pierre
Lawrence, James
Legge, Alexander
Little, George
Lull, Edward Phelps
McCall, Edward Rutledge
McCauley, Charles Stewart
MacDonough, Thomas
MacKenzie, Alexander Slidell
Maclay, Edgar Stanton
Manley, John
Marchand, John Bonnett
Melville, George Wallace
Mervine, William
Michler, Nathaniel
Mills, Enos Abijah
Minnigerode, Lucy
Moore, Edwin Ward
Mullany, James Robert Madison
Murray, Alexander
Nicholson, James
Nicholson, James William
Augustus

Nicholson, Samuel
O'Brien, Jeremiah
O'Shaughnessy, Michael
Maurice
Peabody, Cecil Hobart
Perry, Christopher Raymond
Perry, Matthew Calbraith
Perry, Oliver Hazard
Piez, Charles
Porter, David
Porter, David Dixon
Rainey, Henry Thomas
Raymond, Harry Howard
Rodgers, Christopher Raymond
Perry
Rodgers, George Washington,
1787-1832
Rodgers, George Washington,
1822-1863
Rodgers, John, 1773-1838
Rodgers, John, 1812-1882
Scott, Hugh Lenox
Sloat, John Drake
Smith, Joseph, 1790-1877
Stockton, Charles Herbert
Stockton, Robert Field
Talbot, Silas
Tarbell, Joseph
Tattnall, Josiah
Thatcher, Henry Knox
Thompson, Robert Means
Tucker, Samuel
Turner, Daniel
Tyng, Edward
Wagener, John Andreas
Wainwright, Jonathan Mayhew,
1821-1863
Wainwright, Richard,
1817-1862
Wainwright, Richard,
1849-1926
Warrington, Lewis
Whipple, Abraham
Wilkes, Charles
Williams, John Foster
Woolsey, Melancthon Taylor
Zeilin, Jacob
PAXSON, FREDERICK LOGAN
Alger, Russell Alexander
Altgelt, John Peter
Arthur, Chester Alan
Babcock, Joseph Weeks
Ballinger, Richard Achilles
Barnum, Phineas Taylor
Barstow, William Augustus
Bashford, Coles
Bissell, Wilson Shannon
Brewster, Benjamin Harris
Chandler, William Eaton
Cleveland, Stephen Grover
Conkling, Roscoe
Denby, Edwin
Fair, James Graham
Fairchild, Charles Stebbins
Fairchild, Lucius
Fisk, Clinton Bowen
Flower, Roswell Pettibone
Funston, Frederick
Garfield, James Abram
Grant, Ulysses Simpson
Hazen, William Babcock
Ingersoll, Robert Green
Kohlstaat, Herman Henry

La Follette, Robert Marion
Lamont, Daniel Scott
Lincoln, Robert Todd
Logan, John Alexander
McKinley, William
Morton, Levi Parsons
Morton, Paul
Roosevelt, Theodore
Sawyer, Philetus
Spaulding, Elbridge Gerry
Spooner, John Coit
Stephenson, Isaac
Turner, Frederick Jackson
Vilas, William Freeman
Whitney, William Collins
PAYNE, CECILIA H.
  King, Edward Skinner
PAYNE, CHARLES E.
  Grinnell, Josiah Bushnell
  Jones, George Wallace
  Lacey, John Fletcher
  Lowe, Ralph Phillips
  McCrary, George Washington
  McDill, James Wilson
  Macy, Jesse
  Main, John Hanson Thomas
PEABODY, ROBERT E.
  Derby, Elias Hasket, 1739–1799
  Derby, Richard
PEARCE, HAYWOOD J., JR.
  Hill, Benjamin Harvey
  Iverson, Alfred
  Jenkins, Charles Jones
  Lamar, Lucius Quintus
    Cincinnatus
  Lumpkin, Wilson
  McIntosh, William
PEARCE, KATHARINE S.
  Patrick, Mary Mills
PEARCE, WILLIAM M.
  Mackenzie, Murdo
PEARSON, C. C.
  Abbott, Joseph Carter
  Biggs, Asa
  Bragg, Thomas
  Bridgers, Robert Rufus
  Brown, Bedford
  Carlile, John Snyder
  Carr, Elias
  Clark, Walter
  Cox, William Ruffin
  Daniel, John Warwick
  Davie, William Richardson
  Davis, George
  Dudley, Edward Bishop
  Hoke, Robert Frederick
  Holmes, Theophilus Hunter
  Hughes, Robert William
  Hunter, Eppa
  Jones, Samuel Porter
  Kemper, James Lawson
  Kitchin, William Walton
  Lee, James Wideman
  Lewis, John Francis
  Mahone, William
  Massey, John Edward
  Minor, Lucian
  Ritchie, Thomas
  Roane, Spencer
  Ross, Martin
  Ruffner, Henry
  Ruffner, William Henry
  Wait, Samuel

Walker, Gilbert Carlton
PEARSON, EDMUND L.
  Jenks, George Charles
  Webster, John White
PEARSON, HENRY G.
  Boutwell, George Sewall
  Everett, Alexander Hill
  Everett, Edward
  Forbes, John Murray,
    1813–1898
  McElwaine, William Howe
  Tudor, Frederic
PEARSON, NORMAN HOLMES
  Wright, Robert William
PEASE, ARTHUR STANLEY
  Smyth, Herbert Weir
PEASE, THEODORE CALVIN
  Allen, William Joshua
  Arnold, Isaac Newton
  Browning, Orville Hickman
  Edwards, Ninian Wirt
  Farnsworth, John Franklin
  Farwell, Charles Benjamin
  Ford, Thomas
  Hardin, John J.
  Herndon, William Henry
  Hitt, Robert Roberts
  Hurlbut, Stephen Augustus
  Peck, John Mason
  Raum, Green Berry
PEATTIE, DONALD CULROSS
  Agassiz, Alexander
  Agassiz, Elizabeth Cabot Cary
  Atkinson, George Francis
  Audubon, John James
  Bachman, John
  Barnes, Charles Reid
  Barton, William Paul Crillon
  Bartram, John
  Beal, William James
  Bessey, Charles Edwin
  Bigelow, Jacob
  Brackenridge, William D.
  Brainerd, Ezra
  Brandegee, Townshend Stith
  Bull, Ephraim Wales
  Burrell, Thomas Jonathan
  Chapman, Alvan Wentworth
  Chapman, John
  Clayton, John
  Collins, Frank Shipley
  Curtis, Moses Ashley
  Darlington, William
  Farlow, William Gilson
  Garden, Alexander
PECK, EPAPHRODITUS
  Dunbar, Moses
PECK, LILLIE M.
  Wald, Lillian D.
PECK, MORTON E.
  Luelling, Henderson
PEDDLE, JOHN B.
  Rose, Chauncey
PEEBLES, BERNARD M.
  Rand, Edward Kennard
PEELING, JAMES H.
  Gregg, Andrew
  Hamilton, James, c. 1710–1783
  Hand, Edward
  Harris, John
  Hartley, Thomas
  Hazelwood, John
  Hemphill, Joseph

Hiester, Daniel
Hiester, Joseph
Irvine, James
Kinsey, John
Lacock, Abner
Leib, Michael
Levin, Lewis Charles
Lowrie, Walter
McKean, Joseph Borden
McKean, Samuel
McKean, Thomas
Marshall, Christopher
Mifflin, Thomas
Moore, William, 1735–1793
Morgan, John
Peters, Richard, c. 1704–1776
Peters, Richard, 1744–1828
Pettit, Charles
Pettit, Thomas McKean
Porter, Andrew
Potter, James
Read, George
Roberdeau, Daniel
Ross, George
Ross, James
Salomon, Haym
Smith, James, 1719–1806
Smith, Jonathan Bayard
Snyder, Simon
Tilghman, Edward
Tilghman, William
Tod, John
Van Dyke, Nicholas, 1738–1789
Van Dyke, Nicholas, 1770–1826
Walker, Jonathan Hoge
Wharton, Thomas
Whitehill, Robert
Yeates, Jasper
PEERS, SUSIE M.
  Evermann, Barton Warren
PEIRCE, GEORGE J.
  Goodale, George Lincoln
PELLS, RICHARD H.
  Agee, James Rufus
PENDERGRASS, EUGENE P.
  Pancoast, Henry Khunrath
PENICK, JAMES, JR.
  Pinchot, Gifford
  Smith, George Otis
PENKOWER, MONTY N.
  Flanagan, Hallie
PENNIMAN, JOSIAH H.
  Pepper, William
PENNINGTON, EDGAR LEGARE
  Forbes, John, d. 1783
PENZL, HERBERT
  Prokosch, Eduard
PERKIN, ROBERT L.
  Penrose, Spencer
PERKINS, DEXTER
  Gillet, Ransom Hooker
  Granger, Francis
  Greenleaf, Halbert Stevens
  Hill, David Jayne
  Johnston, Robert Matteson
  Kasson, John Adam
  Monroe, James
  Rochester, Nathaniel
  Rush, Richard
  Seward, Frederick William
  Seward, William Henry
  Sibley, Hiram

PERKINS, EDWIN J.
  Merrill, Charles Edward
PERKINS, ERNEST RALPH
  Wharton, Francis
PERKINS, FRANCIS D.
  Bodanzky, Artur
  Gilman, Lawrence
  Schumann-Heink, Ernestine
PERKINS, HENRY F.
  Thompson, Zadock
PULLMAN, MAIN
  Slichter, Sumner Huber
PERRY, ANNA B.
  McGrath, James Howard
PERRY, CHARNER
  Mead, George Herbert
PERRY, EDWARD DELAVAN
  Wheeler, James Rignall
  Whitehouse, Frederick
PERRY, HELEN SWICK
  Sullivan, Harry Stack
PERRY, HOBART S.
  Converse, John Heman
  Cramp, Charles Henry
  Cramp, William
  Parry, Charles Thomas
  Pearse, John Barnard Swett
  Thomas, David
  Towne, John Henry
  Waln, Robert, 1765–1836.
  Wharton, Joseph
  Widener, Peter Arrell Brown
PERRY, LAWRENCE
  Haughton, Percy Duncan
PERRY, RALPH BARTON
  Eliot, Charles William
  James, Henry, 1811–1882
  James, William
  Royce, Josiah
  Woods, James Haughton
PERSHEY, EDWARD
  Booth, Albert James, Jr.
    ("Albie")
PERSHING, BENJAMIN H.
  Cowan, Edgar
  Sargent, Winthrop, 1753–1820
PERSONS, CHARLES E.
  Hyde, Henry Baldwin
  Park, Trenor William
  Phillips, Thomas Wharton
  Post, Charles William
PERSONS, FREDERICK TORREL
  Adams, Nehemiah
  Adams, William
  Barton, William Eleazar
  Benjamin, Nathan
  Berg, Joseph Frederic
  Bethune, George Washington
  Bidwell, Walter Hilliard
  Blakeslee, Erastus
  Brady, John Green
  Brownlee, William Craig
  Burton, Asa
  Chamberlain, Jacob
  Chapin, Calvin
  Cheever, George Barrell
  Child, Frank Samuel
  Clark, Joseph Sylvester
  Cobb, William Henry
  Coleman, Leighton
  Coleman, Lyman
  Collyer, Robert

Conant, Hannah O'Brien
  Chaplin
Conant, Thomas Jefferson
Conwell, Russell Herman
Cooper, Samuel
Corby, William
Dean, Sidney
Dempster, John
Dewey, Orville
Doane, William Croswell
Dorchester, Daniel
Doty, Elihu
Dunning, Albert Elijah
Everett, Charles Carroll
Fleming, John, 1807–1894
Follett, Mary Parker
Freeman, James
Furness, William Henry
Good, Adolphus Clemens
Goodrich, Chauncey
Hallett, Benjamin
Hiacoomes
Hogue, Wilson Thomas
Jackson, Edward Payson
Jenks, William
Jones, Abner
Lawrance, Uriah Marion
McClure, Alexander Wilson
Newcomb, Harvey
North, Frank Mason
Noyes, George Rapall
Paine, Robert Treat
Parkhurst, Charles
Peloubet, Francis Nathan
Perkins, Justin
Peters, Absalom
Pond, Enoch
Poor, Daniel
Purnell, Benjamin
Rice, Edwin Wilbur
Richards, Charles Herbert
Ripley, Ezra
Ross, Abel Hastings
Sawyer, Leicester Ambrose
Schauffler, Henry Albert
Scudder, John
Shedd, William Ambrose
Smith, Elias
Smyth, Egbert Coffin
Spring, Samuel
Steele, Daniel
Sunday, William Ashley
Talcott, Eliza
Todd, John
Tracy, Joseph
Whiton, James Morris
Williams, William R.
Williston, Samuel
Woods, Leonard, 1774–1854
PETERS, JAMES A.
  Stejneger, Leonhard Hess
PETERS, JEAN
  Melcher, Frederic Gershom
PETERSEN, PETER L.
  Henie, Sonja
  Jensen, Benton Franklin
    ("Ben")
  Reynolds, Quentin James
PETERSON, A. EVERETT
  Aikens, Andrew Jackson
  Alvord, Corydon Alexis
  Appleton, Daniel
  Appleton, William Henry

Appleton, William Worthen
Armstrong, Samuel Turell
Baker, Peter Carpenter
Bartlett, John Sherren
Bayard, Nicholas
Bayard, Samuel
Bell, Robert
Bladen, William
Brewster, Osmyn
Chester, Joseph Lemuel
Cochran, John
Corwin, Edward Tanjore
Crocker, Uriel
Cruger, Henry
De Peyster, Abraham
De Peyster, John Watts
Folsom, George
Francis, Charles Stephen
Fraunces, Samuel
Frissell, Hollis Burke
Gowans, William
Graham, James
Grim, David
Harper, Fletcher
Harper, James
Herring, James
Homes, Henry Augustus
Hooker, William
Hunt, Freeman
Imbert, Antoine
Inglis, Charles
Jay, John
Jay, William
Johnston, Henry Phelps
Johnston, John Taylor
Joline, Adrian Hoffman
Jones, Thomas
Kearny, Philip
Lamb, Martha Joanna Reade
  Nash
Le Roux, Bartholomew
Le Roux, Charles
Leslie, Frank
Leslie, Miriam Florence Folline
Loudon, Samuel
Ludlow, Daniel
O'Callaghan, Edmund Bailey
Osborn, Selleck
Pennington, James W. C.
Stanford, John
PETERSON, F. ROSS
  Chavez, Dennis
  Hatch, Carl A.
  Krug, Julius Albert
  Welker, Herman
PETERSON, HAROLD F.
  Weddell, Alexander Wilbourne
PETERSON, HENRY J.
  Hoyt, John Wesley
  Warren, Francis Emroy
PETERSON, ROBERT
  Gibson, Joshua
PETERSON, THEODORE
  Lane, Gertrude Battles
PETTIJOHN, FRANCIS J.
  Lawson, Andrew Cowper
PFAFF, CAROLINE S.
  Shreve, Henry Miller
PFEFFERKORN, BLANCHE
  Noyes, Clara Dutton
PFEIFFER, ROBERT H.
  Lyon, David Gordon

Mitchell, Hinckley Gilbert
  Thomas
PHALEN, JAMES M.
  Agramonte Y Simoni, Aristides
  Ainsworth, Frederick Crayton
  Allison, Nathaniel
  Allison, Richard
  Ashford, Bailey Kelly
  Barnes, Joseph K.
  Bernays, Augustus Charles
  Billings, Frank
  Brainard, Daniel
  Brown, Samuel
  Bruce, Archibald
  Byford, William Heath
  Carroll, James
  Carter, Henry Rose
  Cooper, Elias Samuel
  Davis, Nathan Smith
  Dennis, Frederic Shepard
  Emerson, Gouverneur
  Engelmann, George Julius
  Eve, Paul Fitzsimons
  Faget, Jean Charles
  Favill, Henry Baird
  Fenger, Christian
  Ferguson, Alexander Hugh
  Finlay, Carlos Juan
  Fletcher, Robert
  Fletcher, William Baldwin
  Forwood, William Henry
  Garrison, Fielding Hudson
  Goldberger, Joseph
  Gorgas, William Crawford
  Gradle, Henry
  Guild, La Fayette
  Guiteras, Juan
  Hammond, William Alexander
  Henrotin, Fernand
  Holmes, Bayard Taylor
  Husk, Charles Ellsworth
  Hyde, James Nevins
  Ingals, Ephraim Fletcher
  Johnston, George Ben
  Jones, Joseph
  Kilty, William
  King, Albert Freeman Africanus
  Kinloch, Robert Alexander
  Lane, Levi Cooper
  Lawson, Leonidas Merion
  Lazear, Jesse William
  Letterman, Jonathan
  Linde, Christian
  Logan, Thomas Muldrup,
    1808–1876
  Lydston, George Frank
  Lyster, Henry Francis Le Hunte
  McCormack, Joseph Nathaniel
  McCreery, Charles
  Manson, Otis Frederick
  Martin, Franklin Henry
  Mastin, Claudius Henry
  Maxwell, George Troup
  Merrill, James Cushing
  Miller, Henry
  Morrow, Thomas Vaughan
  Murphy, John Benjamin
  Nancrède, Charles Beylard
    Guérard de
  Newton, Robert Safford
  Ochsner, Albert John
  O'Reilly, Robert Maitland
  Palmer, Daniel David

Pilcher, Lewis Stephen
Pitcher, Zina
Powell, William Byrd
Quine, William Edward
Reed, Walter
Robinson, Frederick Byron
Rockwell, Alfonso David
Sachs, Theodore Bernard
Salisbury, James Henry
Salmon, Daniel Elmer
Satterlee, Richard Sherwood
Schadle, Jacob Evans
Scudder, John Milton
Semmes, Alexander Jenkins
Senn, Nicholas
Smith, James McCune
Smith, Theobald
Speir, Samuel Fleet
Spitzka, Edward Anthony
Spitzka, Edward Charles
Steiner, Lewis Henry
Stephenson, Benjamin Franklin
Sternberg, George Miller
Stockton, Charles G.
Stone, Richard French
Terry, Marshall Orlando
Tilton, James
Toner, Joseph Meredith
Vance, Ap Morgan
Van Hook, Weller
Von Ruck, Karl
Ward, Richard Halsted
Weil, Richard
Wickes, Stephen
Wilbur, Hervey Backus
Williams, David Hale
Williams, Elkanah
Wood, James Rushmore
Wood, Thomas
Woodhull, Alfred Alexander
Woodruff, Charles Edward
Woodward, Joseph Janvier
Wright, Hamilton, Kemp
Wright, Joseph Jefferson Burr
Yandell, David Wendell
Yandell, Lunsford Pitts
PHELPS, ISAAC KING
  Frear, William
PHELPS, ORME W.
  Millis, Harry Alvin
PHELPS, REGINALD H.
  Fay, Sidney Bradshaw
PHILBRICK, FRANCIS SAMUEL
  Blodgett, Henry Williams
  Boutell, Henry Sherman
  Bowers, Lloyd Wheaton
  Buchanan, William Insco
  Cullom, Shelby Moore
  Dickinson, Jacob McGavock
  Fry, James Barnet
  Fuller, Melville Weston
  Hall, John Elihu
  Harding, George
  Hare, John Innes Clark
  Hoffman, David
  Lockwood, Samuel Drake
  McClain, Emlin
  McKenna, Joseph
  Pennypacker, Samuel Whitaker
  Read, John Meredith,
    1797–1874
  Sharswood, George
  Shiras, George

Strong, William
Wallace, John William
PHILBRICK, NORMAN
  Bates, Blanche
PHILIPSON, DAVID
  Berkowitz, Henry
  Blaustein, David
  Deutsch, Gotthard
  Gratz, Barnard
  Gratz, Michael
  Gratz, Rebecca
  Lilienthal, Max
  Neumark, David
  Wice, Isaac Mayer
PHILLIPS, CLIFTON J.
  Luce, Henry Winters
  McFarland, George Bradley
PHILLIPS, J. O. C.
  Stoddard, Theodore Lothrop
PHILLIPS, PAUL CHRISLER
  Brantley, Theodore
  Carter, Thomas Henry
  Clark, William Andrews
  Craighead, Edwin Boone
  Daly, Marcus
  De Lacy, Walter Washington
  Edgerton, Sidney
  Gibson, Paris
  Hamilton, William Thomas,
    1822–1908
  Haskell, Ella Louise Knowles
  Hauser, Samuel Thomas
  Heinze, Frederick Augustus
  Maginnis, Martin
  Mullan, John
  Nelson, John
  Potts, Benjamin Franklin
  Sanders, Wilbur Fisk
  Toole, Edwin Warren
  Toole, Joseph Kemp
  Wade, Dennis Spear
PHILLIPS, PAUL CHRYSOSTOM
  Hitchcock, Edward, 1828–1911
PHILLIPS, ROBERT
  Schwartz, Delmore David
PHILLIPS, ULRICH BONNELL
  Calhoun, John Caldwell
  Crawford, William Harris
  Hayne, Robert Young
  Stephens, Alexander Hamilton
  Toombs, Robert Augustus
PHILP, KENNETH R.
  Collier, John
PICKENS, DONALD K.
  Johnson, Osa
PIERCE, BESSIE LOUISE
  Cermak, Anton Joseph
PIERSOL, GEORGE MORRIS
  Kelly, Aloysius Oliver Joseph
PIERSON, WILLIAM WHATLEY, JR.
  Branch, John
  Branch, Lawrence O'Bryan
  Burton, Hutchins Gordon
PILCHER, LEWIS FREDERICK
  Caffin, Charles Henry
  Cook, Walter
  Cummings, Charles Amos
PILSBRY, HENRY AUGUSTUS
  Adams, Charles Baker
  Anthony, John Gould
  Binney, Amos
  Brooks, William Keith

Davis, Charles Henry Stanley
Earle, Pliny, 1809–1892
Elsberg, Louis
Evans, George Alfred
Fisher, George Jackson
Flint, Austin, 1812–1886
Flint, Austin, 1836–1915
Foster, Frank Pierce
Fowler, George Ryerson
Francis, John Wakefield
Friedenwald, Aaron
Fuller, Robert Mason
Garcelon, Alonzo
Gerrish, Frederic Henry
Gerster, Arpad Geyza Charles
Gilliam, David Tod
Gray, John Purdue
Guernsey, Egbert
Hall, William Whitty
Hamilton, Allan McLane
Hamilton, Frank Hastings
Hartley, Frank
Haviland, Clarence Floyd
Henry, Morris Henry
Herter, Christian Archibald
Hoch, August
Hosack, Alexander Eddy
Hosack, David
Hutchinson, Woods
Jackson, Abraham Reeves
Jacobi, Abraham
Janeway, Edward Gamaliel
Janeway, Theodore Caldwell
Jarvis, William Chapman
Jones, Calvin
Jones, John
Jones, William Palmer
Judson, Adoniram Brown
Kedzie, Robert Clark
Keeley, Leslie E.
Keyes, Edward Lawrence
Kolle, Frederick Strange
Lee, Charles Alfred
Lefferts, George Morewood
Letchworth, William Pryor
Lincoln, Rufus Pratt
Lozier, Clemence Sophia
    Harned
Lumbrozo, Jacob
Lusk, William Thompson
McBurney, Charles
McCosh, Andrew James
MacNeven, William James
March, Alden
Miller, Edward
Mott, Valentine
PRENTICE, WILLIAM K.
Frothingham, Arthur Lincoln
PRESCOTT, FREDERICK CLARKE
Finch, Francis Miles
PRESCOTT, SAMUEL C.
Stratton, Samuel Wesley
PRICE, DAVID E.
Mahoney, John Friend
PRICHARD, WALTER
Dymond, John
PRIDE, ARMISTEAD S.
Abbott, Robert Sengstacke
PRIDE, LEO B.
Couldock, Charles Walter
PRIESTLEY, HERBERT INGRAM
Alvarado, Juan Bautista
Benavides, Alonzo de

Costansó, Miguel
De Soto, Hernando
Espejo, Antonio de
Fages, Pedro
Hittell, John Shertzer
Hittell, Theodore Henry
Luna Y Arellano, Tristan de
Moscoso De Alvarado, Luis de
PRIMER, BEN
Sloan, Harold Paul
PRINCE, LEON C.
Kline, George
McClure, Alexander Kelly
Nisbet, Charles
PRINGLE, HENRY F.
Taft, Alphonso
Taft, Charles Phelps
Taft, William Howard
PROSCHANSKY, HARRIS
Huebner, Solomon Stephen
PRUITT, BETTYE H.
Frary, Francis Cowles
PUCKETTE, CHARLES McD.
Sulzberger, Cyrus Lindauer
PULLEY, RAYMOND H.
Glass, Carter
PURCELL, EDWARD
Conboy, Martin
PURCELL, EDWARD A., JR.
Clark, Bennett Champ
Wood, Frederick Hill
PURCELL, J. M.
Keeler, Ralph Olmstead
PURCELL, RICHARD J.
Adams, Alvin
Ames, Frederick Lothrop
Ames, Oliver, 1779–1863
Ames, Oliver, 1807–1877
Ames, Oliver, 1831–1895
Armstrong, George Washington
Aspinwall, William Henry
Blanchet, François Norbet
Bradley, Denis Mary
Brondel, John Baptist
Bruté de Rémur, Simon
    William Gabriel
Cabrini, Francis Xavier
Carroll, John
Chatard, Francis Silas
Cheverus, John Louis Ann
    Magdalen Lefebre de
Corrigan, Michael Augustine
Cotton, Joseph Potter
Curtis, Alfred Allen
Daeger, Albert Thomas
David, John Baptist Mary
Dowling, Austin
Doyle, Alexander Patrick
Duffy, Francis Patrick
Engelhardt, Zephyrin
England, John
Feehan, Patrick Augustine
Fenwick, Edward Dominic
Ffrench, Charles Dominic
Fitzgerald, Edward
Flaget, Benedict Joseph
Galberry, Thomas
Gallagher, Hugh Patrick
Gallitzin, Demetrius Augustine
Garrigan, Philip Joseph
Gasson, Thomas Ignatius
Gilmour, Richard
Gmeiner, John

Graessl, Lawrence
Greaton, Joseph
Griffin, Martin Ignatius Joseph
Hassard, John Rose Greene
Heenan, John Carmel
Helbron, Peter
Helmpraecht, Joseph
Hughes, John Joseph
Huntington, Jedediah Vincent
Ireland, John, 1838–1918
Ives, Levi Silliman
Judge, Thomas Augustine
Julia, Sister
Keane, James John
Kelly, Eugene
Kenedy, Patrick John
Kenrick, Francis Patrick
Kirlin, Joseph Louis Jerome
Larkin, John
Lemke, Peter Henry
Levins, Thomas C.
Maas, Anthony J.
McCaffrey, John
McCloskey, John
McCloskey, William George
McElroy, John
McFaul, James Augustine
McGill, John
McGivney, Michael Joseph
McGrath, James
McGuire, Charles Bonaventure
Machebeuf, Joseph Projectus
McHenry, James
McKenna, Charles Hyacinth
McMaster, James Alphonsus
McQuaid, Bernard John
Maes, Camillus Paul
Malone, Sylvester
Maloney, Martin
Maréchal, Ambrose
Marty, Martin
Matignon, Francis Anthony
Meeschaert, Théophile
Menetrey, Joseph
Mengarini, Gregory
Messmer, Sebastian Gebhard
Middleton, Thomas Cooke
Miles, Richard Pius
Ming, John Joseph
Moeller, Henry
Molyneux, Robert
Moore, John, 1834–1901
Moosmüller, Oswald William
Moriarity, Patrick Eugene
Morini, Austin John
Mulry, Thomas Maurice
Murphy, John
Neale, Leonard
Nerinckx, Charles
Neumann, John Nepomucene
Nobili, John
O'Brien, Matthew Anthony
O'Callaghan, Jeremiah
O'Connor, James
O'Connor, Michael
Odin, John Mary
O'Gorman, Thomas
Ortynsky, Stephen Soter
Palladino, Lawrence Benedict
Pardow, William O'Brien
Peter, Sarah Worthington King
Phelan, David Samuel
Pise, Charles Constantine

Portier, Michael
Potamian, Brother
Power, John
Preston, Thomas Scott
Price, Thomas Frederick
Purcell, John Baptist
Quarter, William
Quigley, James Edward
Raffeiner, John Stephen
Ravalli, Antonio
Rese, Frederick
Reuter, Dominic
Richard, Gabriel
Riordan, Patrick William
Robot, Isidore
Roche, James Jeffrey
Rosecrans, Sylvester Horton
Russell, Mother Mary Baptist
Ryan, Abram Joseph
Ryan, Patrick John
Ryan, Stephen Vincent
Sadlier, Denis
Sadlier, Mary Anne Madden
Scanlan, Lawrence
Schneider, Theodore
Schrieck, Sister Louise Van der
Seghers, Charles Jean
Shahan, Thomas Joseph
Shea, John Dawson Gilmary
Shields, James
Shields, Thomas Edward
Shipman, Andrew Jackson
Smith, John Cotton, 1765–1845
Smith, Nathan, 1770–1835
Smith, Nathaniel
Spalding, Catherine
Spalding, John Lancaster
Spalding, Martin John
Stang, William
Starr, Eliza Allen
Stone, James Kent
Swift, Zephaniah
Thayer, John
Thébaud, Augustus J.
Tierney, Richard Henry
Timon, John
Tracy, Uriah
Tyler, William
Vander Wee, John Baptist
Van de Velde, James Oliver
Van Quickenborne, Charles
  Felix
Varela Y Morales, Felix
  Francisco José María de la
  Concepción
Verhaegen, Peter Joseph
Verot, Jean Marcel Pierre
  Auguste
Walsh, Robert
Walworth, Clarence Augustus
White, Andrew
White, Charles Ignatius
Whiting, William
Wigger, Winand Michael
Williams, John Joseph
Wilson, Samuel Thomas
Wood, James Frederick
Yorke, Peter Christopher
Young, Alfred
Young, Josue Maria
PURCELL, SALLEE McNAMARA
  Malone, Dudley Field

PURDY, LAWSON
  Ensley, Enoch
PURSELL, CARROLL
  Borg, George William
  Merriam, John Campbell
  Ritter, William Emerson
  Rust, John Daniel
PUSEY, MERLO J.
  Graham, Philip Leslie
  Meyer, Eugene Isaac

QUAIFE, MILO MILTON
  Barry, John Stewart
  Campau, Joseph
QUIGLEY, MARTIN, JR.
  Rothafel, Samuel Lionel
QUILL, J. MICHAEL
  Bow, Clara Gordon
  Powell, Richard Ewing ("Dick")
  Power, Tyrone
  Waller, Frederic
  Webb, Clifton
  Wong, Anna May
QUINN, ARTHUR HOBSON
  Aiken, George L.
  Baker, Benjamin A.
  Bannister, Nathaniel Harrington
  Barnes, Charlotte Mary Sanford
  Bateman, Sidney Frances
    Cowell
  Bird, Robert Montgomery
  Boker, George Henry
  Campbell, Bartley
  Custis, George Washington
    Parke
  Daly, John Augustin
  Godfrey, Thomas, 1736–1763
  Harrigan, Edward
  Hoyt, Charles Hale
  Mitchell, Langdon Elwyn
  Mitchell, Silas Weir
  Stone, John Augustus
  Tyler, Royall

RAACKE, I. D.
  Nelson, Marjorie Maxine
RABINOWITZ, ISAAC
  Torrey, Charles Cutler
RADBILL, SAMUEL X.
  Brennemann, Joseph
  Gesell, Arnold Lucius
RADER, BENJAMIN G.
  Bell, De Benneville ("Bert")
  Heffelfinger, William Walter
    "Pudge"
  Riddle, Samuel Doyle
  Stewart, Walter Winne
RAE, JOHN B.
  Boeing, William Edward
  Braniff, Thomas Elmer
  Chapin, Roy Dikeman
  Coffin, Howard Earle
  Durant, William Crapo
  Duryea, James Frank
  Fisher, Alfred J.
  Fisher, Charles T.
  Joy, Henry Bourne
  Kellett, William Wallace
  Keys, Clement Melville
  Lawrance, Charles Lanier
  Lockheed, Allan Haines
  Nash, Charles Williams
  Sorensen, Charles

Swasey, Ambrose
Vance, Harold Sines
Wilson, Charles Erwin
RAGATZ, LOWELL JOSEPH
  Hatton, Frank
  McComas, Louis Emory
  Miller, Oliver
  Moran, Benjamin
  Shepherd, Alexander Robey
  Welling, James Clarke
RAINE, JAMES WATT
  Rogers, John Almanza Rowley
RAINGER, RONALD
  Menninger, William Claire
  Osborn, Henry Fairfield
  Sinnott, Edmund Ware
RAINWATER, P. L.
  Watson, John William Clark
RAMAKER, ALBERT J.
  Kendrick, Asahel Clark
RAMMELKAMP, CHARLES HENRY
  Baldwin, Theron
  Beecher, Edward
  Bradley, John Edwin
  Sturtevant, Julian Monson
RAMMELKAMP, JULIAN S.
  McCormick, Robert Rutherford
RAMPERSAD, ARNOLD
  Du Bois, William Edward
    Burghardt
  Hughes, James Langston
RAMSDELL, CHARLES WILLIAM
  Baker, Daniel
  Baker, William Mumford
  Baylor, Robert Emmet Bledsoe
  Bell, Peter Hansborough
  Burleson, Edward
  Burleson, Rufus Clarence
  Burnet, David Gouverneur
  Coke, Richard
  Culberson, Charles Allen
  Culberson, David Browning
  Gorgas, Josiah
  Lubbock, Francis Richard
  Memminger, Christopher
    Gustavus
  Myers, Abraham Charles
  Neighbors, Robert Simpson
RAMSEY, FREDERIC, JR.
  Oliver, Joseph
RAMSEY, GEORGE H.
  Nott, Josiah Clark
RANDALL, J. G.
  Calhoun, John
  Chase, Salmon Portland
  Davis, David
  Lamon, Ward Hill
  Lincoln, Abraham
  Lincoln, Mary Todd
  Logan, Stephen Trigg
  Nicolay, John George
  Reynolds, John, 1788–1865
  Singleton, James Washington
  Stuart, John Todd
  Yates, Richard
RANDALL, JOHN HERMAN, JR.
  Woodbridge, Frederick James
    Eugene
RANDEL, WILLIAM PEIRCE
  Hagedorn, Hermann Ludwig
    Gebhard
  Hart, Moss

RANDOLPH, HARRISON
  Middleton, Nathaniel Russell
RANKIN, BELLE
  Blackburn, Gideon
  Corson, Juliet
  Doak, Samuel
  Farmer, Fannie Merritt
  Gordon, Laura De Force
  Hay, Mary Garrett
  Huntington, Margaret Jane
    Evans
  Low, Juliette Gordon
  Pitman, Benn
  Severance, Caroline Maria
    Seymour
  Skinner, William
RANKIN, DANIEL S.
  Mitchell, Isaac
RAPHAEL, MARC LEE
  Liebman, Joshua Loth
RASKIN, A. H.
  Stark, Louis
RASKIN, EUGENE
  La Farge, Christopher Grant
  Yellin, Samuel
RASMUSSEN, WAYNE D.
  Edwards, Everett Eugene
  Hansen, Niels Ebbesen
  Webber, Herbert John
RATHBONE, PERRY T.
  Sachs, Paul Joseph
RATNER, SIDNEY
  Bentley, Arthur Fisher
RAU, ALBERT G.
  Heckewelder, John Gottlieb
    Ernestus
  Levering, Joseph Mortimer
  Loskiel, George Henry
  Nitschmann, David
  Peter, John Frederick
  Post, Christian Frederick
  Reichel, Charles Gotthold
  Reichel, William Cornelius
  Rondthaler, Edward
  Schultze, Augustus
  Schweinitz, Emil Alexander de
  Schweinitz, Lewis David von
  Spangenberg, Augustus
    Gottlieb
  Zeisberger, David
RAUB, WILLIAM L.
  Gale, George Washington
  Garman, Charles Edward
RAUCHER, ALAN
  Hannagan, Stephen Jerome
RAUP, HUGH M.
  James Thomas Potts
RAVITCH, MARK M.
  Bevan, Arthur Dean
  Finney, John Miller Turpin
RAWLEY, JAMES A.
  Flanders, Ralph Edward
  Ford, Guy Stanton
  Green, Theodore Francis
  Holbrook, Stewart Hall
  Hughes, Rupert
  West, Roy Owen
RAY, P. ORMAN
  Atchison, David Rice
  Brown, Benjamin Gratz
  Davis, Horace
  Donohue, Peter
  Gerstle, Lewis

Haggin, James Ben Ali
Kahn, Julius
Kearney, Denis
King of Williams, James
McAllister, Hall
McAllister, Matthew Hall
Marsh, John
Morrow, William W.
Otis, Harrison Gray
Perkins, George Clement
Phelan, James
Phelan, James Duval
Price, William Cecil
Randolph, Edmund, 1819–1861
Sargent, Aaron Augustus
Sawyer, Lorenzo
Scripps, Ellen Browning
Sloss, Louis
Smith, Francis Marion
Spreckels, Claus
Spreckels, John Diedrich
Stewart, William Morris
Sutro, Adolph Heinrich Joseph
Swift, John Franklin
Weller, John B.
Wilson, Samuel Mountford
RDEN, GEORGE H.
  Burton, William
  Cannon, William
  Gilbert, Eliphalet Wheeler
  McKinly, John
  Purnell, William Henry
  Ridgely, Nicholas
  Rodney, Caesar
  Rodney, Caesar Augustus
  Rodney, Thomas
  White, Samuel
READ, HELEN APPLETON
  Force, Juliana Rieser
READ, PATRICIA
  Eustis, Dorothy Leib Harrison
    Wood
  Frohman, Daniel
  Tanner, Henry Ossawa
READ, THOMAS T.
  Bassett, William Hastings
  Bradley, Frederick Worthen
  Manning, Vannoy Hartrog
  Mathews, John Alexander
  Matthiessen, Frederick William
  Maynard, George William
  Merritt, Leonidas
  Moore, Philip North
  Olcott, Eben Erskine
  Overman, Frederick
  Smith, Hamilton
  Stetefeldt, Carl August
  Vinton, Francis Laurens
  Wellington, Arthur Mellen
  Williams, Gardner Fred
REARDON, M. E.
  McNicholas, John Timothy
REDE, WYLLYS
  Hotz, Ferdinand Carl
  Whittingham, William Rollinson
REDFIELD, RUTH
  Colby, Luther
  Davis, Andrew Jackson
  Dods, John Bovee
REED, AMY LOUISE
  Wilson, William

REED, HENRY HOPE, JR.
  Blashfield, Edwin Howland
REED, JAMES
  Bryant, Louise Frances Stevens
  Pincus, Gregory Goodwin
    ("Goody")
REED, WALT
  Birch, Reginald Bathurst
REEDS, CHESTER A.
  Whitefield, Robert Parr
REESE, LIZETTE, WOODWORTH
  Henderson, Daniel McIntyre
REEVES, JESSE SIDDALL
  Angell, James Burrill
REICH, SHELDON
  Marin, John (Cheri)
REICHELDERFER, F. W.
  McAdie, Alexander George
REICHLE, HERBERT S.
  Mundé, Paul Fortunatus
  Noeggerath, Emil Oscar Jacob
    Bruno
  Peaslee, Edmund Randolph
  Polk, William Mecklenburg
  Richmond, John Lambert
  Smith, Job Lewis
  Starr, Louis
  Weber, Gustav Carl Erich
REID, JOSEPH H.
  Brace, Charles Loring
REID, W. T.
  Bolza, Oskar
REIDER, NORMAN
  Fenichel, Otto
REIFF, ROBERT F.
  Christy, Howard Chandler
  Held, John, Jr.
  Rosenberg, Paul
  Sterne, Maurice
  Szyk, Arthur
  Tchelitchew, Pavel
REITT, BARBARA B.
  Loveman, Amy
REMALEY, PETER P.
  Fowler, Gene
  Service, Robert William
REMINI, ROBERT V.
  James, Marquis
RESTOUT, DENISE
  Landowska, Wanda Aleksandra
  Robinson-Smith, Gertrude
RETHERFORD, J. E.
  Shoup, George Laird
REYNOLDS, CLARK G.
  Adams, Charles Francis
  Barbey, Daniel Edward
  Bloch, Claude Charles
  Brereton, Lewis Hyde
  Burgess, W(illiam) Starling
  Halsey, William Frederick, Jr.
  Kimmel, Husband Edward
  Kirk, Alan Goodrich
  Ricketts, Claude Vernon
  Sherman, Forrest Percival
  Sherman, Frederick Carl
  Spruance, Raymond Ames
  Standley, William Harrison
  Towers, John Henry
REYNOLDS, JOHN HENRY
  Leete, William
RHINELANDER, PHILIP M.
  Satterlee, Henry Yates

RHODES, CHARLES DUDLEY
Averell, William Woods
Birney, David Bell
Blunt, James Gillpatrick
Brannan, John Milton
Brooks, William Thomas
Harbaugh
Buchanan, Robert Christie
Buford, Abraham, 1820–1884
Butterfield, Daniel
Ernst, Oswald Herbert
Farnsworth, Ebon John
Gaillard, David Du Bose
Garrard, Kenner
Gillmore, Quincy Adams
Goethals, George Washington
Graham, William Montrose
Haan, William George
Hancock, Winfield Scott
Hodges, Harry Foote
Howze, Robert Lee
Imboden, John Daniel
Irwin, George Le Roy
Jadwin, Edgar
Johnson, Bushrod Rust
Johnson, Edward
Johnson, Richard W.
Jordan, Thomas
Kautz, August Valentine
Kelton, John Cunningham
Kershaw, Joseph Brevard
Keyes, Erasmus Darwin
Kilpatrick, Hugh Judson
Lander, Frederick West
Lewis, William Gaston
Loring, William Wing
Ludlow, William
McCallum, Daniel Craig
McCawley, Charles Grymes
McCook, Alexander McDowell
McCook, Edward Moody
Magoon, Charles Edward
Meade, Robert Leamy
Meagher, Thomas Francis
Meigs, Montgomery
Cunningham
Menoher, Charles Thomas
Merriam, Henry Clay
Miles, Nelson Appleton
Minty, Robert Horatio George
Morgan, James Dada
Mulholland, St. Clair Augustin
Nicholson, William Jones
Noble, Alfred
Roberts, Benjamin Stone
Rodman, Thomas Jackson
Rogers, John Ignatius
Ruger, Thomas Howard
Sedgwick, John
Shafter, William Rufus
Sheridan, Philip Henry
Simpson, James Hervey
Smith, James Francis
RIBBLE, F. D. G.
Lile, William Minor
RICE, HERBERT W.
Chalmers, William James
Falk, Otto Herbert
Kohler, Walter Jodok
RICE, WILLIAM NORTH
Cummings, Joseph

RICH, DANIEL CATTON
Harshe, Robert Bartholow
RICHARDS, ALFRED E.
Paine, Ralph Delahaye
RICHARDS, ELIZABETH M.
Vattemare, Nicholas Marie
Alexandre
RICHARDS, THOMAS COLE
Calkins, Phineas Wolcott
Chamberlain, Nathan Henry
Chapin, Edwin Hubbell
Chapman, John Wilbur
Clark, George Whitefield
Cobb, Sylvanus
Dike, Samuel Warren
RICHARDSON, EDWARD E.
Sterrett, James Macbride
RICHARDSON, GEORGE L.
Hall, Arthur Crawshay Alliston
Littlejohn, Abram Newkirk
RICHARDSON, HESTER DORSEY
Hamilton, Alexander,
1712–1756
RICHARDSON, LEON B.
Occom, Samson
Sanborn, Edwin David
Smith, Asa Dodge
Tucker, William Jewett
Whitaker, Nathaniel
RICHARDSON, LEON J.
Kellogg, Martin
RICHARDSON, LYON N.
Bradstreet, Anne
Thwing, Charles Franklin
RICHMAN, IRVING BERDINE
Aco, Michel
Alarcón Hernando De
Allefonsce, Jean
Amadas, Philip
Anza, Juan Bautista De
Ayala, Juan Manuel De
Ayllon, Lucas Vasquez De
Black Hawk
Coddington, William
Collins, John
Cranston, Samuel
Fenner, Arthur
Fenner, James
Font, Pedro
Foster, Theodore
Francis, John Brown
Garcés, Francisco Tomás
Hermenegildo
Greene, William, 1695/96–1758
Greene, William, 1731–1809
Groseilliers, Médart Chouart
Hopkins, Stephen
Keokuk
Lisa, Manuel
Ponce de León, Juan
RICKARD, THOMAS A.
Pearce, Richard
RIDEOUT, WALTER B.
Anderson, Sherwood
Calverton, Victor Francis
RIDGELY, JOSEPH V.
Chandler, Raymond Thornton
Erskine, John
Hammett, Samuel Dashiell
Quinn, Arthur Hobson
Roberts, Kenneth Lewis
Van Druten, John William

RIDGEWAY, GEORGE L.
Marvin, Dudley
RIDGLEY, RONALD H.
Bell, Eric Temple
Blair, William Richards
Gunn, Ross
Jeffers, William Martin
Mendelsohn, Samuel
RIEGEL, ROBERT E.
Gould, George Jay
Hubbard, Thomas Hamlin
Jeffery, Edward Turner
Kirkman, Marshall Monroe
Marvin, Dudley
Mellen, Charles Sanger
Moffat, David Halliday
Palmer, William Jackson
Pearson, Edward Jones
Reigel, Robert E.
Smith, Milton Hannibal
Wallace, John Findley
RIESS, STEVEN A.
Heilmann, Harry
Klein, Charles Herbert
("Chuck")
RIFE, CLARENCE W.
Kittson, Norman Wolfred
RILEY, FRANKLIN LAFAYETTE
Alcorn, James Lusk
Barry, William Taylor Sullivan
Brown, Albert Gallatin
Campbell, Josiah A. Patterson
Chalmers, James Ronald
Claiborne, John Francis
Hamtramck
Clark, Charles
Dunbar, William
Fulton, Robert Burwell
RILEY, HARRIS, D., JR.
Papanicolaou, George Nicholas
Rous, Francis Peyton
Smith, Homer William
RINGENBERG, WILLIAM C.
Buchman, Frank Nathan Daniel
Erdman, Charles Rosenbury
Jones, Robert Reynolds
("Bob")
Kagan, Henry Enoch
Ritter, Joseph Elmer
RIPPY, J. FRED
Gadsden, James
Poinsett, Joll Roberts
Thompson, Waddy
Trist, Nicholas Philip
RISCHIN, MOSES
Cahan, Abraham
RISTINE, FRANK H.
Brown, Samuel Gilman
Thompson, James Maurice
RITCHIE, DONALD A.
Duff, James Henderson
Landis, James McCauley
RITCHIE, WILLIAM A.
Parker, Arthur Caswell
RITVO, LUCILLE B.
Meyer, Adolf
ROBBINS, RICHARD
Johnson, Charles Spurgeon
ROBBINS, ROSSELL HOPE
Brown, Carleton
ROBBINS, WILLIAM J.
Crocker, William

ROBERT, JOSEPH C.
  Patterson, Rufus Lenoir
ROBERTS, DONALD A.
  Grinnell, Henry Walton
  Harland, Henry
  Major, Charles
  Moses, Montrose Jonas
  O'Higgins, Harvey Jerrold
  Shepard, Edward Morse
  Tremain, Henry Edwin
  Webb, Alexander Stewart
  Wheeler, Everett Pepperrell
  Youngs, John
ROBERTS, GEORGE B.
  Perkins, James Handasyd
  Peter, Robert
ROBERTS, JOHN D.
  Cope, Arthur Clay
ROBERTSON, DAVID A.
  Goodspeed, Thomas Wakefield
  Gunsaulus, Frank Wakeley
  Leonard, Robert Josselyn
  MacAlister, James
  Mayo, Amory Dwight
ROBERTSON, H. E.
  Wesbrook, Frank Fairchild
ROBERTSON, JAMES ALEXANDER
  Call, Richard Keith
  Narváez, Pánfilo de
  Núñez Cabeza De Vaca, Alvar
  Smith, Buckingham
ROBIE, EDWARD HODGES
  Hammond, John Hays
ROBINETT, PAUL M.
  Chaffee, Adna Romanza
  Craig, Malin
ROBINSON, BENJAMIN L.
  Watson, Sereno
ROBINSON, BURR A.
  Bristol, William Henry
  Church, Irving Porter
  Gotshall, William Charles
  Irving, John Duer
  McCullough, Ernest
  Meyer, Henry Coddington
  Miller, Kempster Blanchard
  Moldenke, Richard George
    Gottlob
  Mulholland, William
  Nettleton, Edwin S.
  Newhouse, Samuel
  Pearson, Fred Stark
  Peters, Edward Dyer
  Rafter, George W.
  Rand, Addison Crittenden
  Randolph, Isham
  Richards, Charles Brinckerhoff
  Richards, Joseph William
  Robb, William Lispenard
  Roberts, Nathan S.
  Robinson, Albert Alonzo
  Serrell, Edward Wellman
  Smith, Jonas Waldo
  Spilsbury, Edmund Gybbon
  Stauffer, David McNeely
  Stearns, Irving Ariel
  Stott, Henry Gordon
  Strong, Charles Lyman
  Stuart, Charles Beebe
  Wegmann, Edward
  Wernag, Lewis
  Williams, Frank Martin
  Williams, Jesse Lynch

  Wilson, Joseph Miller
  Wilson, William Hasell
ROBINSON, C. A., JR.
  Allinson, Francis Greenleaf
ROBINSON, CERVIN
  Corbett, Harvey Wiley
ROBINSON, DAVID MOORE
  Bright, James Wilson
ROBINSON, DOANE
  Fetterman, William Judd
  Kyle, James Henderson
  Ladd, Edwin Freemont
  Loucks, Henry Langford
  Mellette, Arthur Calvin
ROBINSON, EDGAR E.
  Hager, John Sharpenstein
  Haight, Henry Huntly
  Hearst, George
  Hearst, Phoebe Apperson
  Latham, Milton Slocum
  Lick, James
ROBINSON, EDGAR EUGENE
  Requa, Mark Lawrence
ROBINSON, EDWIN ARLINGTON
  Perry, Thomas Sergeant
ROBINSON, ELWYN B.
  Amidon, Charles Fremont
ROBINSON, GEORGE W.
  Emerton, Ephraim
ROBINSON, HENRY MORTON
  Dorgan, Thomas Aloysius
  Rogers, William Allen
  Thomas, Robert Bailey
ROBINSON, HERBERT SPENCER
  Smith, Roswell
  Tomlinson, Everett Titsworth
  Watson, Henry Clay
  Webber, Charles Wilkins
  Zachos, John Celivergos
ROBINSON, MARION O.
  Cushman, Vera Charlotte Scott
ROBINSON, WILLIAM ALEXANDER
  Atherton, Charles Gordon
  Barlett, Ichabod
  Bayard, Thomas Francis
  Bell, Charles Henry
  Bell, Samuel
  Bentley, William
  Berry, Nathaniel Springer
  Bishop, Abraham
  Blair, Henry William
  Bowdoin, James, 1726–1790
  Bowdoin, James, 1752–1811
  Brown, Francis, 1784–1820
  Cheney, Person Colby
  Clark, Daniel
  Corbin, Daniel Chase
  Currier, Moody
  Daggett, David
  Dwight, Theodore, 1764–1846
  Edmunds, George Franklin
  Edwards, Pierpont
  Evans, George
  Fairfield, John
  Fessenden, Francis
  Fessenden, James Deering
  Fessenden, Samuel
  Fessenden, William Pitt
  Fisk, James, 1763–1844
  Fogg, George Gilman
  Folsom, Nathaniel
  Foot, Solomon
  Foster, Abiel

  Foster, Abigail Kelley
  Foster, John Gray
  Foster, Stephen Symonds
  Gallinger, Jacob Harold
  Gilman, John Taylor
  Gilman, Nicholas
  Gilmore, Joseph Albree
  Goodrich, Chauncey
  Goodrich, Elizur
  Goodwin, Ichabod
  Granger, Gideon
  Griswold, Matthew
  Griswold, Roger
  Griswold, Stanley
  Hale, Eugene
  Hale, John Parker
  Hamlin, Hannibal
  Harriman, Walter
  Hill, Isaac
  Hinds, Asher Crosby
  Holman, William Steele
  Langdon, John
  Lincoln, Enoch
  Lincoln, Levi, 1749–1820
  Lincoln, Levi, 1782–1868
  Lord, Nathan
  Lyon, Matthew
  Metcalf, Henry Harrison
  Patterson, James Willis
  Peabody, Nathaniel
  Perley, Ira
  Pickering, John
  Pickering, Timothy
  Plumer, William
  Reed, Thomas Brackett
  Rollins, Edward Henry
  Rollins, Frank West
  Smith, Israel
  Smith, Jeremiah, 1759–1842
  Sullivan, George
  Thornton, Matthew
  Tichenor, Isaac
  Tuck, Amos
  Washburn, Albert Henry
  Weare, Meshech
  Whipple, William
  Wingate, Paine
ROBINSON, WILLIAM M., JR.
  Coxetter, Louis Mitchell
  Lamar, Gazaway Bugg
  Maffitt, John Newland
  Rains, George Washington
  Read, Charles William
  Semmes, Raphael
  Smith, Gustavus Woodson
  Tucker, John Randolph,
    1812–1883
  Wood, John Taylor
ROBISON, DANIEL M.
  McMillin, Benton
  Shields, John Knight
  Witherspoon, John Alexander
ROCHESTER, ANNA
  Woodbury, Helen Laura
    Sumner
ROCKWELL, WILLIAM WALKER
  Prentiss, George Lewis
RODABAUGH, JAMES H.
  Bishop, Robert Hamilton
  Jones, Samuel Milton
RODEN, CARL B.
  McClurg, Alexander Caldwell
  Poole, William Frederick

RODIONOFF, NICHOLAS R.
Shelekhov, Grigorii Ivanovich
ROE, JOSEPH W.
Hartness, James
ROEVER, WILLIAM H.
Chauvenet, William
ROGAN, OCTAVIA F.
Rosenberg, Henry
ROGERS, ALLEN
Sadtler, Samuel Philip
ROGERS, JAMES GRAFTON
Long, Joseph Ragland
Thatcher, Mahlon Daniel
ROGERS, L. HARDING, JR.
Warren, Sir Peter
ROGERS, LINDSAY
Baldwin, Henry
Blatchford, Samuel
ROGERS, MAX GRAY
Moffatt, James
ROGOSIN, WILLIAM DONN
Dundee, Johnny
Langford, Samuel
Leavitt, Frank Simmons (Man
Mountain Dean)
ROHNE, J. MAGNUS
Clausen, Claus Lauritz
Dahl, Theodore Halvorson
Dietrichson, Johannes Wilhelm
Christian
Hoenecke, Gustav Adolf Felix
Theodor
Hove, Elling
Hoyme, Gjermund
Kildahl, Johan Nathan
Koren, Ulrik Vilhelm
Larsen, Peter Laurentius
Lenker, John Nicholas
Lindberg, Conrad Emil
Norelius, Eric
Pieper, Franz August Otto
ROLAND, CHARLES G.
Wilder, Russell Morse
ROLBIECKI, JOHN J.
Barzynski, Vincent
Dabrowski, Joseph
ROLLINS, ALFRED B., JR.
Hopkins, Harry Lloyd
Roper, Daniel Calhoun
ROLLINS, CARL P.
De Vinne, Theodore Low
ROLLINS, REED C.
Fernald, Merritt Lyndon
ROMANOFSKY, PETER
Potter, Ellen Culver
ROMANUS, CHARLES F., SR.
Patch, Alexander McCarrell
ROMASCO, ALBERT U.
Brookhart, Smith Wildman
Watson, James Eli
ROMER, ALFRED S.
Barbour, Thomas
RONSAVILLE, VIRGINIA
Corbin, Margaret
Curwen, Samuel
McCauley, Mary Ludwig Hays
ROONEY, MIRIAM THERESA
Fitzpatrick, John Bernard
ROOT, EDWARD W.
Hooker, Philip
ROOT, ERNEST ROB
Langstroth, Lorenzo Lorraine

ROOT, ROBERT K.
Hudson, Henry Norman
ROOT, WALTER S.
Lee, Frederic Schiller
ROOT, WINFRED TREXLER
Keith, Sir William
ROPES, JAMES H.
Gregory, Caspar René
Moore, George Foot
ROPPOLO, JOSEPH PATRICK
Barry, Philip James Quinn
RORABAUGH, W J
Genovese, Vito
Poling, Daniel Alfred
Ruditsky, Barney
Yellowley, Edward Clements
RUSE, FLORA
Van Rensselaer, Martha
ROSE, GEORGE, III
Alexander, James
Bouvier, John
ROSE, KATHERINE
Gates, Caleb Frank
ROSE, LISLE A.
Messersmith, George Strausser
ROSEBOOM, EUGENE H.
Tod, David
Wood, Reuben
ROSEN, ELLIOTT
Edge, Walter Evans
ROSEN, GEORGE
Baker, Sara Josephine
Blake, Francis Gilman
Park, William Hallock
Rosenau, Milton Joseph
ROSEN, ROBERT S.
Hirschbein, Peretz
ROSENAU, WILLIAM
Mielziner, Moses
ROSENBACH, A. S. W.
Bement, Clarence Sweet
Mackenzie, William
Polock, Moses
ROSENBERG, J. MITCHELL
Frank, Jerome
ROSENBERG, NATHAN
De Leeuw, Adolph Lodewyk
ROSENBERRY, LOIS K. M.
Helmer, Bessie Bradwell
Meeker, Moses
Mosher, Eliza Maria
Nichols, Clarina Irene Howard
Parrish, Celestia Susannah
Sewall, May Eliza Wright
Talbot, Emily Fairbanks
Tiffany, Katrina Brandes Ely
ROSENBERRY, MARVIN B.
Cassoday, John Bolivar
Jenkins, James Graham
Larrabee, Charles Hathaway
Lyon, William Penn
Orton, Harlow South
Ryan, Edward George
Strong, Moses McCure
Winslow, John Bradley
ROSENBLATT, MILTON B.
Wells, Harry Gideon
ROSENFELD, ALBERT
Langmuir, Irving
ROSENFELD, LULLA
Adler, Sara
Schwartz, Maurice

ROSENKRANTZ, BARBARA GUTMANN
Briggs, Lloyd Vernon
Brunswick, Ruth Mack
Gunn, Selskar Michael
ROSENZWEIG, ROY
Brophy, John
Foster, William Z.
Mason, Lucy Randolph
Muste, Abraham Johannes
Steuben, John
ROSEWATER, VICTOR
Creighton, Edward
Hale, William Bayard
McLean, William Leppard
McRae, Milton Alexander
Nelson, William Rockhill
Phillips, Walter Polk
Prime, William Cowper
Singerly, William Miskey
ROSS, BARBARA
Guthrie, Edwin Ray, Jr.
ROSS, DOROTHY
Cattell, James McKeen
ROSS, EARLE DUDLEY
Gear, John Henry
Geddes, James Loraine
Harlan, James, 1820–1899
Haugen, Gilbert Nelson
Herron, Francis Jay
Howell, James Bruen
Kenyon, William Squire
Knapp, Bradford
Pearson, Raymond Allen
Shaw, Leslie Mortier
Wilson, James Falconer
ROSS, ELIZABETH D.
Hill, Patty Smith
Wheelock, Lucy
ROSS, FRANK A.
Giddings, Franklin Henry
ROSS, FRANK EDWARD
Allen, Philip
Austin, James Trecothick
Bland, Thomas
Brown, John Porter
Bryant, Gridley
Burrill, James
Butler, John
Butler, Richard
Butler, Walter N.
Butler, Zebulon
Cathcart, James Leander
Chafin, Eugene Wilder
Childs, Thomas
Clarke, John Sleeper
Cleveland, Benjamin
Cleveland, Chauncey Fitch
Darby, William
Davidson, William Lee
Dickinson, Philemon
Elbert, Samuel
Febiger, Christian
Forman, David
Grayson, William
Gridley, Richard
Gulick, Luther Halsey,
1828–1891
Harlan, Josiah
Hite, Jost
Howard, Volney Erskine
Ives, Joseph Christmas
James, Edwin
Knowlton, Thomas

Lamb, John
Laurens, John
Lewis, William David
McArthur, William Pope
McDowell, Charles
McDowell, Joseph
Neville, John
Ross, HAROLD E.
Van Slyke, Lucius Lincoln
Ross, MARC
Eno, William Phelps
Ross, MARVIN CHAUNCEY
Porter, Arthur Kingsley
Ross, RODNEY A.
Leland, Waldo Gifford
Ross, SUE FIELDS
Bernstein, Aline
ROSSINI, FREDERICK D.
Washburn, Edward Wight
ROSSITER, FRANK R.
Downes (Edwin) Olin
ROSTOW, W. W.
Rogers, James Harvey
ROTH, JOHN K.
Bode, Boyd Henry
Buchanan, Scott Milross
Carnap, Rudolf
Divine, Father
Hocking, William Ernest
Latourette, Kenneth Scott
Montague, William Pepperell
Niebuhr, Helmut Richard
Perry, Ralph Barton
Santayana, George
ROTHENSTEINER, JOHN E.
Hoecken, Christian
Kenrick, Peter Richard
ROUDER, WENDY
Hampden, Walter
Leiber, Fritz
Taylor, Laurette
ROURKE, CONSTANCE M.
Crabtree, Lotta
Keene, Laura
ROUS, PEYTON
Warthin, Aldred Scott
ROWE, HENRY KALLOCH
Anderson, Martin Brewer
Bowne, Borden Parker
Boyce, James Petigru
Bright, Edward
Broadus, John Albert
Brown, Charles Rufus
Brown, John Newton
Callender, John
Campbell, Alexander
Campbell, Thomas
Mitchell, Edward Cushing
Sharp, Daniel
Thomas, Jesse Burgess
ROWE, J. P.
Clapp, Charles Horace
ROWE, ROBERT R.
Barker, James William
Boldt, George C.
Boorman, James
Bruce, George
ROWLAND, DUNBAR
Adams, William Wirt
Brandon, Gerard Chittocque
Gholson, Samuel Jameson
Hardy, William Harris
Harris, Nathaniel Harrison

Harris, Wiley Pope
Harris, William Littleton
Henderson, John
RUBIN, JOAN SHELLEY
Canby, Henry Seidel
Rinehart, Stanley Marshall, Jr.
RUBIN, JOSEPH L.
Murphy, William Walton
RUDOLPH, FREDERICK
Dennett, Tyler (Wilbur)
Garfield, Harry Augustus
RUFUS, W. CARL
Rittenhouse, David
Watson, James Craig
RUHRAH, JOHN
Hemmeter, John Conrad
RUNDELL, WALTER, JR.
Webb, Walter Prescott
RUPPENTHAL, ROLAND G.
Lee, John Clifford Hodges
RUSH, N. ORWIN
Fraser, James Earle
Leigh, William Robinson
RUSK, GEORGE Y.
Miller, John
RUSK, RALPH L.
Bennett, Emerson
Coggeshall, William Turner
Eggleston, Edward
Imlay, Gilbert
RUSK, WILLIAM SENER
Adams, Herbert Samuel
Polk, Willis Jefferson
Rinehart, William Henry
Rogers, John, 1829–1904
Rogers, Randolph
Rumsey, Charles Cary
Simmons, Franklin
Stone, Horatio
Story, Julian Russell
Story, William Wetmore
Thayer, Abbott Handerson
Turner, Charles Yardley
Walter, Thomas Ustick
Weir, John Ferguson
Weir, Robert Walter
RUSSELL, ROSS
Parker, Charlie ("Bird")
RUSSELL, WILLIAM L.
Salmon, Thomas William
RUTLAND, ROBERT A.
Dryfoos, Orvil E.
Kiplinger, Willard Monroe
Scherman, Harry
Scripps, William Edmund
Shuster, W(illiam) Morgan
RUTLAND, ROBERT ALLEN
McClatchy, Charles Kenny
RYAN, EDWIN
Dubois, John
RYAN, JOHN A.
McGlynn, Edward
RYAN, JOHN K.
Pace, Edward Aloysius
Turner, William
RYAN, PAT M.
Allen, Viola Emily
Brice, Fanny
Pemberton, Brock
Perry, Antoinette
Shubert, Lee
Warfield, David

RYDEN, GEORGE H.
Burton, William
Cannon, William
Gilbert, Eliphalet Wheeler
McKinly, John
Purnell, William Henry
Ridgely, Nicholas
Rodney, Caesar
Rodney, Caesar Augustus
Rodney, Thomas
White, Samuel

SABLOSKY, IRVING L.
Damrosch, Walter Johannes
Spalding, Albert
SACHS, BERNARD
Seguin, Edouard
Seguin, Edward Constant
SAFFORD, JEFFREY
Vickery, Howard Leroy
SAFFRON, MORRIS H.
Fowler, Russell Story
Haupt, Alma Cecelia
Rubin, Isidor Clinton
Warbasse, James Peter
SAKOLSKI, A. M.
Hendrix, Joseph Clifford
Hotchkiss, Horace Leslie
Jones, Frank
Keith, Benjamin Franklin
SALES, JANE
McCord, James Bennett
SALMON, WESLEY C.
Reichenbach, Hans
SALMOND, JOHN
McEntee, James Joseph
SALON, MARLENE
Farrand, Beatrix Cadwalader
Jones
SALOUTOS, THEODORE
Butler, Marion
Callimachos, Panos Demetrios
Frazier, Lynn Joseph
Goss, Albert Simon
Hirth, William Andrew
Jardine, William Marion
Johnson, Magnus
Reno, Milo
Sloan, George Arthur
SALSBURY, STEPHEN
Du Pont, Lammot
SALTER, SUMNER
Bartlett, Homer Newton
Bradbury, William Batchelder
SAMINSKY, LAZARE
Rosenblatt, Joseph
SAMSON, VERNE LOCKWOOD
Johnston, Annie Fellows
Rowland, Henry Cottrell
Singleton, Esther
Smith, George Henry
Stein, Evaleen
Stiles, Henry Reed
Tappan, Eva March
Thayer, William Makepeace
Waggaman, Mary Teresa
McKee
Warner, Anne Richmond
Wormley, James
SAMUELSON, PAUL A.
Schumpeter, Joseph Alois

SANBORN, ASHTON ROLLINS
Loeb, James
SANDBURG, CARL
Wentworth, John
Wright, Philip Green
SANDIFER, DURWARD V.
Johnson, William
Jones, Samuel
Kirkpatrick, Andrew
Kneeland, Stillman Foster
Knott, Aloysius Leo
Mitchell, William, 1801–1886
SAPIENZA, MADELINE
Adams, Frank Ramsay
Monteux, Pierre Benjamin
Munch, Charles
Reiner, Fritz
Spaeth, Sigmund
SAPOSS, DAVID J.
Schlesinger, Benjamin
Sigman, Morris
SARASOHN, DAVID
Marcosson, Isaac Frederick
Von Wiegand, Karl Henry
SARGENT, GEORGE HENRY
Mosher, Thomas Bird
SAUL, RICHARD S.
Johnson, George Francis
SAVAGE, CARLTON
Foote, Lucius Harwood
Ide, Henry Clay
Jackson, John Brinckerhoff
SAVAGE, GEORGE
Walter, Eugene
SAVELLE, MAX
Morgan, George
SAWYER, RALPH A.
Lyman, Theodore
SAYRE, WALLACE S.
Kenna, John Edward
Roe, Gilbert Ernstein
SCAASI, ARNOLD
Adrian, Gilbert
Carnegie, Hattie
SCARBOROUGH, DOROTHY
Barr, Amelia Edith Huddleston
SCHAFER, JOSEPH
Abernethy, George
Adams, William Lysander
Applegate, Jesse
Atkinson, George Henry
Boise, Reuben Patrick
Campbell, Prince Lucien
Corbett, Henry Winslow
De Smet, Pierre-Jean
Doolittle, James Rood
Doty, James Duane
Draper, Lyman Copeland
Farnham, Thomas Jefferson
Gaines, John Pollard
Greenhow, Robert
Grover, La Fayette
Jackson, Mortimer Melville
Kelley, Hall Jackson
Keyes, Elisha Williams
Lane, Joseph
McLoughlin, John
Nesmith, James Willis
Parker, Samuel
Randall, Alexander Williams
Rusk, Jeremiah McClain
Smith, Jedediah Strong
Stevens, Isaac Ingalls

Whitman, Marcus
Wyeth, Nathaniel Jarvis
SCHAFFER, ALAN L.
Marcantonio, Vito Anthony
SCHAMBERG, JAY FRANK
Duhring, Louis Adolphus
SCHAPIRO, ISRAEL
Imber, Naphtali Herz
Paley, John
Rombro, Jacob
Rosenberg, Abraham Hayyim
Rosenfeld, Morris
Rosenthal, Herman
Schomer, Nahum Meir
Selikovitsch, Goetzel
Spivak, Charles David
Winchevsky, Morris
Wolf, Simon
Zevin, Israel Joseph
Zunser, Eliakum
SCHARNHORST, GARY
Forester, Cecil Scott
SCHEIN, JEROME D.
Keller, Helen Adams
SCHELL, HERBERT S.
Young, Clark Montgomery
SCHELLENBERG, T. R.
Binkley, Robert Cedric
SCHENE, MICHAEL G.
Stefansson, Vilhjalmur
SCHEVILL, FERDINAND
Holst, Hermann, Eduard Von
SCHEYER, ERNST
Hofmann, Hans
Weber, Max
SCHIEDT, RICHARD C.
Stahr, John Summers
SCHILLER, A. ARTHUR
Smith, Edmund Munroe
SCHILLER, FRANCIS
Kennedy, Robert Foster
SCHLABACH, THERON F.
Ely, Richard Theodore
Witte, Edwin Emil
SCHLESINGER, ARTHUR M., JR.
Kennedy, John Fitzgerald
Kennedy, Robert Francis
SCHLESINGER, FRANK
Elkin, William Lewis
SCHLESINGER, H. I.
Stieglitz, Julius
SCHLUNDT, CHRISTENA L.
Tamiris, Helen
SCHMEHL, LAWRENCE H.
Hinman, Joel
Hosmer, Titus
James, Edward Christopher
Knapp, Martin Augustine
SCHMIDT, DOROTHY S.
Grosvenor, Gilbert Hovey
SCHMIDT, DWIGHT L.
Warner, William Lloyd
SCHMIDT, LESTER F.
Ball, Frank Clayton
SCHMIDT, LOUIS BERNARD
Henderson, David Bremner
Hepburn, William Peters
Meredith, Edwin Thomas
Simpson, John Andrew
Wallace, Henry
Wallace, Henry Cantwell
Wilson, James

SCHNEER, CECIL J.
Bowen, Norman Levi
Spurr, Josiah Edward
SCHNEIDER, DAVID M.
Adie, David Craig
SCHNEIDER, HERBERT W.
Colby, Luther
Davis, Andrew Jackson
Dods, John Bovee
Harris, Thomas Lake
Hudson, Thomas Jay
Hyslop, James Hervey
Lee, Ann
Newbrough, John Ballou
Pratt, James Bissett
Sandeman, Robert
SCHOBINGER, GEORGE
McConnell, Ira Welch
SCHOEN, ELIN
Miranda, Carmen
SCHOENBERGER, H. W.
Hill, Frederic Stanhope
Hillhouse, James Abraham
Ingersoll, Edward
Judah, Samuel Benjamin
    Helbert
Noah, Mordecai Manuel
Smith, Richard Penn
SCHOENFELD, DOROTHY BRIGSTOCK
Kiam, Omar
McCardell, Claire
Maxwell, Elsa
Orry-Kelly
Snow, Carmel White
SCHOFIELD, ANN
Lang, Lucy Fox Robins
SCHOFIELD, CARLETON F.
Dodge, Raymond
SCHOTT, THOMAS E.
Hawley, Paul Ramsey
Pate, Maurice
SCHRADER, FRANZ
Wilson, Edmund Beecher
SCHREIBER, CARL F.
English, Thomas Dunn
Hirst, Henry Beck
Möllhausen, Heinrich Balduin
SCHROEDER, FRED E. H.
Hartmann, Carl Sadakichi
Norris, Charles Gilman Smith
Terhune, Albert Payson
SCHROM, NANCY
Nathan, Maud
SCHRUBEN, FRANCIS W.
Allen, Henry Justin
SCHUCHERT, CHARLES
Gabb, William More
Gibbs, George
Merrill, George Perkins
SCHUETTE, H. A.
Reid, David Boswell
SCHUKER, STEPHEN A.
Avery, Sewell Lee
Davison, George Willets
Goldschmidt, Jakob
Leffingwell, Russell Cornell
Prince, Frederick Henry
SCHULTES, RICHARD EVANS
Ames, Oakes
SCHULTZ, JACK
Bridges, Calvin Blackman

SCHULTZ, STANLEY K.
  Curley, James Michael
  Curran, Thomas Jerome
SCHULZE, ELDOR PAUL
  James, Thomas Lemuel
  Kemble, Gouverneur
SCHUSKY, ERNEST L.
  Cantril, Albert Hadley
  Densmore, Frances
  Heye, George Gustav
  La Farge, Oliver Hazard Perry
  MacIver, Robert Morrison
  Powdermaker, Hortense
  Radin, Paul
  Son of Many Beads
SCHUSKY, MARY SUE DILLIARD
  Abbott, Eleanor Hallowell
  Aldrich, Bess Genevra Streeter
  Anthony, Katharine Susan
  Bailey, (Irene) Temple
  Baum, Hedwig ("Vicki")
  Carr, Charlotte Elizabeth
  Fauset, Jessie Redmon
  Hill, Grace Livingston
  Hobart, Alice Nourse Tisdale
  Orton, Helen Fuller
  Rives, Hallie Erminie
  Wheeler, (George) Post
SCHUYLER, HAMILTON
  Morris, Edmund
  Ogden, Uzal
  Smith, Charles Perrin
SCHUYLER, MONTGOMERY
  Bacon, Robert
  Eidlitz, Cyrus Lazelle Warner
  Eidlitz, Leopold
  Le Brun, Napoléon Eugène
    Henry Charles
SCHUYLER, ROBERT LIVINGSTON
  Beer, George Louis
SCHWANTES, ROBERT S.
  Fleisher, Benjamin Wilfrid
  Gulick, Sidney Lewis
SCHWARTZ, ARTHUR
  Koller, Carl
SCHWARTZ, CHARLES
  Porter, Cole
SCHWARZ, JORDAN A.
  Bunker, Arthur Hugh
  Doughton, Robert Lee
  Guffey, Joseph F.
  Kaiser, Henry John
  Neely, Matthew Mansfield
SCHWARZ, RICHARD W.
  Kellogg, John Harvey
SCOBIE, INGRID WINTHER
  Bloor, Ella Reeve
SCOON, ROBERT
  Spaulding, Edward Gleason
SCOTT, CHARLES F.
  Sprague, Frank Julian
SCOTT, EDITH
  Hanson, James Christian
    Meinich
SCOTT, FRANKLIN WILLIAM
  Brownlow, William Ganaway
  Hall, James, 1793–1868
  Morrison, William Ralls
  Russell, Benjamin
SCOTT, JONATHAN FRENCH
  Backus, Truman Jay
  Bailey, Ebenezer
  Bailey, Rufus William

Barnes, Mary Downing Sheldon
SCOTT, KENNETH
  Fiske, George Converse
SCOTT, LESLIE M.
  Pittock, Henry Lewis
SCROGGS, WILLIAM O.
  Walker, William
SEARS, FREDERIC C.
  Manning, Robert
SEARS, J. D.
  Campbell, Marius Robinson
SEARS, LOUIS M.
  Benton, Thomas Hart,
    1782–1858
  Brown, Ethan Allen
  Cass, Lewis
  Smart, James Henry
SEARS, PAUL B.
  Clements, Frederic Edward
  Cowles, Henry Chandler
SEARS, ROBERT R.
  Hull, Clark Leonard
  Terman, Lewis Madison
SEELIG, M. G.
  Hodgen, John Thompson
  Still, Andrew Taylor
  Whelpley, Henry Milton
SEITZ, DON C.
  Depew, Chauncey Mitchell
SELDEN, SAMUEL
  Koch, Frederick Henry
SELEMENT, GEORGE
  Dodd, Monroe Elmon
SELLARDS, ELIAS HOWARD
  Udden, Johan August
SELLARS, ROY W.
  Morris, George Sylvester
  Tappan, Henry Philip
SELLERS, HORACE WELLS
  McArthur, John, 1823–1890
  Peale, Charles Willson
  Peale, Rembrandt
  Peale, Sarah Miriam
  Peale, Titian Ramsay
SELLERS, JAMES LEE
  Paine, Halbert Eleazer
  Philipp, Emanuel Lorenz
  Sarpy, Peter A.
  Thayer, John Milton
  Van Wyck, Charles Henry
SELLERS, J. L.
  Hitchcock, Gilbert Monell
  Holdrege, George Ward
SELLIN, THORSTEN
  Brockway, Zebulon Reed
  Hart, Hastings Hornell
  Koren, John
  Lewis, Orlando Faulkland
  Lynds, Elam
  Osborne, Thomas Mott
  Pilsbury, Amos
  Vaux, Richard
  Vaux, Roberts
SEMONCHE, JOHN E.
  Phillips, John Sanburn
SENIOR, CLARENCE
  Iglesias, Santiago
SENSABAUGH, GEORGE F.
  Jones, Richard Foster
SENTURIA, JOSEPH J.
  Wanamaker, John
  Wanamaker, Lewis Rodman
  Williams, John Skelton

SERONDE, JOSEPH
  Knapp, William Ireland
SEVERANCE, FRANK HAYWARD
  Alexander, De Alva Stanwood
SEWALL, HENRY
  Vaugham, Victor Clarence
SEYBOLT, ROBERT FRANCIS
  Cook, John Williston
  Grew, Theophilus
  Morrison, John Irwin
  Neef, Francis Joseph Nicholas
  Northend, Charles
  Nott, Eliphalet
  Orcutt, Hiram
  Park, Roswell
  Peabody, Selim Hobart
  Peirce, Cyrus
  Pormort, Philemon
  Russell, William
  Sheldon, Edward Austin
  Sheldon, William Evarts
  Sherwin, Thomas
  Stetson, William Wallace
  Thayer, Gideon French
  Ticknor, Elisha
  Tompkins, Arnold
  Turner, Asa
  Turner, Jonathan Baldwin
  Watson, James Madison
  Wells, William Harvey
  Wickersham, James Pyle
SEYMOUR, CHARLES
  House, Edward Mandell
  Wilson, Woodrow
SEYMOUR, GEORGE DUDLEY
  Austin, Henry
  Hale, Nathan
  Hoadley, David
  Niemeyer, John Henry
  Town, Ithiel
SEYMOUR, HAROLD
  Alexander, Grover Cleveland
  Griffith, Clark Calvin
SHACHTMAN, TOM
  Wilson, Edith Bolling
SHAFER, ROBERT
  Boies, Horace
  Dodge, Grenville Mellen
  Grimes, James Wilson
  Gue, Benjamin F.
  Mason, Charles
  Nichols, George Ward
  Parvin, Theodore Sutton
  Payne, William Morton
SHAMBAUGH, BENJAMIN F.
  Boies, Horace
  Dodge, Grenville Mellen
  Grimes, James Wilson
  Gue, Benjamin F.
  Mason, Charles
  Parvin, Theodore Sutton
SHAMBAUGH, BERTHA M. H.
  Metz, Christian
SHANDS, ALFRED R., JR.
  Whitman, Royal
SHANE, C. D.
  Curtis, Heber Doust
  Moore, Joseph Haines
SHANE, MARY LEA
  Aitken, Robert Grant
SHANKLAND, R. S.
  Allison, Samuel King
  Miller, Dayton Clarence

SHANNON, DAVID A.
  Walling, William English
SHANNON, FRED A.
  Spring, Leverett Wilson
SHANNON, WILLIAM H.
  Merton, Thomas
SHANNON, WILLIAM V.
  Patterson, Joseph Medill
SHAPIRO, EDWARD S.
  Burgess, Frank Gelett
  De Palma, Ralph
  Lambeau, Earl Louis ("Curly")
  Lawson, Robert Ripley
  White, Benjamin Franklin
  Wills, Harry
SHAPIRO, HARRY L.
  Hooton, Earnest Albert
  Weidenreich, Franz
SHAPLEN, ROBERT
  Musica, Philip Mariano Fausto
SHARLIN, HAROLD I.
  Gale, Henry Gordon
SHARP, NICHOLAS A.
  Anthony, John J.
SHAVER, MURIEL
  Baum, Lyman Frank
  Blackwell, Henry Brown
  Bliss, Porter Cornelius
  Brainerd, Erastus
  Bross, William
  Brown, Olympia
  Brown, Simon
  Browne, Francis Fisher
  Bryan, Mary Edwards
  Castle, Vernon Blythe
  Chambers, James Julius
  Chandler, Joseph Ripley
  Child, David Lee
  Cox, Palmer
  Croly, David Goodman
  Croly, Jane Cunningham
  Davidge, William Pleater
  Davis, Paulina Kellogg Wright
  Delavan, Edward Cornelius
  Duff, Mary Ann Dyke
  Farnham, Eliza Woodson
    Burham
  Flower, Lucy Louisa Coues
  Fuller, Loie
  Gilbert, Linda
  Goodnow, Isaac Tichenor
SHAW, ARNOLD
  Armstrong, Henry Worthington
    ("Harry")
  Guthrie, Woody
  Handy, William Christopher
  Hendrix, Jimi
  Silvers, Louis
  Taylor, Joseph Deems
  Washington, Dinah
  Williams, (Hiram) Hank
SHAW, EDWIN B.
  Lewis, Ellis
SHAW, HARRY, JR.
  Joynes, Edward Southey
  Stoddard, Elizabeth Drew
    Bartow
  Stoddard, Richard Henry
  Thomas, Edith Matilda
  Tincker, Mary Agnes
SHAW, ROBERT K.
  Norcross, Orlando Whitney

SHAW, WILFRED B.
  Hutchins, Harry Burns
SHAW, WILLIAM BRISTOL
  Abbey, Henry Eugene
  Aborn, Milton
  Adams, Henry Carter
  Albee, Edward Franklin
  Allis, Edward Phelps
  Andrews, Chauncey Hummason
  Andrews, Stephen Pearl
  Arbuckle, John
  Archbold, John Dustin
  Avery, Samuel Putnam
  Baker, Lorenzo Dow
  Barber, Amzi Lorenzo
  Benjamin, George Hillard
  Bergh, Christian
  Bragg, Edward Stuyvesant
  Brayman, Mason
  Butts, Isaac
  Byrnes. Thomas F.
  Cary, Edward
  Chittenden, Simeon Baldwin
  Claflin, Horace Brigham
  Clark, Jonas Gilman
  Clark, Myron Holley
  Collier, Peter Fenelon
  Corbin, Austin
  Crimmins, John Daniel
  Croker, Richard
  Davey, John
  Davison, Henry Pomeroy
  Day, Horace H.
  De Kay, George Colman
  De Kay, James Ellsworth
  Delafield, John, 1748–1824
  Delafield, John, 1786–1853
  Delmonico, Lorenzo
  Dodd, Frank Howard
  Dodge, David Low
  Dodge, William Earl
  Doremus, Sarah Platt Haines
  Douglass, David Bates
  Dudley, Charles Edward
  Dun, Robert Graham
  Eckford, Henry
  Englis, John
  Faber, John Eberhard
  Fahnestock, Harris Charles
  Fayerweather, Daniel Burton
  Fels, Joseph
  Field, Benjamin Hazard
  Fish, Stuyvesant
  Fisher, Joshua Francis
  Fiske, Haley
  Foster, Judith Ellen Horton
  Francis, Samuel Ward
  Genin, John Nicholas
  Gorham, Jabez
  Grant, Lewis Addison
  Green, Henrietta Howland
    Robinson
  Harris, William
  Hasbrouck, Abraham Bruyn
  Hatch, Rufus
  Havemeyer, Henry Osborne
  Havemeyer, William Frederick
  Heath, Perry Sanford
  Herring, Silas Clark
  Hicks, John, 1847–1917
  Higinbotham, Harlow Niles
  Irene, Sister
  James, Daniel Willis

Jesup, Morris Ketchum
Jones, Alexander
Jordan, William George
Judd, Orange
Juilliard, Augustus D.
Keely, John Ernst Worrell
Keene, James Robert
Kennedy, John Stewart
King, James Gore
King, John Alsop
Lefferts, Marshall
Lexow, Clarence
Loew, Marcus
Lord, David Nevins
Lorillard, Pierre
McCall, John Augustine
McCurdy, Richard Aldrich
Macy, Valentine Everit
Masson, Thomas Lansing
Moskowitz, Belle Lindner
  Israels
Odell, Benjamin Barker
Ogden, Robert Curtis
Packard, Silas Sadler
Paine, Byron
Pond, James Burton
Proctor, Frederick Francis
Putnam, Gideon
Quigg, Lemuel Ely
Reed, Lumar
Rice, Isaac Leopold
Ruggles, Samuel Bulkley
Sabin, Charles Hamilton
Schuyler, Louisa Lee
Scrymser, James Alexander
Sears, Robert
Seney, George Ingraham
Shonts, Theodore Perry
Sloan, Samuel
Smith, Ormond Gerald
Spinner, Francis Elias
Sterling, John William
Stetson, John Batterson
Stettinius, Edward Riley
Stevens, John Austin,
  1795–1874
Stillman, James
Stranahan, James Samuel
  Thomas
Stuart, Robert Leighton
Taylor, Moses
Thompson, John
Thompson, William Boyce
White, Alfred Tredway
Willard, Mary Hatch
Willys, John North
Wolfe, John David
SHEA, WILLIAM E.
  Squiers, Herbert
  Thompson, Richard Wigginton
  Walker, Mary Edwards
  Weeks, John Wingate
  Wheeler, Wayne Bidwell
  Woodford, Stewart Lyndon
  Woolley, John Granville
  Wright, Luke Edward
SHEAFER, LOUIS
  Glaspell, Susan Keating
SHEAFFER, LOUIS
  Douglas, Lloyd Cassel
SHEAR, CORNELIUS LOTT
  Ellis, Job Bicknell

SHEARER, AUGUSTUS H.
  Lacey, John
  Larned, Josephus Nelson
  Severance, Frank Hayward
  Ward, James Warner
SHEDD, SOLON
  Smith, James Perrin
SHEEHAN, DONAL
  Wyckoff, John Henry
SHELDON, HENRY D.
  Hall, Granville Stanley
SHELDON, MARION
  Wright, Silas
SHELLEY, WALTER BROWN
  Pusey, William Allen
SHELTON, SUZANNE
  St. Denis, Ruth
SHENK, HIRAM H.
  Bates, Samuel Penniman
SHENTON, JAMES P.
  Kerby, William Joseph
SHEPARD, ARTHUR MACC.
  Alden, James
  Almy, John Jay
SHEPARD, MORRIS G.
  Ostromislensky, Iwan
    Iwanowich
SHEPHERD, REBECCA
  Mannes, Leopold Damrosch
SHEPHERD, REBECCA ANN
  Rubinstein, Helena
SHEPHERD, WILLIAM R.
  Rives, George Lockhart
  Sloane, William Milligan
SHERMAN, CLIFTON LUCIEN
  Burr, Alfred Edmund
SHERMAN, JAY J.
  Livingstone, William
  Newberry, John Stoughton
  Newberry, Oliver
SHERWOOD, GARRISON P.
  Carter, Caroline Louise Dudley
SHERWOOD, HENRY NOBLE
  Brown, George Pliny
SHERWOOD, MORGAN
  Jones, Lewis Ralph
SHETRONE, H. C.
  Fowke, Gerard
SHEWMAKER, KENNETH E.
  Carlson, Evans Fordyce
  Smedley, Agnes
SHINN, OWEN L.
  Tilghman, Richard Albert
SHIPLER, GUY EMERY
  Hale, Charles Reuben
  Houghton, George Hendric
  Huntington, Frederic Dan
  Langdon, William Chauncy
  McLaren, William Edward
  Odenheimer, William Henry
  Onderdonk, Benjamin Tredwell
  Onderdonk, Henry Ustick
  Provoost, Samuel
  Smith, John Cotton, 1826–1882
  Spencer, Jesse Ames
SHIPMAN, FRED W.
  Gardner, Charles Kitchell
  Hood, Washington
  Kelly, Luther Sage
  Lederer, John
  Loring, Frederick Wadsworth
  Needham, James
  O'Fallon, Benjamin

Ogden, Herbert Gouverneur
SHIPPEE, LESTER BURRELL
  Davis, Cushman Kellogg
  Gorman, Willis Arnold
  Loring, Charles Morgridge
  Lowry, Thomas
  Marshall, William Rainey
  Merriam, William Rush
  Mitchell, William 1832–1900
  Nettleton, Alvred Bayard
  Otis, Charles Eugene
  Peavey, Frank Hutchinson
  Pillsbury, John Sargent
  Smalley, Eugene Virgil
  Stevens, Hiram Fairchild
  Stevens, John Harrington
  Tawney, James Albertus
  Towne, Charles Arnette
  Walker, Thomas Barlow
  Washburn, William Drew
  Wheelock, Joseph Albert
  Windom, William
SHIPTON, CLIFFORD K.
  Pring, Martin
  Willard, Joseph, 1738–1804
  Willard, Joseph, 1798–1865
  Willard, Samuel
  Williams, Nathaniel
  Winthrop, James
SHIRLEY, GLENN
  Lillie, Gordon William
SHIRLEY, WAYNE
  Mannes, Clara Damrosch
SHIVELY, CHARLES
  O'Sullivan, Mary Kenney
SHIVER, PETER, JR.
  Lewis, William Henry
SHOEMAKER, FLOYD CALVIN
  Broadhead, James Overton
  Cockrell, Francis Marion
  Colman, Norman Jay
  Crittenden, Thomas Theodore
SHOR, ELIZABETH NOBLE
  Bigelow, Henry Bryant
  Hubbard, Bernard Rosecrans
  Kofoid, Charles Atwood
SHOREY, PAUL
  Harper, William Rainey
SHOUT, JOHN D.
  Blitzstein, Marc
  Dandridge, Dorothy Jean
  Loesser, Frank
SHOVER, JOHN L.
  Ayres, William Augustus
  Benson, Oscar Herman
  O'Neal, Edward Asbury, III
SHOWALTER, ELAINE C.
  Taggard, Genevieve
SHRIVER, PHILLIP RAYMOND
  Pomerene, Atlee
SHRYOCK, RICHARD H.
  Abbott, Samuel Warren
  Arnold, Richard Dennis
  Deaver, John Blair
  Rush, Benjamin
  Rush, James
  Strudwick, Edmund Charles
    Fox
  Taylor, Charlotte de Bernier
  Wells, William Charles
SHURCLIFF, WILLIAM A.
  Pfund, August Herman

SHUSTER, GEORGE N.
  Donahue, Patrick
  Finn, Francis James
  Kilmer, Alfred Joyce
  Lambert, Louis Aloisius
  Lambing, Andrew Arnold
  Lamy, John Baptist
  Lynch, Patrick Neeson
  Walsh, Henry Collins
  Walsh, Thomas
SICHERMAN, BARBARA
  Coriat, Isador Henry
SICKELS, ELEANOR M.
  Schuyler, Montgomery
  Smalley, George Washburn
  Vallentine, Benjamin Bennaton
  Ward, Thomas
  Wardman, Ervin
  Warman, Cy
  Webb, James Watson
  Welch, Philip Henry
  Wheeler, Andrew Carpenter
SIEBERT, WILBUR H.
  De Brahm, William Gerard
  Graham, John
  Leonard, George
  Moody, James
  Moultrie, John
  Romans, Bernard
  Stuart, John
  Turnbull, Andrew
SIEVERS, HARRY J., S.J.
  Drexel, Katharine Mary
SIKES, E. W.
  Clemson, Thomas Green
SILER, JOSEPH F.
  Garnett, Alexander Yelverton
    Peyton
  Hullihen, Simon P.
SILLS, KENNETH C. M.
  Avery, John
  Goodwin, Daniel Raynes
  Johnson, Henry
  McKeen, Joseph
  Packard, Alpheus Spring
  Smyth, William
  Upham, Thomas Cogswell
  Woods, Leonard, 1807–1878
SILVER, ROLLO G.
  Stokes, Frederick Abbot
SILVERMAN, ALEXANDER
  Owens, Michael Joseph
SILVERMAN, S. RICHARD
  Goldstein, Max Aaron
SILVEUS, MARIAN
  Thompson, Josiah Van Kirk
  Warner, Adoniram Judson
  Weeks, Joseph Dame
SIMKINS, FRANCIS BUTLER
  Gist, William Henry
  Lever, Asbury Francis
  McGowan, Samuel
  Miles, William Porcher
  Montague, Andrew Jackson
  Moses, Franklin J.
  Orr, James Lawrence
  Pickens, Francis Wilkinson
  Rainey, Joseph Hayne
  Scott, Robert Kingston
  Simpson, William Dunlap
  Smalls, Robert
  Thompson, Hugh Smith
  Thornwell, James Henley

Tillman, Benjamin Ryan
Trescot, William Henry
Wilkinson, Robert Shaw
SIMMONS, JEROLD L.
 Burlingham, Charles Culp
 Dickinson, John
 Stryker, Lloyd Paul
SIMMS, L. MOODY, JR.
 Barrymore, Ethel
 Blue, Gerald Montgomery
  ("Monte")
 Darwell, Jane
 Gable, (William) Clark
 Hull, Josephine
 Jackson, Joseph Henry
 Karloff, Boris
 Schildkraut, Joseph
 Stevens, Ashton
 Todd, Mike
 Tone, Stanislas Pascal Franchot
 White, Clarence Cameron
SIMON, GEORGE T.
 Miller, Glenn
SIMONDS, FREDERIC W.
 Roemer, Karl Ferdinand
SIMONS, CORINNE MILLER
 Lloyd, John Uri
SIMPSON, B. M., III
 McCormick, Lynde Dupuy
SIMPSON, GEORGE GAYLORD
 Granger, Walter
 Osborn, Henry Fairfield
SIMPSON, LESLEY BYRD
 Vallejo, Mariano Guadalupe
 Vizcaino, Sebastían
SIMPSON, LEWIS P.
 Bradford, Roark Whitney
  Wickliffe
SIMPSON, SARAH H. J.
 Duane, James
SIMPSON, WILLIAM KELLY
 Winlock, Herbert Eustis
SINCLAIR, BRUCE
 Rice, George Samuel
 Weymouth, Frank Elwin
SINGER, EDGAR A., JR.
 Fullerton, George Stuart
SINGER, JAMES
 Veblen, Oswald
SIOUSSAT, ST GEORGE L.
 Johnson, Andrew
 Smith, Justin Harvey
SIPLEY, LOUIS WALTON
 Ives, Frederic Eugene
SISSON, CHARLES P.
 Moody, William Henry
SITKOFF, HARVARD
 Brownlee, James Forbis
 Cooper, (Leon) Jere
 Dawson, William Levi
 Gaston, Herbert Earle
 Tilson, John Quillin
 Tobin, Maurice Joseph
 Tydings, Millard Evelyn
SIZER, THEODORE
 Jarves, James Jackson
 Parton, Arthur
 Penfield, Edward
 Ross, Denman Waldo
 Smibert, John
 Street, Augustus Russell
 Trumbull, John, 1756–1843

SKEEL, EMILY E. F.
 Weems, Mason Locke
SKEHAN, PATRICK W.
 Hyvernat, Henri
SKILLING, HAZEL
 Ryan, Harris Joseph
SKINNER, CLARENCE A.
 Brace, Dewitt Bristol
SKINNER, CLARENCE R.
 Miner, Alonzo Ames
SKINNER, CONSTANCE LINDSAY
 Franchère, Gabriel
 Stanley, Henry Morton
SKLAR, ROBERT
 Bitzer, George William
 Fields, William Claude
 Flaherty, Robert Joseph
 Griffith, David Wark
 Hart, William Surrey
 Langdon, Harry Philmore
 Lubitsch, Ernst
 Porter, Edwin Stanton
SLADE, MARY B.
 Saunders, Prince
SLADE, WILLIAM ADAMS
 Andrews, Elisha Benjamin
 Carpenter, Edmund Janes
 Hazard, Jonathan J.
 Hazard, Rowland Gibson
 Hazard, Thomas
 Hazard, Thomas Robinson
 Spofford, Ainsworth Rand
SLATTERY, THOMAS C.
 Grainger, George Percy
SLAUGHTER, GERTRUDE
 Allinson, Anne Crosby Emery
SLOCUM, ADELE
 Rhoads, Cornelius Packard
SLONIMSKY, NICOLAS
 Foote, Arthur William
 Ives, Charles Edward
 Korngold, Erich Wolfgang
 Mitropoulos, Dimitri
 Schillinger, Joseph
SMALL, MELVIN
 Davies, Joseph Edward
 Houghton, Alanson Bigelow
SMERTENKO, CLARA MILLERD
 Herron, George Davis
SMITH, ALBERT WILLIAM
 Kerr, Walter Craig
SMITH, ALICE KIMBALL
 Oppenheimer, Julius Robert
SMITH, ALICE R. HUGER
 Fraser, Charles
SMITH, CARLETON SPRAGUE
 Converse, Frederick Shepherd
SMITH, CHARLES FORSTER
 Adams, Charles Kendall
SMITH, DANIEL M.
 Colby, Bainbridge
 Cox, James Middleton
SMITH, DAVID C.
 Eckstorm, Fannie Hardy
SMITH, DAVID EUGENE
 Adrain, Robert
 Bôcher, Maxime
 Cole, Frank Nelson
 Craig, Thomas
 De Forest, Erastus Lyman
 Farrar, John
 Green, Gabriel Marcus
 Greenwood, Isaac

Halsted, George Bruce
Johnson, William Woolsey
Loomis, Elias
McClintock, Emory
Maschke, Heinrich
Newton, Hubert Anson
Runkle, John Daniel
Stringham, Washington Irving
Sylvester, James Joseph
Wentworth, George Albert
SMITH, DAVID STANLEY
 Parker, Horatio William
 Steinert, Morris
SMITH, EDGAR FAHS
 Bache, Franklin
 Boyé, Martin Hans
 Cutbush, James
 Griscom, John
 Hare, Robert
 Lea, Mathew Carey
 Woodhouse, James
SMITH, EDWARD CONRAD
 Hitchcock, Frank Harris
 MacVeagh, Franklin
 Mooney, William
 Nicoll, De Lancey
 Olyphant, Robert Morrison
 Opdyke, George
 Parker, Alton Brooks
 Parker, Amasa Junius
 Parsons, John Edward
 Pierrepont, Edwards
 Robertson, William Henry
 Roosevelt, Robert Barnwell
 Rumsey, William
 Sampson, William
 Sanford, Nathan
 Sedgwick, Arthur George
 Shearman, Thomas Gaskell
 Sherman, James Schoolcraft
 Smith, Charles Emory
 Smith, Erasmus Darwin
 Smith, Truman
 Stanchfield, John Barry
 Sterne, Simon
 Tanner, James
 Tracy, Benjamin Franklin
 Wheeler, William Almon
 Wood, Fernando
 Wood, George
 Woodruff, Timothy Lester
SMITH, EDWIN W.
 Aggrey, James Emman Kwegyir
 Lindley, Daniel
SMITH, FRED M.
 Lucas, Daniel Bedinger
 Post, Melville Davisson
 Strother, David Hunter
SMITH, GERALD BIRNEY
 Anderson, Galusha
SMITH, GERTRUDE
 Merrill, Elmer Truesdell
SMITH, HAROLD S.
 Ghent, William James
SMITH, HARRY WORCESTER
 Troye, Edward
SMITH, HENRY CLAY
 Allport, Gordon Willard
 Bingham, Walter Van Dyke
 Fryer, Douglas Henry
 Maslow, Abraham H.
 Otis, Arthur Sinton

SMITH, J. M. POWIS
Curtiss, Samuel Ives
SMITH, JOE PATTERSON
Grierson, Benjamin Henry
SMITH, JOHN DAVID
Owsley, Frank Lawrence
SMITH, MARION PARRIS
Colden, Jane
Logan, James, 1674–1751
Logan, James Harvey
Marshall, Humphry
Reilly, Marion
Rittenhouse, William
Roberts, Job
Rothrock, Joseph Trimble
SMITH, PAUL A.
Veatch, Arthur Clifford
SMITH, RALPH C.
Adams, Joseph Alexander
Aitken, Robert
Andrews, Joseph
Barber, John Warner
SMITH, RALPH G.
Edmunds, Charles Wallis
SMITH, ROLAND M.
Simmons, Roscoe Conkling
Murray
SMITH, RONALD A.
Berenson, Senda
SMITH, WALTER M.
Dunn, Charles
Durrie, Daniel Steele
SMITH, WARREN HUNTING
Towler, John
SMITH, WILLIAM
Finlay, Hugh
SMITH, WILLIAM E.
Blair, Francis Preston,
1791–1876
Blair, Francis Preston,
1821–1875
Blair, Montgomery
Cassidy, William
Croswell, Edwin
Gales, Joseph, 1761–1841
Gales, Joseph, 1786–1860
King, Preston
Medary, Samuel
Morris, Thomas
Rives, John Cook
Sargent, Nathan
Seaton, William Winston
Smith, Margaret Bayard
Smith, Samuel Harrison
Vallandigham, Clement Laird
Van Buren, John
Van Buren, Martin
Van Ness, William Peter
Venable, William Henry
Walden, John Morgan
Williams, George Washington
Woodbury, Levi
SMITH, WILLIAM ROY
Hazard, Ebenezer
Hazard, Samuel
Holme, Thomas
Lloyd, David
Lloyd, Thomas
Markham, William
Moore, John, 1659–1732
Moore, William, 1699–1783
More, Nicholas
Norris, Isaac, 1671–1735

Norris, Isaac, 1701–1766
Pusey, Caleb
Rawie, Francis, c.
1662–1726/27
Shippen, Edward, 1639–1712
Shippen, Edward,
1728/29–1806
Thomas, George
SMITHER, HARRIET
Smith, Ashbel
SMULLYAN, ARTHUR
Rand, Benjamin
SMYTH, HERBERT WEIR
Lane, George Martin
Morgan, Morris Hicky
Richardson, Rufus Byam
SMYTHE, GEORGE FRANKLIN
Andrews, Lorin
Leonard, William Andrew
McIlvaine, Charles Pettit
SNYDER, JOHN KIMBALL
Abbott, Jacob
SNYDER, LOUIS L.
Hayes, Carlton Joseph Huntley
SNYDER, MERRILL J.
Plotz, Harry
SNYDER, W. E.
Newcomer, Christian
SOARES, JANET
Horst, Louis
SOBEL, ROBERT
Cuppia, Jerome Chester
Young, Robert Ralph
SOBOL, ROBERT
Hopson, Howard Colwell
SOCOLOFSKY, HOMER E.
Bean, Leon Lenwood
Capper, Arthur
Hertz, John Daniel
Schoeppel, Andrew Frank
SOHON, F. W.
Tondorf, Francis Anthony
SOKAL, MICHAEL M.
Scott, Walter Dill
Seashore, Carl Emil
SOLBERG, WINTON U.
Davenport, Eugene
SOLLMAN, TORALD
Stewart, George Neil
SOLOMON, BARBARA MILLER
Brooks, John Graham
SOLOMON, HARRY C.
Campbell, Charles Macfie
SOLOW, HERBERT
Parker, Carleton Hubbell
Seixas, Gershom Mendes
Stephens, Uriah Smith
Sylvis, William H.
Trevellick, Richard F.
Upchurch, John Jordan
Wright, James Lendrew
SOLVICK, STANLEY D.
Hawley, Willis Chatman
Taft, Henry Waters
SOMMER, LEO H.
Whitmore, Frank Clifford
SONNEBORN, T. M.
Jennings, Herbert Spencer
SONNECK, OSCAR G. T.
Heinrich, Antony Philip
SONNICHSEN, ALBERT
Kelly, Edmond

SONTAG, RAYMOND J.
Van Dyke, Paul
SOPER, GEORGE A.
McMath, Robert Emmet
Waring, George Edwin
SOSNA, MORTON
Williams, Aubrey Willis
SOULE, BYRON A.
Acheson, Edward Goodrich
SOULE, SHERROD
Andrews, Samuel James
Andrews, William Watson
Badger, Joseph, 1757–1846
SOUTHALL, JAMES P. C.
Maclaurin, Richard Cockburn
Renwick, James, 1792–1863
Rood, Ogden Nicholas
Troland, Leonard Thompson
Zentmayer, Joseph
SOUTHERN, DAVID W.
Hunton, George Kenneth
Waring, Julius Waties
SOUTHERN, EILEEN
Burleigh, Henry Thacker
SOUVAY, CHARLES L.
Andreis, Andrew James Felix
Bartholomew De
Du Bourg, Louis Guillaume
Valentin
Rosati, Joseph
SPAETH, J. DUNCAN
Hibben, John Grier
Hunt, Theodore Whitefield
Lacy, Ernest
Van Dyke, Henry
SPALDING, JAMES ALFRED
Aspinwall, William
Barker, Jeremiah
Batchelder, John Putnam
SPALDING, M. E.
Neville, Wendell Cushing
SPANTON, A. I.
Buchtel, John Richards
SPARGO, JOHN
Haswell, Anthony
SPAULDING, E. WILDER
Law, Richard
Morris, Lewis Richard
Olds, Robert Edwin
Partridge, James Rudolph
Pendleton, John Strother
Pickett, James Chamberlayne
Pitkin, William, 1635–1694
Pitkin, William, 1694–1769
Pitkin, William, 1725–1789
Plumley, Frank
Roberts, Edmund
Schenck, Robert Cumming
Schuyler, Eugene
Seward, George Frederick
Sharp, William Graves
Storer, Bellamy
Taylor, Hannis
Tower, Charlemagne
Tripp, Bartlett
Vail, Aaron
Van Schaick, Goose
Willard, Joseph Edward
Willett, Marinus
Wilson, Henry Lane
Yates, Abraham
Yates, John Van Ness
Yates Robert

SPAULDING, FRANK E.
  Inglis, Alexander James
SPAULDING, OLIVER L.
  MacArthur, Arthur
SPAULDING, OLIVER L., JR.
  Lawton, Henry Ware
  McClellan, George Brinton
  McDowell, Irvin
  McPherson, James Birdseye
  Marcy, Randolph Barnes
  Otis, Elwell Stephen
  Pope, John
  Porter, Fitz-John
  Rawlins, John Aaron
  Ropes, John Codman
  Rosecrans, William Starke
  Schofield, John McAllister
  Sherman, William Tecumseh
  Slocum, Henry Warner
  Stoneman, George
  Thomas, George Henry
  Weitzel, Godfrey
  Wilcox, Orlando Bolivar
SPAULDING, THOMAS MARSHALL
  Alexander, Barton Stone
  Alexander, William Dewitt
  Allen, Henry Tureman
  Allen, Robert
  Alvord, Benjamin
  Ammen, Jacob
  Anderson, Robert
  Andrews, George Leonard
  Armistead, Lewis Addison
  Arnold, Lewis Golding
  Arnold, Richard
  Ayres, Romeyn Beck
  Baker, Laurence Simmons
  Barksdale, William
  Barringer, Rufus
  Barton, Seth Maxwell
  Battle, Cullen Andrews
  Beale, Richard Lee Turberville
  Beauregard, Pierre Gustave
    Toutant
  Bee, Barnard Elliott
  Bee, Hamilton Prioleau
  Bernard, Simon
  Birge, Henry Warner
  Bomford, George
  Bonaparte, Jerome Napoleon
  Bowers, Theodore Shelton
  Boynton, Edward Carlisle
  Brooke, John Rutter
  Brown, Jacob Jennings
  Burbridge, Stephen Gano
  Bussey, Cyrus
  Canby, Edward Richard Sprigg
  Carr, Eugene Asa
  Carr, Joseph Bradford
  Carroll, Samuel Sprigg
  Casey, Silas
  Chaffee, Adna Romanza
  Cheatham, Benjamin Franklin
  Chetlain, Augustus Louis
  Cist, Henry Martyn
  Colston, Raleigh Edward
  Cooke, Philip St. George
  Cooper, Samuel, 1798–1876
  Corse, John Murray
  Couch, Darius Nash
  Crozet, Claude
  Cullum, George Washington

Dana, Napoleon Jackson
  Tecumseh
Davies, Henry Eugene
Davis, George Whitefield
Davis, Jefferson Columbus
Devin, Thomas Casimer
Dickman, Joseph Theodore
Dodge, Theodore Ayrault
Doubleday, Abner
Duke, Basil Wilson
Early, Jubal Anderson
Evans, Clement Anselm
Evans, Nathan George
Ferrero, Edward
Forrest, Nathan Bedford
Foster, Robert Sanford
Franklin, William Buel
French, William Henry
Fuller, John Wallace
Gardner, John Lane
Getty, George Washington
Gibbon, John
Gilmor, Harry
Graham, Charles Kinnaird
Granger, Gordon
Grant, Frederick Dent
Greene, Francis Vinton
Greene, George Sears
Gregg, John
Griffin, Charles
Griffin, Simon Goodell
King, Edward Leonard
Lee, William Little
Mills, Anson
Partridge, Alden
Ripley, Eleazar Wheelock
Roberdeau, Issac
Smith, Andrew Jackson
Smith, Martin Luther
Smith, Richard Somers
Snelling, Josiah
Steedman, James Blair
Steele, Frederick
Stevens, John Leavitt
Stevens, Walter Husted
Stevenson, Carter Littlepage
Stone, Charles Pomeroy
Sturgis, Samuel Davis
Sumner, Edwin Vose
Swayne, Wager
Swift, Joseph Gardner
Swift, William Henry
Swinton, William
Thomas, Allen
Tucker, Stephen Davis
Van Dorn, Earl
Wadsworth, James Samuel
Webster, Joseph Dana
Wheeler, George Montague
Whipple, Amiel Weeks
Williams, Alpheus Starkey
Winder, William Henry
Woodbury, Daniel Phineas
SPEAR, ALLAN H.
  Jackson, Robert R.
  Williams, Fannie Barrier
SPEAR, JOHN W.
  Heard, Dwight Bancroft
SPECTOR, RONALD
  Knox, Dudley Wright
SPEER, ROBERT ELLIOTT
  Wanless, William James

SPEERT, HAROLD
  Taussig, Frederick Joseph
SPENCE, CLARK C.
  Dwight, Arthur Smith
  Mathewson, Edward Payson
SPENCER, CHARLES WORTHEN
  Benson, Egbert
  Clarke, George
  Clarkson, Matthew
  Coote, Richard
  Cruger, John
  De Lancey, James, 1703–1760
  De Lancey, James, 1732–1800
  De Lancey, James, 1746–1804
  De Lancey, Oliver
  De Lancey, William Heathcote
  Hamilton, Andrew, d. 1741
  Hobart, John Sloss
  Horsmanden, Daniel
  Kennedy, Archibald
  Laurance, John
  Lewis, Francis
  Lewis, Morgan
  Thomas, David
SPIEGEL, SHALOM
  Davidson, Israel
SPILLER, ROBERT E.
  Shelton, Frederick William
  Thomas, Joseph
  Wallace, Horace Binney
SPINGARN, J. E.
  Woodberry, George Edward
SPOFFORD, CHARLES M.
  Freeman, John Ripley
SPRENG, SAMUEL PETER
  Esher, John Jacob
SPRING, LA VERNE WARD
  Kelley, William
SPURLIN, PAUL M.
  Schinz, Albert
SQUIRES, JAMES DUANE
  Sprague, Homer Baxter
SRB, ADRIAN R.
  Emerson, Rollins Adams
STACEY, C. P.
  O'Mahony, John
  O'Neill, John
  Roberts, William Randall
  Smith, Robert, 1722–1777
STANARD, MARY NEWTON
  Archer, William Segar
  Breckenridge, James
STANLEY, GEORGE M.
  Leverett, Frank
STANLEY, PETER W.
  Forbes, William Cameron
  Quezon, Manuel Luis
STANLEY, RICHARD J.
  Waymouth, George
STANTON, TIMOTHY WILLIAM
  White Charles Abiathar
STAROBIN, JOSEPH R.
  Minor, Robert
STARR, HARRIS ELWOOD
  Abbey, Henry
  Abbot, Gorham Dummer
  Abbott, Benjamin
  Adams, Daniel
  Adams, Ebenezer
  Adams, Eliphalet
  Adams, Hannah
  Adams, Jasper
  Aiken, Charles Augustus

Akers, Elizabeth Chase
Alden, Isabella Macdonald
Alden, Joseph
Allen, Paul
Allen, Thomas M.
Allen, William, 1784–1868
Alline, Henry
Altsheler, Joseph Alexander
Anderson, Henry Tompkins
Andrew, Samuel
Anthon, Charles Edward
Anthony, Susan Brownell
Appleton, James
Appleton, Jesse
Appleton, Thomas Gold
Armstrong, George Dod
Atwater, Lyman Hotchkiss
Augustus, John
Austin, David
Austin, Jane Goodwin
Austin, Samuel
Austin, William
Ayres, Anne
Babcock, Maltbie Davenport
Backus, Azel
Bacon, Thomas
Bailey, Jacob
Barnard, Henry
Bartlett, Joseph
Barton, Clara
Beecher, Charles
Beecher, Henry Ward
Beecher, Thomas Kinnicut
Bickel, Luke Washington
Bickerdyke, Mary Ann Ball
Blaikie, William
Bliss, Philip Paul
Bolton Sarah Tittle Barrett
Bonard, Louis
Bouton, John Bell
Bowman, Thomas
Brainerd, David
Brainerd, John
Breckinridge, John
Bridgman, Elijah Coleman
Bronson, Walter Cochrane
Brooks, Charles Timothy
Brown, Phoebe Hinsdale
Brown, Samuel Robbins
Brownell, Henry Howard
Buckley, James Monroe
Burnap, George Washington
Burrell, David James
Burton, Nathaniel Judson
Bush, George
Byrne, Andrew
Cannon, Harriet Starr
Channing, Edward Tyrrell
Channing, William Henry
Chapman, Victor Emmanuel
Cheney, Charles Edward
Clap, Thomas
Clark, Jonas
Clark, Sheldon
Clark, Thomas March
Clay, Joseph, 1764–1811
Colver, Nathaniel
Cone, Spencer Houghton
Connelly, Cornelia
Cooke, George Willis
Cooper, Ezekiel
Cox, Samuel Hanson
Coxe, Arthur Cleveland

Craig, Austin
Creath, Jacob, 1777–1854
Creath, Jacob, 1799–1886
Crittenton, Charles Nelson
Crocker, Hannah Mather
Crooks, George Richard
Cummins, George David
Cutler, Timothy
Cuyler, Theodore Ledyard
Daboll, Nathan
Daggett, Naphtali
Dana, James
Day, Jeremiah
Dearing, John Lincoln
De Forest, John William
Dickins, John
Diman, Jeremiah Lewis
Dix, Morgan
Dole, Nathan Haskell
Dorrell, William
Doyle, Sarah Elizabeth
Drinkwater, Jennie Maria
Duffield, George, 1732–1790
Duffield, George, 1794–1868
Duffield, Samuel Augustus
    Willoughby
Durbin, John Price
Dwight, Timothy, 1752–1817
Dwight, Timothy, 1828–1916
Eaton, Homer
Embury, Philip
Emory, John
Errett, Isaac
Evans, Hugh Davey
Evans, Nathaniel
Ewer, Ferdinand Cartwright
Fallows, Samuel
Fanning, Tolbert
Farley, Harriet
Fenwick, Benedict Joseph
Ferguson, William Porter
    Frisbee
Finley, James Bradley
Finley, Robert
Finley, Samuel
Finney, Charles Grandison
Fisher, Daniel Webster
Fisher, Ebenezer
Fisk, Wilbur
Fiske, Fidelia
Fitton, James
Flickinger, Daniel Kumler
Flower, Benjamin Orange
Floy, James
Follen, Eliza Lee Cabot
Foss, Cyrus David
Foster, Charles James
Foster, Frank Hugh
Foster, Randolph Sinks
Fowler, Orin
Francis, Convers
Franklin, Benjamin, 1812–1878
Gaines, Wesley John
Gammon, Elijah Hedding
Gannett, Ezra Stiles
Gannett, William Channing
Garrettson, Freeborn
Gates, Frederick Taylor
Gay, Ebenezer
Gibbons, Herbert Adams
Gladden, Washington
Goodell, William, 1792–1867
Goodrich, Chauncey Allen

Goodrich, Elizur, 1734–1797
Goodwin, Elijah
Gordon, Andrew
Graham, Isabella Marshall
Grant, Asahel
Green, Lewis Warner
Greenleaf, Benjamin
Greer, David Hummell
Grellet, Stephen
Griswold, Alexander Viets
Gunn, Frederick William
Hall, Charles Henry
Hall, Hazel
Hallowell, Benjamin
Hamline, Leonidas Lent
Hardey, Mother Mary Aloysia
Hare, George Emlen
Hare, William Hobart
Harper, Ida Husted
Harris, William Logan
Harrison, William Pope
Hartranft, Chester David
Hawes, Charles Boardman
Hayden, Amos Sutton
Hayden, William
Haygood, Laura Askew
Headley, Phineas Camp
Heck, Barbara
Hedding, Elijah
Hendrix, Eugene Russell
Hepworth, George Hughes
Herbert, Henry William
Herford, Oliver Brooke
Herrick, Edward Claudius
Hibbard, Freeborn Garrettson
Hooker, Isabella Beecher
Hopkins, Lemuel
Hoshour, Samuel Klinefelter
Hosmer, Frederick Lucian
Hunt, Robert
Hunter, Andrew
Ingalls, Marilla Baker
Inskip, John Swanel
Jarratt, Devereux
Jarvis, Abraham
Jeanes, Anna T.
Johnson, Samuel, 1822–1882
Joyce, Isaac Walton
Judd, Sylvester
Junkin, George
Kelly, Michael J.
King, Thomas Starr
Kingsley, Calvin
Kirk, Edward Norris
Kumler, Henry
Lamont, Hammond
Lane, Tidence
Lard, Moses E.
Lee, Jesse
Lord, John
Lothrop, Harriett Mulford
    Stone
Lufbery, Raoul Gervais Victor
McAuley, Jeremiah
McAuley, Thomas
McCabe, Charles Cardwell
McCalla, William Latta
M'Clintock, John
McDowell, John, 1751–1820
McDowell, John, 1780–1863
McGarvey, John William
McKendree, William
McVickar, William Neilson

MacWhorter, Alexander
Mahan, Milo
Manning, James
Marsh, John, 1788–1868
Meigs, Josiah
Messer, Asa
Milligan, Robert
Moore, James, 1764–1814
Moore, Richard Channing
Nash, Daniel
Nettleton, Asahel
Nott, Samuel
Ochs, Julius
Ogilvie, John, 1724–1774
O'Kelly, James
Osborn, Norris Galpin
Paddock, Benjamin Henry
Paddock, John Adams
Parker, Edwin Pond
Parker, Edwin Wallace
Payson, Edward
Peck, George
Pendleton, William Kimbrough
Phelps, Austin
Pierpont, James
Pierson, Abraham, 1609–1678
Pierson, Abraham, c.
    1645–1707
Pierson, Arthur Tappan
Pierson, Hamilton Wilcox
Pike, Albert
Pinkerton, Lewis Letig
Porter, Noah
Power, Frederick Dunglison
Purviance, David
Reach, Alfred James
Reed, David
Reid, John Morrison
Robbins, Chandler
Roberts, Benjamin Titus
Roberts, Robert Richford
Robinson, Ezekiel Gilman
Rockwell, Kiffin Yates
Rodgers, John, 1727–1811
Rodgers, John, 1881–1926
Rogers, James Blythe
Russell, James Solomon
Ruter, Martin
Sage, Henry Williams
Sankey, Ira David
Sawyer, Thomas Jefferson
Schaff, Philip
Sears, Barnas
Seeger, Alan
Sergeant, John, 1710–1749
Shaw, Elijah
Shuey, William John
Simpson, Matthew
Sims, Charles N.
Slicer, Thomas Roberts
Smith, Oliver
Smith, William, 1727–1803
Smyth, Newman
Spalding, Franklin Spencer
Sparrow, William
Spencer, Elihu
Sprague, William Buell
Stebbins, Horatio
Stiles, Ezra
Stokes, Anson Phelps
Stone, Barton Warren
Storrs, Richard Salter,
    1787–1873

Storrs, Richard Salter,
    1821–1900
Strawbridge, Robert
Sumner, Walter Taylor
Sumner, William Graham
Swain, Clara A.
Swing, David
Taylor, Edward Thompson
Taylor, William Mackergo
Tennent, Gilbert
Tennent, William, 1673–1745
Tennent, William, 1705–1777
Tichenor, Isaac Taylor
Tomkins, Floyd Williams
Twichell, Joseph Hopkins
Tyler, Charles Mellen
Upham, Samuel Foster
Vail, Stephen Montfort
Van Rensselaer, Cortlandt
Varick, James
Vinton, Alexander Hamilton
Vinton, Francis
Wadsworth, James
Wakeley, Joseph Burton
Ware, Henry, 1764–1845
Ware, Henry, 1794–1843
Ware, John Fothergill
    Waterhouse
Ware, William
Warren, Henry White
Washburn, Edward Abiel
Wayman, Alexander Walker
Webb, Thomas
Welles, Noah
Wellons, William Brock
Wharton, Charles Henry
Whedon, Daniel Denison
Whitefield, George
Willard, Sidney
Willey, Samuel Hopkins
Williams, Charles David
Williams, Elisha, 1694–1755
Winchester, Elhanan
Winslow, Hubbard
Wise, Daniel
Woodbridge, William Channing
Woolsey, Theodore Dwight
Worcester, Noah
Worcester, Samuel
Wylie, Samuel Brown
Young, Jessie Bowman
Zollars, Ely Vaughan
STARR, LOUIS M.
    Carvalho, Solomon Solis
    Earhart, Amelia Mary
    Goddard, Morrill
    Johnson, Robert Underwood
    Martin, Edward Sandford
    Means, Gaston Bullock
    Miller, Webb
    Patterson, Eleanor Medill
STARRETT, VINCENT
    Biggers, Earl Derr
STAVE, BRUCE M.
    McLevy, Jasper
STEAD, EUGENE A., JR.
    Weiss, Soma
STEADMAN, J. M., JR.
    Smith, Charles Henry,
        1826–1903
    Stanton, Frank Lebby
    Wilde, Richard Henry

STEARNS, BERTHA MONICA
    Godey, Louis Antoine
    Hale, Sarah Josepha Buell
    Hasbrouck, Lydia Sayer
    Haven, Emily Bradley Neal
    Herrick, Sophia McIlvaine
        Bledsoe
    Hooper, Lucy Hamilton
    Martyn, Sarah Towne Smith
    Mayo, Sarah Carter Edgarton
    Nichols, Mary Sargeant Neal
        Gove
    Nichols, Thomas Low
    Sanders, Elizabeth Elkins
    Sedgwick, Catharine Maria
    Sherwood, Katharine Margaret
        Brownlee
    Spofford, Harriet Elizabeth
        Prescott
    Stephens, Ann Sophia
    Swisshelm, Jane Grey Cannon
    Townsend, Virginia Frances
    Welby, Amelia Ball Coppuck
    Whitcher, Frances Miriam Berry
    Whitney, Adeline Dutton Train
    Whittelsey, Abigail Goodrich
    Woolsey, Sarah Chauncy
STEARNS, HENRY P.
    Bellingham, Richard
    Canonchet
    Church, Benjamin, 1639–1718
    Philip
STEARNS, MARSHALL W.
    Rainey, Gertrude Malissa Nix
        Pridgett
    Smith, Bessie
STEARNS, RAYMOND P.
    Parris, Samuel
    Underhill, John
    Weld, Thomas
    Williams, John, 1664–1729
STEBBINS, JOEL
    Comstock, George Cary
STECK, FRANCIS BORGIA
    Serra, Junipero
STEELE, RICHARD W.
    Early, Stephen Tyree
STEFFEK, EDWIN F.
    Pyle, Robert
STEFFEN, NANCY L.
    Burgess, Thornton Waldo
    Cooper, Kent
    Dreyfus, Max
    Field, Marshall, IV
STEGNER, WALLACE
    DeVoto, Bernard Augustine
    Wister, Owen
STEIN, LEON
    Henry, Alice
STEIN, STANLEY J.
    Haring, Clarence
STEINER, FRED
    Newman, Alfred
STEINER, GOTTHOLD
    Cobb, Nathan Augustus
STEINER, WALTER RALPH
    Baer, William Stevenson
    Brigham, Amariah
    Brinton, John Hill
    Bronson, Henry
STEINER, WILLIAM F., JR.
    Morton, Charles Walter

STEIRER, WILLIAM E., JR.
  Greenslet, Ferris
STEIRER, WILLIAM F.
  Adams, Franklin Pierce
STEIRER, WILLIAM F., JR.
  Howey, Walter Crawford
  O'Brien, Robert Lincoln
  Phillips, Harry Irving
STENERSON, DOUGLAS C.
  Mencken, Henry Louis
STEPHENS, EDNA B.
  Fletcher, John Gould
STEPHENS, FERRIS J.
  Dougherty, Raymond Philip
STEPHENS, GEORGE W.
  Nelson, Nelson Olsen
STEPHENS, JOHN
  Alexander, Hartley Burr
STEPHENSON, GEORGE M.
  Esbjörn, Lars Paul
  Hasselquist, Tuve Nilsson
  Lind, John
  Lindbergh, Charles Augustus
  Mattson, Hans
  Swensson, Carl Aaron
  Thomas, William Widgery
STEPHENSON, MARTHA TUCKER
  Adams, Abigail
  Davis, Varina Anne Jefferson
  Davis, Varina Howell
STEPHENSON, NATHANIEL WRIGHT
  Aldrich, Nelson Wilmarth
  Benjamin, Judah Philip
  Davis, Jefferson
STEPHENSON, WENDELL H.
  Boyd, Thomas Duckett
  Lane, James Henry, 1814–1866
  Mitchell, Robert Byington
  Montgomery, James
  Plumb, Preston B.
  Pomeroy, Samuel Clarke
  Porter, Alexander
  Reeder, Andrew Horatio
  Richardson, Edmund
  Robinson, Charles
  Shannon, Wilson
  Slidell, John
  Stanton, Frederick Perry
  Taylor, Richard
  Taylor, Zachary
STERLING, KEIR B.
  Allen, Arthur Augustus
  Beary, Donald Bradford
  Beebe, (Charles) William
  Chapin, James Paul
  Child, Charles Manning
  Griscom, Ludlow
  Jones, Lynds
  Lear, Ben
  Miller, Gerrit Smith, Jr.
  Oberholser, Harry Church
  Seton, Grace Gallatin
    Thompson
  Smith, Holland McTyeire
  Tate, George Henry Hamilton
STERNSTEIN, JEROME L.
  Diat, Louis Felix
  Rombauer, Irma Louise
  Sardi, Melchiorre Pio Vencenzo
    ("Vincent")
STEVENS, RAYMOND
  Little, Arthur Dehon

STEVENS, S. K.
  Farrell, James Augustine
STEVENS, THOMAS WOOD
  Goodman, Kenneth Sawyer
STEVENS, WALTER B.
  Francis, David Rowland
STEVENS, WAYNE E.
  Coles, Edward
  Dongan, Thomas
  Duncan, Joseph
  Edwards, Ninian
  Hendrick
  Johnson, Guy
  Johnson, Sir John
  Johnson, Sir William
  Munro, Henry
  Trent, William
  Wentworth, John, 1737–1820
  Wharton, Samuel
  Wraxall, Peter
STEVENS, WILLIAM OLIVER
  Adams, William Taylor
STEVENSON, JOHN A.
  Galloway, Beverly Thomas
  Kauffman, Calvin Henry
  Smith, Erwin Frink
STEWARD, HELEN R.
  Rust, Richard Sutton
  Stoddard, Amos
STEWART, DE LISLE
  Vaughan, Daniel
STEWART, EDGAR I.
  Ward, Joseph
STEWART, GEORGE R., JR.
  Derby, George Horatio
  Harte, Francis Brett
  McBurney, Robert Ross
  Thomes, William Henry
  Webb, Charles Henry
  Wells, William Vincent
STEWART, RANDALL
  Kester, Vaughan
  King, William Benjamin Basil
  Ticknor, William Davis
  Upham, Charles Wentworth
STEWART, WILLIAM J.
  McIntire, Ross
STIGLER, GEORGE J.
  Simons, Henry Calvert
STILLWELL, MARGARET B.
  Hawkins, Rush Christopher
STILLWELL, PAUL
  Martin, Johnny Leonard
    Roosevelt ("Pepper")
STINE, JEFFREY K.
  Cone, Russell Glenn
  Houdry, Eugene Jules
  Savage, John Lucian ("Jack")
STOCK, LEO F.
  Pallen, Condé Benoist
STOCKING, GEORGE W., JR.
  Benedict, Ruth Fulton
  Boas, Franz
  Redfield, Robert
  Wissler, Clark
STOKES, ANSON PHELPS
  Dexter, Franklin Bowditch
  Dillard, James Hardy
  Washington, Booker Taliaferro
STONE, ALAN
  Perlman, Philip Benjamin

STONE, DONALD L.
  Hackett, Frank Warren
  Haddock, Charles Brickett
STONE, MARSHALL H.
  Birkhoff, George David
STONE, RICHARD G.
  Weaver, Philip
STONE, WITMER
  Abbott, Charles Conrad
  Brewer, Thomas Mayo
  Brewster, William
  Cassin, John
  Cory, Charles Barney
  Coues, Elliott
  Elliot, Daniel Giraud
  Forbush, Edward Howe
  Lawrence, George Newbold
  Maynard, Charles Johnson
  Nehrling, Henry
  Nuttall, Thomas
  Ord, George
  Ridgway, Robert
  Townsend, John Kirk
  Wilson, Alexander
STONES, ELLEINE H.
  Burton, Clarence Monroe
STORRS, HARRY C.
  Little, Charles Sherman
STORY, RONALD
  Beatty, Clyde Raymond
  Breen, Joseph Ignatius
  Selznick, David O.
  Woolley, Edgar Montillion
    ("Monty")
STOVER, JOHN F.
  Harrison, Fairfax
  Willard, Daniel
STRATTON, DAVID H.
  Fall, Albert Bacon
STRAYER, JOSEPH R.
  Haskins, Charles Homer
STREVEY, TRACY E.
  McCormick, Joseph Medill
  Medill, Joseph
  Scott, James Wilmot
  Seymour, Horatio Winslow
STRICKLAND, ARVARH E.
  Spaulding, Charles Clinton
STRINGFIELD, V. T.
  Meinzer, Oscar Edward
STRITZLER, HELEN S.
  Sullavan, Margaret
STROBEL, MARIAN ELIZABETH
  Wells, Harriet Sheldon
STROUP, HERBERT
  Rutherford, Joseph Franklin
STROUT, CUSHING
  Beard, Charles Austin
STROVEN, CARL G.
  Stoddard, Charles Warren
STRUIK, D. J.
  Van Vleck, Edward Burr
STRUNK, OLIVER
  Zeuner, Charles
STRUNK, WILLIAM, JR.
  Sampson, Martin Wright
STRUVE, OTTO
  Frost, Edwin Brant
STUEWER, ROGER H.
  Compton, Arthur Holly
  Compton, Karl Taylor
  Fermi, Enrico
  Gamow, George

Lawrence, Ernest Orlando
Tate, John Torrence
STUNKARD, HORACE W.
Ward, Henry Baldwin
STURCHIO, JEFFREY L.
Pfister, Alfred
SUBER, EDNA SWENSON
Stratemeyer, Edward
SUDDS, R. H.
Hart, Edmund Hall
Henderson, Peter
Hovey, Charles Mason
McMahon, Bernard
Miller, Samuel, 1820–1901
Parsons, Samuel Bowne
Prince, Willim, c. 1725–1802
Prince William, 1766–1842
Prince, William Robert
Rogers, Edward Staniford
SUID, LAWRENCE H.
Ladd, Alan Walbridge
SULLIVAN, FRANK
Marquis, Donald Robert Perry
SULLIVAN, JAMES
Draper, Andrew Sloan
Leipziger, Henry Marcus
Page, David Perkins
Phelps, William Franklin
Pruyn, John Van Schaick
Lansing
SULMAN, A. MICHAEL
Anderson, Victor Vance
SUMMERS, LIONEL M.
Jones, Leonard Augustus
Southmayd, Charles Ferdinand
Stetson, Francis Lynde
Stillman, Thomas Edgar
Tiedeman, Christopher
Gustavus
Toulmin, Harry Theophilus
Tyler, Ransom Hubert
Wallace, William James
SUMMERS, U. T. MILLER
Matthiessen, Francis Otto
SUMMERSON, WILLIAM H.
Benedict, Stanley Rossiter
SUMNER, WILLIAM A.
Hoard, William Dempster
King, Franklin Hiram
Smith, Hiram
SUSMAN, WARREN I.
Howard, Leslie
SUSSKIND, CHARLES
Conrad, Frank
Page, Leigh
Stone, John Stone
Tesla, Nikola
SUSSKIND, JACOB L.
Carmichael, Oliver Cromwell
Clark, Felton Grandison
Gauss, Christian Frederick
McHale, Kathryn
Patri, Angelo
SUTHERLAND, ARTHUR E.
Beale, Joseph Henry
SUTTIE, ROSCOE H.
Hazen, Allen
SUTTON, WALTER A.
Allen, Florence Ellinwood
SUTTON, WILLIAM SENECA
Baldwin, Joseph

SWAIN, DONALD C.
Allen, Edward Tyson
SWAIN, MARTHA H.
Short, Joseph Hudson, Jr.
SWAIN, ROBERT E.
Franklin, Edward Curtis
SWAN, WILLIAM U.
Herreshoff, John Brown
Lawley, George Frederick
Smith, Archibald Cary
Steers, George
SWANBERG, W. A.
Davies, Marion Cecilia
SWANN, W. F. G.
McClenahan, Howard
SWANSON, FREDERICK C.
Campbell, James Hepburn
Cooper, James
SWARTWOUT, EGERTON
Gilbert, Cass
SWEENEY, J. K.
Dickson, Earle Ensign
Holmes, Julius Cecil
SWEET, ALFRED H.
Dod, Thaddeus
SWEET, WILLIAM WARREN
De Pauw, Washington Charles
Gray, Isaac Pusey
Grose, William
Henderson, Charles Richmond
Hovey, Alvin Peterson
Howard, Timothy Edward
Larrabee, William Clark
McCaine, Alexander
Nast, William
Nevin, John Williamson
Quayle, William Alfred
Scott, Orange
Shinn, Asa
Snethen, Nicholas
Stevens, Abel
Stuart, Charles Macaulay
Taylor, John, 1752–1835
Thomson, Edward
SWEETLAND, WILLIAM VIRGIL
Randall, Samuel
SWEM, EARL GREGG
Blair, James
Blair, John, 1687–1771
Blair, John, 1732–1800
Bland, Richard
Bland, Theodorick
SWIFT, EBEN
Augur, Christopher Columbus
Buford, John
SWIFT, FLETCHER HARPER
Durant, Henry
Mann, Horace
Marwedel, Emma Jacobina
Christiana
SWINDLER, HENRY O.
Neill, Thomas Hewson
Nelson, William, 1824–1862
SWISHER, CARL BRENT
Boyden, Roland William
Gregory, Charles Noble
Taney, Roger Brooke
SYDNOR, CHARLES S.
Featherston, Winfield Scott
Foote, Henry Stuart
George, James Zachariah
Gordon, James
Leflore, Greenwood

McLaurin, Austin Joseph
McLean, Walter
Martin, William Thompson
Mayes, Edward
Money, Hernando De Soto
Orr, Juhu Amaziah
Poindexter, George
Prentiss, Seargent Smith
Sharkey, William Lewis
Stewart, Alexander Peter
Stockdale, Thomas Ringland
Stone, John Marshall
Thompson, Jacob
Turner, Edward
Vardaman, James Kimble
Wailes, Benjamin Leonard
Covington
Walthall, Edward Cary
Williams, John Sharp
Yerger, William
SYRETT, HAROLD C.
McClellan, George Brinton
SZASZ, FERENC M.
Riley, William Bell

TAFT, PHILIP
Frayne, Hugh
Garretson, Austin Bruce
Howard, Charles Perry
Johnston, William Hugh
Maurer, James Hudson
Murray, Philip
Sullivan, James William
Woll, Matthew
TAFT, WILLIAM H.
James, Edwin Leland
TALBERT, CHARLES GANO
McVey, Frank Lerond
TALBOT, HENRY P.
Crafts, James Mason
Drown, Thomas Messinger
TALBOT, MARION
Richards, Ellen Henrietta
Swallow
TALLMADGE, THOMAS E.
Holabird, William
Pond, Allen Bartlit
Shaw, Howard Van Doren
Sullivan, Louis Henri
Van Osdel, John Mills
Wight, Peter Bonnett
TANDY, JEANNETTE R.
Burdette, Robert Jones
Cooper, Susan Fenimore
TANNER, EDWIN PLATT
Anson, Adrian Constantine
Basse, Jeremiah
Beauchamp, William Martin
Carter, William Samuel
Chadwick, Henry
Clarkson, John Gibson
Cornbury, Edward Hyde
Viscount
Cosby, William
Deerfoot
Fenwick, John
Franklin, William
Hamilton, Andrew, d. 1703
TANSELLE, G. THOMAS
Huebsch, Benjamin W.
TANSILL, CHARLES C.
Hurst, John Fletcher

TARBELL, ROBERTA K.
  Young, Mahonri Mackintosh
TARR, JOEL ARTHUR
  Harrison, Carter Henry, Jr.
TASHER, LUCY LUCILE
  Snead, Thomas Lowndes
TATE, MERZE
  Farrington, Joseph Rider
TATLOCK, JOHN S. P.
  Hempl, George
TATUM, GEORGE B.
  Cret, Paul Philippe
TAUSSIG, FRANK WILLIAM
  Young, Allyn Abbott
TAYLOR, FRANK A.
  Appleby, John Francis
  Atwood, Lewis John
  Bachelder, John
  Bacon, Edward Payson
  Ball, Ephraim
  Bissell, George Henry
  Blake, Lyman Reed
  Blodget, Samuel
  Boyden, Seth
  Brooks, Byron Alden
  Brown, Sylvanus
  Coe, Israel
  Crompton, George
  Crompton, William
  Draper, Ira
  Graff, Frederic
  Harper, John Lyell
  Harris, Daniel Lester
  Hayden, Hiram Washington
  Hazard, Augustus George
  Henck, John Benjamin
  Hering, Carl
  Hering, Rudolph
  Hoadley, John Chipman
  Hobbs, Alfred Charles
  Holcomb, Amasa
  Holland, Clifford Milburn
  Holloway, Joseph Flavius
  Holmes, Israel
  Houston, Edwin James
  Hunt, Alfred Ephraim
  Hunt, Charles Wallace
  Hussey, Curtis Grubb
  Hutton, Frederick Remsen
  Ingersoll, Robert Hawley
  Isherwood, Benjamin Franklin
  Jervis, John Bloomfield
  Johnson, Edwin Ferry
  Johnson, John Butler
  Jones, Evan William
  Judson, Egbert Putnam
  Katte, Walter
  Kinnersley, Ebenezer
  Klein, Joseph Frederic
  Knowles, Lucius James
  Latrobe, Benjamin Henry,
    1806–1878
  Laurie, James
  Leonard, Harry Ward
  Lyman, Chester Smith
TAYLOR, FRANK O.
  Takamine, Jokichi
TAYLOR, JOHN R. M.
  Adams, Daniel Weissiger
  Adams, John, 1825–1864
TAYLOR, LLOYD C., JR.
  Holt, Winifred

TAYLOR, RICHARD S.
  Norris, John Franklyn
TAYLOR, WILLIAM A.
  Gideon, Peter Miller
  Kellerman, Karl Frederic
  Lyon, Theodatus Timothy
  Saunders, William
  Thomas, John Jacobs
  Van Fleet, Walter
TAYLOR, WILLIAM S.
  Prince, Morton
TEBBEL, JOHN
  Lorimer, George Horace
TEDLOW, RICHARD S.
  Lasker, Albert Davis
  Link, Henry Charles
TEETER, A. GRACE
  Johnson, Oliver
  Jones, David
TEFFT, SHELDON
  Bigelow, Harry Augustus
TEN HOOR, MARTEN
  Heller, Maximilian
  Lynch, Robert Clyde
TERMAN, FREDERICK EMMONS
  Durand, William Frederick
  Hansen, William Webster
TESAR, ANTHONY V.
  Hessoun, Joseph
THAYER, CHARLES HIRAM
  Stockbridge, Levi
"THE EDITORS"
  Bentley, Elizabeth Terrill
THEOHARIS, ATHAN
  Dennis, Eugene
  Fischer, Ruth
  Perry, Pettis
  Remington, William Walter
THILLY, FRANK
  Creighton, James Edwin
THODY, P. M. W.
  Huxley, Aldous Leonard
  O'Brien, Justin
THOM, CHARLES
  Marbut, Curtis Fletcher
THOMAS, CHARLES M.
  Towne, Benjamin
THOMAS, C. R. WALTHER
  Nies, Konrad
THOMAS, DAVID Y.
  Battle, Burrell Bunn
  Baxter, Elisha
  Berry, James Henderson
  Borland, Solon
  Boudinot, Elias, c. 1803–1839
  Boudinot, Elias Cornelius
  Brough, Charles Hillman
  Churchill, Thomas James
  Clarke, James Paul
  Clayton, Powell
  Cleburne, Patrick Ronayne
  Conway, Elias Nelson
  Conway, James Sevier
  Davis, Jeff
  Dorsey, Stephen Wallace
  English, Elbert Hartwell
  Fagan, James Fleming
  Fishback, William Meade
  Flanagin, Harris
  Garland, Augustus Hill
  Govan, Daniel Chevilette
  Hindman, Thomas Carmichael
  Izard, George

  Johnson, Robert Ward
  Jones, James Kimbrough
  McRae, Thomas Chipman
  Murphy, Isaac
  Parker, Isaac Charles
  Rector, Henry Massey
  Roane, John Selden
  Rose, Uriah Milton
  Sevier, Ambrose Hundley
  Walker, David, 1806–1879
  Watkins, George Claiborne
  Yell, Archibald
THOMAS, EVAN
  Bartlett, William Holmes
    Chambers
THOMAS, LOUIS R.
  Bauer, Harold Victor
  De Paolis, Alessio
  Elman, Mischa
  Katchen, Julius
  Rodzinski, Artur
  Szell, George
  Walter, Bruno
  Warren, Leonard
THOMAS, MILTON HALSEY
  Buckminster, Joesph Stevens
  Jay, Sir James
  Jones, William Alfred
  Kemp, John
  King, Charles
  McVickar, John
  Middleton, Peter
  Moore, Benjamin
  Moore, Nathaniel Fish
  Romayne, Nicholas
  Van Amringe, John Howard
  Vardill, John
THOMAS, NORMAN F.
  Bell, Frederic Somers
THOMAS, ROBERT E.
  Hooker, Elon Huntington
THOMAS, R. S.
  Bell, James Franklin
  Casey, Thomas Lincoln
  Johnston, William Hartshorne
THOMPSON, C. MILDRED
  McPherson, Edward
  Palmer, Bertha Honoré
  Palmer, Potter
  Salmon, Lucy Maynard
THOMPSON, ERNEST TRICE
  Makemie, Francis
  Peck, Thomas Ephraim
  Reid, William Shields
  Rice, John Holt
  Robinson, Stuart
  Smith, Benjamin Mosby
THOMPSON, FREDERIC L.
  Humphrey, Heman
  Morse, Anson Daniel
  Sachs, Julius
  Seelye, Julius Hawley
  Stearns, William Augustus
THOMPSON, GERALD
  Allen, Gracie
  Knight, Goodwin Jess
    ("Goodie")
  McClintic, Guthrie
THOMPSON, HOLLAND
  Durant, Thomas Clark
  Flagler, Henry Morrison
  Flagler, John Haldane
  Forman, Joshua

Hall, Nathan Kelsey
Harris, Ira
Havens, James
Inman, John Hamilton
Inman, Samuel Martin
THOMPSON, HOMER A.
Shear, Theodore Leslie
THOMPSON, J. A.
Gerard, James Watson
THOMPSON, JOHN
Rosenfeld, Paul Leopold
THOMPSON, RANDALL
Mannes, David
THOMPSON, SUSAN OTIS
Adams, Randolph Greenfield
THOMS, HERBERT
Alcott, William Andrus
Graves, William Phillips
Hirst, Barton Cooke
Hooker, Worthington
Ives, Eli
Knight, Jonathan
North, Elisha
Perkins, Elisha
Tully, William
THOMSON, ELIZABETH H.
Fulton, John Farquhar
THOMSON, IRVING L.
Child, Richard Washburn
Egan, Patrick
Heap, Samuel Davies
King, Jonas
McKim, Isaac
McRae, Duncan Kirkland
MacVeagh, Charles
Maxcy, Virgil
Meigs, Return Jonathan
Mitchell, George Edward
Morgan, Edwin Vernon
Nelson, Thomas Henry
Newel, Stanford
Niles, Nathaniel, 1791–1869
O'Brien, Edward Charles
Osborn, Thomas Andrew
Osborn, Thomas Ogden
Stovall, Pleasant Alexander
Strobel, Edward Henry
Terrell, Edwin Holland
Thompson, Thomas Larkin
Todd, Charles Stewart
Tree, Lambert
Vopicka, Charles Joseph
Wallace, Hugh Campbell
Ward, John Elliott
THORINGTON, J. MONROE
Mitchell, Samuel Augustus
THORNTON, HARRISON JOHN
Chandler, Thomas Bradbury
THORP, WILLARD
Tabb, John Banister
THORPE, EDWARD S.
Pepper, William
THWING, CHARLES FRANKLIN
Barnard, Frederick Augustus
Porter
Burton, Ernest DeWitt
Burton, Marion LeRoy
TICKNOR, CAROLINE
Alcott, Louisa May
TILDEN, CHARLES J.
Hughes, Hector James
Roebling, John Augustus

Roebling, Washington Augustus
TILLETT, WILBUR FISK
Alexander, Gross
Andrew, James Osgood
Bascom, Henry Bidleman
TINDALL, GEORGE B.
Parker, John Milliken
TINGLEY, DONALD F.
Humphries, George Rolfe
Mason, Max
Rivers, Lucius Mendel
TINKER, EDWARD LAROCQUE
Hearn, Lafcadio
Latil, Alexandre
Marigny, Bernard
Mazureau, Étienne
Moreau De Saint-Méry,
Médéric-Louis-Élie
Pennell, Joseph
Perché, Napoleon Joseph
Perry, Enoch Wood
Rémy, Henri
Rouquette, Adrien Emmanuel
Rouquette, François Dominique
Séjour, Victor
Testut, Charles
Thierry, Camille
Tousard, Anne Louis de
Viel, François Étienne Bernard
Alexandre
TINSLEY, JAMES A.
Ferguson, James Edward
TIPPLE, EZRA SQUIER
Boehm, Henry
Buttz, Henry Anson
TISHLER, HACE
Johnson, Alexander
TOBEY, JAMES A.
Sedgwick, William Thompson
TOBIN, EUGENE M.
Fagan, Mark Matthew
TODD, ELIZABETH
Ormsby, Waterman Lilly
Outcault, Richard Felton
TODD, FREDERICK P.
Sibert, William Luther
TOEPFER, KENNETH H.
Russell, James Earl
TOLMAN, R. P.
Catlin, George
Chapman, John Gadsby
Cheney, John
Cheney, Seth Wells
Stanley, John Mix
TOLMAN, RUEL P.
Gellatly, John
TOMLINSON, DAVID O.
Fearing, Kenneth Flexner
Jeffers, John Robinson
TOMPKINS, C. DAVID
Vandenberg, Arthur Hendrick
TONDORF, FRANCIS A.
Bayma, Joseph
Rigge, William Francis
Sestini, Benedict
TONKS, OLIVER S.
Hubbard, Richard William
Huntington, Daniel
TOPPIN, EDGAR ALLAN
Haynes, George Edmund
Scott, Emmett Jay

TORODASH, MARTIN
Keyes, Frances Parkinson
Mitchell, Thomas Gregory
Spence, Brent
TORREY, CHARLES C.
Gibbs, Josiah Willard,
1790–1861
Orne, John
Salisbury, Edward Elbridge
Toy, Crawford Howell
TOULMIN, HARRY A., JR.
Patterson, John Henry
TOURSCHER, F. E.
Carr, Thomas Matthew
Conwell, Henry
TOWER, OLIN F.
Morley, Edward Williams
TOWER, WILLIAM B., JR.
Winchester, Caleb Thomas
TOWNER, LAWRENCE W.
Graff, Everett Dwight
Phillips, William
TOWNSEND, LEAH
Eve, Joseph
TOZZER, ALFRED M.
Bowditch, Charles Pickering
TRACHTENBERG, ALAN
Frank, Waldo David
Goldmark, Henry
TRANI, EUGENE
Work, Hubert
TRATTNER, WALTER I.
Folks, Homer
Heckscher, August
Lovejoy, Owen Reed
TRAYNOR, ROGER J.
Costigan, George Purcell
TREADWELL, AARON L.
Orton, James
TREAT, PAYSON J.
Low, Frederick Ferdinand
TREFOUSSE, HANS L.
Milton, George Fort
TREXLER, HARRISON A.
DeBardeleben, Henry Fairchild
Hillman, Thomas Tennessee
Pratt, Daniel
Sloss, James Withers
TRIMBLE, BRUSE R.
Waite, Morrison Remick
TRISCO, ROBERT F.
Meyer, Albert Gregory
TROLANDER, JUDITH ANN
Balch, Emily Greene
Binford, Jessie Florence
Dock, Lavinia Lloyd
Lingelbach, Anna Lane
Peck, Lillie
Riis, Mary Phillips
TRUE, ALFRED CHARLES
Allen, Richard Lamb
Alvord, Henry Elijah
Barry, Patrick
Beatty, Adam
Bordley, John Beale
TRUESDELL, LEON E.
Hill, Joseph Adna
TRUSCOTT, ALAN
Culbertson, Ely
TSCHAN, FRANCIS J.
Chanche, John Mary Joseph
Chapelle, Placide Louis
Harding, Robert

TUCHMAN, BARBARA W.
  Stilwell, Joseph Warren
TUCKER, WILLIAM E.
  Willett, Herbert Lockwood
TUCKERMAN, FREDERICK
  Chadbourne, Paul Ansel
  Clark, Henry James
  Clark, William Smith
  Goodell, Henry Hill
  Gulick, John Thomas
TUGWELL, REXFORD G.
  Seager, Henry Rogers
TULCHIN, JOSEPH S.
  Rowe, Leo Stanton
TUNSTALL, ROBERT B.
  Leigh, Benjamin Watkins
  Taylor, Creed
  Tazewell, Henry
  Tazewell, Littleton Waller
TURCK, CHARLES J.
  Knott, James Proctor
  Young, John Clarke
TURK, MILTON HAIGHT
  Norton, John Nicholas
TURNBULL, ANDREW
  Perkins, Maxwell Evarts
TURNER, ALBERT L.
  Morton, Robert Russa
TURNER, CHARLES W.
  Harahan, William Johnson
TURNER, DARWIN T.
  McKay, Claude
TURNER, JEAN-RAE
  Mich, Daniel Danforth
TURNER, THOMAS B.
  Moore, Joseph Earle
TUTHILL, EDWARD
  Hanson, Roger Weightman
  Hobson, Edward Henry
TUTOROW, NORMAN E.
  Gaxton, William
  Paul, Josephine Bay
  Rockwell, George Lincoln
TUTTLE, ALONZO H.
  Kinkead, Edgar Benton
  Nash, Simeon
  Okey, John Waterman
  Richards, John Kelvey
  Shauck, John Allen
  Spear, William Thomas
  Swan, Joseph Rockwell
  Swayne, Noah Haynes
  Walker, Timothy, 1802–1856
  Wanamaker, Reuben Melville
  Welch, John
  Williams, Marshall Jay
  Woods, William Burnham
TUTTLE, JULIUS H.
  Green, Samuel Abbott
TWEEDY, HENRY H.
  Hoppin, James Mason
  Proctor, Henry Hugh
TWYNHAM, LEONARD
  Sprague, Achsa W.
TYACK, DAVID B.
  Cubberley, Ellwood Patterson
TYLER, ALICE FELT
  Elliott, Charles Burke
TYLER, GUS
  Kelly, Machine Gun (George
    Kelly Barnes, Jr.)
  Wexler, Irving ("Waxey
    Gordon")

TYNER, RICHARD F. F.
  Mayhew, Experience
TYOR, PETER L.
  Goddard, Henry Herbert

UHL, A. H.
  Kremers, Edward
UPSON, LENT DAYTON
  Wilcox, Delos Franklin
UPTON, WILLIAM TREAT
  Beck, Johann Heinrich
  Bird, Arthur
  Burlin, Natalie Curtis
  Burton, Frederick Russell
  Hanby, Benjamin Russell
  Hastings, Thomas
UROFF, MARGARET DICKIE
  Plath, Sylvia
UROFSKY, MELVIN I.
  Ballantine, Arthur Atwood
  Chafee, Zechariah, Jr.
  Cline, Genevieve Rose
  Curtis, Charles Pelham
  Davis, Pauline Morton Sabin
  Dowling, Noel Thomas
  Goldsborough, Thomas Alan
  Grady, Henry Francis
  Greenbaum, Edward Samuel
  Howe, Mark De Wolfe
  Lane, Arthur Bliss
  Llewellyn, Karl Nickerson
  Miller, Nathan Lewis
  Montague, Gilbert Holland
  Musmanno, Michael Angelo
  Rogers, Edith Nourse
  Silver, Abba Hillel
  Snell, Bertrand Hollis
  Vanderbilt, Arthur T.
  Warren, Charles
  Williston, Samuel
USHER, ROLAND GREENE
  Allerton, Isaac
  Brewster, William, 1567–1644
  Carver, John
  Cushman, Robert
  Morton, George
  Morton, Nathaniel
  Standish, Myles
  Weston, Thomas
  Winslow, Edward
  Winslow, Josiah
UTLAUT, ROBERT L.
  Bestor, Arthur Eugene
UTLEY, GEORGE B.
  Gardner, Gilson
  Newberry, Walter Loomis
  Perkins, Frederic Beecher
  Rich, Obadiah
  Scammon, Jonathan Young
  Sharp, Katharine Lucinda
  Strong, Walter Ansel
  Taylor, Benjamin Franklin
  White, Alexander, 1814–1872
  Wilkie, Franc Bangs
  Woolley, Celia Parker
UTTER, WILLIAM T.
  Campbell, John Wilson
  Campbell, Lewis Davis
  Cook, Isaac
  Creighton, William
  Drake, John Burroughs
  Eckels, James Herron
  Goodenow, John Milton

  Groesbeck, William Slocum
  Grosvenor, Charles Henry
  Huntington, Samuel,
    1765–1817
  McArthur, Duncan
  Meigs, Return Jonathan,
    1764–1824
  Morrow, Jeremiah
  Pease, Calvin
  Tiffin, Edward
  Tod, George
  Worthington, Thomas

VAIL, DERRICK T.
  Gifford, Sanford Robinson
  Wood, Casey Albert
VAIL, ROBERT W. G.
  Thomas, Isaiah
VANCE, CLARENCE H.
  Seabury, Samuel, 1729–1796
  Sears, Isaac
VANCE, JOHN R.
  McIntosh, John Baillie
  McLaws, Lafayette
  McMillan, James Winning
  Martindale, John Henry
VANCE, JOHN T.
  Griggs, John William
  Grosscup, Peter Stenger
  Paschal, George Washington
VANCE, MAURICE M.
  Debye, Peter Joseph William
  Kharasch, Morris Selig
  Piccard, Jean Felix
  Thurstone, Louis Leon
  White, Leonard Dupee
VANCE, WILLIAM REYNOLDS
  Woolsey, Theodore Salisbury
VAN CLEVE, EDWARD M.
  Russ, John Dennison
  Wait, William Bell
VAN CLEVE, THOMAS C.
  Pike, James Shepherd
VAN DE KAMP, PETER
  Schlesinger, Frank
VAN DER KLOOT, WILLIAM
  Loewi, Otto
VANDERSEE, CHARLES
  Poole, Ernest Cook
VANDER VELDE, LEWIS G.
  Warner, Fred Maltby
  Woodbridge, William
VAN DEUSEN, JOHN G.
  Hamilton, Paul
  Huger, Benjamin
  Huger, Daniel Elliott
  Huger, Francis Kinloch
  Huger, Isaac
  Huger, John
  Kennedy, John Doby
  Loring, Joshua, 1716–1781
  Loring, Joshua, 1744–1789
  Ludlow, Gabriel George
  Ludlow, George Duncan
  Lynch, Thomas, 1727–1776
  Lynch, Thomas, 1749–1779
  Manning, Richard Irvine
  Middleton, Henry, 1717–1784
  Middleton, Henry, 1770–1846
  Miller, Stephen Decatur
  Taylor, John W.
  Troup, Robert

VANDIVER, FRANK E.
  Pershing, John Joseph
  York, Alvin Cullum
VAN DOREN, CARL
  Brown, Charles Brockden
  Clemens, Samuel Langhorne
  Cooper, James Fenimore
  Hawthorne, Nathaniel
  James, Henry, 1843–1916
  Porter, William Sydney
  Simms, William Gilmore
  Stockton, Frank Richard
  Taylor, Bayard
  Wylie, Elinor Morton Hoyt
VAN DOREN, HAROLD L.
  Koehler, Robert
VAN DOREN, MARK
  Comstock, Anthony
  Dibble, Roy Floyd
  Emerson, Ralph Waldo
  Whitman, Walt
VAN DOREN, SANDRA SHAFFER
  Martin, Warren Homer
  Thomas, Roland Jay
VAN DYKE, PAUL
  Baird, Charles Washington
  Baird, Henry Martyn
  Baird, Robert
VAN FOSSEN, IRENE
  Laimbeer, Nathalie Schenck
  Matheson, William John
  Mulford, Prentice
VAN HOOSEN, BERTHA
  Mergler, Marie Josepha
VAN LAER, ARNOLD J. F.
  Bogardus, Everardus
  De Vries, David Pietersen
  Hudde, Andries
  Krol, Bastiaen Jansen
  Van Ilpendam, Jan Jansen
VAN LENNEP, WILLIAM
  Brady, Alice
  Elliott, Maxine
  Gillette, William Hooker
  Russell, Annie
  Smith, Harry Bache
VAN METER, SONDRA
  Barnard, Chester Irving
VAN PELT, JOHN V.
  Hunt, Richard Morris
VAN RAVENSWAAY, CHARLES
  Barton, David
VAN SANTVOORD, GEORGE
  Buehler, Huber Gray
  Van Schaack, Henry Cruger
  Van Schaack, Peter
VAN SLYCK, DEFOREST
  Harrison, Henry Baldwin
  Hillhouse, James
  Huntington, Samuel,
    1731–1796
VAN TASSEL, DAVID D.
  McHugh, Rose John
  Shepard, James Edward
VAN TINE, WARREN R.
  Frey, John Philip
  Lundeberg, Harry
  Morrison, Frank
  Tobin, Daniel Joseph
VARGA, NICHOLAS
  Cullen, Hugh Roy

VARRELL, H. M.
  Lyman, Theodore, 1833–1897
VAUGHN, VICTOR C.
  Beaumont, William
VECOLI, RUDOLPH J.
  Tresca, Carlo
VEEDER, BORDEN S.
  Marriott, Williams McKim
VEEDER, VAN VECHTEN
  Hough, Charles Merrill
VEITH, ILZA
  Menninger, Charles Frederick
VENABLE, FRANCIS PRESTON
  Mallet, John William
VESTAL, S. C.
  Newton, John
VEYSEY, LAURENCE R.
  Angell, James Rowland
  Reinhardt, Aurelia Isabel Henry
  Schurman, Jacob Gould
  West, Andrew Fleming
  Wilbur, Ray Lyman
VIETS, HENRY R.
  Babcock, James Woods
  Baker, Frank
  Baldwin, William
  Barker, Benjamin Fordyce
  Barton, John Rhea
  Battey, Robert
  Bayley, Richard
  Chadwick, James Read
  Channing, Walter
  Cullis, Charles
  Dix, John Homer
  Edes, Robert Thaxter
  Ellis, Calvin
  Ernst, Harold Clarence
  Fisher, Theodore Willis
  Hale, Enoch
  Harrington, Thomas Francis
  Hunt, Harriot Kezia
  Kimball, Gilman
  Lewis, Dioclesian
  Lloyd, James
  Marcy, Henry Orlando
  Mumford, James Gregory
  Oliver, Fitch Edward
  Putnam, Charles Pickering
  Putnam, James Jackson
  Ramsay, Alexander
  Randolph, Jacob
  Redman, John
  Reese, John James
  Richardson, Maurice Howe
  Richardson, William Lambert
  Rogers, Stephen
  Rotch, Thomas Morgan
  Shattuck, Frederick Cheever
  Shattuck, George Brune
  Shattuck, George Cheyne,
    1783–1854
  Shattuck, George Cheyne,
    1813–1893
  Storer, David Humphreys
  Storer, Horatio Robinson
  Thacher, James
  Tuckerman, Frederick
  Tuckerman, Frederick Goddard
  Tufts, Cotton
  Twitchell, Amos
  Walcott, Henry Pickering
  Ware, John
  Warren, John

Warren, John Collins,
  1778–1856
Warren, John Collins,
  1842–1927
  Waterhouse, Benjamin
  White, James Clarke
  Wigglesworth, Edward
  Williams, Henry Willard
  Williams, Stephen West
  Wood, Edward Stickney
  Wyman, Morrill
  Young, Aaron
  Zakrzewska, Marie Elizabeth
VILES, JONAS
  Allen, Thomas
  Bland, Richard Parks
  Bliss, Philemon
  Boggs, Lillburn W.
VILLARD, HAROLD G.
  Horton, Samuel Dana
  Knox, John Jay
  Nell, William Cooper
  Payne, Christopher Harrison
  Payne, Daniel Alexander
  Perkins, George Walbridge
  Perry, Rufus Lewis
  Powers, Daniel William
  Pratt, Charles
  Pratt, Sereno Stansbury
  Rankine, William Birch
  Ray, Charles Bennett
  Remond, Charles Lenox
  Scarborough, William Saunders
  Slater, John Fox
  Smyth, John Henry
  Still, William
  Tanner, Benjamin Tucker
  Taylor, Marshall William
  Turner, Henry McNeal
  Ward, Samuel, 1786–1839
  White, Stepten Van Culen
VILLARD, OSWALD GARRISON
  Croly, Herbert David
  Curtis, Cyrus Hermann
    Kotzschmar
  Linn, William Alexander
  Munsey, Frank Andrew
  Pulitzer, Joseph
  Ridder, Herman
  Schurz, Carl
  Seitz, Don Carlos
  White, Horace
VINCENT, JOHN MARTIN
  Browne, William Hand
  Huntington, Henry Edwards
  Lieber, Francis
VINOKOUROFF, MICHAEL Z.
  Innokentii
  Ioasaf
  Kuskov, Ivan Aleksandrovich
VIOLETTE, EUGENE M.
  Blanchard, Newton Crain
  Bouligny, Dominique
  Boyd, David French
  Caffery, Donelson
  Conrad, Charles Magill
  Foster, Murphy James
  Gibson, Randall Lee
  La Tour, Le Blond de
  McCaleb, Theodore Howard
  Merrick, Edwin Thomas
  Moore, Thomas Overton
  Mouton, Alexander

Pauger, Adrien de
Sullivan, William Henry
VISELTEAR, ARTHUR J.
Winslow, Charles-Edward
Amory
VITELLI, JAMES R.
Adler, Elmer
Brown, John Mason, Jr.
Seldes, Gilbert Vivian
VIZETELLY, FRANK HORACE
Champlin, John Denison
Funk, Isaac Kauffman
Gregory, Daniel Seelye
VOGEL, MORRIS J.
Cannon, Ida Maud
Simmons, James Stevens
VOIGT, DAVID QUENTIN
Barrow, Edward Grant
Cicotte, Edward Victor
Collins, Edward Trowbridge
Comiskey, Grace Elizabeth
Reidy
Johnson, Walter Perry
Kelly, John Brendan
Landis, Kenesaw Mountain
Mack, Connie
Rickey, Wesley Branch
Ruth, George Herman (Babe)
Spink, John George Taylor
Stevens, Frank Mozley
Stevens, Harry Mozley
Young, Denton True ("Cy")
VOLWILER, ALBERT T.
Croghan, George, d. 1782
Croghan, George, 1791–1849
Harrison, Benjamin, 1833–1901
Miller, William Henry Harrison
Porter, Albert Gallatin
Proctor, Redfield
Swank, James Moore
Swift, Lucius Burrie
VON ECKARDT, WOLF
Mendelsohn, Erich (or Eric)
VOORHEES, DAVID WILLIAM
O'Dwyer, William
VOORHEES, DAYTON
Beasley, Mercer
VOSPER, EDNA
Vaughan, Benjamin
VOSS, FREDERICK
Diller, Burgoyne
Lebrun, Federico ("Rico")
VOSS, FREDERICK S.
Rorimer, James Joseph
Wynn, Ed
VOTH, PAUL D.
Chamberlain, Charles Joseph

WADE, JOHN DONALD
Ashe, Samuel
Ashe, William Shepperd
Avery, William Waigstill
Bass, William Capers
Baylor, Frances Courtenay
Behan, William James
Bellamy, Elizabeth W. Croom
Binns, John
Blake, Mary Elizabeth McGrath
Bloodworth, Timothy
Bohune, Lawrence
Bryan, Thomas Barbour
Bulkeley, Peter
Carleton, Henry Guy

Caruthers, William Alexander
Chappell, Absalom Harris
Clapp, William Warland
Clarke, Mary Bayard Devereux
Clement, Edward Henry
Colburn, Zerah
Conant, Alban Jasper
Cook, Russell S.
Coolbrith, Ina Donna
Corrothers, James David
Corson, Hiram
Crandall, Charles Henry
Crane, Anne Moncure
Crawford, John Martin
Crerar, John
Cromwell, Gladys Louise
Husted
Crosby, John Schuyler
Curwood, James Oliver
Cutler, Lizzie Petit
Dabney, Robert Lewis
Dabney, Virginius
Dalcho, Frederick
Dale, Samuel
Daniel, John Moncure
Davidson, James Wood
Daviess, Maria Thompson
Davis, Jerome Dean
Davis, Mary Evelyn Moore
Davis, Noah Knowles
Deems, Charles Force
De Fontaine, Felix Gregory
De Lamar, Joseph Raphael
Delano, Amassa
De Leon, Thomas Cooper
Derbigny, Pierre Auguste
Charles Bourguignon
De Trobriand, Régis Denis de
Keredern
Diaz, Abby Morton
Didier, Eugene Lemoine
Dimitry, Alexander
Dimitry, Charles Patton
Disturnell, John
Ditson, George Leighton
Donnelly, Eleanor Cecilia
Dorr, Julia Caroline Ripley
Dorsey, Anna Hanson
McKenney
Dorsey, Sarah Anne Ellis
Dow, Lorenzo, 1777–1834
Drake, Francis Samuel
Drake, Samuel Adams
Drumgoole, John Christopher
Du Bois, William Ewing
Early, John
Elliott, Charles
Elliott, William
Ellis, Edward Sylvester
Elwyn, Alfred Langdon
Estabrook, Joseph
Evans, Augusta Jane
Fairfax, Donald McNeill
Few, Ignatius Alphonso
Field, Roswell Martin
Fisher, Sidney George,
1809–1871
Fiske, Amos Kidder
Fitzgerald, Oscar Penn
Flagg, Edmund
Flagg, Thomas Wilson
Ford, Patrick
Forman, Justus Miles

Fosdick, William Whiteman
Foster, David Skaats
Fox, John William
Fuller, Richard
Fulton, Justin Dewey
Furman, James Clement
Galloway, Charles Betts
Gambrell, James Bruton
Garland, Landon Cabell
Gilmore, Joseph Henry
Girardeau, John Lafayette
Goodsell, Daniel Ayres
Goulding, Francis Robert
Grady, Henry Woodfin
Grafton, Charles Chapman
Graves, James Robinson
Graves, John Temple
Graves, Zuinglius Calvin
Green, Alexander Little Page
Grieve, Miller
Grimes, Absalom Carlisle
Gwin, William McKendree
Gwinnett, Button
Harben, William Nathaniel
Hargrove, Robert Kennon
Haughery, Margaret Gaffney
Hays, William Shakespeare
Holcombe, Henry
Hooper, Johnson Jones
Hope, James Barron
Howell, Evan Park
Hubner, Charles William
Jones, Charles Colcock
Lipscomb, Andrew Adgate
Longstreet, Augustus Baldwin
WADE, LOUISE CARROLL
McDowell, Mary Eliza
Taylor, Graham
Terrell, Mary Eliza Church
WAGENKNECHT, EDWARD
Grant, Robert
Paine, Albert Bigelow
WAGGONER, RAYMOND W.
Barrett, Albert Moore
WAGLEY, CHARLES
Lewis, Oscar
WAGNER, CHARLES F.
Fortescue, Charles LeGeyt
WAGNER, R. RICHARD
Everleigh, Ada
Everleigh, Minna
WAGNER, THEODORE B.
Frasch, Herman
WAGNON, WILLIAM O., JR.
Fairburn, William Armstrong
Gates, Thomas Sovereign
Hill, George Washington
James, Arthur Curtiss
WAGONER, C. D.
Faccioli, Giuseppe
Potter, William Bancroft
Rice, Edwin Wilbur
WAIT, WILLIAM CUSHING
Elder, Samuel James
WAITE, FREDERICK C.
Kirtland, Jared Potter
WAITE, J. HERBERT
Howe, Lucien
Jeffries, Benjamin Joy
Knapp, Herman
WALBRIDGE, EARLE F.
Pearson, Edmund Lester
Wright, Willard Huntington

WALCUTT, CHARLES CHILD
  Beer, Thomas
WALD, GEORGE
  Hecht, Selig
WALDEN, DANIEL
  Hecht, Ben
  Hurst, Fannie
WALKER, BUZ M.
  Montgomery, William Bell
WALKER, FRANKLIN DICKERSON
  Wilson, Harry Leon
WALKER, FRANKLIN TRENABY
  Trent, William Peterfield
WALKER, J. SAMUEL
  Wallace, Henry Agard
WALKER, S. JAY
  Hurston, Zora Neale
WALL, ALEXANDER J.
  Moore, Frank
  Moore, George Henry
  Moore, Jacob Bailey
  Robertson, Archibald
  Stevens, John Austin,
    1827–1910
  Trow, John Fowler
WALL, BENNETT H.
  Barden, Graham Arthur
  Johnston, Olin DeWitt
    Talmadge
  Kress, Samuel Henry
WALL, JOSEPH FRAZIER
  Biddle, Francis Beverley
  Hendrick, Burton Jesse
  Humphrey, George Magoffin
  Olds, Irving Sands
  Phipps, Lawrence Cowle
  Taylor, Myron Charles
  Weir, Ernest Tener
WALL, JOSEPH S.
  Foote, John Ambrose
WALLACE, D. D.
  Shipp, Albert Micajah
  Yeadon, Richard
WALLACE, W. STEWART
  Henry, John, 1807–1820
WALLER, INGRID NELSON
  Lipman, Jacob Goodale
WALMSLEY, JAMES ELLIOTT
  Bonham, Milledge Luke
  Botts, John Minor
  Brawley, William Hiram
  Brooks, Preston Smith
  Cheves, Langdon
  Echols, John
  Elzey, Arnold
  Eppes, John Wayles
  Faulkner, Charles James,
    1814–1898
  Floyd, John
  Floyd, John Buchanan
  Lomax, Lunsford Lindsay
  Lowndes, William
  McDowell, James
  Preston, William Ballard
  Pryor, Roger Atkinson
  Smith, William, 1797–1887
  Smith, William Waugh
  Smyth, Alexander
  Staples, Waller Redd
WALSH, JAMES J.
  Farley, John Murphy
  O'Dwyer, Joseph
  Paine, Martyn

Pattison, Granville Sharp
Quinan, John Russell
Ricord, Philippe
Rohé, George Henry
WALSH, J. L.
  Osgood, William Fogg
WALTER, FRANK K.
  Jones, Herschel Vespasian
WALTER, PAUL ALFRED FRANCIS
  Prince, Le Baron Bradford
WALTER, RICHARD D.
  Myerson, Abraham
WALTERS, EVERETT
  Fess, Simeon Davidson
WALTERS, RAYMOND
  Wolle, John Frederick
WALTON, J. BARNARD
  Cresson, Elliott
WARBEKE, JOHN M.
  Scott, Colin Alexander
WARD, CHARLES S.
  Wehle, Louis Brandeis
WARD, ESTELLE FRANCES
  Jones, William Patterson
WARD, HARRY F.
  Rauschenbusch, Walter
WARD, PATRICIA SPAIN
  Aldrich, Charles Anderson
  Cabot, Hugh
  Chapin, Henry Dwight
  Nutting, Mary Adelaide
  Stimson, Julia Catherine
WARE, EDITH E.
  Sage, Margaret Olivia Slocum
  Skinner, Charles Rufus
WARE, EDITH W.
  Breasted, James Henry
WARE, LOUISE
  Peabody, George Foster
WARFEL, HARRY R.
  Carruth, Fred Hayden
  Grosset, Alexander
  Percival, James Gates
  Porter, Gene Stratton
WARNER, HOYT LANDON
  Clarke, John Hessin
  Garfield, James Rudolph
WARNER, LANDON
  Howe, Frederic Clemson
WARNER, LANGDON
  Fenollosa, Ernest Francisco
WARNER, MARJORIE F.
  Brincklé, William Draper
WARNER, ROBERT A.
  Red Jacket
  Smohalla
WARNER, ROBERT M.
  Osborn, Chase Salmon
WARREN, CHARLES H.
  Silliman, Benjamin, 1779–1864
WARREN, DONALD R.
  Tigert, John James, IV
WARREN, SHIELDS
  Christian, Henry Asbury
  Mallory, Frank Burr
WARTHIN, ALDRED S.
  Ohlmacher, Albert Philip
WASHBURN, FREDERIC A.
  Mixter, Samuel Jason
WASHBURN, HENRY B.
  Worcester, Elwood

WASHBURN, MARGARET F.
  Titchener, Edward Bradford
WASHINGTON, JOSEPH R., JR.
  Gregg, John Andrew
WASSERSTROM, WILLIAM
  Brooks, Van Wyck
  Deland, Margaret
WATERHOUSE, EDWARD J.
  Allen, Edward Ellis
WATERMAN, W. RANDALL
  Brisbane, Albert
  Dow, Neal
  Evans, Frederick William
  Gage, Frances Dana Barker
  Gage, Matilda Joslyn
  Goodell, William
  Green, Beriah
  Green, Frances Harriet
    Whipple
  Gurley, Ralph Randolph
  Miller, Jonathan Peckham
  Morse, Jedidiah
  Parish, Elijah
  Payson, Seth
  Robinson, Harriet Jane Hanson
  Robinson, William Stevens
  Stearns, George Luther
WATERS, CAMPBELL EASTER
  Hillebrand, William Francis
WATERS, EDWARD N.
  Engel, Carl
  Nielsen, Alice
  Putnam, (George) Herbert
  Rachmaninoff, Sergei
    Vasilyevich
WATKINS, SAMUEL S.
  Gibbs, George
WATSON, EDWARD H.
  Bascom, Florence
WATSON, MARK S.
  Ritchie, Albert Cabell
WATSON, RICHARD L., JR.
  Gardner, Oliver Maxwell
  Simmons, Furnifold McLendel
WATT, JAMES CRAWFORD
  McMurrich, James Playfair
WATTEL, HAROLD L.
  Chamberlin, Edward Hastings
  Fairchild, Fred Rogers
  Levitt, Abraham
  Overstreet, Harry Allen
WATTS, EMILY STIPES
  Millay, Edna St. Vincent
WATTS, EUGENE J.
  Smith, Bruce
WAY, ROYAL B.
  Harvey, Louis Powell
  Howe, Timothy Otis
WEATHERBY, C. A.
  Robinson, Benjamin Lincoln
WEAVER, RAYMOND
  Allston, Washington
WEAVER, RUFUS W.
  Waller, John Lightfoot
  Whitsitt, William Heth
  Willingham, Robert Josiah
  Winkler, Edwin Theodore
  Yeaman, William Pope
WEBB, GEORGE ERNEST
  Douglass, Andrew Ellicott
  Nicholson, Seth Barnes
  Slipher, Vesto Melvin

WEBB, R. K.
  Schuyler, Robert Livingston
WEBB, ROBERT H.
  Humphreys, Milton Wylie
WEBB, W. P.
  Jones, John B.
  Wharton, William H.
WEBBER, MABEL L.
  Izard, Ralph
  Manigault, Gabriel
  Manigault, Peter
  Manigault, Pierre
WEBER, WILLIAM A.
  Cockerell, Theodore Dru
    Alison
WEBSTER, HUTTON
  Howard, George Elliott
WECHSLER, HARRY L.
  Jackson, Chevalier
WECTER, DIXON
  Rogers, Will
WEEKS, EDWARD
  Allen, Fred
  Allen, Frederick Lewis
WEEKS, MANGUM
  Cheshire, Joseph Blount
WEEMS, JOHN EDWARD
  Henson, Matthew Alexander
WEHLE, LOUIS B.
  McCarthy, Charles
WEIGLE, LUTHER ALLAN
  Clark, Francis Edward
  Mills, Benjamin Fay
  Moody, Dwight Lyman
  Trumbull, Henry Clay
  Valentine, Milton
WEIGLEY, EMMA SEIFRIT
  Marlatt, Abby Lillian
  Rose, Mary Davies Swartz
WEIGLEY, RUSSELL F.
  Merrill, Frank Dow
WEIGOLD, MARILYN E.
  Fitzgerald, Alice Louise
    Florence
  Speer, Emma Bailey
WEINBERG, JULIUS
  Ross, Edward Alsworth
WEINBERG, MEYER
  Carter, Boake
  McNamee, Graham
WEINBERG, SYDNEY STAHL
  Bonsal, Stephen
  Davis, Elmer Holmes
  Lange, Dorothea
  Lardner, John Abbott
  Stokes, Thomas Lunsford, Jr.
WEINBERGER, CASPAR W., JR.
  Curtis, Edward Sheriff
WEINSTEIN, ALLEN
  Rosenberg, Ethel
  Rosenberg, Julius
WEISENBURG, THEODORE H.
  Mills, Charles Karsner
  Potts, Charles Sower
WEISENBURGER, FRANCIS P.
  Hoey, Clyde Roark
  Noyes, Edward Follansbee
  Payne, Henry B.
  Pugh, George Ellis
  Sherwood, Isaac Ruth
  Shuey, Edwin Longstreet
  Tappan, Benjamin
  Taylor, James Wickes

  Trimble, Allen
WEISMAN, AVERY D.
  Sachs, Hanns
WEISS, BENJAMIN P.
  Dercum, Francis Xavier
WEISS, GAIL GARFINKEL
  Henderson, Ray
WEISS, HARRY B.
  Yeager, Joseph
WEISS, NANCY J.
  Caraway, Hattie Ophelia Wyatt
  Kahn, Florence Prag
  Sulzer, William
  White, Walter Francis
WEISS, PAUL
  Peirce, Charles Sanders
WEITENKAMPF, FRANK
  Anthony, Andrew Varick Stout
  Bacher, Otto Henry
  Bellew, Frank Henry Temple
  Bowen, Abel
  Brennan, Alfred Laurens
  Cole, Timothy
  Linton, William James
  Maverick, Peter
  Mielatz, Charles Frederick
    William
  Rollinson, William
  Schoff, Stephen Alonzo
WELCH, WILLIAM HENRY
  Welch, William Wickham
WELKER, ROBERT H.
  Bailey, Florence Augusta
    Merriam
  Chapman, Frank Michler
  Pearson, Thomas Gilbert
  Seton, Ernest Thompson
WELLINGTON, RAYNOR G.
  Beadle, William Henry
    Harrison
WELLS, CHARLES L.
  Otey, James Hervey
  Patillo, Henry
  Pettigrew, Charles
WELLS, F. ESTELLE
  Jayne, Horace Fort
  Marshall, Clara
  Michener, Ezra
  Ott, Isaac
  Pickering, Charles
  Preston, Ann
  Price, Joseph
  Willard, De Forest
WELLS, H. GIDEON
  Ricketts, Howard Taylor
WELLS, JAMES M.
  McMurtrie, Douglas Crawford
WELLS, WALTER A.
  Cutter, Ephraim
WELSH, S. JANE
  Ramsay, Erskine
  Stanley, Robert Crooks
WENTZ, ABDEL ROSS
  Day, David Alexander
  Jacobs, Henry Eyster
WERNER, RAYMOND C.
  Galloway, Joseph
WERTENBAKER, THOMAS JEFFERSON
  Brown, Alexander, 1843–1906
  Byrd, William, 1652–1704
  Byrd, William, 1674–1744
  Dale, Sir Thomas
  Dinwiddie, Robert

  Pocahontas
  Powhatan
  Rolfe, John
WEST, ELIZABETH HOWARD
  Forbes, John, 1769–1823
  Hays, John Coffee
  Panton, William
  Wallace, William Alexander
    Anderson
WESTCOTT, ALLAN
  Ammen, Daniel
  Badger, Charles Johnston
  Barron, Samuel
  Beaumont, John Colt
  Blue, Victor
  Calvert, George Henry
  Champlin, Stephen
  Chester, Colby Mitchell
  Chester, George Randolph
  Coffin, Charles Carleton
  Collier, Hiram Price
  Collins, Napoleon
  Colvocoresses, George Musalas
  Conner, David
  Coontz, Robert Edward
  Crane, Stephen
  Crane, William Montgomery
  Crosby, Peirce
  Davis, Charles Henry,
    1807–1877
  Davis, Charles Henry,
    1845–1921
  Davis, John Lee
  Decatur, Stephen, 1752–1808
  Decatur, Stephen, 1779–1820
  Eberle, Edward Walter
  Egan, Maurice Francis
  Ewell, James
  Ewell, Thomas
  Foote, Andrew Hull
  Forrest, French
  Gillon, Alexander
  Glynn, James
  Gorringe, Henry Honeychurch
  Grant, Albert Weston
  Griffin, Robert Stanislaus
  Hayden, Edward Everett
  Hughes, Charles Frederick
  Ingersoll, Royal Rodney
  Ingraham, Duncan Nathaniel
  Jeffers, William Nicholson
  Jenkins, Thornton Alexander
  Jones, Jacob
  Kelley, James Douglas Jerrold
  Key, Francis Scott
  Kimball, William Wirt
  Landon, Melville de Lancy
  Lanigan, George Thomas
  Lanman, Joseph
  Lardner, James Lawrence
  Leggett, William
  Lester, Charles Edwards
  Loomis, Charles Battell
  Ludlow, Fitz Hugh
  Lynch, William Francis
  McNair, Frederick Vallette
  Mahan, Alfred Thayer
  Mayo, William Kennon
  Meade, Richard Worsam,
    1807–1870
  Meade, Richard Worsam,
    1837–1897
  Milligan, Robert Wiley

Moffett, William Adger
Montgomery, John Berrien
Morris, Charles
Murdock, Joseph Ballard
Olmsted, Gideon
Page, Thomas Jefferson
Palmer, James Croxall
Palmer, John Williamson
Parker, Foxhall Alexander
Parker, William Harwar
Parrott, Enoch Greenleafe
Patterson, Daniel Todd
Patterson, Thomas Harman
Pattison, Thomas
Paulding, Hiram
Pennock, Alexander Mosely
Percival, John
Phelps, Thomas Stowell
Philip, John Woodward
Plunkett, Charles Peshall
Poor, Charles Henry
Preble, George Henry
Pringle, Joel Roberts Poinsett
Quackenbush, Stephen Platt
Raby, James Joseph
Radford, William
Read, George Campbell
Read, Thomas
Reid, Samuel Chester
Remey, George Collier
Revere, Joseph Warren
Ringgold, Cadwalader
Rousseau, Harry Harwood
Sampson, William Thomas
Sands, Benjamin Franklin
Sands, Joshua Ratoon
Schley, Winfield Scott
Shubrick, John Templer
Shubrick, William Branford
Shufeldt, Robert Wilson
Sicard, Montgomery
Simpson, Edward
Smith, Melancton, 1810–1893
Soley, James Russell
Stevens, Thomas Holdup,
    1795–1841
Stevens, Thomas Holdup,
    1819–1896
Stewart, Edwin
Stoddard, John Lawson
Taylor, William Rogers
Taylor, William Vigneron
Temple, William Grenville
Thompson, Egbert
Tingey, Thomas
Truxtun, Thomas
Truxtun, William Talbot
Tyson, George Emory
Upshur, John Henry
Waldo, Samuel Putnam
Walke, Henry
Walker, John Grimes
Waters, Daniel
Watson, John Crittenden
Werden, Reed
Wilde, George Francis Faxon
Wilson, Theodore Delavan
Winslow, Cameron McRae
Worden, John Lorimer
Ziegemeier, Henry Joseph
WESTERFIELD, RAY B.
    Farnam, Henry Walcott

WESTERHOFF, JOHN HENRY, III
    Coe, George Albert
WESTON, ARTHUR D.
    Goodnough, Xanthus Henry
WESTON, WILLIAM H., JR.
    Thaxter, Roland
WETMORE, ALEXANDER
    True, Frederick William
WETTEREAU, JAMES O.
    Willing, Thomas
    Wolcott, Oliver, 1760–1833
WEYEN, EDWARD M.
    Ladd, George Trumbull
    Le Moyne, Francis Julius
WHEELER, GERALD E.
    Pratt, William Veazie
WHEELER, GERARD E.
    Lee, Willis Augustus
WHEELER, JESSIE F.
    Wilson, Samuel
WHEELER, JOSEPH L.
    Mayer, Brantz
WHICHER, GEORGE F.
    Adams, Charles Follen
    Alden, William Livingston
    Arnold, George
    Dennie, Joseph
    Dickinson, Emily Elizabeth
    Genung, John Franklin
    Lewis, Charles Bertrand
    Sewall, Jonathan Mitchell
    Story, Isaac
    Thaxter, Celia Laighton
    Todd, Mabel Loomis
    Turell, Jane
    Tyler, William Seymour
    Underwood, Francis Henry
    Wallace, William Ross
    Ward, Herbert Dickinson
    Whiting, Charles Goodrich
WHIPPLE, THOMAS K.
    London, Jack
WHISNANT, DAVID E.
    Boyd, James
WHITAKER, ARTHUR P.
    Bowles, William Augustus
    Carondelet, Francisco Luis
        Hector, Baron de
    Fanning, Alexander Campbell
        Wilder
    Forbes, John Murray,
        1771–1831
    Gálvez, Bernardo de
    Gayoso de Lemos, Manuel
    Jackson, James, 1757–1806
    McGillivray, Alexander
    McIntosh, Lachlan
    Miró, Esteban Rod
    O'Reilly, Alexander
    Robertson, James Alexander
    Sevier, John
    Ulloa, Antonio de
WHITAKER, CHARLES HARRIS
    Bacon, Henry
WHITE, CHARLES ADAMS
    Elson, Louis Charles
WHITE, COURTLAND Y., III
    Smith, Francis Hopkinson
WHITE, G. EDWARD
    Pound, (Nathan) Roscoe
WHITE, HORATIO S.
    Fiske, Daniel Willard

WHITE, LAURA A.
    Rhett, Robert Barnwell
WHITE, LESLIE A.
    Goldenweiser, Alexander
        Alexandrovich
    Parsons, Elsie Worthington
        Clews
WHITE, MELVIN JOHNSON
    Brown, James, 1766–1835
    Bullard, Henry Adams
    Eustis, George, 1796–1858
    Eustis, George, 1828–1872
    Eustis, James Biddle
    Hahn, George Michael Decker
    Hall, Dominick Augustin
    Hays, Harry Thompson
    Hébert, Paul Octave
    Howe, William Wirt
    Hunt, William Henry
    Johnston, Josiah Stoddard
    Johnston, William Preston
    Kenner, Duncan Farrar
    Lafon, Thomy
    Livermore, Samuel, 1786–1833
    Lucas, John Baptiste Charles
    Ludeling, John Theodore
    McEnery, Samuel Douglas
    Manning, Thomas Courtland
    Morgan, Philip Hicky
    Newcomb, Josephine Louise Le
        Monnier
    Provosty, Olivier Otis
WHITE, ROBERT
    Thomas, John Charles
WHITE, WILLIAM A.
    Nichols, Charles Henry
WHITEHILL, WALTER MUIR
    Browne, Herbert Wheildon
        Cotton
    Carnegie, Mary Crowninshield
        Endicott 021676 Chamberlain
    Colcord, Lincoln Ross
    Connick, Charles Jay
    Coolidge, Julian Lowell
    Coolidge, Thomas Jefferson
    Cram, Ralph Adams
    Edwards, Richard Stanislaus
    Howe, Mark Antony De Wolfe
    Kean, Jefferson Randolph
    King, Ernest Joseph
    Lawrence, William
    Lodge, John Ellerton
    Marquand, John Phillips
    Mayo, Henry Thomas
    Perry, Bliss
    Tyler, Royall
    Updike, Daniel Berkeley
    Wheelwright, Mary Cabot
    Winship, George Parker
WHITELAW, JOHN L.
    Graves, William Sidney
WHITELEY, EMILY STONE
    Hughes, Christopher
WHITEMAN, HAROLD B., JR.
    Davis, Norman Hezekiah
WHITFIELD, STEPHEN J.
    Berg, Gertrude Edelstein
    Cantor, Eddie
    Moore, Victor Frederick
WHITING, BARTLETT JERE
    Kittredge, George Lyman

Nelson, Hugh
Nelson, Thomas
Nelson, William, 1711–1772
Page, John
Page, Mann
Randolph, John, 1728–1784
Randolph, Sir John
Randolph, Peyton
Randolph, William
Ryland, Robert
Taylor, George Boardman
Taylor, James Barnett
Thomson, John
Tupper, Henry Allen
Wood, John
WOODRUFF, CLINTON ROGERS
Blankenburg Rudolph
WOODS, ALAN C.
Wilmer, William Holland
WOODSON, CARTER GODWIN
Allen, Richard
Boyd, Richard Henry
Brown, John Mifflin
Brown, Morris
Brown, William Wells
Bruce, Blanche K.
Cain, Richard Harvey
Clinton, George Wylie
Garnet, Henry Highland
Greener, Richard Theodore
WOODWARD, CARL R.
Nelson, Julius
Read, Charles
Thurber, George
WOODWARD, SHERMAN M.
Davis, Arthur Powell
WOODWARD, VANN
Watson, Thomas Edward
WOODWARD, WALTER C.
Nicholson, Timothy
WOODWORTH, ROBERT S.
Franz, Shepherd Ivory
Ladd-Franklin, Christine
Washburn, Margaret Floy
WOODY, ROBERT H.
Boyd, William Kenneth
Moses, Franklin, Jr.
Simonton, Charles Henry
Sydnor, Charles Sackett
Wright, Jonathan Jasper
WOODY, THOMAS
Alison, Francis
Allen, George
Allen, William Henry
Bishop, Nathan
Burton, Warren
Calhoun, William Barron
Camp, David Nelson
Carter, James Gordon
Cheever, Ezekiel
Cobb, Lyman
Colburn, Dana Pond
Cooley, Edwin Gilbert
Cooper, William John
Dock, Christopher
Downey, John
Furst, Clyde Bowman
Keagy, John Miller
Knox, Samuel
Pennypacker, Elijah Funk
Phelps, Almira Hart Lincoln
Poor, John
Schaeffer, Nathan Christ

Sill, Anna Peck
WOOLLEY, MARY E.
Lyon, Mary
WOOLSEY, GEORGE
Stimson, Lewis Atterbury
WOOSTER, JAMES W., JR.
Harkness, Edward Stephen
WORCESTER, WILLIAM LORING
Barrett, Benjamin Fiske
Giles, Chauncey
WORRELL, WILLIAM H.
Frieze, Henry Simmons
Kelsey, Francis Willey
WORTH, DEAN S.
Wiener, Leo
WORTHY, JAMES C.
Wood, Robert Elkington
WRIGHT, C. P.
Marshall, Benjamin
Thompson, Jeremiah
WRIGHT, ERNEST H.
Boyesen, Hjalmar Hjorth
Canfield, James Hulme
Carpenter, George Rice
Da Ponte, Lorenzo
Drisler, Henry
Duer, William Alexander
Earle, Mortimer Lamson
WRIGHT, FREDERICK E.
Woodward, Robert Simpson
WRIGHT, HARRY A.
Pynchon, John
WRIGHT, HELEN
Benson, Eugene
Brumidi, Constantino
Cassatt, Mary
Coleman, Charles Caryl
Colman, Samuel
Coman, Charlotte Buell
Cropsey, Jasper Francis
Haskell, Ernest
Hyde, Helen
Jones, Alfred
Keith, William
Kingsley, Elbridge
Koehler, Sylvester Rosa
Koopman, Augustus
Kruell, Gustav
Mackubin, Florence
Nicholls, Rhoda Holmes
Plowman, George Taylor
Porter, Russell Williams
Reed, Earl Howell
Ritchey, George Willis
WRIGHT, HERBERT F.
Balch, Thomas Willing
Bidlack, Benjamin Alden
Denby, Charles
Eames, Charles
Farman, Elbert Eli
Fearn, John Walker
Fisher, George Purnell
Fox, Williams Carlton
Gorman, Arthur Pue
Gresham, Walter Quintin
Jones, Walter
Knox, Philander Chase
WRIGHT, JAMES
Tobey, Charles William
WRIGHT, JOHN W.
Hatch, Edward
Howe, Albion Parris
Spaulding, Oliver Lyman

WRIGHT, NELDA E.
Hay, Oliver Perry
WRIGHT, WALTER L., JR.
Bradish, Luther
Brewer, Charles
Carr, Dabney Smith
Carter, Henry Alpheus Peirce
De Forest, David Curtis
English, George Bethune
Ferguson, Thomas Barker
Gibson, Walter Murray
Green, Benjamin Edwards
Gregg, David McMurtrie
Gummere, Samuel René
Hale, Charles
Hamlin, Cyrus
Hassaurek, Friedrich
Hill, John Henry
Hunnewell, James
Marsh, George Perkins
Marshall, James Fowle Baldwin
Offley, David
Peirce, Henry Augustus
Post, George Edward
Prime, Edward Dorr Griffin
Rhind, Charles
Riggs, Elias
Robert, Christopher
Rhinelander
Ryan, Arthur Clayton
Schneider, Benjamin
Shaler, William
Shepard, Fred Douglas
Smith, Azariah
Thurber, Christopher Carson
Van Dyck, Cornelius Van Alen
Van Lennep, Henry John
Washburn, George
Wilson, Samuel Graham
WROTH, LAWRENCE COUNSELMAN
Brown, John, 1736–1803
Brown, John Carter
Brown, Joseph
Brown, Nicholas, 1729
  o.s.–1791
Brown, Nicholas, 1769–1841
Carroll, Charles
Cooke, Ebenezer
Cresap, Michael
Cresap, Thomas
Logan, James, 1725–1780
Nuthead, William
Parks, William
Staples, William Read
Steiner, Bernard Christian
Sterling, James
WUNSCH, WILLIAM F.
Smyth, Julian Kennedy
WYER, JAMES INGERSOLL
Eastman, William Reed
Fairchild, Mary Salome Cutler
Randall, Henry Stephens
Sanders, Charles Walton
Street, Alfred Billings
Thacher, John Boyd
Thompson, Samuel Rankin
Tucker, Gilbert Milligan
Williams, Edwin
Williams, John, 1761–1818
Williams, William, 1787–1850
WYLLIE, JOHN C.
Gordon, William Fitzhugh
Levy, Uriah Phillips

BIRTHPLACES—UNITED STATES

ALABAMA

Allen, Viola Emily
Bankhead, John Hollis, 1842–1920
Bankhead, John Hollis, 1872–1946
Bankhead, Tallulah
Bankhead, William Brockman
Belmont, Alva Ertskin Smith Vanderbilt
Berry, James Henderson
Birney, David Bell
Birney, William
Bozeman, Nathan
Brickell, Robert Coman
Bridgman, Frederic Arthur
Brown, William Garrott
Bullard, Robert Lee
Burleson, Rufus Clarence
Camp, John Lafayette
Campbell, William Edward March
Carmichael, Oliver Cromwell
Clay, Clement Claiborne
Clayton, Henry De Lamar
Clemens, Jeremiah
Cole, Nat ("King")
Comer, Braxton Bragg
Culberson, Charles Allen
Davis, Mary Evelyn Moore
De Bardeleben, Henry Fairchild
De Priest, Oscar Stanton
Dowling, Noel Thomas
Duggar, Benjamin Minge
English, Elbert Hartwell
Fearn, John Walker
Fitzpatrick, Morgan Cassius
Fleming, Walter Lynwood
Fulton, Robert Burwell
Gaines, Reuben Reid
Glass, Franklin Potts
Gorgas, William Crawford
Grant, James Benton
Graves, David Bibb
Greenway, John Campbell
Gregg, John
Guild, La Fayette
Hamilton, Andrew Jackson
Hancock, John
Handy, William Christopher
Harding, William Procter Gould
Hardy, William Harris
Hargrove, Robert Kennon
Heflin, James Thomas
Hitchcock, Ethan Allen, 1835–1909
Hitchcock, Henry
Hobson, Richmond Pearson
Jones, Robert Reynolds ("Bob")
Jones, Samuel Porter
Keller, Helen Adams
Kolb, Reuben Francis
Lambrith, James William
Lile, William Minor
Love, Emanuel King
Lyon, David Gordon
McKellar, Kenneth Douglas

Manly, John Matthews
Mastin, Claudius Henry
Mitchell, Sidney Zollicoffer
Moore, John Trotwood
Morgan, John Hunt
Murphy, Edgar Gardner
Oates, William Calvin
O'Neal, Edward Asbury, 1818–1890
O'Neal, Edward Asbury, III, 1875–1958
Owen, Thomas McAdory
Owsley, Frank Lawrence
Parsons, Albert Richard
Pelham, John
Perry, Pettis
Pettus, Edmund Winston
Pou, Edward William
Riley, Benjamin Franklin
Roddey, Philip Dale
Screws, William Wallace
Sibert, William Luther
Simmons, William Joseph
Sloan, Matthew Scott
Sloss, James Withers
Smith, Eugene Allen
Smith, Holland McTyeire
Steagall, Henry Bascom
Tomochichi
Toulmin, Harry Theophilus
Tutwiler, Julia Strudwick
Valliant, Leroy Branch
Van de Graaff, Robert Jemison
Van Doren, Irita Bradford
Vincent, John Heyl
Walker, Leroy Pope
Wallace, Lurleen Burns
Walthall, Henry Brazeal
Washington, Dinah
Watts, Thomas Hill
Weatherford, William
Williams, Aubrey Willis
Williams, (Hiram) Hank
Winston, John Anthony
Wyeth, John Allan

ARIZONA

Geronimo
Patch, Alexander McCarrell

ARKANSAS

Adler, Cyrus
Anthony, Katharine Susan
Barnes, Julius Howland
Baylor, Frances Courtenay
Bennett, Henry Garland
Biffle, Leslie L
Brady, Mildred Alice Edie
Burns, Bob
Couch, Harvey Crowley
Davis, Jefferson
Fletcher, John Gould
Gray, Carl Raymond
Haynes, George Edmund
Ladd, Alan Walbridge

MacArthur, Douglas
McRae, Thomas Chipman
Perkins, Marion
Powell, Richard Ewing ("Dick")
Robinson, Joseph Taylor
Somervell, Brehon Burke
Sutton, William Seneca

CALIFORNIA

Aborn, Milton
Abrams, Albert
Acosta, Bertram Blanchard ("Bert")
Adams, Annette Abbott
Aitken, Robert Grant
Allen, Gracie
Alvarado, Juan Bautista
Anderson, Mary
Andrus, Ethel Percy
Atherton, Gertrude Franklin (Horn)
Atkinson, Henry Avery
Bacon, Frank
Beatty, Willard Walcott
Belasco, David
Blinn, Holbrook
Bowes, Edward J.
Bradley, Frederick Worthen
Brady, William Aloysius
Brownlee, James Forbis
Burton, Clarence Monroe
Connolly, Maureen Catherine
Cooper, William John
Corbett, Harvey Wiley
Corbett, James John
Cottrell, Frederick Gardner
De Angelis, Thomas Jefferson
Dorgan, Thomas Aloysius
Doyle, Alexander Patrick
Duncan, Isadora
Engle, Clair William Walter
Erlanger, Joseph
Fay, Francis Anthony ("Frank")
Fisher, William Arms
Frost, Robert Lee
Gaxton, William
George, Henry
Gherardi, Bancroft
Giannini, Amadeo Peter
Goldberg, Reuben Lucius ("Rube")
Goodman, Louis Earl
Grady, Henry Francis
Guthrie, William Dameron
Hammond, John Hays
Hansen, William Webster
Hearst, William Randolph
Heilmann, Harry
Hinkle, Beatrice Moses
Hohfeld, Wesley Newcomb
Hopper, Edna Wallace
Howard, Sidney Coe
Hubbard, Bernard Rosecrans
Jackson, Shirley Hardie
Jepson, Willis Linn
Jewett, Frank Baldwin

333

Johnson, Hiram Warren
Jones, Lindley Armstrong ("Spike")
Kirchoff, Charles William Henry
Kohlberg, Alfred
Kuykendall, Ralph Simpson
Kyne, Peter Bernard
Laguna, Theodore de Leo de
Lasky, Jesse Louis
Lawson, Ernest
Leonard, Robert Josselyn
Leonard, Sterling Andrus
Lindley, Curtis Holbrook
Lockheed, Allan Haines
Lockheed, Malcolm
London, Jack
Lord, Pauline
Lydston, George Frank
McClatchy, Charles Kenny
McClintock, James Harvey
McClung, Clarence Erwin
McGeehan, William O'Connell
Mack, Julian William
Mackay, Clarence Hungerford
Magnes, Judah Leon
Mather, Stephen Tyng
Matthiessen, Francis Otto
Maxwell, George Hebard
Meyer, Eugene Isaac
Meyer, Martin Abraham
Mezes, Sidney Edward
Mizner, Addison
Monroe, Marilyn
Morgan, Julia
Moss, Sanford Alexander
Nevada, Emma
Norris, Kathleen Thompson
O'Brien, Willis Harold
O'Doul, Francis Joseph ("Lefty")
Overstreet, Harry Allen
Oxnam, Garfield Bromley
Pacheco, Romualdo
Palón, Francisco
Parker, Carleton Hubbell
Patton, George Smith
Peek, Frank William
Phelan, James Duval
Regan, Agnes Gertrude
Reinhardt, Aurelia Isabel Henry
Ripley, Robert LeRoy
Roberts, Theodore
Roeding, George Christian
Rolph, James
Royce, Josiah
Ruef, Abraham
Sanderson, Sibyl
Sanford, Edmund Clark
Scripps, Robert Paine
Seton, Grace Gallatin Thompson
Smith, James Francis
Spreckels, Rudolph
Standley, William Harrison
Steffens, Lincoln
Steinbeck, John Ernst, Jr.
Stevens, Ashton
Stevenson, Adlai Ewing, II
Suzzallo, Henry
Swain, George Fillmore
Taylor, William Chittenden
Theobald, Robert Alfred
Tibbett, Lawrence Mervil
Toklas, Alice Babette
Vallejo, Mariano Guadalupe

Wanger, Walter
Warfield, David
Warner, William Lloyd
Webb, Harry Howard
White, Stephen Mallory
Whitney, Charlotte Anita
Wigmore, John Henry
Wislocki, George Bernays
Wong, Anna May
Younger, Maud
Zellerbach, James David

COLORADO

Allen, Edgar
Andrews, Bert
Chaney, Lon
Fairbanks, Douglas
Fowler, Gene
Gregg, Alan
Herr, Herbert Thacker
Hoagland, Dennis Robert
Holt, Arthur Erastus
Lea, Homer
Leyner, John George
MacDonald, Betty
May, Morton Jay
Otis, Arthur Sinton
Perry, Antoinette
Ross, Harold Wallace
Sabin, Florence Rena
Smith, Homer William
Whiteman, Paul Samuel ("Pops")

CONNECTICUT

Abbot, Willis John
Abbott, Frank Frost
Abbott, William Hawkins
Adams, Andrew
Adams, John
Adams, William
Adrian, Gilbert
Alcott, Amos Bronson
Alcott, William Andrus
Alexander, Francis
Alford, Leon Pratt
Allen, Edward Tyson
Allen, Ethan
Allen, Ira
Allen, Jeremiah Mervin
Allyn, Robert
Alsop, Richard
Alvord, Corydon Alexis
Andrews, Charles McLean
Andrews, Israel Ward
Andrews, Lorrin
Andrews, Samuel James
Andrews, Sherlock James
Andrews, William Watson
Arnold, Benedict
Arnold, Harold DeForest
Arnold, Leslie Philip
Atwater, Lyman Hotchkiss
Atwood, Lewis John
Augur, Hezekiah
Austin, David
Austin, Henry
Austin, Moses
Austin, Samuel
Ayer, James Cook
Ayres, Leonard Porter
Babcock, Washington Irving

Backus, Azel
Backus, Isaac
Bacon, Alice Mabel
Bacon, Benjamin Wisner
Bacon, David
Bacon, John
Bacon, Leonard Woolsey
Badger, Oscar Charles
Bailey, Anna Warner
Bailey, Ebenezer
Baker, Remember
Baldwin, Abraham
Baldwin, Edward Robinson
Baldwin, Frank Stephen
Baldwin, Henry
Baldwin, John
Baldwin, John Denison
Baldwin, Roger Sherman
Baldwin, Simeon
Baldwin, Simeon Eben
Baldwin, Theron
Bangs, Nathan
Banister, Zilpah Polly Grant
Barber, John Warner
Barbour, Clarence Augustus
Barbour, Henry Gray
Barlow, Joel
Barnard, Daniel Dewey
Barnard, Henry
Barnum, Phineas Taylor
Barstow, William Augustus
Bartholomew, Edward Sheffield
Bartlett, Paul Wayland
Batchelor, George
Bates, Walter
Batterson, James Goodwin
Bayley, Richard
Beach, Moses Yale
Beach, Wooster
Beard, George Miller
Beardsley, Eben Edwards
Beaumont, William
Beecher, Charles
Beecher, Henry Ward
Beecher, Lyman
Beecher, Thomas Kinnicut
Beers, Clifford Whittingham
Begley, Edward James ("Ed")
Belden, Josiah
Bell, Jacob
Bellamy, Joseph
Benedict, David
Benedict, Erastus Cornelius
Bentley, Elizabeth Terrill
Besse, Arthur Lyman
Bidwell, Walter Hilliard
Bingham, Caleb
Birge, Henry Warner
Bishop, Abraham
Bissell, George Edwin
Blakeslee, Erastus
Blatchford, Richard Milford
Blatchford, Samuel
Bliss, Philemon
Boardman, Thomas Danforth
Bolton, Sarah Knowles
Booth, Albert James, Jr. ("Albie")
Bostwick, Arthur Elmore
Bouton, Nathaniel
Bowen, Henry Chandler
Bowers, Elizabeth Crocker
Bowles, Samuel, 1797–1851
Bowles, Samuel, 1826–1878

Bowles, Samuel, 1851–1915
Brace, Charles Loring
Brace, John Pierce
Bradley, Frank Howe
Bradley, Stephen Row
Brainard, John Gardiner Calkins
Brainerd, David
Brainerd, Erastus
Brainerd, John
Brainerd, Lawrence
Brandegee, Frank Bosworth
Brandegee, Townshend Stith
Brewster, James
Dikinton, Clarence Crane
Bristol, William Henry
Brockway, Zebulon Reed
Bromley, Isaac Hill
Bronson, Henry
Brooker, Charles Frederick
Brown, Ethan Allen
Brown, John
Brown, John Newton
Brown, Samuel Robbins
Brown, Solymon
Buck, Daniel
Buck, Dudley
Buckingham, Joseph Tinker
Buckingham, William Alfred
Buckland, Cyrus
Buel, Jesse
Buell, Abel
Bulkeley, Morgan Gardner
Bulkley, John Williams
Bunce, William Gedney
Burleigh, Charles Calistus
Burleigh, George Shepard
Burleigh, William Henry
Burr, Aaron
Burr, Alfred Edmund
Burr, Enoch Fitch
Burr, William Hubert
Burrall, William Porter
Burritt, Elihu
Burton, Asa
Burton, Nathaniel Judson
Burton, Richard Eugene
Bushnell, David
Bushnell, Horace
Butler, John
Butler, Simeon
Butler, Thomas Belden
Cable, Frank Taylor
Calkins, Mary Whiton
Camp, David Nelson
Camp, Hiram
Camp, Walter Chauncey
Candee, Leverett
Carrington, Henry Beebee
Carter, Franklin
Case, William Scoville
Chamberlain, Jacob
Chamberlain, William Isaac
Chandler, Thomas Bradbury
Chapin, Aaron Lucius
Chapin, Alonzo Bowen
Chauncey, Isaac
Cheney, John
Cheney, Seth Wells
Cheney, Ward
Chester, Colby Mitchell
Chester, Joseph Lemuel
Chipman, Daniel
Chipman, Nathaniel

Chittenden, Martin
Chittenden, Russell Henry
Chittenden, Simeon Baldwin
Chittenden, Thomas
Church, Frederick Erwin
Church, Irving Porter
Clark, Charles Hopkins
Clark, Horace Francis
Clark, Sheldon
Clark, William Thomas
Cleaveland, Moses
Cleveland, Chauncey Fitch
Conn, Titus
Coe, Israel
Coggeshall, George
Coit, Thomas Winthrop
Cole, George Watson
Colt, Samuel
Comstock, Anthony
Cooke, Rose Terry
Copeland, Charles W.
Corbin, Austin
Corning, Erastus
Cowles, Henry Chandler
Cox, Jacob Dolson
Crary, Isaac Edwin
Cross, Wilbur Lucius
Croswell, Harry
Curtiss, Samuel Ives
Cushman, George Hewitt
Cutler, Manasseh
Daboll, Nathan
Dana, Edward Salisbury
Dana, Samuel Whittelsey
Danforth, Moseley Isaac
Davenport, Charles Benedict
Davenport, James
Davis, Charles Henry Stanley
Davis, George Whitefield
Day, Henry Noble
Day, Jeremiah
Dean, Sidney
Deane, Silas
De Forest, David Curtis
De Forest, John Kinne Hyde
De Forest, John William
De Koven, Henry Louis Reginald
De Koven, James
Deming, Henry Champion
De Vinne, Theodore Low
Dickinson, Anson
Dickinson, Daniel Stevens
Dike, Samuel Warren
Dillingham, Charles Bancroft
Dixon, James
Dockstader, Lew
Dodge, David Low
Dodge, William Earl
Doolittle, Amos
Douglas, Benjamin
Douglas, William
Dow, Lorenzo
Downer, Eliphalet
Dudley, William Russel
Dunbar, Moses
Dunning, Albert Elijah
Durand, William Frederick
Durkee, John
Dutton, Clarence Edward
Dutton, Henry
Dwight, Benjamin Woodbridge
Dwight, Sereno Edwards
Dwight, Theodore, 1764–1846

Dwight, Theodore, 1796–1866
Dwight, Timothy
Dyer, Eliphalet
Eaton, William
Edwards, Henry Waggaman
Edwards, Jonathan, 1703–1758
Eliot, Jared
Ellsworth, Henry Leavitt
Ellsworth, Henry William
Ellsworth, Oliver
Ellsworth, William Wolcott
Emmons, Nathanael
English, James Edward
Falkner, Roland Post
Fanning, Edmund
Fanning, John Thomas
Fanning, Nathaniel
Farnam, Henry Walcott
Farrell, James Augustine
Fayerweather, Daniel Burton
Ferry, Orris Sanford
Fetterman, William Judd
Field, David Dudley, 1781–1867
Field, David Dudley, 1805–1894
Field, Stephen Johnson
Fillmore, John Comfort
Finney, Charles Grandison
Fiske, John
Fitch, John
Fitch, Samuel
Fitch, Thomas
Flagg, George Whiting
Flagg, Jared Bradley
Fleming, William Maybury
Foot, Samuel Augustus
Foote, Andrew Hull
Foote, William Henry
Ford, Gordon Lester
Forward, Walter
Foster, John Pierrepont Codrington
Foster, Lafayette Sabine
Foulois, Benjamin Delahauf
Fryer, Douglas Henry
Gallaudet, Edward Miner
Gallaudet, Thomas
Gallup, Joseph Adams
Gardner, Leroy Upson
Gary, James Albert
Gauvreau, Emile Henry
Gaylord, Willis
Gibbs, Josiah Willard
Gibson, William Hamilton
Giddings, Franklin Henry
Gilbert, William Lewis
Gillett, Ezra Hall
Gillette, Francis
Gillette, William Hooker
Gilman, Charlotte Perkins Stetson
Gilman, Daniel Coit
Gleason, Frederic Grant
Goddard, William
Goodhue, Bertram Grosvenor
Goodrich, Charles Augustus
Goodrich, Chauncey
Goodrich, Chauncey Allen
Goodrich, Elizur, 1734–1797
Goodrich, Elizur, 1761–1849
Goodrich, Samuel Griswold
Goodyear, Charles
Goodyear, William Henry
Gould, Edward Sherman
Gould, George Jay

Gould, James
Graham, John Andrew
Graham, Sylvester
Granger, Francis
Granger, Gideon
Green, Beriah
Green, Thomas
Griffin, Edward Dorr
Griffing, Josephine Sophie White
Griswold, Alexander Viets
Griswold, Matthew
Griswold, Roger
Griswold, Stanley
Grosvenor, Charles Henry
Grow, Galusha Aaron
Guernsey, Egbert
Gunn, Frederick William
Gurley, Ralph Randolph
Hadley, Arthur Twining
Hale, David
Hale, Nathan
Hall, Asaph
Hall, Isaac Hollister
Hall, Lyman
Halleck, Fitz-Greene
Hamline, Leonidas Lent
Hammett, Samuel Adams
Hammond, Edward Payson
Hand, Daniel
Harding, Abner Clark
Harris, William Torrey
Harrison, Henry Baldwin
Hart, John
Hart, Samuel
Harvey, Louis Powell
Haskell, Ernest
Hastings, Thomas
Haven, Henry Philemon
Hawley, Gideon, 1727–1809
Hawley, Gideon, 1785–1870
Hayden, Horace H.
Hendrick, Burton Jesse
Herrick, Edward Claudius
Herter, Christian Archibald
Hewit, Augustine Francis
Hickok, Laurens Perseus
Higginson, Nathaniel
Hill, Ureli Corelli
Hillhouse, James
Hillhouse, James Abraham
Hinman, Elisha
Hinman, Joel
Hitchcock, Peter
Hoadley, David
Hoadly, George
Hobart, John Sloss
Holbrook, Alfred
Holbrook, Frederick
Holbrook, Josiah
Holcomb, Amasa
Holley, Alexander Lyman
Holley, Horace
Holley, Myron
Hollister, Gideon Hiram
Holmes, Abiel
Holmes, Israel
Hooker, Donald Russell
Hooker, Isabella Beecher
Hopkins, Lemuel
Hopkins, Samuel, 1721–1803
Hosmer, Titus
Hotchkiss, Benjamin Berkeley
Howe, Henry

Howe, John Ireland
Howland, Gardiner Greene
Hubbard, Henry Griswold
Hubbard, Joseph Stillman
Hubbard, Richard William
Hull, Isaac
Hull, William
Humphrey, Heman
Humphreys, David
Hunt, Mary Hannah Hanchett
Hunt, Thomas Sterry
Huntington, Collis Potter
Huntington, Jabez
Huntington, Jedediah
Huntington, Samuel, 1731–1796
Huntington, Samuel, 1765–1817
Hyde, James Nevins
Ingersoll, Jared, 1722–1781
Ingersoll, Jared, 1749–1822
Ingersoll, Simon
Inglis, Alexander James
Ives, Charles Edward
Ives, Chauncey Bradley
Ives, Eli
Ives, Frederic Eugene
Ives, Levi Silliman
Jarvis, Abraham
Jenkins, John, 1728–1785
Jenkins, John, 1751–1827
Jerome, Chauncey
Jesup, Morris Ketchum
Jewett, David
Jewett, William
Jocelyn, Nathaniel
Johnson, Samuel
Johnson, Seth Whitmore
Johnson, Treat Baldwin
Johnson, William
Johnson, William Samuel
Johnston, Josiah Stoddard
Jones, Joel
Judah, Theodore Detton
Keeler, James Edward
Keep, Robert Porter
Kelley, Alfred
Kellogg, Albert
Kellogg, Edward
Kellogg, Martin
Kellogg, William Pitt
Kensett, John Frederick
Kilbourne, James
King, Dan
Kingsbury, John
Kingsley, James Luce
Kirby, Ephraim
Kirkland, Samuel
Kirtland, Jared Potter
Knight, Jonathan
Ladd-Franklin, Christine
Lanman, Charles Rockwell
Lanman, Joseph
Larned, Joseph Gay Eaton
Larrabee, William
Law, Andrew
Law, John
Law, Jonathan
Law, Richard
Leaming, Jeremiah
Leavenworth, Henry
Leavitt, Humphrey Howe
Ledyard, John
Ledyard, William
Lee, Charles Alfred

Leonard, William Andrew
Lester, Charles Edwards
Levermore, Charles Herbert
Lockwood, Ralph Ingersoll
Lockwood, Robert Wilton
Loomis, Arphaxed
Loomis, Dwight
Loomis, Elias
Lord, Daniel
Lord, David Nevins
Lord, Eleazar
Lothrop, Harriett Mulford Stone
Lusk, Graham
Lusk, William Thompson
Lyman, Chester Smith
Lyman, Phineas
Lynds, Elam
Lyon, Nathaniel
McClellan, George, 1796–1847
McGwney, Michael Joseph
MacLean, George Edwin
McLevy, Jasper
McMahon, Brien
Mallary, Rollin Carolas
Mansfield, Edward Deering
Mansfield, Jared
Mansfield, Joseph King Fenno
Mansfield, Richard
Marble, Danforth
Marks, Amasa Abraham
Marsh, John
Marshall, Daniel
Marvin, Dudley
Mason, Jeremiah
Mason, William
Masson, Thomas Lansing
Mather, Frank Jewett, Jr.
Mather, Samuel Livingston
Mather, William Williams
Mattocks, John
Meigs, Josiah
Meigs, Return Jonathan, 1740–1823
Meigs, Return Jonathan, 1764–1824
Merrill, Selah
Miller, Emily Clark Huntington
Miller, Oliver
Mills, Samuel John
Miner, Charles
Mitchell, Donald Grant
Mitchell, Elisha
Mitchell, Samuel Augustus
Mitchell, Stephen Mix
Moody, (Arthur Edson) Blair
Morey, Samuel
Morgan, Charles
Morgan, John Pierpont
Morris, Charles
Morris, Luzon Burritt
Morse, Jedidiah
Moses, Bernard
Moulton, Ellen Louise Chandler
Munson, Walter David
Murdock, James
Murdock, Joseph Ballard
Nettleton, Asahel
Newberry, John Strong
Newberry, Oliver
Newberry, Walter Loomis
Newcomb, Charles Leonard
Newman, Alfred
Niles, John Milton

North, Edward
North, Elisha
North, Simeon, 1765–1852
North, Simeon, 1802–1884
Northrop, Birdsey Grant
Northrop, Cyrus
Norton, Charles Hotchkiss
Nott, Abraham
Nott, Eliphalet
Nott, Samuel
Noyes, Walter Chadwick
Occom, Samson
Olmsted, Denison
Olmsted, Frederick Law
Olmsted, Gideon
Olney, Jesse
Ormsby, Waterman Lilly
Osborn, Henry Fairfield
Osborn, Norris Galpin
Osborn, Selleck
Osborne, Thomas Burr
Owen, Edward Thomas
Packer, Asa
Paddock, Benjamin Henry
Paddock, John Adams
Paine, Elijah
Painter, Gamaliel
Palmer, Albert Marshman
Palmer, Elihu
Palmer, Nathaniel Brown
Palmer, William Adams
Parish, Elijah
Park, Roswell, 1807–1869
Park, Roswell, 1852–1914
Parker, Amasa Junius
Parsons, Samuel Holden
Paterson, John
Pease, Calvin
Pease, Elisha Marshall
Pease, Joseph Ives
Peck, Charles Howard
Peck, Harry Thurston
Peck, John Mason
Peck, Tracy
Peet, Harvey Prindle
Peet, Isaac Lewis
Penfield, Frederic Courtland
Percival, James Gates
Perkins, Elisha
Perkins, Frederic Beecher
Perrin, Bernadotte
Peters, Samuel Andrew
Phelps, Almira Hart Lincoln
Phelps, Anson Greene
Phelps, Guy Rowland
Phelps, John Smith
Phelps, Oliver
Phelps, William Lyon
Phillips, Harry Irving
Picket, Albert
Pierpont, John
Pierrepont, Edwards
Piggott, James
Pinchot, Gifford
Pinney, Norman
Pitkin, Frederick Walker
Pitkin, Timothy
Pitkin, William, 1694–1769
Pitkin, William, 1725–1789
Plant, Henry Bradley
Platt, Charles Adams
Platt, Orville Hitchcock
Platter, Samuel Ball

Pond, Peter
Pond, Samuel William
Porter, Arthur Kingsley
Porter, Ebenezer
Porter, Noah
Porter, Peter Buell
Porter, Samuel
Porter, Sarah
Potter, Edward Clark
Potter, Ellen Culver
Potter, William Bancroft
Pratt, Bela Lyon
Prentice, Samuel Oscar
Prentiss, Samuel
Preston, Thomas Scott
Prudden, Theophil Mitchell
Putnam, Nina Wilcox
Pynchon, Thomas Ruggles
Quintard, Charles Todd
Quintard, George William
Ranney, William Tylee
Raymond, Charles Walker
Raymond, Daniel
Read, John, 1679/80–1749
Redfield, Justus Starr
Redfield, William C.
Reid, Samuel Chester
Remington, Eliphalet
Reynolds, Edwin
Riggs, John Markey
Ripley, James Wolfe
Robbins, Thomas
Robins, Henry Ephraim
Robinson, Edward, 1794–1863
Robinson, Henry Cornelius
Robinson, Solon
Robinson, William Callyhan
Rockwell, Alphonso David
Rogers, John, 1648–1721
Rogers, John Almanza Rowley
Rogers, Moses
Rogers, Thomas
Rogers, William Augustus
Rood, Ogden Nicholas
Root, Erastus
Root, Jesse
Rose, Chauncey
Rosenthal, Toby Edward
Rossiter, Thomas Prichard
Rowland, Thomas Fitch
Ruggles, Samuel Bulkley
Sage, Bernard Janin
Sage, Henry Williams
Saltonstall, Dudley
Sanford, Elias Benjamin
Sanford, Henry Shelton
Sassacus
Saunders, Prince
Savage, Thomas Staughton
Sawyer, Walter Howard
Scoville, Joseph Alfred
Scranton, George Whitfield
Seabury, Samuel, 1729–1796
Seabury, Samuel, 1801–1872
Sedgwick, John
Sedgwick, Theodore, 1746–1813
Sedgwick, William Thompson
Seelye, Julius Hawley
Seelye, Laurenus Clark
Setchell, William Albert
Seymour, Charles
Seymour, Thomas Hart
Shaler, William

Shaw, Nathaniel
Sheffield, Joseph Earl
Sigourney, Lydia Howard Huntley
Sill, Edward Rowland
Silliman, Benjamin, 1779–1864
Silliman, Benjamin, 1816–1885
Sloan, Alfred Pritchard, Jr.
Smith, Abby Hadassah
Smith, Arthur Henderson
Smith, Ashbel
Smith, Charles Emory
Smith, Eli
Smith, Elias
Smith, Elihu Hubbard
Smith, Harry James
Smith, Israel
Smith, James Youngs
Smith, Joel West
Smith, John Cotton, 1765–1845
Smith, Junius
Smith, Nathan, 1770–1835
Smith, Nathaniel
Smith, Roswell
Smith, Truman
Smith, Winchell
Sonnichsen, Albert
Sparks, Jared
Spencer, Ambrose
Spencer, Christopher Miner
Spencer, Elihu
Spencer, Joseph
Sperry, Nehemiah Day
Sprague, Frank Julian
Sprague, William Buell
Stanton, Henry Brewster
Stedman, Edmund Clarence
Steiner, Bernard Christian
Stephens, Ann Sophia
Sterling, John William
Stevens, Clement Hoffman
Stevens, Thomas Holdup, 1819–
 1896
Steward, Ira
Stewart, Philo Penfield
Stiles, Ezra
Stine, Charles Milton Altland
Stoddard, Amos
Stoeckel, Carl
Stone, David Marvin
Stone, Wilbur Fisk
Stone, William Oliver
Stowe, Harriet Elizabeth Beecher
Stratton, Charles Sherwood
Street, Augustus Russell
Strong, William
Stuart, Isaac William
Stuart, Moses
Sturtevant, Julian Monson
Sumner, Francis Bertody
Talcott, Andrew
Talcott, Eliza
Talcott, Joseph
Tarbox, Increase Niles
Tatlock, John Strong Perry
Taylor, Nathaniel William
Terry, Alfred Howe
Terry, Eli
Thacher, Thomas Anthony
Thomas, Seth
Thompson, Charles Oliver
Thurber, Christopher Carson
Ticknor, Elisha
Tiffany, Charles Lewis

Tod, George
Tod, John
Todd, Eli
Totten, George Muirson
Totten, Joseph Gilbert
Toucey, Isaac
Tousey, Sinclair
Town, Ithiel
Townsend, Virginia Frances
Tracy, Uriah
Troland, Leonard Thompson
True, Alfred Charles
True, Frederick William
Trumbull, Benjamin
Trumbull, Henry Clay
Trumbull, James Hammond
Trumbull, John, 1750–1831
Trumbull, John, 1756–1843
Trumbull, Jonathan, 1710–1785
Trumbull, Jonathan, 1740–1809
Trumbull, Joseph
Trumbull, Lyman
Tryon, Dwight William
Tucker, William Jewett
Tully, William
Twichell, Joseph Hopkins
Twining, Alexander Catlin
Tyler, Bennet
Tyler, Daniel
Tyler, Moses Coit
Utley, George Burwell
Van Vleck, Edward Burr
Verrill, Alpheus Hyatt
Vonnoh, Robert William
Wadsworth, James
Wadsworth, Jeremiah
Waite, Morrison Remick
Wakeley, Joseph Burton
Waldo, Samuel Lovett
Waldo, Samuel Putnam
Walker, Amasa
Walworth, Reuben Hyde
Ward, James Harmon
Warner, Jonathan Trumbull
Warner, Olin Levi
Warner, Seth
Warren, Israel Perkins
Washburn, Nathan
Watson, Sereno
Webster, Pelatiah
Welch, Adonijah Strong
Welch, William Henry
Welch, William Wickham
Weld, Theodore Dwight
Welles, Gideon
Welles, Noah
Welles, Roger
Wells, Harry Gideon
Wells, Horace
Wells, Samuel Roberts
Wells, William Harvey
Wheaton, Nathaniel Sheldon
Wheeler, Arthur Leslie
Wheeler, Nathaniel
Wheelock, Eleazar
Wheelock, John
White, William Nathaniel
Whitman, Charles Seymour
Whitney, Asa
Whittelsey, Abigail Goodrich
Wight, Frederick Coit
Wilcox, Reynold Webb
Willard, De Forest

Willard, Emma Hart
Williams, Alpheus Starkey
Williams, Edwin
Williams, Elisha
Williams, Thomas Scott
Williams, William
Williamson, William Durkee
Williston, Seth
Wilson, George Grafton
Winchester, Caleb Thomas
Winthrop, Theodore
Wolcott, Oliver, 1726–1797
Wolcott, Oliver, 1760–1833
Wolcott, Roger
Woodbridge, William
Woodruff, Timothy Lester
Woodruff, Wilford
Woodward, Samuel Bayard
Woolley, Mary Emma
Woolsey, Theodore Salisbury
Wooster, Charles Whiting
Wooster, David
Work, Henry Clay
Wright, Benjamin
Wright, Charles
Wright, Elizur
Wright, Horatio Gouverneur
Wyllys, George

DELAWARE

Bates, Daniel Moore
Bates, George Handy
Bayard, James Asheton
Bayard, Richard Henry
Bayard, Thomas Francis
Beauchamp, William
Bedford, Gunning
Bird, Robert Montgomery
Brown, John Mifflin
Budd, Edward Gowen
Burton, William
Canby, Henry Seidel
Cannon, Annie Jump
Cannon, William
Chandler, Elizabeth Margaret
Clayton, John Middleton
Coit, Henry Augustus
Cummins, George David
Davies, Samuel
Du Pont, Henry
Du Pont, Henry Algernon
Du Pont, Lammot
Du Pont, Pierre Samuel
Emerson, Gouverneur
Evans, Oliver
Fisher, George Purnell
Forwood, William Henry
Garretson, James
Gibbons, James Sloan
Gilpin, Edward Woodward
Gray, George
Harrington, Samuel Maxwell
Howell, Richard
Johns, Clayton
Johns, John
Johns, Kensey
Johnson, Eldridge Reeves
Jones, David
Jones, Jacob
Keating, William Hypolitus
Kollock, Shepard
Lea, Isaac

Learned, Marion Dexter
Lewis, William David
Lord, William Paine
McCullough, John Griffith
Macdonough, Thomas
McKean, Joseph Borden
McKennan, Thomas McKean
   Thompson
McLane, Louis
McLane, Robert Milligan
MacWhorter, Alexander
Marquand, John Phillips
Miller, Edward
Miller, Samuel
Mitchell, Nathaniel
Moore, John Bassett
Newbold, William Romaine
Palmer, William Jackson
Parke, John
Polk, Trusten
Pyle, Howard
Read, John, 1769–1854
Read, Thomas
Ridgely, Nicholas
Rodney, Caesar
Rodney, Caesar Augustus
Rodney, Thomas
Ross, George
Saulsbury, Eli
Saulsbury, Gove
Saulsbury, Willard, 1820–1892
Saulsbury, Willard, 1861–1927
Smyth, Herbert Weir
Squibb, Edward Robinson
Stewart, John George
Sykes, George
Thomas, Lorenzo
Tilton, James
Torbert, Alfred Thomas Ar-
   chimedes
Townsend, George Alfred
Van Dyke, Nicholas, 1738–1789
Van Dyke, Nicholas, 1770–1826
Wales, Leonard Eugene
White, Samuel
Wiley, Andrew Jackson
Wilson, Clarence True

DISTRICT OF COLUMBIA

Ashford, Bailey Kelly
Baker, William Mumford
Barber, Donn
Beale, Edward Fitzgerald
Bowie, Richard Johns
Brannan, John Milton
Breck, George William
Broderick, David Colbreth
Burke, Billie
Carroll, Samuel Sprigg
Cassidy, Marshall Whiting
Colby, Frank Moore
Cook, Will Marion
Corcoran, William Wilson
Cranch, Christopher Pearse
Craven, Thomas Tingey
Da Costa, John Chalmers
Davis, Benjamin Oliver, Sr.
Davis, Watson
Dimitry, Charles Patton
Dorsey, Anna Hanson McKenney
Drew, Charles Richard
Dulles, John Foster

Ewell, Benjamin Stoddert
Ewell, Richard Stoddert
Farrington, Joseph Rider
Fay, Sidney Bradshaw
Fitzpatrick, John Clement
Force, Manning Ferguson
Garrison, Fielding Hudson
Gauss, Clarence Edward
Getty, George Washington
Gibbons, Floyd
Gilliss, James Melville
Goldsborough, Louis Malesherbes
Graham, William Montrose
Graves, Alvin Cushman
Hartley, Frank
Hodes, Henry Irving
Hodgson, William Brown
Holly, James Theodore
Houston, Charles Hamilton
Hunter, David
Hyatt, Alpheus
Janney, Oliver Edward
Johnson, Robert Underwood
Johnston, Eric Allen
Kelser, Raymond Alexander
King of William, James
Lenthall, John
Lewis, Fulton, Jr.
Lipscomb, Andrew Adgate
Lovell, Mansfield
McCormick, Cyrus Hall
McGuire, Joseph Deakins
McLean, Edward Beale
McNamee, Graham
Magruder, George Lloyd
Manning, Marie
Mason, James Murray
Mattingly, Garrett
Maynard, George Willoughby
Meade, Robert Leamy
Nicholson, William Jones
Noyes, Frank Brett
O'Neale, Margaret
Peary, Josephine Diebitsch
Pilling, James Constantine
Pleasonton, Alfred
Plunkett, Charles Peshall
Pollock, Channing
Pratt, Thomas George
Queen, Walter W.
Ramsay, Francis Munroe
Rawlings, Marjorie Kinnan
Richardson, Charles Williamson
Riggs, George Washington
Rodgers, John, 1881–1926
Schroeder, Seaton
Scott, William Lawrence
Seibold, Louis
Semmes, Alexander Jenkins
Semmes, Thomas Jenkins
Shellabarger, Samuel
Shepherd, Alexander Robey
Shuster, W(illiam) Morgan
Slicer, Thomas Roberts
Sousa, John Philip
Southworth, Emma Dorothy Eliza Nevitte
Steers, George
Stoek, Harry Harkness
Swann, Thomas
Towle, George Makepeace
Tree, Lambert
Vance, Louis Joseph

Wainwright, Richard, 1849–1926
Watterson, Henry
Weaver, Aaron Ward
West, James Edward
Willard, Joseph Edward
Winlock, Herbert Eustis
Winslow, Cameron McRae
Wormley, James

FLORIDA

Avery, Isaac Wheeler
Bellamy, Elizabeth Whitfield Croom
Bloxham, William Dunnington
Brooke, John Mercer
Broward, Napoleon Bonaparte
Bryan, Mary Edwards
Davis, Edmund Jackson
Drayton, William
Forbes, John Murray
Geiger, Roy Stanley
Hurston, Zora Neale
Johnson, James Weldon
Kirby-Smith, Edmund
McIntosh, John Bailie
Merrill, Charles Edward
Pace, Edward Aloysius
Raney, George Pettus
Smith, Lillian Eugenia
Summerall, Charles Pelot
Turnbull, Robert James
Zacharias, Ellis Mark

GEORGIA

Abbott, Robert Sengstacke
Alexander, Edward Porter
Allen, Young John
Anderson, George Thomas
Andrew, James Osgood
Andrews, Garnett
Arnold, Richard Dennis
Atkinson, William Yates
Bacon, Augustus Octavius
Baker, Daniel
Barrett, Charles Simon
Barrett, Janie Porter
Bass, William Capers
Battey, Robert
Battle, Cullen Andrews
Benning, Henry Lewis
Benson, William Shepherd
Berry, Martha McChesney
Bibb, William Wyatt
Black, Eugene Robert
Blalock, Alfred
Bleckley, Logan Edwin
Blount, James Henderson
Boudinot, Elias
Boudinot, Elias Cornelius
Bowie, James
Bozeman, John M.
Bulloch, James Dunwody
Callaway, Morgan
Campbell, Henry Fraser
Campbell, John Archibald
Candler, Allen Daniel
Candler, Asa Griggs
Candler, Warren Akin
Cardozo, Jacob Newton
Carnochan, John Murray
Chivers, Thomas Holley

Clay, Joseph
Clements, Judson Claudius
Clopton, David
Cobb, Andrew Jackson
Cobb, Howell
Cobb, Thomas Reade Rootes
Cobb, Tyrus Raymond ("Ty")
Cohen, John Sanford
Collier, John
Colquitt, Alfred Holt
Cook, Philip
Couper, James Hamilton
Cox, Edward Eugene
Crawford, George Walker
Crawford, Martin Jenkins
Culberson, David Browning
Cumming, Alfred
Curry, Jabez Lamar Monroe
Dawson, William Crosby
Dawson, William Levi
Dickson, David
Divine, Father
Doughty, William Henry
Elliott, Sarah Barnwell
Evans, Augusta Jane
Evans, Clement Anselm
Eve, Paul Fitzsimons
Fannin, James Walker
Felton, Rebecca Latimer
Felton, William Harrell
Few, Ignatius Alphonso
Fitzpatrick, Benjamin
Fletcher, Duncan Upshaw
Frémont, John Charles
Furlow, Floyd Charles
Gaines, Wesley John
Gartrell, Lucius Jeremiah
George, James Zachariah
George, Walter Franklin
Gibbons, Thomas
Gibson, Joshua
Gordon, John Brown
Gordon, William Washington
Goulding, Francis Robert
Grady, Henry Woodfin
Grant, John Thomas
Habersham, Joseph
Hadas, Moses
Hale, William Gardner
Hall, Charles Henry
Hammond, Nathaniel Job
Harben, William Nathaniel
Hardee, William Joseph
Hardwick, Thomas William
Hardy, Oliver Norvell
Harris, Joel Chandler
Harris, Julian La Rose
Harris, William Littleton
Harrison George Paul
Harrison, William Pope
Haygood, Atticus Green
Haygood, Laura Askew
Henderson, Fletcher Hamilton
Herring, Augustus Moore
Herty, Charles Holmes
Hill, Benjamin Harvey
Hill, Walter Barnard
Hillyer, Junius
Hodges, Courtney Hicks
Holsey, Lucius Henry
Hope, John
Hopkins, Isaac Stiles
Houston, John

Howell, Evan Park
Howley, Richard
Hubbard, Richard Bennett
Hudson, Claude Silbert
Hughes, Dudley Mays
Hyer, Robert Stewart
Iverson, Alfred
Jackson, Henry Rootes
Jackson, James, 1819–1887
Jacobs, Joseph, 1859–1929
Johnson, Herschel Vespasian
Johnston, Richard Malcolm
Jones, Charles Colcock
Jones, Joseph
Jones, Thomas Goode
Judson, Frederick Newton
Keener, William Albert
Kerneys, Edward
Kilpatrick, William Heard
King, Martin Luther, Jr.
Knight, Lucian Lamar
Lamar, Gazaway Bugg
Lamar, Joseph Rucker
Lamar, Lucius Quintus Cincinnatus
Lamar, Mirabeau Buonaparte
Langworthy, Edward
LeConte, John
LeConte, Joseph
Lee, Ivy Ledbetter
Lee, James Wideman
Lincecum, Gideon
Lomax, Louis Emanuel
Long, Crawford Williamson
Longstreet, Augustus Baldwin
Lumpkin, Joseph Henry
McAdoo, William Gibbs
McAllister, Hall
McAllister, Matthew Hall
McAllister, Samuel Ward
McCullers, Carson
McDaniel, Henry Dickerson
McDuffie, George
McGillivray, Alexander
McIntosh, William
McKinley, Carlyle
McKinstry, Alexander
McLaws, Lafayette
Maxwell, Augustus Emmett
Maxwell, George Troup
Mayes, Joel Bryan
Meigs, Montgomery Cunningham
Mell, Patrick Hues, 1814–1888
Mell, Patrick Hues, 1850–1918
Melton, James
Milledge, John
Millis, Walter
Milner, John Turner
Milton, John
Mitchell, Margaret Munnerlyn
Moore, George Fleming
Morehouse, Ward
Murrow, Joseph Samuel
Nisbet, Eugenius Aristides
Northen, William Jonathan
O'Connor, Mary Flannery
Odum, Howard Washington
Oemler, Arminius
Ogburn, William Fielding
Osceola
Paschal, George Washington
Peabody, George Foster
Pendleton, Edmund Monroe

Perry, William Flake
Phillips, Ulrich Bonnell
Phinizy, Ferdinand
Pierce, George Foster
Pierce, William Leigh
Pinchback, Pinckney Benton Stewart
Rainey, Gertrude Malissa Nix Pridgett
Riegger, Wallingford
Rivers, Thomas Milton
Robinson, Ruby Doris Smith
Root, John Wellborn
Rucker, George ("Nap")
St. John, Isaac Munroe
Sanders, Billington McCarter
Saunders, William Lawrence, 1856–1931
Scarborough, William Saunders
Sherwood, Thomas Adiel
Shorter, John Gill
Silcox, Ferdinand Augustus
Simmons, Thomas Jefferson
Smith, Albert Merriman
Smith, Buckingham
Smith, Charles Henry, 1826–1903
Spalding, Thomas
Speer, Emory
Spencer, Samuel
Stallings, Laurence Tucker
Stephens, Alexander Hamilton
Stephens, Linton
Stokes, Thomas Lunsford, Jr.
Stovall, Pleasant Alexander
Sydnor, Charles Sackett
Talmadge, Eugene
Tattnall, Josiah
Taylor, Charlotte De Bernier
Tensler, Rudolf Bolling
Thomas, Charles Spalding
Ticknor, Francis Orray
Tobias, Channing Heggie
Toombs, Robert Augustus
Towers, John Henry
Towns, George Washington Bonaparte
Troup, George Michael
Tucker, Henry Holcombe
Twiggs, David Emanuel
Upshaw, William David
Wailes, Benjamin Leonard Covington
Walker, William Henry Talbot
Ward, John Elliott
Watie, Stand
Watson, Thomas Edward
Wayne, James Moore
Wheeler, Joseph
White, Walter Francis
Willie, Asa Hoxie
Winkler, Edwin Theodore
Winship, Blanton
Wofford, William Tatum
Wood, John Stephens
Wright, Richard Robert
Yancey, William Lowndes

HAWAII

Alexander, William Dewitt
Armstrong, Samuel Chapman
Baldwin, Henry Perrine
Bingham, Hiram

Carter, Henry Alpheus Peirce
Castle, William Richards, Jr.
Dillingham, Walter Francis
Dole, Sanford Ballard
Gulick, John Thomas
Gulick, Luther Halsey, 1828–1891
Gulick, Luther Halsey, 1865–1918
Hillebrand, William Francis
Kalanianaole, Jonah Kuhio
Lathrop, George Parsons
Thurston, Lorrin Andrews

IDAHO

Borglum John Gutzon de la Mothe
Jardine, William Marion
Kamaiakan
Sacagawea
Welker, Herman

ILLINOIS

Abbott, Emma
Abt, Isaac Arthur
Adams, Cyrus Cornelius
Adams, Frank Ramsay
Adams, Franklin Pierce
Addams, Jane
Alcorn, James Lusk
Allison, Samuel King
Atwood, Wallace Walter
Austin, Mary
Ayres, William Augustus
Bacon, Henry
Baker, James
Bancroft, Edgar Addison
Bancroft, Frederic
Barrett, Albert Moore
Barrow, Edward Grant
Barrows, David Prescott
Barton, William Eleazar
Beaupré, Arthur Matthias
Bendix, Vincent
Bentley, Arthur Fisher
Bernays, Augustus Charles
Bestor, Arthur Eugene
Bettendorf, William Peter
Bevan, Arthur Dean
Black, Greene Vardiman
Black Hawk
Blackstone, Harry
Bliss, Gilbert Ames
Bloom, Sol
Bloomfield, Leonard
Bode, Boyd Henry
Borah, William Edgar
Boring, William Alciphron
Bosworth, Edward Increase
Bovard, Oliver Kirby
Bowen, Louise De Koven
Brann, William Cowper
Breasted, James Henry
Breckinridge, Henry Skillman
Brennemann, Joseph
Brophy, Truman William
Brown, Gertrude Foster
Brunswick, Ruth Mack
Bryan, Charles Wayland
Bryan, William Jennings
Bryant, Ralph Clement
Bumstead, Henry Andrews
Burroughs, Edgar Rice

Bush, Lincoln
Calkins, Earnest Elmo
Capps, Edward
Carpenter, John Alden
Chalmers, William James
Chamberlain, Henry Richardson
Chamberlin, Thomas Chrowder
Chandler, Raymond Thornton
Chase, (Mary) Agnes Merrill
Coghill, George Ellett
Cohn, Alfred A.
Colton, George Radcliffe
Comiskey, Grace Elizabeth Reidy
Conger, Edwin Hurd
Conover, Harry Sayles
Coolbrith, Ina Donna
Coolidge, Elizabeth Penn Sprague
Copley, Ira Clifton
Coquillett, Daniel William
Cort, Edwin Charles
Costigan, George Purcell
Crane, Charles Richard
Crane, Frank
Crothers, Rachel
Crothers, Samuel McChord
Cudahy, Edward Aloysius, Jr.
Cummings, Walter Joseph
Cushman, Vera Charlotte Scott
Danenhower, John Wilson
Davis, Arthur Powell
Davis, Pauline Morton Sabin
Davisson, Clinton Joseph
Dell, Floyd James
Dille, John Flint
Dirksen, Everett McKinley
Disney, Walter Elias ("Walt")
Donaldson, Jesse Monroe
Donoghue, John
Dos Passos, John Roderigo
Doubleday, Neltje de Graff
Downes (Edwin) Olin
Drake, Francis Marion
Dressen, Charles Walter
Dunbar, (Helen) Flanders
Duniway, Abigail Jane Scott
Dunne, Finley Peter
Durkin, Martin Patrick
Duryea, Charles Edgar
Duryea, James Frank
Dyer, Louis
Easley, Ralph Montgomery
East, Edward Murray
Eddy, Manton Sprague
Elliott, John Lovejoy
Ellsworth, Lincoln
Emmett, Burton
Fearing, Kenneth Flexner
Ferris, George Washington Gale
Field, Marshall, III
Finley, John Huston
Fisher, Henry Conroy ("Bud")
Flower, Benjamin Orange
Forbes, Stephen Alfred
Frankfurter, Alfred Moritz
Fry, James Barnet
Fuller, Henry Blake
Fuller, Loie
Gale, Henry Gordon
Gardner, Gilson
Gary, Elbert Henry
Gates, Caleb Frank
Gates, John Warne
Gibbs, George

Gilbert, Charles Henry
Gilman, Arthur
Goodman, Kenneth Sawyer
Goodnight, Charles
Goudy, Frederic William
Graham, Evarts Ambrose
Gray, Glen ("Spike")
Gray, Harold Lincoln
Gray, William Scott, Jr.
Greenlaw, Edwin Almiron
Gunther, John
Hale, George Ellery
Hale, Louise Closser
Hallett, Moses
Hansberry, Lorraine Vivian
Hapgood, Hutchins
Hapgood, Norman
Harbord, James Guthrie
Harlan, James
Harrington, Mark Walrod
Harrison, Carter Henry, Jr.
Hart, George Overbury
Hartzell, Joseph Crane
Hawthorne, Charles Webster
Helmer, Bessie Bradwell
Hemingway, Ernest Miller
Hibben, John Grier
Hickok, James Butler
High, Stanley Hoflund
Higinbotham, Harlow Niles
Hills, Elijah Clarence
Hodge, John Reed
Hoerr, Normand Louis
Hokinson, Helen Elna
Holmes, Elias Burton
Horner, Henry
Hovey, Richard
Howard, Charles Perry
Howard, Leland Ossian
Hubbard, Elbert
Humphrey, Doris
Hunt, Lester Callaway
Huntington, Ellsworth
Huntington, William Edwards
Hurley, Edward Nash
Husk, Charles Ellsworth
Hyde, Charles Cheney
Illington, Margaret
Ingals, Ephraim Fletcher
Jackson, Robert R.
James, Edmund Janes
James, Louis
Jennings, Herbert Spencer
Johnson, Albert
Johnson, Harold Ogden ("Chic")
Jones, Wesley Livsey
Keane, James John
Keefe, Daniel Joseph
Kelly, Edward Joseph
Kelsey, Rayner Wickersham
Kempff, Louis
Keokuk
Kilgallen, Dorothy Mae
Kingsbury, Albert
Kirby, Rollin
Kirkman, Marshall Monroe
Koch, Fred Conrad
Kofoid, Charles Atwood
Kohlsaat, Herman Henry
Lardner, John Abbott
Lathrop, Julia Clifford
Lawson, Victor Freemont
Lee, John Doyle

Lee, William Granville
Leiber, Fritz
Leiter, Joseph
Lenz, Sidney Samuel
Lewis, Dean De Witt
Lillie, Gordon William
Lincoln, Robert Todd
Lindsay, Nicholas Vachel
Lingelbach, Anna Lane
Logan, John Alexander
Loree, Leonor Fresnel
Lowry, Thomas
Lucas, Scott Wike
McAdams, Clark
MacCameron, Robert
McClure, Robert Alexis
McConnel, John Ludlum
McCord, James Bennett
McCormick, Joseph Medill
McCormick, Robert Rutherford
McCoy, Joseph Geating
McCumber, Porter James
McKinley, William Brown
McLaughlin, Andrew Cunningham
Mann, James Robert
Marquis, Donald Robert Perry
Martin, Everett Dean
Martin, Warren Homer
Masterson, William Barclay
Maxwell, Lucien Bonaparte
Mayer, Oscar Gottfried
Maytag, Frederick Louis
Meinzer, Oscar Edward
Mendelsohn, Samuel
Micheaux, Oscar
Miller, Perry Gilbert Eddy
Millikan, Clark Blanchard
Millikan, Robert Andrews
Mitchell, James Tyndale
Mitchell, John, 1870-1919
Mitchell, Lucy Sprague
Mitchell, Wesley Clair
Monroe, Harriet
Mooney, Thomas Joseph
Morgan, Helen
Morrison, William Ralls
Motley, Willard Francis
Mulford, Clarence Edward
Munson, Thomas Volney
Nash, Charles Williams
Newell, Peter Sheaf Hersey
Nicholson, Seth Barnes
Norris, Benjamin Franklin
Norris, Charles Gilman Smith
Novy, Frederick George
Nutting, Charles Cleveland
O'Brien, Justin
Paine, Ralph Delahaye
Palmer, John McAuley
Parkhurst, John Adelbert
Parr, Samuel Wilson
Parrington, Vernon Louis
Patten, James A.
Patten, Simon Nelson
Patterson, Alicia
Patterson, Eleanor Medill
Patterson, Joseph Medill
Pearson, Drew
Pearson, Thomas Gilbert
Peattie, Donald Culross
Peek, George Nelson
Pentecost, George Frederick
Perkins, George Walbridge

Poole, Ernest Cook
Post, Charles William
Powell, Alma Webster
Powell, Maud
Rainey, Henry Thomas
Raum, Green Berry
Rawlins, John Aaron
Raymond, George Lansing
Redfield, Robert
Reed, Earl Howell
Reed, Myrtle
Reeves, Joseph Mason
Revell, Fleming Hewitt
Revell, Nellie MacAleney
Rhees, Rush
Richmond, Mary Ellen
Ridgway, Robert
Robertson, Ashley Herman
Robinson, Benjamin Lincoln
Robinson, Edward Van Dyke
Robinson, James Harvey
Rockwell, George Lincoln
Rogers, John Raphael
Rohde, Ruth Bryan Owen
Rosenwald, Julius
Ross, Edward Alsworth
Rowell, Chester Harvey
Ruby, Jack L.
Ruhl, Arthur Brown
Sandburg, Carl August
Schalk, Raymond William
  ("Cracker")
Schneider, Albert
Schroeder, Rudolph William
Schwatka, Frederick
Scott, Harvey Whitefield
Scott, John Adams
Scott, Walter Dill
Scripps, Edward Wyllis
Selig, William Nicholas
Sharp, Katharine Lucinda
Shaw, Howard Van Doren
Sheil, Bernard James
Short, Walter Campbell
Sills, Milton
Simons, Henry Calvert
Simpson, Charles Torrey
Slade, Joseph Alfred
Smith, Frank Leslie
Smith, Henry Justin
Smith, Robert Sidney
Snow, William Freeman
Snyder, John Francis
Spalding, Albert
Spalding, Albert Goodwill
Stephenson, Benjamin Franklin
Stettinius, Edward Reilly
Stone, Melville Elijah
Stone, Ormond
Stratton, Samuel Wesley
Strawn, Silas Hardy
Strong, Josiah
Strong, Walter Ansel
Stryker, Lloyd Paul
Sturges, Preston
Sunderland, Eliza Jane Read
Symons, George Gardner
Taft, Lorado Zadoc
Talbot, Arthur Newell
Teeple, John Edgar
Thayer, Tiffany Ellsworth
Thomas, Jesse Burgess
Thompson, Seymour Dwight

Thurstone, Louis Leon
Todd, Henry Alfred
Tompkins, Arnold
Townsend, Francis Everett
Turner, George Kibbe
Vanderlip, Frank Arthur
Van Doren, Carl Clinton
Van Horne, William Cornelius
Vincent, George Edgar
Wacker, Charles Henry
Walgreen, Charles Rudolph
Wallace, Henry Cantwell
Waller, Willard Walter
Ward, Arch Burdette
Ward, Lester Frank
Warman, Cy
Warmoth, Henry Clay
Waymack, William Wesley
West, Roy Owen
Westermann, William Linn
Weston, Edward Henry
Weston, Nathan Austin
Weyerhaeuser, Frederick Edward
Willard, Frank Henry
Willcox, Louise Collier
Williams, Jesse Lynch
Wilson, Edmund Beecher
Wilson, Harry Leon
Wilson, Hugh Robert
Wilson, James Harrison
Wolfe, Harry Kirke
Wright, Theodore Paul
Yancey, James Edward ("Jimmy")
Young, Art
Ziegfeld, Florenz
Ziff, William Bernard

INDIANA

Acker, Charles Ernest
Adams, Andy
Ade, George
Allport, Gordon Willard
Anderson, Edwin Hatfield
Andrew, Abram Piatt
Arvin, Newton
Atterbury, William Wallace
Aydelotte, Frank
Barnes, Charles Reid
Bass, Sam
Beadle, William Henry Harrison
Beard, Charles Austin
Beard, Mary Ritter
Beeson, Charles Henry
Bell, Lawrence Dale
Bement, Charles Sweet
Bennett, Richard
Billings, John Shaw
Blackburn, William Maxwell
Blasdel, Henry Goode
Blue, Gerald Montgomery
  ("Monte")
Boisen, Anton Theophilus
Booth, Newton
Bowers, Claude Gernade
Bradley, Lydia Moss
Buley, Roscoe Carlyle
Burnside, Ambrose Everett
Caldwell, Otis William
Calkins, Gary Nathan
Catlett, Sidney
Chapman, John Wilbur
Chase, William Merritt

Coffman, Lotus Delta
Cooper, Henry Ernest
Cooper, Kent
Cope, Arthur Clay
Crawford, Samuel Johnson
Cubberley, Ellwood Patterson
Cuppy, William Jacob (Will)
Curme, George Oliver
Daeger, Albert Thomas
Davis, Elmer Holmes
Davis, Jefferson Columbus
Davis, John Lee
Dean, James Byron
Debs, Eugene Victor
Deemer, Horace Emerson
Denby, Edwin
De Pauw, Washington Charles
Dillinger, John
Dodge, Henry
Doolittle, Charles Leander
Doolittle, Eric
Douglas, Lloyd Cassel
Dreiser, Theodore
Dresser, Louise Kerlin
Dunn, William McKee
Eads, James Buchanan
Eggleston, Edward
Eggleston, George Cary
English, William Hayden
Fazenda, Louise Marie
Fetter, Frank Albert
Fletcher, James Cooley
Fletcher, William Baldwin
Fordney, Joseph Warren
Foster, John Watson
Foster, Robert Sanford
Ghent, William James
Gimbel, Bernard Feustman
Girdler, Tom Mercer
Goode, George Brown
Goudy, William Charles
Green, Norvin
Gresham, Walter Quintin
Gridley, Charles Vernon
Grissom Virgil Ivan ("Gus")
Haan, William George
Hackley, Charles Henry
Haggerty, Melvin Everett
Hale, William Bayard
Hamtrauck, John Francis
Hannagan, Stephen Jerome
Harper, Ida Husted
Hawley, Paul Ramsey
Hay, John Milton
Hay, Mary Garrett
Hay, Oliver Perry
Hays, Will H.
Heath, Perry Sanford
Henderson, Charles Richmond
Herron, George Davis
Hibben, Paxton Pattison
Hill, Edwin Conger
Holcomb, Silas Alexander
Hollis, Ira Nelson
Holman, William Steele
Hornaday, William Temple
Hovey, Alvin Peterson
Howe, Edgar Watson
Howe, Louis McHenry
Hunter, Robert
Ingram, Jonas Howard
Jaquess, James Frazier
Jessup, Walter Albert

Johnston, Annie Fellows
Jones, George Wallace
Juday, Chancey
Julian, George Washington
Kern, John Worth
Kimball, Nathan
Klein, Charles Herbert ("Chuck")
Lane, James Henry
Leavenworth, Francis Preserved
Levinson, Salmon Oliver
Lewis, Lloyd Downs
Lilly, Josiah Kirby
Little Turtle
Logan, James Harvey
Lombard, Carole
Lowes, John Livingston
Lynd, Robert Staughton
McCrary, George Washington
McCutcheon, George Barr
McFarland, John Thomas
McHale, Kathryn
McMurry, Frank Morton
McNutt, Paul Vories
McPherson, Smith
Macy, Jesse
Major, Charles
Marshall, Thomas Riley
Martin, William Alexander Parsons
Mead, Elwood
Meek, Fielding Bradford
Mellette, Arthur Calvin
Menninger, Charles Frederick
Miller, Cincinnatus Hiner
Miller, John Franklin
Millis, Harry Alvin
Mills, Anson
Milroy, Robert Huston
Minton, Sherman
Monroe, Paul
Moody, William Vaughn
Mooney, James
Moore, Addison Webster
Moore, Philip North
Morgan, Thomas Jefferson
Morrow, William W.
Morton, Oliver Perry
Nash, Arthur
Nathan, George Jean
Nelson, William Rockhill
New, Harry Stewart
Newlon, Jesse Homer
Newsom, Herschel David
Niblack, Albert Parker
Niblack, William Ellis
Nicholson, Meredith
Nixon, William Penn
Noll, John Francis
Ogg, Frederic Austin
Oliphant, Herman
Olsen, John Sigvard ("Ole")
Osborn, Chase Salmon
Pearson, Edward Jones
Pearson, Leonard
Pearson, Raymond Allen
Philipson, David
Phillips, David Graham
Piatt, John James
Plummer, Mary Wright
Porter, Albert Gallatin
Porter, Cole
Porter, Gene Stratton
Pyle, Ernest Taylor

Randall, James Garfield
Record, Samuel James
Reisner, George Andrew
Ridpath, John Clark
Riley, James Whitcomb
Riley, William Bell
Ritter, Joseph Elmer
Rodman, Thomas Jackson
Rose, Joseph Nelson
Rovenstine, Emery Andrew
Runcie, Constance Faunt Le Roy
St. John, John Pierce
Schelling, Felix Emanuel
Scott, Fred Newton
Scott, Leroy
Shaw, (Warren) Wilbur
Shelton, Albert Leroy
Shields, Charles Woodruff
Shoup, Francis Asbury
Sims, Charles N.
Skidmore, Louis
Slipher, Vesto Melvin
Sloan, James Forman
Smith, David Roland
Smith, Walter Bedell
Sparks, William Andrew Jackson
Spooner, John Coit
Springer, William McKendree
Starbuck, Edwin Diller
Stein, Evaleen
Stephenson, Carl
Straton, John Roach
Straus, Simon William
Stubbs, Walter Roscoe
Tarkington, Booth
Taylor, Frank Bursley
Terman, Lewis Madison
Terrell, Edwin Holland
Thomas, (John William) Elmer
Thompson, James Maurice
Thompson, Oscar Lee
Thornton, Henry Worth
Thorpe, Rose Alnora Hartwick
Tolley, Howard Ross
Trueblood, Benjamin Franklin
Usher, Nathaniel Reilly
Vanderburgh, William Henry
Van Devanter, Willis
Van Hook, Weller
Veatch, Arthur Clifford
Voris, John Ralph
Wallace, Lewis
Warthin, Aldred Scott
Watson, James Eli
Webb, Clifton
Wharton, Greene Lawrence
Whetzel, Herbert Hice
Whistler, George Washington
Wickard, Claude Raymond
Wiley, Harvey Washington
Williams, Elkanah
Williams, Gaar Campbell
Willkie, Wendell Lewis
Wills, Childe Harold
Wilson, Henry Lane
Wilson, John Lockwood
Wirt, William Albert
Wissler, Clark
Wood, Thomas Bond
Wood, William Robert
Woolman, Collett Everman
Wright, George Grover
Wright, Wilbur

Yohn, Frederick Coffay

IOWA

Adams, Ephraim Douglass
Adams, Henry Carter
Adler, Felix
Alden, Cynthia May Westover
Aldrich, Bess Genevra Streeter
Anson, Adrian Constantine
Baker, Carl Lotus
Ballinger, Richard Achilles
Beer, Thomas
Bell, Frederic Somers
Benson, Oscar Herman
Binford, Jessie Florence
Bingham, Walter Van Dyke
Borg, George William
Botsford, George Willis
Bowen, Thomas Meade
Buckley, Oliver Ellsworth
Buckner, Emory Roy
Budd, Ralph
Burdick, Eugene Leonard
Burton, Marion Le Roy
Byoir, Carl Robert
Campbell, Marius Robinson
Carothers, Wallace Hume
Case, Francis Higbee
Cody, William Frederick
Collier, Hiram Price
Cone, Russell Glenn
Cook, George Cram
Cooley, Edwin Gilbert
Cowles, Gardner
De Forest, Lee
Devaney, John Patrick
Devine, Edward Thomas
Dickinson, Edwin De Witt
Dickson, Leonard Eugene
Ely, Hanson Edward
Emerson, Oliver Farrar
Evermann, Barton Warren
Garretson, Austin Bruce
Gidley, James Williams
Glaspell, Susan Keating
Graff, Everett Dwight
Gregory, Clifford Verne
Hall, James Norman
Hawley, James Henry
Herbst, Josephine Frey
Hillis, Newell Dwight
Hooper, Jessie Annette Jack
Hoover, Herbert Clark
Hope, Clifford Ragsdale
Hopkins, Harry Lloyd
Hough, Emerson
Hove, Elling
Howard, Edgar
Howard, Joseph Kinsey
Howey, Walter Crawford
Hutton, Levi William
Irwin, Robert Benjamin
Jackson, Clarence Martin
Jensen, Benton Franklin ("Ben")
Keenan, James Francis
Kerby, William Joseph
Knapp, Bradford
Koren, John
Langdon, Harry Philmore
Laughlin, Harry Hamilton
Leahy, William Daniel
Leedom, Boyd Stewart

Leopold, (Rand) Aldo
Leverett, Frank
Lewelling, Lorenzo Dow
Lewis, John Llewellyn
Lunn, George Richard
McGee, William John
McKean, James William
MacNider, Hanford
Mall, Franklin Paine
Martin, Glenn Luther ("Cy")
Maxwell, Elsa
Meredith, Edna C. Elliott
Meredith, Edwin Thomas
Merriam, Charles Edward, Jr.
Merriam, John Campbell
Miller, Glenn
Morley, Margaret Warner
Mott, Frank Luther
Nagel, Conrad
Noyes, William Albert
Paul, Josephine Bay
Phillips, John Sanburn
Plumb, Glenn Edward
Pritchard, Frederick John
Quick, John Herbert
Read, George Windle
Remey, George Collier
Reno, Milo
Reynolds, George McClelland
Ringling, Charles
Ross, Lawrence Sullivan
Rowe, Leo Stanton
Ruml, Beardsley
Russell, Charles Edward
Russell, Lillian
Ryan, Arthur Clayton
Salter, William Mackintire
Sherman, Stuart Pratt
Shorey, Paul
Smith, Courtney Craig
Smith, Fred Burton
Smith, Walter Inglewood
Springer, Charles
Springer, Frank
Stone, Warren Sanford
Stong, Phil(lip Duffield)
Stouffer, Samuel Andrew
Sunday, William Ashley
Tate, John Torrence
Tilghman, William Matthew
Van Allen, Frank
Vance, Arthur Charles ("Dazzy")
Van Vechten, Carl
Veblen, Oswald
Wallace, Henry Agard
Wallgren, Mon[rad] C[harles]
Warner, Amos Griswold
Welch, Joseph Nye
Whitcomb, Selden Lincoln
Whitehill, Clarence Eugene
Whitney, Alexander Fell
Wilbur, Curtis Dwight
Wilbur, Ray Lyman
Wilson, Mortimer
Wood, Grant
Young, Karl
Young, Lafayette

KANSAS

Bemis, Harold Edward
Braniff, Thomas Elmer
Capper, Arthur

Chaffee, Adna Romanza
Chaplin, Ralph Hosea
Chrysler, Walter Percy
Clapper, Raymond Lewis
Cobb, Frank Irving
Curry, John Steuart
Curtis, Charles
Earhart, Amelia Mary
Fisher, Dorothea Frances Canfield
Frank, Tenney
Franklin, Edward Curtis
Friday
Gregg, John Andrew
Hadley, Herbert Spencer
Harrington, John Lyle
Hatch, Carl A.
Henderson, Paul
Hinshaw, David Schull
Holmes, Julius Cecil
Johnson, Edwin Carl
Johnson, Hugh Samuel
Johnson, Osa
Johnson, Walter Perry
Johnson, Wendell Andrew Leroy
Keaton, Joseph Francis ("Buster"), V
Kuhn, Joseph Ernst
Latimer, Wendell Mitchell
Lee, John Clifford Hodges
Livingstone, Belle
McDaniel, Hattie
Marlatt, Abby Lillian
Masters, Edgar Lee
Menninger, William Claire
Mills, Enos Abijah
Murdock, Victor
Nichols, Ernest Fox
O'Hare, Kate (Richards) Cunningham
Parker, Charlie ("Bird")
Peabody, Lucy Whitehead
Pemberton, Brock
Pitts, Zasu
Runyon, Damon
Schoeppel, Andrew Frank
Slosson, Edwin Emery
Smith, Harold Dewey
Sprague, Charles Arthur
Starrett, Paul
Starrett, William Aiken
Stewart, Walter Winne
White, William Allen
Willebrandt, Mabel Walker
Woodring, Harry Hines
Wright, Henry
Zook, George Frederick

KENTUCKY

Adams, William Wirt
Alexander, Barton Stone
Alexander, Gross
Allen, Henry Tureman
Allen, James Lane
Altsheler, Joseph Alexander
Anderson, Richard Clough
Anderson, Robert
Anderson, Victor Vance
Anshutz, Thomas Pollock
Applegate, Jesse
Atchison, David Rice
Baker, Jehu
Barkley, Alben William

Baylor, Robert Emmet Bledsoe
Becknell, William
Bell, James Franklin
Bent, Silas
Berryman, Clifford Kennedy
Birney, James
Birney, James Gillespie
Blackburn, Joseph Clay Styles
Blackburn, Luke Pryor
Blair, Francis Preston
Blair, Montgomery
Bland, Richard Parks
Bledsoe, Albert Taylor
Bloch, Claude Charles
Boggs, Lillburn W.
Bolton, Sarah Tittle Barrett
Bowman, John Bryan
Boyle, Jeremiah Tilford
Bradley, William O'Connell
Bramlette, Thomas E.
Brandeis, Louis Dembitz
Breckenridge, Sophonisba Preston
Breckinridge, Desha
Breckinridge, John
Breckinridge, John Cabell
Breckinridge, Robert Jefferson
Brennan, Alfred Laurens
Bristow, Benjamin Helme
Bristow, Joseph Little
Brown, Benjamin Gratz
Brown, John Mason, Jr.
Brown, John Young
Brown, William Wells
Browning, Orville Hickman
Browning, Tod
Buchanan, Joseph Rodes
Buckner, Simon Bolivar, 1823–1914
Buckner, Simon Bolivar, 1886–1945
Buford, Abraham
Buford, John
Buford, Napoleon Bonaparte
Bullitt, Henry Massie
Burbridge, Stephen Gano
Burnam, John Miller
Butler, Burridge Davenal
Butler, William Orlando
California Joe
Canby, Edward Richard Sprigg
Carlisle, John Griffin
Carson, Christopher
Carter, Caroline Louise Dudley
Cawein, Madison Julius
Chilton, William Paris
Churchill, Thomas James
Clark, Champ
Clay, Cassius Marcellus
Cobb, Irvin Shrewsbury
Cofer, Martin Hardin
Coleman, William Tell
Combs, Leslie
Connelly, Henry
Cooper, Joseph Alexander
Corwin, Thomas
Crittenden, George Bibb
Crittenden, John Jordan
Crittenden, Thomas Leonidas
Crittenden, Thomas Theodore
Croghan, George
Cullom, Shelby Moore
Davies, William Augustine
Daviess, Maria Thompson

Davis, Garrett
Davis, Jefferson
Dickey, Theophilus Lyle
Dinwiddie, Albert Bledsoe
Doniphan, Alexander William
Drake, Benjamin
Duke, Basil Wilson
Duncan, Joseph
Dunn, Charles
Dunn, Williamson
Du Pont, Thomas Coleman
Durbin, John Price
Durrett, Reuben Thomas
Duveneck, Frank
Edwards, Ninian Wirt
Evans, Walter
Everleigh, Ada
Everleigh, Minna
Fagan, James Fleming
Fall, Albert Bacon
Fee, John Gregg
Field, Charles William
Flanagan, Webster
Flexner, Abraham
Flexner, Bernard
Flexner, Jennie Maas
Flexner, Simon
Floyd, John
Ford, John Baptiste
Foster, Ephraim Hubbard
Fowke, Gerard
Fox, Fontaine Talbot, Jr.
Fox, John William
Francis, David Rowland
Frazer, Oliver
Garrard, Kenner
Gholson, Samuel Jameson
Gibson, Randall Lee
Gilliss, Walter
Goldman, Edwin Franko
Goodloe, William Cassius
Gorman, Willis Arnold
Greathouse, Clarence Ridgeby
Green, Benjamin Edwards
Green, Duff
Green, Lewis Warner
Greene, George Sears
Griffith, David Wark
Grimes, Absalom Carlisle
Guthrie, James
Haggin, James Ben Ali
Halderman, John A.
Hall, William Whitty
Hanson, Roger Weightman
Hardin, Charles Henry
Hardin, John J.
Harlan, James
Harlan, John Marshall
Harney, Benjamin Robertson
Harrison, Carter Henry
Harrison, Elizabeth
Harrison, James
Hart, Joel Tanner
Hatch, William Henry
Hauser, Samuel Thomas
Hays, William Shakespeare
Helm, John Larue
Henderson, Yandell
Herndon, William Henry
Hill, Patty Smith
Hines, Duncan
Hines, Walker Downer
Hobson, Edward Henry

Hodgen, John Thompson
Holladay, Ben
Holman, Jesse Lynch
Holt, Joseph
Hood, John Bell
Hume, Edgar Erskine
Hunter, William C.
Ireland, John, 1827–1896
Jackson, Claiborne Fox
Jackson, John Davies
Jacob, Richard Taylor
James, Ollie Murray
Jennings, James Hennen
Johnson, Richard Mentor
Johnson, Richard W.
Johnson, Robert Ward
Johnson, Tom Loftin
Johnston, Albert Sidney
Johnston, William Preston
Jones, William Palmer
Jouett, James Edward
Jouett, Matthew Harris
Kimmel, Husband Edward
King, John Pendleton
Klaw, Marc
Knott, James Proctor
Koch, Frederick Henry
Lane, Henry Smith
Lawson, Leonidas Merion
Lee, Willis Augustus
Lewis, Joseph Horace
Lincoln, Abraham
Lincoln, Mary Todd
Linn, Lewis Fields
Logan, Stephen Trigg
Lorimer, George Horace
Lurton, Horace Harmon
McAfee, Robert Breckinridge
McCalla, William Latta
McCann, William Penn
McClernand, John Alexander
McCormack, Joseph Nathaniel
McCreary, James Bennett
McCreery, Charles
McElroy, John
McElroy, Robert McNutt
McGarvey, John William
McMillan, James Winning
McMillin, Benton
McReynolds, James Clark
Magoffin, Beriah
Magoffin, James Wiley
Majors, Alexander
Marcosson, Isaac Frederick
Marshall, Humphrey
Marshall, Thomas Alexander
Marshall, William Louis
Martin, William Thompson
Masquerier, Lewis
Matthews, Claude
Matthews, Joseph Brown
Maury, Francis Fontaine
Maxey, Samuel Bell
Maxwell, David Hervey
May, Andrew Jackson
Meigs, Return Jonathan
Miller, Henry
Miller, Samuel Freeman
Mills, Robert, 1809–1888
Mills, Roger Quarles
Mitchel, Ormsby MacKnight
Moore, William Thomas
Morehead, Charles Slaughter

Morehead, James Turner
Morgan, Thomas Hunt
Morris, Thomas Armstrong
Morrow, Edwin Porch
Morrow, Prince Albert
Morrow, Thomas Vaughan
Moss, Lemuel
Nation, Carry Amelia Moore
Nelson, Thomas Henry
Nelson, William, 1824–1862
Nolan, Philip
Norton, Elijah Hise
O'Fallon, Benjamin
O'Fallon, John
Oglesby, Richard James
O'Hara, Theodore
Palmer, Bertha Honoré
Palmer, John McAuley
Pattie, James Ohio
Peay, Austin
Phillips, Lena Madesin
Piatt, Sarah Morgan Bryan
Polk, Willis Jefferson
Pope, John
Pope, Nathaniel
Poston, Charles Debrill
Powell, Lazarus Whitehead
Powell, William Byrd
Preston, William
Price, William Thompson
Proctor, John Robert
Purnell, Benjamin
Pusey, William Allen
Rachford, Benjamin Knox
Rector, Henry Massey
Reynolds, Charles Alexander
Reynolds, Joseph Jones
Rice, Alice Caldwell Hegan
Rice, Nathan Lewis
Richardson, Tobias Gibson
Ridgely, Daniel Bowly
Rives, Hallie Erminie
Roark, Ruric Nevel
Roberts, Elizabeth Madox
Robertson, George
Robertson, Jerome Bonaparte
Rogers, James Gamble
Rollins, James Sidney
Rose, Uriah Milton
Rousseau, Lovell Harrison
Russell, William Henry
Rutledge, Wiley Blount
Sanders, George Nicholas
Saunders, Alvin
Scopes, John Thomas
Scott, Hugh Lenox
Scott, Walter Edward
Semple, Ellen Churchill
Shaler, Nathaniel Southgate
Shelby, Joseph Orville
Shields, George Howell
Short, Charles Wilkins
Shouse, Jouett
Simms, William Elliott
Smith, Gustavus Woodson
Smith, William Russell
Spalding, John Lancaster
Spalding, Martin John
Speed, James
Spence, Brent
Springer, Reuben Runyan
Stanley, Augustus Owsley
Stayton, John William

Stevenson, Adlai Ewing
Stevenson, James
Stone, Richard French
Stone, William Joel
Stuart, John Todd
Sublette, William Lewis
Switzler, William Franklin
Taylor, Marshall William
Taylor, Richard
Terry, David Smith
Tevis, Lloyd
Tichenor, Isaac Taylor
Todd, Charles Stewart
Towne, Charles Hanson
Traylor, Melvin Alvah
Underwood, Oscar Wilder
Vest, George Graham
Vinson, Fred(erick) Moore
Visscher, William Lightfoot
Walker, David, 1806–1879
Walker, David Shelby
Walker, Pinkney Houston
Walker, Stuart Armstrong
Wallace, William Ross
Waller, John Lightfoot
Walling, William English
Walters, Alexander
Warden, Robert Bruce
Warfield, Benjamin Breckinridge
Watkins, George Claiborne
Watson, John Crittenden
Webber, Charles Wilkins
Wehle, Louis Brandeis
West, William Edward
White, Alma Bridwell
Whitman, Albery Allson
Wickliffe, Charles Anderson
Wickliffe, Robert Charles
Willis, Albert Shelby
Willson, Augustus Everett
Winlock, Joseph
Witherspoon, Alexander Maclaren
Wood, Thomas John
Wrather, William Embry
Yates, Richard
Yeaman, William Pope

LOUISIANA

Aime, Valcour
Basso, (Joseph) Hamilton
Beauregard, Pierre Gustave Toutant
Bechet, Sidney
Behan, William James
Bermudez, Edouard Edmond
Blanchard, Newton Crain
Bouligny, Dominique
Bouvet, Marie Marguerite
Breaux, Joseph Arsenne
Brooks, Overton
Cable, George Washington
Caffery, Donelson
Cahn, Edmond Nathaniel
Canonge, Louis Placide
Celestin, Oscar "Papa"
Chouteau, Jean Pierre
Chouteau, René Auguste
Clark, Felton Grandison
Collens, Thomas Wharton
Connelly, Pierre Francis
Cushman, Pauline
Deléry, François Charles

Dimitry, Alexander
Dugué, Charles Oscar
Edeson, Robert
Elder, Susan Blanchard
Elkin, William Lewis
Eustis, George
Eustis, James Biddle
Faget, Jean Charles
Farrar, Edgar Howard
Fay, Edwin Whitfield
Fiske, Minnie Maddern
Fortier, Alcée
Foster, Murphy James
Gayarré, Charles Étienne Arthur
Gherardi, Bancroft
Goldman, Mayer C.
Gottschalk, Louis Moreau
Hall, Luther Egbert
Harrod, Benjamin Morgan
Hébert, Louis
Hébert, Paul Octave
Herriman, George Joseph
Hunt, Carleton
Hunt, Gaillard
Janin, Louis
Janvier, Margaret Thomson
Kenner, Duncan Farrar
Kennicott, Robert
King, Grace Elizabeth
Koenigsberg, Moses
La Barge, Joseph
Lafon, Thomy
Latil, Alexandre
Ledbetter, Huddie ("Leadbelly")
Lejeune, John Archer
Leslie, Miriam Florence Folline
Lisa, Manuel
Long, Earl Kemp
Long, Huey Pierce
Ludeling, John Theodore
Lynch, John Roy
McEnery, Samuel Douglas
Marigny, Bernard
Matas, Rudolph
Matthews, James Brander
Menken, Adah Isaacs
Mercier, Charles Alfred
Morgan, James Morris
Morgan, Philip Hicky
Morphy, Paul Charles
Morrison, Delesseps Story
Morton, Ferdinand Joseph ("Jelly Roll")
Mouton, Alexander
Nicholls, Francis Redding Tillou
Oliver, Joseph
Osgood, Howard
Oswald, Lee Harvey
Ott, Melvin Thomas ("Mel")
Patterson, Thomas Harman
Pavy, Octave
Perez, Leander Henry
Pope, James Pinckney
Provosty, Olivier Otis
Richardson, Henry Hobson
Roman, André Bienvenu
Rouquette, Adrien Emmanuel
Rouquette, François Dominique
Scarborough, Lee Rutland
Séjour, Victor
Smith, Marcus
Sothern, Edward Hugh
Souchon, Edmond

Stuart, Ruth McEnery
Thierry, Camille
Turpin, Ben
Viel, François Étienne Bernard Alexandre
Vignaud, Henry
Vileré, Jacques Philippe
Walker, Sarah Breedlove
Wells, James Madison
White, Edward Douglass
Wills, Harry
Wiltz, Louis Alfred

MAINE

Abbot, Ezra
Abbot, Gorham Dummer
Abbott, Edward
Abbott, Frank
Abbott, Jacob
Abbott, John Stevens Cabot
Akers, Benjamin Paul
Akers, Elizabeth Chase
Albee, Edward Franklin
Alden, James
Alexander, De Alva Stanwood
Allen, William Henry
Allinson, Anne Crosby Emery
Ames, Adelbert
Anderson, Martin Brewer
Andrew, John Albion
Andrews, George Pierce
Andrews, Israel DeWolf
Bailey, Rufus William
Baker, James Hutchins
Banks, Charles Edward
Barker, Benjamin Fordyce
Barker, Jacob
Barrett, Benjamin Fiske
Bartol, Cyrus Augustus
Bates, Arlo
Bates, James
Beaman, Charles Cotesworth
Bean, Leon Lenwood
Berry, Hiram Gregory
Berry, Nathaniel Springer
Bickmore, Albert Smith
Black, Frank Swett
Blunt, James Gillpatrick
Bogan, Louise Marie
Bond, William Cranch
Boutelle, Charles Addison
Brackett, Edward Augustus
Bradbury, James Ware
Bradbury, William Batchelder
Bradley, Milton
Brannan, Samuel
Brewster, Ralph Owen
Bridges, (Henry) Styles
Brooks, Erastus
Brooks, James
Brooks, Noah
Brooks, Peter Chardon
Brown, Samuel Gilman
Browne, Charles Farrar
Cary, Annie Louise
Cayvan, Georgia
Chadbourne, Paul Ansel
Chamberlain, Joshua Lawrence
Chandler, Peleg Whitman
Chase, George
Cheever, George Barrell
Cheever, Henry Theodore

Clarke, McDonald
Clarke, Rebecca Sophia
Clarkson, Coker Fifield
Cobb, Sylvanus, 1798–1866
Cobb, Sylvanus, 1823–1887
Coburn, Abner
Coffin, Charles Albert
Coffin, Robert Peter Tristram
Colby, Gardner
Cole, Joseph Foxcroft
Colman, Samuel
Cook, Walter Wheeler
Copeland, Charles Townsend
Cross, Arthur Lyon
Cummings, Joseph
Curtis, Cyrus Hermann Kotzschmar
Curtis, Olin Alfred
Cutler, Elliott Carr
Dana, Napoleon Jackson Tecumseh
Daveis, Charles Stewart
Davis, Henry Gassett
Davis, Owen Gould
Davis, Raymond Cazallis
Davis, William Hammatt
Day, Holman Francis
Day, James Roscoe
Deane, Charles
Dearing, John Lincoln
Deering, Nathaniel
Deering, William
Dennison, Aaron Lufkin
Dingley, Nelson
Dix, Dorothea Lynde
Dole, Charles Fletcher
Dow, Lorenzo
Dow, Neal
Drinkwater, Jennie Maria
Dryden, John Fairfield
Dunlap, Robert Pinckney
Eastman, Charles Gamage
Eckstorm, Fannie Hardy
Edes, Robert Thaxter
Elliott, Maxine
Emerson, Ellen Russell
Emerson, George Barrell
Emerson, James Ezekiel
Emery, Henry Crosby
Emery, Lucilius Alonzo
Emery, Stephen Albert
Estes, Dana
Evans, George
Everett, Charles Carroll
Fairfield, John
Farmer, Hannah Tobey Shapleigh
Farrington, Wallace Rider
Felch, Alpheus
Fernald, Charles Henry
Fernald, James Champlin
Fernald, Merritt Lyndon
Fessenden, Francis
Fessenden, James Deering
Fessenden, Samuel
Fillebrown, Thomas
Fisher, Clark
Fisher, Ebenezer
Flagg, Edmund
Flint, Charles Ranlett
Folsom, George
Foster, Benjamin
Freeman, John Ripley
Frye, William Pierce

Fuller, Melville Weston
Gammon, Elijah Hedding
Gannett, Henry
Garcelon, Alonzo
Garman, Charles Edward
George, Gladys
Gerrish, Frederic Henry
Gibson, Paris
Gill, Laura Drake
Ginn, Edwin
Goddard, Henry Herbert
Goddard, Morrill
Goddard, Pliny Earle
Goodale, George Lincoln
Goodale, Stephen Lincoln
Goodwin, Daniel Raynes
Goodwin, Ichabod
Goodwin, John Noble
Gould, George Milbry
Grant, Albert Weston
Grant, Claudius Buchanan
Grant, George Barnard
Greenough, James Bradstreet
Griffin, Eugene
Griswold, William McCrillis
Grover, Cuvier
Grover, La Fayette
Hale, Eugene
Hall, Edwin Herbert
Hamlin, Alfred Dwight Foster
Hamlin, Charles
Hamlin, Cyrus
Hamlin, Hannibal
Harris, George
Harris, Samuel
Hartford, George Huntington
Hartley, Marsden
Hatch, Edward
Hatch, Rufus
Hawkins, Dexter Arnold
Hayes, Edward Carey
Hayes, John Lord
Hill, Frank Alpine
Hill, James
Hillard, George Stillman
Hinds, Asher Crosby
Hitchcock, Roswell Dwight
Holden, Liberty Emery
Howard, Blanche Willis
Howard, Oliver Otis
Howard, Volney Erskine
Howe, Albion Parris
Howe, Lucien
Howe, Timothy Otis
Hubbard, John
Hubbard, Thomas Hamlin
Hughes, Charles Frederick
Hume, William
Hussey, Obed
Ingalls, Melville Ezra
Ingraham, Joseph Holt
Jackson, John Adams
Jewett, Charles Coffin
Jewett, John Punchard
Jewett, Sarah Orne
Johnson, Henry
Johnson, Jonathan Eastman
Jones, Rufus Matthew
Jones, Sybil
Jordan, Edwin Oakes
Kavanagh, Edward
Kellogg, Elijah
Kimball, Sumner Increase

Kimball, William Wirt
King, Henry Melville
King, Horatio
King, Rufus
King, William
Klingelsmith, Margaret Center
Ladd, Edwin Fremont
Lane, Gertrude Battles
Lane, Horace M.
Lapham, William Berry
Larrabee, William Clark
Little, Charles Coffin
Littledale, Clara Savage
Long, John Davis
Longfellow, Henry Wadsworth
Longfellow, Samuel
Longfellow, Stephen
Longfellow, William Pitt Preble
Lord, Herbert Mayhew
Lord, Nathan
Loring, Charles Morgridge
Lovejoy, Elijah Parish
Lovejoy, Owen
Low, Frederick Ferdinand
Lunt, Orrington
Mabery, Charles Frederic
McCulloch, Hugh
McGraw, John Harte
McLellan, Isaac
Magoun, George Frederic
Malcolm, Daniel
Manley, Joseph Homan
Marble, Albert Prescott
Mason, Luther Whiting
Mason, Otis Tufton
Mathews, Shailer
Mathews, William
Maxim, Hiram Stevens
Maxim, Hudson
Mellen, Grenville
Merriam, Henry Clay
Merrick, Samuel Vaughan
Merrill, Elmer Drew
Merrill, George Perkins
Millay, Edna St. Vincent
Mills, Hiram Francis
Mitchell, Edward Page
Moore, Anne Carroll
Morrill, Anson Peaslee
Morrill, Edmund Needham
Morrill, Lot Myrick
Morse, Charles Wyman
Morse, Edward Sylvester
Morse, Freeman Harlow
Morton, Charles Gould
Moses, George Higgins
Mosher, Thomas Bird
Munsey, Frank Andrew
Neal, John
Neal, Josephine Bicknell
Nelson, Charles Alexander
Nichols, Charles Henry
Nichols, George Ward
Noble, Frederick Alphonso
Norcross, Orlando Whitney
Nordica, Lillian
North, William
Noyes, Crosby Stuart
Nye, Edgar Wilson
O'Brien, Jeremiah
O'Brien, Richard
Osgood, Herbert Levi
Packard, Alpheus Spring

Packard, Joseph
Paine, Henry Warren
Paine, John Knowles
Parker, Edwin Pond
Parris, Albion Keith
Parris, Alexander
Parsons, Usher
Parton, Sara Payson Willis
Patten, Gilbert
Peavey, Frank Hutchinson
Pepperrell, Sir William
Perham, Josiah
Perkins, George Clement
Peters, John Andrew
Phelps, Thomas Stowell
Phips, Sir William
Pike, James Shepherd
Pike, Mary Hayden Green
Pingree, Hazen Stuart
Poor, Henry Varnum
Poor, John Alfred
Pratt, William Veazie
Preble, Edward
Preble, George Henry
Preble, William Pitt
Prentiss, Elizabeth Payson
Prentiss, George Lewis
Prentiss, Seargent Smith
Proctor, Frederick Frances
Putnam, George Palmer
Putnam, William Le Baron
Reed, Elizabeth Armstrong
Reed, Thomas Brackett
Richards, Robert Hallowell
Richardson, Charles Francis
Rideout, Henry Milner
Roberts, Kenneth Lewis
Robinson, Edwin Arlington
Rogers, Edith Nourse
Rogers, John Rankin
Rowse, Samuel Worcester
Russell, Osborne
Sargent, Dudley Allen
Savage, Minot Judson
Scammon, Jonathan Young
Sewall, Arthur
Sewall, Frank
Sewall, Harold Marsh
Sewall, Joseph Addison
Sewall, Stephen
Sheldon, Edward Stevens
Sheldon, Henry Newton
Shepley, George Foster
Sibley, John Langdon
Simmons, Franklin
Sleeper, Jacob
Small, Albion Woodbury
Small, Alvan Edmond
Smiley, Albert Keith
Smith, Charles Henry, 1827–1902
Smith, Elizabeth Oakes Prince
Smith, George Otis
Smith, Henry Boynton
Smith, Seba
Smith, Theodate Louise
Smyth, Egbert Coffin
Smyth, Newman
Smyth, William
Soule, Joshua
Southgate, Horatio
Spofford, Harriet Elizabeth Prescott
Stanley, Francis Edgar

Stanwood, Edward
Starrett, Laroy S.
Stearns, Frederic Pike
Stephens, Charles Asbury
Stetson, Augusta Emma Simmons
Stetson, William Wallace
Stevens, John Frank
Stevens, John Leavitt
Stevens, William Bacon
Stickney, Alpheus Beede
Storer, David Humphreys
Sturtevant, Benjamin Franklin
Sullivan, James
Sullivan, Louis Robert
Sullivan, William
Swallow, George Clinton
Swanton, John Reed
Talbot, Emily Fairbanks
Thatcher, Benjamin Bussey
Thatcher, Henry Knox
Thomas, William Widgery
Thomes, William Henry
Thorndike, Ashley Horace
Thornton, John Wingate
Thrasher, John Sidney
Thwing, Charles Franklin
Tincker, Mary Agnes
Townsend, Luther Tracy
Tripp, Bartlett
Tripp, Guy Eastman
Tuck, Amos
Tuttle, Charles Wesley
Tyler, Charles Mellen
Upton, George Bruce
Verrill, Addison Emery
Vinton, Francis Laurens
Vinton, Frederic Porter
Vose, George Leonard
Walker, Williston
Washburn, Cadwallader Colden
Washburn, Israel
Washburn, William Drew
Washburne, Elihu Benjamin
Waters, William Everett
Weymouth, Frank Elwin
Whipple, William
White, Ellen Gould Harmon
White, James Clarke
Whitman, Charles Otis
Whitman, Royal
Wilder, Harris Hawthorne
Willard, Joseph
Williams, Reuel
Willis, Nathaniel Parker
Winslow, Edward Francis
Wood, Frederick Hill
Wood, Sarah Sayward Barrell Keating
Woolson, Abba Louisa Goold
Young, Aaron
Young, Josue Maria

MARYLAND

Adams, Thomas Sewall
Alexander, John Henry
Alvey, Richard Henry
Andrews, John
Archer, James J.
Archer, John
Archer, Stevenson
Bachrach, Louis Fabian
Badger, Charles Johnston

Baer, William Stevenson
Baetjer, Frederick Henry
Baker, John Franklin
Bamberger, Louis
Bannister, Nathaniel Harrington
Barber, Edwin Atlee
Barnett, George Ernest
Barney, Joshua
Bartholow, Roberts
Bassett, Richard
Baxley, Henry Willis
Bayard, James Ash(e)ton
Bayard, John Bubenheim
Beach, Sylvia Woodbridge
Beall, Samuel Wootton
Beatty, Adam
Bonaparte, Charles Joseph
Bonaparte, Elizabeth Patterson
Bonaparte, Jerome Napoleon
Bond, Hugh Lennox
Bond, Shadrach
Bond, Thomas
Bonsal, Stephen
Booth, Edwin Thomas
Booth, John Wilkes
Bordley, John Beale
Boston, Charles Anderson
Bowie, Oden
Bowie, Robert
Bowie, William
Bowles, William Augustus
Bozman, John Leeds
Bradford, Augustus Williamson
Bradford, Edward Green
Breckinridge, William Campbell Preston
Brookings, Robert Somers
Brown, George William
Brown, Lawrason
Browne, William Hand
Buchanan, Franklin
Buchanan, John
Buchanan, Robert Christie
Buckler, Thomas Hepburn
Burns, William John
Bushman, Francis Xavier
Calvert, Charles Benedeict
Calvert, George Henry
Calverton, Victor Francis
Campbell, William Henry
Cannon, James
Carmichael, William
Carroll, Charles
Carroll, Daniel
Carroll, John
Carroll, John Lee
Carvalho, Solomon Solis
Casey, Joseph
Caswell, Richard
Chaillé-Long, Charles
Chambers, Ezekiel Forman
Chanche, John Mary Joseph
Chappell, Absalom Harris
Chase, Samuel
Chatard, Francis Silas
Chester, Colby Mitchell
Chew, Benjamin
Childs, George William
Churchman, William Henry
Clark, Charles Heber
Clarke, John Sleeper
Clayton, Joshua
Clayton, Thomas

Cohen, Mendes
Cone, Claribel
Conway, Martin Franklin
Cooke, Ebenezer
Cooper, Ezekiel
Cooper, James
Cooper, John Montgomery
Councilman, William Thomas
Crane, Anne Moncure
Creamer, David
Creagh, Michael
Creswell, John Angel James
Curtis, Alfred Allen
Davidge, John Beale
Davidson, Robert
Davis, David
Davis, Henry Gassaway
Davis, Henry Winter
Deady, Matthew Paul
Decatur, Stephen
Deems, Charles Force
Dew, Thomas Roderick
Dickinson, John, 1732–1808
Dickinson, John, 1894–1952
Dickinson, Philemon
Didier, Eugene Lemoine
Dorsey, James Owen
Douglass, Frederick
Dulany, Daniel
Duvall, Gabriel
Eberle, John
Edwards, Minian
Elder, William Henry
Elliott, Jesse Duncan
Elzey, Arnold
Emory, John
Emory, William Hemsley
Evans, Hugh Davey
Ewing, John
Fenwick, Benedict Joseph
Fenwick, Edward Dominic
Ferguson, William Jason
Few, William
Flynn, John Thomas
Ford, Henry Jones
Ford, John Thomson
Forrest, French
Foxx, James Emory
Francis, Paul James
Franklin, Philip Albright Small
Frazier, Edward Franklin
French, William Henry
Friedenwald, Aaron
Galloway, Joseph
Gantt, Henry Laurence
Garnet, Henry Highland
Garrett, John Work
Garrettson, Freeborn
Geyer, Henry Sheffie
Gibbons, Herbert Adams
Gibbons, James
Gibson, William
Gilmor, Harry
Gist, Christopher
Gist, Mordecai
Glenn, John Mark
Goddard, Calvin Hooker
Goddard, Paul Beck
Godman, John Davidson
Goldsborough, Charles
Goldsborough, Robert
Goldsborough, Thomas Alan
Goldsmith, Middleton

Gordy, John Pancoast
Gorman, Arthur Pue
Gorrell, Edgar Staley
Graves, Rosewell Hobart
Greene, Samuel Dana
Greenwald, Emanuel
Griffith, Goldsborough Sapping-
ton
Hambleton, Thomas Edward
Hamilton, William Thomas
Hammett, Samuel Bashiell
Hammond, Charles
Hammond, William Alexander
Handy, Alexander Hamilton
Hanson, Alexander Contee, 1749
–1806
Hanson, Alexander Contee, 1786
–1819
Hanson, John
Hardey, Mother Mary Aloysia
Hastings, Daniel Oren
Hemmeter, John Conrad
Henry, John
Henshall, James Alexander
Henson, Josiah
Henson, Matthew Alexander
Hesselius, John
Hicks, Thomas Holliday
Hill, Richard
Hindman, William
Hoffman, David
Holiday, Billie
Hollander, Jacob Harry
Hollins, George Nichols
Holt, Henry
Hopkins, Johns
Howard, Benjamin Chew
Howard, John Eager
Howell, William Henry
Howison, George Holmes
Hubner, Charles William
Hughes, Christopher
Hughes, James
Hurst, John Fletcher
Husbands, Hermon
Iddings, Joseph Paxon
James, Thomas
Jenifer, Daniel of St. Thomas
Jewett, Hugh Judge
Johns, Kensey
Johnson, Reverdy
Johnson, Thomas
Jones, Harry Clary
Jones, Hugh Bolton
Jones, John Beauchamp
Kefauver, Grayson Neikirk
Kennedy, John Pendleton
Kent, Joseph
Kerr, Sophie
Key, Francis Scott
Key, Philip Barton
Kirk, Norman Thomas
Kirkwood, Daniel
Kirkwood, Samuel Jordan
Knott, Aloysius Leo
Lane, Tidence
Latrobe, Charles Hazlehurst
Lazear, Jesse William
Lee, Thomas Sim
Leeds, John
Leiter, Levi Zeigler
Lewis, Estelle Anna Blanche Rob-
inson

Lloyd, Edward, 1744–1796
Lloyd, Edward, 1779–1834
Lockwood, James Booth
Logan, Cornelius Ambrosius
Longcope, Warfield, Theobald
Louis, Morris
McCaffrey, John
McCardell, Claire
McClenahan, Howard
McComas, Louis Emory
McCormick, Lynde Dupuy
McDonogh, John
Machen, John Gresham
McKenney, Thomas Loraine
Mackenzie, John Noland
McMahon, John Van Lear
Marburg, Theodore
Marden, Charles Carroll
Marriott, Williams McKim
Massey, George Betton
Maus, Marion Perry
Mayer, Alfred Marshall
Mayer, Brantz
Mayor, Alfred Goldsborough
Mencken, Henry Louis
Mercer, Margaret
Miles, George Henry
Miles, Richard Pius
Mills, Benjamin
Mitchell, George Edward
Moore, Henry Ludwell
Morawetz, Victor
Murray, Alexander
Murray, John Gardner
Murray, William Vans
Neale, Leonard
Nelson, Roger
Newcomb, Josephine Louise Le
Monnier
Nicholson, James
Nicholson, Joseph Hopper
Nicholson, Samuel
Norris, James Flack
Norris, William
Noyes, Clara Dutton
O'Brien, Frederick
Ord, Edward Otho Cresap
Otis, Elwell Stephen
Oursler, (Charles) Fulton
Paca, William
Painter, William
Palmer, James Croxall
Palmer, John Williamson
Partridge, James Rudolph
Pattison, Robert Emory
Peale, Charles Willson
Peale, James
Peale, Raphael
Pennington, James W. C.
Perlman, Philip Benjamin
Peterkin, George William
Pinkerton, Lewis Letig
Pinkney, Ninian
Pinkney, William
Pise, Charles Constantine
Plater, George
Porter, Nathaniel
Post, Emily Price
Potts, Richard
Price, Bruce
Proctor, William
Purnell, William Henry
Quigg, Lemuel Ely

Randall, Burton Alexander
Randall, James Ryder
Randall, Wyatt William
Rayner, Isidor
Read, George
Reese, Charles Lee
Reese, Lizette Woodworth
Ricketts, Palmer Chamberlaine
Ricord, Philippe
Ridgaway, Henry Bascom
Ridgely, Charles Goodwin
Riley, Bennet
Rinehart, William Henry
Ringgold, Cadwalader
Roberts, Robert Richford
Robinson, George Canby
Robinson, John Mitchell
Robson, Stuart
Rodgers, George Washington, 1787–1832
Rodgers, John, 1773–1838
Rodgers, John, 1812–1882
Rogers, Henry J.
Rogers, Robert Empie
Rohé, George Henry
Rommel, Edwin Americus ("Eddie")
Rose, John Carter
Rous, Francis Peyton
Royall, Anne Newport
Rumsey, James
Russell, John Henry
Ruth, George Herman (Babe)
Ryan, Abram Joseph
Sachs, Bernard
Sachs, Julius
Sadtler, John Philip Benjamin
Sands, Benjamin Franklin
Sappington, John
Saxton, Eugene Francis
Schaeffer, Charles William
Scharf, John Thomas
Schley, Winfield Scott
Schmucker, Samuel Simon
Schroeder, John Frederick
Scott, Irving Murray
Searing, Laura Catherine Redden
Seiss, Joseph Augustus
Sellers, Matthew Bacon
Semmes, Raphael
Shaw, John, 1778–1809
Shelby, Isaac
Shipley, Ruth Bielaski
Sinclair, Upton Beall, Jr.
Singleton, Esther
Skinner, John Stuart
Smallwood, William
Smith, Francis Hopkinson
Spalding, Catherine
Sprecher, Samuel
Spruance, Raymond Ames
Steiner, Lewis Henry
Sterett, Andrew
Stockbridge, Henry
Stoddert, Benjamin
Stone, Barton Warren
Stone, Thomas
Sturgis, Russell
Sutherland, Richard Kerens
Szold, Henrietta
Tammen, Harry Heye
Taney, Roger Brooke
Theobold, Samuel

Thomas, Allen
Thomas, Francis
Thomas, Martha Carey
Thomas, Philip Evan
Thomas, Philip Francis
Thomas, Richard Henry
Thompson, Alfred Wordsworth
Tiffany, Louis McLane
Tilghman, Edward
Tilghman, Matthew
Tilghman, Tench
Tilghman, William
Tipton, John
Trippe, John
Tubman, Harriet
Turner, Charles Yardley
Turner, Edward Raymond
Tydings, Millard Evelyn
Tyler, Samuel
Uhler, Philip Reese
Valentine, Milton
Van Osdel, John Mills
Veazey, Thomas Ward
Waesche, Russell Randolph
Waggaman, Mary Teresa McKee
Wagner, Clinton
Waidner, Charles William
Wallis, Severn Teackle
Walsh, Robert
Walters, Henry
Ward, Samuel Ringgold
Warfield, Solomon Davies
Warrington, Albert Powell
Watson, Henry Clay
Wayman, Alexander Walker
Weems, Mason Locke
Welby, Amelia Ball Coppuck
Wharton, Charles Henry
White, Charles Ignatius
White, Henry
White, Henry Clay
Whitney, Courtney
Wickes, Lambert
Wilkinson, James
Wilkinson, Theodore Stark
Williams, John Whitridge
Williams, Otho Holland
Wilmer, James Jones
Wilmer, William Holland
Winchester, James
Winder, John Henry
Winder, Levin
Winder, William Henry
Winebrenner, John
Wolman, Leo
Wright, Robert
Young, John Richardson

MASSACHUSETTS

Abbot, Benjamin
Abbot, Francis Ellingwood
Abbot, Henry Larcom
Abbot, Joel
Abbott, Austin
Abbott, Benjamin Vaughan
Abbott, Eleanor Hallowell
Abbott, Horace
Abbott, Lyman
Abbott, Samuel Warren
Adams, Abigail
Adams, Abijah
Adams, Brooks

Adams, Charles Baker
Adams, Charles Follen
Adams, Charles Francis, 1807–1886
Adams, Charles Francis, 1835–1915
Adams, Charles Francis, 1866–1954
Adams, Charles R.
Adams, Daniel
Adams, Dudley W.
Adams, Edward Dean
Adams, Edwin
Adams, Eliphant
Adams, Frederick Upham
Adams, Hannah
Adams, Henry Brooks
Adams, Herbert Baxter
Adams, Jasper
Adams, John
Adams, John Coleman
Adams, John Quincy
Adams, Nehemiah
Adams, Samuel
Adams, William Taylor
Agassiz, Elizabeth Cabot Cary
Aiken, George L.
Albro, Lewis Colt
Alden, Ebenezer
Alden, Ichabod
Alden, Timothy
Alden, William Livingston
Aldrich, Charles Anderson
Alger, Cyrus
Alger, Horatio
Alger, William Rounseville
Allen, Alexander Viets Griswold
Allen, Anthony Benezet
Allen, Charles
Allen, David Oliver
Allen, Edward Ellis
Allen, Fred
Allen, Frederick Lewis
Allen, Joel Asaph
Allen, Joseph Henry
Allen, Lewis Falley
Allen, Nathan
Allen, Nathan H.
Allen, Richard Lamb
Allen, Thomas
Allen, William
Allen, William Francis
Alphonsa, Mother
Alvord, Clarence Walworth
Alvord, Henry Elijah
Ames, Charles Gordon
Ames, Edward Raymond
Ames, Ezra
Ames, Fisher
Ames, Frederick Lothrop
Ames, Herman Vandenburg
Ames, James Barr
Ames, James Tyler
Ames, Joseph Alexander
Ames, Nathan Peabody
Ames, Nathaniel
Ames, Oakes, 1804–1873
Ames, Oakes, 1874–1950
Ames, Oliver, 1779–1863
Ames, Oliver, 1807–1877
Ames, Oliver, 1831–1895
Ames, Winthrop
Andrew, Samuel

Andrews, Charles Bartlett
Andrews, George Leonard
Andrews, Joseph
Andrews, Sidney
Andrews, Stephen Pearl
Angell, George Thorndike
Anthony, Susan Brownell
Apes, William
Appleton, Daniel
Appleton, James
Appleton, John
Appleton, Nathaniel Walker
Appleton, Thomas Gold
Appleton, William Henry
Appleton, William Sumner
Apthorp, William Foster
Armsby, Henry Prentiss
Armstrong, George Washington
Armstrong, Henry Worthington
  ("Harry")
Armstrong, Samuel Turell
Ashmun, George
Aspinwall, William
Atherton, George Washington
Atherton, Joshua
Atkinson, Edward
Atkinson, George Henry
Atwater, Caleb
Atwood, Charles B.
Auchmuty, Robert
Auchmuty, Samuel
Augustus, John
Austin, Benjamin
Austin, James Trecothick
Austin, Jane Goodwin
Austin, Jonathan Loring
Austin, William
Avery, John
Babbitt, Irving
Babbitt, Isaac
Babcock, James Francis
Babson, Roger Ward
Bacon, Robert
Badger, Joseph, 1708–1765
Badger, Joseph, 1757–1846
Bailey, Jacob
Bailey, Jacob Whitman
Baker, Benjamin Franklin
Baker, Harvey Humphrey
Baker, Lorenzo Dow
Balch, Emily Greene
Baldwin, Loammi, 1740–1807
Baldwin, Loammi, 1780–1838
Baldwin, William Henry
Ball, Albert
Ball, Thomas
Ballou, Maturin Murray
Bancroft, Aaron
Bancroft, Edward
Bancroft, George
Banks, Nathaniel Prentiss
Barbour, Thomas
Bardeen, Charles William
Barker, Albert Smith
Barker, George Frederick
Barker, Jeremiah
Barker, Josiah
Barlow, Samuel Latham Mitchill
Barnard, Charles
Barnard, Charles Francis
Barnard, Chester Irving
Barnard, Frederick Augustus
  Porter

Barnard, John
Barnard, John Gross
Barnes, Charlotte Mary Sanford
Barnes, James
Barron, Clarence Walker
Barrows, Alice Prentice
Bartlet, William
Bartlett, Francis Alonzo
Bartlett, John
Bartlett, Joseph
Bartlett, Josiah
Barton, Clara
Bascom, Florence
Bass, Edward
Bassett, William Hastings
Bates, Joshua
Bates, Katharine Lee
Bates, Samuel Penniman
Baylies, Francis
Beach, Alfred Ely
Beach, Moses Sperry
Beale, Joseph Henry
Beckwith, Clarence Augustine
Belcher, Jonathan
Belknap, Jeremy
Bellamy, Edward
Bellows, Albert Fitch
Bellows, Henry Whitney
Bemis, George
Benchley, Robert Charles
Benjamin, Asher
Bennett, Emerson
Benson, Frank Weston
Bent, Josiah
Bentley, William
Bernard, William Bayle
Betts, Samuel Rossiter
Bidwell, Barnabas
Bidwell, Marshall Spring
Bigelow, Erastus Brigham
Bigelow, Frank Hagar
Bigelow, Harry Augustus
Bigelow, Henry Bryant
Bigelow, Henry Jacob
Bigelow, Jacob
Bigelow, William Sturgis
Billings, William
Binney, Amos
Bird, Arthur
Bishop, Robert Roberts
Bitzer, George William
Bixby, James Thompson
Blackmur, Richard Palmer
Blake, Eli Whitney
Blake, Francis
Blake, Lyman Reed
Blanchard, Thomas
Bliss, Cornelius Newton
Bliss, George, 1816–1896
Bliss, George, 1830–1897
Bliss, Jonathan
Blodget, Samuel
Blodgett, Benjamin Colman
Blodgett, Henry Williams
Blowers, Sampson Salter
Blunt, George William
Bôcher, Maxine
Bojes, Henry Martyn
Boise, Reuben Patrick
Bolles, Frank
Boltwood, Bertram Borden
Bond, George Phillips
Bonham, Milledge Luke

Borden, Lizzie Andrew
Borden, Richard
Borden, Simeon
Bourne, Jonathan
Boutell, Henry Sherman
Boutwell, George Sewall
Bowditch, Henry Ingersoll
Bowditch, Henry Pickering
Bowditch, Nathaniel
Bowdoin, James, 1726–1790
Bowdoin, James, 1752–1811
Bowen, Francis
Bowers, Lloyd Wheaton
Bowker, Richard Rogers
Boyd, John Parker
Boyden, Roland William
Boyden, Seth
Boyden, Uriah Atherton
Boyle, Thomas
Boylston, Zabdiel
Boynton, Charles Brandon
Brackett, Jeffrey Richardson
Bradbury, Theophilus
Bradford, Alden
Bradford, Edward Hickling
Bradford, Gamaliel, 1831–1911
Bradford, Gamaliel, 1863–1932
Bradford, William
Bradish, Luther
Bradley, John Edwin
Brattle, Thomas
Brattle, William
Brazer, John
Breck, Samuel
Breed, Ebenezer
Brewer, Charles
Brewer, Thomas Mayo
Brewster, Osmyn
Brewster, William
Bridgman, Elijah Coleman
Bridgman, Herbert Lawrence
Bridgman, Percy Williams
Briggs, Charles Frederick
Briggs, George Nixon
Briggs, LeBaron Russell
Briggs, Lloyd Vernon
Brigham, Amariah
Brigham, Mary Ann
Brightman, Edgar Sheffield
Bromfield, John
Bronson, Walter Cochrane
Brooks, Charles
Brooks, Charles Timothy
Brooks, Elbridge Streeter
Brooks, John
Brooks, Maria Gowen
Brooks, Phillips
Brooks, Richard Edwin
Brown, Addison
Brown, Charlotte Emerson
Brown, Ebenezer
Brown, Henry Billings
Brown, Henry Kirke
Brown, James
Brown, John
Brown, John Appleton
Brown, Mather
Brown, Moses
Brown, Percy
Brown, Ralph Hall
Brown, Simon
Brown, William Hill
Browne, Benjamin Frederick

Browne, Charles Albert
Browne, Herbert Wheildon Cotton
Browne, William
Brownell, Thomas Church
Bryant, Gridley
Bryant, John Howard
Bryant, William Cullen
Bulfinch, Charles
Bulfinch, Thomas
Bull, Ephraim Wales
Bullard, Henry Adams
Bumstead, Freeman Josiah
Bumstead, Horace
Burbank, Luther
Burgess, Edward
Burgess, Frank Gelett
Burgess, George Kimball
Burgess, Neil
Burgess, Thornton Waldo
Burgess, W(illiam) Starling
Burlingame, Edward Livermore
Burnett, Joseph
Burnham, Clara Louise Root
Burrage, Henry Sweetser
Burrage, Walter Lincoln
Burrill, Thomas Jonathan
Burroughs, Bryson
Burt, William Austin
Burton, Harold Hitz
Bushnell, George Ensign
Butler, Ezra
Butler, John Wesley
Butler, Zebulon
Butterick, Ebenezer
Byington, Cyrus
Byles, Mather
Cabot, Arthur Tracy
Cabot, Edward Clarke
Cabot, George
Cabot, Godfrey Lowell
Cabot, Hugh
Cabot, Richard Clarke
Cady, Sarah Louise Ensign
Caldwell, Charles Henry Bromedge
Calhoun, William Barron
Callender, John
Canfield, Richard A.
Capen, Elmer Hewitt
Capen, Nahum
Capen, Samuel Billings
Capen, Samuel Paul
Capron, Horace
Carnegie, Mary Crowninshield Endicott
Carpenter, Edmund Janes
Carter, Elias
Carter, James Coolidge
Carter, James Gordon
Carty, John Joseph
Carver, Jonathan
Caswell, Alexis
Chadwick, George Whitefield
Chadwick, James Read
Chadwick, John White
Chamberlain, Daniel Henry
Chamberlain, Nathan Henry
Champney, James Wells
Chandler, Charles Frederick
Chandler, Joseph Ripley
Chandler, Seth Carlo
Channing, Edward

Channing, William Ellery
Channing, William Francis
Channing, William Henry
Chapin, Calvin
Chapin, Chester William
Chaplin, Jeremiah
Chapman, Alvan Wentworth
Chapman, John
Chapman, Maria Weston
Chase, Harry Woodburn
Chase, Pliny Earle
Chase, Thomas
Chauncy, Charles
Checkley, John
Cheney, Ednah Dow Littlehale
Chever, James W.
Child, David Lee
Child, Francis James
Child, Lydia Maria Francis
Child, Richard Washburn
Childe, John
Childs, Thomas
Chipman, Ward
Choate, Joseph Hodges
Choate, Rufus
Church, Benjamin
Church, George Earl
Claflin, Horace Brigham
Claflin, William
Claghorn, George
Clap, Thomas
Clapp, Asa
Clapp, Charles Horace
Clapp, William Warland
Clark, Alvan
Clark, Alvan Graham
Clark, Arthur Hamilton
Clark, Henry James
Clark, John Maurice
Clark, Jonas
Clark, Jonas Gilman
Clark, Joseph Sylvester
Clark, Thomas March
Clark, William Smith
Clarke, Frank Wigglesworth
Clarke, Richard
Clarkson, John Gibson
Cleaveland, Parker
Clement, Edward Henry
Cleveland, Aaron
Cleveland, Horace William Shaler
Cleveland, Richard Jeffry
Cobb, David
Cobb, Elijah
Cobb, Jonathan Holmes
Cobb, Lyman
Cobb, Nathan Augustus
Cobb, William Henry
Cochrane, Gordon Stanley ("Mickey")
Codman, John
Coffin, Charles Fisher
Coffin, Sir Isaac
Coffin, James Henry
Coffin, John
Cogswell, Joseph Green
Colburn, Dana Pond
Colburn, Irving Wightman
Colburn, Warren
Colby, Luther
Cole, Frank Nelson
Coleman, Lyman
Coleman, William

Collins, Edward Knight
Collins, Frank Shipley
Colman, Benjamin
Colman, Henry
Colman, John
Colman, Lucy Newhall
Colt, LeBaron Bradford
Colton, Calvin
Conant, Charles Arthur
Conant, Hannah O'Brien Chaplin
Conant, Hezekiah
Conboy, Sara Agnes McLaughlin
Coney, John
Congdon, Charles Taber
Conly, Jabez
Converse, Charles Crozat
Converse, Edmund Cogswell
Converse, Frederick Shepherd
Conwell, Russell Herman
Cook, Clarence Chatham
Cook, Russell S.
Cook, Zebedee
Cooke, Elisha, 1637–1715
Cooke, Elisha, 1678–1737
Cooke, Josiah Parsons
Coolidge, Archibald Cary
Coolidge, Charles Allerton
Coolidge, Julian Lowell
Coolidge, Thomas Jefferson, 1831 –1920
Coolidge, Thomas Jefferson, 1893 –1959
Cooper, Samuel
Copley, John Singleton
Corbett, Henry Winslow
Corson, Juliet
Corthell, Elmer Lawrence
Cory, Charles Barney
Cowl, Jane
Cox, Lemuel
Coyle, Grace Longwell
Crafts, James Mason
Craigie, Andrew
Cranch, William
Crane, John
Crane, William Henry
Crane, Winthrop Murray
Craven, Frank
Creesy, Josiah Perkins
Crocker, Alvah
Crocker, Hannah Mather
Crocker, Uriel
Cross, Charles Whitman
Crowell, Luther Childs
Crowninshield, Benjamin Williams
Crowninshield, Frederic
Crowninshield, George
Crowninshield, Jacob
Cuffe, Paul
Cullis, Charles
Cummings, Charles Amos
Cummings, E. E.
Cummings, Edward
Cummings, John
Cummins, Maria Susanna
Curley, James Michael
Currier, Nathaniel
Curtis, Benjamin Robbins
Curtis, Charles Pelham
Curtis, Edwin Upton
Curtis, George
Curtis, George Ticknor

Curtis, Moses Ashley
Curwen, Samuel
Cushing, Caleb
Cushing, John Perkins
Cushing, Josiah Nelson
Cushing, Luther Stearns
Cushing, Richard James
Cushing, Thomas
Cushing, William
Cushman, Charlotte Saunders
Cushman, Joseph Augustine
Cushman, Joshua
Cushman, Susan Webb
Cutler, Charles Ammi
Cutler, Ephraim
Cutler, Timothy
Daggett, David
Daggett, Naphtali
Dall, Caroline Wells Healey
Dall, William Healey
Dalton, John Call
Dana, Francis
Dana, James
Dana, Richard
Dana, Richard Henry, 1787–1879
Dana, Richard Henry, 1815–1882
Dane, Nathan
Danforth, Charles
Danforth, Thomas
Darby, John
Davenport, Edward Loomis
Davis, Andrew McFarland
Davis, Arthur Vining
Davis, Charles Harold
Davis, Charles Henry, 1807–1877
Davis, Charles Henry, 1845–1921
Davis, George Breckenridge
Davis, Horace
Davis, John, 1761–1847
Davis, John, 1780–1838
Davis, John Chandler Bancroft
Davis, William Thomas
Dawes, Henry Laurens
Dawes, William
Day, Arthur Louis
Day, Benjamin Henry
Day, Horace H.
Deane, Samuel
De Costa, Benjamin Franklin
De Fontaine, Felix Gregory
Delano Amassa
DeMille, Cecil Blount
Dennie, Joseph
Dennison, Henry Sturgis
Derby, Elias Hasket, 1736–1826
Derby, Elias Hasket, 1766–1799
Derby, Elias Hasket, 1803–1880
Derby, George Horatio
Derby, Richard
Devens, Charles
Dewey, Chester
Dewey, Orville
Dewing, Thomas Wilmer
Dexter, Franklin
Dexter, Franklin Bowditch
Dexter, Henry
Dexter, Henry Martyn
Dexter, Samuel, 1726–1810
Dexter, Samuel, 1761–1816
Dexter, Timothy
Diaz, Abby Morton
Dickinson, Emily Elizabeth
Dickinson, John Woodbridge

Dickinson, Jonathan
Ditson, George Leighton
Ditson, Oliver
Dix, John Homer
Dixon, Joseph
Dixon, Roland Burrage
Doane, Thomas
Doane, William Craswell
Dodge, Ebenezer
Dodge, Grenville Mellon
Dodge, Mary Abigail
Dodge, Raymond
Dodge, Theodore Ayrault
Dole, James Drummond
Dole, Nathan Haskell
Dorchester, Daniel
Douglas, William Lewis
Downer, Samuel
Downes, John
Dowse, Thomas
Drake, Samuel Adams
Draper, Eben Sumner
Draper, Ira
Draper, William Franklin
Du Bois, William Edward Burghardt
Duchin, Edward Frank ("Eddy")
Dudley, Joseph
Dudley, Paul
Duganne, Augustine Joseph Hickey
Dumaine, Frederic Christopher
Dummer, Jeremiah, 1645–1718
Dummer, Jeremiah, 1679–1739
Dunbar, Charles Franklin
Dunham, Henry Morton
Durant, Henry
Durant, Thomas Clark
Durant, William Crapo
Durfee, William Franklin
Durfee, Zobeth Sherman
Durivage, Francis Alexander
Dwight, Arthur Smith
Dwight, Edmund
Dwight, Francis
Dwight, Harrison Gray Otis
Dwight, John Sullivan
Dwight, Nathaniel
Dwight, Theodore
Dwight, Thomas
Dwight, Timothy
Dwight, William
Dyer, Nehemiah Mayo
Eagels, Jeanne
Eames, Charles
Earle, Alice Morse
Earle, James
Earle, Pliny, 1762–1832
Earle, Pliny, 1809–1892
Earle, Ralph, 1751–1801
Earle, Ralph, 1874–1939
Earle, Thomas
Eddy, Clarence
Eddy, Daniel Clarke
Eddy, Harrison Prescott
Eddy, Henry Turner
Edes, Benjamin
Edmonds, John
Edwards, Bela Bates
Edwards, Jonathan, 1745–1801
Edwards, Justin
Edwards, Oliver
Edwards, Pierpont

Eldridge, Shalor Winchell
Eliot, Charles
Eliot, Charles William
Eliot, Samuel
Eliot, Samuel Atkins
Eliot, William Greenleaf
Elliot, James
Ellis, Calvin
Ellis, George Edward
Elman, Robert
Elson, Louis Charles
Elwell, Frank Edwin
Emerson, Edward Waldo
Emerson, Mary Moody
Emerson, Ralph
Emerson, Ralph Waldo
Emerson, William
Emerton, Ephraim
Emerton, James Henry
Emmons, Ebenezer
Emmons, Samuel Franklin
Endicott, Charles Moses
Endicott, William Crowninshield
English, George Bethune
Erving, George William
Eustis, George
Eustis, Henry Lawrence
Eustis, William
Evans, Charles
Evarts, William Maxwell
Everett, Alexander Hill
Everett, David
Everett, Edward
Ewer, Ferdinand Cartwright
Fairbanks, Erastus
Fairbanks, Thaddeus
Fairchild, Blair
Fairchild, James Harris
Fairchild, Mary Salome Cutler
Fairfield, Sumner Lincoln
Fanning, Alexander Campbell Wilder
Farlow, William Gilson
Farmer, Fannie Merritt
Farmer, John
Farnham, Russel
Farnum, Franklyn
Farrar, Geraldine
Farrar, John
Faunce, William Herbert Perry
Fay, Jonas
Felt, Joseph Barlow
Felton, Cornelius Conway
Felton, Samuel Morse
Fenn, William Wallace
Fenno, John
Fenollosa, Ernest Francisco
Fewkes, Jesse Walter
Field, Cyrus West
Field, Henry Martyn
Field, Marshall
Field, Stephen Dudley
Field, Walbridge Abner
Fields, Annie Adams
Filene, Edward Albert
Fisher, Alvan
Fisher, George Park
Fisher, John Dix
Fisher, Theodore Willis
Fisk, James
Fiske, Fidelia
Fiske, George Converse
Fiske, John

Fitton, James
Fitz, Henry
Fitz, Reginald Heber
Fitzgerald, John Francis
Fitzpatrick, John Bernard
Flagg, Josiah
Flagg, Josiah Foster
Flagg, Thomas Wilson
Fletcher, Horace
Flint, Albert Stowell
Flint, Austin, 1812–1886
Flint, Austin, 1836–1915
Flint, Charles Louis
Flint, Timothy
Flower, Lucy Louisa Coues
Folger, Charles James
Folger, Walter
Follen, Eliza Lee Cabot
Follett, Mary Parker
Foote, Arthur William
Forbes, Esther
Forbes, Robert Bennet
Forbes, William Cameron
Forbush, Edward Howe
Ford, Daniel Sharp
Ford, George Burdett
Foster, Abiel
Foster, Abigail Kelley
Foster, Frank Hugh
Foster, Hannah Webster
Foster, John
Foster, Judith Ellen Horton
Foster, Roger Sherman Baldwin
Foster, Theodore
Foster, William Trufant
Foster, William Z.
Fowle, Daniel
Fowle, William Bentley
Fox, Charles Kemble
Fox, George Washington Lafayette
Fox, Gustavus Vasa
Fox, Harry
Francis, Charles Stephen
Francis, Convers
Francis, Joseph
Frankland, Lady Agnes Surriage
Franklin, Benjamin
Franklin, James
Fraser, Leon
Freeman, James
Freeman, Mary Eleanor Wilkins
Freeman, Nathaniel
French, Alice
French, Edwin Davis
Frieze, Henry Simmons
Frisbie, Levi
Frothingham, Arthur Lincoln
Frothingham, Nathaniel Langdon
Frothingham, Octavius Brooks
Frothingham, Paul Revere
Frothingham, Richard
Frye, Joseph
Fullam, Frank L.
Fuller, Hiram
Fuller, Sarah Margaret
Furness, William Henry
Gannett, Ezra Stiles
Gannett, William Channing
Gardiner, John
Gardner, Erle Stanley
Gardner, Henry Joseph
Gardner, John Lane

Garrison, William Lloyd
Gay, Ebenezer
Gay, Frederick Parker
Gay, Sydney Howard
Gay, Winckworth Allan
Gerry, Elbridge
Gibbs, Josiah Willard
Gibson, Charles Dana
Gifford, Robert Swain
Gifford, Walter Sherman
Gilbert, Henry Franklin Belknap
Gilbert, John Gibbs
Giles, Chauncey
Gill, John
Gillett, Frederick Huntington
Gillis, James Martin
Gilman, Arthur Delevan
Gilman, Caroline Howard
Gilman, Samuel
Gilmore, James Roberts
Gilmore, Joseph Henry
Glidden, Charles Jasper
Glover, John
Goddard, John
Goddard, Robert Hutchings
Godfrey, Benjamin
Goldthwaite, George
Goodell, William
Goodhue, Benjamin
Goodnough, Xanthus Henry
Goodrich, Chauncey, 1759–1815
Goodrich, Chauncey, 1798–1858
Goodrich, Frank Boott
Goodrich, William Marcellus
Goodridge, Sarah
Goodwin, Nathaniel Carll
Goodwin, William Watson
Gordon, George Henry
Gorham, John
Gorham, Nathaniel
Gould, Benjamin Apthorp, 1787–1859
Gould, Benjamin Apthorp, 1824–1896
Gould, Hannah Flagg
Gould, Thomas Ridgeway
Grafton, Charles Chapman
Grandgent, Charles Hall
Grant, Percy Stickney
Grant, Robert
Graves, William Phillips
Gray, Francis Calley
Gray, Horace
Gray, John Chipman
Gray, William
Greaton, John
Greely, Adolphus Washington
Green, Andrew Haswell
Green, Asa
Green, Bartholomew
Green, Francis
Green, Francis Matthews
Green, Henrietta Howland Robinson
Green, Jacob
Green, John
Green, Jonas
Green, Joseph
Green, Nathan
Green, Samuel Abbott
Green, Samuel Bowdlear
Green, Samuel Swett
Greene, Charles Ezra

Greene, Daniel Crosby
Greene, Roger Sherman
Greene, Samuel Stillman
Greenleaf, Benjamin
Greenleaf, Moses
Greenleaf, Simon
Greenleaf, Thomas
Greenough, Henry
Greenough, Horatio
Greenough, Richard Saltonstall
Greenwood, Isaac
Greenwood, John
Grew, Joseph Clark
Gridley, Jeremiah
Gridley, Richard
Griffin, Solomon Bulkley
Grimes, James Stanley
Grinnell, Frederick
Grinnell, Henry
Grinnell, Joseph
Grinnell, Moses Hicks
Grosvenor, William Mason
Guild, Curtis, 1827–1911
Guild, Curtis, 1860–1915
Guild, Reuben Aldridge
Guilford, Nathan
Guiney, Louise Imogen
Gurney, Ephraim Whitman
Guthrie, Samuel
Hackett, Horatio Balch
Hadley, Henry Kimball
Hague, Arnold
Hague, James Duncan
Hale, Benjamin
Hale, Charles
Hale, Edward Everett
Hale, Enoch
Hale, Lucretia Peabody
Hale, Nathan
Hale, Philip Leslie
Hall, Arethusa
Hall, Florence Marion Howe
Hall, Granville Stanley
Hall, James
Hall, Samuel, 1740–1807
Hall, Samuel, 1800–1870
Hall, Willard
Hallett, Benjamin
Hallett, Benjamin Franklin
Hallock, Gerard
Hallock, William Allen
Halsey, John
Hamblin, Joseph Eldridge
Hamlin, Charles Sumner
Hammond, George Henry
Hammond, Jabez Delano
Hammond, James Bartlett
Hanaford, Phoebe Ann Coffin
Hancock, John
Hancock, Thomas
Hapgood, Isabel Florence
Haraden, Jonathan
Harahan, James Theodore
Harding, Chester
Harding, Seth
Hardy, Arthur Sherburne
Harkness, Albert
Harnden, William Frederick
Harrington, Charles
Harrington, Thomas Francis
Harris, Thaddeus Mason
Harris, Thaddeus William
Harris, William

Hart, John Seely
Hasket, Elias
Hassam, Frederick Childe
Hastings, Samuel Dexter
Haven, Erastus Otis
Haven, Gilbert
Haven, Joseph
Hawes, Harriet Ann Boyd
Hawley, Joseph
Hawthorne, Julian
Hawthorne, Nathaniel
Hayden, Charles
Hayden, Charles Henry
Hayden, Edward Everett
Hayden, Ferdinand Vaudiveer
Hayden, Hiram Washington
Hayden, Joseph Shepard
Haynes, John Henry
Hayward, George
Hayward, Nathaniel Manley
Hazeltine, Mayo Williamson
Hazen, Moses
Healy, George Peter Alexander
Heard, Augustine
Heard, Dwight Bancroft
Heard, Franklin Fiske
Heath, William
Hedge, Frederic Henry
Hedge, Levi
Henchman, Daniel
Henderson, Lawrence Joseph
Henry, Caleb Sprague
Henshaw, David
Henshaw, Henry Wetherbee
Hentz, Caroline Lee Whiting
Hepworth, George Hughes
Herne, Chrystal Katharine
Herrick, Robert Welch
Herschel, Clemens
Hersey, Evelyn Weeks
Hewes, Robert
Heywood, Ezra Hervey
Heywood, Levi
Hiacoomes
Hichborn, Philip
Higginson, Stephen
Higginson, Thomas Wentworth
Hildreth, Richard
Hildreth, Samuel Prescott
Hill, Frederic Stanhope
Hill, George Handel
Hill, Henry Barker
Hill, Isaac
Hilliard, Francis
Hitchcock, Charles Henry
Hitchcock, Edward, 1793–1864
Hitchcock, Edward, 1828–1911
Hitchcock, Enos
Hitchcock, James Ripley Wellman
Hoar, Ebenezer Rockwood
Hoar, George Frisbie
Hoar, Samuel
Hobbs, Alfred Charles
Hodges, Harry Foote
Holden, Oliver
Holder, Charles Frederick
Holder, Joseph Bassett
Holland, Clifford Milburn
Holland, Josiah Gilbert
Holmes, Ezekiel
Holmes, John
Holmes, Mary Jane Hawes

Holmes, Oliver Wendell, 1809–1894
Holmes, Oliver Wendell, 1841–1935
Holt, Edwin Bissell
Holten, Samuel
Holyoke, Edward Augustus
Holyoke, Samuel
Homer, Winslow
Homes, Henry Augustus
Hooker, Joseph
Hooker, Philip
Hooker, Worthington
Hooper, Samuel
Hooper, William
Hopkins, Edward Washburn
Hopkins, Mark
Horr, George Edwin
Hosmer, Frederick Lucian
Hosmer, Harriet Goodhue
Hosmer, James Kendall
Houghton, Alanson Bigelow
Houghton, George Hendric
House, Edward Howard
Hovey, Charles Mason
Howard, Henry
Howe, Andrew Jackson
Howe, Elias
Howe, Frederick Webster
Howe, George
Howe, Henry Marion
Howe, Mark De Wolfe
Howe, Samuel
Howe, Samuel Gridley
Howe, William
Howe, William F.
Hubbard, Gardiner Greene
Hudson, Charles
Hudson, Daniel Eldred
Hudson, Frederic
Hull, Josephine
Hummel, Abraham Henry
Hunnewell, Horatio Hollis
Hunnewell, James
Hunt, Alfred Ephraim
Hunt, Freeman
Hunt, Harriot Kezia
Hunt, William Gibbes
Huntington, Elisha
Huntington, Frederic Dan
Huntington, William Reed
Hurd, John Codman
Hurd, Nathaniel
Huse, Caleb
Hutchinson, Benjamin Peters
Hutchinson, Charles Lawrence
Hutchinson, Thomas
Hyde, William DeWitt
Ingalls, John James
Ingraham, Joseph
Inman, George
Jackson, Charles
Jackson, Charles Thomas
Jackson, Dunham
Jackson, Helen Maria Fiske Hunt
Jackson, James, 1777–1867
Jackson, Mercy Ruggles Bisbe
Jackson, Patrick Tracy
Jackson, William
Jameson, John Franklin
Jarves, Deming
Jarves, James Jackson
Jarvis, Edward

Jarvis, William
Jefferson, Mark Sylvester William
Jeffries, Benjamin Joy
Jeffries, John
Jenkins, Edward Hopkins
Jenkins, Nathaniel
Jenks, William
Jenney, William Le Baron
Johnson, Allen
Johnson, Ellen Cheney
Johnson, George Francis
Johnson, Joseph French
Johnson, Samuel
Johnston, Thomas
Jones, Abner
Jones, Anson
Jones, Calvin
Jones, Joseph Stevens
Jones, Leonard Augustus
Jordan, Eben Dyer
Judd, Sylvester
Judge, Thomas Augustine
Judson, Adoniram
Judson, Ann Hasseltine
Kalmus, Herbert Thomas
Kehew, Mary Morton Kimball
Kellett, William Wallace
Kelley, Oliver Hudson
Kemp, Robert H.
Kendall, Amos
Kendrick, John
Kennedy, John Fitzgerald
Kennedy, Joseph Patrick
Kennedy, Robert Francis
Kenrick, William
Kerouac, Jack
Kettell, Samuel
Keyes, Erasmus Darwin
Kilby, Christopher
Kimball, (Sidney) Fiske
King, Edward Leonard
King, Edward Smith
King, Jonas
King, Thomas Butter
Kinnicutt, Leonard Parker
Kittredge, George Lyman
Knapp, Philip Coombs
Knapp, Samuel Lorenzo
Kneeland, Abner
Kneeland, Samuel, 1697–1769
Kneeland, Samuel, 1821–1888
Kneeland, Stillman Foster
Knight, Austin Melvin
Knight, Frederick Irving
Knight, Henry Cogswell
Knight, Sarah Kemble
Knowles, Lucius James
Knowlton, Charles
Knowlton, Marcus Perrin
Knowlton, Thomas
Knox, Frank
Knox, Henry
Lahey, Frank Howard
Lamb, Arthur Becket
Lamb, Martha Joanna Reade Nash
Lander, Edward
Lander, Frederick West
Lane, George Martin
Lang, Benjamin Johnson
Langdon, Samuel
Langley, John Williams
Langley, Samuel Pierpont
Larcom, Lucy

Larkin, Thomas Oliver
Lathrop, John
Lawrance, Charles Lanier
Lawrence, Abbott
Lawrence, Amos
Lawrence, Amos Adams
Lawrence, William, 1783–1848
Lawrence, William, 1819–1899
Lawrence, William, 1850–1941
Lawson, Thomas William
Leach, Abby
Leach, Daniel Dyer
Leach, Shepherd
Learned, Ebenezer
Leavitt, Erasmus Darwin
Leavitt, Henrietta Swan
Leavitt, Joshua
Lee, Alfred
Lee, Hannah Farnham Sawyer
Lee, Henry, 1782–1867
Lee, Joseph
Leland, George Adams
Leland, John
Leland, Waldo Gifford
Le Moyne, William J.
Leonard, Charles Lester
Leonard, Daniel
Leonard, George
Leonard, Levi Washburn
Leverett, John, 1662–1724
Lewis, Clarence Irving
Lewis, Gilbert Newton
Lewis, Orlando Faulkland
Lewis, Samuel
Lewis, Winslow
Libbey, Edward Drummond
Lincoln, Benjamin
Lincoln, Enoch
Lincoln, John Larkin
Lincoln, Joseph Crosby
Lincoln, Levi, 1749–1820
Lincoln, Levi, 1782–1868
Lincoln, Mary Johnson Bailey
Lincoln, Rufus Pratt
Lindsey, William
Litchfield, Paul Weeks
Little, Arthur Dehon
Little, George
Livermore, George
Livermore, Mary Ashton Rice
Livermore, Samuel, 1732–1803
Locke, Bessie
Lodge, George Cabot
Lodge, Henry Cabot
Lodge, John Ellerton
Logan, Cornelius Ambrose
Lombard, Warren Plimpton
Longfellow, Ernest Wadsworth
Lord, Otis Phillips
Loring, Charles Harding
Loring, Edward Greely
Loring, Ellis Gray
Loring, Frederick Wadsworth
Loring, George Bailey
Loring, Joshua, 1716–1781
Loring, Joshua, 1744–1789
Lothrop, Alice Louise Higgins
Lothrop, George Van Ness
Lovejoy, Asa Lawrence
Loveland, William Austin Hamilton
Lovell, James
Lovell, John

Lovell, Joseph
Lovering, Joseph
Lovett, Robert Morss
Lovett, Robert Williamson
Low, Abiel Abbot
Low, John Gardner
Lowell, Abbott Lawrence
Lowell, Amy
Lowell, Edward Jackson
Lowell, Francis Cabot
Lowell, Guy
Lowell, James Russell
Lowell, John, 1743–1802
Lowell, John, 1769–1840
Lowell, John, 1799–1836
Lowell, John, 1824–1897
Lowell, Josephine Shaw
Lowell, Percival
Lowell, Robert Traill Spence
Lucas, Frederic Augustus
Lummis, Charles Fletcher
Lunt, George
Lyman, Benjamin Smith
Lyman, Eugene William
Lyman, Joseph Bardwell
Lyman, Theodore, 1792–1849
Lyman, Theodore, 1833–1897
Lyman, Theodore, 1874–1954
Lynde, Benjamin
Lyon, Mary
MacArthur, Arthur
McBurney, Charles
McCarren, Patrick Henry
McCarthy, Charles
McCawley, Charles Laurie
McClure, Alexander Wilson
McElwain, William Howe
McIntire, Samuel
McIntyre, Alfred Robert
Mack, Connie
McKay, Gordon
McKenzie, Alexander
MacNeil, Hermon Atkins
McNeill, Daniel
McNeill, George Edwin
McNulty, John Augustine
Macomber, Mary Lizzie
Macy, Josiah
Maier, Walter Arthur
Main, Charles Thomas
Manley, John
Mann, Horace
Mann, James
Mann, Mary Tyler Peabody
Mann, Newton
Manning, Robert
Maranville, Walter James Vincent
  ("Rabbit")
Marble, Manton Malone
March, Alden
March, Francis Andrew
Marchant, Henry
Marciano, Rocky
Marcy, Henry Orlando
Marcy, Randolph Barnes
Marcy, William Learned
Marsh, John
Marshall, Charles Henry
Marshall, James Fowle Baldwin
Martin, Joseph William, Jr.
Mason, Daniel Gregory
Mason, Frank Stuart
Mason, Henry

Mason, Jonathan
Mason, Lowell
Mason, William
Massasoit
Masury, John Wesley
Mather, Cotton
Mather, Increase
Mather, Samuel
Matthews, Nathan
Maxcy, Jonathan
Maxcy, Virgil
May, Samuel Joseph
Mayhew, Experience
Mayhew, Jonathan
Maynard, Charles Johnson
Mayo, Frank
Mayo, Sarah Carter Edgarton
Mead, George Herbert
Mears, David Otis
Mecom, Benjamin
Melcher, Frederic Gershom
Mellen, Charles Sanger
Mellen, Prentiss
Merriam, Charles
Merrick, Edwin Thomas
Merrick, Frederick
Merrick, Pliny
Merrill, Daniel
Merrill, Elmer Truesdell
Merrill, Frank Dow
Merrill, George Edwards
Merrill, Gretchen Van Zandt
Merrill, James Cushing
Merrill, James Griswold
Merrill, Joshua
Meserve, Frederick Hill
Messer, Asa
Metcalf, Theron
Metcalf, Willard Leroy
Meyer, George Von Lengerke
Miles, Henry Adolphus
Miles, Nelson Appleton
Miller, Kempster Blanchard
Miller, William
Miller, William Snow
Mills, Elijah Hunt
Minot, Charles Sedgwick
Minot, George Richards, 1758–
  1802
Minot, George Richards, 1885–
  1950
Mitchell, Albert Graeme
Mitchell, Edward Cushing
Mitchell, Henry
Mitchell, Maria
Mitchell, Nahum
Mitchell, William, 1791–1869
Mixter, Samuel Jason
Montague, Gilbert Holland
Montague, William Pepperell
Moody, Dwight Lyman
Moody, Paul
Moody, William Henry
Moore, Clifford Herschel
Moore, Zephaniah Swift
Morgan, Edwin Denison
Morgan, James Dada
Morgan, Junius Spencer
Morgan, Justin
Morison, George Shattuck
Morris, Robert, 1818–1888
Morse, Henry Dutton
Morse, John Lovett

Morse, John Torrey
Morse, Samuel Finley Breese
Morse, Sidney Edwards
Morton, Marcus, 1784–1864
Morton, Marcus, 1819–1891
Morton, Sarah Wentworth Apthorp
Morton, William James
Morton, William Thomas Green
Moseley, Edward Augustus
Motley, John Lothrop
Mott, Lucretia Coffin
Mudge, Enoch
Mudge, James
Mulliken, Samuel Parsons
Munn, Orson Desaix
Munroe, Charles Edward
Munsell, Joel
Murdoch, Frank Hitchcock
Murphy, Gerald Clery
Murphy, Michael Charles
Murray, Judith Sargent Stevens
Muzzey, David Saville
Myrick, Herbert
Nash, Charles Sumner
Nash, Daniel
Nash, Simeon
Nason, Elias
Nason, Henry Bradford
Neagle, John
Neal, David Dalhoff
Nell, William Cooper
Newell, William Wells
Newman, Henry
Newman, Samuel Phillips
Nichols, Charles Lemuel
Nichols, James Robinson
Nicholson, James William Augustus
Niles, David K.
Nixon, John, 1727–1815
Northend, Charles
Norton, Andrews
Norton, Charles Eliot
Norton, Mary Alice Peloubet
Norton, William Edward
Noyes, Arthur Amos
Noyes, Edward Follansbee
Noyes, George Rapall
Nutting, Wallace
Oakes, Thomas Fletcher
Ober, Frederick Albion
O'Brien, Robert Lincoln
O'Callahan, Joseph Timothy
O'Connell, William Henry
O'Connor, William Douglas
O'Gorman, Thomas
Oliver, Andrew, 1706–1774
Oliver, Andrew, 1731–1799
Oliver, Fitch Edward
Oliver, Henry Kemble
Oliver, Peter
Olney, Richard
O'Mahoney, Joseph Christopher
Orne, John
Osborn, William Henry
Osgood, Frances Sargent Locke
Osgood, George Laurie
Osgood, Samuel
Osgood, William Fogg
Otis, Bass
Otis, George Alexander
Otis, Harrison Gray

Otis, James
Ouimet, Francis Desales
Packard, Alpheus Spring
Packard, Frederick Adolphus
Packard, Silas Sadler
Page, Charles Grafton
Paine, Albert Bigelow
Paine, Charles Jackson
Paine, Robert Treat, 1731–1814
Paine, Robert Treat, 1773–1811
Paine, Robert Treat, 1835–1910
Palfrey, John Carver
Palfrey, John Gorham
Palmer, George Herbert
Palmer, Walter Walker
Park, Maud Wood
Parker, Henry Taylor
Parker, Horatio William
Parker, Isaac
Parker, James Cutler Dunn
Parker, John
Parker, Peter
Parker, Richard Green
Parker, Samuel
Parker, Theodore
Parker, Theodore Bissell
Parkhurst, Charles Henry
Parkman, Francis
Parsons, Theophilus, 1750–1813
Parsons, Theophilus, 1797–1882
Parsons, Thomas William
Patten, William
Pattison, James William
Paul, Elliot Harold
Paul, Henry Martyn
Payne, Henry Clay
Payne, William Morton
Payson, Seth
Peabody, Andrew Preston
Peabody, Elizabeth Palmer
Peabody, Endicott
Peabody, Francis Greenwood
Peabody, George
Peabody, Joseph
Peabody, Nathaniel
Peabody, Robert Swain
Pearce, Charles Sprague
Pearson, Edmund Lester
Pearson, Eliphalet
Pearson, Fred Stark
Peck, George Washington
Peck, William Dandridge
Peirce, Benjamin
Peirce, Benjamin Osgood
Peirce, Charles Sanders
Peirce, Cyrus
Peirce, Henry Augustus
Peirce, James Mills
Pelham, Henry
Percival, John
Perkins, Charles Callahan
Perkins, Frances
Perkins, George Henry
Perkins, Jacob
Perkins, James Handasyd, 1810–1849
Perkins, James Handasyd, 1876–1940
Perkins, Justin
Perkins, Thomas Handasyd
Perkins, Thomas Nelson
Perley, Ira
Perry, Bliss

Perry, Edward Aylesworth
Perry, Edward Baxter
Perry, Enoch Wood
Perry, Nora
Perry, Walter Scott
Perry, William
Peters, Edward Dyer
Phelps, Austin
Phillips, John
Phillips, Samuel
Phillips, Walter Polk
Phillips, Wendell
Phillips, Willard
Phillips, William, 1750/51–1827
Phillips, William, 1824–1893
Phillips, William Addison
Pickard, Samuel Thomas
Pickering, Edward Charles
Pickering, John
Pickering, Timothy
Pidgin, Charles Felton
Pierce, Benjamin
Pierce, Edward Lillie
Pierce, Henry Lillie
Pierpont, James
Pierson, Abraham
Pike, Albert
Pillsbury, Harry Nelson
Pillsbury, John Elliott
Pillsbury, Parker
Pinkham, Lydia Estes
Plath, Sylvia
Plimpton, George Arthur
Plumer, William
Plummer, Jonathan
Poe, Edgar Allan
Pomeroy, Samuel Clarke
Pomeroy, Seth
Pond, Enoch
Pond, George Edward
Pool, Maria Louise
Poole, Fitch
Poole, William Frederick
Poor, Charles Henry
Poor, Daniel
Poor, Enoch
Poore, Benjamin Perley
Pope, Albert Augustus
Pope, Franklin Leonard
Porter, Benjamin Curtis
Porter, David
Porter, Rufus
Potter, Charles Francis
Potter, William James
Pratt, Charles
Pratt, Daniel, 1809–1887
Pratt, Enoch
Pratt, Thomas Willis
Pray, Isaac Clark
Prendergast, Maurice Brazil
Prentice, George Dennison
Presbrey, Eugene Wiley
Prescott, Oliver
Prescott, Samuel
Prescott, William
Prescott, William Hickling
Preston, Harriet Waters
Priest, Edward Dwight
Prince, Frederick Henry
Prince, Morton
Prince, Thomas
Proctor, Joseph
Putnam, Charles Pickering

Putnam, Eben
Putnam, Frederic Ward
Putnam, Gideon
Putnam, Israel
Putnam, James Jackson
Putnam, Rufus
Quincy, Edmund
Quincy, Josiah, 1744–1775
Quincy, Josiah, 1772–1864
Quincy, Josiah Phillips
Rand, Addison Crittenden
Rand, Edward Kennard
Rand, Edward Sprague
Randall, Samuel
Ranney, Ambrose Loomis
Ranney, Rufus Percival
Rantoul, Robert, 1778–1858
Rantoul, Robert, 1805–1852
Ray, Charles Bennett
Ray, Isaac
Read, Daniel, 1757–1836
Read, Nathan
Reed, David
Reed, James, 1722–1807
Reed, James, 1834–1921
Reed, Sampson
Reed, Simeon Gannett
Reid, Robert
Remond, Charles Lenox
Revere, Joseph Warren
Revere, Paul
Rhoads, Cornelius Packard
Rice, Alexander Hamilton
Rice, Calvin Winsor
Rice, Charles Allen Thorndike
Rice, Luther
Rice, William Marsh
Rice, William North
Rich, Isaac
Rich, Obadiah
Richards, Ellen Henrietta Swallow
Richards, Laura Elizabeth Howe
Richards, William
Richards, Zalmon
Richardson, Albert Deane
Richardson, Maurice Howe
Richardson, Rufus Byam
Richardson, Willard
Richardson, William Adams
Richardson, William Lambert
Richmond, John Lambert
Ricketson, Daniel
Riddell, John Leonard
Riddle, Albert Gallatin
Riddle, George Peabody
Rindge, Frederick Hastings
Ripley, Edward Payson
Ripley, Ezra
Ripley, George
Ripley, William Zebina
Robbins, Chandler
Robinson, Charles
Robinson, Edward, 1858–1931
Robinson, Ezekiel Gilman
Robinson, Harriet Jane Hanson
Robinson, Henry Morton
Robinson, Moses
Robinson, William Stevens
Roche, Arthur Somers
Rodgers, John, 1727–1811
Rogers, Edward Staniford
Rogers, Harriet Burbank
Rogers, Henry Huttleston

Rogers, Isaiah
Rogers, John, 1829–1904
Rogers, Mary Josephine
Rogers, Robert
Rogers, William Crowninshield
Rolfe, William James
Rollins, Alice Marland Wellington
Root, Elisha King
Root, Frederic Woodman
Root, George Frederick
Root, Joseph Pomeroy
Ropes, James Hardy
Ropes, Joseph
Ross, Abel Hastings
Rossiter, William Sidney
Rotch, Abbott Lawrence
Rotch, Arthur
Rotch, William
Roulstone, George
Rugg, Arthur Prentice
Rugg, Harold Ordway
Ruggles, Timothy
Russ, John Dennison
Russell, Benjamin
Russell, Joseph
Russell, William Eustis
Rust, Richard Sutton
Ruter, Martin
Ryder, Albert Pinkham
Sabin, Charles Hamilton
Salisbury, Edward Elbridge
Saltonstall, Gurdon
Samuels, Edward Augustus
Sanders, Daniel Clarke
Sanders, Elizabeth Elkins
Sanders, Thomas
Sanger, Charles Robert
Sanger, George Partridge
Sargent, Aaron Augustus
Sargent, Charles Sprague
Sargent, Epes
Sargent, Fitzwilliam
Sargent, Henry
Sargent, Henry Winthrop
Sargent, John Osborne
Sargent, Lucius Manlius
Sargent, Winthrop, 1753–1820
Sartwell, Henry Parker
Savage, Edward
Savage, James
Savage, Philip Henry
Saville, Marshall Howard
Sawyer, Sylvanus
Scammell, Alexander
Schofield, Henry
Schouler, James
Scudder, Horace Elisha
Scudder, Samuel Hubbard
Sears, Barnas
Sears, Edmund Hamilton
Sears, Isaac
Sears, Richard Dudley
Seccomb, John
Sedgwick, Catharine Maria
Sedgwick, Theodore, 1780–1839
Selfridge, Thomas Oliver
Severance, Frank Hayward
Sewall, Jonathan
Sewall, Jonathan Mitchell
Shattuck, Frederick Cheever
Shattuck, George Brune
Shattuck, George Cheyne, 1783–
   1854

Shattuck, George Cheyne, 1813–
   1893
Shattuck, Lemuel
Shaw, Henry Wheeler
Shaw, Lemuel
Shaw, Mary
Shaw, Oliver
Shaw, Samuel
Shaw, William Smith
Shays, Daniel
Shedd, Joel Herbert
Shedd, William Greenough Thay-
   er
Shepard, William
Shepley, Ether
Sherman, Roger
Short, Charles
Shurtleff, Nathaniel Bradstreet
Sibley, George Champlain
Sibley, Hiram
Sibley, John
Silsbee, Nathaniel
Simkhovitch, Mary Melinda Kings-
   bury
Simmons, Edward
Simonds, Frank Herbert
Simpson, Michael Hodge
Sinnott, Edmund Ware
Sizer, Nelson
Skinner, Aaron Nichols
Skinner, Otis
Smalley, George Washburn
Smith, Caleb Blood
Smith, Charles Sprague
Smith, Edward Hanson
Smith, Gerald Birney
Smith, Harold Babbitt
Smith, Horace
Smith, Horatio Elwin
Smith, John Cotton, 1826–1882
Smith, John Rowson
Smith, Jonas Waldo
Smith, Joseph, 1790–1877
Smith, Judson
Smith, Nathan, 1762–1829
Smith, Oliver
Smith, Samuel Francis
Smith, Sophia
Snelling, Josiah
Snelling, William Joseph
Snow, Eliza Roxey
Snow, Francis Huntington
Snow, Jessie Baker
Soley, James Russell
Southard, Elmer Ernest
Sparrow, William
Spear, Charles
Spellman, Francis Joseph
Spencer, Anna Garlin
Sperry, Willard Learoyd
Spooner, Lysander
Sprague, Charles
Sprague, Homer Baxter
Sprague, Oliver Mitchell Went-
   worth
Sprague, Peleg
Spring, Gardiner
Spring, Samuel
Spurr, Josiah Edward
Stanley, Harold
Starr, Eliza Allen
Stearns, Abel
Stearns, Asahel

Stearns, Eben Sperry
Stearns, Frank Waterman
Stearns, George Luther
Stearns, Harold Edmund
Stearns, Henry Putnam
Stearns, Oliver
Stearns, Robert Edwards Carter
Stearns, Shubal
Stearns, William Augustus
Stebbins, Horatio
Stebbins, Rufus Phineas
Stetson, Charles Augustus
Stetson, Henry Crosby
Stevens, Isaac Ingalls
Stimpson, William
Stimson, Alexander Lovett
Stimson, Frederic Jesup
Stimson, Julia Catherine
Stockbridge, Henry Smith
Stockbridge, Horace Edward
Stockbridge, Levi
Stockwell, John Nelson
Stoddard, David Tappan
Stoddard, Elizabeth Drew Barstow
Stoddard, John Lawson
Stoddard, John Tappan
Stoddard, Richard Henry
Stoddard, Solomon
Stoddard, Theodore Lothrop
Stone, Amasa
Stone, Charles Augustus
Stone, Charles Pomeroy
Stone, Ellen Maria
Stone, James Kent
Stone, John Augustus
Stone, John Seely
Stone, Lucy
Storer, Francis Humphreys
Storer, Horatio Robinson
Storey, Moorfield
Storrow, James Jackson
Storrs, Richard Salter, 1787–1873
Storrs, Richard Salter, 1821–1900
Story, Isaac
Story, Joseph
Story, William Edward
Story, William Wetmore
Stowe, Calvin Ellis
Strong, Caleb
Strong, Charles Augustus
Strong, Theodore
Sturgis, William
Sturtevant, Edward Lewis
Sullivan, John Lawrence
Sullivan, Louis Henri
Sumner, Charles
Sumner, Edwin Vose
Sumner, Increase
Sumner, James Batcheller
Swan, Timothy
Swift, Gustavus Franklin
Swift, Joseph Gardner
Swift, Louis Franklin
Swift, William Henry
Swift, Zephaniah
Sylvester, Frederick Oakes
Talbot, Henry Paul
Talbot, Israel Tisdale
Talbot, Silas
Tappan, Arthur
Tappan, Benjamin
Tappan, Lewis
Tarbell, Edmund Charles

Tarbell, Frank Bigelow
Tarbell, Joseph
Tarr, Ralph Stockman
Taylor, Bert Leston
Taylor, Charles Alonzo
Taylor, Charles Henry
Taylor, William Ladd
Tenney, Charles Daniel
Thacher, George
Thacher, James
Thacher, Peter, 1651–1727
Thacher, Peter, 1752–1802
Thacher, Samuel Cooper
Thaxter, Roland
Thayer, Abbott Handerson
Thayer, Alexander Wheelock
Thayer, Eli
Thayer, Ezra Ripley
Thayer, Gideon French
Thayer, James Bradley
Thayer, John
Thayer, John Milton
Thayer, Joseph Henry
Thayer, Nathaniel
Thayer, Sylvanus
Thayer, Thomas Baldwin
Thayer, Whitney Eugene
Thayer, William Makepeace
Thayer, William Roscoe
Thayer, William Sydney
Thomas, David
Thomas, Isaiah
Thomas, John
Thompson, Benjamin
Thompson, Cephas Giovanni
Thompson, Daniel Pierce
Thompson, Edward Herbert
Thompson, Jerome B.
Thompson, John
Thompson, William Hale
Thoreau, Henry David
Thorndike, Edward Lee
Thorndike, Israel
Thorndike, Lynn
Thorp, John
Thorpe, Thomas Bangs
Thurber, Charles
Thwaites, Reuben Gold
Ticknor, George
Tileston, Thomas
Tingley, Katherine Augusta West-
   cott
Tinkham, George Holden
Tobey, Charles William
Tobey, Edward Silas
Tobin, Maurice Joseph
Todd, Mabel Loomis
Tolman, Edward Chace
Tolman, Herbert Cushing
Tolman, Richard Chace
Tondorf, Francis Anthony
Topliff, Samuel
Torrey, Bradford
Torrey, Charles Turner
Tower, Zealous Bates
Townsend, Edward Davis
Tracy, Nathaniel
Train, Arthur Cheney
Train, Enoch
Train, George Francis
Treadwell, Daniel
Trott, Benjamin
Trow, John Fowler

Trowbridge, Edmund
Trowbridge, John
Tucker, Benjamin Ricketson
Tucker, Samuel
Tuckerman, Edward
Tuckerman, Frederick
Tuckerman, Frederick Goddard
Tuckerman, Henry Theodore
Tuckerman, Joseph
Tudor, Frederic
Tudor, William
Tufts, Charles
Tufts, Cotton
Tufts, James Hayden
Tufts, John
Tupper, Benjamin
Turell, Jane
Turner, Asa
Turner, Jonathan Baldwin
Tyler, Ransom Hubert
Tyler, Royall, 1757–1826
Tyler, Royall, 1884–1953
Tyler, William Seymour
Tyng, Edward
Tyng, Stephen Higginson
Underwood, Francis Henry
Underwood, Loring
Upham, Samuel Foster
Upton, George Putnam
Upton, Winslow
Vaillant, George Clapp
Valentine, Robert Grosvenor
Van Brunt, Henry
Varnum, James Mitchell
Varnum, Joseph Bradley
Very, Jones
Very, Lydia Louisa Ann
Villard, Helen Frances Garrison
Vinton, Frederic
Vinton, Samuel Finley
Wade, Benjamin Franklin
Wadsworth, Eliot
Wadsworth, Peleg
Wainwright, Richard, 1817–1862
Walcot, Charles Melton, 1840–
   1921
Walcott, Henry Pickering
Waldo, Samuel
Walker, Francis Amasa
Walker, Henry Oliver
Walker, Sears Cook
Walker, Timothy, 1705–1782
Walker, Timothy, 1802–1856
Walker, William Johnson
Wallace, John Findley
Walsh, David Ignatius
Walsh, Edmund Aloysius
Walsh, James Anthony
Walter, Thomas, 1696–1725
Ward, Artemas
Ward, Charles Henshaw
Ward, Elizabeth Stuart Phelps
Ward, Frederick Townsend
Ward, Henry Dana
Ward, Herbert Dickinson
Ward, Robert De Courcy
Ward, Thomas Wren
Ward, William Hayes
Ware, Ashur
Ware, Edmund Asa
Ware, Henry, 1764–1845
Ware, Henry, 1794–1843
Ware, John

Ware, John Fothergill Waterhouse
Ware, William
Ware, William Robert
Warner, Charles Dudley
Warner, Hiram
Warner, Langdon
Warner, Worcester Reed
Warren, Charles
Warren, Cyrus Moors
Warren, Francis Emroy
Warren, Henry Clarke
Warren, Henry Ellis
Warren, Henry White
Warren, James
Warren, John
Warren, John Collins, 1778–1856
Warren, John Collins, 1842–1927
Warren, Joseph
Warren, Josiah
Warren, Mercy Otis
Warren, William Fairfield
Washburn, Albert Henry
Washburn, Charles Grenfill
Washburn, Edward Abiel
Washburn, Emory
Washburn, George
Washburn, Ichabod
Waters, Daniel
Watson, Elkanah
Watson, Thomas Augustus
Watson, William
Wayland, Francis, 1826–1904
Webb, Thomas Smith
Webster, Arthur Gordon
Webster, Edwin Sibley
Webster, John White
Webster, Noah
Weeks, Edwin Lord
Weeks, Joseph Dame
Weiss, John
Weld, Arthur Cyril Gordon
Wellington, Arthur Mellen
Wellman, Samuel Thomas
Wells, David Ames
Wells, William Vincent
Wendell, Barrett
Wendte, Charles William
Wesson, Daniel Baird
West, Benjamin
West, Samuel
Wheeler, Benjamin Ide
Wheeler, George Montague
Wheeler, William
Wheeler, William Adolphus
Wheelwright, Edmund March
Wheelwright, Mary Cabot
Wheelwright, William
Whipple, Amiel Weeks
Whipple, Edwin Percy
Whipple, Squire
Whistler, James Abbott McNeill
Whitaker, Daniel Kimball
White, Charles Abiathar
White, Leonard Dupee
Whiting, Arthur Battelle
Whiting, George Elbridge
Whiting, William
Whiting, William Henry Chase
Whitman, Ezekiel
Whitmore, Frank Clifford
Whitmore, William Henry
Whitney, Anne
Whitney, Asa

Whitney, Caspar
Whitney, Eli
Whitney, George
Whitney, James Lyman
Whitney, Josiah Dwight
Whitney, Mary Watson
Whitney, Myron William
Whitney, William Collins
Whitney, William Dwight
Whiton, James Morris
Whittemore, Amos
Whittemore, Thomas, 1800–1861
Whittemore, Thomas, 1871–1950
Whittier, John Greenleaf
Whorf, Benjamin Lee
Wiggin, Albert Henry
Wiggin, James Henry
Wigglesworth, Edward, 1693–1765
Wigglesworth, Edward, 1732–1794
Wigglesworth, Edward, 1840–1896
Wilbur, Hervey Backus
Wilde, George Francis Faxon
Wiley, Ephraim Emerson
Willard, Joseph
Willard, Samuel, 1639/40–1707
Willard, Samuel, 1775–1859
Willard, Sidney
Willard, Simon
Willard, Solomon
Williams, Elisha
Williams, Ephraim
Williams, Francis Henry
Williams, Henry Willard
Williams, Israel
Williams, John, 1664–1729
Williams, John, 1817–1899
Williams, John Foster
Williams, John Joseph
Williams, Jonathan
Williams, Nathaniel
Williams, Stephen West
Williams, William
Willis, Nathaniel
Willis, William
Williston, Samuel, 1795–1874
Williston, Samuel, 1861–1963
Williston, Samuel Wendell
Wilmarth, Lemuel Everett
Wilson, George Francis
Wilson, Samuel
Winchester, Elhanan
Winchester, Oliver Fisher
Wingate, Paine
Winship, Albert Edward
Winship, George Parker
Winslow, Charles-Edward Amory
Winslow, Edward
Winslow, John
Winslow, Josiah
Winslow, Sidney Wilmot
Winslow, William Copley
Winsor, Justin
Winter, William
Winthrop, James
Winthrop, John, 1638–1707
Winthrop, John, 1714–1779
Winthrop, Robert Charles
Wise, John
Wolcott, Edward Oliver
Wood, Edward Stickney

Wood, Jethro
Woodberry, George Edward
Woodbridge, Samuel Merrill
Woodbridge, William Channing
Woodbury, Charles Jeptha Hill
Woodbury, Isaac Baker
Woods, James Haughton
Woods, Leonard, 1774–1854
Woods, Leonard, 1807–1878
Woodward, Calvin Milton
Woodworth, Samuel
Worcester, Samuel Austin
Workman, Fanny Bullock
Worthen, William Ezra
Worthington, John
Wright, Chauncey
Wright, John Stephen
Wright, Philip Green
Wright, Silas
Wyeth, John
Wyeth, Newell Convers
Wyman, Horace
Wyman, Jeffries
Wyman, Morrill
Yale, Elihu
Yeomans, John William
Young, Alexander

MICHIGAN

Ament, William Scott
Anthon, John
Atkinson, George Francis
Atterbury, Grosvenor
Avery, Sewell Lee
Bachmann, Werner Emmanuel
Bacon, Leonard
Bagley, William Chandler
Bailey, James Anthony
Bailey, Liberty Hyde
Baker, Ray Stannard
Barrows, John Henry
Beach, Rex
Beal, William James
Bigelow, Melville Madison
Binga, Jesse
Birkhoff, George David
Blodgett, John Wood
Boeing, William Edward
Bovie, William T.
Brewer, Mark Spencer
Briggs, Lyman James
Brooks, Alfred Hulse
Brower, Jacob Vradenberg
Brown, Olympia
Brucker, Wilber Marion
Bundy, Harvey Hollister
Burton, Frederick Russell
Butterfield, Kenyon Leech
Campaw, Joseph
Campbell, Douglas Houghton
Carleton, Will
Chaffee, Roger Bruce
Chapin, Roy Dikeman
Chessman, Caryl Whittier
Child, Charles Manning
Church, Frederick Stuart
Cicotte, Edward Victor
Clements, William Lawrence
Cobo, Albert Eugene
Comfort, Will Levington
Cooke, George Willis
Cooley, Thomas Benton

Copeland, Royal Samuel
Corby, William
Corrothers, James David
Corwin, Edward Samuel
Curtis, Edward Lewis
Curtis, Heber Doust
Curwood, James Oliver
Darling, Jay Norwood ("Ding")
Davenport, Eugene
De Langlade, Charles Michel
Dennison, Walter
Dodge, Joseph Morrell
Drum, Hugh Aloysius
Eaton, Daniel Cady
Elliott, Walter Hackett Robert
Fairchild, David Grandison
Farnsworth, Elon John
Ferber, Edna Jessica
Ferry, Elisha Peyre
Ferry, Thomas White
Flaherty, Robert Joseph
Folks, Homer
Ford, Edsel Bryant
Ford, Henry
Forsyth, Thomas
Frieseke, Frederick Carl
Gauss, Christian Frederick
Gay, Edwin Francis
Geddes, Norman Bel
Gerber, (Daniel) Frank
Gerber, Daniel (Frank)
Gräbner, August Lawrence
Graham, Ernest Robert
Hale, Frederick
Haynes, Williams
Hill, Louis Clarence
Howard, Brownson Crocker
Howard, Timothy Edward
Howell, Albert Summers
Hubbard, Henry Guernsey
Hulbert, Edwin James
Humphrey, George Magoffin
Hunt, Henry Jackson
Hupp, Louis Gorham
Hutcheson, William Levi
Ingersoll, Robert Hawley
Ingersoll, Royal Rodney
Irwin, George Le Roy
Jenks, Jeremiah Whipple
Joy, Henry Bourne
Kearns, Jack
Kelland, Clarence Budington
Kellogg, John Harvey
Kellogg, Paul Underwood
Kellogg, Will Keith
Kidder, Alfred Vincent
King, Henry Churchill
Kirchwey, George Washington
Kohler, Max James
Krehbiel, Henry Edward
Lacy, William Albert
Lamb, Isaac Wixom
Lamoureux, Andrew Jackson
Lanman, Charles
Lardner, Ringgold Wilmer
Lemmon, John Gill
Levy, Max
Liggett, Louis Kroh
Lindeman, Eduard Christian
Livingston, Burton Edward
Longyear, John Munroe
Lovejoy, Owen Reed
McAndrew, William

McHugh, Rose John
McKinstry, Elisha Williams
Macomb, Alexander
McRae, Milton Alexander
Macy, John Albert
Marsh, Frank Burr
Matthews, Franklin
Mayo, Mary Anne Bryant
Meany, Edmond Stephen
Melchers, Gari
Miller, Webb
Moore, Charles
Morton, Paul
Moulton, Forest Ray
Muir, Charles Henry
Murphy, Frank
Navarre, Pierre
Nestor, Agnes
Newberry, Truman Handy
Noble, Alfred
O'Brien, Thomas James
Otis, Charles Eugene
Pack, Charles Lathrop
Palmer, Thomas Witherell
Penfield, William Lawrence
Pilcher, Lewis Stephen
Pitkin, Walter Boughton
Pond, Allen Bartlit
Pond, Irving Kane
Prall, David Wight
Raby, James Joseph
Roethke, Theodore Huebner
Rolshoven, Julius
Royce, Ralph
Ryan, John Dennis
Ryerson, Martin Antoine
St. John, Charles Edward
Sanderson, Ezra Dwight
Schall, Thomas David
Scripps, William Edmund
Seager, Henry Rogers
Shafter, William Rufus
Shepard, James Henry
Sherman, Frederick Carl
Sibley, Henry Hastings
Sloane, Isabel Cleves Dodge
Squier, George Owen
Taylor, Fred Manville
Thomas, Calvin
Tilzer, Harry Von
Toumey, James William
Towne, Charles Arnette
Vance, Harold Sines
Vandenberg, Arthur Hendrick
Van Tyne, Claude Halstead
Webber, Herbert John
Whelpley, Henry Milton
White, Stewart Edward
Wilbur, Cressy Livingston
Wilcox, Delas Franklin
Willcox, Orlando Bolivar
Willett, Herbert Lockwood
Williams, Gardner Fred
Winchell, Horace Vaughn
Woodward, Robert Simpson

MINNESOTA

Bender, Charles Albert ("Chief")
Bottineau, Pierre
Boyle, Michael J.
Burdick, Usher Lloyd
Burleson, Hugh Latimer

Burnham, Frederick Russell
Butler, Pierce
Carruth, Fred Hayden
Cooper, Hugh Lincoln
Densmore, Frances
Dobie, Gilmour
Dworshak, Henry Clarence
Edwards, Everett Eugene
Farwell, Arthur
Fillmore, Charles
Fitzgerald, Francis Scott Key
Flandrau, Charles Macomb
Frary, Francis Cowles
Fraser, James Earle
Frazier, Lynn Joseph
Frey, John Philip
Fulton, John Farquhar
Garland, Judy
Gillespie, Mabel
Goode, John Paul
Griggs, Everett Gallup
Haines, Lynn
Hall, Hazel
Haupt, Alma Cecelia
Heffelfinger, William Walter "Pudge"
Hodson, William
Hopkins, Cyril George
Hormel, Jay Catherwood
Johnson, John Albert
Judd, Edward Starr
Kerr, Walter Craig
Knappen, Theodore Temple
Langlie, Arthur Bernard
Lemke, William Frederick
Lewis, Harry Sinclair
Liggett, Walter William
Little Crow V
Lloyd, Marshall Burns
Lowden, Frank Orren
McAlexander, Ulysses Grant
McNair, Lesley James
Magoon, Charles Edward
Manship, Paul Howard
Mayo, Charles Horace
Mayo, William James
Mich, Daniel Danforth
Michel, Virgil George
Mitchell, William DeWitt
Olds, Robert Edwin
Olson, Floyd Bjerstjerne
Oppenheim, James
Pegler, Westbrook
Plowman, George Taylor
Plummer, Henry Stanley
Putnam, Helen Cordelia
Pye, Watts Orson
Ranson, Stephen Walter
Red Wing
Rothafel, Samuel Lionel
Ryan, John Augustine
Sears, Richard Warren
Shaughnessy, Clark Daniel
Shields, Thomas Edward
Shipstead, Henrik
Swift, Linton Bishop
Todd, Mike
Townley, Arthur Charles
Volstead, Andrew John
Wabasha
Warner, Anne Richmond
Wood, John Taylor

MISSISSIPPI

Bailey, Joseph Weldon
Barry, William Taylor Sullivan
Baskerville, Charles
Battle, Burrell Bunn
Bilbo, Theodore Gilmore
Black, John Charles
Bodenheim, Maxwell
Boyd, Richard Henry
Brandon, Gerard Chittocque
Brickell, Henry Herschel
Brough, Charles Hillman
Chamberlain, George Earle
Claiborne, John Francis Hamtramck
Clarke, James Paul
Clayton, William Lockhart
Davis, Joseph Robert
Davis, Varina Howell
Dickinson, Jacob McGavock
Dorsey, Sarah Anne Ellis
Evers, Medgar Wiley
Farish, William Stamps
Faulkner (Falkner), William Cuthbert
Finney, John Miller Turpin
Gailor, Thomas Frank
Gaither, Horace Rowan, Jr.
Galloway, Charles Betts
Garner, James Wilford
Gordon, James
Gore, Thomas Pryor
Gregory, Thomas Watt
Harris, Nathaniel Harrison
Harris, Wiley Pope
Harrison, Byron Patton
Harrison, James Albert
Howry, Charles Bowen
Hughes, Henry
Humphreys, Benjamin Grubb
Ingraham, Prentiss
Jeffrey, Rosa Griffith Vertner Johnson
Jones, James Kimbrough
Leflore, Greenwood
Littlefield, George Washington
Lomax, John Avery
MacDowell, Katherine Sherwood Bonner
McLaurin, Anselm Joseph
Manning, Vannoy Hartrog
Mayes, Edward
Money, Hernando De Soto
Morton, Ferdinand Quintin
Mullins, Edgar Young
Newlands, Francis Griffith
Nicholson, Eliza Jane Poitevent Holbrook
Parker, John Milliken
Percy, William Alexander
Phelan, James
Pitchlynn, Peter Perkins
Pittman, Key
Pushmataha
Putnam, Arthur
Rankin, John Elliott
Read, Charles William
Russell, Irwin
Short, Joseph Hudson, Jr.
Simmons, Roscoe Conkling Murray
Stockard, Charles Rupert

Van Dorn, Earl
Warfield, Catherine Ann Ware
Wheeler, George Wakeman
Whitfield, Owen
Williams, Ben Ames
Wright, Fielding Lewis
Wright, Richard Nathaniel
Yellowley, Edward Clements
Young, Stark
Zimmerman, Eugene

MISSOURI

Alexander, Will Winton
Allison, Nathaniel
Anderson, Benjamin McAlester
Arden, Edwin Hunter Pendleton
Armstrong, Paul
Asbury, Herbert
Baldwin, Evelyn Briggs
Bates, John Coalter
Bates, Onward
Beckwith, James Carroll
Beery, Wallace Fitzgerald
Bent, Silas
Bent, William
Blair, Emily Newell
Bliss, Robert Woods
Blow, Susan Elizabeth
Bogy, Lewis Vital
Bonfils, Frederick Gilmer
Boyd, William Kenneth
Brookhart, Smith Wildman
Buchanan, Joseph Ray
Caldwell, Eugene Wilson
Campbell, Prince Lucien
Cannon, Clarence
Caraway, Thaddeus Horatius
Carnegie, Dale
Carver, George Washington
Chetlain, Augustus Louis
Chopin, Kate O'Flaherty
Chouteau, Auguste Pierre
Chouteau, Pierre
Churchill, Winston
Clark, Bennett Champ
Clemens, Samuel Langhorne
Cockrell, Francis Marion
Colby, Bainbridge
Coontz, Robert Edward
Cornoyer, Paul
Craig, Malin
Craighead, Edwin Boone
Creel, George
Crowder, Enoch Herbert
Croy, Homer
Dalton, Robert
Dandy, Walter Edward
Darwell, Jane
Davis, Dwight Filley
Davison, Gregory Caldwell
Dent, Frederick Tracy
De Young, Michel Harry
Dodge, Augustus Caesar
Dooley, Thomas Anthony, III
Eliot, T(homas) S(tearns)
Ellis, George Washington
Engelmann, George Julius
Field, Eugene
Field, Mary Katherine Keemle
Field, Roswell Martin
Finck, Henry Theophilus
Finn, Francis James

Fletcher, Thomas Clement
Fox, Williams Carlton
Frank, Glenn
Galloway, Beverly Thomas
Goldstein, Max Aaron
Gotshall, William Charles
Grant, Frederick Dent
Grant, Harry Johnston
Griffith, Clark Calvin
Hammond, Bray
Hannegan, Robert Emmet
Harlow, Jean
Harshe, Robert Bartholow
Hatcher, Robert Anthony
Hearst, George
Hearst, Phoebe Apperson
Hendrix, Eugene Russell
Hendrix, Joseph Clifford
Hewett, Waterman Thomas
Hildreth, Samuel Clay
Holden, Edward Singleton
Holden, Hale
Holt, William Franklin
Horn, Tom
Horst, Louis
Howell, Thomas Jefferson
Hubbard, Wynant Davis
Hubble, Edwin
Hudson, Manley Ottmer
Hughes, Howard Robard
Hughes, James Langston
Hughes, Rupert
Hunt, George Wylie Paul
Hyde, Arthur Mastick
Jackling, Daniel Cowan
James, Jesse Woodson
James, Marquis
Jones, Benjamin Allyn
Joy, Charles Turner
Keith, Arthur
Kimball, Dan Able
Kroeger, Ernest Richard
Lange, Alexis Frederick
Long, Breckinridge
Love, Robertus Donnell
Lunceford, James Melvin ("Jimmie")
McAfee, John Armstrong
McArthur, William Pope
McCausland, John
McClurg, Joseph Washington
McConnell, Ira Welch
MacCurdy, George Grant
Macfadden, Berharr
McIntyre, Oscar Odd
McManus, George
Malin, Patrick Murphy
Mallinckrodt, Edward
Mallinckrodt, Edward, Jr.
Marbut, Curtis Fletcher
Marmaduke, John Sappington
Marshall, William Rainey
Marvin, Enoch Mather
Mondell, Frank Wheeler
More, Paul Elmer
Morfit, Campbell
Nelson, Donald Marr
Nelson, Marjorie Maxine
Nicholson, James Bartram
Niebuhr, Helmut Richard
Noonan, James Patrick
O'Sullivan, Mary Kenney
Pallen, Condé Benoist

Parker, Edward Brewington
Pendergast, Thomas Joseph
Pershing, John Joseph
Philips, John Finis
Powell, John Benjamin
Pratte, Bernard
Prentis, Henning Webb, Jr.
Pritchett, Henry Smith
Pryor, Arthur W.
Pulitzer, Ralph
Quayle, William Alfred
Rautenstrauch, Walter
Reedy, William Marion
Rickard, George Lewis
Robidon, Antoine
Rombauer, Irma Louise
Ross, Charles Griffith
Russell, Charles Ellsworth ("Pee
  Wee")
Russell, Sol Smith
Rutherford, Joseph Franklin
St. Vrain, Ceran De Hault De
  Lassus de
Sarpy, Peter A.
Shafroth, John Franklin
Shannon, Fred Albert
Smedley, Agnes
Smith, Horton
Smith, James Allen
Smith, Joseph Fielding
Spiering, Theodore
Spillman, William Jasper
Spink, John George Taylor
Stephens, Edwin William
Stettinius, Edward Riley
Stoessel, Albert Frederic
Swift, John Franklin
Swope, Gerard
Swope, Herbert Bayard
Talbot, Ethelbert
Taussig, Frank William
Teasdale, Sara
Thomas, Augustus
Toole, Edwin Warren
Toole, Joseph Kemp
Turner, George
Turner, James Milton
Vaughn, Victor Clarence
Walker, Robert Franklin
Wallace, Charles William
Wallace, Hugh Campbell
Walsh, Francis Patrick
Walton, Lester Aglar
White, Pearl
Wiener, Norbert
Williams, Walter
Wood, Robert Elkington
Yost, Casper Salathiel
Younger, Thomas Coleman

MONTANA

Baker, Dorothy Dodds
Beary, Donald Bradford
Brophy, Thomas D'Arcy
Cooper, Gary
Thompson, William Boyce
Washakie

NEBRASKA

Abbott, Edith
Abbott, Grace

Alexander, Grover Cleveland
Alexander, Hartley Burr
Barrett, Frank Aloysius
Billings, Asa White Kenney
Bright Eyes
Bryson, Lyman Lloyd
Clements, Frederic Edward
Clift, Edward Montgomery
Cloud, Henry Roe
Crawford, Samuel Earl
Dern, George Henry
Embree, Edwin Rogers
Fairchild, Fred Rogers
Gibson, Edmund Richard
  ("Hoot")
Gifford, Sanford Robinson
Gortner, Ross Aiken
Guthrie, Edwin Ray, Jr.
Higgins, Andrew Jackson
Hitchcock, Gilbert Monell
Hoagland, Charles Lee
Hollingworth, Leta Stetter
Hunter, Walter David
Jeffers, William Martin
Malcolm X
Matthews, Francis Patrick
Monsky, Henry
Morton, Charles Walter
Pate, Maurice
Patterson, Richard Cunningham,
  Jr.
Phillips, Frank
Pound, (Nathan) Roscoe
Red Cloud
Rhodes, Eugene Manlove
Rosewater, Victor
Sandoz, Mari
Scott, Allen Cecil
Simpson, John Andrew
Smart, David Archibald
Spencer, Robert
Stevens, Doris
Strong, Anna Louise
Sutherland, Edwin Hardin
Taylor, Robert
Warren, George Frederick
Washburn, Edward Wight
Wherry, Kenneth Spicer

NEVADA

Ashurst, Henry Fountain
Lynch, Robert Clyde
McCarran, Patrick Anthony
McLoughlin, Maurice Evans
Martin, Anne Henrietta
Michelson, Charles
Requa, Mark Lawrence
Winnemucca, Sarah
Wovoka

NEW HAMPSHIRE

Abbott, Joseph Carter
Adams, Ebenezer
Adams, Isaac
Akerman, Amos Tappan
Albee, Ernest
Aldrich, Edgar
Aldrich, Thomas Bailey
Allen, Glover Morrill
Andrews, Christopher Columbus
Andrews, Elisha Benjamin

Appleton, John
Appleton, Nathan
Appleton, Samuel
Atherton, Charles Gordon
Atwood, David
Bachelder, John
Bailey, Solon Irving
Baker, Osmon Cleander
Ballon, Hosea
Bancroft, Cecil Franklin Patch
Barnabee, Henry Clay
Barry, John Stewart
Bartlett, Ichabod
Bartlett, Samuel Colcord
Batchelder, John Putnam
Batchelder, Samuel
Beach, Amy Marcy Cheney
Beard, Mary
Belknap, George Eugene
Bell, Charles Henry
Bell, Louis
Bell, Luther Vose
Bell, Samuel
Benton, James Gilchrist
Bissell, George Henry
Blair, Henry William
Blake, John Lauris
Blodget, Samuel
Blunt, Edmund March
Bonton, John Bell
Bridgman, Laura Dewey
Brooks, John Graham
Brown, Charles Rufus
Brown, Francis, 1784–1820
Brown, Francis, 1849–1916
Brown, George
Browne, Daniel Jay
Buckminster, Joseph Stevens
Bundy, Jonas Mills
Burnap, George Washington
Burnham, William Henry
Burton, Warren
Butler, Benjamin Franklin
Cass, Lewis
Chamberlain, Mellen
Champney, Benjamin
Chandler, Harry
Chandler, John
Chandler, William Eaton
Chandler, Zachariah
Chase, Philander
Chase, Salmon Portland
Cheney, Benjamin Pierce
Cheney, Oren Burbank
Cheney, Person Colby
Chickering, Jonas
Cilley, Joseph
Clark, Daniel
Clark, Greenleaf
Clarke, James Freeman
Clifford, Nathan
Coffin, Charles Carleton
Coffin, Lorenzo S.
Cones, Elliott
Corbin, Daniel Chase
Craig, Daniel H.
Cram, Ralph Adams
Craven, Tunis Augustus Mac-
  donough
Currier, Moody
Cutler, Carroll
Cutting, James Ambrose
Damon, Ralph Shepard

Dana, Charles Anderson
Dana, James Freeman
Dana, Samuel Luther
Daniels, Fred Harris
Darling, Flora Adams
Davis, Noah
Davis, Phineas
Day, Edmund Ezra
Dearborn, Henry
Dearborn, Henry Alexander
    Scammell
Dodge, Jacob Richards
Doe, Charles
Donovan, John Joseph
Drake, Francis Samuel
Drake, Samuel Gardner
Durant, Henry Fowle
Durell, Edward Henry
Dutton, Samuel Train
Eastman, Arthur MacArthur
Eastman, Enoch Worthen
Eastman, John Robie
Eastman, Timothy Corser
Eaton, John
Eddy, Mary Morse Baker
Ellis, Carleton
Elwyn, Alfred Langdon
Emerson, Benjamin Kendall
Emerson, Joseph
Estabrook, Joseph
Estey, Jacob
Farley, Harriet
Farmer, Moses Gerrish
Farnum, Dustin Lancy
Farrar, Timothy
Ferguson, Samuel
Fessenden, Thomas Green
Fessenden, William Pitt
Fields, James Thomas
Fiske, Amos Kidder
Flanders, Henry
Fletcher, William Asa
Flynn, Elizabeth Gurley
Fogg, George Gilman
Folsom, Charles
Folsom, Nathaniel
Foss, Sam Walter
Foster, Frank Pierce
Foster, John Gray
Foster, Stephen Symonds
French, Daniel Chester
French, William Merchant Rich-
    ardson
Fuller, Levi Knight
Gardner, Helen
Gilman, John Taylor
Gilman, Nicholas
Glidden, Joseph Farwell
Goldthwaite, Henry Barnes
Goodenow, John Milton
Goodhue, James Madison
Gordon, George Phineas
Gould, Augustus Addison
Gove, Aaron Estellus
Greeley, Horace
Greene, Nathaniel
Griffin, Appleton Prentiss Clark
Griffin, Simon Goodell
Grimes, James Wilson
Gunnison, John Williams
Hackett, Frank Warren
Haddock, Charles Brickett
Haines, Charles Glidden

Hale, Edwin Moses
Hale, Horatio Emmons
Hale, John Parker
Hale, Sarah Josepha Buell
Hall, Charles Francis
Hall, George Henry
Hall, Samuel Read
Hall, Thomas Seavey
Harlow, Ralph Volney
Harriman, Walter
Haskell, Ella Louise Knowles
Hill, Joseph Adna
Holmes, Nathaniel
Howard, Ada Lydia
Howland, Alfred Cornelius
Hoyt, Albert Harrison
Hoyt, Charles Hale
Hunton, George Kenneth
Hutchins, Harry Burns
Jackson, Hall
Jewell, Harvey
Jewell, Marshall
Jewett, Clarence Frederick
Jones, Frank
Jones, John Taylor
Jones, Robert Edmond
Joy, James Frederick
Judson, Sarah Hall Boardman
Keith, Benjamin Franklin
Kelley, Hall Jackson
Kendall, George Wilkins
Kent, Edward
Kidder, Frederic
Kimball, Gilman
Kimball, Richard Burleigh
Knox, Thomas Wallace
Ladd, William
Langdell, Christopher Columbus
Langdon, John
Langdon, Woodbury
Lear, Tobias
Leavitt, Dudley
Leavitt, Mary Greenleaf Clement
Lee, Eliza Buckminster
Little, Charles Sherman
Livermore, Abiel Abbot
Livermore, Arthur
Livermore, Edward St. Loe
Livermore, Samuel, 1786–1833
Locke, John
Long, Stephen Harriman
Lord, John
Lothrop, Daniel
Lovewell, John
Lowe, Charles
Lowe, Thaddeus Sobieski Coulin-
    court
McKeen, Joseph
Marden, Orison Sweet
Marsh, Sylvester
Martyn, Sarah Towne Smith
Mather, Samuel Holmes
Mathews, William Smythe Bab-
    cock
Mead, Edwin Doak
Mead, Larkin Goldsmith
Merrill, William Bradford
Meserve, Nathaniel
Metalious, Grace
Metcalf, Henry Harrison
Miller, Charles Ransom
Miner, Alonzo Ames
Moore, Frank

Moore, George Henry
Moore, Jacob Bailey
Moore, John Weeks
Morril, David Lawrence
Morrison, Nathan Jackson
Mussey, Reuben Dimond
Neal, Joseph Clay
Nelson, Edward William
Nesmith, John
Nichols, Mary Sargeant Neal
    Gove
Nichols, Thomas Low
Orcutt, Hiram
Ordway, John
Osgood, Jacob
Page, David Perkins
Parker, Francis Wayland
Parker, Joel
Parker, Willard
Parrott, Enoch Greenleafe
Parrott, Robert Parker
Partridge, Richard
Patrick, Mary Mills
Patterson, James Willis
Payson, Edward
Peabody, Oliver William Bourn
Peabody, William Bourn Oliver
Pearl, Raymond
Peaslee, Edmund Randolph
Perkins, George Hamilton
Perry, Arthur Latham
Peters, Absalom
Pickering, John
Pierce, Franklin
Pierce, John Davis
Pike, Nicholas
Pillsbury, Charles Alfred
Pillsbury, John Sargent
Pilsbury, Amos
Plaisted, Harris Merrill
Poor, John
Porter, Fitz-John
Pratt, Daniel, July 20, 1799–May
    13, 1873
Prescott, George Bartlett
Prescott, Samuel Cate
Proctor, Lucien Brock
Quimby, Phineas Parkhurst
Randall, Benjamin
Rankin, Jeremiah Eames
Rice, George Samuel
Richards, Charles Herbert
Richardson, William Merchant
Ripley, Eleazar Wheelock
Roberts, Edmund
Rolfe, Robert Abial ("Red")
Rollins, Edward Henry
Rollins, Frank West
Sabine, Lorenzo
Sanborn, Edwin David
Sanborn, Franklin Benjamin
Sanborn, Katherine Abbott
Sanborn, Walter Henry
Sargent, George Henry
Savage, Henry Wilson
Shahan, Thomas Joseph
Shattuck, Aaron Draper
Shaw, Elijah
Shear, Theodore Leslie
Shedd, Fred Fuller
Shedd, John Graves
Sherman, Forrest Percival
Sherwin, Thomas

Sherwood, Mary Elizabeth Wilson
Shillaber, Benjamin Penhallow
Shurtleff, Roswell Morse
Smart, James Henry
Smith, Asa Dodge
Smith, Hamilton
Smith, Jeremiah, 1759–1842
Smith, Jeremiah, 1837–1921
Smith, Jeremiah, 1870–1935
Smith, Justin Harvey
Smith, Nathan Ryno
Smith, Uriah
Spalding, Lyman
Spaulding, Levi
Spaulding, Oliver Lyman
Spofford, Ainsworth Rand
Stark, John
Stearns, John Newton
Stone, Harlan Fiske
Stow, Baron
Sullivan, George
Sullivan, John
Sumner, Walter Taylor
Swasey, Ambrose
Swett, John
Taylor, Harry
Taylor, Samuel Harvey
Tenney, Edward Payson
Tenney, Tabitha Gilman
Thaxter, Celia Laighton
Thomson, Samuel
Ticknor, William Davis
Tilton, John Rollin
Titcomb, John Wheelock
Treat, Samuel
Twitchell, Amos
Upham, Thomas Cogswell
Upham, Warren
Walker, Asa
Walker, John Grimes
Waterhouse, Sylvester
Weare, Meshech
Webster, Daniel
Webster, Joseph Dana
Weeks, John Wingate
Wentworth, Benning
Wentworth, George Albert
Wentworth, John, 1737 N.S.–1820
Wentworth, John, 1815–1888
Wentworth, Paul
Whipple, Sherman Leland
White, Horace
Wilder, Marshall Pinckney
Willey, Samuel Hopkins
Wilson, Henry
Wilson, William Dexter
Wood, Edith Elmer
Wood, Leonard
Wood, Walter Abbott
Woodbury, Daniel Phineas
Woodbury, Levi
Woolson, Constance Fenimore
Worcester, Joseph Emerson
Worcester, Noah
Worcester, Samuel
Wright, Carroll Davidson
Wyman, Robert Harris
Wyman, Seth
Young, Ammi Burnham
Young, Charles Augustus

NEW JERSEY

Abbott, Charles Conrad
Abeel, David
Adams, Joseph Alexander
Alexander, Samuel Davies
Allen, William Frederick
Allinson, Francis Greenleaf
Archer, Samuel
Armstrong, George Dod
Armstrong, John
Arnold, Lewis Golding
Bailey, Gamaliel
Bainbridge, William
Baird, Charles Washington
Baldwin, Matthias William
Barber, Francis
Bard, John
Barrell, Joseph
Barrett, Lawrence
Barton, James Edward
Bateman, Newton
Beach, Harlan Page
Berrien, John MacPherson
Berry, Edward Wilber
Bishop, William Darius
Blackford, Charles Minor
Blackwell, Alice Stone
Blair, John Insley
Blakeley, George Henry
Bloomfield, Joseph
Boggs, Charles Stuart
Bourne, Randolph Silliman
Brearly, David
Breckinridge, Aida de Acosta
Brewster, Benjamin Harris
Bristol, Mark Lambert
Brooks, Van Wyck
Bross, William
Brown, Isaac Van Arsdale
Buckley, James Monroe
Burlingham, Charles Culp
Burnet, David Gouverneur
Burnet, Jacob
Burnet, William
Burr, Aaron
Butler, Nicholas Murray
Cadwalader, Lambert
Caldwell, Joseph
Campbell, Andrew
Cattell, Alexander Gilmore
Cattell, William Cassaday
Chambers, John
Chapman, Frank Michler
Chase, Edna Woolman
Christie, John Walter
Clark, Abraham
Clark, George Whitefield
Claxton, Kate
Cleveland, Stephen Grover
Coerne, Louis Adolphe
Coit, Henry Leber
Combs, Moses Newell
Condit, John
Cone, Spencer Houghton
Cook, Albert Stanburrough
Cook, George Hammell
Cook, Isaac
Cooke, Robert Anderson
Cooper, James Fenimore
Cooper, Samuel
Corrigan, Michael Augustine
Costello, Lou

Cox, Samuel Hanson
Coxe, Arthur Cleveland
Coxe, John Redman
Coxe, Richard Smith
Craig, Austin
Crane, Jonathan Townley
Crane, Stephen
Crane, William Montgomery
Craven, John Joseph
Darling, Samuel Taylor
Dayton, Elias
Dayton, Jonathan
Dayton, William Lewis
Dennis, Frederic Shepard
Dennis, James Shepard
Dickerson, Edward Nicoll
Dickerson, Mahlon
Dickerson, Philemon
Dickinson, Robert Latou
Dingman, Mary Agnes
Disbrow, William Stephen
Ditmars, Raymond Lee
Doane, George Washington
Dod, Albert Baldwin
Dod, Thaddeus
Dodd, Frank Howard
D'Olier, Franklin
Douglass, David Bates
Drake, Alexander Wilson
Drake, Daniel
Duffy, Edmund
Dunlap, William
Dunning, William Archibald
Du Pont, Samuel Francis
Durand, Asher Brown
Durand, Cyrus
Eames, Wilberforce
Edgar, Charles
Edison, Charles
Edsall, David Linn
Edwards, William
Eilshemius, Louis Michel
Elmer, Ebenezer
Elmer, Jonathan
Elmer, Lucius Quintius Cincinnatus
Endicott, Mordecai Thomas
Entwistle, James
Evans, Anthony Walton Whyte
Ewing, Charles
Fagan, Mark Matthew
Farrand, Livingston
Farrand, Max
Farson, Negley
Fauset, Jessie Redmon
Fay, Edward Allen
Filed, Richard Stockton
Finley, Robert
Fiske, Haley
Fiske, Stephen Ryder
Flanagin, Harris
Force, Peter
Ford, Jacob
Forman, David
Frank, Waldo David
Franz, Shepherd Ivory
Frazee, John
Frelinghuysen, Frederick
Frelinghuysen, Frederick Theodore
Frelinghuysen, Theodore
Gano, John
Gardner, Charles Kitchell

Garrison, Lindley Miller
Gaul, William Gilbert
Gilbert, Seymour Parker
Gilchrist, Robert
Gilchrist, William Wallace
Gilder, Richard Watson
Gitlow, Benjamin
Godwin, Parke
Goetschius, Percy
Goodrich, Annie Warburton
Grace, Eugene Gifford
Green, Ashbel
Green, Henry Woodhull
Green, John Cleve
Green, William Henry
Greenwood, Miles
Griffith, William
Griggs, John William
Griscom, John
Griscom, Lloyd Carpenter
Griswold, Alfred Whitney
Grundy, Joseph Ridgway
Gummere, Francis Barton
Gummere, Samuel James
Gummere, Samuel René
Gummere, William Stryker
Hager John Sharpenstein
Hague, Frank
Hall, Juanita Armethea
Halsey, William Frederick, Jr.
Halsted, George Bruce
Hardenbergh, Henry Janeway
Hare, William Hobart
Hart, James Morgan
Hartford, John Augustine
Hartley, Fred Allen, Jr.
Hatfield, Edwin Francis
Henderson, John
Henderson, Thomas
Henderson, William James
Henry, Alexander
Hewes, Joseph
Higgins, Daniel Paul
Hill, David Jayne
Hill, Ernest Rowland
Hill, Thomas, 1818–1891
Hillyer, Robert Silliman
Hires, Charles Elmer
Hobart, Garret Augustus
Hodge, Archibald Alexander
Hoffman, Josiah Ogden
Hopper, Isaac Tatem
Hornblower, Joseph Coerten
Hornblower, William Butler
Howell, David
Howell, James Bruen
Hubbs, Rebecca
Hunt, Theodore Whitefield
Hunt, Wilson Price
Hutchins, Thomas
Hutchinson, Paul
Imlay, Gilbert
Ivins, Anthony Woodward
Ivins, William Mills
Jackson, Charles Reginald
Jackson, John Brinckerhoff
Jackson, Joseph Henry
Janeway, Edward Gamaliel
Jay, Peter Augustus
Jeffers, William Nicholson
Jennings, Jonathan
Johnson, Elijah
Johnston, Augustus

Jones, Ernest Lester
Kafer, John Christian
Katchen, Julius
Kearney, Francis
Kearney, Lawrence
Kearny, Stephen Watts
Keater, Vaughan
Kelly, Howard Atwood
Kerlin, Isaac Newton
Kerney, James
Kilmer, Alfred Joycen
Kilpatrick, Hugh Judson
Kinney, William Burnet
Kinsey, Alfred Charles
Kinsey, John
Kirkpatrick, Andrew
Klein, August Clarence
Knight, Edward Coleings
Kovacs, Ernie
Kroeber, Alfred Louis
Lafever, Minard
Lake, Simon
Lange, Dorothea
Larned, William Augustus
Lasser, Jacob Kay
Lawrence, James
Leaming, Thomas
Leonard, William Ellery
Lieb, John William
Lindaberry, Richard Vliet
Lindsey, John Berrien
Lindsley, Philip
Linn, William Alexander
Lippincott, Joshua Ballinger
Littell, Eliakim
Littell, Squier
Littell, William
Lloyd, Alfred Henry
Longstreet, William
Longworth, Nicholas, 1782–1863
Low, Isaac
Low, Nicholas
Lozier, Clemence Sophia Harned
Lundy, Benjamin
Lyon, James
McAllister, Charles Albert
McCalla, Bowman Hendry
McCauley, Mary Ludwig Hays
McDowell, John
McEntee, James Joseph
McIlvaine, Charles Pettit
Maclean, John
McLean, John
McLean, Walter
McMichael, Morton
McMurtrie, Douglas Crawford
McMurtrie, William
Madigan, Laverne
Magie, William Jay
Magonigle, Harold Van Buren
Manning, James
Marin, John (Cheri)
Marshall, James Wilson
Marten, Alexander
Marten, Luther
Mason, John
Matlack, Timothy
Meeker, Moses
Messler, Thomas Doremus
Miller, Ezra
Miller, James Alexander
Miller, John
Mills, Benjamin Fay

Mitchell, James Paul
Mitchell, Thomas Gregory
Montgomery, John Berrien
Moody, James
Moody, John
Moore, Edward Mott
Moore, Ely
Moore, Victor Frederick
Moran, Daniel Edward
Morford, Henry
Morgan, Daniel
Morley, Edward Williams
Morris, Edmund
Morris, Robert, 1745–1815
Mott, Gershom
Murphy, Franklin
Myers, Gustavus
Napton, William Barclay
Neilson, John
Nelson, William, 1847–1914
Newton, Isaac, 1800–1867
Nies, James Buchanan
Nixon, John Thompson
Norris, Mary Harriott
Norton, Mary Teresa Hopkins
Noyes, Alexander Dana
Oatman, Johnson
Odell, Jonathan
O'Donnell, Thomas Jefferson
Ogden, Aaron
Ogden, David
Ogden, Francis Barber
Ogden, Samuel
Ogden, Thomas Ludlow
Ogden, Uzal
Olcott, Henry Steel
Opdyke, George
Osborn, Henry Fairfield
Otto, John Conrad
Oxden, Charles Smith
Page, Leigh
Paine, John Alsop
Palmer, James Shedden
Pancoast, Joseph
Parke, Benjamin
Parker, Dorothy Rothschild
Parker, James, c. 1714–1770
Parker, James, 1776–1868
Parker, Joel
Parker, John Cortlandt
Parsons, Frank
Parvin, Theodore Sutton
Patrick, Edwin Hill ("Ted")
Pennington, William
Pennington, William Sandford
Periam, Jonathan
Perrine, Frederic Auten Combs
Perrine, Henry
Pettit, Charles
Pike, Zebulon Montgomery
Pincus, Gregory Goodwin
   ("Goody")
Pitney, Mahlon
Plotz, Harry
Pollak, Walter Heilprin
Post, Louis Freeland
Price, Rodman McCamley
Quinby, Isaac Ferdinand
Ralph, James
Randall, Robert Richard
Randolph, Theodore Fitz
Reed, Joseph
Rellstab, John

Riggs, Elias
Roberts, Nathan S.
Robeson, George Maxwell
Rusby, Henry Hurd
St. Denis, Ruth
Salmon, Daniel Elmer
Sayre, Lewis Albert
Scattergood, Thomas
Schelling, Ernest Henry
Scovell, Melville Amasa
Scudder, John
Scudder, Nathaniel
Sedgwick, Anne Douglas
Seldes, Gilbert Vivian
Sergeant, John, 1710–1749
Sergeant, Jonathan Dickinson
Shafer, Helen Almira
Sharp, Dallas Lore
Shinn, Asa
Shinn, Everett
Shreve, Henry Miller
Sickels, Frederick Ellsworth
Silver, Thomas
Simpson, James Hervey
Sloan, Harold Paul
Smith, James, 1851–1927
Smith, John Jay
Smith, Lloyd Logan Pearsall
Smith, Richard
Somers, Richard
Sonneck, Oscar George Theodore
Southard, Samuel Lewis
Stagg, Amos Alonzo
Stanley, Robert Crooks
Stephens, Alice Barber
Stephens, John Lloyd
Stephens, Uriah Smith
Stetson, John Batterson
Stevens, Edwin Augustus
Stevens, Robert Livingston
Stieglitz, Alfred
Stieglitz, Julius
Still, William
Stillman, Thomas Bliss
Stimson, Lewis Atterbury
Stockton, John Potter
Stockton, Richard, 1730–1781
Stockton, Richard, 1764–1828
Stockton, Robert Field
Stockton, Thomas Hewlings
Stratemeyer, Edward
Sulzer, William
Sumner, William Graham
Sutherland, Joel Barlow
Talmadge, Norma
Talmage, John Van Nest
Talmage, Thomas DeWitt
Taylor, Joseph Wright
Tedyuskung
Terhune, Albert Payson
Thacher, Thomas Day
Thomas, John Parnell
Thompson, John Bodine
Tichenor, Isaac
Tomlinson, Everett Titsworth
Traubel, Horace L.
Tucker, Stephen Davis
Tumulty, Joseph Patrick
Tyson, George Emory
Vail, Alfred
Vanderbilt, Arthur T.
Vanderbilt, William Henry
Van Dyke, John Charles

Van Santvoord, George
Varick, Richard
Veiller, Lawrence Turnure
Voorhees, Edward Burnett
Voorhees, Philip Falkerson
Vroom, Peter Dumont
Warbasse, James Peter
Ward, Aaron Montgomery
Ward, James Warner
Ward, Marcus Lawrence
Ward, Richard Halsted
Ward, Thomas
Warren, Howard Crosby
Washington, Henry Stephens
Watson, John Fanning
Waugh, Frederick Judd
Welling, James Clarke
Westervelt, Jacob Aaron
Wetherill, Samuel
Whitehead, William Adee
Whiteside, Arthur Dare
Willard, Mary Hatch
Williams, William Carlos
Williamson, Isaac Halsted
Winans, Ross
Winans, Thomas De Kay
Wines, Enoch Cobb
Wood, George
Wood, George Bacon
Woodhull, Alfred Alexander
Woollcott, Alexander Humphreys
Woolman, John
Wright, Joseph
Wright, Patience Lovell
Wylie, Elinor Morton Hoyt
Young, David
Zane, Charles Shuster

NEW MEXICO

Beals, Ralph Albert
Bryan, Kirk
Carleton, Henry Guy
Chavez, Dennis
Dodge, Henry Chee
Glassford, Pelham Davis
Hubbell, John Lorenzo
Lyon, Harris Merton
Ouray
Seligman, Arthur
Son of Many Beads

NEW YORK

Abbe, Cleveland
Abbey, Henry
Abernethy, George
Adams, Henry Cullen
Adams, James Truslow
Adams, Samuel Hopkins
Adee, Alvey Augustus
Adler, Elmer
Agate, Alfred T.
Agate, Frederick Styles
Agnew, Cornelius Rea
Agnew, Eliza
Akeley, Carl Ethan
Alden, Isabella Macdonald
Alden, John Ferris
Alden, Joseph
Alden, Raymond MacDonald
Aldridge, Ira Frederick
Alexander, Stephen

Alexander, William
Allaire, James Peter
Allen, Arthur Augustus
Allen, Horatio
Allen, John
Allen, Kelcey
Allerton, Samuel Waters
Allis, Edward Phelps
Allison, Richard
Altman, Benjamin
Amidon, Charles Fremont
Anderson, Alexander
Anderson, Elizabeth Milbank
Anderson, Galusha
Andrews, Charles
Andrews, Edward Gayer
Andrews, William Loring
Angel, Benjamin Franklin
Anthon, Charles
Anthon, Charles Edward
Anthony, Andrew Varick Stout
Anthony, George Tobey
Anthony, John J.
Appleby, John Francis
Appleton, William Worthen
Armour, Philip Danforth
Armstrong, David Maitland
Armstrong, Edwin Howard
Arno, Peter
Arnold, Edward
Arnold, George
Arnold, Isaac Newton
Arnold, Lauren Briggs
Arthony, George Tobey
Arthur, Joseph Charles
Arthur, Timothy Shay
Ashmun, Jehudi
Aspinwall, William Henry
Astor, John Jacob, 1822–1890
Astor, John Jacob, 1864–1912
Astor, William Backhouse
Astor, William Vincent
Astor, William Waldorf
Atkinson, John
Atwater, Wilbur Olin
Auchmuty, Richard Tylden
Auer, John
Augur, Christopher Columbus
Austen, (Elizabeth) Alice
Austen, Peter Townsend
Averell, William Woods
Avery, Benjamin Parke
Avery, Milton Clark
Avery, Samuel Putnam
Ayres, Romeyn Beck
Babbitt, Benjamin Talbot
Babcock, George Herman
Babcock, Howard Edward
Babcock, Maltbie Davenport
Babcock, Stephen Moulton
Bache, Jules Semon
Bacheller, Irving
Bachman, John
Backus, Truman Jay
Bacon, Edward Payson
Bacon, Leonard
Badeau, Adam
Bailey, Florence Augusta Merriam
Bailey, James Montgomery
Bailey, Theodorus
Baker, Benjamin A.
Baker, Frank
Baker, George Augustus

Baker, George Fisher
Baker, La Fayette Curry
Baker, Peter Carpenter
Baker, Sara Josephine
Baker, Walter Ransom Gail
Baldwin, Elihu Whittlesey
Balestier, Charles Wolcott
Bangs, Francis Nehemiah
Bangs, John Kendrick
Banvard, John
Banvard, Joseph
Barbour, Oliver Lorenzo
Barclay, Thomas
Barker, James William
Barlow, Francis Channing
Barlow, John Whitney
Barnes, Albert
Barnes, Mary Downing Sheldon
Barnum, Henry A.
Barrows, Samuel June
Barry, Philip James Quinn
Barry, William Farquhar
Barthelmess, Richard
Bartlett, Homer Newton
Bascom, Henry Bidleman
Bascom, John
Bashford, Coles
Bassett, Edward Murray
Batcheller, George Sherman
Baum, Lyman Frank
Bausch, Edward
Baxter, Henry
Bayard, William
Bayles, James Copper
Bayley, James Roosevelt
Beach, Frederick Converse
Beach, William Augustus
Beadle, Erastus Flavel
Beard, James Henry
Beardsley, Samuel
Beauchamp, William Martin
Beck, John Brodhead
Beck, Lewis Caleb
Beck, Theodric Romeyn
Becker, George Ferdinand
Beebe, (Charles) William
Beecher, Catharine Esther
Beecher, Charles Emerson
Beecher, Edward
Beer, George Louis
Beers, Ethel Lynn
Beers, Henry Augustin
Belknap, William Worth
Bell, Clark
Bell, Isaac
Beman, Nathan Sidney Simth
Bement, Caleb N.
Benedict, Ruth Fulton
Benjamin, George Hillard
Benjamin, Nathan
Benjamin, Park
Bennet, Sanford Fillmore
Bennett, Constance Campbell
Bennett, de Robigne Mortimer
Bennett, Floyd
Bennett, James Gordon
Bennett, Nathaniel
Benson, Eugene
Benton, Allen Richardson
Benton, Joel
Berg, Gertrude Edelstein
Berger, Meyer
Bergh, Christian

Bergh, Henry
Bernet, John Joseph
Bernstein, Aline
Bethune, George Washington
Bidlack, Benjamin Alden
Bidwell, John
Bigelow, John
Biggs, Hermann Michael
Billy The Kid (Bonney, William H.)
Birdseye, Clarence
Birge, Edward Asahel
Bishop, Charles Reed
Bishop, Joel Prentiss
Bishop, Nathan
Bissell, Edwin Cone
Bissell, William Henry
Bissell, Wilson Shannon
Bixby, Horace Ezra
Blackfan, Kenneth Daniel
Blackwell, Antoinette Louisa Brown
Blaikie, William
Blair, Austin
Blake, Homer Crane
Blake, William Phipps
Blakelock, Ralph Albert
Blandy, William Henry Purnell
Blashfield, Edwin Howland
Blatch, Harriot Eaton Stanton
Bleecker, Ann Eliza
Bliss, Aaron Thomas
Bliss, Cornelius Newton
Bliss, Eliphalet Williams
Bliss, Porter Cornelius
Block, Paul
Blodget, Lorin
Blood, Benjamin Paul
Bloomer, Amelia Jenks
Bloor, Ella Reeve
Bogardus, James
Bogart, Humphrey DeForest
Bogart, John
Bogue, Virgil Gay
Boies, Horace
Boissevain, Inez Milholland
Bolton, Henry Carrington
Bomford, George
Bond, Elizabeth Powell
Bonney, Charles Carroll
Bonstelle, Jessie
Booth, Mary Louise
Borchard, Edwin Montefiore
Borden, Gail
Bottome, Margaret McDonald
Bouch, William C.
Bourne, Edward Gaylord
Bow, Clara Gordon
Bowen, Abel
Bowen, Herbert Wolcott
Boyle, John J.
Brace, Charles Loring
Brace, Dewitt Bristol
Brace, Donald Clifford
Brackett, Charles William
Bradford, Alexander Warfield
Bradford, Amory Howe
Bradford, William
Bradley, Joseph P.
Brady, Alice
Brady, James Topham
Brady, John Green
Brady, Mathew B.

Bragg, Edward Stuyvesant
Brainard, Daniel
Brainerd, Thomas
Braslau, Sophie
Brayman, Mason
Breese, Sidney
Brevoort, James Renwick
Brewer, William Henry
Brice, Fanny
Bridges, Calvin Blackman
Briggs, Charles Augustus
Brigham, Albert Perry
Bright, Jesse David
Brill, Nathan Edwin
Brinkerhoff, Jacob
Brinkerhoff, Roeliff
Brisbane, Albert
Brisbane, Arthur
Bristed, Charles Astor
Bristol, John Bunyan
Bristow, George Frederick
Britton, Nathaniel Lord
Brodhead, Daniel
Brooks, Byron Alden
Brooks, James Gordon
Brooks, Thomas Benton
Broun, Heywood Campbell
Browere, John Henri Isaac
Brown, Elmer Ellsworth
Brown, Frederic Tilden
Brown, Margaret Wise
Brown, Phoebe Hinsdale
Brown, William Adams
Brown, William Carlos
Browne, Irving
Browne, Junius Henri
Brownell, William Crary
Brownson, Willard Herbert
Bruce, Archibald
Bruce, Edward Bright
Bruce, Lenny
Brunner, Arnold William
Brush, Edward Nathaniel
Brush, George Jarvis
Bryce, Lloyd Stephens
Buck, Albert Henry
Buck, Gurdon
Buck, Leffert Lefferts
Buck, Philo Melvin
Buckhout, Isaac Craig
Buckley, Samuel Botsford
Budd, Joseph Lancaster
Bulkley, Lucius Duncan
Bullock, Rufus Brown
Bullock, William A.
Bunce, Oliver Bell
Bunker, Arthur Hugh
Bunner, Henry Cuyler
Burchard, Samuel Dickinson
Burdick, Francis Marion
Burke, John Joseph
Burke, Stevenson
Burke, Thomas
Burlin Natalie Curtis
Burlingame, Anson
Burnham, Daniel Hudson
Burr, George Lincoln
Burr, Theodosia
Burrill, Alexander Mansfield
Burroughs, John
Burroughs, John Curtis
Burroughs, William Seward
Burt, John

Bush-Brown, Henry Kirke
Bushnell, Asa Smith
Butler, Benjamin Franklin
Butler, Charles
Butler, Howard Crosby
Butler, Walter N.
Butler, William Allen
Butterfield, Daniel
Butterfield, John
Buttrick, Wallace
Butts, Isaac
Cady, Daniel
Calkins, Norman Allison
Calkins, Phineas Wolcott
Calverley, Charles
Cameron, Robert Alexander
Campbell, Allen
Campbell, George Washington
Campbell, James Valentine
Campbell, Thomas Joseph
Campbell, William W.
Cannon, Charles James
Cannon, James Graham
Cantor, Eddie
Capone, Alphonse
Cardozo, Benjamin Nathan
Carlisle, Floyd Leslie
Carll, John Franklin
Carlson, Evans Fordyce
Carpenter, Francis Bicknell
Carpenter, Stephen Haskins
Carr, Eugene Asa
Carr, Joseph Bradford
Carrier, Willis Haviland
Carrington, Elaine Stern
Carroll, Howard
Carryl, Guy Wetmore
Carter, Jesse Benedict
Carter, Robert
Cary, Edward
Cary, Elisabeth Luther
Case, Jerome Increase
Casey, Thomas Lincoln
Casilear, John William
Cassidy, William
Cassoday, John Bolivar
Castle, Irene Foote
Chaffee, Jerome Bonaparte
Chambers, Robert William
Champlin, John Wayne
Chanfrau, Francis S.
Chapin, Edwin Hubbell
Chapin, James Paul
Chapman, John Jay
Chapman, Victor Emmanuel
Chatterton, Ruth
Cheesman, Forman
Cheney, John Vance
Chesebrough, Caroline
Chevey, Charles Edward
Child, Frank Samuel
Chittenden, Hiram Martin
Choate, Anne Hyde Clarke
Christiancy, Isaac Peckham
Church, John Adams
Church, Pharcellus
Church, William Conant
Churchill, William
Claflin, John
Clark, Grenville
Clark, Lewis Gaylord
Clark, Myron Holley
Clark, Willis Gaylord

Clarke, John Mason
Clarke, Thomas Benedict
Clarke, William Newton
Clarkson, Matthew
Clemmer, Mary
Clifton, Josephine
Clinch, Charles Powell
Clinton DeWitt
Clinton, George
Clinton, James
Clough, John Everett
Clough, William Pitt
Cluett, Sanford Lockwood
Coakley, Cornelius Godfrey
Cochran, Alexander Smith
Cochrane, John
Coe, George Albert
Coffey, James Vincent
Coffin, Henry Sloane
Cogswell, William Browne
Cohen, Felix Solomon
Cohen, Jacob De Silva Solis
Cohn, Alfred Einstein
Cohn, Edwin Joseph
Cohn, Harry
Colden, Cadwallader David
Cole, Chester Cicero
Coleman, Charles Caryl
Colfax, Schuyler
Colgate, James Boorman
Collamer, Jacob
Collier, Peter
Collins, Edward Trowbridge
Collins, Guy N
Colman, Norman Jay
Coman, Charlotte Buell
Comstock, George Franklin
Conboy, Martin
Cone, Hutchinson Ingham
Cone, Orello
Conkling, Alfred
Conkling, Roscoe
Cook, Flavius Josephus
Cook, Frederick Albert
Cook, James Merrill
Cook, John Williston
Cook, Walter
Cooley, Lyman Edgar
Cooley, Mortimer Elwyn
Cooley, Thomas McIntyre
Cooper, Edward
Cooper, James Graham
Cooper, Peter
Cooper, Sarah Brown Ingersoll
Cooper, Susan Fenimore
Cooper, Theodore
Cooper-Poucher, Matilda S.
Corliss, George Henry
Cornell, Alonzo B.
Cornell, Ezra
Cortelyou, George Bruce
Cortissoz, Royal
Corwin, Edward Tanjore
Couch, Darius Nash
Coudert, Frederic René
Courtney, Charles Edward
Cowen, Joshua Lionel
Cozzens, Frederick Swartwout
Crabtree, Lotta
Crandall, Charles Henry
Crane, Frederick Evan
Crane, Thomas Frederick
Crapsey, Adelaide

Cravath, Erastus Milo
Crawford, Thomas
Crerar, John
Crimmins, John Daniel
Crittenton, Charles Nelson
Crocker, Charles
Crocker, Francis Bacon
Croly, Herbert David
Cromwell, Gladys Louise Husted
Cromwell, William Nelson
Cropsey, Jasper Francis
Crosby, Ernest Howard
Crosby, Founy
Crosby, Howard
Crosby, John Schuyler
Crosby, Percy Lee
Croswell, Edwin
Crounse, Lorenzo
Cruger, Henry
Cruger, John
Culbertson, Josephine Murphy
Cullum, George Washington
Cummings, Amos Jay
Cuppia, Jerome Chester
Curran, Thomas Jerome
Curtis, John Green
Curtis, Newton Martin
Curtis, Samuel Ryan
Curtiss, Glenn Hammond
Cutler, James Goold
Cutting, Bronson Murray
Cutting, Robert Fulton
Cuyler, Theodore Ledyard
Daggett, Ellsworth
Dakin, James Harrison
Dale, Chester
Dale, Maud Murray Thompson
Daly, Peter Christopher Arnold
Dalzell, John
Dana, James Dwight
Darton, Nelson Horatio
Davidson, Jo
Davidson, Lucretia Maria
Davidson, Margaret Miller
Davies, Arthur Bowen
Davies, Henry Eugene
Davies, Marion Cecilia
Davis, Alexander Jackson
Davis, Andrew Jackson
Davis, Cushman Kellogg
Davis, Francis Breese, Jr.
Davis, Henry
Davis, Jerome Dean
Davis, Katharine Bement
Davis, Matthew Livingston
Davis, Nathan Smith
Davis, Oscar King
Davis, Paulina Kellogg Wright
Davison, George Willets
Dawley, Almena
Day, Clarence Shepard
Day, George Parmly
Day, Luther
Dean, Bashford
Dean, Julia
Deerfoot
De Forest, Alfred Victor
De Forest, Robert Weeks
De Kay, George Colman
Delafield, Edward
Delafield, Francis
Delafield, John
Delafield, Richard

De Lancey, James, 1703–1760
De Lancey, James, 1732–1800
De Lancey, James, 1746–1804
De Lancey, William Heathcote
Delano, Jane Arminda
Delano, William Adams
Delavan, Edward Cornelius
Delawater, Cornelius Henry
DeLee, Joseph Bolivar
De Long, George Washington
Del Mar, Alexander
Deming, Philander
Dempster, John
Depew, Chauncey Mitchell
De Peyster, Abraham
De Peyster, John Watts
De Rose, Peter
De Sylva, George Gard "Buddy"
Devin, Thomas Casimer
Dewey, Melvil
Dewey, Richard Smith
Dewing, Maria Richards Oakey
De Witt, Simeon
De Wolfe, Elsie
Dexter, Henry
Dibble, Ray Floyd
Dickinson, Charles Monroe
Dickinson, Donald McDonald
Dickinson, Preston
Dietz, Peter Ernest
Dill, James Brooks
Diller, Burgoyne
Dillon, John Forrest
Dillon, Sidney
Disturnell, John
Diven, Alexander Samuel
Dix, Morgan
Dodge, Grace Hoadley
Dodge, Mary Elizabeth Mapes
Dods, John Bovee
Dolph, Joseph Norton
Donaldson, Henry Herbert
Donn-Byrne, Brian Oswald
Donovan, James Britt
Donovan, William Joseph
Doolittle, James Rood
Doremus, Robert Ogden
Doremus, Sarah Platt Haines
Dorn, Harold Fred
Dorsheimer, William Edward
Doty, Elihu
Doty, James Duane
Doubleday, Abner
Doubleday, Frank Nelson
Doubleday, Nelson
Douglas, Amanda Minnie
Dove, Arthur Garfield
Dowling, Austin
Downing, Andrew Jackson
Downing, Charles
Doyle, John Thomas
Drake, Edwin Laurentine
Drake, Francis Ann Denny
Drake, Joseph Rodman
Draper, Andrew Sloan
Draper, Dorothy
Draper, Lyman Copeland
Draper, Ruth
Dreier, Katherine Sophie
Dreier, Mary Elisabeth
Drew, Daniel
Drisler, Henry
Drury, John Benjamin

Dryfoos, Orvil E.
Duane, Alexander
Duane, James
Duane, James Chatham
Duane, William
Dudley, Charles Benjamin
Duer, John
Duffield, Samuel Augustus Willoughby
Dulles, Allen Welsh
Dumont, Allen Balcom
Dumont, Margaret
Durant, Charles Ferson
Durrie, Daniel Steele
Duryea, Hermanes Barkulo
Duryée, Abram
Duyckinck, Evert Augustus
Dwight, Theodore William
Dyar, Harrison Gray
Earle, Edward Mead
Earle, Mortimer Lamson
Eastman, George
Eastman, Harvey Gridley
Eastman, Joseph Bartlett
Eastman, Max Forrester
Eastman, William Reed
Eaton, Amos
Edebohls, George Michael
Edgerton, Alfred Peck
Edgerton, Sidney
Edman, Irwin
Edmonds, Francis William
Edmonds, John Worth
Edwards, William Henry
Eells, Dan Parmelee
Egleston, Thomas
Ehuinger, John Whelten
Eidlitz, Cyrus Lazelle Warner
Ellet, Elizabeth Fries Lummis
Elliot, Daniel Giraud
Elliott, Charles Loring
Ellis, Job Bicknell
Ellsworth, Elmer Ephraim
Elsberg, Charles Albert
Ely, Richard Theodore
Embury, Emma Catherine
Emerson, Haven
Emerson, Rollins Adams
Emery, Albert Hamilton
Emery, Charles Edward
Emmet, William Le Roy
Emott, James, 1771–1850
Emott, James, 1823–1884
Englis, John
Eno, William Phelps
Epstein, Jacob
Epstein, Philip G.
Erdman, Charles Rosenbury
Erlanger, Abraham Lincoln
Errett, Isaac
Erskine, John
Esterly, George
Evans, Edward Payson
Evans, George Alfred
Fairbank, Calvin
Fairchild, Charles Stebbins
Faneuil, Peter
Fanning, Edmund
Fargo, William George
Farman, Elbert Eli
Farmer, John
Farnam, Henry
Farnham, Eliza Woodson Burhans

Farrand, Beatrix Cadwalader Jones
Farwell, Charles Benjamin
Farwell, John Villiers
Fassett, Cornelia Adèle Strong
Fassett, Jacob Sloat
Fawcett, Edgar
Fay, Theodore Sedgwick
Feke, Robert
Fell, John
Fenner, Burt Leslie
Fenton, Reuben Eaton
Ferguson, William Porter Frisbee
Ferris, Isaac
Ferris, Woodbridge Nathan
Field, Benjamin Hazard
Field, Herbert Haviland
Field, Marshall, IV
Field, Maunsell Bradhurst
Field, Thomas Warren
Fields, Lewis Maurice
Fillmore, Millard
Finch, Francis Miles
Fish, Hamilton
Fish, Nicholas
Fish, Stuyvesant
Fisher, George Jackson
Fisher, Harrison
Fisher, Irving
Fisk, Clinton Bowen
Fiske, Bradley Allen
Fiske, Daniel Willard
Fiske, Harrison Grey
Fitch, Asa
Fitch, William Clyde
Fitzgerald, Thomas
Fitzsimmons, James Edward ("Sunny Jim")
Flagg, Ernest
Flagg, James Montgomery
Flagler, Henry Morrison
Flagler, John Haldane
Flandrau, Charles Eugene
Flegenheimer, Arthur
Fletcher, Robert
Flint, Weston
Florence, William Jermyn
Flower, Roswell Pettibone
Floy, James
Floyd, William
Flynn, Edward Joseph
Folger, Henry Clay
Folwell, William Watts
Fonda, John H.
Foote, Lucius Harwood
Forbes, Edwin
Ford, Hannibal Choate
Ford, Paul Leicester
Ford, Worthington Chauncey
Forman, Joshua
Forman, Justus Miles
Forrestal, James Vincent
Forsyth, John
Fosdick, Charles Austin
Fosdick, Harry Emerson
Foshag, William Frederick
Foster, David Skaats
Foulke, William Dudley
Fowler, Frank
Fowler, George Ryerson
Fowler, Orson Squire
Fowler, Russell Story
Fox, Dixon Ryan

Foy, Eddie
Francis, Charles Spencer
Francis, John Morgan
Francis, John Wakefield
Francis, Samuel Ward
Frank, Jerome
Frederic, Harold
Freedman, Andrew
Freer, Charles Lang
Freneau, Philip Morin
Freund, Ernst
Frissell, Hollis Burke
Frost, Holloway Halstead
Fuertes, Louis Agassiz
Fuller, Andrew S.
Fuller, George
Fuller, George Warren
Fuller, Robert Mason
Fulton, Justin Dewey
Funk, Wilfred John
Furman, Richard
Gage, Lyman Judson
Gage, Matilda Joslyn
Gale, Benjamin
Gale, George Washington
Gallagher,
Gally, Merritt
Galpin, Charles Josiah
Gannett, Frank Ernest
Gano, Stephen
Gansevoort, Leonard
Gansevoort, Peter
Gardiner, James Terry
Gardner, Isabella Stewart
Garfield, John
Garis, Howard Roger
Garrett, Edmund Henry
Garrison, Cornelius Kingsland
Gaskill, Harvey Freeman
Gayler, Charles
Gaynor, William Jay
Gear, John Henry
Gehrig, Henry Louis
Gellatly, John
Genin, John Nicholas
Genung, John Franklin
George, Grace
George, William Reuben
Gerard, James Watson, 1794–
1874
Gerard, James Watson, 1867–
1951
Gerry, Elbridge Thomas
Gershwin, George
Gibbs, George
Gibbs, Oliver Wolcott, 1822–1908
Gibbs, (Oliver) Wolcott, 1902–
1958
Gifford, Sanford Robinson
Gilbert, Eliphalet Wheeler
Gilbert, Grove Karl
Gilbert, Linda
Gilbert, Rufus Henry
Gilder, Jeannette Leonard
Gildersleeve, Virginia Crocheron
Gill, Theodore Nicholas
Gillespie, William Mitchell
Gillet, Ransom Hooker
Gillett, Horace Wadsworth
Gilman, Lawrence
Ginter, Lewis
Gleason, Kate
Glynn, Martin Henry

Goddard, Calvin Luther
Goddard, Luther Marcellus
Godey, Louis Antoine
Goethals, George Washington
Goff, Emmet Stull
Goforth, William
Gold, Michael
Golden, John
Goldmark, Henry
Goldmark, Rubin
Goldwater, Sigismund Schulz
Goodell, William
Goodnow, Frank Johnson
Goodrich, Benjamin Franklin
Goodsell, Daniel Ayres
Goodspeed, Thomas Wakefield
Goodwin, Hannibal Williston
Goodyear, Anson Conger
Gorcey, Leo
Gordon, Andrew
Goss, Albert Simon
Gould, Jay
Gracie, Archibald
Graham, Charles Kinnaird
Granger, Gordon
Grant, Asahel
Grant, Madison
Graves, Frederick Rogers
Gray, Asa
Gray, Henry Peters
Green, Gabriel Marcus
Green, Seth
Greenbaum, Edward Samuel
Greene, William Cornell
Greenslet, Ferris
Gregg, Willis Ray
Gregory, Charles Noble
Gregory, Daniel Seelye
Gregory, Eliot
Gregory, John Milton
Griffes, Charles Tomlinson
Griffiths, John Willis
Grinnell, George Bird
Grinnell, Henry Walton
Griscom, Ludlow
Griswold, John Augustus
Groesbeck, William Slocum
Gross, Charles
Gross, Milt
Groves, Leslie Richard, Jr.
Gue, Benjamin F.
Guinzburg, Harold Kleinert
Gunnison, Foster
Guthrie, Alfred
Habberton, John
Habersham, Alexander Wylly
Hackett, James Henry
Hadley, James
Hagedorn, Hermann Ludwig
Gebhard
Hagen, Walter Charles
Haight, Charles Coolidge
Haight, Henry Huntly
Haines, Daniel
Hall, Abraham Oakley
Hall, Charles Cuthbert
Hall, Fitzedward
Hall, Nathan Kelsey
Halleck, Henry Wager
Hallock, Charles
Halsey, Frederick Arthur
Halsted, William Stewart
Hamilton, Alice

Hamilton, Allan McLane
Hamilton, Charles Smith
Hamilton, Clayton
Hamilton, James Alexander
Hamilton, Schuyler
Hamlin, Emmons
Hamlin, Talbot Faulkner
Hammerstein, Oscar, II
Hammon, Jupiter
Hampden, Walter
Hanchett, Henry Granger
Hand, Augustus Noble
Hand, Learned
Hanna, Edward Joseph
Harcourt, Alfred
Hard, William
Hardenbergh, Jacob Rutsen
Hardie, James Allen
Harland, Henry
Harper, Fletcher
Harper, James
Harper, John Lyell
Harrigan, Edward
Harriman, Edward Henry
Harriman, Florence Jaffray Hurst
Harris, Chapin Aaron
Harris, Charles Kassell
Harris, Ira
Harris, Miriam Coles
Harris, Rollin Arthur
Harris, Sam Henry
Harris, Townsend
Harrison, Fairfax
Harrison, Francis Burton
Hart, Edmund Hall
Hart, Lorenz Milton
Hart, Moss
Hart, Virgil Chittenden
Hart, William Surrey
Harte, Francis Brett
Hartford, George Ludlum
Hartley, Jonathan Scott
Hartness, James
Hartsuff, George Lucas
Harvey, Hayward Augustus
Hasbrouck, Abraham Bruyn
Hasbrouck, Lydia Sayer
Hascall, Milo Smith
Hassard, John Rose Greene
Hastings, Charles Sheldon
Hastings, Serranus Clinton
Hastings, Thomas
Haswell, Charles Haynes
Hatch, John Porter
Haughton, Percy Duncan
Hauk, Minnie
Havemeyer, Henry Osborne
Havemeyer, William Frederick
Haven, Emily Bradley Neal
Havens, James Smith
Haviland, Clarence Floyd
Hawes, Charles Boardman
Hayes, Carlton Joseph Huntley
Hayes, Gabby
Hayes, Patrick Joseph
Hayford, John Fillmore
Hays, Arthur Garfield
Hays, William Jacob
Headley, Joel Tyler
Headley, Phineas Camp
Heaton, John Langdon
Hecht, Ben
Hecker, Isaac Thomas

Hedding, Elijah
Heenan, John Carmel
Hegeman, John Rogers
Heintzelman, Stuart
Heinze, Frederick Augustus
Helburn, Theresa
Helm, Charles John
Hemenway, Mary Porter Tileston
Henderson, Ray
Hendrick
Hendrick, Ellwood
Heney, Francis Joseph
Henry, Joseph
Hepburn, Alonzo Barton
Hepburn, Katharine Houghton
Herdic, Peter
Herkimer, Nicholas
Herne, James A.
Hess, Alfred Fabian
Hewitt, Abram Stevens
Hewitt, John Hill
Hewitt, Peter Cooper
Heye, George Gustav
Hibbard, Freeborn Garrettson
Hicks, Elias
Hicks, John, 1847–1917
Higgins, Frank Wayland
Higginson, Henry Lee
Hill, David Bennett
Hill, Frederick Trevor
Hill, George William
Hill, Grace Livingston
Hill, John Henry
Hill, Nathaniel Peter
Hines, James J.
Hinman, George Wheeler
Hirsch, Isaac Seth
Hirth, William Andrew
Hiscock, Frank Harris
Hitchcock, Phineas Warrener
Hitchcock, Raymond
Hoadley, John Chipman
Hoag, Joseph
Hoard, William Dempster
Hobart, Alice Nourse Tisdale
Hodge, William Thomas
Hodges, George
Hoe, Richard March
Hoe, Robert, 1839–1909
Hoff, John Van Rensselaer
Hoffman, Charles Fenno
Hoffman, David Murray
Hoffman, Eugene Augustus
Hoffman, John Thompson
Hoffman, Ogden
Hoffman, Wickham
Hofstadter, Richard
Hogue, Wilson Thomas
Holabird, William
Holcombe, Chester
Holdrege, George Ward
Holland, Edmund Milton
Holland, Joseph Jefferson
Hollerith, Herman
Holley, Marietta
Hollick, Charles Arthur
Holliday, Judy
Holmes, Daniel Henry
Holt, Hamilton Bowen
Holt, Luther Emmett
Holt, Winifred
Hone, Philip
Hooker, Elon Huntington

Hoppe, William Frederick ("Willie")
Hopper, DeWolf
Hopper, Edward
Hormel, George Albert
Horsford, Eben Norton
Horton, Edward Everett, Jr.
Hosack, Alexander Eddy
Hosack, David
Hosmer, Hezekiah Lord
Hosmer, William Howe Cuyler
Hotchkiss, Horace Leslie
Hough, Franklin Benjamin
Hough, George Washington
Houghton, Douglass
House, Henry Alonzo
House, Samuel Reynolds
Hovey, Alvah
Howard, George Elliott
Howe, Herbert Alonzo
Howe, Julia Ward
Howe, William Wirt
Howell, John Adams
Howland, Emily
Howland, John
Hoxie, Robert Franklin
Hoxie, William Dixie
Hoyt, John Sherman
Hubbard, Lucius Frederick
Huebsch, Benjamin W.
Hughes, Charles Evans
Hughes, George Wurtz
Hull, Clark Leonard
Hunt, Benjamin Weeks
Hunt, Charles Wallace
Hunt, Ward
Hunt, Washington
Huntington, Daniel
Huntington, Edward Vermilye
Huntington, Henry Edwards
Huntington, Jedediah Vincent
Huntington, Margaret Jane Evans
Hurlbut, Jesse Lyman
Husing, Edward Britt ("Ted")
Hutton, Edward Francis
Hutton, Frederick Remsen
Hutton, Laurence
Hyatt, John Wesley
Hyde, Helen
Hyde, Henry Baldwin
Hylan, John Francis
Ingalls, Marilla Baker
Ingersoll, Robert Green
Inman, Henry, 1801–1846
Inman, Henry, 1837–1899
Inman, John
Inness, George
Ireland, Joseph Norton
Irving, John Treat
Irving, Peter
Irving, Pierre Munro
Irving, Roland Duer
Irving, Washington
Irving, William
Irwin, Elisabeth Antoinette
Irwin, William Henry
Isaacs, Abram Samuel
Isham, Ralph Heyward
Isham, Samuel
Isherwood, Benjamin Franklin
Ives, Halsey Cooley
Ives, Irving McNeil
Ives, James Merritt

Ives, Joseph Christmas
Jackson, Abraham Valentine Williams
Jackson, Charles Douglas
Jackson, George Thomas
Jackson, James Caleb
Jackson, Mortimer Melville
Jackson, Samuel Macauley
Jackson, Sheldon
Jackson, William Henry
Jacobs, Hirsch
Jacobs, Michael Strauss
James, Arthur Curtiss
James, Edward Christopher
James, Henry, 1811–1882
James, Henry, 1843–1916
James, Thomas Lemuel
James, William
Janeway, Theodore Caldwell
Jay, Sir James
Jay, John, 1745–1829
Jay, John, 1817–1894
Jay, William
Jelliffe, Smith Ely
Jemison, Alice Mae Lee
Jenkins, James Graham
Jenkins, John Stilwell
Jenks, Tudor Storrs
Jerome, William Travers
Jervis, John Bloomfield
Jewett, William Cornell
Johnson, Alexander Smith
Johnson, Benjamin Pierce
Johnson, Elias Henry
Johnson, Helen Louise Kendrick
Johnson, Sir John
Johnson, Levi
Johnson, Owen McMahon
Johnson, Samuel William
Johnson, Virginia Wales
Johnson, William Woolsey
Johnson, Willis Fletcher
Johnston, Alexander
Johnston, John Taylor
Johnston, Samuel
Joline, Adrian Hoffman
Jones, Amanda Theodosia
Jones, George Heber
Jones, Herschel Vespasian
Jones, John
Jones, Samuel, 1734–1819
Jones, Samuel, 1770–1853
Jones, Thomas
Jones, William Alfred
Jordan, David Starr
Jordan, Virgil Justin
Jordan, William George
Judah, Samuel
Judah, Samuel Benjamin Helbert
Judd, Gerrit Parmele
Judd, Norman Buel
Judd, Orange
Judson, Edward Zane Carroll
Judson, Egbert Putnam
Judson, Emily Chubbuck
Judson, Harry Pratt
Kaempffert, Waldemar Bernhard
Kaiser, Henry John
Kane, Helen
Kane, John Kintzing
Kaye, Frederick Benjamin
Kearny, Philip
Kedzie, Robert Clark

Keeley, Leslie E.
Keene, Thomas Wallace
Keep, Henry
Keith, Minor Cooper
Keller, Arthur Ignatius
Kelley, James Douglas Jerrold
Kellogg, Frank Billings
Kellogg, Samuel Henry
Kelly, John
Kelly, Luther Sage
Kelly, Michael J.
Kelsey, Francis Willey
Kemble, Gouverneur
Kemp, James Furman
Kemper, Jackson
Kenedy, Patrick John
Kent, Charles Foster
Kent, James
Kenyon, Josephine Hemenway
Keppel, Frederick Paul
Kern, Jerome David
Kernan, Francis
Kert, Charles Foster
Kidder, Daniel Parish
Kilpatrick, John Reed
King, Carol Weiss
King, Charles
King, Edward Skinner
King, James Gore
King, John
King, John Alsop
King, Preston
King, Richard
King, Rufus
King, Stanley
King, Thomas Starr
Kingsley, Calvin
Kingsley, Elizabeth Seelman
Kingsley, Norman William
Kinne, La Vega George
Kinney, Elizabeth Clementine
    Dodge Stedman
Kip, William Ingraham
Kiphuth, Robert John Herman
Kirk, Edward Norris
Kirkland, Caroline Matilda Stans-
    bury
Kirkland, John Thornton
Kirkland, Joseph
Kirstein, Louis Edward
Klem, William J. (Bill)
Knapp, Joseph Palmer
Knapp, Martin Augustine
Knapp, Seaman Asahel
Knapp, William Ireland
Knauth, Oswald Whitman
Knickerbocker, Herman
Knopf, Blanche Wolf
Knox, George William
Knox, John Jay
Kobbé, Gustav
Koch, Vivienne
Kreymborg, Alfred Francis
Kuhn, Walt
Kunz, George Frederick
Ladd, Carl Edwin
Ladd, Kate Macy
La Farge, Christopher Grant
La Farge, John
La Farge, Oliver Hazard Perry
La Guardia, Fiorello Henry
Lahr, Bert
Laimbeer, Natalie Schenk

Lait, Jacquin Leonard (Jack)
Lamb, John
Lamb, William Frederick
Lamont, Daniel Scott
Lamont, Hammond
Lamont, Thomas William
La Mountain, John
Landon, Melville de Lancey
Lane, Arthur Bliss
Langford, Nathaniel Pitt
Langmuir, Irving
Lansing, Gulian
Lansing, John
Lansing, Robert
Lapchick, Joseph Bohomiel
Lapham, Increase Allen
Larrabee, Charles Hathaway
Lathbury, Mary Artemisia
Lathrop, John Hiram
Law, George
Lawes, Lewis Edward
Lawrence, George Newbold
Lawrence, William Beach
Lawrie, Alexander
Lawson, Robert Ripley
Lay, John Louis
Lazarus, Emma
Le Clear, Thomas
Le Conte, John Lawrence
Leavitt, Frank Simmons (Man
    Mountain Dean)
Lee, Canada
Lee, Frederic Schiller
Lee, James Melvin
Lee, Luther
Lee, Porter Raymond
Lee, William Little
Lefferts, George Morewood
Lefferts, Marshall
Leffingwell, Russell Cornell
Leggett, Mortimer Dormer
Leggett, William
Lehman, Adele Lewisohn
Lehman, Arthur
Lehman, Herbert Henry
Lehman, Irving
Lehman, Robert
Lennox, Charlotte Ramsay
Lenox, James
Le Roux, Charles
Letchworth, William Pryor
Leupp, Francis Ellington
Levitt, Abraham
Lewis, Dioclesian
Lewis, George William
Lewis, James
Lewis, Morgan
Lewis, Oscar
Lewis, Taylor
Lewisohn, Sam Adolph
Lexow, Clarence
L'Hommedieu, Ezra
Libman, Emanuel
Liebling, Abbott Joseph
Liebling, Estelle
Lindsay, Howard
Link, Henry Charles
Lintner, Joseph Albert
Lippincott, Sara Jane Clarke
Litchfield, Electus Backus
Littauer, Lucius Nathan
Littlejohn, Abram Newkirk
Livingston, Edward

Livingston, Henry Brockholst
Livingston, John Henry
Livingston, John William
Livingston, Peter VanBrugh
Livingston, Philip
Livingston, Robert R., 1718–1775
Livingston, Robert R., 1746–1813
Livingston, William
Lloyd, Henry Demarest
Lloyd, James
Lloyd, John Uri
Locke, David Ross
Lockwood, Belva Ann Bennett
Lockwood, Samuel Drake
Loeb, James
Loesser, Frank
Loew, Marcus
Logan, Olive
Lombardi, Vincent Thomas
Loomis, Charles Battell
Loomis, Elmer Howard
Loomis, Mahlon
Loop, Henry Augustus
Lord, Asa Dearborn
Lord, Chester Sanders
Lord, William Wilberforce
Lorillard, Pierre
Lossing, Benson John
Lounsbury, Thomas Raynesford
Loveman, Amy
Low, Seth
Low, Will Hicok
Lowery, Woodbury
Luce, Stephen Bleecker
Luckenbach, J(ohn) Lewis
Ludlow, Daniel
Ludlow, Fitz Hugh
Ludlow, Gabriel George
Ludlow, George Duncan
Ludlow, Noah Miller
Ludlow, Thomas William
Ludlow, William
Luhan, Mabel Dodge
Lynch, James Mathew
Lynde, Francis
Lyon, Caleb
Lyon, Theodatus Timothy
Lyon, William Penn
Mabie, Hamilton Wright
McAdie, Alexander George
McAlpine, William Jarvis
McArthur, Duncan
McCall, John Augustine
McCarthy, Charles Louis (Clem)
McCloskey, John
McCloskey, William George
McComb, John
McCormick, Richard Cunningham
McCullough, Ernest
McCurdy, Richard Aldrich
MacDowell, Edward Alexander
McEntee, Jervis
McGarrah, Gates White
McGiffert, Arthur Cushman
McGlyn, Edward
McGovern, John
McGraw, James Herbert
McGraw, John Joseph
MacKaye, James Morrison Steele
MacKaye, Percy Wallace
Mackenzie, Alexander Slidell
Mackenzie, Ranald Slidell
McLaren, William Edward

McLaughlin, Hugh
Maclay, William Brown
McLeod, Hugh
McMaster, Guy Humphreys
McMaster, James Alphonsus
McMaster, John Bach
McMath, Robert Emmet
MacMonnies, Frederick William
McQuaid, Bernard John
McVickar, William Neilson
McVicker, James Hubert
Macy, Valentine Everit
Maginnis, Martin
Mahan, Alfred Thayer
Mahan, Asa
Mahan, Dennis Hart
Mallory, Clifford Day
Malone, Dudley Field
Mankiewicz, Herman Jacob
Mann, Louis
Mannes, David
Mannes, Leopold Damrosch
Manning, Daniel
Mantle, (Robert) Burns
Mapes, Charles Victor
Mapes, James Jay
Marbury, Elisabeth
Marcantonio, Vito Anthony
Marcus, Bernard Kent
Marquand, Allan
Marquand, Henry Gurdon
Marsh, Grant Prince
Marsh, Othniel Charles
Marshall, Frank James
Marshall, Henry Rutgers
Marshall, Louis
Marshall, William Edgar
Martin, Artemas
Martin, Edward Sandford
Martin, Frederick Townsend
Martin, Homer Dodge
Martindale, John Henry
Marx, Adolf Arthur ("Harpo")
Marx, Leonard ("Chico")
Maslow, Abraham H.
Mason, Charles
Mason, John Mitchell
Mason, William Ernest
Mather, Fred
Mathews, Albert
Mathews, Cornelius
Matteson, Joel Aldrich
Matteson, Tompkins Harrison
Mattice, Asa Martines
Mattison, Hiram
Mattoon, Stephen
Maverick, Peter
Maxim, Hiram Percy
Maxwell, Samuel
Maybeck, Bernard Ralph
Mayer, Emil
Mayer, Philip Frederick
Maynard, Edward
Maynard, George William
Mayo, William Starbuck
Mead, James Michael
Meade, Richard Worsam
Mearns, Edgar Alexander
Mechem, Floyd Russell
Megrue, Roi Cooper
Meiggs, Henry
Melville, George Wallace
Melville, Herman

Mendel, Lafayette Benedict
Meneely, Andrew
Merck, George Wilhelm
Merriam, Augustus Chapman
Merriam, Clinton Hart
Merriam, William Rush
Merrill, Stuart Fitz Randolph
Merritt, Israel John
Merritt, Leonidas
Merry, William Lawrence
Meyer, Agnes Elizabeth Ernst
Meyer, Annie Nathan
Michael, Arthur
Miles, Manly
Milledoler, Philip
Miller, Charles Henry
Miller, David Hunter
Miller, Gerrit Smith, Jr.
Miller, Gilbert Heron
Miller, Harriet Mann
Miller, Kenneth Hayes
Miller, Nathan Lewis
Miller, Warner
Miller, William Henry Harrison
Mills, Clark
Mills, Cyrus Taggart
Mills, Darius Ogden
Mills, Lawrence Heyworth
Millspaugh, Charles Frederick
Miner, Myrtilla
Minor, Robert Crannell
Minturn, Robert Bowne
Mitchel, John Purroy
Mitchell, Hinckley Gilbert
   Thomas
Mitchell, Isaac
Mitchell, John Ames
Mitchell, Margaret Julia
Mitchell, William, 1801–1886
Mitchill, Samuel Latham
Moffat, David Halliday
Moffat, Jay Pierrepont
Moffett, Cleveland Langston
Mollenhauer, Emil
Montgomery, David Henry
Montgomery, Thomas Harrison
Moon, Parker Thomas
Mooney, William
Moore, Benjamin
Moore, Charles Herbert
Moore, Clement Clarke
Moore, Nathaniel Fish
Moore, Richard Channing
Moore, Veranus Alva
Moore, William Henry
Moran, Eugene Francis
Morehouse, Henry Lyman
Morell, George Webb
Morgan, Anne
Morgan, Charles Hill
Morgan, Edwin Barber
Morgan, Edwin Vernon
Morgan, John Pierpont
Morgan, Lewis Henry
Morgenthau, Henry, Jr.
Morrell, Benjamin
Morris, Edward Dafydd
Morris, Gouverneur
Morris, Lewis, 1671–1746
Morris, Lewis, 1726–1798
Morris, Lewis Richard
Morris, Richard
Morris, Richard Valentine

Morris, Robert Hunter
Morris, William Hopkins
Morton, Henry
Morton, Julius Sterling
Moses, Anna Mary Robertson
   ("Grandma")
Moses, Montrose Jonas
Mosher, Eliza Maria
Moskowitz, Belle Lindner Israels
Mosler, Henry
Moss, Frank
Mott, James
Mott, John R.
Mott, Valentine
Mount, William Sidney
Muldoon, William
Mulford, Prentice
Mullany, James Robert Madison
Muller, Hermann Joseph
Mulry, Thomas Maurice
Mumford, James Gregory
Mundelein, George William
Munger, Theodore Thornton
Murphy, Charles Francis
Murphy, Henry Cruse
Murphy, John Francis
Murphy, John W.
Murray, David
Murray, Thomas Edward, 1860–
   1929
Murray, Thomas Edward, 1891–
   1961
Musica, Philip Mariano Fausto
Myer, Albert James
Nack, James M.
Nathan, Maud
Nelson, Henry Loomis
Nelson, Rensselaer Russell
Nelson, Reuben
Nelson, Samuel
Nevins, John Livingston
Newberry, John Stoughton
Newell, Robert Henry
Newhouse, Samuel
Newman, Barnett
Newman, Henry Roderick
Newman, John Philip
Newton, Hubert Anson
Newton, Isaac, 1794–1858
Nichols, Ruth Rowland
Nichols, William Ford
Nicoll, De Lancey
Nicoll, James Craig
Nipher, Francis Eugene
Nitchie, Edward Bartlett
Noble, Gladwyn Kingsley
Norsworthy, Naomi
North, Frank Joshua
North, Frank Mason
North, Simon Newton Dexter
Norton, John Nicholas
Norton, John Pitkin
Nott, Charles Cooper
Noyes, Henry Drury
Noyes, La Verne
Noyes, William Curtis
Nye, James Warren
Oakley, Thomas Jackson
Oberholser, Harry Church
Oberndorf, Clarence Paul
O'Brien, Edward Charles
O'Brien, Morgan Joseph
O'Conor, Charles

Odell, Benjamin Barker
Odell, George Clinton Densmore
Odenbach, Frederick Louis
Ogden, David Bayard
Ogden, Herbert Gouverneur
Ogden, Rollo
Ogden, William Butler
Ogilvie, John
Olcott, Chauncey
Olcott, Eben Erskine
Olds, Leland
Olmstead, Albert Ten Eyck
Olmsted, Frederick Law
Olyphant, Robert Morrison
Onderdonk, Benjamin Tredwell
Onderdonk, Henry
Onderdonk, Henry Ustick
O'Neill, Eugene
Oppenheimer, Julius Robert
Ordronaux, John
Orton, Edward Francis Baxter
Orton, Harlow South
Orton, Helen Fuller
Orton, James
Orton, William
Osborn, Laughton
Osborne, Thomas Mott
O'Shaughnessy, Nelson Jarvis Waterbury
O'Shea, Michael Vincent
Osterhout, Winthrop John Vanleuven
Otis, Charles Rollin
Otis, Fessenden Nott
Ottley, Roi
Paddock, Algernon Sidney
Page, William
Palmer, Alice Elvira Freeman
Palmer, Alonzo Benjamin
Palmer, Erastus Dow
Palmer, Horatio Richmond
Palmer, Innis Newton
Palmer, Potter
Palmer, Walter Launt
Pardee, Ario
Pardow, William O'Brien
Park, William Hallock
Parker, Alton Brooks
Parker, Arthur Caswell
Parker, Ely Samuel
Parker, Foxhall Alexander
Parker, Jane Marsh
Parker, William Harwar
Parsons, Elsie Worthington Clews
Parsons, John Edward
Parsons, Lewis Baldwin
Parsons, Lewis Eliphalet
Parsons, Samuel Bowne
Parsons, William Barclay
Parton, Arthur
Pastor, Antonio
Paton, Lewis Bayles
Patrick, Marsena Rudolph
Patterson, Daniel Todd
Patterson, Robert Porter
Pattison, Thomas
Paulding, Hiram
Paulding, James Kirke
Payne, Henry B.
Payne, John Howard
Payne, Sereno Elisha
Payne, William Harold
Peabody, Josephine Preston

Peck, Charles Horton
Peck, George
Peck, George Record
Peck, George Wilbur
Peck, Jesse Truesdell
Peck, John James
Peck, Lillie
Peckham, George Williams
Peckham, Rufus Wheeler
Peckham, Wheeler Hazard
Peixotto, Benjamin Franklin
Peloubet, Francis Nathan
Pendleton, John B.
Penfield, Edward
Pennoyer, Sylvester
Perin, Charles Page
Perkins, George Douglas
Perkins, Maxwell Evarts
Perry, Clarence Arthur
Perry, Stuart
Peters, John Charles
Peters, John Punnett
Phelps, William Franklin
Philip, John Woodward
Phillips, Philip
Picton, Thomas
Pierce, Gilbert Ashville
Pierson, Arthur Tappan
Pierson, Hamilton Wilcox
Piggot, Robert
Pilcher, Paul Monroe
Pintard, John
Pintard, Lewis
Piper, William Thomas
Pirsson, Louis Valentine
Pitcher, Zina
Platt, Thomas Collier
Polak, John Osborn
Polk, Frank Lyon
Pomeroy, John Norton
Pomeroy, Marcus Mills
Pond, James Burton
Pope, John Russell
Porter, Holbrook Fitz-John
Porter, Jermain Gildersleeve
Porter, John Addison
Post, Augustus
Post, George Adams
Post, George Browne
Post, George Edward
Post, Isaac
Post, Wright
Pott, Francis Lister Hawks
Potter, Alonzo
Potter, Eliphalet Nott
Potter, Henry Codman
Potter, Horatio
Potter, Louis McClellan
Potter, Platt
Potter, Robert Brown
Pound, Cuthbert Winfred
Powell, Edward Payson
Powell, George Harold
Powell, John Wesley
Powell, William Bramwell
Powell, William Henry
Power, Frederick Belding
Powers, Daniel William
Prang, Mary Amelia Dana Hicks
Pratt, Eliza Ann Farman
Pratt, James Bissett
Pratt, Orson
Pratt, Parley Parker

Pratt, Richard Henry
Pratt, Sereno Stansbury
Pratt, Tadock
Prescott, Albert Benjamin
Pressman, Lee
Price, Stephen
Price, Theodore Hazeltine
Prime, Benjamin Youngs
Prime, Edward Dorr Griffin
Prime, Samuel Irenaeus
Prime, William Cowper
Prince, LeBaron Bradford
Prince, William, c. 1725–1802
Prince, William, 1766–1842
Prince, William Robert
Pringle, Henry Fowles
Prosser, Charles Smith
Provoost, Samuel
Pruyn, John Van Schaick Lansing
Pruyn, Robert Hewson
Pulitzer, Joseph, Jr.
Pullman, George Mortimer
Pumpelly, Raphael
Purdy, Lawson
Purple, Samuel Smith
Putnam, (George) Herbert
Putnam, James Osborne
Putnam, Ruth
Quackenbush, Stephen Platt
Quidor, John
Quitman, John Anthony
Radcliff, Jacob
Rafter, George W.
Raines, John
Ralph, Julian
Rambaut, Mary Lucinda Bonney
Rand, James Henry
Randall, Alexander Williams
Randall, Clarence Belden
Randall, Henry Stephens
Randall, Samuel Sidwell
Ranger, Henry Ward
Rankine, William Birch
Raskob, John Jakob
Rathbone, Justus Henry
Rathbun, Richard
Rauschenbusch, Walter
Raymond, Alexander Gillespie
Raymond, Benjamin Wright
Raymond, Henry Jarvis
Raymond, John Howard
Raymond, John T.
Raymond, Miner
Red Jacket
Redfield, Amasa Angell
Redfield, William Cox
Redman, Ben Ray
Reed, Daniel Alden
Reed, Luman
Rees, John Krom
Reeve, Tapping
Reid, Gilbert
Reid, John Morrison
Reid, Ogden Mills
Reid, William Wharry
Reinhardt, Ad
Remington, Frederic
Remington, Philo
Remington, William Walter
Remsen, Ira
Renwick, Edward Sabine
Renwick, Henry Brevoort
Renwick, James, 1818–1895

Reynolds, Quentin James
Rhind, Alexander Colden
Rice, Dan
Rice, Edwin Wilbur
Rice, Elmer
Rice, Thomas Dartmouth
Rice, Victor Moreau
Richards, Charles Brinkerhoff
Richards, Vincent
Richtmyer, Floyd Karker
Ricketts, James Brewerton
Ridder, Herman
Ridgway, Robert
Riggs, William Henry
Riley, Isaac Woodbridge
Rittenhouse, Jessie Belle
Rives, George Lockhart
Robb, William Lispenard
Robert, Christopher Rhinelander
Roberts, Benjamin Titus
Roberts, Ellis Henry
Roberts, Marshall Owen
Robertson, Morgan Andrew
Robertson, William Henry
Robertson, William Schenck
Robins, Margaret Dreier
Robins, Raymond
Robinson, Charles Mulford
Robinson, John Cleveland
Robinson-Smith, Gertrude
Rockefeller, John Davison
Rockefeller, William
Rodgers, Christopher Raymond
   Perry
Rodgers, George Washington,
   1822–1863
Roe, Edward Payson
Roe, Francis Asbury
Rogers, Henry Wade
Rogers, Randolph
Rogers, Stephen
Rohlfs, Anna Katharine Green
Romayne, Nicholas
Rooney, Pat
Roosa, Daniel Bennett St. John
Roosevelt, (Anna) Eleanor
Roosevelt, Franklin Delano
Roosevelt, Hilborne Lewis
Roosevelt, Kermit
Roosevelt, Nicholas J.
Roosevelt, Robert Barnwell
Roosevelt, Theodore, 1858–1919
Roosevelt, Theodore, 1887–1944
Root, Elihu
Root, Frank Albert
Rosa, Edward Bennett
Rose, Billy
Rosenberg, Ethel
Rosenberg, Julius
Rosenfeld, Paul Leopold
Rossen, Robert
Rousseau, Harry Harwood
Rowland, Henry Cottrell
Rudge, William Edwin
Rudkin, Margaret Fogarty
Ruger, Thomas Howard
Rumsey, Charles Cary
Rumsey, Mary Harriman
Rumsey, William
Runkle, John Daniel
Ruppert, Jacob
Russell, David Allen
Russell, Henry Norris

Russell, Israel Cook
Russell, James Earl
Rutgers, Henry
Rutherfurd, Lewis Morris
Sachs, Paul Joseph
Sackett, Henry Woodward
Sage, Margaret Olivia Slocum
Sage, Russell
Salisbury, James Henry
Salmon, Lucy Maynard
Salmon, Thomas William
Salter, William
Saltus, Edgar Evertson
Sampson, William Thomas
Sanders, Charles Walton
Sanders, Wilbur Fisk
Sands, Comfort
Sands, David
Sands, Joshua Ratoon
Sands, Robert Charles
Sanford, Nathan
Sanger, Margaret Higgins
Sangster, Margaret Elizabeth
   Munson
Satterlee, Henry Yates
Satterlee, Richard Sherwood
Sawyer, Leicester Ambrose
Sawyer, Lorenzo
Sayles, John
Sayre, Reginald Hall
Sayre, Stephen
Schell, Augustus
Schenck, Ferdinand Schureman
Schirmer, Rudolph Edward
Schlesinger, Frank
Schofield, John McAllister
Schoolcraft, Henry Rowe
Schuyler, Eugene
Schuyler, George Washington
Schuyler, James Dix
Schuyler, Louisa Lee
Schuyler, Margarita
Schuyler, Montgomery
Schuyler, Peter
Schuyler, Philip John
Schuyler, Robert Livingston
Schwab, John Christopher
Schwartz, Delmore David
Scollard, Clinton
Scott, John Morin
Scott, John Prindle
Scribner, Charles, 1821–1871
Scribner, Charles, 1854–1930
Scribner, Charles, 1890–1952
Scrymser, James Alexander
Scullin, John
Seabury, George John
Seabury, Samuel
Searle, James
Searle, John Preston
Sedgwick, Arthur George
Sedgwick, Ellery
Sedgwick, Theodore, 1811–1859
Seeger, Alan
Seixas, Gershom Mendes
Selden, George Baldwin
Seligman, Edwin Robert Ander-
   son
Seligman, Isaac Newton
Seney, George Ingraham
Sennett, George Burritt
Sergeant, Henry Clark
Sessions, Henry Howard

Seton, Elizabeth Ann Bayley
Seton, William
Severance, Caroline Maria Sey-
   mour
Seward, Frederick William
Seward, George Frederick
Seward, Theodore Frelinghuysen
Seward, William Henry
Seymour, George Franklin
Seymour, Horatio
Seymour, Horatio Winslow
Seymour, William
Shaw, Edward Richard
Shea, John Dawson Gilmary
Sheffield, Devello Zelotes
Sheldon, Charles Monroe
Sheldon, Edward Austin
Shelton, Frederick William
Shepard, Edward Morse
Shepard, Fred Douglas
Sheridan, Philip Henry
Sherman, Frank Dempster
Sherman, James Schoolcraft
Sherwood, Adiel
Sherwood, Isaac Ruth
Sherwood, Robert Emmet
Sherwood, William Hall
Shipherd, John Jay
Shrady, George Frederick
Shrady, Henry Merwin
Shufeldt, Robert Wilson
Sibley, Joseph Crocker
Sicard, Montgomery
Sickles, Daniel Edgar
Sidell, William Henry
Sigsbee, Charles Dwight
Sikes, William Wirt
Sill, Anna Peck
Silverman, Sime
Silvers, Louis
Simon, Richard Leo
Simonton, James William
Simpson, Edward
Simpson, William Kelly
Sims, Winfield Scott
Singer, Isaac Merrit
Skaniadariio
Skinner, Alanson Buck
Skinner, Charles Rufus
Slidell, John
Sloat, John Drake
Slocum, Henry Warner
Smillie, George Henry
Smillie, James David
Smillie, Ralph
Smith, Alfred Emanuel
Smith, Archibald Cary
Smith, Azariah
Smith, Bruce
Smith, David Eugene
Smith, Edmund Munroe
Smith, Erasmus Darwin
Smith, Erminnie Adelle Platt
Smith, Erwin Frink
Smith, Gerrit
Smith, Giles Alexander
Smith, Harry Bache
Smith, Hezekiah
Smith, James McCune
Smith, Jedediah Strong
Smith, Job Lewis
Smith, John Bernhard
Smith, Martin Luther

Smith, Melancton, 1744–1798
Smith, Melancton, 1810–1893
Smith, Milton Hannibal
Smith, Morgan Lewis
Smith, Ormond Gerald
Smith, Peter
Smith, Solomon Franklin
Smith, Stephen
Smith, Theobald
Smith, William, 1728–1793
Smith, William Henry, 1833–1896
Smith, William Stephens
Smyth, Julian Kennedy
Snell, Bertrand Hollis
Snelling, Henry Hunt
Snethen, Nicholas
Snowden, Thomas
Sokolsky, George Ephraim
Solomons, Adolphus Simeon
Sooysmith, Charles
Soulé, George
Southmayd, Charles Ferdinand
Spalding, Volney Morgan
Spaulding, Elbridge Gerry
Speck, Frank Gouldsmith
Speir, Samuel Fleet
Spencer, Cornelia Phillips
Spencer, Jesse Ames
Spencer, John Canfield
Spencer, Platt Rogers
Sperry, Elmer Ambrose
Speyer, James Joseph
Spier, Leslie
Spingarn, Joel Elias
Spinner, Francis Elias
Spitzka, Edward Anthony
Spitzka, Edward Charles
Sprague, Charles Ezra
Squier, Ephraim George
Squire, Watson Carvosso
Stager, Anson
Staley, Cady
Stanbery, Henry
Stanchfield, John Barry
Stanford, Leland
Stanley, John Mix
Stanley, William
Stansbury, Howard
Stanton, Elizabeth Cady
Starin, John Henry
Starr, Frederick
Starr, Merritt
Starr, Moses Allen
Stearns, Irving Ariel
Steele, Daniel
Steele, Frederick
Steele, Joel Dorman
Steinhardt, Laurence Adolph
Steinman, David Barnard
Stelzle, Charles
Sterling, George
Stern, Joseph William
Sternberg, George Miller
Stetson, Francis Lynde
Stevens, Alexander Hodgdon
Stevens, Emily
Stevens, George Barker
Stevens, George Washington
Stevens, John
Stevens, John Austin
Stevens, Walter Husted
Stevenson, John James
Stewart, Alvan

Stewart, Edwin
Stewart, John Aikman
Stewart, Robert Marcellus
Stewart, William Morris
Stewart, William Rhinelander
Stiles, Charles Wardell
Stiles, Henry Reed
Stillman, Thomas Edgar
Stillman, William James
Stilwell, Joseph Warren
Stilwell, Silas Moore
Stimson, Henry Lewis
Stoddard, Charles Warren
Stoddard, John Fair
Stoddard, William Osborn
Stokes, Anson Phelps, 1838–1913
Stokes, Anson Phelps, 1874–1958
Stokes, Caroline Phelps
Stokes, Frederick Abbot
Stokes, Isaac Newton Phelps
Stokes, Olivia Egleston Phelps
Stokes, William Earl Dodge
Stone, Horatio
Stone, William Leete, 1792–1844
Stone, William Leete, 1835–1908
Stoneman, George
Straight, Willard Dickermam
Stranahan, James Samuel Thomas
Strang, James Jesse
Strange, Michael
Straus, Jesse Isidor
Straus, Percy Selden
Straus, Roger W(illiams)
Street, Alfred Billings
Streeter, George Linius
Stringham, Silas Horton
Stringham, Washington Irving
Strong, Augustus Hopkins
Strong, Benjamin
Strong, Harriet Williams Russell
Strong, James
Strong, James Hooker
Stryker, Melancthon Woolsey
Stuart, Charles Beebe
Stuart, Robert Leighton
Sullivan, Harry Stack
Sullivan, James Edward
Sullivan, Timothy Daniel
Sulzberger, Arthur Hays
Swain, Clara A.
Swain, James Barrett
Swan, Joseph Rockwell
Swartwout, Samuel
Sweeny, Peter Barr
Sweet, John Edson
Swift, Lewis
Swift, Lucius Burrie
Swing, Raymond Edwards (Gram)
Symmes, John Cleves
Symons, Thomas William
Taber, John
Tallmadge, Benjamin
Tallmadge, James
Tamiris, Helen
Tanner, Benjamin
Tanner, Henry Schenck
Tanner, James
Tappan, Henry Philip
Tappen, Frederick Dobbs
Taussig, Frederick Joseph
Taylor, Benjamin Franklin
Taylor, Graham
Taylor, Henry Osborn

Taylor, James Monroe
Taylor, James Wickes
Taylor, John W.
Taylor, Joseph Deems
Taylor, Laurette
Taylor, Moses
Taylor, Myron Charles
Taylor, Stevenson
Teall, Francis Augustus
Teller, Henry Moore
Ten Broeck, Abraham
Ten Broeck, Richard
Terry, Marshall Orlando
Terry, Milton Spenser
Thacher, Edwin
Thacher, John Boyd
Thalberg, Irving Grant
Thayer, Amos Madden
Thomas, Amos Russell
Thomas, George Allison
Thomas, John Jacobs
Thomas, Joseph
Thompson, Dorothy
Thompson, Egbert
Thompson, Malvina Cynthia
Thompson, Martin E.
Thompson, Smith
Thompson, William Gilman
Thomson, Mortimer Neal
Thorne, Charles Robert, 1814–1893
Thorne, Charles Robert, 1840–1883
Throop, Enos Thompson
Throop, Montgomery Hunt
Thurber, Jeannette Meyer
Thursby, Emma Cecilia
Tiebout, Cornelius
Tierney, Richard Henry
Tiffany, Louis Comfort
Tilden, Samuel Jones
Tilney, Frederick
Tilton, Edward Lippincott
Tilton, Theodore
Tilyou, George Cornelius
Timby, Theodore Ruggles
Timme, Walter
Todd, Sereno Edwards
Tomkins, Floyd Williams
Tomlin, Bradley Walker
Tompkins, Daniel D.
Tone, Stanislas Pascal Franchot
Torrey, John
Townsend, Mary Ashley
Townsend, Robert
Tracy, Benjamin Franklin
Trask, James Dowling
Travers, Jerome Dunstan
Treat, Samuel Hubbel
Trelease, William
Tremain, Henry Edwin
Tremaine, Henry Barnes
Trenchard, Stephen Decatur
Trowbridge, Augustus
Trowbridge, John Townsend
Trowbridge, William Petit
Trude, Alfred Samuel
Trudeau, Edward Livingston
Truxtun, Thomas
Tucker, Allen
Tucker, Gilbert Milligan
Tuckerman, Bayard
Turner, Daniel

Turner, John Wesley
Turner, Ross Sterling
Tuthill, William Burnet
Tuttle, Daniel Sylvester
Tweed, Harrison
Tweed, William Marcy
Tyler, Robert Ogden
Underhill, Franklin Pell
Underwood, Benjamin Franklin
Underwood, John Curtiss
Underwood, Lucien Marcus
Upton, Emory
Usher, John Palmer
Vail, Robert William Glenroie
Vail, Stephen Montfort
Valentine, David Thomas
Van Buren, John
Van Buren, Martin
Van Cortlandt, Philip
Van Cortlandt, Pierre
Van Cortlandt, Stephanus
Van Dam, Rip
Vanderbilt, Cornelius, 1794–1877
Vanderbilt, Cornelius, 1843–1899
Vanderbilt, George Washington
Vanderbilt, Grace Graham Wilson
Vanderbilt, William Kissam
Vanderlyn, John
Vander Veer, Albert
Van de Warker, Edward Ely
Van Dyck, Cornelius Van Alen
Van Dyke, Paul
Van Fleet, Walter
Van Name, Addison
Van Ness, William Peter
Van Nest, Abraham Rynier
Van Nostrand, David
Van Rensselaer, Cortlandt
Van Rensselaer, Mariana Griswold
Van Rensselaer, Martha
Van Rensselaer, Solomon
Van Rensselaer, Stephen
Van Schaack, Henry Cruger
Van Schaack, Peter
Van Schaick, Goose
Van Slyke, Lucius Lincoln
Van Vechten, Abraham
Van Winkle, Peter Godwin
Van Wyck, Charles Henry
Vardill, John
Varick, James
Vedder, Edward Bright
Vedder, Elihu
Vedder, Henry Clay
Verplanck, Julian Crommelin
Vesey, William
Vibbard, Chauncey
Victor, Frances Fuller
Viele, Aernout Cornelissen
Viele, Egbert Ludovicus
Vincent, Frank
Vincent, Marvin Richardson
Volk, Leonard Wells
Vorse, Mary Heaton
Vought, Chance Milton
Wade, Jeptha Homer
Wadsworth, James Samuel
Wadsworth, James Wolcott, Jr.
Wagner, Webster
Wainwright, Jonathan Mayhew,
  1821–1863
Wait, Samuel
Wait, William

Wait, William Bell
Walcott, Charles Doolittle
Walden, Jacob Treadwell
Walker, Gilbert Carlton
Walker, James John
Walker, Mary Edwards
Wallace, William James
Wallack, Lester
Waller, Frederic
Waller, Thomas Macdonald
Waller, Thomas Wright
Walsh, Blanche
Walsh, Thomas
Walworth, Clarence Augustus
Ward, Cyrenus Osborne
Ward, Genevieve
Ward, Henry Augustus
Ward, Henry Baldwin
Ward, James Edward
Ward, Joseph
Ward, Samuel, 1814–1884
Waring, George Edwin
Warner, Adoniram Judson
Warner, Anna Bartlett
Warner, Glenn Scobey ("Pop")
Warner, Susan Bogert
Warren, Gouverneur Kemble
Warren, Leonard
Warren, Richard Henry
Washburn, Margaret Floy
Waterman, Alan Tower
Waterman, Lewis Edson
Waterman, Robert H.
Waterman, Thomas Whitney
Watson, James Madison
Watson, Thomas John
Watterston, George
Wayland, Francis, 1796–1865
Webb, Alexander Stewart
Webb, Charles Henry
Webb, James Watson
Webb, William Henry
Weber, Joseph Morris
Webster, Alice Jane Chandler
Weed, Thurlow
Weigel, Gustave
Weil, Richard
Weir, John Ferguson
Weir, Julian Alden
Weir, Robert Fulton
Weir, Robert Walter
Welch, Ashbel
Welch, Charles Clark
Welch, Philip Henry
Welles, (Benjamin) Sumner
Wells, Erastus
Wells, Harriet Sheldon
Wells, John
Wende, Ernest
Wende, Grover William
Wentworth, Cecile de
Westcott, Edward Noyes
Westinghouse, George
Westley, Helen
Wexler, Irving ("Waxey Gordon")
Whalen, Grover Aloysius
Wharton, Edith Newbold Jones
Wheatley, William
Whedon, Daniel Denison
Wheeler, Andrew Carpenter
Wheeler, Everett Pepperrell
Wheeler, (George) Post
Wheeler, Schuyler Skaats

Wheeler, William Almon
Whipple, Henry Benjamin
Whitaker, Nathaniel
Whitcher, Frances Miriam Berry
White, Alfred Tredway
White, Andrew Dickson
White, Canvass
White, David
White, George
White, George Leonard
White, Joseph Malachy
White, Richard Grant
White, Stanford
White, William Alanson
Whitehouse, Frederic Cope
Whitfield, Robert Parr
Whitman, Marcus
Whitman, Walt
Whitney, Gertrude Vanderbilt
Whitney, Harry Payne
Whitney, Willis Rodney
Whittingham, William Rollinson
Wickes, Stephen
Wickham, John
Wickson, Edward James
Wiechmann, Ferdinand Gerhard
Wigger, Winand Michael
Wiggins, Carleton
Wight, Peter Bonnett
Wilder, Alexander
Wilder, John Thomas
Wilkes, Charles
Wilkes, George
Wilkie, Franc Bangs
Willard, Frances Elizabeth Caro-
  line
Willet, William
Willett, Marinus
Williams, Charles Richard
Williams, Fannie Barrier
Williams, Frank Martin
Williams, George Henry
Williams, George Huntington
Williams, Henry Shaler
Williams, Linsly Rudd
Williams, Samuel Wells
Williams, William R.
Willis, Bailey
Willis, Henry Parker
Willys, John North
Wilson, Allen Benjamin
Wilson, Theodore Delavan
Winant, John Gilbert
Winchell, Alexander
Winchell, Newton Horace
Wing, Joseph Elwyn
Winslow, John Bradley
Wise, Henry Augustus
Wisner, Henry
Witherspoon, Herbert
Witmark, Isidore
Witthaus, Rudolph August
Wolfe, Catharine Lorillard
Wolfe, John David
Wolheim, Louis Robert
Wood, Craig Ralph
Wood, Henry Alexander Wise
Wood, James, 1799–1867
Wood, James, 1839–1925
Wood, James Rushmore
Wood, Joseph
Wood, Mary Elizabeth
Wood, Samuel

Woodford, Stewart Lyndon
Woodhull, Nathaniel
Woodruff, Lorande Loss
Woodruff, Theodore Tuttle
Woodruff, William Edward
Woodward, Augustus Brevoort
Woodward, William
Woodworth, Jay Backus
Wool, John Ellis
Woolley, Edgar Montillion ("Monty")
Woolsey, Melancthon Taylor
Woolsey, Theodore Dwight
Woolworth, Frank Winfield
Worcester, Edwin Dean
Worden, John Lorimer
Worth, William Jenkins
Worthington, Henry Rossiter
Wright, George
Wright, George Frederick
Wright, Harold Bell
Wright, William
Yale, Linus
Yates, Abraham
Yates, Herbert John
Yates, John Van Ness
Yates, Robert
Youmans, Edward Livingston
Youmans, Vincent Millie
Youmans, William Jay
Young, Ella Flagg
Young, Owen D.
Young, Thomas
Zimmerman, Henry ("Heinie")
Zinsser, Hans

NORTH CAROLINA

Alderman, Edwin Anderson
Allen, George Venable
Allen, William
Ammons, Elias Milton
Andrews, Alexander Boyd
Armistead, Lewis Addison
Arrington, Alfred W.
Ashe, John
Ashe, John Baptista
Ashe, Samuel
Ashe, Thomas Samuel
Ashe, William Shepperd
Atkinson, Henry
Avery, William Waigstill
Aycock, Charles Brantley
Badger, George Edmund
Bailey, Josiah William
Baker, Laurence Simmons
Barden, Graham Arthur
Barringer, Daniel Moreau
Barringer, Rufus
Bassett, John Spencer
Battle, Kemp Plummer
Battle, William Horn
Baxter, Elisha
Baxter, John
Beasley, Frederick
Bell, Henry Haywood
Belo, Alfred Horatio
Bennett, Hugh Hammond
Benton, Thomas Hart
Bickett, Thomas Walter
Biggs, Asa
Bingham, Robert Worth
Bingham, William

Blake, Lillie Devereux
Blalock, Nelson Gates
Bloodworth, Timothy
Blount, Thomas
Blount, Willie
Blue, Victor
Bonner, John Henry
Bragg, Braxton
Bragg, Thomas
Branch, John
Branch, Lawrence O'Bryan
Bridgers, Robert Rufus
Brinkley, John Richard
Brooks, George Washington
Brown, Bedford
Burgevine, Henry Andrea
Burleson, Edward
Burns, Otway
Burton, Hutchins Gordon
Butler, Marion
Bynum, William Preston
Cain, William
Caldwell, Charles
Cambreleng, Churchill Caldom
Cannon, Joseph Gurney
Cannon, Newton
Carr, Elias
Carson, Simeon Lewis
Cheshire, Joseph Blount
Clark, John
Clark, Walter
Clarke, Francis Devereux
Clarke, Mary Bayard Devereux
Clement, Rufus Early
Clewell, John Henry
Clingman, Thomas Lanier
Coffin, Levi
Colton, Elizabeth Avery
Coltrane, John William
Connor, Henry Graves
Connor, Robert Digges Wimberly
Cox, William Ruffin
Craven, Braxton
Daly, John Augustin
Daniels, Josephus
Dargan, Edmund Strother
Davis, George
De Mille, Henry Churchill
Denny, George Vernon, Jr.
De Rosset, Moses John
Dick, Robert Paine
Dixon, Thomas
Dobbin, James Cochran
Dodd, William Edward
Donnell, Robert
Doughton, Robert Lee
Dudley, Edward Bishop
Duke, Benjamin Newton
Duke, James Buchanan
Eaton, John Henry
Edwards, Weldon Nathaniel
Elliott, Aaron Marshall
Ellis, John Willis
Fels, Samuel Simeon
Finley, James Bradley
Fitzgerald, Oscar Penn
Forney, William Henry
Fries, Francis
Fuller, Thomas Charles
Gaines, George Strother
Gardner, Oliver Maxwell
Gaston, William
Gatling, Richard Jordan

Gilmer, John Adams
Gould, Robert Simonton
Govan, Daniel Chevilette
Graham, Edward Kidder
Graham, William Alexander
Gray, George Alexander
Hale, Edward Joseph
Harnett, Cornelius
Harrell, John
Hawkins, Benjamin
Hawks, Francis Lister
Hawley, Joseph Roswell
Haywood, John
Heineman, Daniel Webster ("Dannie")
Helper, Hinton Rowan
Henderson, Archibald
Henderson, James Pinckney
Henderson, Leonard
Henkel, Paul
Hill, Robert Andrews
Hilliard, Henry Washington
Hoey, Clyde Roark
Hoke, Robert Frederick
Holden, William Woods
Holmes, Theophilus Hunter
Holt, Edwin Michael
Hooper, Johnson Jones
Houston, David Franklin
Houston, William Churchill
Howe, Robert
Howell, Robert Boyté Crawford
Hunt, Nathan
Jarvis, Thomas Jordan
Jasper, William
Johnson, Andrew
Johnson, Edward Austin
Johnson, William Ransom
Johnston, Joseph Forney
Jones, Alexander
Jones, Allen
Jones, Willie
Kerr, Washington Caruthers
King, William Rufus Devane
Kirby, George Hughes
Kitchin, Claude
Kitchin, William Walton
Koopman, Augustus
Lane, Joseph
Lanier, James Franklin Doughty
Law, Sallie Chapman Gordon
Lewis, Exum Percival
Lewis, William Gaston
Long, James
Loring, William Wing
Luelling, Henderson
Lyon, Francis Strother
McGilvary, Daniel
McIver, Charles Duncan
McKay, James Iver
McLean, Angus Wilton
McNeill, William Gibbs
Macon, Nathaniel
McRae, Duncan Kirkland
Madison, Dolly Payne
Mangum, Willie Person
Manly, Basil
Manning, Thomas Courtland
Martin, James Green
Means, Gaston Bullock
Mercer, Jesse
Merrimon, Augustus Summerfield
Moore, Alfred

Moore, Bartholomew Figures
Moore, Gabriel
Moore, James, 1737–1777
Moore, Maurice
Moore, Thomas Overton
Mordecai, Alfred
Morehead, John Motley
Murphey, Archibald De Bow
Murphy, James Bumgardner
Murrow, Edward (Egbert) Roscoe
Nash, Frederick
Nicholson, Timothy
Osborn, Charles
Osborne, James Walker
Overman, Lee Slater
Page, Walter Hines
Paine, Robert
Parker, John Johnston
Patterson, Rufus Lenoir
Payne, Bruce Ryburn
Pearson, Richmond Mumford
Pegram, George Braxton
Pender, William Dorsey
Pettigrew, James Johnston
Pickens, Israel
Pickett, Albert James
Polk, James Knox
Polk, Leonidas
Polk, Leonidas Lafayette
Polk, Lucius Eugene
Polk, William
Pool, John
Porter, William Sydney
Potter, Robert
Price, Thomas Frederick
Purviance, David
Rains, Gabriel James
Rains, George Washington
Ramseur, Stephen Dodson
Ransom, Matt Whitaker
Rayner, Kenneth
Reade, Edwin Godwin
Reichel, William Cornelius
Reid, David Settle
Revels, Hiram Rhoades
Reynolds, Robert Rice
Richardson, Edmund
Rivers, Lucius Mendel
Ross, Martin
Royster, James Finch
Ruark, Robert Chester
Saunders, Romulus Mitchell
Saunders, William Laurence, 1835
–1891
Sawyer, Lemuel
Schweinitz, Emil Alexander de
Scott, Thomas Fielding
Scott, W(illiam) Kerr
Sellers, Isaiah
Settle, Thomas
Shepard, James Edward
Shipp, Albert Micajah
Simmons, Furnifold McLendel
Simmons, James Stevens
Skinner, Harry
Skinner, Thomas Harvey
Smith, Charles Alphonso
Smith, Henry Louis
Smith, Hoke
Smith, Robert Hardy
Smith, William, 1762–1840
Smith, William Nathan Harrell
Spaight, Richard Dobbs

Spaulding, Charles Clinton
Stacy, Walter Parker
Stanly, Edward
Steele, John
Steele, Wilbur Daniel
Stitt, Edward Rhodes
Stone, David
Strudwick, Edmund Charles Fox
Stuart, Elbridge Amos
Swain, David Lowry
Taylor, Hannis
Thompson, Jacob
Tiernan, Frances Christine Fisher
Truett, George Washington
Turner, Josiah
Tyson, Lawrence Davis
Upchurch, John Jordan
Vance, Zebulon Baird
Waddel, Moses
Waddell, Alfred Moore
Waddell, James Iredell
Walker, David, 1785–1830
Webb, William Robert
Weeks, Stephen Beauregard
Wheeler, John Hill
White, Hugh Lawson
White, James
White, Stephen Van Culen
Wilcox, Cadmus Marcellus
Wiley, Calvin Henderson
Williams, Jesse Lynch
Williams, John
Winslow, John Ancrum
Wolfe, Thomas Clayton
Worth, Jonathan
Yell, Archibald
Yount, George Concepcíon

NORTH DAKOTA

Aandahl, Fred George
Durstine, Roy Sarles
Flannagan, John Bernard
Hunter, Croil
Langer, William

OHIO

Abbey, Henry Eugene
Abel, John Jacob
Adams, William Lysander
Adkins, Homer Burton
Akeley, Mary Leonore
Aldrich, Louis
Alger, Russell Alexander
Allen, Frederic de Forest
Allen, Robert
Allen, William Vincent
Allison, William Boyd
Anderson, Sherwood
Andrews, Chauncey Hummason
Andrews, Lorin
Archbold, John Dustin
Ashmore, William
Axtell, Samuel Beach
Bacher, Otto Henry
Bacon, Delia Salter
Bailey, Joseph
Baird, Samuel John
Baker, James Heaton
Baker, Oliver Edwin
Ball, Ephraim
Ball, Frank Clayton

Ball, George Alexander
Ballantine, Arthur Atwood
Bancroft, Hubert Howe
Bara, Theda
Barber, Ohio Columbus
Barus, Carl
Bauer, Louis Agricola
Beard, Daniel Carter
Beard, James Carter
Beard, Thomas Francis
Beard, William Holbrook
Beardshear, William Miller
Beatty, Clyde Raymond
Beatty, John
Beatty, William Henry
Beavers, Louise
Beck, Johann Heinrich
Bell, Bernard Iddings
Bell, James Madison
Bellows, George Wesley
Bender, George Harrison
Benedict, Stanley Rossiter
Bessey, Charles Edwin
Bettman, Alfred
Beveridge, Albert Jeremiah
Bevier, Isabel
Bickel, Luke Washington
Bickerdyke, Mary Ann Ball
Biddle, Horace P.
Bierce, Ambrose Gwinett
Biggers, Earl Derr
Bingham, Amelia
Binkley, Wilfred Ellsworth
Blum, Robert Frederick
Boardman, Mabel Thorp
Bohm, Max
Boole, Ella Alexander
Bosworth, Francke Huntington
Boyd, Thomas Alexander
Bragdon, Claude Fayette
Brett, William Howard
Brice, Calvin Stewart
Brigham, Joseph Henry
Bromfield, Louis
Brooks, William Keith
Brooks, William Thomas Harbaugh
Brough, John
Brown, Carleton
Brown, Clarence James
Brown, Fayette
Brown, George Pliny
Brown, Henry Cordis
Brown, John Porter
Brown, Walter Folger
Brush, Charles Francis
Buchanan, William Insco
Buchtel, John Richards
Buckland, Ralph Pomeroy
Buell, Don Carlos
Burchfield, Charles Ephraim
Burnett, Henry Lawrence
Burton, Ernest De Witt
Burton, Theodore Elijah
Bussey, Cyrus
Butterworth, Benjamin
Byford, William Heath
Callahan, Patrick Henry
Callender, Guy Stevens
Campbell, Lewis Davis
Campbell, William Wallace
Canaga, Alfred Bruce
Canfield, James Hulme

Carney, Thomas
Carpenter, Frank George
Carr, Charlotte Elizabeth
Carr, Wilbur John
Carter, Thomas Henry
Cary, Alice
Cary, Phoebe
Case, Leonard
Cass, George Washington
Catherwood, Mary Hartwell
Chaffee, Adna Romanza
Chamberlain, Charles Joseph
Chamberlain, Joseph Perkins
Chambers, James Julius
Chapin, Henry Dwight
Cherrington, Ernest Hurst
Chester, George Randolph
Christy, David
Christy, Howard Chandler
Cist, Henry Martyn
Clark, Bobby
Clark, Charles
Clarke, John Hessin
Clevenger, Shobal Vail
Cline, Genevieve Rose
Cockerill, John Albert
Coffin, Howard Earle
Coit, Stanton
Colver, William Byron
Commons, John Rogers
Compton, Arthur Holly
Compton, Karl Taylor
Conklin, Edwin Grant
Conover, Obadiah Milton
Cooke, Henry David
Cooke, Jay
Cooper, Elias Samuel
Cooper, Jacob
Cooper, Oswald Bruce
Corbin, Henry Clark
Coulter, Ernest Kent
Cowen, John Kissig
Cowles, Edwin
Cox, Georges Barnsdale
Cox, James Middleton
Cox, Kenyon
Cox, Samuel Sullivan
Craig, Winchell McKendree
Crane, Harold Hart
Cranston, Earl
Crapsey, Algernon Sidney
Cratty, Mabel
Cravath, Paul Drennan
Creighton, Edward
Creighton, John Andrew
Crile, George Washington
Crissinger, Daniel Richard
Crocker, William
Crook, George
Crosby, William Otis
Crosley, Powel, Jr.
Crouse, Russel McKinley
Crozier, William
Curtis, William Eleroy
Cushing, Harvey Williams
Custer, George Armstrong
Dahlgren, Sarah Madeleine Vinton
Dandridge, Dorothy Jean
Daniels, Frank Albert
Daniels, Winthrop More
Darrow, Clarence Seward
Daugherty, Harry Micajah

Davis, Edwin Hamilton
Dawes, Charles Gates
Dawes, Rufus Cutler
Day, David Talbot
Day, James Gamble
Day, William Rufus
De Camp, Joseph Rodefer
Dellenbaugh, Frederick Samuel
Dennison, William
Dickman, Joseph Theodore
Dinwiddie, Edwin Courtland
Dittemore, John Valentine
Doherty, Henry Latham
Dorsey, George Amos
Doyle, Alexander
Drake, John Burroughs
Du Bois, Augustus Jay
Dun, Robert Graham
Dunbar, Paul Laurence
Dwenger, Joseph
Dwiggins, William Addison
Dykstra, Clarence Addison
Eaton, Benjamin Harrison
Eaton, Joseph Oriel
Eckart, William Roberts
Eckert, Thomas Thompson
Edison, Thomas Alva
Edwards, Clarence Ransom
Eichelberger, Robert Lawrence
Elkins, Stephen Benton
Elliott, Charles Burke
Ellis, Edward Sylvester
Ellis, John Washington
Ellis, Seth Hockett
Elwell, John Johnson
Emmett, Daniel Decatur
Enneking, John Joseph
Ernst, Harold Clarence
Ernst, Oswald Herbert
Evans, John
Evans, Lawrence Boyd
Ewing, Hugh Boyle
Ewing, Thomas
Fairbanks, Charles Warren
Fairchild, George Thompson
Fairchild, Lucius
Fairless, Benjamin F.
Faran, James John
Fenneman, Nevin Melancthon
Ferree, Clarence Errol
Fess, Simeon Davidson
Finley, Martha Farquharson
Firestone, Harvey Samuel
Fisher, Alfred J.
Fisher, Charles T.
Fisher, Frederic John
Fleming, John Adam
Flickinger, Daniel Kumler
Foraker, Joseph Benson
Fordyce, John Addison
Fosdick, William Whiteman
Foster, Charles
Foster, Randolph Sinks
Fowler, Joseph Smith
Frank, Lawrence Kelso
Franklin, Benjamin
Freas, Thomas Bruce
French, Aaron
Frohman, Charles
Frohman, Daniel
Funk, Isaac Kauffman
Funston, Frederick
Furnas, Robert Wilkinson

Gable, (William) Clark
Gage, Frances Dana Barker
Galbreath, Charles Burleigh
Garey, Thomas Andrew
Garfield, Harry Augustus
Garfield, James Abram
Garfield, James Rudolph
Gavin, Frank Stanton Burns
Gideon, Peter Miller
Gilbert, Cass
Gilliam, David Tod
Gillmore, Quincy Adams
Gish, Dorothy
Goodrich, Alfred John
Goodwin, Elijah
Granger, Alfred Hoyt
Grant, Ulysses Simpson
Grasselli, Caesar Augustin
Gray, Elisha
Green, William
Greene, Charles Sumner
Greene, Henry Mather
Greer, James Augustin
Grey, Zane
Griffin, Charles
Grose, William
Gross, Samuel Weissell
Grosscup, Peter Stenger
Gunn, James Newton
Gunn, Ross
Gunsaulus, Frank Wakeley
Hall, Charles Martin
Halstead, Murat
Hammond, Percy Hunter
Hanby, Benjamin Russel
Handerson, Henry Ebenezer
Hanna, Marcus Alonzo
Hannegan, Edward Allen
Harding, Warren Gamaliel
Harkness, Edward Stephen
Harmon, Judson
Harper, Robert Francis
Harper, William Rainey
Harris, James Arthur
Harris, Merriman Colbert
Harris, William Logan
Harrison, Benjamin
Hart, Edwin Bret
Hart, Hastings Hornell
Haskell, Charles Nathaniel
Haskell, Henry Jospeh
Hatton, Frank
Hayden, Amos Sutton
Hayes, Charles Willard
Hayes, Max Sebastian
Hayes, Rutherford Birchard
Hayes, William Henry
Hendricks, Thomas Andrews
Henri, Robert
Henry, William Arnon
Hepburn, William Peters
Herrick, Myron Timothy
Herrick, Sophia McIlvaine Bledsoe
Hickenlooper, Andrew
Hinsdale, Burke Aaron
Hitchcock, Frank Harris
Hitt, Robert Roberts
Hocking, William Ernest
Holloway, Joseph Flavius
Holmes, William Henry
Hooper, Claude Ernest
Hoover, Charles Franklin

Hoover, Herbert William
Hopwood, Avery
Horton, Samuel Dana
Howard, Roy Wilson
Howe, William Henry
Howells, William Dean
Hoyt, John Wesley
Hubbard, Frank McKinney
Hudson, Thomson Jay
Huggins, Miller James
Humiston, William Henry
Hunt, Reid
Hurley, Joseph Patrick
Hurst, Fannie
Hussey, William Joseph
Hyslop, James Hervey
Jackman, Wilbur Samuel
Janis, Elsie
Janney, Russell Dixon
Jay, Allen
Jefferson, Charles Edward
Jeffrey, Joseph Andrew
Jeffries, James Jackson
Johnson, Bushrod Rust
Johnson, Byron Bancroft
Johnson, Franklin
Johnson, George
Johnson, John Butler
Johnston, William Hartshorne
Jones, Lynds
Joyce, Isaac Wilson
Kalisch, Samuel
Keeler, Ralph Olmstead
Keifer, Joseph Warren
Kellor, Frances (Alice)
Kennan, George
Kennedy, Robert Patterson
Kennedy, William Sloane
Kenyon, William Squire
Kerr, John Glasgow
Kester, Paul
Kettering, Charles Franklin
Keyt, Alonzo Thrasher
King, Ernest Joseph
King, Henry
Kingsley, Elbridge
Kinkead, Edgar Benton
Kiplinger, Willard Monroe
Klippart, John Hancock
Knox, Rose Markward
Krapp, George Philip
Kroger, Bernhard Henry
Kyle, David Braden
Kyle, James Henderson
Ladd, George Trumbull
Lamme, Benjamin Garver
Landis, Henry Robert Murray
Landis, Kenesaw Mountain
Lane, Levi Cooper
Lanston, Tolbert
Latham, Milton Slocum
Latta, Alexander Bonner
Laughlin, James Laurence
Lawrance, Uriah Marion
Lawrence, William, 1819–1899
Lawton, Henry Ware
Leaming, Jacob Spicer
Leavitt, Frank McDowell
Le Duc, William Gates
Leonard, Harry Ward
Lewis, Alfred Henry
Lewis, Charles Bertrand
Liebman, Joshua Loth

Loeb, Louis
Loeb, Morris
Long, John Harper
Long, Perrin Hamilton
Longley, Alcander
Longworth, Nicholas, 1869–1931
Lord, Henry Curwen
Lowe, Ralph Phillips
Lower, William Edgar
Lowry, Hiram Harrison
Lydenberg, Harry Miller
Lytle, William Haines
McBride, F(rancis) Scott
McCabe, Charles Cardwell
McClain, Emlin
McConnell, Francis John
McCook, Alexander McDowell
McCook, Anson George
McCook, Edward Moody
McCook, Henry Christopher
McCook, John James
MacCracken, Henry Mitchell
McCulloch, Oscar Carleton
McDill, James Wilson
McDonald, James Grover
MacDonald, James Wilson Alexander
McDonald, Joseph Ewing
McDougal, David Stockton
McDowell, Irvin
McDowell, Mary Eliza
McDowell, William Fraser
MacGahan, Januarius Aloysius
McKinley, William
McPherson, James Birdseye
McPherson, Logan Grant
McVey, Frank Lerond
Main, John Hanson Thomas
Mallory, Frank Burr
Manatt, James Irving
Marquett, Turner Mastin
Marquis, Albert Nelson
Marvin, Charles Frederick
Mather, Samuel
Matthews, Stanley
Mayo-Smith, Richmond
Meeker, Ezra
Meeker, Jotham
Meeker, Nathan Cook
Mees, Arthur
Mendenhall, Charles Elwood
Mendenhall, Thomas Corwin
Merrill, Stephen Mason
Miller, Dayton Clarence
Miller, Lewis
Miller, Willoughby Dayton
Millikin, Eugene Donald
Mitchell, Edwin Knox
Mitchell, Robert Byington
Moeller, Henry
Montgomery, James
Moore, Clarence Lemuel Elisha
Moore, Eliakim Hastings
Moore, Joseph Haines
Moore, Richard Bishop
Moorehead, William Gallogly
Mussey, Ellen Spencer
Nash, Henry Sylvester
Nettleton, Alvred Bayard
Nettleton, Edwin S.
Newbrough, John Ballou
Newell, Robert
Newell, William Augustus

Newsam, Albert
Newton, Robert Safford
Nichols, Dudley
Niehaus, Charles Henry
Noble, John Willock
Norris, George William
Norton, William Warder
Notestein, Wallace
Nugent, John Frost
Oakes, George Washington Ochs
Oakley, Annie
O'Daniel, Wilbert Lee ("Pappy")
O'Dwyer, Joseph
Ohlmacher, Albert Philip
Okey, John Waterman
Oldfield, ("Barney") Berna Eli
Olds, Ransom Eli
Oliver, Charles Augustus
Opper, Frederick Burr
Osborn, Thomas Ogden
Otis, Harrison Gray
Outcault, Richard Felton
Packard, James Ward
Paine, Byron
Paine, Halbert Eleazer
Pardee, Don Albert
Parker, Isaac Charles
Parker, Samuel Chester
Parsons, Albert Ross
Patrick, Hugh Talbot
Patterson, John Henry
Pattison, John M.
Payne, Oliver Hazard
Pease, Alfred Humphreys
Peet, Stephen Denison
Pendleton, George Hunt
Perkins, Charles Elliott
Perrine, Charles Dillon
Peter, Sarah Worthington King
Plumb, Preston B.
Poe, Orlando Metcalfe
Pomerene, Atlee
Porter, Stephen Geyer
Porter, William Townsend
Potts, Benjamin Franklin
Power, Tyrone
Pratt, Donn
Proctor, William Cooper
Pugh, George Ellis
Quantrill, William Clarke
Ralston, Samuel Moffett
Ralston, William Chapman
Ransohoff, Joseph
Rarey, John Solomon
Raymond, Rossiter Worthington
Read, Daniel, 1805–1878
Reed, James Alexander
Reed, Mary
Reeves, Arthur Middleton
Reid, James L.
Reid, Whitelaw
Resor, Stanley Burnet
Rhodes, James Ford
Rice, Felelon Bird
Richards, John Kelvey
Rickert, Martha Edith
Ricketts, Howard Taylor
Rickey, Wesley Branch
Rigge, William Francis
Riggs, Stephen Return
Ripley, Roswell Sabine
Ritchey, George Willis
Robinson, Edward Stevens

Rockefeller, John Davison, Jr.
Rogers, William Allen
Root, Amos Ives
Rorimer, James Joseph
Rose, Mary Davies Swartz
Rosecrans, Sylvester Horton
Rosecrans, William Starke
Ross, Alexander Coffman
Ross, Denman Waldo
Ross, Edmund Gibson
Rourke, Constance Mayfield
Roye, Edward James
Rusk, Jeremiah McClain
Sabine, Wallace Clement Ware
Safford, James Merrill
Safford, William Edwin
Sampson, Martin Wright
Sanders, James Harvey
Schenck, James Findlay
Schenck, Robert Cumming
Schevill, Rudolph
Schlesinger, Arthur Meier
Schuchert, Charles
Scott, Austin
Scott, Samuel Parsons
Scott, William Berryman
Scudder, John Milton
Seiberling, Frank Augustus
Seitz, Don Carlos
Severance, Louis Henry
Seymour, Thomas Day
Shabonee
Shannon, Wilson
Sharp, William Graves
Shauck, John Allen
Shaw, Albert
Sherman, John, 1823–1900
Sherman, William Tecumseh
Sherwood, Katharine Margaret
  Brownlee
Shields, George Oliver
Short, Sidney Howe
Shuey, Edwin Longstreet
Shuey, William John
Shull, George Harrison
Silverman, Joseph
Simms, Ruth Hanna McCormick
Simpson, Matthew
Skinner, Halcyon
Sloan, Richard Elihu
Sloane, William Milligan
Smalley, Eugene Virgil
Smith, Alfred Holland
Smith, Byron Caldwell
Smith, Henry Preserved
Smith, Joseph, 1832–1914
Smith, Preserved
Smith, William Sooy
Snider, Denton Jaques
Snow, Lorenzo
Spahr, Charles Barzillai
Sparks, Edwin Erle
Speaks, Oley
Spear, William Thomas
Sprague, Kate Chase
Stanley, David Sloane
Stanton, Edwin McMasters
Stearns, Frank Ballou
Stephenson, Nathaniel Wright
Stevens, William Arnold
Stewart, Eliza Daniel
Stewart, Robert
Stockton, Charles G.

Stone, John Wesley
Storer, Bellamy
Stratemeyer, George Edward
Strauss, Joseph Baermann
Strobel, Charles Louis
Strong, William Lafayette
Stuhldreher, Harry A.
Stutz, Harry Clayton
Sullivant, William Starling
Swayne, Wager
Sweeney, Martin Leonard
Swing, David
Taft, Charles Phelps
Taft, Henry Waters
Taft, Robert Alphonso
Taft, William Howard
Talbott, Harold Elstner
Tappan, Eli Todd
Tatum, Art
Taylor, Archibald Alexander Ed-
  ward
Tecumseh
Tenskwatawa
Thatcher, Roscoe Wilfred
Thilly, Frank
Thoburn, Isabella
Thoburn, James Mills
Thomas, Edith Matilda
Thomas, Norman Mattoon
Thomas, Roland Jay
Thompson, David P.
Thompson, William Oxley
Thompson, William Tappan
Thomson, William McClure
Thurber, James Grover
Thurston, Howard
Tibbles, Thomas Henry
Tittle, Ernest Fremont
Tod, David
Todd, Walter Edmond Clyde
Torrence, Frederick Ridgely
Tourgée, Albion Winegar
Townsend, Willard Saxby, Jr.
Twachtman, John Henry
Tyler, George Crouse
Tytus, John Butler
Ulrich, Edward Oscar
Updegraff, David Brainard
Vail, Theodore Newton
Vallandigham, Clement Laird
Van Anda, Carr Vattel
Van Deman, Esther Boise
Van Sweringen, Mantis James
Venable, William Henry
Verity, George Matthew
Vickery, Howard Leroy
Victor, Orville James
Voorhees, Daniel Wolsey
Wade, Decius Spear
Wade, Jeptha Homer
Waite, Henry Matson
Wald, Lillian D.
Walden, John Morgan
Wales, James Albert
Walker, Thomas Barlow
Walter, Eugene
Wambaugh, Sarah
Wanamaker, Reuben Melville
Ward, Charles Alfred
Ward, John Quincy Adams
Weaver, James Baird
Weber, Henry Adam
Weed, Lewis Hill

Weeks, John Elmer
Weitzel, Godfrey
Welch, John
Weller, John B.
Wellman, Walter
Wheeler, Wayne Bidwell
White, Emerson Elbridge
White Eyes
Whitehead, Wilbur Cherrier
Whitlock, Brand
Whittredge, Worthington
Widney, Joseph Pomeroy
Wilder, Russell Morse
Wildman, Murray Shipley
Williams, Charles David
Williams, Edward Thomas
Williams, Harrison Charles
Williams, James Douglas
Williams, John Elias
Williams, John Fletcher
Williams, Marshall Jay
Wilson, Charles Erwin
Wilson, James Falconer
Wilson, Samuel Mountford
Wilson, Samuel Ramsay
Windom, William
Wolfson, Erwin Service
Woodhull, Victoria Claflin
Woods, Charles Robert
Woods, William Burnham
Woolley, Celia Parker
Woolley, John Granville
Woolsey, Sarah Chauncy
Worcester, Elwood
Wright, Hamilton Kemp
Wright, Orville
Wright, William
Wyant, Alexander Helwig
Young, Allyn Abbott
Young, Clark Montgomery
Young, Denton True ("Cy")
Young, John Wesley
Zahm, John Augustine
Zollars, Ely Vaughan

OKLAHOMA

Armstrong, Frank C.
Billingsley, John Sherman
Francis, Kay
Guthrie, Woody
Hamilton, Maxwell McGaughey
Hastings, William Wirt
Hurley, Patrick Jay
Jansky, Karl Guthe
Jones, William
Kerr, Robert Samuel
Kirkwood, John Gamble
Martin, Johnny Leonard Roose-
  velt ("Pepper")
Owen, Stephen Joseph
Posey, Alexander Lawrence
Robertson, Alice Mary
Rogers, Will
Stigler, William Grady
Thorpe, James Francis
Waner, Paul Glee

OREGON

Barbey, Daniel Edward
Bates, Blanche
Cromwell, Dean Bartlett

Davenport, Homer Calvin
Gaston, Herbert Earle
Gilbert, Alfred Carlton
Hawley, Willis Chatman
Joseph
Latourette, Kenneth Scott
MacDonald, Ranald
McIntire, Ross
McKay, (James) Douglas
McNary, Charles Linza
Markham, Edwin
Neuberger, Richard Lewis
Poling, Daniel Alfred
Reed, John, 1887–1920
Robinson, Claude Everett
Turner, Richmond Kelly

PENNSYLVANIA

Abbett, Leon
Abbey, Edwin Austin
Abbott, Benjamin
Acheson, Edward Goodrich
Adams, Randolph Greenfield
Adams, Robert
Addicks, John Edward O'Sullivan
Adlum, John
Agnew, David Hayes
Albright, Jacob
Alcott, Louisa May
Alexander, John White
Alexander, Joseph Addison
Allen, Andrew
Allen, Harrison
Allen, Henry Justin
Allen, Hervey
Allen, Richard
Allen, William
Allibone, Samuel Austin
Alter, David
Anderson, John Alexander
Anderson, Joseph
Anderson, Maxwell
Angela, Mother
Appenzeller, Henry Gerhard
Apple, Thomas Gilmore
Arbuckle, John
Arensberg, Walter Conrad
Armstrong, John
Arnold, Henry Harley
Asch, Morris Joseph
Ashburner, Charles Albert
Ashhurst, John
Ashley, James Mitchell
Ashmead, Isaac
Ashmead, William Harris
Atkinson, William Biddle
Atkinson, Wilmer
Atlee, John Light
Atlee, Washington Lemuel
Awl, William Maclay
Bache, Alexander Dallas
Bache, Benjamin Franklin
Bache, Franklin
Baer, George Frederick
Bailey, Francis
Bailey, Frank Harvey
Bailey, Lydia R.
Baird, Absalom
Baird, Henry Carey
Baird, Henry Martyn
Baird, Robert
Baird, Spencer Fullerton

Baldwin, Joseph
Baldwin, William
Bard, Samuel
Bard, William
Barker, James Nelson
Barker, Wharton
Barnard, George Grey
Barnes, Albert Coombs
Barnes, Joseph K.
Barnum, Zenus
Barrymore, Ethel
Barrymore, Georgiana Emma Drew
Barrymore, John
Barrymore, Lionel
Bartlett, William Holmes Chambers
Bartley, Mordecai
Barton, Benjamin Smith
Barton, John Rhea
Barton, Thomas Pennant
Barton, William Paul Crillon
Bartram, John
Bartram, William
Baugher, Henry Louis
Bausman, Benjamin
Bayard, Samuel
Baziotes, William
Bean, Tarleton Hoffman
Beasley, Mercer
Beatty, John
Beaumont, John Colt
Beaux, Cecilia
Beaver, James Addams
Beck, James Montgomery
Bedford, Gunning
Bedinger, George Michael
Bell, De Benneville ("Bert")
Bell, James Ford
Bell, James Stroud
Benbridge, Henry
Benner, Philip
Bennett, Caleb Prew
Berger, Daniel
Berkowitz, Henry
Berwind, Edward Julius
Biddle, Anthony Joseph Drexel, Jr.
Biddle, Clement
Biddle, James
Biddle, Nicholas, 1750–1778
Biddle, Nicholas, 1786–1844
Bigler, John
Bigler, William
Bingham, Anne Willing
Bingham, John Armor
Bingham, William
Binkley, Robert Cedric
Binney, Horace
Bird, Frederic Mayer
Bisphan, David Scull
Black, James
Black, Jeremiah Sullivan
Black, William Murray
Blaine, James Gillespie
Blake, Francis Gilman
Bliss, Philip Paul
Bliss, Tasker Howard
Blitzstein, Marc
Boehm, Henry
Boker, George Henry
Boller, Alfred Pancoast
Bomberger, John Henry Augustus

Boone, Daniel
Booth, James Curtis
Boreman, Arthur Ingram
Borie, Adolph Edward
Borie, Adolphe
Boring, Edwin Garrigues
Boudinot, Elias
Bourke, John Gregory
Bowers, Theodore Shelton
Bowman, Thomas
Boyd, James
Brackenridge, Henry Marie
Bradford, William
Brady, Cyrus Townsend
Brashear, John Alfred
Breck, James Lloyd
Breen, Joseph Ignatius
Breese, Kidder Randolph
Brennan, Francis James
Brereton, Lewis Hyde
Brewster, Frederick Carroll
Bridges, Robert
Bright, James Wilson
Brinton, Daniel Garrison
Brinton, John Hill
Brodhead, John Romeyn
Brooke, John Rutter
Brown, Charles Brockden
Brown, David Paul
Brown, Jacob Jennings
Brown, William Henry
Brown, William Hughey
Buchanan, James
Buchman, Frank Nathan Daniel
Buckalew, Charles Rollin
Bucknell, William
Buehler, Huber Gray
Bullard, William Hannum Grubb
Bullitt, William Christian
Burdette, Robert Jones
Burleigh, Henry Thacker
Burnett, Charles Henry
Burrell, David James
Burrowes, Thomas Henry
Burrows, Julius Caesar
Burrows, William
Burson, William Worth
Butler, Smedley Darlington
Buttz, Henry Anson
Byerly, William Elwood
Cadman, Charles Wakefield
Cadwalader, John, 1742–1786
Cadwalader, John, 1805–1879
Cadwalader, Thomas
Calder, Alexander Stirling
Caldwell, Alexander
Caldwell, David
Calhoun, William James
Cameron, James Donald
Cameron, Simon
Campbell, Bartley
Campbell, James
Campbell, James Hepburn
Carey, Henry Charles
Carnahan, James
Carpenter, Cyrus Clay
Carrick, Samuel
Carroll, Earl
Carroll, William
Carson, Hampton Lawrence
Carson, John Renshaw
Carson, Joseph
Carson, Rachel Louise

Carter, John
Case, Leonard
Cassatt, Alexander Johnston
Cassatt, Mary
Cassin, John
Catlin, George
Catron, John
Cattell, James McKeen
Chambers, George
Chambers, Talbot Wilson
Chambers, Whittaker
Chanfrau, Henrietta Baker
Chapman, Henry Cadwalader
Chauvenet, William
Cheyney, Edward Potts
Childs, Cephas Grier
Chorpenning, George
Christy, Edwin P.
Cist, Charles
Cist, Jacob
Clark, Walter Leighton
Clark, William Andrews
Clarke, Helen Archibald
Clarke, Thomas Shields
Clay, Albert Thomas
Clay, Edward Williams
Clayton, Powell
Clement, Martin Withington
Clemson, Thomas Green
Cliffton, William
Clothier, William Jackson
Clymer, George
Clymer, George E.
Coates, Florence Earle
Coates, Samuel
Cochran, John
Cochrane, Henry Clay
Coffin, William Anderson
Coggeshall, William Turner
Coleman, Leighton
Collins, Napoleon
Connelly, Cornelia
Conner, David
Connick, Charles Jay
Connolly, John
Conrad, Frank
Conrad, Robert Taylor
Converse, James Booth
Cook, Martha Elizabeth Duncan
    Walker
Cook, Robert Johnson
Cooke, Morris Llewellyn
Coombe, Thomas
Cooper, William
Cope, Caleb
Cope, Edward Drinker
Cope, Thomas Pym
Cope, Walter
Corbin, Margaret
Corey, William Ellis
Coriat, Isador Henry
Cornstalk
Corse, John Murray
Corson, Hiram
Corson, Robert Rodgers
Cowan, Edgar
Cox, Hannah Peirce
Cox, Rowland
Coxe, Eckley Brinton
Coxe, Tench
Coxe, William
Coxey, Jacob Sechler
Craig, Thomas

Cramp, Charles Henry
Cramp, William
Crawford, James Pyle Wickersham
Crawford, John Martin
Cresson, Elliott
Cresson, Ezra Townsend
Crooks, George Richard
Crosby, Peirce
Crozer, John Price
Crumbine, Samuel Jay
Cullinan, Joseph Stephen
Cummins, Albert Baird
Cupples, Samuel
Curran, John Joseph
Curry, George Law
Curtin, Andrew Gregg
Cushing, Frank Hamilton
Cutbush, James
Dahlgren, John Adolphus Bernard
Dallas, George Mifflin
Darby, William
Darke, William
Darley, Felix Octavius Carr
Darling, Henry
Darlington, William
Davenport, Russell Wheeler
Davidson, William Lee
Davis, Ernest R. ("Ernie")
Davis, John Wesley
Davis, Noah Knowles
Davis, Rebecca Blaine Harding
Davis, Richard Harding
Davis, Stuart
Davis, William Morris
Davison, Henry Pomeroy
Day, David Alexander
Day, Frank Miles
Deaver, John Blair
De Haren, Edwin Jesse
Deitzler, George Washington
Del Ruth, Roy
Deland, Margaret
Demuth, Charles
Dercum, Francis Xavier
Desha, Joseph
Dewees, William Potts
Dick, Elisha Cullen
Dickinson, Anna Elizabeth
Diller, Joseph Silas
Dock, Lavinia Lloyd
Dodd, Lee Wilson
Dodd, Samuel Calvin Tate
Doddridge, Joseph
Doddridge, Philip
Dolan, Thomas
Donnelly, Eleanor Cecilia
Donnelly, Ignatius
Dorsey, John Syng
Dorsey, Thomas Francis ("Tom-
    my")
Dos Passas, John Randolph
Dougherty, Dennis Joseph
Dougherty, Raymond Philip
Doughty, Thomas
Downey, John
Drew, John
Drexel, Anthony Joseph
Drexel, Joseph William
Drexel, Katharine Mary
Drinker, Cecil Kent
Dropsie, Moses Aaron
Drown, Thomas Messinger
Duane, William

Dubbs, Joseph Henry
Du Bois, William Ewing
Duff, James Henderson
Duffield, George, 1732–1790
Duffield, George, 1794–1868
Dunlop, James
Dunwoody, William Hood
Durant, Thomas Jefferson
Durham, Caleb Wheeler
Dye, William McEntyre
Eakins, Thomas
Eckels, James Herron
Eddy, Thomas
Edge, Walter Evans
Edwards, Richard Stanislaus
Egan, Maurice Francis
Egle, William Henry
Eichholtz, Jacob
Eisenhart, Luther Pfahler
Elder, William
Ellet, Charles
Ellicott, Andrew
Ellicott, Joseph
Ellicott, Washington Lafayette
Ellmaker, (Emmett) Lee
Elman, Harry ("Ziggy")
English, Thomas Dunn
Espy, James Pollard
Eustis, Dorothy Leib Harrison
    Wood
Evans, Henry Clay
Evans, Lewis
Evans, Nathaniel
Evans, Thomas
Evans, Thomas Wiltberger
Eve, Joseph
Ewing, James, 1736–1806
Ewing, James, 1866–1943
Ewing, James Caruthers Rhea
Eytinge, Rose
Fahnestock, Harris Charles
Fairlamb, James Remington
Falk, Maurice
Farabee, William Curtis
Farquhar, Percival
Faulk, Andrew Jackson
Ferguson, Elizabeth Graeme
Ferrel, William
Ferris, Jean Léon Gérôme
Ffoulke, Charles Mather
Fields, William Claude
Filson, John
Findlay, James
Fine, Henry Burchard
Fischer, Louis
Fisher, Clarence Stanley
Fisher, Daniel Webster
Fisher, Frederick Bohn
Fisher, Hammond Edward
Fisher, Joshua Francis
Fisher, Sidney George
Fisher, Sydney George
Fite, Warner
Fitler, Edwin Henry
Flather, John Joseph
Fleisher, Benjamin Wilfrid
Fleming, John
Fletcher, Henry Prather
Flick, Lawrence Francis
Florence, Thomas Birch
Folwell, Samuel
Foote, John Ambrose
Force, Juliana Rieser

Ford, Thomas
Forepaugh, Adam
Forney, John Wien
Forney, Matthias Nace
Forrest, Edwin
Forten, James
Foster, Stephen Collins
Foster, Thomas Jefferson
Foulk, George Clayton
Fraley, Frederick
Francis, John Brown
Franklin, William
Franklin, William Buel
Frayne, Hugh
Frazer, John Fries
Frazer, Persifor, 1736–1792
Frazer, Persifor, 1844–1909
Frazier, Charles Harrison
Frear, William
Freed, Alan J.
French, Paul Comly
Frick, Henry Clay
Fries, John
Fritz, John
Frost, Arthur Burdett
Fry, William Henry
Fulton, Robert
Furness, Horace Howard, 1732–1790
Furness, Horace Howard, 1794–1868
Furst, Clyde Bowman
Fussell, Bartholomew
Gabb, William More
Gallagher, William Davis
Gallaudet, Thomas Hopkins
Galloway, Samuel
Garman, Samuel
Garrett, Thomas
Gass, Patrick
Gates, Thomas Sovereign
Gayley, James
Geary, John White
Geddes, James
George, Henry
Gerhard, William Wood
Gerhart, Emanuel Vogel
Gibbon, John
Gibbons, Abigail Hopper
Gibbons, William
Gibson, George
Gibson, John
Gibson, John Bannister
Giddings, Joshua Reed
Gihon, Albert Leary
Gilder, William Henry
Gilpin, William
Girty, Simon
Glackens, William James
Gladden, Washington
Glynn, James
Gobrecht, Christian
Godfrey, Thomas, 1704–1749
Godfrey, Thomas, 1736–1763
Goebel, William
Good, Adolphus Clemens
Good, James Isaac
Good, Jeremiah Haak
Goodman, Charles
Goodyear, Charles
Gordon, Laura De Force
Gorgas, Josiah
Gostelowe, Jonathan

Goucher, John Franklin
Gouge, William M.
Gowen, Franklin Benjamin
Graff, Frederic
Graff, Frederick
Grafly, Charles
Graham, George Rex
Graham, Joseph
Gratz, Rebecca
Gray, Isaac Pusey
Gray, John Purdue
Graydon, Alexander
Green, Jacob
Green, William Joseph, Jr.
Greener, Richard Theodore
Gregg, Andrew
Gregg, David McMurtrie
Gregory, Casper René
Gregory, Thomas Barger
Grier, Robert Cooper
Grierson, Benjamin Henry
Griffin, Martin Ignatius Joseph
Griffis, William Elliot
Griscom, Clement Acton
Gross, Samuel David
Guffey, James McClurg
Guffey, Joseph F.
Guggenheim, Daniel
Guggenheim, Simon
Guggenheim, Solomon Robert
Guilday, Peter Keenan
Gummere, John
Guthrie, George Wilkins
Hagner, Peter
Haid, Leo
Haldeman, Samuel Steman
Haldeman-Julius, Emanuel
Hale, Charles Reuben
Hall, Baynard Rush
Hall, James, 1744–1826
Hall, James, 1793–1868
Hall, John Elihu
Hall, Sarah Ewing
Hall, Thomas
Hallowell, Benjamin
Hallowell, Richard Price
Hamer, Thomas Lyon
Hamilton, Peter
Hammer, William Joseph
Hancock, Winfield Scott
Happer, Andrew Patton
Harbaugh, Henry
Hardin, Ben
Hardin, Martin D.
Harding, George
Harding, Jesper
Harding, William White
Hare, George Emlen
Hare, John Innes Clark
Hare, Robert
Haring, Clarence
Harkins, William Draper
Harlan, Josiah
Harlan, Richard
Harmar, Josiah
Harpster, John Henry
Harrah, Charles Jefferson
Harris, George Washington
Harris, John
Harrison, Charles Custis
Harrison, Gabriel
Harrison, John
Harrison, Joseph

Harrison, Lovell Birge
Harrison, Ross Granville
Harrison, Thomas Alexander
Harrod, James
Harshberger, John William
Hart, Abraham
Hart, Albert Bushnell
Hart, Charles Henry
Hart, Edward
Hartley, Thomas
Hartranft, Chester David
Hartranft, John Frederick
Hartshorne, Henry
Haseltine, James Henry
Haskins, Charles Homer
Haupt, Herman
Haverly, Christopher
Hay, Charles Augustus
Hayden, William
Hayes, Isaac Israel
Hayes, John William
Hays, Alexander
Hays, Isaac
Hazard, Ebenezer
Hazard, Samuel
Heap, Samuel Davies
Heath, Thomas Kurton
Heintzelman, Samuel Peter
Heinz, Henry John
Helmuth, William Tod
Hemphill, Joseph
Hench, Philip Showalter
Henck, John Benjamin
Hendricks, William
Henrici, Arthur Trautwein
Henry, Andrew
Henry, William
Hepburn, James Curtis
Hergesheimer, Joseph
Hering, Carl
Hering, Rudolph
Herr, John
Herron, Francis Jay
Hershey, Milton Snavely
Hicks, John, 1823–1890
Hiester, Daniel
Hiester, Joseph
Hill, George Washington
Hillegas, Michael
Hillis, David
Himes, Charles Francis
Hirst, Barton Cooke
Hirst, Henry Beck
Hise, Elijah
Hittell, John Shertzer
Hittell, Theodore Henry
Hobart, John Henry
Hodge, Charles
Hodge, Hugh Lenox
Hoffman, Clare Eugene
Hogan, John Vincent Lawless
Holliday, Cyrus Kurtz
Holls, George Frederick William
Holmes, David
Holmes, John Haynes
Homer, Louise Dilworth Beatty
Hood, James Walker
Hood, Washington
Hooper, Lucy Hamilton
Hoover, James Matthews
Hopkins, Edward Augustus
Hopkinson, Francis
Hopkinson, Joseph

Hopper, Hedda
Horn, Edward Traill
Horn, George Henry
Horsfield, Thomas
Hoshour, Samuel Klinefelter
Hough, Charles Merrill
Houston, Henry Howard
Howe, Frederic Clemson
Hoyt, Henry Martyn
Hughes, Hector James
Huidekoper, Frederic
Hullihen, Simon P.
Humphreys, Andrew Atkinson
Humphreys, James
Humphreys, Joshua
Humphries, George Rolfe
Huneker, James Gibbons
Hunt, Robert Woolston
Hunter, Andrew
Hussey, Curtis Grubb
Huston, Charles
Hutchinson, James
Ickes, Harold Le Clair
Ingersoll, Charles Jared
Ingersoll, Edward
Ingham, Samuel Delucenna
Ingraham, Edward Duffield
Irvine, James
Irvine, William Mann
Jackson, Abraham Reeves
Jackson, Chevalier
Jackson, David
Jackson, Dugald Caleb
Jackson, Edward
Jackson, Robert Houghwout
Jackson, Samuel
Jacobs, Henry Eyster
Jacobs, Michael
Jadwin, Edgar
Jaggar, Thomas Augustus, Jr.
James, Thomas Chalkley
James, Thomas Potts
Jameson, Horatio Gates
Janvier, Catharine Ann
Janvier, Thomas Allibone
Jarvis, Charles H.
Jayne, Horace Fort
Jeanes, Anna T.
Jeffers, John Robinson
Jefferson, Joseph
Jenkins, Howard Malcolm
Jennings, John
Jessup, Henry Harris
Johnson, John Graver
Johnston, David Claypoole
Johnston, William Andrew
Jones, Benjamin Franklin
Jones, George
Jones, Jehu Glancy
Jones, John Price
Jones, William
Jones, William Patterson
Jones, William Richard
Jordon, John Woolf
Junkin, George
Kagan, Henry Enoch
Kane, Elisha Kent
Kane, Thomas Leiper
Kauffman, Calvin Henry
Kaufman, George S.
Kay, Edgar Boyd
Keagy, John Miller
Keating, John Marie

Keely, John Ernst Worrell
Keen, Morris Longstreth
Keen, William Williams
Keller, Kaufman Thuma
Kelley, Florence
Kelley, William Darrah
Kelly, Aloysius Oliver Joseph
Kelly, John Brendan
Kelly, William
Kelton, John Cunningham
Kemmerer, Edwin Walter
Kennedy, Joseph Camp Griffith
Kent, William
Kephart, Ezekial Boring
Kephart, Isaiah La Fayette
Kephart, John William
Kier, Samuel M.
King, Samuel Archer
Kirk, Alan Goodrich
Kirkbride, Thomas Story
Kirlin, Joseph Louis Jerome
Klauder, Charles Zeller
Kline, Franz Josef
Kneass, Samuel Honeyman
Kneass, Strickland
Kneass, William
Knight, Daniel Ridgway
Knight, Jonathan
Knox, Philander Chase
Kohler, Elmer Peter
Kraemer, Henry
Krause, Allen Kramer
Krauth, Charles Philip
Kresge, Sebastian Spering
Kress, Samuel Henry
Kuhn, Adam
Kumler, Henry
Kurtz, Benjamin
Kynett, Alpha Jefferson
Lacey, John
Lacy, Ernest
Lambdin, James Reid
Lambert, Louis Aloisius
Lamberton, Benjamin Jeffer
Lambing, Andrew Arnold
Landis, Walter Savage
Lane, William Carr
Langstroth, Lorenzo Lorraine
Lardner, James Lawrence
La Roche, Rene
Latrobe, Benjamin Henry, 1806–1878
Latrobe, John Hazlehurst Boneval
Lawrence, David Leo
Lea, Henry Charles
Lea, Mathew Carey
Lease, Mary Elizabeth Clyens
Le Brun, Napoléon Eugène Henry Charles
Leffler, Isaac
Leffler, Shepherd
Leffmann, Henry
Leib, Michael
Leidy, Joseph
Leishman, John G. A.
Leland, Charles Godfrey
LeMoyne, Francis Julius
Lenker, John Nicholas
Leonard, Zenas
Lesley, Peter
Leslie, Eliza
Letterman, Jonathan
Levy, Uriah Phillips

Lewis, Charlton Thomas
Lewis, Edmund Darch
Lewis, Ellis
Lewis, Enoch
Lewis, Isaac Newton
Lewis, Lawrence
Lewis, Wilfred
Lewis, William
Lewis, William Draper
Lick, James
Liggett, Hunter
Lightburn, Joseph Andrew Jackson
Linderman, Henry Richard
Lindley, Daniel
Lindley, Jacob
Linn, John Blair
Linton, Ralph
Lippard, George
Lippincott, James Starr
Little, Charles Joseph
Liveright, Horace Brisbin
Lochman, John George
Locke, Alain Leroy
Locke, Matthew
Lockrey, Sarah Hunt
Logan, Deborah Norris
Logan, George
Logan, James, c. 1725–1780
Long, John Luther
Longacre, James Barton
Love, Alfred Henry
Loy, Matthias
Loyd, Samuel
Lucas, James H.
Luce, Henry Winters
Lukens, Rebecca Webb Pennock
Luks, George Benjamin
Lutz, Frank Eugene
Lybrand, William Mitchell
Lyon, James Benjamin
Macalester, Charles, 1798–1873
MacArthur, Charles Gordon
McBride, Henry
McCall, Samuel Walker
McCann, Alfred Watterson
McCartee, Divie Bethune
McCarthy, Daniel Joseph
McCartney, Washington
McCauley, Charles Stewart
MacCauley, Clay
McCauley, Edward Yorke
McCawley, Charles Grymes
McCay, Charles Francis
McCay, Henry Kent
McClellan, George, 1849–1913
McClellan, George Brinton
McClellan, Henry Brainerd
McClellan, Robert
McClelland, Robert
McClintock, Emory
McClintock, John
McClintock, Oliver
McClure, Alexander Kelly
McClurg, Alexander Caldwell
McCormick, Samuel Black
McCoy, Isaac
McCracken, Joan
McCreery, James Work
MacDonald, Jeanette Anna
McDowell, John
McElrath, Thomas
McFadden, Louis Thomas

McFarland, John Horace
McFarland, Samuel Gamble
McFarland, Thomas Bard
Macfarlane, Charles William
McGiffin, Philo Norton
McGill, John
McGranery, James Patrick
McGready, James
McGuffey, William Holmes
McKean, Samuel
McKean, Thomas
McKean, William Wister
McKechnie, William Boyd
McKenna, Joseph
Mackenzie, William
McKim, Charles Follen
McKim, Isaac
McKim, James Miller
McKinley, Albert Edward
McLane, Allan
Maclay, Robert Samuel
Maclay, Samuel
Maclay, William
McLean, William Lippard
McMinn, Joseph
McNair, Alexander
McNair, Frederick Valette
MacNair, Harley Farnsworth
McPherson, Edward
McQuillen, John Hugh
MacVeagh, Charles
MacVeagh, Franklin
MacVeagh, Isaac Wayne
Madden, John Edward
Magee, Christopher Lyman
Magill, Edward Hicks
Mailly, William
Malcolm, James Peller
Malcom, Howard
Mallery, Garrick
Manderson, Charles Frederick
Mansfield, Jayne
March, Francis Andrew
March, Peyton Conway
Marchand, John Bonnett
Marland, Ernest Whitworth
Marquis, John Abner
Marshall, Clara
Marshall, George Catlett, Jr.
Marshall, Humphry
Martin, Elizabeth Price
Martin, John Alexander
Martin, John Hill
Mast, Phineas Price
Mateer, Calvin Wilson
Mathews, John Alexander
Mathewson, Christopher
Matthews, Joseph Merritt
Maurer, James Hudson
Mayer, Lewis
Meade, George
Meade, Richard Worsam
Mears, John William
Mease, James
Medary, Milton Bennett
Medary, Samuel
Meigs, Arthur Vincent
Meigs, James Aitken
Meigs, John
Meigs, John Forsyth
Meigs, William Montgomery
Mellon, Andrew William
Mellon, William Larimer

Menjou, Adolphe Jean
Menoher, Charles Thomas
Mercer, Henry Chapman
Mercer, Lewis Pyle
Mercur, Ulysses
Meredith, Samuel
Meredith, William Morris
Merritt, Anna Lea
Mervine, William
Messersmith, George Strausser
Metcalf, Joel Hastings
Metcalf, William
Michener, Ezra
Michler, Nathaniel
Middleton, Thomas Cooke
Midgley, Thomas
Mifflin, Lloyd
Mifflin, Thomas
Milburn, William Henry
Miller, George
Miller, George Abram
Miller, James Russell
Miller, Samuel
Milligan, Robert Wiley
Mills, Charles Karsner
Mitchell, John Hipple
Mitchell, Langdon Elwyn
Mitchell, Silas Weir
Mitchell, Thomas Duché
Mix, Tom
Montgomery, James Alan
Moore, Annie Aubertine Wood-
   ward
Moore, George Foot
Moore, James Edward
Moore, Joseph Earle
Moore, William, 1699–1783
Moore, William, 1735–1793
Moorhead, James Kennedy
Moran, Benjamin
Morgan, George
Morgan, George Washington
Morgan, John
Morley, Christopher Darlington
Morley, Sylvanus Griswold
Morris, Anthony, 1766–1860
Morris, Cadwalader
Morris, Caspar
Morris, Edward Joy
Morris, George Pope
Morris, John Gottlieb
Morris, Thomas
Morrison, John Irwin
Morrison, William
Morrow, Jeremiah
Morton, James St. Clair
Morton, John
Morton, Samuel George
Moss, John Calvin
Muhlenberg, Frederick Augustus
Mühlenberg, Frederick Augustus
   Conrad
Mühlenberg, Gotthilf Henry Er-
   nest
Mühlenberg, Henry Augustus Phi-
   lip
Muhlenberg, John Peter Gabriel
Muhlenberg, William Augustus
Mulford, Elisha
Murdock, James Edward
Murphy, Dominic Ignatius
Murphy, Isaac
Murray, John, 1737–1808

Murray, Lindley
Murray, Louise Shipman Welles
Musmanno, Michael Angelo
Nancrède, Charles Beylard Gué-
   rard de
Nassau, Robert Hamill
Neely, Thomas Benjamin
Negley, James Scott
Neill, Edward Duffield
Neill, John
Neill, Thomas Hewson
Neill, William
Neilson, William George
Nesbit, Evelyn Florence
Nevin, Alfred
Nevin, Edwin Henry
Nevin, Ethelbert Woodbridge
Nevin, George Balch
Nevin, John Williamson
Nevin, Robert Peebles
Newcomer, Christian
Newell, Frederick Haynes
Newton, Henry Jotham
Newton, Richard Heber
Newton, William Wilberforce
Niles, Hezekiah
Nixon, John, 1733–1808
Noah, Mordecai Manuel
Nock, Albert Jay
Nolen, John
Norris, George Washington
Norris, Isaac, 1701–1766
Norris, William Fisher
Noss, Theodore Bland
Oberholtzer, Ellis Paxson
Oberholtzer, Sara Louisa Vickers
Odenheimer, William Henry
Odets, Clifford
Oehmler, Leo Carl Martin
Offley, David
Ogden, Robert Curtis
O'Hara, John Henry
Olds, Irving Sands
Olmsted, Marlin Edgar
O'Malley, Frank Ward
O'Neill, Rose Cecil
Ord, George
O'Reilly, Robert Maitland
Ortle, Godlove Stein
Osborn, Henry Stafford
Osborn, Thomas Andrew
Ott, Isaac
Otto, William Tod
Outerbridge, Alexander Ewing
Outerbridge, Eugenius Harvey
Packard, John Hooker
Packer, William Fisher
Palmer, Alexander Mitchell
Palmer, Henry Wilbur
Pancoast, Henry Khunrath
Pancoast, Seth
Park, James
Park, Robert Ezra
Parke, John Grubb
Parker, George Howard
Parkinson, Thomas Ignatius
Parrish, Anne
Parrish, Charles
Parrish, Edward
Parrish, Joseph
Parrish, Maxfield
Parry, Charles Thomas
Parry, John Stubbs

Passavant, William Alfred
Patterson, Morris
Patterson, Robert Mayne
Patton, William
Peale, Anna Claypoole
Peale, Rembrandt
Peale, Sarah Miriam
Peale, Titian Ramsay
Pearse, John Barnard Swett
Peary, Robert Edwin
Peffer, William Alfred
Pemberton, Israel
Pemberton, James
Pemberton, John
Pemberton, John Clifford
Penington, Edward
Penn, John
Penn, Richard
Pennell, Joseph
Pennypacker, Elijah Funk
Pennypacker, Galusha
Pennypacker, Samuel Whitaker
Penrose, Boies
Penrose, Charles Bingham
Penrose, Richard Alexander Fullerton
Penrose, Spencer
Pepper, George Seckel
Pepper, George Wharton
Pepper, William, 1810–1864
Pepper, William, 1843–1898
Pepper, William, III, 1874–1947
Peters, Madison Clinton
Peters, Richard, 1744–1828
Peters, Richard, 1810–1889
Peterson, Charles Jacobs
Peterson, Henry
Pettigrew, Charles
Pettit, Thomas McKean
Pew, Joseph Newton, Jr.
Pfahler, George Edward
Phelps, William Walter
Phillips, Francis Clifford
Phillips, Henry
Phillips, Thomas Wharton
Phipps, Henry
Phipps, Lawrence Cowle
Physick, Philip Syng
Pickens, Andrew
Pickering, Charles
Pippin, Horace
Plumer, William Swan
Polk, Thomas
Polock, Moses
Porter, Andrew
Porter, David Dixon
Porter, David Rittenhouse
Porter, Edwin Stanton
Porter, Horace
Porter, James Madison
Porter, Thomas Conrad
Potts, Charles Sower
Potts, Jonathan
Poulson, Zachariah
Powderly, Terence Vincent
Powdermaker, Hortense
Powel, John Hare
Pratt, Matthew
Pratt, Waldo Selden
Presser, Theodore
Preston, Ann
Preston, Jonas
Preston, Margaret Junkin

Preston, William Campbell
Price, Eli Kirk, 1797–1884
Price, Eli Kirk, 1860–1933
Price, Hiram
Pugh, Evan
Purdue, John
Pyle, Robert
Pyle, Walter Lytle
Quay, Matthew Stanley
Quinan, John Russell
Quinn, Arthur Hobson
Quinn, Edmond Thomas
Raguet, Condy
Ramsay, David
Ramsay, Erskine
Ramsay, Nathaniel
Ramsey, Alexander
Randall, Samuel Jackson
Randolph, Jacob
Rauch, John Henry
Rawle, Francis, 1846–1930
Rawle, William
Rawle, William Henry
Rea, Samuel
Read, Charles
Read, Conyers
Read, John Meredith, 1797–1874
Read, John Meredith, 1837–1896
Read, Thomas Buchanan
Ream, Norman Bruce
Redman, John
Reed, David Aiken
Reed, Henry Hope
Reed, James Hay
Reed, William Bradford
Reeder, Andrew Horatio
Reese, John James
Rehn, Frank Knox Morton
Reick, William Charles
Reid, William Shields
Reilly, Marion
Reinhart, Benjamin Franklin
Reinhart, Charles Stanley
Remington, Joseph Price
Repplier, Agnes
Reynolds, John
Reynolds, John Fulton
Reynolds, William
Rhees, William Jones
Rhoades, James E.
Rich, Robert
Richards, Theodore William
Richards, William Trost
Richardson, Joseph
Richardson, Robert
Richter, Conrad Michael
Riddle, Matthew Brown
Riddle, Samuel Doyle
Rigdon, Sidney
Rinehart, Mary Roberts
Rinehart, Stanley Marshall, Jr.
Ritner, Joseph
Rittenhouse, David
Roane, Archibald
Robb, James
Roberdeau, Isaac
Roberts, Elizabeth Wentworth
Roberts, George Brooke
Roberts, Howard
Roberts, Job
Roberts, Jonathan
Roberts, Owen Josephus
Roberts, Solomon White

Roberts, William Milnor
Robertson, James Alexander
Robinson, Edward Mott
Rockhill, William Woodville
Rodenbough, Theophilus Francis
Roebling, Washington Augustus
Rogers, Henry Darwin
Rogers, James Blythe
Rogers, John Ignatius
Rogers, Robert William
Rogers, William Barton
Rondthaler, Edward
Rosenau, Milton Joseph
Rosenbach, Abraham Simon Wolf
Rosenbach, Philip Hyman
Ross, Betsy
Ross, James
Rossiter, Clinton Lawrence, III
Rotch, Thomas Morgan
Rothermel, Peter Frederick
Rothrock, Joseph Trimble
Rowan, John
Rowland, Henry Augustus
Rupp, Israel Daniel
Rupp, William
Rush, Benjamin
Rush, James
Rush, Richard
Rush, William
Russell, Charles Taze
Ryan, Harris Joseph
Sachse, Julius Friedrich
Sadtler, Samuel Philip
Samuels, Samuel
Sanderson, John
Sankey, Ira David
Sargent, Winthrop, 1825–1870
Sartain, Emily
Sartain, Samuel
Sartain, William
Savery, William, 1750–1804
Saxton, Joseph
Say, Benjamin
Say, Thomas
Sayre, Robert Heysham
Schadle, Jacob Evans
Schaeffer, Charles Frederick
Schaeffer, David Frederick
Schaeffer, Frederick Christian
Schaeffer, Nathan Christ
Schamberg, Jay Frank
Schmauk, Theodore Emanuel
Schmucker, Beale Melanchthon
Schneider, Benjamin
Schneider, Herman
Schodde, George Henry
Schriver, Edmund
Schwab, Charles Michael
Schweinitz, Edmund Alexander de
Schweinitz, George Edmund de
Schweinitz, Lewis David von
Scott, Robert Kingston
Scott, Thomas Alexander
Scovel, Henry Sylvester
Scull, John
Seaman, Elizabeth Cochrane
See, Horace
Seidel, George Lukas Emil
Seip, Theodore Lorenzo
Sellers, Coleman
Sellers, William
Selznick, David O.
Sergeant, John, 1779–1852

Sergeant, Thomas
Servoss, Thomas Lowery
Seybert, Adam
Seybert, Henry
Seybert, John
Sharpless, Isaac
Sharswood, George
Shaw, Thomas
Sheeler, Charles R., Jr.
Shippen, Edward, 1728/29–1806
Shippen, William
Shiras, George
Shiras, Oliver Perry
Sholes, Christopher Latham
Shonts, Theodore Perry
Shoup, George Laird
Shulze, John Andrew
Shunk, Francis Rawn
Simpson, Stephen
Singerly, William Miskey
Skillern, Ross Hall
Slattery, Charles Lewis
Sloan, John French
Smedley, William Thomas
Smith, Albert Holmes
Smith, Andrew Jackson
Smith, Charles Ferguson
Smith, Charles Perrin
Smith, Charles Shaler
Smith, Daniel B.
Smith, Edgar Fahs
Smith, Hannah Whitall
Smith, Hiram
Smith, James, 1737–1814
Smith, John Blair
Smith, Jonathan Bayard
Smith, Lloyd Pearsall
Smith, Margaret Bayard
Smith, Oliver Hampton
Smith, Persifor Frazer
Smith, Richard Penn
Smith, Richard Somers
Smith, Robert, 1757–1842
Smith, Samuel
Smith, Samuel Harrison
Smith, Samuel Stanhope
Smith, Xanthus Russell
Smyth, Albert Henry
Snowden, James Ross
Snyder, Edwin Reagan
Snyder, Simon
Sower, Christopher, 1754–1799
Spaeth, John Duncan
Spaeth, Sigmund
Spalding, Franklin Spencer
Spangler, Henry Wilson
Speer, Emma Bailey
Speer, Robert Elliott
Speer, William
Sproul, William Cameron
Sproull, Thomas
Stahr, John Summers
Starr, Louis
Statler, Ellsworth Milton
Stauffer, David McNeely
Steedman, James Blair
Stehle, Aurelius Aloysius
Stein, Gertrude
Stein, Leo Daniel
Stengel, Alfred
Sterling, John Whalen
Sterne, Simon
Sterrett, James Macbride

Stevens, Abel
Stevens, Wallace
Stewardson, John
Stewart, Andrew
Stillé, Alfred
Stillé, Charles Janeway
Stillman, Samuel
Stockdale, Thomas Ringland
Stockton, Charles Herbert
Stockton, Frank Richard
Stoddart, Joseph Marshall
Stoever, Martin Luther
Stokes, Maurice
Stone, Witmer
Stotesbury, Edward Townsend
Strain, Isaac G.
Strawn, Jacob
Strickland, William
Studebaker, Clement
Sturgis, Samuel Davis
Sullivan, James William
Sullivan, Mark
Sulzberger, Cyrus Lindauer
Swallow, Silas Comfort
Swank, James Moore
Swensson, Carl Aaron
Swisshelm, Jane Grey Cannon
Sylvis, William H.
Talbot, Francis Xavier
Tanner, Benjamin Tucker
Tanner, Henry Ossawa
Tarbell, Ida Minerva
Tawney, James Albertus
Taylor, Bayard
Taylor, Francis Henry
Taylor, Frank Walter
Taylor, Frederick Winslow
Thatcher, Mahlon Daniel
Thaw, Harry Kendall
Thaw, William
Thomas, George Clifford
Thomas, John Charles
Thompson, Arthur Webster
Thompson, Denman
Thompson, Joseph Parrish
Thompson, Josiah Van Kirk
Thompson, Robert Means
Thompson, Samuel Rankin
Thompson, Will Lamartine
Thomson, Frank
Thomson, John Edgar
Thomson, William
Tiffany, Katrina Brandes Ely
Tilden, William Tatem ("Big
  Bill")
Tilghman, Richard Albert
Timon, John
Tome, Jacob
Toner, Joseph Meredith
Torrence, Joseph Thatcher
Tower, Charlemagne
Towne, Henry Robinson
Towne, John Henry
Townsend, John Kirk
Townsend, Mira Sharpless
Trautwine, John Cresson
Trent, William
Trumbauer, Horace
Truxtun, William Talbot
Tryon, George Washington
Turnbull, William
Turner, Samuel Hulbeart
Tyndale, Hector

Tyson, James
Tyson, Job Roberts
Tyson, Stuart Lawrence
Unangst, Erias
Van Amringe, John Howard
Van Buren, William Holme
Vandergrift, Jacob Jay
Van Dyke, Henry
Van Dyke, John Wesley
Van Horn, Robert Thompson
Van Meter, John Blackford
Vanuxem, Lardner
Vare, William Scott
Vauclain, Samuel Matthews
Vaux, Richard
Vaux, Roberts
Vezin, Hermann
Von Moschzisker, Robert
Wagner, John Peter
Wagner, William
Wahl, William Henry
Walker, Frank Comerford
Walker, James Barr
Walker, John Brisben
Walker, Jonathan Hoge
Walker, Robert John
Wallace, David
Wallace, Henry
Wallace, Horace Binney
Wallace, John Hankins
Wallace, John William
Waln, Nicholas
Waln, Robert, 1765–1836
Waln, Robert, 1794–1825
Walsh, Edward Augustine
Walsh, Thomas Joseph
Walter, Francis Eugene
Walter, Thomas Ustick
Walters, William Thompson
Walworth, Jeannette Ritchie
  Hodermann
Wanamaker, John
Wanamaker, Lewis Rodman
Warden, John Aston
Warner, Edward Pearson
Warren, William, 1812–1888
Watson, David Thompson
Watts, Frederick
Wayne, Anthony
Weaver, William Dixon
Webb, John Burkitt
Weems, Ted
Weidner, Revere Franklin
Weir, Ernest Tener
Welsh, John
Wenner, George Unangst
Werdin, Reed
West, Andrew Fleming
West, Benjamin
Westcott, Thompson
Wetherill, Charles Mayer
Wetherill, Samuel
Wetzel, Lewis
Wharton, Anne Hollingsworth
Wharton, Francis
Wharton, Joseph
Wharton, Robert
Wharton, Samuel
Wharton, Thomas
Wharton, Thomas Isaac
Wherry, Elwood Morris
White, James William
White, John De Haven

White, Samuel Stockton
White, William
Whitehill, Robert
Wickersham, George Woodward
Wickersham, James Pyle
Widener, Harry Elkins
Widener, Peter Arrell Brown
Wieland, George Reber
Wiggin, Kate Douglas
Wikoff, Henry
Wiley, David
Wilkins, Ross
Wilkins, William
Willard, James Field
Williams, Daniel Hale
Williams, George Washington
Williamson, Hugh
Willing, Thomas
Wilmot, David
Wilson Bird
Wilson, Francis
Wilson, John Fleming
Wilson, Joseph Miller
Wilson, Louis Blanchard
Wilson, Robert Burns
Wilson, Samuel Graham
Wilson, Warren Hugh
Winans, Williams
Wines, Frederick Howard
Wise, John
Wistar, Caspar
Wister, Owen
Wister, Sarah
Wolf, George
Wolle, John Frederick
Wood, Charles Erskine Scott
Wood, David Duffle
Wood, Fernando
Wood, Horatio Charles
Wood, James Frederick
Woodhouse, James
Woodin, William Hartman
Woodruff, Charles Edward
Woods, Robert Archey
Woodward, Joseph Janvier
Work, Hubert
Work, Milton Cooper
Wormley, Theodore George
Wright, Charles Barstow
Wright, Hendrick Bradley
Wright, Jonathan Jasper
Wright, Joseph Albert
Wright, Joseph Jefferson Burr
Wrigley, William
Wurtz, Henry
Wylie, Andrew
Wynn, Ed
Yeager, Joseph
Yeates, Jasper
Yerkes, Charles Tyson
Yerkes, Robert Mearns
Young, Jesse Bowman
Young, John Clarke
Young, Samuel Hall
Zahniser, Howard Clinton
Zeilin, Jacob
Ziegemeier, Henry Joseph
Ziegler, William

RHODE ISLAND

Abell, Arunah Shepherdson
Aldrich, Chester Holmes

Aldrich, Nelson Wilmarth
Aldrich, Richard
Allen, Paul
Allen, Philip
Allen, William Henry
Allen, Zachariah
Alline, Henry
Almy, John Jay
Ames, Samuel
Angell, Israel
Angell, James Burrill
Angell, Joseph Kinnicutt
Angell, William Gorham
Anthony, Henry Bowen
Anthony, John Gould
Anthony, William Arnold
Arnold, Aza
Arnold, Jonathan
Arnold, Richard
Arnold, Samuel Greene
Bacon, Edwin Munroe
Baker, George Pierce
Baldwin, Henry Porter
Ballou, Adin
Bancroft, Wilder Dwight
Bartlett, Elisha
Bartlett, John Russell
Barton, William
Bennett, Charles Edwin
Boss, Lewis
Bourne, Benjamin
Brayton, Charles Ray
Brown, Goold
Brown, James Salisbury
Brown, John
Brown, John Carter
Brown, Joseph
Brown, Joseph Rogers
Brown, Moses
Brown, Nicholas, 1729–1791
Brown, Nicholas, 1769–1841
Brown, Obadiah
Brown, Sylvanus
Brownell, Henry Howard
Buffum, Arnold
Bull, William Tillinghast
Burgess, Alexander
Burgess, George
Burrill, James
Butterworth, Hezekiah
Casey, Silas
Chace, Elizabeth Buffum
Chafee, Zechariah, Jr.
Champlin, John Denison
Champlin, Stephen
Channing, Edward Tyrell
Channing, Walter
Channing, William Ellery
Chapin, Charles Value
Church, Benjamin
Clark, John Bates
Clarke, Walter
Clifford, John Henry
Coe, George Simmons
Cohan, George Michael
Collins, John
Colvin, Stephen Sheldon
Cornell, Ezekiel
Cotton, Joseph Potter
Cottrell, Calvert Byron
Crandall, Prudence
Cranston, Samuel
Cross, Samuel Hazzard

Curtis, George William
Davis, Harvey Nathaniel
Dearth, Henry Golden
Decatur, Stephen
De Wolf, James
Diman, Jeremiah Lewis
Dorr, Thomas Wilson
Doyle, Sarah Elizabeth
Duffy, Hugh
Durfee, Job
Durfee, Thomas
Eddy, Nelson
Elder, Samuel James
Ellery, Frank
Ellery, William
Fenner, Arthur
Fenner, James
Fish, Carl Russell
Fish, Preserved
Gardiner, Silvester
Gardner, Caleb
Gibbs, George
Gorham, Jabez
Green, Theodore Francis
Greene, Albert Gorton
Greene, Christopher
Greene, Edward Lee
Greene, Francis Vinton
Greene, George Sears
Greene, George Washington
Greene, Nathanael
Greene, William, 1695/96–1758
Greene, William, 1731–1809
Hague, Robert Lincoln
Halsey, Thomas Lloyd
Hamlin, William
Hammond, William Gardiner
Harris, Caleb Fiske
Harris, Daniel Lester
Hatlo, Jimmy
Haworth, Joseph
Hazard, Augustus George
Hazard, Jonathan J.
Hazard, Rowland Gibson
Hazard, Thomas
Hazard, Thomas Robinson
Herreshoff, James Brown
Herreshoff, John Brown
Herreshoff, Nathanael Greene
Himes, Joshua Vaughan
Hood, Raymond Mathewson
Hopkins, Esek
Hopkins, John Burroughs
Hopkins, Stephen
Hoppin, Augustus
Hoppin, James Mason
Hoppin, Joseph Clark
Hoppin, William Warner
Howe, Mark Anthony De Wolfe
Howe, Mark Antony De Wolfe
Howe, Percy Rogers
Hunter, William
Ide, John Jay
James, Charles Tillinghast
Janes, Lewis George
Jenckes, Joseph
Jenckes, Thomas Allen
Jones, William
King, Charles William
King, Clarence
King, Samuel
King, Samuel Ward
Ladd, Joseph Brown

La Farge, Christopher Grant
LaFarge, John
Lajoie, Napoleon ("Larry")
Lippitt, Henry
Little, William Lawson, Jr.
Lomax, Lunsford Lindsay
Luther, Seth
Malbone, Edward Greene
Mauran, John Lawrence
McGrath, James Howard
Melville, David
Mills, Ogden Livingston
Morgan, Morris Hicky
Munro, Dana Carleton
Newel, Stanford
Nicholson, William Thomas
Niles, Nathaniel, 1741–1828
Niles, Samuel
O'Connor, Edwin Greene
Olyphant, David Washington Cincinnatus
Palmer, Ray
Park, Edwards Amasa
Patch, Sam
Peckham, Stephen Farnum
Pendleton, Ellen Fitz
Perry, Christopher Raymond
Perry, Matthew Calbraith
Perry, Oliver Hazard
Perry, Thomas Sergeant
Perry, William Stevens
Pinchot, Cornelia Elizabeth Bryce
Potter, Elisha Reynolds
Reynolds, Samuel Godfrey
Richmond, John Wilkes
Robinson, Christopher
Rockefeller, Abby Greene Aldrich
Rodman, Isaac Peace
Round, William Marshall Fitts
Russell, Jonathan
Scott, Job
Shepard, Charles Upham
Sherman, Thomas West
Slater, John Fox
Slocum, Frances
Slocum, Samuel
Southwick, Solomon
Sprague, William, 1773–1836
Sprague, William, 1830–1915
Stanley, Albert Augustus
Staples, William Read
Stetson, Charles Walter
Stiness, John Henry
Stuart, Gilbert
Sully, Daniel John
Sunderland, La Roy
Taylor, William Rogers
Taylor, William Vigneron
Tenney, William Jewett
Thomas, Frederick William
Thurber, George
Thurston, Robert Henry
Thurston, Robert Lawton
Tourjée, Eben
Truman, Benjamin Cummings
Updike, Daniel
Updike, Daniel Berkeley
Vernon, Samuel
Vernon, William
Vinton, Alexander Hamilton
Vinton, Francis
Wanton, Joseph
Ward, Richard

Ward, Samuel, 1725–1776
Ward, Samuel, 1756–1832
Ward, Samuel, 1786–1839
Warren, Minton
Warren, Russell
Waterhouse, Benjamin
Weaver, Philip
Weeden, William Babcock
Welling, Richard Ward Greene
Weston, Edward Payson
Wheaton, Frank
Wheaton, Henry
Whipple, Abraham
Whitaker, Charles Harris
Whitman, Sarah Helen Power
Wilbur, John
Wilcox, Stephen
Wilkinson, David
Wilkinson, Jemima
Wilkinson, Jeremiah
Williams, Catharine Read Arnold
Williams, Samuel May

SOUTH CAROLINA

Adair, John
Adams, Joseph Quincy
Aiken, David Wyatt
Aiken, William
Allston, Robert Francis Withers
Allston, Washington
Alston, Joseph
Anderson, David Lawrence
Anderson, Richard Heron
Babcock, James Woods
Baldwin, James Mark
Barnwell, Robert Woodward
Baruch, Bernard Mannes
Bee, Barnard Elliott
Bee, Hamilton Prioleau
Bethune, Mary McLeod
Blease, Coleman Livingston
Bounethean, Henry Brintnell
Boyce, James Petigru
Bratton, John
Brawley, William Hiram
Brooks, Preston Smith
Brown, Albert Gallatin
Brown, Charlotte Hawkins
Brown, Joseph Emerson
Brown, Morris
Brumby, Richard Trapier
Bull, William, 1683–1755
Bull, William, 1710–1791
Bulloch, Archibald
Butler, Andrew Pickens
Butler, Matthew Calbraith
Butler, Pierce Mason
Calhoun, John Caldwell
Calhoun, Patrick
Campbell, Josiah A. Patterson
Cannon, Harriet Starr
Capers, Ellison
Capers, William
Cash, Wilbur Joseph
Charlton, Thomas Usher Pulaski
Chestnut, James
Cheves, Langdon
Chisolm, Alexander Robert
Chisolm, John Julian
Clarke, Elijah
Clinton, George Wylie
Cloud, Noah Bartlett

Cogdell, John Stevens
Cohen, Octavus Roy
Coker, David Robert
Coker, James Lide
Conner, James
Corcoran, James Andrew
Crafts, William
Cunningham, Ann Pamela
Davidson, James Wood
Deas, Zachariah Cantey
De Bow, James Dunwoody Brownson
De Leon, Thomas Cooper
De Saussure, Henry William
Dickson, Samuel Henry
Dorr, Julia Caroline Ripley
Drayton, John
Drayton, Percival
Drayton, Thomas Fenwich
Drayton, William
Drayton, William Henry
Du Bose, William Porcher
Elbert, Samuel
Elliott, Benjamin
Elliott, Stephen
Elliott, William
Elmore, Franklin Harper
Evans, Nathan George
Fayssoux, Peter
Ferguson, Thomas Barker
Few, William Preston
Fraser, Charles
Fuller, Richard
Furman, James Clement
Gadsden, Christopher
Gadsden, James
Gaillard, David Du Bose
Gaillard, Edwin Samuel
Gaillard, John
Gambrell, James Bruton
Garden, Alexander
Gary, Martin Witherspoon
Gaston, James McFadden
Gayle, John
Gibbes, Robert Wilson
Gibbes, William Hasell
Gibbons, William
Gildersleeve, Basil Lanneau
Girardeau, John Lafayette
Gist, William Henry
Gonzales, Ambrose Elliott
Gorrie, John
Gossett, Benjamin Brown
Graves, John Temple
Gregg, Maxcy
Grimké, Angelina Emily
Grimké, Archibald Henry
Grimké, John Faucheraud
Grimké, Sara Moore
Grimké, Thomas Smith
Hagood, Johnson
Hall, Dominick Augustin
Hamilton, James
Hamilton, Paul
Hammett, Henry Pinckney
Hammond, James Henry
Hampton, Wade
Harper, William
Hayne, Isaac
Hayne, Paul Hamilton
Hayne, Robert Young
Hemphill, John
Henry, Edward Lamson

Henry, Robert
Herbert, Hilary Abner
Heyward, DuBose
Heyward, Thomas
Hill, Daniel Harvey
Hill, Joshua
Hitchcock, Thomas
Holbrook, John Edwards
Holland, Edwin Clifford
Holmes, Isaac Edward
Holmes, Joseph Austin
Howell, Clark
Huger, Benjamin
Huger, Daniel Elliott
Huger, Francis Kinloch
Huger, Isaac
Huger, John
Hunt, William Henry
Hurlbert, William Henry
Hurlbut, Stephen Augustus
Hutson, Richard
Hyrne, Edmund Massingberd
Ingraham, Duncan Nathaniel
Ioor, William
Irving, John Beaufain
Izard, Ralph
Jackson, Andrew
Jacobs, William Plumer
Jamison, David Flavel
Jenkins, Charles Jones
Jenkins, Micah
Johnson, Joseph
Johnson, William
Johnson, William Bullein
Johnston, Henrietta
Johnston, Olin DeWitt Talmadge
Johnstone, Job
Jones, David Rumph
Jones, John B.
Just, Ernest Everett
Keitt, Lawrence Massillon
Kellogg, Clara Louise
Kennedy, John Doby
Kershaw, Joseph Brevard
Keyes, Edward Lawrence
Kinloch, Cleland
Kirkland, James Hampton
La Borde, Maximilian
Laurens, Henry
Laurens, John
Law, Evander McIvor
Lawton, Alexander Robert
Lee, Stephen Dill
Lee, Thomas
Legaré, Hugh Swinton
Lever, Asbury Francis
Levin, Lewis Charles
Lipscomb, Abner Smith
Logan, Thomas Muldrup, 1808–1876
Logan, Thomas Muldrup, 1840–1914
Longstreet, James
Loughridge, Robert McGill
Lowndes, William
Lowry, Robert
Lubbock, Francis Richard
Lynch, Thomas, 1727–1776
Lynch, Thomas, 1749–1779
McBryde, John McLaren
McCaleb, Theodore Howard
McCall, Edward Rutledge
McCord, David James

McCord, Louisa Susanna Cheves
McCrady, Edward
McDonald, Charles James
McGowan, Samuel
Mackey, Albert Gallatin
McTyeire, Holland Nimmons
Magrath, Andrew Gordon
Manigault, Arthur Middleton
Manigault, Gabriel
Manigault, Peter
Manly, Basil
Manly, Basil Maxwell
Manning, Richard Irvine, 1789–1836
Manning, Richard Irvine, 1859–1931
Marion, Francis
Marks, Elias
Mathews, John
Maybank, Burnet Rhett
Meek, Alexander Beaufort
Michel, William Middleton
Middleton, Arthur, 1681–1737
Middleton, Arthur, 1742–1787
Middleton, Henry
Middleton, John Izard
Middleton, Nathaniel Russell
Mignot, Louis Remy
Miles, William Porcher
Miller, Kelly
Miller, Stephen Decatur
Mills, Robert, 1781–1855
Moffett, William Adger
Moïse, Penina
Montgomery, William Bell
Mood, Francis Asbury
Moore, Samuel Preston
Mordecai, Moses Cohen
Moses, Franklin J.
Moultrie, John
Moultrie, William
Murphy, William Sumter
Murray, James Ormsbee
Myers, Abraham Charles
Newman, Albert Henry
Northrop, Lucius Bellinger
Nott, Henry Junius
Nott, Josiah Clark
O'Neall, John Belton
Orr, Gustavus John
Orr, James Lawrence
Orr, John Amaziah
Palmer, Benjamin Morgan
Payne, Daniel Alexander
Peck, Thomas Ephraim
Perry, Benjamin Franklin
Peterkin, Julia Mood
Petigru, James Louis
Philips, Martin Wilson
Pickens, Francis Wilkinson
Pickens, William
Pinckney, Charles
Pinckney, Charles Cotesworth
Pinckney, Henry Laurens
Pinckney, Thomas
Poinsett, Joel Roberts
Porcher, Francis Peyre
Pratt, John
Pringle, Joel Roberts Poinsett
Pringle, John Julius
Rainey, Joseph Hayne
Ravenel, Edmund
Ravenel, Harriott Horry Rutledge

Ravenel, Henry William
Ravenel, St. Julien
Read, Jacob
Requier, Augustus Julian
Rhett, Robert Barnwell
Rice, John Andrew
Richardson, Anna Euretta
Rivers, William James
Robert, Henry Martyn
Roberts, Oran Milo
Rogers, James Harvey
Roper, Daniel Calhoun
Rusk, Thomas Jefferson
Rutledge, Edward
Rutledge, John
Sanders, Daniel Jackson
Scarbrough, William
Shecut, John Linnaeus Edward Whitridge
Shepherd, William Robert
Shubrick, John Templer
Shubrick, William Branford
Simms, William Gilmore
Simonton, Charles Henry
Simpson, William Dunlap
Sims, James Marion
Smalls, Robert
Smith, Charles Forster
Smith, Ellison DuRant
Smith, Henry Augustus Middleton
Smith, James Perrin
Smith, John Lawrence
Smith, William Loughton
Spreckels, John Diedrich
Stanton, Frank Lebby
Steedman, Charles
Stevens, Thomas Holdup, 1795–1841
Strobel, Edward Henry
Stuart, Francis Lee
Thomas, Theodore Gaillard
Thompson, Hugh Smith
Thompson, Waddy
Thornwell, James Henley
Tiedeman, Christopher Gustavus
Tillman, Benjamin Ryan
Timrod, Henry
Toland, Hugh Huger
Tompkins, Daniel Augustus
Travis, William Barret
Trenholm, George Alfred
Trescot, William Henry
Trott, Nicholas
Tupper, Henry Allen
Turner, Henry McNeal
Waddel, John Newton
Waring, Julius Waties
Watson, John Broadus
Wayne, Arthur Trezevant
Wells, William Charles
White, George
White, John Blake
White, Josh
Wigfall, Louis Trezevant
Wilkinson, Robert Shaw
Williams, David Rogerson
Willingham, Robert Josiah
Wilson, John Leighton
Wilson, William Hasell
Woolsey, John Munro
Wragg, William
Yeadon, Richard
Young, Pierce Manning Butler

Zogbaum, Rufus Fairchild

SOUTH DAKOTA

Flanagan, Hallie
Gall
Graham, Philip Leslie
Grass, John
Lawrence, Ernest Orlando
Lundeen, Ernest
Norbeck, Peter
Sande, Earl
Schmidt, Carl Louis August
Sitting Bull
Thye, Edward John

TENNESSEE

Adams, John
Agee, James Rufus
Allen, William Joshua
Anderson, James Patton
Anderson, Paul Y.
Andrews, Frank Maxwell
Austell, Alfred
Ayres, Brown
Balch, George Beall
Barksdale, William
Barnard, Edward Emerson
Barrow, Washington
Barton, Bruce Fairchild
Barton, David
Bate, William Brimage
Beard, Richard
Bell, John
Benton, Thomas Hart
Berry, George Leonard
Bewley, Anthony
Boyd, Lynn
Bradford, Joseph
Bradford, Roark Whitney Wick-
    liffe
Branner, John Casper
Brantley, Theodore
Bridges, Thomas Jefferson Davis
    ("Tommy")
Brown, John Calvin
Brown, Neill Smith
Brush, George de Forest
Burgess, John William
Burnet, Peter Hardeman
Burnett, Swan Moses
Byrns, Joseph Wellington
Campbell, Francis Joseph
Campbell, William Bowen
Caraway, Hattie Ophelia Wyatt
Carmack, Edward Ward
Carter, Samuel Powhatan
Catchings, Waddill
Cheatham, Benjamin Franklin
Chisum, John Simpson
Clement, Frank Goad
Collier, Barron Gift
Cone, Moses Herman
Conway, Elias Nelson
Conway, James Sevier
Cooper, (Leon) Jere
Crockett, David
Crump, Edward Hull
Davis, Norman Hezekiah
Davis, Reuben
Dibrell, George Gibbs
Dickson, Earle Ensign

Dodd, Monroe Elmon
Dorset, Marion
Dromgoole, William Allen
Edmondson, William
Embree, Elihu
Ensley, Enoch
Fanning, Tolbert
Farragut, David Glasgow
Featherston, Winfield Scott
Fenner, Charles Erasmus
Folk, Joseph Wingate
Forrest, Nathan Bedford
Fuller, Joseph Vincent
Garland, Augustus Hill
Garrett, Finis James
Garvin, Lucius Fayette Clark
Gaut, John McReynolds
Geers, Edward Franklin
Gillem, Alvan Cullem
Gilmer, Elizabeth Meriwether
    ("Dorothy Dix")
Gleaves, Albert
Gordon, George Washington
Green, Alexander Little Page
Gregg, Josiah
Gwin, William McKendree
Hamilton, Walton Hale
Harahan, William Johnson
Harney, William Selby
Harris, Isham Green
Harrison, Henry Sydnor
Hays, Harry Thompson
Hays, John Coffee
Hillman, Thomas Tennessee
Hindman, Thomas Carmichael
Hogg, James Stephen
Houk, Leonidas Campbell
Houston, George Smith
Howze, Robert Lee
Hull, Cordell
Humes, Thomas William
Humphreys, West Hughes
Inman, John Hamilton
Inman, Samuel Martin
Isom, Mary Frances
Jackson, Howell Edmunds
Jackson, William Hicks
Jarrell, Randall
Johnson, Cave
Johnson, David Bancroft
Jones, James Chamberlayne
Jones, Jesse Holman
Kefauver, (Carey) Estes
Kelly, Machine Gun (George Kel-
    ly Barnes, Jr.)
Key, David McKendree
King, Austin Augustus
Krutch, Joseph Wood
Lard, Moses E.
Lea, Luke
Levering, Joseph Mortimer
Lindsey, Benjamin Barr
Littleton, Martin Wiley
Loguen, Jermain Wesley
Lowrey, Mark Perrin
McAnally, David Rice
McCulloch, Ben
McFerrin, John Berry
McGhee, Charles McClung
McGill, Ralph Emerson
McGlothlin, William Joseph
McReynolds, Samuel Davis
Malone, Walter

Maney, George Earl
Markham, Charles Henry
Marling, John Leake
Milton, George Fort
Moore, (Austin) Merrill
Moore, Grace
Morgan, John Tyler
Murfree, Mary Noailles
Murrell, John A.
Nelson, David
Newman, William Truslow
Nicholson, Alfred Osborne Pope
Nielsen, Alice
Oconostota
Oldham, Williamson Simpson
Palmore, William Beverly
Peck, James Hawkins
Perkins, Dwight Heald
Perry, Rufus Lewis
Pillow, Gideon Johnson
Poindexter, Miles
Polk, William Mecklenburg
Porter, James Davis
Pritchard, Jeter Connelly
Proctor, Henry Hugh
Ramsey, James Gettys McGready
Raulston, John Tate
Rayburn, Samuel Taliaferro
    ("Sam")
Read, Opie Pope
Reagan, John Henninger
Reece, Brazilla Carroll
Reed, Richard Clark
Reynolds, Richard Samuel, Sr.
Rice, (Henry) Grantland
Richardson, James Daniel
Richberg, Donald Randall
Ridge, Major
Riis, Mary Phillips
Roane, John Selden
Roberts, Issachar Jacob
Rockwell, Kiffin Yates
Rogers, James Harris
Rose, Edward
Rose, Wickliffe
Ross, John
Sanford, Edward Terry
Scott, William Anderson
Scruggs, William Lindsay
Sequoyah
Sevier, Ambrose Hundley
Sharkey, William Lewis
Shields, John Knight
Shook, Alfred Montgomery
Sloan, George Arthur
Smith, Bessie
Smith, George Henry
Stilwell, Simpson Everett
Stone, John Marshall
Stribling, Thomas Sigismund
Stritch, Samuel Alphonsus
Sumners, Hatton, William
Taylor, Alfred Alexander
Taylor, Robert Love
Temple, Oliver Perry
Terrell, Mary Eliza Church
Thomas, Cyrus
Thomas, John Wilson
Tigert, John James, IV
Tilson, John Quillin
Tipton, John
Turner, Fennell Parrish
Turney, Peter

Vance, Ap Morgan
Walker, William
Ward, Nancy
Warner, James Cartwright
Watterson, Harvey Magee
White, Clarence Cameron
White, Edward Douglass
Whitsitt, William Heth
Williams, James
Williams, John Sharp
Wilson, J(ames) Finley
Witherspoon, John Alexander
Woods, William Allen
Wright, Luke Edward
Wright, Marcus Joseph
Yandell, David Wendell
Yandell, Lunsford Pitts
Yeatman, James Erwin
Yerger, William
Yoakum, Henderson
York, Alvin Cullum
Young, Ewing
Zollicoffer, Felix Kirk

TEXAS

Batts, Robert Lynn
Beaty, Amos Leonidas
Buck, Franklyn Howard
Burleson, Albert Sidney
Camp, John Lafayette
Carter, William Samuel
Chennault, Claire Lee
Connally, Thomas Terry ("Tom")
Cordon, Guy
Cullen, Hugh Roy
Dobie, J(ames) Frank
Dyer, Isadore
Eberle, Edward Walter
Eisenhower, Dwight David
Ferguson, James Edward
Ferguson, Miriam Amanda Wallace
Fly, James Lawrence
Frye, William John ("Jack")
Garner, John Nance
Graves, William Sidney
Hirsch, Maximilian Justice
Hobby, William Pettus
Holly, Charles Hardin ("Buddy")
Hornsby, Rogers
House, Edward Mandell
Johnson, Jack
Jones, Richard Foster
Joplin, Janis Lyn
Kendrick, John Benjamin
Key, Valdimer Orlando, Jr.
Lanham, Frederick Garland ("Fritz")
Lasater, Edward Cunningham
Lovett, Robert Scott
Maverick, (Fontaine) Maury
McMillin Alvin Nugent ("Bo")
Mills, Charles Wright
Minor, Robert
Moser, Christopher Otto
Munger, Robert Sylvester
Murchison, Clinton Williams
Murray, William Henry David
Newton, Joseph Fort
Neyland, Robert Reese, Jr.
Nimitz, Chester William
Norris, John Franklyn

Page, Oran Thaddeus ("Lips")
Parker, Alvin Pierson
Pool, Joe Richard
Post, Wiley
Quanah
Richardson, Sid Williams
Richardson, Wilds Preston
Rister, Carl Coke
Rowe, Lynwood Thomas
Rust, John Daniel
Samaroff, Olga
Scarborough, Dorothy
Scott, Emmett Jay
Shepard, Seth
Sheppard, John Morris
Siringo, Charles A.
Smith, Thomas Vernor
Speaker, Tris E.
Sterling, Ross Shaw
Stevenson, Matilda Coxe Evans
Stillman, James
Tansill, Charles Callan
Teagarden, Weldon Leo ("Jack")
Van Der Stucken, Frank Valentin
Vardaman, James Kimble
Vaughan, Thomas Wayland
Walker, Walton Harris
Webb, Walter Prescott
White, Edward Higgins, II
Yoakum, Benjamin Franklin
Young, Hugh Hampton
Young, Robert Ralph
Zaharias, Mildred ("Babe") Didrikson

UTAH

Adams, Maude
Allen, Florence Ellinwood
Borglum, Solon Hannibal
Borzage, Frank
Browning, John Moses
Cantril, Albert Hadley
Clark, Joshua Reuben, Jr.
Dallin, Cyrus Edwin
DeVoto, Bernard Augustine
Gilbert, John
Haywood, William Dudley
Held, John, Jr.
Hines, Frank Thomas
Kahn, Florence Prag
Knight, Goodwin Jess ("Goodie")
McKay, David Oman
Smith, George Albert
Smoot, Reed Owen
Thomas, Elbert Duncan
Wardman, Ervin
Young, Mahonri Mackintosh

VERMONT

Adams, Alvin
Adams, Charles Kendall
Adams, George Burton
Adams, Herbert Samuel
Aiken, Charles Augustus
Aikens, Andrew Jackson
Ainsworth, Frederick Crayton
Alden, Henry Mills
Allen, Elisha Hunt
Allen, George
Allen, Timothy Field
Alvord, Benjamin

Ames, Joseph Sweetman
Angell, James Rowland
Arthur, Chester Alan
Atkins, Jearum
Austin, Warren Robinson
Babcock, Joseph Weeks
Babcock, Orville E.
Ballou, Hosea
Barber, Amzi Lorenzo
Barrett, John
Barton, James Levi
Bennett, Edmund Hatch
Bentley, Wilson Alwyn
Benton, Josiah Henry
Billings, Charles Ethan
Billings, Frederick
Bingham, Harry
Bingham, Hiram
Blaine, Anita (Eugenie) McCormick
Blanchard, Jonathan
Bliss, Daniel
Bliss, Edwin Elisha
Botta, Anne Charlotte Lynch
Bowen, George
Boynton, Edward Carlisle
Bradley, William Czar
Bradwell, Myra
Brainerd, Ezra
Browne, Francis Fisher
Brownson, Orestes Augustus
Burnham, Sherburne Wesley
Bush, George
Carpenter, Matthew Hale
Chase, Irah
Church, Alonzo
Clark, Charles Edgar
Clark, William Bullock
Closson, William Baxter
Coates, George Henry
Colburn, Zerah
Collins, John Anderson
Colton, Gardner Quincy
Colton, Walter
Colver, Nathaniel
Conant, Alban Jasper
Conant, Thomas Jefferson
Converse, John Heman
Coolidge, Calvin
Dana, Charles Loomis
Dana, John Cotton
Davenport, Herbert Joseph
Davenport, Thomas
Dean, Amos
Deere, John
Delano, Columbus
Dewey, George
Dewey, John
Dillingham, William Paul
Dixon, Luther Swift
Dorsey, Stephen Wallace
Douglas, Stephen Arnold
Douglass, Andrew Ellicott
Eaton, Dorman Bridgman
Eaton, Homer
Edmunds, George Franklin
Emmons, George Foster
Evans, Warren Felt
Evarts, Jeremiah
Fairbanks, Henry
Farnham, Thomas Jefferson
Field, Fred Tarbell
Fisk, James

Fisk, Wilbur
Flagg, Azariah Cutting
Flanders, Ralph Edward
Fletcher, Calvin
Fletcher, Richard
Foot, Solomon
Frost, Edwin Brant
Gale, Elbridge
Garlick, Theodatus
Gates, George Augustus
Gilmore, Joseph Albree
Going, Jonathan
Goodall, Harvey L.
Goodnow, Isaac Tichenor
Granger, Walter
Grant, Lewis Addison
Graves, James Robinson
Graves, Zuinglius Calvin
Gray, Joseph W.
Green, Horace
Greenleaf, Halbert Stevens
Grinnell, Josiah Bushnell
Griswold, Rufus Wilmot
Hale, Philip
Hale, Robert Safford
Hall, Hiland
Hall, Sherman
Hamilton, Frank Hastings
Hammond, Edwin
Harmon, Daniel Williams
Harris, Elisha
Harvey, George Brinton McClellan
Haselton, Seneca
Haskell, Dudley Chase
Hawkins, Rush Christopher
Hayes, Augustus Allen
Hazen, Allen
Hazen, William Babcock
Herring, Silas Clark
Hitchcock, Ethan Allen, 1798–1870
Hoisington, Henry Richard
Holbrook, Stewart Hall
Holmes, Bayard Taylor
Hopkins, James Campbell
Horton, Valentine Baxter
Houghton, Henry Oscar
House, Royal Earl
Hovey, Charles Edward
Hovey, Otis Ellis
Howard, Jacob Merritt
Howard, William Alanson
Hubbard, Gurdon Saltonstall
Hudson, Henry Norman
Hulbert, Archer Butler
Hunt, Richard Morris
Hunt, William Morris
Ide, Henry Clay
Jackson, William Alexander
James, Edwin
Jameson, John Alexander
Jewett, Milo Parker
Johnson, Edwin Ferry
Johnson, Oliver
Jones, George
Kasson, John Adam
Kendrick, Asahel Clark
Kent, Arthur Atwater
Keyes, Elisha Williams
Kimball, Heber Chase
Kingsley, Darwin Pearl
Knowlton, Frank Hall

Ladd, William Sargent
Lampson, Sir Curtis Miranda
Langdon, William Chauncy
Langworthy, James Lyon
Lawrence, Richard Smith
Lull, Edward Phelps
Lyman, Albert Josiah
Marsh, George Perkins
Marsh, James
Mayo, Henry Thomas
Mead, Charles Marsh
Mead, William Rutherford
Merrill, Samuel
Miller, Jonathan Peckham
Miller, Leslie William
Mills, Susan Lincoln Tolman
Morrill, Justin Smith
Morris, George Sylvester
Morse, Anson Daniel
Morse, Harmon Northrop
Morton, Levi Parsons
Mower, Joseph Anthony
Mozier, Joseph
Newcomb, Harvey
Nichols, Clarina Irene Howard
Niles, Nathaniel, 1791–1869
Noyes, John Humphrey
Olin, Stephen
Otis, Elisha Graves
Paine, Charles
Paine, Martyn
Park, Trenor William
Parker, Edwin Wallace
Parker, Joel
Parkhurst, Charles
Parmly, Eleazar
Partridge, Alden
Peabody, Cecil Hobart
Peabody, Selim Hobart
Pearsons, Daniel Kimball
Peirce, Bradford Kinney
Perkins, Samuel Elliott
Perry, Ralph Barton
Pettigrew, Richard Franklin
Phelps, Charles Edward
Phelps, Edward John
Picknell, William Lamb
Pilkington, James
Plumley, Frank
Poland, Luke Potter
Porter, Russell Williams
Porter, William Trotter
Post, Truman Marcellus
Powell, Thomas Reed
Powers, Hiram
Pratt, Francis Ashbury
Pratt, Silas Gamaliel
Pringle, Cyrus Guernsey
Proctor, Redfield
Prouty, Charles Azro
Ransom, Thomas Edward Greenfield
Redfield, Isaac Fletcher
Rice, Edmund
Rice, Henry Mower
Richardson, Israel Bush
Richmond, Dean
Ripley, Edward Hastings
Rix, Julian Walbridge
Roberts, Benjamin Stone
Robinson, Albert Alonzo
Robinson, Charles Seymour
Robinson, Rowland Evans

Robinson, Stillman Williams
Robinson, Theodore
Rowell, George Presbury
Rublee, Horace
Russell, William Hepburn
Safford, Truman Henry
Salm-Salm, Agnes Elisabeth Winona Leclercq Joy, Princess
Sargent, Frank Pierce
Sargent, James
Sargent, Nathan
Sawyer, Philetus
Sawyer, Thomas Jefferson
Saxe, John Godfrey
Schoff, Stephen Alonzo
Scott, Orange
Seymour, Truman
Shaw, Leslie Mortier
Sheldon, Walter Lorenzo
Sheldon, William Evarts
Sherry, Louis
Slade, William
Slafter, Edmund Farwell
Smith, Chauncey
Smith, John Gregory
Smith, Joseph, 1805–1844
Smith, William Farrar
Southard, Lucien H.
Spaulding, Edward Gleason
Spooner, Shearjashub
Sprague, Achsa W.
Spring, Leverett Wilson
Stevens, Benjamin Franklin
Stevens, Henry
Stevens, Hiram Fairchild
Stevens, Thaddeus
Stoddard, Joshua C.
Stone, Warren
Storey, Wilbur Fisk
Stoughton, Edwin Wallace
Strong, Charles Lyman
Strong, James Woodward
Strong, Moses McCure
Strong, William Barstow
Tabor, Horace Austin Warner
Taft, Alphonso
Taylor, Charles Fayette
Temple, William Grenville
Thompson, Zadock
Todd, John
Torrey, Charles Cutler
Tracy, Joseph
Tucker, Luther
Tuttle, Herbert
Tyler, William
Vilas, William Freeman
Wade, Martin Joseph
Wells, Henry
Wheeler, James Rignall
Wheeler, John Martin
Wheeler, Royall Tyler
Wheelock, Lucy
Whitcomb, James
Whiting, Charles Goodrich
Willard, Daniel
Wilson, Halsey William
Winslow, Hubbard
Winslow, John Flack
Winslow, Miron
Wood, Reuben
Woods, Alva
Worthen, Amos Henry
Wright, Robert William

Yale, Caroline Ardelia
Young, Brigham
Young, John

VIRGINIA

Abert, John James
Adams, Daniel Weissiger
Adams, James Hopkins
Ainslie, Peter
Alexander, Archibald
Allen, Henry Watkins
Allen, John James
Allen, Thomas M.
Ambler, James Markham Marshall
Ammen, Daniel
Ammen, Jacob
Anderson, Henry Tompkins
Anderson, Joseph Reid
Anderson, Richard Clough
Anderson, William
Archer, Branch Tanner
Archer, William Segar
Armistead, George
Armstrong, Edward Cooke
Armstrong, Robert
Ashby, Turner
Ashley, William Henry
Atkinson, George Wesley
Atkinson, Thomas
Austin, Stephen Fuller
Bagby, Arthur Pendleton
Bagby, George William
Bailey, (Irene) Temple
Baldwin, John Brown
Baldwin, Joseph Glover
Ballard, Bland Williams
Bangs, Frank C.
Banister, John
Barbour, James
Barbour, John Strode, Jr.
Barbour, Philip Pendleton
Barrett, Kate Waller
Barron, James
Barron, Samuel
Barry, William Taylor
Barton, Robert Thomas
Barton, Seth Maxwell
Bates, Edward
Bates, Frederick
Baylor, George
Bayly, Thomas Henry
Beale, Richard Lee Turberville
Beall, John Yates
Beckwourth, James P.
Bell, Peter Hansborough
Beverley, Robert
Bibb, George Mortimer
Bingham, George Caleb
Binns, John Alexander
Bitter, Karl Theodore Francis
Blackburn, Gideon
Blair, Francis Preston
Blair, John, 1687–1771
Blair, John, 1732–1800
Bland, Richard
Bland, Theodorick
Blow, Henry Taylor
Bocock, Thomas Stanley
Borland, Solon
Botts, Charles Tyler
Botts, John Minor
Boyd, Belle

Boyd, David French
Boyd, Thomas Duckett
Boyle, John
Bradford, John
Brannon, Henry
Braxton, Carter
Breckenridge, James
Breckenridge, John
Bridger, James
Broadhead, Garland Carr
Broadus, John Albert
Brodhead, James Overton
Brooke, Francis Taliaferro
Brown, Aaron Venable
Brown, James
Brown, John, 1757–1837
Brown, Samuel
Brownlow, William Gannaway
Bruce, Blanche K.
Bruce, Philip Alexander
Bruce, William Cabell
Bryan, John Stewart
Bryan, Thomas Barbour
Buchanan, Joseph
Buford, Abraham
Bullitt, Alexander Scott
Burns, Anthony
Burrow, Trigant
Butler, William
Byrd, Richard Evelyn
Byrd, William
Cabell, James Branch
Cabell, James Lawrence
Cabell, Joseph Carrington
Cabell, Nathaniel Francis
Cabell, Samuel Jordan
Cabell, William
Cabell, William H.
Cabell, William Lewis
Cain, Richard Harvey
Caldwell, Henry Clay
Caldwell, James
Call, Richard Keith
Camden, Johnson Newlon
Cameron, William Evelyn
Campbell, Charles
Campbell, John Wilson
Campbell, William
Capps, Washington Lee
Carleton, Henry
Carlile, John Snyder
Carlisle, James Mandeville
Carr, Dabney
Carr, Dabney Smith
Carrington, Paul
Carter, Henry Rose
Carter, John
Carter, Landon
Carter, Robert
Cartwright, Peter
Caruthers, William Alexander
Cary, Archibald
Cary, Lott
Cather, Willa
Chalmers, James Ronald
Chandler, Julian Alvin Carroll
Chapman, John Gadsby
Chapman, Reuben
Christian, Henry Asbury
Christian, William
Claiborne, Nathaniel Herbert
Claiborne, William Charles Coles
Clark, George Rogers

Clark, James
Clark, William
Clay, Clement Comer
Clay, Green
Clay, Henry
Clay, Matthew
Clayton, Augustin Smith
Cleghorn, Sarah Norcliffe
Cleveland, Benjamin
Clopton, John
Clyman, James
Cocke, John Hartwell
Cocke, Philip St. George
Cocke, William
Coke, Richard
Coles, Edward
Collier, Henry Watkins
Colquitt, Walter Terry
Colter, John
Colwell, Stephen
Cone, Etta
Conrad, Charles Magill
Conrad, Holmes
Conway, Moncure Daniel
Cooke, John Esten
Cooke, Philip St. George
Cooper, Mark Anthony
Costigan, Edward Prentiss
Crawford, William
Crawford, William Harris
Creath, Jacob
Creighton, William
Cross, Edward
Crump, William Wood
Cutler, Lizzie Petit
Dabney, Charles William
Dabney, Richard
Dabney, Robert Lewis
Dabney, Thomas Smith Gregory
Dabney, Virginius
Dagg, John Leodley
Dale, Richard
Dale, Samuel
Daniel, John Moncure
Daniel, John Warwick
Daniel, Peter Vivian
Dare, Virginia
Dargan, Edwin Preston
Daveiss, Joseph Hamilton
Davidson, John Wynn
Davis, John Staige
Davis, Varina Anne Jefferson
Dawson, John
Dean, William Henry, Jr.
De Lacy, Walter Washington
Denby, Charles
Denver, James William
Dillard, James Hardy
Dinwiddie, Courtenay
Doak, Samuel
Dod, Daniel
Dodge, William De Leftwich
Dowell, Greensville
Dudley, Benjamin Winslow
Dupuy, Eliza Ann
Duval, William Pope
Dyer, Alexander Brydie
Early, John
Early, Jubal Anderson
Early, Peter
Early, Stephen Tyree
Echols, John
Edwards, John, 1748–1837

Ellis, Powhatan
Emmet, Thomas Addis
Eppes, John Wayles
Evans, Robley Dunglison
Ewell, James
Ewell, Thomas
Ewing, Finis
Ewing, Thomas
Ezekiel, Moses Jacob
Fackler, David Parks
Fairfax, Donald McNeill
Fanning, David
Faulkner, Charles James, 1806–1884
Faulkner, Charles James, 1847–1929
Fels, Joseph
Fifer, Joseph Wilson
Fishback, William Meade
Fitzhugh, George
Fleming, Aretas Brooks
Floyd, John Buchanan
Foote, Henry Stuart
Forsyth, John
Franklin, Jesse
Freeman, Allen Weir
Freeman, Douglas Southall
Freeman, Frederick Kemper
Frémont, Jessie Benton
French, Lucy Virginia Smith
Frost, Wade Hampton
Fry, Birkett Davenport
Gaines, Edmund Pendleton
Gaines, John Pollard
Gamble, Hamilton Rowan
Gardener, Helen Hamilton
Garland, Landon Cabell
Garnett, Alexander Yelverton Peyton
Garnett, James Mercer, 1770–1843
Garnett, James Mercer, 1840–1916
Garnett, Muscoe Russell Hunter
Garnett, Robert Selden
Garrard, James
Garrett, William Robertson
Gholson, Thomas Saunders
Gholson, William Yates
Gibbs, James Ethan Allen
Giles, William Branch
Gilmer, Francis Walker
Gilmer, George Rockingham
Gilmer, Thomas Walker
Gilpin, Charles Sidney
Glasgow, Ellen Anderson Gholson
Glass, Carter
Glenn, Hugh
Glover, Samuel Taylor
Goode, John
Gordon, William Fitzhugh
Goss, James Walker
Graham, James Duncan
Graham, John
Grasty, Charles Henry
Grayson, William
Green, James Stephens
Green, William
Greene, Belle Da Costa
Greenhow, Robert
Greenup, Christopher
Griffin, Cyrus

Griffin, Robert Stanislaus
Grigsby, Hugh Blair
Grundy, Felix
Hall, Willard Preble
Hamilton, James
Hammond, Samuel
Hampton, Wade
Hardin, John
Hardy, Samuel
Harper, Robert Goodloe
Harris, John Woods
Harris, William Alexander
Harrison, Benjamin
Harrison, Constance Cary
Harrison, Gessner
Harrison, William Henry
Harvie, John
Hatcher, Orie Latham
Hatcher, William Eldridge
Hay, George
Heath, James Ewell
Henderson, John Brooks
Henderson, Richard
Hening, William Waller
Henley, Robert
Henry, Patrick
Henry, William Wirt
Herndon, William Lewis
Heth, Henry
Hill, Ambrose Powell
Hine, Charles De Lano
Hoge, Moses
Hoge, Moses Drury
Holcombe, Henry
Holcombe, James Philemon
Holcombe, William Henry
Holt, John
Hope, James Barron
Hopkins, Arthur Francis
Hopkins, Juliet Ann Opie
Hopkins, Samuel, 1753–1819
Horner, William Edmonds
Hough, Theodore
Hough, Warwick
Houston, Edwin James
Houston, Samuel
Howard, Benjamin
Howard, William Travis
Hubbard, David
Hughes, Robert William
Humphreys, Milton Wylie
Hunter, Robert Mercer Taliaferro
Hunton, Eppa
Imboden, John Daniel
Innes, Harry
Innes, James
Jackson, Charles Samuel
Jackson, John George
James, Edwin Leland
Janney, Eli Hamilton
Janney, Samuel McPherson
Jarratt, Devereux
Jarvis, William Chapman
Jefferson, Thomas
Jenkins, Albert Gallatin
Jenkins, Thornton Alexander
Jesse, Richard Henry
Jesup, Thomas Sidney
Jeter, Jeremiah Bell
Johnson, Ames
Johnson, Chapman
Johnson, Charles Spurgeon
Johnson, Edward

Johnson, Louis Arthur
Johnston, George Ben
Johnston, Joseph Eggleston
Johnston, Mary
Johnston, Peter
Johnston, Zachariah
Jones, Catesby ap Roger
Jones, Gabriel
Jones, Hilary Pollard
Jones, John William
Jones, John Winston
Jones, Joseph
Jones, Thomas ap Catesby
Jones, Walter
Jordan, Thomas
Jouett, John
Joynes, Edward Southey
Kalmus, Natalie Mabelle Dunfee
Kean, Jefferson Randolph
Keith, James
Kemper, James Lawson
Kemper, Reuben
Kenna, John Edward
Kenton, Simon
Keyes, Frances Parkinson
Kilgore, Harley Martin
Klipstein, Louis Frederick
Krauth, Charles Porterfield
Lackaye, Wilton
Lacock, Abner
Lacy, Drury
Ladd, Catherine
Lamon, Ward Hill
Lancaster, Henry Carrington
Lane, James Henry
Lane, John
Langston, John Mercer
Lanier, Sidney
Lattimore, William
Laws, Samuel Spahr
Lawson, Thomas
Lay, Henry Champlin
Leathers, Waller Smith
Lee, Arthur
Lee, Charles, 1758–1815
Lee, Fitzhugh
Lee, Francis Lightfoot
Lee, George Washington Custis
Lee, Henry, 1756–1818
Lee, Henry, 1787–1837
Lee, Jesse
Lee, Richard Bland
Lee, Richard Henry
Lee, Robert Edward
Lee, Samuel Phillips
Lee, William
Lee, William Henry Fitzhugh
Leffel, James
Leigh, Benjamin Watkins
Letcher, John
Letcher, Robert Perkins
Lewis, Dixon Hall
Lewis, Fielding
Lewis, James Hamilton
Lewis, John Francis
Lewis, Meriwether
Lewis, William Berkeley
Lewis, William Henry
Ligon, Thomas Watkins
Lindsay, William
Littlepage, Lewis
Logan, Benjamin
Lomax, John Tayloe

Long, Armistead Lindsay
Long, Joseph Ragland
Low, Juliette Gordon
Lukeman, Henry Augustus
Lumpkin, Wilson
Lynch, Charles
Lynch, James Daniel
Lynch, William Francis
McCabe, John Collins
McCabe, William Gordon
McCaw, James Brown
McClurg, James
McCormick, Cyrus Hall
McCormick, Leander James
McCormick, Robert
McCormick, Robert Sanderson
McCormick, Stephen
McDowell, Charles
McDowell, Ephraim
McDowell, James
McDowell, Joseph
McGuire, Hunter Holmes
McIlwaine, Richard
McKee, John
McKinley, John
McKnight, Robert
McNeill, John Hanson
Macrae, John
Madison, James
Magruder, John Bankhead
Magruder, Julia
Mahan, Milo
Mahone, William
Manly, Charles Matthews
Mann, Ambrose Dudley
Manson, Otis Frederick
Marshall, Humphrey
Marshall, James Markham
Marshall, John
Marshall, Louis
Marshall, Thomas
Martin, Thomas Staples
Mason, Claibourne Rice
Mason, George
Mason, John Young
Mason, Lucy Randolph
Mason, Richard Barnes
Mason, Samuel
Mason, Stevens Thomson, 1760–1803
Mason, Stevens Thomson, 1811–1843
Mason, Thomson
Massey, John Edward
Mathews, George
Maury, Dabney Herndon
Maury, Matthew Fontaine
Maxwell, William
Mayo, William Kennon
Meade, Richard Kidder
Meade, William
Meason, Isaac
Meek, Joseph L.
Mercer, Charles Fenton
Mercer, James
Mercer, John Francis
Metcalfe, Samuel Lytler
Metcalfe, Thomas
Mettauer, John Peter
Michaux, Lightfoot Solomon
Mifflin, Warner
Minnigerode, Lucy
Minor, Benjamin Blake

Minor, John Barbee
Minor, Lucian
Minor, Raleigh Colston
Minor, Virginia Louisa
Mitchell, David Dawson
Mitchell, John Kearsley
Moncure, Richard Cassius Lee
Monette, John Wesley
Monroe, James
Montague, Andrew Jackson
Moore, Andrew
Moore, Edwin Ward
Moore, Frederick Randolph
Moore, James, 1764–1814
Moore, Thomas Patrick
Morehead, John Motley
Morgan, William
Morrison, William McCutchan
Morton, Robert Russa
Mosby, John Singleton
Mullan, John
Munford, Robert
Munford, William
Murfee, James Thomas
Murray, Mae
Myers, Jerome
Nash, Abner
Nash, Francis
Neighbors, Robert Simpson
Nelson, Hugh
Nelson, Thomas
Nelson, William, 1711–1772
Neville, John
Neville, Wendell Cushing
Newman, Robert Loftin
Newman, William H.
Newton, John
Newton, Thomas, 1768–1847
Nicholas, George
Nicholas, John
Nicholas, Philip Norborne
Nicholas, Robert Carter
Nicholas, Wilson Cary
Noble, James
O'Donovan, William Rudolf
O'Ferrall, Charles Triplett
Otey, James Hervey
Overton, John
Owen, Robert Latham
Owsley, William
Page, John
Page, Mann
Page, Richard Lucian
Page, Thomas Jefferson
Page, Thomas Nelson
Page, Thomas Walker
Parker, Josiah
Parker, Richard Elliot
Parrish, Celestia Susannah
Patton, John Mercer
Pearce, James Alfred
Peers, Benjamin Orrs
Pelham, Robert A.
Pendleton, Edmund
Pendleton, James Madison
Pendleton, John Strother
Pendleton, William Kimbrough
Pendleton, William Nelson
Penick, Charles Clifton
Penn, John
Penniman, James Hosmer
Pennock, Alexander Mosely
Person, Thomas

Peyton, John Lewis
Pick, Lewis Andrew
Pickett, George Edward
Pickett, James Chamberlayne
Pierpont, Francis Harrison
Pilcher, Joshua
Pleasants, James
Pleasants, John Hampden
Pocahontas
Poindexter, George
Pollard, Edward Alfred
Porter, John Luke
Posey, Thomas
Powell, Adam Clayton, Sr.
Powell, Lucien Whiting
Power, Frederick Dunglison
Prentiss, Benjamin Mayberry
Preston, John Smith
Preston, William Ballard
Price, Joseph
Price, Sterling
Price, Thomas Lawson
Price, Thomas Randolph
Price, William Cecil
Pryor, Nathaniel
Pryor, Roger Atkinson
Puryear, Bennet
Radford, William
Ramsay, George Douglas
Randolph, Alfred Magill
Randolph, Edmund, 1753–1813
Randolph, Edmund, 1819–1861
Randolph, Epes
Randolph, George Wythe
Randolph, Isham
Randolph, Sir John
Randolph, John, 1727 or 1728–1784
Randolph, John, 1773–1833
Randolph, Peyton
Randolph, Sarah Nicholas
Randolph, Thomas Jefferson
Randolph, Thomas Mann
Ravenscroft, John Stark
Reed, Walter
Reid, Ira De Augustine
Reid, Mont Rogers
Renick, Felix
Reynolds, Alexander Welch
Reynolds, William Neal
Rice, David
Rice, John Holt
Richard, James William
Ritchie, Albert Cabell
Ritchie, Thomas
Rives, John Cook
Rives, William Cabell
Roane, Spencer
Roberts, Joseph Jenkins
Robertson, James, 1742–1814
Robertson, John
Robertson, Thomas Bolling
Robertson, William Joseph
Robertson, Wyndham
Robinson, Beverley
Robinson, Bill (Bojangles)
Robinson, Conway
Robinson, John
Robinson, Moncure
Rochester, Nathaniel
Rodes, Robert Emmett
Rorer, David
Ross, Erskine Mayo

Rosser, Thomas Lafayette
Ruffin, Edmund
Ruffin, Thomas
Ruffner, Henry
Ruffner, William Henry
Russell, James Solomon
Ryan, Thomas Fortune
Ryland, Robert
Saunders, Clarence
Scott, Charles
Scott, Dred
Scott, Gustavus
Scott, William
Scott, Winfield
Seaton, William Winston
Seawell, Molly Elliot
Sebastian, Benjamin
Seddon, James Alexander
Seevers, William Henry
Sevier, John
Sherman, Henry Clapp
Shipman, Andrew Jackson
Shipp, Scott
Short, William
Shreve, Thomas Hopkins
Shuck, John Lewis
Silver, Gray
Singleton, James Washington
Slaughter, Philip
Slemp, Campbell Bascom
Smith, Benjamin Mosby
Smith, Daniel
Smith, Francis Henney
Smith, John, 1735–1824
Smith, John Augustine
Smith, Lucy Harth
Smith, Meriwether
Smith, Thomas Adams
Smith, William, 1797–1887
Smith, William Andrew
Smith, William Waugh
Smythe, John Henry
Snead, Thomas Lowndes
Southall, James Cocke
Spencer, Pitman Clemens
Stanard, Mary Mann Page Newton
Stanard, William Glover
Stanton, Frederick Perry
Stanton, Richard Henry
Staples, Waller Redd
Sterrett, John Robert Sitlington
Stevenson, Andrew
Stevenson, Carter Littlepage
Stevenson, John White
Still, Andrew Taylor
Stith, William
Stokes, Montfort
Stone, George Washington
Stone, John Stone
Street, Joseph Montfort
Stringfellow, Franklin
Strong, Richard Pearson
Stuart, Alexander Hugh Holmes
Stuart, Archibald
Stuart, Granville
Stuart, James Ewell Brown
Sullavan, Margaret
Summers, George William
Sumner, Jethro
Sumter, Thomas
Swanson, Claude Augustus
Swayne, Noah Haynes
Tabb, John Banister

Tait, Charles
Taliaferro, Lawrence
Taliaferro, William Booth
Taylor, Creed
Taylor, David Watson
Taylor, Edward Thompson
Taylor, George Boardman
Taylor, John, 1752–1835
Taylor, John, 1753–1824
Taylor, Robert Tunstall
Taylor, William
Taylor, Zachary
Tazewell, Henry
Tazewell, Littleton Waller
Terhune, Mary Virginia Hawes
Thomas, George Henry
Thomas, Jesse Burgess
Thomas, William Isaac
Thompson, John Reuben
Thompson, Richard Wigginton
Thompson, Thomas Larkin
Thompson, Wiley
Thomson, John
Thornton, Jesse Quinn
Thurman, Allen Granberry
Timberlake, Gideon
Timberlake, Henry
Todd, Thomas
Tompkins, Sally Louisa
Toy, Crawford Howell
Trent, William Peterfield
Trimble, Allen
Trimble, Isaac Ridgeway
Trimble, Robert
Trist, Nicholas Philip
Tucker, Henry St. George, 1780–1848
Tucker, Henry St. George, 1853–1932
Tucker, Henry St. George, 1874–1959
Tucker, John Randolph, 1812–1883
Tucker, John Randolph, 1823–1897
Tucker, Nathaniel Beverley, 1784–1851
Tucker, Nathaniel Beverley, 1820–1890
Turner, Edward
Turner, Nat
Tutwiler, Henry
Tyler, John, 1747–1813
Tyler, John, 1790–1862
Tyler, Lyon Gardiner
Tyler, Robert
Underwood, Joseph Rogers
Untermyer, Samuel
Upshur, Abel Parker
Upshur, John Henry
Valentine, Edward Virginius
Venable, Charles Scott
Venable, Francis Preston
Walke, Henry
Walker, Alexander
Walker, Joseph Reddeford
Walker, Reuben Lindsay
Walker, Thomas
Wallace, William Alexander Anderson
Walthall, Edward Cary
Walton, George
Ward, Lydia Arms Avery Cooney

Warrington, Lewis
Washington, Booker Taliaferro
Washington, Bushrod
Washington, George
Washington, John Macrae
Watkins, John Elfreth
Watson, John William Clark
Waugh, Beverly
Weddell, Alexander Wilbourne
Wellons, William Brock
Wells, Robert William
Wertenbaker, Charles Christian
Wertenbaker, Thomas Jefferson
Wharton, William H.
White, Alexander
White, Thomas Willis
Wilkinson, John
Will, Allen Sinclair
Williams, Channing Moore
Williams, John Skelton
Willoughby, Westel Woodbury
Wilmer, Joseph Pére Bell
Wilmer, Richard Hooker
Wilmer, William Holland
Wilson, Edith Bolling
Wilson, James Southall
Wilson, Joshua Lacy
Wilson, William
Wilson, Woodrow
Winn, Richard
Winston, Joseph
Wise, Henry Alexander
Woodford, William
Woodson, Carter Godwin
Wootton, Richens Lacy
Wright, Willard Huntington
Wythe, George
Young, George

WASHINGTON

Bailey, Mildred
Bartlett, Edward Lewis ("Bob")
Blakeslee, Howard Walter
Buchanan, Scott Milross
Carlson, Chester Floyd
Cayton, Horace Roscoe
Chamberlin, Edward Hastings
Dean, Gordon Evans
Dennis, Eugene
Fairchild, Muir Stephen
Faust, Frederick Shiller
Garry, Spokane
Hendrix, Jimi
Knox, Dudley Wright
Lee, Gypsy Rose
Leschi
Llewellyn, Karl Nickerson
McClintic, Guthrie
Pangborn, Clyde Edward
Seattle
Smohalla
Taggard, Genevieve
Wainwright, Jonathan Mayhew

WEST VIRGINIA

Baker, Newton Diehl
Bent, Charles
Bishop, John Peale
Brooke, Charles Frederick Tucker
Brown, Charles Reynolds
Byrd, Harry Flood

Carpenter, Franklin Reuben
Chadwick, French Ensor
Cooke, Philip Pendleton
Davis, John William
Delany, Martin Robinson
Dixon, William
Dolliver, Jonathan Prentiss
Douglas, Henry Kyd
Elkins, William Lukens
Fairfield, Edmund Burke
Fisher, Walter Lowrie
Foster, George Burman
Greer, David Hummell
Gregg, William
Hamilton, John William
Harvey, William Hope
Hines, John Leonard ("Birdie")
Hough, Walter
Hughes, Edwin Holt
Humphreys, Wiliam Jackson
Jackson, Thomas Jonathan
Johnson, Douglas Wilson
Johnston, Frances Benjamin
Lacey, John Fletcher
Lashley, Karl Spencer
Leigh, William Robinson
Lowndes, Lloyd
Lucas, Daniel Bedinger
Lucas, Robert
Miller, John
Morrow, Dwight Whitney
Nadal, Ehrman Syme
Neely, Matthew Mansfield
Owens, Michael Joseph
Patrick, Mason Mathews
Payne, Christopher Harrison
Payne, John Barton
Post, Melville Davisson
Reno, Jesse Lee
Reuther, Walter Philip
Russell, Charles Wells
Sinclair, Harry Ford
Strother, David Hunter
Tidball, John Caldwell
Vawtor, Charles Erastus
Waldo, David
Webster, Harold Tucker
White, Israel Charles
Willey, Wartman Thomas
Wilson, William Lyne
Worthington, Thomas
Yost, Fielding Harris
Zane, Ebenezer

WISCONSIN

Adams, Alva
Ames, Edward Scribner
Andrews, John Bertram
Andrews, Roy Chapman
Ayer, Edward Everett
Baker, Hugh Potter
Bashford, James Whitford
Billings, Frank
Bishop, Seth Scott
Blaine, John James
Bleyer, Willard Grosvenor
Bloodgood, Joseph Colt
Bolton, Herbert Eugene
Bond, Carrie Jacobs
Briggs, Clare A.
Bryant, Joseph Decatur
Burt, Mary Elizabeth

Cannon, Ida Maud
Cannon, Walter Bradford
Catt, Carrie Clinton Lane Chapman
Chafin, Eugene Wilder
Chapelle, Dickey
Coburn, Foster Dwight
Comstock, George Cary
Comstock, John Henry
Curtin, Jeremiah
Curtis, Edward Sheriff
Cushing, William Barker
Davies, Joseph Edward
Dawson, Thomas Cleland
Dennett, Tyler (Wilbur)
Dexter, Wirt
Doheny, Edward Laurence
Eklund, Carl Robert
Elvehjem, Conrad Arnold
Esch, John Jacob
Falk, Otto Herbert
Favill, Henry Baird
Fitzpatrick, Daniel Robert
Ford, Guy Stanton
Gale, Zona
Garland, Hamlin
Gasser, Herbert Spencer
Gesell, Arnold Lucius
Gillette, King Camp
Goetz, George Washington
Grabau, Amadeus William
Haas, Francis Joseph
Hansen, Marcus Lee
Hanson, Ole
Harris, Paul Percy
Haugen, Gilbert Nelson
Hazelton, George Cochrane
Hempl, George
Hine, Lewis Wickes
Hoan, Daniel Webster
Hooton, Earnest Albert
Hopson, Howard Colwell
Houdini, Harry
Hoxie, Vinnie Ream
Huebner, Solomon Stephen
Husting, Paul Oscar
Irving, John Duer
Jones, Lewis Ralph
Kaltenborn, Hans Von
Kelley, Edgar Stillman
King, Franklin Hiram
Kohler, Walter Jodok
Kremers, Edward
Krug, Julius Albert
La Follette, Philip Fox
La Follette, Robert Marion
La Follette, Robert Marion, Jr.
Lambeau, Earl Louis ("Curly")
Legge, Alexander
Lennon, John Brown
Lenroot, Irvine Luther
Lewis, Ed ("Strangler")
Libby, Orin Grant
Lutkin, Peter Christian
McCarthy, Joseph Raymond
McIntyre, James
McNair, Fred Walter
Macune, Charles William
Mahoney, John Friend
Manville, Thomas Franklyn ("Tommy"), Jr.
Martin, Franklin Henry
Mason, Max

Matheson, William John
Mears, Helen Farnsworth
Merrill, William Emery
Meyer, Albert Gregory
Mitscher, Marc Andrew
Moldenke, Richard George Gottlob
Murphy, Frederick E.
Murphy, John Benjamin
Nehrling, Henry
Newell, Edward Theodore
Nieman, Lucius William
Ochsner, Albert John
Older, Fremont
Pammel, Louis Hermann
Perkins, James Breck
Persons, Warren Milton
Pfund, August Herman
Philipp, Emanuel Lorenz
Pond, Frederick Eugene
Preus, Christian Keyser
Purdy, Corydon Tyler
Reid, Helen Miles Rogers
Reinsch, Paul Samuel
Rice, Edwin Wilbur
Richmond, Charles Wallace
Ritter, William Emerson
Robinson, Frederick Byron
Roe, Gilbert Ernstein
Rublee, George
Salisbury, Albert
Salisbury, Rollin D.
Savage, John Lucian ("Jack")
Sawyer, Wilbur Augustus
Schwellenbach, Lewis Baxter
Scidmore, Eliza Ruhamah
Scott, James Wilmot
Sewall, May Eliza Wright
Showerman, Grant
Simmons (Szymanski), Aloysius Harry
Simons, Algie Martin
Slichter, Sumner Huber
Smith, Francis Marion
Starks, Edwin Chapin
Stromme, Peer Olsen
Stub, Hans Gerhard
Tracy, Spencer Bonaventure
Turner, Frederick Jackson
Underwood, Frederick Douglas
U'Ren, William Simon
Vandenberg, Hoyt Sanford
Van Hise, Charles Richard
Veblen, Thorstein Bunde
Walsh, Thomas James
Warner, William
West, Allen Brown
Wheeler, William Morton
Wilcox, Ella Wheeler
Wilder, Laura Ingalls
Wiley, Alexander
Willard, Josiah Flint
Witte, Edwin Emil
Woodbury, Helen Laura Sumner
Wright, Frank Lloyd
Wright, Theodore Lyman

WYOMING

Arnold, Thurman Wesley
Downey, June Etta
Downey, Sheridan
Pollock, (Paul), Jackson

Snyder, Howard McCrum
Spotted Tail

STATE NOT SPECIFIED

Attucks, Crispus
Baynham, William
Glass, Hugh
Grew, Theophilus
Johnson, Robert
Kicking Bird
Plummer, Henry
Pontiac
Powhatan
Squanto
Tammany
Uncas
Vesey, Denmark
Ware, Nathaniel A.

BIRTHPLACES—FOREIGN COUNTRIES

ARGENTINA

Parvin, Theophilus

AUSTRALIA

Booth, Agnes
Errol, Leon
Flynn, Errol Leslie
Grainger, George Percy
Henry, Alice
Jacobs, Joseph, 1854–1916
Mason, Arthur John
Mayo, George Elton
Orry-Kelly
Robson, May
Travis, Walter John

AUSTRIA

(Including Austria–Hungary)

Baraga, Frederic
Baum, Hedwig ("Vicki")
Berger, Victor Louis
Bloomfield, Maurice
Bodanzky, Artur
Brill, Abraham Arden
Carnegie, Hattie
Conried, Heinrich
Deutsch, Gotthard
Drexel, Francis Martin
Fall, Bernard B.
Fenichel, Otto
Frank, Philipp G.
Frankfurter, Felix
Gericke, Wilhelm
Goldberger, Joseph
Grau, Maurice
Grossmann, Louis
Grund, Francis Joseph
Hassaurek, Friedrich
Herbert, Frederick Hugh
Hess, Victor Franz
Katzer, Frederic Xavier
Keppler, Joseph
King, Alexander
Korngold, Erich Wolfgang
Kreisler, Fritz
Landsteiner, Karl
Lowie, Robert Harry
Lucas, Anthony Francis
Malter, Henry
Muni, Paul
Neutra, Richard Joseph
Ortynsky, Stephen Soter
Pierz, Franz
Pilat, Ignaz Anton
Pollak, Gustav
Pupin, Michael Idvorsky
Raffeiner, John Stephen
Reik, Theodor
Rubin, Isidor Clinton
Sachs, Hanns
Sakel, Manfred Joshua
Schildkraut, Joseph
Schindler, Rudolph Michael

Schnabel, Artur
Schoenberg, Arnold
Schuster, Max Lincoln
Stark, Edward Josef
Urban, Joseph
Von Sternberg, Josef
Von Stroheim, Erich
Weisenburg, Theodore Herman
Zeisler, Fannie Bloomfield
Zeisler, Sigmund

BELGIUM

(Including Flanders)

Baekeland, Leo Hendrik
Bouquillon, Thomas Joseph
Brondel, John Baptist
Carondelet, Francisco Luis Hector, Baron de
Coppens, Charles
Croix, Teodoro de
De Smet, Pierre-Jean
Hennepin, Louis
Heurotin, Charles
Heurotin, Fernand
Janssens, Francis
Lefevere, Peter Paul
Maes, Camillus Paul
Meerschaert, Théophile
Musin, Ovide
Nerinckx, Charles
Nieuwland, Julius Arthur
Parmentier, Andrew
Rau, Charles
Sauveur, Albert
Seghers, Charles Jean
Van Depoele, Charles Joseph
Vander Wee, John Baptist
Van de Velde, James Oliver
Van Quickenborne, Charles Felix
Verbrugghen, Henri
Verhaegen, Peter Joseph

BERMUDA

Cooke, John Esten
Cooke, John Rogers
Meigs, Charles Delucena
Patton, Francis Landey
Tucker, George
Tucker, St. George

BOHEMIA

Heinrich, Antony Philip
Heller, Maximilian
Herrman, Augustine
Hessoun, Joseph
Janauschek, Franziska Magdalena Romance
Levy, Louis Edward
Neumann, John Nepomucene
Prokosch, Eduard
Rosewater, Edward
Steinitz, William
Taussig, William

Vopicka, Charles Joseph
Wise, Isaac Mayer

BRAZIL

Carrère, John Merven
Glover, Townend
Wegmann, Edward
Wise, John Sergeant

BRITISH GUIANA

Benjamin, Park
Holmes, George Frederick
Vethake, Henry

BULGARIA

Arlen, Michael

BURMA

Seagrave, Gordon Stifler

CANADA

Anglin, Margaret Mary
Arden, Elizabeth
Avery, Oswald Theodore
Aylwin, John Cushing
Barton, George Aaron
Bassett, James
Beattie, Francis Robert
Becket, Frederick Mark
Belcourt, George Antoine
Benham, Henry Washington
Bensley, Robert Russell
Bingay, Malcolm Wallace
Blake, William Rufus
Blanchet, François Norbert
Bowen, Norman Levi
Bowman, Isaiah
Brent, Charles Henry
Brokenshire, Norman Ernest
Brunton, David William
Burk, Frederic Lister
Burrowes, Edward Thomas
Callaway, Samuel Rodger
Carpenter, George Rice
Carson, Jack
Case, Shirley Jackson
Céloron de Blainville, Pierre Joseph de
Cerré, Jean Gabriel
Chisholm, Hugh Joseph
Clark, Francis Edward
Colpitts, Edwin Henry
Comstock, Henry Tompkins Paige
Copway, George
Costain, Thomas Bertram
Couzens, James
Cox, Palmer
Coxetter, Louis Mitchell
Creath, Jacob
Creelman, James
Creighton, James Edwin
Crouter, Albert Louis Edgerton

403

Crowe, Francis Trenholm
Cullen, Thomas Stephen
Cutter, George Washington
Daly, Reginald Aldworth
Dett, Robert Nathaniel
Doran, George Henry
Douglas, James
Doull, James Angus
Dow, Herbert Henry
Dressler, Marie
Dubuque, Julien
Duffy, Francis Patrick
Duncan, Robert Kennedy
Dymond, John
Eaton, Charles Aubrey
Eaton, Wyatt
Faribault, Jean Baptiste
Farnsworth, John Franklin
Ferguson, Alexander Hugh
Ferguson, John Calvin
Fessenden, Reginald Aubrey
Finn, Henry James William
Fleming, Arthur Henry
Fortescue, Charles LeGeyt
Fowler, Charles Henry
Fox, Margaret
Franchére, Gabriel
Freeman, James Edwards
Frizell, Joseph Palmer
Gallinger, Jacob Harold
Garrison, William Re Tallack
Gibault, Pierre
Goddu, Louis
Gordon, George Byron
Gould, Elgin Ralston Lovell
Grosset, Alexander
Hackett, James Keteltas
Hambidge, Jay
Harrison, Richard Berry
Hill, James Jerome
Hunton, William Lee
Huston, Walter
Iberville, Pierre Le Moyne, Sieur d'
Ironside, Henry Allan
Irwin, May
James, Will Roderick
Jamison, Cecilia Viets Dakin Hamilton
Jeffrey, Edward Charles
Johnson, Edward
Johnston, William Hugh
Johnstone, Edward Ransom
Jolliet, Louis
Juneau, Solomon Laurent
Kelley, Edith Summers
Keys, Clement Melville
Kimball, Dexter Simpson
King, William Benjamin Basil
Kinzie, John
Kirk, John Foster
Kittson, Norman Wolfred
Koyl, Charles Herschel
Kraft, James Lewis
Lane, Franklin Knight
Langford, Samuel
Lanigan, George Thomas
Laramie, Jacques
Larned, Josephus Nelson
La Ronde, Louis Denis, Sieur de
Lear, Ben
Leary, John
Lee, Jason

Léry, Joseph Gaspard Chaussegros de
Lewis, Francis Park
Lillie, Frank Rattray
Livingston, James
Livingstone, William
Lorimier, Pierre Louis
Loucks, Henry Langford
MacArthur, Robert Stuart
McBain, Howard Lee
MacCallum, William George
McCoy, Elijah
McCrae, Thomas
Macdonald, Charles Blair
McKay, Donald
McKenzie, Robert Tait
McLaughlin, James
McLean, Archibald
McLeod, Martin
McLoughlin, John
McMillan, James
McMurrich, James Playfair
McPherson, Aimee Semple
Mahler, Herbert
Marling, Alfred Erskine
Marsh, Charles Wesley
Marsh, William Wallace
Mason, Walt
Mathewson, Edward Payson
Matthew, William Diller
Medill, Joseph
Menard, Michel Branamour
Menard, Pierre
Mitchell, William, 1832–1900
Morgan, John Harcourt Alexander
Morris, Clara
Morrison, Frank
Moxom, Philip Stafford
Munro, George
Munro, William Bennett
Murphy, William Walton
Murray, James Edward
Naismith, James
Nash, John Henry
Nesmith, James Willis
Newcomb, Simon
Nicholson, Samuel Danford
Norwood, Robert Winkworth
Noyan, Pierre-Jacques Payen de
Nutting, Mary Adelaide
Ogden, Peter Skene
O'Higgins, Harvey Jerrold
Osler, William
Palmer, Daniel David
Palmer, Joel
Pearce, Richard Mills
Phelan, David Samuel
Piper, Charles Vancouver
Price, George Edward McCready
Provost, Etienne
Quigley, James Edward
Rand, Benjamin
Rankin, McKee
Raymond, Harry Howard
Riordan, Patrick William
Robinson, Boardman
Rolette, Jean Joseph
Rose, Walter Malins
Ross, James Delmage McKenzie
Rothwell, Richard Pennefather
Ryan, Stephen Vincent
Ryan, Walter D'Arcy

St. Ange De Bellerive, Louis
St. Denis (Denys), Louis Juchereau de
Sandham, Henry
Sauganash
Scherman, Harry
Schofield, William Henry
Schurman, Jacob Gould
Scott, Colin Alexander
Scott, James Brown
Sears, Robert
Sennett, Mack
Shikellamy
Shotwell, James Thomson
Simpson, Albert Benjamin
Simpson, Jerry
Sims, William Sowden
Slocum, Joshua
Squiers, Herbert Goldsmith
Stefansson, Vilhjalmur
Stephenson, Isaac
Stevens, John Harrington
Stewart, George Neil
Storrow, Charles Storer
Sullivan, William Henry
Tanguay, Eva
Thompson, Slason
Thomson, Edward William
Truteau, Jean Baptiste
Upham, Charles Wentworth
Vaudreuil-Cavagnal, Pierre de Rigaud, Marquis de
Vincennes, Jean Baptiste Bissot
Viner, Jacob
Waddell, John Alexander Low
Wanless, William James
Warren, Samuel Prowse
Watson, James Craig
Wesbrook, Frank Fairchild
West, Oswald
Wheelock, Joseph Albert
White, Benjamin Franklin
Williams, Eleazar
Wood, Casey Albert
Wood, William Burke
Woodbridge, Frederick James Eugene

CEYLON

Coomaraswamy, Ananda Kentish
Sanders, Frank Knight

CHILE

De Cuevas, Marquis
Murrieta, Joaquin

CHINA

Coulter, John Merle
Lambuth, Walter Russell
Lowrie, James Walter
Luce, Henry Robinson
Lyon, David Willard
Maclay, Edgar Stanton
Ng Poon Chew
Stuart, John Leighton
Sydenstricker, Edgar
Williams, Frederick Wells
Yung Wing

CUBA

Agramonte Y Simoni, Aristides

CZECHOSLOVAKIA

(See also Bohemia; Moravia; Silesia)

Cermak, Anton Joseph
Cori, Gerty Theresa Radnitz
Gerster, Arpad Geyza Charles
Hertz, John Daniel
Koller, Carl
Ottendorfer, Oswald
Sabath, Adolph J.
Schumann-Heink, Ernestine
Schumpeter, Joseph Alois
Steuer, Max David
Wertheimer, Max

DENMARK

Bjerregaard, Carl Henrik Andreas
Blichfeldt, Hans Frederik
Boyé, Martin Hans
Clausen, Claus Lauritz
Febiger, Christian
Fenger, Christian
Gronlund, Laurence
Hansen, Niels Ebbesen
Hovgaard, William
Isbrandtsen, Hans Jeppesen
Jacobson, John Christian
Jensen, Jens
Jensen, Peter Laurits
Knudsen, William S.
Linde, Christian
Nelson, Julius
Nelson, Nels Christian
Poulson, Niels
Riis, Jacob August
Rybner, Martin Cornelius
Sorensen, Charles
Westergaard, Harald Malcolm

DUTCH GUIANA

Matzeliger, Jan Ernst

EGYPT

Forester, Cecil Scott
Mowbray, Henry Siddons
Watson, Charles Roger

ENGLAND

(Including Channel Islands, Isle of Man, Isle of Wight, Orkney Islands, Scilly Isles)

Abel-Henderson, Annie Heloise
Alden, John
Allen, John F.
Allerton, Isaac
Alsop, George
Altham, John
Amadas, Philip
Amherst, Jeffery
Andros, Sir Edmund
Archdale, John
Archer, Frederic
Argall, Sir Samuel

Arliss, George
Asbury, Francis
Asher, Joseph Mayor
Ayer, Francis Wayland
Ayres, Anne
Bache, Richard
Bache, Theophylact
Bacon, Nathaniel
Bacon, Thomas
Bailey, Ann
Baker, Edward Dickinson
Banister, John
Banner, Peter
Barr, Amelia Edith Huddleston
Barradall, Edward
Barrett, George Horton
Bartlett, John Sherren
Bateman, Harry
Bates, Barnabas
Bauer, Harold Victor
Baxter, William
Bazett, Henry Cuthbert
Beer, William
Bellingham, Richard
Berkeley, John
Berkeley, Sir William
Bernard, John
Bernard, Sir Francis
Bertram, John
Birch, Reginald Bathurst
Birch, Thomas
Birch, William Russell
Birchall, Frederick Thomas
Birkbeck, Morris
Blackstone, William
Blackton, James Stuart
Blackwell, Elizabeth
Blackwell, Henry Brown
Bladen, William
Bland, Thomas
Blennerhassett, Harman
Blitz, Antonio
Bollan, William
Boorman, James
Booth, Ballington
Booth, Evangeline Cory
Booth, Junius Brutus
Booth-Tucker, Emma Moss
Boucher, Jonathan
Bourne, George
Bourne, Nehemiah
Bowler, Metcalf
Bowne, John
Bradford, William, 1589/90–1657
Bradford, William, 1663–1752
Bradstreet, Anne
Bradstreet, Simon
Bradwell, James Bolesworth
Bray, Thomas
Brent, Margaret
Brett, George Platt
Brewster, William
Brierton, John
Bright, Edward
Brightly, Frederick Charles
Bristed, John
Brooks, William Robert
Brophy, John
Brown, Ernest William
Brown, John George
Browne, John
Bulkeley, Peter
Burgis, William

Burnett, Frances Eliza Hodgson
Burrington, George
Burton, William Evans
Byrd, William
Cadman, Samuel Parkes
Caffin, Charles Henry
Calef, Robert
Calvert, Charles
Calvert, George
Calvert, Leonard
Cameron, Andrew Carr
Camm, John
Campbell, Lord William
Campbell, William
Cannon, George Quayle
Carbutt, John
Carr, Benjamin
Carroll, James
Carteret, Philip
Castle, Vernon Blythe
Catesby, Mark
Chadwick, Henry
Chalkley, Thomas
Chamberlain, Alexander Francis
Chauncy, Charles, 1592–1671/72
Cheetham, James
Cheever, Ezekiel
Child, Robert
Chovet, Abraham
Clagett, Wyseman
Claiborne, William
Clarke, George
Clarke, John
Clay, Joseph
Claypole, Edward Waller
Clayton, John
Clews, Henry
Clinton, George
Cobbett, William
Cockerell, Theodore Dru Alison
Coddington, William
Coghlan, Rose
Cole, Thomas
Cole, Timothy
Colgate, William
Collier, Constance
Collyer, Robert
Colman, Ronald Charles
Comstock, Elizabeth L.
Conant, Roger
Connolly, Thomas H.
Conway, Frederick Bartlett
Cooper, Myles
Cooper, Thomas
Cooper, Thomas Abthorpe
Copley, Lionel
Coram, Thomas
Cornbury, Edward Hyde, Viscount
Cornwallis, Kinahan
Cotton, John
Couldock, Charles Walter
Cowley, Charles
Coxe, Daniel
Cranston, John
Cresop, Thomas
Crisp, Charles Frederick
Croly, Jane Cunningham
Crompton, George
Crompton, William
Crowne, John
Crowne, William
Crunden, Frederick Morgan

Culpeper, Thomas, Lord
Cuming, Sir Alexander
Cummings, Thomas Seirs
Cunliffe-Owen, Philip Frederick
Cushman, Robert
Daft, Leo
Dakin, Henry Drysdale
Dalcho, Frederick
Danforth, Thomas
Davenport, Fanny Lily Gypsy
Davenport, George
Davenport, John
Davey, John
Davidge, William Pleater
Davidson, George
Davie, William Richardson
Dawkins, Henry
Dawson, Francis Warrington
Dawson, Henry Barton
Day, Stephen
Dealey, George Bannerman
De Berdt, Dennys
Delafield, John
De La Warr, Thomas West, Baron
Dennis, Graham Barclay
Dickins, John
Dickson, Thomas
Disston, Henry
Dixwell, John
Dorrell, William
Dove, David James
Dow, Henry
Downing, George
Drake, Samuel
Draper, John William
Dudley, Charles Edward
Dudley, Thomas
Duer, William
Duff, Mary Ann Dyke
Dunglison, Robley
Dunster, Henry
Duranty, Walter
Dyer, Mary
Dyott, Thomas W.
Eaton, Nathaniel
Eaton, Samuel
Eaton, Theophilus
Eddis, William
Eden, Charles
Eden, Robert
Edmunds, Charles Wallis
Edwards, Charles
Edwards, John, 1671–1746
Edwards, Julian
Edwards, Morgan
Edwards, Talmadge
Edwin, David
Eliot, John
Elliot, Jonathan
Elliott, John
Ellis, Henry
Endecott, John
Estaugh, Elizabeth Haddon
Esterbrook, Richard
Evans, Frederick William
Evans, George Henry
Everendon, Walter
Ewbank, Thomas
Fairburn, William Armstrong
Fairfax, Thomas
Fallows, Samuel
Farrer, Henry

Fauquier, Francis
Faversham, William Alfred
Fechter, Charles Albert
Fendall, Josias
Fennell, James
Fenwick, George
Fenwick, John
Field, Robert
Fisher, Clara
Fitzhugh, William
Fitzsimmons, Robert Prometheus
Fleet, Thomas
Fletcher, Benjamin
Fletcher, Robert
Flower, George
Flower, Richard
Folger, Peter
Foster, Charles James
Fox, Gilbert
Foxall, Henry
Francis, James Bicheno
Fry, Joshua
Fry, Richard
Fuller, John Wallace
Gage, Thomas
Gales, Joseph, 1761–1841
Gales, Joseph, 1786–1860
Gardiner, Sir Christopher
Gardiner, Harry Norman
Gardiner, Lion
Gardiner, Robert Hallowell
Gasson, Thomas Ignatius
Gates, Horatio
Gates, Sir Thomas
Gibbs, Arthur Hamilton
Gilbert, Anne Hartley
Gillam, Bernhard
Gilpin, Henry Dilworth
Gladwin, Henry
Glass, Montague Marsden
Godbe, William Samuel
Goffe, William
Gompers, Samuel
Gooch, Sir William
Goodall, Thomas
Gookin, Daniel
Gordon, William
Gorton, Samuel
Gosnold, Bartholomew
Gottheil, Richard James Horatio
Gough, John Bartholomew
Graham, David
Greaton, Joseph
Green, Samuel
Greenhalge, Frederic Thomas
Greenstreet, Sydney Hughes
Grierson, Francis
Grote, Augustus Radcliffe
Guest, Edgar Albert
Gunn, Selskar Michael
Gunter, Archibald Clavering
Gunton, George
Guy, Seymour Joseph
Gwinnett, Button
Haas, Jacob Judah Aaron de
Habersham, James
Hall, Arthur Crawshay Alliston
Hall, Henry Bryan
Hallam, Lewis
Hallidie, Andrew Smith
Hamblin, Thomas Sowerby
Hamilton, Andrew
Hamilton, William Thomas

Harding, Robert
Hardwicke, Cedric Webster
Hare, James H.
Harland, Thomas
Harris, Benjamin
Harris, Joseph
Harris, Maurice Henry
Harris, Thomas Lake
Harrison, Peter
Harvard, John
Harvey, Sir John
Haswell, Anthony
Hathorne, William
Havell, Robert
Haviland, John
Hawks, John
Haynes, John
Haywood, Allan Shaw
Hazelwood, John
Heathcote, Caleb
Heckewelder, John Gottlieb Ernestus
Henningsen, Charles Frederick
Henry, Morris Henry
Herbert, Henry William
Herford, Oliver Brooke
Herring, James
Hewitt, James
Hibbins, Ann
Higginson, Francis
Higginson, John
Hill, John
Hill, Thomas, 1829–1908
Hoar, Leonard
Hodgkinson, Francis
Hodgkinson, John
Hoe, Robert, 1784–1833
Hoffman, Richard
Hogg, George
Holland, George
Holloway, John
Hollyer, Samuel
Holme, Thomas
Hooker, Samuel Cox
Hooker, Thomas
Hooker, William
Hoover, Herbert Clark, Jr.
Hopkins, Edward
Horlick, William
Hornblower, Josiah
Horrocks, James
Horsmanden, Daniel
Howard, Leslie
Howe, George Augustus, Viscount
Hubbard, William
Hudson, Henry
Hudson, William Smith
Hughes, David Edward
Hughes, Robert Ball
Hull, John
Hunt, Robert
Hutchinson, Anne
Hutchinson, Woods
Huxley, Aldous Leonard
Hyde, Edward
Ingle, Richard
Inskip, John Swanel
Insull, Samuel
Iredell, James
Irene, Sister
Izard, George
Jackson, George K.

Jackson, James, 1757–1806
Jackson, William
Jacobi, Mary Corinna Putnam
James, Charles
James, Daniel Willis
James, George Wharton
Jarvis, John Wesley
Jefferson, Joseph
Jeffery, Edward Turner
Jenckes, Joseph
Jenks, George Charles
Jenks, Joseph
Johnson, Alexander
Johnson, Alexander Bryan
Johnson, Edward
Johnson, Marmaduke
Johnson, Sir Nathaniel
Jones, Alfred
Jones, Hugh
Jones, John Percival
Jones, Noble Wymberley
Jones, Thomas P.
Josselyn, Hugh
Joy, Thomas
Karloff, Boris
Katte, Walter
Kearsley, John
Keene, James Robert
Keene, Laura
Keimer, Samuel
Kemble, Frances Anne
Kempster, Walter
Kilty, William
King, Albert Freeman Africanus
Kingsford, Thomas
Kinnersley, Ebenezer
Klein, Charles
Knight, Edward Henry
Lake, Kirsopp
Lander, Jean Margaret Davenport
Landreth, David
Lane, Sir Ralph
Larkin, John
Latimer, Mary Elizabeth Wormeley
Latrobe, Benjamin Henry, 1764–1820
Laughton, Charles
Laurance, John
Laurel, Stan
Lawley, George Frederick
Lawrence, Gertrude
Lawson, John
Lay, Benjamin
Lechford, Thomas
Lee, Ann
Lee, Charles, 1731–1782
Lee, Richard
Leeds, Daniel
Leete, William
Leipziger, Henry Marcus
Leney, William Satchwell
Leslie, Charles Robert
Leslie, Frank
Leverett, John, 1616–1679
Levy, Joseph Leonard
Lewis, Arthur
Linton, William James
Locke, Richard Adams
Lorimer, William
Lothropp, John
Lovelace, Francis
Lovell, John Epy

Lucas, Jonathan, 1754–1821
Lucas, Jonathan, 1775–1832
Ludlow, Roger
Ludwell, Philip
Lyttelton, William Henry
McCormick, Anne Elizabeth O'Hare
McDougall, William
McLaglen, Victor
Madden, Martin Barnaby
Madden, Owen Victor ("Owney")
Manners, John Hartley
Manning, William Thomas
Markham, William
Marlowe, Julia
Marshall, Benjamin
Martin, Henry Austin
Martin, Thomas Commerford
Mason, Francis
Mason, George
Mason, John
Mather, Richard
Mathews, Samuel
Matthews, John
Maverick, Samuel
May, Edward Harrison
Mayhew, Thomas, 1593–1682
Mayhew, Thomas, 1621–1657
Mayo, William
Mayo, William Worrell
Meehan, Thomas
Mees, Charles Edward Kenneth
Meiklejohn, Alexander
Mendes, Henry Pereira
Merry, Ann Brunton
Middleton, Henry
Middleton, Peter
Miles, Edward
Miller, Henry
Millington, John
Mitchell, John, d. 1768
Mitchell, Jonathan
Mitchell, William, 1798–1856
Mitten, Thomas Eugene
Molyneux, Robert
Monckton, Robert
Montague, Henry James
Montefiore, Joshua
Moore, John, c. 1569–1732
Moran, Edward
Moran, Peter
Moran, Thomas
More, Nicholas
Morgan, Matthew Somerville
Morley, Frank
Morris, Anthony, 1654–1721
Morris, Elizabeth
Morris, Robert, 1734–1806
Morris, Roger
Mortimer, Mary
Morton, Charles
Morton, George
Morton, Thomas
Moulton, Richard Green
Mowbray, George Mordey
Murray, John, 1741–1815
Muybridge, Eadweard
Myles, John
Needham, James
Nelson, John
Newport, Christopher
Newton, Richard
Newton, Thomas, 1660–1721

Nicholls, Rhoda Holmes
Nichols, Edward Leamington
Nicholson, Francis
Nicolls, Matthias
Nicolls, Richard
Nicolls, William
Noble, Samuel
Nordhoff, Charles Bernard
Norman, John
Norris, Edward
Norris, Isaac, 1671–1735
Norton, John
Nurse, Rebecca
Nuthead, William
Nuttall, Thomas
Oakes, Urian
Ogle, Samuel
Oglethorpe, James Edward
Oldham, John
Owens, John Edmond
Paine, Thomas
Palmer, Joseph
Palmer, William Henry
Paris, Walter
Parks, William
Parris, Samuel
Parry, Charles Christopher
Parton, James
Pasco, Samuel
Pearce, Richard
Pearce, Stephen Austen
Pedder, James
Peirce, William
Pelham, Peter
Pellew, Henry Edward
Penhallow, Samuel
Penington, Edward
Penn, Thomas
Penn, William
Peter, Hugh
Peter, Robert
Peters, Richard
Peters, William Cumming
Phillips, George
Pierson, Abraham
Pike, Robert
Pilmore, Joseph
Pine, Robert Edge
Pinkney, Edward Coote
Pitkin, William, 1635–1694
Pitman, Benn
Pittock, Henry Lewis
Popham, George
Pormort, Philemon
Porter, Robert Percival
Pory, James
Pott, John
Potter, Paul Meredith
Pound, Thomas
Powell, Thomas
Power, Frederick Tyrone
Pownall, Thomas
Priestley, James
Priestley, Joseph
Pring, Martin
Proud, Robert
Pusey, Caleb
Putnam, George Haven
Pynchon, John
Pynchon, William
Quelch, John
Quine, William Edward
Rains, Claude

Randolph, Edward
Randolph, William
Ransome, Frederick Leslie
Rawle, Francis, 1662–1726/27
Rawlinson, Frank Joseph
Reach, Alfred James
Realf, Richard
Reinagle, Alexander
Renwick, James, 1792–1863
Restarick, Henry Bond
Reynolds, John
Richards, Joseph William
Richards, Thomas Addison
Richings, Peter
Rideing, William Henry
Riley, Charles Valentine
Rimmer, William
Rivington, James
Roberts, Brigham Henry
Rogers, Clara Kathleen Barnett
Rolfe, John
Rollinson, William
Rose, Aquila
Rowlands, William
Rowlandson, Mary White
Rowson, Susanna Haswell
Ruditsky, Barney
Russell, Annie
Sabin, Joseph
Saltonstall, Richard
Sanderson, Robert
Sandys, George
Sargent, Frederick
Sartain, John
Saunders, Frederick
Savery, William, 1721–1787
Scott, John
Scripps, Ellen Browning
Scripps, James Edmund
Searle, Arthur
Sedgwick, Robert
Seed, Miles Ainscough
Selby, William
Serrell, Edward Wellman
Service, Robert William
Seton, Ernest Thompson
Sewall, Samuel
Sharp, Daniel
Sharpe, Horatio
Sharples, James
Shaw, Anna Howard
Shaw, Henry
Shearman, Thomas Gaskell
Shelton, Edward Mason
Shepard, Thomas
Sheppard, Samuel Edward
Sherman, John, 1613–1685
Shippen, Edward, 1639–1712
Shirley, William
Shute, Samuel
Simmons, George Henry
Simpson, Edmund Shaw
Skinner, William
Slater, Samuel
Smith, John, 1579–1631
Smith, John Merlin Powis
Smith, John Rubens
Smith, Robert, 1732–1801
Smith, Robert Alexander
Smith, William, 1697–1769
Sothern, Edward Askew
Southack, Cyprian
Spargo, John

Spilsbury, Edmund Gybbon
Standish, Myles
Stanford, John
Stansbury, Joseph
Staughton, William
Stevens, Frank Mozley
Stevens, Harry Mozley
Stewart, Humphrey John
Stoddart, James Henry
Stone, Samuel
Stone, William
Story, Julian Russell
Stott, Henry Gordon
Stoughton, William
Strachey, William
Stuck, Hudson
Sully, Thomas
Summers, Thomas Osmond
Sutherland, George
Sylvester, James Joseph
Syms, Benjamin
Tait, Arthur Fitzwilliam
Talbot, John
Talmage, James Edward
Tate, George Henry Hamilton
Tatham, William
Taylor, Edward
Taylor, James Barnett
Taylor, John
Taylor, John Louis
Taylor, Raynor
Taylor, Richard Cowling
Tennent, John
Thompson, David
Thompson, Jeremiah
Thomson, Elihu
Tiffin, Edward
Tingey, Thomas
Titchener, Edward Bradford
Todd, Thomas Wingate
Tomlins, William Lawrence
Toulmin, Harry
Towler, John
Towne, Benjamin
Treat, Robert
Trevellick, Richard F.
Troup, Robert
Tryon, William
Tuckey, William
Turner, Walter Victor
Underhill, John
Underwood, Horace Grant
Underwood, John Thomas
Upjohn, Richard
Upjohn, Richard Michell
Vallentine, Benjamin Bennaton
Vandenhoff, George
Van Druten, John William
Vane, Sir Henry
Vasey, George
Vassall, John
Vassar, Matthew
Vaughan, Charles
Vaux, Calvert
Vick, James
Vincent, Mary Ann
Vizetelly, Frank Horace
Wainwright, Jonathan Mayhew, 1792–1854
Walcot, Charles Melton, 1816–1868
Walderne, Richard
Wallace, William

Wallack, Henry John
Wallack, James William, 1795–1864
Wallack, James William, 1818–1873
Waller, Emma
Walsh, Benjamin Dann
Walter, Thomas, c. 1740–1789
Ward, George Gray
Ward, Harry Frederick
Ward, Nathaniel
Warde, Frederick Barkham
Warner, Fred Maltby
Warren, Herbert Langford
Warren, William, 1767–1832
Waterhouse, Frank
Watson, Henry Cood
Waymouth, George
Webb, Daniel
Webb, George James
Webb, Thomas
Weightman, William
Weld, Thomas
Wemyss, Francis Courtney
West, Francis
West, George
West, Joseph
Weston, Edward
Weston, Thomas
Weston, William
Whalley, Edward
Wharton, Richard
Whatcoat, Richard
Wheelwright, John
Whitaker, Alexander
White, Andrew
White, John
Whitefield, George
Whitehead, Alfred North
Whitfield, Henry
Whitworth, George Frederic
Wigglesworth, Michael
Wignell, Thomas
Wilbur, Samuel
Willard, Simon
Williams, John
Williams, Robert
Williams, Roger
Wilson, Ernest Henry
Wilson, John
Wilson, Samuel Thomas
Wingfield, Edward Maria
Winslow, Edward
Winthrop, John, 1587/88–1649
Winthrop, John, 1605/06 o.s.–1676
Wise, Daniel
Wise, Thomas Alfred
Withers, Frederick Clarke
Wood, Abraham
Wood, William
Woodbridge, John
Woodrow, James
Woolf, Benjamin Edward
Wormeley, Katharine Prescott
Wraxall, Peter
Wright, Henry
Wyatt, Sir Francis
Wylie, Robert
Yeamans, Sir John
Yeardley, Sir George
Young, Alfred
Youngs, John

ESTONIA

Holst, Hermann Eduard von, 1841–1904
Leiserson, William Morris

FINLAND

Nordberg, Bruno Victor
Saarinen, Eero
Saarinen, Gottlieb Eliel

FRANCE

Aca, Michel
Agnus, Felix
Allefonsce, John
Allouez, Claude Jean
André, Louis
Badin, Stephen Theodore
Bailly, Joseph Alexis
Bedaux, Charles Eugene
Benezet, Anthony
Bernard, Simon
Biard, Pierre
Biddle, Francis Beverley
Bienville, Jean Baptiste le Moyne, Sieur de
Blanc, Antoine
Bonard, Louis
Bonneville, Benjamin Louis Eulalie de
Bouvier, John
Brady, Anthony Nicholas
Brulé, Étienne
Bruté de Rémur, Simon William Gabriel
Bryant, Louise Frances Stevens
Cabet, Étienne
Cadillac, Antoine de la Mothe
Carrel, Alexis
Champlain, Samuel de
Chanute, Octave
Chapelle, Placide Louis
Charlevoix, Pierre François Xavier de
Chaumonot, Pierre Joseph Marie
Cheverus, John Louis Ann Magdalen Lefebre de
Clerc, Laurent
Colston, Raleigh Edward
Considérant, Victor Prosper
Cortambert, Louis Richard
Coutard, Henri
Cret, Paul Philippe
Crétin, Joseph
Crèvecoeur, Michel-Guillaume Jean de
Crowninshield, Francis Welch
Crozet, Claude
Dablon, Claude
Dannreuther, Gustav
David, John Baptist Mary
Delmas, Delphin Michael
De Mézières Y Clugny, Athanase
Derbigny, Pierre Auguste Charles Bourguignon
De Trobriand, Régis Denis De Keredern
De Vries, David Pietersen
Diat, Louis Felix
Du Bois, John
Duchesne, Rose Philippine

Dugdale, Richard Louis
Duluth, Daniel Greysolon, Sieur
Du Ponceau, Pierre Etienne
Du Pont, Eleuthère Irénée
Du Pont, Victor Marie
Durand, Élie Magloire
Engel, Carl
Esher, John Jacob
Flaget, Benedict Joseph
Forbes, John Murray
Gaillardet, Théodore Frédéric
Garreau, Armand
Genet, Edmond Charles
Girard, Stephen
Gravier, Jacques
Grellet, Stephen
Groseilliers, Médart Chouart, Sieur de
Guérin, Anne-Thérèse
Guignas, Michel
Hallet, Étienne Sulpice
Harrisse, Henry
Herrmann, Alexander
Herter, Christian Archibald
Hite, Jost
Houdry, Eugene Jules
Humbert, Jean Joseph Amable
Hyvernat, Henri
Imbert, Antoine
Jogues, Isaac
Johnston, Robert Matteson
Joubert de la Maraille, James Hector Marie Nicholas
Joutel, Henri
Jumel, Stephen
Kelly, Edmond
Klein, Joseph Frederic
Kohlmann, Anthony
Lachaise, Gaston
Laclede, Pierre
Lafayette, Marie Joseph Paul Yves Roch Gilbert du Motier, Marquis de
Laffite, Jean
Lahontan, Louis-Armand de Lom D'Arce, Baron de
Lamy, John Baptist
Landais, Pierre
Larpenteur, Charles
La Salle, Robert Cavelier, Sieur de
La Tour, Le Blond de
Laudonnière, René Goulaine de
Le Gendre, Charles William
Le Jau, Francis
L'Enfant, Pierre Charles
Lesueur, Charles Alexandre
Le Sueur, Pierre
L'Halle, Constantin de
Loeffler, Charles Martin
Loos, Charles Louis
Loras, Jean Mathias Pierre
Lucas, John Baptiste Charles
Lufbery, Raoul Gervais Victor
Machebeuf, Joseph Projectus
Mangin, Joseph François
Manigault, Pierre
Marcow, Jules
Maréchal, Ambrose
Marest, Pierre Gabriel
Marquette, Jacques
Marsh, Reginald
Martin, François-Xavier

Martiny, Philip
Matignon, Francis Anthony
Maurin, Peter Aristide
Mayer, Constant
Mazureau, Étienne
Membré, Zenobius
Ménard, René
Merton, Thomas
Michaux, André
Michaux, François André
Mitchell, William
Monteux, Pierre Benjamin
Mowatt, Anna Cora Ogden
Murat, Achille
Nancrède, Paul Joseph Guérard de
Neef, Francis Joseph Nicholas
Nicola, Lewis
Nicolet, Jean
Nicollet, Joseph Nicolas
Niza, Marcos de
Noailles, Louis Marie, Vicomte de
Noyan, Gilles-Augustin Payen de
Odin, John Mary
Partridge, William Ordway
Pascalis-Ouvrière, Felix
Pauger, Adrien de
Perché, Napoleon Joseph
Perrot, Nicolas
Petri, Angelo
Pinchot, Amos Richards Eno
Portier, Michael
Poydras, Julien De Lelande
Prevost, François Marie
Quartley, Arthur
Quesnay, Alexandre-Marie
Radisson, Pierre Esprit
Râle, Sébastien
Ramée, Joseph Jacques
Ravoux, Augustin
Rémy, Henri
Ribaut, Jean
Richard, Gabriel
Ritter, Frédéric Louis
Robot, Isidore
Rochambeau, Jean Baptiste Donatien De Vimeur, Comte de
Rosenberg, Paul
Ruckstull, Frederick Wellington
St. Lusson, Simon François Daumont, Sieur de
Saint-Mémin, Charles Balthazar Julien Fevret de
Saugrain De Vigni, Antoine François
Schussele, Christian
Seguin, Edouard
Seguin, Edward Constant
Sigerist, Henry Ernest
Sorin, Edward Frederick
Soulé, Pierre
Stevenson, Sara Yorke
Testut, Charles
Thébaud, Augustus J.
Timothy, Lewis
Tonty, Henry de
Tousard, Anne Louis de
Tulane, Paul
Urso, Camilla
Vail, Aaron
Vattemare, Nicolas Marie Alexandre
Verot, Jean Marcel Pierre Auguste

Wolf, Henry
You, Dominique

GALICIA

Imber, Naphtali Herz
Neumark, David
Sembrich, Marcella
Speiser, Ephraim Avigdor
Zach, Max Wilhelm

GERMANY

(Including Bavaria and Prussia)

Adams, Charles
Adler, Felix
Adler, George J.
Adler, Samuel
Ameringer, Oscar
Antes, Henry
Arents, Albert
Astor, John Jacob
Baade, Wilhelm Heinrich Walter
Baermann, Carl
Balbach, Edward
Balch, Thomas Willing
Bartholdt, Richard
Beck, Carl
Beck, Charles
Behrendt, Walter Curt
Behrens, Henry
Beissel, Johann Conrad
Belmont, August
Bergmann, Max
Berkenmeyer, Wilhelm Christoph
Berliner, Emile
Bien, Julius
Bierstadt, Albert
Bimeler, Joseph Michael
Blankenburg, Rudolph
Blenk, James Hubert
Bloede, Gertrude
Bluemner, Oscar Florians
Boas, Emil Leopold
Boas, Franz
Boehler, Peter
Boehm, John Philip
Boldt, George C.
Bollman, Justus Erich
Bolza, Oskar
Bonzano, Adolphus
Brachvogel, Udo
Brentano, Lorenz
Brokmeyer, Henry C.
Brühl, Gustav
Busch, Adolphus
Cammerhoff, John Christopher
  Frederick
Carnap, Rudolf
Carus, Paul
Damrosch, Walter Johannes
Dancel, Christian
Deindörfer, Johannes
Demme, Charles Rudolph
Detmold, Christian Edward
Dielman, Frederick
Dold, Jacob
Dorsch, Eduard
Dresel, Otto
Dreyfus, Max
Duhring, Louis Adolphus
Eckstein, John

Eichberg, Julius
Eickemeyer, Rudolf
Eigenmann, Carl H.
Eilers, Frederic Anton
Eimbeck, William
Einhorn, David
Einstein, Albert
Eisler, Gerhart
Elsberg, Louis
Engelhardt, Zephyrin
Engelmann, George
Ettwein, John
Faber, John Eberhard
Falckner, Daniel
Falckner, Justus
Farmer, Ferdinand
Felsenthal, Bernhard
Fernow, Bernhard Eduard
Fernow, Berthold
Feuchtwanger, Lion
Fink, Albert
Fischer, Emil Friedrick August
Fischer, Ruth
Flad, Henry
Flügel, Ewald
Follen, Charles
Franck, James
Francke, Kuno
Frasch, Herman
Frelinghuysen, Theodorus Jaco-
  bus
Frey, Joseph Samuel Christian
  Frederick
Friedlaender, Walter Ferdinand
Fritschel, Conrad Sigmund
Fritschel, Gottfried Leonhard Wil-
  helm
Fromm-Reichmann, Frieda
Ganso, Emil
Ganss, Henry George
Gemünder, August Martin Lud-
  wig
Genth, Frederick Augustus
Genthe, Arnold
Gerstle, Lewis
Giesler-Anneke, Mathilde Franzis-
  ka
Girsch, Frederick
Gmeiner, John
Goessmann, Charles Anthony
Goldbeck, Robert
Goldschmidt, Jakob
Gottheil, Gustav
Grabau, Johannes Andreas Au-
  gust
Gradle, Henry
Graessl, Lawrence
Graupner, Johann Christian Gott-
  lieb
Grim, David
Gropius, Walter Adolf Georg
Gros, John Daniel
Grossmann, Georg Martin
Grosz, George
Grube, Bernhard Adam
Gruening, Emil
Gunther, Charles Frederick
Guthe, Karl Eugen
Haarstick, Henry Christian
Hack, George
Hagen, Hermann August
Hahn, Georg Michael Decker
Haish, Jacob

Hamilton, Edith
Hammerstein, Oscar
Hansen, George
Hanus, Paul Henry
Hartwig, Johann Christoph
Hasenclever, Peter
Haupt, Paul
Hazelius, Ernest Lewis
Hecker, Friedrich Karl Franz
Heckscher, August
Heinemann, Ernst
Heinrich, Max
Heinzen, Karl Peter
Heiss, Michael
Helbron, Peter
Helffenstein, John Albert Conrad
Helmpraecht, Joseph
Helmuth, Justus Henry Christian
Hempel, Charles Julius
Hendel, John William
Herbermann, Charles George
Hering, Constantine
Herman, Lebrecht Frederick
Herter, Christian
Hertz, Alfred
Heyer, John Christian Frederick
Hilgard, Eugene Woldemar
Hilgard, Julius Erasmus
Hilgard, Theodor Erasmus
Hilprecht, Herman Volrath
Hirsch, Emil Gustav
Hoecken, Christian
Hoen, August
Hoenecke, Gustav Adolf Felix
  Thedor
Hoffman, Frederick Ludwig
Hoffmann, Francis Arnold
Hofman, Heinrich Oscar
Hofmann, Hans
Horney, Karen Danielssen
Hotz, Ferdinand Carl
Howard, Willie
Husmann, George
Jacobi, Abraham
Jacoby, Ludwig Sigmund
Jaeger, Werner Wilhelm
Juengling, Frederick
Jungman, John George
Kahn, Albert
Kahn, Gustav Gerson
Kahn, Julius
Kahn, Otto Herman
Kalb, Johann
Kalisch, Isidor
Kapp, Friedrich
Kautz, August Valentine
Keller, Mathias
Kellerman, Karl Frederic
Kelpius, Johann
Kiehbiel, Christian
Kirchmayer, John
Klein, Bruno Oscar
Kline, George
Klopsch, Louis
Knab, Frederick
Knabe, Valentine Wilhelm Ludwig
Knapp, Herman
Kober, George Martin
Kocherthal, Josua von
Koehler, Robert
Koehler, Sylvester Rosa
Koemmenich, Louis
Koenig, George Augustus

Koffka, Kurt
Kohler, Kaufmann
Kolb, Dielman
Kolle, Frederick Strange
Korner, Gustav Philipp
Kracauer, Siegfried
Kraus, John
Fraus-Boelté, Maria
Krauskopf, Joseph
Krez, Konrad
Krimmel, John Lewis
Kroeger, Adolph Ernst
Kruell, Gustav
Kunze, John Christopher
Kunze, Richard Ernest
Laemmle, Carl
Lange, Louis
Lasker, Albert Davis
Laufer, Berthold
Lederer, John
Leeser, Isaac
Lehmann, Frederick William
Leisler, Jacob
Lemke, Peter Henry
Leutze, Emanuel
Lewin, Kurt
Lewisohn, Adolph
Lewisohn, Ludwig
Ley, Willy
Leyendecker, Joseph Christian
Leypoldt, Frederick
Lieber, Francis
Liebling, Emil
Lienau, Detlef
Lilienthal, Max
Lindenkohl, Adolph
Lindheimer, Ferdinand Jacob
List, Georg Friedrich
Listemann, Bernhard
Loeb, Jacques
Loeb, Leo
Loewi, Otto
Lovejoy, Arthur Oncken
Lubitsch, Ernst
Ludwick, Christopher
Maas, Anthony J.
McClellan, George Brinton
Maisch, John Michael
Mann, William Julius
Mansfield, Richard
Marwedel, Emma Jacobina Christiana
Maschke, Heinrich
Mattheissen, Frederick William
Melsheimer, Friedrick Valentin
Memminger, Christopher Gustavus
Mendelsohn, Erich (or Eric)
Mergenthaler, Ottmar
Mergler, Marie Josepha
Merz, Karl
Metz, Christian
Meyer, Henry Coddington
Meyerhof, Otto
Michaelis, Leonor
Michelson, Albert Abraham
Mies van der Rohe, Ludwig
Miller, John Henry
Miller, John Peter
Mohr, Charles Theodore
Moldehuke, Edward Frederick
Möllhausen, Heinrich Baldwin
Mombert, Jacob Isidor

Moosmüller, Oswald William
Morgenthau, Henry
Morris, Nelson
Morwitz, Edward
Most, Johann Joseph
Mühlenberg, Henry Melchior
Müller, Wilhelm Max
Munch, Charles
Mundé, Paul Fortunatus
Münsterberg, Hugo
Nast, Thomas
Nast, William
Neidhard, Charles
Nessler, Karl Ludwig
Neuendorff, Adolph Heinrich Anton Magnus
Ney, Elisabet
Nicolay, John George
Niedringhaus, Frederick Gottlieb
Niemeyer, John Henry
Nies, Konrad
Noeggerath, Emil Oscar Jacob Bruno
Nordheimer, Isaac
Nordhoff, Charles
Notz, Frederick William Augustus
Oberhoffer, Emil Johann
Ochs, Julius
Oertel, Johannes Adam Simon
Orthwein, Charles F.
Osterhaus, Peter Joseph
Ottendorfer, Anna Behr Uhl
Otterbein, Philip William
Otto, Bodo
Overman, Frederick
Panofsky, Erwin
Pastorius, Francis Daniel
Perabo, Johann Ernst
Peters, Christian Henry Frederick
Phisterer, Frederick
Pieper, Franz August Otto
Piez, Charles
Pollard, Joseph Percival
Post, Christian Fredrick
Preetorius, Emil
Priber, Christian
Pulte, Joseph Hippolyt
Pursh, Frederick
Rademacher, Hans
Raht, August Wilhelm
Rapp, George
Rapp, Wilhelm
Rattermann, Heinrich Armin
Rauch, Frederick Augustus
Raue, Charles Gottlieb
Reed, John, 1757–1845
Reichenbach, Hans
Reisinger, Hugo
Reitzel, Robert
Rese, Frederick
Reuling, George
Reuter, Dominic
Rice, Charles
Rice, Isaac Leopold
Rieger, Johann Georg Joseph Anton
Rittenhouse, William
Robinson, Therese Albertine Louise Von Jakob
Rock, John
Roebling, John Augustus
Roemer, Karl Ferdinand
Roselius, Christian

Rummel, Joseph Francis
Saenderl, Simon
Sapir, Edward
Schaeberle, John Martin
Schaeffer, Frederick David
Schauffler, William Gottlieb
Scheel, Fritz
Schem, Alexander Jacob
Scheve, Edward Benjamin
Schieren, Charles Adolph
Schiff, Jacob Henry
Schilling, Hugo Karl
Schindler, Kurt
Schindler, Solomon
Schirmer, Gustav
Schmidt, Arthur Paul
Schmidt, Friedrich August
Schmucker, John George
Schnauffer, Carl Heinrich
Schneider, George
Schneider, Theodore
Schneller, George Otto
Schnerr, Leander
Schoenheimer, Rudolf
Schoenhof, Jacob
Schöpf, Johann David
Schott, Charles Anthony
Schradieck, Henry
Schrembs, Joseph
Schultze, Augustus
Schurz, Carl
Schuttler, Peter
Seidensticker, Oswald
Seligman, Jesse
Seligman, Joseph
Seyffarth, Gustavus
Shean, Albert
Sieber, Al
Sigel, Franz
Sloss, Louis
Sobolewski, J. Friedrich Eduard
Soldan, Frank Louis
Solger, Reinhold
Sorge, Friedrich Adolph
Sower, Christopher, 1693–1758
Sower, Christopher, 1721–1784
Spaeth, Adolph
Spangenberg, Augustus Gottlieb
Spicker, Max
Spreckels, Claus
Stahlman, Edward Bushrod
Stallo, Johann Bernard
Stang, William
Steck, George
Steinert, Morris
Steinmetz, Charles Proteus
Steinway, Christian Friedrich Theodore
Steinway, Henry Engelhard
Steinway, William
Stern, Kurt Guenter
Stern, Otto
Stetefeldt, Carl August
Steuben, Friedrich Wilhelm Ludolf Gerhard Augustin, Baron von
Stiegel, Henry William
Stock, Frederick August
Stockhardt, Karl Georg
Stolberg, Benjamin
Straus, Isidor
Straus, Nathan
Straus, Oscar Solomon

Strubberg, Friedrich Armand
Struve, Gustav
Stuckenberg, John Henry Wilbrandt
Sulzberger, Mayer
Tannenberger, David
Taussig, Joseph Knefler
Thomas, Christian Friedrich Theodore
Tillich, Paul
Timken, Henry
Timm, Henry Christian
Tobani, Theodore Moses
Viereck, George Sylvester
Villard, Henry
Villard, Oswald Garrison
Volck, Adalbert John
Von Wiegand, Karl Henry
Wachsmuth, Charles
Wagener, John Andreas
Wagner, Robert Ferdinand
Walter, Albert G.
Walter, Bruno
Walther, Carl Ferdinand Wilhelm
Warburg, Felix Moritz
Warburg, James Paul
Warburg, Paul Moritz
Waxman, Franz
Weber, Albert
Weber, Gustav Carl Erich
Weidenreich, Franz
Weidig, Adolf
Weill, Kurt
Weiser, Johann Conrad
Wernawag, Lewis
Wesselhoeft, Conrad
Weyl, Hermann
Wilczynski, Ernest Julius
Wimar, Carl
Wimmer, Boniface
Wislizenus, Frederick Adolph
Wistar, Caspar
Woerner, John Gabriel
Wolf, Innocent William
Wolf, Simon
Wolff, Kurt August Paul
Wolfsohn, Carl
Zakrzewska, Marie Elizabeth
Zenger, John Peter
Zentmayer, Joseph
Zeuner, Charles
Ziegler, David
Ziehn, Bernhard
Zinzendorf, Nicolaus Ludwig
Zuppke, Robert Carl

GHANA

Aggrey, James Emman Kwegyir

GIBRALTAR

Montrésor, John

GREECE

Anagnos, Michael
Benjamin, Samuel Greene Wheeler
Colvocoresses, George Musalas
Hearn, Lafcadio
Mitropoulos, Dimitri
Papanicolaou, George Nicholas

Skouras, George Panagiotes
Sophocles, Evangelinus Apostolides

GUATEMALA

Sarg, Tony

HONG KONG

Higgins, Marguerite

HUNGARY

Alexander, Franz Gabriel
Asboth, Alexander Sandor
Beck, Martin
Curtiz, Michael
Ditrichstein, Leo
Fejos, Paul
Fleischmann, Charles Louis
Fox, William
Franklin, Fabian
Haraszthy de Mokcsa, Agoston
Heilprin, Angelo
Joseffy, Rafael
Kaiser, Alvis
Karfiol, Bernard
Kiss, Max
Kohnt, Alexander
Kohut, George Alexander
Lorre, Peter
Lugosi, Bela
Pulitzer, Joseph
Rapaport, David
Reiner, Fritz
Roheim, Geza
Romberg, Sigmund
Schwimmer, Rosika
Seidl, Anton
Stahel, Julius
Stark, Louis
Szell, George
Szilard, Leo
Szold, Benjamin
Thorek, Max
Von Neumann, John
Weiss, Soma
Wise, Aaron
Wise, Stephen Samuel
Xántus, Jánas

ICELAND

Cahill, Holger

INDIA

Barrymore, Maurice
Bellew, Frank Henry Temple
Bruce, Andrew Alexander
Chandler, John Scudder
Fullerton, George Stuart
Hazen, Henry Allen
Huber, Gotthelf Carl
Hume, Robert Allen
Judd, Charles Hubbard
Judson, Adoniram Brown
Judson, Edward
Kennelly, Arthur Edwin
Leigh, Vivien
Mansell, William Albert
Oldham, William Fitzjames

Scudder, (Julia) Vida Dutton
Wyckoff, John Henry
Wyckoff, Walter Augustus

INDONESIA

(See Java)

IRAN

(See Persia)

IRELAND

Adair, James
Adrain, Robert
Alison, Francis
Amory, Thomas
Anthony, Sister
Argall, Philip
Armstrong, George Buchanan
Armstrong, John
Arthur, William
Azarias, Brother
Baird, Matthew
Barnwell, John
Barry, John
Barry, Patrick
Beatty, Charles Clinton
Binns, John
Blair, Samuel
Blair, William Richards
Blake, Mary Elizabeth McGrath
Blakely, Johnston
Bonner, Robert
Boucicault, Dion
Bowden, John
Breen, Patrick
Brenon, Herbert
Brougham, John
Brown, Alexander
Brown, George
Brown, James
Brown, John A.
Browne, John Ross
Bryan, George
Burk, John Daly
Burke, AEdanus
Burke, Thomas
Butler, Pierce
Butler, Richard
Butler, William
Byrne, Andrew
Byrne, John
Byrnes, Thomas F.
Campbell, Alexander
Campbell, Robert
Campbell, Thomas
Carey, Mathew
Carpenter, Stephen Cullen
Carr, Thomas Matthew
Cathcart, James Leander
Cathcart, William
Charless, Joseph
Clark, Daniel
Clarke, Sir Caspar Purdon
Clarke, Joseph Ignatius Constantine
Clarke, Mary Francis
Cleburne, Patrick Ronayne
Coate, Richard
Cockran, William Bourke
Colden, Cadwallader

Colles, Christopher
Collier, Peter Fenelon
Collins, Patrick Andrew
Conaty, Thomas James
Condon, Thomas
Connolly, John
Connor, Patrick Edward
Conway, Thomas
Conwell, Henry
Conyngham, Gustavus
Cosby, William
Cox, Henry Hamilton
Crawford, John
Crawford, John Wallace
Croghan, George
Croker, Richard
Croly, David Goodman
Cudahy, Michael
Cuming, Fortescue
Daly, Charles Patrick
Daly, Marcus
Dalzell, Robert M.
Delany, Patrick Bernard
Devoy, John
Digges, Dudley
Dinsmoor, Robert
Dobbs, Arthur
Donahue, Patrick
Dongan, Thomas
Donnelly, Charles Francis
Dornin, Thomas Aloysius
Drew, John
Dripps, Isaac L.
Drumgoole, John Christopher
Duane, William John
Dulany, Daniel
Dunlap, John
Egan, Michael
Elliott, Charles
Embury, Philip
Emmet, Thomas Addis
England, John
Erskine, John
Evans, William Thomas
Fair, James Graham
Farley, John Murphy
Feehan, Patrick Augustine
Ffrench, Charles Dominic
Field, Joseph M.
Findley, William
Finley, Samuel
Fitzgerald, Edward
Fitzpatrick, John
Fitzpatrick, Thomas
Fitzsimmons or Fitzsimins,
   Thomas
Flanagan, Edward Joseph
Flannery, John
Ford, Patrick
Fox, Richard Kyle
Francis, Tench
Gaine, Hugh
Galberry, Thomas
Gallagher, Hugh Patrick
Gallier, James
Garrett, Robert
Garrigan, Philip Joseph
Gillman, Henry
Gilmore, Patrick Sarsfield
Glennon, John Joseph
Godkin, Edwin Lawrence
Goff, John William
Good, John

Grace, William Russell
Gregg, John Robert
Hackett, Francis
Hall, Bolton
Hall, John
Halpine, Charles Graham
Hamilton, Edward John
Hand, Edward
Harpur, Robert
Haughery, Margaret Gaffney
Heck, Barbara
Hennessy, John
Hennessy, William John
Henry, John, 1746–1794
Henry, John, fl. 1807–1820
Herbert, Victor
Heron, Matilda Agnes
Heron, William
Hill, William
Hoban, James
Hogan, John
Hogun, James
Holland, John Philip
Hopkins, John Henry
Hovenden, Thomas
Hudson, Edward
Hughes, John Joseph
Hunter, Thomas
Hunter, Whiteside Godfrey
Ingham, Charles Cromwell
Inglis, Charles
Ireland, John, 1838–1918
Irvine, William
Johnson, Guy
Johnson, Sir William
Jones, Mary Harris
Jordan, Kate
Judge, William Quan
Julia, Sister
Keane, John Joseph
Kearney, Denis
Keating, John McLeod
Kelley, Eugene
Kelly, Myra
Kennedy, Robert Foster
Kenrick, Francis Patrick
Kenrick, Peter Richard
Keppel, Frederick
Kerens, Richard C.
Kerfoot, John Barrett
Kinsella, Thomas
Knox, Samuel
Laffan, William Mackay
Lane, Walter Paye
Leighton, William
Levins, Thomas C.
Lewis, Andrew
Logan, James, 1674–1751
Loudon, Samuel
Lynch, Patrick Neeson
Lyon, Matthew
Lyons, Peter
Lyster, Henry Francis Le Hunte
McAuley, Jeremiah
McAuley, Thomas
McBurney, Robert Ross
McCaine, Alexander
McCarroll, James
McClure, George
McClure, Samuel Sidney
McCormack, John Francis
McCosh, Andrew James
McCullagh, Joseph Burbridge

McCullough, John
McDonald, John Bartholomew
McElroy, John
McFaul, James Augustine
McGrath, James
McGrath, Matthew J.
McGuire, Charles Bonaventure
McHenry, James, 1753–1816
McHenry, James, 1785–1845
Mackay, John William
McKenna, Charles Hyacinth
Mackenzie, Robert Shelton
McKinly, John
McMahon, Bernard
McManes, James
McNeill, Hector
MacNeven, William James
McNicholas, John Timothy
McNulty, Frank Joseph
McNutt, Alexander
MacSparran, James
McVickar, John
Maginnis, Charles Donagh
Makemie, Francis
Mallet, John William
Malone, Sylvester
Maloney, Martin
Marshall, Christopher
Martin, Henry Newell
Matthews, Washington
Maxwell, William
Maxwell, William Henry
Meagher, Thomas Francis
Milligan, Robert
Milmore, Martin
Minty, Robert Horatio George
Mitchel, John
Montgomery, Richard
Moore, James, d. 1706
Moore, John, 1834–1901
Moriarity, Patrick Eugene
Morrissey, John
Moylan, Stephen
Mulholland, St. Clair Augustin
Mulholland, William
Mulligan, Charles J.
Murphy, Francis
Murphy, John
Murray, Joseph
Nesbitt, John Maxwell
Niblo, William
O'Brien, Fitz-James
O'Brien, Matthew Anthony
O'Brien, William Shoney
O'Callaghan, Edmund Bailey
O'Callaghan, Jeremiah
O'Connor, James
O'Connor, Michael
O'Dwyer, William
O'Fallon, James
O'Hara, James
O'Leary, Daniel
Oliver, George Tener
Oliver, Henry William
O'Mahony, John
O'Neill, James
O'Neill, John
O'Reilly, Alexander
O'Reilly, Henry
O'Reilly, John Boyle
Orr, Alexander Ector
O'Shaughnessy, Michael Maurice
Owen, William Florence

Paterson, William
Patterson, Robert, 1743–1824
Patterson, Robert, 1792–1881
Patterson, Thomas MacDonald
Patterson, William
Phelan, James
Pollock, Oliver
Porter, Alexander
Potamian, Brother
Potter, James
Power, John
Purcell, John Baptist
Quarter, William
Quill, Michael Joseph
Rainsford, William Stephen
Ramage, John
Read, George Campbell
Rehan, Ada
Reid, Thomas Mayne
Rhea, John
Roach, John
Roberts, William Randall
Robinson, Stuart
Robinson, William
Robinson, William Erigena
Roche, James Jeffrey
Rowan, Stephen Clegg
Russell, Mother Mary Baptist
Ryan, Edward George
Ryan, Patrick John
Sadlier, Denis
Sadlier, Mary Anne Madden
Saint-Gaudens, Augustus
Sampson, William
Savage, John
Scanlan, Lawrence
Sewall, William Joyce
Shaw, John, 1773–1823
Sheedy, Dennis
Shields, James
Sloan, Samuel
Smith, James, 1719–1806
Smyth, Alexander
Smyth, Thomas
Snow, Carmel White
Sproule, William
Stephenson, John
Sterling, James
Stewart, Alexander Turney
Strawbridge, Robert
Sweeny, Thomas William
Syng, Philip
Taggart, Thomas
Teggart, Frederick John
Tennent, Gilbert
Tennent, William, 1673–1745
Tennent, William, 1705–1777
Teresa, Mother
Thompson, Hugh Miller
Thompson, Launt
Thompson, Robert Ellis
Thompson, William
Thomson, Charles
Thornton, Matthew
Tobin, Daniel Joseph
Turner, William
Vaughan, Daniel
Waddel, James
Waddell, Hugh
Walsh, Michael
Warden, David Bailie
Warren, Sir Peter
Wilde, Richard Henry

Williams, Barney
Wood, James J.
Wright, James Lendrew
Wylie, Samuel Brown
Yorke, Peter Christopher
Young, John Russell

ITALY

Amateis, Louis
Andreis, Andrew James Felix Bartholomew de
Baccaloni, Salvatore
Barsotti, Charles
Bayma, Joseph
Bellanca, Giuseppe Mario
Bemelmans, Ludwig
Botta, Vincenzo
Boucher, Horace Edward
Brumidi, Constantino
Cabrini, Francis Xavier
Caruso, Enrico
Cataldo, Joseph Maria
Cesnola, Luigi Palma di
Chiera, Edward
Clevenger, Shobal Vail
Corey, Lewis
Crawford, Francis Marion
Da Ponte, Lorenzo
De Luca, Giuseppe
De Palma, Ralph
De Paolis, Alessio
Dodd, Bella Visono
Dundee, Johnny
Faccioli, Giuseppe
Fermi, Enrico
Finotti, Joseph Maria
Fitzgerald, Alice Louise Florence
Foresti, Eleutario Felice
Galli-Curci, Amelita
Gatti-Casazza, Giulio
Genovese, Vito
Giovannitti, Arturo
Hadfield, George
Kino, Eusebio Francisco
Langdon, Courtney
Lebrun, Federico ("Rico")
Legler, Henry Eduard
Luchese, Thomas
Luciano, Charles ("Lucky")
Mackubin, Florence
Martinelli, Giovanni
Marzo, Eduardo
Mazzachelli, Samuel Charles
Mazzei, Philip
Mengarini, Gregory
Morais, Sabato
Morini, Austin John
Nobili, John
Palladino, Lawrence Benedict
Patri, Angelo
Pinza, Ezio
Profaci, Joseph
Ravalli, Antonio
Rosati, Joseph
Sacco, Nicola
Sardi, Melchiorre Pio Vencenzo ("Vincent")
Sargent, John Singer
Sestini, Benedict
Seton, Robert
Stella, Joseph
Tagliabue, Giuseppe

Toscanini, Arturo
Trajetta, Philip
Tresca, Carlo
Vanzetti, Bartolomeo
Vigo, Joseph Maria Francesco
Vitale, Ferruccio
Walsh, Henry Collins
Yon, Pietro Alessandro

JAMAICA

Garvey, Marcus Moziah
McKay, Claude

JAPAN

Greene, Jerome Davis
Hartmann, Carl Sadakichi
Kuniyoshi, Yasuo
Landis, James McCauley
Noguchi, Hideyo
Takamine, Jokichi
Verbeck, William

JAVA

Norden, Carl Lukas

LATVIA

Bellanca, Dorothy Jacobs
Moisseiff, Leon Solomon
Sterne, Maurice

LITHUANIA

Berenson, Bernard
Berenson, Senda
Bloomgarden, Solomon
Godowsky, Leopold
Goldman, Emma
Hillman, Sidney
Myerson, Abraham
Sack, Israel
Schereschewsky, Samuel Isaac Joseph
Schlesinger, Benjamin
Shahn, Benjamin ("Ben")
Silver, Abba Hillel
Winchevsky, Morris
Zorach, William

LUXEMBOURG

Gernsback, Hugo
Woll, Matthew

MARSHALL ISLANDS

Gulick, Sidney Lewis

MEXICO

Font, Pedro
Kiam, Omar
Larrazolo, Octaviano Ambrosio
Novarro, Ramon
Oñate, Juan de

MORAVIA

Lindenthal, Gustav
Maretzek, Max

Nitschmann, David
Sealsfield, Charles
Zeisberger, David

NETHERLANDS

Bayard, Nicholas
Behrends, Adolphus Julius Frederick
Block, Adriaen
Boelen, Jacob
Bogardus, Everardus
Bok, Edward William
Burnet, William
Cazenove, Théophile
Covode, John
Cuyler, Theodore
Debye, Peter Joseph William
De Haas, John Philip
De Lamar, Joseph Raphael
De Leeuw, Adolph Lodewyk
D'ooge, Martin Luther
Dupratz, Antoine Simon Le Page
Dusser de Barenne, Joannes Gregorius
Freeman, Bernardus
Gallitzin, Demetrius Augustine
Henny, David Christiaan
Hudde, Andries
Huidekoper, Harm Jan
Isaacs, Samuel Myer
Jansen, Reinier
Kieft, Willem
Krol, Bastiaen Jansen
Le Roux, Bartholomew
Mappa, Adam Gerard
Matthes, Gerard Hendrik
Megapolensis, Johannes
Michaëlius, Jonas
Minuit, Peter
Morton, Nathaniel
Muste, Abraham Johannes
Peter, John Frederick
Philipse, Frederick
Romans, Bernard
Scholte, Hendrik Peter
Schrieck, Sister Louise Van Der
Selijns, Henricus
Steendam, Jacob
Steenwyck, Cornelis
Stuyvesant, Petrus
Troost, Gerard
Van Beuren, Johannes
Van Cortlandt, Oloff Stevenszen
Van Curler, Arent
Van Der Donck, Adriaen
Van Der Kemp, Francis Adrian
Van Ilpendam, Jan Jansen
Van Loon, Hendrik Willem
Van Raalte, Albertus Christiaan
Van Rensselaer, Nicholas
Van Twiller, Wouter
Verbeck, Guido Herman Fridolin
Verwyst, Chrysostom Adrian
Voorsanger, Jacob

NORWAY

Barth, Carl Georg Lange
Boyesen, Hjalmar Hjorth
Dahl, Theodor Halvorson
Dietrichson, Johannes Wilhelm Christian

Eielsen, Elling
Furuseth, Andrew
Hanson, James Christian Meinich
Haugen, Nils Pederson
Henie, Sonja
Hoyme, Gjermund
Janson, Kristofer Nagel
Johnsen, Erik Kristian
Kildahl, Johan Nathan
Knutson, Harold
Koren, Ulrik Vilhelm
Larsen, Peter Laurentius
Larson, Laurence Marcellus
Lie, Jonas
Lundeberg, Harry
Mallory, Anna Margrethe ("Molla") Bjurstedt
Nelson, Knute
Nelson, Nelson Olsen
Oftedal, Sven
Owre, Alfred
Peerson, Cleng
Reiersen, Johan Reinert
Rockne, Knute Kenneth
Rölvaag, Ole Edvart
Rynning, Ole
Stejneger, Leonhard Hess
Sverdrup, Georg
Tapper, Bertha Feiring
Tou, Erik Hansen
Wergeland, Agnes Mathilde

PALESTINE

Hirschensohn, Chaim

PERSIA

Mitchell, Lucy Myers Wright
Oldfather, William Abbott
Shedd, William Ambrose
Wright, John Henry

PERU

Peñalosa Briceño, Diego Dioniso de

PHILIPPINES

Quezon, Manuel Luis

POLAND

(See also Silesia)

Baruch, Simon
Barzynski, Vincent
Blaustein, David
Dabrowski, Joseph
Damrosch, Leopold
Friedlaender, Israel
Funk, Casimir
Goldin, Horace
Gray, Gilda
Gurowski, Adam
Hecht, Selig
Heilprin, Michael
Hodur, Francis
Hofmann, Josef Casimir
Jastrow, Joseph
Jastrow, Marcus
Jastrow, Morris

Kosciuszko, Tadeusz Andrzej Bonawentura
Krueger, Walter
Landowska, Wanda Aleksandra
Loewenthal, Isidor
London, Meyer
Lotka, Alfred James
Lubin, David
Modjeska, Helena
Modjeski, Ralph
Nadelman, Elie
Neumann, Franz Leopold
Perlman, Selig
Poznanski, Gustavus
Pulaski, Casimir
Radin, Max
Radin, Paul
Rose, Ernestine Louise Siismondi Potowski
Rosenblatt, Bernard Abraham
Rosenfeld, Morris
Rosenthal, Max
Rubinstein, Helena
Salomon, Haym
Schultz, Henry
Schwidetzky, Oscar Otto Rudolf
Singer, Israel Joshua
Stokes, Rose Harriet Pastor
Szyk, Arthur
Warner, Harry Morris
Wiener, Leo
Znaniecki, Florian Witold

PORTUGAL

Benavides, Alonzo de
Cabrillo, Juan Rodriguez
De Kay, James Ellsworth
Lopez, Aaron
Lumbrozo, Jacob
Miranda, Carmen

ROMANIA

Bloomfield, Meyer
Covici, Pascal ("Pat")
Culbertson, Ely
Gluck, Alma
Kneisel, Franz
Schechter, Solomon

RUSSIA

Adler, Polly
Adler, Sara
Annenberg, Moses Louis
Antin, Mary
Archipenko, Alexander
Artzybasheff, Boris
Baranov, Alexander Andreevich
Berkman, Alexander
Bernstein, Herman
Billikopf, Jacob
Blavatsky, Helena Petrovna Hahn
Bolm, Adolph Rudolphovitch
Boudin, Louis Boudinoff
Brenner, Victor David
Cahan, Abraham
Carter, Boake
Casanowicz, Immanuel Moses
Chotzinoff, Samuel
Cist, Charles
Cohen, Morris Raphael

Cooke, Samuel
Davidson, Israel
Duke, Vernon
Ehrlich, Arnold Bogamil
Elman, Mischa
Enelow, Hyman Gerson
Epstein, Abraham
Fokine, Michel
Freeman, Joseph
Friedman, William Frederick
Gabrilowitsch, Ossip
Gamow, George
Gest, Morris
Goerz, David
Goldenweiser, Alexander Alexandrovich
Goldenweiser, Emanuel Alexander
Golder, Frank Alfred
Goldfine, Bernard
Gomberg, Moses
Gordin, Jacob
Guzik, Jack
Halpert, Edith Gregor
Hillquit, Morris
Hindus, Maurice Gerschon
Hirschbein, Peretz
Hourwich, Isaac Aaronovich
Hubert, Conrad
Ioasaf
Innokentïi
Jolson, Al
Kharasch, Morris Selig
Koussevitzky, Serge Alexandrovich
Kuskov, Ivan Aleksandrovich
Lang, Lucy Fox Robins
Launitz, Robert Eberhard Schmidt Von Der
Leonty, Metropolitan
Levene, Phoebus Aaron Theodore
Lipman, Jacob Goodale
Loeb, Sophie Irene Simon
Loskiel, George Henry
Margalis, Max Leopold
Masliansky, Zvi Hirsch
Mayer, Louis Burt
Mears, Otto
Meltzer, Samuel James
Mosessohn, David Nehemiah
Nazimova, Alla
Osten Sacken, Carl Robert Romanovich Von Der
Ostromislensky, Iwan Iwanowich
Paley, John
Pasvolsky, Leo
Price, George Moses
Rachmaninoff, Sergei Vasilyevich
Revel, Bernard
Rezanov, Nikolai Petrovich
Rombro, Jacob
Romeike, Henry
Ropes, John Codman
Rosen, Joseph A.
Rosenberg, Abraham Hayyim
Rosenblatt, Joseph
Rosenthal, Herman
Rostovtzeff, Michael Ivanovitch
Rothko, Mark
Rubinow, Isaac Max
Sachs, Theodore Bernard
Sandler, Jacob Koppel

Saslavsky, Alexander
Schenck, Nicholas Michael
Schillinger, Joseph
Schomer, Nahum Meir
Schwartz, Maurice
Selikovitsch, Goetzel
Shelekhov, Grigorii Ivanovich
Shubert, Lee
Sidis, Boris
Siloti, Alexander Ilyitch
Spivak, Charles David
Sternberg, Constantin Ivanovich Edler von
Steuben, John
Stone, Abraham
Strunsky, Simeon
Struve, Otto
Tamarkin, Jacob David
Tchelitchew, Pavel
Tucker, Sophie
Vasiliev, Alexander Alexandrovich
Vladeck, Baruch Charney
Vladimiroff, Pierre
Vogrich, Max Wilhelm Karl
Weber, Max
Woytinsky, Wladimir Savelievich
Yellin, Samuel
Zevin, Israel Joseph
Zilboorg, Gregory
Zunser, Eliakum

SCOTLAND

Abercromby, James
Adie, David Craig
Affleck, Thomas
Ainslie, Hew
Aitken, Robert
Alexander, Abraham
Alexander, James
Allan, John
Armour, Thomas Dickson ("Tommy")
Arthur, Peter M.
Auchmuty, Robert
Audsley, George Ashdown
Bain, George Luke Scobie
Barr, Charles
Bell, Alexander Graham
Bell, Alexander Melville
Bell, Eric Temple
Bell, Robert
Bennett, James Gordon
Bishop, Robert Hamilton
Blair, James
Brackenridge, Hugh Henry
Brackenridge, William D.
Brown, William
Brownlee, William Craig
Bruce, George
Bruce, Robert
Buchanan, Thomas
Burden, Henry
Callender, James Thomson
Calvin, Samuel
Cameron, Archibald
Campbell, Charles Macfie
Campbell, George Washington
Campbell, John
Carnegie, Andrew
Clarke, Robert
Craik, James
Crooks, Ramsay

Crosser, Robert
Cushny, Arthur Robertson
Davidson, Thomas
Dickie, George William
Dickson, Robert
Dollar, Robert
Donahue, Peter
Douglass, William
Dow, Alex
Dowie, John Alexander
Dunbar, Robert
Dunbar, William
Duncan, James
Dunmore, John Murray
Dunwiddie, Robert
Eckford, Henry
Elmslie, George Grant
Erskine, Robert
Fairlie, John Archibald
Finlay, Hugh
Fleming, John
Fleming, William
Fleming, Williamina Paton Stevens
Forbes, John, 1710–1759
Forbes, John, d. 1783
Forbes, John, 1769–1823
Forgan, James Berwick
Garden, Alexander
Garden, Mary
Geddes, James Loraine
Gilmour, Richard
Goold, William A.
Gordon, George Angier
Gowans, William
Graham, Isabella Marshall
Graham, James
Graham, John
Grieve, Miller
Hall, David
Hamilton, Alexander
Hamilton, Andrew
Harkness, William
Hart, James MacDougal
Hart, William
Henderson, Daniel McIntyre
Henderson, David Bremner
Henderson, Peter
Hewat, Alexander
Humphreys, Alexander Crombie
Hunter, Robert
Jamison, David
Johnston, Gabriel
Johnston, John, 1791–1880
Johnston, John, 1881–1950
Johnston, Samuel
Jones, John Paul
Kane, John
Keith, George
Keith, Sir William, 1680–1749
Keith, William, 1839–1911
Kemp, James
Kemp, John
Kennedy, Archibald
Kennedy, John Stewart
Kidd, William
Laurie, James
Lawson, Alexander
Lawson, Andrew Cowper
Lawson, James
Leiper, Thomas
Lining, John
Livingston, Robert

Lockhart, Charles
Lorimer, George Claude
Loudoun, John Campbell, Earl of
Lowrie, Walter
Lundie, John
Lyall, James
Macalester, Charles, 1765–1832
MacAlister, James
McArthur, John, 1823–1890
McArthur, John, 1826–1906
McCallum, Daniel Craig
McCosh, James
McDougall, Alexander, 1732–1786
McDougall, Alexander, 1845–1923
Macintosh, Douglas Clyde
McIntosh, Lachlan
MacIver, Robert Morrison
Mackay, James
Mackellar, Patrick
Mackenzie, Donald
Mackenzie, George Henry
Mackenzie, James Cameron
Mackenzie, Kenneth
Mackenzie, Murdo
McLaren, John
Maclaurin, Richard Cockburn
Maclean, John
McLeod, Alexander
Maclure, William
McTammany, John
MacVicar, Malcolm
Mantell, Robert Bruce
Matthews, William
Maxwell, Hugh
Melish, John
Mercer, Hugh
Michie, Peter Smith
Minto, Walter
Mitchell, Alexander
Mitchell, David Brydie
Moffat, James Clement
Moffatt, James
Montgomery, Edmund Duncan
Montrésor, James Gabriel
Muir, John
Munro, Henry
Murray, Philip
Murray, Robert
Nairne, Thomas
Neilson, William Allan
Nisbet, Charles
Ogilvie, James
Oliver, James
Orr, Hugh
Owen, David Dale
Owen, Robert Dale
Panton, William
Patillo, Henry
Patterson, James Kennedy
Pattison, Granville Sharp
Phillips, William Addison
Phyfe, Duncan
Pinkerton, Allan
Pitcairn, John, 1722–1775
Pitcairn, John, 1841–1916
Rae, John
Ramsay, Alexander
Redpath, James
Reid, David Boswell
Rhind, Charles
Ritchie, Alexander Hay

Robertson, Archibald
Robertson, James, b. 1740
Robertson, William Spence
Ross, Alexander
Russell, William
St. Clair, Arthur
Sandeman, Robert
Saunders, William
Schouler, William
Scott, Walter
Seth, James
Sharp, John
Shirlaw, Walter
Skene, Alexander Johnston Chalmers
Smibert, John
Smillie, James
Smith, Alexander
Smith, George
Smith, Robert, 1722–1777
Smith, Russell
Smith, William, 1727–1803
Smith, William, 1754–1821
Sprunt, James
Stephens, Henry Morse
Stobo, Robert
Stuart, Charles Macaulay
Stuart, John
Stuart, Robert
Swan, James
Swinton, John
Swinton, William
Taylor, William Mackergo
Telfair, Edward
Thomson, John
Thorburn, Grant
Turnbull, Andrew
Vetch, Samuel
Watson, Andrew
Wenley, Robert Mark
White, Alexander
William, Charles
Williamson, Andrew
Williamson, Charles
Wilson, Alexander
Wilson, James, 1742–1798
Wilson, James, 1836–1920
Wilson, James Grant
Wilson, Peter
Wilson, William
Wilson, William Bauchop
Winton, Alexander
Witherspoon, John
Wood, John
Wright, Frances

SIAM

Chang and Eng

SILESIA

Damrosch, Frank Heino
Gratz, Barnard
Gratz, Michael
Mannes, Clara Damrosch
Pelz, Paul Johannes
Prang, Louis
Reichel, Charles Gotthold
Schwarz, Eugene Amandus

SOUTH AFRICA

Rathbone, Basil

SOVIET UNION

(See Russia)

SPAIN

Alemany, José Sadoc
Antoine, Père
Anza, Juan Bautista de
Ayala, Juan Manuel de
Ayllon, Lucas Vasquez de
Bori, Lucrczia
Cárdenas, García Lópéz de
Copley, Thomas
Coronado, Francisco Vásquez
Costansó, Miguel
Cubero, Pedro Rodríquez
De Soto, Hernando
De Vargas, Zapata y Lujan Ponce De Leon, Diego
Escalante, Silvestre Velez de
Espejo, Antonio de
Fages, Pedro
Ferrero, Edward
Garcés, Francisco Tomás Hermenegildo
Gálvez, Bernardo de
Gayoso de Lemos, Manuel
Iglesias, Santiago
Luna y Arellano, Tristan de
Meade, George Gordon
Meade, Richard Worsam
Menéndez, De Aviles Pedro
Miró, Esteban Rodríquez
Montgomery, George Washington
Moscoso De Alvarado, Luis de
Narváez, Panfilo de
Núñez, Cabeza De Vaca, Alvar
Nunó, Jaime
Ponce De León, Juan
Portolá, Gaspar de
Santayana, George
Tamarón, Pedro
Ulloa, Antonio de
Villagrá, Gaspar Pérez de
Viccaíno, Sebastián

SRI LANKA

(See Ceylon)

SURINAM

(See Dutch Guiana)

SWEDEN

Acrelius, Israel
Anderson, Mary
Campanius, John
Carlson, Anton Julius
Cesare, Oscar Edward
Dylander, John
Edgren, August Hjalmar
Ericsson, John
Esbjörn, Lars Paul
Fersen, Hans Axel, Count Von
Folin, Otto Knut Olof
Hasselquist, Tuve Nilsson

Hesselius, Gustavus
Johnson, Magnus
Leipzig, Nate
Lind, John
Lindberg, Charles Augustus
Lindberg, Conrad Emil
Lindgren, Waldemar
Lundin, Carl Axel Robert
Mattson, Hans
Norelius, Eric
Ockerson, John Augustus
Printz, Johan Björnsson
Raphall, Morris Jacob
Reuterdahl, Henry
Rising, Johan Classon
Rydberg, Per Axel
Schele De Vere, Maximilian
Schmidt, Nathaniel
Seashore, Carl Emil
Sellstedt, Lars Gustaf
Swenson, David Ferdinand
Thulstrup, Bror Thure
Udden, Johan August
Widforss, Gunnar Mauritz

SWITZERLAND

Agassiz, Alexander
Agassiz, Jean Louis Rodolphe
Ammann, Othmar Hermann
Bandelier, Adolph Francis Alphonse
Bapst, John
Behrend, Bernard Arthur
Bloch, Ernest
Boll, Jacob
Bouquet, Henry
Bucher, John Conrad
Cajori, Florian
Cramer, Michael John
Delmonico, Lorenzo
Dufour, John James
Du Simitière, Pierre Eugène
Faesch, John Jacob
Gallatin, Abraham Alfonse Albert
Gatschet, Albert Samuel
Goetschius, John Henry
Graffenried, Christopher
Gratiot, Charles
Guggenheim, Meyer
Gutherz, Carl
Guyot, Arnold Henry
Hailmann, William Nicholas
Hassler, Ferdinand Rudolph
Henni, John Martin
Hoch, August
Kruesi, John
Krüsi, Johann Heinrich Hermann
Lang, Henry Roseman
Lesquereux, Leo
Martel, Charles
Marty, Martin
Menetrey, Joseph
Messmer, Sebastian Gebhard
Meyer, Adolf
Ming, John Joseph
Nef, John Ulric
Olmsted, John Charles
Pfister, Alfred
Piccard, Jean Félix
Pourtalès, Louis François de
Purry, Jean Pierre
Rosenberg, Henry

Schaff, Philip
Schinz, Albert
Schlatter, Michael
Seiler, Carl
Senn, Nicholas
Shaw, Pauline Agassiz
Smith, John Eugene
Sterki, Victor
Theus, Jeremiah
Troye, Edward
Vanderbilt, Gloria Morgan
Weidenmann, Jacob
Wirt, William
Zimmerman, Eugene
Zubly, John Joachim

SYRIA

Adams, Walter Sydney
Bliss, Frederick Jones
Bliss, Howard Sweetser
Dennis, Alfred Lewis Pinneo
Smith, Benjamin Eli

THAILAND

(See also Siam)

McFarland, George Bradley

TURKEY

Bliss, Edwin Munsell
Bliss, William Dwight Porter
Brewer, David Josiah
Callimachos, Panos Demetrios
Dwight, Henry Otis
Frame, Alice Seymour Browne
Goodell, Henry Hill
Gorky, Arshile
Gregory, Menas Sarkas Boulgourjian
Grosvenor, Edwin Prescott
Grosvenor, Gilbert Hovey
Jackson, Edward Payson
Johnston, Henry Phelps
Rafinesque, Constantine Samuel
Schauffler, Henry Albert
Van Lennep, Henry John
Van Lennep, William Bird
Von Ruck, Karl
Williams, Talcott
Zachos, John Celivergos

VIRGIN ISLANDS

Behn, Sosthenes
Crosswaith, Frank Rudolph

WALES

Coke, Thomas
Davies, John Vipond
Davis, James John
Easton, John
Easton, Nicholas
Evans, Evan
Evans, John
Everett, Robert
Gardiner, John Sylvester John
Griffith, Benjamin
Hughes, Price
Jones, Evan William

Jones, Jenkin Lloyd
Jones, John Peter
Jones, Samuel Milton
Langner, Lawrence
Lewis, Francis
Lloyd, David
Lloyd, Thomas
Morgan, Abel
Moxham, Arthur James
Nicholson, John
Owen, Griffith
Plumbe, John
Powell, Snelling
Pugh, Ellis
Rees, James
Reese, Abram
Reese, Isaac
Reese, Jacob
Rhees, Morgan John
Roberts, William Charles
Roberts, William Henry
Shelby, Evan
Smith, William Henry, 1806–1872
Stanley, Henry Morton
Templeton, Alec Andrew
Thomas, David
Williams, John Elias

WEST INDIES

Alarcón, Hernando De
Audubon, John James
Benjamin, Judah Philip
Berg, Joseph Frederic
Currier, Charles Warren
Da Costa, Jacob Mendez
Dallas, Alexander James
D'avezac, Auguste Geneviève Valentin
Davis, John
Du Bourg, Louis Guillaume Valentin
Finlay, Carlos Juan
Fitzgerald, Desmond
Fletcher, Alice Cunningham
Fraunces, Samuel
Fuertes, Estevan Antonio
Gorringe, Henry Honeychurch
Guiteras, Juan
Hamilton, Alexander
Holland, William Jacob
Hunt, Isaac
Larrínaga, Tulio
Lowndes, Rawlins
Mallory, Stephen Russell
Markoe, Abraham
Markoe, Peter
Martin, Josiah
Mendes, Frederic De Sola
Menocal, Aniceto Garcia
Moore, Sir Henry
Moreau de Saint-méry, Médéric-Louis-Élie
Moreau-Lislet, Louis Casimir Elisabeth
Muñoz-Rivera, Luis
Pinckney, Elizabeth Lucas
Prud'homme, John Francis Eugene
Redwood, Abraham
Ricord, Frederick William
Roberdeau, Daniel
Russwurm, John Brown

Stuart, Charles
Thomas, George
Thornton, William
Varela y Morales, Félix Francisco
  José María de la Concepción
Vaughan, Benjamin
Williams, Bert
Woodward, Henry
Yulee, David Levy

YUGOSLAVIA

Adamic, Louis
Rodzinski, Artur
Tesla, Nikola

AT SEA

Colcord, Lincoln Ross
Gibson, Walter Murray
Jemison, Mary
Juilliard, Augustus D.
Kirby, J. Hudson
Lathrop, Francis Augustus
McFee, William
Sajous, Charles Euchariste De
  Médicis

SCHOOLS AND COLLEGES

Listed below are the Schools, Colleges, and Universities, followed, in each case, by the names of those persons in the Dictionary who have attended the respective institutions.

ACADEMIC AND COMMERCIAL COLLEGE (WIS.)
Haugen, Gilbert Nelson
ACADEMIE CARMEN (FRANCE)
Frieseke, Frederick Carl
ACADEMIE COLAROSSI (FRANCE)
Robinson, Boardman
ACADEMIE DELACLUSE (FRANCE)
Young, Mahonri Mackintosh
ACADEMIE JULIEN (FRANCE)
Benson, Frank Weston
Borglum John Gutzon de la Mothe
Calder, Alexander Stirling
Eilshemius, Louis Michel
Karfiol, Bernard
MacNeil, Hermon Atkins
Ruckstull, Frederick Wellington
Szyk, Arthur
Weber, Max
Wood, Grant
Young, Art
ACADEMIE OZENFANT (FRANCE)
Bouché, René Robert
ACADEMY OF FINE ARTS IN ROME (ITALY)
Baccaloni, Salvatore
ACADIA UNIVERSITY (CANADA)
Case, Shirley Jackson
Eaton, Charles Aubrey
Rand, Benjamin
Graduate Study
Case, Shirley Jackson
Eaton, Charles Aubrey
ADELPHI ACADEMY (BROOKLYN, N.Y.)
Folger, Henry Clay
Fowler, Frank
Harland, Henry
Ivins, William Mills
Kemp, James Furman
Nitchie, Edward Bartlett
Partridge, William Ordway
AGRICULTURAL COLLEGE OF UTAH
Hines, Frank Thomas
Jardine, William Marion
ALABAMA POLYTECHNIC INSTITUTE
Fleming, Walter Lynwood
Owsley, Frank Lawrence
Sloan, Matthew Scott
Graduate Study
Duggar, Benjamin Minge
Fleming, Walter Lynwood
Sloan, Matthew Scott
ALABAMA PRESBYTERIAN COLLEGE
Carmichael, Oliver Cromwell
ALBANY ACADEMY (N.Y.)
Bogart, John
Boltwood, Bertram Borden
Bradford, Alexander Warfield
Brodhead, John Romeyn
Campbell, Allen
Cassidy, William
Cutler, James Goold

Draper, Andrew Sloan
Durrie, Daniel Steele
Hartley, Jonathan Scott
Henry, Joseph
Isherwood, Benjamin Franklin
James, Henry 1811–1882
Marble, Manton Malone
Martin, Frederick Townsend
Pruyn, Robert Hewson
Smith, Charles Emory
Tucker, Gilbert Milligan
Viele, Egbert Ludovicus
Welch, Ashbel
ALBANY LAW SCHOOL (N.Y.)
Benjamin, Park, 1849–1922
Benton, Josiah Henry
Brewer, David Josiah
Brown, Irving
Cassoday, John Bolivar
Converse, Charles Crozat
Deming, Philander
Draper, Andrew Sloan
Eckels, James Herron
Jackson, Robert Houghwout
Kirchwey, George Washington
Kneeland, Stillman Foster
MacAlister, James
McKinley, William
Manley, Joseph Homan
Martin, Frederick Townsend
Parker, Alton Brooks
Peckham, George Williams
Peckham, Wheeler Hazard
Pitkin, Frederick Walker
Plaisted, Harris Merrill
Raines, John
Schenck, Ferdinand Schureman
Stone, William Leete
Tripp, Bartlett
ALBANY MEDICAL COLLEGE (N.Y.)
Benjamin, George Hillard
Blackfan, Kenneth Daniel
Duane, Alexander
Durant, Thomas Clark
Fuller, Robert Mason
Gregory, Menas Sarkas Boulgourjian
Hayden, Ferdinand Vandiveer
House, Samuel Reynolds
Salisbury, James Henry
Salmon, Thomas William
Smith, Theobald
ALBERTUS UNIVERSITY (GERMANY)
Fromm-Reichmann, Frieda
ALBION COLLEGE (MICH.)
Adams, Henry Cullen
Bovie, William T.
Folks, Homer
Greene, Edward Lee
Lovejoy, Owen Reed
Moulton, Forest Ray
Nelson, Knute
Shaw, Anna Howard
Shepard, James Henry

Graduate Study
Lovejoy, Owen Reed
ALCORN AGRICULTURAL AND MECHANICAL COLLEGE (MISS.)
Evers, Medgar Wiley
ALFRED ACADEMY (See ALFRED UNIVERSITY)
ALFRED UNIVERSITY (N.Y.)
Anderson, Galusha
Cassoday, John Bolivar
Flint, Weston
Rogers, William Augustus
Stillman, Thomas Bliss
Stillman, Thomas Edgar
Willson, Augustus Everett
Graduate Study
Pearson, Raymond Allen
ALLEGHENY COLLEGE (PA.)
Allison, William Boyd
Cooke, Henry David
Darrow, Clarence Seward
Dibble, Roy Floyd
Gary, James Albert
Harris, Merriman Colbert
Haskins, Charles Homer
Hays, Alexander
Holliday, Cyrus Kurtz
Howe, Frederic Clemson
Jackman, Wilbur Samuel
Jones, William Patterson
Kennedy, Joseph Camp Griffith
Kingsley, Calvin
Lowndes, Lloyd
McKinley, William
Metcalf, Joel Hastings
Oldham, William Fitzjames
Pierpont, Francis Harrison
Rice, Victor Moreau
Tarbell, Ida Minerva
Thoburn, James Mills
Thompson, Arthur Webster
ALLEGHENY SEMINARY (See WESTERN THEOLOGICAL SEMINARY)
ALLEGHENY THEOLOGICAL SEMINARY
Miller, James Russell
Moorehead, William Gallogly
ALLENTOWN SEMINARY (See MUHLENBERG COLLEGE)
ALMA COLLEGE (MICH.)
Knox, Frank
ALMA COLLEGE (N.Y.)
Hull, Clark Leonard
AMENIA SEMINARY (N.Y.)
Benton, Joel
Foss, Cyrus David
Pirsson, Louis Valentine
Winchell, Alexander
AMERICAN ACADEMY IN ROME (ITALY)
Graduate Study
Van Deman, Esther Boise

421

AMERICAN ACADEMY OF DRAMATIC
    ARTS (N.Y.)
  DeMille, Cecil Blount
  Lindsay, Howard
  McClintic, Guthrie
  Schildkraut, Joseph
  Tracy, Spencer Bonaventure
AMERICAN BUSINESS COLLEGE
    (MINN.)
  Thye, Edward John
AMERICAN CONSERVATORY OF MU-
    SIC (ILL.)
  Gray, Glen
AMERICAN UNIVERSITY (D.C.)
  Graduate Study
  Lomax, Louis Emanuel
  Zahniser, Howard Clinton
AMHERST ACADEMY (MASS.)
  Blodgett, Henry Williams
  Chamberlain, Daniel Henry
  Clark, Joseph Sylvester
  Dickinson, Emily Elizabeth
  Graham, Sylvester
  Hitchcock, Edward, 1828–1911
  Loomis, Dwight
  Lyon, Mary
  Pope, Franklin Leonard
  Riggs, Elias
AMHERST COLLEGE (MASS.)
  Adams, Charles Baker
  Adams, Herbert Baxter
  Allen, David Oliver
  Allen, Nathan
  Allen, Timothy Field
  Ames, Herman Vandenburg
  Andrews, Charles Bartlett
  Andrews, Israel Ward
  Avery, John
  Bancroft, Frederic
  Barton, Bruce Fairchild
  Bassett, Edward Murray
  Bayley, James Roosevelt
  Beecher, Henry Ward
  Birdseye, Clarence
  Bissell, Edwin Cone
  Bliss, Daniel
  Bliss, Edwin Elisha
  Bliss, Edwin Munsell
  Bliss, Frederick Jones
  Bliss, Howard Sweetser
  Bliss, William Dwight Porter
  Bridgman, Elijah Coleman
  Bridgman, Herbert Lawrence
  Broun, Addison
  Brownell, William Crary
  Buchanan, Scott Milross
  Burgess, John William
  Chapman, Alvan Wentworth
  Clark, George Whitefield
  Clark, John Bates
  Clark, John Maurice
  Clark, Joseph Sylvester
  Clark, Thomas March
  Clark, William Bullock
  Clark, William Smith
  Clarke, John Mason
  Cobb, William Henry
  Codman, John
  Coffin, James Henry
  Cohn, Edwin Joseph
  Coit, Stanton
  Coolidge, Calvin

Cross, Charles Whitman
Curtiss, Samuel Ives
Darling, Henry
Davis, Arthur Vining
Dewey, Melvil
Drew, Charles Richard
Eastman, Joseph Bartlett
Edwards, Bela Bates
Emerson, Benjamin Kendall
Ewing, James
Farman, Elbert Eli
Fitch, William Clyde
Flint, Austin
Folger, Henry Clay
Fowler, Orson Squire
Gardiner, Harry Norman
Garman, Charles Edward
Garvin, Lucius Fayette Clark
Gillett, Frederick Huntington
Goodale, George Lincoln
Goodell, Henry Hill
Goodhue, James Madison
Goodnow, Frank Johnson
Grosvenor, Edwin Prescott
Grosvenor, Gilbert Hovey
Grow, Galusha Aaron
Hackett, Horatio Balch
Hallock, Charles
Hamlin, Alfred Dwight Foster
Hamlin, Talbot Faulkner
Hammond, William Gardiner
Hardy, Arthur Sherburne
Harris, George
Haven, Joseph
Hewett, Waterman Thomas
Hewit, Augustine Francis
Hitchcock, Charles Henry
Hitchcock, Edward, 1828–1911
Hitchcock, Roswell Dwight
Holland, William Jacob
Holt, Edwin Bissell
Hooper, Claude Ernest
Houston, Charles Hamilton
Humphries, George Rolfe
Huntington, Frederick Dan
Jackson, Edward Payson
James, Arthur Curtiss
Jameson, John Franklin
Jerome, William Travers
Johnson, Allen
Jones, John Taylor
Kemp, James Furman
King, Stanley
Landis, Henry Robert Murray
Lansing, Robert
Leland, George Adams
Lewis, William Henry
Lincoln, Rufus Pratt
Lord, Otis Phillips
Lyman, Eugene William
McClure, Alexander Wilson
March, Francis Andrew, 1825–
    1911
Marcy, Henry Orlando
Maynard, Horace
Mayo, Amory Dwight
Mayo-Smith, Richmond
Mead, William Rutherford
Mears, David Otis
Mell, Patrick Hues, 1814–1888
Merrill, Charles Edward
Merrill, James Griswold

Moore, William Henry
Morrow, Dwight Whitney
Morse, Anson Daniel
Morse, Harmon Northrop
Nash, Charles Sumner
Nash, Simeon
Nason, Henry Bradford
Neill, Edward Duffield
Nitchie, Edward Bartlett
Northend, Charles
Noyes, Alexander Dana
Olds, Leland
Orne, John
Osgood, Herbert Levi
Palmer, Benjamin Morgan
Palmer, Walter Walker
Parker, Peter
Parkhurst, Charles Henry
Perkins, Justin
Plimpton, George Arthur
Pomeroy, Samuel Clarke
Potter, Edward Clark
Pray, Isaac Clark
Rainey, Henry Thomas
Rhees, Rush
Riggs, Elias
Robinson, Charles Mulford
Robinson, Stuart
Rolfe, William James
Rossiter, William Sidney
Rugg, Arthur Prentice
Schneider, Benjamin
Seelye, Julius Hawley
Shepard, Charles Upham
Smith, Benjamin Eli
Smith, Charles Sprague
Smith, Edward Munroe
Smith, Henry Preserved
Smith, Horatio Elwin
Smith, Judson
Smith, Preserved
Snell, Bertrand Hollis
Sophocles, Evangelinus Aposto-
    lides
Spahr, Charles Barzillai
Stanchfield, John Barry
Stearns, Frank Waterman
Stebbins, Rufus Phineas
Stockbridge, Henry
Stockbridge, Henry Smith
Stoddard, John Tappan
Stone, Harlan Fiske
Storrs, Richard Salter, 1821–
    1900
Swinton, William
Taft, Alphonso
Tufts, James Hayden
Tyler, William Seymour
Van Lennep, Henry John
Vinton, Frederic
Walker, Francis Amasa
Walker, Williston
Ward, Herbert Dickinson
Ward, John Elliott
Ward, William Hayes
Washburn, George
Whipple, Amiel Weeks
Wilbur, Hervey Backus
Wilder, Harris Hawthorne
Williams, George Huntington
Williams, Talcott

Woodbridge, Frederick James Eugene
Woods, Robert Archey
Graduate Study
Bliss, Frederick Jones
Clark, George Whitefield
Grosvenor, Edwin Prescott
Grosvenor, Gilbert Hovey
March, Francis Andrew, 1825–1911
Osgood, Herbert Levi
Post, Augustus
Rainey, Henry Thomas
Wilbur, Henry Backus
AMMENDALE COLLEGE (MD.)
Bushman, Francis Xavier
ANDOVER (See PHILLIPS ACADEMY, ANDOVER)
ANDOVER THEOLOGICAL SEMINARY (MASS.)
Abbott, Edward
Abbott, Gorham Dummer
Abbott, Jacob
Abbott, John Stevens Cabot
Adams, Charles Baker
Adams, Henry Carter
Adams, Jasper
Adams, Nehemiah
Adams, William
Aiken, Charles Augustus
Alden, Henry Mills
Allen, David Oliver
Ament, William Scott
Atkinson, George Henry
Bacon, Leonard
Bacon, Leonard Woolsey
Baldwin, Elihu Whittlesey
Barrows, John Henry
Bartlett, Samuel Colcord
Beach, Harlan Page
Beecher, Edward
Benjamin, Nathan
Bingham, Hiram, 1789–1869
Bingham, Hiram, 1831–1908
Blakeslee, Erastus
Blanchard, Jonathan
Bliss, Daniel
Bliss, Edwin Elisha
Bouton, Nathaniel
Brainerd, Ezra
Brainerd, Thomas
Bridgman, Elijah Coleman
Brown, Carleton
Brown, Samuel Gilman
Bumstead, Horace
Byington, Cyrus
Chase, Irah
Cheever, George Barrell
Cheever, Henry Theodore
Clark, Francis Edward
Clark, Joseph Sylvester
Cobb, William Henry
Coit, Thomas Winthrop
Collins, John Anderson
Colton, Calvin
Colton, Walter
Cook, Flavius Josephus
Dewey, Orville
Dike, Samuel Warren
Diman, Jeremiah Lewis
Dole, Charles Fletcher
Dunning, Albert Elijah

Dwight, Harrison Gray Otis
Eaton, John
Edwards, Bela Bates
Edwards, Justin
Fairbanks, Henry
Farrar, John
Fisher, George Park
Foster, Frank Hugh
Gallaudet, Thomas Hopkins
Gates, George Augustus
Gibbs, Josiah Willard, 1790–1861
Goodell, William, 1792–1867
Goodrich, Chauncey, 1836–1925
Goodwin, Daniel Raynes
Green, Beriah
Greene, Daniel Crosby
Hackett, Horatio Balch
Haddock, Charles Brickett
Hale, Benjamin
Hall, Sherman
Hallock, Gerard
Hallock, William Allen
Harris, George
Harris, Samuel
Hart, Hastings Hornell
Hatfield, Edwin Francis
Haven, Joseph
Henry, Caleb Sprague
Hitchcock, Charles Henry
Hitchcock, Roswell Dwight
Homes, Henry Augustus
Hoppin, James Mason
Howe, George
Hume, Robert Allen
Jewett, Chas. Coffin
Jones, John Taylor
Judson, Adoniram
Kellogg, Elijah
Kellogg, Martin
King, Jones
Ladd, George Trumbull
Lawrence, William, 1850–1941
Leach, Daniel Dyer
Loomis, Elias
Lord, Eleazar
Lord, John
Lord, Nathan
McClure, Alexander Wilson
McKenzie, Alexander
McKim, James Miller
Magoun, George Frederic
Mahan, Asa
Marsh, James
Mead, Charles Marsh
Merrill, James Griswold
Mulford, Elisha
Munger, Theodore Thornton
Murray, James Ormsbee
Neill, Edward Duffield
Noble, Frederick Alphonso
Noyes, John Humphrey
Ogden, Rollo
Orton, James
Packard, Joseph
Paine, John Alsop
Palmer, George Herbert
Park, Edwards Amasa
Parker, Samuel
Parkhurst, Charles
Peet, Stephen Denison

Perkins, Justin
Pillsbury, Parker
Post, Truman Marcellus
Rankin, Jeremiah Eames
Richards, William
Riggs, Elias
Ropes, James Hardy
Ross, Abel Hastings
Sanborn, Edwin David
Schauffler, Henry Albert
Schneider, Benjamin
Shedd, William Greenough Thayer
Sheldon, Charles Monroe
Sherwood, Adiel
Slafter, Edmund Farwell
Smith, Arthur Henderson
Smith, Asa Dodge
Smith, Eli
Smith, Henry Boynton
Smyth, Newman
Smyth, William
Snow, Francis Huntington
Southgate, Horatio
Spaulding, Levi
Spring, Gardiner
Spring, Leverett Wilson
Stearns, William Augustus
Stoddard, David Tappan
Storrs, Richard Salter, 1787–1873
Storrs, Richard Salter, 1821–1900
Stowe, Calvin Ellis
Taylor, Samuel Harvey
Thayer, Joseph Henry
Thwing, Charles Franklin
Todd, John
Torrey, Charles Cutler
Torrey, Charles Turner
Townsend, Luther Tracy
Winship, Albert Edward
Winslow, Hubbard
Winslow, Miron
Woods, Alva
Woods, Leonard, 1807–1878
Woods, Robert Archey
Worcester, Samuel Austin
Yeomans, John William
ANNAPOLIS (See UNITED STATES NAVAL ACADEMY)
ANTIOCH COLLEGE (OHIO)
Binkley, Wilfred Ellsworth
Brown, Olympia
Herford, Oliver Brooke
Jay, Allen
Keifer, Joseph Warren
Lawrance, Uriah Marion
Sherwood, Isaac Ruth
Shull, George Harrison
Terrell, Mary Eliza Church
Wilson, Edmund Beecher
APPLETON ACADEMY (N.H.)
Bancroft, Cecil Franklin Patch
Champney, Benjamin
Fiske Amos Kidder
Mathews, William Smythe Babcock
Shattuck, Lemuel
ARMOUR INSTITUTE OF TECHNOLOGY (ILL.)
Howell, Albert Summers

Lardner, Ringgold Wilmer
ARMY MEDICAL SCHOOL
  Ashford, Bailey Kelly
ARNOLD COLLEGE (ENGLAND)
  Vizetelly, Frank Horace
ART INSTITUTE OF CHICAGO
  Leyendecker, Joseph Christian
  Williams, Gaar Campbell
  Ziff, William Bernard
ARTISTS' AND ARTISANS' INSTITUTE
  (N.Y.)
  McBride, Henry
ART STUDENTS' LEAGUE (D.C.)
  Johnston, Frances Benjamin
ART STUDENTS' LEAGUE (N.Y.)
  Bachrach, Louis Fabian
  Barrymore, John
  Barrymore, Lionel
  Beard, Daniel Carter
  Breck, George William
  Burroughs, Bryson
  Chambers, Robert William
  Christy, Howard Chandler
  Clarke, Thomas Shields
  Curry, John Steuart
  Davidson, Jo
  Dickinson, Preston
  Dreier, Katherine Sophie
  Duffy, Edmund
  Eilshemius, Louis Michel
  Epstein, Jacob
  French, Edwin Davis
  Frieseke, Frederick Carl
  Gág, Wanda (Hazel)
  Gaul, William Gilbert
  Gibson, Charles Dana
  Gilman, Lawrence
  Hambidge, Jay
  Hartley, Marsden
  Hawthorne, Charles Webster
  Holt, Winifred
  Hyde, Helen
  Juengling, Frederick
  Kirby, Rollin
  Koehler, Robert
  Kuniyoshi, Yasuo
  Lawson, Ernest
  Lie, Jonas
  Lockwood, Robert Wilton
  Loeb, Louis
  McBride, Henry
  MacMonnies, Frederick William
  Manship, Paul Howard
  Marsh, Reginald
  Meière, Marie Hildreth
  Miller, Kenneth Hayes
  Newman, Barnett
  O'Malley, Frank Ward
  Penfield, Edward
  Pollock, (Paul), Jackson
  Potter, Ellen Culver
  Pratt, Bela Lyon
  Pyle, Howard
  Reid, Robert
  Remington, Frederic
  Rothko, Mark
  Smith, David Roland
  Stella, Joseph
  Taylor, William Ladd
  Tucker, Allen
  Vance, Louis Joseph
  Yohn, Frederic Coffay

  Young, Art
  Zogbaum, Rufus Fairchild
ASBURY COLLEGE (KY.)
  Matthews, Joseph Brown
ASBURY UNIVERSITY (See DE PAUW
  UNIVERSITY)
ASHFIELD ACADEMY (MASS.)
  Fowler, Orson Squire
  Hall, Granville Stanley
  Lyon, Mary
ATHENEE ROYALE (BELGIUM)
  Sauveur, Albert
ATHENS CONSERVATORY OF MUSIC
  (GREECE)
  Mitropoulos, Dimitri
ATHENS ACADEMY (GA.)
  English, Elbert Hartwell
  Paschal, George Washington
  Wright, Charles Barstow
ATKINSON ACADEMY (N.H.)
  Brown, Francis 1784–1820
  Clark, Greenleaf
  Woodbury, Levi
ATLANTA CONSERVATORY OF MUSIC
  (GA.)
  Hardy, Oliver Norvell
ATLANTA UNIVERSITY (GA.)
  Henderson, Fletcher Hamilton
  Johnson, Edward Austin
  Johnson, James Weldon
  White, Walter Francis
  Wright, Richard Robert
AUBURN THEOLOGICAL SEMINARY
  (N.Y.)
  Babcock, Maltbie Davenport
  Bascom, John
  Benjamin, Nathan
  Cloud, Henry Roe
  Coan, Titus
  Condon, Thomas
  Cook, Russell S.
  Darling, Henry
  Fisher, George Park
  Gally, Merritt
  Grinnell, Josiah Bushnell
  Headley, Joel Tyler
  Headley, Phineas Camp
  Hoisington, Henry Richard
  Knox, George William
  Logan, Cornelius Ambrose,
    1832–1899
  Lord, William Wilberforce
  Morris, George Sylvester
  Parker, Joel, 1799–1873
  Roe, Edward Payson
  Seelye, Julius Hawley
  Sheffield, Devello Zelotes
  Stryker, Melancthon Woolsey
  Tappan, Henry Philip
  Williams, John Elias, 1871–
    1927
AUBURN UNIVERSITY (ALA.)
  Bullard, Robert Lee
  Heflin, James Thomas
  Smith, Holland McTyeire
AUGSBURG COLLEGE (MINN.)
  Wiley, Alexander
AUGUSTA COLLEGE (KY.)
  Browning, Orville Hickman
  Doniphan, Alexander William
  Fee, John Gregg
  Foster, Randolph Sinks

  Groesbeck, William Slocum
  Preston, William
  Wickliffe, Robert Charles
AUGUSTA COLLEGE (See WASHING-
  TON AND LEE)
AUGUSTANA COLLEGE (ILL.)
  Borg, George William
  Carlson, Anton Julius
Graduate Study
  Carlson, Anton Julius

BABSON INSTITUTE OF BUSINESS
  ADMINISTRATION (MASS.)
  Gerber, Daniel (Frank)
BACON ACADEMY (MAINE)
  Bartholomew, Edward Sheffield
  Crary, Isaac Edwin
  Fowler, Orin
  Gillett, Ezra Hall
  Morgan, Edwin Denison
  Trumbull, Lyman
BACONE COLLEGE (OKLA.)
  Hurley, Patrick Jay
BAKER UNIVERSITY (KANS.)
  Allen, Henry Justin
  Bristow, Joseph Little
BALDWIN COLLEGE (OHIO)
  Miller, Dayton Clarence
Graduate Study
  Miller, Dayton Clarence
BALDWIN-WALLACE COLLEGE
  (OHIO)
  Cline, Genevieve Rose
  Norris, George William
  Ulrich, Edward Oscar
Law
  Sweeney, Martin Leonard
BALTIMORE CITY COLLEGE
  Adams, Thomas Sewall
  Boston, Charles Anderson
  Gorrell, Edgar Staley
  Hemmeter, John Conrad
  Kennedy, John Pendleton
  Latané, John Holladay
  Perlman, Philip Benjamin
  Rose, John Carter
  Ryan, Harris Joseph
  Slicer, Thomas Roberts
  Uhler, Philip Reese
  Van Meter, John Blackford
  Williams, John Whitridge
BALTIMORE POLYTECHNIC INSTI-
  TUTE
  Bachrach, Louis Fabian
  Hammett, Samuel Dashiell
BANGOR THELOGICAL SEMINARY
  (MAINE)
  Beckwith, Clarence Augustine
  Chamberlain, Joshua Lawrence
  Chandler, Peleg Whitman
  Cheever, Henry Theodore
  Hamlin, Cyrus
  Parker, Edwin Pond
  Peloubet, Francis Nathan
  Savage, Minot Judson
  Smyth, Egbert Coffin
  Tenney, Edward Payson
BAPTIST COLLEGE (IOWA)
  Springer, Charles
BAPTIST COLLEGE (MO.)
  Asbury, Herbert

BARBER-SCOTIA COLLEGE (N.C.)
Bethune, Mary McLeod
BARD COLLEGE (N.Y.)
Francis, Paul James
Nock, Albert Jay
Graduate Study
Francis, Paul James
BARNARD COLLEGE (N.Y.)
Antin, Mary
Gildersleeve, Virginia Crocheron
Hurston, Zora Neale
King, Carol Weiss
Lehman, Adele Lewisohn
Loveman, Amy
Meyer, Agnes Elizabeth Ernst
Parsons, Elsie Worthington Clews
Reid, Helen Miles Rogers
Rumsey, Mary Harriman
BATES COLLEGE (MAINE)
Baker, James Hutchins
Dennett, Tyler (Wilbur)
Haskell, Ella Louise Knowles
Hayes, Edward Carey
Hewett, Waterman Thomas
Howe, Percy Rogers
Neal, Josephine Bicknell
Simmons, Franklin
Sullivan, Louis Robert
BATTLE CREEK COLLEGE (MICH.)
Price, George Edward McCready
BAYLOR FEMALE COLLEGE (TEX.)
Ferguson, Miriam Amanda Wallace ("Ma")
BAYLOR UNIVERSITY (TEX.)
Burleson, Albert Sidney
Connally, Thomas Terry ("Tom")
Norris, John Franklyn
Scarborough, Dorothy
Scarborough, Lee Rutland
Truett, George Washington
Graduate Study
Eaton, Charles Aubrey
Scarborough, Dorothy
BEAUMONT COLLEGE (ENGLAND)
Mackay, Clarence Hungerford
BELLEVUE COLLEGE (NEBR.)
Lunn, George Richard
BELLEVUE HOSPITAL MEDICAL COLLEGE (See NEW YORK UNIVERSITY, *Medicine*)
BELLEVUE TRAINING SCHOOL FOR NURSES (N.Y.)
Dock, Lavinia Lloyd
BELMONT COLLEGE (OHIO)
Cist, Henry Martyn
Halstead, Murat
Harrison, Benjamin, 1833–1901
Nixon, William Penn
Walden, John Morgan
Zimmerman, Eugene
BELOIT ACADEMY (WIS.)
Bishop, Seth Scott
Keyes, Elisha Williams
Williams, Jesse Lynch, 1871–1929
BELOIT COLLEGE (WIS.)
Adams, George Burton
Andrews, Roy Chapman

Bingham, Walter Van Dyke
Bishop, Seth Scott
Bundy, Jonas Mills
Bushnell, George Ensign
Chamberlin, Thomas Chrowder
Clark, Felton Grandison
Curtis, Edward Lewis
Davis, Jerome Dean
Gates, Caleb Frank
Hallett, Moses
Huntington, Ellsworth
Mellizer, Oscar Edward
Peet, Stephen Denison
Pettigrew, Richard Franklin
Salisbury, Rollin D.
Scott, James Wilmot
Skinner, Aaron Nichols
Smith, Arthur Henderson
Strong, James Woodward
Strong, Walter Ansel
White, Horace
Wright, Theodore Lyman
BEREA COLLEGE (KY.)
Barton, Bruce Fairchild
Barton, William Eleazar
Woodson, Carter Godwin
BERKELEY DIVINITY SCHOOL (CONN.)
Hart, Samuel
Leonard, William Andrew
Nichols, William Ford
Nock, Albert Jay
Potter, Eliphalet Nott
BERKSHIRE MEDICAL INSTITUTION (MASS.)
Green, Asa
Hopkins, Mark
Lee, Charles Alfred
Root, Joseph Pomeroy
Stone, Warren
BERLIN-CHARLOTTENBURG TECHNISCHE HOCHSCHULE (GERMANY)
Graduate Study
Kracauer, Siegfried
BERLIN POLYTECHNICUM (GERMANY)
Wiener, Leo
BETHANY COLLEGE (W.VA.)
Adams, William Lysander
Baldwin, Joseph
Baxter, William
Benton, Allen Richardson
Clark, Champ
Dennis, Graham Barclay
Ferrel, William
Hodgen, John Thompson
Lamar, Joseph Rucker
Lard, Moses E.
Loos, Charles Louis
McGarvey, John William
McLean, Archibald
Mayes, Edward
Moore, William Thomas
Odell, Benjamin Barker
Oliver, George Tener
Power, Frederick Dunglison
Wharton, Greene Lawrence
Willett, Herbert Lockwood
Williams, Edward Thomas
Zollars, Ely Vaughan

BETHEL COLLEGE (KY.)
Dargan, Edwin Preston
McGlothlin, William Joseph
BETHEL COLLEGE (TENN.)
Garrett, Finis James
BIALYSTOK SCHOOL OF COMMERCE (POLAND)
Perlman, Selig
BINGHAM SCHOOL (N.C.)
Ashe, Thomas Samuel
Dobbin, James Cochran
Page, Walter Hines
Waddell, Alfred Moore
Webb, William Robert
BIRMINGHAM SOUTHERN UNIVERSITY (ALA.)
Jones, Robert Reynolds ("Bob")
BIRMINGHAM UNIVERSITY (ENGLAND)
Lotka, Alfred James
Graduate Study
Lotka, Alfred James
BISHOP PAINE DIVINITY SCHOOL (VA.)
Russell, James Solomon
BISHOP'S COLLEGE (CANADA)
Fessenden, Reginald Aubrey
BLACKBURN UNIVERSITY (ILL.)
Austin, Mary
BLACK HILLS COLLEGE (S.D.)
Gidley, James Williams
BLACK HILLS TEACHERS COLLEGE (S.DAK.)
Leedom, Boyd Stewart
BLOOMFIELD ACADEMY (MAINE)
Coburn, Abner
Coffin, Charles Albert
Howard, Volney Erskine
BLOOMFIELD ACADEMY (N.J.)
Dodd, Frank Howard
Hoisington, Henry Richard
Peloubet, Francis Nathan
Ward, Richard Halsted
BLOOMSBURG STATE NORMAL SCHOOL (PA.)
Pfahler, George Edward
BOLOGNA CONSERVATORY OF MUSIC (ITALY)
Spalding, Albert
BONEBRAKE THEOLOGICAL SEMINARY (OHIO)
Dougherty, Raymond Philip
BOSTON, ENGLISH HIGH SCHOOL
Ballou, Maturin Murray
Chandler, Seth Carlo
Child, Francis James
Cummings, Charles Amos
Green, Francis Mathews
Guild, Curtis, 1827–1911
Sullivan, Louis Henri
Whitmore, William David
BOSTON COLLEGE
Cushing, Richard James
O'Connell, William Henry
Tobin, Maurice Joseph
Walsh, James Anthony
BOSTON CONSERVATORY OF MUSIC
Berenson, Senda
BOSTON GIRLS' LATIN SCHOOL
Berenson, Senda
Scudder, (Julia) Vida Dutton

BOSTON LATIN SCHOOL
Abbot, Henry Larcom
Adams, Charles Francis, 1807–1886
Adams, Charles Francis, 1835–1915
Ames, James Barr
Appleton, Thomas Gold
Austin, James Trecothick
Austin, Jonathan Loring
Barnard, Charles Francis
Barnes, James
Beecher, Charles
Bigelow, Henry Jacob
Blaikie, William
Bowditch, Henry Ingersoll
Breck, Samuel
Brooks, Phillips
Bulfinch, Thomas
Bumstead, Horace
Butler, John Wesley
Byles, Mather
Channing, William Ellery, 1818–1901
Channing, William Henry
Chauncy, Charles
Checkley, John
Child, Francis James
Clark, Arthur Hamilton
Clarke, James Freeman
Coerne, Louis Adolphe
Coffin, Sir Isaac
Converse, Edmund Cogswell
Crafts, James Mason
Craigie, Andrew
Crowninshield, Frederic
Dall, William Healey
Davis, Charles Henry, 1807–1877
Derby, Elias Hasket, 1803–1880
Devens, Charles
Dwight, John Sullivan
Eliot, Charles William
Ellis, George Edward
Emerson, Ralph Waldo
Eustis, William
Evarts, William Maxwell
Fenn, William Wallace
Fiske, George Converse
Fitzpatrick, John Bernard
Ford, Patrick
Foster, Roger Sherman Baldwin
Fowle, William Bentley
Freeman, James
Furness, William Henry
Gardiner, Robert Hallowell
Goldthwaite, George
Gould, Benjamin Apthorp
Grafton, Charles Chapman
Gray, John Chipman
Greenough, James Bradstreet
Greenough, Richard Saltonstall
Hale, Charles
Hale, Edward Everett
Hammond, James Bartlett
Hancock, John, 1736–1793
Hardy, Arthur Sherburne
Hayden, Edward Everett
Hepworth, George Hughes
Hodges, Harry Foote
Hooper, William
Howe, Henry Marion

Hunt, Richard Morris
Jackson, Charles
Jackson, James, 1777–1867
Jenks, William
Kneeland, Samuel
Langley, Samuel Pierpont
Leland, George Adams
Leverett, John, 1662–1724
Lincoln, John Larkin
Loring, Edward Greely
Loring, Ellis Gray
McClure, Alexander Wilson
Mather, Cotton
Merrill, William Bradford
Milmore, Martin
Morton, William James
Mundé, Paul Fortunatus
Oliver, Henry Kemble
Osgood, William Fogg
Otis, George Alexander
Otis, Harrison Gray, 1765–1848
Paine, Charles Jackson
Paine, Robert Treat, 1731–1814
Paine, Robert Treat, 1773–1811
Paine, Robert Treat, 1835–1910
Palfrey, John Carver
Parker, Isaac
Parker, James Cutler Dunn
Parker, Richard Green
Parsons, Thomas William
Peabody, Selim Hobart
Pearce, Charles Sprague
Pearce, Richard Mills
Pelham, Henry
Phillips, Wendell
Phillips, William
Pickering, Edward Charles
Pond, George Edward
Pynchon, Thomas Ruggles
Quincy, Josiah Phillips
Reed, James, 1834–1921
Richardson, William Lambert
Robinson, Edward, 1858–1931
Salisbury, Edward Elbridge
Sargent, Epes
Sargent, Henry Winthrop
Sargent, John Osborne
Scudder, Horace Elisha
Shattuck, Frederick Cheever
Shattuck, George Cheyne, 1813–1893
Shurtleff, Nathaniel Bradstreet
Smith, Samuel Francis
Southard, Elmer Ernest
Stimpson, William
Storey, Moorfield
Sumner, Charles
Thayer, Joseph Henry
Thayer, Thomas Baldwin
Townsend, Edward Davis
True, Alfred Charles
Tuckerman, Edward
Tuckerman, Henry Theodore
Tuckerman, Joseph
Van Brunt, Henry
Waldo, Samuel
Warren, John Collins, 1778–1856
Warren, John Collins, 1842–1927
Washburn, Edward Abiel
Wellington, Arthur Mellen

Whitmore, William David
Whiton, James Morris
Wigglesworth, Edward, c. 1693–1765
Wigglesworth, Edward, 1840–1896
Williams, Henry Willard
Willis, Nathaniel Parker
Winslow, William Copley
Winsor, Justin
Winthrop, John, 1714–1779
BOSTON NORMAL SCHOOL
Rogers, Mary Josephine
BOSTON NORMAL SCHOOL OF GYMNASTICS
Berenson, Senda
BOSTON SCHOOL OF ART
Kalmus, Natalie Mabelle Dunfee
BOSTON SCHOOL OF ORATORY
Blatch, Harriot Eaton Stanton
BOSTON (SIMMONS) SCHOOL OF SOCIAL WORK
Cannon, Ida Maud
BOSTON UNIVERSITY
Ayres, Leonard Porter
Bailey, Solon Irving
Bartlett, Francis Alonzo
Blackwell, Alice Stone
Bogan, Louise Marie
Brace, Dewitt Bristol
Cochrane, Gordon Stanley ("Mickey")
Drum, Hugh Aloysius
Ferguson, John Calvin
Hale, William Bayard
Jefferson, Mark Sylvester William
Kline, Franz Josef
Leonard, William Ellery
Libbey, Edward Drummond
Maier, Walter Arthur
Marden, Orison Swett
Myrick, Herbert
Oldham, William Fitzjames
Oxnam, Garfield Bromley
Simkhovitch, Mary Melinda Kingsbury
Tuckerman, Frederick
Graduate Study
Ayres, Leonard Porter
Bailey, Solon Irving
Brightman, Edgar Sheffield
King, Martin Luther, Jr.
McConnell, Francis John
Stockbridge, Horace Edward
Law
Bloomfield, Meyer
Cooper, Henry Ernest
Emerton, Ephraim
McGrath, James Howard
Morton, Ferdinand Quintin
Roche, Arthur Somers
Rugg, Arthur Prentice
Russell, William Eustis
Stoddard, Theodore Lothrop
Walsh, David Ignatius
Young, Owen D.
Medicine
Shaw, Anna Howard
Music
Dunham, Henry Morton

Theology
Bashford, James Whitford
Brightman, Edgar Sheffield
Brown, Charles Reynolds
Butler, John Wesley
Coe, George Albert
Curtis, Olin Alfred
Ferguson, John Calvin
Fisher, Frederick Bohn
Hamilton, John William
High, Stanley Hoflund
Hughes, Edwin Holt
Huntington, William Edwards
Jefferson, Charles Edward
McDowell, William Fraser
McFarland, John Thomas
Mansell, William Albert
Mitchell, Hinckley Gilbert
  Thomas
Mudge, James
Sharp, Dallas Lore
Shaw, Anna Howard
BOWDOIN COLLEGE (MAINE)
Abbot, Ezra
Abbot, Gorham Dummer
Abbott, Jacob
Abbott, John Stevens Cabot
Alexander, De Alva Stanwood
Allen, William Henry
Andrew, John Albion
Appleton, John, 1804–1891
Appleton, John, 1815–1864
Barker, Benjamin Fordyce
Barrett, Benjamin Fiske
Bartol, Cyrus Augustus
Bates, Arlo
Beecher, Charles
Bell, Luther Vose
Bradbury, James Ware
Brewster, Ralph Owen
Burton, Harold Hitz
Chamberlain, Joshua Lawrence
Chandler, Peleg Whitman
Cheever, George Barrell
Cheever, Henry Theodore
Coffin, Robert Peter Tristram
Curtis, Edwin Upton
Davies, Charles Stewart
Day, James Roscoe
Dean, William Henry, Jr.
Dunlap, Robert Pinckney
Emery, Henry Crosby
Emery, Lucilius Alonzo
Evans, George
Everett, Charles Carroll
Felch, Alpheus
Fernald, Charles Henry
Fessenden, Francis
Fessenden, James Deering
Fessenden, William Pitt
Fillebrown, Thomas
Flagg, Edmund
Frye, William Pierce
Fuller, Melville Weston
Garcelon, Alonzo
Gardner, Henry Joseph
Gerrish, Frederic Henry
Gibson, Paris
Goddard, Morrill
Goodwin, Daniel Raynes
Grover, La Fayette
Hale, Benjamin

Hale, John Parker
Hall, Edwin Herbert
Hamlin, Charles
Hamlin, Cyrus
Harrington, Charles
Harris, Samuel
Hawes, Charles Boardman
Hawkins, Dexter Arnold
Hawthorne, Nathaniel
Hill, Frank Alpine
Howard, Oliver Otis
Howe, Lucien
Hubbard, Thomas Hamlin
Ingalls, Melville Ezra
Ingraham, Joseph Holt
Johnson, Henry
Kellogg, Elijah
Kimball, Sumner Increase
King, Henry Melville
Kinsey, Alfred Charles
Larrabee, William Clark
Longfellow, Henry Wadsworth
Lord, Nathan
Lovejoy, Owen
McCulloch, Hugh
McLellan, Isaac
Magoun, George Frederic
Mitchell, Edward Page
Morse, Charles Wyman
Packard, Alpheus Spring, 1798–
  1884
Packard, Alpheus Spring, 1839–
  1905
Packard, Joseph
Parker, Edwin Pond
Peary, Robert Edwin
Pierce, Franklin
Poor, Henry Varnum
Prentiss, George Lewis
Prentiss, Seargent Smith
Putnam, William Le Baron
Ray, Isaac
Reed, Thomas Brackett
Rhoads, Cornelius Packard
Russwurm, John Brown
Sargent, Dudley Allen
Sewall, Frank
Sheldon, Henry Newton
Smith, Henry Boynton
Smith, John Cotton, 1826–1882
Smith, Seba
Smyth, Egbert Coffin
Smyth, William
Southgate, Horatio
Stanwood, Edward
Stephens, Charles Asbury
Storer, David Humphreys
Stowe, Calvin Ellis
Sturtevant, Edward Lewis
Swallow, George Clinton
Thatcher, Benjamin Bussey
Thomas, William Widgery
Torrey, Charles Cutler
Vail, Stephen Montfort
Washburn, William Drew
Wheeler, William Adolphus
Whitman, Charles Otis
Young, Aaron
Graduate Study
Hall, Edwin Herbert
Packard, Alpheus Spring, 1839–
  1905

Sewall, Frank
Medicine
Barker, Benjamin Fordyce
Everett, Charles Carroll
Gerrish, Frederic Henry
Holmes, Ezekiel
Ray, Isaac
BOWLING GREEN BUSINESS COL-
  LEGE (KY.)
Hines, Duncan
BRADFORD ACADEMY (MASS.)
Atkinson, George Henry
Judson, Ann Hesseltine
Perley, Ira
Poole, Fitch
BRADFORD ACADEMY (VT.)
Benton, Josiah Henry
Jewett, Milo Parker
Pearsons, Daniel Kimball
Worthen, Amos Henry
BRADLEY UNIVERSITY (ILL.)
Hoerr, Normand Louis
Skidmore, Louis
BRECKINRIDGE COLLEGE (IOWA)
Haugen, Gilbert Nelson
BRIDGEWATER ACADEMY (MASS.)
Leach, Daniel Dyer
Phillips, Willard
Pierce, Edward Lillie
Pierce, Henry Lillie
Sanger, George Partridge
Shedd, Joel Herbert
BRIDGEWATER STATE NORMAL
  SCHOOL (MASS.)
Cushman, Joseph Augustine
O'Brien, Robert Lincoln
BRIDGTON
Grant, George Barnard
Hamlin, Charles
Hamlin, Cyrus
Hawkins, Dexter Arnold
Ingalls, Melville Ezra
BRIGHAM YOUNG UNIVERSITY
  (UTAH)
Smith, George Albert
Smoot, Reed Owen
BRIMMER SCHOOL (BOSTON,
  MASS.)
Ames, James Barr
Crane, William Henry
Milmore, Martin
Pearce, Charles Sprague
Sullivan, Louis Henri
BRISTOL ACADEMY (MASS.)
Baylies, Francis
Brownell, Thomas Church
Hill, George Handel
Shaw, Oliver
BROOKLYN LAW SCHOOL (N.Y.)
Reynolds, Quentin James
BROOKLYN POLYTECHNIC INSTITUTE
  (N.Y.)
Adams, James Truslow
Babcock, Washington Irving
Bowen, Herbert Wolcott
Brown, Alexander Ephraim
Canfield, James Hulme
Chambers, Robert William
Davenport, Charles Benedict
Dickinson, Robert Latou
Doubleday, Frank Nelson
Dwight, Arthur Smith

Field, Herbert Haviland
Flint, Charles Ranlett
Ford, Worthington Chauncey
Fowler, Russell Story
Gherardi, Bancroft
Gibson, William Hamilton
Hamilton, Clayton
Hampden, Walter
Hegeman, John Rogers
Heinze, Frederick Augustus
Hill, Frederick Trevor
Jelliffe, Smith Ely
Jenks, Tudor Storrs
Johnston, Alexander
Knapp, Joseph Palmer
Loomis, Charles Battell
Low, Seth
Melville, George Wallace
Pilcher, Paul Monroe
Post, Augustus
Raymond, Rossiter Worthington
Scollard, Clinton
Sloan, Alfred Pritchard, Jr.
Speir, Samuel Fleet
Waller, Frederic
Wegmann, Edward
Wood, James J.

BROOKS MILITARY ACADEMY (OHIO)
Gregory, Thomas Barger

BROWN UNIVERSITY (R.I.)
Abbott, Samuel Warren
Adams, Jasper
Alden, Joseph
Allen, Edgar
Allen, Paul
Allen, Philip
Allen, Zachariah
Ames, Oliver, 1831–1895
Ames, Samuel
Andrews, Elisha Benjamin
Angell, George Thorndike
Angell, James Burrill
Angell, Joseph Kinnicutt
Anthony, Henry Bowen
Anthony, William Arnold
Arnold, Samuel Greene
Barbour, Clarence Augustus
Bates, Samuel Penniman
Benedict, David
Bennett, Charles Edwin
Binney, Amos
Bishop, Nathan
Blake, John Lauris
Blaustein, David
Boyce, James Petigru
Brayton, Charles Ray
Brightman, Edgar Sheffield
Brockett, Linus Pierpont
Brokmeyer, Henry C.
Bronson, Walter Cochrane
Brooks, Erastus
Brown, Nicholas, 1769–1841
Brownell, Thomas Church
Burgess, Alexander
Burgess, George
Burrage, Henry Sweetser
Burrill, James
Carpenter, Edmund Janes
Caswell, Alexis
Chafee, Zechariah, Jr.

Chapin, Charles Value
Chaplin, Jeremiah
Claflin, William
Clark, John Bates
Clifford, John Henry
Coghill, George Ellett
Colvin, Stephen Sheldon
Congdon, Charles Taber
Corthill, Elmer Lawrence
Cox, Samuel Sullivan
Cushing, Josiah Nelson
Davis, Harvey Nathaniel
Dexter, Henry Martyn
Dinau, Jeremiah Lewis
Dodge, Ebenezer
Durfee, Job
Durfee, Thomas
Durrett, Reuben Thomas
Ewing, Thomas
Fairfield, Sumner Lincoln
Faunce, William Herbert Perry
Fenner, James
Field, Fred Tarbell
Fish, Carl Russell
Fisher, George Park
Fisher, John Dix
Fisk, Wilbur
Fletcher, James Cooley
Foss, Sam Walter
Foster, Lafayette Sabine
Foster, Theodore
Francis, John Brown
French, Edwin Davis
Frieze, Henry Simmons
Fryer, Douglas Henry
Gale, Elbridge
Gaston, William, 1820–1894
Gifford, Sanford Robinson
Gilmore, Joseph Henry
Going, Jonathan
Gorky, Arshile
Green, Theodore Francis
Greene, Albert Gorton
Greene, George Washington
Greene, Samuel Stillman
Guild, Reuben Aldridge
Hallett, Benjamin Franklin
Halsey, Thomas Lloyd
Harkness, Albert
Harris, Caleb Fiske
Hay, John Milton
Herreshoff, James Brown
Heywood, Ezra Hervey
Hill, Nathaniel Peter
Himes, Joshua Vaughan
Holbrook, John Edwards
Holley, Alexander Lyman
Holmes, Ezekiel
Holmes, John
Hood, Raymond Mathewson
Hope, John
Hoppin, Augustus
Horr, George Edwin
Howe, Mark Anthony de Wolfe
Howe, Samuel Gridley
Hughes, Charles Evans
Hunter, William
Jenckes, Thomas Allen
Jewett, Charles Coffin
Jones, John Taylor
Judson, Adoniram
Judson, Adoniram Brown

Judson, Edward
Keen, William Williams
King, Charles William
King, Samuel Ward
Kingsbury, John
Knight, Henry Cogswell
Krause, Allen Kramer
Law, Andrew
Leach, Daniel Dyer
Leland, Waldo Gifford
Lincoln, John Larkin
Lothrop, George Van Ness
MacAlister, James
McCarthy, Charles
Magill, Edward Hicks
Mann, Horace
Marcy, William Learned
Maxcy, Jonathan
Maxcy, Virgil
Meiklejohn, Alexander
Messer, Asa
Metcalf, Theron
Miles, Henry Adolphus
Montgomery, David Henry
Moody, (Arthur Edson) Blair
Morton, Marcus, 1784–1864
Morton, Marcus, 1819–1891
Mowry, William Augustus
Munro, Dana Carleton
Murray, James Ormsbee
Nason, Elias
Nichols, Charles Lemuel
Nott, Eliphalet
Olney, Richard
Osterhout, Winthrop John Vanleuven
Park, Edwards Amasa
Peck, George Washington
Peckham, Stephen Farnum
Perry, William Stevens
Pierce, Edward Lillie
Pierce, John Davis
Pond, Enoch
Prentice, George Dennison
Randall, Samuel
Read, John Meredith, 1837–1896
Reed, David
Reynolds, Quentin James
Richmond, John Wilkes
Robinson, Christopher
Robinson, Ezekiel Gilman
Rockefeller, John Davison, Jr.
Rockwell, George Lincoln
Rogers, William Augustus
Russell, Jonathan
Sears, Barnas
Sharp, Dallas Lore
Sheldon, Charles Monroe
Shepard, Charles Upham
Smith, Gerald Birney
Smith, Roswell
Staples, William Read
Stiness, John Henry
Stone, William Leete
Tallmadge, James
Thayer, Eli
Thayer, John Milton
Thayer, William Makepeace
Thurber, Charles
Thurston, Robert Henry
Upton, George Putnam

Upton, Winslow
Utley, George Burwell
Varnum, James Mitchell
Ward, Joseph
Ward, Samuel, 1756–1832
Wayland, Francis, 1826–1904
Wheaton, Frank
Wheaton, Henry
Wheeler, Benjamin Ide
Whitman, Ezekiel
Williams, David Rogerson
Williamson, William Durkee
Wilson, George Grafton
Winkler, Edwin Theodore
Woolley, Mary Emma
Graduate Study
Allen, Edgar
Brightman, Edgar Sheffield
Coghill, George Ellett
Colvin, Stephen Sheldon
Davis, Harvey Nathaniel
Green, Theodore Francis
Howell, David
Krause, Allen Kramer
Magill, Edward Hicks
Maxcy, Virgil
Meiklejohn, Alexander
Osterhout, Winthrop John Van-
  leuven
Rogers, William Augustus
Thurber, Charles
Thurston, Robert Henry
Wilson, George Grafton
Woolley, Mary Emma
Medicine
Allen, Zachariah
Bartlett Elisha
Green, Asa
March, Alden
BRYANT AND STRATTON BUSINESS
  COLLEGE (ILL.)
Sabath, Adolph J.
BRYN MAWR COLLEGE (PA.)
Allinson, Anne Crosby Emery
Balch, Emily Greene
Dunbar, (Helen) Flanders
Hamilton, Edith
Helburn, Theresa
Hepburn, Katharine Houghton
Reilly, Marion
Speer, Emma Bailey
Strong, Anna Louise
Tiffany, Katrina Brandes Ely
Graduate Study
Akeley, Mary Leonore
Allinson, Anne Crosby Emery
Hepburn, Katharine Houghton
Kenyon, Josephine Hemenway
BUCKNELL UNIVERSITY (PA.)
Bliss, Tasker Howard
Frear, William
Golder, Frank Alfred
Gregg, David McMurtrie
Hall, Thomas
Hill, David Jayne
Mathewson, Christopher
  ("Christy")
Potter, Charles Francis
Rawlinson, Frank Joseph
Thomas, Norman Mattoon
Graduate Study
Hill, David Jayne

Potter, Charles Francis
BUDAPEST ACADEMY OF MUSIC
  (HUNGARY)
Reiner, Fritz
BUDAPEST INSTITUTE OF TECH-
  NOLOGY (HUNGARY)
Szilard, Leo
BUFFALO MEDICAL COLLEGE (N.Y.)
Brush, Edward Nathaniel
Myer, Albert James
Smith, Stephen
BURLESON COLLEGE (TEX.)
Neyland, Robert Reese, Jr.
BURR AND BURTON SEMINARY
  (MANCHESTER, VT.)
Cheney, John Vance
Roe, Edward Payson
Sheldon, William Evarts
Spring, Leverett Wilson
BUTLER UNIVERSITY (IND.)
Cope, Arthur Clay
Randall, James Garfield

CALIFORNIA INSTITUTE OF TECH-
  NOLOGY
Acosta, Bertram Blanchard
  ("Bert")
Carlson, Chester Floyd
Jewett, Frank Baldwin
Kirkwood, John Gamble
Graduate Study
Millikan, Clark Blanchard
CALIFORNIA STATE NORMAL
  SCHOOL AT CHICO
Adams, Annette Abbott
CAMBRIDGE HIGH AND LATIN
  SCHOOL (MASS.)
Bixby, James Thompson
Bôcher, Maxime
Greene, Charles Ezra
Holland, Clifford Milburn
Merrill, George Edmands
Nelson, Charles Alexander
Peirce Charles Sanders
CAMBRIDGE UNIVERSITY (ENGLAND)
Bateman, Harry
Boyd, James
Brown, Ernest William
Buchman, Frank Nathan Daniel
Carter, Boake
Child, Robert
Duranty, Walter
Field, Marshall, III
McDougall, William
Morley, Frank
Peabody, Endicott
Rainsford, William Stephen
Seymour, Charles
Whitehead, Alfred North
Graduate Study
Brown, Ernest William
Farrand, Livingston
McDougall, William
Morley, Frank
Osborn, Henry Fairfield
Russell, Henry Norris
Whitehead, Alfred North
CANANDAIGUA ACADEMY (N.Y.)
Ball, Frank Clayton
Ball, George Alexander
Bennett, Nathaniel
Chesebrough, Caroline

Clarke, John Mason
Emery, Charles Edward
Rafter, George W.
Rankine, William Birch
Squires, Herbert Goldsmith
CANISIUS COLLEGE (N.Y.)
Odenbach, Frederick Louis
CAPITAL UNIVERSITY (OHIO)
Loy, Matthias
Norelius, Eric
Piatt, John James
Schodde, George Henry
Short, Sidney Howe
CARLETON COLLEGE (MINN.)
Brown, Carleton
Burton, Marion Le Roy
Butler, Pierce
Carson, Jack
Dickinson, Edwin De Witt
Edwards, Everett Eugene
Eklund, Carl Robert
Holmes Bayard Taylor
Lundeen, Ernest
Pye, Watts Orson
Veblen, Thorstein Bunde
CARLETON COLLEGE (MO.)
Asbury, Herbert
CARLISLE INDIAN SCHOOL (PA.)
Bender, Charles Albert
  ("Chief")
Thorpe, James Francis
CARNEGIE INSTITUTE OF TECH-
  NOLOGY (PA.)
Wilson, Charles Erwin
Graduate Study
Robinson, Edward Stevens
CARROLL COLLEGE (WIS.)
Curtin, Jeremiah
Davis, Cushman Kellogg
Fairchild, Lucius
Showerman, Grant
Watson, Andrew
CARSON-NEWMAN COLLEGE
  (TENN.)
Reece, Brazilla Carroll
Tilson, John Quillin
CASE INSTITUTE OF TECHNOLOGY
  (OHIO)
Stearns, Frank Ballou
CASE SCHOOL OF APPLIED SCIENCE
  (OHIO)
Bevier, Isabel
Dow, Herbert Henry
East, Edward Murray
CASE-WESTERN RESERVE UNIVERSI-
  TY (OHIO)
Hughes, Rupert
Graduate Study
Hughes, Rupert
CATHOLIC UNIVERSITY OF AMERICA
  (D.C.)
Dietz, Peter Ernest
Dowling, Austin
Duffy, Francis Patrick
Grady, Henry Francis
Tansill, Charles Callan
Graduate Study
Burke, John Joseph
Haas, Francis Joseph
Hayes, Patrick Joseph
Johnson, George
Kerby, William Joseph

Michel, Virgil George
Nieuwland, Julius Arthur
Ryan, John Augustine
Tansill, Charles Callan
CATHOLIC UNIVERSITY OF LOUVAIN (BELGIUM)
Graduate Study
  Kerby, William Joseph
CATHOLIC UNIVERSITY OF SANTIAGO (CHILE)
  De Cuevas, Marquis
CAZENOVIA SEMINARY (N.Y.)
  Andrews, Charles
  Andrews, Edward Gayer
  Armsur, Philip Danforth
  Blair, Austin
  Bowman, Thomas
  Burdick, Francis Marion
  Clarke, William Newton
  Condon, Thomas
  Cone, Orello
  Cooper, Sarah Brown Ingersoll
  Davis, Nathan Smith
  Dexter, Wirt
  Fairchild, Charles Stebbins
  Fiske, Daniel Willard
  Longyear, John Munroe
  Mann, Newton
  Newman, John Philip
  Peck, Jesse Truesdell
  Remington, Philo
  Slocum, Henry Warner
  Stanford, Leland
  Stranahan, James Samuel Thomas
  Throop, Montgomery Hunt
  Underwood, Lucien Marcus
  Vail, Stephen Montfort
CENTENARY COLLEGE (N.J.)
  McClenahan, Howard
CENTRAL COLLEGE (MO.)
  Craighead, Edwin Boone
  Hendrix, Joseph Clifford
  Hirth, William Andrew
  Parker, Edwin Brewington
  Shafroth, John Franklin
  Stuart, John Todd
  Vest, George Graham
  Wickliffe, Robert Charles
  Yandell, David Wendell
CENTRAL HIGH SCHOOL (PHILA.)
  Abbett, Leon
  Allen, Harrison
  Ashburner, Charles Albert
  Atkinson, William Biddle
  Bell, James Stroud
  Brown, William Henry
  Cochrane, Henry Clay
  Cohen, Jacob Da Silva Solis
  Cramp, Charles Henry
  Davidson, George
  Ffoulke, Charles Mather
  Gabb, William More
  Gihon, Albert Leary
  Hartranft, Chester David
  Houston, Edwin James
  Jackson, Abraham Reeves
  Leffmann, Henry
  Macfarlane, Charles William
  Mills, Charles Karsner
  Mitchell, James Tyndale
  Murphy, Dominic Ignatius

Newhouse, Samuel
Oliver, Charles Augustus
Patterson, Robert Mayne
Pattison, Robert Emory
Potts, Charles Sower
Pyle, Walter Lytle
Rhees, William Jones
Rice, Edwin Wilbur
Rogers, John Ignatius
Rogers, Robert William
Smith, Eugene Allen
Smyth, Albert Henry
Stockton, Frank Richard
Sulzberger, Cyrus Lindauer
Sulzberger, Mayer
Townsend, George Alfred
Tryon, George Washington
Tyson, James
Widener, Peter Arrell Brown
Woodruff, Charles Edward
Woodward, Joseph Janvier
Yerkes, Charles Tyson
CENTRAL NORMAL COLLEGE (ILL.)
  Thomas, (John William) Elmer
CENTRAL NORMAL COLLEGE (IND.)
  Menninger, Charles Frederick
CENTRAL NORMAL SCHOOL (IND.)
  Terman, Lewis Madison
CENTRAL TURKEY COLLEGE (TURKEY)
  Gregory, Menas Sarkas Boulgourjian
CENTRE COLLEGE (KY.)
  Baird, Samuel John
  Birney, James
  Blackburn, Joseph Clay Styles
  Boyle, Jeremiah Tilford
  Breckinridge, John Cabell
  Breckinridge, William Campbell Preston
  Brown, John Young
  Buford, Abraham, 1820–1884
  Burchard, Samuel Dickinson
  Crittenden, Thomas Theodore
  Duke, Basil Wilson
  Green, Lewis Warner
  Hall, William Whitty
  Harlan, John Marshall
  Holt, Joseph
  Hume, Edgar Erskine
  Jackson, John Davies
  Johnston, William Preston
  Lewis, Joseph Horace
  McCreary, James Bennett
  McMillin Alvin Nugent ("Bo")
  Magoffin, Beriah
  Martin, William Thompson
  Matthews, Claude
  Maury, Francis Fontaine
  Norton, Elijah Hise
  Peay, Austin
  Philips, John Finis
  Rice, Nathan Lewis
  Stanley, Augustus Owsley
  Stevenson, Adlai Ewing
  Vinson, Fred(erick) Moore
  West, Andrew Fleming
Graduate Study
  Hume, Edgar Erskine
CHAFFEE JUNIOR COLLEGE (CAL.)
  Jones, Lindley Armstrong ("Spike")

CHARLESTON COLLEGE (S.C.)
  Boyce, James Petigru
  Frémont, John Charles
  Hayne, Paul Hamilton
  Jacobs, William Plumer
  Johnson, Joseph
  Kinlock, Robert Alexander
  Logan, Thomas Muldrup, 1808–1876
CHATHAM COLLEGE (PA.)
  Carson, Rachel Louise
CHAUNCY HALL SCHOOL (MASS.)
  Bacon, Henry
  Bumstead, Freeman Josiah
  Guild, Curtis, 1860–1915
  Jarves, James Jackson
  Lovett, Robert Williamson
  Riddle, George Peabody
  Ropes, John Codman
  Thayer, Abbott Handerson
  Towne, John Henry
CHEROKEE MALE SEMINARY (OKLA.)
  Hastings, William Wirt
CHESTER ACADEMY
  Burnett, Henry Lawrence
  Evans, Warren Felt
  Forwood, William Henry
  Grant, Lewis Addison
CHICAGO ACADEMY OF FINE ARTS
  Hokinson, Helen Elna
CHICAGO ART INSTITUTE
  Barnard, George Grey
  Chaplin, Ralph Hosea
  Curry, John Steuart
  Fraser, James Earle
  Frieseke, Frederick Carl
  Harshe, Robert Bartholow
  Howey, Walter Crawford
CHICAGO COLLEGE OF LAW
  Levinson, Salmon Oliver
  Sabath, Adolph J.
CHICAGO COLLEGE OF MEDICINE AND SURGERY
  Sullivan, Harry Stack
CHICAGO COLLEGE OF PHARMACY
  Breasted, James Henry
CHICAGO CONSERVATORY OF MUSIC
  Henderson, Ray
CHICAGO-KENT COLLEGE OF LAW
  Horner, Henry
CHICAGO-KENT SCHOOL OF LAW
  Dawson, William Levi
CHICAGO MEDICAL COLLEGE
  Billings, Frank
  Holmes, Bayard Taylor
  Quine, William Edward
  Senn, Nicholas
CHICAGO THEOLOGICAL SCHOOL
  Gates, Caleb Frank
CHICAGO THEOLOGICAL SEMINARY
  Breasted, James Henry
  Davis, Jerome Dean
  Greene, Daniel Crosby
  Lyman, Albert Josiah
  McCulloch, Oscar Carleton
CHRISTIAN COLLEGE (CAL.)
  Markham, Edwin
CINCINNATI ART SCHOOL
  Hill, Grace Livingston

CINCINNATI COLLEGE
Chase, Salmon Portland
Durbin, John Price
Fosdick, William Whiteman
Lytle, William Haines
Pendleton, George Hunt
Pugh, George Ellis
Law
Butterworth, Benjamin
Cannon, Joseph Gurney
Case, Leonard
Clark, Champ
Crawford, Samuel Johnson
Dawson, Thomas Cleland
Day, James Gamble
Denver, James William
Edgerton, Sidney
Ewing, Thomas
Goebel, William
Hine, Charles de Lano
Holmes, Daniel Henry
Hoyt, John Wesley
Lawrence, William, 1819–1899
Longworth, Nicholas
Morton, Oliver Perry
Noble John Willock
Noyes, Edward Follansbee
Sherwood, Thomas Adiel
Storer, Bellamy
Swayne, Wager
Taft, William Howard
CINCINNATI COLLEGE OF MEDICINE
AND SURGERY
Crumbine, Samuel Jay
CINCINNATI LAW SCHOOL
Crosser, Robert
Dawes, Charles Gates
Pomerene, Atlee
Van Devanter, Willis
CLAFLIN UNIVERSITY (S.C.)
Abbott, Robert Sengstacke
CLARK UNIVERSITY (MASS.)
Dibble, Roy Floyd
Fryer, Douglas Henry
Goddard, Robert Hutchings
Harris, Rollin Arthur
Graduate Study
Albee, Ernest
Burk, Frederic Lister
Calkins, Mary Whiton
Chamberlain, Alexander Francis
Chase, Harry Woodburn
Duncan, Robert Kennedy
Frazier, Edward Franklin
Fryer, Douglas Henry
Gesell, Arnold Lucius
Goddard, Henry Herbert
Jordan, Edwin Oakes
Odum, Howard Washington
Smith, Theodate Louise
Starbuck, Edwin Diller
Terman, Lewis Madison
CLEMSON COLLEGE (S.C.)
Cohen, Octavus Roy
Gossett, Benjamin Brown
CLEVELAND MEDICAL COLLEGE
Elwell, John Johnson
Goodrich, Benjamin Franklin
Newberry, John Strong
CLEVELAND SCHOOL OF ART
(OHIO)
Burchfield, Charles Ephraim

CLINTON LIBERAL INSTITUTE (N.Y.)
Gage, Matilda Joslyn
McEntee, Jervis
Scollard Clinton
Skinner, Charles Rufus
Stanford, Leland
COAST GUARD ACADEMY (N.Y.)
Waesche, Russell Randolph
COBB DIVINITY SCHOOL (MAINE)
Hayes, Edward Carey
COE COLLEGE (IOWA)
Reed, James Alexander
Ross, Edward Alsworth
COKESBURY INSTITUTE (S.C.)
Bass, William Capers
Capers, Ellison
De Bow, James Dunwoody
Brownson
Gary, Martin Witherspoon
McTyeire, Holland Nimmons
Pratt, John
White, Samuel
COLBY COLLEGE (MAINE)
Anderson, Martin Brewer
Brooks, James
Butler, Benjamin Franklin, 1818
–1893
Day, Holman Francis
Dearing, John Lincoln
Dingley, Nelson
Emery, Stephen Albert
Hinds, Asher Crosby
Holden, Liberty Emery
Howard, Volney Erskine
Lapham, William Berry
Lord, Herbert Mayhew
Lovejoy, Elijah Parish
McNulty, John Augustine
Marble, Albert Prescott
Mathews, Shailer
Mathews, William
Merriam, Henry Clay
Mitchell, Edward Cushing
Morrill, Lot Myrick
Paine, Henry Warren
Plaistead, Harris Merrill
Scammon, Jonathan Young
Sheldon, Edward Stevens
Small, Albion Woodbury
Smith, Charles Henry, 1827–
1902
Smith, George Otis
Tripp, Bartlett
Graduate Study
Smith, Charles Henry, 1827–
1902
COLGATE UNIVERSITY
Avery, Oswald Theodore
Bonney, Charles Carroll
Brigham, Albert Perry
Brown, John Newton
Burroughs, John Curtis
Carpenter, Stephen Haskins
Church, Pharcellus
Clarke, William Newton
Davis, Oscar King
Fosdick, Harry Emerson
Galpin, Charles Josiah
Hindus, Maurice Gerschon
Hughes, Charles Evans
Judson, Edward
Knapp, William Ireland

Landon, Melville de Lancey
Loomis, Elmer Howard
Orton, Harlow South
Rathbone, Justus Henry
Stillman, Thomas Edgar
Taylor, Benjamin Franklin
Tupper, Henry Allen
Utley, George Burwell
Williams, Frank Martin
Graduate Study
Davis, Oscar King
Fosdick, Harry Emerson
Galpin, Charles Josiah
Hindus, Maurice Gerschon
Schmidt, Nathaniel
Theology
Brigham, Albert Perry
Clarke, William Newton
Johnson, Franklin
Raymond, John Howard
COLLEGE DE GENEVE (SWITZER-
LAND)
Bacon, Benjamin Wisner
COLLEGE OF CHARLESTON (S.C.)
De Bow, James Dunwoody
Brownson
Fraser, Charles
Furman, James Clement
Gildersleeve, Basil Lanneau
Girardeau, John Lafayette
Lewisohn, Ludwig
McCrady, Edward
Maybank, Burnet Rhett
Middleton, Nathaniel Russell
Miles, William Porcher
Mills, Robert, 1781–1855
Mood, Francis Asbury
Rivers, Lucius Mendel
Silcox, Ferdinand Augustus
Simonton, Charles Henry
Smith, Henry Augustus Middle-
ton
Smith, John Lawrence
Tiedeman, Christopher Gus-
tavus
Trescot, William Henry
Waring, Julius Waties
Graduate Study
Lewisohn, Ludwig
Mood, Francis Asbury
COLLEGE OF EMPORIA (KANS.)
Pemberton, Brock
COLLEGE OF MEDICAL EVANGE-
LISTS (CAL.)
Price, George Edward
McCready
COLLEGE OF NEW JERSEY (See
PRINCETON UNIVERSITY)
COLLEGE OF NEW ROCHELLE
(N.Y.)
Kilgallen, Dorothy Mae
COLLEGE OF PHARMACY OF NEW
YORK
Kunze, Richard Ernest
Mayer, Emil
Ziegler, William
COLLEGE OF PHILADELPHIA (See
UNIVERSITY OF PENNSYLVANIA)
COLLEGE OF PHYSICIANS AND SUR-
GEONS (MD.)
Hunt, Reid

COLLEGE OF PHYSICIANS AND SUR-
GEONS (See COLUMBIA UNI-
VERSITY,
COLLEGE OF ST. FRANCIS XAVIER
Malone, Dudley Field
COLLEGE OF ST. MARY OF THE
SPRINGS (OHIO)
McCormick, Anne Elizabeth
O'Hare
COLLEGE OF ST. XAVIER (N.Y.) See
also ST. FRANCIS XAVIER COL-
LEGE)
Campbell, Thomas Joseph
Crimmins, John Daniel
Drumgoole, John Christopher
Duffy, Francis Patrick
Edebohls, George Michael
Herbermann, Charles George
Keane, James John
McFaul, James Augustine
Moeller, Henry
Pardow, William O'Brien
Tierney, Richard Henry
Wigger, Winand Michael
COLLEGE OF SOUTH CAROLINA
(See UNIVERSITY OF SOUTH
CAROLINA)
COLLEGE OF THE CITY OF NEW
YORK
Abbe, Cleveland
Agramonte y Simoni, Aristides
Bangs, Francis Nehemiah
Baruch, Bernard Mannes
Blackton, James Stuart
Bloomfield, Meyer
Borchard, Edwin Montefiore
Bowker, Richard Rogers
Brill, Abraham Arden
Brill, Nathan Edwin
Brooks, Elbridge Streeter
Brown, George, 1823–1892
Carvalho, Solomon Solis
Claflin, John
Coakley, Cornelius Godfrey
Cohen, Felix Solomon
Cohen, Morris Raphael
Corwin, Edward Tanjore
Croly, Herbert David
Damrosch, Frank Heino
Davidson, Israel
Dean, Bashford
Elsberg, Charles Albert
Epstein, Philip G.
Evans, William Thomas
Fackler, David Parks
Fletcher, Robert
Frankfurter, Felix
Glass, Montague Marsden
Goethals, George Washington
Goldberger, Joseph
Goldmark, Rubin
Grau, Maurice
Green, Gabriel Marcus
Grinnell, Henry Walton
Hackett, James Keteltas
Harland, Henry
Hays, Arthur Garfield
Hecht, Selig
Hirsch, Isaac Seth
Jackson, George Thomas
Jackson, Samuel Macauley
Jordan, Virgil Justin

Jordon, William George
Kaempffert, Waldemar Bern-
hard
Kohler, Max James
Leipziger, Henry Marcus
Lewis, Oscar
Libman, Emanuel
Lowie, Robert Harry
McAdie, Alexander George
McMaster, John Bach
Maslow, Abraham H.
Maybeck, Bernard Ralph
Mayer, Emil
Morgenthau, Henry
Moses, Montrose Jonas
Moss, Frank
Newman, Barnett
Olcott, Eben Erskine
Park, William Hallock
Pasvolsky, Leo
Patri, Angelo
Pope, John Russell
Post, George Edward
Radin, Max
Radin, Paul
Remsen, Ira
Rice, George Samuel
Roberts, William Henry
Rosenberg, Julius
Rubin, Isidor Clinton
Schlesinger, Frank
Schultz, Henry
Shahn, Benjamin ("Ben")
Shepard, Edward Morse
Sinclair, Upton Beall, Jr.
Spier, Leslie
Spingarn, Joel Elias
Spitzka, Edward Anthony
Spitzka, Edward Charles
Steinman, David Barnard
Steuer, Max David
Stieglitz, Alfred
Stillman, Thomas Edgar
Sturgis, Russell
Taylor, Bert Leston
Taylor, Stevenson
Tilton, Theodore
Timme, Walter
Towne, Charles Hanson
Tremain, Henry Edwin
Tuthill, William Burnet
Untermyer, Samuel
Veiller, Lawrence Turnure
Viereck, George Sylvester
Wagner, Robert Ferdinand
Weir, Robert Fulton
Wheeler, Everett Pepperrell
Wight, Peter Bonnett
Wise, Stephen Samuel
Wolheim, Louis Robert
Woodruff, Lorande Loss
Graduate Study
Coakley, Cornelius Godfrey
McAdie, Alexander George
COLLEGE OF THE PACIFIC (CAL.)
Kuykendall, Ralph Simpson
Widney, Joseph Pomeroy
COLLEGE OF WILLIAM AND MARY
(VA.)
Anderson, Richard Clough
Archer, William Segar
Barbour, Philip Pendleton

Barry, William Taylor
Bibb, George Mortimer
Blair, John, 1687–1771
Blair, John, 1732–1800
Bland, Richard
Bloxham, William Dunnington
Brandon, Gerard Chittocque
Braxton, Carter
Breckenridge, James
Breckinridge, John, 1760–1806
Brown, James, 1766–1835
Brown, John, 1757–1837
Cabell, James Branch
Cabell, Joseph Carrington
Cabell, Samuel Jordan
Cabell, William H.
Cary, Archibald
Chandler, Julian Alvin Carroll
Claiborne, William Charles
Coles
Cocke, John Hartwell
Coke, Richard
Coles, Edward
Crittenden, John Jordan
Croghan, George, 1791–1849
Crump, William Wood
Dabney, Thomas Smith Grego-
ry
Dearborn, Henry Alexander
Sammell
Dew, Thomas Roderick
Garrett, William Robertson
Gilmer, Francis Walker
Greenhow, Robert
Hardy, Samuel
Harrison, Benjamin, 1726–1791
Henley, Robert
Hope, James Barron
Innes, James
Jefferson, Thomas
Johnson, Chapman
Jones, John Winston
Lee, Henry, 1787–1837
Leigh, Benjamin Watkins
Littlepage, Lewis
McRae, Duncan Kirkland
Madison, James, 1749–1812
Mason, Stevens Thomson, 1760
–1803
Mercer, James
Mercer, John Francis
Minor, Benjamin Blake
Minor, Lucian
Monroe, James
Munford, William
Nelson, Hugh
Nelson, Roger
Newton, Thomas, 1768–1847
Nicholas, George
Nicholas, John
Nicholas, Philip Norborne
Nicholas, Robert Carter
Nicholas, Wilson Cary
Page, John
Plater, George
Pleasants, James
Pleasants, John Hampden
Randolph, Alfred Magill
Randolph, Edmund, 1753–1813
Randolph, Edmund, 1819–1861
Randolph, Sir John
Randolph, Peyton

Randolph, Thomas Mann
Rives, William Cabell
Roane, Spencer
Robertson, John
Robertson, Thomas Bolling
Robertson, Wyndham
Robinson, John
Robinson Moncure
Rogers, James Blythe
Rogers, William Barton
Ruffin, Edmund
Scott, Winfield
Short, William
Smith, Daniel
Smith, John Augustine
Stanard, William Glover
Staples, Walter Redd
Stevenson, Andrew
Stuart, Alexander Hugh
  Holmes
Stuart, Archibald
Taliaferro, William Booth
Taylor, John
Taylor, John Louis
Tazewell, Henry
Tazewell, Littleton Waller
Thomson, John, 1776–1799
Todd, Charles Stewart
Tucker, George
Tucker, Henry St. George
Tucker, Nathaniel Beverley
Tucker, St. George
Tyler, John, 1747–1813
Tyler, John, 1790–1862
Tyler, Robert
Walker, Thomas
Warrington, Lewis
Washington, Bushrod
Williams, Channing Moore
Wilson, James Southall
Wythe, George
Graduate Study
  Chandler, Julian Alvin Carroll
  Garrett, William Robertson
Law
  Cooke, John Rogers
  Ellis, Powhatan
  Marshall, John
  Mason, James Murray
  Ravenscroft, John Stark
COLLEGE OF WOOSTER (OHIO)
  Bevier, Isabel
  Boole, Ella Alexander
  Compton, Arthur Holly
  Compton, Karl Taylor
  Fairless, Benjamin F.
  Lyon, David Willard
  Notestein, Wallace
  Patrick, Hugh Talbot
  Thomas, Roland Jay
Graduate Study
  Bevier, Isabel
  Boole, Ella Alexander
  Compton, Karl Taylor
COLLEGE ST. GERVAIS (BELGIUM)
  Feininger, Lyonel (Charles Léo-
    nell Adrian)
COLLEGIATE INSTITUTE OF CHA-
  THAM (CANADA)
  Ross, James Delmage McKenzie

COLORADO COLLEGE
  Holt, Arthur Erastus
  Leverett, Frank
  Paul, Josephine Bay
COLORADO SCHOOL OF MINES
  Fairbanks, Douglas
COLORADO STATE COLLEGE OF
  AGRICULTURE
  Jones, Benjamin Allyn
COLUMBIA COLLEGE (S.C.)
  Peterkin, Julia Mood
COLUMBIAN UNIVERSITY (See
  GEORGE WASHINGTON UNI-
  VERSITY)
COLUMBIA THEOLOGICAL SEMINARY
  (S.C.)
  Jacobs, William Plumer
  McKinley, Carlyle
  Palmer, Benjamin Morgan
  Wilson, John Leighton
COLUMBIA UNIVERSITY (N.Y.)
  Adler, Felix
  Aggrey, James Emman Kwegyir
  Allen, Horatio
  Anthon, Charles
  Anthon, Charles Edward
  Anthon, John
  Armstrong, Edwin Howard
  Astor, John Jacob, 1822–1890
  Auchmuty, Richard Tylden
  Bangs, John Kendrick
  Barclay, Thomas
  Bard, Samuel
  Bard, William
  Beck, John Brodhead
  Beebe, (Charles) William
  Beer, George Louis
  Benson, Egbert
  Bergh, Henry
  Bethune, George Washington
  Blatchford, Samuel
  Blount, Willie
  Bolton, Henry Carrington
  Borchard, Edwin Montefiore
  Bourne, Randolph Silliman
  Bowden, John
  Brace, Donald Clifford
  Bridges, Calvin Blackman
  Browere, John Henri Isaac
  Brown, Margaret Wise
  Bruce, Archibald
  Bruce, Edward Bright
  Burrill, Alexander Mansfield
  Butler, Nicholas Murray
  Cahill, Holger
  Cardozo, Benjamin Nathan
  Carrington, Elaine Stern
  Carryl, Guy Wetmore
  Chambers, Whittaker
  Chapin, James Paul
  Chisolm, Alexander Robert
  Chotzinoff, Samuel
  Clinton, De Witt
  Cohn, Alfred Einstein
  Coit, Stanton
  Colby, Frank Moore
  Cole, George Watson
  Collins, Edward Trowbridge
  Cook, Walter Wheeler
  Cooper, Edward
  Copeland, Charles W.
  Coudert, Frederic René

Cowen, Joshua Lionel
Cruger, Henry
Cutting, Robert Fulton
Davies, Henry Eugene
De Koven, James
Delafield, John, 1786–1853
De Mille, Henry Churchill
De Peyster, John Watts
Dix, Morgan
Doremus, Robert Ogden
Drisler, Henry
Dunning, William Archibald
Duyckinck, Evert Augustus
Earhart, Amelia Mary
Earle, Edward Mead
Earle, Mortimer Lamson
Edman, Irwin
Ehninger, John Whetten
Ely, Richard Theodore
Emott, James, 1823–1884
Erskine, John
Fawcett, Edgar
Ferris, Isaac
Fish, Hamilton
Fish, Stuyvesant
Floy, James
Ford, Worthington Chauncey
Foulke, William Dudley
Fox, Dixon Ryan
Francis, John Wakefield
Francis, Samuel Ward
Frank, Lawrence Kelso
Franz, Shepherd Ivory
Fraser, Leon
Freeman, Joseph
Gehrig, Henry Louis
Gerard, James Watson
Gerard, James Watson
Gerry, Elbridge Thomas
Gibbs, Oliver Wolcott
Gillespie, William Mitchell
Goldenweiser, Alexander Alex-
  androvich
Goldenweiser, Emanuel Alex-
  ander
Goldwater, Sigismund Schulz
Gottheil, Richard James
  Horatio
Graham, John, 1774–1820
Griscom, Ludlow
Hackett, James Henry
Haight, Charles Coolidge
Hamilton, Alexander, 1757–
  1804
Hamilton, James Alexander
Hammerstein, Oscar, II
Harcourt, Alfred
Harris, Maurice Henry
Harrison, Fairfax
Harrison, Henry Sydnor
Hart, Lorenz Milton
Hastings, Thomas, 1860–1929
Havemeyer, William Frederick
Hayes, Carlton Joseph Huntley
Hays, Arthur Garfield
Hewitt, Abram Stevens
Hewitt, Peter Cooper
Hill, John Henry
Hine, Lewis Wickes
Hoffman, Charles Fenno
Hoffman, David Murray
Hoffman, Ogden

Holls, George Frederick William
Holt, Hamilton Bowen
Hopkins, Edward Washburn
Horton, Edward Everett, Jr.
Hosack, David
Hughes, James Langston
Hurd, John Codman
Hutton, Frederick Remsen
Irving, John Duer
Irving, John Treat
Irving, Pierre Munro
Irving, Roland Duer
Jackson, Abraham Valentine Williams
Jackson, George Thomas
Jay, John, 1745–1829
Jay, John, 1817–1894
Jay, Peter Augustus
Jenks, Tudor Storrs
Johnson, Allen
Jones, Samuel
Jones, William
Jones, William Alfred
Kearny, Philip
Kearny, Stephen Watts
Kellogg, Paul Underwood
Kelly, Edmond
Kemble, Gouverneur
Kemp, James Furman
Kemper, Jackson
Keppel, Frederick Paul
Kerouac, Jack
Kilmer, Alfred Joyce
Knapp, Joseph Palmer
Kobbé, Gustav
Kroeber, Alfred Louis
Langer, William
Lathrop, Francis Augustus
Lawrence, William Beach
Lee, Ivy Ledbetter
Lehman, Irving
Lenox, James
Leonard, Robert Josselyn
Linn, John Blair
Livingston, Robert R., 1746–1813
Lloyd, Henry Demarest
Locke, Bessie
Low, Seth
Ludlow, Thomas William
McCartee, Divie Bethune
McHale, Kathryn
McNulty, John Augustine
McVickar, John
McVickar, William Neilson
Macy, Valentine Everit
Mahan, Alfred Thayer
Mankiewicz, Herman Jacob
Marcus, Bernard Kent
Margolis, Max Leopold
Marshall, Henry Rutgers
Mason, John, 1858–1919
Mason, John Mitchell
Matthews, James Brander
Maxwell, Hugh
Mayer, Philip Frederick
Maynard, George William
Megrue, Roi Cooper
Merriam, Augustus Chapman
Merton, Thomas
Meyer, Annie Nathan

Milledoler, Philip
Mitchel, John Purroy
Mitchell, William, 1801–1886
Moisseiff, Leon Solomon
Moldenke, Richard George Gottlob
Moon, Parker Thomas
Moore, Benjamin
Moore, Clement Clarke
Moore, Nathaniel Fish
Morris, Gouverneur
Muller, Hermann Joseph
Murphy, Henry Cruse
Nadal, Ehrman Syme
Nies, James Buchanan
Oberholser, Harry Church
Odell, Benjamin Barker
Odell, George Clinton Densmore
Ogden, Thomas Ludlow
Olyphant, Robert Morrison
O'Mahoney, Joseph Christopher
Onderdonk, Benjamin Tredwell
Onderdonk, Henry
Onderdonk, Henry Ustick
Oppenheim, James
Osborn, Laughton
O'Sullivan, John Louis
Parsons, William Barclay
Partridge, William Ordway
Pasvolsky, Leo
Patterson, Richard Cunningham, Jr.
Peck, Harry Thurston
Plotz, Harry
Pollak, Walter Heilprin
Pott, Francis Lister Hawks
Price, Stephen
Provoost, Samuel
Pupin, Michael Idvorsky
Raymond, John Howard
Redman, Ben Ray
Rees, John Krom
Reinhardt, Ad
Renwick, Edward Sabine
Renwick, Henry Brevoort
Renwick, James, 1792–1863
Renwick, James, 1818–1895
Reynolds, Richard Samuel, Sr.
Richardson, Anna Euretta
Rives, George Lockhart
Robb, William Lispenard
Robinson, Henry Morton
Rosenblatt, Bernard Abraham
Rosewater, Victor
Rubinow, Isaac Max
Rutgers, Henry
Sachs, Julius
Sands, Robert Charles
Sapir, Edward
Satterlee, Henry Yates
Sayre, Reginald Hall
Schlesinger, Arthur Meier
Schuster, Max Lincoln
Schuyler, Robert Livingston
Sedgwick, Theodore, 1811–1859
Seligman, Edwin Robert Anderson
Seligman, Isaac Newton
Seymour, George Franklin
Shepherd, William Robert

Sherman, Frank Dempster
Shrady, Henry Merwin
Simkhovitch, Mary Melinda Kingsbury
Simon, Richard Leo
Slidell, John
Sloane, William Milligan
Smillie, Ralph
Smith, Bruce
Sokolsky,
Sparrow, William
Speck, Frank Gouldsmith
Spencer, Jesse Ames
Spingarn, Joel Elias
Steinhardt, Laurence Adolph
Stephens, John Lloyd
Stevens, John
Stewart, John Aikman
Stokes, Isaac Newton Phelps
Straus, Oscar Solomon
Strunsky, Simeon
Sulzberger, Arthur Hays
Sweeny, Peter Barr
Tate, George Henry Hamilton
Terhune, Albert Payson
Tompkins, Daniel D.
Troup, Robert
Trowbridge, Augustus
Trudeau, Edward Livingston
Tucker, Allen
Tuttle, Daniel Sylvester
Van Amringe, John Howard
Van Ness, William Peter
Verplanck, Julian Crommelin
Vethake, Henry
Vincent, Marvin Richardson
Vroom, Peter Dumont
Weil, Richard
Weiss, Soma
Wheeler, Schuyler Skaats
Whitehouse, Frederic Cope
Williams, William R.
Willis, Bailey
Wise, Stephen Samuel
Witthaus, Rudolph August
Woodford, Stewart Lyndon
Woodward, Augustus Brevoort
Worcester, Elwood
Youmans, William Jay
Young, John Clarke
Zilboorg, Gregory
Zinsser, Hans
Architecture
Atterbury, Grosvenor
Delano, William Adams
Hamlin, Talbot Faulkner
Ide, John Jay
Lamb, William Frederick
Porter, Arthur Kingsley
Graduate Study
Akeley, Mary Leonore
Alexander, Hartley Burr
Ames, Herman Vandenburg
Anderson, Benjamin McAlester
Andrews, Roy Chapman
Baker, Carl Lotus
Baker, Oliver Edwin
Bancroft, Frederic
Barber, Donn
Barrows, Alice Prentice
Beard, Charles Austin
Beary, Donald Bradford

Becket, Frederick Mark
Bell, Eric Temple
Benedict, Ruth Fulton
Bentley, Elizabeth Terrill
Borchard, Edwin Montefiore
Boyd, William Kenneth
Britton, Nathaniel Lord
Butler, Howard Crosby
Butler, Nicholas Murray
Calkins, Gary Nathan
Campbell, William
Chapin, James Paul
Clark, Felton Grandison
Clark, John Maurice
Coffman, Lotus Delta
Cohen, Morris Raphael
Cutting, Robert Fulton
Davidson, Israel
Dean, Bashford
Dennis, Alfred Lewis Pinneo
Dibble, Roy Floyd
Dobie, J(ames) Frank
Dodd, Bella Visono
Dowling, Noel Thomas
Dunbar, (Helen) Flanders
Dunning, William Archibald
Dyar, Harrison Gray
Earle, Edward Mead
Earle, Mortimer Lamson
Eastman, Max Forrester
Edman, Irwin
Emery, Henry Crosby
Erskine, John
Fairlie, John Archibald
Fauset, Jessie Redmon
Fisher, Dorothea Frances Canfield
Fleming, Walter Lynwood
Ford, Guy Stanton
Fox, Dixon Ryan
Franz, Shepherd Ivory
Fraser, Leon
Furst, Clyde Bowman
Garner, James Wilford
Gavin, Frank Stanton Burns
Gerard, James Watson
Gildersleeve, Virginia Crocheron
Goldenweiser, Alexander Alexandrovich
Gortner, Ross Aiken
Grady, Henry Francis
Graham, Edward Kidder
Green, Gabriel Marcus
Greenslet, Ferris
Hadas, Moses
Hamilton, Clayton
Hayes, Carlton Joseph Huntley
Hofstadter, Richard
Holt, Edwin Bissell
Hourwich, Isaac Aaronovich
Inglis, Alexander James
Irving, John Duer
Irwin, Elisabeth Antoinette
Jackson, Abraham Valentine Williams
Jelliffe, Smith Ely
Johnson, Douglas Wilson
Jones, Richard Foster
Jordan, Virgil Justin
Kagan, Henry Enoch
Kelly, Myra

Knauth, Oswald Whitman
Koch, Vivienne
Kohler, Max James
Kroeber, Alfred Louis
Krutch, Joseph Wood
La Farge, Oliver Hazard Perry
Lee, Porter Raymond
Leiserson, William Morris
Leonard, Robert Josselyn
Leonard, Sterling Andrus
Leonard, William Ellery
Lewis, Oscar
Lewisohn, Ludwig
Linton, Ralph
Lowie, Robert Harry
McBain, Howard Lee
McClung, Clarence Erwin
McHale, Kathryn
MacNair, Harley Farnsworth
Malin, Patrick Murphy
Margolis, Max Leopold
Marshall, Henry Rutgers
Martin, Anne Henrietta
Mathews, John Alexander
Matthew, William Diller
Matthews, Joseph Brown
Maxwell, Hugh
Menninger, William Claire
Merriam, Charles Edward, Jr.
Merton, Thomas
Millikan, Robert Andrews
Moldenke, Richard George Gottlob
Moon, Parker Thomas
Mott, Frank Luther
Muller, Hermann Joseph
Muzzey, David Saville
Nies, James Buchanan
Noble, Gladwyn Kingsley
Odell, George Clinton Densmore
Odum, Howard Washington
Ogburn, William Fielding
Olds, Leland
O'Sullivan, John Louis
Parker, Samuel Chester
Parsons, Elsie Worthington Clews
Patri, Angelo
Payne, Bruce Ryburn
Peck, Harry Thurston
Pegram, George Braxton
Phillips, Ulrich Bonnell
Pope, John Russell
Powell, Thomas Reed
Radin, Max
Radin, Paul
Reinhardt, Ad
Remington, William Walter
Renwick, Edward Sabine
Ripley, William Zebina
Robinson, Claude Everett
Robinson, Henry Morton
Rosenblatt, Bernard Abraham
Rosewater, Victor
Sachs, Julius
Sapir, Edward
Scarborough, Dorothy
Schlesinger, Arthur Meier
Schlesinger, Frank
Schultz, Henry
Schuyler, Robert Livingston

Seligman, Edwin Robert Anderson
Shepherd, William Robert
Sherman, Henry Clapp
Shotwell, James Thomson
Sinclair, Upton Beall, Jr.
Smith, Bruce
Smith, Preserved
Snyder, Edwin Reagan
Spahr, Charles Barzillai
Spaulding, Edward Gleason
Speck, Frank Gouldsmith
Spier, Leslie
Spingarn, Joel Elias
Steinhardt, Laurence Adolph
Steinman, David Barnard
Stimson, Julia Catherine
Stockard, Charles Rupert
Stong, Phil(lip Duffield)
Sullivan, Louis Robert
Sumner, Francis Bertody
Suzzallo, Henry
Swenson, David Ferdinand
Thorndike, Lynn
Van Doren, Carl Clinton
Van Doren, Irita Bradford
Voris, John Ralph
Whitcomb, Selden Lincoln
White, Israel Charles
Whitehouse, Frederic Cope
Wiechmann, Ferdinand Gerhard
Wilcox, Delos Franklin
Wise, Stephen Samuel
Wissler, Clark
Woodruff, Lorande Loss
Young, Stark
Zinsser, Hans

Journalism
Bromfield, Louis
Higgins, Marguerite
Liebling, Abbott Joseph
Richards, Vincent
Rosenfeld, Paul Leopold

Law
Astor, William Waldorf
Bancroft, Edgar Addison
Bassett, Edward Murray
Beer, Thomas
Bowen, Herbert Wolcott
Bowers, Lloyd Wheaton
Bruce, Edward Bright
Burlingham, Charles Culp
Byoir, Carl Robert
Cardozo, Benjamin Nathan
Chase, George
Clark, Walter
Cohen, Felix Solomon
Colby, Bainbridge
Colt, LeBaron Bradford
Cook, Walter Wheeler
Coudert, Frederic René
Crane, Frederick Evan
Crane, Thomas Frederick
Cravath, Paul Drennan
Cromwell, William Nelson
Crosby, Ernest Howard
De Forest, Robert Weeks
De Leon, Daniel
Dickinson, Jacob McGavock
Donovan, William Joseph
Dowling, Noel Thomas

Folger, Henry Clay
Foster, Roger Sherman Baldwin
Foulke, William Dudley
Fox, John William
Garfield, Harry Augustus
Garfield, James Rudolph
Goodnow, Frank Johnson
Grant, Madison
Grau, Maurice
Greenbaum, Edward Samuel
Grosvenor, Edwin Prescott
Guthrie, William Dameron
Hale, Frederick
Hall, Bolton
Hall, Isaac Hollister
Hoffman, David Murray
Holls, George Frederick William
Hornblower, William Butler
Hughes, Charles Evans
Ivins, William Mills
Jerome, William Travers
Joline, Adrian Hoffman
Kalisch, Samuel
Kelly, Edmond
Kobbé, Gustav
Kohler, Max James
Lea, Luke
Leffingwell, Russell Cornell
Lehman, Irving
Leipziger, Henry Marcus
Leupp, Francis Ellington
Lewisohn, Sam Adolph
Lexow, Clarence
Lowery, Woodbury
Mabie, Hamilton Wright
MacVeagh, Charles
MacVeagh, Franklin
Marshall, Louis, 1856–1929
Matthews, James Brander
Mitchell, Langdon Elwyn
Morgenthau, Henry
Morrow, Dwight Whitney
Nelson, Henry Loomis
Nicoll, De Lancey
O'Brien, Morgan Joseph
Osborne, James Walker
Phelps, William Walter
Pinchot, Amos Richards Eno
Polk, Frank Lyon
Pratt, James Bissett
Prince, Le Baron Bradford
Putnam, (George) Herbert
Rice, Charles Allen Thorndike
Rice, Isaac Leopold
Rives, George Lockhart
Roosevelt, Franklin Delano
Rosenblatt, Bernard Abraham
Saltus, Edgar Evertson
Schirmer, Rudolph Edward
Schuyler, Eugene
Smith, Edmund Munroe
Sterling, John William
Steuer, Max David
Stevens, Hiram Fairchild
Stevens, John
Stewart, William Rhinelander
Stone, Harlan Fiske
Straus, Oscar Solomon
Taft, Charles Phelps
Taft, Henry Waters
Taylor, Henry Osborn

Thurston, Lorrin Andrews
Tiedeman, Christopher Gustavus
Tremain, Henry Edwin
Untermyer, Samuel
Vanderbilt, Arthur T.
Van Dyke, John Charles
White, Stewart Edward
Whitney, Harry Payne
Wood, Charles Erskine Scott
Woolsey, John Munro
Medicine
Agnew, Cornelius Rea
Agramonte y Simoni, Aristides
Avery, Oswald Theodore
Beach, Wooster
Beard, George Miller
Beck, John Brodhead
Beck, Lewis Caleb
Beck, Theodric Romeyn
Brill, Abraham Arden
Brown, Frederic Tilden
Bruce, Archibald
Buck, Albert Henry
Buck, Gurdon
Buckley, Samuel Botsford
Bulkley, Lucius Duncan
Bull, William Tillinghast
Carnochan, John Murray
Chamberlain, Jacob
Chapin, Charles Value
Chapin, Henry Dwight
Cohn, Alfred Einstein
Cook, Frederick Albert
Cooke, Robert Anderson
Cooper, James Graham
Curtis, John Green
Dana, Charles Loomis
Delafield, Edward
Delafield, Francis
Duane, Alexander
Edebohls, George Michael
Elsberg, Charles Albert
Emerson, Haven
Ewing, James
Farrand, Livingston
Fletcher, William Baldwin
Foster, Frank Pierce
Fowler, Russell Story
Francis, John Wakefield
Gibbs, Oliver Wolcott
Gilbert, Rufus Henry
Goldsmith, Middleton
Gorrie, John
Greenhow, Robert
Gruening, Emil
Guthrie, Samuel
Halsted, William Stewart
Hamilton, Allan McLane
Hamilton, Frank Hastings
Handerson, Henry Ebenezer
Harris, Elisha
Hartley, Frank
Herter, Christian Archibald
Hess, Alfred Fabian
Hirsch, Isaac Seth
Hoff, John Van Rensselaer
Holmes, Bayard Taylor
House, Samuel Reynolds
Howe, John Ireland
Husk, Charles Ellsworth
Hyde, James Nevins

Irving, Peter
Janeway, Edward Gamaliel
Janeway, Theodore Caldwell
Jelliffe, Smith Ely
Johnstone, Job
Judson, Adoniram Brown
Lazear, Jesse William
Le Conte, John
Le Conte, John Lawrence
Le Conte, Joseph
Lefferts George Morewood
Levene, Phoebus Aaron Theodore
Lewis, Dean De Witt
Libman, Emanuel
Lincoln, Rufus Pratt
McBurney, Charles
McCosh, Andrew James
Marks, Elias
Mayo, William Starbuck
Mearns, Edgar Alexander
Merriam, Clinton Hart
Miller, James Alexander
Moore, Edward Mott
Mott, Valentine
Myerson, Abraham
Nott, Josiah Clark
Noyes, Henry Drury
O'Dwyer, Joseph
Osborn, Henry Fairfield
Owre, Alfred
Palmer, Alonzo Benjamin
Park, William Hallock
Parry, Charles Christopher
Peck, Charles Howard
Pilcher, Paul Monroe
Plotz, Harry
Remsen, Ira
Romayne, Nicholas
Rubin, Isidor Clinton
Rubinow, Isaac Max
Rusby, Henry Hurd
Sayre, Lewis Albert
Schneider, Albert
Seguin, Edward Constant
Shrady, George Frederick
Simpson, William Kelly
Smith, Arthur Henderson
Smith, Stephen
Spitzka, Edward Anthony
Spooner, Shearjashub
Starr, Moses Allen
Sternberg, George Miller
Streeter, George Linius
Taylor, Robert Tunstall
Thompson, William Gilman
Timme, Walter
Torrey, John
Warbasse, James Peter
West, Henry Sergeant
Whitman, Marcus
Williams, Linsly Rudd
Williams, Stephen West
Wood, James Rushmore
Zilboorg, Gregory
Pharmacy
Kiss, Max
School of Mines
Aldrich, Chester Holmes
Austen, Peter Townsend
Barus, Carl
Britton, Nathaniel Lord

Church, John Adams
Crocker, Francis Bacon
Dwight, Arthur Smith
Ellsworth, Lincoln
Ferguson, Samuel
Heinze, Frederick Augustus
Heye, George Gustav
Hollerith, Herman
Hollick, Charles Arthur
Hoyt, John Sherman
Hutton, Frederick Remsen
Irving, Roland Duer
Kraemer, Henry
Langmuir, Irving
Levene, Phoebus Aaron Theodore
Lusk, Graham
Matthew, William Diller
Moldenke, Richard George Gottlob
Moore, Philip North
Moran, Daniel Edward
Olcott, Eben Erskine
Paine, John Alsop
Parsons, William Barclay
Piez, Charles
Rees, John Krom
Rice, George Samuel
Russell, Israel Cook
Stanley, Robert Crooks
Stone, John Stone
Thompson, William Boyce
Wiechmann, Ferdinand Gerhard
Woodin, William Hartman
CONCORDIA SEMINARY (MO.)
Gräbner, August Lawrence
Hanson, James Christian Meinich
Hoenecke, Gustav Adolf Felix Theodor
Hove, Elling
Koren, John
Pieper, Franz August Otto
Preus, Christian Keyser
Schmidt, Friedrich August
Stromme, Peer Olsen
Stub, Hans Gerhard
CONCORDIA THEOLOGICAL SEMINARY (MO.)
Maier, Walter Arthur
CONNECTICUT LITERARY INSTITUTE
(See SUFFIELD SCHOOL)
CONVERSE COLLEGE (S.C.)
Peterkin, Julia Mood
COOK COUNTY NORMAL SCHOOL
(ILL.)
Nelson, Edward William
COOPERATIVE SCHOOL FOR STUDENT TEACHERS (N.Y.)
Brown, Margaret Wise
COOPER MEDICAL COLLEGE (CAL.)
Snow, William Freeman
Wilbur, Ray Lyman
COOPER UNION (N.Y.)
Bitzer, George William
Christie, John Walter
Cowen, Joshua Lionel
Deland, Margaret
King, Alexander
Kunz, George Frederick
Lukeman, Henry Augustus

Opper, Frederick Burr
CORCORAN SCIENTIFIC SCHOOL
(D.C.)
Davis, William Hammatt
CORNELL COLLEGE (IOWA)
Baker, Carl Lotus
Devine, Edward Thomas
CORNELL UNIVERSITY (N.Y.)
Acker, Charles Ernest
Allen, Arthur Augustus
Atkinson, George Francis
Babcock, Stephen Moulton
Balestier, Charles Wolcott
Bausch, Edward
Berkowitz, Henry
Biggs, Herman Michael
Boring, Edwin Garrigues
Botsford, George Willis
Branner, John Casper
Bromfield, Louis
Bryant, Ralph Clement
Burr, George Lincoln
Carlisle, Floyd Leslie
Carrier, Willis Haviland
Chambers, James Julius
Chittenden, Hiram Martin
Church, Irving Porter
Comstock, John Henry
Creighton, James Edwin
Cushing, Frank Hamilton
Dorn, Harold Fred
Dove, Arthur Garfield
Dudley, William Russel
Edgren, August Hjalmar
Eilshemius, Louis Michel
Elliott, John Lovejoy
Fauset, Jessie Redmon
Flather, John Joseph
Foraker, Joseph Benson
Ford, Hannibal Choate
Francis, Charles Spencer
Fuertes, Louis Agassiz
Gannett, Frank Ernest
Gherardi, Bancroft
Gifford, Sanford Robinson
Gillett, Horace Wadsworth
Gleason, Kate
Grant, James Benton
Gregg, Willis Ray
Halsey, Frederick Arthur
Harper, John Lyell
Harris, Rollin Arthur
Hayford, John Fillmore
Hendrix, Joseph Clifford
Henry, William Arnon
Hill, Ernest Rowland
Hillebrand, William Francis
Hills, Elijah Clarence
Hiscock, Frank Harris
Holmes, Joseph Austin
House, Edward Mandell
Howard, Leland Ossian
Hoxie, Robert Franklin
Isham, Ralph Heyward
Jackson, Dugald Caleb
Jordan, David Starr
Kellerman, Karl Frederic
Kelley, Florence
Kellor, Frances (Alice)
Kerr, Walter Craig
King, Franklin Hiram
Kingsbury, Albert

Knight, Goodwin Jess ("Goodie")
Ladd, Carl Edwin
Laguna, Theodore de Leo de
Lamoureux, Andrew Jackson
Larned, William Augustus
Lee, Porter Raymond
Lewis, George William
McAllister, Charles Albert
McConnell, Ira Welch
Matthews, Franklin
Menjou, Adolphe Jean
Midgley, Thomas
Miller, Kempster Blanchard
Millspaugh, Charles Frederick
Moore, Veranus Alva
Morgenthau, Henry, Jr.
Mott, John R.
Nathan, George Jean
Nichols, Edward Leamington
Noyes, Walter Chadwick
Oberndorf, Clarence Paul
Olmstead, Albert Ten Eyck
O'Shea, Michael Vincent
Parsons, Frank
Pearson, Edward Jones
Pearson, Leonard
Pearson, Raymond Allen
Perry, Clarence Arthur
Pew, Joseph Newton, Jr.
Pincus, Gregory Goodwin ("Goody")
Pound, Cuthbert Winfred
Powell, George Harold
Pressman, Lee
Pringle, Henry Fowles
Prosser, Charles Smith
Putnam, Ruth
Rafter, George W.
Rathbun, Richard
Reed, Daniel Alden
Reeves, Arthur Middleton
Richtmyer, Floyd Karker
Riegger, Wallingford
Roberts, Kenneth Lewis
Rossiter, Clinton Lawrence, III
Russell, James Earl
Ryan, Harris Joseph
Sackett, Henry Woodward
Salmon, Daniel Elmer
Sanderson, Ezra Dwight
Severance, Frank Haywood
Shepard, Fred Douglas
Simpson, William Kelly
Smith, Harold Babbitt
Smith, Theobald
Sperry, Elmer Ambrose
Stevens, George Barker
Straight, Willard Dickerman
Sullivan, Harry Stack
Teeple, John Edgar
Thomas, Martha Carey
Thurstone, Louis Leon
Tone, Stanislas Pascal Franchot
Trelease, William
Vail, Robert William Glenroie
Van Loon, Hendrik Willem
Veatch, Arthur Clifford
Warner, Glenn Scobey ("Pop")
Washburn, Albert Henry
White, David
White, William Alanson

Wolheim, Louis Robert
Graduate Study
Adams, Joseph Quincy
Albee, Ernest
Allen, Arthur Augustus
Arthur, Joseph Charles
Bagley, William Chandler
Bode, Boyd Henry
Boring, Edwin Garrigues
Bronson, Walter Cochrane
Buckley, Oliver Ellsworth
Dorn, Harold Fred
Emerson, Oliver Farrar
Ferree, Clarence Errol
Fetter, Frank Albert
Friedman, William Frederick
Gherardi, Bancroft
Gillett, Horace Wadsworth
Goldenweiser, Emanuel Alexander
Griscom, Ludlow
Hanson, James Christian Meinich
Hewett, Waterman Thomas
Hooker, Elon Huntington
Hopkins, Cyril George
Howard, Leland Ossian
Kemmerer, Edwin Walter
Ladd, Carl Edwin
Lewis, George William
Lipman, Jacob Goodale
Lotka, Alfred James
Manly, Charles Matthews
Meiklejohn, Alexander
Moore, Addison Webster
Moore, Clarence Lemuel Elisha
Morgan, John Harcourt Alexander
Moss, Sanford Alexander
Nichols, Ernest Fox
Olmstead, Albert Ten Eyck
Parr, Samuel Wilson
Pearson, Raymond Allen
Pincus, Gregory Goodwin ("Goody")
Powell, George Harold
Pritchard, Frederick John
Prosser, Charles Smith
Rautenstrauch, Walter
Richtmyer, Floyd Karker
Smith, Theobald
Thilly, Frank
Warren, George Frederick
Washburn, Margaret Floy
Whetzel, Herbert Hice
Whitcomb, Selden Lincoln
Wiener, Norbert
Young, John Wesley
Zook, George Frederick
Law
Mussey, Ellen Spencer
Reed, Daniel Alden
Rose, Walter Malins
Taylor, Myron Charles
Warner, Glenn Scobey ("Pop")
Medicine
Marriott, Williams McKim
Menninger, William Claire
Muller, Hermann Joseph
Neal, Josephine Bicknell
Oberndorf, Clarence Paul
Trask, James Dowling

Weiss, Soma
CORTLAND STATE TEACHERS COLLEGE (N.Y.)
Ladd, Carl Edwin
CREIGHTON UNIVERSITY (NEB.)
Barrett, Frank Aloysius
Cudahy, Edward Aloysius, Jr.
Matthews, Francis Patrick
Law
Barrett, Frank Aloysius
Monsky, Henry
CROZER THEOLOGICAL SEMINARY (PA.)
Chiera, Edward
King, Martin Luther, Jr.
Sloan, Harold Paul
CULVER MILITARY ACADEMY (IND.)
Ingram, Jonas Howard
CUMBERLAND COLLEGE (KY.)
Alcorn, James Lusk
Morrow, Edwin Porch
Roane, John Selden
Scott, William Anderson
Watterson, Harvey Magee
CUMBERLAND UNIVERSITY (TENN.)
Battle, Burrell Bunn
Beard, Richard
Brantley, Theodore
Clement, Frank Goad
Ensley, Enoch
Foster, Murphy James
Hardy, William Harris
Hatch, Carl A.
McReynolds, Samuel Davis
Graduate Study
Miller, George Abram
Peck, Harry Thurston
Law
Bate, William Brimage
Clements, Judson Claudius
Cooper, (Leon) Jere
Davis, Jeff
Fitzpatrick, Morgan Cassius
Gaines, Reuben Reid
Gordon, George Washington
Gore, Thomas Pryor
Hull, Cordell
Lurton, Horace Harmon
McCreary, James Bennett
Valliant, Leroy Branch
CURRY SCHOOL OF EXPRESSIONISM (MASS.)
Kalmus, Natalie Mabelle Dunfee
CURTIS INSTITUTE (PA.)
Blitzstein, Marc
CUTLER SCHOOL (N.Y.)
Carryl, Guy Wetmore
Coffin, Henry Sloane
Howland, John
Janeway, Theodore Caldwell

DAKOTA WESLEYAN UNIVERSITY (S.DAK.)
Case, Francis Higbee
DALHOUSIE UNIVERSITY (CANADA)
Doull, James Angus
Medicine
Doull, James Angus
DALLAS COLLEGE (ORE.)
Poling, Daniel Alfred

DANE LAW SCHOOL (See HARVARD UNIVERSITY *Law*)
DANISH NAVAL ACADEMY (DENMARK)
Hovgaard, William
DARTMOUTH COLLEGE (N.H.)
Adams, Daniel
Adams, Ebenezer
Adams, Henry Carter
Adams, Walter Sydney
Aiken, Charles Augustus
Akerman, Amos Tappan
Angell, George Thorndike
Appleton, Jesse
Atkinson, George Henry
Bailey, Rufus William
Bancroft, Cecil Franklin Patch
Barlow, Joel
Barrett, John
Bartlett, Ichabod
Bartlett, Samuel Colcord
Bell, Charles Henry
Bell, Louis
Bell, Samuel
Bickmore, Albert Smith
Bingham, Caleb
Bingham, Harry
Bissell, George Henry
Black, Frank Swett
Blake, Francis Gilman
Boss, Lewis
Bouton, John Bell
Brown, Francis, 1784–1820
Brown, Francis, 1849–1916
Brown, George William
Brown, Samuel Gilman
Burton, Asa
Bush, George
Cantril, Albert Hadley
Chamberlain, Mellen
Chase, Harry Woodburn
Chase, Philander
Chase, Salmon Portland
Cheney, Oren Burbank
Chipman, Daniel
Choate, Rufus
Clark, Daniel, 1809–1891
Clark, Francis Edward
Clark, Greenleaf
Cluttenden, Martin
Colman, Henry
Currier, Moody
Dana, Charles Loomis
Dana, John Cotton
Day, Edmund Ezra
Dingley, Nelson
Doe, Charles
Dryfoos, Orvil E.
Dunning, William Archibald
Eastman, John Robie
Eaton, John
Eaton, William
Ely, Richard Theodore
Estabrook, Joseph
Evans, Warren Felt
Everett, David
Fairbanks, Henry
Farmer, Moses Gerrish
Farrar, Timothy
Felt, Joseph Barlow
Fessenden, Samuel
Fessenden, Thomas Green

Field, Walbridge Abner
Fletcher, Horace
Fletcher, Richard
Fogg, George Gilman
Forrestal, James Vincent
Foster, Stephen Symonds
Frost, Edwin Brant
Frost, Robert Lee
Gates, George Augustus
Goddard, Morrill
Goodell, William 1709-1867
Goodwin, John Noble
Grant, George Barnard
Greene, Daniel Crosby
Greenleaf, Benjamin
Grimes, James Wilson
Gulick, Sidney Lewis
Haddock, Charles Brickett
Hall, Sherman
Hayes, John Lord
Hazen, Henry Allen
Henry, Caleb Sprague
Hough, Charles Merrill
House, Samuel Reynolds
Hovey, Alvah
Hovey, Charles Edward
Hovey, Otis Ellis
Hovey, Richard
Hubbard, Gardiner Greene
Hubbard, John
Huntington, Samuel 1765-1817
Huntington Elisha
Hutchins, Harry Burns
Ide, Henry Clay
Jackson, Edward Payson
Jewell, Harvey
Jewett, Milo Parker
Joy, James Frederick
Just, Ernest Everett
Kendall, Amos
Kimball, Richard Burleigh
Knapp, Samuel Lorenzo
Ledyard, John
Liebling, Abbott Joseph
Little, Charles Sherman
Long, Stephen Harriman
Lord, John
McCall, Samuel Walker
McKeen, Joseph
Marsh, George Perkins
Marsh, James
Mather, Samuel Holmes
Merrill, Daniel
Merrill, Samuel
Miller, Charles Ransom
Miller, Jonathan Peckham
Miller, Oliver
Moore, George Henry
Moore, Zephaniah Swift
Morris, George Sylvester
Morrison, Nathan Jackson
Moses, George Higgins
Mussey, Reuben Dimond
Nichols, Thomas Low
Noyes, Edward Follansbee
Noyes, John Humphrey
O'Brien, Robert Lincoln
Oliver, Fitch Edward
Oliver, Henry Kemble
Orcutt, Hiram
Ordronaux, John
Palmer, Elihu

Parish, Elijah
Parker, Joel, 1795-1875
Parris, Albion Keith
Partridge, Alden
Patterson, James Willis
Patterson, John Henry
Paul, Henry Martyn
Pearl, Raymond
Pearsons, Daniel Kimball
Peaslee, Edmund Randolph
Perley, Ira
Peters, Absalom
Pillsbury, Charles Alfred
Poor, Daniel
Porter, Ebenezer
Procter, Redfield
Prouty, Charles Azro
Ranney, Ambrose Loomis
Redfield, Isaac Fletcher
Remington, William Walter
Richardson, Charles Francis
Ripley, Eleazar Wheelock
Robinson, William Callyhan
Rolfe, Robert Abial ("Red")
Root, Erastus
Rugg, Harold Ordway
Ruml, Beardsley
Sanborn, Edwin David
Sanborn, Walter Henry
Shattuck, George Cheyne, 1783
   -1854
Shepley, Ether
Shepley, George Foster
Shurtleff, Roswell Morse
Slafter, Edmund Farwell
Smith, Asa Dodge
Smith, Justin Harvey
Spaulding, Levi
Stevens, Thaddeus
Strong, Moses McCure
Sumner, Walter Taylor
Talbot, Ethelbert
Taylor, Samuel Harvey
Tenney, Charles Daniel
Tenney, Edward Payson
Thompson, Charles Oliver
Ticknor, Elisha
Ticknor, George
Townsend, Luther Tracy
Tracy, Joseph
Tuck, Amos
Tucker, William Jewett
Twitchell, Amos
Upham, Thomas Cogswell
Upham, Warren
Wanger, Walter
Webster, Daniel
Webster, Joseph Dana
Wentworth, John, 1815-1888
Wheelock, John
White, Leonard Dupee
Willey, Samuel Hopkins
Williams, Ben Ames
Williston, Seth
Woodbury, Daniel Phineas
Woodbury, Levi
Woods, Leonard, 1807-1878
Worcester, Samuel
Wright, John Henry
Young, Charles Augustus
Graduate Study
Andrews, John Bertram

Chase, Harry Woodburn
Day, Edmund Ezra
Dickinson, Edwin De Witt
Hale, Nathan, 1784-1863
Paul, Henry Martyn
White, Leonard Dupee
Medicine
Adams, Daniel
Alden, Ebenezer
Banks, Charles Edward
Bell, Luther Vose
Cheney, Oren Burbank
Dana, Charles Loomis
Gallup, Joseph Adams
Garcelon, Alonzo
Hayes, Augustus Allen
Kimball, Gilman
Knowlton, Charles
Little, Charles Sherman
Nichols, James Robinson
Peaslee, Edmund Randolph
DAVIDSON COLLEGE (N.C.)
Bynum, William Preston
Campbell, Josiah A. Patterson
Carter, Landon
Osborne, James Walker
Ramseur, Stephen Dodson
Simmons, James Stevens
Smith, Charles Alphonso
Smith, Henry Louis
Wilson, Woodrow
DAY'S ACADEMY (MASS.)
Parker, Peter
Pond, Enoch
Sunderland, La Roy
Towle, George Makepeace
DECORAH INSTITUTE (MINN.)
Volstead, Andrew John
DEERFIELD ACADEMY (MASS.)
Allen, Charles
Fuller, George
Howe, Samuel
Mayo, Amory Dwight
Williamson, William Durkee
DELAWARE COLLEGE (DEL.)
Blandy, William Henry Purnell
DELAWARE LITERARY INSTITUTE
   (N.Y.)
Champlin, John Wayne
Jones, Herschel Vespasian
White, William Nathaniel
DELAWARE STATE COLLEGE (DEL.)
Messersmith, George Strausser
DENISON UNIVERSITY (OHIO)
Adkins, Homer Burton
Ashmore, William
Behrends, Adolphus Julius
   Frederick
Burton, Ernest De Witt
Dorsey, George Amos
Fairfield, Edmund Burke
Harmon, Judson
Johnson, Douglas Wilson
Kerr, John Glasgow
Larrabee, Charles Hathaway
Rose, Mary Davies Swartz
Seagrave, Gordon Stifler
Stevens, William Arnold
DEPAUW UNIVERSITY (IND.)
Beard, Charles Austin
Beard, Mary Ritter
Beveridge, Albert Jeremiah

Booth, Newton
Curme, George Oliver
Eggleston, George Cary
Fisher, Frederick Bohn
Harlan, James, 1820–1899
Hitt, Robert Roberts
Jaquess, James Frazier
McDonald, Joseph Ewing
Moore, Addison Webster
Ogg, Frederic Austin
Patterson, Thomas MacDonald
Phillips, David Graham
Porter, Albert Gallatin
Ridpath, John Clark
Shoup, Francis Asbury
Sims, Charles N.
Stephenson, Carl
Stone, Wilbur Fisk
Terrell, Edwin Holland
Van Devanter, Willis
Voorhees, Daniel Wolsey
Watson, James Eli
West, Roy Owen
Williams, Elkanah
Wirt, William Albert
Wood, Thomas Bond
Graduate Study
Curme, George Oliver
Stephenson, Carl
West, Roy Owen
Wirt, William Albert
Law
West, Roy Owen
DERBY ACADEMY (MASS.)
Carter, James Coolidge
Gardiner, Robert Hallowell
Savage, James
DES MOINES COLLEGE (IOWA)
McVey, Frank Lerond
DETROIT COLLEGE OF LAW (MICH.)
Kelland, Clarence Budington
DETROIT JUNIOR COLLEGE (MICH.)
Bachmann, Werner Emmanuel
DICKINSON COLLEGE (PA.)
Allen, John James
Baird, Spencer Fullerton
Bates, Daniel Moore
Baugher, Henry Louis
Beale, Richard Lee Turberville
Bender, Charles Albert
("Chief")
Bethune, George Washington
Bigler, John
Bowman, Thomas
Bridges, Robert, 1806–1882
Brown, Samuel
Buchanan, James
Campbell, William Henry
Chambers, Talbot Wilson
Conway, Moncure Daniel
Creighton, William
Creswell, John Angel James
Crooks, George Richard
Cummins, George David
Deems, Charles Force
Dunlop, James
Edwards, Ninian
Elliott, Washington Lafayette
Ellis, Powhatan
Fisher, George Purnell
Fisher, Sidney George
Floyd, John

Furst, Clyde Bowman
Gerhard, William Wood
Gibson, John Bannister
Goucher, John Franklin
Grier, Robert Cooper
Haldeman, Samuel Steman
Hare, George Emlen
Himes, Charles Francis
Hurst, John Fletcher
Lamberton, Benjamin Peffer
Lane, William Carr
Learned, Marion Dexter
MacCauley, Clay
McClelland, Robert, 1807–1880
McComas, Louis Emory
McKim, James Miller
Maclay, Robert Samuel
Neely, Thomas Benjamin
Palmer, James Croxall
Ridgaway, Henry Bascom
Robinson, John Mitchell
Saulsbury, Eli
Saulsbury, Willard, 1820–1892
Snowden, James Ross
Taney, Roger Brooke
Thomas, Philip Francis
Wahl, William Henry
Walker, Jonathan Hodge
Watts, Frederick
Wilkins, Ross
Wilkins, William
Wormley, Theodore George
Wright, Hendrick Brodley
Young, Jesse Bowman
Young, John Clarke
Graduate Study
Furst, Clyde Bowman
Gray, John Purdue
Law
Curtin, Andrew Gregg
Kephart, John William
Nevin, Alfred
Medicine
Campbell, James Hepburn
DICKINSON SEMINARY (PA.)
Parker, Arthur Caswell
DICKSON COLLEGE (TENN.)
Caraway, Thaddeus Horatius
DICKSON NORMAL COLLEGE
(TENN.)
Caraway, Hattie Ophelia Wyatt
DIXWELL'S LATIN SCHOOL (MASS.)
Adams, Henry Brooks
Emmons, Samuel Franklin
Lodge, Henry Cabot
Longfellow, Ernest Wadsworth
Lowell, Edward Jackson
Matthews, Nathan
Peabody, Robert Swain
Peirce, Charles Sanders
Rotch, Arthur
Stone, James Kent
DOANE COLLEGE (NEB.)
Fairchild, Fred Rogers
Taylor, Robert
DRAKE UNIVERSITY (IOWA)
Ames, Edward Scribner
Glaspell, Susan Keating
Larson, Laurence Marcellus
Nicholson, Seth Barnes
Stong, Phil(lip Duffield)

DREW THEOLOGICAL SEMINARY
(N.J.)
Alexander, Gross
Appenzeller, Henry Gerhard
Ferguson, William Porter Frisbee
Murray, John Gardner
Sloan, Harold Paul
Tittle, Ernest Fremont
Tobias, Channing Heggie
DREW UNIVERSITY (N.J.)
Matthews, Joseph Brown
DREXEL UNIVERSITY (PA.)
Cable, Frank Taylor
DROPSIE COLLEGE (PA.)
Graduate Study
Revel, Bernard
Speiser, Ephraim Avigdor
DUKE UNIVERSITY (N.C.)
Allen, George Venable
Boyd, William Kenneth
Payne, Bruce Ryburn
Pegram, George Braxton
Roper, Daniel Calhoun
Simmons, Furnifold McLendel
Graduate Study
Boyd, William Kenneth
DULWICH COLLEGE (ENGLAND)
Chandler, Raymond Thornton
DUMMER ACADEMY (MASS.)
Bromfield, John
Cleaveland, Parker
Emerson, George Barrell
Jackson, Charles
Jackson, James, 1777–1867
Jackson, Patrick Tracy
King, Rufus, 1755–1827
Knight, Henry Cogswell
Lander, Frederick West
Parsons, Theophilus, 1750–1813
Phillips, Samuel
Poore, Benjamin Perley
Preble, Edward
Smyth, Egbert Coffin
DURHAM UNIVERSITY COLLEGE OF
SCIENCE (ENGLAND)
Campbell, William

EARLHAM COLLEGE (IND.)
Goddard, Pliny Earle
Jessup, Walter Albert
Johnson, Robert Underwood
Kelsey, Rayner Wickersham
Nixon, William Penn
Trueblood, Benjamin Franklin
Wildman, Murray Shipley
EAST CENTRAL NORMAL SCHOOL
(OKLA.)
Kerr, Robert Samuel
EAST FLORIDA MILITARY AND
AGRICULTURAL COLLEGE
Cone, Hutchinson Ingham
EAST GREENWICH ACADEMY (R. I.)
Aldrich, Nelson Wilmarth
Tourjée, Eben
Upham, Samuel Foster
Warren, William Fairfield
Winship, Albert Edward
EASTMAN BUSINESS COLLEGE
(N.Y.)
Kresge, Sebastian Spering

EAST TEXAS STATE UNIVERSITY
Rayburn, Samuel Taliaferro ("Sam")
ECLECTIC MEDICAL COLLEGE (N.Y.)
Hrdlicka, Ales
ECLECTIC MEDICAL INSTITUTE (OHIO)
Henshall, James Alexander
Hoyt, John Wesley
Kunze, Richard Ernest
Morrow, Prince Albert
Scudder, John Milton
ECLECTIC MEDICAL UNIVERSITY OF KANSAS
Brinkley, John Richard
ECOLE BERNARD PALISSY (FRANCE)
Lachaise, Gaston
ECOLE DES ARTS ET METIERS (FRANCE)
Houdry, Eugene Jules
ECOLE DES BEAUX-ARTS (FRANCE)
Aldrich, Chester Holmes
Atterbury, Grosvenor
Barnard, George Grey
Borglum John Gutzon de la Mothe
Brush, George de Forest
Burroughs, Bryson
Calder, Alexander Stirling
Corbett, Harvey Wiley
Cret, Paul Philippe
Davidson, Jo
Dickinson, Preston
Flagg, Ernest
Fraser, James Earle
Granger, Alfred Hoyt
Hood, Raymond Mathewson
Ide, John Jay
Lachaise, Gaston
Lamb, William Frederick
Lawrance, Charles Lanier
Lukeman, Henry Augustus
MacMonnies, Frederick William
MacNeil, Hermon Atkins
Maybeck, Bernard Ralph
Morgan, Julia
Robinson, Boardman
Rogers, James Gamble
Stokes, Isaac Newton Phelps
Taft, Lorado Zadoc
ECOLE DES HAUTES ETUDES (FRANCE)
Mather, Frank Jewett, Jr.
ECOLE DES MINES (BELGIUM)
Sauveur, Albert
ECOLE DES MINES (FRANCE)
Perin, Charles Page
ECOLE DES PONTS ET CHAUSEES (FRANCE)
Modjeski, Ralph
ECOLE LIBRE DES SCIENCES POLITIQUES (FRANCE)
Wilson, Hugh Robert
EDEN THEOLOGICAL SEMINARY (MO.)
Niebuhr, Helmut Richard
EDGEFIELD ACADEMY (S.C.)
Bonham, Milledge Luke
La Borde, Maximilian
Tompkins, Daniel Augustus

EDGEHILL SCHOOL (N.J.)
Bagby, George William
Miller, John, 1819–1895
Stillé, Charles Janeway
EDINBURGH UNIVERSITY (SCOTLAND)
Campbell, Charles Macfie
MacIver, Robert Morrison
Neilson, William Allan
Graduate Study
MacIver, Robert Morrison
Medicine
Campbell, Charles Macfie
ELGIN ACADEMY (ILL.)
Boyd, Thomas Alexander
ELMHURST COLLEGE (ILL.)
Niebuhr, Helmut Richard
ELMIRA COLLEGE (N.Y.)
Hill, Grace Livingston
ELMIRA FREE ACADEMY (N.Y.)
Farwell, Charles Benjamin
Goff, Emmet Stull
Roe, Francis Asbury
Stanchfield, John Barry
Wing, Joseph Elwyn
EMORY AND HENRY COLLEGE (VA.)
Allen, Young John
Comer, Braxton Bragg
Goode, John
Lambuth, Walter Russell
Stuart, James Ewell Brown
Vawter, Charles Erastus
EMORY COLLEGE (GA.)
Allen, Young John
Barkley, Alben William
Bass, William Capers
Callaway, Morgan
Candler, Warren Akin
Hadas, Moses
Harrison, William Pope
Haygood, Atticus Green
Hopkins, Isaac Stiles
Hyer, Robert Stewart
Keener, William Albert
Lamar, Lucius Quintus Cincinnatus
Lee, Ivy Ledbetter
Lee, James Wideman
Odum, Howard Washington
Orr, Gustavus John
Rivers, Thomas Milton
EPISCOPAL ACADEMY (PHILA.)
Boller, Alfred Pancoast
Coleman, Leighton
Decatur, Stephen, 1779–1820
Drew, John, 1853–1927
George, Henry, 1839–1897
Harrison, Charles Custis
Hirsch, Emil Gustav
Hobart, John Henry
Lewis, Lawrence
Montgomery, Thomas Harrison
Morton, Henry
Outerbridge, Alexander Ewing
Penrose, Boies
Wheaton, Nathaniel Sheldon
EPISCOPAL THEOLOGICAL SCHOOL (MASS.)
Bigelow, Frank Hagar
Lawrence, William
Livermore, Abiel Abbot
Nash, Henry Sylvester

Peabody, Endicott
Rand, Edward Kennard
Slattery, Charles Lewis
Sterrett, James MacBride
Woods, James Haughton
EPWORTH SEMINARY AND JUNIOR COLLEGE (IOWA)
Benson, Oscar Herman
ERSKINE COLLEGE (S.C.)
Montgomery, William Bell
Orr, Jehu Amaziah
Riley, Benjamin Franklin
EWING COLLEGE (ILL.)
Martin, Warren Homer
EXCELSIOR COLLEGE (TEXAS)
Batts, Robert Lynn
EXETER ACADEMY (See PHILLIPS EXETER ACADEMY)
FAIRFIELD ACADEMY (N.Y.)
Arnold, Lauren Briggs
Dickinson, Charles Monroe
Dwight, Harrison Gray Otis
Gray, Asa
Hadley, James
Kelley, Alfred
Loomis, Arphaxed
Lord, Chester Sanders
Satterlee, Richard Sherwood
Whipple, Squire
FARMER'S COLLEGE (See BELMONT COLLEGE)
FEDERAL INSTITUTE OF TECHNOLOGY (SWITZERLAND)
Norden, Carl Lukas
FEMALE MEDICAL COLLEGE (See WOMAN'S MEDICAL COLLEGE)
FERRIS INSTITUTE (MICH.)
Bowman, Isaiah
FIRST STATE COLLEGE OF BRNO (CZECHOSLOVAKIA)
Sakel, Manfred Joshua
FISK UNIVERSITY (TENN.)
Dawson, William Levi
Du Bois, William Edward Burghardt
Haynes, George Edmund
Lunceford, James Melvin ("Jimmie")
Wilson, J(ames) Finley
Graduate Study
Pickens, William
FLORIDA STATE COLLEGE FOR WOMEN
Van Doren, Irita Bradford
Graduate Study
Van Doren, Irita Bradford
FLORIDA STATE NORMAL SCHOOL
Geiger, Roy Stanley
FORDHAM UNIVERSITY (N.Y.)
Burrow, Trigant
Coppens, Charles
Curran, Thomas Jerome
Donovan, James Britt
Drumgoole, John Christopher
Edebohls, George Michael
Farley, John Murphy
Flynn, Edward Joseph
Glynn, Martin Henry
Hassard, John Rose Greene
Herbermann, Charles George
La Farge, John
Lombardi, Vincent Thomas

McMahon, Brien
O'Brien, Morgan Joseph
Richards, Vincent
Rosecrans, Sylvester Horton
Seton, William
Shea, John Dawson Gilmary
Spellman, Francis Joseph
Wigger, Winand Michael
Law
Hunton, George Kenneth
Lombardi, Vincent Thomas
O'Dwyer, William
FORT WORTH POLYTECHNIC INSTI-
TUTE (TEX.)
Speaker, Tris E.
FRAMINGHAM ACADEMY (MASS.)
Clark, Thomas March
Gordon, George Henry
Peirce, Cyrus
Pike, Albert
Weiss, John
FRANK HOLME SCHOOL OF ILLUS-
TRATION (ILL.)
Dwiggins, William Addison
FRANKLIN AND MARSHALL COLLEGE
(PA.)
Appenzeller, Henry Gerhard
Apple, Thomas Gilmore
Baer, George Frederick
Bausman, Benjamin
Black, William Murray
Bomberger, John Henry Augus-
tus
Clay, Albert Tobias
Douglas, Henry Kyd
Dubbs, Joseph Henry
Ferrel, William
Gerhart, Emanuel Vogel
Harbaugh, Henry
Hartranft, John Frederick
McFarland, Thomas Bard
Miller, George Abram
Peters, Madison Clinton
Rupp, William
Schaeffer, Nathan Christ
Stahr, John Summers
Stauffer, David McNeely
Steiner, Lewis Henry
FRANKLIN COLLEGE (See UNIVERSI-
TY OF GEORGIA)
FRANKLIN COLLEGE (IND.)
Caldwell, Otis William
Davis, Elmer Holmes
Monroe, Paul
Voris, John Ralph
FRANKLIN COLLEGE (OHIO)
Hammond, Percy Hunter
FREDERICKSBURG COLLEGE (VA.)
Sydenstricker, Edgar
FREDONIA ACADEMY (N. Y.)
Barbour, Oliver Lorenzo
Houghton, Douglass
Orton, Edward Francis Baxter
Strang, James Jesse
FREMONT NORMAL COLLEGE (NEB.)
Dern, George Henry
FRIEDRICH-WILHELMS UNIVERSITY
(GERMANY)
Jaeger, Werner Wilhelm
Stern, Kurt Guenter

FRIENDS' UNIVERSITY (KANS.)
Ayres, William Augustus
Graduate Study
Ayres, William Augustus
FURMAN UNIVERSITY (S.C.)
Watson, John Broadus
Graduate Study
Manly, John Matthews

GARRETT BIBLE INSTITUTE (CAL.)
Atkinson, Henry Avery
GARRETT BIBLICAL INSTITUTE
(ILL.)
Clement, Rufus Early
Fowler, Charles Henry
Hart, Virgil Chittenden
Hartzell, Joseph Crane
Hutchinson, Paul
Stuart, Charles Macaulay
GENERAL THEOLOGICAL SEMINARY
(N.Y.)
Bradley, Charles William
Breck, James Lloyd
Burgess, Alexander
Burleson, Hugh Latimer
Coleman, Leighton
Crapsey, Algernon Sidney
De Koven, James
Dix, Morgan
Doane, George Washington
Fite, Warner
Francis, Paul James
Gailor, Thomas Frank
Gavin, Frank Stanton Burns
Goodwin, Hannibal Williston
Graves, Frederick Rogers
Hall, Charles Henry
Hare, George Emlen
Hoffman, Eugene Augustus
Kip, William Ingraham
Lee, Alfred
McVickar, William Neilson
Murphy, Edgar Gardner
Newton, Richard
Nies, James Buchanan
Odenheimer, William Henry
Paddock, Benjamin Henry
Paddock, John Adams
Pott, Francis Lister Hawks
Preston, Thomas Scott
Robinson, William Callyhan
Schroeder, John Frederick
Seymour, George Franklin
Spalding, Franklin Spencer
Spencer, Jesse Ames
Stone, John Seely
Talbot, Ethelbert
Whitehouse, Frederic Cope
Whittingham, William Rollinson
Winslow, William Copley
Worcester, Elwood
GENESEE COLLEGE (See SYRACUSE
UNIVERSITY)
GENESEE WESLEYAN SEMINARY
(N.Y.)
Rittenhouse, Jessie Belle
GENEVA COLLEGE (N.Y.) (See HO-
BART COLLEGE)
GENEVA COLLEGE (PA.)
Curry, John Steuart

GENEVA MEDICAL SCHOOL (N.Y.)
Blackwell, Elizabeth
Purple, Samuel Smith
Smith, Azariah
Smith, Stephen
GEORGETOWN COLLEGE (KY.)
Breaux, Joseph Arsenne
Golden, Frank Alfred
Lorimer, George Claude
Loring, William Wing
Pentecost, George Frederick
GEORGETOWN UNIVERSITY (D.C.)
Ashford, Bailey Kelly
Beale, Edward Fitzgerald
Blease, Coleman Livingston
Bowie, Richard Johns
Bradley, Denis Mary
Bryce, Lloyd Stephens
Burbridge, Stephen Gano
Childe, John
Corcoran, William Wilson
De Leon, Thomas Cooper
Denby, Charles
Dimitry, Alexander
Dimitry, Charles Patton
Doyle, John Thomas
Egan, Maurice Francis
Faulkner, Charles James
Fenwick, Benedict Joseph
Foote, John Ambrose
Gaston, William, 1778–1844
Green, Benjamin Edwards
Heth, Henry
Kavaugh, Edward
Kober, George Martin
Lackaye, Wilton
Latrobe, Benjamin Henry
Latrobe, John Hazlehurst Bone-
val
Leggett, William
Longyear, John Munroe
Magruder, George Lloyd
Mengarini, Gregory
Mouton, Alexander
Musmanno, Michael Angelo
Nast, Condé Montrose
O'Shaughnessy, Nelson Jarvis
Waterbury
Pallen, Condé Benoist
Pise, Charles Constantine
Provosty, Olivier Otis
Randall, James Ryder
Russell, Charles Wells
Saxton, Eugene Francis
Semmes, Alexander Jenkins
Semmes, Thomas Jenkins
Shipman, Andrew Jackson
Walsh, Henry Collins
Walsh, Thomas
Walters, Henry
White, Edward Douglass, 1845–
1921
Whiting, William Henry Chase
Graduate Study
Musmanno, Michael Angelo
Nast, Condé Montrose
Law
Bankhead, John Hollis
Bankhead, William Brockman
Carr, Wilbur John
Chavez, Dennis
Conboy, Martin

Cortelyou, George Bruce
Flynn, John Thomas
Lever, Asbury Francis
Musmanno, Michael Angelo
Walter, Francis Eugene
Medicine
Dana, Charles Loomis
Foote, John Ambrose
Garrison, Fielding Hudson
GEORGE WASHINGTON UNIVERSITY
(D.C.)
Alden, Raymond MacDonald
Baker, Frank
Coves, Elliott
Cranch, Christopher Pearse
Davis, Arthur Powell
Davis, Watson
Eliot, William Greenleaf
Franklin, Fabian
Harris, William Alexander
Hazelton, George Cochrane
Hitchcock, Frank Harris
Howell, Robert Boyte Crawford
Kelser, Raymond Alexander
Lewis, Exum Percival
Mason, Otis Tufton
Mitchell, William
Morfit, Campbell
Richardson, Charles Williamson
Ryland, Robert
Shuster, W(illiam) Morgan
Stanton, Frederick Perry
Stow, Baron
Tucker, Henry Holcombe
Walter, Francis Eugene
Weddell, Alexander Wilbourne
Wheeler, John Hill
Wilson, William Lyne
Graduate Study
Clark, Bennett Champ
Gidley, James Williams
Moore, Charles
Munroe, Charles Edward
Rister, Carl Coke
Simmons, James Stevens
Wilkinson, Theodore Stark
Zahniser, Howard Clinton
Law
Carr, Wilbur John
Cortelyou, George Bruce
Davis, William Hammatt
Dulles, John Foster
Flint, Weston
Guthrie, George Wilkins
Hastings, Daniel Oren
Hopson, Howard Colwell
McCawley, Charles Laurie
Newlands, Francis Griffith
Robins, Raymond
Weddell, Alexander Wilbourne
Wilson, William Lyne
Medicine
Bean, Tarleton Hoffman
Coues, Elliott
Dana, Charles Loomis
Dorset, Marion
Moore, Veranus Alva
Vander Veer, Albert
GEORGIA COLLEGE
O'Connor, Mary Flannery

GEORGIA LAW SCHOOL
Black, Eugene Robert
GEORGIA MILITARY INSTITUTE
Harrison, George Paul
Howell, Evan Park
Spencer, Samuel
Young, Pierce Manning Butler
GEORGIA SCHOOL OF TECHNOLOGY
Towers, John Henry
GERMANTOWN ACADEMY (PA.)
Bird, Robert Montgomery
Downey, John
Schaeffer, Charles William
Schaeffer, Frederick Christian
Stockton, Charles Herbert
GERMAN UNIVERSITY OF PRAGUE
(CZECHOSLOVAKIA)
Cori, Gerty Theresa Radnitz
Prokosch, Eduard
GETTYSBURG COLLEGE (PA.)
Buehler, Huber Gray
Clay, Albert Tobias
Eisenhart, Luther Pfahler
Hay, Charles Augustus
Horn, Edward Traill
Hunton, William Lee
Jacobs, Henry Eyster
McPherson, Edward
Muhlenberg, Frederick Augustus
Orth, Godlove Stein
Payne, Daniel Alexander
Richard, James William
Sadtler, John Philip Benjamin
Sadtler, Samuel Philip
Schmucker, Beale Melancthon
Seip, Theodore Lorenzo
Seiss, Joseph Augustus
Smith, Edgar Fahs
Sprecher, Samuel
Stine, Charles Milton Altland
Stoever, Martin Luther
Unangst, Erias
Valentine, Milton
Graduate Study
Stine, Charles Milton Altland
GETTYSBURG THEOLOGICAL SEMINARY (PA.)
Harpster, John Henry
Hay, Charles Augustus
Jacobs, Henry Eyster
Morris, John Gottlieb
Passavant, William Alfred
Richard, James William
Schaeffer, Charles William
GLASGOW UNIVERSITY (SCOTLAND)
Capps, Washington Lee
GONZAGA COLLEGE (D.C.)
Conboy, Martin
GONZAGA COLLEGE (WASH.)
Brophy, Thomas D'Arcy
GONZAGA UNIVERSITY (WASH.)
Hubbard, Bernard Rosecrans
Walker, Frank Comerford
GORHAM ACADEMY (MAINE)
Andrew, John Albion
Bradbury, James Ware
Peters, John Andrew
Prentiss, George Lewis
Smyth, William
Stowe, Calvin Ellis
Young, Aaron

GOUCHER COLLEGE (MD.)
Blair, Emily Newell
Phillips, Lena Madesin
Powdermaker, Hortense
Graduate Study
Adams, Joseph Quincy
GRAND ISLAND COLLEGE (NEB.)
Abbott, Grace
Sutherland, Edwin Hardin
GRAND SEMINARY, MONTREAL
(CANADA)
Schrembs, Joseph
GRAND SEMINARY (CANADA)
Curran, John Joseph
GRANVILLE COLLEGE (See DENISON
UNIVERSITY)
GREENSBORO LAW SCHOOL (N.C.)
Dixon, Thomas
GREENVILLE ACADEMY (TENN.)
Barton, David
GREENVILLE COLLEGE (ILL.)
Zahniser, Howard Clinton
GREENVILLE MILITARY INSTITUTE
(S.C.)
Manly, John Matthews
GREYLOCK INSTITUTE (MASS.)
Davison, Henry Pomeroy
Dickinson, John Woodbridge
Hazelton, George Cochrane
Sabin, Charles Hamilton
GRINNELL COLLEGE (IOWA)
Adams, Ephraim Douglass
Buckley, Oliver Ellsworth
Burton, Theodore Elijah
Cooper, Gary
Cowles, Gardner
Emerson, Oliver Farrar
Flanagan, Hallie
Hall, James Norman
Hopkins, Harry Lloyd
Hughes, Edwin Holt
Jones, Lynds
Kenyon, William Squire
Macy, Jesse
Manatt, James Irving
Noyes, William Albert
Ryan, Arthur Clayton
Shaw, Albert
Welch, Joseph Nye
Whitcomb, Selden Lincoln
Wilson, James
Graduate Study
Noyes, William Albert
GRISWOLD COLLEGE (IOWA)
Restarick, Henry Bond
GROTON SCHOOL (MASS.)
Allen, Frederick Lewis
Burnap, George Washington
Carter, James Gordon
Cutting, Bronson Murray
Farrar, Timothy
Haughton, Percy Duncan
Heintzelman, Stuart
Holbrook, Alfred
Hoppin, Joseph Clark
McCormick, Joseph Medill
McCormick, Robert Rutherford
Parker, Joel, 1795–1875
Todd, Sereno Edwards
GUILFORD COLLEGE (N.C.)
Pearson, Thomas Gilbert

GUSTAVUS ADOLPHUS COLLEGE (MINN.)
Seashore, Carl Emil

HAHNEMANN MEDICAL SCHOOL (ILL.)
Menninger, Charles Frederick
Simmons, George Henry

HALLOWELL ACADEMY (MAINE)
Abbott, Jacob
Abbott, John Stevens Cabot
Cheever, George Barrell
Cheever, Henry Theodore
Hubbard, Thomas Hamlin
Williams, Reuel

HAMBURG SCHOOL OF APPLIED ARTS (GERMANY)
Feininger, Lyonel (Charles Léonell Adrian)

HAMILTON ACADEMY (N.Y.)
Bishop, Nathan
Bonney, Charles Carroll
Cogswell, William Browne
Maynard, Edward
Orton, Harlow South
Park, Roswell, 1807–1869
Smith, Erasmus Darwin
Sterling, John Whalen

HAMILTON COLLEGE (N.Y.)
Adams, Samuel Hopkins
Amidon, Charles Fremont
Barnes, Albert
Bassett, Edward Murray
Bennett, Nathaniel
Blair, Austin
Bliss, Philemon
Bliss, Porter Cornelius
Bradford, Amory Howe
Breese, Sidney
Burdick, Francis Marion
Child, Frank Samuel
Cochrane, John
Dwight, Benjamin Woodbridge
Dwight, Harrison Gray Otis
Dwight, Theodore William
Eells, Dan Parmelee
Fiske, Daniel Willard
Grant, Asabel
Hall, Isaac Hollister
Hawley, Joseph Roswell
Hinman, George Wheeler
Hodges, George
Howe, William Wirt
Hunt, Ward
Huntington, Daniel
Ives, Irving McNeil
Ives, Levi Silliman
Jenkins, John Stilwell
Kendrick, Asahel Clark
Kidder, Daniel Parish
King, Edward Skinner
Knox, George William
Knox, John Jay
Lathrop, John Hiram
Lord, Chester Sanders
McMaster, Guy Humphreys
Mahan, Asa
Miller, William Henry Harrison
North, Edward
North, Simon Newton Dexter
Orton, Edward Francis Baxter
Paine, John Alsop

Parker, Joel, 1799–1873
Payne, Henry B.
Pierson, Arthur Tappan
Pomeroy, John Norton
Porter, Jermain Gildersleeve
Powell, Edward Payson
Putnam, James Osborne
Randall, Samuel Sidwell
Reid, Gilbert
Robinson, Edward, 1794–1863
Root, Elihu
Sawyer, Leicester Ambrose
Sayles, John
Schneider, Benjamin
Scollard, Clinton
Shaw, Henry Wheeler
Sheldon, Edward Austin
Sherman, James Schoolcraft
Sherman, James Schoolcraft
Smith, Erasmus Darwin
Smith, Gerrit
Stryker, Lloyd Paul
Stryker, Melancthon Woolsey
Taylor, James Wickes
Thayer, Amos Madden
Underwood, John Curtiss
Walker, Gilbert Carlton
Wallace, William James
Warner, Charles Dudley
Whedon, Daniel Denison
White, William Nathaniel
Wickson, Edward James
Winslow, William Copley
Woollcott, Alexander Humphreys
Graduate Study
Stryker, Lloyd Paul

HAMILTON LITERARY AND THEOLOGICAL INSTITUTION (See COLGATE UNIVERSITY)

HAMLINE UNIVERSITY (MINN.)
Schall, Thomas David

HAMMA SCHOOL OF THEOLOGY OF WITTENBERG UNIVERSITY
Douglas, Lloyd Cassel
Graduate Study
Douglas, Lloyd Cassel

HAMPDEN-SYDNEY COLLEGE (VA.)
Atkinson, Thomas
Baker, Daniel
Bibb, George Mortimer
Bocock, Thomas Stanley
Cabell, Nathaniel Francis
Cabell, William H.
Carr, Dabney
Coles, Edward
Dabney, Charles William
Dabney, Robert Lewis
Gamble, Hamilton Rowan
Giles, William Branch
Harrison, William Henry
Howard, William Travis
Johnston, Peter
Klipstein, Louis Frederick
Ligon, Thomas Watkins
McGready, James
McIlwaine, Richard
Manson, Otis Frederick
Mettauer, John Peter
Penick, Charles Clifton
Pollard, Edward Alfred
Preston, John Smith

Preston, William Ballard
Price, Sterling
Pryor, Roger Atkinson
Rives, William Cabell
Smith, Benjamin Mosby
Stevenson, John White
Stuart, John Leighton
Sydnor, Charles Sackett
Venable, Charles Scott
Waddel, Moses
Theology
Lindley, Daniel

HAMPTON INSTITUTE (VA.)
Abbott, Robert Sengstacke
Barrett, Janie Porter
Morton, Robert Russa
Smith, Lucy Harth

HANNIBAL-LA GRANGE COLLEGE (MO.)
Cannon, Clarence

HANOVER COLLEGE (IND.)
Barnes, Charles Reid
Blackburn, William Maxwell
Coulter, John Merle
Dawson, Thomas Cleland
English, William Hayden
Fisher, Walter Lowrie
Goldsmith, Middleton
Hamilton, Edward John
Hendricks, Thomas Andrews
Jacob, Richard Taylor
Monroe, Paul
Oldfather, William Abbott
Patterson, James Kennedy
Porter, Albert Gallatin
Riley, William Bell
Wallace, William Ross
Whitworth, George Frederic
Wiley, Harvey Washington
Wilson, Samuel Ramsey
Graduate Study
Jessup, Walter Albert

HARDIN-SIMMONS UNIVERSITY (TEX.)
Richardson, Sid Williams
Rister, Carl Coke

HARTFORD THEOLOGICAL SEMINARY (CONN.)
Barton, James Levi
Frame, Alice Seymour Browne
Nutting, Wallace
Pitkin, Walter Boughton
Rhees, Rush

HARVARD UNIVERSITY (MASS.)
Abbot, Benjamin
Abbot, Francis Ellingwood
Adams, Brooks
Adams, Charles Francis, 1807–1886
Adams, Charles Francis, 1835–1915
Adams, Eliphalet
Adams, Henry Brooks
Adams, John, 1735–1826
Adams, John Quincy
Adams, Nehemiah
Adams, Samuel
Agassiz, Alexander
Agee, James Rufus
Alden, Ebenezer
Alden, Timothy
Aldrich, Richard

Alger, Horatio
Allen, Charles
Allen, Edward Ellis
Allen, Frederick Lewis
Allen, Glover Morrill
Allen, Joel Asaph
Allen, Joseph Henry
Allen, William
Allen, William Francis
Allison, Nathaniel
Allport, Gordon Willard
Allston, Washington
Ames, Fisher
Ames, Frederick Lothrop
Ames, James Barr
Ames, Oakes
Ames, Winthrop
Andrew, Samuel
Appleton, Nathaniel Walker
Appleton, Thomas Gold
Appleton, William Sumner
Apthorp, William Foster
Arensberg, Walter Conrad
Arvin, Newton
Aspinwall, William
Astor, John Jacob, 1864–1912
Astor, William Vincent
Atherton, Charles Gordon
Atherton, Joshua
Atwood, Charles B.
Auchmuty, Samuel
Austin, James Trecothick
Austin, Jonathan Loring
Austin, William
Babbitt, Irving
Babcock, James Francis
Babcock, James Woods
Bacon, Robert
Bailey, Jacob
Baker, George Pierce
Baker, Harvey Humphrey
Balch, Thomas Willing
Baldwin, Loammi, 1780–1838
Baldwin, William Henry
Ballantine, Arthur Atwood
Bancroft, Aaron
Bancroft, Wilder Dwight
Bancroft. George
Barbour, Thomas
Barlow, Francis Channing
Barnard, Charles Francis
Barnard, Chester Irving
Barnard, John
Barnes, Joseph K.
Barnwell, Robert Woodward
Bartlett, Joseph
Bass, Edward
Batchelor, George
Beal, William James
Beale, Joseph Henry
Beaman, Charles Cotesworth
Becker, George Ferdinand
Belcher, Jonathan
Belknap, Jeremy
Bellows, Henry Whitney
Bemis, George
Benchley, Robert Charles
Benjamin, Park, 1809–1864
Bentley, William
Berenson, Bernard
Besse, Arthur Lyman
Bettman, Alfred

Bickmore, Albert Smith
Biddle, Francis Beverley
Bigelow, Frank Hagar
Bigelow, Harry Augustus
Bigelow, Henry Bryant
Bigelow, Henry Jacob
Bigelow, Jacob
Bigelow, William Sturgis
Biggers, Earl Derr
Billings, Asa White Kenney
Binney, Horace
Birkhoff, George David
Bixby, James Thompson
Blaikie, William
Blaustein, David
Bliss, Cornelius Newton
Bliss, George, 1830–1897
Bliss, Jonathan
Bliss, Robert Woods
Bloomfield, Leonard
Bloomfield, Meyer
Blowers, Sampson Salter
Bôcher, Maxime
Bonaparte, Charles Joseph
Bonaparte, Jerome Napoleon
Bond, George Phillips
Boott, Kirk
Bourne, Benjamin
Bourne, Jonathan
Boutell, Henry Sherman
Bowditch, Charles Pickering
Bowditch, Henry Ingersoll
Bowditch, Henry Pickering
Bowdoin, James, 1726–1790
Bowdoin, James, 1752–1811
Bowen, Francis
Bowman, Isaiah
Boyden, Roland William
Brackett, Jeffrey Richardson
Bradford, Alden
Bradford, Edward Hickling
Bradford, Gamaliel
Bradley, Milton
Bradley, Theophilus
Brainerd, Erastus
Brattle, Thomas
Brattle, William
Brazer, John
Brewer, Thomas Mayo
Bridgman, Percy Williams
Briggs, LeBaron Russell
Brinton, Clarence Crane
Brooks, Alfred Hulse
Brooks, Charles
Brooks, Charles Timothy
Brooks, Phillips
Brooks, Van Wyck
Broun, Heywood Campbell
Brown, Addison
Brown, Charles Rufus
Brown, Frederic Tilden
Brown, John Mason, Jr.
Brown, Walter Folger
Brown, William Garrott
Browne, Daniel Jay
Browne, William
Brownlee, James Forbis
Buckminster, Joseph Stevens
Bulfinch, Charles
Bulfinch, Thomas
Bull, William Tillinghast
Bullard, Henry Adams

Burgess, Edward
Burgess, W(illiam) Starling
Burlingame, Edward Livermore
Burlingham, Charles Culp
Burnap, George Washington
Burnham, William Henry
Burrage, Walter Lincoln
Burton, Frederick Russell
Burton. Warren
Byerly, William Elwood
Byles, Mather
Cabot, Arthur Tracy
Cabot, George
Cabot, Godfrey Lowell
Cabot, Hugh
Cabot, Richard Clarke
Callender, John
Calvert, George Henry
Campbell, Prince Lucien
Cannon, Walter Bradford
Capen, Samuel Paul
Carpenter, George Rice
Carpenter, John Alden
Carter, James Coolidge
Carter, James Gordon
Castle, William Richards, Jr.
Catchings, Waddill
Chadwick, James Read
Chamberlain, Joseph Perkins
Chamberlain, Nathan Henry
Chandler, Charles Frederick
Chandler, Seth Carlo
Channing, Edward
Channing, Edward Tyrrell
Channing, Walter
Channing, William Ellery, 1780
–1842
Channing, William Ellery, 1818
–1901
Channing, William Francis
Channing, William Henry
Chapman, John Jay
Chapman, Victor Emmanuel
Chase, Pliny Earle
Chase, Thomas
Chauncy, Charles
Child, David Lee
Child, Francis James
Child, Richard Washburn
Chipman, Ward
Choate, Joseph Hodges
Clap, Thomas
Clark, Grenville
Clark, Henry James
Clark, Jonas
Clarke, Frank Wigglesworth
Clarke, James Freeman
Clarke, Richard
Cleaveland, Parker
Cleveland, Aaron
Clothier, William Jackson
Cobb, David
Cobb, Jonathan Holmes
Coerne, Louis Adolphe
Cogswell, Joseph Green
Coker, James Lide
Colburn, Warren
Cole, Frank Nelson
Colman, Benjamin
Colpitts, Edwin Henry
Converse, Frederick Shepherd
Cook, Clarence Chatham

Cook, Flavius Josephus
Cook, George Cram
Cook, Walter
Cooke, Elisha, 1637–1715
Cooke, Elisha, 1678–1737
Cooke, Josiah Parsons
Coolidge, Archibald Cary
Coolidge, Charles Allerton
Coolidge, Julian Lowell
Coolidge, Thomas Jefferson
Cooper, Samuel, 1725–1783
Copeland, Charles Townsend
Cory, Charles Barney
Costigan, Edward Prentiss
Costigan, George Purcell
Cotton, Joseph Potter
Crafts, James Mason
Crafts, William
Cranch, Christopher Pearse
Cranch, William
Croly, Herbert David
Cross, Arthur Lyon
Cross, Samuel Hazzard
Crowne, John
Crowninshield, Frederic
Cummings, Edward
Cummings, E. E.
Curtin, Jeremiah
Curtis, Benjamin Robbins
Curtis, Charles Pelham
Curtis, George Ticknor
Curtis, John Green
Curwen, Samuel
Cushing, Caleb
Cushing, Luther Stearns
Cushing, Thomas
Cushing, William
Cushman, Joseph Augustine
Cushman, Joshua
Cutler, Elliott Carr
Cutler, Timothy
Cutter, Charles Ammi
Cutting, Bronson Murray
Dalton, John Coll
Damon, Ralph Shepard
Dana, Charles Anderson
Dana, Francis
Dana, James
Dana, James Freeman
Dana, Richard
Dana, Richard Henry, 1787–1879
Dana, Richard Henry, 1815–1882
Dana, Samuel Luther
Dane, Nathan
Danforth, Thomas, 1703–c. 1786
Davenport, Charles Benedict
Davies, Henry Eugene
Davis, Andrew McFarland
Davis, Charles Henry, 1807–1877
Davis, Dwight Filley
Davis, Horace
Davis, John, 1761–1847
Davis, John Chandler Bancroft
Davis, Owen Gould
Davis, William Morris
Davis, William Thomas
Dawson, John
Deane, Samuel

Deering, Nathaniel
Dennie, Joseph
Dennison, Henry Sturgis
Derby, Elias Hasket, 1766–1826
Derby, Elias Hasket, 1803–1880
Dett, Robert Nathaniel
Devens, Charles
DeVoto, Bernard Augustine
Dexter, Franklin
Dexter, Samuel, 1761–1816
Diller, Joseph Silas
Dillingham, Walter Francis
Dix, John Homer
Dixon, Roland Burrage
Doe, Charles
Dole, Charles Fletcher
Dole, James Drummond
Dole, Nathan Haskell
Dorr, Thomas Wilson
Dorsheimer, William Edward
Dos Passos, John Roderigo
Downing, George
Dudley, Joseph
Dudley, Paul
Dummer, Jeremiah, c. 1679–1739
Dunbar, Charles Franklin
Durant, Henry Fowle
Durell, Edward Henry
Durfee, William Franklin
Dwight, Francis
Dwight, John Sullivan
Dwight, Thomas
Dyer, Louis
Eames, Charles
Earhart, Amelia Mary
Edes, Robert Thaxter
Eliot, Charles
Eliot, Charles William
Eliot, Samuel
Eliot, Samuel Atkins
Eliot, T(homas) S(tearns)
Elleny, William
Elliott, Aaron Marshall
Elliott, William
Ellis, Calvin
Ellis, George Edward
Elman, Robert
Elwyn, Alfred Langdon
Emerson, Edward Waldo
Emerson, George Barrell
Emerson, Haven
Emerson, Joseph
Emerson, Ralph Waldo
Emerson, William
Emerton, Ephraim
Emmons, Samuel Franklin
Endicott, William Crowninshield
English, George Bethune
Ernst, Harold Clarence
Ernst, Oswald Herbert
Eustis, George, 1796–1858
Eustis, George, 1828–1872
Eustis, Henry Lawrence
Eustis, James Biddle
Eustis, William
Everett, Alexander Hill
Everett, Edward
Ewer, Ferdinand Cartwright
Fairchild, Blair
Fairchild, Charles Stebbins

Fairlie, John Archibald
Farlow, William Gilson
Farrar, John
Fay, Sidney Bradshaw
Felton, Cornelius Conway
Felton, Samuel Morse
Fenn, William Wallace
Fenollosa, Ernest Francisco
Fernald, James Champlin
Fernald, Merritt Lyndon
Fessenden, Francis
Fewkes, Jesse Walter
Field, Herbert Haviland
Field, Marshall, IV
Finck, Henry Theophilus
Fisher, Joshua Francis
Fiske, Amos Kidder
Fiske, George Converse
Fiske, John
Fitz, Reginald Heber
Flagg, Thomas Wilson
Flandrau, Charles Macomb
Fletcher, John Gould
Flint, Albert Stowell
Flint, Austin
Flint, Charles Louis
Flint, Timothy
Folsom, Charles
Folsom, George
Foote, Arthur William
Forbes, John Murray
Forbes, William Cameron
Force, Manning Ferguson
Ford, George Burdett
Foster, Abiel
Foster, Frank Hugh
Foster, John
Foster, John Watson
Foster, William Trufant
Fox, John William
Francis, Convers
Frear, William
Freeman, James
French, William Merchant Richardson
Frisbie, Levi
Frothingham, Nathaniel Langdon
Frothingham, Octavius Brooks
Frothingham, Paul Revere
Fullam, Frank L.
Fuller, Joseph Vincent
Fuller, Richard
Fulton, John Farquhar
Furness, Horace Howard, 1833–1912
Furness, Horace Howard, 1865–1930
Furness, William Henry
Gannett, Ezra Stiles
Gannett, Henry
Gannett, William Channing
Gardiner, Robert Hallowell
Garrard, Kenner
Garrison, Lindley Miller
Gary, Martin Witherspoon
Gay, Ebenezer
Gay, Frederick Parker
Gay, Sydney Howard
Gerry, Elbridge
Gibbs, George, 1815–1873
Gifford, Walter Sherman

Gilman, Samuel
Golder, Frank Alfred
Goldmark, Henry
Goodhue, Benjamin
Goodnough, Xanthus Henry
Goodrich, Frank Boott
Goodwin, William Watson
Gordon, George Angier
Gordon, George Byron
Gorham, John
Gould, Augustus Addison
Gould, Benjamin Apthorp,
    1787–1859
Grandgent, Charles Hall
Grant, George Barnard
Grant, Harry Johnston
Grant, Percy Stickney
Grant, Robert
Gray, Francis Calley
Gray, Horace
Gray, John Chipman
Green, Francis
Green, Jacob, 1722–1790
Green, John
Green, Joseph
Green, Samuel Abbott
Green, Samuel Swett
Greene, Charles Ezra
Greene, George Sears
Greene, Jerome Davis
Greene, Roger Sherman
Greener, Richard Theodore
Greenhalge, Frederic Thomas
Greenlaw, Edwin Almiron
Greenough, Henry
Greenough, Horatio
Greenough, James Bradstreet
Greenwood, Isaac
Gregg, Alan
Grew, Joseph Clark
Gridley, Jeremiah
Griswold, William McCrillis
Guild, Curtis, 1860–1915
Guinzburg, Harold Kleinert
Gummere, Francis Barton
Gurney, Ephraim Whitman
Hackett, Frank Warren
Hagedorn, Hermann Ludwig
    Gebhard
Hague, James Duncan
Hale, Charles
Hale, Edward Everett
Hale, Frederick
Hale, Horatio Emmons
Hale, William Bayard
Hale, William Gardner
Hall, Fitzedward
Hall, Willard
Hamlin, Charles Sumner
Hancock, John, 1736–1793
Hand, Augustus Noble
Hand, Learned
Hapgood, Hutchins
Hapgood, Norman
Haring, Clarence
Harrington, Charles
Harris, Thaddeus Mason
Harris, Thaddeus William
Harris, William
Harrod, Benjamin Morgan
Hart, Albert Bushnell
Haughton, Percy Duncan

Hawthorne, Julian
Hayward, George
Hazeltine, Mayo Williamson
Heard, Franklin Fiske
Hearst, William Randolph
Hedge, Frederic Henry
Hedge, Levi
Henck, John Benjamin
Henderson, Lawrence Joseph
Herrick, Robert Welch
Herschel, Clemens
Herter, Christian Archibald
Hess, Alfred Fabian
Higginson, Henry Lee
Higginson, Nathaniel
Higginson, Thomas Wentworth
Hildreth, Richard
Hill, Henry Barker
Hill, Joseph Adna
Hill, Thomas, 1818–1891
Hillard, George Stillman
Hillyer, Robert Silliman
Hitchcock, Enos
Hitchcock, Frank Harris
Hitchcock, James Ripley Well-
    man
Hitchcock, Thomas
Hoar, Ebenezer Rockwood
Hoar, George Frisbie
Hoar, Leonard
Hoar, Samuel
Hocking, William Ernest
Hoer, Ebenezer Rockwood
Hoffman, Wickham
Holdrege, George Ward
Holland, Clifford Milburn
Holmes, John Haynes
Holmes, Nathaniel
Holmes, Oliver Wendell, 1809–
    1894
Holmes, Oliver Wendell, 1841–
    1935
Holt, Edwin Bissell
Holyoke, Edward Augustus
Holyoke, Samuel
Hooper, William
Hoover, Charles Franklin
Hoppin, Joseph Clark
Horton, Samuel Dana
Hosmer, Frederick Lucian
Hosmer, James Kendall
Houghton, Alanson Bigelow
Howe, Andrew Jackson
Howe, Henry Marion
Howe, Mark De Wolfe
Hubbard, Henry Guernsey
Hubbard, William
Hubbard, Wynant Davis
Hughes, Hector James
Hughes, Howard Robard
Huidekoper, Frederic
Hunt, Carleton
Hunt, William Gibbes
Hunt, William Morris
Huntington, Edward Vermilye
Huntington, Jeddediah
Huntington, William Reed
Hurlbert, William Henry
Hutchinson, Thomas
Hyatt, Alpheus
Hyde, William DeWitt
Inman, George

Jackman, Wilbur Samuel
Jackson, Charles
Jackson, Dunham
Jackson, James, 1777–1867
Jaggar, Thomas Augustus, Jr.
James, Edmund Janes
James, William
Jarvis, Edward
Jeffries, Benjamin Joy
Jeffries, John
Jenks, William
Jenney, William LeBaron
Jennings, James Herman
Johns, Clayton
Johnson, Joseph French
Johnson, Samuel
Jones, John Price
Jones, Leonard Augustus
Jones, Robert Edmond
Jones, William
Jordan, Eben Dyer
Kauffman, Calvin Henry
Keith, Arthur
Kennedy, John Fitzgerald
Kennedy, Joseph Patrick
Kennedy, Robert Francis
Kent, Edward
Kerr, Washington Caruthers
Kidder, Alfred Vincent
Kimball, (Sidney) Fiske
King, Henry Churchill
King, James Gore
King, Rufus, 1755–1827
Kirkland, John Thornton
Kittredge, George Lyman
Knapp, Philip Coombs
Knauth, Oswald Whitman
Kneeland, Samuel
Knight, Henry Cogswell
Ladd, William
La Farge, Christopher Grant
LaFarge, John
La Farge, Oliver Hazard Perry
Lamont, Hammond
Lamont, Thomas William
Lander, Edward
Lane, George Martin
Langdell, Christopher Colum-
    bus
Langdon, Courtney
Langley, John Williams
Lardner, John Abbott
Lathrop, John
Laughlin, James Laurence
Law, Jonathan
Lawrence, Amos Adams
Lawrence, William
Lear, Tobias
Lee, Alfred
Lee, Joseph
Lee, William Henry Fitzhugh
Lehman, Arthur
Leiter, Joseph
Leonard, Charles Lester
Leonard, Daniel
Leonard, Levi Washburn
Leverett, John, 1662–1724
Lewis, Clarence Irving
Lewis, Gilbert Newton
Lincoln, Enoch
Lincoln, Levi, 1749–1820
Lincoln, Levi, 1782–1868

Lincoln, Robert Todd
Lindsay, Howard
Littauer, Lucius Nathan
Livermore, Abiel Abbot
Livermore, Samuel, 1786–1833
Lloyd, Alfred Henry
Locke, Alain Leroy
Lodge, George Cabot
Lodge, John Ellerton
Loeb, James
Loeb, Morris
Lombard, Warren Plimpton
Long, John Davis
Longfellow, Ernest Wadsworth
Longfellow, Samuel
Longfellow, Stephen
Longfellow, William Pitt Preble
Longworth, Nicholas
Loring, Edward Greely
Loring, Ellis Gray
Loring, Frederick Wadsworth
Loring, George Bailey
Lovell, James
Lovell, John
Lovell, Joseph
Lovering, Joseph
Lovett, Robert Morss
Lovett, Robert Williamson
Lowe, Charles
Lowell, Abbott Lawrence
Lowell, Edward Jackson
Lowell, Francis Cabot
Lowell, Guy
Lowell, James Russell
Lowell, John, 1743–1802
Lowell, John, 1769–1840
Lowell, John, 1799–1836
Lowell, John, 1824–1897
Lowell, Percival
Lowell, Robert Traill Spence
Lowery, Woodbury
Lummis, Charles Fletcher
Lunt, George
Lydenberg, Harry Miller
Lyman, Benjamin Smith
Lyman, Theodore, 1792–1849
Lyman, Theodore, 1833–1897
Lynde, Benjamin
Mabery, Charles Frederic
McBurney, Charles
MacCurdy, George Grant
McIntyre, Alfred Robert
McKenzie, Alexander
McKim, Charles Follen
MacNider, Hanford
MacVeagh, Charles
Macy, John Albert
Mallinckrodt, Edward, Jr.
Mallory, Frank Burr
Mann, James
Mannes, Leopold Damrosch
Mapes, Charles Victor
Marmaduke, John Sappington
Marquand, John Phillips
Marsh, John, 1799–1856
Martin, Edward Sandford
Mason, Daniel Gregory
Mather, Cotton
Mather, Increase
Mather, Samuel, 1706–1785
Matthews, Nathan
Mattingly, Garrett

Mayer, Oscar Gottfried
Mayhew, Jonathan
Mead, George Herbert
Mellen, Grenville
Mellen, Prentiss
Mercer, Henry Chapman
Merck, George Wilhelm
Merrick, Pliny
Merrill, George Edmands
Merrill, William Bradford
Meyer, George von Lengerke
Mezes, Sidney Edward
Miller, Gerrit Smith, Jr.
Millet, Francis Davis
Mills, Ogden Livingston
Minot, George Richards
Mitchell, James Tyndale
Mitchell, John Ames
Mitchell, Jonathan
Mitchell, Nahum
Moffat, Jay Pierrepont
Montague, Gilbert Holland
Montague, William Pepperell
Moody, William Henry
Moody, William Vaughn
Moore, Charles
Moore, Clifford Herschel
Morgan, Edwin Vernon
Morgan, John Pierpont
Morgan, Morris Hicky
Morison, George Shattuck
Morley, Sylvanus Griswold
Morris, Edward Joy
Morse, Edward Sylvester
Morse, John Lovett
Morse, John Torrey
Morton, Ferdinand Quintin
Morton, William James
Motley, John Lothrop
Mumford, James Gregory
Munro, William Bennett
Munroe, Charles Edward
Muzzey, David Saville
Nash, Henry Sylvester
Nef, John Ulric
Nelson, Charles Alexander
Newell, William Wells
Newman, Henry
Newman, Samuel Phillips
Niles, Nathaniel, 1741–1828
Niles, Samuel
Noble, Gladwyn Kingsley
Nordhoff, Charles Bernard
Norton, Andrews
Norton, Charles Eliot
Noyes, George Repall
Nutting, Wallace
O'Brien, Robert Lincoln
Olds, Robert Edwin
Oliver, Andrew, 1706–1774
Oliver, Andrew, 1731–1799
Oliver, Henry Kemble
Oliver, Peter
Olmsted, Frederick Law
Oppenheimer, Julius Robert
Osborne, Thomas Mott
Osgood, George Laurie
Osgood, Howard
Osgood, Samuel
Osgood, William Fogg
Otis, Harrison Gray, 1765–1848
Otis, James

Packard, Frederick Adolphus
Page, Charles Grafton
Paine, Charles
Paine, Charles Jackson
Paine, Elijah
Paine, Martyn
Paine, Robert Treat, 1731–1814
Paine, Robert Treat, 1773–1811
Paine, Robert Treat, 1835–1910
Palfrey, John Carver
Palfrey, John Gorham
Palmer, George Herbert
Parker, Carleton Hubbell
Parker, George Howard
Parker, Henry Taylor
Parker, Isaac
Parker, James Cutler Dunn
Parker, Richard Green
Parker, Theodore
Parker, Willard
Parkman, Francis
Parrington, Vernon Louis
Parris, Samuel
Parsons, Samuel Holden
Parsons, Theophilus, 1750–
    1813
Parsons, Theophilus, 1797–
    1882
Partridge, James Rudolph
Pasco, Samuel
Patten, William
Payson, Edward
Payson, Seth
Peabody, Andrew Preston
Peabody, Francis Greenwood
Peabody, Oliver William Bourn
Peabody, Robert Swain
Peabody, William Bourn Oliver
Pearson, Edmund Lester
Pearson, Eliphalet
Peattie, Donald Culross
Peck, William Dandridge
Peirce, Benjamin
Peirce, Benjamin Osgood
Peirce, Charles Sanders
Peirce, Cyrus
Peirce, James Mills
Penrose, Boies
Penrose, Richard Alexander
    Fullerton
Penrose, Spencer
Perin, Charles Page
Perkins, Charles Callahan
Perkins, James Handasyd
Perkins, Maxwell Evarts
Perkins, Thomas Nelson
Perry, Thomas Sergeant
Perry, William
Perry, William Stevens
Phillips, John
Phillips, John Sanburn
Phillips, Samuel
Phillips, Wendell
Phillips, Willard
Phillips, William
Pickering, Charles
Pickering, Edward Charles
Pickering, John, c. 1738–1805
Pickering, John, 1777–1846
Pickering, Timothy
Pierpont, James

Pierson, Abraham, c. 1645–1707
Pike, Albert
Pike, Nicolas
Piper, William Thomas
Pollak, Walter Heilprin
Pond, George Edward
Poor, John
Potter, Elisha Reynolds
Pray, Isaac Clark
Preble, William Pitt
Prescott, Oliver
Prescott, William Hickling
Prince, Frederick Henry
Prince, Morton
Prince, Thomas
Pulitzer, Joseph, Jr.
Pulitzer, Ralph
Putnam, Charles Pickering
Putnam, Frederic Ward
Putnam, (George) Herbert
Putnam, Helen Cordelia
Putnam, James Jackson
Pynchon, Thomas Ruggles
Quincy, Edmund
Quincy, Josiah, 1744–1775
Quincy, Josiah, 1772–1864
Quincy, Josiah Phillips
Rand, Benjamin
Rand, Edward Kennard
Randall, Clarence Belden
Rantoul, Robert, 1805–1852
Rawle, Francis, 1846–1930
Read, Conyers
Read, John, 1679/80–1749
Read, Nathan
Reed, James, 1834–1921
Reed, John, 1887–1920
Reed, Sampson
Reisner, George Andrew
Richards, John Kelvey
Richards, Theodore William
Richardson, Henry Hobson
Richardson, William Adams
Richardson, William Merchant
Riddle, George Peabody
Rideout, Henry Milner
Rindge, Frederick Hastings
Rinehart, Stanley Marshall, Jr.
Ripley, Ezra
Ripley, George
Robbins, Chandler
Robinson, Benjamin Lincoln
Robinson, Edward, 1858–1931
Robinson, Edwin Arlington
Robinson, James Harvey
Roethke, Theodore Huebner
Rogers, William Crowninshield
Roosevelt, Franklin Delano
Roosevelt, Kermit
Roosevelt, Theodore
Ropes, James Hardy
Ropes, John Codman
Rorimer, James Joseph
Ross, Denman Waldo
Rotch, Arthur
Rotch, Thomas Morgan
Rothrock, Joseph Trimble
Rublee, George
Ruggles, Timothy
Ruhl, Arthur Brown
Rumsey, Charles Cary

Runkle, John Daniel
Russell, William Eustis
Sachs, Bernard
Sachs, Paul Joseph
Safford, Truman Henry
Saltonstall, Gurdon
Sanborn, Franklin Benjamin
Sanders, Daniel Clarke
Sanford, Edward Terry
Sanger, Charles Robert
Sanger, George Partridge
Santayana, George
Sargent, Charles Sprague
Sargent, Henry Winthrop
Sargent, John Osborne
Sargent, Lucius Manlius
Sargent, Winthrop, 1753–1820
Savage, Henry Wilson
Savage, James
Savage, Philip Henry
Sawyer, Wilbur Augustus
Scammell, Alexander
Schofield, Henry
Schouler, James
Scott, James Brown
Searle, Arthur
Sears, Richard Dudley
Seccomb, John
Sedgwick, Arthur George
Sedgwick, Ellery
Seeger, Alan
Seldes, Gilbert Vivian
Sewall, Harold Marsh
Sewall, Jonathan
Sewall, Jonathan Mitchell
Sewall, Joseph Addison
Sewall, Samuel
Sewall, Stephen
Shaler, Nathaniel Southgate
Sharpless, Isaac
Shattuck, Frederick Cheever
Shattuck, George Brune
Shattuck, George Cheyne, 1783–1854
Shattuck, George Cheyne, 1813–1893
Shaw, Lemuel
Shaw, William Smith
Sheldon, Edward Stevens
Shepley, George Foster
Sherwin, Thomas
Sherwood, Robert Emmet
Shorey, Paul
Short, Charles
Shubrick, William Branford
Shurtleff, Nathaniel Bradstreet
Sibley, John Langdon
Sidis, Boris
Simmons, Edward
Simonds, Frank Herbert
Sinnott, Edmund Ware
Slattery, Charles Lewis
Smith, Courtney Craig
Smith, Jeremiah, 1759–1842
Smith, Jeremiah, 1837–1921
Smith, Lloyd Logan Pearsall
Smith, Ormond Gerald
Smith, Samuel Francis
Smyth, Herbert Weir
Soley, James Russell
Southard, Elmer Ernest
Spalding, Lyman

Sparks, Jared
Spearns, William Augustus
Spencer, Ambrose
Sprague, Oliver Mitchell Wentworth
Sprague, Peleg
Spurr, Josiah Edward
Starr, Merritt
Stearns, Asahel
Stearns, Eben Sperry
Stearns, Harold Edmund
Stearns, Oliver
Stearns, William Augustus
Stebbins, Horatio
Stein, Leo Daniel
Stephenson, Nathaniel Wright
Stetson, Henry Crosby
Stevens, John Austin, 1827–1910
Stevens, Wallace
Stewardson, John
Stimson, Frederic Jesup
Stoddard, Solomon
Stoddard, Theodore Lothrop
Stokes, Isaac Newton Phelps
Stolberg, Benjamin
Stone, James Kent
Storer, Bellamy
Storer, Francis Humphreys
Storer, Horatio Robinson
Storey, Moorfield
Storrow, Charles Storer
Storrow, James Jackson
Story, Isaac
Story, Joseph
Story, William Edward
Story, William Wetmore
Stoughton, William
Straus, Jesse Isidor
Straus, Percy Selden
Stringham, Washington Irving
Strobel, Edward Henry
Strong, Caleb
Strong, Charles Augustus
Sullivan, George
Sullivan, Mark
Sullivan, William
Sumner, Charles
Sumner, James Batcheller
Swanton, John Reed
Tarr, Ralph Stockman
Tatlock, John Strong Perry
Taussig, Frank William
Taussig, Frederick Joseph
Taylor, Edward
Taylor, Frank Bursley
Taylor, Henry Osborn
Taylor, Richard
Thacher, George
Thacher, Peter, 1651–1727
Thacher, Peter, 1752–1802
Thacher, Samuel Cooper
Thaw, Harry Kendall
Thaxter, Roland
Thayer, Alexander Wheelock
Thayer, Ezra Ripley
Thayer, James Bradley
Thayer, Joseph Henry
Thayer, William Roscoe
Thayer, William Sydney
Thompson, Benjamin
Thoreau, Henry David

Thorndike, Edward Lee
Thwing, Charles Franklin
Tinkham, George Holden
Tompkins, Floyd Williams
Tompson, Benjamin
Tower, Charlemagne
Townsend, Edward Davis
Tracy, Nathaniel
Train, Arthur Cheney
Treat, Samuel
Trowbridge, Edmund
Trowbridge, John
Trumbull, John, 1756–1843
Trumbull, Jonathan, 1710–1785
Trumbull, Jonathan, 1740–1809
Trumbull, Joseph
Tuckerman, Bayard
Tuckerman, Edward
Tuckerman, Frederick Goddard
Tuckerman, Henry Theodore
Tuckerman, Joseph
Tudor, William
Tufts, Cotton
Tufts, John
Tweed, Harrison
Tyler, Royall
Tyng, Stephen Higginson
Underwood, Loring
Upham, Charles Wentworth
Vaillant, George Clapp
Valentine, Robert Grosvenor
Van Brunt, Henry
Vaughan, Thomas Wayland
Veblen, Oswald
Verrill, Addison Emery
Very, Jones
Vesey, William
Villard, Oswald Garrison
Wadsworth, Eliot
Wadsworth, James Samuel
Wadsworth, Peleg
Wainwright, Jonathan Mayhew
Walcott, Henry Pickering
Walker, James
Walker, Sears Cook
Walker, Timothy, 1705–1782
Walker, Timothy, 1802–1856
Walker, William Johnson
Walsh, James Anthony
Walter, Thomas
Walters, Henry
Warburg, James Paul
Ward, Artemas
Ward, Henry Dana
Ward, Robert DeCourcey
Wardman, Ervin
Ware, Ashur
Ware, Henry, 1764–1845
Ware, Henry, 1794–1843
Ware, John
Ware, John Fothergill Water-
  house
Ware, William
Ware, William Robert
Warner, Edward Pearson
Warner, Langdon
Warren, Charles
Warren, Cyrus Moors
Warren, Henry Clarke
Warren, Herbert Langford
Warren, James
Warren, John

Warren, John Collins, 1778–
  1856
Warren, John Collins, 1842–
  1927
Warren, Joseph
Washburn, Charles Grenfill
Washburn, Edward Abiel
Watson, William
Wehle, Louis Brandeis
Welles, (Benjamin) Sumner
Welling, Richard Ward Greene
White, David
Whiting, William
Whitmore, Frank Clifford
Whitney, George
Wigmore, John Henry
Williston, Samuel
Winlock, Herbert Eustis
Winship, George Parker
Wister, Owen
Woods, James Haughton
Woodward, William
Wright, Willard Huntington

Divinity School
Alger, Horatio
Alger, William Rounseville
Bancroft, George
Barnard, Charles Francis
Barrett, Benjamin Fiske
Barrows, Samuel June
Bartol, Cyrus Augustus
Bass, Edward
Bellows, Henry Whitney
Bixby, James Thompson
Bronson, Walter Cochrane
Brooks, Charles Timothy
Brooks, John Graham
Burnap, George Washington
Burton, Warren
Chadwick, John White
Chamberlain, Nathan Henry
Channing, William Henry
Clarke, James Freeman
Collier, Hiram Price
Conway, Moncure Daniel
Cranch, Christopher Pearse
Crothers, Samuel McChord
Cummings, Edward
Cutler, Charles Ammi
Dwight, John Sullivan
Eliot, Samuel Atkins
Eliot, William Greenleaf
Ellis, George Edward
Emerson, Ralph Waldo
English, George Bethune
Everett, Charles Carroll
Everett, Edward
Fenn, William Wallace
Frothingham, Octavius Brooks
Gannett, Ezra Stiles
Gannett, William Channing
Gould, George Milbry
Green, Samuel Swett
Harland, Henry
Hedge, Frederic Henry
Hepworth, George Hughes
Holmes, John Haynes
Hosmer, Frederick Lucian
Hosmer, James Kendall
Huidekoper, Frederic
Huntington, Frederic Dan
Hurlbert, William Henry

Johnson, Samuel
Judd, Sylvester
Kennedy, William Sloane
Leonard, Levi Washburn
Longfellow, Samuel
Lovering, Joseph
Lowe, Charles
Maier, Walter Arthur
Metcalf, Joel Hastings
Miles, Henry Adolphus
Montgomery, David Henry
Newell, William Wells
Noyes, George Rapall
Parker, Theodore
Peabody, Andrew Preston
Peabody, Francis Greenwood
Peabody, William Bowin Oliver
Peirce, Cyrus
Peirce, James Mills
Potter, William James
Rand, Edward Kennard
Reed, Sampson
Ripley, George
Robbins, Chandler
Salter William Mackintire
Sibley, John Langdon
Sparks, Jared
Stearns, Oliver
Stebbins, Horatio
Stebbins, Rufus Phineas
Stevens, William Arnold
Wendte, Charles William
Wigglesworth, Edward, *c.* 1693–
  1765
Willard, Sidney
Wilson, William Dexter
Young, Alexander

Graduate Study
Allen, Frederick Lewis
Allen, George Venable
Allen, Glover Morrill
Allen, Hervey
Allinson, Francis Greenleaf
Allport, Gordon Willard
Ames, Herman Vandenburg
Ames, Oakes
Andrew, Abram Piatt
Angell, James Rowland
Appleton, William Sumner
Arensberg, Walter Conrad
Babbitt, Irving
Bailey, Liberty Hyde
Barbour, Thomas
Barton, George Aaron
Bazett, Henry Cuthbert
Beals, Ralph Albert
Bennett, Charles Edwin
Bigelow, Henry Bryant
Billings, Asa White Kenney
Bingham, Hiram
Bingham, Walter Van Dyke
Binkley, Wilfred Ellsworth
Birge, Edward Asahel
Birkhoff, George David
Bovie, William T.
Bowditch, Charles Pickering
Bridgman, Percy Williams
Briggs, LeBaron Russell
Brigham, Albert Perry
Brooks, William Keith
Brown, Carleton
Buchanan, Scott Milross

Burrage, Walter Lincoln
Byerly, William Elwood
Byles, Mather
Calkins, Mary Whiton
Cannon, Walter Bradford
Cantril, Albert Hadley
Carpenter, John Alden
Chamberlin, Edward Hastings
Channing, Edward
Chauncy, Charles
Christian, Henry Asbury
Cohen, Felix Solomon
Cohen, Morris Raphael
Cole, Frank Nelson
Collender, Guy Stevens
Colman, Benjamin
Colpitts, Edwin Henry
Cook, Walter
Cope, Arthur Clay
Crafts, William
Cross, Arthur Lyon
Cross, Samuel Hazzard
Cullen, Countée Porter
Cummings, Edward
Cummings, E. E.
Curtis, John Green
Daly, Reginald Aldworth
Davenport, Charles Benedict
Davis, Harvey Nathaniel
Day, Edmund Ezra
Dean, William Henry, Jr.
Dickinson, Edwin De Witt
Dixon, Roland Burrage
Dorsey, George Amos
Duane, William
Du Bois, William Edward Burg-
  hardt
Eaton, Daniel Cady
Edwards, Everett Eugene
Eigenmann, Carl H.
Eliot, T(homas) S(tearns)
Emery, Henry Crosby
Fairlie, John Archibald
Farabee, William Curtis
Fay, Sidney Bradshaw
Few, William Preston
Fish, Carl Russell
Folks, Homer
Foster, William Trufant
Frothingham, Paul Revere
Fuller, Joseph Vincent
Galpin, Charles Josiah
Gilman, Daniel Coit
Gilman, Samuel
Goode, George Brown
Goode, John Paul
Goodwin, William Watson
Grabau, Amadeus William
Grant, Percy Stickney
Grant, Robert
Green, John
Greene, Roger Sherman
Greenlaw, Edwin Almiron
Gummere, Francis Barton
Haggerty, Melvin Everett
Hall, Fitzeward
Hansen, Marcus Lee
Hapgood, Hutchins
Hawes, Charles Boardman
Hecht, Selig
Hibben, Paxton Pattison
Hill, Joseph Adna

Hillard, George Stillman
Hindus, Maurice Gerschon
Hitchcock, James Ripley Well-
  man
Hoar, Leonard
Hocking, William Ernest
Hoffman, Eugene Augustus
Holt, Edwin Bissell
Hooper, Claude Ernest
Hoover, Herbert Clark, Jr.
Horton, Samuel Dana
Hough, George Washington
Houston, David Franklin
Howe, Mark Antony De Wolfe
Huntington, Edward Vermilye
Huntington, Ellsworth
Hutchinson, Thomas
Hyde, Charles Cheney
Irwin, Robert Benjamin
Jackson, Dunham
Jaggar, Thomas Augustus, Jr.
Jefferson, Mark Sylvester Wil-
  liam
Jeffrey, Edward Charles
Jennings, Herbert Spencer
Johnson, William Samuel
Keith, Arthur
Kidder, Alfred Vincent
Kinsey, Alfred Charles
Koch, Frederick Henry
Kofoid, Charles Atwood
La Farge, Oliver Hazard Perry
Lamb, Arthur Becket
Lander, Edward
Lathrop, John
Laughlin, James Laurence
Law, Jonathan
Lawrence, William
Leland, Waldo Gifford
Leonard, William Ellery
Leverett, John
Lewis, Clarence Irving
Lewis, Gilbert Newton
Linton, Ralph
Lloyd, Alfred Henry
Locke, Alain Leroy
Locy, William Albert
Lodge, Henry Cabot
Lomax, John Avery
Longfellow, William Pitt Preble
Lovejoy, Arthur Oncken
Lovell, James
Lowery, Woodbury
Lowes, John Livingston
Lyman, Theodore, 1833–1897
McAdie, Alexander George
MacCurdy, George Grant
McDonald, James Grover
McKeen, Joseph
Maier, Walter Arthur
Mallinckrodt, Edward, Jr.
Manly, John Matthews
Marbut, Curtis Fletcher
Mather, Cotton
Matthiessen, Francis Otto
Mattingly, Garrett
Mayor, Alfred Goldsborough
Mezes, Sidney Edward
Minot, Charles Sedgwick
Minot, George Richards
Montague, Gilbert Holland
Montague, William Pepperell

Moody, William Vaughn
Morgan, Edwin Vernon
Morgan, Morris Hicky
Morley, Sylvanus Griswold
Munro, William Bennett
Neilson, William Allan
Nelson, Charles Alexander
Newman, Henry
O'Brien, Justin
Ogg, Frederic Austin
Oldfather, William Abbott
Olds, Leland
Osgood, William Fogg
Otis, Harrison Gray, 1765–1848
Oxnam, Garfield Bromley
Parker, George Howard
Parsons, Samuel Holden
Peirce, Charles Sanders
Penrose, Richard Alexander
  Fullerton
Perin, Charles Page
Perry, Ralph Barton
Phelps, William Lyon
Phillips, John
Pike, Nicholas
Pratt, James Bissett
Procter, John Robert
Quincy, Edmund
Quincy, Josiah, 1744–1775
Rand, Benjamin
Read, Conyers
Reisner, George Andrew
Richards, Theodore William
Richardson, William Lambert
Ritter, William Emerson
Robinson, James Harvey
Ross, Denman Waldo
Runkle, John Daniel
Sabine, Wallace Clement Ware
Sadtler, Samuel Philip
St. John, Charles Edward
Sanger, Charles Robert
Santayana, George
Schofield, William Henry
Schwartz, Delmore David
Scollard, Clinton
Scott, James Brown
Scudder, Samuel Hubbard
Setchell, William Albert
Shellabarger, Samuel
Sherman, Frank Dempster
Sherman, Stuart Pratt
Sidis, Boris
Simmons, James Stevens
Sinnott, Edmund Ware
Smith, Charles Forster
Smith, Courtney Craig
Smith, Harry James
Southard, Elmer Ernest
Sparks, Jared
Sprague, Oliver Mitchell Went-
  worth
Spurr, Josiah Edward
Starbuck, Edwin Diller
Stearns, Eben Sperry
Stefansson, Vilhjalmur
Stephenson, Carl
Stetson, Henry Crosby
Stoddard, Theodore Lothrop
Storer, Francis Humphreys
Stouffer, Samuel Andrew
Sumner, James Batcheller

Swanton, John Reed
Tatlock, John Strong Perry
Taussig, Frank William
Thaxter, Roland
Thayer, William Roscoe
Thorndike, Ashley Horace
Tolman, Edward Chace
Tracy, Nathaniel
Trelease, William
Troland, Leonard Thompson
Vaillant, George Clapp
Vaughan, Thomas Wayland
Villard, Oswald Garrison
Viner, Jacob
Ward, Harry Frederick
Ward, Henry Baldwin
Waterhouse, Sylvester
Wheeler, James Rignall
Whitaker, Daniel Kimball
Whitcomb, Selden Lincoln
White, John Williams
Whitmore, Frank Clifford
Whittemore, Thomas
Wiener, Norbert
Wigglesworth, Edward, 1732–
   1794
Wigglesworth, Michael
Wigmore, John Henry
Willard, Samuel, 1639–1707
Wolfe, Thomas Clayton
Woodrow, James
Woodson, Carter Godwin
Woodward, William
Woolley, Edgar Montillion
   ("Monty")
Wright, Philip Green
Wright, Theodore Lyman
Wurtz, Henry
Yerkes, Robert Mearns
Young, Karl
Landscape Architecture
Murphy, Gerald Clery
Law School
Abbott, Benjamin Vaughan
Adams, Brooks
Adams, Charles Francis
Allen, Charles
Allen, Henry Watkins
Ames, James Barr
Andrews, Christopher Colum-
   bus
Appleton, John, 1815–1864
Arnold, Samuel Greene
Arnold, Thurman Wesley
Astor, John Jacob, 1822–1890
Baker, Harvey Humphrey
Ballantine, Arthur Atwood
Batcheller, George Sherman
Bates, George Handy
Beale, Joseph Henry
Beaman, Charles Cotesworth
Bemis, George
Benjamin, Park, 1809–1864
Bettman, Alfred
Biddle, Francis Beverley
Bigelow, Harry Augustus
Bishop, Robert Roberts
Blaikie, William
Bliss, George, 1830–1897
Bolles, Frank
Bonaparte, Charles Joseph
Boyden, Roland William

Brackett, Charles William
Brandeis, Louis Dembitz
Breckinridge, Henry Skillman
Brewster, Ralph Owen
Brown, Addison
Brown, Henry Billings
Brown, Walter Folger
Bruce, Philip Alexander
Bryan, John Stewart
Bryan, Thomas Barbour
Buckner, Emory Roy
Buford, Napoleon Bonaparte
Bundy, Harvey Hollister
Bundy, Jonas Mills
Burlingame, Anson
Burton, Harold Hitz
Cabell, Nathaniel Francis
Carroll, John Lee
Carter, James Coolidge
Catchings, Waddill
Chafee, Zechariah, Jr.
Chamberlain, Daniel Henry
Chamberlain, Mellen
Chandler, Peleg Whitman
Chandler, William Eaton
Chapman, John Jay
Child, Richard Washburn
Choate, Joseph Hodges
Choate, Rufus
Clark, Greenleaf
Clark, Grenville
Cole, Chester Cicero
Copeland, Charles Townsend
Corbin, Austin
Costigan, George Purcell
Cotton, Joseph Potter
Curry, Jabez Lamar Monroe
Curtis, Benjamin Robbins
Curtis, Charles Pelham
Curtis, George Ticknor
Cushing, Caleb
Davenport, Herbert Joseph
Davis, Horace
Deming, Henry Champion
Dennis, James Shepard
Devens, Charles
Dickinson, John
Doe, Charles
Donnelly, Charles Francis
Donovan, James Britt
Dunbar, Charles Franklin
Dwight, Francis
Eames, Charles
Eaton, Dorman Bridgman
Echols, John
Endicott, William Crownin-
   shield
Evans, Lawrence Boyd
Evarts, William Maxwell
Fairchild, Charles Stebbins
Field, Fred Tarbell
Field, Walbridge Abner
Fisher, Sydney George
Fly, James Lawrence
Fogg, George Gilman
Frankfurter, Felix
Fuller, Melville Weston
Gilbert, Seymour Parker
Gillett, Frederick Huntington
Gordon, George Henry
Grafton, Charles Chapman
Graham, Philip Leslie

Gray, George
Gray, Horace
Gray, John Chipman
Green, Theodore Francis
Greene, Jerome Davis
Grimké, Archibald Henry
Hackett, Frank Warren
Hall, Abraham Oakey
Hamlin, Charles Sumner
Hand, Augustus Noble
Hand, Learned
Hapgood, Norman
Hawkins, Dexter Arnold
Hayes, John Lord
Hayes, Rutherford Birchard
Hillard, George Stillman
Hilliard, Francis
Hoadly, George
Hoar, Ebenezer Rockwood
Hoar, George Frisbie
Hodson, William
Hohfeld, Wesley Newcomb
Holden, Hale
Holmes, Nathaniel
Holmes, Oliver Wendell
Hoppin, Augustus
Hoppin, James Mason
Horton, Samuel Dana
Houston, Charles Hamilton
Howe, Mark De Wolfe
Hudson, Manley Ottmer
Ingalls, Melville Ezra
James, Henry, 1843–1916
Jenkins, Albert Gallatin
Jones, Charles Colcock
Jones, Leonard Augustus
Joy, James Frederick
Keener, William Albert
King, Stanley
Lander, Edward
Landis, James McCauley
Langdell, Christopher Colum-
   bus
Lawton, Alexander Robert
Lawton, Henry Ware
Lee, Ivy Ledbetter
Lee, Joseph
Lee, William Little
Lewis, William Henry
Lincoln, Robert Todd
Lodge, Henry Cabot
Long, John Davis
Longworth, Nicholas
Lord, Otis Phillips
Lowell, Abbott Lawrence
Lowell, James Russell
McCurdy, Richard Aldrich
Mack, Julian William
McNutt, Paul Vories
Magrath, Andrew Gordon
Matthews, Albert
Matthews, William
Mellen, Grenville
Mills, Ogden Livingston
Mitchell, Langdon Elwyn
Montague, Gilbert Holland
Moody, William Henry
Morawetz, Victor
Morison, George Shattuck
Morton, Marcus, 1819–1891
Newel, Stanford
Olds, Irving Sands

Olds, Robert Edwin
Olney, Richard
Ordronaux, John
Otis, Elwell Stephen
Paine, Henry Warren
Paine, Robert Treat, 1835–1910
Parkman, Francis
Parsons, Lewis Baldwin
Partridge, James Rudolph
Patterson, Robert Porter
Peabody, Oliver William Bourn
Peirce, James Mills
Pennoyer, Sylvester
Percy, William Alexander
Perkins, Thomas Nelson
Peters, John Andrew
Phelps, Charles Edward
Phillips, Wendell
Phillips, William
Pierce, Edward Lillie
Plimpton, George Arthur
Plumb, Glenn Edward
Pollak, Walter Heilprin
Post, Augustus
Pound, (Nathan) Roscoe
Powell, Thomas Reed
Pressman, Lee
Preston, John Smith
Preston, William
Quincy, Josiah Phillips
Randall, Clarence Belden
Rawle, Francis, 1846–1930
Richardson, William Adams
Richberg, Donald Randall
Rollins, Frank West
Ropes, John Codman
Rublee, George
Ryerson, Martin Antoine
Sanford, Edward Terry
Sanger, George Partridge
Sargent, Winthrop, 1825–1870
Schauffler, Henry Albert
Schofield, Henry
Sedgwick, Arthur George
Sellers, Matthew Bacon
Semmes, Thomas Jenkins
Shattuck, George Cheyne, 1813
  –1893
Shellabarger, Samuel
Simpson, William Dunlap
Smalley, George Washburn
Smith, Buckingham
Smith, Jeremiah
Smith, Jeremiah, 1837–1921
Spear, William Thomas
Starr, Merritt
Stevens, Henry
Stevenson, Adlai Ewing, II
Stimson, Frederic Jesup
Stimson, Henry Lewis
Storey, Moorfield
Storrow, James Jackson
Story, William Wetmore
Strobel, Edward Henry
Sullivan, Mark
Sumner, Charles
Taft, Robert Alphonso
Taliaferro, William Booth
Taussig, Frank William
Taylor, Frederick Winslow
Terrell, Edwin Holland
Thayer, Alexander Wheelock

Thayer, Ezra Ripley
Thayer, James Bradley
Thompson, Robert Means
Thornton, John Wingate
Tinkham, George Holden
Towle, George Makepeace
Train, Arthur Cheney
Tuttle, Charles Wesley
Tweed, Harrison
Warren, Charles
Wehle, Louis Brandeis
Welch, Joseph Nye
Welling, Richard Ward Greene
Wheeler, Everett Pepperrell
Wherry, Kenneth Spicer
White, David
Whiting, William
Whitney, William Collins
Whyte, William Pinkney
Wigmore, John Henry
Willard, Joseph, 1798–1865
Williston, Samuel
Willson, Augustus Everett
Winter, William
Wolcott, Edward Oliver
Medical School
Abbott, Samuel Warren
Allen, Edward Ellis
Allison, Nathaniel
Babcock, James Woods
Batchelder, John Putnam
Bates, James
Bigelow, Henry Jacob
Bigelow, William Sturgis
Binney, Amos
Blake, Francis Gilman
Bowditch, Henry Ingersoll
Bowditch, Henry Pickering
Bradford, Edward Hickling
Brewer, Thomas Mayo
Brown, Percy
Bumstead, Freeman Josiah
Burrage, Walter Lincoln
Cabot, Arthur Tracy
Cabot, Hugh
Cabot, Richard Clarke
Cannon, Walter Bradford
Chadwick, James Read
Channing, Walter
Cushing, Harvey Williams
Cutler, Elliott Carr
Cutter, Ephraim
Dall, William Healey
Dalton, John Call
Dixon, John Homer
Edes, Robert Thaxter
Ellis, Calvin
Ernst, Harold Clarence
Farlow, William Gilson
Fillebrown, Thomas
Finney, John Miller Turpin
Fisher, John Dix
Fisher, Theodore Willis
Fitzgerald, John Francis
Flagg, Thomas Wilson
Garvin, Lucius Fayette Clark
Goodale, George Lincoln
Gorham, John
Gould, Augustus Addison
Graves, William Phillips
Green, John
Green, Samuel Abbott

Gregg, Alan
Hale, Enoch
Harrington, Charles
Harrington, Thomas Francis
Henderson, Lawrence Joseph
Holder, Joseph Bassett
Hooker, Worthington
Hoover, Charles Franklin
Howe, Lucien
Jackson, Charles Thomas
Jackson, James, 1777–1867
James, William
Jarvis, Edward
Jeffries, Benjamin Joy
Judson, Adoniram Brown
Knapp, Philip Coombs
Lahey, Frank Howard
Leland, George Adams
Lewis, Dioclesian
Lincoln, Rufus Pratt
Lombard, Warren Plimpton
Loring, Edward Greely
Loring, George Bailey
Lovell, Joseph
Lovett, Robert Williamson
Mallory, Frank Burr
Marcy, Henry Orlando
Marden, Orison Swett
Martin, Henry Austin
Minot, Charles Sedgwick
Minot, George Richards
Mixter, Samuel Jason
Morse, John Lovett
Morton, William James
Morton, William Thomas Green
Mumford, James Gregory
Mundé, Paul Fortunatus
Nichols, Charles Lemuel
Niles, Nathaniel, 1791–1869
Norton, William Edward
Oliver, Fitch Edward
Paine, Martyn
Palmer, Walter Walker
Parker, Willard
Parsons, Thomas William
Pearce, Richard Mills
Perry, William
Peters, Edward Dyer
Pickering, Charles
Prince, Morton
Putnam, Charles Pickering
Putnam, James Jackson
Rhoads, Cornelius Packard
Richardson, Maurice Howe
Richardson, William Lambert
Rotch, Thomas Morgan
Round, William Marshall Fitts
Sawyer, Wilbur Augustus
Shattuck, Frederick Cheever
Shattuck, George Brune
Shattuck, George Cheyne, 1813
  –1893
Shurtleff, Nathaniel Bradstreet
Smith, Nathan, 1762–1829
Southard, Elmer Ernest
Spalding, Lyman
Stearns, Henry Putnam
Storer, David Humphreys
Storer, Horatio Robinson
Sturtevant, Edward Lewis
Talbot, Israel Tisdale
Taylor, Robert Tunstall

Thaxter, Roland
Thayer, William Sydney
Weare, Meshech
Webster, Arthur Gordon
Webster, John White
Weiss, John
Wendell, Barrett
Wentworth, Benning
Wentworth, George Albert
Wentworth, John, 1737–1820
Wesselhoeft, Conrad
West, Samuel
Wheelwright, Edmund March
Whitaker, Daniel Kimball
White, James Clarke
Whitman, Royal
Widener, Harry Elkins
Wigglesworth, Edward, c. 1693–1765
Wigglesworth, Edward, 1732–1794
Wigglesworth, Edward, 1840–1896
Wigglesworth, Michael
Wilcox, Reynold Webb
Wiley, Harvey Washington
Willard, Joseph, 1738–1804
Willard, Joseph, 1798–1865
Willard, Samuel, 1639–1707
Willard, Samuel, 1775–1859
Willard, Sidney
Williams, Elisha, 1694–1755
Williams, Francis Henry
Williams, Henry Willard
Williams, Israel
Williams, John, 1664–1729
Williams, John, 1817–1899
Williams, Nathaniel
Williams, William, 1731–1811
Willis, William
Willson, Augustus Everett
Wingate, Paine
Winslow, Josiah
Winsor, Justin
Winthrop, James
Winthrop, John, 1638–1707
Winthrop, John, 1714–1779
Winthrop, Robert Charles
Wise, John
Wood, Edward Stickney
Wood, Leonard
Woodberry, George Edward
Woods, Alva
Woods, Leonard, 1774–1854
Woodward, Calvin Milton
Woodworth, Jay Backus
Worthen, William Ezra
Wright, Chauncey
Wyman, Jeffries
Wyman, Morrill
Wyman, Morrill
Young, Alexander
HAVERFORD COLLEGE (PA.)
Allinson, Francis Greenleaf
Barton, George Aaron
Drinker, Cecil Kent
Elliott, Aaron Marshall
Fite, Warner
Gates, Thomas Sovereign
Goddard, Henry Herbert
Gummere, Francis Barton
Hallowell, Richard Price

Hartshorne, Henry
Hinshaw, David Schull
Jones, Rufus Matthew
Katchen, Julius
Lewis, William Draper
Lippincott, James Storr
Lutz, Frank Eugene
Morley, Christopher Darlington
Parrish, Maxfield
Richards, Theodore William
Rogers, Robert William
Smiley, Albert Keith
Smith, Lloyd Logan Pearsall
Smith, Lloyd Pearsall
Spaeth, Sigmund
Starr, Louis
Thomas, Richard Henry
Tyson, James
Updegraff, David Brainard
Wood, James, 1839–1925
Graduate Study
Goddard, Henry Herbert
Jones, Rufus Matthew
Spaeth, Sigmund
HEATHERLEY'S ART SCHOOL (ENGLAND)
Kline, Franz Josef
HEBREW UNION COLLEGE (OHIO)
Berkowitz, Henry
Enelow, Hyman Gerson
Gavin, Frank Stanton Burns
Grossmann, Louis
Heller, Maximilian
Krauskopf, Joseph
Liebman, Joshua Loth
Magnes, Judah Leon
Meyer, Martin Abraham
Philipson, David
Silver, Abba Hillel
Silverman, Joseph
Graduate Study
Liebman, Joshua Loth
Philipson, David
Theology
Kagan, Henry Enoch
HEBRON ACADEMY (MAINE)
Hale, Eugene
Hamlin, Hannibal
Long, John Davis
HEIDELBERG COLLEGE (OHIO)
Fenneman, Nevin Melancthon
Seiberling, Frank Augustus
HEIDELBERG UNIVERSITY (OHIO)
Baker, Oliver Edwin
Graduate Study
Baker, Oliver Edwin
HIGHLAND PARK COLLEGE (IOWA)
Budd, Ralph
Nagel, Conrad
HILLSDALE COLLEGE (MICH.)
Carleton, Will
King, Henry Churchill
Rice, Fenelon Bird
Wilbur, Cressy Livingston
HIRAM COLLEGE (OHIO)
Garfield, James Abram
Hinsdale, Burke Aaron
Hoover, Herbert William
Lindsay, Nicholas Vachel
Young, Allyn Abbott
Young, Clark Montgomery

HOBART COLLEGE (N.Y.)
Blodget, Lorin
Brogg, Edward Stuyvesant
Brooks, William Keith
Cheney, Charles Edward
Doolittle, James Rood
Dove, Arthur Garfield
Duyckinck, George Long
Folger, Charles James
Folwell, William Watts
Graves, Frederick Rogers
Handerson, Henry Ebenezer
Hosmer, William Howe Cuyler
Myer, Albert James
Norton, John Nicholas
Phelps, Austin
Randall, Henry Stephens
Rankine, William Birch
Ricord, Frederick William
Schuyler, Montgomery
Seymour, Horatio
Throop, Montgomery Hunt
HOCHSCHULE FUR MUSICK, BERLIN (GERMANY)
Stoessel, Albert Frederic
HOLLINS COLLEGE (VA.)
Brown, Margaret Wise
HOLY CROSS COLLEGE (MASS.)
Armstrong, Frank C.
Bradley, Denis Mary
Conaty, Thomas James
Hudson, Daniel Eldred
Hunton, George Kenneth
McNulty, John Augustine
Walsh, David Ignatius
HOMEOPATHIC MEDICAL COLLEGE (PA.)
Helmuth, William Tod
Hilgard, Eugene Woldemar
Talbot, Israel Tisdale
HOMER ACADEMY (N.Y.)
Harris, Ira
Nye, James Warren
Pennoyer, Sylvester
Salisbury, James Henry
Sanders, Charles Walton
Smith, Job Lewis
Smith, Stephen
Sterling, John Whalen
Stoddard, William Osborn
HOOD COLLEGE (MD.)
Kerr, Sophie
McCardell, Claire
HOPE COLLEGE (MICH.)
Muste, Abraham Johannes
HOPEWELL ACADEMY
Howell, David
Jewett, Hugh Judge
Jones, David
Smith, Hezekiah
HOPEWELL ACADEMY (PA.)
Jewett, Hugh Judge
HOPKINS ACADEMY (MASS.)
Hooker, Joseph
Judd, Sylvester
Kingsley, Elbridge
Nash, Simeon
Stockbridge, Levi
HOPKINS GRAMMAR SCHOOL (CONN.)
Baldwin, Roger Sherman
Baldwin, Simeon Eben

Barnard, Henry
Camp, Walter Chauncey
Case, William Scoville
Champlin, John Denison
Cutler, Charles Ammi
Day, Henry Noble
Dwight, Sereno Edwards
Dwight, Timothy, 1828–1916
Hadley, Arthur Twining
Holmes, Isaac Edward
Hunt, Gaillard
Huntington, Frederick Dan
Levermore, Charles Herbert
Mansfield, Richard, 1723–1820
Osborn, Norris Galpin
Stoeckel, Carl
Thacher, Thomas Anthony
Thompson, William Gilman
Totten, George Muirson
Wales, Leonard Eugene
Williams, Frederick Wells
Woolsey, Theodore Dwight

HOPKINTON ACADEMY (N.H.)
Currier, Moody
Gunnison, John Williams
Harriman, Walter
Perkins, George Hamilton
Woodbury, Daniel Phineas

HOWARD COLLEGE (ALA.)
Brown, William Garrott
Johnson, John Butler
Lyon, David Gordon
Moore, John Trotwood

HOWARD COLLEGE (IND.)
Evermann, Barton Warren

HOWARD UNIVERSITY (D.C.)
Davis, Benjamin Oliver, Sr.
Frazier, Edward Franklin
Hurston, Zora Neale
Miller, Kelly
Pelham, Robert A.
White, Clarence Cameron
Graduate Study
Miller, Kelly

HUDSON RIVER INSTITUTE (N.Y)
Abbey, Henry
Draper, Lyman Copeland
Evans, George Alfred
Sherwood, Isaac Ruth

HUNTER COLLEGE (N.Y.)
Bernstein, Aline
Dodd, Bella Visono

IGNATIUS COLLEGE (AUSTRIA)
Hubbard, Bernard Rosecrans

ILLINOIS COLLEGE
Bateman, Newton
Beecher, Thomas Kinnicut
Bryan, William Jennings
Capps, Edward
Carson, Jack
Goudy, William Charles
Greenlaw, Edwin Almiron
Martin, Everett Dean
Smith, Byron Caldwell
Yates, Richard

ILLINOIS COLLEGE OF PHOTOGRAPHY
Weston, Edward Henry

ILLINOIS INDUSTRIAL UNIVERSITY
(See UNIVERSITY OF ILLINOIS)

ILLINOIS INSTITUTE OF TECHNOLOGY
Andrus, Ethel Percy
Chaffee, Roger Bruce
Lait, Jacquin Leonard (Jack)

ILLINOIS NORMAL UNIVERSITY
Crocker, William

ILLINOIS STATE NORMAL SCHOOL
Burrill, Thomas Jonathan
Cook, John Williston
Garman, Samuel
Gove, Aaron Estellus
Jennings, Herbert Spencer
McMurry, Frank Morton
Scott, Walter Dill

ILLINOIS STATE NORMAL UNIVERSITY
Gray, William Scott, Jr.

ILLINOIS WESLEYAN COLLEGE
Fifer, Joseph Wilson

ILLINOIS WESLEYAN UNIVERSITY
Crane, Frank
Frear, William
Gray, Glen
Hogue, Wilson Thomas
Hunt, Lester Callaway
Illington, Margaret
Lucas, Scott Wike
Stevenson, Adlai Ewing
Talmage, James Edward

IMPERIAL COLLEGE OF SCIENCE AND TECHNOLOGY (ENGLAND)
Tate, George Henry Hamilton

IMPERIAL CONSERVATORY AT ST. PETERSBURG (RUSSIA)
Gabrilowitsch, Ossip
Schillinger, Joseph

IMPERIAL INSTITUTE OF ENGINEERING (AUSTRIA)
Schindler, Rudolph Michael

IMPERIAL MILITARY MEDICAL ACADEMY (RUSSIA)
Levene, Phoebus Aaron Theodore

INDIANA STATE NORMAL SCHOOL
Howard, George Elliott
Juday, Chancey
McCreery, James Work
Tompkins, Arnold

INDIANA STATE TEACHERS COLLEGE
Shannon, Fred Albert

INDIANA STATE UNIVERSITY
Dunn, William McKee
Eigenmann, Carl H.
Evermann, Barton Warren
Foster, John Watson
Gresham, Walter Quintin
Hardin, Charles Henry
Harper, Ida Husted
Leavenworth, Francis Preserved
Martin, William Alexander Parsons
Mellette, Arthur Calvin
Niblack, William Ellis
Parvin, Theophilus
Rollins, James Sidney
Scott, Leroy
Springer, William McKendree
Stone, Wilbur Fisk
Tompkins, Arnold
Warthin, Alfred Scott

Wright, George Grover
Wright, Joseph Albert
Graduate Study
Coulter, John Merle
Eigenmann, Carl H.
Evermann, Barton Warren
Gilbert, Charles Henry
Law
Gorman, Willis Arnold
Mellette, Arthur Calvin

INDIANA UNIVERSITY
Aydelotte, Frank
Beeson, Charles Henry
Boisen, Anton Theophilus
Buley, Roscoe Carlyle
Coffman, Lotus Delta
Cooper, Kent
Cubberley, Ellwood Patterson
Dreiser, Theodore
Edmunds, Charles Wallis
Fetter, Frank Albert
Fox, Fontaine Talbot, Jr.
Haggerty, Melvin Everett
Hawley, Paul Ramsey
Hill, Edwin Conger
Hunter, Robert
Juday, Chancey
Lingelbach, Anna Lane
McDonald, James Grover
McNutt, Paul Vories
Millis, Harry Alvin
Minton, Sherman
Newlon, Jesse Homer
Newsom, Herschel David
Oliphant, Herman
Pyle, Ernest Taylor
Slipher, Vesto Melvin
Starbuck, Edwin Diller
Stephenson, Nathaniel Wright
Tolley, Howard Ross
Veatch, Arthur Clifford
Willkie, Wendell Lewis
Wissler, Clark
Graduate Study
Beeson, Charles Henry
Buley, Roscoe Carlyle
Coffman, Lotus Delta
Juday, Chancey
Lingelbach, Anna Lane
McDonald, James Grover
Millis, Harry Alvin
Ogg, Frederic Austin
Shannon, Fred Albert
Slipher, Vesto Melvin
Terman, Lewis Madison
Wissler, Clark
Law
Willkie, Wendell Lewis
Medicine
Rovenstine, Emery Andrew

INSTITUTE FOR ART HISTORY (GERMANY)
Frankfurter, Alfred Moritz

INSTITUTE OF MUSICAL ART (N.Y.)
Riegger, Wallingford

INTERNATIONAL SCHOOL FOR SOCIAL AND RELIGIOUS STUDIES (ENGLAND)
Pyle, Robert

INTERNATIONAL YMCA COLLEGE (MASS.)
Stagg, Amos Alonzo

IOWA, UNIVERSITY OF (See UNIVERSITY OF IOWA)
IOWA COLLEGE OF LAW
  Howard, Edgar
IOWA COLLEGE (See GRINNELL COLLEGE)
IOWA STATE AGRICULTURAL COLLEGE
  Hornaday, William Temple
IOWA STATE COLLEGE
  Catt, Carrie Clinton Lane Chapman
  Hansen, Niels Ebbesen
Graduate Study
  Hansen, Niels Ebbesen
IOWA STATE COLLEGE OF AGRICULTURE
  Arthur, Joseph Charles
  Bemis, Harold Edward
  Carver, George Washington
  Fairchild, David Grandison
  Gregory, Clifford Verne
Graduate Study
  Arthur, Joseph Charles
  Carver, George Washington
IOWA STATE TEACHERS COLLEGE
  Benson, Oscar Herman
IOWA STATE UNIVERSITY
  Barrett, Albert Moore
  Dykstra, Clarence Addison
  Hansen, Marcus Lee
  Leverett, Frank
  Mead, Elwood
  Meredith, Edna C. Elliott
  Smith, Fred Burton
  Veblen, Oswald
  Wallace, Henry Agard
Graduate Study
  Hansen, Marcus Lee
Law
  Harris, Paul Percy
  Kenyon, William Squire
  Springer, Charles
Medicine
  Barrett, Albert Moore
IOWA WESLEYAN COLLEGE
Graduate Study
  Cowles, Gardner
ISTITUTO TECNICO OF MILAN (ITALY)
  Bellanca, Giuseppe Mario
ITHACA ACADEMY (N.Y.)
  Brewer, William Henry
  Finch, Francis Miles
  Sackett, Henry Woodward
  Stevens, George Barker

JAGIELLONIAN UNIVERSITY OF KRAKOW (POLAND)
  Znaniecki, Florian Witold
JEFFERSON COLLEGE (LA.)
  Eustis, George, 1828–1872
  Hébert, Louis
  Hébert, Paul Octave
JEFFERSON COLLEGE (MISS.)
  Brown, Albert Gallatin
  Ingraham, Prentiss
  Wailes, Benjamin Leonard Covington
JEFFERSON MEDICAL COLLEGE (PA.)
  Asch, Morris Joseph
  Atkinson, William Biddle

Atlee, Washington Lemuel
Bailey, Gamaliel
Battey, Robert
Bissell, William Henry
Blalock, Nelson Gales
Bonwill, William Gibson Arlington
Brainard, Daniel
Brinton, Daniel Garrison
Brinton, John Hill
Brown, George, 1823–1892
Cohen, Jacob Da Silva Solis
Da Costa, Jacob Mendez
Da Costa, John Chalmers
Dix, John Homer
Dowell, Greensville
Elder, William
Elsberg, Louis
Emmet, Thomas Addis, 1828–1919
Evans, Thomas Wiltberger
Finlay, Carlos Juan
Flick, Lawrence Francis
Flint, Austin
Gould, George Milbuy
Green, Samuel Abbott
Gross, Samuel David
Gross, Samuel Weissell
Guild, La Fayette
Heap, Samuel Davies
Howard, William Travis
Howe, Andrew Jackson
Huston, Charles
Jackson, Chevalier
Jones, Anson
Judson, Adoniram Brown
Keen, William Williams
Kerr, John Glasgow
Kyle, David Braden
Landis, Henry Robert Murray
Lane, Levi Cooper
Leffmann, Henry
Le Moyne, Francis Julius
Letterman, Jonathan
McClellan, George, 1849–1913
McGuire, Hunter Holmes
McQuillen, John Hugh
Maury, Francis Fontaine
Meigs, James Aitken
Mitchell, Silas Weir
Nicholson, Alfred Osborne Pope
Northrop, Lucius Bellinger
Pinkney, Ninian
Richardson, Robert
Riggs, John Mankey
Sajous, Charles Euchariste de Médicis
Schadle, Jacob Evans
Sims, James Marion
Snyder, Howard McCrum
Spitka, Edward Anthony
Squibb, Edward Robinson
Stockton, Thomas Hewlings
Thomson, Edward
Tiffin, Edward
Toner, Joseph Meredith
Van Dyck, Cornelius Van Alen
Warder, John Aston
White, John De Haven
Willard, De Forest
Woodruff, Charles Edward

Young, Aaron
JEWISH THEOLOGICAL SEMINARY
Graduate Study
  Hadas, Moses
JOHN CARROLL UNIVERSITY (OHIO)
  Hurley, Joseph Patrick
JOHNS HOPKINS UNIVERSITY (MD.)
  Abt, Isaac Arthur
  Adams, Thomas Sewall
  Ames, Joseph Sweetman
  Auer, John
  Baer, William Stevenson
  Baetjer, Frederick Henry
  Baker, Newton Diehl
  Bassett, John Spencer
  Bell, Louis
  Bentley, Arthur Fisher
  Berry, Edward Wilber
  Boston, Charles Anderson
  Botsford, George Willis
  Brown, Lawrason
  Bumstead, Henry Andrews
  Calverton, Victor Francis
  Casanowicz, Immanuel Moses
  Cattell, James McKeen
  Davis, Richard Harding
  Day, David Talbot
  Dickinson, John
  Fall, Bernard B.
  Fay, Edwin Whitfield
  Fitzgerald, Alice Louise Florence
  Flexner, Abraham
  Gantt, Henry Laurence
  Garrison, Fielding Hudson
  Goddard, Calvin Hooker
  Halsted, George Bruce
  Harrison, Ross Granville
  Hoerr, Normand Louis
  Hollander, Jacob Harry
  Hough, Theodore
  Howell, William Henry
  Hunt, Reid
  Jayne, Horace Fort
  Jones, Harry Clary
  Keeler, James Edward
  Koyl, Charles Herschel
  Ladd-Franklin, Christine
  Latané, John Holladay
  Lazear, Jesse William
  Longcope, Warfield, Theobald
  Machen, John Gresham
  Marburg, Theodore
  Marden, Charles Carroll
  Marquand, Allan
  Nelson, Edward William
  Norris, James Flack
  Noyes, Clara Dutton
  Perlman, Philip Benjamin
  Reese, Charles Lee
  Ritchie, Albert Cabell
  Robinson, George Canby
  Rogers, Robert William
  Rosewater, Victor
  Rous, Francis Peyton
  Smyth, Albert Henry
  Stein, Leo Daniel
  Stone, John Stone
  Stringham, Washington Irving
  Talmage, James Edward
  Taylor, Robert Tunstall
  Tondorf, Francis Anthony

Waidner, Charles William
Williams, John Whitridge
Willoughby, Westel Woodbury
Wolman, Leo
Graduate Study
Abel, John Jacob
Adams, Thomas Sewall
Adler, Cyrus
Allinson, Francis Greenleaf
Ames, Joseph Sweetman
Andrews, Charles McLean
Armstrong, Edward Cooke
Baer, William Stevenson
Baetjer, Frederick Henry
Barnett, George Ernest
Bascom, Florence
Bateman, Harry
Bentley, Arthur Fisher
Bloomfield, Maurice
Brackett, Jeffrey Richardson
Briggs, Lyman James
Bright, James Wilson
Brough, Charles Hillman
Burnham, William Henry
Burrow, Trigant
Burton, Richard Eugene
Cajori, Florian
Calverton, Victor Francis
Carson, Rachel Louise
Chandler, Julian Alvin Carroll
Commons, John Rogers
Conklin, Edwin Grant
Craig, Thomas
Dargan, Edwin Preston
Dewey, John
Dixon, Thomas
Donaldson, Henry Herbert
Eisenhart, Luther Pfahler
Finley, John Huston
Franklin, Edward Curtis
Franklin, Fabian
Freeman, Douglas Southall
Frothingham, Arthur Lincoln
Furst, Clyde Bowman
Glenn, John Mark
Gould, Elgin Ralston Lovell
Hall, Edwin Herbert
Hamilton, Alice
Harrison, Ross Granville
Hart, Edward
Haskins, Charles Homer
Hayes, Charles Willard
Hemmeter, John Conrad
Herter, Christian Archibald
Herty, Charles Holmes
Hollander, Jacob Harry
Howe, Frederic Clemson
Howell, William Henry
Humphreys, Wiliam Jackson
Hunt, Reid
Jameson, John Franklin
Jarvis, William Chapman
Jastrow, Joseph
Kilpatrick, William Heard
Kohler, Elmer Peter
Krapp, George Philip
Lancaster, Henry Carrington
Lashley, Karl Spencer
Latané, John Holladay
Learned, Marion Dexter
Lee, Frederic Schiller
Levermore, Charles Herbert

Lewis, Exum Percival
Machen, John Gresham
McMurrich, James Playfair
Main, John Hanson Thomas
Marden, Charles Carroll
Marquand, Allan
Mather, Frank Jewett, Jr.
Mendenhall, Charles Elwood
Miller, Kelly
Moore, Henry Ludwell
Moore, Joseph Haines
Morgan, Thomas Hunt
Nichols, Edward Leamington
Norris, James Flack
Noyes, William Albert
Page, Walter Hines
Pfund, August Herman
Philipson, David
Pratt, Waldo Selden
Randall, Wyatt William
Rosa, Edward Bennett
Ross, Edward Alsworth
Royce, Josiah
Ruhräh, John
Sanford, Edmund Clark
Scott, John Adams
Seager, Henry Rogers
Shaw, Albert
Shear, Theodore Leslie
Shields, Thomas Edward
Smith, Charles Alphonso
Smith, George Otis
Smith, Homer William
Smith, Horatio Elwin
Smith, Theobald
Squier, George Owen
Steiner, Bernard Christian
Stine, Charles Milton Altland
Sydnor, Charles Sackett
Thomas, Martha Carey
Thomas, Richard Henry
Timberlake, Gideon
Trent, William Peterfield
Van Vleck, Edward Burr
Willoughby, Westel Woodbury
Wilson, Edmund Beecher
Wilson, Woodrow
Wolman, Leo
Medical School
Barbour, Henry Gray
Blalock, Alfred
Brown, Lawrason
Callaway, Morgan
Christian, Henry Asbury
Cort, Edwin Charles
Craig, Winchell McKendree
Dandy, Walter Edward
Davis, John Staige
Elman, Robert
Erlanger, Joseph
Flexner, Simon
Freeman, Allen Weir
Gasser, Herbert Spencer
Gay, Frederick Parker
Goddard, Calvin Hooker
Hooker, Donald Russell
Hume, Edgar Erskine
Kenyon, Josephine Hemenway
Krause, Allen Kramer
Longcope, Warfield, Theobald
MacCallum, William George
Moore, Joseph Earle

Murphy, James Bumgardner
Reid, Mont Rogers
Rivers, Thomas Milton
Robinson, George Canby
Rous, Francis Peyton
Sabin, Florence Rena
Seagrave, Gordon Stifler
Stein, Gertrude
Strong, Richard Pearson
Weed, Lewis Hill
Wislocki, George Bernays
JOHNSON COLLEGE (ILL.)
Easley, Ralph Montgomery
JURIDICIAL SEMINARY OF ST. APOL-
LINAIRE (ITALY)
Brennan, Francis James

KANSAS, UNIVERSITY OF (SEE UNI-
VERSITY OF KANSAS)
KANSAS CITY BAPTIST THEOLOGI-
CAL SEMINARY (KAN.)
Graduate Study
Martin, Warren Homer
KANSAS CITY UNIVERSITY
Brady, Mildred Alice Edie
KANSAS STATE AGRICULTURAL COL-
LEGE
Harbord, James Guthrie
Graduate Study
Harbord, James Guthrie
KANSAS STATE COLLEGE OF
AGRICULTURE
Fairchild, David Grandison
Marlatt, Abby Lillian
Graduate Study
Fairchild, David Grandison
Marlatt, Abby Lillian
KANSAS STATE NORMAL SCHOOL
Davis, Arthur Powell
KANSAS WESLEYAN UNIVERSITY
Martin, Glenn Luther ("Cy")
KENT COLLEGE OF LAW (ILL.)
Abbott, Robert Sengstacke
KENTUCKY, UNIVERSITY OF (See
UNIVERSITY OF KENTUCKY)
KENTUCKY AGRICULTURAL AND ME-
CHANICAL COLLEGE
McMillin, Benton
Stanley, Augustus Owsley
KENTUCKY MILITARY INSTITUTE
Burbridge, Stephen Gano
Hoke, Robert Frederick
McClure, Robert Alexis
Phelan, James, 1856–1891
Williams, John Sharp
KENTUCKY STATE COLLEGE
Smith, Lucy Harth
KENYON COLLEGE (OHIO)
Allen, Alexander Viets Griswold
Andrews, Lorin
Bledsoe, Albert Taylor
Buckland, Ralph Pomeroy
Crosser, Robert
Davis, David
Davis, Edwin Hamilton
Davis, Henry Winter
Ellis, John Washington
Goebel, William
Granger, Alfred Hoyt
Hayes, Rutherford Birchard
Jones, Jehu Glancy
Le Duc, William Gates

McKinstry, Elisha Williams
Marshall, William Louis
Matthews, Stanley
Minor, John Barbee
Pease, Alfred Humphreys
Piatt, John James
Rockwell, Alphonso David
Rosecrans, Sylvester Horton
Smith, John Cotton, 1826–1882
Speer, William
Stanton, Edwin McMasters
Thomas, Jesse Burgess, 1832–1915
Trenchard, Stephen Decatur
Williams, Charles David
Zachos, John Celivergos
KEYSTONE STATE NORMAL SCHOOL (PA.)
Messersmith, George Strausser
KIEV ART INSTITUTE (RUSSIA)
Archipenko, Alexander
KIEV THEOLOGICAL ACADEMY (RUSSIA)
Leonty, Metropolitan
KIMBALL UNION ACADEMY (N.H.)
Bissell, George Henry
Clark, Francis Edward
Dillingham, William Paul
Field, Walbridge Abner
Flanders, Henry
Hall, Samuel Read
Hough, Charles Merrill
Just, Ernest Everett
Mather, Samuel Holmes
Miller, Charles Ransom
Morris, George Sylvester
Noble, Frederick Alphonso
Parkhurst, Charles
Richards, Charles Herbert
Smith, Asa Dodge
Stevens, Hiram Fairchild
Tucker, William Jewett
KING COLLEGE (TENN.)
Reynolds, Richard Samuel, Sr.
Reynolds, William Neal
KING'S COLLEGE (See COLUMBIA UNIVERSITY)
KIRKLAND SCHOOL (ILL.)
Blaine, Anita (Eugenie) McCormick
KITCHENER COLLEGE (CANADA)
Murray, James Edward
KNOX COLLEGE (ILL.)
Bancroft, Edgar Addison
Bancroft, Frederic
Bradwell, James Bolesworth
Calkins, Earnest Elmo
Field, Eugene
Finley, John Huston
Foote, Lucius Harwood
McClure, Samuel Sidney
McCoy, Joseph Gesting
Perkins, George Henry
Phillips, John Sanburn
Rainey, Henry Thomas
Revels, Hiram Rhoades
Salter, William Mackintire
Scripps, Ellen Browning
Severance, Frank Hayward
White, Stephen Van Culen

KONIGLICHE AKADEMIE DER TONKUNST (GERMANY)
Converse, Frederick Shepherd
KONIGLICHE BERGAKADEMIE AT FREIBERG (GERMANY)
Lindgren, Waldemar

LAFAYETTE COLLEGE (PA.)
Barber, Edwin Atlee
Bright, James Wilson
Cattell, James McKeen
Craig, Austin
Craig, Thomas
Crawford, John Martin
Garrett, John Work
Gayley, James
Good, James Isaac
Green, William Henry
Griggs, John William
Harkness, William
Hart, Edward
Hench, Philip Showalter
Hoyt, Henry Martyn
Hutchinson, Paul
Jackson, Joseph Henry
Jadwin, Edgar
Macfarlane, Charles William
Mackenzie, James Cameron
McMurtrie, William
March, Francis Andrew, 1863–1928
March, Peyton Conway
Meigs, John
Michler, Nathaniel
Nassau, Robert Hamill
Nevin, George Balch
Ott, Isaac
Porter, Thomas Conrad
Ramsey, Alexander
Rodenbough, Theophilus Francis
Shaw, Edward Richard
Starr, Frederick
Watkins, John Elfreth
Graduate Study
March, Francis Andrew, 1863–1928
Meigs, John
Shaw, Edward Richard
LAKE ERIE COLLEGE FOR WOMEN (PA.)
Mussey, Ellen Spencer
LAKE FOREST COLLEGE (ILL.)
Chapman, John Wilbur
Graff, Everett Dwight
Hillis, Newell Dwight
Humiston, William Henry
Lewis, Dean De Witt
Mills, Benjamin Fay
Sabath, Adolph J.
Law
Woll, Matthew
LAKE FOREST UNIVERSITY
Law
Morrison, Frank
LAMAR STATE COLLEGE OF TECHNOLOGY (TEX.)
Joplin, Janis Lyn
LANE THEOLOGICAL SEMINARY (OHIO)
Andrews, Samuel James
Bateman, Newton

Beecher, Charles
Beecher, Henry Ward
Beecher, Thomas Kinnicut
Blanchard, Jonathan
Chapman, John Wilbur
Fee, John Gregg
Howison, George Holmes
Noble, Frederick Alphonso
Orton, Edward Francis Baxter
Smith, Henry Preserved
Stanton, Henry Brewster
Strong, Josiah
LAWRENCE ACADEMY (MASS.)
Barker, George Frederick
Beecher, Charles
Green, Samuel Abbott
Jones, Leonard Augustus
Richardson, Rufus Byam
Richardson, William Adams
Tarbell, Frank Bigelow
Towle, George Makepeace
Walker, James
LAWRENCE SCIENTIFIC SCHOOL
Brown, Percy
LAWRENCE UNIVERSITY (WIS.)
Curtis, Olin Alfred
Davis, Jerome Dean
Hooton, Earnest Albert
Huntington, Margaret Jane Evans
LAWRENCEVILLE SCHOOL (N.J.)
Besse, Arthur Lyman
Borie, Adolphe
Breckinridge, Desha
Green, Henry Woodhull
Green, John Cleve
Gross, Samuel David
Gummere, Samuel René
Gummere, William Stryker
Maclean, John, 1800–1886
Mallory, Clifford Day
Porter, Horace
Price, Rodman McCamley
Rodgers, John, 1881–1926
Woodhull, Alfred Alexander
LEBANON SCHOOL OF LAW (TENN.)
Bailey, Joseph Weldon
LEBANON VALLEY COLLEGE (PA.)
Dougherty, Raymond Philip
Ryan, Harris Joseph
Graduate Study
Dougherty, Raymond Philip
LEHIGH UNIVERSITY (PA.)
Barrell, Joseph
Cooke, Morris Llewellyn
Davis, Richard Harding
Doolittle, Eric
Girdler, Tom Mercer
Grace, Eugene Gifford
Howe, Mark Antony De Wolfe
Landis, Walter Savage
Macfarlane, Charles William
Packard, James Ward
Patch, Alexander McCarrell
Porter, Holbrook Fitz-John
Richards, Joseph William
Schneider, Herman
Stoek, Harry Harkness
Talmage, James Edward
Walter, Francis Eugene
Wickersham, George Woodward

Graduate Study
Bowie, William
Landis, Walter Savage
Richards, Joseph Williams
Sadtler, Samuel Philip
LEICESTER ACADEMY (MASS.)
Ames, Oliver, 1831–1895
Davis, John, 1787–1854
Eames, Charles
Earle, Pliny, 1809–1892
Earle, Thomas
Guilford, Nathan
Henshaw, David
Hill, Thomas, 1818–1891
Knowles, Lucius James
Marcy, William Learned
Merrick, Pliny
Morton, William Thomas Green
Olney, Richard
Poole, William Frederick
Rice, Luther
Washburn, Emory
Whitney, Eli
Woods, Leonard, 1774–1854
LEIPZIG INSTITUTE FOR THE HISTORY OF MEDICINE (GERMANY)
Sigerist, Henry Ernest
LELAND STANFORD UNIVERSITY (CAL.)
Blinn, Holbrook
Freas, Thomas Bruce
Harper, Ida Husted
Lea, Homer
Peek, Frank William
LENOX COLLEGE (IOWA)
McKean, James William
Merriam, Charles Edward, Jr.
Merriam, John Campbell
LIBERTY HALL ACADEMY (See WASHINGTON AND LEE UNIVERSITY)
LINFIELD COLLEGE (OREG.)
Latourette, Kenneth Scott
LITCHFIELD LAW SCHOOL (CONN.)
Angell, Joseph Kinnicutt
Baldwin, Roger Sherman
Blake, Eli Whitney
Brace, John Pierce
Bradley, Stephen Row
Burrall, William Porter
Calhoun, John Caldwell
Clayton, John Middleton
Edwards, Henry Waggaman
Ellsworth, Henry Leavitt
Ellsworth, William Wolcott
Francis, John Brown
Gould, James
Green, Henry Woodhull
Hasbrouck, Abraham Bruyn
Hawks, Francis Lester
Hollister, Gideon Hiram
Howe, Samuel
Hull, William
Hunt, Ward
Johns, Kensey
King, James Gore
Lawrence, William Beach
Longstreet, Augustus Baldwin
Lord, Daniel
Mann, Horace
Mansfield, Edward Deering
Mason, John Young

Metcalf, Theron
Morse, Sidney Edwards
Morton, Marcus, 1784–1864
Nisbet, Eugenius Aristides
Pierpont, John
Platt, Orville Hitchcock
Porter, Peter Buell
Raymond, Daniel
Schell, Augustus
Smith, Junius
Smith, Nathan, 1770–1835
Smith, Nathaniel
Smith, Truman
Sprague, Peleg
Stephens, John Lloyd
Strong, Moses McCure
Tod, George
Williams, Elisha, 1773–1833
Williams, Thomas Scott
Wolcott, Oliver
Woodbridge, William
Woodbury, Levi
LITTLE ROCK COLLEGE (ARK.)
Powell, Richard Ewing ("Dick")
LIVINGSTONE COLLEGE (N.C.)
Aggrey, James Emman Kwegyir
Clement, Rufus Early
LOMBARD COLLEGE (ILL.)
Sandburg, Carl August
Wright, Theodore Paul
LONDON SCHOOL OF ECONOMICS (ENGLAND)
Abbott, Edith
Neumann, Franz Leopold
Graduate Study
Powdermaker, Hortense
Schultz, Henry
LONDON SCHOOL OF MINES (ENGLAND)
Herbert, Frederick Hugh
LONG ISLAND COLLEGE HOSPITAL (N.Y.)
Medicine
Tilney, Frederick
White, William Alanson
LONG ISLAND COLLEGE OF MEDICINE (N.Y.)
Dickinson, Robert Latou
LONG ISLAND MEDICAL COLLEGE (N.Y.)
Kirby, George Hughes
LORAS COLLEGE (IOWA)
Kerby, William Joseph
Ward, Arch Burdette
LOS ANGELES COLLEGE (CAL.)
Hubbard, Bernard Rosecrans
LOS ANGELES SCHOOL OF ART
Kuniyoshi, Yasuo
LOUISIANA, UNIVERSITY OF (See TULANE UNIVERSITY)
LOUISIANA POLYTECHNIC INSTITUTE
Pope, James Pinckney
LOUISIANA STATE UNIVERSITY
Boyd, Thomas Duckett
Brooks, Overton
Chennault, Claire Lee
Harrison, Byron Patton
Morrison, Delesseps Story
Perez, Leander Henry
Law
Brooks, Overton
Morrison, Delesseps Story

LOUISVILLE, UNIVERSITY OF (See UNIVERSITY OF LOUISVILLE)
LOUISVILLE COLLEGE OF PHARMACY (KY.)
Flexner, Simon
LOUISVILLE COLLEGIATE INSTITUTE (KY.)
Hill, Patty Smith
LOUISVILLE LAW SCHOOL (KY.)
Klaw, Marc
LOWELL TEXTILE INSTITUTE
Dickson, Earle Ensign
LOWVILLE ACADEMY (N.Y.)
Bartlett, John Russell
Dickinson, Charles Monroe
Doty, James Duane
Hough, Franklin Benjamin
Johnson, Samuel William
Strong James
LOYOLA COLLEGE (MD.)
Saxton, Eugene Francis
LOYOLA UNIVERSITY (CAL.)
Wright, Willard Huntington
LOYOLA UNIVERSITY (LA.)
Law
Long, Earl Kemp
LOYOLA UNIVERSITY OF CHICAGO
Harrison, Carter Henry, Jr.
LUTHERAN THEOLOGICAL SEMINARY (See GETTYSBURG COLLEGE)
LUTHER COLLEGE (IOWA)
Hanson, James Christian Meinich
Haugen, Nils Pederson
Kildahl, John Nathan
Koren, John
Preus, Christian Keyser
Stromme, Peer Olsen
Stub, Hans Gerhard
LYONS COLLEGIATE INSTITUTE (IOWA)
Patrick, Mary Mills

MACALESTER COLLEGE (MINN.)
Baker, Hugh Potter
McCORMICK THEOLOGICAL SEMINARY (ILL.)
Holt, Arthur Erastus
Lyon, David Willard
Martin, Everett Dean
Scott, Walter Dill
McGEE COLLEGE (MO.)
Hirth, William Andrew
McGILL UNIVERSITY (CANADA)
Becket, Frederick Mark
McKenzie, Robert Tait
Mathewson, Edward Payson
Naismith, James
Viner, Jacob
Graduate Study
Harrington, John Lyle
Medicine
Drew, Charles Richard
McKenzie, Robert Tait
Wood, Casey Albert
McKENDREE COLLEGE (ILL.)
Baker, Jehu
Bernays, Augustus Charles
Loveland, William Austin Hamilton
Morrison, William Ralls
Snyder, John Francis

Sparks, William Andrew Jackson
Waller, Willard Walter
Wilson, James Harrison
Zane, Charles Shuster
MCMASTER UNIVERSITY (CANADA)
Eaton, Charles Aubrey
Macintosh, Douglas Clyde
Graduate Study
Eaton, Charles Aubrey
MCMURRY COLLEGE (TEX.)
Key, Valdimer Orlando, Jr.
MCPHERSON COLLEGE (KANS.)
Johnson, Wendell Andrew Leroy
MADISON UNIVERSITY (See COLGATE UNIVERSITY)
MADRAS CHRISTIAN COLLEGE (INDIA)
Oldham, William Fitzjames
MAINE STATE SEMINARY (See BATES COLLEGE)
MAINE WESLEYAN SEMINARY
Burrowes, Edward Thomas
Fernald, Charles Henry
Fillebrown, Thomas
Howe, Timothy Otis
Maxim, Hudson
Stevens, John Leavitt
MANHATTAN COLLEGE (N.Y.)
Dowling, Austin
Hayes, Patrick Joseph
Mundelein, George William
MARIAHILFE MILITARY ACADEMY (AUSTRIA)
Von Stroheim, Erich
MARIETTA COLLEGE (OHIO)
Bosworth, Francke Huntington
Dawes, Charles Gates
Dawes, Rufus Cutler
Elliott, Charles Burke
Fairfield, Edmund Burke
Howison, George Holmes
Hulbert, Archer Butler
Johnson, Byron Bancroft
Kinkead, Edgar Benton
Mitchell, Edwin Knox
Quinan, John Russell
Shedd, William Ambrose
Williams, John Elias, 1871–1927
Graduate Study
Dawes, Charles Gates
MARION (ALA.) INSTITUTE
Short, Joseph Hudson, Jr.
MARQUETTE UNIVERSITY (WIS.)
McCarthy, Joseph Raymond
Medicine
Mahoney, John Friend
MARSHALL COLLEGE (See FRANKLIN AND MARSHALL COLLEGE)
MARSHALL COLLEGE (W.VA.)
Harvey, William Hope
MARVIN COLLEGE (KY.)
Barkley, Alben William
MARYLAND INSTITUTE, COLLEGE OF ART
Leigh, William Robinson
MARYLAND INSTITUTE OF FINE AND APPLIED ARTS
Louis, Morris

MARYVILLE COLLEGE (TENN.)
Rutledge, Wiley Blount
Williams, Aubrey Willis
MASSACHUSETTS AGRICULTURAL COLLEGE
Bartlett, Francis Alonzo
Stone, Harlan Fiske
MASSACHUSETTS COLLEGE OF PHARMACY
Duchin, Edward Frank ("Eddy")
MASSACHUSETTS INSTITUTE OF TECHNOLOGY
Adams, Edward Dean
Babson, Roger Ward
Bassett, William Hastings
Blashfield, Edwin Howland
Bowen, Norman Levi
Brophy, Thomas D'Arcy
Browne, Herbert Wheildon Cotton
Brunner, Arnold William
Burgess, Frank Gelett
Burgess, George Kimball
Cabot, Godfrey Lowell
Calkins, Gary Nathan
Chapelle, Dickey
Clapp, Charles Horace
Coolidge, Charles Allerton
De Forest, Alfred Victor
Draper, Eben Sumner
Du Pont, Alfred Irénée
Du Pont, Irénée
Du Pont, Lammot
Du Pont, Pierre Samuel
Du Pont, Thomas Coleman
Dyar, Harrison Gray
Edison, Charles
Ellis, Carleton
Farwell, Arthur
Fenner, Burt Leslie
Flint, Albert Stowell
Ford, George Burdett
Freeman, John Ripley
French, Daniel Chester
French, William Merchant Richardson
Fuller, George Warren
Gilbert, Cass
Grabau, Amadeus William
Granger, Alfred Hoyt
Greene, Charles Ezra
Greene, Charles Sumner
Greene, Henry Mather
Groves, Leslie Richard, Jr.
Gunn, Selskar Michael
Hale, George Ellery
Hamlin, Alfred Dwight Foster
Harkins, William Draper
Hayden, Charles
Hazen, Allen
Herreshoff, Nathanael Greene
Hood, Raymond Mathewson
Howard, Henry
Howe, Henry Marion
Hunt, Alfred Ephraim
Jordan, Edwin Oakes
Kalmus, Herbert Thomas
Kinnicutt, Leonard Parker
La Farge, Christopher Grant
Leonard, Harry Ward
Lewis, Wilfred

Litchfield, Paul Weeks
Little, Arthur Dehon
Lowell, Guy
McMurtrie, Douglas Crawford
Main, Charles Thomas
Matthes, François Emile
Matthes, Gerard Hendrik
Mauran, John Lawrence
Maxim, Hiram Percy
Merrill, Frank Dow
Meserve, Frederick Hill
Minot, Charles Sedgwick
Mixter, Samuel Jason
Mulliken, Samuel Parsons
Newell, Frederick Haynes
Noyes, Arthur Amos
Parker, Theodore Bissell
Peabody, Cecil Hobart
Pearson, Fred Stark
Perkins, Dwight Heald
Prescott, Samuel Cate
Rice, Calvin Winsor
Richards, Ellen Henrietta Swallow
Richards, Robert Hallowell
Ripley, William Zebina
Rollins, Frank West
Rotch, Abbott Lawrence
Rotch, Arthur
Sauveur, Albert
Shaw, Howard Van Doren
Sherman, Forrest Percival
Skidmore, Louis
Sloan, Alfred Pritchard, Jr.
Smith, Edward Hanson
Smith, Jonas Waldo
Smith, Jonas Waldo
Stone, Charles Augustus
Sullivan, Louis Henry
Swain, George Fillmore
Swope, Gerard
Talbot, Henry Paul
Taylor, William Chittenden
Tolman, Edward Chace
Tolman, Richard Chace
Troland, Leonard Thompson
Tucker, Benjamin Ricketson
Vickery, Howard Leroy
Waite, Henry Matson
Warner, Edward Pearson
Warren, Henry Ellis
Warren, Herbert Langford
Washburn, Edward Wight
Webster, Edwin Sibley
Wheelwright, Edmund March
Whitney, Willis Rodney
Whorf, Benjamin Lee
Williams, Francis Henry
Winslow, Charles-Edward Amory
Woodbury, Charles Jeptha Hill
Wright, Theodore Paul
Graduate Study
Clapp, Charles Horace
Du Pont, Irénée
Ford, George Burdett
Gorrell, Edgar Staley
Graves, Alvin Cushman
Kalmus, Herbert Thomas
Kirkwood, John Gamble
Oxnam, Garfield Bromley
Ripley, William Zebina

Tolman, Richard Chace
Whitney, Willis Rodney
Winslow, Charles-Edward Amory
MASSACHUSETTS NORMAL ART
SCHOOL
Adams, Herbert Samuel
MacNeil, Hermon Atkins
Metcalf, Willard Leroy
Miller, Leslie William
Perry, Walter Scott
Robinson, Boardman
Sylvester, Frederick Oakes
Vonnoh, Robert William
MASSACHUSETTS STATE COLLEGE
Brown, Ralph Hall
Green, Samuel Bowdlear
Myrick, Herbert
Stockbridge, Horace Edward
Tuckerman, Frederick
Tydings, Millard Evelyn
Wheeler, William
MASSACHUSETTS STATE NORMAL
SCHOOL
Cortelyou, George Bruce
MASSACHUSETTS STATE NORMAL
SCHOOL AT WESTFIELD
Diller, Joseph Silas
MAYVILLE STATE COLLEGE (N.D.)
Burdick, Usher Lloyd
MEADVILLE THEOLOGICAL SCHOOL
(PA.)
Abbot, Francis Ellingwood
Batchelor, George
Cooke, George Willis
Jones, Jenkin Lloyd
Kennedy, William Sloane
Metcalf, Joel Hastings
Wiggin, James Henry
MECHANICS' INSTITUTE (N.Y.)
Rose, Mary Davies Swartz
MEDICAL COLLEGE OF OHIO
Billings, John Shaw
Newton, Robert Safford
Oliver, Fitch Edward
Rachford, Benjamin Knox
Ransohoff, Joseph
MEDICAL COLLEGE OF SOUTH
CAROLINA
Chisolm, John Julian
Logan, Thomas Muldrup, 1808
–1876
Massey, George Betton
Pendleton, Edmund Monroe
Ravenel, Mazyck Porcher
Smith, John Lawrence
Stevens, William Bacon
Thomas, Theodore Gaillard
MEDICAL COLLEGE OF VIRGINIA
Briggs, Lloyd Vernon
MEDICO-CHIRURGICAL COLLEGE OF
PHILADELPHIA
Pfahler, George Edward
MELBOURNE CONSERVATORY (AUS-
TRALIA)
Grainger, George Percy
MERCERSBURG THEOLOGICAL
SEMINARY (PA.)
Bausman, Benjamin
Gerhart, Emanuel Vogel
Harbaugh, Henry

MERCER UNIVERSITY (GA.)
Candler, Allen Daniel
Cox, Edward Eugene
Crawford, Martin Jenkins
Davis, Noah Knowles
George, Walter Franklin
Hardwick, Thomas William
Hubbard, Richard Bennett
Johnston, Richard Malcolm
Kilpatrick, William Heard
Kilpatrick, William Heard
McDaniel, Henry Dickerson
Murrow, Joseph Samuel
Newman, Albert Henry
Ogburn, William Fielding
Sherwood, Thomas Adiel
Straton, John Roach
Upshaw, William David
Winship, Blanton
Wood, John Stephens
Law
George, Walter Franklin
METROPOLITAN BUSINESS COL-
LEGE, CHICAGO (ILL.)
Thompson, William Hale
MEXICO ACADEMY (N.Y.)
Emery, Albert Hamilton
Moore, Veranus Alva
Skinner, Charles Rufus
Watson, James Madison
MIAMI UNIVERSITY (OHIO)
Anderson, John Alexander
Billings, John Shaw
Birney, James
Brice, Calvin Stewart
Davis, Joseph Robert
Dennison, William
Dickey, Theophilus Lyle
Durbin, John Price
Faran, James John
Fee, John Gregg
Galloway, Samuel
Groesbeck, William Slocum
Hardin, Charles Henry
Harrison, Benjamin, 1833–1901
Hittell, John Shertzer
Hittell, Theodore Henry
Howell, James Bruen
Kennedy, William Sloane
Kenner, Duncan Farrar
Laws, Samuel Spahr
Loughridge, Robert McGill
Lowe, Ralph Phillips
McClurg, Alexander Caldwell
McClurg, Joseph Washington
McCracken, Henry Mitchell
McDill, James Wilson
Moore, Philip North
Morrison, John Irwin
Morton, Oliver Perry
Noble, John Willock
Patterson, John Henry
Reid, Whitelaw
Schenck, Robert Cumming
Scott, Samuel Parsons
Smith, Caleb Blood
Swing, David
Thomson, William McClure
Torrence, Frederick Ridgely
Venable, William Henry
Weller, John B.
Wilson, Samuel Ramsay

Medicine
Burnett, Swan Moses
McCormack, Joseph Nathaniel
Zachos, John Celivergos
MICHIGAN, UNIVERSITY OF (See
UNIVERSITY OF MICHIGAN)
MICHIGAN AGRICULTURAL COLLEGE
Bagley, William Chandler
Baker, Hugh Potter
Baker, Ray Stannard
Friedman, William Frederick
Sanderson, Ezra Dwight
MICHIGAN COLLEGE OF MINES
Flaherty, Robert Joseph
MICHIGAN STATE AGRICULTURAL
COLLEGE
Bessey, Charles Edwin
Butterfield, Kenyon Leech
Davenport, Eugene
Lewis, Charles Bertrand
Lindeman, Eduard Christian
St. John, Charles Edward
Shelton, Edward Mason
Symons, Thomas William
Toumey, James William
Graduate Study
Davenport, Eugene
MICHIGAN STATE NORMAL COL-
LEGE
Bowman, Isaiah
MICHIGAN STATE NORMAL SCHOOL
Kellogg, John Harvey
St. John, Charles Edward
MICHIGAN STATE UNIVERSITY
Bailey, Liberty Hyde
Briggs, Lyman James
Copeland, Royal Samuel
Diller, Burgoyne
Graduate Study
McAndrew, William
MIDDLEBURY COLLEGE (VT.)
Ashmun, Jehudi
Barton, James Levi
Beman, Nathan Sidney Smith
Bingham, Hiram, 1789–1869
Blanchard, Jonathan
Brainerd, Ezra
Chase, Irah
Church, Alonzo
Collins, John Anderson
Conant, Thomas Jefferson
Day, Luther
Evans, Warren Felt
Foot, Solomon
Glidden, Joseph Farwell
Green, Beriah
Haines, Charles Glidden
Hall, Thomas Seavey
Hatfield, Edwin Francis
Hepburn, Alonzo Barton
Howard, William Alanson
Howe, George
Howe, Mark Anthony de Wolfe
Hudson, Henry Norman
James, Edwin
Kelley, Hall Jackson
Knowlton, Frank Hall
Mallary, Rollin Carolas
Mead, Charles Marsh
Nelson, Samuel
Olin, Stephen
Patton, William

Phelps, Edward John
Pitcher, Zina
Post, Truman Marcellus
Rankin, Jeremiah Eames
Sawyer, Thomas Jefferson
Saxe, John Godfrey
Schoolcraft, Henry Rowe
Sheffield, Devello Zelotes
Sheldon, Walter Lorenzo
Sheldon, William Evarts
Sherwood, Adiel
Slade, William
Stevens, Henry
Strong, Moses McCure
Thompson, Daniel Pierce
Tyler, Samuel
Ward, Henry Augustus
Wines, Enoch Cobb
Winslow, Hubbard
Winslow, Miron
Wright, Silas
MILAN CONSERVATORY (ITALY)
Galli-Curci, Amelita
MILAN POLITECNICO (ITALY)
Bellanca, Giuseppe Mario
MILLERSBURG FEMALE COLLEGE
(KY.)
White, Alma Bridwell
MILLER SCHOOL OF COMMERCE
(N.Y.)
Watson, Thomas John
MILLS COLLEGE (CAL.)
Nevada, Emma
MILTON COLLEGE (WIS.)
West, Allen Brown
MILTON ACADEMY (MASS.)
Child, Richard Washburn
Cobb, Jonathan Holmes
Forbes, Robert Bennet
Pierce, Henry Lillie
MILWAUKEE NORMAL SCHOOL
(WIS.)
Bolton, Herbert Eugene
MILWAUKEE NORMAL SCHOOL
(WIS.)
Zuppke, Robert Carl
MILWAUKEE UNIVERSITY
Mahoney, John Friend
MISSISSIPPI AGRICULTURAL AND
MECHANICAL COLLEGE
Stockard, Charles Rupert
MISSISSIPPI COLLEGE
Brough, Charles Hillman
MISSISSIPPI STATE COLLEGE
Duggar, Benjamin Minge
MISSISSIPPI STATE UNIVERSITY
Garner, James Wilford
MISSOURI, UNIVERSITY OF (See
UNIVERSITY OF MISSOURI)
MISSOURI SCHOOL OF MINES
Jackling, Daniel Cowan
MISSOURI STATE TEACHERS COL-
LEGE
Smith, Horton
MISSOURI WESLEYAN COLLEGE
Jones, Benjamin Allyn
MONMOUTH COLLEGE (ILL.)
Howard, Oliver Otis
Shonts, Theodore Perry
Sloan, Richard Elihu
Sprague, Charles Arthur
Wallace, John Findley

MONSON ACADEMY (MASS.)
Barnard, Henry
Bennett, Emerson
Bissell, Edwin Cone
Brown, Samuel Robbins
Colton, Calvin
Knowlton, Marcus Perrin
Loomis, Dwight
Munn, Orson Desaix
Sophocles, Evangelinus Aposto-
lides
Storrs, Richard Salter, 1821–
1900
Yung, Wing
MONTVALE INSTITUTE (TENN.)
Hull, Cordell
MOODY BIBLE INSTITUTE (ILL.)
Stelzle, Charles
MOORE'S HILL COLLEGE (IND.)
Main, John Hanson Thomas
Graduate Study
Main, John Hanson Thomas
MORAVIAN COLLEGE AND THEO-
LOGICAL SEMINARY (PA.)
Clewell, John Henry
Holland, William Jacob
Levering, Joseph Mortimer
Reichel, William Cornelius
Thursby, Emma Cecilia
MORAVIAN COLLEGE (PA.)
Badè, William Frederic
Beck, James Montgomery
Schweinitz, George Edmund de
MOREHOUSE COLLEGE (GA.)
King, Martin Luther, Jr.
Reid, Ira De Augustine
MORNINGSIDE COLLEGE (IOWA)
Stouffer, Samuel Andrew
Waymack, William Wesley
MOSCOW CONSERVATORY (RUSSIA)
Rachmaninoff, Sergei Vasilye-
vich
MOSCOW PHILHARMONIC SCHOOL
(RUSSIA)
Koussevitzky, Serge Alexan-
drovich
MOUNT ALLISON UNIVERSITY
(CANADA)
Colpitts, Edwin Henry
MOUNT HOLYOKE COLLEGE
(MASS.)
Brigham, Mary Ann
Colton, Elizabeth Avery
Dickinson, Emily Elizabeth
Fairchild, Mary Salome Cutler
Fiske, Fidelia
Frame, Alice Seymour Browne
Freeman, Mary Eleanor Wilkins
Hersey, Evelyn Weeks
Howard, Ada Lydia
Mills, Susan Lincoln Tolman
Mitchell, Lucy Myers Wright
Perkins, Frances
Sunderland, Eliza Jane Read
Yale, Caroline Ardelia
MOUNT PLEASANT CLASSICAL INSTI-
TUTE (MASS.)
Beecher, Henry Ward
Clark, Horace Francis
Frick, Henry Clay
Prime, William Cowper

MOUNT PLEASANT COLLEGE (See
OTTERBEIN COLLEGE)
MOUNT ST. MARY'S COLLEGE (MD.)
Chatard, Francis Silas
Cooper, James
Corrigan, Michael Augustine
Elder, William Henry
Fitzgerald, Edward
Flanagan, Edward Joseph
Fry, William Henry
Gilmour, Richard
La Farge, John
Le Conte, John Lawrence
McCann, Alfred Watterson
McCloskey, John
McCloskey, William George
McCoffery, John
Miles, George Henry
Pise, Charles Constantine
Purcell, John Baptist
Quarter, William
Seton, Robert
Seton, William
Toner, Joseph Meredith
White, Charles Ignatius
White, Edward Douglass, 1845–
1921
Graduate Study
Flanagan, Edward Joseph
MOUNT ST. MARY'S OF THE WEST
(OHIO)
Dwenger, Joseph
Enneking, John Joseph
Fitzgerald, Edward
Noll, John Francis
Rosecrans, Sylvester Horton
Spalding, John Lancaster
MOUNT UNION COLLEGE (OHIO)
Atkinson, George Wesley
Galbreath, Charles Burleigh
Hamilton, John William
Knox, Philander Chase
Laughlin, James Laurence
Presser, Theodore
Thompson, Will Lamartine
Tibbles, Thomas Henry
MOUNT WASHINGTON COLLEGIATE
INSTITUTE (N.Y.)
Conkling, Roscoe
Miller, Charles Henry
Mitchell, Edward Page
Phelps, William Walter
Pierson, Arthur Tappan
MOUNT ZION ACADEMY (S.C.)
Aiken, David Wyatt
Bratton, John
Chappell, Absalom Harris
Du Bose, William Porcher
Gaillard, David Du Bose
Jones, John B.
Lewis, Dixon Hall
Porcher, Francis Peyre
MT. AIRY LUTHERAN THEOLOGICAL
SEMINARY
Buchman, Frank Nathan Daniel
MUHLENBERG COLLEGE (PA.)
Buchman, Frank Nathan Daniel
Kohler, Elmer Peter
Peters, Madison Clinton
Rupp, William
Weidner, Revere Franklin

Graduate Study
Miller, George Abram
MUNGRET COLLEGE (IRELAND)
Turner, William
MUSEUM OF FINE ARTS SCHOOL
(MASS.)
Benson, Frank Weston
Davis, Charles Harold
Tarbell, Edmund Charles
MUSKINGUM COLLEGE (OHIO)
Harper, Robert Francis
Harper, William Rainey
Kyle, David Braden
McBride, F(rancis) Scott
Moorehead, William Gallogly
Thompson, William Oxley

NAPLES ACADEMY OF FINE ARTS
(ITALY)
Lebrun, Federico ("Rico")
NASSAU HALL (See PRINCETON
UNIVERSITY)
NATIONAL ACADEMY OF DESIGN
(N.Y.)
Anshutz, Thomas Pollock
Baziotes, William
Beckwith, James Carroll
Benson, Eugene
Brevoort, James Renwick
Brush, George de Forest
Bush-Brown, Henry Kirke
Chase, William Merritt
Christy, Howard Chandler
Dewing, Maria Richards Oakey
Eaton, Wyatt
Freeman, James Edwards
Gaul, William Gilbert
Gray, Henry Peters
Hartley, Marsden
Hennessy, William John
Hicks, John 1823-1890
Jones, Alfred
Karfiol, Bernard
Keller, Arthur Ignatius
Koehler, Robert
Lawrie, Alexander
Lie, Jonas
Lukeman, Henry Augustus
MacMonnies, Frederick William
Maynard, George Willoughby
Ormsby, Waterman Lilly
Page, William
Platt, Charles Adams
Reinhart, Benjamin Franklin
Richards, Thomas Addison
Robinson, Theodore
Ryder, Albert Pinkham
Shattuck, Aaron Draper
Shurtleff, Roswell Morse
Spencer, Robert
Sterne, Maurice
Wiggins, Carleton
NATIONAL CONSERVATORY OF MU-
SIC (N.Y.)
Burleigh, Henry Thacker
Cook, Will Marion
Downes, (Edwin) Olin
Goldman, Edwin Franko
NATIONAL NORMAL UNIVERSITY
(OHIO)
Hull, Cordell

NATIONAL TECHNICAL INSTITUTE,
NAPLES (ITALY)
Lebrun, Federico ("Rico")
NATIONAL UNIVERSITY (D.C.)
West, James Edward
Whitney, Courtney
Law
West, James Edward
NATURAL SCIENCE ESTABLISHMENT
(N.Y.)
Wheeler, William Morton
NAVAL ENGINEERING SCHOOL (IT-
ALY)
Gatti-Casazza, Giulio
NAVAL TECHNICAL SCHOOL (NOR-
WAY)
Barth, Carl Georg Lange
NAZARETH HALL (PA.)
Berg, Joseph Frederic
Cist, Jacob
Fries, Francis
McCalla, Bowman Hendry
McCawley, Charles Grymes
Mallory, Stephen Russell
Rondthaler, Edward
Schweinitz, Edmund Alexander
Schweinitz, Emil Alexander de
NEBRASKA WESLEYAN UNIVERSITY
Gortner, Ross Aiken
High, Stanley Hoflund
Hope, Clifford Ragsdale
NEOPHEGEN COLLEGE (TENN.)
Read, Opie Pope
NEWARK ACADEMY (N.J.)
Clayton, Thomas
Frelinghuysen, Frederick Theo-
dore
Gregg, Andrew
Hamilton, Peter
Jones, Ernest Lester
Lieb, John William
Murphy, Franklin
Parke, John
Platner, Samuel Ball
Shields, Charles Woodruff
Whitehead, William Adee
Wiley, Andrew Jackson
NEWBERRY COLLEGE (S.C.)
Blease, Coleman Livingston
Lever, Asbury Francis
NEW BRUNSWICK THEOLOGICAL
SEMINARY (N.J.)
Chambers, Talbot Wilson
Corwin, Edward Tanjore
Drury, John Benjamin
Ferris, Isaac
Muste, Abraham Johannes
Schenck, Ferdinand Schureman
Searle, John Preston
Talmage, John Van Nest
Talmage, Thomas De Witt
Woodbridge, Samuel Merrill
NEWBURY SEMINARY (VT.)
Dillingham, William Paul
Flanders, Henry
Hoyt, Albert Harrison
Pearsons, Daniel Kimball
NEW COLLEGE OF EDINBURGH
(SCOTLAND)
Coffin, Henry Sloane

NEW ENGLAND CONSERVATORY OF
MUSIC (MASS.)
Brady, Alice
Brown, Gertrude Foster
Chadwick, George Whitefield
Cortelyou, George Bruce
Daniels, Frank Albert
Dunham, Henry Morton
Gilbert, Henry Franklin Belk-
nap
Hadley, Henry Kimball
Hull, Josephine
Lodge, John Ellerton
Mason, Frank Stuart
Nordica, Lillian
Presser, Theodore
Williams, Fannie Barrier
NEW HAMPSHIRE COLLEGE OF
AGRICULTURE AND MECHANI-
CAL ARTS
Hazen, Allen
NEW HAMPTON ACADEMY (N.H.)
Fogg, George Gilman
Haven, Emily Bradley Neal
Morrison, Nathan Jackson
Plaisted, Harris Merrill
Robinson, Ezekiel Gilman
NEW HAMPTON LITERARY AND
THEOLOGICAL INSTITUTION
(N.H.)
Cheney, Oren Burbank
Eddy, Daniel Clarke
Gale, Elbridge
McCall, Samuel Walker
Marden, Orison Swett
NEW IPSWICH ACADEMY (N.H.)
Allen, David Oliver
Bell, Samuel
Everett, David
Howard, Ada Lydia
Payson, Edward
Sherwin, Thomas
Stearns, John Newton
Stearns, Oliver
Wilder, Marshall Pinckney
Worcester, Samuel
NEW PALTZ STATE NORMAL
SCHOOL (N.Y.)
Harcourt, Alfred
NEW SALEM ACADEMY (MASS.)
Allen, David Oliver
Going, Jonathan
Heywood, Levi
Howe, Samuel
NEW SCHOOL FOR SOCIAL RE-
SEARCH
Cahill, Holger
NEW SCHOOL OF DESIGN (MASS.)
Gorky, Arshile
NEWTON COLLEGIATE INSTITUTE
(N.J.)
Warbasse, James Peter
NEWTON THEOLOGICAL INSTITU-
TION (MASS.)
Anderson, Martin Brewer
Andrews, Elisha Benjamin
Banvard, Joseph
Brown, Charles Rufus
Burrage, Henry Sweetser
Cushing, Josiah Nelson
Dearing, John Lincoln
Dodge, Ebenezer

Eaton, Charles Aubrey
Faunce, William Herbert Perry
Fernald, James Champlin
Gilmore, Joseph Henry
Horr, George Edwin
Hovey, Alvah
Jones, John Taylor
King, Henry Melville
Lincoln, John Larkin
Manly, Basil, 1825–1892
Mason, Francis
Mathews, Shailer
Merrill, George Edmands
Mitchell, Edward Cushing
Robins, Henry Ephraim
Robinson, Ezekiel Gilman
Small, Albion Woodbury
Stevens, William Arnold
Williams, George Washington
Winkler, Edwin Theodore
NEW YORK COLLEGE OF PHARMA-
  CY
Coit, Henry Leber
Disbrow, William Stephen
Jacobi, Mary Corinna Putnam
NEW YORK FREE ACADEMY (See
  COLLEGE OF CITY OF NEW
  YORK)
NEW YORK HOMEOPATHIC MEDI-
  CAL COLLEGE
Gallinger, Jacob Harold
Hanchett, Henry Granger
Harkness, William
Hrdlicka, Ales
Miller, Charles Henry
Millspaugh, Charles Frederick
NEW YORK HOSPITAL SCHOOL OF
  NURSING
Beard, Mary
Goodrich, Annie Warburton
NEW YORK HOSPITAL TRAINING
  SCHOOL FOR NURSES
Stimson, Julia Catherine
Wald, Lillian D.
NEW YORK LAW SCHOOL
Borchard, Edwin Montefiore
Chester, Colby Mitchell
Colby, Bainbridge
Coulter, Ernest Kent
Dodd, Lee Wilson
Griscom, Lloyd Carpenter
Harrison, Francis Burton
Hylan, John Francis
McClellan, George Brinton
Miller, David Hunter
Pinchot, Amos Richards Eno
Purdy, Lawson
Rice, Elmer
Seabury, Samuel
Stevens, Wallace
Taber, John
Wagner, Robert Ferdinand
Walker, James John
Whalen, Grover Aloysius
NEW YORK MEDICAL COLLEGE
Byrne, John
Lapham, William Berry
Otis, Fessenden Nott
Spooner, Shearjashub
Taylor, Charles Fayette

NEW YORK SCHOOL FOR APPLIED
  DESIGN
Bernstein, Aline
NEW YORK SCHOOL OF APPLIED
  DESIGN FOR WOMEN
Meière, Marie Hildreth
NEW YORK SCHOOL OF ART
Hopper, Edward
Miller, Kenneth Hayes
Stella, Joseph
NEW YORK SCHOOL OF FINE AND
  APPLIED ARTS
Adrian, Gilbert
Lawson, Robert Ripley
NEW YORK SCHOOL OF PHILAN-
  THROPY
Perkins, Frances
Graduate Study
Billikopf, Jacob
NEW YORK SCHOOL OF SOCIAL
  WORK
Coyle, Grace Longwell
NEW YORK SCHOOL OF THEATER
Kovacs, Ernie
NEW YORK STATE LIBRARY SCHOOL
  AT ALBANY
Anderson, Edwin Hatfield
Pearson, Edmund Lester
NEW YORK TRAINING SCHOOL FOR
  TEACHERS
Lange, Dorothea
Stark, Louis
NEW YORK UNIVERSITY
Abbott, Austin
Abbott, Benjamin Vaughan
Abbott, Edward
Abbott, Lyman
Adler, George J.
Baird, Charles Washington
Baird, Henry Martyn
Bond, Hugh Lennox
Bowne, Borden Parker
Brill, Abraham Arden
Buehler, Huber Gray
Butler, William Allen
Carter, Jesse Benedict
Clark, Henry James
Clay, Albert Tobias
Coxe, Arthur Cleveland
Croly, David Goodman
Crosby, Ernest Howard
Crosby, Howard
Crosby, John Schuyler
Cullen, Countée Porter
Doubleday, Nelson
Duyckinck, George Long
Fiske, Harrison Grey
Goodsell, Daniel Ayres
Hall, Abraham Oakey
Hay, Charles Augustus
Higgins, Daniel Paul
Hine, Lewis Wickes
Horn, Edward Traill
Houghton, George Hendric
Huntington, Jedediah Vincent
Hunton, William Lee
Isaacs, Abram Samuel
Johnson, Willis Fletcher
Johnston, Jalen Taylor
Koch, Vivienne
Lasser, Jacob Kay
Ludlow, William

Maclay, William Brown
Madigan, Laverne
Mathews, Cornelius
Mills, Lawrence Heyworth
Moore, George Henry
Noyes, Henry Drury
Olcott, Henry Steel
Orth, Godlove Stein
Parsons, John Edward
Paton, Lewis Bayles
Payne, Daniel Alexander
Picton, Thomas
Post, George Browne
Pressman, Lee
Redfield, Amasa Angell
Reid, John Morrison
Rossen, Robert
Russell, Israel Cook
Salter, William
Schuyler, George Washington
Shahn, Benjamin ("Ben")
Shear, Theodore Leslie
Sickles, Daniel Edgar
Smillie, James David
Speir, Samuel Fleet
Sprecher, Samuel
Stevenson, John James
Stoever, Martin Luther
Taylor, Joseph Deems
Tilden, Samuel Jones
True, Frederick William
Unangst, Erias
Underwood, Horace Grant
Vail, Alfred
Valentine, Milton
Wegmann, Edward
White, Richard Grant
Whitman, Charles Seymour
Woodbridge, Samuel Merrill
Youmans, William Jay
Young, Alfred
Graduate Study
Davison, George Willets
Hine, Lewis Wickes
Isaacs, Abram Samuel
Kingsley, Elizabeth Seelman
Madigan, Laverne
Noyes, Henry Drury
Parsons, John Edward
Reece, Brazilla Carroll
Revel, Bernard
Shaw, Edward Richard
Shear, Theodore Leslie
Stevenson, John James
Stoddard, John Fair
Law
Allen, Florence Ellinwood
Boissevain, Inez Milholland
Boudin, Louis Boudinoff
Dill, James Brooks
Dodd, Bella Visono
Glass, Montague Marsden
Golden, John
Goldman, Mayer C.
Hillquit, Morris
Kaempffert, Waldemar Bern-
  hard
King, Carol Weiss
La Guardia, Fiorello Henry
Levitt, Abraham
Marcantonio, Vito Anthony
Murray, James Edward

Palmer, Albert Marshman
Radin, Max
Root, Elihu
Talmage, Thomas DeWitt
Thomas, John Parnell
Tilden, Samuel Jones
Medicine
Abbott, Frank
Ainsworth, Frederick Crayton
Allen, Timothy Field
Biggs, Hermann Michael
Bishop, Seth Scott
Bosworth, Franke Huntington
Brill, Nathan Edwin
Bryant, Joseph Decatur
Burnett, Swan Moses
Caldwell, Eugene Wilson
Carroll, James
Chapin, Charles Value
Coakley, Cornelius Godfrey
Davis, Charles Henry Stanley
Dennis, Frederic Shepard
De Rosset, Moses John
Disbrow, William Stephen
Doremus, Robert Ogden
Draper, Henry
Evans, George Alfred
Fisher, George Jackson
Fowler, George Ryerson
Francis, Samuel Ward
Goldberger, Joseph
Goldwater, Sigismund Schulz
Guernsey, Egbert
Gulick, Luther Halsey, 1828–1891
Gulick, Luther Halsey, 1865–1918
Hammond, William Alexander
Hempel, Charles Julius
Howland, John
Johnston, George Ben
Kellogg, John Harvey
Lambuth, Walter Russell
Lydston, George Frank
McCaw, James Brown
McKean, James William
Mackenzie, John Noland
Maxwell, George Troup
Mayer, Emil
Mendes, Henry Pereira
Morrow, Prince Albert
Nichols, Charles Henry
Osborn, Henry Fairfield
Patrick, Hugh Talbot
Price, George Moses
Purple, Samuel Smith
Pusey, William Allen
Quintard, Charles Todd
Ranney, Ambrose Loomis
Reed, Walter
Rockwell, Alphonso David
Roosa, Daniel Bennett St. John
Rubinow, Isaac Max
Rusby, Henry Hurd
Sayre, Reginald Hall
Spitka, Edward Charles
Stiles, Henry Reed
Stone, Abraham
Wanless, William James
Wilbur, Cressy Livingston
Witthaus, Rudolph August
Wyckoff, John Henry

Wyeth, John Allan
NIAGARA UNIVERSITY (N.Y.)
Donovan, William Joseph
NOBLE AND GREENOUGH SCHOOL (MASS.)
Lovett, Robert Williamson
Lowell, Guy
Lowell, Percival
Underwood, Loring
Ward, Robert De Courcy
NORMAL SCHOOL OF MARYVILLE (N.DAK.)
Frazier, Lynn Joseph
NORTH AMERICAN COLLEGE, ROME (ITALY)
Spellman, Francis Joseph
Stritch, Samuel Alphonsus
Turner, William
Graduate Study
Pace, Edward Aloysius
NORTH AMERICAN COLLEGE (ITALY)
Dougherty, Dennis Joseph
Meyer, Albert Gregory
O'Connell, William Henry
Rummel, Joseph Francis
Theology
Cooper, John Montgomery
NORTH CAROLINA MILITARY AND POLYTECHNIC INSTITUTE
Cain, William
NORTH CAROLINA STATE UNIVERSITY
Scott, W(illiam) Kerr
NORTH CAROLINA STATE UNIVERSITY AT RALEIGH
Gardner, Oliver Maxwell
NORTH CENTRAL COLLEGE (ILL.)
Baldwin, Evelyn Briggs
Breasted, James Henry
Link, Henry Charles
NORTHEASTERN STATE COLLEGE (OKLA.)
Stigler, William Grady
NORTHEAST MISSOURI STATE COLLEGE
Laughlin, Harry Hamilton
NORTH GEORGIA AGRICULTURAL COLLEGE
Wood, John Stephens
NORTH GEORGIA COLLEGE
Morehouse, Ward
NORTHWESTERN MILITARY AND NAVAL ACADEMY (WIS.)
Tracy, Spencer Bonaventure
NORTHWESTERN UNIVERSITY (ILL.)
Aldrich, Charles Anderson
Bemis, Harold Edward
Boutell, Henry Sherman
Corrothers, James David
Emmett, Burton
Frank, Glenn
Gates, John Warne
Greenlaw, Edwin Almiron
Hard, William
Harrington, Mark Walrod
Hart, Virgil Chittenden
Helmer, Bessie Bradwell
Hoffman, Clare Eugene
James, Edmund Janes
Johnson, Harold Ogden ("Chic")

Johnson, Joseph French
Olsen, John Sigvard ("Ole")
Patten, Simon Nelson
Peek, George Nelson
Pieper, Franz August Otto
Ricketts, Howard Taylor
Scott, John Adams
Scott, Walter Dill
Sewall, May Eliza Wright
Shipstead, Henrik
Taylor, Fred Manville
Ward, Harry Frederick
Graduate Study
Case, Francis Higbee
Clement, Rufus Early
Greenlaw, Edwin Almiron
Helmer, Bessie Bradwell
Sharp, Katharine Lucinda
Law
Dawson, William Levi
Gardner, Gilson
Hadley, Herbert Spencer
McCormick, Robert Rutherford
Olson, Floyd Bjerstjerne
Plumb, Glenn Edward
Zeisler, Sigmund
Medicine
Abt, Isaac Arthur
Aldrich, Charles Anderson
Bishop, Seth Scott
Brennemann, Joseph
DeLee, Joseph Bolivar
Fordyce, John Addison
Gradle, Henry
McCord, James Bennett
Martin, Franklin Henry
Mayo, Charles Horace
Ohlmacher, Albert Philip
Park, Roswell, 1852–1914
Plummer, Henry Stanley
Ricketts, Howard Taylor
Williams, Daniel Hale
NORTHWICK COLLEGE (ENGLAND)
Mendes, Henry Pereira
NORWALK ACADEMY (OHIO)
Gilmore, Quincy Adams
Harris, William Logan
Hayes, Rutherford Birchard
Victor, Orville James
NORWICH FREE ACADEMY (CONN.)
Bourne, Edward Gaylord
Bryant, Joseph Decatur
Colvocoresses, George Musalas
Dorchester, Daniel
Gilman, Daniel Coit
Prentice, Samuel Oscar
Thurber, Christopher Carson
Ware, Edmund Asa
NORWICH UNIVERSITY (VT.)
Adams, Edward Dean
Adams, James Hopkins
Alvord, Henry Elijah
Beach, William Augustus
Boggs, Charles Stuart
Bragg, Thomas
Dixon, Luther Swift
Dodge, Grenville Mellen
Frazer, John Fries
Hatch, Edward
Hayes, Augustus Allen
Horton, Valentine Baxter
Hubbard, Henry Griswold

Huntington, William Reed
Kellogg, William Pitt
Lee, William Little
Lyon, Caleb
Milroy, Robert Huston
Morgan, Junius Spencer
Mower, Joseph Anthony
Porter, Russell Williams
Ransom, Thomas Edward
    Greenfield
Seymour, Horatio
Seymour, Thomas Hart
Seymour, Truman
Totten, George Muirson
Ward, Frederick Townsend
Ward, James Harmon
Welles, Gideon
Wellman, Samuel Thomas
Wheeler, William Adolphus
NOTRE DAME CONVENT (MD.)
Johnston, Frances Benjamin
NOTRE DAME UNIVERSITY
Corby, William
Dooley, Thomas Anthony, III
Elliott, Walter Hackett Robert
Howard, Timothy Edward
Lambeau, Earl Louis ("Curly")
Murphy, Frederick E.
Nelson, William Rockhill
Nieuwland, Julius Arthur
O'Connor, Edwin Greene
Riordan, Patrick William
Rockne, Knute Kenneth
Stuhldreher, Harry A.
Ward, Arch Burdette
Zahm, John Augustine
Law
Walker, Frank Comerford

OAHU COLLEGE (HAWAII)
Baldwin, Henry Perrine
OBERLIN ACADEMY (OHIO)
Ament, William Scott
Gray, Elisha
Gulick, Luther Halsey
Haskell, Henry Jospeh
Herrick, Myron Timothy
Powell, William Bramwell
OBERLIN COLLEGE (OHIO)
Allen, Frederic de Forest
Ament, William Scott
Barber, Amzi Lorenzo
Bickerdyke, Mary Ann Ball
Blackwell, Antoinette Louisa
    Brown
Bosworth, Edward Increase
Brooks, John Graham
Brown, John Mifflin
Bruce, Blanche K.
Burns, Anthony
Burt, Mary Elizabeth
Burton, Theodore Elijah
Callender, Guy Stevens
Chamberlain, Charles Joseph
Chapman, John Wilbur
Cloud, Henry Roe
Coffin, Lorenzo S.
Commons, John Rogers
Cowles, Henry Chandler
Cravath, Erastus Milo
Cravath, Paul Drennan
Dawley, Almena

Dill, James Brooks
Ells, Dan Parmelee
Fairbanks, Calvin
Fairchild, George Thompson
Fairchild, James Harris
Fairfield, Edmund Burke
Fillmore, John Comfort
Gray, Elisha
Gunn, Ross
Hall, Charles Martin
Hart, Hastings Hornell
Haskell, Henry Jospeh
Hayden, Ferdinand Vandiveer
Hayes, Charles Willard
Johnson, Byron Bancroft
Jones, Lynds
Kedzie, Robert Clark
King, Henry Churchill
Kofoid, Charles Atwood
Kyle, James Henderson
Langston, John Mercer
McCord, James Bennett
Mead, George Herbert
Miller, Emily Clark Huntington
Millikan, Robert Andrews
Nettleton, Alvred Bayard
Nettleton, Edwin S.
Plumb, Glenn Edward
Powell, John Wesley
Rogers, John Almanza Rowley
Rogers, John Raphael
Ross, Abel Hastings
Roye, Edward James
Ryan, Arthur Clayton
Scarborough, William Saunders
Scidmore, Eliza Ruhamah
Scott, John Prindle
Shafer, Helen Almira
Smith, Judson
Snider, Denton Jaques
Snow, Lorenzo
Spaulding, Oliver Lyman
Starr, Merritt
Stevens, Doris
Stone, Lucy
Strong, Anna Louise
Swing, Raymond Edwards
    (Gram)
Terrell, Mary Eliza Church
Thomas, Edith Matilda
Turner, James Milton
Wheeler, Wayne Bidwell
Whipple, Henry Benjamin
Wilkinson, Robert Shaw
Willard, Frances Elizabeth
    Caroline
Wilson, Warren Hugh
Wright, George Frederick
Graduate Study
Chamberlain, Charles Joseph
Jones, Lynds
Millikan, Robert Andrews
Plumb, Glenn Edward
Terrell, Mary Eliza Church
Music
Cook, Will Marion
Densmore, Frances
Dett, Robert Nathaniel
Theology
Blackwell, Antoinette Louisa
    Brown
Bosworth, Edward Increase

Fairchild, George Thompson
Fairchild, James Harris
Fairfield, Edmund Burke
King, Henry Churchill
Morrison, Nathan Jackson
Pye, Watts Orson
Rogers, John Almanza Rowley
Ryan, Arthur Clayton
Smith, Judson
Tenney, Charles Daniel
Wright, George Frederick
OBERLIN CONSERVATORY OF MUSIC
    (OHIO)
White, Clarence Cameron
OBERLIN THEOLOGICAL SEMINARY
    (OHIO)
Barton, William Eleazar
OCCIDENTAL COLLEGE (CAL.)
Baker, Dorothy Dodds
Cromwell, Dean Bartlett
Jeffers, John Robinson
OGDEN COLLEGE (KY.)
Bent, Silas
Bloch, Claude Charles
Hines, Walker Downer
Witherspoon, Alexander Ma-
    claren
OGLETHORPE UNIVERSITY (GA.)
Smith, Albert Merriman
OHIO MEDICAL COLLEGE
Byford, William Heath
Gates, Richard Jordan
Gilliam, David Tod
Jones, William Palmer
Keyt, Alonzo Thrasher
Owen, David Dale
OHIO NORTHERN UNIVERSITY
Binkley, Wilfred Ellsworth
Bromfield, Louis
Crile, George Washington
Fairless, Benjamin F.
Fess, Simeon Davidson
Lower, William Edgar
Yost, Fielding Harris
Law
Fess, Simeon Davidson
OHIO STATE NORMAL SCHOOL
Reed, Mary
OHIO STATE UNIVERSITY
Ames, Edward Raymond
Bellows, George Wesley
Brough, John
Butterworth, Benjamin
Campbell, Marius Robinson
Coulter, Ernest Kent
Cox, Samuel Sullivan
Dickey, Theophilus Lyle
Eichelberger, Robert Lawrence
Fisher, Dorothea Frances Can-
    field
Fowke, Gerard
Freed, Alan J.
Kellerman, Karl Frederic
Kettering, Charles Franklin
Kingsbury, Albert
Kiplinger, Willard Monroe
Lamme, Benjamin Carver
Landis, Henry Robert Murray
Lord, Henry Curwen
Marquett, Turner Mastin
Marvin, Charles Frederick

Moore, Clarence Lemuel Elisha
Norton, William Warder
Osborn, Thomas Ogden
Read, Daniel, 1805-1878
Sabine, Wallace Clement Ware
Safford, James Merrill
Shannon, Wilson
Shiras, George
Shiras, Oliver Perry
Short, Sidney Howe
Smith, William Sooy
Sparks, Edwin Erle
Sullivant, William Starling
Summers, George William
Thurber, James Grover
Young, John Wesley
Graduate Study
Adkins, Homer Burton
Homeopathic Medicine
Lewis, Francis Park
Law
Colver, William Byron
Cox, Samuel Sullivan
OHIO UNIVERSITY
Cranston, Earl
Lindley, Daniel
Smith, David Roland
OHIO WESLEYAN COLLEGE
Hughes, Edwin Holt
Tittle, Ernest Fremont
OHIO WESLEYAN UNIVERSITY
Atkinson, George Wesley
Baker, James Heaton
Bingham, Amelia
Burke, Stevenson
Conklin, Edwin Grant
Craig, Winchell McKendree
Cramer, Michael John
Cratty, Mabel
Dwight, Henry Otis
Fairbanks, Charles Warren
Foraker, Joseph Benson
Freas, Thomas Bruce
Gould, George Milbry
Gunsaulus, Frank Wakeley
Henry, William Arnon
Herrick, Myron Timothy
Hoyt, John Wesley
Jefferson, Charles Edward
Koch, Frederick Henry
Lowry, Hiram Harrison
McCabe, Charles Cordwell
McConnell, Francis John
McDowell, William Fraser
McVey, Frank Lerond
Mansell, William Albert
Mast, Phineas Price
Pattison, John M.
Rickey, Wesley Branch
Sparks, Edwin Erle
White, John Williams
Williams, John Fletcher
Williams, Marshall Jay
Woolley, John Granville
Graduate Study
Ferree, Clarence Errol
McDowell, William Fraser
OKOLONA COLLEGE (MISS.)
Whitfield, Owen
OLIVET COLLEGE (MICH.)
Beckwith, Clarence Augustine
Sperry, Willard Learoyd

OMAHA MEDICAL COLLEGE (NEB.)
Townsend, Francis Everett
ONEIDA INSTITUTE (N.Y.)
Bishop, Joel Prentiss
Bliss, Philemon
Brainard, Daniel
Garnet, Henry Highland
Grinnell, Josiah Bushnell
Janney, Eli Hamilton
Warner, Charles Dudley
Weld, Theodore Dwight
ONEIDA SEMINARY (N.Y.)
Alden, Isabella Macdonald
OREGON STATE UNIVERSITY
McKay, (James) Douglas
OSKALOOSA COLLEGE (IOWA)
Hornaday, William Temple
Reno, Milo
OTTERBEIN COLLEGE (OHIO)
Beardshear, William Miller
Frick, Henry Clay
Hanby, Benjamin Russel
Kephart, Isaiah Lafayette
Shauck, John Allen
Shuey, Edwin Longstreet
Weber, Henry Adam
OUACHITA BAPTIST UNIVERSITY
(ARK.)
Bennett, Henry Garland
OWEGO ACADEMY (N.Y.)
Genung, John Franklin
Gladden, Washington
Pumpelly, Raphael
Rockefeller, William
Tracy, Benjamin Franklin
OXFORD ACADEMY (N.Y.)
Park, Roswell, 1807-1869
Randall, Samuel Sidwell
Robinson, John Cleveland
Seymour, Horatio
OXFORD UNIVERSITY (ENGLAND)
Bazett, Henry Cuthbert
Brinton, Clarence Crane
Brooke, Charles Frederick
Tucker
Buchanan, Scott Milross
Burdick, Eugene Leonard
Campbell, William
Coffin, Robert Peter Tristram
Coolidge, Julian Lowell
Fulton, John Farquhar
Gibbs, Arthur Hamilton
Hooton, Earnest Albert
Hubble, Edwin
Huxley, Aldous Leonard
Lake, Kirsopp
Locke, Alain Leroy
Luce, Henry Robinson
O'Shaughnessy, Nelson Jarvis
Waterbury
Overstreet, Harry Allen
Rice, John Andrew
Smith, Lloyd Logan Pearsall
Tyler, Royall
Graduate Study
Beard, Charles Austin
Berenson, Bernard
Davis, Elmer Holmes
Haring, Clarence
Lake, Kirsopp
MacIver, Robert Morrison
Matthiessen, Francis Otto

Morley, Christopher Darlington
Page, Thomas Walker
Scarborough, Dorothy
Scudder, (Julia) Vida Dutton
Smith, Courtney Craig
Sperry, Willard Learoyd
Tigert, John James, IV
Van de Graaff, Robert Jemison
West, Allen Brown
Medicine
Bazett, Henry Cuthbert

PACIFIC METHODIST COLLEGE
(CAL.)
Atkinson, Henry Avery
PACIFIC UNIVERSITY (OREG.)
Gilbert, Alfred Carlton
PACKARD BUSINESS COLLEGE
(N.Y.)
Norton, Mary Teresa Hopkins
PACKARD COMMERCIAL COLLEGE
(N.Y.)
Whalen, Grover Aloysius
PAINE COLLEGE (GA.)
Lomax, Louis Emanuel
Tobias, Channing Heggie
PALATINE JOSEPH POLYTECHNIC
((HUNGARY)
Kármán, Theodore (Todor)
Von
PARIS CONSERVATORY (FRANCE)
Kreisler, Fritz
Varèse, Edgard
Wister, Owen
PARK COLLEGE (MO.)
Willebrandt, Mabel Walker
PARMA CONSERVATORY (ITALY)
Toscanini, Arturo
PARSONS SCHOOL OF DESIGN
(N.Y.)
McCardell, Claire
PARTRIDGE'S MILITARY ACADEMY
(See NORWICH UNIVERSITY)
PATON CONGREGATIONAL COLLEGE
(ENGLAND)
Booth, Ballington
PEABODY CONSERVATORY (MD.)
Smith, Lillian Eugenia
PEABODY CONSERVATORY OF MUSIC
(MD.)
Thomas, John Charles
PEABODY INSTITUTE OF MUSIC
(MD.)
Phillips, Lena Madesin
PEABODY NORMAL COLLEGE
(TENN.)
Anthony, Katharine Susan
Bilbo, Theodore Gilmore
PEIRCE BUSINESS COLLEGE (PA.)
Stotesbury, Edward Townsend
PEMBROKE ACADEMY (N.H.)
Alger, William Rounseville
Bell, Charles Henry
Brown, Simon
Chamberlain, Mellen
Eastman, Enoch Worthen
Swett, John
Tenney, Edward Payson
PENN CHARTER SCHOOL (PA.)
Allison, Nathaniel

PENNINGTON SEMINARY (N.J.)
Bowne, Borden Parker
Buckley, James Monroe
Taylor, Alfred Alexander
Taylor, Robert Love
PENNSYLVANIA ACADEMY OF FINE
   ARTS
Abbey, Edwin Austin
Anshutz, Thomas Pollock
Bingham, George Caleb
Borie, Adolphe
Boyle, John J.
Calder, Alexander Stirling
Chapman, John Gadsby
Cox, Kenyon
Demuth, Charles
Eakins, Thomas
Frost, Arthur Burdett
Grafly, Charles
Harrison, Lovell Birge
Harrison, Thomas Alexander
Haseltine, James Henry
Henri, Robert
Henry, Edward Lamson
Hergesheimer, Joseph
Hicks, John, 1823–1890
Hill, Thomas, 1829–1908
Korpman, Augustus
Luks, George Benjamin
Marin, John (Cheri)
Mifflin, Lloyd
O'Malley, Frank Ward
Parton, Arthur
Pennell, Joseph
Rehn, Frank Knox Morton
Roberts, Elizabeth Wentworth
Roberts, Howard
Rothermel, Peter Frederick
Sartain, Emily
Sartain, William
Sheeler, Charles R., Jr.
Shinn, Everett
Smedley, William Thomas
Smith, Xanthus Russell
Smyth, John Henry
Stephens, Alice Barber
Stetson, Charles Walter
Tanner, Henry Ossawa
Taylor, Frank Walter
Waugh, Frederick Judd
Wilmarth, Lemuel Everett
PENNSYLVANIA MILITARY COLLEGE
Morley, Sylvanus Griswold
PENNSYLVANIA SCHOOL OF SOCIAL
   WORK
Hersey, Evelyn Weeks
PENNSYLVANIA STATE COLLEGE
Lasser, Jacob Kay
Graduate Study
Lasser, Jacob Kay
PENNSYLVANIA STATE NORMAL
   SCHOOL AT SHIPPENSBURG
Hoover, James Matthews
PENNSYLVANIA STATE UNIVERSITY
Epstein, Philip G.
Jackson, Dugald Caleb
Wieland, George Reber
Graduate Study
Jackson, Dugald Caleb
PHILADELPHIA COLLEGE OF PHAR-
   MACY (PA.)
Battey, Robert

Hatcher, Robert Anthony
Jacobs, Joseph, 1859–1929
Kraemer, Henry
Lilly, Josiah Kirby
Parrish, Edward
Power Frederick Belding
Procter, William
Remington, Joseph Price
Stitt, Edward Rhodes
PHILADELPHIA DENTAL COLLEGE
   (PA.)
Howe, Percy Rogers
PHILADELPHIA DIVINITY SCHOOL
Montgomery, James Alan
PHILADELPHIA SCHOOL OF INDUS-
   TRIAL ART (PA.)
Sheeler, Charles R., Jr.
PHILADELPHIA SCHOOL OF PEDAGO-
   GY (PA.)
Fischer, Louis
PHILLIPS ACADEMY (ANDOVER,
   MASS.)
Abbot, Benjamin
Abbott, Joseph Carter
Abbott, Samuel Warren
Adams, Charles Baker
Adams, Henry Carter
Alden, Timothy
Allen, Nathan H.
Alvord, Clarence Walworth
Ames, Samuel
Austin, James Trecothick
Battey, Robert
Beard, George Miller
Benjamin, George Hillard
Birney, David Bell
Bishop, Robert Roberts
Bliss, William Dwight Porter
Brown, George, 1823–1892
Burrell, David James
Carpenter, George Rice
Carter, Franklin
Chamberlain, Daniel Henry
Clark, Thomas March
Coleman, William
Cook, Flavius Josephus
Cook, Robert Johnson
Cutler, Carroll
Daveis, Charles Stewart
De Forest, John Kinne Hyde
Dennis, Frederic Shepard
Doe, Charles
Dole, Nathan Haskell
Dorsheimer, William Edward
Durant, Henry
Edmands, John
Emerson, Ralph
Farmer, Moses Gerrish
Farrar, Timothy
Fisher, Theodore Willis
Fitzgerald, Desmond
Flagg, Thomas Wilson
Flint, Charles Louis
Flint, Timothy
Fox, Gustavus Vasa
Frisbie, Levi
Frissell, Hollis Burke
Gannett, Ezra Stiles
Gardiner, Robert Hallowell
Gilmore, Joseph Henry
Goodell, William, 1792–1867
Grafton, Charles Chapman

Graves, William Phillips
Greener, Richard Theodore
Greenway, John Campbell
Guernsey, Egbert
Hackett, Horatio Balch
Hall, Charles Henry
Hall, Sherman
Halsted, William Stewart
Hammond, Edward Payson
Hammond, James Bartlett
Hardy, Arthur Sherburne
Harris, William Torrey
Hewit, Augustine Francis
Hildreth, Samuel Prescott
Holmes, Oliver Wendell
Homes, Henry Augustus
Howe, Mark Anthony de Wolfe
Hyde, James Nevins
Isham, Samuel
Jackson, Edward Payson
Jenkins, Edward Hopkins
Jenney, William Le Baron
Johnson, Henry
Jones, William
Kaye, Frederick Benjamin
King, William
Kirkland, John Thornton
Knight, Henry Cogswell
Lawson, Victor Freemont
Lee, Henry, 1782–1867
Leonard, William Andrew
Linn, William Alexander
Loring, Frederick Wadsworth
McKenzie, Alexander
McLellan, Isaac
Marsh, John, 1799–1856
Marsh, Othniel Charles
Mears, David Otis
Mills, Benjamin Fay
Moody, William Henry
Morse, Samuel Finley Breese
Mowry, William Augustus
Newman, Samuel Phillips
Oliver, Henry Kemble
Orcutt, Hiram
Packard, Joseph
Palmer, George Herbert
Palmer, Ray
Payne, Oliver Hazard
Peet, Harvey Prindle
Poor, Daniel
Quincy, Edmund
Quincy, Josiah, 1772–1864
Rantoul, Robert, 1805–1852
Ray, Isaac
Raymond, George Lansing
Reid, Robert
Ropes, James Hardy
Rowland, Henry Augustus
Rust, Richard Sutton
Short, Charles
Smith, Charles Sprague
Smith, John Cotton, 1826–1882
Smith, Jonas Waldo
Smith, Jonas Waldo
Smyth, Newman
Stearns, Eben Sperry
Stearns, William Augustus
Stevens, Isaac Ingalls
Stevens, William Bacon
Stewart, Edwin
Storrow, James Jackson

Taft, Charles Phelps
Thayer, Alexander Wheelock
Torrey, Charles Turner
Trow, John Fowler
Tyler, Charles Mellen
Van Name, Addison
Walker, William Johnson
Ward, Herbert Dickinson
Ward, Joseph
Ward, William Hayes
Ware, Henry, 1794–1843
Washburn, George
Wheelwright, William
Whitney, Josiah Dwight
Willis, Nathaniel Parker
Williston, Samuel
Winslow, Hubbard
Woods, Alva
Woods, Leonard, 1807–1878
Worcester, Joseph Emerson
PHILLIPS EXETER ACADEMY (N.H.)
Abbot, Ezra
Akerman, Amos Tappan
Ames, Frederick Lothrop
Angel, Benjamin Franklin
Atherton, George Washington
Babcock, James Wood
Bancroft, George
Bell, Charles Henry
Bell, Louis
Blake, John Lauris
Bowen, Francis
Boyden, Roland William
Brown, Charles Rufus
Buckminster, Joseph Stevens
Bulfinch, Thomas
Cass, Lewis
Chadbourne, Paul Ansel
Chadwick, John White
Cogswell, Joseph Green
Coolidge, Julian Lowell
Curtin, Jeremiah
Dana, James Freeman
Deering, Nathaniel
Dix, John Adams
Doe, Charles
Dorr, Thomas Wilson
Dunbar, Charles Franklin
Durell, Edward Henry
Dwight, Francis
Elwyn, Alfred Langdon
Felch, Alpheus
Field, Roswell Martin
Fletcher, James Cooley
Folsom, Charles
Folsom, George
French, William Merchant Richardson
Gardner, Henry Joseph
Garrison, Lindley Miller
Greene, Charles Ezra
Griswold, William McCrillis
Hackett, Frank Warren
Hale, John Parker
Hale, William Gardner
Heard, Augustine
Hildreth, Richard
Holmes, Nathaniel
Howland, John
Hyde, William DeWitt
Irwine, William Mann

Langdell, Christopher Columbus
Lincoln, Robert Todd
Lincoln, Rufus Pratt
Livermore, Abiel Abbot
Lowe, Charles
Lunt, George
Lyman, Theodore, 1792–1849
McCaleb, Theodore Howard
Mackenzie, James Cameron
MacVeagh, Charles
Mitchell, John Ames
Morison, George Shattuck
Morril, David Lawrence
Moses, George Higgins
Nutting, Wallace
Packard, Alpheus Spring, 1798–1884
Paine, Charles
Palfrey, John Gorham
Peabody, William Bourn Oliver
Perkins, James Handasyd
Porter, Fitz-John
Rawle, Francis, 1846–1930
Sanborn, Franklin Benjamin
Sargent, Lucius Manlius
Sibley, John Langdon
Sill, Edward Rowland
Smith, Jeremiah
Smith, Jeremiah, 1837–1921
Smith, Uriah
Sparks, Jared
Stebbins, Horatio
Sullivan, George
Taylor, Frederick Winslow
Thompson, William Boyce
Titcomb, John Wheelock
Tower, Charlemagne
Wardman, Ervin
Ware, William Robert
Waterhouse, Sylvester
Webster, Daniel
Wentworth, George Albert
Willard, Joseph, 1798–1865
Willis, William
Woodberry, George Edward
Woodruff, Timothy Lester
Wyman, Jeffries
Wyman, Morrill
PHILLIPS UNIVERSITY (OKLA.)
James, Marquis
Owen, Stephen Joseph
PIEDMONT COLLEGE (GA.)
Smith, Lillian Eugenia
PINKERTON ACADEMY (N.H.)
Bartlett, Samuel Colcord
Derby, Elias Hasket, 1803–1880
Fairbanks, Henry
Richardson, William Adams
Spofford, Harriet Elizabeth Prescott
Taylor, Samuel Harvey
PITTSBURGH THEOLOGICAL SEMINARY (PA.)
McBride, F(rancis) Scott
PITTSBURGH TRAINING SCHOOL FOR NURSES (PA.)
Rinehart, Mary Roberts
PITTSBURG STATE UNIVERSITY (KAN.)
Haldeman-Julius, Emanuel

PLAINFIELD ACADEMY (CONN.)
Burleigh, Charles Calistus
Burleigh, William Henry
Gaston, William, 1820–1894
Harris, Daniel Lester
Kingsley, James Luce
Moore, Addison Webster
Nott, Eliphalet
Parish, Elijah
Slater, John Fox
Smith, William, 1797–1887
Tyler, Daniel
POLYTECHNIC INSTITUTE IN HELSINKI (FINLAND)
Saarinen, Gottlieb Eliel
POLYTECHNIC INSTITUTE OF CHARLOTTENBURG (GERMANY)
Behrend, Bernard Arthur
POLYTECHNIC SCHOOL OF DELFT (NETHERLANDS)
Henny, David Christiaan
POLYTECHNICUM OF MOSCOW (RUSSIA)
Ostromislensky, Iwan Iwanowich
POMONA COLLEGE (CAL.)
Barrows, David Prescott
Taylor, Robert
Ward, Charles Henshaw
Wright, Willard Huntington
PONTIFICAL BIBLICAL INSTITUTE (ITALY)
Graduate Study
Meyer, Albert Gregory
PONTIFICAL GREGORIAN UNIVERSITY (ITALY)
Graduate Study
Weigel, Gustave
PORTER'S SCHOOL, FARMINGTON, CONN.
Dodge, Grace Hoadley
Hapgood, Isabel Florence
Stokes, Caroline Phelps
Talcott, Eliza
PORTLAND ACADEMY (MAINE)
Abbott, John Stevens Cabot
Fessenden, Francis
Longfellow, Samuel
Mellen, Grenville
Peary, Robert Edwin
PRATT INSTITUTE (N.Y.)
Hill, Ernest Rowland
Karfiol, Bernard
Luckenbach, J(ohn) Lewis
Moore, Anne Carroll
Rockwell, George Lincoln
Weber, Max
PRESBYTERIAN COLLEGE (CANADA)
Naismith, James
PRINCETON THEOLOGICAL SEMINARY (N.J.)
Cannon, James
Foote, William Henry
Gibbons, Herbert Adams
Hibben, John Grier
Holland, William Jacob
Knight, Lucian Lamar
Luce, Henry Winters
Lunn, George Richard
Machen, John Gresham
Speer, Robert Elliott
Watson, Charles Roger

PRINCETON UNIVERSITY (N.J.)
Alexander, Joseph Addison
Alexander, Samuel Davies
Alston, Joseph
Andrew, Abram Piatt
Archer, James J.
Archer, John
Archer, Stevenson
Armstrong, George Dod
Armstrong, John, 1758–1843
Arnold, Richard Dennis
Arnold, Thurman Wesley
Bacon, John
Baker, Daniel
Baker, William Mumford
Baldwin, James Mark
Barber, Francis
Barton, William Paul Crillon
Bayard, James Asheton, 1767–1815
Bayard, James Asheton, 1799–1880
Bayard, Richard Henry
Bayard, Samuel
Beasley, Frederick
Beasley, Mercer
Beatty, John, 1749–1826
Bedford, Gunning
Belknap, William Worth
Berrien, John Macpherson
Biddle, Nicholas, 1786–1844
Birney, James Gillespie
Bishop, John Peale
Blair, Francis Preston, 1821–1875
Blount, Willie
Boker, George Henry
Boteler, Alexander Robinson
Bowden, John
Boyd, James
Boyle, Jeremiah Tilford
Brackenridge, Hugh Henry
Bradford, William, 1755–1795
Branch, Lawrence O'Bryan
Brandon, Gerard Chittocque
Breckinridge, Desha
Breckinridge, Henry Skillman
Breckinridge, John, 1797–1841
Breckinridge, John Cabell
Brewster, Benjamin Harris
Brincklé, William Draper
Brown, Isaac Van Arsdale
Burnet, Jacob
Burnet, William, 1730–1791
Burr, Aaron, 1756–1836
Butler, Howard Crosby
Buttz, Henry Anson
Caldwell, David
Caldwell, James
Caldwell, Joseph
Cameron, James Donald
Campbell, Charles
Campbell, George Washington, 1769–1848
Carnahan, James
Carson, John Renshaw
Carter, Jesse Benedict
Carter, Samuel Powhatan
Cattell, William Cassaday
Chambers, George
Chapin, Henry Dwight
Chavis, John

Chesnut, James
Clarke, Thomas Shields
Clay, Joseph, 1764–1811
Colquitt, Alfred Holt
Colquitt, Walter Terry
Cone, Spencer Houghton
Conover, Obadiah Milton
Converse, James Booth
Cooke, Philip Pendleton
Cowen, John Kissig
Cox, Rowland
Coxe, Richard Smith
Crane, Jonathan Townley
Crane, Thomas Frederick
Crawford, George Walker
Crothers, Samuel McChord
Custis, George Washington Parke
Cuyler, Theodore Ledyard
Dallas, George Mifflin
Daniel, Peter Vivian
Daniels, Winthrop More
Dayton, Jonathan
Dayton, William Lewis
Dennis, Alfred Lewis Pinneo
Dennis, James Shepard
Dickerson, Edward Nicoll
Dickerson, Mahlon
Doak, Samuel
Dod, Albert Baldwin
Dod, Thaddeus
D'Olier, Franklin
Drayton, John
Duff, James Henderson
Duffield, George, 1732–1790
Dulles, Allen Welsh
Dulles, John Foster
Durstine, Roy Sarles
Early, Peter
Edsall, David Linn
Edwards, Henry Waggaman
Edwards, Jonathan, 1745–1801
Edwards, Pierpont
Elliott, Benjamin
Ellsworth, Oliver
Erdman, Charles Rosenbury
Ewing, Charles
Ewing, John
Farrand, Livingston
Farrand, Max
Few, Ignatius Alphonso
Field, Richard Stockton
Fine, Henry Burchard
Finley, Robert
Finn, Henry James William
Finney, John Miller Turpin
Fish, Nicholas
Fitzgerald, Francis Scott Key
Flint, Albert Stowell
Forman, David
Forrestal, James Vincent
Forsyth, John
Frankfurter, Alfred Moritz
Frelinghuysen, Frederick
Frelinghuysen, Theodore
Freneau, Philip Morin
Funk, Wilfred John
Gano, John
Gaston, William, 1778–1844
Gholson, William Yates
Gibson, William
Gidley, James Williams

Gildersleeve, Basil Lanneau
Giles, William Branch
Glass, Franklin Potts
Godwin, Parke
Goodman, Kenneth Sawyer
Graham, Evarts Ambrose
Gray, George
Green, Ashbel
Green, Henry Woodhull
Gregory, Daniel Seelye
Guffey, Joseph F.
Gummere, Samuel René
Gummere, William Stryker
Hager, John Sharpenstein
Haines, Daniel
Hall, Bolton
Hall, James, 1744–1826
Hall, John Elihu
Halsted, George Bruce
Hamilton, Maxwell McGaughey
Hamilton, Peter
Harper, Robert Goodloe
Hart, James Morgan
Hart, John Seely
Hartley, Frank
Hawkins, Benjamin
Hazard, Ebenezer
Henderson, Thomas
Henderson, William James
Henry, John, 1750–1798
Hepburn, James Curtis
Hibben, John Grier
Hibben, Paxton Pattison
Hobart, John Henry
Hodge, Archibald Alexander
Hodge, Charles
Hodge, Hugh Lenox
Hormel, Jay Catherwood
Hornblower, William Butler
Hosack, David
Houston, William Churchill
Howard, Benjamin Chew
Howell, David
Hudson, Claude Silbert
Huger, Daniel Elliott
Hunt, Theodore Whitefield
Hunter, Andrew
Hutson, Richard
Ingersoll, Charles Jared
Inman, Samuel Martin
Irvine, William Mann
Iverson, Alfred
Jackson, Charles Douglas
Johns, John
Johns, Kensey
Johnson, Bradley Tyler
Johnson, William, 1771–1834
Joline, Adrian Hoffman
Jones, Charles Colcock
Jones, Joseph
Kellett, William Wallace
Kellogg, Samuel Henry
Kirk, Edward Norris
Kirkland, Samuel
Kirkpatrick, Andrew
Landis, James McCauley
Lee, Charles
Lee, Henry, 1756–1818
Lee, Ivy Ledbetter
Leland, Godfrey Charles
Lewis, Morgan
Lewisohn, Sam Adolph

Lindley, Jacob
Lindsley, Philip
Livermore, Samuel, 1732–1803
Livingston, Edward
Livingston, Henry Brockholst
Long, Breckinridge
Lowrie, James Walter
Luckenbach, J(ohn) Lewis
Ludlow, Fitz Hugh
Lumpkin, Joseph Henry
Lynd, Robert Staughton
Lyon, James
McAllister, Matthew Hall
MacCauley, Clay
McCay, Henry Kent
McClellan, George Brinton
McClenahan, Howard
McCormick, Cyrus Hall
McCosh, Andrew James
McDowell, James
McDowell, John, 1780–1863
McElroy, Robert McNutt
McGuire, Joseph Deakins
McIlvaine, Charles Pettit
Maclean, John, 1800–1886
McMahon, John Van Lear
Macon, Nathaniel
MacWhorter, Alexander
Madison, James, 1750/51–1836
Magie, William Jay
Manning, James
Mansfield, Edward Deering
Marquand, Allan
Martin, Alexander
Martin, Luther
Mason, Jonathan
Meade, William
Mercer, Charles Fenton
Miller, James Alexander
Miller, John, 1819–1895
Moffat, James Clement
Montgomery, William Bell
Morris, John Gottlieb
Napton, William Barclay
Nash, Frederick
Nassau, Robert Hamill
Neill, William
Nicoll, DeLancey
Niles, Nathaniel, 1741–1828
Nixon, John Thompson
Odell, Jonathan
O'Neill, Eugene
Orr, Jehu Amaziah
Osborn, Henry Fairfield
Osborn, Henry Fairfield
Otis, George Alexander
Otto, John Conrad
Parker, Joel, 1816–1888
Pate, Maurice
Paterson, William
Patton, John Mercer
Pearce, James Alfred
Pennington, William
Pepper, William, 1810–1864
Perrine, Frederic Auten Combs
Perry, Ralph Barton
Phelps, Charles Edward
Phillips, David Graham
Pintard, John
Pitney, Mahlon
Pollock, James
Pomerene, Atlee

Poole, Ernest Cook
Potter, Nathaniel
Pratt, Thomas George
Price, Bruce
Price, Rodman McCamley
Prime, Benjamin Youngs
Prime, William Cowper
Proctor, William Cooper
Radcliff, Jacob
Ramsay, David
Ramsay, Nathaniel
Read, John, 1769–1854
Reed, David Aiken
Reed, Joseph
Reeve, Tapping
Reid, William Shields
Rhea, John
Rice, David
Roberts, William Charles
Robeson, George Maxwell
Rood, Ogden Nicholas
Root, Jesse
Ruffin, Thomas
Rush, Benjamin
Rush, James
Rush, Richard
Russell, Henry Norris
Sayre, Stephen
Schenck, Ferdinand Schureman
Schirmer, Rudolph Edward
Schroeder, John Frederick
Scott, William Berryman
Scribner, Charles, 1821–1871
Scribner, Charles, 1854–1930
Scribner, Charles, 1890–1952
Scudder, John
Scudder, Nathaniel
Sergeant, John, 1779–1852
Sergeant, Jonathan Dickinson
Sergeant, Thomas
Sheldon, Walter Lorenzo
Shellabarger, Samuel
Shelton, Frederick William
Shields, Charles Woodruff
Shippen, William
Skinner, Thomas Harvey
Smith, Hezekiah
Smith, John Blair
Smith, Jonathan Bayard
Smith, Persifor Frazer
Smith, Samuel Stanhope
Smith, William Stephens
Southard, Samuel Lewis
Spalding, Franklin Spencer
Speer, Robert Elliott
Spring, Samuel
Starr, Moses Allen
Sterling, John Whalen
Stevenson, Adlai Ewing, II
Stockton, John Potter
Stockton, Richard, 1730–1781
Stockton, Richard, 1764–1828
Stockton, Robert Field
Stone, David
Straus, Roger W(illiams)
Tarkington, Booth
Taylor, Archibald Alexander
    Edward
Thomas, Allen
Thomas, Norman Mattoon
Thompson, Smith
Tichenor, Isaac

Todd, Henry Alfred
Torrence, Frederick Ridgely
Troup, George Michael
Van Dyke, Henry
Van Dyke, Nicholas
Van Dyke, Paul
Van Lennep, William Bird
Wallace, Horace Binney
Wanamaker, Lewis Rodman
Ward, Thomas
Warfield, Benjamin Breckin-
    ridge
Warren, Howard Crosby
Waterman, Alan Tower
Watson, Charles Roger
Wayne, James Moore
Welling, James Clarke
Wells, John
West, Andrew Fleming
Wheeler, (George) Post
Whitaker, Nathaniel
Whiteside, Arthur Dare
Wiley, David
Williams, Charles Richard
Williams, Jesse Lynch, 1871–
    1929
Williams, Linsly Rudd
Wilson, Henry Parke Custis
Wilson, John Fleming
Wilson, Samuel Graham
Wilson, Woodrow
Winant, John Gilbert
Wood, George
Woodhull, Alfred Alexander
Wurtz, Henry
Wyckoff, Walter Augustus
Young, Alfred
Young, John Richardson
Graduate Study
Baldwin, James Mark
Brackenridge, Hugh Henry
Butler, Howard Crosby
Cannon, James
Carson, John Renshaw
Coffin, Robert Peter Tristram
Compton, Arthur Holly
Compton, Karl Taylor
Crane, Thomas Frederick
Daniels, Winthrop More
Davisson, Clinton Joseph
Dickinson, John
Farrand, Max
Fullerton, George Stuart
Gummere, William Stryker
Hibben, John Grier
Hudson, Claude Silbert
Irvine, William Mann
Laughlin, Harry Hamilton
Lord, William Wilberforce
Lowrie, James Walter
McElroy, Robert McNutt
Miller, Dayton Clarence
Miller, James Alexander
Otis, George Alexander
Paterson, William
Perrine, Frederic Auten Combs
Rossiter, Clinton Lawrence, III
Russell, Henry Norris
Shellabarger, Samuel
Spaeth, Sigmund
Taylor, Francis Henry
Waterman, Alan Tower

Wheeler, (George) Post
Wilson, James Southall
Woodhull, Alfred Alexander
Theology
Alden, Joseph
Alexander, Samuel Davies
Andrews, Lorrin
Baird, Henry Martyn
Baird, Robert
Baker, William Mumford
Barnes, Albert
Baugher, Henry Louis
Bethune, George Washington
Blackburn, William Maxwell
Boyce, James Petigru
Breckinridge, John, 1797–1841
Bush, George
Campbell, William Henry
Cattell, William Cassaday
Chambers, Talbot Wilson
Clark, Thomas March
Cobb, William Henry
Conover, Obadiah Milton
Cuyler, Theodore Ledyard
Dennis, James Shepard
Dod, Albert Baldwin ,
Estabrook, Joseph
Fleming, John
Fletcher, James Cooley
Gale, George Washington
Galloway, Samuel
Gilbert, Eliphalet Wheeler
Green, Lewis Warner
Green, William Henry
Gregory, Caspar René
Gregory, Daniel Seelye
Hall, Baynard Rush
Hart, John Seely
Hodge, Archibald Alexander
Hodge, Charles
Howard, Benjamin Chew
Humes, Thomas William
Hunt, Theodore Whitefield
Jackson, Samuel Macauley
Jackson, Sheldon
James, Henry, 1811–1882
Kellogg, Samuel Henry
Kirk, Edward Norris
Laws, Samuel Spahr
Lesley, Peter
Lindsley, Philip
Lord, Eleazer
Lord, William Wilberforce
Loughridge, Robert McGill
Lovejoy, Elijah Parish
Lowrie, James Walter
MacCracken, Henry Mitchell
McGilvary, Daniel
McIlvaine, Charles Pettit
McKim, James Miller
Maclean, John, 1800–1886
Manly, Basil, 1825–1892
Marquand, Allan
Mattoon, Stephen
Merrill, James Griswold
Miller, John, 1819–1895
Morris, John Gottlieb
Muhlenberg, Frederick Augustus
Nassau, Robert Hamill
Nevin, Edwin Henry
Nevin, John Williamson

Parvin, Theophilus
Paton, Lewis Bayles
Patterson, Robert Mayne
Patton, Francis Landey
Patton, William
Peers, Benjamin Orrs
Peters, Absalom
Pierce, John Davis
Plumer, William Swan
Porter, Thomas Conrad
Prime, Edward Dorr Griffin
Prime, Samuel Irenaeus
Raymond, George Lansing
Roberts, William Charles
Roberts, William Henry
Robinson, Charles Seymour
Robinson, Stuart
Ruffner, William Henry
Sawyer, Leicester Ambrose
Scott, William Anderson
Shedd, William Ambrose
Shields, Charles Woodruff
Smyth, Thomas
Sprague, William Buell
Sterling, John Whalen
Taylor, Archibald Alexander
   Edward
Wilson, Samuel Graham
Wilson, Samuel Ramsay
Wines, Frederick Howard
Wood, James, 1799–1867
Woodbridge, William Channing
Woolsey, Theodore Dwight
Wyckoff, Walter Augustus
Young, John Clarke
Young, Samuel Hall
PRITCHETT COLLEGE (MO.)
Kenyon, Josephine Hemenway
Pritchett, Henry Smith
Graduate Study
Kenyon, Josephine Hemenway
PROVIDENCE COLLEGE (R.I.)
McGrath, James Howard
PURDUE UNIVERSITY (IND.)
Ade, George
Chaffee, Roger Bruce
Gray, Harold Lincoln
Grissom Virgil Ivan ("Gus")
Hannagan, Stephen Jerome
Mead, Elwood
Osborn, Chase Salmon
Tarkington, Booth
Waesche, Russell Randolph
Wickard, Claude Raymond

QUEEN'S COLLEGE (See RUTGERS
   UNIVERSITY)
QUEEN'S MUSEUM COLLEGE (N.C.)
Davidson, William Lee
Davie, William Richardson
Graham, Joseph
Polk, William
QUEEN'S UNIVERSITY (CANADA)
Bowen, Norman Levi
Fortescue, Charles LeGeyt
Graduate Study
Fortescue, Charles LeGeyt
QUEEN'S UNIVERSITY (IRELAND)
Kennedy, Robert Foster

RACINE COLLEGE (WIS.)
Burleson, Hugh Latimer
Gailor, Thomas Frank
RADCLIFFE COLLEGE (MASS.)
Abbott, Eleanor Hallowell
Balch, Emily Greene
Brunswick, Ruth Mack
Cleghorn, Sarah Norcliffe
Follett, Mary Parker
Gillespie, Mabel
Hull, Josephine
Keller, Helen Adams
Leavitt, Henrietta Swan
Mitchell, Lucy Sprague
Park, Maud Wood
Peabody, Josephine Preston
Simkhovitch, Mary Melinda
   Kingsbury
Stein, Gertrude
Wambaugh, Sarah
Graduate Study
Flanagan, Hallie
RANDOLPH-MACON COLLEGE (VA.)
Armstrong, Edward Cooke
Barnett, George Ernest
Cannon, James
Christian, Henry Asbury
Clopton, David
Craven, Braxton
Ellis, John Willis
Evans, Nathan George
Gartrell, Lucius Jeremiah
Howard, William Travis
James, Edwin Leland
Jarvis, Thomas Jordan
McTyeire, Holland Nimmons
Moore, Henry Ludwell
Page, Thomas Walker
Page, Walter Hines
Puryear, Bennet
Smith, William Waugh
Swanson, Claude Augustus
Taylor, David Watson
RAND SCHOOL OF SOCIAL SCIENCE
   (N.Y.)
Crosswaith, Frank Rudolph
RENSSELAER POLYTECHNIC INSTITUTE (N.Y.)
Alden, John Ferris
Bogue, Virgil Gay
Boller, Alfred Pancoast
Booth, James Curtis
Buck, Leffert Lefferts
Burr, William Hubert
Cassatt, Alexander Johnston
Cluett, Sanford Lockwood
Cogswell, William Browne
Cook, George Hammell
Cooley, Lyman Edgar
Cooper, Theodore
Cummings, Charles Amos
Dumont, Allen Balcom
Emery, Albert Hamilton
Emmons, Ebenezer
Endicott, Mordecai Thomas
Evans, Anthony Walton Whyte
Ferris, George Washington
   Gale
Fisher, Clark
Fitch, Asa
Fuertes Estevan Antonio
Gardiner, James Terry

Grinnell, Frederick
Hall, Fitzedward
Hall, James, 1811–1898
Horsford, Eben Norton
Houghton, Douglass
House, Samuel Reynolds
Judah, Theodore Dehone
Kay, Edgar Boyd
Knappen, Theodore Temple
Kneass, Strickland
Larrínaga, Tulio
Menocal, Aniceto Garcia
Metcalf, William
Mills, Hiram Francis
Moore, Edward Mott
Murphy, John W.
Peter, Robert
Pratt, Thomas Willis
Ricketts, Palmer Chamberlaine
Riddell, John Leonard
Roberts, George Brooke
Roebling, Washington Augustus
Rousseau, Henry Harwood
Rowland, Henry Augustus
Salisbury, James Henry
Sooysmith, Charles
Stearns, Irving Ariel
Thacher, Edwin
Thomas, Joseph
Tompkins, Daniel Augustus
Van de Warker, Edward Ely
Waddell, John Alexander Low
White, Alfred Tredway
Wickes, Stephen
Williams, Samuel Wells
Wilson, Joseph Miller

RHODE ISLAND COLLEGE (See BROWN UNIVERSITY)

RHODE ISLAND SCHOOL OF DESIGN
Gorky, Arshile

RICHMOND COLLEGE (VA.)
Freeman, Allen Weir
Freeman, Douglas Southall
Long, Joseph Ragland
McBain, Howard Lee
Montague, Andrew Jackson

RIPON COLLEGE (WIS.)
Jones, Lewis Ralph
Tracy, Spencer Bonaventure

RIVERSIDE JUNIOR COLLEGE (CAL.)
Carlson, Chester Floyd

ROANOKE COLLEGE (VA.)
Reid, Mont Rogers

ROCHESTER INSTITUTE OF TECHNOLOGY (N.Y.)
Hooker, Elon Huntington

ROCHESTER THEOLOGICAL SCHOOL (MO.)
Ruckstull, Frederick Wellington

ROCHESTER THEOLOGICAL SEMINARY (N.Y.)
Anderson, Galusha
Barbour, Clarence Augustus
Behrends, Adolphus Julius Frederick
Burton, Ernest De Witt
Buttrick, Wallace
Clark, George Whitefield
Foster, George Burman
Fulton, Justin Dewey
Gates, Frederick Taylor
Genung, John Franklin

Goodspeed, Thomas Wakefield
Johnson, Elias Henry
MacArthur, Robert Stuart
Morehouse, Henry Lyman
Moss, Lemuel
Moxom, Philip Stafford
Newman, Albert Henry
Rawlinson, Frank Joseph
Stevens, George Barker
Stevens, William Arnold
Strong, Augustus Hopkins
Strong, Charles Augustus
Taylor, James Monroe
Thomas, Jesse Burgess, 1832–1915
Vedder, Henry Clay

ROCKFORD COLLEGE (ILL.)
Binford, Jessie Florence
Mussey, Ellen Spencer

ROCK RIVER SEMINARY (ILL.)
Hallett, Moses
Hitt, Robert Roberts
Ingals, Ephraim Fletcher
Jones, William Patterson
Rawlins, John Aaron
Thompson, Seymour Dwight

ROLLINS COLLEGE (FLA.)
Beach, Rex

ROSE-HULLMAN INSTITUTE OF TECHNOLOGY (IND.)
Mendenhall, Charles Elwood

ROUND HILL SCHOOL (MASS.)
Appleton, Thomas Gold
Barnes, Joseph K.
Bellows, Henry Whitney
Ellis, George Edward
Gibbs, George, 1815–1873
Hillard, George Stillman
Kearny, Philip
Lowell, Robert Traill Spence
Perkins, James Handasyd
Riggs, George Washington
Shattuck, George Cheyne, 1813–1893
Shurtleff, Nathaniel Bradstreet
Stoddard, David Tappan
Storrow, Charles Storer
Ward, Samuel
Whitney, Josiah Dwight

ROXBURY LATIN SCHOOL (MASS.)
Allen, William Francis
Baker, Harvey Humphrey
Baldwin, William Henry
Bancroft, Wilder Dwight
Bradford, Edward Hickling
Cabot, Hugh
Dyar, Harrison Gray
Grant, Percy Stickney
Hale, Philip Leslie
Hunt, Alfred Ephraim
McBurney, Charles
Scudder, Horace Elisha
Soley, James Russell
Sumner, Increase
Sumner, James Batcheller
Thorndike, Ashley Horace
Tobey, Charles William
Upton, George Bruce
Wheelwright, Edmund March
Williams, John, 1664–1729

ROYAL ACADEMY AT MUNICH (GERMANY)
Birch, Reginald Bathurst
Dielman, Frederick

ROYAL ACADEMY AT TAIN (SCOTLAND)
Mackenzie, Murdo

ROYAL ACADEMY OF ART IN BERLIN (GERMANY)
Feininger, Lyonel (Charles Leonell Adrian)

ROYAL ACADEMY OF DESIGN (GERMANY)
Bluemner, Oscar Florians

ROYAL ACADEMY OF DRAMATIC ARTS (ENGLAND)
Hardwicke, Cedric Webster
Laughton, Charles
Leigh, Vivien

ROYAL ACADEMY OF FINE ARTS IN MUNICH (GERMANY)
Leigh, William Robinson

ROYAL ACADEMY OF THEATER AND ART (HUNGARY)
Curtiz, Michael

ROYAL ARTS AND CRAFTS SCHOOL IN BERLIN (GERMANY)
Grosz, George

ROYAL CENTRAL INSTITUTE OF GYMNASTICS (SWEDEN)
Berenson, Senda

ROYAL COLLEGE OF SCIENCE, TORONTO (CANADA)
Townsend, Willard Saxby, Jr.

ROYAL CONSERVATORY OF MUSIC (BELGIUM)
Bloch, Ernest

ROYAL HUNGARIAN MEDICAL UNIVERSITY (HUNGARY)
Fejos, Paul

ROYAL HUNGARIAN UNIVERSITY (HUNGARY)
Graduate Study
Rapaport, David

ROYAL INSTITUTE OF TECHNOLOGY, STUTTGART (GERMANY)
Strobel, Charles Louis

ROYAL IRISH UNIVERSITY
Kennedy, Robert Foster
O'Shaughnessy, Michael Maurice

ROYAL NAVAL COLLEGE (ENGLAND)
Hovgaard, William

ROYAL POLYTECHNIC INSTITUTE OF MILAN (ITALY)
Faccioli, Giuseppe

ROYAL POLYTECHNIC SCHOOL AT STUTTGART (GERMANY)
Elkin, William Lewis

ROYAL SAXON ACADEMY OF THE FINE ARTS IN DRESDEN (GERMANY)
Grosz, George

ROYAL SCHOOL OF MINES AT FREIBERG (GERMANY)
Hammond, John Hays

ROYAL SCHOOL OF MINES (LONDON)
Graduate Study
Webb, Harry Howard

ROYAL TECHNICAL COLLEGE (DENMARK)
Westergaard, Harald Malcolm
ROYAL UNIVERSITY OF IRELAND
Hackett, Francis
Turner, William
RUSH MEDICAL COLLEGE (ILL.)
Bevan, Arthur Dean
Brophy, Truman William
Cameron, Robert Alexander
Favill, Henry Baird
Forbes, Stephen Alfred
Graham, Evarts Ambrose
Henrotin, Fernand
Ingals, Ephraim Fletcher
Keeley, Leslie E.
Lewis, Dean De Witt
Miles, Manly
Murphy, John Benjamin
Ochsner, Albert John
Ranson, Stephen Walter
Robinson, Frederick Byron
Stephenson, Benjamin Franklin
Thorek, Max
Wells, Harry Gideon
White, Charles Abiathar
Wilder, Russell Morse
RUSSELL'S MILITARY SCHOOL
(CONN.)
Bogue, Virgil Gay
Daggett, Ellsworth
Lusk, William Thompson
Penfield, Frederic Courtland
RUTGERS UNIVERSITY (N.J.)
Blakeley, George Henry
Bogart, John
Bradley, Joseph P.
Brodhead, John Romeyn
Brown, George William
Chamberlain, Jacob
Chambers, Talbot Wilson
Cook, Albert Stanburrough
Cook, Walter Wheeler
Cooke, Robert Anderson
De Witt, Simeon
Dod, Daniel
Doty, Elihu
Drury, John Benjamin
Fairchild, David Grandison
Fiske, Haley
Fiske, Stephen Ryder
Fitch, Asa
Forsyth, John
Frelinghuysen, Frederick Theodore
Frelinghuysen, Theodore
Gaut, John McReynolds
Gilbert, Seymour Parker
Griffis, William Elliot
Hartley, Fred Allen, Jr.
Hill, George William
Hobart, Garret Augustus
Hoffman, Eugene Augustus
Janeway, Edward Gamaliel
Johnston, Alexander
Judah, Samuel
Kilmer, Alfred Joyce
Kip, William Ingraham
Lipman, Jacob Goodale
Loree, Leonor Fresnel
Newell, William Augustus
Parker, John Cortlandt

Polak, John Osborn
Pruyn, Robert Hewson
Ricord, Frederick William
Searle, John Preston
Smith, Jeremiah, 1759–1842
Stillman, Thomas Bliss
Talmage, John Van Nest
Taylor, Graham
Thompson, John Bodine
Van Nest, Abraham Rynier
Van Wyck, Charles Henry
Voorhees, Edward Burnett
Wilson, Peter
Wyckoff, John Henry
Graduate Study
Cooke, Robert Anderson
Loree, Leonor Fresnel

ST. ANSELM'S COLLEGE (N.H.)
Rummel, Joseph Francis
ST. BERNARD SEMINARY (N.Y.)
Hurley, Joseph Patrick
ST. BONAVENTURE COLLEGE (N.Y.)
Dietz, Peter Ernest
Walsh, Thomas Joseph
Graduate Study
Walsh, Thomas Joseph
ST. CHARLES BORROMEO SEMINARY (PA.)
Brennan, Francis James
Guilday, Peter Keenan
ST. CHARLES COLLEGE (MD.)
Cooper, John Montgomery
Garrigan, Philip Joseph
Gibbons, James
Gillis, James Martin
Keane, John Joseph
O'Connell, William Henry
Pace, Edward Aloysius
Price, Thomas Frederick
Sterling, George
ST. CHARLES SEMINARY (PA.)
Dougherty, Dennis Joseph
ST. FRANCIS COLLEGE (PA.)
Stokes, Maurice
ST. FRANCIS SEMINARY (WIS.)
Haas, Francis Joseph
Kerby, William Joseph
ST. FRANCIS SERAPHIC COLLEGE (OHIO)
Daeger, Albert Thomas
Engelhardt, Zephyrin
ST. FRANCIS XAVIER COLLEGE (N.Y.)
Burke, John Joseph
Dietz, Peter Ernest
Walker, James John
Graduate Study
O'Brien, Morgan Joseph
ST. GREGORY'S PREPARATORY SEMINARY (OHIO)
Stritch, Samuel Alphonsus
ST. JOHNSBURY ACADEMY (VT.)
Coolidge, Calvin
Fairbanks, Henry
Gates, George Augustus
Lloyd, Alfred Henry
Parker, Edwin Wallace
Russell, Charles Edward
ST. JOHN'S COLLEGE (LA.)
Harahan, William Johnson

ST. JOHN'S COLLEGE (MD.)
Alexander, John Henry
Brereton, Lewis Hyde
Chester, Colby Mitchell
Councilman, William Thomas
Davidge, John Beale
Gibson, William
Hanson, Alexander Contee, 1786–1819
Hoffman, David
Johnson, Reverdy
Key, Francis Scott
Lockwood, James Booth
Lomax, John Tayloe
Mullan, John
Pinkney, Ninian
Randall, Burton Alexander
Randall, Wyatt William
Shaw, John, 1778–1809
Thomas, Francis
Turner, Edward Raymond
Will, Allen Sinclair
Wilson, Clarence True
ST. JOHN'S COLLEGE (See FORDHAM UNIVERSITY)
ST. JOHN'S SEMINARY (MASS.)
Cushing, Richard James
Dowling, Austin
Gillis, James Martin
Walsh, James Anthony
ST. JOHN'S UNIVERSITY (MINN.)
Michel, Virgil George
Graduate Study
Michel, Virgil George
ST. JOHN'S UNIVERSITY (N.Y.)
Law
Curran, Thomas Jerome
ST. JOHN'S UNIVERSITY (OHIO)
Johnson, George
ST. JOSEPH'S COLLEGE (AUSTRALIA)
Errol, Leon
ST. JOSEPH'S COLLEGE (KY.)
Clay, Cassius Marcellus
Garland, Augustus Hill
Holt, Joseph
Johnson, Robert Ward
McGill, John
O'Hara, Theodore
Powell, Lazarus Whitehead
Preston, William
Speed, James
Wells, James Madison
Wickliffe, Robert Charles
ST. JOSEPH'S COLLEGE (PA.)
Breen, Joseph Ignatius
Green, William Joseph, Jr.
ST. JOSEPH'S PROVINCIAL SEMINARY (N.Y.)
Hayes, Patrick Joseph
ST. JOSEPH'S SEMINARY (N.Y.)
Rummel, Joseph Francis
ST. LAWRENCE COLLEGE (WIS.)
Noll, John Francis
ST. LAWRENCE UNIVERSITY (N.Y.)
Bacheller, Irving
Gunnison, Foster
Heaton, John Langdon
Lee, Frederic Schiller
Young, Owen D.
Graduate Study
Lee, Frederic Schiller

ST. LOUIS UNIVERSITY (MO.)
Blow, Henry Taylor
Coleman, William Tell
Cooper, Elias Samuel
Coppens, Charles
Finn, Francis James
Ludeling, John Theodore
Pallen, Condé Benoist
Reedy, William Marion
Russell, Irwin
Snyder, John Francis
Stettinius, Edward Riley
Taussig, William
Dentistry
Hunt, Lester Callaway
Law
Hannegan, Robert Emmet
Medicine
Dooley, Thomas Anthony, III
ST. MARKS SCHOOL (MASS.)
Duane, Alexander
Mather, Samuel, 1851–1931
Morgan, Morris Hicky
ST. MARY'S COLLEGE (CAL.)
Heilmann, Harry
ST. MARY'S COLLEGE (KY.)
Morrow, Edwin Porch
ST. MARY'S COLLEGE (MD.)
Baxley, Henry Willis
Bowie, Oden
Bradford, Augustus Williamson
Buckler, Thomas Hepburn
Caffery, Donelson
Chanche, John Mary Joseph
Churchill, Thomas James
Corrigan, Michael Augustine
De Lacy, Walter Washington
Dornin, Thomas Aloysius
Fisher, George Purnell
Gibbons, James
Graves, Rosewell Hobart
Hambleton, Thomas Edward
Hays, Harry Thompson
Kavanagh, Edward
Knott, Aloysius Leo
La Barge, Joseph
Latrobe, Benjamin Henry
Latrobe, Charles Hazlehurst
Latrobe, John Hazlehurst Boneval
Logan, Cornelius Ambrosius, 1806–1853
McGivney, Michael Joseph
Mayer, Alfred Marshall
Mayer, Brantz
Meade, Richard Worsam, 1807–1870
Norris, William
Pinkney, Edward Coote
Rogers, Henry J.
Roman, André Bienvenu
Smith, James, 1851–1927
Spalding, John Lancaster
Spalding, Martin John
Tappan, Eli Todd
Wallis, Severn Teackle
ST. MARY'S COLLEGE (PA.)
Dietz, Peter Ernest
ST. MARY'S SEMINARY (MD.)
Chapelle, Placide Louis
Curtis, Alfred Allen
Dietz, Peter Ernest

Keane, John Joseph
Portier, Michael
Price, Thomas Frederick
Shields, Thomas Edward
Tabb, John Banister
Walsh, Robert
Yorke, Peter Christopher
ST. MARY'S SEMINARY (OHIO)
Hurley, Joseph Patrick
ST. MARY'S UNIVERSITY (MD.)
Grady, Henry Francis
ST. MATTHEW'S COLLEGE (CAL.)
Whitney, Caspar
ST. MEINRAD COLLEGE (IND.)
Ritter, Joseph Elmer
ST. MEINRAD SCHOOL OF THEOLOGY (IND.)
Ritter, Joseph Elmer
ST. OLAF COLLEGE (MINN.)
Lawrence, Ernest Orlando
Volstead, Andrew John
ST. PAUL COLLEGE OF LAW
Schall, Thomas David
ST. PAUL COLLEGE OF LAW (MINN.)
Swift, Linton Bishop
ST. PAUL SEMINARY (MINN.)
Ryan, John Augustine
ST. PAUL'S SCHOOL (N.H.)
Bonsal, Stephen
Brown, William Adams
Chapman, John Jay
Chapman, Victor Emmanuel
Crawford, Francis Marion
Fisher, Sydney George
Garfield, Harry Augustus
Hearst, William Randolph
Hoyt, John Sherman
Kirlin, Joseph Louis Jerome
Leiter, Joseph
Marquand, Allan
Mitchell, Langdon Elwyn
Mumford, James Gregory
Nicoll, De Lancey
Norton, William Warder
Porter, Holbrook Fitz-John
Saltus, Edgar Evertson
Shattuck, George Brune
Thayer, William Roscoe
Thornton, Henry Worth
ST. PETERSBURG UNIVERSITY (RUSSIA)
Vasiliev, Alexander Alexandrovich
Graduate Study
Vasiliev, Alexander Alexandrovich
ST. PETER'S COLLEGE (N.J.)
Tumulty, Joseph Patrick
ST. STEPHEN'S NORMAL TRAINING SCHOOL (VA.)
Russell, James Solomon
ST. VIATOR'S COLLEGE (ILL.)
Sheil, Bernard James
ST. VIATOR'S SEMINARY (ILL.)
Sheil, Bernard James
ST. VINCENT'S COLLEGE (PA.)
Curran, John Joseph
Flick, Lawrence Francis
Ganss, Henry George
Lambert, Louis Aloisius
McFaul, James Augustine
Ramsay, Erskine

Stehle, Aurelius Aloysius
Wolf, Innocent William
ST. VINCENT SEMINARY (PA.)
Hodur, Francis
Judge, Thomas Augustine
Mundelein, George William
ST. XAVIER COLLEGE (OHIO)
Browne, Junius Henri
Hickenlooper, Andrew
Piatt, Donn
Pugh, George Ellis
Rigge, William Francis
SAINTE-MARIE COLLEGE (CANADA)
Dougherty, Dennis Joseph
SALADO COLLEGE (TEX.)
Ferguson, Miriam Amanda Wallace
SALEM COLLEGIATE INSTITUTE (N.J.)
Baldwin, James Mark
SALEM LATIN SCHOOL (MASS.)
Adams, Nehemiah
Brooks, Charles Timothy
Dodge, Ebenezer
Endicott, William Crowninshield
Rogers, William Crowninshield
Williams, Henry Willard
SALT LAKE COLLEGE (UTAH)
Allen, Florence Ellinwood
SAN FRANCISCO NORMAL SCHOOL
Regan, Agnes Gertrude
SAN JOAQUIN VALLEY COLLEGE
Wilson, Clarence True
SANTA CLARA COLLEGE (CAL.)
Carleton, Henry Guy
Delmas, Delphin Michael
Hubbard, Bernard Rosecrans
Smith, James Francis
White, Stephen Mallory
SANTA CLARA UNIVERSITY (CAL.)
McClatchy, Charles Kenny
SANTA MONICA COLLEGE (CAL.)
Burdick, Eugene Leonard
SCARRITT-MORRISVILLE COLLEGE (TENN.)
Alexander, Will Winton
SCHOOL OF FINE ARTS (D.C.)
Williams, Fannie Barrier
SCHOOL OF INDUSTRIAL ART OF THE PENNSYLVANIA MUSEUM
Yellin, Samuel
SCHOOL OF PHILANTHROPY (N.Y.)
Dreier, Mary Elisabeth
SCIO COLLEGE (OHIO)
Akeley, Mary Leonore
SENECA COLLEGIATE INSTITUTE (N.Y.)
Alden, Isabella Macdonald
SETON HALL COLLEGE (N.J.)
Barrymore, John
Keating, John Marie
Kelley, James Douglas Jerrold
McFaul, James Augustine
Messmer, Sebastian Gebhard
Wigger, Winand Michael
SEWARD INSTITUTE (N.Y.)
Baker, George Fisher
SHAW UNIVERSITY (N.C.)
Shepard, James Edward
Law
Johnson, Edward Austin

SHURTLEFF COLLEGE (ILL.)
Applegate, Jesse
Coghill, George Ellett
Loveland, William Austin
  Hamilton
McAdams, Clark
Moxom, Philip Stafford
Palmer, John McAuley
Sherwood, Thomas Adiel
SIMMONS COLLEGE (MASS.)
Peck, Lillie
SIMPSON COLLEGE (IOWA)
Carver, George Washington
Mott, Frank Luther
SMITH COLLEGE (MASS.)
Bailey, Florence Augusta Merriam
Binford, Jessie Florence
Bryant, Louise Frances Stevens
Calkins, Mary Whiton
Cushman, Vera Charlotte Scott
Eckstorm, Fannie Hardy
Gill, Laura Drake
Hawes, Harriet Ann Boyd
Irwin, Elisabeth Antoinette
Littledale, Clara Savage
Norton, Mary Alice Peloubet
Plath, Sylvia
Rogers, Mary Josephine
Sabin, Florence Rena
Scudder, (Julia) Vida Dutton
Smith, Theodate Louise
Wood, Edith Elmer
Graduate Study
Calkins, Mary Whiton
Scudder, (Julia) Vida Dutton
SORBONNE (FRANCE)
Babbitt, Irving
Eliot, T(homas) S(tearns)
King, Alexander
Lingelbach, Anna Lane
Morawetz, Victor
Van de Graaff, Robert Jemison
Znaniecki, Florian Witold
Graduate Study
Liebling, Abbott Joseph
Lovejoy, Arthur Oncken
Marsh, Frank Burr
Steffens, Lincoln
Wheeler, (George) Post
SOUTH BERWICK ACADEMY (MAINE)
Goodwin, Daniel Raynes
Goodwin, Ichabod
Hayes, John Lord
Lord, John
Lord, Nathan
Tripp, Guy Eastman
SOUTH CAROLINA COLLEGE (See UNIVERSITY OF SOUTH CAROLINA)
SOUTH CAROLINA MEDICAL COLLEGE
Bratton, John
Gaillard, Edwin Samuel
Gaston, James McFadden
La Borde, Maximilian
Mackey, Albert Gallatin
Michael, William Middleton
Moore, Samuel Preston
SOUTH CAROLINA MILITARY INSTITUTE
Capers, Ellison

Coker, James Lide
Ferguson, Thomas Barker
Jenkins, Micah
SOUTHEAST ALABAMA AGRICULTURAL SCHOOL
Steagall, Henry Bascom
SOUTHERN BAPTIST THEOLOGICAL SEMINARY (KY.)
Coghill, George Ellett
Lyon, David Gordon
McGlothlin, William Joseph
Newton, Joseph Fort
Norris, John Franklyn
Riley, William Bell
Scarborough, Lee Rutland
SOUTHERN BAPTIST THEOLOGICAL SEMINARY (S.C.)
Newman, Albert Henry
SOUTHERN ILLINOIS TEACHERS COLLEGE
Hodge, John Reed
SOUTHERN ILLINOIS UNIVERSITY
Jones, Wesley Livsey
SOUTHERN METHODIST UNIVERSITY (TEX.)
Pool, Joe Richard
SOUTHERN NORMAL COLLEGE (TENN.)
Stribling, Thomas Sigismund
SOUTHERN NORMAL UNIVERSITY LAW SCHOOL (TENN.)
May, Andrew Jackson
SOUTHERN UNIVERSITY (ALA.)
Heflin, James Thomas
Hobson, Richmond Pearson
SOUTHWESTERN PRESBYTERIAN UNIVERSITY (TENN.)
Dinwiddie, Courtenay
Gregory, Thomas Watt
Pittman, Key
SOUTHWESTERN UNIVERSITY (TEX.)
Dobie, J(ames) Frank
SOUTHWEST MISSOURI STATE TEACHERS COLLEGE
Hoagland, Charles Lee
SPELMAN COLLEGE (GA.)
Robinson, Ruby Doris Smith
SPRING GARDEN INSTITUTE (N.J.)
Shinn, Everett
SPRING HILL COLLEGE (ALA.)
Bermudez, Edouard Edmond
Gordon, William Fitzhugh
McEnery, Samuel Douglas
Morphy, Paul Charles
STANFORD UNIVERSITY (CAL.)
Andrews, Bert
Bell, Eric Temple
Binkley, Robert Cedric
Blichfeldt, Hans Frederik
Burdick, Eugene Leonard
Burk, Frederic Lister
Davis, Norman Hezekiah
Hammond, Bray
Hansen, William Webster
Harkins, William Draper
Hoagland, Dennis Robert
Hoover, Herbert Clark
Hoover, Herbert Clark, Jr.
Humphries, George Rolfe
Irwin, William Henry
Kimball, Dexter Simpson

Knight, Goodwin Jess ("Goodie")
Kuykendall, Ralph Simpson
Little, William Lawson, Jr.
McNary, Charles Linza
Martin, Anne Henrietta
Nordhoff, Charles Bernard
Otis, Arthur Sinton
Perry, Clarence Arthur
Rose, Walter Malins
Snow, William Freeman
Starks, Edwin Chapin
Steinbeck, John Ernst, Jr.
Suzzallo, Henry
Teggart, Frederick John
Wilbur, Ray Lyman
Graduate Study
Anderson, Maxwell
Binkley, Robert Cedric
Blichfeldt, Hans Frederik
Hansen, William Webster
Harkins, William Draper
Kefauver, Grayson Neikirk
Otis, Arthur Sinton
Snow, William Freeman
Wilbur, Ray Lyman
Medicine
Hinkle, Beatrice Moses
STATE NORMAL SCHOOL, FARMINGTON (MAINE)
Stevens, John Frank
STATE NORMAL SCHOOL AT CALIFORNIA (PA.)
Wilson, Louis Blanchard
STATE NORMAL SCHOOL AT FREDONIA (N.Y.)
McGraw, James Herbert
STATE NORMAL SCHOOL (ILL.)
Brown, Elmer Ellsworth
STATE NORMAL SCHOOL IN KIRKSVILLE (MO.)
Pershing, John Joseph
STATE NORMAL SCHOOL IN WARRENSBURG (MO.)
MacCurdy, George Grant
STATE NORMAL SCHOOL (MASS.)
Brown, Charlotte Hawkins
STATE NORMAL SCHOOL (WIS.)
Ritter, William Emerson
STATE TEACHERS COLLEGE (ARIZ.)
McClintock, James Harvey
STATE TEACHERS COLLEGE AT ADA (OKLA.)
Waner, Paul Glee
STATE TEACHERS COLLEGE AT WARRENSBURG (MO.)
Carnegie, Dale
STATE UNIVERSITY OF IOWA
Benson, Oscar Herman
Merriam, Charles Edward, Jr.
Law
Hyde, Arthur Mastick
STATE UNIVERSITY OF KENTUCKY
Morgan, Thomas Hunt
STE. BARBE COLLEGE (FRANCE)
Behn, Sosthenes
STETSON UNIVERSITY (FLA.)
Geiger, Roy Stanley
Kalmus, Natalie Mabelle Dunfee
STEVENS INSTITUTE OF TECHNOLOGY (N.J.)
Ayres, Brown

Bristol, William Henry
De Palma, Ralph
Gantt, Henry Laurence
Gibbs, George
Herring, Augustus Moore
Hewitt, Peter Cooper
Hoxie, William Dixie
Humphreys, Alexander Crombie
Kent, William
Klvin, August Clarence
Leavitt, Frank McDowell
Lieb, John William
Marin, John (Cheri)
Mayor, Alfred Goldsborough
Rice, Richard Henry
Stanley, Robert Crooks
STOCKHOLM UNIVERSITY (SWEDEN)
Schmidt, Nathaniel
STOCKTON BUSINESS COLLEGE (CAL.)
Ashurst, Henry Fountain
SUFFIELD SCHOOL (CONN.)
Andrews, Elisha Benjamin
Brockett, Linus Pierpont
French, Edwin Davis
Weeden, William Babock
SULLINS COLLEGE (VA.)
Sullavan, Margaret
SWARTHMORE COLLEGE
Clothier, William Jackson
Grundy, Joseph Ridgway
Lewis, Lloyd Downs
Linton, Ralph
Palmer, Alexander Mitchell
Pearson, Drew
Pyle, Robert
Richards, John Kelvey
Smyth, Herbert Weir
Sproul, William Cameron
SWISS FEDERAL POLYTECHNIC INSTITUTE IN ZURICH
Ammann, Othmar Hermann
SWISS INSTITUTE OF TECHNOLOGY
Piccard, Jean Felix
SYDNEY UNIVERSITY (AUSTRALIA)
Errol, Leon
SYRACUSE UNIVERSITY
Babcock, Howard Edward
Babcock, Maltbie Davenport
Brokenshire, Norman Ernest
Collins, Guy N
Davis, Ernest R. ("Ernie")
Dolph, Joseph Norton
Farman, Elbert Eli
Fowler, Charles Henry
Haviland, Clarence Floyd
Jackson, Charles Reginald
Jackson, Shirley Hardie
Kelly, Luther Sage
Kidder, Daniel Parish
Lockwood, Belva Bennett
Lozier, Clemence Sophia Harned
Maclay, Edgar Stanton
Morehouse, Henry Lyman
Noss, Theodore Bland
Ranger, Henry Ward
Raymond, Henry Jarvis
Smith, David Eugene
Steele, Joel Dorman
Thomas, Amos Russell

Thompson, Dorothy
Tomlin, Bradley Walker
Underwood, Lucien Marcus
Wilder, Alexander
Williams, Frank Martin
Graduate Study
Brokenshire, Norman Ernest
Fall, Bernard B.
Smith, David Eugene

TABOR COLLEGE (IOWA)
Simmons, George Henry
TALLADEGA COLLEGE (ALA.)
Pickens, William
TARKIO COLLEGE (MO.)
Carothers, Wallace Hume
TEACHERS COLLEGE, COLUMBIA UNIVERSITY (N.Y.)
Antin, Mary
Ayres, Leonard Porter
Cubberley, Ellwood Patterson
Dingman, Mary Agnes
Gray, William Scott, Jr.
Harshe, Robert Bartholow
Jessup, Walter Albert
Moskowitz, Belle Lindner Israels
Newlon, Jesse Homer
Rose, Mary Davies Swartz
Graduate Study
Hollingworth, Leta Stetter
Payne, Bruce Ryburn
TECHNICAL UNIVERSITY IN AACHEN (GERMANY)
Debye, Peter Joseph William
Graduate Study
Debye, Peter Joseph William
TECHNICAL UNIVERSITY OF KARLSRUHE (GERMANY)
Harkins, William Draper
TECHNISCHE HOCHSCHULE, VIENNA (AUSTRIA)
Neutra, Richard Joseph
TECHNISCHE HOCHSCHULE IN BERLIN (GERMANY)
Mendelsohn, Erich (*or* Eric)
TECHNISCHE HOCHSCHULE IN STUTTGART (GERMANY)
Reichenbach, Hans
TECHNISCHE HOCHSCHULE IN ZURICH (SWITZERLAND)
Graduate Study
Von Neumann, John
TEMPLE UNIVERSITY
McKinley, Albert Edward
Law
McGranery, James Patrick
TENNESEE A. & M. COLLEGE
Kelly, Machine Gun (George Kelly Barnes, Jr.)
TENNESSEE WESLEYAN COLLEGE
Raulston, John Tate
TEXAS AGRICULTURAL AND MECHANICAL COLLEGE
Burleson, Albert Sidney
Mills, Charles Wright
Moser, Christopher Otto
Neyland, Robert Reese, Jr.
THEOLOGICAL SEMINARY OF THE REFORMED CHURCH IN AMERICA (N.J.)
Taylor, Graham

THEOLOGICAL SEMINARY OF VIRGINIA
Kip, William Ingraham
Lay, Henry Champlin
Perry, William Stevens
Peterkin, George William
Randolph, Alfred Magill
Savage, Thomas Staughton
Slaugher, Philip
Tucker, Henry St. George
Williams, Channing Moore
Wilmer, Joseph Père Bell
Wilmer, Richard Hooker
THETFORD ACADEMY (VT.)
Eaton, John
Leavitt, Mary Greenleaf Clement
Perry, Arthur Latham
Slafter, Edmund Farwell
TRANSYLVANIA COLLEGE (KY.)
Allen, James Lane
Atchison, David Rice
Austin, Stephen Fuller
Birney, James Gillespie
Blair, Francis Preston, 1791–1876
Bogy Lewis Vital
Breckinridge, John Cabell
Brown, Benjamin Gratz
Buchanan, Joseph
Butler, William Orlando
Cameron, Archibald
Chambers, John
Clay, Cassius Marcellus
Connelly, Henry
Cooke, Henry David
Crittenden, George Bibb
Davis, Jefferson
Espy, James Pollard
Ford, Thomas
Fosdick, William Whiteman
Fox, John William
Goodloe, William Cassius
Green, Lewis Warner
Hardin, John J.
Hardin, Martin D.
Hise, Elijah
Humphreys, West Hughes
Johnston, Josiah Stoddard
Jones, George Wallace
Kellogg, Albert
Kerr, John Glasgow
Langdon, William Chauncey
McAfee, Robert Breckinridge
Mason, Stevens Thomson, 1811–1843
Monette, John Wesley
Morehead, Charles Slaughter
Morehead, James Turner
Morrow, Thomas Vaughan
Peers, Benjamin Orrs
Pope, Nathaniel
Powell, Lazarus Whitehead
Powell, William Byrd
Robertson, George
Sayre, Lewis Albert
Shannon, Wilson
Shelby, Joseph Orville
Short, Charles Wilkins
Todd, Charles Stewart
Turner, Edward
Underwood, Joseph Rogers

Vest, George Graham
Waldo, David
Whitcomb, James
Law
Allen, Thomas M.
Barry, William Taylor
Blair, Francis Preston, 1821–1875
Blair, Montgomery
Boyle, Jeremiah Tilford
Churchill, Thomas James
Clemens, Jeremiah
Donelson, Andrew Jackson
Duke, Basil Wilson
Edwards, Minian Wirt
Harlan, John Marshall
Harrison, Carter Henry
Long, Crawford Williamson
McConnel, John Ludlum
Magoffin, Beriah
Morehead, Charles Slaughter
Norton, Elijah Hise
Rollins, James Sidney
Rose, Uriah Milton
Simms, William Elliott
Speed, James
Yates, Richard
Medicine
Blackburn, Luke Pryor
Chivers, Thomas Holley
Gwin, William McKendree
Hall, William Whitty
Lawson, Leonidas Merion
Metcalfe, Samuel Lytler
Miller, Henry, 1800–1874
Miller, Samuel Freeman
Peter, Robert
Robertson, Jerome Bonaparte
Toland, Hugh Huger
Yandell, Lunsford Pitts
TRANSYLVANIA COLLEGE (VA.)
Ainslie, Peter
TRENTON ACADEMY (N.J.)
Abbott, Benjamin Vaughan
Fisher, Clark
Gummere, Samuel René
Roebling, Washington Augustus
Welling, James Clarke
TRINITY COLLEGE (CANADA)
Brent, Charles Henry
TRINITY COLLEGE (CONN.)
Andrews, Charles McLean
Armstrong, David Maitland
Ashe, William Shepperd
Barbour, Henry Gray
Barthelmess, Richard
Bayley, James Roosevelt
Beardsley, Eben Edwards
Benjamin, Park, 1809–1864
Bowie, William
Bradley, Charles William
Buck, Dudley
Burton, Richard Eugene
Cheshire, Joseph Blount
Clement, Martin Withington
Crary, Isaac Edwin
Douglass, Andrew Ellicott
Ferguson, Samuel
Fisher, Sydney George
Flagg, Jared Bradley
Gallaudet, Edward Miner
Gallaudet, Thomas

Gilman, Arthur Delevan
Goddard, Paul Beck
Hart, Samuel
Nichols, William Ford
Nies, James Buchanan
Paddock, Benjamin Henry
Paddock, John Adams
Phelps, John Smith
Preston, Thomas Scott
Purdy, Lawson
Pynchon, Thomas Ruggles
Riggs, John Mankey
Sanford, Henry Shelton
Smith, Buckingham
Southard, Lucien H.
Thurber, Christopher Carson
Williams, John, 1817–1899
Graduate Study
Purdy, Lawson
TRINITY COLLEGE (N.C.)
Reynolds, William Neal
TROY FEMALE ACADEMY (N.Y.)
Rohlfs, Anna Katharine Green
TROY FEMALE SEMINARY (N.Y.)
Cooper, Sarah Brown Ingersoll
Davidson, Lucretia Maria
Lewis, Estelle Anna Blanche Robinson
Moulton, Ellen Louise Chandler
Phelps, Almira Hart Lincoln
Rambaut, Mary Lucinda Bonney
Sage, Margaret Olivia Slocum
Smith, Erminnie Adelle Platt
Stanton, Elizabeth Cady
TUFTS UNIVERSITY (MASS.)
Adams, John Coleman
Babcock, Stephen Moulton
Capen, Elmer Hewitt
Capen, Samuel Paul
Clement, Edward Henry
Ginn, Edwin
Lamb, Arthur Becket
Lewis, Orlando Faulkland
Pearce, Richard Mills
Pearson, Fred Stark
Warren, Minton
Whittemore, Thomas
Wiener, Norbert
Wiggin, James Henry
Wright, Philip Green
Graduate Study
Lamb, Arthur Becket
Medicine
Brunswick, Ruth Mack
Coriat, Isador Henry
Myerson, Abraham
TULANE UNIVERSITY (LA.)
Basso, (Joseph) Hamilton
Behan, William James
Breaux, Joseph Arsenne
Cahn, Edmond Nathaniel
Farrar, Edgar Howard
Foster, Murphy James
Hall, Luther Egbert
Harris, Nathaniel Harrison
Lynch, Robert Clyde
Matas, Rudolph
Rice, John Andrew
Toulmin, Harry Theophilus
Vaughan, Thomas Wayland

Law
Bermudez, Edouard Edmond
Blanchard, Newton Crain
Cahn, Edmond Nathaniel
Fenner, Charles Erasmus
Gibson, Randall Lee
Hahn, Georg Michael Decker
Hunt, Carleton
Long, Huey Pierce
Lyman, Joseph Bardwell
Morphy, Paul Charles
Perez, Leander Henry
Provosty, Olivier Otis
Medicine
Dyer, Isadore
Handerson, Henry Ebenezer
Hatcher, Robert Anthony
Lynch, Robert Clyde
Riddell, John Leonard
Souchon, Edmond
TUSKEGEE INSTITUTE (ALA.)
Simmons, Roscoe Conkling
Murray

UNION COLLEGE (KY.)
Anderson, Victor Vance
UNION COLLEGE (N.Y.)
Alden, Joseph
Alexander, Stephen
Allen, David Oliver
Allen, Thomas
Allis, Edward Phelps
Andrews, Sherlock James
Arnold, Lauren Briggs
Arthur, Chester Alan
Baker, Walter Ransom Gail
Baldwin, Frank Stephen
Bayard, James Asheton, 1799–1880
Beall, Samuel Wootton
Beck, Lewis Caleb
Beck, Theodric Romeyn
Bellamy, Edward
Benjamin, George Hillard
Bigelow, John
Blair, Austin
Blatchford, Richard Milford
Blood, Benjamin Paul
Bradford, Alexander Warfield
Breckinridge, Robert Jefferson
Breese, Sidney
Brooks, James Gordon
Brooks, Thomas Benton
Brownell, Thomas Church
Butterfield, Daniel
Campbell, William W.
Carey, Joseph Maull
Cary, Edward
Cassidy, William
Cochrane, John
Comstock, George Franklin
Conkling, Alfred
Dean, Amos
Doane, George Washington
Duane, Alexander
Duane, James Chatham
Edmonds, John Worth
Ellis, Job Bicknell
Flint, Weston
Forman, Joshua
Fuller, Robert Mason
Gale, George Washington

Genung, John Franklin
Giddings, Franklin Henry
Gilbert, Eliphalet Wheeler
Goodwin, Hannibal Williston
Gregory, John Milton
Hall, Baynard Rush
Halleck, Henry Wager
Hamilton, Frank Hastings
Hare, George Emlen
Harris, Ira
Hartrantt, John Frederick
Hawley, Gideon, 1785–1870
Headley, Joel Tyler
Hickok, Laurens Perseus
Hoff, John Van Rensselacr
Hoffman, John Thompson
Holcombe, Chester
Hough, Franklin Benjamin
Hough, George Washington
House, Samuel Reynolds
Hunt, Ward
Jackson, Edward
Jackson, Sheldon
James, Henry, 1811–1882
Jenkins, Charles Jones
Johnson, Benjamin Pierce
King, Preston
Knapp, Seaman Asahel
Lamont, Daniel Scott
Landon, Milville de Lancey
Lane, Levi Cooper
Lewis, Tayler
Littlejohn, Abram Newkirk
Ludlow, Fitz Hugh
McAuley, Thomas
McLeod, Alexander
McMaster, James Alphonsus
Mattoon, Stephen
Miller, Warner
Morgan, Lewis Henry
Morton, Julius Sterling
Murray, David
Nevin, John Williamson
Nevius, John Livingston
Nott, Charles Cooper
Paddock, Algernon Sidney
Park, Roswell, 1807–1869
Parker, Amasa Junius
Parry, Charles Christopher
Patterson, Robert Porter
Peck, Charles Horton
Peckham, Wheeler Hazard
Perry, Stuart
Perry, William
Pierson, Hamilton Wilcox
Potter, Alonzo
Potter, Eliphalet Nott
Potter, Horatio
Potter, Robert Brown
Price, Joseph
Prime, Edward Dorr Griffin
Randall, Henry Stephens
Rankine, William Birch
Raymond, John Howard
Reid, William Wharry
Rice, Alexander Hamilton
Rice, Edwin Wilbur
Ripley, Edward Hastings
Robertson, William Schenck
Salisbury, James Henry
Schell, Augustus
Schoolcraft, Henry Rowe

Sears, Edmund Hamilton
Seward, Frederick William
Seward, George Frederick
Seward, William Henry
Sherwood, Adiel
Smith, Charles Emory
Snow, Jessie Baker
Spencer, John Canfield
Sprague, Charles Ezra
Staley, Cady
Stillman, William James
Stone, John Seely
Streeter, George Linius
Tappan, Henry Philip
Taylor, John W.
Thomas, John Wilson
Toombs, Robert Augustus
Townsend, Robert
Tuckerman, Edward
Van de Warker, Edward Ely
Van Santvoord, George
Walworth, Clarence Augustus
Wayland, Francis, 1796–1865
Westinghouse, George
Whipple, Squire
White, Albert Smith
Whitsitt, William Heth
Wickes, Stephen
Wikoff, Henry
Wilkie, Franc Bangs
Wilson, John Leighton
Wood, James, 1799–1867
Woods, Leonard, 1807–1878
UNION COLLEGE OF LAW (ILL.)
Copley, Ira Clifton
Landis, Kenesaw Mountain
Lowden, Frank Orren
Rainey, Henry Thomas
UNION THEOLOGICAL SEMINARY
(N.Y.)
Ament, William Scott
Armstrong, George Dod
Baird, Charles Washington
Baird, Henry Martyn
Bancroft, Cecil Franklin Patch
Barrows, John Henry
Bird, Frederic Mayer
Bissell, Edwin Cone
Bliss, Howard Sweetser
Boisen, Anton Theophilus
Bowen, George
Brady, John Green
Briggs, Charles Augustus
Brown, Charles Rufus
Brown, Francis, 1849–1916
Brown, Samuel Robbins
Brown, William Adams
Burrell, David James
Calkins, Phineas Wolcott
Chamberlain, Jacob
Chapin, Aaron Lucius
Child, Frank Samuel
Clewell, John Henry
Coffin, Henry Sloane
Converse, James Booth
Crothers, Samuel McChord
Curtis, Edward Lewis
Curtiss, Samuel Ives
Cutler, Carroll
Dabney, Robert Lewis
Darling, Henry
Dennett, Tyler (Wilbur)

D'Ooge, Martin Luther
Eastman, William Reed
Fosdick, Harry Emerson
Foster, Stephen Symonds
Gardiner, Harry Norman
Gillett, Ezra Hall
Gladden, Washington
Good, James Isaac
Goodrich, Chauncey, 1836–
1925
Gulick, John Thomas
Gulick, Sidney Lewis
Hall, Charles Cuthbert
Hall, Granville Stanley
Hamilton, Edward John
Hammond, Edward Payson
Hammond, James Bartlett
Haven, Joseph
Hendrix, Eugene Russell
Hoge, Moses Drury
Hoppin, James Mason
Horr, George Edwin
Hunt, Theodore Whitefield
Hyde, William De Witt
Jackson, Samuel Macauley
Kellogg, Martin
Klipstein, Louis Frederick
Luce, Henry Winters
Lunn, George Richard
Lyman, Albert Josiah
Lyman, Chester Smith
Lynd, Robert Staughton
McGiffert, Arthur Cushman
McIlwaine, Richard
McMaster, James Alphonsus
Marquand, Allan
Mills, Cyrus Taggart
Mitchell, Edwin Knox
Moore, George Foot
Morris, George Sylvester
Mulford, Elisha
Muste, Abraham Johannes
Muzzey, David Saville
Nutting, Wallace
Ogden, Rollo
Olds, Leland
Osborn, Henry Stafford
Peet, Isaac Lewis
Phelps, Austin
Pierson, Arthur Tappan
Pierson, Hamilton Wilcox
Post, George Edward
Powell, Edward Payson
Reed, Richard Clark
Reid, Gilbert
Reid, John Morrison
Richards, Charles Herbert
Robinson, Charles Seymour
Robinson, Stuart
Salter, William
Schuyler, George Washington
Smith, Arthur Henderson
Smith, Benjamin Mosby
Smith, Gerald Birnev
Strong, James Woodward
Stuart, John Leighton
Thomas, Norman Mattoon
Willey, Samuel Hopkins
Wilson, Warren Hugh
Woodbridge, Frederick James
Eugene

Graduate Study
Matthews, Joseph Brown
UNION UNIVERSITY (TENN.)
Dodd, Monroe Elmon
UNITED STATES COAST GUARD
ACADEMY (CONN.)
Smith, Edward Hanson
UNITED STATES MILITARY ACADE-
MY (N.Y.)
Abbot, Henry Larcom
Abert, John James
Adams, John, 1825–1864
Alexander, Barton Stone
Alexander, Edward Porter
Allen, Henry Tureman
Allen, Robert
Allison, Nathaniel
Allston, Robert Francis Withers
Alvord, Benjamin
Ames, Adelbert
Ammen, Daniel
Ammen, Jacob
Anderson, Joseph Reid
Anderson, Richard Heron
Anderson, Robert
Andrews, Frank Maxwell
Andrews, George Leonard
Armistead, Lewis Addison
Arnold, Henry Harley
Arnold, Lewis Golding
Arnold, Richard
Augur. Christopher Columbus
Averell. William Woods
Avres, Romeyn Beck
Babcock. Orville E.
Bache, Alexander Dallas
Bailey, Jacob Whitman
Baird, Absalom
Baker, Laurence Simmons
Barlow, John Whitney
Barnard, John Gross
Barnes, James
Barry, William Farquhar
Bartlett, William Holmes
Chambers
Barton, Seth Maxwell
Beauregard, Pierre Gustave
Toutant
Bee, Barnard Elliott
Bell, James Franklin
Benham, Henry Washington
Benton, James Gilchrist
Black, William Murray
Blair, Montgomery
Bledsoe, Albert Taylor
Bliss, Tasker Howard
Bonaparte, Jerome Napoleon
Bonfils, Frederick Gilmer
Bonneville, Benjamin Louis Eu-
lalie de
Bourke, John Gregory
Boynton, Edward Carlisle
Bragg, Braxton
Brannan, John Milton
Brooks, William Thomas Har-
baugh
Buchanan, Robert Christie
Buckner, Simon Bolivar
Buckner, Simon Bolivar
Buell, Don Carlos
Buford, Abraham, 1820–1884
Buford, John

Buford, Napoleon Bonaparte
Bullard, Robert Lee
Burnside, Ambrose Everett
Cabell, William Lewis
Camden, Johnson Newlon
Campbell, John Archibald
Canby, Edward Richard Sprigg
Carpenter, Matthew Hale
Carr, Eugene Asa
Carroll, Samuel Sprigg
Casey, Silas
Casey, Thomas Lincoln
Cass, George Washington
Chaffee, Adna Romanza
Childe, John
Childs, Thomas
Chittenden, Hiram Martin
Chouteau, Auguste Pierre
Cocke, Philip St. George
Cooke, Philip St. George
Cooper, Samuel
Coppée, Henry
Couch, Darius Nash
Craig, Malin
Crittenden, George Bibb
Crook, George
Crowder, Enoch Herbert
Crozier, William
Cullum, George Washington
Curtis, Samuel Ryan
Custer, George Armstrong
Dana, Napoleon Jackson
Tecumseh
Davidson, John Wynn
Davis, George Breckinridge
Davis, Jefferson
Delafield, Richard
Dent, Frederick Tracy
Derby, George Horatio
Dickman, Joseph Theodore
Donelson, Andrew Jackson
Doubleday, Abner
Drayton, Thomas Fenwick
Duane, James Chatham
Du Pont, Henry
Du Pont, Henry Algernon
Dwight, William
Dye, William McEntyre
Dyer, Alexander Brydie
Early, Jubal Anderson
Edwards, Clarence Ransom
Eichelberger, Robert Lawrence
Eisenhower, Dwight David
Elliott, Washington Lafayette
Ely, Hanson Edward
Elzey, Arnold
Emory, William Hemsley
Ernst, Oswald Herbert
Eustis, Henry Lawrence
Evans, Nathan George
Ewell, Benjamin Stoddert
Ewell, Richard Stoddert
Ewing, Hugh Boyle
Fannin, James Walker
Fanning, Alexander Campbell
Wilder
Field, Charles William
Fletcher, Robert
Foote, Andrew Hull
Foster, John Gray
Franklin, William Buel
French, William Henry

Fry, Birkett Davenport
Fry, James Barnet
Gaillard, David Du Bose
Garnett, Robert Selden
Garrard, Kenner
Getty, George Washington
Gibbon, John
Gillem, Alvan Cullem
Gillmore, Quincy Adams
Gilpin, William
Glassford, Pelham Davis
Goethals, George Washington
Goldthwaite, George
Gordon, George Henry
Gordon, William Washington
Gorgas, Josiah
Gorrell, Edgar Staley
Gracie, Archibald
Graham, James Duncan
Granger, Gordon
Grant, Frederick Dent
Grant, Ulysses Simpson
Graves, William Sidney
Greene, Francis Vinton
Greene, George Sears
Gregg, David McMurtrie
Griffin, Charles
Griffin, Eugene
Grover, Cuvier
Groves, Leslie Richard, Jr.
Gunnison, John Williams
Haan, William George
Halleck, Henry Wager
Hamilton, Charles Smith
Hamilton, Schuyler
Hamtramck, John Francis
Hancock, Winfield Scott
Hardee, William Joseph
Hardie, James Allen
Hardy, Arthur Sherburne
Hartsuff, George Lucas
Hascall, Milo Smith
Hatch, John Porter
Haupt, Herman
Hays, Alexander
Hazen, William Babcock
Hébert, Louis
Hébert, Paul Octave
Heintzelman, Samuel Peter
Heintzelman, Stuart
Heth, Henry
Hewitt, John Hill
Hill, Ambrose Powell
Hill, Daniel Harvey
Hine, Charles de Lano
Hines, John Leonard ("Birdie")
Hitchcock, Ethan Allen, 1798–
1870
Hodes, Henry Irving
Hodges, Courtney Hicks
Hodges, Harry Foote
Holabird, William
Holden, Edward Singleton
Holmes, Theophilus Hunter
Hood, John Bell
Hood, Washington
Hooker, Joseph
Howe, Albion Parris
Howze, Robert Lee
Huger, Benjamin
Hughes, George Wurtz
Humphreys, Andrew Atkinson

Humphreys, Benjamin Grubb
Hunt, Henry Jackson
Hunter, David
Huse, Caleb
Irwin, George Le Roy
Ives, Joseph Christmas
Jackson, Thomas Jonathan ("Stonewall")
Jackson, William Hicks
Jadwin, Edgar
Johnson, Bushrod Rust
Johnson, Edward
Johnson, Hugh Samuel
Johnson, Richard W.
Johnston, Albert Sidney
Johnston, Joseph Eggleston
Jones, David Rumph
Jordan, Thomas
Kautz, August Valentine
Kelton, John Cunningham
Keyes, Erasmus Darwin
Kilpatrick, Hugh Judson
King, Edward Leonard
King, Rufus, 1814–1876
Kinney, William Burnet
Kirby-Smith, Edmund
Knappen, Theodore Temple
Kuhn, Joseph Ernst
Lawton, Alexander Robert
Lee, Fitzhugh
Lee, George Washington Custis
Lee, John Clifford Hodges
Lee, Robert Edward
Lee, Stephen Dill
Lewis, Isaac Newton
Liggett, Hunter
Lomax, Lunsford Lindsay
Long, Armistead Lindsay
Longstreet, James
Lovell, Mansfield
Ludlow, William
Lyon, Nathaniel
McAlexander, Ulysses Grant
MacArthur, Douglas
McClellan, George Brinton
McCook, Alexander McDowell
McDowell, Irvin
Mackenzie, Ranald Slidell
McLane, Robert Milligan
McLaws, Lafayette
McLeod, Hugh
McNair, Lesley James
McNeill, William Gibbs
McPherson, James Birdseye
Magruder, John Bankhead
Mahan, Dennis Hart
Mann, Ambrose Dudley
Mansfield, Edward Deering
Mansfield, Joseph King Fenno
March, Peyton Conway
Marmaduke, John Sappington
Marshall, Humphrey
Marshall, William Louis
Martin, James Green
Martin, John Hill
Martindale, John Henry
Mason, Charles
Mather, William Williams
Maury, Dabney Herndon
Maus, Marion Perry
Maxey, Samuel Bell
Maynard, Edward

Meade, George Gordon
Meigs, Montgomery Cunningham
Menoher, Charles Thomas
Merrill, Frank Dow
Merrill, William Emery
Merritt, Wesley
Michie, Peter Smith
Michler, Nathaniel
Mills, Anson
Mitchel, Ormsby MacKnight
Mordecai, Alfred
Morell, George Webb
Morris, Thomas Armstrong
Morris, William Hopkins
Morton, Charles Gould
Morton, James St. Clair
Mowbray, Henry Siddons
Muir, Charles Henry
Mullan, John
Myers, Abraham Charles
Neill, Thomas Hewson
Newton, John
Neyland, Robert Reese, Jr.
Nicholls, Francis Redding Tillow
Northrop, Lucius Bellinger
Ord, Edward Otho Cresap
Palfrey, John Carver
Palmer, Innis Newton
Palmer, John McAuley
Park, Roswell, 1807–1869
Parke, John Grubb
Parrott, Robert Parker
Partridge, Alden
Patch, Alexander McCarrell
Patrick, Marsena Rudolph
Patrick, Mason Mathews
Patton, George Smith
Peck, John James
Pelham, John
Pemberton, John Clifford
Pender, William Dorsey
Pendleton, William Nelson
Pershing, John Joseph
Pickett, George Edward
Pleasonton, Alfred
Poe, Edgar Allan
Poe, Orlando Metcalfe
Polk, Leonidas
Pope, John
Porter, Fitz-John
Quinby, Isaac Ferdinand
Rains, Gabriel James
Rains, George Washington
Ramsay, George Douglas
Ramseur, Stephen Dodson
Raymond, Charles Walker
Read, George Windle
Reno, Jesse Lee
Reynolds, Alexander Welch
Reynolds, John Fulton
Reynolds, Joseph Jones
Richardson, Israel Bush
Richardson, Wilds Preston
Ricketts, James Brewerton
Ripley, James Wolfe
Ripley, Roswell Sabine
Robert, Henry Martyn
Roberts, Benjamin Stone
Robinson, John Cleveland
Rodman, Thomas Jackson

Rosecrans, William Starke
Rosser, Thomas Lafayette
Royce, Ralph
Ruger, Thomas Howard
Russell, David Allen
Schenck, James Findlay
Schofield, John McAllister
Schriver, Edmund
Schwatka, Frederick
Scott, Hugh Lenox
Sedgwick, John
Seymour, Truman
Sheridan, Philip Henry
Sherman, Thomas West
Sherman, William Tecumseh
Shoup, Francis Asbury
Sibert, William Luther
Sidell, William Henry
Simpson, James Hervey
Slocum, Henry Warner
Smith, Charles Ferguson
Smith, Francis Henney
Smith, Gustavus Woodson
Smith, Martin Luther
Smith, Richard Somers
Smith, Robert Hardy
Smith, William Farrar
Smith, William Sooy
Snelling, William Joseph
Somervell, Brehon Burke
Squier, George Owen
Stanley, David Sloane
Steele, Frederick
Stevens, Isaac Ingalls
Stevens, Walter Husted
Stevenson, Carter Littlepage
Stewart, Alexander Peter
Stilwell, Joseph Warren
Stone, Charles Pomeroy
Stoneman, George
Stratemeyer, George Edward
Stuart, James Ewell Brown
Sturgis, Samuel Davis
Summerall, Charles Pelot
Swift, Joseph Gardner
Swift, William Henry
Sykes, George
Symons, Thomas William
Talcott, Andrew
Taylor, Harry
Ten Broeck, Richard
Thatcher, Henry Knox
Thayer, Sylvanus
Thomas, George Henry
Thomas, Lorenzo
Tidball, John Caldwell
Torbert, Alfred Thomas Archimedes
Totten, Joseph Gilbert
Tower, Zealous Bates
Townsend, Edward Davis
Trimble, Isaac Ridgeway
Trist, Nicholas Philip
Trowbridge, William Petit
Turnbull, William
Turner, John Wesley
Tyler, Daniel
Tyler, Robert Ogden
Tyson, Lawrence Davis
Vandenberg, Hoyt Sanford
Vanderburgh, William Henry
Van Dorn, Earl

Vinton, Francis
Vinton, Francis Laurens
Wainwright, Jonathan Mayhew
Walker, John Brisben
Walker, Walton Harris
Walker, William Henry Talbot
Wallace, David
Warren, Gouverneur Kemble
Washington, John Macrae
Webb, Alexander Stewart
Weitzel, Godfrey
Wheeler, George Montague
Wheeler, Joseph
Whipple, Amiel Weeks
Whistler, George Washington
Whistler, James Abbott McNeill
White, Edward Higgins, II
Whiting, William Henry Chase
Wilcox, Cadmus Marcellus
Willcox, Orlando Bolivar
Wilson, James Harrison
Winder, John Henry
Wood, Charles Erskine Scott
Wood, Robert Elkington
Wood, Thomas John
Woodbury, Daniel Phineas
Woods, Charles Robert
Wright, Horatio Gouverneur
Yoakum, Henderson
Young, Pierce Manning Butler
Zeilin, Jacob

UNITED STATES NAVAL ACADEMY (MD.)

Allen, Hervey
Badger, Charles Johnston
Badger, Oscar Charles
Bailey, Frank Harvey
Barbey, Daniel Edward
Barker, Albert Smith
Beale, Edward Fitzgerald
Beary, Donald Bradford
Benjamin, Park, 1849–1922
Benson, William Shepherd
Berwind, Edward Julius
Blake, Homer Crane
Blandy, William Henry Purnell
Bloch, Claude Charles
Blue, Victor
Bradford, Joseph
Brady, Cyrus Townsend
Brereton, Lewis Hyde
Bristol, Mark Lambert
Brown, Charles Rufus
Brownson, Willard Herbert
Bullard, William Hannum Grubb
Byrd, Richard Evelyn
Canaga, Alfred Bruce
Capps, Washington Lee
Chadwick, French Ensor
Chester, Colby Mitchell
Churchill, Winston
Clark, Charles Edgar
Cohen, John Sanford
Cone, Hutchinson Ingham
Cooley, Mortimer Elwyn
Coontz, Robert Edward
Danenhower, John Wilson
Davis, Andrew McFarland
Davis, Charles Henry, 1845–1921
Davis, John Lee

Davison, Gregory Caldwell
De Long, George Washington
Dewey, George
Drake, Charles Daniel
Durand, William Frederick
Earle, Ralph
Eberle, Edward Walter
Edwards, Richard Stanislaus
Emmet, William Le Roy
Evans, Robley Dunglison
Fiske, Bradley Allen
Fly, James Lawrence
Foulk, George Clayton
Fox, Gustavus Vasa
Frost, Holloway Halstead
Gherodi, Bancroft
Gleaves, Albert
Gossett, Benjamin Brown
Grant, Albert Weston
Greene, Samuel Dana
Greer, James Augustin
Gridley, Charles Vernon
Griffin, Robert Stanislaus
Gunnison, Foster
Habersham, Alexander Wylly
Halsey, William Frederick, Jr.
Hayden, Edward Everett
Hobson, Richmond Pearson
Holder, Charles Frederick
Hollis, Ina Nelson
Howell, John Adams
Hughes, Charles Frederick
Ingersoll, Royal Rodney
Ingram, Jonas Howard
Jackson, John Brinckerhoff
Jeffers, William Nicholson
Jones, Hilary Pollard
Jouett, James Edward
Joy, Charles Turner
Kelley, James Douglas Jerrold
Kempff, Louis
Kimball, William Wirt
Kimmel, Husband Edward
King, Ernest Joseph
Kirk, Alan Goodrich
Knight, Austin Melvin
Knox, Dudley Wright
Lamberton, Benjamin Peffer
Leahy, William Daniel
Lee, Willis Augustus
Lejeune, John Archer
Luce, Stephen Bleecker
Lull, Edward Phelps
McCalla, Bowman Henry
McCauley, Edward Yorke
McCormick, Lynde Dupuy
McEnery, Samuel Douglas
McGiffin, Philo Norton
McLean, Walter
McNair, Frederick Vallette
Mahan, Alfred Thayer
Mattice, Asa Martines
Maury, Matthew Fontaine
Mayo, Henry Thomas
Mayo, William Kennon
Meade, Richard Worsam, 1837–1897
Meade, Robert Leamy
Michelson, Albert Abraham
Mitchell, Sidney Zollicoffer
Mitscher, Marc Andrew
Moffett, William Adger

Morgan, James Morris
Murdock, Joseph Ballard
Neville, Wendell Cushing
Niblack, Albert Parker
Nimitz, Chester William
Pardee, Don Albert
Parker, William Harwar
Perkins, George Hamilton
Phelps, Thomas Stowell
Philip, John Woodward
Pillsbury, John Elliott
Plunkett, Charles Peshall
Pratt, William Veazie
Raby, James Joseph
Ramsay, Francis Munroe
Read, Charles William
Reeves, Joseph Mason
Remey, George Collier
Ricketts, Claude Vernon
Robertson, Ashley Herman
Rockwell, Kiffin Yates
Rodgers, John, 1881–1926
Roe, Francis Asbury
Russell, John Henry
Safford, William Edwin
Sampson, William Thomas
Schley, Winfield Scott
Schroeder, Seaton
Selfridge, Thomas Oliver
Sherman, Forrest Percival
Sherman, Frederick Carl
Sicard, Montgomery
Sigsbee, Charles Dwight
Simpson, Edward
Sims, William Sowden
Smyth, Newman
Snowden, Thomas
Spangler, Henry Wilson
Sprague, Frank Julian
Spruance, Raymond Ames
Standley, William Harrison
Stockton, Charles Herbert
Taussig, Joseph Knefler
Taylor, David Watson
Theobald, Robert Alfred
Thompson, Robert Means
Towers, John Henry
Townsend, Robert
Trenchard, Stephen Decatur
Turner, Richmond Kelly
Vickery, Howard Leroy
Wainwright, Richard
Walker, Asa
Walker, John Grimes
Watson, John Crittenden
Weaver, Aaron Ward
Weaver, William Dixon
Weeks, John Wingate
Welles, Roger
Wilbur, Curtis Dwight
Wilde, George Francis Faxon
Wilkinson, Theodore Stark
Winslow, Cameron McRae
Wood, John Taylor
Woodruff, Charles Edward
Zacharias, Ellis Mark
Ziegemier, Henry Joseph

UNIVERSITY COLLEGE, LONDON (ENGLAND)

Mees, Charles Edward Kenneth
Sheppard, Samuel Edward
Sigerist, Henry Ernest

Graduate Study
Sheppard, Samuel Edward
UNIVERSITY COLLEGE (ENGLAND)
Mendes, Henry Pereira
UNIVERSITY MEDICAL COLLEGE
(N.Y.)
Cook, Frederick Albert
UNIVERSITY OF ADELAIDE (AUS-
TRALIA)
Mayo, George Elton
Graduate Study
Mayo, George Elton
UNIVERSITY OF AKRON (OHIO)
Crissinger, Daniel Richard
Kingsbury, Albert
UNIVERSITY OF ALABAMA
Bankhead, John Hollis
Bankhead, William Brockman
Battle, Cullen Andrews
Campbell, William Edward
March
Carmichael, Oliver Cromwell
Clay, Clement Claiborne
Clayton, Henry De Lamar
Clemens, Jeremiah
Comer, Braxton Bragg
Duggar, Benjamin Minge
Forney, William Henry
Gaines, Reuben Reid
Gould, Robert Simonton
Graves, David Bibb
Guild, La Fayette
Harding, William Procter Gould
Hargrove, Robert Kennon
Herbert, Hilary Abner
McKellar, Kenneth Douglas
Manly, Basil, 1825–1892
Meek, Alexander Beaufort
Moore, George Fleming
Owen, Thomas McAdory
Roberts, Oran Milo
Sibert, William Luther
Smith, Eugene Allen
Smith, William Russell
Toulmin, Harry Theophilus
Van de Graaff, Robert Jemison
Graduate Study
Carmichael, Oliver Cromwell
McKellar, Kenneth Douglas
Van de Graaff, Robert Jemison
Law
Clayton, Henry De Lamar
Smith, Holland McTyeire
Steagall, Henry Bascom
Wright, Fielding Lewis
UNIVERSITY OF ALASKA
Bartlett, Edward Lewis ("Bob")
UNIVERSITY OF AMSTERDAM (NETH-
ERLANDS)
Medicine
Dusser de Barenne, Joannes
Gregorius
UNIVERSITY OF ARIZONA
Kefauver, Grayson Neikirk
UNIVERSITY OF ARKANSAS
Burns, Bob
Robinson, Joseph Taylor
UNIVERSITY OF ATHENS (GREECE)
Callimachos, Panos Demetrios
Medicine
Papanicolaou, George Nicholas

UNIVERSITY OF BASEL (SWITZER-
LAND)
Pfister, Alfred
Piccard, Jean Felix
UNIVERSITY OF BERLIN (GERMANY)
Bauer, Louis Agricola
Beckwith, Clarence Augustine
Behrend, Bernard Arthur
Bolza, Oskar
Brightman, Edgar Sheffield
Coe, George Albert
Franck, James
Freund, Ernst
Friedlaender, Walter Ferdinand
Fuller, George Warren
Hammer, William Joseph
Horney, Karen Danielssen
Koffka, Kurt
Köhler, Wolfgang
Laufer, Berthold
Lewin, Kurt
Ley, Willy
Mather, Frank Jewett, Jr.
Mead, George Herbert
Michael, Arthur
Santayana, George
Schindler, Kurt
Simkhovitch, Mary Melinda
Kingsbury
Stieglitz, Alfred
Stiles, Charles Wardell
Tillich, Paul
Von Neumann, John
Willard, Josiah Flint
Graduate School
Brown, William Adams
Graduate Study
Allen, Florence Ellinwood
Balch, Emily Greene
Bentley, Arthur Fisher
Bergmann, Max
Coit, Stanton
Falkner, Roland Post
Franklin, Edward Curtis
Gay, Edwin Francis
Gottheil, Richard James
Horatio
Hayes, Edward Carey
Herty, Charles Holmes
Hibben, John Grier
Hoyt, John Sherman
Merrill, Elmer Truesdell
Millikan, Robert Andrews
Morgan, Edwin Vernon
Muzzey, David Saville
Rhees, Rush
Robb, William Lispenard
Schinz, Albert
Schmidt, Nathaniel
Stieglitz, Julius
Szilard, Leo
Tate, John Torrence
Thilly, Frank
Westermann, William Linn
Woods, James Haughton
Medicine
Michaelis, Leonor
Schoenheimer, Rudolf
UNIVERSITY OF BERN (SWITZER-
LAND)
Funk, Casimir

UNIVERSITY OF BONN (GERMANY)
De Forest, Robert Weeks
Wolff, Kurt August Paul
Graduate Study
Coolidge, Julian Lowell
Harrison, Ross Granville
Spaulding, Edward Gleason
UNIVERSITY OF BORDEAUX
(FRANCE)
Williams, Aubrey Willis
UNIVERSITY OF BRESLAU (GERMA-
NY)
Graduate Study
Tillich, Paul
UNIVERSITY OF BUDAPEST (HUN-
GARY)
Moholy-Nagy, László
Rapaport, David
Reiner, Fritz
Roheim, Geza
Graduate Study
Von Neumann, John
Medicine
Alexander, Franz Gabriel
UNIVERSITY OF BUFFALO (N.Y.)
Fisher, George Jackson
Hofstadter, Richard
Holt, Luther Emmett
Stockton, Charles G.
Wende, Ernest
Wende, Grover William
UNIVERSITY OF CALIFORNIA
Beals, Ralph Albert
Beatty, Willard Walcott
Bradley, Frederick Worthen
Burk, Frederic Lister
Chamberlain, Joseph Perkins
Cooper, William John
Corbett, Harvey Wiley
Cottrell, Frederick Gardner
Erlanger, Joseph
Faust, Frederick Shiller
Foshag, William Frederick
Gaither, Horace Rowan, Jr.
Gaxton, William
Goldberg, Reuben Lucius
("Rube")
Goodman, Louis Earl
Gunter, Archibald Clavering
Heney, Francis Joseph
Herbst, Josephine Frey
Higgins, Marguerite
Hohfield, Wesley Newcomb
Howard, Sidney Coe
Jepson, Willis Linn
Johnson, Hiram Warren
Kahn, Florence Prag
Knappen, Theodore Temple
Kohlberg, Alfred
Laguna, Theodore de Leo de
Lane, Franklin Knight
Lindley, Curtis Holbrook
Lovejoy, Arthur Oncken
McLoughlin, Maurice Evans
Mann, Louis
Mather, Stephen Tyng
Merriam, John Campbell
Meyer, Eugene Isaac
Mezes, Sidney Edward
Morgan, Julia
Moss, Sanford Alexander
Nelson, Nels Christian

Norris, Benjamin Franklin
Norris, Charles Gilman Smith
Overstreet, Harry Allen
Parker, Carleton Hubbell
Phelan, James Duval
Ransome, Frederick Leslie
Reinhardt, Aurelia Isabel Henry
Ritter, William Emerson
Royce, Josiah
Ruef, Abraham
Sajous, Charles Euchariste de
   Médicis
Sanford, Edmund Clark
Sawyer, Wilbur Augustus
Schmidt, Carl Louis August
Steffens, Lincoln
Stein, Leo Daniel
Stoddard, Charles Warren
Taggard, Genevieve
Theobald, Robert Alfred
Warner, William Lloyd
Webb, Harry Howard
Williams, Gardner Fred
Zellerbach, James David
Graduate Study
Baker, Dorothy Dodds
Barrows, David Prescott
Cooper, William John
Foshag, William Frederick
Grady, Henry Francis
Jepson, Willis Linn
Kelsey, Rayner Wickersham
Kuykendall, Ralph Simpson
Latimer, Wendell Mitchell
MacNair, Harley Farnsworth
Moss, Sanford Alexander
Nelson, Marjorie Maxine
Nelson, Nels Christian
Nicholson, Seth Barnes
Prall, David Wight
Ransome, Frederick Leslie
Schmidt, Carl Louis August
Thomas, Elbert Duncan
Hastings College of Law
Chamberlain, Joseph Perkins
Law
Adams, Annette Abbott
Engle, Clair William Walter
Gaither, Horace Rowan, Jr.
Goodman, Louis Earl
Heney, Francis Joseph
Ruef, Abraham
Medicine
Widney, Joseph Pomeroy
UNIVERSITY OF CALIFORNIA, LOS
  ANGELES
Baker, Dorothy Dodds
Bartlett, Edward Lewis ("Bob")
UNIVERSITY OF CHATTANOOGA
Raulston, John Tate
UNIVERSITY OF CHICAGO (ILL.)
Adams, Cyrus Cornelius
Adams, Frank Ramsay
Allison, Samuel King
Andrus, Ethel Percy
Anthony, Katharine Susan
Atwood, Wallace Walter
Beal, William James
Bell, Bernard Iddings
Benson, Oscar Herman
Bestor, Arthur Eugene
Billikopf, Jacob

Birkhoff, George David
Blair, William Richards
Bliss, Gilbert Ames
Bloomfield, Maurice
Bryan, Charles Wayland
Chase, (Mary) Agnes Merrill
Cohn, Edwin Joseph
Covici, Pascal ("Pat")
Cuppy, William Jacob (Will)
Davenport, Herbert Joseph
Davisson, Clinton Joseph
Dille, John Flint
Enelow, Hyman Gerson
Fisher, Henry Conroy ("Bud")
Frank, Jerome
Gale, Henry Gordon
Gardner, Helen
Gaston, Herbert Earle
Goodspeed, Thomas Wakefield
Graham, Evarts Ambrose
Gray, William Scott, Jr.
Greenlaw, Edwin Almiron
Gunther, John
Harper, Robert Francis
Henderson, Charles Richmond
Hine, Lewis Wickes
Hobart, Alice Nourse Tisdale
Howe, Herbert Alonzo
Hubble, Edwin
Ickes, Harold Le Clair
Johnson, Charles Spurgeon
Kellor, Frances (Alice)
Kharasch, Morris Selig
Kirkwood, John Gamble
Levinson, Salmon Oliver
Lurton, Horace Harmon
McHugh, Rose John
McKinley, Albert Edward
Miller, Perry Gilbert Eddy
Millikan, Clark Blanchard
Mitchell, Wesley Clair
Moore, Richard Bishop
Mott, Frank Luther
O'Brien, Justin
Peattie, Donald Culross
Redfield, Robert
Richberg, Donald Randall
Sills, Milton
Smith, Henry Justin
Stone, Ormond
Thorek, Max
Van Vechten, Carl
Walling, William English
Wilder, Russell Morse
Wilson, Edmund Beecher
Graduate Study
Abbott, Edith
Abbott, Grace
Adams, Joseph Quincy
Adams, Walter Sydney
Allison, Samuel King
Alvord, Clarence Walworth
Atwood, Wallace Walter
Balch, Emily Greene
Barrows, David Prescott
Beeson, Charles Henry
Bestor, Arthur Eugene
Billikopf, Jacob
Bingham, Walter Van Dyke
Birkhoff, George David
Blair, William Richards
Bliss, Gilbert Ames

Bloomfield, Leonard
Breckenridge, Sophonisba Pres-
  ton
Brooke, Charles Frederick
  Tucker
Caldwell, Otis William
Cayton, Horace Roscoe
Chamberlain, Charles Joseph
Cohn, Edwin Joseph
Cowles, Henry Chandler
Crocker, William
Cuppy, William Jacob (Will)
Davis, Katharine Bement
Dawley, Almena
Dickson, Leonard Eugene
Doolittle, Eric
Downey, June Etta
Dykstra, Clarence Addison
Evans, Lawrence Boyd
Fenneman, Nevin Melancthon
Folin, Otto Knut Olof
Frank, Tenney
Frazier, Edward Franklin
Gale, Henry Gordon
Gardner, Helen
Garner, James Wilford
Goode, John Paul
Graves, Alvin Cushman
Gray, William Scott, Jr.
Hatcher, Orie Latham
Hayes, Edward Carey
Hoerr, Normand Louis
Hoxie, Robert Franklin
Hubble, Edwin
Jewett, Frank Baldwin
Jones, Lynds
Just, Ernest Everett
Key, Valdimer Orlando, Jr.
Kharasch, Morris Selig
Koch, Fred Conrad
Lillie, Frank Rattray
Lingelbach, Anna Lane
Livingston, Burton Edward
Locy, William Albert
Lutz, Frank Eugene
McClung, Clarence Erwin
Macintosh, Douglas Clyde
Meinzer, Oscar Edward
Millis, Harry Alvin
Mitchell, Wesley Clair
Monroe, Paul
Moulton, Forest Ray
Owsley, Frank Lawrence
Parker, Samuel Chester
Prokosch, Eduard
Randall, James Garfield
Ranson, Stephen Walter
Rice, John Andrew
Rickert, Martha Edith
Robinson, Edward Stevens
Rogers, James Harvey
Royster, James Finch
Ruml, Beardsley
Scarborough, Dorothy
Shull, George Harrison
Sills, Milton
Simons, Henry Calvert
Skinner, Aaron Nichols
Slichter, Sumner Huber
Slosson, Edwin Emery
Smith, John Merlin Powis
Smith, Thomas Vernor

Stolberg, Benjamin
Stone, Ormond
Stouffer, Samuel Andrew
Strong, Anna Louise
Struve, Otto
Sutherland, Edwin Hardin
Sydenstricker, Edgar
Thurstone, Louis Leon
Van Deman, Esther Boise
Veblen, Oswald
Waller, Willard Walter
Walling, William English
Watson, John Broadus
Webb, Walter Prescott
Wells, Harry Gideon
Whitcomb, Selden Lincoln
White, Leonard Dupee
Wilder, Russell Morse
Wildman, Murray Shipley
Willett, Herbert Lockwood
Willis, Henry Parker
Wirt, William Albert
Woodson, Carter Godwin
Young, Ella Flagg
Law
Allen, Florence Ellinwood
Breckenridge, Sophonisba Preston
Frank, Jerome
Goddard, Luther Marcellus
Ickes, Harold Le Clair
Oliphant, Herman
Pierce, Gilbert Ashville
Pope, James Pinckney
Redfield, Robert
Wrather, William Embry
Theology
Holt, Arthur Erastus
McClung, Clarence Erwin
Voris, John Ralph
UNIVERSITY OF CINCINNATI (OHIO)
Bara, Theda
Bauer, Louis Agricola
Benedict, Stanley Rossiter
Berkowitz, Henry
Crosley, Powel, Jr.
Fleming, John Adam
Gavin, Frank Stanton Burns
Grossmann, Louis
Heller, Maximilian
Howe, Herbert Alonzo
Huggins, Miller James
Kagan, Henry Enoch
Liebman, Joshua Loth
Magnes, Judah Leon
Meyer, Martin Abraham
Parker, Samuel Chester
Philipson, David
Ritchey, George Willis
Robinson, Edward Stevens
Sampson, Martin Wright
Silver, Abba Hillel
Silverman, Joseph
Sloan, Richard Elihu
Spence, Brent
Stephenson, Nathaniel Wright
Strauss, Joseph Baermann
Thilly, Frank
Walker, Stuart Armstrong
Williams, Aubrey Willis
Wolfson, Erwin Service

Graduate Study
Prentis, Henning Webb, Jr.
Law
Crissinger, Daniel Richard
Morrow, Edwin Porch
Medicine
Hawley, Paul Ramsey
UNIVERSITY OF CITY OF NEW YORK
(See NEW YORK UNIVERSITY)
UNIVERSITY OF COLORADO
Alden, Cynthia May Westover
Fowler, Gene
May, Morton Jay
Miller, Glenn
Millikin, Eugene Donald
Snyder, Howard McCrum
Graduate Study
Hills, Elijah Clarence
Law
Rutledge, Wiley Blount
Medicine
Naismith, James
UNIVERSITY OF CRACOW (POLAND)
(See UNIVERSITY OF KRAKOW)
UNIVERSITY OF DELAWARE
Agnew, David Hayes
Bagby, George William
Bradford, Edward Green
Joynes, Edward Southey
McCullough, John Griffith
Mears, John William
Purnell, William Henry
Saulsbury, Willard, 1820–1892
Stewart, John George
Townsend, George Alfred
Wiley, Andrew Jackson
UNIVERSITY OF DENVER (COLO.)
Smith, Homer William
Steele, Wilbur Daniel
UNIVERSITY OF EDINBURGH (SCOTLAND)
Arlen, Michael
Bishop, Robert Hamilton
Loeb, Leo
UNIVERSITY OF FLORENCE (ITALY)
Graduate Study
Bentley, Elizabeth Terrill
UNIVERSITY OF FLORIDA
Graham, Philip Leslie
Melton, James
UNIVERSITY OF FRANKFURT (GERMANY)
Neumann, Franz Leopold
UNIVERSITY OF FREIBURG (GERMANY)
Horney, Karen Danielssen
Panofsky, Erwin
Graduate Study
Hart, Albert Bushnell
Robinson, James Harvey
Tufts, James Hayden
Webb, Harry Howard
UNIVERSITY OF GENEVA (SWITZERLAND)
Znaniecki, Florian Witold
Graduate Study
Rogers, James Harvey
UNIVERSITY OF GEORGIA
Bacon, Augustus Octavius
Benning, Henry Lewis
Black, Eugene Robert
Blalock, Alfred

Blount, James Henderson
Campbell, Henry Fraser
Campbell, John Archibald
Carleton, Henry
Clayton, Augustin Smith
Cobb, Andrew Jackson
Cobb, Howell
Cobb, Thomas Reade Rootes
Comer, Braxton Bragg
Cooper, Mark Anthony
Curry, Jabez Lamar Munroe
Dawson, William Crosby
Doughty, William Henry
Eve, Paul Fitzsimons
Felton, William Harrell
Fowler, Joseph Smith
Gartrell, Lucius Jeremiah
Gordon, John Brown
Grady, Henry Woodfin
Grant, John Thomas
Graves, John Temple
Hammond, Nathaniel Job
Hardy, Oliver Norvell
Harris, William Littleton
Herty, Charles Holmes
Hill, Benjamin Harvey
Hill, Walter Barnard
Hillyer, Junius
Hopkins, Isaac Stiles
Howell, Clark
Hughes, Dudley Mayo
Jackson, James, 1819–1887
Jacobs, Joseph, 1859–1929
Johnson, Herschel Vespasian
Knight, Lucian Lamar
Lamar, Joseph Rucker
Lane, John
Le Conte, John
Le Conte, Joseph
Long, Crawford Williamson
Lumpkin, Joseph Henry
Meigs, Charles Delucena
Mell, Patrick Hues, 1850–1918
Milner, John Turner
Nisbet, Eugenius Aristides
Orr, Gustavus John
Palmer, Benjamin Morgan
Phillips, Ulrich Bonnell
Phinizy, Ferdinand
Pickens, Francis Wilkinson
Pierce, George Foster
Sanders, Billington McCarter
Scott, Thomas Fielding
Shorter, John Gill
Smith, Charles Henry, 1826–1903
Speer, Emory
Spencer, Samuel
Stephens, Alexander Hamilton
Stephens, Linton
Stokes, Thomas Lunsford, Jr.
Stovall, Pleasant Alexander
Talmadge, Eugene
Timrod, Henry
Toombs, Robert Augustus
Waddel, John Newton
Willingham, Robert Josiah
Graduate Study
McCarthy, Charles
Mell, Patrick Hues, 1850–1918
Phillips, Ulrich Bonnell

Law
Andrews, Garnett
Atkinson, William Yates
Cobb, Andrew Jackson
Hardwick, Thomas William
Howell, Evan Park
Knight, Lucian Lamar
Winship, Blanton
UNIVERSITY OF GHENT (BELGIUM)
Baekeland, Leo Hendrik
Sarton, George Alfred Léon
Graduate Study
Baekeland, Leo Hendrik
UNIVERSITY OF GLASGOW (SCOT-
LAND)
Fairburn, William Armstrong
Moffatt, James
UNIVERSITY OF GOTTINGEN (GER-
MANY)
Alexander, Franz Gabriel
Baade, Wilhelm Heinrich Wal-
ter
Browne, Charles Albert
Horney, Karen Danielssen
Rademacher, Hans
Graduate Study
Babcock, Stephen Moulton
Bliss, Gilbert Ames
Bolza, Oskar
Dabney, Charles William
Emerson, Benjamin Kendall
Jackson, Dunham
Kármán, Theodore (Todor)
Von
Kremers, Edward
Langmuir, Irving
McCrae, Thomas
Mason, Max
Nichols, Edward Leamington
Oppenheimer, Julius Robert
Osgood, William Fogg
Rademacher, Hans
Smyth, Herbert Weir
Van Vleck, Edward Burr
Weyl, Hermann
UNIVERSITY OF GRAZ (AUSTRIA)
Hess, Victor Franz
UNIVERSITY OF GRENOBLE
(FRANCE)
Stigler, William Grady
UNIVERSITY OF HALLE (GERMANY)
Elliott, John Lovejoy
Graduate Study
Dodge, Raymond
Ely, Richard Theodore
Falkner, Roland Post
Fetter, Frank Albert
Hill, Joseph Adna
Howe, Frederic Clemson
Jackson, Abraham Valentine
Williams
McMurry, Frank Morton
Peabody, Francis Greenwood
Rowe, Leo Stanton
UNIVERSITY OF HEIDELBERG (GER-
MANY)
Bonsal, Stephen
Franck, James
Freund, Ernst
Gurowski, Adam
Hart, Edwin Bret
Michael, Arthur

Graduate Study
Clark, John Bates
Ely, Richard Theodore
Magnes, Judah Leon
Reese, Charles Lee
Scott, William Berryman
Seligman, Edwin Robert Ander-
son
Thilly, Frank
Medicine
Meyerhof, Otto
UNIVERSITY OF IDAHO
Pangborn, Clyde Edward
Welker, Herman
Law
Welker, Herman
UNIVERSITY OF ILLINOIS
Boring, William Alciphron
Bryant, Ralph Clement
Bush, Lincoln
Cone, Russell Glenn
Crocker, William
East, Edward Murray
Fearing, Kenneth Flexner
Hodge, John Reed
Koch, Fred Conrad
Kyle, James Henderson
McKinley, William Brown
Mann, James Robert
Ockerson, John Augustus
Parr, Samuel Wilson
Post, Charles William
Sachs, Theodore Bernard
Scopes, John Thomas
Scovell, Melville Amasa
Short, Walter Campbell
Stratton, Samuel Wesley
Taft, Lorado Zadoc
Talbot, Arthur Newell
Vanderlip, Frank Arthur
Van Doren, Carl Clinton
Van Hook, Weller
Waller, Willard Walter
Weston, Nathan Austin
Woolman, Collett Everman
Graduate Study
Anderson, Benjamin McAlester
Carothers, Wallace Hume
Crocker, William
East, Edward Murray
Koch, Fred Conrad
O'Neal, Edward Asbury, III
Rugg, Harold Ordway
Taft, Lorado Zadoc
Westergaard, Harald Malcolm
UNIVERSITY OF INNSBRUCK
(AUSTRIA)
Flanagan, Edward Joseph
LaFarge, John
UNIVERSITY OF IOWA
Brown, Charles Reynolds
Byoir, Carl Robert
Chamberlin, Edward Hastings
Cook, George Cram
Hough, Emerson
Johnson, Wendell Andrew
Leroy
Johnston, Annie Fellows
Lowden, Frank Orren
McClain, Emlin
Nipher, Francis Eugene
Springer, Frank

Stefansson, Vilhjalmur
Wade, Martin Joseph
Graduate Study
Johnson, Wendell Andrew
Leroy
McClain, Emlin
Nipher, Francis Eugene
Shannon, Fred Albert
Law
Elliott, Charles Burke
Hughes, Howard Robard
McPherson, Smith
Medicine
Dillon, John Forrest
Matthews, Washington
UNIVERSITY OF JENA (GERMANY)
Genthe, Arnold
Graduate Study
Cobb, Nathan Augustus
McMurry, Frank Morton
UNIVERSITY OF KANSAS
Abel-Henderson, Annie Heloise
Bingham, Walter Van Dyke
Borah, William Edgar
Brady, Mildred Alice Edie
Caldwell, Eugene Wilson
Ellis, George Washington
Frank, Tenney
Franklin, Edward Curtis
Gregg, John Andrew
Hadley, Herbert Spencer
Harrington, John Lyle
Harris, James Arthur
Holmes, Julius Cecil
Latimer, Wendell Mitchell
Long, John Harper
McClung, Clarence Erwin
Moore, Joseph Earle
Pemberton, Brock
Schoeppel, Andrew Frank
Simpson, John Andrew
Slosson, Edwin Emery
Smith, Harold Dewey
White, William Allen
Wood, Frederick Hill
Zook, George Frederick
Graduate Study
Abel-Henderson, Annie Heloise
Frank, Tenney
Franklin, Edward Curtis
Zook, George Frederick
Law
Wood, Frederick Hill
Medicine
Menninger, Charles Frederick
UNIVERSITY OF KENTUCKY
Carr, Wilbur John
Clark, Champ
Flower, Benjamin Orange
Goulding, Francis Robert
Munson, Thomas Volney
Scopes, John Thomas
Shelton, Albert Leroy
Skinner, Harry
UNIVERSITY OF KHARKOV (RUSSIA)
Struve, Otto
UNIVERSITY OF KONIGSBURG (GER-
MANY)
Ley, Willy
UNIVERSITY OF KRAKOW (POLAND)
Hodur, Francis
Rubinstein, Helena

UNIVERSITY OF KRISTIANA (NOR-
WAY)
Stejneger, Leonhard Hess
Law
Stejneger, Leonhard Hess
UNIVERSITY OF LEIPZIG (GERMANY)
Bancroft, Wilder Dwight
Mead, George Herbert
Schoenheimer, Rudolf
Graduate Study
Abel, John Jacob
Blichfeldt, Hans Frederik
Cattell, James McKeen
Child, Charles Manning
Cross, Charles Whitman
Daniels, Winthrop More
Dodd, William Edward
Emerton, Ephraim
Foster, Frank Hugh
Gottheil, Richard James
Horatio
Hopkins, Edward Washburn
Judd, Charles Hubbard
Kirkland, James Hampton
Laufer, Berthold
Lotka, Alfred James
Lyon, David Gordon
Mulliken, Samuel Parsons
Noyes, Arthur Amos
Pace, Edward Aloysius
Page, Thomas Walker
Prokosch, Eduard
Scott, Walter Dill
Smyth, Herbert Weir
Spaeth, John Duncan
Stiles, Charles Wardell
Thomas, Martha Carey
Worcester, Elwood
UNIVERSITY OF LENINGRAD
(RUSSIA)
Gamow, George
UNIVERSITY OF LEWISBURG (See
BUCKNELL UNIVERSITY)
UNIVERSITY OF LEYDEN (NETHER-
LANDS)
De Leeuw, Adolph Lodewyk
UNIVERSITY OF LONDON (CANADA)
Schurman, Jacob Gould
Graduate Study
Schurman, Jacob Gould
UNIVERSITY OF LONDON (ENGLAND)
Adams, Joseph Quincy
Brenon, Herbert
Cadman, Samuel Parkes
Coomaraswamy, Ananda Kent-
ish
Davies, John Vipond
Van Druten, John William
Graduate Study
Coomaraswamy, Ananda Kent-
ish
Reece, Brazilla Carroll
Schultz, Henry
UNIVERSITY OF LOUISVILLE (KY.)
Dowell, Greensville
Flint, Austin
Visscher, William Lightfoot
Law
Bingham, Robert Worth
Bozeman, Nathan
Breckinridge, William Campbell
Preston

Colman, Norman Jay
Durrett, Reuben Thomas
Flexner, Bernard
Johnston, William Preston
Shields, George Howell
Stayton, John William
Strubberg, Friedrich Armand
Willis, Albert Shelby
Medicine
Anderson, Victor Vance
Buchanan, Joseph Rodes
Flexner, Simon
Green, Norvin
Jackson, John Davies
Richardson, Tobias Gibson
Vance, Ap Morgan
Williams, Elkanah
Wyeth, John Allan
Yandell, David Wendell
UNIVERSITY OF LVOV (POLAND)
Rodzinski, Artur
UNIVERSITY OF LYONS (FRANCE)
Medicine
Carrel, Alexis
UNIVERSITY OF MADRID (SPAIN)
Law
Houston, Charles Hamilton
UNIVERSITY OF MAINE
Bridges, (Henry) Styles
Colcord, Lincoln Ross
Crowe, Francis Trenholm
Farrington, Wallace Rider
Fernald, Merritt Lyndon
Merrill, Elmer Drew
Paul, Elliot Harold
Weymouth, Frank Elwin
Graduate Study
Merrill, Elmer Drew
UNIVERSITY OF MARBURG (GERMA-
NY)
Brightman, Edgar Sheffield
Coffin, Henry Sloane
Hart, Edwin Bret
Wolff, Kurt August Paul
Graduate Study
McGiffert, Arthur Cushman
UNIVERSITY OF MARYLAND
Browne, William Hand
Buckler, Thomas Hepburn
Carroll, James
Carter, Henry Rose
Godman, John Davidson
Krauth, Charles Philip
Palmer, James Croxall
Rayner, Isidor
Rose, John Carter
Sherman, Henry Clapp
Yandell, Lunsford Pitts
Graduate Study
Koch, Vivienne
Law
Boston, Charles Anderson
Bruce, William Cabell
Glenn, John Mark
Goldsborough, Thomas Alan
Mayer, Brantz
Perlman, Philip Benjamin
Ritchie, Albert Cabell
Steiner, Bernard Christian
Stockbridge, Henry
Tydings, Millard Evelyn

Medicine
Ambler, James Markham Mar-
shall
Bartholow, Roberts
Baxley, Henry Willis
Cabell, James Lawrence
Chatard, Francis Silas
Councilman, William Thomas
Davis, Charles Henry Stanley
Davis, John Wesley
Freidenwald, Aaron
Fussell, Bartholomew
Garlick, Theodatus
Graves, Rosewell Hobart
Hemmeter, John Conrad
Hoch, August
Jameson, Horatio Gates
Janney, Oliver Edward
Jarvis, William Chapman
Kirk, Norman Thomas
Palmer, John Williamson
Rogers, James Blythe
Rohé, George Henry
Ruhräh, John
Theobald, Samuel
Thomas, Richard Henry
Tiffany, Louis McLane
Wagner, Clinton
Williams, John Whitridge
Wilson, Henry Parke Custis
UNIVERSITY OF MICHIGAN
Abbot, Willis John
Abel, John Jacob
Adams, Charles Kendall
Adams, Ephraim Douglass
Adams, Franklin Pierce
Aldrich, Edgar
Andrews, Sidney
Angell, James Rowland
Auer, John
Baker, Marcus
Barnes, Mary Downing Sheldon
Beadle, William Henry Harri-
son
Beal, William James
Beecher, Charles Emerson
Bell, Frederic Somers
Bennett, Sanford Fillmore
Bigelow, Melville Madison
Blakeslee, Howard Walter
Bovie, William T.
Brennemann, Joseph
Brett, William Howard
Brown, Elmer Ellsworth
Brunton, David William
Brush, Charles Francis
Bryson, Lyman Lloyd
Burlingame, Anson
Burton, Clarence Monroe
Campbell, Douglas Houghton
Campbell, William Wallace
Carson, Simeon Lewis
Cassoday, John Bolivar
Chapin, Roy Dikeman
Clements, William Lawrence
Coffin, Howard Earle
Comstock, George Cary
Cooley, Thomas Benton
Corwin, Edward Samuel
Covici, Pascal ("Pat")
Curme, George Oliver
Curtis, Heber Doust

Curwood, James Oliver
Davis, Cushman Kellogg
Davis, Raymond Cazallis
Day, William Rufus
Denby, Edwin
Dennison, Walter
D'Ooge, Martin Luther
Doolittle, Charles Leander
Durham, Caleb Wheeler
Edmunds, Charles Wallis
Evans, Edward Payson
Evans, Lawrence Boyd
Farnsworth, Elon John
Fay, Edward Allen
Ferris, Woodbridge Nathan
Fulton, Justin Dewey
Gauss, Christian Frederick
Gay, Edwin Francis
Gomberg, Moses
Grant, Claudius Buchanan
Gunn, Ross
Hall, Asaph
Hamilton, Alice
Hanus, Paul Henry
Hapgood, Hutchins
Harrington, Mark Walrod
Hart, Edwin Bret
Hempl, George
Hill, Louis Clarence
Holden, Liberty Emery
Hopwood, Avery
Howard, Timothy Edward
Hull, Clark Leonard
Humphrey, George Magoffin
Hupp, Louis Gorham
Hussey, William Joseph
Hutchins, Harry Burns
Hyde, Arthur Mastick
Jenks, Jeremiah Whipple
Jennings, Herbert Spencer
Kinne, La Vega George
Lange, Alexis Frederick
Lemmon, John Gill
Leonard, Sterling Andrus
Lindbergh, Charles Augustus
Livingston, Burton Edward
Locy, William Albert
Long, Perrin Hamilton
Lyster, Peter Francis Le Hunte
McAndrew, William
McLaughlin, Andrew Cunning-
  ham
McMurry, Frank Morton
Mall, Franklin Paine
Marland, Ernest Whitworth
Marsh, Frank Burr
Miller, Willoughby Dayton
Morton, Julius Sterling
Moses, Bernard
Newberry, John Stoughton
Nichols, Dudley
Noble, Alfred
Novy, Frederick George
Otis, Charles Eugene
Palmer, Alice Elvira Freeman
Park, Robert Ezra
Penfield, William Lawrence
Pilcher, Lewis Stephen
Pilcher, Paul Monroe
Pitkin, Walter Boughton
Plumley, Frank
Pond, Allen Bartlit

Pond, Irving Kane
Prall, David Wight
Robinson, Albert Alonzo
Robinson, Edward Van Dyke
Robinson, Stillman Williams
Roethke, Theodore Huebner
Rogers, Henry Wade
Rosen, Joseph A.
Rowell, Chester Harvey
Salmon, Lucy Maynard
Schaeberle, John Martin
Scott, Fred Newton
Scovel, Henry Sylvester
Seager, Henry Rogers
Shafroth, John Franklin
Shepard, Fred Douglas
Shepard, James Henry
Simons, Henry Calvert
Skene, Alexander Johnston
  Chalmers
Smith, Erwin Frank
Spalding, Volney Morgan
Starrett, William Aiken
Swift, Lucius Burrie
Thomas, Calvin
Thomson, Mortimer Neal
Towne, Charles Arnette
Van Deman, Esther Boise
Vandenberg, Arthur Hendrick
Van Hook, Weller
Van Slyke, Lucius Lincoln
Vaughan, Victor Clarence
Von Ruck, Karl
Watson, James Craig
Webb, John Burkitt
Welch, Adonijah Strong
White, Stewart Edward
Wilbur, Cressy Livingston
Wilcox, Delos Franklin
Winchell, Horace Vaughn
Winchell, Newton Horace
Woodward, Robert Simpson
Woolley, John Granville
Work, Hubert
Young, Karl
Graduate Study
Adams, Ephraim Douglass
Angell, James Rowland
Bachmann, Werner Emmanuel
Briggs, Lyman James
Bryson, Lyman Lloyd
Butterfield, Kenyon Leech
Campbell, Douglas Houghton
Chamberlin, Edward Hastings
Chamberlin, Thomas Chrowder
Curtis, Heber Doust
Gauss, Christian Frederick
Gomberg, Moses
Gunn, Ross
Harrington, Mark Walrod
Holden, Liberty Emery
Kimball, (Sidney) Fiske
Leonard, Sterling Andrus
Lyster, Henry Francis Le Hunte
Marsh, Frank Burr
Pearl, Raymond
Pilcher, Lewis Stephen
Robinson, Albert Alonzo
Robinson, Edward Van Dyke
Roethke, Theodore Huebner
Rogers, Henry Wade
St. John, Charles Edward

Salmon, Lucy Maynard
Scott, Austin
Scott, Fred Newton
Shepard, James Henry
Smith, Erwin Frank
Smith, Harold Dewey
Taylor, Fred Manville
Van Deman, Esther Boise
White, Edward Higgins, II
Law
Abbot, Willis John
Ashurst, Henry Fountain
Avery, Sewell Lee
Beadle, William Henry Harri-
  son
Bigelow, Melville Madison
Bilbo, Theodore Gilmore
Brice, Calvin Stewart
Brooks, John Graham
Browne, Francis Fisher
Brucker, Wilber Marion
Burke, Thomas, 1849–1925
Burton, Clarence Monroe
Cowen, John Kissig
Darrow, Clarence Seward
Daugherty, Harry Micajah
Day, William Rufus
Dickinson, Donald McDonald
Downey, Sheridan
Haselton, Seneca
Haugen, Nils Pederson
Hitchcock, Gilbert Monell
Humphrey, George Magoffin
Kern, John Worth
Knapp, Bradford
McCumber, Porter James
McLaughlin, Andrew Cunning-
  ham
Metcalf, Henry Harrison
Murphy, Frank
O'Brien, Thomas James
Rickey, Wesley Branch
Sharp, William Graves
Shauck, John Allen
Smith, James Allen
Sutherland, George
Wood, William Robert
Medicine
Carson, Simeon Lewis
Cooley, Thomas Benton
Copeland, Royal Samuel
Dewey, Richard Smith
Edmunds, Charles Wallis
Huber, Gotthelf Carl
Hutchinson, Woods
Kellogg, John Harvey
Long, Perrin Hamilton
Mall, Franklin Paine
Mayo, William James
Moore, James Edward
Mosher, Eliza Maria
Novy, Frederick George
Peckham, George Williams
Pilcher, Lewis Stephen
Prescott, Albert Benjamin
Rockwell, Alphonso David
Weeks, John Elmer
White, Charles Abiathar
UNIVERSITY OF MINNESOTA
Adams, Cyrus Cornelius
Bell, James Ford
Cannon, Ida Maud

Carruth, Fred Hayden
Devaney, John Patrick
Dobie, Gilmour
Folin, Otto Knut Olof
Forman, Justus Miles
Frary, Francis Cowles
Fulton, John Farquhar
Goode, John Paul
Haupt, Alma Cecelia
Hodson, William
Liggett, Walter William
Mitchell, William DeWitt
Olson, Floyd Bjerstjerne
Owre, Alfred
Park, Robert Ezra
Plowman, George Taylor
Plummer, Henry Stanley
Ranson, Stephen Walter
Schall, Thomas David
Shaughnessy, Clark Daniel
Sumner, Francis Bertody
Swenson, David Ferdinand
Swift, Linton Bishop
Wilson, Halsey William
Winchell, Horace Vaughn
Dentistry
Owre, Alfred
Graduate Study
Elliott, Charles Burke
Frary, Francis Cowles
Kefauver, Grayson Neikirk
Lawrence, Ernest Orlando
Swenson, David Ferdinand
Law
Burdick, Usher Lloyd
Devaney, John Patrick
Dobie, Gilmour
Lundeen, Ernest
Medicine
Judd, Edward Starr
Wilson, Louis Blanchard
UNIVERSITY OF MISSISSIPPI
Bailey, Joseph Weldon
Baskerville, Charles
Brickell, Henry Herschel
Fulton, Robert Burwell
Galloway, Charles Betts
Gordon, James
Howry, Charles Bowen
Lambuth, James William
Malone, Walter
Manning, Vannoy Hartrog
Mayes, Edward
Valliant, Leroy Branch
Wright, Luke Edward
Young, Stark
Graduate Study
Odum, Howard Washington
Law
Brough, Charles Hillman
Farish, William Stamps
Mayes, Edward
Money, Hernando de Soto
Rankin, John Elliott
Stockdale, Thomas Ringland
UNIVERSITY OF MISSOURI
Anderson, Benjamin McAlester
Brady, Mildred Alice Edie
Broadhead, Garland Carr
Clark, Bennett Champ
Croy, Homer
Dandy, Walter Edward

Elkins, Stephen Benton
Field, Eugene
Field, Roswell Martin
Galloway, Beverly Thomas
Grasty, Charles Henry
Hodgen, John Thompson
Hough, Warwick
Jackson, Clarence Martin
Lyon, Harris Merton
Manly, Basil Maxwell
Marbut, Curtis Fletcher
Mayo, William Worrell
Nelson, Donald Marr
Powell, John Benjamin
Prentis, Henning Webb, Jr.
Rautenstrauch, Walter
Ross, Charles Griffith
Shouse, Jouett
Smith, James Allen
Spillman, William Jasper
Stewart, Walter Winne
Stone, William Joel
Walker, Robert Franklin
Graduate Study
Rautenstrauch, Walter
Law
Cannon, Clarence
Crowder, Enoch Herbert
Medicine
Jackson, Clarence Martin
UNIVERSITY OF MONTREAL (CANA-
DA)
Graduate Study
Tate, George Henry Hamilton
UNIVERSITY OF MUNICH (GERMA-
NY)
Bergmann, Max
Schindler, Kurt
Shellabarger, Samuel
Weidenreich, Franz
Weyl, Hermann
Wolff, Kurt August Paul
Graduate Study
Baker, Hugh Potter
Hooker, Samuel Cox
Noyes, William Albert
Oldfather, William Abbott
Piccard, Jean Felix
Pritchett, Henry Smith
Quinn, Arthur Hobson
Rand, Edward Kennard
Schevill, Rudolph
Van Loon, Hendrik Willem
UNIVERSITY OF MUNSTER (GERMA-
NY)
Baade, Wilhelm Heinrich Wal-
ter
UNIVERSITY OF NASHVILLE (TENN.)
Barksdale, William
Bell, John
Dickinson, Jacob McGavock
Donelson, Andrew Jackson
Fanning, Tolbert
Foster, Ephraim Hubbard
Hitchcock, Henry
Johnson, Cave
Lindsley, John Berrien
Maney, George Earle
Paine, Robert
Pillow, Gideon Johnson
Porter, James Davis
Rose, Wickliffe

Walker, William
Winston, John Anthony
Yerger, William
Graduate Study
Rose, Wickliffe
UNIVERSITY OF NEBRASKA
Abbott, Edith
Alexander, Hartley Burr
Botsford, George Willis
Briggs, Clare A.
Buckner, Emory Roy
Cather, Willa
Clements, Frederic Edward
Dern, George Henry
Emerson, Rollins Adams
Fisher, Dorothea Frances Can-
field
Guthrie, Edwin Ray, Jr.
Hollingworth, Leta Stetter
Howard, George Elliott
Hunter, Walter David
Lewis, Gilbert Newton
Magoon, Charles Edward
Patterson, Richard Cunning-
ham, Jr.
Pound, (Nathan) Roscoe
Pritchard, Frederick John
Ricketts, Howard Taylor
Rohde, Ruth Bryan Owen
Rydberg, Per Axel
Simmons, George Henry
Tate, John Torrence
Thatcher, Roscoe Wilfred
Wallace, Charles William
Warner, Amos Griswold
Warren, George Frederick
Webber, Herbert John
Westermann, William Linn
Wherry, Kenneth Spicer
Wolfe, Harry Kirke
Graduate Study
Abbott, Grace
Clements, Frederic Edward
Guthrie, Edwin Ray, Jr.
Pearson, Raymond Allen
Pound, (Nathan) Roscoe
Tate, John Torrence
Webber, Herbert John
Westermann, William Linn
Law
Schoeppel, Andrew Frank
Medicine
Gifford, Sanford Robinson
UNIVERSITY OF NEUCHATEL (SWIT-
ZERLAND)
Schinz, Albert
UNIVERSITY OF NEVADA
McCarran, Patrick Anthony
Martin, Anne Henrietta
UNIVERSITY OF NEW MEXICO
Bryan, Kirk
Johnson, Douglas Wilson
Graduate Study
Coghill, George Ellett
UNIVERSITY OF NORTH CAROLINA
Alderman, Edwin Anderson
Ashe, Thomas Samuel
Avery, William Waigstill
Aycock, Charles Brantley
Barden, Graham Arthur
Barringer, Daniel Moreau
Barringer, Rufus

Baskerville, Charles
Battle, Kemp Plummer
Battle, William Horn
Bennett, Hugh Hammond
Benton, Thomas Hart
Bingham, Robert Worth
Bingham, William, 1835–1873
Blakely, Johnston
Branch, John
Branch, Lawrence O'Bryan
Bridgers, Robert Rufus
Brown, Aaron Venable
Brown, Bedford
Burton, Hutchins Gordon
Butler, Marion
Carr, Elias
Clark, Walter
Clingman, Thomas Lanier
Connor, Robert Digges Wimberly
Denny, George Vernon, Jr.
Dick, Robert Paine
Dobbin, James Cochran
Eaton, John Henry
Ellis, John Willis
Fuller, Thomas Charles
Gales, Joseph
Graham, Edward Kidder
Graham, William Alexander
Hale, Edward Joseph
Hawks, Francis Lister
Henderson, James Pinckney
Hoey, Clyde Roark
Hopkins, Arthur Francis
King, William Rufus Devane
Kirby, George Hughes
Kolb, Reuben Francis
Lewis, William Gaston
Lynch, James Daniel
McIver, Charles Duncan
McRae, Duncan Kirkland
Mangum, Willie Person
Manning, Thomas Courtland
Marriott, Williams McKim
Mason, John Young
Means, Gaston Bullock
Moore, Bartholomew Figures
Morehead, John Motley
Murphey, Archibald De Bow
Murphy, James Bumgardner
Nicholson, Alfred Osborne Pope
Otey, James Hervey
Parker, John Johnston
Patterson, Rufus Lenoir
Pearson, Richmond Mumford
Pearson, Thomas Gilbert
Pettigrew, James Johnston
Polk, James Knox
Polk, Leonidas
Pool, John
Pou, Edward William
Ransom, Matt Whitaker
Reynolds, Robert Rice
Ruark, Robert Chester
Saunders, Romulus Mitchell
Saunders, William Laurence, 1835–1891
Sawyer, Lemuel
Schweinitz, Emil Alexander de
Settle, Thomas
Shipp, Albert Micajah

Stacy, Walter Parker
Staples, Waller Redd
Swain, David Lowry
Taylor, Hannis
Thompson, Jacob
Waddell, Alfred Moore
Webb, William Robert
Weeks, Stephen Beauregard
Wiley, Calvin Henderson
Wolfe, Thomas Clayton
Graduate Study
Wheeler, John Hill
Law
Battle, Kemp Plummer
Bickett, Thomas Walter
Gardner, Oliver Maxwell
McLean, Angus Wilton
Parker, John Johnston
Reynolds, Robert Rice
Vance, Zebulon Baird
Medicine
Simmons, James Stevens
UNIVERSITY OF NORTH DAKOTA
Aandahl, Fred George
Anderson, Maxwell
Frazier, Lynn Joseph
Lemke, William Frederick
Law
Langer, William
UNIVERSITY OF NORTHERN IOWA
Aldrich, Bess Genevra Streeter
UNIVERSITY OF OKLAHOMA
Kerr, Robert Samuel
Stigler, William Grady
Law
Long, Huey Pierce
UNIVERSITY OF OREGON
Neuberger, Richard Lewis
Robinson, Claude Everett
Medicine
McIntire, Ross
UNIVERSITY OF PADUA (ITALY)
Child, Robert
UNIVERSITY OF PARIS (FRANCE)
Chamberlain, Joseph Perkins
Graduate Study
Hills, Elijah Clarence
Page, Thomas Walker
Medicine
Coutard, Henri
UNIVERSITY OF PENNSYLVANIA
Abbott, Charles Conrad
Adams, Randolph Greenfield
Adams, Robert
Adler, Cyrus
Alden, Raymond MacDonald
Alexander, Hartley Burr
Allen, Andrew
Andrews, John
Asch, Morris Joseph
Ashhurst, John
Bache, Franklin
Barker, Wharton
Barton, Benjamin Smith
Bates, George Handy
Battey, Robert
Bell, De Benneville ("Bert")
Bibb, William Wyatt
Biddle, James
Biddle, Nicholas, 1786–1844
Bingham, William, 1752–1804
Bird, Frederic Mayer

Blitzstein, Marc
Bloor, Ella Reeve
Boller, Alfred Pancoast
Booth, James Curtis
Borie, Adolphe
Borie, Adolph Edward
Bozman, John Leeds
Bradford, Thomas
Breck, James Lloyd
Brewster, Frederick Carroll
Brinton, John Hill
Brooks, Thomas Benton
Brown, Ralph Hall
Buehler, Huber Gray
Bullitt, Henry Massie
Cadwalader, John, 1742–1786
Cadwalader, John, 1805–1879
Cadwalader, Lambert
Carson, Hampton Lawrence
Carson, Joseph
Chandler, Joseph Ripley
Chapman, Henry Cadwalader
Cheyney, Edward Potts
Clayton, Joshua
Clopton, John
Coit, Henry Augustus
Coombe, Thomas
Cope, Edward Drinker
Coxe, Eckley Brinton
Coxe, Tench
Crawford, James Pyle Wickersham
Cuyler, Theodore
Da Costa, John Chalmers
Davidson, Robert
Decatur, Stephen, 1779–1820
Dewees, William Potts
Dick, Elisha Cullen
Dickinson, Philemon
Duane, William
Duché, Jacob
Duffield, George 1794–1868
Duhring, Louis Adolphus
Du Pont, Francis Irénée
Du Pont, Henry Algernon
Durant, Thomas Jefferson
Eberle, John
Elmer, Lucius Quintius Cincinnatus
Falkner, Roland Post
Farson, Negley
Fisher, Clarence Stanley
Fleisher, Benjamin Wilfrid
Floyd, John
Frazer, John Fries
Frazer, Persifor
Frazier, Charles Harrison
Fullerton, George Stuart
Furness, Horace Howard, 1865–1930
Garnett, Alexander Yelverton Peyton
Garrison, Lindley Miller
Gibbons, Herbert Adams
Gilpin, Henry Dilworth
Gilpin, William
Goldsborough, Charles
Graydon, Alexander
Grayson, William
Green, Jacob, 1790–1841
Gregory, Caspar René
Grey, Zane

Griscom, Lloyd Carpenter
Hagner, Peter
Hale, Charles Reuben
Hanson, Alexander Contee,
1749–1806
Harding, George
Hare, John Innes Clark
Hare, William Hobart
Harrison, Charles Custis
Harshberger, John William
Hart, Charles Henry
Hartranft, Chester David
Hays, Isaac
Hemphill, Joseph
Hering, Carl
Hindman, William
Hirsch, Emil Gustav
Hirst, Barton Cooke
Hobart, John Henry
Hoch, August
Hodge, Hugh Lenox
Hopkinson, Francis
Hopkinson, Joseph
Humphreys, James
Hunt, Isaac
Huston, Charles
Hutchinson, James
Ingersoll, Edward
Jackson, David
James, Thomas Chalkley
Jastrow, Joseph
Jastrow, Morris
Jayne, Horace Fort
Keating, John Marie
Keating, William Hypolitus
Kelly, Aloysius Oliver Joseph
Kelly, Howard Atwood
Lane, William Carr
La Roche, René
Leonard, Charles Lester
Lesley, Peter
Leslie, Charles Robert
Lewis, Lawrence
Little, Charles Joseph
Lochman, John George
Long, Joseph Ragland
McClellan, George, 1849–1913
McClellan, George Brinton
M'Clintock, John
McDowell, John, 1751–1820
McGuire, Hunter Holmes
McKean, Joseph Borden
Malin, Patrick Murphy
Marchant, Henry
Mason, James Murray
Matthews, Joseph Merritt
Mease, James
Medary, Milton Bennett
Meigs, Arthur Vincent
Meigs, John Forsyth
Meigs, Montgomery Cunning-
ham
Meigs, William Montgomery
Meredith, William Morris
Merrill, James Cushing
Mifflin, Thomas
Miller, Samuel, 1769–1850
Mitchell, Silas Weir
Montgomery, James Alan
Montgomery, Thomas Harrison
Morgan, John
Morris, Anthony, 1766–1860

Morris, Edward Joy
Morton, Henry
Morton, James St. Clair
Muhlenberg, William Augustus
Neidhard, Charles
Neill, Edward Duffield
Neill, John
Neill, Thomas Hewson
Newbold, William Romaine
Newton, Richard
Newton, Richard Heber
Newton, William Wilberforce
Nichols, Charles Henry
Nolen, John
Norris, George Washington
Norris, William Fisher
North, Elisha
Oberholtzer, Ellis Paxson
Odenheimer, William Henry
Ogden, David Bayard
Osborn, Henry Stafford
Otto, John Conrad
Otto, William Tod
Paca, William
Packard, John Hooker
Pancoast, Henry Khunrath
Parke, John
Parke, John Grubb
Pemberton, Brock
Pepper, George Wharton
Pepper, William, III
Pepper, William, 1843–1898
Peters, Richard
Peterson, Charles Jacobs
Pettit, Thomas McKean
Phelps, Austin
Phillips, Francis Clifford
Phillips, Henry
Physick, Philip Syng
Piñero Jiménez, JesÚs Toribio
Price, Eli Kirk
Procter, John Robert
Quinn, Arthur Hobson
Rawle, William Henry
Read, John Meredith, 1797–
1874
Reed, Henry Hoke
Reed, William Bradford
Reese, John James
Revel, Bernard
Roberts, Owen Josephus
Rodney, Caesar Augustus, 1772
–1824
Rogers, Robert William
Rosenbach, Abraham Simon
Wolf
Sargent, Winthrop, 1825–1870
Saunders, William Lawrence,
1856–1931
Schaeffer, Charles Frederick
Schaeffer, Charles William
Schaeffer, David Frederick
Schelling, Ernest Henry
Schelling, Felix Emanuel
Scherman, Harry
Schmauk, Theodore Emanuel
Schmucker, Samuel Simon
Sergeant, Jonathan Dickinson
Sharswood, George
Skillern, Ross Hall
Sloan, Harold Paul
Smith, Albert Holmes

Smith, Samuel Harrison
Smith, Xanthus Russell
Spaeth, John Duncan
Speiser, Ephraim Avigdor
Stengel, Alfred
Stillé, Alfred
Stone, Witmer
Taylor, Francis Henry
Thomas, John Parnell
Thompson, Robert Ellis
Thornton, Henry Worth
Tilden, William Tatem ("Big
Bill")
Tilghman, Edward
Tilghman, Richard Albert
Tilghman, Tench
Tilghman, William
Towne, Henry Robinson
Turner, Samuel Hulbeart
Vezin, Hermann
Walker, Robert John
Wallace, John William
Weems, Ted
Weisenburg, Theodore Herman
Wetherill, Charles Mayer
Wetherill, Samuel, 1821–1890
Wharton, Thomas Isaac
White, William
Willard, De Forest
Willard, James Field
Williamson, Hugh
Wilson, Bird
Wood, George Bacon
Woodhouse, James
Work, Milton Cooper
Wright, Henry

Architecture
La Farge, Christopher Grant

Graduate Study
Adams, Randolph Greenfield
Bolton, Herbert Eugene
Capen, Samuel Paul
Chiera, Edward
Clay, Albert Tobias
Corwin, Edward Samuel
Coxe, Eckley Brinton
Crawford, James Pyle Wicker-
sham
Day, Frank Miles
Devine, Edward Thomas
Fauset, Jessie Redmon
Fite, Warner
Goldsborough, Charles
Goode, John Paul
Guthrie, Edwin Ray, Jr.
Huebner, Solomon Stephen
Lee, Porter Raymond
Lewis, Lawrence
Lewis, Orlando Faulkland
Lewis, William Draper
Lingelbach, Anna Lane
Linton, Ralph
Locy, William Albert
Macfarlane, Charles William
McKinley, Albert Edward
Matthews, Joseph Merritt
Meigs, William Montgomery
Miller, Edward
Miller, Willoughby Dayton
Mills, Charles Karsner
Montgomery, James Alan
Munro, Dana Carleton

Newbold, William Romaine
Oberholtzer, Ellis Paxson
Parke, John
Pearson, Leonard
Perkins, Frances
Quinn, Arthur Hobson
Ravenel, Mazyck Porcher
Reese, John James
Rosenbach, Abraham Simon
   Wolf
Schelling, Felix Emanuel
Speck, Frank Gouldsmith
Vedder, Edward Bright
Waller, Willard Walter
Wheeler, (George) Post
White, James Williams
Wieland, George Reber
Willard, James Field
Woodhouse, James
Law
Balch, Thomas Willing
Carey, Joseph Maull
Carson, Hampton Lawrence
Duff, James Henderson
Gates, Thomas Sovereign
Johnson, John Graver
Klingelsmith, Margaret Center
Lewis, William Draper
Long, Crawford Williamson
Lowndes, Lloyd
McCullough, John Griffith
Mitchell, James Tyndale
Nixon, William Penn
Parkinson, Thomas Ignatius
Pennypacker, Samuel Whitaker
Pepper, George Wharton
Price, Eli Kirk
Roberts, Owen Josephus
Schelling, Felix Emanuel
Sterne, Simon
Wickersham, George Wood-
   ward
Work, Milton Cooper
Medicine
Agnew, David Hayes
Alden, Ebenezer
Allen, Harrison
Allen, Nathan
Archer, John
Arnold, Richard Dennis
Ashhurst, John
Atlee, John Light
Awl, William Maclay
Ayer, James Cook
Bagby, George William
Baldwin, William
Barnes, Albert Coombs
Barnes, Joseph K.
Barton, John Rhea
Barton, William Paul Crillon
Bigelow, Jacob
Bird, Robert Montgomery
Bloodgood, Joseph Colt
Boyé, Martin Hans
Bridges, Robert, 1806–1882
Brincklé, William Draper
Burnett, Charles Henry
Burton, William
Caldwell, Charles
Carson, Joseph
Channing, Walter
Channing, William Francis

Chapman, Henry Cadwalader
Chapman, Nathaniel
Cohen, Jacob Da Silva Solis
Cooke, John Esten
Coxe, John Redman
Cutter, Ephraim
Darlington, William
Deaver, John Blair
Dercum, Francis Xavier
Dewees, William Potts
Dickson, Samuel Henry
Dorset, Marion
Dorsey, John Syng
Drake, Daniel
Drinker, Cecil Kent
Drown, Thomas Messenger
Dudley, Benjamin Winslow
Earle, Pliny
Edsall, David Linn
Egle, William Henry
Elmer, Jonathan
Elwyn, Alfred Langdon
Emerson, Gouverneur
English, Thomas Dunn
Eve, Paul Fitzsimons
Ewell, Thomas
Forwood, William Henry
Frazier, Charles Harrison
Garretson, James Edmund
Gerhard, William Wood
Gibbons, William, 1781–1845
Gibson, William
Gihon, Albert Leary
Goddard, Paul Beck
Gray, John Purdue
Guiteras, Juan
Guthrie, Samuel
Hamilton, Frank Hastings
Happer, Andrew Patton
Harlan, Richard
Hartshorne, Henry
Hayes, Isaac Israel
Hays, Isaac
Hayward, George
Hepburn, James Curtis
Holbrook, John Edwards
Horn, George Henry
Horner, William Edmonds
Horsfield, Thomas
Hosack, Alexander Eddy
House, Samuel Reynolds
Hubbard, John
Huger, Francis Kinloch
Huntington, Jedediah Vincent
Jackson, Abraham Reeves
Jackson, Edward
Jackson, Henry Rootes
Jackson, John Davies
Jackson, Samuel
Johnson, Joseph
Jones, Alexander
Jones, Jacob
Jones, Joseph
Kane, Elisha Kent
King, Albert Freeman Africanus
Kinloch, Robert Alexander
Kirkbride, Thomas Story
Kutland, Jared Potter
Leidy, Joseph
Leonard, Charles Lester
Lindsley, John Berrien
Littell, Squier

McCartee, Divie Bethune
McCarthy, Daniel Joseph
McClellan, George, 1796–1847
McFarland, George Bradley
McMahon, Bernard
Massey, George Betton
Mastin, Claudius Henry
Mease, James
Meigs, Arthur Vincent
Meigs, Charles Delucena
Meigs, William Montgomery
Mettauer, John Peter
Michener, Ezra
Miller, Edward
Mills, Charles Karsner
Mitchell, Albert Graeme
Mitchell, George Edward
Mitchell, John Kearsley
Mitchell, Thomas Duché
Moore, Edward Mott
Morris, Caspar
Morton, Samuel George
Mussey, Reuben Dimond
Nancrède, Charles Beylard
   Guérard de
Nassau, Robert Hamill
Neill, John
Newell, William Augustus
Norris, George Washington
Norris, William Fisher
Oliver, Charles Augustus
O'Reilly, Robert Maitland
Otis, George Alexander
Ott, Isaac
Packard, John Hooker
Pancoast, Henry Khunrath
Pancoast, Joseph
Pancoast, Seth
Parrish, Joseph
Parry, John Stubbs
Patton, John Mercer
Peale, Titian Ramsay
Pepper, William, III
Pepper, William, 1810–1864
Percival, James Gates
Philips, Martin Wilson
Potter, Nathaniel
Potts, Charles Sower
Potts, Jonathan
Pyle, Walter Lytle
Ramsey, James Gettys
   McGready
Randall, Burton Alexander
Randolph, Jacob
Rauch, John Henry
Ravenel, Edmund
Richardson, Charles Williamson
Richardson, Robert
Rogers, Robert Empie
Rosenau, Milton Joseph
Rush, James
Sargent, Fitz William
Saulsbury, Gove
Schamberg, Jay Frank
Schweinitz, George Edmund de
Seiler, Carl
Seybert, Adam
Shattuck, George Cheyne, 1783
   –1854
Short, Charles Wilkins
Simmons, James Stevens
Skillern, Ross Hall

Small, Alvan Edmond
Smith, Albert Holmes
Spencer, Pitman Clemens
Starr, Louis
Steiner, Lewis Henry
Stengel, Alfred
Stevens, Alexander Hodgdon
Stitt, Edward Rhodes
Strudwick, Edmund Charles
    Fox
Sutherland, Joel Barlow
Taylor, Joseph Wright
Thomas, Amos Russell
Thomas, Joseph
Ticknor, Francis Orray
Van Buren, William Holme
White, James William
Wickes, Stephen
Williams, William Carlos
Wistar, Caspar, 1761–1818
Witherspoon, John Alexander
Wood, George Bacon
Wood, Horatio Charles
Wood, Thomas
Woodhouse, James
Woodhull, Alfred Alexander
Woodward, Joseph Janvier
Work, Hubert·
Wormley, Theodore George
Wright, Joseph Jefferson Burr
Young, John Richardson
Wharton School of Economics
Gimbel, Bernard Feustman
Wharton School of Finance
Cheyney, Edward Potts
Gates, Thomas Sovereign
Rowe, Leo Stanton
UNIVERSITY OF PISA (ITALY)
Fermi, Enrico
Graduate Study
Fermi, Enrico
UNIVERSITY OF PITTSBURGH (PA.)
Allen, Hervey
Epstein, Abraham
Guthrie, George Wilkins
Herron, Francis Jay
Jackson, Chevalier
Jeffers, John Robinson
Johnston, William Andrew
Kaufman, George S.
Mellon, Andrew William
Negley James Scott
Oehmler, Leo Carl Martin
Reed, James Hay
Thaw, Harry Kendall
Thaw, William
Graduate Study
Epstein, Abraham
Lashley, Karl Spencer
Reid, Ira De Augustine
Law
Duff, James Henderson
Reed, David Aiken
Medicine
Hench, Philip Showalter
Henrici, Arthur Trautwein
UNIVERSITY OF PUERTO RICO
Piñero Jiménez, Jesús Toribio
UNIVERSITY OF RAVENNA (ITALY)
Pinza, Ezio

UNIVERSITY OF REDLANDS (CAL.)
Dean, Gordon Evans
MacNair, Harley Farnsworth
UNIVERSITY OF RICHMOND (VA.)
Day, James Gamble
Eggleston, George Cary
Hatcher, William Eldridge
Massey, John Edward
Snead, Thomas Lowndes
Stanard, William Glover
Taylor, George Boardman
UNIVERSITY OF ROCHESTER (N.Y.)
Anderson, Galusha
Ayer, Francis Wayland
Backus, Truman Jay
Carpenter, Stephen Haskins
Coe, George Albert
Fassett, Jacob Sloat
Fenner, Burt Leslie
Fulton, Justin Dewey
Gally, Merritt
Gates, Frederick Taylor
Gilbert, Grove Karl
Goodspeed, Thomas Wakefield
Harkness, William
Holt, Luther Emmett
Hooker, Elon Huntington
Jackson, Shirley Hardie
Johnson, Elias Henry
Kelsey, Francis Willey
MacArthur, Robert Stuart
MacVicar, Malcolm
Marble, Manton Malone
Morehouse, Henry Lyman
Moss, Lemuel
Moxom, Philip Stafford
Otis, Elwell Stephen
Payne, Sereno Elisha
Perkins, James Breck
Rauschenbusch, Walter
Robinson, Charles Mulford
Selden, George Baldwin
Sterrett, James MacBride
Stevens, George Parker
Stoddard, William Osborn
Strong, Charles Augustus
Taylor, James Monroe
Tourgée, Albion Winegar
Vedder, Edward Bright
Vedder, Henry Clay
Williams, Charles Richard
UNIVERSITY OF ST. ANDREWS
    (SCOTLAND)
Johnston, John
Graduate Study
Johnston, John
UNIVERSITY OF ST. PETERSBURG
    (RUSSIA)
Rostovtzeff, Michael Ivanovitch
Tamarkin, Jacob David
Woytinsky, Wladimir Savelie-
    vich
UNIVERSITY OF SANTO TOMAS
    (PHILIPPINES)
Quezon, Manuel Luis
UNIVERSITY OF SOUTH CAROLINA
Aiken, David Wyatt
Aiken, William
Bonham, Milledge Luke
Bratton, John
Brawley, William Hiram
Brooks, Preston Smith

Brumby, Richard Trapier
Butler, Andrew Pickens
Butler, Matthew Calbraith
Capers, William
Clinton, George Wylie
Coker, David Robert
Conner, James
Cooper, Mark Anthony
Davidson, James Wood
Davis, George
Elmore, Franklin Harper
Floyd, John Buchanan
Gaillard, Edwin Samuel
Gary, Martin Witherspoon
Gaston, James McFadden
Gayle, John
Gibbes, Robert Wilson
Gist, William Henry
Gordon, George Byron
Govan, Daniel Chevilette
Hammond, James Henry
Hampton, Wade, 1818–1902
Harper, William
Harrisse, Henry
Hilliard, Henry Washington
Houston, David Franklin
Jamison, David Flavel
Johnstone, Job
Jones, Charles Colcock
Keitt, Lawrence Massillon
Kennedy, John Doby
Kerr, Washington Caruthers
La Borde, Maximilian
Legaré, Hugh Swinton
Levin, Lewis Charles
Lewis, Dixon Hall
Logan, Thomas Muldrup, 1840
    –1914
McBryde, John McLaren
McCord, David James
McDonald, Charles James
McDuffie, George
McGowan, Samuel
McGrath, Andrew Gordon
Manly, Basil, 1798–1868
Manning, Richard Irvine, 1789–
    1836
Miller, Stephen Decatur
Moses, Franklin J.
Nisbet, Eugenius Aristides
Nott, Henry Junius
Nott, Josiah Clark
O'Neall, John Belton
Petigru, James Louis
Philips, Martin Wilson
Pickens, Francis Wilkinson
Pinckney, Henry Laurens
Porcher, Francis Peyre
Preston, William Campbell
Ravenel, Henry William
Richardson, Willard
Rivers, William James
Rogers, James Harvey
Sanders, Billington McCarter
Simonton, Charles Henry
Simpson, William Dunlap
Sims, James Marion
Smith, Ellison DuRant
Stitt, Edward Rhodes
Thompson, Waddy
Thornwell, James Henley
Tompkins, Daniel Augustus

Wigfall, Louis Trezevant
Yeadon, Richard
Graduate Study
Johnston, Olin DeWitt Talmadge
Rogers, James Harvey
Law
Blease, Coleman Livingston
Rivers, Lucius Mendel
UNIVERSITY OF SOUTH DAKOTA
Davenport, Herbert Joseph
Lawrence, Ernest Orlando
Norbeck, Peter
Law
Leedom, Boyd Stewart
UNIVERSITY OF SOUTHERN CALIFORNIA
De Sylva, George Gard "Buddy"
Earhart, Amelia Mary
Oxnam, Garfield Bromley
Wilson, Clarence True
Wright, Willard Huntington
Graduate Study
Andrus, Ethel Percy
Law
Dean, Gordon Evans
Willebrandt, Mabel Walker
Medicine
Jeffers, John Robinson
Theology
Wilson, Clarence True
UNIVERSITY OF STRASBOURG (FRANCE/GERMANY)
Graduate Study
Elkin, William Lewis
Huntington, Edward Vermilye
Lang, Henry Roseman
Sachs, Bernard
Torrey, Charles Cutler
Woods, James Haughton
Medicine
Abel, John Jacob
Loewi, Otto
UNIVERSITY OF TENNESSEE
Bridges, Thomas Jefferson Davis ("Tommy")
Camp, John Lafayette, 1828–1891
Clay, Clement Comer
Davis, Owen Gould
Dorset, Marion
Kefauver, (Carey) Estes
Krutch, Joseph Wood
McAdoo, William Gibbs
McGhee, Charles McClung
Milton, George Fort
Oakes, George Washington Ochs
Sanford, Edward Terry
Thomas, William Isaac
Graduate Study
Thomas, William Isaac
UNIVERSITY OF TEXAS
Batts, Robert Lynn
Dickson, Leonard Eugene
Hamilton, Walton Hale
Jones, Richard Foster
Joplin, Janis Lyn
Key, Valdimer Orlando, Jr.
Lanham, Frederick Garland ("Fritz")

Lomax, John Avery
Maverick, (Fontaine) Maury
Mills, Charles Wright
Pool, Joe Richard
Sheppard, John Morris
Smith, Thomas Vernor
Webb, Walter Prescott
Graduate Study
Burleson, Albert Sidney
Dickson, Leonard Eugene
Key, Valdimer Orlando, Jr.
Lomax, John Avery
Mills, Charles Wright
Smith, Thomas Vernor
Webb, Walter Prescott
Law
Connally, Thomas Terry ("Tom")
Graves, David Bibb
Gregory, Thomas Watt
Lanham, Frederick Garland ("Fritz")
Rayburn, Samuel Taliaferro ("Sam")
Sheppard, John Morris
UNIVERSITY OF THE PACIFIC (CAL.)
Rhodes, Eugene Manlove
UNIVERSITY OF THE SOUTH
Gorgas, William Crawford
Lea, Luke
Manning, William Thomas
Murphy, Edgar Gardner
Percy, William Alexander
Ravenel, Mazyck Porcher
Williams, John Sharp
Graduate Study
Lea, Luke
UNIVERSITY OF TORONTO (CANADA)
Bensley, Robert Russell
Cullen, Thomas Stephen
Daly, Reginald Aldworth
Duffy, Francis Patrick
Jeffrey, Edward Charles
Kelley, Edith Summers
Keys, Clement Melville
Lawson, Andrew Cowper
Lillie, Frank Rattray
MacCallum, William George
McCrae, Thomas
McMurrich, James Playfair
Morgan, John Harcourt Alexander
Shotwell, James Thomson
Townsend, Willard Saxby, Jr.
Graduate Study
Gortner, Ross Aiken
Jeffrey, Edward Charles
Lawson, Andrew Cowper
McCrae, Thomas
McMurrich, James Playfair
Smith, Theobald
Medicine
Bensley, Robert Russell
McCrae, Thomas
UNIVERSITY OF TUBINGEN (GERMANY)
Graduate Study
Gottheil, Richard James Horatio
UNIVERSITY OF UTAH
Clark, Joshua Reuben, Jr.
DeVoto, Bernard Augustine

McKay, David Oman
Smith, George Albert
Thomas, Elbert Duncan
UNIVERSITY OF VERMONT
Albee, Ernest
Allen, George
Ashmun, Jehudi
Atwater, Wilbur Olin
Austin, Warren Robinson
Bennett, Edmund Hatch
Brown, George, 1823–1892
Collamer, Jacob
Converse, John Heman
Deming, Philander
Dewey, John
Ditson, George Leighton
Eastman, Charles Gamage
Eaton, Dorman Bridgman
Fisk, Wilbur
Hale, Robert Safford
Hammond, James Bartlett
Harris, Paul Percy
Haselton, Seneca
Houghton, Henry Oscar
Jameson, John Alexander
Kasson, John Adam
Kingsley, Darwin Pearl
Miller, Jonathan Peckham
Peabody, Selim Hobart
Polak, John Osborn
Porter, Russell Williams
Powell, Thomas Reed
Pratt, Sereno Stansbury
Raymond, Henry Jarvis
Shedd, William Greenough Thayer
Smith, Chauncey
Smith, John Gregory
Spaulding, Edward Gleason
Stevens, Benjamin Franklin
Stevens, Hiram Fairchild
Stevens, Thaddeus
Stewart, Alvan
Thompson, Zadock
Tuttle, Herbert
Wheeler, James Rignall
Wheeler, John Martin
Wheeler, William Almon
Worcester, Samuel Austin
Graduate Study
Kerr, Sophie
Medicine
Wheeler, John Martin
UNIVERSITY OF VIENNA (AUSTRIA)
Bonsal, Stephen
Fenichel, Otto
Frank, Philipp G.
Grund, Francis Joseph
Koller, Carl
Landsteiner, Karl
Prokosch, Eduard
Reik, Theodor
Schumpeter, Joseph Alois
Graduate Study
Moore, Henry Ludwell
Park, William Hallock
Reik, Theodor
Medicine
Sakel, Manfred Joshua
UNIVERSITY OF VIRGINIA
Adams, Daniel Weissiger
Bailey, Joseph Weldon

Baldwin, John Brown
Barbour, John Strode, Jr.
Bayly, Thomas Henry
Beale, Richard Lee Turberville
Beall, John Yates
Beatty, William Henry
Blackford, Charles Minor
Boyd, David French
Brannon, Henry
Breckinridge, Desha
Briggs, Charles Augustus
Broadhead, James Overton
Broadus, John Albert
Bruce, Philip Alexander
Bruce, William Cabell
Bryan, John Stewart
Byrd, Richard Evelyn
Cabell, James Lawrence
Calvert, Charles Benedict
Carr, Elias
Carter, Henry Rose
Chalmers, James Ronald
Cocke, Philip St. George
Conrad, Holmes
Dabney, Robert Lewis
Dabney, Virginius
Davis, William Augustine
Dinwiddie, Albert Bledsoe
Farrar, Edgar Howard
Faulkner, Charles James
Fenner, Charles Erasmus
Fishback, William Meade
Fleming, Aretas Brooks
Fortier, Alcée
Frost, Wade Hampton
Garnett, James Mercer
Garnett, Muscoe Russell Hunt-
er
Gholson, Thomas Saunders
Gilliss, James Melville
Goss, James Walker
Graves, Alvin Cushman
Greenway, John Campbell
Halsey, William Frederick, Jr.
Harris, John Woods
Harris, Wiley Pope
Harrison, Gessner
Harrison, James Albert
Henry, William Wirt
Herbert, Hilary Abner
Holcombe, James Philemon
Humphreys, Wiliam Jackson
Hunter, Robert Mercer Talia-
ferro
Jackson, Howell Edmunds
Jesse, Richard Henry
Johnston, George Ben
Jones, John William
Joynes, Edward Southey
Kane, Elisha Kent
Keith, James
Lancaster, Henry Carrington
Lane, James Henry
Lay, Henry Champlin
Leathers, Waller Smith
Lewis, Fulton, Jr.
Lewis, James Hamilton
Ligon, Thomas Watkins
Lucas, Daniel Bedinger
McBryde, John McLaren
McCabe, William Gordon
McCausland, John

McCormick, Robert Sanderson
McEnery, Samuel Douglas
Mackenzie, John Noland
Manning, Richard Irvine
Martin, Thomas Staples
Mastin, Claudius Henry
Mathews, Henry Mason
Maury, Dabney Herndon
Maxwell, Augustus Emmett
Milton, George Fort
Minor, Benjamin Blake
Minor, John Barbee
Minor, Raleigh Colston
Moore, John Bassett
Mosby, John Singleton
Page, Thomas Walker
Pendleton, William Kimbrough
Peterkin, George William
Poe, Edgar Allan
Polk, Lucius Eugene
Pollard, Edward Alfred
Preston, John Smith
Randolph, George Wythe
Raney, George Pettus
Reed, Walter
Reese, Charles Lee
Robertson, William Joseph
Rodgers, John, 1812–1882
Rood, Ogden Nicholas
Saulsbury, Willard, 1861–1927
Slaughter, Philip
Smith, John Lawrence
Smith, William Waugh
Southall, James Cocke
Sterrett, John Robert Sitlington
Stettinius, Edward Reilly
Stevenson, John White
Stuart, Alexander Hugh
Holmes
Swann, Thomas
Taylor, George Boardman
Thompson, John Reuben
Timberlake, Gideon
Toulmin, Harry Theophilus
Toy, Crawford Howell
Trent, William Peterfield
Tucker, Henry St. George
Tucker, John Randolph
Tucker, Nathaniel Beverley
Tutwiler, Henry
Underwood, Oscar Wilder
Vawter, Charles Erastus
Venable, Charles Scott
Venable, Francis Preston
Walker, Alexander
Watson, John William Clark
Watts, Thomas Hill
Wertenbaker, Charles Christian
Wertenbaker, Thomas Jefferson
White, Henry Clay
Whitsitt, William Heth
Wigfall, Louis Trezevant
Wilson, William Lyne
Young, Hugh Hampton
Young, Robert Ralph
Graduate Study
Bryan, John Stewart
Cabell, James Lawrence
Curtis, Heber Doust
Dabney, Charles William
Dargan, Edwin Preston
Dinwiddie, Albert Bledsoe

Dinwiddie, Courtenay
Du Bose, William Porcher
Lancaster, Henry Carrington
Mathews, Henry Mason
Smith, Henry Louis
Spencer, Samuel
Taylor, Robert Tunstall
Trent, William Peterfield
Tyler, Lyon Gardiner
Wertenbaker, Thomas Jefferson
Wilson, James Southall
Young, Hugh Hampton
Law
Bingham, Robert Worth
Blackford, Charles Minor
Clarke, James Paul
Clay, Clement Claiborne
Cook, Philip
Culberson, Charles Allen
Davis, Henry Winter
Field, Marshall, IV
Flexner, Bernard
Garnett, Muscoe Russell Hunt-
er
Grady, Henry Woodfin
Green, Benjamin Edwards
Gregory, Thomas Watt
Hines, Walker Downer
Hubbard, Richard Bennett
Johnson, Louis Arthur
Kennedy, Robert Francis
Lile, William Minor
Long, Joseph Ragland
McIlwaine, Richard
McReynolds, James Clark
Minor, Raleigh Colston
Montague, Andrew Jackson
Moore, George Fleming
Orr, James Lawrence
Page, Thomas Nelson
Peyton, John Lewis
Preston, William Ballard
Pryor, Roger Atkinson
Randolph, Edmund, 1819–1861
Reynolds, Richard Samuel, Sr.
Seddon, James Alexander
Slemp, Campbell Bascom
Snead, Thomas Lowndes
Stephens, Linton
Swanson, Claude Augustus
Thornton, Jessy Quinn
Tree, Lambert
Tyler, Lyon Gardiner
Warrington, Albert Powell
Willard, Joseph Edward
Williams, John Sharp
Wilson, Woodrow
Wise, John Sergeant
Medicine
Burrow, Trigant
Dyer, Isadore
Frost, Wade Hampton
Kean, Jefferson Randolph
Leathers, Waller Smith
Mackenzie, John Noland
Reed, Walter
Wilmer, William Holland
Young, Hugh Hampton
UNIVERSITY OF WARSAW (POLAND)
Wiener, Leo
Znaniecki, Florian Witold

UNIVERSITY OF WASHINGTON
Bartlett, Edward Lewis ("Bob")
Bell, Eric Temple
Cayton, Horace Roscoe
Fairchild, Muir Stephen
Gaston, Herbert Earle
Groves, Leslie Richard, Jr.
Irwin, Robert Benjamin
Langlie, Arthur Bernard
MacDonald, Betty
Meany, Edmond Stephen
Toklas, Alice Babette
Graduate Study
Jeffers, John Robinson
Meany, Edmond Stephen
Nelson, Marjorie Maxine
Law
Johnston, Eric Allen
Langlie, Arthur Bernard
Schwellenbach, Lewis Baxter
UNIVERSITY OF WESTERN ONTARIO
(CANADA)
Johnson, Edward
UNIVERSITY OF WISCONSIN
Adams, Henry Cullen
Andrews, John Bertram
Baker, Carl Lotus
Bascom, Florence
Bashford, James Whitford
Bleyer, Willard Grosvenor
Bloodgood, Joseph Colt
Bolton, Herbert Eugene
Bruce, Andrew Alexander
Cajori, Florian
Chafin, Eugene Wilder
Davies, Joseph Edward
Elvehjem, Conrad Arnold
Esch, John Jacob
Fallows, Samuel
Farrington, Joseph Rider
Favill, Henry Baird
Fearing, Kenneth Flexner
Ford, Guy Stanton
Gale, Zona
Gasser, Herbert Spencer
Gesell, Arnold Lucius
Goetz, George Washington
Gregory, Charles Noble
Gregory, Stephen Strong
Hansberry, Lorraine Vivian
Hoan, Daniel Webster
Hooton, Earnest Albert
Hopson, Howard Colwell
Hoyme, Gjermund
Huebner, Solomon Stephen
Huntington, William Edmonds
Jansky, Karl Guthe
Johnson, Hugh Samuel
Kremers, Edward
Krug, Julius Albert
La Follette, Philip Fox
La Follette, Robert Marion
La Follette, Robert Marion, Jr.
Leiserson, William Morris
Libby, Orin Grant
Lord, Henry Curwen
McNair, Fred Walter
Maslow, Abraham H.
Mason, Max
Mich, Daniel Danforth
Muir, John
Nelson, Julius

Ochsner, Albert John
Pammel, Louis Hermann
Perlman, Selig
Persons, Warren Milton
Pfund, August Herman
Purdy, Corydon Tyler
Rawlings, Marjorie Kinnan
Reinsch, Paul Samuel
Robertson, William Spence
Robinson, Frederick Byron
Roe, Gilbert Ernstein
Rublee, Horace
Rutledge, Wiley Blount
Savage, John Lucian ("Jack")
Schwartz, Delmore David
Showerman, Grant
Simons, Algie Martin
Slichter, Sumner Huber
Spooner, John Coit
Turner, Frederick Jackson
Van Hise, Charles Richard
Vilas, William Freeman
Walsh, Thomas James
Wilcox, Ella Wheeler
Witte, Edwin Emil
Wright, Frank Lloyd
Zuppke, Robert Carl
Graduate Study
Andrews, John Bertram
Bagley, William Chandler
Baker, Carl Lotus
Baker, Oliver Edwin
Bascom, Florence
Bleyer, Willard Grosvenor
Bloomfield, Leonard
Bolton, Herbert Eugene
Brown, Ralph Hall
Buley, Roscoe Carlyle
Cope, Arthur Clay
Dorn, Harold Fred
Elvehjem, Conrad Arnold
Ford, Guy Stanton
Gale, Zona
Hoagland, Dennis Robert
Hooton, Earnest Albert
Huebner, Solomon Stephen
Hull, Clark Leonard
Jansky, Karl Guthe
Johnson, Hugh Samuel
Jordan, Virgil Justin
Krug, Julius Albert
Libby, Orin Grant
McCarthy, Charles
Maslow, Abraham H.
Mills, Charles Wright
Nelson, Julius
Perlman, Selig
Persons, Warren Milton
Pritchard, Frederick John
Purdy, Corydon Tyler
Reinsch, Paul Samuel
Robertson, William Spence
Showerman, Grant
Slichter, Sumner Huber
West, Allen Brown
Willard, James Field
Witte, Edwin Emil
Woodbury, Helen Laura Sumner
Young, Allyn Abbott
Law
Bruce, Andrew Alexander

Comstock, George Cary
Davies, Joseph Edward
Esch, John Jacob
Gregory, Charles Noble
Gregory, Stephen Strong
La Follette, Philip Fox
Pettigrew, Richard Franklin
Roe, Gilbert Ernstein
Tawney, James Albertus
Wiley, Alexander
Winslow, John Bradley
UNIVERSITY OF WURZBURG (GERMANY)
Barus, Carl
Wertheimer, Max
Graduate Study
Robb, William Lispenard
UNIVERSITY OF WYOMING
Downey, June Etta
Downey, Sheridan
UNIVERSITY OF ZURICH (SWITZERLAND)
Cabot, Godfrey Lowell
Loeb, Leo
Sigerist, Henry Ernest
Znaniecki, Florian Witold
Graduate Study
Clark, John Bates
Herty, Charles Holmes
Ostromislensky, Iwan Iwanowich
Medicine
Ostromislensky, Iwan Iwanowich
UPPER IOWA UNIVERSITY
Mott, John R.
URBANA UNIVERSITY (OHIO)
Du Pont, Thomas Coleman
URBAN COLLEGE OF PROPAGANDA, ROME (ITALY)
Mundelein, George William
URBANIA COLLEGE OF THE SACRED CONGREGATION DE PROPAGANDA FIDE (ITALY)
Meyer, Albert Gregory
URSINUS ACADEMY AND COLLEGE (PA.)
Yerkes, Robert Mearns
UTICA ACADEMY (N.Y.)
Butterfield, Daniel
Caton, John Dean
Dwight, Harrison Gray Otis
Hoadley, John Chipman
James, Thomas Lemuel
Seymour, Horatio
Stevens, George Washington
Walcott, Charles Doolittle
Williams, George Huntington

VALPARAISO NORMAL SCHOOL (IND.)
Gerber, (Daniel) Frank
VALPARAISO UNIVERSITY (IND.)
Blaine, John James
Campbell, William Edward March
Norris, George William
Teeple, John Edgar
VANCEBURG SEMINARY (KY.)
White, Alma Bridwell

VANDERBILT UNIVERSITY (TENN.)
Alexander, Will Winton
Altsheler, Joseph Alexander
Barnard, Edward Emerson
Craighead, Edwin Boone
Davis, Jeff
Davis, Norman Hezekiah
Dowling, Noel Thomas
Fletcher, Duncan Upshaw
Folk, Joseph Wingate
Hamilton, Walton Hale
Jarrell, Randall
Knapp, Bradford
Lanham, Frederick Garland
  ("Fritz")
McGill, Ralph Emerson
McReynolds, James Clark
Melton, James
Moore, (Austin) Merrill
Pusey, William Allen
Rice, (Henry) Grantland
Sloan, George Arthur
Smith, James Perrin
Tigert, John James
Tigert, John James, IV
Turner, Fennell Parrish
Graduate Study
Jarrell, Randall
Pusey, William Allen
Law
Bilbo, Theodore Gilmore
Byrns, Joseph Wellington
Clement, Frank Goad
Fletcher, Duncan Upshaw
Hastings, William Wirt
Medicine
Moore, (Austin) Merrill
VASSAR COLLEGE (N.Y.)
Barrows, Alice Prentice
Benedict, Ruth Fulton
Bentley, Elizabeth Terrill
Blatch, Harriot Eaton Stanton
Boissevain, Inez Milholland
Carr, Charlotte Elizabeth
Crapsey, Adelaide
Davis, Katharine Bement
Hatcher, Orie Latham
Ladd-Franklin, Christine
Lathrop, Julia Clifford
Leach, Abby
Millay, Edna St. Vincent
Norris, Mary Harriott
Putnam, Helen Cordelia
Richards, Ellen Henrietta Swallow
Rickert, Martha Edith
Rourke, Constance Mayfield
Semple, Ellen Churchill
Stimson, Julia Catherine
Tappan, Eva March
Tutwiler, Julia Strudwick
Washburn, Margaret Floy
Webster, Alice Jane Chandler
Whitney, Mary Watson
VICTORIA COLLEGE (ENGLAND)
Graduate Study
Dakin, Henry Drysdale
VICTORIA UNIVERSITY (ENGLAND)
Todd, Thomas Wingate
**VIENNA ACADEMY OF FINE ARTS
  (AUSTRIA)**
Mestrovic, Ivan

Schindler, Rudolph Michael
**VIENNA ACADEMY OF MUSIC
  (AUSTRIA)**
Rodzinski, Artur
VIENNA CONSERVATORY (AUSTRIA)
Bodanzky, Artur
Goldmark, Rubin
**VILNA TEACHERS INSTITUTE
  (RUSSIA)**
Cahan, Abraham
VIRGINIA MILITARY INSTITUTE
Buckner, Simon Bolivar
Colston, Raleigh Edward
Conrad, Holmes
Culberson, Charles Allen
Echols, John
Ezekiel, Moses Jacob
Faulkner, Charles James
Fry, Birkett Davenport
Harris, William Alexander
Jones, Thomas Goode
Kemper, James Lawson
Lane, James Henry
McCausland, John
Mahone, William
Marshall, George Catlett, Jr.
Martin, Thomas Staples
Maverick, (Fontaine) Maury
Murfee, James Thomas
Patton, George Smith
Peyton, John Lewis
Polk, William Mechlenburg
Rockwell, Kiffin Yates
Rodes, Robert Emmett
Ross, Erskine Mayo
Shipp, Scott
Short, Joseph Hudson, Jr.
Slemp, Campbell Bascom
Walker, Reuben Lindsay
Willard, Joseph Edward
Wise, John Sergeant
VIRGINIA POLYTECHNIC INSTITUTE
Dodd, William Edward
Pick, Lewis Andrew
Graduate Study
Dodd, William Edward
VIRGINIA UNION UNIVERSITY
Johnson, Charles Spurgeon
Powell, Adam Clayton, Sr.
VOLHYNIAN THEOLOGICAL SEMINARY (RUSSIA)
Leonty, Metropolitan

WABASH COLLEGE (IND.)
Acker, Charles Ernest
Anderson, Edwin Hatfield
Arnold, Thurman Wesley
Bassett, James
Black, John Charles
Hays, Will H.
McDonald, Joseph Ewing
Marshall, Thomas Riley
Patterson, Thomas MacDonald
Record, Samuel James
Reynolds, Joseph Jones
Rose, Joseph Nelson
Rovenstine, Emery Andrew
Whetzel, Herbert Hice
Wilson, Henry Lane
Wilson, John Lockwood
Woods, William Allen

WADDEL'S ACADEMY (S.C.)
Butler, Andrew Pickens
Calhoun, John Caldwell
Collier, Henry Watkins
Curry, Jabez Lamar Monroe
Gilmer, George Rockingham
Legaré, Hugh Swinton
Longstreet, Augustus Baldwin
Petigru, James Louis
WAKE FOREST COLLEGE (N.C.)
Adams, Joseph Quincy
Bailey, Josiah William
Bickett, Thomas Walter
Cash, Wilbur Joseph
Dixon, Thomas
Kitchin, Claude
Kitchin, William Walton
Royster, James Finch
Simmons, Furnifold McLendel
Stallings, Laurence Tucker
Yates, Matthew Tyson
Graduate Study
Adams, Joseph Quincy
Law
Cash, Wilbur Joseph
WARSAW CONSERVATORY (POLAND)
Landowska, Wanda Aleksandra
WASHBURN COLLEGE
Menninger, William Claire
WASHBURN UNIVERSITY (KAN.)
Hope, Clifford Ragsdale
**WASHINGTON ACADEMY (See
  WASHINGTON AND LEE UNIVERSITY)**
WASHINGTON AND JEFFERSON COLLEGE (PA.)
Agnew, David Hayes
Alden, William Livingston
Andrews, Lorrin
Baird, Absalom
Baird, Robert
Beaver, James Addams
Bissell, George Henry
Blaine, James Gillespie
Breckinridge, Robert Jefferson
Breckinridge, William Campbell
  Preston
Bristow, Benjamin Helm
Brown, Fayette
Chambers, Ezekiel Forman
Colwell, Stephen
Cooper, James
Cort, Edwin Charles
Dodd, Samuel Calvin Tate
Ewing, James Caruthers Rhea
Fisher, Daniel Webster
Fleming, John
Foster, Stephen Collins
Fry, Birkett Davenport
Geary, John White
Gildersleeve, Basil Lanneau
Good, Adolphus Clemens
Greer, David Hummell
Hamilton, Maxwell McGaughey
Hamilton, William Thomas
Hemphill, John
Hendricks, William
Imboden, John Daniel
Jacobs, Michael
Jenkins, Albert Gallatin
Kemper, James Lawson
Lane, William Carr

Latham, Milton Slocum
Leffler, Shepherd
Letterman, Jonathan
Lowes, John Livingston
Lowndes, Lloyd
Lucas, James H.
Lyon, James Benjamin
McCartney, Washington
McCay, Charles Francis
McCook, Henry Christopher
McCook, John James
McCormick, Samuel Black
McFarland, George Bradley
McFarland, Samuel Gamble
McGuffey, William Holmes
McKennan, Thomas McKean
   Thompson
McLaren, William Edward
Marquis, John Abner
Mateer, Calvin Wilson
Mathews, John Alexander
Mercur, Ulysses
Milligan, Robert
Mitchell, William, 1832–1900
Morgan, George Washington
Muhlenberg, Frederick Augus-
   tus
Nevin, Alfred
Nevin, Edwin Henry
Nevin, Robert Peebles
Passavant, William Alfred
Pickens, Israel
Quay, Matthew Stanley
Riddle, Matthew Brown
Riggs, Stephen Return
Rollins, James Sidney
Sargent, Fitz William
Speer, William
Stanbery, Henry
Stewart, Robert
Stockdale, Thomas Ringland
Strother, David Hunter
Swank, James Moore
Thompson, Josiah Van Kirk
Vallandigham, Clement Laird
Wallace, Henry
Watson, David Thompson
Wherry, Elwood Morris
Wines, Frederick Howard
Wise, Henry Alexander
Woodrow, James
Wright, Joseph Jefferson Burr
Wylie, Andrew
Graduate Study
Cort, Edwin Charles
Lowes, John Livingston
WASHINGTON AND LEE UNIVERSITY
Alexander, Archibald
Allen, John James
Ambler, James Markham Mar-
   shall
Anderson, David Lawrence
Ayres, Brown
Brown, Clarence James
Caruthers, William Alexander
Chamberlain, George Earle
Chavis, John
Davis, John William
Dillard, James Hardy
Echols, John
Ellis, Powhatan
Foote, Henry Stuart

Foster, Murphy James
Glenn, John Mark
Hall, Luther Egbert
Harris, John Woods
Hoge, Moses
Holcombe, William Henry
Humphreys, Milton Wylie
Humphreys, Wiliam Jackson
Lamar, Joseph Rucker
Le Moyne, Francis Julius
Letcher, John
McDowell, James
McKee, John
McRae, Thomas Chipman
Manly, Basil Maxwell
Moore, Andrew
Morrison, William McCutchan
Nelson, David
O'Ferrall, Charles Triplett
O'Neal, Edward Asbury, III
Owen, Robert Latham
Page, Thomas Nelson
Parker, Richard Elliott
Plumer, William Swan
Poindexter, Miles
Preston, William Campbell
Priestley, James
Rice, John Holt
Ruffner, Henry
Ruffner, William Henry
Shepard, Seth
Summers, George William
Sydenstricker, Edgar
Tucker, Henry St. George
Graduate Study
Davis, John William
Dillard, James Hardy
Glenn, John Mark
Sydenstricker, Edgar
Law
Baker, Newton Diehl
Dillard, James Hardy
WASHINGTON COLLEGE (CONN.)
   (See TRINITY COLLEGE)
WASHINGTON COLLEGE (MD.)
Emory, John
Goldsborough, Thomas Alan
Harrington, Samuel Maxwell
Townsend, George Alfred
Veazey, Thomas Ward
Wilmer, William Holland
WASHINGTON COLLEGE (TENN.)
Carter, Samuel Powhatan
Ramsey, James Gettys
   McGready
Temple, Oliver Perry
Vance, Zebulon Baird
WASHINGTON COLLEGIATE INSTI-
   TUTE (N.Y.)
Clarke, Thomas Benedict
WASHINGTON STATE COLLEGE
Murrow, Edward (Egbert)
   Roscoe
WASHINGTON STATE SCHOOL OF
   OPTOMETRY
Wallgren, Mon[rad] C[harles]
WASHINGTON UNIVERSITY (MO.)
Anderson, Paul Y.
Bates, John Coalter
Burman, John Miller
Cameron, William Evelyn
Crunden, Frederick Morgan

Engelmann, George Julius
Fox, William Carlton
Francis, David Rowland
Harris, James Arthur
Hoagland, Charles Lee
Holden, Edward Singleton
Hurst, Fannie
Johnston, William Hartshorne
More, Paul Elmer
Stolberg, Benjamin
Taussig, Frank William
Wislocki, George Bernays
Graduate Study
More, Paul Elmer
Niebuhr, Helmut Richard
Webber, Herbert John
Law
Davis, Dwight Filley
Long, Breckinridge
Nast, Condé Montrose
Medicine
Goldstein, Max Aaron
Hoagland, Charles Lee
Porter, William Townsend
Taussig, Frederick Joseph
WATERVILLE COLLEGE (See COLBY
   COLLEGE)
WAYNE STATE UNIVERSITY (MICH.)
Reuther, Walter Philip
WEATHERFORD COLLEGE (TEX.)
Lanham, Frederick Garland
   ("Fritz")
WEBB INSTITUTE OF NAVAL ARCHI-
   TECTURE (N.Y.)
Ward, Charles Alfred
WELLESLEY COLLEGE
Bates, Katharine Lee
Breckenridge, Sophonisba Pres-
   ton
Cannon, Annie Jump
Coyle, Grace Longwell
Davies, Maria Thompson
Isom, Mary Frances
Kingsley, Elizabeth Seelman
Nichols, Ruth Rowland
Pendleton, Ellen Fitz
Plummer, Mary Wright
Whitney, Charlotte Anita
Woodbury, Helen Laura Sumn-
   er
Graduate Study
Bates, Katharine Lee
Pendleton, Ellen Fitz
WESLEYAN COLLEGE (ENGLAND)
Davies, John Vipond
WESLEYAN COLLEGE (MONT.)
Cooper, Gary
WESLEYAN UNIVERSITY (CONN.)
Allyn, Robert
Andrews, Edward Gayer
Arnold, Harold DeForest
Atwater, Wilbur Olin
Baker, Osmon Cleander
Bangs, Francis Nehemiah
Brewer, David Josiah
Brooks, Byron Alden
Buckley, James Monroe
Buckley, Samuel Botsford
Burrowes, Edward Thomas
Burton, Nathaniel Hudson
Child, Charles Manning
Cummings, Joseph

Davison, George Willets
Dorchester, Daniel
Dow, Lorenzo
Foss, Cyrus David
Goode, George Brown
Gordy, John Pancoast
Greenslet, Ferris
Harris, Daniel Lester
Haven, Erastus Otis
Haven, Gilbert
Hendrix, Eugene Russell
Hoyt, Albert Harrison
Hubbard, Henry Griswold
Hurlbut, Jesse Lyman
Inglis, Alexander James
Judd, Charles Hubbard
Judd, Orange
Kemmerer, Edwin Walter
Kidder, Daniel Parish
Knapp, Martin Augustine
Lee, James Melvin
Mather, Samuel Livingston
Merrick, Frederick
Merrill, Elmer Truesdell
Mitchell, Hinckley Gilbert
  Thomas
Mudge, James
Peirce, Bradford Kinney
Pitkin, Frederick Walker
Ray, Charles Bennett
Rice, William North
Roberts, Benjamin Titus
Robinson, William
Robinson William Callyhan
Rosa, Edward Bennett
Rust, Richard Sutton
Sanford, Elias Benjamin
Saxe, John Godfrey
Smith, Bruce
Squire, Watson Carvosso
Steele, Daniel
Stevens, Abel
Stiles, Charles Wardell
Strong, James
Thorndike, Ashley Horace
Thorndike, Edward Lee
Thorndike, Lynn
Thorpe, Thomas Bangs
True, Alfred Charles
Upham, Samuel Foster
Vanderbilt, Arthur T.
Van Vleck, Edward Burr
Warren, Henry White
Warren, William Fairfield
Weeks, Joseph Dame
Wiley, Ephraim Emerson
Winchell, Alexander
Winchester, Caleb Thomas
Wood, Thomas Bond
Graduate Study
  Child, Charles Manning
  Merrill, Elmer Truesdell
WESTERN COLLEGE (N.MEX.)
  Rust, John Daniel
WESTERN COLLEGIATE INSTITUTE
  (IOWA)
  Howard, Edgar
WESTERN RESERVE ECLECTIC IN-
  STITUTE (See HIRAM COL-
  LEGE)

WESTERN RESERVE UNIVERSITY
  (OHIO)
Allen, Florence Ellinwood
Allison, William Boyd
Axtell, Samel Beach
Brett, William Howard
Chamberlain, Jacob
Chamberlain, William Isaac
Clarke, John Hessin
Curtis, William Eleroy
Elwell, John Johnson
Flexner, Jennie Maas
Foote, Lucius Harwood
Hanna, Marcus Alonzo
Harvey, Louis Powell
Hoadly, George
Hough, Franklin Benjamin
Ladd, George Trumbull
Leggett, Mortimer Dormer
Lord, Asa Dearborn
McGiffert, Arthur Cushman
Newberry, John Strong
Paine, Halbert Eleazer
Ranney, Ruffus Percival
Robertson, James Alexander
Seymour, Thomas Day
Strong, Josiah
Wheeler, Wayne Bidwell
Willis, Henry Parker
Woods, William Burnham
Graduate Study
  Allen, Florence Ellinwood
Medicine
  Crile, George Washington
  Lower, William Edgar
WESTERN THEOLOGICAL SEMINARY
  (ILL.)
  Bell, Bernard Iddings
  Sumner, Walter Taylor
WESTERN THEOLOGICAL SEMINARY
  (OHIO)
Ewing, James Caruthers Rhea
Fisher, Daniel Webster
Good, Adolphus Clemens
Happer, Andrew Patton
Jones, John Percival
Kyle, James Henderson
Lowes, John Livingston
McCook, Henry Christopher
McCormick, Samuel Black
McFarland, Samuel Gamble
Marquis, John Abner
Mateer, Calvin Wilson
Nevin, Alfred
Nevin, Edwin Henry
Riddle, Matthew Brown
Riggs, Stephen Return
Schereschewsky, Samuel Isaac
  Joseph
Speer, William
Tanner, Benjamin Tucker
Thompson, William Oxley
Wilson, Samuel Graham
Young, Samuel Hall
WESTFIELD ACADEMY (MASS.)
Allen, Jeremiah Mervin
Allen, Richard Lamb
Chapin, Chester William
Clemmer, Mary
Ditson, George Leighton
Goodrich, Benjamin Franklin
Hall, Arethusa

King, Thomas Butler
Orton, Edward Francis Baxter
Pease, Elisha Marshall
Perkins, Justin
Stockton, Charles G.
Thayer, Amos Madden
Williston, Samuel
WESTMINSTER COLLEGE (MO.)
McAfee, John Armstrong
Shields, George Howell
Shipp, Scott
WESTMINSTER COLLEGE (PA.)
Miller, James Russell
Potts, Benjamin Franklin
Thompson, Samuel Rankin
WESTON COLLEGE (MASS.)
O'Callahan, Joseph Timothy
Graduate Study
O'Callahan, Joseph Timothy
WEST POINT (See UNITED STATES
  MILITARY ACADEMY)
WESTTOWN BOARDING SCHOOL
  (PA.)
Cope, Edward Drinker
Cox, Hannah Peirce
Cox, Samuel Hanson
Emerson, Gouverneur
Gummere, John
Hayes, Isaac Israel
Hazard, Rowland Gibson
Hazard, Thomas Robinson
Magill, Edward Hicks
Morton, Samuel George
Say, Thomas
Sharpless, Isaac
Smith, Albert Holmes
Smith, John Joy
Wood, James, 1839–1925
WEST VIRGINIA UNIVERSITY
Brooke, Charles Frederick
  Tucker
Hough, Walter
Kilgore, Harley Martin
Lashley, Karl Spencer
Neely, Matthew Mansfield
Graduate Study
Brooke, Charles Frederick
  Tucker
Hough, Walter
Kagan, Henry Enoch
Law
Yost, Fielding Harris
WHEATON COLLEGE (MASS.)
Lincoln, Mary Johnson Bailey
Parkhurst, John Adelbert
Stoddard, Elizabeth Drew Bar-
  stow
Woolley, Mary Emma
WHITESTOWN SEMINARY (N.Y.)
Child, Frank Samuel
Deming, Philander
Gaynor, William Jay
Morris, Edward Dafydd
Roberts, Ellis Henry
WHITMAN COLLEGE (WASH.)
Nelson, Marjorie Maxine
WIDENER COLLEGE (PA.)
Riddle, Samuel Doyle
WILBRAHAM ACADEMY (MASS.)
Andrews, Elisha Benjamin
Baker, Lorenzo Dow
Baker, Osmon Cleander

Bowman, Thomas
Brown, John Mifflin
Burton, Nathaniel Judson
Conwell, Russell Herman
Crane, Winthrop Murray
Dean, Sidney
Goodnow, Isaac Tichenor
Haven, Gilbert
Ladd-Franklin, Christine
Lee, Jason
Marcy, Henry Orlando
Merrick, Edwin Thomas
Peirce, Bradford Kinney
Phelps, Austin
Pratt, Charles
Prudden, Theophil Mitchell
Ray, Charles Bennett
Raymond, Miner
Rust, Richard Sutton
Slater, John Fox
Stebbins, Rufus Phineas
Steele, Daniel
Stevens, Abel
Warren, Henry White
Winchester, Caleb Thomas
WILEY UNIVERSITY (TEX.)
Scott, Emmett Jay
WILLAMETTE UNIVERSITY (OREG.)
Hawley, Willis Chatman
Graduate Study
Hawley, Willis Chatman
WILLARD'S FEMALE SEMINARY (See
TROY FEMALE SEMINARY)
WILLIAM AND MARY (See COLLEGE
OF WILLIAM AND MARY)
WILLIAM JEWELL COLLEGE (MO.)
Hudson, Manley Ottmer
Martin, Warren Homer
Graduate Study
Cannon, Clarence
Hudson, Manley Ottmer
WILLIAMS COLLEGE (MASS.)
Aitken, Robert Grant
Alden, Henry Mills
Allen, David Oliver
Allen, Elisha Hunt
Alvord, Clarence Walworth
Andrews, Israel Ward
Andrews, Samuel James
Armstrong, Samuel Chapman
Atwater, Caleb
Bachman, John
Ballinger, Richard Achilles
Barnard, Daniel Dewey
Bascom, John
Beman, Nathan Sidney Smith
Benedict, Erastus Cornelius
Benjamin, Nathan
Benjamin, Samuel Greene
Wheeler
Betts, Samuel Rossiter
Birge, Edward Asahel
Boise, Reuben Patrick
Boynton, Charles Brandon
Brace, John Pierce
Brackett, Charles William
Bradish, Luther
Bradley, John Edwin
Brooks, William Keith
Bross, William
Browne, Charles Albert
Bryant, William Cullen

Bumstead, Freeman Josiah
Canfield, James Hulme
Carter, Franklin
Chadbourne, Paul Ansel
Clark, Horace Francis
Colby, Bainbridge
Curtis, Moses Ashley
Darby, John
Davies, Henry Eugene
Dearborn, Henry Alexander
Scammell
Dennett, Tyler (Wilbur)
Dewey, Chester
Dewey, Orville
Dickinson, John Woodbridge
Dike, Samuel Warren
Dixon, James
Dodge, Raymond
Dole, Sanford Ballard
Eastman, Max Forrester
Eaton, Amos
Edmonds, John Worth
Edwards, Bela Bates
Edwards, Justin
Edwards, William Henry
Emmons, Ebenezer
Field, David Dudley, 1805–1894
Field, Eugene
Field, Henry Martyn
Field, Stephen Dudley
Field, Stephen Johnson
Fowler, Orin
Gardner, Gilson
Garfield, Harry Augustus
Garfield, James Abram
Garfield, James Rudolph
Giles, Chauncey
Gladden, Washington
Goodrich, Chauncey, 1836–
1925
Green, Asa
Greenbaum, Edward Samuel
Griffin, Solomon Bulkley
Gross, Charles
Gulick John Thomas
Hale, Nathan, 1784–1863
Hall, Charles Cuthbert
Hall, Granville Stanley
Hallock, Gerard
Hallock, William Allen
Hammond, Edward Payson
Haynes, John Henry
Hill, George Washington
Hitchcock, Phineas Warrener
Hoisington, Henry Richard
Holden, Hale
Holley, Myron
Hopkins, Mark
Howard, Jacob Merritt
Howe, Samuel
Hoyt, Henry Martyn
Ingalls, John James
Jackson, William Alexander
Judson, Harry Pratt
Kellogg, Samuel Henry
King, Jonas
Kingsley, James Luce
Lamb, William Frederick
Lee, Charles Alfred
Lehman, Herbert Henry
Leupp, Francis Ellington
Mabie, Hamilton Wright

McClellan, Henry Brainerd
MacLean, George Edwin
McMath, Robert Emmet
Mather, Frank Jewett, Jr.
Mills, Cyrus Taggart
Mills, Elijah Hunt
Mills, Samuel John
Morton, Charles Walter
Nelson, Henry Loomis
Ogden, Rollo
Orton, James
Parker, Samuel
Peloubet, Francis Nathan
Perry, Arthur Latham
Perry, Bliss
Pratt, James Bissett
Pratt, Waldo Selden
Prime, Samuel Irenaeus
Raymond, George Lansing
Rice, Luther
Richards, William
Richards, Zalmon
Robbins, Thomas
Robinson, Benjamin Lincoln
Robinson, Charles Seymour
Roe, Edward Payson
Rowland, Henry Cottrell
Rumsey, William
Rutherford, Lewis Morris
Schauffler, Henry Albert
Scudder, Horrace Elisha
Scudder, Samuel Hubbard
Sherman, Stuart Pratt
Smith, Harry James
Snow, Francis Huntington
Spencer, John Canfield
Spring, Leverett Wilson
Stetson, Francis Lynde
Stewart, Edwin
Stiles, Henry Reed
Stoddard, David Tappan
Stoddard, John Lawson
Storrs, Richard Salter, 1787–
1873
Thacher, John Boyd
Tomlinson, Everett Tilsworth
Tucker, Gilbert Milligan
Turner, George Kibbe
Vinton, Samuel Finley
Ward, Henry Augustus
Ward, Henry Baldwin
Ward, Richard Halsted
Washburn, Emory
Wells, David Ames
Whitman, Charles Seymour
Whitney, William Dwight
Williamson, William Durkee
Yancey, William Lowndes
Yeomans, John William
Graduate Study
Pratt, Waldo Selden
WILLISTON SEMINARY (MASS.)
Andrews, George Pierce
Avery, John
Barber, Edwin Atlee
Bingham, Hiram, 1831–1908
Blakeslee, Erastus
Clark, William Smith
Crane, Winthrop Murray
Dexter, Franklin Bowditch
Dickinson, John Woodbridge
Durham, Caleb Wheeler

Goodell, Henry Hill
Hall, Granville Stanley
Hitchcock, Charles Henry
Hitchcock, Edward, 1828–1911
Hume, Robert Allen
Kellogg, Martin
Lincoln, Rufus Pratt
Lyman, Albert Josiah
Magill, Edward Hicks
Merrill, Selah
Nason, Henry Bradford
Northrop, Cyrus
Peck, Tracy
Smith, Judson
Spofford, Ainsworth Rand
Stanley, William
Stockbridge, Henry
Strong, Charles Lyman
Swinton, John
Wheeler, George Wakeman

WILMINGTON COLLEGE (OHIO)
Moore, Joseph Haines

WINONA STATE TEACHERS COLLEGE (IND.)
Rovenstine, Emery Andrew

WISCONSIN STATE NORMAL SCHOOL
Libby, Orin Grant

WITTENBERG COLLEGE (OHIO)
Anderson, Sherwood
Crothers, Samuel McChord
Dinwiddie, Edwin Courtland
Douglas, Lloyd Cassel
Funk, Isaac Kauffman
Grosscup, Peter Stenger
Krapp, George Philip
Lenker, John Nicholas
Marquett, Turner Mastin
Stuckenberg, John Henry Wilbrandt
Tittle, Ernest Fremont

WOFFORD COLLEGE (S.C.)
Cash, Wilbur Joseph
Few, William Preston
Johnston, Olin DeWitt Talmadge
Kirkland, James Hampton
Lever, Asbury Francis
Roper, Daniel Calhoun
Smith, Ellison DuRant

WOMAN'S MEDICAL COLLEGE (MD.)
Cone, Claribel

WOMAN'S MEDICAL COLLEGE (N.Y.)
Baker, Sara Josephine

WOMAN'S MEDICAL COLLEGE (PA.)
Addams, Jane
Jacobi, Mary Corinna Putnam
Lockrey, Sarah Hunt
Marshall, Clara
Potter, Ellen Culver
Putnam, Helen Cordelia
Swain, Clara A.

WOODSTOCK COLLEGE (MD.)
Campbell, Thomas Joseph
Rigge, William Francis
Talbot, Francis Xavier
Tondorf, Francis Anthony
Walsh, Edmund Aloysius
Weigel, Gustave

Graduate Study
LaFarge, John

Walsh, Edmund Aloysius

WOODWARD COLLEGE (OHIO)
Clarke, Robert
Hickenlooper, Andrew
Parvin, Theodore Sutton

WORCESTER ACADEMY (MASS.)
Bates, Samuel Penniman
Colvin, Stephen Sheldon
Fullam, Frank L.
Green, Andrew Haswell
Harris, William Torrey
Lord, Chester Sanders
Meade, Richard Worsam, 1837–1897
Talbot, Israel Tisdale
Thayer, Eli

WORCESTER POLYTECHNIC INSTITUTE (MASS.)
Adams, Herbert Samuel
Alford, Leon Pratt
Armsby, Henry Prentiss
Coates, George Henry
Cobb, Nathan Augustus
Daniels, Fred Harris
Donovan, John Joseph
Eddy, Harrison Prescott
Furlow, Floyd Charles
Goddard, Robert Hutchings
Hague, Robert Lincoln
Kent, Arthur Atwater
Newcomb, Charles Leonard
Priest, Edward Dwight
Thompson, Edward Herbert
Washburn, Charles Grenfill

WORRALL'S ACADEMY (KY.)
Beard, Daniel Carter

YALE UNIVERSITY (CONN.)
Abbott, Frank Frost
Adams, Andrew
Adams, Charles Baker
Adams, James Hopkins
Adams, John, 1772–1863
Adams, William
Alexander, William Dewitt
Alsop, Richard
Andrews, George Pierce
Andrews, William Watson
Anthony, William Arnold
Armsby, Henry Prentiss
Arno, Peter
Ashmun, George
Atherton, George Washington
Atkinson, Thomas
Atterbury, Grosvenor
Atterbury, William Wallace
Atwater, Lyman Hotchkiss
Austin, David
Austin, Samuel
Backus, Azel
Bacon, Benjamin Wisner
Bacon, Leonard
Bacon, Leonard Woolsey
Badger, George Edmund
Badger, Joseph, 1757–1846
Bailey, Ebenezer
Baldwin, Abraham
Baldwin, Elihu Whittlesey
Baldwin, Henry
Baldwin, John Denison
Baldwin, Roger Sherman
Baldwin, Simeon

Baldwin, Simeon Eben
Baldwin, Theron
Barber, Donn
Bardeen, Charles William
Barker, George Frederick
Barlow, Joel
Barnard, Frederick Augustus Porter
Barnard, Henry
Barry, Philip James Quinn
Barry, William Taylor Sullivan
Beach, Frederick Converse
Beach, Harlan Page
Beard, George Miller
Beecher, Edward
Beecher, Lyman
Beer, Thomas
Beers, Clifford Whittingham
Beers, Henry Augustin
Bellamy, Joseph
Benét, Stephen Vincent
Benham, Henry Washington
Benjamin, Judah Philip
Bennett, Nathaniel
Bevan, Arthur Dean
Bidwell, Barnabas
Bidwell, Walter Hilliard
Bingham, Hiram, 1831–1908
Bishop, Abraham
Bishop, William Darius
Bissell, Wilson Shannon
Blake, Eli Whitney
Blake, William Phipps
Blakeslee, Erastus
Bliss, Porter Cornelius
Boies, Henry Martyn
Boisen, Anton Theophilus
Boltwood, Bertram Borden
Bostwick, Arthur Elmore
Bosworth, Edward Increase
Bosworth, Francke Huntington
Bourne, Edward Gaylord
Bouton, Nathaniel
Bowen, Herbert Wolcott
Bowers, Lloyd Wheaton
Bowles, Samuel, 1851–1915
Brace, Charles Loring
Bradley, Frank Howe
Bradley, Stephen Row
Bradley, William Czar
Brady, John Green
Brainard, John Gardiner Calkins
Brainerd, John
Brandegee, Frank Bosworth
Brandegee, Townshend Stith
Breckinridge, Robert Jefferson
Brewer, David Josiah
Brewer, William Henry
Brinton, Daniel Garrison
Bristead, Charles Astor
Bromley, Isaac Hill
Brown, Benjamin Gratz
Brown, Henry Billings
Brown, John, 1744–1780
Brown, Samuel Robbins
Brown, Solyman
Brown, William Adams
Bryan, Kirk
Buck, Albert Henry
Bulkley, Lucius Duncan
Bullitt, William Christian

Bumstead, Horace
Bundy, Harvey Hollister
Bunker, Arthur Hugh
Burnam, John Miller
Burnett, Charles Henry
Burr, Aaron, 1715/16–1757
Burr, Enoch Fitch
Burrall, William Porter
Burrell, David James
Burroughs, John Curtis
Burrowes, Thomas Henry
Bushnell, David
Bushnell, George Ensign
Bushnell, Horace
Calhoun, John Caldwell
Calhoun, William Barron
Calkins, Phineas Wolcott
Camp, Walter Chauncey
Carleton, Henry
Carrington, Henry Beebee
Carter, Franklin
Case, Leonard
Case, William Scoville
Chamberlain, Daniel Henry
Champlin, John Denison
Chandler, John Scudder
Chandler, Thomas Bradbury
Chapin, Aaron Lucius
Chapin, Calvin
Chase, George
Chauvenet, William
Chester, Colby Mitchell
Chipman, Nathaniel
Chittenden, Russell Henry
Churchill, William
Clark, Charles Hopkins
Clark, Sheldon
Clark, Thomas March
Clay, Cassius Marcellus
Clayton, John Middleton
Cleaveland, Moses
Cloud, Henry Roe
Cochran, Alexander Smith
Coffin, Henry Sloane
Coffin William Anderson
Coit, Thomas Winthrop
Coleman, Lyman
Collier, Peter
Colt, LeBaron, Bradford
Colton, Calvin
Colton, Walter
Conwell, Russell Herman
Cook, Flavius Josephus
Cook, Robert Johnson
Cook, Walter
Cooper, Jacob
Cooper, James Fenimore
Copley, Ira Clifton
Coppée, Henry
Couper, James Hamilton
Cross, Wilbur Lucius
Culbertson, Ely
Curtis, Edward Lewis
Cushing, Harvey Williams
Cutler, Carroll
Cutler, Manasseh
Cutter, Ephraim
Daggett, David
Daggett, Ellsworth
Daggett, Naphtali
Dalzell, John
Dana, Edward Salisbury

Dana, James Dwight
Dana, Samuel Whittelsey
Davenport, James
Davenport, Russell Wheeler
Davis, Henry
Davis, John, 1787–1854
Dawes, Henry Laurens
Day, Clarence Shepard
Day, George Parmly
Day, Henry Noble
Day, Jeremiah
Deane, Silas
De Forest, Erastus Lyman
De Forest, John Kinne Hyde
De Forest, Robert Weeks
Delafield, Edward
Delafield, Francis
De Lancey, William Heathcote
Delano, William Adams
Deming, Henry Champion
Dennis, Frederic Shepard
Depew, Chauncey Mitchell
Dexter, Franklin Bowditch
Dexter, Henry Martyn
Dickinson, Jonathan
Dickson, Earle Ensign
Dickson, Samuel Henry
Dill, James Brooks
Dodd, Lee Wilson
Donaldson, Henry Herbert
Douglass, David Bates
Dryden, John Fairfield
Dubois, Augustus Jay
Dudley, Charles Benjamin
Duffield, Samuel Augustus Willoughby
Dunning, Albert Elijah
Du Pont, Francis Irénée
Durant, Henry
Dutton, Clarence Edward
Dutton, Henry
Dutton, Samuel Train
Dwight, Edmund
Dwight, Sereno Edwards
Dwight, Theodore
Dwight, Timothy, 1752–1817
Dwight, Timothy, 1828–1916
Dyer, Eliphalet
Dyer, Isadore
Eastman, William Reed
Eaton, Daniel Cady
Eddy, Henry Turner
Edmands, John
Edwards, Jonathan, 1703–1758
Egleston, Thomas
Elder, Samuel James
Eliot, Jared
Elliott, Stephen
Ellsworth, Henry Leavitt
Ellsworth, Henry William
Ellsworth, Oliver
Ellsworth, William Wolcott
Embree, Edwin Rogers
Emmons, Nathaniel
Eno, William Phelps
Evarts, Jeremiah
Evarts, William Maxwell
Fanning, Edmund, 1739–1818
Farnam, Henry Walcott
Farquhar, Percival
Farragut, David Glasgow
Fearn, John Walker

Ferry, Orris Sanford
Field, David Dudley, 1781–1867
Field, Maunsell Bradhurst
Finch, Francis Miles
Fisher, Irving
Fitch, Samuel
Fitch, Thomas
Flather, John Joseph
Foot, Samuel Augustus
Foote, William Henry
Forman, Justus Miles
Foster, John Pierrepont Codrington
Foster, Roger Sherman Baldwin
Fowler, Orin
Frank, Waldo David
Frissell, Hollis Burke
Gadsden, James
Gale, Benjamin
Gallaudet, Thomas Hopkins
Gardiner, James Terry
Gardner, Leroy Upson
Gibbs, Josiah Willard, 1790–1861
Gibbs, Josiah Willard, 1839–1903
Gibson, Randall Lee
Gillett, Ezra Hall
Gillette, Francis
Gilman, Daniel Coit
Goddard, Calvin Luther
Goodrich, Charles Augustus
Goodrich, Chauncey, 1759–1815
Goodrich, Chauncey Allen
Goodrich, Elizur, 1734–1797
Goodrich, Elizur, 1761–1849
Goodyear, Anson Conger
Goodyear, William Henry
Gould, James
Granger, Francis
Granger, Gideon
Grant, Madison
Graves, William Phillips
Greenway, John Campbell
Gregory, Eliot
Gregory, Samuel
Griffin, Edward Dorr
Griggs, Everett Gallup
Grigsby, Hugh Blair
Grimké, Thomas Smith
Grinnell, George Bird
Griswold, Alfred Whitney
Griswold, Roger
Griswold, Stanley
Grosvenor, William Mason
Guilford, Nathan
Gunn, Frederick William
Gurley, Ralph Randolph
Hadley, Arthur Twining
Hadley, James
Hague, Arnold
Haight, Henry Huntly
Hale, Nathan, 1755–1776
Hale, Philip
Hall, Charles Henry
Hall, Lyman
Hall, Willard Preble
Hallock, Charles
Halsted, William Stewart
Harkness, Edward Stephen
Harlow, Ralph Volney

Harper, William Rainey
Harris, William Torrey
Harrison, Carter Henry
Harrison, Fairfax
Harrison, Francis Burton
Harrison, Henry Baldwin
Hasbrouck, Abraham Bruyn
Haskell, Dudley Chase
Hastings, Charles Sheldon
Havens, James Smith
Hawley, Gideon, 1727–1807
Hawley, Joseph
Hazard, Thomas
Henderson, Yandell
Hendrick, Burton Jesse
Herr, Herbert Thacker
Herrick, Edward Claudius
Hill, Frederick Trevor
Hillhouse, James
Hillhouse, James Abraham
Hitchcock, Henry
Hitchcock, Peter
Hittell, Theodore Henry
Hobart, John Sloss
Holbrook, Josiah
Holley, Horace
Hollister, Gideon Hiram
Holmes, Abiel
Holmes, Isaac Edward
Holt, Hamilton Bowen
Holt, Henry
Hooker, Donald Russell
Hooker, Worthington
Hopkins, Samuel, 1721–1803
Hoppin, James Mason
Hoppin, William Warner
Hosmer, Titus
Howland, John
Hubbard, Joseph Stillman
Hubbard, Richard William
Hull, William
Hume, Robert Allen
Humphrey, Heman
Humphreys, David
Hunt, Thomas Sterry
Hunt, William Henry
Hunter, Croil
Huntington, Daniel
Huntington, Jabez
Huntington, Jedediah Vincent
Huntington, Samuel, 1765–
1817
Hurd, John Codman
Hyatt, Alphaeus
Hyde, Charles Cheney
Hyde, James Nevins
Iddings, Joseph Paxon
Ingersoll, Jared, 1722–1781
Ingersoll, Jared, 1749–1822
Isham, Ralph Heyward
Isham, Samuel
Ives, Charles Edward
Ives, Eli
Jackson, Henry Rootes
Janeway, Theodore Caldwell
Janney, Russell Dixon
Jarvis, Abraham
Jay, William
Jenkins, Edward Hopkins
Jenks, Tudor Storrs
Jessup, Henry Harris
Johnson, ALexander Smith

Johnson, Owen McMahon
Johnson, Samuel
Johnson, Samuel William
Johnson, William, 1769–1848
Johnson, William Samuel
Johnson, William Woolsey
Johnston, Henry Phelps
Johnston, William Preston
Jones, George
Jones, Joel
Jones, Samuel
Jones, Thomas
Judd, Orange
Judd, Sylvester
Judson, Frederick Newton
Kane, John Kintzing
Kaye, Frederick Benjamin
Keep, Robert Porter
Kellogg, Martin
Kennedy, William Sloane
Kent, Charles Foster
Kent, James
Keyes, Edward Lawrence
Kilpatrick, John Reed
King, Clarence
Kingsley, James Luce
Kip, William Ingraham
Kirchwey, George Washington
Klein, Joseph Frederic
Knight, Frederick Irving
Knight, Jonathan
Knowlton, Marcus Perrin
Lane, Arthur Bliss
Lanman, Charles Rockwell
Larned, Joseph Gay Eaton
Lathrop, John Hiram
Latourette, Kenneth Scott
Law, John
Law, Richard
Lawrance, Charles Lanier
Leaming, Jeremiah
Leavitt, Joshua
Leffingwell, Russell Cornell
Lehman, Robert
Levermore, Charles Herbert
Levinson, Salmon Oliver
Lewis, Charlton Thomas
Lewis, Harry Sinclair
L'Hommedieu, Ezra
Link, Henry Charles
Linn, William Alexander
Livingston, John Henry
Livingston, Peter Van Brugh
Livingston, Philip
Livingston, William, 1723–1790
Llewellyn, Karl Nickerson
Locke, John
Lockwood, Ralph Ingersoll
Longstreet, Augustus Baldwin
Loomis, Elias
Lord, Daniel
Lord, David Nevins
Lorimer, George Horace
Lounsbury, Thomas Raynesford
Luce, Henry Robinson
Luce, Henry Winters
Lusk, William Thompson
Lyman, Chester Smith
Lyman, Joseph Bardwell
Lyman, Phineas
McAllister, Hall
McCaleb, Theodore Howard

McClellen, George, 1796–1847
McClure, Alexander Wilson
McCormick, Joseph Medill
McCormick, Robert Rutherford
McDowell, James
MacVeagh, Franklin
MacVeagh, Isaac Wayne
Magill, Edward Hicks
Mallery, Garrick
Mansfield, Jared
Mansfield, Richard, 1723–1820
Marmaduke, John Sappington
Marsh, John, 1788–1868
Marsh, Othniel Charles
Marsh, Reginald
Marshall, Thomas Alexander
Mason, Jeremiah
Mathews, Albert
Matthiessen, Francis Otto
Maxwell, William, 1784–1857
Meigs, Josiah
Meigs, Return Jonathan, 1764–
1824
Mendel, Lafayette Benedict
Merrill, Selah
Millikan, Clark Blanchard
Millis, Walter
Mitchell, Donald Grant
Mitchell, Elisha
Mitchell, Stephen Mix
Mitchell, William DeWitt
Moffett, Cleveland Langston
Moore, Eliakim Hastings
Moore, George Foot
Morris, Edward Dafydd
Morris, Lewis 1726–1798
Morris, Luzon Burritt
Morris, Richard
Morse, Jedidiah
Morse, Samuel Finlay Breese
Morse, Sidney Edwards
Mulford, Elisha
Munger, Theodore Thornton
Murdock, James
Murphy, Gerald Clery
Nadal, Ehrman Syme
Nash, Daniel
Nelson, Rensselaer Russell
Nettleton, Asahel
Newel, Stanford
Newell, Edward Theodore
Newlands, Francis Griffith
Newton, Hubert Anson
Noble, Frederick Alphonso
Noble, John Willock
North, Simeon, 1802–1884
Northrop, Birdsey Grant
Northrop, Cyrus
Norton, John Pitkin
Nott, Abraham
Nott, Samuel
Oakley, Thomas Jackson
Ogden, David
Ogilvie, John
Olds, Irving Sands
Olmsted, Denison
Olmsted, John Charles
Osborn, Norris Galpin
Osborne, Thomas Burr
Owen, Edward Thomas
Paine, Ralph Delahaye
Palmer, Ray

Parker, Peter
Parsons, Lewis Baldwin
Paterson, John
Patterson, Joseph Medill
Payne, Oliver Hazard
Pearse, John Barnard Swett
Peck, Tracy
Peet, Harvey Prindle
Peet, Isaac Lewis
Penniman, James Hosmer
Perkins, Elisha
Perkins, Frederic Beecher
Perkins, George Henry
Perrin, Bernadotte
Perry, Edward Aylesworth
Peters, John Andrew
Peters, John Punnett
Peters, Samuel Andrew
Phelps, William Lyon
Phelps, William Walter
Pickens, William
Pierpont, John
Pierrepont, Edwards
Pinchot, Amos Richards Eno
Pinchot, Gifford
Pinney, Norman
Pirsson, Louis Valentine
Pitkin, Timothy
Platner, Samuel Ball
Platt, Thomas Collier
Polk, Frank Lyon
Polk, Trusten
Poole, William Frederick
Porter, Arthur Kingsley
Porter, Cole
Porter, John Addison
Porter, Noah
Porter, Peter Buell
Porter, Samuel
Pratt, Bela Lyon
Prentice, Samuel Oscar
Prudden, Theophil Mitchell
Putnam, James Osborne
Reid, Ogden Mills
Remington, Frederic
Resor, Stanley Burnet
Richards, Charles Herbert
Richardson, Rufus Byam
Riley, Isaac Woodbridge
Robbins, Thomas
Roberts, Ellis Henry
Robinson, Henry Cornelius
Robinson, William Erigena
Rogers, James Gamble
Rogers, James Harvey
Rood, Ogden Nicholas
Rosenfeld, Paul Leopold
Rothko, Mark
Rowland, Henry Cottrell
Ruggles, Samuel Bulkley
Russ, John Dennison
Saarinen, Eero
St. John, Isaac Munroe
Salisbury, Edward Elbridge
Saltus, Edgar Evertson
Savage, Thomas Staughton
Schevill, Rudolph
Schuyler, Eugene
Schwab, John Christopher
Scott, Austin
Scott, John Morin
Seabury, Samuel, 1729–1796

Sedgwick, Theodore, 1746–
1813
Sedgwick, Theodore, 1780–
1839
Sedgwick, William Thompson
Selden, George Baldwin
Sergeant, John, 1710–1749
Setchell, William Albert
Seymour, Charles
Shaw, Howard Van Doren
Shiras, George
Sill, Edward Rowland
Silliman, Benjamin, 1779–1864
Silliman, Benjamin, 1816–1885
Smalley, George Washburn
Smillie, Ralph
Smith, Ashbel
Smith, Azariah
Smith, Eli
Smith, Elihu Hubbard
Smith, George Henry
Smith, Israel
Smith, Job Lewis
Smith, John Cotton, 1765–1845
Smith, Junius
Smith, Nathan Ryno
Smith, Truman
Smith, William, 1697–1769
Smith, William, 1728–1793
Smith, William Nathan Harrell
Spencer, Ambrose
Spencer, Elihu
Sprague, Homer Baxter
Sprague, William Buell
Spring, Gardiner
Stagg, Amos Alonzo
Stanley, Harold
Stanley, William
Stearns, Henry Putnam
Stedman, Edmund Clarence
Steiner, Bernard Christian
Sterling, John William
Stevens, Alexander Hodgdon
Stevens, Henry
Stevens, John Austin, 1795–
1874
Stewart, William Morris
Stiles, Ezra
Stillé, Alfred
Stillé, Charles Janeway
Stimson, Henry Lewis
Stimson, Lewis Atterbury
Stoddard, David Tappan
Stokes, Anson Phelps
Stokes, Frederick Abbot
Stokes, William Earl Dodge
Storrs, Richard Salter, 1787–
1873
Street, Augustus Russell
Strong, Augustus Hopkins
Strong, Theodore
Strong, William
Stuart, Isaac William
Stuart, Moses
Sturtevant, Julian Monson
Sullivant, William Starling
Sumner, William Graham
Sutherland, Richard Kerens
Swayne, Wager
Swift, Zephaniah
Taber, John
Taft, Alphonso

Taft, Charles Phelps
Taft, Henry Waters
Taft, Robert Alphonso
Taft, William Howard
Tallmadge, Benjamin
Tarbell, Frank Bigelow
Tarbox, Increase Niles
Taylor, Nathaniel William
Taylor, Richard
Tenney, William Jewett
Thacher, Thomas Anthony
Thacher, Thomas Day
Thayer, John
Thomas, Joseph
Thompson, Joseph Parrish
Thompson, William Gilman
Thwaites, Reuben Gold
Tilden, Samuel Jones
Tilson, John Quillin
Tod, George
Todd, Eli
Todd, John
Tolman, Herbert Cushing
Torrey, Charles Turner
Towle, George Makepeace
Tracy, Uriah
Trumbull, Benjamin
Trumbull, James Hammond
Trumbull, John, 1750 o.s.–1831
Tully, William
Turner, Asa
Turner, Jonathan Baldwin
Twichell, Joseph Hopkins
Twining, Alexander Catlin
Tyler, Bennet
Tyler, Charles Mellen
Tyler, Moses Coit
Tytus, John Butler
Underhill, Frank Pell
Van Allen, Frank
Van Buren, John
Van Buren, William Holme
Van Name, Addison
Van Rensselaer, Cortlandt
Veblen, Thorstein Bunde
Verrill, Alpheus Hyatt
Vincent, Frank
Vincent, George Edgar
Vinton, Alexander Hamilton
Wadsworth, James
Wadsworth, James Wolcott, Jr.
Waite, Morrison Remick
Wales, Leonard Eugene
Ware, Edmund Asa
Warren, Israel Perkins
Washington, Henry Stephens
Waterman, Thomas Whitney
Waters, William Everett
Watson, Sereno
Webster, Noah
Webster, Pelatiah
Weed, Lewis Hill
Welch, William Henry
Welch, William Wickham
Welles, Noah
Wenner, George Unangst
West, Henry Sergeant
Weyerhaeuser, Frederick Edward
Wharton, Francis
Wheaton, Nathaniel Sheldon
Wheeler, Arthur Leslie

Wheeler, George Wakeman
Wheelock, Eleazar
Wheelock, John
Whipple, Sherman Leland
White, Andrew Dickson
Whitney, Eli
Whitney, Harry Payne
Whitney, James Lyman
Whitney, Josiah Dwight
Whitney, William Collins
Whitney, William Dwight
Whiton, James Morris
Wikoff, Henry
Wilcox, Reynold Webb
Willard, De Forest
Williams, Alpheus Starkey
Williams, Frederick Wells
Williams, Henry Shaler
Williams, Thomas Scott
Willis, Nathaniel Parker
Wilmer, Richard Hooker
Wilson, Hugh Robert
Winslow, Hubbard
Winthrop, Theodore
Witherspoon, Alexander Maclaren
Witherspoon, Herbert
Wolcott, Edward Oliver
Wolcott, Oliver, 1726–1797
Wolcott, Oliver, 1760–1833
Woodbridge, William Channing
Woodruff, Timothy Lester
Woods, William Burnham
Woolley, Edgar Montillion ("Monty")
Woolsey, John Munro
Woolsey, Theodore Dwight
Woolsey, Theodore Salisbury
Wooster, David
Worcester, Joseph Emerson
Worthington, John
Wright, Charles
Wright, Elizur
Wright, Robert William
Wyllys, George
Youmans, William Jay
Yung, Wing

Forestry
Baker, Oliver Edwin
Record, Samuel James

Graduate Study
Abel-Henderson, Annie Heloise
Adams, James Truslow
Baker, Hugh Potter
Benedict, Stanley Rossiter
Benét, Stephen Vincent
Bloomfield, Maurice
Bostwick, Arthur Elmore
Bourne, Edward Gaylord
Bowman, Isaiah
Brown, William Adams
Bryan, Kirk
Bumstead, Henry Andrews
Burnam, John Miller
Burr, Aaron 1715/16–1757
Canby, Henry Seidel
Capps, Edward
Case, Shirley Jackson
Chittenden, Russell Henry
Cloud, Henry Roe
Collier, Peter
Cross, Wilbur Lucius

Cutler, Manasseh
Dana, Edward Salisbury
Day, Arthur Louis
De Forest, Lee
Dougherty, Raymond Philip
Dubois, Augustus Jay
Dudley, Charles Benjamin
Eastman, William Reed
Eddy, Henry Turner
Edgren, August Hjalmar
Embree, Edwin Rogers
Fairchild, Fred Rogers
Farnam, Henry Walcott
Fisher, Irving
Frank, Waldo David
Fullerton, George Stuart
Grinnell, George Bird
Griswold, Alfred Whitney
Gunn, Ross
Hadley, Arthur Twining
Hadley, James
Harlow, Ralph Volney
Hastings, Charles Sheldon
Hay, Oliver Perry
Haynes, George Edmund
Henderson, Yandell
Hendrick, Burton Jesse
Hillhouse, James Abraham
Hooker, Donald Russell
Hume, Robert Allen
Humphreys, David
Huntington, Ellsworth
Hyde, Charles Cheney
Jackson, William Alexander
Jenkins, Edward Hopkins
Johnson, Treat Baldwin
Kent, Charles Foster
Lanman, Charles Rockwell
Latourette, Kenneth Scott
Lawrence, Ernest Orlando
Leopold, (Rand) Aldo
Link, Henry Charles
Lomax, Louis Emanuel
MacCurdy, George Grant
McVey, Frank Lerond
Manatt, James Irving
Marsh, Othniel Charles
Mendel, Lafayette Benedict
Merrill, Elmer Truesdell
Moore, Eliakim Hastings
Newell, Edward Theodore
Niebuhr, Helmut Richard
Notestein, Wallace
Olmsted, Denison
Osborne, Thomas Burr
Owen, Edward Thomas
Page, Leigh
Paine, John Alsop
Peck, Tracy
Perkins, George Henry
Peters, John Punnett
Peters, Samuel Andrew
Phelps, William Lyon
Pirsson, Louis Valentine
Platner, Samuel Ball
Reid, Ogden Mills
Reinhardt, Aurelia Isabel Henry
Richardson, Rufus Byam
Riley, Isaac Woodbridge
Robertson, William Spence
Rogers, James Harvey
Rogers, William Augustus

Rood, Ogden Nicholas
Rose, Mary Davies Swartz
Safford, James Merrill
Salisbury, Edward Elbridge
Schuyler, Eugene
Seashore, Carl Emil
Seymour, Charles
Silcox, Ferdinand Augustus
Smalley, George Washburn
Smillie, Ralph
Smith, Theodate Louise
Smith, William, 1697–1769
Sperry, Willard Learoyd
Steiner, Bernard Christian
Taft, Charles Phelps
Tarbell, Frank Bigelow
Tolman, Herbert Cushing
Ward, Charles Henshaw
Wheeler, Arthur Leslie
White, Andrew Dickson
Whitney, James Lyman
Whiton, James Morris
Wieland, George Reber
Williams, Henry Shaler
Williston, Samuel Wendell
Witherspoon, Alexander Maclaren

Law
Baldwin, Simeon Eben
Bangs, Francis Nehemiah
Birney, James
Brown, Henry Billings
Brown, Joseph Emerson
Carrington, Henry Beebee
Cummings, Homer Stillé
Davis, David
Delmas, Delphin Michael
Dwight, Theodore William
Goodrich, Chauncey, 1759–1815
Goodwin, Hannibal Williston
Graves, David Bibb
Harrison, Carter Henry, Jr.
Hoppin, William Warner
Hunt, William Henry
Hurd, John Codman
Johnston, John Taylor
Kefauver, (Carey) Estes
Lathrop, John Hiram
Lemke, William Frederick
Ligon, Thomas Watkins
Llewellyn, Karl Nickerson
Loomis, Dwight
McMahon, Brien
Minton, Sherman
Phelps, Edward John
Prentice, Samuel Oscar
Scarborough, Lee Rutland
Sheppard, John Morris
Shiras, George
Shiras, Oliver Perry
Strong, William
Thacher, Thomas Day
Tilson, John Quillin
Wheeler, George Wakeman
Whipple, Sherman Leland
Williams, Alpheus Starkey
Woolsey, Theodore Salisbury

Medicine
Bacon, Leonard Woolsey
Baldwin, Edward Robinson
Brockett, Linus Pierpont

Bronson, Henry
Bushnell, George Ensign
Butler, Thomas Belden
Camp, Walter Chauncey
Cutter, Ephraim
Davidson, Jo
Davis, Henry Gassett
Gardner, Leroy Upson
Gilbert, Alfred Carlton
Gregory, Samuel
Homes, Henry Augustus
Huntington, Elisha
King, Dan
Kirtland, Jared Potter
Locke, John
Miller, William Snow
Parker, Peter
Peaslee, Edmund Randolph
Percival, James Gates
Phelps, Guy Rowland
Prudden, Theophil Mitchell
Rowland, Henry Cottrell
Russ, John Dennison
Sargent, Dudley Allen
Savage, Thomas Staughton
Smith, Ashbel
Smith, Azariah
Smith, Nathan Ryno
Stearns, Henry Putnam
Williston, Samuel Wendell

Sheffield Scientific School
Benét, William Rose
Boeing, William Edward
Booth, Albert James, Jr. ("Albie")
Brace, Charles Loring
Canby, Henry Seidel
Cummings, Homer Stillé
Davis, Francis Breese, Jr.
Davis, John Staige
Day, Arthur Louis
De Forest, Lee
Ellsworth, Lincoln
Hammond, John Hays
Heffelfinger, William Walter "Pudge"
Hogan, John Vincent Lawless
Johnson, Treat Baldwin
Joy, Henry Bourne
Leopold, (Rand) Aldo
Merriam, Clinton Hart
Murray, Thomas Edward
Newberry, Truman Handy
Page, Leigh
Strong, Richard Pearson
Talbott, Harold Elstner
Trask, James Dowling
Wells, Harry Gideon
Wilson, Edmund Beecher

Theology
Adams, George Burton
Ames, Edward Scribner
Atwater, Lyman Hotchkiss
Badè, William Frederic
Baldwin, John Denison
Baldwin, Theron
Barrows, John Henry
Beardshear, William Miller
Beckwith, Clarence Augustine
Beecher, Lyman
Bidwell, Walter Hilliard
Bliss, Edwin Munsell

Brace, Charles Loring
Brainerd, David
Burr, Enoch Fitch
Burton, Marion Le Roy
Burton, Nathaniel Judson
Bushnell, Horace
Case, Shirley Jackson
Chandler, John Scudder
Coleman, Lyman
De Forest, John Kinne Hyde
Durant, Henry
Dwight, Benjamin Woodbridge
Dwight, Timothy, 1828–1916
Edmands, John
Edwards, Jonathan, 1703–1758
Fisher, George Park
Garman, Charles Edward
Green, Lewis Warner
Hadley, James
Henry, Caleb Sprague
Hitchcock, Charles Henry
Hitchcock, Edward, 1793–1864
Hume, Robert Allen
Lyman, Chester Smith
Lyman, Eugene William
MacLean, George Edwin
Magoun, George Frederick
Mears, John William
Merrill, Selah
Munger, Theodore Thornton
North, Simeon, 1802–1884
Northdrop, Birdsey Grant
Noyes, John Humphrey
Olmsted, Denison
Parker, Peter
Patterson, James Willis
Peet, Stephen Denison
Perrin, Bernadotte
Peters, John Punnett
Phelps, Austin
Powell, Adam Clayton, Sr.
Proctor, Henry Hugh
Salter, William Mackintire
Sanders, Frank Knight
Smith, Azariah
Stevens, George Barker
Stoddard, John Lawson
Sturtevant, Julian Monson
Tarbox, Increase Niles
Terry, Milton Spenser
Tufts, James Hayden
Wheelock, Eleazar
Willett, Herbert Lockwood
Winslow, Hubbard
Woolsey, Theodore Dwight

YANKTON COLLEGE (S.D.)
Bode, Boyd Henry
Darling, Jay Norwood ("Ding")

YORKSHIRE COLLEGE (ENGLAND)
Dakin, Henry Drysdale

YOUNG LADIES INSTITUTE (N.Y.)
Alden, Isabella Macdonald

ZURICH EIDGENOSSICHE TECHNISCHE HOCHSCHULE (SWITZERLAND)
Einstein, Albert

ZURICH POLYTECHNICUM (SWITZERLAND)
Cabot, Godfrey Lowell

OCCUPATIONS

ABOLITIONIST
Bailey, Gamaliel
Birney, James Gillespie
Bourne, George
Bowditch, Henry Ingersoll
Brown, John
Buffum, Arnold
Burleigh, Charles Calistus
Chace, Elizabeth Buffum
Child, Lydia Maria Francis
Christy, David
Clay, Cassius Marcellus
Coffin, Levi
Coles, Edward
Collins, John Anderson
Colman, Lucy Newhall
Cooper, Thomas
Cox, Hannah Peirce
Deitzler, George Washington
Douglass, Frederick
Edgerton, Sidney
Embree, Elihu
Fairbank, Calvin
Fee, John Gregg
Fessenden, Samuel
Follen, Charles
Follen, Eliza Lee Cabot
Foster, Abigail Kelley
Foster, Stephen Symonds
Garnet, Henry Highland
Garrett, Thomas
Gibbons, Abigail Hopper
Gibbons, James Sloan
Giddings, Joshua Reed
Grimké, Angelina Emily
Grimké, Sarah Moore
Grinnell, Josiah Bushnell
Hallowell, Richard Price
Haven, Gilbert
Hazard, Thomas
Holley, Myron
Hopper, Isaac Tatem
Jackson, James Caleb
Johnson, Oliver
Julian, George Washington
Leavitt, Joshua
Lee, Luther
LeMoyne, Francis Julius
Loring, Ellis Gray
Lovejoy, Elijah Parish
Lovejoy, Owen
Lundy, Benjamin
McKim, James Miller
Mercer, Margaret
Miller, Jonathan Peckham
Mott, James
Nelson, David
Osborn, Charles
Post, Issac
Realf, Richard
Sands, David
Scott, Orange
Stewart, Alvan
Stuart, Charles
Sumner, Charles
Sunderland, La Roy
Tappan, Arthur

Tappan, Benjamin
Tappan, Lewis
Taylor, John W.
Torrey, Charles Turner
Tubman, Harriet
Ward, Samuel Ringgold
Weld, Theodore Dwight
Whittier, John Greenleaf
Woolman, John

ACCOUNTANT (See also TAX EXPERT)
Lasser, Jacob Kay
Lybrand, William Mitchell

ACTOR (See also ENTERTAINER)
Adams, Edwin
Aiken, George L.
Aldrich, Louis
Aldridge, Ira Frederick
Arden, Edwin Hunter Pendleton
Arliss, George
Arnold, Edward
Bacon, Frank
Baker, Benjamin A.
Bangs, Frank C.
Bannister, Nathaniel Harrington
Barnabee, Henry Clay
Barrett, George Horton
Barrett, Lawrence
Barrymore, John
Barrymore, Lionel
Barrymore, Maurice
Barthelmess, Richard
Beery, Wallace Fitzgerald
Begley, Edward James ("Ed")
Belasco, David
Benchley, Robert Charles
Bennett, Richard
Bernard, John
Blake, William Rufus
Blinn, Holbrook
Blue, Gerald Montgomery ("Monte")
Bogart, Humphrey DeForest
Booth, Edwin Thomas
Booth, John Wilkes
Booth, Junius Brutus
Boucicault, Dion
Bradford, Joseph
Brougham, John
Browning, Tod
Burgess, Neil
Burke, Charles St. Thomas
Burns, Bob
Burton, William Evans
Bushman, Francis Xavier
Carson, Jack
Chaney, Lon
Chanfrau, Francis S.
Clarke, John Sleeper
Clift, Edward Montgomery
Cohan, George Michael
Colman, Ronald Charles
Conried, Heinrich
Conway, Frederick Bartlett
Cooper, Gary
Cooper, Thomas Abthorpe

Couldock, Charles Walter
Crane, William Henry
Craven, Frank
Daly, Peter Christopher Arnold
Davenport, Edward Loomis
Davidge, William Pleater
Dean, James Byron
De Angelis, Thomas Jefferson
DeMille, Cecil Blount
Digges, Dudley
Ditrichstein, Leo
Dockstader, Lew
Drake, Samuel
Drew, John, 1827–1862
Drew, John, 1853–1927
Eddy, Nelson
Edeson, Robert
Fairbanks, Douglas
Farnum, Charles Albert
Farnum, Dustin Lancy
Farnum, Franklyn
Faversham, William Alfred
Fay, Francis Anthony ("Frank")
Fennell, James
Ferguson, William Jason
Field, Joseph M.
Finn, Henry James William
Fitzsimmons, Robert Prometheus
Fleming, William Maybury
Florence, William Jermyn
Flynn, Errol Leslie
Forrest, Edwin
Fox, Charles Kemble
Fox, George Washington Lafayette
Fox, Gilbert
Gable, (William) Clark
Garfield, John
Gaxton, William
Gibson, Edmund Richard ("Hoot")
Gilbert, John
Gilbert, John Gibbs
Gillette, William Hooker
Gilpin, Charles Sidney
Goodwin, Nathaniel Carll
Gorcey, Leo
Greenstreet, Sydney Hughes
Hackett, James Henry
Hackett, James Keteltas
Hallam, Lewis
Hamblin, Thomas Sowerby
Hampden, Walter
Hardwicke, Cedric Webster
Harrigan, Edward
Harrison, Gabriel
Harrison, Richard Berry
Hart, William Surrey
Haworth, Joseph
Hayes, Gabby
Hazelton, George Cochrane
Henry, John, 1746–1794
Herne, James A.
Hill, Frederic Stanhope
Hill, George Handel
Hitchcock, Raymond

Hodge, William Thomas
Hodgkinson, John
Holland, Edmund Milton
Holland, Joseph Jefferson
Hopper, DeWolf
Horton, Edward Everett, Jr.
Howard, Leslie
Huston, Walter
James, Louis
Jefferson, Joseph, 1774–1832
Jefferson, Joseph, 1829–1905
Johnston, David Claypoole
Jones, Joseph Stevens
Karloff, Boris
Keenan, James Francis
Keene, Thomas Wallace
Kirby, J. Hudson
Lackaye, Wilton
Ladd, Alan Walbridge
Lahr, Bert
Laughton, Charles
Leavitt, Frank Simmons ("Man
   Mountain Dean")
Lee, Canada
Leiber, Fritz
Le Moyne, William J.
Lewis, Arthur
Lewis, James
Lindsay, Howard
Logan, Cornelius Ambrosius
Lorre, Peter
Ludlow, Noah Miller
Lugosi, Bela
McCullough, John
MacKaye, James Morrison
   Steele
McLaglen, Victor
McVicker, James Hubert
Mann, Louis
Manners, John Hartley
Mansfield, Richard
Mantell, Robert Bruce
Marble, Danforth
Mason, John
Mayo, Frank
Menjou, Adolphe Jean
Miller, Henry
Mitchell, Thomas Gregory
Mitchell, William, 1798–1856
Mix, Tom
Montague, Henry James
Moore, Victor Frederick
Muni, Paul
Murdoch, Frank Hitchcock
Murdoch, James Edward
Nagel, Conrad
Novarro, Ramon
Odets, Clifford
Olcott, Chauncey
O'Neill, James
Owen, William Florence
Owens, John Edmond
Pastor, Antonio
Payne, John Howard
Placide, Henry
Powell, Richard Ewing ("Dick")
Powell, Snelling
Power, Frederick Tyrone
Power, Tyrone
Pray, Isaac Clark
Proctor, Joseph
Rains, Claude

Rankin, McKee
Rathbone, Basil
Raymond, John T.
Richings, Peter
Riddle, George Peabody
Roberts, Theodore
Robson, Stuart
Rogers, Will
Rooney, Pat
Russell, Sol Smith
Schildkraut, Joseph
Schwartz, Maurice
Sennett, Mack
Seymour, William
Shean, Albert
Sills, Milton
Simpson, Edmund Shaw
Skinner, Otis
Smith, Marcus
Smith, William Henry,
   1806–1872
Sothern, Edward Askew
Sothern, Edward Hugh
Stoddart, James Henry
Stone, John Agustus
Taylor, Robert
Thayer, Tiffany Ellsworth
Thompson, Denman
Thorne, Charles Robert,
   1814–1893
Thorne, Charles Robert,
   1840–1883
Tone, Stanislas Pascal Franchot
Tracy, Spencer Bonaventure
Vandenhoff, George
Vezin, Hermann
Visscher, William Lightfoot
Von Stroheim, Erich
Walcot, Charles Melton,
   1816–1868
Walcot, Charles Melton,
   1840–1921
Wallack, Henry John
Wallack, James William
   1795–1864
Wallack, James William,
   1818–1873
Wallack, Lester
Walthall, Henry Brazeal
Warde, Frederick Barkham
Warfield, David
Warren, William, 1767–1832
Warren, William, 1812–1888
Webb, Clifton
Wemyss, Francis Courtney
Wheatley, William
White, George
Wignell, Thomas
Williams, Barney
Williams, Bert
Wilson, Francis
Wise, Thomas Alfred
Wolheim, Louis Robert
Wood, William Burke
Woolley, Edgar Montillion
   ("Monty")
Wynn, Ed
ACTRESS (See also ENTERTAINER)
Adams, Maude
Adler, Sara
Allen, Viola Emily
Anderson, Mary

Anglin, Margaret Mary
Bankhead, Tallulah
Bara, Theda
Barnes, Charlotte Mary Sanford
Barrymore, Ethel
Barrymore, Georgiana Emma
   Drew
Bateman, Kate Josephine
Bateman, Sidney Francis Cowell
Bates, Blanche
Beavers, Louise
Bennett, Constance Campbell
Berg, Gertrude Edelstein
Bingham, Amelia
Bonstelle, Jessie
Booth, Agnes
Bow, Clara Gordon
Bowers, Elizabeth Crocker
Brady, Alice
Burke, Billie
Carter, Caroline Louise Dudley
Castle, Irene Foote
Cayvan, Georgia
Chanfrau, Henrietta Baker
Chatterton, Ruth
Claxton, Kate
Clifton, Josephine
Coghlan, Rose
Collier, Constance
Cowl, Jane
Crabtree, Lotta
Cushman, Charlotte Saunders
Cushman, Pauline
Cushman, Susan Webb
Dandridge, Dorothy Jean
Darwell, Jane
Davenport, Fanny Lily Gypsy
Davies, Marion Cecilia
Dean, Julia
De Wolfe, Elsie
Dickinson, Anna Elizabeth
Drake, Frances Ann Denny
Dresser, Louise Kerlin
Dressler, Marie
Duff, Mary Ann Dyke
Dumont, Margaret
Eagels, Jeanne
Elliott, Maxine
Eytinge, Rose
Fazenda, Louise Marie
Field, Mary Katherine Kemble
Fisher, Clara
Fiske, Minnie Maddern
Francis, Kay
Garland, Judy
George, Gladys
George, Grace
Gilbert, Anne Hartley
Gish, Dorothy
Hale, Louise Closser
Hall, Juanita Armethea
Harlow, Jean
Henie, Sonja
Herne, Chrystal Katharine
Heron, Matilda Agnes
Holliday, Judy
Hopper, Hedda
Hull, Josephine
Illington, Margaret
Irwin, May
Jananschek, Franziska
   Magdalena Romance

Kane, Helen
Keene, Laura
Kemble, Frances Anne
Lander, Jean Margaret
   Davenport
Lawrence, Gertrude
Leigh, Vivien
Logan, Olive
Lombard, Carole
Lord, Pauline
McCracken, Joan
McDaniel, Hattie
MacDonald, Jeanette Anna
Mansfield, Jayne
Marlowe, Julia
Menken, Adah Isaacs
Merry, Ann Brunton
Mitchell, Margaret Julia
Modjeska, Helena
Monroe, Marilyn
Morgan, Helen
Morris, Clara
Morris, Elizabeth
Mowatt, Anna Cora Ogden
Murray, Mae
Nazimova, Alla
Perry, Antoinette
Pitts, Zasu
Rehan, Ada
Robson, May
Rowson, Susanna Haswell
Russell, Annie
Shaw, Mary
Stevens, Emily
Strange, Michael
Sullavan, Margaret
Talmadge, Norma
Taylor, Laurette
Tucker, Sophie
Vincent, Mary Ann
Waller, Emma
Walsh, Blanche
Ward, Genevieve
Western, Lucille
Westley, Helen
White, Pearl
Wong, Anna May
ACTUARY (See also INSURANCE EX-
   ECUTIVE)
Fackler, David Parks
McCay, Charles Francis
McClintock, Emory
Wright, Elizur
ADMINISTRATOR (See also COL-
   LEGE ADMINISTRATOR, PRISON
   ADMINISTRATOR)
Abernethy, George
Adams, Jasper
Cloud, Henry Roe
Coburn, Foster Dwight
Crafts, James Mason
Dinwiddie, Robert
Geddes, James Loraine
Goethals, George Washington
Goode, George Brown
Hatfield, Edwin Francis
Hawley, Gideon, 1785–1870
King, Clarence
Landis, James McCauley
Lynds, Elam
Magoon, Charles Edward
Mendenhall, Thomas Corwin

Nelson, Reuben
Perkins, George Henry
Pickering, Timothy
Pilsbury, Amos
Powell, John Wesley
Randall, Alexander Williams
Richmond, Mary Ellen
Runkle, John Daniel
Sargent, Winthrop, 1753–1820
Smith, Edgar Fahs
Smith, James Francis
Taylor, James Barnett
Thacher, Thomas Anthony
Tompkins, Sally Louisa
Valentine, Robert Grosvenor
Vaughan, Victor Clarence
Walcott, Charles Doolittle
Wilson, Peter
Woodward, Robert Simpson
ADVENTURER (See also COLONIZ-
   ER, EXPLORER, FILIBUSTER,
   FUR TRADER, PRIVATEER, SPY,
   SWINDLER, TRADER, TRAVEL-
   ER)
Argall, Sir Samuel
Bartlett, Joseph
Bowles, William Augustus
Boyd, John Parker
Burgevine, Henry Andrea
Clarke, Elijah
Coode, John
Crowne, William
Gibson, Walter Murray
Graffenried, Christopher, Baron
   de
Harlan, Josiah
Hayes, William Henry ("Bully")
Henry, John, fl. 1807–1820
Judson, Edward Zane Carroll
Laffite, Jean
Long, James
MacDonald, Ranald
Morton, Thomas
Peñalosa Briceño, Diego
   Dioniso de
Revere, Joseph Warren
Scott, John
Smith, John, 1579/80–1631
Thrasher, John Sidney
Walker, William
Ward, Frederick Townsend
Wikoff, Henry
Wingfield, Edward Maria
Yeardley, Sir George
ADVENTURESS
Livingstone, Belle
ADVERTISING AGENT
Ayer, Francis Wayland
Post, Charles William
Rowell, George Presbury
ADVERTISING EXECUTIVE
Ayer, Francis Wayland
Barton, Bruce Fairchild
Block, Paul
Brophy, Thomas D'Arcy
Calkins, Earnest Elmo
Durstine, Roy Sarles
Emmett, Burton
Lasker, Albert Davis
Resor, Stanley Burnet
Watson, John Broadus

AERONAUT (See also AVIATOR,
   BALLOONIST)
Chanute, Octave
Durant, Charles Ferson
Herring, Augustus Moore
King, Samuel Archer
La Mountain, John
Langley, Samuel Pierpont
Lowe, Thaddeus Sobieski
   Coulincourt
Sellers, Matthew Bacon
Vought, Chance Milton
Wellman, Walter
AERONAUTICAL CONSULTANT
Ide, John Jay
AERONAUTICAL DESIGNER
Bellanca, Giuseppe Mario
AEROSPACE PIONEER
Bell, Lawrence Dale
AGITATOR (See also PAMPHLETEER,
   PROPAGANDIST, RADICAL,
   REVOLUTIONIST)
Beach, Wooster
Cooper, Thomas
McCord, David James
McDougall, Alexander
Paine, Thomas
Struve, Gustav
AGRARIAN LEADER (See also
   AGRICULTURAL LEADER,
   AGRICULTURIST, FARM LEAD-
   ER)
Johnson, Magnus
Lemke, William Frederick
AGRICULTURAL CHEMIST (See
   ALSO AGRICULTURIST, CHEM-
   IST)
Armsby, Henry Prentiss
Atwater, Wilbur Olin
Babcock, Stephen Moulton
Carver, George Washington
Collier, Peter
Frear, William
Hopkins, Cyril George
Jenkins, Edward Hopkins
Johnson, Samuel William
King, Franklin Hiram
Mapes, Charles Victor
Ravenel, St. Julien
Stockbridge, Horace Edward
Thatcher, Roscoe Wilfred
Van Slyke, Lucius Lincoln
AGRICULTURAL ECONOMIST (See
   also ECONOMIST)
Tolley, Howard Ross
Warren, George Frederick
AGRICULTURAL EDUCATOR (See
   also AGRICULTURIST, EDUCA-
   TOR)
Babcock, Howard Edward
Davenport, Eugene
Ladd, Carl Edwin
AGRICULTURAL HISTORIAN (See
   also HISTORIAN)
Edwards, Everett Eugene
AGRICULTURAL JOURNALIST (See
   also AGRICULTURIST, JOURNAL-
   IST)
Gregory, Clifford Verne
Sanders, James Harvey
Tucker, Luther
Wallace, Henry Cantwell

Wing, Joseph Elwyn
AGRICULTURAL LEADER (See also
  AGRARIAN LEADER, FARM
  LEADER)
  Goss, Albert Simon
  Haugen, Gilbert Nelson
  Lowden, Frank Orren
  Newsom, Herschel David
AGRICULTURAL SCIENTIST
  Wallace, Henry Agard
AGRICULTURE, COMMISSIONER OF
  (See also **AGRICULTURIST**)
  Le Duc, William Gates
  Newton, Isaac, 1800–1867
  Pearson, Raymond Allen
AGRICULTURIST (See also
  AGRICULTURAL CHEMIST, EDI-
  TOR, EDUCATOR, JOURNALIST;
  AGRICULTURE, COMMISSIONER
  OF; AGRONOMIST; ARBORICUL-
  TURIST; BOTANIC PHYSICIAN;
  BOTANIST; FARM COOPERATIVE
  LEADER; FARMER; FORESTER;
  GRANGER; HORTICULTURIST;
  NURSERYMAN; PLANT BREED-
  ER; PLANTER; POMOLOGIST;
  SECRETARY OF AGRICULTURE;
  SEEDSMAN; SILVICULTURIST;
  SOIL EXPERT; SOIL SCIENTIST;
  SUGAR PLANTER; TREE SUR-
  GEON; TREE-CARE EXPERT;
  VITICULTURIST
  Allen, Richard Lamb
  Bement, Caleb N.
  Blalock, Nelson Gales
  Bordley, John Beale
  Brigham, Joseph Henry
  Buel, Jesse
  Capron, Horace
  Chamberlain, William Isaac
  Coker, David Robert
  Dabney, Charles William
  Eaton, Benjamin Harrison
  Ellsworth, Henry Leavitt
  Emerson, Gouverneur
  Flint, Charles Louis
  Furnas, Robert Wilkinson
  Gardiner, Robert Hallowell
  Garnett, James Mercer
  Goodale, Stephen Lincoln
  Hazard, Thomas Robinson
  Henry, William Arnon
  Holmes, Ezekiel
  Jarvis, William
  Johnson, Benjamin Pierce
  Johnston, John
  Knapp, Bradford
  Knapp, Seaman Asahel
  Landreth, David
  Leaming, Jacob Spicer
  Le Duc, William Gates
  L'Hommedieu, Ezra
  Loring, George Bailey
  Lubin, David
  Lyman, Joseph Bardwell
  McBryde, John McLaren
  Mapes, James Jay
  Mason, Arthur John
  Miles, Manly
  Mitchell, Donald Grant
  Montgomery, William Bell
  Morton, Julius Sterling

Murphy, Frederick E.
Oemler, Arminius
O'Neal, Edward Asbury, III
Patrick, Marsena Rudolph
Pedder, James
Peters, Richard, 1810–1889
Powel, John Hare
Randall, Henry Stephens
Roberts, Job
Robinson, Solon
Ruffin, Edmund
Shelton, Edward Mason
Smith, Hiram
Stockbridge, Levi
Sturtevant, Edward Lewis
Taylor, John
Todd, Sereno Edwards
Trimble, Allen
True, Alfred Charles
Turner, Jonathan Baldwin
Vanderbilt, George Washington
Vaughan, Benjamin
Voorhees, Edward Burnett
Waring, George Edwin
Watson, Elkanah
Watts, Frederick
Wilder, Marshall Pinckney
Wilson, James
AGRONOMIST (See also **AGRICUL-**
  TURIST)
  Cobb, Nathan Augustus
  Hopkins, Cyril George
  Piper, Charles Vancouver
  Rosen, Joseph A.
AIR FORCE CHIEF OF STAFF
  Vandenberg, Hoyt Sanford
AIR FORCE OFFICER
  Chennault, Claire Lee
  Fairchild, Muir Stephen
  Grissom, Virgil Ivan ("Gus")
  Royce, Ralph
  Stratemeyer, George Edward
  White, Edward Higgins, II
AIRLINE EXECUTIVE (See **AVIATION**
  EXECUTIVE)
AIRMAIL PIONEER
  Henderson, Paul
ALIENIST (See also **PHYSICIAN;**
  PSYCHIATRIST; PSY-
  CHOANALYST)
  Awl, William Maclay
  Flint, Austin
  Gray, John Purdue
  Hamilton, Allan McLane
ALMANAC MAKER
  Ames, Nathaniel
  Daboll, Nathan
  Franklin, Benjamin
  Leavitt, Dudley
  Leeds, Daniel
  Pierce, William
  West, Benjamin
  Young, David
AMERICAN INDIAN RIGHTS ADVO-
  CATE
  Madigan, Laverne
AMERICAN RED CROSS OFFICIAL
  Boardman, Mabel Thorp
  Olds, Robert Edwin
  Payne, John Barton

AMUSEMENT PARK CREATOR
  Disney, Walter Elias ("Walt")
ANARCHIST
  Berkman, Alexander
  Goldman, Emma
  Most, Johann Joseph
  Parsons, Albert Richard
  Tucker, Benjamin Ricketson
  Warren, Josiah
ANATOMIST (See also **PHYSICIAN**)
  Allen, Edgar
  Allen, Harrison
  Baker, Frank
  Bensley, Robert Russell
  Brödel, Max
  Chovet, Abraham
  Coghill, George Ellett
  Davidge, John Beale
  Dorsey, John Syng
  Dwight, Thomas
  Gerrish, Frederic Henry
  Goddard, Paul Beck
  Godman, John Davidson
  Horner, William Edmonds
  Huber, Gotthelf Carl
  Jackson, Clarence Martin
  McClellan, George, 1796–1847
  McClellan, George, 1849–1913
  McMurrich, James Playfair
  Mall, Franklin Paine
  March, Alden
  Miller, William Snow
  Nelson, Marjorie Maxine
  Pancoast, Joseph
  Pancoast, Seth
  Papanicolaou, George Nicholas
  Pattison, Granville Sharp
  Ramsay, Alexander
  Ranson, Stephen Walter
  Robinson, Frederick Byron
  Sabin, Florence Rena
  Souchon, Edmond
  Spitzka, Edward Anthony
  Stockard, Charles Rupert
  Todd, Thomas Wingate
  Tuckerman, Frederick
  Weed, Lewis Hill
  Wislocki, George Bernays
  Wyman, Jeffries
ANESTHESIOLOGIST (**PHYSICIAN**)
  Colton, Gardner Quincy
  Long, Crawford Williamson
  Morton, William Thomas Green
  Rovenstine, Emery Andrew
  Wells, Horace
ANIMAL PSYCHOLOGIST
  Yerkes, Robert Mearns
ANIMATOR
  Disney, Walter Elias ("Walt")
ANTHOLOGIST
  Bronson, Walter Cochrane
  Griswold, Rufus Wilmot
  Kennedy, William Sloane
  Tappan, Eva March
ANTHROPOGEOGRAPHER (See also
  ANTHROPOLOGIST)
  Semple, Ellen Churchill
ANTHROPOLOGIST (See also **ETH-**
  NOLOGIST, FOLKLORIST)
  Alexander, Hartley Burr
  Bandelier, Adolph Francis
  Alphonse

Barrows, David Prescott
Benedict, Ruth Fulton
Boas, Franz
Brinton, Daniel Garrison
Chamberlain, Alexander Francis
Dixon, Roland Burrage
Dorsey, George Amos
Farabee, William Curtis
Farrand, Livingston
Fejos, Paul
Goldenweiser, Alexander
   Alexandrovich
Hooton, Earnest Albert
Hough, Walter
Hrdlicka, Ales
Hurston, Zora Neale
Kroeber, Alfred Louis
La Farge, Oliver Hazard Perry
Lewis, Oscar
Linton, Ralph
MacCurdy, George Grant
McGee, William John
McGuire, Joseph Deakins
Meigs, James Aitken
Nelson, Nels Christian
Parker, Arthur Caswell
Parsons, Elsie Worthington
   Clews
Powdermaker, Hortense
Radin, Paul
Redfield, Robert
Roheim, Geza
Sapir, Edward
Skinner, Alanson Buck
Spier, Leslie
Starr, Frederick
Sullivan, Louis Robert
Swanton, John Reed
Todd, Thomas Wingate
Warner, William Lloyd
Weidenreich, Franz
Wheelwright, Mary Cabot
Wissler, Clark

ANTIQUARIAN
Alden, Timothy
Appleton, William Sumner
Arthur, William
Bartlett, John Russell
Campbell, Charles
Chester, Joseph Lemuel
Davis, Andrew McFarland
Dexter, Franklin Bowditch
Drake, Samuel Gardner
Du Simitière, Pierre Eugène
Earle, Alice Morse
Endicott, Charles Moses
Farmer, John
Felt, Joseph Barlow
Folsom, George
Green, Samuel Abbott
Grim, David
Hazard, Samuel
Hoyt, Albert Harrison
Jordan, John Woolf
Livermore, George
McCabe, John Collins
Malcolm, James Peller
Mercer, Henry Chapman
Munsell, Joel
Nutting, Wallace
Robbins, Thomas
Sachse, Julius Friedrich

Sargent, Lucius Manlius
Savage, James
Shurtleff, Nathaniel Bradstreet
Smith, Buckingham
Stanard, William Glover
Stevens, Benjamin Franklin
Taylor, Richard Cowling
Van Schaack, Henry Cruger
Watson, John Fanning
Whitmore, William Henry
Young, Alexander

ANTIQUE DEALER
Rosenbach, Abraham Simon
   Wolf
Rosenbach, Philip Hyman
Sack, Israel

ANTISUFFRAGIST
Meyer, Annie Nathan

APIARIST
Langstroth, Lorenzo Lorraine
Root, Amos Ives

APOTHECARY (See also DRUGGIST,
   PHARMACIST)
Craigie, Andrew
Jackson, David

ARACHNOLOGIST
Emerton, James Henry

ARBORICULTURIST (See also
   AGRICULTURIST, BOTANIST,
   FORESTER, HORTICULTURIST,
   NURSERYMAN, PLANT BREED-
   ER, POMOLOGIST, SILVICUL-
   TURIST, TREE-CARE EXPERT,
   TREE SURGEON)
Sargent, Charles Sprague

ARCHABBOT (See also RELIGIOUS
   LEADER)
Schnerr, Leander
Stehle, Aurelius Aloysius

ARCHBISHOP (See also RELIGIOUS
   LEADER)
Alemany, José Sadoc
Blanc, Antoine
Blanchet, François Norbert
Blenk, James Hubert
Chapelle, Placide Louis
Corrigan, Michael Augustine
Dowling, Austin
Feehan, Patrick Augustine
Glennon, John Joseph
Hanna, Edward Joseph
Janssens, Francis
McNicholas, John Timothy
O'Connell, William Henry
Rummel, Joseph Francis
Stritch, Samuel Alphonsus

ARCHEOLOGIST (See also SCHOL-
   AR)
Abbott, Charles Conrad
Badè, William Frederic
Barber, Edwin Atlee
Beauchamp, William Martin
Bliss, Frederick Jones
Bowditch, Charles Pickering
Breasted, James Henry
Brower, Jacob Vradenberg
Butler, Howard Crosby
Casanowicz, Immanuel Moses
Cesnola, Luigi Palma di
Clarke, Sir Caspar Purdon
Conant, Alban Jasper
Davis, Edwin Hamilton

Fisher, Clarence Stanley
Fowke, Gerard
Goodyear, William Henry
Gordon, George Byron
Hawes, Harriet Ann Boyd
Haynes, John Henry
Holmes, William Henry
Hoppin, Joseph Clark
Kelsey, Francis Willey
Kidder, Alfred Vincent
MacCurdy, George Grant
Mercer, Henry Chapman
Merriam, Augustus Chapman
Merrill, Selah
Middleton, John Izard
Morley, Sylvanus Griswold
Murray, Louise Shipman Welles
Nies, James Buchanan
Paine, John Alsop
Parker, Arthur Caswell
Paton, Lewis Bayles
Peet, Stephen Denison
Peters, John Punnett
Porter, Arthur Kingsley
Putnam, Frederic Ward
Rau, Charles
Richardson, Rufus Byam
Rostovtzeff, Michael Ivanovitch
Saville, Marshall Howard
Seyffarth, Gustavus
Shear, Theodore Leslie
Snyder, John Francis
Speiser, Ephraim Avigdor
Squier, Ephraim George
Sterrett, John Robert Sitlington
Stevenson, Sara Yorke
Tarbell, Frank Bigelow
Thompson, Edward Herbert
Upham, Warren
Vaillant, George Clapp
Van Deman, Esther Boise
Wheeler, James Rignall
Whitehouse, Frederic Cope
Whittemore, Thomas
Winchell, Newton Horace
Winslow, William Copley

ARCHITECT (See also NAVAL AR-
   CHITECT)
Albro, Lewis Colt
Aldrich, Chester Holmes
Atterbury, Grosvenor
Atwood, Charles B.
Audsley, George Ashdown
Austin, Henry
Bacon, Henry
Banner, Peter
Barber, Donn
Behrendt, Walter Curt
Benjamin, Asher
Blodget, Samuel
Bluemner, Oscar Florians
Boring, William Alciphron
Boucher, Horace Edward
Bragdon, Claude Fayette
Browne, Herbert Wheildon
   Cotton
Brunner, Arnold William
Bulfinch, Charles
Burnham, Daniel Hudson
Cabot, Edward Clarke
Carrère, John Merven
Carter, Elias

Clarke, Sir Caspar Purdon
Cook, Walter
Coolidge, Charles Allerton
Cope, Walter
Corbett, Harvey Wiley
Cram, Ralph Adams
Cret, Paul Philippe
Culter, James Goold
Cummings, Charles Amos
Dakin, James Harrison
Davis, Alexander Jackson
Day, Frank Miles
Delano, William Adams
Downing, Andrew Jackson
Eidlitz, Cyrus Lazelle Warner
Eidlitz, Leopold
Elmslie, George Grant
Fenner, Burt Leslie
Flagg, Ernest
Ford, George Burdett
Gallier, James
Gilbert, Cass
Gilman, Arthur Delevan
Godefroy, Maximilian
Goodhue, Bertram Grosvenor
Graham, Ernest Robert
Granger, Alfred Hoyt
Greene, Charles Sumner
Greene, Henry Mather
Greenough, Henry
Gropius, Walter Adolf Georg
Hadfield, George
Haight, Charles Coolidge
Hallet, Étienne Sulpice
Hamlin, Alfred Dwight Foster
Hamlin, Talbot Faulkner
Hardenberg, Henry Janeway
Harrison, Peter
Hastings, Thomas
Haviland, John
Hawks, John
Higgins, Daniel Paul
Hoadley, David
Hoban, James
Holabird, William
Hood, Raymond Mathewson
Hooker, Philip
Hunt, Richard Morris
Jefferson, Thomas
Jenney, William Le Baron
Joy, Thomas
Kahn, Albert
Kearsley, John
Kimball, (Sidney) Fiske
Klauder, Charles Zeller
Kneass, Samuel Honeyman
La Farge, Christopher Grant
Lafever, Minard
Lamb, William Frederick
Latrobe, Benjamin Henry,
  1764–1820
Le Brun, Napoléon Eugène
  Henry Charles
Lienau, Detlef
Longfellow, William Pitt Preble
Lowell, Guy
McArthur, John, 1823–1890
McComb, John
McIntire, Samuel
McKim, Charles Folley
Maginnis, Charles Donagh
Magonigle, Harold Van Buren

Mangin, Joseph François
Marshall, Henry Rutgers
Mauran, John Lawrence
Maybeck, Bernard Ralph
Mazzuchelli, Samuel Charles
Mead, William Rutherford
Medary, Milton Bennett
Mendelsohn, Erich (*or* Eric)
Mies van der Rohe, Ludwig
Mills, Robert, 1781–1855
Mizner, Addison
Morgan, Julia
Neutra, Richard Joseph
Parris, Alexander
Peabody, Robert Swain
Pelz, Paul Johannes
Perkins, Dwight Heald
Platt, Charles Adams
Polk, Willis, Jefferson
Pond, Allen Bartlit
Pond, Irving Kane
Pope, John Russell
Post, George Browne
Poulson, Niels
Price, Bruce
Ramée, Joseph Jacques
Renwick, James, 1818–1895
Richardson, Henry Hobson
Rogers, Isaiah
Rogers, James Gamble
Root, John Wellborn
Rotch, Arthur
Saarinen, Eero
Saarinen, Gottlieb Eliel
Schindler, Rudolph Michael
Shaw, Howard Van Doren
Sherman, Frank Dempster
Skidmore, Louis
Smith, Robert, 1722–1777
Starrett, William Aiken
Stewardson, John
Stewart, John George
Stokes, Isaac Newton Phelps
Strickland, William
Sturgis, Russell
Sullivan, Louis Henri
Thompson, Martin E.
Thornton, William
Tilton, Edward Lippincott
Town, Ithiel
Trumbauer, Horace
Tucker, Allen
Tuthill, William Burnet
Upjohn, Richard
Upjohn, Richard Michell
Urban, Joseph
Van Brunt, Henry
Van Osdel, John Mills
Walter, Thomas Ustick
Ware, William Robert
Warren, Herbert Langford
Warren, Russell
Wheelwright, Edmund March
White, Stanford
Wight, Peter Bonnett
Willard, Soloman
Wilson, Joseph Miller
Withers, Frederick Clarke
Wright, Frank Lloyd
Wright, Henry
Young, Ammi Burnham

ARCHIVIST (See also LIBRARIAN,
  SCHOLAR)
Connor, Robert Digges
  Wimberly
Fernow, Berthold
Force, Peter
Ford, Worthington Chauncey
Knight, Lucian Lamar
Leland, Waldo Gifford
Owen, Thomas McAdory
ARMOR EXPERT
Dean, Bashford
ARMY AIR CORPS OFFICER
Andrews, Frank Maxwell
ARMY MEDICAL OFFICER (See also
  PHYSICIAN, SOLDIER)
Hume, Edgar Erskine
Simmons, James Stevens
ARMY OFFICER (See also GENERAL,
  SOLDIER)
Ainsworth, Frederick Crayton
Ames, Adelbert
Arnold, Henry Harley
Bell, James Franklin
Black, William Murray
Brereton, Lewis Hyde
Buckner, Simon Bolivar
Bullard, Robert Lee
Casey, Thomas Lincoln
Chaffee, Adna Romanza
Craig, Malin
Crowder, Enoch Herbert
Crozier, William
Davis, Benjamin Oliver, Sr.
Drum, Hugh Aloysius
Eddy, Manton Sprague
Edwards, Clarence Ransom
Eichelberger, Robert Lawrence
Eisenhower, Dwight David
Ely, Hanson Edward
Fairchild, Muir Stephen
Foulois, Benjamin Delahauf
Glassford, Pelham Davis
Graves, William Sidney
Groves, Leslie Richard, Jr.
Guild, La Fayette
Harbord, James Guthrie
Hawley, Paul Ramsey
Heintzelman, Stuart
Hines, Frank Thomas
Hines, John Leonard ("Birdie")
Hodes, Henry Irving
Hodge, John Reed
Hodges, Courtney Hicks
Johnson, Hugh Samuel
Johnston, William Hartshorne
King, Edward Leonard
Krueger, Walter
Kuhn, Joseph Ernst
Lear, Ben
Lee, John Clifford Hodges
Liggett, Hunter
Lynch, John Roy
McAlexander, Ulysses Grant
MacArthur, Arthur
MacArthur, Douglas
McClure, Robert Alexis
McNair, Lesley James
MacNider, Hanford
Marshall, George Catlett, Jr.
Michler, Nathaniel
Mitchell, William

Morton, Charles Gould
Muir, Charles Henry
Neyland, Robert Reese, Jr.
Palmer, John McAuley
Patch, Alexander McCarrell
Patrick, Mason Mathews
Patton, George Smith
Pick, Lewis Andrew
Read, George Windle
Roosevelt, Kermit
Roosevelt, Theodore
Schroeder, Rudolph William
Scott, Hugh Lenox
Short, Walter Campbell
Smith, Walter Bedell
Snyder, Howard McCrum
Somervell, Brehon Burke
Stilwell, Joseph Warren
Sutherland, Richard Kerens
Vedder, Edward Bright
Wagener, John Andreas
Wainwright, Jonathan Mayhew
Walker, Walton Harris
Whitney, Courtney
Winship, Blanton
Wood, Charles Erskine Scott
Wood, Robert Elkington

ART COLLECTOR (See also COL-
   LECTOR)
Arensberg, Walter Conrad
Bache, Jules Semon
Barnes, Albert Coombs
Berenson, Bernard
Cone, Claribel
Cone, Etta
Dale, Chester
Dale, Maud Murray Thompson
Emmett, Burton
Freer, Charles Lang
Gardner, Isabella Stewart
Gellatly, John
Goodyear, Anson Conger
Jarves, James Jackson
Johnson, John Graver
Johnston, John Taylor
Kress, Samuel Henry
Lasker, Albert Davis
Lehman, Adele Lewisohn
Lewisohn, Adolph
Mellon, Andrew William
Reisinger, Hugo
Rosenberg, Paul
Ross, Denman Waldo
Ryerson, Martin Antoine
Walker, Thomas Barlow
Walters, Henry
Walters, William Thompson
White, Alexander

ART CONNOISSEUR
Avery, Samuel Putnam
Berenson, Bernard
Cahill, Holger
Clarke, Sir Caspar Purdon
Frankfurter, Alfred Moritz
Hart, Charles Henry
Laffan, William Mackay
Lyon, Caleb

ART CRITIC
Berenson, Bernard
Cary, Elisabeth Luther
Coffin, William Anderson
Cook, Clarence Chatham

Cortissoz, Royal
Cox, Kenyon
Foster, Benjamin
Frankfurter, Alfred Moritz
Hartmann, Carl Sadakichi
Hitchcock, James Ripley
   Wellman
Keppel, Frederick
Perkins, Charles Callahan
Rosenfeld, Paul Leopold
Stein, Leo Daniel
Van Dyke, John Charles
Van Rensselaer, Mariana
   Griswold
Wallace, Horace Binney

ART DEALER
Avery, Samuel Putnam
Halpert, Edith Gregor
Rosenberg, Paul

ART EDUCATOR
Sachs, Paul Joseph

ART HISTORIAN
Berenson, Bernard
Coomaraswamy, Ananda
   Kentish
Friedlaender, Walter Ferdinand
Gardner, Helen
Kimball, (Sidney) Fiske
Panofsky, Erwin
Warner, Langdon

ART PATRON
Altman, Benjamin
Crowninshield, Francis Welch
De Cuevas, Marquis
Dreier, Katherine Sophie
Evans, William Thomas
Kahn, Otto Herman
Lewisohn, Sam Adolph
Libbey, Edward Drummond
Luhan, Mabel Dodge
Murphy, Gerald Clery
Reed, Luman
Stieglitz, Alfred
Whitney, Gertrude Vanderbilt
Wolfe, Catharine Lorillard

ARTIST (CARTOONIST, CRAFTSMAN,
   GRAPHIC ARTIST, ILLUSTRA-
   TOR, MODELER, MURALIST,
   PAINTER, SCULPTOR)
Allston, Washington
Appleton, Thomas Gold
Artzybasheff, Boris
Audubon, John James
Avery, Milton Clark
Baziotes, William
Beard, James Henry
Beard, William Holbrook
Bemelmans, Ludwig
Birch, Reginald Bathurst
Burroughs, Bryson
Cassatt, Mary
Catlin, George
Cesare, Oscar Edward
Chaplin, Ralph Hosea
Chase, William Merritt
Cheney, Seth Wells
Cole, Thomas
Coman, Charlotte Buell
Conant, Alban Jasper
Connick, Charles Jay
Crosby, Percy Lee
Davis, Charles Harold

Davis, Stuart
Dellenbaugh, Frederick Samuel
Demuth, Charles
Dodge, William de Leftwich
Drake, Alexander Wilson
Dreier, Katherine Sophie
Du Simitière, Pierre Eugène
Emerton, James Henry
Flagg, Josiah Foster
Fuertes, Louis Agassiz
Fulton, Robert
Gág, Wanda (Hazel)
Gibson, William Hamilton
Gutherz, Carl
Hambridge, Jay
Harshe, Robert Bartholow
Hassam, Frederick Childe
Hokinson, Helen Elna
Holmes, William Henry
Howland, Alfred Cornelius
Hyde, Helen
Imbert, Antoine
Isham, Samuel
Ives, Halsey Cooley
James, Will Roderick
Jamison, Cecilia Viets Dakin
   Hamilton
Johnston, Henrietta
Koehler, Sylvester Rosa
Lanman, Charles
Lawrie, Alexander
Lesueur, Charles Alexandre
Leyendecker, Joseph Christian
Louis, Morris
Low, Will Hicok
Marin, John (Cheri)
Mitchell, John Ames
Moholy-Nagy, László
Moore, Charles Herbert
Morse, Samuel Finley Breese
Nicholls, Rhoda Holmes
Niemeyer, John Henry
Oertel, Johannes Adam Simon
Outcault, Richard Felton
Parrish, Maxfield
Peale, Titian Ramsay
Perry, Walter Scott
Pippin, Horace
Pyle, Howard
Rehn, Frank Knox Morton
Ripley, Robert LeRoy
Robinson, Boardman
Robinson, Theodore
Rothermel, Peter Frederick
Saint-Mémin, Charles Balthazar
   Julien Fevret de
Shahn, Benjamin ("Ben")
Sheeler, Charles R., Jr.
Smibert, John
Smith, Francis Hopkinson
Stein, Evaleen
Stillman, William James
Thorpe, Thomas Bangs
Thulstrup, Bror Thure
Tiffany, Louis Comfort
Weber, Max
Weir, John Ferguson
White, John
White, John Blake
Widforss, Gunnar Mauritz
Willet, William

ASSASSIN
  Booth, John Wilkes
  Oswald, Lee Harvey
  Ruby, Jack L.
ASSYRIOLOGIST (See also SCHOL-
    AR)
  Dougherty, Raymond Philip
  Harper, Robert Francis
  Haupt, Paul
  Hilprecht, Herman Volrath
ASTRONAUT (See ALSO, AERONAUT,
    AVIATOR, BALLOONIST)
  Chaffee, Roger Bruce
  Grissom, Virgil Ivan ("Gus")
  White, Edward Higgins, II
ASTRONOMER
  Abbe, Cleveland
  Adams, Walter Sydney
  Aitken, Robert Grant
  Alexander, Stephen
  Baade, Wilhelm Heinrich
    Walter
  Bailey, Solon Irving
  Barnard, Edward Emerson
  Bond, George Phillips
  Bond, William Cranch
  Boss, Lewis
  Bowditch, Nathaniel
  Brooks, William Robert
  Burnham, Sherburne Wesley
  Campbell, William Wallace
  Cannon, Annie Jump
  Chandler, Seth Carlo
  Chauvenet, William
  Clark, Alvan
  Clark, Alvan Graham
  Comstock, George Cary
  Curtis, Heber Doust
  Davidson, George
  Doolittle, Charles Leander
  Doolittle, Eric
  Douglass, Andrew Ellicott
  Draper, Henry
  Eastman, John Robie
  Elkin, William Lewis
  Farrar, John
  Fleming, Williamina Paton
    Stevens
  Flint, Albert Stowell
  Freeman, Thomas
  Frost, Edwin Brant
  Gilliss, James Melville
  Gould, Benjamin Apthorp
  Grew, Theophilus
  Hale, George Ellery
  Hall, Asaph
  Harkness, William
  Harrington, Mark Walrod
  Holden, Edward Singleton
  Hough, George Washington
  Howe, Herbert Alonzo
  Hubbard, Joseph Stillman
  Hubble, Edwin
  Hussey, William Joseph
  Keeler, James Edward
  King, Edward Skinner
  Kirkwood, Daniel
  Leavenworth, Francis Preserved
  Leavitt, Henrietta Swan
  Leeds, John
  Loomis, Elias
  Lord, Henry Curwen

Lowell, Percival
Lyman, Chester Smith
Metcalf, Joel Hastings
Mitchel, Ormsby MacKnight
Mitchell, Maria
Mitchell, William, 1791–1869
Moore, Joseph Haines
Moulton, Forest Ray
Newcomb, Simon
Nicholson, Seth Barnes
Parkhurst, John Adelbert
Paul, Henry Martyn
Peirce, Benjamin
Perrine, Charles Dillon
Peters, Christian Henry
  Frederick
Pickering, Edward Charles
Porter, Jermain Gildersleeve
Pritchett, Henry Smith
Rees, John Krom
Rigge, William Francis
Ritchey, George Willis
Rittenhouse, David
Rogers, William Augustus
Russell, Henry Norris
Safford, Truman Henry
St. John, Charles Edward
Schaeberle, John Martin
Schlesinger, Frank
Searle, Arthur
Sestini, Benedict
Skinner, Aaron Nichols
Slipher, Vesto Melvin
Stockwell, John Nelson
Stone, Ormond
Struve, Otto
Swift, Lewis
Tuttle, Charles Wesley
Twining, Alexander Catlin
Upton, Winslow
Vaughan, Daniel
Walker, Sears Cook
Watson, James Craig
West, Benjamin
Whitney, Mary Watson
Winlock, Joseph
Winthrop, John
Young, Charles Augustus
Young, David
ASTRONOMICAL LENSMAKER
  Brashear, John Alfred
  Clark, Alvan
  Clark, Alvan Graham
ASTRONOMICAL PHOTOGRAPHER
  (See also ASTRONOMER, PHO-
  TOGRAPHER)
  Draper, Henry
ASTROPHYSICIST (See also AS-
  TRONOMER, PHYSICIST)
  Mason, Max
  Rutherfurd, Lewis Morris
ATHLETE (See also SPECIFIC
  SPORTS)
  Blaikie, William
  Clothier, William Jackson
  McGrath, Matthew J.
  Pilkington, James
  Thorpe, James Francis
  Zaharias, Mildred ("Babe")
    Didrikson

ATHLETIC COACH
  Lapchick, Joseph Bohomiel
ATHLETIC TRAINER
  Murphy, Michael Charles
ATTORNEY (See LAWYER)
ATTORNEY GENERAL (CONFEDER-
    ATE)
  Benjamin, Judah Philip
  Davis, George
  Watts, Thomas Hill
ATTORNEY GENERAL (FEDERAL)
  Beck, James Montgomery
  Biddle, Francis Beverley
  Black, Jeremiah Sullivan
  Bonaparte, Charles Joseph
  Brewster, Benjamin Harris
  Cummings, Homer Stillé
  Daugherty, Harry Micajah
  Devens, Charles
  Garland, Augustus Hill
  Gilpin, Henry Dilworth
  Gregory, Thomas Watt
  Harmon, Judson
  Hoar, Ebenezer Rockwood
  Kennedy, Robert Francis
  Lee, Charles, 1758–1815
  Legaré, Hugh Swinton
  McGranery, James Patrick
  McGrath, James Howard
  Miller, William Henry Harrison
  Moody, William Henry
  Murphy, Frank
  Olney, Richard
  Palmer, Alexander Mitchell
  Perlman, Philip Benjamin
  Pierrepont, Edwards
  Randolph, Edmund, 1753–1813
  Speed, James
  Stanbery, Henry
  Stanton, Edwin McMasters
  Stockton, John Potter
  Taft, Alphonso
  Taney, Roger Brooke
  Thacher, Thomas Day
  Toucey, Isaac
  Wickersham, George
    Woodward
  Williams, George Henry
  Wirt, William
ATTORNEY GENERAL (STATE)
  Conner, James
  Gilchrist, Robert
  Johnston, Augustus
  Martin, Luther
  Pringle, John Julius
  Robeson, George Maxwell
  Trott, Nicholas
  Updike, Daniel
AUTHOR (See also BIOGRAPHER,
    CRITIC, DIARIST, DRAMATIST,
    ESSAYIST, LITTERATEUR, NOV-
    ELIST, POET, WRITER)
  Abbot, Willis John
  Abbott, Austin
  Abbott, Benjamin Vaughan
  Abbott, Charles Conrad
  Abbott, Edith
  Abbott, Jacob
  Abbott, Lyman
  Acrelius, Israel
  Adair, James
  Adams, Andy

Adams, Frederick Upham
Adams, John Coleman
Adams, Samuel Hopkins
Ade, George
Adler, Polly
Akeley, Mary Leonore
Akers, Elizabeth Chase
Alcott, Amos Bronson
Alcott, Louisa May
Alden, Henry Mills
Alden, Isabella Macdonald
Alden, Joseph
Alexander, Archibald
Alexander, Edward Porter
Alexander, Joseph Addison
Alger, William Rounseville
Allen, Alexander Viets Griswold
Allen, Anthony Benezet
Allen, Ethan
Allen, George
Allen, Joel Asaph
Allen, Joseph Henry
Allen, William
Allen, Zachariah
Allston, Washington
Alsop, Charles
Altsheler, Joseph Alexander
Anderson, Sherwood
Anderson, Victor Vance
Andrews, Christopher
  Columbus
Andrews, Roy Chapman
Antin, Mary
Apes, William
Arthur, Timothy Shay
Artzybasheff, Boris
Ashhurst, John
Atkinson, George Wesley
Atwater, Caleb
Audsley, George Ashdown
Austin, Jane Goodwin
Austin, Mary
Austin, William
Azarias, Brother
Babbitt, Irving
Babcock, Maltbie Davenport
Babson, Roger Ward
Bacon, Alice Mabel
Bacon, Delia Salter
Bacon, Edwin Munroe
Badeau, Adam
Bagby, George William
Baird, Samuel John
Baker, Ray Stannard
Baker, William Mumford
Baldwin, Joseph
Baldwin, Joseph Glover
Baldwin, Loammi
Balestier, Charles Wolcott
Ballou, Hosea
Ballou, Maturin Murray
Bancroft, Aaron
Bancroft, Edward
Banvard, John
Banvard, Joseph
Barbour, Oliver Lorenzo
Bardeen, Charles William
Barnard, Charles
Barnes, Albert
Barr, Amelia Edith Huddleston
Bartholow, Roberts
Bartlett, Elisha

Bartlett, Joseph
Barton, Bruce Fairchild
Barton, Robert Thomas
Bates, Arlo
Bates, Katharine Lee
Baum, Lyman Frank
Bausman, Benjamin
Baylor, Frances Courtenay
Beard, Daniel Carter
Beard, James Carter
Beard, Mary Ritter
Beatty, John
Beers, Henry Augustin
Bell, Bernard Iddings
Bell, Charles Henry
Bell, Eric Temple
Bellamy, Edward
Bellamy, Elizabeth Whitfield
  Croom
Benét, William Rose
Benezet, Anthony
Benjamin, Asher
Benjamin, Park
Benjamin, Samuel Greene
  Wheeler
Bennett, Charles Edwin
Bentley, William
Berg, Gertrude Edelstein
Berger, Meyer
Berkman, Alexander
Biddle, Horace P.
Bidwell, Barnabas
Bierce, Ambrose Gwinett
Bigelow, John
Binkley, Wilfred Ellsworth
Binns, John
Bishop, John Peale
Bixby, James Thompson
Blackmur, Richard Palmer
Blake, John Lauris
Blake, Lillie Devereux
Blake, Mary Elizabeth McGrath
Bledsoe, Albert Taylor
Bleyer, Willard Grosvenor
Bloomgarden, Solomon
Bodenheim, Maxwell
Bok, Edward William
Bolton, Sarah Knowles
Bond, Elizabeth Powell
Bonsal, Stephen
Booth, Mary Louise
Botta, Anne Charlotte Lynch
Bottome, Margaret McDonald
Botts, John Minor
Boudin, Louis Boudinoff
Bouton, John Bell
Bouvet, Marie Marguerite
Bowen, Herbert Wolcott
Bowker, Richard Rogers
Boyesen, Hjalmar Hjorth
Boynton, Charles Brandon
Brace, John Pierce
Brachvogel, Udo
Brackenridge, Henry Marie
Brackenridge, Hugh Henry
Brackett, Charles William
Bradford, Alden
Brady, Cyrus Townsend
Bragdon, Claude Fayette
Brierton, John
Briggs, Charles Frederick
Brigham, Amariah

Brightly, Frederick Charles
Bristed, Charles Astor
Bristed, John
Brockett, Linus Pierpont
Bromfield, Louis
Brooks, Elbridge Streeter
Brooks, Noah
Broun, Heywood Campbell
Brown, Addison
Brown, Benjamin Frederick
Brown, Margaret Wise
Brown, William Garrott
Brown, William Hill
Browne, John Ross
Browne, William Hand
Brownson, Orestes Augustus
Bruce, Andrew Alexander
Brühl, Gustav
Bryan, Mary Edwards
Bryce, Lloyd Stephens
Bryson, Lyman Lloyd
Buchanan, Joseph Rodes
Buchanan, Scott Milross
Buckminster, Joseph Stevens
Bulfinch, Thomas
Bunce, Oliver Bell
Bunner, Henry Cuyler
Buntline, Ned (*See* Judson,
  Edward Zane Carroll)
Burdick, Usher Lloyd
Burgess, John William
Burgess, Thornton Waldo
Burnap, George Washington
Burnett, Frances Eliza Hodgson
Burnham, Clara Louisa Root
Burrage, Walter Lincoln
Burrill, Alexander Mansfield
Burroughs, Edgar Rice
Burroughs, John
Burt, Mary Elizabeth
Burton, William Evans
Butler, William Allen
Butterworth, Hezekiah
Byrd, William
Cabell, Nathaniel Francis
Cable, George Washington
Caffin, Charles Henry
Cahill, Holger
Cain, William
Caines, George
Calef, Robert
Calkins, Earnest Elmo
Calkins, Norman Allison
Callimachos, Panos Demetrios
Cannon, Charles James
Capen, Nahum
Carleton, Henry
Carlson, Evans Fordyce
Carnegie, Dale
Carpenter, Edmund Janes
Carpenter, Frank George
Carpenter, George Rice
Carrington, Henry Beebee
Carroll, Howard
Carruth, Fred Hayden
Carryl, Guy Wetmore
Carter, Robert
Caruthers, William Alexander
Cash, Wilbur Joseph
Castle, William Richards, Jr.
Cather, Willa
Catlin, George

Chadwick, John White
Chamberlain, Nathan Henry
Champlin, John Denison
Chandler, Elizabeth Margaret
Chandler, Raymond Thornton
Charlton, Thomas Usher
  Pulaski
Cheney, Ednah Dow Littlehale
Cheney, John Vance
Chesebrough, Caroline
Chessman, Caryl Whittier
Chester, George Randolph
Child, Frank Samuel
Child, Lydia Maria Francis
Child, Richard Washburn
Chipman, Daniel
Chopin, Kate O'Flaherty
Church, Benjamin
Church, George Earl
Church, Irving Porter
Clapp, William Warland
Clark, Charles Heber
Clarke, Helen Archibald
Clarke, Mary Bayard Devereux
Clemmer, Mary
Cleveland, Horace William
  Shaler
Clews, Henry
Clinch, Charles Powell
Cobb, Irvin Shrewsbury
Cobb, Lyman
Coburn, Foster Dwight
Codman, John
Coffin, Charles Carleton
Coggeshall, George
Coggeshall, William Turner
Colburn, Warren
Colby, Frank Moore
Collens, Thomas Wharton
Collier, Hiram Price
Colton, Calvin
Colton, Walter
Colvin, Stephen Sheldon
Conant, Charles Arthur
Conant, Hannah O'Brien
  Chaplin
Cone, Orello
Congdon, Charles Taber
Conkling, Alfred
Converse, James Booth
Conway, Moncure Daniel
Cook, Clarence Chatham
Cook, Martha Elizabeth Duncan
  Walker
Cooke, George Willis
Cooke, Josiah Parsons
Cooke, Philip St. George
Copway, George
Cornwallis, Kinahan
Corson, Hiram
Cortambert, Louis Richard
Cory, Charles Barney
Cotton, John
Cowley, Charles
Cox, Jacob Dolson
Cox, Palmer
Cox, Rowland
Cox, Samuel Sullivan
Coxe, Arthur Cleveland
Cozzens, Frederick Swartwout
Crafts, William
Crane, Anne Moncure

Crane, Stephen
Crane, Thomas Frederick
Crapsey, Algernon Sidney
Crocker, Hannah Mather
Croly, Herbert David
Crosby, Ernest Howard
Crothers, Samuel McChord
Crouse, Russel McKinley
Crowninshield, Frederic
Cullum, George Washington
Cuming, Fortescue
Cummins, Maria Susanna
Currier, Charles Warren
Curry, Jabez Lamar Monroe
Curtis, Charles Pelham
Curtis, George Ticknor
Curtis, George William
Curwen, Samuel
Cushing, Luther Stearns
Cutler, Lizzie Petit
Cuyler, Theodore Ledyard
Dabney, Robert Lewis
Dabney, Virginius
Dagg, John Leadley
Dahlgren, Sarah Madeleine
  Vinton
Dall, Caroline Wells Healey
Daly, Charles Patrick
Dana, John Cotton
Dana, Richard Henry
Darby, John
Darling, Flora Adams
Davenport, John
Davidson, James Wood
Davies, Joseph Edward
Davies, Maria Thompson
Davis, Andrew McFarland
Davis, Mary Evelyn Moore
Davis, Noah Knowles
Davis, Oscar King
Davis, Richard Harding
Davis, Varina Anne Jefferson
Davis, Varina Howell
Davis, William Thomas
Day, Clarence Shepard
Dean, Sidney
Dearborn, Henry Alexander
  Scammell
De Costa, Benjamin Franklin
Deems, Charles Force
Deering, Nathaniel
De Fontaine, Felix Gregory
De Forest, John William
De Kay, James Ellsworth
Deland, Margaret
Delano, Amassa
De Leon, Thomas Cooper
Deléry, François Charles
Dellenbaugh, Frederick Samuel
Deming, Philander
De Peyster, John Watts
Detmold, Christian Edward
De Trobriand, Régis Denis de
  Keredern
Dewey, Orville
Diat, Louis Felix
Diaz, Abby Morton
Dibble, Roy Floyd
Didier, Eugene Lemoine
Dimitry, Charles Patton
Ditson, George Leighton
Dixon, Thomas

Dodd, Lee Wilson
Doddridge, Joseph
Dodge, Mary Abigail
Dodge, Mary Elizabeth Mapes
Dole, Nathan Haskell
Donnelly, Eleanor Cecilia
Dorchester, Daniel
Dorr, Julia Caroline Ripley
Dorsey, Anna Hanson
  McKenney
Dorsey, George Amos
Dorsey, Sarah Anne Ellis
Douglas, Amanda Minnie
Downey, June Etta
Downing, Charles
Drayton, John
Dromgoole, William Allen
Duganne, Augustine Joseph
  Hickey
Dummer, Jeremiah
Dunlop, James
Du Ponceau, Pierre Étienne
Durfee, Job
Durivage, Francis Alexander
Dwight, Benjamin Woodbridge
Dwight, Theodore, 1764–1846
Dwight, Theodore, 1796–1866
Dwight, Timothy
Dyer, Louis
Earle, Alice Morse
Eckstorm, Fannie Hardy
Eddy, Daniel Clarke
Edes, Robert Thaxter
Edwards, Charles
Egan, Maurice Francis
Elder, Susan Blanchard
Elder, William
Eliot, Charles
Ellet, Elizabeth Fries Lummis
Elliott, Benjamin
Elliott, Sarah Barnwell
Elliott, Walter Hackett Robert
Ellis, Edward Sylvester
Ellis, George Washington
Elson, Louis Charles
Embree, Edwin Rogers
Embury, Emma Catherine
Emerson, Edward Waldo
Emerson, Ellen Russell
Erskine, John
Evans, Augusta Jane
Evans, Warren Felt
Everett, David
Ewbank, Thomas
Ewing, Hugh Boyle
Eytinge, Rose
Fairchild, David Grandison
Farley, Harriet
Farnham, Eliza Woodson
  Burhans
Farnham, Thomas Jefferson
Farrar, Timothy
Farwell, Arthur
Faust, Frederick Shiller
Fawcett, Edgar
Fay, Edwin Whitefield
Fay, Theodore Sedgwick
Felton, Rebecca Latimer
Fernald, James Champlin
Fernow, Bernhard Eduard
Feuchtwanger, Lion
Field, Eugene

Field, Henry Martyn
Field, Mary Katherine Kemble
Field, Maunsell Bradhurst
Field, Richard Stockton
Field, Roswell Martin
Field, Thomas Warren
Fields, Annie Adams
Fields, James Thomas
Fillebrown, Thomas
Finck, Henry Theophilus
Finley, John Huston
Finley, Martha Farquharoon
Finn, Francis James
Fisher, Dorothea Frances
  Canfield
Fisher, Sidney George
Fiske, Amos Kidder
Fitzgerald, Oscar Penn
Flagg, Edmund
Flagg, James Montgomery
Flagg, Thomas Wilson
Flanders, Henry
Flandrau, Charles Eugene
Flint, Timothy
Florence, William Jermyn
Floy, James
Follen, Eliza Lee Cabot
Follett, Mary Parker
Folsom, George
Forbes, Edwin
Forbes, Robert Bennett
Force, Manning Ferguson
Forman, Justus Miles
Fortier, Alcée
Fosdick, Charles Austin
Fosdick, Harry Emerson
Fosdick, William Whiteman
Foster, David Skaats
Foster, Hannah Webster
Foster, Roger Sherman Baldwin
Foulke, William Dudley
Fowle, Daniel
Fowler, Gene
Francis, Samuel Ward
Frank, Jerome
Frank, Lawrence Kelso
Franklin, Benjamin
Freeman, James Edwards
Freeman, Mary Eleanor Wilkins
Frémont, Jessie Benton
French, Alice
French, Lucy Virginia Smith
Frothingham, Arthur Lincoln
Frothingham, Octavius Brooks
Frothingham, Paul Revere
Fry, James Barnet
Fulton, John Farquhar
Gage, Frances Dana Barker
Gage, Matilda Joslyn
Gaillardet, Théodore Frédéric
Gale, Zona
Garden, Alexander
Gardener, Helen Hamilton
Garis, Howard Roger
Garretson, James
Garrett, Edmund Henry
Gass, Patrick
Gay, Sydney Howard
Gernsback, Hugo
Ghent, William James
Gholson, William Yates
Gibbes, Robert Wilson

Gibbons, Herbert Adams
Gibbons, James Sloan
Gibbs, Arthur Hamilton
Gibbs, (Oliver) Wolcott
Giesler-Anneke, Mathilde
  Franziska
Gildersleeve, Basil Lanneau
Giles, Chauncey
Gillett, Ezra Hall
Gillman, Henry
Gilman, Arthur
Gilman, Caroline Howard
Gilman, Daniel Coit
Gilman, Samuel
Gilmer, Francis Walker
Gilmer, George Rockingham
Gilmore, James Roberts
Gilpin, Henry Dilworth
Gitlow, Benjamin
Glaspell, Susan Keating
Glass, Montague Marsden
Godwin, Parke
Goode, George Brown
Goodrich, Alfred John
Goodrich, Charles Augustus
Goodrich, Frank Boott
Goodrich, Samuel Griswold
Goodyear, William Henry
Gordon, George Angier
Gordon, George Henry
Gordon, William
Gould, Edward Sherman
Gould, George Milbry
Goulding, Francis Robert
Graham, David
Graham, John Andrew
Gray, John Chipman
Graydon, Alexander
Greely, Adolphus Washington
Green, Asa
Green, Frances Harriet
  Whipple
Green, Joseph
Green, Samuel Abbott
Greene, George Washington
Greenleaf, Moses
Greenleaf, Simon
Greenough, Henry
Gregg, Josiah
Grew, Joseph Clark
Grey, Zane
Grierson, Francis
Griffis, William Elliot
Grimké, Archibald Henry
Griswold, Rufus Wilmot
Gross, Milt
Gross, Samuel David
Grund, Francis Joseph
Guild, Curtis, 1827–1911
Gulick, Luther Halsey,
  1865–1918
Gunther, John
Gurowski, Adam
Habberton, John
Hackett, Frank Warren
Haines, Charles Glidden
Haldeman-Julius, Emanuel
Hale, Louise Closser
Hale, Lucretia Peabody
Hale, Sarah Josepha Buell
Hales, Edward Everett
Hall, Abraham Oakey

Hall, Arethusa
Hall, Baynard Rush
Hall, Florence Marion Howe
Hall, James, 1793–1868
Hall, James Norman
Halleck, Henry Wager
Hallock, Charles
Hamilton, Allan McLane
Hamilton, Edith
Hammett, Samuel Adams
Hammett, Samuel Dashiell
Hanaford, Phoebe Ann Coffin
Hanchett, Henry Granger
Hapgood, Hutchins
Hapgood, Isabel Florence
Harbaugh, Henry
Harland, Henry
Harper, Ida Husted
Harris, Benjamin
Harris, Joel Chandler
Harris, Joseph
Harrison, Constance Cary
Harrison, Gabriel
Hart, Charles Henry
Harte, Francis Brett
Hartmann, Carl Sadakichi
Hatcher, William Eldridge
Haupt, Herman
Haven, Emily Bradley Neal
Hawthorne, Julian
Hayes, John Lord
Hays, Arthur Garfield
Hazard, Thomas Robinson
Headley, Joel Tyler
Hearn, Lafcadio
Heath, James Ewell
Heilprin, Michael
Heinzen, Karl Peter
Helmuth, William Tod
Helper, Hinton Rowan
Hempel, Charles Julius
Henderson, Peter
Hendrick, Ellwood
Hennepin, Louis
Henningsen, Charles Frederick
Henry, Caleb Sprague
Hentz, Caroline Lee Whiting
Herbermann, Charles George
Herbert, Henry William
Herford, Oliver Brooke
Herrick, Sophia McIlvaine
  Bledsoe
Herron, George Davis
Higginson, Thomas Wentworth
Hildreth, Richard
Hilgard, Theodor Erasmus
Hill, Frederick Trevor
Hill, Grace Livingston
Hilliard, Henry Washington
Hillis, Newell Dwight
Hillquit, Morris
Hine, Charles De Lano
Hinsdale, Burke Aaron
Hinshaw, David Schull
Hirst, Barton Cooke
Hitchcock, Enos
Hitchcock, Ethan Allen,
  1798–1870
Hitchcock, James Ripley
  Wellman
Hittell, John Shertzer
Hittell, Theodore Henry

Hodges, George
Hofstadter, Richard
Hogue, Wilson Thomas
Hoisington, Henry Richard
Holcombe, William Henry
Holder, Joseph Bassett
Holland, Edwin Clifford
Holland, Josiah Gilbert
Holley, Alexander Lyman
Hollister, Gideon Hiram
Holmes, George Frederick
Holt, Henry
Hooker, Worthington
Hopkinson, Francis
Hosmer, Hezekiah Lord
Hosmer, James Kendall
Houdini, Harry
Hough, Emerson
House, Edward Howard
Howard, Blanche Willis
Howe, Edgar Watson
Howe, Julia Ward
Hoyt, Henry Martyn
Hubbard, Elbert
Hubbard, Wynant Davis
Hudson, Charles
Hudson, Thomson Jay
Hughes, Henry
Hughes, Rupert
Huneker, James Gibbons
Hunt, Isaac
Hunt, Theodore Whitefield
Hunter, William C.
Huntington, William Reed
Hunton, William Lee
Hurlbert, William Henry
Hurlbut, Jesse Lyman
Husmann, George
Hutchinson, Woods
Hutton, Laurence
Hyde, William De Witt
Ickes, Harold Le Clair
Ide, John Jay
Imlay, Gilbert
Ingersoll, Charles Jared
Ingersoll, Edward
Inglis, Alexander James
Ingraham, Edward Duffield
Ingraham, Joseph Holt
Ingraham, Prentiss
Inman, Henry
Irving, John Treat
Irving, Peter
Irving, Pierre Munro
Irving, Washington
Irwin, William Henry
Isham, Samuel
Jackson, Edward Payson
Jacobi, Mary Cerinna Putnam
James, Marquis
James, Thomas
James, Will Roderick
Jamison, Cecilia Viets Dakin
  Hamilton
Jamison, David Flavel
Janes, Lewis George
Janney, Russell Dixon
Janney, Samuel McPherson
Janvier, Catharine Ann
Janvier, Margaret Thomson
Janvier, Thomas Allibone
Jarves, James Jackson

Jay, John
Jay, William
Jefferson, Thomas
Jenkins, John Stilwell
Jenks, Tudor Storrs
Jewett, Sarah Orne
Johnson, Alexander Bryan
Johnson, Franklin
Johnson, Helen Louise
  Kendrick
Johnson, James Weldon
Johnson, Joseph
Johnson, Osa
Johnson, Richard W.
Johnson, Samuel
Johnson, Samuel William
Johnson, Viriginia Wales
Johnston, Richard Malcolm
Johnston, William Andrew
Joline, Adrian Hoffman
Jones, Alexander
Jones, Amanda Theodosia
Jones, George
Jones, John Beauchamp
Jones, William Alfred
Jordan, William George
Josselyn, John
Joutel, Henri
Joynes, Edward Southey
Judah, Samuel Benjamin
  Helbert
Judd, Sylvester
Judson, Edward Zane Carroll
  ("Ned Buntline")
Judson, Emily Chubbuck
Kaempffert, Waldemar
  Bernhard
Kaye, Frederick Benjamin
Keating, John McLeod
Keating, John Marie
Keener, William Albert
Keller, Helen Adams
Kelley, Edith Summers
Kelley, James Douglas Jerrold
Kellogg, Elijah
Kelly, Aloysius Oliver Joseph
Kelly, Myra
Kemble, Frances Anne
Kennan, George
Kennedy, John Pendleton
Kent, Charles Foster
Kidder, Frederic
Kimball, Richard Burleigh
King, Alexander
King, Clarence
King, Edward Smith
King, Grace Elizabeth
King, Thomas Starr
Kinsey, Alfred Charles
Kirk, John Foster
Kirkland, Caroline Matilda
  Stansbury
Kirkland, Joseph
Kirkman, Marshall Monroe
Kirlin, Joseph Louis Jerome
Klingelsmith, Margaret Center
Knapp, Samuel Lorenzo
Knapp, William Ireland
Kneeland, Stillman Foster
Knight, Edward Henry
Knight, Henry Cogswell
Knox, George William

Knox, Thomas Wallace
Kobbé, Gustav
Koebler, Sylvester Rosa
Kohler, Max James
Krapp, George Philip
Krauth, Charles Porterfield
Krehbiel, Henry Edward
Kyne, Peter Bernard
La Borde, Maximilian
La Farge, John
La Farge, Oliver Hazard Perry
Lamb, Martha Joanna Reade
  Nash
Lambert, Louis Aloisius
Landon, Melville de Lancey
Landreth, David
Lane, Arthur Bliss
Langley, Samuel Pierpont
Lanman, Charles
Larcom, Lucy
Lardner, Ringgold Wilmer
Larned, Josephus Nelson
Larpenteur, Charles
Lathbury, Mary Artemisia
Lathrop, George Parsons
Latimer, Mary Elizabeth
  Wormeley
Lawson, James
Lawson, John
Lawson, Robert Ripley
Lawson, Thomas William
Lea, Homer
Leach, Daniel Dyer
Leavitt, Dudley
Lee, Eliza Buckminster
Lee, Hannah Farnham Sawyer
Lee, Henry, 1787–1837
Lee, James Melvin
Lee, James Wideman
Leeds, Daniel
Leeser, Isaac
Legler, Henry Eduard
Leigh, William Robinson
Leland, Charles Godfrey
Leonard, Sterling Andrus
Leonard, Zenas
Leslie, Charles Robert
Leslie, Eliza
Lester, Charles Edwards
Levy, Louis Edward
Lewis, Alfred Henry
Lewis, Estelle Anna Blanche
  Robinson
Lewis, Lawrence
Lewis, Orlando Faulkland
Liebling, Abbott Joseph
Liebman, Joshua Loth
Lincoln, John Larkin
Lincoln, Mary Johnson Bailey
Lindsey, William
Linn, William Alexander
Lippincott, Sara Jane Clarke
Littell, William
Little, Arthur Dehon
Livermore, Abiel Abbot
Livermore, Mary Ashton Rice
Lloyd, Henry Demarest
Lockwood, Ralph Ingersoll
Lodge, Henry Cabot
Loeb, Sophie Irene Simon
Logan, Olive
Lomax, Louis Emanuel

London, Jack
Long, John Luther
Longfellow, William Pitt Preble
Longstreet, Augustus Baldwin
Lord, Eleazar
Loring, Frederick Wadsworth
Lossing, Benson John
Lounsbury, Thomas Raynesford
Love, Robertus Donnell
Loveman, Amy
Lowell, James Russell
Lowell, Percival
Lowell, Robert Traill Spence
Lucas, Daniel Bedinger
Ludlow, Fitz Hugh
Ludlow, Noah Miller
Luhan, Mabel Dodge
Lummis, Charles Fletcher
Lunt, George
Lyman, Albert Josiah
Lyman, Theodore, 1792–1849
Lynch, James Daniel
Lynd, Robert Staughton
Lyon, Harris Merton
Lyttelton, William Henry
MacArthur, Robert Stuart
McCabe, William Gordon
McClure, Alexander Wilson
McClure, Samuel Sidney
McConnel, John Ludlum
McCrae, Thomas
McCullough, Ernest
MacDonald, Betty
McGarvey, John William
McGovern, John
McKenney, Thomas Loraine
Mackenzie, Alexander Slidell
Mackenzie, Robert Shelton
Maclay, Edgar Stanton
McLeod, Alexander
McPherson, Edward
McQuillen, John Hugh
MacVicar, Malcolm
Macy, John Albert
Malcolm, James Peller
Malcom, Howard
Mann, Mary Tyler Peabody
Mann, Newton
Mann, William Julius
Mansfield, Edward Deering
Marble, Albert Prescott
Marden, Orison Swett
Margalis, Max Leopold
Marshall, Henry Rutgers
Martin, Anne Henrietta
Martin, François-Xavier
Martin, Frederick Townsend
Martin, John Hill
Martin, Thomas Commerford
Martin, William Alexander
  Parsons
Martyn, Sarah Towne Smith
Mason, Daniel Gregory
Mather, Cotton
Mather, Frank Jewett, Jr.
Mather, Fred
Mather, Increase
Mather, Richard
Mather, Samuel
Mathews, Albert
Mathews, Cornelius
Mathews, William

Matthews, Franklin
Matthews, Joseph Brown
Maxwell, Elsa
Maxwell, Samuel
Mayer, Brantz
Mayes, Edward
Mayhew, Experience
Mayo, Sarah Carter Edgarton
Mayo, William Starbuck
Mead, Edwin Doak
Mears, John William
Mease, James
Mechem, Floyd Russell
Meehan, Thomas
Meek, Alexander Beaufort
Meigs, Arthur Vincent
Meigs, Charles Deluccna
Meigs, John Forsyth
Mell, Patrick Hues
Mellen, Grenville
Melville, Herman
Mercier, Charles Alfred
Merrill, Stephen Mason
Metcalf, Henry Harrison
Micheaux, Oscar
Mielziner, Moses
Miller, Emily Clark Huntington
Miller, Harriet Mann
Miller, James Russell
Miller, Samuel
Millet, Francis Davis
Mills, Enos Abijah
Minor, Raleigh Colston
Mitchell, Donald Grant
Mitchell, John, d. 1768
Mitchell, Margaret Munnerlyn
Mitchell, Nahum
Moffett, Cleveland Langston
Möllhausen, Heinrich Baldwin
Mombert, Jacob Isidor
Montefiore, Joshua
Moore, Annie Aubertine
  Woodward
Moore, Frank
Moore, Jacob Bailey
Moore, John Trotwood
Moran, Benjamin
Morford, Henry
Morgan, James Morris
Morley, Christopher Darlington
Morley, Margaret Warner
Morris, Edward Joy
Morris, William Hopkins
Morse, Sidney Edwards
Morton, Charles Walter
Morton, Nathaniel
Mott, Frank Luther
Moulton, Richard Green
Mowatt, Anna Cora Ogden
Mowry, William Augustus
Mulford, Clarence Edward
Mulford, Elisha
Mullins, Edgar Young
Mumford, James Gregory
Murat, Achille
Murdock, James
Murray, David
Murray, Judith Sargent Stevens
Nadal, Ehrman Syme
Nash, Henry Sylvester
Nash, Simeon
Nason, Elias

Nathan, George Jean
Neal, John
Neely, Thomas Benjamin
Nelson, Henry Loomis
Neuberger, Richard Lewis
Nevin, Alfred
Nevin, Edwin Henry
Newcomb, Harvey
Newman, Samuel Phillips
Newton, Joseph Fort
Nichols, Charles Lemuel
Nichols, Mary Sargeant Neal
  Gove
Nichols, Thomas Low
Nicholson, Meredith
Niza, Marcos de
Nock, Albert Jay
Nordhoff, Charles
Nordhoff, Charles Bernard
Norris, Mary Harriott
Northen, William Jonathan
Norton, Charles Eliot
Nott, Henry Junius
Oberholtzer, Sara Louisa
  Vickers
O'Brien, Fitz-James
O'Brien, Frederick
O'Callaghan, Jeremiah
O'Connor, William Douglas
Ogg, Frederic Austin
Okey, John Waterman
O'Malley, Frank Ward
O'Neall, John Belton
O'Neill, Rose Cecil
O'Reilly, Henry
Orton, Helen Fuller
Osborn, Henry Stafford
Osgood, Howard
O'Shea, Michael Vincent
Otis, Arthur Sinton
Ott, Isaac
Ottley, Roi
Owen, Robert Dale
Oxnam, Garfield Bromley
Paine, Ralph Delahaye
Paine, Thomas
Paley, John
Pallen, Condé Benoist
Palmer, Horatio Richmond
Palmer, Joel
Palmer, John McAuley
Palmer, John Williamson
Parish, Elijah
Parker, Jane Marsh
Parker, William Harwar
Parton, James
Parton, Sara Payson Willis
Partridge, William Ordway
Paschal, George Washington
Pastorius, Francis Daniel
Patterson, Robert Mayne
Pattie, James Ohio
Pattison, James William
Patton, William
Paulding, James Kirke
Peabody, Andrew Preston
Peabody, Elizabeth Palmer
Pearson, Edmund Lester
Peattie, Donald Culross
Peck, George Washington
Peck, John Mason
Pedder, James

Peloubet, Francis Nathan
Penfield, Edward
Penfield, Frederic Courtland
Penniman, James Hosmer
Pennington, James W. C.
Pentecost, George Frederick
Percy, George
Percy, William Alexander
Perkins, Frederic Beecher
Perkins, James Handasyd
Perry, Bliss
Perry, Edward Baxter
Perry, Thomas Sergeant
Peterkin, Julia Mood
Peters, Absalom
Peters, Madison Clinton
Peterson, Charles Jacobs
Peyton, John Lewis
Phelan, James, 1856–1891
Phelps, Almira Hart Lincoln
Phelps, Charles Edward
Phillips, Willard
Phillips, William Addison
Phisterer, Frederick
Pickard, Samuel Thomas
Picket, Albert
Pidgin, Charles Felton
Pierce, Gilbert Ashville
Pierson, Arthur Tappan
Pierson, Hamilton Wilcox
Pike, Albert
Pike, James Shepherd
Pise, Charles Constantine
Pollard, Edward Alfred
Pollard, Joseph Percival
Pollock, Channing
Pond, Enoch
Pond, Frederick Eugene
Pool, Maria Louise
Poore, Benjamin Perley
Porter, Robert Percival
Post, Louis Freeland
Poston, Charles Debrill
Potter, Elisha Reynolds
Powel, John Hare
Powell, Edward Payson
Prang, Mary Amelia Dana Hicks
Pratt, Sereno Stansbury
Preble, George Henry
Prentiss, George Lewis
Prescott, George Bartlett
Preston, Harriet Waters
Preston, Margaret Junkin
Preston, Thomas Scott
Price, William Thompson
Prime, Edward Dorr Griffin
Prime, Samuel Irenaeus
Prime, William Cowper
Proctor, William
Pugh, Ellis
Pulte, Joseph Hippolyt
Putnam, George Haven
Putnam, Nina Wilcox
Putnam, Ruth
Pyle, Howard
Quick, John Herbert
Quincy, Edmund
Quincy, Josiah Phillips
Rains, George Washington
Ramsey, James Gettys
  McGready
Randall, Henry Stephens

Randolph, Sarah Nicholas
Randolph, Thomas Jefferson
Ravenel, Harriott Horry
  Rutledge
Rawle, Francis, 1846–1930
Raymond, George Lansing
Read, Opie Pope
Redfield, Isaac Fletcher
Redman, Ben Ray
Reed, Earl Howell
Reed, Myrtle
Reed, Richard Clark
Reed, William Bradford
Reid, Gilbert
Reiersen, Johan Reinert
Remington, Frederic
Rémy, Henri
Renwick, James, 1792–1863
Reuterdahl, Henry
Revere, Joseph Warren
Reynolds, Quentin James
Rhodes, Eugene Manlove
Rice, Alice Caldwell Hegan
Rice, Nathan Lewis
Richards, Laura Elizabeth Howe
Richards, Thomas Addison
Richardson, Charles Francis
Richardson, Robert
Richmond, Mary Ellen
Rickert, Martha Edith
Riddle, Albert Gallatin
Rideing, William Henry
Rideout, Henry Milner
Riis, Jacob August
Riley, Benjamin Franklin
Rivers, William James
Roberts, Elizabeth Madox
Roberts, Kenneth Lewis
Robertson, George
Robertson, John
Robertson, Morgan Andrew
Robinson, Charles Mulford
Robinson, Conway
Robinson, Henry Morton
Robinson, Rowland Evans
Robinson, Solon
Robinson, Stillman Williams
Robinson, Therese Albertine
  Louise Von Jakob
Robinson, William Callyhan
Rodenbough, Theophilus
  Francis
Roe, Edward Payson
Roe, Gilbert Ernstein
Rogers, Clara Kathleen Barnett
Rollins, Alice Marland
  Wellington
Rölvaag, Ole Edvart
Romans, Bernard
Rombro, Jacob
Roosevelt, Robert Barnwell
Root, Frank Albert
Rose, John Carter
Rosenberg, Abraham Hayyim
Rosenthal, Herman
Ross, Alexander
Rowland, Henry Cottrell
Rowlandson, Mary White
Royall, Anne Newport
Ruffner, Henry
Rugg, Harold Ordway
Ruhl, Arthur Brown

Russell, Charles Edward
Russell, Osborne
Rynning, Ole
Sachs, Hanns
Sachse, Julius Friedrich
Sadlier, Mary Anne Madden
Sadtler, Samuel Philip
Sage, Bernard Janin
Salter, William
Salter, William Mackintire
Sanborn, Franklin Benjamin
Sanborn, Katherine Abbott
Sanders, Elizabeth Elkins
Sanders, Frank Knight
Sanderson, John
Sands, Robert Charles
Sangster, Margaret Elizabeth
  Munson
Sarg, Tony
Sargent, Epes
Sargent, John Osborne
Sargent, Lucius Manlius
Sargent, Winthrop, 1825–1870
Saunders, Frederick
Saunders, Prince
Savage, Minot Judson
Sawyer, Lemuel
Schechter, Solomon
Schofield, William Henry
Schroeder, John Frederick
Schultze, Augustus
Schuyler, George Washington
Schuyler, Montgomery
Scidmore, Eliza Ruhamah
Scott, Leroy
Scott, Samuel Parsons
Scott, William Anderson
Scruggs, William Lindsay
Scudder, Horace Elisha
Sears, Edmund Hamilton
Seawell, Molly Elliot
Sedgwick, Catharine Maria
Sedgwick, Theodore,
  1780–1839
Sedgwick, Theodore,
  1811–1859
Seiss, Joseph Augustus
Selikovitsch, Goetzel
Semmes, Raphael
Seton, Grace Gallatin
  Thompson
Seton, William
Severance, Frank Hayward
Sewall, Jonathan
Seward, Theodore
  Frelinghuysen
Shaler, William
Sharp, Dallas Lore
Shecut, John Linnaeus Edward
  Whitridge
Shedd, William Greenough
  Thayer
Sheldon, Charles Monroe
Shelton, Frederick William
Sherwood, Katharine Margaret
  Brownlee
Sherwood, Mary Elizabeth
  Wilson
Shields, Charles Woodruff
Shields, George Oliver
Showerman, Grant
Shreve, Thomas Hopkins

Shuey, Edwin Longstreet
Sigourney, Lydia Howard
  Huntley
Sikes, William Wirt
Simpson, James Hervey
Simpson, Stephen
Singleton, Esther
Siringo, Charles A.
Skinner, John Stuart
Skinner, Thomas Harvey
Slafter, Edmund Farwell
Sloan, Harold Paul
Sloan, Richard Elihu
Slocum, Joshua
Slosson, Edwin Emery
Smedley, Agnes
Smith, Alexander
Smith, Arthur Henderson
Smith, Charles Alphonso
Smith, Edmund Munroe
Smith, Elias
Smith, Elihu Hubbard
Smith, Elizabeth Oakes Prince
Smith, Francis Hopkinson
Smith, Hannah Whitall
Smith, Henry Justin
Smith, James McCune
Smith, James 1737–1814
Smith, John, 1579–1631
Smith, John Augustine
Smith, John Cotton, 1826–1882
Smith, Margaret Bayard
Smith, Richard Penn
Smith, Samuel Harrison
Smith, William Andrew
Smith, William Russell
Smythe, Albert Henry
Smythe, Thomas
Snead, Thomas Lowndes
Snider, Denton Jaques
Snyder, John Francis
Sobolewski, J. Friedrich Eduard
Sokolsky, George Ephraim
Solger, Reinhold
Sounichsen, Albert
Spalding, Thomas
Spangler, Henry Wilson
Spencer, Cornelia Phillips
Spencer, Jesse Ames
Spivak, Charles David
Spofford, Harriet Elizabeth
  Prescott
Sprague, Achsa W.
Sprague, Oliver Mitchell
  Wentworth
Sprunt, James
Starr, Eliza Allen
Stauffer, David McNeely
Steele, Daniel
Steffens, Lincoln
Stein, Evaleen
Stein, Gertrude
Stein, Leo Daniel
Stephens, Ann Sophia
Stephens, Charles Asbury
Stephens, John Lloyd
Sterling, James
Stevens, George Washington
Stevens, John Austin,
  1827–1910
Stimson, Alexander Lovett
Stimson, Frederic Jesup

Stitt, Edward Rhodes
Stoddard, Charles Warren
Stoddard, John Lawson
Stoddard, William Osborn
Stoever, Martin Luther
Stong, Phil(lip Duffield)
Storey, Moorfield
Story, Isaac
Stowe, Harriet Elizabeth
  Beecher
Straus, Oscar Solomon
Strömme, Peer Olsen
Strong, Josiah
Strother, David Hunter
Stuart, Charles Beebe
Stuart, Ruth McEnery
Sturgis, Russell
Sullivan, James William
Sullivan, William
Sunderland, Eliza Jane Read
Swensson, Carl Aaron
Swift, Lucius Burrie
Swinton, William
Tappan, Eli Todd
Tarbox, Increase Niles
Taylor, Bert Leston
Taylor, George Boardman
Taylor, James Wickes
Taylor, Joseph Deems
Temple, Oliver Perry
Tennent, John
Tenney, Edward Payson
Terhune, Albert Payson
Terhune, Mary Virginia Hawes
Thacher, John Boyd
Thacher, Samuel Cooper
Thatcher, Benjamin Bussey
Thayer, Thomas Baldwin
Thayer, William Makepeace
Thomas, John Jacobs
Thomas, Richard Henry
Thomes, William Henry
Thompson, Benjamin
Thompson, Daniel Pierce
Thompson, Edward William
Thompson, James Maurice
Thompson, Joseph Parrish
Thompson, Richard Wigginton
Thompson, Slason
Thorburn, Grant
Thorpe, Rose Alnora Hartwick
Thorpe, Thomas Bangs
Thrasher, John Sidney
Thurber, George
Ticknor, George
Tiernan, Frances Christine
  Fisher
Todd, John
Todd, Mabel Loomis
Todd, Sereno Edwards
Tolman, Herbert Cushing
Tomlinson, Everett Titsworth
Toner, Joseph Meredith
Topliff, Samuel
Torrey, Bradford
Tourgée, Albion Winegar
Towle, George Makepeace
Towne, Charles Hanson
Townsend, George Alfred
Townsend, Luther Tracy
Townsend, Mary Ashley
Townsend, Virginia Frances

Tracy, Joseph
Train, Arthur Cheney
Train, George Francis
Traubel, Horace L.
Trowbridge, John Townsend
Truman, Benjamin Cummings
Trumbull, Henry Clay
Tucker, George
Tucker, Gilbert Milligan
Tucker, Nathaniel Beverley,
  1784–1851
Tuckerman, Bayard
Tudor, William
Turner, George Kibbe
Turner, Henry McNeal
Turner, William
Tyler, Samuel
Underwood, Francis Henry
Upham, Thomas Cogswell
Upton, Emory
Upton, George Putnam
Van Brunt, Henry
Vance, Louis Joseph
Van Der Kemp, Francis Adrian
Van Dyke, Henry
Van Rensselaer, Mariana
  Griswold
Van Schaack, Henry Cruger
Venable, William Henry
Verplanck, Gulian Crommelin
Verrill, Alpheus Hyatt
Very, Lydia Louisa Ann
Victor, Frances Fuller
Victor, Orville James
Villard, Oswald Garrison
Vincent, Frank
Vorse, Mary Heaton
Waddell, Alfred Moore
Waggaman, Mary Teresa
  McKee
Wakeley, Joseph Burton
Walden, Jacob Treadwell
Waldo, Samuel Putnam
Walker, Alexander
Wallace, John William
Wallace, Lewis
Wallis, Severn Teackle
Waln, Robert, 1794–1825
Walsh, Edmund Aloysius
Walsh, Henry Collins
Walworth, Jeannette Ritchie
  Hadermann
Warburg, James Paul
Ward, Cyrenus Osborne
Ward, Elizabeth Stuart Phelps
Ward, Harry Frederick
Ward, Herbert Dickinson
Ward, James Harmon
Ward, James Warner
Ward, Lydia Arms Avery
  Coonley
Ward, Nathaniel
Ward, Samuel, 1814–1884
Warden, David Bailie
Warden, Robert Bruce
Ware, Nathaniel A.
Ware, William
Waring, George Edwin
Warman, Cy
Warren, Israel Perkins
Washburn, Charles Grenfill
Washburn, Emory

Watson, Thomas Edward
Webb, Charles Henry
Webber, Charles Wilkins
Webster, Alice Jane Chandler
Weems, Mason Locke
Wehle, Louis Brandeis
Weiss, John
Welby, Amelia Ball Coppuck
Wells, William Vincent
Wendte, Charles William
Wertenbaker, Charles Christian
West, Samuel
Westcott, Edward Noyes
Wharton, Anne Hollingsworth
Wharton, Francis
Wharton, Thomas Isaac
Wheeler, Andrew Carpenter
Wheeler, (George) Post
Whipple, Edwin Percy
Whipple, Squire
Whitcher, Frances Miram Berry
Whitcomb, Selden Lincoln
White, Emerson Elbridge
White, George
White, Stewart Edward
White, William Allen
Whitlock, Brand
Whitney, Adeline Dutton Train
Whitney, Caspar
Whiton, James Morris
Whittelsey, Abigail Goodrich
Whittemore, Thomas
Wiggin, Kate Douglas
Wigglesworth, Michael
Wikoff, Henry
Wilder, Laura Ingalls
Willard, Sidney
William, John
Williams, Charles Richard
Williams, Edwin
Williams, Frederick Wells
Williams, George Washington
Williams, Jesse Lynch
Williams, John
Williams, William R.
Wilson, George Grafton
Wilson, James Grant
Wilson, James Harrison
Wilson, James Southall
Wilson, John
Wilson, John Fleming
Wilson, Samuel Graham
Winchell, Alexander
Winkler, Edwin Theodore
Winslow, Edward
Winslow, Hubbard
Winthrop, Theodore
Wise, Daniel
Wise, Henry Augustus
Wister, Owen
Woerner, John Gabriel
Wood, Charles Erskine Scott
Wood, William
Woodbridge, John
Woodbury, Helen Laura
  Sumner
Woollcott, Alexander
  Humphreys
Woolley, Celia Parker
Woolsey, Sarah Chauncy
Woolson, Abba Louisa Goold
Woolson, Constance Fenimore

Workman, Fanny Bullock
Wormeley, Katherine Prescott
Wright, Marcus Joseph
Wright, Richard Nathaniel
Wright, Willard Huntington
Wright, William
Wyckoff, Walter Augustus
Youmans, Edward Livingston
Young, Art
Young, Jesse Bowman
Zachos, John Celivergos
Ziff, William Bernard
Zinsser, Hans

AUTHOR'S AGENT
Marbury, Elisabeth

AUTOMOBILE EXECUTIVE (See also
  MANUFACTURER, AUTOMOBILE)
Keller, Kaufman Thuma

AUTOMOBILE RACER
Oldfield, Berna Eli ("Barney")
Shaw, (Warren) Wilbur

AUTOMOTIVE DESIGNER
Wills, Childe Harold

AVIATION EXECUTIVE
Arnold, Leslie Philip
Boeing, William Edward
Chennault, Claire Lee
Damon, Ralph Shepard
Frye, William John ("Jack")
Hunter, Croil
Kellett, William Wallace
Keys, Clement Melville
Schroeder, Rudolph William
Woolman, Collett Everman

AVIATOR
Acosta, Bertram Blanchard
  ("Bert")
Arnold, Henry Harley ("Hap")
Arnold, Leslie Philip
Bennett, Floyd
Brereton, Lewis Hyde
Byrd, Richard Evelyn
Castle, Vernon Blythe
Chapman, Victor Emmanuel
Chennault, Claire Lee
Curtiss, Glenn Hammond
Earhart, Amelia Mary
Foulois, Benjamin Delahauf
Geiger, Roy Stanley
Glidden, Charles Jasper
Gorrell, Edgar Staley
Hitchcock, Thomas
Lufbery, Raoul Gervais Victor
Martin, Glenn Luther ("Cy")
Mitchell, William
Mitscher, Marc Andrew
Nichols, Ruth Rowland
Pangborn, Clyde Edward
Patrick, Mason Mathews
Post, Augustus
Post, Wiley
Rockwell, Kiffin Yates
Rodgers, John, 1881–1926
Royce, Ralph
Schroeder, Rudolph William
Wright, Orville
Wright, Wilbur

BACTERIOLOGIST (See also PHYSI-
  CIAN, SCIENTIST)
Avery, Oswald Theodore
Carroll, James

Ernst, Harold Clarence
Gay, Frederick Parker
Henrici, Arthur Trautwein
Jordan, Edwin Oakes
Libman, Emanuel
Moore, Veranus Alva
Noguchi, Hideyo
Park, William Hallock
Plotz, Harry
Prescott, Samuel Cate
Prudden, Theophil Mitchell
Ravenel, Mazyck Porcher
Schneider, Albert
Simmons, James Stevens
Smith, Erwin Frink
Sternberg, George Miller
Winslow, Charles-Edward
  Amory
Zinsser, Hans

BAKER
Ludwick, Christopher

BALLADIST (See also COMPOSER,
  LYRICIST, MUSICIAN, SONG-
  WRITER)
Haswell, Anthony
Hays, William Shakespeare
Plummer, Jonathan
Prime, Benjamin Youngs

BALLET IMPRESARIO
De Cuevas, Marquis

BALLOONIST (See also AERONAUT,
  AVIATOR)
Wise, John

BANDIT (See also BRIGAND, BUC-
  CANEER, BURGLAR, DE-
  SPERADO, OUTLAW, PIRATE)
Dillinger, John
Plummer, Henry

BANDLEADER (See also CONDUC-
  TOR, MUSICIAN)
Dorsey, Thomas Francis
  ("Tommy")
Elman, Harry ("Ziggy")
Gilmore, Patrick Sarsfield
Goldman, Edwin Franko
Gray, Glen
Handy, William Christopher
Henderson, Fletcher Hamilton
Jones, Lindley Armstrong
  ("Spike")
Lunceford, James Melvin
  ("Jimmie")
Miller, Glenn
Page, Oran Thaddeus ("Lips")
Pryor, Arthur W.
Sousa, John Philip
Teagarden, Weldon Leo
  ("Jack")
Weems, Ted
Whiteman, Paul Samuel
  ("Pops")

BANKER (See also CAPITALIST, FIN-
  ANCIER)
Adams, Edward Dean
Appleton, Nathan
Armstrong, Samuel Turell
Bacon, Robert
Baker, George Fisher
Beatty, John
Belmont, August
Binga, Jesse
Bingham, William

Bishop, Charles Reed
Black, Eugene Robert
Bliss, George
Bradford, Gamaliel
Brinkerhoff, Roeliff
Brown, Alexander
Brown, Fayette
Brown, James
Brown, John A.
Cannon, James Graham
Catchings, Waddill
Cattell, Alexander Gilmore
Chaffee, Jerome Bonaparte
Chetlain, Augustus Louis
Clark, Horace Francis
Coe, George Simmons
Cooke, Henry David
Cooke, Jay
Corbett, Henry Winslow
Corcoran, William Wilson
Creighton, Edward
Cummings, Walter Joseph
Cutler, James Goold
Dale, Chester
Davis, Norman Hezekiah
Davison, George Willets
Davison, Henry Pomeroy
Dawes, Charles Gates
De Coppet, Edward J.
Dodge, Joseph Morrell
Drexel, Anthony Joseph
Drexel, Francis Martin
Drexel, Joseph William
Eells, Dan Parmelee
Ellis, John Washington
Elmore, Franklin Harper
Fahnestock, Harris Charles
Fenton, Reuben Eaton
Few, William
Fish, Stuyvesant
Flannery, John
Fletcher, Calvin
Forbes, William Cameron
Forgan, James Berwick
Forrestal, James Vincent
Fraley, Frederick
Fraser, Leon
Gage, Lyman Judson
Garrett, John Work
Gaston, Herbert Earle
Gates, Thomas Sovereign
Giannini, Amadeo Peter
Goldschmidt, Jakob
Grant, James Benton
Greene, Jerome Davis
Hall, James 1793–1868
Hammond, Bray
Hammond, Samuel
Harding, William Procter Gould
Hascall, Milo Smith
Heard, Dwight Bancroft
Hendrix, Joseph Clifford
Henrotin, Charles
Hepburn, Alonzo Barton
Herrick, Myron Timothy
Higginson, Henry Lee
Hunnewell, Horatio Hollis
Hutchinson, Charles Lawrence
Jeffrey, Joseph Andrew
Johnson, Alexander Bryan
Jones, Jesse Holman
Kahn, Otto Herman

Kelly, Eugene
Ladd, William Sargent
Laimbeer, Nathalie Schenck
Lamar, Gazaway Bugg
Lamont, Thomas William
Lee, Thomas
Leffingwell, Russell Cornell
Lehman, Arthur
Lehman, Herbert Henry
Lehman, Robert
Lewis, William David
Littlefield, George Washington
Livingstone, William
Loeb, James
Low, Frederick Ferdinand
Lucas, James H.
Ludlow, Daniel
McFadden, Louis Thomas
McGarrah, Gates White
Marcus, Bernard Kent
Mather, Samuel Holmes
Merriam, William Rush
Merrill, Charles Edward
Meyer, Eugene Isaac
Mills, Darius Ogden
Mitchell, Alexander
Morgan, James Dada
Morgan, John Pierpont
Morgan, Junius Spencer
Morrow, Dwight Whitney
Newberry, Walter Loomis
Peabody, George Foster
Perkins, George Clement
Perkins, George Walbridge
Perkins, James Handasyd
Powers, Daniel William
Price, Hiram
Prince, Frederick Henry
Ralston, William Chapman
Reynolds, George McClelland
Riggs, George Washington
Robb, James
Rollins, Frank West
Rosenberg, Henry
Sabin, Charles Hamilton
Salomon, Haym
Sayre, Stephen
Schneider, George
Seligman, Arthur
Seligman, Isaac Newton
Seligman, Jesse
Seney, George Ingraham
Shaw, Leslie Mortier
Smith, George
Smith, Samuel Harrison
Spaulding, Charles Clinton
Spaulding, Elbridge Gerry
Sprague, Charles
Sprague, Charles Ezra
Spreckels, Rudolph
Stanley, Harold
Stevens, John Austin,
    1795–1874
Stewart, John Aikman
Stillman, James
Stokes, Anson Phelps
Stotesbury, Edward Townsend
Straus, Simon William
Strong, Benjamin
Taggart, Thomas
Tappen, Frederick Dobbs
Taylor, Moses

Thatcher, Mahlon Daniel
Thomas, George Clifford
Thompson, David P.
Thompson, John
Thompson, Josiah Van Kirk
Tome, Jacob
Traylor, Melvin Alvah
Vanderlip, Frank Arthur
Waldo, David
Warburg, Paul Moritz
Ward, Samuel, 1786–1839
Westcott, Edward Noyes
White, Stephen Van Culen
Whitney, George
Wiggin, Albert Henry
Williams, Samuel May
Willing, Thomas
Woodward, William
Wright, Richard Robert
Yeatman, James Erwin

BARITONE (See SINGER)

BASEBALL CLUB OWNER
Comiskey, Grace Elizabeth
    Reidy
Crosley, Powel, Jr.

BASEBALL COMMISSIONER
Landis, Kenesaw Mountain

BASEBALL EXECUTIVE
Barrow, Edward Grant
Griffith, Clark Calvin
Johnson, Byron Bancroft
Rickey, Wesley Branch

BASEBALL MANAGER
Collins, Edward Trowbridge
Dressen, Charles Walter
Griffith, Clark Calvin
McGraw, John Joseph
Mack, Connie
McKechnie, William Boyd
Rolfe, Robert Abial ("Red")

BASEBALL ORIGINATOR
Doubleday, Abner

BASEBALL PLAYER
Alexander, Grover Cleveland
Anson, Adrian Constantine
Baker, John Franklin
Bender, Charles Albert
    ("Chief")
Bridges, Thomas Jefferson
    Davis ("Tommy")
Cicotte, Edward Victor
Clarkson, John Gibson
Cobb, Tyrus Raymond ("Ty")
Cochrane, Gordon Stanley
    ("Mickey")
Collins, Edward Trowbridge
Crawford, Samuel Earl
Dressen, Charles Walter
    ("Chuck")
Duffy, Hugh
Foxx, James Emory
Gehrig, Henry Louis ("Lou")
Gibson, Joshua
Griffith, Clark Calvin
Heilmann, Harry
Hornsby, Rogers
Huggins, Miller James
Johnson, Walter Perry
Kelly, Michael J.
Klein, Charles Herbert
    ("Chuck")
Lajoie, Napoleon ("Larry")

McGraw, John Joseph
Maranville, Walter James Vincent ("Rabbit")
Martin, Johnny Leonard Roosevelt ("Pepper")
Mathewson, Christopher ("Christy")
O'Doul, Francis Joseph ("Lefty")
Ott, Melvin Thomas ("Mel")
Reach, Alfred James
Rolfe, Robert Abial ("Red")
Rommel, Edwin Americus ("Eddie")
Rowe, Lynwood Thomas
Rucker, George ("Nap")
Ruth, George Herman ("Babe")
Schalk, Raymond William ("Cracker")
Simmons (Szymanski), Aloysius Harry
Speaker, Tris E.
Vance, Arthur Charles ("Dazzy")
Wagner, John Peter
Walsh, Edward Augustine
Waner, Paul Glee
Wright, George
Wright, Henry
Young, Denton True ("Cy")
Zimmerman, Henry ("Heinie")
BASEBALL UMPIRE
Connolly, Thomas H.
Klem, William J. (Bill)
BASKETBALL ORIGINATOR
Naismith, James
BASKETBALL PLAYER
Lapchick, Joseph Bohomiel
Stokes, Maurice
BEAUTY EXPERT
Arden, Elizabeth
Rubinstein, Helena
BELL FOUNDER (See IRON FOUNDER)
BIBLICAL SCHOLAR
Barton, George Aaron
Lake, Kirsopp
Moffatt, James
Montgomery, James Alan
Speiser, Ephraim Avigdor
Willett, Herbert Lockwood
BIBLIOGRAPHER (See also SCHOLAR)
Bartlett, John Russell
Bolton, Henry Carrington
Bowker, Richard Rogers
Cole, George Watson
Eames, Wilberforce
Evans, Charles
Field, Herbert Haviland
Finotti, Joseph Maria
Fletcher, Robert
Ford, Worthington Chauncey
Garrison, Fielding Hudson
Greene, Belle Da Costa
Griffin, Appleton Prentiss Clark
Griswold, William McCrillis
Harrisse, Henry
Jackson, William Alexander
Jewett, Charles Coffin
Leypoldt, Frederick
McMurtrie, Douglas Crawford

Moore, George Henry
Nelson, Charles Alexander
Rand, Benjamin
Rhees, William Jones
Rich, Obadiah
Sabin, Joseph
Sargent, George Henry
Trumbull, James Hammond
Vail, Robert William Glenroie
Weeks, Stephen Beauregard
Wilson, Halsey William
Winship, George Parker
BIBLIOPHILE (See also BOOK COLLECTOR, COLLECTOR)
Adler, Elmer
Alden, Ebenezer
Andrews, William Loring
Ayer, Edward Everett
Barton, Thomas Pennant
Dowse, Thomas
Fisher, George Jackson
Ford, Gordon Lester
Fulton, John Farquhar
Gowans, William
Harris, Caleb Fiske
Hoe, Robert, 1839–1909
Hutton, Laurence
Jones, Herschel Vespasian
Mackenzie William
Nichols, Charles Lemuel
Penniman, James Hosmer
Pennypacker, Samuel Whitaker
Polock, Moses
Prince, Thomas
Sabin, Joseph
Thacher, John Boyd
Wood, Casey Albert
Young, George
BILLIARD PLAYER
Hoppe, William Frederick ("Willie")
BIOCHEMIST (See also CHEMIST, PHYSICIAN, SCIENTIST)
Bergmann, Max
Chittenden, Russell Henry
Cohn, Edwin Joseph
Cori, Gerty Theresa Radnitz
Dakin, Henry Drysdale
Elvehjem, Conrad Arnold
Funk, Casimir
Gortner, Ross Aiken
Hart, Edwin Bret
Henderson, Lawrence Joseph
Herter, Christian Archibald
Hoagland, Charles Lee
Koch, Fred Conrad
Levene, Phoebus Aaron Theodore
Marriott, Williams McKim
Meyerhof, Otto
Osborne, Thomas Burr
Schmidt, Carl Louis August
Schoenheimer, Rudolf
Schweinitz, Emil Alexander de
Stern, Kurt Guenter
Sumner, James Batcheller
Vaughan, Victor Clarence
BIOGRAPHER (See also AUTHOR, WRITER)
Allen, Hervey
Anthony, Katharine Susan
Atkinson, William Biddle

Beer, Thomas
Bernard, William Bayle
Bradford, Gamaliel
Brooks, Van Wyck
Bruce, William Cabell
Drake, Benjamin
Duyckinck, Evert Augustus
Duyckinck, George Long
Forester, Cecil Scott
Greenslet, Ferris
Hagedorn, Hermann Ludwig Gebhard
Hendrick, Burton Jesse
Hergesheimer, Joseph
Howe, Mark Antony De Wolfe
Johnson, Allen
Kennedy, William Sloane
Lewis, Lloyd Downs
Long, Armistead Lindsay
Morse, John Torrey
Nicolay, John George
Paine, Albert Bigelow
Parton, James
Pickard, Samuel Thomas
Pierce, Edward Lillie
Pringle, Henry Fowles
Proctor, Lucien Brock
Quinn, Arthur Hobson
Sandburg, Carl August
Shellabarger, Samuel
Sprague, William Buell
Thayer, Alexander Wheelock
Thayer, William Roscoe
Van Doren, Carl Clinton
BIOLOGIST (See also BOTANIST, SCIENTIST, ZOOLOGIST)
Carrel, Alexis
Chapman, Henry Cadwalader
Coghill, George Ellett
Conklin, Edwin Grant
Davenport, Charles Benedict
Harrison, Ross Granville
Jayne, Horace Fort
Jennings, Herbert Spencer
Lillie, Frank Rattray
Loeb, Leo
McClung, Clarence Erwin
McMurrich, James Playfair
Mayor, Alfred Goldsborough
Minot, Charles Sedgwick
Nelson, Julius
Noble, Gladwyn Kingsley
Pearl, Raymond
Pincus, Gregory Goodwin ("Goody")
Sedgwick, William Thompson
Stockard, Charles Rupert
Whitman, Charles Otis
Wilson, Edmund Beecher
Woodruff, Lorande Loss
BIOMETRICIAN (See also BIOLOGIST, PHYSICIAN, SCIENTIST, STATISTICIAN)
Harris, James Arthur
BIOPHYSICIST (See also BIOLOGIST, PHYSICIST, SCIENTIST)
Bovie, William T.
Hecht, Selig
BIRTH CONTROL ADVOCATE
Hepburn, Katharine Houghton
Sanger, Margaret Higgins
Stone, Abraham

BISHOP (See also RELIGIOUS LEAD-
ER)
African Methodist Episcopal
Allen, Richard
Brown, John Mifflin
Brown, Morris
Clinton, George Wylie
Gaines, Wesley John
Gregg, John Andrew
Holsey, Lucius Henry
Hood, James Walker
Loguen, Jermain Wesley
Payne, Daniel Alexander
Tanner, Benjamin Tucker
Turner, Henry McNeal
Walters, Alexander
Wayman, Alexander Walker
Anglican
Inglis, Charles
Episcopal
Atkinson, Thomas
Bass, Edward
Brooks, Phillips
Brownell, Thomas Church
Burgess, Alexander
Burgess, George
Burleson, Hugh Latimer
Capers, Ellison
Chase, Philander
Cheney, Charles Edward
Clark, Thomas March
Coleman, Leighton
Coxe, Arthur Cleveland
De Lancey, William Heathcote
Doane, George Washington
Doane, William Croswell
Fallows, Samuel
Grafton, Charles Chapman
Graves, Frederick Rogers
Greer, David Hummell
Griswold, Alexander Viets
Hale, Charles Reuben
Hall, Arthur Crawshay Alliston
Hare, William Hobart
Hobart, John Henry
Holly, James Theodore
Hopkins, John Henry
Howe, Mark Anthony De Wolfe
Huntington, Frederic Dan
Ives, Levi Silliman
Jarvis, Abraham
Johns, John
Kemp, James
Kemper, Jackson
Kerfoot, John Barrett
Kip, William Ingraham
Lay, Henry Champlin
Lee, Alfred
Leonard, William Andrew
Littlejohn, Abram Newkirk
McIlvaine, Charles Pettit
McLaren, William Edward
McVickar, William Neilson
Madison, James
Meade, William
Moore, Benjamin
Moore, Richard Channing
Murray, John Gardner
Nichols, William Ford
Odenheimer, William Henry
Onderdonk, Benjamin Tredwell
Onderdonk, Henry Ustick

Otey, James Hervey
Paddock, Benjamin Henry
Paddock, John Adams
Penick, Charles Clifton
Perry, William Stevens
Peterkin, George William
Polk, Leonidas
Potter, Alonzo
Potter, Henry Codman
Potter, Horatio
Provoost, Samuel
Quintard, Charles Todd
Randolph, Alfred Magill
Ravenscroft, John Stark
Satterlee, Henry Yates
Schereschewsky, Samuel Isaac
Joseph
Scott, Thomas Fielding
Seabury, Samuel, 1729–1796
Seymour, George Franklin
Slattery, Charles Lewis
Smith, Robert, 1732–1801
Spalding, Franklin Spencer
Stevens, William Bacon
Talbot, Ethelbert
Thompson, Hugh Miller
Tucker, Henry St. George
Tuttle, Daniel Sylvester
Wainwright, Jonathan Mayhew,
1792–1854
Whipple, Henry Benjamin
White, William
Whittingham, William Rollinson
Williams, Channing Moore
Williams, Charles David
Williams, John, 1817–1899
Wilmer, Joseph Père Bell
Wilmer, Richard Hooker
Evangelical
Esher, John Jacob
Seybert, John
German Baptist Brethren
Sower, Christopher, 1721–1784
Mennonite
Boehm, Martin
Methodist
Ames, Edward Raymond
Andrew, James Osgood
Andrews, Edward Gayer
Asbury, Francis
Baker, Osmon Cleander
Bascom, Henry Bidleman
Bashford, James Whitford
Bowman, Thomas
Capers, William
Coke, Thomas
Early, John
Emory, John
Fitzgerald, Oscar Penn
Foss, Cyrus David
Foster, Randolph Sinks
Fowler, Charles Henry
Galloway, Charles Betts
Goodsell, Daniel Ayres
Hamline, Leonidas Lent
Hargrove, Robert Kennon
Harris, Merriman Colbert
Harris, William Logan
Hartzell, Joseph Crane
Haven, Erastus Otis
Haven, Gilbert
Haygood, Atticus Green

Hedding, Elijah
Hendrix, Eugene Russell
Hurst, John Fletcher
Joyce, Isaac Wilson
Kingsley, Calvin
Lambuth, Walter Russell
McCabe, Charles Cardwell
McKendree, William
McTyeire, Holland Nimmons
Marvin, Enoch Mather
Merrill, Stephen Mason
Neely, Thomas Benjamin
Newman, John Philip
Oxnam, Garfield Bromley
Paine, Robert
Parker, Edwin Wallace
Peck, Jesse Truesdell
Pierce, George Foster
Quayle, William Alfred
Roberts, Robert Richford
Simpson, Matthew
Soule, Joshua
Taylor, William
Thoburn, James Mills
Thomson, Edward
Tigert, John James
Vincent, John Heyl
Walden, John Morgan
Warren, Henry White
Waugh, Beverly
Whatcoat, Richard
Methodist Episcopal
Cranston, Earl
Fisher, Frederick Bohn
Hamilton, John William
Hughes, Edwin Holt
McConnell, Francis John
McDowell, William Fraser
Oldham, William Fitzjames
Moravian
Boehler, Peter
Boehm, Martin
Ettwein, John
Jacobson, John Christian
Kephart, Ezekiel Boring
Kumler, Henry
Laskiel, George Henry
Levering, Joseph Mortimer
Nitschmann, David
Reichel, Charles Gotthold
Rondthaler, Edward
Schweinitz, Edmund Alexander
de
Spangenberg, Augustus
Gottlieb
Polish National Catholic
Hodur, Francis
Protestant Episcopal
Brent, Charles Henry
Cheshire, Joseph Blount
Gailor, Thomas Frank
Lawrence, William
Manning, William Thomas
Restarick, Henry Bond
Southgate, Horatio
Sumner, Walter Taylor
Roman Catholic
Bayley, James Roosevelt
Bradley, Denis Mary
Byrne, Andrew
Carroll, John
Chanche, John Mary Joseph

Chatard, Francis Silas
Cheverus, John Louis Ann
    Magdalen Lefebre de
Connolly, John
Conwell, Henry
Crétin, Joseph
Curtis, Alfred Allen
David, John Baptist Mary
Dougherty, Dennis Joseph
Du Bois, John
Egan, Michael
England, John
Fenwick, Edward Dominic
Fitzpatrick, John Bernard
Flaget, Benedict Joseph
Galberry, Thomas
Haas, Francis Joseph
Haid, Leo
Heiss, Michael
Lefevere, Peter Paul
McQuaid, Bernard John
Noll, John Francis
Stritch, Samuel Alphonsus
Tamarón, Pedro
Russian
    Ioasaf
BLIND, DEAF, MUTE
    Bridgman, Laura Dewey
BLOCKADE RUNNER (See also NA-
    VAL OFFICER)
    Hambleton, Thomas Edward
BOOKBINDER
    Matthews, William
    Nicholson, James Bartram
BOOK COLLECTOR (See also AN-
    TIQUARIAN, COLLECTOR)
    Adler, Elmer
    Ayer, Edward Everett
    Brown, John Carter
    Carson, Hampton Lawrence
    Clements, William Lawrence
    Emmett, Burton
    Fiske, Daniel Willard
    Folger, Henry Clay
    Graff, Everett Dwight
    Greene, Albert Gorton
    Gunther, Charles Frederick
    Jacobs, Joseph
    Joline, Adrian Hoffman
    Lenox, James
    Mackenzie, William
    Montague, Gilbert Holland
    Pancoast, Seth
    Plimpton, George Arthur
    Toner, Joseph Meredith
    Warden, David Bailie
    Widener, Harry Elkins
    Young, George
BOOK DESIGNER
    Dwiggins, William Addison
    Seton, Grace Gallatin
       Thompson
BOOKSELLER (See also PUBLISHER)
    Beach, Sylvia Woodbridge
    Bell, Robert
    Brown, James
    Francis, Charles Stephen
    Fry, Richard
    Gaine, Hugh
    Goodrich, Chauncey
    Green, Asa
    Hall, David

Harris, Benjamin
Henchman, Daniel
Henderson, Daniel McIntyre
Kenedy, Patrick John
McClurg, Alexander Caldwell
Melcher, Frederic Gershom
Nancrède, Paul Joseph Guérard
    de
Polock, Moses
Rivington, James
Stevens, Benjamin Franklin
Stevens, Henry
Trow, John Fowler
Weems, Mason Locke
Wilson, William
BOOTLEGGER
    Capone, Alphonse ("Al")
    Wexler, Irving ("Waxey
       Gordon")
BOTANIC PHYSICIAN (See also
    AGRICULTURIST, BOTANIST,
    PHYSICIAN)
    Bickerdyke, Mary Ann Ball
    Thomson, Samuel
BOTANICAL EXPLORER
    Rusby, Henry Hurd
BOTANIST (See also AGRICULTUR-
    IST, BIOLOGIST)
    Allen, Timothy Field
    Alvan, Wentworth Chapman
    Ames, Oakes
    Arthur, Joseph Charles
    Atkinson, George Francis
    Bailey, Jacob Whitman
    Bailey, Liberty Hyde
    Baldwin, William
    Banister, John
    Barnes, Charles Reid
    Barton, William Paul Crillon
    Bartram, John
    Beal, William James
    Bessey, Charles Edwin
    Bigelow, Jacob
    Brackenridge, William D.
    Brainerd, Ezra
    Brandegee, Townshend Stith
    Bridges, Robert
    Britton, Nathaniel Lord
    Buckley, Samuel Botsford
    Burrill, Thomas Jonathan
    Campbell, Douglas Houghton
    Carver, George Washington
    Chamberlain, Charles Joseph
    Chase, (Mary) Agnes Merrill
    Clark, Henry James
    Clayton, John
    Clements, Frederic Edward
    Colden, Jane
    Collins, Frank Shipley
    Coulter, John Merle
    Cowles, Henry Chandler
    Curtis, Moses Ashley
    Cutler, Manasseh
    Darlington, William
    Dudley, William Russel
    Duggar, Benjamin Minge
    Durand, Élie Magloire
    Eaton, Daniel Cady
    Elliott, Stephen
    Ellis, Job Bicknell
    Engelmann, George
    Fairchild, David Grandison

Farlow, William Gilson
Fernald, Merritt Lyndon
Goodale, George Lincoln
Gray, Asa
Greene, Edward Lee
Harris, James Arthur
Harshberger, John William
Hollick, Charles Arthur
Howell, Thomas Jefferson
James, Thomas Potts
Jeffrey, Edward Charles
Jepson, Willis Linn
Kauffman, Calvin Henry
Kellogg, Albert
Knowlton, Frank Hall
Kraemer, Henry
Kuhn, Adam
Lemmon, John Gill
Lindheimer, Ferdinand Jacob
Marshall, Humphry
Meehan, Thomas
Michaux, André
Michaux, François André
Michener, Ezra
Millspaugh, Charles Frederick
Mitchell, Elisha
Mitchell, John, d. 1768
Mohr, Charles Theodore
Mühlenberg, Gotthilf Henry
    Ernest
Nieuwland, Julius Arthur
Nuttall, Thomas
Paine, John Alsop
Pammel, Louis Hermann
Parry, Charles Christopher
Porcher, Francis Peyre
Porter, Thomas Conrad
Pound, (Nathan) Roscoe
Pursh, Frederick
Ravenel, Henry William
Riddell, John Leonard
Robinson, Benjamin Lincoln
Rose, Joseph Nelson
Rothrock, Joseph Trimble
Rydberg, Per Axel
Safford, William Edwin
Sartwell, Henry Parker
Schweinitz, Lewis David von
Setchell, William Albert
Shecut, John Linnaeus Edward
    Whitridge
Short, Charles Wilkins
Sinnott, Edmund Ware
Smith, Edwin Frink
Spalding, Volney Morgan
Sullivant, William Starling
Thaxter, Roland
Thurber, George
Torrey, John
Trelease, William
Tuckerman, Edward
Underwood, Lucien Marcus
Vasey, George
Walter, Thomas, *c.* 1740–1789
Watson, Sereno
White, David
Wilson, Ernest Henry
Wright, Charles
BOXER (See also ATHLETE, PUGIL-
    IST)
    Dundee, Johnny
    Jeffries, James Jackson

Johnson, Jack
Langford, Samuel
Marciano, Rocky
Wills, Harry
BOY SCOUT LEADER
West, James Edward
BREEDER OF DOGS
Sloane, Isabel Cleves Dodge
BREEDER OF RACEHORSES (See
also HORSEMAN)
Jones, Benjamin Allyn
Lorillard, Pierre
Madden, John Edward
White, Benjamin Franklin
BREWER
Busch, Adolphus
Jones, Frank
Ruppert, Jacob
Vassar, Matthew
Wacker, Charles Henry
BRIDGE BUILDER (See also ENGI-
NEER îBRIDGEî, ENGINEER
îCIVILî)
Harrington, John Lyle
Lindenthal, Gustav
BRIDGE PLAYER (CONTRACT)
Culbertson, Ely
Culbertson, Josephine Murphy
Lenz, Sidney Samuel
Whitehead, Wilbur Cherrier
Work, Milton Cooper
BRIGAND (See also BANDIT, DE-
SPERADO, OUTLAW)
Murrieta, Joaquin
BROADCAST AUDIENCE ANALYST
Hooper, Claude Ernest
BRONZE FOUNDER (See also IRON
FOUNDER)
Mills, Clark
BRYOLOGIST (See also BOTANIST,
BIOLOGIST)
BUCCANEER (See also BANDIT,
BRIGAND, CRIMINAL, DE-
SPERADO, OUTLAW, PIRATE)
You, Dominique
BUCK ROGERS ORIGINATOR
Dille, John Flint
BUILDER (See also CANAL BUILD-
ER, RAILROAD BUILDER, SHIP-
BUILDER)
Allaire, James Peter
Hawks, John
Hoban, James
Hooker, Philip
Joy, Thomas
Macfarlane, Charles William
Parris, Alexander
Starrett, Paul
Starrett, William Aiken
Wolfson, Erwin Service
BUILDING CONTRACTOR (See also
CONTRACTOR)
Kelly, John Brendan
BURGLAR (See also BANDIT, BRIG-
AND, BUCCANEER, CRIMINAL,
DESPERADO, OUTLAW, PIRATE)
Wyman, Seth
BUSINESS FORECASTER
Babson, Roger Ward

BUSINESSMAN (See also BUSINESS-
WOMAN, CAPITALIST, ENTRE-
PRENEUR EXECUTIVE, FACTOR,
INDUSTRIALIST, MANUFACTUR-
ER, MERCHANT)
Abernethy, George
Adams, Charles Francis
Aldrich, Nelson Wilmarth
Baldwin, Henry Porter
Batterson, James Goodwin
Bean, Leon Lenwood
Delm, Costhenes
Bement, Clarence Sweet
Besse, Arthur Lyman
Bliss, Cornelius Newton
Borg, George William
Brady, Anthony Nicholas
Bruce, Edward Bright
Buchanan, William Insco
Buchtel, John Richards
Bucknell, William
Bunker, Arthur Hugh
Caldwell, Alexander
Camden, Johnson Newlon
Caroll, Howard
Chester, Colby Mitchell
Cobo, Albert Eugene
Coburn, Abner
Comer, Braxton Bragg
Cooke, Samuel
Cooper, Mark Anthony
Coxey, Jacob Sechler
Crane, Charles Richard
Dana, Napoleon Jackson
Tecumseh
Dawes, Rufus Cutler
Dexter, Henry
Dow, Lorenzo
Early, Stephen Tyree
Eastman, Harvey Gridley
Edison, Charles
Emery, Henry Crosby
Farwell, Charles Benjamin
Forbes, John Murray
Franklin, William Buel
Goldfine, Bernard
Gorham, Nathaniel
Grady, Henry Francis
Hamlin, Charles
Hartford, George Huntington
Hartford, George Ludlum
Hartford, John Augustine
Haugen, Gilbert Nelson
Hiester, Daniel
Hogan, John
Holt, William Franklin
Hoyt, John Sherman
Huidekoper, Harm Jan
Keyes, Erasmus Darwin
Kimball, Dan Able
Knauth, Oswald Whitman
Kraft, James Lewis
Ladd, William Sargent
Lasater, Edward Cunningham
Lowell, Percival
McCormick, Richard
Cunningham
MacNider, Hanford
Manigault, Peter
Matthews, Francis Patrick
Miller, David Hunter
Millikin, Eugene Donald

Mills, Cyrus Taggart
Mitchell, James Paul
Morton, Paul
Mosessohn, David Nehemiah
Murphy, Gerald Clery
Newberry, Truman Handy
Niles, Nathaniel, 1741–1828
O'Daniel, Wilbert Lee
("Pappy")
Olds, Irving Sands
Pate, Maurice
Peek, George Moloon
Petri, Angelo
Phelps, William Walter
Rand, James Henry
Reece, Brazilla Carroll
Rich, Robert
Richmond, Dean
Roosevelt, Theodore
Scammon, Jonathan Young
Schell, Augustus
Scott, Allen Cecil
Shuey, Edwin Longstreet
Sibley, Hiram
Smoot, Reed Owen
Snell, Bertrand Hollis
Sprunt, James
Strawn, Silas Hardy
Stuart, Elbridge Amos
Taussig, William
Thomas, John Parnell
Thomas, (John William) Elmer
Walker, Amasa
Whalen, Grover Aloysius
Wherry, Kenneth Spicer
BUSINESSWOMAN
Arden, Elizabeth
Gleason, Kate
Rubinstein, Helena
Walker, Sarah Breedlove
Willard, Mary Hatch
BYZANTINE SCHOLAR
Vasiliev, Alexander
Alexandrovich

CABALIST (See also RELIGIOUS
LEADER)
Pancoast, Seth
CABINETMAKER (See CARPENTER)
CABLE PROMOTER
Eastman, Arthur MacArthur
Field, Cyrus West
Scrymser, James Alexander
CALLIGRAPHER
Dwiggins, William Addison
CANAL BUILDER
Goethals, George Washington
Lacock, Abner
Moorhead, James Kennedy
CANAL PROMOTER
Shonts, Theodore Perry
Watson, Elkanah
CANNON MAKER (See also IRON
FOUNDER)
Denning, William
CANTOR (See also SINGER)
Kaiser, Alois
Rosenblatt, Joseph
Stark, Edward Josef
CAPITALIST (See also FINANCIER)
Allerton, Samuel Waters
Ames, Frederick Lothrop

Ames, Oakes
Ames, Oliver
Archbold, John Dustin
Astor, John Jacob, 1763–1848
Astor, John Jacob, 1822–1890
Astor, John Jacob, 1864–1914
Astor, William Backhouse
Astor, William Waldorf
Ayer, James Cook
Baldwin, Henry Perrine
Barber, Amzi Lorenzo
Barnum, Zenus
Bennett, James Gordon
Berwind, Edward Julius
Blair, John Insley
Blow, Henry Taylor
Boies, Henry Martyn
Brainerd, Lawrence
Brown, Henry Cordis
Burt, John
Campbell, Robert
Collier, Barron Gift
Converse, Edmund Cogswell
Cook, James Merrill
Corbin, Austin
Cornell, Ezra
Crimmins, John Daniel
Crocker, Charles
Daly, Marcus
De Lamar, Joseph Raphael
Dennis, Graham Barclay
Dickson, Thomas
Dolan, Thomas
Donahue, Peter
Drew, Daniel
Du Pont, Thomas Coleman
Eells, Dan Parmelee
Elkins, William Lukens
Field, Cyrus West
Fisk, James
Fiske, John
Flagler, Henry Morrison
Flagler, John Haldane
Fleischmann, Charles Louis
Folger, Henry Clay
Freedman, Andrew
Frick, Henry Clay
Gerstle, Lewis
Gilbert, William Lewis
Glidden, Joseph Farwell
Grace, William Russell
Grant, John Thomas
Guggenheim, Daniel
Haggin, James Ben Ali
Halleck, Henry Wager
Hanna, Marcus Alonzo
Harrah, Charles Jefferson
Hauser, Samuel Thomas
Havemeyer, Henry Osborne
Havemeyer, William Frederick
Huntington, Collis Potter
Jesup, Morris Ketchum
Jones, Frank
Juilliard, Augustus D.
Keith, Minor Cooper
Kennedy, John Stewart
Knight, Edward Collings
Leach, Shepherd
Leary, John
Leiter, Joseph
Lewisohn, Adolph

Logan, Thomas Muldrup,
  1840–1914
Longyear, John Munroe
Lowry, Thomas
Lucas, James H.
Mackay, Clarence Hungerford
Mackay, John William
Macy, Valentine Everit
Markoe, Abraham
Marquand, Henry Gurdon
Mather, Samuel Livingston
Moffat, David Halliday
Moore, William Henry
O'Brien, William Shoney
Paine, Charles Jackson
Patten, James A.
Payne, Oliver Hazard
Phelan, James, 1824–1892
Pratt, Enoch
Ralston, William Chapman
Raymond, Benjamin Wright
Ream, Norman Bruce
Reed, Simeon Gannett
Roberts, Marshall Owen
Rogers, Henry Huttleston
Ryan, John Dennis
Ryerson, Martin Antoine
Scrymser, James Alexander
Severance, Louis Henry
Sheedy, Dennis
Simpson, Michael Hodge
Sloss, Louis
Smith, Francis Marion
Smith, Robert Alexander C.
Spreckels, Claus
Spreckels, John Diedrich
Squire, Watson Carvosso
Stewart, William Rhinelander
Stillman, James
Stokes, William Earl Dodge
Stone, Amasa
Stranahan, James Samuel
  Thomas
Taylor, Moses
Tevis, Lloyd
Thaw, William
Tobey, Edward Silas
Tod, David
Upton, George Bruce
Vanderbilt, George Washington
Vanderbilt, William Kissam
Vibbard, Chauncey
Waldo, Samuel
Walters, Henry
Waterhouse, Frank
Welch, Charles Clark
Winslow, Sidney Wilmot
Zimmerman, Eugene

CARDINAL
Brennan, Francis James
Cushing, Richard James
Glennon, John Joseph
Meyer, Albert Gregory
Ritter, Joseph Elmer
Spellman, Francis Joseph
CARDIOLOGIST (See also PHYSI-
  CIAN)
Libman, Emanuel
CARE EXECUTIVE DIRECTOR
French, Paul Comly

CARICATURIST (See CARTOONIST)
CARPENTER
Goddard, John
Gostelowe, Jonathan
Holden, Oliver
Luther, Seth
Phyfe, Duncan
Savery, William, 1721–1787
CARPETBAGGER (See also ADVEN-
  TURER, SPECULATOR)
Clarke, William Thomas
Tourgée, Albion Winegar
CARRIAGE BUILDER
Brewster, James
CARTOGRAPHER (See also MAPMAK-
  ER)
Farmer, John
Herrman, Augustine
Kino, Eusebio Francisco
Lindenkohl, Adolph
Ogden, Herbert Gouverneur
Pelham, Henry
Pound, Thomas
Romans, Bernard
Southack, Cyprian
Tanner, Henry Schenck
White, John
CARTOONIST (See also ARTIST, IL-
  LUSTRATOR)
Arno, Peter
Bellew, Frank Henry Temple
Berryman, Clifford Kennedy
Briggs, Clare A.
Cesare, Oscar Edward
Charles, William
Clay, Edward Williams
Crosby, Percy Lee
Darling, Jay Norwood ("Ding")
Davenport, Homer Calvin
Dorgan, Thomas Aloysius
Duffy, Edmund
Fisher, Hammond Edward
Fisher, Henry Conroy ("Bud")
Fitzpatrick, Daniel Robert
Fox, Fontaine Talbot, Jr.
Gibson, Charles Dana
Gillam, Bernhard
Goldberg, Reuben Lucius
  ("Rube")
Gray, Harold Lincoln
Gross, Milt
Grosz, George
Hatlo, Jimmy
Held, John, Jr.
Herriman, George Joseph
Hubbard, Frank McKinney
Keppler, Joseph
Kirby, Rollin
McManus, George
Minor, Robert
Morgan, Matthew Somerville
Nast, Thomas
Newell, Peter Sheaf Hersey
Opper, Frederick Burr
Raymond, Alexander Gillespie
Rogers, William Allen
Smith, Robert Sidney
Szyk, Arthur
Thurber, James Grover
Volck, Adalbert John
Wales, James Albert
Webster, Harold Tucker

Willard, Frank Henry
Williams, Gaar Campbell
Young, Art
Zimmerman, Eugene
CATERER (See RESTAURATEUR)
CATTLEMAN (See also DAIRY HUS-
    BANDMAN, RANCHER, STOCK
    BREEDER)
Chisum, John Simpson
Goodnight, Charles
Lasater, Edward Cunningham
Littlefield, George Washington
McCoy, Joseph Geating
Mackenzie, Murdo
Renick, Felix
Springer, Charles
Strawn, Jacob
CENSUS DIRECTOR
Kennedy, Joseph Camp Griffith
Merriam, William Rush
CHANCELLOR (STATE)
Harrington, Samuel Maxwell
Livingston, Robert R.,
    1746–1813
Saulsbury, Willard, 1820–1892
Walworth, Reuben Hyde
CHANDLER
Jackson, William, 1783–1855
CHAPLAIN (See also CLERGYMAN,
    RELIGIOUS LEADER)
Hunter, Andrew
Jones, David
Jones, George
Munro, Henry
CHEF
Diat, Louis Felix
CHEMIST (See also BIOCHEMIST,
    SCIENTIST)
Abel, John Jacob
Adkins, Homer Burton
Austen, Peter Townsend
Babcock, James Francis
Bache, Franklin
Bailey, Jacob Whitman
Bancroft, Wilder Dwight
Barker, George Frederick
Baskerville, Charles
Beck, Lewis Caleb
Benedict, Stanley Rossiter
Bolton, Henry Carrington
Boltwood, Bertram Borden
Booth, James Curtis
Boyé, Martin Hans
Browne, Charles Albert
Burnett, Joseph
Carothers, Wallace Hume
Chandler, Charles Frederick
Clarke, Frank Wigglesworth
Cooke, Josiah Parsons
Cope, Arthur Clay
Cottrell, Frederick Gardner
Crafts, James Mason
Cutbush, James
Dabney, Charles William
Dana, James Freeman
Dana, Samuel Luther
Day, David Talbot
Debye, Peter Joseph William
Doremus, Robert Ogden
Dorset, Marion
Dow, Herbert Henry
Draper, John William

Drown, Thomas Messinger
Dudley, Charles Benjamin
Duncan, Robert Kennedy
Du Pont, Francis Irénée
Ellis, Carleton
Folin, Otto Knut Olof
Franklin, Edward Curtis
Freas, Thomas Bruce
Fullam, Frank L.
Genth, Frederick Augustus
Gibbs, Oliver Wolcott
Goessmann, Charles Anthony
Gomberg, Moses
Gorham, John
Grasselli, Caesar Augustin
Green, Jacob
Griscom, John
Guthrie, Samuel
Hall, Charles Martin
Hare, Robert
Harkins, William Draper
Hart, Edward
Hayes, Augustus Allen
Hendrick, Ellwood
Herty, Charles Holmes
Hill, Henry Barker
Hillebrand, William Francis
Hooker, Samuel Cox
Horsford, Eben Norton
Hudson, Claude Silbert
Hunt, Thomas Sterry
Jackson, Charles Thomas
James, Charles
Jarves, Deming
Johnson, Treat Baldwin
Johnston, John
Jones, Harry Clary
Keating, William Hypolitus
Kedzie, Robert Clark
Kharasch, Morris Selig
Kinnicutt, Leonard Parker
Kirkwood, John Gamble
Koenig, George Augustus
Kohler, Elmer Peter
Ladd, Edwin Fremont
Lamb, Arthur Becket
Langley, John Williams
Langmuir, Irving
Latimer, Wendell Mitchell
Lea, Mathew Carey
Leffmann, Henry
Levy, Louis Edward
Lewis, Gilbert Newton
Loeb, Morris
Long, John Harper
Mabery, Charles Frederic
Maclean, John
McMurtrie, William
Mallet, John William
Mallinckrodt, Edward, Jr.
Matheson, William John
Matthews, Joseph Merritt
Merrill, Joshua
Metcalfe, Samuel Lytler
Michael, Arthur
Michaelis, Leonor
Midgley, Thomas
Mitchell, John Kearsley
Moore, Richard Bishop
Morfit, Campbell
Morley, Edward Williams
Mulliken, Samuel Parsons

Munroe, Charles Edward
Nef, John Ulric
Nichols, James Robinson
Nieuwland, Julius Arthur
Norris, James Flack
Norton, John Pitkin
Noyes, Arthur Amos
Noyes, William Albert
Ostromislensky, Iwan
    Iwanowich
Parr, Samuel Wilson
Peckham, Stephen Farnum
Pendleton, Edmund Monroe
Peter, Robert
Phillips, Francis Clifford
Piccard, Jean Felix
Porter, John Addison
Power, Frederick Belding
Prescott, Albert Benjamin
Pugh, Evan
Randall, Wyatt William
Reese, Charles Lee
Reid, David Boswell
Remsen, Ira
Rice, Charles
Richards, Ellen Henrietta
    Swallow
Richards, Theodore William
Rogers, James Blythe
Rogers, Robert Empie
Sadtler, Samuel Philip
Sanger, Charles Robert
Scovell, Melville Amasa
Seabury, George John
Shepard, James Henry
Sheppard, Samuel Edward
Silliman, Benjamin, 1816–1885
Slosson, Edwin Emery
Smith, Alexander
Smith, Edgar Fahs
Smith, John Lawrence
Squibb, Edward Robinson
Stern, Otto
Stieglitz, Julius
Stillman, Thomas Bliss
Stine, Charles Milton Altland
Stoddard, John Tappan
Storer, Francis Humphreys
Takamine, Jokichi
Talbot, Henry Paul
Taylor, William Chittenden
Teeple, John Edgar
Tilghman, Richard Albert
Tolman, Richard Chace
Torrey, John
Vaughan, Daniel
Warren, Cyrus Moors
Washburn, Edward Wight
Weber, Henry Adam
Weightman, William
Wetherill, Charles Mayer
White, Henry Clay
Whitmore, Frank Clifford
Whitney, Josiah Dwight
Whitney, Willis Rodney
Wiechmann, Ferdinand
    Gerhard
Wiley, Harvey Washington
Witthaus, Rudolph August
Wood, Edward Stickney
Woodhouse, James
Wurtz, Henry

CHESS PLAYER
Loyd, Samuel
Mackenzie, George Henry
Marshall, Frank James
Morphy, Paul Charles
Pillsbury, Harry Nelson
Rice, Isaac Leopold
Steinitz, William
CHIEF JUSTICE (STATE) (See also JUDGE, JURIST, LAWYER, SUPREME COURT JUSTICE)
De Lancey, James
Gaines, Reuben Reid
Horsmanden, Daniel
Livermore, Arthur
Lloyd, David
Lowe, Ralph Phillips
Lumpkin, Joseph Henry
Mellen, Prentiss
More, Nicholas
Morris, Lewis, 1671–1746
Morris, Robert Hunter
Morton, Marcus, 1819–1891
Nicholls, Francis Redding Tillon
Read, George
Rusk, Thomas Jefferson
Shippen, Edward, 1728–1806
Simpson, William Dunlap
CHINESE ART SPECIALIST
Ferguson, John Calvin
CHOIRMASTER (See also CONDUCTOR)
Dett, Robert Nathaniel
Tuckey, William
CHOREOGRAPHER
Bolm, Adolph Rudolphovitch
Fokine, Michel
Humphrey, Doris
Tamiris, Helen
CHRISTIAN SCIENCE LEADER (See also RELIGIOUS LEADER)
Eddy, Mary Morse Baker
Stetson, Augusta Emma Simmons
CHRONICLER (See also DIARIST, HISTORIAN)
Clyman, James
Johnson, Edward
CHURCH HISTORIAN (See also HISTORIAN)
Dubbs, Joseph Henry
Edwards, Morgan
Guilday, Peter Keenan
Jackson, Samuel Macauley
Moffatt, James
Perry, William Stevens
Schaff, Philip
Walker, Williston
Whitsitt, William Heth
CIRCUS CLOWN (See CLOWN)
CIRCUS PROPRIETOR (See SHOWMAN)
CITY PLANNER
Atterbury, Grosvenor
Bassett, Edward Murray
Bettman, Alfred
Brunner, Arnold William
Ford, George Burdett
Moore, Charles
Nolen, John
Robinson, Charles Mulford

Saarinen, Gottlieb Eliel
Wacker, Charles Henry
Wright, Henry
CIVIC LEADER
Adams, Charles Francis, 1835–1915
Blodgett, John Wood
Breckinridge, Desha
Burlingham, Charles Culp
Chandler, Harry
Clement, Rufus Early
Cutting, Robert Fulton
Dawes, Rufus Cutler
Donovan, John Joseph
Fallows, Samuel
Fortier, Alcée
Foulke, William Dudley
Haskell, Henry Jospeh
Hay, Mary Garrett
Hirsch, Emil Gustav
Jackson, Robert R.
Kirstein, Louis Edward
Lingelbach, Anna Lane
Loring, Charles Morgridge
Marburg, Theodore
Martin, Elizabeth Price
Mosher, Eliza Maria
Ochs, Julius
O'Connor, William Douglas
Outerbridge, Eugenius Harvey
Price, Eli Kirk
Seligman, Isaac Newton
Seligman, Joseph
Sloan, George Arthur
Spaulding, Oliver Lyman
Stranahan, James Samuel Thomas
Strong, Harriet Williams Russell
Sullivan, William Henry
Sulzberger, Cyrus Lindauer
Taussig, William
Thacher, Thomas Day
Tiffany, Katrina Brandes Ely
Wagener, John Andreas
Waterhouse, Sylvester
Widney, Joseph Pomeroy
Williams, Fannie Barrier
CIVIC REFORMER (See also POLITICAL REFORMER, REFORMER, SOCIAL REFORMER)
Coulter, Ernest Kent
CIVIL LIBERTARIAN
Chafee, Zechariah, Jr.
Flynn, Elizabeth Gurley
Malin, Patrick Murphy
CIVIL RIGHTS LEADER
Evers, Medgar Wiley
Garvey, Marcus Moziah
Houston, Charles Hamilton
Howe, Mark De Wolfe
Hunton, George Kenneth
Jackson, Robert R.
Johnson, James Weldon
King, Martin Luther, Jr.
Malcolm X
Remond, Charles Lenox
Robinson, Ruby Doris Smith
Smith, Lillian Eugenia
Still, William
Terrell, Mary Eliza Church
Turner, James Milton

Walker, David, 1785–1830
Waring, Julius Waties
White, Walter Francis
CIVIL SERVICE REFORMER (See also REFORMER)
Bonaparte, Charles Joseph
Eaton, Dorman Bridgman
Proctor, John Robert
Swift, Lucius Burrie
Wheeler, Everett Pepperrell
CLASSICIST (See also SCHOLAR)
Allinson, Francis Greenleaf
Beeson, Charles Henry
Capps, Edward
Ezekiel, Cheever
Fiske, George Converse
Frank, Tenney
Hadas, Moses
Hamilton, Edith
Harrison, Gessner
Jaeger, Werner Wilhelm
Kelsey, Francis Willey
Kendall, Asabel Clark
Lane, George Martin
Leach, Abby
Lewis, Charlton Thomas
Manatt, James Irving
Moore, Clifford Herschel
Morgan, Morris Hicky
Munford, William
North, Edward
Oldfather, William Abbott
Peck, Tracy
Rand, Edward Kennard
Scott, John Adams
Sewall, Stephen
Seymour, Thomas Day
Shorey, Paul
Showerman, Grant
Sophocles, Evangelinus Apostolides
Thacher, Thomas Anthony
Waters, William Everett
West, Andrew Fleming
Wheeler, Arthur Leslie
Wheeler, James Rignall
CLERGYMAN (See also ARCHABBOT, ARCHBISHOP, BISHOP, CARDINAL, CHAPLAIN, EVANGELIST, RELIGIOUS LEADER)
Adventist
Himes, Joshua Vaughan
Miller, William
Ward, Henry Dana
White, Ellen Gould Harmon
African Methodist Episcopal
Gaines, Wesley John
Gregg, John Andrew
Whitman, Albery Allson
Anglican (See also Episcopal)
Auchmuty, Samuel
Bacon, Thomas
Boucher, Jonathan
Bowden, John
Bray, Thomas
Camm, John
Chandler, Thomas Bradbury
Checkley, John
Coombe, Thomas
Davenport, John
Duché, Jacob
Evans, Evan

Evans, Nathaniel
Forbes, John, d. 1783
Heathcote, Caleb
Hunt, Isaac
Hunt, Robert
Inglis, Charles
Johnson, Samuel
Le Jau, Francis
Munro, Henry
Ogilvie, John
Peters, Richard, c. 1704–1776
Peters, Samuel Andrew
Smith, William, 1727–1803
Sterling, James
Talbot, John
Vesey, William
Whitaker, Alexander
Baptist
Anderson, Galusha
Arthur, William
Backus, Isaac
Banvard, Joseph
Barbour, Clarence Augustus
Benedict, David
Boyce, James Petigru
Boyd, Richard Henry
Broadus, John Albert
Brown, Charles Rufus
Brown, John Newton
Burdette, Robert Jones
Burleson, Rufus Clarence
Burroughs, John Curtis
Buttrick, Wallace
Callender, John
Cathcart, William
Chaplin, Jeremiah
Cheney, Oren Burbank
Church, Pharcellus
Clark, George Whitefield
Clarke, John
Clarke, William Newton
Clay, Joseph
Colver, Nathaniel
Cone, Spencer Houghton
Conwell, Russell Herman
Creath, Jacob, 1777–1854
Creath, Jacob, 1799–1886
Dagg, John Leadley
Dixon, Thomas
Dodge, Ebenezer
Eaton, Charles Aubrey
Eddy, Daniel Clarke
Edwards, Morgan
Faunce, William Herbert Perry
Fermald, James Champlin
Fosdick, Harry Emerson
Foster, George Burman
Frey, Joseph Samuel Christian
    Frederick
Fuller, Richard
Fulton, Justin Dewey
Furman, James Clement
Furman, Richard
Gale, Elbridge
Gambrell, James Bruton
Gano, John
Gano, Stephen
Garrard, James
Gilmore, Joseph Henry
Going, Jonathan
Goodspeed, Thomas Wakefield
Graves, James Robinson

Gregory, John Milton
Griffith, Benjamin
Hatcher, William Eldridge
Henderson, Charles Richmond
Holcombe, Henry
Holman, Jesse Lynch
Horr, George Edwin
Hovey, Alvah
Howell, Robert Boyté Crawford
Jeter, Jeremiah Bell
Johnson, Franklin
Johnson, William Bullein
Jones, David
Judson, Edward
King, Henry Melville
King, Martin Luther, Jr.
Lamb, Isaac Wixom
Lane, Tidence
Leland, John
Lightburn, Joseph Andrew
    Jackson
Lorimer, George Claude
Love, Emanuel King
Lowrey, Mark Perrin
MacArthur, Robert Stuart
McGlothlin, William Joseph
Macintosh, Douglas Clyde
Malcolm, Howard
Manly, Basil, 1798–1868
Manly, Basil, 1825–1892
Manning, James
Marshall, Daniel
Martin, Warren Homer
Massey, John Edward
Mell, Patrick Hues
Mercer, Jesse
Merrill, Daniel
Merrill, George Edmands
Morehouse, Henry Lyman
Morgan, Abel
Morgan, Thomas Jefferson
Moss, Lemuel
Moxom, Philip Stafford
Mullins, Edgar Young
Myles, John
Osgood, Howard
Payne, Christopher Harrison
Peck, John Mason
Pendleton, James Madison
Pentecost, George Frederick
Perry, Rufus Lewis
Potter, Charles Francis
Powell, Adam Clayton, Sr.
Rauschenbusch, Walter
Rhees, Morgan John
Rhees, Rush
Rice, Luther
Richmond, John Lambert
Riley, Benjamin Franklin
Riley, William Bell
Robins, Henry Ephraim
Robinson, Ezekiel Gilman
Ross, Martin
Ryland, Robert
Sanders, Billington McCarter
Sears, Barnas
Sharp, Daniel
Sherwood, Adiel
Smith, Hezekiah
Smith, John, c. 1735–c. 1824
Smith, Samuel Francis
Stanford, John

Staughton, William
Stearns, Shubal
Stillman, Samuel
Stow, Baron
Straton, John Roach
Taylor, George Boardman
Taylor, James Barnett
Taylor, James Monroe
Taylor, John
Thomas, Jesse Burgess
Tichenor, Isaac Taylor
Tomlinson, Everett Titsworth
Tucker, Henry Holcombe
Tupper, Henry Allen
Vedder, Henry Clay
Waller, John Lightfoot
Wayland, Francis, 1796–1865
Whitfield, Owen
Whitsitt, William Heth
Williams, George Washington
Williams, William R.
Willingham, Robert Josiah
Winchester, Elhanan
Winkler, Edwin Theodore
Woods, Alva
Yeaman, William Pope
Campbellite (See Disciples of Christ)
Catholic (See Roman Catholic)
Christian Connection
Shaw, Elijah
Smith, Elias
Wellons, William Brock
Church of England (See Anglican)
Church of God
Michaux, Lightfoot Solomon
Church of the New Jerusalem (See
    Swedenborgian)
Congregational
Abbott, Edward
Abbott, Jacob
Abbott, John Stevens Cabot
Abbott, Lyman
Adams, Nehemiah
Alden, Timothy
Allen, William
Ament, William Scott
Andrew, Samuel
Atkinson, George Henry
Atkinson, Henry Avery
Atwater, Lyman Hotchkiss
Austin, David
Austin, Samuel
Backus, Azel
Bacon, Benjamin Wisner
Bacon, David
Bacon, John
Bacon, Leonard
Bacon, Leonard Woolsey
Bailey, Rufus William
Bancroft, Aaron
Barnard, John
Barrows, John Henry
Bartlett, Samuel Colcord
Barton, James Levi
Barton, William Eleazar
Beecher, Charles
Beecher, Edward
Beecher, Henry Ward
Beecher, Thomas Kinnicut
Behrends, Adolphus Julius
    Frederick
Belknap, Jeremy

Bissell, Edwin Cone
Blakeslee, Erastus
Bosworth, Edward Increase
Boynton, Charles Brandon
Bradford, Amory Howe
Brattle, William
Brown, Charles Reynolds
Bumstead, Horace
Burr, Enoch Fitch
Burton, Asa
Burton, Marion Le Roy
Burton, Nathaniel Judson
Bushnell, Horace
Byles, Mather
Calkins, Phineas Wolcott
Chapin, Aaron Lucius
Chapin, Calvin
Cheever, George Barrell
Child, Frank Samuel
Clap, Thomas
Clark, Francis Edward
Clark, Jonas
Clark, Joseph Sylvester
Cleveland, Aaron
Cobb, William Henry
Condon, Thomas
Cook, Russell S.
Cooper, Samuel, 1725–1783
Crane, Frank
Cravath, Erastus Milo
Cushman, Joshua
Cutler, Carroll
Cutler, Manasseh
Daggett, Naphtali
Dana, James
Davenport, James
Davis, Jerome Dean
Day, Henry Noble
Deane, Samuel
Dewey, Chester
Dexter, Henry Martyn
Dike, Samuel Warren
Diman, Jeremiah Lewis
Dole, Charles Fletcher
Douglas, Lloyd Cassel
Dunning, Albert Elijah
Durant, Henry
Dwight, Sereno Edwards
Dwight, Timothy, 1752–1817
Dwight, Timothy, 1828–1916
Eastman, William Reed
Edwards, Jonathan
Edwards, Justin
Eliot, Jared
Emerson, Joseph
Emmons, Nathanael
Everett, Robert
Fairbanks, Henry
Field, David Dudley
Fisher, George Park
Fowler, Orin
Gay, Ebenezer
Gladden, Washington
Goodrich, Charles Augustus
Goodrich, Chauncey Allen
Goodrich, Elizur
Gordon, George Angier
Gordon, William
Griffin, Edward Dorr
Griffis, William Elliot
Grinnell, Josiah Bushnell
Gulick, Sidney Lewis

Gunsaulus, Frank Wakeley
Hall, Sherman
Harris, George
Haven, Joseph
Hepworth, George Hughes
Herron, George Davis
Hiacoomes
Higginson, John
Hillis, Newell Dwight
Hitchcock, Edward, 1793–1864
Hitchcock, Enos
Hitchcock, Roswell Dwight
Hoisington, Henry Richard
Holmes, Abiel
Holt, Arthur Erastus
Hooker, Thomas
Hubbard, William
Hume, Robert Allen
Humphrey, Heman
Jefferson, Charles Edward
Jenks, William
Kellogg, Elijah
Kellogg, Martin
Kyle, James Henderson
Langdon, Samuel
Leavitt, Joshua
L'Halle, Constantin de
Lord, Nathan
Lovejoy, Owen Reed
Lyman, Albert Josiah
McCulloch, Oscar Carleton
McKeen, Joseph
McKenzie, Alexander
Magoun, George Frederic
Mahan, Asa
Marsh, John
Mather, Samuel
Mayhew, Thomas
Mead, Charles Marsh
Mears, David Otis
Merrill, Selah
Mills, Samuel John
Mitchell, Jonathan
Moore, Zephaniah Swift
Morril, David Lawrence
Morrison, Nathan Jackson
Morse, Jedidiah
Munger, Theodore Thornton
Murdock, James
Nash, Charles Sumner
Nason, Elias
Newcomb, Harvey
Newman, Samuel Phillips
Niles, Samuel
Noble, Frederick Alphonso
Norris, Edward
North, Simeon, 1802–1884
Nott, Samuel
Nutting, Wallace
Oakes, Urian
Palmer, Ray
Parish, Elijah
Parker, Edwin Pond
Parker, Samuel
Payson, Edward
Payson, Seth
Peet, Stephen Denison
Peloubet, Francis Nathan
Pennington, James W. C.
Peter, Hugh
Phelps, Austin
Phillips, George

Pierce, John Davis
Pierpont, James
Pierson, Abraham, 1645–1707
Pond, Enoch
Porter, Ebenezer
Porter, Noah
Post, Truman Marcellus
Proctor, Henry Hugh
Rankin, Jeremiah Eames
Rice, Edwin Wilbur
Richards, Charles Herbert
Robbins, Thomas
Rogers, John Almanza Rowley
Ross, Abel Hastings
Salter, William
Saltonstall, Gurdon
Sanders, Daniel Clarke
Sanford, Elias Benjamin
Schauffler, Henry Albert
Seccomb, John
Sheldon, Charles Monroe
Shepard, Thomas
Smyth, Egbert Coffin
Smyth, Newman
Sperry, Willard Learoyd
Sprague, William Buell
Spring, Leverett Wilson
Spring, Samuel
Stearns, William Augustus
Stiles, Ezra
Stoddard, Solomon
Storrs, Richard Salter,
    1787–1873
Storrs, Richard Salter,
    1821–1900
Strong, James Woodward
Strong, Josiah
Stuart, Moses
Sturtevant, Julian Monson
Tappan, Henry Philip
Tarbox, Increase Niles
Taylor, William Mackergo
Tenney, Edward Payson
Thacher, Peter
Thayer, Joseph Henry
Thayer, William Makepeace
Thompson, Joseph Parrish
Todd, John
Tracy, Joseph
Trumbull, Benjamin
Tucker, William Jewett
Tufts, John
Turner, Asa
Twichell, Joseph Hopkins
Tyler, Charles Mellen
Walker, Timothy, 1705–1782
Walter, Thomas, 1696–1725
Ward, Joseph
Ware, Henry, 1764–1845
Warren, Israel Perkins
Welles, Noah
Wheelock, Eleazar
Whiton, James Morris
Willard, Samuel, 1775–1859
Williams, Elisha
Williams, John, 1664–1729
Williston, Seth
Wines, Enoch Cobb
Wingate, Paine
Winship, Albert Edward
Winslow, Hubbard
Wise, John

Woods, Leonard, 1774–1854
Worcester, Noah
Worcester, Samuel
Wright, George Frederick
Yeomans, John William
Disciples of Christ
Adams, William Lysander
Ainslie, Peter
Allen, Thomas M.
Ames, Edward Scribner
Anderson, Henry Tompkins
Baxter, William
Campbell, Alexander
Creath, Jacob, 1777–1854
Creath, Jacob, 1799–1886
Errett, Isaac
Fanning, Tolbert
Franklin, Benjamin
Goodwin, Elijah
Goss, James Walker
Hayden, Amos Sutton
Hoshour, Samuel Klinefelter
Lard, Moses E.
Loos, Charles Louis
McGarvey, John William
McLean, Archibald
Milligan, Robert
Moore, William Thomas
Pendleton, William Kimbrough
Pinkerton, Lewis Letig
Power, Frederick Dunglison
Scott, Walter
Willett, Herbert Lockwood
Zollars, Ely Vaughn
Dutch Reformed
Berg, Joseph Frederic
Bethune, George Washington
Bourne, George
Chambers, Talbot Wilson
Corwin, Edward Tanjore
Drury, John Benjamin
Ferris, Isaac
Freeman, Bernardus
Frelinghuysen, Theodorus
 Jacobus
Goetschius, John Henry
Hardenbergh, Jacob Rutsen
Hartranft, Chester David
Livingston, John Henry
McClure, Alexander Wilson
Megapolensis, Johannes
Michaëlius, Jonas
Milledoler, Philip
Riddle, Matthew Brown
Seelye, Julius Hawley
Selijns, Henricus
Talmage, Thomas DeWitt
Taylor, Graham
Van Rensselaer, Nicholas
Episcopal (See also Anglican)
Abbott, Edward
Adams, Jasper
Allen, Alexander Viets Griswold
Allen, George
Andrews, John
Beardsley, Eben Edwards
Beasley, Frederick
Bell, Bernard Iddings
Bird, Frederic Mayer
Blake, John Lauris
Brady, Cyrus Townsend
Breck, James Lloyd

Briggs, Charles Augustus
Bristed, John
Chamberlain, Nathan Henry
Chapin, Alonzo Bowen
Coit, Henry Augustus
Coit, Thomas Winthrop
Cooper, Myles
Crapsey, Algernon Sidney
Croswell, Harry
Cummins, George David
Curtis, Moses Ashley
Cutler, Timothy
Dalcho, Frederick
De Costa, Benjamin Franklin
De Koven, James
Dix, Morgan
Doddridge, Joseph
Ewer, Ferdinand Cartwright
Flagg, Jared Bradley
Francis, Paul James
Gavin, Frank Stanton Burns
Goodwin, Hannibal Williston
Grant, Percy Stickney
Griswold, Alexander Viets
Hall, Charles Henry
Hare, George Emlen
Harris, William
Hawks, Francis Lister
Henry, Caleb Sprague
Hodges, George
Hoffman, Eugene Augustus
Houghton, George Hendric
Humes, Thomas William
Huntington, William Reed
Ingraham, Joseph Holt
Jarratt, Devereux
Jarvis, Abraham
Jones, Hugh
Kilbourne, James
King, William Benjamin Basil
Knight, Henry Cogswell
Langdon, William Chauncy
Leach, Daniel Dyer
Leaming, Jeremiah
Le Jau, Francis
Lord, William Wilberforce
Lowell, Robert Traill Spence
McCabe, John Collins
McCook, John James
MacSparran, James
McVickar, John
Mahan, Milo
Mansfield, Richard
Mombert, Jacob Isidor
Montgomery, James Alan
Moore, James, 1764–1814
Muhlenberg, William Augustus
Mulford, Elisha
Murphy, Edgar Gardner
Nash, Daniel
Nash, Henry Sylvester
Newton, Richard
Newton, Richard Heber
Newton, William Wilberforce
Nies, James Buchanan
Norton, John Nicholas
Norwood, Robert Winkworth
Oertel, Johannes Adam Simon
Ogden, Uzal
Packard, Joseph
Park, Roswell
Pendleton, William Nelson

Penick, Charles Clifton
Peterkin, George William
Peters, John Punnett
Pettigrew, Charles
Piggot, Robert
Pilmore, Joseph
Pinney, Norman
Pott, Francis Lister Hawks
Potter, Eliphalet Nott
Pynchon, Thomas Ruggles
Rainsford, William Stephen
Russell, James Solomon
Satterlee, Henry Yates
Savage, Thomas Staughton
Schroeder, John Frederick
Scott, Thomas Fielding
Seabury, Samuel, 1801–1872
Shelton, Frederick William
Shields, Charles Woodruff
Shoup, Francis Asbury
Slafter, Edmund Farwell
Slaughter, Philip
Smith, John Cotton, 1826–1882
Smith, William, 1754–1821
Sparrow, William
Spencer, Jesse Ames
Sterrett, James Macbride
Stokes, Anson Phelps
Stone, John Seely
Stuck, Hudson
Tolman, Herbert Cushing
Tomkins, Floyd Williams
Tucker, Henry St. George
Turner, Samuel Hulbeart
Tyng, Stephen Higginson
Tyson, Stuart Lawrence
Vesey, William
Vinton, Alexander Hamilton
Vinton, Francis
Walden, Jacob Treadwell
Ward, Henry Dana
Washburn, Edward Abiel
Weems, Mason Locke
Wharton, Charles Henry
Wharton, Francis
Wheaton, Nathaniel Sheldon
White, George
Wilmer, James Jones
Wilmer, William Holland
Wilson, Bird
Wilson, William Dexter
Winslow, William Copley
Worcester, Elwood
Evangelical Lutheran
Dinwiddie, Edwin Courtland
Friends (See Quaker)
German Reformed
Bausman, Benjamin
Boehm, John Philip
Bomberger, John Henry
Bucher, John Conrad
Dubbs, Joseph Henry
Good, James Isaac
Good, Jeremiah Haak
Gros, John Daniel
Harbaugh, Henry
Helffenstein, John Albert
 Conrad
Hendel, John William
Herman, Lebrecht Frederick
Mayer, Lewis
Miller, John Peter

Otterbein, Philip William
Rupp, William
Schlatter, Michael
Stahr, John Summers
Greek Orthodox
Callimachos, Panos Demetrios
Jewish
Adler, Samuel
Asher, Joseph Mayor
Berkowitz, Henry
Blaustein, David
Einhorn, David
Enelow, Hyman Gerson
Felsenthal, Bernhard
Gottheil, Gustav
Grossmann, Louis
Harris, Maurice Henry
Heller, Maximilian
Hirsch, Emil Gustav
Hirschensohn, Chaim
Isaacs, Samuel Myer
Jastrow, Marcus
Kagan, Henry Enoch
Kalisch, Isidor
Kohler, Kaufmann
Kohut, Alexander
Kohut, George Alexander
Krauskopf, Joseph
Leeser, Isaac
Levy, Joseph Leonard
Liebman, Joshua Loth
Lilienthal, Max
Magnes, Judah Leon
Mendes, Frederic De Sola
Mendes, Henry Pereira
Meyer, Martin Abraham
Mielziner, Moses
Morais, Sabato
Philipson, David
Raphall, Morris Jacob
Schindler, Solomon
Seixas, Gershom Mendes
Silver, Abba Hillel
Silverman, Joseph
Szold, Benjamin
Voorsanger, Jacob
Wise, Aaron
Wise, Isaac Mayer
Wise, Stephen Samuel
Latter-Day Saints (*See* Mormon)
Lutheran
Acrelius, Israel
Bachman, John
Baugher, Henry Louis
Berkenmeyer, Wilhelm
  Christoph
Bird, Frederic Mayer
Boltzius, Johann Martin
Campanius, John
Clausen, Claus Lauritz
Dahl, Theodor Halvorson
Deindörfer, Johannes
Demme, Charles Rudolph
Dietrichson, Johannes Wilhelm
  Christian
Douglas, Lloyd Cassel
Dylander, John
Eielsen, Elling
Esbjörn, Lars Paul
Falckner, Daniel
Falckner, Justus
Funk, Isaac Kauffman

Grabau, Johannes Andreas
  August
Greenwald, Emanuel
Grossmann, Georg Martin
Hartwig, Johann Christoph
Hasselquist, Tuve Nilsson
Hay, Charles Augustus
Hayme, Gjermund
Hazelius, Ernest Lewis
Helmuth, Justus Henry
  Christian
Henkel, Paul
Hoenecke, Gustav Adolf Felix
  Theodor
Hoffmann, Francis Arnold
Horn, Edward Traill
Hunton, William Lee
Jacobs, Michael
Kildahl, Johan Nathan
Kocherthal, Josua von
Koren, John
Koren, Ulrik Vihelm
Krauth, Charles Philip
Krauth, Charles Porterfield
Kunze, John Christopher
Kurtz, Benjamin
Larsen, Peter Laurentius
Lenker, John Nicholas
Lindberg, Conrad Emil
Lochman, John George
Loy, Matthias
Maier, Walter Arthur
Mann, William Julius
Mayer, Philip Frederick
Melsheimer, Friedrich Valentin
Moldehnke, Edward Frederick
Morris, John Gottlieb
Muhlenberg, Frederick
  Augustus
Muhlenberg, Frederick
  Augustus Conrad
Mühlenberg, Gotthilf Henry
  Ernest
Muhlenberg, Henry Augustus
  Philip
Mühlenberg, Henry Melchior
Muhlenberg, John Peter Gabriel
Norelius, Eric
Oftedal, Sven
Passavant, William Alfred
Preus, Christian Keyser
Richard, James William
Sadtler, John Philip Benjamin
Schaeffer, Charles Frederick
Schaeffer, Charles William
Schaeffer, David Frederick
Schaeffer, Frederick Christian
Schaeffer, Frederick David
Schmauk, Theodore Emanuel
Schmucker, Beale Melanchthon
Schmucker, John George
Schmucker, Samuel Simon
Schodde, George Henry
Seip, Theodore Lorenzo
Seiss, Joseph Augustus
Spaeth, Adolph
Sprecher, Samuel
Stöckhardt, Karl Georg
Stub, Hans Gerhard
Swensson, Carl Aaron
Walther, Carl Ferdinand
  Wilhelm

Wenner, George Unangst
Mennonite
Goerz, David
Kolb, Dielman
Krehbiel, Christian
Rittenhouse, William
Methodist
Alexander, Gross
Asbury, Francis
Atkinson, John
Bangs, Nathan
Beauchamp, William
Bewley, Anthony
Boehm, Henry
Brown, Ebenezer
Buckley, James Monroe
Buttz, Henry Anson
Cadman, Samuel Parkes
Cain, Richard Harvey
Candler, Warren Akin
Cannon, James
Cartwright, Peter
Collyer, Robert
Cooper, Ezekiel
Cramer, Michael John
Crane, Frank
Crane, Jonathan Townley
Crooks, George Richard
Cummings, Joseph
Day, James Roscoe
Dean, Sidney
Deems, Charles Force
Dickins, John
Dorchester, Daniel
Durbin, John Price
Eaton, Homer
Elliott, Charles
Embury, Philip
Evans, Warren Felt
Fairbank, Calvin
Finley, James Bradley
Fisk, Wilbur
Floy, James
Foss, Cyrus David
Gammon, Elijah Hedding
Garrettson, Freeborn
Green, Alexander Little Page
Hamline, Leonidas Lent
Harrell, John
Harrison, William Pope
Hibbard, Freeborn Garrettson
Hogan, John
Hogue, Wilson Thomas
Hopkins, Isaac Stiles
Huntington, William Edwards
Hurlbut, Jesse Lyman
Inskip, John Swanel
Jaquess, James Frazier
Kidder, Daniel Parish
Kynett, Alpha Jefferson
Lane, John
Larrabee, William Clark
Lee, Jesse
Lee, Luther
Lipscomb, Andrew Adgate
McAnally, David Rice
McCaine, Alexander
M'Clintock, John
McFarland, John Thomas
McFerrin, John Berry
Mattison, Hiram
Merrick, Frederick

Milburn, William Henry
Mitchell, Hinckley Gilbert
  Thomas
Mood, Francis Asbury
Mudge, Enoch
Mudge, James
Nast, William
Nelson, Reuben
O'Kelly James
Olin, Stephen
Palmore, William Beverly
Parkhurst, Charles
Peck, George
Peirce, Bradford Kinney
Ray, Charles Bennett
Reid, John Morrison
Revels, Hiram Rhoades
Ridgaway, Henry Bascom
Roberts, Benjamin Titus
Rowlands, William
Rust, Richard Sutton
Ruter, Martin
Shaw, Anna Howard
Shinn, Asa
Shipp, Albert Micajah
Sims, Charles N.
Sloan, Harold Paul
Smith, William Andrew
Snethen, Nicholas
Steele, Daniel
Stevens, Abel
Stockton, Thomas Hewlings
Strawbridge, Robert
Stuart, Charles Macaulay
Summers, Thomas Osmond
Swallow, Silas Comfort
Taylor, Marshall William
Terry, Milton Spenser
Tigert, John James
Tittle, Ernest Fremont
Townsend, Luther Tracy
Upham, Samuel Foster
Vail, Stephen Montfort
Van Meter, John Blackford
Wakeley, Joseph Burton
Warren, William Fairfield
Webb, Thomas
Whedon, Daniel Denison
Wiley, Ephraim Emerson
Williams, Robert
Winans, William
Wise, Daniel
Young, Jesse Bowman
Methodist Episcopal
North, Frank Mason
Wilson, Clarence True
Moravian (See United Brethren)
Mormon
Cannon, George Quayle
Clark, Joshua Reuben, Jr.
Godbe, William Samuel
Kimball, Heber Chase
Lee, John Doyle
Pratt, Parley Parker
Rigdon, Sidney
Roberts, Brigham Henry
Sharp, John
Smith, Joseph, 1805–1844
Smith, Joseph, 1832–1914
Snow, Lorenzo
Strang, James Jesse
Taylor, John

Whitmer, David
Woodruff, Wilford
Young, Brigham
Nonconformist
Chauncy, Charles 1592–1671/2
Chauncy, Charles 1705–1787
Eaton, Samuel
Higginson, Francis
Lothropp, John
Ward, Nathaniel
Presbyterian
Abbot, Gorham Dummer
Adams, William
Alexander, Archibald
Alexander, Samuel Davies
Alison, Francis
Anderson, John Alexander
Armstrong, George Dod
Babcock, Maltbie Davenport
Baird, Charles Washington
Baird, Henry Martyn
Baird, Robert
Baird, Samuel John
Baker, Daniel
Baker, William Mumford
Baldwin, Elihu Whittlesey
Barnes, Albert
Beard, Richard
Beattie, Francis Robert
Beatty, Charles Clinton
Beecher, Lyman
Beman, Nathan Sidney Smith
Bishop, Robert Hamilton
Blackburn, Gideon
Blackburn, William Maxwell
Blair, Samuel
Blanchard, Jonathan
Bourne, George
Boynton, Charles Brandon
Brainerd, Thomas
Breckinridge, John, 1797–1841
Breckinridge, Robert Jefferson
Brown, Isaac Van Arsdale
Brown, William Adams
Brownlee, William Craig
Bruce, Robert
Burchard, Samuel Dickinson
Burr, Aaron
Burrell, David James
Bush, George
Caldwell, David
Caldwell, James
Cameron, Archibald
Campbell, William Henry
Carrick, Samuel
Cattell, William Cassaday
Chavis, John
Coffin, Henry Sloane
Colman, Benjamin
Converse, James Booth
Corrothers, James David
Cox, Samuel Hanson
Crosby, Howard
Curtis, Edward Lewis
Cuyler, Theodore Ledyard
Darling, Henry
Davidson, Robert
Doak, Samuel
Dod, Albert Baldwin
Dod, Thaddeus
Donnell, Robert
Duffield, George, 1732–1790

Duffield, George, 1794–1868
Duffield, Samuel Augustus
  Willoughby
Dwight, Benjamin Woodbridge
Ewing, John
Field, Henry Martyn
Finley, Robert
Finley, Samuel
Fisher, Daniel Webster
Foote, William Henry
Frey, Joseph Samuel Christian
  Frederick
Frissell, Hollis Burke
Gale, George Washington
Gally, Merritt
Garnet, Henry Highland
Gaut, John McReynolds
Gilbert, Eliphalet Wheeler
Gillett, Ezra Hall
Girardeau, John Lafayette
Goulding, Francis Robert
Green, Ashbel
Green, Jacob
Green, Lewis Warner
Gregory, Daniel Seelye
Hall, Baynard Rush
Hall, Charles Cuthbert
Hall, James, 1744–1826
Hall, John
Hatfield, Edwin Francis
Headley, Phineas Camp
Henry, Robert
Hewat, Alexander
Hickok, Laurens Perseus
Hoge, Moses
Hoge, Moses Drury
House, Samuel Reynolds
Howe, George
Hunter, Andrew
Jackson, Samuel Macauley
Jacobs, William Plumer
Junkin, George
Kellogg, Samuel Henry
Kirk, Edward Norris
Knox, Samuel
Lacy, Drury
Lindley, Daniel
Lindsley, John Berrien
Lindsley, Philip
Linn, John Blair
Lunn, George Richard
Lyon, James
McAfee, John Armstrong
McAuley, Thomas
McBride, F(rancis) Scott
McCalla, William Latta
McCook, Henry Christopher
McCormick, Samuel Black
MacCracken, Henry Mitchell
McDowell, John
McFarland, Samuel Gamble
McGready, James
McIlwaine, Richard
McLeod, Alexander
MacWhorter, Alexander
Makemie, Francis
Marquis, John Abner
Mason, John Mitchell
Mattoon, Stephen
Mears, David Otis
Mears, John William
Miller, James Russell

Miller, John
Miller, Samuel
Mitchell, Edwin Knox
Moorehead, William Gallogly
Morris, Edward Dafydd
Morrison, William McCutchan
Murray, James Ormsbee
Neill, Edward Duffield
Neill, William
Nelson, David
Nevin, Alfred
Nevin, Edwin Henry
Nisbet, Charles
Noble, Frederick Alphonso
Nott, Eliphalet
Osborn, Henry Stafford
Palmer, Benjamin Morgan
Parker, Joel
Parker, Thomas
Parkhurst, Charles Henry
Patillo, Henry
Patterson, Robert Mayne
Patton, Francis Landey
Patton, William
Peck, Thomas Ephraim
Peters, Absalom
Peters, Madison Clinton
Pierson, Arthur Tappan
Pierson, Hamilton Wilcox
Plumer, William Swan
Prentiss, George Lewis
Prime, Edward Dorr Griffin
Prime, Samuel Irenaeus
Purviance, David
Reed, Richard Clark
Reid, William Shields
Rice, David
Rice, John Holt
Rice, Nathan Lewis
Roberts, William Charles
Roberts, William Henry
Robinson, Charles Seymour
Robinson, Stuart
Rodgers, John, 1727–1811
Ruffner, Henry
Ruffner, William Henry
Sanders, Daniel Jackson
Sawyer, Leicester Ambrose
Scott, William Anderson
Simpson, Albert Benjamin
Skinner, Thomas Harvey
Smith, Asa Dodge
Smith, Benjamin Mosby
Smith, Henry Boynton
Smith, Henry Preserved
Smith, John Blair
Smith, Samuel Stanhope
Smyth, Thomas
Speer, Robert Elliott
Spencer, Elihu
Spring, Gardiner
Sproull, Thomas
Stelzle, Charles
Stryker, Melancthon Woolsey
Swing, David
Taylor, Archibald Alexander
  Edward
Tennent, Gilbert
Tennent, William, 1673–1745
Tennent, William, 1705–1777
Thacher, Peter
Thompson, William Oxley

Thornwell, James Henley
Van Dyke, Henry
Van Rensselaer, Cortlandt
Vincent, Marvin Richardson
Voris, John Ralph
Waddel, James
Waddel, John Newton
Waddel, Moses
Walker, James Barr
Warfield, Benjamin
  Breckinridge
Whitaker, Nathaniel
Whitworth, George Frederic
Wiley, David
Willey, Samuel Hopkins
Wilson, Joshua Lacy
Wilson, Samuel Ramsay
Wilson, Warren Hugh
Witherspoon, John
Wood, James
Woodrow, James
Woods, Leonard, 1807–1878
Yeomans, John William
Young, John Clarke
Zubly, John Joachim
Protestant Episcopal (See Episcopal)
Puritan
Bulkeley, Peter
Cotton, John
Holden, Oliver
Mather, Cotton
Mather, Increase
Mather, Richard
Mayhew, Jonathan
Morton, Charles
Norton, John
Parris, Samuel
Sherman, John, 1613–1685
Stone, Samuel
Taylor, Edward
Weld, Thomas
Whitfield, Henry
Wigglesworth, Michael
Williams, Roger
Wilson, John
Woodbridge, John
Quaker
Chalkley, Thomas
Coffin, Charles Fisher
Comstock, Elizabeth L.
Evans, Thomas
Grellet, Stephen
Hallowell, Benjamin
Hicks, Elias
Hoag, Joseph
Hubbs, Rebecca
Hunt, Nathan
Janney, Samuel McPherson
Jay, Allen
Jones, Sybil
Kelsey, Rayner Wickersham
Mott, Lucretia Coffin
Muste, Abraham Johannes
Owen, Griffith
Pemberton, John
Pugh, Ellis
Sands, David
Savery, William, 1750–1804
Scattergood, Thomas
Scott, Job
Updegraff, David Brainard
Waln, Nicholas

Wilbur, John
Reformed Church in America
Schenck, Ferdinand Schureman
Searle, John Preston
Thompson, John Bodine
Van Nest, Abraham Rynier
Woodbridge, Samuel Merrill
Roman Catholic
Alphonsa, Mother
Andreis, Andrew James Felix
  Bartholomew de
Andrews, Samuel James
Andrews, William Watson
Angela, Mother
Antoine, Père
Ayres, Anne
Barzy*ndski, Vincent
Bayma, Joseph
Behrens, Henry
Benavides, Alonzo de
Burke, John Joseph
Campbell, Thomas Joseph
Carr, Thomas Matthew
Clarke, Mary Francis
Conaty, Thomas James
Cooper, John Montgomery
Coppens, Charles
Corcoran, James Andrew
Cosby, William
Curran, John Joseph
Currier, Charles Warren
Cushing, Richard James
Dabrowski, Joseph
Dietz, Peter Ernest
Dougherty, Dennis Joseph
Drumgoole, John Christopher
Du Bois, John
Du Bourg, Louis Guillaume
  Valentin
Duffy, Francis Patrick
Dwenger, Joseph
Elder, William Henry
Elliott, Walter Hacket Robert
Farley, John Murphy
Fenwick, Benedict Joseph
Ffrench, Charles Dominic
Finn, Francis James
Finotti, Joseph Maria
Fitzgerald, Edward
Flanagan, Edward Joseph
Francis, Paul James
Gallagher, Hugh Patrick
Ganss, Henry George
Garrigan, Philip Joseph
Gasson, Thomas Ignatius
Gibbons, James
Gilmour, Richard
Gmeiner, John
Goupil, René
Greaton, Joseph
Guérin, Anne-Thérèse
Guilday, Peter Keenan
Haid, Leo
Hardey, Mother Mary Aloysia
Harding, Robert
Hayes, Patrick Joseph
Hecker, Isaac Thomas
Hennepin, Louis
Hennessy, John
Henni, John Martin
Hessoun, Joseph
Hewit, Augustine Francis

Hubbard, Bernard Rosecrans
Hudson, Daniel Eldred
Hughes, John Joseph
Hurley, Joseph Patrick
Ireland, John, 1838–1918
Johnson, George
Joubert de la Muraille, James
    Hector Marie Nicholas
Judge, Thomas Augustine
Katzer, Frederic Xavier
Keane, James John
Keane, John Joseph
Kenrick, Francis Patrick
Kenrick, Peter Richard
Kerby, William Joseph
Kirlin, Joseph Louis Jerome
Kohlmann, Anthony
LaFarge, John
Lambert, Louis Aloisius
Lambing, Andrew Arnold
Lamy, John Baptist
Larkin, John
Lee, James Wideman
Levins, Thomas C.
Loras, Jean Mathias Pierre
Lynch, Patrick Neeson
Maas, Anthony J.
McCaffrey, John
McCloskey, John
McCloskey, William George
McElroy, John, 1782–1877
McFaul, James Augustine
McGill, John
McGivney, Michael Joseph
McGlynn, Edward
McGrath, James
McGuire, Charles Bonaventure
Machebeuf, Joseph Provectus
Maes, Camillus Paul
Malone, Sylvester
Maréchal, Ambrose
Marest, Pierre Gabriel
Marty, Martin
Matignon, Francis Anthony
Meerschaert, Théophile
Merton, Thomas
Messmer, Sebastian Gebhard
Meyer, Albert Gregory
Michel, Virgil George
Miles, Richard Pius
Ming, John Joseph
Moeller, Henry
Molyneux, Robert
Moore, John, 1834–1901
Moosmüller, Oswald William
Moriarity, Patrick Eugene
Morini, Austin John
Mundelein, George William
Neale, Leonard
Nerinckx, Charles
Neumann, John Nepomucene
Nieuwland, Julius Arthur
Nobili, John
O'Brien, Matthew Anthony
O'Callaghan, Jeremiah
O'Callahan, Joseph Timothy
O'Connor, James
O'Connor, Michael
Odenbach, Frederick Louis
Odin, John Mary
O'Gorman, Thomas
Ortynsky, Stephen Soter

Pace, Edward Aloysius
Pardow, William O'Brien
Patrick, John Ryan
Perché, Napoleon Joseph
Phelan, David Samuel
Pise, Charles Constantine
Portier, Michael
Power, John
Preston, Thomas Scott
Price, Thomas Frederick
Purcell, John Baptist
Quarter, William
Quigley, James Edward
Rese, Frederick
Reuter, Dominic
Rigge, William Francis
Riordan, Patrick William
Ritter, Joseph Elmer
Robot, Isidore
Rosati, Joseph
Rosecrans, Sylvester Horton
Rouquette, Adrien Emmanuel
Ryan, Abram Joseph
Ryan, John Augustine
Ryan, Patrick John
Ryan, Stephen Vincent
Saenderl, Simon
Scanlan, Lawrence
Schnerr, Leander
Schrembs, Joseph
Seghers, Charles Jean
Semmes, Alexander Jenkins
Sestini, Benedict
Seton, Robert
Shahan, Thomas Joseph
Sheil, Bernard James
Shields, Thomas Edward
Sorin, Edward Frederick
Spalding, Catherine
Spalding, John Lancaster
Spalding, Martin John
Spellman, Francis Joseph
Stang, William
Stehle, Aurelius Aloysius
Stone, James Kent
Tabb, John Banister
Talbot, Francis Xavier
Thébaud, Augustus J.
Tierney, Richard Henry
Timon, John
Tondorf, Francis Anthony
Turner, William
Tyler, William
Van de Velde, James Oliver
Varela y Morales, Félix
    Francisco José María de la
    Concepción
Verot, Jean Marcel Pierre
    Auguste
Viel, François Étienne Bernard
    Alexandre
Walsh, Edmund Aloysius
Walsh, James Anthony
Walsh, Thomas Joseph
White, Charles Ignatius
Wigger, Winand Michael
Williams, John Joseph
Wilson, Samuel Thomas
Wimmer, Boniface
Wolf, Innocent William
Wood, James Frederick
Yorke, Peter Christopher

Young, Alfred
Young, Josue Maria
Zahm, John Augustine
Russion Orthodox
    Leonty, Metropolitan
Society of Friends (*See* Quaker)
Southern Baptist
    Dodd, Monroe Elmon
    Norris, John Franklyn
    Rawlinson, Frank Joseph
    Scarborough, Lee Rutland
    Truett, George Washington
Swedenborgian
    Barrett, Benjamin Fiske
    Brown, Solyman
    Giles, Chauncey
    Mercer, Lewis Pyle
    Reed, James, 1834–1921
    Sewall, Frank
    Smyth, Julian Kennedy
Unaffiliated
    Craig, Austin
    Newton, Joseph Fort
    Spencer, Anna Garlin
Unitarian
    Abbot, Francis Ellingwood
    Alger, William Rounseville
    Allen, Joseph Henry
    Ames, Charles Gordon
    Barnard, Charles Francis
    Barrows, Samuel June
    Bartol, Cyrus Augustus
    Batchelor, George
    Bellows, Henry Whitney
    Bentley, William
    Bixby, James Thompson
    Brazer, John
    Brooks, Charles
    Brooks, Charles Timothy
    Buckminster, Joseph Stevens
    Burnap, George Washington
    Burton, Warren
    Chadwick, John White
    Channing, William Ellery
    Channing, William Henry
    Clarke, James Freeman
    Colman, Henry
    Conway, Moncure Daniel
    Cooke, George Willis
    Cranch, Christopher Pearse
    Crothers, Samuel McChord
    Cummings, Edward
    Dewey, Orville
    Ellis, George Edward
    Emerson, William
    Everett, Edward
    Fenn, William Wallace
    Follen, Charles
    Francis, Convers
    Freeman, James
    Frothingham, Nathaniel
      Langdon
    Frothingham, Octavius Brooks
    Frothingham, Paul Revere
    Furness, William Henry
    Gannett, Ezra Stiles
    Gannett, William Channing
    Gilman, Samuel
    Hale, Edward Everett
    Harris, Thaddeus Mason
    Hedge, Frederic Henry
    Hill, Thomas

Holley, Horace
Holmes, John Haynes
Hosmer, Frederick Lucian
Huntington, Frederic Dan
Janson, Kristofer Nagel
Jones, Jenkin Lloyd
Judd, Sylvester
King, Thomas Starr
Leonard, Levi Washburn
Livermore, Abiel Abbot
Longfellow, Samuel
Lowe, Charles
MacCauley, Clay
Mann, Newton
May, Samuel Joseph
Mayo, Amory Dwight
Metcalf, Joel Hastings
Miles, Henry Adolphus
Noyes, George Rapall
Palfrey, John Gorham
Parker, Theodore
Peabody, Andrew Preston
Peabody, Francis Greenwood
Peabody, Oliver William Bourn
Peabody, William Bourn Oliver
Pierpont, John
Potter, William James
Powell, Edward Payson
Reed, David
Ripley, Ezra
Robbins, Chandler
Savage, Minot Judson
Sears, Edmund Hamilton
Slicer, Thomas Roberts
Stearns, Oliver
Stebbins, Horatio
Stebbins, Rufus Phineas
Tuckerman, Joseph
Upham, Charles Wentworth
Walker, James
Ware, Henry 1794–1843
Ware, John Fothergill
   Waterhouse
Ware, William
Weiss, John
Wendte, Charles William
West, Samuel
Wheelwright, John
Wiggin, James Henry
Willard, Samuel, 1775–1859
Woolley, Celia Parker
Young, Alexander
Zachos, John Celivergos
United Brethren
Beardshear, William Miller
Berger, Daniel
Clewell, John Henry
Flickinger, Daniel Kumler
Holland, William Jacob
Jungman, John George
Kephart, Isaiah Lafayette
Peter, John Frederick
Reichel, William Cornelius
Schultze, Augustus
Schweinitz, Lewis David von
Shuey, William John
Zinzendorf, Nicolaus Ludwig
United Evangelical
Poling, Daniel Alfred
Universalist
Adams, John Coleman
Ballou, Adin

Ballou, Hosea
Cobb, Sylvanus
Edwin, Hubbell Chapin
Ferguson, William Porter
   Frisbee
Fisher, Ebenezer
Hanaford, Phoebe Ann Coffin
Hudson, Charles
Kneeland, Abner
Miner, Alonzo Ames
Sawyer, Thomas Jefferson
Spear, Charles
Thayer, Thomas Baldwin
Whittemore, Thomas
CLIMATOLOGIST (See also
   METEOROLOGIST)
De Brahm, William Gerard
Logan, Thomas Muldrup,
   1808–1876
Ward, Robert De Courcy
CLOCKMAKER (See also MANUFAC-
   TURER, WATCH)
Camp, Hiram
Harland, Thomas
Jerome, Chauncey
Terry, Eli
Thomas, Seth
Willard, Simon
CLOWN
Adler, Felix
Rice, Dan
CLUB WOMAN
Choate, Anne Hyde Clarke
COAL MERCHANT
Clothier, William Jackson
COAL MINER
Haywood, Allan Shaw
COAL OPERATOR (See also INDUS-
   TRIALIST)
Brown, William Hughey
Horton, Valentine Baxter
Pardee, Ario
Parrish, Charles
Scott, William Lawrence
Thompson, Josiah Van Kirk
COAST GUARD OFFICER (See also
   NAVAL OFFICER)
Smith, Edward Hanson
Waesche, Russell Randolph
COLLECTOR (See also ART COL-
   LECTOR, BOOK COLLECTOR,
   NUMISMATIST)
Bement, Clarence Sweet
   (minerals)
Clarke, Thomas Benedict (art)
Cone, Claribel (art)
Cone, Etta (art)
Disbrow, William Stephen
   (misc.)
Draper, Lyman Copeland
   (frontier history)
Emmett, Burton (prints)
Ffoulke, Charles Mather
   (tapestries)
Fisher, George Jackson
   (anatomical illustrations)
Folger, Henry Clay
   (Shakespeareana)
Guggenheim, Solomon Robert
   (art)
Hawkins, Rush Christopher
   (incunabula)

Horner, Henry (Lincolniana)
Isham, Ralph Heyward
   (manuscripts)
Jacobs, Joseph, 1859–1929
   (Burnsiana)
Lewis, Edmund Darch (misc.)
Lomax, John Avery (folk songs)
Lowery, Woodbury (maps)
Meserve, Frederick Hill
   (Lincolniana)
Nutting, Wallace (antiques)
Pringle, Cyrus Guernsey
   (plants)
Riggs, William Henry (armor)
Rindge, Frederick Hastings
   (coins)
Scharf, John Thomas
   (Americana)
Sprague, William Buell
   (autographs)
Stauffer, David McNeely
   (autographic historical
   material)
Steinert, Morris (musical
   instruments)
Thomas, George Clifford
   (autographic historical
   material)
Vincent, Frank (antiquities)
Wilson, Ernest Henry (plants)
COLLEGE ADMINISTRATOR
Fulton, Robert Burwell
Geddes, James Lorraine
Keppel, Frederick Paul
Perkins, George Henry
Royster, James Finch
Small, Albion Woodbury
COLLEGE PRESIDENT
Adams, Charles Kendall
Adams, Jasper
Alden, Timothy
Alderman, Edwin Anderson
Allen, William Henry
Ames, Joseph Sweetman
Anderson, Galusha
Anderson, John Alexander
Anderson, Martin Brewer
Andrews, Elisha Benjamin
Andrews, Israel Ward
Andrews, Lorin
Angell, James Burrill
Angell, James Rowland
Atherton, George Washington
Atwood, Wallace Walter
Aydelotte, Frank
Ayres, Brown
Backus, Azel
Bailey, Rufus William
Baker, Hugh Potter
Baker, James Hutchins
Baldwin, Elihu Whittlesey
Ballou, Hosea
Barnard, Frederick Augustus
   Porter
Barrows, David Prescott
Barrows, John Henry
Bartlett, Samuel Colcord
Bascom, Henry Bidleman
Bascom, John
Bashford, James Whitford
Bass, William Capers
Battle, Kemp Plummer

Baugher, Henry Louis
Beardshear, William Miller
Beecher, Edward
Beman, Nathan Sidney Smith
Bennett, Henry Garland
Benton, Allen Richardson
Bethune, Mary McLeod
Blackburn, Gideon
Blackburn, William Maxwell
Blanchard, Jonathan
Domberger, John Henry
　Augustus
Bowman, Isaiah
Bradley, John Edwin
Breckinridge, Robert Jefferson
Brown, Elmer Ellsworth
Brown, Francis
Brown, Samuel Gilman
Brownell, Thomas Church
Bryan, John Stewart
Burr, Aaron
Burton, Ernest DeWitt
Burton, Marion Le Roy
Butler, Nicholas Murray
Butterfield, Kenyon Leech
Cain, Richard Harvey
Caldwell, Joseph
Camm, John
Campbell, Prince Lucien
Campbell, William Henry
Candler, Warren Akin
Capen, Elmer Hewitt
Carnahan, James
Carrick, Samuel
Carter, Franklin
Caswell, Alexis
Cattell, William Cassaday
Chadbourne, Paul Ansel
Chandler, Julian Alvin Carroll
Chapin, Aaron Lucius
Chaplin, Jeremiah
Chase, Harry Woodburn
Chase, Thomas
Chauncey, Charles
Cheney, Oren Burbank
Clapp, Charles Horace
Clark, William Smith
Coffman, Lotus Delta
Compton, Karl Taylor
Cooper, Myles
Corby, William
Crafts, James Mason
Cravath, Erastus Milo
Craven, Braxton
Cummings, Joseph
Cutler, Carroll
Daggett, Naphtali
Darling, Henry
Davies, Samuel
Davis, Harvey Nathaniel
Davis, Henry
Day, Jeremiah
Dennett, Tyler (Wilbur)
Dickinson, Jonathan
Dunster, Henry
Durant, Henry
Dwight, Timothy, 1752–1817
Dwight, Timothy, 1828–1916
Dykstra, Clarence Addison
Eaton, Nathaniel
Eisenhower, Dwight D.
Eliot, Charles William

Estabrook, Joseph
Fairchild, George Thompson
Fairchild, James Harris
Farrand, Livingston
Faunce, William Herbert Perry
Ferris, Isaac
Few, Ignatius Alphonso
Fisher, Daniel Webster
Folwell, William Watts
Foster, William Trufant
Fox, Dixon Ryan
Fraley, Samuel
Frank, Glenn
Frelinghuysen, Theodore
Frieze, Henry Simmons
Furman, James Clement
Garfield, Harry Augustus
Garland, Landon Cabell
Gates, Caleb Frank
Gates, Thomas Sovereign
Gerhart, Emanuel Vogel
Gilbert, Eliphalet Wheeler
Gilman, Daniel Coit
Goodell, Henry Hill
Goodnow, Frank Johnson
Goodwin, Daniel Raynes
Goucher, John Franklin
Graham, Edward Kidder
Graves, Zuinglius Calvin
Green, Ashbel
Gregg, John Andrew
Gregory, John Milton
Griffin, Edward Dorr
Griswold, Alfred Whitney
Gummere, Samuel James
Hadley, Arthur Twining
Hadley, Herbert Spencer
Hardenbergh, Jacob Rutsen
Harris, William
Hasbrouck, Abraham Bruyn
Hibben, John Grier
Hickok, Laurens Perseus
Hill, David Jayne
Hill, Thomas
Hinman, George Wheeler
Hoar, Leonard
Holt, Hamilton Bowen
Horrocks, James
Howard, Ada Lydia
Humes, Thomas William
Humphrey, Heman
Huntington, William Edwards
Hutchins, Harry Burns
Hyer, Robert Stewart
James, Edmund Janes
Jessup, Walter Albert
Johns, John
Johnson, Samuel
Jordan, David Starr
Kephart, Ezekiel Boring
King, Charles
King, Stanley
Kirkland, James Hampton
Kirkland, John Thornton
Knapp, Bradford
Krauth, Charles Philip
Langdon, Samuel
Lathrop, John Hiram
Leverett, John, 1662–1724
Lipscomb, Andrew Adgate
Livermore, Abiel Abbot
Loos, Charles Louis

Lord, Nathan
Low, Seth
Lowell, Abbott Lawrence
McBryde, John McLaren
McCosh, James
McGlothlin, William Joseph
McIlwaine, Richard
McKeen, Joseph
Maclean, John
McNair, Fred Walter
McVey, Frank Lerond
Madison, James
Magill, Edward Hicks
Magnes, Judah Leon
Magoun, George Frederic
Malian, Asa
Main, John Hanson Thomas
Manning, James
Marquis, John Abner
Marsh, James
Maxcy, Jonathan
Maxwell, William
Mayes, Edward
Mendenhall, Thomas Corwin
Merrill, George Edmands
Middleton, Nathaniel Russell
Miner, Alonzo Ames
Mitchell, Edward Cushing
Moore, Benjamin
Moore, Nathaniel Fish
Moore, Zephaniah Swift
Morgan, John Harcourt
　Alexander
Morrison, Nathan Jackson
Mortimer, Mary
Morton, Henry
Muhlenberg, Frederick
　Augustus
Neilson, William Allan
Nichols, Ernest Fox
Nisbet, Charles
Northrop, Cyrus
Nott, Eliphalet
Oakes, Urian
Parrish, Edward
Patrick, Mary Mills
Patton, Francis Landey
Payne, Bruce Ryburn
Payne, Daniel Alexander
Pearson, Raymond Allen
Pendleton, Ellen Fitz
Pendleton, William Kimbrough
Porter, Noah
Pott, Francis Lister Hawks
Potter, Eliphalet Nott
Preus, Christian Keyser
Pritchett, Henry Smith
Pugh, Evan
Purnell, William Henry
Pynchon, Thomas Ruggles
Quincy, Josiah, 1772–1864
Rankin, Jeremiah Eames
Raymond, John Howard
Reid, John Morrison
Reinhardt, Aurelia Isabel Henry
Rhees, Rush
Rhoades, James E.
Robinson, Ezekiel Gilman
Runkle, John Daniel
Sadtler, John Philip Benjamin
Sanford, Edmund Clark

Scarborough, William Saunders
Schurman, Jacob Gould
Scott, Austin
Scott, Walter Dill
Seelye, Laurenus Clark
Seip, Theodore Lorenzo
Sewall, Joseph Addison
Seymour, Charles
Shafer, Helen Almira
Sharpless, Isaac
Shepard, James Edward
Sims, Charles N.
Smart, James Henry
Smith, Asa Dodge
Smith, John Augustine
Smith, John Blair
Smith, Samuel Stanhope
Smith, William Andrew
Smith, William Waugh
Sparks, Edwin Erle
Stearns, William Augustus
Stewart, Alexander Peter
Stiles, Ezra
Stith, William
Stockbridge, Horace Edward
Strong, James Woodward
Stryker, Melancthon Woolsey
Stuart, John Leighton
Swain, David Lowry
Tappan, Henry Philip
Taylor, James Monroe
Thatcher, Roscoe Wilfred
Thomas, Martha Carey
Thompson, William Oxley
Thomson, Edward
Thornwell, James Henley
Thwing, Charles Franklin
Tigert, John James, IV
Tyler, Lyon Gardiner
Van Hise, Charles Richard
Venable, Francis Preston
Vincent, George Edgar
Waddel, Moses
Wait, Samuel
Walker, James
Warren, William Fairfield
Wayland, Francis, 1796–1865
Webb, Alexander Stewart
Wheeler, Benjamin Ide
Wheelock, Eleazar
Wheelock, John
White, Andrew Dickson
White, Henry Clay
Whitsitt, William Heth
Wilbur, Ray Lyman
Willard, Joseph
Willard, Samuel
Williams, Walter
Wilson, Woodrow
Woods, Alva
Woods, Leonard
Woolley, Mary Emma
Woolsey, Theodore Dwight
Wylie, Andrew

COLONIAL AGENT
Argall, Sir Samuel
Ashmun, Jehudi
Barnwell, John
Bollan, William
De Berdt, Dennys
Dummer, Jeremiah
Partridge, Richard

Randolph, Edward
Sebastian, Benjamin
Vassall, John
Weld, Thomas

COLONIAL LEADER
Bacon, Nathaniel
Byrd, William
Carter, Robert
Clarke, George
Dinwiddie, Robert
Gayoso de Lemos, Manuel
Habersham, James
Hathorne, William
Holloway, John
Jenifer, Daniel of St. Thomas
Kennedy, Archibald
Minuit, Peter
Moore, John, c. 1659–1732
Newton, Thomas, 1660–1721
Nicholas, Robert Carter
Norris, Isaac, 1671–1735
Núñez Cabeza De Vaca, Alvar
Owen, Griffith
Pike, Robert
Randolph, William
Schuyler, Peter
Stuyvesant, Petrus
Van Cortlandt, Stephanus
Weare, Meshech
Wharton, Richard
Wingfield, Edward Maria
Wragg, William
Yeardley, Sir George
Youngs, John

COLONIST
Blackstone, William
Claiborne, William
Fenwick, George
Fenwick, John
Gardiner, Lion
Gookin, Daniel
Gorton, Samuel
Hack, George
Lane, Sir Ralph
Mason, George
Maverick, George
Oldham, John
Popham, George
Rolfe, John
Saltonstall, Richard
Sandys, George
Scholte, Hendrik Peter
Sedgwick, Robert
Van Curler, Arent
Van Der Donck, Adriaen
Weston, Thomas
Wilbur, Samuel
Willard, Simon

COLONIZER
Cameron, Robert Alexander
Coram, Thomas
Cutler, Manasseh
Dale, Sir Thomas
De Vries, David Pietersen
Durkee, John
Eaton, Theophilus
Finley, Robert
Gosnold, Bartholomew
Graffenried, Christopher, Baron
de
Henderson, Richard
Hite, Jost

Krehbiel, Christian
Oñate, Juan de
Peerson, Cleng
Purry, Jean Pierre
Ribaut, Jean
St. Denis (Denys), Louis
Juchereau de
Smith, Robert, 1722–1777
Turnbull, Andrew
Wingfield, Edward Maria
Young, Brigham

COLOR CINEMATOGRAPHER
Kalmus, Natalie Mabelle Dunfee

COMEDIAN (See also ACTOR,
CLOWN, COMEDIENNE, ENTER-
TAINER, HUMORIST, WIT)
Allen, Fred
Barton, James Edward
Bruce, Lenny
Cantor, Eddie
Carson, Jack
Costello, Lou
Daniels, Frank Albert
Errol, Leon
Fields, Lewis Maurice
Fields, William Claude
Foy, Eddie
Hardy, Oliver Norvell
Hayes, Gabby
Holland, George
Howard, Willie
Johnson, Harold Ogden
("Chic")
Jones, Lindley Armstrong
("Spike")
Keaton, Joseph Francis, V
("Buster")
Langdon, Harry Philmore
Laurel, Stan
Marx, Adolf Arthur ("Harpo")
Marx, Leonard ("Chico")
Olsen, John Sigvard ("Ole")
Shean, Albert
Smith, Solomon Franklin
Turpin, Ben
Weber, Joseph Morris
Wynn, Ed

COMEDIENNE (See also ACTRESS,
ENTERTAINER, HUMORIST)
Brice, Fanny
Fazenda, Louise Marie

COMIC ARTIST (See CARTOONIST)

COMMERCIAL COUNSELOR
Kuskov, Ivan Aleksandrovich

COMMISSIONER OF EDUCATION
Tigert, John James, IV

COMMUNIST (See also MARXIST
THEORIST)
Cabet, Étienne
Dennis, Eugene
Eisler, Gerhart
Fischer, Ruth
Minor, Robert

COMMUNIST LEADER
Bloor, Ella Reeve
Foster, William Z.
Perry, Pettis

COMMUNITY BUILDER (See also
CITY PLANNER, CIVIC LEADER)
Atkinson, George Henry
Kelley, Alfred
Wadsworth, James

COMMUNITY ORGANIZER
Collier, John
COMPILER (See also BIBLIOGRA-
PHER, SCHOLAR)
Adams, Hannah
Disturnell, John
Law, Andrew
Sears, Robert
Swan, Timothy
Tenney, Tabitha Gilman
Tutts, John
Valentine, David Thomas
COMPOSER (See also HYMNOLO-
GIST, MUSICIAN, SONGWRITER)
Allen, Nathan H.
Armstrong, Henry Worthington
("Harry")
Baker, Benjamin Franklin
Bartlett, Homer Newton
Beach, Amy Marcy Cheney
Beck, Johann Heinrich
Bird, Arthur
Blitzstein, Marc
Bloch, Ernest
Blodgett, Benjamin Colman
Bond, Carrie Jacobs
Bristow, George Frederick
Buck, Dudley
Burleigh, Henry Thacker
Burton, Frederick Russell
Cadman, Charles Wakefield
Carpenter, John Alden
Carr, Benjamin
Chadwick, George Whitefield
Coerne, Louis Adolphe
Cohan, George Michael
Coltrane, John William
Converse, Charles Crozat
Converse, Frederick Shepherd
Cook, Will Marion
Damrosch, Leopold
Damrosch, Walter Johannes
De Koven, Henry Louis
Reginald
De Rose, Peter
Dett, Robert Nathaniel
Dresel, Otto
Duke, Vernon
Dunham, Henry Morton
Edwards, Julian
Eichberg, Julius
Elman, Harry ("Ziggy")
Emery, Stephen Albert
Engel, Carl
Fairchild, Blair
Fairlamb, James Remington
Farwell, Arthur
Fisher, William Arms
Foote, Arthur William
Foster, Stephen Collins
Fry, William Henry
Ganss, Henry George
Gershwin, George
Gilbert, Henry Franklin
Belknap
Gilchrist, William Wallace
Gleason, Frederic Grant
Godowsky, Leopold
Goldbeck, Robert
Goldman, Edwin Franko
Goldmark, Rubin
Gottschalk, Louis Moreau

Grainger, George Percy
Griffes, Charles Tomlinson
Hadley, Henry Kimball
Hammerstein, Oscar
Harney, Benjamin Robertson
Hastings, Thomas
Hays, William Shakespeare
Heinrich, Antony Philip
Hemmeter, John Conrad
Henderson, Ray
Hewitt, James
Hoffman, Richard
Hofmann, Josef Casimir
Holyoke, Samuel
Humiston, William Henry
Ives, Charles Edward
Jackson, George K.
Johns, Clayton
Jones, Lindley Armstrong
("Spike")
Kaiser, Alois
Keller, Mathias
Kelley, Edgar Stillman
Kern, Jerome David
Klein, Bruno Oscar
Koemmenich, Louis
Korngold, Erich Wolfgang
Kreisler, Fritz
Kroeger, Ernest Richard
Landowska, Wanda Aleksandra
Lang, Benjamin Johnson
Law, Andrew
Ledbetter, Huddie
("Leadbelly")
Liebling, Emil
Liebling, Estelle
Loeffler, Charles Martin
Loesser, Frank
Lutkin, Peter Christian
MacDowell, Edward Alexander
Mannes, Leopold Damrosch
Maretzek, Max
Marzo, Eduardo
Mason, Daniel Gregory
Mason, William
Mitchell, Nahum
Mitropoulos, Dimitri
Morton, Ferdinand Joseph
("Jelly Roll")
Musin, Ovide
Nevin, Ethelbert Woodbridge
Nevin, George Balch
Newman, Alfred
Nunó, Jaime
Oehmler, Leo Carl Martin
Oliver, Joseph
Osgood, George Laurie
Paine, John Knowles
Palmer, Horatio Richmond
Parker, Charlie ("Bird")
Parker, Horatio William
Parker, James Cutler Dunn
Pease, Alfred Humphreys
Perabo, Johann Ernst
Phillips, Philip
Porter, Cole
Pratt, Silas Gamaliel
Pryor, Arthur W.
Rachmaninoff, Sergei
Vasilyevich
Reinagle, Alexander
Riegger, Wallingford

Ritter, Frédéric Louis
Rogers, Clara Kathleen Barnett
Romberg, Sigmund
Root, Frederic Woodman
Root, George Frederick
Rosenblatt, Joseph
Runcie, Constance Faunt Le
Roy
Rybner, Martin Cornelius
Sandler, Jacob Koppel
Schelling, Ernest Henry
Schillinger, Joseph
Schindler, Kurt
Schnabel, Artur
Schoenberg, Arnold
Scott, John Prindle
Selby, William
Shaw, Oliver
Sherwood, William Hall
Silvers, Louis
Sobolewski, J. Friedrich Eduard
Sousa, John Philip
Southard, Lucien H.
Speaks, Oley
Spicker, Max
Stanley, Albert Augustus
Stark, Edward Josef
Sternberg, Constantin
Ivanovich, Edler von
Stewart, Humphrey John
Stoessel, Albert Frederic
Swan, Timothy
Taylor, Joseph Deems
Taylor, Raynor
Thayer, Whitney Eugene
Tilzer, Harry Von
Tobani, Theodore Moses
Trajetta, Philip
Tuckey, William
Van Der Stucken, Frank
Valentin
Varèse, Edgard
Vogrich, Max Wilhelm Karl
Waller, Thomas Wright
("Fats")
Warren, Richard Henry
Warren, Samuel Prowse
Waxman, Franz
Webb, George James
Weems, Ted
Weidig, Adolf
Weill, Kurt
Weld, Arthur Cyril Gordon
White, Clarence Cameron
White, Joseph Malachy
Whiting, Arthur Battelle
Whiting, George Elbridge
Wight, Frederick Coit
Wilson, Mortimer
Witmark, Isidore
Wolle, John Frederick
Woodbury, Isaac Baker
Woolf, Benjamin Edward
Yon, Pietro Alessandro
Youmans, Vincent Millie
Zach, Max Wilhelm
Zeuner, Charles
COMPTROLLER OF CURRENCY (See
also BANKER, ECONOMIST,
FINANCIER)
Crissinger, Daniel Richard
Eckels, James Herron

Knox, John Jay
McCulloch, Hugh
Steele, John
CONCESSIONAIRE
Grace, William Russell
Tilyou, George Cornelius
CONCHOLOGIST (See also BIOLOGIST, ZOOLOGIST)
Gould, Augustus Addison
Say, Thomas
Tryon, George Washington
CONDUCTOR (See also BANDLEADER, MUSICIAN)
Barrère, Georges
Beck, Johann Heinrich
Bergman, Carl
Bodanzky, Artur
Damrosch, Leopold
Damrosch, Walter Johannes
Dannreuther, Gustav
Duchin, Edward Frank ("Eddy")
Gabrilowitsch, Ossip
Gericke, Wilhelm
Gilchrist, William Wallace
Gould, Nathaniel Duren
Hadley, Henry Kimball
Hertz, Alfred
Hill, Ureli Corelli
Koussevitzky, Serge Alexandrovich
Kroeger, Ernest Richard
Lang, Benjamin Johnson
Listemann, Bernhard
Lunceford, James Melvin ("Jimmie")
Lutkin, Peter Christian
Mannes, David
Mees, Arthur
Miller, Glenn
Mitropoulos, Dimitri
Mollenhauer, Emil
Monteux, Pierre Benjamin
Munch, Charles
Neuendorff, Adolph Heinrich Anton Magnus
Newman, Alfred
Nunó, Jaime
Oberhoffer, Emil Johann
Osgood, George Laurie
Palmer, Horatio Richmond
Pratt, Silas Gamaliel
Rachmaninoff, Sergei Vasilyevich
Reiner, Fritz
Rodzinski, Artur
Root, Frederic Woodman
Saslavsky, Alexander
Scheel, Fritz
Schelling, Ernest Henry
Schradieck, Henry
Seidl, Anton
Siloti, Alexander Ilyitch
Silvers, Louis
Sobolewski, J. Friedrich Eduard
Spicker, Max
Spiering, Theodore
Stanley, Albert Augustus
Stock, Frederick August
Stoessel, Albert Frederic
Szell, George

Thomas, Christian Friedrich Theodore
Timm, Henry Christian
Toscanini, Arturo
Van Der Stucken, Frank Valentin
Verbrugghen, Henri
Walter, Bruno
Waxman, Franz
Weidig, Adolf
White, George Leonard
Whiteman, Paul Samuel ("Pops")
Wilson, Mortimer
Woolle, John Frederick
Zach, Max Wilhelm
Zerralin, Carl
CONFEDERATE AGENT (See also SPY)
Bulloch, James Dunwody
Clay, Clement Claiborne
Helm, Charles John
Holcombe, James Philemon
Kenner, Duncan Farrar
Lamar, Gazaway Bugg
Peyton, John Lewis
Sanders, George Nicholas
Thompson, Jacob
Tucker, Nathaniel Beverley, 1820–1890
CONGRESSMAN (CONFEDERATE) (See also CONGRESSMAN)
Bridgers, Robert Rufus
Shorter, John Gill
Smith, Robert Hardy
Staples, Waller Redd
CONGRESSMAN (CONTINENTAL) (See also CONGRESSMAN)
Burnet, William
Clay, Joseph
Deane, Silas
Goldsborough, Robert
Grayson, William
Griffin, Cyrus
Hanson, John
Henry, John, 1750–1798
Howell, David
Huntington, Samuel, 1731–1796
Johnson, Thomas
Jones, Allen
Langworthy, Edward
Low, Isaac
Lynch, Thomas, 1727–1776
McClurg, James
Marchant, Henry
Mathews, John
Mercer, James
Middleton, Henry
Mifflin, Thomas
Nash, Abner
Neilson, John
Pierce, William Leigh
Randolph, Peyton
Read, Jacob
Root, Jesse
Scudder, Nathaniel
Searle, James
Smith, Jonathan Bayard
Smith, Melancton, 1744–1798
Smith, Richard
Telfair, Edward

Tilghman, Matthew
Van Dyke, Nicholas, 1738–1789
Ward, Samuel, 1725–1776
Wisner, Henry
Zubly, John Joachim
CONGRESSMAN (See also CONGRESSMAN, CONFEDERATE; CONGRESSMAN, CONTINENTAL; CONGRESSWOMAN)
Aandahl, Fred George
Adams, Henry Cullen
Aiken, David Wyatt
Alexander, de Alva Stanwood
Allen, Elisha Hunt
Allen, Thomas
Allen, William
Allen, William Joshua
Allison, William Boyd
Anderson, John Alexander
Andrew, Abram Piatt
Andrews, Sherlock James
Appleton, John
Archer, William Segar
Arnold, Isaac Newton
Ashe, William Shepperd
Ashley, James Mitchell
Ashley, William Henry
Ashmun, George
Ayres, William Augustus
Babcock, Joseph Weeks
Bailey, Joseph Weldon
Baker, Jehu
Banks, Nathaniel Prentiss
Barbour, John Strode
Barden, Graham Arthur
Barkley, Alben William
Barksdale, William
Barrett, Frank Aloysius
Barringer, Daniel Moreau
Barrow, Washington
Bartholdt, Richard
Barton, Bruce Fairchild
Bates, James
Bayly, Thomas Henry
Beardsley, Samuel
Beck, James Montgomery
Bedinger, George Michael
Bell, Peter Hansborough
Bender, George Harrison
Berger, Victor Louis
Berrien, John Macpherson
Bissell, William Henry
Blair, Henry William
Bland, Richard Parks
Bliss, Philemon
Bloom, Sol
Blount, James Henderson
Blow, Henry Taylor
Bocock, Thomas Stanley
Boteler, Alexander Robinson
Botts, John Minor
Boutelle, Charles Addison
Boyd, Lynn
Bradley, William Czar
Bragg, Edward Stuyvesant
Branch, Lawrence O'Bryan
Brawley, William Hiram
Breckenridge, James
Breckinridge, William Campbell Preston
Brewer, Mark Spencer
Broadhead, James Overton

Brooks, Overton
Brooks, Preston Smith
Brown, Aaron Venable
Brown, Albert Gallatin
Brown, Clarence James
Brown, John Young
Burdick, Usher Lloyd
Burke, Aedanus
Burleson, Albert Sidney
Burling, Anson
Burton, Theodore Elijah
Butler, Benjamin Franklin
Butler, Ezra
Butler, William
Butler, William Orlando
Cabell, Samuel Jordan
Calvert, Charles Benedict
Cambreleng, Churchill Caldom
Campbell, James Hepburn
Campbell, John Wilson
Campbell, Lewis Davis
Campbell, William Bowen
Campbell, William W.
Candler, Allen Daniel
Cannon, Clarence
Cannon, Joseph Gurney
Cannon, Newton
Case, Francis Higbee
Chalmers, James Ronald
Chambers, John
Chandler, Joseph Ripley
Cheves, Langdon
Chittenden, Simeon Baldwin
Claiborne, John Francis
    Hamtramck
Claiborne, Nathaniel Herbert
Clark, James
Clay, Henry
Clay, Matthew
Clayton, Augustin Smith
Clayton, Henry De Lamar
Clements, Judson Claudius
Cleveland, Chauncey Fitch
Clopton, John
Cockran, William Bourke
Condit, John
Conger, Edwin Hurd
Conkling, Alfred
Connally, Thomas Terry
    ("Tom")
Conway, Martin Franklin
Cook, Philip
Cooper, (Leon) Jere
Copley, Ira Clifton
Covode, John
Cox, Edward Eugene
Cox, Samuel Sullivan
Crawford, Martin Jenkins
Creighton, William
Crisp, Charles Frederick
Crosser, Robert
Crowninshield, Jacob
Crump, Edward Hull
Cummings, Amos Jay
Curtis, Charles
Cushman, Joshua
Dalzell, John
Davis, Garret
Davis, Horace
Davis, John Wesley
Davis, John William
Dawes, Henry Laurens

Dawson, William Levi
Dayton, Jonathan
Dean, Sidney
Dearborn, Henry
Delano, Columbus
De Priest, Oscar Stanton
Desha, Joseph
Dickinson, Philemon
Dingley, Nelson
Dirksen, Everett McKinley
Dixon, James
Doughton, Robert Lee
Drayton, William
Dudley, Edward Bishop
Dunn, William McKee
Duval, William Pope
Duvall, Gabriel
Dworshak, Henry Clarence
Eaton, Charles Aubrey
Edgerton, Sidney
Edwards, Henry Waggaman
Ellsworth, William Wolcott
Engle, Clair William Walter
English, William Hayden
Eppes, John Wayles
Esch, John Jacob
Evans, Walter
Ewing, Thomas
Ferry, Orris Sanford
Fess, Simeon Davidson
Findlay, James
Findley, William
Fitzpatrick, Morgan Cassius
Fitzsimmons, Thomas
Florence, Thomas Birch
Floyd, William
Foot, Samuel Augustus
Fordney, Joseph Warren
Forney, William Henry
Forward, Walter
Foster, Abiel
Foster, Charles
Fowler, Orin
Frye, William Pierce
Galloway, Samuel
Garfield, James Abram
Garrett, Finis James
Gear, John Henry
Gillett, Frederick Huntington
Gilmer, George Rockingham
Gilmer, John Adams
Glynn, Martin Henry
Goldsborough, Charles
Goldsborough, Thomas Alan
Goodenow, John Milton
Green, James Stephens
Green, William Joseph, Jr.
Greenhalge, Frederic Thomas
Greenup, Christopher
Griswold, John Augustus
Groesbeck, William Slocum
Grosvenor, Charles Henry
Hahn, Georg Michael Decker
Hale, Robert Safford
Hamer, Thomas Lyon
Hamilton, William Thomas
Hampton, Wade, 1751–1835
Hancock, John, 1824–1893
Hanson, Alexander Contee,
    1786–1819
Hardin, Ben
Hardin, John J.

Harding, Abner Clark
Hardwick, Thomas William
Harlan, James
Harris, Wiley Pope
Harrison, Byron Patton
Harrison, Francis Burton
Hartley, Fred Allen, Jr.
Hartley, Thomas
Hasbrouck, Abraham Bruyn
Hastings, William Wirt
Hatch, William Henry
Haugen, Gilbert Nelson
Haugen, Nils Pederson
Havens, James Smith
Hawley, Willis Chatman
Heflin, James Thomas
Hemphill, Joseph
Henderson, Archibald
Hendricks, Thomas Andrews
Hendricks, William
Hendrix, Joseph Clifford
Hepburn, William Peters
Herbert, Hilary Abner
Herter, Christian Archibald
Hiester, Daniel
Hiester, Joseph
Hillhouse, James
Hilliard, Henry Washington
Hillyer, Junius
Hinds, Asher Crosby
Hitt, Robert Roberts
Hoar, Ebenezer Rockwood
Hoar, George Frisbie
Hoar, Samuel
Hobson, Richmond Pearson
Hoey, Clyde Roark
Hoffman, Clare Eugene
Hoffman, Ogden
Hogan, John
Holman, William Steele
Holmes, Isaac Edward
Hope, Clifford Ragsdale
Hopkinson, Joseph
Houghton, Alanson Bigelow
Houk, Leonidas Campbell
Howard, Benjamin
Howard, Jacob Merritt
Howard, Volney Erskine
Hubbard, David
Hughes, Dudley Mays
Hull, Cordell
Hunt, Carleton
Hunter, Whiteside Godfrey
Hurlbut, Stephen Augustus
Ingersoll, Charles Jared
Ingham, Samuel Delucenna
Iverson, Alfred
Jackson, James, 1819–1887
Jackson, John George
Jackson, William, 1783–1855
James, Ollie Murray
Jenkins, Albert Gallatin
Jensen, Benton Franklin
    ("Ben")
Johns, Kensey
Johnson, Cave
Johnson, James
Johnson, Magnus
Johnson, Robert Ward
Johnson, Tom Loftin
Jones, Frank
Jones, Jehu Glancy

Jones, John Winston
Jones, William
Judd, Norman Buel
Kahn, Julius
Keifer, Joseph Warren
Keitt, Lawrence Massillon
Kelley, William Darrah
Kelly, John
Kenna, John Edward
Kennedy, John Fitzgerald
Kennedy, Robert Patterson
Kent, Joseph
Key, Philip Barton
Kilbourne, James
King, Austin Augustus
King, John Alsop
King, Thomas Butler
King, William Rufus Devane
Kitchin, Claude
Kitchin, William Walton
Knickerbocker, Herman
Knott, James Proctor
Knutson, Harold
Lacey, John Fletcher
Lacock, Abner
La Guardia, Fiorello Henry
Lane, Henry Smith
Lanham, Frederick Garland
    ("Fritz")
Lattimore, William
Law, John
Lawrence, William, 1819–1899
Leavitt, Humphrey Howe
Lee, William Henry Fitzhugh
Leffler, Isaac
Leffler, Shepherd
Leib, Michael
Lemke, William Frederick
Lenroot, Irvine Luther
Letcher, John
Letcher, Robert Perkins
Lever, Asbury Francis
Levin, Lewis Charles
Lewis, Dixon Hall
Lewis, James Hamilton
Lewis, Joseph Horace
Ligon, Thomas Watkins
Lind, John
Lindbergh, Charles Augustus
Littauer, Lucius Nathan
Littleton, Martin Wiley
Livermore, Arthur
Livermore, Edward St. Loe
Livermore, Samuel, 1732–1803
Lloyd, Edward, 1779–1834
Locke, Matthew
Long, John Davis
Longfellow, Stephen
Loomis, Arphaxed
Loomis, Dwight
Lorimer, William
Lowndes, William
Lucas, John Baptiste Charles
Lucas, Scott Wike
Lundeen, Ernest
Lynch, John Roy
Lyon, Francis Strother
McArthur, Duncan
McCall, Samuel Walker
McClelland, Robert
McClernand, John Alexander
McClurg, Joseph Washington

McComas, Louis Emory
McCook, Anson George
McCrary, George Washington
McCreary, James Bennett
McFadden, Louis Thomas
McGranery, James Patrick
McKay, James Iver
McKean, Samuel
McKee, John
McKennan, Thomas McKean
    Thompson
McKim, Isaac
McKinley, John
McKinley, William Brown
McLane, Robert Milligan
Maclay, Samuel
McLean, John
McMillin, Benton
McNulty, Frank Joseph
McPherson, Edward
McPherson, Smith
McRae, Thomas Chipman
McReynolds, Samuel Davis
Madden, Martin Barnaby
Maginnis, Martin
Mallary, Rollin Carolas
Mann, James Robert
Marcantonio, Vito Anthony
Marland, Ernest Whitworth
Marshall, Thomas Alexander
Martin, Joseph William, Jr.
Marvin, Dudley
Mason, John Young
Mathews, George
Mattocks, John
Maverick, (Fontaine) Maury
Maxwell, Augustus Emmett
Maxwell, Samuel
May, Andrew Jackson
Maynard, Horace
Mercee, John Francis
Mercer, Charles Fenton
Mercier, Ulysses
Miles, William Porcher
Miller, John
Mills, Elijah Hunt
Mills, Roger Quarles
Miner, Charles
Mitchell, Alexander
Mitchell, George Edward
Mitchell, Nahum
Mitchill, Samuel Latham
Mondell, Frank Wheeler
Money, Hernando De Soto
Montague, Andrew Jackson
Moody, William Henry
Moore, Andrew
Moore, Ely
Moore, Gabriel
Moore, Thomas Patrick
Moorhead, James Kennedy
Morehead, Charles Slaughter
Morgan, George Washington
Morrill, Anson Peaslee
Morrill, Edmund Needham
Morrill, Justin Smith
Morris, Lewis Richard
Morrison, William Ralls
Morrissey, John
Morrow, Jeremiah
Morrow, William W.
Morse, Freeman Harlow

Murdock, Victor
Murray, William Henry David
Neely, Matthew Mansfield
Negley, James Scott
Nelson, Roger
Newberry, John Stoughton
Newell, William Augustus
Newlands, Francis Griffith
Newton, Thomas, 1768–1847
Niblack, William Ellis
Nicholas, John
Nicholas, Wilson Cary
Nicholson, Joseph Hopper
Niedringhaus, Frederick
    Gottlieb
Nisbet, Eugenius Aristides
Norris, George William
Norton, Elijah Hise
Nott, Abraham
Oates, William Calvin
O'Ferrall, Charles Triplett
Olmsted, Marlin Edgar
Orth, Godlove Stein
Pacheco, Romualdo
Packer, Asa
Page, John
Paine, Halbert Eleazer
Palmer, Alexander Mitchell
Palmer, Henry Wilbur
Parker, Isaac Charles
Pattison, John M.
Payne, Henry B.
Pearce, James Alfred
Pendleton, George Hunt
Pennington, William
Perkins, George Douglas
Perkins, James Breck
Phelan, James, 1856–1891
Phelps, Charles Edward
Phelps, John Smith
Phelps, William Walter
Philips, John Finis
Phillips, Thomas Wharton
Phillips, William Addison
Pickens, Francis Wilkinson
Pierce, Henry Lillie
Pinckney, Henry Laurens
Plaisted, Harris Merrill
Plumley, Frank
Poindexter, George
Poland, Luke Potter
Pollock, James
Pool, Joe Richard
Porter, Albert Gallatin
Porter, Peter Buell
Porter, Stephen Geyer
Potter, Elisha Reynolds
Potter, Robert
Pou, Edward William
Pratt, Zadock
Prentiss, Seargent Smith
Preston, William
Preston, William Ballard
Price, Hiram
Price, Sterling
Price, Thomas Lawson
Pryor, Roger Atkinson
Pujo, Arsène Paulin
Quigg, Lemuel Ely
Rainey, Joseph Hayne
Randall, Samuel Jackson
Randolph, Thomas Mann

Rankin, John Elliott
Rayner, Kenneth
Read, Nathan
Reagan, John Henninger
Reece, Brazilla Carroll
Reed, Daniel Alden
Rhea, John
Rice, Alexander Hamilton
Rice, Edmund
Rich, Robert
Riddle, Albert Gallatin
Rivers, Lucius Mendel
Roberts, Ellis Henry
Roberts, Jonathan
Roberts, William Randall
Robertson, Alice Mary
Robertson, George
Robertson, John
Robinson, Joseph Taylor
Rollins, James Sidney
Rousseau, Lovell Harrison
Rowan, John
Rusk, Jeremiah McClain
Sabath, Adolph J.
Sage, Russell
Saunders, Romulus Mitchell
Sawyer, Lemuel
Schenck, Robert Cumming
Seddon, James Alexander
Sergeant, John, 1779–1852
Sergeant, Jonathan Dickinson
Sevier, Ambrose Hundley
Seybert, Adam
Seymour, Thomas Hart
Shafroth, John Franklin
Shepard, William
Sheppard, John Morris
Sherwood, Isaac Ruth
Shouse, Jouett
Sibley, Joseph Crocker
Sickles, Daniel Edgar
Simms, William Elliott
Simpson, Jerry
Singleton, James Washington
Skinner, Harry
Slemp, Campbell Bascom
Smalls, Robert
Smith, Caleb Blood
Smith, Jeremiah, 1759–1842
Smith, Oliver Hampton
Smith, Truman
Smith, Walter Inglewood
Smith, William, 1797–1887
Smith, William Loughton
Smith, William Nathan Harrell
Smith, William Russell
Smyth, Alexander
Snell, Bertrand Hollis
Spaight, Richard Dobbs
Spalding, Thomas
Sparks, William Andrew
  Jackson
Spaulding, Elbridge Gerry
Speer, Emory
Spence, Brent
Spencer, Ambrose
Spencer, John Canfield
Sperry, Nehemiah Day
Springer, William McKendree
Stanley, Augustus Owsley
Stanly, Edward
Stanton, Frederick Perry

Stanton, Richard Henry
Starin, John Henry
Steagall, Henry Bascom
Steele, John
Stephens, Alexander Hamilton
Stephenson, Andrew
Stephenson, Isaac
Stevens, Thaddeus
Stevenson, Adlai Ewing
Stevenson, John White
Stewart, Andrew
Stigler, William Grady
Stockdale, Thomas Ringland
Stone, David
Stone, William Joel
Storer, Bellamy
Stuart, Alexander Hugh
  Holmes
Stuart, John Todd
Sullivan, George
Sulzer, William
Summers, George William
Sumners, Hatton, William
Sumter, Thomas
Sutherland, Joel Barlow
Swann, Thomas
Swanson, Claude Augustus
Sweeney, Martin Leonard
Taber, John
Tallmadge, Benjamin
Tawney, James Albertus
Taylor, Alfred Alexander
Thacher, George
Thayer, Eli
Thomas, David
Thomas, Francis
Thomas, John Parnell
Thomas, Philip Francis
Thompson, Jacob
Thompson, Thomas Larkin
Thompson, Waddy
Thompson, Wiley
Throop, Enos Thompson
Thurman, Allen Granberry
Tilson, John Quillin
Tinkham, George Holden
Tod, John
Toucey, Isaac
Towne, Charles Arnette
Towns, George Washington
  Bonaparte
Tracy, Uriah
Troup, George Michael
Trumbull, Jonathan, 1740–1809
Tuck, Amos
Tucker, Henry St. George,
  1853–1932
Tucker, John Randolph,
  1823–1897
Tyson, Job Roberts
Upham, Charles Wentworth
Van Cortlandt, Philip
Van Horn, Robert Thompson
Van Rensselaer, Solomon
Van Rensselaer, Stephen
Verplanck, Julian Crommelin
Vibbard, Chauncey
Vinson, Fred(erick) Moore
Vinton, Samuel Finley
Volstead, Andrew John
Vroom, Peter Dumont
Waddell, Alfred Moore

Wadsworth, James Wolcott, Jr.
Wadsworth, Jeremiah
Wadsworth, Peleg
Walker, Amasa
Walker, Gilbert Carlton
Wallace, David
Wallgren, Mon(rad) C(harles)
Walter, Francis Eugene
Ward, Marcus Lawrence
Warner, Adoniram Judson
Warner, Hiram
Warner, William
Washburn, Cadwallader Colden
Washburn, Charles Grenfill
Washburn, Israel
Washburn, William Drew
Washburne, Elihu Benjamin
Watson, James Eli
Watterson, Harvey Magee
Weaver, James Baird
Weeks, John Wingate
Welch, John
Weller, John B.
Wells, Erastus
Wentworth, John, 1815–1888
West, George
Wheeler, Joseph
White, Alexander
White, Stephen Van Culen
Whitehill, Robert
Whitman, Ezekiel
Wickliffe, Charles Anderson
Wilde, Richard Henry
Williams, David Rogerson
Willis, Albert Shelby
Wilmot, David
Wilson, James
Wilson, James Falconer
Wilson, William Bauchop
Wilson, William Lyne
Windom, William
Winn, Richard
Winthrop, Robert Charles
Wise, Henry Alexander
Wolf, George
Wood, Fernando
Wood, John Stephens
Wood, William Robert
Wright, Hendrick Bradley
Wright, Joseph Albert
Wright, Robert
Yates, Abraham
Yell, Archibald
Young, Pierce Manning Butler
Zollicoffer, Felix Kirk
CONGRESSWOMAN
  Kahn, Florence Prag
  Norton, Mary Teresa Hopkins
  Rogers, Edith Nourse
  Rohde, Ruth Bryan Owen
  Simms, Ruth Hanna
    McCormick
CONSERVATIONIST (See also
  ECOLOGIST)
  Darling, Jay Norwood ("Ding")
  Grinnell, George Bird
  McAdams, Clark
  McFarland, John Horace
  Maxwell, George Hebard
  Merriam, John Campbell
  Olmsted, Frederick Law
  Osborn, Henry Fairfield

Pack, Charles Lathrop
Pammel, Louis Hermann
Pearson, Thomas Gilbert
Pinchot, Gifford
Roosevelt, Robert Barnwell
Shields, George Oliver
Silcox, Ferdinand Augustus
Zahniser, Howard Clinton
CONSTITUTIONAL SCHOLAR
Warren, Charles
CONSUL (See also DIPLOMAT,
STATESMAN)
Andrews, Israel DeWolf
Cathcart, James Leander
De Forest, David Curtis
Foresti, Eleutario Felice
Gillman, Henry
Hale, Charles
Halsey, Thomas Lloyd
Heap, Samuel Davies
Helm, Charles John
Jarvis, William
Jones, William Patterson
King, Jonas
Lear, Tobias
McRae, Duncan Kirkland
Magoffin, James Wiley
Merrill, Selah
Morse, Freeman Harlow
Murphy, Dominic Ignatius
Murphy, William Walton
O'Brien, Richard
Offley, David
Ogden, Francis Barber
Osterhaus, Peter Joseph
Shaler, William
Stahel, Julius
Taylor, James Wickes
Thayer, Alexander Wheelock
Underwood, Francis Henry
Wood, Leonard
CONSUMER ADVOCATE
Brady, Mildred Alice Edie
CONTRACTOR (See also BUILDING
CONTRACTOR)
Crimmins, John Daniel
Faesch, John Jacob
Fox, Harry
Glenn, Hugh
Haish, Jacob
Law, George
Levitt, Abraham
Stubbs, Walter Roscoe
Thompson, David P.
Vare, William Scott
Wolfson, Erwin Service
CONTROVERSIALIST (See also
CLERGYMAN, PAMPHLETEER,
PROPAGANDIST, WRITER)
Breckinridge, John, 1797–1841
Graves, James Robinson
McCaine, Alexander
McCalla, William Latta
Niles, Samuel
Ogden, Uzal
Pickering, Timothy
Yorke, Peter Christopher
CORNETIST
Handy, William Christopher
Oliver, Joseph

COSMOGRAPHER
Constansó, Miguel
COUNCILLOR (COLONIAL)
Nelson, William, 1711–1772
Page, Mann
Peters, Richard, c. 1704–1776
COURT REPORTER
Deming, Philander
Munford, William
Otto, William Tod
COWBOY (See also RANGER)
Adams, Andy
Gibson, Edmund Richard
("Hoot")
Rhodes, Eugene Manlove
Rogers, Will
Siringo, Charles A.
CRAFTSMAN (See also ARTIST,
CABINETMAKER, DIAMOND
CUTTER, GOLDSMITH, PEWTER-
ER, SILVERSMITH, TOOLMAKER,
VIOLIN MAKER, WOOD-CARV-
ER, WOOD-ENGRAVER)
Armstrong, David Maitland
Fitch, John
Hubbard, Elbert
La Farge, John
Revere, Paul
Wright, Philip Green
CRIMINAL (See also BOOTLEGGER,
GANGSTER, ORGANIZED CRIME
LEADER, RACKETEER)
Capone, Alphonse ("Al")
Chessman, Caryl Whittier
Wexler, Irving ("Waxey
Gordon")
CRIMINOLOGIST (See also PENOLO-
GIST, PRISON REFORMER,
SOCIOLOGIST)
Goddard, Calvin Hooker
Kirchwey, George Washington
Smith, Bruce
Spitzka, Edward Anthony
Sutherland, Edwin Hardin
CRITIC (See also ART, DRAMATIC,
LITERARY, MUSIC, POLITICAL,
SOCIAL CRITIC)
Agee, James Rufus
Bacon, Leonard
Bent, Silas
Bogan, Louise Marie
Bradford, Gamaliel
Brooks, Van Wyck
Brownell, William Crary
Cranch, Christopher Pearse
DeVoto, Bernard Augustine
Fowler, Frank
Fuller, Sarah Margaret
Gilder, Jeannette Leonard
Hale, Philip Leslie
Hamilton, Clayton
Hillyer, Robert Silliman
Humiston, William Henry
Huneker, James Gibbons
Jacobs, Joseph, 1854–1916
Jarves, James Jackson
Kilmer, Alfred Joyce
Kobbé, Gustav
Koch, Vivienne
Lanier, Sidney
Lowell, Amy
Mabie, Hamilton Wright

Magonigle, Harold Van Buren
Mencken, Henry Louis
Morehouse, Ward
Nathan, George Jean
Parker, Dorothy Rothschild
Poe, Edgar Allan
Pollak, Gustav
Price, William Thompson
Redman, Ben Ray
Reitzel, Robert
Rittenhouse, Jessie Belle
Seldes, Gilbert Vivian
Stedman, Edmund Clarence
Stoddard, Richard Henry
Sturgis, Russell
Tuckerman, Henry Theodore
Van Vechten, Carl
Wallace, Horace Binney
Walsh, Thomas
Wheeler, Andrew Carpenter
Whitaker, Charles Harris
Willcox, Louise Collier
Williams, John
Woodberry, George Edward
Woollcott, Alexander
Humphreys
CRYPTOLOGIST
Friedman, William Frederick
CURATOR (See also MUSEUM DI-
RECTOR)
Burroughs, Bryson
Fitzpatrick, John Clement
Goodyear, William Henry
Koehler, Sylvester Rosa
Lutz, Frank Eugene
Rau, Charles
Todd, Walter Edmond Clyde
Watkins, John Elfreth
CUSTOMS EXPERT
Colton, George Radcliffe
Keith, Sir William
Sterling, James
CYTOLOGIST
Wilson, Edmund Beecher

DAIRY HUSBANDMAN (See also
CATTLEMAN)
Alvord, Henry Elijah
Arnold, Lauren Briggs
Hoard, William Dempster
DANCE EDUCATOR
Horst, Louis
DANCER
Barton, James Edward
Bolm, Adolph Rudolphovitch
Castle, Irene Foote
Castle, Vernon Blythe
Duncan, Isadora
Fokine, Michel
Fuller, Loie
Gilbert, Anne Hartley
Gray, Gilda
Humphrey, Doris
McCracken, Joan
Murray, Mae
Robinson, Bill ("Bojangles")
Rooney, Pat
St. Denis, Ruth
Tamiris, Helen
Vladimiroff, Pierre
Webb, Clifton

DEAF EDUCATION SCHOLAR
  Goldstein, Max Aaron
DEMOGRAPHER (See also STATISTI-
    CIAN)
  Lotka, Alfred James
DENDROCHRONOLOGIST
  Douglass, Andrew Ellicott
DENTIST (See also PHYSICIAN)
  Abbott, Frank
  Allen, John
  Black, Greene Vardiman
  Bonwill, William Gibson
    Arlington
  Brown, Solyman
  Evans, Thomas Wiltberger
  Fillebrown, Thomas
  Flagg, Josiah Foster
  Garretson, James
  Greenwood, John
  Harris, Chapin Aaron
  Hayden, Horace H.
  Howe, Percy Rogers
  Hudson, Edward
  Hullihen, Simon P.
  Kingsley, Norman William
  Loomis, Mahlon
  McQuillen, John Hugh
  Miller, Willoughby Dayton
  Morton, William Thomas Green
  Owre, Alfred
  Parsons, Thomas William
  Riggs, John Mankey
  Spooner, Shearjashub
  Volck, Adalbert John
  Wells, Horace
  White, John de Haven
DEPARTMENT STORE EXECUTIVE
  Straus, Percy Selden
DERMATOLOGIST (See also PHYSI-
    CIAN)
  Duhring, Louis Adolphus
  Jackson, George Thomas
  Pusey, William Allen
  Schamberg, Jay Frank
  Wende, Ernest
  Wende, Grover William
  White, James Clarke
  Wigglesworth, Edward
DESIGNER (CINEMATOGRAPHIC
    EQUIPMENT)
  Howell, Albert Summers
DESIGNER (COSTUME)
  Bernstein, Aline
DESIGNER (FASHION)
  Adrian, Gilbert
  Carnegie, Hattie
  Kiam, Omar
  McCardell, Claire
  Orry-Kelly
DESIGNER (INTERIOR)
  Herter, Christian
DESIGNER (SCENIC)
  Bernstein, Aline
DESPERADO (See also BANDIT,
    BRIGAND, BUCCANEER, BUR-
    GLAR, CRIMINAL, OUTLAW, PI-
    RATE)
  Bass, Sam
  Billy the Kid
  Dalton, Robert
  James, Jesse Woodson
  Mason, Samuel

  Slade, Joseph Alfred
  Younger, Thomas Coleman
DETECTIVE
  Burns, William John
  Means, Gaston Bullock
  Pinkerton, Allan
  Ruditsky, Barney
  Siringo, Charles A.
DIAMOND CUTTER (See also
    CRAFTSMAN)
  Morse, Henry Dutton
DIARIST (See also CHRONICLER)
  Breen, Patrick
  Hone, Philip
  Knight, Sarah Kemble
  Laudonnière, René Goulaine de
  Maclay, William
  Marshall, Christopher
  Sewall, Samuel
  Smith, Richard
  Wister, Sarah
DIESINKER (See also ENGRAVER)
  Gobrecht, Christian
  Kneass, William
  Wright, Joseph
DIETICIAN (See also NUTRITIONIST,
    PHYSICIAN)
  Nichols, Thomas Low
DIPLOMAT (See also CONSUL,
    STATESMAN)
  Adams, Charles
  Adams, Charles Francis
  Adee, Alvey Augustus
  Allen, Elisha Hunt
  Allen, George Venable
  Anderson, Richard Clough
  Angel, Benjamin Franklin
  Angell, James Burrill
  Appleton, John
  Armstrong, John
  Avery, Benjamin Parke
  Bacon, Robert
  Badeau, Adam
  Bagby, Arthur Pendleton
  Baker, Jehu
  Bancroft, Edgar Addison
  Bancroft, George
  Barrett, John
  Barringer, Daniel Moreau
  Barton, Thomas Pennant
  Bayard, James Ach(e)ton
  Bayard, Thomas Francis
  Beaupré, Arthur Matthias
  Belmont, August
  Benjamin, Samuel Greene
    Wheeler
  Bernstein, Herman
  Biddle, Anthony Joseph Drexel,
    Jr.
  Bidlack, Benjamin Alden
  Bigelow, John
  Bingham, Robert Worth
  Birney, James
  Bliss, Robert Woods
  Bliss, Tasker Howard
  Blount, James Henderson
  Blow, Henry Taylor
  Bogardus, Everardus
  Boker, George Henry
  Bonsal, Stephen
  Borland, Solon
  Boutell, Henry Sherman

  Bowdoin, James
  Bowen, Herbert Wolcott
  Bowers, Claude Gernade
  Bradish, Luther
  Bradley, Charles William
  Bristol, Mark Lambert
  Broadhead, James Overton
  Brown, James
  Brown, John Porter
  Buchanan, William Insco
  Bullitt, William Christian
  Burlingame, Anson
  Calhoun, William James
  Cambreleng, Churchill Caldom
  Cameron, Simon
  Campbell, George Washington
  Campbell, Lewis Davis
  Carmichael, William
  Carr, Dabney Smith
  Carter, Henry Alpheus Peirce
  Cass, Lewis
  Castle, William Richards, Jr.
  Child, Richard Washburn
  Choate, Joseph Hodges
  Clark, Joshua Reuben, Jr.
  Clay, Clement Claiborne
  Conger, Edwin Hurd
  Coolidge, Thomas Jefferson
  Cooper, Henry Ernest
  Cramer, Michael John
  Crowder, Enoch Herbert
  Dallas, George Mifflin
  Dana, Francis
  Daniel, John Moncure
  Daniels, Josephus
  D'Avezac, Auguste Geneviève
    Valentin
  Davies, Joseph Edward
  Davis, John Chandler Bancroft
  Davis, John William
  Davis, Norman Hezekiah
  Dawson, Thomas Cleland
  Dayton, William Lewis
  Deane, Silas
  Denby, Charles
  Dickinson, Charles Monroe
  Dodd, William Edward
  Dodge, Augustus Caesar
  Donelson, Andrew Jackson
  Donovan, William Joseph
  Draper, William Franklin
  Dulles, Allen Welsh
  Dulles, John Foster
  Du Pont, Victor Marie
  Eames, Charles
  Eaton, William
  Edge, Walter Evans
  Egan, Maurice Francis
  Egan, Patrick
  Ellis, Powhatan
  Ellsworth, Henry William
  Erving, George William
  Eustis, George
  Eustis, James Biddle
  Eustis, William
  Everett, Alexander Hill
  Fairchild, Lucius
  Farman, Elbert Eli
  Fay, Theodore Sedgwick
  Fearn, John Walker
  Ferguson, Thomas Barker
  Flagg, Edmund

Fletcher, Henry Prather
Fogg, George Gilman
Foote, Lucius Harwood
Forbes, John Murray
Foster, John Watson
Foulk, George Clayton
Fox, Williams Carleton
Francis, Charles Spencer
Francis, John Morgan
Franklin, Benjamin
Gadsden, James
Gallatin, Abraham Alfonse Albert
Gauss, Clarence Edward
Genet, Edmond Charles
Gerard, James Watson
Gifford, Walter Sherman
Grady, Henry Francis
Graham, John
Gray, Isaac Pusey
Greathouse, Clarence Ridgeby
Green, Benjamin Edwards
Greene, Roger Sherman
Grew, Joseph Clark
Grieve, Miller
Griscom, Lloyd Carpenter
Gummere, Samuel René
Guthrie, George Wilkins
Halderman, John A.
Hale, Edward Joseph
Hale, John Parker
Hamilton, Maxwell McGaughey
Hardy, Arthur Sherburne
Harriman, Florence Jaffray Hurst
Harris, Townsend
Harvey, George Brinton McClellan
Hassaurek, Friedrich
Hay, Joh Milton
Hayes, Carlton Joseph Huntley
Herrick, Myron Timothy
Hibben, Paxton Pattison
Hicks, John, 1847–1917
Hill, David Jayne
Hise, Elijah
Hoffman, Wickham
Holcombe, Chester
Holmes, Julius Cecil
Hoover, Herbert Clark, Jr.
Hopkins, Harry Lloyd
Houghton, Alanson Bigelow
Hughes, Christopher
Hunt, William Henry
Hunter, William
Hurley, Patrick Jay
Ide, Henry Clay
Izard, Ralph
Jackson, Charles Douglas
Jackson, Henry Rootes
Jackson, John Brinckerhoff
Jackson, Mortimer Melville
Jardine, William Marion
Jay, John, 1745–1829
Jay, John, 1817–1894
Jefferson, Thomas
Johnson, Reverdy
Judd, Norman Buel
Kasson, John Adam
Kavanagh, Edward
Kilpatrick, Hugh Judson
King, Rufus

King, Thomas Butler
King, William Rufus Devane
Kinney, William Burnet
Kirk, Alan Goodrich
Lane, Arthur Bliss
Langston, John Mercer
Larkin, Thomas Oliver
Larrínaga, Tulio
Laurens, John
Lawrence, Abbott
Lee, Arthur
Lee, William
LeGendre, Charles William
Leishman, John G. A.
Lincoln, Robert Todd
Lind, John
Livingston, Robert R., 1746–1813
Long, Breckinridge
Lothrop, George Van Ness
Low, Frederick Ferdinand
McCartee, Divie Bethune
McCook, Edward Moody
McCormick, Robert Sanderson
McDonald, James Grover
McLane, Louis
McLane, Robert Milligan
McMillin, Benton
McNutt, Paul Vories
MacVeagh, Charles
MacVeagh, Isaac Wayne
Maney, George Earl
Mann, Ambrose Dudley
Marling, John Leake
Marsh, George Perkins
Marshall, Humphrey
Marshall, James Fowle Baldwin
Mason, James Murray
Mason, John Young
Maxcy, Virgil
Merry, William Lawrence
Messersmith, George Strausser
Meyer, George Von Lengerke
Miller, David Hunter
Moffat, Jay Pierrepont
Montgomery, George Washington
Moore, Thomas Patrick
Moran, Benjamin
Morgan, Edwin Vernon
Morgan, Philip Hicky
Morgenthau, Henry
Morris, Edward Joy
Morris, Gouverneur
Morris, Richard Valentine
Morrison, Delesseps Story
Morrow, Dwight Whitney
Morton, Levi Parsons
Motley, John Lothrop
Muhlenberg, Henry Augustus Philip
Muñoz-Rivera, Luis
Murray, William Vans
Nelson, Donald Marr
Nelson, Hugh
Nelson, Thomas Henry
Newel, Stanford
Nicholson, Meredith
Niles, Nathaniel, 1791–1869
Noyes, Edward Follansbee
O'Brien, Edward Charles
O'Brien, Thomas James

Offley, David
Osborn, Thomas Andrew
Osborn, Thomas Ogden
O'Shaughnessy, Nelson Jarvis Waterbury
Osten Sacken, Carl Robert Romanovich von der
O'Sullivan, John Louis
Pacheco, Romualdo
Page, Thomas Nelson
Page, Walter Hines
Palmer, Thomas Witherell
Parker, Peter
Partridge, James Rudolph
Patterson, Richard Cunningham, Jr.
Payne, John Howard
Peirce, Henry Augustus
Peixotto, Benjamin Franklin
Pendleton, George Hunt
Pendleton, John Strother
Penfield, Frederic Courtland
Phelps, Edward John
Phelps, William Walter
Phillips, William
Pickett, James Chamberlayne
Pierrepont, Edwards
Pinckney, Charles
Pinckney, Charles Cotesworth
Pinckney, Thomas
Pinkney, William
Poinsett, Joel Roberts
Polk, Frank Lyon
Porter, Horace
Preble, William Pitt
Preston, William
Pruyn, Robert Hewson
Putnam, James Osborne
Putnam, William LeBaron
Randolph, Sir John
Read, John Meredith, 1837–1896
Reed, William Bradford
Reid, Whitelaw
Reinsch, Paul Samuel
Rhind, Charles
Richards, William
Rives, William Cabell
Roberts, Edmund
Robinson, Christopher
Rockhill, William Woodville
Rodney, Caesar Augustus
Rohde, Ruth Bryan Owen
Root, Joseph Pomeroy
Rowe, Leo Stanton
Rublee, Horace
Rush, Richard
Russell, Charles Wells
Russell, Jonathan
Sanford, Henry Shelton
Saunders, Romulus Mitchell
Sayre, Stephen
Schenck, Robert Cumming
Schurman, Jacob Gould
Schurz, Carl
Schuyler, Eugene
Scruggs, William Lindsay
Sedgwick, Theodore, 1811–1859
Sewall, Harold Marsh
Seward, Frederick William
Seward, George Frederick

Seymour, Charles
Seymour, Thomas Hart
Shannon, Wilson
Sharp, William Graves
Short, William
Sickles, Daniel Edgar
Slidell, John
Smith, Charles Emory
Smith, Walter Bedell
Smith, William Loughton
Smyth, John Henry
Soulé, Pierre
Squier, Ephraim George
Squiers, Herbert Goldsmith
Stallo, Johann Bernhard
Standley, William Harrison
Steinhardt, Laurence Adolph
Stevens, John Leavitt
Stevenson, Andrew
Stillman, William James
Stimson, Frederic Jesup
Storer, Bellamy
Stovall, Pleasant Alexander
Straight, Willard Dickerman
Straus, Jesse Isidor
Straus, Oscar Solomon
Strobel, Edward Henry
Stuart, John Leighton
Swift, John Franklin
Taft, Alphonso
Taylor, Hannis
Taylor, Myron Charles
Tenney, Charles Daniel
Terrell, Edwin Holland
Thomas, Allen
Thomas, William Widgery
Thompson, Thomas Larkin
Thompson, Waddy
Tod, David
Todd, Charles Stewart
Torbert, Alfred Thomas
    Archimedes
Tower, Charlemagne
Tree, Lambert
Trescot, William Henry
Tripp, Bartlett
Trist, Nicholas Philip
Turner, James Milton
Vail, Aaron
Van Dyke, Henry
Vaughan, Benjamin
Vignaud, Henry
Vopicka, Charles Joseph
Wallace, Hugh Campbell
Walton, Lester Aglar
Ward, John Elliott
Warden, David Bailie
Washburn, Albert Henry
Washburne, Elihu Benjamin
Webb, James Watson
Weddell, Alexander Wilbourne
Welles, (Benjamin) Sumner
Wheaton, Henry
Wheeler, (George) Post
Wheeler, John Hill
White, Andrew Dickson
White, Henry
Whitlock, Brand
Wikoff, Henry
Wilkins, William
Willard, Joseph Edward
Williams, Edward Thomas

Williams, James
Williams, John
Williams, Samuel Wells
Willis, Albert Shelby
Wilson, Henry Lane
Wilson, Hugh Robert
Winant, John Gilbert
Woodford, Stewart Lyndon
Wright, Joseph Albert
Young, Owen D.
Zollerbach, James David

DIRECTOR (See also **MOTION PIC-
    TURE DIRECTOR, STAGE DI-
    RECTOR, THEATRICAL
    DIRECTOR**)
Brenon, Herbert
Craven, Frank
DeMille, Cecil Blount
Griffith, David Wark
Hampden, Walter
Hart, William Surrey
Lindsay, Howard
Lubitsch, Ernst
Miller, Gilbert Heron
Mitchell, Thomas Gregory
Nagel, Conrad
Nichols, Dudley
Pemberton, Brock
Perry, Antoinette
Rice, Elmer
Rossen, Robert
Schwartz, Maurice
Von Sternberg, Josef
White, George

DIRECTOR OF U. S. MINT (See also
    COMPTROLLER OF CURRENCY)
DeSaussure, Henry William
Linderman, Henry Richard
Snowden, James Ross

DISARMAMENT ADVOCATE
Dingman, Mary Agnes

DISK JOCKEY
Freed, Alan J.

DISCOVERER (See also **EXPLORER,
    FRONTIERSMAN, GUIDE, PIO-
    NEER, SCOUT**)
Cárdenas, García López de
De Soto, Hernando
Gray, Robert
Ingraham, Joseph
Ponce, Juan de León

DIVER
Patch, Sam

DRAFTSMAN
Sterne, Maurice

DRAMA CRITIC
Allen, Kelcey
Benchley, Robert Charles
Brown, John Mason, Jr.
Gibbs, (Oliver) Wolcott
Hale, Philip
Hammond, Percy Hunter
Laffan, William Mackay
Mailly, William
Mantle, (Robert) Burns
Moses, Montrose Jonas
Parker, Henry Taylor
Pollard, Joseph Percival
Stevens, Ashton
Winter, William
Young, Stark

DRAMATIST
Adams, Frank Ramsay
Ade, George
Aiken, George L.
Akins, Zoë
Anderson, Maxwell
Arden, Edwin Hunter
    Pendleton
Arliss, George
Armstrong, Paul
Bacon, Frank
Baker, Benjamin A.
Bannister, Nathaniel Harrington
Barker, James Nelson
Barnes, Charlotte Mary Sanford
Barry, Philip James Quinn
Bateman, Sidney Frances
    Cowell
Baum, Lyman Frank
Belasco, David
Bernard, William Bayle
Biggers, Earl Derr
Bird, Robert Montgomery
Blitzstein, Marc
Boker, George Henry
Boucicault, Dion
Bradford, Gamaliel
Bradford, Joseph
Brougham, John
Brown, David Paul
Burgess, Frank Gelett
Burk, John Daly
Burke, Charles St. Thomas
Campbell, Bartley
Canonge, Louis Placide
Carleton, Henry Guy
Clarke, Joseph Ignatius
    Constantine
Cohan, George Michael
Cohen, Octavus Roy
Conrad, Robert Taylor
Cowl, Jane
Craven, Frank
Crothers, Rachel
Crouse, Russel McKinley
Crowne, John
Custis, George Washington
    Parke
Daly, John Augustin
Davis, Owen Gould
Davis, Richard Harding
Deering, Nathaniel
Dell, Floyd James
DeMille, Cecil Blount
De Mille, Henry Churchill
Dickinson, Anna Elizabeth
Ditrichstein, Leo
Dodd, Lee Wilson
Dunlap, William
Durivage, Francis Alexander
Elliott, Sarah Barnwell
English, Thomas Dunn
Epstein, Philip G.
Ferber, Edna Jessica
Field, Joseph M.
Finn, Henry James William
Fitch, William Clyde
Fitzgerald, Thomas
Flanagan, Hallie
Gayler, Charles
Gillette, William Hooker
Godfrey, Thomas

Golden, John
Goodman, Kenneth Sawyer
Goodrich, Frank Boott
Gordin, Jacob
Gunter, Archibald Clavering
Hamilton, Clayton
Hansberry, Lorraine Vivian
Harby, Isaac
Harrigan, Edward
Hart, Moss
Hazelton, George Cochrane
Hecht, Ben
Helburn, Theresa
Herbert, Frederick Hugh
Herne, James A.
Heyward, DuBose
Hill, Frederic Stanhope
Hirschbein, Peretz
Hodge, William Thomas
Hopwood, Avery
Howard, Bronson Crocker
Howard, Sidney Coe
Hoyt, Charles Hale
Hughes, James Langston
Ioor, William
Jones, Joseph Stevens
Jordan, Kate
Judah, Samuel Benjamin
     Helbert
Kaufman, George S.
Kester, Paul
Klein, Charles
Kreymborg, Alfred Francis
Lacy, Ernest
Langner, Lawrence
Lennox, Charlotte Ramsay
Lindsay, Howard
Lindsey, William
Logan, Cornelius Ambrosius
Long, John Luther
MacArthur, Charles Gordon
McCarroll, James
McCullers, Carson
MacKaye, James Morrison
     Steele
MacKaye, Percy Wallace
Mankiewicz, Herman Jacob
Mann, Louis
Manners, John Hartley
Markoe, Peter
Marquis, Donald Robert Perry
Megrue, Roi Cooper
Miles, George Henry
Mitchell, Langdon Elwyn
Mitchell, Thomas Gregory
Mitchell, William, 1798–1856
Moody, William Vaughn
Morehouse, Ward
Munford, Robert
Murdoch, Frank Hitchcock
Noah, Mordecai Manuel
Odets, Clifford
O'Neill, Eugene
Osborn, Laughton
Parker, Dorothy Rothschild
Payne, John Howard
Peabody, Josephine Preston
Pollock, Channing
Potter, Paul Meredith
Powell, Thomas
Pray, Isaac Clark
Presbrey, Eugene Wiley

Price, William Thompson
Randall, Samuel
Rice, Elmer
Sargent, Epes
Schomer, Nahum Meir
Séjour, Victor
Sherwood, Robert Emmet
Smith, Harry James
Smith, Richard Penn
Smith, Winchell
Stone, John Augustus
Sturges, Preston
Tarkington, Booth
Thomas, Augustus
Thompson, Denman
Torrence, Frederick Ridgely
Tyler, Royall
Vallentine, Benjamin Bennaton
Van Druten, John William
Walcott, Charles Melton,
     1816–1868
Walker, Stuart Armstrong
Wallack, Lester
Walter, Eugene
Ward, Thomas
Warren, Mercy Otis
White, John Blake
Williams, Jesse Lynch
Willis, Nathaniel Parker
Wilson, Harry Leon
Woodworth, Samuel
Young, Stark

DRUGGIST (See also APOTHECARY,
     PHARMACIST)
Browne, Benjamin Frederick
Lawrence, George Newbold

DRUMMER
Jones, Lindley Armstrong
     ("Spike")

EAST ASIAN AFFAIRS EXPERT
Greene, Roger Sherman

ECOLOGIST (See also CONSERVA-
     TIONIST)
Carson, Rachel Louise
Clements, Frederic Edward
Leopold, (Rand) Aldo

ECONOMIST (See also HOME
     ECONOMIST)
Adams, Henry Carter
Adams, Thomas Sewall
Anderson, Benjamin McAlester
Andrew, Abram Piatt
Andrews, John Bertram
Atkinson, Edward
Ayres, Leonard Porter
Barnett, George Ernest
Bigelow, Eratus Brigham
Blodget, Samuel
Callender, Guy Stevens
Cardozo, Jacob Newton
Carey, Henry Charles
Carey, Mathew
Catchings, Waddill
Chamberlin, Edward Hastings
Clark, John Bates
Clark, John Maurice
Commons, John Rogers
Conant, Charles Arthur
Corey, Lewis
Daniels, Winthrop More
Davenport, Herbert Joseph

Day, Edmund Ezra
Dean, William Henry, Jr.
Del Mar, Alexander
Dew, Thomas Roderick
Dunbar, Charles Franklin
Ely, Richard Theodore
Emery, Henry Crosby
Ensley, Enoch
Fairchild, Fred Rogers
Falkner, Roland Post
Farnam, Henry Walcott
Fetter, Frank Albert
Fisher, Irving
Foster, William Trufant
George, Henry
Goldenweiser, Emanuel
     Alexander
Gould, Elgin Ralston Lovell
Gunton, George
Hadley, Arthur Twining
Hamilton, Walton Hale
Haynes, Williams
Hollander, Jacob Harry
Horton, Samuel Dana
Hoxie, Robert Franklin
James, Edmund James
Jenks. Jeremiah Whipple
Jordan, Virgil Justin
Kemmerer, Edwin Walter
Knauth, Oswald Whitman
Laughlin, James Laurence
Leiserson, William Morris
List, Georg Friedrich
Macfarlane, Charles WIlliam
McPherson, Logan Grant
McVey, Frank Lerond
McVickar. John
Mayo-Smith, Richmond
Millis, Harry Alvin
Mitchell, Wesley Clair
Moore, Henry Ludwell
Olds, Leland
Page, Thomas Walker
Parker, Carleton Hubbell
Pasvolsky, Leo
Patten, Simon Nelson
Perlman, Selig
Perry, Arthur Latham
Persons, Warren Milton
Pitkin, Timothy
Poor, Henry Varnum
Rae, John
Raguet, Condy
Remington, William Walter
Ripley, William Zebina
Robinson, Edward Van Dyke
Rogers, James Harvey
Schoenhof, Jacob
Schultz, Henry
Schumpeter, Joseph Alois
Schwab, John Christopher
Seager, Henry Rogers
Seligman, Edwin Robert
     Anderson
Shearman, Thomas Gaskell
Simons, Algie Martin
Simons, Henry Calvert
Slichter, Sumner Huber
Spahr, Charles Brazillai
Spillman, William Jasper
Stewart, Walter Winne
Sumner, William Graham

Gibbs, (Oliver) Wolcott
Gilder, Jeannette Leonard
Gilder, Richard Watson
Gildersleeve, Basil Lanneau
Giles, Chauncey
Gillis, James Martin
Gilpin, Henry Dilworth
Glass, Franklin Potts
Glynn, Martin Henry
Godkin, Edwin Lawrence
Godman, John Davison
Godwin, Parke
Goodhue, James Madison
Goodwin, Elijah
Gordon, Laura De Force
Gould, George Milbry
Graham, George Rex
Grasty, Charles Henry
Greeley, Horace
Green, Thomas
Greene, Nathaniel
Gregory, Daniel Seelye
Griffin, Solomon Bulkley
Griswold, Stanley
Grosvenor, Gilbert Hovey
Gunton, George
Habberton, John
Hackett, Francis
Hahn, Georg Michael Decker
Haines, Lynn
Haldeman-Julius, Emanuel
Hale, Edward Joseph
Hale, Sarah Josepha Buell
Hall, John Elihu
Hall, William Whitty
Hallett, Benjamin Franklin
Hanson, Alexander Contee,
    1786–1819
Hapgood, Norman
Harris, Chapin Aaron
Harris, Joseph
Hart, Edward
Hart, John Seely
Harvey, George Brinton
    McClellan
Hasbrouck, Lydia Sayer
Hasselquist, Tuve Nilsson
Haswell, Anthony
Haven, Emily Bradley Neal
Hawley, Joseph Roswell
Hayes, Max Sebastian
Hays, Isaac
Hazard, Ebenezer
Hazard, Samuel
Heaton, John Langdon
Helmer, Bessie Bradwell
Hepworth, George Hughes
Herbermann, Charles George
Herrick, Sophia McIlvaine
    Bledsoe
Hewett, Waterman Thomas
Hicks, John, 1847–1917
High, Stanley Hoflund
Hildreth, Richard
Hill, Isaac
Hinman, George Wheeler
Hinsdale, Burke Aaron
Hoard, William Dempster
Hobby, William Pettus
Hoffman, Charles Fenno
Holland, Josiah Gilbert
Holmes, Ezekiel

Holt, Hamilton Bowen
Hooker, Donald Russell
Hooper, Lucy Hamilton
Horr, George Edwin
Howard, Edgar
Howe, Mark Antony De Wolfe
Howell, Evan Park
Howell, James Bruen
Hubbard, Elbert
Hudson, Daniel Eldred
Hughes, Robert William
Hunt, Freeman
Hunt, William Gibbes
Huntington, Jedediah Vincent
Hunton, George Kenneth
Hunton, William Lee
Hurlbut, Jesse Lyman
Hutchinson, Paul
Hutton, Laurence
Inman, John
Jackson, Henry Rootes
Jackson, Joseph Henry
Jameson, John Franklin
Jarves, James Jackson
Jenkins, Howard Malcolm
Jenkins, John Stilwell
Jeter, Jeremiah Bell
Johnson, Allen
Johnson, John Albert
Johnson, Oliver
Johnson, Robert Underwood
Johnson, Willis Fletcher
Jones, Jenkins Lloyd
Jones, Thomas P.
Jordan, John Woolf
Jordan, William George
Joseffy, Rafael
Kaempffert, Waldemar
    Bernhard
Keating, John Marie
Kellogg, Paul Underwood
Kent, William
Kephart, Isaiah Lafayette
Kerney, James
Kettell, Samuel
Keyes, Frances Parkinson
King, Alexander
King, Charles
King, Horatio
King, Rufus
King of William, James
Kinsella, Thomas
Kirchoff, Charles William
    Henry
Kirk, John Foster
Kline, George
Knopf, Blanche Wolf
Kohlsaat, Herman Henry
Kreymborg, Alfred Francis
Kurtz, Benjamin
LaFarge, John
Lamb, Martha Joanna Reade
    Nash
Lamont, Hammond
Lane, Gertrude Battles
Lange, Louis
Lathrop, George Parsons
Lawson, James
Learned, Marion Dexter
Leavitt, Joshua
Lee, James Melvin
Lee, James Wideman

Leeser, Isaac
Levin, Lewis Charles
Lewis, Charlton Thomas
Lewis, Enoch
Lewisohn, Ludwig
Liggett, Walter William
Linn, William Alexander
Littell, Eliakim
Littledale, Clara Savage
Loos, Charles Louis
Lord, Chester Sanders
Lossing, Benson John
Loveman, Amy
Lovett, Robert Morss
Luce, Henry Robinson
Lummis, Charles Fletcher
Mabie, Hamilton Wright
McAdams, Clark
MacArthur, Robert Stuart
McCaw, James Brown
M'Clintock, John
McClure, Alexander Kelly
McClure, Alexander Wilson
McClure, Samuel Sidney
McCord, David James
McCullough, Ernest
McElroy, John
McKelway, St. Clair
McKinley, Albert Edward
Maclay, William Brown
McLeod, Alexander
McMichael, Morton
McPherson, Edward
McQuillen, John Hugh
Mansfield, Edward Deering
Marble, Manton Malone
Marsh, Charles Wesley
Martin, Franklin Henry
Martin, Thomas Commerford
Masson, Thomas Lansing
Mead, Edwin Doak
Medary, Samuel
Meigs, Josiah
Melcher, Frederic Gershom
Mencken, Henry Louis
Merrill, William Bradford
Metcalf, Henry Harrison
Mich, Daniel Danforth
Miller, Charles Ransom
Miller, David Hunter
Miller, Emily Clark Huntington
Miller, James Russell
Miller, John Henry
Miner, Charles
Minor, Benjamin Blake
Mitchell, Edward Page
Mitchell, Isaac
Mitchell, John Ames
Money, Hernando De Soto
Monroe, Harriet
Montgomery, William Bell
Moody, John
Moore, Frank
Moore, John Weeks
Morley, Christopher Darlington
Morris, Edmund
Morse, John Torrey
Morton, Charles Walter
Moses, Montrose Jonas
Mosessohn, David Nehemiah
Moss, Lemuel
Munn, Orson Desaix

Muñoz-Rivera, Luis
Nancrède, Paul Joseph Guérard de
Nast, William
Nathan, George Jean
Neal, John
Nelson, Henry Loomis
Nevin, Alfred
Newcomb, Harvey
Newell, William Wells
Newton, Robert Safford
Ng Poon Chew
Nichols, Clarina Irene Howard
Nichols, Thomas Low
Nicola, Lewis
Nieman, Lucius William
Niles, Hezekiah
Niles, John Milton
Nock, Albert Jay
North, Simon Newton Dexter
Northen, William Jonathan
Norton, Charles Eliot
Oakes, George Washington Ochs
O'Brien, Robert Lincoln
Ogg, Frederic Austin
Older, Fremont
O'Reilly, Henry
O'Reilly, John Boyle
Osborn, Norris Galpin
Otis, George Alexander
Oursler, (Charles) Fulton
Packard, Frederick Adolphus
Packer, William Fisher
Paley, John
Palfrey, John Gorham
Pallen, Condé Benoist
Palmore, William Beverly
Parkhurst, Charles
Passavant, William Alfred
Patterson, Robert Mayne
Patterson, Thomas MacDonald
Paul, Elliot Harold
Payne, John Howard
Peck, George
Peck, Harry Thurston
Pedder, James
Peirce, Bradford Kinney
Peloubet, Francis Nathan
Pendleton, William Kimbrough
Perché, Napoleon Joseph
Perkins, Frederic Beecher
Perkins, George Douglas
Perkins, Maxwell Evarts
Perry, Bliss
Peters, Absalom
Peterson, Charles Jacobs
Peterson, Henry
Phillips, John Sanburn
Pickard, Samuel Thomas
Pierson, Arthur Tappan
Pilcher, Lewis Stephen
Pinckney, Henry Laurens
Pinkerton, Lewis Letig
Pinkney, Edward Coote
Polk, Leonidas Lafayette
Pollak, Gustav
Pomeroy, Marcus Mills
Pond, George Edward
Poore, Benjamin Perley
Potter, William James
Powell, John Benjamin

Pratt, Eliza Anna Farman
Pratt, Sereno Stansbury
Presser, Theodore
Price, Thomas Frederick
Prime, Samuel Irenaeus
Pulitzer, Joseph, Jr.
Purple, Samuel Smith
Putnam, Eben
Quick, John Herbert
Raguet, Condy
Raymond, Henry Jarvis
Raymond, Rossiter Worthington
Redman, Ben Ray
Redpath, James
Reed, David
Reid, Gilbert
Reid, John Morrison
Reiersen, Johan Reinert
Reitzel, Robert
Rémy, Henri
Rhoades, James E.
Rice, Edwin Wilbur
Rideing, William Henry
Ripley, George
Robertson, James Alexander
Robinson, Charles Seymour
Robinson, Stuart
Rombro, Jacob
Ross, Charles Griffith
Ross, Harold Wallace
Rothwell, Richard Pennefather
Rowlands, William
Rublee, Horace
Rupp, William
Sanders, Daniel Jackson
Sanger, George Partridge
Sangster, Margaret Elizabeth Munson
Saunders, William Laurence
Sawyer, Thomas Jefferson
Saxton, Eugene Francis
Schem, Alexander Jacob
Schnauffer, Carl Heinrich
Schouler, William
Schultze, Augustus
Schuster, Max Lincoln
Schuyler, Robert Livingston
Schwimmer, Rosika
Scott, Harvey Whitefield
Screws, William Wallace
Scudder, Horace Elisha
Scull, John
Seymour, Horatio Winslow
Shattuck, George Brune
Shea, John Dawson Gilmary
Sherwood, Isaac Ruth
Shields, George Oliver
Shreve, Thomas Hopkins
Sigel, Franz
Silverman, Sime
Simpson, Stephen
Singerly, William Miskey
Singleton, Esther
Sloan, Harold Paul
Smalley, Eugene Virgil
Smith, Benjamin Eli
Smith, Charles Perrin
Smith, Edmund Munroe
Smith, Elias
Smith, Elihu Hubbard
Smith, John Augustine

Smith, John Cotton, 1826–1882
Smith, John Jay
Smith, Lillian Eugenia
Smith, Lloyd Pearsall
Smith, Samuel Francis
Smith, Uriah
Smyth, Albert Henry
Snow, Carmel White
Spahr, Charles Barzillai
Sparks, Jared
Spivak, Charles David
Spooner, Shearjashub
Sprague, Charles Arthur
Stanard, William Glover
Stanwood, Edward
Stauffer, David McNeely
Stedman, Edmund Clarence
Stephens, Ann Sophia
Stephens, Edwin William
Steuben, John
Stevens, Abel
Stoddard, Richard Henry
Stoddart, Joseph Marshall
Stone, David Marvin
Stone, Richard French
Storey, Wilbur Fisk
Stovall, Pleasant Alexander
Street, Joseph Montfort
Stuart, Charles Macaulay
Summers, Thomas Osmond
Swisshelm, Jane Grey Cannon
Talmage, Thomas De Witt
Taylor, Marshall William
Teall, Francis Augustus
Tenney, William Jewett
Thatcher, Benjamin Bussey
Thayer, Thomas Baldwin
Thayer, William Makepeace
Thomas, John Jacobs
Thomas, Robert Bailey
Thompson, John Reuben
Thompson, Joseph Parrish
Thompson, Thomas Larkin
Thompson, William Tappan
Thomson, Edward
Thomson, Edward William
Thrasher, John Sidney
Thurber, George
Thurston, Lorrin Andrews
Thwaites, Reuben Gold
Tigert, John James
Tilton, Theodore
Todd, Henry Alfred
Torrence, Frederick Ridgely
Towne, Charles Hanson
Tracy, Joseph
Trumbull, Henry Clay
Tucker, Gilbert Milligan
Turner, George Kibbe
Turner, Henry McNeal
Turner, Josiah
Tyler, Robert
Underwood, Benjamin Franklin
Updegraff, David Brainard
Vanderlip, Frank Arthur
Van Doren, Irita Bradford
Villard, Oswald Garrison
Vizetelly, Frank Horace
Vogrich, Max Wilhelm Karl
Walker, James Barr
Wallace, Henry
Waller, John Lightfoot

Walsh, Henry Collins
Walsh, Michael
Walsh, Thomas
Ward, Cyrenus Osborne
Ware, Ashur
Ware, John
Warner, Charles Dudley
Warren, Israel Perkins
Watson, Henry Clay
Watson, Henry Cood
Watterson, Harvey Magee
Watterson, Henry
Wellington, Arthur Mellen
Wentworth, John, 1815-1888
Wertenbaker, Charles Christian
Wharton, Francis
Whedon, Daniel Denison
Wheelock, Joseph Albert
Whelpley, Henry Milton
Whitaker, Charles Harris
Whitaker, Daniel Kimball
White, Charles Ignatius
White, William Allen
White, William Nathaniel
Whitney, Caspar
Whittelsey, Abigail Goodrich
Whittemore, Thomas
Wiggin, James Henry
Willcox, Louise Collier
Williams, Charles Richard
Williams, Jesse Lynch
Willis, Henry Parker
Willis, Nathaniel
Willis, Nathaniel Parker
Wilson, George Grafton
Wilson, James Grant
Wilson, James Southall
Winchester, Caleb Thomas
Winchevsky, Morris
Winkler, Edwin Theodore
Winship, Albert Edward
Wise, Daniel
Woodruff, Lorande Loss
Woodruff, William Edward
Worcester, Noah
Wright, John Stephen
Wright, Marcus Joseph
Wright, Robert William
Wurtz, Henry
Wyeth, John
Yeadon, Richard
Yost, Casper Salathiel
Youmans, Edward Livingston
Youmans, William Jay
Young, Jesse Bowman
Young, Lafayette
Zahniser, Howard Clinton
Zevin, Israel Joseph
Ziff, William Bernard

**EDITOR (AGRICULTURAL) (See also
AGRICULTURIST)**
Aiken, David Wyatt
Brown, Simon
Coburn, Foster Dwight
Gaylord, Willis
Judd, Orange
Myrick, Herbert
Skinner, John Stuart
Stockbridge, Horace Edward
Wiley, David

EDITOR (ANARCHIST)
Goldman, Emma
EDITOR (MAGAZINE)
Brady, Mildred Alice Edie
Lorimer, George Horace
Patrick, Edwin Hill ("Ted")
Patterson, Alicia
Sedgwick, Ellery
Woodward, Robert Simpson
EDITOR (MEDICAL)
Jelliffe, Smith Ely
Simmons, George Henry
EDITOR (NEWSPAPER)
Abbott, Robert Sengstacke
Bingay, Malcolm Wallace
Bovard, Oliver Kirby
Brokenshire, Norman Ernest
Freeman, Douglas Southall
Gauvreau, Emile Henry
Goddard, Morrill
Howard, Joseph Kinsey
Howe, Edgar Watson
Howell, Clark
Johnson, Albert
Lait, Jacquin Leonard (Jack)
McClatchy, Charles Kenny
Ogden, Rollo
Patterson, Eleanor Medill
Pulitzer, Ralph
Reid, Ogden Mills
Shedd, Fred Fuller
Smith, Henry Justin
EDITOR (SCIENCE)
Blakeslee, Howard Walter
Cattell, James McKeen
Woodward, Robert Simpson
**EDUCATOR (See also COLLEGE
PRESIDENT, PROFESSOR,
SCHOLAR, TEACHER)**
Abbot, Benjamin
Abbot, Gorham Dummer
Abbott, Edith
Abbott, Jacob
Adams, Daniel
Adams, Ebenezer
Adams, John
Adler, Felix
Agassiz, Elizabeth Cabot Cary
Aggrey, James Emman Kwegyir
Aiken, Charles Augustus
Akeley, Mary Leonore
Alcott, Amos Bronson
Alcott, William Andrus
Alden, Joseph
Alderman, Edwin Anderson
Aldrich, Charles Anderson
Alexander, Archibald
Alexander, Joseph Addison
Alison, Francis
Allen, Alexander Viets Griswold
Allen, George
Allen, William
Allen, Young John
Allinson, Anne Crosby Emery
Allyn, Robert
Alvord, Henry Elijah
Ames, Herman Vandenburg
Ames, James Barr
Anderson, David Lawrence
Anderson, Victor Vance
Andrews, John
Andrews, Lorrin

Andrus, Ethel Percy
Angela, Mother
Anthon, Charles Edward
Apple, Thomas Gilmore
Appleton, Jesse
Armstrong, Samuel Chapman
Arnold, Thurman Wesley
Atkinson, George Henry
Atwater, Lyman Hotchkiss
Azarias, Brother
Backus, Truman Jay
Bagley, William Chandler
Bailey, Ebenezer
Bailey, Liberty Hyde
Baker, Daniel
Baldwin, Elihu Whittlesey
Baldwin, Joseph
Baldwin, Theron
Bancroft, Cecil Franklin Patch
Banister, Zilpah Polly Grant
Bapst, John
Barbour, Clarence Augustus
Bardeen, Charles William
Barnard, Henry
Barnes, Mary Downing Sheldon
Barnwell, Robert Woodward
Barrett, Janie Porter
Bateman, Newton
Bates, Arlo
Bates, Katharine Lee
Bates, Samuel Penniman
Baxter, William
Beadle, William Henry
   Harrison
Beals, Ralph Albert
Beard, Mary
Beard, Richard
Beatty, Willard Walcott
Beckwith, Clarence Augustine
Beecher, Catharine Esther
Beers, Henry Augustin
Bell, Alexander Graham
Bell, Alexander Melville
Bell, Bernard Iddings
Bell, Eric Temple
Bemis, Harold Edward
Benedict, Erastus Cornelius
Benson, Oscar Herman
Benton, Thomas Hart
Berry, Edward Wilber
Berry, Martha McChesney
Bestor, Arthur Eugene
Bickmore, Albert Smith
Bigelow, Harry Augustus
Bigelow, Melville Madison
Bingham, William
Binkley, Wilfred Ellsworth
Bishop, Nathan
Bishop, Robert Hamilton
Blalock, Alfred
Blaustein, David
Bliss, Daniel
Bliss, Gilbert Ames
Bliss, Howard Sweetser
Bode, Boyd Henry
Bond, Elizabeth Powell
Bonney, Charles Carroll
Bosworth, Edward Increase
Bourne, Edward Gaylord
Bowden, John
Bowman, Thomas
Boyce, James Petigru

Boyd, David French
Boyd, Thomas Duckett
Boyesen, Hjalmar Hjorth
Brace, John Pierce
Brackett, Anna Callender
Brackett, Jeffrey Richardson
Bradford, Edward Hickling
Bradley, Charles Henry
Brainard, Daniel
Brainerd, Ezra
Brattle, William
Breaux, Joseph Arsenne
Briggs, LeBaron Russell
Brigham, Mary Ann
Brightman, Edgar Sheffield
Bronson, Walter Cochrane
Brookings, Robert Somers
Brooks, Charles
Brough, Charles Hillman
Brown, Charles Rufus
Brown, Charlotte Hawkins
Brown, George
Brown, George Pliny
Brown, Samuel Robbins
Browne, William Hand
Bruce, Robert
Brumby, Richard Trapier
Bryant, Joseph Decatur
Bryant, Ralph Clement
Bryson, Lyman Lloyd
Buchanan, Joseph
Buchanan, Scott Milross
Buehler, Huber Gray
Bulkley, John Williams
Bumstead, Horace
Burk, Frederic Lister
Burleson, Rufus Clarence
Burnam, John Miller
Burr, William Hubert
Burroughs, John Curtis
Burrowes, Thomas Henry
Burt, Mary Elizabeth
Buttrick, Wallace
Buttz, Henry Anson
Cabell, James Lawrence
Cady, Sarah Louise Ensign
Caldwell, Otis William
Calhoun, William Barron
Calkins, Norman Allison
Camp, David Nelson
Canby, Henry Seidel
Canfield, James Hulme
Cannon, James
Capen, Samuel Paul
Carmichael, Oliver Cromwell
Carnap, Rudolf
Carpenter, George Rice
Carpenter, Stephen Haskins
Carter, James Gordon
Carver, George Washington
Chamberlain, Joshua Lawrence
Chamberlin, Edward Hastings
Chandler, Julian Alvin Carroll
Channing, Edward Tyrrell
Chase, Harry Woodburn
Chase, Irah
Chavis, John
Cheever, Ezekiel
Church, Alonzo
Church, Irving Porter
Clark, Felton Grandison
Claypole, Edward Waller

Clement, Rufus Early
Clewell, John Henry
Cloud, Henry Roe
Cobb, Lyman
Coe, George Albert
Coffin, Henry Sloane
Coffman, Lotus Delta
Colburn, Dana Pond
Coleman, Lyman
Colton, Elizabeth Avery
Colvin, Stephen Sheldon
Conklin, Edwin Grant
Conover, Obadiah Milton
Cook, George Hammell
Cook, John Williston
Cooley, Edwin Gilbert
Cooley, Mortimer Elwyn
Cooper, Thomas
Cooper, William John
Cooper-Poucher, Matilda S.
Coppée, Henry
Coppens, Charles
Cox, Samuel Hanson
Craig, Austin
Craighead, Edwin Boone
Crandall, Prudence
Crary, Isaac Edwin
Crooks, George Richard
Crunden, Frederick Morgan
Cubberley, Ellwood Patterson
Curry, Jabez Lamar Monroe
Curtis, Edwards Lewis
Dagg, John Leadley
Darby, John
Dawley, Almena
Day, Edmund Ezra
Day, Henry Noble
Day, James Roscoe
Day, Jeremiah
Dean, Amos
Denny, George Vernon, Jr.
Deutsch, Gotthard
Dewey, Chester
Dewey, John
Dickinson, John
Dickinson, John Woodbridge
Dickson, Leonard Eugene
Dillard, James Hardy
Diman, Jeremiah Lewis
Dimitry, Alexander
Dinwiddie, Albert Bledsoe
Doak, Samuel
Dod, Thaddeus
Dodge, Ebenezer
Donovan, James Britt
Dorchester, Daniel
Dove, David James
Downey, John
Draper, Andrew Sloan
Drinker, Cecil Kent
Drisler, Henry
Drown, Thomas Messinger
Dunham, Henry Morton
Dutton, Samuel Train
Dwight, Benjamin Woodbridge
Dwight, Francis
Dwight, Nathaniel
Dwight, Sereno Edwards
Dwight, Theodore, 1796–1866
Dwight, Theodore William
Dwight, Timothy
Dyer, Isadore

Dykstra, Clarence Addison
Earle, Edward Mead
Earle, Mortimer Lamson
Earle, Ralph
Eastman, Harvey Gridley
Eaton, Amos
Eaton, John
Edwards, Ninian Wirt
Eigenmann, Carl H.
Eliot, Charles William
Elman, Robert
Elvehjem, Conrad Arnold
Emerson, Benjamin Kendall
Emerson, George Barrell
Emerson, Joseph
Emerton, Ephraim
Erdman, Charles Rosenbury
Esbjörn, Lars Paul
Espy, James Pollard
Ewell, Benjamin Stoddert
Fairchild, Fred Rogers
Fairchild, George Thompson
Fairchild, James Harris
Fairfield, Edmund Burke
Fairlie, John Archibald
Fanning, Tolbert
Fay, Sidney Bradshaw
Ferguson, John Calvin
Ferris, Woodbridge Nathan
Fess, Simeon Davidson
Few, William Preston
Fillebrown, Thomas
Finley, John Huston
Finley, Robert
Finn, Francis James
Finney, Charles Grandison
Fisher, Ebenezer
Fisk, Wilbur
Fiske, George Converse
Fite, Warner
Fitzpatrick, Morgan Cassius
Fleming, Walter Lynwood
Fletcher, Robert
Flexner, Abraham
Follen, Charles
Ford, Guy Stanton
Fortier, Alcée
Foss, Cyrus David
Foster, George Burman
Fowle, William Bentley
Frame, Alice Seymour Browne
Francis, Convers
Frank, Philipp G.
Frazier, Edward Franklin
Frear, William
Friedlaender, Walter Ferdinand
Frissell, Hollis Burke
Fuertes, Estevan Antonio
Furman, Richard
Furst, Clyde Bowman
Gale, George Washington
Galloway, Samuel
Gambrell, James Bruton
Garland, Landon Cabell
Garnet, Henry Highland
Garnett, James Mercer
Garrett, William Robertson
Gasson, Thomas Ignatius
Gates, George Augustus
Gauss, Christian Frederick
Giddings, Franklin Henry

Giesler-Anneke, Mathilde Franziska
Gildersleeve, Virginia Crocheron
Gill, Laura Drake
Gillespie, William Mitchell
Gillett, Ezra Hall
Gilman, Arthur
Gilmer, Francis Walker
Going, Jonathan
Goldbeck, Robert
Goodale, George Lincoln
Goodell, Henry Hill
Goodnow, Isaac Tichenor
Goodrich, Annie Warburton
Goodrich, Chauncey Allen
Goodrich, Elizur
Goodspeed, Thomas Wakefield
Gordy, John Pancoast
Goss, James Walker
Gove, Aaron Estellus
Grady, Henry Francis
Graham, Evarts Ambrose
Gray, John Chipman
Gray, William Scott, Jr.
Green, Lewis Warner
Green, Samuel Bowdlear
Greene, Charles Ezra
Greene, George Washington
Greene, Samuel Stillman
Greener, Richard Theodore
Greenlaw, Edwin Almiron
Greenleaf, Benjamin
Gregg, Alan
Gregory, Charles Noble
Gregory, Daniel Seelye
Gregory, John Milton
Griffis, William Elliot
Grimké, Thomas Smith
Gros, John Daniel
Gross, Charles
Grossmann, Louis
Guérin, Anne-Thérèse
Guilford, Nathan
Gurney, Ephraim Whitman
Guthe, Karl Eugen
Haas, Francis Joseph
Haddock, Charles Brickett
Hale, Benjamin
Hall, Arethusa
Hall, Baynard Rush
Hall, Granville Stanley
Hall, Samuel Read
Hall, Willard
Hallowell, Benjamin
Hamlin, Cyrus
Hamlin, Talbot Faulkner
Hammond, William Gardiner
Hanus, Paul Henry
Hare, George Emlen
Harlow, Ralph Volney
Harper, William Rainey
Harpur, Robert
Harrell, John
Harrington, Charles
Harris, George
Harris, Samuel
Harris, William Torrey
Harrison, Charles Custis
Hart, Edward
Hart, John Seely
Hartranft, Chester David

Hasselquist, Tuve Nilsson
Haven, Erastus Otis
Hawkins, Dexter Arnold
Hawley, Gideon, 1785–1870
Hawley, Willis Chatman
Hayden, Amos Sutton
Haygood, Atticus Green
Heiss, Michael
Henck, John Benjamin
Henry, Caleb Sprague
Henry, Robert
Hewett, Waterman Thomas
Hibben, John Grier
Hill, Daniel Harvey
Hill, Frank Alpine
Hill, Henry Barker
Hill, John Henry
Hill, Patty Smith
Hill, Walter Barnard
Hills, Elijah Clarence
Himes, Charles Francis
Hinman, George Wheeler
Hinsdale, Burke Aaron
Hitchcock, Edward, 1793–1864
Hitchcock, Edward, 1828–1911
Hitchcock, Roswell Dwight
Hocking, William Ernest
Hoerr, Normand Louis
Hoffman, Eugene Augustus
Hoge, Moses
Hogue, Wilson Thomas
Holbrook, Alfred
Holcombe, James Philemon
Holland, William Jacob
Holley, Horace
Hollis, Ira Nelson
Holmes, Ezekiel
Holmes, George Frederick
Hope, John
Hopkins, Isaac Stiles
Hopkins, Mark
Horr, George Edwin
Hoshour, Samuel Klinefelter
Houston, David Franklin
Houston, Edwin James
Hovey, Alvah
Hovey, Charles Edward
Howard, Ada Lydia
Howe, George
Howe, Herbert Alonzo
Howland, Emily
Hoyt, John Wesley
Huber, Gotthelf Carl
Humphreys, Alexander Crombie
Hunt, Carleton
Hunt, Mary Hannah Hanchett
Hunt, Nathan
Hunter, Thomas
Huntington, Margaret Jane Evans
Hutchins, Harry Burns
Hyde, William DeWitt
Inglis, Alexander James
Irvine, William Mann
Irwin, Elisabeth Antoinette
Irwin, Robert Benjamin
Jackman, Wilbur Samuel
Jackson, Dugald Caleb
Jackson, Edward Payson
Jackson, Mercy Ruggles Bisbe
Jacobi, Mary Corinna Putnam

Jacobs, Michael
Jacobson, John Christian
Janes, Lewis George
Jaquess, James Frazier
Jardine, William Marion
Jay, Allen
Jeffrey, Edward Charles
Jesse, Richard Henry
Jessup, Walter Albert
Jewett, Milo Parker
Johnson, Charles Spurgeon
Johnson, David Bancroft
Johnson, Edward Austin
Johnson, Ellen Cheney
Johnson, Franklin
Johnson, George
Johnson, James Weldon
Johnson, Joseph French
Johnson, Wendell Andrew Leroy
Johnson, William Bullein
Johnston, Henry Phelps
Johnston, Richard Malcolm
Johnston, Robert Matteson
Johnston, William Preston
Johnstone, Edward Ransom
Jones, Richard Foster
Jones, William Patterson
Joynes, Edward Southey
Judson, Harry Pratt
Julia, Sister
Junkin, George
Kafer, John Christian
Keagy, John Miller
Keener, William Albert
Keep, Robert Porter
Kefauver, Grayson Neikirk
Kent, Charles Foster
Key, Valdimer Orlando, Jr.
Kidder, Daniel Parish
Kilpatrick, William Heard
Kimball, Dexter Simpson
King, Henry Churchill
Kingsbury, John
Kingsley, James Luce
Kinnicutt, Leonard Parker
Kirby-Smith, Edmund
Kirchwey, George Washington
Kirkland, James Hampton
Knox, George William
Knox, Samuel
Kohlmann, Anthony
Krapp, George Philip
Kraus, John
Kraus-Boelté, Maria
Krauth, Charles Porterfield
Krüsi, Johann Heinrich Hermann
La Borde, Maximilian
Lacy, Drury
Lacy, Ernest
Lamont, Hammond
Lane, James Henry
Langdon, Courtney
Lange, Alexis Frederick
Langley, John Williams
Langston, John Mercer
Larkin, John
Larrabee, William Clark
Larsen, Peter Laurentius
Latané, John Holladay
Lathrop, John Hiram

Latourette, Kenneth Scott
Law, Evander McIvor
Laws, Samuel Spahr
Lawson, Andrew Cowper
Leach, Daniel Dyer
Leathers, Waller Smith
Lee, George Washington Custis
Lee, Stephen Dill
Leipziger, Henry Marcus
Leland, George Adams
Leonard, Levi Washburn
Leonard, Robert Josselyn
Leonard, Sterling Andrus
Levermore, Charles Herbert
Lewis, Clarence Irving
Lewis, Enoch
Lewis, Exum Percival
Lewis, Oscar
Lewis, Samuel
Lieber, Francis
Lindeman, Eduard Christian
Lindsley, John Berrien
Lindsley, Philip
Lipman, Jacob Goodale
Listemann, Bernhard
Littlefield, George Washington
Livingston, John Henry
Locke, Alain Leroy
Locke, Bessie
Longcope, Warfield Theobald
Longstreet, Augustus Baldwin
Lord, Asa Dearborn
Lord, Chester Sanders
Loughridge, Robert McGill
Lovell, John Epy
Lovett, Robert Morss
Lowes, John Livingston
Lowrey, Mark Perrin
Luce, Henry Winters
Lutkin, Peter Christian
Lyon, David Gordon
Lyon, Mary
Maas, Anthony J.
McAfee, John Armstrong
MacAlister, James
McAnally, David Rice
McAndrew, William
McAuley, Thomas
McCaleb, Theodore Howard
McCartee, Divie Bethune
McCartney, Washington
McClellan, Henry Brainerd
McClenahan, Howard
M'Clintock, John
McCook, John James
McCormick, Samuel Black
MacCracken, Henry Mitchell
McDonald, James Grover
McDowell, John
McFarland, John Thomas
McFarland, Samuel Gamble
McGarvey, John William
McGuffey, William Holmes
McHale, Kathryn
McIver, Charles Duncan
Mackenzie, James Cameron
McKenzie, Robert Tait
MacLean, George Edwin
Maclean, John
McMurry, Frank Morton
MacVicar Malcolm
Mahan, Dennis Hart

Mahan, Milo
Main, John Hanson Thomas
Malcom, Howard
Manly, Basil, 1798–1868
Manly, Basil, 1825–1892
Mann, Horace
Mann, Mary Tyler Peabody
Mannes, Clara Damrosch
Mannes, David
Marble, Albert Prescott
Marks, Elias
Marshall, James Fowle Baldwin
Martin, Everett Dean
Martin, William Alexander
  Parsons
Mason, John Mitchell
Maxwell, William Henry
Mayo, Amory Dwight
Meany, Edmond Stephen
Mears, John William
Meigs, John
Meigs, Josiah
Meiklejohn, Alexander
Mell, Patrick Hues
Mendenhall, Thomas Corwin
Menetrey, Joseph
Mengarini, Gregory
Mercer, Margaret
Merrick, Frederick
Merrill, James Griswold
Messer, Asa
Mezes, Sidney Edward
Michel, Virgil George
Michie, Peter Smith
Middleton, Thomas Cooke
Milledoler, Philip
Miller, Emily Clark Huntington
Miller, Kelly
Miller, Leslie William
Miller, Samuel
Milligan, Robert
Millikan, Robert Andrews
Mills, Cyrus Taggart
Mills, Susan Lincoln Tolman
Miner, Myrtilla
Minor, Benjamin Blake
Minot, Charles Sedgwick
Mitchell, Albert Graeme
Mitchell, Lucy Sprague
Molyneux, Robert
Monis, Judah
Monroe, Paul
Montague, William Pepperell
Mood, Francis Asbury
Moody, William Vaughn
Moore, James, 1764–1814
Moore, Joseph Earle
Morgan, Thomas Jefferson
Morley, Margaret Warner
Morris, Edward Dafydd
Morris, George Sylvester
Morrison, John Irwin
Morse, Anson Daniel
Morton, Robert Russa
Mosher, Eliza Maria
Moss, Lemuel
Mott, Frank Luther
Mowry, William Augustus
Mullins, Edgar Young
Munro, William Bennett
Murfee, James Thomas
Murray, David

Muste, Abraham Johannes
Muzzey, David Saville
Nash, Charles Sumner
Nason, Henry Bradford
Neef, Francis Joseph Nicholas
Neill, Edward Duffield
Neill, William
Nelson, David
Nelson, Reuben
Nevin, Edwin Henry
Nevin, John Williamson
Newlon, Jesse Homer
Newman, Albert Henry
Nicholls, Rhoda Holmes
Niebuhr, Helmut Richard
Nobili, John
Norris, Mary Harriott
Norsworthy, Naomi
North, Edward
North, Simeon, 1802–1884
Northend, Charles
Northrop, Birdsey Grant
Norton, John Pitkin
Noss, Theodore Bland
Notestein, Wallace
Nott, Henry Junius
Notz, Frederick William
  Augustus
Noyes, Clara Dutton
Nutting, Mary Adelaide
O'Callahan, Joseph Timothy
Odell, George Clinton
  Densmore
Ogden, Robert Curtis
O'Gorman, Thomas
Olin, Stephen
Orcutt, Hiram
Orr, Gustavus John
Orton, Edward Francis Baxter
Orton, James
Osborn, Henry Fairfield
O'Shea, Michael Vincent
Overstreet, Harry Allen
Owen, Edward Thomas
Owre, Alfred
Pace, Edward Aloysius
Packard, Silas Sadler
Page, David Perkins
Page, Leigh
Palmer, Alice Elvira Freeman
Palmer, Walter Walker
Pardow, William O'Brien
Park, Roswell
Parker, Amasa Junius
Parker, Francis Wayland
Parker, Samuel Chester
Parrish, Celestia Susannah
Partridge, Alden
Patri, Angelo
Patterson, James Kennedy
Patterson, James Willis
Payne, Bruce Ryburn
Payne, William Harold
Peabody, Cecil Hobart
Peabody, Elizabeth Palmer
Peabody, Endicott
Peabody, Selim Hobart
Pearce, Richard Mills
Pearson, Eliphalet
Peers, Benjamin Orrs
Peirce, Cyrus
Peirce, James Mills

Pendleton, James Madison
Penniman, James Hosmer
Pepper, William
Perkins, George Henry
Perry, Ralph Barton
Perry, Rufus Lewis
Perry, Thomas Sergeant
Perry, Walter Scott
Perry, William Flake
Phelps, Almira Hart Lincoln
Phelps, William Franklin
Pickens, William
Pierce, George Foster
Pierce, John Davis
Pinney, Norman
Poor, John
Porter, Ebenezer
Porter, James Davis
Porter, Noah
Post, Truman Marcellus
Potamian, Brother
Powell, John Wesley
Powell, William Bramwell
Pratt, Richard Henry
Priestley, James
Priestley, Joseph
Prosser, Charles Smith
Proud, Robert
Puryear, Bennet
Putnam, Helen Cordelia
Quinby, Isaac Ferdinand
Quinn, Arthur Hobson
Rademacher, Hans
Rambaut, Mary Lucinda
   Bonney
Randall, Henry Stephens
Randall, Samuel Sidwell
Rauch, Frederick Augustus
Rautenstrauch, Walter
Raymond, George Lansing
Raymond, Miner
Read, Daniel, 1805–1878
Redfield, Robert
Regan, Agnes Gertrude
Reichel, Charles Gotthold
Reichel, William Cornelius
Reichenbach, Hans
Reid, David Boswell
Reid, Ira De Augustine
Reid, William Shields
Reilly, Marion
Reinsch, Paul Samuel
Remsen, Ira
Reuter, Dominic
Revel, Bernard
Revels, Hiram Rhoades
Rice, John Holt
Rice, Luther
Rice, Victor Moreau
Rice, William North
Richard, Gabriel
Richard, James William
Richards, Zalmon
Richardson, Tobias Gibson
Ricketts, Palmer Chamberlaine
Ridpath, John Clark
Riley, Benjamin Franklin
Roark, Rurio Nevel
Robb, William Lispenard
Roberts, William Charles
Robertson, Alice Mary
Robertson, William Schenck

Robins, Henry Ephraim
Robinson, Ezekiel Gilman
Robinson, George Canby
Robinson, Stillman Williams
Robinson, William Callyhan
Rogers, Henry Darwin
Rogers, Henry Wade
Rogers, James Blythe
Rogers, John Almanza Rowley
Rogers, Robert Empie
Rogers William Barton
Rohé, George Henry
Rölvaag, Ole Edvart
Ross, Denman Waldo
Rowson, Susanna Haswell
Ruffner, Henry
Ruffner, William Henry
Rugg, Harold Ordway
Russell, James Earl
Russell, James Solomon
Russell, William
Russwurm, John Brown
Rust, Richard Sutton
Ruter, Martin
Ryland, Robert
Saarinen, Gottlieb Eliel
Sachs, Julius
Safford, James Merrill
St. John, Charles Edward
Salisbury, Albert
Salisbury, Rollin D.
Salmon, Lucy Maynard
Sanborn, Edwin David
Sanders, Billington McCarter
Sanders, Charles Walton
Sanders, Daniel Clarke
Sanders, Daniel Jackson
Sartain, Emily
Sawyer, Thomas Jefferson
Scarborough, Lee Rutland
Schaeffer, Nathan Christ
Schlatter, Michael
Schmucker, Samuel Simon
Schodde, George Henry
Schultze, Augustus
Schuyler, Robert Livingston
Scopes, John Thomas
Scott, Austin
Scott, Emmett Jay
Scott, Walter Dill
Scott, William Anderson
Scovell, Melville Amasa
Sears, Barnas
Seelye, Julius Hawley
Shafer, Helen Almira
Shahan, Thomas Joseph
Shaler, Nathaniel Southgate
Sharp, Dallas Lore
Shaw, Edward Richard
Sheldon, Edward Austin
Sheldon, William Evarts
Shellabarger, Samuel
Sherman, Stuart Pratt
Sherwin, Thomas
Sherwood, Adiel
Shields, Thomas Edward
Shipp, Albert Micajah
Shipp, Scott
Shoup, Francis Asbury
Skinner, Charles Rufus
Skinner, Thomas Harvey
Slade, William

Sloane, William Milligan
Smart, James Henry
Smiley, Albert Keith
Smith, Alexander
Smith, Benjamin Mosby
Smith, Charles Alphonso
Smith, Charles Sprague
Smith, Courtney Craig
Smith, Daniel B.
Smith, David Eugene
Smith, Francis Henney
Smith, Harold Babbitt
Smith, Henry Louis
Smith, Judson
Smith, Lucy Harth
Smith, Richard Somers
Smith, William, 1727–1803
Smith, William Waugh
Smyth, Albert Henry
Smyth, John Henry
Snider, Denton Jaques
Snow, Francis Huntington
Snyder, Edwin Reagan
Soldan, Frank Louis
Son of Many Beads
Sorin, Edward Frederick
Soulé, George
Spaeth, John Duncan
Spalding, John Lancaster
Spangler, Henry Wilson
Sparrow, William
Spencer, Anna Garlin
Spencer, Jesse Ames
Sperry, Willard Learoyd
Sprague, Homer Baxter
Sprecher, Samuel
Stahr, John Summers
Stang, William
Stanley, Albert Augustus
Staughton, William
Stearns, Eben Sperry
Steele, Joel Dorman
Stengel, Alfred
Stephens, Henry Morse
Sterling, John Whalen
Stetson, William Wallace
Stevens, George Barker
Stevens, George Washington
Stillé, Charles Janeway
Stillman, Thomas Bliss
Stockbridge, Levi
Stoddard, John Fair
Stoek, Harry Harkness
Stoever, Martin Luther
Stokes, Anson Phelps
Stone, James Kent
Stone, John Seely
Stowe, Calvin Ellis
Strong, Richard Pearson
Stuart, Charles Macaulay
Sturtevant, Julian Monson
Summerall, Charles Pelot
Sumner, William Graham
Sunderland, Eliza Jane Read
Sutton, William Seneca
Suzzallo, Henry
Sverdrup, Georg
Swensson, Carl Aaron
Swett, John
Talbot, Arthur Newell
Tappan, Eli Todd

Taylor, Archibald Alexander
 Edward
Taylor, Nathaniel William
Taylor, Samuel Harvey
Tenney, Charles Daniel
Tenney, Edward Payson
Terrell, Mary Eliza Church
Terry, Milton Spenser
Thayer, Eli
Thayer, Gideon French
Thayer, Sylvanus
Thébaud, Augustus J.
Thoburn, Isabella
Thomas, Elbert Duncan
Thomas, Joseph
Thomas, Martha Carey
Thompson, Benjamin
Thompson, Charles Oliver
Thompson, Hugh Smith
Thompson, John Bodine
Thompson, Robert Ellis
Thompson, Samuel Rankin
Thurston, Robert Henry
Tichenor, Isaac Taylor
Ticknor, Elisha
Ticknor, George
Tomlinson, Everett Titsworth
Tompkins, Arnold
Toulmin, Harry
Townsend, Luther Tracy
Trowbridge, John
Trowbridge, William Petit
Trueblood, Benjamin Franklin
Tucker, William Jewett
Turner, Asa
Turner, Jonathan Baldwin
Turner, Samuel Hulbeart
Turner, William
Tutwiler, Henry
Tutwiler, Julia Strudwick
Tyler, Bennet
Tyler, Moses Coit
Vail, Stephen Montfort
Valentine, Milton
Van Lennep, Henry John
Van Meter, John Blackford
Van Quickenborne, Charles
 Felix
Varela y Morales, Félix
 Francisco José María de la
 Concepción
Vawtor, Charles Erastus
Venable, Charles Scott
Verbeck, William
Verhaegen, Peter Joseph
Vincent, George Edgar
Vincent, John Heyl
Vose, George Leonard
Waddel, John Newton
Wadsworth, James
Walker, Francis Amasa
Wallace, Charles William
Walsh, Edmund Aloysius
Ward, Harry Frederick
Ward, Joseph
Ware, Edmund Asa
Ware, John
Warren, William Fairfield
Warthin, Aldred Scott
Washburn, Edward Wight
Washburn, George
Washington, Booker Taliaferro

Waterhouse, Sylvester
Waters, William Everett
Watson, Charles Roger
Watson, William
Wayland, Francis, 1796–1865
Webb, William Robert
Welch, Adonijah Strong
Welling, James Clarke
Welling, Richard Ward Greene
Wells, William Harvey
Wergeland, Agnes Mathilde
Wesbrook, Frank Fairchild
Wesselhoeft, Conrad
Wheaton, Nathaniel Sheldon
Wheeler, William
White, Emerson Elbridge
Whiton, James Morris
Whitworth, George Frederic
Wickersham, James Pyle
Widney, Joseph Pomeroy
Wigglesworth, Edward,
 1693–1765
Wigglesworth, Edward,
 1732–1794
Wigmore, John Henry
Wilbur, Hervey Backus
Wilczynski, Ernest Julius
Wilder, Russell Morse
Wiley, Calvin Henderson
Wiley, Ephraim Emerson
Wilkinson, Robert Shaw
Will, Allen Sinclair
Willard, Emma Hart
Willard, Samuel
Willard, Sidney
Willebrandt, Mabel Walker
Willey, Samuel Hopkins
Williams, John Elias
Williams, Robert
Williston, Samuel
Wilson, James Southall
Wilson, Peter
Wilson, William Dexter
Wilson, William Lyne
Wines, Enoch Cobb
Wirt, William Albert
Witherspoon, Alexander
 Maclaren
Witherspoon, John Alexander
Wolfe, Harry Kirke
Wood, James
Wood, Thomas Bond
Woodbridge, Frederick James
 Eugene
Woodbridge, William Channing
Woodward, Calvin Milton
Woolsey, Theodore Dwight
Woolsey, Theodore Salisbury
Wright, Jonathan Jasper
Wright, Richard Robert
Wyckoff, John Henry
Wyeth, John Allan
Wylie, Andrew
Wylie, Samuel Brown
Yale, Caroline Ardelia
Yeomans, John William
Youmans, Edward Livingston
Young, Clark Montgomery
Young, Ella Flagg
Young, John Clarke
Zachos, John Celivergos
Zollars, Ely Vaughn

Zook, George Frederick
EFFICIENCY EXPERT
Fascist Collaborator
 Bedaux, Charles Eugene
EGYPTOLOGIST (See also SCHOLAR)
 Breasted, James Henry
 McCauley, Edward Yorke
 Reisner, George Andrew
 Selikovitsch, Goetzel
 Winlock, Herbert Eustis
ELECTRIC POWER ADMINISTRATOR
 Ross, James Delmage McKenzie
ELECTRICAL ENGINEER (See ENGINEER, ELECTRICAL)
ELECTRICIAN (See also ENGINEER, ELECTRICAL)
 Farmer, Moses Gerrish
 Pope, Franklin Leonard
ELECTROTHERAPIST (See also PHYSICIAN)
 Rockwell, Alphonso David
EMBRYOLOGIST (See also BIOLOGIST, PHYSICIAN, ZOOLOGIST)
 Mall, Franklin Paine
 Streeter, George Linius
 Wilson, Edmund Beecher
EMIGRATION AGENT
 Mattson, Hans
ENCYCLOPEDIST (See also COMPILER, SCHOLAR)
 Heilprin, Michael
 Mackey, Albert Gallatin
 Schem, Alexander Jacob
ENDOCRINOLOGIST (See also PHYSICIAN)
 Timme, Walter
ENGINEER (See also SPECIFIC TYPES)
 Allen, Jeremiah Mervin
 Allen, John F.
 Argall, Philip
 Babcock, George Herman
 Babcock, Orville E.
 Bailey, Frank Harvey
 Bailey, Joseph
 Ball, Albert
 Barnes, James
 Barrell, Joseph
 Bayles, James Copper
 Bell, Louis
 Benham, Henry Washington
 Benjamin, George Hillard
 Black, William Murray
 Bogart, John
 Bonzano, Adolphus
 Boyden, Uriah Atherton
 Broadhead, Garland Carr
 Burr, William Hubert
 Cass, George Washington
 Colles, Christopher
 Coney, Jabez
 Crozet, Claude
 Curtis, Samuel Ryan
 Daniels, Fred Harris
 Davis, George Whitefield
 De Lacy, Walter Washington
 De Leeuw, Adolph Lodewyk
 Dickie, George William
 Dod, Daniel
 Douglass, David Bates
 Dripps, Isaac L.
 Dunbar, Robert

Durfee, William Franklin
Durham, Caleb Wheeler
Eads, James Buchanan
Eastman, William Reed
Eckart, William Roberts
Eimbeck, William
Ellicott, Joseph
Emery, Albert Hamilton
Emery, Charles Edward
Ericsson, John
Ernst, Oswald Herbert
Eustis, Henry Lawrence
Field, Charles William
Flad, Henry
Ford, Hannibal Choate
Forney, Matthias Nace
Frasch, Herman
Fuertes, Estevan Antonio
Furlow, Floyd Charles
Gaillard, David Du Bose
Gantt, Henry Laurence
Gardiner, James Terry
Gaskill, Harvey Freeman
Gayley, James
Goethals, George Washington
Graff, Frederick
Greene, Francis Vinton
Grinnell, Frederick
Guthrie, Alfred
Hallidie, Andrew Smith
Hamilton, Schuyler
Harris, Daniel Lester
Haswell, Charles Haynes
Hebert, Louis
Henck, John Benjamin
Hickenlooper, Andrew
Hornblower, Josiah
Humphreys, Andrew Atkinson
Hunt, Alfred Ephraim
Hutton, Frederick Remsen
Jadwin, Edgar
James, Charles Tillinghast
Jervis, John Bloomfield
Jones, William Richard
Judah, Theodore Dehone
Kafer, John Christian
Kármán, Theodore (Todor)
    Von
Kerr, Walter Craig
Lamme, Benjamin Garver
La Tour, Le Blond de
Latrobe, Benjamin Henry,
    1764–1820
Lefferts, Marshall
L'Enfant, Pierre Charles
Léry, Joseph Gaspard
    Chaussegros de
Lewis, William Gaston
Long, Stephen Harriman
Lucas, Anthony Francis
Ludlow, William
Lundie, John
McCallum, Daniel Craig
Macfarlane, Charles William
Mangin, Joseph François
Marshall, William Louis
Mason, Arthur John
Maxim, Hiram Stevens
Meigs, Montgomery
    Cunningham
Merrill, William Emery
Miller, Ezra

Millington, John
Mills, Robert, 1781–1855
Mitchell, Henry
Mordecai, Alfred
Morell, George Webb
Morgan, Charles Hill
Morris, Thomas Armstrong
Morton, James St. Clair
Murray, Thomas Edward
Newton, John
Ockerson, John Augustus
Ogden, Francis Barber
Packard, James Ward
Painter, William
Palfrey, John Carver
Pardee, Ario
Parker, Ely Samuel
Parsons, William Barclay
Patterson, Richard
    Cunningham, Jr.
Pauger, Adrien de
Paul, Henry Martyn
Pearson, Fred Stark
Peters, Edward Dyer
Poe, Orlando Metcalfe
Reid, David Boswell
Renwick, Henry Brevoort
Renwick, James, 1792–1863
Reynolds, Edwin
Rice, Richard Henry
Ricketts, Palmer Chamberlaine
Roberts, Benjamin Stone
Robinson, Stillman Williams
Robinson, William
Roebling, John Augustus
Roosevelt, Nicholas J.
Rosser, Thomas Lafayette
Rousseau, Harry Harwood
Ryan, Walter D'Arcy
St. John, Isaac Munroe
Sargent, Frederick
Saunders, William Lawrence
Sawyer, Walter Howard
Scovel, Henry Sylvester
Sellers, Coleman
Sidell, William Henry
Simpson, James Hervey
Smith, Francis Hopkinson
Smith, William Farrar
Spangler, Henry Wilson
Sperry, Elmer Ambrose
Starrett, William Aiken
Stevens, Edwin Augustus
Stevens, John
Stevens, Robert Livingston
Storrow, Charles Storer
Strickland, William
Strong, Harriet Williams Russel
Stuart, Charles Beebe
Swift, Joseph Gardner
Swift, William Henry
Talcott, Andrew
Thompson, Charles Oliver
Thurston, Robert Henry
Tompkins, Daniel Augustus
Totten, George Muirson
Totten, Joseph Gilbert
Tower, Zealous Bates
Towne, Henry Robinson
Towne, John Henry
Trautwine, John Cresson
Trimble, Isaac Ridgeway

Troland, Leonard Thompson
Trowbridge, William Petit
Turnbull, William
Turner, Walter Victor
Twining, Alexander Catlin
Viele, Egbert Ludovicus
Vose, George Leonard
Ward, George Gray
Warren, Gouverneur Kemble
Warren, Russell
Watkins, John Elfreth
Watson, William
Webb, John Burkitt
Webster, Joseph Dana
Weitzel, Godfrey
Wellman, Samuel Thomas
Wheeler, William
Whistler, George Washington
White, Canvass
Wilcox, Stephen
Wilson, James Harrison
Winans, Thomas De Kay
Wood, James J.
Woodbury, Daniel Phineas
Woodward, Robert Simpson
Worthington, Henry Rossiter
Wright, Horatio Gouverneur

ENGINEER (AERONAUTICAL)
Acosta, Bertram Blanchard
    ("Bert")
Durand, William Frederick
Lawrance, Charles Lanier
Lewis, George William
Millikan, Clark Blanchard
Piccard, Jean Felix
Warner, Edward Pearson
Wright, Theodore Paul

ENGINEER (ARMY)
Casey, Thomas Lincoln
Robert, Henry Martyn
Sibert, William Luther

ENGINEER (AUTOMOTIVE)
Coffin, Howard Earle

ENGINEER (BRIDGE)
Cooper, Theodore
Cox, Lemuel
Hovey, Otis Ellis
Mason, Claibourne Rice
Modjeski, Ralph
Moisseiff, Leon Solomon
Morison, George Shattuck
Murphy, John. W.
Roebling, John Augustus
Smith, Charles Shaler
Steinman, David Barnard
Strauss, Joseph Baermann
Wernwag, Lewis

ENGINEER (CHEMICAL)
Frary, Francis Cowles
Howard, Henry
Landis, Walter Savage
Little, Arthur Dehon
Morehead, John Motley
Whorf, Benjamin Lee

ENGINEER (CIVIL)
Alden, John Ferris
Allen, Horatio
Ammann, Othmar Hermann
Baldwin, Loammi, 1740–1807
Baldwin, Loammi, 1780–1838
Bates, Onward
Billings, Asa White Kenney

Bogue, Virgil Gay
Boller, Alfred Pancoast
Borden, Simeon
Brown, William Henry
Bryant, Gridley
Buck, Leffert Lefferts
Buckhout, Isaac Craig
Bush, Lincoln
Cambpell, Allen
Carll, John Franklin
Cassatt, Alexander Johnston
Chanute, Octave
Childe, John
Church, George Earl
Cohen, Mendes
Cone, Russell Glenn
Cooley, Lyman Edgar
Cooper, Theodore
Corthell, Elmer Lawrence
Crowe, Francis Trenholm
Davies, John Vipond
Detmold, Christian Edward
Devereux, John Henry
Dodge, Grenville Mellon
Duane, James Chatham
Dubois, Augustus Jay
Ellet, Charles
Ellsworth, Lincoln
Evans, Anthony Walton Whyte
Felton, Samuel Morse
Ferris, George Washington
  Gale
Freeman, John Ripley
Freeman, Thomas
Fulton, Robert
Geddes, James
Gillespie, William Mitchell
Goldmark, Henry
Graff, Frederic
Graham, Charles Kinnaird
Greene, Charles Ezra
Greene, George Sears,
  1801–1899
Greene, George Sears,
  1837–1922
Harrington, John Lyle
Harrod, Benjamin Morgan
Haupt, Herman
Hayford, John Fillmore
Hill, Louis Clarence
Hoadley, John Chipman
Holland, Clifford Milburn
Hooker, Elon Huntington
Hovey, Otis Ellis
Hughes, Hector James
Johnson, Edwin Ferry
Johnson, John Butler
Katte, Walter
Knappen, Theodore Temple
Kneass, Samuel Honeyman
Kneass, Strickland
Knight, Jonathan
Koyl, Charles Herschel
Latrobe, Benjamin Henry,
  1806–1878
Latrobe, Charles Hazlehurst
Laurie, James
Lindenthal, Gustav
Lovell, Mansfield
McAlpine, William Jarvis
McConnell, Ira Welch
McCullough, Ernest

McMath, Robert Emmet
McNeill, William Gibbs
Menocal, Aniceto Garcia
Milner, John Turner
Moran, Daniel Edward
Nettleton, Edwin S.
Newell, Frederick Haynes
Noble, Alfred
Norcross, Orlando Whitney
Parker, Theodore Bissell
Peters, Richard, 1810–1889
Pick, Lewis Andrew
Pratt, Thomas Willis
Rafter, George W.
Randolph, Isham
Rea, Samuel
Ridgway, Robert
Roberdeau, Isaac
Roberts, Nathan S.
Roberts, Solomon White
Roberts, William Milnor
Robinson, Albert Alonzo
Robinson, Moncure
Roebling, Washington Augustus
Romans, Bernard
Rugg, Harold Ordway
Savage, John Lucian ("Jack")
Sayre, Robert Heysham
Schneider, Herman
Serrell, Edward Wellman
Silver, Thomas
Smillie, Ralph
Smith, Gustavus Woodson
Smith, Jonas Waldo
Smith, Jonas Waldo
Smith, William Sooy
Snow, Jessie Baker
Sooysmith, Charles
Staley, Cady
Stauffer, David McNeely
Stearns, Frederic Pike
Stevens, John Frank
Strobel, Charles Louis
Stuart, Francis Lee
Swain, George Fillmore
Talbot, Arthur Newell
Tatham, William
Thacher, Edwin
Waddell, John Alexander Low
Waite, Henry Matson
Walker, Reuben Lindsay
Wallace, John Findley
Wegmann, Edward
Welch, Ashbel
Wellington, Arthur Mellen
Westergaard, Harald Malcolm
Weston, William
Whipple, Squire
Williams, Frank Martin
Williams, Jesse Lynch
Wilson, Joseph Miller
Wilson, William Hasell
Worthen, William Ezra
Wright, Benjamin
ENGINEER (COMMUNICATIONS)
  Colpitts, Edwin Henry
Business Man
  Hoover, Herbert Clark, Jr.
ENGINEER (ELECTRICAL)
  Anthony, William Arnold
  Armstrong, Edwin Howard
  Baker, Walter Ransom Gail

Behrend, Bernard Arthur
Billings, Asa White Kenney
Cable, Frank Taylor
Carson, John Renshaw
Carty, John Joseph
Conrad, Frank
Crocker, Francis Bacon
Daft, Leo
Delaney, Patrick Bernard
Dumont, Allen Balcom
Emmet, William Le Roy
Faccioli, Giuseppe
Field, Stephen Dudley
Fortescue, Charles LeGeyt
Gotshall, William Charles
Griffin, Eugene
Hammer, William Joseph
Harper, John Lyell
Heineman, Daniel Webster
  ("Dannie")
Hering, Carl
Hill, Ernest Rowland
Hogan, John Vincent Lawless
Houston, Edwin James
Jackson, Dugald Caleb
Jansky, Karl Guthe
Kennelly, Arthur Edwin
Kettering, Charles Franklin
Leonard, Harry Ward
Loomis, Mahlon
Moorhead, James Kennedy
O'Reilly, Henry
Peek, Frank William
Perrine, Frederic Anten Combs
Potter, William Bancroft
Prescott, George Bartlett
Priest, Edward Dwight
Rice, Edwin Wilbur
Robb, William Lispenard
Rogers, Henry J.
Rosenberg, Julius
Ross, James Delmage McKenzie
Ryan, Harris Joseph
Sargent, Frederick
Short, Sidney Howe
Smith, Harold Babbitt
Sprague, Frank Julian
Squier, George Owen
Stanley, William
Steinmetz, Charles Proteus
Stone, Charles Augustus
Stott, Henry Gordon
Swope, Gerard
Tesla, Nikola
Van Depoele, Charles Joseph
Weaver, William Dixon
Webster, Edwin Sibley
Weston, Edward
ENGINEER (HIGHWAY)
  Merrill, Frank Dow
ENGINEER (HYDRAULIC)
  Davis, Arthur Powell
  Fanning, John Thomas
  Fitzgerald, Desmond
  Francis, James Bicheno
  Frizell, Joseph Palmer
  Hazen, Allen
  Henny, David Christiaan
  Herschel, Clemens
  Hill, Louis Clarence
  Knappen, Theodore Temple
  Matthes, Gerard Hendrik

Mills, Hiram Francis
O'Shaughnessy, Michael
   Maurice
Schuyler, James Dix
Shedd, Joel Herbert
Weymouth, Frank Elwin
ENGINEER (HYDROELECTRIC)
Cooper, Hugh Lincoln
ENGINEER (INDUSTRIAL)
Gunn, James Newton
Hine, Charles De Lano
Porter, Holbrook Fitz-John
Rautenstrauch, Walter
Taylor, Frederick Winslow
Woodbury, Charles Jeptha Hill
ENGINEER (IRRIGATION)
Eaton, Benjamin Harrison
Mead, Elwood
Nettleton, Edwin S.
Wiley, Andrew Jackson
ENGINEER (MARINE)
Fairburn, William Armstrong
Herreshoff, Nathanael Greene
ENGINEER (MECHANICAL)
Barth, Carl Georg Lange
Bristol, William Henry
Carrier, Willis Haviland
Clark, Walter Leighton
Cooke, Morris Llewellyn
Delamater, Cornelius Henry
Doane, Thomas
Durand, William Frederick
Emmet, William Le Roy
Faccioli, Giuseppe
Flanders, Ralph Edward
Flather, John Joseph
Fritz, John
Gibbs, George
Grant, George Barnard
Halsey, Frederick Arthur
Harper, John Lyell
Harrington, John Lyle
Harrison, Joseph
Herr, Herbert Thacker
Hoadley, John Chipman
Hobbs, Alfred Charles
Hodgkinson, Francis
Holley, Alexander Lyman
Holloway, Joseph Flavius
Hudson, William Smith
Humphreys, Alexander
   Crombie
Hunt, Charles Wallace
Isherwood, Benjamin Franklin
Jones, Evan William
Kent, William
Kimball, Dexter Simpson
Kingsbury, Albert
Klein, August Clarence
Klein, Joseph Frederic
Leavitt, Erasmus Darwin
Leavitt, Frank McDowell
Lewis, Wilfred
Lieb, John William
Main, Charles Thomas
Manly, Charles Matthews
Mattice, Asa Martines
Miller, Kempster Blanchard
Moss, Sanford Alexander
Murray, Thomas Edward
Newcomb, Charles Leonard
Nordberg, Bruno Victor

Norden, Carl Lukas
Norton, Charles Hotchkiss
Porter, Holbrook Fitz-John
Rice, Calvin Winsor
Richards, Charles Brinckerhoff
Sessions, Henry Howard
Swasey, Ambrose
Sweet, John Edson
ENGINEER (METALLURGICAL)
Bassett, William Hastings
Dwight, Arthur Smith
ENGINEER (MILITARY)
Abbot, Henry Larcom
Barlow, John Whitney
Bernard, Simon
Chittenden, Hiram Martin
Costansó, Miguel
De Brahm, William Gerard
Delafield, Richard
Duane, James Chatham
Gardiner, Lion
Gillmore, Quincy Adams
Godefroy, Maximilian
Gridley, Richard
Gunnison, John Williams
Hodges, Harry Foote
Hutchins, Thomas
Mackellar, Patrick
Mansfield, Joseph King Fenno
Montrésor, James Gabriel
Montrésor, John
Raymond, Charles Walker
Roberdeau, Isaac
Serrell, Edward Wellman
Smith, Gustavus Woodson
Symons, Thomas William
Thayer, Sylvanus
ENGINEER (MINING)
Blake, William Phipps
Bradley, Frederick Worthen
Brooks, Thomas Benton
Brunton, David William
Carpenter, Franklin Reuben
Clemson, Thomas Green
Cogswell, William Browne
Coxe, Eckley Brinton
Daggett, Ellsworth
Del Mar, Alexander
Douglas, James
Dwight, Arthur Smith
Emmons, Samuel Franklin
Greenway, John Campbell
Hague, James Duncan
Hammond, John Hays
Holmes, Joseph Austin
Hoover, Herbert Clark
Hulbert, Edwin James
Irving, Roland Duer
Jackling, Daniel Cowan
Janin, Louis
Jennings, James Hennen
Kemp, James Furman
King, Clarence
Lyman, Benjamin Smith
Manning, Vannoy Hartrog
Mathewson, Edward Payson
Maynard, George William
Moore, Philip North
Neilson, William George
Olcott, Eben Erksine
Peters, Edward Dyer
Ramsay, Erskine

Raymond, Rossiter
   Worthington
Requa, Mark Lawrence
Rice, George Samuel
Richards, Robert Hallowell
Rothwell, Richard Pennefather
Smith, Hamilton
Spilsbury, Edmund Gybbon
Stearns, Irving Ariel
Stoek, Harry Harkness
Strong, Charles Lyman
Vinton, Francis Laurens
Webb, Harry Howard
Williams, Gardner Fred
Winchell, Horace Vaughn
ENGINEER (NAVAL)
Canaga, Alfred Bruce
Copeland, Charles W.
Endicott, Mordecai Thomas
Entwistle, James
Fisher, Clark
Hollis, Ira Nelson
Hoxie, William Dixie
McAllister, Charles Albert
Taylor, Stevenson
ENGINEER (PUBLIC UTILITY)
Doherty, Henry Latham
ENGINEER (RADIO)
Conrad, Frank
Stone, John Stone
ENGINEER (RESEARCH)
Buckley, Oliver Ellsworth
ENGINEER (SANITARY)
Eddy, Harrison Prescott
Fuller, George Warren
Goodnough, Xanthus Henry
Hazen, Allen
Hering, Rudolph
Kay, Edgar Boyd
Kinnicutt, Leonard Parker
Meyer, Henry Coddington
Mills, Hiram Francis
Shedd, Joel Herbert
Waring, George Edwin
ENGINEER (STEEL)
Blakeley, George Henry
Perin, Charles Page
ENGINEER (STRUCTURAL)
Pond, Irving Kane
Purdy, Corydon Tyler
ENGINEER (TELEPHONE)
Gherardi, Bancroft
Jewett, Frank Baldwin
Stone, John Stone
ENGINEER (TOPOGRAPHICAL)
Abert, John James
Hood, Washington
Hughes, George Wurtz
Wheeler, George Montague
Whipple, Amiel Weeks
ENGINEER (WATER-SUPPLY)
Mulholland, William
ENGRAVER (See also ARTIST, DIE-
   SINKER, ETCHER, PHOTOEN-
   GRAVER)
Aitken, Robert
Alexander, Anderson
Andrews, Joseph
Barber, John Warner
Birch, William Russell
Buell, Abel
Burgis, William

Casilear, John William
Charles, William
Cheney, John
Cheney, Seth Wells
Childs, Cephas Grier
Clay, Edward Williams
Closson, William Baxter
Cushman, George Hewitt
Danforth, Moseley Isaac
Dawkins, Henry
Dewing, Francis
Doolittle, Amos
Dummer, Jeremiah
Durand, Asher Brown
Durand, Cyrus
Eckstein, John
Edwin, David
Field, Robert
Folwell, Samuel
Foster, John
Fox, Gilbert
French, Edwin Davis
Girsch, Frederick
Gobrecht, Christian
Goodman, Charles
Hall, Henry Bryan
Hamlin, William
Havell, Robert
Hill, John
Hollyer, Samuel
Hooker, William
Hurd, Nathaniel
Jocelyn, Nathaniel
Johnston, David Claypoole
Johnston, Thomas
Jones, Alfred
Kearny, Francis
Keith, William
Kensett, John Frederick
Kingsley, Elbridge
Kneass, William
Lawson, Alexander
Leney, William Satchwell
Le Roux, Charles
Longacre, James Barton
Malcolm, James Peller
Maverick, Peter
Norman, John
Ormsby, Waterman Lilly
Otis, Bass
Pease, Joseph Ives
Pelham, Henry
Pelham, Peter
Piggot, Robert
Prud'homme, John Francis
 Eugene
Ritchie, Alexander Hay
Rollinson, William
Rosenthal, Max
Saint-Mémin, Charles Balthazar
 Julien Fevret de
Sartain, Emily
Sartain, John
Sartain, Samuel
Savage, Edward
Schoff, Stephen Alonzo
Shirlaw, Walter
Smillie, James
Smillie, James David
Smith, John Rubens
Strickland, William
Tanner, Benjamin

Tiebout, Cornelius
Yeager, Joseph
ENGRAVER (WOOD; SEE ALSO ART-
 IST)
Adams, Joseph Alexander
Anthony, Andrew Varick Stout
Bowen, Abel
Cole, Timothy
Drake, Alexander Wilson
Heinemann, Ernst
Juengling, Frederick
Kruell, Gustav
Leslie, Frank
Linton, William James
Lossing, Benson John
Wolf, Henry
ENTERTAINER (See also ACTOR,
 ACTRESS, CLOWN, COMEDIAN,
 COMEDIENNE, HUMORIST,
 WIT)
Allen, Gracie
Clark, Bobby
Gray, Gilda
Hopper, Edna Wallace
Janis, Elsie
Lee, Gypsy Rose
Mansfield, Jayne
Maxwell, Elsa
Nesbit, Evelyn Florence
Palmer, William Henry
Rooney, Pat
Waller, Thomas Wright
 ("Fats")
ENTOMOLOGIST (See also ZOOLO-
 GIST)
Ashmead, William Harris
Burgess, Edward
Comstock, John Henry
Coquillett, Daniel William
Cresson, Ezra Townsend
Dyar, Harrison Gray
Edwards, William Henry
Fernald, Charles Henry
Fitch, Asa
Forbes, Stephen Alfred
Glover, Townend
Grote, Augustus Radcliffe
Hagen, Hermann August
Harris, Thaddeus William
Horn, George Henry
Howard, Leland Ossian
Hubbard, Henry Guernsey
Hunter, Walter David
Kinsey, Alfred Charles
Knab, Frederick
LeConte, John Lawrence
Lintner, Joseph Albert
Lutz, Frank Eugene
Melsheimer, Friedrich Valentin
Morgan, John Harcourt
 Alexander
Osten Sacken, Carl Robert
 Romanovich von der
Packard, Alpheus Spring
Peckham, George Williams
Riley, Charles Valentine
Sanderson, Ezra Dwight
Say, Thomas
Schwarz, Eugene Amandus
Scudder, Samuel Hubbard
Smith, John Bernhard
Taylor, Charlotte De Bernier

Thomas, Cyrus
Uhler, Philip Reese
Walsh, Benjamin Dann
Wheeler, William Morton
Williston, Samuel Wendell
ENTREPRENEUR (See also BUSI-
 NESSMAN, CAPITALIST, INDUS-
 TRIALIST, MANUFACTURER,
 MERCHANT)
Farquhar, Percival
Kennedy, Joseph Patrick
Pincus, Gregory Goodwin
 ("Goody")
EPIDEMIOLOGIST (See also PHYSI-
 CIAN)
Carter, Henry Rose
Chapin, Charles Value
Doull, James Angus
Frost, Wade Hampton
Rosenau, Milton Joseph
Sedgwick, William Thompson
Sternberg, George Miller
ESSAYIST (See also AUTHOR, WRIT-
 ER)
Agee, James Rufus
Appleton, Thomas Gold
Bourne, Randolph Silliman
Calvert, George Henry
Crèvecoeur, Michel-Guillaume
 Jean de
Crothers, Samuel McChord
Dana, Richard Henry
Dennie, Joseph
Douglas, Lloyd Cassel
Downey, John
Emerson, Ralph Waldo
Gregory, Eliot
Guiney, Louise Imogen
Hall, Sarah Ewing
Holley, Marietta
Holmes, Oliver Wendell
Kinney, Elizabeth Clementine
 Dodge Stedman
Lazarus, Emma
McKinley, Carlyle
Saltus, Edgar Evertson
Sperry, Willard Learoyd
Story, William Wetmore
Thoreau, Henry David
Tuckerman, Henry Theodore
Warner, Charles Dudley
Willcox, Louise Collier
Winchevsky, Morris
Winter, William
ETCHER (See also ARTIST, EN-
 GRAVER)
Bacher, Otto Henry
Bellows, Albert Fitch
Benson, Frank Weston
Charles, William
Clay, Edward Williams
Dielman, Frederick
Duveneck, Frank
Farrer, Henry
Forbes, Edwin
Garrett, Edmund Henry
Gifford, Robert Swain
Hart, George Overbury
Haskell, Ernest
Koopman, Augustus
Merritt, Anna Lea

Mielatz, Charles Frederick
William
Miller, Charles Henry
Moran, Peter
Moran, Thomas
Nicoll, James Craig
Pennell, Joseph
Platt, Charles Adams
Plowman, George Taylor
Reed, Earl Howell
Rix, Julian Walbridge
Smillie, James David
Whistler, James Abbott McNeill
Young, Mahonri Mackintosh
ETHICAL CULTURE LEADER
Coit, Stanton
Elliott, John Lovejoy
ETHNOLOGIST (See also AN-
THROPOLOGIST)
Bourke, John Gregory
Churchill, William
Cooper, John Montgomery
Cushing, Frank Hamilton
Dorsey, James Owen
Emerson, Ellen Russell
Farabee, William Curtis
Fewkes, Jesse Walter
Fletcher, Alice Cunningham
Gatschet, Albert Samuel
Gibbs, George
Goddard, Pliny Earle
Hale, Horatio Emmons
Henshaw, Henry Wetherbee
Jones, William
Lowie, Robert Harry
Mallery, Garrick
Mason, Otis Tufton
Matthews, Washington
Mooney, James
Morgan, Lewis Henry
Nott, Josiah Clark
Pilling, James Constantine
Safford, William Edwin
Schoolcraft, Henry Rowe
Skinner, Alanson Buck
Smith, Erminnie Adelle Platt
Speck, Frank Gouldsmith
Stevenson, James
Stevenson, Matilda Coxe Evans
Thomas, Cyrus
Woodruff, Charles Edward
Wyman, Jeffries
ETHNOMUSICOLOGIST
Densmore, Frances
ETIQUETTE AUTHORITY
Post, Emily Price
ETYMOLOGIST
Vizetelly, Frank Horace
EUGENICIST
Davenport, Charles Benedict
Laughlin, Harry Hamilton
EVANGELIST (See also CLERGYMAN,
RELIGIOUS LEADER)
Chapman, John Wilbur
Crittenden, Charles Nelson
Dow, Lorenzo
Durant, Henry Fowle
Hammond, Edward Payson
Hayden, William
Ironside, Henry Allan
Jones, Robert Reynolds
("Bob")

Jones, Samuel Porter
McPherson, Aimee Semple
Miller, George
Mills, Benjamin Fay
Moody, Dwight Lyman
Nettleton, Asahel
Rieger, Johann Georg Joseph
Anton
Riley, William Bell
Smith, Fred Burton
Stone, Barton Warren
Sunday, William Ashley
("Billy")
Taylor, William
Updegraff, David Brainard
Upshaw, William David
Whitefield, George
EXECUTIVE (See also BUSINESS-
MAN, BUSINESSWOMAN, CAPI-
TALIST, ENTREPRENEUR,
INDUSTRIALIST, MANUFACTUR-
ER, MERCHANT)
Avery, Sewell Lee
Barton, Bruce Fairchild
Berwind, Edward Julius
Boeing, William Edward
Braniff, Thomas Elmer
Brookings, Robert Somers
Brownlee, James Forbis
Brush, George Jarvis
Carpenter, John Alden
Clayton, William Lockhart
Copley, Ira Clifton
Davis, Francis Breese, Jr.
Dean, Gordon Evans
Dillingham, Walter Francis
Dittemore, John Valentine
D'Olier, Franklin
Drum, Hugh Aloysius
Dyer, Isadore
Fairburn, William Armstrong
Ferguson, Samuel
Flint, Charles Ranlett
French, Paul Comly
Gherardi, Bancroft
Gifford, Walter Sherman
Gossett, Benjamin Brown
Green, Norvin
Gregory, Thomas Barger
Guggenheim, Simon
Harbord, James Guthrie
Hartford, George Huntington
Hartford, George Ludlum
Hartford, John Augustine
Henderson, Paul
Hill, George Washington
Hopson, Howard Colwell
Hutton, Edward Francis
Johnson, Eldridge Reeves
Lawrance, Charles Lanier
Marshall, Charles Henry
Mellon, William Larimer
Mitchell, Sidney Zollicoffer
Murray, Thomas Edward
Nelson, Donald Marr
Olcott, Eben Erskine
Orton, William
Patterson, Richard
Cunningham, Jr.
Prentis, Henning Webb, Jr.
Reid, Helen Miles Rogers
Reynolds, Richard Samuel, Sr.

Rudkin, Margaret Fogarty
Schenck, Nicholas Michael
Simmons, George Henry
Sloan, George Arthur
Sloan, Matthew Scott
Somervell, Brehon Burke
Stettinius, Edward Reilly
Swope, Gerard
Talbott, Harold Elstner
Thalberg, Irving Grant
Vail, Theodore Newton
Vance, Harold Sines
Wacker, Charles Henry
Watson, Thomas John
Whiteside, Arthur Dare
Willkie, Wendell Lewis
Wilson, Charles Erwin
Yates, Herbert John
Yerkes, Charles Tyson
EXPERIMENTER (See also AGRICUL-
TURIST, AGRICULTURAL CHEM-
IST, CHEMIST, PHYSIOLOGIST,
PHYSICIST, SCIENTIST)
Johnson, Samuel William
Kinnersley, Ebenezer
Lining, John
Livingston, Robert R.,
1746–1813
Loomis, Mahlon
Page, Charles Grafton
Reid, James L.
Thatcher, Roscoe Wilfred
EXPLORER (See also DISCOVERER,
FRONTIERSMAN, GUIDE, PIO-
NEER, SCOUT)
Aco, Michel
Akeley, Carl Ethan
Akeley, Mary Leonore
Alarcón, Hernando de,
Ambler, James Markham
Marshall
Andrews, Roy Chapman
Anza, Juan Bautista de,
Armstrong, John
Ashley, William Henry
Ayllon, Lucas Vasquez de
Baldwin, Evelyn Briggs
Bandelier, Adolph Francis
Alphonse
Becknell, William
Bingham, Hiram
Bourgmont, Étienne Venyard,
Sieur de
Bridgman, Herbert Lawrence
Brower, Jacob Vradenberg
Brulé, Étienne
Burnham, Frederick Russell
Byrd, Richard Evelyn
Cabrillo, Juan Rodriguez
Céloron de Blainville, Pierre
Joseph de
Chaillé-Long, Charles
Champlain, Samuel de
Charlevoix, Pierre François
Xavier de
Church, George Earl
Clark, William
Colter, John
Cook, Frederick Albert
Coronado, Francisco Vázquez
Crespi, Juan
Danenhower, John Wilson

De Long, George Washington
De Mézières y Clugny, Athauase
Du Chaillu, Paul Belloni
Duluth, Daniel Greysolon, Sieur de
Eklund, Carl Robert
Ellsworth, Lincoln
Escalante, Silvestre Velez de
Fanning, Edmund
Filson, John
Forsyth, Thomas
Freeman, Thomas
Frémont, John Charles
Garcés, Francisco Tomás Hermenegildo
Gass, Patrick
Gist, Christopher
Greely, Adolphus Washington
Groseilliers, Médart Chouart, Sieur de
Hall, Charles Francis
Harmon, Daniel Williams
Hayes, Isaac Israel
Heilprin, Angelo
Henry, Alexander
Henson, Matthew Alexander
Horsfield, Thomas
Hubbard, Bernard Rosecrans
Iberville, Pierre Le Moyne, Sieur d'
Ives, Joseph Christmas
James, Edwin
Johnson, Osa
Jolliet, Louis
Kane, Elisha Kent
Kennan, George
Kennicott, Robert
Kino, Eusebio Francisco
Lander, Frederick West
Langford, Nathaniel Pitt
Lanman, Charles
La Salle, Robert Cavelier, Sieur de
La Vérendrye, Pierre Gaultier de Varennes, Sieur de
Lederer, John
Ledyard, John
Le Sueur, Pierre
Lewis, Meriwether
Lockwood, James Booth
Long, Stephen Harriman
Luna y Arellano, Tristan de
Mackay, James
Marquette, Jacques
Menéndez de Avilés, Pedro
Michaux, André
Morrell, Benjamin
Muir, John
Mullan, John
Needham, James
Nicolet, Jean
Nicollet, Joseph Nicolas
Niza, Marcos de
Núñez Cabeza de Vaca, Alvar
Ogden, Peter Skene
Ordway, John
Orton, James
Page, Thomas Jefferson
Palmer, Nathaniel Brown
Parker, Samuel
Pavy, Octave

Peary, Robert Edwin
Perrot, Nicolas
Pike, Zebulon Montgomery
Ponce de León, Juan
Pond, Peter
Porter, Russell Williams
Poston, Charles Debrill
Pring, Martin
Pumpelly, Raphael
Pursh, Frederick
Radisson, Pierre Esprit
Roosevelt, Kermit
Ross, Alexander
St. Denis (Denys), Louis Juchereau de
St. Lusson, Simon François Daumont, Sieur de
Schoolcraft, Henry Rowe
Sibley, George Champlain
Smith, Jedediah Strong
Smith, John, 1579–1631
Stanley, Henry Morton
Stansbury, Howard
Stefansson, Vilhjalmur
Stevenson, James
Strain, Isaac G.
Thompson, David
Thompson, Edward Herbert
Tonty, Henry de
Truteau, Jean Baptiste
Tyson, George Emory
Verrill, Alpheus Hyatt
Vincennes, Jean Baptiste Bissot, Sieur de
Vizcaíno, Sabastián
Walker, Joseph Reddeford
Walker, Thomas
Walsh, Henry Collins
Waymouth, George
Webber, Charles Wilkins
Welles, Roger
Wellman, Walter
Wilkes, Charles
Wood, Abraham
Workman, Fanny Bullock
Wyeth, Nathaniel Jarvis

EXPRESSMAN (See also TRANSPORTER)
Adams, Alvin
Armstrong, George Washington
Butterfield, John
Cheney, Benjamin Pierce
Fargo, William George
Harnden, William Frederick
Stimson, Alexander Lovett
Wells, Henry

FACTOR (See also MERCHANT)
Flannery, John
McLoughlin, John
Richardson, Edmund
FARM COOPERATIVE LEADER
Babcock, Howard Edward
FARMER (See also AGRICULTURIST)
Allen, Anthony Benezet
Binns, John Alexander
Bromfield, Louis
Clark, Abraham
Clayton, John Middleton
Cox, Henry Hamilton
Delafield, John
Dickson, David

Frazier, Lynn Joseph
Glidden, Joseph Farwell
Gregg, Andrew
Harris, Joseph
Hart, John
Haugen, Gilbert Nelson
Heard, Dwight Bancroft
Hecker, Friedrich Karl Franz
Hiester, Daniel
Hughes, Dudley Mays
Jardine, William Marion
Johnson, Edward
Lacock, Abner
Leaming, Jacob Spicer
Livingston, Robert R., 1746–1813
Magoffin, Beriah
Northen, William Jonathan
Paine, Elijah
Palmer, William Adams
Peters, Richard, 1744–1828
Polk, Leonidas Lafayette
Potter, James
Reed, John, 1757–1845
Rodney, Thomas
Silver, Gray
Stockton, Richard
Strawn, Jacob
Wadsworth, James Wolcott, Jr.
Wilkinson, Jeremiah
Wing, Joseph Elwyn
Wood, James
FARM LEADER (See also AGRICULTURAL LEADER, AGRICULTURIST)
Barrett, Charles Simon
Butler, Marion
Gregory, Clifford Verne
Hirth, William Andrew
Kolb, Reuben Francis
Macune, Charles William
Moser, Christopher Otto
Peek, George Nelson
Reno, Milo
Silver, Gray
Simpson, John Andrew
FASHION AUTHORITY
Snow, Carmel White
FASHION RETAILER
Carnegie, Hattie
FBI INFORMER
Bentley, Elizabeth Terrill
FEDERAL ART ADMINISTRATOR
Bruce, Edward Bright
FEDERAL ART PROJECT DIRECTOR
Cahill, Holger
FEDERAL OFFICIAL
Carr, Wilbur John
Matthews, Francis Patrick
Willebrandt, Mabel Walker
Williams, Aubrey Willis
Wrather, William Embry
FEDERAL RESERVE BOARD GOVERNOR
Crissinger, Daniel Richard
FEDERAL RESERVE BOARD MEMBER
Hamlin, Charles Sumner
FEDERAL THEATRE PROJECT DIRECTOR
Flanagan, Hallie

FEDERAL TRADE COMMISSIONER
Ayres, William Augustus
FEMINIST
Allen, Florence Ellinwood
Anthony, Katharine Susan
Bloor, Ella Reeve
Breen, Margaret
Brown, Charlotte Emerson
Brown, Olympia
Catt, Carrie Clinton Lane
  Chapman
Chace, Elizabeth Buffum
Crocker, Hannah Mather
Doyle, Sarah Elizabeth
Duniway, Abigail Jane Scott
Foster, Abigail Kelley
Gage, Matilda Joslyn
Grimké, Angelina Emily
Grimké, Sarah Moore
Harper, Ida Husted
Haskell, Ella Louise Knowles
Hepburn, Katharine Houghton
Hooker, Isabella Beecher
Huntington, Margaret Jane
  Evans
Kehew, Mary Morton Kimball
Lozier, Clemence Sophia
  Harned
Martin, Anne Henrietta
Mussey, Ellen Spencer
Nathan, Maud
Park, Maud Wood
Robinson, Harriet Jane Hanson
Schwimmer, Rosika
Sewall, May Eliza Wright
Sill, Anna Peck
Smith, Abby Hadassah
Snow, Eliza Roxey
Stanton, Elizabeth Cady
Stevens, Doris
Stone, Lucy
Terrell, Mary Eliza Church
Walker, Mary Edwards
Zakrzewska, Maria Elizabeth
FENCER
Hewes, Robert
FENIAN LEADER
Devoy, John
O'Mahony, John
O'Neill, John
Roberts, William Randall
Sweeny, Thomas William,
FILIBUSTER
Walker, William
Ward, Frederick Townsend
FILM ANIMATOR
O'Brien, Willis Harold
FILM CENSOR
Breen, Joseph Ignatius
FILMMAKER (See also MOTION PIC-
  TURE DIRECTOR)
Flaherty, Robert Joseph
Micheaux, Oscar
Porter, Edwin Stanton
Selig, William Nicholas
FINANCIER (See also BANKER,
  CAPITALIST, STOCKBROKER)
Adams, Charles Francis
Aldrich, Nelson Wilmarth
Astor, William Vincent
Austell, Alfred
Bache, Jules Semon

Barbour, John Strode
Barker, Jacob
Barker, Wharton
Baruch, Bernard Mannes
Bates, Joshua
Biddle, Nicholas
Borie, Adolph Edward
Brooker, Charles Frederick
Butterfield, John
Calhoun, Patrick
Canfield, Richard H.
Carlisle, Floyd Leslie
Cazenove, Théophile
Cheves, Langdon
Chisolm, Alexander Robert
Chouteau, Pierre
Clews, Henry
Cooke, Jay
Coolidge, Thomas Jefferson
Corbin, Daniel Chase
Craigie, Andrew
Crerar, John
Currier, Moody
Cutting, Robert Fulton
Day, George Parmly
Dillon, Sidney
Duer, William
Dunwoody, William Hood
Durant, William Crapo
Eckels, James Herron
Fair, James Graham
Fairchild, Charles Stebbins
Fessenden, William Pitt
Garrett, Robert
Garrison, Cornelius Kingsland
Garrison, William Re Tallack
Gary, Elbert Henry
Giannini, Amadeo Peter
Gilbert, Seymour Parker
Gilman, John Taylor
Girard, Stephen
Godfrey, Benjamin
Goodwin, Ichabod
Gould, George Jay
Gould, Jay
Green, Henrietta Howland
  Robinson
Green, John Cleve
Griscom, Clement Acton
Guggenheim, Meyer
Hambleton, Thomas Edward
Harding, Abner Clark
Harding, William Procter Gould
Harrison, Charles Custis
Harvie, John
Hatch, Rufus
Hayden, Charles
Hertz, John Daniel
Hill, James Jerome
Holden, Liberty Emery
Holladay, Ben
Hopson, Howard Colwell
Hotchkiss, Horace Leslie
Huntington, Henry Edwards
Inman, John Hamilton
James, Arthur Curtiss
Joy, Henry Bourne
Keep, Henry
Keys, Clement Melville
King, James Gore
Knox, John Jay
Lamont, Daniel Scott

Lamont, Thomas William
Lanier, James Franklin Doughty
Lewisohn, Sam Adolph
Lord, Herbert Mayhew
Ludlow, Thomas William
Macalester, Charles, 1798–1873
McGhee, Charles McClung
Mather, Samuel
Matheson, William John
Mellon, Andrew William
Meredith, Samuel
Mitchell, Alexander
Morgan, John Pierpont
Morgan, Junius Spencer
Morris, Robert, 1734–1806
Nettleton, Alvred Bayard
Newhouse, Samuel
Nixon, John, 1733–1808
Park, Trenor William
Peabody, George
Pearsons, Daniel Kimball
Peters, Richard, 1810–1889
Phinizy, Ferdinand
Pollock, Oliver
Randolph, Thomas Jefferson
Raskob, John Jakob
Rice, Isaac Leopold
Ripley, Edward Hastings
Roberts, Ellis Henry
Rockefeller, William
Rollins, Edward Henry
Rose, Chauncey
Ryan, Thomas Fortune
Sage, Russell
Salomon, Haym
Sanders, Thomas
Scarbrough, William
Schiff, Jacob Henry
Seligman, Joseph
Shuster, W(illiam) Morgan
Smith, George
Smith, Jeremiah
Speyer, James Joseph
Sprague, Oliver Mitchell
  Wentworth
Starrett, William Aiken
Stevens, Edwin Augustus
Stevens, John Austin,
  1827–1910
Straight, Willard Dickerman
Straus, Simon William
Swan, James
Taylor, Myron Charles
Thatcher, Mahlon Daniel
Thayer, Nathaniel
Thompson, Robert Means
Thompson, William Boyce
Trenholm, George Alfred
Vanderbilt, Cornelius,
  1794–1877
Vanderbilt, Cornelius,
  1843–1899
Vanderbilt, William Henry
Villard, Henry
Wade, Jeptha Homer
Wadsworth, Eliot
Walker, William Johnson
Wallace, Hugh Campbell
Warburg, Felix Moritz
Warburg, James Paul
Ward, Samuel, 1814–1884
Warfield, Solomon Davies

Watson, John Fanning
Weightman, William
Weyerhaeuser, Frederick
  Edward
Whitney, Harry Payne
Whitney, William Collins
Whittemore, Thomas
Widener, Peter Arrell Brown
Williams, John Skelton
Wright, Charles Barston
Yerkes, Charles Tyson

FIRE PREVENTION EXPERT
Woodbury, Charles Jeptha Hill

FIRST LADY
Adams, Abigail
Lincoln, Mary Todd
Madison, Dolly Payne
Roosevelt, (Anna) Eleanor
Wilson, Edith Bolling

FISH CULTURIST (See PISCICULTURIST)

FLORIST (See NURSEYMAN)

FLUTIST
Barrère, Georges

FOLKLORIST (See also ANTHROPOLOGIST, ETHNOLOGIST)
Dobie, J(ames) Frank
Hurston, Zora Neale
Jacobs, Joseph, 1854–1916
Newell, William Wells
Rourke, Constance Mayfield
Sandburg, Carl August
Scarborough, Dorothy
Swanton, John Reed

FOLK PLAYS SPECIALIST
Koch, Frederick Henry

FOOD ADMINISTRATOR
Lasater, Edward Cunningham

FOOD CHEMIST (See also CHEMIST)
Sherman, Henry Clapp

FOOTBALL COACH (See also ATHLETIC DIRECTOR)
Dobie, Gilmour
Haughton, Percy Duncan
Lambeau, Earl Louis ("Curly")
Lombardi, Vincent Thomas
McMillin, Alvin Nugent ("Bo")
Murphy, Michael Charles
Neyland, Robert Reese, Jr.
Owen, Stephen Joseph
Rockne, Knute Kenneth
Shaughnessy, Clark Daniel
Stagg, Amos Alonzo
Warner, Glenn Scobey ("Pop")
Yost, Fielding Harris
Zuppke, Robert Carl

FOOTBALL PLAYER
Bell, De Benneville ("Bert")
Booth, Albert James, Jr.
  ("Albie")
Davis, Ernest R. ("Ernie")
Heffelfinger, William Walter
  "Pudge"
Lambeau, Earl Louis ("Curly")
Leavitt, Frank Simmons ("Man
  Mountain Dean")
McMillin Alvin Nugent ("Bo")
Stuhldreher, Harry A.

FOOTBALL PROMOTER
Camp, Walter Chauncey

FOREIGN CORRESPONDENT (See also JOURNALIST, NEWSPAPER CORRESPONDENT, NEWSPAPER REPORTER)
Gibbons, Herbert Adams
Miller, Webb
Swing, Raymond Edwards
  (Gram)
Von Wiegand, Karl Henry

FOREIGN POLICY ADVISER
Coudert, Frederic René

FORESTER (See also AGRICULTURIST, SILVICULTURIST)
Allen, Edward Tyson
Baker, Hugh Potter
Bryant, Ralph Clement
Fernow, Bernhard Eduard
Hough, Franklin Benjamin
Pinchot, Gifford
Record, Samuel James
Rothrock, Joseph Trimble
Silcox, Ferdinand Augustus
Toumey, James William
Vanderbilt, George Washington
Warder, John Aston

FOUNDATION EXECUTIVE
Embree, Edwin Rogers
Gaither, Horace Rowan, Jr.
Glenn, John Mark
Greene, Roger Sherman
Keppel, Frederick Paul
Scott, James Brown

FOUNDER
Addams, Jane (Hull-House,
  Chicago, Ill.)
Allen, Richard (African
  Methodist Episcopal Church)
Andrew, Samuel (Yale College)
Andrus, Ethel Percy (American
  Association of Retired
  Persons, National Retired
  Teachers Association)
Anza, Juan Bautista de (San
  Francisco, Cal.)
Archer, John (Medical and
  Chirurgical Faculty of
  Maryland)
Austin, Stephen Fuller (Texas)
Baker, George Pierce (47
  Workshop)
Baldwin, John (Baldwin-Wallace
  College, Baker University)
Ballou, Adin (Hopedale
  Community)
Beers, Clifford Whittingham
  (mental hygiene movement)
Black, James (National
  Prohibition Party)
Blair, James (College of
  William and Mary)
Blavatsky, Helena Petrovna
  Hahn (Theosophical Society)
Bliss, Daniel (Syrian Protestant
  College)
Boisen, Anton Theophilus
  (clinincal pastoral education
  movement)
Booth, Ballington (Volunteers
  of America)
Bowman, John Bryan (Kentucky
  University)

Buchman, Frank Nathan Daniel
  (Moral Re-Armament)
Cabell, Joseph Carrington
  (University of Virginia)
Cabrini, Francis Xavier (Mother
  Cabrini) (Missionary Sisters
  of the Sacred Heart)
Cadillac, Antoine de la Mothe
  (Detroit, Mich.)
Campbell, Thomas (Disciples of
  Christ)
Cannon, Harriet Starr
  (Sisterhood of St. Mary)
Champlain, Samuel de
  (Canada)
Clark, Francis Edward (Young
  People's Society of Christian
  Endeavor)
Coit, Stanton (America's first
  social settlement)
Connelly, Cornelia (Society of
  the Holy Child Jesus)
Conover, Harry Sayles (Harry
  Conover Modeling Agency)
Considérant, Victor Prosper
  (utopian community in
  Texas)
Cook, George Cram
  (Provincetown Players)
Cooke, Samuel (Penn Fruit
  Company)
Cooper, Sarah Brown Ingersoll
  (kindergartens)
Cornell, Ezra (Cornell
  University)
Coulter, Ernest Kent (Big
  Brother Movement)
Crittenton, Charles Nelson
  (Florence Crittenton
  Missions)
Cummins, George David
  (Reformed Episcopal Church)
Cunningham, Ann Pamela
  (Mount Vernon Ladies'
  Association of the Union)
Dabrowski, Joseph (S.S. Cyril
  and Methodius Seminary)
Darling, Flora Adams (patriotic
  organizations)
Davenport, George (Davenport,
  Iowa)
Davidge, John Beale (Univ. of
  Maryland)
Dempster, John (Methodist
  theological seminaries)
Dodge, David Low (New York
  Peace Society)
Dole, James Drummond
  (Hawaiian Pineapple
  Company)
Donahue, Peter (Union Iron
  Workers)
Dooley, Thomas Anthony, III
  (Medical International
  Corporation Organization,
  MEDICO)
Dorrell, William (Dorrellites)
Dowie, John Alexander
  (Christian Catholic Apostolic
  Church in Zion)
Drexel, Katharine Mary (Sisters
  of the Blessed Sacrament for

Indians and Colored People)

Dufour, John James (Swiss vineyards in America)

Easley, Ralph Montgomery (National Civic Federation)

Eddy, Mary Morse Baker (Christian Science)

Eggleston, Thomas (School of Mines, Columbia Univ.)

Eielsen, Elling (Norwegian Evangelical Church of North America)

Eliot, William Greenleaf (Washington University of St. Louis)

Estaugh, Elizabeth Haddon (Haddonfield home for travelling ministers)

Eustis, Dorothy Leib Harrison Wood (The Seeing Eye)

Evans, John (Northwestern University, Colorado Seminary)

Ewing, Finis (Cumberland Presbyterian Church)

Fee, John Gregg (Berea College)

Few, Ignatius Alphonso (Emory College)

Fillmore, Charles (Unity School of Christianity)

Flanagan, Edward Joseph (Boys Town)

Foster, Thomas Jefferson (International Correspondence Schools)

Francis, Paul James (Society of the Atonement)

George, William Reuben (George Junior Republic)

Goodall, Harvey L. (livestock market paper)

Guérin, Anne-Thérèse (Mother Theodore) (Sisters of Providence of Saint Mary-of-the-Woods)

Hallett, Benjamin (Seamen's Bethels)

Harris, John (Harrisburg, Pa.)

Harris, Paul Percy (Rotary International)

Harvard, John (Harvard College)

Haynes, George Edmund (Urban League)

Hecker, Isaac Thomas (Paulists)

Herr, John (Reformed Mennonites)

Higginson, Henry Lee (Boston Symphony Orchestra)

Hodur, Francis (Polish National Catholic Church in America)

Holmes, Joseph Austin (U. S. Bureau of Mines)

Houghton, George Hendric (Church of the Transfiguration, N.Y.C.)

Hubbard, Gardiner Greene (National Geographic Society)

Huidekoper, Harm Jan (Meadville Theological School)

Huntington, Henry Edwards (Hungington Library and Art Gallery)

Hyde, Henry Baldwin (Equitable Life Assurance Society of the U.S.)

Jackson, Patrick Tracy (cotton factories at Lowell, Mass.)

Jansky, Karl Guthe (science of radio astronomy)

Jenckes, Joseph (Pawtucket, R.I.)

Johnson, Elijah (Liberia)

Jones, Robert Reynolds ("Bob") (Bob Jones University)

Joubert de la Muraille, James Hector Marie Nicholas (Oblate Sisters of Providence)

Juneau, Solomon Laurent (Milwaukee, Wis.)

Kalmus, Herbert Thomas (Technicolor Incorporated)

Keeley, Oliver Hudson (Grange)

Keith, George ("Christian Quakers")

Keith, Minor Cooper (American Fruit Company)

Keppler, Joseph (*Puck*)

King, John (eclectic school of medicine)

King, Richard (ranch)

Kneisel, Franz (Kneisel Quartet)

Knight, Jonathan (American Medical Association, Yale Medical School)

Kroger, Bernhard Henry (Kroger grocery store chain)

Kuskov, Ivan Aleksandrovich (Russian settlement in California)

Laclede, Pierre (St. Louis, Mo.)

Lambeau, Earl Louis ("Curly") (Green Bay Packers football team)

Lane, John (Vicksburg, Miss.)

Lee, Ann (Shakers in America)

Lewis, Samuel (free public school system of Ohio)

Liggett, Louis Kroh (United Drug Company)

Lindley, Jacob (Ohio University)

Lippard, George (Brotherhood of the Union)

Lorimier, Pierre Louis (Cape Girardeau, Mo.)

Lovejoy, Asa Lawrence (Portland, Oreg.)

Low, Juliette Gordon (Girl Scouts of America)

Lowell, John, 1799–1836 (Lowell Institute)

Lyon, David Willard (YMCA in China)

McClellan, George, 1796–1847 (Jefferson Medical College)

Maclay, Robert Samuel (colleges)

McPherson, Aimee Semple (International Church of the Foursquare Gospel)

Mannes, David (Mannes College of Music)

Marquis, Albert Nelson (*Who's Who in America*)

Maslow, Abraham H. (humanistic psychology)

Maurin, Peter Aristide (Catholic Worker Movement)

Meeker, Nathan Cook (Union Colony of Colorado)

Menninger, Charles Frederick (Menninger Clinic)

Meyer, Annie Nathan (Barnard College)

Mooney, William (New York Society of Tammany)

Morgan, John (University of Penn. Medical School)

Muller, Hermann Joseph (radiation genetics)

Murray, John, 1741–1815 (Universalism in America)

Myer, Albert James (Weather Bureau)

Nast, William (first German Methodist church in the U.S.)

Newbrough, John Ballou (Shalam religious community)

Newcomer, Christian (Church of the United Brethren in Christ)

Noble, Samuel (Anniston, Ala.)

Noyes, John Humphrey (Oneida Community)

Oglethorpe, James Edward (colony of Georgia)

Osgood, Jacob (Osgoodites)

Otterbein, Philip William (Church of the United Brethren in Christ)

Painter, Gamaliel (Middlebury College)

Palmer, Daniel David (chiropractic)

Parmly, Eleazer (dentistry, as an organized profession)

Pastorius, Francis Daniel (Germantown, Pa.)

Peirce, Charles Sanders (pragmatism)

Penn, William (Pennsylvania)

Peralta, Pedro de (Santa Fé, New Mex.)

Phelps, Guy Rowland (Connecticut Mutual Life Insurance Company)

Phillips, Frank (Phillips Petroleum Company)

Phillips, John (Phillips Exeter Academy)

Phillips, Lena Madesin (International Federation of Business and Professional Women, National Federation of Business and Professional Women's Clubs)

Phillips, Samuel (Phillips Academy, Andover)

Pierpont, James (Yale College)

Plant, Henry Bradley (Plant system of railroads)
Porter, James Madison (Lafayette College)
Porter, Rufus (*Scientific American*)
Portolá, Gaspar de (San Diego and Monterey, Cal.)
Purnell, Benjamin (House of David)
Purviance, David (Christian denomination)
Putnam, Gideon (Saratoga Springs, N.Y.)
Quimby, Phineas Parkhurst (mental healing)
Radcliff, Jacob (Jersey City, N.J.)
Randall, Benjamin (Free-Will Baptists)
Rapp, George (Harmony Society)
Rathbone, Justus Henry (Order of Knights of Pythias)
Rezanov, Nikolai Petrovich (Russian-American Company)
Rice, John Andrew (Black Mountain College)
Rice, William Marsh (William Marsh Rice Institute)
Robinson-Smith, Gertrude (Berkshire Symphony Festival, Inc., Tanglewood)
Rochester, Nathaniel (Rochester, N.Y.)
Rogers, John, 1648–1721 (Rogerenes)
Rogers, Mary Josephine (Maryknoll Sisters)
Ross, Harold Wallace (*New Yorker*)
Rowell, George Presbury (*Printer's Ink*)
Russell, Mother Mary Baptist (Sisters of Mercy in California)
Russell, William Hepburn (Pony Express)
Sanford, Henry Shelton (Sanford, Fla.)
Scherman, Harry (Book-of-the-Month Club)
Schneider, Herman (cooperative system of education)
Schrieck, Sister Louise Van der (Sisters of Notre Dame de Namur)
Seton, Elizabeth Ann Bayley (American Society of Charity)
Severance, Caroline Maria Seymour (women's clubs)
Shaw, Henry (Missouri Botanical Garden)
Shelekhov, Grigori Ivanovich (first Russian colony in America)
Shinn, Asa (Methodist Protestant Church)
Shipherd, John Jay (Oberlin College)
Simmons, William Joseph (Ku Klux Klan)

Simpson, Albert Benjamin (Christian and Missionary Alliance)
Slater, Samuel (American cotton industry)
Smith, Sophia (Smith College)
Snethen, Nicholas (Methodist Protestant Church)
Sorin, Edward Frederick (University of Notre Dame)
Spalding, Catherine (Sisters of Charity of Nazareth)
Spring, Samuel (American Board of Commissioners for Foreign Missions)
Spring, Samuel (Andover Theological Seminary)
Stephenson, Benjamin Franklin (Grand Army of the Republic)
Stewart, Philo Penfield (Oberlin College)
Still, Andrew Taylor (osteopathy)
Taylor, Joseph Wright (Bryn Mawr College)
Teresa, Mother (Visitation Order in U.S.)
Teusler, Rudolf Bolling (St. Luke's Hospital, Tokyo)
Thomas, Isaiah (American Antiquarian Society)
Thomas, Robert Bailey (*Farmer's Almanack*)
Tonty, Henry de (Mississippi Valley settlements)
Tourjée, Eben (New England Conservatory of Music)
Townley, Arthur Charles (Nonpartisan League)
Townsend, Francis Everett (Old Age Revolving Pension Plan)
Tufts, Charles (Tufts College)
Upchurch, John Jordan (Ancient Order of United Workmen)
Valentine, Robert Grosvenor (industrial counseling)
Van Raalte, Albertus Christiaan (Dutch settlement in Holland, Mich.)
Varick, James (African Methodist Episcopal Zion Church)
Vassar, Matthew (Vassar College)
Vattemare, Nicholas Marie Alexandre (system of international exchanges)
Vincennes, François Marie Bissot, Sieur de (Vincennes Ind.)
Wade, Jeptha Homer (American commercial telegraph system)
Walgreen, Charles Rudolph (Walgreen drugstore chain)
Wertheimer, Max (Gestalt movement)
Wetherill, Samuel (Free Quakers)
White, Alma Bridwell (Pillar of Fire Church)

White, Thomas Willis (*Southern Literary Messenger*)
FRATERNAL ORDER LEADER
Davis, James John
Wilson, J(ames) Finley
FREEMASON
Morgan, William
Pike, Albert
FREE-SOILER
Stearns, George Luther
FREE-STATE ADVOCATE
Conway, Martin Franklin
Pomeroy, Samuel Clarke
FREETHINKER
Bennett, De Robigne Mortimer
Underwood, Benjamin Franklin
Wright, Frances
FREIGHTER (See also TRANSPORTER)
Majors, Alexander
Russell, William Hepburn
FRONTIERSMAN (See also DISCOVERER, EXPLORER, GUIDE, PIONEER, SCOUT)
Bridger, James
Burleson, Edward
California Joe
Crockett, David
Dixon, William
Fonda, John H.
Hughes, Price
Kenton, Simon
Lillie, Gordon William
Maxwell, Lucien Bonaparte
North, Frank Joshua
Oñate, Juan de
Shelby, Evan
Wallace, William Alexander Anderson
FROZEN FOOD PROCESS INVENTOR
Birdseye, Clarence
FUNDAMENTALIST ADVOCATE
Price, George Edward McCready
FUND RAISER
Jones, John Price
FUR TRADER (See also FUR TRAPPER, MERCHANT, TRADER, TRAPPER)
Ashely, William Henry
Astor, John Jacob
Baranov, Alexander Andreevich
Bent, Charles
Bent, William
Bridger, James
Cerré, Jean Gabriel
Chouteau, Auguste Pierre
Chouteau, Jean Pierre
Chouteau, Pierre
Crooks, Ramsay
Dickson, Robert
Farnham, Russel
Franchère, Gabriel
Gray, Robert
Harmon, Daniel Williams
Henry, Alexander
Hubbard, Gurdon Saltonstall
Kinzie, John
Kittson, Norman Wolfred
La Barge, Joseph
Larpenteur, Charles
Lisa, Manuel

Mackenzie, Donald
Mackenzie, Kenneth
McLeod, Martin
Menard, Pierre
Mitchell, David Dawson
Morton, Thomas
Navarre, Pierre
Ogden, Peter Skene
Pilcher, Joshua
Pond, Peter
Pratte, Bernard
Provost, Etienne
Rolette, Jean Joseph
Ross, Alexander
Sarpy, Peter A.
Sibley, Henry Hastings
Stuart, Robert
Sublette, William Lewis
Thompson, David
Vanderburgh, William Henry
Willard, Simon
FUR TRAPPER (See also FUR TRAD-
ER, MERCHANT, TRADER,
TRAPPER)
Campbell, Robert
Henry, Andrew

GAMBLER
Canfield, Richard A.
Morrissey, John
GANGSTER (See also BOOTLEGGER,
CRIMINAL)
Capone, Alphonse ("Al")
Flegenheimer, Arthur
Kelly, Machine Gun (George
Kelly Barnes, Jr.)
Madden, Owen Victor
("Owney")
GAS PRODUCER
Gregory, Thomas Barger
GEMOLOGIST
Kunz, George Frederick
GENEALOGIST
Alden, Ebenezer
Banks, Charles Edward
Chester, Joseph Lemuel
Farmer, John
Lapham, William Berry
Putnam, Eben
Shattuck, Lemuel
Sherman, Frank Dempster
Smith, Charles Perrin
Stiles, Henry Reed
Tyler, Lyon Gardiner
GENERAL (See also AVIATOR, SOL-
DIER)
Abercromby, James
Allen, Henry Tureman
Arnold, Henry Harley
Arnold, Lewis Golding
Braddock, Edward
Colston, Raleigh Edward
Conway, Thomas
Cooper, Samuel
Corse, John Murray
Couch, Darius Nash
Cox, Jacob Dolson
Eisenhower, Dwight David
Evans, Clement Anselm
Evans, Nathan George
Floyd, John Buchanan
Forrest, Nathan Bedford

Gartrell, Lucius Jeremiah
Grant, Ulysses Simpson
Greene, Nathaniel
Gregg, John
Hanson, Roger Weightman
Herron, Francis Jay
Hodges, Courtney Hicks
Howe, George Augustus, third
Viscount Howe
Humbert, Jean Joseph Amable
Jackson, William Hicks
Kalb, Johann
Kelser, Raymond Alexander
Knox, Henry
Krueger, Walter
Lee, Charles, 1731–1782
Logan, Thomas Muldrup,
1840–1914
Loudoun, John Campbell,
Fourth Earl of
MacArthur, Douglas
McIntosh, William
Manigault, Arthur Middleton
March, Peyton Conway
Marion, Francis
Maxey, Samuel Bell
Monckton, Robert
Moultrie, William
Nicholls, Francis Redding
Tillou
Patton, George Smith
Pershing, John Joseph
Polk, Leonidas
Porter, Peter Buell
St. John, Isaac Munroe
Slocum, Henry Warner
Steuben, Friedrich Wilhelm
Ludolf Gerhard Augustin,
Baron von
Stevenson, Carter Littlepage
Sullivan, John
Trumbull, Joseph
Van Dorn, Earl
Wadsworth, Peleg
Wainwright, Jonathan Mayhew
Walthall, Edward Cary
Ward, Artemas
Watie, Stand
Webb, Daniel
Wigfall, Louis Trezevant
Wise, Henry Alexander
Woodhull, Nathaniel
Wooster, David
GENETICIST (See also BIOLOGIST,
CYTOLOGIST, ZOOLOGIST)
Bridges, Calvin Blackman
Collins, Guy N.
Emerson, Rollins Adams
Morgan, Thomas Hunt
Muller, Hermann Joseph
Sinnott, Edmund Ware
GEODESIST (See also SURVEYOR)
Bowie, William
Davidson, George
Hassler, Ferdinand Rudolph
Hayford, John Fillmore
Hilgard, Julius Erasmus
Rees, John Krom
GEOGRAPHER (See also CARTOGRA-
PHER, MAPMAKER)
Atwood, Wallace Walter
Baker, Marcus

Baker, Oliver Edwin
Bowman, Isaiah
Brigham, Albert Perry
Brooks, Alfred Hulse
Brown, Ralph Hall
Cowles, Henry Chandler
Darby, William
Davidson, George
Davis, William Morris
De Brahm, William Gerard
Erskine, Robert
Evans, Lewis
Fenneman, Nevin Melancthon
Gannett, Henry
Goode, John Paul
Guyot, Arnold Henry
Huntington, Ellsworth
Hutchins, Thomas
Jefferson, Mark Sylvester
William
Johnson, Douglas Wilson
Melish, John
Mitchell, Samuel Augustus
Morse, Jedidiah
Pory, John
Robinson, Edward, 1794–1863
Schott, Charles Anthony
Tanner, Henry Schenck
Tarr, Ralph Stockman
Tatham, William
Thompson, David
Worcester, Joseph Emerson
GEOLOGIST (See also GEOMOR-
PHOLOGIST, GEOPHYSICIST)
Agassiz, Jean Louis Rodolphe
Ashburner, Charles Albert
Atwood, Wallace Walter
Bailey, Jacob Whitman
Barrell, Joseph
Bascom, Florence
Becker, George Ferdinand
Blake, William Phipps
Boll, Jacob
Bowen, Norman Levi
Boyé, Martin Hans
Bradley, Frank Howe
Brainerd, Ezra
Branner, John Casper
Broadhead, Garland Carr
Brooks, Alfred Hulse
Brooks, Thomas Benton
Bryan, Kirk
Calvin, Samuel
Campbell, Marius Robinson
Carll, John Franklin
Chamberlin, Thomas Chrowder
Christy, David
Clapp, Charles Horace
Clark, William Bullock
Claypole, Edward Waller
Condon, Thomas
Cook, George Hammell
Crosby, William Otis
Cross, Charles Whitman
Daly, Reginald Aldworth
Dana, James Dwight
Darton, Nelson Horatio
Davis, William Morris
Day, David Talbot
Diller, Joseph Silas
Dutton, Clarence Edward
Emerson, Benjamin Kendall

Emmons, Ebenezer
Emmons, Samuel Franklin
Fenneman, Nevin Melancthon
Foshag, William Frederick
Gilbert, Grove Karl
Grabau, Amadeus William
Hague, Arnold
Hall, James, 1811–1898
Hayden, Ferdinand Vandiveer
Hayden, Horace H.
Hayes, Charles Willard
Heilprin, Angelo
Hilgard, Eugene Woldemar
Hitchcock, Charles Henry
Hitchcock, Edward, 1793–1864
Houghton, Douglass
Hunt, Thomas Sterry
Iddings, Joseph Paxon
Irving, John Duer
Irving, Roland Duer
Jackson, Charles Thomas
Jaggar, Thomas Augustus, Jr.
Johnson, Douglas Wilson
Keith, Arthur
Kemp, James Furman
Kerr, Washington Caruthers
King, Clarence
Lawson, Andrew Cowper
LeConte, Joseph
Lesley, Peter
Leverett, Frank
Lindgren, Waldemar
Lucas, Anthony Francis
Lyman, Benjamin Smith
McGee, William John
Maclure, William
Marbut, Curtis Fletcher
Marcou, Jules
Mather, William Williams
Matthes, François Emile
Meinzer, Oscar Edward
Merrill, George Perkins
Mitchell, Elisha
Newberry, John Strong
Orton, Edward Francis Baxter
Owen, David Dale
Penrose, Richard Alexander
  Fullerton
Percival, James Gates
Perin, Charles Page
Perkins, George Henry
Pirsson, Louis Valentine
Powell, John Wesley
Price, George Edward
  McCready
Proctor, John Robert
Prosser, Charles Smith
Pumpelly, Raphael
Ransome, Frederick Leslie
Rice, William North
Roemer, Karl Ferdinand
Rogers, Henry Darwin
Rogers, William Barton
Russell, Israel Cook
Safford, James Merrill
Salisbury, Rollin D.
Scopes, John Thomas
Scott, William Berryman
Shaler, Nathaniel Southgate
Smith, Erminnie Adelle Platt
Smith, Eugene Allen
Smith, George Otis

Smith, James Perrin
Spurr, Josiah Edward
Stetson, Henry Crosby
Stevenson, John James
Swallow, George Clinton
Talmage, James Edward
Tarr, Ralph Stockman
Taylor, Frank Bursley
Taylor, Richard Cowling
Troost, Gerard
Udden, Johan August
Ulrich, Edward Oscar
Upham, Warren
Van Hise, Charles Richard
Vanuxem, Lardner
Vaughan, Thomas Wayland
Veatch, Arthur Clifford
White, Charles Abiathar
White, David
White, Israel Charles
Whitney, Josiah Dwight
Willis, Bailey
Winchell, Alexander
Winchell, Horace Vaughn
Winchell, Newton Horace
Woodworth, Jay Backus
Worthen, Amos Henry
Wright, George Frederick
GEOMORPHOLOGIST
  Bryan, Kirk
  Johnson, Douglas Wilson
GEOPHYSICIST
  Day, Arthur Louis
  Fleming, John Adam
GIRL SCOUT LEADER
  Choate, Anne Hyde Clarke
  Low, Juliette Gordon
GLASSMAKER (See also GLAZIER)
  Hewes, Robert
  Leighton, William
  Libbey, Edward Drummond
  Stiegel, Henry William
  Tiffany, Louis Comfort
GLAZIER (See also GLASSMAKER)
  Godfrey, Thomas
GOLDSMITH (See also CRAFTSMAN)
  Le Roux, Bartholomew
GOLF-COURSE DESIGNER
  Macdonald, Charles Blair
GOLFER
  Armour, Thomas Dickson
    ("Tommy")
  Hagen, Walter Charles
  Little, William Lawson, Jr.
  Macdonald, Charles Blair
  Ouimet, Francis Desales
  Smith, Horton
  Travers, Jerome Dunstan
  Travis, Walter John
  Wood, Craig Ralph
GOVERNMENT OFFICIAL (See also
    PUBLIC OFFICIAL)
  Ames, Joseph Sweetman
  Arnold, Thurman Wesley
  Ballantine, Arthur Atwood
  Bennett, Henry Garland
  Bethune, Mary McLeod
  Biffle, Leslie L.
  Breckinridge, Henry Skillman
  Bundy, Harvey Hollister
  Bunker, Arthur Hugh
  Clayton, William Lockhart

Coolidge, Thomas Jefferson
Cooper, William John
Creel, George
Dennett, Tyler (Wilbur)
Dodge, Joseph Morrell
Dorn, Harold Fred
Early, Stephen Tyree
Flint, Weston
Fly, James Lawrence
Gaston, Herbert Earle
Haas, Francis Joseph
Hannegan, Robert Emmet
Herrick, Robert Welch
Hines, Frank Thomas
Hopkins, Harry Lloyd
Hunt, Gaillard
Johnson, Hugh Samuel
Kennedy, Joseph Patrick
Knudsen, William S.
Krug, Julius Albert
Leffingwell, Russell Cornell
Legge, Alexander
McEntee, James Joseph
Manly, Basil Maxwell
Merriam, Charles Edward, Jr.
Meyer, Eugene Isaac
Mitchell, William DeWitt
Nelson, Donald Marr
Niles, David K.
Pasvolsky, Leo
Payne, Christopher Harrison
Pelham, Robert A.
Pickens, William
Post, Louis Freeland
Powderly, Terence Vincent
Richberg, Donald Randall
Russell, Charles Wells
Sargent, Frank Pierce
Sherwood, Robert Emmet
Talbott, Harold Elstner
Vance, Harold Sines
Vanderlip, Frank Arthur
Wadsworth, Eliot
Warburg, James Paul
Warner, Edward Pearson
Waterman, Alan Tower
Waymack, William Wesley
Wharton, Francis
Zook, George Frederick
GOVERNOR (ACTING)
  Argall, Sir Samuel (Va.)
  Blair, John (Va.)
  Danforth, Thomas (Mass.)
  Evans, John (Pa.)
  Hamilton, Andrew, d.1703 (Pa.)
  Hamilton, Andrew Jackson
    (Tex.)
  Hamilton, James, 1710–1783
    (Pa.)
  Lloyd, Thomas (Pa.)
  Nelson, William, 1711–1722
    (Va.)
  Paddock, Algernon Sidney
    (Nebr.)
  Parsons, Lewis Eliphalet (Ala.)
  St. Ange de Bellerive, Louis
    (La.)
  Sharkey, William Lewis (Miss.)
  Shippen, Edward, 1639–1712
    (Pa.)
  Stanton, Frederick Perry
    (Kans.)

Stoddard, Amos (La.)
GOVERNOR (COLONIAL)
Andros, Sir Edmund
Archdale, John
Basse, Jeremiah
Belcher, Jonathan
Bellingham, Richard
Berkeley, Sir William
Bernard, Sir Francis
Botetourt, Norborne Berkeley,
   Baron de
Burnet, William
Burrington, George
Calvert, Leonard
Campbell, Lord William
Clarke, Walter
Clinton, George
Coote, Richard
Copley, Lionel
Cosby, William
Cranston, John
Cranston, Samuel
Cubero, Pedro Rodriguez
Culpeper, Thomas, Lord
Dobbs, Arthur
Dongan, Thomas
Dudley, Joseph
Dudley, Thomas
Dunmore, John Murray, Earl of
Eden, Robert
Ellis, Henry
Fendall, Josias
Fitch, Thomas
Fletcher, Benjamin
Franklin, William
Gage, Thomas
Gates, Sir Thomas
Gooch, Sir William
Greene, William
Hamilton, Andrew, d. 1703
Harvey, Sir John
Hopkins, Stephen
Hunter, Robert
Hutchinson, Thomas
Hyde, Edward
Johnson, Robert
Johnson, Sir Nathaniel
Johnston, Gabriel
Keith, Sir William
Kieft, Willem
Law, Jonathan
Leete, William
Leverett, John, 1616–1679
Lovelace, Francis
Ludwell, Philip
Lyttelton, William Henry
Markham, William
Martin, Josiah
Mayhew, Thomas
Middleton, Arthur
Miró, Esteban Rodríguez
Moore, James, d. 1706
Moore, Sir Henry
Nicholson, Francis
Nicolls, Richard
Ogle, Samuel
Phips, Sir William
Pierpont, Francis Harrison
Pott, John
Pownall, Thomas
Printz, Johan Björnsson
Reynolds, John

Rising, Johan Classon
Russwurm, John Brown
Saltonstall, Gurdon
Sharpe, Horatio
Shirley, William
Shute, Samuel
Stone, William
Talcott, Joseph
Thomas, George
Treat, Robert
Trumbull, Jonathan, 1710–1785
Tryon, William
Ulloa, Antonio de
Vane, Sir Henry
Van Twiller, Wouter
Villeré, Jacques Philippe
Ward, Richard
Ward, Samuel, 1725–1776
Wentworth, Benning
Wentworth, John, 1737
   N.S.–1820
West, Joseph
Winslow, Josiah
Winthrop, John, 1587/88
   O.S.–1649
Winthrop, John, 1605/06
   O.S.–1676
Winthrop, John, 1638–1707
Wolcott, Oliver, 1726–1797
Wolcott, Roger
Wyatt, Sir Francis
Yeamans, Sir John
Yeardley, Sir George
GOVERNOR (GENERAL)
Alvarado, Juan Bautista
   (Mexican California)
Brown, William (Bermuda)
Coddington, William
   (Aquidneck)
Colton, George Radcliffe
   (Puerto Rico)
Corondo, Francisco Vázquez
   (Nueva Galicia)
Hasket, Elias (Bahamas)
Minuit, Peter (New Sweden)
Vandreuli-Cavagnal, Pierre de
   Riguad, Marquis de (Canada)
Wright, Luke Edward
   (Philippines)
GOVERNOR (STATE)
Aandahl, Fred George (N.Dak.)
Abbett, Leon (N.J.)
Adams, Alva (Colo.)
Adams, James Hopkins (S.C.)
Alcorn, James Lusk (Miss.)
Alger, Russell Alexander
   (Mich.)
Allen, Henry Justin (Kans.)
Allen, Henry Watkins (La.)
Allen, Philip (R.I.)
Allen, William (Ohio)
Allston, Robert Francis Withers
   (S.C.)
Altgeld, John Peter (Ill.)
Ames, Adelbert (Miss.)
Ames, Oliver (Mass.)
Ammons, Elias Milton (Colo.)
Andrew, John Albion (Mass.)
Anthony, George Tobey (Kans.)
Ashe, Samuel (N.C.)
Atkinson, William Yates (Ga.)

Aycock, Charles Brantley (N.C.)
Bagby, Arthur Pendleton (Ala.)
Baldwin, Henry Porter (Mich.)
Baldwin, Roger Sherman
   (Conn.)
Baldwin, Simeon Eben (Conn.)
Banks, Nathaniel Prentiss
   (Mass.)
Barrett, Frank Aloysius (Wyo.)
Barry, John Stewart (Mich.)
Barstow, William Augustus
   (Wis.)
Bartlett, Josiah (N.H.)
Bartley, Mordecai (Ohio)
Bashford, Coles (Wis.)
Bate, William Brimage (Tenn.)
Bates, Frederick (Mo.)
Beaver, James Addams (Pa.)
Bell, Peter Hansborough (Tex.)
Bell, Samuel (N.H.)
Bennett, Caleb Prew (Del.)
Berry, James Henderson (Ark.)
Berry, Nathaniel Springer
   (N.H.)
Bibb, William Wyatt (Ala.)
Bickett, Thomas Walter (N.C.)
Bienville, Jean Baptiste Le
   Moyne, Sieur de (La.)
Bigler, John (Calif.)
Bigler, William (Pa.)
Bilbo, Theodore Gilmore
   (Miss.)
Bissell, William Henry (Ill.)
Black, Frank Swett (N.Y.)
Blackburn, Luke Pryor (Ky.)
Blaine, John James (Wis.)
Blair, Austin (Mich.)
Blanchard, Newton Crain (La.)
Blasdel, Henry Goode (Nev.)
Blease, Coleman Livingston
   (S.C.)
Bliss, Aaron Thomas (Mich.)
Blount, Willie (Tenn.)
Bloxham, William Dunnington
   (Fla.)
Boggs, Lillburn W. (Mo.)
Boies, Horace (Iowa)
Bond, Shadrach (Ill.)
Bonham, Milledge Lake (S.C.)
Booth, Newton (Calif.)
Boreman, Arthur Ingram
   (W.Va.)
Bouck, William C. (N.Y.)
Bowdoin, James (Mass.)
Bowie, Oden (Md.)
Bowie, Robert (Md.)
Bradford, Augustus Williamson
   (Md.)
Bradly, William O'Connell (Ky.)
Bramlette, Thomas E. (Ky.)
Branch, John (N.C.)
Brandon, Gerard Chittocque
   (Miss.)
Brewster, Ralph Owen (Maine)
Bridges, (Henry) Styles (N.H.)
Brough, John (Ohio)
Broward, Napoleon Bonaparte
   (Fla.)
Brown, Aaron Venable (Tenn.)
Brown, Albert Gallatin (Miss.)
Brown, Benjamin Gratz (Mo.)
Brown, John Calvin (Tenn.)

Brown, John Young (Ky.)
Brownlow, William Gannaway (Tenn.)
Bryan, Charles Wayland (Nebr.)
Buckingham, William Alfred (Conn.)
Bulkeley, Morgan Gardner (Conn.)
Bull, William (S.C.)
Bullock, Rufus Brown (Ga.)
Burke, Thomas (N.C.)
Burton, Hutchins Gordon (N.C.)
Burton, William (Del.)
Bushnell, Asa Smith (Ohio)
Butler, Benjamin Franklin (Mass.)
Butler, Ezra (Vt.)
Butler, Pierce Mason (S.C.)
Byrd, Harry Flood (Va.)
Cabell, William H. (Va.)
Cadillac, Antoine de la Mothe (La.)
Call, Richard Keith (Fla.)
Cameron, William Evelyn (Va.)
Campbell, William Bowen (Tenn.)
Candler, Allen Daniel (Ga.)
Cannon, Newton (Tenn.)
Cannon, William (Del.)
Capper, Arthur (Kans.)
Carney, Thomas (Kans.)
Carondelet, Francisco Luis Hector, Baron de (La.)
Carpenter, Cyrus Clay (Iowa)
Carr, Elias (N.C.)
Carroll, John Lee (Md.)
Carroll, William (Tenn.)
Carteret, Philip (N.J.)
Chamberlain, Daniel Henry (S.C.)
Chamberlain, George Earle (Oreg.)
Chamberlain, Joshua Lawrence (Maine)
Chambers, John (Iowa)
Chapman, Reuben (Ala.)
Cheney, Person Colby (N.H.)
Chittenden, Martin (Vt.)
Chittenden, Thomas (Vt.)
Churchill, Thomas James (Ark.)
Claflin, William (Mass.)
Claiborne, William Charles Coles (La.)
Clark, Charles (Miss.)
Clark, James (Ky.)
Clark, John (Ga.)
Clark, Myron Holley (N.Y.)
Clarke, James Paul (Ark.)
Clay, Clement Comer (Ala.)
Clayton, Joshua (Del.)
Clayton, Powell (Ark.)
Clement, Frank Goad (Tenn.)
Cleveland, Chauncey Fitch (Conn.)
Cleveland, Stephen Grover (N.Y.)
Coburn, Abner (Maine)
Coke, Richard (Tex.)
Coles, Edward (Ill.)
Collier, Henry Watkins (Ala.)
Comer, Braxton Bragg (Ala.)

Conway, James Sevier (Ark.)
Cornbury, Edward Hyde (N.Y. and N.J.)
Cornell, Alonzo B. (N.Y.)
Corwin, Thomas (Ohio)
Cox, Jacob Dolson (Ohio)
Crane, Winthrop Murray (Mass.)
Crawford, George Walker (Ga.)
Crawford, Samuel Johnson (Kans.)
Crittenden, Thomas Theodore (Mo.)
Cross, Wilbur Lucius (Conn.)
Crounse, Lorenzo (Nebr.)
Curtin, Andrew Gregg (Pa.)
Davie, William Richardson (N.C.)
Davis, Cushman Kellogg (Minn.)
Davis, Edmund Jackson (Tex.)
Davis, Jeff (Ark.)
De La Warr, Thomas West, Baron (Va.)
Dennison, William (Ohio)
Derbigny, Pierre Auguste Charles Bourguignon (La.)
Dern, George Henry (Utah)
Desha, Joseph (Ky.)
Dickerson, Mahlon (N.J.)
Dingley, Nelson (Maine)
Dix, John Adams (N.Y.)
Douglas, William Lewis (Mass.)
Drake, Francis Marion (Iowa)
Drayton, John (S.C.)
Dudley, Edward Bishop (N.C.)
Duff, James Henderson (Pa.)
Duncan, Joseph (Ill.)
Dunlap, Robert Pinckney (Maine)
Duval, William Pope (Fla.)
Easton, John (R.I.)
Easton, Nicholas (R.I.)
Eden, Charles (N.C.)
Edge, Walter Evans (N.J.)
Edison, Charles (N.J.)
Edwards, Henry Waggaman (Conn.)
Edwards, Ninian (Ill.)
Elbert, Samuel (Ga.)
Ellis, John Willis (N.C.)
Ellsworth, William Wolcott (Conn.)
Endecott, John (Mass.)
Fages, Pedro (Calif.)
Fairbanks, Erastus (Vt.)
Fairchild, Lucius (Wis.)
Fauquier, Francis (Va.)
Felch, Alpheus (Mich.)
Fenner, Arthur (R.I.)
Fenner, James (R.I.)
Fenton, Reuben Eaton (N.Y.)
Ferguson, James Edward (Tex.)
Ferguson, Miriam Amanda Wallace (Tex.)
Ferris, Woodbridge Nathan (Mich.)
Ferry, Elisha Peyre (Wash.)
Fifer, Joseph Wilson (Ill.)
Fishback, William Meade (Ark.)
Fitzpatrick, Benjamin (Ala.)
Flanagin, Harris (Ark.)

Fleming, Aretas Brooks (W. Va.)
Flower, Roswell Pettibone (N.Y.)
Floyd, John (Va.)
Floyd, John Buchanan (Va.)
Folk, Joseph Wingate (Mo.)
Foot, Samuel Augustus (Conn.)
Foote, Henry Stuart (Miss.)
Foraker, Joseph Benson (Ohio)
Ford, Thomas (Ill.)
Foster, Charles (Ohio)
Foster, Murphy James (La.)
Francis, David Rowland (Mo.)
Francis, John Brown (R.I.)
Frazier, Lynn Joseph (N.Dak.)
Fuller, Levi Knight (Vt.)
Furnas, Robert Wilkinson (Nebr.)
Gamble, Hamilton Rowan (Mo.)
Gardner, Henry Joseph (Mass.)
Gardner, Oliver Maxwell (N.C.)
Garrard, James (Ky.)
Garvin, Lucius Fayette Clark (R.I.)
Gayle, John (Ala.)
Gear, John Henry (Iowa)
Geary, John White (Pa.)
Gilmer, George Rockingham (Ga.)
Gilmore, Joseph Albree (N.H.)
Gist, William Henry (S.C.)
Glynn, Martin Henry (N.Y.)
Goebel, William (Ky.)
Goldsborough, Charles (Md.)
Grant, James Benton (Colo.)
Graves, David Bibb (Ala.)
Gray, Isaac Pusey (Ind.)
Green, Theodore Francis (R.I.)
Greene, William (R.I.)
Greenhalge, Frederic Thomas (Mass.)
Greenup, Christopher (Ky.)
Grimes, James Wilson (Iowa)
Griswold, Matthew (Conn.)
Guild, Curtis, 1860–1915 (Mass.)
Hadley, Herbert Spencer (Mo.)
Hagood, Johnson (S.C.)
Hahn, Georg Michael Decker (La.)
Haight, Henry Huntly (Calif.)
Haines, Daniel (N.J.)
Hall, Hiland (Vt.)
Hall, Luther Egbert (La.)
Hall, Willard Preble (Mo.)
Hamilton, James, 1786–1857 (S.C.)
Hamilton, Paul (S.C.)
Hamilton, William Thomas (Md.)
Hammond, James Henry (S.C.)
Hampton, Wade, 1818–1902 (S.C.)
Hardin, Charles Henry (Mo.)
Hardwick, Thomas William (Ga.)
Harmon, Judson (Ohio)
Harriman, Walter (N.H.)
Harrison, Benjamin, 1726–1791 (Va.)

Harrison, Henry Baldwin (Conn.)
Hartness, James (Vt.)
Harvey, Louis Powell (Wis.)
Haskell, Charles Nathaniel (Okla.)
Hawley, James Henry (Idaho)
Hayne, Robert Young (S.C.)
Haynes, John (Conn. & Mass.)
Hébert, Paul Octave (La.)
Helm, John Larue (Ky.)
Henderson, James Pinckney (Tex.)
Hendricks, Thomas Andrews (Ind.)
Hendricks, William (Ind.)
Henry, John, 1750–1798 (Md.)
Herter, Christian Archibald (Mass.)
Hicks, Thomas Holliday (Md.)
Hiester, Joseph (Pa.)
Hoadly, George (Ohio)
Hoard, William Dempster (Wis.)
Hobby, William Pettus (Tex.)
Hoey, Clyde Roark (N.C.)
Hoffman, John Thompson (N.Y.)
Hogg, James Stephen (Tex.)
Holbrook, Frederick (Vt.)
Holden, William Woods (N.C.)
Holmes, David (Miss.)
Hopkins, Edward (Conn.)
Hoppin, William Warner (R.I.)
Horner, Henry (Ill.)
Houston, George Smith (Ala.)
Houstoun, John (Ga.)
Hovey, Alvin Peterson (Ind.)
Howell, Richard (N.J.)
Hubbard, John (Maine)
Hubbard, Lucius Frederick (Minn.)
Hubbard, Richard Bennett (Tex.)
Hughes, Charles Evans (N.Y.)
Humphreys, Benjamin Grubb (Miss.)
Hunt, George Wylie Paul (Ariz.)
Hunt, Lester Callaway (Wyo.)
Hunt, Washington (N.Y.)
Huntington, Samuel, 1731–1796 (Conn.)
Huntington, Samuel, 1765–1817 (Ohio)
Hyde, Arthur Mastick (Mo.)
Ireland, John, 1827–1896 (Tex.)
Jackson, Claiborne Fox (Mo.)
Jackson, James 1757–1806 (Ga.)
Jarvis, Thomas Jordan (N.C.)
Jenckes Joseph (R.I.)
Jenkins, Charles Jones (Ga.)
Jennings, Jonathan (Ind.)
Jewell, Marshall (Conn.)
Johnson, Edwin Carl (Colo.)
Johnson, Hiram Warren (Calif.)
Johnson, John Albert (Minn.)
Johnson, Thomas (Md.)
Johnston, Joseph Forney (Ala.)
Jones, James Chamberlayne (Tenn.)

Jones, Thomas Goode (Ala.)
Jones, William (R.I.)
Kavanagh, Edward (Maine)
Kellogg, William Pitt (La.)
Kemper, James Lawson (Va.)
Kendrick, John Benjamin (Wyo.)
Kent, Edward (Maine)
Kent, Joseph (Md.)
Kerr, Robert Samuel (Okla.)
King, Austin Augustus (Mo.)
King, John Alsop (N.Y.)
King, Samuel Ward (R.I.)
King, William (Maine)
Kirkwood, Samuel Jordan (Iowa)
Kitchin, William Walton (N.C.)
Knight, Goodwin Jess ("Goodie") (Calif.)
Knott, James Proctor (Ky.)
Kohler, Walter Jodok (Wis.)
La Follette, Philip Fox (Wis.)
La Follette, Robert Marion (Wis.)
Langlie, Arthur Bernard (Wash.)
Larrabee, William (Iowa)
Larrazolo, Octaviano Ambrosio (N.Mex.)
Lawrence, David Leo (Pa.)
Lee, Thomas Sim (Md.)
Lehman, Herbert Henry (N.Y.)
Letcher, John (Va.)
Letcher, Robert Perkins (Ky.)
Lewelling, Lorenzo Dow (Kans.)
Lewis, Morgan (N.Y.)
Ligon, Thomas Watkins (Md.)
Lind, John (Minn.)
Lippitt, Henry (R.I.)
Lloyd, Edward, 1779–1834 (Md.)
Long, Earl Kemp (La.)
Long, Huey Pierce (La.)
Long, John Davis (Mass.)
Lord, William Paine (Oreg.)
Low, Frederick Ferdinand (Calif.)
Lowden, Frank Orren (Ill.)
Lowe, Ralph Phillips (Iowa)
Lowndes, Lloyd (Md.)
Lowry, Robert (Miss.)
Lubbock, Francis Richard (Tex.)
Lucas, Robert (Ohio)
McArthur, Duncan (Ohio)
McCall, Samuel Walker (Mass.)
McClelland, Robert (Mich.)
McClurg, Joseph Washington (Mo.)
McCreary, James Bennett (Ky.)
McCullough, John Griffith (Vt.)
McDaniel, Henry Dickerson (Ga.)
McDonald, Charles James (Ga.)
McDowell, James (Va.)
McEnery, Samuel Douglas (La.)
McGrath, James Howard (R.I.)
McGraw, John Harte (Wash.)
McKay, (James) Douglas (Oreg.)

McLaurin, Anselm Joseph (Miss.)
McLean, Angus Wilton (N.C.)
McMillin, Benton (Tenn.)
McMinn, Joseph (Tenn.)
McNair, Alexander (Mo.)
McNutt, Paul Vories (Ind.)
McRae, Thomas Chipman (Ark.)
Magoffin, Beriah (Ky.)
Magrath, Andrew Gordon (S.C.)
Manning, Richard Irvine, 1789–1836 (S.C.)
Manning, Richard Irvine, 1859–1931 (S.C.)
Marland, Ernest Whitworth (Okla.)
Marmaduke, John Sappington (Mo.)
Marshall, Thomas Riley (Ind.)
Marshall, William Rainey (Minn.)
Martin, Alexander (N.C.)
Martin, John Alexander (Kans.)
Mason, Richard Barnes (Calif.)
Mason, Stevens Thomson (Mich.)
Mathews, Henry Mason (W. Va.)
Mathews, John (S.C.)
Mathews, Samuel (Va.)
Matteson, Joel Aldrich (Ill.)
Matthews, Claude (Ind.)
Mattocks, John (Vt.)
Maybank, Burnet Rhett (S.C.)
Meigs, Return Jonathan (Ohio)
Mellette, Arthur Calvin (S. D.)
Mercer, John Francis (Md.)
Metcalfe, Thomas (Ky.)
Mifflin, Thomas (Pa.)
Milledge, John (Ga.)
Miller, John (Mo.)
Miller, Nathan Lewis (N.Y.)
Milton, John (Fla.)
Mitchell, David Brydie (Ga.)
Mitchell, Nathaniel (Del.)
Montague, Andrew Jackson (Va.)
Moore, Gabriel (Ala.)
Moore, Thomas Overton (La.)
Morehead, Charles Slaughter (Ky.)
Morehead, James Turner (Ky.)
Morehead, John Motley (N.C.)
Morgan, Edwin Denison (N.Y.)
Morril, David Lawrence (N.H.)
Morrill, Anson Peaslee (Maine)
Morrill, Edmund Needham (Kans.)
Morrill, Lot Myrick (Maine)
Morris, Lewis, 1671–1746 (N.J.)
Morris, Luzon Burritt (Conn.)
Morris, Robert Hunter (Pa.)
Morrow, Edwin Porch (Ky.)
Morrow, Jeremiah (Ohio)
Morton, Levi Parsons (N.Y.)
Morton, Marcus, 1784–1864 (Mass.)
Morton, Oliver Perry (Ind.)
Moses, Franklin J. (S.C.)
Moultrie, William (S.C.)

Mouton, Alexander (La.)
Murphy, Franklin (N.J.)
Murphy, Frank (Mich.)
Murphy, Isaac (Ark.)
Nash, Abner (N.C.)
Neely, Matthew Mansfield
  (W.Va.)
Nelson, Knute (Minn.)
Nelson, Thomas (Va.)
Newell, William Augustus (N.J.)
Nicholas, Wilson Cary (Va.)
Nicholls, Francis Redding
  Tillou (La.)
Norbeck, Peter (S.Dak.)
Northen, William Jonathan
  (Ga.)
Noyes, Edward Follansbee
  (Ohio)
Oates, William Calvin (Ala.)
O'Daniel, Wilbert Lee
  ("Pappy") (Tex.)
Odell, Benjamin Barker (N.Y.)
O'Ferrall, Charles Triplett (Va.)
Ogden, Aaron (N.J.)
Oglesby, Richard James (Ill.)
Olden, Charles Smith (N.J.)
Olson, Floyd Bjerstjerne
  (Minn.)
O'Neal, Edward Asbury (Ala.)
Orr, James Lawrence (S.C.)
Osborn, Chase Salmon (Mich.)
Otermín, Antonio de (N.Mex.)
Owsley, William (Ky.)
Paca, William (Md.)
Pacheco, Romualdo (Calif.)
Page, John (Va.)
Paine, Charles (Vt.)
Palmer, John McAuley (Ill.)
Parker, John Milliken (La.)
Parris, Albion Keith (Maine)
Pattison, John M. (Ohio)
Pease, Elisha Marshall (Tex.)
Peay, Austin (Tenn.)
Peck, George Wilbur (Wis.)
Peñalosa Briceño, Diego
  Dioniso de (N.Mex.)
Pennington, William (N.J.)
Pennington, William Sandford
  (N.J.)
Pennoyer, Sylvester (Oreg.)
Pennypacker, Samuel Whitaker
  (Pa.)
Peralta, Pedro de (N.Mex.)
Percy, George (Va.)
Perkins, George Clement
  (Calif.)
Perry, Benjamin Franklin (S.C.)
Perry, Edward Aylesworth (Fla.)
Phelps, John Smith (Mo.)
Philipp, Emanuel Lorenz (Wis.)
Pickens, Francis Wilkinson
  (S.C.)
Pickens, Israel (Ala.)
Pierce, Benjamin (N.H.)
Pillsbury, John Sargent (Minn.)
Pinchot, Gifford (Pa.)
Pinckney, Charles (S.C.)
Pinckney, Thomas (S.C.)
Pingree, Hazen Stuart (Mich.)
Pitkin, Frederick Walker (Colo.)
Pitkin, William, 1694–1769
  (Conn.)

Plaisted, Harris Merrill (Maine)
Plater, George (Md.)
Pleasants, James (Va.)
Pollock, James (Pa.)
Porter, Albert Gallatin (Ind.)
Porter, James Davis (Tenn.)
Pratt, Thomas George (Md.)
Price, Rodman McCamley (N.J.)
Price, Sterling (Mo.)
Proctor, Redfield (Vt.)
Ralston, Samuel Moffett (Ind.)
Ramsey, Alexander (Minn.)
Randall, Alexander Williams
  (Wis.)
Randolph, Theodore Fitz (N.J.)
Randolph, Thomas Mann (Va.)
Rector, Henry Massey (Ark.)
Reid, David Settle (N.C.)
Reynolds, John (Ill.)
Rice, Alexander Hamilton
  (Mass.)
Ritchie, Albert Cabell (Md.)
Ritner, Joseph (Pa.)
Roane, Archibald (Tenn.)
Robertson, Thomas Bolling
  (La.)
Robertson, Wyndham (Va.)
Robinson, Charles (Kans.)
Rogers, John Rankin (Wash.)
Roman, André Bienvenu (La.)
Ross, Lawrence Sullivan (Tex.)
Rusk, Jeremiah McClain (Wis.)
Russell, William Eustis (Mass.)
Rutledge, Edward (S.C.)
St. John, John Pierce (Kans.)
Saulsbury, Gove (Del.)
Scott, Charles (Ky.)
Scott, Robert Kingston (S.C.)
Scott, W(illiam) Kerr (N.C.)
Seligman, Arthur (N.Mex.)
Sevier, John (Tenn.)
Seymour, Horatio (N.Y.)
Seymour, Thomas Hart (Conn.)
Shafroth, John Franklin (Colo.)
Shaw, Leslie Mortier (Iowa)
Shelby, Isaac (Ky.)
Shorter, John Gill (Ala.)
Shoup, George Laird (Idaho)
Shulze, John Andrew (Pa.)
Shunk, Francis Rawn (Pa.)
Sibley, Henry Hastings (Minn.)
Simpson, William Dunlap (S.C.)
Smallwood, William (Md.)
Smith, Alfred Emanuel (N.Y.)
Smith, Hoke (Ga.)
Smith, James Youngs (R.I.)
Smith, Jeremiah, 1759–1842
  (N.H.)
Smith, John Cotton, 1765–1845
  (Conn.)
Smith, John Gregory (Vt.)
Smith, William, 1797–1887
  (Va.)
Snyder, Simon (Pa.)
Southard, Samuel Lewis (N.J.)
Spaight, Richard Dobbs (N.C.)
Sprague, Charles Arthur
  (Oreg.)
Sprague, William, 1830–1915
  (R.I.)
Sproul, William Cameron (Pa.)
Stanford, Leland (Calif.)

Sterling, Ross Shaw (Tex.)
Stevenson, Adlai Ewing, II (Ill.)
Stevenson, John White (Ky.)
Stewart, Robert Marcellus (Mo.)
Stokes, Montfort (N.C.)
Stone, John Marshall (Miss.)
Stone, William Joel (Mo.)
Stoneman, George (Calif.)
Stubbs, Walter Roscoe (Kans.)
Sulzer, William (N.Y.)
Sumner, Increase (Mass.)
Swain, David Lowry (N.C.)
Swann, Thomas (Md.)
Swanson, Claude Augustus
  (Va.)
Talmadge, Eugene (Ga.)
Taylor, Alfred Alexander
  (Tenn.)
Taylor, Robert Love (Tenn.)
Tazewell, Littleton Waller (Va.)
Telfair, Edward (Ga.)
Thomas, Francis (Md.)
Thomas, Philip Francis (Md.)
Thompson, Hugh Smith (S.C.)
Throop, Enos Thompson
  (N.Y.)
Thye, Edward John (Minn.)
Tiffin, Edward (Ohio)
Tilden, Samuel Jones (N.Y.)
Tillman, Benjamin Ryan (S.C.)
Tobey, Charles William (N.H.)
Tobin, Maurice Joseph (Mass.)
Tod, David (Ohio)
Tompkins, Daniel D. (N.Y.)
Toole, Joseph Kemp (Mont.)
Toucey, Isaac (Conn.)
Towns, George Washington
  Bonaparte (Ga.)
Trimble, Allen (Ohio)
Trumbull, Jonathan, 1740–1809
  (Conn.)
Turney, Peter (Tenn.)
Tyler, John, 1747–1813 (Va.)
Vance, Zebulon Baird (N.C.)
Vardaman, James Kimble
  (Miss.)
Veazey, Thomas Ward (Md.)
Vroom, Peter Dumont (N.J.)
Walker, David Shelby (Fla.)
Walker, Gilbert Carlton (Va.)
Wallace, David (Ind.)
Wallace, Lurleen Burns (Ala.)
Waller, Thomas Macdonald
  (Conn.)
Wallgren, Mon(rad) C(harles)
  (Wash.)
Walsh, David Ignatius (Mass.)
Wanton, Joseph (R.I.)
Ward, Marcus Lawrence (N.J.)
Warmoth, Henry Clay (La.)
Warner, Fred Maltby (Mich.)
Washburn, Cadwallader Colden
  (Wis.)
Washburn, Emory (Mass.)
Washburn, Israel (Maine)
Watts, Thomas Hill (Ala.)
Weller, John B. (Calif.)
Wells, James Madison (La.)
West, Francis (Va.)
West, Oswald (Oreg.)
Whitcomb, James (Ind.)
White, John (Va.)

Whitman, Charles Seymour
(N.Y.)
Wickliffe, Robert Charles (La.)
Williams, David Rogerson
(S.C.)
Williams, James Douglas (Ind.)
Williamson, Isaac Halsted (N.J.)
Williamson, William Durkee
(Maine)
Willson, Augustus Everett (Ky.)
Wiltz, Louis Alfred (La.)
Winant, John Gilbert (N.H.)
Winder, Levin (Md.)
Winston, John Anthony (Ala.)
Wise, Henry Alexander (Va.)
Wolcott, Oliver, 1760–1833
(Conn.)
Wolf, George (Pa.)
Wood, Reuben (Ohio)
Woodbridge, William (Mich.)
Woodring, Harry Hines (Kans.)
Worth, Jonathan (N.C.)
Worthington, Thomas (Ohio)
Wright, Fielding Lewis (Miss.)
Wright, Joseph Albert (Ind.)
Wright, Robert (Md.)
Wright, Silas (N.Y.)
Yates, Richard (Ill.)
Yell, Archibald (Ark.)
GOVERNOR (TERRITORIAL)
Blount, William (Tenn.)
Brady, John Green (Alaska)
Clark, William (Mo.)
Cotton, George Radcliff (P.R.)
Connelly, Henry (N.Mex.)
Cumming, Alfred (Utah)
Curry, George Law (Oreg.)
Davis, Dwight Filley
(Philippines)
De Vargas Zapata y Lujan
Ponce De Leon, Diego
(N.Mex.)
Dodge, Henry (Wis.)
Dole, Sanford Ballard (Hawaii)
Edgerton, Sidney (Mont.)
Farrington, Wallace Rider
(Hawaii)
Forbes, William Cameron
(Philippines)
Gaines, John Pollard (Oreg.)
Geary, John White (Kans.)
Gilpin, William (Colo.)
Gorman, Willis Arnold (Minn.)
Hammond, Samuel (Mo.)
Hauser, Samuel Thomas
(Mont.)
Howard, Benjamin (La.)
Hoyt, John Wesley (Wyo.)
Izard, George (Ark.)
Lane, Joseph (Oreg.)
Lewis, Meriwether (La.)
Lyon, Caleb (Idaho)
McCook, Edward Moody
(Colo.)
Magoon, Charles Edward (C.Z.)
Mathews, George (Miss.)
Mitchell, Robert Byington
(N.Mex.)
Murphy, Frank (Philippines)
Nye, James Warren (Nev.)
Peñalosa Briceñ, Deigo Dionisio
(N.Mex.)

Pierce, Gilbert Ashville
(Dakota)
Piñero Jiménez, Jesús Toribio
(P.R.)
Portolá, Gaspar de (Upper
Calif.)
Posey, Thomas (Indian Terr.)
Potts, Benjamin Franklin
(Mont.)
Prince, Le Baron Bradford
(N.Mex.)
Reeder, Andrew Horatio
(Kans.)
St. Clair, Arthur (Northwest)
Sargent, Winthrop, 1753–1820
(Miss.)
Saunders, Alvin (Nebr.)
Shepherd, Alexander Robey
(D.C.)
Shepley, George Foster (La.)
Sloan, Richard Elihu (Ariz.)
Squire, Watson Carvosso
(Wash.)
Stevens, Isaac Ingalls (Wash.)
Walker, Robert John (Kans.)
Winship, Blanton (P.R.)
GRAMMARIAN
Brown, Goold
Murray, Lindley
Scott, Fred Newton
GRANGE, (See also AGRICULTUR-
IST)
Adams, Dudley W.
Ellis, Seth Hockett
Mayo, Mary Anne Bryant
GRAPHIC ARTIST
Archipenko, Alexander
Marsh, Reginald
GUERRILLA CHIEFTAIN
Quantrill, William Clarke
Sumter, Thomas
GUIDE (See also SCOUT)
Baker, James
Bottineau, Pierre
Carson, Christopher ("Kit")
Fitzpatrick, Thomas
Provost, Etienne
Reynolds, Charles Alexander
Rose, Edward
Walker, Joseph Reddeford
Williams, William Sherley
GUITARIST
Hendrix, Jimi
White, Josh
Williams, (Hiram) Hank
GUNSMITH (See also ORDNANCE
EXPERT)
Henry, William
Lawrence, Richard Smith
Pomeroy, Seth
Whittemore, Amos
GYNECOLOGIST (See also PHYSI-
CIAN)
Byford, William Heath
Cullen, Thomas Stephen
Dickinson, Robert Latou
Engelmann, George Julius
Gilliam, David Tod
Graves, William Phillips
Howard, William Travis
Jackson, Abraham Reeves
Kelly, Howard Atwood

Marcy, Henry Orlando
Parry, John Stubbs
Parvin, Theophilus
Polak, John Osborn
Rubin, Isidor Clinton
Sims, James Marion
Skene, Alexander Johnston
Chalmers
Smith, Albert Holmes
Storer, Horatio Robinson
Taussig, Frederick Joseph
Thomas, Theodore Gaillard
Van de Warker, Edward Ely
Wilson, Henry Parke Custis

HARNESS MAKER (See MANUFAC-
TURER, *Harness Maker*)
HARNESS RACER
White, Benjamin Franklin
HARPSICHORDIST
Landowska, Wanda Aleksandra
HATTER (See MANUFACTURER, *Hat-
ter*)
HEALTH CARE ADMINISTRATOR
Fitzgerald, Alice Louise
Florence
HEALTH PROPAGANDIST
Kellogg, John Harvey
HEBRAIST (See also SEMITIST,
SCHOLAR)
Davidson, Israel
Harper, William Rainey
Revel, Bernard
Schechter, Solomon
Sewall, Stephen
HELLENIST (See also CLASSICIST,
SCHOLAR)
Callimachos, Panos Demetrios
Goodwin, William Watson
Smyth, Herbert Weir
White, John William
Wright, John Henry
HEROINE
Bailey, Anna Warner
Corbin, Margaret
McCauley, Mary Ludwig Hays
HERPETOLOGIST (See also ZOOLO-
GIST)
Barbour, Thomas
Ditmars, Raymond Lee
HISPANIST
Crawford, James Pyle
Wickersham
HISTOLOGIST (See also ANATO-
MIST, PHYSICIAN)
Hoerr, Normand Louis
HISTORIAN (See also CHRONICLER,
CHURCH HISTORIAN, LITERARY
HISTORIAN, MEDICAL HISTORI-
AN, MEDIEVALIST)
Abbott, John Stevens Cabot
Abel-Henderson, Annie Heloise
Absalom, Harris Chappell
Adams, Brooks
Adams, Charles Francis
Adams, Charles Kendall
Adams, Ephraim Douglass
Adams, George Burton
Adams, Henry Brooks
Adams, James Truslow
Adams, Randolph Greenfield
Alexander, de Alva Stanwood

Alexander, William Dewitt
Allen, Frederick Lewis
Alvord, Clarence Walworth
Ames, Herman Vandenburg
Andrews, Charles McLean
Arnold, Isaac Newton
Arnold, Samuel Greene
Asbury, Herbert
Atkinson, John
Backus, Isaac
Baird, Charles Washington
Baird, Henry Martyn
Baker, Carl Lotus
Baker, Frank
Bancroft, Frederic
Bancroft, George
Bancroft, Hubert Howe
Bandelier, Adolph Francis
    Alphonse
Banks, Charles Edward
Barber, John Warner
Bassett, John Spencer
Bayley, James Roosevelt
Beard, Charles Austin
Beard, Mary Ritter
Beauchamp, William Martin
Beer, George Louis
Benedict, David
Berenson, Bernard
Beveridge, Albert Jeremiah
Beverley, Robert
Binkley, Robert Cedric
Bolton, Herbert Eugene
Botsford, George Willis
Bourne, Edward Gaylord
Bouton, Nathaniel
Bowers, Claude Gernade
Boyd, William Kenneth
Bozman, John Leeds
Breasted, James Henry
Brinton, Clarence Crane
Brodhead, John Romeyn
Bronson, Henry
Brown, Alexander
Brown, William Wells
Bruce, Philip Alexander
Buley, Roscoe Carlyle
Burr, George Lincoln
Burrage, Henry Sweetser
Burton, Clarence Monroe
Cabell, James Branch
Cajori, Florian
Callender, Guy Stevens
Campbell, Charles
Campbell, William W.
Carson, Hampton Lawrence
Case, Shirley Jackson
Cathcart, William
Chamberlain, Mellen
Channing, Edward
Charlevoix, Pierre François
    Xavier de
Cheyney, Edward Potts
Chittenden, Hiram Martin
Cist, Henry Martyn
Claiborne, John Francis
    Hamtramck
Clark, Arthur Hamilton
Colcord, Lincoln Ross
Connor, Robert Digges
    Wimberly
Cooke, John Esten

Coolidge, Archibald Cary
Corwin, Edward Samuel
Corwin, Edwin Tanjore
Crawford, Francis Marion
Cross, Arthur Lyon
Dart, Henry Paluché
Dawson, Henry Barton
Deane, Charles
Del Mar, Alexander
Dennett, Tyler (Wilbur)
Dennis, Alfred Lewis Pinneo
Dennis, James Shepard
DeVoto, Bernard Augustine
Dexter, Franklin Bowditch
Dodd, William Edward
Dodge, Theodore Ayrault
Dos Passos, John Roderigo
Drake, Francis Samuel
Drake, Samuel Adams
Drake, Samuel Gardner
Draper, John William
Draper, Lyman Copeland
Du Bois, William Edward
    Burghardt
Dunlap, William
Dunning, William Archibald
Dupratz, Antoine Simon Le
    Page
Durrett, Reuben Thomas
Eggleston, Edward
Egle, William Henry
Eliot, Samuel
Elliott, Charles
Ellis, George Edward
Emerton, Ephraim
Engelhardt, Zephyrin
English, William Hayden
Evans, Clement Anselm
Fall, Bernard B.
Farrand, Max
Fay, Sidney Bradshaw
Fernow, Berthold
Field, David Dudley
Filson, John
Finney, Charles Grandison
Fish, Carl Russell
Fisher, George Park
Fisher, Sydney George
Fiske, John
Fleming, Walter Lynwood
Folwell, William Watts
Forbes, Esther
Force, Peter
Ford, Henry Jones
Ford, Paul Leicester
Fortier, Alcée
Fox, Dixon Ryan
Francis, Joshua Francis
Francke, Kuno
Frank, Tenney
Freeman, Douglas Southall
Frothingham, Richard
Fulton, John Farquhar
Garrett, William Robertson
Garrison, Fielding Hudson
Gavin, Frank Stanton Burns
Gay, Edwin Francis
Gayarré, Charles Étienne
    Arthur
Goddard, Calvin Hooker
Golder, Frank Alfred
Good, James Isaac

Gordy, John Pancoast
Gräbner, August Lawrence
Greene, Francis Vinton
Greenhow, Robert
Griffin, Martin Ignatius Joseph
Grigsby, Hugh Blair
Gross, Charles
Hall, Hiland
Hamilton, Alexander,
    1712–1756
Hammond, Bray
Hammond, Jabez Delano
Hansen, Marcus Lee
Haring, Clarence
Harlow, Ralph Volney
Harrisse, Henry
Hart, Albert Bushnell
Haskins, Charles Homer
Hawks, Francis Lister
Hay, John Milton
Hayes, Carlton Joseph Huntley
Haynes, Williams
Haywood, John
Hendrick, Burton Jesse
Henry, William Wirt
Hewat, Alexander
Hildreth, Samuel Prescott
Hill, Frederick Trevor
Hoffman, David
Hofstadter, Richard
Holbrook, Stewart Hall
Holmes, Abiel
Holst, Hermann Eduard von
Howard, Joseph Kinsey
Howe, George
Howe, Henry
Howe, Mark De Wolfe
Hubbard, William
Hulbert, Archer Butler
Hunt, Gaillard
Ireland, Joseph Norton
Jacobs, Joseph, 1854–1916
Jameson, John Franklin
Jenkins, Howard Malcolm
Jewett, Clarence Frederick
Johnson, Allen
Johnston, Alexander
Johnston, Henry Phelps
Johnston, Robert Matteson
Jones, Charles Colcock
Jones, Hugh
Kapp, Friedrich
Kelsey, Rayner Wickersham
Knight, Lucian Lamar
Knox, Dudley Wright
Kobbé, Gustav
Körner, Gustav Philip
Krehbiel, Henry Edward
Kuykendall, Ralph Simpson
Lacy, William Albert
Lambing, Andrew Arnold
Larson, Laurence Marcellus
Latané, John Holladay
Latourette, Kenneth Scott
Lea, Henry Charles
Learned, Marion Dexter
Lee, Jesse
Leland, Waldo Gifford
Lenker, John Nicholas
Levering, Joseph Mortimer
Libby, Orin Grant
Lingelbach, Anna Lane

Logan, Deborah Norris
Lovejoy, Arthur Oncken
Lowell, Edward Jackson
Lowery, Woodbury
McAfee, Robert Breckinridge
McCrady, Edward
McElroy, Robert McNutt
McGiffert, Arthur Cushman
McKinley, Albert Edward
McLaughlin, Andrew
  Cunningham
McMahon, John Van Lear
McMaster, John Bach
MacNair, Harley Farnsworth
Mahan, Alfred Thayer
Marquand, Allan
Marsh, Frank Burr
Marshall, Humphrey
Mattingly, Garrett
Meigs, William Montgomery
Merrill, Elmer Truesdell
Miles, Henry Adolphus
Miller, David Hunter
Miller, William Snow
Milton, George Fort
Minot, George Richards
Mitchell, Lucy Myers Wright
Moffat, James Clement
Monette, John Wesley
Moon, Parker Thomas
Moore, George Foot
Moore, George Henry
Moreau De Saint-Méry,
  Médéric-Louis-Elie
Morse, Anson Daniel
Moses, Bernard
Motley, John Lothrop
Munro, Dana Carleton
Murray, Louise Shipman Welles
Muzzey, David Saville
Myers, Gustavus
Neill, Edward Duffield
Nelson, William, 1847–1914
Newman, Albert Henry
Niles, Samuel
Notestein, Wallace
Oberholtzer, Ellis Paxson
O'Callaghan, Edmund Bailey
Odell, George Clinton
  Densmore
Oliver, Fitch Edward
Olmstead, Albert Ten Eyck
Onderdonk, Henry
Osgood, Herbert Levi
Owen, Thomas McAdory
Owsley, Frank Lawrence
Palfrey, John Gorham
Palón, Francisco
Parkman, Francis
Parrington, Vernon Louis
Penhallow, Samuel
Pennypacker, Samuel Whitaker
Perkins, James Breck
Phillips, Ulrich Bonnell
Pickett, Albert James
Pitkin, Timothy
Poole, William Frederick
Prescott, William Hickling
Proud, Robert
Putnam, Eben
Quincy, Josiah Phillips
Quinn, Arthur Hobson

Ramsay, David
Rand, Edward Kennard
Randall, James Garfield
Rattermann, Heinrich Armin
Read, Conyers
Reeves, Arthur Middleton
Reichel, William Cornelius
Rhodes, James Ford
Ricketson, Daniel
Ridpath, John Clark
Rister, Carl Coke
Rives, George Lockhart
Robertson, James Alexander
Robertson, William Spence
Robinson, James Harvey
Ropes, John Codman
Rostovtzeff, Michael Ivanovitch
Rourke, Constance Mayfield
Rupp, Israel Daniel
Sabine, Lorenzo
Salmon, Lucy Maynard
Salter, William
Sandoz, Mari
Sarton, George Alfred Léon
Saunders, William Laurence
Scharf, John Thomas
Schlesinger, Arthur Meier
Schmidt, Nathaniel
Schouler, James
Schouler, William
Schuyler, Robert Livingston
Schweinitz, Edmund Alexander
  de
Seidensticker, Oswald
Severance, Frank Hayward
Seymour, Charles
Shannon, Fred Albert
Shea, John Dawson Gilmary
Shepherd, William Robert
Shotwell, James Thomson
Simonds, Frank Herbert
Slaughter, Philip
Sloane, William Milligan
Smith, David Eugene
Smith, Henry Augustus
  Middleton
Smith, Justin Harvey
Smith, Preserved
Smith, William, 1728–1793
Sonneck, Oscar George
  Theodore
Spargo, John
Sparks, Edwin Erle
Sparks, Jared
Spring, Leverett Wilson
Stanard, Mary Mann Page
  Newton
Stanwood, Edward
Staples, William Read
Steiner, Bernard Christian
Stephens, Henry Morse
Stephenson, Nathaniel Wright
Stevens, Abel
Stevens, William Bacon
Stiles, Henry Reed
Stillé, Charles Janeway
Stith, William
Stone, William Leete,
  1792–1844
Stone, William Leete,
  1835–1908
Strachey, William

Stuart, Isaac William
Swank, James Moore
Switzler, William Franklin
Sydnor, Charles Sackett
Tansill, Charles Callan
Taylor, Henry Osborn
Teggart, Frederick John
Thacher, James
Thayer, William Roscoe
Thomas, Isaiah
Thompson, Zadock
Thornton, John Wingate
Trent, William Peterfield
Trescot, William Henry
Trumbull, Benjamin
Trumbull, James Hammond
Turner, Edward Raymond
Turner, Frederick Jackson
Tuttle, Charles Wesley
Tuttle, Herbert
Tyler, Lyon Gardiner
Tyler, Moses Coit
Tyler, Royall
Tyson, Job Roberts
Upham, Charles Wentworth
Upham, Warren
Vail, Robert William Glenroie
Van Dyke, Paul
Van Loon, Hendrik Willem
Van Tyne, Claude Halstead
Vedder, Henry Clay
Victor, Frances Fuller
Vignaud, Henry
Warren, Charles
Warren, Herbert Langford
Warren, Mercy Otis
Washburne, Elihu Benjamin
Webb, Walter Prescott
Weeden, William Babcock
Weeks, Stephen Beauregard
Wergeland, Agnes Mathilde
Wertenbaker, Thomas Jefferson
West, Allen Brown
Westcott, Thompson
Westermann, William Linn
Wheaton, Henry
Wheeler, John Hill
White, Andrew Dickson
White, Leonard Dupee
Whitehead, William Adee
Wickes, Stephen
Wiener, Leo
Willard, James Field
Willard, Joseph
Williamson, William Durkee
Willis, William
Winsor, Justin
Woodson, Carter Godwin
Worcester, Joseph Emerson
Yoakum, Henderson
Zook, George Frederick
HOME ECONOMIST (See also
  ECONOMIST)
Bevier, Isabel
Marlatt, Abby Lillian
Norton, Mary Alice Peloubet
Richards, Ellen Henrietta
  Swallow
Richardson, Anna Euretta
Van Rensselaer, Martha

HOMEOPATHIST (See also PHYSI-CAN)
Hering, Constantine
Neidhard, Charles
Thomas, Amos Russell

HORSE BREEDER (See also HORSE-MAN)
Jacobs, Hirsch

HORSEMAN (See also HORSE BREEDER, RACEHORSE OWNER)
Breckinridge, Drahn
Ten Broeck, Richard
Woodward, William

HORSE TAMER (See also COWBOY, HORSEMAN)
Rarey, John Solomon

HORSE TRAINER
Fitzsimmons, James Edward ("Sunny Jim")
Hirsch, Maximilian Justice
Jacobs, Hirsch
Jones, Benjamin Allyn
Sande, Earl
White, Benjamin Franklin

HORTICULTURIST (See also AGRICULTURIST)
Adams, Dudley W.
Bailey, Liberty Hyde
Barry, Patrick
Budd, Joseph Lancaster
Bull, Ephraim Wales
Burrill, Thomas Jonathan
Campbell, George Washington
Cook, Zebedee
Downing, Andrew Jackson
Downing, Charles
Fuller, Andrew S.
Gale, Elbridge
Garey, Thomas Andrew
Goff, Emmet Stull
Goodrich, Chauncey
Green, Samuel Bowdlear
Hansen, George
Hansen, Niels Ebbesen
Haraszthy De Mokcsa, Agoston
Hart, Edmund Hall
Henderson, Peter
Hilgard, Theodor Erasmus
Hovey, Charles Mason
Hunnewell, Horatio Hollis
Hunt, Benjamin Weeks
Lippincott, James Starr
Logan, James Harvey
Longworth, Nicholas, 1782–1863
McFarland, John Horace
McLaren, John
McMahon, Bernard
Mazzei, Philip
Meehan, Thomas
Miller, Samuel
Munson, Thomas Volney
Nehrling, Henry
Parmentier, Andrew
Parsons, Samuel Bowne
Periam, Jonathan
Powell, George Harold
Pursh, Frederick
Pyle, Robert
Roeding, George Christian
Rogers, Edward Staniford
Sargent, Henry Winthrop

Saunders, William
Strong, Harriet Williams Russell
Thurber, George
Van Fleet, Walter
Warder, John Aston
White, Wiliam Nathaniel
Wickson, Edward James

HOSPITAL ADMINISTRATOR
Goldwater, Sigismund Schulz
McFarland, George Bradley
White, William Alanson

HOSTESS (See also SOCIALITE)
Botta, Anne Charlotte Lynch
Carnegie, Mary Crowninshield Endicott Chamberlain
De Wolfe, Elsie
Madison, Dolly Payne
Maxwell, Elsa
Meredith, Edna C. Elliott
Schuyler, Margarita
Sprague, Kate Chase

HOTELMAN
Barnum, Zenus
Boldt, George C.
Drake, John Burroughs
Fraunces, Samuel
Grim, David
Niblo, William
Statler, Ellsworth Milton
Stetson, Charles Augustus
Stokes, William Earl Dodge
Taggart, Thomas
Wormley, James

HOUSING EXPERT
Veiller, Lawrence Turnure

HOUSING REFORMER
Stokes, Isaac Newton Phelps
Wood, Edith Elmer

HUMANIST
Loeb, James

HUMANITARIAN (See ALSO REFORMER, SETTLEMENT WORKER, SOCIAL REFORMER, SOCIAL WORKER)
Blackwell, Alice Stone
Carson, Robert Rodgers
Dix, Dorothea Lynde
Eustis, Dorothy Leib Harrison Wood
Fisher, Joshua Francis
Hopper, Isaac Tatem
Howe, Samuel Gridley
Klopsch, Louis
Nicholson, Timothy
Pond, Allen Bartlit
Roosevelt, (Anna) Eleanor
Rush, Benjamin
Seward, Theodore Frelinghuysen
Smiley, Albert Keith
Smith, George Albert
Stanford, John
Stewart, Eliza Daniel
Stowe, Harriet Elizabeth Beecher

HUMAN RELATIONS ADVISER
Anthony, John J.

HUMORIST (See also CLOWN, COMEDIAN, COMEDIENNE, WIT)
Bangs, John Kendrick

Benchley, Robert Charles
Brown, Charles Farrar
Burdette, Robert Jones
Burgess, Frank Gelett
Clemens, Samuel Langhorne
Cobb, Irvin Shrewsbury
Cuppy, William Jacob ("Will")
Derby, George Horatio
Dunne, Finley Peter
Foss, Sam Walter
Frost, Arthur Burdett
Harris, George Washington
Holley, Marietta
Hooper, Johnson Jones
Hubbard, Frank McKinney
Landon, Melville de Lancey
Lewis, Charles Bertrand
Loomis, Charles Battell
McAdams, Clark
Marquis, Donald Robert Perry
Mason, Walt
Masson, Thomas Lansing
Neal, Joseph Clay
Newell, Robert Henry
Nye, Edgar Wilson
Peck, George Wilbur
Pomeroy, Marcus Mills
Poole, Fitch
Read, Opie Pope
Rogers, Will
Shaw, Henry Wheeler (Josh Billings)
Shillaber, Benjamin Penhallow
Smith, Charles Henry ("Bill Arp"), 1826–1903
Thompson, William Tappan
Thomson, Mortimer Neal
Thorpe, Thomas Bangs
Welch, Philip Henry
Williams, Gaar Campbell
Zevin, Israel Joseph

HUNTER (See also FRONTIERSMAN, GUIDE, SCOUT)
Beckwourth, James P.
Provost, Etienne
Reynolds, Charles Alexander
Tinkham, George Holden

HYDROGRAPHER (See also GEODESIST, SURVEYOR)
Blunt, Edmund March
Blunt, George William
Ellis, Henry
Green, Francis Mathews
McArthur, William Pope
Mitchell, Henry

HYDROLOGIST (See also GEOLOGIST)
McGee, William John

HYDROTHERAPIST (See also PHYSICIAN)
Nichols, Thomas Low

HYGIENIST (See also PHYSICIAN)
Harrington, Thomas Francis
Ravenel, Mazyck Porcher
Thompson, William Gilman
Vaughan, Victor Clarence

HYMNOLOGIST (See also COMPOSER, LYRICIST, MUSICIAN)
Beissel, Johann Conrad
Billings, William
Bird, Frederic Mayer
Brown, Phoebe Hinsdale

Creamer, David
Crosby, Fanny
Duffield, Samuel Augustus
    Willoughby
Floy, James
Gilmore, Joseph Henry
Hastings, Thomas
Hatfield, Edwin Francis
Hosmer, Frederick Lucian
Lathbury, Mary Artemisia
Mason, Lowell
Oatman, Johnson
Palmer, Ray
Robinson, Charles Seymour
Thompson, Will Lamartine
Wendte, Charles William
Willard, Samuel

ICE SKATER
Henie, Sonja
Merrill, Gretchen Van Zandt
ICHTHYOLOGIST (See also PIS-
    CICULTURIST, ZOOLOGIST)
Bean, Tarleton Hoffman
Evermann, Barton Warren
Goode, George Brown
Starks, Edwin Chapin
ILLUSTRATOR (See also ARTIST,
    CARTOONIST, PAINTER)
Agate, Alfred T.
Artzybasheff, Boris
Bacher, Otto Henry
Beard, Daniel Carter
Beard, James Carter
Beard, Thomas Francis
Bellew, Frank Henry Temple
Bellows, George Wesley
Birch, Reginald Bathurst
Bouché, René Robert
Brennan, Alfred Laurens
Burgess, Frank Gelett
Chambers, Robert William
Champney, James Wells
Christy, Howard Chandler
Cox, Palmer
Curry, John Steuart
Darley, Felix Octavius Carr
Dielman, Frederick
Ehninger, John Whetton
Fisher, Harrison
Flagg, James Montgomery
Frost, Arthur Burdett
Garrett, Edmund Henry
Gaul, William Gilbert
Gibson, Charles Dana
Gifford, Robert Swain
Glackens, William James
Gross, Milt
Held, John, Jr.
Hennessy, William John
Herford, Oliver Brooke
Hoppin, Augustus
Keller, Arthur Ignatius
King, Alexander
Kirby, Rollin
Lawson, Robert Ripley
Leigh, William Robinson
Leyendecker, Joseph Christian
Loeb, Louis
Newell, Peter Sheaf Hersey
O'Neill, Rose Cecil
Penfield, Edward

Raymond, Alexander Gillespie
Reinhart, Charles Stanley
Remington, Frederic
Reuterdahl, Henry
Richards, Thomas Addison
Rowse, Samuel Worcester
Sandham, Henry
Sarg, Tony
Seton, Ernest Thompson
Shinn, Everett
Smedley, William Thomas
Stephens, Alice Barber
Strother, David Hunter
Taylor, Frank Walter
Taylor, William Ladd
Van Loon, Hendrik Willem
Vedder, Elihu
Verrill, Alpheus Hyatt
Wyeth, Newell Convers
Yohn, Frederick Coffay
Zogbaum, Rufus Fairchild
IMMIGRATION LEADER (See also
    LABOR LEADER)
Keefe, Daniel Joseph
Peerson, Cleng
Reiersen, Johan Reinert
Rynning, Ole
IMMIGRATION RESTRICTION ADVO-
    CATE
Grant, Madison
IMMUNOLOGIST (See also PHYSI-
    CIAN)
Avery, Oswald Theodore
Foster, Frank Pierce
Landsteiner, Karl
Noguchi, Hideyo
IMPERSONATOR
Vattemare, Nicolas Marie
    Alexandre
IMPORTER
Kohlberg, Alfred
IMPOSTER
Keely, John Ernst Worrell
IMPRESARIO (See also THEATRICAL
    MANAGER)
Abbey, Henry Eugene
Aborn, Milton
Beck, Martin
Conried, Heinrich
Grau, Maurice
Hammerstein, Oscar
Maretzek, Max
Neuendorff, Adolph Heinrich
    Anton Magnus
Nunó, Jaime
INDEXER
Nelson, Charles Alexander
INDIAN AGENT
Butler, John
Butler, Richard
Carson, Christopher ("Kit")
Chouteau, Jean Pierre
Clark, William
Cocke, William
Croghan, George
De Mézières y Clugny,
    Athanase
Fitzpatrick, Thomas
Forsyth, Thomas
Gaines, George Strother
Hamtramck, John Francis
Hawkins, Benjamin

McCoy, Isaac
McKee, John
McLaughlin, James
Meeker, Nathan Cook
Milroy, Robert Huston
Mitchell, David Brydie
Morgan, George
Nairne, Thomas
Neighbors, Robert Simpson
O'Fallon, Benjamin
Pryor, Nathaniel
Sibley, George Champlain
Sibley, John
Street, Joseph Montfort
Taliaferro, Lawrence
Thompson, Wiley
Weiser, Johann Conrad
INDIAN AUTHORITY
Curtis, Edward Sheriff
McKenney, Thomas Loraine
INDIAN CAPTIVE
Rowlandson, Mary White
Slocum, Frances
INDIAN CHIEF
Black Hawk
Brant, Joseph
Canonchet
Canonicus
Captain Jack
Comstalk
Copway, George
Crazy Horse
Friday
Gall
Garakonthie, Daniel
Geronimo
Hendrick
Joseph
Kamaiakan
Keokuk
Kicking Bird
Leflore, Greenwood
Leschi
Little Crow V
Little Turtle
McGillwray, Alexander
McIntosh, William
Massassoit
Mayes, Joel Bryan
Menewa
Miantonomo
Oconostota
Ouray
Outacity
Parker, Ely Samuel
Philip
Pitchlynn, Peter Perkins
Pontiac
Powhatan
Pushmataha
Quanah
Red Cloud
Red Jacket
Red Wing
Ross, John
Sanganash
Sassacus
Seattle
Shabonee
Shikellamy
Sitting Bull
Skaniadariio

Spotted Tail
Tammany
Tecumseh
Tedyskung
Thomas, George Allison
Tomochichi
Uncas
Wabasha
Washakie
Weatherford, William
White Eyes
INDIAN FIGHTER (See also PIO-
  NEER, SOLDIER)
Ballard, Bland Williams
Boone, Daniel
Connor, Patrick Edward
Gilpin, William
Hardin, John
Kenton, Simon
Lovewell, John
Sieber, Al
Wetzel, Lewis
INDIAN INTERPRETER (See INTER-
  PRETER)
INDIAN LEADER
Dodge, Henry Chee
Son of Many Beads
Ward, Nancy
Watie, Stand
Williams, Eleazar
Wraxall, Peter
INDIAN MUSIC TRANSCRIBER
Burlin, Natalie Curtis
Burton, Frederick Russell
INDIAN NEGOTIATOR (See also DIP-
  LOMAT)
Ridge, Major
Viele, Aermont Cornelissen
INDIAN PROPHET (See also RELI-
  GIOUS LEADER)
Smohalla
Tenskwatawa
Wovoka
INDIAN RUNNER (See also ATH-
  LETE)
Deerfoot
INDIAN TRADER (See TRADER)
INDUSTRIAL CHEMIST
Baekeland, Leo Hendrik
INDUSTRIAL CONSULTANT
Sokolsky, George Ephraim
INDUSTRIAL DESIGNER
Geddes, Norman Bel
INDUSTRIAL ENGINEER (See ENGI-
  NEER, INDUSTRIAL)
INDUSTRIALIST (See also BUSINESS-
  MAN, BUSINESSWOMAN, CAPI-
  TALIST, EXECUTIVE,
  MANUFACTURER)
Adams, Edward Dean
Atkinson, Edward
Ball, Frank Clayton
Barnes, Julius Howland
Bausch, Edward
Bell, James Ford
Bendix, Vincent
Budd, Edward Gowen
Cabot, Godfrey Lowell
Clements, William Lawrence
Cluett, Sanford Lockwood
Coffin, Charles Albert
Coffin, Howard Earle

Cummings, Walter Joseph
Davis, Arthur Vining
De Bardeleben, Henry Fairchild
Dibrell, George Gibbs
Douglas, James
Drake, Edwin Laurentine
Duke, Benjamin Newton
Duke, James Buchanan
Dumaine, Frederic Christopher
Du Pont, Henry Algernon
Du Pont, Irénée
Du Pont, Lammot
Du Pont, Pierre Samuel
Elkins, Stephen Benton
Evans, Henry Clay
Fairless, Benjamin F.
Falk, Maurice
Falk, Otto Herbert
Ford, Henry
Gantt, Henry Laurence
Gates, John Warne
Girdler, Tom Mercer
Goldfine, Bernard
Goodrich, Benjamin Franklin
Goodyear, Anson Conger
Goodyear, Charles
Grace, Eugene Gifford
Green, Duff
Greenleaf, Halbert Stevens
Grinnell, Frederick
Heineman, Daniel Webster
  ("Dannie")
Heinze, Frederick Augustus
Higgins, Andrew Jackson
Hillman, Thomas Tennessee
Hooker, Elon Huntington
Houdry, Eugene Jules
Hume, William
Humphrey, George Magoffin
Hurley, Edward Nash
Jackling, Daniel Cowan
Johnson, Tom Loftin
Jones, Benjamin Franklin
Jones, William Richard
Joy, Henry Bourne
Kaiser, Henry John
Kier, Samuel M.
King, Stanley
Larned, Joseph Gay Eaton
Lewisohn, Sam Adolph
McDaniel, Henry Dickerson
McKay, Gordon
Maloney, Martin
Mellon, Andrew William
Milner, John Turner
Morehead, John Motley
Murchison, Clinton Williams
Patterson, Robert
Peavey, Frank Hutchinson
Pew, Joseph Newton, Jr.
Phipps, Lawrence Cowle
Pratt, Daniel, July 20,
  1799–May 13, 1873
Prince, Frederick Henry
Pullman, George Mortimer
Pynchon, John
Randall, Clarence Belden
Rockefeller, John Davison
Rockefeller, John Davison, Jr.
Rockefeller, William
Roebling, Washington Augustus
Schwab, Charles Michael

Shook, Alfred Montgomery
Sloan, Alfred Pritchard, Jr.
Sloss, James Withers
Sorensen, Charles
Stettinius, Edward Riley
Straus, Roger W(illiams)
Swank, James Moore
Takamine, Jokichi
Tompkins, Daniel Augustus
Tripp, Guy Eastman
Tudor, Frederic
Tyler, Daniel
Valentine, Robert Grosvenor
Vance, Harold Sines
Warner, Adoniram Judson
Warner, James Cartwright
Washburn, Cadwallader Colden
Weston, Edward
Wetherill, Samuel
Wilder, John Thomas
Willys, John North
Winslow, John Flack
Young, Owen D.
Zellerbach, James David
INDUSTRIAL PIONEER, ELECTRO-
  THERMAL
Acheson, Edward Goodrich
INDUSTRIAL PSYCHOLOGIST
Link, Henry Charles
INDUSTRIAL RELATIONS CONSULT-
  ANT
Eaton, Charles Aubrey
INDUSTRIAL RESEARCH PIONEER
Little, Arthur Dehon
INFLUENCE PEDDLER
Goldfine, Bernard
INSTRUMENT MAKER (See MANU-
  FACTURER)
INSURANCE EXECUTIVE
Kingsley, Darwin Pearl
Parkinson, Thomas Ignatius
Spaulding, Charles Clinton
INSURANCE EXPERT (See also STAT-
  ISTICIAN)
Allen, Jeremiah Mervin
Bard, William
Cook, Zebedee
D'Olier, Franklin
Dryden, John Fairfield
Epstein, Abraham
Fiske, Haley
Hegeman, John Rogers
Lawson, James
McCall, John Augustine
McCurdy, Richard Aldrich
INSURGENT (See also AGITATOR,
  REBEL, REVOLUTIONIST)
Fries, John
Shays, Daniel
INTELLIGENCE OFFICIAL
Dulles, Allen Welsh
INTERIOR DECORATOR (See also
  ARTIST, LANDSCAPE GARDEN-
  ER)
De Wolfe, Elsie
Draper, Dorothy
Herter, Christian
INTERNATIONALIST
Catt, Carrie Clinton Lane
  Chapman
Crane, Charles Richard
Holt, Hamilton Bowen

McDonald, James Grover
Marburg, Theodore
Shotwell, James Thomson
Wambaugh, Sarah
INTERNATIONAL LAW SCHOLAR
Wilson, George Grafton
INTERPRETER (See also LINGUIST)
Dorian, Marie
Horn, Tom
Lorimier, Pierre Louis
Sacagawea
Squanto
Viele, Clermont Cornelissen
Winnemucca, Sarah
INTERSTATE COMMERCE COMMISSIONER
Lane, Franklin Knight
Morrison, William Ralls
Prouty, Charles Azro
INTERSTATE COMMERCE COMMISSION MEMBER
Daniels, Winthrop More
Esch, John Jacob
INTERVIEWER
Marcosson, Isaac Frederick
INVENTOR (See also EXPERIMENTER)
Acheson, Edward Goodrich
Acker, Charles Ernest
Adams, Frederick Upham
Adams, Isaac
Adams, Joseph Alexander
Akeley, Carl Ethan
Alger, Cyrus
Allen, Horatio
Allen, John F.
Allen, Zachariah
Angell, William Gorham
Appleby, John Francis
Armstrong, Edwin Howard
Arnold, Aza
Astor, John Jacob
Atkins, Jearum
Atwood, Lewis John
Babbitt, Benjamin Talbot
Babbitt, Isaac
Babcock, George Herman
Bachelder, John
Baekeland, Leo Hendrik
Baldwin, Frank Stephen
Ball, Albert
Ball, Ephraim
Bancroft, Edward
Barnes, Albert Coombs
Batchelder, John Putnam
Batchelder, Samuel
Bausch, Edward
Beach, Moses Yale
Bell, Alexander Graham
Bement, Caleb N.
Bendix, Vincent
Berliner, Emile
Bettendorf, William Peter
Bigelow, Erastus Brigham
Blair, William Richards
Blake, Eli Whitney
Blake, Francis
Blake, Lyman Reed
Blanchard, Thomas
Bogardus, James
Bonard, Louis

Bonwill, William Gibson Arlington
Bonzano, Adolphus
Borden, Gail
Borg, George William
Bovie, William T.
Boyden, Seth
Boyden, Uriah Atherton
Brooks, Byron Alden
Brown, Alexander Ephraim
Brown, Fayette
Brown, James Salisbury
Brown, Joseph Rogers
Brown, Sylvanus
Browning, John Moses
Brunton, David William
Brush, Charles Francis
Bryant, Gridley
Buchanan, Joseph
Buckland, Cyrus
Bullock, William A.
Burden, Henry
Burgess, W(illiam) Starling
Burroughs, William Seward
Burrowes, Edward Thomas
Burson, William Worth
Burt, John
Burt, William Austin
Bushnell, David
Butterick, Ebenezer
Campbell, Andrew
Carlson, Chester Floyd
Carothers, Wallace Hume
Channing, William Francis
Christie, John Walter
Cist, Jacob
Cluett, Sanford Lockwood
Clymer, George E.
Coates, George Henry
Colburn, Irving Wightman
Colles, Christopher
Colt, Samuel
Conant, Hezekiah
Converse, Edmund Cogswell
Cooper, Peter
Corliss, George Henry
Cottrell, Calvert Byron
Cottrell, Frederick Gardner
Cowen, Joshua Lionel
Craven, John Joseph
Crompton, George
Crompton, William
Crowell, Luther Childs
Crozier, William
Curtiss, Glenn Hammond
Cutler, James Goold
Cutting, James Ambrose
Daft, Leo
Dahlgren, John Adolphus Bernard
Dalzell, Robert M.
Dancel, Christian
Danforth, Charles
Daniels, Fred Harris
Davenport, Thomas
Davis, Phineas
Davis, William Augustine
Davison, Gregory Caldwell
De Forest, Lee
Delany, Patrick Bernard
Dickson, Earle Ensign
Dixon, Joseph

Dod, Daniel
Doremus, Robert Ogden
Dow, Lorenzo
Draper, Ira
Dripps, Isaac L.
Dunbar, Robert
Du Pont, Francis Irénée
Durand, Cyrus
Durfee, William Franklin
Durfee, Zoheth Sherman
Durham, Caleb Wheeler
Duryea, Charles Edgar
Duryea, James Frank
Dymond, John
Eads, James Buchanan
Earle, Pliny
Eastman, George
Edgar, Charles
Edison, Thomas Alva
Edwards, Oliver
Edwards, William
Eickemeyer, Rudolf
Ellis, Carleton
Emerson, James Ezekiel
Emerson, Ralph
Emery, Albert Hamilton
Ericsson, John
Esterly, George
Evans, Oliver
Eve, Joseph
Ewbank, Thomas
Fairbanks, Henry
Fairbanks, Thaddeus
Farmer, Moses Gerrish
Ferris, George Washington Gale
Fessenden, Reginald Aubrey
Fessenden, Thomas Green
Field, Stephen Dudley
Fisher, Clark
Fitch, John
Flad, Henry
Ford, Hannibal Choate
Ford, John Baptiste
Forney, Matthias Vace
Fortescue, Charles LeGeyt
Francis, Joseph
Franklin, Benjamin
Frash, Herman
French, Aaron
Fuller, Levi Knight
Fuller, Robert Mason
Fulton, Robert
Furlow, Floyd Charles
Gally, Merritt
Gaskill, Harvey Freeman
Gatling, Richard Jordan
Gayley, James
Gernsback, Hugo
Gibbs, James Ethan Allen
Gilbert, Alfred Carlton
Gilbert, Rufus Henry
Gillette, King Camp
Glidden, Joseph Farwell
Goddard, Calvin Luther
Goddu, Louis
Godfrey, Thomas
Good, John
Goodwin, Hannibal Williston
Goodyear, Charles
Gordon, George Phineas
Grant, George Barnard

Gray, Elisha
Grinnell, Frederick
Haish, Jacob
Hall, Thomas
Hall, Thomas Seavey
Hallidie, Andrew Smith
Hamlin, Emmons
Hammerstein, Oscar
Hammond, James Bartlett
Harvey, Hayward Augustus
Haupt, Herman
Hayden, Hiram Washington
Hayden, Joseph Shepard
Hayward, Nathaniel Manley
Herdic, Peter
Herreshoff, James Brown
Hewitt, Peter Cooper
Heywood, Levi
Hoe, Richard March
Hogan, John Vincent Lawless
Holland, John Philip
Hollerith, Herman
Hotchkiss, Benjamin Berkeley
Houdry, Eugene Jules
House, Henry Alonzo
House, Royal Earl
Howe, Elias
Howe, Frederick Webster
Howe, John Ireland
Howe, William
Howell, Albert Summers
Howell, John Adams
Howey, Walter Crawford
Hoxie, William Dixie
Hubbard, Henry Griswold
Hubert, Conrad
Hudson, William Smith
Hughes, David Edward
Hughes, Howard Robard
Hussey, Obed
Hyatt, John Wesley
Ingersoll, Simon
Ives, Frederic Eugene
Janney, Eli Hamilton
Jarves, Deming
Jenkins, Nathaniel
Jenks, Joseph
Jenney, William Le Baron
Jerome, Chauncey
Johnson, Eldridge Reeves
Johnson, Tom Loftin
Johnston, Samuel
Jones, Amanda Theodosia
Jones, Evan William
Jones, Samuel Milton
Judson, Egbert Putnam
Kalmus, Herbert Thomas
Kalmus, Natalie Mabelle Dunfee
Keely, John Ernst Worrell
Keen, Morris Longstreth
Kelly, William
Kent, Arthur Atwater
Kettering, Charles Franklin
Kingsford, Thomas
Knight, Edward Collings
Knowles, Lucius James
Knox, Thomas Wallace
Kraft, James Lewis
Kruesi, John
Lake, Simon
Lamb, Isaac Wixom
Lamme, Benjamin Garver

Lanston, Tolbert
Larned, Joseph Gay Eaton
Latrobe, John Hazlehurst
  Boneval
Latta, Alexander Bonner
Lawrence, Richard Smith
Lay, John Louis
Leavitt, Frank McDowell
Leffel, James
Leonard, Harry Ward
Levy, Louis Edward
Levy, Max
Lewis, Isaac Newton
Leyner, John George
Lloyd, Marshall Burns
Locke, John
Lockheed, Malcolm
Longstreet, William
Lowe, Thaddeus Sobieski
  Coulincourt
Lucas, Jonathan, 1775–1832
Lundie, John
Lyall, James
McCarroll, James
McCormick, Cyrus Hall
McCormick, Robert
McCormick, Stephen
McCoy, Elijah
McDougall, Alexander
McKay, Gordon
McTammany, John
Manly, Charles Matthews
Mannes, Leopold Damrosch
Marks, Amasa Abraham
Marsh, Charles Wesley
Marsh, Sylvester
Marsh, William Wallace
Mason, Arthur John
Mason, William
Mast, Phineas Price
Masury, John Wesley
Matthews, John
Matzeliger, Jan Ernst
Maxim, Hiram Percy
Maxim, Hiram Stevens
Maxim, Hudson
Maynard, Edward
Melville, David
Mendelsohn, Samuel
Mercer, Henry Chapman
Mergenthaler, Ottmar
Merritt, Israel John
Midgley, Thomas
Miller, Ezra
Miller, Lewis
Mills, Anson
Moody, Paul
Morehead, John Motley
Morey, Samuel
Morgan, Charles Hill
Morse, Samuel Finley Breese
Morse, Sidney Edwards
Mowbray, George Mordey
Munger, Robert Sylvester
Murray, Thomas Edward
Nesmith, John
Nessler, Karl Ludwig
Newcomb, Charles Leonard
Newton, Henry Jotham
Nicholson, William Thomas
Niles, Nathaniel, 1741–1828
Norden, Carl Lukas

Nott, Eliphalet
Noyes, La Verne
Olds, Ransom Eli
Oliver, James
Oliver, Paul Ambrose
Orr, Hugh
Otis, Charles Rollin
Otis, Elisha Graves
Owens, Michael Joseph
Packard, James Ward
Painter, William
Parr, Samuel Wilson
Parrott, Robert Parker
Patterson, Rufus Lenoir
Perkins, Jacob
Perry, Stuart
Pidgin, Charles Felton
Pitts, Hiram Avery
Pope, Franklin Leonard
Porter, Rufus
Potter, William Bancroft
Pratt, Francis Ashbury
Pratt, John
Pratt, Thomas Willis
Prince, Frederick Henry
Pullman, George Mortimer
Rains, George Washington
Ramsay, Erskine
Rand, James Henry
Read, Nathan
Rees, James
Reese, Abram
Reese, Isaac
Reese, Jacob
Renwick, Edward Sabine
Reynolds, Edwin
Reynolds, Samuel Godfrey
Rice, Richard Henry
Riddell, John Leonard
Roberts, Benjamin Stone
Robinson, Stillman Williams
Robinson, William
Rodman, Thomas Jackson
Rogers, Henry J.
Rogers, James Harris
Rogers, John Raphael
Rogers, Thomas
Roosevelt, Hilborne Lewis
Roosevelt, Nicholas J.
Root, Elisha King
Rowland, Thomas Fitch
Rumsey, James
Rust, John Daniel
Sargent, James
Saunders, William Lawrence
Sawyer, Sylvanus
Saxton, Joseph
Schieren, Charles Adolph
Schneller, George Otto
See, Horace
Seiberling, Frank Augustus
Selden, George Baldwin
Sellers, Coleman
Sellers, William
Sergeant, Henry Clark
Sessions, Henry Howard
Shaw, Thomas
Sholes, Christopher Latham
Short, Sidney Howe
Sickles, Frederick Ellsworth
Silver, Thomas
Simpson, Michael Hodge

Sims, Winfield Scott
Singer, Isaac Merrit
Skinner, Halcyon
Slocum, Samuel
Smith, Horace
Spencer, Christopher Miner
Sperry, Elmer Ambrose
Sprague, Frank Julian
Stanley, Francis Edgar
Stanley, William
Starrett, Laroy S.
Stearns, Frank Ballou
Stetefeldt, Carl August
Stevens, Edwin Augustus
Stevens, John
Stevens, Robert Livingston
Stewart, Philo Penfield
Stoddard, Joshua C.
Stoddard, William Osborn
Sturtevant, Benjamin Franklin
Tagliabue, Giuseppe
Taylor, Frederick Winslow
Terry, Eli
Tesla, Nikola
Thomson, Elihu
Thomson, John
Thornton, William
Thorp, John
Thurber, Charles
Timby, Theodore Ruggles
Timken, Henry
Treadwell, Daniel
Troland, Leonard Thompson
Tucker, Stephen Davis
Turner, Walter Victor
Twining, Alexander Catlin
Tytus, John Butler
Van de Graaff, Robert Jemison
Van Depoele, Charles Joseph
Van Dyke, John Wesley
Vauclain, Samuel Matthews
Verbeck, William
Wait, William Bell
Wallace, William
Waller, Frederic
Warren, Cyrus Moors
Warren, Henry Ellis
Warren, Josiah
Washburn, Nathan
Waterman, Lewis Edson
Webb, John Burkitt
Wellman, Samuel Thomas
Wesson, Daniel Baird
Westinghouse, George
Wetherill, Samuel
Wheeler, Nathaniel
Wheeler, Schuyler Skaats
Whipple, Squire
Whitney, Asa
Whitney, Eli
Whittemore, Amos
Wilcox, Stephen
Wilkinson, David
Wilkinson, Jeremiah
Wilson, Allen Benjamin
Wilson, George Francis
Winans, Ross
Winans, Thomas De Kay
Wood, Henry Alexander Wise
Wood, James J.
Wood, Jethro
Wood, Walter Abbott

Woodruff, Theodore Tuttle
Worthington, Henry Rossiter
Wright, Orville
Wyman, Horace
Yale, Linus
Zachos, John Celivergos
Zentmayer, Joseph
INVESTMENT EXECUTIVE
  Paul, Josephine Bay
INVESTOR
  Ball, George Alexander
IRONFOUNDER (See also TYPE-
    FOUNDER)
  Ames, Nathan Peabody
  Foxall, Henry
  Leach, Shepherd
  Meneely, Andrew
  Ogden, Samuel
IRONMASTER (See MANUFACTURER)
IRRIGATION ENGINEER (See ENGI-
    NEER, IRRIGATION)
ITALIAN CULTURE PROMOTER
  Da Ponte, Lorenzo

JAYHAWKER (See also OUTLAW,
    VIGILANTE)
  Montgomery, James
JAZZ BAND LEADER
  Celestin, Oscar ("Papa")
  Oliver, Joseph
JAZZ CORNET PLAYER
  Celestin, Oscar ("Papa")
JAZZ DRUMMER
  Catlett, Sidney
JAZZ MUSICIAN
  Morton, Ferdinand Joseph
    ("Jelly Roll")
  Parker, Charlie ("Bird")
JAZZ PIANIST
  Tatum, Art
  Waller, Thomas Wright
JAZZ SINGER
  Bailey, Mildred
  Holiday, Billie
JAZZ TRUMPET PLAYER
  Celestin, Oscar "Papa"
JEWELER (See also CRAFTSMAN,
    GOLDSMITH, SILVERSMITH)
  Belden, Josiah
  Ross, Alexander Coffman
  Tiffany, Charles Lewis
JEWISH LEADER (See also CLERGY-
    MAN, ZIONIST LEADER)
  Lehman, Irving
  Mack, Julian William
  Monsky, Henry
  Philipson, David
  Vladeck, Baruch Charney
JOCKEY (See also ATHLETE,
    HORSEMAN, TURFMAN)
  Sande, Earl
  Sloan, James Forman
JOURNALIST (See also FOREIGN
    CORRESPONDENT, NEWSPAPER
    CORRESPONDENT, NEWSPAPER
    REPORTER)
  Abbot, Willis John
  Abbott, Joseph Carter
  Abell, Arunah Shepherdson
  Adamic, Louis
  Adams, Abijah
  Adams, Franklin Pierce

Adams, Samuel Hopkins
Agee, James Rufus
Agnus, Felix
Alden, Cynthia May Westover
Alden, William Livingston
Anderson, Paul Y.
Andrews, Sidney
Angell, James Burrill
Anthony, Henry Bowen
Astor, William Waldorf
Atkinson, Wilmer
Avery, Benjamin Parke
Avery, Isaac Wheeler
Bache, Benjamin Franklin
Bacon, Edwin Munroe
Bailey, Francis
Bailey, Gamaliel
Bailey, James Montgomery
Baker, James Heaton
Baker, Ray Stannard
Baldwin, John Denison
Ballou, Maturin Murray
Barrows, David Prescott
Bartlett, John Sherren
Basso, (Joseph) Hamilton
Beach, Moses Yale
Belo, Alfred Horatio
Bent, Silas
Benton, Joel
Berger, Victor Louis
Bernstein, Herman
Bierce, Ambrose Gwinett
Binns, John
Birchall, Frederick Thomas
Blair, Francis Preston
Bliss, Porter Cornelius
Bonsal, Stephen
Boutelle, Charles Addison
Bowers, Claude Gernade
Bradford, Joseph
Bradford, Roark Whitney
  Wickliffe
Brentano, Lorenz
Briggs, Charles Frederick
Bromley, Isaac Hill
Brooks, Erastus
Brooks, James
Brooks, Noah
Bross, William
Brown, Charles Brockden
Browne, Junius Henri
Bryan, Mary Edwards
Bundy, Jonas Mills
Burleigh, William Henry
Butterworth, Hezekiah
Cahan, Abraham
Callimachos, Panos Demetrios
Campbell, Bartley
Campbell, John
Canonge, Louis Placide
Carpenter, Edmund Janes
Carpenter, Frank George
Carpenter, Stephen Cullen
Carr, Dabney Smith
Carter, Boake
Case, Francis Higbee
Cash, Wilbur Joseph
Cassidy, William
Cesare, Oscar Edward
Chamberlain, Henry
  Richardson
Chambers, James Julius

Chambers, Whittaker
Chandler, Joseph Ripley
Cheetham, James
Child, David Lee
Clapp, William Warland
Clarke, Joseph Ignatius
  Constantine
Clement, Edward Henry
Cobbett, William
Cockerill, John Albert
Coffin, Charles Carleton
Coggeshall, William Turner
Colcord, Lincoln Ross
Coleman, William
Colton, Calvin
Colton, Walter
Conant, Charles Arthur
Conrad, Robert Taylor
Cook, Clarence Chatham
Cooke, Henry David
Cooper, Kent
Cortambert, Louis Richard
Cowles, Edwin
Craig, Daniel H.
Crane, Frank
Creel, George
Creelman, James
Croly, David Goodman
Croly, Jane Cunningham
Croswell, Edwin
Croy, Homer
Cummings, Amos Jay
Curtis, William Eleroy
Daniel, John Moncure
Davidson, James Wood
Davis, Matthew Livingston
Davis, Oscar King
Davis, Richard Harding
Dawson, Francis Warrington
Day, Benjamin Henry
Day, Holman Francis
De Fontaine, Felix Gregory
DeVoto, Bernard Augustine
Devoy, John
Dickinson, Charles Monroe
Dimitry, Charles Patton
Dodge, Jacob Richards
Dorsheimer, William Edward
Douglass, Frederick
Draper, John
Dromgoole, William Allen
Duane, William
Duranty, Walter
Durivage, Francis Alexander
Eastman, Charles Gamage
Eaton, Charles Aubrey
Edes, Benjamin
Eggleston, George Cary
Everett, David
Farson, Negley
Fessenden, Thomas Green
Field, Joseph M.
Field, Mary Katherine Kemble
Fischer, Louis
Fiske, Harrison Grey
Fiske, Stephen Ryder
Flynn, John Thomas
Ford, Patrick
Forney, John Wien
Foss, Sam Walter
Foster, Thomas Jefferson
Fowler, Gene

Fox, Richard Kyle
Franklin, Fabian
Frederic, Harold
Freeman, Joseph
Fry, William Henry
Fuller, Hiram
Fuller, Sarah Margaret
Gaillard, Edwin Samuel
Gaillardet, Théodore Frédéric
Gales, Joseph, 1761–1841
Gales, Joseph, 1786–1860
Gannett, Frank Ernest
Gardner, Charles Kitchell
Gardner, Gilson
Garis, Howard Roger
Gaston, Herbert Earle
Gay, Sydney Howard
George, Henry
Gilder, Jeannette Leonard
Gilder, William Henry
Gill, John
Goddard, William
Gold, Michael
Goodall, Harvey L.
Goodrich, Frank Boott
Grady, Henry Woodfin
Graham, Philip Leslie
Graves, John Temple
Gray, Joseph W.
Greathouse, Clarence Ridgeby
Green, Bartholomew
Green, Duff
Green, Jonas
Greenleaf, Thomas
Grieve, Miller
Griffin, Martin Ignatius Joseph
Griswold, Rufus Wilmot
Grosvenor, William Mason
Grund, Francis Joseph
Gue, Benjamin F.
Guild, Curtis, 1827–1911
Gunther, John
Hale, Charles
Hale, David
Hale, Nathan
Hale, William Bayard
Hall, Abraham Oakey
Hallock, Charles
Hallock, Gerard
Halpine, Charles Graham
Halstead, Murat
Hammond, Charles
Hapgood, Isabel Florence
Harby, Isaac
Hard, William
Hardy, William Harris
Harper, Ida Husted
Harris, Joel Chandler
Harris, Julian La Rose
Harrison, Henry Sydnor
Harvey, George Brinton
  McClellan
Haskell, Henry Jospeh
Hassard, John Rose Greene
Hassaurek, Friedrich
Hatton, Frank
Hay, John Milton
Hazeltine, Mayo Williamson
Heath, Perry Sanford
Hecht, Ben
Heinzen, Karl Peter
Hendrick, Burton Jesse

Herbst, Josephine Frey
Hewitt, John Hill
Hibben, Paxton Pattison
Higgins, Marguerite
Hill, Edwin Conger
Hirth, William Andrew
Hitchcock, James Ripley
  Wellman
Hittell, John Shertzer
Holbrook, Stewart Hall
Holden, Liberty Emery
Holden, William Woods
Holt, John
Hooper, Lucy Hamilton
Hough, Emerson
House, Edward Howard
Howell, James Bruen
Howey, Walter Crawford
Hudson, Charles
Hudson, Frederic
Hunt, William Gibbes
Hurlbert, William Henry
Ickes, Harold Le Clair
Inman, John
Irwin, William Henry
Isaacs, Samuel Myer
Jackson, Charles Douglas
James, Edwin Leland
Janvier, Thomas Allibone
Jemison, Alice Mae Lee
Jenks, George Charles
Johnston, William Andrew
Jones, Alexander
Jones, Herschel Vespasian
Jones, John Beauchamp
Jones, John Price
Jordan, Thomas
Keating, John McLeod
Keeler, Ralph Olmstead
Kendall, Amos
Kendall, George Wilkins
Kennan, George
Kester, Vaughan
Keys, Clement Melville
King, Edward Smith
King, Henry
Kinney, William Burnet
Kiplinger, Willard Monroe
Knapp, George
Knox, Frank
Knox, Thomas Wallace
Koenigsberg, Moses
Kollock, Shepard
Kroeger, Adolph Ernst
Laffan, William Mackay
Lamoureux, Andrew Jackson
Lanigan, George Thomas
Lapham, William Berry
Lardner, John Abbott
Lardner, Ringgold Wilmer
Lawson, Victor Freemont
Leggett, William
Leupp, Francis Ellington
Lewis, Alfred Henry
Lewis, Lloyd Downs
Liebling, Abbott Joseph
List, Georg Friedrich
Littledale, Clara Savage
Lloyd, Henry Demarest
Locke, David Ross
Locke, Richard Adams
Loeb, Sophie Irene Simon

Logan, Olive
Lomax, Louis Emanuel
Loring, Frederick Wadsworth
Love, Robertus Donnell
Lunt, George
McAnally, David Rice
MacArthur, Charles Gordon
McBride, Henry
McCann, Alfred Watterson
McCarroll, James
McCormick, Anne Elizabeth
    O'Hare
McCormick, Joseph Medill
McCormick, Richard
    Cunningham
McCullagh, Joseph Burbridge
MacGahan, Januarius Aloysius
McGeehan, William O'Connell
McGill, Ralph Emerson
McGovern, John
Mackenzie, Robert Shelton
McKinley, Carlyle
McMaster, James Alphonsus
McNulty, John Augustine
Mailly, William
Manley, Joseph Homan
Marcosson, Isaac Frederick
Marden, Orison Swett
Marling, John Leake
Martin, John Alexander
Mathews, William
Matthews, Franklin
Medill, Joseph
Meeker, Nathan Cook
Mencken, Henry Louis
Meredith, Edwin Thomas
Meyer, Agnes Elizabeth Ernst
Meyer, Eugene Isaac
Michelson, Charles
Milton, George Fort
Mitchel, John
Moffett, Cleveland Langston
Moody, (Arthur Edson) Blair
Moore, Charles
Moore, Frederick Randolph
Moore, Jacob Bailey
Moore, John Trotwood
Morford, Henry
Morris, George Pope
Mott, Frank Luther
Mulford, Prentice
Murdock, Victor
Neal, Joseph Clay
Nelson, William Rockhill
Nettleton, Alvred Bayard
Nevin, Robert Peebles
New, Harry Stewart
Newell, Robert Henry
Nixon, William Penn
Noah, Mordecai Manuel
Nordhoff, Charles
Norris, Benjamin Franklin
Noyes, Alexander Dana
Noyes, Crosby Stuart
Nye, Edgar Wilson
Oberholtzer, Ellis Paxson
O'Brien, Fitz-James
O'Brien, Frederick
O'Brien, Robert Lincoln
O'Connor, William Douglas
O'Hara, Theodore
O'Higgins, Harvey Jerrold

O'Mahoney, Joseph Christopher
Osborn, Chase Salmon
Osborn, Selleck
O'Sullivan, John Louis
Otis, Harrison Gray
Ottley, Roi
Page, Walter Hines
Paine, Ralph Delahaye
Parker, Henry Taylor
Parker, James
Paschal, George Washington
Paul, Elliot Harold
Pearson, Drew
Peck, George Washington
Peck, George Wilbur
Peffer, William Alfred
Pegler, Westbrook
Peixotto, Benjamin Franklin
Pelham, Robert A.
Penfield, Frederic Courtland
Perry, Nora
Perry, Rufus Lewis
Phelan, David Samuel
Phillips, David Graham
Phillips, Harry Irving
Phillips, Walter Polk
Piatt, Donn
Piatt, John James
Picton, Thomas
Pike, James Shepherd
Pleasants, John Hampden
Plumb, Preston B.
Pollard, Edward Alfred
Pond, George Edward
Poole, Ernest Cook
Poole, Fitch
Poor, Henry Varnum
Poore, Benjamin Perley
Porter, Robert Percival
Porter, William Trotter
Posey, Alexander Lawrence
Powell, Thomas
Pratt, John
Pratt, Sereno Stansbury
Pray, Isaac Clark
Preetorius, Emil
Prentice, George Dennison
Prime, William Cowper
Pringle, Henry Fowles
Pulitzer, Joseph
Quigg, Lemuel Ely
Ralph, Julian
Randall, James Ryder
Randall, Samuel
Rapp, Wilhelm
Ray, Charles Bennett
Redpath, James
Reed, John, 1887–1920
Reedy, William Marion
Reick, William Charles
Reid, Whitelaw
Revell, Nellie MacAleney
Rice, Charles Allen Thorndike
Richardson, Albert Deane
Richardson, Willard
Riis, Jacob August
Ritchie, Thomas
Rives, John Cook
Rivington, James
Robertson, James, b. 1740
Robinson, Charles Mulford
Robinson, William Erigena

Robinson, William Stevens
Roche, James Jeffrey
Rosewater, Edward
Rosewater, Victor
Ross, Edmund Gibson
Round, William Marshall Fitts
Rowell, Chester Harvey
Ruark, Robert Chester
Ruhl, Arthur Brown
Runyon, Damon
Russell, Benjamin
Russell, Charles Edward
Sanborn, Franklin Benjamin
Sandburg, Carl August
Sands, Robert Charles
Sargent, Epes
Sargent, George Henry
Sargent, John Osborne
Sargent, Nathan
Savage, John
Schneider, George
Schuyler, Montgomery
Scott, James Wilmot
Scovel, Henry Sylvester
Scoville, Joseph Alfred
Scripps, Ellen Browning
Seaman, Elizabeth Cochrane
Searing, Laura Catherine
    Redden
Seaton, William Winston
Sedgwick, Arthur George
Seibold, Louis
Seitz, Don Carlos
Seldes, Gilbert Vivian
Selikovitsch, Goetzel
Seward, Frederick William
Shaw, Albert
Shillaber, Benjamin Penhallow
Sholes, Christopher Latham
Short, Joseph Hudson, Jr.
Shrady, George Frederick
Sikes, William Wirt
Simmons, Roscoe Conkling
    Murray
Simonds, Frank Herbert
Simons, Algie Martin
Simonton, James William
Sinclair, Upton Beall, Jr.
Smalley, Eugene Virgil
Smalley, George Washburn
Smedley, Agnes
Smith, Albert Merriman
Smith, Charles Emory
Smith, Charles Henry ("Bill
    Arp"), 1826–1903
Smith, George Henry
Smith, Samuel Harrison
Smith, William Henry,
    1833–1896
Snelling, William Joseph
Sonnichsen, Albert
Southall, James Cocke
Southwick, Solomon
Spencer, Anna Garlin
Squier, Ephraim George
Stanton, Frank Lebby
Stanton, Henry Brewster
Stearns, Harold Edmund
Steffens, Lincoln
Stevens, John Leavitt
Stillman, William James
Stokes, Thomas Lunsford, Jr.

Stolberg, Benjamin
Stone, Melville Elijah
Stone, William Leete,
    1792–1844
Stone, William Leete,
    1835–1908
Stromme, Peer Olsen
Strong, Anna Louise
Strong, Walter Ansel
Strunsky, Simeon
Sullivan, Mark
Swain, James Barrett
Swinton, John
Swinton, William
Switzler, William Franklin
Swope, Herbert Bayard
Taylor, Benjamin Franklin
Taylor, Bert Leston
Taylor, Charles Henry
Taylor, James Wickes
Testut, Charles
Thomas, Frederick William
Thompson, Dorothy
Thompson, Slason
Tibbles, Thomas Henry
Tierney, Richard Henry
Todd, Sereno Edwards
Towle, George Makepeace
Towne, Benjamin
Townsend, George Alfred
Tresca, Carlo
Truman, Benjamin Cummings
Turner, George Kibbe
Upton, George Putnam
Vallentine, Benjamin Bennaton
Van Anda, Carr Vattel
Vandenberg, Arthur Hendrick
Van Horn, Robert Thompson
Vedder, Henry Clay
Vignaud, Henry
Villard, Henry
Visscher, William Lightfoot
Vorse, Mary Heaton
Walker, Alexander
Walsh, Robert
Walton, Lester Aglar
Wardman, Ervin
Warman, Cy
Waymack, William Wesley
Webb, James Watson
Webber, Charles Wilkins
Weed, Thurlow
Weeks, Joseph Dame
Welch, Philip Henry
Welling, James Clarke
Wellman, Walter
Westcott, Thompson
Wheeler, Andrew Carpenter
White, Horace
Whiting, Charles Goodrich
Wilkes, George
Wilkie, Franc Bangs
Will, Allen Sinclair
Williams, Edwin
Williams, James
Williams, Talcott
Williams, Walter
Willis, Nathaniel
Willis, Nathaniel Parker
Woodworth, Samuel
Wright, William
Young, John Russell

Zenger, John Peter
Zollicoffer, Felix Kirk
JUDGE (See also CHIEF JUSTICE
    [STATE], JURIST, LAWYER,
    MAGISTRATE, SUPREME COURT
    JUSTICE)
Adams, Annette Abbott
Baker, Harvey Humphrey
Beardsley, Samuel
Biddle, Francis Beverley
Bouvier, John
Bowler, Metcalf
Boyle, John
Brantley, Theodore
Brawley, William Hiram
Brooks, George Washington
Brown, George William
Browne, William
Camp, John Lafayette
Cilley, Joseph
Clark, Bennett Champ
Clark, James
Clayton, Henry De Lamar
Clements, Judson Claudius
Cline, Genevieve Rose
Cobb, David
Collamer, Jacob
Conkling, Alfred
Connor, Henry Groves
Cox, Edward Eugene
Crane, Frederick Evan
Crawford, Martin Jenkins
Davis, George Breckenridge
Derbigny, Pierre Auguste
    Charles Bourguignon
Dole, Sanford Ballard
Dunn, William McKee
Early, Peter
Fell, John
Foster, Lafayette Sabine
Frank, Jerome
Fuller, Thomas Charles
Gamble, Hamilton Rowan
Gansevoort, Leonard
Garrett, Finis James
George, Walter Franklin
Goldsborough, Thomas Alan
Goodman, Louis Earl
Grant, Robert
Grose, William
Hager, John Sharpenstein
Halderman, John A.
Hall, Dominick Augustin
Hamtramck, John Francis
Hand, Augustus Noble
Hand, Learned
Hardy, William Harris
Harper, William
Harris, Wiley Pope
Hatch, Carl A.
Hedding, Elijah
Hemphill, Joseph
Hill, Richard
Hiscock, Frank Harris
Hise, Elijah
Hobart, John Sloss
Holman, Jesse Lynch
Holmes, Nathaniel
Holt, Joseph
Hopkins, James Campbell
Hornblower, Josiah
Horner, Henry

Hosmer, Hezekiah Lord
Hough, Warwick
Hudson, Manley Ottmer
Huger, Daniel Elliott
Hughes, James
Innes, Harry
Jay, William
Jenkins, James Graham
Key, David McKendree
King, Austin Augustus
Larrabee, Charles Hathaway
Laurance, John
Law, John
Lenroot, Irvine Luther
Lindsey, Benjamin Barr
McGranery, James Patrick
McPherson, Smith
McReynolds, Samuel Davis
Miller, Nathan Lewis
Mitchell, William, 1832–1900
Moore, George Fleming
Morris, Robert, 1745–1815
Musmanno, Michael Angelo
Nash, Simeon
Newman, William Truslow
Niblack, William Ellis
Nisbet, Eugenius Aristides
Ogden, David
Okey, John Waterman
Paine, Byron
Parker, Isaac Charles
Patterson, Robert Porter
Peckham, Rufus Wheeler
Penhallow, Samuel
Pennypacker, Samuel Whitaker
Perkins, Samuel Elliott
Peters, Richard, 1744–1828
Pickering, John
Pitkin, William, 1635–1694
Pitkin, William, 1694–1769
Pitney, Mahlon
Pritchard, Jeter Connelly
Randall, Samuel
Raulston, John Tate
Redfield, Isaac Fletcher
Rellstab, John
Richardson, William Merchant
Ross, Erskine Mayo
Ruggles, Timothy
Sanborn, Walter Henry
Sharswood, George
Shepley, George Foster
Sloan, Richard Elihu
Smith, William Nathan Harrell
Taft, Alphonso
Taylor, Creed
Tazewell, Henry
Thacher, Thomas Day
Thomas, Jesse Burgess
Toulmin, Harry
Tyler, John, 1747–1813
Van Devanter, Willis
Wales, Leonard Eugene
Waring, Julius Waties
JURIST (See also CHIEF JUSTICE
    [STATE], JUDGE, LAWYER,
    MAGISTRATE, SUPREME COURT
    JUSTICE)
Adams, Andrew
Aldrich, Edgar
Allen, Charles
Allen, Florence Ellinwood

Allen, John James
Allen, William
Allen, William Joshua
Alvey, Richard Henry
Ames, Samuel
Amidon, Charles Fremont
Anderson, Joseph
Andrews, Charles
Andrews, Charles Bartlett
Andrews, George Pierce
Archer, Stevenson
Ashe, Samuel
Atkinson, George Wesley
Auchmuty, Robert, d. 1750
Auchmuty, Robert, d. Nov. 1788
Axtell, Samuel Beach
Badger, George Edmund
Baldwin, Joseph Glover
Baldwin, Simeon
Baldwin, Simeon Eben
Barbour, Philip Pendleton
Bassett, Richard
Bates, Daniel Moore
Battle, Burrell Bunn
Battle, William Horn
Batts, Robert Lynn
Baxter, Elisha
Bayard, Samuel
Baylor, Robert Emmet Bledsoe
Bayly, Thomas Henry
Beasley, Mercer
Beatty, William Henry
Bennett, Edmund Hatch
Bennett, Nathaniel
Benning, Henry Lewis
Bermudez, Edouard Edmond
Betts, Samuel Rossiter
Biddle, Horace P.
Biggs, Asa
Bishop, Robert Roberts
Blair, John
Blatchford, Samuel
Bleckley, Logan Edwin
Bliss, Jonathan
Bliss, Philemon
Blount, Willie
Blowers, Sampson Salter
Boise, Reuben Patrick
Bond, Hugh Lennox
Bourne, Benjamin
Brackenridge, Hugh Henry
Bradbury, Theophilus
Bradford, Edward Green
Bradford, William
Bradley, Stephen Row
Brannon, Henry
Brearly, David
Breaux, Joseph Arsenne
Breese, Sidney
Brennan, Francis James
Brewer, David Josiah
Brewster, Frederick Carroll
Brickell, Robert Coman
Brinkerhoff, Jacob
Brooke, Francis Taliaferro
Brown, Addison
Brown, Henry Billings
Bruce, Andrew Alexander
Bryan, George
Buchanan, John
Bullard, Henry Adams

Burke, Aedanus
Butler, Thomas Belden
Bynum, William Preston
Cadwalader, John
Cady, Daniel
Caldwell, Henry Clay
Campbell, James Valentine
Campbell, John Wilson
Campbell, Josiah A. Patterson
Campbell, William W.
Cardozo, Benjamin Nathan
Carleton, Henry
Carr, Dabney
Carrington, Paul
Case, William Scoville
Casey, Joseph
Cassoday, John Bolivar
Caton, John Dean
Catron, John
Chambers, Ezekiel Forman
Champlin, John Wayne
Charlton, Thomas Usher Pulaski
Chew, Benjamin
Chilton, William Paris
Chipman, Nathaniel
Clark, Daniel
Clark, Greenleaf
Clark, Walter
Clay, Joseph
Clayton, Thomas
Clifford, Nathan
Clopton, David
Cobb, Andrew Jackson
Cofer, Martin Hardin
Coffey, James Vincent
Cole, Chester Cicero
Collens, Thomas Wharton
Collier, Henry Watkins
Colt, Le Baron Bradford
Comstock, George Franklin
Conrad, Robert Taylor
Cooley, Thomas McIntyre
Cooper, William
Cranch, William
Cross, Edward
Crounse, Lorenzo
Crump, William Wood
Curtis, Benjamin Robbins
Cushing, Luther Stearns
Cushing, William
Daly, Charles Patrick
Dana, Francis
Daniel, Peter Vivian
Dargan, Edmund Strother
Davis, David
Davis, John
Davis, Noah
Day, James Gamble
Day, Luther
Deady, Matthew Paul
Deemer, Horace Emerson
Devaney, John Patrick
Devens, Charles
Dick, Robert Paine
Dickerson, Philemon
Dickey, Theophilus Lyle
Dickinson, John
Dill, James Brooks
Dillon, John Forrest
Dixon, Luther Swift
Doe, Charles

Doggett, David
Drake, Charles Daniel
Drayton, John
Drayton, William
Duane, James
Dudley, Paul
Duer, John
Dunn, Charles
Durell, Edward Henry
Durfee, Job
Durfee, Thomas
Dutton, Henry
Dyer, Eliphalet
Edmonds, John Worth
Edwards, Pierpont
Elliott, Charles Burke
Ellis, Powhatan
Elmer, Jonathan
Elmer, Lucius Quintus Cincinnatus
Emery, Lucilius Alonzo
Emott, James, 1771–1850
Emott, James, 1823–1884
Endicott, William Crowninshield
Erskine, John
Eustis, George
Evans, Walter
Ewing, Charles
Farman, Elbert Eli
Farrar, Timothy
Fenner, Charles Erasmus
Field, Fred Tarbell
Field, Richard Stockton
Field, Walbridge Abner
Finch, Francis Miles
Fisher, George Purnell
Flandrau, Charles Eugene
Fleming, Aretas Brooks
Fletcher, Richard
Fletcher, William Asa
Folger, Charles James
Force, Manning Ferguson
Gaston, William
Gaynor, William Jay
George, James Zachariah
Gholson, Samuel Jameson
Gholson, Thomas Saunders
Gholson, William Yates
Gibson, John Bannister
Gilpin, Edward Woodward
Goddard, Luther Marcellus
Goff, John William
Goldthwaite, George
Goldthwaite, Henry Barnes
Goodenow, John Milton
Gould, James
Gould, Robert Simonton
Grant, Claudius Buchanan
Gray, George
Gray, Horace
Green, Henry Woodhull
Greene, Albert Gorton
Gresham, Walter Quintin
Griffin, Cyrus
Grimké, John Faucheraud
Griswold, Matthew
Groesbeck, William Slocum
Grosscup, Peter Stenger
Grundy, Felix
Gummere, William Stryker
Haines, Daniel

Hall, Hiland
Hall, James, 1793–1868
Hall, Nathan Kelsey
Hall, Willard
Hallett, Moses
Hamilton, Walton Hale
Handy, Alexander Hamilton
Hanson, Alexander Contee,
  1749–1806
Hare, John Innes Clark
Harlan, John Marshall
Harmon, Judson
Harrington, Samuel Maxwell
Harris, Ira
Harris, William Littleton
Haselton, Seneca
Hastings, Serranus Clinton
Hay, George
Haywood, John
Hemphill, John
Henderson, Leonard
Heyward, Thomas
Hill, Robert Andrews
Hinman, Joel
Hitchcock, Peter
Hoadly, George
Hoar, Ebenezer Rockwood
Hoffman, David Murray
Hopkinson, Joseph
Hornblower, Joseph Coerten
Hornblower, William Butler
Hough, Charles Merrill
Hovey, Alvin Peterson
Howard, Timothy Edward
Howe, Samuel
Howe, William Wirt
Howell, David
Howry, Charles Bowen
Hughes, Robert William
Humphreys, West Hughes
Hunt, William Henry
Hutson, Richard
Iredell, James
Iverson, Alfred
Jackson, Howell Edmunds
Jackson, James, 1819–1887
Jackson, John George
Jackson, Mortimer Melville
Jackson, Robert Houghwout
Jameson, John Alexander
Jenckes, Thomas Allen
Jenkins, Charles Jones
Johns, Kensey, 1759–1848
Johns, Kensey, 1791–1857
Johnson, Alexander Smith
Johnson, Herschel Vespasian
Johnson, William
Johnson, William Samuel
Johnston, Job
Johnston, Peter
Jones, Joseph
Jones, Leonard Augustus
Jones, Samuel
Jones, Thomas
Jones, Thomas Goode
Kalisch, Samuel
Kane, John Kintzing
Keith, James
Kent, Edward
Kent, James
Kenyon, William Squire
Kephart, John William

Kershaw, Joseph Brevard
Kilty, William
Kinkead, Edgar Benton
Kinne, La Vega George
Kinsey, John
Kirkpatrick, Andrew
Knapp, Martin Augustine
Knowlton, Marcus Perrin
Körner, Gustav Philip
Lamar, Joseph Rucker
Lander, Edward
Landis, Kenesaw Mountain
Lansing, John
Larrazolo, Octaviano Ambrosio
Law, Richard
Lawrence, William, 1819–1899
Leavitt, Humphrey Howe
Lee, Charles, 1758–1815
Lee, Thomas
Lee, William Little
Lehman, Irving
Lewis, Ellis
Lewis, Joseph Horace
Lewis, Morgan
Lindley, Curtis Holbrook
Lindsay, William
Lipscomb, Abner Smith
Livermore, Samuel, 1732–1803
Livingston, Henry Brockholst
Livingston, Robert R.,
  1718–1775
Lockwood, Samuel Drake
Logan, James Harvey
Logan, Stephen Trigg
Lomax, John Tayloe
Longstreet, Augustus Baldwin
Loomis, Dwight
Lord, Otis Phillips
Lord, William Paine
Lowell, John, 1743–1802
Lowell, John, 1824–1897
Lucas, Daniel Bedinger
Lucas, John Baptiste Charles
Ludeling, John Theodore
Ludlow, George Duncan
Lurton, Horace Harmon
Lynde, Benjamin
Lyon, William Penn
Lyons, Peter
McAllister, Matthew Hall
McCaleb, Theodore Howard
McCarran, Patrick Anthony
McCay, Henry Kent
McComas, Louis Emory
McCrary, George Washington
McDonald, Charles James
McEnery, Samuel Douglas
McFarland, Thomas Bard
McGowan, Samuel
Mack, Julian William
McKean, Joseph Borden
McKenna, Joseph
McKinstry, Elisha Williams
McLean, John
McMaster, Guy Humphreys
Magie, William Jay
Magrath, Andrew Gordon
Malone, Walter
Manning, Thomas Courtland
Marchant, Henry
Marshall, Thomas Alexander
Martin, François-Xavier

Mason, Charles
Mason, John Young
Matthews, Stanley
Maxwell, Augustus Emmett
Maxwell, Samuel
Mercur, Ulysses
Merrick, Edwin Thomas
Merrick, Pliny
Merrimon, Augustus
  Summerfield
Metcalf, Theron
Miller, Oliver
Mills, Benjamin
Minot, George Richards
Mitchell, James Tyndale
Mitchell, Nahum
Mitchell, Stephen Mix
Mitchell, William, 1801–1886
Moncure, Richard Cassius Lee
Moody, William Henry
Moore, John Bassett
Moore, Maurice
Moore, William, 1699–1783
Moore, William, 1735–1793
Moreau-Lislet, Louis Casimir
  Elisabeth
Morgan, Philip Hicky
Morris, Richard
Morrow, William W.
Morton, Marcus, 1784–1864
Murphey, Archibald De Bow
Napton, William Barclay
Nash, Frederick
Nelson, Hugh
Nelson, Rensselaer Russell
Nelson, Roger
Nelson, Samuel
Nicholas, Philip Norborne
Nicholson, Alfred Osborne
  Pope
Nicholson, Joseph Hopper
Nicolls, Matthias
Nixon, John Thompson
Norton, Elijah Hise
Nott, Abraham
Nott, Charles Cooper
Noyes, Walter Chadwick
Oakley, Thomas Jackson
O'Brien, Morgan Joseph
Oldham, Williamson Simpson
Oliver, Andrew
O'Neall, John Belton
Orton, Harlow South
Otis, Charles Eugene
Otto, William Tod
Overton, John
Owsley, William
Paca, William
Paine, Elijah
Paine, Robert Treat
Pardee, Don Albert
Parke, Benjamin
Parker, Alton Brooks
Parker, Amasa Junius
Parker, Edwin Brewington
Parker, Isaac
Parker, Joel, 1795–1875
Parker, Joel, 1816–1888
Parker, John Johnston
Parker, Richard Elliot
Parsons, Theophilus
Paschal, George Washington

Paterson, William
Pearson, Richmond Mumford
Pease, Calvin
Peck, James Hawkins
Pendleton, Edmund
Penfield, William Lawrence
Pennington, William Sandford
Perley, Ira
Pettit, Thomas McKean
Phelps, Charles Edward
Philips, John Finis
Pitkin, William, 1725–1789
Plumley, Frank
Poland, Luke Potter
Porter, Alexander
Porter, James Madison
Potter, Elisha Reynolds
Potter, Platt
Potts, Richard
Pound, Cuthbert Winfred
Pound, (Nathan) Roscoe
Preble, William Pitt
Prentice, Samuel Oscar
Prentiss, Samuel
Prince, Le Baron Bradford
Provosty, Olivier Otis
Pryor, Roger Atkinson
Putnam, William Le Baron
Raney, George Pettus
Ranney, Rufus Percival
Read, Edwin Godwin
Read, John Meredith,
    1797–1874
Reeve, Tapping
Requier, Augustus Julian
Richards, John Kelvey
Richardson, William Adams
Ridgely, Nicholas
Roane, Spencer
Roberts, Oran Milo
Robertson, George
Robertson, John
Robinson, John Mitchell
Robinson, Moses
Rodney, Thomas
Rogers, Henry Wade
Root, Jesse
Rose, John Carter
Rose, Uriah Milton
Ross, George
Rowan, John
Ruffin, Thomas
Rugg, Arthur Prentice
Rumsey, William
Rutledge, John
Ryan, Edward George
Sanford, Edward Terry
Sanford, Nathan
Sawyer, Lorenzo
Scott, William
Seabury, Samuel
Sebastian, Benjamin
Sedgwick, Theodore,
    1746–1813
Seevers, William Henry
Sergeant, Thomas
Settle, Thomas
Shauck, John Allen
Shaw, Lemuel
Sheldon, Henry Newton
Shepard, Seth
Shepley, Ether

Sherwood, Thomas Adiel
Shields, George Howell
Shields, John Knight
Shiras, George
Shiras, Oliver Perry
Shorter, John Gill
Simmons, Thomas Jefferson
Simonton, Charles Henry
Smith, Erasmus Darwin
Smith, Henry Augustus
    Middleton
Smith, James Francis
Smith, Jeremiah, 1759–1842
Smith, Jeremiah, 1837–1921
Smith, Nathan, 1770–1835
Smith, Nathaniel
Smith, Walter Inglewood
Smith, William, 1697–1769
Smith, William, 1728–1793
Soulé, Pierre
Southard, Samuel Lewis
Spear, William Thomas
Speer, Emory
Spencer, Ambrose
Sprague, Peleg
Stacy, Walter Parker
Stanton, Richard Henry
Staples, Waller Redd
Stayton, John William
Stephens, Linton
Stiness, John Henry
Stockbridge, Henry
Stone, George Washington
Stone, John Wesley
Stone, Wilbur Fisk
Story, Joseph
Stuart, Archibald
Sulzberger, Mayer
Sumner, Increase
Swan, Joseph Rockwell
Swayne, Noah Haynes
Swift, Zephaniah
Tait, Charles
Tappan, Benjamin
Taylor, John Louis
Ten Broeck, Abraham
Terry, David Smith
Thacher, George
Thayer, Amos Madden
Thompson, Seymour Dwight
Thompson, Smith
Throop, Enos Thompson
Throop, Montgomery Hunt
Tichenor, Isaac
Tilghman, William
Tod, George
Toulmin, Harry Theophilus
Treat, Samuel
Treat, Samuel Hubbel
Tree, Lambert
Trimble, Robert
Tripp, Bartlett
Trott, Nicholas
Troup, Robert
Trowbridge, Edmund
Trumbull, John, 1750–1831
Trumbull, Lyman
Tucker, Henry St. George,
    1780–1848
Tucker, St. George
Turner, Edward
Turney, Peter

Tyler, Royall
Underwood, John Curtiss
Underwood, Joseph Rogers
Upshur, Abel Parker
Valliant, Leroy Branch
Vanderbilt, Arthur T.
Van Ness, William Peter
Van Santvoord, George
Von Moschzisker, Robert
Wade, Decius Spear
Wade, Martin Joseph
Walker, David, 1806–1879
Walker, David Shelby
Walker, Jonathan Hoge
Walker, Pinkney Houston
Walker, Robert Franklin
Walker, Timothy, 1802–1856
Wallace, William James
Walworth, Reuben Hyde
Wanamaker, Reuben Melville
Warden, Robert Bruce
Ware, Ashur
Warner, Hiram
Watkins, George Claiborne
Weare, Meshech
Welch, John
Wells, Robert William
Wheaton, Henry
Wheeler, George Wakeman
Wheeler, Royal Tyler
White, Albert Smith
White, Edward Douglass
White, Hugh Lawson
Whitman, Ezekiel
Wilbur, Curtis Dwight
Wilkins, Ross
Wilkins, William
Williams, Marshall Jay
Williams, Thomas Scott
Willie, Asa Hoxie
Wilson, Bird
Wilson, James
Wilson, William
Wingate, Paine
Winslow, John Bradley
Winthrop, James
Woerner, John Gabriel
Wood, Reuben
Woodbury, Levi
Woods, William Allen
Woods, William Burnham
Woodward, Augustus Brevoort
Woolsey, John Munro
Woolsey, Theodore Salisbury
Wright, George Grover
Wright, Jonathan Jasper
Yates, Robert
Yeates, Jaster
Yerger, William
Zane, Charles Shuster

KINDERGARTEN EDUCATOR (See
    also EDUCATOR, TEACHER)
Blow, Susan Elizabeth
Hailmann, William Nicholas
Harrison, Elizabeth
Marwedel, Emma Jacobina
    Christiana
Wheelock, Lucy
Wiggin, Kate Douglas

LABOR ACTIVIST
Bloor, Ella Reeve
Lang, Lucy Fox Robins
Mooney, Thomas Joseph
Vorse, Mary Heaton
LABOR ARBITRATOR (See also LABOR MEDIATOR)
Billikopf, Jacob
Millis, Harry Alvin
Stacy, Walter Parker
LABOR ECONOMIST (See also ECONOMIST)
Witte, Edwin Emil
LABOR EXPERT
Andrews, John Bertram
Silcox, Ferdinand Augustus
LABOR LEADER
Arthur, Peter M.
Bellanca, Dorothy Jacobs
Berry, George Leonard
Bloor, Ella Reeve
Boyle, Michael J.
Brophy, John
Buchanan, Joseph Ray
Cahan, Abraham
Cameron, Andrew Carr
Duncan, James
Durkin, Martin Patrick
Fitzpatrick, John
Frayne, Hugh
Frey, John Philip
Furuseth, Andrew
Garretson, Austin Bruce
Gillespie, Mabel
Gompers, Samuel
Green, William
Harnden, William Frederick
Hayes, John William
Haywood, Allan Shaw
Haywood, William Dudley
Henry, Alice
Hillman, Sidney
Howard, Charles Perry
Hutcheson, William Levi
Iglesias, Santiago
Johnston, William Hugh
Jones, Mary Harris
Kearney, Denis
Keefe, Daniel Joseph
Lee, William Granville
Lewis, John Llewellyn
London, Meyer
Lundeberg, Harry
Lynch, James Mathew
McNeill, George Edwin
McNulty, Frank Joseph
Maurer, James Hudson
Mitchell, John, 1870–1919
Moore, Ely
Morrison, Frank
Murray, Philip
Muste, Abraham Johannes
Nestor, Agnes
Noonan, James Patrick
Oliver, Henry Kemble
Olson, Floyd Bjerstjerne
O'Sullivan, Mary Kenney
Parker, Carleton Hubbell
Post, Charles William
Powderly, Terence Vincent
Quill, Michael Joseph
Reuther, Walter Philip

Robins, Margaret Dreier
Rombro, Jacob
Sargent, Frank Pierce
Schlesinger, Benjamin
Sigman, Morris
Sorge, Friedrich Adolph
Stephens, Uriah Smith
Steward, Ira
Sylvis, William H.
Tobin, Daniel Joseph
Townsend, Willard Saxby, Jr.
Tresca, Carlo
Trevellick, Richard F.
Ward, Cyrenus Osborne
Whitney, Alexander Fell
Wilson, William Bauchop
Woll, Matthew
Wright, James Lendrew
LABOR MEDIATOR (See also LABOR ARBITRATOR)
Davis, William Hammatt
Leiserson, William Morris
McEntee, James Joseph
LABOR ORGANIZER
Ameringer, Oscar
Anderson, Mary
Crosswaith, Frank Rudolph
Dennis, Eugene
Flynn, Elizabeth Gurley
Foster, William Z.
Giovannitti, Arturo
Mahler, Herbert
LABOR REFORMER
Perkins, Frances
Walling, William English
LAND AGENT
Case, Leonard
Ellicott, Joseph
Mappa, Adam Gerard
LANDOWNER
Cooper, William
Coxe, Daniel
Gardiner, Silvester
Herrman, Augustine
Read, Charles
Rutgers, Henry
Smith, Peter
Wood, Abraham
LAND PROMOTER (See also PROMOTER)
McNutt, Alexander
Nicholson, John
Ogden, Samuel
Phelps, Oliver
Vaughan, Charles
Williamson, Charles
LAND PROPRIETOR
Marshall, James Markham
Philipse, Frederick
LANDSCAPE ARCHITECT
Cleveland, Horace William Shales
Downing, Andrew Jackson
Eliot, Charles
Farrand, Beatrix Cadwalader Jones
Hansen, George
Jensen, Jens
McLaren, John
Mitchell, Donald Grant
Nolen, John
Olmsted, Frederick Law

Olmsted, John Charles
Parmentier, Andrew
Parsons, Samuel Bowne
Pilat, Ignaz Anton
Platt, Charles Adams
Ramée, Joseph Jacques
Sargent, Henry Winthrop
Saunders, William
Underwood, Loring
Vaux, Calvert
Vitale, Ferruccio
Weidenmann, Jacob
LANDSCAPE DESIGNER
Wright, Henry
LAND SPECULATOR (See also SPECULATOR)
Croghan, George
Crowne, William
Low, Nicholas
Morgan, George
Scott, John
Trent, William
Wharton, Samuel
LARYNGOLOGIST (See also PHYSICIAN)
Asch, Morris Joseph
Bishop, Seth Scott
Bosworth, Francke Huntington
Coakley, Cornelius Godfrey
Elsberg, Louis
Green, Horace
Jarvis, William Chapman
Knight, Frederick Irving
Kyle, David Braden
Lefferts, George Morewood
Lincoln, Rufus Pratt
Mackenzie, John Noland
Mayer, Emil
Schadle, Jacob Evans
Seiler, Carl
Simpson, William Kelly
Skillern, Ross Hall
Wagner, Clinton
LAWYER (SEE ALSO CHIEF JUSTICE [STATE], JUDGE, JURIST, MAGISTRATE, SUPREME COURT JUSTICE)
Abbett, Leon
Abbott, Austin
Abbott, Benjamin Vaughan
Absalom, Harris Chappelle
Adams, Annette Abbott
Adams, Daniel Weissiger
Adams, Robert
Akerman, Amos Tappan
Alexander, James
Alston, Joseph
Andrews, Christopher Columbus
Andrews, Garnett
Andrews, Sherlock James
Angel, Benjamin Franklin
Anthon, John
Appleton, John
Arnold, Isaac Newton
Arnold, Thurman Wesley
Arrington, Alfred W.
Atchison, David Rice
Atherton, Charles Gordon
Atherton, Joshua
Austin, James Trecothick
Avery, William Waigstill

Axtell, Samuel Beach
Bacon, Augustus Octavius
Baer, George Frederick
Baker, Jehu
Baker, Newton Diehl
Baldwin, John Brown
Baldwin, Loammi
Baldwin, Roger Sherman
Ballantine, Arthur Atwood
Ballinger, Richard Achilles
Bancroft, Edgar Addison
Bangs, Francis Nehemiah
Bankhead, John Hollis
Barbour, John Strode, Jr.
Barbour, Oliver Lorenzo
Barbour, Philip Pendleton
Barden, Graham Arthur
Barker, Jacob
Barlow, Samuel Latham Mitchill
Barnard, Daniel Dewey
Barradall, Edward
Barringer, Daniel Moreau
Barry, William Taylor
Bartlett, Ichabod
Bartlett, Joseph
Barton, Robert Thomas
Bassett, Edward Murray
Bates, George Handy
Battle, William Horn
Bayard, James Asheton
Bayard, Richard Henry
Beach, William Augustus
Beaman, Charles Cotesworth
Beatty, Adam
Beaty, Amos Leonidas
Beck, John Brodhead
Belknap, William Worth
Bell, Charles Henry
Bell, Clark
Bell, Samuel
Bemis, George
Benedict, Erastus Cornelius
Benjamin, George Hillard
Benjamin, Judah Philip
Benjamin, Park
Bennett, Nathaniel
Benton, Josiah Henry
Bermudez, Edouard Edmond
Bettman, Alfred
Bibb, George Mortimer
Bickerdyke, Mary Ann Ball
Biddle, Francis Beverley
Bidwell, Barnabas
Bidwell, Marshall Spring
Billings, Frederick
Bingham, Harry
Bingham, John Armor
Binney, Horace
Birney, James
Birney, James Gillespie
Bishop, Joel Prentiss
Bishop, Robert Roberts
Bissell, Wilson Shannon
Black, Frank Swett
Black, James
Black, John Charles
Blackford, Charles Minor
Blaikie, William
Blair, Montgomery
Blanchard, Newton Crane
Blatchford, Richard Milford
Blatchford, Samuel

Bliss, George
Blodgett, Henry Williams
Bloomfield, Joseph
Bloomfield, Meyer
Blount, James Henderson
Bogy, Lewis Vital
Bollan, William
Bonaparte, Charles Joseph
Bonney, Charles Carroll
Bordley, John Beale
Boston, Charles Anderson
Botts, John Minor
Boudin, Louis Boudinoff
Boudinot, Elias Cornelius
Boutell, Henry Sherman
Bowen, Thomas Meade
Bowers, Lloyd Wheaton
Boyd, Lynn
Boyden, Roland William
Bozman, John Leeds
Brackenridge, Henry Marie
Bradbury, James Ware
Bradford, Alexander Warfield
Bradwell, James Bolesworth
Bradwell, Myra
Brady, James Topham
Bragg, Thomas
Branch, Lawrence O'Bryan
Brandeis, Louis Dembitz
Brandon, Gerard Chittocque
Brayman, Mason
Breckenridge, James
Breckinridge, Henry Skillman
Breckinridge, John
Breckinridge, Robert Jefferson
Breckinridge, William Campbell
    Preston
Brennan, Francis James
Brewster, Frederick Carroll
Brewster, Ralph Owen
Briggs, George Nixon
Brightly, Frederick Charles
Brinkerhoff, Roeliff
Bristow, Benjamin Helm
Brown, David Paul
Brown, George William
Brown, Joseph Emerson
Brown, Neill Smith
Brown, Walter Folger
Browning, Orville Hickman
Bruce, Edward Bright
Buck, Daniel
Buckland, Ralph Pomeroy
Buckner, Emory Roy
Bundy, Harvey Hollister
Burdick, Usher Lloyd
Burke, Stevenson
Burke, Thomas
Burlingham, Charles Culp
Burnet, Jacob
Burnett, Henry Lawrence
Burr, Aaron
Burrall, William Porter
Burrell, Alexander Mansfield
Burrill, James
Burton, Clarence Monroe
Butler, Andrew Pickens
Butler, Benjamin Franklin
Butler, Charles
Butler, Pierce
Butler, William Allen
Butler, William Orlando

Butterworth, Benjamin
Byran, Thomas Barbour
Cabell, William Lewis
Cahn, Edmond Nathaniel
Caines, George
Calhoun, Patrick
Calhoun, William Barron
Camp, John Lafayette
Campbell, John Archibald
Cardozo, Benjamin Nathan
Carlile, John Snyder
Carlisle, James Mandeville
Carlson, Chester Floyd
Carpenter, Matthew Hale
Carrington, Henry Beebee
Carson, Hampton Lawrence
Carter, James Coolidge
Case, Leonard
Case, William Scoville
Chalmers, James Ronald
Chamberlain, George Earle
Chamberlain, Joseph Perkins
Chambers, George
Chandler, Peleg Whitman
Chavez, Dennis
Chester, Colby Mitchell
Chestnut, James
Chipman, Daniel
Choate, Joseph Hodges
Choate, Rufus
Christiancy, Isaac Peckham
Clagett, Wyseman
Clark, Abraham
Clark, Horace Francis
Clark, Joshua Reuben, Jr.
Clarke, John Hessin
Clay, Clement Claiborne
Clay, Joseph
Clayton, Augustin Smith
Clayton, John Middleton
Cleveland, Chauncey Fitch
Clifford, John Henry
Cline, Genevieve Rose
Clough, William Pitt
Cobb, Jonathan Holmes
Cobb, Thomas Reade Rootes
Cochran, William Bourke
Cogdell, John Stevens
Cohen, Felix Solomon
Colby, Bainbridge
Colden, Cadwallader David
Colquitt, Walter Terry
Conboy, Martin
Connally, Thomas Terry
    ("Tom")
Conner, James
Conover, Obadiah Milton
Conrad, Charles Magill
Conrad, Holmes
Converse, Charles Crozat
Cook, Philip
Cooke, John Rogers
Cooper, Henry Ernest
Cooper, James
Cornwallis, Kinahan
Costigan, Edward Prentiss
Cotton, Joseph Potter
Coudert, Frederic René
Cowen, John Kissig
Cowles, Charles
Cox, Edward Eugene
Cox, Rowland

Crafts, William
Crane, Frederick Evan
Cravath, Paul Drennan
Creighton, William
Crittenden, John Jordan
Crittenden, Thomas Leonidas
Cromwell, William Nelson
Crowder, Enoch Herbert
Culberson, Charles Allen
Culberson, David Browning
Cullom, Shelby Moore
Cummins, Albert Baird
Curran, Thomas Jerome
Curtis, Charles Pelham
Curtis, George Ticknor
Curtis, Samuel Ryan
Cuyler, Theodore
Daggett, David
Dallas, Alexander James
Dana, Richard
Dana, Richard Henry
Dana, Samuel Whittelsey
Dane, Nathan
Darrow, Clarence Seward
Dart, Henry Paluché
Daugherty, Harry Micajah
Daveis, Charles Stewart
Daveiss, Joseph Hamilton
D'Avezac, Auguste Geneviève
    Valentin
Davies, Joseph Edward
Davis, Cushman Kellogg
Davis, Garret
Davis, George
Davis, John
Davis, John William
Davis, Reuben
Davis, William Thomas
Davison, George Willets
Dayton, William Lewis
Dean, Amos
Dean, Gordon Evans
De Forest, Robert Weeks
Delmas, Delphin Michael
Deming, Henry Champion
Deming, Philander
Denby, Charles
Denver, James William
Depew, Chauncey Mitchell
Derby, Elias Hasket
De Saussure, Henry William
Devaney, John Patrick
Dexter, Franklin
Dexter, Samuel
Dexter, Wirt
Dickerson, Edward Nicoll
Dickinson, Daniel Stevens
Dickinson, Donald McDonald
Dickinson, Jacob McGavack
Dillingham, William Paul
Diven, Alexander Samuel
Dodd, Samuel Calvin Tate
Doddridge, Philip
Donelson, Andrew Jackson
Donnelly, Charles Francis
Donovan, James Britt
Donovan, William Joseph
Doolittle, James Rood
Dorsheimer, William Edward
Dos Passos, John Randolph
Douglas, Henry Kyd
Dow, Neal

Doyle, John Thomas
Drake, Benjamin
Drake, Charles Daniel
Drayton, William
Dropsie, Moses Aaron
Duane, William John
Duff, James Henderson
Dulany, Daniel, 1685–1753
Dulany, Daniel, 1722–1797
Dulles, Allen Welsh
Dulles, John Foster
Dunlop, James
Dunn, Charles
Du Ponceau, Pierre Étienne
Durant, Henry Fowle
Durant, Thomas Jefferson
Durrett, Reuben Thomas
Duval, William Pope
Dwight, Francis
Dwight, Theodore
Dwight, Theodore William
Eames, Charles
Earle, Thomas
Eaton, Dorman Bridgman
Eaton, John Henry
Echols, John
Eckels, James Herron
Edmunds, George Franklin
Edwards, Charles
Edwards, Henry Waggaman
Edwards, Pierpont
Elder, Samuel James
Elliott, Benjamin
Elliott, Charles Burke
Ellis, George Washington
Ellsworth, Henry William
Ellsworth, William Wolcott
Elwell, John Johnson
Emmet, Thomas Addis
Evans, George
Evans, Hugh Davey
Evans, Lawrence Boyd
Evarts, Jeremiah
Evarts, William Maxwell
Everett, David
Ewing, Thomas
Fairfield, John
Fall, Albert Bacon
Farnham, Thomas Jefferson
Farrar, Edgar Howard
Fearn, John Walker
Featherston, Winfield Scott
Felch, Alpheus
Ferry, Elisha Peyre
Fessenden, Francis
Fessenden, James Deering
Fessenden, Samuel
Fessenden, William Pitt
Field, David Dudley
Field, Maunsell Bradhurst
Fisher, George Purnell
Fisher, Sidney George
Fisher, Sydney George
Fisher, Walter Lowrie
Fisk, James
Fiske, Haley
Fitch, Samuel
Fitch, Thomas
Fitzhugh, George
Fitzhugh, William
Flanders, Henry
Fletcher, Calvin

Fletcher, Thomas Clement
Flexner, Bernard
Fly, James Lawrence
Fogg, George Gilman
Folger, Henry Clay
Folger, Walter
Folk, Joseph Wingate
Foot, Solomon
Foote, Lucius Harwood
Forbes, John Murray
Ford, Gordon Lester
Forney, William Henry
Foster, John Watson
Foster, Judith Ellen Horton
Foster, Murphy James
Foster, Roger Sherman Baldwin
Foulke, William Dudley
Freeman, Nathaniel
Frelinghuysen, Frederick
Frelinghuysen, Theodore
Freund, Ernst
Fry, Birkett Davenport
Gaines, John Pollard
Gaither, Horace Rowan, Jr.
Gamble, Hamilton Rowan
Gansevoort, Leonard
Gardiner, John
Garfield, Harry Augustus
Garfield, James Rudolph
Garrison, Lindley Miller
Gartrell, Lucius Jeremiah
Gary, Elbert Henry
Gaut, John McReynolds
Gerard, James Watson
Gerry, Elbridge Thomas
Geyer, Henry Sheffie
Gibbes, William Hasell
Gibbons, Thomas
Gibbons, William
Gibson, Randall Lee
Gilbert, Seymour Parker
Gilchrist, Robert
Gilmer, Francis Walker
Gilpin, Henry Dilworth
Glover, Samuel Taylor
Goldman, Mayer C.
Goldsborough, Robert
Goldsborough, Thomas Alan
Goode, John
Goodhue, James Madison
Goodman, Charles
Goodrich, Chauncey
Goodrich, Elizur
Goodwin, John Noble
Gordon, George Washington
Gordon, Laura De Force
Gordon, William Fitzhugh
Gordon, William Washington
Gorman, Willis Arnold
Goudy, William Charles
Gowen, Franklin Benjamin
Graham, David
Graham, John Andrew
Graham, William Alexander
Granger, Gideon
Grant, Madison
Gray, John Chipman
Greathouse, Clarence Ridgeby
Green, Andrew Haswell
Green, Benjamin Edwards
Green, William
Greenbaum, Edward Samuel

Greener, Richard Theodore
Greenleaf, Simon
Greenup, Christopher
Gregory, Charles Noble
Gregory, Thomas Watt
Gridley, Jeremiah
Griffith, William
Griggs, John William
Grimes, James Wilson
Grimké, Archibald Henry
Griscom, Lloyd Carpenter
Griswold, Roger
Grosvenor, Edwin Prescott
Grover, La Fayette
Grundy, Felix
Gummere, Samuel René
Guthrie, George Wilkins
Guthrie, William Dameron
Hackett, Frank Warren
Hager, John Sharpenstein
Haggin, James Ben Ali
Haight, Henry Huntly
Haines, Charles Glidden
Hale, Eugene
Hale, John Parker
Hale, Robert Safford
Hall, Abraham Oakey
Hall, John Elihu
Hall, Willard Preble
Halleck, Henry Wager
Hamilton, Andrew, d. 1741
Hamilton, James, 1710–1783
Hamilton, James Alexander
Hamilton, Peter
Hamlin, Charles
Hamlin, Charles Sumner
Hammond, Charles
Hammond, Nathaniel Job
Hammond, William Gardiner
Hancock, John, 1824–1893
Hardin, Ben
Hardin, Martin D.
Harding, George
Hardy, William Harris
Harlan, James
Harris, John Woods
Harris, Nathaniel Harrison
Harris, Wiley Pope
Harrison, Fairfax
Hart, Charles Henry
Hartley, Thomas
Hasbrouck, Abraham Bruyn
Hascall, Milo Smith
Haskell, Ella Louise Knowles
Havens, James Smith
Hawkins, Dexter Arnold
Hawley, Gideon, 1785–1870
Hawley, James Henry
Hawley, Joseph
Hayes, John Lord
Hayne, Robert Young
Hays, Arthur Garfield
Hays, Harry Thompson
Hays, Will H.
Hazelton, George Cochrane
Helmer, Bessie Bradwell
Hemphill, Joseph
Henderson, Archibald
Henderson, John
Heney, Francis Joseph
Henry, John, 1750–1798
Henry, William Wirt

Herndon, William Henry
Herrick, Myron Timothy
Hildreth, Richard
Hilgard, Theodor Erasmus
Hill, David Bennett
Hill, Frederick Trevor
Hill, Walter Barnard
Hillard, George Stillman
Hilliard, Henry Washington
Hillquit, Morris
Hillyer, Junius
Hindman, Thomas Carmichael
Hindman, William
Hines, Walker Downer
Hirst, Henry Beck
Hiscock, Frank Harris
Hise, Elijah
Hitchcock, Henry
Hittell, Theodore Henry
Hoadly, George
Hoar, George Frisbie
Hoar, Samuel
Hoffman, David
Hoffman, John Thompson
Hoffman, Josiah Ogden
Hoffman, Ogden
Holcomb, Silas Alexander
Holcombe, James Philemon
Holden, Hale
Hollister, Gideon Hiram
Holls, George Frederick
  William
Holmes, Daniel Henry
Holmes, John
Hopkins, Arthur Francis
Hoppin, William Warner
Hornblower, Joseph Coerten
Hosmer, Titus
Hough, Warwick
Hourwich, Isaac Aaronovich
Houston, Charles Hamilton
Howard, Benjamin Chew
Howard, Volney Erskine
Howe, Frederic Clemson
Howe, Samuel
Howe, William F.
Hoyt, Henry Martyn
Hubbard, Richard Bennett
Hubbard, Thomas Hamlin
Hughes, Charles Evans
Hughes, Henry
Hughes, James
Hummel, Abraham Henry
Humphrey, George Magoffin
Hunt, Carleton
Hunter, Robert Mercer
  Taliaferro
Hunton, Eppa
Hunton, George Kenneth
Hurley, Patrick Jay
Hutchins, Harry Burns
Hyde, Charles Cheney
Ickes, Harold Le Clair
Ide, Henry Clay
Ingersoll, Charles Jared
Ingersoll, Edward
Ingersoll, Jared, 1722–1781
Ingersoll, Jared, 1749–1822
Ingersoll, Robert Green
Ingraham, Edward Duffield
Innes, James
Ireland, John, 1827–1896

Irving, Pierre Munro
Ivins, William Mills
Jackson, Charles
Jackson, Henry Rootes
Jackson, Robert Houghwout
James, Edward Christopher
Jamison, David
Jay, John
Jay, Peter Augustus
Jenkins, James Graham
Jenkins, John Stilwell
Jerome, William Travers
Jewell, Harvey
Johnson, Chapman
Johnson, Edward Austin
Johnson, John Graver
Johnson, Louis Arthur
Johnson, Reverdy
Johnson, Robert Ward
Johnston, Augustus
Johnston, Josiah Stoddard
Johnston, William Preston
Joline, Adrian Hoffman
Jones, Gabriel
Jones, Joel
Jones, Samuel
Jones, Walter
Joy, James Frederick
Judah, Samuel
Judd, Norman Buel
Judson, Frederick Newton
Keener, William Albert
Kefauver, (Carey) Estes
Keifer, Joseph Warren
Kellogg, Frank Billings
Kelly, Edmond
Kennedy, Robert Patterson
Kent, Edward
Kernan, Francis
Key, David McKendree
Key, Francis Scott
Keyes, Elisha Williams
Kimball, Richard Burleigh
King, Carol Weiss
King, Horatio
King, John Pendleton
King, Thomas Butler
Kinsey, John
Kirby, Ephraim
Kneeland, Stillman Foster
Knickerbocker, Herman
Knight, Goodwin Jess
  ("Goodie")
Knott, Aloysius Leo
Knott, James Proctor
Knox, Philander Chase
Kohler, Max James
Lacey, John Fletcher
Lamon, Ward Hill
Landis, James McCauley
Langlie, Arthur Bernard
Lanham, Frederick Garland
  ("Fritz")
Larned, Joseph Gay Eaton
Larrabee, Charles Hathaway
Lathrop, George Parsons
Lathrop, John
Latrobe, John Hazlehurst
  Boneval
Law, Jonathan
Lawton, Alexander Robert
Leaming, Thomas

Lechford, Thomas
Leffingwell, Russell Cornell
Leffler, Isaac
Legaré, Hugh Swinton
Leggett, Mortimer Dormer
Lehmann, Frederick William
Leigh, Benjamin Watkins
Leonard, Daniel
Levin, Lewis Charles
Levinson, Salmon Oliver
Levitt, Abraham
Lewis, Charlton Thomas
Lewis, James Hamilton
Lewis, Lawrence
Lewis, William
Lewis, William Draper
Lewis, William Henry
Lexow, Clarence
L'Hommedieu, Ezra
Lile, William Minor
Lincoln, Enoch
Lincoln, Levi, 1749–1820
Lincoln, Levi, 1782–1868
Lind, John
Lindabury, Richard Vliet
Lindley, Curtis Holbrook
Lipscomb, Abner Smith
Littell, William
Littleton, Martin Wiley
Livermore, Edward St. Loe
Livermore, Samuel, 1786–1833
Livingston, William
Lloyd, David
Lockwood, Belva Ann Bennett
Lockwood, Ralph Ingersoll
Logan, Stephen Trigg
Long, Joseph Ragland
Longfellow, Stephen
Lord, Daniel
Loring, Ellis Gray
Lovejoy, Asa Lawrence
Lovett, Robert Scott
Lowden, Frank Orren
Lowell, John, 1769–1840
Lowery, Woodbury
Lowry, Robert
Lucas, Scott Wike
Ludlow, Thomas William
Lynch, John Roy
Mabie, Hamilton Wright
McAdoo, William Gibbs
McAllister, Hall
McCarran, Patrick Anthony
McCartney, Washington
McClain, Emlin
McClure, Alexander Kelly
McCord, David James
McCrady, Edward
McCreery, James Work
McCullough, John Griffith
McCumber, Porter James
McDaniel, Henry Dickerson
McDonald, Joseph Ewing
McDowell, John
Mack, Julian William
McKinstry, Alexander
McLane, Robert Milligan
Maclay, William
Maclay, William Brown
McLean, Angus Wilton
McMahon, Brien
McMahon, John Van Lear

McNutt, Paul Vories
McRae, Duncan Kirkland
McRae, Thomas Chipman
MacVeagh, Charles
MacVeagh, Isaac Wayne
Magoffin, Beriah
Magoon, Charles Edward
Malone, Dudley Field
Manderson, Charles Frederick
Maney, George Earl
Mann, James Robert
Marcy, William Learned
Marquett, Turner Mastin
Marsh, George Perkins
Marshall, Louis
Martin, John Hill
Martindale, John Henry
Mason, Jeremiah
Mather, Samuel Holmes
Matthews, Francis Patrick
Maxcy, Virgil
Maxwell, George Hebard
Maxwell, Hugh
Maxwell, William
Mayer, Brantz
Mazureau, Étienne
Meagher, Thomas Francis
Mechem, Floyd Russell
Meigs, Josiah
Meigs, Return Jonathan
Meigs, William Montgomery
Meredith, William Morris
Miller, Nathan Lewis
Millikin, Eugene Donald
Mills, Elijah Hunt
Mills, Ogden Livingston
Minor, Benjamin Blake
Mitchel, John Purroy
Mitchell, John Hipple
Mitchell, William DeWitt
Money, Hernando De Soto
Monsky, Henry
Montague, Gilbert Holland
Montefiore, Joshua
Moore, Bartholomew Figures
Moore, John Bassett
Morawetz, Victor
Morell, George Webb
Morgan, George Washington
Morgenthau, Henry
Morris, Luzon Burritt
Morrow, Dwight Whitney
Morrow, Edwin Porch
Morton, Ferdinand Quintin
Moseley, Edward Augustus
Mosessohn, David Nehemiah
Murphy, Henry Cruse
Murray, Joseph
Murray, William Henry David
Mussey, Ellen Spencer
Nelson, Thomas Henry
Nelson, William, 1847–1914
Nesmith, James Willis
Neumann, Franz Leopold
Newberry, John Stoughton
Newel, Stanford
Nicoll, De Lancey
Nicolls, William
Noah, Mordecai Manuel
Noble, John Willock
Noyes, William Curtis
O'Brien, Morgan Joseph

O'Brien, Thomas James
O'Conor, Charles
O'Donnell, Thomas Jefferson
O'Dwyer, William
Ogden, Aaron
Ogden, David
Ogden, David Bayard
Ogden, Thomas Ludlow
Olds, Irving Sands
Olds, Robert Edwin
Oliver, George Tener
Olmsted, Marlin Edgar
Olney, Richard
Ordronaux, John
Orr, Jehu Amaziah
Orton, Harlow South
Osborn, Thomas Andrew
Osborn, Thomas Ogden
Osborne, James Walker
Owen, Thomas McAdory
Paine, Halbert Eleazer
Paine, Henry Warren
Palmer, Alexander Mitchell
Palmer, Henry Wilbur
Palmer, William Adams
Park, Trenor William
Parker, Amasa Junius
Parker, John Cortlandt
Parkinson, Thomas Ignatius
Parsons, John Edward
Parsons, Lewis Baldwin
Parvin, Theodore Sutton
Pastorius, Francis Daniel
Patterson, Robert Porter
Patterson, Thomas MacDonald
Pattison, Robert Emory
Patton, John Mercer
Payne, Christopher Harrison
Payne, John Barton
Peabody, Oliver William Bourn
Peck, George Record
Peckham, Wheeler Hazard
Pennypacker, Samuel Whitaker
Penrose, Boies
Penrose, Charles Bingham
Pepper, George Wharton
Perkins, James Breck
Perkins, Thomas Nelson
Perley, Ira
Perlman, Philip Benjamin
Peters, John Andrew
Peters, Richard, 1744–1828
Petigru, James Louis
Pettigrew, James Johnston
Phelps, Edward John
Phelps, William Walter
Phillips, Willard
Pickering, John
Pierce, Edward Lillie
Pierrepont, Edwards
Piexotto, Benjamin Franklin
Pike, Albert
Pinchot, Amos Richards Eno
Pinkney, William
Pitkin, Frederick Walker
Pitkin, William, 1635–1694
Plumb, Glenn Edward
Polk, Frank Lyon
Pollak, Walter Heilprin
Pomerene, Atlee
Pool, Joe Richard
Poor, John Alfred

Pope, James Pinckney
Post, Melville Davisson
Powell, Thomas Reed
Pressman, Lee
Price, Eli Kirk
Prouty, Charles Azro
Pruyn, John Van Schaick
   Lansing
Pruyn, Robert Hewson
Pujo, Arsène Paulin
Purnell, William Henry
Putnam, (George) Herbert
Putnam, James Osborne
Quick, John Herbert
Quincy, Josiah, 1744–1775
Quitman, John Anthony
Radcliff, Jacob
Radin, Max
Raines, John
Ralston, Samuel Moffett
Randall, Alexander Williams
Randolph, Edmund, 1819–1861
Randolph, George Wythe
Rankine, William Birch
Raulston, John Tate
Rawle, Francis, 1846–1930
Rawle, William
Rawle, William Henry
Raymond, Daniel
Rayner, Isidor
Read, Charles
Read, George
Read, John, 1679/80–1749
Read, John, 1769–1854
Rector, Henry Massey
Redfield, Amasa Angell
Reed, David Aiken
Reed, James Hay
Reed, Joseph
Reed, Thomas Brackett
Reed, William Bradford
Rellstab, John
Rice, Isaac Leopold
Richberg, Donald Randall
Riddle, Albert Gallatin
Ritchie, Albert Cabell
Rives, George Lockhart
Roane, John Selden
Roberts, Oran Milo
Robertson, William Joseph
Robinson, Christopher
Robinson, Conway
Robinson, Henry Cornelius
Rodney, Caesar Augustus
Roe, Gilbert Ernstein
Rogers, John Ignatius
Root, Elihu
Root, Erastus
Rorer, David
Roselius, Christian
Ross, James
Rublee, George
Ruggles, Samuel Bulkley
Rush, Richard
Russell, Charles Wells
Rutherford, Joseph Franklin
Rutledge, Wiley Blount
Sackett, Henry Woodward
Sage, Bernard Janin
Sampson, William
Sanders, Wilbur Fisk
Sanger, George Partridge

Sargent, John Osborne
Sayles, John
Scammon, Jonathan Young
Schell, Augustus
Schoeppel, Andrew Frank
Schouler, James
Scott, Gustavus
Scott, James Brown
Scott, John Morin
Scott, Samuel Parsons
Seabury, Samuel
Sedgwick, Arthur George
Sedgwick, Theodore,
   1780–1839
Sedgwick, Theodore,
   1811–1859
Semmes, Thomas Jenkins
Sergeant, John, 1779–1852
Sergeant, Jonathan Dickinson
Sewall, Jonathan
Sewall, Jonathan Mitchell
Shannon, Wilson
Shearman, Thomas Gaskell
Shepard, Edward Morse
Shipman, Andrew Jackson
Shuster, W(illiam) Morgan
Simms, William Elliott
Smith, Buckingham
Smith, Caleb Blood
Smith, Chauncey
Smith, Israel
Smith, James Francis
Smith, Jeremiah
Smith, Junius
Smith, Melancton, 1744–1798
Smith, Oliver Hampton
Smith, Richard
Smith, Richard Penn
Smith, Robert Hardy
Smith, Roswell
Smith, Truman
Smith, William, 1762–1840
Smith, William Russell
Smyth, John Henry
Snowden, James Ross
Soley, James Russell
Southmayd, Charles Ferdinand
Sparks, William Andrew
   Jackson
Speed, James
Spencer, John Canfield
Spooner, Lysander
Springer, Charles
Springer, Frank
Springer, William McKendree
Stallo, Johann Bernhard
Stanbery, Henry
Stanchfield, John Barry
Stanley, Augustus Owsley
Stanton, Henry Brewster
Starr, Merritt
Stearns, Asahel
Steinhardt, Laurence Adolph
Sterling, John William
Sterne, Simon
Stetson, Francis Lynde
Steuer, Max David
Stevens, Hiram Fairchild
Stevens, Thaddeus
Stewart, Alvan
Stewart, William Morris
Stickney, Alpheus Beede

Stillman, Thomas Edgar
Stilwell, Silas Moore
Stimson, Frederic Jesup
Stockbridge, Henry Smith
Stockton, Richard, 1730–1781
Stockton, Richard, 1764–1828
Stoddard, Amos
Stone, John Wesley
Storey, Moorfield
Storrow, James Jackson
Stoughton, Edwin Wallace
Straus, Oscar Solomon
Strawn, Silas Hardy
Street, Alfred Billings
Strong, Caleb
Strong, Moses McCure
Stryker, Lloyd Paul
Stuart, John Todd
Sullivan, George
Sullivan, William
Sumners, Hatton William
Swayne, Wager
Sweeney, Martin Leonard
Swift, John Franklin
Swift, Lucius Burrie
Taber, John
Taft, Charles Phelps
Taft, Henry Waters
Taft, Robert Alphonso
Tallmadge, James
Taylor, Hannis
Tazewell, Henry
Tazewell, Littleton Waller
Teller, Henry Moore
Temple, Oliver Perry
Tench, Francis
Terrell, Edwin Holland
Thatcher, Benjamin Bussey
Thayer, John Milton
Thomas, Charles Spalding
Thomas, William Widgery
Thompson, Daniel Pierce
Thompson, Richard Wigginton
Thompson, Robert Means
Thurston, Lorrin Andrews
Tichenor, Isaac
Tilden, Samuel Jones
Tilghman, Edward
Tilson, John Quillin
Todd, Charles Stewart
Toole, Edwin Warren
Towne, Charles Arnette
Tracy, Benjamin Franklin
Train, Arthur Cheney
Tremain, Henry Edwin
Trude, Alfred Samuel
Tucker, Henry St. George,
   1853–1932
Tucker, John Randolph,
   1823–1897
Turner, George
Tuttle, Charles Wesley
Tweed, Harrison
Tydings, Millard Evelyn
Tyler, Robert
Tyler, Samuel
Tyson, Job Roberts
Underwood, Francis Henry
Untermyer, Samuel
Usher, John Palmer
Van Buren, John
Vandenhoff, George

Vanderbilt, Arthur T.
Van Der Donck, Adriaen
Van Devanter, Willis
Van Dyke, Nicholas, 1770–1826
Van Schaack, Peter
Van Vechten, Abraham
Van Winkle, Peter Godwin
Van Wyck, Charles Henry
Varnum, James Mitchell
Vaux, Richard
Vilas, William Freeman
Vinton, Samuel Finley
Vroom, Peter Dumont
Wait, William
Walker, Frank Comerford
Wallace, Lewis
Waller, Thomas Macdonald
Wallis, Severn Teackle
Waln, Nicholas
Walsh, Francis Patrick
Walter, Francis Eugene
Ward, John Elliott
Waring, Julius Waties
Warmoth, Henry Clay
Warner, William
Washburn, Albert Henry
Washburn, Israel
Waterman, Thomas Whitney
Watson, David Thompson
Watson, John William Clark
Wayland, Francis, 1826–1904
Wehle, Louis Brandeis
Welch, Joseph Nye
Welker, Herman
Wells, John
West, James Edward
Westcott, Thompson
Wharton, Francis
Wharton, Thomas Isaac
Wheeler, Everett Pepperrell
Wheeler, John Hill
Wheeler, Wayne Bidwell
Wherry, Kenneth Spicer
Whipple, Sherman Leland
White, Albert Smith
White, Alexander
White, John Blake
White, Samuel
White, Stephen Mallory
Whiting, William
Whyte, William Pinkney
Wickersham, George
  Woodward
Wickham, John
Wiley, Alexander
Wilkins, Ross
Willard, Joseph
Willard, Joseph Edward
Williams, Elisha
Williamson, Isaac Halstead
Williston, Samuel
Willkie, Wendell Lewis
Wilson, James Falconer
Wilson, John Lockwood
Wilson, Samuel Mountford
Winder, William Henry
Wise, John Sergeant
Wolf, Simon
Wood, Charles Erskine Scott
Wood, Frederick Hill
Wood, George
Work, Milton Cooper

Worthington, John
Wright, Robert William
Yates, John Van Ness
Yeadon, Richard
Yeates, Jasper
Yerger, William
Young, Owen D.
Zeisler, Sigmund
LEAGUE OF NATIONS OFFICIAL
Tyler, Royall
LECTURE PROMOTER (See also
  PROMOTER)
Pond, James Burton
Redpath, James
LECTURER (See also ORATOR)
Antin, Mary
Atkinson, George Wesley
Bacon, Alice Mabel
Bangs, John Kendrick
Bell, James Madison
Bragdon, Claude Fayette
Brough, Charles Hillman
Brown, John Mason, Jr.
Burton, Richard Eugene
Coffin, Robert Peter Tristram
Colman, Lucy Newhall
Cook, Flavius Josephus
Cooke, George Willis
Dinwiddie, Edwin Courtland
Dixon, Thomas
Dyer, Louis
Elson, Louis Charles
Erskine, John
Farmer, Fannie Merritt
Field, Mary Katherine Kemble
Fletcher, Horace
Gibbons, Herbert Adams
Gilman, Charlotte Perkins
  Stetson
Goldman, Emma
Gronlund, Laurence
Hall, Florence Marion Howe
Herron, George Davis
Holmes, Elias Burton
Hubbard, Bernard Rosecrans
Ingersoll, Robert Green
James, George Wharton
James, Henry, 1811–1882
Johnson, John Albert
Keller, Helen Adams
King, Thomas Starr
Krehbiel, Henry Edward
Lease, Mary Elizabeth Clyens
Leipziger, Henry Marcus
Lockwood, Belva Ann Bennett
Logan, Olive
Lord, John
Morris, Robert, 1818–1888
Moulton, Richard Green
Murdoch, James Edward
Nason, Elias
Ng Poon Chew
Nicholson, Meredith
Ogilvie, James
Pattison, James William
Perry, Edward Baxter
Peters, Madison Clinton
Phelps, William Lyon
Pollock, Channing
Rossiter, Clinton Lawrence, III
Salter, William Mackintire
Sanborn, Katherine Abbott

Savage, Minot Judson
Schaeffer, Nathan Christ
Seton, Ernest Thompson
Slocum, Joshua
Slosson, Edwin Emery
Smith, Elizabeth Oakes Prince
Soulé, George
Starr, Eliza Allen
Stoddard, John Lawson
Stone, Ellen Maria
Strong, Anna Louise
Sunderland, Eliza Jane Read
Talmage, Thomas De Witt
Taylor, Benjamin Franklin
Taylor, Robert Love
Towle, George Makepeace
Underwood, Benjamin Franklin
Vasiliev, Alexander
  Alexandrovich
Warde, Frederick Barkham
Whipple, Edwin Percy
Wiley, Harvey Washington
Williams, Fannie Barrier
Winnemucca, Sarah
Winship, Albert Edward
Woolson, Abba Louisa Goold
LEGAL ANNOTATOR
Kirby, Ephraim
Lowery, Woodbury
Rose, Walter Malins
LEGAL PHILOSOPHER
Cahn, Edmond Nathaniel
Llewellyn, Karl Nickerson
LEGISLATOR (See also CONGRESS-
  MAN, SENATOR)
Adams, Robert
Anderson, William
Applegate, Jesse
Ashe, Thomas Samuel
Bacon, John
Beatty, John
Bingham, William
Bouligny, Dominique
Brinkerhoff, Jacob
Brown, John
Buck, Daniel
Clay, Green
Cocke, William
Curtis, Newton Martin
Edwards, Weldon Nathaniel
Elmer, Ebenezer
Elmer, Jonathan
Elmer, Lucius Quintius
  Cincinnatus
Fell, John
Garnett, James Mercer,
  1770–1843
Garvin, Lucius Fayette Clark
Goebel, William
Green, Norvin
Grimes, James Wilson
Grose, William
Halderman, John A.
Hale, Eugene
Hamer, Thomas Lyon
Harlan, James
Hart, John
Hill, James
Hill, Richard
Holman, Jesse Lynch
Holmes, Ezekiel
Hooper, Samuel

Hoppin, William Warner
Hornblower, Josiah
Huntington, Jabez
Jenckes, Thomas Allen
Johnson, Chapman
Johnston, Peter
Jones, George Wallace
Lane, Joseph
Leffler, Isaac
Leffler, Shepherd
L'Hommedieu, Ezra
Lord, Otis Phillips
Low, Nicholas
Lowell, John, 1743–1802
Lyon, William Penn
McClure, Alexander Kelly
McCreery, James Work
Maclay, William Brown
Marshall, Thomas
Mason, Thomson
Maxcy, Virgil
Maxwell, David Hervey
Maxwell, George Troup
Memminger, Christopher
  Gustavus
Mills, Benjamin
Morris, Edward Joy
Munford, William
Nesmith, James Willis
Nisbet, Eugenius Aristides
Northen, William Jonathan
Orr, Jehu Amaziah
Osgood, Samuel
Parker, James
Pendleton, John Strother
Pitney, Mahlon
Pruyn, Robert Hewson
Purviance, David
Raines, John
Raney, George Pettus
Ridgely, Nicholas
Robinson, Henry Cornelius
Rodman, Isaac Peace
Rollins, Edward Henry
Sanford, Nathan
Sedgwick, Theodore,
  1746–1813
Seevers, William Henry
Silver, Gray
Spalding, Thomas
Stephens, Linton
Strong, Moses McCure
Stuart, Archibald
Van Wyck, Charles Henry
White, James
Wingate, Paine
Wofford, William Tatum

LETTERING ARTIST
Goudy, Frederic William

LEXICOGRAPHER (See also
  PHILOLOGIST)
Allibone, Samuel Austin
Foster, Frank Pierce
Funk, Wilfred John
Goodrich, Chauncey Allen
Jastrow, Marcus
Kohut, Alexander
McFarland, George Bradley
March, Francis Andrew
Sheldon, Edward Stevens
Thomas, Joseph
Vizetelly, Frank Horace

Webster, Noah
Wheeler, William Adolphus
Worcester, Joseph Emerson

LIBRARIAN
Adams, Randolph Greenfield
Allibone, Samuel Austin
Anderson, Edwin Hatfield
Beals, Ralph Albert
Beer, William
Billings, John Shaw
Binkley, Robert Cedric
Bjerregaard, Carl Henrik
  Andreas
Bostwick, Arthur Elmore
Brett, William Howard
Burr, George Lincoln
Canfield, James Hulme
Chadwick, James Read
Cheney, John Vance
Cobb, William Henry
Cogswell, Joseph Green
Cole, George Watson
Crunden, Frederick Morgan
Cutter, Charles Ammi
Dana, John Cotton
Davis, Raymond Cazallis
Dewey, Melvil
Draper, Lyman Copeland
Durrie, Daniel Steele
Eames, Wilberforce
Eastman, William Reed
Edmonds, John
Evans, Charles
Fairchild, Mary Salome Cutler
Farrand, Max
Fiske, Daniel Willard
Flexner, Jennie Maas
Flint, Weston
Folsom, Charles
Foss, Sam Walter
Galbreath, Charles Burleigh
Green, Samuel Abbott
Green, Samuel Swett
Greene, Belle Da Costa
Griffin, Appleton Prentiss Clark
Guild, Reuben Aldridge
Hamlin, Talbot Faulkner
Hanson, James Christian
  Meinich
Harris, Thaddeus William
Herrick, Edward Claudius
Holden, Edward Singleton
Homes, Henry Augustus
Hosmer, James Kendall
Isom, Mary Frances
Jackson, William Alexander
Jewett, Charles Coffin
Jordan, John Woolf
Klingelsmith, Margaret Center
Lamoureux, Andrew Jackson
Larned, Josephus Nelson
Legler, Henry Eduard
Lydenberg, Harry Miller
Martel, Charles
Moore, Anne Carroll
Moore, George Henry
Moore, Nathaniel Fish
Nelson, Charles Alexander
Parvin, Theodore Sutton
Pearson, Edmund Lester
Peckham, George Williams
Perkins, Frederic Beecher

Plummer, Mary Wright
Poole, Fitch
Poole, William Frederick
Putnam, (George) Herbert
Robertson, James Alexander
Rosenthal, Herman
Saunders, Frederick
Schwab, John Christopher
Sharp, Katharine Lucinda
Shaw, William Smith
Sibley, John Langdon
Skinner, Charles Rufus
Smith, John J.
Smith, Lloyd Pearsall
Sonneck, Oscar George
  Theodore
Spofford, Ainsworth Rand
Steiner, Bernard Christian
Steiner, Lewis Henry
Street, Alfred Billings
Thwaites, Reuben Gold
Uhler, Philip Reese
Utley, George Burwell
Vail, Robert William Glenroie
Van Dyke, John Charles
Van Name, Addison
Vinton, Frederic
Ward, James Warner
Watterston, George
Whitney, James Lyman
Williams, John Fletcher
Winship, George Parker
Winsor, Justin
Winthrop, James
Wood, Mary Elizabeth

LIBRARY PROMOTER
Bowker, Richard Rogers

LIBRETTIST
Da Ponte, Lorenzo
Hammerstein, Oscar, II
Smith, Harry Bache

LIEUTENANT GOVERNOR
Bull, William (S.C.)
Bullitt, Alexander Scott (Ky.)
Carlisle, John Griffin (Ky.)
Colden, Cadwallader (N.Y.)
De Lancey, James (N.Y.)
Eastman, Enoch Worthen
  (Iowa)
Gray, William (Mass.)
Gue, Benjamin F. (Iowa)
Hamilton, James, 1710–1783
  (Pa.)
Hoffmann, Francis Arnold (Ill.)
Leisler, Jacob (N.Y.)
McKinstry, Alexander (Ala.)
Moultrie, John (East Fla.)
Oliver, Andrew (Mass.)
Penn, John (Pa.)
Penn, Richard (Pa.)
Phillips, William (Mass.)
Spotswood, Alexander (Va.)
Van Cortlandt, Pierre (N.Y.)
Woodruff, Timothy Lester
  (N.Y.)

LIGHTHOUSE BUILDER
Lewis, Winslow

LIMNOLOGIST (See also BIOLOGIST,
  HYDROGRAPHER, HYDROLO-
  GIST)
Birge, Edward Asahel
Juday, Chancey

LINGUIST (See also INTERPRETER)
André, Louis
Avery, John
Bloomfield, Leonard
Bouvet, Marie Marguerite
Burritt, Elihu
Curtin, Jeremiah
Gatschet, Albert Samuel
Greenhow, Robert
McFarland, George Bradley
Radin, Paul
Riggs, Elias
Sapir, Edward
Speiser, Ephraim Avigdor
Verwyst, Chrysostom Adrian
Whitney, William Dwight
Whorf, Benjamin Lee

LITERARY CRITIC (See also CRITIC, SCHOLAR)
Arvin, Newton
Blackmur, Richard Palmer
Burton, Richard Eugene
Canby, Henry Seidel
Cuppy, William Jacob ("Will")
Goldman, Emma
Hackett, Francis
Hazeltine, Mayo Williamson
Jackson, Joseph Henry
Lewisohn, Ludwig
Lowes, John Livingston
Macy, John Albert
Matthiessen, Francis Otto
More, Paul Elmer
Payne, William Morton
Peck, Harry Thurston
Phelps, William Lyon
Pollard, Joseph Percival
Ripley, George
Rosenfeld, Paul Leopold
Sherman, Stuart Pratt
Spingarn, Joel Elias
Van Doren, Carl Clinton
Wallace, Horace Binney

LITERARY HISTORIAN (See also HISTORIAN)
Brooks, Van Wyck
Lancaster, Henry Carrington

LITHOGRAPHER (See also ARTIST, ENGRAVER, ENGRAVER óWOO-DÔ, ETCHER)
Alexander, Francis
Bellows, George Wesley
Bien, Julius
Haskell, Ernest
Hoen, August
Imbert, Antoine
Ives, James Merritt
Johnston, David Claypoole
Newsam, Albert
Otis, Bass
Pendleton, John B.
Prang, Louis
Rosenthal, Max
Rowse, Samuel Worcester

LITHOTOMIST (See also PHYSICIAN)
Spencer, Pitman Clemens

LITTERATEUR (See also AUTHOR, WRITER)
Biddle, Nicholas
Eliot, Samuel Atkins
Evans, Edward Payson
Hassard, John Rose Greene

Hillard, George Stillman
Lowell, James Russell
Matthews, James Brander
Norton, Andrews
Page, Thomas Nelson
Palmer, George Herbert
Peabody, Oliver William Bourn
Rae, John
Rattermann, Heinrich Armin
Reed, Henry Hope
Ricord, Frederick William
Simms, William Gilmore
Taylor, Bayard
Walsh, Robert
Wendell, Barrett
White, Richard Grant

LOBBYIST (See also POLITICIAN)
Tanner, James
Ward, Samuel, 1814–1884

LOCK EXPERT (See MANUFACTURER)

LOCOMOTIVE BUILDER (See MANUFACTURER)

LOGICIAN (See also MATHEMATICIAN, PHILOSOPHER, SCHOLAR)
Ladd-Franklin, Christine
Peirce, Charles Sanders
Reichenbach, Hans

LOYALIST (See also PATRIOT)
Allen, Andrew
Atherton, Joshua
Auchmuty, Robert
Auchmuty, Samuel
Bailey, Jacob
Barclay, Thomas
Bates, Walter
Boucher, Jonathan
Browne, William
Butler, John
Butler, Walter N.
Chandler, Thomas Bradbury
Chipman, Ward
Clarke, Richard
Coffin, John
Colden, Cadwallader
Connolly, John
Coombe, Thomas
Cooper, Myles
Curwen, Samuel
De Lancy, James
Duché, Jacob
Eddis, William
Fanning, David
Fanning, Edmund
Fitch, Samuel
Fleming, John
Galloway, Joseph
Graham, John
Green, Francis
Hewat, Alexander
Inglis, Charles
Johnson, Guy
Johnson, Sir John
Jones, Thomas
Leonard, Daniel
Leonard, George
Loring, Joshua, 1716–1781
Loring, Joshua, 1744–1789
Low, Isaac
Ludlow, Gabriel George
Morris, Roger
Moultrie, John

Munro, Henry
Odell, Jonathan
Ogden, David
Oliver, Peter
Peters, Samuel Andrew
Randolph, John, 1727 or 1728–1784
Robinson, Beverley
Ruggles, Timothy
Sewall, Jonathan
Smith, William, 1728–1793
Sower, Christopher, 1754–1799
Stansbury, Joseph
Wentworth, John, 1737 N.S.–1820
White, Henry
Williams, Israel
Wragg, William

LUMBERMAN (See also MANUFACTURER)
Ayer, Edward Everett
Bell, Frederic Somers
Blodgett, John Wood
Donovan, John Joseph
Edgar, Charles
Fleming, Arthur Henry
Fordney, Joseph Warren
Griggs, Everett Gallup
Hackley, Charles Henry
Herdic, Peter
Jones, Jesse Holman
Sawyer, Philetus
Stephenson, Isaac
Sullivan, William Henry
Walker, Thomas Barlow
Weyerhaeuser, Frederick Edward

LYRICIST (See also BALLADIST, COMPOSOR, SONGWRITER)
Adams, Frank Ramsay
Cohan, George Michael
De Sylva, George Gard ("Buddy")
Hammerstein, Oscar, II
Hart, Lorenz Milton
Kahn, Gustav Gerson
Loesser, Frank
Porter, Cole
White, George
White, Joseph Malachy

MACHINE DESIGNER
De Leeuw, Adolph Lodewyk
Norton, Charles Hotchkiss

MADAM
Adler, Polly
Everleigh, Ada
Everleigh, Minna

MAGAZINE PUBLISHER (See also PUBLISHER)
Lane, Gertrude Battles
Nast, Condé Montrose
Phillips, John Sanburn
Sedgwick, Ellery
Smart, David Archibald

MAGICIAN
Blackstone, Harry
Goldin, Horace
Herrmann, Alexander
Houdini, Harry
Leipzig, Nate
Thurston, Howard

MAGISTRATE (See also **JUDGE**)
Boise, Reuben Patrick
Bridges, Robert
Browne, John
Dummer, Jeremiah
Forbes, John
Freeman, Nathaniel
Gookin, Daniel
Ludlow, Roger
Mason, John
Masterson, William Barclay
Pynchon, William
Sewall, Samuel
Stilwell, Simpson Everett
Stoughton, William
Tilghman, William Matthew
Underhill, John
Woodbridge, John

MAGNETICIAN (See also **PHYSICIST**)
Schott, Charles Anthony

MAIL RUNNER (See also **TRANSPORTER**)
Grimes, Absalom Carlisle

MALACOLOGIST (See also **ZOOLOGIST**)
Lea, Isaac

MAMMALOGIST (See also **ZOOLOGIST**)
Miller, Gerrit Smith, Jr.
Tate, George Henry Hamilton

MANHATTAN PROJECT DIRECTOR
Groves, Leslie Richard, Jr.

MAN OF AFFAIRS
Barker, James Nelson
Neal, John
Noailles, Louis Marie, Viscomte de
Peck, John James

MANUFACTURER (**GENERAL**)
Acker, Charles Ernest
Allen, Anthony Benezet
Allen, Philip
Allen, Richard Lamb
Allis, Edward Phelps
Ames, James Tyler
Ames, Nathan Peabody
Ames, Oakes
Ames, Oliver, 1779–1863
Ames, Oliver, 1807–1877
Anderson, Joseph Reid
Andrews, Chauncey Hummason
Appleton, Nathan
Atwood, Lewis John
Babbitt, Benjamin Talbot
Bachelder, John
Baldwin, Matthias William
Ball, Ephraim
Barber, Ohio Columbus
Batchelder, Samuel
Bent, Josiah
Bettendorf, William Peter
Billings, Charles Ethan
Blake, Eli Whitney
Bliss, Eliphalet Williams
Boott, Kirk
Borden, Richard
Boyden, Seth
Bradley, Milton
Bridgers, Robert Rufus
Brooker, Charles Frederick
Brown, Alexander Ephraim
Brown, Fayette

Brown, James Salisbury
Brown, Joseph
Brown, Joseph Rogers
Brown, Moses
Bullock, William A.
Burrowes, Edward Thomas
Burson, William Worth
Campbell, Andrew
Candler, Asa Griggs
Carnegie, Andrew
Case, Jerome Increase
Cheney, Person Colby
Coates, George Henry
Cochran, Alexander Smith
Coker, James Lide
Colburn, Irving Wightman
Colt, Samuel
Combs, Moses Newell
Conant, Hezekiah
Cone, Moses Herman
Cooper, Edward
Cooper, Peter
Corliss, George Henry
Cottrell, Calvert Byron
Crane, Winthrop Murray
Crocker, Alvah
Crompton, George
Crompton, William
Crozer, John Price
Cuppler, Samuel
Danforth, Charles
Davis, Horace
Deere, John
Deering, William
Dennison, Henry Sturgis
De Pauw, Washington Charles
De Wolf, James
Disston, Henry
Dixon, Joseph
Douglas, Benjamin
Downer, Samuel
Draper, Eben Sumner
Draper, Ira
Draper, William Franklin
Du Pont, Eleuthère Irénée
Du Pont, Henry
Du Pont, Victor Marie
Durfee, Zoheth Sherman
Dwight, Edmund
Dwight, William
Eickemeyer, Rudolf
Emerson, Ralph
Ensley, George
Esterbrook, Richard
Esterby, George
Ewbank, Thomas
Fairbanks, Henry
Fitler, Edwin Henry
Flagler, John Haldane
Fleischmann, Charles Louis
Ford, John Baptiste
Francis, Joseph
Fries, Francis
Fuller, Levi Knight
Gammon, Elijah Hedding
Gary, James Albert
Good, John
Goodall, Thomas
Griffin, Eugene
Grinnell, Joseph
Griswold, John Augustus
Grover, La Fayette

Haish, Jacob
Hall, Charles Martin
Hall, Thomas Seavey
Hamlin, Emmons
Hammond, James Bartlett
Harvey, Hayward Augustus
Hayden, Joseph Shepard
Hayward, Nathaniel Manley
Hazard, Augustus George
Hazard, Rowland Gibson
Hazard, Thomas Robinson
Heywood, Levi
Hoadley, John Chipman
Hobbs, Alfred Charles
Hoe, Richard March
Hoe, Robert, 1784–1833
Hoe, Robert, 1839–1909
Hogg, George
Hoover, Herbert William
Hotchkiss, Benjamin Berkeley
House, Henry Alonzo
Howe, John Ireland
Hubbard, Henry Griswold
Hughes, Howard Robard
Hunt, Charles Wallace
Hussey, Curtis Grubb
Ingersoll, Robert Hawley
Ingham, Samuel Delucenna
Jeffrey, Joseph Andrew
Jenkins, Nathaniel
Jewell, Marshall
Johnston, Samuel
Kemble, Gouverneur
Kingsford, Thomas
Knowles, Lucius James
Latta, Alexander Bonner
Lawrence, Abbott
Leffel, James
Leymer, John George
Lindsey, William
Lippitt, Henry
Lloyd, Marshall Burns
Lyall, James
McArthur, John, 1826–1906
McCormick, Cyrus Hall
McCormick, Leander James
McCormick, Stephen
Mapes, Charles Victor
Marks, Amasa Abraham
Marsh, Charles Wesley
Marsh, William Wallace
Marshall, Benjamin
Mason, William
Mast, Phineas Price
Masury, John Wesley
Matthews, John
Matthiessen, Frederick William
Merrick, Samuel Vaughan
Miller, Lewis
Munger, Robert Sylvester
Murphy, Franklin
Nelson, Nelson Olsen
Nesmith, John
Newberry, John Stoughton
Newton, Henry Jotham
Nicholson, William Thomas
Niedringhaus, Frederick Gottlieb
Noyes, La Verne
O'Hara, James
Oliver, James
Oliver, Paul Ambrose

Otis, Charles Rollin
Otis, Elisha Graves
Packard, James Ward
Paine, Charles
Paine, Elijah
Palmer, Joseph
Parrott, Robert Parker
Phipps, Henry
Pingree, Hazen Stuart
Pitcairn, John
Pitkin, William, 1725–1789
Post, George Adams
Pratt, Zadock
Rand, Edward Sprague
Redfield, William Cox
Reese, Abram
Remington, Eliphalet
Remington, Philo
Rice, Alexander Hamilton
Richardson, Edmund
Roebling, John Augustus
Rowland, Thomas Fitch
Schieren, Charles Adolph
Schneller, George Otto
Scullin, John
Seed, Miles Ainscough
Seiberling, Frank Augustus
Simpson, Michael Hodge
Slater, John Fox
Slocum, Samuel
Smith, Horace
Smith, James Youngs
Spencer, Christopher Miner
Sproul, William Cameron
Stanley, Francis Edgar
Starrett, Laroy S.
Stearns, Frank Ballou
Sturtevant, Benjamin Franklin
Sweet, John Edson
Thomson, John
Thurber, Charles
Timken, Henry
Tompkins, Daniel Augustus
Towne, Henry Robinson
Tucker, Stephen Davis
Vought, Chance Milton
Wallace, William
Waller, Frederic
Waln, Robert, 1765–1836
Warner, Worcester Reed
Warren, Cyrus Moors
Washburn, Charles Grenfill
Washburn, Ichabod
Washburn, Nathan
Waterman, Lewis Edson
Weeden, William Babcock
Weightman, William
Wesson, Daniel Baird
Westinghouse, George
Wetherill, Samuel
Wharton, Joseph
Wheeler, Nathaniel
White, Samuel Stockton
Whitney, Asa
Wilkinson, David
Williams, David Rogerson
Wilson, George Francis
Winchester, Oliver Fisher
Winslow, Sidney Wilmot
Woodruff, Theodore Tuttle
Wright, John Stephen
Wright, William

Yale, Linus
Ziegler, William
MANUFACTURER (SPECIFIC)
Adding Machines
Burroughs, William Seward
Agricultural Equipment
Legge, Alexander
Agricultural Machinery
Wood, Walter Abbott
Aircraft
Martin, Glenn Luther ("Cy")
Airplanes
Bellanca, Giuseppe Mario
Burgess, W(illiam) Starling
Lockheed, Allan Haines
Lockheed, Malcolm
Piper, William Thomas
Automobiles
Chapin, Roy Dikeman
Chrysler, Walter Percy
Couzens, James
Durant, William Crapo
Duryea, Charles Edgar
Duryea, James Frank
Fisher, Frederic John
Ford, Edsel Bryant
Ford, Henry
Hupp, Louis Gorham
Knudsen, William S.
Nash, Charles Williams
Olds, Ransom Eli
Pope, Albert Augustus
Stutz, Harry Clayton
Wills, Childe Harold
Winton, Alexander
Automobile Bodies
Fisher, Alfred J.
Fisher, Charles T.
Baby Food
Gerber, (Daniel) Frank
Gerber, Daniel (Frank)
Brass
Coe, Israel
Hayden, Hiram Washington
Holmes, Israel
Bricks
Reese, Isaac
Business Machines
Watson, Thomas John
Candy
Gunther, Charles Frederick
Cash Registers
Patterson, John Henry
Cereal
Kellogg, John Harvey
Kellogg, Will Keith
Chemicals
Dow, Herbert Henry
Mallinckrodt, Edward
Merck, George Wilhelm
Pfister, Alfred
Chewing Gum
Wrigley, William
Chocolate
Hershey, Milton Snavely
Cigarettes
Hill, George Washington
Cocoa
Pierce, Henry Lillie
Collars (Detachable)
Brown, Ebenezer

Conveying Equipment
Piez, Charles
Cosmetics
Arden, Elizabeth
Rubinstein, Helena
Cotton
Fry, Birkett Davenport
Gray, George Alexander
Gregg, William
Hammett, Henry Pinckney
Holt, Edwin Michael
Lowell, Francis Cabot
Oliver, Henry Kamble
Sprague, William, 1773–1836
Weaver, Philip
Cotton Machinery
Earle, Pliny
Drugs
Lloyd, John Uri
Explosives
Du Pont, Irénée
Everendon, Walter
Judson, Egbert Putnam
Farm Machinery
McCormick, Cyrus Hall
Firearms
Eastman, Arthur MacArthur
North, Simeon, 1765–1852
Wisner, Henry
Flashbulbs
Mendelsohn, Samuel
Flour
Bell, James Stroud
Pillsbury, Charles Alfred
Pillsbury, John Sargent
Washburn, William Drew
Food (Prepared)
Heinz, Henry John
Horlick, William
Post, Charles William
Gelatin
Knox, Rose Markward
Glass
Dyott, Thomas W.
Houghton, Alanson Bigelow
Lyon, James Benjamin
Owens, Michael Joseph
Wistar, Caspar
Glass Jars
Ball, George Alexander
Gloves
Edwards, Talmage
Littauer, Lucius Nathan
Grindstones
Baldwin, John
Gunpowder
Du Pont, Alfred Irénée
Hats
Genin, John Nicholas
Stetson, John Batterson
Iron
Abbott, Horace
Alger, Cyrus
Benner, Philip
Berkeley, John
Bridges, Robert
Burden, Henry
Faesch, John Jacob
Fritz, John
Greenwood, Miles
Harrison, James
Hasenclever, Peter

Hewitt, Abram Stevens
Hill, William
Huston, Charles
Jenckes, Joseph
Lukens, Rebecca Webb
   Pennock
Meason, Isaac
Noble, Samuel
Oliver, Henry William
Porter, David Rittenhouse
Poulson, Niels
Read, Charles
Read, Nathan
Scranton, George Whitfield
Stiegel, Henry William
Taylor, George
Thomas, David
Torrence, Joseph Thatcher
Lighting Equipment
   Thomson, Elihu
Locks
   Hobbs, Alfred Charles
Locomotives
   Baird, Matthew
   Converse, John Heman
   Norris, William
   Parry, Charles Thomas
   Rogers, Thomas
   Vauclain, Samuel Matthews
Lumber (See also Lumberman)
   Sage, Henry Williams
   Washburn, William Drew
Machinery
   Chalmers, William James
Marine Engines
   Quintard, George William
Meat Packing
   Cudahy, Edward Aloysius, Jr.
   Hormel, George Albert
Nautical Instruments
   King, Samuel
Newspaper Printing Machinery
   Wood, Henry Alexander Wise
Oil Well Equipment
   Jones, Samuel Milton
Organs
   Audsley, George Ashdown
   Estey, Jacob
   Goodrich, William Marcellus
   Hesselius, Gustavus
   Roosevelt, Hilborne Lewis
   Tanneberger, David
Paint
   Callahan, Patrick Henry
Paper
   Chisholm, Hugh Joseph
   Fry, Richard
   Miller, Warner
   Pittock, Henry Lewis
   Rittenhouse, William
   West, George
Patent Medicine
   Ayer, James Cook
   Pinkham, Lydia Estes
Pencils
   Faber, John Eberhard
Pharmaceuticals
   Kiss, Max
   Lilly, Josiah Kirby
Photographic Equipment
   Eastman, George

Pianos
   Bradbury, William Batchelder
   Chickering, Jonas
   Knabe, Valentine Wilhelm
      Ludwig
   Mason, Henry
   Steck, George
   Steinway, Christian Friedrich
      Theodore
   Steinway, Henry Engelhard
   Steinway, William
   Tremaine, Henry Barnes
   Weber, Albert
Plumbing Fixtures
   Kohler, Walter Jodok
Precision Instruments
   Swasey, Ambrose
Prefabricated Housing
   Gunnison, Foster
Radios
   Crosley, Powel, Jr.
   Kent, Arthur Atwater
Railroad Equipment
   French, Aaron
   Wagner, Webster
Razors/Razor Blades
   Gillette, King Camp
Recording Instruments
   Bristol, William Henry
Rubber
   Candee, Leverett
   Day, Horace H.
   Firestone, Harvey Samuel
   Litchfield, Paul Weeks
Saddles and Harnesses
   Redfield, William C.
Safes
   Herring, Silas Clark
Scientific Instruments
   Zentmayer, Joseph
Screws
   Angell, William Gorham
Shoes
   Douglas, William Lewis
   Johnson, George Francis
   McElwain, William Howe
Silk
   Cheney, Ward
   Cobb, Jonathan Holmes
   Skinner, William
Soap
   Colgate, William
   Fels, Joseph
   Fels, Samuel Simeon
   Proctor, William Cooper
Soft Drinks
   Hires, Charles Elmer
Sound Reproduction Equipment
   Jensen, Peter Laurits
Sporting Goods
   Reach, Alfred James
   Spalding, Albert Goodwill
Starch
   Perry, William
Steam Engines
   Thurston, Robert Lawton
Steel
   Carnegie, Andrew
   Corey, William Ellis
   Fairless, Benjamin F.
   Frick, Henry Clay
   Leishman, John G. A.

   Metcalf, William
   Moxham, Arthur James
   Oliver, George Tener
   Park, James
   Verity, George Matthew
   Weir, Ernest Tener
Sugar
   Spreckels, Claus
   Spreckels, Rudolph
Tabulating Machines
   Hollerith, Herman
Telescopes
   Fitz, Henry
   Holcomb, Amasa
   Lundin, Carl Axel Robert
   Rittenhouse, David
   Warner, Worcester Reed
Television Receivers
   Dumont, Allen Balcom
Thermometers
   Tagliabue, Giuseppe
Tobacco
   Reynolds, William Neal
Tools
   Billings, Charles Ethan
   Howe, Frederick Webster
   Lawrence, Richard Smith
   Pratt, Francis Ashbury
   Rand, Addison Crittenden
   Sellers, William
Toys
   Gilbert, Alfred Carlton
Toy Trains
   Cowen, Joshua Lionel
Typewriters
   Underwood, John Thomas
Violins
   Gemünder, August Martin
      Ludwig
Wagons
   Studebaker, Clement
Washing Machines
   Maytag, Frederick Louis
Watches
   Dennison, Aaron Lufkin
   Harland, Thomas
MAPMAKER (See also CARTOGRA-
   PHER)
   Bien, Julius
   Bonner, John
   Greenleaf, Moses
   Hoen, August
   Holme, Thomas
   Mitchell, John, d. 1768
   Osborn, Henry Stafford
   Wood, John
MARINE ALGAE AUTHORITY (See
   also ZOOLOGIST)
   Setchell, William Albert
MARINE BIOLOGIST (See also BI-
   OLOGIST, ZOOLOGIST)
   Carson, Rachel Louise
MARINE CORPS OFFICER
   Butler, Smedley Darlington
   Geiger, Roy Stanley
   Lejeune, John Archer
   McCawley, Charles Laurie
   Smith, Holland McTyeire
MARINER (See also NAVIGATOR,
   SEA CAPTAIN, STEAMBOAT OP-
   ERATOR)
   Bickel, Luke Washington

Bonner, John
Clapp, Asa
Clark, Arthur Hamilton
Coxetter, Louis Mitchell
Douglas, William
Feke, Robert
Freneau, Philip Morin
Levy, Uriah Phillips
Lewis, Winslow
Newport, Christopher
O'Brien, Richard
Peabody, Joseph
Peirce, William
Samuels, Samuel
Slocum, Joshua
Thorndike, Israel
MARKSWOMAN
Oakley, Annie
MARXIST THEORIST
Corey, Lewis
MATHEMATICIAN
Adrain, Robert
Bartlett, William Holmes
Chambers
Bateman, Harry
Bayma, Joseph
Becker, George Ferdinand
Bell, Eric Temple
Birkhoff, George David
Blichfeldt, Hans Frederik
Bliss, Gilbert Ames
Bôcher, Maxime
Bolza, Oskar
Bowditch, Nathaniel
Brown, Ernest William
Byerly, William Elwood
Cain, William
Caldwell, Joseph
Chauvenet, William
Coffin, James Henry
Colburn, Zerah
Cole, Frank Nelson
Coolidge, Julian Lowell
Craig, Thomas
De Forest, Erastus Lyman
Dickson, Leonard Eugene
Eddy, Henry Turner
Eisenhart, Luther Pfahler
Ellicott, Andrew
Farrar, John
Fine, Henry Burchard
Frank, Philipp G.
Franklin, Fabian
Gibbs, Josiah Willard
Godfrey, Thomas
Green, Gabriel Marcus
Greenwood, Isaac
Grew, Theophilus
Gummere, John
Halsted, George Bruce
Hardy, Arthur Sherburne
Harris, Rollin Arthur
Hassler, Ferdinand Rudolph
Hill, George William
Hull, Clark Leonard
Huntington, Edward Vermilye
Jackson, Dunham
Johnson, William Woolsey
Jones, Hugh
Kármán, Theodore (Todor) Von
Leavitt, Dudley

Leeds, John
Lewis, Enoch
Loomis, Elias
McCartney, Washington
McCay, Charles Francis
McClintock, Emory
Martin, Artemas
Maschke, Heinrich
Mason, Max
Miller, George Abram
Minto, Walter
Moore, Clarence Lemuel Elisha
Moore, Eliakim Hastings
Morley, Frank
Moulton, Forest Ray
Newton, Hubert Anson
Nicollet, Joseph Nicolas
Osgood, William Fogg
Patterson, Robert
Peirce, Benjamin
Peirce, Benjamin Osgood
Peirce, James Mills
Pike, Nicolas
Rademacher, Hans
Rittenhouse, David
Rogers, William Augustus
Runkle, John Daniel
Safford, Truman Henry
Sestini, Benedict
Sherman, Frank Dempster
Sherman, John, 1613–1685
Soulé, George
Steinmetz, Charles Proteus
Story, William Edward
Stringham, Washington Irving
Strong, Theodore
Sylvester, James Joseph
Tamarkin, Jacob David
Thompson, Zadock
Van Vleck, Edward Burr
Vaughan, Daniel
Veblen, Oswald
Venable, Charles Scott
Von Neumann, John
Walker, Sears Cook
Weyl, Hermann
Wiener, Norbert
Wilczynski, Ernest Julius
Winlock, Joseph
Winthrop, John
Young, John Wesley
MAYOR
Baker, Newton Diehl (Cleveland)
Blankenburg, Rudolph (Philadelphia)
Cermak, Anton Joseph (Chicago)
Cobo, Albert Eugene (Detroit)
Colden, Cadwallader David (New York)
Couzens, James (Detroit)
Cruger, John (New York)
Crump, Edward Hull (Memphis)
Curtis, Edwin Upton (Boston)
Fagan, Mark Matthew (Jersey City)
Gaynor, William Jay (New York)
Harrison, Carter Henry (Chicago)

Harrison, Carter Henry, Jr. (Chicago)
Havemeyer, William Frederick (New York)
Hoffman, John Thompson (New York)
Hylan, John Francis (New York City)
Johnson, Tom Loftin (Cleveland)
Kelly, Edward Joseph (Chicago)
La Guardia, Fiorello Henry (New York)
Lawrence, David Leo (Pittsburgh)
Lunn, George Richard (Schenectady)
Lyman, Theodore, 1792–1849 (Boston)
McMichael, Morton (Philadelphia)
Maverick, (Fontaine) Maury (San Antonio)
Mitchel, John Purroy (New York)
Murphy, Frank (Detroit)
Norris, Isaac, 1671–1735 (Philadelphia)
O'Dwyer, William (New York)
Phelan, James Duval (San Francisco)
Pierce, Henry Lillie (Boston)
Pinckney, Henry Laurens (Charleston)
Pingree, Hazen Stuart (Detroit)
Radcliff, Jacob (New York)
Seidel, George Lukas Emil (Milwaukee)
Shippen, Edward, 1639–1712 (Philadelphia)
Shurtleff, Nathaniel Bradstreet (Boston)
Strong, William Lafayette (New York)
Swann, Thomas (Baltimore)
Thompson, William Hale (Chicago)
Tobin, Maurice Joseph (Boston)
Walker, James John (New York)
Wentworth, John, 1815–1888 (Chicago)
Westervelt, Jacob Aaron (New York)
Wharton, Robert (Philadelphia)
Whitlock, Brand (Toledo)
Wood, Fernando (New York)
MEAT PACKER (See also INDUSTRIALIST, MANUFACTURER)
Armour, Philip Danforth
Cudahy, Michael
Dold, Jacob
Eastman, Timothy Corser
Hammond, George Henry
Hormel, Jay Catherwood
Hubbard, Gurdon Saltonstall
Hutchinson, Benjamin Peters
Mayer, Oscar Gottfried
Morris, Nelson
Swift, Gustavus Franklin
Swift, Louis Franklin
Wilson, Samuel

MECHANIC
Allaire, James Peter
Ames, James Tyler
Borden, Simeon
Cox, Lemuel
Emerson, James Ezekiel
Knight, Edward Henry
Kruesi, John
Peale, Titian Ramsay
Root, Elisha King
Winans, Ross
MEDALIST (See also CRAFTSMAN, GOLDSMITH, JEWELER, SILVERSMITH)
Brenner, Victor David
MEDICAL ADMINISTRATOR
Weed, Lewis Hill
MEDICAL CHARLATAN
Brinkley, John Richard
MEDICAL EDUCATOR (See also EDUCATOR)
Cabot, Hugh
Edsall, David Linn
Vaughan, Victor Clarence
Wilson, Louis Blanchard
MEDICAL HISTORIAN (See also HISTORIAN, PHYSICIAN)
Alden, Ebenezer
Buck, Albert Henry
Handerson, Henry Ebenezer
Sigerist, Henry Ernest
Williams, Stephen West
MEDICAL ILLUSTRATOR (See also ILLUSTRATOR)
Brödel, Max
MEDICAL INSTRUMENT MAKER
Schwidetzky, Oscar Otto Rudolf
MEDICAL REFORMER
Cabot, Hugh
MEDICAL RESEARCH WORKER (See also PHYSICIAN)
Agramonte y Simoni, Aristides
Ashford, Bailey Kelly
Goldberger, Joseph
Rous, Francis Peyton
Sawyer, Wilbur Augustus
Trask, James Dowling
Weil, Richard
MEDICAL SCIENTIST (See also BACTERIOLOGIST, PATHOLOGIST)
Smith, Theobald
MEDICAL STATISTICIAN (See also STATISTICIAN)
Dorn, Harold Fred
MEDIEVALIST (See also HISTORIAN)
Beeson, Charles Henry
Rand, Edward Kennard
Stephenson, Carl
Tatlock, John Strong Perry
Thorndike, Lynn
Young, Karl
MEDIUM (See SPIRITUALIST)
MENTAL HYGIENIST (See also PHYSICIAN)
Burnham, William Henry
Salmon, Thomas William
MERCANTILE AGENT (See also MERCHANT)
Dun, Robert Graham
MERCENARY
Boyd, John Parker
Burgevine, Henry Andrea

MERCHANT (See also BUSINESSMAN, EXECUTIVE, FACTOR, MERCANTILE AGENT)
Abernethy, George
Allen, William
Altman, Benjamin
Amory, Thomas
Appleton, Samuel
Arbuckle, John
Archer, Samuel
Aspinwall, William Henry
Austin, Jonathan Loring
Austin, Moses
Bache, Richard
Bache, Theophylact
Bain, George Luke Scobie
Baker, Lorenzo Dow
Bamberger, Louis
Barker, Jacob
Barker, James William
Bartlet, William
Bayard, John Bubenheim
Bayard, William
Belcher, Jonathan
Bell, Isaac
Benner, Philip
Bertram, John
Biddle, Clement
Bliss, Cornelius Newton
Bliss, George
Blodget, Samuel
Blount, Thomas
Boorman, James
Borie, Adolph Edward
Bowdoin, James, 1726–1790
Bowdoin, James, 1752–1811
Bowen, Henry Chandler
Brattle, Thomas
Brewer, Charles
Bromfield, John
Brooks, Peter Chardon
Brown, John
Brown, Moses
Brown, Nicholas
Brown, Nicolas
Brown, Obadiah
Buchanan, Thomas
Byrd, William
Cabot, George
Calef, Robert
Capen, Samuel Billings
Carter, Henry Alpheus Peirce
Cerré, Jean Gabriel
Chalkley, Thomas
Chittenden, Simeon Baldwin
Chouteau, Pierre
Claflin, Horace Brigham
Claflin, John
Clapp, Asa
Clark, Daniel
Clarke, Richard
Clay, Joseph
Cleveland, Richard Jeffry
Coates, Samuel
Colby, Gardner
Coleman, William Tell
Colman, John
Cone, Moses Herman
Cook, Isaac
Coolidge, Thomas Jefferson
Cope, Thomas Pym
Coram, Thomas

Corbett, Henry Winslow
Corson, Robert Rodgers
Cozzens, Frederick Swartwout
Cresson, Elliott
Crocker, Charles
Crowninshield, Benjamin Williams
Crowninshield, George
Crowninshield, Jacob
Cruger, Henry
Cupples, Samuel
Cushing, John Perkins
Cushing, Thomas
Deane, Charles
Deas, Zachariah Cantey
De Forest, David Curtis
Delafield, John
De Peyster, Abraham
Derby, Elias Hasket, 1739–1799
Derby, Elias Hasket, 1766–1826
Derby, Richard
De Vries, David Pietersen
Dexter, Samuel
Dexter, Timothy
Dibrell, George Gibbs
Dodge, David Low
Dodge, William Earl
Duer, William
Dunwoody, William Hood
Duryée, Abram
Dwight, Edmund
Eaton, Theophilus
Espejo, Antonio de
Faneuil, Peter
Fell, John
Field, Cyrus West
Field, Marshall
Filene, Edward Albert
Finlay, Hugh
Fish, Preserved
Forbes, John
Forbes, Robert Bennet
Foster, Charles
Fraley, Frederick
Francis, David Rowland
Gadsden, Christopher
Gaines, George Strother
Gardner, Caleb
Garrett, Robert
Genin, John Nicholas
Gillon, Alexander
Gimbel, Bernard Feustman
Girard, Stephen
Glenn, Hugh
Godfrey, Benjamin
Goodhue, Benjamin
Goodwin, Ichabod
Gorham, Jabez
Gould, Benjamin Apthorp
Grace, William Russell
Gratz, Barnard
Gratz, Michael
Gray, William
Green, John Cleve
Green, Joseph
Grim, David
Grinnell, Henry
Grinnell, Joseph
Grinnell, Moses Hicks
Habersham, Alexander Wylly
Habersham, James
Hack, George

Hallowell, Richard Price
Hancock, John, 1736–1793
Hancock, Thomas
Hand, Daniel
Harris, Caleb Fiske
Harris, Townsend
Harrison, James
Haven, Henry Philemon
Hazard, Augustus George
Heard, Augustine
Heathcote, Caleb
Henchman, Daniel
Henderson, Peter
Herrman, Augustine
Hiester, Joseph
Higginson, Nathaniel
Higginson, Stephen
Higinbotham, Harlow Niles
Hill, Richard
Hillegas, Michael
Hogg, George
Hooper, Samuel
Hopkins, Johns
Howland, Gardiner Greene
Hubbard, Gurdon Saltonstall
Hull, John
Hunnewell, James
Hunter, William C.
Huntington, Jabez
Hutchinson, Charles Lawrence
Ingersoll, Robert Hawley
Inman, John Hamilton
Inman, Samuel Martin
Irving, William
James, Daniel Willis
Jarvis, William
Jones, George Wallace
Jordon, Eben Dyer
Juilliard, Augustus D.
Jumel, Stephen
Kemp, Robert H.
Kilby, Christopher
King, Charles
King, Charles William
Kirstein, Louis Edward
Kresge, Sebastian Spering
Kress, Samuel Henry
Ladd, William Sargent
Lamar, Gazaway Bugg
Lampson, Sir Curtis Miranda
Landreth, David
Langdon, John
Langdon, Woodbury
Larkin, Thomas Oliver
Laurens, Henry
Lawrence, Abbott
Lawrence, Amos
Lawrence, Amos Adams
Lawrence, William, 1783–1848
Leaming, Thomas
Lee, Henry, 1782–1867
Lee, William
Leiper, Thomas
Leiter, Levi Zeigler
Lewis, Francis
Lewis, William David
Livingston, Peter Van Brugh
Livingston, Philip
Lopez, Aaron
Lord, David Nevins
Lorillard, Pierre
Loudon, Samuel

Loveland, William Austin
 Hamilton
Low, Abiel Abbot
Low, Isaac
Low, Nicholas
Low, Seth
Ludlow, Daniel
Lumbrozo, Jacob
Macalester, Charles, 1765–1832
McClintock, Oliver
McDonogh, John
Mackenzie, Kenneth
McKim, Isaac
Macy, Josiah
Malcolm, Daniel
Manigault, Gabriel
Manigault, Pierre
Marshall, Benjamin
Marshall, James Fowle Baldwin
Mather, Samuel
May, Morton Jay
Mazzei, Philip
Meade, George
Meade, Richard Worsam
Melish, John
Menard, Pierre
Merry, William Lawrence
Mifflin, Thomas
Mills, Darius Ogden
Mills, Robert, 1809–1888
Minturn, Robert Bowne
Moore, William, 1735–1793
Mordecai, Moses Cohen
Morgan, Edwin Barber
Morgan, James Dada
Morris, Anthony, 1766–1860
Morris, Cadwalader
Morrison, William
Murray, John, 1737–1808
Murray, Robert
Nash, Arthur
Nelson, Thomas
Nelson, William, 1711–1772
Nesbitt, John Maxwell
Nesmith, John
Newberry, Oliver
Newberry, Walter Loomis
Nicola, Lewis
Nixon, John, 1733–1808
Norris, Isaac, 1671–1735
Norris, Isaac, 1701–1766
O'Brien, Edward Charles
Ochs, Julius
O'Fallon, John
Offley, David
Ogden, Robert Curtis
Olyphant, David Washington
 Cincinnatus
Olyphant, Robert Morrison
Opdyke, George
Orr, Alexander Ector
Orthwein, Charles F.
Outerbridge, Eugenius Harvey
Palmer, Potter
Partridge, Richard
Patten, James A.
Patterson, Morris
Patterson, William
Peabody, George
Peabody, Joseph
Peirce, Henry Augustus
Pemberton, Israel

Pemberton, James
Penhallow, Samuel
Penington, Edward
Pepperrell, Sir William
Perkins, Thomas Handasyd
Pettit, Charles
Phelan, James, 1824–1892
Phelps, Anson Greene
Phelps, Oliver
Phillips, William
Phinizy, Ferdinand
Pintard, John
Pintard, Lewis
Pinto, Isaac
Pratt, Charles
Pratte, Bernard
Price, Theodore Hazeltine
Purdue, John
Rand, Edward Sprague
Randall, Robert Richard
Randolph, William
Rawle, Francis, 1662–1726/27
Raymond, Benjamin Wright
Redwood, Abraham
Reed, Luman
Reed, Simeon Gannett
Reisinger, Hugo
Rhind, Charles
Rice, William Marsh
Rich, Isaac
Roberdeau, Daniel
Robert, Christopher
 Rhinelander
Roberts, Edmund
Robinson, Edward Mott
Rochester, Nathaniel
Roddey, Philip Dale
Ropes, Joseph
Rosenberg, Henry
Rosenwald, Julius
Rotch, William
Russell, Joseph
Sage, Henry Williams
St. Vrain, Ceran de Hault de
 Lassus de
Salomon, Haym
Sands, Comfort
Saunders, Clarence
Sayre, Stephen
Searle, James
Sears, Richard Warren
Seligman, Arthur
Servoss, Thomas Lowery
Sewall, Samuel
Shaw, Nathaniel
Shedd, John Graves
Sheedy, Dennis
Sheffield, Joseph Earl
Shelekhov, Grigorii Ivanovich
Silsbee, Nathaniel
Sleeper, Jacob
Smith, John, 1735–1824
Smith, Jonathan Bayard
Smith, Junius
Smith, Melancton, 1744–1798
Spalding, Albert Goodwill
Spreckels, John Diedrich
Stearns, Frank Waterman
Steenwyck, Cornelis
Stewart, Alexander Turney
Stokes, Anson Phelps
Straus, Isidor

Straus, Jesse Isidor
Strong, William Lafayette
Sturgis, William
Sublette, William Lewis
Sulzberger, Cyrus Lindauer
Swartwout, Samuel
Tappan, Lewis
Taylor, Joseph Wright
Telfair, Edward
Thatcher, Mahlon Daniel
Thompson, Jeremiah
Thorndike, Israel
Ticknor, Elisha
Tileston, Thomas
Tobey, Edward Silas
Tome, Jacob
Tracy, Nathaniel
Train, Enoch
Train, George Francis
Tulane, Paul
Tyndale, Hector
Upton, George Bruce
Van Cortlandt, Oloff
  Stevenszen
Van Cortlandt, Stephanus
Van Dam, Rip
Vassar, Matthew
Vaughan, Charles
Vernon, William
Vigo, Joseph Maria Francesco
Wagner, William
Waldo, Samuel
Waln, Robert, 1765–1836
Walters, William Thompson
Wanamaker, John
Wanamaker, Lewis Rodman
Ward, Aaron Montgomery
Ward, Samuel, 1756–1832
Ward, Thomas Wren
Watson, Elkanah
Weston, Thomas
Wharton, Richard
Wharton, Robert
Wharton, Samuel
Wharton, Thomas
White, Alexander
Whitney, Asa
Wilbur, Samuel
Wilder, Marshall Pinckney
Williams, Jonathan
Wolfe, John David
Wood, Robert Elkington
Woodruff, Timothy Lester
Woolworth, Frank Winfield
MESSENGER (See also TRANSPORT-
  ER)
Bailey, Ann
METAL DESIGNER
Yellin, Samuel
METALLOGRAPHER
Sauveur, Albert
METALLURGIST (See also CHEMIST,
  GEOLOGIST, MINERALOGIST)
Arents, Albert
Argall, Philip
Balback, Edward
Becket, Frederick Mark
Campbell, William
Church, John Adams
Daggett, Ellsworth
Daniels, Fred Harris
De Forest, Alfred Victor

Douglas, James
Eilers, Frederic Anton
Gayley, James
Gillett, Horace Wadsworth
Goetz, George Washington
Grant, James Benton
Hill, Nathaniel Peter
Hofman, Heinrich Oscar
Holley, Alexander Lyman
Howe, Henry Marion
Hunt, Alfred Ephraim
Hunt, Robert Woolston
Jackling, Daniel Cowan
Johnston, John
Mathews, John Alexander
Mathewson, Edward Payson
Matthiessen, Frederick William
Metcalf, William
Moldenke, Richard George
  Gottlob
Outerbridge, Alexander Ewing
Overman, Frederick
Pearce, Richard
Pearse, John Barnard Swett
Raht, August Wilhelm
Reese, Jacob
Richards, Joseph William
Sauveur, Albert
Spilsbury, Edmund Gybbon
Stanley, Robert Crooks
Stetefeldt, Carl August
Wahl, William Henry
Wills, Childe Harold
METAPHYSICIAN (See also
  PHILOSOPHER, RELIGIOUS
  LEADER)
Coomaraswamy, Ananda
  Kentish
Upham, Thomas Cogswell
METEOROLOGIST (See also
  CLIMATOLOGIST)
Abbe, Cleveland
Bentley, Wilson Alwyn
Bigelow, Frank Hagar
Coffin, James Henry
De Brahm, William Gerard
Engelmann, George
Espy, James Pollard
Ferrel, William
Gregg, Willis Ray
Harrington, Mark Walrod
Hayden, Edward Everett
Hazen, Henry Allen
Humphreys, William Jackson
Lippincott, James Starr
Lowe, Thaddeus Sobieski
  Coulincourt
McAdie, Alexander George
Marvin, Charles Frederick
Odenbach, Frederick Louis
Redfield, William C.
Rotch, Abbott Lawrence
Upton, Winslow
MICROBIOLOGIST
Gifford, Sanford Robinson
Henrici, Arthur Trautwein
Kelser, Raymond Alexander
Novy, Frederick George
MICROPALEONTOLOGIST (See also
  PALEONTOLOGIST)
Cushman, Joseph Augustine

MICROSCOPIST (See also PHYSI-
  CIAN)
Ward, Richard Halsted
MIDGET
Stratton, Charles Sherwood
MILITARY ENGINEER (See ENGI-
  NEER, MILITARY)
MILLER (See MANUFACTURER)
MILLWRIGHT (See also ENGINEER)
Brown, Sylvanus
Coney, Jabez
Dalzell, Robert M.
Lucas, Jonathan, 1754–1821
Lucas, Jonathan, 1775–1832
MINE OPERATOR (See also MINE
  OWNER, MINER)
Dern, George Henry
Harvey, William Hope
Mondell, Frank Wheeler
Penrose, Spencer
MINE OWNER (See also MINER)
Guggenheim, Solomon Robert
Heckscher, August
Scott, Walter Edward
MINER (See also INDUSTRIALIST,
  METALLURGIST, MINE OPERA-
  TOR, MINE OWNER, PROSPEC-
  TOR)
Agassiz, Alexander
Andrews, Chauncey Hummason
Austin, Moses
Bowen, Thomas Meade
Cist, Jacob
Daly, Marcus
Fleming, Aretas Brooks
Godbe, William Samuel
Goold, William A.
Greene, William Cornell
Hauser, Samuel Thomas
Hearst, George
Henry, Andrew
Hussey, Curtis Grubb
Hutton, Levi William
Imboden, John Daniel
Jones, George Wallace
Mackay, John William
McKnight, Robert
Meeker, Moses
Newhouse, Samuel
Nicholson, Samuel Danford
O'Brien, William Shoney
Reed, John, 1757–1845
Ryan, John Dennis
Tabor, Horace Austin Warner
Thompson, William Boyce
Welch, Charles Clark
MINERALOGIST (See also GEOLO-
  GIST)
Bruce, Archibald
Brush, George Jarvis
Dana, Edward Salisbury
Eggleston, Thomas
Koenig, George Augustus
Seybert, Henry
Shepard, Charles Upham
Smith, John Lawrence
Williams, George Huntington
MINIATURIST (See PAINTER)
MINING ENGINEER (See ENGINEER,
  [MINING])

MINING PROMOTER (See MINER)
MINSTREL (See also BALLADIST,
    FOLKLORIST, SINGER)
Christy, Edwin P.
Dockstader, Lew
Heath, Thomas Kurton
McIntyre, James
Rice, Thomas Dartmouth
MISSIONARY (See also CLERGYMAN,
    RELIGIOUS LEADER)
Abeel, David
Agnew, Eliza
Alemany, José Sadoc
Allen, David Oliver
Allen, Young John
Allonez, Claude Jean
Altham, John
Anderson, David Lawrence
André, Louis
Andrews, Lorrin
Apes, William
Appenzeller, Henry Gerhard
Ashmore, William
Bacon, David
Badger, Joseph
Badin, Stephen Theodore
Bailey, Jacob
Baldwin, Theron
Bapst, John
Baraga, Frederic
Barton, James Levi
Bashford, James Whitford
Bassett, James
Beach, Harlan Page
Belcourt, George Antoine
Benjamin, Nathan
Biard, Pierre
Bickel, Luke Washington
Bingham, Hiram, 1789–1869
Bingham, Hiram, 1831–1908
Blackburn, Gideon
Blanchet, François Norbert
Bliss, Daniel
Bliss, Edwin Elisha
Bliss, Edwin Munsell
Bliss, Howard Sweetser
Bowen, George
Brainerd, David
Brainerd, John
Bridgman, Elijah Coleman
Brondel, John Baptist
Brown, Samuel Robbins
Buck, Philo Melvin
Butler, John Wesley
Butler, William
Byington, Cyrus
Cammerhoff, John Christopher
    Frederick
Campanius, John
Cary, Lott
Cataldo, Joseph Maria
Chamberlain, Jacob
Chandler, John Scudder
Clough, John Everett
Coan, Titus
Copley, Thomas
Copway, George
Cort, Edwin Charles
Crespi, Juan
Cushing, Josiah Nelson
Dablon, Claude
Daeger, Albert Thomas

David, John Baptist Mary
Davis, Jerome Dean
Day, David Alexander
Dearing, John Lincoln
De Forest, John Kinne Hyde
Dennis, James Shepard
De Smet, Pierre-Jean
Doty, Elihu
Dougherty, Raymond Philip
Doyle, Alexander Patrick
Druillettes, Gabriel
Dwight, Harrison Gray Otis
Dwight, Henry Otis
Eliot, John
Elliott, Walter Hackett Robert
Engelhardt, Zephyrin
Ewing, James Caruthers Rhea
Farmer, Ferdinand
Ferguson, John Calvin
Filton, James
Fiske, Fidelia
Fleming, John
Fletcher, James Cooley
Flint, Timothy
Fout, Pedro
Frame, Alice Seymour Browne
Gallitzin, Demetrius Augustine
Garcés, Francisco Tomás
    Hermenegildo
Garry, Spokane
Gates, Caleb Frank
Gibault, Pierre
Going, Jonathan
Good, Adolphus Clemens
Goodell, William
Goodrich, Chauncey
Gordon, Andrew
Goupil, René
Graessl, Lawrence
Grant, Asahel
Graves, Rosewell Hobart
Greaton, Joseph
Greene, Daniel Crosby
Grube, Bernhard Adam
Guignas, Michel
Gulick, John Thomas
Gulick, Luther Halsey,
    1828–1891
Gulick, Sidney Lewis
Hall, Sherman
Hamlin, Cyrus
Happer, Andrew Patton
Harding, Robert
Harpster, John Henry
Hart, Virgil Chittenden
Hawley, Gideon, 1727–1807
Haygood, Laura Askew
Heckewelder, John Gottlieb
    Ernestus
Heiss, Michael
Helbron, Peter
Hepburn, James Curtis
Heyer, John Christian Frederick
Hill, John Henry
Hoecken, Christian
Hoisington, Henry Richard
Holcombe, Chester
Homes, Henry Augustus
Hoover, James Matthews
Hume, Robert Allen
Ingalls, Marilla Baker
Innokentii

Jackson, Sheldon
Jacoby, Ludwig Sigmund
Jessup, Henry Harris
Jogues, Isaac
Jones, George Heber
Jones, John Peter
Jones, John Taylor
Judge, Thomas Augustine
Judson, Adoniram
Judson, Ann Hasseltine
Judson, Emily Chubbuck
Judson, Sarah Hall Boardman
Keith, George
Kellogg, Samuel Henry
King, Jonas
Kino, Eusebio Francisco
Kirkland, Samuel
Kohlmann, Anthony
Lambuth, James William
Lambuth, Walter Russell
Lane, Horace M.
Lansing, Gulian
Lee, Jason
Lefevere, Peter Paul
Lemke, Peter Henry
Lindley, Daniel
Loewenthal, Isidor
Loughridge, Robert McGill
Lowrie, James Walter
Lowrie, Walter
Lowry, Hiram Harrison
Luce, Henry Winters
McCartee, Divie Bethune
MacCauley, Clay
McCord, James Bennett
McCoy, Isaac
McElroy, John
McFarland, Samuel Gamble
McGilvary, Daniel
McKay, David Oman
McKean, James William
McKenna, Charles Hyacinth
Maclay, Robert Samuel
MacSparran, James
Mansell, William Albert
Marquette, Jacques
Martin, William Alexander
    Parsons
Marty, Martin
Mason, Francis
Mateer, Calvin Wilson
Mayhew, Experience
Mayhew, Thomas, 1593–1682
Mayhew, Thomas, 1621–1657
Mazzuchelli, Samuel Charles
Meeker, Jotham
Meerschaert, Théophile
Membré, Zenobius
Ménard, René
Menetrey, Joseph
Mengarini, Gregory
Mills, Cyrus Taggart
Mills, Susan Lincoln Tolman
Morrison, William McCutchan
Mott, John R.
Mudge, James
Murrow, Joseph Samuel
Nash, Daniel
Nassau, Robert Hamill
Nevins, John Livingston
Niza, Marcos de
O'Brien, Matthew Anthony

Occom, Samson
Padilla, Juan de
Palladino, Lawrence Benedict
Palóu, Francisco
Parker, Alvin Pierson
Parker, Edwin Wallace
Parker, Peter
Parker, Samuel
Perkins, Justin
Perry, Rufus Lewis
Pierre, Joseph Marie
  Chaumonot
Pierson, Arthur Tappan
Pierz, Franz
Pond, Samuel William
Poor, Daniel
Post, Christian Frederick
Post, George Edward
Pott, Francis Lister Hawks
Price, Thomas Frederick
Pye, Watts Orson
Raffeimer, John Stephen
Râle, Sébastien
Ravalli, Antonio
Ravoux, Augustin
Rawlinson, Frank Joseph
Reed, Mary
Reid, Gilbert
Reid, John Morrison
Rice, Luther
Richard, Gabriel
Richards, William
Riggs, Elias
Riggs, Stephen Return
Roberts, Issachar Jacob
Robot, Isidore
Ruter, Martin
Ryan, Arthur Clayton
Saenderl, Simon
Savage, Thomas Staughton
Schauffler, Henry Albert
Schauffler, William Gottlieb
Schereschewsky, Samuel Isaac
  Joseph
Schneider, Benjamin
Schneider, Theodore
Scudder, John
Seagrave, Gordon Stifler
Seghers, Charles Jean
Sergeant, John, 1710–1749
Serra, Junípero
Shedd, William Ambrose
Sheffield, Devello Zelotes
Shelton, Albert Leroy
Shepard, Fred Douglas
Shipherd, John Jay
Shuck, Jehu Lewis
Smith, Arthur Henderson
Smith, Azariah
Smith, Eli
Smith, Judson
Spaulding, Levi
Speer, William
Stewart, Philo Penfield
Stewart, Robert
Stoddard, David Tappan
Stone, Ellen Maria
Stuart, John Leighton
Swain, Clara A.
Talbot, John
Talcott, Eliza
Talmage, John Van Nest

Taylor, George Boardman
Taylor, William
Tenney, Charles Daniel
Thayer, John
Thoburn, Isabella
Thomson, William McClure
Tichenor, Isaac Taylor
Tou, Erik Hansen
Trumbull, Henry Clay
Tupper, Henry Allen
Turner, Fennell Parrish
Unangst, Erias
Underwood, Horace Grant
Van Allen, Frank
Van Dyck, Cornelius Van Alen
Van Lennep, Henry John
Van Quickenborne, Charles
  Felix
Verbeck, Guido Herman
  Fridolin
Verwyst, Chrysostom Adrian
Walworth, Clarence Augustus
Wanless, William James
Washburn, George
Watson, Andrew
Watson, Charles Roger
West, Henry Sergeant
Wharton, Greene Lawrence
Wherry, Elwood Morris
White, Andrew
Whitman, Marcus
Williams, Channing Moore
Williams, Edward Thomas
Williams, Eleazar
Williams, John Elias
Williams, Samuel Wells
Willingham, Robert Josiah
Williston, Seth
Wilson, John Leighton
Wilson, Samuel Graham
Winslow, Miron
Wood, Thomas Bond
Worcester, Samuel Austin
Yates, Matthew Tyson
Young, Samuel Hall
Zeisberger, David

MODELER (See also ARTIST,
  CRAFTSMAN, SCULPTOR)
Wright, Patience Lovell
MONOLOGUIST
Draper, Ruth
MORALIST
Fisher, Dorothea Frances
  Canfield
MOTION PICTURE CAMERAMAN
Bitzer, George William
MOTION PICTURE DIRECTOR (See
  also DIRECTOR, FILMMAKER)
Borzage, Frank
Browning, Tod
Curtiz, Michael
Del Ruth, Roy
Fejos, Paul
Sennett, Mack
Sturges, Preston
Von Stroheim, Erich
MOTION PICTURE DISTRIBUTOR
Laemmle, Carl
MOTION PICTURE EXECUTIVE
Johnston, Eric Allen
Mayer, Louis Burt
Warner, Harry Morris

MOTION PICTURE PIONEER
Blackton, James Stuart
Lasky, Jesse Louis
MOTION PICTURE PRODUCER
Borzage, Frank
Fox, William
Selznick, David O.
Sennett, Mack
Sturges, Preston
Todd, Mike
Waller, Frederic
Yates, Herbert John
MOTORIST (See also TRANSPORT-
  ER)
Glidden, Charles Jasper
MUCKRAKER (See AUTHOR, JOUR-
  NALIST, WRITER)
MURALIST (See also ARTIST,
  PAINTER)
Christy, Howard Chandler
Lebrun, Federico ("Rico")
Meière, Marie Hildreth
Sterne, Maurice
MURDERESS (ALLEGED)
Borden, Lizzie Andrew
MUSEUM DIRECTOR (See also
  CURATOR)
Barbour, Thomas
Cesnola, Luigi Palma di
Clarke, Sir Caspar Purdon
Dana, John Cotton
D'Harnoncourt, René
Force, Juliana Rieser
French, William Merchant
  Richardson
Harshe, Robert Bartholow
Heye, George Gustav
Ives, Halsey Cooley
Johnston, John Taylor
Lodge, John Ellerton
Lucas, Frederic Augustus
Mather, Frank Jewett, Jr.
Miller, Gerrit Smith, Jr.
Morse, Edward Sylvester
Osborn, Henry Fairfield
Parker, Arthur Caswell
Putnam, Frederic Ward
Rathbun, Richard
Robinson, Edward, 1858–1931
Rorimer, James Joseph
Spargo, John
Stevens, George Washington
Taylor, Francis Henry
Vaillant, George Clapp
Winlock, Herbert Eustis
MUSEUM FOUNDER
Guggenheim, Solomon Robert
MUSICAL SATIRIST
Templeton, Alec Andrew
MUSIC ARRANGER
Henderson, Fletcher Hamilton
MUSIC CRITIC (See also CRITIC)
Aldrich, Richard
Apthorp, William Foster
Chotzinoff, Samuel
Downes, (Edwin) Olin
Dwight, John Sullivan
Elson, Louis Charles
Finck, Henry Theophilus
Fry, William Henry
Gilman, Lawrence
Gleason, Frederic Grant

Hale, Philip
Henderson, William James
Krehbiel, Henry Edward
Parker, Henry Taylor
Peck, George Washington
Rosenfeld, Paul Leopold
Singleton, Esther
Taylor, Joseph Deems
Thompson, Oscar Lee
Upton, George Putnam
Van Vechten, Carl
Watson, Henry Cood
Woolf, Benjamin Edward
MUSIC EDUCATOR (See also
    EDUCATOR)
Bauer, Harold Victor
Damrosch, Frank Heino
Farwell, Arthur
Goldmark, Rubin
Mannes, Leopold Damrosch
White, Clarence Cameron
MUSICIAN (See also SPECIFIC IN-
    STRUMENTS)
Adgate, Andrew
Allen, Nathan H.
Baker, Benjamin Franklin
Bechet, Sidney
Brown, Gertrude Foster
Clarke, Helen Archibald
Coltrane, John William
Cook, Will Marion
Duchin, Edward Frank
    ("Eddy")
Elman, Harry ("Ziggy")
Elman, Mischa
Erskine, John
Fillmore, John Comfort
Flagg, Josiah
Gericke, Wilhelm
Gleason, Frederic Grant
Graupner, Johann Christian
    Gottlieb
Grierson, Francis
Hale, Philip
Herbert, Victor
Hewitt, John Hill
Holden, Oliver
Holly, Charles Hardin
    ("Buddy")
Holmes, Daniel Henry
Hopkinson, Francis
Horst, Louis
House, Edward Howard
Humiston, William Henry
Huneker, James Gibbons
Koemmenich, Louis
Kroeger, Ernest Richard
Lanier, Sidney
Mason, Frank Stuart
Mathews, William Smythe
    Babcock
Merz, Karl
Moore, Annie Aubertine
    Woodward
Neuendorff, Adolph Heinrich
    Anton Magnus
Oberhoffer, Emil Johann
Oehmler, Leo Carl Martin
Oliver, Henry Kemble
Parsons, Albert Ross
Pearce, Stephen Austen
Peter, John Frederick

Peters, William Cumming
Pryor, Arthur W.
Read, Daniel, 1757–1836
Reinagle, Alexander
Russell, Charles Ellsworth
    ("Pee Wee")
Scheve, Edward Benjamin
Schindler, Kurt
Seidl, Anton
Selby, William
Seward, Theodore
    Frelinghuysen
Shaw, Oliver
Sonneck, Oscar George
    Theodore
Southard, Lucien H.
Spicker, Max
Taylor, Raynor
Thomas, Christian Friedrich
    Theodore
Timm, Henry Christian
Tourjée, Eben
Trajetta, Philip
Ward, Thomas
Webb, George James
Weber, Max
Weld, Arthur Cyril Gordon
Wight, Frederick Coit
Wolfsohn, Carl
Yancey, James Edward
    ("Jimmy")
Young, Alfred
Zerralin, Carl
Ziehn, Bernhard
MUSICOLOGIST
Engel, Carl
Landowska, Wanda Aleksandra
Pratt, Waldo Selden
Spaeth, Sigmund
MUSIC PATRON (See also PHILAN-
    THROPIST)
Coolidge, Elizabeth Penn
    Sprague
De Coppet, Edward J.
Frieze, Henry Simmons
Jordan, Eben Dyer
Juilliard, Augustus D.
Nichols, George Ward
Robinson-Smith, Gertrude
Scherman, Harry
Sloan, George Arthur
Stoeckel, Carl
Thurber, Jeannette Meyer
Webb, Thomas Smith
MUSIC PUBLISHER (See also EDI-
    TOR, PUBLISHER)
Bloom, Sol
Ditson, Oliver
Dreyfus, Max
Fisher, William Arms
Handy, William Christopher
Harris, Charles Kassell
Peters, William Cumming
Presser, Theodore
Schirmer, Gustav
Schirmer, Rudolph Edward
Schmidt, Arthur Paul
Stern, Joseph William
Witmark, Isidore
MUSIC THEORIST
Goetschius, Percy
Schillinger, Joseph

MYCOLOGIST (See also BOTANIST)
Ellis, Job Bicknell
Peck, Charles Horton
Schweinitz, Lewis David von
Whetzel, Herbert Hice
MYSTIC (See also RELIGIOUS
    LEADER)
Alcott, Amos Bronson
Blood, Benjamin Paul
Harris, Thomas Lake
Kelpius, Johann
Very, Jones

NATIONAL FOOTBALL LEAGUE COM-
    MISSIONER
Bell, De Benneville ("Bert")
NATIONAL LABOR RELATIONS
    BOARD CHAIRMAN
Leedom, Boyd Stewart
NATURALIST (See also BIOLOGIST,
    BOTANIST, ECOLOGIST, ZOOLO-
    GIST)
Abbott, Charles Conrad
Adams, Charles Baker
Agassiz, Jean Louis Rodolphe
Akeley, Carl Ethan
Allen, Glover Morrill
Bachman, John
Barbour, Thomas
Barton, Benjamin Smith
Bartram, William
Beebe, (Charles) William
Bland, Thomas
Boll, Jacob
Buckley, Samuel Botsford
Catesby, Mark
Cist, Jacob
Cockerell, Theodore Dru
    Alison
Cooper, James Graham
Dall, William Healey
De Brahm, William Gerard
De Kay, James Ellsworth
Doubleday, Neltje de Graff
Du Simitière, Pierre Eugène
Emerton, James Henry
Flagg, Thomas Wilson
Forbes, Stephen Alfred
Garden, Alexander
Gibson, William Hamilton
Godman, John Davidson
Good, Adolphus Clemens
Goode, George Brown
Grant, Madison
Green, Jacob
Grinnell, George Bird
Grosvenor, Gilbert Hovey
Gulick, John Thomas
Harlan, Richard
Harshberger, John William
Henshall, James Alexander
Henshaw, Henry Wetherbee
Hildreth, Samuel Prescott
Holder, Charles Frederick
Holder, Joseph Bassett
Holland, William Jacob
Hornaday, William Temple
Horsfield, Thomas
Hubbard, Wynant Davis
James, Edwin
Jordan, David Starr
Kennicott, Robert

Kirtland, Jared Potter
Kunze, Richard Ernest
Leidy, Joseph
Lesueur, Charles Alexandre
Lincecum, Gideon
Lucas, Frederick Augustus
McCook, Henry Christopher
Maynard, Charles Johnson
Mearns, Edgar Alexander
Merriam, Clinton Hart
Miles, Manly
Miller, Harriet Mann
Mills, Enos Abijah
Morton, Samuel George
Muir, John
Nelson, Edward William
Osborn, Henry Fairfield
Pavy, Octave
Peale, Charles Willson
Peale, Titian Ramsay
Peck, William Dandridge
Pickering, Charles
Pitcher, Zina
Putnam, Frederic Ward
Rafinesque, Constantine Samuel
Ravenel, Edmund
Ritter, William Emerson
Romans, Bernard
Samuels, Edward Augustus
Saugraïn de Vigni, Antoine
  François
Savage, Thomas Staughton
Seton, Ernest Thompson
Sharp, Dallas Lore
Snow, Francis Huntington
Stearns, Robert Edwards Carter
Stimpson, William
Stone, Witmer
Storer, David Humphreys
Thompson, Zadock
Tuckerman, Frederick
Verrill, Alpheus Hyatt
Ward, Henry Augustus
Webber, Charles Wilkins
White, Charles Abiathar

NAVAL ARCHITECT (See also AR-
  CHITECT)
Babcock, Washington Irving
Burgess, W(illiam) Starling
Eckford, Henry
Fairburn, William Armstrong
Forman, Cheesman
Griffiths, John Willis
Herreshoff, Nathanael Greene
Hovgaard, William
Humphreys, Joshua
Isherwood, Benjamin Franklin
Lenthall, John
McKay, Donald
Newton, Isaac, 1794–1858
Porter, John Luke
See, Horace
Steers, George
Stevens, Robert Livingston
Ward, Charles Alfred
Wilson, Theodore Delavan
NAVAL AVIATOR
Towers, John Henry
NAVAL CONSTRUCTOR
Taylor, David Watson

NAVAL ENGINEER (See ENGINEER,
  NAVAL)
NAVAL OFFICER
Abbot, Joel
Alden, James
Allen, William Henry
Almy, John Jay
Ammen, Daniel
Astor, William Vincent
Aylwin, John Cushing
Badger, Charles Johnston
Badger, Oscar Charles
Bailey, Frank Harvey
Bailey, Theodorus
Bainbridge, William
Balch, George Beall
Barbey, Daniel Edward
Barker, Albert Smith
Barney, Joshua
Barron, James
Barron, Samuel
Barry, John
Beary, Donald Bradford
Beaumont, John Colt
Belknap, George Eugene
Bell, Henry Haywood
Benson, William Shepherd
Bent, Silas
Biddle, James
Biddle, Nicholas
Blake, Homer Crane
Blakely, Johnston
Blandy, William Henry Purnell
Bloch, Claude Charles
Blue, Victor
Boggs, Charles Stuart
Bourne, Nehemiah
Boutelle, Charles Addison
Breese, Kidder Randolph
Bristol, Mark Lambert
Brooke, John Mercer
Brownson, Willard Herbert
Buchanan, Franklin
Bullard, William Hannum
  Grubb
Bulloch, James Dunwody
Burrows, William
Caldwell, Charles Henry
  Bromedge
Capps, Washington Lee
Carter, Samuel Powhatan
Chadwick, French Ensor
Chaffee, Roger Bruce
Champlin, Stephen
Chauncey, Isaac
Chester, Colby Mitchell
Clark, Charles Edgar
Coffin, Sir Isaac
Collins, Napoleon
Colvocoresses, George Musalas
Cone, Hutchinson Ingham
Conner, David
Conyngham, Gustavus
Coontz, Robert Edward
Crane, William Montgomery
Craven, Thomas Tingey
Craven, Tunis Augustus
  MacDonough
Crosby, Peirce
Cushing, William Baker
Dahlgren, John Adolphus
  Bernard

Dale, Richard
Dale, Sir Thomas
Davis, Charles Henry,
  1807–1877
Davis, Charles Henry,
  1845–1921
Davis, John Lee
Davison, Gregory Caldwell
Decatur, Stephen
Decatur, Stephen (son of
  Stephen)
De Haven, Edwin Jesse
Delano, Amassa
Dewey, George
Dornin, Thomas Aloysius
Downes, John
Drayton, Percival
Du Pont, Samuel Francis
Dyer, Nehemiah Mayo
Earle, Ralph
Eberle, Edward Walter
Edwards, Richard Stanislaus
Elliott, Jesse Duncan
Emmons, George Foster
Evans, Robley Dunglison
Fairfax, Donald McNeill
Fanning, Nathaniel
Farragut, David Glasgow
Farragut, George
Fiske, Bradley Allen
Fiske, John
Foote, Andrew Hull
Forrest, French
Foulk, George Clayton
Frost, Holloway Halstead
Gherardi, Bancroft
Gillon, Alexander
Gleaves, Albert
Glynn, James
Goldsborough, Louis
  Malesherbes
Gorringe, Henry Honeychurch
Grant, Albert Weston
Greene, Samuel Dana
Greer, James Augustin
Gridley, Charles Vernon
Griffin, Robert Stanislaus
Grinnell, Henry Walton
Habersham, Alexander Wylly
Halsey, William Frederick
  ("Bull"), Jr.
Haraden, Jonathan
Harding, Seth
Hayden, Edward Everett
Hazelwood, John
Henley, Robert
Herndon, William Lewis
Hichborn, Philip
Hinman, Elisha
Hobson, Richmond Pearson
Hollins, George Nichols
Hopkins, Esek
Hopkins, John Burroughs
Howell, John Adams
Hudde, Andries
Hughes, Charles Frederick
Hull, Isaac
Ingersoll, Royal Rodney
Ingraham, Duncan Nathaniel
Ingram, Jonas Howard
Jeffers, William Nicholson
Jenkins, Thornton Alexander

Jewett, David
Jones, Catesby Ap Roger
Jones, Hilary Pollard
Jones, Jacob
Jones, John Paul
Jones, Thomas Ap Catesby
Jouett, James Edward
Joy, Charles Turner
Kane, Elisha Kent
Kearney, Lawrence
Kelley, James Douglas Jerrold
Kempff, Louis
Kimball, William Wirt
Kimmel, Husband Edward
King, Ernest Joseph
Kirk, Alan Goodrich
Knight, Austin Melvin
Knox, Dudley Wright
Lamberton, Benjamin Peffer
Landais, Pierre
Lanman, Joseph
Lardner, James Lawrence
La Ronde, Louis Denis, Sieur de
Lawrence, James
Leahy, William Daniel
Lee, Samuel Phillips
Lee, Willis Augustus
Little, George
Livingston, John William
Loring, Charles Harding
Loring, Joshua, 1716–1781
Luce, Stephen Bleecker
Lull, Edward Phelps
Lynch, William Francis
McArthur, William Pope
McCall, Edward Rutledge
McCalla, Bowman Hendry
McCann, William Penn
McCauley, Charles Stewart
McCauley, Edward Yorke
McCormick, Lynde Dupuy
Macdonough, Thomas
McDougal, David Stockton
McGiffin, Philo Norton
McKean, William Wister
Mackenzie, Alexander Slidell
McLean, Walter
McNair, Frederick Vallette
McNeill, Daniel
McNeill, Hector
Maffitt, John Newland
Mahan, Alfred Thayer
Manley, John
Marchand, John Bonnett
Mattice, Asa Martines
Maury, Matthew Fontaine
Mayo, Henry Thomas
Mayo, William Kennon
Meade, Richard Worsam
Melville, George Wallace
Mervine, William
Milligan, Robert Wiley
Mitscher, Marc Andrew
Moffett, William Adger
Montgomery, John Berrien
Moore, Edwin Ward
Morgan, James Morris
Morris, Charles
Morris, Richard Valentine
Mullany, James Robert Madison
Murdock, Joseph Ballard

Murray, Alexander
Nelson, William, 1824–1862
Niblack, Albert Parker
Nicholson, James
Nicholson, James William Augustus
Nicholson, Samuel
Nimitz, Chester William
O'Brien, Jeremiah
Page, Richard Lucian
Page, Thomas Jefferson
Palmer, James Shedden
Parker, Foxhall Alexander
Parker, William Harwar
Parrott, Enoch Greenleafe
Patterson, Daniel Todd
Patterson, Thomas Harman
Pattison, Thomas
Paulding, Hiram
Paulding, James Kirke
Pennock, Alexander Mosely
Percival, John
Perkins, George Hamilton
Perry, Christopher Raymond
Perry, Matthew Calbraith
Perry, Oliver Hazard
Phelps, Thomas Stowell
Philip, John Woodward
Pillsbury, John Elliott
Plunkett, Charles Peshall
Poor, Charles Henry
Porter, David
Porter, David Dixon
Pound, Thomas
Pratt, William Veazie
Preble, Edward
Preble, George Henry
Price, Rodman McCamley
Pring, Martin
Pringle, Joel Robert Poinsett
Quackenbush, Stephen Platt
Queen, Walter W.
Raby, James Joseph
Radford, William
Ramsay, Francis Munroe
Read, Charles William
Read, George Campbell
Read, Thomas
Reeves, Joseph Mason
Remey, George Collier
Revere, Joseph Warren
Reynolds, William
Rhind, Alexander Colden
Ribaut, Jean
Ricketts, Claude Vernon
Ridgely, Charles Goodwin
Ridgely, Daniel Bowly
Ringgold, Cadwalader
Robertson, Ashley Herman
Rodgers, Christopher Raymond Perry
Rodgers, George Washington, 1787–1832
Rodgers, George Washington, 1822–1863
Rodgers, John, 1773–1838
Rodgers, John, 1812–1882
Rodgers, John, 1881–1926
Roe, Francis Asbury
Rousseau, Harry Harwood
Rowan, Stephen Clegg
Russell, John Henry

Saltonstall, Dudley
Sampson, William Thomas
Sands, Benjamin Franklin
Sands, Joshua Ratoon
Schenck, James Findlay
Schley, Winfield Scott
Schroeder, Seaton
Selfridge, Thomas Oliver
Semmes, Raphael
Shaw, John, 1773–1823
Shaw, Nathaniel
Sherman, Forrest Percival
Sherman, Frederick Carl
Shubrick, John Templer
Shubrick, William Branford
Shufeldt, Robert Wilson
Sicard, Montgomery
Sigsbee, Charles Dwight
Simpson, Edward
Sims, William Sowden
Sloat, John Drake
Smith, Joseph, 1790–1877
Smith, Melancton, 1810–1893
Snowden, Thomas
Somers, Richard
Spruance, Raymond Ames
Standley, William Harrison
Steedman, Charles
Sterett, Andrew
Stevens, Thomas Holdup, 1795–1841
Stevens, Thomas Holdup, 1819–1896
Stewart, Edwin
Stockton, Charles Herbert
Stockton, Robert Field
Strain, Isaac G.
Stringham, Silas Horton
Strong, James Hooker
Tabot, Silas
Tarbell, Joseph
Tattnall, Josiah
Taussig, Joseph Knefler
Taylor, David Watson
Taylor, William Rogers
Taylor, William Vigneron
Temple, William Grenville
Thatcher, Henry Knox
Theobald, Robert Alfred
Thompson, Egbert
Tingey, Thomas
Towers, John Henry
Townsend, Robert
Trenchard, Stephen Decatur
Trippe, John
Trott, Nicholas
Truxtun, Thomas
Truxtun, William Talbot
Tucker, John Randolph, 1812–1883
Tucker, Samuel
Turner, Daniel
Turner, Richmond Kelly
Tyng, Edward
Upshur, John Henry
Usher, Nathaniel Reilly
Vickery, Howard Leroy
Voorhees, Philip Falkerson
Waddell, James Iredell
Wainwright, Jonathan Mayhew, 1821–1863

Wainwright, Richard,
  1817–1862
Wainwright, Richard,
  1849–1926
Walke, Henry
Walker, Asa
Walker, John Grimes
Ward, James Harmon
Warren, Sir Peter
Warrington, Lewis
Waters, Daniel
Watson, John Crittenden
Weaver, Aaron Ward
Welles, Roger
Werder, Reed
Whipple, Abraham
Wickes, Lambert
Wilde, George Francis Faxon
Wilkes, Charles
Wilkinson, John
Wilkinson, Theodore Stark
Williams, John Foster
Winslow, Cameron McRae
Winslow, John Ancrum
Wise, Henry Augustus
Wood, John Taylor
Woolsey, Melancthon Taylor
Wooster, Charles Whiting
Worden, John Lorimer
Wyman, Robert Harris
Zacharias, Ellis Mark
Ziegemeier, Henry Joseph
NAVIGATOR (See also MARINER,
  STEAMBOAT OPERATOR)
Allefonsce, Jean
Amadas, Philip
Ayala, Juan Manuel de
De Brahm, William Gerard
Gosnold, Bartholomew
Gray, Robert
Hudson, Henry
Ingraham, Joseph
Kendrick, John
Waymouth, George
NAVY SURGEON GENERAL
McIntire, Ross
NAZI PARTY (AMERICAN) LEADER
Rockwell, George Lincoln
NEMATOLOGIST (See also ANATO-
  MIST)
Cobb, Nathan Augustus
NEUROANATOMIST (See also
  ANATOMIST)
Hoerr, Normand Louis
NEUROBIOLOGIST
Loewi, Otto
NEUROLOGIST (See also PHYSI-
  CIAN)
Coriat, Isador Henry
Dana, Charles Loomis
Donaldson, Henry Herbert
Hammond, William Alexander
Jelliffe, Smith Ely
Kennedy, Robert Foster
Knapp, Philip Coombs
McCarthy, Daniel Joseph
Mills, Charles Karsner
Mitchell, Silas Weir
Morton, William James
Patrick, Hugh Talbot
Potts, Charles Sower
Putnam, James Jackson

Ranson, Stephen Walter
Sachs, Bernard
Seguin, Edward Constant
Spitzka, Edward Charles
Starr, Moses Allen
Tilney, Frederick
Timme, Walter
Weisenburg, Theodore Herman
NEUROPATHOLOGIST (See also PA-
  THOLOGIST)
Barrett, Albert Moore
Southard, Elmer Ernest
NEUROPHARMACOLOGIST (See also
  PHARMACOLOGIST)
Loewi, Otto
NEUROPHYSIOLOGIST (See also
  PHYSIOLOGIST)
Fulton, John Farquhar
NEUROPSYCHIATRIST (See also PSY-
  CHIATRIST)
Myerson, Abraham
NEUROSURGEON (See also SUR-
  GEON)
Craig, Winchell McKendree
NEWSAGENT (See also PUBLICIST)
Topliff, Samuel
Tousey, Sinclair
NEWS COMMENTATOR
Swing, Raymond Edwards
  (Gram)
NEWSPAPER COLUMNIST
Berger, Meyer
Broun, Heywood Campbell
Clapper, Raymond Lewis
Crouse, Russel McKinley
Gilmer, Elizabeth Meriwether
  ("Dorothy Dix")
Guest, Edgar Albert
Hopper, Hedda
Kilgallen, Dorothy Mae
Lewis, Fulton, Jr.
McIntyre, Oscar Odd
Morehouse, Ward
Patri, Angelo
Pyle, Ernest Taylor
Stevens, Ashton
NEWSPAPER CORRESPONDENT (See
  also FOREIGN CORRESPOND-
  ENT, JOURNALIST, NEWSPAPER
  REPORTER)
Andrews, Bert
Ross, Charles Griffith
Stark, Louis
NEWSPAPER EXECUTIVE
Carvalho, Solomon Solis
Dryfoos, Orvil E.
Grant, Harry Johnston
Howard, Roy Wilson
Laffan, William Mackay
NEWSPAPERMAN (See also JOUR-
  NALIST)
Asbury, Herbert
Cobb, Irvin Shrewsbury
Early, Stephen Tyree
Farrington, Wallace Rider
Hapgood, Hutchins
Mankiewicz, Herman Jacob
Neuberger, Richard Lewis
Wilson, J(ames) Finley
NEWSPAPER OWNER
Bingham, Robert Worth
Chandler, Harry

Farrington, Joseph Rider
Grasty, Charles Henry
Knutson, Harold
Lea, Luke
Livingstone, William
McCormick, Robert Rutherford
Nicholson, Eliza Jane Poitevent
  Holbrook
Patterson, Alicia
Pulitzer, Joseph, Jr.
Scripps, William Edmund
NEWSPAPER PUBLISHER (See also
  PUBLISHER)
Abbott, Robert Sengstacke
Annenberg, Moses Louis
Block, Paul
Bryan, John Stewart
Copley, Ira Clifton
Cowles, Gardner
Cox, James Middleton
Dealey, George Bannerman
Fitzgerald, John Francis
Fleisher, Benjamin Wilfrid
Glass, Carter
McClatchy, Charles Kenny
McLean, Edward Beale
Murphy, Frederick E.
Noyes, Frank Brett
Patterson, Eleanor Medill
Patterson, Joseph Medill
Pulitzer, Ralph
Reid, Ogden Mills
Scripps, Robert Paine
Sulzberger, Arthur Hays
NEWSPAPER REPORTER (See also
  FOREIGN CORRESPONDENT,
  JOURNALIST, NEWSPAPER COR-
  RESPONDENT)
Berger, Meyer
Kilgallen, Dorothy Mae
Manning, Marie
Powell, John Benjamin
Stark, Louis
NEWSPAPER SYNDICATOR
Dille, John Flint
NIGHTCLUB OWNER
Billingsley, John Sherman
Livingstone, Belle
Rose, Billy
NOVELIST (See also AUTHOR,
  WRITER)
Abbott, Eleanor Hallowell
Adamic, Louis
Adams, Frank Ramsay
Agee, James Rufus
Aldrich, Bess Genevra Streeter
Allen, Hervey
Allen, James Lane
Arlen, Michael
Atherton, Gertrude Franklin
  (Horn)
Bacheller, Irving
Bailey, (Irene) Temple
Baker, Dorothy Dodds
Basso, (Joseph) Hamilton
Baum, Hedwig ("Vicki")
Beach, Rex
Beer, Thomas
Benét, Stephen Vincent
Bennett, Emerson
Biggers, Earl Derr
Bird, Robert Montgomery

Boyd, James
Boyd, Thomas Alexander
Bradford, Roark Whitney
  Wickliffe
Brown, Charles Brockden
Buntline, Ned (*See* Judson,
  Edward Zane Carroll)
Burgess, Frank Gelett
Cabell, James Branch
Cahan, Abraham
Campbell, William Edward
  March
Catherwood, Mary Hartwell
Chambers, Robert William
Chatterton, Ruth
Churchill, Winston
Cleghorn, Sarah Norcliffe
Clemens, Jeremiah
Clemens, Samuel Langhorne
Cobb, Sylvanus
Cohen, Octavus Roy
Comfort, Will Levington
Cooke, John Esten
Cooper, James Fenimore
Costain, Thomas Bertram
Crawford, Francis Marion
Croy, Homer
Cullen, Countée Porter
Curwood, James Oliver
Davis, Rebecca Blaine Harding
Day, Holman Francis
Dell, Floyd James
Donn-Byrne, Brian Oswald
Dos Passos, John Roderigo
Douglas, Lloyd Cassel
Dreiser, Theodore
Dupuy, Eliza Ann
Eggleston, Edward
Eggleston, George Cary
Faulkner (Falkner), William
  Cuthbert
Fearing, Kenneth Flexner
Ferber, Edna Jessica
Fitzgerald, Francis Scott Key
Forbes, Esther
Ford, Paul Leicester
Forester, Cecil Scott
Fox, John William
Frederic, Harold
Freeman, Joseph
Fuller, Henry Blake
Garland, Hamlin
Garreau, Armand
Glasgow, Ellen Anderson
  Gholson
Grant, Robert
Gunter, Archibald Clavering
Hackett, Francis
Hagedorn, Hermann Ludwig
  Gebhard
Harben, William Nathaniel
Hardy, Arthur Sherburne
Harris, Miriam Coles
Harrison, Constance Cary
Harrison, Henry Sydnor
Hawthorne, Nathaniel
Hazelton, George Cochrane
Hemingway, Ernest Miller
Herbert, Frederick Hugh
Herbst, Josephine Frey
Hergesheimer, Joseph
Herrick, Robert Welch

Heyward, DuBose
Hirschbein, Peretz
Hobart, Alice Nourse Tisdale
Hoffman, Charles Fenno
Holley, Marietta
Holmes, Mary Jane Hawes
Howells, William Dean
Hughes, James Langston
Huntington, Jedediah Vincent
Hurst, Fannie
Hurston, Zora Neale
Jackson, Charles Reginald
Jackson, Helen Maria Fiske
  Hunt
Jackson, Shirley Hardie
James, Henry, 1843–1916
Janson, Kristofer Nagel
Johnson, Owen McMahon
Johnston, Mary
Jordan, Kate
Judson, Edward Zane Carroll
  ("Ned Buntline")
Kelland, Clarence Budington
Kerouac, Jack
Kerr, Sophie
Kester, Vaughan
King, William Benjamin Basil
Koch, Vivienne
La Farge, Christopher Grant
Lennox, Charlotte Ramsay
Lewis, Harry Sinclair
Lewisohn, Ludwig
Lincoln, Joseph Crosby
Lippard, George
Lloyd, John Uri
Lynde, Francis
McCullers, Carson
McCutcheon, George Barr
MacDowell, Katherine
  Sherwood Bonner
McHenry, James
McKay, Claude
Magruder, Julia
Major, Charles
Marquand, John Phillips
Masters, Edgar Lee
Melville, Herman
Mitchell, Isaac
Mitchell, John Ames
Mitchell, Margaret Munnerlyn
Mitchell, Silas Weir
Morley, Christopher Darlington
Motley, Willard Francis
Murfree, Mary Noailles
Norris, Benjamin Franklin
Norris, Charles Gilman Smith
Norris, Kathleen Thompson
O'Connor, Edwin Greene
O'Connor, Mary Flannery
O'Hara, John Henry
O'Higgins, Harvey Jerrold
Oppenheim, James
Patten, Gilbert
Paul, Elliot Harold
Phillips, David Graham
Pike, Mary Hayden Green
Poole, Ernest Cook
Porter, Gene Stratton
Post, Melville Davisson
Rawlings, Marjorie Kinnan
Reid, Thomas Mayne
Rice, Elmer

Rinehart, Mary Roberts
Rives, Hallie Erminie
Roche, Arthur Somers
Rowson, Susanna Haswell
Ruark, Robert Chester
Saltus, Edgar Evertson
Sandoz, Mari
Scarborough, Dorothy
Schomer, Nahum Meir
Scoville, Joseph Alfred
Sealsfield, Charles
Sedgwick, Anne Douglas
Shellabarger, Samuel
Simms, William Gilmore
Sinclair, Upton Beall, Jr.
Singer, Israel Joshua
Smith, Harry James
Southworth, Emma Dorothy
  Eliza Nevitte
Stockton, Frank Richard
Stoddard, Elizabeth Drew
  Barstow
Stribling, Thomas Sigismund
Strubberg, Friedrich Armand
Tarkington, Booth
Tenney, Tabitha Gilman
Thayer, Tiffany Ellsworth
Thomas, Frederick William
Tincher, Mary Agnes
Twain, Mark (*See* Clemens,
  Samuel Longhorne)
Tyler, Royall
Vance, Louis Joseph
Van Vechten, Carl
Warfield, Catherine Ann Ware
Warner, Anna Bartlett
Warner, Charles Dudley
Warner, Susan Bogert
Wharton, Edith Newbold Jones
Williams, Ben Ames
Williams, Catharine Read
  Arnold
Wilson, Harry Leon
Wilson, Robert Burns
Wolfe, Thomas Clayton
Wright, Harold Bell
Wylie, Elinor Morton Hoyt
Young, Stark
NUCLEAR PHYSICIST
Graves, Alvin Cushman
NUMISMATIST (See also COLLEC-
  TOR)
Anthon, Charles Edward
Du Bois, William Ewing
Newell, Edward Theodore
Phillips, Henry
Snowden, James Ross
Storer, Horatio Robinson
NURSE
Anthony, Sister
Barton, Clara
Delano, Jane Armindo
Dock, Lavinia Lloyd
Fitzgerald, Alice Louise
  Florence
Goodrich, Annie Warburton
Haupt, Alma Cecelia
Hopkins, Juliet Ann Opie
Law, Sallie Chapman Gordon
Minnigerode, Lucy
Noyes, Clara Dutton
Nutting, Mary Adelaide

Stimson, Julia Catherine
Wald, Lillian D.
NURSERYMAN (See also AGRICUL-
    TURIST)
Kenrick, William
Luelling, Henderson
Parsons, Samuel Bowne
Prince, William, c. 1725–1802
Prince, William, 1766–1842
Prince, William Robert
Pyle, Robert
Rock, John
Roeding, George Christian
Vick, James
NURSING EDUCATOR (See also
    EDUCATOR)
Stimson, Julia Catherine
NUTRITIONAL BIOCHEMIST (See
    also BIOCHEMIST, NUTRITION-
    IST)
Nelson, Marjorie Maxine
NUTRITIONIST (See also DIETI-
    CIAN)
Hart, Edwin Bret
Rose, Mary Davies Swartz

OARSMAN (See also ATHLETE,
    ROWING CHAMPION, ROWING
    COACH)
Cook, Robert Johnson
Courtney, Charles Edward
OBSTETRICIAN (See also PHYSI-
    CIAN)
Atkinson, William Biddle
DeLee, Joseph Bolivar
Dewees, William Potts
Engelmann, George Julius
Hirst, Barton Cooke
Hodge, Hugh Lenox
Lloyd, James
Lusk, William Thompson
Parry, John Stubbs
Parvin, Theophilus
Polak, John Osborn
Richardson, William Lambert
Smith, Albert Holmes
Storer, David Humphreys
Thomas, Theodore Gaillard
Williams, John Whitridge
OCCULTIST
Comfort, Will Levington
OCEANOGRAPHER (See also HY-
    DROGRAPHER)
Agassiz, Alexander
Beebe, (Charles) William
Bent, Silas
Bigelow, Henry Bryant
Harris, Rollin Arthur
Lindenkohl, Adolph
Maury, Matthew Fontaine
Pillsbury, John Elliott
Smith, Edward Hanson
Vaughan, Thomas Wayland
OCULIST (See also PHYSICIAN)
Chisolm, John Julian
OFFICIAL GREETER
Whalen, Grover Aloysius
OIL COMPANY EXECUTIVE
Beaty, Amos Leonidas
Cullen, Hugh Roy
Cullinan, Joseph Stephen
Farish, William Stamps

Gallagher, Ralph W.
Kerr, Robert Samuel
Richardson, Sid Williams
Rockefeller, John Davison
Rockefeller, John Davison, Jr.
Van Dyke, John Wesley
OIL PRODUCER (See also INDUS-
    TRIALIST)
Abbott, William Hawkins
Bissell, George Henry
Doheny, Edward Laurence
Donnell, James C.
Gregory, Thomas Barger
Guffey, James McClurg
Lockhart, Charles
Marland, Ernest Whitworth
Mellon, William Larimer
Murchison, Clinton Williams
Phillips, Frank
Phillips, Thomas Wharton
Sinclair, Harry Ford
Sterling, Ross Shaw
Vandergrift, Jacob Jay
OIL REFINER (See also INDUSTRI-
    ALIST)
Kier, Samuel M.
Lockhart, Charles
Merrill, Joshua
Mowbray, George Mordey
Nevin, Robert Peebles
Rockefeller, John Davison
Rockefeller, John Davison, Jr.
Sibley, Joseph Crocker
ONCOLOGIST (See also PHYSICIAN)
Papanicolaou, George Nicholas
OOLOGIST (See also NATURALIST)
Brewer, Thomas Mayo
OPERA MANAGER (See also IMPRE-
    SARIO, THEATRICIAL MANAG-
    ER)
Gatti-Casazza, Giulio
Johnson, Edward
OPERA SINGER (See SINGER)
OPHTHALMOLOGIST (See also
    OCULIST, PHYSICIAN)
Agnew, Cornelius Rea
Delafield, Edward
Dix, John Homer
Duane, Alexander
Friedenwald, Aaron
Gifford, Sanford Robinson
Gould, George Milbry
Green, John
Gruening, Emil
Hays, Isaac
Hotz, Ferdinand Carl
Howe, Lucien
Jackson, Edward
Knapp, Herman
Koller, Carl
Lewis, Francis Park
Loring, Edward Greely
Norris, William Fisher
Noyes, Henry Drury
Oliver, Charles Augustus
Pyle, Walter Lytle
Randall, Burton Alexander
Reuling, George
Schweinitz, George Edmund de
Theobald, Samuel
Weeks, John Elmer
Wheeler, John Martin

Williams, Elkanah
Williams, Henry Willard
Wilmer, William Holland
Wood, Casey Albert
OPTICAL EXPERT
Ritchey, George Willis
OPTICIAN (See also OCULIST,
    OPHTHALMOLOGIST, PHYSI-
    CIAN)
Lundin, Carl Axel Robert
Porter, Russell Williams
ORATOR (See also LECTURER)
Alderman, Edwin Anderson
Bancroft, Edgar Addison
Bowers, Claude Gernade
Curtis, George William
Dickinson, Anna Elizabeth
Douglass, Frederick
Gillis, James Martin
Grady, Henry Woodfin
Graves, John Temple
Henry, Patrick
Innes, James
Logan, James, 1725–1780
Phillips, Wendell
Prentiss, Seargent Smith
Preston, John Smith
Randolph, John, 1773–1833
Russell, Jonathan
Simmons, Roscoe Conkling
    Murray
Stuart, Isaac William
Thomson, John
ORCHESTRAL CONDUCTOR (See
    CONDUCTOR)
ORDNANCE EXPERT
Benton, James Gilchrist
ORGAN BUILDER (See MANUFAC-
    TURER)
ORGANIC CHEMIST (See also
    CHEMIST)
Bachmann, Werner Emmanuel
ORGANIST (See also MUSICIAN, PI-
    ANIST)
Archer, Frederic
Blodgett, Benjamin Colman
Buck, Dudley
Cadman, Charles Wakefield
Dunham, Henry Morton
Eddy, Clarence
Fairlamb, James Remington
Hale, Philip
Jackson, George K.
Marzo, Eduardo
Mees, Arthur
Paine, John Knowles
Parker, James Cutler Dunn
Root, Frederic Woodman
Stewart, Humphrey John
Thayer, Whitney Eugene
Tuckey, William
Warren, Richard Henry
Warren, Samuel Prowse
Whiting, George Elbridge
Wolle, John Frederick
Wood, David Duffle
Yon, Pietro Alessandro
Zeuner, Charles
ORGANIZATION EXECUTIVE
Breckinridge, Aida de Acosta

ORGANIZED CRIME LEADER (See
   also CRIMINAL, GANGSTER)
   Luchese, Thomas
   Luciano, Charles ("Lucky")
   Profaci, Joseph
ORGANIZER (See PROMOTER)
ORIENTALIST (See also SCHOLAR,
   SINOLOGUE)
   Adler, Cyrus
   Barton, George Aaron
   Bigelow, William Sturgis
   Bloomfield, Maurice
   Brown, John Porter
   Casanowicz, Immanuel Moses
   Chiera, Edward
   Clay, Albert Tobias
   Davis, Charles Henry Stanley
   Gibbs, Josiah Willard
   Hall, Isaac Hollister
   Hodgson, William Brown
   Hopkins, Edward Washburn
   Hyvernat, Henri
   Jackson, Abraham Valentine
     Williams
   Lanman, Charles Rockwell
   Lewis, Tayler
   Lyon, David Gordon
   Moore, George Foot
   Müller, Wilhelm Max
   Newbold, William Romaine
   Nordheimer, Isaac
   Olmstead, Albert Ten Eyck
   Orne, John
   Rockhill, William Woodville
   Rogers, Robert William
   Salisbury, Edward Elbridge
   Schmidt, Nathaniel
   Smith, Eli
   Toy, Crawford Howell
   Ward, William Hayes
   Warren, Henry Clarke
ORNITHOLOGIST (See also NATU-
   RALIST, ZOOLOGIST)
   Allen, Arthur Augustus
   Audubon, John James
   Bailey, Florence Augusta
     Merriam
   Brewer, Thomas Mayo
   Brewster, William
   Cassin, John
   Chapin, James Paul
   Chapman, Frank Michler
   Cory, Charles Barney
   Coues, Elliott
   Eckstorm, Fannie Hardy
   Eklund, Carl Robert
   Forbush, Edward Howe
   Griscom, Ludlow
   Henshaw, Henry Wetherbee
   Jones, Lynds
   Lawrence, George Newbold
   Nehrling, Henry
   Nuttall, Thomas
   Nutting, Charles Cleveland
   Ober, Frederick Albion
   Oberholser, Harry Church
   Pearson, Thomas Gilbert
   Richmond, Charles Wallace
   Ridgway, Robert
   Samuels, Edward Augustus
   Sennett, George Burritt
   Todd, Walter Edmond Clyde

Torrey, Bradford
Townsend, John Kirk
Wayne, Arthur Trezevant
Wilson, Alexander
Wood, Casey Albert
Xántus, János
OTOLOGIST (See also PHYSICIAN)
   Buck, Albert Henry
   Burnett, Charles Henry
   Gruening, Emil
   Leland, George Adams
   Randall, Burton Alexander
OUTLAW (See also BANDIT, JAY-
   HAWKER, VIGILANTE)
   Laffite, Jean
   Murrell, John A.
OYSTER CULTURIST
   Nelson, Julius
   Oemler, Arminius

PAINTER (See also ARTIST, ILLUS-
   TRATOR, MURALIST)
   Abbey, Edwin Austin
   Agate, Alfred T.
   Agate, Frederick Styles
   Alexander, Francis
   Alexander, John White
   Ames, Ezra
   Ames, Joseph Alexander
   Anshutz, Thomas Pollock
   Archipenko, Alexander
   Armstrong, David Maitland
   Badger, Joseph
   Baker, George Augustus
   Banvard, John
   Beaux, Cecilia
   Beckwith, James Carroll
   Bellows, Albert Fitch
   Bellows, George Wesley
   Benbridge, Henry
   Benjamin, Samuel Greene
     Wheeler
   Benson, Eugene
   Benson, Frank Weston
   Bierstadt, Albert
   Bingham, George Caleb
   Birch, Thomas
   Birch, William Russell
   Blackburn, Joseph
   Blakelock, Ralph Albert
   Blashfield, Edwin Howland
   Bluemner, Oscar Florians
   Blum, Robert Frederick
   Bohm, Max
   Borglum, John Gutzon de la
     Mothe
   Borie, Adolphe
   Bouché, René Robert
   Bounetheau, Henry Brintnell
   Bradford, William
   Breck, George William
   Brevoort, James Renwick
   Bridgman, Frederick Arthur
   Bristol, John Bunyan
   Brown, John Appleton
   Brown, John George
   Brown, Mather
   Bruce, Edward Bright
   Brumidi, Constantino
   Brush, George de Forest
   Bunce, William Gedney
   Burchfield, Charles Ephraim

Carpenter, Francis Bicknell
Casilear, John William
Champney, Benjamin
Champney, James Wells
Chapman, John Gadsby
Church, Frederick Edwin
Church, Frederick Stuart
Clarke, Thomas Shields
Closson, William Baxter
Coffin, William Anderson
Cogdell, John Stevens
Cole, Joseph Foxcroft
Coleman, Charles Caryl
Colman, Samuel
Copley, John Singleton
Cornoyer, Paul
Cox, Kenyon
Cranch, Christopher Pearse
Cropsey, Jaspar Francis
Crowninshield, Frederic
Cummings, Thomas Seir
Curry, John Steuart
Cushman, George Hewitt
Danforth, Moseley Isaac
Davies, Arthur Bowen
Daviess, Maria Thompson
Dearth, Henry Golden
De Camp, Joseph Rodefer
Dewing, Maria Richards Oakey
Dewing, Thomas Wilmer
Dickinson, Anson
Dickinson, Preston
Dielman, Frederick
Diller, Burgoyne
Doughty, Thomas
Dove, Arthur Garfield
Dummer, Jeremiah
Dunlap, William
Durand, Asher Brown
Duveneck, Frank
Eakins, Thomas
Earle, James
Earle, Ralph
Eaton, Joseph Oriel
Eaton, Wyatt
Eckstein, John
Edmonds, Francis William
Ehninger, John Whetten
Eichholtz, Jacob
Eilshemius, Louis Michel
Elliott, Charles Loring
Elliott, John
Ennecking, John Joseph
Farrer, Henry
Feininger, Lyonel (Charles
   Léonell Adrian)
Feke, Robert
Ferris, Jean Léon Gérôme
Field, Robert
Fisher, Alvan
Flagg, George Whiting
Flagg, Jared Bradley
Folwell, Samuel
Forbes, Edwin
Foster, Benjamin
Fowler, Frank
Fraser, Charles
Frazer, Oliver
Freeman, James Edwards
Frieseke, Frederick Carl
Fuller, George
Ganso, Emil

Garrett, Edmund Henry
Gaul, William Gilbert
Gay, Winckworth Allan
Gifford, Robert Swain
Gifford, Sanford Robinson
Glackens, William James
Godefroy, Maximilian
Goodridge, Sarah
Gorky, Arshile
Gray, Henry Peters
Greenough, Henry
Gregory, Eliot
Grosz, George
Guy, Seymour Joseph
Hale, Philip Leslie
Hall, George Henry
Hall, Henry Bryan
Harding, Chester
Harrison, Gabriel
Harrison, Lovell Birge
Harrison, Thomas Alexander
Hart, George Overbury
Hart, James MacDougal
Hart, William
Hartley, Marsden
Haskell, Ernest
Havell, Robert
Hawthorne, Charles Webster
Hayden, Charles Henry
Hays, William Jacob
Healy, George Peter Alexander
Hennessy, William John
Henri, Robert
Henry, Edward Lamson
Herring, James
Hesselius, Gustavus
Hesselius, John
Hicks, John, 1823–1890
Hill, Thomas
Hofmann, Hans
Homer, Winslow
Hopper, Edward
Hovenden, Thomas
Howe, William Henry
Hubbard, Richard William
Hunt, William Morris
Huntington, Daniel
Ingham, Charles Cromwell
Inman, Henry
Inness, George
Irving, John Beaufain
Jackson, William Henry
Janvier, Catharine Ann
Jarvis, John Wesley
Jewett, William
Jocelyn, Nathaniel
Johnson, Jonathan Eastman
Johnston, Thomas
Jones, Hugh Bolton
Jouett, Matthew Harris
Kane, John
Karfiol, Bernard
Keith, William
Keller, Arthur Ignatius
Kensett, John Frederick
King, Samuel
Kingsley, Elbridge
Kline, Franz Josef
Knight, Daniel Ridgway
Koehler, Robert
Koopman, Augustus
Krimmel, John Lewis

Kuhn, Walt
Kuniyoshi, Yasuo
La Farge, John
Lambdin, James Reid
Lathrop, Francis Augustus
Lawrie, Alexander
Lawson, Ernest
Lebrun, Federico ("Rico")
Le Clear, Thomas
Lehman, Adele Lewisohn
Leigh, William Robinson
Leslie, Charles Robert
Leutze, Emanuel
Lewis, Edmund Darch
Lie, Jonas
Lockwood, Robert Wilton
Loeb, Louis
Longfellow, Ernest Wadsworth
Loop, Henry, Augustus
Low, John Gardner
Luks, George Benjamin
MacCameron, Robert
McEntee, Jervis
Mackubin, Florence
Macomber, Mary Lizzie
Malbone, Edward Greene
Marsh, Reginald
Marshall, William Edgar
Martin, Homer Dodge
Matteson, Tompkins Harrison
May, Edward Harrison
Mayer, Constant
Maynard, George Willoughby
Melchers, Gari
Merritt, Anna Lea
Metcalf, Willard Leroy
Mifflin, Lloyd
Mignot, Louis Remy
Miles, Edward
Miller, Charles Henry
Miller, Kenneth Hayes
Millet, Francis Davis
Minor, Robert Crannell
Moran, Edward
Moran, Peter
Moran, Thomas
Morgan, Matthew Somerville
Moses, Anna Mary Robertson
  ("Grandma")
Mosler, Henry
Mount, William Sidney
Mowbray, Henry Siddons
Murphy, Gerald Clery
Murphy, John Francis
Myers, Jerome
Neagle, John
Neal, David Dalhoff
Newman, Barnett
Newman, Henry Roderick
Newman, Robert Loftin
Nicoll, James Craig
Norton, William Edward
O'Donovan, William Rudolf
Otis, Bass
Page, William
Palmer, Walter Launt
Paris, Walter
Parton, Arthur
Pattison, James William
Peale, Anna Claypoole
Peale, Charles Willson
Peale, James

Peale, Raphael
Peale, Rembrandt
Peale, Sarah Miriam
Pearce, Charles Sprague
Pelham, Henry
Penfield, Edward
Perry, Enoch Wood
Picknell, William Lamb
Pine, Robert Edge
Platt, Charles Adams
Pollock, (Paul), Jackson
Porter, Benjamin Curtis
Powell, Lucien Whiting
Powell, William Henry
Pratt, Matthew
Prendergast, Maurice Brazil
Quartley, Arthur
Quidor, John
Quinn, Edmond Thomas
Ramage, John
Ranger, Henry Ward
Ranney, William Tylee
Read, Thomas Buchanan
Reid, Robert
Reinhardt, Ad
Reinhart, Benjamin Franklin
Reinhart, Charles Stanley
Remington, Frederic
Reuterdahl, Henry
Richards, Thomas Addison
Richards, William Trost
Ritchie, Alexander Hay
Rix, Julian Walbridge
Roberts, Elizabeth Wentworth
Robertson, Archibald
Rolshoven, Julius
Rosenthal, Toby Edward
Rossiter, Thomas Prichard
Rothko, Mark
Rowse, Samuel Worcester
Ryder, Albert Pinkham
Sandham, Henry
Sargent, Henry
Sargent, John Singer
Sartain, Emily
Sartain, William
Savage, Edward
Schussele, Christian
Sellstedt, Lars Gustaf
Shahn, Benjamin ("Ben")
Sharples, James
Shattuck, Aaron Draper
Shinn, Everett
Shirlaw, Walter
Shurtleff, Roswell Morse
Simmons, Edward
Sloan, John French
Smedley, William Thomas
Smillie, George Henry
Smith, Archibald Cary
Smith, John Rowson
Smith, John Rubens
Smith, Russell
Smith, Xanthus Russell
Spencer, Robert
Stanley, John Mix
Stella, Joseph
Sterne, Maurice
Stetson, Charles Walter
Stone, William Oliver
Story, Julian Russell
Stuart, Gilbert

Sully, Thomas
Sylvester, Frederick Oakes
Symons, George Gardner
Szyk, Arthur
Tait, Arthur Fitzwilliam
Tanner, Henry Ossawa
Tarbell, Edmund Charles
Taylor, Frank Walter
Tchelitchew, Pavel
Thayer, Abbott Handerson
Theus, Jeremiah
Thompson, Alfred Wordsworth
Thompson, Cephas Giovanni
Thompson, Jerome B.
Thulstrup, Bror Thure
Tilton, John Rollin
Tomlin, Bradley Walker
Trott, Benjamin
Troye, Edward
Trumbull, John 1756–1843
Tryon, Dwight William
Tucker, Allen
Turner, Charles Yardley
Turner, Ross Sterling
Twachtman, John Henry
Vanderlyn, John
Vedder, Elihu
Vinton, Frederic Porter
Vonnoh, Robert William
Waldo, Samuel Lovett
Walker, Henry Oliver
Waugh, Frederick Judd
Weeks, Edwin Lord
Weir, Julian Alden
Weir, Robert Walter
Wentworth, Cecile de
West, Benjamin
West, William Edward
Whistler, James Abbott McNeill
Whitteredge, Worthington
Wiggins, Carleton
Wilmarth, Lemuel Everett
Wilson, Robert Burns
Wimar, Carl
Wood, Grant
Wood, Joseph
Wright, Joseph
Wyant, Alexander Helwig
Wyeth, Newell Convers
Wylie, Robert
Yohn, Frederick Coffay
Young, Mahonri Mackintosh
PALEOBOTANIST (See also BOTA-
  NIST, GEOLOGIST)
Berry, Edward Wilber
Lesquereux, Leo
PALEOGRAPHER
Beeson, Charles Henry
PALEONTOLOGIST (See also GEOLO-
  GIST)
Beecher, Charles Emerson
Clarke, John Mason
Cope, Edward Drinker
Gabb, William More
Gidley, James Williams
Grabau, Amadeus William
Granger, Walter
Hall, James, 1811–1898
Hay, Oliver Perry
Heilprin, Angelo
Hyatt, Alpheus
Knowlton, Frank Hall

Marsh, Othniel Charles
Matthew, William Diller
Meek, Fielding Bradford
Merriam, John Campbell
Newberry, John Strong
Osborn, Henry Fairfield
Patten, William
Schuchert, Charles
Scott, William Berryman
Smith, James Perrin
Springer, Frank
Ulrich, Edward Oscar
Vaughan, Thomas Wayland
Wachsmuth, Charles
Walcott, Charles Doolittle
White, Charles Abiathar
Whitfield, Robert Parr
Wieland, George Reber
Williams, Henry Shaler
Williston, Samuel Wendell
Yandell, Lunsford Pitts
PAMPHLETEER (See also PUBLICIST)
Dove, David James
Heywood, Ezra Hervey
King, Dan
Paine, Thomas
Penington, Edward
Pickering, Timothy
Smith, William Loughton
Wood, John
Yates, Abraham
Zubly, John Joachim
PAPYROLOGIST
Westermann, William Linn
PARACHUTE DESIGNER
Scott, Allen Cecil
PARASITOLOGIST (See also ZOOLO-
  GIST)
Noguchi, Hideyo
Ward, Henry Baldwin
PARLIAMENTARIAN
Dalzell, John
Hinds, Asher Crosby
Reed, Thomas Brackett
Robert, Henry Martyn
PASSPORT DIVISION CHIEF
Shipley, Ruth Bielaski
PATENT COMMISSIONER
Ellsworth, Henry Leavitt
Leggett, Mortimer Dormer
Paine, Halbert Eleazer
PATENT EXPERT
Benjamin, George Hillard
Hall, Thomas
Knight, Edward Henry
Langner, Lawrence
Renwick, Edward Sabine
Renwick, Henry Brevoort
Selden, George Baldwin
PATENT LAWYER
Davis, William Hammatt
"PATENT MEDICINE KING"
Dyott, Thomas W.
PATHOLOGIST (See also PHYSICIAN)
Biggs, Herman Michael
Bloodgood, Joseph Colt
Carroll, James
Councilman, William Thomas
Darling, Samuel Taylor
Delafield, Francis
Ewing, James
Fenger, Christian

Fitz, Reginald Heber
Flexner, Simon
Gardner, Leroy Upson
Hess, Alfred Fabian
Landsteiner, Karl
Libman, Emanuel
Loeb, Leo
MacCallum, William George
Mallory, Frank Burr
Moore, Veranus Alva
Murphy, James Bumgardner
Ohlmacher, Albert Philip
Pearce, Richard Mills
Prudden, Theophil Mitchell
Ricketts, Howard Taylor
Stengel, Alfred
Welch, William Henry
Wells, Harry Gideon
Wesbrook, Frank Fairchild
Wilson, Louis Blanchard
PATRIOT (See also LOYALIST,
  REVOLUTIONARY PATRIOT)
Alexander, James
Anagnos, Michael
Boker, George Henry
Clark, Jonas
Dawes, William
Emmet, Thomas Addis
Freeman, Nathaniel
Gurowski, Adam
Henry, William
Hitchcock, Enos
Hudson, Edward
Jackson, David
Kosciuszko, Tadeusz Andrzej
  Bonawentura
Law, Richard
Levy, Uriah Phillips
MacNeven, William James
Malcolm, Daniel
Markoe, Abraham
Mitchel, John
O'Reilly, John Boyle
Orr, Hugh
Peale, Charles Willson
Pinto, Isaac
Prescott, Samuel
Pulaski, Casimir
Quincy, Josiah, 1744–1775
Revere, Paul
Rush, Benjamin
Sampson, William
Scott, Gustavus
Thacher, James
Tracy, Nathaniel
Varela y Morales, Félix
  Francisco José Maria de la
  Concepción
PEACE ADVOCATE (See also RE-
  FORMER)
Abbot, Willis John
Balch, Emily Greene
Bok, Edward William
Clark, Grenville
Culbertson, Ely
Dingman, Mary Agnes
Dutton, Samuel Train
Garry, Spokane
Hooper, Jessie Annette Jack
Jewett, William Cornell
Jordan, David Starr
Levermore, Charles Herbert

Levinson, Salmon Oliver
Love, Alfred Henry
Muste, Abraham Johannes
Scott, Winfield
Trueblood, Benjamin Franklin
Woolley, Mary Emma
PEDDLER (See also MERCHANT)
Plummer, Jonathan
PEDIATRICIAN (See also PHYSICIAN)
Abt, Isaac Arthur
Aldrich, Charles Anderson
Blackfan, Kenneth Daniel
Brennemann, Joseph
Chapin, Henry Dwight
Cooley, Thomas Benton
Hess, Alfred Fabian
Holt, Luther Emmett
Howland, John
Jacobi, Abraham
Kenyon, Josephine Hemenway
Marriott, Williams McKim
Mitchell, Albert Graeme
Morse, John Lovett
Rachford, Benjamin Knox
Rotch, Thomas Morgan
Ruhräh, John
Trask, James Dowling
PENMAN
Spencer, Platt Rogers
PENOLOGIST (See also PRISON RE-
FORMER, REFORMER)
Brinkerhoff, Roeliff
Brockway, Zebulon Reed
Hart, Hastings Hornell
Kirchwey, George Washington
Lewis, Orlando Faulkland
Lewisohn, Sam Adolph
Lynds, Elam
Pilsbury, Amos
Russ, John Dennison
Vaux, Richard
PENSION COMMISSIONER
Murphy, Dominic Ignatius
Tanner, James
PERSONNEL MANAGEMENT PIONEER
Bloomfield, Meyer
PETROLEUM GEOLOGIST (See also
GEOLOGIST, PETROLOGIST)
Wrather, William Embry
PETROLOGIST (See also GEOLO-
GIST, PETROLEUM GEOLOGIST)
Bowen, Norman Levi
Cross, Charles Whitman
Daly, Reginald Aldworth
Iddings, Joseph Paxon
Washington, Henry Stephens
Williams, George Huntington
PEWTERER (See also CRAFTSMAN)
Boardman, Thomas Danforth
Danforth, Thomas
Melville, David
PHARMACEUTICAL CHEMIST (See
also CHEMIST)
Kremers, Edward
PHARMACIST (See also APOTHE-
CARY, DRUGGIST)
Durand, Élie Magloire
Frasch, Herman
Fuller, Robert Mason
Jacobs, Joseph, 1859–1929
Kiss, Max
Lloyd, John Uri

Maisch, John Michael
Marshall, Christopher
Parrish, Edward
Proctor, William
Remington, Joseph Price
Rice, Charles
Seabury, George John
Smith, Daniel B.
Squibb, Edward Robinson
Whelpley, Henry Milton
PHARMACOGNOSIST (See also
PHARMACOLOGIST)
Rusby, Henry Hurd
PHARMACOLOGIST (See also PHAR-
MACOGNOSIST, PHYSICIAN)
Abel, John Jacob
Auer, John
Barbour, Henry Gray
Edmunds, Charles Wallis
Hatcher, Robert Anthony
Hunt, Reid
Kraemer, Henry
Underhill, Franklin Pell
Weiss, Soma
PHILANTHROPIST
Adams, Charles Francis
Aiken, William
Alden, Cynthia May Westover
Alphonsa, Mother
Altman, Benjamin
Anderson, Elizabeth Milbank
Appleton, Samuel
Archer, Samuel
Auchmuty, Richard Tylden
Augustus, John
Avery, Samuel Putnam
Baker, George Fisher
Baldwin, Matthias William
Ball, Frank Clayton
Ball, George Alexander
Bamberger, Louis
Bancroft, Frederic
Barnard, Charles Francis
Barrett, Kate Waller
Barsotti, Charles
Bartlet, William
Barton, Clara
Bates, Joshua
Benezet, Anthony
Billings, Frederick
Bishop, Charles Reed
Bishop, Nathan
Blaine, Anita (Eugenie)
McCormick
Blair, John Insley
Bliss, Cornelius Newton
Blodgett, John Wood
Bok, Edward William
Bowen, Louise De Koven
Brace, Charles Loring
Bradley, Lydia Moss
Breckinridge, Aida de Acosta
Bromfield, John
Brookings, Robert Somers
Brown, Moses, 1738–1836
Brown, Moses, 1742–1827
Brown, Nicholas
Brown, Obadiah
Buchtel, John Richards
Bucknell, William
Burrett, Joseph
Butler, Charles

Cabot, Godfrey Lowell
Camp, Hiram
Candler, Asa Griggs
Carnegie, Andrew
Case, Leonard
Childs, George William
Clark, Jonas Gilman
Clarkson, Matthew
Clinton, De Witt
Coates, Samuel
Coburn, Abner
Cochran, Alexander Smith
Coffin, Lorenzo S.
Coker, David Robert
Coker, James Lide
Colby, Gardner
Colgate, James Boorman
Combs, Moses Newell
Comstock, Elizabeth L.
Converse, Edmund Cogswell
Cooper, Peter
Cooper, Sarah Brown Ingersoll
Cope, Thomas Pym
Corcoran, William Wilson
Crane, Charles Richard
Creighton, Edward
Creighton, John Andrew
Crerar, John
Cresson, Elliott
Crozer, John Price
Cullen, Hugh Roy
Cupples, Samuel
Cushing, John Perkins
Cutting, Robert Fulton
Davis, Arthur Vining
De Forest, Robert Weeks
De Pauw, Washington Charles
Dodge, Grace Hoadley
Drake, Francis Marion
Dreier, Mary Elisabeth
Drexel, Anthony Joseph
Drexel, Joseph William
Duke, Benjamin Newton
Durant, Henry Fowle
Dwight, Edmund
Dyer, Isadore
Eastman, George
Eliot, Samuel
Eustis, Dorothy Leib Harrison
Wood
Evans, Thomas Wiltberger
Evarts, Jeremiah
Fahnestock, Harris Charles
Falk, Maurice
Farmer, Hannah Tobey
Shapleigh
Farnam, Henry
Farnam, Henry Walcott
Farnham, Eliza Woodson
Burhans
Fels, Samuel Simeon
Field, Benjamin Hazard
Field, Marshall, III
Fleming, Arthur Henry
Flexner, Bernard
Flower, Lucy Louisa Coues
Folger, Henry Clay
Ford, Daniel Sharp
Franklin Benjamin
Gammon, Elijah Hedding
Gardiner, Robert Hallowell
George, William Reuben

Gerard, James Watson
Gerry, Elbridge Thomas
Gibbons, Abigail Hopper
Gilbert, Linda
Ginn, Edwin
Ginter, Lewis
Girard, Stephen
Gleason, Kate
Godfrey, Benjamin
Goucher, John Franklin
Graff, Everett Dwight
Graham, Isabella Marshall
Grasselli, Caesar Augustin
Gratz, Rebecca
Gray, Francis Calley
Green, Francis
Green, John Cleve
Griffith, Goldsborough
  Sappington
Grinnell, Henry
Griscom, John
Guggenheim, Daniel
Guggenheim, Simon
Gurley, Ralph Randolph
Hackley, Charles Henry
Hand, Daniel
Hardin, Charles Henry
Harkness, Edward Stephen
Hart, Abraham
Haughery, Margaret Gaffney
Hayden, Charles
Hearst, Phoebe Apperson
Heckscher, August
Heilprin, Michael
Hemenway, Mary Porter
  Tileston
Hepburn, Alonzo Barton
Hershey, Milton Snavely
Hewitt, Abram Stevens
Heye, George Gustav
Higinbotham, Harlow Niles
Hopkins, Johns
Horlick, William
Hoyt, John Sherman
Hutton, Levi William
Inman, Samuel Martin
Irene, Sister
Jackson, Helen Maria Fiske
  Hunt
Jackson, Samuel Macauley
Jacobs, Joseph, 1859–1929
James, Arthur Curtiss
James, Daniel Willis
Janney, Oliver Edward
Jeanes, Anna T.
Jesup, Morris Ketchum
Kelly, Eugene
Kennedy, John Stewart
Knapp, Joseph Palmer
Kresge, Sebastian Spering
Kress, Samuel Henry
Ladd, Kate Macy
Lafon, Thomy
Lamont, Thomas William
Lasker, Albert Davis
Lawrence, Abbott
Lawrence, Amos
Lawrence, Amos Adams
Lawrence, William, 1783–1848
Lehman, Adele Lewisohn
Lenox, James
Letchworth, William Pryor

Lewisohn, Adolph
Lewisohn, Sam Adolph
Libbey, Edward Drummond
Lick, James
Littauer, Lucius Nathan
Loeb, James
Lowell, Josephine Shaw
Ludwick, Christopher
Lunt, Orrington
Lyman, Theodore, 1792–1849
McCormick, Cyrus Hall
McCormick, Leander James
McDonogh, John
Mackay, Clarence Hungerford
McKinley, William Brown
McLean, William Lippard
Maclure, William
Macy, Valentine Everit
Magee, Christopher Lyman
Mallinckrodt, Edward
Mallinckrodt, Edward, Jr.
Maloney, Martin
Marquand Henry Gurdon
Martin, Frederick Townsend
Mather, Samuel
Matheson, William John
Matthiessen, Frederick William
Mercer, Jesse
Meyer, Agnes Elizabeth Ernst
Miller, Lewis
Mills, Darius Ogden
Morehead, John Motley
Morgan, Edwin Barber
Newberry, Walter Loomis
Newcomb, Josephine Louise Le
  Monnier
Newman, Henry
O'Fallon, John
Oglethorpe, James Edward
Olyphant, David Washington
  Cincinnatus
Osborn, William Henry
Ottendorfer, Anna Behr Uhl
Ottendorfer, Oswald
Packer, Asa
Paine, Robert Treat
Pardee, Ario
Parrish, Anne
Passavant, William Alfred
Patten, James A.
Patterson, Morris
Peabody, George
Peabody, George Foster
Pearsons, Daniel Kimball
Pellew, Henry Edward
Pemberton, Israel
Pemberton, James
Penrose, Spencer
Pepper, George Seckel
Pepper, William
Perkins, Thomas Handasyd
Peter, Sarah Worthington King
Phelps, Anson Greene
Phillips, Thomas Wharton
Phillips, William
Phipps, Henry
Pintard, John
Pitcairn, John
Poulson, Niels
Poulson, Zachariah
Poydras, Julien De Lelande
Pratt, Charles

Pratt, Enoch
Presser, Theodore
Proctor, William Cooper
Purdue, John
Rachford, Benjamin Knox
Ramsay, Erskine
Randall, Robert Richard
Rawle, William
Redwood, Abraham
Reilly, Marion
Reisinger, Hugo
Reynolds, William Neal
Rhoades, James E.
Rich, Isaac
Richardson, Sid Williams
Rindge, Frederick Hastings
Robert, Christopher
Rhinelander
Rockefeller, Abby Greene
  Aldrich
Rockefeller, John Davison
Rockefeller, John Davison, Jr.
Rose, Chauncey
Rosenberg, Henry
Rosenwald, Julius
Rutgers, Henry
Ryerson, Martin Antoine
Sachs, Paul Joseph
Sage, Henry Williams
Sage, Margaret Olivia Slocum
Sanborn, Franklin Benjamin
Say, Benjamin
Schiff, Jacob Henry
Scripps, Ellen Browning
Seligman, Jesse
Seney, George Ingraham
Severance, Louis Henry
Seybert, Henry
Shattuck, George Cheyne,
  1783–1854
Shattuck, George Cheyne,
  1813–1893
Shaw, Pauline Agassiz
Shedd, John Graves
Sheffield, Joseph Earl
Slater, John Fox
Sleeper, Jacob
Sloan, Alfred Pritchard, Jr.
Sloss, Louis
Smith, Daniel B.
Smith, Gerrit
Smith, Oliver
Solomons, Adolphus Simeon
Speyer, James Joseph
Springer, Reuben Runyan
Sprunt, James
Sterling, John William
Stetson, John Batterson
Stewart, William Rhinelander
Stoeckel, Carl
Stokes, Caroline Phelps
Stokes, Olivia Egleston Phelps
Stone, Amasa
Straus, Nathan
Straus, Roger W(illiams)
Street, Augustus Russell
Stuart, Robert Leighton
Sulzberger, Cyrus Lindauer
Swasey, Ambrose
Syms, Benjamin
Taft, Charles Phelps
Talbot, Emily Fairbanks

Tappan, Arthur
Taylor, Joseph Wright
Thaw, William
Thayer, Nathaniel
Thomas, George Clifford
Thompson, Benjamin
Thompson, William Boyce
Tiffany, Louis Comfort
Tome, Jacob
Tompkins, Sally Louisa
  ("Captain Sally")
Towne, John Henry
Townsend, Mira Sharpless
Tracy, Nathaniel
Tulane, Paul
Vanderbilt, Cornelius,
  1843–1899
Vaux, Roberts
Wade, Jeptha Homer
Wadsworth, Eliot
Wagner, William
Walker, William Johnson
Warburg, Felix Moritz
Ward, Marcus Lawrence
Weddell, Alexander Wilbourne
Welsh, John
Wharton, Joseph
Widener, Peter Arrell Brown
Williston, Samuel
Wolfe, Catharine Lorillard
Wolfe, John David
Wormeley, Katherine Prescott
Yeatman, James Erwin

PHILOLOGIST (See also SCHOLAR)
Adler, George J.
Alden, Raymond MacDonald
Armstrong, Edward Cooke
Bloomfield, Maurice
Bright, James Wilson
Brown, Carleton
Callaway, Morgan
Child, Francis James
Churchill, William
Conant, Thomas Jefferson
Davis, Charles Henry Stanley
Elliott, Aaron Marshall
Emerson, Oliver Farrar
Flügel, Ewald
Francke, Kuno
Garnett, James Mercer
Gibbs, Josiah Willard
Gildersleeve, Basil Lanneau
Grandgent, Charles Hall
Greenough, James Bradstreet
Gummere, Francis Barton
Hadley, James
Haldeman, Samuel Steman
Hall, Fitzedward
Harrison, James Albert
Hart, James Morgan
Haupt, Paul
Hempl, George
Hills, Elijah Clarence
Hopkins, Edward Washburn
Jackson, Abraham Valentine
  Williams
Klipstein, Louis Frederick
Lang, Henry Roseman
Learned, Marion Dexter
Lounsbury Thomas Raynesford
Manly, John Matthews
March, Francis Andrew

Marden, Charles Carroll
Merriam, Augustus Chapman
Ord, George
Parrington, Vernon Louis
Peck, Harry Thurston
Phillips, Henry
Pickering, John
Price, Thomas Randolph
Prokosch, Eduard
Radin, Max
Reeves, Arthur Middleton
Rice, Charles
Rickert, Martha Edith
Robinson, Edward, 1794–1863
Robinson, Thérèse Albertine
  Louise von Jakob
Rolfe, William James
Royster, James Finch
Safford, William Edwin
Schele de Vere, Maximilian
Schilling, Hugo Karl
Seidensticker, Oswald
Sheldon, Edward Stevens
Short, Charles
Smith, Byron Caldwell
Smith, Charles Forster
Smith, Lloyd Logan Pearsall
Todd, Henry Alfred
Trumbull, James Hammond
Van Name, Addison
Wiener, Leo
Wilson, Peter

PHILOMATH (See also SCHOLAR)
Daboll, Nathan

PHILOSOPHER (See also SCHOLAR)
Abbot, Francis Ellingwood
Albee, Ernest
Alexander, Hartley Burr
Ames, Edward Scribner
Andrews, Stephen Pearl
Bascom, John
Beasley, Frederick
Bentley, Arthur Fisher
Bjerregaard, Carl Henrik
  Andreas
Blood, Benjamin Paul
Bode, Boyd Henry
Bowen, Francis
Bowne, Borden Parker
Bridgman, Percy Williams
Brightman, Edgar Sheffield
Brokmeyer, Henry C.
Buchanan, Joseph
Buchanan, Scott Milross
Calhoun, John Caldwell
Calkins, Mary Whiton
Carnap, Rudolf
Carus, Paul
Cohen, Morris Raphael
Creighton, James Edwin
Davidson, Thomas
Dewey, John
Edwards, Jonathan
Fiske, John
Fite, Warner
Frank, Philipp G.
Fullerton, George Stuart
Gardiner, Harry Norman
Gordy, John Pancoast
Grimes, James Stanley
Gros, John Daniel
Hall, Granville Stanley

Hamilton, Edward John
Harris, William Torrey
Hedge, Levi
Hibben, John Grier
Hickok, Laurens Perseus
Hocking, William Ernest
Howison, George Holmes
Hyslop, James Hervey
James, William
Jones, Rufus Matthew
Kroeger, Adolph Ernst
Ladd, George Trumbull
Laguna, Theodore de Leo de
Lewis, Clarence Irving
Lloyd, Alfred Henry
Locke, Alain Leroy
Longfellow, Samuel
Lovejoy, Arthur Oncken
Lyman, Eugene William
Macy, Jesse
Marsh, James
Mead, George Herbert
Michel, Virgil George
Montague, William Pepperell
Montgomery, Edmund Duncan
Moore, Addison Webster
More, Paul Elmer
Morris, George Sylvester
Mulford, Prentice
Neumark, David
Newbold, William Romaine
Overstreet, Harry Allen
Pace, Edward Aloysius
Palmer, George Herbert
Peirce, Charles Sanders
Perry, Ralph Barton
Powell, John Wesley
Prall, David Wight
Pratt, James Bissett
Radin, Max
Rauch, Frederick Augustus
Reichenbach, Hans
Riley, Isaac Woodbridge
Royce, Josiah
Salter, William Mackintire
Santayana, George
Saugrain de Vigni, Antoine
  François
Schurman, Jacob Gould
Seth, James
Smith, Thomas Vernor
Spaulding, Edward Gleason
Sterrett, James Macbride
Strong, Charles Augustus
Swenson, David Ferdinand
Tappan, Henry Philip
Thilly, Frank
Tillich, Paul
Tufts, James Hayden
Wenley, Robert Mark
Whitehead, Alfred North
Wilder, Alexander
Woodbridge, Frederick James
  Eugene
Woodward, Augustus Brevoort
Wright, Chauncey
Znaniecki, Florian Witold

PHONETIC SPELLING PIONEER
Masquerier, Lewis

PHONOGRAPHER
Pitman, Benn

PHOTOENGRAVER (See also EN-
GRAVER)
Levy, Max
Moss, John Calvin
PHOTOGRAPHER
Austen, (Elizabeth) Alice
Bachrach, Louis Fabian
Brady, Mathew B.
Carbutt, John
Curtis, Edward Sheriff
Genthe, Arnold
Goddard, Paul Beck
Hare, James H.
Hine, Lewis Wickes
Hubbard, Bernard Rosecrans
Jackson, William Henry
Johnston, Frances Benjamin
Lange, Dorothea
Muybridge, Eadweard
Plumbe, John
Sheeler, Charles R., Jr.
Stieglitz, Alfred
Van Vechten, Carl
Weston, Edward Henry
PHOTOGRAPHIC SCIENTIST
Mees, Charles Edward Kenneth
PHOTOJOURNALIST
Chapelle, Dickey
PHRENOLOGIST
Fowler, Orson Squire
Sizer, Nelson
Wells, Samuel Roberts
PHYLOBIOLOGIST
Burrow, Trigant
PHYSICAL CULTURIST
Macfadden, Bernarr
PHYSICAL EDUCATION LEADER (See
also PHYSICIAN)
Alcott, William Andrus
Berenson, Senda
Blaikie, William
Gulick, Luther Halsey,
1865–1918
Kiphuth, Robert John Herman
Lewis, Dioclesian
Naismith, James
Sargent, Dudley Allen
PHYSICAL TRAINER
Muldoon, William
PHYSICIAN (See also ALIENIST,
ANESTHESIOLOGIST, ANATO-
MIST, APOTHECARY, BACTERI-
OLOGIST, BIOCHEMIST,
BIOMETRICIAN, DENTIST, DER-
MATOLOGIST, DIETICIAN,
DRUGGIST, ELECTRO-THERA-
PIST, EMBRYOLOGIST, EPIDEMI-
OLOGIST, GYNECOLOGIST,
HOMEOPATHIST, HYDROTHERA-
PIST, HYGIENIST, IMMUNOLO-
GIST, LARYNGOLOGIST,
LITHOTOMIST, MEDICAL HIS-
TORIAN, MEDICAL RESEARCH
WORKER, MENTAL HYGIENIST,
MICROSCOPIST, NEUROLOGIST,
NEUROPATHOLOGIST, NURSE,
OBSTETRICIAN, OCULIST, OPH-
THALMOLOGIST, OPTICIAN,
OTOLOGIST, PATHOLOGIST,
PEDIATRICIAN, PHARMACIST,
PHARMACOLOGIST, PHYSICAL
EDUCATION LEADER, PHYSI-

OLOGIST, PSYCHIATRIST, PHY-
CHOANALYST, PSYCHOPATHOLO-
GIST, PUBLIC HEALTH
OFFICIAL, RADIOGRAPHER,
RHINOLOGIST, ROENTGENOLO-
GIST, SANITARIAN, SURGEON,
TOXICOLOGIST, UROLOGIST,
VACCINATOR, VETERINARIAN)
Abbott, Samuel Warren
Abrams, Albert
Adams, Daniel
Adams, William Lysander
Allen, Harrison
Allen, Nathan
Allen, Timothy Field
Allison, Richard
Alter, David
Ames, Nathaniel
Anderson, Victor Vance
Appleton, Nathaniel Walker
Arnold, Richard Dennis
Aspinwall, William
Ayer, James Cook
Bache, Franklin
Baetjer, Frederick Henry
Baker, Sara Josephine
Baldwin, Edward Robinson
Baldwin, William
Bard, John
Bard, Samuel
Barker, Benjamin Fordyce
Barker, Jeremiah
Bartholow, Roberts
Bartlett, Elisha
Bartlett, John Sherren
Bartlett, Josiah
Barton, Benjamin Smith
Baruch, Simon
Batchelder, John Putnam
Bates, James
Battey, Robert
Baxley, Henry Willis
Bayley, Richard
Beach, Wooster
Beard, George Miller
Beck, John Brodhead
Beck, Lewis Caleb
Beck, Theodric Romeyn
Bell, Luther Vose
Bennet, Sanford Fillmore
Bigelow, Jacob
Bigelow, William Sturgis
Biggs, Hermann Michael
Billings, Frank
Bird, Robert Montgomery
Blackburn, Luke Pryor
Blackwell, Elizabeth
Blake, Francis Gilman
Blalock, Nelson Gales
Blunt, James Gillpatrick
Bohune, Lawrence
Bond, Thomas
Bowditch, Henry Ingersoll
Boylston, Zabdiel
Bozeman, Nathan
Bridges, Robert
Brigham, Amariah
Brill, Nathan Edwin
Brinckle, William Draper
Brockett, Linus Pierpont
Bronson, Henry
Brown, George

Brown, Lawrason
Brown, Percy
Brown, Samuel
Brown, William
Bruce, Archibald
Brühl, Gustav
Buchanan, Joseph Rodes
Buckler, Thomas Hepburn
Bulkley, Lucius Duncan
Bullitt, Henry Massie
Burnett, Swan Moses
Burrage, Walter Lincoln
Burton, William
Bushnell, George Ensign
Byrne, John
Cabell, James Lawrence
Cabot, Richard Clarke
Cadwalader, Thomas
Caldwell, Charles
Campbell, Henry Fraser
Carson, Joseph
Carson, Simeon Lewis
Chadwick, James Read
Channing, Walter
Chapman, Alvan Wentworth
Chapman, Henry Cadwalader
Chapman, Nathaniel
Child, Robert
Christian, Henry Asbury
Church, Benjamin
Clayton, Joshua
Cochran, John
Cohen, Jacob da Silva Solis
Cohn, Alfred Einstein
Coit, Henry Leber
Cook, Frederick Albert
Cooke, Elisha
Cooke, John Esten
Cooke, Robert Anderson
Copeland, Royal Samuel
Craik, James
Cranston, John
Craven, John Joseph
Crawford, John
Crawford, John Martin
Crumbine, Samuel Jay
Cullis, Charles
Cushny, Arthur Robertson
Cutler, Ephraim
Da Costa, Jacob Mendez
Dalcho, Frederick
Darling, Samuel Taylor
Davis, Charles Henry Stanley
Davis, Edwin Hamilton
Davis, Nathan Smith
Delafield, Francis
Deléry, François Charles
Dercum, Francis Xavier
De Rosset, Moses John
Dewees, William Potts
Dick, Elisha Cullen
Dickson, Samuel Henry
Disbrow, William Stephen
Doddridge, Joseph
Dooley, Thomas Anthony, III
Dorsch, Eduard
Doughty, William Henry
Douglass, William
Drake, Daniel
Dwight, Nathaniel
Dyer, Isadore
Earle, Pliny

Eberle, John
Edder, William
Edes, Robert Thaxter
Edsall, David Linn
Eliot, Charles
Ellis, Calvin
Elmer, Ebenezer
Elmer, Jonathan
Elwell, John Johnson
Elwyn, Alfred Langdon
Emerson, Gouverneur
Emmet, Thomas Addis
Emmons, Ebenezer
Engelmann, George
Evans, George Alfred
Evans, John
Ewell, James
Ewell, Thomas
Faget, Jean Charles
Favill, Henry Baird
Fay, Jonas
Fayssoux, Peter
Finlay, Carlos Juan
Fisher, George Jackson
Fisher, John Dix
Fletcher, William Baldwin
Flick, Lawrence Francis
Flint, Austin, 1812–1886
Flint, Austin, 1836–1915
Foote, John Ambrose
Fordyce, John Addison
Forwood, William Henry
Foster, Frank Pierce
Foster, John Pierrepont
    Codrington
Francis, John Wakefield
Francis, Samuel Ward
Freeman, Nathaniel
Friedenwald, Aaron
Fuller, Robert Mason
Fussell, Bartholomew
Gale, Benjamin
Gallinger, Jacob Harold
Gallup, Joseph Adams
Garcelon, Alonzo
Garden, Alexander
Gardiner, Silvester
Garnett, Alexander Yelverton
    Peyton
Garvin, Lucius Fayette Clark
Gerhard, William Wood
Gibbes, Robert Wilson
Gibbons, William
Gilbert, Rufus Henry
Girard, Charles Frédéric
Goddard, Paul Beck
Goforth, William
Goldsmith, Middleton
Goldstein, Max Aaron
Goodrich, Benjamin Franklin
Gorham, John
Gorrie, John
Gould, Augustus Addison
Gould, George Milbry
Gradle, Henry
Grant, Asahel
Gray, John Purdue
Green, Asa
Green, Horace
Green, Norvin
Green, Samuel Abbott
Greenhow, Robert

Guernsey, Egbert
Guild, La Fayette
Guiteras, Juan
Guthrie, Samuel
Hack, George
Hale, Edwin Moses
Hale, Enoch
Hall, William Whitty
Hamilton, Alexander,
    1712–1756
Hamilton, Alice
Hamilton, Allan McLane
Hand, Edward
Harlan, Richard
Harrington, Thomas Francis
Hartshorne, Henry
Haviland, Clarence Floyd
Hawley, Paul Ramsey
Hayes, Isaac Israel
Hays, Isaac
Hempel, Charles Julius
Hench, Philip Showalter
Henderson, Thomas
Henry, Morris Henry
Henshall, James Alexander
Hering, Constantine
Herter, Christian Archibald
Hewes, Robert
Hildreth, Samuel Prescott
Hoagland, Charles Lee
Hoff, John Van Rensselaer
Holcombe, William Henry
Holder, Joseph Bassett
Holten, Samuel
Holyoke, Edward Augustus
Hooker, Worthington
Hoover, Charles Franklin
Hopkins, Lemuel
Horn, George Henry
Horsfield, Thomas
Hosack, David
Hough, Franklin Benjamin
House, Samuel Reynolds
Hubbard, John
Huger, Francis Kinloch
Hunt, Harriot Kezia
Huntington, Elisha
Husk, Charles Ellsworth
Huston, Charles
Hutchinson, James
Hutchinson, Woods
Hyde, James Nevins
Ingals, Ephraim Fletcher
Ives, Eli
Jackson, Abraham Reeves
Jackson, Chevalier
Jackson, David
Jackson, Hall
Jackson, James, 1777–1867
Jackson, James Caleb
Jackson, John Davies
Jackson, Mercy Ruggles Bisbe
Jackson, Samuel
Jacobi, Abraham
Jacobi, Mary Corinna Putnam
James, Edwin
James, Thomas Chalkley
Jameson, Horatio Gates
Janeway, Edward Gamaliel
Janeway, Theodore Caldwell
Janney, Oliver Edward
Jarvis, Edward

Jarvis, Wiliam Chapman
Jay, Sir James
Jeffries, John
Johnson, Joseph
Jones, Alexander
Jones, Calvin
Jones, Joseph
Jones, William Palmer
Kane, Elisha Kent
Keagy, John Miller
Kearsley, John
Keating, John Marie
Kedzie, Robert Clark
Keeley, Leslie E.
Kellogg, Albert
Kelly, Aloysius Oliver Joseph
Kempster, Walter
Kerr, John Glasgow
Keyt, Alonzo Thrasher
King, Albert Freeman Africanus
King, Dan
King, John
King, Samuel Ward
Kirkbride, Thomas Story
Kirkland, Jared Potter
Kneeland, Samuel
Knight, Frederick Irving
Knight, Jonathan
Knowlton, Charles
Kober, George Martin
Kolle, Frederick Strange
Krause, Allen Kramer
Kuhn, Adam
Kunze, Richard Ernest
La Borde, Maximilian
Ladd, Joseph Brown
Landis, Henry Robert Murray
Lane, William Carr
Lapham, William Berry
La Roche, René
Lattimore, William
Lawson, Leonidas Merion
Lazear, Jesse William
Leathers, Waller Smith
Le Conte, John Lawrence
Lee, Charles Alfred
Leib, Michael
Leland, George Adams
Le Moyne, Francis Julius
Leonard, Charles Lester
Letterman, Jonathan
Lincecum, Gideon
Lincoln, Rufus Pratt
Linde, Christian
Lindsley, John Berrien
Lining, John
Linn, Lewis Fields
Littell, Squier
Lloyd, Thomas
Locke, John
Logan, Cornelius Ambrose
Logan, George
Long, Perrin Hamilton
Longcope, Warfield, Theobald
Loring, George Bailey
Lozier, Clemence Sophia
    Harned
Lumbrozo, Jacob
Lydston, George Frank
Lynch, Robert Clyde
Lyster, Henry Francis Le Hunte
McCaw, James Brown

McClellan, George, 1849–1913
McClurg, James
McCormack, Joseph Nathaniel
McCrae, Thomas
McCreery, Charles
McDowell, Ephraim
McFarland, George Bradley
McIntire, Ross
Mackenzie, John Noland
McKenzie, Robert Tait
MacNeven, William James
Magruder, George Lloyd
Mahoney, John Friend
Manson, Otis Frederick
Marks, Elias
Marshall, Clara
Marshall, Louis
Massey, George Betton
Matas, Rudolph
Maxwell, David Hervey
Maxwell, George Troup
Mayo, William Starbuck
Mayo, William Worrell
Mazzei, Philip
Mease, James
Meeker, Moses
Meigs, Arthur Vincent
Meigs, Charles Delucena
Meigs, James Aitken
Meigs, John Forsyth
Meltzer, Samuel James
Menninger, Charles Frederick
Mergler, Marie Josepha
Metcalfe, Samuel Lytler
Mettauer, John Peter
Michel, William Middleton
Michener, Ezra
Middleton, Peter
Miles, Manly
Miller, Edward
Miller, Henry
Miller, James Alexander
Minot, George Richards
Mitchell, George Edward
Mitchell, John, d. 1768
Mitchell, John Kearsley
Mitchell, Silas Weir
Mitchell, Thomas Duché
Mitchill, Samuel Latham
Monette, John Wesley
Moore, Joseph Earle
Morgan, John
Morril, David Lawrence
Morris, Caspar
Morrow, Prince Albert
Morrow, Thomas Vaughan
Morton, Samuel George
Morwitz, Edward
Mosher, Eliza Maria
Moultrie, John
Mundé, Paul Fortunatus
Neal, Josephine Bicknell
Neidhard, Charles
Newton, Robert Safford
Nichols, Charles Henry
Nichols, Charles Lemuel
Nichols, Mary Sargeant Neal
  Gove
Noeggerath, Emil Oscar Jacob
  Bruno
North, Elisha
Nott, Josiah Clark

O'Callaghan, Edmund Bailey
O'Dwyer, Joseph
Oemler, Arminius
O'Fallon, James
Ohlmacher, Albert Philip
Oliver, Fitch Edward
Ordronaux, John
Osler, William
Otis, Fessenden Nott
Ott, Isaac
Otto, John Conrad
Page, Charles Grafton
Paine, Martyn
Palmer, Alonzo Benjamin
Palmer, Walter Walker
Pancoast, Seth
Parrish, Joseph
Parsons, Usher
Pascalis-Ouvrière, Felix
Pavy, Octave
Peabody, Nathaniel
Pearsons, Daniel Kimball
Peaslee, Edmund Randolph
Pendleton, Edmund Monroe
Pepper, William, 1810–1864
Pepper, William, 1843–1898
Pepper, William, III
Perkins, Elisha
Perrine, Henry
Perry, William
Peter, Robert
Peters, John Charles
Pickering, Charles
Pitcher, Zina
Plotz, Harry
Plummer, Henry Stanley
Polk, William Mecklenburg
Porcher, Francis Peyre
Post, George Edward
Pott, John
Potter, Ellen Culver
Potter, Nathaniel
Potts, Charles Sower
Potts, Jonathan
Powell, William Byrd
Prescott, Oliver
Prescott, Samuel
Preston, Ann
Preston, Jonas
Price, George Moses
Price, Joseph
Prime, Benjamin Youngs
Prince, Morton
Pulte, Joseph Hippolyt
Purple, Samuel Smith
Putnam, Charles Pickering
Putnam, Helen Cordelia
Quine, William Edward
Quintard, Charles Todd
Ramsay, David
Ramsey, James Gettys
  McGready
Ranney, Ambrose Loomis
Rauch, John Henry
Raue, Charles Gottlieb
Ravenel, Edmund
Ravenel, St. Julien
Redman, John
Reed, Walter
Rhoads, Cornelius Packard
Richardson, Charles Williamson
Richardson, Robert

Richmond, John Lambert
Richmond, John Wilkes
Ricord, Philippe
Riddell, John Leonard
Rivers, Thomas Milton
Robertson, Jerome Bonaparte
Robinson, George Canby
Romayne, Nicholas
Roosa, Daniel Bennett St. John
Root, Joseph Pomeroy
Rothrock, Joseph Trimble
Rous, Francis Peyton
Rovenstine, Emery Andrew
Rowland, Henry Cottrell
Rubinow, Isaac Max
Rush, Benjamin
Rush, James
Russ, John Dennison
Russell, Bartholomew
Sachs, Theodore Bernard
Sajous, Charles Euchariste de
  Médicis
Salisbury, James Henry
Salmon, Thomas William
Sappington, John
Sargent, Dudley Allen
Sargent, Fitzwilliam
Sartwell, Henry Parker
Saugrain de Vigni, Antoine
  François
Saulsbury, Gove
Savage, Thomas Staughton
Say, Benjamin
Schöpf, Johann David
Scudder, John Milton
Semmes, Alexander Jenkins
Seybert, Adam
Shattuck, Frederick Cheever
Shattuck, George Brune
Shattuck, George Cheyne,
  1783–1854
Shattuck, George Cheyne,
  1813–1893
Shaw, Anna Howard
Shaw, John, 1778–1809
Shecut, John Linnaeus Edward
  Whitridge
Shepard, Fred Douglas
Shippen, William
Short, Charles Wilkins
Sibley, John
Small, Alvan Edmond
Smith, Elihu Hubbard
Smith, James McCune
Smith, Job Lewis
Smith, John Augustine
Smith, Nathan, 1762–1829
Snyder, Howard McCrum
Snyder, John Francis
Spalding, Lyman
Speir, Samuel Fleet
Spivak, Charles David
Squibb, Edward Robinson
Starr, Louis
Stearns, Henry Putnam
Steiner, Lewis Henry
Stephenson, Benjamin Franklin
Stiles, Henry Reed
Stillé, Alfred
Stockton, Charles G.
Stone, Abraham
Stone, Richard French

Stone, Warren
Strong, Richard Pearson
Strudwick, Edmund Charles Fox
Talbot, Israel Tisdale
Taussig, William
Taylor, Joseph Wright
Taylor, Robert Tunstall
Tennent, John
Terry, Marshall Orlando
Testut, Charles
Thacher, James
Thayer, William Sydney
Thomas, Joseph
Thomas, Richard Henry
Thompson, William Gilman
Thomson, Samuel
Thornton, Matthew
Ticknor, Francis Orray
Timberlake, Gideon
Timme, Walter
Todd, Eli
Toner, Joseph Meredith
Townsend, Francis Everett
Trudeau, Edward Livingston
Tufts, Cotton
Tully, William
Turnbull, Andrew
Tyson, James
Van Allen, Frank
Van Beuren, Johannes
Van Buren, William Holme
Van Fleet, Walter
Vedder, Edward Bright
Von Ruck, Karl
Walcott, Henry Pickering
Waldo, David
Walker, Mary Edwards
Walker, Thomas
Walker, William Johnson
Ward, Richard Halsted
Warder, John Aston
Ware, John
Warren, Joseph
Warthin, Aldred Scott
Waterhouse, Benjamin
Weber, Gustav Carl Erich
Weil, Richard
Welch, William Wickham
Wells, William Charles
Werde, Grover. William
Wesselhoeft, Conrad
West, Henry Sergeant
White, Charles Abiathar
Whitman, Marcus
Wickes, Stephen
Widney, Joseph Pomeroy
Wilbur, Ray Lyman
Wilcox, Reynold Webb
Wilder, Alexander
Wilder, Russell Morse
Willard, De Forest
Williams, Francis Henry
Williams, John Whitridge
Williams, Linsly Rudd
Williams, Nathanael
Williams, William Carlos
Wistar, Caspar
Witherspoon, John Alexander
Wood, Edward Stickney
Wood, George Bacon
Wood, Horatio Charles

Woodhouse, James
Woodruff, Charles Edward
Woodward, Joseph Janvier
Woodward, Samuel Bayard
Work, Hubert
Wormley, Theodore George
Wright, Joseph Jefferson Burr
Wyckoff, John Henry
Wyman, Morrill
Yandell, David Wendell
Yandell, Lunsford Pitts
Young, Thomas
Zakrgewska, Marie Elizabeth
Zinsser, Hans

PHYSICIST (See also SCIENTIST)

Allison, Samuel King
Alter, David
Ames, Joseph Sweetman
Anthony, William Arnold
Bache, Alexander Dallas
Barker, George Frederick
Barus, Carl
Bauer, Louis Agricola
Bayma, Joseph
Becker, George Ferdinand
Bell, Louis
Blair, William Richards
Blake, Francis
Boltwood, Bertram Borden
Boyé, Martin Hans
Brace, Dewitt Bristol
Bridgman, Percy Williams
Briggs, Lyman James
Buckley, Oliver Ellsworth
Bumstead, Henry Andrews
Burgess, George Kimball
Cohen, Jacob da Silva Solis
Compton, Arthur Holly
Compton, Karl Taylor
Davis, Harvey Nathaniel
Davisson, Clinton Joseph
Debye, Peter Joseph William
Duane, William
Eddy, Henry Turner
Einstein, Albert
Farrar, John
Fermi, Enrico
Franck, James
Frank, Philipp G.
Gale, Henry Gordon
Gamow, George
Gibbs, Josiah Willard
Goddard, Robert Hutchings
Gunn, Ross
Guthe, Karl Eugen
Hall, Edwin Herbert
Hansen, William Webster
Harkins, William Draper
Hastings, Charles Sheldon
Henry, Joseph
Hess, Victor Franz
Humphreys, Wiliam Jackson
Kármán, Theodore (Todor) von
Langmuir, Irving
Lawrence, Ernest Orlando
Lewis, Exum Percival
Loomis, Elmer Howard
Lyman, Chester Smith
Lyman, Theodore
Maclaurin, Richard Cockburn
Mayer, Alfred Marshall
Mendenhall, Charles Elwood

Mendenhall, Thomas Corwin
Michelson, Albert Abraham
Miller, Dayton Clarence
Millikan, Clark Blanchard
Millikan, Robert Andrews
Morley, Edward Williams
Nichols, Edward Leamington
Nichols, Ernest Fox
Nipher, Francis Eugene
Oppenheimer, Julius Robert
Page, Leigh
Pegram, George Braxton
Peirce, Benjamin Osgood
Pfund, August Herman
Pupin, Michael Idvorsky
Richtmyer, Floyd Karker
Rogers, William Augustus
Rood, Ogden Nicholas
Rosa, Edward Bennett
Rowland, Henry Augustus
Sabine, Wallace Clement Ware
Stern, Otto
Szilard, Leo
Tate, John Torrence
Thompson, Benjamin
Tolman, Richard Chace
Troland, Leonard Thompson
Trowbridge, Augustus
Trowbridge, John
Van de Graaff, Robert Jemison
Von Neumann, John
Waidner, Charles William
Waterman, Alan Tower
Webster, Arthur Gordon
Wells, William Charles
Winthrop, John
Woodward, Robert Simpson

PHYSIOGRAPHER (See also GEOG-RAPHER, NATURALIST)

Campbell, Marius Robinson

PHYSIOLOGICAL CHEMIST (See also CHEMIST, PHYSIOLOGIST)

Mendel, Lafayette Benedict

PHYSIOLOGIST (See also PHYSI-CIAN)

Allen, Edgar
Auer, John
Bazett, Henry Cuthbert
Bowditch, Henry Pickering
Cannon, Walter Bradford
Carlson, Anton Julius
Curtis, John Green
Dalton, John Call
Drinker, Cecil Kent
Dusser de Barenne, Joannes Gregorius
Erlanger, Joseph
Flint, Austin
Gasser, Herbert Spencer
Hecht, Selig
Hemmeter, John Conrad
Henderson, Lawrence Joseph
Henderson, Yandell
Hooker, Donald Russell
Hough, Theodore
Howell, William Henry
Keyt, Alonzo Thrasher
Lee, Frederic Schiller
Lining, John
Loeb, Jacques
Lombard, Warren Plimpton
Lusk, Graham

Martin, Henry Newell
Meltzer, Samuel James
Mitchell, John Kearsley
Osterhout, Winthrop John
    Vanleuven
Porter, William Townsend
Rachford, Benjamin Knox
Smith, Homer William
Stewart, George Neil
Troland, Leonard Thompson
Vaughan, Daniel
Weiss, Soma

PIANIST (See also JAZZ PIANIST,
    MUSICIAN)
Armstrong, Henry Worthington
    ("Harry")
Baermann, Carl
Bauer, Harold Victor
Beach, Amy Marcy Cheney
Blodgett, Benjamin Colman
Cadman, Charles Wakefield
Chotzinoff, Samuel
Cole, Nat ("King")
Dresel, Otto
Duchin, Edward Frank
    ("Eddy")
Gabrilowitsch, Ossip
Godowsky, Leopold
Goldbeck, Robert
Gottschalk, Louis Moreau
Grainger, George Percy
Griffes, Charles Tomlinson
Hanchett, Henry Granger
Henderson, Fletcher Hamilton
Hoffman, Richard
Hofmann, Josef Casimir
Jarvis, Charles H.
Joseffy, Rafael
Katchen, Julius
Klein, Bruno Oscar
Landowska, Wanda Aleksandra
Lang, Benjamin Johnson
Lhévinne, Josef
Liebling, Emil
Mannes, Clara Damrosch
Mannes, Leopold Damrosch
Mason, William
Mitropoulos, Dimitri
Pease, Alfred Humphreys
Perabo, Johann Ernst
Perry, Edward Baxter
Pratt, Silas Gamaliel
Rachmaninoff, Sergei
    Vasilyevich
Runcie, Constance Faunt Le
    Roy
Rybner, Martin Cornelius
Samaroff, Olga
Schelling, Ernest Henry
Schnabel, Artur
Sherwood, William Hall
Siloti, Alexander Ilyitch
Sternberg, Constantin
    Ivanovich, Edler von
Tapper, Bertha Feiring
Templeton, Alec Andrew
Vogrich, Max Wilhelm Karl
Washington, Dinah
Whiting, Arthur Battelle
Zeisler, Fannie Bloomfield

PILGRIM
Alden, John
Allerton, Isaac
Brewster, William
Morton, George
Morton, Nathaniel
Standish, Myles
Winslow, Edward

PIONEER (See also FRONTIERSMAN,
    GUIDE, SCOUT)
Atwater, Caleb
Ballard, Bland Williams
Bedinger, George Michael
Belden, Josiah
Birkbeck, Morris
Boone, Daniel
Bozeman, John M.
Brannan, Samuel
Bryant, John Howard
Burnett, Peter Hardeman
Carter, John
Carter, Landon
Chapman, John
Clark, George Rogers
Cleaveland, Moses
Connor, Patrick Edward
Cresap, Thomas
Dale, Samuel
Doddridge, Joseph
Duchesne, Rose Philippine
Dunn, Williamson
Dupratz, Antoine Simon Le
    Page
Dustin, Hannah
Faribault, Jean Baptiste
Flower, George
Flower, Richard
Folger, Peter
Fry, Joshua
Gaines, George Strother
Gerstle, Lewis
Gibson, Paris
Goodnow, Isaac Tichenor
Gross, Samuel David
Haraszthy de Mokcsa, Agoston
Harrod, James
Henderson, David Bremner
Hillis, David
Hitchcock, Phineas Warrener
Jenkins, John, 1728–1785
Jenkins, John, 1751–1827
Langworthy, James Lyon
Lee, Jason
Logan, Benjamin
Lyon, Matthew
McLeod, Martin
Magoffin, James Wiley
Marsh, Grant Prince
Marsh, John
Mattson, Hans
Mears, Otto
Meeker, Ezra
Meigs, Return Jonathan
Neighbors, Robert Simpson
Nesmith, James Willis
Newell, Robert
Nicholas, George
Overton, John
Palmer, Joel
Peary, Josephine Diebitsch
Piggott, James
Potter, Robert

Pryor, Nathaniel
Putnam, Rufus
Renick, Felix
Rice, Henry Mower
Robertson, James, 1742–1814
Robinson, Charles
Robinson, Solon
Russell, Osborne
Russell, William Henry
Sargent, Winthrop, 1753–1820
Sawyer, Lorenzo
Scholte, Hendrik Peter
Sevier, John
Stearns, Abel
Stevens, John Harrington
Stone, Wilbur Fisk
Stuart, Granville
Symmes, John Cleves
Thornton, Jesse Quinn
Tupper, Benjamin
Walderne, Richard
Warner, Jonathan Trumbull
Warren, Francis Emroy
White, James
Whitman, Marcus
Wilkeson, Samuel
Williams, Samuel May
Wolfskill, William
Young, Ewing
Zane, Ebenezer
Ziegler, David

PIRATE (See also BUCCANEER)
Halsey, John
Ingle, Richard
Kidd, William
Laffite, Jean
Mason, Samuel
Pound, Thomas
Quelch, John

PISCICULTURIST (See also ICH-
    THYOLOGIST, ZOOLOGIST
Garlick, Theodatus
Green, Seth
Mather, Fred
Titcomb, John Wheelock

PLANT BREEDER (See also
    AGRICULTURIST, BOTANIST)
Burbank, Luther
Coker, David Robert
Perrine, Henry
Pringle, Cyrus Guernsey
Pritchard, Frederick John

PLANTER (See AGRICULTURIST,
    FARMER, SUGAR PLANTER)
Aiken, William
Aime, Valcour
Allston, Robert Francis Withers
Alston, Joseph
Baker, Lorenzo Dow
Baldwin, Henry Perrine
Brandon, Gerard Chittocque
Byrd, William, 1652–1704
Byrd, William, 1674–1744
Cary, Archibald
Chesnut, James
Cloud, Noah Bartlett
Cocke, John Hartwell
Cocke, Philip St. George
Couper, James Hamilton
Dabney, Thomas Smith
    Gregory
Dibrell, George Gibbs

Drayton, Thomas Fenwick
Dunbar, William
Dymond, John
Edwards, John
Edwards, Weldon Nathaniel
Ensley, Enoch
Fagan, James Fleming
Gaines, George Strother
Gibson, Randall Lee
Habersham, James
Hampton, Wade, 1751–1835
Kermer, Duncan Farrar
King, Thomas Butler
Kinloch, Cleland
Kolb, Reuben Francis
Laurens, Henry
Leflore, Greenwood
Lewis, William Berkeley
Lumbrozo, Jacob
Lynch, Charles
Lynch, Thomas 1727–1776
Manigault, Gabriel
Manigault, Peter
Marigny, Bernard
Mason, George
Matthews, Samuel
Mills, Robert, 1809–1888
Nelson, William, 1711–1772
Page, Mann
Philips, Martin Wilson
Pollock, Oliver
Porter, Alexander
Randolph, William
Ravenel, Edmund
Rector, Henry Massey
Richardson, Edmund
Roane, John Selden
Sibley, John
Spalding, Thomas
Syms, Benjamin
Wailes, Benjamin Leonard
  Covington
Winston, John Anthony
Wofford, William Tatum
Yeardley, Sir George
PLANT GENETICIST (See also BOTA-
  NIST, GENETICIST)
East, Edward Murray
Shull, George Harrison
PLANT PATHOLOGIST (See also
  BOTANIST, PATHOLOGIST)
Duggar, Benjamin Minge
Galloway, Beverly Thomas
Jones, Lewis Ralph
Whetzel, Herbert Hice
PLANT PHYSIOLOGIST (See also
  BOTANIST, PHYSIOLOGIST)
Crocker, William
Hoagland, Dennis Robert
Kellerman, Karl Frederic
Livingston, Burton Edward
Webber, Herbert John
PLAYWRIGHT (See DRAMATIST)
PLEBISCITE AUTHORITY
Wambaugh, Sarah
POET (See also AUTHOR, WRITER)
Abbey, Henry
Adams, Charles Follen
Agee, James Rufus
Ainslie, Hew
Akins, Zoë
Aldrich, Thomas Bailey

Allen, Hervey
Allen, Paul
Alsop, Richard
Appleton, Thomas Gold
Arensberg, Walter Conrad
Arnold, George
Arrington, Alfred W.
Bacon, Leonard
Barlow, Joel
Bates, Katharine Lee
Beers, Ethel Lynn
Bell, James Madison
Benét, Stephen Vincent
Benét, William Rose
Benjamin, Park
Bennett, Emerson
Benton, Joel
Bleecker, Ann Eliza
Bloede, Gertrude
Blood, Benjamin Paul
Bogan, Louise Marie
Boker, George Henry
Bolton, Sarah Tittle Bartlett
Boner, John Henry
Bradford, Gamaliel
Bradford, Joseph
Bradstreet, Anne
Brainard, John Gardiner
  Calkins
Brooks, Charles Timothy
Brooks, James Gordon
Brooks, Maria Gowen
Brown, Sólyman
Brownell, Henry Howard
Bryant, William Cullen
Burgess, Frank Gelett
Burgess, W(illiam) Starling
Burleigh, George Shepard
Burton, Richard Eugene
Calvert, George Henry
Carleton, Will
Carrothers, James David
Cary, Alice
Cary, Phoebe
Cawein, Madison Julius
Channing, William Ellery
Chaplin, Ralph Hosea
Chapman, John Jay
Chivers, Thomas Holley
Church, Benjamin
Clark, Willis Gaylord
Clarke, McDonald
Cleghorn, Sarah Norcliffe
Cliffton, William
Coates, Florence Earle
Coffin, Robert Peter Tristram
Cole, Thomas
Congdon, Charles Taber
Cooke, Ebenezer
Cooke, Philip Pendleton
Cooke, Rose Terry
Coolbrith, Ina Donna
Coombe, Thomas
Cox, Henry Hamilton
Cranch, Christopher Pearse
Crandall, Charles Henry
Crane, Harold Hart
Crapsey, Adelaide
Crawford, John Wallace
  ("Captain Jack")
Cromwell, Gladys Louise
  Husted

Cullen, Countée Porter
Cullum, George Washington
Cummings, E. E.
Dabney, Richard
Dana, Richard Henry
Da Ponte, Lorenzo
Davidson, Lucretia Maria
Davidson, Margaret Miller
Day, Holman Francis
Dickinson, Emily Elizabeth
Dinsmoor, Robert
Drake, Joseph Rodman
Duganne, Augustine Joseph
  Hickey
Dugué, Charles Oscar
Dunbar, Paul Laurence
Eastman, Charles Gamage
Eliot, T(homas) S(tearns)
Emerson, Ralph Waldo
Evans, Nathaniel
Eve, Joseph
Fairfield, Sumner Lincoln
Faust, Frederick Shiller
Fearing, Kenneth Flexner
Fenollosa, Ernest Francisco
Ferguson, Elizabeth Graeme
Fessenden, Thomas Green
Field, Eugene
Finch, Francis Miles
Fletcher, John Gould
Foss, Sam Walter
Freeman, Joseph
Freneau, Philip Morin
Frost, Robert Lee
Gallagher, William Davis
Gilder, Richard Watson
Giovannitti, Arturo
Godfrey, Thomas
Gould, Hannah Flagg
Greene, Albert Gorton
Guiney, Louise Imogen
Hagedorn, Hermann Ludwig
  Gebhard
Hall, Hazel
Halleck, Fitz-Greene
Halpine, Charles Graham
Hammon, Jupiter
Harris, Thomas Lake
Hartley, Marsden
Hay, John Milton
Hayne, Paul Hamilton
Henderson, Daniel McIntyre
Hewitt, John Hill
Heyward, DuBose
Hillhouse, James Abraham
Hillyer, Robert Silliman
Hirst, Henry Beck
Hoffman, Charles Fenno
Holley, Marietta
Holmes, Daniel Henry
Holmes, Oliver Wendell
Hope, James Barron
Hosmer, William Howe Cuyler
Hovey, Richard
Hubner, Charles William
Hughes, James Langston
Humphreys, David
Humphries, George Rolfe
Imber, Naphtali Herz
Irving, William
Jackson, Helen Maria Fiske
  Hunt

Janson, Kristofer Nagel
Jarrell, Randall
Jeffers, John Robinson
Jeffrey, Rosa Griffith Vertner
   Johnson
Johnson, Henry
Johnson, Robert Underwood
Kerouac, Jack
Kilmer, Alfred Joyce
Kinney, Elizabeth Clementine
   Dodge Stedman
Kreymborg, Alfred Francis
Krez, Konrad
Lacy, Ernest
Ladd, Joseph Brown
La Farge, Christopher Grant
Lander, Frederick West
Lanier, Sidney
Lathrop, John
Latil, Alexandre
Lazarus, Emma
Leonard, William Ellery
Lindsay, Nicholas Vachel
Linn, John Blair
Linton, William James
Lodge, George Cabot
Longfellow, Henry Wadsworth
Longfellow, Samuel
Lord, William Wilberforce
Lowell, Amy
Lucas, Daniel Bedinger
Lytle, William Haines
McCarroll, James
McHenry, James
McKay, Claude
MacKaye, Percy Wallace
MacKellar, Thomas
McKinley, Carlyle
McLellan, Isaac
McMaster, Guy Humphreys
Macy, John
Malone, Walter
Markham, Edwin
Markoe, Peter
Marquis, Donald Robert Perry
Martin, Edward Sandford
Masters, Edgar Lee
Menken, Adah Isaacs
Merrill, Stuart FitzRandolph
Mifflin, Lloyd
Miles, George Henry
Millay, Edna St. Vincent
Miller, Cincinnatus Hiner
Mitchell, Langdon Elwyn
Mitchell, Silas Weir
Moïse, Penina
Monroe, Harriet
Moody, William Vaughn
Moore, (Austin) Merrill
Morris, George Pope
Morton, Sarah Wentworth
   Apthorp
Munford, William
Muñoz-Rivera, Luis
Nack, James M.
Newell, Robert Henry
Nicholson, Eliza Jane Poitevent
   Holbrook
Nies, Konrad
Niles, Nathaniel
Oakes, Urian
Oppenheim, James

O'Reilly, John Boyle
Osborn, Laughton
Osborn, Selleck
Osgood, Frances Sargent Locke
Paine, Robert Treat
Parke, John
Parker, Dorothy Rothschild
Parsons, Thomas William
Peabody, Josephine Preston
Percival, James Gates
Perry, Nora
Peterson, Henry
Piatt, John James
Piatt, Sarah Morgan Bryan
Pierpont, John
Pinkney, Edward Coote
Plath, Sylvia
Plummer, Jonathan
Plummer, Mary Wright
Poe, Edgar Allan
Posey, Alexander Lawrence
Powell, Thomas
Poydras, Julien de Lelande
Preston, Margaret Junkin
Randall, James Ryder
Rankin, Jeremiah Eames
Read, Thomas Buchanan
Realf, Richard
Reed, John, 1887–1920
Reese, Lizette Woodworth
Reitzel, Robert
Requier, Augustus Julian
Ricketson, Daniel
Riley, James Whitcomb
Rittenhouse, Jessie Belle
Robinson, Edwin Arlington
Roche, James Jeffrey
Roethke, Theodore Huebner
Rose, Aquila
Rosenfeld, Morris
Rouquette, Adrien Emmanuel
Rouquette, François Dominique
Russell, Irwin
Ryan, Abram Joseph
Saltus, Edgar Evertson
Sandburg, Carl August
Sandys, George
Santayana, George
Sargent, Epes
Savage, Philip Henry
Saxe, John Godfrey
Schnauffer, Carl Heinrich
Scollard, Clinton
Searing, Laura Catherine
   Redden
Seeger, Alan
Service, Robert William
Sewall, Jonathan Mitchell
Shaw, John, 1778–1809
Sherman, Frank Dempster
Shillaber, Benjamin Penhallow
Sill, Edward Rowland
Smith, Samuel Francis
Snow, Eliza Roxey
Spingarn, Joel Elias
Sprague, Charles
Stanton, Frank Lebby
Stedman, Edmund Clarence
Steendam, Jacob
Stein, Evaleen
Sterling, George
Stevens, Wallace

Stoddard, Elizabeth Drew
   Barstow
Stoddard, Richard Henry
Story, Isaac
Story, William Wetmore
Strange, Michael
Street, Alfred Billings
Sylvester, Frederick Oakes
Tabb, John Banister
Taggard, Genevieve
Taylor, Benjamin Franklin
Taylor, Edward
Teasdale, Sara
Testut, Charles
Thaxter, Celia Laighton
Thierry, Camille
Thomas, Edith Matilda
Thompson, James Maurice
Thompson, John Reuben
Thomson, Edward William
Thoreau, Henry David
Thorpe, Rose Alnora Hartwick
Ticknor, Francis Orray
Timrod, Henry
Torrence, Frederick Ridgely
Townsend, Mary Ashley
Trumbull, John, 1750–1831
Tuckerman, Frederick Goddard
Tuckerman, Henry Theodore
Turell, Jane
Van Dyke, Henry
Villagrá, Gasper Pérez de
Wallace, William Ross
Walsh, Thomas
Ward, Thomas
Warfield, Catherine Ann Ware
Warren, Mercy Otis
Wheatley, Phillis
Whitman, Albery Allson
Whitman, Sarah Ellen Power
Whitman, Walt
Whitney, Anne
Whittier, John Greenleaf
Wilcox, Ella Wheeler
Wilde, Richard Henry
Williams, Catharine Read
   Arnold
Williams, William Carlos
Willis, Nathaniel Parker
Wilson, Robert Burns
Wilson, William
Winchevsky, Morris
Winter, William
Woodberry, George Edward
Woodworth, Samuel
Wright, Philip Green
Wylie, Elinor Morton Hoyt
Young, David
Zunser, Eliakum
POLICE CONSULTANT
   Smith, Bruce
POLICE EXECUTIVE
   Byrnes, Thomas F.
   Curtis, Edwin Upton
POLICE OFFICER
   Glassford, Pelham Davis
   McGrath, Matthew J.
   Ruditsky, Barney
POLITICAL ACTIVIST
   Du Bois, William Edward
   Burghardt

Harriman, Florence Jaffray
   Hurst
Whitney, Charlotte Anita
POLITICAL ADVISER
Bryan, Charles Wayland
Young, Owen D.
POLITICAL AIDE
Hinshaw, David Schull
POLITICAL BOSS
Hague, Frank
Kelly, Edward Joseph
Pendergast, Thomas Joseph
Tweed, William Marcy
POLITICAL COMMENTATOR
Dunne, Finley Peter
Gillis, James Martin
POLITICAL CRITIC (See also **CRITIC**)
Howard, Joseph Kinsey
POLITICAL ECONOMIST (See also **ECONOMIST**)
Colwell, Stephen
Coxe, Tench
Rawle, Francis, 1662–1726/27
POLITICAL LEADER
Raskob, John Jakob
POLITICAL ORGANIZER
Kohlberg, Alfred
POLITICAL PHILOSOPHER
MacIver, Robert Morrison
POLITICAL REFORMER (See also **REFORMER**)
Churchill, Winston
Hawkins, Dexter Arnold
Kelly, Edmond
Linton, William James
McClintock, Oliver
MacVeagh, Isaac Wayne
Moskowitz, Belle Lindner
   Israels
Pinchot, Amos Richards Eno
Roosevelt, Robert Barnwell
Shepard, Edward Morse
U'Ren, William Simon
Welling, Richard Ward Greene
POLITICAL SCIENTIST
Barrows, David Prescott
Beard, Charles Austin
Bentley, Arthur Fisher
Burgess, John William
Corwin, Edward Samuel
Eastman, Max Forrester
Fairlie, John Archibald
Garner, James Wilford
Goodnow, Frank Johnson
Key, Valdimer Orlando, Jr.
Lieber, Francis
McBain, Howard Lee
McCarthy, Charles
Macy, Jesse
Merriam, Charles Edward, Jr.
Moses, Bernard
Ogg, Frederic Austin
Parsons, Frank
Reinsch, Paul Samuel
Rossiter, Clinton Lawrence, III
Rowe, Leo Stanton
Smith, James Allen
Smith, Thomas Vernor
Thomas, Elbert Duncan
White, Leonard Dupee
Willoughby, Westel Woodbury

POLITICAL THEORIST
Burdick, Eugene Leonard
Neumann, Franz Leopold
POLITICIAN (See also **CONGRESSMAN, CONGRESSWOMAN, DIPLOMAT, LOBBYIST, POLITICAL LEADER, SENATOR, STATESMAN**)
Abbott, Joseph Carter
Adair, John
Addicks, John Edward
   O'Sullivan
Alexander, James
Allen, Ira
Ames, Oakes
Anthony, Henry Bowen
Appleton, Nathan
Archer, Branch Tanner
Armstrong, John
Arnold, Richard Dennis
Ashe, John
Ashe, John Baptista
Atherton, Charles Gordon
Atwood, David
Austin, Benjamin
Austin, James Trecothick
Avery, Isaac Wheeler
Axtell, Samuel Beach
Baker, James Heaton
Baldwin, John Brown
Bartlett, Ichabod
Bartlett, Joseph
Battle, Cullen Andrews
Beale, Richard Lee Turberville
Beall, Samuel Wootton
Beatty, John
Bedford, Gunning
Behan, William James
Bell, Charles Henry
Bell, Isaac
Bell, Luther Vose
Bidwell, John
Bidwell, Marshall Spring
Biggs, Asa
Bingham, Harry
Bingham, John Armor
Binns, John
Bishop, Abraham
Blair, Emily Newell
Blair, Francis Preston
Bliss, Cornelius Newton
Bloodworth, Timothy
Blount, Thomas
Blunt, James Gillpatrick
Boutwell, George Sewall
Bowen, Thomas Meade
Bowie, Richard Johns
Brady, James Topham
Brandegee, Frank Bosworth
Brayton, Charles Ray
Breese, Sidney
Bright, Jesse David
Broderick, David Colbreth
Brooks, Erastus
Brown, Neill Smith
Brown, Walter Folger
Browning, Orville Hickman
Bryan, George
Bryan, William Jennings
Bryce, Lloyd Stephens
Burnet, David Gouverneur
Burrill, James

Burrowes, Thomas Henry
Butler, Benjamin Franklin
Butterworth, Benjamin
Cain, Richard Harvey
Caldwell, Alexander
Calhoun, John
Calhoun, William Barron
Camp, John Lafayette
Carr, Joseph Bradford
Cassidy, William
Caswell, Richard
Cattell, Alexander Gilmore
Chaffee, Jerome Bonaparte
Chandler, Zachariah
Christian, William
Cilley, Joseph
Clark, Daniel
Clarke, John Hessin
Clayton, Powell
Clingman, Thomas Lanier
Cloud, Noah Bartlett
Cobb, David
Cochrane, John
Collins, Patrick Andrew
Colton, Calvin
Combs, Leslie
Cook, Isaac
Cook, James Merrill
Cooke, Elisha
Cooper, Mark Anthony
Corbett, Henry Winslow
Cornell, Alonzo B.
Cox, George Barnsdale
Cox, James Middleton
Cox, William Ruffin
Coxe, Daniel
Crocker, Alvah
Croker, Richard
Croswell, Edwin
Crowninshield, Benjamin
   Williams
Cruger, Henry
Cruger, John
Crump, Edward Hull
Curley, James Michael
Curran, Thomas Jerome
Currier, Moody
Cushing, Thomas
Daggett, David
Daugherty, Harry Micajah
Davis, Henry Winter
Davis, Matthew Livingston
Davis, Pauline Morton Sabin
Dawson, William Levi
Dayton, William Lewis
Dearborn, Henry Alexander
   Scammell
De Lancey, James, 1703–1760
De Lancey, James, 1732–1800
De Lancey, Oliver
Deming, Henry Champion
Devaney, John Patrick
Dibrell, George Gibbs
Dickinson, Daniel Stevens
Doddridge, Philip
Dodge, Grenville Mellon
Donelson, Andrew Jackson
Donnelly, Ignatius
Dorr, Thomas Wilson
Dorsheimer, William Edward
Doty, James Duane
Douglas, Stephen Arnold

Draper, Andrew Sloan
Draper, Eben Sumner
Duane, William
Dudley, Charles Edward
Duncan, Joseph
Durant, Thomas Jefferson
Early, Peter
Eastman, Charles Gamage
Eastman, Enoch Worthen
Eastman, Harvey Gridley
Eaton, John Henry
Edgerton, Alfred Peck
Edwards, Pierpont
Egan, Patrick
Elliot, James
Ellis, Seth Hockett
English, Thomas Dunn
Evans, George
Evans, Henry Clay
Fairfield, John
Faran, James John
Farnsworth, John Franklin
Farwell, Charles Benjamin
Fay, Jonas
Felton, William Harrell
Fessenden, William Pitt
Fisk, James
Fitzgerald, John Francis
Flagg, Azariah Cutting
Flanagan, Webster
Flynn, Edward Joseph
Folsom, Nathaniel
Foot, Solomon
Frazier, Lynn Joseph
Frémont, John Charles
Gallinger, Jacob Harold
Gansevoort, Leonard
Gartrell, Lucius Jeremiah
Gary, James Albert
Gibbons, Thomas
Gibson, Walter Murray
Gillet, Ransom Hooker
Gilman, John Taylor
Gilman, Nicholas
Gitlow, Benjamin
Goodloe, William Cassius
Goodrich, Elizur
Goodwin, Ichabod
Goodwin, John Noble
Gordon, George Washington
Granger, Francis
Granger, Gideon
Greeley, Horace
Green, Duff
Greene, Nathaniel
Gregg, Andrew
Gregg, Maxcy
Griswold, Roger
Griswold, Stanley
Grover, La Fayette
Grow, Galusha Aaron
Grund, Francis Joseph
Grundy, Felix
Gwin, William McKendree
Hague, Frank
Haines, Charles Glidden
Hale, Charles
Hale, Eugene
Hale, John Parker
Hall, Abraham, Oakey
Hallett, Benjamin Franklin
Hamilton, James Alexander

Hammond, Jabez Delano
Hancock, John, 1736–1793
Hanna, Marcus Alonzo
Hannegan, Robert Emmet
Hanson, Ole
Harper, Robert Goodloe
Harris, Isham Green
Harris, Townsend
Harrison, Carter Henry, Jr.
Harrison, George Paul
Hartranft, John Frederick
Haskell, Dudley Chase
Haskell, Ella Louise Knowles
Hassaurck, Friedrich
Hays, Will H.
Hazard, Jonathan J.
Heath, Perry Sanford
Heney, Francis Joseph
Henshaw, David
Higgins, Frank Wayland
Hill, David Bennett
Hill, Isaac
Hines, James J.
Hitchcock, Phineas Warrener
Hoan, Daniel Webster
Hoey, Clyde Roark
Hoffman, John Thompson
Holcomb, Silas Alexander
Howard, Benjamin Chew
Howard, Edgar
Howard, William Alanson
Howell, Clark
Hoyt, Henry Martyn
Hubbard, David
Hughes, James
Hunter, Whiteside Godfrey
Husting, Paul Oscar
Imlay, Gilbert
Irving, William
Jackson, Robert R.
Jardine, William Marion
Johnson, Albert
Johnson, Bradley Tyler
Johnson, Edward Austin
Kelly, Edward Joseph
Kelly, John
Kelly, John Brendan
Kennedy, John Doby
Kerens, Richard C.
Kerman, Francis
Keyes, Elisha Williams
King, Preston
Kinsella, Thomas
Kinsey, John
Knott, Aloysius Leo
Knox, Frank
Lane, James Henry
Langdon, John
Lasker, Albert Davis
Lewis, William Berkeley
Lexow, Clarence
Lincoln, Enoch
Lincoln, Levi, 1749–1820
Lincoln, Levi, 1782–1868
Lloyd, David
Logan, Cornelius Ambrose
Lorimer, William
Loring, George Bailey
Loucks, Henry Langford
Lovell, James
Lunn, George Richard
Lyon, Caleb

Lyon, Matthew
McAfee, Robert Breckinridge
McCarren, Patrick Henry
McClellan, George Brinton
McCormick, Richard
  Cunningham
McCumber, Porter James
McDonald, Joseph Ewing
McDowell, Joseph
McLaughlin, Hugh
McLevy, Jasper
McMahon, Brien
McManes, James
McNutt, Paul Vories
Magee, Christopher Lyman
Maginnis, Martin
Manigault, Peter
Manley, Joseph Homan
Marcantonio, Vito Anthony
Massey, John Edward
Mather, Increase
Meagher, Thomas Francis
Merriam, William Rush
Mills, Ogden Livingston
Minor, Robert
Moore, Andrew
Moreau-Lislet, Louis Casimir
  Elisabeth
Morrissey, John
Morton, Ferdinand Quintin
Moses, George Higgins
Muhlenberg, Frederick
  Augustus Conrad
Muhlenberg, Henry Augustus
  Philip
Muhlenberg, John Peter Gabriel
Muñoz-Rivera, Luis
Murphy, Charles Francis
Murphy, Henry Cruse
Nairne, Thomas
Nelson, Hugh
New, Harry Stewart
Nicholas, George
Nicholas, Philip Norborne
Nicolls, William
Niles, David K.
Niles, Nathaniel
Norris, Isaac, 1701–1766
O'Dwyer, William
O'Fallon, James
Orth, Godlove Stein
Osgood, Samuel
Otis, James
Overton, John
Packer, William Fisher
Palmer, William Adams
Parker, John Milliken
Parker, Josiah
Partridge, James Rudolph
Patterson, James Willis
Payne, Sereno Elisha
Pelham, Robert A.
Penrose, Boies
Penrose, Charles Bingham
Perez, Leander Henry
Petigru, James Louis
Pew, Joseph Newton, Jr.
Pickering, Timothy
Pinchback, Pinckney Benton
  Stewart
Platt, Thomas Collier
Pleasants, John Hampden

Pomeroy, Marcus Mills
Porter, James Madison
Pringle, John Julius
Pusey, Caleb
Quay, Matthew Stanley
Quick, John Herbert
Quincy, Josiah, 1772–1864
Ramsay, Nathaniel
Randall, Alexander Williams
Randolph, John, 1728–1784
Ranney, Rufus Percival
Raum, Green Berry
Raymond, Henry Jarvis
Requa, Mark Lawrence
Richmond, Dean
Ritchie, Thomas
Rives, William Cabell
Roberts, William Randall
Robertson, William Henry
Robins, Raymond
Robinson, William Erigena
Rollins, Edward Henry
Rollins, Frank West
Root, Erastus
Rosewater, Edward
Rosewater, Victor
Rowell, Chester Harvey
Ruef, Abraham
Russell, William Henry
Schell, Augustus
Schoeppel, Andrew Frank
Seidel, George Lukas Emil
Settle, Thomas
Sewell, William Joyce
Shannon, Wilson
Shields, George Howell
Shippen, Edward, 1639–1712
Sibley, John
Simmons, Roscoe Conkling
   Murray
Simons, Algie Martin
Skinner, Charles Rufus
Slidell, John
Smith, Buckingham
Smith, Charles Perrin
Smith, Frank Leslie
Smith, Israel
Smith, James, 1851–1927
Smith, Nathan, 1770–1835
Smith, Thomas Vernor
Springer, Charles
Steedman, James Blair
Stevens, Thaddeus
Stevenson, Adlai Ewing, II
Stockton, Richard
Sullivan, Timothy Daniel
Swartwout, Samuel
Sweeny, Peter Barr
Swensson, Carl Aaron
Switzler, William Franklin
Taggart, Thomas
Terry, David Smith
Thayer, John Milton
Thomas, David
Thomas, Elbert Duncan
Thomas, (John William) Elmer
Thomas, William Widgery
Thompson, Richard Wigginton
Tichenor, Isaac
Tipton, John
Tumulty, Joseph Patrick
Tweed, William Marcy

Tyler, Robert
Upshaw, William David
Vallandigham, Clement Laird
Van Buren, John
Van Dam, Rip
Van Ness, William Peter
Vare, William Scott
Wagner, Robert Ferdinand
Walcott, Edward Oliver
Waldo, Samuel
Walker, Frank Comerford
Wallace, Hugh Campbell
Waln, Robert, 1765–1836
Walsh, Michael
Ward, John Elliott
Warren, James
Watson, Thomas Edward
Weed, Thurlow
West, Roy Owen
White, Edward Douglass
Williams, Elisha
Wilson, J(ames) Finley
Wise, John Sergeant
POLO PLAYER
Rumsey, Charles Cary
POMOLOGIST (See also AGRICUL-
   TURIST)
Brincklé, William Draper
Coxe, William
Downing, Charles
Gideon, Peter Miller
Lyon, Theodatus Timothy
Manning, Robert
Thomas, John Jacobs
PORTRAITIST
Bachrach, Louis Fabian
Christy, Howard Chandler
POSTAL PIONEER
Bates, Barnabas
Chorpenning, George
Davis, William Augustine
Holt, John
Majors, Alexander
POSTMASTER GENERAL (CONFEDER-
   ATE)
Reagan, John Henninger
POSTMASTER GENERAL (See also
   POSTAL PIONEER)
Brown, Walter Folger
Burleson, Albert Sidney
Campbell, James
Collamer, Jacob
Cortelyou, George Bruce
Creswell, John Angel James
Dickinson, Donald McDonald
Donaldson, Jesse Monroe
Gary, James Albert
Habersham, Joseph
Hatton, Frank
Hazard, Ebenezer
Hitchcock, Frank Harris
Holt, Joseph
Howe, Timothy Otis
James, Thomas Lemuel
Jewell, Marshall
Johnson, Cave
Kendall, Amos
King, Horatio
McLean, John
Meigs, Return Jonathan
Meyer, George von Lengerke
Niles, John Milton

Payne, Henry Clay
Randall, Alexander Williams
Smith, Charles Emory
Vilas, William Freeman
Walker, Frank Comerford
Wickliffe, Charles Anderson
Wilson, William Lyne
POTTER (See also CRAFTSMAN)
Low, John Gardner
Rellstab, John
POWDER MAKER (See also MANU-
   FACTURER, *Explosives*)
Keppel, Frederick
PRESIDENT, COLLEGE (See COL-
   LEGE PRESIDENT)
PRESIDENT (COMMONWEALTH OF
   THE PHILIPPINES)
Quezon, Manuel Luis
PRESIDENT (CONFEDERATE STATES)
Davis, Jefferson
PRESIDENTIAL ADVISER
House, Edward Mandell
Howe, Louis McHenry
PRESIDENTIAL CANDIDATE
Adams, Samuel
Babson, Roger Ward
Bell, John
Bidwell, John
Birney, James Gillespie
Blaine, James Gillespie
Brenckinridge, John Cabell
Brown, Benjamin Gratz
Bryan, William Jennings
Burr, Aaron
Butler, Benjamin Franklin
Cass, Lewis
Chafin, Eugene Wilder
Clay, Henry
Clinton, De Witt
Clinton, George, 1739–1812
Cooper, Peter
Cox, James Middleton
Crawford, William Harris
Davis, David
Davis, John William
Debs, Eugene Victor
Douglas, Stephen Arnold
Dow, Neal
Ellsworth, Oliver
Ferguson, James Edward
Fisk, Clinton Bowen
Floyd, John
Foster, William Z.
Frémont, John Charles
Greeley, Horace
Hale, John Parker
Hancock, Winfield Scott
Harvey, William Hope
Hendricks, Thomas Andres
Hughes, Charles Evans
Iredell, James
Jay, John
Jenkins, Charles Jones
King, Rufus, 1755–1827
La Follette, Robert Marion
Lemke, William Frederick
MacArthur, Douglas
Magnum, Willie Person
O'Connor, Charles
Palmer, John McAuley
Parker, Atlon Brooks
Pinckney, Charles Cotesworth

Pnckney, Thomas
St. John, John Pierce
Scott, Winfield
Seymour, Haratio, 1810–1886
Smith, Alfred Emanuel
Stevenson, Adlai Ewing, II
Swallow, Silas Comfort
Taft, Robert Alphonso
Thomas, Norman Mattoon
Tilden, Samuel Jones
Upshaw, William David
Wallace, Henry Agard
Watson, Thomas Edward
Weaver, James Baird
Webster, Daniel
White, Hugh Lawson
Willkie, Wendell Lewis
Wirt, William
PRESIDENT OF UNITED STATES
Adams, John
Adams, John Quincy
Arthur, Chester Alan
Buchanan, James
Cleveland, Stephen Grover
Coolidge, Calvin
Eisenhower, Dwight David
Fillmore, Millard
Garfield, James Abram
Grant, Ulysses Simpson
Harding, Warren Gamaliel
Harrison, Benjamin, 1833–1901
Harrison, William Henry
Hayes, Rutherford Birchard
Hoover, Herbert Clark
Jackson, Andrew
Jefferson, Thomas
Johnson, Andrew
Kennedy, John Fitzgerald
Lincoln, Abraham
McKinley, William
Madison, James
Monroe, James
Pierce, Franklin
Polk, James Knox
Roosevelt, Franklin Delano
Roosevelt, Theodore
Taft, William Howard
Taylor, Zachary
Tyler, John, 1790–1862
Van Buren, Martin
Washington, George
Wilson, Woodrow
PRESS AGENT
Thompson, Slason
PRESS SECRETARY (PRESIDENTIAL)
Early, Stephen Tyree
Ross, Charles Griffith
Short, Joseph Hudson, Jr.
PRINTER (See also PUBLISHER)
Adler, Elmer
Aitken, Robert
Alvord, Corydon Alexis
Ashmead, Isaac
Bailey, Francis
Bailey, Lydia R.
Baker, Peter Carpenter
Beadle, Erastus Flavel
Bradford, Andrew
Bradford, John
Bradford, Thomas
Bradford, William
Brewster, Osmyn

Carter, John
Charless, Joseph
Cist, Charles
Crocker, Uriel
Currier, Nathaniel
Dana, John Cotton
Day, Benjamin Henry
Day, Stephen
De Vinne, Theodore Low
Draper, Richard
Dunlap, John
Fleet, Thomas
Fleming, John
Foster, John
Fowle, Daniel
Franklin, Benjamin
Franklin, James
Gaine, Hugh
Gilliss, Walter
Goddard, William
Gordon, George Phineas
Goudy, Frederic William
Green, Bartholomew
Green, Jonas
Green, Samuel
Green, Thomas
Greenleaf, Thomas
Hall, David
Hall, Samuel, 1740–1807
Harper, Fletcher
Harper, James
Haswell, Anthony
Holt, John
Humphreys, James
Jansen, Reinier
Johnson, Marmaduke
Keimer, Samuel
Kneeland, Samuel
Linton, William James
Loudon, Samuel
MacKellar, Thomas
Mecom, Benjamin
Meeker, Jotham
Miller, John Henry
Moore, Jacob Bailey
Munsell, Joel
Nancrède, Paul Joseph Guérard de
Nash, John Henry
Nuthead, William
Parker, James
Parks, William
Pickard, Samuel Thomas
Pomeroy, Marcus Mills
Rivington, James
Robertson, James, b. 1740
Roulstone, George
Rudge, William Edwin
Sholes, Christopher Latham
Sower, Christopher, 1693–1758
Sower, Christopher, 1721–1784
Thomas, Isaiah
Tileston, Thomas
Timothy, Lewis
Towne, Benjamin
Trow, John Fowler
Updike, Daniel Berkeley
White, Thomas Willis
Williams, William
Zamorano, Augustin Juan Vicente
Zenger, John Peter

PRINTMAKER (See also ARTIST, ENGRAVER, ETCHER, LITHOGRAPHER)
Ganso, Emil
Sloan, John French
PRISON ADMINISTRATOR
Lawes, Lewis Edward
Lynds, Elam
Pilsbury, Amos
PRISON REFORMER (See also PENOLOGIST, REFORMER)
Davis, Katharine Bement
Gibbons, Abigail Hopper
Johnson, Ellen Cheney
Older, Fremont
Osborne, Thomas Mott
Round, William Marshall Fitts
Spear, Charles
Wines, Enoch Cobb
PRIVATEER (See also ADVENTURER, NAVAL OFFICER, NAVIGATOR)
Burns, Otway
Chever, James W.
Fanning, Nathaniel
Green, Nathan
Haraden, Jonathan
McNeill, Daniel
McNeill, Hector
Maffitt, David
Olmsted, Gideon
Peabody, Joseph
Randall, Robert Richard
Ropes, Joseph
Southack, Cyprian
PROBATION OFFICER
Augustus, John
PRODUCER (See also DIRECTOR, FILMMAKER, MOTION PICTURE DIRECTOR, MOTION PICTURE PRODUCER, THEATRICAL MANAGER)
Ames, Winthrop
Belasco, David
Berg, Gertrude Edelstein
Bonstelle, Jessie
Brackett, Charles William
Brady, William Aloysius
Brenon, Herbert
Carroll, Earl
Cohan, George Michael
Cohn, Harry
Conried, Heinrich
Crouse, Russel McKinley
Daly, John Augustin
DeMille, Cecil Blount
De Sylva, George Gard ("Buddy")
Dillingham, Charles Bancroft
Disney, Walter Elias ("Walt")
Dixon, Thomas
Faversham, William Alfred
Fiske, Harrison Grey
Frohman, Daniel
Gest, Morris
Golden, John
Hampden, Walter
Harrigan, Edward
Harris, Sam Henry
Helburn, Theresa
Janney, Russell Dixon
Klaw, Marc
Laemmle, Carl

Langner, Lawrence
Leiber, Fritz
Liveright, Horace Brisbin
Loew, Marcus
MacArthur, Charles Gordon
McClintic, Guthrie
Mayer, Louis Burt
Miller, Gilbert Heron
Nichols, Dudley
Pemberton, Brock
Rice, Elmer
Rose, Billy
Rossen, Robert
Savage, Henry Wilson
Schwartz, Maurice
Selig, William Nicholas
Shubert, Lee
Taylor, Charles Alonzo
Thalberg, Irving Grant
Tyler, George Crouse
Walker, Stuart Armstrong
Wanger, Walter
White, George
Youmans, Vincent Millie
Ziegfeld, Florenz
PROFESSOR (See also EDUCATOR,
    SCHOLAR, TEACHER)
Abel-Henderson, Annie Heloise
Adams, George Burton
Adams, Herbert Baxter
Adams, Thomas Sewall
Allinson, Francis Greenleaf
Babbitt, Irving
Bachmann, Werner Emmanuel
Baker, Carl Lotus
Baker, George Pierce
Barus, Carl
Beach, Harlan Page
Beale, Joseph Henry
Bleyer, Willard Grosvenor
Borchard, Edwin Montefiore
Boring, Edwin Garrigues
Briggs, Charles Augustus
Brigham, Albert Perry
Brinton, Clarence Crane
Bristol, William Henry
Brown, Carleton
Brown, Francis
Bruce, Andrew Alexander
Burgess, John William
Cain, William
Calkins, Mary Whiton
Capps, Edward
Case, Shirley Jackson
Chafee, Zechariah, Jr.
Chamberlain, Joseph Perkins
Chase, George
Child, Charles Manning
Christian, Henry Asbury
Clarke, Frank Wigglesworth
Cook, Walter Wheeler
Cooper, Jacob
Cooper, Thomas
Copeland, Charles Townsend
Costigan, George Purcell
Crafts, James Mason
Crawford, James Pyle
    Wickersham
Cross, Arthur Lyon
Cross, Samuel Hazzard
Cross, Wilbur Lucius
Curme, George Oliver

Daggett, Naphtali
Da Ponte, Lorenzo
Dargan, Edwin Preston
Davis, William Morris
Dickinson, Edwin De Witt
Dod, Albert Baldwin
Dowling, Noel Thomas
Dubbs, Joseph Henry
Edman, Irwin
Elvehjem, Conrad Arnold
Fish, Carl Russell
Flather, John Joseph
Fleming, Walter Lynwood
Foresti, Elentario Felice
Forsyth, John
Franklin, Edward Curtis
Freund, Ernst
Friedlaender, Walter Ferdinand
Frieze, Henry Simmons
Frisbie, Levi
Fry, Joshua
Genung, John Franklin
Gildersleeve, Basil Lanneau
Gilmore, Joseph Henry
Greenlaw, Edwin Almiron
Gregory, Charles Noble
Hamilton, Alice
Hanson, James Christian
    Meinich
Haring, Clarence
Hart, Albert Bushnell
Herrick, Robert Welch
Hitchcock, Edward, 1828–1911
Hohfeld, Wesley Newcomb
Hovgaard, William
Hudson, Manley Ottmer
Hulbert, Archer Butler
Hunt, Theodore Whitefield
Hyvernat, Henri
Johnson, Samuel William
Jones, Lynds
Jones, Rufus Matthew
Kelsey, Rayner Wickersham
Kemp, John
Kilpatrick, William Heard
Kittredge, George Lyman
Koch, Frederick Henry
Ladd, Carl Edwin
Lake, Kirsopp
Landis, James McCauley
Langdell, Chrisopher Columbus
Latané, John Holladay
Leonard, William Ellery
Lile, William Minor
Lincoln, John Larkin
Long, Joseph Ragland
Lovering, Joseph
Lowell, Abbott Lawrence
Lyman, Eugene William
Lyon, David Gordon
McCarthy, Daniel Joseph
McClellan, George Brinton
McGlothlin, William Joseph
Marquand, Allan
Marsh, Frank Burr
Mason, Daniel Gregory
Matthews, James Brander
Mead, George Herbert
Mendenhall, Thomas Corwin
Meyer, Adolf
Miller, George Abram
Mitchell, Edwin Knox

Mitchell, Langdon Elwyn
Moore, Eliakim Hastings
Moore, Nathaniel Fish
Morse, Harmon Northrop
Moulton, Richard Green
Muller, Hermann Joseph
Naismith, James
Neilson, William Allan
Noyes, George Rapall
Ogg, Frederic Austin
Oldfather, William Abbott
Osgood, William Fogg
Owsley, Frank Lawrence
Packard, Alpheus Spring
Panofsky, Erwin
Parker, George Howard
Parsons, Theophilus
Parvin, Theodore Sutton
Peabody, Andrew Preston
Peabody, Francis Greenwood
Perrin, Bernadotte
Perry, Bliss
Phelps, Austin
Phelps, William Lyon
Phillips, Ulrich Bonnell
Pirsson, Louis Valentine
Pond, Enoch
Pound, (Nathan) Roscoe
Prime, William Cowper
Putnam, Frederic Ward
Quine, William Edward
Rand, Edward Kennard
Randall, James Garfield
Rauschenbusch, Walter
Ravenel, Edmund
Read, Conyers
Reed, Richard Clark
Richardson, Robert
Rister, Carl Coke
Ritter, Frédéric Louis
Robertson, William Spence
Robinson, Edward, 1794–1863
Rostovtzeff, Michael Ivanovitch
Rupp, William
Russell, James Earl
Rutledge, Wiley Blount
Sampson, Martin Wright
Schelling, Felix Emanuel
Schevill, Rudolph
Schinz, Albert
Schlesinger, Arthur Meier
Schmidt, Nathaniel
Scott, Walter Dill
Scudder, (Julia) Vida Dutton
Searle, John Preston
Shannon, Fred Albert
Sherman, Henry Clapp
Shields, Charles Woodruff
Silliman, Benjamin, 1779–1864
Smith, Charles Forster
Smith, David Eugene
Smith, Edgar Fahs
Smith, Edmund Munroe
Smith, Henry Louis
Smith, Horatio Elwin
Smith, Nathan, 1762–1829
Smyth, Egbert Coffin
Smyth, Herbert Weir
Smyth, William
Sprague, Oliver Mitchell
    Wentworth
Spring, Leverett Wilson

Stephenson, Carl
Sumner, James Batcheller
Tansill, Charles Callan
Tatlock, John Strong Perry
Thacher, Thomas Anthony
Thayer, Ezra Ripley
Thayer, James Bradley
Thorndike, Lynn
Thurstone, Louis Leon
Tiedeman, Christopher
    Gustavus
Tigert, John James, IV
Timberlake, Gideon
Towler, John
Treadwell, Daniel
Trent, William Peterfield
Tucker, Nathaniel Beverley,
    1784–1851
Tuttle, Herbert
Tyler, Charles Mellen
Tyler, William Seymour
Van Amringe, John Howard
Vasiliev, Alexander
    Alexandrovich
Venable, Francis Preston
Vincent, Marvin Richardson
Ward, Robert De Courcy
Ware, Henry, 1764–1845
Warner, Langdon
Webb, John Burkitt
Webster, John White
Weed, Lewis Hill
Weiss, Soma
Wertenbaker, Thomas Jefferson
West, Allen Brown
West, Andrew Fleming
Weyl, Hermann
Wheeler, Arthur Leslie
Willard, James Field
Williams, Edward Thomas
Willis, Henry Parker
Wilson, Bird
Wilson, George Grafton
Wilson, Peter
Woodbridge, Samuel Merrill
Woods, James Haughton
Woods, Leonard
Young, Karl

PROHIBITION ADMINISTRATOR
Yellowley, Edward Clements

PROHIBITIONIST (See also REFORM-
    ER, TEMPERANCE REFORMER)
Carmack, Edward Ward
Fisk, Clinton Bowen
Poling, Daniel Alfred
St. John, John Pierce
Wheeler, Wayne Bidwell
Wilson, Clarence True
Woolley, John Granville

PROMOTER (See also LAND PRO-
    MOTER, LECTURE PROMOTER,
    PRODUCER, SHOWMAN)
Addicks, John Edward
    O'Sullivan
Agnew, Cornelius Rea
Andrews, Israel DeWolf
Brady, Anthony Nicholas
Brown, Charlotte Emerson
Collier, Barron Gift
Durant, Henry
Fanning, Edmund
Flagler, Henry Morrison

Gates, John Warne
    ("Bet–you–a–million")
Goerz, David
Goldschmidt, Jakob
Green, Benjamin Edwards
Harrah, Charles Jefferson
Harvey, William Hope
Hatch, Rufus
Holladay, Ben
Holliday, Cyrus Kurtz
Hopkins, Edward Augustus
Hotchkiss, Horace Leslie
Hubbard, Gardiner Greene
Kearns, Jack
Law, Sallie Chapman Gordon
Lawrance, Uriah Marion
Moore, William Henry
Morgan, Anne
Morse, Charles Wyman
Patterson, John Henry
Penrose, Spencer
Perkins, Charles Callahan
Rankine, William Birch
Reed, James Hay
Rickard, George Lewis
Ryan, Thomas Fortune
Sanders, George Nicholas
Seiberling, Frank Augustus
Sheedy, Dennis
Sibley, Hiram
Smart, David Archibald
Smith, Junius
Smith, Robert Alexander C.
Thompson, Benjamin
Train, George Francis
Whalen, Grover Aloysius
Wharton, Richard
Wright, John Stephen

PROPAGANDIST (See also AGITA-
    TOR, REFORMER)
Bergh, Henry
Goldman, Emma
Kelley, Hall Jackson
Lovejoy, Owen Reed
Pomeroy, Marcus Mills
Viereck, George Sylvester

PROSPECTOR (See also MINER)
Broderick, David Colbreth
Fair, James Graham
Goold, William A.
La Ronde, Louis Denis, Sieur
    de
Marshall, James Wilson
Merritt, Leonidas
Osborn, Chase Salmon
Scott, Walter Edward

PROTESTANT SPOKESMAN
Lyman, Eugene William

PSYCHIATRIC HISTORIAN (See also
    HISTORIAN, PSYCHIATRIST)
Zilboorg, Gregory

PSYCHIATRIST (See also PSY-
    CHOANALYST, PSYCHOLOGIST,
    PHYSICIAN)
Anderson, Victor Vance
Babcock, James Woods
Barrett, Albert Moore
Briggs, Lloyd Vernon
Brush, Edward Nathaniel
Burrow, Trigant
Campbell, Charles Macfie
Clevenger, Shobal Vail

Dewey, Richard Smith
Earle, Pliny
Fisher, Theodore Willis
Fromm-Reichmann, Frieda
Gregory, Menas Sarkas
    Boulgourjian
Haviland, Clarence Floyd
Hinkle, Beatrice Moses
Hoch, August
Jones, William Parker
Kempster, Walter
Kerlin, Isaac Newton
Kirby, George Hughes
Little, Charles Sherman
Menninger, William Claire
Meyer, Adolf
Moore, (Austin) Merrill
Nichols, Charles Henry
Ray, Isaac
Rohé, George Henry
Sakel, Manfred Joshua
Salmon, Thomas William
Seguin, Edouard
Southard, Elmer Ernest
Spitzka, Edward Charles
White, William Alanson

PSYCHOANALYST (See also ALIE-
    NIST, PHYSICIAN, PSYCHIA-
    TRIST, PSYCHOLOGIST)
Alexander, Franz Gabriel
Brill, Abraham Arden
Brunswick, Ruth Mack
Coriat, Isador Henry
Dunbar, (Helen) Flanders
Fenichel, Otto
Fromm-Reichmann, Frieda
Hinkle, Beatrice Moses
Horney, Karen Danielssen
Jelliffe, Smith Ely
Oberndorf, Clarence Paul
Rapaport, David
Reik, Theodor
Roheim, Geza
Sachs, Hanns
Zilboorg, Gregory

PSYCHOLOGIST (See also ALIE-
    NIST, EDUCATOR, PHYSICIAN,
    PSYCHIATRIST, PSY-
    CHOANALYST, PSYCHOPATHOLO-
    GIST, PROFESSOR, SCHOLAR)
Allport, Gordon Willard
Angell, James Rowland
Baldwin, James Mark
Bingham, Walter Van Dyke
Boisen, Anton Theophilus
Boring, Edwin Garrigues
Burnham, William Henry
Cattell, James McKeen
Dodge, Raymond
Downey, June Etta
Farrand, Livingston
Franz, Shepherd Ivory
Fryer, Douglas Henry
Gesell, Arnold Lucius
Goddard, Henry Herbert
Guthrie, Edwin Ray, Jr.
Haggerty, Melvin Everett
Hall, Granville Stanley
Hollingworth, Leta Stetter
Holt, Edwin Bissell
Hull, Clark Leonard
Hyslop, James Hervey

James, William
Jastrow, Joseph
Johnson, Wendell Andrew
  Leroy
Judd, Charles Hubbard
Kagan, Henry Enoch
Koffka, Kurt
Köhler, Wolfgang
Ladd, George Trumbull
Ladd-Franklin, Christine
Lashley, Karl Spencer
Lewin, Kurt
McDougall, William
McHale, Kathryn
Marshall, Henry Rutgers
Maslow, Abraham H.
Münsterberg, Hugo
Newbold, William Romaine
Norsworthy, Naomi
Otis, Arthur Sinton
Pace, Edward Aloysius
Prince, Morton
Robinson, Edward Stevens
Rush, James
Sandford, Edmund Clark
Scott, Colin Alexander
Scott, Walter Dill
Seashore, Carl Emil
Smith, Theodate Louise
Starbuck, Edwin Diller
Strong, Charles Augustus
Terman, Lewis Madison
Thorndike, Edward Lee
Thurstone, Louis Leon
Titchener, Edward Bradford
Tolman, Edward Chace
Troland, Leonard Thompson
Warren, Howard Crosby
Washburn, Margaret Floy
Watson, John Broadus
Wertheimer, Max
Wolfe, Harry Kirke
PSYCHOPATHOLOGIST (See also AL-
  IENIST, PHYSICIAN, PSYCHIA-
  TRIST, PSYCHOANALYST,
  PSYCHOLOGIST)
Sidis, Boris
PSYCHOSOMATIC MOVEMENT LEAD-
  ER
Dunbar, (Helen) Flanders
PUBLIC ADMINISTRATOR
Abbott, Grace
Eastman, Joseph Bartlett
Hoover, Herbert Clark
PUBLIC ADVISER
Baruch, Bernard Mannes
PUBLIC AFFAIRS BROADCASTER
Murrow, Edward (Egbert)
  Roscoe
PUBLIC DEFENDER ADVOCATE
Goldman, Mayer C.
PUBLIC HEALTH ADMINISTRATOR
Baker, Sara Josephine
PUBLIC HEALTH EXPERT
Winslow, Charles-Edward
  Amory
PUBLIC HEALTH LEADER
Abbott, Samuel Warren
Beard, Mary
Emerson, Haven
Mahoney, John Friend
Price, George Moses

Ravenel, Mazyck Porcher
Rosenau, Milton Joseph
Smith, Stephen
Stiles, Charles Wardell
Strong, Richard Pearson
Walcott, Henry Pickering
PUBLIC HEALTH OFFICIAL (See
  also PHYSICIAN)
Banks, Charles Edward
Chapin, Charles Value
Copeland, Royal Samuel
Crumbine, Samuel Jay
Goldwater, Sigismund Schulz
Gunn, Selskar Michael
Park, William Hallock
Rose, Wickliffe
Sawyer, Wilbur Augustus
Snow, William Freeman
Wende, Ernest
PUBLICIST (See also EDITOR,
  NEWSAGENT, PAMPHLETEER)
Alford, Leon Pratt
Ames, Fisher
Applegate, Jesse
Balch, Thomas Willing
Barker, Wharton
Barrett, John
Bates, George Handy
Beck, James Montgomery
Beer, George Louis
Bement, Caleb N.
Bemis, George
Birkbeck, Morris
Bradford, Gamaliel
Carnegie, Andrew
Clark, Willis Gaylord
Cobbett, William
Cocke, John Hartwell
Cohn, Alfred A.
Cunliffe-Owen, Philip Frederick
Curtis, William Eleroy
Elliot, Jonathan
Fisher, Joshua Francis
Ford, Henry Jones
Francis, John Morgan
Frank, Glenn
Franklin, Fabian
Freeman, Joseph
Gilman, Daniel Colt
Gmeiner, John
Grimké, Archibald Henry
Grosvenor, William Mason
Haines, Lynn
Hannagan, Stephen Jerome
Hapgood, Norman
Harvey, William Hope
Hinman, George Wheeler
Holls, George Frederick
  William
House, Edward Howard
Hurd, John Codman
Ives, Levi Silliman
Jewett, William Cornell
Kapp, Friedrich
Knox, Dudley Wright
Kohler, Max James
Lea, Henry Charles
Lee, Henry, 1782–1867
Lee, Ivy Ledbetter
Lewis, Charlton Thomas
Lewis, Enoch
McCarthy, Charles

MacCauley, Clay
McElroy, Robert McNutt
Manly, Basil Maxwell
Marburg, Theodore
Marshall, Louis
Mason, Lucy Randolph
Michelson, Charles
Minor, Raleigh Colston
Murphy, Edgar Gardner
Myrick, Herbert
Nichols, Clarina Irene Howard
Opdyke, George
Otis, James
Pallen, Condé Benoist
Parker, Theodore
Peixotto, Benjamin Franklin
Pinchot, Amos Richards Eno
Plumbe, John
Preetorius, Emil
Puryear, Bennet
Rauch, John Henry
Revell, Nellie MacAleney
Richmond, John Wilkes
Ruml, Beardsley
Scott, Emmett Jay
Seelye, Julius Hawley
Spink, John George Taylor
Stoddard, Theodore Lothrop
Stokes, Anson Phelps
Storey, Moorfield
Straight, Willard Dickerman
Struve, Gustav
Sumner, William Graham
Trueblood, Benjamin Franklin
Tucker, Gilbert Milligan
Turnbull, Robert James
Upshur, Abel Parker
Van Hise, Charles Richard
Ward, Herbert Dickinson
Ward, William Hayes
Waterhouse, Sylvester
Wolf, Simon
Wood, Henry Alexander Wise
Woolsey, Theodore Salisbury
Wright, John Stephen
PUBLIC OFFICIAL
Akerman, Amos Tappan
Allen, George Venable
Anderson, Mary
Beall, Samuel Wootton
Bulfinch, Charles
Carter, Landon
Cotton, Joseph Potter
Crosby, John Schuyler
Davis, Dwight Filley
De Peyster, Abraham
Dickinson, John
Dimitry, Alexander
Dykstra, Clarence Addison
Earle, Edward Mead
Fagan, James Fleming
Fairlie, John Archibald
Gallagher, William Davis
Garfield, Harry Augustus
Graham, James
Greenleaf, Halbert Stevens
Hawley, Joseph
Henderson, Thomas
Hoan, Daniel Webster
Holten, Samuel
Huntington, Elisha
Ingersoll, Jared, 1722–1781

Jennings, John
Jones, Jesse Holman
Kirtland, Jared Potter
Lacey, John
Latrobe, John Hazlehurst
  Boneval
Lawrence, William Beach
Lewis, William Henry
Lowell, James Russell
Macy, Valentine Everit
Meigs, Josiah
Morrison, Delesseps Story
Moseley, Edward Augustus
Murray, Thomas Edward
Newberry, Truman Handy
Nicola, Lewis
Olds, Leland
Page, Thomas Walker
Paterson, John
Poydras, Julien de Lelande
Pynchon, John
Ricord, Frederick William
Roane, John Selden
Rolph, James
Roosevelt, Theodore
Smith, George Otis
Smith, Harold Dewey
Thacher, John Boyd
Thompson, David P.
Thornton, William
Vaux, Richard
Waite, Henry Matson
Walsh, Francis Patrick
Ware, Nathaniel A.
Wehle, Louis Brandeis
Whiting, William
Williams, John Skelton
Winston, Joseph
Woytinsky, Wladimir
  Savelievich
Wright, Carroll Davidson

**PUBLIC OPINION RESEARCH SPE-
  CIALIST**
Robinson, Claude Everett

PUBLIC RELATIONS COUNSEL
Byoir, Carl Robert
Hinshaw, David Schull

PUBLIC SPEAKING EXPERT
Carnegie, Dale

PUBLIC UTILITIES EXPERT
Cooley, Mortimer Elwyn
Couch, Harvey Crowley
Dow, Alex
Mitchell, Sidney Zollicoffer
Sloan, Matthew Scott

PUBLIC UTILITY EXECUTIVE
Carlisle, Floyd Leslie
Cortelyou, George Bruce
Doherty, Henry Latham
Insull, Samuel

PUBLIC WELFARE LEADER
Rumsey, Mary Harriman

**PUBLISHER (See also EDITOR,
  MAGAZINE PUBLISHER, NEWS-
  PAPER PUBLISHER)**
Adler, Elmer
Aiken, Andrew Jackson
Aitkin, Robert
Allen, Henry Justin
Appleton, Daniel
Appleton, William Henry
Appleton, William Worthen

Armstrong, Samuel Turell
Baird, Henry Carey
Baker, Peter Carpenter
Balestier, Charles Wolcott
Bancroft, Hubert Howe
Bardeen, Charles William
Barron, Clarence Walker
Barsotti, Charles
Bartlett, John
Beach, Sylvia Woodbridge
Beadle, Erastus Flavel
Bell, Robert
Bidwell, Walter Hilliard
Bladen, William
Bonfils, Frederick Gilmer
Bonner, Robert
Bowen, Abel
Bowen, Henry Chandler
Bowker, Richard Rogers
Brace, Donald Clifford
Bradford, Andrew
Bradford, Thomas
Bradford, William
Breckinridge, Desha
Brett, George Platt
Brewster, Osmyn
Bridgman, Herbert Lawrence
Brown, James
Bunce, Oliver Bell
Butler, Burridge Davenal
Butler, Simeon
Cameron, Andrew Carr
Capper, Arthur
Carey, Henry Charles
Carey, Mathew
Charless, Joseph
Childs, Aphas Grier
Childs, George William
Cist, Charles
Clarke, Robert
Collier, Peter Fenelon
Cook, Robert Johnson
Covici, Pascal ("Pat")
Crocker, Uriel
Currier, Nathaniel
Curtis, Cyrus Hermann
  Kotzschmar
Day, George Parmly
Delavan, Edward Cornelius
De Young, Michel Harry
Dodd, Frank Howard
Doran, George Henry
Doubleday, Frank Nelson
Doubleday, Nelson
Draper, Margaret Green
Dworshak, Henry Clarence
Ellmaker, (Emmett) Lee
Estes, Dana
Everett, Robert
Field, Marshall, III
Field, Marshall, IV
Fields, James Thomas
Fitzgerald, Thomas
Ford, Daniel Sharp
Francis, Charles Stephen
Funk, Isaac Kauffman
Funk, Wilfred John
Gannett, Frank Ernest
Gernsback, Hugo
Ginn, Edwin
Glass, Franklin Potts
Godey, Louis Antoine

Gonzales, Ambrose Elliott
Goodrich, Samuel Griswold
Gowans, William
Graham, George Rex
Graham, Philip Leslie
Grasty, Charles Henry
Greenslet, Ferris
Griscom, Lloyd Carpenter
Grosset, Alexander
Guinzburg, Harold Kleinert
Gunter, Archibald Clavering
Haldeman-Julius, Emanuel
Harcourt, Alfred
Harding, Jesper
Harding, William White
Harper, Fletcher
Harper, James
Harris, Benjamin
Harris, Julian La Rose
Hart, Abraham
Haynes, Williams
Heard, Dwight Bancroft
Hearst, William Randolph
Helmer, Bessie Bradwell
Hill, David Jayne
Hitchcock, Gilbert Monell
Hobby, William Pettus
Holt, Henry
Houghton, Henry Oscar
Huebsch, Benjamin W.
Humphreys, James
Hunt, Freeman
Jackson, Charles Samuel
Jewett, John Punchard
Jones, George
Judd, Orange
Kenedy, Patrick John
Kiplinger, Willard Monroe
Kline, George
Klopch, Louis
Knapp, Joseph Palmer
Kneeland, Samuel
Knopf, Blanche Wolf
Kohlberg, Alfred
Kollock, Shepard
Lange, Louis
Langlie, Arthur Bernard
Lea, Henry Charles
Lea, Isaac
Leslie, Frank
Leslie, Miriam Florence Folline
Leypoldt, Frederick
Lippincott, Joshua Ballinger
Littell, Eliakim
Little, Charles Coffin
Liveright, Horace Brisbin
Longley, Alcander
Lothrop, Daniel
Loudon, Samuel
Luce, Henry Robinson
McClurg, Alexander Caldwell
McCook, Anson George
McElrath, Thomas
Macfadden, Bernarr
McGraw, James Herbert
McIntyre, Alfred Robert
McLean, William Lippard
Macrae, John
McRae, Milton Alexander
Marble, Manton Malone
Marquis, Albert Nelson
Mattson, Hans

Maxwell, William
Melcher, Frederic Gershom
Meredith, Edna C. Elliott
Meredith, Edwin Thomas
Merriam, Charles
Miller, John Henry
Mitchell, Samuel Augustus
Moody, John
Moreau de Saint-Méry,
   Médéric-Louis-Élie
Morwitz, Edward
Mosher, Thomas Bird
Munn, Orson Desaix
Munro, George
Munsey, Frank Andrew
Murphy, John
Myrick, Herbert
Nieman, Lucius William
Norman, John
Norton, William Warder
Oliver, George Tener
Parks, William
Patterson, Alicia
Peterson, Charles Jacobs
Pittock, Henry Lewis
Plimpton, George Arthur
Polock, Moses
Pomeroy, Marcus Mills
Poulson, Zachariah
Prang, Louis
Pulitzer, Joseph, Jr.
Putnam, Eben
Putnam, George Haven
Putnam, George Palmer
Redfield, Justus Starr
Revell, Fleming Hewitt
Rice, Edwin Wilbur
Ridder, Herman
Rinehart, Stanley Marshall, Jr.
Root, Frank Albert
Rossiter, William Sidney
Rowell, George Presbury
Rudge, William Edwin
Ruffin, Edmund
Sadlier, Denis
Sartain, John
Saxton, Eugene Francis
Scherman, Harry
Schuster, Max Lincoln
Scribner, Charles, 1821–1871
Scribner, Charles, 1854–1930
Scribner, Charles, 1890–1952
Scripps, Edward Wyllis
Scripps, James Edmund
Sears, Robert
Shuster, W(illiam) Morgan
Silverman, Sime
Simon, Richard Leo
Singerly, William Miskey
Smith, Lloyd Pearsall
Smith, Ormond Gerald
Smith, Roswell
Sower, Christopher, 1693–1758
Sower, Christopher, 1721–1784
Sower, Christopher, 1754–1799
Stahlman, Edward Bushrod
Stephens, Edwin William
Stoddart, Joseph Marshall
Stokes, Frederick Abbot
Stone, David Marvin
Strong, Walter Ansel
Taft, Charles Phelps

Tammen, Harry Heye
Thomas, Robert Bailey
Thompson, John
Ticknor, William Davis
Trow, John Fowler
Tyson, Lawrence Davis
Van Nostrand, David
Vick, James
Victor, Orville James
Walker, John Brisben
Watson, John Fanning
Williams, William
Wilson, Halsey William
Wilson, John Lockwood
Wilson, William
Wolff, Kurt August Paul
Wood, Samuel
Woodruff, William Edward
Wyeth, John
Yeager, Joseph
Young, Lafayette
Ziff, William Bernard
PUGILIST (See also ATHLETE, BOX-
   ER)
Corbett, James John
Fitzsimmons, Robert
   Prometheus
Heenan, John Carmel
Morrissey, John
Sullivan, John Lawrence
PUPPETEER
Sarg, Tony
PUZZLEMAKER
Kingsley, Elizabeth Seelman

QUAKER HISTORIAN (See also
   CLERGYMAN, *Quaker*)
Jones, Rufus Matthew

RACEHORSE OWNER
Sloane, Isabel Cleves Dodge
RACE RELATIONS EXPERT
Alexander, Will Winton
Haynes, George Edmund
RACING CAR DRIVER
De Palma, Ralph
RACING-NEWS ENTREPRENEUR
Annenberg, Moses Louis
RACING OFFICIAL
Cassidy, Marshall Whiting
RACKETEER (See also BOOTLEG-
   GER, CRIMINAL, GANSTER, OR-
   GANIZED CRIME LEADER)
Luciano, Charles ("Lucky")
Madden, Owen Victor
   ("Owney")
RACONTEUR (See also HUMORIST,
   LECTURER, READER, WIT)
Beckwourth, James P.
King, Alexander
RADICAL (See also AGITATOR, IN-
   SURGENT, REVOLUTIONIST, SO-
   CIALIST ADVOCATE)
Chaplin, Ralph Hosea
Gurowski, Adam
Mahler, Herbert
Steuben, John
Stokes, Rose Harriet Pastor
RADIO ANNOUNCER
Brokenshire, Norman Ernest
Husing, Edward Britt ("Ted")
McNamee, Graham

RADIO BROADCASTER
Bryson, Lyman Lloyd
Denny, George Vernon, Jr.
Murrow, Edward (Egbert)
   Roscoe
RADIO COMMENTATOR
Carter, Boake
Davis, Elmer Holmes
Gibbons, Floyd
Hill, Edwin Conger
Kaltenborn, Hans Von
Lewis, Fulton, Jr.
Woollcott, Alexander
   Humphreys
RADIO COMMUNICATIONS PIONEER
Fessenden, Reginald Aubrey
RADIOGRAPHER (See also PHYSI-
   CIAN, RADIOLOGIST, ROENT-
   GENOLOGIST)
Kolle, Frederick Strange
RADIOLOGIST (See also PHYSICIAN,
   ROENTGENOLOGIST)
Coutard, Henri
Hirsch, Isaac Seth
Pancoast, Henry Khunrath
Pfahler, George Edward
RADIO PERSONALITY
Adams, Franklin Pierce
Allen, Fred
Allen, Gracie
Burns, Bob
Kilgallen, Dorothy Mae
Revell, Nellie MacAleney
Woollcott, Alexander
   Humphreys
RADIO SPORTSCASTER
McCarthy, Charles Louis
   ("Clem")
RAILROAD BUILDER
Allen, Thomas
Andrews, Chauncey Hummason
Barnum, Zenus
Brice, Calvin Stewart
Crocker, Alvah
Crocker, Charles
Davis, Henry Gassaway
Dillon, Sidney
Donovan, John Joseph
Drake, Francis Marion
Durant, Thomas Clark
Evans, John
Farnam, Henry
Grant, John Thomas
Holdrege, George Ward
Holliday, Cyrus Kurtz
Joy, James Frederick
Judah, Theodore Dehone
Keith, Minor Cooper
Kerens, Richard C.
Litchfield, Electus Backus
McDonald, John Bartholomew
Martin, William Thompson
Mason, Claibourne Rice
Meiggs, Henry
Mitchell, Alexander
Packer, Asa
Price, Thomas Lawson
Robinson, Albert Alonzo
Rose, Chauncey
Scullin, John
Stanford, Leland
Stickney, Alpheus Beede

Stone, Amasa
Welch, Charles Clark
Winslow, Edward Francis
RAILROAD ENGINEER
Cohen, Mendes
Fink, Albert
Pearson, Edward Jones
Schuyler, James Dix
Spencer, Samuel
RAILROAD EXECUTIVE
Ashe, William Shepperd
Atterbury, William Wallace
Baer, George Frederick
Baldwin, William Henry
Bernet, John Joseph
Billings, Frederick
Bishop, William Darius
Boorman, James
Borden, Richard
Bridgers, Robert Rufus
Brown, William Carlos
Budd, Ralph
Burrall, William Porter
Callaway, Samuel Rodger
Cameron, James Donald
Cass, George Washington
Cassatt, Alexander Johnston
Clark, Horace Francis
Clement, Martin Withington
Clifford, John Henry
Clough, William Pitt
Colby, Gardner
Corbin, Austin
Corbin, Daniel Chase
Cowen, John Kissig
Depew, Chauncey Mitchell
Devereux, John Henry
Drayton, Thomas Fenwick
Dudley, Edward Bishop
Echols, John
Fink, Albert
Fish, Stuyvesant
Gadsden, James
Garrett, John Work
Gordon, William Washington
Gould, George Jay
Gowen, Franklin Benjamin
Gray, Carl Raymond
Harahan, James Theodore
Harahan, William Johnson
Harriman, Edward Henry
Harrington, Samuel Maxwell
Harrison, Fairfax
Hayne, Robert Young
Hill, James Jerome
Hine, Charles de Lano
Holden, Hale
Houston, Henry Howard
Hubbard, Thomas Hamlin
Huntington, Collis Potter
Huntington, Henry Edwards
Ingalls, Melville Ezra
Jeffers, William Martin
Jeffrey, Edward Turner
Jewett, Hugh Judge
Johnston, John Taylor
Jones, Frank
King, John Pendleton
Kirkman, Marshall Monroe
Kneass, Strickland
Lord, Eleazar
Loree, Leonor Fresnel

Lovett, Robert Scott
Lucas, James H.
McCullough, John Griffith
McKennan, Thomas McKean
 Thompson
Mahone, William
Markham, Charles Henry
Mellen, Charles Sanger
Merrick, Samuel Vaughan
Messler, Thomas Doremus
Minty, Robert Horatio George
Negley, James Scott
Newman, William H.
Oakes, Thomas Fletcher
Ogden, William Butler
Olyphant, Robert Morrison
Osborn, William Henry
Palmer, William Jackson
Parsons, Lewis Baldwin
Payne, Henry Clay
Pearson, Edward Jones
Perham, Josiah
Perkins, Charles Elliott
Peters, Richard, 1810–1889
Plumbe, John
Poor, John Alfred
Porter, Horace
Preble, William Pitt
Randolph, Epes
Rea, Samuel
Rice, Edmund
Ripley, Edward Payson
Robb, James
Roberts, George Brooke
Sayre, Robert Heysham
Scott, Thomas Alexander
Scott, William Lawrence
Sewell, William Joyce
Shonts, Theodore Perry
Sloan, Samuel
Smith, Alfred Holland
Smith, John Gregory
Smith, Milton Hannibal
Spencer, Samuel
Sproule, William
Stahlman, Edward Bushrod
Stephens, John Lloyd
Stevens, John Frank
Stewart, Robert Marcellus
Strong, William Barstow
Thomas, John Wilson
Thompson, Arthur Webster
Thomson, Frank
Thomson, John Edgar
Thornton, Henry Worth
Underwood, Frederick Douglas
Vanderbilt, William Henry
Van Horne, William Cornelius
Van Sweringen, Mantis James
Vibbard, Chauncey
Wallace, John Findley
Walters, William Thompson
Willard, Daniel
Worcester, Edwin Dean
Wright, Charles Barston
Yeager, Joseph
Yoakum, Benjamin Franklin
Young, Robert Ralph
Zimmerman, Eugene
RAILROAD EXPERT
Adams, Charles Francis
Allen, William Frederick

Reagan, John Henninger
RAILROAD OWNER
James, Arthur Curtiss
Morgan, Charles
Starin, John Henry
RAILROAD PROMOTER (See also
 PROMOTER)
Ames, Oliver
Andrews, Alexander Boyd
Brewster, James
Brown, George
Burke, Stevenson
Chapin, Chester William
Corbett, Henry Winslow
Diven, Alexander Samuel
Guthrie, James
Hardy, William Harris
Jackson, William, 1783–1855
Law, George
Le Duc, William Gates
Loveland, William Austin
 Hamilton
Paine, Charles
Rice, Edmund
Thomas, Philip Evan
Vanderbilt, Cornelius,
 1794–1877
Villard, Henry
Whitney, Asa
Yulee, David Levy
RANCHER (See also COWBOY, CAT-
 TLEMAN, RANGER, STOCK
 BREEDER)
Ammons, Elias Milton
Haggin, James Ben Ali
Jardine, William Marion
Kendrick, John Benjamin
Maxwell, Lucien Bonaparte
RANGER (See also RANCHER)
McNeill, John Hanson
Mosby, John Singleton
Rogers, Robert
Wallace, William Alexander
 Anderson
RARE BOOK DEALER (See also BIB-
 LIOPHILE)
Rosenbach, Abraham Simon
 Wolf
Rosenbach, Philip Hyman
READER (See also LECTURER,
 RACONTEUR)
Kemble, Frances Anne
Riddle, George Peabody
READING DEVELOPMENT EXPERT
Gray, William Scott, Jr.
REAL-ESTATE DEVELOPER
Chandler, Harry
REAL-ESTATE OPERATOR (See also
 LAND AGENT)
Binga, Jesse
Bloom, Sol
Bowes, Edward J.
Hanson, Ole
Heckscher, August
Marling, Alfred Erskine
Morgenthau, Henry
Palmer, Potter
Savage, Henry Wilson
Wright, John Stephen
REALTOR
De Priest, Oscar Stanton

REBEL (See also AGITATOR, INSUR-
   GENT, RADICAL, REVOLUTION-
   IST)
Ingle, Richard
Vesey, Denmark
REFORMER (See also AGITATOR,
   FEMINIST, HUMANITARIAN,
   PEACE ADVOCATE, POLITICAL
   REFORMER, PRISON REFORM-
   ER, PROHIBITIONIST, PROPA-
   GANDIST, SOCIAL REFORMER,
   TEMPERANCE REFORMER)
Allen, Zachariah
Andrews, Stephen Pearl
Angell, George Thorndike
Anthony, Susan Brownell
Appleton, James
Ballou, Adin
Barrows, Samuel June
Beecher, Catharine Esther
Bishop, Robert Hamilton
Blackwell, Antoinette Louisa
   Brown
Blake, Lillie Devereux
Bloomer, Amelia Jenks
Boissevain, Inez Milholland
Bolton, Sarah Knowles
Bonney, Charles Carroll
Bright Eyes
Brooks, John Graham
Brown, William Wells
Bruce, William Cabell
Burleigh, George Shepard
Burleigh, William Henry
Burritt, Elihu
Cabet, Étienne
Cannon, Ida Maud
Chapman, Maria Weston
Cheever, George Barrell
Cheney, Ednah Dow Littlehale
Cleghorn, Sarah Norcliffe
Collier, John
Colver, Nathaniel
Comstock, Anthony
Coxey, Jacob Sechler
Crandall, Prudence
Dall, Caroline Wells Healey
Delavan, Edward Cornelius
Dewey, Melvil
Dike, Samuel Warren
Dinwiddie, Edwin Courtland
Donnelly, Ignatius
Dorr, Thomas Wilson
Easley, Ralph Montgomery
Eastman, Joseph Bartlett
Eddy, Thomas
Ely, Richard Theodore
Evans, Frederick William
Evans, George Henry
Farnam, Henry Walcott
Ferguson, William Porter
   Frisbee
Field, David Dudley
Filene, Edward Albert
Flower, Benjamin Orange
Fussell, Bartholomew
Gage, Frances Dana Barker
Gales, Joseph
Garrison, William Lloyd
George, Henry
Giesler-Anneke, Mathilde
   Franziska

Goodell, William
Gould, Elgin Ralston Lovell
Graham, Sylvester
Green, Beriah
Green, Frances Harriet
   Whipple
Griffing, Josephine Sophie
   White
Grimké, Thomas Smith
Hall, Bolton
Hapgood, Norman
Harriman, Florence Jaffray
   Hurst
Hastings, Samuel Dexter
Hepburn, William Peters
Higginson, Thomas Wentworth
Himes, Joshua Vaughan
Holbrook, Josiah
Hooker, Isabella Beecher
Howe, Frederic Clemson
Howe, Julia Ward
Howland, Emily
Hunt, Harriot Kezia
Ivins, William Mills
Jay, William
Johnson, Magnus
Jones, Samuel Milton
Kellor, Frances (Alice)
Kynett, Alpha Jefferson
Lay, Benjamin
Leavitt, Joshua
Lewelling, Lorenzo Dow
Livermore, Mary Ashton Rice·
Loomis, Arphaxed
Lowell, Josephine Shaw
Luther, Seth
McCann, Alfred Watterson
Marsh, John
Masquerier, Lewis
Matthews, Joseph Brown
Matthews, Nathan
Mattison, Hiram
May, Samuel Joseph
Mead, Edwin Doak
Mifflin, Warner
Moss, Frank
Mott, James
Mott, Lucretia Coffin
Murphey, Archibald de Bow
Myers, Gustavus
Nichols, Clarina Irene Howard
Nichols, Mary Sargeant Neal
   Gove
Noyes, John Humphrey
Opdyke, George
O'Sullivan, Mary Kenney
Parkhurst, Charles Henry
Pennypacker, Elijah Funk
Philips, Martin Wilson
Phillips, Wendell
Pierpont, John
Pillsbury, Parker
Polk, Frank Lyon
Post, Louis Freeland
Poznanski, Gustavus
Price, Eli Kirk
Quincy, Edmund
Quincy, Josiah, 1772–1864
Rambaut, Mary Lucinda
   Bonney
Rantoul, Robert, 1778–1858
Rantoul, Robert, 1805–1852

Riis, Jacob August
Ripley, George
Rose, Ernestine Louise
   Siismondi Potowski
Rose, John Carter
Russell, Charles Edward
Sanders, Elizabeth Elkins
Saunders, Prince
Scott, Colin Alexander
Scott, Walter
Seidel, George Lukas Emil
Shaw, Albert
Shaw, Anna Howard
Sherwood, Katharine Margaret
   Brownlee
Sims, William Sowden
Smith, Elizabeth Oakes Prince
Smith, Fred Burton
Smith, Gerrit
Smith, Hannah Whitall
Spargo, John
Spencer, Anna Garlin
Spingarn, Joel Elias
Spreckels, Rudolph
Stanton, Elizabeth Cady
Stanton, Henry Brewster
Steffens, Lincoln
Sterne, Simon
Still, William
Stone, Lucy
Straton, John Roach
Sunderland, Eliza Jane Read
Swallow, Silas Comfort
Swisshelm, Jane Grey Cannon
Sylvis, William H.
Thomas, Norman Mattoon
Tutwiler, Julia Strudwick
Villard, Helen Frances Garrison
Villard, Oswald Garrison
Ward, Henry Dana
Warren, Josiah
Weber, Henry Adam
Whipple, Henry Benjamin
White, Alfred Tredway
Wiley, Harvey Washington
Willard, Frances Elizabeth
   Caroline
Woodhull, Victoria Claflin
Woods, Robert Archey
Wright, Elizur
Wright, Frances
REGICIDE
Dixwell, John
Goffe, William
Whalley, Edward
REGIONAL PLANNER
Behrendt, Walter Curt
RELIEF ORGANIZER
Morgan, Anne
RELIGIOUS ACTIVIST
Robins, Raymond
RELIGIOUS LEADER (See also AR-
   CHABBOT, ARCHBISHOP, BISH-
   OP, CABALIST, CHAPLAIN,
   CHRISTIAN SCIENCE LEADER,
   CLERGYMAN, EVANGELIST, IN-
   DIAN PROPHET, METAPHYSI-
   CIAN, MISSIONARY, MYSTIC,
   REVIVALIST, SPIRITUALIST,
   THEOLOGIAN, THEOSOPHIST,
   TRANSCENDENTALIST
Abbott, Benjamin

Adler, Cyrus
Adler, Felix
Albright, Jacob
Antes, Henry
Backus, Isaac
Bowne, John
Coe, George Albert
Coffin, Henry Sloane
Cox, Henry Hamilton
Dittemore, John Valentine
Divine, Father
Drexel, Katharine Mary
Eddy, Mary Morse Baker
Haven, Henry Philemon
Hodur, Francis
Hutchinson, Anne
Ivins, Anthony Woodward
Jones, Abner
McKay, David Oman
Metz, Christian
Middleton, Arthur
Mills, Benjamin Fay
Morris, Anthony, 1654–1721
Norris, Isaac, 1701–1766
Osgood, Jacob
Poznanski, Gustavus
Pratt, Orson
Rapp, George
Russell, Charles Taze
Rutherford, Joseph Franklin
Sharpless, Isaac
Skaniadariio
Smith, George Albert
Smith, Uriah
Thomas, Richard Henry
Tobias, Channing Heggie
Wilkinson, Jemima
Wood, James
Woolman, John
REMONSTRANT
Child, Robert
RESETTLEMENT EXPERT
Rosen, Joseph A.
RESTAURANT CRITIC
Hines, Duncan
RESTAURATEUR
Delmonico, Lorenzo
Kohlsaat, Herman Henry
Sardi, Melchiorre Pio Vencenzo
("Vincent")
Sherry, Louis
Stevens, Frank Mozley
REVIVALIST (See also EVANGELIST,
RELIGIOUS LEADER)
Alline, Henry
Finney, Charles Grandison
Kirk, Edward Norris
Wormley, James
REVOLUTIONARY HEROINE (See
HEROINE)
REVOLUTIONARY LEADER (See also
PATRIOT, REVOLUTIONARY PA-
TRIOT, SOLDIER, STATESMAN)
Benson, Egbert
Carroll, Charles
Chase, Samuel
Drayton, William Henry
Gadsden, Christopher
Hanson, John
Hindman, William
Hobart, John Sloss
Houston, William Churchill

Houstoun, John
Huger, Isaac
Huger, John
Johnston, Samuel
Jones, Willie
Person, Thomas
Scott, John Morin
Sears, Isaac
Tilghman, Matthew
REVOLUTIONARY PATRIOT (See also
PATRIOT, REVOLUTIONARY
LEADER, SOLDIER)
Alexander, Abraham
Arnold, Benedict
Arnold, Jonathan
Banister, John
Bartlett, Josiah
Cabell, William
Frelinghuysen, Frederick
Habersham, Joseph
Harvie, John
Howell, Richard
Howley, Richard
Izard, Ralph
Jones, Noble Wymberley
Jouett, John
Lamb, John
Leaming, Thomas
Lewis, Andrew
Lewis, Fielding
Livingston, Robert R.,
1718–1775
Marshall, Christopher
Mason, Thomson
Matlock, Timothy
Mercer, James
Milledge, John
Moore, Maurice
Moore, William, 1735–1793
Nicholas, Robert Carter
Nixon, John, 1733–1808
Page, John
Parsons, Samuel Holden
Peabody, Nathaniel
Pendleton, Edmund
Peters, Richard, 1744–1828
Pettit, Charles
Roberdeau, Daniel
Sands, Comfort
Smith, Robert, 1732–1801
Thornton, Matthew
Tyler, John, 1747–1813
Warren, Joseph
Weare, Meshech
Whipple, William
Yates, Abraham
Yates, Robert
Young, Thomas
REVOLUTIONIST (See also AGITA-
TOR, INSURGENT, RADICAL)
Hecker, Friedrich Karl Franz
Heinzen, Karl Peter
Lee, Francis Lightfoot
Rapp, Wilhelm
Reed, John, 1887–1920
Sanders, George Nicholas
Wharton, William H.
RHEUMATOLOGIST (See also PHYSI-
CIAN)
Hench, Philip Showalter

RHINOLOGIST (See also PHYSICIAN)
Jarvis, William Chapman
ROAD BUILDER
Mears, Otto
Mullan, John
ROCKET PIONEER
Goddard, Robert Hutchings
ROCKET SCIENTIST
Ley, Willy
ROENTGENOLOGIST (See also
PHYSICIAN, RADIOGRAPHER,
RADIOLOGIST)
Baetjer, Frederick Henry
Brown, Percy
Caldwell, Eugene Wilson
Williams, Francis Henry
ROWING CHAMPION (See also
OARSMAN)
Kelly, John Brendan
ROWING COACH (See also ATH-
LETE, OARSMAN)
Cook, Robert Johnson
Courtney, Charles Edward

SAILMAKER
Forten, James
SAILOR (See MARINER)
SALVAGE EXPERT
Merritt, Israel John
SALVATION ARMY GENERAL
Booth, Evangeline Cory
SANITARIAN (See also ENGINEER,
SANITARY)
Carter, Henry Rose
Freeman, Allen Weir
Gorgas, William Crawford
Harrington, Charles
Harris, Elisha
Jones, Joseph
Jordan, Edwin Oakes
Kedzie, Robert Clark
Logan, Thomas Muldrup,
1808–1876
McCormack, Joseph Nathaniel
Magruder, George Lloyd
Richards, Ellen Henrietta
Swallow
Souchon, Edmond
SATIRIST (See also HUMORIST,
WIT)
Alsop, Richard
Hopkins, Lemuel
Locke, David Ross
Smith, Seba
Snelling, William Joseph
Wright, Robert William
SAXOPHONIST
Gray, Glen
SCENARIST
Beach, Rex
SCHOLAR (See also ARCHAEOLO-
GIST, ASSYRIOLOGIST, CLASSI-
CIST, EGYPTOLOGIST,
GENEALOGIST, GRAMMARIAN,
HEBRAIST, HELLENIST, LOGI-
CIAN, ORIENTALIST, PHILOLO-
GIST, PHILOSOPHER, SEMITIST,
SINOLOGUE)
Abbot, Ezra
Abbott, Frank Frost
Adams, Jasper
Allen, Frederic de Forest

Allen, William Francis
Anderson, Henry Tompkins
Anthon, Charles
Baylies, Francis
Beck, Charles
Beeson, Charles Henry
Bennett, Charles Edwin
Biddle, Nicholas
Bliss, Tasker Howard
Botta, Vincenzo
Carter, Jesse Benedict
Chase, Thomas
Clinton, DeWitt
Coe, George Albert
Cook, Albert Stanburrough
Crane, Thomas Frederick
Cross, Wilbur Lucius
Curme, George Oliver
Currier, Charles Warren
Curtin, Jeremiah
Dargan, Edwin Preston
Davidson, Thomas
Dennison, Walter
D'Ooge, Martin Luther
Dowling, Noel Thomas
Dunbar, (Helen) Flanders
Dyer, Louis
Edgren, August Hjalmar
Eliot, Samuel
Fay, Edwin Whitefield
Felton, Cornelius Conway
Fenollosa, Ernest Francisco
Fletcher, Robert
Frothingham, Arthur Lincoln
Furness, Horace Howard,
  1833–1912
Furness, Horace Howard,
  1865–1930
Grandgent, Charles Hall
Green, William Henry
Griswold, Alfred Whitney
Gruening, Emil
Hale, William Gardner
Harkness, Albert
Haven, Joseph
Heilprin, Michael
Hirsch, Emil Gustav
Hohfeld, Wesley Newcomb
Holmes, George Frederick
Hudson, Henry Norman
Humphreys, Milton Wylie
Humphries, George Rolfe
Isaacs, Abram Samuel
Jastrow, Morris
Kaye, Frederick Benjamin
Kendrick, Asahel Clark
Knapp, William Ireland
Kohut, George Alexander
Lewis, William Draper
Lincoln, John Larkin
Logan, James, 1674–1751
MacLean, George Edwin
Malter, Henry
Margolis, Max Leopold
Marsh, George Perkins
Mather, Cotton
Matthiessen, Francis Otto
Merrill, Elmer Truesdell
Miller, Perry Gilbert Eddy
Mills, Lawrence Heyworth
Mitchell, Hinckley Gilbert
  Thomas

Monis, Judah
Moore, Clement Clarke
Murphy, Henry Cruse
Newell, William Wells
O'Brien, Justin
Perrin, Bernadotte
Perry, Thomas Sergeant
Pinto, Isaac
Platner, Samuel Ball
Prince, Thomas
Richardson, Rufus Byam
Rorimer, James Joseph
Schinz, Albert
Schofield, William Henry
Schuyler, Eugene
Scott, Samuel Parsons
Shipman, Andrew Jackson
Soldan, Frank Louis
Solger, Reinhold
Sprecher, Samuel
Stiles, Ezra
Sulzberger, Mayer
Tait, Charles
Taylor, Hannis
Thomas, Calvin
Thorndike, Ashley Horace
Tolman, Herbert Cushing
Torrey, Charles Cutler
Trent, William Peterfield
Updike, Daniel Berkeley
Van der Kemp, Francis Adrian
Van Dyck, Cornelius van Alen
Viel, François Étienne Bernard
  Alexandre
Wallace, Charles William
Wallace, John William
Warren, Minton
Wiener, Leo
Wigmore, John Henry
Wilde, Richard Henry
Woolsey, Theodore Dwight
SCHOLAR (BIBLICAL)
Cone, Orello
Gregory, Caspar René
Hackett, Horatio Balch
Kent, Charles Foster
Mead, Charles Marsh
Mitchell, Edward Cushing
Moorehead, William Gallogly
Morgan, Abel
Norton, Andrews
Packard, Joseph
Paton, Lewis Boyles
Riddle, Matthew Brown
Ropes, James Hardy
Rosenberg, Abraham Hayyim
Sanders, Frank Knight
Sawyer, Leicester Ambrose
Smith, Henry Preserved
Smith, John Merlin Powis
Stevens, William Arnold
Strong, James
Stuart, Moses
Thayer, Joseph Henry
SCHOLAR (LAW)
Cook, Walter Wheeler
SCHOOL BUILDING SPECIALIST
Barrows, Alice Prentice
SCHOOLMASTER (See also EDUCA-
  TOR, TEACHER)
Coit, Henry Augustus
Dock, Christopher

Gould, Benjamin Apthorp
Gummere, John
Gunn, Frederick William
Keith, George
Ladd, Catherine
Lovell, James
Lovell, John
McCabe, William Gordon
Mazzuchelli, Samuel Charles
Morton, Charles
Nason, Elias
Peter, John Frederick
Pormort, Philemon
Truteau, Jean Baptiste
Williams, Nathanael
SCIENCE ADMINISTRATOR
Merriam, John Campbell
Ritter, William Emerson
SCIENCE HISTORIAN (See also HIS-
  TORIAN)
Thorndike, Lynn
SCIENTIFIC MANAGEMENT CON-
  SULTANT
Cooke, Morris Llewellyn
SCIENTIST (See also SPECIFIC
  SCIENCES)
Agassiz, Jean Louis Rodolphe
Alexander, John Henry
Alexander, William Dewitt
Allen, Zachariah
Arnold, Harold DeForest
Birdseye, Clarence
Brashear, John Alfred
Brewer, William Henry
Brooke, John Mercer
Caswell, Alexis
Clark, William Smith
Cleaveland, Parker
Cooper, Thomas
Dewey, Chester
Drake, Daniel
Dunbar, William
Durant, Charles Ferson
Eaton, Amos
Emerson, Rollins Adams
Eve, Joseph
Ferguson, Thomas Barker
Ferree, Clarence Errol
Folger, Walter
Franklin, Benjamin
Frazer, John Fries
Frazer, Persifor
Gibbes, Robert Wilson
Gillman, Henry
Greely, Adolphus Washington
Greenhow, Robert
Haldeman, Samuel Steman
Hallock, Charles
Hayes, John Lord
Herrick, Edward Claudius
Hewitt, Peter Cooper
Hill, Thomas
Himes, Charles Francis
Humphreys, Andrew Atkinson
Hyer, Robert Stewart
Jefferson, Thomas
Jeffries, John
Lapham, Increase Allen
LeConte, John
Lee, Charles Alfred
Locke, John
Mease, James

Mell, Patrick Hues
Michaelis, Leonor
Minot, George Richards
Mitchill, Samuel Latham
Morton, Henry
Oliver, Andrew
Olmsted, Denison
Palmer, Walter Walker
Peirce, Charles Sanders
Pliny, Earle Chase
Potamian, Brother
Priestley, Joseph
Rhoads, Cornelius Packard
Saugrain de Vigni, Antoine
    François
Schöpf, Johann David
Seybert, Adam
Sheppard, Samuel Edward
Simpson, Charles Torrey
Spillman, William Jasper
Squier, George Owen
Stallo, Johann Bernhard
Thompson, Samuel Rankin
Thomson, Elihu
Totten, Joseph Gilbert
Trowbridge, William Petit
Van Depoele, Charles Joseph
Wailes, Benjamin Leonard
    Covington
Westergaard, Harald Malcolm
Wilder, Russell Morse
Williamson, Hugh
Wright, Hamilton Kemp
SCOUT (See also GUIDE, FRON-
    TIERSMAN, PIONEER)
Bailey, Ann
Bridger, James
Burnham, Frederick Russell
Cody, William Frederick
Dixon, William
Grouard, Frank
Hamilton, William Thomas
Hickok, James Butler
Horn, Tom
Kelly, Luther Sage
McClellan, Robert
Navarre, Pierre
North, Frank Joshua
Reynolds, Charles Alexander
Sieber, Al
Stilwell, Simpson Everett
Stringfellow, Franklin
SCREENWRITER (See AUTHOR,
    DRAMATIST, WRITER)
SCULPTOR (See also ARTIST, MOD-
    ELER)
Adams, Herbert Samuel
Akers, Benjamin Paul
Amateis, Louis
Archipenko, Alexander
Augur, Hezekiah
Bailly, Joseph Alexis
Ball, Thomas
Barnard, George Grey
Bartholomew, Edward Sheffield
Bartlett, Paul Wayland
Bissell, George Edwin
Bitter, Karl Theodore Francis
Borglum, John Gutzon de la
    Mothe
Borglum, Solon Hannibal
Boyle, John J.

Brackett, Edward Augustus
Brenner, Victor David
Brooks, Richard Edwin
Browere, John Henri Isaac
Brown, Henry Kirke
Bush-Brown, Henry Kirke
Calder, Alexander Stirling
Calverley, Charles
Clarke, Thomas Shields
Clevenger, Shobal Vail
Cogdell, John Stevens
Connelly, Pierce Francis
Crawford, Thomas
Dallin, Cyrus Edwin
Davidson, Jo
Dexter, Henry
Diller, Burgoyne
Donoghue, John
Doyle, Alexander
Duveneck, Frank
Eakins, Thomas
Eckstein, John
Edmondson, William
Elwell, Frank Edwin
Epstein, Jacob
Ezekiel, Moses Jacob
Flannagan, John Bernard
Fraser, James Earle
Frazee, John
French, Daniel Chester
Garlick, Theodatus
Goldberg, Reuben Lucius
    ("Rube")
Gould, Thomas Ridgeway
Grafly, Charles
Greenough, Horatio
Greenough, Richard Saltonstall
Hart, Joel Tanner
Hartley, Jonathan Scott
Haseltine, James Henry
Hosmer, Harriet Goodhue
Hoxie, Vinnie Ream
Hughes, Robert Ball
Ives, Chauncey Bradley
Jackson, John Adams
Kemeys, Edward
Kingsley, Norman William
Lachaise, Gaston
Launitz, Robert Eberhard
    Schmidt von der
Lebrun, Federico ("Rico")
Lukeman, Henry Augustus
MacDonald, James Wilson
    Alexander
McKenzie, Robert Tait
MacMonnies, Frederick William
MacNeil, Hermon Atkins
Magonigle, Harold Van Buren
Manship, Paul Howard
Martiny, Philip
Mead, Larkin Goldsmith
Mears, Helen Farnsworth
Mestrovic, Ivan
Mills, Clark
Milmore, Martin
Mozier, Joseph
Mulligan, Charles J.
Nadelman, Elie
Newman, Barnett
Ney, Elisabet
Niehaus, Charles Henry
O'Donovan, William Rudolf

Palmer, Erastus Dow
Partridge, William Ordway
Perkins, Marion
Potter, Edward Clark
Potter, Louis McClellan
Powers, Hiram
Pratt, Bela Lyon
Putnam, Arthur
Quinn, Edmond Thomas
Remington, Frederic
Rimmer, William
Rinehart, William Henry
Roberts, Howard
Rogers, John, 1829–1904
Rogers, Randolph
Ruckstull, Frederick Wellington
Rumsey, Charles Cary
Rush, William
Saint-Gaudens, Augustus
Shrady, Henry Merwin
Simmons, Franklin
Smith, David Roland
Sterne, Maurice
Stone, Horatio
Story, William Wetmore
Taft, Lorado Zadoc
Thompson, Launt
Valentin, Edward Virginius
Volk, Leonard Wells
Ward, John Quincy Adams
Warner, Olin Levi
Whitney, Gertrude Vanderbilt
Whitney, Anne
Willard, Solomon
Young, Mahonri Mackintosh
Zorach, William
SEA CAPTAIN (See also MARINER,
    WHALING CAPTAIN)
Baker, Lorenzo Dow
Bertram, John
Boyle, Thomas
Brewer, Charles
Chever, James W.
Cobb, Elijah
Codman, John
Coggeshell, George
Creesy, Josiah Perkins
Crowninshield, George
Crowninshield, Jacob
Endicott, Charles Moses
Fanning, Edmund
Forbes, Robert Bennet
Godfrey, Benjamin
Harvey, Sir John
Heard, Augustine
Hunnewell, James
Malcolm, Daniel
Marshall, Charles Henry
Merry, William Lawrence
Morrell, Benjamin
Olmsted, Gideon
Palmer, Nathaniel Brown
Reid, Samuel Chester
Rogers, William Crowninshield
Shaler, William
Tompkins, Sally Louisa
Waterman, Robert H.
SECESSIONIST
Edwards, Weldon Nathaniel
Yancey, William Lowndes

SECRETARY
Thompson, Malvina Cynthia
SECRETARY OF AGRICULTURE (See
also AGRICULTURIST)
Colman, Norman Jay
Houston, David Franklin
Hyde, Arthur Mastick
Jardine, William Marion
Meredith, Edwin Thomas
Morton, Julius Sterling
Rusk, Jeremiah McClain
Wallace, Henry Agard
Wallace, Henry Cantwell
Wickard, Claude Raymond
Wilson, James
SECRETARY OF ARMY
Brucker, Wilber Marion
SECRETARY OF COMMERCE
Chapin, Roy Dikeman
Redfield, William Cox
Roper, Daniel Calhoun
Wallace, Henry Agard
SECRETARY OF DEFENSE (See also
SECRETARY OF WAR)
Forrestal, James Vincent
Johnson, Louis Arthur
Wilson, Charles Erwin
SECRETARY OF LABOR
Davis, James John
Mitchell, James Paul
Perkins, Frances
Schwellenbach, Lewis Baxter
Tobin, Maurice Joseph
Wilson, William Bauchop
SECRETARY OF NAVY
Badger, George Edmund
Chandler, William Eaton
Daniels, Josephus
Denby, Edwin
Dickerson, Mahlon
Dobbin, James Cochran
Edison, Charles
Forrestal, James Vincent
Hamilton, Paul
Henshaw, David
Herbert, Hilary Abner
Hunt, William Henry
Jones, William, 1760–1831
Kimball, Dan Able
Knox, Frank
Long, John Davis
Meyer, George von Lengerke
Morton, Paul
Preston, William Ballard
Robeson, George Maxwell
Smith, Robert, 1757–1842
Southard, Samuel Lewis
Stoddert, Benjamin
Swanson, Claude Augustus
Tracy, Benjamin Franklin
Upshur, Abel Parker
Welles, Gideon
Whitney, William Collins
Wilbur, Curtis Dwight
SECRETARY OF NAVY (CONFEDER-
ATE)
Mallory, Stephen Russell
SECRETARY OF STATE
Adams, John Quincy
Bacon, Robert
Bayard, Thomas Francis
Black, Jeremiah Sullivan

Blaine, James Gillespie
Bryan, William Jennings
Buchanan, James
Calhoun, John Caldwell
Cass, Lewis
Clay, Henry
Clayton, John Middleton
Colby, Bainbridge
Day, William Rufus
Dulles, John Foster
Evarts, William Maxwell
Everett, Edward
Fish, Hamilton
Forsyth, John
Foster, John Watson
Frelinghuysen, Frederick
Theodore
Gresham, Walter Quintin
Hay, John Milton
Herter, Christian Archibald
Hughes, Charles Evans
Hull, Cordell
Jay, John
Jefferson, Thomas
Kellogg, Frank Billings
Knox, Philander Chase
Lansing, Robert
Legaré, Hugh Swinton
Livingston, Edward
McLane, Louis
Madison, James
Marcy, William Learned
Marshall, John
Monroe, James
Olney, Richard
Pickering, Timothy
Randolph, Edmund, 1753–1813
Root, Elihu
Seward, William Henry
Sherman, John
Smith, Robert, 1757–1842
Stettinius, Edward Reilly
Stimson, Henry Lewis
Upshur, Abel Parker
Van Buren, Martin
Washburne, Elihu Benjamin
Webster, Daniel
SECRETARY OF STATE (CONFEDER-
ATE)
Benjamin, Judah Philip
Hunter, Robert Mercer
Taliaferro
SECRETARY OF THE INTERIOR
Ballinger, Richard Achilles
Bliss, Cornelius Newton
Browning, Orville Hickman
Chandler, Zachariah
Cox, Jacob Dolson
Delano, Columbus
Ewing, Thomas
Fall, Albert Bacon
Fisher, Walter Lowrie
Francis, David Rowland
Garfield, James Rudolph
Harlan, James
Hitchcock, Ethan Allen,
1835–1909
Ickes, Harold Le Clair
Kirkwood, Samuel Jordan
Lamar, Lucius Quintus
Cincinatus
Lane, Franklin Knight

McClelland, Robert
McKay, (James) Douglas
McKennan, Thomas McKean
Thompson
Noble, John Willock
Payne, John Barton
Schurz, Carl
Smith, Caleb Blood
Smith, Hoke
Stuart, Alexander Hugh
Holmes
Teller, Henry Moore
Thompson, Jacob
Usher, John Palmer
Vilas, William Freeman
West, Roy Owen
Wilbur, Ray Lyman
Work, Hubert
SECRETARY OF TREASURY
Campbell, George Washington
Carlisle, John Griffin
Chase, Salmon Portland
Corwin, Thomas
Dallas, Alexander James
Dix, John Adams
Ewing, Thomas
Fairchild, Charles Stebbins
Folger, Charles James
Forward, Walter
Gage, Lyman Judson
Gallatin, Abraham Alfonse
Albert
Glass, Carter
Guthrie, James
Hamilton, Alexander
Humphrey, George Magoffin
Ingham, Samuel Delucenna
McAdoo, William Gibbs
McCulloch, Hugh
MacVeagh, Franklin
Manning, Daniel
Mellon, Andrew William
Meredith, William Morris
Mills, Ogden Livingston
Morgenthau, Henry, Jr.
Morrill, Lot Myrick
Richardson, William Adams
Shaw, Leslie Mortier
Spencer, John Canfield
Taney, Roger Brooke
Thomas, Philip Francis
Vinson, Fred(erick) Moore
Walker, Robert John
Wolcott, Oliver
Woodbury, Levi
Woodin, William Hartman
SECRETARY OF TREASURY (CONFED-
ERATE)
Trenholm, George Alfred
SECRETARY OF WAR (See also
SECRETARY OF DEFENSE)
Alger, Russell Alexander
Baker, Newton Diehl
Belknap, William Worth
Calhoun, John Caldwell
Cameron, James Donald
Cameron, Simon
Crawford, William Harris
Davis, Dwight Filley
Dearborn, Henry
Dern, George Henry
Dickinson, Jacob McGavack

Elkins, Stephen Benton
Endicott, William
  Crowninshield
Floyd, John Buchanan
Garrison, Lindley Miller
Holt, Joseph
Knox, Henry
Lamont, Daniel Scott
Lincoln, Robert Todd
McHenry, James
Patterson, Robert Porter
Porter, Peter Buell
Proctor, Redfield
Ramsey, Alexander
Spencer, John Canfield
Stanton, Edwin McMasters
Stimson, Henry Lewis
Taft, Alphonso
Weeks, John Wingate
Wilkins, William
Woodring, Harry Hines
Wright, Luke Edward
SECRETARY OF WAR (CONFEDER-
  ATE)
  Benjamin, Judah Philip
SECURITIES EXPERT
  Stanley, Harold
SEEDSMAN (See also AGRICULTUR-
  IST)
  Thorburn, Grant
  Vick, James
SEGREGATIONIST LEADER
  Perez, Leander Henry
SEISMOLOGIST
  Tondorf, Francis Anthony
SEMITIST (See also SCHOLAR)
  Friedlaender, Israel
  Gottheil, Richard James
    Horatio
  Meyer, Martin Abraham
  Torrey, Charles Cutler
SENATOR
  Alcorn, James Lusk
  Allen, Philip
  Allen, William Vincent
  Anderson, Joseph
  Ashurst, Henry Fountain
  Atchison, David Rice
  Austin, Warren Robinson
  Bacon, Augustus Octavius
  Badger, George Edwin
  Bagby, Arthur Pendleton
  Bailey, Joseph Weldon
  Bailey, Josiah William
  Baker, Edward Dickinson
  Baldwin, Henry Porter
  Baldwin, Roger Sherman
  Bankhead, John Hollis
  Barkley, Alben William
  Barrett, Frank Aloysius
  Bartlett, Edward Lewis ("Bob")
  Barton, David
  Bayard, James Asheton
  Bayard, Richard Henry
  Bender, George Harrison
  Berry, George Leonard
  Berry, James Henderson
  Beveridge, Albert Jeremiah
  Bibb, George Mortimer
  Bigler, William
  Bilbo, Theodore Gilmore
  Bingham, Hiram

Blackburn, Joseph Clay Styles
Blaine, John James
Blease, Coleman Livingston
Blount, William
Bogy, Lewis Vital
Booth, Newton
Borah, William Edgar
Boreman, Arthur Ingram
Borland, Solon
Bourne, Jonathan
Bradbury, James Ware
Bradley, Stephen Row
Bradley, William O'Connell
Brainerd, Lawrence
Brewster, Ralph Owen
Brice, Calvin Stewart
Bridges, (Henry) Styles
Bristow, Joseph Little
Brookhart, Smith Wildman
Brown, Bedford
Brown, Benjamin Gratz
Brown, James
Brown, John
Bruce, Blanche K.
Bruce, William Cabell
Buckalew, Charles Rollin
Buckingham, William Alfred
Bulkeley, Morgan Gardner
Burnet, Jacob
Burr, Aaron
Burrows, Julius Caesar
Burton, Theodore Elijah
Butler, Marion
Butler, Matthew Calbraith
Butler, Pierce
Butler, William Pickens
Byrd, Harry Flood
Cabat, George
Caffery, Donelson
Camden, Johnson Newlon
Cameron, James Donald
Cameron, Simon
Campbell, George Washington
Capper, Arthur
Caraway, Hattie Ophelia Wyatt
Caraway, Thaddeus Horatius
Carlile, John Snyder
Carlisle, John Griffin
Carpenter, Matthew Hale
Carter, Thomas Henry
Case, Francis Higbee
Chamberlain, George Earle
Chandler, John
Chandler, William Eaton
Chandler, Zachariah
Chavez, Dennis
Chesnut, James
Christiancy, Isaac Peckham
Clark, Bennett Champ
Clark, William Andrews
Clarke, James Paul
Clay, Clement Claiborne
Clay, Clement Comer
Clay, Henry
Clemens, Jeremiah
Cobb, Howell
Cockrell, Francis Marion
Cohen, John Sanford
Coke, Richard
Collamer, Jacob
Colt, Le Baron Bradford
Conkling, Roscoe

Connally, Thomas Terry
  ("Tom")
Cooper, James
Copeland, Royal Samuel
Cordon, Guy
Corwin, Thomas
Costigan, Edward Prentiss
Couzens, James
Crane, Winthrop Murray
Crawford, William Harris
Curtis, Charles
Cutting, Bronson Murray
Daniel, John Warwick
Davis, Cushman Kellogg
Davis, Garret
Davis, Henry Gassaway
Davis, James John
Davis, Jeff
Dawes, Henry Laurens
Dawson, William Crosby
Depew, Chauncey Mitchell
De Wolf, James
Dickerson, Mahlon
Dirksen, Everett McKinley
Dodge, Augustus Caesar
Dodge, Henry
Dolph, Joseph Norton
Dorsey, Stephen Wallace
Douglas, Stephen Arnold
Downey, Sheridan
Drake, Charles Daniel
Dryden, John Fairfield
Duff, James Henderson
Du Pont, Henry Algernon
Dworshak, Henry Clarence
Edge, Walter Evans
Edmunds, George Franklin
Edwards, John
Edwards, Ninian
Elkins, Stephen Benton
Ellis, Powhatan
Elmore, Franklin Harper
Engle, Clair William Walter
Eppes, John Wayles
Ewing, Thomas
Fairbanks, Charles Warren
Fall, Albert Bacon
Felch, Alpheus
Felton, Rebecca Latimer
Fenton, Reuben Eaton
Ferris, Woodbridge Nathan
Ferry, Orris Sanford
Ferry, Thomas White
Fess, Simeon Davidson
Field, Richard Stockton
Fitzpatrick, Benjamin
Flanders, Ralph Edward
Fletcher, Duncan Upshaw
Foot, Samuel Augustus
Foote, Henry Stuart
Foraker, Joseph Benson
Foster, Ephraim Hubbard
Foster, Lafayette Sabine
Foster, Theodore
Fowler, Joseph Smith
Francis, John Brown
Franklin, Jesse
Frazier, Lynn Joseph
Frelinghuysen, Frederick
Frelinghuysen, Theodore
Frye, William Pierce
Gaillard, John

Gear, John Henry
George, James Zachariah
George, Walter Franklin
Geyer, Henry Sheffie
Gibson, Paris
Gillett, Frederick Huntington
Glass, Carter
Goldthwaite, George
Goodhue, Benjamin
Goodrich, Chauncey
Gordon, James
Gore, Thomas Pryor
Gorman, Arthur Pue
Grayson, William
Green, James Stephens
Green, Theodore Francis
Grimes, James Wilson
Grundy, Joseph Ridgway
Guffey, Joseph F.
Guggenheim, Simon
Hager, John Sharpenstein
Hale, Frederick
Hamilton, William Thomas
Hamlin, Hannibal
Hammond, James Henry
Hampton, Wade, 1818–1902
Hanna, Marcus Alonzo
Hannegan, Edward Allen
Hanson, Alexander Contee,
   1786–1819
Hardin, Martin D.
Hardwick, Thomas William
Harlan, James
Harris, William Alexander
Harrison, Byron Patton
Hastings, Daniel Oren
Hatch, Carl A.
Hawkins, Benjamin
Hawley, Joseph Roswell
Hayne, Robert Young
Hearst, George
Heflin, James Thomas
Henderson, John
Henderson, John Brooks
Hendricks, Thomas Andrews
Henry, John, 1750–1798
Hill, Joshua
Hill, Nathaniel Peter
Hindman, William
Hoar, George Frisbie
Holmes, John
Hopkins, Samuel, 1753–1819
Houston, George Smith
Howard, Jacob Merritt
Howe, Timothy Otis
Hull, Cordell
Hunt, Lester Callaway
Hunter, William
Hunton, Eppa
Ingalls, John James
Iverson, Alfred
Ives, Irving McNeil
Izard, Ralph
Jackson, Howell Edmunds
Jackson, James, 1757–1806
James, Charles Tillinghast
James, Ollie Murray
Johnson, Edwin Carl
Johnson, Hiram Warren
Johnson, Magnus
Johnston, Joseph Forney

Johnston, Olin DeWitt
   Talmadge
Jones, James Chamberlayne
Jones, James Kimbrough
Jones, John Percival
Jones, Wesley Livsey
Kefauver, (Carey) Estes
Kellogg, Frank Billings
Kellogg, William Pitt
Kendrick, John Benjamin
Kenna, John Edward
Kennedy, John Fitzgerald
Kennedy, Robert Francis
Kent, Joseph
Kenyon, William Squire
Kerr, Robert Samuel
Key, David McKendree
Kilgore, Harley Martin
King, John Pendleton
Kirkwood, Samuel Jordan
Knox, Philander Chase
Kyle, James Henderson
Lacock, Abner
Lad, Edwin Fremont
La Follette, Robert Marion
La Follette, Robert Marion, Jr.
Lamar, Lucius Quintus
   Cincinnatus
Lane, Henry Smith
Langer, William
Larrazolo, Octaviano Ambrosio
Latham, Milton Slocum
Laurence, John
Lea, Luke
Lehman, Herbert Henry
Leib, Michael
Lenroot, Irvine Luther
Lewis, Dixon Hall
Lewis, John Francis
Lindsay, William
Linn, Lewis Fields
Livermore, Samuel, 1732–1803
Lodge, Henry Cabot
Logan, George
Logan, John Alexander
Long, Huey Pierce
Lorimer, William
Lowrie, Walter
Lucas, Scott Wike
Lundeen, Ernest
McCarran, Patrick Anthony
McCarthy, Joseph Raymond
McComas, Louis Emory
McCormick, Joseph Medill
McCreary, James Bennett
McDill, James Wilson
McDuffie, George
McEnery, Samuel Douglas
McGrath, James Howard
McKean, Samuel
McKellar, Kenneth Douglas
McKinley, John
McKinley, William Brown
McLauren, Anselm Joseph
Maclay, Samuel
Maclay, William
McMillan, James
McNary, Charles Linza
Macon, Nathaniel
Manderson, Charles Frederick
Mangum, Willie Person
Marshall, Humphrey

Martin, Alexander
Martin, Thomas Staples
Mason, James Murray
Mason, Jonathan
Mason, Stevens Thomson
Mason, William Ernest
Maxey, Samuel Bell
Maybank, Burnet Rhett
Mead, James Michael
Meigs, Return Jonathan
Mellen, Prentiss
Metcalfe, Thomas
Milledge, John
Miller, John Franklin
Miller, Stephen Decatur
Miller, Warner
Mills, Roger Quarles
Minton, Sherman
Mitchell, John Hipple
Mitchell, Samuel Latham
Money, Hernando De Soto
Moody, (Arthur Edson) Blair
Moore, Andrew
Moore, Gabriel
Morehead, James Turner
Morgan, Edwin Denison
Morgan, John Tyler
Morril, David Lawrence
Morrill, Justin Smith
Morrill, Lot Myrick
Morris, Thomas
Morrow, Jeremiah
Morton, Oliver Perry
Mouton, Alexander
Murray, James Edward
Neely, Matthew Mansfield
Nelson, Knute
Neuberger, Richard Lewis
Newberry, Truman Handy
Newlands, Francis Griffith
Nicholas, Wilson Cary
Nicholson, Alfred Osborne
   Pope
Nicholson, Samuel Danford
Niles, John Milton
Noble, James
Norbeck, Peter
Norris, George William
Nugent, John Frost
Nye, James Warren
O'Daniel, Wilbert Lee
   ("Pappy")
Ogden, Aaron
Oglesby, Richard James
Oliver, George Tener
O'Mahoney, Joseph Christopher
Overman, Lee Slater
Owen, Robert Latham
Paddock, Algernon Sidney
Palmer, John McAuley
Palmer, Thomas Witherell
Parris, Albion Keith
Pasco, Samuel
Patterson, Thomas MacDonald
Payne, Henry B.
Pearce, James Alfred
Peffer, William Alfred
Pendleton, George Hunt
Penrose, Boies
Pepper, George Wharton
Perkins, George Clement
Pettigrew, Richard Franklin

Pettus, Edmund Winston
Phelan, James Duval
Phipps, Lawrence Cowle
Pierce, Gilbert Ashville
Pinckney, Charles
Pittman, Key
Platt, Orville Hitchcock
Plumb, Preston B.
Plumer, William
Poindexter, George
Poindexter, Miles
Poland, Luke Potter
Polk, Trusten
Pomerene, Atlee
Pomeroy, Samuel Clarke
Pool, John
Pope, James Pinckney
Porter, Alexander
Potts, Richard
Prentiss, Samuel
Preston, William Campbell
Pritchard, Jeter Connelly
Pugh, George Ellis
Ralston, Samuel Moffett
Ramsey, Alexander
Randolph, Theodore Fitz
Ransom, Matt Whitaker
Rayner, Isidor
Read, George
Read, Jacob
Reagan, John Henninger
Reed, David Aiken
Reed, James Alexander
Revels, Hiram Rhoades
Reynolds, Robert Rice
Rice, Henry Mower
Roberts, Jonathan
Robinson, Joseph Taylor
Ross, Edmund Gibson
Ross, James
Rowan, John
Rusk, Thomas Jefferson
Sanders, Wilbur Fisk
Sargent, Aaron Augustus
Saulsbury, Eli
Saulsbury, Willard, 1820–1892
Saulsbury, Willard, 1861–1927
Saunders, Alvin
Sawyer, Philetus
Schall, Thomas David
Schurz, Carl
Schwellenbach, Lewis Baxter
Scott, W(illiam) Kerr
Sevier, Ambrose Hundley
Shafroth, John Franklin
Shepley, Ether
Sheppard, John Morris
Shields, James
Shields, John Knight
Shipstead, Henrik
Simmons, Furnifold McLendel
Smith, Ellison DuRant
Smith, Hoke
Smith, James, 1851–1927
Smith, John, 1735–1824
Smith, Nathan, 1770–1835
Smith, Oliver Hampton
Smith, William, 1762–1840
Smoot, Reed Owen
Southard, Samuel Lewis
Spooner, John Coit
Sprague, William, 1830–1915

Squire, Watson Carvosso
Stanford, Leland
Stanley, Augustus Owsley
Stephenson, Isaac
Stevenson, John White
Stewart, William Morris
Stockton, John Potter
Stokes, Montfort
Stone, David
Stone, William Joel
Sumner, Charles
Sumter, Thomas
Sutherland, George
Swanson, Claude Augustus
Taft, Robert Alphonso
Tait, Charles
Tappan, Benjamin
Tazewell, Littleton Waller
Taylor, Robert Love
Tazewell, Henry
Teller, Henry Moore
Thomas, Charles Spalding
Thomas, Elbert Duncan
Thomas, Jesse Burgess
Thurman, Allen Granberry
Thye, Edward John
Tillman, Benjamin Ryan
Tipton, John
Tobey, Charles William
Toombs, Robert Augustus
Toucey, Isaac
Tracy, Uriah
Troup, George Michael
Trumbull, Jonathan, 1740–1809
Trumbull, Lyman
Turner, George
Tydings, Millard Evelyn
Tyson, Lawrence Davis
Underwood, Joseph Rogers
Underwood, Oscar Wilder
Vance, Zebulon Baird
Vandenberg, Arthur Hendrick
Van Dyke, Nicholas, 1770–1826
Van Winkle, Peter Godwin
Vardaman, James Kimble
Varnum, Joseph Bradley
Vest, George Graham
Vilas, William Freeman
Voorhees, Daniel Wolsey
Wade, Benjamin Franklin
Wadsworth, James Wolcott, Jr.
Wagner, Robert Ferdinand
Walker, Robert John
Wallgren, Mon(rad) C(harles)
Walsh, David Ignatius
Walsh, Thomas James
Walthall, Edward Cary
Walton, George
Warner, William
Warren, Francis Emroy
Washburn, William Drew
Watson, James Eli
Webb, William Robert
Weeks, John Wingate
Welker, Herman
Weller, John B.
Wherry, Kenneth Spicer
Whitcomb, James
White, Albert Smith
White, Hugh Lawson
White, Samuel
White, Stephen Mallary

Whyte, William Pinkney
Wigfall, Louis Frezevant
Wiley, Alexander
Wilkins, William
Willey, Waitman Thomas
Williams, George Henry
Williams, John
Williams, John Sharp
Williams, Reuel
Wilson, Henry
Wilson, James Falconer
Wilson, John Lockwood
Windom, William
Winthrop, Robert Charles
Wolcott, Edward Oliver
Woodbury, Levi
Worthington, Thomas
Wright, George Grover
Wright, Robert
Wright, Silas
Wright, William
Yulee, David Levy
SENATOR (CONFEDERATE)
Johnson, Herschel Vespasian
Maxwell, Augustus Emmett
Oldham, Williamson Simpson
Orr, James Lawrence
Semmes, Thomas Jenkins
Simms, William Elliott
Thomson, Charles
Vest, George Graham
Watson, John William Clark
SETTLEMENT HOUSE FOUNDER
Addams, Jane
Taylor, Graham
Wald, Lillian D.
SETTLEMENT WORKER
Simkhovitch, Mary Melinda
 Kingsbury
Woods, Robert Archey
Woolley, Celia Parker
SETTLER (See also PIONEER)
Baker, James
Clyman, James
Conant, Roger
Dubuque, Julien
Otto, Bodo
Whitfield, Henry
Woodward, Henry
Wootton, Richens Lacy
SHAKESPEAREAN SCHOLAR
Adams, Joseph Quincy
Brooke, Charles Frederick
 Tucker
SHIPBUILDER
Bourne, Nehemiah
Burns, Otway
Cheesman, Forman
Claghorn, George
Cramp, Charles Henry
Cramp, William
Dickie, George William
Eckford, Henry
Englis, John
Hague, Robert Lincoln
Hall, Samuel, 1800–1870
Herreshoff, John Brown
Herreshoff, Nathanael Greene
Higgins, Andrew Jackson
Hill, James
Humphreys, Joshua
Johnson, Levi

Johnson, Seth Whitmore
McDougall, Alexander
McKay, Donald
Newberry, Oliver
Roach, John
Scott, Irving Murray
Sewall, Arthur
Vickery, Howard Leroy
Watson, Thomas Augustus
Webb, William Henry
Westervelt, Jacob Aaron
SHIPMASTER (See MARINER)
SHIP MODELER
Boucher, Horace Edward
SHIPOWNER
Collins, Edward Knight
Derby, Elias Hasket
Derby, Richard
Dollar, Robert
Fish, Preserved
Forbes, Robert Bennet
Grinnell, Moses Hicks
Griscom, Clement Acton
King, William
Lamar, Gazaway Bugg
Livingstone, William,
1844–1925
Moredecai, Moses Cohen
Morgan, Charles
Munson, Walter David
Perkins, George Clement
Russell, Joseph
Servoss, Thomas Lowery
Thompson, Jeremiah
Tileston, Thomas
Train, Enoch
Ward, James Edward
SHIPPING EXECUTIVE
Franklin, Philip Albright Small
Isbrandtsen, Hans Jeppesen
Luckenbach, J(ohn) Lewis
Mallory, Clifford Day
Moran, Eugene Francis
SHIPPING OFFICIAL
Boas, Emil Leopold
Borden, Richard
Cone, Hutchinson Ingham
McAllister, Charles Albert
Munson, Walter David
Raymond, Harry Howard
Roosevelt, Kermit
Smith, Robert Alexander C.
SHORTHAND INVENTOR
Gregg, John Robert
SHOWMAN (See also CONCES-
SIONAIRE, IMPRESARIO, PRO-
MOTER, THEATRICAL
MANAGER)
Bailey, James Anthony
Barnum, Phineas Taylor
Beatty, Clyde Raymond
Bowes, Edward J.
Buck, Franklyn Howard
Cody, William Frederick
("Buffalo Bill")
Forepaugh, Adam
Lillie, Gordon William
Perham, Josiah
Rice, Dan
Ringling, Charles
Rothafel, Samuel Lionel

SIGNER OF DECLARATION OF IN-
DEPENDENCE
Adams, John
Adams, Samuel
Bartlett, Josiah
Braxton, Carter
Carroll, Charles
Chase, Samuel
Clark, Abraham
Clymer, George
Ellery, William
Floyd, William
Franklin, Benjamin
Gerry, Elbridge
Gwinnett, Button
Hall, Lyman
Hancock, John
Harrison, Benjamin
Hart, John
Hewes, Joseph
Heyward, Thomas
Hooper, William
Hopkins, Stephen
Hopkinson, Francis
Huntington, Samuel,
1731–1796
Jefferson, Thomas
Lee, Francis Lightfoot
Lee, Richard Henry
Lewis, Francis
Livingston, Philip
Lynch, Thomas, 1749–1779
McKean, Thomas
Middleton, Arthur
Morris, Lewis, 1726–1798
Morris, Robert, 1734–1806
Morton, John
Nelson, Thomas
Paca, William
Paine, Robert Treat
Penn, John
Read, George
Rodney, Caesar
Ross, George
Rush, Benjamin
Rutledge, Edward
Sherman, Roger
Smith, James, 1719–1806
Stockton, Richard
Stone, Thomas
Taylor, George
Thornton, Matthew
Walton, George
Whipple, William
Williams, William
Wilson, James, 1742–1798
Witherspoon, John
Wolcott, Oliver
Wythe, George
SILVERSMITH (See also CRAFTS-
MAN, JEWELER, GOLDSMITH)
Boelen, Jacob
Buell, Abel
Dummer, Jeremiah
Edward, John
Gorham, Jabez
Harland, Thomas
Hull, John
Hurd, Nathaniel
Le Roux, Bartholomew
Le Roux, Charles
Richardson, Joseph

Sanderson, Robert
Syng, Philip
Verhaegen, Peter Joseph
Winslow, Edward
SILVICULTURIST (See also
AGRICULTURIST, FORESTER)
Michaux, André
Michaux, François André
SINGER (See also CANTOR, MIN-
STREL)
Abbott, Emma
Adams, Charles R.
Baccaloni, Salvatore
Barnabee, Henry Clay
Barton, James Edward
Bispham, David Scull
Bori, Lucrezia
Braslau, Sophie
Brice, Fanny
Burleigh, Henry Thacker
Caruso, Enrico
Cary, Annie Louise
Cole, Nat ("King")
Dandridge, Dorothy Jean
De Luca, Giuseppe
De Paolis, Alessio
Eddy, Nelson
Farrar, Geraldine
Fischer, Emil Friedrich August
Fisher, Clara
Fox, Gilbert
Galli-Curci, Amelita
Garden, Mary
Garland, Judy
Gluck, Alma
Guthrie, Woody
Hall, Juanita Armethea
Hauk, Minnie
Heinrich, Max
Hendrix, Jimi
Homer, Louise Dilworth Beatty
Johnson, Edward
Jolson, Al
Joplin, Janis Lyn
Kane, Helen
Kellogg, Clara Louise
Lawrence, Gertrude
Ledbetter, Huddie
("Leadbelly")
Liebling, Estelle
McCormack, John Francis
McCracken, Joan
McDaniel, Hattie
MacDonald, Jeanette Anna
Martinelli, Giovanni
Melton, James
Miranda, Carmen
Moore, Grace
Morgan, Helen
Nevada, Emma
Nielsen, Alice
Nordica, Lillian
Olcott, Chauncey
Osgood, George Laurie
Page, Oran Thaddeus ("Lips")
Pinza, Ezio
Powell, Alma Webster
Rainey, Gertrude Malissa Nix
Pridgett
Rogers, Clara Kathleen Barnett
Rosenblatt, Joseph
Russell, Lillian

Sanderson, Sibyl
Schumann-Heink, Ernestine
Sembrich, Marcella
Smith, Bessie
Tanguay, Eva
Thomas, John Charles
Thursby, Emma Cecilia
Tibbett, Lawrence Mervil
Tucker, Sophie
Warren, Leonard
Washington, Dinah
Webb, Clifton
White, Joseph Malachy
White, Josh
Whitehill, Clarence Eugene
Whitney, Myron William
Williams, (Hiram) Hank
Witherspoon, Herbert

SINGING EVANGELIST
Bliss, Philip Paul
Phillips, Philip
Sankey, Ira David

SINGLE TAX ADVOCATE (See also
  AGITATOR, REFORMER)
Fels, Joseph

SINOLOGUE (See also ORIENTALIST,
  SCHOLAR)
Bradley, Charles William
Laufer, Berthold
Williams, Samuel Wells

SLAVE
Burns, Anthony
Henson, Josiah
Scott, Dred
Tubman, Harriet
Turner, Nat

SLAVE TRADER
De Wolf, James

SLAVIC LANGUAGE SCHOLAR
Cross, Samuel Hazzard

SOCIAL ACTIVIST
Michaux, Lightfoot Solomon

SOCIAL ANALYST
Arnold, Thurman Wesley

SOCIAL COMMENTATOR
Dunne, Finley Peter

SOCIAL CRITIC (See also CRITIC)
Dell, Floyd James
Howard, Joseph Kinsey
Martin, Anne Henrietta
Mills, Charles Wright
Stearns, Harold Edmund
Ward, Harry Frederick

SOCIAL ECONOMIST (See also
  ECONOMIST)
Dugdale, Richard Louis
Sydenstricker, Edgar
Veblen, Thorstein Bunde
Wright, Carroll Davidson

SOCIAL ETHICS SPECIALIST
Holt, Arthur Erastus

SOCIAL INSURANCE EXPERT
Epstein, Abraham

SOCIALIST
Berger, Victor Louis
Bliss, William Dwight Porter
Bloor, Ella Reeve
Corey, Lewis
Debs, Eugene Victor
DeLeon, Daniel
Ghent, William James
Gronlund, Laurence

Hayes, Max Sebastian
Hillquit, Morris
Hoan, Daniel Webster
Hunter, Robert
London, Meyer
McLevy, Jasper
Mailly, William
Maurer, James Hudson
Mooney, Thomas Joseph
O'Hare, Kate (Richards)
  Cunningham
Russell, Charles Edward
Seidel, George Lukas Emil
Sorge, Friedrich Adolph
Spargo, John
Thomas, Norman Mattoon
Vladeck, Baruch Charney
Walling, William English
Young, Art

SOCIALITE
Belmont, Alva Ertskin Smith
  Vanderbilt
Bingham, Anne Willing
Gardner, Isabella Stewart
Harriman, Florence Jaffray
  Hurst
McAllister, Samuel Ward
Mackay, Clarence Hungerford
Manville, Thomas Franklyn
  ("Tommy"), Jr.
Palmer, Bertha Honoré
Rublee, George
Smith, Margaret Bayard
Thaw, Harry Kendall
Vanderbilt, Gloria Morgan
Vanderbilt, Grace Graham
  Wilson

SOCIAL PHILOSOPHER (See also
  PHILOSOPHER)
Lindeman, Eduard Christian

SOCIAL PSYCHOLOGIST (See also
  PSYCHOLOGIST)
Cantril, Albert Hadley
Martin, Everett Dean
Overstreet, Harry Allen

SOCIAL REFORMER (See also RE-
  FORMER)
Addams, Jane
Andrews, John Bertram
Bellanca, Dorothy Jacobs
Blatch, Harriot Eaton Stanton
Brisbane, Albert
Chapin, Henry Dwight
Collins, John Anderson
Crosby, Ernest Howard
Darrow, Clarence Seward
Dennison, Henry Sturgis
Dietz, Peter Ernest
Dock, Lavinia Lloyd
Dreier, Mary Elisabeth
Fuller, Sarah Margaret
Gillette, King Camp
Gilman, Charlotte Perkins
  Stetson
Hamilton, Alice
Hazard, Thomas Robinson
Holmes, John Haynes
Jemison, Alice Mae Lee
Jones, Rufus Matthew
Kellogg, Paul Underwood
Lindsey, Benjamin Barr
Longley, Alcander

McBride, F(rancis) Scott
McClure, Samuel Sidney
Mussey, Ellen Spencer
Nathan, Maud
O'Hare, Kate (Richards)
  Cunningham
Owen, Robert Dale
Oxnam, Garfield Bromley
Peck, Lillie
Pinchot, Cornelia Elizabeth
  Bryce
Poling, Daniel Alfred
Regan, Agnes Gertrude
Robins, Margaret Dreier
Robins, Raymond
Roosevelt, (Anna) Eleanor
Ryan, John Augustine
Simkhovitch, Mary Melinda
  Kingsbury
Strong, Josiah
Swinton, John
Taylor, Graham
Tibbles, Thomas Henry
Tiffany, Katrina Brandes Ely
Voris, John Ralph

SOCIAL RESEARCHER
Bryant, Louise Frances Stevens

SOCIAL SCIENTIST (See also SPE-
  CIFIC SOCIAL SCIENCES)
Frank, Lawrence Kelso
Kracauer, Siegfried
Mayo, George Elton
Merriam, Charles Edward, Jr.
Mitchell, Wesley Clair
Sullivan, Harry Stack
Sumner, William Graham

SOCIAL WELFARE LEADER
Brackett, Jeffrey Richardson
Mack, Julian William
Swift, Linton Bishop

SOCIAL WORKER (See also SETTLE-
  MENT WORKER)
Abbott, Edith
Abbott, Grace
Adie, David Craig
Antin, Mary
Balch, Emily Greene
Barrett, Janie Porter
Billikopf, Jacob
Binford, Jessie Florence
Blaustein, David
Bloomfield, Meyer
Bowen, Louise De Koven
Brace, Charles Loring
Breckenridge, Sophonisba
  Preston
Cabot, Richard Clarke
Cannon, Ida Maud
Carr, Charlotte Elizabeth
Coyle, Grace Longwell
Cratty, Mabel
Devine, Edward Thomas
Dinwiddie, Courtenay
Dodge, Grace Hoadley
Doremus, Sarah Platt Haines
Dyott, Thomas W.
Elliott, John Lovejoy
Hart, Hastings Hornell
Hersey, Evelyn Weeks
Hopkins, Harry Lloyd
Hunter, Robert
Johnson, Alexander

Kelley, Florence
Kober, George Martin
Lathrop, Alice Louise Higgins
Lathrop, Julia Clifford
Lee, Joseph
Lee, Porter Raymond
Lewis, Orlando Faulkland
Loeb, Sophie Irene Simon
Lovejoy, Owen Reed
McDowell, Mary Eliza
McHugh, Rose John
Mason, Lucy Randolph
Park, Maud Wood
Peirce, Bradford Kinney
Perkins, James Handasyd
Perry, Clarence Arthur
Potter, Ellen Culver
Richmond, Mary Ellen
Robertson, Alice Mary
Rubinow, Isaac Max
Schuyler, Louisa Lee
Shuey, Edwin Longstreet
Thurber, Christopher Carson
Veiller, Lawrence Turnure
West, James Edward
Willard, Mary Hatch
Williams, Aubrey Willis
SOCIAL WORK LEADER
 Glenn, John Mark
SOCIOLOGIST
 Bentley, Arthur Fisher
 Brooks, John Graham
 Butterfield, Kenyon Leech
 Cayton, Horace Roscoe
 Davis, Katharine Bement
 Dawley, Almena
 Dike, Samuel Warren
 Du Bois, William Edward
  Burghardt
 Ellis, George Washington
 Fitzhugh, George
 Frazier, Edward Franklin
 Galpin, Charles Josiah
 Giddings, Franklin Henry
 Hayes, Edward Carey
 Haynes, George Edmund
 Henderson, Charles Richmond
 Johnson, Charles Spurgeon
 Kellor, Frances (Alice)
 Kelly, Edmond
 Kerby, William Joseph
 Lynd, Robert Staughton
 MacIver, Robert Morrison
 Mills, Charles Wright
 Morrow, Prince Albert
 Odum, Howard Washington
 Ogburn, William Fielding
 Park, Robert Ezra
 Parsons, Elsie Worthington
  Clews
 Reid, Ira De Augustine
 Ross, Edward Alsworth
 Sanderson, Ezra Dwight
 Small, Albion Woodbury
 Stouffer, Samuel Andrew
 Stuckenberg, John Henry
  Wilbrandt
 Sutherland, Edwin Hardin
 Teggart, Frederick John
 Thomas, William Isaac
 Vincent, George Edgar
 Waller, Willard Walter

Warbasse, James Peter
Ward, Lester Frank
Warner, Amos Griswold
Wilson, Warren Hugh
Wing, John Joseph
Woods, Robert Archey
Wyckoff, Walter Augustus
Znaniecki, Florian Witold
SOIL CHEMIST (See also CHEMIST)
 Hoagland, Dennis Robert
SOIL CONSERVATIONIST
 Bennett, Hugh Hammond
SOIL EXPERT (See also AGRICUL-
 TURIST)
 Hilgard, Eugene Woldemar
 Marbut, Curtis Fletcher
SOIL SCIENTIST (See also
 AGRICULTURIST)
 Lipman, Jacob Goodale
SOLDIER OF FORTUNE (See also
 ADVENTURER)
 Burnham, Frederick Russell
 Lee, Charles, 1731–1782
 Littlepage, Lewis
 Picton, Thomas
SOLDIER (See also ARMY OFFICER,
 GENERAL, INDIAN CHIEF, JAY-
 HAWKER)
 Adair, John
 Adams, Charles
 Adams, Daniel Weissiger
 Adams, John
 Adams, William Wirt
 Agnus, Felix
 Alden, Ichabod
 Alexander, Barton Stone
 Alexander, Edward Porter
 Alexander, William
 Alger, Russell Alexander
 Allan, John
 Allen, Ethan
 Allen, Henry Tureman
 Allen, Henry Watkins
 Allen, Robert
 Allison, Richard
 Alvord, Benjamin
 Amherst, Jeffery
 Ammen, Jacob
 Anderson, George Thomas
 Anderson, James Patton
 Anderson, Joseph Reid
 Anderson, Richard Clough
 Anderson, Richard Heron
 Anderson, Robert
 Anderson, William
 Andrews, Garnett
 Andrews, George Leonard
 Angell, Israel
 Archer, James J.
 Armistead, George
 Armistead, Lewis Addison
 Armstrong, Frank C.
 Armstrong, John, 1717–1795
 Armstrong, John, 1755–1816
 Armstrong, John, 1758–1843
 Armstrong, Robert
 Arnold, Richard
 Asboth, Alexander Sandor
 Asch, Morris Joseph
 Ashby, Turner
 Ashe, John
 Ashe, John Baptista

Atkinson, Henry
Augur, Christopher Columbus
Austin, Jonathan Loring
Averell, William Woods
Avery, Isaac Wheeler
Ayres, Romeyn Beck
Babcock, Orville E.
Bacon, Robert
Badeau, Adam
Bailey, Joseph
Baird, Absalom
Baker, Edward Dickinson
Baker, James Heaton
Baker, Laurence Simmons
Baker, Remember
Baldwin, Loammi
Banks, Nathaniel Prentiss
Barber, Francis
Barksdale, William
Barlow, Francis Channing
Barnard, John Gross
Barnes, James
Barnum, Henry A.
Barnwell, John
Barringer, Rufus
Barry, William Farquhar
Barry, William Taylor Sullivan
Barton, Seth Maxwell
Barton, William
Batcheller, George Sherman
Bate, William Brimage
Bates, John Coalter
Battle, Cullen Andrews
Baxter, Henry
Baylor, George
Beale, Richard Lee Turberville
Beall, John Yates
Beatty, John
Beauregard, Pierre Gustave
 Toutant
Beaver, James Addams
Bedford, Gunning
Bedinger, George Michael
Bee, Barnard Elliott
Bee, Hamilton Prioleau
Bell, Peter Hansborough
Belo, Alfred Horatio
Bemis, Harold Edward
Benham, Henry Washington
Bennett, Caleb Prew
Benning, Henry Lewis
Berry, Hiram Gregory
Biddle, Clement
Birge, Henry Warner
Birney, David Bell
Birney, William
Black, John Charles
Blackburn, Joseph Clay Styles
Blair, Francis Preston
Bland, Theodorick
Bliss, Tasker Howard
Bloomfield, Joseph
Blount, Thomas
Blunt, James Gillpatrick
Bomford, George
Bonaparte, Jerome Napoleon
Bonham, Milledge Luke
Bonneville, Benjamin Louis
 Eulalie de
Borland, Solon
Boteler, Alexander Robinson
Bouquet, Henry

Bourke, John Gregory
Bourne, Benjamin
Bowers, Theodore Shelton
Bowie, James
Boyle, Jeremiah Tilford
Boynton, Edward Carlisle
Bradstreet, John
Bragg, Braxton
Bragg, Edward Stuyvesant
Branch, Lawrence O'Bryan
Brannan, John Milton
Bratton, John
Brayman, Mason
Breckenridge, James
Breckinridge, John Cabell
Brodhead, Daniel
Brooke, Francis Taliaferro
Brooke, John Rutter
Brooks, John
Brooks, William Thomas
    Harbaugh
Brown, Jacob Jennings
Brown, John
Browne, Thomas
Buchanan, Robert Christie
Bucher, John Conrad
Buckland, Ralph Pomeroy
Buckner, Simon Bolivar
Buell, Don Carlos
Buford, Abraham, 1749–1833
Buford, Abraham, 1820–1884
Buford, John
Buford, Napoleon Bonaparte
Burbridge, Stephen Gano
Burleson, Edward
Burnett, Henry Lawrence
Burnside, Ambrose Everett
Burr, Aaron
Bussey, Cyrus
Butler, Benjamin Franklin
Butler, John
Butler, Matthew Calbraith
Butler, Richard
Butler, Walter N.
Butler, William
Butler, William Orlando
Butler, Zebulon
Butterfield, Daniel
Cabell, Samuel Jordan
Cabell, William Lewis
Cadwalader, John
Cadwalader, Lambert
Cameron, Robert Alexander
Camp, John Lafayette
Campbell, William
Canby, Edward Richard Sprigg
Capers, Ellison
Carlson, Evans Fordyce
Carr, Eugene Asa
Carr, Joseph Bradford
Carroll, Samuel Sprigg
Carson, Christopher
Casey, Silas
Cass, Lewis
Caswell, Richard
Cesnola, Luigi Palma di
Chaffee, Adna Romanza
Chalmers, James Ronald
Chamberlain, Joshua Lawrence
Chandler, John
Cheatham, Benjamin Franklin
Chesnut, James

Chetlain, Augustus Louis
Childs, Thomas
Chisolm, Alexander Robert
Christian, William
Church, Benjamin
Churchill, Thomas James
Cilley, Joseph
Cist, Henry Martin
Claghorn, George
Clark, Charles
Clark, William Smith
Clark, William Thomas
Clarke, Elijah
Clarkson, Matthew
Clay, Green
Clay, Joseph
Cleburne, Patrick Ronayne
Clemens, Jeremiah
Cleveland, Benjamin
Clinton, George
Clinton, James
Cobb, David
Cobb, Thomas Reade Rootes
Cochrane, Henry Clay
Cocke, Philip St. George
Cocke, William
Cockrell, Francis Marion
Cofer, Martin Hardin
Colquitt, Alfred Holt
Combs, Leslie
Conger, Edwin Hurd
Conner, James
Connor, Patrick Edward
Cook, Philip
Cooke, Philip St. George
Cooper, Joseph Alexander
Coppée, Henry
Corbin, Henry Clark
Cornell, Ezekiel
Cox, William Ruffin
Crane, John
Crawford, Martin Jenkins
Crawford, Samuel Johnson
Crawford, William
Cresap, Michael
Crittenden, George Bibb
Crittenden, Thomas Leonidas
Croghan, George
Croix, Teodore de
Crook, George
Crosby, John Schuyler
Crozet, Claude
Cullum, George Washington
Curtis, Newton Martin
Curtis, Samuel Ryan
Custer, George Armstrong
Dale, Samuel
Dale, Sir Thomas
Dana, Napoleon Jackson
    Tecumseh
Darke, William
Davenport, George
Davidson, John Wynn
Davidson, William Lee
Davie, William Richardson
Davies, Henry Eugene
Davis, George Breckenridge
Davis, George Whitefield
Davis, Jefferson Columbus
Davis, Joseph Robert
Dayton, Elias
Dayton, Jonathan

Dearborn, Henry
Deas, Zachariah Cantey
De Haas, John Philip
De Lacy, Walter Washington
De Lancey, James
De Lancey, Oliver
Delany, Martin Robinson
De Mézières y Clugny,
    Athanase
Dent, Frederick Tracy
Denver, James William
De Peyster, John Watts
De Trobriand, Régis Denis de
    Keredern
Devens, Charles
Devin, Thomas Casimer
Dibrell, George Gibbs
Dickey, Theophilus Lyle
Dickinson, Philemon
Dickman, Joseph Theodore
Diven, Alexander Samuel
Dix, John Adams
Dodge, Henry
Donelson, Andrew Jackson
Dongan, Thomas
Doniphan, Alexander William
Donovan, William Joseph
Doubleday, Abner
Douglas, Henry Kyd
Douglas, William
Douglass, David Bates
Dow, Henry
Draper, William Franklin
Drayton, Thomas Fenwick
Drayton, William
Duke, Basil Wilson
Du Pont, Henry Algernon
Durkee, John
Duryée, Abram
Dutton, Clarence Edward
Dwight, William
Dye, William McEntyre
Dyer, Alexander Brydie
Early, Jubal Anderson
Eaton, William
Echols, John
Edgren, August Hjalmar
Edwards, Oliver
Elbert, Samuel
Elliott, Washington Lafayette
Ellsworth, Elmer Ephraim
Elmer, Ebenezer
Elzey, Arnold
Emory, William Hensley
Ernst, Oswald Herbert
Eustis, Henry Lawrence
Ewell, Benjamin Stoddert
Ewell, Richard Stoddert
Ewing, Hugh Boyle
Ewing, James
Ewing, Thomas
Fagan, James Fleming
Fairchild, Lucius
Falk, Otto Herbert
Fannin, James Walker
Fanning, Alexander Campbell
    Wilder
Farnsworth, Elon John
Farnsworth, John Franklin
Farragut, George
Featherston, Winfield Scott
Febiger, Christian

Fenner, Charles Erasmus
Ferguson, Thomas Barker
Ferrero, Edward
Fersen, Hans Axel
Fessenden, Francis
Fessenden, James Deering
Fetterman, William Judd
Few, William
Field, Charles William
Findlay, James
Fish, Nicholas
Fiske, John
Flandrau, Charles Eugene
Fleming, William
Fleming, William Maybury
Fletcher, Benjamin
Fletcher, Thomas Clement
Folsom, Nathaniel
Forbes, John
Force, Manning Ferguson
Ford, Jacob
Forman, David
Forney, William Henry
Foster, John Gray
Foster, John Watson
Foster, Robert Sanford
Franklin, William Buel
Frazer, Persifor
Frémont, John Charles
French, William Henry
Fry, Birkett Davenport
Fry, James Barnet
Frye, Joseph
Fuller, John Wallace
Funston, Frederick
Furnas, Robert Wilkinson
Gaillard, David Du Bose
Gaines, Edmund Pendleton
Gaines, John Pollard
Gálvez, Bernardo de
Gansevoort, Peter
Garden, Alexander
Gardner, Charles Kitchell
Gardner, John Lane
Garfield, James Abram
Garnett, Robert Selden
Garrard, Kenner
Gary, Martin Witherspoon
Gates, Horatio
Geary, John White
Geddes, James Loraine
George, James Zachariah
Getty, George Washington
Gholson, Samuel Jameson
Gibbon, John
Gibson, George
Gibson, John
Gibson, Randall Lee
Gillem, Alvan Cullem
Gillmore, Quincy Adams
Gilmor, Harry
Gist, Christopher
Gist, Mordecai
Gladwin, Henry
Glover, John
Goethals, George Washington
Gookin, Daniel
Gordon, George Henry
Gordon, George Washington
Gordon, John Brown
Gorgas, Josiah
Gorman, Willis Arnold

Govan, Daniel Chevilette
Gracie, Archibald
Graham, Charles Kinnaird
Graham, James Duncan
Graham, Joseph
Graham, William Montrose
Granger, Gordon
Grant, Frederick Dent
Grant, Lewis Addison
Gray, Isaac Pusey
Grayson, William
Greaton, John
Greely, Adolphus Washington
Greene, Christopher
Greene, Francis Vinton
Greene, George Sears
Gregg, David McMurtrie
Gregg, Maxcy
Gresham, Walter Quintin
Gridley, Richard
Grierson, Benjamin Henry
Griffin, Charles
Griffin, Eugene
Griffin, Simon Goodell
Grose, William
Grosvenor, Charles Henry
Grover, Cuvier
Guild, Curtis, 1860–1915
Haan, William George
Hagood, Johnson
Halderman, John A.
Hall, Willard Preble
Halleck, Henry Wager
Hamblin, Joseph Eldridge
Hamer, Thomas Lyon
Hamilton, Charles Smith
Hamilton, Schuyler
Hamlin, Charles
Hammond, Samuel
Hampton, Wade, 1751–1835
Hampton, Wade, 1818–1902
Hamtramck, John Francis
Hancock, Winfield Scott
Hand, Edward
Hardee, William Joseph
Hardie, James Allen
Hardin, John
Hardin, John J.
Hardin, Martin D.
Harding, Abner Clark
Harlan, Josiah
Harmar, Josiah
Harney, William Selby
Harriman, Walter
Harris, Nathaniel Harrison
Harrison, George Paul
Harrod, James
Hartley, Thomas
Hartranft, John Frederick
Hartsuff, George Lucas
Hascall, Milo Smith
Hatch, Edward
Hatch, John Porter
Hawkins, Rush Christopher
Hawley, Joseph Roswell
Hayne, Isaac
Hays, Alexander
Hays, Harry Thompson
Hays, John Coffee
Hazen, Moses
Hazen, William Babcock
Heath, William

Hébert, Louis
Hébert, Paul Octave
Hecker, Friedrich Karl Franz
Heintzelman, Samuel Peter
Henderson, David Bremner
Henderson, Thomas
Henningsen, Charles Frederick
Herbert, Hilary Abner
Herkimer, Nicholas
Heth, Henry
Heyward, Thomas
Hibben, Paxton Pattison
Hickenlooper, Andrew
Hickok, James Butler
Hiester, Joseph
Higginson, Henry Lee
Higginson, Thomas Wentworth
Hill, Ambrose Powell
Hill, Daniel Harvey
Hill, James
Hill, William
Hindman, Thomas Carmichael
Hitchcock, Ethan Allen,
   1798–1870
Hitchcock, Henry
Hobson, Edward Henry
Hodes, Henry Irving
Hodges, Courtney Hicks
Hoffman, Wickham
Hogun, James
Hoke, Robert Frederick
Holmes, Julius Cecil
Holmes, Theophilus Hunter
Hood, John Bell
Hooker, Joseph
Hopkins, Samuel, 1753–1819
Hough, Warwick
Houston, Samuel
Hovey, Alvin Peterson
Hovey, Charles Edward
Howard, Benjamin
Howard, John Eager
Howard, Oliver Otis
Howe, Albion Parris
Howe, Robert
Howe, William Wirt
Howze, Robert Lee
Hubbard, Lucius Frederick
Hubbard, Richard Bennett
Hubbard, Thomas Hamlin
Huger, Benjamin
Huger, Francis Kinloch
Hughes, George Wurtz
Hull, William
Humbert, Jean Joseph Amable
Humphreys, Andrew Atkinson
Humphreys, Benjamin Grubb
Humphreys, David
Hunt, Henry Jackson
Hunter, David
Huntington, Jedediah
Hunton, Eppa
Hurlbut, Stephen Augustus
Huse, Caleb
Hyrne, Edmund Massingberd
Imboden, John Daniel
Ingraham, Prentiss
Inman, George
Inman, Henry
Ireland, John, 1827–1896
Irvine, James
Irvine, William

Irwin, George Le Roy
Ives, Joseph Christmas
Izard, George
Jackson, Henry Rootes
Jackson, Thomas Jonathan
Jackson, William, 1759–1828
Jacob, Richard Taylor
Jadwin, Edgar
Jaquess, James Frazier
Jasper, William
Jenkins, Albert Gallatin
Jenkins, John
Jenkins, Micah
Jennings, John
Jesup, Thomas Sidney
Johnson, Bradley Tyler
Johnson, Bushrod Rust
Johnson, Edward
Johnson, James
Johnson, Richard W.
Johnston, Albert Sidney
Johnston, Joseph Eggleston
Johnston, Peter
Johnston, William Preston
Johnston, Zachariah
Jones, Allen
Jones, David Rumph
Jones, John B.
Jones, William
Jordan, Thomas
Kane, Thomas Leiper
Kautz, August Valentine
Kearney, Philip
Kearney, Stephen Watts
Keifer, Joseph Warren
Keitt, Lawrence Massillon
Kelton, John Cunningham
Kemper, James Lawson
Kennedy, John Doby
Kennedy, Robert Patterson
Kershaw, Joseph Brevard
Key, David McKendree
Keyes, Erasmus Darwin
Kilmer, Alfred Joyce
Kilpatrick, Hugh Judson
Kimball, Nathan
King, Rufus
Kirby-Smith, Edmund
Knowlton, Thomas
Kosciuszko, Tadeusz Andrzej
  Bonawentura
Lacey, John
Lacey, John Fletcher
Lafayette, Marie Joseph Paul
  Yves Roch Gilbert du Motier,
  Marquis de
Lamb, John
Lander, Frederick West
Lane, James Henry, 1814–1866
Lane, James Henry, 1833–1907
Lane, Joseph
Lane, Walter Paye
Larrabee, Charles Hathaway
Laurance, John
Laurens, John
Law, Evander McIvor
Lawton, Alexander Robert
Lawton, Henry Ware
Lea, Homer
Leaming, Thomas
Learned, Ebenezer
Leavenworth, Henry

Le Duc, William Gates
Ledyard, William
Lee, Fitzhugh
Lee, George Washington Custis
Lee, Henry ("Light-Horse
  Harry"), 1756–1818
Lee, Henry, 1787–1837
Lee, Robert Edward
Lee, Stephen Dill
Lee, William Henry Fitzhugh
Le Gendre, Charles William
Leggett, Mortimer Dormer
L'Enfant, Pierre Charles
Lewis, Andrew
Lewis, Isaac Newton
Lewis, Joseph Horace
Lewis, Morgan
Lewis, William Gaston
Liggett, Hunter
Lightburn, Joseph Andrew
  Jackson
Lincoln, Benjamin
Livingston, James
Locke, Matthew
Lockwood, James Booth
Logan, John Alexander
Lomax, Lunsford Lindsay
Longstreet, James
Lorimier, Pierre Louis
Loring, William Wing
Lovell, Mansfield
Lowrey, Mark Perrin
Lowry, Robert
Lubbock, Francis Richard
Ludlow, William
Lynch, Charles
Lynch, James Daniel
Lyon, Matthew
Lyon, Nathaniel
Lytle, William Haines
McArthur, John, 1826–1906
McCausland, John
McCawley, Charles Grymes
McCay, Henry Kent
McClellan, George Brinton
McClellan, Henry Brainerd
McClernand, John Alexander
McClintock, James Harvey
McClure, George
McClurg, Alexander Caldwell
McClurg, James
McCook, Alexander McDowell
McCook, Anson George
McCook, Edward Moody
McCrady, Edward
McCulloch, Ben
McCullough, Ernest
McDaniel, Henry Dickerson
McDougall, Alexander
McDowell, Charles
McDowell, Irvin
McDowell, Joseph
McElroy, John
McGowan, Samuel
McHenry, James
McIntosh, John Baillie
McIntosh, Lachlan
Mackenzie, Ronald Slidell
McKinstry, Alexander
McLane, Allan
McLaws, Lafayette
McLeod, Hugh

McMillan, James Winning
Macomb, Alexander
Macon, Nathaniel
McPherson, James Birdseye
McRae, Duncan Kirkland
Maginnis, Martin
Magruder, John Bankhead
Mahan, Dennis Hart
Mahone, William
Mallery, Garrick
Manderson, Charles Frederick
Maney, George Earl
Mappa, Adam Gerard
March, Peyton Conway
Marcy, Randolph Barnes
Marmaduke, John Sappington
Marshall, George Catlett, Jr.
Marshall, Humphrey
Marshall, Thomas
Marshall, William Louis
Marshall, William Rainey
Martin, Alexander
Martin, James Green
Martin, John Alexander
Martin, William Thompson
Martindale, John Henry
Mason, John
Mason, Richard Barnes
Matthews, George
Maury, Dabney Herndon
Maus, Marion Perry
Maxwell, William
Meade, George Gordon
Meade, Richard Kidder
Meade, Robert Leamy
Meagher, Thomas Francis
Meigs, Montgomery
  Cunningham
Meigs, Return Jonathan
Menoher, Charles Thomas
Mercer, Hugh
Mercer, John Francis
Merriam, Henry Clay
Merrill, Frank Dow
Merrill, William Emery
Merritt, Wesley
Meserve, Nathaniel
Michie, Peter Smith
Miles, Nelson Appleton
Mills, Anson
Milroy, Robert Huston
Minty, Robert Horatio George
Mitchel, Ormsby MacKnight
Mitchell, David Dawson
Mitchell, George Edward
Mitchell, Nathaniel
Mitchell, Robert Byington
Montefiore, Joshua
Montgomery, James
Montgomery, Richard
Moore, Alfred
Moore, James, 1737–1777
Mordecai, Alfred
Morell, George Webb
Morgan, Daniel
Morgan, George Washington
Morgan, James Dada
Morgan, James Morris
Morgan, John Hunt
Morgan, Thomas Jefferson
Morris, Roger
Morris, William Hopkins

Morton, James St. Clair
Mott, Gershom
Mower, Joseph Anthony
Moylan, Stephen
Muhlenberg, John Peter Gabriel
Mulholland, St. Clair Augustin
Munford, Robert
Myer, Albert James
Myers, Abraham Charles
Nancrède, Paul Joseph Guérard de
Narváez, Pánfilo de
Nash, Francis
Negley, James Scott
Neill, Thomas Hewson
Neilson, John
Nelson, Roger
Nelson, Thomas
Nelson, William, 1824–1862
Nesmith, James Willis
Nettleton, Alvred Bayard
Neville, John
Neville, Wendell Cushing
Newton, John
Nicholson, William Jones
Nicola, Lewis
Nixon, John, 1727–1815
Noailles, Louis Marie, Vicomte de
Noble, John Willock
North, William
Northen, William Jonathan
Northrop, Lucius Bellringer
Noyan, Gilles-Augustin Payen de
Noyen, Pierre-Jacques Payen de
Oates, William Calvin
O'Fallon, James
O'Fallon, John
Ogden, Aaron
Oglethorpe, James Edward
O'Hara, James
O'Hara, Theodore
Oliver, Paul Ambrose
O'Neal, Edward Asbury
O'Neill, John
Ord, Edward Otho Cresap
O'Reilly, Alexander
Osborn, Thomas Ogden
Osceola
Osgood, Samuel
Osterhaus, Peter Joseph
Otis, Elwell Stephen
Otis, Harrison Gray
Page, Richard Lucian
Paine, Charles Jackson
Paine, Halbert Eleazer
Painter, Gamaliel
Palfrey, John Carver
Palmer, Innis Newton
Palmer, John McAuley
Palmer, Joseph
Palmer, William Jackson
Pardee, Don Albert
Parke, Benjamin
Parke, John
Parke, John Grubb
Parker, Ely Samuel
Parker, John
Parker, Josiah
Parker, Richard Elliot
Parsons, Lewis Baldwin

Parsons, Samuel Holden
Paterson, John
Patrick, Marsena Rudolph
Patterson, Robert
Peck, John James
Pelham, John
Pemberton, John Clifford
Peñalosa Briceño, Diego Dionisio
Pender, William Dorsey
Pendleton, William Nelson
Pennypacker, Galusha
Pepperrell, Sir William
Perry, Edward Aylesworth
Pettigrew, James Johnston
Pettus, Edmund Winston
Phelps, Charles Edward
Philips, John Finis
Phillips, William Addison
Phisterer, Frederick
Pickens, Andrew
Pickering, Timothy
Pickett, George Edward
Pierce, William Leigh
Pike, Albert
Pike, Zebulon Montgomery
Pillow, Gideon Johnson
Pinckney, Charles Cotesworth
Pinckney, Thomas
Pitcairn, John
Plaisted, Harris Merrill
Pleasonton, Alfred
Plumb, Preston B.
Poe, Orlando Metcalfe
Polk, Lucius Eugene
Polk, Thomas
Polk, William
Pomeroy, Seth
Pond, Peter
Poor, Enoch
Pope, John
Porter, Andrew
Porter, Fitz-John
Porter, Horace
Posey, Thomas
Potter, James
Potter, Robert Brown
Potts, Benjamin Franklin
Powel, John Hare
Pratt, Richard Henry
Prentiss, Benjamin Mayberry
Prescott, Oliver
Prescott, William
Preston, John Smith
Preston, William
Price, Sterling
Pryor, Nathaniel
Pryor, Roger Atkinson
Pulaski, Casimir
Putnam, Eben
Putnam, George Haven
Putnam, Israel
Putnam, Rufus
Quesnay, Alexandre-Marie
Quimby, Isaac Ferdinand
Quitman, John Anthony
Rains, Gabriel James
Rains, George Washington
Ramsay, George Douglas
Ramsay, Nathaniel
Ramseur, Stephen Dodson
Ransom, Matt Whitaker

Ransom, Thomas Edward Greenfield
Raum, Green Berry
Rawlins, John Aaron
Read, Jacob
Reed, James, 1772–1807
Reed, John, 1757–1845
Reed, Joseph
Reno, Jesse Lee
Revere, Joseph Warren
Reynolds, Alexander Welch
Reynolds, John Fulton
Reynolds, Joseph Jones
Richardson, Israel Bush
Richardson, Wilds Preston
Ricketts, James Brewerton
Riley, Bennet
Ripley, Edward Hastings
Ripley, Eleazar Wheelock
Ripley, James Wolfe
Ripley, Roswell Sabine
Roane, John Selden
Roberts, Benjamin Stone
Roberts, Oran Milo
Robertson, Jerome Bonaparte
Robinson, John Cleveland
Robinson, Moses
Rochambeau, Jean Baptiste Donatien Vimeur, Comte de
Rockwell, Kiffin Yates
Roddey, Philip Dale
Rodenbough, Theophilus Francis
Rodes, Robert Emmett
Rodman, Isaac Peace
Rodman, Thomas Jackson
Rodney, Thomas
Romans, Bernard
Rosecrans, William Starke
Ross, Lawrence Sullivan
Rosser, Thomas Lafayette
Rousseau, Lovell Harrison
Ruger, Thomas Howard
Ruggles, Timothy
Rusk, Thomas Jefferson
Russell, David Allen
Rutgers, Henry
St. Ange Bellerive, Louis de
St. Clair, Arthur
St. Denis (Denys), Louis Juchereau de
St. Lusson, Simon François Daumont, Sieur de
St. Vrain, Ceran de Hault de Lassus de
Sargent, Henry
Sargent, Winthrop, 1753–1820
Scammell, Alexander
Scharf, John Thomas
Schenck, Robert Cumming
Schnauffer, Carl Heinrich
Schofield, John McAllister
Schriver, Edmund
Schurz, Carl
Schuyler, Peter
Schuyler, Philip John
Scott, Charles
Scott, Robert Kingston
Scott, Winfield
Scudder, Nathaniel
Sedgwick, John
Sedgwick, Robert

Seeger, Alan
Sevier, John
Sewell, William Joyce
Seymour, Truman
Shafter, William Rufus
Shaw, Samuel
Shays, Daniel
Shelby, Evan
Shelby, Isaac
Shelby, Joseph Orville
Shepard, William
Shepley, George Foster
Sheridan, Philip Henry
Sherman, Thomas West
Sherman, William Tecumseh
Sherwood, Isaac Ruth
Shields, James
Shipp, Scott
Shoup, Francis Asbury
Sickles, Daniel Edgar
Sidell, William Henry
Sigel, Franz
Simmons, Thomas Jefferson
Simms, William Elliott
Simonton, Charles Henry
Simpson, James Hervey
Smallwood, William
Smith, Andrew Jackson
Smith, Charles Ferguson
Smith, Charles Henry,
    1827–1902
Smith, Daniel
Smith, Francis Henney
Smith, Giles Alexander
Smith, Gustavus Woodson
Smith, James, 1737–1814
Smith, James Francis
Smith, John Eugene
Smith, Martin Luther
Smith, Morgan Lewis
Smith, Persifor Frazer
Smith, Richard Somers
Smith, Samuel
Smith, Thomas Adams
Smith, Walter Bedell
Smith, William, 1797–1887
Smith, William Farrar
Smith, William Sooy
Smith, William Stephens
Smyth, Alexander
Snead, Thomas Lowndes
Snelling, Josiah
Snyder, John Francis
Spaulding, Oliver Lyman
Spencer, Joseph
Squier, George Owen
Squiers, Herbert Goldsmith
Stahel, Julius
Standish, Myles
Stanley, David Sloane
Stansbury, Howard
Stark, John
Steedman, James Blair
Steele, Frederick
Stephens, Linton
Steuben, Friedrich Wilhelm
    Ludolf Gerhard Augustin,
    Baron von
Stevens, Clement Hoffman
Stevens, Isaac Ingalls
Stevens, Walter Husted
Stewart, Alexander Peter

Stobo, Robert
Stoddard, Amos
Stone, Charles Pomeroy
Stoneman, George
Strother, David Hunter
Struve, Gustav
Stuart, Archibald
Stuart, James Ewell Brown
Sturgis, Samuel Davis
Summerall, Charles Pelot
Sumner, Edwin Vose
Sumner, Jethro
Sumter, Thomas
Swartwout, Samuel
Swayne, Wager
Sweeny, Thomas William
Swift, Joseph Gardner
Swift, William Henry
Sykes, George
Talcott, Andrew
Taliaferro, William Booth
Tallmadge, Benjamin
Taylor, Harry
Taylor, Richard
Taylor, Zachary
Ten Broeck, Abraham
Terry, Alfred Howe
Terry, David Smith
Thayer, John Milton
Thomas, Allen
Thomas, David
Thomas, George Henry
Thomas, John
Thomas, Lorenzo
Thompson, William
Thomson, William
Tidball, John Caldwell
Tilghman, Tench
Timberlake, Henry
Tipton, John, 1730–1813
Tipton, John, 1786–1839
Todd, Charles Stewart
Torbert, Alfred Thomas
    Archimedes
Totten, Joseph Gilbert
Toulmin, Harry Theophilus
Tousard, Anne Louis de
Tower, Zealous Bates
Townsend, Edward Davis
Tracy, Benjamin Franklin
Travis, William Barret
Tremain, Henry Edwin
Trimble, Isaac Ridgeway
Troup, Robert
Trumbull, Jonathan, 1740–1809
Tupper, Benjamin
Turnbull, William
Turner, John Wesley
Turney, Peter
Twiggs, David Emanuel
Tyler, Daniel
Tyler, Robert Ogden
Tyndale, Hector
Tyson, Lawrence Davis
Underhill, John
Upton, Emory
Vallejo, Mariano Guadalupe
Van Cortlandt, Philip
Van Rensselaer, Solomon
Van Rensselaer, Stephen
Van Schaick, Goose
Van Wyck, Charles Henry

Varick, Richard
Varnum, James Mitchell
Varnum, Joseph Bradley
Venable, Charles Scott
Vetch, Samuel
Vigo, Joseph Maria Francesco
Villagrá, Gasper Pérez de
Vincennes, Jean Baptiste Bissot,
    Sieur de
Vinton, Francis
Vinton, Francis Laurens
Waddell, Hugh
Wadsworth, James Samuel
Wadsworth, Jeremiah
Walderne, Richard
Walker, Reuben Lindsay
Walker, Thomas
Walker, William Henry Talbot
Wallace, Lewis
Ward, Samuel, 1756–1832
Warmoth, Henry Clay
Warner, Adoniram Judson
Warner, Seth
Warner, William
Warren, Gouverneur Kemble
Washburn, Cadwallader Colden
Washington, John Macrae
Wayne, Anthony
Weaver, James Baird
Webb, Alexander Stewart
Webb, Thomas
Webber, Charles Wilkins
Webster, Joseph Dana
Weitzel, Godfrey
Wetherill, Samuel
Wheaton, Frank
Wheeler, Joseph
Whipple, Amiel Weeks
Whistler, George Washington
White, James
Whiting, William Henry Chase
Wilcox, Cadmus Marcellus
Wilder, John Thomas
Wilkinson, James
Willcox, Orlando Bolivar
Willett, Marinus
Williams, Alpheus Starkey
Williams, Ephraim
Williams, George Washington
Williams, Jonathan
Williams, Otho Holland
Williamson, Andrew
Wilson, James Grant
Wilson, James Harrison
Winchester, James
Winder, John Henry
Winder, Levin
Winder, William Henry
Winn, Richard
Winslow, Edward Francis
Winslow, John
Winston, Joseph
Winthrop, John
Wofford, William Tatum
Wood, Leonard
Wood, Thomas John
Woodbury, Daniel Phineas
Woodford, Stewart Lyndon
Woodford, William
Woods, Charles Robert
Wool, John Ellis
Worth, William Jenkins

Wraxall, Peter
Wright, Horatio Gouveneur
Wright, Marcus Joseph
Wyatt, Aiken David
Yell, Archibald
York, Alvin Cullum
Young, Pierce Manning Butler
Youngs, John
Zeilin, Jacob
Ziegler, David
Zollicoffer, Felix Kirk
SONGWRITER (See also COMPOSER,
   HYMNOLOGIST, LYRICIST,
   MUSICIAN)
Bennet, Sanford Fillmore
Chaplin, Ralph Hosea
Emmett, Daniel Decatur
Golden, John
Guthrie, Woody
Hanby, Benjamin Russel
Handy, William Christopher
Harris, Charles Kassell
Hendrix, Jimi
Hopkinson, Joseph
Key, Francis Scott
Maxwell, Elsa
Randall, James Ryder
Rooney, Pat
Rose, Billy
Ross, Alexander Coffman
Speaks, Oley
Stern, Joseph William
Williams, Bert
Williams, (Hiram) Hank
Work, Henry Clay
SONNETEER (See also BALLADIST,
   POET)
Very, Jones
SOPRANO (See SINGER)
SOVIET AGENT (See also SPY)
Bentley, Elizabeth Terrill
Chambers, Whittaker
SPACE PIONEER
Goddard, Robert Hutchings
SPEAKER OF HOUSE OF BURGESSES
Randolph, Sir John
Randolph, Peyton
Robinson, John
SPEAKER OF HOUSE OF REPRESEN-
   TATIVES
Bankhead, William Brockman
Byrns, Joseph Wellington
Clark, Champ
Henderson, David Bremner
Longworth, Nicholas,
   1869–1931
Macon, Nathaniel
Martin, Joseph William, Jr.
Muhlenberg, Frederick
   Augustus Conrad
Orr, James Lawrence
Rainey, Henry Thomas
Randall, Samuel Jackson
Rayburn, Samuel Taliaferro
   ("Sam")
Reed, Thomas Brackett
Stevenson, Andrew
Varnum, Joseph Bradley
SPECULATOR (See also LAND
   SPECULATOR, REAL-ESTATE
   OPERATOR)
Craigie, Andrew

Doty, James Duane
Drew, Daniel
Fisk, James
Gates, John Warne
   ("Bet-you-a-million")
Hutchinson, Benjamin Peters
Keene, James Robert
Morse, Charles Wyman
Sully, Daniel John
Swartwout, Samuel
Wilson, James
SPIRITUALIST (See also RELIGIOUS
   LEADER)
Colby, Luther
Davenport, Ira Erastus
Davis, Andrew Jackson
Dods, John Bovee
Fox, Margaret
King, William Benjamin Basil
Post, Isaac
Sargent, Epes
Sprague, Achsa W.
SPORTS CONCESSIONAIRE
Stevens, Frank Mozley
SPORTS ENTHUSIAST
Biddle, Anthony Joseph Drexel,
   Jr.
SPORTS EXECUTIVE
Kilpatrick, John Reed
SPORTS JOURNALIST
Rice, (Henry) Grantland
SPORTSMAN (See also ATHLETE,
   SPECIFIC SPORTS)
Astor, William Vincent
Chadwick, Henry
Cochran, Alexander Smith
Davis, Dwight Filley
Duryea, Hermanes Barkulo
Greenslet, Ferris
Hitchcock, Thomas
Holder, Charles Frederick
Lasker, Albert Davis
Lorillard, Pierre
McLellan, Isaac
Reynolds, William Neal
Riddle, Samuel Doyle
Ruppert, Jacob
Samuels, Edward Augustus
Spalding, Albert Goodwill
Thompson, Robert Means
Vanderbilt, William Kissam
Wharton, Robert
Whitney, Harry Payne
Whitney, William Collins
SPORTS PROMOTER
Fox, Richard Kyle
Jacobs, Michael Strauss
Rickard, George Lewis ("Tex")
Sullivan, James Edward
Ward, Arch Burdette
SPORTS WRITER (See also JOUR-
   NALIST)
Dorgan, Thomas Aloysius
Elliott, William
Masterson, William Barclay
Ward, Arch Burdette
SPY (See also SOVIET AGENT)
Boyd, Belle
Cushman, Pauline
Eisler, Gerhart
Hale, Nathan
Heron, William

Moody, James
Rosenberg, Ethel
Rosenberg, Julius
Scott, John
Vardill, John
Wentworth, Paul
Wright, Patience Lovell
STAGE DESIGNER (See THEATRICAL
   DESIGNER)
STAGE DIRECTOR (See THEATRICAL
   DIRECTOR)
STAINED GLASS ARTIST
Connick, Charles Jay
STATE OFFICIAL
De Saussure, Henry William
Heath, James Ewell
Lloyd, Edward, 1744–1796
Matlack, Timothy
Mazureau, Étienne
Murphy, William Sumter
Robertson, Jerome Bonaparte
Schuyler, George Washington
Whitehill, Robert
Wickliffe, Charles Anderson
Wyllys, George
Yates, John Van Ness
STATESMAN (See also DIPLOMAT)
Adams, Charles Francis
Adams, Samuel
Aiken, William
Aldrich, Nelson Wilmarth
Alexander, James
Alston, Joseph
Ames, Fisher
Anderson, Richard Clough
Armstrong, Samuel Turell
Baldwin, Abraham
Barbour, James
Barbour, Philip Pendleton
Barker, Josiah
Barlow, Joel
Barnard, Daniel Dewey
Barnwell, Robert Woodward
Barry, William Taylor
Barry, William Taylor Sullivan
Barton, David
Bassett, Richard
Batcheller, George Sherman
Bates, Edward
Baxter, Henry
Bayard, James Ash(e)ton
Bayard, John Bubenheim
Bayard, Thomas Francis
Baylies, Francis
Bedford, Gunning
Belknap, William Worth
Bell, Jacob
Bell, John
Benjamin, Judah Philip
Benning, Henry Lewis
Benton, Thomas Hart
Bergh, Christian
Bergh, Henry
Biddle, Nicholas
Blaine, James Gillespie
Blair, Francis Preston
Blair, Montgomery
Bland, Richard
Boudinot, Elias
Bowdoin, James
Boyden, Roland William
Bradish, Luther

Bradstreet, Simon
Bragg, Thomas
Braxton, Carter
Brearly, David
Breckenridge, John
Breckinridge, John Cabell
Brentano, Lorenz
Briggs, George Nixon
Bristow, Benjamin Helm
Brown, Joseph Emerson
Cary, Archibald
Cass, Lewis
Chase, Salmon Portland
Choate, Rufus
Clarke, John
Clayton, John Middleton
Clinton, De Witt
Clinton, George
Colquitt, Alfred Holt
Colquitt, Walter Terry
Conrad, Charles Magill
Cooke, Elisha
Crittenden, John Jordan
Culberson, Charles Allen
Culberson, David Browning
Cullom, Shelby Moore
Cummings, Albert Baird
Curry, Jabez Lamar Monroe
Cushing, Caleb
Dana, Samuel Whittelsey
Dane, Nathan
Davis, Henry Winter
Davis, John
Dawson, John
Dickinson, John
Dillingham, William Paul
Dolliver, Jonathan Prentiss
Doniphan, Alexander William
Doolittle, James Rood
Dow, Henry
Eaton, Charles Aubrey
Eliot, Samuel Atkins
Ellsworth, Oliver
Emerson, Haven
Eustis, George
Eustis, James Biddle
Evarts, William Maxwell
Everett, Edward
Fersen, Hans Axel
Few, William
Fish, Hamilton
Fleming, William
Forsyth, John
Franklin, Benjamin
Frelinghuysen, Frederick
  Theodore
Galloway, Joseph
Garnett, Muscoe Russell
  Hunter
Gerry, Elbridge
Gholson, Thomas Saunders
Gibson, Randall Lee
Giles, William Branch
Gillette, Francis
Gilmer, Thomas Walker
Goode, John
Gordon, John Brown
Gordon, William Fitzhugh
Gorham, Nathaniel
Graham, William Alexander
Gresham, Walter Quintin
Griffin, Cyrus

Griggs, John William
Hall, Lyman
Hamilton, Alexander,
  1757–1804
Hardy, Samuel
Harnett, Cornelius
Harpur, Robert
Harrison, Benjamin, 1726–1791
Harvie, John
Heathcote, Caleb
Henry, Patrick
Hewitt, Abram Stevens
Hill, Benjamin Harvey
Hindman, Thomas Carmichael
Hopkinson, Francis
Hosmer, Titus
Houston, Samuel
Humphreys, David
Hunter, Robert Mercer
  Taliaferro
Ide, Henry Clay
Iredell, James
Jay, John
Jefferson, Thomas
Jenifer, Daniel of St. Thomas
Johnson, William Samuel
Johnston, Josiah Stoddard
Johnston, Zachariah
Jones, Joseph
Judd, Gerrit Parmele
Kennedy, John Pendleton
Kern, John Worth
Körner, Gustav Philip
Lafayette, Marie Joseph Paul
  Yves Roch Gilbert du Motier
  Marquis de
Lamar, Lucius Quintus
  Cincinnatus
Laurens, Henry
Lawrence, Abbott
Lee, Francis Lightfoot
Lee, Henry, 1756–1818
Lee, Richard
Lee, Richard Bland
Lee, Richard Henry
Leigh, Benjamin Watkins
Livingston, Edward
Livingston, Robert R.,
  1746–1813
Logan, James, 1674–1751
Lovejoy, Owen
Lumpkin, Wilson
McKean, Thomas
Marcy, William Learned
Marshall, George Catlett, Jr.
Mason, George
Menard, Pierre
Mitchell, Stephen Mix
Morris, Gouverneur
Morris, Lewis Richard
Nelson, John
Osborn, Thomas Andrew
Otis, Harrison Gray
Parker, Joel
Parker, Richard Elliot
Pattison, Robert Emory
Patton, John Mercer
Pinckney, Charles Cotesworth
Pinkney, William
Pitkin, Timothy
Poinsett, Joel Roberts
Porter, David Rittenhouse

Powel, John Hare
Randolph, John, 1773–1833
Reed, Joseph
Rhett, Robert Barnwell
Richardson, James Daniel
Roberts, Oran Milo
Robinson, Moses
Rodney, Caesar
Rodney, Caesar Augustus
Rublee, George
Rush, Richard
Rutledge, John
Schuyler, Philip John
Seward, William Henry
Sherman, John, 1823–1900
Sherman, Roger
Silsbee, Nathaniel
Slade, William
Smith, Meriwether
Smith, Samuel
Strong, Caleb
Sullivan, James
Sullivan, John
Tallmadge, James
Vane, Sir Henry
Watterson, Henry
Webster, Daniel
Williamson, Hugh
STATES RIGHTS ADVOCATE (See
  also AGITATOR, REFORMER)
Paine, Byron
Quitman, John Anthony
STATISTICIAN (See also INSURANCE
  EXPERT)
Abbott, Samuel Warren
Adams, Henry Carter
Ayres, Leonard Porter
Babson, Roger Ward
Day, David Talbot
De Bow, James Dunwoody
  Brownson
Dennis, James Shepard
Dodge, Jacob Richards
Dorchester, Daniel
Falkner, Roland Post
Hill, Joseph Adna
Hittell, John Shertzer
Hoffman, Frederick Ludwig
Hourwich, Isaac Aaronovich
Jarvis, Edward
Kennedy, Joseph Camp Griffith
Koren, John
McPherson, Logan Grant
Mayo-Smith, Richmond
North, Simon Newton Dexter
Ogburn, William Fielding
Pearl, Raymond
Persons, Warren Milton
Pidgin, Charles Felton
Rossiter, William Sidney
Rubinow, Isaac Max
Schem, Alexander Jacob
Shattuck, Lemuel
Stouffer, Samuel Andrew
Swank, James Moore
Sydenstricker, Edgar
Walker, Francis Amasa
Weeks, Joseph Dame
Wilbur, Cressy Livingston
Woytinsky, Wladimir
  Savelievich
Wright, Carroll Davidson

STEAMBOAT BUILDER
  Rees, James
STEAMBOAT CAPTAIN (See also
  SHIP CAPTAIN)
  Bixby, Horace Ezra
  Ford, John Baptiste
  King, Richard
  Marsh, Grant Prince
  Rogers, Moses
  Sellers, Isaiah
  Shreve, Henry Miller
  Vandergrift, Jacob Jay
STEAMBOAT OPERATOR
  Gibbons, Thomas
  La Barge, Joseph
  Ogden, Aaron
  Reed, Simeon Gannett
STEAMSHIP OWNER (See also SHIP-
  OWNER)
  Grace, William Russell
  Hallett, Benjamin
  Newton, Isaac, 1794–1858
  Ralston, William Chapman
STEEL COMPANY EXECUTIVE
  Farrell, James Augustine
  Graff, Everett Dwight
STOCK BREEDER (See also CATTLE-
  MAN)
  Allen, Lewis Falley
  Buford, Abraham
  Hammond, Edwin
  Harris, William Alexander
  Jackson, William Hicks
  McNeill, John Hanson
  Matthews, Claude
  Morris, Nelson
  Sheedy, Dennis
STOCKBROKER (See also BANKER,
  CAPITALIST, FINANCIER)
  Colgate, James Boorman
  Cuppia, Jerome Chester
  Du Pont, Francis Irénée
  Hendrick, Ellwood
  Hutton, Edward Francis
  Lawson, Thomas William
  Merrill, Charles Edward
  Ouimet, Francis Desales
  Riis, Mary Phillips
STONEMASON
  Edmondson, William
STREET RAILWAY BUILDER
  Stephenson, John
  Wells, Erastus
STREET RAILWAY OPERATOR
  Johnson, Tom Loftin
  Mitten, Thomas Eugene
  Scullin, John
SUBMARINE PIONEER
  Lake, Simon
SUFFRAGIST (See also FEMINIST)
  Belmont, Alva Ertskin Smith
    Vanderbilt
  Blackwell, Alice Stone
  Brown, Gertrude Foster
  Catt, Carrie Clinton Lane
    Chapman
  Flynn, Elizabeth Gurley
  Hooper, Jessie Annette Jack
  Stevens, Doris
  Wells, Harriet Sheldon
  Whitney, Charlotte Anita
  Younger, Maud

SUGAR PLANTER (See also
  AGRICULTURIST, FARMER,
  PLANTER)
  Behan, William James
  Boré, Jean Étienne
SUGAR REFINER
  Havemeyer, Henry Osborne
  Havemeyer, William Frederick
  Stuart, Robert Leighton
SUGAR TECHNOLOGIST
  Hooker, Samuel Cox
SUPERINTENDENT OF INDIAN AF-
  FAIRS
  Johnson, Guy
  Johnson, Sir John
  Johnson, Sir William
  Mitchell, David Dawson
  Pilcher, Joshua
  Stuart, John
SUPREME COURT CHIEF JUSTICE
  Chase, Salmon Portland
  Ellsworth, Oliver
  Fuller, Melville Weston
  Hughes, Charles Evans
  Jay, John
  Marshall, John
  Stone, Harlan Fiske
  Taft, William Howard
  Taney, Roger Brooke
  Vinson, Fred(erick) Moore
  Waite, Morrison Remick
  White, Edward Douglass
SUPREME COURT JUSTICE
  Baldwin, Henry
  Barbour, Philip Pendleton
  Blair, John
  Blatchford, Samuel
  Bradley, Joseph P.
  Brandeis, Louis Dembitz
  Brewer, David Josiah
  Brown, Henry Billings
  Burton, Harold Hitz
  Butler, Pierce
  Campbell, John Archibald
  Cardozo, Benjamin Nathan
  Catron, John
  Chase, Samuel
  Clarke, John Hessin
  Clifford, Nathan
  Curtis, Benjamin Robbins
  Cushing, William
  Daniel, Peter Vivian
  Davis, David
  Day, William Rufus
  Duvall, Gabriel
  Field, Stephen Johnson
  Frankfurter, Felix
  Gray, Horace
  Grier, Robert Cooper
  Harlan, John Marshall
  Holmes, Oliver Wendell
  Hughes, Charles Evans
  Hunt, Ward
  Iredell, James
  Jackson, Howell Edmunds
  Jackson, Robert Houghwout
  Johnson, Thomas
  Johnson, William
  Lamar, Lucius Quintus
    Cincinnatus
  Livingston, Henry Brockholst
  Lurton, Horace Harmon

  McKenna, Joseph
  McKinley, John
  McLean, John
  McReynolds, James Clark
  Matthews, Stanley
  Miller, Samuel Freeman
  Minton, Sherman
  Moody, William Henry
  Moore, Alfred
  Murphy, Frank
  Nelson, Samuel
  Peckham, Rufus Wheeler
  Pitney, Mahlon
  Roberts, Owen Josephus
  Rutledge, John
  Rutledge, Wiley Blount
  Sanford, Edward Terry
  Shiras, George
  Stone, Harlan Fiske
  Story, Joseph
  Strong, William
  Sutherland, George
  Swayne, Noah Haynes
  Thompson, Smith
  Todd, Thomas
  Trimble, Robert
  Van Devanter, Willis
  Washington, Bushrod
  Wayne, James Moore
  White, Edward Douglass
  Wilson, James
  Woodbury, Levi
  Woods, William Burnham
SURGEON (See also PHYSICIAN)
  Agnew, David Hayes
  Allison, Nathaniel
  Ambler, James Markham
    Marshall
  Ashhurst, John
  Atlee, John Light
  Atlee, Washington Lemuel
  Baer, William Stevenson
  Barnes, Joseph K.
  Barton, John Rhea
  Barton, William Paul Crillon
  Batchelder, John Putnam
  Battey, Robert
  Baxley, Henry Willis
  Beaumont, William
  Beck, Carl
  Bernays, Augustus Charles
  Bevan, Arthur Dean
  Bigelow, Henry Jacob
  Billings, John Shaw
  Blackburn, Luke Pryor
  Blalock, Alfred
  Bloodgood, Joseph Colt
  Bradford, Edward Hickling
  Brainard, Daniel
  Brinton, John Hill
  Brophy, Truman William
  Brown, Frederic Tilden
  Bryant, Joseph Decatur
  Buck, Gurdon
  Bull, William Tillinghast
  Bumstead, Freeman Josiah
  Burnet, William
  Cabot, Arthur Tracy
  Cabot, Hugh
  Carnochan, John Murray
  Carrel, Alexis
  Carson, Simeon Lewis

Chisolm, John Julian
Chovet, Abraham
Condit, John
Cooper, Elias Samuel
Crile, George Washington
Cushing, Harvey Williams
Cutler, Elliott Carr
Da Costa, John Chalmers
Dandy, Walter Edward
Davidge, John Beale
Davis, Henry Gassett
Davis, John Staige
Deaver, John Blair
Delafield, Edward
Dennis, Frederic Shepard
Dorsey, John Syng
Dowell, Greensville
Downer, Eliphalet
Drew, Charles Richard
Dudley, Benjamin Winslow
Edebohls, George Michael
Elman, Robert
Elsberg, Charles Albert
Eve, Paul Fitzsimons
Fayssoux, Peter
Fenger, Christian
Ferguson, Alexander High
Finney, John Miller Turpin
Floyd, John
Fowler, George Ryerson
Fowler, Russell Story
Frazier, Charles Harrison
Gaillard, Edwin Samuel
Garlick, Theodatus
Garretson, James
Gaston, James McFadden
Gerrish, Frederic Henry
Gerster, Arpad Geyza Charles
Gibson, William
Gihon, Albert Leary
Gilliam, David Tod
Goldsmith, Middleton
Gorgas, William Crawford
Graham, Evarts Ambrose
Gross, Samuel David
Gross, Samuel Weissell
Halsted, William Stewart
Hamilton, Frank Hastings
Hammond, William Alexander
Hartley, Frank
Hays, John Coffee
Hayward, George
Heap, Samuel Davies
Helmuth, William Tod
Henrotin, Fernand
Hodgen, John Thompson
Holmes, Bayard Taylor
Hosack, Alexander Eddy
Howe, Andrew Jackson
Hullihen, Simon P.
Jackson, Edward
Jackson, Hall
Jameson, Horatio Gates
Jeffries, Benjamin Joy
Johnston, George Ben
Jones, John
Judd, Edward Starr
Judson, Adoniram Brown
Kean, Jefferson Randolph
Keen, William Williams
Kellogg, John Harvey
Kelly, Howard Atwood

Keyes, Edward Lawrence
Kilty, William
Kimball, Gilman
Kinloch, Robert Alexander
Kirk, Norman Thomas
Kolle, Frederick Strange
Lahey, Frank Howard
Lane, Levi Cooper
Lawson, Thomas
Lefferts, George Morewood
Lewis, Dean De Witt
Lincoln, Rufus Pratt
Lloyd, James
Lockrey, Sarah Hunt
Long, Crawford Williamson
Lovell, Joseph
Lovett, Robert Williamson
Lower, William Edgar
McBurney, Charles
McClellan, George, 1796–1847
McCosh, Andrew James
McDowell, Ephraim
McGuire, Hunter Holmes
Mann, James
March, Alden
Marcy, Henry Orlando
Martin, Franklin Henry
Martin, Henry Austin
Mastin, Claudius Henry
Matas, Rudolph
Maury, Francis Fontaine
Maynard, Edward
Mayo, Charles Horace
Mayo, William James
Mayo, William Worrell
Mearns, Edgar Alexander
Merrill, James Cushing
Mettauer, John Peter
Mixter, Samuel Jason
Moore, Edward Mott
Moore, James Edward
Moore, Samuel Preston
Mott, Valentine
Mumford, James Gregory
Murphy, John Benjamin
Mussey, Reuben Dimond
Nancrède, Charles Beylard
  Guérard de
Neill, John
Norris, George Washington
Ochsner, Albert John
O'Reilly, Robert Maitland
Otto, Bodo
Owen, Griffith
Packard, John Hooker
Palmer, James Croxall
Pancoast, Joseph
Park, Roswell
Parker, Willard
Parsons, Usher
Peck, Charles Howard
Physick, Philip Syng
Pilcher, Lewis Stephen
Pilcher, Paul Monroe
Pinkney, Ninian
Post, Wright
Prevost, François Marie
Price, Joseph
Randolph, Jacob
Ransohoff, Joseph
Reid, Mont Rogers
Reid, William Wharry

Richardson, Maurice Howe
Richardson, Tobias Gibson
Robinson, Frederick Byron
Rogers, Stephen
Satterlee, Richard Sherwood
Sayre, Lewis Albert
Sayre, Reginald Hall
Senn, Nicholas
Shrady, George Frederick
Smith, Ashbel
Smith, Nathan, 1762–1829
Smith, Nathan Ryno
Smith, Stephen
Souchon, Edmond
Spalding, Lyman
Spencer, Pitman Clemens
Sternberg, George Miller
Stevens, Alexander Hodgdon
Stimson, Lewis Atterbury
Stitt, Edward Rhodes
Stone, Warren
Taylor, Charles Fayette
Teusler, Rudolf Bolling
Thorek, Max
Tiffany, Louis McLane
Tilton, James
Toland, Hugh Huger
Twitchell, Amos
Van Buren, William Holme
Vance, Ap Morgan
Vander Veer, Albert
Van Hook, Weller
Van Lennep, William Bird
Walter, Albert G.
Warbasse, James Peter
Warren, John
Warren, John Collins,
  1778–1856
Warren, John Collins,
  1842–1927
Weir, Robert Fulton
White, James William
Whitman, Royal
Willard, De Forest
Williams, Daniel Hale
Wilson, Henry Parke Custis
Wood, James Rushmore
Wood, Thomas
Woodhull, Alfred Alexander
Woodward, Henry
Wyeth, John Allan
SURVEYOR (See also GEODESIST,
  HYDROGRAPHER)
Applegate, Jesse
Borden, Gail
Burt, William Austin
Clark, Abraham
De Brahm, William Gerard
De Witt, Simeon
Ellicott, Andrew
Fry, Joshua
Holme, Thomas
Hooker, Philip
Hudde, Andries
Hulbert, Edwin James
Jenkins, John, 1728–1785
Jenkins, John, 1751 o.s.–1827
Kilbourne, James
Leeds, Daniel
Marshall, Thomas
Mayo, William
Penington, Edward

Porter, Andrew
Strong, Moses McCure
SWIMMING COACH
Kiphuth, Robert John Herman
SWINDLER (See also CRIMINAL)
Means, Gaston Bullock
Musica, Philip Mariano Fausto
Scott, John
SYPHILOLOGIST (See also PHYSICIAN)
Pusey, William Allen

TANK (MILITARY) DESIGNER
Christie, John Walter
TANNER
Cummings, John
Easton, Nicholas
Edwards, William
TARIFF EXPERT
O'Brien, Robert Lincoln
TAVERN KEEPER (See HOTELMAN)
TAX COMMISSIONER
Haugen, Nils Pederson
TAX EXPERT (See also ACCOUNTANT)
Lasser, Jacob Kay
Purdy, Lawson
TAXIDERMIST
Akeley, Carl Ethan
Maynard, Charles Johnson
TAXONOMIST (See also BOTANIST, ZOOLOGIST)
Gill, Theodore Nicholas
Merrill, Elmer Drew
TEACHER (See also EDUCATOR, PROFESSOR, SCHOLAR)
General
Agnew, David Hayes
Allen, Hervey
Archer, John
Arvin, Newton
Bache, Franklin
Bacon, Alice Mabel
Baermann, Carl
Bailey, Florence Augusta Merriam
Baker, Benjamin Franklin
Barrows, Alice Prentice
Bartlett, Elisha
Barton, William Paul Crillon
Beal, William James
Beck, Johann Heinrich
Blackmur, Richard Palmer
Blodgett, Benjamin Colman
Bradbury, William Batchelder
Brooks, Byron Alden
Brown, Solyman
Bumstead, Harry Andrews
Cobb, Andrew Jackson
Coerne, Louis Adolphe
Coffin, Robert Peter Tristram
Cogswell, Joseph Green
Cole, Chester Cicero
Cooke, Josiah Parsons
Corson, Hiram
Crafts, James Mason
Crane, Thomas Frederick
Dabney, Robert Lewis
Dabney, Virginius
Dannreuther, Gustav
Davis, Noah Knowles
Delano, Jane Arminda

Dennison, Walter
Douglass, David Bates
Doyle, Sarah Elizabeth
Duchesne, Rose Philippine
Dunglison, Robley
Dunning, William Archibald
Durant, Henry
Duveneck, Frank
Eakins, Thomas
Edman, Irwin
Eichbery, Julius
Elson, Louis Charles
Emery, Henry Crosby
Emery, Stephen Albert
Emmons, Ebenezer
Erskine, John
Estabrook, Joseph
Eustis, Henry Lawrence
Everett, Edward
Eytinge, Rose
Fauset, Jessie Redmon
Fay, Edwin Whitefield
Fernald, Charles Henry
Fernow, Bernhard Eduard
Flint, Austin
Folsom, Charles
Francke, Kuno
Frazer, John Fries
Frothingham, Arthur Lincoln
Fulton, Robert Burwell
Gallaudet, Edward Miner
Garman, Charles Edward
Garry, Spokane
Gaston, James McFadden
Gibbs, Josiah Willard
Goessmann, Charles Anthony
Goodrich, Alfred John
Gorgas, Josiah
Gould, Nathaniel Duren
Gould, Robert Simonton
Green, Jacob
Griffes, Charles Tomlinson
Griscom, John
Gross, Samuel David
Gross, Samuel Weissell
Gruening, Emil
Hale, Philip Leslie
Hamilton, Edith
Hamlin, Alfred Dwight Foster
Hanchett, Henry Granger
Harrison, Gessner
Harshberger, John William
Haven, Joseph
Henri, Robert
Herbermann, Charles George
Hodge, Archibald Alexander
Hoffman, David
Hoffman, Richard
Holmes, Nathaniel
Holmes, Oliver Wendell
Holyoke, Samuel
Hoppin, James Mason
Houston, William Churchill
Howard, George Elliott
Humphreys, Milton Wylie
Hyde, Charles Cheney
Inglis, Alexander James
Ives, Halsey Cooley
Jackson, George K.
James, Thomas Chalkley
Jameson, Horatio Gates
Jarrell, Randall

Jarvis, Charles H.
Jenks, Jeremiah Whipple
Johnson, Allen
Johnson, Henry
Jordan, David Starr
Joseffy, Rafael
Kay, Edgar Boyd
Kearsley, John
Kelly, Aloysius Oliver Joseph
Kinnersley, Ebenezer
Kirkwood, Daniel
Klein, Bruno Oscar
Klein, Joseph Frederic
Knapp, Seaman Asabel
Knapp, William Ireland
Kneisel, Franz
Knight, Sarah Kemble
Larcom, Lucy
Law, Andrew
Leavenworth, Francis Preserved
Leavitt, Dudley
LeConte, John
Lee, James Melvin
Le Jan, Francis
Lewisohn, Ludwig
Liebling, Emil
Lincoln, John Larkin
Lincoln, Mary Johnson Bailey
Lockwood, Belva Ann Bennett
Locy, William Albert
Lomax, John Taylor
Longfellow, Samuel
Lowell, James Russell
McCaw, James Brown
McClain, Emlin
MacDonald, Ronald
Magill, Edward Hicks
Malin, Patrick Murphy
Malter, Henry
Mansfield, Jared
Margolis, Max Leopold
Marshall, Louis
Marzo, Eduardo
Mason, Lowell
Mason, Luther Whiting
Mason, William
Mathews, William
Mathews, William Smythe Babcock
Mechem, Floyd Russell
Mees, Arthur
Meigs, James Aitken
Mell, Patrick Hues
Mielziner, Moses
Miles, George Henry
Miller, Kenneth Hayes
Millington, John
Minor, John Barbee
Minor, Raleigh Colston
Mitchell, Maria
Montgomery, Thomas Harrison
Moore, Charles Herbert
Mortimer, Mary
Muhlenberg, Frederick Augustus
Mulford, Elisha
Nancrède, Paul Joseph Guérard de
Nash, Henry Sylvester
Nelson, Henry Loomis
Newman, Samuel Phillips
Nichols, Ernest Fox

Niemeyer, John Henry
Northen, William Jonathan
Norton, Charles Eliot
Ogilvie, James
Oliver, Henry Kemble
Olmsted, Denison
Onderdonk, Henry
Osgood, George Laurie
Osgood, Howard
Packard, Alpheus Spring
Paine, John Knowles
Palmer, Alonzo Benjamin
Palmer, George Herbert
Parker, James Cutler Dunn
Parker, Richard Green
Parr, Samuel Wilson
Parrington, Vernon Louis
Parrish, Edward
Parrish, Joseph
Parsons, Albert Ross
Paul, Henry Martyn
Payne, William Morton
Peck, Thomas Ephraim
Peck, Tracy
Peckham, George Williams
Pennington, James W. C.
Pepper, William
Perabo, Johann Ernst
Pickett, Albert
Pike, Nicolas
Pitkin, Walter Boughton
Platner, Samuel Ball
Plummer, Mary Wright
Pomeroy, John Norton
Porter, Andrew
Porter, Sarah
Powell, Alma Webster
Powell, Edward Payson
Prang, Mary Amelia Dana Hicks
Prentiss, George Lewis
Price, William Thompson
Proctor, William
Pyle, Howard
Randolph, Sarah Nicholas
Reeve, Tapping
Renwick, James, 1792–1863
Rice, Fenelon Bird
Rice, Nathan Lewis
Richards, Joseph William
Richards, Thomas Addison
Richardson, Charles Francis
Riddle, Matthew Brown
Rivers, William James
Roethke, Theodore Huebner
Rolfe, William James
Root, Frederic Woodman
Root, George Frederick
Royce, Josiah
Rybner, Martin Cornelius
Sadtler, Samuel Philip
Safford, Truman Henry
Salisbury, Edward Elbridge
Sanborn, Katherine Abbott
Sanderson, John
Schofield, Henry
Schradieck, Henry
Schussele, Christian
Sedgwick, William Thompson
Sherwood, William Hall
Shippen, William
Short, Charles Wilkins
Sill, Edward Rowland

Small, Albion Woodbury
Smith, James Perrin
Smith, Jeremiah, 1837–1921
Smith, John Augustine
Smith, Lucy Harth
Smith, Nathan Ryno
Soley, James Russell
Southard, Elmer Ernest
Spiering, Theodore
Sprague, Charles Ezra
Sproull, Thomas
Stanford, John
Steele, Daniel
Steiner, Bernard Christian
Sternberg, Constantin
  Ivanovich, Edler von
Stoddard, John Tappan
Suzzallo, Henry
Tapper, Bertha Feiring
Tarr, Ralph Stockman
Taylor, Creed
Thayer, Amos Madden
Thomas, Amos Russell
Thurber, Charles
Thursby, Emma Cecilia
Tomlins, William Lawrence
Toumey, James William
Toy, Crawford Howell
Treat, Samuel
Tucker, John Randolph,
  1823–1897
Turner, Ross Sterling
Tyson, James
Upham, Thomas Cogswell
Van Dyke, Henry
Venable, William Henry
Vethake, Henry
Waddel, Moses
Walker, Timothy, 1802–1856
Warren, Minton
Washburn, Emory
Weidig, Adolf
Weir, John Ferguson
Weir, Robert Walter
Wendell, Barrett
Wentworth, George Albert
Wharton, Francis
Whedon, Daniel Denison
Whelpley, Henry Milton
Whitcomb, Selden Lincoln
White, George
White, Henry Clay
Whitney, Mary Watson
Wiley, Harvey Washington
Williams, Frederick Wells
Williams, George Huntington
Wilmarth, Lemuel Everett
Winchell, Alexander
Winchester, Caleb Thomas
Winship, Albert Edward
Winslow, Hubbard
Wood, Horatio Charles
Woodberry, George Edward
Woolson, Abba Louisa Goold
Wright, Philip Green
Wright, Theodore Lyman
Young, David
Zehn, Bernhard
Of American Literature
  Miller, Perry Gilbert Eddy
Of Art
  Gardner, Helen

McBride, Henry
Tarbell, Edmund Charles
Of Blind
  Allen, Edward Ellis
  Anagnos, Michael
  Campbell, Francis Joseph
  Churchman, William Henry
  Holt, Winifred
  Russ, John Dennison
  Smith, Joel West
  Wait, William Bell
Of Cooking
  Carson, Juliet
Of Deaf
  Clarke, Francis Devereux
  Clerc, Laurent
  Crouter, Albert Louis Edgerton
  Fay, Edward Allen
  Fisher, John Dix
  Gallaudet, Edward Miner
  Gallaudet, Thomas
  Gallaudet, Thomas Hopkins
  Hubbard, Gardiner Greene
  Nitchie, Edward Bartlett
  Peet, Harvey Prindle
  Peet, Isaac Lewis
  Porter, Samuel
  Rogers, Harriet Burbank
Of Elocution
  Murdock, James Edward
Of Insurance
  Huebner, Solomon Stephen
Of Law
  Llewellyn, Karl Nickerson
  Oliphant, Herman
Of Navigation
  Daboll, Nathan
Of Piano
  Lhévinne, Josef
  Samaroff, Olga
Of Theater
  Hamilton, Clayton
Of Voice
  Liebling, Estelle
TELEGRAPHER (INCLUDING TELE-
  PHONE)
  Creighton, Edward
  Eckert, Thomas Thompson
  Glidden, Charles Jasper
  Lefferts, Marshall
  Phillips, Walter Polk
  Stager, Anson
  Vail, Alfred
  Watson, Thomas Augustus
TELEPHONE EXECUTIVE
  Barnard, Chester Irving
TELESCOPE MAKER
  Porter, Russell Williams
TELEVISION COMMENTATOR
  Murrow, Edward (Egbert)
  Roscoe
TELEVISION PERSONALITY
  Kilgallen, Dorothy Mae
  Kovacs, Ernie
TEMPERANCE REFORMER (See also
  PROHIBITIONIST, REFORMER)
  Boole, Ella Alexander
  Cannon, James
  Chafin, Eugene Wilder
  Cherrington, Ernest Hurst
  Dow, Neal
  Dyott, Thomas W.

Foster, Judith Ellen Horton
Gough, John Bartholomew
Hunt, Mary Hannah Hanchett
Leavitt, Mary Greenleaf
   Clement
Lewis, Dioclesian
Minor, Lucian
Murphy, Francis
Nation, Carry Amelia Moore
Sargent, Lucius Manlius
Stearns, John Newton
Stewart, Eliza Daniel

TENNIS PLAYER (See also **ATH-LETE**)
Connolly, Maureen Catherine
Larned, William Augustus
McLoughlin, Maurice Evans
Mallory, Anna Margrethe
   ("Molla") Bjurstedt
Richards, Vincent
Sears, Richard Dudley
Tilden, William Tatem ("Big
   Bill")

TERRITORIAL DELEGATE (See also
   CONGRESSMAN, SENATOR)
Clark, Daniel
Kalanianaole, Jonah Kuhio
Pettigrew, Richard Franklin
Poindexter, George
Pope, Nathaniel
Poston, Charles Debrill
Sibley, Henry Hastings

TERRITORIAL GOVERNOR (See
   GOVERNOR, TERRITORIAL)

TEST PILOT
Royce, Ralph

THEATER ANNALIST
Mantle, (Robert) Burns

THEATER EXECUTIVE
Skouras, George Panagiotes

THEATER OPERATOR
Rothafel, Samuel Lionel

THEATER OWNER
Keith, Benjamin Franklin
Loew, Marcus
Proctor, Frederick Francis

THEATRE GUILD DIRECTOR
Helburn, Theresa

THEATRICAL AGENT
Marbury, Elisabeth

THEATRICAL DESIGNER
Geddes, Norman Bel
Jones, Robert Edmond
Tchelitchew, Pavel
Urban, Joseph

THEATRICAL DIRECTOR (See also
   DIRECTOR)
Carroll, Earl
Cowl, Jane
De Sylva, George Gard
   "Buddy"
Digges, Dudley
Fiske, Harrison Grey
Howard, Leslie
Jones, Robert Edmond
Kaufman, George S.
McClintic, Guthrie
Seymour, William
Smith, Winchell
Woolley, Edgar Montillion
   ("Monty")

THEATRICAL MANAGER (See also
   IMPRESARIO)
Abbey, Henry Eugene
Albee, Edward Franklin
Ames, Winthrop
Arden, Edwin Hunter
   Pendleton
Baker, Benjamin A.
Bateman, Sidney Frances
   Cowell
Beck, Martin
Bernard, John
Blake, William Rufus
Brady, William Aloysius
Buchanan, William Insco
Campbell, Bartley
Clarke, John Sleeper
Cooper, Thomas Abthorpe
Davis, John
Dunlap, William
Erlanger, Abraham Lincoln
Fiske, Stephen Ryder
Fleming, William Maybury
Ford, John Thomson
Fox, George Washington
   Lafayette
Frohman, Charles
Frohman, Daniel
Hallam, Lewis
Hamblin, Thomas Sowerby
Hammerstein, Oscar
Harrison, Gabriel
Haverly, Christopher
Henry, John, 1746–1794
Hodgkinson, John
Keith, Benjamin Franklin
Klaw, Marc
Lewis, Arthur
Logan, Cornelius Ambrosius
Ludlow, Noah Miller
McVicker, James Hubert
Merry, Ann Brunton
Miller, Henry
Mitchell, William, 1798–1856
Niblo, William
Palmer, Albert Marshman
Pastor, Antonio
Powell, Snelling
Pray, Isaac Clark
Presbrey, Eugene Wiley
Price, Stephen
Proctor, Frederick Francis
Proctor, Joseph
Rankin, McKee
Richings, Peter
Seymour, William
Simpson, Edmund Shaw
Smith, Solomon Franklin
Thorne, Charles Robert
Tyler, George Crouse
Warren, William, 1767–1832
Wemyss, Francis Courtney
Wheatley, William
Wignell, Thomas
Wikoff, Henry
Wood, William Burke

THEATRICAL PRODUCER (See also
   PRODUCER)
Todd, Mike

THEOLOGIAN (See also **RELIGIOUS
   LEADER**)
Apple, Thomas Gilmore

Appleton, Jesse
Beckwith, Clarence Augustine
Bellamy, Joseph
Boisen, Anton Theophilus
Bouquillon, Thomas Joseph
Brown, William Adams
Bruté de Rémur, Simon
   William Gabriel
Bushnell, Horace
Chambers, Talbot Wilson
Cheever, Henry Theodore
Clarke, William Newton
Coit, Thomas Winthrop
Colton, Walter
Corcoran, James Andrew
Curtis, Olin Alfred
Curtiss, Samuel Ives
Dabney, Robert Lewis
David, John Baptist Mary
Dempster, John
Dodge, Ebenezer
Du Bose, William Porcher
Edwards, Jonathan, 1703–1758
Edwards, Jonathan, 1745–1801
Emmons, Nathanael
Erdman, Charles Rosenbury
Evans, Hugh Davey
Everett, Charles Carroll
Fenn, William Wallace
Foster, Frank Hugh
Fritschel, Conrad Sigmund
Fritschel, Gottfried Leonhard
   Wilhelm
Gerhart, Emanuel Vogel
Gillis, James Martin
Girardeau, John Lafayette
Gräbner, August Lawrence
Hall, Charles Cuthbert
Harris, Samuel
Hart, Samuel
Hodge, Charles
Hoenecke, Gustav Adolf Felix
   Theodor
Hopkins, Mark
Hopkins, Samuel, 1721–1803
Hoye, Elling
Huidekoper, Frederic
Huidekoper, Harm Jan
Jacobs, Henry Eyster
Johnson, Elias Henry
Johnson, Erik Kristian
King, Henry Churchill
Knox, George William
Krauth, Charles Porterfield
Ladd, George Trumbull
Little, Charles Joseph
Lord, David Nevins
McCaffrey, John
Machen, John Gresham
Macintosh, Douglas Clyde
Mathews, Shailer
Monis, Judah
Moore, George Foot
Nevin, John Williamson
Niebuhr, Helmut Richard
Niles, Nathaniel, 1741–1828
Oftedal, Sven
Park, Edwards Amasa
Parker, Theodore
Patton, Francis Landey
Pieper, Franz August Otto
Prince, Thomas

Raymond, Miner
Richard, James William
Ridgaway, Henry Bascom
Ropes, James Hardy
Schmidt, Friedrich August
Schmucker, Samuel Simon
Seyffarth, Gustavus
Shedd, William Greenough
   Thayer
Smith, Gerald Birney
Smith, Henry Boynton
Smyth, Newman
Sperry, Willard Learoyd
Stearns, Oliver
Stevens, George Barker
Strong, Augustus Hopkins
Stuckenberg, John Henry
   Wilbrandt
Sverdrup, Georg
Talmage, James Edward
Taylor, Nathaniel William
Thacher, Peter
Thacher, Samuel Cooper
Tillich, Paul
Tyler, Bennet
Valentine, Milton
Walther, Carl Ferdinand
   Wilhelm
Watson, Charles Roger
Weidner, Revere Franklin
Weigel, Gustave
Wigglesworth, Edward,
   1693–1765
Wigglesworth, Edward,
   1732–1794
Woodbridge, Samuel Merrill
THEOSOPHIST (See also RELIGIOUS
   LEADER)
Judge, William Quan
Tingley, Katherine Augusta
   Westcott
Warrington, Albert Powell
TOBACCONIST
Ginter, Lewis
TOOL BUILDER
Hartness, James
TOPOGRAPHER (See also CARTOG-
   RAPHER, MAPMAKER)
Ogden, Herbert Gouverneur
TOPOGRAPHICAL ENGINEER (See
   ENGINEER, TOPOGRAPHICAL)
TOXICOLOGIST (See also PHYSI-
   CIAN)
Henderson, Yandell
Reese, John James
Underhill, Franklin Pell
Witthaus, Rudolph August
Wormley, Theodore George
TRACK AND FIELD COACH
Cromwell, Dean Bartlett
TRADER (See also FUR TRADER,
   TRAPPER)
Allerton, Isaac
Becknell, William
Campau, Joseph
Chouteau, René Auguste
Davenport, George
Glenn, Hugh
Gratiot, Charles
Gregg, Josiah
Hamilton, William Thomas
Harrison, James

Hayes, William Henry
Hubbell, John Lorenzo
Ingraham, Joseph
James, Thomas
Johnson, Levi
Kendrick, John
Laclede, Pierre
Le Sueur, Pierre
Magoffin, James Wiley
Morton, Thomas
Nelson, John
Nolan, Philip
O'Fallon, Benjamin
Oldham, John
Pollock, Oliver
Pryor, Nathaniel
Pynchon, William
Robidou, Antoine
St. Vrain, Ceran de Hault de
   Lassus de
Smith, Jedediah Strong
Vetch, Samuel
Waldo, David
Wyeth, Nathaniel Jarvis
TRADER (GRAIN) (See also
   SPECULATOR)
Armour, Philip Danforth
Bacon, Edward Payson
Hutchinson, Benjamin Peters
TRADER (INDIAN)
Adair, James
Byrd, William
Croghan, George
Harris, John
Lorimier, Pierre Louis
McClellan, Robert
Menard, Michel Branamour
Panton, William
Rice, Henry Mower
Trent, William
Truteau, Jean Baptiste
TRADE UNIONIST
Sullivan, James William
Younger, Maud
TRAFFIC REGULATION EXPERT
Eno, William Phelps
TRAITOR
Arnold, Benedict
Church, Benjamin
TRANSCENDENTALIST (See also
   RELIGIOUS LEADER)
Hedge, Frederic Henry
Thoreau, Henry David
Very, Jones
TRANSLATOR (See also LINGUIST)
Anderson, Henry Tompkins
Bingham, Hiram
Booth, Mary Louise
Conant, Hannah O'Brien
   Chaplin
Conant, Thomas Jefferson
Cook, Martha Elizabeth Duncan
   Walker
Crawford, John Martin
Dole, Nathan Haskell
Ferguson, Elizabeth Graeme
George, Grace
Greene, Nathaniel
Hadas, Moses
Hapgood, Isabel Florence
Hedge, Frederic Henry
Hempel, Charles Julius

Humphries, George Rolfe
Johnson, Henry
Kroeger, Adolph Ernst
Lenker, John Nicholas
Lennox, Charlotte Ramsay
Leonard, William Ellery
Mayhew, Experience
Montgomery, George
   Washington
Moore, Annie Aubertine
   Woodward
O'Brien, Justin
Parsons, Thomas William
Payne, William Morton
Phillips, Henry
Preston, Harriet Waters
Robinson, Thérèse Albertine
   Louise von Jakob
Rupp, Israel Daniel
Schereschewsky, Samuel Isaac
   Joseph
Taylor, Bayard
Worcester, Samuel Austin
TRANSPORTATION EXECUTIVE
Hertz, John Daniel
TRANSPORTER (See EXPRESSMAN,
   MESSENGER, MAIL-RUNNER)
TRAPPER (See also FUR TRADER,
   TRADER)
Baker, James
Carson, Christopher ("Kit")
Clyman, James
Colter, John
Fitzpatrick, Thomas
Glass, Hugh
Hamilton, William Thomas
James, Thomas
Laramie, Jacques
Leonard, Zenas
Meek, Joseph L.
Newell, Robert
Pattie, James Ohio
Robidou, Antoine
Russell, Osborne
Walker, Joseph Reddeford
Williams, William Sherley
Wolfskill, William
Wootton, Richens Lacy
Young, Ewing
TRAVELER (See also ADVENTURER,
   EXPLORER)
Ballou, Maturin Murray
Bartram, William
Browne, John Ross
Carpenter, Frank George
Carver, Jonathan
Catesby, Mark
Cuming, Fortescue
Curtis, William Eleroy
Estes, Dana
Farnham, Thomas Jefferson
Flandrau, Charles Macomb
Josselyn, John
Knox, Thomas Wallace
Lahontan, Louis-Armand de
   Lom D'Arce, Baron de
Lawson, John
Lederer, John
Melish, John
Michaux, François André
Möllhausen, Heinrich Baldwin
Pory, John

Rowland, Henry Cottrell
Royall, Anne Newport
Scattergood, Thomas
Schöpf, Johann David
Scidmore, Eliza Ruhamah
Stephens, John Lloyd
Taylor, Bayard
Vincent, Frank
Wislizenus, Frederick Adolph
TREASURER OF UNITED STATES
  (See also COMPTROLLER OF
  CURRENCY, SECRETARY OF
  TREASURY)
Hillegas, Michael
Spinner, Francis Elias
TREE-CARE EXPERT
Bartlett, Francis Alonzo
TREE SURGEON
Davey, John
TROMBONIST
Dorsey, Thomas Francis
  ("Tommy")
Teagarden, Weldon Leo
  ("Jack")
TRUMPETER
Elman, Harry ("Ziggy")
Page, Oran Thaddeus ("Lips")
TUBERCULOSIS RESEARCHER
Baldwin, Edward Robinson
TURFMAN (See also ATHLETE,
  BREEDER OF RACEHORSES,
  HORSE BREEDER, HORSE
  TRAINER, HORSEMAN, RACE-
  HORSE OWNER)
Bonner, Robert
De Lancey, James, 1732–1800
Geers, Edward Franklin
Hildreth, Samuel Clay
Johnson, William Ransom
Keene, James Robert
TYPE DESIGNER
Dwiggins, William Addison
Goudy, Frederic William
TYPEFOUNDER (See also IRON-
  FOUNDER)
Bruce, George
Buell, Abel
Mappa, Adam Gerard
TYPOGRAPHER
McMurtrie, Douglas Crawford
TYPOGRAPHIC DESIGNER
Cooper, Oswald Bruce

UNDERWORLD FIGURE (See also
  CRIMINAL, GANGSTER, ORGA-
  NIZED CRIME LEADER, RACK-
  ETEER)
Genovese, Vito
Guzik, Jack
Luchese, Thomas
UNION OFFICIAL
Besse, Arthur Lyman
Carter, William Samuel
Stone, Warren Sanford
UNION ORGANIZER
Martin, Warren Homer
Steuben, John
Thomas, Roland Jay
Whitfield, Owen
UNION REPRESENTATIVE
Dodd, Bella Visono

UNITED NATIONS AMBASSADOR
Austin, Warren Robinson
Stevenson, Adlai Ewing, II
UNITED NATIONS DIPLOMAT
Roosevelt, (Anna) Eleanor
UNITED NATIONS OFFICIAL
Pate, Maurice
UNIVERSITY ADMINISTRATOR
Birge, Edward Asahel
Case, Shirley Jackson
Day, George Parmly
Simmons, James Stevens
Sydnor, Charles Sackett
UNIVERSITY PRESIDENT (See COL-
  LEGE PRESIDENT)
UROLOGIST (See also PHYSICIAN)
Pilcher, Paul Monroe
Timberlake, Gideon
Young, Hugh Hampton
UTILITIES EXECUTIVE
McKinley, William Brown
Williams, Harrison Charles

VACCINATOR (See also PHYSICIAN)
Martin, Henry Austin
Waterhouse, Benjamin
VAGRANT
Pratt, Daniel, 1809–1887
VENTRILOQUIST (See also ENTER-
  TAINER)
Vattemare, Nicholas Marie
  Alexandre
VETERINARIAN (See also PHYSI-
  CIAN)
Bemis, Harold Edward
Kelser, Raymond Alexander
Moore, Veranus Alva
Pearson, Leonard
Salmon, Daniel Elmer
VICE-PRESIDENT OF CONFEDERACY
Stephens, Alexander Hamilton
VICE-PRESIDENT OF UNITED
  STATES
Adams, John
Arthur, Chester Alan
Barkley, Alben William
Breckinridge, John Cabell
Burr, Aaron
Calhoun, John Caldwell
Clinton, George
Colfax, Schuyler
Coolidge, Calvin
Curtis, Charles
Dallas, George Mifflin
Dawes, Charles Gates
Fairbanks, Charles Warren
Fillmore, Millard
Garner, John Nance
Gerry, Elbridge
Hamlin, Hannibal
Hendricks, Thomas Andrews
Hobart, Garret Augustus
Jefferson, Thomas
Johnson, Andrew
Johnson, Richard Mentor
King, William Rufus Devane
Marshall, Thomas Riley
Morton, Levi Parsons
Roosevelt, Theodore
Sherman, James Schoolcraft
Stevenson, Adlai Ewing
Tompkins, Daniel D.

Tyler, John
Van Buren, Martin
Wallace, Henry Agard
Wheeler, William Almon
Wilson, Henry
VIGILANTE (See also JAYHAWKER,
  OUTLAW)
Langford, Nathaniel Pitt
VINTNER
Petri, Angelo
VIOLINIST
Beck, Johann Heinrich
Bristow, George Frederick
Damrosch, Leopold
Dannreuther, Gustav
Eichburg, Julius
Elman, Mischa
Hill, Ureli Corelli
Kneisel, Franz
Kreisler, Fritz
Listemann, Bernhard
Loeffler, Charles Martin
Mannes, David
Mollenhauer, Emil
Musin, Ovide
Powell, Maud
Saslavsky, Alexander
Scheel, Fritz
Schradieck, Henry
Spalding, Albert
Spiering, Theodore
Stoessel, Albert Frederic
Urso, Camilla
Verbrugghen, Henri
White, Clarence Cameron
VIROLOGIST
Rivers, Thomas Milton
VITICULTURIST (See also AGRICUL-
  TURIST)
Adlum, John
Dufour, John James
Husmann, George
Munson, Thomas Volney
VOCATIONAL GUIDANCE PIONEER
Hatcher, Orie Latham
VOLCANOLOGIST
Jaggar, Thomas Augustus, Jr.

WALKER (See also ATHLETE)
O'Leary, Daniel
Weston, Edward Payson
WAR CORRESPONDENT (See also
  FOREIGN CORRESPONDENT,
  JOURNALIST, NEWSPAPER COR-
  RESPONDENT, NEWSPAPER RE-
  PORTER, PHOTOJOURNALIST)
Chapelle, Dickey
Comfort, Will Levington
Fall, Bernard B.
Gibbons, Floyd
Hare, James H.
Higgins, Marguerite
Pyle, Ernest Taylor
Reynolds, Quentin James
Whitney, Caspar
WAR HERO (See also SOLDIER)
York, Alvin Cullum
WELFARE ADMINISTRATOR
Hodson, William
WELFARE PLANNER
Dennison, Henry Sturgis

WELFARE WORKER (See also SO-CIAL WORKER)
Billikopf, Jacob
Folks, Homer
Moskowitz, Belle Lindner Israels
WHALING CAPTAIN (SEE ALSO SEA CAPTAIN)
Tyson, George Emory
WILD ANIMAL TRAINER
Beatty, Clyde Raymond
WILDLIFE CONSERVATIONIST
Hornaday, William Temple
WIT (See also COMEDIAN, COME-DIENNE, HUMORIST, SATIRIST)
Depew, Chauncey Mitchell
Herford, Oliver Brooke
Hughes, Christopher
WITCHCRAFT VICTIM
Hibbins, Ann
WOMEN'S FOREIGN MISSIONS LEADER
Peabody, Lucy Whitehead
WOOD CARVER (See also CRAFTS-MAN)
Kirchmayer, John
McIntire, Samuel
Morse, Freeman Harlow
WRESTLER
Leavitt, Frank Simmons ("Man Mountain Dean")
Lewis, Ed ("Strangler")
Muldoon, William
WRITER (NOTE: THE FOLLOWING ARE CLASSIFIED UNDER WRIT-ERS BECAUSE THE SPECIFIC FIELD IN WHICH THEY WROTE WAS SO DESIGNATED AT HEAD OF THE ARTICLE. FOR COM-PLETE LIST OF WRITERS SEE, IN ADDITION, AUTHOR, BIOGRA-PHER, DIARIST, DRAMATIST, ESSAYIST, HISTORIAN, JOUR-NALIST, LITERATEUR)
Abbott, Eleanor Hallowell (short story)
Adamic, Louis
Adams, Abigail (letter)
Adams, Cyrus Cornelius (geographical)
Adams, Frank Ramsay (screen)
Adams, Hannah (history)
Adams, William Taylor (juvenile)
Affleck, Thomas (agricultural)
Agee, James Rufus (screen)
Akins, Zoë (screen)
Aldrich, Bess Genevra Streeter (short story)
Aldrich, Thomas Bailey (story)
Alger, Horatio (juvenile)
Allen, James Lane (short story)
Allen, Lewis Falley (agricultural)
Allinson, Anne Crosby Emery
Ames, James Barr (legal)
Ammen, Daniel (naval)
Angell, Joseph Kinnicutt (legal)
Anthony, Katharine Susan
Arlen, Michael (short story)
Armstrong, George Dod (controversial)

Bailey, Florence Augusta Merriam
Bailey, (Irene) Temple (short story)
Baird, Henry Carey (economics)
Bard, Samuel (midwifery)
Barrett, Benjamin Fiske (religious)
Beatty, Adam (agricultural)
Beer, Thomas (short story)
Bemelmans, Ludwig
Benchley, Robert Charles
Benét, Stephen Vincent (short story)
Bennett, Edmund Hatch (legal)
Bigelow, Melville Madison (legal)
Blair, Emily Newell
Blakeslee, Howard Walter (science)
Blatch, Harriot Eaton Stanton (woman suffrage, peace)
Bogan, Louise Marie (short story)
Bolles, Frank (nature)
Bouvier, John (legal)
Bradford, Roark Whitney Wickliffe (short story)
Brickell, Henry Herschel
Brisbane, Arthur
Brown, John Mason, Jr.
Browne, Daniel Jay (agricultural)
Browne, Irving (legal)
Browning, Tod
Burdick, Eugene Leonard
Burdick, Francis Marion (legal)
Burgess, Thornton Waldo (juvenile)
Cabell, James Branch (essayist)
Callender, James Thomson (political)
Calverton, Victor Francis
Campbell, William Edward March (short story)
Carrington, Elaine Stern (magazine, radio script)
Carson, Rachel Louise (nature)
Catchings, Waddill
Cayton, Horace Roscoe
Chambers, Whittaker
Chapman, John Jay (essayist)
Checkley, John (controversial)
Clarke, Rebecca Sophia (juvenile)
Cocke, Philip St. George (agricultural)
Cohen, Octavus Roy (screen)
Cohn, Alfred A. (magazine, screen)
Colburn, Dana Pond (textbook)
Coleman, Lyman (religious)
Colman, Henry (agricultural)
Cooke, Philip Pendleton (story)
Cooke, Rose Terry (story)
Cullen, Countée Porter (essayist)
Da Ponte, Lorenzo (librettist)
Davenport, Russell Wheeler
Davis, Elmer Holmes (magazine)

Davis, Watson (science)
Deane, Samuel (agricultural)
Dercum, Francis Xavier (medical)
Dickson, David (agricultural)
Dobie, J(ames) Frank
Drinkwater, Jennie Maria (juvenile)
Dunglison, Robley (medical)
Eastman, Max Forrester
Edman, Irwin (philosophy)
Elliott, Charles Burke (legal)
Epstein, Philip G. (screen)
Faulkner (Falkner), William Cuthbert (short story)
Fauset, Jessie Redmon
Ferguson, Elizabeth Graeme (letter)
Fischer, Louis
Fischer, Ruth
Flandrau, Charles Macomb (essayist)
Fletcher, Alice Cunningham (Indian music)
Fletcher, Horace (nutrition)
Frank, Waldo David
Gág, Wanda (Hazel) (juvenile)
Gale, Benjamin (political)
Gardner, Erle Stanley (detective fiction)
Gaylord, Willis (agricultural)
Genung, John Franklin (religious)
Gilman, Charlotte Perkins Stetson
Gold, Michael
Goldbeck, Robert (music)
Gonzales, Ambrose Elliott (Negro dialect story)
Gouge, William M. (financial)
Greene, Samuel Stillman (textbook)
Greenleaf, Benjamin (mathematical textbook)
Guest, Edgar Albert (popular verse)
Gulick, John Thomas (evolution)
Hall, Bolton
Hammett, Samuel Dashiell (detective fiction)
Hawes, Charles Boardman (adventure)
Hazard, Rowland Gibson (philosophy)
Headley, Phineas Camp (biography)
Heard, Franklin Fiske (legal)
Heaton, John Langdon (editorial)
Hecht, Ben (screen)
Held, John, Jr.
Hemingway, Ernest Miller (short story)
Hening, William Waller (legal)
Henshall, James Alexander (angling)
Herbert, Frederick Hugh (screen)
Hergesheimer, Joseph (short story)

High, Stanley Hoflund
  (magazine)
Hilliard, Francis (legal)
Hindus, Maurice Gerschon
Hobart, Alice Nourse Tisdale
Hoffman, Frederick Ludwig
Hoffmann, Francis Arnold
  (agricultural)
Horner, William Edmonds
  (medical)
Huebner, Solomon Stephen
Hunter, Robert
Hutchinson, Paul (religious
  subjects)
Huxley, Aldous Leonard
Jackson, Charles Reginald
  (short story)
Jackson, Joseph Henry
Jackson, Shirley Hardie (short
  story)
James, George Wharton
  (Southwest)
James, Henry, 1811–1882
  (religious)
Jarrell, Randall (essayist)
Jenks, George Charles (dime
  novel)
Johnson, Joseph French
  (financial)
Johnson, Owen McMahon
  (short story)
Johnston, Annie Fellows
  (juvenile)
Jones, Leonard Augustus (legal)
Judson, Frederick Newton
  (legal)
Kaufman, George S. (screen)
Kellogg, Edward (commercial
  reform)
Kent, James (legal)
Kerouac, Jack (essayist)
Kerr, Sophie (short story)
Keyes, Frances Parkinson
Klippart, John Hancock
  (agricultural)
Kracauer, Siegfried
Krutch, Joseph Wood
Lahontan, Louis-Armand de
  Lom D'Arce, Baron de
  (travel)
Laimbeer, Nathalie Schenck
  (financial)
Lait, Jacquin Leonard (Jack)
  (newspaper)
Langdell, Christopher
  Columbus (legal)
Lathrop, Harriett Mulford
  Stone (juvenile)
Lawrence, William Beach
  (legal)
Lease, Mary Elizabeth Clyens
Lee, Gypsy Rose
Ley, Willy
Liggett, Walter William
Linton, Ralph (popular)
Livermore, Samuel, 1786–1833
  (legal)
Long, Joseph Ragland (legal)
Lowell, John, 1769–1840
  (political)
McClintock, James Harvey
  (historical)

McCord, Louisa Susanna
  Cheves (Antebellum South)
McCullers, Carson (short story)
MacDowell, Katherine
  Sherwood Bonner (short
  story)
McFee, William (essayist,
  novelist)
MacKaye, Percy Wallace
  (essayist)
Mackey, Albert Gallatin
  (Masonic)
McNulty, John Augustine (short
  story)
Magruder, Julia (short story)
Mankiewicz, Herman Jacob
  (screen)
Martin, Edward Sandford
  (essayist)
Mathews, William Smythe
  Babcock (music)
Merton, Thomas (religious)
Metalious, Grace
Meyer, Agnes Elizabeth Ernst
Meyer, Annie Nathan
Millay, Edna St. Vincent
  (poetry)
Millington, John (scientific)
Millis, Walter
Minor, John Barbee (legal)
Montgomery, David Henry
  (textbook)
Moore, Charles Herbert (fine
  arts)
Moore, John Weeks (music)
Morley, Christopher Darlington
  (essayist)
Morris, Edmund (agricultural)
Morris, Robert, 1818–1888
  (Masonic)
Morton, James St, Clair
  (engineering)
Moulton, Ellen Louise Chandler
  (juvenile)
Mulford, Clarence Edward
  (magazine)
Murfree, Mary Noailles (short
  story)
Musmanno, Michael Angelo
Nichols, Dudley (screen)
Nitchie, Edward Bartlett
  (lip-reading)
O'Connor, Mary Flannery
  (short story)
Odets, Clifford (screen)
O'Hara, John Henry (short
  story)
Olney, Jesse (textbook)
Oursler, (Charles) Fulton
Paine, Albert Bigelow (light
  fiction)
Palmer, Alonzo Benjamin
  (medical)
Parker, Dorothy Rothschild
  (short story)
Parker, Henry Taylor (essayist)
Parker, Richard Green
  (textbook)
Peabody, Francis Greenwood
  (religious thought)
Pearson, Edmund Lester (crime
  stories)

Peary, Josephine Diebitsch
Peattie, Donald Culross
  (magazine)
Periam, Jonathan (agricultural)
Perkins, Samuel Elliott (legal)
Perry, Nora (juvenile)
Peterkin, Julia Mood (short
  story)
Peters, John Charles (medical)
Philips, Martin Wilson
  (agricultural)
Phillips, Thomas Wharton
  (religious)
Pitkin, Walter Boughton
Poe, Edgar Allan (short story)
Pomeroy, John Norton (legal)
Porter, Gene Stratton (nature)
Porter, William Sydney (short
  story)
Post, Augustus
Post, Melville Davisson (short
  story)
Powell, John Benjamin
Pratt, Eliza Anna Farman
  (juvenile)
Prentiss, Elizabeth Payson,
  (juvenile)
Priestley, Joseph (religious)
Prince, William Robert
  (agricultural)
Proctor, Lucien Brock (legal)
Pusey, Caleb (Quaker
  controversial)
Quinan, John Russell (medical)
Ralph, James (political)
Rauschenbusch, Walter
  (religious)
Ravenel, Henry William
  (agricultural)
Rawle, William Henry (legal)
Redfield, Amasa Angell (legal)
Reed, Elizabeth Armstrong
  (Oriental literature)
Reed, Sampson
  (Swedenborgian)
Reeve, Tapping, (legal)
Reid, Thomas Mayne, (juvenile)
Reik, Theodor (psychology)
Repplier, Agnes
Richter, Conrad Michael
Rinehart, Mary Roberts
  (mystery story)
Ritter, Frédéric Louis (music)
Roane, Spencer (political)
Rohlfs, Anna Katharine Green
  (detective stories)
Rombauer, Irma Louise
  (cookbook)
Rorer, David
Rossen, Robert (screen)
Rumsey, William (legal)
Runyon, Damon (short story)
Sayles, John (legal)
Schofield, Henry (legal)
Schwartz, Delmore David
  (poetry)
Schwimmer, Rosika
Scudder, (Julia) Vida Dutton
Sergeant, Thomas (legal)
Seton, Ernest Thompson
  (nature)

Sherwood, Robert Emmet
(dramatist)
Smith, George Henry (juvenile)
Smith, Lillian Eugenia
Smith, Lloyd Logan Pearsall
(essayist)
Soley, James Russell (naval)
Spooner, Lysander (political)
Sprague, Charles Ezra
(accountancy)
Stallings, Laurence Tucker
Stanton, Richard Henry (legal)
Stark, Louis (editorial)
Steele, Joel Dorman (textbook)
Steele, Wilbur Daniel
Steinbeck, John Ernst, Jr.
Stilwell, Silas Moore (financial)
Stockton, Frank Richard (story)
Stoddard, John Fair (textbook)
Stratemeyer, Edward (juvenile)
Stribling, Thomas Sigismund
(short story)
Strunsky, Simeon (essayist)
Swan, Joseph Rockwell (legal)
Talbot, Francis Xavier
Tappan, Eva March (juvenile)
Tarbell, Ida Minerva
Taylor, Charles Alonzo
Taylor, John (political)
Terhune, Mary Virginia Hawes
(household management)
Thomson, John (political)
Thurber, James Grover
(humor)
Tiedeman, Christopher
Gustavus (legal)
Toklas, Alice Babette
Towler, John (photography)
Tyler, Ransom Hubert (legal)
Upshaw, William David
Viereck, George Sylvester
(magazine, newspaper)
Wahl, William Henry (science)
Wait, William (legal)
Walker, James Barr (religious)
Walker, Timothy, 1802–1856
(legal)
Wallace, Henry (agricultural)
Ward, Charles Henshaw
Warner, Anna Bartlett
(juvenile)
Warner, Anne Richmond
(fiction)
Watson, Henry Clay (editorial,
historical, juvenile)
Watson, James Madison
(textbook)
Wentworth, George Albert
(mathematics textbooks)
Will, Allen Sinclair (biography)
Willard, Josiah Flint (vagrancy,
criminology)
Williams, Ben Ames (short
story)
Williams, Catharine Read
Arnold (biography)
Wood, Sarah Sayward Barrell
Keating (fiction)
Wright, Willard Huntington
(detective fiction)
Youmans, William Jay
(scientific)

Zevin, Israel Joseph (story)

YACHT DESIGNER (See also SHIP-
BUILDER)
Burgess, Edward
Herreshoff, John Brown
Lawley, George Frederick
Smith, Archibald Cary
Steers, George
YACHTSMAN (See also ATHLETE)
Adams, Charles Francis
Barr, Charles
Crowninshield, George
Paine, Charles Jackson
YMCA OFFICIAL
Mott, John R.
Tobias, Channing Heggie
YOUTH LEADER
Beard, Daniel Carter
Smith, George Albert
YWCA OFFICIAL
Cushman, Vera Charlotte Scott
Speer, Emma Bailey

ZIONIST LEADER
Flexner, Bernard
Haas, Jacob Judah Aaron de
Lewisohn, Ludwig
Masliansky, Zvi Hirsch
Rosenblatt, Bernard Abraham
Silver, Abba Hillel
Szold, Henrietta
Wise, Stephen Samuel
ZONING EXPERT
Purdy, Lawson
ZOOLOGIST (See also APIARIST,
ARACHNOLOGIST, CONCHOLO-
GIST, ENTOMOLOGIST, HER-
PETOLOGIST, ICHTHYOLOGIST,
MALACOLOGIST, MAMMALO-
GIST, MARINE ALGAE AU-
THORITY, MARINE BIOLOGIST,
MICROBIOLOGIST, NATURALIST,
ORNITHOLOGIST, PARASITOLO-
GIST, PISCICULTURIST, TAX-
ONOMIST, VIROLOGIST)
Agassiz, Alexander
Agassiz, Jean Louis Rodolphe
Allen, Joel Asaph
Andrews, Roy Chapman
Anthony, John Gould
Baird, Spencer Fullerton
Binney, Amos
Brooks, William Keith
Calkins, Gary Nathan
Child, Charles Manning
Clark, Henry James
Cope, Edward Drinker
Dana, James Dwight
Dean, Bashford
Eigenmann, Carl H.
Elliot, Daniel Giraud
Field, Herbert Haviland
Garmon, Samuel
Gilbert, Charles Henry
Gill, Theodore Nicholas
Girard, Charles Frédéric
Holbrook, John Edwards
Hyatt, Alpheus
Just, Ernest Everett
Kinsey, Alfred Charles
Kneeland, Samuel

Kofoid, Charles Atwood
Locy, William Albert
Lyman, Theodore, 1833–1897
Montgomery, Thomas Harrison
Morgan, Thomas Hunt
Morse, Edward Sylvester
Nutting, Charles Cleveland
Orton, James
Parker, George Howard
Patten, William
Pourtalès, Louis François de
Rathbun, Richard
Stejneger, Leonhard Hess
Stiles, Charles Wardell
Sumner, Francis Bertody
True, Frederick William
Verrill, Addison Emery
Ward, Henry Baldwin
Wheeler, William Morton
Wilder, Harris Hawthorne

TOPICS

Under this heading have been included distinctive topics about which there are definite statements and discussions and not merely the mention of the topic.

A

AAA. See Agricultural Adjustment Administration
Aandahl, Sam, reference to, **Supp. 8,** 1
A&P. See Great Atlantic and Pacific Tea Co.
AARP. See American Association of Retired Persons
Abbe, Dorothy, reference to, **Supp. 6,** 186
Abbot, Willis J., reference to, **Supp. 3,** 851
Abbott, Edith, reference to, **Supp. 4,** 106, 107
Abbott, Grace, reference to, **Supp. 6,** 1
Abbott, Lyman, reference to, **Vol. 6, Part 1,** 541
Abbott, Robert S., reference to, **Supp. 5,** 633; **Supp. 6,** 490
Abbott and Costello (comedy team), **Supp. 6,** 12
ABC. See American Broadcasting Co.
ABC Conference (1914), **Vol. 2, Part 1,** 195; **Vol. 10, Part 2,** 357
Abel, Rudolf, reference to, **Supp. 8,** 135
Abele, Julian, reference to, **Supp. 2,** 668
Abelson, Phillip H., reference to, **Supp. 8,** 232
Abingdon, Va., skirmish at, **Vol. 7, Part 1,** 174
Abolition movement, **Vol. 1, Part 1,** 200, 205, 279, 297, 481, 496, 542, 568, 628; **Vol. 1, Part 2,** 292 f., 375, 382, 399, 485, 493; Vol. 2, Part 1, 43, 49, 105, 118, 132, 146, 161, 241, 284 f., 584; **Vol. 2, Part 2,** 19, 28, 68, 280, 296 f., 308, 313, 324, 407, 474 f.; **Vol. 3, Part 1,** 124 f., 406 f., 569 f., 597; **Vol. 3, Part 2,** 20, 65, 68, 82, 95, 106, 113, 118, 124, 168, 216, 227, 247, 278, 284, 297, 298, 310, 346, 360, 381, 416, 478, 481, 491 f., 514, 542, 551, 558, 561; **Vol. 4, Part 1,** 80 f., 85, 115, 118, 154, 165, 169 f., 195, 238, 260 f., 529, 539, 542, 622, 634; **Vol. 4, Part 2,** 34, 51, 56, 105, 160, 196 f., 386, 407, 421, 473, 564, 569; **Vol. 5, Part 1,** 17, 19, 150, 217, 292, 297, 328, 384, 547; **Vol. 5, Part 2,** 74, 112, 245 f., 399; **Vol. 6, Part 1,** 84 f., 163, 189, 237, 368, 416, 435 f., 459 f., 506 f.; **Vol. 6, Part 2,** 103, 363, 545, 633; **Vol. 7, Part 1,** 22 f., 227, 228 f., 413, 415, 447, 521 f.; **Vol. 7, Part 2,** 160, 546; **Vol. 8, Part 1,** 117, 306, 499; **Vol. 8, Part 2,** 44, 58, 84, 103, 120, 150, 175, 253, 343, 497 f., 551, 616 f.; **Vol. 9, Part 1,** 271, 466, 486, 525, 621; **Vol. 9, Part 2,** 5, 116 f., 298 f., 300, 303, 335, 493 f., 495, 595; **Vol. 10, Part 1,** 27, 112, 440, 625 f.; **Vol. 10, Part 2,** 174, 323, 548; **Supp. 1,** 83, 244; American Anti-Slavery Society, **Vol. 1, Part 2,** 292; **Vol. 2, Part 1,** 284; **Vol. 4, Part 1,** 169 f., 539, 634; **Vol. 7, Part 1,** 289, 415; **Vol. 7, Part 2,** 546; **Vol. 9, Part 1,** 525; **Vol. 9, Part 2,** 5, 299, 303; **Vol. 10, Part 1,** 625 f.; "Beecher Bible and Rifle Colony," **Vol. 8, Part 2,** 150; California, **Vol. 2, Part 1,** 62; District of Columbia, **Vol. 5, Part 2,** 12; foreign interest in, **Vol. 1, Part 2,** 350; **Vol. 4, Part 2,** 384, 502, 509, 564; **Vol. 5, Part 2,** 496; **Vol. 8, Part 2,** 87; hymns, **Vol. 4, Part 2,** 396; Illinois, **Vol. 1, Part 2,** 128; **Vol. 6, Part 1,** 435; Kansas, **Vol. 5, Part 2,** 576; manuscript material on, **Vol. 10, Part 1,** 42; Massachusetts, **Vol. 2, Part 2,** 308; **Vol. 3, Part 1,** 407; **Vol. 5, Part 1,** 86 f., 89; **Vol. 6, Part 1,** 263; **Vol. 8, Part 2,** 326; Missouri, **Vol. 2, Part 1,** 105; Nat Turner insurrection, **Vol. 10, Part 1,** 70; National movement, disruption of, 1840, **Vol. 9, Part 2,** 5; New Jersey, **Vol. 1, Part 2,** 386; Ohio, **Vol. 6, Part 1,** 224; Pennsylvania, **Vol. 7, Part 2,** 413; **Vol. 8, Part 1,** 452; **Vol. 10, Part 2,** 517; press support, **Vol. 4, Part**
1, 195, 390; **Vol. 5, Part 2,** 112, 410; State Society, first, **Vol. 1, Part 2,** 128; Tennessee, **Vol. 5, Part 2,** 83; Texas, **Vol. 1, Part 1,** 298; "Underground Railroad," **Vol. 2, Part 2,** 268 f.; **Vol. 3, Part 2,** 247; **Vol. 4, Part 1,** 195, 622; **Vol. 5, Part 1,** 224, 576; **Vol. 5, Part 2,** 258; **Vol. 6, Part 1,** 163, 368; **Vol. 8, Part 1,** 403; **Vol. 8, Part 2,** 84, 315; **Vol. 9, Part 1,** 288, 379; **Vol. 9, Part 2,** 23, 304; **Vol. 10, Part 1,** 27; Webster's speech on, **Vol. 4, Part 1,** 170; writings on, **Vol. 1, Part 1,** 496; **Vol. 2, Part 1,** 285, 613; **Vol. 2, Part 2,** 68, 97, 364 f.; **Vol. 3, Part 1,** 407; **Vol. 4, Part 1,** 169, 310, 385, 390, 632, 634 f.; **Vol. 4, Part 2,** 572; **Vol. 5, Part 1,** 213; **Vol. 5, Part 2,** 112, 410; **Vol. 6, Part 1,** 85, 225, 434 f., 507; **Vol. 8, Part 1,** 499 f.; **Vol. 8, Part 2,** 58, 228; **Vol. 9, Part 2,** 5, 117 f., 595; **Vol. 10, Part 1,** 42, 625 f.
Abortion: therapeutic advocacy, **Supp. 3,** 763; writings on, **Vol. 9, Part 2,** 96
Abraham, Karl, reference to, **Supp. 5,** 315
Abraham Lincoln High School (Los Angeles), **Supp. 8,** 7–8
Abrams, Jacob, reference to, **Supp. 6,** 105
Absalom, Absalom!, **Supp. 7,** 233
Absentee Voting Act (1944), **Supp. 8,** 223
Abstract of the Suffering of the People Called Quakers, An, **Vol. 8, Part 1,** 399
Abyssinian Baptist Church (New York City), **Supp. 5,** 548
Academic freedom: Clark University, **Supp. 4,** 32; Columbia University, **Supp. 3,** 151; **Supp. 4,** 62, 135; Cornell University, **Supp. 3,** 698; Harvard University, **Supp. 3,** 471; Johns Hopkins University, **Supp. 5,** 410; Kentucky, University of, **Supp. 5,** 461; loyalty issues, **Supp. 7,** 542; Scopes trial, **Supp. 8,** 582–84; Stanford University, **Supp. 7,** 481; University of Wisconsin, **Supp. 3,** 249; **Supp. 7,** 450; writings on, **Supp. 7,** 264, 481; **Supp. 8,** 272
Academician, educational periodical, one of first, **Vol. 7, Part 2,** 568
Academy Awards, **Supp. 7,** 32; first black winner, **Supp. 5,** 451
Academy of Motion Picture Arts and Sciences, **Supp. 6,** 476; **Supp. 8,** 46, 678; founding of, **Supp. 7,** 32; **Supp. 8,** 459, 460
Academy of Music (Boston), **Vol. 3, Part 2,** 81
Academy of Natural Sciences (Philadelphia), **Vol. 6, Part 2,** 136; **Vol. 7, Part 2,** 351
Academy of Political and Social Science, **Vol. 5, Part 1,** 574
Academy of the U.S.A., project for an, **Vol. 8, Part 1,** 300 f.
Acadians, **Vol. 5, Part 2,** 370; arrival of, **Vol. 4, Part 2,** 221; befriended by Quakers, **Vol. 1, Part 2,** 178; in South Carolina, **Vol. 6, Part 1,** 538 f.
Accardo, Tony, reference to, **Supp. 6,** 264
Accounting: modernization of, **Vol. 7, Part 2,** 478; professional organizations, **Supp. 6,** 397–98; tax forms, **Supp. 5,** 412
Ace bandage, **Supp. 7,** 678
Acetylcholine, **Supp. 3,** 136; **Supp. 4,** 411; **Supp. 7,** 476
Acetylene gas, **Supp. 7,** 553–54
ACF Industries, predecessor, **Supp. 5,** 324

416; Chautauqua movement, **Supp. 3,** 64–65, 792–93; for immigrants, **Supp. 8,** 9; Great Books programs, **Supp. 8,** 58; New School for Social Research, **Supp. 2,** 563; People's Institute, **Supp. 3,** 511, 563; radio and television, **Supp. 6,** 83, 160; teaching programs, **Supp. 8, 488;** women, **Supp. 6,** 203, 412; writings on, **Supp. 5,** 431–32. *See also* Education

Adult Education Association, **Supp. 6,** 203

Ad valorem tax, **Supp. 1,** 385

Advance (brig), North Pole, **Vol. 5, Part 2,** 256

Advance, The, editing of, **Vol. 7, Part 1,** 538

Adventist movement, **Vol. 1, Part 1,** 432; **Vol. 5, Part 1,** 60; **Vol. 7, Part 1,** 589; **Vol. 9, Part 1,** 350; **Vol. 10, Part 1,** 422 f.; **Vol. 10, Part 2,** 98, founding and doctrines of, **Vol. 6, Part 2,** 642. *See also* Seventh-day Adventists

Adventists. *See* Adventist movement; Seventh-day Adventists

Advent Review, founding of, **Vol. 9, Part 1,** 350

Adventure Galley, Kidd's ship, **Vol. 5, Part 2,** 368

Adventures of Ideas, **Supp. 4,** 883

Advertising and marketing, **Vol. 1, Part 1,** 413, 449; **Vol. 3, Part 1,** 405; **Vol. 4, Part 1,** 209, 318; **Vol. 4, Part 2,** 591; **Vol. 7, Part 2,** 251; **Vol. 8, Part 2,** 197; **Vol. 9, Part 1,** 138; agencies, **Supp. 7,** 101, 211–12, 641–42; **Supp. 8,** 27; "Arrow Collar Man," **Supp. 5,** 428, 429; art illustraton, **Supp. 8,** 494; automobiles, **Supp. 8,** 599; chewing gum, **Supp. 1,** 715; cigarettes, **Supp. 4,** 371; **Supp. 5,** 411; copywriting, **Supp. 1,** 287–88; **Supp. 5,** 411; **Supp. 6,** 627; cosmetics, **Supp. 8,** 13; cotton and tobacco cooperatives, **Supp. 2,** 39, 79; Ex-Lax, **Supp. 8,** 339; farmers' cooperatives, **Supp. 2,** 307; flour products, **Supp. 7,** 47; illustration, **Supp. 5,** 428–29; **Supp. 7,** 66–67; industrial, **Supp. 6,** 519; layout and design, **Supp. 6,** 186; "List system," **Vol. 8, Part 2,** 197; newspaper, **Supp. 3,** 80; pioneers in, **Supp. 6,** 519, 614; pipe tobacco, **Supp. 5,** 565, 567; poster, **Supp. 2,** 112; product distribution, **Supp. 2,** 333; psychology of, **Supp. 5,** 433, 611–12; **Supp. 6,** 672–73; radio, **Supp. 3,** 103–4; **Supp. 8,** 52; retail trades, **Supp. 2,** 105; Reynolds Wrap, **Supp. 5,** 566; sign painting, **Vol. 7, Part 1,** 576; trade books, **Supp. 8,** 536; truth in, early advocacy of, **Vol. 8, Part 2,** 197

Advocate of Peace, editing of, **Vol. 10, Part 1,** 6

AEC. *See* Atomic Energy Commission

AEF. *See* American Expeditionary Force

Aeolian Co., **Vol. 9, Part 2,** 637; **Supp. 6,** 297

Aerial Experiment Association, **Vol. 1, Part 2,** 152; founding of, **Supp. 1,** 214

Aerial Navigation Co., **Vol. 4, Part 1,** 330

Aerial photography. *See* Photography, aerial

Aero Club of America, founding of, **Supp. 5,** 547

Aerodynamics, **Vol. 5, Part 2,** 596 f.; **Vol. 8, Part 2,** 576; first academic courses in, **Supp. 8,** 439–40

Aerojet General Corporation, founding of, **Supp. 7,** 411; **Supp. 8,** 440

Aeronautical engineering: air-cooled engine research, **Supp. 4,** 473–74; 486–87; balloon research, **Supp. 7,** 619–20; short-takeoff-and-landing (STOL) airplane, **Supp. 8,** 709

Aeronautics, **Vol. 6, Part 1,** 452; **Vol. 8, Part 2,** 79; balloon, **Vol. 5, Part 2,** 565; kites, **Vol. 8, Part 2,** 184. *See also* Aviation

Aeronautics, **Supp. 5,** 760–61

Aesthetics, **Vol. 4, Part 1,** 588; **Vol. 8, Part 1,** 408; **Vol. 8, Part 2,** 36; in conservation movement, **Supp. 4,** 522–23; order of merit rating scale, **Supp. 3,** 149; quantitative bases for, **Supp. 3,** 71; standards, **Supp. 2,** 540; writings on, **Supp. 5,** 39, 601–2

Aetna Explosives Co., **Vol. 7, Part 1,** 301

Aetna Life Insurance Co., **Vol. 2, Part 1,** 248

AFL. *See* American Federation of Labor

AFL-CIO. *See* American Federation of Labor-Congress of Industrial Organizations

Africa: colonization, **Vol. 6, Part 1,** 28; **Vol. 8, Part 2,** 349; "Dark Continent," first called the, **Vol. 9, Part 1,** 511; education, **Supp. 1,** 14; experts on, **Supp. 7,** 372; exploration, **Vol. 2, Part 1,** 591; **Vol. 6, Part 1,** 28; **Vol. 8, Part 2,** 112, 340; **Vol. 9, Part 1,** 509 f.; **Supp. 5,** 370–71; missions in, **Vol. 4, Part 1,** 375; **Vol. 4, Part 2,** 371; **Vol. 5, Part 2,** 561; **Vol. 7, Part 1,** 231, 390 f.; **Vol. 8, Part 1,** 243 f.; **Vol. 8, Part 2,** 391; **Vol. 10, Part 2,** 338; **Supp. 1,** 499; music, **Supp. 5,** 436; ornithology, **Supp. 7,** 117; scouting, **Supp. 4,** 126–27; slave-trading, investigation of, **Vol. 3, Part 1,** 220; U.S. blacks' relationship with, **Supp. 2,** 222; **Supp. 6,** 716–17; **Supp. 7,** 509; writings on, **Supp. 4,** 878

African-Americans. *See* Blacks

African Methodist Episcopal Zion Church, **Vol. 1, Part 1,** 204 f.; **Vol. 2, Part 2,** 229; **Vol. 4, Part 1,** 96; **Vol. 5, Part 1,** 192 f.; **Vol. 6, Part 1,** 368; **Vol. 7, Part 2,** 324; **Vol. 9, Part 2,** 296; **Vol. 10, Part 1,** 65 f., 398 f.; leadership, **Supp. 5,** 258–59; **Supp. 8,** 94

African Protestant Episcopal Church, **Vol. 1, Part 1,** 204

Afro-American League, **Vol. 10, Part 1,** 398 f.; founding of, **Supp. 3,** 596

Afro-American Realty Co., **Supp. 3,** 535

After Dark, **Supp. 4,** 103

"After the Ball," **Vol. 4, Part 2,** 306

Agassiz, Alexander: biography of, **Vol. 1, Part 1,** 114; Garman, Samuel, **Vol. 4, Part 1,** 154; Le Conte, Joseph, **Vol. 6, Part 1,** 90; Lesquereux, **Vol. 6, Part 1,** 188; references to, **Vol. 1, Part 1,** 318, 514; **Vol. 3, Part 2,** 352; **Vol. 4, Part 2,** 63; **Vol. 5, Part 1,** 12, 141, 446, 591; **Vol. 5, Part 2,** 212; **Vol. 7, Part 1,** 606; **Vol. 9, Part 1,** 18

Agassiz, Louis, reference to, **Supp. 4,** 52

Agassiz Museum (Cambridge, Mass.), **Supp. 4,** 51–52

Age, founding of, **Supp. 1,** 363

Age of Mammals in Europe, Asia and North America, The, **Supp. 1,** 586

Age of Reason, **Vol. 7, Part 2,** 162 f.

Age of Reform: From Bryan to F.D.R., The, **Supp. 8,** 271, 272, 273

Age of the Reformation, The, **Supp. 3,** 726

Agee, James, reference to, **Supp. 7,** 114

Aging and aged: advocacy organizations, **Supp. 8,** 10; group activities, **Supp. 7,** 151; social work, **Supp. 5,** 454; Townsend Plan, **Supp. 6,** 646–47. *See also* Social Security

Aglipayanism, **Supp. 5,** 178–79

Agnes Scott College, **Vol. 5, Part 1,** 485

Agora excavations, **Supp. 3,** 705

Agrarianism, **Supp. 3,** 363

Agricultural Adjustment Acts (1933 and 1938), **Supp. 3,** 100, 319; **Supp. 4,** 50, 407, 795; **Supp. 5,** 358, 572–73; **Supp. 7,** 760; **Supp. 8,** 277, 508

Agricultural Adjustment Administration, **Supp. 6,** 215–16, 487, 638; **Supp. 7,** 36; **Supp. 8,** 699–700; founding of, **Supp. 3,** 594, 650, 651–52; tenant farming under, **Supp. 7,** 781

Agricultural Credit Corporation, founding of, **Supp. 2,** 480

Agricultural Credits Act (1923), **Supp. 4,** 482

Agricultural Economics, Bureau of, **Vol. 10, Part 1,** 370; research, **Supp. 6,** 638

Agricultural History, founding of, **Supp. 5,** 201

Agricultural Marketing Act (1929), passage of, **Supp. 7,** 360–61

Agricultural Trade Development and Assistance Act (1954), **Supp. 7**, 678; **Supp. 8**, 278

Agriculture (general), **Vol. 1, Part 1**, 110, 316, 392, 408; **Vol. 1, Part 2**, 172, 283, 460; **Vol. 2, Part 1**, 25, 43; **Vol. 2, Part 2**, 185, 250; **Vol. 3, Part 1**, 304; **Vol. 3, Part 2**, 45, 128, 268, 424, 479; **Vol. 4, Part 1**, 200, 379, 595; **Vol. 4, Part 2**, 204, 207 f., 473 f.; **Vol. 5, Part 1**, 90, 128, 207, 348, 624; **Vol. 5, Part 2**, 45, 90, 142 f., 231 f., 446, 452 f.; **Vol. 6, Part 1**, 134, 163, 418, 465, 481 f., 501, 516, 554 f.; **Vol. 7, Part 1**, 170, 205, 257, 629, f.; **Vol. 7, Part 2**, 464; **Vol. 8, Part 1**, 239; **Vol. 8, Part 2**, 15, 335; **Vol. 9, Part 1**, 69, 146, 148, 180, 200; **Vol. 9, Part 2**, 134, 333, 396, 574, 641; **Vol. 10, Part 1**, 68, 174, 180, 370, 444, 617; **Vol. 10, Part 2**, 460; aerial crop-dusting, **Supp. 8**, 707–8; agrarian movement, **Vol. 4, Part 1**, 529; **Vol. 5, Part 2**, 28; alfalfa, introduction of, **Vol. 10, Part 2**, 387; apple-raising, **Vol. 6, Part 1**, 535 f.; **Vol. 7, Part 1**, 197; biochemical research, **Supp. 3**, 145–46, 315; **Supp. 4**, 114; "Bloomsdale Farm," **Vol. 5, Part 2**, 571–72; boll weevil, Mexican, **Vol. 5, Part 2**, 453; chemistry, as applied to, **Vol. 1, Part 1**, 109, 349, 417; **Vol. 2, Part 1**, 238, 484; **Vol. 2, Part 2**, 304; **Vol. 3, Part 1**, 61, 210; **Vol. 4, Part 1**, 5; **Vol. 5, Part 1**, 22, 207; **Vol. 5, Part 2**, 45, 120, 231 f., 388 f.; **Vol. 6, Part 2**, 223, 263 f.; **Vol. 7, Part 1**, 574 f.; **Vol. 7, Part 2**, 388, 509; **Vol. 8, Part 1**, 96 f., 154 f., 257 f., 272 f., 397; **Vol. 8, Part 2**, 512; **Vol. 9, Part 2**, 37, 395, 514; **Vol. 10, Part 2**, 22, 104, 491; cold-resistant crop development, **Supp. 4**, 357; colonial, **Vol. 8, Part 1**, 419; colonies of Russian Jews, **Vol. 8, Part 2**, 168; cooperatives, **Vol. 7, Part 1**, 377; **Supp. 2**, 39, 79, 307, 426; **Supp. 4**, 36–37, 853; **Supp. 5**, 365; **Supp. 7**, 361; corn culture, **Vol. 1, Part 1**, 533; **Vol. 6, Part 1**, 74; **Vol. 8, Part 1**, 477 f.; correspondence course in, **Vol. 1, Part 1**, 236; cotton, **Vol. 3, Part 1**, 304; **Vol. 3, Part 2**, 482; **Vol. 8, Part 1**, 565 f.; **Vol. 9, Part 1**, 427; credit, **Supp. 4**, 406, 482; crop breeding, **Supp. 4**: 252–53, 862–63; **Supp. 5**, 629; crop quota system, **Supp. 6**, 639; dairy, **Supp. 1**, 37, 444; diversification, **Vol. 3, Part 2**, 411; **Supp. 2**, 480; domestic allotment, **Supp. 6**, 559; drainage, **Vol. 5, Part 2**, 143; economic relief legislation, **Supp. 2**, 492; economics, **Supp. 1**, 152, 384, 491; **Supp. 2**, 696; **Supp. 4**, 45; **Supp. 6**, 459, 638–39; education, **Vol. 1, Part 1**, 236, 592; **Vol. 1, Part 2**, 321, 568; **Vol. 2, Part 1**, 378, 428; **Vol. 2, Part 2**, 147, 165, 201; **Vol. 3, Part 1**, 242; **Vol. 3, Part 2**, 252, 351, 473; **Vol. 4, Part 1**, 139, 379, 383, 395; **Vol. 4, Part 2**, 34; **Vol. 5, Part 1**, 163; **Vol. 5, Part 2**, 453, 501, 525; **Vol. 6, Part 1**, 555; **Vol. 6, Part 2**, 613; **Vol. 7, Part 2**, 197, 282; **Vol. 8, Part 1**, 143 f., 175 f., 257 f.; **Vol. 8, Part 2**, 180, 512 f.; **Vol. 9, Part 2**, 78; **Vol. 10, Part 1**, 4, 139, 370, 617 f.; electrification, **Supp. 3**, 192–93; experimental, **Supp. 1**, 444; **Supp. 2**, 387; **Supp. 6**, 77–78; experiment stations established, **Vol. 1, Part 1**, 238, 417; **Vol. 2, Part 1**, 25; **Vol. 5, Part 2**, 120; **Vol. 9, Part 2**, 39; **Vol. 10, Part 1**, 4; extension service, **Supp. 1**, 144; **Supp. 2**, 217, 364; **Supp. 3**, 145–46; Federal Farm Loan Board, **Supp. 6**, 453; fertilizers, **Vol. 7, Part 2**, 419; **Vol. 8, Part 1**, 397; **Vol. 9, Part 2**, 39; 4-H clubs, **Supp. 5**, 51; geography, **Supp. 4**, 45; government aid, recognition of principle of, **Vol. 3, Part 2**, 110; **Vol. 4, Part 2**, 394; government assistance, attitudes on, **Supp. 1**, 197; Grange movement, **Vol. 5, Part 2**, 299; **Supp. 4**, 340–41; historical writings on, **Supp. 5**, 201–2; **Supp. 7**, 685; insects, injuries to crops by, **Vol. 8, Part 1**, 609 f.; international organizations, **Supp. 4**, 341; journalism on, **Supp. 3**, 319; **Supp. 6**, 676–77; legislation, **Supp. 2**, 321, 380, 492; **Supp. 4**, 309, 479–80; **Supp. 8**, 277–78; machinery, invention and development of, **Vol. 1, Part 1**, 130, 178, 185, 406; **Vol. 1, Part 2**, 172, 230; **Vol. 2, Part 1**, 337, 557; **Vol. 3, Part 1**, 193 f., 195; **Vol. 3, Part 2**, 110, 188, 251; **Vol. 4, Part 1**, 98; **Vol. 4, Part 2**, 94; **Vol. 5, Part 2**, 53; **Vol. 6, Part 1**, 607 f., 614; **Vol. 6, Part 2**, 296, 303 f., 383, 635; **Vol. 7, Part 1**, 177, 590; **Vol. 7, Part 2**, 21, 471, 493, 537, 644; **Vol. 8, Part 1**, 101 f., 496, 498 f., 505; **Vol. 8, Part 2**, 9; **Vol. 9, Part 2**, 439; **Vol. 10, Part 2**, 464, 475; **Supp. 2**, 402; migrant workers, **Supp. 8**, 301; New Deal policies, **Supp. 3**, 434, 651–52; **Supp. 6**, 12, 638–39; **Supp. 7**, 760–61; **Supp. 8**, 445, 700; North Carolina programs, **Supp. 6**, 569; organizations, **Supp. 1**, 51, 645, 660; **Supp. 2**, 307, 426, 552; **Supp. 8**, 468; personal writings on, **Supp. 6**, 409; pest control, **Supp. 4**, 399, 601; physics application, **Supp. 7**, 76; political activity, **Supp. 3**, 108, 468, 723–24; **Supp. 6**, 86–87; price supports, **Supp. 6**, 487–88, 639; **Supp. 8**, 277–78; publications, **Supp. 1**, 461–62; **Supp. 4**, 132; **Supp. 7**, 527; radio programs, **Supp. 4**, 132; regulation of, early attempts at, **Vol. 5, Part 2**, 120; research in, **Supp. 1**, 183, 395; rice growing, **Vol. 1, Part 1**, 128, 224; **Vol. 5, Part 2**, 453; rotation of crops, **Vol. 1, Part 2**, 460; seed production, **Vol. 6, Part 1**, 74; socialist view of, **Supp. 4**, 746, 747; soil bacteriology, **Supp. 1**, 461; soil conservation, **Supp. 3**, 656; **Supp. 6**, 52–53, 639; soil erosion, **Vol. 8, Part 1**, 146 f.; Southern interests, **Supp. 4**, 50; Soviet Jewish resettlement, **Supp. 4**, 699–700; statistical information, early collection of, **Vol. 3, Part 1**, 349 f.; sugar, **Vol. 9, Part 1**, 427; sugar beet experimentation, **Vol. 8, Part 1**, 239 f.; surplus sales, **Supp. 1**, 384; **Supp. 3**, 496, 594; **Supp. 4**, 51; **Supp. 8**, 278; teaching of, **Supp. 3**, 216–17, 433–34; **Supp. 5**, 31; tenant farming, **Supp. 4**, 50, 251; **Supp. 5**, 511; **Supp. 7**, 781–82; voluntary allotment plant, **Supp. 7**, 760–61; wheat, **Vol. 6, Part 1**, 92; writings on, **Vol. 1, Part 1**, 185, 205, 413; **Vol. 1, Part 2**, 100, 172, 460; **Vol. 2, Part 1**, 155, 164, 238, 388, **Vol. 2, Part 2**, 254 f., 312, 314; **Vol. 3, Part 1**, 172 f., 304, 579 f.; **Vol. 3, Part 2**, 347; **Vol. 4, Part 1**, 200; **Vol. 4, Part 2**, 315; **Vol. 5, Part 1**, 118, 163; **Vol. 5, Part 2**, 90, 231, 445 f., 453, 501; **Vol. 6, Part 1**, 284, 377, 426, 516; **Vol. 7, Part 1**, 376 f.; **Vol. 7, Part 2**, 464, 537; **Vol. 8, Part 1**, 40 f., 143 f., 145 f., 347 f., 419; **Vol. 8, Part 2**, 9, 51, 215; **Vol. 9, Part 1**, 199 f., 201, 427; **Vol. 9, Part 2**, 38 f., 309, 396, 439, 514, 574; **Vol. 10, Part 1**, 4, 35 f., 369 f., 456 f.; **Vol. 10, Part 2**, 214, 387, 617. *See also* Agriculture, Department of (U.S.); Agriculture (by state); Farming; Food; Horticulture

Agriculture (by state): Alabama, **Vol. 2, Part 2**, 232; **Vol. 9, Part 2**, 524; Arizona, **Vol. 4, Part 2**, 483; **Vol. 6, Part 1**, 611; **Vol. 8, Part 1**, 121 f.; Colorado, **Vol. 3, Part 1**, 606; Connecticut, **Vol. 5, Part 2**, 45; Florida, **Vol. 9, Part 2**, 38; Georgia, **Vol. 5, Part 1**, 348; **Vol. 7, Part 1**, 564; Illinois, **Vol. 1, Part 2**, 289; Indiana, **Vol. 3, Part 1**, 419 f.; **Vol. 5, Part 1**, 55; Iowa, **Vol. 1, Part 2**, 96; **Vol. 2, Part 2**, 165; **Vol. 4, Part 2**, 34; **Vol. 7, Part 2**, 197; **Vol. 10, Part 1**, 617 f.; Kansas, **Vol. 1, Part 1**, 267, 316; **Vol. 3, Part 2**, 252; **Vol. 5, Part 2**, 504; **Vol. 7, Part 2**, 393; Kentucky, **Vol. 3, Part 1**, 491 f.; **Vol. 9, Part 1**, 18; Louisiana, **Vol. 3, Part 1**, 585 f.; Maine, **Vol. 4, Part 1**, 379; **Vol. 5, Part 1**, 163; Massachusetts, **Vol. 4, Part 1**, 383; **Vol. 10, Part 1**, 541 f.; Michigan, **Vol. 6, Part 2**, 613; Mississippi, **Vol. 7, Part 1**, 100; **Vol. 9, Part 2**, 78; Nebraska, **Vol. 4, Part 1**, 77; New England, **Vol. 3, Part 2**, 473; **Vol. 6, Part 1**, 418; **Vol. 7, Part 2**, 567; **Vol. 10, Part 2**, 210; New Hampshire, **Vol. 8, Part 2**, 120; New York, **Vol. 3, Part 1**, 210, 605 f.; **Vol. 5, Part 2**, 90; **Vol. 6, Part 1**, 232;

Alamo, Texas, massacre at (March 6, 1836), **Vol. 1,
Part 2,** 510; **Vol. 2, Part 1,** 293; **Vol. 2, Part 2,** 555;
Vol. 5, Part 1, 265; **Vol. 9, Part 2,** 630
Alaska: birds, **Supp. 1,** 572; bishopric of, **Vol. 5, Part
1,** 491; boundary surveys, **Vol. 3, Part 1,** 35 f., 92,
298, 315; **Vol. 5, Part 2,** 167; **Vol. 6, Part 1,** 348;
Vol. 7, Part 1, 640; **Vol. 9, Part 1,** 492; **Vol. 10, Part
1,** 540 f.; cataloging of names in, **Vol. 7, Part 1,** 640;
coal lands controversy, **Supp. 1,** 300; **Supp. 3,** 96,
321; **Supp. 4,** 665; **Supp. 5,** 666, 699; **Supp. 7,** 606;
development of, **Vol. 3, Part 1,** 35 f.; **Vol. 9, Part 1,**
220; **Supp. 1,** 108; education, **Vol. 5, Part 1,** 555;
ethnology, **Supp. 1,** 572; exploration, **Vol. 8, Part
2,** 481; **Supp. 4,** 674; **Supp. 7,** 371; flora of, **Vol. 8,
Part 2,** 188; fur trade, **Vol. 6, Part 2,** 631; geography of, **Vol. 2, Part 1,** 73; geological expeditions,
Vol. 2, Part 1, 73; **Vol. 8, Part 2,** 243; gold rush,
Supp. 5, 578; governmental code, **Vol. 7, Part 2,** 31;
governors, **Supp. 1,** 108; history, early, **Vol. 5, Part
1,** 489; Indian policy, **Vol. 5, Part 2,** 573; missions
in, **Vol. 5, Part 1,** 489; **Vol. 8, Part 2,** 559; **Vol. 10,
Part 2,** 634; mountain climbing in, **Vol. 8, Part 2,**
243; novels about, **Supp. 4,** 60; politics, **Supp. 8,**
25–26; purchase of, 1867, **Vol. 5, Part 2,** 88; **Vol. 8,
Part 2,** 620; Roads Commission, U.S., **Vol. 8, Part
1,** 576; Russian colonization, **Vol. 5, Part 2,** 515;
Vol. 8, Part 1, 523 f.; statehood, **Supp. 7,** 50, 590;
Supp. 8, 26; trade with, **Vol. 4, Part 1,** 229; **Vol. 9,
Part 1,** 67; **Vol. 10, Part 1,** 532 f.; World War II
operations, **Supp. 3,** 118; Yukon, first steam vessel
to go up, **Vol. 8, Part 1,** 406. *See also* Eskimos
Alaska-Canadian boundary arbitration (1903), **Vol. 3,
Part 2,** 552; **Vol. 4, Part 2,** 435; **Vol. 6, Part 1,** 348;
Vol. 8, Part 2, 139
Alaska Statehood Act (1958), passage of, **Supp. 8,** 25–
26
Albany, Ga., civil rights demonstrations, **Supp. 8,** 334
Albany, N.Y.: Buffalo, connection of, by railroad, **Vol.
8, Part 1,** 582; capitol, construction of, **Vol. 9, Part
2,** 657; early history of, **Vol. 7, Part 1,** 333; educa-
tion, **Vol. 1, Part 2,** 571; Episcopal diocese of, **Vol.
3, Part 1,** 334 f.; public service, **Vol. 4, Part 2,** 310;
Vol. 5, Part 1, 198; **Vol. 9, Part 2,** 388
Albany Congress (1754), **Vol. 5, Part 2,** 125
Albany Free Academy (N.Y.), **Vol. 1, Part 2,** 570
Albany Institute, **Vol. 7, Part 1,** 333
Albany Law Journal, **Vol. 2, Part 1,** 166
Albany Law School, founding of, **Vol. 7, Part 2,** 215
Albany Medical College, **Vol. 3, Part 1,** 169
Albany Patriot, **Vol. 9, Part 2,** 596
"Albany Regency," **Vol. 10, Part 1,** 153
Albee, Ernest F., reference to, **Supp. 3,** 697
Albemarle and *Sassacus,* **Vol. 1, Part 2,** 487
Albemarle Sound, N.C., battle of, **Vol. 6, Part 2,** 393;
Vol. 8, Part 2, 85; **Vol. 9, Part 1,** 321
Albert, Heinrich, reference to, **Supp. 7,** 757
Albino, famous, **Vol. 4, Part 2,** 388
Albion Village, social experiment of, **Vol. 3, Part 2,**
478
Albright, William Foxwell, reference to, **Supp. 4,** 595
Alchemy, **Supp. 1,** 174
Alcoa. *See* Aluminum Co. of America
Alcohol: addictive quality, **Supp. 3,** 354; liquor indus-
try, **Supp. 7,** 780; physiologic effects, **Supp. 3,** 163.
See also Prohibition
Alcoholism: cure for, **Vol. 5, Part 2,** 280; fictional
writings on, **Supp. 8,** 298; liver involvement, **Supp.
3,** 503; psychiatric view of, **Supp. 3,** 320
Alcorn University, presidency of, **Vol. 8, Part 1,** 513
Aldrich, Chester Holmes, reference to, **Supp. 6,** 157,
158

Aldrich, Mary M., reference to, **Supp. 4,** 8
Aldrich, Nelson W., references to, **Vol. 7, Part 1,** 463;
Vol. 10, Part 1, 412 f.; **Supp. 5,** 745
Aldrich Currency Bill, **Vol. 1, Part 1,** 157; **Vol. 2, Part
2,** 154
Aldrich Plan, formulation of, **Supp. 2,** 15, 544, 555
Aleichem, Sholom, reference to, **Supp. 6,** 567
Alert, capture of, in War of 1812, **Vol. 8, Part 1,** 83 f.
Aleutian Islands, **Supp. 6,** 629; survey of, **Vol. 3, Part
1,** 36
Alexander, Annie M., reference to, **Supp. 3,** 519
Alexander, Archibald, reference to, **Vol. 7, Part 1,** 439
Alexander, Samuel T., reference to, **Supp. 1,** 48
Alexander, William C., reference to, **Vol. 5, Part 1,**
450
Alexandria, La., operation at, **Vol. 1, Part 1,** 579
Alexandria, Va., skirmish at, **Vol. 3, Part 2,** 110
Alfalfa: hybridization, **Supp. 4,** 357; introduction of,
Vol. 10, Part 2, 387
Alfred, first to fly Continental flag, **Vol. 5, Part 2,** 184
Alfred University, **Vol. 8, Part 2,** 114
Alfred Observatory, **Vol. 8, Part 2,** 114
Algae, marine, **Supp. 3,** 703–4
Alger, Horatio, books, **Vol. 1, Part 1,** 178 f.
Algiers: naval attack on, **Vol. 5, Part 1,** 152; **Vol. 8,
Part 2,** 73; **Vol. 9, Part 1,** 19; **Vol. 9, Part 2,** 310;
treaty with (1796), **Vol. 1, Part 1,** 611; **Vol. 5, Part
1,** 374. *See also* Tripoli, war with
Algonquian Indians, **Supp. 4,** 179
Algonquin Round Table, **Supp. 3,** 54, 841–42; **Supp.
5,** 464, 623; **Supp. 7,** 413, 516; **Supp. 8,** 491, 622
Alice in Wonderland: illustrations for, **Vol. 7, Part 1,**
458; original manuscript, **Supp. 5,** 587
Alien and Sedition Acts, **Vol. 1, Part 1,** 78; **Vol. 3, Part
1,** 54; **Vol. 4, Part 2,** 177; **Vol. 5, Part 2,** 27, 148;
Vol. 6, Part 2, 33, 188, 319
Aliens. *See* Immigration
Alimony, **Supp. 8,** 10. *See also* Divorce
Alinsky, Saul, reference to, **Supp. 8,** 589
Allaire, James P., reference to, **Vol. 9, Part 2,** 520
All-American Conference (football), **Supp. 6,** 48
Allatoona, Ga., battle of, **Vol. 2, Part 2,** 453; **Vol. 9,
Part 1,** 95
Alleghany Corporation, **Supp. 6,** 721
Allegheny River, traffic on, **Vol. 8, Part 1,** 464
Allen, Ethan, references to, **Vol. 1, Part 1,** 526 f.; **Vol.
8, Part 2,** 49; **Vol. 10, Part 1,** 468
Allen, Fred, reference to, **Supp. 8,** 477
Allen, Frederick Lewis, reference to, **Supp. 6,** 571
Allen, Hervey, reference to, **Supp. 8,** 536
Allen, Moses, references to, **Supp. 4,** 510, 511
Allen, Richard Day, reference to, **Supp. 3,** 6
Allen, Robert S., reference to, **Supp. 8,** 496
Allergies: anaphylactic shock from, **Supp. 4,** 701; first
clinic, **Supp. 6,** 123; first recorded observation of,
Supp. 1, 666; studies of, **Supp. 5,** 438
Alliance Book Corporation, **Supp. 5,** 761
Alliance College (Ohio), presidency of, **Vol. 1, Part 2,**
208
Alliance for Labor Action, founding of, **Supp. 8,** 528
Alliance for Progress, **Supp. 7,** 421
Alliance for the Guidance of Rural Youth, founding of,
Supp. 4, 365–66
"Alliancemen," **Vol. 5, Part 2,** 492
Allied Chemical Co., **Supp. 6,** 452
Allied Jewish Appeal, founding of, **Supp. 4,** 262
Alliluyeva, Svetlana, reference to, **Supp. 8,** 224
Allis-Chalmers Manufacturing Co., **Supp. 5,** 597
Allison, Jerry, reference to, **Supp. 6,** 301
Allison Engineering Co., **Supp. 7,** 793
"Allison" letters, **Vol. 9, Part 2,** 351 f.

All My Sons, **Supp. 8,** 31
Alloys: experiments with, **Vol. 1, Part 1,** 456; property requirements, **Supp. 2,** 91
Almanacs, **Vol. 1, Part 1,** 250, 413; **Vol. 3, Part 1,** 23; **Vol. 3, Part 2,** 89, 489, 549, 587; **Vol. 4, Part 1,** 609; **Vol. 4, Part 2,** 43, 123, 390; **Vol. 5, Part 1,** 131; **Vol. 6, Part 1,** 16, 81, 135; **Vol. 9, Part 1,** 88, 416; **Vol. 9, Part 2,** 444, 480; **Vol. 10, Part 2,** 5, 625; computations of, **Vol. 8, Part 2,** 287; first in America, **Vol. 7, Part 1,** 488; nautical, **Vol. 7, Part 1,** 450; *New England, The,* **Vol. 3, Part 1,** 23; **Vol. 4, Part 2,** 390; phrenological, **Vol. 3, Part 2,** 565; *Poor Richard's,* **Vol. 1, Part 1,** 413; **Vol. 3, Part 2,** 587; **Vol. 4, Part 2,** 123; revolving, **Vol. 8, Part 1,** 101 f.; *Solomon Thrifty's,* **Vol. 4, Part 2,** 43
Alone, **Supp. 6,** 93
Alpine Club, founding of, **Vol. 4, Part 2,** 501
Al Serena scandal, **Supp. 6,** 416
Alsop, Stewart, reference to, **Supp. 7,** 724
Alternating current, **Supp. 3,** 231, 251
Altgeld, John P., references to, **Supp. 2,** 142; **Supp. 3,** 852
Altmann, Richard, reference to, **Supp. 6,** 53, 54
Alton Observer, abolitionist paper, **Vol. 6, Part 1,** 434 f.
Altoona Conference, **Vol. 1, Part 1,** 280
Altruist, **Vol. 6, Part 1,** 389
Alum, first manufacture of, **Vol. 9, Part 2,** 648
Aluminum, **Vol. 5, Part 1,** 382; automobile industry use of, **Supp. 8,** 309; electrolytic refining process studies, **Supp. 8,** 193–94; foil wrap, **Supp. 5,** 565–66; manufacturing, **Vol. 4, Part 2,** 122; **Supp. 7,** 166; solder, first successful, **Vol. 8, Part 1,** 555; World War II production, **Supp. 5,** 566; **Supp. 7,** 92
Aluminum Co. of America: founding of, **Supp. 2,** 446; **Supp. 7,** 166; product diversification, **Supp. 5,** 565–66; research, **Supp. 8,** 193–94
Alvarez, Luis, reference to, **Supp. 7,** 275
Alvey Resolution, **Vol. 1, Part 1,** 235
Alvord, C. A., reference to, **Vol. 7, Part 1,** 613
Amahl and the Night Visitors, **Supp. 7,** 124
Amalgamated Clothing Workers of America, **Supp. 4,** 69, 279; **Supp. 7,** 801; founding of, **Supp. 4,** 375–76
Amalgamated Copper Co., **Vol. 6, Part 1,** 60; **Vol. 8, Part 2,** 95, 263; **Vol. 9, Part 2,** 589 f.
Amalgamated Textile Workers Union, **Supp. 8,** 457
Amana Society, founding of, **Vol. 6, Part 2,** 586
Amateur Cinema League, founding of, **Supp. 2,** 436
"Amateur Hour." *See* "Major Bowes Amateur Hour"
Amateur Telescope Making, **Supp. 4,** 675
Amazing Stories, founding of, **Supp. 8,** 209
Amazon River, exploration, **Vol. 4, Part 1,** 481; **Vol. 4, Part 2,** 580
Ambassador Bridge (Detroit-Windsor), **Supp. 7,** 136
Amelia Court House, Va., in Civil War, **Vol. 6, Part 1,** 127
America, attempted transatlantic flight in, **Vol. 10, Part 1,** 635 f.
America, Jesuit publication, **Vol. 9, Part 2,** 532; **Supp. 5,** 677; **Supp. 7,** 448
America (ship), presented to French government, **Vol. 5, Part 2,** 186
America (aircraft), **Supp. 5,** 3
America First Committee, **Supp. 4,** 303, 480; **Supp. 5,** 339–40, 674–77, 689–90; **Supp. 7,** 249, 451; **Supp. 8,** 410, 650, 705; founding of, **Supp. 3,** 605
America-Japan Society of Tokyo, **Supp. 4,** 284
American, **Supp. 3,** 556, 816
Americana: art, **Supp. 7,** 556–57; bibliographies, **Supp. 1,** 375; **Supp. 2,** 111; 162–63; collections of, **Vol. 3, Part 2,** 514; **Vol. 6, Part 1,** 157; **Vol. 8, Part 1,** 51 f., 549; **Vol. 8, Part 2,** 275, 420; **Vol. 9, Part 1,** 432; **Vol. 9, Part 2,** 499; **Vol. 10, Part 1,** 443;

Supp. 1, 139–40, 154, 180; Ford museum and restorations, **Supp. 4,** 302
Americana, **Supp. 7,** 436
American Academy in Rome, **Vol. 2, Part 1,** 306, 539; **Vol. 6, Part 2,** 101; architecture, **Supp. 1,** 322; founding of, **Supp. 2,** 402. *See also* American School of Classical Studies (Rome)
American Academy of Allergy: founding of, **Supp. 5,** 438; predecessor, **Supp. 6,** 123
American Academy of Arts and Letters, founding of, **Supp. 2,** 349
American Academy of Arts and Sciences, **Vol. 1, Part 2,** 492, 501; **Vol. 2, Part 2,** 633; **Vol. 5, Part 1,** 185; **Vol. 6, Part 1,** 465; **Vol. 7, Part 2,** 15, 157; Faulkner Farm, **Supp. 4,** 115
American Academy of Christian Democracy, founding of, **Supp. 4,** 232, 233
American Academy of Fine Arts, **Vol. 6, Part 1,** 325; **Vol. 7, Part 2,** 82, 350; **Vol. 8, Part 2,** 21
American Academy of Medicine, **Vol. 9, Part 1,** 563; American Academy of Pediatrics: founding of, **Supp. 4,** 8; predecessors, **Supp. 5,** 553
American Academy of Political and Social Science, founding of, **Supp. 2,** 175
American Academy of Teachers of Singing, founding of, **Supp. 1,** 712
American Action, **Supp. 6,** 679
American Agriculturist, **Vol. 1, Part 1,** 185; **Vol. 5, Part 2,** 231; **Vol. 9, Part 2,** 514; **Supp. 3,** 434; **Supp. 8,** 445
American Airlines, **Supp. 6,** 145; predecessor, **Supp. 8,** 367
American Alliance for Labor and Democracy, founding of, **Supp. 8,** 611
American and Foreign Bible Society, **Vol. 2, Part 2,** 342
American Anthropological Association, founding of, **Supp. 3,** 84, 85; **Supp. 6,** 534
American Antiquarian and Oriental Journal, **Vol. 7, Part 2,** 392
American Antiquarian Society, **Vol. 5, Part 2,** 54; **Vol. 7, Part 2,** 384; **Vol. 9, Part 2,** 436; **Supp. 8,** 664
American Anti-Slavery Society, **Vol. 1, Part 2,** 292; **Vol. 2, Part 1,** 284; **Vol. 4, Part 1,** 169 F., 539, 634; **Vol. 7, Part 1,** 289, 415; **Vol. 7, Part 2,** 546; **Vol. 9, Part 1,** 525; **Vol. 9, Part 2,** 5, 299, 303; **Vol. 10, Part 1,** 625 f.
American Anti-Slavery Standard, **Vol. 4, Part 1,** 195
American Appeal, **Vol. 3, Part 1,** 184
American Architect, The, **Vol. 6, Part 1,** 389
American Archives, **Vol. 3, Part 2,** 513
American Artists' Congress, founding of, **Supp. 7,** 171
American Art Review, **Vol. 5, Part 2,** 485
American Association for Adult Education: first black president, **Supp. 5,** 437; founding of, **Supp. 3,** 677
American Association for Cancer Research, founding of, **Supp. 3,** 258, 503
American Association for Labor Legislation, founding of, **Supp. 3,** 18, 178
American Associatian for Old Age Security, founding of, **Supp. 3,** 255
American Association for Social Security, **Supp. 3,** 255
American Association for the Advancement of Science, **Vol. 1, Part 2,** 530; **Vol. 7, Part 2,** 207, 471; **Vol. 8, Part 1,** 442; **Supp. 3,** 150; **Supp. 5,** 509
American Association for the Study and Prevention of Infant Mortality, founding of, **Supp. 5,** 553
American Association of Advertising Agencies, **Supp. 8,** 53
American Association of Anatomists, **Supp. 6,** 296; first woman president, **Supp. 5,** 600

American Association of Cartoonists and Caricaturists, founding of, **Supp. 1**, 718

American Association of Collegiate Alumnae, **Vol. 4, Part 2**, 514; **Vol. 7, Part 2**, 174; **Vol. 8, Part 1**, 554; **Vol. 9, Part 2**, 276

American Association of Economic Entomologists, founding of, **Supp. 4**, 400

American Association of Hospital Social Workers, **Supp. 6**, 98

American Association of Labor Legislation, **Supp. 1**, 294

American Association of Marriage Counselors, founding of, **Supp. 6**, 602

American Association of Museums, founding of, **Supp. 1**, 415

American Association of Pathologists and Bacteriologists, founding of, **Supp. 3**, 503

American Association of Petroleum Geologists, founding of, **Supp. 7**, 804

American Association of Physical Anthropologists, founding of, **Supp. 3**, 372

American Association of Plastic Surgery, founding of, **Supp. 4**, 221

American Association of Retired Persons, founding of, **Supp. 8**, 9–10

American Association of Social Workers, founding of, **Supp. 2**, 376

American Association of Teachers of Italian, founding of, **Supp. 2**, 254

American Association of Teachers of Journalism, **Supp. 1**, 87

American Association of University Professors, founding of, **Supp. 1**, 683; **Supp. 3**, 151; **Supp. 6**, 467; **Supp. 7**, 481

American Association of University Women, **Vol. 4, Part 2**, 514; **Vol. 7, Part 2**, 174; **Vol. 9, Part 2**, 276; **Supp. 6**, 412, 413

American Association to Promote the Teaching of Speech to the Deaf, **Vol. 2, Part 2**, 574

American Astronomical Society, **Vol. 7, Part 2**, 563; **Supp. 1**, 187; first woman officer, **Supp. 3**, 131

American Automobile Association, **Vol. 4, Part 1**, 330

American Bandmasters Association, **Supp. 6**, 242

American Bank Note Co., **Vol. 3, Part 2**, 22

American Baptist Education Society, **Vol. 4, Part 1**, 182

American Baptist Home Mission Society, **Vol. 4, Part 1**, 603; **Vol. 7, Part 1**, 160; **Vol. 8, Part 1**, 543

American Baptist Missionary Union, **Vol. 9, Part 2**, 143

American Bar Association, **Vol. 1, Part 1**, 544; **Vol. 5, Part 1**, 383; **Vol. 8, Part 1**, 400; **Vol. 8, Part 2**, 177; **Vol. 9, Part 1**, 612; **Supp. 6**, 651; **Supp. 8**, 662; blacks' membership in, **Supp. 4**, 493; first woman committee chairman, **Supp. 7**, 785

American Bar Association Journal, founding of, **Supp. 2**, 500

American Battle Monuments Commission, **Supp. 3**, 199

American Bell Telephone Co. *See* American Telephone & Telegraph Co.

American Bible League, **Vol. 4, Part 1**, 602

American Bible Society, **Vol. 1, Part 1**, 512; **Vol. 1, Part 2**, 136, 568; **Vol. 2, Part 2**, 299; **Vol. 3, Part 2**, 215; **Vol. 4, Part 1**, 619; **Vol. 5, Part 2**, 9, 12; **Vol. 7, Part 1**, 2, 16, 245 f., 411; **Vol. 7, Part 2**, 591; **Vol. 8, Part 1**, 542; **Vol. 8, Part 2**, 261; **Vol. 9, Part 1**, 204, 300; **Vol. 9, Part 2**, 11, 303

American Bibliography, **Supp. 1**, 290

American Bimetallic League, **Vol. 10, Part 1**, 459 f.

American Birth Control League, founding of, **Supp. 8**, 569

American Board of Anesthesia, founding of, **Supp. 6**, 554

American Board of Foreign Missions, **Vol. 2, Part 2**, 13; **Vol. 3, Part 1**, 573 f.; **Vol. 3, Part 2**, 215; **Vol. 5, Part 2**, 234

American Board of Obstetrics and Gynecology, founding of, **Supp. 6**, 555

American Board of Plastic Surgery, founding of, **Supp. 2**, 707

American Board of Psychiatry and Neurology, founding of, **Supp. 4**, 572

American Board of Radiology, founding of, **Supp. 2**, 512

American Board of Surgery, founding of, **Supp. 6**, 246

American Book Co., **Vol. 4, Part 2**, 503

American Booksellers Association, **Supp. 7**, 524, 525

American Bridge Co., **Supp. 3**, 367

American-British Mixed Claims Commission, **Vol. 4, Part 2**, 111

American Broadcasting Co.: founding of, **Supp. 8**, 179; news commentary, **Supp. 6**, 148

American Bureau of Shipping, **Vol. 9, Part 2**, 344; **Supp. 5**, 440

American Cancer Society, **Supp. 4**, 617; predecessor, **Supp. 3**, 258; **Supp. 4**, 385

American Can Co., **Vol. 7, Part 1**, 144

American Car and Foundry Co., founding of, **Supp. 5**, 324

American Catholic Historical Association, founding of, **Supp. 4**, 353

American Catholic Historical Society of Philadelphia, founding of, **Vol. 6, Part 2**, 604; **Supp. 2**, 197

American Catholic Philosophical Association, founding of, **Supp. 2**, 506

American Chemical Journal, **Vol. 8, Part 1**, 501 f.

American Chemical Society, **Vol. 1, Part 2**, 34; **Vol. 7, Part 2**, 540; founding of, **Supp. 1**, 178; history division, **Supp. 4**, 114; publications, **Supp. 3**, 566

American Child Health Association, publications and promotion, **Supp. 7**, 70

American China Policy Association, founding of, **Supp. 6**, 350

American Citizen, **Vol. 2, Part 2**, 47

American Citizenship Foundation, founding of, **Supp. 2**, 637

American Civil Liberties Union, **Supp. 4**, 539, 542, 837; **Supp. 6**, 392; **Supp. 7**, 262, 356; administration, **Supp. 7**, 510; expulsion of Communists from, **Supp. 7**, 248–49; founding of, **Supp. 3**, 246; **Supp. 4**, 904; **Supp. 6**, 330; **Supp. 7**, 248, 375; Jehovah's Witnesses' case, **Supp. 3**, 679; legal counsel, **Supp. 5**, 280; national board, **Supp. 8**, 35, 681; predecessor, **Supp. 3**, 604; **Supp. 8**, 649; Scopes trial, **Supp. 6**, 528; **Supp. 8**, 583–84

American Classical League, founding of, **Supp. 3**, 810

American Climatological Society, **Vol. 7, Part 2**, 454

American College for Girls at Constantinople, founding of, **Supp. 2**, 517

American College of Physicians, reorganization, **Supp. 2**, 628

American College of Surgeons: criticism of, **Supp. 6**, 246, 632; directorship, **Supp. 7**, 329; founding of, **Supp. 1**, 408, 542; **Supp. 2**, 722; **Supp. 3**, 67, 202; **Supp. 6**, 215

American Colonization Society, **Vol. 2, Part 2**, 540; **Vol. 4, Part 2**, 56, 286, 524; **Vol. 5, Part 2**, 204; **Vol. 6, Part 1**, 163; **Vol. 8, Part 2**, 10; **Vol. 9, Part 1**, 288, 330; **Vol. 9, Part 2**, 506, 623; **Vol. 10, Part 1**, 508 f.; **Vol. 10, Part 2**, 509

American Committee for Democracy and Intellectual Freedom, **Supp. 3**, 85

American Committee for Relief in Ireland, founding of, **Supp. 2,** 497

American Committee for the Outlawry of War, founding of, **Supp. 3,** 457

American Committee for the Revision of the Bible, **Vol. 2, Part 2,** 38

American Congress on Tuberculosis, **Vol. 1, Part 2,** 154

American Cotton Growers Exchange, founding of, **Supp. 1,** 566

American Council of Learned Societies, **Vol. 7, Part 1,** 331; **Supp. 3,** 22; founding of, **Supp. 2,** 186, 342; **Supp. 8,** 369, 370

American Council on Educaton, **Supp. 5,** 761

American Country Life Association, **Supp. 1,** 145; founding of, **Supp. 3,** 684

American Cyanamid Co., **Supp. 3,** 439–40

American Cyclopaedia, **Vol. 4, Part 2,** 503

American Dance Festival, Connecticut College, **Supp. 6,** 313

American De Forest Wireless Telegraph Co., founding of, **Supp. 7,** 175

American Dialect Society, **Vol. 9, Part 1,** 64

American Dispensatory, **Vol. 5, Part 2,** 394

American Documentation Institute, founding of, **Supp. 8,** 120

American Drawing Book, **Vol. 2, Part 2,** 18

American Economic Association, **Vol. 5, Part 1,** 574; **Vol. 7, Part 2,** 300; **Supp. 3,** 248; founding of, **Supp. 2,** 106, 608

American Electric Co., founding of, **Supp. 2,** 658

American Electro-Chemical Society, **Vol. 10, Part 1,** 570 f.

American Electrotherapeutic Association, **Vol. 6, Part 2,** 381

American Engineering Council, waste-inefficiency studies, **Supp. 3,** 189

American Equal Rights Association, **Vol. 7, Part 2,** 609

American Ethnological Society, **Vol. 1, Part 2,** 7; **Vol. 2, Part 2,** 540 f.; **Vol. 3, Part 2,** 228; **Vol. 4, Part 2,** 417

American Ethnology, Bureau of **Vol. 4, Part 1,** 192; **Vol. 7, Part 2,** 603

American Eugenics Society, **Supp. 4,** 413

American Expeditionary Force, **Vol. 5, Part 1,** 571; **Vol. 9, Part 2,** 327; **Supp. 2,** 460; **Supp. 4,** 123, 656–57, 702; **Supp. 5,** 160, 186, 468–69; 530–31; 668–69; **Supp. 8,** 262, 705

American Export Lines, **Supp. 7,** 604

American Express Co., **Vol. 2, Part 2,** 50; **Vol. 3, Part 2,** 271; **Vol. 10, Part 1,** 639 f.

American Farm Book, **Vol. 1, Part 1,** 205

American Farm Bureau Federation, founding of, **Supp. 1,** 660; **Supp. 3,** 319; **Supp. 4,** 37

American Farmer, **Vol. 9, Part 1,** 200

American Farm Foundation, founding of, **Supp. 1,** 645

American Federation of Catholic Societies, Social Service Commission, **Supp. 4,** 232

American Federation of Labor (AFL), **Vol. 2, Part 2,** 338, 612; **Vol. 3, Part 1,** 510; **Vol. 4, Part 1,** 370 f.; **Vol. 5, Part 2,** 278; **Vol. 6, Part 1,** 170, 521; **Vol. 6, Part 2,** 150; **Vol. 7, Part 1,** 545; **Vol. 8, Part 1,** 142 f.; administration, **Supp. 2,** 218–19; **Supp. 3,** 347; **Supp. 4,** 606–7; **Supp. 5,** 253–54, 339–40, 691; **Supp. 6,** 706, 707; auto industry unions, **Supp. 8,** 418, 419, 526; blacks and, **Supp. 6,** 648; CIO v., **Supp. 6,** 219, 379, 707; conservatism, **Supp. 6,** 218–19; **Supp. 7,** 455; craft v. industrial union issue, **Supp. 2,** 325; **Supp. 5,** 254–55, 339–40, 510, 654, 691; **Supp. 6,** 218–19; **Supp. 7,** 255; first woman organizers, **Supp. 3,** 576; **Supp. 7,** 455; founding of, **Supp. 1,** 317; mass production workers' unionization, **Supp. 4,** 279–80; Metal Trade Department, **Supp. 6,** 218–19; organizers, **Supp. 8,** 374, 375; presidential endorsements by, **Supp. 5,** 255; socialist movement and, **Supp. 3,** 347–48, 373; theory behind, **Supp. 6,** 503

American Federation of Labor-Congress of Industrial Organizations (AFL-CIO): awards, **Supp. 8,** 309; founding of, **Supp. 8,** 508

American Federation of Radio Artists, **Supp. 6,** 159–60

American Federation of Teachers, **Supp. 8,** 132

American Field Service, organization of, **Supp. 2,** 15

American Fisheries Society, **Vol. 4, Part 2,** 562

American Folklore Society, **Vol. 1, Part 2,** 423; **Vol. 7, Part 1,** 460; **Supp. 3,** 83

American Forestry Association, **Vol. 10, Part 1,** 444 f.

American Foundation for the Blind: founding of, **Supp. 5,** 347; fund-raising, **Supp. 8,** 318

American Foundation, Inc., **Supp. 1,** 93

American Friends of France, founding of, **Supp. 5,** 506

American Friends of the Middle East, **Supp. 7,** 740

American Friends' Peace Association, **Vol. 5, Part 2,** 4

American Friends Service Committee, founding of, **Supp. 4,** 442

American Fur Co., **Vol. 1, Part 1,** 397, 401; **Vol. 2, Part 2,** 565; **Vol. 5, Part 1,** 326; **Vol. 8, Part 2,** 117; **Vol. 9, Part 1,** 144

American Game Association, founding of, **Supp. 2,** 265

American Gas and Electric Co., founding of, **Supp. 5,** 750

American Geographical Society, **Vol. 4, Part 2,** 2, 417, 445; **Supp. 4,** 99

American Geologists and Naturalists Association, **Vol. 8, Part 2,** 94

American Geophysical Union, **Supp. 6,** 206

"American Gothic" (painting), **Supp. 3,** 841

American Greek War Relief Association, founding of, **Supp. 7,** 692

American Guild of Musical Artists, **Supp. 6,** 633

American Guild of Organists, **Vol. 10, Part 1,** 480; founding of, **Supp. 2,** 198

American Gynecological Society, **Vol. 9, Part 2,** 446; founding of, **Supp. 1,** 437

American Hebrew, **Vol. 6, Part 2,** 532; founding of, **Supp. 2,** 453

American Heritage (magazine), predecessor, **Supp. 8,** 328

American Heritage Foundation, founding of, **Supp. 8,** 53

American Historical Association, **Vol. 1, Part 1,** 309; **Vol. 3, Part 1,** 523 f.; **Vol. 7, Part 1,** 331; **Vol. 8, Part 2,** 312; **Vol. 10, Part 1,** 93; **Supp. 4,** 162–63; **Supp. 6,** 531; **Supp. 7,** 253; **Supp. 8,** 369, 370; founding of, **Supp. 2,** 340

American Historical Review, **Supp. 6,** 310; **Supp. 7,** 253; **Supp. 8,** 169; founding of, **Supp. 2,** 341

American history. *See* Colonial Period; History; *specific events*

American History Told by Contemporaries, **Supp. 3,** 336

American Home Economics Association, **Vol. 7, Part 1,** 576; **Vol. 8, Part 1,** 554; founding of, **Supp. 3,** 507; predecessor, **Supp. 3,** 68

American Home Missionary Society, **Vol. 7, Part 2,** 318, 502

American Homes, **Vol. 9, Part 2,** 319, 329

American Hospital. *See* Thorek Hospital and Medical Center

American Humane Educational Society, **Vol. 1, Part 1,** 303

American Humor, **Supp. 3,** 672

American Ice Co., **Vol. 7, Part 1,** 240

American Imago, The, founding of, **Supp. 4,** 717

American Indian Day, **Supp. 5,** 662

American Indian Federation, **Supp. 7,** 393

American Indians. *See* Indians, American (general); Indians, American (by state); Indians, American (by tribe)

American Individualism, **Supp. 7,** 359

American Institute for Social Service, **Vol. 9, Part 2,** 150 f.

American Institute of Aeronautics and Astronautics, predecessor, **Supp. 6,** 666

American Institute of Architects, **Vol. 3, Part 1,** 104; **Vol. 4, Part 2,** 413; **Vol. 7, Part 2,** 342; **Vol. 10, Part 1,** 125 f., 397 f.; first woman member, **Supp. 6,** 463

American Institute of Christian Philosophy, **Vol. 3, Part 1,** 193

American Institute of Christian Sociology, **Supp. 3,** 177

American Institute of Civics, **Vol. 6, Part 1,** 424

American Institute of Electrical Engineers, **Vol. 3, Part 1,** 221; **Vol. 8, Part 1,** 75 f.; **Vol. 10, Part 1,** 570 f.

American Institute of Graphic Arts, **Vol. 8, Part 2,** 214

American Institute of Homeopathy, **Vol. 4, Part 2,** 516; **Vol. 8, Part 1,** 264

American Institute of Instruction, **Vol. 5, Part 2,** 408 f.; **Vol. 7, Part 2,** 18 f.; **Vol. 8, Part 2,** 250; **Vol. 10, Part 1,** 558 f.

American Institute of International Law: first woman elected to, **Supp. 7,** 718; founding of, **Supp. 3,** 700

American Institute of Mining and Metallurgical Engineers, **Supp. 7,** 804

American Institute of Mining Engineers, **Vol. 2, Part 2,** 486; **Vol. 3, Part 1,** 460 f.; **Vol. 7, Part 2,** 354; **Vol. 8, Part 1,** 415; **Vol. 8, Part 2,** 189

American Institute of Physics, founding, of, **Supp. 4,** 818; **Supp. 5,** 126; **Supp. 6,** 500

American Institute of Planners, predecessors, **Supp. 4,** 56

American Institute of Public Opinion, **Supp. 7,** 649

American Iron and Steel Association, **Vol. 7, Part 2,** 206

"Americanism," coining of the term, **Vol. 10, Part 2,** 438

American Issue Publishing Co., **Supp. 4,** 161

"Americanizers," **Vol. 8, Part 2,** 124

American Jewish Committee, **Supp. 2,** 6; **Supp. 3,** 85; **Supp. 4,** 603; founding of, **Supp. 4, 539;** Joint Distribution Committee, **Supp. 4,** 699–700

American Jewish Conference, founding of, **Supp. 4,** 593–94

American Jewish Congress, **Supp. 4,** 905, 906; first, **Supp. 2,** 266; founding of, **Supp. 3,** 488

American Jewish Historical Society, **Vol. 9, Part 2,** 131; **Supp. 1,** 473; **Supp. 5,** 587

American-Jewish Joint Distribution Committee, founding of, **Supp. 4,** 539

American Jewish League Against Communism, **Supp. 6,** 350

American Joint Agricultural Society, **Supp. 4,** 699

American Journal of Dental Science, pioneer dental periodical, **Vol. 7, Part 2,** 251

American Journal of Education, **Vol. 1, Part 1,** 624

American Journal of International Law, **Vol. 5, Part 2,** 609; founding of, **Supp. 1,** 358; **Supp. 5,** 751–52

American Journal of Mathematics, **Vol. 9, Part 2,** 109, 257

American Journal of Mining, **Vol. 8, Part 1,** 415

American Journal of Nursing, **Supp. 6,** 167; founding of, **Supp. 4,** 632

American Journal of Obstetrics, **Vol. 7, Part 1,** 325

American Journal of Philology, **Vol. 4, Part 1,** 281

American Journal of Physical Anthropology, founding of, **Supp. 3,** 372

American Journal of Physiology: editing of, **Supp. 4,** 390; founding of, **Supp. 4,** 676

American Journal of Police Science, founding of, **Supp. 5,** 245

American Journal of Psychology, **Vol. 4, Part 2,** 128; **Vol. 8, Part 2,** 346; **Supp. 8,** 44

American Journal of Public Health, **Supp. 3,** 324; **Supp. 4,** 684; **Supp. 6,** 703

American Journal of Science and Arts, **Vol. 4, Part 1,** 245; **Vol. 9, Part 1,** 161 f., 163 f.

American Journal of Sociology, **Vol. 9, Part 1,** 222; **Supp. 6,** 482–83

American Labor Legislation Review, **Supp. 3,** 18

American Labor party, **Supp. 5,** 466–67; **Supp. 7,** 156; **Supp. 8,** 512; founding of, **Supp. 2,** 684; **Supp. 4,** 69–70

American Laboratory Theater, **Supp. 8,** 54

American Language, The, **Supp. 6,** 445, 446

American Laryngological Association, **Vol. 1, Part 1,** 191; **Vol. 5, Part 2,** 465

American Law Institute, **Supp. 8,** 662; founding of, **Supp. 2,** 471; **Supp. 4,** 491–92; **Supp. 6,** 87; **Supp. 7,** 317; presidency, **Supp. 8,** 662

American Law Journal, **Vol. 4, Part 2,** 138

American Law Magazine, **Vol. 9, Part 1,** 29

American Law Register, **Vol. 7, Part 1,** 49

American Law Review, **Vol. 4, Part 1,** 520

American League Against War and Fascism, founding of, **Supp. 8,** 425, 681

American League (baseball), founding and development of, **Supp. 5,** 261; **Supp. 6,** 415; **Supp. 7,** 139

American Legal History Society, founding of, **Supp. 3,** 43

American Legion, **Supp. 5,** 363, 459; **Supp. 7,** 744; founding of, **Supp. 2,** 15; **Supp. 3,** 449, 668; **Supp. 5,** 113, 177; **Supp. 7,** 808; **Supp. 8,** 495; national commander, **Supp. 8,** 302; organization of, **Vol. 8, Part 1,** 276; state commander, **Supp. 8,** 410; subversives, investigation of, **Supp. 8,** 426

American Leprosy Foundation, **Supp. 7,** 195

American Liberty League, **Supp. 3,** 653, 720; **Supp. 8,** 593; founding of, **Supp. 4,** 171, 683; **Supp. 5,** 156, 494, 715

American Liberty Oil Co., founding of, **Supp. 8,** 454, 455

American Library Association, **Vol. 2, Part 1,** 20; **Vol. 2, Part 2,** 583; **Vol. 3, Part 1,** 15; **Vol. 3, Part 2,** 22; **Vol. 4, Part 1,** 557; **Vol. 4, Part 2,** 42; **Vol. 8, Part 1,** 66 f.; **Vol. 9, Part 1,** 24; **Vol. 10, Part 1,** 426; administration, **Supp. 4,** 846; **Supp. 5,** 554; founding of, **Supp. 1,** 101, 242, 290; uniform catalog code, **Supp. 3,** 326–27; **Supp. 6,** 554

American Literary, Scientific and Military Society. *See* Norwich University

American literature, **Supp. 2,** 189–90, 703–5, 730–33; **Supp. 3,** 234–38; **Supp. 7,** 334–39; **Supp. 8,** 491–93, 563–64, 581–82, 625–26; beat generation, **Supp. 8,** 326–27; bibliography, **Supp. 8,** 663–64; Buddhist influence, **Supp. 8,** 327; Chicago Renaissance, **Supp. 8,** 124; comprehensive library of, **Supp. 7,** 797; first novel, **Supp. 1,** 125; Golden Age of Indiana, **Supp. 4,** 629–30; grotesque tradition, **Supp. 7,** 231–35, 582–83; novel of manners, **Supp. 8,** 480–82; scholarship in, **Supp. 7,** ; teaching of, **Supp. 5,** 542; writings on, **Supp. 3,** 72; **Supp. 6,** 6.445, 523. *See also* English literature and language; *specific genres,*

works, and writers
American Locomotive Co., **Vol. 2, Part 1,** 424
American Longshoremen's Union, founding of, **Supp. 2,** 272
American Machine and Foundry Co., **Supp. 3,** 587
American Machinist, **Supp. 3,** 5
American Magazine, **Vol. 9, Part 1,** 354; **Supp. 3,** 762; **Supp. 4,** 47; founding of, **Supp. 4,** 518, 662
American Mathematical Society, **Vol. 5, Part 2,** 134; **Vol. 10, Part 1,** 149; **Vol. 10, Part 2,** 632
American Mechanic, first scientific newspaper in U.S., **Vol. 8, Part 1,** 101 f.
American Medical Association, **Vol. 2, Part 2,** 20; **Vol. 3, Part 1,** 139 f., 595 f.; **Vol. 4, Part 2,** 20; **Vol. 5, Part 2,** 468; **Vol. 6, Part 1,** 606; **Vol. 7, Part 2,** 276, 286; antitrust action against, **Supp. 3,** 122; birth control sanction, **Supp. 8,** 569; on medical care costs, **Supp. 6,** 702–3; on medical quackery, **Supp. 3,** 104. *See also Journal of the American Medical Association*
American Medical Biography, **Vol. 9, Part 2,** 388
American Medical Missionary College, **Supp. 3,** 411
American Medical Recorder, **Vol. 3, Part 1,** 615 f.
American Medical Weekly, **Vol. 4, Part 1,** 90
American Medico-Psychological Association, **Vol. 3, Part 1,** 595 f.
American Men of Science, **Supp. 3,** 150
American Mercury: contributors, **Supp. 3,** 147; **Supp. 5,** 4; **Supp. 7,** 20; **Supp. 8,** 426; covers, **Supp. 7,** 3; founding of, **Supp. 6,** 445, 470, 471, 571
American Messenger, **Vol. 4, Part 2,** 159
American Metal Co., **Supp. 3,** 214
American Methodist Conference, **Vol. 9, Part 2,** 133
American Metropolis, **Vol. 7, Part 1,** 280
American Microscopical Society, **Vol. 10, Part 1,** 435 f.; **Supp. 3,** 40
American Midland Naturalist, founding of, **Supp. 2,** 488
American Mining Co., **Vol. 7, Part 2,** 461
American Missionary Association, **Vol. 4, Part 2,** 223; **Vol. 8, Part 2,** 103; **Supp. 6,** 321
American Missionary Society, **Vol. 1, Part 2,** 552; **Vol. 9, Part 2,** 299
American Museum of Natural History (New York City), **Vol. 1, Part 1,** 198; **Vol. 1, Part 2,** 239; **Vol. 2, Part 2,** 84; **Vol. 3, Part 2,** 356; **Vol. 4, Part 1,** 341; **Vol. 4, Part 2,** 437; **Vol. 5, Part 2,** 62; **Vol. 6, Part 1,** 484; **Vol. 6, Part 2,** 412; **Vol. 10, Part 2,** 135; administration, **Supp. 8,** 485; African Hall, **Supp. 5,** 420; **Supp. 8,** 3–4; anthropology division, **Supp. 3,** 83, 84; **Supp. 4,** 867, 907–8; **Supp. 6,** 392–93; archaeological halls, **Supp. 7,** 570; architecture of, **Supp. 5,** 300; arctic expeditions, **Supp. 7,** 716; exhibit design, **Supp. 1,** 585–86; insects and spiders collections, **Supp. 3,** 478; **Supp. 6,** 341; mammals curation, **Supp. 5,** 678; Mexican archaeology collection, **Supp. 3,** 786; ornithology division, **Supp. 3,** 161; **Supp. 6,** 255; **Supp. 7,** 116–17; paleontology division, **Supp. 3,** 316–17; public health exhibits, **Supp. 6,** 701; sculptures of Indians, **Supp. 6,** 720; whale collection, **Supp. 6,** 17–18
American Musical Fund Association, **Vol. 10, Part 1,** 543
American Musical Magazine, **Vol. 8, Part 1,** 421
American Musicological Society, founding of, **Supp. 3,** 253
American Naturalist, **Vol. 5, Part 1,** 447; **Vol. 7, Part 1,** 242; **Vol. 7, Part 2,** 126
American Nazi party, founding of, **Supp. 8,** 540–41
American Neurological Association, **Vol. 8, Part 1,** 282 f.
American News Co., **Vol. 3, Part 1,** 278 f.; **Vol. 7, Part 1,** 332; **Vol. 9, Part 2,** 606 f.

American Newspaper Guild: founding of, **Supp. 2,** 14, 67; Hearst organization opposition to, **Supp. 5,** 287
American Newspaper Publishers Association, **Vol. 2, Part 1,** 37
American Newspapers, Inc., founding of, **Supp. 5,** 287
American Normal School Association, **Vol. 7, Part 2,** 532
American Nurses Association, founding of, **Supp. 1,** 556
American Opera Company, **Vol. 9, Part 2,** 425; **Supp. 4,** 834
American Ophthalmological Society, **Vol. 3, Part 1,** 207; **Vol. 5, Part 2,** 38
American Oriental Society, **Vol. 1, Part 2,** 387; **Vol. 2, Part 2,** 168 f.; **Vol. 5, Part 2,** 54; **Vol. 7, Part 2,** 56, 476; **Vol. 8, Part 2,** 308
American Ornithologists' Union, **Vol. 2, Part 1,** 31; **Vol. 2, Part 2,** 459, 465; **Vol. 8, Part 1,** 598
American Orthopaedic Association, **Vol. 1, Part 2,** 556; **Vol. 5, Part 2,** 236
American Orthopsychiatric Association, founding of, **Supp. 6,** 17
American Otological Society, **Vol. 8, Part 2,** 132
American Oxonian, **Supp. 6,** 30
American Palestine Exploration Society, **Vol. 7, Part 2,** 150
American Park Association, **Vol. 8, Part 2,** 37
American Patriot, **Vol. 5, Part 1,** 34
American Peace Award, **Supp. 1,** 93
American Peace Society, **Vol. 3, Part 1,** 345; **Vol. 4, Part 1,** 170; **Vol. 5, Part 2,** 527; **Vol. 9, Part 1,** 271, 635
American Peace Society of Japan, **Supp. 3,** 322
American Pediatric Society, founding of, **Supp. 3,** 160
American Pharmaceutical Association, **Vol. 7, Part 2,** 259; **Vol. 8, Part 1,** 242, 259
American Philological Association, **Vol. 2, Part 2,** 535; **Vol. 3, Part 1,** 372
American Philosophical Association, founding of, **Supp. 1,** 332
American Philosophical Society, **Vol. 1, Part 2,** 434; **Vol. 4, Part 2,** 385, 561; **Vol. 5, Part 1,** 220; **Vol. 5, Part 2,** 205; **Vol. 7, Part 1,** 510; **Vol. 7, Part 2,** 306; **Vol. 9, Part 1,** 355 f.; **Vol. 10, Part 1,** 433
American Physical Society, **Vol. 7, Part 2,** 397; **Vol. 10, Part 1,** 584 f.; founding of, **Supp. 2,** 488; **Supp. 3,** 11
American Physiological Society, **Vol. 1, Part 2,** 496; **Vol. 2, Part 2,** 617; founding of, **Supp. 2,** 391
American Place, An (New York City gallery), **Supp. 4,** 781
American Political Parties, **Supp. 7,** 54
American Political Science Association, **Vol. 8, Part 1,** 491; founding of, **Supp. 2,** 250; **Supp. 3,** 831; **Supp. 4,** 260; **Supp. 5,** 485
American Political Science Review, **Supp. 3,** 831; **Supp. 5,** 522
American Political Tradition and the Men Who Made It, The, **Supp. 8,** 271, 272
American Pomological Society, **Vol. 4, Part 2,** 356; **Vol. 9, Part 2,** 439
American Presidency, The, **Supp. 8,** 552
American President Line, **Supp. 6,** 244
American Press Association, **Vol. 3, Part 1,** 220, 278; **Vol. 7, Part 1,** 332; **Vol. 9, Part 2,** 606 f.
American Psychiatric Association, **Vol. 4, Part 2,** 411
American Psychoanalytic Association, **Supp. 4,** 572; founding of, **Supp. 4,** 131; reorganization, **Supp. 5,** 518
American Psychological Association, **Vol. 5, Part 2,** 526; **Supp. 8,** 8; presidency, **Supp. 6,** 672, 718

American Theatre Wing, "Tony" awards, **Supp. 4,** 653

American Theological Society, founding of, **Supp. 3,** 111

American Tin Plate Co., **Vol. 7, Part 1,** 143

American Tobacco Co., **Vol. 3, Part 1,** 496 f.; **Vol. 4, Part 1,** 318; **Vol. 7, Part 1,** 591; **Vol. 7, Part 2,** 330; **Vol. 8, Part 2,** 266; advertising, **Supp. 5,** 411; antitrust case, **Supp. 3,** 587; Lucky Strike cigarettes, **Supp. 4,** 371; Reynolds' competition with, **Supp. 5,** 166, 166–67

American Tobacco Co. v. *United States*, **Supp. 7,** 96

American Tract Society, **Vol. 2, Part 2,** 378 f.; **Vol. 4, Part 2,** 158; **Vol. 6, Part 1,** 183; **Vol. 8, Part 1,** 89 f.; **Vol. 8, Part 2,** 43

American Tragedy, An, **Supp. 3,** 235, 237

American Tree Association, founding of, **Supp. 2,** 507

American Trotting Register, **Vol. 10, Part 1,** 373 f.

American Union Against Militarism, **Supp. 7,** 356; **Supp. 8,** 649; founding of, **Supp. 6,** 664

American Unitarian Association, **Vol. 1, Part 1,** 561; **Vol. 9, Part 1,** 551; **Vol. 10, Part 1,** 448 f.; **Supp. 7,** 356

American University (Beirut, Lebanon), **Vol. 1, Part 2,** 370, 372; **Vol. 8, Part 1,** 116 f.

American University (Cairo, Egypt), predecessor, **Supp. 4,** 860

American University (Washington, D.C.), **Vol. 5, Part 1,** 426; **Vol. 6, Part 1,** 558; history studies, **Supp. 7,** 735; physics studies, **Supp. 8,** 231

American Vindicator, **Supp. 7,** 644

American Volunteer Group. *See* Flying Tigers

American Watchman, **Vol. 2, Part 2,** 47

American Weekly, circulation, **Supp. 2,** 242

American Weekly Mercury, **Vol. 1, Part 2,** 553

American Wine Co., **Vol. 2, Part 2,** 374 f.

American Woman Suffrage Association, **Vol. 1, Part 1,** 320; **Vol. 1, Part 2,** 581; **Supp. 4,** 85

American Women's Association, predecessor, **Supp. 5,** 506

American Wood Paper Co., **Vol. 5, Part 2,** 281 f.

American Woolen Co., **Supp. 3,** 577

American Youth Congress, **Supp. 7,** 660

American Zionist Emergency Council, **Supp. 7,** 689

America's Coming of Age, **Supp. 7,** 79–80

America's Cup, **Supp. 4,** 124, **Supp. 5,** 6

"America's Town Meeting of the Air" (radio program), **Supp. 6,** 160–61; **Supp. 8,** 488

"America the Beautiful" (song), **Supp. 1,** 59

Ames, Adelbert, Jr., reference to, **Supp. 8,** 69–70

Ames, Blanche, reference to, **Supp. 4,** 17

Ames, James Barr, reference to, **Vol. 9, Part 2,** 404

Ames, Winthrop, references to, **Supp. 3,** 685; **Supp. 7,** 495, 496

Amherst, General, reference to, **Vol. 6, Part 1,** 517; **Vol. 7, Part 1,** 647

Amherst College, **Vol. 4, Part 1,** 210; **Vol. 4, Part 2,** 308; **Vol. 5, Part 1,** 70 f., 369; **Vol. 8, Part 2,** 556; **Vol. 9, Part 1,** 549; **Vol. 10, Part 1,** 99; economics studies, **Supp. 6,** 271; founding of, **Vol. 7, Part 1,** 146; **Vol. 10, Part 1,** 594 f.; presidency, **Supp. 5,** 390–91; **Supp. 7,** 523

Amino acids: chain synthesis, **Supp. 3,** 441–42; chemistry of, **Supp. 3,** 61; cystine as, **Supp. 5,** 623; definition and preparation of, **Supp. 4,** 720; nutrition research on, **Supp. 6,** 190; **Supp. 7,** 476; research on, **Supp. 5,** 122, 149

Amistad case, **Vol. 1, Part 1,** 542; **Vol. 8, Part 2,** 383

Ammann, Othmar H., reference to, **Supp. 6,** 594

Ammann and Whitney, founding of, **Supp. 7,** 12

Ammonia, isolation of, **Vol. 8, Part 1,** 223 f.

"Amnesty oath," Texas, **Vol. 1, Part 1,** 111

Amoskeag Manufacturing Co., **Supp. 5,** 190

Amplification. *See* Audio systems

Amsterdam News, **Supp. 6,** 490

Amundsen, Roald, reference to, **Supp. 2,** 115; **Supp. 5,** 206

Amusement parks, **Vol. 9, Part 2,** 553; first in U. S., **Vol. 10, Part 1,** 48

Amyotrophic lateral sclerosis (Gehrig's disease), **Supp. 3,** 294–96

Anaconda Copper Co., **Vol. 8, Part 2,** 263; **Supp. 4,** 556–57; **Supp. 5,** 273

Anagnos, Michael, reference to, **Supp. 8,** 316

Analysts. *See* Psychoanalysis

Anaphylaxis, **Supp. 4,** 34, 701; **Supp. 6,** 481

Anarchist movement, **Supp. 2,** 37, 246, 670; **Supp. 7,** 254, 454–55

Anastasia, Albert, reference to, **Supp. 7,** 585; **Supp. 8,** 208, 397

Anatomy: comparative and functional, **Supp. 6,** 704; embryological studies, **Supp. 5,** 600; endocrinology and reproduction hormones studies, **Supp. 3,** 6; neuroanatomy, **Supp. 1,** 439, 584; **Supp. 6,** 295–95; plant, **Supp. 2,** 488; research in, **Supp. 4,** 419–20; **Supp. 6,** 53–54; skeletal development, **Supp. 2,** 665 –66; teaching of, **Supp. 2,** 422; **Supp. 3,** 619; techniques of study, **Supp. 6,** 53–54; writings on, **Supp. 2,** 423. *See also* Medicine; Physiology

Anatomy of Revolution, The, **Supp. 8,** 50–51

Anatomy of the Nervous System, **Supp. 3,** 620

Anderson, Carl D., references to, **Supp. 5,** 496; **Supp. 7,** 344

Anderson, D. C., reference to, **Vol. 1, Part 2,** 445

Anderson, Ernest G., reference to, **Supp. 3,** 540

Anderson, George W., reference to, **Supp. 3,** 98

Anderson, Henry W., reference to, **Supp. 3,** 304

Anderson, Jack, reference to, **Supp. 8,** 497

Anderson, John F., reference to, **Supp. 4,** 701

Anderson, John W., reference to, **Supp. 4,** 294

Anderson, Marian, reference to, **Supp. 5,** 343; **Supp. 8,** 328

Anderson, Maxwell, references to, **Supp. 5,** 100; **Supp. 8,** 255, 529, 622

Anderson, Olaf, reference to, **Supp. 6,** 71

Anderson, Paul Y., reference to, **Supp. 3,** 92

Anderson, Robert B., reference to, **Supp. 6,** 540

Anderson, Sherwood, references to, **Supp. 4,** 131; **Supp. 7,** 231, 306, 334, 335

Anderson, Clayton and Co., founding of, **Supp. 8,** 89

Anderson School (Staatsburg, N.Y.), **Supp. 6,** 17

Andersonville prison, **Vol. 5, Part 1,** 194; **Vol. 6, Part 1,** 162; **Vol. 7, Part 1,** 567; **Vol. 10, Part 2,** 381

Andover Academy. *See* Phillips Academy, Andover

Andover Review, founding of, **Vol. 9, Part 1,** 374

Andover Theological Seminary, **Vol. 1, Part 2,** 31; **Vol. 3, Part 1,** 573 f.; **Vol. 3, Part 2,** 40; **Vol. 7, Part 2,** 204 f., 548; controversy concerning, **Vol. 4, Part 2,** 308; **Vol. 7, Part 2,** 526; **Vol. 8, Part 2,** 46; **Vol. 9, Part 1,** 374, 377; **Vol. 10, Part 1,** 41; founding of, **Vol. 2, Part 1,** 147; **Vol. 7, Part 1,** 245; **Vol. 7, Part 2,** 358; **Vol. 9, Part 1,** 481; heterodoxy, charges of, **Vol. 3, Part 1,** 571 f.; **Supp. 5,** 649

André, John, references to, **Vol. 5, Part 1,** 295, 417; **Vol. 6, Part 1,** 31, 314; **Vol. 8, Part 2,** 34, 239, 407; **Vol. 9, Part 2,** 387

Andrews, John, **Vol. 1, Part 1,** 245, 294

Andrews, John B., references to, **Supp. 3,** 178, 255, 256

Andrews, Roy Chapman, reference to, **Supp. 3,** 316

Andrews, Yvette, reference to, **Supp. 6,** 18

Andromeda, nebula, **Supp. 6,** 31

Andros, Sir Edmund, references to, **Vol. 1, Part 2,** 336; **Vol. 3, Part 1,** 481 f.; **Vol. 7, Part 1,** 500

Androscoggin River, power development, **Vol. 8, Part 2,** 399

Androsterone, **Supp. 4,** 460

Anemia: childhood, **Supp. 3,** 190; hypoplastic, **Supp. 3,** 75; iron treatment for, **Supp. 5,** 276; liver extract for pernicious, **Supp. 5,** 122, 149; nutritional deficiency and, **Supp. 4,** 580–82; treatment of, **Supp. 3,** 242; tropical, **Supp. 1,** 32

Anesthesia: childbirth, **Supp. 3,** 223; cocaine as, **Supp. 3,** 430–31; cyclopropane, **Supp. 6,** 334; ether production and packaging, **Supp. 8,** 411; ethylene, **Supp. 3,** 458; first ethylene-oxygen use, **Supp. 3,** 67; local and regional, **Supp. 6,** 435; shockless, **Supp. 3,** 201–2; side-effect counteraction, **Supp. 4,** 34; spinal, **Supp. 4,** 507; **Supp. 7,** 679; training in, **Supp. 6,** 553–54. *See also* Medicine

Angell, James Burrill, reference to, **Supp. 4,** 20

Angell, James Rowland, references to, **Supp. 6,** 559, 600, 671

Angelus Temple (Los Angeles), **Supp. 3,** 498

Anger (emotion), hypothalamus relationship, **Supp. 3,** 135

Anglican church. *See* Church of England; Protestant Episcopal church

Anglo-American Telegraph Co., **Vol. 3, Part 1,** 600

Anglo-Catholicism, **Supp. 3,** 195; **Supp. 6,** 45–46; **Supp. 7,** 220

Anglo-Chinese College, **Vol. 1, Part 1,** 263; **Vol. 7, Part 2,** 214

Anglo-Roman Union, founding of, **Supp. 2,** 201–2

Anheuser, Eberhard, reference to, **Supp. 1,** 142

Anhydremia syndrome, **Supp. 2,** 432

Animal Industry, Bureau of **Vol. 6, Part 1,** 92; **Vol. 8, Part 2,** 311

Animals: antivivisectionism, **Supp. 6,** 113; behavior studies, **Supp. 2,** 489, 699; biochemical studies, **Supp. 5,** 275, 276; coloration, **Vol. 9, Part 2,** 400; diseases, research in, **Supp. 1,** 258; diseases of, **Vol. 7, Part 1,** 140; **Vol. 8, Part 2,** 311; game surveys, **Supp. 4,** 483; geographic distribution of, **Supp. 4,** 52; husbandry, **Vol. 4, Part 1,** 380; **Vol. 6, Part 1,** 163; **Vol. 7, Part 2,** 510 f.; **Vol. 8, Part 2,** 335 f.; locomotion, photography of, **Vol. 7, Part 1,** 373; Mexican survey, **Supp. 1,** 572; movie use of, **Supp. 4,** 735; nutrition, **Vol. 1, Part 1,** 349 f.; **Supp. 1,** 37; paintings of, **Vol. 1, Part 2,** 95; **Vol. 4, Part 2,** 463 f.; **Vol. 5, Part 1,** 299 f.; **Vol. 7, Part 1,** 152; **Vol. 9, Part 2,** 399 f.; **Vol. 10, Part 2,** 191; psychological studies, **Supp. 8,** 343; sculpture of, **Vol. 1, Part 2,** 11; **Vol. 5, Part 2,** 317 f.; **Vol. 8, Part 1,** 125 f.; seeing-eye dogs, **Supp. 4,** 253–55; shelters, **Supp. 8,** 78; stories about, **Supp. 3,** 767; **Supp. 4,** 736; use in research studies, **Supp. 2,** 157; **Supp. 4,** 832; welfare of, **Vol. 1, Part 1,** 303; **Vol. 1, Part 2,** 215, 424. *See also* Livestock; Psychology, comparative; Veterinary medicine; Wild animals; Zoology; *specific kinds*

Animal World, **Vol. 1, Part 1,** 304

Animated cartoons, first, **Supp. 3,** 76

Anna Christie, **Supp. 4,** 503

Annal of the New York Stage, **Supp. 4,** 634

Annals of Mathematics, founding of, **Supp. 1,** 675

Annals of Surgery, editing of, **Supp. 1,** 599

Annals of the American Academy of Political and Social Science, founding of, **Supp. 2,** 175

Annapolis. *See* United States Naval Academy

Annapolis Convention (1786), **Vol. 1, Part 2,** 204

Anne (ship), **Vol. 7, Part 1,** 43

Annenberg, Max, reference to, **Supp. 3,** 19

Annenberg, Moses, references to, **Supp. 4,** 613; **Supp. 6,** 232

Annenberg, Walter, reference to, **Supp. 3,** 21

Anniston, Ala., founding of, **Vol. 7, Part 1,** 540

Annual Cyclopaedia, **Vol. 3, Part 2,** 416

Ansonia, Conn., history of, **Vol. 7, Part 2,** 526

Antarctica: birds, **Supp. 7,** 217; exploration, **Supp. 2,** 115; **Supp. 6,** 92–93; Ford, Edsel, commemoration, **Supp. 3,** 284; mapping, **Supp. 7,** 217; Palmer Peninsula exploration, **Supp. 5,** 206–7. *See also* Exploration

Antarctican Society, founding of, **Supp. 7,** 217

Anthologies, **Vol. 2, Part 1,** 263; **Vol. 3, Part 1,** 224; **Vol. 4, Part 2,** 11; **Vol. 5, Part 2,** 337, 361, 614; **Vol. 9, Part 1,** 259; **Vol. 9, Part 2,** 374

Anthology Club, founding of, **Vol. 6, Part 2,** 138

Anthony, Katharine, reference to, **Supp. 3,** 376

Anthony, Susan B., references to, **Vol. 5, Part 1,** 150, 195, 196, 312; **Vol. 9, Part 1,** 36; **Supp. 4,** 85, 86; **Supp. 5,** 532; **Supp. 6,** 1

Anthony Adverse, **Supp. 4,** 13–14; **Supp. 8,** 536

Anthracosis, research in, **Supp. 2,** 371

Anthropogeography, **Vol. 8, Part 2,** 583

Anthropologists. For complete list, *see* Occupations Index

Anthropology, **Vol. 1, Part 1,** 537, 571; **Vol. 2, Part 1,** 51, 594; **Vol. 3, Part 1,** 384 f.; **Vol. 4, Part 1,** 421; **Vol. 4, Part 2,** 105; **Vol. 5, Part 2,** 205 f.; **Vol. 6, Part 2,** 47, 60, 373; **Vol. 7, Part 1,** 242, 265 f.; **Vol. 7, Part 2,** 392; **Vol. 8, Part 1,** 276 f., 388 f.; **Vol. 8, Part 2,** 391,; **Vol. 9, Part 1,** 197, 532 f.; academic, **Supp. 7,** 710–11; American community studies, **Supp. 8,** 684–85; American Indians, **Supp. 2,** 9, 176, 593; black folklore, **Supp. 6,** 313–14; cranial indices, **Supp. 1,** 252; cultural, **Supp. 5,** 435; cultural age-area theory, **Supp. 4,** 907–8; cultural reconstruction, **Supp. 6,** 524–25; cultural relativity, **Supp. 3,** 82–86; **Supp. 4,** 71–72; dean of American, **Supp. 6,** 352–53; education in, **Supp. 4,** 521; ethnographic films, **Supp. 7,** 241; field research, **Supp. 1,** 259, 436; fieldwork by women, **Supp. 8,** 509–10; first American Ph.D., **Supp. 3,** 83; folk cultures, **Supp. 6,** 532–34, 611–13; geological relationship to, **Supp. 4,** 119; historical reconstruction, **Supp. 4,** 179; Mexican Tepoztlán study, **Supp. 8,** 378; museum collections, **Supp. 1,** 435–36; Navajo Indian museum, **Supp. 6,** 688; North American Indian, **Supp. 2,** 9, 176; **Supp. 6,** 611–13; physical, **Supp. 3,** 371–72; **Supp. 4,** 866–67; physical human types, **Supp. 5,** 312; primitive religious symbolism, **Supp. 6,** 688; professional master plan, **Supp. 3,** 83; psychoanalytic theory in, **Supp. 5,** 583–84; psychological, writings on, **Supp. 8,** 345; social, **Supp. 8,** 683–85; worker fatigue, **Supp. 8,** 684; writings on, **Supp. 3,** 632

Antibiotics, aureomycin, **Supp. 6,** 176

Antibodies, **Supp. 3,** 440–42

Antietam, battle of, **Vol. 2, Part 1,** 310; **Vol. 2, Part 2,** 476, 563; **Vol. 5, Part 1,** 25, 193, 197, 371, 559; **Vol. 6, Part 1,** 124, 253–254, 392, 583; **Vol. 6, Part 2,** 257; **Vol. 7, Part 2,** 408; **Vol. 8, Part 1,** 570; **Vol. 8, Part 2,** 72, 548; **Vol. 9, Part 1,** 224; **Vol. 9, Part 2,** 215, 591

Antifederalism, **Vol. 2, Part 1,** 189; **Vol. 3, Part 2,** 385; **Vol. 9, Part 2,** 320, 356; **Vol. 10, Part 2,** 598, 601

Antigens, **Supp. 3,** 440–42

Anti-Imperialist League, **Vol. 1, Part 2,** 490

Anti-intellectualism in American Life, **Supp. 8,** 271, 272–73

Anti-Liturgical party, **Vol. 1, Part 2,** 426

Anti-Masonic movement, **Vol. 2, Part 2,** 177, 224; **Vol. 4, Part 1,** 482; **Vol. 4, Part 2,** 155; **Vol. 5, Part 2,** 158; **Vol. 6, Part 2,** 128; **Vol. 7, Part 1,** 188–89; **Vol. 8, Part 2,** 233, 615; **Vol. 9, Part 1,** 621; **Vol. 9,**

Part 2, 89, 454; **Vol. 10, Part 1,** 422, 598; **Vol. 10, Part 2,** 420

Antin, Mary, reference to, **Supp. 4,** 343

Anti-Nazi League, founding of, **Supp. 8,** 492

Antinomians, **Vol. 7, Part 1,** 573; **Vol. 10, Part 1,** 627 f.

Antioch College, Ohio, **Vol. 1, Part 2,** 169; **Vol. 5, Part 1,** 46

Antiquarian studies, **Vol. 1, Part 1,** 149, 379; **Vol. 3, Part 1,** 172, 276 f., 433 f.; **Vol. 3, Part 2,** 157, 316, 494, 559; **Vol. 4, Part 1,** 356, 556, 629; **Vol. 4, Part 2,** 472, 562; **Vol. 5, Part 1,** 320; **Vol. 6, Part 1,** 305 f.; **Vol. 7, Part 1,** 333; **Vol. 8, Part 2,** 367, 387 f.; **Vol. 9, Part 1,** 142, 243, 607; **Vol. 10, Part 1,** 74, 546; **Vol. 10, Part 2,** 154

Antiques: books on, **Vol. 9, Part 1,** 190; Metropolitan Museum American Wing, **Supp. 6,** 562; reproductions, **Supp. 3,** 567. *See also* Americana; Rare books and manuscripts

Anti-Race-Track Gambling League, **Vol. 6, Part 1,** 269

Anti-Saloon League of America, **Vol. 4, Part 2,** 253; **Vol. 6, Part 1,** 171, 276; **Vol. 6, Part 2,** 483; **Vol. 10, Part 2,** 55; factions in, **Supp. 5,** 442; founding of, **Vol. 5, Part 2,** 517; Ohio, **Supp. 4,** 161; Virginia, **Supp. 3,** 132

Anti-Semitism. *See* Holocaust; Judaism and Jews, anti-Semitism

Antiseptics: Argyrol, **Supp. 5,** 39; for childbirth, **Supp. 3,** 223; Dakin's solution, **Supp. 5,** 149; mercurochrome development, **Supp. 3,** 854; research in, **Supp. 4,** 435; wound cleansing technique, **Supp. 3,** 141. *See also* Surgery

Antislavery movement. *See* Abolition movement

Antitrust actions: aluminum manufacturing, **Supp. 7,** 167; Brandeis views, **Supp. 3,** 95, 97; chain stores, **Supp. 5,** 278; federal regulation advocacy, **Supp. 4,** 317; inequities, allegations of, **Supp. 4,** 268; International Business Machines, **Supp. 6,** 675; investment banking, **Supp. 7,** 715; legal experts, **Supp. 5,** 174; legislation, **Vol. 1, Part 2,** 428; **Vol. 3, Part 1,** 342; **Vol. 4, Part 1,** 217; **Vol. 4, Part 2,** 25; **Vol. 7, Part 2,** 32; **Vol. 8, Part 2,** 65; **Supp. 1,** 179; **Supp. 5,** 27, 174; **Supp. 6,** 556; **Supp. 7,** 547; motion pictures, **Supp. 6,** 668; New Deal policy, **Supp. 3,** 168; **Supp. 8,** 17; New York state prosecution, **Supp. 4,** 536, 785; organized medicine, **Supp. 3,** 122; radio networks, **Supp. 8,** 179; Senate committee on, **Supp. 7,** 416; Standard Oil case, **Supp. 2,** 355, 573, 714; **Supp. 4,** 317; steel industry, **Supp. 3,** 263; **Supp. 6,** 591; temporary National Economic Committee, **Supp. 7,** 590; theaters, **Supp. 3,** 276–77; **Supp. 5,** 628; tobacco industry, **Supp. 3,** 587; **Supp. 4,** 536; **Supp. 5,** 567; **Supp. 7,** 96; trade unions, **Supp. 5,** 340; Wilson v. Roosevelt, T., views, **Supp. 3,** 97. *See also* Federal Trade Commission; Sherman Antitrust Act

Antivivisectionism, **Supp. 6,** 113

Ants, study of, **Vol. 6, Part 1,** 242, 603; **Supp. 2,** 708

Anything Goes, **Supp. 8,** 108, 383

Apache Indians, **Vol. 2, Part 2,** 563; **Supp. 1,** 660; **Supp. 6,** 720

Apartment houses: first in U. S., **Vol. 3, Part 1,** 327. *See also* Tenements

Aphasia: rehabilitation methods, **Supp. 1,** 317; studies on, **Supp. 4,** 570

Apollo Club, **Vol. 5, Part 2,** 584; **Vol. 8, Part 1,** 177 f.; **Vol. 9, Part 2,** 579

Apollo project, **Supp. 8,** 81, 225, 694

Appalachian Mountain Club, founding of, **Vol. 5, Part 1,** 447; **Vol. 7, Part 2,** 563

Appalachian Mountains, **Supp. 3,** 407–8; geology of, **Vol. 6, Part 1,** 189; **Vol. 8, Part 2,** 94, 115

Apparel. *See* Clothing manufacture; Fashion

Apparel Arts, **Supp. 5,** 637

Appeal to Reason (Socialist weekly), **Vol. 3, Part 1,** 184; **Supp. 5,** 264

Appendectomy, procedures, **Supp. 1,** 236. *See also* Surgery

Appia, Dr. Louis, reference to, **Vol. 1, Part 2,** 30

Appleton & Co., founding of, **Vol. 2, Part 2,** 554

Appleton-Century-Crofts (publishing), **Supp. 6,** 580

Appleton's Annual Cyclopaedia, **Vol. 9, Part 2,** 375

Appliances. *See* Home appliances; *specific types*

Appointment in Samarra, **Supp. 8,** 480

Appomattox Court House, surrender at, **Vol. 4, Part 1,** 424, 497; **Vol. 5, Part 2,** 202; **Vol. 6, Part 1,** 104, 127, 392; **Vol. 7, Part 2,** 49

Apprentice system, **Vol. 4, Part 2,** 275; **Vol. 8, Part 2,** 238 f.

"April in Paris" (song), **Supp. 8,** 145

"April Showers" (song), **Supp. 5,** 630

Aptitude tests: correlation machine for, **Supp. 5,** 329; for learning, **Supp. 4,** 833; for music, **Supp. 4,** 731

Aquacade, **Supp. 8,** 547

Aquariums, New York, **Supp. 8,** 485–86

Aqueducts: Potomac River, **Vol. 9, Part 2,** 260; **Vol. 10, Part 1,** 57; Rochester, **Vol. 8, Part 2,** 13

Arab-Israeli conflict. *See* Palestine; Zionism

Arachnology. *See* Spiders

Arbeiter Zeitung, **Supp. 5,** 95

Arbor Day, origin of, **Vol. 4, Part 1,** 78; **Vol. 7, Part 1,** 258, 565 f.

Arboriculture, **Vol. 8, Part 2,** 354

Arbuckle, Roscoe ("Fatty"), reference to, **Supp. 8,** 314

Arcadia Conference (1941-42), **Supp. 6,** 339–40

Arcaro, Eddie, reference to, **Supp. 7,** 400

Arc de Triomphe (Paris), one-way traffic, **Supp. 3,** 254

Archaeological Institute of America, **Vol. 4, Part 2,** 460; **Vol. 7, Part 2,** 249; **Vol. 10, Part 2,** 113

Archaeologists. For complete list, *see* Occupations Index

Archaeology, **Vol. 1, Part 1,** 571, 588; **Vol. 1, Part 2,** 492, **Vol. 2, Part 1,** 361, 556, 583; **Vol. 3, Part 1,** 113, 240, 594 f.; **Vol. 3, Part 2,** 161; **Vol. 4, Part 1,** 42 f., 416, 421; **Vol. 4, Part 2,** 460, 519; **Vol. 5, Part 1,** 226; **Vol. 5, Part 2,** 313 f.; **Vol. 6, Part 2,** 292, 551, 564, 601; **Vol. 7, Part 1,** 56, 366, 519; **Vol. 7, Part 2,** 506; **Vol. 8, Part 1,** 388 f., 574; **Vol. 9, Part 1,** 4, 10 f., 482, 489, 594, 635; **Vol. 9, Part 2,** 306; **Vol. 10, Part 1,** 442 f.; **Vol. 10, Part 2,** 49, 132, 402; American Indian artifacts, **Supp. 6,** 289–90; Asia, **Supp. 6,** 18; ceramic chronology, **Supp. 2,** 44; Crete, **Supp. 3,** 343–44; Egypt, **Supp. 1,** 111; **Supp. 3,** 272, 375, 626–28; **Supp. 4,** 901–2; first system of scientific excavation, **Supp. 3,** 626; geological relationship, **Supp. 4,** 119; Greece, **Supp. 3,** 705; Latin America, **Supp. 1,** 648; **Supp. 5,** 711; medieval, **Supp. 1,** 601; Mesopotamia (Iraq), **Supp. 7,** 709; Mexico, **Supp. 4,** 605–6; Middle East, **Supp. 3,** 37; Palestine, **Supp. 3,** 272; pre-Columbian Mexico, **Supp. 3,** 786; prehistoric, **Supp. 4,** 520–21; research in, **Supp. 1,** 428; Sidon excavation, **Supp. 6,** 641; southern Russia, **Supp. 5,** 595; Southwestern U.S., **Supp. 7,** 432; stratigraphic method of excavation, **Supp. 7,** 570; United States, **Vol. 1, Part 1,** 588; **Vol. 2, Part 1,** 50, 97; **Vol. 3, Part 1,** 113, 553 f.; **Vol. 3, Part 2,** 353; **Vol. 6, Part 1,** 193 f.; **Vol. 7, Part 1,** 366; **Vol. 7, Part 2,** 392; **Vol. 8, Part 1,** 276 f.; **Vol. 9, Part 1,** 389; **Vol. 10, Part 2,** 376; writings on, **Vol. 2, Part 1,** 51, 183, 361; **Vol. 3, Part 1,** 113, 226, 240 f.; **Vol. 4, Part 1,** 42, 421; **Vol. 7, Part 1,** 519; **Vol. 8, Part 1,** 161 f., 229 f., 252 f., 389, 574;

Area Redevelopment Act (1961), **Supp. 7**, 424
Arevalo, Juan José, reference to, **Supp. 8**, 495
Argentina: astronomy in, **Supp. 5**, 541; diplomacy with U.S., **Vol. 3, Part 1**, 197; **Vol. 7, Part 2**, 283; **Vol. 8, Part 2**, 83; **Supp. 3**, 740; **Supp. 4**, 864; **Supp. 5**, 332; **Supp. 6**, 451–52; **Supp. 7**, 60; missions in, **Vol. 9, Part 2**, 76; protection of American interests in, **Vol. 7, Part 2**, 71 f.; sea fighting in service of, **Vol. 3, Part 1**, 202 f.; Treaty of Friendship, Commerce and Navigation, **Vol. 7, Part 2**, 422; writings on, **Vol. 9, Part 2**, 122
Argentine National Observatory, **Supp. 5**, 541
Arginase, **Supp. 5**, 149
Argon (rare gas), **Supp. 3**, 439
Argus, naval exploits of, **Vol. 1, Part 1**, 212
Argyrol, **Supp. 5**, 39
Arizona: agriculture, **Vol. 4, Part 2**, 483; **Vol. 6, Part 1**, 611; **Vol. 8, Part 1**, 121 f.; botany, **Vol. 6, Part 1**, 162; constitutional convention, **Supp. 1**, 445; cowpunching, **Vol. 4, Part 1**, 577; governors, **Supp. 1**, 144; historical writings on, **Supp. 1**, 524; history of, **Vol. 9, Part 1**, 213; Indians, **Vol. 8, Part 1**, 121 f.; irrigation, **Vol. 8, Part 1**, 121 f.; land claims, **Vol. 9, Part 2**, 87; legal service, **Vol. 9, Part 1**, 212; political service, **Vol. 4, Part 1**, 409; **Vol. 6, Part 1**, 611; **Vol. 8, Part 1**, 121; politics, **Supp. 7**, 21–22; railroad development, **Vol. 8, Part 1**, 357 f.; statehood, admission into, **Vol. 9, Part 1**, 213; **Vol. 9, Part 2**, 270; Taliesin West, **Supp. 6**, 714; territorial, **Vol. 8, Part 1**, 121 f.
Arkansas: carpetbagging in, **Vol. 8, Part 1**, 33 f.; Civil War period, **Vol. 3, Part 2**, 454; **Vol. 5, Part 1**, 60; "criminal intruders," **Vol. 7, Part 2**, 225; exploration, **Vol. 3, Part 1**, 507 f.; frontier justice, **Vol. 8, Part 2**, 161; governors, **Vol. 1, Part 2**, 226 f.; **Vol. 2, Part 2**, 105 f., 154, 187 f., 363; **Vol. 3, Part 1**, 122 f.; **Vol. 3, Part 2**, 403, 454; **Vol. 6, Part 2**, 166 f.; **Vol. 7, Part 1**, 352; **Vol. 8, Part 1**, 436; **Vol. 10, Part 2**, 607 f.; **Supp. 1**, 124; "Johnson Family," **Vol. 5, Part 2**, 118; land claims in, **Vol. 2, Part 2**, 363; **Vol. 8, Part 1**, 436; legal service, **Vol. 1, Part 2**, 56, 506; **Vol. 7, Part 2**, 225, 594; **Vol. 8, Part 1**, 436; **Vol. 8, Part 2**, 161; **Vol. 10, Part 1**, 538 f.; missions in, **Vol. 7, Part 1**, 625; pioneer days in, **Vol. 10, Part 2**, 500, 607; political service, **Vol. 1, Part 2**, 227, 465, 479, 506; **Vol. 2, Part 2**, 154; **Vol. 3, Part 1**, 122, 389; **Vol. 3, Part 2**, 403, 454; **Vol. 4, Part 1**, 150; **Vol. 5, Part 1**, 523; **Vol. 6, Part 2**, 167; **Vol. 7, Part 1**, 352; **Vol. 7, Part 2**, 12; **Vol. 8, Part 1**, 436, 641; **Vol. 10, Part 2**, 608; public service, **Vol. 2, Part 2**, 362, 570; railroad scandal in, **Vol. 3, Part 1**, 387; Reconstruction, **Vol. 1, Part 2**, 61; **Vol. 2, Part 1**, 408; **Vol. 2, Part 2**, 187; **Vol. 4, Part 1**, 150; **Vol. 8, Part 1**, 33 f., 436; roads, state system of, in, **Vol. 8, Part 1**, 641; school desegregation, **Supp. 8**, 57–58, 157; stories of, **Vol. 9, Part 2**, 509; Territory, organizing of, **Vol. 9, Part 2**, 335; writings on, **Supp. 4**, 286
Arkansas College, **Vol. 1, Part 2**, 63
Arkansas Folklore Society, founding of, **Supp. 4**, 286
Arkansas Institute for the Deaf, **Vol. 2, Part 2**, 151
Arkansas Light & Power Co., **Supp. 3**, 192–93
Arkansas Post, battle of, **Vol. 2, Part 2**, 105; **Vol. 6, Part 1**, 588; **Vol. 9, Part 1**, 95, 237, 556; **Vol. 10, Part 1**, 458
Arkansas Traveler, founding of, **Supp. 2**, 550
Arlington, Va., **Vol. 3, Part 1**, 9; **Vol. 4, Part 2**, 77; **Vol. 6, Part 1**, 127
Arlington Memorial Bridge (Washington, D.C.-Va.), **Supp. 3**, 534
Arliss, George, references to, **Vol. 3, Part 1**, 590; **Supp. 3**, 277

ARMCO. *See* American Rolling Mill Co.
Armed forces and defense: aircraft development, **Supp. 3**, 314; **Supp. 6**, 182–83, 618; Army Corps of Engineers, **Supp. 6**, 508–9; Army War College, founding of, **Supp. 1**, 89; aviation, **Supp. 2**, 460–61; **Supp. 3**, 314; black, first general, **Supp. 8**, 118–19; budget reduction, **Supp. 7**, 795; **Supp. 8**, 157; chaplains, **Supp. 8**, 505–6; civilian v. military authority, **Supp. 6**, 432; congressional interests, **Supp. 8**, 538; contracts investigations, **Supp. 6**, 618; **Supp. 7**, 764; conventional weapons v. nuclear, **Supp. 7**, 277; **Supp. 8**, 157–58; counterinsurgency, **Supp. 7**, 422; draft, **Supp. 1**, 211; **Supp. 5**, 482–531; gun carriage design, **Supp. 3**, 204; Joint Chiefs of Staff, **Supp. 5**, 706; **Supp. 6**, 374; **Supp. 8**, 156; "military-industrial complex" warning, **Supp. 8**, 159; preparedness and mobilization issues, **Supp. 2**, 18; **Supp. 6**, 335; prison reform, **Supp. 1**, 211; segregation and desegregation, **Supp. 3**, 661; **Supp. 5**, 741; **Supp. 8**, 118–19; tactical bombing, **Supp. 8**, 185; tanks and armored vehicles, **Supp. 3**, 165–66; training, **Supp. 1**, 211, 392; unification of branches, **Supp. 4**, 305–6; **Supp. 5**, 478; **Supp. 8**, 303; universal military training advocacy, **Supp. 5**, 531, 715; **Supp. 7**, 78; writings on strategy, **Supp. 5**, 196. *See also* Biological and chemical warfare; Nuclear weapons and energy; *specific branches of the armed forces; names of specific wars*
Armenia: language, **Vol. 3, Part 1**, 565 f.; literature, cataloguing, of, **Vol. 3, Part 1**, 565 f.; missions in, **Vol. 1, Part 2**, 187, 270; Turkish massacre in, **Supp. 4**, 604
Armor: bibliography of, **Vol. 3, Part 1**, 170; collections of, **Vol. 3, Part 1**, 170; **Vol. 8, Part 1**, 606; Indian wars, use of in, **Vol. 4, Part 2**, 560; plate, Harvey process, **Vol. 4, Part 2**, 374; ships, use of for, **Vol. 9, Part 1**, 608, 620
Armory Show (1913), **Supp. 2**, 239, 372, 483; **Supp. 4**, 463, 464, 774; **Supp. 5**, 20, 184, 376, 635; **Supp. 7**, 15, 486, 494, 686, 754; **Supp. 8**, 279, 714
Armour and Co., reorganization, **Supp. 5**, 551
Armour Institute, founding of, **Vol. 4, Part 2**, 53
Armour Institute of Technology. *See* Illinois Institute of Technology
Arms. *See* Firearms; *specific types*
Arms control and disarmament: civil disobedience to promote, **Supp. 8**, 458; federal agency for, **Supp. 8**, 680; Geneva Conference (1927), **Supp. 4**, 685; Geneva Conference (1932), **Supp. 3**, 219; **Supp. 7**, 186, 362; Geneva Protocol (1925), **Supp. 7**, 537; Kellogg-Briand Pact, **Supp. 2**, 52, 356; **Supp. 3**, 219; **Supp. 4**, 137; **Supp. 7**, 112, 113, 688; mutual security agreement advocacy, **Supp. 3**, 219; naval limitation, **Supp. 3**, 219, 397, 668; **Supp. 4**, 405–6, 786; **Supp. 6**, 518, 519; nuclear inspection advocacy, **Supp. 7**, 750–51; nuclear scientists' advocacy, **Supp. 8**, 483–84; nuclear test-ban treaty, **Supp. 7**, 424; nuclear weapons' control plan, **Supp. 7**, 37; Pugwash Conferences on Sciences and World Affairs, **Supp. 7**, 732; reduction moves (1950s), **Supp. 5**, 455; women's organizations advocating, **Supp. 7**, 186. *See also* Peace, international
Armstrong, John, reference to, **Vol. 5, Part 1**, 523
Armstrong, Louis, references to, **Supp. 5**, 105, 293, 529
Armstrong, Samuel C., reference to, **Vol. 7, Part 1**, 641
Armstrong Cork Co., **Supp. 6**, 519–20
Armstrong Transfer Co., **Vol. 1, Part 1**, 353
Army, Department of the, administration, **Supp. 8**, 57–58
Army, United States, armored force development, **Supp. 3**, 152; cavalry, **Supp. 3**, 152; chaplains,

Supp. 4, 463–64; Supp. 6, 720; Supp. 8, 63–64, 280–81; regionalism, Supp. 3, 340, 840–41; Supp. 4, 204–5; Supp. 5, 580; religious, Supp. 2, 649; representational, Supp. 6, 625; "Rural," Vol. 3, Part 1, 418; school, oldest in America, Vol. 3, Part 1, 590 f.; selling, Vol. 5, Part 2, 143, 352; Vol. 9, Part 1, 229; semiabstract, Supp. 7, 560, 561; "Signing the Constitution," Supp. 5, 112; social realism, Supp. 5, 580; Supp. 8, 586–87; stained glass, Supp. 3, 183–84; still-life, Supp. 1, 338; surrealism, Supp. 5, 184–85; Supp. 6, 512–13; Supp. 8, 467–68; teaching of, Vol. 3, Part 1, 558 f., 590 f.; Vol. 4, Part 2, 110; Vol. 5, Part 1, 225 f.; Vol. 5, Part 2, 287, 485; Vol. 7, Part 1, 488; Vol. 8, Part 1, 166; Vol. 9, Part 1, 532; Vol. 10, Part 1, 70; Supp. 1, 596, 641; Supp. 2, 288, 647; Supp. 3, 292; Supp. 4, 591; Supp. 5, 39, 50, 492–93; Supp. 7, 15, 39, 773; Supp. 8, 271; technical bases of, Vol. 4, Part 2, 166; Vol. 8, Part 1, 408; Vol. 9, Part 2, 29; "Ten, The," Supp. 1, 382; Supp. 2, 149, 649; Supp. 8, 553; urban realism, Supp. 1, 516; Supp. 4, 463–64; Supp. 5, 472–73; 492–93, 624–25, 635–36; Supp. 7, 170; "Veils" technique, Supp. 7, 480; Western themes, Supp. 3, 382–83; Supp. 5, 420; Whistlerian, Supp. 5, 470–71; writings on, Vol. 1, Part 1, 423; Vol. 2, Part 1, 37, 403; Vol. 2, Part 2, 371, 479; Vol. 3, Part 1, 169, 274; Vol. 3, Part 2, 563; Vol. 4, Part 1, 11, 65; Vol. 5, Part 2, 352, 485 f., 534, 539; Vol. 6, Part 1, 185; Vol. 6, Part 2, 292; Vol. 7, Part 1, 56; Vol. 7, Part 2, 285; Vol. 8, Part 1, 165 f., 408; Vol. 9, Part 1, 307, 532; Vol. 9, Part 2, 29; Supp. 1, 641; Supp. 4, 290; Supp. 5, 427; Supp. 6, 96. See also Armory Show (1913); Illustrations; Landscape painting; Mural painting; Museums; Oriental painting; Portrait painting; Sculpture; specific museum names

Art deco, Supp. 5, 134; Supp. 7, 308
Arthritis, cortisone treatment, Supp. 7, 340–41
Arthur, Chester A., references to, Vol. 2, Part 1, 26; Vol. 5, Part 1, 589; Vol. 7, Part 1, 169
Articles of Confederation, Vol. 3, Part 1, 465 f.; Vol. 4, Part 2, 330 f., 375; Vol. 5, Part 1, 220, 245; Vol. 5, Part 2, 398; Vol. 6, Part 1, 119 f.; Vol. 7, Part 1, 221, 257; Vol. 8, Part 1, 423; Vol. 8, Part 2, 49
Artificial insemination, Supp. 8, 502–3
Artificial organ transplants, Supp. 3, 140–41
Art Institute of Chicago, Vol. 4, Part 1, 26; Vol. 7, Part 1, 321 f.; architecture, Supp. 2, 117; development of, Supp. 2, 288; lecture course, Supp. 4, 313; sculpture instruction, Supp. 2, 647
Artists. For complete list, see Occupations Index
Artists' Union, founding of, Supp. 7, 171
Art News, Supp. 7, 260
Art of This Century gallery (New York City), Supp. 6, 512, 513
Art Students League (New York City), Vol. 1, Part 2, 121; Vol. 2, Part 2, 102; Vol. 4, Part 2, 366, 423; Vol. 8, Part 2, 54; Supp. 3, 113; Supp. 5, 492; Supp. 6, 257, 511–12
Art Through the Ages, Supp. 4, 313
Aruch, rabbinical dictionary, Vol. 5, Part 2, 490 f.
Arundel, Supp. 6, 545
Arvey, Jacob M., reference to, Supp. 7, 721
Asbury, Francis, references to, Vol. 2, Part 2, 280; Vol. 5, Part 1, 617; Vol. 6, Part 1, 560; Vol. 7, Part 2, 7; Vol. 9, Part 1, 382
ASCAP. See American Society of Composers, Authors, and Publishers
Ashburton Treaty, Vol. 3, Part 1, 79 f. See also Webster–Ashburton Treaty
Asia: Christianity studies, Supp. 8, 360; diplomacy with U.S., Vol. 8, Part 2, 4; Supp. 6, 269–70; diplomatic history studies, Supp. 4, 224, 225; English-

language journals in, Supp. 4, 679; forerunner of journal Asia, Vol. 9, Part 2, 121; historical studies, Supp. 4, 532–33; missions, Supp. 3, 323; religions of, Supp. 8, 431; scientific expeditions, Supp. 6, 18; secret American agency in, Vol. 8, Part 2, 4; studies programs in U.S. universities, Supp. 8, 360; trade with U.S., Vol. 8, Part 2, 4; Supp. 1, 257. See also individual country names
Asia Minor, exploration in, Vol. 9, Part 1, 594
Asphalt, early use of, Vol. 1, Part 1, 500; Vol. 10, Part 1, 471
Asphyxia, theories of, Supp. 3, 353
Assassination attempts on: Congress, Supp. 8, 300; Frick, H. C., Supp. 2, 37; Mitchel, J. P., Supp. 3, 605; Roosevelt, F. D., Supp. 1, 160; Supp. 3, 648; Supp. 6, 23
Assassination of: Evers, Medgar, Supp. 7, 227; Kennedy, J. F., Supp. 7, 227, 425, 593–94; Supp. 8, 323, 557–58, 607; Kennedy, R. F., Supp. 8, 324; King, M. L., Jr., Supp. 8, 324, 335; McKinley, W., Supp. 5, 285, 286; Malcolm X, Supp. 7, 509; Oswald, L. H., Supp. 8, 557–58; Rockwell, G. L., Supp. 8, 541; Tresca, C., Supp. 3, 778; underworld leaders, Supp. 8, 208
Assay Office, establishment of, Vol. 9, Part 2, 597
Assembly line, moving, Supp. 4, 296, 456; Supp. 8, 609
Associated Catholic Charities, founding of, Supp. 2, 478
Associated Dress Industries, Vol. 7, Part 1, 276 f.
Associated Dry Goods Corporation, Supp. 7, 440–41
Associated Gas and Electric Co. of New York, Supp. 4, 394–95
Associated Hospital Service Corporation, Supp. 3, 122, 313
Associated Negro Press, Supp. 5, 544
Associated Press (AP), Vol. 1, Part 2, 84; Vol. 3, Part 1, 294; Vol. 4, Part 2, 158; Vol. 5, Part 1, 347; Vol. 5, Part 2, 331; Vol. 6, Part 1, 61; Vol. 7, Part 1, 428; Vol. 7, Part 2, 545; Vol. 8, Part 2, 518; Vol. 9, Part 1, 176 f., 364 f.; Vol. 9, Part 2, 74, 82, 592; Supp. 5, 65, 286, 626; Supp. 6, 202; administration, Supp. 4, 630–31; first executive committee, Supp. 1, 441; growth of, Supp. 7, 145; libel suit, Supp. 3, 852
Associated Refugees, Vol. 3, Part 2, 265
Association for Defense of the Constitution, Supp. 6, 75
Association for Prevention of Heart Disease, Supp. 6, 117
Association for Research in Nervous and Mental Disease, founding of, Supp. 2, 665
Association for the Advancement of Psychoanalysis, founding of, Supp. 5, 316
Association for the Improvement of Colored People, Vol. 1, Part 2, 432
Association for the Protection of Industry and for the Promotion of National Education, Vol. 7, Part 2, 119
Association for the Study of Negro Life and History, Supp. 6, 313; founding of, Supp. 4, 911
Association of All Classes of All Nations, Vol. 8, Part 2, 158
Association of American Geographers, Supp. 1, 119
Association of American Geologists and Naturalists, Vol. 8, Part 2, 94
Association of American Law Schools, founding of, Supp. 1, 358
Association of American Painters and Sculptors, founding of, Supp. 4, 463
Association of American Physicians, Vol. 3, Part 1, 208; Vol. 8, Part 1, 79

Vol. 8, Part 1, 30 f., 630 f.; **Vol. 8, Part 2,** 341, 412; **Vol. 10, Part 1,** 470 f.; time observations by, **Vol. 5, Part 2,** 594; variable stars, **Vol. 2, Part 1,** 616; Venus, **Vol. 3, Part 1,** 602 f.; **Vol. 6, Part 1,** 516; **Vol. 7, Part 1,** 454; **Vol. 8, Part 1,** 630; **Vol. 9, Part 2,** 18. *See also* Astrophysics

Astrophysical Journal, **Supp. 7,** 726; founding of, **Supp. 2,** 271

Astrophysics: foundations for, **Supp. 2,** 92; research in, **Supp. 2,** 271; spectroscopic, **Supp. 3,** 291; **Supp. 7,** 726–27; universe origin theories, **Supp. 8,** 199. *See also* Astronomy

Aswan Dam, **Supp. 8,** 276

Atalanta and *Wasp,* naval engagement, **Vol. 1, Part 2,** 348

AT&T. *See* American Telephone & Telegraph Co.

Ataturk, Mustapha Kemal, reference to, **Supp. 5,** 562–63

Atchison Daily Globe, founding of, **Supp. 2,** 325

Atchison, Topeka & Santa Fe Railroad, **Vol. 5, Part 1,** 151; **Vol. 7, Part 2,** 375

"At Dawning" (song), **Supp. 4,** 138, 139

Atherton, Gertrude, reference to, **Supp. 6,** 309

Athletes. For complete list, *see* Occupations Index

Athletics: coaching, **Vol. 2, Part 1,** 444; **Vol. 4, Part 2,** 398; **Vol. 7, Part 1,** 355 f.; **Vol. 8, Part 2,** 68; colleges, athletic policy, **Vol. 3, Part 2,** 74; **Vol. 8, Part 2,** 67; Olympic Games, **Vol. 7, Part 1,** 356; writings on, **Vol. 2, Part 1,** 587; **Vol. 3, Part 2,** 545, 572; **Vol. 4, Part 2,** 570; **Vol. 7, Part 2,** 573; **Vol. 8, Part 1,** 58 f., 107 f.; **Vol. 10, Part 2,** 218. *See also* specific sports

Atkins' Garden (Cuba), **Supp. 4,** 16, 52

Atkinson, George F., reference to, **Supp. 6,** 175, 176

Atkinson, Henry, reference to, **Vol. 5, Part 2,** 273

Atlanta, naval prize, Civil War, **Vol. 3, Part 1,** 529 f.

Atlanta, Ga.: battles about, **Vol. 1, Part 1,** 267; **Vol. 4, Part 2,** 240; **Vol. 5, Part 1,** 193–94, 197; **Vol. 5, Part 2,** 145–46; **Vol. 6, Part 1,** 364; **Vol. 8, Part 2,** 160; **Vol. 8, Part 2,** 453; **Vol. 9, Part 1,** 95, 217; **Vol. 9, Part 2,** 434; first black education board member, **Supp. 8,** 95; library service, **Vol. 5, Part 1,** 335; public service, **Vol. 5, Part 1,** 302; **Vol. 7, Part 2,** 511; **Vol. 9, Part 1,** 282

Atlanta Constitution, **Vol. 5, Part 1,** 302, 485; **Vol. 9, Part 1,** 249; editorial policy, **Supp. 8,** 404–5

Atlanta Journal, **Vol. 9, Part 1,** 281; **Supp. 1,** 184

Atlanta University: founding of, **Vol. 2, Part 2,** 516; **Vol. 10, Part 1,** 446 f.; presidency, **Supp. 2,** 315; **Supp. 8,** 94–95; sociological studies of blacks, **Supp. 7,** 202, 203, 204; **Supp. 8,** 522

Atlantic & St. Lawrence Railroad Co., **Vol. 8, Part 1,** 71 f., 184 f.

Atlantic Charter (1941), **Supp. 3,** 660; **Supp. 7,** 778

Atlantic Coast Line Railroad Co., **Vol. 10, Part 1,** 399 f.

Atlantic, Gulf & West Indies Steamship Lines, **Supp. 3,** 501

Atlantic Improvement Co., founding of, **Vol. 10, Part 1,** 399 f.

Atlantic Monthly, **Vol. 1, Part 1,** 159, 335; **Vol. 3, Part 2,** 379; **Vol. 5, Part 1,** 173 f., 307, 580; **Vol. 6, Part 1,** 15, 461; **Vol. 7, Part 1,** 570; **Vol. 7, Part 2,** 143; **Vol. 8, Part 2,** 522; **Vol. 9, Part 2,** 529; **Supp. 3,** 719; **Supp. 6,** 252, 306, 571–72; **Supp. 8,** 476; editing of, **Supp. 5,** 16, 542; **Supp. 8,** 447–48; founding of, **Vol. 10, Part 1,** 112; Little, Brown association, **Supp. 4,** 526–27

Atlantic Ocean: early map of, **Vol. 3, Part 1,** 183; deepest recorded spot, **Supp. 2,** 239; first steam vessel to cross, **Vol. 3, Part 1,** 339; **Vol. 8, Part 1,** 214 f.; **Vol. 8, Part 2,** 106

Atlantic Refining Co., management, **Supp. 2,** 679

Atlantic Union, **Supp. 8,** 90

Atomic bomb: development of, **Supp. 3,** 664; **Supp. 4,** 453–54; **Supp. 5,** 204, 220–21, 663; **Supp. 6,** 166, 371, 501, 656; **Supp. 7,** 10–11, 76, 91, 135, 732; **Supp. 8,** 229–31, 411, 483–84; first explosion, **Supp. 8,** 230; scientists' concerns on use of, **Supp. 7,** 732, 733; test of first, **Supp. 7,** 10–11; testing, **Supp. 7,** 136, 300. *See also* Arms control and disarmament; Nuclear weapons and energy

Atomic Energy Act (1946), passage of, **Supp. 5,** 455

Atomic Energy Commission: civilian v. military control of, **Supp. 5,** 455; **Supp. 8,** 230, 484; first commissioners, **Supp. 6,** 676–77; first engineer appointed to, **Supp. 7,** 565; first weapons' test series, **Supp. 7,** 300; hydrogen bomb development, **Supp. 6,** 156; Lilienthal appointment, **Supp. 6,** 419; mathematicians, **Supp. 6,** 656; nuclear power advocates, **Supp. 6,** 650

Atoms: electron chemical bond theory, **Supp. 4,** 488; far-ultraviolet spectra of, **Supp. 5,** 496; motion of suspended objects research, **Supp. 5,** 202; "octet" structure theory, **Supp. 6,** 365; particle accelerator, **Supp. 8,** 665–66; research technique, **Supp. 8,** 627–28; statistical model, **Supp. 5,** 219; weights, **Supp. 1,** 178

"Atticus," letter of, **Vol. 7, Part 1,** 134

Attitude testing. *See* Public opinion

Attorney generals. For complete list, *see* Occupations Index

Attorneys. For complete list, *see* Occupations Index

Attucks, Crispus, erection of monument to memory of, **Vol. 7, Part 1,** 413

Atwater, W. O., reference to, **Supp. 5,** 622

Atwater Kent Manufacturing Works, founding of, **Supp. 4,** 452

Atzerodt, George A., reference to, **Vol. 1, Part 2,** 449

Auburn, N.Y., **Vol. 7, Part 2,** 330

Auburn Declaration, **Vol. 6, Part 1,** 554

Auburn Theological Seminary, founding of, **Vol. 6, Part 1,** 406; **Vol. 9, Part 2,** 299

Auction bridge, history of, **Vol. 10, Part 2,** 130, 533

Audiology, **Supp. 7,** 395–96. *See also* Deaf and deafness

Audion tube, **Supp. 5,** 21

Audio systems: high-fidelity reproduction, **Supp. 5,** 324; microphone invention, **Supp. 1,** 75; speaker development, **Supp. 7,** 395

Audubon, John James, references to, **Vol. 1, Part 1,** 467, 513; **Vol. 2, Part 1,** 24; **Vol. 5, Part 2,** 300, 517; **Vol. 6, Part 1,** 49; **Vol. 10, Part 1,** 580 f.

Audubon movement, **Supp. 3,** 592–93

Audubon Society, **Vol. 5, Part 2,** 62; founding of, **Supp. 2,** 265

Auer, Leopold, reference to, **Supp. 8,** 164

Augsburg Seminary (Minneapolis), controversy at, **Vol. 7, Part 1,** 635

Augusta, Ga., attack on, **Vol. 6, Part 1,** 107; **Vol. 10, Part 1,** 83

Augusta College (Ky.), **Vol. 3, Part 1,** 544 f.

Auk (publication), **Supp. 3,** 9

Aural surgery. *See* Surgery

Aureomycin, **Supp. 6,** 176

Auriol, Vincent, reference to, **Supp. 5,** 589

Aurora, Jeffersonian organ, **Vol. 1, Part 1,** 462; **Vol. 3, Part 1,** 467 f.

Aurora borealis. *See* Astronomy

Austin College (Tex.), **Vol. 1, Part 1,** 501, 517

Austin Riggs Center (Stockbridge), **Supp. 6,** 527

Australia, water reclamation, **Supp. 2,** 444

Australian ballot system, **Vol. 4, Part 1,** 215

Aydelotte, Frank, reference to, **Supp. 3**, 321–22

Ayllón, Lucus Vásquez de, reference to, **Vol. 3, Part 1**, 257

Azana, Manuel, reference to, **Supp. 6**, 72–73

B

Baade, Fritz, reference to, **Supp. 6**, 708–9

Babbitt, Frank L., Jr., reference to, **Supp. 6**, 665

Babbitt, Irving, references to, **Supp. 7**, 218, 624

Babcock, H. W., reference to, **Supp. 7**, 170

Babcock, John, reference to, **Vol. 9, Part 2**, 521

Babies. *See* Children; Pediatrics

Babies Hospital (New York City), **Supp. 7**, 427

Babson College, predecessor, **Supp. 8**, 19

Babson Statistical Organization, Inc., founding of, **Supp. 8**, 18–19

"Baby, It's Cold Outside" (song), **Supp. 5**, 529

Babylonia, archaeological research, **Vol. 7, Part 2**, 506; **Vol. 10, Part 1**, 442 f.; tablets, **Supp. 1**, 261; Yale Collection, **Vol. 2, Part 2**, 168

"Baby Snooks" (fictional character), **Supp. 5**, 88

Bacall, Lauren, reference to, **Supp. 6**, 66

Bach, Johann Sebastian, harpsichord works, **Supp. 6**, 357–58

Bache, J. S., & Co., **Supp. 3**, 24

Bachrach, David, Jr., references to, **Supp. 7**, 25, 26

Back of the Yards Council, founding of, **Supp. 8**, 589

Back Stage Club, **Supp. 8**, 546

Bacon, Augustus O., reference to, **Supp. 3**, 330

Bacon, Francis, Foundation, **Supp. 5**, 20

Bacon, Nathaniel, reference to, **Vol. 1, Part 2**, 218; **Vol. 6, Part 1**, 496; writings on, **Supp. 8**, 692, 693

Bacon, Roger, manuscript, decipherment of, **Vol. 7, Part 1**, 448

Bacone College, foundation of, **Vol. 7, Part 1**, 371

Baconian theory, Shakespeare, **Vol. 1, Part 1**, 475; **Vol. 5, Part 1**, 169, 244; **Vol. 7, Part 1**, 620

Bacon's Rebellion, **Vol. 1, Part 1**, 482; **Vol. 1, Part 2**, 218; **Vol. 6, Part 2**, 361

Bacq, Z. M., reference to, **Supp. 3**, 136

Bacteria: as animal disease carriers, **Supp. 5**, 383; conjunctivitis-causing, **Supp. 4**, 865; food preservation and spoilage, **Supp. 7**, 629–31; tuberculosis-causing, **Supp. 4**, 435, 684; typhus-causing, **Supp. 4**, 468

Bacteriology, **Vol. 3, Part 1**, 478 f.; **Vol. 3, Part 2**, 177 f.; **Vol. 6, Part 1**, 66; **Vol. 7, Part 1**, 140, 542; **Vol. 8, Part 1**, 252 f., 391, 460 f.; **Vol. 8, Part 2**, 445, 483; **Vol. 9, Part 1**, 263, 591 f.; **Vol. 10, Part 1**, 621 f.; communicable diseases, **Supp. 6**, 481; development as discipline, **Supp. 2**, 513; disease relationship, **Supp. 4**, 287, 494; microscope use for, **Supp. 4**, 790; ophthalmic, **Supp. 3**, 302; plant pathology, **Supp. 3**, 400–1; preventive medicine, **Supp. 5**, 632; public health, **Supp. 6**, 701; research in, **Supp. 3**, 832; **Supp. 5**, 25–26; sanitary science, **Supp. 3**, 158; soil, **Supp. 1**, 461; surgery laboratory, **Supp. 6**, 664; teaching of, **Supp. 1**, 665; **Supp. 2**, 225, 353, 744; variation and order in, **Supp. 3**, 354; veterinary, **Supp. 5**, 382–83. *See also* Bacteria; Microbiology

Bad Axe, battle of. *See* Black Hawk War

Badlands National Monument, establishment of, **Supp. 2**, 492

Bad Seed, The, **Supp. 5**, 99, 100

Baehr, George, reference to, **Supp. 4**, 468

Baekeland, Leo, reference to, **Supp. 3**, 247

Baffin Land, Eskimo studies, **Supp. 3**, 82

Bahamas: governorship of, **Vol. 4, Part 1**, 296; **Vol. 4, Part 2**, 382; zoölogical expedition, **Vol. 7, Part 1**, 598

Bailey, Mildred, reference to, **Supp. 8**, 697

Bailey, Pearce, reference to, **Supp. 4**, 249

Bailey, Pearl, reference to, **Supp. 5**, 529

Bailey, Thomas, reference to, **Supp. 6**, 710

Bailey, Vernon, reference to, **Supp. 4**, 41

Bain, Alexander, reference to, **Supp. 3**, 149

"Baines, Scattergood" (fictional character), **Supp. 7**, 417

Baird, Bil, reference to, **Supp. 3**, 685

Baked goods: manufacturing and marketing, **Supp. 8**, 560–61; nutrient enriched, **Supp. 7**, 223

Bakelite (plastic), **Supp. 3**, 26–27

Baker, George Barr, reference to, **Supp. 6**, 514

Baker, George Pierce, references to, **Supp. 3**, 426, 448, 454, 471; **Supp. 4**, 54; **Supp. 6**, 286, 622; **Supp. 7**, 803; **Supp. 8**, 53

Baker, Helen Cody, reference to, **Supp. 6**, 1

Baker, Howard, Jr., reference to, **Supp. 8**, 92

Baker, James P., reference to, **Supp. 3**, 805

Baker, Newton D., references to, **Vol. 9, Part 1**, 601; **Supp. 3**, 168; **Supp. 5**, 468; **Supp. 7**, 370

Baker, Ray Stannard, reference to, **Supp. 3**, 762, 816; **Supp. 4**, 518, 662

Baker's Creek, battle of, **Vol. 4, Part 1**, 495; **Vol. 5, Part 1**, 271; **Vol. 6, Part 1**, 130, 420; **Vol. 8, Part 2**, 631; **Vol. 9, Part 1**, 631

Baker Street Irregulars, **Supp. 6**, 465

Baker University, **Vol. 1, Part 1**, 536; **Vol. 8, Part 1**, 298

Baking Powder, manufacture of, **Vol. 10, Part 2**, 655

Balanchine, George, reference to, **Supp. 8**, 670

Balch, Emily Greene, reference to, **Supp. 5**, 508

Balchen, Bernt, reference to, **Supp. 5**, 3

Baldwin, E. J. ("Lucky"), reference to, **Supp. 3**, 155

Baldwin, Edward R., reference to, **Supp. 3**, 431

Baldwin, James, reference to, **Supp. 7**, 719

Baldwin, Roger, references to, **Supp. 3**, 532; **Supp. 6**, 664

Baldwin, Ruth Standish, reference to, **Supp. 6**, 284

"Baldwin's Rules," **Vol. 1, Part 1**, 536

Baldwin University, founding of, **Vol. 1, Part 1**, 535 f.

Baldwin-Wallace College, **Vol. 7, Part 1**, 393

Balfour Declaration (1917), **Supp. 3**, 97; **Supp. 4**, 660

Ball, Thomas, references to, **Vol. 7, Part 1**, 18; **Supp. 3**, 266

Ballads, **Vol. 2, Part 1**, 492; **Vol. 4, Part 2**, 48, 390, 432, 464; **Vol. 6, Part 1**, 159; **Vol. 7, Part 1**, 23; **Vol. 8, Part 2**, 608; **Vol. 9, Part 1**, 245 f.; study of, **Supp. 3**, 423

Ball Brothers Co., **Supp. 3**, 29

Ball Grain Explosives Co., **Supp. 3**, 239

Ballet, **Vol. 4, Part 1**, 59 f.; **Supp. 5**, 74–76; **Supp. 7**, 173–74, 548, 560; **Supp. 8**, 669–70; American jazz, **Supp. 5**, 103–4; choreography, **Supp. 3**, 281–82; music, **Supp. 8**, 145, 146

Ballet International, **Supp. 7**, 173

Ballet Intime, **Supp. 5**, 75

Ballet Russe (Diaghilev company), **Supp. 5**, 75; **Supp. 7**, 173, 548, 560;

Ballet Russe de Monte Carlo (de Basil company), **Supp. 7**, 173

Ballinger, Richard A., references to, **Supp. 1**, 300; **Supp. 3**, 96, 321, 605, 724–25; **Supp. 4**, 664–66; **Supp. 5**, 666, 699; **Supp. 6**, 556; **Supp. 7**, 606

Ballinger-Pinchot controversy, **Vol. 1, Part 1**, 555; **Vol. 9, Part 2**, 269

Ballistics, **Vol. 10, Part 1**, 584 f. *See also* Firearms

Balloons: flights, **Supp. 5**, 547; motors for, **Supp. 1**, 214; naval experimentation, **Supp. 1**, 561; scientific research with, **Supp. 7**, 619. *See also* Aviation

Ballroom dancing, **Supp. 7**, 563; **Supp. 8**, 77–78; **Supp. 8**, 690

Bearden, J. A., reference to, **Supp. 7,** 134
Beards, **Supp. 6,** 636
Bear Flag Revolt, **Vol. 4, Part 1,** 21; **Vol. 9, Part 2,** 49
Bearings, roller, **Vol. 5, Part 1,** 448; **Vol. 9, Part 2,** 555; tilting-pad thrust, **Supp. 3,** 419
Bear Mountain Bridge, construction of, **Vol. 8, Part 2,** 90
Beat generation, **Supp. 7,** 239; **Supp. 8,** 56, 326–27
Beaufort, S.C., attack on, **Vol. 2, Part 1,** 310; **Vol. 7, Part 1,** 293
Beaumarchais, Caron de, munitions for Revolutionary War supplied by, **Vol. 3, Part 1,** 174
Beaumont Enterprise, **Supp. 7,** 349, 350
Beauregard, General Pierre, reference to, **Vol. 6, Part 1,** 127 f.
Beauty products. *See* Cosmetics
Beaux-arts Apartments (New York City), architecture, **Supp. 1,** 430
Beaux-Arts architecture, **Supp. 1,** 341; **Supp. 4,** 281–82; **Supp. 5,** 133–34
Beaver: study of the, **Vol. 7, Part 1,** 185; trade, **Vol. 8, Part 1,** 320 f.
Beaver Club, founding of, **Supp. 1,** 394
Beaver Dam Creek, Va., **Vol. 5, Part 1,** 558; **Vol. 6, Part 1,** 123. *See also* Peninsular campaign
Bebop (jazz style), **Supp. 5,** 534
Bechet, Sidney, reference to, **Supp. 3,** 188
Bechtel Corporation, founding of, **Supp. 8,** 308–9
Beck, Dave, reference to, **Supp. 7,** 119
Beck, Marshall, reference to, **Supp. 6,** 67
Becker, Carl L., reference to, **Supp. 4,** 63
Becker, Charles, reference to, **Supp. 4,** 885–86
Becker, G. F., reference to, **Vol. 5, Part 1,** 457
Becker, Marion Rombauer, references to, **Supp. 7,** 656, 657
Beckham, John C., reference to, **Supp. 6,** 591
Becky Sharp (movie), **Supp. 7,** 407
Becton, Dickinson and Co., **Supp. 7,** 678
Bedford, N.Y., public service, **Vol. 7, Part 2,** 410
Bedloe's Island, purchase of, **Vol. 1, Part 1,** 597
Bed springs, manufacture of, **Vol. 6, Part 1,** 334
Beebe, William, reference to, **Supp. 3,** 835
Beech, importation of purple tree, **Vol. 5, Part 2,** 341
Beecham, Sir Thomas, reference to, **Supp. 6,** 324
Beecher, Catharine, reference to, **Vol. 7, Part 1,** 252
Beecher, Charles Emerson, reference to, **Supp. 3,** 695
Beecher, Henry Ward, references to, **Vol. 1, Part 1,** 336, 641; **Vol. 1, Part 2,** 505; **Vol. 7, Part 1,** 36; **Vol. 8, Part 1,** 60 f.; **Vol. 8, Part 2,** 290, 398; **Vol. 9, Part 1,** 52, 588; **Vol. 9, Part 2,** 551 f., 622
Beecher, Lyman: reference to, **Vol. 1, Part 2,** 129; writings on, **Supp. 3,** 672
Beecher Bible and Rifle Colony (Kans.), **Vol. 8, Part 2,** 150
Beef, shipping methods revolutionized, **Vol. 1, Part 1,** 111; **Vol. 3, Part 1,** 603
Beef Steak Club, **Vol. 5, Part 2,** 456
Beef Trust case, **Vol. 7, Part 1,** 108
Beer: legalization, **Supp. 3,** 649; pasteurization of, **Supp. 1,** 142
Beers, Clifford, reference to, **Supp. 4,** 571
Bees, **Vol. 3, Part 1,** 17, 343; **Vol. 5, Part 2,** 598; **Vol. 8, Part 2,** 144; **Supp. 4,** 167
Beeson, Mabel Banta, reference to, **Supp. 4,** 67–68
Beethoven, Ludwig van: biographer of, **Vol. 9, Part 2,** 401; piano interpretation of, **Supp. 5,** 607
Beethoven Association, founding of, **Supp. 5,** 45–46
Beethoven Society, **Vol. 5, Part 2,** 486
Beet sugar industry, **Vol. 2, Part 2,** 66; **Vol. 5, Part 2,** 277; **Supp. 1,** 431
Beginnings of Christianity, The, **Supp. 4,** 468

Behavior and behaviorism: animal studies, **Supp. 2,** 699; conditioned reflex, application to education, **Supp. 3,** 119; conditioned-reflex studies, **Supp. 5,** 329–30; criminology theory, **Supp. 4,** 809; goal-directed, **Supp. 6,** 640; habit inventory for kindergartens, **Supp. 4,** 374; lower organisms, **Supp. 4,** 425; modification studies, **Supp. 6,** 17, 262, 528; neurological research, **Supp. 2,** 664; physiology of, **Supp. 3,** 172; **Supp. 6,** 367–68; political science studies, **Supp. 5,** 485–86; **Supp. 7,** 430, 431; stimulus and response studies, **Supp. 4,** 832–33; **Supp. 6,** 262, 672; synthesis with Freudian theory, **Supp. 4,** 387; writings on, **Supp. 8,** 489
Behemoth, **Supp. 5,** 514
Behn Brothers, **Supp.** 6, 49
Behrens, Peter, references to, **Supp. 8,** 226, 435
Behrman, S. N., reference to, **Supp. 8,** 529
Beiderbecke, Leon ("Bix"), reference to, **Supp. 8,** 20
Beirne, Michael J., reference to, **Supp. 3,** 181
Bekker, Paul, reference to, **Supp. 6,** 351
Belasco, David, references to, **Vol. 6, Part 1,** 379; **Supp. 3,** 39, 40, 297; **Supp. 5,** 726–27; **Supp. 6,** 305, 306, 369
Bel Geddes, Norman, & Co., **Supp. 6,** 233
Belgium: Confederate relations with, **Vol. 6, Part 2,** 240; diplomacy with, **Vol. 1, Part 2,** 464; **Vol. 6, Part 1,** 145; **Vol. 8, Part 2,** 349; **Vol. 9, Part 2,** 93, 377, 635; **Supp. 7,** 438
Belknap, Jeremy, reference to, **Vol. 9, Part 2,** 391
Bell, Alexander Graham, references to, **Vol. 5, Part 1,** 325; **Vol. 8, Part 2,** 534; **Vol. 10, Part 1,** 548 f.; **Supp. 8,** 228, 316
Bell, Don J., reference to, **Supp. 5,** 321
Bell, John, reference to, **Vol. 9, Part 2,** 363
Bell, Theodore, reference to, **Supp. 3,** 394
Bell Aircraft Corporation, **Supp. 6,** 50
Bellanca, August, reference to, **Supp. 4,** 69; **Supp. 6,** 51
Bell and Howell Co., founding of, **Supp. 5,** 321–22
Bellefonte, Pa., founding of, **Vol. 1, Part 2,** 190
Belleville, N.Y., sociological study of, **Supp. 4,** 312
Bellevue Hospital (New York City): **Vol. 5, Part 1,** 240; **Vol. 10, Part 1,** 150; **Vol. 10, Part 2,** 463; anesthesia program, **Supp. 6,** 553, 554; first nurses' training school in America, **Vol. 8, Part 2,** 474; Medical College, **Vol. 8, Part 2,** 403 f.; psychiatric facilities, **Supp. 3,** 320; tuberculosis clinic, **Supp. 4,** 578; X-ray department, **Supp. 3,** 360
Bellinger, Clarence, reference to, **Supp. 4,** 808
Bell-making, **Vol. 6, Part 2,** 533
Bellows, George: reference to, **Supp. 5,** 636; sculpture, **Supp. 3,** 124
Bellows, Henry W., reference to, **Vol. 1, Part 2,** 20
Bell System. *See* American Telephone & Telegraph Co.
Bell Telephone Co., **Vol. 1, Part 2,** 151; **Vol. 9, Part 1,** 253; patent litigations, **Vol. 9, Part 2,** 99
Bell Telephone Laboratories, **Supp. 6,** 84, 152; founding of, **Supp. 4,** 430. *See also* American Telephone & Telegraph Co.
Belluschi, Pietro, reference to, **Supp. 7,** 800
Belmont, Mo., engagement at, **Vol. 4, Part 1,** 493; **Vol. 6, Part 1,** 587; **Vol. 7, Part 2,** 604; **Vol. 8, Part 1,** 40; **Vol. 9, Part 2,** 3
Belmont, Mrs. O. H. P., references to, **Supp. 7,** 717, 718
Beloit College, founding of, **Vol. 2, Part 2,** 12
Beltrami, Eugenio, reference to, **Supp. 7,** 216
Bemis Heights, N.Y., battle of, **Vol. 1, Part 1,** 365; **Vol. 4, Part 1,** 185; **Vol. 7, Part 1,** 166
Ben Ami, Jacob, reference to, **Supp. 6,** 566

Biographers. For complete list, *see* Occupations Index

Biograph Studios, **Supp. 4,** 349–50; **Supp. 6,** 573; **Supp. 8,** 214

Biography, **Supp. 2,** 475, 509, 266; **Supp. 8,** 181; City Beautiful movement, **Supp. 3,** 534; historical, **Supp. 4,** 489–90, 556, 848; **Supp. 5,** 364; juvenile, **Supp. 3,** 630; literary, **Supp. 4,** 13, 14; of women, **Supp. 7,** 13; popular, **Supp. 4,** 368; psychobiography, **Supp. 1,** 106; **Supp. 7,** 80; **Supp. 8,** 61; theatrical, **Supp. 8,** 54

Biological Abstracts, **Supp. 4,** 516

Biological and chemical warfare: development of, **Supp. 6,** 448; gas mask design, **Supp. 3,** 353; napalm, **Supp. 7,** 617; poison gas studies, **Supp. 5,** 710; World War I studies, **Supp. 4,** 838; World War II studies, **Supp. 4,** 6

Biological Experiment Station (Woods Hole, Mass.). *See* Marine Biological Laboratory

Biology: animal form, **Supp. 6,** 281; cell lineage, **Supp. 2,** 723; engineering, **Supp. 8,** 502–3; experimental, **Supp. 3,** 540; **Supp. 4,** 425–27; first use of laboratory methods in high-school teaching of, **Vol. 7, Part 2,** 384; historical writings on, **Supp. 4,** 910; marine, **Vol. 6, Part 2,** 468; **Vol. 8, Part 1,** 387; molecular, **Supp. 8,** 450; philosophy of, **Supp. 4,** 427; protozoa immortality study, **Supp. 4,** 910; psychological problems arising from, **Supp. 3,** 172; reproductive cycle, **Supp. 2,** 632; research, **Supp. 4,** 515–16; statistical methodology, **Supp. 2,** 521; **Supp. 3,** 214–15; **Supp. 3,** 477; teaching of, **Supp. 4,** 253; tissue culture experiments, **Supp. 6,** 282. *See also* Biochemistry; Botany; Natural history; Zoology. For complete list of biologists, *see* Occupations Index

Biometry, **Vol. 4, Part 2,** 312. *See also* Biostatistics

Biophysics, development of, **Supp. 6,** 69–70; photoreception studies, **Supp. 4,** 367

Biostatistics, **Supp. 2,** 251; **Supp. 3,** 214–15, 477

Bird, William, reference to, **Supp. 7,** 335

"Bird in a Gilded Cage, A" (song), **Supp. 4,** 835

Bird-Lore, **Supp. 7,** 8

Birds: Alaskan studies, **Supp. 1,** 572; Antarctica, **Supp. 7,** 217; Audubon movement, **Supp. 3,** 592–93; children's books on, **Vol. 6, Part 2,** 625; collections, **Vol. 1, Part 1,** 513; **Vol. 3, Part 2,** 91; **Vol. 4, Part 2,** 564; **Vol. 9, Part 1,** 385; colored engravings, **Vol. 6, Part 1,** 56; clubs, **Vol. 3, Part 2,** 511; counts, **Supp. 5,** 374; distribution survey, **Supp. 3,** 517; **Supp. 8,** 655; drawings of, **Vol. 1, Part 1,** 427; eyes, studies of, **Supp. 3,** 835; field identification, **Supp. 6,** 255–56; identification and classification of, **Vol. 8, Part 1,** 598; **Supp. 7,** 578; illustrations of, **Supp. 4,** 736; 737; Maine, writings on, **Supp. 4,** 248–49; museum displays, **Supp. 3,** 161; song recordings, **Supp. 7,** 8; studies of, **Vol. 6, Part 1,** 49; **Vol. 7, Part 1,** 406; **Vol. 9, Part 2,** 617–18; Texas and Louisiana, **Supp. 7,** 578–79; western, writings on, **Supp. 4,** 41; writings on, **Vol. 1, Part 1,** 426; **Vol. 3, Part 2,** 511; **Vol. 4, Part 1,** 367; **Vol. 8, Part 2,** 324; **Vol. 9, Part 1,** 32; **Vol. 9, Part 2,** 595; **Supp. 3,** 162. *See also* Ornithology

Birds of the Belgian Congo, **Supp. 7,** 117

Birmingham, Ala.: civil rights demonstrations, **Supp. 8,** 334; development of, **Vol. 3, Part 1,** 179; **Vol. 5, Part 1,** 57; **Vol. 8, Part 1,** 170; **Vol. 9, Part 1,** 125, 219

Birney, J. G., reference to, **Vol. 2, Part 2,** 28

Birth control. *See* Family planning

Birth control pills. *See* Oral contraceptives

Birth Control Review, founding of, **Supp. 8,** 568

Birth defects: nutrition linked, **Supp. 7,** 569; pathology of, **Supp. 4,** 801, 802; Rh-negative blood type,

Supp. 3, 441

Birth of a Nation, The, **Supp. 3,** 73, 535, 708; **Supp. 4,** 235, 350, 351; **Supp. 6,** 657; production of, **Supp. 2,** 693

Birthrate, **Supp. 4,** 45

Births, first English, in America, **Vol. 3, Part 1,** 73 f.; first registration of, **Vol. 9, Part 1,** 33

BIS. *See* Bank for International Settlements

Bishop, Bernice P., Museum, **Supp. 1,** 82

Bishop, Isabel, reference to, **Supp. 5,** 493

Bishop, James W., reference to, **Supp. 4,** 292

Bishop, William Sutton, reference to, **Supp. 3,** 170

Bixby, Mrs., Lincoln's letter to, **Vol. 6, Part 1,** 256

Black, Harry S., reference to, **Supp. 6,** 593

Black, Hugo L., references to, **Supp. 3,** 80; **Supp. 5,** 294, 358, 574, 575, 576, 713; **Supp. 7,** 541

Black, Newton Henry, reference to, **Supp. 5,** 154

Blackberries, raising of, **Vol. 6, Part 1,** 363

"Black-birding," in South Seas, **Vol. 4, Part 2,** 451

Blackboards in school, first use of, **Vol. 4, Part 2,** 142

Black Boy, **Supp. 6,** 716

Black Cat Minstrels, **Supp. 6,** 89

"Black Cockade" forces in Pennsylvania, **Vol. 6, Part 1,** 154

Black Code. *See* Blacks

Black Crook, production of, **Vol. 7, Part 1,** 482

Blackfan, Kenneth D., references to, **Supp. 3,** 244; **Supp. 4,** 213

Blackfoot Indians, **Supp. 2,** 265; **Supp. 4,** 907

"Black Friday" (1869), **Vol. 1, Part 1,** 489; **Vol. 3, Part 2,** 415; **Vol. 4, Part 1,** 454, 499; **Vol. 9, Part 2,** 304; **Vol. 10, Part 1,** 81

"Black Hawk": locomotive, **Vol. 7, Part 1,** 556; references to, **Vol. 1, Part 2,** 314; **Vol. 5, Part 2,** 350

Black Hawk War, service in, **Vol. 1, Part 1,** 410; **Vol. 1, Part 2,** 314; **Vol. 2, Part 2,** 389; **Vol. 3, Part 1,** 123, 349, 510, 520; **Vol. 3, Part 2,** 497; **Vol. 4, Part 1,** 93; **Vol. 5, Part 2,** 135, 172, 350, 583, 600; **Vol. 6, Part 1,** 114, 587; **Vol. 6, Part 2,** 373; **Vol. 8, Part 1,** 609; **Vol. 8, Part 2,** 251, 507; **Vol. 9, Part 2,** 350, 437; Lincoln's service in, **Vol. 6, Part 1,** 244

Black Kettle's Village, Okla., attack on, **Vol. 3, Part 1,** 8

Blacklisting. *See* Loyalty issues; Motion pictures

Black literature, **Supp. 5,** 490; **Supp. 6,** 715–17; **Supp. 8,** 286–89; collections of, **Supp. 1,** 717; *Crisis* influence on, **Supp. 7,** 203–4; middle-class society depiction, **Supp. 7,** 236; playwriting, **Supp. 7,** 319. *See also* Harlem Renaissance

Black markets, **Supp. 5,** 737

Blackmer, Harry M., reference to, **Supp. 6,** 455

Black Metropolis, **Supp. 8,** 81

Black Mountain College, founding of, **Supp. 8,** 530–31

Black Muslims, **Supp. 7,** 507–9; **Supp. 8,** 388

Black Power, **Supp. 6,** 716

Black Power movement, **Supp. 8,** 335, 383

"Black Republicanism," **Vol. 6, Part 1,** 200

"Black-Robe" Fathers, **Vol. 8, Part 2,** 192

Blacks, **Vol. 1, Part 1,** 23, 549, 562; **Vol. 1, Part 2,** 554; **Vol. 2, Part 1,** 161; **Vol. 3, Part 2,** 536; **Vol. 4, Part 1,** 578 f.; **Vol. 5, Part 2,** 546; **Vol. 7, Part 2,** 324; **Vol. 8, Part 2,** 212, 382, 409; **Vol. 9, Part 1,** 225; acting, **Vol. 1, Part 1,** 160; **Vol. 4, Part 1,** 314; advancement of, **Vol. 2, Part 1,** 180; **Vol. 4, Part 1,** 633; **Vol. 8, Part 1,** 171 f.; **Vol. 10, Part 2,** 264; agriculture, **Supp. 3,** 145–46; anti-Communism by, **Supp. 7,** 156; art, major survey exhibit of, **Supp. 8,** 240; arts participation, **Supp. 5,** 436–37; awards, **Supp. 2,** 623; "Back to Africa" movement, **Supp. 2,** 222; baseball, **Supp. 8,** 142; baseball, Negro League, **Supp. 3,** 378; **Supp. 4,** 327–28; biological

Blake, Francis G., references to, **Supp. 3,** 774, 775
Blake, Tiffany, reference to, **Supp. 7,** 309
Bland-Allison Act, **Vol. 1, Part 2,** 355; **Vol. 9, Part 1,** 86 f.
Blanshard, Paul, reference to, **Supp. 8,** 614
Blashfield, E. H., reference to, **Vol. 7, Part 1,** 299
Blast furnaces, **Vol. 8, Part 1,** 517, 544; **Vol. 9, Part 1,** 428; **Vol. 10, Part 1,** 465 f., 602 f.; feat, reduction of, **Vol. 8, Part 1,** 326; turboblower for, **Vol. 8, Part 1,** 544
Blasting powder, manufacture of, **Vol. 3, Part 1,** 528
Blatchford, Thomas W., reference to, **Vol. 10, Part 1,** 435 f.
Blavatsky, Mme., references to, **Vol. 5, Part 2,** 233; **Vol. 7, Part 2,** 10 f.
Bledsoe, Jules, reference to, **Supp. 3,** 418
"Bleeding Kansas," **Vol. 6, Part 1,** 534; **Vol. 9, Part 2,** 13
Blegen, Carl, reference to, **Supp. 4,** 144
Blennerhasset Papers, **Vol. 8, Part 2,** 288
Bleuler, Eugen, references to, **Supp. 4,** 107, 108
Blind and blindness: books and magazines for, **Vol. 3, Part 1,** 512 f.; **Vol. 5, Part 2,** 288; **Vol. 9, Part 1,** 294; care of, **Vol. 2, Part 2,** 107; **Vol. 5, Part 1,** 296; **Vol. 6, Part 1,** 296, 404; **Vol. 7, Part 2,** 305; **Vol. 8, Part 2,** 238; **Supp. 1,** 19; dog guides, **Supp. 4,** 253–55; education, **Vol. 1, Part 1,** 261; **Vol. 2, Part 1,** 38, 451; **Vol. 2, Part 2,** 106 f.; **Vol. 3, Part 2,** 409 f.; **Vol. 9, Part 1,** 294; **Vol. 10, Part 2,** 455; **Supp. 4,** 10–11; **Supp. 5,** 347–48; **Supp. 8,** 316–17; eye banks, **Supp. 7,** 70; federal aid programs, **Supp. 5,** 347; first blind U.S. senator, **Supp. 4,** 338; Lighthouse organization, **Supp. 3,** 364–65; prevention, **Supp. 2,** 381; **Supp. 3,** 364–65, 377. *See also* Color blindness; Vision
Bliss, Eleanor, reference to, **Supp. 7,** 477
Bliss, George, reference to, **Vol. 10, Part 1,** 637 f.
Bliss, Gilbert A., reference to, **Supp. 3,** 87
Bliss, Mildred Barnes. *See* Barnes, Mildred
Bliss, Robert Woods, reference to, **Supp. 5,** 700
Blizzard of 1888, **Vol. 8, Part 1,** 393
Bloch, Felix, reference to, **Supp. 4,** 358
Bloch, Louis, reference to, **Supp. 8,** 586
Bloch, Suzanne, reference to, **Supp. 6,** 62
Block, Paul, & Associates, **Supp. 3,** 80
Blockade-running in Civil War, **Vol. 3, Part 1,** 60; **Vol. 5, Part 2,** 550; **Vol. 8, Part 1,** 47 f.; **Vol. 8, Part 2,** 149, 341
Block Island, discovery of, **Vol. 1, Part 2,** 378
Block signals. *See* Railroads
Blondell, Joan, reference to, **Supp. 6,** 637
Blood: abnormalities, **Supp. 3,** 75; clotting, **Supp. 3,** 369–70; component interaction, **Supp. 3,** 350–51; Cooley's anemia, **Supp. 3,** 190; culture studies, **Supp. 4,** 494; embryological cell studies, **Supp. 5,** 600; hypoplastic anemia, **Supp. 3,** 75; physiology of circulation, **Supp. 3,** 352–53; plasma, **Supp. 5,** 122–23; plasma preservation, **Supp. 4,** 242–243; research on, **Supp. 4,** 580–81; Rh-negative factor, **Supp. 3,** 441; writings on, **Supp. 4,** 866. *See also* Anemia
Blood cells: hemoglobin determination, **Supp. 4,** 643; role of white, **Supp. 4,** 616
Blood pressure: choline relationship to lowering, **Supp. 4,** 411; measurement, **Supp. 2,** 137; **Supp. 7,** 226; monitoring in surgery, **Supp. 3,** 201
Blood transfusions: blood banks, **Supp. 4,** 242; **Supp. 6,** 547; **Supp. 8,** 556; blood type, **Supp. 3,** 440; donor program, **Supp. 6,** 547; first blood bank, **Supp. 4,** 242; first clinical studies, **Supp. 4,** 494; heparin use, **Supp. 3,** 370; plasma development, **Supp. 5,** 122–23; plasma for burn patients, **Supp. 6,**

190; regional donor centers, **Supp. 6,** 414; surgical use of, **Supp. 3,** 201; **Supp. 7,** 59
Blood vessels: clots and heparin, **Supp. 3,** 370; surgery of, **Supp. 3,** 140; 626; temperature effect on, **Supp. 4,** 59. *See also* Cardiovascular system; Circulatory system
"Bloody Angle," **Vol. 3, Part 2,** 230; **Vol. 5, Part 2,** 96; **Vol. 6, Part 1,** 126; **Vol. 10, Part 1,** 129
"Bloody Monday," **Vol. 7, Part 1,** 158
"Bloody Shirt," **Vol. 9, Part 2,** 540
Bloomer costume, **Vol. 1, Part 1,** 319; **Vol. 4, Part 2,** 376
Bloomfield, N.J., early history of, **Vol. 1, Part 2,** 385
Bloomsbury group, **Supp. 7,** 219
Blount, William, references to, **Vol. 1, Part 2,** 64, 390; **Vol. 3, Part 1,** 613; **Vol. 5, Part 1,** 527 f.; **Vol. 8, Part 2,** 128
Blount conspiracy. *See* Conspiracy, Blount (1797)
Blow, Henry T., case of Dred Scott, **Vol. 8, Part 2,** 488 f.
"Blue and the Gray," **Vol. 3, Part 2,** 383
Blue Angel, The, **Supp. 8,** 672, 688
Blue Cross and Blue Shield: development of, **Supp. 4,** 251; predecessors, **Supp. 3,** 122
"Blue Eagle." *See* National Recovery Administration
Blue Hill Observatory, **Vol. 8, Part 2,** 183 f.
Bluemont Central College, founding of, **Vol. 4, Part 1,** 395
Blue Mountain College, founding of, **Vol. 6, Part 1,** 475
Blue Mountain Valley, capture of, **Vol. 1, Part 1,** 175
Blues music, **Supp. 2,** 547, 616; **Supp. 6,** 275; boogie-woogie, **Supp. 5,** 758
Bluffton movement, **Vol. 7, Part 2,** 59
Blum, René, reference to, **Supp. 3,** 283
Blumenthal, George, reference to, **Supp. 3,** 24
Blunt, E. M., reference to, **Vol. 5, Part 1,** 201
B'nai B'rith, **Supp. 4,** 593–94
Boag, Gil, reference to, **Supp. 6,** 247
Board of Jewish Ministers (New York City), founding of, **Supp. 2,** 453
Board of Missionary Preparation, **Vol. 10, Part 1,** 62
Board of Missions, for Freedmen, **Vol. 8, Part 2,** 332
Board of Navy Commissioners, **Vol. 7, Part 2,** 321
Board of Regents of New York, **Vol. 4, Part 2,** 419
Board of Temperance, Prohibition and Public Morals, **Vol. 5, Part 2,** 517
Boas, Franz, references to, **Supp. 4,** 71, 72, 907; **Supp. 5,** 435; **Supp. 6,** 314, 352, 353, 393, 524, 611; **Supp. 7,** 710, 711
Boas, Sophie Meyer, reference to, **Supp. 3,** 81
Boat building, **Vol. 3, Part 2,** 582; **Vol. 4, Part 2,** 585; **Vol. 5, Part 1,** 155; first iron boat, **Vol. 3, Part 1,** 211
Bob Jones University, founding of, **Supp. 8,** 304
Boccia, Ferdinand ("The Shadow"), reference to, **Supp. 8,** 208
Bôcher, Maxime, reference to, **Supp. 3,** 70, 575
Bodleian Library, **Vol. 7, Part 2,** 86
Body, human: anthropological study of types, **Supp. 5,** 312; heat and temperature, **Supp. 3,** 32; **Supp. 4,** 58–59. *See also* Anatomy; Physiology
Boeing Aircraft, founding of, **Supp. 6,** 63–64
Boer War, **Supp. 4,** 126–27
Bogalusa Paper Co., **Supp. 7,** 293
Bogan, Louise, references to, **Supp. 7,** 654, 655
Bogardus, Emory S., reference to, **Supp. 3,** 578
Boggs, Hale, reference to, **Supp. 7,** 555
Bohemian church, first in U.S., **Vol. 4, Part 2,** 599
Bohemian Roman Catholic Union, **Vol. 4, Part 2,** 600
Bohemians, The: activities of, **Vol. 10, Part 2,** 406; founding of, **Supp. 2,** 250

Bohlen, Charles E., references to, **Supp. 7,** 212; **Supp. 8,** 90

Bohr, Niels, references to, **Supp. 6,** 501; **Supp. 7,** 133, 134, 258; **Supp. 8,** 199, 483

Boilers: inventions relating to, **Vol. 1, Part 1,** 457; **Vol. 8, Part 1,** 429; **Vol. 10, Part 2,** 205; plate manufacture, **Vol. 5, Part 1,** 434; for steamers and battleships, **Vol. 5, Part 1,** 318

Bok, Edward W., peace prize, **Vol. 6, Part 1,** 199; reference to, **Supp. 3,** 573

Boldini, Giovanni (portraitist), reference to, **Supp. 6,** 552

Bolivia, diplomatic relations with, **Vol. 1, Part 1,** 329

Boll weevil, **Vol. 5, Part 1,** 406; **Vol. 5, Part 2,** 453; **Supp. 4,** 601

Bolles, H. Eugene, reference to, **Supp. 6,** 562

Bolshevik Bureau of Information, founding of, **Supp. 5,** 135

Bolshevik Revolution. *See* Russian Revolution (1917)

Bolshevism. *See* Communism; Communist party; Loyalty issues

Bolton, Guy, reference to, **Supp. 3,** 417

Bolton, Herbert Eugene, reference to, **Supp. 4,** 824

Bolts, invention and manufacture of, **Vol. 4, Part 2,** 374

Boltzius, I. M., reference to, **Vol. 7, Part 1,** 310

Boltzmann, Ludwig, reference to, **Supp. 8,** 190

Bombings and terrorism: *Los Angeles Times* unionization issue, **Supp. 3,** 156; San Francisco Preparedness Day (1916), **Supp. 3,** 532–33; St. Valentine's Day massacre, **Supp. 4,** 141

Bonaparte, Napoleon, biography of, **Vol. 9, Part 1,** 214

Bonar, Ronald E., reference to, **Supp. 3,** 289

Bond, Dr. Thomas E., Jr., reference to, **Vol. 1, Part 2,** 61

Bonds, coupon, **Vol. 8, Part 1,** 322 f.; government, **Vol. 2, Part 2,** 383 f.

Bone surgery *See* Surgery

Bonfils, Frederick G., reference to, **Supp. 3,** 851

Bonhomme Richard, and the *Serapis,* naval engagement, **Vol. 5, Part 2,** 185

Boni, Albert, reference to, **Supp. 8,** 577

Boni, Charles, reference to, **Supp. 8,** 577

Boni Brothers Bookshop, **Supp. 8,** 349

Bonsack Machines, perfection of, **Vol. 3, Part 1,** 497 f.

Bonstelle, Jessie, references to, **Supp. 3,** 796; **Supp. 6,** 311

Bonus army (1932), **Supp. 5,** 502; **Supp. 6,** 239–40; **Supp. 7,** 363, 377, 488; **Supp. 8,** 497

Boogie-woogie (musical style), **Supp. 5,** 758

Book clubs. *See* Book-of-the-Month Club; Literary Guild

Bookman, The, **Vol. 3, Part 1,** 341; **Vol. 7, Part 2,** 378; **Vol. 9, Part 1,** 607; **Supp. 6,** 172

Book of Common Prayer, **Vol. 1, Part 2,** 564; **Vol. 5, Part 1,** 421; **Vol. 9, Part 1,** 207, 359; **Supp. 3,** 785

Book of Daniel (Old Testament), **Supp. 4,** 595–96

Book of Mormon, The, **Vol. 9, Part 1,** 310 f.; authorship of, **Vol. 8, Part 1,** 600 f.; translations of, **Vol. 9, Part 2,** 334

Book-of-the-Month Club: editorial board, **Supp. 5,** 439; founding of, **Supp. 8,** 577–78; judges, **Supp. 6,** 203, 465; **Supp. 7,** 104; lawsuit, **Supp. 3,** 500

Book reviews. *See* Criticism, literature

Books: art reproduction, **Supp. 6,** 583; auctioneering, **Vol. 1, Part 2,** 161; authors' agents, **Supp. 1,** 539; baby-care, **Supp. 7,** 528; binding, **Vol. 1, Part 1,** 131; **Vol. 4, Part 1,** 445; **Vol. 6, Part 2,** 421; **Vol. 7, Part 1,** 503; blind, for the use of, **Vol. 3, Part 1,** 512 f.; **Vol. 5, Part 2,** 288; **Vol. 9, Part 1,** 294; braille, **Supp. 5,** 347; cataloguing, **Vol. 4, Part 1,** 460; **Vol.**

6, Part 1, 231; **Vol. 8, Part 2,** 275; censorship, **Supp. 7,** 98, 149, 292, 293; **Supp. 8,** 605; child guidance, **Supp. 7,** 601; child-care, **Supp. 4,** 8; children's, *see* Children's literature; collecting, **Vol. 1, Part 2,** 173; **Vol. 2, Part 1,** 137; **Vol. 3, Part 2,** 158, 363, 407, 417; **Vol. 4, Part 1,** 561; **Vol. 4, Part 2,** 305; **Vol. 5, Part 1,** 445; **Vol. 5, Part 2,** 155 f., 174 f.; **Vol. 6, Part 1,** 110, 308; **Vol. 6, Part 2,** 97; **Vol. 8, Part 1,** 51 f., 232 f.; **Vol. 9, Part 1,** 256; **Vol. 9, Part 2,** 586; **Vol. 10, Part 1,** 443; **Vol. 10, Part 2,** 185; collections, *see* Collections; Rare books and manuscripts; cooking, **Supp. 7,** 528, 656–57; Copyright Act of 1909, **Vol. 8, Part 1,** 279 f.; design, *see* Typographical design; dime novel, **Supp. 3,** 586; editing, **Supp. 3,** 686; **Supp. 4,** 651–52; first movie-rights contract clause, **Supp. 4,** 60; hoax, **Supp. 7,** 643; illustrations, **Vol. 5, Part 2,** 139, *see also* Illustration; indexes to, **Supp. 5,** 752–53; "inside" genre, **Supp. 8,** 232–33; inspirational novels, **Supp. 5,** 182; limited editions, **Supp. 4,** 622; litigation, **Supp. 8,** 224; muckraking, **Supp. 8,** 594–95; novels about emancipated women, **Supp. 4,** 31; paperback, **Supp. 5,** 264–65; **Supp. 6,** 583; **Supp. 7,** 307; **Supp. 8,** 579; plates, **Vol. 5, Part 1,** 424; **Vol. 8, Part 1,** 361 f.; popular adventure, **Supp. 4,** 60; popular culture, **Supp. 3,** 846–47; popular fiction, **Supp. 4,** 372; popular psychology, **Supp. 3,** 384; **Supp. 4,** 495–96; popular romance, **Supp. 5,** 33; popular sensations, **Supp. 7,** 531–32; preservation of, **Supp. 2,** 40; **Supp. 6,** 399; pulp fiction, **Supp. 3,** 264; reviews of, *see* Criticism, literature; self-improvement, **Supp. 5,** 102; technical, **Supp. 4,** 523–24; trade, **Vol. 1, Part 2,** 161; **Vol. 2, Part 1,** 367; **Vol. 2, Part 2,** 162; **Vol. 3, Part 2,** 188, 576; **Vol. 4, Part 1,** 91 f., 398, 460, 536; **Vol. 4, Part 2,** 303, 525; **Vol. 5, Part 2,** 66 f., 444; **Vol. 6, Part 1,** 565 f.; **Vol. 7, Part 1,** 156, 278, 352 f., 508; **Vol. 8, Part 1,** 279 f.; **Vol. 9, Part 2,** 652; **Vol. 10, Part 1,** 604 f.; *Ulysees* censorship, **Supp. 3,** 844; vocabulary-building, **Supp. 7,** 275; Westerns, **Supp. 2,** 262–63, 729; **Supp. 3,** 382–83. *See also* Bibliographies; Biography; Detective stories; Dictionaries; Illustration; Libraries and library work; Literature; Publishing; Rare books and manuscripts; Textbooks; types of literature and genre; Typographical design

Bookstores: associations, **Supp. 7,** 524–25; English language in Paris, **Supp. 7,** 40–41; small retail v. discount, **Supp. 3,** 499–500

Boone, Daniel, first account of, **Vol. 3, Part 2,** 382; references to, **Vol. 3, Part 2,** 475; **Vol. 5, Part 1,** 482; **Vol. 5, Part 2,** 349

Boone and Crockett Club, founding of, **Supp. 2,** 265

Booneville, Mo., engagement at, **Vol. 6, Part 2,** 290

Booth, Bramwell, reference to, **Supp. 4,** 95, 96

Booth, Edwin, references to, **Vol. 1, Part 1,** 647; **Vol. 2, Part 2,** 157; **Vol. 4, Part 2,** 542; **Vol. 5, Part 1,** 605; **Supp. 3,** 713

Booth, George Gough, reference to, **Supp. 7,** 670

Booth, Henry S., reference to, **Supp. 4,** 714, 715

Booth, John Wilkes, **Vol. 5, Part 1,** 182; assassination of Lincoln, **Vol. 6, Part 1,** 257; capture of, **Vol. 1, Part 1,** 523; false accusation of association with, **Vol. 3, Part 1,** 396

Booth, Maud Ballington, reference to, **Supp. 2,** 48–49

Booth, Sherman M., reference to, **Vol. 7, Part 2,** 145 f.

Bootlegging. *See* Prohibition

Boott, Kirk, reference to, **Vol. 5, Part 1,** 553

Borah, William E., references to, **Supp. 3,** 457, 561; **Supp. 5,** 579

Borax, discovery of, **Vol. 9, Part 1,** 267

Bordeaux mixture, **Supp. 3,** 400–1

Bordello. *See* Prostitution

Borden, Lizzie, murder case, **Vol. 7, Part 1,** 107
Border City During the Civil War, **Vol. 1, Part 1,** 264
Borderline personality, **Supp. 6,** 724
Bordes, Charles, reference to, **Supp. 6,** 357
Bordin, Michael, reference to, **Supp. 8,** 564
Boré, Étienne de, reference to, **Vol. 1, Part 1,** 130
Borg, Max, reference to, **Supp. 8,** 482
Borgana (synthetic fabric), **Supp. 6,** 67
Borglum, Lincoln, reference to, **Supp. 3,** 89
Borglum, Solon, reference to, **Supp. 8,** 414
Borg-Warner Corporation, **Supp. 6,** 67
Bori, Lucrezia, references to, **Supp. 6,** 323, 324
Born, Gustav, reference to, **Supp. 6,** 282
Born, Max, references to, **Supp. 7,** 258–59, 411
Borneo, missions in, **Vol. 3, Part 1,** 389
Born Yesterday, **Supp. 7,** 355
Borodin, Mikhail, reference to, **Supp. 8,** 635
Borrow, George, biography of, **Vol. 5, Part 2,** 454
Bosis, Lauro de, reference to, **Supp. 6,** 174
Boston, Mass., Academy of Music, **Vol. 3, Part 2,** 81; Adams House, **Vol. 1, Part 1,** 102; apartment house, site of first in U.S., **Vol. 3, Part 1,** 327; architectural firms, **Supp. 3,** 195–97; Arnold Arboretum, **Vol. 8, Part 2,** 355; Associated Charities, **Vol. 6, Part 1,** 423; **Vol. 7, Part 2,** 158 f.; **Vol. 8, Part 1,** 275 f.; Beacon Hill, development of, **Vol. 6, Part 2,** 371; book publishing, **Supp. 4,** 526–27; Boylston Club, **Vol. 7, Part 2,** 78; Brattle Street Church, **Vol. 2, Part 2,** 311, 410 f.; British evacuation of, **Vol. 6, Part 1,** 77; Castle Square Theatre, **Vol. 8, Part 2,** 386; Catholic church, **Vol. 3, Part 1,** 361; **Vol. 6, Part 2,** 37, 408; **Vol. 8, Part 2,** 63; **Vol. 10, Part 2,** 277; censorship, **Supp. 7,** 20; **Supp. 8,** 605; Chamber of Commerce, **Supp. 2,** 183; charter for, **Vol. 8, Part 1,** 230 f.; **Vol. 9, Part 1,** 42; **Supp. 5,** 730; Church of the Advent, founding of, in Boston, **Vol. 9, Part 1,** 33; Church of the Disciples, **Vol. 2, Part 2,** 153; Church of the New Jerusalem, **Vol. 8, Part 1,** 448 f.; city form of government, adoption of, **Vol. 8, Part 1,** 308 f.; city ordinances, digest of, **Vol. 2, Part 1,** 615; city planning, 1855, **Vol. 4, Part 2,** 523; civic service, **Vol. 1, Part 1,** 361; **Vol. 3, Part 1,** 501 f.; **Vol. 3, Part 2,** 81; **Vol. 7, Part 2,** 582; **Vol. 8, Part 1,** 308 f., 534; **Vol. 9, Part 1,** 31, 33, 142; **Vol. 10, Part 2,** 395; commerce, **Vol. 5, Part 1,** 16; **Vol. 5, Part 2,** 370; Common, movement for perservation of, **Vol. 4, Part 2,** 41; Directory of Nurses, **Vol. 8, Part 1,** 275 f.; education, public, **Vol. 1, Part 2,** 274, 297; **Vol. 2, Part 1,** 482; **Vol. 7, Part 2,** 221; **Vol. 8, Part 1,** 80; **Vol. 9, Part 2,** 276, 524; Emmanuel Church, **Vol. 6, Part 1,** 278; engineering, **Vol. 1, Part 1,** 540; engraved map of harbor, first, **Vol. 8, Part 1,** 140 f.; engravings, **Vol. 2, Part 1,** 278; Eye & Ear Infirmary, founding of, **Vol. 3, Part 1,** 207; faith-cure movement, **Vol. 2, Part 2,** 588; Faneuil Hall, **Vol. 3, Part 2,** 263; **Vol. 6, Part 1,** 439; **Vol. 8, Part 1,** 308 f.; **Vol. 9, Part 1,** 229; Faneuil Hall Market built, **Vol. 8, Part 1,** 308 f.; fire-alarm, first electric, **Vol. 2, Part 2,** 265; fire department, first organized, **Vol. 8, Part 1,** 308 f.; fish horn, first, **Vol. 8, Part 1,** 548; Franklin Park, **Vol. 7, Part 2,** 26 f.; Franklin Square House, **Vol. 1, Part 1,** 560; Free Bridges party, **Vol. 4, Part 2,** 563; Gardner Museum, **Vol. 4, Part 1,** 143; Handel and Haydn Society, **Vol. 5, Part 2,** 584; **Vol. 10, Part 1,** 577 f.; Hide and Leather National Bank, **Vol. 2, Part 2,** 111; hotel building, **Vol. 8, Part 2,** 98; housing, improvements, in, **Vol. 6, Part 1,** 45 f.; Howard Athenaeum, **Vol. 6, Part 1,** 164; ice, exportation, **Vol. 10, Part 1,** 47 f.; journalism, **Vol. 4, Part 2,** 41; **Vol. 5, Part 2,** 458; **Vol. 9, Part 2,** 609; **Vol. 10, Part 2,** 306; King's Chapel, **Vol. 4, Part 1,** 10; **Vol. 5, Part 1,**

414; letter boxes, introduction of, **Vol. 2, Part 1,** 482; library, public, **Vol. 1, Part 2,** 24, 53; **Vol. 4, Part 1,** 617; **Vol. 5, Part 2,** 66; **Vol. 6, Part 2,** 100; **Vol. 7, Part 2,** 241; **Vol. 9, Part 2,** 405, 528; **Vol. 10, Part 2,** 161, 403; life in early nineteenth century, **Vol. 4, Part 2,** 603; literary fame of, in the nineteenth century, **Vol. 1, Part 2,** 17; **Vol. 7, Part 1,** 283; magazines, **Vol. 8, Part 2,** 203; Manufacturer's Mutual Insurance Co., **Vol. 1, Part 1,** 406; mayors, **Supp. 6,** 139–141; municipal improvements, **Supp. 2,** 183; music, **Vol. 3, Part 1,** 513; **Vol. 8, Part 2,** 567; newspapers, early, **Vol. 3, Part 2,** 458; Old Corner Bookstore, **Vol. 9, Part 2,** 529; Old South Church, **Vol. 5, Part 1,** 88; **Vol. 9, Part 2,** 390, 392; Opera House, **Vol. 5, Part 2,** 264; Park Commission, **Supp. 6,** 485; parks, **Vol. 3, Part 2,** 70; Park Street Church, **Vol. 1, Part 1,** 581; philanthropy in, **Vol. 3, Part 1,** 321, 368; **Vol. 7, Part 2,** 158 f.; **Vol. 9, Part 2,** 393; **Vol. 10, Part 1,** 46; pirates, hanging of, in, **Vol. 8, Part 1,** 299 f.; police strike, **Supp. 1,** 194–95; **Supp. 3,** 471; political irregularities, **Supp. 8,** 219; political service, **Vol. 2, Part 2,** 612; **Vol. 7, Part 2,** 101 f.; politics, **Supp. 4,** 277–78; **Supp. 6,** 139–41; pre-Revolutionary War agitation, **Vol. 4, Part 1,** 87 f.; **Vol. 6, Part 2,** 455; printing, **Vol. 3, Part 2,** 460; **Vol. 5, Part 2,** 110; **Vol. 9, Part 2,** 435; psychoanalysis in, **Supp. 4,** 717; Public Franchise League, **Vol. 8, Part 1,** 230 f.; **Supp. 3,** 240; public health, **Vol. 4, Part 2,** 303; **Vol. 9, Part 1,** 543; public service, **Vol. 2, Part 2,** 52 f.; **Vol. 3, Part 1,** 361; **Vol. 6, Part 2,** 370, 418, 587; real estate, **Vol. 2, Part 2,** 136; reforms, **Vol. 2, Part 2,** 595; **Vol. 8, Part 1,** 308 f.; Republican mayor, first, **Vol. 8, Part 1,** 534; Revolutionary War period, **Vol. 2, Part 1,** 381, 395; **Vol. 9, Part 2,** 476; Roman Catholic diocese, **Supp. 3,** 568–71; **Supp. 8,** 114–16, 612–13; rural free delivery, introduction of, **Vol. 2, Part 1,** 482; Saturday Club, **Vol. 5, Part 1,** 86 173; settlement houses in, **Vol. 10, Part 1,** 41; sewer systems, **Vol. 8, Part 1,** 308 f.; shipbuilding, **Vol. 4, Part 2,** 142; siege of, **Vol. 4, Part 1,** 184, 569; **Vol. 4, Part 2,** 490; **Vol. 10, Part 1,** 415, 514; **Vol. 10, Part 2,** 222; social service, **Vol. 8, Part 1,** 275 f.; south, development of, **Vol. 1, Part 1,** 177; South End House founded, **Vol. 10, Part 1,** 41; street cleaning, **Vol. 8, Part 1,** 308 f.; town hall, first, **Vol. 5, Part 2,** 225; trade, colonial period, **Vol. 4, Part 2,** 220; Tremont Temple, **Vol. 6, Part 1,** 412; Trinity Church, **Vol. 2, Part 1,** 85 f.; **Vol. 4, Part 1,** 137; **Vol. 7, Part 2,** 223, 228; water system, **Vol. 4, Part 2,** 109; **Vol. 8, Part 1,** 308 f.; **Vol. 9, Part 1,** 543; West Church, **Vol. 1, Part 2,** 17; Wintergreen Club, **Vol. 8, Part 2,** 45; Women's Educational and Industrial Union, **Vol. 5, Part 2,** 287; writings about, **Vol. 1, Part 1,** 477; **Vol. 3, Part 1,** 433; **Vol. 10, Part 2,** 403; **Supp. 6,** 307
Boston & Lowell Railroad, **Vol. 5, Part 1,** 552; **Vol. 9, Part 2,** 98
Boston & Maine Railroad, **Vol. 5, Part 2,** 169; N.Y. Central merger, **Supp. 3,** 95
Boston & Westchester Railroad, **Vol. 8, Part 1,** 71 f.
Boston Art Club, **Vol. 8, Part 2,** 339
Boston Athenæum, **Vol. 2, Part 1,** 233; **Vol. 3, Part 1,** 15 f.; **Vol. 5, Part 2,** 431; **Vol. 7, Part 2,** 272; **Vol. 8, Part 2,** 388; **Vol. 9, Part 1,** 49; **Supp. 6,** 307; architecture of, **Vol. 2, Part 1,** 394;
Boston Braves (baseball), **Supp. 5,** 465
Boston Children's Hospital, **Supp. 3,** 75
Boston City Club, founding of, **Supp. 2,** 626
Boston City Hospital, first clinical research laboratory, **Supp. 4,** 581–82; pathology laboratory, **Supp. 3,** 502–3, 805

pathology, **Supp. 3,** 814–15; popularization of, **Vol. 3, Part 1,** 78 f.; **Vol. 10, Part 1,** 116; professorship, first in U.S., **Vol. 5, Part 2,** 511, publication of U.S. flora, first complete, **Vol. 8, Part 1,** 271; South Carolina, **Vol. 10, Part 1,** 396 f.; southern states, **Vol. 3, Part 1,** 72; teaching of, **Vol. 4, Part 1,** 98, **Vol. 5, Part 1,** 240, 305; **Vol. 5, Part 2,** 262; **Vol. 7, Part 1,** 17; **Vol. 9, Part 1,** 127, 427; **Vol. 9, Part 2,** 398, 514, 603; Texas, **Vol. 6, Part 1,** 274; **Vol. 10, Part 2,** 546; Vermont, **Vol. 1, Part 2,** 593; West, American, **Vol. 7, Part 2,** 262; writings on, **Vol. 1, Part 2,** 18, 229; **Vol. 2, Part 1,** 100, 232; **Vol. 3, Part 1,** 268, 417, 485, 538, 605 f., 615 f.; **Vol. 4, Part 1,** 378, 511, 565; **Vol. 5, Part 2,** 263, 472, 499; **Vol. 7, Part 1,** 18, 50, 72, 309; **Vol. 8, Part 1,** 104, 116, 239 f., 249, 271, 396; **Vol. 8, Part 2,** 270, 288; **Vol. 9, Part 1,** 53; **Vol. 9, Part 2,** 398, 488; **Vol. 10, Part 1,** 43, 52, 116, 396 f., 435, 547 f.; **Supp. 3,** 776; **Supp. 6,** 450. *See also* Horticulture
Bothe, Walter, reference to, **Supp. 7,** 134
Bottles, manufacture of, **Vol. 7, Part 2,** 122
Bottle-stopper, invention of, **Vol. 7, Part 2,** 167
Boudinot, Elias, reference to, **Vol. 6, Part 1,** 419
Boulder Dam. *See* Hoover Dam
Boundary questions, **Vol. 5, Part 2,** 344; **Vol. 6, Part 1,** 261; **Vol. 7, Part 1,** 51; **Vol. 8, Part 1,** 426; Alaska, **Vol. 3, Part 1,** 35 f., 92, 298, 315; **Vol. 5, Part 2,** 167; **Vol. 6, Part 1,** 348; **Vol. 7, Part 1,** 640; **Vol. 9, Part 1,** 492; **Vol. 10, Part 1,** 540 f.; British Guiana, **Vol. 1, Part 1,** 235; Canada, **Vol. 1, Part 2,** 576; **Vol. 5, Part 2,** 167, 455; **Vol. 8, Part 1,** 506; **Vol. 8, Part 2,** 507 f.; **Vol. 9, Part 2,** 455; Connecticut, **Vol. 5, Part 2,** 41; **Vol. 8, Part 1,** 290 f., 426; **Vol. 9, Part 2,** 633; **Vol. 10, Part 1,** 121; Delaware, **Vol. 1, Part 2,** 460; **Vol. 5, Part 2,** 42; Florida, **Vol. 3, Part 1,** 557 f.; Illinois, **Vol. 8, Part 1,** 77 f.; Iowa, **Vol. 3, Part 1,** 601 f.; Kentucky, **Vol. 4, Part 2,** 513; Maine, **Vol. 3, Part 1,** 79, 515 f.; **Vol. 3, Part 2,** 258 f.; **Vol. 8, Part 1,** 71 f., 100, 505; Massachusetts, **Vol. 1, Part 2,** 460; **Vol. 5, Part 2,** 41, 150, 608; **Vol. 8, Part 1,** 290 f., 422, 423, 426; **Vol. 10, Part 1,** 121; Mexico, **Vol. 1, Part 2,** 7; **Vol. 8, Part 1,** 353 f.; **Vol. 9, Part 2,** 260; Michigan, **Vol. 2, Part 2,** 185; Mississippi, **Vol. 6, Part 1,** 29; New Brunswick, **Vol. 3, Part 1,** 515 f.; **Vol. 8, Part 1,** 71 f., 100, 505; New Hampshire, **Vol. 5, Part 1,** 439; **Vol. 8, Part 1,** 426; New Jersey, **Vol. 5, Part 2,** 6, 11; **Vol. 7, Part 1,** 363; **Vol. 7, Part 2,** 228; New York, **Vol. 5, Part 2,** 6, 11, 150, 608; **Vol. 8, Part 1,** 426, 633; North Carolina, **Vol. 5, Part 1,** 449; **Vol. 5, Part 2,** 140; **Vol. 8, Part 1,** 42; Ohio, **Vol. 2, Part 2,** 185; Oregon, **Vol. 7, Part 2,** 119; **Vol. 8, Part 1,** 34 f.; Pennsylvania, **Vol. 1, Part 2,** 17; **Vol. 5, Part 2,** 42, 47; **Vol. 8, Part 1,** 82 f.; Rhode Island, **Vol. 1, Part 2,** 460; **Vol. 8, Part 1,** 426; **Vol. 10, Part 1,** 121; South Carolina, **Vol. 5, Part 2,** 140; **Vol. 8, Part 1,** 42; Spain, **Vol. 3, Part 1,** 507 f.; **Vol. 5, Part 2,** 423; territorial, **Vol. 8, Part 1,** 78; Texas, **Vol. 1, Part 2,** 125; **Vol. 8, Part 2,** 237; Vermont, **Vol. 5, Part 2,** 608; Virginia, **Vol. 3, Part 2,** 298
Bounties, military, **Vol. 8, Part 1,** 281 f., 284 f.
Bounty, Mutiny on the, **Vol. 9, Part 2,** 592; **Supp. 5,** 266–67
"Bounty jumping," **Vol. 6, Part 1,** 252
Bourke-White, Margaret, reference to, **Supp. 4,** 806
Bourne, Jonathan, reference to, **Supp. 4,** 844
Bourne, Randolph, references to, **Supp. 4,** 702; **Supp. 6,** 557, 572
Bovard, Oliver K., reference to, **Supp. 5,** 552
Boveri, Theodore, reference to, **Supp. 4,** 516
Bovine tuberculosis, **Supp. 4,** 684

Bow, Clara, reference to, **Supp. 8,** 678
Bowditch, Henry Pickering, references to, **Vol. 10, Part 1,** 481 f.; **Supp. 3,** 133; **Supp. 4,** 676
Bowditch, Nathaniel, reference to, **Vol. 7, Part 2,** 394
Bowdoin College, **Vol. 1, Part 1,** 328; **Vol. 3, Part 1,** 515 f.; **Vol. 4, Part 2,** 319; **Vol. 5, Part 1,** 332, 452; **Vol. 7, Part 1,** 586; **Vol. 7, Part 2,** 125; **Vol. 9, Part 1,** 78, 379; **Vol. 10, Part 2,** 503; English literature and language studies, **Supp. 5,** 118; founding of, **Vol. 1, Part 2,** 501; growth of, **Vol. 1, Part 1,** 209; **Vol. 6, Part 2,** 83; influence of Newman, **Vol. 7, Part 1,** 466; "Phi Chi" Song, **Vol. 7, Part 1,** 43
Bowdoin Scientific Review, **Vol. 4, Part 1,** 378
Bowen, Ira S., reference to, **Supp. 5,** 496
Bowen, Norman L., reference to, **Supp. 6,** 144
"Bowery Boys" (fictional characters), **Supp. 8,** 220
Bowie, James, reference to, **Vol. 9, Part 2,** 630
Bowie knife, origin of, **Vol. 1, Part 2,** 510
Bowker, R. R., Co., **Supp. 7,** 525
Bowles, Chester, reference to, **Supp. 7,** 723
Bowles, Samuel, reference to, **Vol. 5, Part 1,** 147
Bowling Green, Ky., operation about (1861-62), **Vol. 2, Part 1,** 235, 240; **Vol. 4, Part 1,** 494; **Vol. 5, Part 2,** 136
Bowne, Borden Parker, references to, **Supp. 5,** 90, 91
Bowron, Fletcher, reference to, **Supp. 3,** 156
Boxer Rebellion (1900), **Vol. 1, Part 1,** 106, 241, 263; **Vol. 2, Part 1,** 589–90; **Vol. 3, Part 1,** 110; **Vol. 4, Part 2,** 434; **Vol. 5, Part 2,** 324; **Vol. 6, Part 1,** 475; **Vol. 6, Part 2,** 108; **Vol. 9, Part 1,** 238; **Vol. 9, Part 2,** 372; **Vol. 10, Part 2,** 335; **Supp. 7,** 358
Boxing, **Vol. 8, Part 1,** 222; black heavyweights, **Supp. 6,** 362–63, 699–700; cartoons, **Vol. 3, Part 1,** 378 f.; featherweight, **Supp. 7,** 209; first black heavyweight champion, **Supp. 4,** 432–34; first white heavyweight champion since 1937, **Supp. 8,** 417–18; "Great White Hope," **Supp. 5,** 368–69; left hook, **Supp. 1,** 201; middleweight, **Supp. 5,** 418; promotion, **Vol. 8, Part 1,** 585 f.; **Supp. 5,** 359–60; **Supp. 7,** 414–15; radio broadcasts, **Supp. 7,** 494–95
Boyce Thompson Institute, founding of, **Supp. 4,** 191
Boyd, Ernest, reference to, **Supp. 6,** 471
Boyd, William, reference to, **Supp. 6,** 466
Boyden, Allen, reference to, **Supp. 4,** 420
Boylston Medical School, founding of, **Vol. 5, Part 2,** 459
Boys Brotherhood Republic, founding of, **Supp. 4,** 870
Boy Scouts of America, **Vol. 8, Part 2,** 432; administration, **Supp. 4,** 871–72; founding of, **Supp. 4,** 737; **Supp. 5,** 138, 325; rural services, **Supp. 5,** 51; uniform design, **Supp. 3,** 44–45
Boys, Inc., **Supp. 6,** 541
Boy's King Arthur, **Vol. 5, Part 2,** 604
Boys' Life, **Supp. 3,** 45
Boys Town (Nebr.), **Supp. 4,** 594; founding of, **Supp. 4,** 282–83
Boy's Will, The, **Supp. 7,** 271, 272
Bozeman Trail, **Vol. 1, Part 2,** 538; **Vol. 8, Part 1,** 437
Brachiopods, **Supp. 3,** 696
Brackenridge, H. H., reference to, **Vol. 8, Part 2,** 526
Bradbury, Ray, reference to, **Supp. 6,** 166
Bradbury, William B., reference to, **Vol. 7, Part 1,** 470
Braddock Expedition, **Vol. 1, Part 2,** 550; **Vol. 3, Part 1,** 317; **Vol. 4, Part 1,** 87, 184, 327; **Vol. 6, Part 2,** 183; **Vol. 7, Part 1,** 100, 226; **Vol. 9, Part 1,** 59, 121; **Vol. 10, Part 1,** 525
Bradford, William, references to, **Vol. 7, Part 1,** 254; **Vol. 9, Part 2,** 503; writings of, **Supp. 3,** 286
Bradley, F. H., reference to, **Vol. 5, Part 1,** 594 f.
Bradley, Omar N., reference to, **Supp. 8,** 267–68

Bradley Polytechnic Institute, **Vol. 1, Part 2,** 574
Brady, James B. ("Diamond Jim"), reference to, **Supp. 3,** 854; **Supp. 6,** 22
Brady, William A., reference to, **Supp. 6,** 65
Bragg, Braxton, reference to, **Vol. 1, Part 1,** 266
Brahms, Johannes, reference to, **Supp. 7,** 444
Braille, **Supp. 3,** 365; **Supp. 4,** 11; **Supp. 5,** 347
Brain: behavior relationship, **Supp. 2,** 664; damage, rehabilitation for, **Supp. 1,** 316–17; embryological development of, **Supp. 4,** 801, 802; functional organization studies, **Supp. 2,** 162; growth studies, **Supp. 2,** 156; metabolism studies, **Supp. 4,** 618; prefrontal lobotomy, **Supp. 6,** 223; research in, **Supp. 2,** 406; studies of, **Vol. 5, Part 2,** 325; **Vol. 9, Part 1,** 461; surgery, **Supp. 6,** 70, 130–31, 223–24; tumor diagnosis, **Supp. 4,** 214, 250; **Supp. 5,** 384. *See also* Intelligence; Nervous system
Brain Trust, **Supp. 3,** 399–400; **Supp. 4,** 136; **Supp. 8,** 679; formation, **Supp. 3,** 647
Brakes: bicycle, **Vol. 8, Part 2,** 56; elevator, **Vol. 7, Part 2,** 93
Brancusi, Constantin, reference to, **Supp. 6,** 194
Brandegee, Frank, reference to, **Supp. 6,** 59
Brandeis, Louis D.: Public Franchise League, **Supp. 3,** 240; railroad rate-setting, **Supp. 3,** 212; references to, **Supp. 2,** 266; **Supp. 3,** 472; **Supp. 5,** 571, 573, 574; **Supp. 6,** 35, 271, 556, 591, 677; **Supp. 7,** 261, 262, 263, 264; Zionism, **Supp. 3,** 279–80, 489
Brandeis University: original faculty, **Supp. 5,** 425, 426; psychology studies, **Supp. 8,** 423
Brandenburg v. Ohio, **Supp. 7,** 317
Brandt, Carl, reference to, **Supp. 3,** 57
Brandt, Raymond P., reference to, **Supp. 3,** 92
Brandy Station, Va., operation at (1863), **Vol. 6, Part 1,** 134; **Vol. 8, Part 1,** 8; **Vol. 9, Part 2,** 171
Brandywine, battle of, **Vol. 1, Part 1,** 176; **Vol. 1, Part 2,** 356; **Vol. 5, Part 2,** 536; **Vol. 8, Part 1,** 259; **Vol. 9, Part 2,** 193; **Vol. 10, Part 1,** 517, 563
Branford, Conn., early land grant, **Vol. 3, Part 1,** 611
Braniff Airways, founding of, **Supp. 5,** 86
Braque, Georges, references to, **Supp. 6,** 552, 553
Brass manufacture, **Vol. 2, Part 1,** 72; **Vol. 2, Part 2,** 261 f.; **Vol. 3, Part 2,** 425; **Vol. 4, Part 2,** 440; **Vol. 5, Part 2,** 166; **Vol. 8, Part 2,** 448; **Supp. 1,** 58
Braunell Ltd., **Supp. 8,** 397
Brave New World, **Supp. 7,** 380
Brazil: diplomacy, **Vol. 1, Part 1,** 285; **Vol. 1, Part 2,** 392; **Vol. 9, Part 2,** 473, 567; **Vol. 10, Part 1,** 49; diplomacy with U.S., **Supp. 1,** 563; **Supp. 5,** 345; **Supp. 6,** 254; education, **Vol. 5, Part 2,** 575; geological survey, **Vol. 1, Part 2,** 603; **Vol. 8, Part 1,** 387; hydroelectric power, **Supp. 4,** 80–81; missions, **Vol. 5, Part 2,** 561, 575; Navy, **Vol. 5, Part 2,** 67 f.; Presbyterian church, **Vol. 5, Part 2,** 575; railroad development, **Vol. 4, Part 2,** 294; **Vol. 8, Part 2,** 19; transit systems, **Supp. 5,** 215; writings on, **Vol. 1, Part 1,** 114; **Vol. 4, Part 1,** 180; **Vol. 5, Part 2,** 565 f.
Brazilian Traction, Light and Power Co., **Supp. 4,** 81–82
Bread, regulations concerning, **Vol. 4, Part 1,** 480
"Bread Crust" papers, **Vol. 6, Part 1,** 285
Bread Loaf School of English, **Supp. 7,** 797
Bread Loaf Writers' Conference (Middlebury, Vt.), **Supp. 4,** 13
Bread-Winners' College, **Vol. 3, Part 1,** 96 f.; **Vol. 7, Part 2,** 266
Brearley School (New York City), **Supp. 4,** 847
Breast: cancer treatment, **Supp. 6,** 70; reconstruction of, **Supp. 6,** 631–32
Breasted, James Henry, reference to, **Supp. 4,** 902
Breast-feeding, maternal milk collection stations, **Supp. 3,** 159

Breathitt County, Ky., demonstration school, **Supp. 4,** 365
Brecht, Bertolt, references to, **Supp. 4,** 868; **Supp. 7,** 61
Breckinridge, Sophonisba, reference to, **Supp. 6,** 1
Breed's Hill (Boston). *See* Bunker Hill (Boston)
Breitmann Ballads, **Vol. 6, Part 1,** 159
Brent, Charles H., reference to, **Supp. 3,** 111
Brero, Vittorio, references to, **Supp. 7,** 511, 512
Bresnahan, Lawrence J., reference to, **Supp. 8,** 421
Breton, André, reference to, **Supp. 6,** 512
Bretton Woods Agreements Act (1945), **Supp. 8,** 616
Brewing, **Vol. 5, Part 2,** 168 f.
Brewster, William, references to, **Vol. 7, Part 1,** 254; **Vol. 9, Part 1,** 500
Brice, Fanny, references to, **Supp. 8,** 546, 547
Brice's Crossroads, Miss., engagement at, **Vol. 3, Part 2,** 532; **Vol. 9, Part 2,** 183
Brick, manufacture of, **Vol. 4, Part 2,** 77, 506; **Vol. 8, Part 1,** 395, 466 f.
Bricker, John W., reference to, **Supp. 7,** 84; **Supp. 8,** 157
Bricker Amendment, **Supp. 6,** 336, 361
Bridge: auction, **Vol. 5, Part 2,** 153; **Vol. 10, Part 2,** 130, 533; contract, **Supp. 5,** 146; **Supp. 6,** 134, 380
Bridge, The, **Supp. 1,** 207
Bridgeport, Conn., Socialist mayor, **Supp. 7,** 503
Bridges: bascule, **Supp. 2,** 637; caissons, **Vol. 8, Part 2,** 90; collapse of, **Vol. 9, Part 2,** 70; covered, etchings of, **Vol. 8, Part 1,** 9; design and construction, **Vol. 1, Part 1,** 147, 194; **Vol. 1, Part 2,** 421, 441; **Vol. 2, Part 1,** 227; **Vol. 2, Part 2,** 110, 413 f., 497; **Vol. 3, Part 1,** 459 f., 587 f., 602; **Vol. 3, Part 2,** 387, 445, 539; **Vol. 4, Part 2,** 307; **Vol. 5, Part 1,** 298; **Vol. 5, Part 2,** 59, 261, 455; **Vol. 6, Part 1,** 27, 549, 565 f.; **Vol. 7, Part 1,** 191, 351, 355; **Vol. 8, Part 1,** 179; **Vol. 8, Part 2,** 19, 48, 52, 88 f., 577, 592 f.; **Vol. 9, Part 1,** 251, 368, 538; **Vol. 9, Part 2,** 70, 385, 611; **Vol. 10, Part 1,** 372 f.; **Vol. 10, Part 2,** 2, 71, 339; **Supp. 1,** 136, 498; **Supp. 2,** 29, 463; **Supp. 3,** 77, 530–31; **Supp. 6,** 331–32, 367, 594; **Supp. 7,** 11–12; foundation work, **Supp. 2,** 469–70; Hell-Gate Bridge, **Vol. 8, Part 1,** 418; "Latrobe's Folly," **Vol. 6, Part 2,** 26; navigable streams, **Vol. 8, Part 1,** 253 f.; Newburyport, Mass., **Vol. 8, Part 1,** 179; railroad, **Supp. 2,** 638; St. Louis, **Vol. 3, Part 1,** 587 f.; Schuylkill River, **Vol. 3, Part 1,** 549 f.; subaqueous foundations, **Vol. 9, Part 1,** 397; suspension, **Vol. 3, Part 2,** 87; **Vol. 4, Part 2,** 156; **Vol. 8, Part 2,** 88; **Supp. 7,** 135–36; turntable for swing, **Supp. 3,** 367; truss, **Vol. 3, Part 2,** 387; **Vol. 8, Part 1,** 179; **Vol. 9, Part 2,** 70; **Vol. 10, Part 1,** 487 f.; vertical lift, **Supp. 2,** 686; **Supp. 3,** 332. *See also* Tunnels; *specific bridge names*
Bridges, Calvin B., references to, **Supp. 3,** 539–40; **Supp. 8,** 448
Bridges, Harry, references to, **Supp. 6,** 396; **Supp. 7,** 73, 96, 119, 292, 609
Bridges, Robert, reference to, **Supp. 4,** 755–56
Bridges, Styles, references to, **Supp. 5,** 338, 690
Bridgewater, Canada. *See* Lundy's Lane
Bridgewater Collection, **Vol. 7, Part 1,** 59
Bridge World, founding of, **Supp. 5,** 146; **Supp. 6,** 134, 135
Bridgman, Laura, reference to, **Vol. 5, Part 1,** 296; **Supp. 8,** 316
Bridgman, Percy W., references to, **Supp. 4,** 807; **Supp. 8,** 482
Brieux, Eugene, reference to, **Supp. 3,** 58
Brigandage, **Vol. 7, Part 1,** 370; **Vol. 9, Part 2,** 74; **Vol. 10, Part 2,** 636

Briggs, Charles A., reference to, **Supp. 3,** 110
Briggs, Le Baron R., reference to, **Supp. 3,** 470
Briggs v. *Elliot,* **Supp. 8,** 682
Brighton, Mass., early history of, **Vol. 3, Part 1,** 430
Brill, Abraham A., references to, **Supp. 3,** 236, 386; **Supp. 5,** 517
Brill's disease, **Supp. 4,** 667
Brine, electrolysis of, **Supp. 2,** 314
Brines, commercial processing of, **Supp. 1,** 261
Brinkley, John, reference to, **Supp. 8,** 706
Brisbane, Arthur, references to, **Supp. 3,** 504; **Supp. 5,** 284; **Supp. 6,** 232
Brisbane, Walter, reference to, **Supp. 3,** 19–20
Brissot, scheme to seize Louisiana, **Vol. 5, Part 1,** 461 f.
Bristol, R.I., **Vol. 3, Part 1,** 275, 312
Bristol Itinerant Society, founding of, **Supp. 1,** 332
British, captive seamen, **Vol. 8, Part 2,** 175; colonial policy, **Vol. 1, Part 2,** 137; Indian support, **Vol. 9, Part 2,** 359 f.; severity to Continentals, **Vol. 4, Part 2,** 454; spies, **Vol. 7, Part 1,** 106; war with, averted, **Vol. 8, Part 2,** 508
British Museum, mammalogy collection, **Supp. 6,** 454
Broadcasting. *See* Radio; Television
Broadhurst, George, reference to, **Supp. 3,** 198
Broad Seal War, **Vol. 7, Part 2,** 443
Broadus, John, reference to, **Supp. 6,** 671
Broadway. *See* Theater
Brobeck, William, reference to, **Supp. 6,** 370
Brödel, Max, reference to, **Supp. 3,** 412; **Supp. 5,** 147
Broderick, David, reference to, **Vol. 9, Part 2,** 380
Broderick, Johnny, reference to, **Supp. 7,** 667
Brokerage houses. *See* Stock market
Bromine, Dow process, **Supp. 1,** 261
Bromley, Dorothy Dunbar, reference to, **Supp. 8,** 520
Bronchoscope, development of, **Supp. 6,** 317
Broneer, Oscar, reference to, **Supp. 4,** 144
Brontosaurus skeleton, **Supp. 3,** 316
Bronx (New York City), politics, **Supp. 5,** 227–28
Bronx House (New York City), founding of, **Supp. 4,** 603
Bronxville (N.Y.), individualized education system, **Supp. 7,** 42
Bronx-Whitestone Bridge (New York City), **Supp. 3,** 531; **Supp. 7,** 12
Bronx Zoo. *See* New York Zoological Park
Bronze casting, **Vol. 7, Part 1,** 5; **Vol. 8, Part 1,** 274 f.
Brooke, John R., reference to, **Supp. 2,** 332
Brookes, Norman, reference to, **Supp. 6,** 421
Brook Farm, **Vol. 3, Part 1,** 49, 284, 567 f.; **Vol. 3, Part 2,** 137; **Vol. 4, Part 1,** 351; **Vol. 5, Part 1,** 578; **Vol. 8, Part 1,** 623 f.; Hawthorne at, **Vol. 4, Part 2,** 426; journal of, **Vol. 3, Part 1,** 567 f., 624
Brookhaven National Laboratory (N.Y.), **Supp. 6,** 501
Brookings, Robert S., references to, **Supp. 6,** 250, 271
Brookings Institution, **Vol. 10, Part 2,** 563; **Supp. 5,** 537, 538; **Supp. 6,** 271, 586, 600; founding of, **Supp. 1,** 123; Indian affairs survey, **Supp. 4,** 165–66
Brooklyn, N.Y.: battle of, **Vol. 1, Part 1,** 175–76; **Vol. 4, Part 1,** 332; **Vol. 7, Part 2,** 270; **Vol. 8, Part 1,** 281–82; **Vol. 9, Part 2,** 192; **Vol. 10, Part 1,** 515; civic service, **Vol. 1, Part 2,** 372; **Vol. 4, Part 2,** 121, 537; **Vol. 7, Part 1,** 351; **Vol. 8, Part 2,** 430; **Vol. 9, Part 2,** 123; **Vol. 10, Part 2,** 87; "common school revival" in, **Vol. 2, Part 1,** 250; consolidation of, with New York City, **Vol. 9, Part 2,** 123; drama, **Vol. 4, Part 2,** 339 f.; Gothic churches, **Supp. 1,** 480; Greenwood Cemetery, **Vol. 3, Part 1,** 406; medical service, **Vol. 9, Part 1,** 443; modern paving introduced, **Vol. 8, Part 1,** 442; Plymouth Institute, **Vol. 5, Part 1,** 56; Prospect Park, **Vol. 6, Part 1,** 294; **Vol. 7, Part 2,** 26 f.; **Vol. 9, Part 2,** 123; religious service,

Vol. 3, Part 1, 19; **Vol. 8, Part 1,** 322; **Vol. 8, Part 2,** 240; street railways, **Vol. 3, Part 2,** 480; **Vol. 6, Part 1,** 294; **Vol. 7, Part 2,** 358
Brooklyn Academy of Design, **Vol. 4, Part 2,** 361 f.
Brooklyn Anatomical and Surgical Society, founding of, **Supp. 1,** 599
Brooklyn-Battery Tunnel, **Supp. 6,** 587
Brooklyn Bridge: **Vol. 1, Part 1,** 194; **Vol. 7, Part 1,** 351; **Vol. 8, Part 2,** 88 f., 577; modernization, **Supp. 6,** 594
Brooklyn City Planning Committee, founding of, **Supp. 4,** 56
Brooklyn College, psychology studies, **Supp. 8,** 423
Brooklyn Collegiate and Polytechinc Institute, **Vol. 4, Part 1,** 416; **Vol. 6, Part 1,** 484; **Vol. 8, Part 1,** 412; **Vol. 10, Part 2,** 462
Brooklyn Daily Eagle: founding of, **Vol. 7, Part 1,** 351; growth of, **Vol. 6, Part 2,** 85; **Vol. 7, Part 1,** 351
Brooklyn Daily Times, founding of, **Vol. 4, Part 2,** 35
Brooklyn Dodgers (baseball), **Supp. 8,** 142, 558–59; black players, **Supp. 8,** 142; predecessor, **Supp. 7,** 751–52
Brooklyn Eagle, **Supp. 7,** 409
Brooklyn Edison Co., **Supp. 3,** 716
Brooklyn Ethical Association, **Vol. 5, Part 1,** 606
Brooklyn Museum, Exposition of Indian Tribal Arts, **Supp. 6,** 355
Brooklyn Robins (baseball), **Supp. 7,** 751–52
Brooklyn Philharmonic Society, **Vol. 9, Part 2,** 424
"Brooklyn Ring," **Vol. 5, Part 1,** 522
"Brooklyn Tabernacle," **Vol. 8, Part 2,** 240
Brooklyn *Union,* **Vol. 9, Part 2,** 552
Brookmeade Stable, **Supp. 7,** 695–96
Brooks, Alexander, reference to, **Supp. 3,** 278
Brooks, Joseph, reference to, **Vol. 1, Part 2,** 62
Brooks, Phillips: biography of, **Supp. 6,** 306; references to, **Vol. 5, Part 1,** 12; **Supp. 3,** 221, 591
Brooks, Van Wyck, references to, **Supp. 4,** 702; **Supp. 6,** 557; **Supp. 7,** 18
Brooks, William K., reference to, **Supp. 6,** 281
Brooks and Baxter War (1868), **Vol. 1, Part 2,** 62; **Vol. 2, Part 2,** 187; **Vol. 3, Part 2,** 244
Brookwood Labor College (Katonah, N.Y.), founding of, **Supp. 8,** 458
Broom: An International Magazine of the Arts, **Supp. 8,** 350
Brothels. *See* Prostitution
Brotherhood of Locomotive Engineers, **Vol. 9, Part 2,** 86
Brotherhood of Locomotive Firemen, **Vol. 2, Part 1,** 545; **Vol. 3, Part 1,** 183
Brotherhood of Railroad Trainmen, **Vol. 6, Part 1,** 133; leadership, **Supp. 4,** 889–90
Brotherhood of Railway Trainmen, dispute arbitration, **Supp. 5,** 651
Brotherhood of Sleeping Car Porters, **Supp. 6,** 648; **Supp. 7,** 155
Brotherhood of the Kingdom, **Vol. 8, Part 1,** 393
Brotherhood of the Union, **Vol. 6, Part 1,** 286
Brothers of the Christian Schools **Vol. 1, Part 1,** 454
Broun, Heywood, references to, **Supp. 7,** 369, 370, 413; **Supp. 8,** 622
Browder, Earl, references to, **Supp. 5,** 70, 500; **Supp. 7,** 255, 751; **Supp. 8,** 192
Brown, A. Page, reference to, **Supp. 6,** 438
"Brown, Buster" (fictional character), **Vol. 7, Part 2,** 112
Brown, Charles Brockden reference to, **Vol. 9, Part 1,** 259
Brown, Edmund G., reference to, **Supp. 6,** 111
Brown, F. Donaldson, reference to, **Supp. 4,** 682
Brown, Gould, influence of, **Vol. 8, Part 1,** 412

56; interior design, **Supp. 8,** 140–41; New York City, **Supp. 6,** 593; **Supp. 7,** 691, 799–800; public, **Supp. 3,** 656; public works projects, **Supp. 5,** 342–43; skyscrapers, *see* Skyscrapers; steel-framed, **Supp. 3,** 611 –12; steel sections, **Supp. 3,** 77; steel structural beam, **Supp. 6,** 243; Supreme Court, **Supp. 3,** 99; theater, **Supp. 1,** 18. *See also* Architecture

Bukharin, Nikolai, reference to, **Supp. 8,** 162

Bulfinch, Charles, reference to, **Vol. 7, Part 1,** 10

Bulgaria: diplomacy, **Vol. 3, Part 1,** 294; missions, **Vol. 9, Part 2,** 74

Bullard, Dexter, reference to, **Supp. 6,** 220

Bullitt, William C., reference to, **Supp. 7,** 536

Bull Moose party, **Vol. 1, Part 2,** 232; **Vol. 8, Part 2,** 142; **Vol. 9, Part 2,** 270

Bull Run: first battle of, **Vol. 1, Part 2,** 111, 124; **Vol. 4, Part 2,** 214; **Vol. 5, Part 1,** 556; **Vol. 5, Part 2,** 144, 216, 425; **Vol. 6, Part 1,** 253, 391; **Vol. 6, Part 2,** 29; **Vol. 8, Part 1,** 77, 91; **Vol. 9, Part 1,** 94; **Vol. 9, Part 2,** 255; **Vol. 10, Part 1,** 87; second battle of, **Vol. 2, Part 1,** 244; **Vol. 4, Part 2,** 214; **Vol. 5, Part 1,** 558; **Vol. 6, Part 1,** 124, 253, 391; **Vol. 6, Part 2,** 29; **Vol. 7, Part 2,** 307; **Vol. 8, Part 1,** 204

Bundy, McGeorge, reference to, **Supp. 7,** 91

Bunker, George M., reference to, **Supp. 5,** 476

Bunker Hill, battle of, **Vol. 4, Part 2,** 490; **Vol. 6, Part 1,** 44; **Vol. 7, Part 2,** 635; **Vol. 8, Part 1,** 195 f., 282; **Vol. 10, Part 1,** 415, 483; munitions, source of, **Vol. 8, Part 1,** 515

Bunker Hill Monument, **Vol. 1, Part 1,** 540 f.; **Vol. 6, Part 1,** 145; **Vol. 10, Part 2,** 242; designing of, **Vol. 7, Part 1,** 12

Bunts, Frank E., reference to, **Supp. 4,** 507

Burbank, Luther, reference to, **Supp. 7,** 592

Burch, George E., reference to, **Supp. 6,** 117

Burdick, Quentin, references to, **Supp. 6,** 85, 86, 87

Burgess, Charles Paine, reference to, **Supp. 4,** 124

Burgess, Ernest W., reference to, **Supp. 3,** 578

Burgess, John W., reference to, **Supp. 4,** 133

Burgess-Dunne seaplane, **Supp. 4,** 124

Burglar on the Roof, The (first "posed" movie), **Supp. 3,** 75

Burgoyne, General John, references to, **Vol. 1, Part 1,** 365; **Vol. 9, Part 2,** 365

Burial alive, escape from, **Vol. 9, Part 2,** 371

Burk, Frederic, reference to, **Supp. 7,** 42

Burke, John J., references to, **Supp. 3,** 325; **Supp. 6,** 85

Burke, Kenneth, reference to, **Supp. 7,** 654

Burke-Wadsworth Act. *See* Selective Service Act

Burleigh, Harry T., reference to, **Supp. 4,** 834

Burlesque, **Vol. 6, Part 1,** 217; **Vol. 8, Part 2,** 247; comedy, **Supp. 3,** 803–4; **Supp. 4,** 739; **Supp. 5,** 726; **Supp. 6,** 112; **Supp. 8,** 355; dance teams, **Supp. 8,** 694; dialect, **Supp. 3,** 803–4; **Supp. 5,** 726; striptease, **Supp. 8,** 363–65

Burley (Idaho) *Bulletin,* **Supp. 7,** 212

Burley Tobacco Growers Cooperative Association, organization of, **Supp. 2,** 39

Burlingame Treaty (1868), **Vol. 2, Part 1,** 289–90; **Vol. 4, Part 2,** 450

Burlington, N.J.: founding of, **Vol. 7, Part 2,** 434; founding of St. Mary's Hall for girls at, **Vol. 3, Part 1,** 333; political service, **Vol. 1, Part 2,** 386

Burlington College (N.J.), **Vol. 3, Part 1,** 333

Burlington Railroad, **Vol. 5, Part 1,** 38 f.

Burma: medical missions, **Supp. 7,** 680–81; missions in, **Vol. 2, Part 2,** 631; **Vol. 5, Part 2,** 236, 242 f.; **Vol. 6, Part 2,** 359; World War II action, **Supp. 4,** 782–83; **Supp. 6,** 508

Burnelli Co., **Supp. 6,** 493

Burnett, Frances Hodgson, reference to, **Supp. 3,** 69

Burney, Leroy E., reference to, **Supp. 7,** 192

Burnham, Daniel H., references to, **Vol. 8, Part 1,** 45 f.; **Supp. 3,** 533, 534, 771–72; **Supp. 6,** 593

Burns, Allen, reference to, **Supp. 4,** 810

Burns, Anthony, case of, **Vol. 5, Part 1,** 17

Burns, Arthur F., reference to, **Supp. 4,** 587

Burns, George, reference to, **Supp. 7,** 9

Burns, Lucy, reference to, **Supp. 7,** 717

Burns, Tommy, reference to, **Supp. 4,** 433

Burns, blood plasma for, **Supp. 6,** 190

Burns, collecting of works on, **Vol. 5, Part 1,** 567

Burns and Allen (comedy team), **Supp. 7,** 9

Burns Mantle Yearbook of the Theatre, The, **Supp. 4,** 549

Burnt Coat Islands, purchase of, **Vol. 9, Part 2,** 234

Burr, Aaron, **Vol. 1, Part 2,** 386, 422; **Vol. 2, Part 2,** 47; **Vol. 3, Part 1,** 138; **Vol. 5, Part 1,** 486, 504; **Vol. 7, Part 1,** 636; **Vol. 8, Part 2,** 544, 604; **Vol. 9, Part 1,** 41, 297; **Vol. 9, Part 2,** 536, 601,, 651; Burr, Theodosia, relations with, **Vol. 1, Part 1,** 229; **Vol. 2, Part 1,** 322; Clay, relations with, **Vol. 2, Part 2,** 174; conspiracy, *see* Conspiracy, Burr; duel with Hamilton, **Vol. 4, Part 2,** 178; **Vol. 5, Part 1,** 240; Latrobe, relations with, **Vol. 6, Part 1,** 23; Livingston, relations with, **Vol. 6, Part 1,** 309 f.; Martin, relations with, **Vol. 6, Part 2,** 344; Ohio expedition, **Vol. 3, Part 1,** 166; presidential election disputed, **Vol. 1, Part 2,** 64; "Spanish Conspiracy," **Vol. 1, Part 1,** 229; **Vol. 3, Part 1,** 80; trial of, **Vol. 1, Part 2,** 368; **Vol. 2, Part 1,** 317; **Vol. 3, Part 1,** 166, 613; **Vol. 4, Part 2,** 430; **Vol. 5, Part 1,** 507, 528; **Vol. 5, Part 2,** 30; **Vol. 6, Part 2,** 324, 345; **Vol. 8, Part 1,** 353 f.; **Vol. 8, Part 2,** 505; **Vol. 9, Part 2,** 238; **Vol. 10, Part 2,** 182, 225, 420; Wickham, relations with, **Vol. 10, Part 2,** 181; Wilkinson, relations with, **Vol. 10, Part 2,** 224; Wood, relations with, **Vol. 10, Part 2,** 464

Burrage, Walter, reference to, **Supp. 3,** 412

Burrill, Thomas J., reference to, **Supp. 3,** 400

Burroughs, John, references to, **Vol. 5, Part 2,** 293; **Supp. 4,** 737

Burroughs, William, references to, **Supp. 8,** 325, 326

Burroughs Adding Machine Co., **Supp. 6,** 114–15

Busch, Fritz, reference to, **Supp. 6,** 324

Bush, Vannevar, references to, **Supp. 5,** 355; **Supp. 7,** 275; **Supp. 8,** 229

"Bush-lopers," **Vol. 7, Part 1,** 417

Bushman, Francis X., reference to, **Supp. 6,** 440

Bushnell, Horace, references to, **Vol. 10, Part 1,** 605 f.; **Supp. 4,** 512

Bushwick, N.Y. *See* Brooklyn, N.Y., battle of

Bushy Run, battle of, **Vol. 1, Part 2,** 481

Business: black-owned, **Supp. 3,** 535; **Supp. 4,** 82–83; **Supp. 5,** 548, 647–48, 741; businessmen, studies of, **Supp. 2,** 651; capitalization of, **Supp. 2,** 446; company towns, **Supp. 2,** 366; competition and economy, **Supp. 8,** 82; consolidation of, **Supp. 1,** 306; corporate finance methods, **Supp. 4,** 681–82; corporate investment, **Supp. 8,** 78–79, 367–68; Cromwell salvage plan, **Supp. 4,** 193; cycles studies, **Vol. 8, Part 1,** 325 f.; **Supp. 4,** 585–86, 587, 722, 723; financial reorganization, **Supp. 3,** 456–57; forecasting, **Supp. 8,** 18–19; government regulation, **Supp. 2,** 31, 553; high school, first in U.S., **Vol. 8, Part 1,** 152; influence on society, **Supp. 8,** 685; interlocking directorates, **Vol. 3, Part 1,** 356; law, **Supp. 1,** 223; **Supp. 4,** 192–93; **Supp. 7,** 792; mergers, **Supp. 2,** 674; modern methods, introduction of, **Vol. 3, Part 2,** 367; **Vol. 6, Part 1,** 608; National Survey Conference (1929-31), **Supp. 6,** 37; New Deal relationship, **Supp. 6,** 520, 615, 675; organized-crime fronts, **Supp. 7,** 632; **Supp. 8,** 208, 397, 546; politics and,

f.; education, **Vol. 5, Part 2,** 591; **Vol. 8, Part 1,** 52 f.; **Vol. 9, Part 1,** 388; **Vol. 9, Part 2,** 244; environmentalism, **Supp. 6,** 486; EPIC campaign (1934), **Supp. 8,** 595; Episcopal church, **Vol. 5, Part 2,** 422 f.; exploration, **Vol. 1, Part 1,** 322; **Vol. 2, Part 1,** 396; **Vol. 3, Part 1,** 252; **Vol. 3, Part 2,** 244; **Vol. 4, Part 1,** 132; **Vol. 5, Part 2,** 419; **Vol. 6, Part 1,** 180; **Vol. 7, Part 2,** 310; **Vol. 8, Part 1,** 109 f.; **Vol. 8, Part 2,** 32; **Vol. 9, Part 1,** 290 f.; financial history of, **Vol. 8, Part 1,** 333 f.; first woman high school principal, **Supp. 8,** 9; forest preservation, **Vol. 3, Part 1,** 485; **Vol. 6, Part 1,** 162; Franciscan Order, **Vol. 7, Part 2,** 197; Frémont regime, **Vol. 8, Part 2,** 252; fruit-growing, **Vol. 6, Part 1,** 481; **Vol. 8, Part 1,** 145 f.; geology of, **Vol. 2, Part 1,** 25; **Supp. 4,** 896–97; **Supp. 5,** 416; Gold Rush, **Vol. 1, Part 1,** 396, 446; **Vol. 1, Part 2,** 228; **Vol. 2, Part 1,** 62, 300; **Vol. 4, Part 1,** 22, 168; **Vol. 4, Part 2,** 363, 387; **Vol. 5, Part 1,** 81; **Vol. 5, Part 2,** 188, 407; **Vol. 6, Part 1,** 516; **Vol. 6, Part 2,** 314; **Vol. 7, Part 1,** 6, 612; **Vol. 8, Part 2,** 11, 35, 205, 248; **Vol. 9, Part 2,** 315, 384; governors, **Vol. 1, Part 2,** 263 f., 455 f.; **Vol. 3, Part 2,** 244; **Vol. 4, Part 2,** 90; **Vol. 6, Part 1,** 445 f.; **Vol. 6, Part 2,** 373 f.; **Vol. 7, Part 2,** 124 f., 468 f.; **Vol. 9, Part 1,** 501 f.; **Vol. 9, Part 2,** 92 f.; **Vol. 10, Part 1,** 628 f.; **Supp. 1,** 639; **Supp. 3,** 393–96; **Supp. 8,** 340–41; history of, **Vol. 3, Part 1,** 40 f.; **Vol. 6, Part 1,** 82; **Vol. 6, Part 2,** 372; **Vol. 8, Part 1,** 109 f., 214 f., 355 f.; **Vol. 10, Part 1,** 146; **Vol. 10, Part 2,** 246; horticulture, **Vol. 1, Part 2,** 599; **Vol. 4, Part 2,** 229; **Vol. 5, Part 2,** 300; **Vol. 6, Part 1,** 162, 498; **Vol. 8, Part 2,** 90; **Vol. 9, Part 1,** 548; Indian insurrections, **Vol. 2, Part 1,** 485; iron foundries, **Vol. 3, Part 1,** 362; Japanese current, **Vol. 3, Part 1,** 394; Jesuit activities, **Vol. 3, Part 1,** 422; **Vol. 5, Part 2,** 420; **Vol. 8, Part 1,** 109 f.; journalism in, **Vol. 1, Part 1,** 443 f.; **Vol. 2, Part 2,** 323; **Vol. 5, Part 1,** 81 f.; **Vol. 9, Part 1,** 175; judiciary, **Supp. 7,** 292–93; kindergarten movement, **Vol. 6, Part 2,** 355; Know-Nothing party, **Vol. 8, Part 2,** 248; land titles, **Vol. 6, Part 1,** 547; legal service, **Vol. 1, Part 2,** 102, 202, 265, 472; **Vol. 3, Part 1,** 226, 422; **Vol. 3, Part 2,** 373; **Vol. 4, Part 2,** 387; **Vol. 6, Part 1,** 546; **Vol. 6, Part 2,** 11, 42, 110; **Vol. 8, Part 1,** 52, 214, 355; **Vol. 8, Part 2,** 176; **Vol. 10, Part 2,** 344; library, first public, **Vol. 3, Part 1,** 121; meteorology, **Supp. 3,** 479; mission preservation, **Supp. 3,** 88; missions in, **Vol. 1, Part 1,** 161, 322; **Vol. 3, Part 1,** 422; **Vol. 3, Part 2,** 497; **Vol. 5, Part 1,** 577; **Vol. 7, Part 1,** 536; **Vol. 8, Part 1,** 109 f.; **Vol. 8, Part 2,** 591 f.; National Guard, **Supp. 5,** 43; newspaper, first in, **Vol. 2, Part 2,** 323; newspapers, **Supp. 4,** 283–84; normal schools, **Vol. 2, Part 1,** 279; **Vol. 7, Part 1,** 578; oil, **Vol. 7, Part 2,** 386; packet boats, **Vol. 8, Part 2,** 42; painting, **Vol. 5, Part 1,** 46; **Vol. 5, Part 2,** 293; **Vol. 9, Part 1,** 597; penal reform, **Supp. 4,** 636; pioneer life, **Vol. 1, Part 2,** 247, 602; **Vol. 4, Part 1,** 229; **Vol. 6, Part 2,** 301, 621; **Vol. 8, Part 2,** 395; **Vol. 9, Part 1,** 540 f.; **Vol. 10, Part 2,** 245, 452, 637; political service, **Vol. 1, Part 1,** 234, 263, 455; **Vol. 1, Part 2,** 247, 410; **Vol. 3, Part 1,** 121, 243; **Vol. 4, Part 2,** 90, 487; **Vol. 6, Part 1,** 13, 445; **Vol. 6, Part 2,** 631; **Vol. 7, Part 2,** 124, 468, 524; **Vol. 8, Part 1,** 109, 355; **Vol. 9, Part 1,** 502, 505; **Vol. 9, Part 2,** 92; **Vol. 10, Part 1,** 466, 628; **Vol. 10, Part 2,** 119; politics, **Supp. 3,** 394–96; **Supp. 4,** 446–47; **Supp. 7,** 224–25; **Supp. 8,** 595; printing, pioneer, **Vol. 10, Part 2,** 643; probate administration, **Vol. 2, Part 2,** 264; progressive movement, **Supp. 4,** 707; public health, **Supp. 5,** 604; public service, **Vol. 1, Part 2,** 602; **Vol. 2, Part 2,** 552; **Vol. 3, Part 1,** 121 f.; **Vol. 4, Part 2,** 64 f., 83, 463; **Vol. 5, Part 1,** 81 f.; **Vol.**

5, Part 2, 250, 405; **Vol. 7, Part 1,** 238; **Vol. 7, Part 2,** 100 f., 124 f., 522, 523 f.; **Vol. 9, Part 1,** 550; **Vol. 9, Part 2,** 147, 379, 473; public utilities, development of, **Vol. 3, Part 1,** 362; railroad development, **Vol. 5, Part 1,** 408 f.; **Vol. 9, Part 2,** 92; real estate operations, **Vol. 6, Part 1,** 234; redwoods conservation, **Supp. 3,** 520; **Supp. 4,** 429; relics, collection of, **Vol. 6, Part 1,** 502; Royce, Josiah, influence on, **Vol. 8, Part 2,** 206; Russian settlements, **Vol. 5, Part 2,** 514 f.; slavery question, **Vol. 2, Part 1,** 62; **Vol. 3, Part 1,** 125; southern, development of, **Supp. 3,** 154–56; **Supp. 5,** 309–10; Spanish enterprise in, **Vol. 8, Part 1,** 109 f.; state forests, **Supp. 3,** 7; statehood, admission to, **Vol. 8, Part 1,** 609; **Vol. 9, Part 2,** 353; teacher training, **Vol. 7, Part 1,** 578; venereal disease prevention, **Supp. 4,** 758; vigilantes, **Vol. 6, Part 1,** 282; vineyards, **Vol. 4, Part 2,** 236; water supply, **Supp. 3,** 155; **Supp. 6,** 3–4; **Supp. 7,** 224; wheat exportation, **Vol. 7, Part 2,** 522; wineries, **Supp. 7,** 613–14; woman suffrage, **Supp. 5,** 742; wool exportation, **Vol. 7, Part 2,** 522; writings on, **Vol. 4, Part 1,** 425; **Vol. 5, Part 1,** 81 f.; **Vol. 9, Part 2,** 473

California Botanical Garden (Los Angeles), **Supp. 6,** 450

California Club, **Vol. 8, Part 2,** 177

California Institute of Technology: aerodynamics studies, **Supp. 8,** 439–40; astrophysical laboratory, **Supp. 4,** 675; development of, **Supp. 2,** 271, 494; **Supp. 3,** 157; experimental biology studies, **Supp. 3,** 540; financing of, **Supp. 2,** 193; Guggenheim Aeronautical Laboratory, **Supp. 7,** 411; mathematics studies, **Supp. 6,** 49; Observatory Council, **Supp. 7,** 516–17; physical chemistry studies, **Supp. 4,** 838–39; physics studies, **Supp. 4,** 57–58; **Supp. 5,** 496–97; **Supp. 8,** 482–84; predecessor, **Supp. 3,** 157; theoretical physics studies, **Supp. 8,** 482–84; World War II research, **Supp. 5,** 497

California Star, **Vol. 1, Part 2,** 602

Calkins, Richard W., reference to, **Supp. 6,** 166

Calkins and Holden, founding of, **Supp. 7,** 101

Callahan, James, reference to, **Supp. 8,** 109

Calligraphy, **Supp. 5,** 693; **Supp. 6,** 185–86

Calliope, invention of, **Vol. 9, Part 2,** 57

Call of the Wild, The, **Vol. 6, Part 1,** 371

Calorimetry, **Vol. 1, Part 1,** 417; **Vol. 2, Part 1,** 144; **Vol. 7, Part 2,** 252; **Supp. 1,** 517–18

Calumet Farm (Lexington, Ky.), **Supp. 7,** 399–400

Calumet-Hecla Co., **Vol. 5, Part 1,** 360

Calvinism, **Vol. 2, Part 1,** 354; **Vol. 3, Part 2,** 130; **Vol. 4, Part 2,** 560; **Vol. 7, Part 1,** 339, 390

Cambria Iron Works, **Vol. 5, Part 2,** 312

Cambridge, Mass.: college, committee to consider establishment of, **Vol. 3, Part 1,** 484 f.; Congregational church, **Vol. 6, Part 2,** 90; founding of, **Vol. 8, Part 1,** 66 f.; Germanic Museum, **Vol. 8, Part 1,** 493; printing in, **Vol. 5, Part 2,** 110; printing press, first in America, **Vol. 3, Part 1,** 163; public service, **Vol. 1, Part 2,** 258; social life, **Vol. 5, Part 1,** 307; Washington Elm, **Vol. 6, Part 1,** 381

Cambridge History of American Literature, **Supp. 4,** 847

Cambridge Platform, **Vol. 7, Part 1,** 573

Cambridge School of Drama, founding of, **Supp. 2,** 11

Cambridge Theological School, **Vol. 5, Part 1,** 101

Camden, S.C., battle of, **Vol. 2, Part 1,** 571; **Vol. 4, Part 1,** 187, 324, 571; **Vol. 5, Part 2,** 254; **Vol. 7, Part 1,** 421; **Vol. 9, Part 1,** 226, 603

Camel cigarettes, **Supp. 5,** 567; **Supp. 7,** 267

Camel experiment (1858), **Vol. 1, Part 2,** 88; **Vol. 3, Part 1,** 126

Cameo cutting, **Vol. 8, Part 2,** 296

246; **Vol. 5, Part 2,** 164, 317; **Vol. 7, Part 2,** 58; **Vol. 8, Part 1,** 172 f.; **Vol. 9, Part 2,** 632 f.; wrought iron, first use of, **Vol. 3, Part 1,** 237

Canon law, **Vol. 3, Part 1,** 368

Cantatas, composition of, **Vol. 5, Part 2,** 251; **Vol. 7, Part 1,** 441

Cantor, Eddie, reference to, **Supp. 3,** 406

Cantors, **Vol. 8, Part 2,** 167; **Vol. 9, Part 1,** 530

Canyons, paintings of, **Vol. 7, Part 1,** 153

Cape Cod ballads, **Supp. 3,** 461

Cape Girardeau, settlement of, **Vol. 6, Part 1,** 413

Capitalism: "enlightened," **Supp. 6,** 615; Nazism related to, **Supp. 5,** 514; new, **Supp. 7,** 809; welfare, **Supp. 3,** 762–63, 792; writings on, **Supp. 3,** 179, 180

Capitalism, Socialism, and Democracy, **Supp. 4,** 722, 723

Capital punishment, **Vol. 2, Part 1,** 285; **Vol. 3, Part 2,** 166; **Vol. 4, Part 1,** 529; arguments against, **Supp. 3,** 103; **Supp. 4,** 472; biblical authority for, **Vol. 3, Part 1,** 339; Chessman case, **Supp. 6,** 111; **Supp. 7,** 292–93; electric chair, first use of, **Vol. 8, Part 2,** 69; in Kansas, **Supp. 7,** 678; Massachusetts, early move toward abolition of, in, **Vol. 8, Part 1,** 381; state opposition, **Supp. 8,** 92

Capital Transit Co. (Washington, D.C.), **Supp. 4,** 397

Capital University, **Vol. 4, Part 1,** 590–91; **Vol. 6, Part 1,** 479

Capitol, Washington, D.C., **Vol. 1, Part 2,** 380; **Vol. 6, Part 1,** 86; architecture of, **Vol. 6, Part 1,** 599; **Supp. 8,** 629–30; burning of, by British (1814), **Vol. 6, Part 1,** 23; cane-fight in corridors of, **Vol. 8, Part 2,** 195; "Columbus Doors," **Vol. 8, Part 2,** 107; erection of, **Vol. 6, Part 1,** 22; extensions to, **Vol. 10, Part 1,** 397 f.; landscape gardening, **Vol. 7, Part 2,** 26; plans for, **Vol. 9, Part 2,** 505; restoration of (1815), **Vol. 6, Part 1,** 23

Capitol Magazine, collapse of, **Vol. 4, Part 2,** 364

Capitol Records Co., **Supp. 7,** 131; founding of, **Supp. 4,** 226

Capitol Theatre (New York City), **Supp. 4,** 97

Capone, Al, references to, **Supp. 3,** 772; **Supp. 6,** 58, 263, 264; **Supp. 7,** 806

Capp, Al, reference to, **Supp. 5,** 223

Capper, Arthur, reference to, **Supp. 3,** 106

Capper-Ketchum Act (1928), **Supp. 5,** 101

Capper-Volstead Cooperative Marketing Act (1922), **Supp. 4,** 853; **Supp. 5,** 101

Capps, Richard B., reference to, **Supp. 3,** 806

Capra, Frank, references to, **Supp. 3,** 443–44; **Supp. 6,** 118, 119

Captain from Castile, **Supp. 5,** 620

Capuchin Order, **Vol. 1, Part 1,** 321

Carbines, manufacture of, **Vol. 3, Part 1,** 600; **Vol. 7, Part 1,** 228

Carbobenzoxy method, **Supp. 3,** 61

Carbohydrates: chemistry of, **Supp. 3,** 61; research in, **Supp. 2,** 379

Carbon black, **Supp. 7,** 98

Carbon dioxide, plant interaction, **Supp. 4,** 192

Carbonic acid, **Supp. 3,** 350

Carbon monoxide, isolation of, **Vol. 8, Part 1,** 223 f.

Carbon-ratio hypothesis, **Supp. 1,** 703

Carborundum. *See* Silicon carbide

Carcinoma. *See* Cancer

Cardiology. *See* Heart; Heart disease

Cardiovascular system, **Supp. 6,** 117

Cardozo, Benjamin, references to, **Supp. 5,** 572, 573, 574; **Supp. 6,** 88

CARE (Cooperative for American Remittances to Everywhere), **Supp. 6,** 217–18

Carey, William F., reference to, **Supp. 6,** 337

Carhart, Arthur, reference to, **Supp. 4,** 483

Caricatures. *See* Cartoons and caricatures

Caricography, writings on, **Vol. 3, Part 1,** 268

Carlen, Robert, reference to, **Supp. 4,** 667

Carles, Arthur B., reference to, **Supp. 5,** 470

Carleton College, **Vol. 9, Part 2,** 149 f.

Carleton Opera Company, **Vol. 5, Part 1,** 78

Carlisle, F. L., and Co., founding of, **Supp. 3,** 138

Carlisle, Kitty, reference to, **Supp. 7,** 325

Carlisle Indian School, **Vol. 8, Part 1,** 176; football team, **Supp. 5,** 683, 727–28

Carlson, George A., reference to, **Supp. 6,** 455

Carlson's Raiders, **Supp. 4,** 147

Carlyle, Thomas, references to, **Vol. 1, Part 1,** 140, 475; **Vol. 7, Part 1,** 570

Carmack, Edward W., references to, **Supp. 1,** 656; **Supp. 3,** 449

Carman, Bliss, reference to, **Vol. 5, Part 1,** 273

Carmen Jones, **Supp. 7,** 162–63; **Supp. 8,** 547

Carmody, John M., references to, **Supp. 6,** 122, 437

Carnap, Rudolf, reference to, **Supp. 5,** 563

Carnation Co., founding of, **Supp. 3,** 750

Carnegie, Andrew: biography of, **Supp. 4,** 368; references to, **Vol. 4, Part 1,** 30, 189; **Vol. 6, Part 1,** 155; **Vol. 7, Part 1,** 143; **Vol. 7, Part 2,** 171, 550; **Vol. 9, Part 2,** 237, 386; **Supp. 3,** 90, 129; **Supp. 6,** 25, 506–7

Carnegie Corporation, **Supp. 6,** 559; administration philosophy, **Supp. 3,** 416–17

Carnegie Endowment for International Peace, **Supp. 1,** 123; **Supp. 3,** 366; **Supp. 7,** 91, 114, 688; founding of, **Supp. 3,** 700; **Supp. 4,** 136–37; funding for, **Supp. 5,** 308

Carnegie Foundation for the Advancement of Teaching, **Supp. 1,** 327; **Supp. 3,** 387; **Supp. 6,** 208; **Supp. 8,** 72; founding of, **Supp. 2,** 542

Carnegie Hall (New York City): architecture of, **Vol. 10, Part 1,** 73; founding of, **Supp. 4,** 211; jazz concert (1938), **Supp. 8,** 163; organ design, **Supp. 3,** 850

Carnegie-Illinois Steel Corporation, **Supp. 5,** 510

Carnegie Institute of Technology: library school, **Supp. 4,** 19; psychology studies, **Supp. 5,** 58

Carnegie Institution, **Vol. 4, Part 1,** 302; **Vol. 4, Part 2,** 606; **Vol. 8, Part 2,** 98; **Vol. 10, Part 2,** 92; archaeological studies, **Supp. 4,** 605–6; **Supp. 7,** 432; archives, **Supp. 8,** 369; ecology studies, **Supp. 3,** 169; embryology studies, **Supp. 4,** 801–2; genetics department, **Supp. 3,** 215–16; 445–46; geophysical laboratory, **Supp. 6,** 70–71, 153, 154; historical research department, **Supp. 2,** 341; **Supp. 4,** 530–31; presidency, **Supp. 3,** 519; terrestrial magnetism department, **Supp. 6,** 205, 206; trustees, **Supp. 6,** 211

Carnegie Laboratory of Medical Research, **Supp. 1,** 240

Carnegie Museum (Pittsburgh, Pa.): curator of birds, **Supp. 8,** 654; growth of, **Supp. 1,** 414

Carnegie Steel Co., **Supp. 1,** 203

Carney, Robert B., reference to, **Supp. 8,** 157–58

Carnochan, J. M., reference to, **Vol. 9, Part 2,** 318

Carolina Playmakers, **Supp. 3,** 426–27; **Supp. 5,** 109

Carolinas, the: colonial government, **Vol. 5, Part 2,** 111, 116 f.; **Vol. 6, Part 1,** 496; division of, into North and South, **Vol. 5, Part 2,** 117; Sherman's campaign in, **Vol. 1, Part 2,** 587; **Vol. 5, Part 2,** 146; **Vol. 8, Part 2,** 453; **Vol. 9, Part 1,** 96; writings on, **Vol. 5, Part 2,** 484

Carothers, Wallace Hume, reference to, **Supp. 5,** 663

Carpenter, Rhys, reference to, **Supp. 4,** 144

Carpet-Bag, **Vol. 9, Part 1,** 110

Carpetbagging, **Vol. 1, Part 1,** 133, 138; **Vol. 2, Part 2,** 148; **Vol. 3, Part 2,** 403; **Vol. 5, Part 1,** 624; **Vol.**

5, **Part 2**, 305 f., 492; **Vol. 9, Part 1**, 110; **Vol. 9, Part 2**, 592, 603 f.; **Vol. 10, Part 1**, 94; Arkansas, **Vol. 8, Part 1**, 33 f.; Florida, **Vol. 8, Part 1**, 372 f.; Louisiana, **Vol. 3, Part 2**, 554; Mississippi, **Vol. 9, Part 2**, 78; North Carolina, **Vol. 10, Part 1**, 69; South Carolina, **Vol. 1, Part 1**, 127

Carpet manufacture, **Vol. 2, Part 2**, 250; **Vol. 9, Part 2**, 183, 198

Carr, Harvey, reference to, **Supp. 4**, 21

Carr, Julian ?, reference to, **Supp. 3**, 507

Carr, Ralph A., reference to, **Supp. 6**, 455

Carrel, Alexis, references to, **Supp. 4**, 287, 288; **Supp. 6**, 386

Carriage manufacturing, **Vol. 2, Part 1**, 28; **Vol. 8, Part 2**, 9; **Vol. 9, Part 2**, 555; **Supp. 7**, 245

Carrick's Ford, W.Va., engagement at, **Vol. 4, Part 1**, 159; **Vol. 7, Part 1**, 228

Carrier Corporation, founding of, **Supp. 4**, 149

Carroll, B. H., references to, **Supp. 3**, 687, 688

Carroll, Coleman F., reference to, **Supp. 8**, 295

Carroll, John, references to, **Vol. 7, Part 1**, 400, 429; **Vol. 9, Part 2**, 376

Carroll, Lewis, reference to, **Supp. 5**, 587

Carson, Christopher, references to, **Vol. 4, Part 1**, 20; **Vol. 7, Part 1**, 560; **Vol. 7, Part 2**, 111

Carson's Private Hospital (Washington, D.C.), **Supp. 5**, 104

Cartan, Elie Joseph, reference to, **Supp. 7**, 216

Cartography, **Vol. 1, Part 2**, 250; **Vol. 3, Part 2**, 497; **Vol. 4, Part 2**, 592; **Vol. 5, Part 1**, 107; **Vol. 5, Part 2**, 157, 419 f.; **Vol. 6, Part 1**, 272; **Vol. 7, Part 1**, 61; **Vol. 8, Part 2**, 39; **Vol. 9, Part 1**, 409; **Vol. 9, Part 2**, 296 f.; **Vol. 10, Part 2**, 404; agricultural regions, **Supp. 4**, 45; Antarctic, **Supp. 7**, 217; commercial maps, **Supp. 1**, 350; geological, **Supp. 3**, 407–8, 696; **Supp. 4**, 896; Indian trails, **Supp. 1**, 443; topographical of West, **Supp. 4**, 558; writings on, **Supp. 2**, 56. *See also* Maps; Topography

Cartoons and caricatures, **Vol. 2, Part 2**, 22; **Vol. 5, Part 1**, 324; **Vol. 5, Part 2**, 352 f.; **Vol. 7, Part 1**, 186, 391 f.; **Vol. 8, Part 2**, 113; animated, **Supp. 3**, 76; **Supp. 8**, 129–30; boxing, **Vol. 3, Part 1**, 378 f.; Civil War, **Vol. 7, Part 1**, 186; comic strips, **Vol. 3, Part 1**, 378 f.; **Vol. 7, Part 2**, 112; correspondence school, **Supp. 1**, 718; editorial, **Supp. 1**, 707; **Supp. 4**, 76; **Supp. 7**, 205–6; **Supp. 8**, 173–74; first animated, **Supp. 3**, 76; "flapper," **Supp. 6**, 278–88; German political, **Supp. 6**, 256; Gibson Girl, **Supp. 3**, 300–1; Goldberg, Rube, inventions, **Supp. 8**, 217; "hot dog," **Supp. 7**, 719; humorous, **Supp. 5**, 732; legislation against, attempted, **Vol. 3, Part 1**, 83; *New Yorker*, **Supp. 7**, 743; **Supp. 8**, 15–16; one-line caption, **Supp. 8**, 15; painting style, **Supp. 6**, 199–200; political, **Vol. 3, Part 1**, 83 f., 378 f.; **Vol. 4, Part 1**, 286 f.; **Vol. 5, Part 2**, 139; **Vol. 7, Part 1**, 392; **Vol. 8, Part 1**, 514; **Vol. 8, Part 2**, 113; **Supp. 1**, 718; **Supp. 3**, 852; **Supp. 4**, 159–60; **Supp. 5**, 391–92, 499, 580, 672; **Supp. 7**, 164; **Supp. 8**, 218; *Puck*, in, **Vol. 8, Part 2**, 31; "Ripley's Believe It or Not!," **Supp. 4**, 693; Sardi's display of, **Supp. 8**, 571; satiric, **Supp. 4**, 386; syndicate, first, **Vol. 8, Part 2**, 113. *See also* Comic strips

Cartridge belt, invention of, **Vol. 7, Part 1**, 1

Carty, John J., references to, **Supp. 3**, 299; **Supp. 4**, 430

Caruso, Enrico, references to, **Supp. 3**, 742; **Supp. 6**, 323

Carvalho, S. S., references to, **Supp. 3**, 427; **Supp. 5**, 284

Casablanca, **Supp. 5**, 209; **Supp. 7**, 160

Casablanca Conference (1942), **Supp. 3**, 662; **Supp. 5**, 334

Casa del Libro, La (Puerto Rico), **Supp. 7**, 3

Casa Loma Orchestra, **Supp. 7**, 300–1

Cascade Tunnel, **Supp. 3**, 735, 737

Case School of Applied Science, **Vol. 2, Part 1**, 558; **Vol. 3, Part 1**, 262; **Vol. 9, Part 1**, 495; **Vol. 9, Part 2**, 50; physics studies, **Supp. 3**, 523

"Case system" of law, **Vol. 3, Part 1**, 571 f.; **Vol. 3, Part 2**, 75; **Vol. 5, Part 2**, 285

Cash registers, manufacture of, **Vol. 7, Part 2**, 304; **Vol. 9, Part 1**, 198, electrification of, **Supp. 6**, 331

Cassady, Neal, reference to, **Supp. 8**, 326

"Cassidy, Hopalong" (fictional character), **Supp. 6**, 466; **Supp. 8**, 248

Castellammare war (organized crime), **Supp. 7**, 632; **Supp. 8**, 396–97

Castle, Vernon, reference to, **Supp. 8**, 77

Castle, William B., reference to, **Supp. 4**, 582

Castro, Fidel, references to, **Supp. 7**, 116, 421, 422; **Supp. 8**, 135, 323

CAT. *See* Civil Air Transport

Catalases (enzymes), **Supp. 6**, 595

Catalogs: library, **Supp. 1**, 242; **Supp. 3**, 326–27, 375, 510, 664; of rare books, **Supp. 7**, 387. *See also* Bibliographies

Catalogue of Incipits of Mediaeval Scientific Writings in Latin, **Supp. 7**, 742

Catalogue sales. *See* Mail order houses

Cataloguing, **Vol. 1, Part 1**, 218; **Vol. 3, Part 1**, 15 f.; **Vol. 7, Part 1**, 414; **Vol. 8, Part 2**, 114, 275; **Vol. 10, Part 1**, 107

Catamarans, design of, **Supp. 2**, 298

Cataract, pioneer operations for removal of, **Vol. 3, Part 1**, 478 f.; **Vol. 5, Part 1**, 541

Catchings, Waddill, reference to, **Supp. 4**, 307

Catechism of Money, **Vol. 8, Part 2**, 150

Catena, Gerardo (Jerry), **Supp. 8**, 208, 209

Catering industry, sporting events, **Supp. 7**, 719

Cathcart, James, reference to, **Vol. 3, Part 1**, 613

Cathedral: administration, **Vol. 3, Part 1**, 335; Episcopal, first, **Vol. 5, Part 2**, 422

Cathedral College, **Vol. 8, Part 1**, 303 f.; establishment of, **Supp. 2**, 293

Cathedral of St. John the Divine (New York City), **Vol. 3, Part 2**, 354; **Vol. 4, Part 2**, 389; **Vol. 5, Part 1**, 421; architecture, **Supp. 2**, 369; **Supp. 3**, 196–97; design and building, **Supp. 4**, 547; sculpture, **Supp. 3**, 88; stained glass windows, **Supp. 3**, 183

Cather, Willa, references to, **Supp. 4**, 518; **Supp. 6**, 251

Cathode ray: oscilloscope, **Supp. 7**, 226, 280; tubes, **Supp. 1**, 646; **Supp. 7**, 206

Catholic Action, **Supp. 6**, 607, 608

Catholic Association for International Peace, founding of, **Supp. 2**, 87

Catholic Book Exchange, **Vol. 3, Part 1**, 421

Catholic Charities, founding of, **Supp. 2**, 294; **Supp. 6**, 608

Catholic Charities Review, founding of, **Supp. 2**, 360; **Supp. 3**, 680

Catholic church (general; for specific priests, bishops, etc., *see* Occupations Index): Anglican reunification issue, **Supp. 2**, 201; Anglo-Catholicism, **Supp. 3**, 195; **Supp. 6**, 46; apologetical journalism, **Supp. 6**, 478–79; appointments in, early, **Vol. 8, Part 2**, 155; as presidential campaign issue, **Supp. 3**, 719–20; **Supp. 6**, 572; **Supp. 7**, 361; **Supp. 8**, 115–16; beatification, **Supp. 1**, 147–48; bishop, first in United States, **Vol. 2, Part 1**, 527; bookselling, **Vol. 5, Part 2**, 329 f.; Cahensly movement, **Vol. 4, Part 1**, 241; California, **Vol. 3, Part 1**, 421; **Vol. 4, Part 1**, 102; **Vol. 8, Part 1**, 619; **Vol. 8, Part 2**, 248; civil rights support by, **Supp. 1**, 159; **Supp. 7**, 448, 533; **Supp.**

Chain stores, **Vol. 1, Part 2,** 582; **Vol. 5, Part 1,** 122; **Vol. 7, Part 1,** 334; first long-lasting, **Supp. 5,** 277–78. *See also* Retail trades; *specific types and names*

Chairs, making of, **Vol. 4, Part 2,** 611; **Vol. 8, Part 2,** 392

Chalasinski, Joseph, reference to, **Supp. 6,** 726

Chalmers, T. A., reference to, **Supp. 7,** 731

Chamberlain, J. Austen, reference to, **Supp. 5,** 160

Chamberlain, Joseph P., references to, **Supp. 3,** 19; **Supp. 6,** 101–2

Chamberlain, Neville, reference to, **Supp. 6,** 101; **Supp. 7,** 89

Chamberlin, Clarence D., reference to, **Supp. 6,** 51

Chamberlin, Thomas C., reference to, **Vol. 5, Part 2,** 389 f.; **Supp. 3,** 265; **Supp. 3,** 455

Chamberlin Observatory, **Vol. 5, Part 1,** 290

Chamber music, **Vol. 3, Part 1,** 70 f.; **Vol. 5, Part 2,** 460 f.; **Vol. 8, Part 1,** 149 f.; **Vol. 9, Part 2,** 305, 424; **Supp. 4,** 545; **Supp. 7,** 511–12; Library of Congress concerts, **Supp. 3,** 252; **Supp. 5,** 555; promotion of, **Supp. 5,** 128–29; woodwind, **Supp. 3,** 33

Chambers, J. J., reference to, **Vol. 8, Part 2,** 533

Chambers, Whittaker, references to, **Supp. 5,** 19, 665; **Supp. 7,** 269–70, 291; **Supp. 8,** 176, 511

Chambersburg, Pa., burning of, **Vol. 6, Part 1,** 575

Chambers of Commerce: development of, **Supp. 2,** 184; International, **Supp. 5,** 634, 675; Los Angeles, **Vol. 7, Part 2,** 100; New York, **Vol. 2, Part 2,** 582; **Vol. 6, Part 1,** 445, 450; **Vol. 7, Part 2,** 56; **Vol. 8, Part 1,** 348 f.; U.S., **Supp. 2,** 184; **Supp. 5,** 479; **Supp. 6,** 37, 660; **Supp. 7,** 397

Champion, Albert, reference to, **Supp. 4,** 244

Champion's Hill. *See* Baker's Creek, battle of

"Chan, Charlie" (fictional character), **Supp. 1,** 79

Chancellorsville, Va., battle of, **Vol. 2, Part 2,** 463; **Vol. 3, Part 2,** 230; **Vol. 5, Part 1,** 25, 197, 279, 559; **Vol. 6, Part 1,** 125; **Vol. 6, Part 2,** 475; **Vol. 8, Part 1,** 520; **Vol. 8, Part 2,** 72; **Vol. 9, Part 1,** 150; **Vol. 9, Part 2,** 171

Chandler, A. B. ("Happy"), references to, **Supp. 6,** 35; **Supp. 8,** 352

Chandler, Charles Frederick, reference to, **Supp. 3,** 26

Chandler, Thomas B., reference to, **Vol. 8, Part 2,** 528

Chandler, William E., reference to, **Supp. 3,** 543

Chandlery, **Vol. 4, Part 1,** 463; **Vol. 5, Part 1,** 561

Chaney, Lon, reference to, **Supp. 7,** 87

Changing Times, founding of, **Supp. 8,** 338

Channing, Edward, reference to, **Supp. 3,** 336

Channing, William Ellery, references to, **Vol. 3, Part 1,** 323 f.; **Vol. 5, Part 1,** 217; **Vol. 9, Part 2,** 298, 303, 391

Chantilly (or Ox Hill), Va., battle of, **Vol. 2, Part 2,** 147; **Vol. 5, Part 2,** 272; **Vol. 6, Part 1,** 124; **Vol. 9, Part 1,** 613

Chapin, Alfred Clark, reference to, **Supp. 7,** 387

Chapin, Charles V., reference to, **Supp. 3,** 324

Chaplin, Charlie, references to, **Supp. 3,** 238; **Supp. 4,** 350; **Supp. 5,** 523; **Supp. 6,** 573; **Supp. 7,** 462; **Supp. 8,** 282

Chaplins' Aid Association, founding of, **Supp. 2,** 73

Chapman, Frank M., references to, **Supp. 6,** 255; **Supp. 7,** 7

Chappell and Co., **Supp. 7,** 199

Chapultepec, Mexico, battle of, **Vol. 2, Part 1,** 560; **Vol. 6, Part 1,** 121; **Vol. 7, Part 2,** 604; **Vol. 8, Part 2,** 509; **Vol. 9, Part 1,** 331; **Vol. 10, Part 2,** 537

Character education. *See* Ethics

Charcoal Sketches, **Vol. 7, Part 1,** 400

Charitable organizations, **Supp. 1,** 237; financing of, **Supp. 1,** 695; Jewish, **Supp. 3,** 488; **Supp. 4,** 79–80; relief aid, **Supp. 4,** 87, 100–1. *See also* Philanthropy; Welfare; *names of specific organizations*

Charities. *See* Survey

Charity Hospital (New Orleans, La.), **Supp. 3,** 313

Charity organization, first state, **Vol. 5, Part 1,** 297

Charity Organization Society of Baltimore, **Supp. 4,** 333

Charity Organization Society of Buffalo, **Supp. 3,** 4

Charity Organization Society of New York, **Vol. 6, Part 1,** 468; **Vol. 7, Part 2,** 410; **Supp. 1,** 237; **Supp. 3,** 743–44; **Supp. 6,** 654

Charles V, contract for conquest of Florida, **Vol. 3, Part 1,** 256

Charles Scribner's Sons. *See* Scribner's, Charles, Sons

Charleston, S.C.: antebellum history of, **Vol. 4, Part 2,** 455; **Vol. 8, Part 1,** 395; black education, **Vol. 7, Part 2,** 324; civic service, **Vol. 5, Part 1,** 444; **Vol. 6, Part 2,** 234; **Vol. 7, Part 1,** 154; **Vol. 7, Part 2,** 617; **Vol. 9, Part 1,** 53, 173 f., 365; **Vol. 10, Part 2,** 602; commerce, **Vol. 2, Part 1,** 487; **Vol. 5, Part 1,** 345; **Vol. 6, Part 1,** 32; defense installations, **Supp. 8,** 538; defense of, **Vol. 4, Part 2,** 455; **Vol. 8, Part 1,** 626; Democratic Convention (1860), **Vol. 5, Part 2,** 552; earthquake (1886), **Vol. 8, Part 1,** 395; first Museum of Natural History in U.S., **Vol. 3, Part 2,** 307; Jackson at, **Vol. 5, Part 1,** 526; Jacobinism, **Vol. 4, Part 2,** 285; Medical College, **Vol. 3, Part 1,** 305; piracy near, **Vol. 5, Part 2,** 116 f.; political reform, **Supp. 5,** 481–82; Reconstruction, **Vol. 6, Part 2,** 602; Reform Judaism, birthplace of, in America, **Vol. 8, Part 1,** 164 f.; siege of (1780), **Vol. 4, Part 1,** 572; **Vol. 4, Part 2,** 454; **Vol. 5, Part 1,** 454; **Vol. 6, Part 1,** 260, 280; **Vol. 6, Part 2,** 405, 600; **Vol. 7, Part 1,** 293; **Vol. 8, Part 2,** 259; **Vol. 9, Part 1,** 61; **Vol. 10, Part 2,** 297, 299; siege of (1863), **Vol. 1, Part 1,** 274; **Vol. 1, Part 2,** 111; **Vol. 3, Part 1,** 31, 532; **Vol. 4, Part 1,** 295; **Vol. 4, Part 2,** 240; **Vol. 7, Part 2,** 560; **Vol. 9, Part 1,** 12; **Vol. 9, Part 2,** 378; Scots Church, **Vol. 4, Part 2,** 601; site of, **Vol. 10, Part 2,** 604; water supply of, **Vol. 8, Part 1,** 397

Charleston College, **Vol. 1, Part 1,** 72

Charleston Mercury, **Vol. 7, Part 2,** 617; **Vol. 8, Part 1,** 527

Charlotte, a Tale of Truth, **Vol. 8, Part 2,** 203

Charlotte, N.C.: branch mint established at, **Vol. 8, Part 1,** 450; founding of, **Vol. 8, Part 1,** 42

Charlotte, raising of, **Vol. 3, Part 1,** 210

Charlotte Daily Observer, **Vol. 9, Part 2,** 582

Charlotte News, **Supp. 3,** 148

Charm Magazine, founding of, **Supp. 3,** 30

Chase, Edna Woolman, reference to, **Supp. 3,** 547

Chase, Ilka, reference to, **Supp. 6,** 108

Chase, Mary Coyle, references to, **Supp. 4,** 649, 653

Chase, Mary Ellen, reference to, **Supp. 6,** 311

Chase, Salmon P., references to, **Vol. 6, Part 1,** 249 f.; **Vol. 8, Part 1,** 54 f.

Chase, Samuel, references to, **Vol. 3, Part 1,** 599; **Vol. 7, Part 2,** 123 f., 599, 626 f.

Chase, William Merritt, reference to, **Supp. 7,** 685–86

Chase Economic Bulletin, **Supp. 4,** 18

Chase National Bank, **Supp. 5,** 744–45; founding of, **Vol. 9, Part 2,** 463

Chasins, Abram, reference to, **Supp. 6,** 297

Chatham House Conference (1935), **Supp. 4,** 137

Chattahoochee River, Ga., operations on. *See* Atlanta campaign

Chattanooga, Tenn., **Vol. 3, Part 2,** 202

Chattanooga Daily Times, **Vol. 7, Part 1,** 601

Chattanooga News, **Supp. 5,** 497–98

Chattanooga Ringgold campaign, **Vol. 1, Part 2,** 587; **Vol. 2, Part 2,** 190; **Vol. 3, Part 1,** 50–51; **Vol. 3, Part 2,** 532; **Vol. 4, Part 1,** 484, 496; **Vol. 4, Part 2,** 240; **Vol. 5, Part 1,** 193, 197, 280; **Vol. 8, Part 2,** 631; **Vol. 9, Part 1,** 80, 95, 363; **Vol. 9, Part 2,** 433

Chatterton, Ruth, reference to, **Supp. 7**, 591
Chattopadhyaya, Virendraneth, reference to, **Supp. 4**, 749
Chaucer, Geoffrey: scholarship on, **Supp. 2**, 558; **Supp. 3**, 474–75, 855; **Supp. 4**, 819–20; studies in, **Vol. 2, Part 2**, 66; **Vol. 3, Part 2**, 485; **Vol. 6, Part 1**, 430
Chauncy-Hall School, **Vol. 9, Part 2**, 405
Chautauqua Institution and Movement, **Vol. 4, Part 1**, 288; **Vol. 5, Part 1**, 425; **Vol. 6, Part 1**, 14; **Vol. 6, Part 2**, 635; **Vol. 7, Part 2**, 184; **Vol. 9, Part 1**, 104; **Supp. 3**, 64–65, 249; lecture circuit, **Supp. 8**, 317; Music Festival, **Supp. 3**, 742; presidency, **Supp. 3**, 792–93
Checkley, John, reference to, **Vol. 10, Part 1**, 395 f.
Cheek, Jim, reference to, **Supp. 6**, 135
Cheese, processing of, **Supp. 5**, 399–400
Cheetham, James, reference to, **Vol. 10, Part 1**, 642 f.
Chefs. *See* Cooking
Chemical Abstracts, founding of, **Supp. 2**, 494
Chemical engineering. *See* Engineering, chemical
Chemical industry: diversification, **Supp. 5**, 191–94; **Supp. 6**, 447–48; **Supp. 7**, 210; drug manufacturing, **Supp. 6**, 447; dyes, **Supp. 7**, 616; explosives manufacture, **Supp. 1**, 271; historical writings on, **Supp. 8**, 249–50; manufacturing, **Supp. 8**, 411; plant design and construction, **Supp. 1**, 682; sulfuric acid production, **Supp. 5**, 319–20
Chemical Pathology, **Supp. 3**, 807
Chemical Society of Philadelphia, **Vol. 10, Part 2**, 491
Chemical transmitters. *See* Neurotransmitter
Chemicals, manufacture of, **Vol. 2, Part 1**, 299; **Vol. 6, Part 2**, 224; **Vol. 7, Part 1**, 495; **Vol. 9, Part 1**, 488; **Vol. 10, Part 2**, 23
Chemical warfare. *See* Biological and chemical warfare
Chemical Who's Who, founding of, **Supp. 8**, 249
Chemistry (for complete list of chemists, *see* Occupations Index): agricultural, **Vol. 1, Part 1**, 349, 417; **Vol. 2, Part 2**, 304; **Vol. 5, Part 2**, 45, 120, 231 f.; **Vol. 6, Part 2**, 223, 263; **Vol. 7, Part 1**, 574 f.; **Vol. 8, Part 1**, 96 f., 154 f., 239 f., 257 f., 272 f., 397; **Vol. 9, Part 2**, 395; **Vol. 10, Part 2**, 22, 104, 491; **Supp. 3**, 145–46; alloys, experiments with, **Vol. 1, Part 1**, 456; ammonia, isolation of, **Vol. 8, Part 1**, 223 f.; ammonia-cobalt bases, **Vol. 4, Part 1**, 210; analytical, **Vol. 3, Part 1**, 376; **Vol. 4, Part 1**, 210; **Vol. 9, Part 2**, 27; atomic weights, **Vol. 8, Part 1**, 556 f.; **Supp. 1**, 178; book collections on, **Supp. 1**, 431; carbon monoxide, isolation of, **Vol. 8, Part 1**, 223 f.; catalytic reactions, **Supp. 4**, 6; colloids, **Supp. 4**, 743–44; crystals, artificial, **Vol. 5, Part 2**, 487; cyanamide process of nitrogen fixation, **Supp. 3**, 439–40; dyes, synthetic, **Vol. 6, Part 2**, 401; elements, search for rare, **Vol. 5, Part 1**, 572; fluorine, discovery of, **Vol. 9, Part 1**, 3; food, application to, **Vol. 1, Part 1**, 457; **Vol. 1, Part 2**, 448; **Vol. 5, Part 1**, 237; **Vol. 5, Part 2**, 524; **Vol. 8, Part 1**, 192 f., 553 f; **Vol. 9, Part 2**, 28; free-radical, **Supp. 6**, 334–35; Gomberg-Bachmann reaction, **Supp. 5**, 28; historical studies, **Supp. 4**, 114; home economics and, **Supp. 3**, 68; hydrogen bond characteristics, **Supp. 5**, 413; hydrochloric acid, isolation of, **Vol. 8, Part 1**, 223 f.; hydrocyanic acid gas, **Vol. 2, Part 2**, 434; hydrolysis, **Vol. 9, Part 2**, 544; industrial, **Vol. 2, Part 1**, 612; **Vol. 3, Part 1**, 70, 157, 479 f.; **Vol. 4, Part 1**, 502; **Vol. 4, Part 2**, 344, 443; **Vol. 6, Part 2**, 147; **Vol. 7, Part 1**, 162; **Vol. 8, Part 2**, 110; **Vol. 10, Part 1**, 607 f.; **Vol. 10, Part 2**, 572; **Supp. 3**, 25–26, 239, 247, 521–22; **Supp. 4**, 184–85; **Supp. 5**, 235, 319–20; **Supp. 6**, 623–24; ionization, **Supp. 2**, 631; medical, **Vol. 10, Part 2**, 455; mineralogical, **Vol. 5, Part 2**, 276; mohawkite, discovery of, **Vol. 5, Part 2**,

487; nitric oxide, isolation of, **Vol. 8, Part 1**, 223 f.; nitrogen, discovery of, **Vol. 5, Part 1**, 50; nitrogen peroxide, isolation of, **Vol. 8, Part 1**, 233 f.; nitrogen system of compounds, **Supp. 2**, 205–6; nitroglycerine, **Vol. 7, Part 1**, 297; nitrous oxide, isolation of, **Vol. 8, Part 1**, 223 f.; Nobel Prize, **Supp. 5**, 670; **Supp. 8**, 123; of nutrition, **Supp. 5**, 622–23; organic, *see* Organic chemistry; organic compound identification, **Supp. 1**, 571; oxygen, discovery of, **Vol. 8, Part 1**, 223 f.; oxygen, experiments with, **Vol. 8, Part 1**, 376; **Vol. 7, Part 1**, 102; patent litigation, **Vol. 6, Part 1**, 143; **Vol. 8, Part 2**, 285; **Vol. 9, Part 2**, 28; pharmaceutical, **Vol. 8, Part 1**, 154 f.; photo, **Vol. 6, Part 1**, 71; physical, **Vol. 5, Part 2**, 173 f.; **Vol. 6, Part 1**, 353 f.; *see also* Physical Chemistry; physiological, **Supp. 1**, 549; plant, **Vol. 8, Part 1**, 154 f.; proteins, **Vol. 7, Part 2**, 74; **Supp. 6**, 346; research techniques, **Supp. 6**, 695; silicon fluoride, isolation of, **Vol. 8, Part 1**, 223 f.; structural, **Supp. 4**, 488–89; sugar, **Supp. 5**, 327–28; sulphur, researches in, **Vol. 8, Part 1**, 223 f.; **Vol. 9, Part 1**, 235; surface, **Supp. 6**, 365; teaching of, **Vol. 3, Part 1**, 10; **Vol. 4, Part 2**, 7, 96; **Vol. 5, Part 1**, 33, 236, 394, 438, 527; **Vol. 5, Part 2**, 277, 418, 486, 593; **Vol. 6, Part 1**, 143, 378, 540, 576; **Vol. 6, Part 2**, 126; **Vol. 7, Part 1**, 66, 69 f., 136, 162, 192, 243, 404; **Vol. 8, Part 2**, 99 f., 350; **Vol. 9, Part 1**, 74, 160, 163, 235, 255 f., 304, 562; **Vol. 9, Part 2**, 56, 278, 596 f.; textbooks on, **Vol. 3, Part 1**, 10; **Vol. 9, Part 1**, 256; **Supp. 1**, 376; theoretical physical, **Supp. 6**, 345–46; thermodynamics, **Supp. 4**, 488–89; writings on, **Supp. 3**, 565–66; **Supp. 5**, 407. *See also* Biochemistry; Organic chemistry; Petrochemistry; Pharmacology; Physical chemistry
Chemistry of Paper Making, The, **Supp. 1**, 500
Chemists' Club of New York, **Vol. 6, Part 1**, 353
Cheney, Russell, references to, **Supp. 4**, 559, 560, 561
Cherkassky, Shura, reference to, **Supp. 6**, 297
Cherokee Indians, **Vol. 7, Part 1**, 401, 622; **Vol. 10, Part 1**, 67; appropriations to, **Vol. 10, Part 1**, 67; Bible translation, **Vol. 1, Part 2**, 478; Confederacy, relations with, **Vol. 8, Part 2**, 179; England, visit to, **Vol. 9, Part 2**, 554; government relations, **Supp. 2**, 291; land, ceding of, **Vol. 8, Part 1**, 595; language, syllabary of, **Vol. 8, Part 2**, 586; negotiations with, **Vol. 2, Part 2**, 96; **Vol. 8, Part 2**, 508; removal of, **Vol. 6, Part 1**, 504; **Vol. 8, Part 2**, 179; **Vol. 9, Part 2**, 615; Revolutionary War, leader among, during, **Vol. 10, Part 1**, 433
Cherokee Phoenix, **Vol. 1, Part 2**, 478
Cherrington, Ernest H., reference to, **Supp. 5**, 442
Cherry Valley (Pa.) Massacre (1779), **Vol. 1, Part 2**, 604; **Vol. 2, Part 1**, 362, 368, 372
Chesapeake: engagements, **Vol. 1, Part 1**, 650; **Vol. 5, Part 2**, 30; **Vol. 6, Part 1**, 50; **Vol. 7, Part 1**, 477, 486; surrender, **Vol. 3, Part 2**, 96; writings on, **Vol. 1, Part 1**, 80
Chesapeake & Ohio Canal, **Vol. 5, Part 2**, 348; **Vol. 9, Part 2**, 249
Chesapeake & Ohio Railroad, **Vol. 3, Part 2**, 1; **Vol. 5, Part 1**, 411, 464; **Vol. 6, Part 1**, 445; **Supp. 6**, 721; management, **Supp. 2**, 282
Chesney, Alan M., reference to, **Supp. 6**, 460–61
Chess, **Vol. 1, Part 1**, 190; **Vol. 3, Part 2**, 417; **Vol. 6, Part 1**, 479; **Vol. 6, Part 2**, 92; **Vol. 7, Part 1**, 193 f.; **Vol. 7, Part 2**, 606; **Vol. 8, Part 1**, 541; **Vol. 9, Part 1**, 564; **Supp. 3**, 509; **Supp. 5**, 20
Chessman, Caryl, reference to, **Supp. 7**, 292
Chester, Colby M., reference to, **Supp. 7**, 379
Chevrolet, Louis, reference to, **Supp. 4**, 244
Chevrolet car, **Supp. 4**, 301, 302, 457

Chevrolet Motor Car Co., founding of, **Supp. 4,** 244
Chewing gum, manufacture of, **Supp. 1,** 715
Cheyenne Indians: revolt of (1879), **Vol. 2, Part 2,** 530, 563; **Vol. 7, Part 1,** 1; **Vol. 8, Part 1,** 520; **Vol. 9, Part 2,** 379; studies on, **Supp. 2,** 265
Chiang Kai-shek, references to, **Supp. 4,** 147, 750, 782–83; **Supp. 6,** 109, 110, 230–31, 350; **Supp. 7,** 377, 761; **Supp. 8,** 395, 506
Chiaotung University, forerunner, **Supp. 3,** 268
Chicago, Ill.: architecture, **Vol. 8, Part 2,** 149 f.; **Supp. 2,** 117, 537–38, 598–99; **Supp. 6,** 712–13; **Supp. 8,** 463; art, **Vol. 1, Part 1,** 448 f.; **Vol. 9, Part 1,** 53; **Vol. 10, Part 2,** 86; Bauhaus school, **Supp. 4,** 591; banking, **Vol. 1, Part 1,** 217; **Vol. 5, Part 1,** 118; **Vol. 7, Part 1,** 645; **Vol. 9, Part 2,** 631; **Vol. 10, Part 2,** 611; baseball, White Stockings, **Vol. 5, Part 2,** 310; black art projects, **Supp. 7,** 611; black community, studies of, **Supp. 8,** 81; black entrepreneurs, **Supp. 4,** 82–83; black politicians, **Supp. 3,** 378; **Supp. 5,** 166; **Supp. 8,** 121; business development, **Vol. 3, Part 2,** 295, 366 f.; **Vol. 5, Part 1,** 326; **Vol. 6, Part 1,** 157, 508 f.; **Vol. 7, Part 1,** 447; **Vol. 10, Part 1,** 414; Catholic church, **Vol. 8, Part 1,** 295; **Supp. 7,** 533; Century of Progress Exposition, **Vol. 10, Part 1,** 133; charter, first, **Vol. 5, Part 2,** 230; civil rights movement, **Supp. 8,** 335; commercial growth of, **Vol. 8, Part 1,** 405; Debs, Eugene V., demonstration for, **Vol. 3, Part 1,** 184; detective, first on police force in, **Vol. 7, Part 2,** 622; development of, **Vol. 1, Part 1,** 217; **Vol. 1, Part 2,** 486; **Vol. 2, Part 1,** 360, 575; **Vol. 2, Part 2,** 537; **Vol. 3, Part 1,** 431; **Vol. 3, Part 2,** 262 f., 302; **Vol. 4, Part 2,** 53, 55, 336, 545; **Vol. 5, Part 1,** 438, 452; **Vol. 6, Part 1,** 61, 157, 612; **Vol. 6, Part 2,** 244; **Vol. 7, Part 2,** 191, 362; **Vol. 8, Part 1,** 405, 435 f.; **Vol. 8, Part 2,** 171, 272; **Vol. 10, Part 1,** 131, 414; **Vol. 10, Part 2,** 86, 557; drainage canal, **Vol. 8, Part 1,** 359 f.; drama movement, **Vol. 4, Part 1,** 393; education, **Vol. 1, Part 1,** 289; **Vol. 2, Part 2,** 221; **Vol. 8, Part 2,** 408; **Vol. 10, Part 1,** 645 f.; **Supp. 1,** 191; **Supp. 4,** 451; Field Museum of Natural History, **Vol. 1, Part 1,** 448 f.; fire, **Vol. 3, Part 1,** 283; **Vol. 8, Part 1,** 390; **Vol. 8, Part 2,** 84; **Vol. 9, Part 2,** 82, 98, Fire Department, **Vol. 10, Part 1,** 657 f.; Gas Trust, **Vol. 1, Part 1,** 104; Haymarket riot, **Vol. 1, Part 1,** 231; **Vol. 7, Part 2,** 264 f.; **Vol. 10, Part 2,** 648; **Supp. 2,** 142; hospital, first general, **Vol. 1, Part 2,** 589; hotel management, **Vol. 3, Part 1,** 431; Immanuel Hall, **Vol. 7, Part 2,** 207; jazz, **Supp. 3,** 541–42; **Supp. 8,** 561; Jewish community, **Supp. 3,** 488; juvenile social work, **Supp. 8,** 40; labor movement, **Supp. 4,** 279–80, 606; **Supp. 6,** 73–74; **Supp. 7,** 254; lake front, litigation over, **Vol. 4, Part 1,** 605; law, **Vol. 4, Part 1,** 61; libraries, **Vol. 1, Part 1,** 448; **Vol. 6, Part 1,** 148; **Supp. 4,** 846; Marshall Fields', **Vol. 6, Part 1,** 157; mayors, **Vol. 7, Part 1,** 644; **Supp. 3,** 771–72; **Supp. 4,** 450–51; **Supp. 5,** 274–75, 323; Methodist church, **Supp. 4,** 837; music, **Vol. 4, Part 1,** 328; **Vol. 6, Part 1,** 512; **Vol. 8, Part 1,** 177 f.; **Vol. 8, Part 2,** 146 f.; **Vol. 9, Part 2,** 579; **Vol. 10, Part 1,** 131; newspapers, **Vol. 5, Part 2,** 489; **Vol. 6, Part 1,** 60 f.; **Supp. 5,** 285–86, 323, 449; **Supp. 6,** 400; Norton, as idealized by, **Vol. 7, Part 1,** 571; organized crime, **Supp. 4,** 140–42; **Supp. 6,** 263–64; parks, **Vol. 2, Part 1,** 306; **Vol. 8, Part 1,** 405; **Supp. 5,** 369–70; pediatrics practice, **Supp. 5,** 1–2; philanthropy, **Vol. 3, Part 2,** 295; **Vol. 5, Part 1,** 18; **Vol. 6, Part 1,** 508 f.; **Vol. 7, Part 1,** 218; **Vol. 7, Part 2,** 72; **Vol. 8, Part 2,** 272; **Vol. 9, Part 1,** 55; pioneer days in, **Vol. 10, Part 2,** 557; playground system, **Supp. 1,** 595; political machines (1890-1900), **Vol. 6, Part 2,** 180; politics, **Supp. 5,** 448, 450, 598;

Supp. 6, 683–84; **Supp. 8,** 121; Prohibition enforcement, **Supp. 7,** 805–6; prostitution, **Supp. 4,** 255–56; **Supp. 5,** 274–75; public health, **Vol. 3, Part 1,** 139; **Vol. 7, Part 2,** 175; **Vol. 8, Part 2,** 281; race riots (1919), **Supp. 6,** 321; railway development, **Vol. 3, Part 1,** 399; **Vol. 7, Part 1,** 594, 645; **Vol. 8, Part 1,** 405; real estate, **Vol. 7, Part 1,** 644; **Vol. 7, Part 2,** 191; reform politics, **Supp. 2,** 166; **Supp. 5,** 485, 579, 698, 699; restaurant business, **Vol. 5, Part 2,** 489; Roman Catholic diocese, **Supp. 6,** 607–8; **Supp. 8,** 588–89; sanitation, **Vol. 4, Part 1,** 605; **Vol. 6, Part 1,** 378; **Vol. 8, Part 1,** 390; settlement houses, **Supp. 2,** 655–56; skyscrapers in, **Vol. 9, Part 1,** 368; **Supp. 3,** 611–12; social life, **Vol. 7, Part 2,** 176 f.; social service, **Vol. 8, Part 1,** 57 f.; steel strike massacre, **Supp. 5,** 510; stockyards, **Supp. 4,** 279–80; **Supp. 5,** 70; surveying of, **Vol. 3, Part 1,** 520 f.; theater, **Supp. 7,** 1; topographical reconstruction, **Vol. 3, Part 2,** 569; "Traction Tangle," **Vol. 10, Part 2,** 610; transit systems, **Supp. 8,** 112; Tuberculosis Institute, **Vol. 7, Part 2,** 298; World's Fair, *see* World's Columbian Exposition
Chicago Academy of Sciences, **Vol. 5, Part 2,** 338; **Vol. 9, Part 2,** 32
Chicago Agricultural and Horticultural Society, **Vol. 7, Part 2,** 464
Chicago American, **Supp. 3,** 427–28; **Supp. 5,** 285
Chicago & Alton Railroad, **Vol. 7, Part 1,** 144 f.
Chicago & Calumet Railroad, **Vol. 9, Part 2,** 594
Chicago & Northwestern Railroad, **Vol. 1, Part 2,** 382; **Vol. 7, Part 1,** 645
Chicago & Rock Island Railroad, **Vol. 3, Part 2,** 281; **Vol. 5, Part 2,** 60
Chicago Art Institute, **Vol. 5, Part 1,** 438; **Vol. 8, Part 2,** 272
Chicago Bible Institute, **Vol. 7, Part 1,** 104
Chicago Board of Trade, **Vol. 7, Part 2,** 297
Chicago, Burlington & Quincy Railroad, **Vol. 7, Part 2,** 466; **Supp. 3,** 381, 823; **Supp. 7,** 90
Chicago Century of Progress Exposition (1933), **Vol. 10, Part 1,** 133; administration, **Supp. 2,** 147; All-Star baseball game, **Supp. 5,** 724; architectural commission, **Supp. 5,** 134; art exhibition, **Supp. 2,** 288; design, **Supp. 7,** 690; Hall of Science, **Supp. 3,** 199; structural design, **Supp. 3,** 531
Chicago City Mission Society, **Vol. 2, Part 2,** 621
Chicago Civic Opera Company, predecessor, **Supp. 8,** 201
Chicago Civic Shakespeare Society, founding of, **Supp. 4,** 478
Chicago College of Pharmacy, **Vol. 8, Part 1,** 390
Chicago College of Physicians and Surgeons, **Vol. 5, Part 1,** 526
Chicago Commons, founding of, **Supp. 2,** 655–56
Chicago Cubs (baseball), **Supp. 5,** 411; **Supp. 6,** 347
Chicago Daily News, **Supp. 2,** 620; **Supp. 3,** 425; **Supp. 4,** 489–90; **Supp. 6,** 197–98, 202; **Supp. 7,** 243, 244, 331; **Supp. 8,** 563–64; first penny newspaper, **Vol. 6, Part 1,** 60; **Vol. 9, Part 2,** 82
Chicago Daily Times, **Vol. 2, Part 2,** 374
Chicago Daily Tribune, **Vol. 10, Part 1,** 131
Chicago Defender, **Supp. 5,** 633; **Supp. 8,** 287–88, 605; founding of, **Supp. 2,** 3
Chicago Dial, **Vol. 7, Part 2,** 332 f.
Chicago Evening Journal, **Vol. 10, Part 1,** 131
Chicago Evening Post, **Supp. 8,** 124; literary editor, **Supp. 7,** 309–10
Chicago Examiner, drama criticism, **Supp. 5,** 658
Chicago Federation of Churches, founding of, **Supp. 3,** 825
Chicago Federation of Labor, **Supp. 4,** 279

ָ: *Millions of Cats*, **Supp. 4,** 310; mysteries, **Supp. 5,** 526; Pansy books, **Supp. 1,** 20; publishing of, **Supp. 2,** 59; **Supp. 7,** 307; space stories, **Supp. 8,** 380; Uncle Wiggily stories, **Supp. 7,** 279

Children's Medical and Surgical Center (Baltimore, Md.), **Supp. 7,** 59

Children's Memorial Hospital (Chicago, Ill.), **Supp. 3,** 101

Childrens' Museum (Brooklyn, N.Y.), **Vol. 4, Part 1,** 416

Childs, Cephas G., reference to, **Vol. 7, Part 1,** 469

Childs, Marquis W., reference to, **Supp. 3,** 92

Chile: diplomacy, **Vol. 5, Part 2,** 375; **Vol. 6, Part 1,** 358; **Vol. 7, Part 1,** 425; **Vol. 8, Part 2,** 150; **Vol. 9, Part 2,** 141; **Supp. 6,** 73, 207; independence, agitation for, **Vol. 8, Part 1,** 30 f.; Patagonian dispute, **Vol. 7, Part 2,** 71 f.; public service, **Vol. 8, Part 2,** 150; writings on, **Vol. 9, Part 2,** 122

"Chillicotte Junto," **Vol. 9, Part 2,** 536, 568

Chilton Press, **Supp. 7,** 615

China: air force, **Supp. 6,** 109; American mission universities, **Supp. 4,** 677–78; American University, **Vol. 5, Part 2,** 208; anthropological studies, **Supp. 4,** 867; armed landing force, first U.S., **Vol. 8, Part 1,** 183 f.; art, **Supp. 3,** 268–69, 465; art history, **Supp. 5,** 729; Bible translation, **Vol. 4, Part 1,** 399; **Vol. 7, Part 2,** 214; **Vol. 8, Part 2,** 428 f.; **Vol. 9, Part 1,** 58; Boxer Rebellion, **Vol. 1, Part 1,** 106, 241, 263; **Vol. 2, Part 1,** 589 f.; **Vol. 3, Part 1,** 110; **Vol. 4, Part 2,** 434; **Vol. 5, Part 2,** 324; **Vol. 6, Part 1,** 475; **Vol. 6, Part 2,** 108; **Vol. 9, Part 1,** 238; **Vol. 9, Part 2,** 372; **Vol. 10, Part 2,** 335; **Supp. 7,** 358; Catholic University, **Vol. 9, Part 1,** 560; Communist, journalism on, **Supp. 8,** 635; Communist movement in, **Supp. 4,** 749–51; **Supp. 6,** 110, 270, 350; Communist-Nationalist split, **Supp. 4,** 147; **Supp. 5,** 544, 705; **Supp. 6,** 230–31, 350; **Supp. 7,** 728; **Supp. 8,** 158; cultural studies, **Supp. 1,** 486; diplomacy, **Vol. 1, Part 1,** 308, 443; **Vol. 1, Part 2,** 241; **Vol. 3, Part 1,** 234; **Vol. 5, Part 1,** 133; **Vol. 5, Part 2,** 324; **Vol. 6, Part 1,** 146, 446; **Vol. 6, Part 2,** 348; **Vol. 7, Part 2,** 34, 235; **Vol. 8, Part 1,** 121 f., 477, 491 f.; **Vol. 8, Part 2,** 66, 613; **Vol. 9, Part 1,** 140, 491, 493; **Vol. 9, Part 2,** 310, 371, 640; **Vol. 10, Part 1,** 426 f., 437 f., 585 f.; **Supp. 2,** 129; **Supp. 3,** 699, 826; **Supp. 6,** 229–31; **Supp. 7,** 377, 728; education, **Vol. 9, Part 1,** 58; **Vol. 9, Part 2,** 372; education modernization, **Supp. 4,** 592; English-language journals, **Supp. 4,** 679; Exclusion Act, constitutionality of, **Vol. 9, Part 2,** 246; explorations, **Vol. 8, Part 2,** 244; first American exchange professor, **Supp. 6,** 410; Formosa defense, **Supp. 6,** 235; geological expeditions, **Supp. 4,** 344, 896; government advisers, **Supp. 3,** 831; historical writings on, **Supp. 8,** 360; history studies, **Supp. 4,** 532; immigration from, **Vol. 1, Part 1,** 308; **Vol. 5, Part 2,** 269; **Vol. 9, Part 2,** 642; insane, care of, **Vol. 5, Part 2,** 357; Korean War, **Supp. 6,** 327; loan, negotiations for international, **Vol. 9, Part 2,** 121; medical education, **Supp. 4,** 346–47; medicine and public health, **Supp. 3,** 324; metallurgical operations, **Vol. 2, Part 2,** 103 f.; Methodist church, **Vol. 7, Part 2,** 214;; **Supp. 6,** 315; military adviser, unofficial, **Vol. 6, Part 1,** 70; missions in, **Vol. 1, Part 1,** 215, 263, 392; **Vol. 1, Part 2,** 34; **Vol. 2, Part 1,** 36, 154; **Vol. 4, Part 1,** 399, 509 f.; **Vol. 4, Part 2,** 234, 361, 453 f.; **Vol. 5, Part 1,** 132; **Vol. 5, Part 2,** 357, 560 f.; **Vol. 6, Part 1,** 475 f., 570; **Vol. 6, Part 2,** 122, 347, 385; **Vol. 7, Part 1,** 444; **Vol. 7, Part 2,** 34 f., 214, 235; **Vol. 8, Part 1,** 286 f., 476 f.; **Vol. 8, Part 2,** 8, 428 f.; **Vol. 9, Part 1,** 57 f., 68 f., 137, 238, 314, 442; **Vol. 10, Part 2,** 250, 274, 290, 469, 599; **Supp. 1,**

433; **Supp. 2,** 548; **Supp. 3,** 268–69, 288–89, 476–77; **Supp. 4,** 514–15; motion pictures, **Supp. 8,** 495; newspaper, first, **Vol. 7, Part 1,** 480; "Open Door" policy, **Vol. 4, Part 2,** 434; Protestant Christianity, introduction of, **Vol. 8, Part 1,** 286 f.; public libraries, **Supp. 3,** 91; Quemoy and Matsu defense, **Supp. 8,** 223; students from, in U.S., **Vol. 10, Part 2,** 639; Taiping rebellion, **Vol. 10, Part 1,** 419 f.; tariff conferences (1925), **Supp. 4,** 800; trade, **Vol. 2, Part 1,** 66, 129, 149, 289 f.; **Vol. 3, Part 2,** 507 f.; **Vol. 4, Part 1,** 523, 551; **Vol. 4, Part 2,** 324, 482; **Vol. 5, Part 1,** 408; **Vol. 5, Part 2,** 271, 383 f.; **Vol. 6, Part 1,** 444 f.; **Vol. 7, Part 2,** 34; **Vol. 9, Part 2,** 499; **Vol. 10, Part 1,** 585 f.; translations, **Vol. 1, Part 1,** 215; **Vol. 7, Part 1,** 444; treaty, first with, 1846, **Vol. 1, Part 2,** 241; Treaty of Tientsin (1858), **Vol. 2, Part 1,** 289; **Vol. 4, Part 2,** 324; **Vol. 8, Part 1,** 462; U.S. China lobby, **Supp. 8,** 506; U.S. military in, **Supp. 4,** 782–83; **Supp. 6,** 429; writings on, **Vol. 3, Part 1,** 234; **Vol. 5, Part 1,** 133; **Vol. 8, Part 1,** 477; **Vol. 9, Part 1,** 58, 138, 238 f.; **Vol. 10, Part 1,** 387 f.; **Vol. 10, Part 2,** 261; **Supp. 8,** 264–65. *See also* Sino-Japanese War

China Christian Advocate, **Supp. 6,** 315

China Medical Board, founding of, **Supp. 4,** 346–47

China Weekly Review, founding of, **Supp. 4,** 679

Chinese-Americans: movie depictions of, **Supp. 7,** 802; San Francisco Chinatown photographs, **Supp. 3,** 295

Chinese Christian Advocate, **Vol. 7, Part 2,** 214

Chinese Recorder, founding of, **Supp. 2,** 549

Chippewa Indians, **Supp. 6,** 162; language of, **Vol. 1, Part 1,** 585; missionary work, **Vol. 1, Part 2,** 145; Sioux, peace with, **Vol. 3, Part 1,** 500 f.

Chiropractic, founding and development of, **Vol. 7, Part 2,** 177

Chisholm v. *Georgia*, **Vol. 5, Part 2,** 8

Chivington Massacre, **Vol. 2, Part 2,** 620; **Vol. 3, Part 2,** 205

Chlorine, **Supp. 3,** 26; commercial production of, **Supp. 1,** 262; use as disinfectant, **Vol. 3, Part 1,** 377

Chloroform, **Vol. 4, Part 2,** 59, 62

Choate, Joseph H., reference to, **Vol. 6, Part 1,** 270

Choate, Hall and Stewart, **Supp. 7,** 91

Chocolates, **Supp. 3,** 357–58

Choctaw Academy, **Vol. 5, Part 2,** 115

Choctaw Indians, **Vol. 5, Part 2,** 115; **Vol. 7, Part 2,** 638; **Supp. 7,** 376

Chocura, **Vol. 7, Part 2,** 308

Cholera, **Vol. 1, Part 1,** 383, 413; **Vol. 2, Part 1,** 68, 231; **Vol. 3, Part 1,** 204; **Vol. 5, Part 1,** 234 546, 553; **Vol. 5, Part 2,** 517; **Vol. 6, Part 1,** 59, 282; **Vol. 7, Part 1,** 628; **Vol. 7, Part 2,** 110; **Vol. 9, Part 1,** 606; **Vol. 9, Part 2,** 311; chlorine, use of as disinfectant, **Vol. 3, Part 1,** 377; Cincinnati, **Vol. 3, Part 1,** 615 f.; epidemic of 1830, **Vol. 8, Part 2,** 238; investigation by *New York Times*, **Vol. 4, Part 1,** 7; Jacksonville, Ill., **Vol. 8, Part 1,** 120 f.; New Orleans, La., **Vol. 9, Part 2,** 85; Pittsburgh, Pa., **Vol. 3, Part 1,** 220

Cholesterol, **Supp. 3,** 693

Choral music: black, **Supp. 3,** 225–26; conducting, **Vol. 10, Part 2,** 453; New York Choral Society, **Vol. 4, Part 2,** 505; singing, **Vol. 7, Part 2,** 78; **Vol. 10, Part 1,** 46 f.

Choreographers. For complete list, *see* Occupations Index

Chorus line, first, **Supp. 6,** 305

Christ and Culture, **Supp. 7,** 575

Christensen, Parley, reference to, **Supp. 3,** 347

Christian Advocate, **Vol. 2, Part 1,** 231; **Vol. 3, Part 2,** 436; **Vol. 9, Part 1,** 605; **Vol. 9, Part 2,** 482

727; opposition to, **Supp. 1,** 217; parochial school aid, **Supp. 8,** 25, 115–16; Supreme Court decisions on, **Supp. 4,** 713, 796; **Supp. 5,** 358

Church Temperance Society, **Vol. 3, Part 1,** 191

CIA. *See* Central Intelligence Agency

Cicero, Ill., organized crime in, **Supp. 4,** 141–42; **Supp. 6,** 263–64

Cicognani, Amleto, reference to, **Supp. 8,** 46

Cicotte, Ed, reference to, **Supp. 8,** 574, 575

Cigarettes: advertising and promotion of, **Supp. 4,** 371; **Supp. 5,** 411, 567; cancer link, **Supp. 6,** 246; **Supp. 8,** 7; manufacture of, **Vol. 3, Part 1,** 496 f.; **Vol. 4, Part 1,** 318

Cigars, **Supp. 7,** 614; selling of, **Vol. 3, Part 1,** 497 f.

Cinaudagraph Corporation, founding of, **Supp. 5,** 324

Cincinnati, Ohio: "Bibles in the schools" case, **Vol. 6, Part 1,** 241; cholera outbreak, **Vol. 3, Part 1,** 615 f.; civic service, **Vol. 3, Part 1,** 426 f.; **Vol. 3, Part 2,** 458; **Vol. 5, Part 1,** 464; **Vol. 6, Part 1,** 241; **Vol. 6, Part 2,** 255, 419; **Vol. 7, Part 2,** 475; **Vol. 8, Part 1,** 317 f.; **Vol. 8, Part 2,** 462; **Vol. 9, Part 1,** 135; educational service, **Vol. 9, Part 1,** 496; fire prevention, early, **Vol. 4, Part 1,** 593; German singing societies, **Vol. 8, Part 1,** 388; history of, **Vol. 2, Part 2,** 108; **Vol. 3, Part 1,** 424, 426 f.; **Vol. 3, Part 2,** 382; **Vol. 9, Part 2,** 259; **Vol. 10, Part 2,** 655; legal service, **Vol. 9, Part 1,** 498; municipal management of, **Supp. 4,** 246–47; music in, **Vol. 7, Part 1,** 494; **Vol. 8, Part 1,** 633; **Vol. 9, Part 1,** 483; **Vol. 9, Part 2,** 265, 424; Phonography Institute, **Vol. 7, Part 2,** 642; planning of, **Supp. 1,** 311; political reform, **Supp. 5,** 674; public library, **Vol. 8, Part 1,** 66 f.; real estate, **Vol. 6, Part 1,** 394; railroad development, **Vol. 5, Part 1,** 464; Roman Catholic diocese, **Supp. 4,** 535–36; Sunday school, first in, **Vol. 2, Part 2,** 108; university, bequest for free, **Vol. 9, Part 2,** 264

Cincinnati, Society of the. *See* Society of the Cincinnati

Cincinnati Chronicle, **Vol. 3, Part 1,** 424

Cincinnati Convention, **Vol. 1, Part 2,** 517

Cincinnati Enquirer, **Vol. 2, Part 1,** 94; **Vol. 3, Part 2,** 270; **Vol. 4, Part 2,** 163; **Vol. 7, Part 2,** 557; **Supp. 3,** 491

Cincinnati Gazette, **Vol. 8, Part 1,** 482

Cincinnati General Hospital, surgery training, **Supp. 3,** 626

Cincinnati, Hamilton, and Dayton Railroad, **Supp. 5,** 550

Cincinnati Medical College, **Vol. 7, Part 1,** 237

Cincinnati Post, cartoons, **Supp. 5,** 732

Cincinnati Reds (baseball), **Supp. 7,** 155, 502; **Supp. 8,** 141

Cincinnati Repertory Company, **Supp. 3,** 797

Cincinnati Social Unit, **Supp. 3,** 227

Cincinnati Times, **Vol. 7, Part 1,** 532

Cincinnati Union Terminal Co., **Supp. 3,** 795

Cinema. *See* Motion pictures

CinemaScope, **Supp. 7,** 692, 693

Cinematography, **Supp. 3,** 73–74; first mass-market inexpensive camera, **Supp. 5,** 322

Cinerama, **Supp. 5,** 721–22; **Supp. 6,** 638

CIO. *See* Congress of Industrial Organizations

"Cipher Despatches," **Vol. 8, Part 1,** 457, 484; **Vol. 9, Part 2,** 541

Circle of Russian Culture, founding of, **Supp. 2,** 505

Circuit riding, **Vol. 1, Part 1,** 574 f.; **Vol. 1, Part 2,** 31; **Vol. 4, Part 2,** 497; **Vol. 5, Part 2,** 169, 226, 579; **Vol. 6, Part 1,** 113; **Vol. 6, Part 2,** 86; **Vol. 8, Part 2,** 13, 15, 315; **Vol. 9, Part 1,** 4, 382

Circulating libraries, **Vol. 4, Part 2,** 591; **Vol. 6, Part 1,** 427; **Vol. 7, Part 1,** 510; **Vol. 9, Part 2,** 445

Circulatory system, writings on, **Supp. 4,** 390. *See also* Blood vessels; Heart; Lungs

Circumstantial evidence, famous definitions of, **Vol. 10, Part 1,** 592 f.

Circus, **Vol. 1, Part 1,** 498, 636 f.; **Vol. 3, Part 2,** 522; **Vol. 8, Part 1,** 536 f., 618 f.; art depicting, **Supp. 4,** 289, 463–64; calliope, invention of, **Vol. 9, Part 2,** 57; clowns, **Supp. 6,** 8, 112; Madison Square Garden, **Vol. 1, Part 1,** 638; management, **Vol. 1, Part 1,** 499; publicity for, **Supp. 6,** 536; Tom Thumb, **Vol. 9, Part 2,** 126; wild animal collections, **Supp. 4,** 120; **Supp. 7,** 41–42

Citadel, The (S.C.), presidency, **Supp. 5,** 669

Cities: architecture, **Supp. 6,** 593; Cincinnati model, **Supp. 4,** 247; City Beautiful movement, **Supp. 3,** 533–34; engineering projects, **Supp. 4,** 756; first major social survey of, **Supp. 6,** 329–30; geography studies, **Supp. 4,** 424; historical writings on, **Supp. 7,** 676; housing, **Supp. 5,** 630, 631; medieval, studies of, **Supp. 5,** 655–56; neighborhood unit concept, **Supp. 3,** 601; planning studies, *see* City planning; political reform, **Supp. 6,** 467–68; quality of life in, **Supp. 2,** 374; recreation planning, **Supp. 2,** 375; slum clearance, **Supp. 2,** 684; sociological studies, **Supp. 3,** 578; **Supp. 8,** 398–99. *See also* City planning; Model communities; Municipal government; Zoning; *specific city names*

Cities Service, management of, **Supp. 2,** 154

Citizen Kane, **Supp. 3,** 93; **Supp. 5,** 287–88, 464; **Supp. 6,** 441; **Supp. 7,** 166

Citizens and Southern Bank and Trust Co., founding of, **Supp. 4,** 916

Citizens' Association of Chicago, founding of, **Supp. 1,** 535

Citizens' Federal Research Bureau, founding of, **Supp. 2,** 678

Citizenship: diplomatic protection for aliens, **Supp. 5,** 81; dual, **Vol. 8, Part 2,** 124; for Indians, **Vol. 8, Part 1,** 175 f., 335 f.; literacy tests, **Vol. 5, Part 2,** 32; passport issuance, **Supp. 8,** 590–91; Supreme Court decisons, **Supp. 4,** 727; woman's right of choice, **Supp. 5,** 532

Citizens' Industrial Alliance, **Vol. 8, Part 1,** 112 f.

Citizens Union, founding of, **Supp. 1,** 216

Citizen Training Corps, founding of, **Supp. 2,** 637

Citric acid, first manufacture of, **Vol. 10, Part 1,** 607 f.

Citrus fruit industry, **Vol. 4, Part 1,** 144; **Vol. 8, Part 1,** 145 f.; canker disease, **Supp. 1,** 462; diseases, **Supp. 4,** 862–63

City charters, model for, **Vol. 3, Part 1,** 168

City College. *See* College of the City of New York

City Hall (Philadelphia, Pa.), sculpture, **Supp. 3,** 123

City Missionary Society, **Vol. 5, Part 2,** 54

City of New York, airship, **Vol. 6, Part 1,** 452

City planning, **Vol. 3, Part 1,** 168; **Vol. 3, Part 2,** 323; **Vol. 4, Part 2,** 389; **Vol. 5, Part 1,** 56, 108; **Vol. 6, Part 1,** 167; **Vol. 7, Part 2,** 435; **Vol. 8, Part 1,** 45 f.; **Vol. 8, Part 2,** 36; **Supp. 1,** 311; **Supp. 2,** 158, 490, 738; **Supp. 3,** 51–52, 66, 533–34; **Supp. 6,** 486, 522; Baltimore, **Supp. 4,** 550–51; Boston, 1855, **Vol. 4, Part 2,** 523; first national conference on, **Supp. 5,** 631; New York, **Supp. 4,** 56; Washington, D.C., **Vol. 2, Part 1,** 305; **Vol. 6, Part 1,** 167; **Vol. 8, Part 1,** 647. *See also* Model communities; Zoning

City Planning, founding of, **Supp. 1,** 311

City Temple (London), **Supp. 4,** 628

Civic design, first chair of, **Vol. 8, Part 2,** 37

Civic Federation of Chicago, organization of, **Supp. 2,** 166

Civics. *See* Municipal goverment; Political science

Civil Aeronautics Administration (U.S.), administration of, **Supp. 8,** 709

Civil Aeronautics Board (CAB), **Supp. 6,** 666; chairmanship, **Supp. 7,** 453, 454; predecessor, **Supp. 5,** 444

Civil Air Transport (CAT), **Supp. 6,** 110

Civil defense, World War II, **Supp. 4,** 466; **Supp. 7,** 453, 780

Civil engineering. *See* Engineering, civil

Civil Engineering, founding of, **Supp. 2,** 170

Civilian Conservation Corps (CCC): camps, **Supp. 6,** 429–30; founding of, **Supp. 3,** 652; **Supp. 6,** 411–12

Civil liberties, "clear and present danger" test, **Supp. 3,** 99, 168; **Supp. 6,** 495; **Supp. 7,** 317; congressional support for, **Supp. 5,** 480–81; defendants' rights decisions, **Supp. 3,** 755; free speech issues, **Supp. 6,** 104–5, 651; Jehovah's Witnesses cases, **Supp. 3,** 679; judicial support, **Supp. 7,** 317; legal defense, **Supp. 2,** 534; **Supp. 5,** 280; **Supp. 8,** 18, 35; legislation, **Supp. 4,** 407; National Civil Liberties Bureau, founding of, **Supp. 3,** 604; New Deal policies, **Supp. 5,** 343; New York State judicial decisions, **Supp. 3,** 451; organizations, **Supp. 7,** 510–11; preferred freedoms concept, **Supp. 4,** 796–97; press freedom landmark decision (1941), **Supp. 3,** 157; Scopes trial, **Supp. 6,** 528–29; Supreme Court decisions, **Supp. 4,** 537, 614, 713, 796; **Supp. 5,** 358, 389, 574–75, 714; **Supp. 7,** 96, 263–64, 291, 541–42; World War I issues, **Supp. 4,** 62, 542, 613, 636; **Supp. 7,** 248, 356; World War II issues, **Supp. 3,** 93; **Supp. 4,** 614; writings on, **Supp. 4,** 851; **Supp. 8,** 408

Civil Rights Act (1865), **Vol. 5, Part 2,** 86;

Civil Rights Act (1964), **Supp. 8,** 323, 334

Civil Rights Congress, **Supp. 7,** 315

Civil rights movement: American Indian advocacy, **Supp. 5,** 119–20; black criticism of, **Supp. 8,** 435; black indifference to, **Supp. 6,** 314; **Supp. 8,** 121; black leadership, **Supp. 8,** 332–35; black organizations, **Supp. 8,** 539–40; "black power" advocacy, **Supp. 8,** 335; black professional race-relations training, **Supp. 6,** 284–85; black women in, **Supp. 3,** 827–28; Catholic church involvement, **Supp. 7,** 533; **Supp. 8,** 293–94; Communist support for, **Supp. 5,** 499, 500; congressional support, **Supp. 6,** 636; Democratic 1948 proposals, **Supp. 6,** 710–11; early activism, **Supp. 2,** 315, 346; **Supp. 7,** 155, 201–5; early leadership, **Supp. 5,** 680, 740–41; editorial support, **Supp. 8,** 404–5; federal support, **Supp. 8,** 406; financial support, **Supp. 8,** 88; labor involvement, **Supp. 6,** 648; legal action, **Supp. 4,** 397–98; **Supp. 8,** 285; legislation, **Supp. 4,** 407, 493; **Supp. 7,** 425; **Supp. 8,** 323, 333–34; legislation opposition, **Supp. 8,** 68; martyrs, **Supp. 7,** 227; **Supp. 8,** 335–36; mid-1960s intensification, **Supp. 7,** 319, 425; **Supp. 8,** 333–35; militancy, **Supp. 7,** 508–9; New York State legislation, **Supp. 3,** 391; nonviolence tactics, **Supp. 7,** 781; **Supp. 8,** 86, 332, 333–35, 408, 606; pioneer work in, **Supp. 4,** 493, 850–51; real estate restrictive covenants, **Supp. 6,** 502; religious support, **Supp. 6,** 649; school desegregation, **Supp. 5,** 156; "separate but equal" doctrine, **Supp. 6,** 495, 502; southern, 1930s, **Supp. 6,** 11–12; southern activism, **Supp. 8,** 322–23, 333–35; southern resistance to, **Supp. 8,** 500; southern white advocacy, **Supp. 7,** 235, 788; **Supp. 8,** 682–83; student sit-ins, **Supp. 8,** 86; Supreme Court decisions, **Supp. 4,** 796; **Supp. 5,** 713–14; **Supp. 7,** 96; **Supp. 8,** 406; Truman policies, **Supp. 5,** 479; **Supp. 5,** 515, 741; **Supp. 7,** 748; urban North activism, **Supp. 8,** 335; writings on, **Supp. 8,** 387–88. *See also* Racism; School desegregation; Segregation

Civil service, **Vol. 1, Part 1,** 375; **Vol. 1, Part 2,** 169, 427; **Vol. 2, Part 2,** 616; **Vol. 3, Part 1,** 607 f.; **Vol.** **3, Part 2,** 26; **Vol. 4, Part 1,** 401; **Vol. 4, Part 2,** 192, 333 f., 397, 450; **Vol. 5, Part 1,** 81; **Vol. 5, Part 2,** 41 f.; **Vol. 6, Part 1,** 67; **Vol. 7, Part 2,** 420; **Vol. 8, Part 1,** 241 f.; **Vol. 8, Part 2,** 136, 468 f.; **Vol. 9, Part 2,** 248 f.; **Vol. 10, Part 2,** 46; women in, **Vol. 9, Part 1,** 460; writings on, **Vol. 9, Part 2,** 249

Civil Service Chronicle, **Vol. 9, Part 2,** 249

Civil Service Commission, United States, **Vol. 2, Part 2,** 208; **Vol. 3, Part 2,** 475; **Vol. 4, Part 1,** 135, 604; Loyalty Review Board, **Supp. 6,** 60; professional exams, **Supp. 6,** 690; reforms in, **Supp. 1,** 101, 294, 315. *See also* Government employees

Civil Service Reform Association, **Supp. 1,** 101

Civil service reform (1883), **Vol. 2, Part 2,** 208, 616; **Vol. 3, Part 1,** 607; **Vol. 4, Part 2,** 833; **Vol. 5, Part 1,** 81; **Vol. 5, Part 2,** 41, 260; **Vol. 7, Part 2,** 420, 533; **Vol. 8, Part 2,** 137, 469

Civil War, Spanish. *See* Spanish Civil War

Civil War (U.S.; general): allegiance, divided, **Vol. 3, Part 2,** 403, 410; arbitration, international, resulting from, **Vol. 3, Part 1,** 135; biographical writings on, **Supp. 4,** 490; British, diplomacy, **Vol. 1, Part 1,** 43 f.; **Vol. 7, Part 2,** 520; **Supp. 1,** 9; cartoons, **Vol. 7, Part 1,** 186; chaplain, first black, **Vol. 10, Part 1,** 65; Confederate financial agents, **Supp. 1,** 690; conscientious objectors, **Vol. 8, Part 1,** 236 f.; cotton, **Vol. 1, Part 1,** 45; **Vol. 3, Part 1,** 182, 592 f.; Cuba, **Vol. 4, Part 2,** 513; *De Bow's Review,* **Vol. 3, Part 1,** 181; draft methods, **Vol. 3, Part 2,** 580; **Vol. 5, Part 1,** 129; **Vol. 8, Part 1,** 202 f., 358 f.; events leading to, **Vol. 2, Part 1,** 78; **Vol. 3, Part 1,** 399 f.; **Vol. 8, Part 1,** 34 f.; financing of, **Vol. 2, Part 2,** 383; **Vol. 3, Part 1,** 326; **Vol. 5, Part 1,** 129; **Vol. 8, Part 2,** 572; fort construction, **Supp. 1,** 157; France, diplomacy, **Vol. 1, Part 2,** 259; **Vol. 3, Part 1,** 167; "Frank Leslie's" artists, **Vol. 6, Part 1,** 186; historical writings on, **Supp. 1,** 303; **Supp. 5,** 234–35; **Supp. 5,** 498; Indians, part played by, **Vol. 5, Part 1,** 322; **Vol. 10, Part 1,** 537 f.; journalism, **Vol. 1, Part 2,** 199; **Vol. 4, Part 2,** 259; **Vol. 6, Part 2,** 5, 267; **Vol. 8, Part 1,** 482; **Vol. 9, Part 1,** 409 f.; **Vol. 9, Part 2,** 253; **Vol. 10, Part 1,** 6; **Supp. 1,** 441; Kentucky, early neutrality of, **Vol. 2, Part 1,** 235; **Vol. 8, Part 1,** 39 f., 148 f.; laundries, military, **Vol. 1, Part 2,** 238; legal issues, **Vol. 4, Part 1,** 121; Lincolniana collection, **Supp. 7,** 529–30; Lincoln's Cabinet, **Vol. 3, Part 2,** 568; lithographic sketches, **Vol. 8, Part 2,** 169; Louisiana's attempt to organize as free state, **Vol. 3, Part 1,** 543 f.; "Loyal League," **Vol. 4, Part 1,** 623; Lutheran attitude toward, **Vol. 4, Part 2,** 529; medical care, **Vol. 1, Part 1,** 124, 318, 389, 631; **Vol. 4, Part 1,** 238, 319; **Vol. 5, Part 2,** 439; **Vol. 6, Part 1,** 42, 194, 576; **Vol. 9, Part 1,** 426; **Vol. 10, Part 2,** 492, 509, 607; **Supp. 1,** 364; munitions, **Vol. 1, Part 1,** 248, 269; **Vol. 2, Part 2,** 56; **Vol. 4, Part 1,** 593; **Vol. 7, Part 2,** 45 f.; **Vol. 8, Part 1,** 328 f., 496, 625; **Vol. 8, Part 2,** 303; novels about, **Supp. 4,** 583; **Supp. 5,** 747–48; official records of, **Supp. 1,** 17; Ohio steamboat service during, **Vol. 3, Part 2,** 516; peace, efforts toward, **Vol. 5, Part 2,** 73; **Vol. 9, Part 1,** 191; personal writings on, **Supp. 1,** 418; Peru, diplomatic relations during, **Vol. 8, Part 2,** 38; photographic records of, **Vol. 1, Part 2,** 585; play, first based on, **Vol. 6, Part 1,** 483; political issues, **Vol. 3, Part 1,** 119 f.; **Vol. 4, Part 2,** 534; **Vol. 6, Part 1,** 238; prisons, **Vol. 1, Part 1,** 214; **Vol. 2, Part 1,** 168; **Vol. 5, Part 2,** 603; profiteering, **Vol. 8, Part 2,** 11; Quakers, **Vol. 8, Part 1,** 236 f.; religious movement among Confederate soldiers, **Vol. 7, Part 2,** 424; revisionist historical studies of, **Supp. 5,** 557; sanitation, **Vol. 9, Part 2,** 4; **Vol. 10, Part 2,** 607; songs, **Vol. 8, Part 2,** 148; Spanish sympathy

363, 645 f.; **Vol. 10, Part 1,** 89 f., 585 f.; statue of, **Vol. 4, Part 2,** 358

Clay, Jakob, reference to, **Supp. 7,** 134

Clay, Lucius, reference to, **Supp. 6,** 431

Clayton, Buck, reference to, **Supp. 6,** 300

Clayton, Henry D., reference to, **Supp. 3,** 729

Clayton, John M., reference to, **Vol. 9, Part 2,** 352 f.

Clayton, William L., reference to, **Supp. 7,** 36

Clayton Antitrust Act (1914), **Supp. 2,** 213; **Supp. 5,** 27; **Supp. 6,** 591

Clayton-Bulwer Treaty, **Vol. 1, Part 2,** 328; **Vol. 2, Part 1,** 211, 564; **Vol. 2, Part 2,** 186; **Vol. 3, Part 1,** 39; **Vol. 7, Part 2,** 578; **Vol. 9, Part 2,** 353

Clearing, the, founding of, **Supp. 5,** 370

Clemens, Samuel L. *See* Twain, Mark

Clements Library of American History, **Supp. 5,** 9–10

Clemson, Thomas Green, reference to, **Vol. 9, Part 2,** 547

Clemson College, **Vol. 2, Part 2,** 201; **Vol. 9, Part 2,** 548

Cleopatra, **Supp. 8,** 678

"Cleopatra's Needle" (N.Y.), **Vol. 3, Part 1,** 377; **Vol. 3, Part 2,** 276; **Vol. 4, Part 1,** 437

Clergue, Francis H., reference to, **Supp. 3,** 534

Clergy. For complete list, *see* Occupations Index

Clermont, **Vol. 4, Part 1,** 71; **Vol. 8, Part 2,** 106

"C" Letters, **Vol 9, Part 2,** 604

Cleveland, Frank E., reference to, **Supp. 3,** 196

Cleveland, Grover: biography of, **Supp. 6,** 410; references to, **Vol. 2, Part 1,** 199, 495; **Vol. 5, Part 1,** 28, 85; **Vol. 6, Part 2,** 249; **Vol. 7, Part 1,** 176; **Vol. 7, Part 2,** 32 f.; **Vol. 8, Part 2,** 450, 520; **Vol. 9, Part 1,** 281, 598, 629; **Vol. 9, Part 2,** 548; **Supp. 1,** 459; **Supp. 5,** 518; election, news reports of, **Vol. 6, Part 1,** 283; Hawaii, opposition to annexation of, **Vol. 3, Part 1,** 358 f.; monetary adviser to, **Vol. 9, Part 2,** 129; nomination of, **Vol. 3, Part 1,** 388

Cleveland, Ohio: financial history, **Vol. 6, Part 2,** 397; founding of, **Vol. 5, Part 2,** 296; history and growth, **Vol. 2, Part 1,** 557; industrial history, **Vol. 5, Part 2,** 297; **Vol. 6, Part 2,** 398; medical college, **Vol. 5, Part 2,** 438; municipal facilities improvements, **Supp. 2,** 17; municipal government, **Supp. 7,** 95; Museum of Natural History, **Vol. 5, Part 2,** 439; orphanage, **Vol. 7, Part 2,** 407; philanthropy, **Vol. 2, Part 1,** 558; politics, **Supp. 3,** 167–68; public service, **Vol. 5, Part 1,** 137; **Vol. 5, Part 2,** 123 f.; **Vol. 7, Part 2,** 325 f.; railroads, financing of, by city, **Vol. 3, Part 1,** 262; Roman Catholic diocese, **Supp. 3,** 694–95

Cleveland Blues (baseball), **Supp. 6,** 356

Cleveland Citizen, **Supp. 3,** 347

Cleveland Clinic Foundation, founding of, **Supp. 4,** 508

Cleveland Heights, Ohio, **Supp. 3,** 126

Cleveland Indians (baseball), **Supp. 6,** 589

Cleveland Institute of Music, **Supp. 6,** 62

Cleveland Municipal Association, **Supp. 3,** 292

Cleveland Museum of Art, founding of, **Supp. 1,** 695

Cleveland Naps (baseball), **Supp. 6,** 356–57

Cleveland Orchestra, **Supp. 6,** 550; **Supp. 8,** 642

Cleveland Plain Dealer, **Vol. 5, Part 1,** 137

Cliburn, Van, reference to, **Supp. 7,** 512

Cliff-dwelling materials, collecting of, **Vol. 8, Part 1,** 252 f.

Clifford, Clark, reference to, **Supp. 5,** 515;

Clifton Springs Sanitarium, **Vol. 7, Part 1,** 324

Climatology, **Vol. 1, Part 2,** 379; **Vol. 2, Part 2,** 27, 267; **Vol. 3, Part 1,** 394, 427, 507 f.; **Vol. 3, Part 2,** 160, 185, 338; **Vol. 4, Part 2,** 64, 301, 477; **Vol. 6, Part 1,** 287, 367, 452; **Vol. 7, Part 2,** 454; **Vol. 8, Part 1,** 441 f., 573; **Vol. 8, Part 2,** 184; **Vol. 10, Part**

1, 594 f.; hurricanes, study of, **Vol. 8, Part 1,** 441 f.; professorship, first in U.S., **Vol. 10, Part 1,** 436; rain-making, experiments in, **Vol. 8, Part 1,** 112 f.; Weather Bureau, U.S., establishment of, **Vol. 3, Part 1,** 149; wind measurement, **Vol. 5, Part 1,** 252; **Vol. 7, Part 1,** 526; writings on, **Vol. 2, Part 1,** 367; **Vol. 10, Part 1,** 436. *See also* Meteorology; Weather

Clinton, DeWitt: references to, **Vol. 5, Part 1,** 356; **Vol. 9, Part 1,** 444; writings on, **Supp. 2,** 399

Clinton, George, references to, **Vol. 7, Part 1,** 210, 364; **Vol. 9, Part 1,** 320

Clinton, Henry reference to, **Vol. 7, Part 1,** 106

Clinton, Mass., development of, **Vol. 1, Part 2,** 255

Clinton, N.Y., **Vol. 3, Part 1,** 563

Clipper ships. *See* Ships, clipper

Clocks and watches: astronomic, **Vol. 3, Part 2,** 489; "grandfather," **Vol. 9, Part 2,** 394; manufacture of, **Vol. 1, Part 2,** 407; **Vol. 2, Part 1,** 144, 442; **Vol. 3, Part 2,** 166, 489; **Vol. 4, Part 1,** 272; **Vol. 4, Part 2,** 275; **Vol. 5, Part 2,** 58; **Vol. 8, Part 1,** 101 f., 631; **Vol. 9, Part 2,** 380 f., 445; **Vol. 10, Part 2,** 240; synchronous electrical clock, **Vol. 9, Part 2,** 394; **Supp. 6,** 668–69; writings on, **Vol. 5, Part 2,** 58

Cloete, Stuart, reference to, **Supp. 6,** 251

Cloisters (New York City): landscape architecture for, **Supp. 6,** 486; medieval art collection, **Supp. 6,** 549; opening of, **Supp. 4,** 902; planning and building of, **Supp. 2,** 22; **Supp. 8,** 545

Clorindy: The Origin of the Cakewalk (musical), **Supp. 3,** 834

"Closed shop," 1810, **Vol. 8, Part 2,** 321

Clothing manufacture, **Vol. 6, Part 1,** 513; **Vol. 7, Part 1,** 384 f.; **Vol. 7, Part 2,** 45; **Vol. 9, Part 1,** 208; gloves, **Supp. 3,** 463–64; health and sanitation, **Supp. 3,** 609–10; sport shoes, **Supp. 8,** 28; strike (1910), **Supp. 3,** 96; Triangle Shirtwaist fire, **Supp. 5,** 718; unionization, **Supp. 1,** 403; **Supp. 4,** 69, 375–76; **Supp. 5,** 95; **Supp. 7,** 801. *See also* Fashion

Cloud seeding, **Supp. 6,** 364, 365

Clover Leaf Newspapers, **Supp. 4,** 132

Clowns, circus, **Vol. 3, Part 2,** 522; **Vol. 8, Part 1,** 536 f.; **Supp. 6,** 8, 112; paintings of, **Supp. 4,** 463–64

Clubs, group process concept, **Supp. 7,** 151

Cluett, Peabody and Co., **Supp. 5,** 428; **Supp. 8,** 97

Clurman, Harold, reference to, **Supp. 5,** 10

Clutch, automotive, **Supp. 6,** 67

Coal: anthracite, use of, **Vol. 7, Part 1,** 23; by-products, **Supp. 5,** 556; classification of, **Supp. 1,** 703; coke, use of, **Vol. 4, Part 1,** 29 f.; **Vol. 9, Part 1,** 124 f.; **Vol. 10, Part 1,** 400 f.; gas, first use of, for illumination, **Vol. 6, Part 2,** 520; mapping of, **Supp. 2,** 90; stove, invention of, **Vol. 2, Part 2,** 110

Coal Conservation Act, unconstitutionality of, **Supp. 5,** 573

Coal industry, **Vol, 8, Part 1,** 170; **Vol. 10, Part 1,** 465 f.; conveyors in, **Vol. 2, Part 1,** 103; distribution, **Vol. 7, Part 2,** 20; Ludlow massacre, **Supp. 2,** 124; mine ownership, **Supp. 2,** 38; mining, **Vol. 1, Part 2,** 338; **Vol. 2, Part 1,** 160; **Vol. 2, Part 2,** 108, 110; **Vol. 3, Part 1,** 179, 306; **Vol. 3, Part 2,** 47, 84, 459; **Vol. 4, Part 1,** 9, 136, 418; **Vol. 4, Part 2,** 226; **Vol. 5, Part 1,** 238, 383; **Vol. 6, Part 1,** 79, 189; **Vol. 7, Part 2,** 305, 330; **Vol. 8, Part 1,** 170; **Vol. 8, Part 2,** 48, 189, 504; **Vol. 9, Part 1,** 124 f., 273; mining machinery, manufacture of, **Supp. 5, Part 2,** 36; mining safety, **Supp. 4,** 690; mining technology, **Supp. 5,** 556; strikes, **Vol. 1, Part 1,** 260; surveys, **Vol. 6, Part 1,** 189; **Vol. 9, Part 2,** 341; unionization, **Supp. 5,** 282–83; **Supp. 7,** 81–82; **Supp. 8,** 374–77

Coast and Geodetic Survey, United States, **Vol. 1, Part 1,** 1, 119, 169, 461 f.; **Vol. 1, Part 2,** 342; **Vol.**

3, **Part 2**, 64; **Vol. 4, Part 1**, 481; **Vol. 4, Part 2**, 385, 452; **Vol. 5, Part 1**, 23, 303; **Vol. 5, Part 2**, 167, 256; **Vol. 6, Part 1**, 272, 553; **Vol. 6, Part 2**, 531; **Vol. 7, Part 1**, 47, 640; **Vol. 7, Part 2**, 395, 399 f.; **Vol. 8, Part 1**, 617; **Vol. 8, Part 2**, 400, 459; **Vol. 9, Part 1**, 156; **Vol. 9, Part 2**, 656; nonmagnetic observatories, **Supp. 6**, 205

Coast defenses, **Vol. 1, Part 2**, 223; **Vol. 2, Part 2**, 222; **Vol. 3, Part 1**, 210; **Vol. 3, Part 2**, 159; **Vol. 6, Part 2**, 160; **Vol. 7, Part 2**, 160, 610; **Vol. 9, Part 2**, 608

Coast Guard, United States, **Vol. 6, Part 1**, 545; arctic oceanographic studies, **Supp. 7**, 698–99; establishment of, **Vol. 5, Part 2**, 379; **Supp. 2**, 123; **Supp. 4**, 854; *Tars and Spars* revue, **Supp. 8**, 145–6

Cobb, Ty, references to, **Supp. 3**, 438; **Supp. 5**, 291–92; **Supp. 6**, 356–57, 589; **Supp. 7**, 139; **Supp. 8**, 106

Cobbett, William, references to, **Vol. 1, Part 2**, 559; **Vol. 7, Part 1**, 614

Cobbling, **Vol. 9, Part 1**, 88

Coca-Cola, manufacture of, **Vol. 2, Part 1**, 471

Cocaine, **Vol. 4, Part 2**, 165; **Vol. 5, Part 1**, 625; as anesthetic, **Supp. 3**, 430–31

Cochran, Welker, reference to, **Supp. 6**, 304

Cochran, William F., reference to, **Supp. 3**, 734

"Cockrell's Brigade," **Vol. 2, Part 2**, 257

Cockcroft, John D., reference to, **Supp. 8**, 199

Cockran, Bourke, reference to, **Supp. 3**, 532

Cocktail Party, The, **Supp. 7**, 222

Cocoa, manufacture of, **Vol. 7, Part 2**, 582

Cocoanuts, The, **Supp. 7**, 515

Codes and ciphers. *See* Cryptology

Cody, "Buffalo Bill," origin of nickname, **Vol. 5, Part 2**, 238; references to, **Vol. 2, Part 2**, 260 f., 522 f.; **Vol. 5, Part 1**, 480, 483; **Vol. 5, Part 2**, 238; **Vol. 7, Part 1**, 603 f.; **Supp. 3**, 460

Coe, George, reference to, **Supp. 4**, 766

Coe College (Iowa), **Vol. 6, Part 1**, 613; **Vol. 6, Part 2**, 295

Coeducation. *See* Education

Coffin, Charles, reference to, **Supp. 3**, 527

Coffin, Howard E., reference to, **Supp. 2**, 102

Cognitive psychology. *See* Learning, theory

Cohan, George M., references to, **Supp. 3**, 333; **Supp. 5**, 524

Cohen, Benjmain V., reference to, **Supp. 7**, 263

Cohen, Felix S., reference to, **Supp. 8**, 99

Cohens v. Virginia, **Vol. 7, Part 1**, 638 f.

Cohn, Edwin J., references to, **Supp. 3**, 350; **Supp. 4**, 581

Cohn, Roy, McCarthy hearings, **Supp. 6**, 405, 680

Coils, electric, **Vol. 4, Part 2**, 551

Coinage, **Vol. 3, Part 1**, 533 f.; **Vol. 6, Part 1**, 273; **Vol. 8, Part 1**, 49 f.; **Vol. 9, Part 2**, 94; buffalo nickel design, **Supp. 5**, 231; changes in, **Vol. 8, Part 2**, 301; collecting of coins, **Vol. 1, Part 2**, 173; collections of Greek and Roman, **Supp. 3**, 551; designs on early, **Vol. 6, Part 1**, 381; free, **Vol. 1, Part 2**, 355; free silver, **Supp. 2**, 289; **Supp. 5**, 381; gold, first, **Vol. 3, Part 1**, 254; Liberty head dime, **Supp. 5**, 659; Liberty quarter design, **Supp. 4**, 534; pine tree shilling, **Vol. 6, Part 1**, 363; writings on, **Supp. 3**, 551, 564

"Coin's Financial School," **Vol. 7, Part 1**, 533

Coit, Margaret L., reference to, **Supp. 7**, 37

Coke, use of, **Vol. 4, Part 1**, 29 f.; **Vol. 9, Part 1**, 124 f.; **Vol. 10, Part 1**, 400 f.

Coker College, **IVol. 3, Part 1**, 281

Cokesbury College, **Vol. 3, Part 1**, 293

Colbert, Claudette, reference to, **Supp. 6**, 225

Colby College, **Vol. 2, Part 2**, 15, 285; **Vol. 6, Part 2**, 558; **Vol. 8, Part 2**, 32, 114; **Vol. 9, Part 1**, 221

Cold Harbor, Va., attack at, **Vol. 1, Part 1**, 273; **Vol. 4, Part 1**, 496 f.; **Vol. 6, Part 1**, 127; **Vol. 6, Part 2**, 349

Cold storage, **Vol. 8, Part 1**, 145 f.

Cold Spring Harbor (Long Island, N.Y.), **Supp. 3**, 215–16; **Supp. 3**, 445–46, 477–78

Cold war: China policy, **Supp. 6**, 231; containment policy, **Supp. 4**, 306; Eisenhower administration policies, **Supp. 8**, 157–60; hard-line policy, **Supp. 6**, 178–79; McCarthyism, *see* Loyalty issues; nuclear policies, **Supp. 7**, 565; **Supp. 8**, 230–31; propaganda, **Supp. 7**, 438; **Supp. 8**, 6–7; term coined, **Supp. 6**, 617; Truman administration policies, **Supp. 6**, 374, 431–32; Truman-Wallace split over, **Supp. 7**, 762–63; U.S. intelligence activities, **Supp. 8**, 147; U.S. policies, opposition to, **Supp. 4**, 147; **Supp. 5**, 675, 677; U.S.-Soviet confrontations, **Supp. 7**, 423–44, 426. *See also* Korean War; Loyalty issues; Soviet Union

Colds, cause studies, **Supp. 7**, 194

Cole, Frank N., references to, **Vol. 10, Part 1**, 655 f. **Supp. 5**, 491

Cole, Rufus, reference to, **Supp. 6**, 546

Cole, Thomas, reference to, **Vol. 2, Part 2**, 101

Coleman, A. P., reference to, **Supp. 6**, 143

Coleman, Charles Caryl, reference to, **Supp. 3**, 573

Coleman, George W., reference to, **Supp. 5**, 515

Coleman, William, reference to, **Vol. 10, Part 1**, 642 f.

Coleoptera, collection of, **Vol. 4, Part 1**, 54; **Vol. 5, Part 1**, 329; **Vol. 8, Part 2**, 481

Coleridge, Samuel Taylor, scholarship on, **Supp. 3**, 475

Colfax, Schuyler, reference to, **Vol. 9, Part 2**, 334

Colgate University, **Vol. 2, Part 2**, 299; **Vol. 6, Part 2**, 559; **Vol. 8, Part 1**, 412

Coll, Vincent ("Mad Dog"), reference to, **Supp. 7**, 5

Collages, **Supp. 4**, 774

Collars, detachable, **Vol. 2, Part 1**, 112

Collections: Acadians, material on, **Vol. 5, Part 2**, 370; American antiques, **Supp. 3**, 567; **Supp. 6**, 562; American Indian artifacts, **Supp. 6**, 289–90; Americana, **Vol. 3, Part 2**, 514; **Vol. 6, Part 1**, 157; **Supp. 1**, 139, 154, 180; archaeological specimens, **Vol. 2, Part 2**, 168; architectural writings, **Supp. 4**, 116; armor, **Vol. 8, Part 1**, 606; art, **Vol. 1, Part 1**, 232; **Vol. 1, Part 2**, 170; **Vol. 3, Part 2**, 84, 354; **Vol. 4, Part 1**, 14, 143; **Vol. 4, Part 2**, 53, 55; **Vol. 5, Part 1**, 618 f; **Vol. 5, Part 2**, 106 f., 142 f., 411; **Vol. 6, Part 1**, 210 f., 233; **Vol. 8, Part 1**, 157 f.; **Vol. 10, Part 1**, 399f; **Supp. 1**, 337; **Supp. 3**, 24; **Supp. 4**, 174–75, 696–97; **Supp. 5**, 39, 401; **Supp. 7**, 161–62, 466; **Supp. 8**, 367–68; art, American, **Supp. 4**, 290; art, Byzantine, **Supp. 5**, 700; **Supp. 7**, 60; art, French, **Supp. 5**, 150–51; art, Indian and Islamic, **Supp. 4**, 177; art, modern, **Supp. 4**, 351–52, 768, 771; **Supp. 5**, 20, 184–85, 427; **Supp. 7**, 294; art, portrait paintings, **Supp. 1**, 178; as a hobby, discussion of, **Vol. 2, Part 1**, 318; autographs, **Vol. 3, Part 2**, 147; **Vol. 5, Part 1**, 445; **Vol. 5, Part 2**, 156; **Vol. 9, Part 1**, 476; **Vol. 9, Part 2**, 432; ballads, **Vol. 9, Part 1**, 245 f.; Bermudiana, **Supp. 2**, 111; Bibles, **Vol. 6, Part 1**, 172, 305; **Vol. 8, Part 1**, 298; birds, **Vol. 1, Part 1**, 513; **Vol. 3, Part 2**, 91; **Vol. 4, Part 2**, 564; **Vol. 4, Part 1**, 385; black folk songs, **Supp. 4**, 476–77, 502; black literature, **Supp. 1**, 717; books, **Vol. 1, Part 2**, 173; **Vol. 2, Part 1**, 137; **Vol. 3, Part 2**, 158, 363, 407, 419; **Vol. 4, Part 1**, 561; **Vol. 4, Part 2**, 305; **Vol. 5, Part 1**, 445; **Vol. 5, Part 2**, 155 f., 174 f.; **Vol. 6, Part 1**, 110, 308; **Vol. 6, Part 2**, 97; **Vol. 8, Part 1**, 232 f.; **Vol. 9, Part 1**, 256; **Vol.**

9, **Part 2,** 586; **Vol. 10, Part 1,** 443; **Vol. 10, Part 2,** 185; botanical specimens, **Vol. 8, Part 1,** 104 f., 236 f.; botany writings, **Supp. 2,** 390; butterflies, **Vol. 3, Part 2,** 46 f.; **Vol. 3, Part 2,** 525 f.; **Supp. 1,** 414; Catholic publications, **Vol. 3, Part 2,** 396; chemistry books, **Supp. 1,** 431; children's books, **Vol. 8, Part 1,** 51 f.; children's sayings, **Vol. 8, Part 1,** 183 f.; cliff-dwelling materials, **Vol. 8, Part 1,** 252 f.; coins, **Vol. 1, Part 2,** 173; coins, ancient Greek and Roman, **Supp. 3,** 551; coleoptera, **Vol. 4, Part 1,** 54; **Vol. 5, Part 1,** 329; **Vol. 8, Part 2,** 481; criminology writings, **Supp. 2,** 522–23; economic writings, **Supp. 2,** 607; educational historical writings, **Supp. 2,** 532; Egyptology, **Supp. 4,** 900–1; electricity writings, **Supp. 2,** 38; elements, specimens of, **Supp. 1,** 477; English common law, **Supp. 1,** 154; engravings, **Vol. 9, Part 1,** 538; fishes, **Vol. 9, Part 2,** 94; flints, **Vol. 3, Part 2,** 161; flutes, **Supp. 3,** 524; folk songs, **Supp. 1,** 651; **Supp. 8,** 564; French Revolution, publications on, **Vol. 10, Part 1,** 570 f.; fungi, **Vol. 3, Part 2,** 105; **Vol. 8, Part 1,** 396; **Supp. 3,** 815; furniture, period, **Vol. 6, Part 1,** 210 f.; gall wasp, **Supp. 6,** 342; glass flowers, **Vol. 4, Part 1,** 378; glassware, Stiegel, **Vol. 9, Part 2,** 17; historical source material, **Vol. 10, Part 1,** 566 f.; human crania, **Vol. 8, Part 1,** 152, f.; hymns, **Vol. 4, Part 2,** 387; **Vol. 5, Part 1,** 186; **Vol. 6, Part 1,** 530; illustrated works, **Vol. 5, Part 1,** 445; **Vol. 8, Part 1,** 228 f.; incunabula, **Vol. 4, Part 2,** 415; legal decision, **Vol. 8, Part 1,** 439; Lincolniana, **Supp. 2,** 318; **Supp. 7, 529, 530;** magic, apparatus relating to, **Vol. 5, Part 1,** 249; manuscripts, **Vol. 3, Part 2,** 519; **Supp. 4,** 5, 345; **Supp. 5,** 349–50; maps, **Vol. 6, Part 1,** 471; Marshall's legal writings, **Vol. 3, Part 1,** 311; masks, portrait, **Vol. 5, Part 1,** 445; Masonry, **Vol. 9, Part 2,** 389; mathematical writings, **Supp. 3,** 722; medical journals, **Vol. 8, Part 1,** 269 f.; medicinal plants, **Supp. 2,** 591; medieval armor, **Supp. 2,** 415; meteorites, **Vol. 9, Part 1,** 71, 304; **Vol. 10, Part 1,** 421 f.; minerals, **Vol. 1, Part 1,** 248; **Vol. 1, Part 2,** 173; **Vol. 4, Part 1,** 245; **Vol. 6, Part 1,** 71; **Vol. 8, Part 2,** 90; **Vol. 9, Part 1,** 262; **Vol. 9, Part 2,** 629; mollusks, **Vol. 6, Part 1,** 71; Morrisiana, **Vol. 7, Part 1,** 213 f., 218 f., 224, f.; music, **Supp. 2,** 8; music, black, **Vol. 2, Part 1,** 288; **Vol. 5, Part 2,** 505; music, Indian, **Vol. 2, Part 1,** 288, 342; musical instruments, **Vol. 9, Part 1,** 563; natural science, in field of, **Vol. 6, Part 1,** 71; newspapers and pamphlets, Revolutionary period, **Vol. 3, Part 1,** 553 f.; **Vol. 3, Part 2,** 519; orchids, **Supp. 4,** 16–17; paintings, **Vol. 3, Part 2,** 158, 407, 535, 437; **Vol. 8, Part 1,** 493; periodicals, early, **Vol. 6, Part 1,** 110; petrographic, **Supp. 4,** 194; pharmacological writings, **Supp. 2,** 390; phonograph records, **Vol. 7, Part 1,** 136 f.; plants, **Vol. 8, Part 2,** 484; poetry, American, **Vol. 4, Part 1,** 561; **Vol. 4, Part 2,** 305; porcelain, **Vol. 3, Part 2,** 435; **Vol. 6, Part 1,** 210; **Vol. 8, Part 1,** 228 f.; postcards, **Supp. 2,** 112; pottery, **Vol. 3, Part 2,** 161, 435; **Vol. 6, Part 1,** 210; prints, **Vol. 3, Part 2,** 147, 519; **Vol. 9, Part 1,** 256; Quakeriana, **Supp. 1,** 463; rare books, **Supp. 4,** 5; **Supp. 5,** 586–87; **Supp. 7,** 2–3, 295, 387, 547; rare books on ophthalmology, **Supp. 3,** 836; relics, **Vol. 6, Part 1,** 502; scientific materials, **Vol. 10, Part 1,** 421 f.; sermons, **Vol. 1, Part 1,** 501; Shakespeariana, **Vol. 3, Part 2,** 487; **Vol. 9, Part 1,** 372; **Vol. 9, Part 2,** 432; shells, **Vol. 3, Part 2,** 269; **Vol. 6, Part 1,** 71; **Vol. 8, Part 1,** 192, 394 f.; **Vol. 9, Part 2,** 94; silver, old, **Vol. 6, Part 1,** 210; songs, **Vol. 5, Part 2,** 101; synagogic music, **Vol. 5, Part 2,** 251; tapestries, **Vol. 6, Part 1,** 210; tracts, historical, **Vol. 3, Part 2,** 512; transportation, early models, **Vol 10, Part 1,** 539; tree

specimens, **Supp. 3,** 621; Washingtonia, **Vol. 8, Part 1,** 51 f.; wild animals, **Supp. 4,** 120; Wisconsin historical material concerning, **Vol. 3, Part 1,** 551 f.; women writers' works, **Supp. 6,** 576; woodcuts, **Vol. 8, Part 1,** 228 f.; zoological specimens, **Vol. 6, Part 1,** 190; **Supp. 3,** 667–69. *See also* Archives; Art; Libraries and library work; Museums; *specific museums*

College: administration, **Vol. 3, Part 2,** 71, 300, 317, 386, 496, 540; **Vol. 4, Part 2,** 96, 288 f., 376, 384 f., 406 f., 409, 453; **Vol. 5, Part 1,** 153; **Vol. 6, Part 1,** 106, 278, 280, 290, 303, 328; **Vol. 8, Part 2,** 17, 32, 43, 97, 346; **Vol. 9, Part 2,** 392, 479; admission, **Vol. 3, Part 2,** 74; **Vol. 10, Part 1,** 537; architecture, **Vol. 9, Part 1,** 335; black graduate, first, **Vol. 8, Part 2,** 253; fraternity, first national, **Vol. 8, Part 2,** 176; municipal, first in U.S., **Vol. 7, Part 2,** 617

College Association of Pennsylvania, **Vol. 7, Part 2,** 455

College Entrance Examination Board, founding of, **Supp. 4,** 134

College Equal Suffrage League, founding of, **Supp. 5,** 532

College of Agriculture and Mechanics (Ohio), **Vol. 7, Part 2,** 62 f.

College of California, **Vol. 3, Part 1,** 540 f.

College of Charleston, **Vol. 6, Part 2,** 602; **Vol. 9, Part 1,** 336

College of Medicine of Maryland, **Vol. 3, Part 1,** 91

College of Music, Cincinnati (Ohio), **Vol. 7, Part 1,** 494; **Vol. 9, Part 1,** 483

College of New Jersey. *See* Princeton University

College of New Rochelle (N.Y.), architecture of, **Supp. 6,** 272

College of Pharmacy of the City of New York, **Vol. 6, Part 1,** 49

College of Philadelphia, **Vol. 5, Part 1,** 220; **Vol. 5, Part 2,** 4; **Vol. 9, Part 1,** 354 f.

College of Physicians (Philadelphia), **Vol. 2, Part 2,** 96; **Vol. 8, Part 1,** 443

College of Physicians and Surgeons (New York City), **Vol. 3, Part 2,** 581; **Vol. 7, Part 2,** 242; **Vol. 8, Part 1,** 121; **Vol. 8, Part 2,** 127; **Vol. 9, Part 1,** 606

College of St. Francis Xavier, **Vol. 5, Part 2,** 616

College of St. James, **Vol. 5, Part 2,** 354

College of the City of New York, **Vol. 1, Part 2,** 177; **Vol. 6, Part 2,** 589; **Vol. 8, Part 1,** 500; **Vol. 9, Part 1,** 72; founded with free tuition, **Vol. 4, Part 2,** 324; Museum of, **Vol. 5, Part 2,** 142; philosophy and psychology studies, **Supp. 8,** 488; philosophy studies, **Supp. 2,** 168; presidency, **Supp. 2,** 185

College of the Fathers of the Precious Blood, **Vol. 8, Part 1,** 266f

College of the Pacific (Stockton, Calif.), football team, **Supp. 7,** 713

College of William and Mary, **Vol. 2, Part 1,** 440; **Vol. 3, Part 1,** 266; **Vol. 8, Part 1,** 371 f.; **Vol. 9, Part 2,** 34; founding of, **Vol. 1, Part 2,** 335; **Vol. 7, Part 1,** 500; presidency, **Vol. 1, Part 2,** 335; **Vol. 3, Part 2,** 228 f.; **Vol. 5, Part 1,** 235; **Vol. 5, Part 2,** 75; **Vol. 9, Part 1,** 297; **Supp. 1,** 164; **Supp. 3,** 115–16; reorganization after Revolutionary War, **Vol. 6, Part 2,** 183; restoration of, **Supp. 1,** 164; Thomas Jefferson and, **Vol. 5, Part 2,** 32

College Settlements Association, founding of, **Supp. 5,** 616

Colleges and universities. *See* Universities and colleges; *specific institutions*

Collegiate Institute (New York City), **Vol. 3, Part 1,** 268

Collier, John, references to, **Supp. 4,** 238; **Supp. 5,** 342; **Supp. 7,** 122, 393, 486

Collier, Robert J., reference to, **Supp. 5**, 666–67
Collier's, **Supp. 7**, 643; cartoons, **Supp. 3**, 300–1; cover art, **Supp. 5**, 428
Collier's Weekly, **Vol. 2, Part 2**, 305; **Supp. 3**, 96; **Supp. 5**, 666–67
Colliery Engineer, founding of, **Supp. 2**, 200
Collins, Eddie, reference to, **Supp. 8**, 713
Collins, Frank S., reference to, **Supp. 3**, 703
Collins, Joseph, reference to, **Supp. 4**, 249
Collinson, Peter, celebrated correspondence with, **Vol. 1, Part 2**, 26
Collodion, making of, **Vol. 3, Part 1**, 329
Colloids, **Supp. 4**, 743–44; **Supp. 5**, 36
Collyer, Robert, **Vol. 6, Part 1**, 573
Colman, Samuel, **Vol. 9, Part 2**, 534
Colombia: cultural exchange, **Supp. 5**, 89; diplomacy with U.S., **Vol. 1, Part 1**, 271; **Vol. 8, Part 2**, 520; **Vol. 9, Part 2**, 570; **Supp. 6**, 556, 557
Colonel Carter of Cartersville, **Vol. 9, Part 1**, 266
Colonel Crockett's Exploits and Adventures in Texas, authorship of, **Vol. 9, Part 1**, 334
Colonial period: administration, **Vol. 2, Part 2**, 419; **Vol. 3, Part 1**, 316 f.,; **Vol. 3, Part 2**, 16, 204, 301, 329 f., 438, 506, 584; **Vol. 4, Part 1**, 119 f., 138; **Vol. 5, Part 1**, 604; **Vol. 5, Part 2**, 111, 116 f.; **Vol. 7, Part 1**, 573; **Vol. 8, Part 1**, 356 f.; **Vol. 8, Part 2**, 549, 611; **Vol. 9, Part 1**, 587; agents, **Supp. 1**, 467–68; architectural preservation and restoration, **Supp. 4**, 24, 115, 696; **Supp. 5**, 388; chronicles, **Vol. 5, Part 2**, 95; church, **Vol. 6, Part 2**, 167; **Vol. 8, Part 2**, 75; **Vol. 10, Part 2**, 237; commerce, **Vol. 4, Part 2**, 379; **Vol. 6, Part 1**, 215; **Vol. 8, Part 2**, 406; **Vol. 10, Part 2**, 30; furniture reproduction, **Supp. 3**, 567; governors, **Supp. 1**, 304, 380; historical bibliographies, **Supp. 1**, 375; historical view of, **Supp. 3**, 15–16; historical writings on, **Supp. 4**, 848; **Supp. 8**, 552; Jewish commerce in, **Supp. 1**, 473; land patents, **Vol. 5, Part 1**, 80; lawmaking, **Vol. 4, Part 2**, 549; **Vol. 6, Part 1**, 493; poetry, **Vol. 7, Part 1**, 602 f.; population of, estimate of, **Vol. 3, Part 1**, 277; pre-Revolutionary activities, **Vol. 1, Part 2**, 468; **Vol. 3, Part 1**, 173 f., 299 f.; **Vol. 4, Part 1**, 438; **Vol. 7, Part 1**, 267; press, political importance of, in, **Vol. 3, Part 1**, 212; Puritanism studies, **Supp. 7**, 538; reports on, **Vol. 8, Part 1**, 356 f.; social historical writings on, **Supp. 8**, 692, 693; writings on, **Vol. 8, Part 2**, 126f; **Vol. 10, Part 1**, 93, 104; **Vol. 10, Part 2**, 476
Colonization (general): American Colonization Society, **Vol. 2, Part 2**, 540; **Vol. 4, Part 2**, 56, 286, 524; **Vol. 5, Part 2**, 98, 204; **Vol. 6, Part 1**, 163; **Vol. 8, Part 2**, 10; **Vol. 9, Part 1**, 288, 330; **Vol. 9, Part 2**, 506, 623; **Vol. 10, Part 1**, 508 f.; blacks, **Vol. 4, Part 2**, 56; **Vol. 5, Part 2**, 12; **Vol. 6, Part 1**, 28; **Vol. 6, Part 2**, 545; **Vol. 7, Part 2**, 487; **Vol. 8, Part 2**, 349; **Vol. 9, Part 2**, 393; French, **Vol. 8, Part 1**, 533 f.; London Co., **Vol. 3, Part 1**, 34; "military adventurers," **Vol. 6, Part 1**, 517; Swiss exiles, **Vol. 4, Part 1**, 468; **Vol. 5, Part 2**, 117, 491; writings on, **Vol. 8, Part 1**, 270 f.
Colonization (by state): Florida, **Vol. 10, Part 1**, 55; Louisiana, **Vol. 5, Part 2**, 453; Maine, **Vol. 10, Part 2**, 397; New Jersey, **Vol. 9, Part 2**, 48; New Mexico, **Vol. 5, Part 2**, 554; New York, **Vol. 3, Part 1**, 265; North Carolina, **Vol. 1, Part 1**, 239; **Vol. 4, Part 1**, 468; **Vol. 10, Part 2**, 110; Pennsylvania, **Vol. 5, Part 2**, 47; **Vol. 10, Part 2**, 32; South Carolina, **Vol. 2, Part 1**, 252; **Vol. 10, Part 2**, 11; Utah, **Vol. 6, Part 1**, 115; **Vol. 9, Part 1**, 386; **Vol. 10, Part 2**, 621; Vermont, **Vol. 7, Part 2**, 148; Virginia, **Vol. 3, Part 1**, 34; **Vol. 4, Part 1**, 190; **Vol. 5, Part 2**, 581; **Vol. 8, Part 2**, 117; **Vol. 10, Part 2**, 9, 80, 110, 388, 574

Colony Club (New York City), **Supp. 4**, 229; founding of, **Supp. 5**, 505; **Supp. 8**, 243
Colophon: A Book Collector's Quarterly, founding of, **Supp. 1**, 288; **Supp. 7**, 3
Color, nomenclature for, established, **Vol. 8, Part 1**, 598; photography, **Vol. 9, Part 2**, 647; reproduction of, **Vol. 8, Part 1**, 287 f.
Colorado: agriculture, **Vol. 3, Part 1**, 606; botany in, **Vol. 7, Part 2**, 262; business, **Vol. 9, Part 1**, 57; coal strikes, **Vol. 1, Part 1**, 260; **Vol. 5, Part 2**, 196; education, **Vol. 4, Part 1**, 459; **Vol. 10, Part 1**, 619 f.; finance, **Vol. 9, Part 2**, 395; gold mining, **Vol. 3, Part 1**, 210; **Vol. 4, Part 1**, 316; **Vol. 9, Part 2**, 87; governors of, **Vol. 1, Part 1**, 36 f., 259 f.; **Vol. 4, Part 1**, 488 f.; **Vol. 7, Part 2**, 638 f.; **Vol. 9, Part 1**, 14 f.; **Supp. 8**, 301; health, **Vol. 9, Part 1**, 462; historical writings on, **Supp. 1**, 705; history of, **Vol. 1, Part 1**, 522; **Vol. 1, Part 2**, 207; **Vol. 2, Part 1**, 437, 590; **Vol. 6, Part 2**, 61, 383, 485; **Vol. 7, Part 2**, 638; **Vol. 10, Part 1**, 619 f.; **Vol. 10, Part 2**, 525; Indians, Ute, **Vol. 7, Part 2**, 111, 638; irrigation, **Vol. 3, Part 1**, 605; **Vol. 7, Part 1**, 434; **Vol. 10, Part 1**, 619 f.; judiciary, **Supp. 3**, 462–63; Kansas, separation from, **Vol. 3, Part 1**, 243; law, mining, **Vol. 9, Part 2**, 423; legal service, **Vol. 1, Part 2**, 507; **Vol. 4, Part 2**, 155; **Vol. 7, Part 1**, 626; **Vol. 7, Part 2**, 308; mining, **Vol. 2, Part 1**, 186, 511, 590; **Vol. 3, Part 1**, 210; **Vol. 5, Part 1**, 619 f.; missions, **Vol. 6, Part 2**, 61; **Vol. 8, Part 1**, 349 f.; paleontology, **Vol. 10, Part 2**, 310; political service, **Vol. 1, Part 1**, 259; **Vol. 1, Part 2**, 507; **Vol. 3, Part 1**, 606; **Vol. 3, Part 2**, 205; **Vol. 4, Part 1**, 316, 489; **Vol. 6, Part 1**, 602; **Vol. 7, Part 2**, 309, 638; **Vol. 9, Part 1**, 14; **Vol. 9, Part 2**, 362, 373, 423; **Vol. 10, Part 1**, 619 f.; **Vol. 10, Part 2**, 441; politics, **Supp. 3**, 321; **Supp. 6**, 455, 507; public health committee, **Supp. 5**, 601; railroad promotion, **Vol. 6, Part 1**, 437 f.; **Vol. 10, Part 1**, 619 f.; Republican party, **Vol. 1, Part 1**, 260; **Vol. 10, Part 2**, 441; road building, **Vol. 6, Part 2**, 484; Supreme Court of, **Vol. 4, Part 1**, 339; University of, **Vol. 8, Part 2**, 609
Colorado Biological Association, founding of, **Supp. 4**, 167
Colorado Coal and Iron Co., **Vol. 7, Part 2**, 196
Colorado Colleges, **Vol. 7, Part 1**, 434; **Vol. 7, Part 2**, 196; **Vol. 9, Part 2**, 373
Colorado Fuel and Iron Co., **Supp. 6**, 548
Colorado River, **Supp. 6**, 182; **Supp. 7**, 22, 360; conservation of flood waters, **Vol. 9, Part 2**, 147; exploration of, **Vol. 5, Part 1**, 521; **Vol. 7, Part 1**, 445; **Vol. 8, Part 1**, 146 f.; levees, **Vol. 7, Part 1**, 617
Colorado River Aqueduct, **Supp. 3**, 814
Colorado River Land Co., **Supp. 3**, 155
Colorado Springs, Colo., **Vol. 7, Part 2**, 196; development of, **Supp. 2**, 525
Colorado State School of Mines, **Vol. 10, Part 1**, 619 f.
Color blindness, **Supp. 3**, 270
Colored American, second black weekly in U.S., **Vol. 8, Part 1**, 403
Colored Methodist Episcopal Church in America, **Vol. 6, Part 2**, 170; **Vol. 7, Part 2**, 155; founding of, **Vol. 6, Part 2**, 170
Colored Presbyterian Church, **Vol. 8, Part 2**, 332
Colored Woman in a White World, A, **Supp. 5**, 680
Colorimeter, invention of, **Supp. 2**, 36
Color photography, **Supp. 3**, 296
Color television, standards, **Supp. 6**, 32–33
Colosimo, James ("Big Jim"), references to, **Supp. 4**, 140, 142; **Supp. 6**, 263
Colt, Samuel, **Vol. 8, Part 1**, 101 f.
Colton, D. D., **Vol. 5, Part 1**, 410 f.

Colt Patent Fire Arms Co., **Vol. 4, Part 1,** 191; **Vol. 8, Part 2,** 145

Columbia, and *Shamrock,* **Vol. 1, Part 1,** 641

Columbia, S.C., invasion of, during Civil War, **Vol. 8, Part 1,** 395

Columbia Athenaeum, **Vol. 5, Part 2,** 518

Columbia Broadcasting System (CBS): education programs, **Supp. 6,** 83; Lindbergh kidnapping coverage, **Supp. 3,** 142; news and special affairs commentary, **Supp. 6,** 148; **Supp. 7,** 566–67; sports broadcasting, **Supp. 7,** 378

Columbia Dictionary of Modern European Literature, **Supp. 4,** 755

Columbia Gas and Electric Corporation, founding of, **Supp. 5,** 260

Columbia Historical Society, **Vol. 9, Part 2,** 587

Columbian College. *See* George Washington University

Columbian Star, **Vol. 8, Part 1,** 543

Columbia Pictures, **Supp. 6,** 118–19

Columbia-Presbyterian Medical Center (New York City): building architecture, **Supp. 4,** 698; founding of, **Supp. 5,** 325; ophthalmology institute, **Supp. 2,** 706

Columbia River: discovery of, **Vol. 4, Part 1,** 522 f.; survey of, **Vol. 9, Part 2,** 260, 455

Columbia Springs plantation, **Vol. 1, Part 2,** 600

Columbia Telescope, nullification paper, **Vol. 6, Part 1,** 604

Columbia Theological Seminary, **Vol. 8, Part 1,** 454

Columbia University, **Vol. 1, Part 1,** 620 f.; **Vol. 2, Part 2,** 408; **Vol. 4, Part 2,** 293; **Vol. 5, Part 2,** 4; **Vol. 6, Part 1,** 492; **Vol. 7, Part 1,** 364; **Vol. 8, Part 2,** 220, 528; academic freedom, **Supp. 4,** 135; administration, **Supp. 1,** 133; **Supp. 2,** 734; **Supp. 6,** 675; anthropology studies, **Supp. 3,** 83–84; **Supp. 4,** 907–8; **Supp. 5,** 435; **Supp. 6,** 393; architecture studies, **Supp. 5,** 133; **Supp. 6,** 272; Barnard College, **Supp. 2,** 532, 488; **Supp. 7,** 288–89; baseball team, **Supp. 3,** 294; biochemistry studies, **Supp. 3,** 693; biophysics studies, **Supp. 4,** 367; charter of 1787, **Vol. 8, Part 2,** 127; chemistry studies, **Supp. 5,** 622–23; classical studies, **Supp. 5,** 736; **Supp. 8,** 236; Columbia College administration, **Supp. 3,** 416; contemporary drama courses, **Supp. 4,** 354; dean, first, **Vol. 3, Part 1,** 458 f.; economic studies, **Supp. 4,** 586–87; **Supp. 6,** 459; **Supp. 7,** 801; embryology studies, **Supp. 3,** 539–40; engineering department, **Vol. 2, Part 2,** 553; English literature and language studies, **Supp. 4,** 634, 847; **Supp. 5,** 211–12; first black doctorate recipient, **Supp. 6,** 284; first industrial engineering department, **Supp. 5,** 558; first protozoology course, **Supp. 3,** 126–27; first Zionist society, **Supp. 8,** 549; football abolishment, **Supp. 4,** 135; founding of, **Vol. 5, Part 2,** 118 f.; **Vol. 6, Part 1,** 317, 326; French literature and language studies, **Supp. 4,** 754–55; **Supp. 8,** 475–76; geomorphology studies, **Supp. 3,** 389–90; gifts to, **Supp. 3,** 32; growth of, **Vol. 1, Part 1,** 620; **Vol. 6, Part 2,** 369; **Vol. 7, Part 2,** 377; **Vol. 8, Part 1,** 506, 634; **Vol. 10, Part 1,** 149; **Vol. 10, Part 2,** 479; history studies, **Supp. 2,** 563, 564; **Supp. 3,** 287; **Supp. 4,** 61–62; **Supp. 6,** 40–41; **Supp. 7,** 329–30, 518, 567–68; **Supp. 8,** 271–73, 580–81; Institute of Arts and Sciences, **Supp. 6,** 160; Institute of Social Research, **Supp. 5,** 514; international law studies, **Supp. 5,** 341; Journalism, School of, **Vol. 8, Part 1,** 260 f.; **Supp. 1,** 391; Law School, **Vol. 3, Part 1,** 571 f.; **Vol. 5, Part 2,** 486; **Supp. 3,** 185–86, 700; **Supp. 4,** 598, 793, 794; **Supp. 7,** 474–75; **Supp. 8,** 139; law school case-study method, **Supp. 3,** 420; library school, **Supp. 1,** 242; **Supp. 4,** 19; Medicine, School

of, **Vol. 6, Part 2,** 603; **Supp. 4,** 643; **Supp. 5,** 438, 512; Medicine, School of, Teaching Hospital, **Supp. 2,** 284; medieval studies, **Supp. 7,** 741–42; Mines, School of, **Vol. 4, Part 1,** 612; **Vol. 3, Part 2,** 56; **Vol. 7, Part 1,** 446; music studies, **Vol. 6, Part 2,** 26; **Supp. 5,** 477; nuclear research, **Supp. 5,** 220–21; **Supp. 6,** 501; obstetrics and gynecology, **Supp. 6,** 555; pathology studies, **Supp. 3,** 483; philosophy studies, **Supp. 2,** 734; **Supp. 5,** 171–72, 198–99, 503; **Supp. 6,** 45; physics studies, **Supp. 6,** 500–1; political science studies, **Supp. 1,** 132–33; **Supp. 5,** 107; presidency, **Vol. 1, Part 1,** 620 f.; **Vol. 4, Part 2,** 325 f.; **Vol. 5, Part 2,** 118 f., 133, 382 f.; **Vol. 6, Part 1,** 449 f.; **Vol. 7, Part 1,** 115, 134; **Supp. 4,** 133–37; **Supp. 8,** 156; psychology studies, **Supp. 3,** 149; psychosomatic medicine studies, **Supp. 6,** 180–81; public health school, **Supp. 6,** 193; research institutes, **Supp. 2,** 60; rhetoric department, **Vol. 2, Part 1,** 511; "Riot of 1811," **Vol. 6, Part 2,** 441; social work school, **Supp. 4,** 227; sociology, first professorship, **Supp. 1,** 339–40; sociology studies, **Supp. 6,** 482–83, 726–27, 539; **Supp. 8,** 399, 407; Teachers College, **Vol. 3, Part 1,** 346 f.; **Supp. 3,** 206, 552, 671, 677, 721–22, 729; **Supp. 4,** 40, 134, 139, 373–74, 832; **Supp. 5,** 171–72, 251; **Supp. 6,** 83, 208, 557; **Supp. 7,** 427, 435; Teachers College nursing education, **Supp. 4,** 632–33

Columbus, Christopher: biography of, **Vol. 5, Part 1,** 509; landing place, location of, claimed, **Vol. 10, Part 1,** 635 f.; reference to, **Supp. 8,** 457; tomb, discovery of, **Vol. 7, Part 1,** 156

Columbus, Ga. *Enquirer-Sun,* **Supp. 7,** 324

Columbus, Ky., seizure of, **Vol. 2, Part 1,** 235; **Vol. 4, Part 1,** 493; **Vol. 8, Part 1,** 40

Columbus, Ohio, **Vol. 6, Part 1,** 404

Columbus Circle (New York City), one-way traffic, **Supp. 3,** 254

Columbus College (S.Dak.), **Vol. 7, Part 2,** 3

Columbus Dispatch, **Supp. 6,** 422

Columbus Doors of Capitol, Washington, D.C., **Vol. 8, Part 2,** 107

Columbus Savings and Loan Society, **Supp. 4,** 324–25

Columnist, one of first in U.S., **Vol. 5, Part 1,** 320

Colver Institute, **Vol. 2, Part 2,** 324

Comanduras, Peter, reference to, **Supp. 7,** 191

Comden, Betty, reference to, **Supp. 7,** 354

Comedians. For complete list, *see* Occupations Index

Comedy: acting, **Vol. 1, Part 1,** 645; **Vol. 4, Part 2,** 73; **Vol. 5, Part 1,** 143 f., 146; eccentric, **Vol. 3, Part 2,** 393; Irish-American, **Vol. 3, Part 2,** 476 f.; musical, **Vol. 3, Part 2,** 573; of manners, **Vol. 3, Part 1,** 516 f.. *See also* Burlesque; Humor; Motion pictures; Satire; Theater; Vaudeville

"Come-outism," **Vol. 7, Part 1,** 22

Comer, Braxton Bragg, reference to, **Supp. 3,** 729

Comets, **Vol. 1, Part 1,** 618; **Vol. 5, Part 1,** 329; **Vol. 5, Part 2,** 419; **Vol. 9, Part 2,** 248; **Supp. 5,** 540; discovery of, **Vol. 2, Part 1,** 91; **Vol. 9, Part 2,** 18; writings on, **Vol. 5, Part 2,** 419, 436

Comic opera: acting, **Vol. 8, Part 2,** 246; composition, **Vol. 4, Part 2,** 573; **Vol. 9, Part 1,** 408

Comic strips, **Vol. 3, Part 1,** 378 f.; "Bringing Up Father," **Supp. 5,** 456–57; "Buck Rogers," **Supp. 6,** 165–66; color press, **Supp. 2,** 242; "Flash Gordon," **Supp. 6,** 530; "Gumps," **Supp. 1,** 665; "Happy Hooligan," **Supp. 2,** 504; "Joe Palooka," **Supp. 5,** 222; "Jungle Jim," **Supp. 6,** 530, 531; "Krazy Kat," **Supp. 3,** 356–57; "Krazy Kat and Ignatz," **Supp. 3,** 356–57; "Lala Palooza," **Supp. 8,** 218; "Little Orphan Annie," **Supp. 8,** 221–22; "Moon Mullins," **Supp. 6,** 698–99; "Mutt and Jeff," **Supp. 5,** 223–24; "Nize Baby," **Supp. 5,** 262; origin of, **Vol. 7, Part**

545; **Vol. 6, Part 1,** 42; **Vol. 9, Part 1,** 90; **Vol. 9, Part 2,** 250; legal cases, **Supp. 6,** 137; legal service, **Vol. 1, Part 1,** 543; **Vol. 2, Part 1,** 559; **Vol. 3, Part 1,** 230, 555, 581; **Vol. 5, Part 1,** 66, 154; **Vol. 6, Part 1,** 39 f., 41 f.; **Vol. 7, Part 1,** 65; **Vol. 7, Part 2,** 639, 641; **Vol. 8, Part 1,** 187, 426, 468; **Vol. 8, Part 2,** 45, 148; **Vol. 10, Part 1,** 11, 384 f., 560 f.; **Vol. 10, Part 2,** 48; Loyalists, **Vol. 1, Part 2,** 54; medical service, **Vol. 10, Part 1,** 52; **Vol. 10, Part 2,** 511; military expeditions of 1745-47, **Vol. 6, Part 1,** 41; missions, **Vol. 3, Part 1,** 573 f.; **Vol. 8, Part 1,** 645; money, engraving of, **Vol. 3, Part 1,** 501 f.; Pennsylvania, relations with, **Vol. 1, Part 2,** 566; political service, **Vol. 1, Part 1,** 542, 544; **Vol. 1, Part 2,** 295, 298, 569, 598; **Vol. 2, Part 1,** 228; **Vol. 3, Part 1,** 26, 62, 171, 173, 230, 328, 395, 555, 569, 581; **Vol. 3, Part 2,** 343, 427, 498, 538, 553; **Vol. 4, Part 2,** 9, 341, 459; **Vol. 5, Part 1,** 207, 418; **Vol. 5, Part 2,** 132; **Vol. 6, Part 1,** 41, 138; **Vol. 7, Part 1,** 216, 522; **Vol. 7, Part 2,** 32, 639, 641; **Vol. 8, Part 1,** 2, 187; **Vol. 8, Part 2,** 45, 145, 317; **Vol. 9, Part 1,** 11, 300; **Vol. 9, Part 2,** 600 f., 633; **Vol. 10, Part 1,** 8, 11, 16, 18, 384, 624, 629; **Vol. 10, Part 2,** 414, 443, 445, 582; politics, **Supp. 5,** 70, 455-56; powder-mill, first, **Vol. 7, Part 2,** 641; printing, 18th century, **Vol. 10, Part 1,** 10; public health department, **Supp. 6,** 702; public service, **Vol. 2, Part 2,** 139; **Vol. 3, Part 1,** 108, 502 f.; **Vol. 3, Part 2,** 498; **Vol. 4, Part 2,** 9 f., 341, 421; **Vol. 5, Part 1,** 52, 207 f., 245, 416, 419; **Vol. 7, Part 2,** 69; **Vol. 8, Part 2,** 148; **Vol. 9, Part 1,** 300, 327; **Vol. 10, Part 1,** 560 f.; **Vol. 10, Part 2,** 293; railway building and consolidation, **Vol. 1, Part 2,** 298; **Vol. 2, Part 1,** 324; religious history, **Vol. 3, Part 1,** 54 f., 84 f.; **Vol. 5, Part 1,** 620; **Vol. 8, Part 2,** 101; **Vol. 10, Part 1,** 85, 632; **Vol. 10, Part 2,** 42; Republican party, organization of, **Vol. 4, Part 2,** 421; Republican-Tolerationist, revolution in, **Vol. 9, Part 2,** 250; Revolutionary War period, **Vol. 3, Part 2,** 112; **Vol. 5, Part 1,** 416; **Vol. 10, Part 2,** 293, 442; separation of Springfield from, **Vol. 8, Part 1,** 292 f.; Sons of Liberty, **Vol. 3, Part 1,** 550; theocratic government, **Vol. 3, Part 1,** 611; verse, first volume written in, **Vol. 10, Part 2,** 446; woman suffrage, **Supp. 5,** 296, 297, 742

Connecticut Academy of Sciences, **Vol. 1, Part 2,** 341
Connecticut Birth Control Movement, founding of, **Supp. 5,** 297
Connecticut Civil Service Reform Association, **Vol. 7, Part 2,** 69
Connecticut College for Women, **Vol. 7, Part 2,** 647
Connecticut Compromise, **Vol. 3, Part 1,** 98
Connecticut Forestry Association, **Vol. 5, Part 2,** 45
Connecticut Gazette, **Vol. 5, Part 1,** 180
Connecticut Historical Society, **Vol. 8, Part 1,** 646
Connecticut Land Co., **Vol. 2, Part 2,** 189
Connecticut Medical College, **Vol. 7, Part 2,** 466
Connecticut Medical Society, **Vol. 5, Part 2,** 468
Connecticut Mutual Life Insurance Co., **Vol. 7, Part 2,** 529
Connecticut Nutmeg, founding of, **Supp. 2,** 68
Connecticut Society for Mental Hygiene, **Supp. 3,** 51
Connecticut Society of the Cincinnati, **Vol. 5, Part 2,** 423
Connecticut Sound Money League, **Vol. 7, Part 2,** 69
Connelly, Marc, references to, **Supp. 4,** 102; **Supp. 7,** 412-13
Conner, Fox, reference to, **Supp. 8,** 154
Connolly, Maurice E., prosecution of, **Supp. 3,** 117
Connor, Eugene ("Bull"), reference to, **Supp. 8,** 334
Conover, Harry, Modeling Agency, **Supp. 7,** 140-41
Conrad, Johannes, references to, **Vol. 7, Part 2,** 298; **Supp. 3,** 248

Conrad and Jones Co., **Supp. 5,** 555
Conscientious objectors, **Supp. 4,** 441, 526, 794; **Supp. 6,** 217; **Supp. 7,** 597; Civil War, **Vol. 8, Part 1,** 236 f.; Revolutionary War, **Vol. 8, Part 1,** 139 f.
Conscription: draft riots, **Vol. 3, Part 2,** 580; **Vol. 4, Part 1,** 238; Civil War, **Vol. 3, Part 2,** 580; **Vol. 5, Part 1,** 129; **Vol. 8, Part 1,** 202 f., 358 f.; World War I, **Vol. 5, Part 2,** 251. *See also* Draft
Conservation, **Vol. 1, Part 1,** 555; **Vol. 3, Part 2,** 403; **Vol. 4, Part 2,** 157, 354; **Vol. 5, Part 1,** 74 f., 167, 250, 433; **Vol. 5, Part 2,** 520, 573; **Vol. 7, Part 1,** 315 f., 457; **Vol. 8, Part 2,** 45, 134; **Vol. 9, Part 1,** 106; **Vol. 9, Part 2,** 565; aesthetic approach to, **Supp. 4,** 522-23; Alaska, **Supp. 3,** 96; Audubon movement, **Supp. 3,** 592-93; Benbrook Reservoir (Tex.), **Supp. 6,** 540; California redwoods, **Supp. 3,** 520; **Supp. 4,** 429; **Supp. 6,** 486; congressional advocacy, **Supp. 6,** 475; **Supp. 7,** 212, 224-25; ecology, terminology established, **Supp. 3,** 168-70; ecology, writings on, **Supp. 7,** 109-10; federal policies, **Supp. 1,** 300; **Supp. 2,** 553; **Supp. 5,** 342; **Supp. 6,** 416-17; forest preserves, **Supp. 1,** 555; **Supp. 2,** 128, 264, 507, 610; **Supp. 3,** 78; **Supp. 4,** 663-66; **Supp. 6,** 486; fossil sites, **Supp. 5,** 743-44; legislation, **Supp. 4,** 666; **Supp. 7,** 225; Oregon, **Supp. 6,** 682; organizations, **Supp. 7,** 164-65; petroleum, **Supp. 7,** 771-72, 804; popular writings on, **Supp. 8,** 486; Prairie Club, **Supp. 3,** 599; public lands, **Supp. 4,** 317-18; Rockefeller preserves, **Supp. 6,** 549; Roosevelt, Teddy, efforts toward, **Vol. 2, Part 2,** 145; **Vol. 7, Part 1,** 316; shade trees, **Supp. 7,** 33; Washington (state), **Supp. 7,** 353; water supply, **Supp. 4,** 563-64; wilderness areas, **Supp. 6,** 486; **Supp. 7,** 164, 225, 813-14; wildlife, **Supp. 2,** 265; **Supp. 8,** 3-4; writings on, **Supp. 5,** 169; **Vol. 8, Part 2,** 134 f. *See also* Natural history
Conservation Foundation, founding of, **Supp. 8,** 486
Conservatism, writings on, **Supp. 8,** 552
Conservator, **Vol. 9, Part 2,** 628
Consolidated Edison Co.: founding of, **Supp. 3,** 138; management, **Supp. 2,** 123; predecessors, **Supp. 3,** 716
Consolidated Film Industries, founding of, **Supp. 8,** 712
Consolidated Gas Co., **Vol. 8, Part 2,** 95
Consolidated Shipping Co., **Vol. 7, Part 1,** 240
Consolidated Virginia Mine, **Vol. 3, Part 2,** 246
Conspiracies: Blount (1797), **Vol. 1, Part 1,** 78; **Vol. 1, Part 2,** 390; **Vol. 5, Part 1,** 469; **Vol. 6, Part 2,** 82, 403; **Vol. 8, Part 2,** 604; Burr (1806-7), **Vol. 1, Part 1,** 34; **Vol. 1, Part 2,** 369; **Vol. 2, Part 1,** 317-19; **Vol. 2, Part 2,** 116, 125, 174; **Vol. 3, Part 1,** 80, 166, 613; **Vol. 5, Part 1,** 528; **Vol. 5, Part 2,** 30; **Vol. 6, Part 2,** 310; **Vol. 8, Part 2,** 84; **Vol. 9, Part 2,** 238, 536; **Vol. 10, Part 1,** 22; **Vol. 10, Part 2,** 225, 298; Grey (1755), **Vol. 8, Part 1,** 518; Pontiac (1763), **Vol. 1, Part 2,** 481, 579, 604; **Vol. 2, Part 2,** 556; **Vol. 4, Part 1,** 253, 327; **Vol. 8, Part 1,** 63, 578; **Vol. 9, Part 1,** 59; **Vol. 10, Part 2,** 103, 126
Constantinople, foreign missions in, **Vol. 8, Part 2,** 261
Constantinople Woman's College. *See* American College for Girls at Constantinople
Constellation (airplane), **Supp. 6,** 221
Constellation, refractory officers on, **Vol. 8, Part 1,** 424
Constitution ("Old Ironsides"), **Vol. 1, Part 1,** 506 f., 606; **Vol. 5, Part 1,** 360 f.; **Vol. 6, Part 1,** 500; **Vol. 7, Part 1,** 506; **Vol. 8, Part 1,** 424; **Vol. 8, Part 2,** 74; **Vol. 9, Part 1,** 135; **Vol. 9, Part 2,** 7, 306
Constitution (Confederate), **Vol. 9, Part 1,** 130
Constitution (U.S.), **Vol. 1, Part 1,** 91, 405; **Vol. 1, Part 2,** 501; **Vol. 3, Part 1,** 153; **Vol. 3, Part 2,** 374;

Vol. 4, Part 1, 104, 224 f., 304 f., 479; **Vol. 4, Part 2,** 330 f., 366; **Vol. 5, Part 1,** 492 f.; **Vol. 5, Part 2,** 24, 88; **Vol. 7, Part 1,** 215, 218, 222, 412; **Vol. 9, Part 1,** 322; **Vol. 10, Part 1,** 35; Adams, John Quincy, views of, on, **Vol. 1, Part 1,** 91; amendments, *see* Constitutional amendments; antifederalism, **Vol. 2, Part 1,** 189; **Vol. 3, Part 2,** 385; **Vol. 9, Part 2,** 320, 356; **Vol. 10, Part 2,** 598, 601; Bearer of, in procession of July 23, 1788, **Vol. 6, Part 1,** 32; Bible and, **Vol. 4, Part 2,** 272, Delaware, prompt ratification by, **Vol. 1, Part 2,** 39; **Vol. 8, Part 1,** 423; drafting of, **Vol. 1, Part 2,** 338, 499; **Vol. 5, Part 1,** 94 f.; **Vol. 10, Part 1,** 597 f.; interpretation of, **Vol. 4, Part 2,** 270 f.; **Vol. 6, Part 2,** 322 f.; **Vol. 7, Part 2,** 628; Jefferson's approval of, **Vol. 5, Part 2,** 23; Louisiana Purchase and, **Vol. 5, Part 2,** 29; making of, **Vol. 10, Part 2,** 329; nationalistic theory refuted, **Vol. 10, Part 1,** 127; opposition to, **Vol. 2, Part 2,** 227; **Vol. 6, Part 1,** 472 f.; Pinckney draft, **Vol. 7, Part 2,** 612; ratification of, **Vol. 1, Part 2,** 39, 483; **Vol. 2, Part 1,** 280; **Vol. 4, Part 2,** 230; **Vol. 6, Part 2,** 187; **Vol. 8, Part 1,** 138, 237 f., 312, 423; **Vol. 8, Part 2,** 49; **Vol. 9, Part 1,** 320; **Vol. 10, Part 1,** 509 f.; scholarship on, **Supp. 8,** 139; sesquicentennial, **Supp. 4,** 88; signing of, **Vol. 2, Part 2,** 235; **Vol. 9, Part 1,** 90; Webster's theory concerning, **Vol. 10, Part 1,** 585 f.; writings on, **Vol. 5, Part 2,** 8, 260; **Vol. 8, Part 1,** 401; **Supp. 1,** 154, 424–26; **Supp. 2,** 399; **Supp. 4,** 64; 530–31, 680; **Supp. 5,** 429, 549; **Supp. 7,** 146–47

Constitutional amendments: equal rights proposal, **Supp. 5,** 474, 532, 543; First, preferred freedoms of, **Supp. 4,** 796–97; *see also* Civil liberties; Fifth, **Supp. 6,** 105; Sixth, **Supp. 3,** 755; Tenth, **Supp. 5,** 573; Twelfth, **Vol. 9, Part 2,** 332; Thirteenth, **Vol. 10, Part 1,** 19 f.; Fourteenth, **Vol. 1, Part 2,** 489; **Vol. 4, Part 1,** 499; **Vol. 5, Part 1,** 139; **Vol. 5, Part 2,** 86, 88; **Vol. 7, Part 2,** 209; **Vol. 9, Part 1,** 624; **Supp. 3,** 415; Fifteenth, **Vol. 1, Part 2,** 489; **Vol. 5, Part 2,** 86; **Vol. 9, Part 1,** 624; **Vol. 9, Part 2,** 14; Seventeenth, **Supp. 3,** 105; Eighteenth, **Vol. 4, Part 1,** 112; **Vol. 7, Part 1,** 235; **Supp. 3,** 132, 181, 706; **Supp. 4,** 136, 161; **Supp. 6,** 3, 480, 548; Nineteenth, **Vol. 4, Part 1,** 112; **Vol. 6, Part 1,** 341; **Supp. 4,** 158, 861–62; **Supp. 7,** 779; Twentieth, **Supp. 3,** 559, **Supp. 7,** 363; Twenty-second, **Supp. 8,** 421; Twenty-fourth, **Supp. 7,** 416

Constitutional Convention (1787), **Vol. 1, Part 2,** 123, 390; **Vol. 2, Part 1,** 1; **Vol. 3, Part 1,** 166; **Vol. 3, Part 2,** 113; **Vol. 4, Part 1,** 479; **Vol. 5, Part 2,** 133, 398; **Vol. 6, Part 1,** 308; **Vol. 6, Part 2,** 186; **Vol. 7, Part 2,** 584; **Vol. 8, Part 1,** 354; **Vol. 10, Part 2,** 601; Hamilton's part in, **Vol. 4, Part 2,** 174; history of its proceedings, **Vol. 5, Part 1,** 602; record of, **Vol. 5, Part 1,** 560; South Carolina's part in, **Vol. 2, Part 1,** 365

Constitutional History of the United States, **Supp. 4,** 530–31
Constitutional Jeffersonian Democratic party, founding of, **Supp. 4,** 813
Constitutional Union party, **Vol. 1, Part 2,** 158; **Vol. 9, Part 2,** 590
Constitution and What It Means Today, The, **Supp. 7,** 146
Constitution Hall (Washington, D.C.): architecture, **Supp. 5,** 300; racial policy, **Supp. 5,** 343; **Supp. 8,** 328
Constitutions (state). *See specific states*
Construction industry: first multinational firm, **Supp. 8,** 308–9; government-funded works projects, **Supp. 8,** 308; mass construction techniques, **Supp. 1,** 349; New York City, **Supp. 6,** 337, 593; Philadelphia, **Supp. 6,** 331; skyscrapers, **Supp. 6,** 593; **Supp. 7,** 799–800; unionization, **Supp. 5,** 339;

Supp. 6, 73–74
Consular Service, United States, merit system, **Supp. 3,** 139, 467
Consular system, regulation of, **Vol. 3, Part 1,** 294; **Vol. 8, Part 1,** 634
Consumer Distribution Corporation, organization of, **Supp. 2,** 184
Consumerism: boycotts, **Supp. 4,** 623–24; cooperatives, **Supp. 2,** 184; economic theory and, **Supp. 4,** 585; **Supp. 8,** 79; public education in, **Supp. 4,** 307–8; writings on, **Supp. 4,** 267–68; **Supp. 7,** 69; **Supp. 8,** 425
Consumer price index, **Supp. 7,** 794
Consumer Reports, **Supp. 7,** 69
Consumers' cooperatives, **Vol. 9, Part 1,** 396
Consumers' League of Ohio, founding of, **Supp. 3,** 347
Consumers' League of the City of New York, **Supp. 4,** 623–24
Consumers' research, **Supp. 8,** 425
Consumers Union, **Supp. 7,** 69
Contact, **Supp. 7,** 790
Contact dermititis, **Supp. 3,** 442
Containers: for tobacco, **Supp. 5,** 565; glass canning jars, **Supp. 3,** 29; **Supp. 5,** 343. *See also* Canning and canned goods; Packaging
Contemporary Psychology, **Supp. 8,** 44
Continental Association, **Vol. 6, Part 1,** 119
Continental Bank Note Co., **Vol. 7, Part 2,** 55
Continental Bank of New York, **Vol. 2, Part 2,** 613
Continental Congress, **Vol. 1, Part 1,** 73 f.; **Vol. 1, Part 2,** 354, 477; **Vol. 2, Part 1,** 296, 523; **Vol. 3, Part 1,** 174, 581 f.; **Vol. 3, Part 2,** 352; **Vol. 4, Part 1,** 366, 525, 618; **Vol. 4, Part 2,** 219, 232, 260, 279; **Vol. 5, Part 1,** 204, 220 f., 245, 267 f., 301, 314, 385, 418, 469, 539; **Vol. 5, Part 2,** 6, 42, 121 f., 159, 192, 587, 590, 599; **Vol. 6, Part 1,** 34, 105, 108, 132, 215, 232, 307, 318, 321, 438, 446, 464, 472, 523; **Vol. 6, Part 2,** 405, 600; **Vol. 7, Part 1,** 128 f., 210, 220, 307, 383, 411 f., 424; **Vol. 7, Part 2,** 417; **Vol. 8, Part 1,** 138, 338, 340 f., 533 f.; **Vol. 8, Part 2,** 257, 524, 535; **Vol. 9, Part 1,** 89, 307, 319, 322, 333, 451; **Vol. 9, Part 2,** 46, 84, 258, 361, 386, 481, 504, 543, 545; **Vol. 10, Part 1,** 17 f.; **Vol. 10, Part 2,** 327, 431, 442; "Americanus" articles, **Vol. 5, Part 2,** 599; comptroller of treasury under, **Vol. 10, Part 1,** 17 f.; diary of, **Vol. 9, Part 1,** 333; journals of, **Vol. 5, Part 1,** 385; negotiations with France, **Vol. 3, Part 1,** 174; political factions, **Vol. 6, Part 1,** 34; **Vol. 8, Part 2,** 257; president of, **Vol. 4, Part 1,** 618; **Vol. 5, Part 1,** 418

Continental currency, **Vol. 3, Part 1,** 281 f.
Continental drift, **Supp. 2,** 654
Continental League (baseball), **Supp. 7,** 646–47
Continental Oil Co., Marland merger, **Supp. 3,** 505
Continental shelf, **Supp. 5,** 656–57
Contraband, trade in, **Vol. 7, Part 1,** 543
Contraceptives. *See* Family planning; *specific types*
Contract bridge, authorities on, **Supp. 5,** 146; **Supp. 6,** 134–35, 380
Convent of St. Elizabeth, **Vol. 8, Part 2,** 597
Convent of the Sisters of Notre Dame de Nemours, **Vol. 8, Part 1,** 266 f.
Convention of 1787. *See* Constitutional Convention
"Convention of Slaveholders," **Vol. 9, Part 2,** 596
Converse, Harriet Maxwell, reference to, **Supp. 5,** 533
Convulsions, **Supp. 1,** 241
Conway cabal, **Vol. 1, Part 1,** 176; **Vol. 2, Part 1,** 315, 398; **Vol. 2, Part 2,** 498; **Vol. 3, Part 1,** 486 f.; **Vol. 4, Part 1,** 186, 570; **Vol. 5, Part 2,** 100, 537; **Vol. 6, Part 1,** 34, 36, 439; **Vol. 6, Part 2,** 120, 607; **Vol. 8, Part 2,** 228; **Vol. 10, Part 1,** 509, 517–18; **Vol. 10,**

Part 2, 223

Cook, Frederick A., **Vol. 6, Part 1,** 529; **Vol. 7, Part 2,** 366; **Vol. 10, Part 1,** 390; reference to, **Supp. 4,** 674

Cook, George Cram, reference to, **Supp. 4,** 330

Cook, Nancy, references to, **Supp. 7,** 659, 660

Cook, Will Marion, reference to, **Supp. 3,** 834

Cookbooks, **Vol. 6, Part 1,** 185; **Vol. 9, Part 2,** 377; **Supp. 4,** 455; **Supp. 7,** 528, 656–57; **Supp. 8,** 656

Cooke, Jay, **Vol. 7, Part 1,** 176, 436

Cooking: cake mixes, **Supp. 6,** 292; Pyrex ovenware, **Supp. 6,** 624; recipe innovation, **Supp. 6,** 165; teaching of, **Vol. 2, Part 2,** 454; **Vol. 3, Part 2,** 276; **Vol. 6, Part 1,** 265. *See also* Diet and nutrition; Restaurants

Cooley, Charles H., reference to, **Supp. 3,** 601

Cooley's anemia, **Supp. 3,** 190

Coolidge, Archibald Cary, reference to, **Supp. 5,** 130

Coolidge, Calvin: biography of, **Supp. 3,** 817; references to, **Vol. 5, Part 2,** 546; **Vol. 7, Part 1,** 234; **Supp. 1,** 636; **Supp. 6,** 507; **Supp. 7,** 211; **Supp. 8,** 420; Stearns relationship, **Supp. 2,** 624; Teapot Dome scandal, **Supp. 3,** 715; West, R.O., relationship, **Supp. 6,** 684

Coolidge, Elizabeth Sprague: chamber-music concerts, **Supp. 3,** 252; references to, **Supp. 5,** 76, 554; **Supp. 8,** 443

Coolidge, Elizabeth Sprague, Foundation, founding of, **Supp. 5,** 129

Coolidge, Ellen W., reference to, **Supp. 6,** 499

Coolidge, Shepley, Bulfinch & Abbott, **Supp. 2,** 117

"Coon songs," **Supp. 3,** 187

Cooper, Gary, reference to, **Supp. 8,** 649

Cooper, James Fenimore, references to, **Vol. 7, Part 1,** 423; **Vol. 9, Part 1,** 136, 261

Cooper, Kent, reference to, **Supp. 4,** 631

Cooper, Merian C., reference to, **Supp. 7,** 580

Cooper, Peter, references to, **Vol. 5, Part 1,** 347; **Vol. 9, Part 2,** 640

Cooper, Tom, reference to, **Supp. 4,** 293

Cooperative communities, **Vol. 6, Part 2,** 136, 497

Cooperative Education Association of Virginia, founding of, **Supp. 3,** 115

Cooperative for American Remittances to Everywhere. *See* CARE

Cooperative Grange League Federation Exchange, founding of, **Supp. 4,** 37

Cooperative League of America, **Supp. 6,** 664

Cooperative Marketing Act (1926), **Supp. 5,** 365

Cooperatives: agricultural, **Supp. 2,** 307, 426; **Supp. 4,** 36–37, 340–41, 853; **Supp. 5,** 365; **Supp. 7,** 361; consumer, **Supp. 2,** 184; housing, **Supp. 6,** 615; organizations, **Supp. 6,** 664; tobacco, **Supp. 2,** 39, 79; utopian, **Supp. 1,** 345

Cooperative School for Teachers, founding of, **Supp. 8,** 443

Cooper Medical College, **Vol. 5, Part 2,** 580

Coopers and Lybrand, **Supp. 6,** 397

Cooperstown, N.Y., baseball, origin of, at, **Vol. 3, Part 1,** 391

Cooper Union (New York City), **Vol. 2, Part 2,** 410; **Vol. 4, Part 2,** 605; **Vol. 6, Part 1,** 248; **Vol. 7, Part 1,** 579; **Vol. 8, Part 2,** 467; **Vol. 9, Part 1,** 252

Cooper Union Forum, **Supp. 3,** 511, 563

Coote, Richard, reference to, **Vol. 7, Part 1,** 517

Copacabana (nightclub, New York City), **Supp. 5,** 501

Copland, Aaron, reference to, **Supp. 5,** 398

Copper: engraving, **Vol. 3, Part 1,** 272 f.; **Vol. 5, Part 1,** 424; exploitation, **Vol. 4, Part 2,** 507; extraction, **Vol. 3, Part 1,** 396; in electrical conduction, **Supp. 2,** 383; mining, *see* Mining, copper; porphyry deposits development, **Supp. 6,** 315–16; processing,

Supp. 1, 58; rolling, **Vol. 6, Part 1,** 60; **Vol. 8, Part 2,** 95, 263; selling, **Vol. 3, Part 1,** 353; stock trading, **Supp. 2,** 292

"Copperheads," **Vol. 5, Part 2,** 437; **Vol. 6, Part 1,** 251, 336; **Vol. 7, Part 1,** 263; **Vol. 10, Part 1,** 144

Copper House, **Supp. 1,** 31

Coptic studies, **Supp. 3,** 374–75

Copy editing, **Supp. 6,** 236

Copying machines, **Supp. 8,** 71–72

Copyright: Act of 1891, **Vol. 1, Part 1,** 335; Act of 1909, **Vol. 8, Part 1,** 279 f.; book publishing reform, **Supp. 3,** 773; Copyright League, American Publishers', **Vol. 1, Part 1,** 334; international, **Vol. 1, Part 1,** 537; **Vol. 1, Part 2,** 329; **Vol. 2, Part 2,** 149; **Vol. 3, Part 2,** 189; **Vol. 4, Part 1,** 73; **Vol. 5, Part 1,** 417; **Vol. 6, Part 1,** 15; **Vol. 8, Part 1,** 2 f., 19 f., 278 f.; **Vol. 8, Part 2,** 381; **Vol. 10, Part 1,** 594 f.; **Supp. 2,** 348; laws governing, authority on, **Vol. 3, Part 2,** 66; **Supp. 1,** 101; music publishing, **Supp. 3,** 834; news syndicate suit, **Supp. 5,** 223; songwriting, **Supp. 8,** 546; theatrical, **Supp. 6,** 150; writings on, **Vol. 8, Part 1,** 278 f.

Coquelin, Benoît-Constant, reference to, **Supp. 5,** 124

Coral: reefs, **Supp. 3,** 704; **Supp. 6,** 144; study of, **Vol. 1, Part 1,** 113

Corals, **Supp. 5,** 709

Coral Sea, battle of the (1942), **Supp. 6,** 577

Corcoran, Thomas G., references to, **Supp. 7,** 72, 263

Corcoran, W. W., reference to, **Vol. 10, Part 1,** 633 f.

Corcoran Gallery of Art, **Vol. 2, Part 2,** 440; **Vol. 3, Part 2,** 214

Cordmaking machine, invention of, **Vol. 8, Part 1,** 101 f.

Cordoba Observatory, **Vol. 4, Part 1,** 448

Cori cycle, **Supp. 6,** 126

Corinth, Miss., operation about (1862-63), **Vol. 1, Part 2,** 112; **Vol. 4, Part 1,** 495; **Vol. 4, Part 2,** 151; **Vol. 6, Part 2,** 160, 427; **Vol. 7, Part 1,** 76; **Vol. 7, Part 2,** 48; **Vol. 8, Part 1,** 216; **Vol. 8, Part 2,** 163; **Vol. 9, Part 1,** 94; **Vol. 10, Part 1,** 185

Corinth excavations, **Supp. 3,** 705

Corliss engines, **Vol. 7, Part 1,** 546–47

Corn: culture, **Vol. 6, Part 1,** 74; **Vol. 8, Part 1,** 477 f.; first hybrid commercial, **Supp. 7,** 760; genetic studies, **Supp. 2,** 114; growing, **Vol. 6, Part 1,** 74; hybridization, **Supp. 2,** 167; **Supp. 4,** 252–53; **Supp. 5,** 629; **Supp. 7,** 760; milling, **Vol. 8, Part 1,** 273 f.; planting machine, **Vol. 1, Part 1,** 533

"Corn-cob capitals," style of architecture, **Vol. 6, Part 1,** 22

Corneal tissue transplants, **Supp. 7,** 70

Cornell, Katharine, references to, **Supp. 6,** 286, 517; **Supp. 7,** 496

Cornell Greenland Expedition, **Vol. 9, Part 2,** 308

Cornell-Guggenheim Aviation Safety Center, **Supp. 8,** 709

Cornell University, **Vol. 1, Part 1,** 53; **Vol. 1, Part 2,** 419; **Vol. 8, Part 2,** 320; **Vol. 10, Part 2,** 349; agricultural extension service, **Supp. 3,** 433–34; **Supp. 4,** 36–37; agricultural studies, **Supp. 4,** 252–53; **Supp. 5,** 31; biochemistry studies, **Supp. 5,** 670; biology studies, **Supp. 4,** 253; botany studies, **Supp. 3,** 815; **Supp. 6,** 176; chemistry studies, **Supp. 5,** 35–36; engineering studies, **Vol. 4, Part 1,** 52; **Vol. 9, Part 2,** 519; **Supp. 1,** 31, 175; **Supp. 5,** 387; English drama studies, **Supp. 4,** 4–5; first black woman admitted, **Supp. 7,** 236; football team, **Supp. 4,** 236; **Supp. 5,** 727–28; founding of, **Vol. 3, Part 1,** 445 f.; **Vol. 3, Part 2,** 326, 383; **Vol. 7, Part 2,** 296; **Vol. 9, Part 1,** 146; **Vol. 10, Part 2,** 89; gifts to, **Vol. 8, Part 2,** 283, 290; **Supp. 6,** 623; historical library, **Supp. 2,** 75; history studies, **Supp. 3,** 47–48, 726; horticul-

Court martials, military manual revision, **Supp. 1**, 211

Court of Claims, United States, **Vol. 1, Part 1**, 409; **Vol. 2, Part 1**, 559; **Vol. 6, Part 1**, 219; **Vol. 7, Part 1**, 580

Courts, coercion of, **Vol. 3, Part 1**, 160. *See also* Judicial system; Judiciary; Supreme Court

Court stories, **Supp. 3**, 773–74

Couzens, James, references to, **Supp. 4**, 293, 294, 295, 297, 298

Coventry, R.I., site of one of earliest cotton mills in U.S., **Vol. 3, Part 1**, 275

Covered Wagon, **Vol. 5, Part 1**, 250

Covici, Pascal, reference to, **Supp. 7**, 307

Covici-Friede, **Supp. 7**, 307; founding of, **Supp. 7**, 148–49

Covington, Burling, Rublee, Acheson and Shorb, **Supp. 6**, 556, 557

Covode investigations (1857), **Vol. 2, Part 1**, 212

Cowboy Songs and Other Frontier Ballads, **Supp. 4**, 502

Cowboys: fiction on, **Supp. 2**, 729–30; **Supp. 3**, 383; movie, **Supp. 4**, 363–64, 734–35; **Supp. 7**, 286–87; songs of, **Supp. 4**, 502. *See also* West (U.S.)

Cowles, Henry C., reference to, **Supp. 3**, 169

Cowles Foundation, predecessors, **Supp. 4**, 275

Cowley Fathers (Society of St. John the Evangelist), establishment of, **Vol. 4, Part 1**, 470

Cowpens, battle of, **Vol. 4, Part 1**, 572; **Vol. 7, Part 1**, 167; **Vol. 7, Part 2**, 559

Cowpox vaccination, first demonstration of, in U.S., **Vol. 10, Part 1**, 479 f. 529

Cox, Archibald, reference to, **Supp. 8**, 322

Cox, Eugene, reference to, **Supp. 7**, 276

Cox, George B., reference to, **Vol. 6, Part 1**, 394

Cox, James M., references to, **Supp. 3**, 21, 643; **Supp. 5**, 697; **Supp. 8**, 404

Crackers, water, first manufacturing of, **Vol. 1, Part 2**, 205

Craddock, Charles Egbert, reference to, **Vol. 7, Part 1**, 344

Cradle Will Rock, The, **Supp. 7**, 61, 62

Crafts: American Indian, **Supp. 1**, 437–38; **Supp. 8**, 126; museum interest in, **Supp. 6**, 96–97; youth training in, **Supp. 3**, 44. *See also specific crafts*

Craig, Samuel, reference to, **Supp. 7**, 306

Craig headrest, **Supp. 6**, 131

Cram, Ralph Adams, references to, **Supp. 3**, 183, 183–84; **Supp. 4**, 547

Cram and Ferguson (architects), **Supp. 3**, 183

Cram and Goodhue (architects), **Supp. 3**, 195–97

Cramer, Stuart W., reference to, **Supp. 4**, 148

Crampton, Henry E., reference to, **Supp. 3**, 478

Cranbrook Foundation, **Supp. 4**, 714–15; **Supp. 7**, 670

Crandall, Eddie, reference to, **Supp. 6**, 301

Crandall, Prudence, case, **Vol. 3, Part 1**, 27

Crandon, Margery, reference to, **Supp. 8**, 44

Crane, Stephen, reference to, **Supp. 4**, 38

Cranes, building of, **Vol. 9, Part 2**, 613

Cravath, de Gersdorff, Swaine, and Wood, **Supp. 3**, 839

Craven, Avery, reference to, **Supp. 7**, 685

Crawford, Harry J., reference to, **Supp. 5**, 260

Crawford, Jimmy, reference to, **Supp. 4**, 510, 511

Crawford, William H., reference to, **Vol. 5, Part 1**, 531

Crawfordsville, Ind., **Vol. 3, Part 1**, 522

Crayon, publication of, **Vol. 9, Part 2**, 29

Crayon portraits, **Vol. 6, Part 1**, 54; **Vol. 8, Part 2**, 54, 202

Crazy Horse, Indian chief, references to, **Vol. 2, Part 2**, 530 f.; **Vol. 4, Part 2**, 28; **Vol. 7, Part 1**, 560

Credit: for securities purchases, **Supp. 1**, 84; auto-industry-related, **Supp. 4**, 682; economy, relation-

ship to, **Supp. 6**, 599; farm, **Supp. 4**, 341, 480, 482; interest-rate theory, **Supp. 4**, 272–73; ratings, **Supp. 6**, 693–94; rediscount rates, **Supp. 3**, 730; World War I loans, **Supp. 4**, 469–70

Credit Mobilier scandal (1867), **Vol. 1, Part 1**, 251, 580; **Vol. 1, Part 2**, 78, 148; **Vol. 2, Part 1**, 78, 298; **Vol. 4, Part 1**, 146, 500, 539; **Vol. 5, Part 1**, 87; **Vol. 5, Part 2**, 42; **Vol. 8, Part 1**, 33–34

Credit Union Act (1934), **Supp. 3**, 706

Credit unions, **Supp. 2**, 184

Creek Indians, **Vol. 1, Part 2**, 520; **Vol. 7, Part 2**, 569; **Vol. 9, Part 2**, 580, 650; disturbances (1836-37), **Vol. 2, Part 1**, 423; **Vol. 4, Part 1**, 93; **Vol. 5, Part 1**, 73; **Vol. 5, Part 2**, 63; **Vol. 9, Part 2**, 350; treaty with Carolina, **Vol. 5, Part 2**, 111; war (1813-14), **Vol. 1, Part 2**, 391; **Vol. 2, Part 2**, 253; **Vol. 4, Part 2**, 414; **Vol. 5, Part 1**, 263, 529; **Vol. 6, Part 2**, 70, 538; **Vol. 8, Part 1**, 274; **Vol. 10, Part 1**, 567; **Vol. 10, Part 2**, 106, 108

Creel, George, references to, **Supp. 3**, 39, 396

Creighton, James Edwin, reference to, **Supp. 3**, 697

Creighton University, **Vol. 2, Part 2**, 535 f.; **Vol. 7, Part 1**, 618

cremation, **Vol. 6, Part 1**, 163 f.; **Vol. 7, Part 1**, 470

Crenshaw, Daniel, reference to, **Vol. 7, Part 1**, 369

Creole, case of, **Vol. 1, Part 1**, 90; **Vol. 4, Part 2**, 446

Creole Indians, **Vol. 2, Part 1**, 480; **Vol. 6, Part 2**, 283; **Vol. 8, Part 2**, 192 f.

Crescent City Democratic Association, **Supp. 7**, 555, 556

Crete: archaeology in, **Supp. 3**, 343–44; diplomacy, **Vol. 9, Part 2**, 29

Crichton, Kyle, reference to, **Supp. 7**, 52

Crickets, chirps as temperature measurement, **Supp. 1**, 325

Crickets (singing group), **Supp. 6**, 301

Criger, Lou, reference to, **Supp. 5**, 759

Crile, George, references to, **Supp. 4**, 507, 508

Crime: body traits of criminals, **Supp. 5**, 312; criminal administration methodology, **Supp. 3**, 65–66; federal campaigns against, **Supp. 4**, 613; first U.S. government officer convicted of, **Supp. 3**, 259–60; investigative techniques, **Supp. 5**, 245; prevention, **Supp. 1**, 173; psychiatric evaluation of defendants, **Supp. 3**, 102; sociological theory of, **Supp. 4**, 808–9; statistical survey, **Supp. 5**, 639; tax evasion, **Supp. 3**, 21; white collar, **Supp. 4**, 809. *See also* Assassinations; Bombings and terrorism; Capital punishment; Judicial system; Kidnapping; Law; Murders; Organized crime; Prisons

Crimean War, **Vol. 6, Part 1**, 611; **Vol. 7, Part 2**, 578 f.

Criminal law. *See* Law, criminal

Criminology, **Vol. 2, Part 1**, 386; early studies in, **Vol. 3, Part 1**, 493; statistics, **Vol. 5, Part 2**, 495; writings on, **Vol. 3, Part 1**, 493; **Vol. 7, Part 1**, 389

Cripple Creek, **Vol. 7, Part 1**, 75

Crisis, **Supp. 5**, 741; **Supp. 7**, 202, 203, 236

Criterion, **Supp. 7**, 219

Criticism: architecture, **Supp. 2**, 708–9; **Supp. 3**, 52–53; art, **Supp. 2**, 99, 740; **Supp. 3**, 341–42; **Supp. 4**, 182–83, 702; **Supp. 5**, 478–79; **Supp. 7**, 260, 493–94; **Supp. 8**, 489–90; botany, **Supp. 4**, 267; dramatic, **Vol. 8, Part 1**, 132; **Vol. 10, Part 2**, 44, 406; literary, **Vol. 2, Part 1**, 173; **Vol. 4, Part 2**, 11 f.; **Vol. 5, Part 1**, 310, 379; **Vol. 6, Part 1**, 459 f., 540 f.; **Vol. 7, Part 1**, 359, 398; **Vol. 8, Part 1**, 19 f., 46 f., 48 f., 623 f.; **Vol. 9, Part 1**, 91; Vol. 10, Part 1, 45, 387 f., 392 f.; **Vol. 10, Part 2**, 480; **Supp. 2**, 100, 471, 623; **Supp. 3**, 72; **Supp. 4**, 559–61, 702, 847; **Supp. 5**, 89–90, 168–69, 356, 425, 542; **Supp. 7**, 18, 55–56, 79–80, 103–4, 219–22, 309–10, 638, 754; **Supp. 8**, 124, 353–54, 492, 493, 584–85, 667–68; Marxist literary, **Supp. 7,** 268; motion picture, **Supp. 5,** 12, 623; **Supp. 8,** 491, 584–85; music, **Vol. 4, Part 1,** 50; **Vol. 5, Part 1,** 379; **Supp. 1,** 369, 592; **Supp. 2,** 237, 295; **Supp. 3,** 770–71; **Supp. 4,** 702; **Supp. 5,** 183; **Supp. 7,** 124, 754; New Criticism, **Supp. 7,** 55, 219, 347, 442; **Supp. 8,** 325–27; of press, **Supp. 3,** 59–60; **Supp. 7,** 473; poetry, **Supp. 3,** 475; **Supp. 4,** 694, 812; **Supp. 7,** 391; **Supp. 8,** 42, 43; popular entertainment, **Supp. 8,** 584–85; restaurant, **Supp. 6,** 291 –92; social, **Supp. 6,** 445–47, 557–58; **Supp. 7,** 80– 81; 539–40; television, **Supp. 6,** 366; theater, **Supp.** **1,** 369, 591, 643; **Supp. 2,** 76, 277; **Supp. 3,** 53–54, 841–42; **Supp. 4,** 354, 548–49; **Supp. 5,** 17–18, 425, 463–64, 657–58; **Supp. 6,** 237, 470–71; **Supp. 7,** 412, 811–12; **Supp. 8,** 53–55, 353, 444–45, 491, 492, 584–85

Crittenden Compromise (1860), **Vol. 2, Part 1,** 9; **Vol. 2, Part 2,** 548; **Vol. 3, Part 1,** 403; **Vol. 6, Part 2,** 249; **Vol. 7, Part 2,** 420; **Vol. 8, Part 1,** 485; **Vol. 8, Part 2,** 618; **Vol. 10, Part 1,** 304

Crittenton Mission for Wayward Girls, **Vol. 1, Part 1,** 646

"Croaker & Co.," secret authorship of, **Vol. 3, Part 1,** 203

"Crocker, Betty" (fictional character), **Supp. 7,** 47; **Supp. 8,** 27

Crockett, David, reference to, **Vol. 2, Part 2,** 555 f.

"Croghan Hall" (Pittsburgh), **Vol. 2, Part 2,** 556

Croker, Richard, references to, **Vol. 5, Part 2,** 309; **Supp. 3,** 717; **Supp. 6,** 294

Croly, Herbert, reference to, **Supp. 7,** 310, 316

Crop Improvement Bureau (Chicago), founding of, **Supp. 1,** 142

Crops, rotation of, **Vol. 1, Part 2,** 460; insect injuries, **Vol. 8, Part 1,** 609 f.

Crosby, Bing, reference to, **Supp. 5,** 32–33

Crosby, Maunsell, reference to, **Supp. 6,** 255

Crosley Radio Corporation, founding of, **Supp. 7,** 154

Cross, Wilbur, reference to, **Supp. 7,** 103

Cross Keys, Va., battle of, **Vol. 4, Part 1,** 23; **Vol. 5, Part 1,** 557–58

Crossley, Archibald M., reference to, **Supp. 5,** 311

Crossword puzzles, **Supp. 6,** 583

Crothers, Samuel McChord, reference to, **Vol. 6, Part 1,** 423

Croup, treatment of, **Vol. 1, Part 2,** 74

Crouse, Russel, reference to, **Supp. 8,** 383

Crow Indians, **Supp. 6,** 392–93

Crowe, Pat, reference to, **Supp. 8,** 109

Crowell-Collier Publishing Co., **Supp. 5,** 394

Crowell Publishing Co., **Supp. 3,** 442–43

Crowley, Jim, references to, **Supp. 7,** 451, 729

Crown Cork & Seal Co., **Vol. 7, Part 2,** 168

Crowninshield, Frank, reference to, **Supp. 3,** 547; **Supp. 8,** 491

Crown Point, N.Y., operation at (1775-77), **Vol. 1, Part 1,** 257, 363–64; **Vol. 3, Part 2,** 185; **Vol. 8, Part 2,** 477–78; **Vol. 9, Part 1,** 531

Crown Zellerbach Corporation, organization of, **Supp. 7,** 814

Crozier, William, references to, **Supp. 8,** 502, 503

Cruickshank, Bobby, reference to, **Supp. 8,** 14

Crump, Edward Hull ("Boss"), references to, **Supp. 6,** 419; **Supp. 7,** 415

Cryptograms, **Vol. 3, Part 1,** 370; **Vol. 8, Part 1,** 19 f.

Cryptography, literary, **Supp. 5,** 20

Cryptology, **Supp. 8,** 195–96

Crystallography, **Supp. 3,** 38

Crystals, artificial, **Vol. 5, Part 2,** 487

Cry, the Beloved Country, **Supp. 5,** 419

CTR. *See* Computing-Tabulating-Recording Co.,

Cuba, **Vol. 4, Part 2,** 527; **Vol. 8, Part 1,** 315 f.; **Vol. 8, Part 2,** 511; **Vol. 9, Part 2,** 326; annexation of, **Vol. 2, Part 1,** 212 f.; **Vol. 3, Part 1,** 329; **Vol. 9, Part 1,** 406; Bay of Pigs, **Supp. 7,** 421–22, 723–24; **Supp. 8,** 135, 147; civil administration following Spanish-American War, **Vol. 6, Part 2,** 201; conditions in, famous speech on, **Vol. 8, Part 1,** 245 f.; diplomatic relations with U.S., **Vol. 1, Part 1,** 485; **Vol. 3, Part 2,** 224; **Vol. 4, Part 2,** 513; **Vol. 6, Part 1,** 104; **Vol. 8, Part 1,** 2 f.; **Vol. 9, Part 1,** 491; **Vol. 10, Part 2,** 467 f.; **Supp. 1,** 89; **Supp. 6,** 451; explorations, **Vol. 7, Part 1,** 382 f.; filibustering expeditions, **Vol. 2, Part 1,** 96; **Vol. 4, Part 1,** 233; **Vol. 4, Part 2,** 527; **Vol. 9, Part 2,** 510; independence of, **Vol. 4, Part 2,** 527, 543; **Vol. 9, Part 2,** 363; intervention in, **Vol. 3, Part 1,** 110; **Vol. 6, Part 2,** 108; **Vol. 8, Part 1,** 302 f.; insurrection, **Vol. 2, Part 2,** 211; **Vol. 3, Part 2,** 399; **Vol. 7, Part 2,** 154; Isle of Pines ceded to, **Vol. 8, Part 1,** 333; Platt Amendment, **Vol. 6, Part 2,** 108; prisoner exhange with U.S., **Supp. 8,** 135; public relations, **Supp. 6,** 90; revolution (1959), **Supp. 7,** 116; soil conservation, **Supp. 6,** 52; Soviet missiles in, **Supp. 7,** 423, 724; **Supp. 8,** 323; Spanish-American War, **Vol. 1, Part 1,** 154, 180; **Vol. 2, Part 2,** 145; **Vol. 6, Part 1,** 377; **Vol. 6, Part 2,** 107; **Vol. 8, Part 1,** 136–37; **Vol. 9, Part 1,** 16; **Vol. 10, Part 2,** 467; sugar plantations, **Vol. 9, Part 2,** 338; trade, **Vol. 7, Part 1,** 336; **Vol. 9, Part 1,** 338; **Vol. 10, Part 1,** 424 f.; transportation systems, **Supp. 5,** 215; U.S. intervention in, **Supp. 7,** 777; U.S. presence in, **Supp. 2,** 579; **Supp. 6,** 206

Cuban Telephone Co., **Supp. 6,** 43

Cudahy, Edward, Sr., reference to, **Supp. 8,** 109

Cudahy Packing Co., **Supp. 8,** 109–10

Culbertson, Ely, references to, **Supp. 6,** 134–35, 380

Cullen, Countee, reference to, **Supp. 6,** 321

Cullen, Thomas S., reference to, **Supp. 3,** 106

Cullen Foundation, **Supp. 6,** 136

Cultural history. *See* Ethnology

Cultural relativity, **Supp. 4,** 71–72

Cultures. *See* Anthropology; Ethnology; Sociology

Cumberland, command of, **Vol. 9, Part 1,** 310

Cumberland College, **Vol. 7, Part 2,** 591

"Cumberland Compact," **Vol. 8, Part 2,** 24 f.

Cumberland Gap, Tenn., capture of, **Vol. 7, Part 1,** 171

Cumberland Road, **Vol. 7, Part 1,** 90

Cumberland University, **Vol. 3, Part 1,** 368

Cummings, Homer S., references to, **Supp. 6,** 4, 156

Cummings Act (1896), **Supp. 3,** 276

Cummings and Lockwood, **Supp. 6,** 137

Cummins, Albert B., references to, **Supp. 3,** 107; **Supp. 6,** 256

Cumulative Book Index, **Supp. 5,** 752

Cuneiform, studies in, **Supp. 1,** 171, 261

Cuney, Norris, reference to, **Supp. 6,** 567

Cunow, John G., reference to, **Vol. 6, Part 1,** 421

Curators. For complete list, *see* Occupations Index

Curie, Marie, reference to, **Vol. 3, Part 1,** 511 f.

Curie, Pierre, reference to, **Vol. 3, Part 1,** 511 f.

Curley, James M., references to, **Supp. 5,** 692; **Supp. 8,** 219

Curran, Pearl Lenore Pollard, reference to, **Supp. 3,** 851

Currency, **Vol. 1, Part 1,** 510; **Vol. 3, Part 1,** 553 f.; **Vol. 3, Part 2,** 3, 188; **Vol. 5, Part 1,** 203; **Vol. 6, Part 1,** 273, 406; **Vol. 8, Part 1,** 49 f., 325 f.; **Vol. 8, Part 2,** 301; **Vol. 9, Part 1,** 89; Aldrich Plan v. Federal Reserve Act, **Vol. 4, Part 2,** 567; Bland-Allison Act, **Vol. 1, Part 2,** 355; coinage, free, **Vol. 1, Part 2,** 355; counterfeiting, **Vol. 3, Part 1,** 151, 273, 535 f.; designing and printing of first issue,

Vol. 8, Part 1, 515; engraving of, Vol. 2, Part 2, 343; Vol. 5, Part 2, 456; Massachusetts experiments with, Vol. 3, Part 1, 106; minting of, Vol. 1, Part 2, 478; Vol. 3, Part 1, 254; Vol. 5, Part 1, 362; Vol. 5, Part 2, 456; Vol. 6, Part 1, 90, 273; Vol. 8, Part 1, 49 f., 450, 631; Vol. 8, Part 2, 100, 110, 400; Vol. 9, Part 1, 387; paper, Vol. 1, Part 2, 564; Vol. 9, Part 2, 84; paper money based on cotton, Vol. 10, Part 1, 451; publication of valuation of, Vol. 9, Part 2, 462; speculation in continental, Vol. 3, Part 1, 281 f. *See also* Coinage; Monetary system

Current Anthropology, founding of, Supp. 7, 241
Current Events, Vol. 7, Part 1, 377
Current History, Supp. 6, 410
Currier and Ives (lithographers), Vol. 2, Part 2, 604; Vol. 5, Part 1, 520
Curry, John Steuart, reference to, Supp. 3, 841
Curtain manufacture, Vol. 3, Part 2, 279
Curtis, Charles, references to, Supp. 3, 106, 251; Supp. 7, 361
Curtis, George William, references to, Vol. 7, Part 1, 33, 569
Curtis, Richard Cary, reference to, Supp. 6, 143
Curtis, S. R., reference to, Vol. 7, Part 1, 560
Curtis Institute, directors, Supp. 6, 297
Curtis Publishing Co., Supp. 1, 212–13; Supp. 7, 602
Curtiss, Glen, reference to, Supp. 5, 2
Curtiss Aeroplane and Motor Co., Supp. 6, 145
Curtiss-Wright Corporation: founding of, Supp. 5, 384–85; project-engineer system, Supp. 8, 709
Cushing, Caleb, reference to, Vol. 5, Part 2, 256
Cushing, Harvey, references to, Supp. 3, 201; Supp. 4, 208, 209, 213; Supp. 6, 70, 223, 224
Cushing's disease, studies of, Supp. 2, 139
Cushman, Charlotte, reference to, Vol. 5, Part 1, 242
Custer, George A., references to, Vol. 8, Part 2, 181; Vol. 9, Part 1, 192
Custer Hill, battle of, Vol. 3, Part 1, 8; Vol. 9, Part 2, 379
Custis, John Parker, reference to, Vol. 1, Part 2, 474
Custody, child, Supp. 7, 753
Customs Court, United States, Supp. 6, 114
Customs houses, architecture, Supp. 1, 716
Cutlery, manufacturing of, Vol. 1, Part 1, 248
Cutting, Bronson F., reference to, Supp. 7, 121
Cvetic, Matthew, reference to, Supp. 6, 681
CWA. *See* Civil Works Administration
Cyanamide, Supp. 3, 438–39
Cybernetics, Supp. 3, 137; Supp. 7, 785
Cycads, Supp. 3, 153–54
Cyclooctatetraene, Supp. 8, 103
Cyclopedia of Education, Supp. 4, 592
Cyclopropane, Supp. 6, 334
Cyclotron, Supp. 5, 273, 274; invention of, Supp. 6, 370–71
Cygnus A (galaxy), Supp. 6, 31
"Cy-près", doctrine of, Vol. 10, Part 1, 620
Cystoscope, Supp. 3, 854
Cytochemistry, term coined, Supp. 6, 295–96
Cytology, Supp. 6, 53–54; chromosome behavior, Supp. 4, 515–16
Cytosine, synthesis of, Supp. 4, 434
Czechoslovakia, diplomacy with U.S., Supp. 4, 773
Czolgosz, Leon, reference to, Supp. 5, 285, 286

D

Dabney, Virginius, reference to, Supp. 3, 115
Dacron, Supp. 5, 191
Dadaism, Supp. 5, 20; Supp. 6, 256
Daguerreotype, Vol. 1, Part 2, 529; Vol. 7, Part 1, 280 f.; Vol. 8, Part 2, 174, 362; Vol. 9, Part 1, 514

Dahl, Francis, reference to, Supp. 8, 448
Dahl, Nikolai, reference to, Supp. 3, 616
Dahlberg, Mae, reference to, Supp. 7, 462
Dahl-Wolfe, Louise, reference to, Supp. 5, 200
Daily Chicago Herald, Vol. 2, Part 2, 374
Daily Chronicle (Minneapolis), Vol. 2, Part 2, 367
"Daily dozen" exercises, origin of, Vol. 2, Part 1, 445
Daily Evening Bulletin, San Francisco, Vol. 5, Part 2, 408
Daily Graphic, first illustrated daily paper in U.S., Vol. 8, Part 1, 332 f.
Daily News. See New York *Daily News*
Daily News Building, architecture, Supp. 1, 430
Daily Pioneer Press, St. Paul, Vol. 10, Part 2, 60
Daily Racing Form, Supp. 3, 20
Daily Southern Carolinian, Vol. 3, Part 1, 196
Daily Times, Louisville, first newspaper of its kind west of Alleghenies, Vol. 9, Part 2, 607
Daily Worker, Supp. 7, 113, 256; columnists, Supp. 8, 216, 217; editing of, Supp. 5, 499–500; Harlem editor, Supp. 6, 715
Dairy, farming, Vol. 1, Part 1, 238, 370; Vol. 8, Part 2, 512; Vol. 9, Part 1, 280; Supp. 1, 37, 444; herd improvement, Supp. 3, 750; school, first in U.S., Vol. 9, Part 1, 280; promotion, Wisconsin, Vol. 5, Part 1, 90. *See also* Milk
Dairy industry: cheese processing, Supp. 5, 399–400; chemistry of production, Supp. 5, 275–76. *See also* Milk
Dairymen's Associations of the West, Vol. 5, Part 1, 90
Dakin, Henry B., reference to, Supp. 3, 141
Dakota language, readers in the, Vol. 8, Part 1, 61 f., 605
Dakota Playhouse, Supp. 3, 426
Dakota Territory: division of, Vol. 7, Part 2, 517; governorship of, Vol. 3, Part 2, 297; Vol. 5, Part 1, 283; Vol. 7, Part 2, 581; surveying of, Vol. 1, Part 2, 86
Dakota Ruralist, Vol. 6, Part 1, 426
Dale, Chester, references to, Supp. 5, 150, 151
Dale, Henry H., references to, Supp. 3, 134, 136, 137
Dale, Maud, reference to, Supp. 7, 161
Dale, Sir Thomas, reference to, Vol. 7, Part 1, 468
Daley, Richard, reference to, Supp. 8, 121
Dalhousie University, Vol. 7, Part 1, 332
Dallas-Clarendon Treaty, Vol. 3, Part 1, 39; Vol. 7, Part 2, 579
Dallas Morning News, Supp. 4, 222
Dallas News, Vol. 1, Part 2, 171
Dallas *Times-Herald*, Supp. 7, 434
Dalton, Ga., operation at (1863-64), Vol. 1, Part 2, 487; Vol. 4, Part 2, 240; Vol. 5, Part 1, 193; Vol. 9, Part 1, 95; Vol. 9, Part 2, 3
Daly, Augustin, references to, Vol. 5, Part 1, 586, 605; Vol. 8, Part 1, 471 f.
Daly, Marcus, reference to, Vol. 2, Part 2, 145
Daly, Maurice, reference to, Supp. 6, 303
Daly, William M., reference to, Supp. 8, 465
Damaged Goods, Supp. 3, 58
Damrosch, Clara, reference to, Supp. 6, 426
Damrosch, Frank, reference to, Supp. 3, 309
Damrosch, Leopold, references to, Vol. 8, Part 2, 562; Supp. 4, 210, 213, 544, 545
Damrosch, Walter, references to, Supp. 3, 33, 742; Supp. 5, 646; Supp. 6, 20, 426
Damrosch Opera Company, founding of, Supp. 4, 210–11
Damrosch Park (New York City), Supp. 4, 213
Dams: collapse, Supp. 1, 570; design and construction of, Vol. 2, Part 2, 570; Vol. 8, Part 1, 359 f.; Vol. 8, Part 2, 474; Supp. 1, 225, 393, 700; Supp. 2,

304-5; **Supp. 3,** 814; **Supp. 4,** 198–99; **Supp. 6,** 182; **Supp. 8,** 572–73; federal, **Supp. 2,** 119; **Supp. 3,** 397; geological determination of sites, **Supp. 4,** 119; Hetch Hetchy Valley, **Supp. 4,** 522. *See also* Tennessee Valley Authority

Dana, Charles A., references to, **Vol. 2, Part 1,** 99; **Vol. 5, Part 1,** 65; **Vol. 7, Part 1,** 44; **Supp. 1,** 509–10

Dana, Charles R., reference to, **Supp. 5,** 301

Dana, Henry W. L., references to, **Supp. 4,** 62, 135

Dana, John Cotton, references to, **Supp. 3,** 301 **Supp. 6,** 96

Dana, R. H., reference to, **Vol. 7, Part 1,** 107

Danbury, Conn.: *Danbury News Man,* **Vol. 1, Part 1,** 499; "Sandemanians," Scotch religious sect, **Vol. 8, Part 2,** 329; writings on, **Vol. 1, Part 1,** 499

Dance: ballet, **Vol. 4, Part 1,** 59 f.; **Supp. 5,** 74–76; **Supp. 8,** 669–70; ballet companies, **Supp. 7,** 173–74; ballet scores, **Supp. 8,** 145, 146; ballet sets and costumes, **Supp. 6,** 625; ballroom, **Vol. 2, Part 1,** 569; **Supp. 7,** 563; **Supp. 8,** 77–78, 690; black bottom, **Supp. 8,** 694, 695; burlesque, **Supp. 8,** 694; cakewalk, **Supp. 3,** 187; Charleston, **Supp. 8,** 695; choreography, **Supp. 6,** 312–13; creative art, as a, **Vol. 3, Part 1,** 508 f.; first chorus line, **Supp. 6,** 305; "Hootchy Kootchy," **Supp. 4,** 88; modern, **Supp. 5,** 129; **Supp. 6,** 312–13; **Supp. 8,** 620–21, 643–44; modern ballet choreography, **Supp. 3,** 281–82; modern, teaching of, **Supp. 7,** 366–67; musical revues, **Supp. 8,** 694–95; photographs, **Supp. 3,** 296; set designs, **Supp. 7,** 560; shimmy popularization, **Supp. 6,** 247; tap, **Supp. 4,** 695; theatrical musicals and revues, **Supp. 7,** 34, 497, 563; teaching of, **Vol. 4, Part 1,** 60; turkey trot, **Supp. 8,** 694, 695; waltz clog, **Supp. 7,** 657–58; writings on, **Vol. 4, Part 1,** 60

Dance bands, **Supp. 3,** 524–25; **Supp. 5,** 187–88; **Supp. 7,** 300–1, 774; **Supp. 8,** 697–98. *See also* Swing bands

Dance Observer, founding of, **Supp. 7,** 367

Dance Repertory Theatre, **Supp. 6,** 312; **Supp. 8,** 643

Dancing Rabbit Creek, Treaty of (1830), **Vol. 6, Part 2,** 82

Daniels, Josephus, references to, **Supp. 3,** 275, 642, 643; **Supp. 5,** 332

Danielson, Jacques, reference to, **Supp. 8,** 296

Dante, translations and studies of, **Vol. 3, Part 1,** 72; **Vol. 3, Part 2,** 303; **Vol. 6, Part 1,** 383; **Vol. 7, Part 1,** 570; **Vol. 7, Part 2,** 274 f.; **Supp. 2,** 254; **Supp. 5,** 19, 20

Danville, Ky., political club at (1789), **Vol. 5, Part 1,** 486; **Vol. 8, Part 2,** 543

DAR. *See* Daughters of the American Revolution

Darboux, Gaston, reference to, **Supp. 7,** 216

Dargan, E. Preston, reference to, **Supp. 3,** 22

"Dark Continent," first use of name, **Vol. 9, Part 1,** 511

"Dark horse," use of term, in politics, **Vol. 8, Part 1,** 34 f.

Darlan, François, reference to, **Supp. 8,** 274–75

Darling Nelly Gray, **Vol. 4, Part 2,** 217

Darmstädter und Nationalbank (Danatbank), founding of, **Supp. 5,** 249–50

Darrow, Clarence, references to, **Vol. 8, Part 1,** 9 f.; **Supp. 3,** 156, 822; **Supp. 4,** 542; **Supp. 6,** 528, 529; **Supp. 7,** 624, 631; **Supp. 8,** 583, 660

Dartmouth College, **Vol. 1, Part 1,** 56, 126; **Vol. 3, Part 1,** 180; **Vol. 4, Part 1,** 304; **Vol. 5, Part 1,** 166; **Vol. 7, Part 2,** 301, 303, 478; **Vol. 8, Part 2,** 325; **Vol. 10, Part 1,** 585 f., 656; **Vol. 10, Part 2,** 59, 81; architectural studies, **Supp. 3,** 52–53; engineering school, **Supp. 2,** 195; gifts to, **Supp. 6,** 549; gradu-

ates, sketches of early, **Vol. 3, Part 2,** 278; "Laureate" of, **Vol. 5, Part 1,** 273; master plan, **Supp. 2,** 539; medical school, founding of, **Vol. 9, Part 1,** 324; presidency of, **Vol. 1, Part 2,** 15; **Vol. 2, Part 1,** 114; **Vol. 6, Part 1,** 409; **Vol. 7, Part 1,** 493; **Vol. 9, Part 1,** 239; **Vol. 10, Part 1,** 41, 85

Darwin, Charles, references to, **Vol. 1, Part 1,** 112, 120; **Vol. 4, Part 1,** 513; **Vol. 8, Part 1,** 624; **Vol. 10, Part 1,** 644 f.; **Supp. 3,** 697, 704; **Supp. 4,** 691

Darwinism. *See* Evolutionism

Dashiell, Alfred Sheppard, reference to, **Supp. 5,** 614

Daugherty, Harry M., references to, **Supp. 3,** 117, 489

Daughter of Earth, **Supp. 4,** 749, 750

Daughters of the American Revolution (DAR): Constitution Hall, **Supp. 5,** 300, 343; **Supp. 8,** 328; founding of, **Vol. 3, Part 1,** 76

Daughters of the United States of the War of 1812, founding of, **Vol. 3, Part 1,** 76

Davenport, Charles B., references to, **Supp. 3,** 133, 477–78; **Supp. 6,** 241

Davenport, Frances G., reference to, **Supp. 3,** 16

Davenport, James, reference to, **Vol. 7, Part 1,** 614

Davenport, John, reference to, **Vol. 5, Part 1,** 200

Davenport, Russell, reference to, **Supp. 8,** 394

Davenport, Iowa, founding of, **Vol. 3, Part 1,** 83

David, Donald K., reference to, **Supp. 7,** 276

David Harum, writing of, **Vol. 10, Part 2,** 13

Davidson, Thomas, reference to, **Supp. 4,** 168

Davies, A. Powell, reference to, **Supp. 4,** 712

Davies, Arthur B., references to, **Supp. 3,** 278, 340; **Supp. 5,** 635

Davies, John Paton, references to, **Supp. 6,** 230, 231

Davies, Joseph E., reference to, **Supp. 6,** 184

Davies, Marion, references to, **Supp. 5,** 286–88; **Supp. 6,** 440; **Supp. 7,** 759

Davis, Arthur Powell, references to, **Supp. 3,** 813–14, 845–46

Davis, Arthur V., reference to, **Supp. 5,** 565–66

Davis, Bergen, reference to, **Supp. 7,** 10

Davis, Bernard G., reference to, **Supp. 5,** 760

Davis, Bette, reference to, **Supp. 7,** 591

Davis, Chester C., references to, **Supp. 6,** 638, 639

Davis, Donald, reference to, **Supp. 6,** 149

Davis, Dwight F., reference to, **Supp. 3,** 152

Davis, Glenn R., reference to, **Supp. 8,** 701

Davis, Harry Phillips, reference to, **Supp. 3,** 184–85

Davis, James J., reference to, **Supp. 7,** 305

Davis, Jefferson, **Vol. 1, Part 1,** 523; **Vol. 1, Part 2,** 182 f.; **Vol. 3, Part 2,** 483; **Vol. 5, Part 1,** 176, 183, 193, 404; **Vol. 5, Part 2,** 210; **Vol. 6, Part 1,** 106, 122, 481, 522, 581; **Vol. 7, Part 1,** 375, 567 f., 620; **Vol. 8, Part 2,** 545; **Vol. 9, Part 1,** 130, 573; **Vol. 9, Part 2,** 351 f.; amanuensis for, **Vol. 3, Part 1,** 386; biography of, **Vol. 8, Part 2,** 420; **Supp. 6,** 410; capture of, **Vol. 7, Part 1,** 33; trial of, **Vol. 8, Part 2,** 290; **Vol. 10, Part 1,** 114

Davis, Jefferson Columbus, reference to, **Vol. 7, Part 1,** 426

Davis, John W., references to, **Supp. 3,** 114, 481, 606, 644

Davis, Miles, reference to, **Supp. 8,** 100

Davis, Mrs. Jefferson, reference to, **Vol. 5, Part 1,** 85

Davis, Richard Harding, references to, **Supp. 3,** 300–1; **Supp. 6,** 253

Davis, William Morris, references to, **Supp. 3,** 389–90; **Supp. 4,** 98, 423–24, 765, 766

Davis-Bacon Act (1930), **Supp. 4,** 220

Davis, Hoxie, Faithfull and Hapgood, founding of, **Supp. 7,** 172

Davison, Henry P., references to, **Supp. 4,** 469; **Supp. 6,** 27

Vol. **3, Part 2,** 211; **Vol. 6, Part 2,** 458; inventions relating to, **Vol. 1, Part 1,** 19; **Vol. 1, Part 2,** 309, 440; **Vol. 5, Part 2,** 412; laughing gas, first use of, **Vol. 8, Part 1,** 604; machinery, use of, **Vol. 4, Part 1,** 161; nitrous oxide, use of, **Vol. 10, Part 1,** 640 f.; oral surgery, first to make specialty of, **Vol. 4, Part 1,** 161; orthodontics, **Supp. 2,** 666; profession, founding of, **Vol. 2, Part 1,** 155; **Vol. 4, Part 2,** 305; **Vol. 7, Part 2,** 251; pyorrhea, early treatment of, **Vol. 8, Part 1,** 604; research in, **Supp. 4,** 401–3; teaching of, **Vol. 1, Part 2,** 61; **Vol. 3, Part 2,** 212; **Vol. 4, Part 2,** 441; **Vol. 6, Part 2,** 164; Washington, George, **Vol. 4, Part 1,** 592; writings on, **Vol. 1, Part 2,** 309; **Vol. 2, Part 1,** 156; **Vol. 4, Part 1,** 161; **Vol. 4, Part 2,** 306; **Vol. 5, Part 1,** 541; **Vol. 5, Part 2,** 412; **Vol. 7, Part 2,** 251; **Vol. 8, Part 1,** 604; **Vol. 10, Part 1,** 640

Denver, Colo.: growth of, **Vol. 9, Part 2,** 263; life in 1860s, **Vol. 2, Part 1,** 121; Moffat, service of, **Vol. 7, Part 1,** 75; naming of, **Vol. 3, Part 1,** 243; public education, **Supp. 2,** 140

Denver & Rio Grande Railroad, **Vol. 5, Part 2,** 36; **Vol. 7, Part 2,** 195

Denver Post, **Supp. 1,** 94

De Palma Manufacturing Co., **Supp. 6,** 164

Department stores: advertising, **Supp. 5,** 433; air-conditioning of, **Supp. 4,** 149; Bamberger's, **Supp. 3,** 30; Christmas window decoration, **Supp. 3,** 685; discount, **Supp. 8,** 348–49; executives, **Supp. 7,** 440–41; Federated, **Supp. 3,** 421–22; Filene's, **Supp. 2,** 183; Gimbels, **Supp. 8,** 212–13; Macy's, **Supp. 2,** 636; **Supp. 3,** 748–49; management, **Vol. 9, Part 2,** 129 f.; **Vol. 10, Part 1,** 407 f.; May's, **Supp. 8,** 427–28; Sears, Roebuck, **Supp. 8,** 705; women's working conditions, **Supp. 4,** 623–24

De Pauw University, **Vol. 1, Part 2,** 521; **Vol. 3, Part 1,** 244; **Vol. 9, Part 1,** 181; presidency, **Supp. 4,** 408; **Supp. 7,** 597

Depew Memorial Fountain (Indianapolis), **Supp. 3,** 124

Deportation. *See* Immigration; Loyalty issues

Depression, economic. *See* Economics; Great Depression; Welfare

Dermatology, **Vol. 2, Part 1,** 251; **Vol. 3, Part 1,** 494 f.; **Vol. 3, Part 2,** 521; **Vol. 5, Part 1,** 451, 540 f.; **Vol. 5, Part 2,** 364; **Vol. 7, Part 1,** 237; **Vol. 8, Part 2,** 418 f.; **Vol. 10, Part 1,** 648 f.; **Vol. 10, Part 2,** 193; first school of, in U.S., **Vol. 10, Part 2,** 109. *See also* Skin

De Sapio, Carmine, reference to, **Supp. 6,** 142

Desch, Cecil H., reference to, **Supp. 6,** 70

Desegregation. *See* Civil rights movement; School desegregaton

Deseret, state of, **Vol. 5, Part 2,** 377; **Vol. 8, Part 1,** 175

Desert, description of early crossing, **Vol. 8, Part 2,** 251; plants, study of, **Vol. 9, Part 1,** 427

Design. *See subject areas, e.g.,* Art; Fashion

Des Moines *Register and Leader,* **Supp. 4,** 189; **Supp. 6,** 676; **Supp. 7,** 164

Desperadoes of the South West, **Vol. 1, Part 1,** 373

De Sylva, Buddy, reference to, **Supp. 8,** 250–51

Detective agency, private, first in U.S., **Vol. 7, Part 2,** 622 f.

Detective stories, **Vol. 5, Part 2,** 153; **Vol. 8, Part 1,** 119 f.; **Supp. 1,** 80, 635, 637, 692; **Supp. 2,** 740; **Supp. 6,** 106–7, 116; **Supp. 7,** 314, 315; **Supp. 8,** 202–3

Detective work, **Supp. 7,** 667–68

Detroit, Mich.: auto industry, **Supp. 3,** 550; **Supp. 4,** 291–304; 293–94; capture of, **Vol. 2, Part 1,** 563; **Vol. 3, Part 1,** 175; **Vol. 5, Part 1,** 363; **Vol. 6, Part 1,** 550; Catholic bishop, first, **Vol. 8, Part 1,** 510; civic and public service, **Vol. 3, Part 1,** 490 f.; **Vol. 6, Part 1,** 396; **Vol. 6, Part 2,** 144; **Vol. 7, Part 1,** 445; **Vol. 7, Part 2,** 192, 621, 637; **Vol. 8, Part 2,** 519 f.; commercial and industrial architecture, **Supp. 3,** 404–5; electric plant, **Supp. 3,** 231; founding of, **Vol. 2, Part 1,** 397; French colony of Father Constantin, **Vol. 6, Part 1,** 231; history, of early, **Vol. 10, Part 2,** 507; Hull's army at, surrender of, **Vol. 3, Part 1,** 175; Indians, trading with, **Vol. 2, Part 1,** 446; international vehicular tunnel, **Vol. 7, Part 2,** 278; mayors, **Supp. 2,** 126; **Supp. 4,** 611–12; **Supp. 6,** 115; Museum of Art, founding of, **Vol. 7, Part 2,** 192; newspaper, first to be printed in, **Vol. 8, Part 1,** 550; pediatrics; **Supp. 3,** 189–90; Polish immigrants, **Vol. 3, Part 1,** 24; public schools, first free, **Vol. 7, Part 2,** 637

Detroit, the, capture of, **Vol. 3, Part 2,** 96

Detroit Aircraft Corporation, founding of, **Supp. 8,** 385

Detroit Automobile Co., founding of, **Supp. 4,** 292–93

Detroit Bank and Trust Co., **Supp. 7,** 189, 190

Detroit Edison Co., **Supp. 3,** 231

Detroit Evening News, **Supp. 5,** 615

Detroit Free Press, **Vol. 9, Part 2,** 97; **Supp. 5,** 58; **Supp. 6,** 258

Detroit Lions (football), **Supp. 5,** 458

Detroit News, **Supp. 5,** 55–56, 504

Detroit River, Indian council at mouth of, **Vol. 8, Part 1,** 437

Detroit Symphony Orchestra, development of, **Supp. 2,** 214

Detroit Tigers (baseball), **Supp. 5,** 291–92; **Supp. 7,** 128, 130, 139, 663; **Supp. 8,** 49–50, 106–7, 142, 542–43

Deuterium, **Supp. 3,** 693; **Supp. 4,** 488–89

Deutsche Pionier, **Vol. 8, Part 1,** 388

Deutscher Werkbund, **Supp. 8,** 226

De Veaux College, founding of, **Vol. 3, Part 1,** 216

Development theory, **Supp. 4,** 805, 807–8

Dever, Paul A., reference to, **Supp. 8,** 219

De Voto, Bernard, reference to, **Supp. 7,** 517, 518

De Vries, Hugo, reference to, **Supp. 3,** 539

Dewey, Admiral George: biography of, **Supp. 2,** 25; relations with Gridley, **Vol. 4, Part 1,** 610

Dewey, John, references to, **Supp. 1,** 548; **Supp. 2,** 728; **Supp. 3,** 363, 457, 555, 577, 677, 780; **Supp. 4,** 20, 21, 374, 584, 585, 809; **Supp. 5,** 39, 71, 199, 549, 630, 664; **Supp. 6,** 46, 54, 55, 96, 261, 671; **Supp. 7,** 435

Dewey, Thomas E.: biography of, **Supp. 6,** 310; Curran relationship, **Supp. 6,** 141, 142; law practice, **Supp. 6,** 34; organized crime indictments by, **Supp. 5,** 665; **Supp. 6,** 295; **Supp. 7,** 485; presidential bids, **Supp. 3,** 664, 830; **Supp. 8,** 143, 144; references to, **Supp. 5,** 343; Straus relationship, **Supp. 6,** 607; Talbott relationship, **Supp. 6,** 618

Dewey, Ballantine, Bushby, Palmer and Wood, **Supp. 6,** 33

Dewing, Thomas, reference to, **Vol. 9, Part 2,** 400

DeWitt, John L., reference to, **Supp. 6,** 629

De Wolfe, Elsie, reference to, **Supp. 1,** 539

Dewson, Mary Williams, reference to, **Supp. 6,** 4

Diabetes: treatment of, **Supp. 6,** 698; urine analysis for, **Supp. 2,** 36

Diaghilev, Sergei, references to, **Supp. 3,** 282; **Supp. 5,** 75; **Supp. 7,** 548, 549, 560; **Supp. 8,** 145, 669–70

Dial, The, founding of, **Vol. 2, Part 1,** 165; **Vol. 3, Part 1,** 567 f.; **Vol. 8, Part 1,** 596; **Vol. 8, Part 1,** 623; **Supp. 7,** 158, 219, 494; **Supp. 8,** 584

Dialect: American Dialect Society, **Vol. 9, Part 1,** 64; American, pioneer scientific study of, **Vol. 4, Part 2,**

522; black, use of, in literature, **Vol. 4, Part 1,** 373; Indian, **Vol. 4, Part 2,** 94; Pennsylvania-German, **Vol. 6, Part 1,** 78; use of, in writing, **Vol. 4, Part 2,** 314

"Diamond Dick" (dime novel character), **Vol. 5, Part 2,** 51

Diamond Horseshoe (New York City nightclub), **Supp. 8,** 547

Diamond Match Co., **Vol. 1, Part 1,** 590; **Vol. 7, Part 1,** 143; **Vol. 9, Part 1,** 600; safety matches, **Supp. 4,** 257–58

Diamonds: cutting, **Vol. 7, Part 1,** 244; discovered in meteoric iron, **Vol. 5, Part 2,** 487; Dewey diamond, **Vol. 7, Part 1,** 244; mining, **Vol. 10, Part 2,** 261; **Supp. 2,** 701

Diaries, **Vol. 1, Part 1,** 513; **Vol. 2, Part 1,** 5, 64; **Vol. 3, Part 1,** 135, 152, 229; **Vol. 3, Part 2,** 92, 131; **Vol. 4, Part 1,** 116, 130, 133, 183, 378, 424, 461, 470, 497; **Vol. 4, Part 2,** 34 f., 248, 276, 538, 612; **Vol. 5, Part 1,** 192; **Vol. 5, Part 2,** 459, 468 f.; **Vol. 6, Part 1,** 182, 468; **Vol. 7, Part 1,** 150 f.; **Vol. 8, Part 1,** 12 f.; **Vol. 9, Part 1,** 147, 501; **Vol. 9, Part 2,** 20; **Vol. 10, Part 1,** 97, 99, 509 f., 629 f.; Adams, John Quincy, **Vol. 1, Part 1,** 84; Bentley, William, **Vol. 1, Part 2,** 207; Civil War, military diary, **Vol. 10, Part 1,** 95; colonial life, **Vol. 10, Part 1,** 362 f.; Continental Congress, **Vol. 9, Part 1,** 333; Ferguson, E. G., **Vol. 3, Part 2,** 331; Leaming, Aaron, **Vol. 8, Part 1,** 420; Lickford, Thomas, **Vol. 6, Part 1,** 87; McClure, David, **Vol. 3, Part 1,** 277; Ravenel, H. W., **Vol. 8, Part 1,** 396; Read, Daniel, **Vol. 8, Part 1,** 421; Reeder, Andrew Horatio, **Vol. 8, Part 1,** 463; Revolutionary War period, **Vol. 10, Part 2,** 434; Riddle, George Peabody, **Vol. 8, Part 1,** 592; Rieger, Joseph, **Vol. 8, Part 1,** 600; Robbins, Thomas, **Vol. 8, Part 1,** 646; Roebling, J. A., **Vol. 8, Part 2,** 87; Rogers, Robert, **Vol. 8, Part 2,** 109; Root, F. A., **Vol. 8, Part 2,** 146; Royce, Sarah Eleanor, **Vol. 8, Part 2,** 205; Rupp, Israel D., **Vol. 8, Part 2,** 226; Russell, Jonathan, **Vol. 8, Part 2,** 245; Russell, Osborne, trapper, **Vol. 8, Part 2,** 248; Sewall, **Vol. 8, Part 2,** 610 f.; Seybert, **Vol. 9, Part 1,** 4; Spanish expedition into California, **Vol. 8, Part 1,** 109 f.; Stiles, Ezra, **Vol. 3, Part 1,** 277; trip by ox team from Connecticut to Ohio, **Vol. 8, Part 1,** 441; Tudor, Frederic, **Vol. 10, Part 1,** 48; Welles, Gideon, **Vol. 8, Part 1,** 618. *See also* Journals and memoirs

Diarrhea: causes of, **Supp. 4,** 494; infant treatment, **Supp. 5,** 1

"Diary of a Public Man," **Vol. 5, Part 2,** 327

"Dick and Jane" reading textbooks, **Supp. 6,** 248

Dickens, Charles, references to, **Vol. 7, Part 1,** 400; **Vol. 8, Part 1,** 19 f.

Dickerman, Marion, reference to, **Supp. 7,** 659, 660

Dickey, Bill, reference to, **Supp. 7,** 130

Dickinson, Emily, references to, **Vol. 5, Part 1,** 542; **Vol. 9, Part 2,** 573; **Supp. 7,** 547; writings on, **Supp. 4,** 812

Dickinson, Robert L., references to, **Supp. 6,** 81–82; **Supp. 8,** 569

Dickinson College: founding of, **Vol. 3, Part 1,** 544 f.; **Vol. 7, Part 1,** 526; **Vol. 8, Part 2,** 228; first elective laboratory courses, **Vol. 5, Part 1,** 59; presidency of, **Vol. 7, Part 1,** 411

Dickmann, Bernard F., reference to, **Supp. 4,** 355

Dictionaries: Century, **Vol. 9, Part 1,** 241; English-German, **Vol. 7, Part 1,** 272; making of, **Vol. 3, Part 2,** 484 f.; **Vol. 10, Part 2,** 527; modern European literature, **Supp. 4,** 755; music, of, **Vol. 6, Part 1,** 239; *New Standard Dictionary,* **Supp. 2,** 682; publication, **Vol. 6, Part 1,** 287; Thai-English, **Supp. 3,** 486; "War of the Dictionaries," **Vol. 10, Part 1,** 594 f.;

Webster's, first edition of, **Vol. 5, Part 1,** 288; *Webster's New International,* **Supp. 4,** 624

Dictionary of American Biography, **Vol. 3, Part 1,** 430; **Vol. 5, Part 2,** 80 f.; **Vol. 8, Part 2,** 517; **Supp. 5,** 614; **Supp. 8,** 370, 580; planning of, **Supp. 2,** 186, 342

Dictionary of American Medical Biography, **Supp. 3,** 413

Dictionary of Philosophy and Psychology, **Supp. 1,** 50

Dictionary of the United States Congress, **Vol. 5, Part 2,** 606

"Die Hard" Republicanism, **Vol. 3, Part 2,** 581

Die-sinking, **Vol. 5, Part 2,** 456

Die tote Stadt (opera), **Supp. 6,** 351–52

Dielectric constants, **Supp. 6,** 346

Diem, Ngo Dinh, reference to, **Supp. 7,** 422

Dies, Martin, Committee, **Supp. 6,** 392; reference to, **Supp. 5,** 544

Diesel power, development of, **Supp. 6,** 333

Diet and nutrition: animal, **Supp. 1,** 37; baby food, **Supp. 5,** 242–43; biochemical studies, **Supp. 3,** 243, 244; **Supp. 5,** 275–76, 622–23; calorimetry studies, **Supp. 1,** 517–18; cancer-link studies, **Supp. 3,** 141; children, **Supp. 3,** 28, 159; **Supp. 6,** 81; dental disease relationship, **Supp. 4,** 402; disease relationship studies, **Supp. 1,** 398; **Supp. 4,** 580–52; **Supp. 5,** 710; **Supp. 8,** 197–98; fetal development studies, **Supp. 7,** 568–69; growth relationship, **Supp. 4,** 420; health foods, **Supp. 5,** 378–79, 452–53; infants', **Vol. 3, Part 2,** 464; **Vol. 8, Part 2,** 186; **Supp. 2,** 432; infant's appestat, **Supp. 4,** 7–8; low-protein diets, **Supp. 3,** 163; natural products, **Supp. 3,** 409–10; nutrient deficiency research, **Supp. 7,** 223; protein studies, **Supp. 6,** 190; **Supp. 7,** 476; spas, **Supp. 8,** 13; study of, **Vol. 10, Part 2,** 630; teaching of, **Supp. 3,** 671; **Supp. 4,** 37; UNICEF program, **Supp. 7,** 600; vegetarianism, **Supp. 6,** 113, 409–10; vitamins, **Supp. 1,** 398, 560; writings on, **Supp. 3,** 68. *See also* Cookbooks; Cooking; Food

Dietrich, Marlene, reference to, **Supp. 8,** 672

Diffraction gratings, **Supp. 3,** 291

Digestion, contributions to study of, **Vol. 1, Part 2,** 106

Dighton Rock, inscriptions on, **Vol. 1, Part 2,** 7

Digitalis, **Supp. 2,** 741; **Supp. 3,** 343; first experimental analysis, **Vol. 3, Part 1,** 6

Dillard University, founding of, **Supp. 6,** 11

Diller, Burgoyne, reference to, **Supp. 6,** 512

Dillingham, Charles B., reference to, **Supp. 6,** 318

Dillingham, William P., reference to, **Supp. 6,** 320

Dillon, C. Douglas, reference to, **Supp. 7,** 421

Dillon, Read and Co., **Supp. 4,** 305

Dilworth, Dewees, reference to, **Supp. 6,** 337

Di Maggio, Joe, references to, **Supp. 7,** 546, 668; **Supp. 8,** 479

"Dime" novels, **Vol. 3, Part 2,** 102; **Vol. 5, Part 1,** 480; **Vol. 5, Part 2,** 51, 238; **Vol. 7, Part 1,** 331 f.; **Supp. 3,** 585–86

Dime stores. *See* Five and dime stores

Dingley Act, tariff, **Vol. 3, Part 1,** 315; **Vol. 8, Part 1,** 2 f.

Dinkeloo, John, reference to, **Supp. 7,** 671

Dinner at Antoine's, **Supp. 8,** 328

Dinner at the White House, **Supp. 5,** 5

Dinosaur National Monument, **Supp. 7,** 814; **Supp. 8,** 412

Dinosaurs: egg findings, **Supp. 3,** 316; **Supp. 6,** 18; North American, **Supp. 3,** 316–17

Diphtheria: antitoxin, **Supp. 2,** 353; epidemiology of, **Supp. 7,** 194; research in, **Supp. 2,** 513; Schick test for determining, **Supp. 4,** 701; vaccine, **Supp. 5,** 1; treatment of, **Vol. 1, Part 2,** 263; **Vol. 7, Part 1,** 628; **Vol. 8, Part 1,** 252 f., 460, 565

Dominican Order, **Vol. 3, Part 2,** 328, f.; **Vol. 7, Part 1,** 611

"Dominion" movement, in Massachusetts Colony, **Vol. 1, Part 1,** 301; **Vol. 10, Part 2,** 31

Donahey, James H., reference to, **Supp. 6,** 233

Donahue's Magazine, **Vol. 3, Part 1,** 361

Donaldson, H. H., reference to, **Supp. 6,** 671

Donaldson, Walter, reference to, **Supp. 3,** 406

Donham, Wallace, reference to, **Supp. 4,** 565

Doniphan's Expedition, **Vol. 3, Part 1,** 365

Donkey, origin of, as Democratic symbol, **Vol. 7, Part 1,** 392

Donovan, William J., reference to, **Supp. 6,** 531

"Don't give up the ship," **Vol. 6, Part 1,** 50; **Vol. 7, Part 2,** 491

Doolittle, James, references to, **Supp. 4,** 589; **Supp. 6,** 267–68

Doors, architectural design, **Supp. 3,** 2

Doran, George H., reference to, **Supp. 4,** 239–40

Doran, George H., Co., reference to, **Supp. 8,** 535

Dorchester, Mass., founding of, **Vol. 6, Part 1,** 494

Dorchester Heights, attack on, **Vol. 9, Part 2,** 438

Dorgan, Thomas A. ("Tad"), references to, **Supp. 5,** 262; **Supp. 7,** 719

Dorland Advertising Co., **Supp. 6,** 187

Dorman-Smith, Eric, reference to, **Supp. 7,** 335

Dornberger, Walter, reference to, **Supp. 6,** 50

"Dorothy Dix Talks" (column), **Supp. 5,** 244

Dorr, Thomas W., reference to, **Vol. 5, Part 2,** 402

Dorr Rebellion, **Vol. 3, Part 1,** 176, 382, 546; **Vol. 3, Part 2,** 324; **Vol. 5, Part 2,** 386, 402; **Vol. 8, Part 1,** 126 f.; **Vol. 10, Part 1,** 91

Dorrellites, Massachusetts, **Vol. 3, Part 1,** 382 f.

Dorsey, Jimmy, references to, **Supp. 3,** 524–25, **Supp. 6,** 172–73

Dorsey, Tommy, references to, **Supp. 3,** 524–25; **Supp. 8,** 163

Dos Passos, John, references to, **Supp. 7,** 335, 560

Double Agent, The, **Supp. 7,** 55

Double-crostic puzzle, **Supp. 6,** 342

Doubleday, Frank, references to, **Supp. 3,** 234; **Supp. 4,** 239; **Supp. 6,** 465

Doubleday, Nelson, references to, **Supp. 7,** 307; **Supp. 8,** 535

Doubleday, Doran and Co., **Supp. 4,** 239–40; founding of, **Supp. 6,** 172; **Supp. 8,** 535

Doubleday, Page & Co., **Vol. 7, Part 2,** 143; **Supp. 8,** 594

Doubrovska, Felia, reference to, **Supp. 8,** 670

Dougherty, Denis Cardinal, reference to, **Supp. 7,** 71

Douglas, Aaron, reference to, **Supp. 6,** 321

Douglas, Donald W., references to, **Supp. 3,** 157; **Supp. 6,** 221

Douglas, Helen Gahagan, reference to, **Supp. 8,** 282

Douglas, James, reference to, **Vol. 7, Part 1,** 641; **Supp. 3,** 258

Douglas, John, reference to, **Supp. 6,** 426

Douglas, Paul H., reference to, **Supp. 3,** 255; **Supp. 7,** 814

Douglas, Stephen A., **Vol. 2, Part 1,** 15, 175; **Vol. 4, Part 2,** 528; **Vol. 8, Part 2,** 467; **Vol. 9, Part 1,** 570; Lincoln's debates with, **Vol. 6, Part 1,** 247 f.; Pendleton's support of, **Vol. 7, Part 2,** 420; nomination of, **Vol. 8, Part 1,** 582; relations with Henry B. Payne, **Vol. 7, Part 2,** 325

Douglas, William O., references to, **Supp. 5,** 575, 576, 589, 714; **Supp. 6,** 216; **Supp. 7,** 453; **Supp. 8,** 36

Douglas, Ariz., naming of, **Vol. 3, Part 1,** 396

Douglas Aircraft Co., **Supp. 6,** 666

Douglas DC airplane design, **Supp. 6,** 64, 221

Douglass, Frederick, references to, **Vol. 7, Part 1,** 24, 180, 413; **Supp. 3,** 827–28

Dow, Ada, reference to, **Supp. 4,** 551

Dow Chemical Co., antiknock gasoline, **Supp. 3,** 522

Down Argentine Way, **Supp. 5,** 501

Downes, Edward, reference to, **Supp. 5,** 183

Downey, E. H., reference to, **Supp. 6,** 598

Downey, Hal, reference to, **Supp. 4,** 420

Downing Street, London, origin of name, **Vol. 3, Part 1,** 419

Downtown Gallery (New York City), **Supp. 8,** 239–40

Doyle, Arthur Conan, reference to, **Supp. 6,** 465

Doyle, Thomas J., Co., **Supp. 7,** 189

D'Oyly Carte, Richard, reference to, **Vol. 9, Part 2,** 62

Dracula (play and movie), **Supp. 6,** 395

Draft: boards, establishment of, **Supp. 1,** 211; legal basis, **Supp. 3,** 399; legislation, **Supp. 5,** 715; post-World War II, **Supp. 7,** 78; universal military training proposals, **Supp. 5,** 531; World War II, **Supp. 4,** 247; **Supp. 5,** 482, 531. *See also* Conscription

Dragon in the Dust, **Supp. 6,** 686

Drainage, **Vol. 3, Part 1,** 210; **Vol. 5, Part 2,** 143; **Vol. 6, Part 1,** 505; Dismal Swamp, **Vol. 7, Part 1,** 426; Florida Everglades, **Vol. 2, Part 1,** 96; **Vol. 8, Part 1,** 359 f.; house, **Vol. 3, Part 1,** 549; New Orleans, **Vol. 1, Part 2,** 111; Philadelphia, **Vol. 5, Part 2,** 456; Chicago canal, **Vol. 8, Part 1,** 359 f. *See also* Irrigation

Drake, Alexander Wilson, reference to, **Vol. 9, Part 1,** 340

Drake, Charles D., reference to, **Vol. 6, Part 1,** 598

Drake, Edwin L., first oil well drilled by, **Vol. 7, Part 1,** 297, 443

Drake, Joseph, references to, **Vol. 3, Part 1,** 203; **Vol. 4, Part 2,** 159

Drake University, early history of, **Vol. 3, Part 1,** 429

Drama. *See* Theater; *specific play titles*

Drama League of America, founding of, **Supp. 2,** 76

Drama of the Medieval Church, The, **Supp. 3,** 855

Dramatic Technique, **Supp. 1,** 45

Dramatists. For complete list, *see* Occupations Index

Dranesville, Va., action at, **Vol. 7, Part 2,** 48

Draper, Andrew S., reference to, **Supp. 3,** 216

Draper, Dorothy, and Co., founding of, **Supp. 8,** 140–41

Draper, Lyman C., reference to, **Vol. 9, Part 2,** 521

Draper, Paul, reference to, **Supp. 6,** 174

Draper, William Henry, reference to, **Vol. 8, Part 2,** 560

Drawing: birds, **Vol. 1, Part 1,** 427; **Vol. 4, Part 1,** 259; comic, **Vol. 2, Part 2,** 480; Booth, Edwin, **Vol. 4, Part 2,** 542; pen, **Vol. 1, Part 2,** 396; teaching of, **Vol. 7, Part 1,** 518; **Vol. 8, Part 1,** 165 f.; writings on, **Vol. 2, Part 2,** 18. *See also* Cartoons; Comic strips; Illustration

Dreamer religion, **Vol. 9, Part 1,** 342, 372

Dredging, steam, **Vol. 3, Part 2,** 569; **Vol. 9, Part 1,** 156

Dreier, Margaret, reference to, **Supp. 5,** 578–79

Dreier, Mary, reference to, **Supp. 3,** 639; **Supp. 5,** 380

Dreiser, Theodore, references to, **Vol. 6, Part 1,** 529; **Supp. 6,** 444, 445, 471; **Supp. 7,** 198

"Dress Circular" (1856), **Vol. 6, Part 2,** 277

Dress patterns: paper, **Vol. 2, Part 1,** 375; reform for women, **Vol. 1, Part 2,** 385; **Vol. 4, Part 2,** 376; **Vol. 10, Part 2,** 521; of United States envoys, **Vol. 8, Part 2,** 348; Vogue Pattern Co., **Supp. 3,** 547. *See also* Clothing; Fashion

Dresser, Paul, references to, **Supp. 3,** 233–35; **Supp. 7,** 197, 198

Drew, Daniel, reference to, **Vol. 7, Part 1,** 471

Drew, John, reference to, **Supp. 6,** 38

Drew, Louisa Lane, reference to, **Supp. 3,** 34

Drew Theological Seminary, **Vol. 2, Part 1,** 379; **Vol. 5, Part 1,** 426; **Vol. 6, Part 1,** 590

Drexel and Co., **Supp. 4,** 320

Drexel Institute, **Vol. 3, Part 1,** 455 f.; **Vol. 6, Part 1,** 544

Dreyfus, Louis, reference to, **Supp. 7,** 199

Drills: manufacture of, **Vol. 6, Part 1,** 230; steam, **Vol. 2, Part 2,** 544

Drinking cups, disposable, **Supp. 5,** 144

Dr. Jekyll and Mr. Hyde (movie), **Supp. 3,** 35

"Dr. Kildare" series (movies), **Supp. 3,** 164

Drop hammer, invention of, **Vol. 8, Part 2,** 145

Dropsie College for Hebrew and Cognate Learning, **Vol. 3, Part 1,** 459 f.

Drosophila. See Fruit fly studies

Drug addiction. *See* Narcotics

Drug Merchants of America, founding of, **Supp. 4,** 496

Drugs: antibacterial sulfonamide, **Supp. 7,** 477; barbiturates, **Supp. 8,** 102; bioassay methods for standardization of, **Supp. 3,** 242; body temperature relationship, **Supp. 3,** 32; cold-still extraction, **Supp. 2,** 389; custom inspection, **Vol. 8, Part 1,** 242; digitalis, **Supp. 3,** 343; government supervision of, **Vol. 8, Part 1,** 103 f.; laxatives, **Supp. 8,** 339; opium trade, **Vol. 1, Part 1,** 308; **Vol. 3, Part 2,** 508 f.; **Vol. 4, Part 2,** 369; **Vol. 5, Part 2,** 270, 384; **Vol. 6, Part 1,** 491; **Vol. 8, Part 1,** 103 f.; **Vol. 10, Part 2,** 553; patent medicines, **Supp. 5,** 143, 666; pharmacology, **Supp. 3,** 805–6; physiological action of, **Vol. 3, Part 1,** 6; **Vol. 8, Part 1,** 317 f.; plant extracts, **Supp. 2,** 591; prescription, manufacture of, **Supp. 4,** 499–500; research and development, **Supp. 3,** 343; **Supp. 6,** 447–48; venereal disease therapy, **Supp. 3,** 854; **Supp. 6,** 424, 460. *See also* Narcotics; Pharmacology; *specific kinds*

Drugstore (painting), **Supp. 8,** 339

Drugstores: chain founding, **Supp. 4,** 496–97; father of modern, **Supp. 2,** 688

Drug traffic. *See* Narcotics

Drummond, Henry, reference to, **Vol. 7, Part 1,** 105

Drury College, presidency of, **Vol. 7, Part 1,** 230

Dry-goods trade, **Vol. 1, Part 2,** 372; **Vol. 2, Part 2,** 110, 285; **Vol. 5, Part 2,** 214; **Vol. 7, Part 2,** 191; **Vol. 9, Part 1,** 135

Dual citizenship, **Vol. 8, Part 2,** 124

Duane, William, references to, **Vol. 6, Part 2,** 81; **Supp. 6,** 69; **Supp. 7,** 10, 134

Duanesburg, N. Y., founding of, **Vol. 3, Part 1,** 465 f.

DuBois, Eugene F., reference to, **Supp. 3,** 805

Du Bois, W. E. B., references to, **Supp. 3,** 828; **Supp. 4,** 200–1; **Supp. 5,** 467, 544, 741; **Supp. 6,** 284, 285, 322, 567–68; **Supp. 8,** 95, 522

DuBose, William P., reference to, **Supp. 4,** 546

DuBridge, Lee, reference to, **Supp. 7,** 275

Duchamp, Marcel, references to, **Supp. 3,** 245; **Supp. 5,** 20, 184, 185

Duchin Orchestra, **Supp. 5,** 187–88

Dudley, Dorothy, reference to, **Supp. 3,** 236

Dudley, H. W., reference to, **Supp. 5,** 149

Dudley Observatory, **Vol. 5, Part 1,** 252; **Vol. 7, Part 1,** 39

Duelling, laws against, **Vol. 3, Part 1,** 152; **Vol. 7, Part 1,** 40; **Vol. 8, Part 1,** 190 f.

Duels, **Vol. 1, Part 1,** 650; **Vol. 1, Part 2,** 210; **Vol. 2, Part 1,** 62, 316; **Vol. 2, Part 2,** 116, 125, 177; **Vol. 3, Part 1,** 131; **Vol. 3, Part 2,** 96 f., 373, 448, 501, 529, 533, 571; **Vol. 4, Part 1,** 186; **Vol. 4, Part 2,** 66, 178, 188, 232, 260; **Vol. 5, Part 2,** 526; **Vol. 6, Part 1,** 33, 36, 200, 204, 227, 266; **Vol. 6, Part 2,** 35; **Vol. 7, Part 1,** 426; **Vol. 8, Part 1,** 34 f., 37 f., 220, 365, 425, 526; **Vol. 8, Part 2,** 233, 343; **Vol. 9, Part 1,** 153, 170, 395, 420; **Vol. 9, Part 2,** 48, 366, 380; Barron, James, v. the secretary to the governor of Malta, **Vol. 3, Part 1,** 187; Broderick v. Terry, **Vol. 10, Part 1,** 628 f.; Brown v. Reynolds, **Vol. 7, Part 1,** 41; Burr v. Hamilton, **Vol. 3, Part 1,** 573 f.; **Vol. 5, Part 1,** 240; Cadwalader v. Conway, **Vol. 3, Part 1,** 303; Cilley v. Graves, **Vol. 5, Part 2,** 172; Clay v. Randolph, **Vol. 5, Part 2,** 63; Decatur v. Barron, **Vol. 3, Part 1,** 187 f.; Denver v. Gilbert, **Vol. 3, Part 1,** 243; De Trobriand, **Vol. 3, Part 1,** 258; Dickinson v. Jackson, **Vol. 5, Part 1,** 528; Dudley v. Richardson, **Vol. 3, Part 1,** 478 f.; Du Pont v. rival suitor, **Vol. 3, Part 1,** 526 f.; Durrett v. Prentice, **Vol. 3, Part 1,** 550 f.; Gadsden v. Howe, **Vol. 5, Part 1,** 295; Hughes v. Cameron, **Vol. 5, Part 1,** 357; Jackson v. Avery, **Vol. 5, Part 1,** 527; Jackson v. Wells, **Vol. 5, Part 1,** 545; Laurens v. Lee, C., **Vol. 6, Part 1,** 100; Leggett v. Banks, **Vol. 6, Part 1,** 147; McIntosh v. Gwinnett, **Vol. 10, Part 1,** 403 f.; Perry v. marine officer, **Vol. 3, Part, 1,** 189; Pleasants v. Ritchie, **Vol. 8, Part 1,** 7 f.; Poe v. Daniel, **Vol. 8, Part 1,** 19 f.; Poindexter v. Hunt, **Vol. 8, Part 1,** 29 f.; Poor v. junior officer, **Vol. 8, Part 1,** 69; Porter v. fellow officer, **Vol. 8, Part 1,** 82 f.; Porter v. Smyth, **Vol. 8, Part 1,** 99 f.; Price v. Thomas, **Vol. 9, Part 2,** 429; Pryor, Roger Atkinson, **Vol. 8, Part 1,** 255 f.; Queen v. Byrd, **Vol. 8, Part 1,** 298 f.; Randolph v. Clay, **Vol. 8, Part 1,** 363 f.; Randolph v. Taylor, **Vol. 8, Part 1,** 363 f.; Slidell, **Vol. 9, Part 1,** 210; Snipes v. Simons, **Vol. 8, Part 1,** 425; Tattnall, **Vol. 9, Part 2,** 310; Van Allen v. Crawford, **Vol. 9, Part 2,** 274; Walker, William, **Vol. 10, Part 1,** 363 f.; Webb, James Watson, **Vol. 10, Part 1,** 574 f.; Webb v. fellow officers, **Vol. 10, Part 1,** 574 f.; Wilkinson v. Gates, **Vol. 4, Part 1,** 186

Duff, James H., reference to, **Supp. 7,** 305

Duffy, Richard, reference to, **Supp. 6,** 514

Dugan, Raymond Smith, reference to, **Supp. 6,** 560

Duke, James B., references to, **Supp. 3,** 587; **Supp. 4,** 370, 371; **Supp. 5,** 566–67

Duke University, **Vol. 1, Part 2,** 38; **Vol. 2, Part 2,** 516 f.; **Vol. 3, Part 1,** 496 f.; endowment and establishment of, **Supp. 2,** 181, 668; **Supp. 5,** 567

Duke's Laws, legal code, **Vol. 7, Part 1,** 515 f.

Dulles, Allen W., references to, **Supp. 6,** 170; **Supp. 8,** 159

Dulles, John Foster, references to, **Supp. 6,** 235; **Supp. 7,** 35, 420, 467; **Supp. 8,** 147, 157, 160, 223, 276

Dulles International Airport (Va.), architectural design, **Supp. 7,** 671, 672

Dumbarton Oaks (Washington, D.C.): Byzantine art collection, **Supp. 5,** 700, 708; **Supp. 7,** 60, 673; gardens, **Supp. 6,** 197; UN conference (1944), **Supp. 5,** 537

Dumont Laboratories, **Supp. 7,** 206

Dun and Bradstreet, Inc., founding of, **Supp. 6,** 693–94

Dunbar, Paul Laurence, references to, **Supp. 3,** 187, 834

Duncan, Isadora, photographs of, **Supp. 3,** 296

Duncan, Otis Dudley, reference to, **Supp. 6,** 483

Duncan Hines cake mixes, **Supp. 6,** 292

Duncker, Karl, reference to, **Supp. 3,** 808

Dunglison, Robley, reference to, **Vol. 1, Part 2,** 108

Dunkers, leadership of, **Vol. 9, Part 1,** 416

Dunlap, William, references to, **Vol. 5, Part 1,** 103, 498; **Vol. 8, Part 2,** 386; **Vol. 9, Part 1,** 260

Dunmore's War (1774–75), **Vol. 4, Part 2** 353; **Vol. 5, Part 2,** 433; **Vol. 6, Part 1,** 206, 357, 362 f.; **Vol. 9, Part 2,** 563; **Supp. 1,** 189. *See also* Indians, American (by tribe), Oneida; Point Pleasant, battle of

Dunne, Edward F., reference to, **Supp. 3**, 599

Dunne, Finley Peter, reference to, **Supp. 3**, 762

Dunning, John R., reference to, **Supp. 6**, 501

Dunning, William A., reference to, **Supp. 5**, 498

Dun's Review, inaugurated, **Vol. 3, Part 1**, 503

Dunster, Henry, reference to, **Vol. 7, Part 1**, 55

Dunster House Book Shop (Cambridge, Mass.), **Supp. 7**, 55

Du Pont, Alfred I., references to, **Supp. 5**, 192, 193

Du Pont, Coleman, reference to, **Supp. 5**, 192–93

Du Pont, Ernest, reference to, **Supp. 3**, 239;

Du Pont, Pierre S., references to, **Supp. 1**, 270–71; **Supp. 4**, 244, 681, 682, 683, 684; **Supp. 5**, 191, 192; **Supp. 7**, 169, 210; **Supp. 8**, 598–600

Du Pont, E. I., de Nemours & Co., **Supp. 1**, 270–71; **Supp. 4**, 681; **Supp. 5**, 191–92, 235, 662–63; **Supp. 7**, 11, 169, 210; antiknock gasoline, **Supp. 3**, 522; research laboratories, **Supp. 2**, 551; **Supp. 3**, 239

Du Pont Powder Co., **Vol. 7, Part 1**, 301; **Supp. 1**, 270

DuPre, George, reference to, **Supp. 7**, 643

Duran, Carolus, reference to, **Vol. 1, Part 2**, 120

Durant, Henry F., references to, **Vol. 5, Part 1**, 274; **Vol. 7, Part 1**, 104

Durant, Will, reference to, **Supp. 8**, 579

Durant, William C., references to, **Supp. 3**, 273–74; **Supp. 4**, 295, 620, 681–82; **Supp. 5**, 193; **Supp. 7**, 246; **Supp. 8**, 598

Durant-Dort Carriage Co., **Supp. 4**, 620

Durante, Jimmy, reference to, **Supp. 8**, 547

Durham, N.C., development of, **Vol. 3, Part 1**, 496 f., 549 f.

Durkin, Martin P., reference to, **Supp. 8**, 156

Durocher, Leo, reference to, **Supp. 6**, 489

Durstine, Roy, reference to, **Supp. 8**, 27

Durstine, Roy S., Inc., **Supp. 7**, 211

Duryea, Charles, references to, **Supp. 4**, 292; **Supp. 8**, 148

Duryea, J. Frank, reference to, **Supp. 4**, 292

Duse, Eleanora, reference to, **Supp. 3**, 297

Dutch East India Co., **Vol. 5, Part 1**, 339

Dutch elm disease, **Supp. 7**, 33

Dutch Reformed church, **Vol. 4, Part 2**, 241, 367, 376; **Vol. 6, Part 1**, 314; **Vol. 6, Part 2**, 591; **Vol. 8, Part 2**, 572 f.; **Vol. 9, Part 2**, 366 f.; **Supp. 8**, 457

Dutch settlements in America, **Vol. 5, Part 1**, 503; **Vol. 6, Part 1**, 156; **Vol. 7, Part 1**, 284, 613; **Vol. 8, Part 2**, 455

Dutton, E. P., & Co., Everyman's Library, **Supp. 3**, 499

Duveen, Joseph, references to, **Supp. 3**, 24; **Supp. 5**, 401

Duveen brothers (art dealers), **Supp. 6**, 56

Duxbury, Mass., founding of, **Vol. 9, Part 1**, 500

Dvořák, Antonin, references to, **Supp. 4**, 125, 276, 834, 835; **Supp. 5**, 218

Dvorak, Frank, reference to, **Supp. 6**, 27

Dwight, James, reference to, **Supp. 3**, 701

Dwight, Timothy, references to, **Vol. 9, Part 2**, 338, 392

Dwight and Lloyd Metallurgical Co., founding of, **Supp. 4**, 246

Dworshak, Henry, reference to, **Supp. 6**, 681

Dyes, **Vol. 1, Part 1**, 563; **Vol. 6, Part 2**, 43, 401, 417; **Vol. 7, Part 1**, 404; **Vol. 7, Part 2**, 616; industry development, **Supp. 2**, 301, 631

Dylan, Bob, reference to, **Supp. 8**, 235

Dynamite, first use of, **Vol. 5, Part 2**, 239; **Vol. 7, Part 2**, 22

Dynamos, electric, **Vol. 5, Part 2**, 509; **Vol. 8, Part 2**, 198; **Vol. 10, Part 1**, 376 f.; **Vol. 10, Part 2**, 462

Dynel (synthetic fabric), **Supp. 6**, 67

Dysentery, bacillus discovery, **Supp. 4**, 287

E

Eads, James Buchanan, references to, **Vol. 7, Part 1**, 617; **Vol. 9, Part 2**, 311

Eads Bridge (St. Louis), **Vol. 3, Part 2**, 445; **Vol. 6, Part 1**, 549; **Vol. 8, Part 2**, 19

Eagels, Jeanne, reference to, **Supp. 8**, 444

Eakins, Thomas, reference to, **Vol. 7, Part 1**, 627

Eames, Charles, references to, **Supp. 4**, 715; **Supp. 7**, 670, 671

Eames, Emma, reference to, **Supp. 3**, 42

Eames, Wilberforce, references to, **Supp. 8**, 663, 664

Earhart, Amelia, references to, **Supp. 6**, 477, 478

Earle, Ellis B., reference to, **Supp. 6**, 187

Earle, George H., references to, **Supp. 3**, 20; **Supp. 8**, 360

Early chilhood education. *See* Preschool education; Kindergartens

Earthquakes, **Vol. 8, Part 1**, 395; **Vol. 9, Part 2**, 308, 586; research on, **Supp. 4**, 897; **Supp. 6**, 154; San Andreas Fault map, **Supp. 4**, 558; San Francisco, **Supp. 1**, 638; **Supp. 4**, 325, 417; **Supp. 5**, 416; San Francisco photographs, **Supp. 3**, 295; seismological observatories, **Supp. 1**, 579–80

East, Edward M., reference to, **Supp. 4**, 252

Eastern Airlines, **Supp. 7**, 16

Eastern Livestock Cooperative Marketing Association, founding of, **Supp. 1**, 644

Eastern Railroads Presidents Conference, **Supp. 6**, 91

Eastern religions, **Supp. 8**, 431

East India: exploration, **Vol. 5, Part 1**, 236; trade, **Vol. 2, Part 1**, 83, 149; **Vol. 4, Part 1**, 523; **Vol. 4, Part 2**, 482; **Vol. 6, Part 1**, 108

East India Co., **Vol. 3, Part 1**, 467 f.; **Vol. 10, Part 2**, 591

East India Marine Society, founding of, **Vol. 8, Part 2**, 153

Eastman, Crystal, reference to, **Supp. 5**, 631

Eastman, Edward R., reference to, **Supp. 3**, 434

Eastman, George, references to, **Supp. 3**, 26, 41; **Supp. 4**, 105

Eastman, Max, references to, **Supp. 3**, 852; **Supp. 6**, 664; **Supp. 7**, 269

Eastman Kodak Co., **Vol. 4, Part 2**, 410; **Vol. 8, Part 2**, 554; Nepera Chemical Co. acquisition, **Supp. 3**, 26; research laboratory, **Supp. 4**, 743–44; **Supp. 6**, 442; **Supp. 7**, 511, 512

Eastman School of Music, founding of, **Supp. 1**, 276

Eastman's National Business College, **Vol. 3, Part 1**, 602

East River (New York City), bridges, **Supp. 3**, 530–31

Easy Chair, **Vol. 5, Part 1**, 310

Eaton, Cyrus, reference to, **Supp. 7**, 289

Eaton, John H., references to, **Vol. 5, Part 1**, 532; **Vol. 7, Part 2**, 41 f.

Eaton, Theophilus, reference to, **Vol. 5, Part 1**, 207

Ebbetts, Charles, reference to, **Supp. 7**, 752

Eben Holden, **Supp. 4**, 38

Eberhardt, Ernest G., reference to, **Supp. 4**, 499

Eberhart, Nelle Richmond, reference to, **Supp. 4**, 138

Eccles, Marriner, reference to, **Supp. 8**, 446

Echo Park (Colo.), **Supp. 7**, 31

Eckhart, Percy B., reference to, **Supp. 6**, 683

Eckstine, Billy, Orchestra, **Supp. 5**, 534

Eclectic Medical College, founding of, **Vol. 7, Part 1**, 476; **Vol. 8, Part 2**, 524

Eclectic Medical Journal, founding of, **Vol. 1, Part 2**, 86; **Vol. 8, Part 2**, 524

Eclectic medicine, **Supp. 2**, 389; pioneer works in, **Vol. 5, Part 2**, 393; **Vol. 7, Part 1**, 237, 475 f.; **Vol. 8, Part 2**, 524

10, **Part 2,** 455; **Supp. 3,** 364; **Supp. 4,** 10–11; **Supp. 5,** 347–48; boards, **Supp. 5,** 432; Catholic, **Vol. 1, Part 1,** 302; **Vol. 2, Part 2,** 337 f.; **Vol. 3, Part 2,** 440; **Vol. 4, Part 2,** 541; **Vol. 6, Part 2,** 163; **Vol. 7, Part 1,** 74; **Vol. 8, Part 2,** 265; **Supp. 3,** 325–26, 393; character development, **Supp. 4,** 767; child-oriented, **Supp. 7,** 600–1; child-study, early, **Vol. 6, Part 1,** 276; church-state separation issues, **Supp. 4,** 796; **Supp. 5,** 358, 461; classical approach to, **Supp. 3,** 810; **Supp. 6,** 46; coeducation, **Vol. 1, Part 2,** 430; **Vol. 3, Part 1,** 423; **Vol. 3, Part 2,** 95; commercial, **Vol. 3, Part 1,** 602; **Vol. 7, Part 2,** 130 f.; Committee of Ten of the National Education Association, **Vol. 5, Part 2,** 60; corporal punishment, abandonment of, **Vol. 3, Part 1,** 409; **Vol. 8, Part 1,** 412; correspondence courses, **Vol. 8, Part 1,** 126; **Supp. 2,** 199; curriculum determination, **Supp. 3,** 552; day nurseries, **Vol. 1, Part 2,** 471; deaf, of the, **Vol. 1, Part 2,** 139, 149 f.; **Vol. 2, Part 1,** 38; **Vol. 2, Part 2,** 150 f., 201 f.; **Vol. 4, Part 1,** 110 f.; **Vol. 8, Part 2,** 94; **Supp. 3,** 311–12; Eaton's system, **Vol. 3, Part 1,** 608 f.; elective system, **Vol. 3, Part 2,** 73; **Vol. 7, Part 2,** 405; **Vol. 8, Part 1,** 308 f.; elementary, **Vol. 1, Part 1,** 621 f.; **Vol. 4, Part 1,** 574 f.; **Vol. 4, Part 2,** 91; **Vol. 9, Part 1,** 141; evening classes, **Supp. 2,** 45; field schools, **Vol. 5, Part 2,** 149; financing of, **Supp. 8,** 166; first business course in academic institution, **Vol. 7, Part 2,** 299; first business high school in U.S., **Vol. 8, Part 1,** 152; first college to offer graduate work to women, **Vol. 8, Part 1,** 531; first free school west of the Mississippi, **Vol. 3, Part 1,** 477 f.; first institution designed primarily for research, **Vol. 8, Part 1,** 501; first primary school, **Vol. 8, Part 1,** 80; **Vol. 9, Part 1,** 524; first public school nursing, **Supp. 2,** 687; first state charter to be granted for girls' education in U.S., **Vol. 8, Part 1,** 71; first survey of U.S. theological, **Supp. 3,** 111; first university to have school of education, **Vol. 9, Part 1,** 37; first university to open all its professional schools to women, **Vol. 10, Part 1,** 490 f.; first work-study plan, **Supp. 3,** 63; first women's school in South, **Vol. 6, Part 2,** 289; food programs, **Supp. 3,** 28; **Supp. 6,** 81; foreign exchange students, **Supp. 4,** 592–93; free schools, **Vol. 2, Part 2,** 108; **Vol. 3, Part 2,** 99; **Vol. 4, Part 2,** 314, 415; **Vol. 9, Part 1,** 63; **Vol. 9, Part 2,** 261; for freedmen, **Vol. 9, Part 2,** 11; **Vol. 10, Part 1,** 27; general science courses, **Supp. 4,** 139–40; German system, **Supp. 3,** 676; gifted students, **Supp. 2,** 110; **Supp. 4,** 732; health standards in schools, **Supp. 5,** 553; Herbartian method, **Supp. 2,** 424; higher education, public support of, **Vol. 2, Part 1,** 462; **Vol. 3, Part 2,** 319; **Vol. 10, Part 1,** 558 f.; high school administration, **Vol. 9, Part 1,** 37; historical studies on, **Supp. 2,** 532, 663; **Supp. 4,** 592; home, **Supp. 5,** 437–38; honor system, **Vol. 5, Part 2,** 148; **Vol. 10, Part 1,** 32; Indian, **Vol. 1, Part 1,** 238; **Vol. 1, Part 2,** 478 f.; **Vol. 2, Part 1,** 446; **Vol. 3, Part 1,** 376; **Vol. 4, Part 1,** 101; **Vol. 4, Part 2,** 332, 380, 414; **Vol. 5, Part 2,** 115, 176, 428, 504; **Vol. 6, Part 1,** 428 f.; **Vol. 6, Part 2,** 453, 471, 496; **Vol. 7, Part 1,** 336; **Vol. 8, Part 1,** 111, 175; **Vol. 8, Part 2,** 30; **Vol. 10, Part 2,** 58; individualism in, **Vol. 6, Part 2,** 325; industrial, **Vol. 1, Part 1,** 421; **Vol. 3, Part 1,** 319, 455 f.; **Vol. 3, Part 2,** 479; **Vol. 4, Part 2,** 518; **Vol. 5, Part 1,** 130; **Vol. 6, Part 1,** 178; **Vol. 7, Part 2,** 398; **Vol. 9, Part 2,** 282; **Vol. 10, Part 1,** 68, 407 f., 617 f.; inspection of private schools, **Vol. 3, Part 1,** 369; international meetings on, **Supp. 4,** 449; intuitive-thinking emphasis, **Supp. 3,** 429; journals, **Supp. 1,** 103; junior high school and junior college movements, **Vol. 1, Part 1,** 522; **Vol. 5, Part 2,** 591;

Vol. 8, Part 2, 42; kindergartens, **Vol. 1, Part 2,** 392, 393, 575; **Vol. 2, Part 2,** 412; **Vol. 4, Part 2,** 90, 338; **Vol. 5, Part 2,** 499 f.; **Vol. 6, Part 2,** 355; **Vol. 7, Part 2,** 336; **Vol. 8, Part 2,** 560; **Vol. 9, Part 1,** 47; **Vol. 10, Part 2,** 180; **Supp. 1,** 13, 407; **Supp. 4,** 373–74; **Supp. 4,** 874–75; **Supp. 5,** 437–38; laboratory courses, **Supp. 1,** 30; Lancastrian system, **Vol. 2, Part 2,** 224; **Vol. 6, Part 1,** 440; land grants for, **Vol. 9, Part 2,** 261; law school, first in America, **Vol. 8, Part 1,** 469; legal issues, **Supp. 2,** 143; libraries, popularizing, **Supp. 3,** 90–91; Little Red School House, **Supp. 3,** 376; Lyceum system, **Vol. 5, Part 2,** 149; McGuffey Readers, effect of, **Vol. 6, Part 2,** 58; mentally retarded, **Vol. 2, Part 1,** 117; **Vol. 10, Part 2,** 199; **Supp. 3,** 389; **Supp. 4,** 438–39; **Supp. 6,** 241; **Supp. 7,** 284; military, **Vol. 2, Part 2,** 581; **Vol. 4, Part 1,** 206; **Vol. 5, Part 2,** 49, 91, 115; **Vol. 6, Part 1,** 39; **Vol. 7, Part 2,** 281 f.; **Vol. 8, Part 1,** 49 f.; **Vol. 9, Part 1,** 115, 264, 600; mission schools, **Supp. 3,** 476–77; **Supp. 5,** 185–86; "modern methods" in eighteenth century, **Vol. 3, Part 1,** 332 f.; Montessori method, **Vol. 9, Part 1,** 349; national department of, **Vol. 4, Part 2,** 415; **Vol. 8, Part 1,** 562; naval, **Supp. 3,** 275; New York centralization, **Supp. 4,** 134; "object teaching," **Vol. 5, Part 2,** 510; parent-teacher associations, **Vol. 2, Part 1,** 345; Peabody Fund, for promotion of Southern, **Vol. 2, Part 2,** 606; **Vol. 7, Part 2,** 57, 337; **Vol. 8, Part 2,** 537 f.; pedagogy, first chair of, **Vol. 7, Part 2,** 332; Pestalozzian principles, **Vol. 5, Part 2,** 510; philanthropic gifts for, **Supp. 2,** 375; **Supp. 5,** 61; philosophical approaches to, **Supp. 5,** 71–72; physical, **Vol. 1, Part 2,** 322; **Vol. 4, Part 2,** 47; **Vol. 5, Part 1,** 71; **Vol. 6, Part 1,** 160, 209, 353; **Vol. 7, Part 1,** 277; **Vol. 8, Part 2,** 355; **Vol. 10, Part 1,** 92; **Supp. 5,** 553; physical, introduction to Japan, **Vol. 6, Part 1,** 160; physical, teaching of, **Vol. 7, Part 1,** 277–78; physical, for women, **Supp. 5,** 51–52; platoon (work-study-play) system, **Supp. 2,** 728; popular, **Vol. 4, Part 1,** 217; preceptorial system, Princeton, **Vol. 10, Part 2,** 354; private schools, **Vol. 6, Part 2,** 93; **Supp. 3,** 591–92; progressive, **Vol. 1, Part 1,** 139, 142; **Vol. 2, Part 1,** 538; **Vol. 3, Part 1,** 337 f.; **Vol. 3, Part 2,** 468; **Vol. 8, Part 1,** 97 f., 152; **Vol. 8, Part 2,** 42; **Vol. 9, Part 1,** 64, 67, 600; **Vol. 10, Part 2,** 626; **Supp. 3,** 375–76, 552, 677; **Supp. 4,** 139, 373–74; **Supp. 5,** 71–72; **Supp. 6,** 208, 558; **Supp. 8,** 443; progressive, criticism of, **Supp. 3,** 555; **Supp. 4,** 40; progressive, Gary system, **Supp. 2,** 728; progressive, individualized, **Supp. 7,** 42–43, 435; progressive, opposition to, **Supp. 4,** 40; progressive, Lincoln School, **Supp. 3,** 552; **Supp. 4,** 139; progressive, training in, **Supp. 8,** 443; project method, **Vol. 8, Part 2,** 312; psychology and, **Supp. 3,** 119; **Supp. 4,** 832–33; **Supp. 6,** 17; public, pioneering in, **Vol. 1, Part 1,** 621 f.; **Vol. 1, Part 2,** 335, 570; **Vol. 2, Part 1,** 538; **Vol. 3, Part 1,** 314, 416 f., 556, 597 f., 608 f.; **Vol. 4, Part 1,** 117 f.; **Vol. 7, Part 2,** 332; **Vol. 8, Part 2,** 217; **Vol. 9, Part 1,** 353; **Vol. 10, Part 2,** 392; public school system, **Vol. 4, Part 2,** 43, 146, 315; **Vol. 5, Part 1,** 353 f.; **Vol. 8, Part 2,** 388, 616; Quaker, **Vol. 5, Part 2,** 4; Quincy system, **Vol. 1, Part 1,** 50; reading, **Supp. 6,** 248; reform proposals, **Supp. 1,** 200; religious, **Vol. 2, Part 2,** 26, 98 f., 611; **Vol. 3, Part 1,** 522 f.; **Vol. 4, Part 1,** 99; **Vol. 6, Part 2,** 40, 242, 461; **Vol. 10, Part 1,** 653; research in, **Supp. 3,** 677; Rockefeller Foundation, **Vol. 2, Part 1,** 378; rural schools, **Vol. 7, Part 2,** 257; school keeping, earliest treatise on, **Vol. 3, Part 1,** 337; school libraries, **Vol. 8, Part 1,** 17; school readers, **Vol. 8, Part 2,** 357; school survey, **Supp. 3,** 328; science popularization programs,

844–45; militia marched to polls, **Vol. 5, Part 2,** 519; presidential primary, **Supp. 2,** 55; primaries, **Supp. 5,** 575; public opinion surveys, **Supp. 8,** 70; Ross election bill, **Vol. 3, Part 1,** 467 f.; senatorial primaries, **Supp. 2,** 54; violence in Baltimore (1857), **Vol. 6, Part 1,** 240; voting tabulating machines, **Supp. 1,** 415. *See also presidential election headings;* Voting rights; Woman suffrage

Electoral commission, **Vol. 1, Part 2,** 572; **Vol. 4, Part 1,** 449

Electoral Court Act, **Vol. 3, Part 2,** 25

Electrical engineering. *See* Engineering, electrical

Electrical industry: Bakelite uses in, **Supp. 3,** 27; chemical research techniques, **Supp. 6,** 695; labor movement, **Supp. 6,** 73–74

Electric Boat Co., **Supp. 3,** 120

Electric Bond & Share Co., **Supp. 3,** 192, 527

Electricity: agricultural use, **Supp. 3,** 192–93; alternating current, **Supp. 1,** 292; **Supp. 3,** 231, 768–69; arc light, early demonstration of, **Vol. 3, Part 1,** 376; arc lighting, **Supp. 1,** 129; **Supp. 2,** 658; authority on, **Vol. 4, Part 2,** 58; automobile, **Supp. 2,** 436; automobile ignition and starter, **Supp. 6,** 332; book collections on, **Supp. 2,** 38; bulb improvement, **Supp. 6,** 624, 695; cash register, **Supp. 6,** 332; chair, first use of electric, **Vol. 8, Part 2,** 69; circuit theory, **Supp. 2,** 98, 358; coils, early investigation with, **Vol. 4, Part 2,** 551; communication, **Supp. 1,** 613–14; copper conduction, **Supp. 2,** 383; development of, **Vol. 3, Part 2,** 372; **Vol. 4, Part 2,** 550; **Vol. 7, Part 1,** 388; **Vol. 9, Part 2,** 644; dielectric constants, **Supp. 6,** 346; dynamos, **Vol. 10, Part 2,** 462; economics of, **Supp. 2,** 333; electrostatic doublet theory, **Supp. 1,** 297; elevators, **Vol. 4, Part 1,** 75; energy, studies in, **Vol. 7, Part 1,** 268; equipment, making of, **Vol. 5, Part 2,** 509; **Vol. 10, Part 2,** 54, 462; experiments with (1750), **Vol. 6, Part 1,** 280; **Vol. 7, Part 2,** 136; first indoor lighted movie, **Supp. 3,** 73; furnace, **Vol. 4, Part 2,** 575; gas lighter, **Vol. 5, Part 1,** 335; high-frequency transmission, **Supp. 2,** 98; high-power transmission, **Supp. 2,** 199; high-tension transmission, **Supp. 1,** 292; high voltage, **Supp. 1,** 646; high-voltage measurement, **Supp. 2,** 199; hydroelectric power, **Supp. 2,** 118, 583; illumination, science of, **Vol. 8, Part 2,** 268; incandescent lamp, **Supp. 1,** 270; inventions, **Vol. 1, Part 1,** 443; **Vol. 3, Part 1,** 220; **Vol. 3, Part 2,** 59, 279; **Vol. 5, Part 1,** 259; **Vol. 5, Part 2,** 562; **Vol. 6, Part 1,** 176, 400; **Vol. 10, Part 1,** 168 f.; lamps, **Vol. 3, Part 2,** 280; **Vol. 7, Part 2,** 128; **Vol. 9, Part 1,** 514; lighting fixtures, **Supp. 7,** 308; lighting plant, first municipal, **Vol. 7, Part 1,** 450; lighting studies, **Supp. 3,** 269–70; long-distance transmission, **Supp. 1,** 614, 646; magnetic reaction, **Supp. 2,** 273; motor, invention of, **Vol. 3, Part 1,** 87 f.; motors, **Supp. 1,** 669–70; naval use of, **Supp. 3,** 275; Niagara Falls as source of, **Vol. 8, Part 1,** 375 f.; open-hearth charging machine, **Vol. 10, Part 1,** 635; organ, electric, **Vol. 8, Part 2,** 133; pioneer work with, **Vol. 3, Part 1,** 25; plant financing and operating, **Supp. 3,** 745–47; power, first underground conduit for electrical, **Vol. 9, Part 2,** 485; power plants, **Vol. 3, Part 1,** 355; **Vol. 5, Part 1,** 415; **Vol. 7, Part 1,** 367 f.; **Vol. 8, Part 2,** 359; public utility uniformity, **Supp. 3,** 716; railroads, **Vol. 6, Part 1,** 176; **Vol. 7, Part 2,** 358; **Vol. 9, Part 1,** 128; **Supp. 1,** 34, 351; **Supp. 4,** 370; **Supp. 8,** 93; research in, **Vol. 6, Part 1,** 235; **Supp. 2,** 658; "round-type" meter, **Supp. 3,** 184; rural, **Supp. 3,** 193, 560; **Supp. 6,** 122; **Supp. 8,** 700; science of, **Vol. 4, Part 2,** 550 f.; smelting, **Vol. 2, Part 2,** 472; stage lighting, **Supp. 6,** 233; steam turbine use for, **Supp. 4,** 383–84; synchronous clock,

Supp. 6, 668–69; tests in, **Vol. 7, Part 1,** 342 f.; textbooks, **Vol. 5, Part 1,** 261; thermo, **Supp. 2,** 273; tractor, **Vol. 6, Part 1,** 505; traffic lights, **Supp. 3,** 254; transmission lines, lighting protection, **Supp. 2,** 199; turbine generation, **Supp. 3,** 251; units and standards, **Vol. 8, Part 2,** 154; **Supp. 2,** 358, 702; use of, in medicine, **Vol. 9, Part 1,** 53; valve, **Vol. 8, Part 2,** 133; writings on, **Vol. 8, Part 1,** 73 f., 122 f., 193 f., 223. *See also* Public utilities

Electrocardiography, **Supp. 6,** 117

Electrochemistry, **Vol. 8, Part 1,** 558 f.; **Vol. 10, Part 1,** 570; commercial applications, **Supp. 1,** 262; **Supp. 2,** 314

Electrodynamical theory, **Supp. 4,** 58

Electrodynamics, **Supp. 5,** 529

Electrolytes, physical chemistry of, **Supp. 8,** 123

Electromagnetic field: emission theory, **Supp. 5,** 528–29; infrared, **Supp. 4,** 658; separation, **Supp. 4,** 453–54

Electromagnets, **Vol. 9, Part 1,** 188; **Vol. 10, Part 1,** 635

Electro Metallurgical Co., **Supp. 3,** 48

Electronic music, **Supp. 3,** 690

Electronics: circuit inventions, **Supp. 5,** 21–22; device patents, **Supp. 8,** 209; instruments, **Supp. 7,** 756; microwave development, **Supp. 4,** 358–59; transistors, **Supp. 6,** 85; **Supp. 7,** 175

Electrons: change measurement, **Supp. 5,** 495; photoelectrons, **Supp. 6,** 370; "spinning" concept, **Supp. 5,** 496; temperature concept, **Supp. 6,** 365; wave nature of, **Supp. 6,** 151–52

Electrophysiology, **Supp. 7,** 281

Electroplating, dynamos, **Supp. 2,** 702

Electrostatics, **Vol. 8, Part 1,** 223 f.

Electrosurgical knife, **Supp. 6,** 69–70

Electrotherapeutics, **Vol. 1, Part 2,** 93; **Vol. 3, Part 1,** 354; **Vol. 6, Part 2,** 381; **Vol. 8, Part 2,** 68

Electrothermal processes, **Supp. 1,** 5

Electrotyping, **Vol. 1, Part 1,** 93; **Vol. 9, Part 2,** 652

Elementary Economics, **Supp. 8,** 165

Elementary School Teacher, **Vol. 5, Part 1,** 525

Elements: chemical analysis, **Supp. 2,** 493; rare, researches in, **Vol. 5, Part 1,** 572; specimen collections, **Supp. 1,** 477

Elements of Analytical Mechanics, **Supp. 1,** 53

Elements of Logick, **Vol. 4, Part 2,** 499

Elevated railways, **Vol. 2, Part 2,** 544; **Vol. 4, Part 1,** 172, 272

Elevators: building of, **Vol. 7, Part 2,** 93 f., 371; **Vol. 8, Part 1,** 115 f.; first electric control of, **Vol. 6, Part 1,** 176; first safety appliance for, **Vol. 7, Part 2,** 93 f.; manufacture of, **Supp. 1,** 669

Elgar, Edward, reference to, **Supp. 5,** 103

Eliot, Charles W., references to, **Vol. 4, Part 2,** 57; **Vol. 5, Part 1,** 169, 591; **Vol. 7, Part 1,** 570; **Supp. 3,** 327–28, 336, 422–23, 457, 470; **Supp. 6,** 208, 249, 485

Eliot, John, references to, **Vol. 5, Part 1,** 199; **Vol. 7, Part 1,** 328; **Vol. 10, Part 1,** 627 f.

Eliot, T. S.: critical analysis of, **Supp. 4,** 559, 560; references to, **Supp. 7,** 339, 347, 790; **Supp. 8,** 176, 584

Eliot School case, **Vol. 3, Part 1,** 541 f.

Elitcher, Max, reference to, **Supp. 5,** 589

Elizabeth, early boat to America (1634), **Vol. 6, Part 1,** 531

Elizabeth and Mary, seventeenth-century ship, **Vol. 9, Part 2,** 542, 543

Elizabethan history studies, **Supp. 6,** 531–32

Elk Hills, Calif., oil scandal of, **Vol. 8, Part 2,** 194; **Vol. 10, Part 1,** 393 f. *See also* Teapot Dome scandal

Elkhorn Tavern (or Pea Ridge), Ark., **Vol. 2, Part 2,** 620; **Vol. 6, Part 2,** 6, 427; **Vol. 10, Part 1,** 185

Elkins, William M., reference to, **Supp. 5,** 586

Elkins, W.Va., founding of, **Vol. 3, Part 2,** 84

Elks (fraternal order), **Supp. 5,** 754

Ellender, Allen J., reference to, **Supp. 5,** 719

Ellicott, Andrew, reference to, **Vol. 7, Part 1,** 544

Ellington, Duke, references to, **Supp. 3,** 188; **Supp. 6,** 42, 43

Elliott, A. Marshall, reference to, **Supp. 3,** 22

Elliott, John Lovejoy, reference to, **Supp. 3,** 175

Elliott, Maud Howe, reference to, **Supp. 3,** 630

Elliott, Thomas Renton, reference to, **Supp. 3,** 134

Elliott Monograph, **Supp. 3,** 22

Ellis, Emory, reference to, **Supp. 3,** 540

Ellis, Havelock, reference to, **Supp. 8,** 568

Ellis, John Tracy, reference to, **Supp. 6,** 600

Ellis-Foster Co., founding of, **Supp. 3,** 247

Ellis Island, **Vol. 7, Part 1,** 432; **Vol. 8, Part 2,** 169, 313; **Vol. 9, Part 2,** 549

Ellison, Ralph, reference to, **Supp. 5,** 529

Ellsworth, Oliver, reference to, **Vol. 7, Part 1,** 369

Elmer's Digest, **Vol. 7, Part 1,** 531

Elmhurst College, presidency, **Supp. 7,** 574

Elmira, N.Y., battle of, **Vol. 2, Part 1,** 362; **Vol. 2, Part 2,** 229; **Vol. 4, Part 2,** 223; **Vol. 8, Part 1,** 69; **Vol. 9, Part 2,** 193

Elm trees. *See* Dutch elm disease

El Salvador, diplomatic relations, **Vol. 3, Part 1,** 296

Elsie series, **Vol. 3, Part 2,** 390

Elwyn Institution, **Vol. 5, Part 2,** 355

Ely, Richard T., references to, **Supp. 3,** 18, 175–78, 176–77, 514, 680; **Supp. 4,** 738, 746, 747; **Supp. 5,** 591

Emancipation of slaves. *See* Slavery

Emancipator, founding of, **Vol. 5, Part 2,** 12; **Vol. 9, Part 2,** 299

"Embalmed beef" scandals, **Vol. 1, Part 1,** 348

Embargo Act (1807), **Vol. 4, Part 1,** 107; **Vol. 5, Part 2,** 30, 405; **Vol. 7, Part 2,** 89; **Vol. 8, Part 1,** 365; **Vol. 8, Part 2,** 76

Embryo. *See* Fetus

Embryology, **Vol. 6, Part 2,** 221; **Vol. 7, Part 1,** 30; blood cell and lymph vessel studies, **Supp. 5,** 600; cell lineage, **Supp. 2,** 723; cytoplasm studies, **Supp. 5,** 127; descriptive, **Supp. 4,** 801–2; experimental, **Supp. 3,** 403, 539–40; fertilization studies, **Supp. 4,** 497–98; marine organisms, **Supp. 3,** 403; nervous system development, **Supp. 6,** 282–83; nutritional studies, **Supp. 7,** 569; textbooks, **Supp. 4,** 573; uriniferous tubule, **Supp. 1,** 439

Emergency Banking Relief Act (1933), **Supp. 4,** 810; **Supp. 5,** 158

Emergency Fleet Corporation, World War, **Vol. 8, Part 2,** 194

Emergency Relief Administration, founding of, **Supp. 3,** 652

Emerson, John, owner of Dred Scott, **Vol. 8, Part 2,** 488 f.; reference to, **Supp. 6,** 657

Emerson, Joseph, reference to, **Vol. 6, Part 1,** 531

Emerson, Ralph Waldo, references to, **Vol. 1, Part 1,** 139 f., 475; **Vol. 4, Part 1,** 43; **Vol. 5, Part 1,** 606; **Vol. 6, Part 1,** 65; **Vol. 8, Part 1,** 455 f.; **Vol. 9, Part 2,** 492 f.; bust of, **Supp. 1,** 321; works editing, **Supp. 5,** 542; writings on, **Supp. 7,** 18–19

Emerson Radio and Phonograph Co., **Supp. 7,** 207

Emery, discovery of deposits of, **Vol. 9, Part 1,** 304

Emigrants' Guide to New Mexico, California, and Oregon, **Vol. 3, Part 1,** 319

Emigrant wagon train, first, **Vol. 8, Part 2,** 32

Emmanuel movement, **Vol. 7, Part 1,** 324; **Supp. 2,** 736; **Supp. 3,** 190–91

Emma Willard School, founding and history of, **Vol. 10, Part 2,** 232

Emmett, Burton, reference to, **Supp. 3,** 14

Emmet conspiracy, **Vol. 5, Part 1,** 337

Emmons, Samuel F., references to, **Supp. 4,** 765, 766

Emory and Henry College, history of, **Vol. 10, Part 2,** 214

Emory College, **Vol. 2, Part 1,** 471; **Vol. 5, Part 1,** 210; **Vol. 6, Part 1,** 390

Emory University, founding of, **Supp. 3,** 129

Emotions, studies of **Supp. 3,** 134–37; **Supp. 6,** 527

Empire Athletic Association, founding of, **Vol. 7, Part 2,** 602

Empire State Building (New York City): architectural design, **Supp. 5,** 408; construction, **Supp. 6,** 593; construction photographs, **Supp. 2,** 306; corporation, **Supp. 3,** 720–21; investors in, **Supp. 4,** 682

Empire Theater (New York City), **Supp. 6,** 306

Empiricism, theological, **Supp. 4,** 525–26

Employees and employers. *See* Labor and labor movement; Management

Employment. *See* Labor and labor movement; Management; Occupational safety and health; Public works; Trade unions; Unemployment; Wages and hours

Employment Act (1946), **Supp. 7,** 562, 590

Employment Managers' Association, founding of, **Supp. 2,** 45

Emporia Gazette, **Supp. 3,** 816–17

Empyema, **Supp. 6,** 246

Emulsions: photographic, **Supp. 4,** 744; synthetic rubber, **Supp. 5,** 273

Encephalitis, research on, **Supp. 5,** 512

Encyclopaedia Americana, **Vol. 6, Part 1,** 236

Encyclopaedia Britannica, first American on editorial board, **Supp. 5,** 245; first edition, **Vol. 6, Part 1,** 56

Encyclopedia of Materia Medica, **Vol. 1, Part 1,** 208

Encyclopedia of the Social Sciences, **Supp. 2,** 244

Enders, John, reference to, **Supp. 4,** 468

Endicott-Johnson Corporation, founding of, **Supp. 4,** 431–32

Endocarditis, subacute bacterial, **Supp. 4,** 494

Endocrine glands: cancer-resistance research, **Supp. 4,** 616; emotions study, **Supp. 3,** 134–37; pharmacological research, **Supp. 2,** 4; research on, **Supp. 3,** 6; **Supp. 6,** 100, 186, 386; sex hormone research, **Supp. 4,** 498. *See also* Hormones

Endocrinology, **Vol. 8, Part 2,** 306

"End of the Trail" (sculpture), **Supp. 5,** 231

Engineering (for complete list of engineers, *see* Occupations Index), **Vol. 1, Part 1,** 344, 457, 630, 642 f.; **Vol. 2, Part 2,** 460 f., 580 f.; **Vol. 3, Part 1,** 587 f.; **Vol. 3, Part 2,** 7, 178, 192; **Vol. 4, Part 1,** 75, 129, 136, 178, 565 f.; **Vol. 4, Part 2,** 492; **Vol. 5, Part 1,** 3, 371, 570, 572; **Vol. 5, Part 2,** 59, 208, 229, 249 f., 358; **Vol. 6, Part 1,** 23, 414; **Vol. 6, Part 2,** 9; **Vol. 8, Part 1,** 415; **Vol. 8, Part 2,** 12 f., 15 f., 359, 385, 398 f., 574; **Vol. 9, Part 1,** 179, 265, 363; **Vol. 9, Part 2,** 628 f., 656; **Vol. 10, Part 1,** 487 f., 539, 551; applications research, **Supp. 1,** 627; architectural, **Vol. 6, Part 1,** 166; bridge, **Vol. 1, Part 1,** 147; **Vol. 2, Part 2,** 110; **Vol. 3, Part 1,** 587 f.; **Vol. 4, Part 2,** 156, 400; **Vol. 5, Part 2,** 59; **Vol. 8, Part 1,** 418; **Vol. 8, Part 2,** 90, 592; **Vol. 9, Part 1,** 251; chemical, **Vol. 3, Part 2,** 603; **Vol. 9, Part 2,** 28; **Supp. 8,** 193–94; chemical (calcium carbide), **Supp. 7,** 553–54; civil, **Vol. 1, Part 1,** 193 f., 539 f.; **Vol. 1, Part 2,** 421, 441; **Vol. 2, Part 1,** 227; **Vol. 2, Part 2,** 69, 102, 187, 391, 413 f., 456 f., 479 f.; **Vol. 3, Part 1,** 258, 262, 334, 406, 459, 602; **Vol. 3, Part 2,** 339, 357, 387, 445, 569; **Vol. 4, Part 1,** 13, 52, 68, 205, 289, 471, 562, 567; **Vol. 4, Part 2,** 307, 452; **Vol. 5, Part 1,** 142,

298, 349; **Vol. 5, Part 2,** 91, 96, 106, 261, 454 f., 467, 498, 569; **Vol. 6, Part 1,** 27, 36, 380, 441, 505, 548, 549, 565; **Vol. 6, Part 2,** 142, 647; **Vol. 7, Part 1,** 255, 433, 456, 473, 536, 617; **Vol. 8, Part 1,** 19, 52, 179, 406, 417 f., 647; **Vol. 8, Part 2,** 48, 71, 88 f., 577, 592; **Vol. 9, Part 1,** 151, 165, 251, 272, 307, 319, 334, 368, 538, 543; **Vol. 9, Part 2,** 70, 98 f., 249, 309, 385, 519, 598, 611, 614; **Vol. 10, Part 1,** 2, 364, 372 f., 618 f., 634; **Vol. 10, Part 2,** 71, 260, 268, 339, 350, 538; civil (Army Corps of Engineers), **Supp. 6,** 508–9; civil (bridges and tunnels), **Supp. 1,** 135–36; **Supp. 3,** 331–32, 367; **Supp. 4,** 756–57; **Supp. 6,** 587; **Supp. 7,** 11–12; civil (canals), **Supp. 3,** 310–11; civil (dams), **Supp. 4,** 198–99; **Supp. 8,** 572–73; civil (foundations), **Supp. 2,** 469–70; civil (public works), **Supp. 3,** 795; civil (railroads), **Supp. 3,** 735–37, 759; civil (stress analysis), **Supp. 4,** 873–74; civil (structural), **Supp. 1,** 680; **Supp. 2,** 77; civil (teaching of), **Vol. 4, Part 1,** 52; **Vol. 5, Part 2,** 91; **Supp. 2,** 598; civil (textbooks on), **Supp. 1,** 148; civil (TVA project), **Supp. 3,** 580–81; civil (writings on), **Vol. 4, Part 1,** 289, 562; **Vol. 5, Part 2,** 106; **Vol. 6, Part 2,** 647; efficiency, **Vol. 9, Part 2,** 324; electrical, **Vol. 2, Part 2,** 553; **Vol. 3, Part 1,** 87, 220 f.; **Vol. 4, Part 1,** 620; **Vol. 4, Part 2,** 574; **Vol. 5, Part 1,** 261; **Vol. 6, Part 1,** 176; **Vol. 7, Part 1,** 526; **Vol. 7, Part 2,** 358, 480; **Vol. 8, Part 1,** 75, 221; **Vol. 8, Part 2,** 56, 154; **Vol. 9, Part 1,** 128, 275, 454, 490, 504, 514; **Vol. 9, Part 2,** 111; **Vol. 10, Part 1,** 57, 570; **Supp. 3,** 120, 184–85, 251–52, 744–47, 768–70; **Supp. 4,** 81–82; electrical (radio), **Supp. 4,** 422; **Supp. 5,** 21–22; electrical (railroads), **Supp. 3,** 369–70; electrical (studies, in), **Supp. 2,** 357; electrical (teaching of), **Supp. 1,** 31, 630; **Supp. 5,** 354–55; electrical (telephones), **Supp. 4,** 430; hydraulic, **Vol. 1, Part 2,** 529; **Vol. 3, Part 1,** 585 f., 587; **Vol. 3, Part 2,** 2, 228, 267, 434, 579; **Vol. 4, Part 1,** 39, 40, 467; **Vol. 4, Part 2,** 59, 283 f., 576 f., 595 f.; **Vol. 5, Part 1,** 349 f., 371; **Vol. 8, Part 1,** 324 f., 375 f.; **Vol. 8, Part 2,** 398 f., 473; **Vol. 9, Part 1,** 54, 273; illuminating, **Vol. 8, Part 2,** 268; insurance covering, **Supp. 1,** 319; journals, **Supp. 1,** 552; marine, **Vol. 1, Part 1,** 193 f.; **Vol. 2, Part 1,** 468; **Vol. 2, Part 2,** 500; **Vol. 3, Part 1,** 211, 288, 292; **Vol. 3, Part 2,** 143; **Vol. 5, Part 1,** 318; **Vol. 6, Part 1,** 545; **Vol. 8, Part 1,** 314, 639; **Vol. 9, Part 2,** 344; mechanical, **Vol. 3, Part 1,** 142, 288; **Vol. 3, Part 2,** 456; **Vol. 4, Part 1,** 38, 488; **Vol. 4, Part 2,** 345; **Vol. 5, Part 1,** 84, 127, 153, 155, 342, 370, 383, 444, 515; **Vol. 5, Part 2,** 168, 348, 443; **Vol. 6, Part 1,** 81, 235; **Vol. 6, Part 2,** 422; **Vol. 7, Part 1,** 449, 546; **Vol. 8, Part 1,** 172 f., 517, 551; **Vol. 8, Part 2,** 52; **Vol. 9, Part 1,** 429; **Vol. 9, Part 2,** 243, 518, 581; **Vol. 10, Part 1,** 470 f., 575; mechanical (air conditioning), **Supp. 4,** 148–49; mechanical (bridge design), **Supp. 3,** 331–32; mechanical (hydroelectric power plants), **Supp. 3,** 500; mechanical (inspection and testing), **Supp. 3,** 220; mechanical (lubrication and bearing design), **Supp. 3,** 419; mechanical (machine design), **Supp. 5,** 386–87; mechanical (machine tools), **Supp. 3,** 561–62; mechanical (Manhattan Project plant), **Supp. 4,** 453–54; mechanical (steam tables for), **Supp. 5,** 154; mechanical (teaching of), **Supp. 3,** 188, 331–32; **Supp. 6,** 181–82; mechanical (turbines), **Supp. 4,** 383–84; mechanical (turbosupercharger engine), **Supp. 4,** 609; metallurgical, **Vol. 7, Part 2,** 504; military, **Vol. 1, Part 1,** 163, 500, 626; **Vol. 2, Part 2,** 78; **Vol. 3, Part 1,** 210; **Vol. 3, Part 2,** 153 f., 550; **Vol. 4, Part 1,** 138, 343, 612; **Vol. 4, Part 2,** 52, 151; **Vol. 5, Part 1,** 101 f.; **Vol. 6, Part 1,** 182, 495, 496; **Vol. 6, Part 2,** 257; **Vol. 7, Part 1,** 100 f., 154; **Vol. 8, Part 1,** 406, 647; **Vol. 9, Part 2,**

247, 260, 327; mining, **Vol. 2, Part 1,** 511; **Vol. 2, Part 2,** 200, 274, 485 f.; **Vol. 3, Part 1,** 27, 225 f., 396 f., 460; **Vol. 3, Part 2,** 2; **Vol. 4, Part 2,** 87; **Vol. 6, Part 1,** 167, 360, 608 f.; **Vol. 5, Part 2,** 55, 319; **Vol. 6, Part 1,** 482 f., 515; **Vol. 6, Part 2,** 458; **Vol. 7, Part 1,** 135, 412; **Vol. 7, Part 2,** 9 f., 354; **Vol. 8, Part 1,** 412, 414; **Vol. 8, Part 2,** 189; **Vol. 9, Part 1,** 273, 459, 545; **Vol. 9, Part 2,** 64, 146; **Vol. 10, Part 2,** 261; municipal, **Vol. 8, Part 1,** 415; naval, **Vol. 1, Part 1,** 495; **Vol. 2, Part 2,** 423; **Vol. 3, Part 2,** 158, 170, 405; **Vol. 4, Part 2,** 391; **Vol. 5, Part 1,** 153; **Vol. 7, Part 1,** 639; **Vol. 7, Part 2,** 487; **Vol. 8, Part 1,** 640; **Vol. 8, Part 2,** 194; **Vol. 9, Part 2,** 613; railway, **Vol. 2, Part 1,** 562; **Vol. 2, Part 2,** 275 f.; **Vol. 3, Part 1,** 348; **Vol. 5, Part 2,** 292; **Vol. 8, Part 1,** 417 f.; **Vol. 8, Part 2,** 19, 33; **Vol. 9, Part 2,** 642; **Vol. 10, Part 1,** 372; research, **Supp. 2,** 104; sanitary, **Vol. 1, Part 1,** 597; **Vol. 3, Part 1,** 78; **Vol. 4, Part 1,** 433; **Vol. 4, Part 2,** 576 f.; **Vol. 5, Part 2,** 193, 265, 275, 277, 418 f.; **Vol. 8, Part 1,** 390 f., 475, 553 f.; **Vol. 8, Part 2,** 553, 606; **Vol. 9, Part 1,** 495; **Vol. 10, Part 1,** 456 f.; structural, **Supp. 3,** 611–12; structural steel, **Supp. 3,** 77; teaching of, **Supp. 1,** 175, 629, 680; **Supp. 3,** 188; **Supp. 5,** 154; telephone, **Supp. 3,** 298–99; topographical, **Vol. 3, Part 1,** 251 f.; **Vol. 4, Part 1,** 476; **Vol. 5, Part 1,** 348; **Vol. 10, Part 1,** 473 f.; writings on, **Vol. 1, Part 1,** 627; **Vol. 3, Part 1,** 292, 470, 547 f., 587 f.; **Vol. 4, Part 1,** 295; **Vol. 5, Part 1,** 444; **Vol. 5, Part 2,** 60, 106, 443 f.; **Vol. 8, Part 1,** 28 f., 91 f., 329 f., 552; **Vol. 9, Part 1,** 495; **Vol. 9, Part 2,** 520; **Vol. 10, Part 1,** 539, 618 f., 634. *See also specific types of engineering*

Engineering and Mining Journal, **Vol. 8, Part 2,** 189
Engineering Foundation, founding of, **Supp. 2,** 643
Engineering Record, founding of, **Supp. 1,** 552
Engineering Researches, **Vol. 5, Part 1,** 516
Engineers. For complete list, *see* Occupations Index
"Engineers' Bible," **Vol. 4, Part 2,** 391
Engineers' Club (New York City), **Vol. 8, Part 1,** 343
Engineers Group, Inc., **Supp. 6,** 140
Engineers' Pocket Book, **Vol. 9, Part 2,** 629
Engineers Public Service Corporation, founding of, **Supp. 3,** 747
Engines: air-cooled, **Supp. 4,** 473–74, 486; diesel for automobiles, **Supp. 5,** 654; internal-combustion, **Supp. 6,** 332; train, **Supp. 1,** 397; turbine, **Supp. 1,** 65; **Supp. 4,** 383–84; turbosupercharger, **Supp. 4,** 609
England. *See* Great Britain
English literature and language: Chaucer studies, **Supp. 3,** 475, 855; **Supp. 4,** 819–20; Coleridge scholarship, **Supp. 3,** 475; Elizabethan studies, **Supp. 4,** 4–5, 110, 624, 634; grammar, writing on, **Supp. 4,** 203; Jewish immigrants' adaptation, **Supp. 5,** 95–96; manuscript collections, **Supp. 5,** 349–50; Middle English studies, **Supp. 3,** 109; Old English syntax, **Supp. 2,** 88; popularization of, **Supp. 3,** 601–3; rare book catalogs, **Supp. 7,** 387; scholarship, seventeenth- and eighteenth-century, **Supp. 7,** 402–3, 798; Shakespearean scholarship, **Supp. 3,** 423; Society for Pure English, founding of, **Supp. 4,** 755–56; Sterne and Fielding scholarship, **Supp. 4,** 197; studies, **Supp. 1,** 474; teaching of, **Supp. 1,** 356; **Supp. 3,** 422–23, 454–55, 624; **Supp. 5,** 131–32, 211–12, 645–46; **Supp. 7,** 56, 797, 798; textbooks on, **Supp. 1,** 697; usage, writings on, **Supp. 2,** 683; words coined, **Supp. 5,** 94, 480, 481; writings on, **Supp. 3,** 689; **Supp. 4,** 559–61. *See also* American literature; Criticism; Poetry; Reading
English-Speaking Union, founding of American branch, **Vol. 8, Part 1,** 278 f.

English, Thomas Dunn, reference to, **Vol. 9, Part 2,** 314

Engraving, **Vol. 1, Part 1,** 131, 589; **Vol. 1, Part 2,** 284; **Vol. 2, Part 1,** 278; **Vol. 2, Part 2,** 55, 172, 231; **Vol. 3, Part 1,** 3, 66, 150 f., 272, 372 f., 535 f., 538; **Vol. 3, Part 2,** 5, 47, f., 370, 495, 567; **Vol. 4, Part 1,** 286, 336, 432; **Vol. 4, Part 2,** 131, 198; **Vol. 5, Part 1,** 41, 157, 200 f.; **Vol. 5, Part 2,** 73 f., 139, 152, 159, 293 f., 342, 411, 456; **Vol. 6, Part 1,** 56, 165, 186, 285, 381; **Vol. 6, Part 2,** 219, 432; **Vol. 7, Part 1,** 550; **Vol. 7, Part 1,** 141 f., 453, 511, 617; **Vol. 8, Part 2,** 305, 370 f., 386, 451; **Vol. 9, Part 1,** 119 f., 232 f., 307; **Vol. 9, Part 2,** 137, 295, 530; **Vol. 10, Part 1,** 12 f.; **Supp. 3,** 292; aquatint, **Vol. 4, Part 2,** 403; **Vol. 5, Part 2,** 269 f., 456; bank notes, **Vol. 1, Part 2,** 502; **Vol. 2, Part 1,** 56; **Vol. 2, Part 2,** 343; **Vol. 3, Part 1,** 501, 535, 538; **Vol. 4, Part 1,** 322 f.; **Vol. 5, Part 1,** 165; **Vol. 5, Part 2,** 74, 159, 243, 456; **Vol. 6, Part 1,** 284, 422; **Vol. 7, Part 2,** 55, 370, 472; **Vol. 8, Part 1,** 253, 515; **Vol. 8, Part 2,** 122, 451; **Vol. 9, Part 1,** 232; **Vol. 9, Part 2,** 43, 295; bookplates, **Vol. 5, Part 1,** 424; **Vol. 8, Part 1,** 361 f.; Boston, pictorial plates of early, **Vol. 2, Part 1,** 278; colored, **Vol. 6, Part 1,** 56; collecting, **Vol. 9, Part 1,** 538; copper, **Vol. 3, Part 1,** 272 f.; **Vol. 5, Part 1,** 424; first U.S. coins, **Vol. 6, Part 1,** 381; "golden age of American reproductive engraving," **Vol. 4, Part 2,** 503; line, **Vol. 2, Part 2,** 52; **Vol. 4, Part 1,** 392; **Vol. 5, Part 2,** 269 f., 456; **Vol. 6, Part 1,** 56; **Vol. 7, Part 2,** 369 f., 592; **Vol. 8, Part 2,** 122; lithographic, **Vol. 3, Part 1,** 170; **Vol. 7, Part 2,** 421; machines, invention of, **Vol. 1, Part 2,** 407; magazines, early use of, in, **Vol. 3, Part 1,** 613 f.; maps, **Vol. 5, Part 2,** 152; **Vol. 8, Part 1,** 140 f.; **Vol. 9, Part 2,** 295; mezzotint, **Vol. 7, Part 2,** 409; **Vol. 8, Part 2,** 169; miniatures, **Vol. 8, Part 2,** 305; photoengraving, **Vol. 6, Part 1,** 203; portraits, **Vol. 3, Part 1,** 535 f.; **Vol. 5, Part 2,** 509; **Vol. 6, Part 1,** 165; **Vol. 6, Part 2,** 331; **Vol. 10, Part 2,** 603; postage stamps, **Vol. 5, Part 2,** 159; stipple, **Vol. 5, Part 2,** 456; wood, **Vol. 1, Part 1,** 93, 262, 315; **Vol. 3, Part 1,** 423 f.; **Vol. 3, Part 2,** 549; **Vol. 4, Part 2,** 321; **Vol. 6, Part 1,** 56; **Vol. 9, Part 2,** 43; **Vol. 10, Part 2,** 447; **Supp. 1,** 185

Engraving and Printing, Bureau of, **Vol. 3, Part 1,** 535 f., 538

ENIAC computer, **Supp. 6,** 675

Enormous Room, The, **Supp. 7,** 157, 158

Entailed Hat, **Vol. 9, Part 2,** 617

Enterprise (schooner), **Vol. 5, Part 2,** 541; **Vol. 9, Part 1,** 41

Enterprise (steamboat), **Vol. 5, Part 2,** 110; **Vol. 9, Part 1,** 134

Enterprise (yacht), **Supp. 4,** 124

Entertainers. For complete list, *see* Occupations Index

Entertaining, social, **Supp. 7,** 519, 527

Entomological Commission, United States, **Vol. 8, Part 1,** 610

Entomological Society of America, founding of, **Supp. 3,** 478

Entomologists. For complete list, *see* Occupations Index

Entomology, **Vol. 1, Part 1,** 392, 575; **Vol. 2, Part 2,** 433, 541; **Vol. 3, Part 1,** 578 f.; **Vol. 3, Part 2,** 334, 424, 510; **Vol. 4, Part 1,** 333; **Vol. 4, Part 2,** 27, 82, 586; **Vol. 5, Part 1,** 229, 327, 406; **Vol. 5, Part 2,** 448; **Vol. 6, Part 1,** 89, 283; **Vol. 6, Part 2,** 519; **Vol. 7, Part 2,** 87 f., 384; **Vol. 8, Part 1,** 610; **Vol. 8, Part 2,** 401 f., 525; **Vol. 9, Part 1,** 298, 385; **Vol. 9, Part 2,** 319, 426; **Vol. 10, Part 1,** 106 f., 388 f.; agricultural, **Supp. 4,** 601; "agricultural" ants, **Vol. 6, Part 1,** 241 f.; bees, taxonomy of, **Supp. 4,** 167; economic,

Vol. 8, Part 1, 609 f.; popularization of, **Supp. 4,** 399–400; practical use of first, **Vol. 4, Part 2,** 321; research in, **Supp. 1,** 187, 414; writings on, **Supp. 3,** 683. *See also* Insects

Entwhistle, Frederick I., reference to, **Supp. 7,** 577

Environment: health relationship, **Supp. 2,** 646; pioneer in protection movement, **Supp. 4,** 484; radiation-level control, **Supp. 8,** 26. *See also* Conservation; Ecology; Natural history; Pollution

Environment v. heredity. *See* Genetics

Enzymes: biochemical studies of, **Supp. 5,** 26, 140, 489, 622, 623, 670–71; **Supp. 6,** 127, 295–96, 595

Ephemeris, computation of the, **Vol. 7, Part 1,** 453

Epic Mythology, **Supp. 1,** 434

Epidemics: American aid in European, **Vol. 3, Part 2,** 572; cholera, *see* Cholera; control of, **Supp. 2,** 212; **Supp. 4,** 700–1; meningitis, **Supp. 4,** 287; pneumonia, **Supp. 3,** 483; poliomyelitis, **Supp. 4,** 287–88; **Supp. 6,** 192; study of, **Vol. 3, Part 2,** 128; **Vol. 5, Part 2,** 325; **Vol. 8, Part 1,** 131 f.; **Vol. 8, Part 2,** 552 f.; **Vol. 9, Part 1,** 190 f., 590 f.; typhus, **Supp. 4,** 668, 803; **Supp. 5,** 336; yellow fever, *see* Yellow fever

Epidemiology: family concept of, **Supp. 3,** 775; infectious disease studies, **Supp. 7,** 194; preventive measures, **Supp. 3,** 158; **Supp. 5,** 143–44; statistics used in, **Supp. 7,** 192. *See also* Public health; *specific disease names*

Epigraphy, writings on, **Vol. 9, Part 1,** 594

Epileptics, care of, **Vol. 3, Part 1,** 478 f.; **Vol. 6, Part 1,** 194; **Vol. 7, Part 2,** 6

Epinephrine, surgical shock, **Supp. 3,** 201

Episcopal Academy of Connecticut, founding of, **Vol. 1, Part 2,** 491

Episcopal church. *See* Protestant Episcopal church

Epstein, Abraham, reference to, **Supp. 3,** 19, 517

Epstein, Jacob, reference to, **Supp. 3,** 329

Epstein, Julius J., reference to, **Supp. 5,** 209

Epworth League: adoption of, in India, **Vol. 7, Part 2,** 219; organized in China, **Supp. 6,** 315

Equality League of Self-Supporting Women, founding of, **Supp. 2,** 43

Equal rights, **Vol. 1, Part 2,** 581; **Vol. 2, Part 1,** 19, 151; **Vol. 6, Part 1,** 480; **Vol. 9, Part 2,** 253 f.; Amendment, **Supp. 5,** 474, 532, 543; cosponsor, **Supp. 4,** 145; initiation of, **Supp. 7,** 717

Equal Rights Association, American, **Vol. 7, Part 2,** 609

Equal Rights Society, organization of, in Oregon, **Vol. 3, Part 1,** 513 f.

Equations: differential, **Supp. 3,** 70; linear difference, **Supp. 3,** 70; linear integral, **Supp. 3,** 87

Equilenin, synthesis of, **Supp. 5,** 28

Equilibrium, studies in, **Supp. 2,** 373

Equitable Life Assurance Society, **Vol. 5, Part 1,** 450; **Vol. 7, Part 1,** 265; **Supp. 6,** 497

"Equivalent Lands," **Vol. 8, Part 1,** 426

Erasmus, writings on, **Supp. 3,** 726

Erdmann, Benno, references to, **Supp. 3,** 81, 229

Erector Set (toy), **Supp. 7,** 287–88

Ergodic theorem (1931), **Supp. 3,** 70–71

Ergotocin, **Supp. 6,** 334

Ericsson, John, use of revolving battery, **Vol. 9, Part 2,** 554; **Vol. 10, Part 1,** 618 f.

Ericsson, Leif: reference to, **Supp. 8,** 457; sculpture of, **Supp. 3,** 124

Erie Canal, **Vol. 3, Part 2,** 15, 90, 195, 525; **Vol. 5, Part 1,** 83, 150, 395; **Vol. 5, Part 2,** 59, 120, 320; **Vol. 6, Part 1,** 323; **Vol. 7, Part 1,** 212, 355, 563, 604; **Vol. 8, Part 2,** 12; **Vol. 9, Part 1,** 7; **Vol. 9, Part 2,** 651; **Vol. 10, Part 2,** 40, 93; opening (1825), **Vol. 8, Part 2,** 21; writings on, **Vol. 9, Part 2,** 89

1, **Part** 1, 579; **Vol. 5, Part** 2, 441; Rocky Mountains, **Vol. 5, Part** 1, 576; **Vol. 7, Part** 1, 81, 319; **Vol. 8, Part** 1, 250; South America, **Vol. 2, Part** 2, 103; **Vol. 3, Part** 2, 465 f.; **Vol. 7, Part** 1, 594; **Vol. 7, Part** 2, 140; South Carolina, **Vol. 10, Part** 2, 509; South Seas, **Vol. 7, Part** 2, 562; Southwest, **Vol. 2, Part** 2, 449 f.; space, **Supp. 7**, 424, 429; Spanish, **Vol. 1, Part** 1, 135, 322, 451; **Vol. 2, Part** 2, 449 f.; **Vol. 6, Part** 1, 504; Syria, **Vol. 9, Part** 1, 258; Virginia, **Vol. 10, Part** 2, 154; West, **Vol. 2, Part** 2, 234; **Vol. 3, Part** 2, 496; **Vol. 4, Part** 1, 13, 132, 327, 329; **Vol. 6, Part** 1, 180, 380; **Vol. 6, Part** 2, 332; **Vol. 7, Part** 1, 315, 641; **Vol. 7, Part** 2, 481, 599; **Vol. 9, Part** 1, 516, 631 f.; Wilkes expedition, **Vol. 3, Part** 1, 55, 200; **Vol. 7, Part** 2, 185; **Vol. 9, Part** 2, 457; Wisconsin, **Vol. 3, Part** 1, 500 f.; writings on, **Vol. 3, Part** 1, 475 f., 507 f.; **Vol. 4, Part** 1, 18, 20; **Vol. 5, Part** 2, 606; **Vol. 6, Part** 1, 91; Yosemite Valley, **Vol. 6, Part** 1, 180; zoological collections, **Supp. 3**, 667–69. *See also specific states, regions*

Explorations, Journal of, **Vol. 6, Part** 1, 221

Explorers. For complete list, *see* Occupations Index

Explorers' Club of New York, **Vol. 10, Part** 1, 390; founding of, **Supp. 1**, 238

Explosives, **Vol. 3, Part** 1, 528; **Vol. 5, Part** 2, 239; **Vol. 6, Part** 2, 438; **Vol. 7, Part** 2, 22; dynamite, use of, **Vol. 5, Part** 2, 239; **Vol. 7, Part** 2, 22; industry research, **Supp. 2**, 479; manufacturing, **Supp. 1**, 271; **Supp. 2**, 551; **Supp. 3**, 239; **Supp. 4**, 681; **Supp. 5**, 191–93; **Supp. 7**, 169, 210; RDX (cyclonite), **Supp. 5**, 28; safe transportation of, **Vol. 3, Part** 1, 479 f.; smokeless powder, **Supp. 5**, 235

Export-Import Bank, **Supp. 6**, 229, 231, 325; **Supp. 8**, 66

Export trade, **Vol. 3, Part** 1, 429; **Vol. 7, Part** 2, 62

Express business, **Vol. 1, Part** 1, 37, 354; **Vol. 2, Part** 1, 375; **Vol. 2, Part** 2, 50; **Vol. 3, Part** 2, 271; **Vol. 4, Part** 2, 278; **Vol. 9, Part** 2, 385; Post Office and, **Vol. 10, Part** 1, 639 f.; writings on, **Vol. 9, Part** 2, 32, 385

Expressways. *See* Road building

Exter, Alexandra, reference to, **Supp. 6**, 624

Extragalactic nebulae, **Supp. 5**, 326

Extrasensory perception, **Supp. 2**, 407; **Supp. 6**, 612

Eye-Bank for Sight Restoration, founding of, **Supp. 7**, 70

Eyes: astigmatism, **Supp. 3**, 377; belladonna, use of, **Vol. 10, Part** 1, 644 f.; bird and reptile studies, **Supp. 3**, 835; color blindness, **Supp. 3**, 270; color heredity, **Supp. 3**, 215; diseases of, **Vol. 3, Part** 1, 207, 253, 327; **Vol. 5, Part** 1, 293; **Vol. 5, Part** 2, 38; **Vol. 8, Part** 1, 510, 565; **Supp. 2**, 604; **Supp. 3**, 835; **Supp. 4**, 865; dispensary, first in U.S., **Vol. 7, Part** 1, 559; operations on, **Vol. 3, Part** 1, 478 f.; **Vol. 5, Part** 1, 248, 541; **Vol. 7, Part** 1, 557; reading movement of, **Supp. 3**, 229–30; surgery, **Supp. 3**, 301–2; surgery anesthetic, **Supp. 3**, 430–31; visual acuity testing, **Supp. 3**, 269–70. *See also* Blind and blindness; Ophthalmology; Vision

Ezra Church, battle of, **Vol. 1, Part** 1, 266; **Vol. 5, Part** 1, 280; **Vol. 6, Part** 1, 130; **Vol. 9, Part** 2, 3

F

Faber and Faber (publishers), **Supp. 7**, 220

Fabian Society, **Vol. 3, Part** 1, 96

Fabrics. *See* Textiles; *specific types*

Fabulist, The, **Supp. 6**, 185

Factorage, Indian, **Vol. 2, Part** 2, 565; **Vol. 4, Part** 1, 94; **Vol. 6, Part** 2, 89; **Vol. 7, Part** 1, 633

Fagan, Mark, reference to, **Supp. 6**, 265

Fagan, Ruth, reference to, **Supp. 5**, 74

Fail-Safe, **Supp. 7**, 93, 94

Fair, James G., reference to, **Vol. 7, Part** 1, 612

Fairbanks, Douglas, Sr., reference to, **Supp. 4**, 350

Fairchild Tropical Garden (Fla.), **Supp. 5**, 214

Fair Employment Practices Commission, **Supp. 7**, 122; founding of, **Supp. 5**, 120

Fairfax, Beatrice, column of, **Supp. 3**, 504

Fairfax, Sally, reference to, **Supp. 6**, 310

Fairfax Court-House, Va., capture of, **Vol. 7, Part** 1, 272

Fairfax proprietary, **Vol. 3, Part** 2, 256

Fairfield, Calif., founding of, **Vol. 10, Part** 1, 534 f.

Fairfield, Conn., **Vol. 2, Part** 2, 67; settlement of, **Vol. 6, Part** 1, 494

"Fair Harvard," **Vol. 4, Part** 1, 305

Fair Labor Standards Act (1938), **Supp. 3**, 228; **Supp. 4**, 376, 614; **Supp. 5**, 358; **Supp. 6**, 480; **Supp. 7**, 609; passage of, **Supp. 3**, 655–56

Fairless, Benjamin, reference to, **Supp. 7**, 587

Fairmount College, presidency of, **Vol. 7, Part** 1, 230

Fair Oaks, Va., battle of. *See* Seven Pines, battle of

Fairs, county, beginning of American, **Vol. 10, Part** 1, 542; state, **Vol. 8, Part** 1, 347; **Vol. 10, Part** 1, 36

Faith-cure movement, **Vol. 2, Part** 2, 588; **Supp. 4**, 271–72

Falk, Stanley L., reference to, **Supp. 6**, 268

Falk Foundation, founding of, **Supp. 4**, 261–62

Fall, Albert B., reference to, **Supp. 3**, 491, 715; **Supp. 6**, 584

Falla, Manuel de, reference to, **Supp. 6**, 358

Fallingwater (Mill Run, Pa.), **Supp. 6**, 714

Fallopian tubes, **Supp. 6**, 555

Fall River, Mass., **Vol. 1, Part** 2, 459

Fall River Line, **Vol. 1, Part** 2, 459; **Vol. 9, Part** 2, 344

Fallen Timbers, battle of, **Vol. 2, Part** 2, 142; **Vol. 4, Part** 2, 216, 348; **Vol. 5, Part** 2, 8–9; **Vol. 6, Part** 1, 300; **Vol. 8, Part** 2, 487; **Vol. 10, Part** 1, 210, 524, 564

Families: anthropological study of, **Supp. 8**, 378; pioneer in study of, **Vol. 3, Part** 1, 308; popular writings on, **Supp. 8**, 189; situation comedies, **Supp. 7**, 9; social work, **Supp. 4**, 810–11; sociology of black, **Supp. 7**, 266

Family Circle, **Supp. 6**, 449

Family Digest, **Supp. 6**, 478–79

Family Magazine, founding of, **Vol. 8, Part** 1, 440

Family planning: birth control advocacy, **Supp. 5**, 297; **Supp. 6**, 602; first birth control clinic in U.S., **Supp. 8**, 568; oral contraceptive development, **Supp. 8**, 503; Planned Parenthood associations, **Supp. 4**, 391; religious objections to contraception, **Supp. 8**, 116; social research in, **Supp. 6**, 82

Family School for Young Ladies, **Vol. 9, Part** 2, 621

Family Service Association of America, predecessors, **Supp. 4**, 810

Famous-Barr Co., **Supp. 8**, 427

Famous Players Film Co., **Supp. 3**, 607; **Supp. 6**, 369

Faneuil Hall (Boston), **Vol. 3, Part** 2, 263; **Vol. 6, Part** 1, 439; building of, **Vol. 8, Part** 1, 308 f.; designs for, **Vol. 9, Part** 1, 229

Fanning's Islands, discovery of, **Vol. 3, Part** 2, 266

Fanny, fastest merchant vessel of the time, **Vol. 6, Part** 1, 543

FAO. *See* Food and Agriculture Organization

Far Eastern Commission, **Supp. 6**, 270

Fargo, William G., reference to, **Vol. 10, Part** 1, 639 f.

Farish, William S., reference to, **Supp. 4**, 775–76

Farley, James A., references to, **Supp. 3**, 560, 646, 647, 659

Farley, Thomas M., reference to, **Supp. 6**, 570

Farlow, William G., reference to, **Vol. 9, Part 2,** 398

Farm, The, **Supp. 6,** 78

Farm and Home, **Vol. 7, Part 1,** 377

Farm Bankruptcy Act (1934), Frazier-Lemke amendment, **Supp. 4,** 309

Farm Bureau Federation. *See* American Farm Bureau Federation

Farm Bureau system, **Supp. 4,** 36–37

Farm Credit Act (1953), **Supp. 8,** 278

Farm Credit Administration, **Supp. 8,** 445–46; land banks, **Supp. 4,** 341

Farmer, Moses G., references to, **Vol. 2, Part 2,** 9; **Vol. 10, Part 1,** 376 f.

Farmer-Labor party, **Supp. 3,** 347; **Supp. 6,** 577, 645; Democratic party fusion, **Supp. 3,** 227; founding of, **Supp. 4,** 280, 542

Farmer-Labor Reconstruction League, founding of, **Supp. 3,** 10

Farmers' Alliance, **Vol. 1, Part 1,** 522; **Vol. 9, Part 1,** 199; **Supp. 6,** 468

Farmers' Alliance Exchange of Texas, founding of, **Supp. 2,** 426

Farmers' Almanack, founding of, **Vol. 9, Part 2,** 444 f.

Farmers' Club of Pennsylvania, **Vol. 5, Part 2,** 572

Farmers' Educational and Cooperative Union (Farmers' Union), **Supp. 1,** 51; **Supp. 2,** 426; **Supp. 6,** 86, 645

Farmers' Institutes, plan for, **Vol. 10, Part 1,** 617 f.

Farmers' Museum, publication of, **Vol. 3, Part 1,** 236

Farmers' Political League, **Vol. 7, Part 1,** 377

Farmers' Protective Association, **Vol. 2, Part 2,** 165

Farmers' Register, publication of, **Vol. 8, Part 2,** 215

Farmers' Tribune, **Supp. 7,** 527

Farmer's Union, **Vol. 9, Part 1,** 180. *See also* Farmers' Educational and Cooperative Union

Farmer's Wife, **Supp. 7,** 615

Farm Foundation, founding of, **Supp. 1,** 491

Farm Holiday Association, **Supp. 4,** 480; **Supp. 6,** 86, 645; founding of, **Supp. 2,** 552

Farming, **Vol. 1, Part 1,** 316; **Vol. 1, Part 2,** 183; **Vol. 2, Part 1,** 25; **Vol. 2, Part 2,** 185; **Vol. 4, Part 1,** 595; **Vol. 4, Part 2,** 207 f.; **Vol. 6, Part 1,** 482; **Vol. 7, Part 2,** 148; **Vol. 9, Part 1,** 458; **Vol. 9, Part 2,** 134; **Vol. 10, Part 2,** 460; colonial, **Vol. 8, Part 1,** 419; cooperative, **Vol. 7, Part 1,** 377; dairy, **Vol. 1, Part 1,** 370; **Vol. 5, Part 1,** 90; **Vol. 8, Part 2,** 512; **Vol. 9, Part 1,** 280; drainage, **Vol. 3, Part 1,** 210; "dry," **Vol. 1, Part 1,** 408; fertilizers, **Vol. 7, Part 2,** 419; **Vol. 8, Part 1,** 397; **Vol. 9, Part 2,** 37; machinery, **Vol. 1, Part 1,** 178, 185, 284, 551; **Vol. 1, Part 2,** 172, 230; **Vol. 2, Part 1,** 337; **Vol. 3, Part 1,** 437; **Vol. 3, Part 2,** 110, 132; **Vol. 4, Part 1,** 122; **Vol. 5, Part 2,** 53, 151 f.; **Vol. 6, Part 1,** 230, 505, 607, 610 f.; **Vol. 6, Part 2,** 304, 383; **Vol. 7, Part 1,** 590; **Vol. 7, Part 2,** 644; **Vol. 8, Part 1,** 101 f.; **Vol. 9, Part 2,** 439; **Vol. 10, Part 2,** 464, 475; rotation of crops, **Vol. 1, Part 2,** 460; schools, **Vol. 1, Part 2,** 568; **Vol. 3, Part 2,** 351; **Vol. 4, Part 1,** 379; soil analysis, **Vol. 3, Part 1,** 210; writings on, **Vol. 1, Part 1,** 110 f., 205; **Vol. 6, Part 2,** 547; **Vol. 9, Part 1,** 200; **Vol. 9, Part 2,** 388. *See also* Agriculture

Farmington, Conn., early history of, **Vol. 8, Part 1,** 97 f., 102 f.

Farm Journal, **Vol. 1, Part 1,** 413; **Supp. 7,** 615

Farm Mortgage Moratorium Act (1935), **Supp. 4,** 480

Farm Security Administration, **Supp. 4,** 50; **Supp. 6,** 12; **Supp. 7,** 456; founding of, **Supp. 4,** 251; photographs, **Supp. 8,** 586

Farragut, David Glasgow, references to, **Vol. 1, Part 1,** 146, 502; **Vol. 5, Part 2,** 221; **Vol. 7, Part 1,** 320, 402; **Vol. 9, Part 1,** 321

Farragut, Loyall, reference to, **Vol. 7, Part 2,** 186

Farrar, John, reference to, **Supp. 8,** 535–36

Farrar and Rinehart, **Supp. 6,** 543; founding of, **Supp. 8,** 535

Farrell, Charles, reference to, **Supp. 7,** 65

Farrell, Edelmiro, reference to, **Supp. 5,** 332

Farrell, James T., reference to, **Supp. 6,** 663

Farwell, J. V., reference to, **Vol. 7, Part 1,** 103

Fascism: Anti-Fascist Alliance, **Supp. 6,** 239; Italian-American opposition to, **Supp. 3,** 777–78; journalism opposing, **Supp. 5,** 447; opposition, **Supp. 6,** 237, 359, 643; sympathy with, **Supp. 3,** 50; **Supp. 4,** 518. *See also* Nazism

Fashion: design, **Supp. 5,** 385–86; **Supp. 6,** 9, 100–101, 402; **Supp. 7,** 591; **Supp. 8,** 14; entertainers' influence on, **Supp. 5,** 501; illustration, **Supp. 7,** 66–67; jeans, **Supp. 5,** 386; liberated women's, **Supp. 4,** 231; **Supp. 7,** 634; **Supp. 8,** 77; Little Lord Fauntleroy style, **Supp. 3,** 69; magazines, **Supp. 3,** 547; **Supp. 6,** 107–8; **Supp. 7,** 704–5; Metropolitan Museum Costume Institute, **Supp. 6,** 621; theatrical costume design, **Supp. 5,** 52–53; women's trend-setting, **Supp. 8,** 77. *See also* Clothing; Dress

Fashion; or, Life in New York, **Vol. 7, Part 1,** 296

Fassett Committee, **Vol. 3, Part 2,** 297

Fast Day Proclamation (N.H., 1899), **Vol. 8, Part 2,** 121

Fatigue: muscular, **Supp. 2,** 391; physiological studies in, **Supp. 3,** 351; studies, **Supp. 2,** 373–74; **Supp. 4,** 565; **Supp. 8,** 684

Faubus, Orval E., reference to, **Supp. 8,** 157

Faucets, invention of, **Vol. 5, Part 2,** 49 f.

Faulconer, Robert C., reference to, **Supp. 3,** 562

Faulkner, William, references to, **Supp. 3,** 14; **Supp. 6,** 106

Faulkner Farm (Brookline, Mass.), **Supp. 4,** 115

Fauna, history of American, **Vol. 5, Part 1,** 141; deep sea, **Vol. 8, Part 1,** 141 f.

Faust, Clarence, reference to, **Supp. 7,** 276

FBI. *See* Federal Bureau of Investigation

FCA. *See* Farm Credit Administration

FCC. *See* Federal Communications Commission

FDIC. *See* Federal Deposit Insurance Corporation

Fechner, Robert, reference to, **Supp. 6,** 411

Federal Art Commission, **Vol. 4, Part 2,** 389

Federal Art Project, **Supp. 6,** 96, 97

Federal Bureau of Investigation (FBI), **Supp. 7,** 52; **Supp. 8,** 322, 323, 335, 489; administration, **Supp. 4,** 794; congressional support, **Supp. 4,** 446; crime laboratory, **Supp. 5,** 245; World War I growth, **Supp. 1,** 359

"Federal City," designs for Washington, D.C., **Vol. 6, Part 1,** 167

Federal Communications Commission (FCC), chairmanship, **Supp. 8,** 179–80

Federal Convention. *See* Constitutional Convention

Federal Council of Churches, **Vol. 7, Part 1,** 160

Federal Council of the Churches of Christ in America, **Vol. 2, Part 2,** 229; **Vol. 4, Part 2,** 536; **Vol. 8, Part 2,** 348; **Vol. 9, Part 2,** 151; **Vol. 10, Part 1,** 653; **Supp. 5,** 446; Oriental race relations, **Supp. 3,** 322, 323; peace commission, **Supp. 6,** 178; presidency, **Supp. 6,** 649; race relations commission, **Supp. 6,** 285; religion and medicine committee, **Supp. 6,** 180 –81; World War I activities, **Supp. 3,** 110

Federal Deposit Insurance Act, **Supp. 8,** 616

Federal Deposit Insurance Corporation (FDIC), **Supp. 3,** 730; first chairman, **Supp. 8,** 112; founding of, **Supp. 3,** 650; **Supp. 4,** 332; **Supp. 8,** 207; legislation creating, **Supp. 5,** 248

Federal Emergency Relief Act (1933), **Supp. 2,** 170

Federal Emergency Relief Administration, **Supp. 5,** 515; **Supp. 8,** 301

Federal Farm Loan Act (1916), **Vol. 7, Part 1,** 377; **Supp. 8,** 592

Federal Farm Loan Board, **Supp. 6,** 453; **Supp. 7,** 361

Federal Gazette, **Vol. 5, Part 2,** 24

Federalism, attitudes on, **Supp. 1,** 210

"Federalist" papers, **Vol. 4, Part 2,** 174 f.; **Vol. 5, Part 2,** 8

Federalist party, **Vol. 1, Part 1,** 77 f., 245; **Vol. 1, Part 2,** 64; **Vol. 2, Part 1,** 395; **Vol. 3, Part 1,** 569 f.; **Vol. 4, Part 1,** 208, 225, 365, 397 f.; **Vol. 4, Part 2,** 10, 202, 224, 524; **Vol. 6, Part 1,** 101; **Vol. 7, Part 1,** 7; **Vol. 9, Part 1,** 365, 444; **Vol. 9, Part 2,** 144 f.; abuse of, **Vol. 4, Part 2,** 231; Adams, J. Q., and, **Vol. 1, Part 1,** 87 f.; "Indian summer" of, **Vol. 2, Part 1,** 80; Jefferson, T., and, **Vol. 5, Part 2,** 26 f.; New Hampshire, **Vol. 7, Part 2,** 575; North Carolina, **Vol. 4, Part 2,** 414; passing of, **Vol. 7, Part 2,** 99; Pennsylvania, **Vol. 4, Part 2,** 521; **Vol. 8, Part 2,** 178; publications, **Vol. 1, Part 1,** 87, 244; **Vol. 7, Part 2,** 566 f.; **Vol. 9, Part 2,** 136 f.; South Carolina, **Vol. 4, Part 2,** 286; states' rights, attitude toward, **Vol. 4, Part 2,** 458; Virginia, **Vol. 4, Part 2,** 557 f.; **Vol. 6, Part 1,** 117; **Vol. 6, Part 2,** 318

Federal League (baseball), **Supp. 8,** 106

Federal Loan Agency, **Supp. 6,** 325

Federal Orrery, founding of, **Vol. 7, Part 2,** 157

Federal Power Commission (FPC), **Supp. 4,** 544; forming of, **Supp. 6,** 484; private ownership advocacy, **Supp. 3,** 725

Federal Radio Commission, license renewal denial, **Supp. 3,** 104

Federal Reserve Act (1913), **Vol. 1, Part 1,** 157; **Vol. 4, Part 2,** 567; **Supp. 3,** 480; preliminaries to, **Vol. 2, Part 1,** 336

Federal Reserve Act (1933), sponsorship of, **Supp. 4,** 641; writing of, **Supp. 2,** 719

Federal Reserve Bank of New York, **Supp. 3,** 290; **Supp. 6,** 559; growth of, **Vol. 9, Part 2,** 143 f.

Federal Reserve Bank of Philadelphia, architecture, **Supp. 3,** 199

Federal Reserve Board, **Vol. 4, Part 2,** 258; analytical and statistical reports, **Supp. 6,** 599; governors, **Supp. 3,** 203; **Supp. 6,** 453

Federal Reserve Board Building, architecture, **Supp. 3,** 199

Federal Reserve System, credit control, **Supp. 6,** 599; discussion of, **Vol. 9, Part 2,** 144; economic research and analysis, **Supp. 5,** 247–48; events leading to creation of, **Vol. 3, Part 1,** 148; federal government control of, **Supp. 3,** 97; founding of, **Vol. 10, Part 1,** 412 f.; **Supp. 2,** 274, 719; **Supp. 4,** 331, 332; precursor to, **Vol. 8, Part 1,** 34 f.; publications, **Supp. 8,** 242; role limitation, **Supp. 8,** 79; state bank membership, **Supp. 3,** 730

Federal Security Agency, **Supp. 5,** 459–60

Federal Telegraph Co., **Supp. 7,** 394

Federal Theatre Project, **Supp. 8,** 176–77

Federal Trade Commission (FTC), **Vol. 2, Part 2,** 325; **Supp. 1,** 446; **Supp. 3,** 97; **Supp. 5,** 27; **Supp. 7,** 521; **Supp. 8,** 219–20; administration, **Supp. 1,** 446; first chairman, **Supp. 6,** 146; powers, **Supp. 6,** 556; price-fixing actions, **Supp. 4,** 268

Federal Trade Commission Act (1914), **Supp. 3,** 97

Federated Department Stores, founding of, **Supp. 3,** 421–22

Federated Organization of Colored People, **Supp. 5,** 755

Federation for Jewish Philanthropies, **Supp. 7,** 466

Federation for the Support of Jewish Philanthropic Societies, founding of, **Supp. 2,** 695

Federation of American Zionists, **Supp. 2,** 252; **Supp. 3,** 756–57; founding of, **Supp. 4,** 905

Federation of Children's Agencies (New York City), **Supp. 3,** 28

Federation of Jewish Charities, **Vol. 8, Part 2,** 171; **Supp. 4,** 80; founding of, **Supp. 4,** 262

Federation of Organized Trades and Labor Unions, dissolution of, **Vol. 3, Part 1,** 510

Federation of Palestinian Jews in America, founding of, **Supp. 1,** 407

Feeney, Leonard, reference to, **Supp. 8,** 115

Feeney, T. L., reference to, **Vol. 7, Part 2,** 238

Feet, treatment for flat, **Supp. 4,** 887

Feldspar, measurement, **Supp. 6,** 153

Fellenberg Manual Labor Institution, **Vol. 2, Part 2,** 267

Fellowship of Reconciliation, **Supp. 7,** 356; **Supp. 8,** 425, 458, 649

Fels Fund, founding of, **Supp. 4,** 262–63

Fels Naptha soap, **Supp. 4,** 262

Felton, Rebecca Latimer, reference to, **Supp. 4,** 144–45

Female Medical College of Pennsylvania, earliest medical college for women, **Vol. 4, Part 1,** 81; **Vol. 8, Part 1,** 201

Female Medical Education Society, **Vol. 4, Part 1,** 604

Feminism, **Vol. 2, Part 1,** 19, 151; **Vol. 6, Part 1,** 480; **Vol. 9, Part 2,** 253 f. *See also* Woman suffrage; Women's rights

Feminist fiction, **Supp. 7,** 386

"Fencibles," use of the term, **Vol. 8, Part 1,** 315 f.

Fenian Brotherhood, **Vol. 3, Part 1,** 264 f.; **Vol. 5, Part 2,** 88; **Vol. 8, Part 2,** 389; **Vol. 9, Part 2,** 242; founding of, **Vol. 7, Part 2,** 36; militant character of, **Vol. 8, Part 2,** 19 f.; organization of, in Tennessee, **Vol. 7, Part 2,** 45; raids, **Vol. 7, Part 2,** 45; **Vol. 9, Part 2,** 242

Ferber, Edna, references to, **Supp. 3,** 418; **Supp. 7,** 413

Ferguson, Bob, reference to, **Supp. 7,** 168

Ferguson, Frank W., reference to, **Supp. 3,** 195–96

Ferguson, Homer, reference to, **Supp. 7,** 72

Ferguson, James E., references to, **Supp. 4,** 776; **Supp. 7,** 242, 349

Ferguson, Miriam A. ("Ma"), reference to, **Supp. 4,** 776

Fermi, Enrico, references to, **Supp. 6,** 501; **Supp. 7,** 10, 11, 135, 732; **Supp. 8,** 627

Fermi-Dirac statistics, **Supp. 5,** 219, 221

Fernald, Walter E., reference to, **Vol. 5, Part 1,** 296

Fernow, Bernhard E., reference to, **Supp. 4,** 43

Ferns, study of, **Vol. 3, Part 1,** 606 f.; **Vol. 10, Part 1,** 116

Ferris, Eugene B., Jr., reference to, **Supp. 3,** 805–6

Ferris wheel, designing of, **Vol. 3, Part 2,** 339

Ferryboats, early, **Vol. 9, Part 1,** 615, 619; horsepower, New York Harbor (1814), **Vol. 8, Part 2,** 106; Mississippi River, **Vol. 3, Part 1,** 249; St. Louis, **Vol. 7, Part 2,** 593; steam, first on Mississippi River, **Vol. 3, Part 1,** 249; *Susquehanna* (1748), **Vol. 4, Part 2,** 314; Weehawken, N.J., to New York City, **Vol. 8, Part 1,** 214 f.

Fertility. *See* Gynecology; Infertility; Obstetrics; Reproductive system

Fertilization: artificial insemination, **Supp. 8,** 502; studies in, **Supp. 4,** 498

Fertilizer, **Vol. 9, Part 2,** 39; ammoniated, discovery and manufacturing of, **Vol. 8, Part 1,** 397; first use of cotton seed in manufacture of, **Vol. 7, Part 2,** 419

Fessenden, Reginald A., reference to, **Supp. 7,** 175

Fetterman Massacre (Wyo., 1866), **Vol. 2, Part 1,** 521; **Vol. 3, Part 2,** 350; **Vol. 8, Part 1,** 437

Fire insurance company, first in America, **Vol. 8, Part 1,** 139 f.
Fire Island, N.Y., **Supp. 6,** 236, 237
Fire prevention: alarm systems, **Vol. 2, Part 2,** 9, 265; **Vol. 3, Part 2,** 280; **Vol. 8, Part 1,** 101 f.; **Supp. 1,** 554; Baltimore, **Vol. 9, Part 2,** 238; Boston, **Vol. 8, Part 1,** 308 f.; Cincinnati, **Vol. 4, Part 1,** 593; fire engines, **Vol. 1, Part 1,** 540; **Vol. 3, Part 1,** 211; **Vol. 4, Part 1,** 593; **Vol. 4, Part 2,** 1, 275; **Vol. 5, Part 2,** 53; **Vol. 6, Part 1,** 1, 29; fire extinguishers, **Vol. 3, Part 1,** 377; fire nozzles, **Vol. 7, Part 1,** 450; fireproof stairs, **Vol. 8, Part 1,** 138 f.; libraries, **Vol. 8, Part 1,** 138 f.; New York, **Vol. 3, Part 1,** 248; study of, **Vol. 3, Part 1,** 248
Fires: Apollo spacecraft, **Supp. 8,** 694; San Francisco, **Supp. 4,** 325, 417; Triangle Shirtwaist Co., **Supp. 3,** 355–56, 717–18; **Supp. 5,** 718; **Supp. 7,** 608
Fireside Companion, **Vol. 7, Part 1,** 331
Firestone Tire and Rubber Co., establishment of, **Supp. 2,** 187
Firpo, Luis Angel, reference to, **Supp. 6,** 700
First aid, introduction into class work, of, **Vol. 3, Part 2,** 563;
First American, The, **Supp. 7,** 393, 394
First Baptist Church of Dallas (Tex.), **Supp. 3,** 778–79
First Baptist Church of Fort Worth (Tex.), **Supp. 5,** 516
First Century Christian Fellowship. *See* Oxford Group
First Church of Christ Scientist (Berkeley, Calif.), **Supp. 6,** 438
First Humanist Society (N.Y.), founding of, **Supp. 7,** 624
"First in war, first in peace," etc., origin of phrase, **Vol. 6, Part 1,** 108
First National Bank of New York, **Supp. 3,** 290; founding of, **Supp. 1,** 44
First National City Bank (New York City), **Supp. 6,** 24
First National Corporation, **Supp. 3,** 443–44
First National Pictures. *See* Warner Brothers
First Presbyterian Church (New York City), **Supp. 8,** 183;
First Presbyterian Church (Princeton, N.J.), **Supp. 6,** 195
Firuski, Maurice, reference to, **Supp. 7,** 55
Fischer, Carl, reference to, **Supp. 6,** 242
Fischer, Emil, reference to, **Supp. 3,** 60–61
Fish, Hamilton, references to, **Vol. 7, Part 1,** 286–87; **Supp. 1,** 327
Fish: Birdseye quick-frozen, **Supp. 6,** 61; colored plates of, **Vol. 5, Part 1,** 129; culture, **Vol. 4, Part 1,** 558; **Vol. 4, Part 2,** 562; **Vol. 6, Part 2,** 390; **Vol. 9, Part 2,** 565; osteology research, **Supp. 1,** 672–73; preservation of, **Vol. 1, Part 2,** 92; protective coloration and pigmentation, **Supp. 3,** 753; studies of, **Vol. 1, Part 1,** 515; **Vol. 3, Part 1,** 170; **Vol. 3, Part 2,** 63; **Vol. 6, Part 1,** 191; **Vol. 7, Part 1,** 70
Fisher, Albert, reference to, **Supp. 7,** 245
Fisher, Alfred, reference to, **Supp. 7,** 246
Fisher, Charles, reference to, **Supp. 3,** 273–74
Fisher, Dorothy Canfield, references to, **Supp. 5,** 439; **Supp. 6,** 113, 114
Fisher, Edward F., reference to, **Supp. 7,** 246
Fisher, Frederick G., Jr., reference to, **Supp. 6,** 680
Fisher, Irving, references to, **Supp. 4,** 18, 550
Fisher, John S., reference to, **Supp. 7,** 305
Fisher, Lawrence, reference to, **Supp. 3,** 273–74
Fisher, William, reference to, **Supp. 3,** 273–74
Fisher Body Corporation: founding of, **Supp. 3,** 273–74; **Supp. 7,** 245–46; General Motors' acquistion of, **Supp. 4,** 244
Fisheries, **Vol. 1, Part 1,** 309; **Vol. 3, Part 2,** 333; **Vol. 4, Part 2,** 562; **Vol. 8, Part 1,** 387; Connecticut

River, **Vol. 8, Part 2,** 45; reports on (1853), **Vol. 8, Part 2,** 276
Fish horn, first recorded use of, in U.S., **Vol. 8, Part 1,** 548
Fishing equipment, sport, **Supp. 8,** 28–29
Fishing rights, **Vol. 1, Part 1,** 309; negotiations with Great Britain concerning, **Vol. 1, Part 2,** 71; **Vol. 3, Part 1,** 251; **Vol. 8, Part 1,** 285 f.; U.S. coastline extension, **Supp. 8,** 25–26
Fisk, James, reference to, **Vol. 7, Part 1,** 175 f.
Fiske, John, reference to, **Supp. 3,** 160
Fisk University, **Vol. 4, Part 1,** 184; founding of, **Vol. 2, Part 2,** 516; **Vol. 3, Part 2,** 413; growth of, **Vol. 6, Part 2,** 561; Jubilee singers, **Vol. 10, Part 2,** 100; race relations studies, **Supp. 6,** 321, 322
Fitch, John, reference to, **Vol. 8, Part 2,** 401; **Vol. 9, Part 1,** 614; **Vol. 9, Part 2,** 594
Fitchburg Railroad, **Vol. 2, Part 2,** 551
Fitz, Reginald Heber, reference to, **Supp. 5,** 111
Fitzgerald, F. Scott, references to, **Supp. 3,** 72; **Supp. 4,** 651; **Supp. 5,** 614; **Supp. 6,** 21, 287; **Supp. 7,** 335, 336, 339, 560
Fitzgerald, John Francis ("Honey Fitz"), references to, **Supp. 5,** 23, 730; **Supp. 6,** 139; **Supp. 8,** 320
Fitzpatrick, Daniel R., reference to, **Supp. 5,** 552
Fitzsimmons, Bob, reference to, **Supp. 5,** 368
Fitzsimmons, James ("Sunny"), reference to, **Supp. 5,** 757
Five and dime stores, **Supp. 5,** 400–401; **Supp. 8,** 347–49
Five Forks, battle of, **Vol. 1, Part 1,** 454; **Vol. 4, Part 1,** 597, 618; **Vol. 5, Part 1,** 25; **Vol. 6, Part 1,** 104, 134; **Vol. 7, Part 2,** 570; **Vol. 9, Part 1,** 80; **Vol. 10, Part 1,** 474
Five Little Peppers and How They Grew, **Vol. 6, Part 1,** 425
Flack, Marjorie, reference to, **Supp. 4,** 74
Flag, American: compulsory salute issue, **Supp. 3,** 451; **Supp. 4,** 796; **Supp. 5,** 358, 575; **Supp. 7,** 264; design of, **Vol. 5, Part 1,** 222; **Vol. 8, Part 1,** 481 f.; **Vol. 8, Part 2,** 174; first appearance of, in British port, **Vol. 8, Part 2,** 186; first use of, in battle, **Vol. 9, Part 1,** 128; first use of thirteen stripes, **Vol. 6, Part 2,** 287
Flagler, Henry M., references to, **Vol. 7, Part 1,** 132; **Supp. 2,** 569, 572, 573; **Supp. 4,** 211
Flanagan, Edward J., references to, **Supp. 4,** 594; **Supp. 8,** 659
Flanders, Ralph, McCarthy censure resolution, **Supp. 6,** 405
Flanders, Walter E., reference to, **Supp. 4,** 294
"Flapper" (term), **Supp. 5,** 372; **Supp. 6,** 287
Flashlights, battery-powered, **Supp. 7,** 149–50
Flatiron Building (New York City), steel framing, **Supp. 3,** 611
Flaxseed, exporting to Ireland, following Revolution, **Vol. 7, Part 2,** 631
Fleetwood, battle of. *See* Brandy Station, Va.
Flegenheimer, Arthur. *See* Schultz, Dutch
Fleischer, Andrew W., reference to, **Supp. 7,** 678
Fleischmann, Raoul, reference to, **Supp. 5,** 593–94
Fleming, John Ambrose, reference to, **Supp. 7,** 176
Fletcher, Alice, reference to, **Supp. 6,** 162
Fletcher, Horace, reference to, **Supp. 3,** 163, 410
"Fletcherism," **Vol. 3, Part 2,** 465
Flexner, Abraham, references to, **Supp. 2,** 574–75; **Supp. 3,** 31, 67, 279, 280, 555, 676; **Supp. 4,** 139, 286; **Supp. 6,** 30
Flexner, Bernard, references to, **Supp. 3,** 280; **Supp. 4,** 286
Flexner, James T., reference to, **Supp. 6,** 310
Flexner, Simon, references to, **Vol. 10, Part 1,** 621 f.; **Supp. 3,** 141, 279, 441; **Supp. 6,** 537; **Supp. 8,** 556

Vol. 1, Part 2, 458; Delmonico, influence of, on, **Vol. 3, Part 1,** 227; edible wild plants, **Supp. 4,** 266; frozen, **Supp. 6,** 61; health, **Supp. 5,** 378–79; **Supp. 5,** 452–53; hunger studies, **Supp. 3,** 133–34; **Supp. 6,** 100; intravenous feeding, **Supp. 6,** 190; irradiation of, **Supp. 1,** 398; pineapple industry, **Supp. 6,** 168–69; poisoning, research on, **Supp. 2,** 353; preservation and additives, **Supp. 3,** 164; **Supp. 7,** 629–30; strained canned for babies, **Supp. 5,** 242–43. *See also* Canning and canned goods; Cooking; Diet and nutrition; Grocery industry; Restaurants; *specific foods and products*

Food administration: Confederate army, **Vol. 7, Part 2,** 580; World War I, **Vol. 6, Part 1,** 12, 275; **Vol. 8, Part 1,** 145 f.

Food Administration, United States, **Vol. 6, Part 1,** 12; **Supp. 7,** 358–59

Food aid: CARE, **Supp. 6,** 217–18; India, **Supp. 8,** 468; underdeveloped countries, **Supp. 7,** 421; World War I and aftermath, **Supp. 6,** 36–37; **Supp. 7,** 358–59; World War II and aftermath, **Supp. 7,** 492; **Supp. 8,** 90

Food and Agriculture Act (1965), **Supp. 8,** 468

Food and Agriculture Organization (FAO), founding of, **Supp. 6,** 639

Fool, The, **Supp. 4,** 671

Fool's Errand, A, **Vol. 9, Part 2,** 604

Football, **Vol. 2, Part 1,** 444; **Vol. 4, Part 2,** 398; **Vol. 8, Part 2,** 68; All-American Conference founding, **Supp. 5,** 725; All-American team, **Supp. 1,** 704; black players, **Supp. 7,** 167–68; coaching, **Supp. 5,** 458, 727–28; **Supp. 6,** 728; **Supp. 8,** 389–91, 587–88; collegiate, **Supp. 4,** 492, 893, 917; **Supp. 5,** 288–89, 568, 683–84; **Supp. 6,** 66; **Supp. 7,** 167–68; collegiate coaching, **Supp. 4,** 236–37; **Supp. 7,** 571–72, 712–13; headgear, **Supp. 2,** 484; huddle origination, **Supp. 7,** 712; intercollegiate abolishment, **Supp. 4,** 135; management, **Supp. 7,** 451–52; "Notre Dame shift," **Supp. 7,** 729; "point-a-minute" teams, **Supp. 4,** 917; professional leagues, **Supp. 5,** 684; **Supp. 6,** 47–48; professional player-coaches, **Supp. 7,** 595–96; single-wing formation, **Supp. 5,** 289; **Supp. 7,** 571, 572; spiral forward pass, **Supp. 6,** 336; televised games, **Supp. 6,** 48; T formation, **Supp. 8,** 588. *See also* National Football League

Foote, Cone, and Belding, predecessor, **Supp. 5,** 411

Foraker, Joseph B., reference to, **Supp. 5,** 286

Foraker Act (1900), **Vol. 7, Part 2,** 31

Foraminifera, **Supp. 4,** 205–6; **Supp. 5,** 710

Forbes, J. M., and Co., **Supp. 6,** 210

Forbes, Stephen A., reference to, **Supp. 3,** 802

"Forbes Purchase," **Vol. 3, Part 2,** 506

Force, Juliana, reference to, **Supp. 3,** 818

"Forces bill," **Vol. 2, Part 1,** 415; **Vol. 2, Part 2,** 177, 185; **Vol. 3, Part 2,** 534; **Vol. 5, Part 1,** 533; **Vol. 6, Part 1,** 347; **Vol. 6, Part 2,** 233; **Vol. 10, Part 1,** 90, 589; **Vol. 10, Part 2,** 221; only vote recorded against, **Vol. 10, Part 1,** 90

Ford, Charles-Henri, reference to, **Supp. 6,** 625

Ford, Edsel, references to, **Supp. 3,** 550; **Supp. 4,** 292, 298, 301, 303; **Supp. 6,** 92; **Supp. 8,** 610

Ford, Franklin, reference to, **Supp. 3,** 577

Ford, Gerald R., reference to, **Supp. 7,** 140

Ford, Henry: automobile manufacture, **Supp. 4,** 243; museum, **Supp. 4,** 302; peace expedition, **Supp. 4,** 725–26; politics, **Supp. 3,** 550; references to, **Supp. 1,** 78, 280; **Supp. 3,** 63, 283–84, 555, 559, 562, 762; **Supp. 4,** 518, 637; **Supp. 5,** 40; **Supp. 6,** 148, 562, 614; **Supp. 7,** 29; **Supp. 8,** 419, 609–10

Ford, Henry, II, references to, **Supp. 3,** 284; **Supp. 4,** 303; **Supp. 7,** 275, 276; **Supp. 8,** 610

Ford, John, references to, **Supp. 6,** 420, 421, 476; **Supp. 7,** 286; **Supp. 8,** 117

Ford, Nathan, reference to, **Vol. 7, Part 1,** 643

Ford, Paul, reference to, **Supp. 3,** 285

Ford Foundation, **Supp. 6,** 639; directorship and policy; **Supp. 7,** 275–76; finances of, **Supp. 4,** 303; founding, **Supp. 3,** 284

Ford Hall Forum, **Supp. 5,** 515

Fordham University, **Vol. 7, Part 2,** 171

Ford Instrument Co., founding of, **Supp. 5,** 228–29

Ford Motor Co.: founding and growth of, **Supp. 2,** 125; **Supp. 4,** 294–304; General Motors' competition, **Supp. 4,** 301–2, 456–57; **Supp. 8,** 599; modernization and expansion, **Supp. 3,** 283–84; plant architecture, **Supp. 3,** 404; **Supp. 6,** 405; predecessors, **Supp. 4,** 293; unionization, **Supp. 8,** 419, 652; Willow Run aviation plant, **Supp. 8,** 610

Ford Peace Ship Mission, **Vol. 5, Part 2,** 180

Ford stock valuation tax case (1927-28), **Supp. 6,** 146

Forecasting the Yield and Price of Cotton, **Supp. 6,** 459

Foreign Affairs, **Supp. 3,** 219; founding of, **Supp. 4,** 322

Foreign aid. *See* Food aid; Marshall Plan; Truman Doctrine

Foreign and Domestic Commerce, Bureau of, **Vol. 8, Part 1,** 443

Foreign Christian Missionary Society, formed, **Vol. 7, Part 1,** 145 f.

Foreign correspondents. For complete list, *see* Occupations Index

Foreign Missions Conference of North America, **Vol. 8, Part 2,** 333

Foreign Policy Association, founding of, **Supp. 6,** 330; **Supp. 7,** 498

Foreign relations: academic seminars on, **Supp. 5,** 195; antifascism, **Supp. 5,** 343; bipartisan, **Supp. 5,** 505, 704–5; **Supp. 6,** 235; **Supp. 7,** 138, 326; **Supp. 8,** 701; Bricker amendment, **Supp. 6,** 336; China lobby, **Supp. 6,** 350; China policy, **Supp. 6, 230–31;** containment policy, **Supp. 6,** 178–79, 406; Council on Foreign Relations, **Supp. 6,** 377; Cuban missile crisis, **Supp. 8,** 323; "domino theory," **Supp. 7,** 422; economic aid, **Supp. 8,** 89–90; economic sanctions policy, **Supp. 4,** 786–87; Eisenhower administration policies, **Supp. 8,** 157–58; Good Neighbor policy, **Supp. 4,** 706; **Supp. 7,** 777; internationalism, **Supp. 1,** 483–84; **Supp. 3,** 219, 829–30; **Supp. 4,** 136, 332, 550–51, 598–99; **Supp. 5,** 198; **Supp. 7,** 23–24, 687–88, 761–63; **Supp. 8,** 508; isolationism, **Supp. 3,** 396–98; **Supp. 5,** 396–97, 450, 674–77, 689–90, 739; **Supp. 6,** 87, 361, 455, 578, 613–14, 636; **Supp. 8,** 268–69, 373; Japanese expansionism, **Supp. 3,** 657–59; **Supp. 6,** 269–70; Marshall Plan, **Supp. 6,** 431, 432; Migratory Bird Treaty (1916), **Supp. 3,** 593; "military-industrial complex" warning, **Supp. 8,** 159; neutrality advocacy, **Supp. 4,** 63; **Supp. 5,** 81–82, 114; New Deal policies, **Supp. 3,** 657–59; nonrecognition policy, **Supp. 4,** 898; **Supp. 7,** 112–13; particularism, **Supp. 2,** 51–52; Persian-Russian-British dispute, **Supp. 6,** 579; political geography studies, **Supp. 4,** 99; professional organizations, **Supp. 7,** 498; psychological studies of, **Supp. 8,** 70; study of, **Supp. 6,** 662; teaching of, **Supp. 4,** 224; transitional policy, **Supp. 7,** 421; Truman Doctrine, **Supp. 6,** 431, 432; **Supp. 8,** 680; writings on, **Supp. 1,** 173. *See also* Arms control and disarmament; Cold war; Diplomacy; Foreign Service; Peace, international; *specific countries, organizations, and wars*

Foreign Service Act (1946), **Supp. 3,** 139

Foreign Service Institute, **Supp. 8,** 7

Foreign Service, United States: career officers, **Supp. 7,** 60; first career diplomat, **Supp. 6,** 686–87; first woman diplomat, **Supp. 5,** 582; founding of, **Supp.**

Free-radical chemistry, **Supp. 4**, 336–37, 573–74; **Supp. 6**, 334–35
Free Religious Association, **Vol. 8, Part 1**, 135; **Vol. 10, Part 1**, 615 f.
Freer Gallery of Art (Washington, D.C.): **Vol. 4, Part 1**, 14; concerts, **Supp. 3**, 252; Oriental art collection, **Supp. 3**, 465
Free Silver movement, **Vol. 1, Part 1**, 221; **Vol. 1, Part 2**, 355–56; **Vol. 2, Part 1**, 192, 495; **Vol. 2, Part 2**, 211; **Vol. 3, Part 1**, 69; **Vol. 3, Part 2**, 578; **Vol. 4, Part 2**, 334; **Vol. 5, Part 1**, 93, 182; **Vol. 5, Part 2**, 146, 189, 552, 571; **Vol. 6, Part 1**, 268; **Vol. 6, Part 2**, 106; **Vol. 7, Part 1**, 15; **Vol. 8, Part 2**, 87, 251; **Vol. 9, Part 1**, 148, 180; **Vol. 9, Part 2**, 14, 612; **Vol. 10, Part 2**, 441
Free Soil movement, **Vol. 1, Part 1**, 279, 368, 537; **Vol. 1, Part 2**, 48, 258, 489; **Vol. 2, Part 1**, 204; **Vol. 2, Part 2**, 29; **Vol. 3, Part 1**, 375; **Vol. 3, Part 2**, 227, 485, 565, 580; **Vol. 4, Part 1**, 394, 530 f.; **Vol. 4, Part 2**, 106; **Vol. 5, Part 2**, 356; **Vol. 6, Part 1**, 1; **Vol. 7, Part 1**, 645; **Vol. 9, Part 1**, 271, 544; **Vol. 10, Part 1**, 151, 156; **Vol. 10, Part 2**, 323; convention of 1848, **Vol. 8, Part 2**, 58; Iowa, **Vol. 4, Part 2**, 268; Kansas, **Vol. 3, Part 1**, 570 f.; **Vol. 4, Part 1**, 394; Massachusetts, **Vol. 2, Part 2**, 111; **Vol. 5, Part 1**, 86 f., 89; Missouri, **Vol. 1, Part 2**, 332; **Vol. 2, Part 1**, 105; Ohio, **Vol. 8, Part 1**, 591
Free speech. *See* Censorship; Civil liberties; Libel
Free State movement, **Vol. 3, Part 1**, 202; **Vol. 3, Part 2**, 69; **Vol. 5, Part 2**, 576; **Vol. 8, Part 2**, 36, 175
Free Synagogue (New York City), founding of, **Supp. 4**, 603, 904
Freethinkers, writers, **Supp. 3**, 329–30, 341–42, 454–55, 554–55
Freethinkers Colony, Iowa, **Vol. 5, Part 2**, 457 f.
Free trade, **Vol. 1, Part 2**, 134; **Vol. 2, Part 1**, 488; **Vol. 3, Part 1**, 289; **Vol. 6, Part 1**, 109, 292, 609; **Vol. 8, Part 1**, 325 f.; **Vol. 8, Part 2**, 450 f.; **Vol. 10, Part 1**, 387, 637 f.
Free-Will Baptists, origin of, **Vol. 8, Part 1**, 345 f.
Freeze-drying technique, **Supp. 6**, 54
Frege, Gottlob, reference to, **Supp. 8**, 74
Freight: carrying of, **Vol. 9, Part 2**, 396; Atlantic seaboard, **Vol. 7, Part 1**, 336; Great Lakes, **Vol. 6, Part 1**, 327; **Vol. 6, Part 2**, 23; ox and wagon, **Vol. 2, Part 1**, 405; **Vol. 6, Part 2**, 214; stagecoach, **Vol. 8, Part 2**, 252; **Vol. 9, Part 1**, 203
Freiheit, anarchist paper, **Vol. 7, Part 1**, 282
Frelinghuysen, T. J., reference to, **Vol. 7, Part 1**, 366
Frémont, Jessie Benton, reference to, **Supp. 3**, 87–88
Frémont, John, references to, **Vol. 1, Part 1**, 206; **Vol. 1, Part 2**, 333; **Vol. 5, Part 2**, 273
French, Daniel Chester, references to, **Vol. 1, Part 1**, 478; **Vol. 7, Part 1**, 19; **Supp. 3**, 1
French: alliance with U.S., **Vol. 1, Part 1**, 74–75; **Vol. 3, Part 1**, 174; **Vol. 3, Part 2**, 593–94; **Vol. 5, Part 2**, 536; **Vol. 6, Part 1**, 98; **Vol. 7, Part 2**, 210, 221; **Vol. 10, Part 1**, 518; biographies, translation of, **Vol. 8, Part 1**, 217 f.; colonization, **Vol. 8, Part 1**, 533 f.; exploration, **Vol. 1, Part 1**, 183; **Vol. 6, Part 1**, 4, 10, 37, 182; **Vol. 7, Part 1**, 511 f.; **Vol. 8, Part 2**, 293, 304; Huguenot colonies, **Vol. 6, Part 1**, 30; influence of Isham's art, **Vol. 5, Part 1**, 514; Jesuits, political influence of, **Vol. 3, Part 1**, 364; Louisiana, political affairs of, **Vol. 6, Part 1**, 19; Ohio Valley, **Vol. 3, Part 1**, 317; **Vol. 8, Part 2**, 293; painting, influence on American, **Vol. 7, Part 1**, 29; spoliation claims, **Vol. 1, Part 2**, 23; **Vol. 8, Part 2**, 241; translations, **Vol. 6, Part 1**, 171; Treaty of 1801, **Vol. 8, Part 2**, 77; voyageurs, **Vol. 8, Part 2**, 117; withdrawal of, from Mexico, **Vol. 5, Part 2**, 88. *See also* France; French literature and language

French and Indian War, **Vol. 1, Part 2**, 550; **Vol. 7, Part 2**, 457; **Vol. 8, Part 1**, 62 f.; **Vol. 8, Part 2**, 34; **Vol. 9, Part 1**, 26; **Vol. 10, Part 2**, 543; history of, **Vol. 8, Part 2**, 369; *Niagara*, capture of, **Vol. 5, Part 2**, 126; North Carolina's support in, **Vol. 3, Part 1**, 337; Rhode Island and, **Vol. 4, Part 1**, 575 f.; service in, **Vol. 1, Part 2**, 379; **Vol. 2, Part 2**, 251; **Vol. 3, Part 1**, 74, 216, 550, 581 f.; **Vol. 3, Part 2**, 505; **Vol. 4, Part 2**, 420, 478; **Vol. 5, Part 2**, 100, 181; **Vol. 6, Part 1**, 77, 98; **Vol. 8, Part 1**, 55, 61, 62 f., 69 f., 129 f., 161 f., 195 f., 281 f., 284 f., 419, 448; **Vol. 8, Part 2**, 108 f., 221; **Vol. 9, Part 2**, 476, 553 f.; **Vol. 10, Part 1**, 52, 360 f., 415 f., 509 f., 614 f.; **Vol. 10, Part 2**, 397; writings on, **Vol. 9, Part 2**, 35
French-Indian alliances (1670), **Vol. 8, Part 2**, 304
French literature and language: Alexander corpus, **Supp. 3**, 22; classical drama scholarship, **Supp. 5**, 409–10; Rousseau scholarship, **Supp. 3**, 691; studies in, **Supp. 1**, 36; **Supp. 2**, 141; **Supp. 3**, 22; teaching of, **Supp. 4**, 754–55; translations, **Supp. 8**, 475–76
French Revolution: collections on, **Supp. 2**, 75; effect of, on American politics, **Vol. 1, Part 1**, 245; neutrality toward, **Vol. 5, Part 2**, 25; Paine, Thomas, **Vol. 7, Part 2**, 162 f.; studies of, **Supp. 3**, 47
Frenzied Finance, **Vol. 6, Part 1**, 60; **Vol. 8, Part 2**, 65
Freon, development of, **Supp. 3**, 522; **Supp. 6**, 333
Fresco art, **Supp. 5**, 473
Fresno Republican (Calif.), **Supp. 4**, 707
Freud, Sigmund: Clark University lectures, **Supp. 3**, 190–91; cocaine studies, **Supp. 3**, 430; collaboration with, **Supp. 4**, 117–18; influence of, **Supp. 4**, 130; psychoanalytic theory, **Supp. 6**, 527–28, 724–25; references to, **Supp. 3**, 151, 385; relationships with, **Supp. 4**, 716–17; **Supp. 8**, 7, 61, 523; theories of, **Supp. 4**, 387, 572; **Supp. 5**, 301, 315–17, 583; **Supp. 7**, 6, 7; training by, **Supp. 5**, 517; translations of, **Supp. 4**, 108, 109; **Supp. 5**, 108
Freudian Wish and Its Place in Ethics, The, **Supp. 4**, 387
Freund, John Cristian, reference to, **Supp. 8**, 465
"Friar lands," Catholic church, **Vol. 4, Part 1**, 241
Friars Club, **Supp. 5**, 629
Frick, Henry Clay, assassination attempt, **Supp. 2**, 37; references to, **Vol. 2, Part 1**, 502 f.; **Vol. 7, Part 1**, 143; **Supp. 6**, 507
Frick Collection (New York City), building architecture, **Supp. 5**, 301
Friday Literary Review, **Supp. 8**, 124
Friede, Donald, reference to, **Supp. 7**, 148–49
Friedenwald, Harry, reference to, **Supp. 4**, 905
Friedman, Alexander Alexandrovich, reference to, **Supp. 3**, 760
Friedman, Elizabeth Smith, reference to, **Supp. 8**, 195–96
Friedman, Hugo, reference to, **Supp. 6**, 491
Friend, colonial ship, **Vol. 7, Part 1**, 369
Friendly, Fred W., reference to, **Supp. 7**, 566
Friendly Sons of St. Patrick, **Vol. 7, Part 1**, 430
Friends. *See* Society of Friends
Friends' Expositor, **Vol. 10, Part 1**, 120
Friends' Historical Association, founding of, **Vol. 9, Part 1**, 28
Friends of Music in the Library of Congress, founding of, **Supp. 3**, 252
Friends of Negro Freedom, **Supp. 7**, 155
Friends of the Young Artists, founding of, **Supp. 4**, 289–90
Friends' Review, **Vol. 6, Part 1**, 212; **Vol. 8, Part 1**, 531
Fries's Rebellion (1799), **Vol. 1, Part 1**, 79; **Vol. 4, Part 1**, 34
Frigates. For complete list of frigates, *see* Ships

3, 63; writings on, **Vol. 4, Part 1,** 307; **Vol. 4, Part 2,** 238; **Vol. 5, Part 2,** 165; **Vol. 6, Part 1,** 390; **Vol. 9, Part 1,** 249; **Vol. 9, Part 2,** 479 f.

Georgia Female College. *See* Wesleyan College

"Georgia platform," **Vol. 9, Part 2,** 615

Georgia Railroad, surveying and building of, **Vol. 7, Part 2,** 510

Georgia School of Technology, **Vol. 5, Part 1,** 210

Georgia State Industrial College, founding of, **Supp. 4,** 916

Georgia Warm Springs Foundation, founding of, **Supp. 3,** 644

Gerber, Daniel F., reference to, **Supp. 5,** 242–43

Gerber Products Co., founding of, **Supp. 5,** 242–43

Gerlach, Walther, reference to, **Supp. 8,** 628

German American Annals, **Vol. 6, Part 1,** 78

German-American Reform Union, one of the founders of, **Vol. 8, Part 1,** 46 f.

German-Americans: California, **Vol. 8, Part 2,** 90; Illinois, **Vol. 5, Part 2,** 496; "Latin farmer" community, Belleville, Ill., **Vol. 6, Part 1,** 274; Missouri, **Vol. 5, Part 2,** 496; organizations, **Vol. 8, Part 1,** 46 f.; **Vol. 8, Part 2,** 91; **Supp. 1,** 696; pioneers, information concerning, **Vol. 8, Part 1,** 388; Pennsylvania, **Vol. 6, Part 1,** 292; **Vol. 7, Part 1,** 309, 529; **Vol. 7, Part 2,** 108 f.; **Vol. 8, Part 1,** 113 f.; **Vol. 8, Part 2,** 225 f., 282, 447; political influences, **Supp. 1,** 363; political journalism, **Supp. 7,** 757–58; priest, first in Northwest, **Vol. 8, Part 1,** 509; Texas, communist colony, **Vol. 6, Part 1,** 274; World War I policies, **Supp. 5,** 279; writers, **Supp. 3,** 232–33; **Supp. 6,** 443, 444

German Evangelical church, **Supp. 7,** 574

German Reformed church, **Vol. 4, Part 1,** 219, 375 f.; **Vol. 4, Part 2,** 15, 237, 523; **Vol. 7, Part 2,** 107 f.; **Vol. 8, Part 1,** 389 f.; **Vol. 8, Part 2,** 435; Pennsylvania, **Vol. 1, Part 2,** 404; **Vol. 2, Part 1,** 220; **Vol. 4, Part 2,** 578; **Vol. 8, Part 2,** 227, 436

Germantown, Pa.: battle of, **Vol. 4, Part 1,** 570; **Vol. 7, Part 1,** 87; **Vol. 8, Part 1,** 259; **Vol. 10, Part 1,** 517, 564; settlement of, **Vol. 3, Part 2,** 260; **Vol. 7, Part 2,** 291; **Vol. 8, Part 1,** 632

Germany: abstract art movement, **Supp. 8,** 270; architectural design, **Supp. 5,** 483; **Supp. 8,** 226, 435–36; art, modern, first exhibition of, in U.S., **Vol. 8, Part 1,** 493; banking, **Supp. 5,** 249–50; Berlin airlift, **Supp. 6,** 431; Berlin Wall, **Supp. 7,** 423; book publishing, **Supp. 7,** 799; Catholic church, **Vol. 4, Part 2,** 515, 542; Catholic newspaper in U.S. (1837), **Vol. 4, Part 2,** 542; Communist party, **Supp. 7,** 244; **Supp. 8,** 162; culture, devotion to, **Vol. 5, Part 2,** 506; de-Nazification, **Supp. 6,** 407; diplomacy with U.S., **Vol. 5, Part 1,** 548 f.; **Vol. 7, Part 2,** 88, 420, 533; **Vol. 9, Part 2,** 316, 608; **Supp. 3,** 366, 699; **Supp. 4,** 898; **Supp. 5,** 241; education, **Supp. 3,** 676; **Supp. 6,** 207, 208; emigration, **Vol. 5, Part 2,** 484, 491; **Vol. 8, Part 2,** 87; ethnological study of, **Supp. 6,** 394; food relief, **Supp. 7,** 359; Great Depression in, **Supp. 6,** 708–9; housing programs (1920s), **Supp. 3,** 52; immigration, **Vol. 3, Part 2,** 260; **Vol. 4, Part 2,** 383; **Vol. 5, Part 2,** 496; **Vol. 8, Part 1,** 392; **Vol. 8, Part 2,** 87; *Lied,* **Vol. 4, Part 2,** 505; literature and language, grammar studies, **Supp. 4,** 203; Methodism, **Vol. 7, Part 1,** 393; newspapers, German-language, **Vol. 2, Part 1,** 19; **Vol. 4, Part 1,** 262; **Vol. 4, Part 2,** 509, 542; **Vol. 5, Part 2,** 259, 592; **Vol. 6, Part 1,** 274; **Vol. 8, Part 2,** 446 f.; philosophy, conveyed into fashionable English, **Vol. 5, Part 2,** 507; political cartoons, **Supp. 6,** 256; post-World War II occupation of, **Supp. 4,** 900; **Supp. 8,** 275, 446; press in America, **Vol. 7, Part 1,** 271 f.; radicalism, **Vol. 4, Part 2,** 508 f.; refugees, **Vol. 4,**

Part 2, 383; **Vol. 6, Part 1,** 237, 292; **Vol. 8, Part 2,** 444; reparations payments, **Supp. 2,** 234, 356; **Supp. 7,** 809–10; rocket development, **Supp. 3,** 306, 307–8; satirical cabaret, **Supp. 4,** 867–68; scholarship, **Vol. 3, Part 2,** 491 f., 584 f.; **Vol. 8, Part 2,** 55; sentiment, **Vol. 9, Part 1,** 153; study, influence of, **Vol. 1, Part 1,** 564; teaching of German, **Vol. 5, Part 1,** 244, 513; **Vol. 5, Part 2,** 227; Third Humanism, **Supp. 7,** 388; translations, **Vol. 4, Part 2,** 520; **Vol. 6, Part 1,** 103; **Vol. 8, Part 1,** 188 f.; **Vol. 8, Part 2,** 362 f.; universities, **Vol. 9, Part 2,** 526; writings on, **Supp. 4,** 851. *See also* German-Americans; Nazism; War crimes; World War I; World War II

Germer, Lester H., reference to, **Supp. 6,** 151

Germicides. *See* Antiseptics

Germ theory of disease, **Vol. 4, Part 1,** 464; **Vol. 8, Part 2,** 309

Geronimo, reference to, **Vol. 6, Part 1,** 62

Gerontological Society, founding of, **Supp. 5,** 454

Gerrymandering, **Vol. 4, Part 1,** 226; Illinois, **Vol. 3, Part 1,** 398; Massachusetts, **Vol. 9, Part 2,** 145; origin of the word, **Vol. 8, Part 2,** 239; **Vol. 9, Part 2,** 499

Gerry Society, **Vol. 4, Part 1,** 228; **Supp. 8,** 314

Gersh, Isidore, reference to, **Supp. 6,** 54

Gershwin, George, references to, **Supp. 2,** 303; **Supp. 3,** 690; **Supp. 4,** 211, 226; **Supp. 7,** 199; **Supp. 8,** 697, 698

Gershwin, Ira, reference to, **Supp. 5,** 415

Gerstenfeld, Norman, reference to, **Supp. 6,** 600

Gesell, Arnold, reference to, **Supp. 6,** 626

Gesell Institute of Child Development, **Supp. 7,** 284

Gestalt psychology, **Supp. 3,** 428–30; **Supp. 4,** 485; **Supp. 8,** 343–45; founding of, **Supp. 3,** 808–9

Get Rich Quick Wallingford (stories), **Vol. 2, Part 2,** 58

Gettysburg, Pa., **Vol. 1, Part 1,** 165, 524; **Vol. 2, Part 1,** 71, 373; **Vol. 3, Part 2,** 230, 254, 284; **Vol. 4, Part 2,** 152, 168, 194, 214, 222, 235, 243, 600; **Vol. 5, Part 1,** 25, 193, 279 f., 283, 372, 386 f., 422; **Vol. 5, Part 2,** 209, 258, 359, 375; **Vol. 6, Part 1,** 39, 125, 159, 370, 392, 430; **Vol. 6, Part 2,** 193, 476; **Vol. 7, Part 1,** 20, 228, 350, 410, 473, 552, 605; **Vol. 7, Part 2,** 8, 516, 570; **Vol. 8, Part 1,** 520; **Vol. 8, Part 2,** 47, 71, 72, 152, 219, 285, 463, 468, 548; **Vol. 9, Part 1,** 115, 150, 216, 249, 471; **Vol. 9, Part 2,** 66, 171, 255, 530, 593, 621, 636, 642; **Vol. 10, Part 1,** 571; address, Everett, **Vol. 3, Part 2,** 225; address, Lincoln, **Vol. 6, Part 1,** 256; history of, **Vol. 5, Part 1,** 371; **Vol. 10, Part 2,** 628; monuments, **Vol. 4, Part 1,** 471; painting of, battle, **Vol. 8, Part 2,** 187; Pickett's charge, **Vol. 5, Part 2,** 322; religious service in connection with dedication, **Vol. 9, Part 2,** 50; sculpture on battlefield, **Vol. 8, Part 1,** 125 f.

Gettysburg College (formerly Pennsylvania College), **Vol. 1, Part 2,** 59; **Vol. 5, Part 2,** 502; **Vol. 8, Part 2,** 443

Gewandhaus Orchestra of Leipzig, **Supp. 8,** 450

Ghana, **Supp. 7,** 205

Ghent, Treaty of, **Vol. 1, Part 1,** 85; **Vol. 1, Part 2,** 66; **Vol. 2, Part 2,** 175; **Vol. 4, Part 1,** 106; **Vol. 5, Part 1,** 346, 529; **Vol. 6, Part 2,** 192; **Vol. 7, Part 1,** 90; **Vol. 8, Part 2,** 245

"Ghetto" (New York City), **Vol. 8, Part 2,** 165, 168

"Ghost Dance," origin of, **Vol. 10, Part 2,** 541

Giannini Foundation for Agricultural Economics, founding of, **Supp. 6,** 638

Giant Powder Co., **Vol. 5, Part 2,** 239

Giants in the Earth, **Supp. 4,** 172

Giauque, William, reference to, **Supp. 8,** 122

Gibbons, Thomas, reference to, **Vol. 7, Part 1,** 637

Gibbs, George, reference to, **Vol. 9, Part 1,** 161

Gray, Asa, references to, **Vol. 3, Part 2,** 274 f.; **Vol. 6, Part 1,** 162; **Vol. 8, Part 2,** 354; **Vol. 9, Part 2,** 597; **Vol. 10, Part 1,** 547 f.

Gray, Horace, reference to, **Supp. 3,** 94

Gray, John S., reference to, **Supp. 4,** 294

Gray, L. C., reference to, **Supp. 4,** 45

Gray, William, reference to, **Vol. 1, Part 2,** 52

Graybar Electric Co., **Supp. 8,** 211

Gray-Bell controversy, **Vol. 4, Part 1,** 514

Gray Herbarium, **Supp. 1,** 632; **Supp. 4,** 266

Gray Ladies, founding of, **Supp. 4,** 93

Graymoor. *See* Society of the Atonement

Gray's Manual of Botany, **Supp. 4,** 266

Grayson, Cary, reference to, **Supp. 6,** 413

Grayson, David (pseudonym), **Supp. 4,** 47

Great Atlantic and Pacific Tea Co., **Supp. 6,** 90–91; founding of, **Supp. 5,** 277–78

"Great Awakening," **Vol. 3, Part 2,** 391; **Vol. 4, Part 1,** 17; **Vol. 7, Part 1,** 614; **Vol. 8, Part 2,** 545; **Vol. 9, Part 2,** 367

Great Books studies, **Supp. 5,** 211–12; **Supp. 8,** 59

Great Britain: *Alabama,* and, **Vol. 5, Part 2,** 114; American cataloguing code, **Supp. 3,** 327; American distrust of, **Supp. 6,** 361, 614; American fishermen in Canadian waters, **Vol. 8, Part 1,** 285 f.; American Revolution studies, **Supp. 3,** 15–16; antislavery interests, **Vol. 4, Part 2,** 564; armed forces and defense, **Supp. 3,** 166; atomic bomb project, **Supp. 8,** 230; Confederate relations with, **Vol. 1, Part 1,** 43; **Vol. 6, Part 2,** 240, 365; **Vol. 10, Part 2,** 267; controversy with, on Civil War commerce, **Vol. 3, Part 2,** 398; diplomacy during U.S. Civil War, **Supp. 1,** 9; diplomacy with, **Vol. 1, Part 1,** 85, 567; **Vol. 1, Part 2,** 327; **Vol. 3, Part 1,** 39, 134; **Vol. 5, Part 2,** 7 f., 8 f., 398, 403, 566; **Vol. 6, Part 1,** 4, 463; **Vol. 6, Part 2,** 114; **Vol. 7, Part 1,** 150, 286; **Vol. 7, Part 2,** 143, 528, 587, 618; 627; **Vol. 8, Part 1,** 353 f., 485; **Vol. 8, Part 2,** 232; 245; **Vol. 9, Part 2,** 484; **Vol. 10, Part 1,** 136, 154; **Vol. 10, Part 2,** 102; **Supp. 3,** 366; **Supp. 4,** 900; **Supp. 5,** 155, 160; **Supp. 7,** 437–38; **Supp. 8,** 320–21; educational system, **Supp. 4,** 880; Elizabethan history, **Supp. 6,** 531–32; ethical culture movement in, **Supp. 3,** 175–76; expatriates in, **Supp. 4,** 755–56; **Supp. 6,** 101–4; historical writings on, **Supp. 8,** 472–73; law, collections of, **Supp. 1,** 154; Massachusetts Colony relations with, **Vol. 6, Part 2,** 391 f.; **Vol. 10, Part 2,** 412; Mohawk Indians, relations with, **Vol. 4, Part 2,** 532; printing of first penny postage stamps in, **Vol. 7, Part 2,** 472; oil dispute with Iran, **Supp. 8,** 276; Russian agreement on Persia, **Supp. 6,** 579; theater, **Supp. 8,** 21–22; trade with U.S., **Supp. 2,** 39; **Supp. 8,** 90; woman suffrage movement, **Supp. 5,** 473. *See also* Suez crisis (1956); World War I; World War II

Great Chain of Being, The, **Supp. 7,** 482

Great Depression: art reflecting, **Supp. 5,** 580; banking crisis, **Supp. 5,** 158, 469–70; **Supp. 6,** 33–34; bonus army, **Supp. 5,** 502; **Supp. 6,** 239–40; **Supp. 7,** 488; Detroit relief measures, **Supp. 4,** 611–12; economic views of, **Supp. 4,** 36; federal intervention advocacy, **Supp. 5,** 403; Glass-Steagall Act, **Supp. 3,** 730; Hoover policies, **Supp. 7,** 362–63; impact on agriculture, **Supp. 7,** 361, 760–61; journalistic analysis of, **Supp. 4,** 704; National Business Survey Conference, **Supp. 6,** 37; photographic documentation of, **Supp. 7,** 456; **Supp. 8,** 586; public relations to counter, **Supp. 5,** 304; **Supp. 6,** 90; relief programs, **Supp. 6,** 103; religious interpretation of, **Supp. 7,** 761; Roosevelt, F. D., policies, **Supp. 3,** 647–58; social legislation, **Supp. 6,** 378–79; sociological surveys in, **Supp. 6,** 605; Stage Relief Fund, **Supp. 6,** 133; unemployment economics, **Supp. 6,** 708–9;

wealth during, **Supp. 5,** 550. *See also* New Deal; Welfare

Great Eastern: laying of cable by, **Vol. 5, Part 2,** 566; repairing of, while afloat, **Vol. 8, Part 1,** 505;

Greater New York Racing Association, **Supp. 8,** 76

Greatest Story Ever Told, The, **Supp. 5,** 528

Great Frontier, The, **Supp. 7,** 771

Great Gatsby, The, **Supp. 2,** 189, 190

Great Kanawa, battle of. *See* Point Pleasant, battle of

Great Lakes: exploration of, **Vol. 2, Part 1,** 183, 606; **Vol. 5, Part 2,** 156 f.; **Vol. 6, Part 2,** 295; glacial history, **Supp. 2,** 654; lunar tides on, **Vol. 4, Part 1,** 476; report on projected opening of, to ocean shipping, **Vol. 9, Part 2,** 260; shipbuilding, **Vol. 5, Part 2,** 110, 120; shipping on, **Vol. 6, Part 1,** 327; **Vol. 6, Part 2,** 23; **Vol. 7, Part 1,** 472; strategic importance of, for the British against the French, **Vol. 8, Part 1,** 161 f.; survey of, **Vol. 8, Part 2,** 52

Great Lakes Steel Corporation, **Supp. 6,** 678

Great Northern Railroad, **Vol. 3, Part 1,** 183; **Vol. 5, Part 1,** 37 f.; **Vol. 5, Part 2,** 498; **Supp. 7,** 89–90; Pacific extension construction, **Supp. 3,** 735, 736

Great Plains, The, **Supp. 7,** 771

Great Salt Lake: steamboat, first on, **Vol. 2, Part 2,** 353; white man first to visit, **Vol. 8, Part 1,** 250 f.

"Great Seal War" (New Jersey), **Vol. 3, Part 1,** 290

Great Southern Lumber Co., **Supp. 7,** 293

Great Train Robbery, The, **Supp. 3,** 607

Great Western, early steamship, **Vol. 9, Part 1,** 315

Greco-Turkish War, refugee resettlement, **Supp. 4,** 604

Greece: ancient coins collection, **Supp. 3,** 551; ancient slave system, **Supp. 5,** 736; archaeology in, **Vol. 3, Part 1,** 594 f.; **Vol. 8, Part 1,** 574; **Supp. 3,** 705; classical studies, **Supp. 1,** 24, 657, 701; **Supp. 2,** 621, 701; **Supp. 7,** 313–14, 388; classical studies, American School, **Supp. 4,** 143–44; classical studies, Loeb Classical Library, **Supp. 1,** 503; diplomatic relations with, **Vol. 5, Part 1,** 548; **Vol. 5, Part 2,** 396; **Vol. 8, Part 1,** 428 f.; **Vol. 8, Part 2,** 77; **Supp. 6,** 245; expeditions to aid Greek patriots, **Vol. 8, Part 2,** 238; historical writings on, **Supp. 5,** 595–96; independence from Turkey, **Vol. 5, Part 1,** 296, 312; Kallinean Free Schools, **Vol. 1, Part 1,** 261; Marshall Plan, **Supp. 6,** 431; missions in, **Vol. 1, Part 2,** 187; **Vol. 5, Part 1,** 41 f. *See also* Greco-Turkish War; Greek

Greed, **Supp. 6,** 657

Greek: art, **Vol. 4, Part 2,** 166; drama studies, **Supp. 4,** 143; Homeric studies, **Supp. 4,** 728–29; music, **Vol. 1, Part 1,** 189; plays, production of, **Vol. 8, Part 1,** 592; scholarship, **Vol. 3, Part 1,** 372; **Vol. 5, Part 2,** 328; **Vol. 9, Part 2,** 576 f.; teaching Greek, **Vol. 6, Part 1,** 72; **Vol. 7, Part 1,** 584; **Vol. 9, Part 1,** 398, 449, 594; **Vol. 10, Part 1,** 99; **Vol. 10, Part 2,** 556, 567; translations, **Vol. 5, Part 2,** 287; **Vol. 6, Part 1,** 229; **Vol. 10, Part 2,** 519; **Supp. 8,** 236; vases, **Vol. 5, Part 1,** 227; writings on, **Vol. 4, Part 1,** 412; **Vol. 9, Part 1,** 398; **Vol. 10, Part 2,** 113, 556

Greek-Americans, Panhellenism, **Supp. 7,** 702

Greek Catholics, protection in the U.S., **Vol. 7, Part 2,** 66

Greek Orthodox Church in America, **Supp. 7,** 102

Greek Revival architecture, **Vol. 6, Part 1,** 20 f.; **Vol. 8, Part 2,** 99; **Vol. 9, Part 2,** 137 f.; **Vol. 10, Part 1,** 487 f.; **Supp. 6,** 272

Greek Way, The, **Supp. 7,** 313

Greeley, A. W., references to, **Vol. 5, Part 2,** 256; **Vol. 7, Part 2,** 323; **Vol. 8, Part 2,** 438

Greeley, Horace, **Vol. 4, Part 2,** 4; **Vol. 5, Part 2,** 112, 260; **Vol. 6, Part 2,** 36; **Vol. 7, Part 1,** 205; **Vol. 8, Part 1,** 408 f., 483; **Vol. 8, Part 2,** 468 f.; **Vol. 9, Part**

Harbach, Otto, reference to, **Supp. 3,** 418
Harbinger, Brook Farm periodical, **Vol. 3, Part 1,** 567 f., 624
Harbor Association, **Vol. 1, Part 2,** 84
Harbors: engineering, **Supp. 1,** 157; improvements, **Vol. 8, Part 1,** 406; **Vol. 9, Part 1,** 179; surveying of, **Vol. 3, Part 1,** 92; **Vol. 9, Part 2,** 247
Harcourt, Alfred, reference to, **Supp. 5,** 85
Harcourt, Brace and Co., founding of, **Supp. 5,** 85, 272
Hardin College for Women, **Vol. 4, Part 2,** 245
Harding, Warren G.: Daugherty relationship, **Supp. 3,** 213–14; Fall relationship, **Supp. 3,** 259–60; League of Nations, **Supp. 3,** 472–73; presidential candidacy, **Supp. 3,** 643, 129; **Supp. 7,** 86, 305; references to, **Supp. 1,** 173; **Supp. 3,** 203; **Supp. 6,** 114, 291; Sutherland relationship, **Supp. 3,** 754; writings on, **Supp. 6,** 6. *See also* Teapot Dome scandal
"Harding Bible," **Vol. 4, Part 2,** 259
Hardware, manufacture of, **Vol. 1, Part 2,** 341
Hardy, Oliver, references to, **Supp. 7,** 462, 463–64
Hare-Hawes-Cutting Act (1933), **Supp. 3,** 614; **Supp. 4,** 612
Harinck, early Dutch boat, **Vol. 5, Part 2,** 371
Harkins, W. D., reference to, **Supp. 7,** 10
Harkness, Edward S., references to, **Supp. 3,** 262, 471; **Supp. 4,** 22
Harlan, John Marshall, references to, **Supp. 3,** 15, 117
Harlan, Richard, reference to, **Vol. 7, Part 1,** 265
Harlem (New York City): development as community, **Supp. 3,** 535; jazz, **Supp. 3,** 798; libraries, **Supp. 3,** 281; political leadership, **Supp. 5,** 548; Protestant Episcopal churches in, **Supp. 4,** 547
Harlem Hospital (New York City), founding of, **Supp. 1,** 240
Harlem Renaissance, **Supp. 4,** 200–1; **Supp. 4,** 527–28, 436; **Supp. 6,** 314, 321, 489; **Supp. 7,** 203, 236, 754; **Supp. 8,** 286
Harlem River Drive (New York City), construction of, **Supp. 1,** 136
Harlem River-155th Street Bridge (New York City), **Supp. 3,** 77
Harmar's defeat (1790), **Vol. 2, Part 1,** 366; **Vol. 4, Part 2,** 276; **Vol. 6, Part 1,** 300; **Vol. 8, Part 2,** 294; **Vol. 10, Part 1,** 523
Harmonium, **Supp. 5,** 660
Harmony Society, **Vol. 8, Part 1,** 383
Harms, T. B., reference to, **Supp. 3,** 417
Harms, T. B., Inc., **Supp. 7,** 198
Harmsworth, Sir Leicester, reference to, **Supp. 4,** 5
Harnack, Adolf, reference to, **Supp. 3,** 110
Harness making, **Vol. 10, Part 2,** 571
Harness racing, **Supp. 5,** 567; **Supp. 6,** 688–89
Harper, William Rainey, references to, **Vol. 5, Part 1,** 67; **Vol. 5, Part 2,** 241 f.; **Vol. 10, Part 1,** 606 f.; **Supp. 3,** 64, 153, 793, 824; **Supp. 5,** 171; **Supp. 7,** 712
Harper & Bros., publishing house, **Vol. 4, Part 2,** 281 f.; **Vol. 5, Part 1,** 76, 187, 308; **Supp. 3,** 686
Harper and Row, **Supp. 8,** 224
Harper's Bazaar, **Vol. 8, Part 2,** 352; **Supp. 4,** 842; **Supp. 5,** 286; **Supp. 7,** 704
Harper's Dictionary of Classical Literature and Antiquities, **Vol. 7, Part 2,** 378
Harpers Ferry, W.Va., **Vol. 1, Part 2,** 339; **Vol. 2, Part 1,** 133; **Vol. 4, Part 2,** 163; **Vol. 5, Part 1,** 386, 460, 556; **Vol. 6, Part 1,** 122; **Vol. 6, Part 2,** 120; **Vol. 9, Part 1,** 153; **Vol. 10, Part 1,** 144
Harper's magazine, **Vol. 1, Part 1,** 144 f.; **Vol. 4, Part 2,** 283, 486; **Vol. 5, Part 1,** 445; **Vol. 7, Part 1,** 457, 608; **Supp. 5,** 16–17, 168, 169

Harper's Monthly, **Vol. 5, Part 1,** 308
Harper's New Monthly Magazine, **Vol. 8, Part 1,** 409, 624
Harper's Weekly, **Vol. 1, Part 1,** 3, 573 f.; **Vol. 4, Part 2,** 372; **Vol. 5, Part 1,** 187, 201; **Vol. 7, Part 1,** 392, 416; **Vol. 8, Part 2,** 469; **Vol. 9, Part 1,** 227; **Vol. 10, Part 1,** 81
Harpsichord, revival of, **Supp. 6,** 357–58
Harriet Lane Home (Baltimore, Md.), **Supp. 3,** 74
Harriman, Edward H., references to, **Vol. 5, Part 1,** 38; **Vol. 7, Part 1,** 177; **Supp. 1,** 457; **Supp. 3,** 728, 736
Harriman, Job, reference to, **Supp. 3,** 347
Harriman, Mary Williamson, reference to, **Supp. 3,** 215
Harriman, W. Averell, reference to, **Supp. 8,** 69–70
Harriman Alaska expedition, **Supp. 1,** 237
Harriman State Park (N.Y.), nature trail, **Supp. 3,** 478
Harrington, Mark R., reference to, **Supp. 5,** 533
Harrington, Michael, reference to, **Supp. 3,** 373
Harris, Bucky, reference to, **Supp. 8,** 49
Harris, James Arthur, reference to, **Supp. 3,** 315
Harris, Joel Chandler, references to, **Vol. 5, Part 1,** 302; **Vol. 9, Part 1,** 523; **Supp. 7,** 323, 324
Harris, Roy, reference to, **Supp. 3,** 359
Harris, Sam H., reference to, **Supp. 3,** 173–74
Harris, Townsend, reference to, **Vol. 5, Part 1,** 613
Harris, William J., reference to, **Supp. 3,** 331
Harris, W. T., references to, **Vol. 5, Part 1,** 311; **Vol. 9, Part 1,** 66, 383, 391, 593
Harrison, Benjamin, **Vol. 8, Part 1,** 296 f.; **Vol. 10, Part 1,** 88; nomination of, **Vol. 3, Part 1,** 246; **Vol. 8, Part 1,** 80 f.
Harrison, Carter H., references to, **Supp. 4,** 256; **Supp. 5,** 273
Harrison, Francis Burton, reference to, **Supp. 3,** 614
Harrison, Marie L., reference to, **Supp. 6,** 107
Harrison, Pat, reference to, **Supp. 6,** 35
Harrison, Richard, reference to, **Supp. 8,** 444
Harrison, Ross G., references to, **Supp. 3,** 140; **Supp. 6,** 386
Harrison, Samuel, reference to, **Supp. 6,** 281
Harrison, Wallace K., reference to, **Supp. 5,** 133
Harrison, William Henry, references to, **Vol. 5, Part 1,** 158; **Vol. 7, Part 1,** 633; **Vol. 9, Part 2,** 359, 375 f., 570
Harrison Act (1914), **Supp. 5,** 138
Harrison Narcotics Act (1914), **Supp. 6,** 280
Harrison's Landing, Va., operation at, **Vol. 6, Part 1,** 583. *See also* Peninsular Campaign
Harrod's Fort, **Vol. 1, Part 2,** 442; **Vol. 4, Part 2,** 353, 531; **Vol. 6, Part 1,** 357
Harshbarger, Dema, reference to, **Supp. 8,** 282
Har Sinai Temple (Baltimore, Md.), **Supp. 4,** 659
Hart, Lorenz, reference to, **Supp. 8,** 481, 547
Hart, Moss, references to, **Supp. 3,** 333, 842; **Supp. 4,** 374; **Supp. 5,** 415; **Supp. 6,** 311; **Supp. 7,** 413, 803
Hart, William S., references to, **Supp. 4,** 240
Hartford, Conn.: civic service, **Vol. 4, Part 2,** 600 f.; **Vol. 6, Part 1,** 604; **Vol. 7, Part 2,** 217 f., 529, 641; **Vol. 8, Part 1,** 187 f.; **Vol. 10, Part 1,** 82; deaf, school for, in, **Vol. 1, Part 2,** 139; **Vol. 2, Part 2,** 201 f.; **Vol. 8, Part 1,** 102 f.; industrial development, **Vol. 8, Part 1,** 74 f., 172 f.; newspapers, **Vol. 7, Part 1,** 522; philanthropy, **Vol. 7, Part 1,** 182; settlement of, **Vol. 5, Part 1,** 200; **Vol. 8, Part 1,** 175; social reform in, **Supp. 5,** 296–97; "Wits," *see* "Hartford Wits"
Hartford Accident and Indemnity Co., **Supp. 5,** 659–61
Hartford Convention (1814–15), **Vol. 4, Part 1,** 304; **Vol. 7, Part 1,** 212, 523; **Vol. 7, Part 2,** 99; **Vol. 8, Part 1,** 310; **Vol. 9, Part 1,** 300, 329; **Vol. 9, Part 2,**

145
Hartford Courant, **Supp. 6,** 231–32
Hartford Electric Co. (HELCO), **Supp. 4,** 265
Hartford Female Seminary, **Vol. 1, Part 2,** 541
Hartford Theological Foundation, **Supp. 3,** 477
Hartford Theological Seminary, **Vol. 4, Part 2,** 367; **Vol. 7, Part 1,** 433; **Vol. 7, Part 2,** 295 f.; forerunner of, **Vol. 10, Part 1,** 85
"Hartford Wits," **Vol. 1, Part 1,** 228, 610; **Vol. 3, Part 1,** 236, 573 f.; **Vol. 7, Part 1,** 559; **Vol. 9, Part 1,** 259; **Vol. 10, Part 1,** 11
Hartley, Frank, reference to, **Vol. 9, Part 2,** 535
Hartley, Marsden, reference to, **Supp. 6,** 552
Hartmann, Heinz, reference to, **Supp. 6,** 528
Hart, Shaffner and Marx, strike (1910), **Supp. 4,** 375
Harvard Advertising Awards, establishment of, **Supp. 1,** 93
Harvard Alumni Association, **Supp. 6,** 659
Harvard Alumni Bulletin, **Supp. 6,** 249, 306
Harvard Apparatus Co., founding of, **Supp. 4,** 676
Harvard Classics, **Vol. 3, Part 2,** 78
Harvard Club, **Vol. 1, Part 2,** 169
"Harvard Commemoration Ode," **Vol. 6, Part 1,** 462
Harvard Cooperative Society, **Vol. 1, Part 2,** 421
Harvard Corporation, **Supp. 3,** 448; **Supp. 6,** 249, 250; youngest elected to, **Supp. 6,** 143
Harvard Crimson, founding of, **Vol. 9, Part 1,** 168; **Supp. 6,** 249, 677
Harvard Endowment Fund, **Supp. 6,** 659
Harvard Lampoon, **Supp. 5,** 283; founding of, **Supp. 2,** 434
Harvard Law Review: Brandeis article, **Supp. 3,** 94, 95; founding of, **Vol. 1, Part 1,** 247; **Supp. 3,** 43, 821
Harvard Monthly, founding of, **Supp. 1,** 592
Harvard Philosophical Club, founding of, **Supp. 2,** 639
Harvard Research in International Law, **Supp. 6,** 308
Harvard Theological Review, **Vol. 7, Part 1,** 124; **Vol. 8, Part 2,** 151
Harvard Trade Union Fellowship, **Supp. 6,** 586
Harvard University, **Vol. 1, Part 1,** 51; **Vol. 1, Part 2,** 421; **Vol. 2, Part 2,** 42; **Vol. 3, Part 1,** 611; **Vol. 3, Part 2,** 72 f.; **Vol. 4, Part 1,** 411; **Vol. 4, Part 2,** 57, 499; **Vol. 5, Part 1,** 333, 535, 592; **Vol. 5, Part 2,** 431; **Vol. 6, Part 1,** 198, 383 f., 461 f.; **Vol. 6, Part 2,** 387, 391; **Vol. 7, Part 1,** 119, 124, 253; **Vol. 7, Part 2,** 335; **Vol. 8, Part 2,** 355 f.; **Vol. 9, Part 2,** 526 f.; **Vol. 10, Part 1,** 649 f.; **Vol. 10, Part 2,** 192 f., 235, 238, 415; administration, **Supp. 5,** 5, 6; alumni directory, **Supp. 6,** 249; American literature and language studies, **Supp. 5,** 542; **Supp. 7,** 538; "Annex," *see* Radcliffe College; anthropology, first chair of, **Vol. 8, Part 1,** 276 f.; anthropology studies, **Supp. 5,** 312; **Supp. 8,** 684; Appleton Chapel, **Vol. 1, Part 1,** 332 f.; architecture studies, **Supp. 8,** 227; astronomical observatories, **Supp. 1,** 43; **Supp. 3,** 130–31; astronomy, **Vol. 7, Part 2,** 563; "Augustan Age," **Vol. 5, Part 2,** 431; biological chemistry studies, **Supp. 3,** 350; biological laboratories, **Supp. 4,** 16; black, first degree awarded to, **Vol. 4, Part 1,** 578; Boston School for Social Workers, **Supp. 4,** 101; botanical facilities, **Supp. 4,** 16; botanical garden, **Vol. 7, Part 1,** 597; botany, first professorship of, **Vol. 4, Part 1,** 512; business school, **Supp. 1,** 45; business school, business economics, **Supp. 6,** 585; business school, fatigue laboratory, **Supp. 3,** 351; business school, founding of, **Supp. 3,** 448, 471; business school, Kresge Hall, **Supp. 8,** 349; Cancer Commission, **Supp. 6,** 69; Center for Italian Renaissance Studies, **Supp. 6,** 57; chemical engineering studies, **Supp. 2,** 479; chemistry studies, **Vol. 2, Part 2,** 387; **Supp. 5,** 407; climatology, first profes-

sorship in, **Vol. 7, Part 2,** 436; curriculum reform, **Supp. 3,** 328, 470–74; Dante course, **Supp. 2,** 254; dean, first, **Vol. 3, Part 1,** 503 f.; dental school, founding of, **Supp. 4,** 402; divinity school, **Vol. 1, Part 2,** 306; **Vol. 3, Part 2,** 75, 221; **Vol. 7, Part 1,** 588; **Vol. 8, Part 2,** 151; **Vol. 10, Part 1,** 447 f.; **Supp. 5,** 649; **Supp. 7,** 747; Dumbarton Oaks Research Library and Collection, **Supp. 5,** 700, 708; **Supp. 7,** 60, 673; ecclesiastical history studies, **Supp. 4,** 467–68; economic history studies, **Supp. 4,** 321, 322; economics studies, **Supp. 4,** 721–23; **Supp. 6,** 585–86; **Supp. 8,** 82–83; education graduate studies, **Supp. 3,** 327–28, 471; Egyptology collection, **Supp. 4,** 902; elective system, **Vol. 7, Part 2,** 405; **Vol. 8, Part 1,** 308 f.; endowment fund, **Supp. 7,** 401; engineering school, **Vol. 5, Part 1,** 349; engineering studies, **Supp. 4,** 873; English literature and language studies, **Supp. 3,** 422, 423, 474–76; **Supp. 4,** 560; **Supp. 5,** 131–32; English 12 course, **Supp. 5,** 131–32; exchange professorships inaugurated, **Vol. 10, Part 1,** 649 f.; fatigue laboratory, **Supp. 3,** 551; **Supp. 5,** 565; first woman professor, **Supp. 8,** 242; Five-Foot Bookshelf classics series, **Supp. 4,** 624; Fogg Museum, **Vol. 7, Part 1,** 116;; **Supp. 1,** 641; **Supp. 5,** 729; **Supp. 7,** 673–74; football team, **Supp. 4,** 492; founding of, **Vol. 1, Part 2,** 166; **Vol. 3, Part 1,** 419, 484 f., 524; **Vol. 4, Part 2,** 372; French literature and language studies, **Supp. 1,** 36; geology studies, **Supp. 6,** 144; gifts to, **Vol. 4, Part 1,** 515; **Vol. 5, Part 1,** 13; **Vol. 9, Part 2,** 113; **Supp. 3,** 464, 471; Gore Hall, **Vol. 9, Part 2,** 632; government studies, **Supp. 3,** 337, 469–470; graduate of, first class, **Vol. 1, Part 2,** 166; graduates, biographical sketches of, **Vol. 3, Part 1,** 277; Gray Herbarium, **Vol. 9, Part 1,** 632; **Supp. 4,** 266, 428; **Supp. 6,** 450; Gray's Hall, **Vol. 4, Part 1,** 515; "Great Rebellion" of 1823, **Vol. 5, Part 2,** 431; Hasty Pudding Club, **Vol. 7, Part 2,** 247; **Vol. 10, Part 1,** 480 f.; **Supp. 5,** 629; history, **Vol. 9, Part 1,** 147, 433; history of science studies, **Supp. 3,** 351; **Supp. 6,** 564–65; history studies, **Supp. 3,** 336–37; **Supp. 7,** 676; **Supp. 8,** 50, 169–70; Holyoke Center mural, **Supp. 8,** 554; Houghton Library, **Supp. 7,** 387; house plan, **Supp. 2,** 284; **Supp. 3,** 471; **Supp. 5,** 130; international law studies, **Supp. 5,** 751; international relations studies, **Supp. 8,** 167; I Tatti Foundation, **Supp. 7,** 673; Jefferson Laboratory, **Vol. 9, Part 2,** 655; Jew, first, to receive degree, **Vol. 7, Part 1,** 87; John Harvard sculpture, **Supp. 1,** 321; landscape architecture studies, **Supp. 6,** 485; Latin American studies, **Supp. 6,** 277; Latin studies, **Supp. 3,** 617–18; Lawrence Scientific School, **Vol. 3, Part 2,** 192; **Vol. 5, Part 1,** 237; **Vol. 8, Part 1,** 74 f.; **Vol. 9, Part 1,** 18; law school, **Vol. 1, Part 1,** 247; **Vol. 3, Part 2,** 75; **Vol. 4, Part 1,** 520, 584; **Vol. 5, Part 1,** 169; **Vol. 5, Part 2,** 585 f.; **Vol. 7, Part 2,** 225; **Vol. 8, Part 1,** 308 f.; **Vol. 9, Part 1,** 541; **Vol. 9, Part 2,** 106, 404, 406; **Supp. 3,** 43, 94; **Supp. 5,** 549; **Supp. 6,** 104–6; **Supp. 7,** 261, 453, 626–27, 792; **Supp. 8,** 285; liberal traditions challenged, **Vol. 8, Part 1,** 308 f.; libraries, **Vol. 1, Part 2,** 273; **Vol. 4, Part 2,** 321; **Vol. 7, Part 1,** 463, 568; **Vol. 8, Part 1,** 308 f.; **Vol. 9, Part 1,** 147; **Vol. 9, Part 2,** 391; **Vol. 10, Part 2,** 403; **Supp. 5,** 756; mammalogy studies, **Supp. 3,** 9; Mark I automatic calculator, **Supp. 6,** 675; Massachusetts Hall, building of, **Vol. 6, Part 1,** 198; mathematics studies, **Vol. 4, Part 1,** 591; **Vol. 7, Part 2,** 394, 405; **Supp. 3,** 70, 575; **Supp. 5,** 130–31, 338; medical school, **Vol. 1, Part 2,** 556; **Vol. 3, Part 2,** 76, 102, 178, 434; **Vol. 4, Part 2,** 303, 465; **Vol. 5, Part 1,** 172, 546; **Vol. 7, Part 1,** 324; **Vol. 8, Part 2,** 186; **Vol. 9, Part 1,** 33; **Vol. 10,**

Part 1, 474, 479 f., 529 f.; **Supp. 1,** 206; **Supp. 3,** 121, 502, 806; **Supp. 4,** 208–9, 582, 676; **Supp. 5,** 122; **Supp. 6,** 175; **Supp. 8,** 241–42; medical school, pediatrics, **Supp. 3,** 75; medical school, psychiatry studies, **Supp. 3,** 128; **Supp. 4,** 617–18, 717; medical school, research, **Supp. 3,** 243–44; medical school, teaching hospital, **Supp. 2,** 138; meteorology studies, **Supp. 3,** 479; Museum of Comparative Zoology, **Vol. 1, Part 1,** 119, 198; **Vol. 8, Part 1,** 141 f.; **Supp. 4,** 51–52; **Supp. 5,** 656; **Supp. 6,** 255; music, **Vol. 3, Part 1,** 567 f.; **Vol. 7, Part 2,** 151; neuropsychology studies, **Supp. 6,** 367; observatory, **Vol. 1, Part 2,** 431, 435; **Vol. 7, Part 1,** 39; **Vol. 7, Part 2,** 394; **Vol. 8, Part 1,** 308 f.; **Vol. 8, Part 2,** 535; **Vol. 10, Part 2,** 390; oceanography studies, **Supp. 8,** 37; organic chemistry studies, **Supp. 3,** 520–21; Oriental series, **Supp. 3,** 445; overseers, **Supp. 3,** 448; **Supp. 6,** 125, 250, 659; Peabody Museum, **Vol. 1, Part 2,** 492; **Vol. 7, Part 1,** 242; **Vol. 7, Part 2,** 337; **Vol. 8, Part 1,** 276 f., 583; pharmacology studies, **Supp. 4,** 411; Philharmonic Society, **Vol. 3, Part 1,** 567 f.; Phillips Brooks House, **Vol. 7, Part 2,** 159; philosophy studies, **Vol. 7, Part 1,** 338; **Vol. 7, Part 2,** 181; **Supp. 1,** 713–14; **Supp. 4,** 880–81, 883; **Supp. 5,** 601–2; **Supp. 6,** 504–5; **Supp. 7,** 471; **Supp. 8,** 266; physics studies, **Vol. 9, Part 2,** 654; **Vol. 10, Part 1,** 529 f.; **Supp. 5,** 441–42; **Supp. 7,** 74–75; **Supp. 8,** 191; physiography studies, **Supp. 4,** 32; physiology studies, **Supp. 3,** 133; **Supp. 4,** 676; political economy, **Vol. 3, Part 1,** 503 f.; presidency, **Vol. 3, Part 1,** 524; **Vol. 3, Part 2,** 71, 317; **Vol. 5, Part 1,** 46, 87 f.; **Vol. 5, Part 2,** 431, 588 f.; **Vol. 6, Part 1,** 197 f.; **Vol. 7, Part 1,** 343, 603; **Vol. 8, Part 1,** 308 f.; **Vol. 9, Part 1,** 433; **Vol. 9, Part 2,** 391; **Supp. 3,** 468–74; president, first, **Vol. 3, Part 1,** 524; press sold to, **Vol. 4, Part 1,** 555; psychology studies, **Supp. 6,** 718–19; **Supp. 8,** 7, 44; public administration school, **Supp. 3,** 464; public health school, **Supp. 3,** 244; **Supp. 4,** 701; **Supp. 5,** 632; quota system, **Supp. 3,** 472, 489; **Supp. 6,** 250; Radcliffe College, **Supp. 1,** 146; Robbins Philosophical Library, **Supp. 1,** 619; Sanskrit studies, **Supp. 3,** 444–45; Saunders Theatre, **Vol. 8, Part 2,** 332; scholarship fund, first, **Vol. 10, Part 1,** 627 f.; Semitic Museum, founding of, **Supp. 1,** 519; Slavic language studies, **Supp. 2,** 717; **Supp. 4,** 195–96; social relations laboratory, **Supp. 6,** 605; Society of Fellows, **Supp. 3,** 351, 352, 473, 476; **Supp. 4,** 884; Soldiers Field, **Vol. 5, Part 1,** 153; stadium, first, in U.S., **Vol. 5, Part 1,** 143; theater studies, **Supp. 1,** 45; tropical medicine studies, **Supp. 4,** 803; tutorial and reading period, **Supp. 3,** 470; Widener collection, **Supp. 5,** 756; Yard, use of, by Revolutionary soldiers, **Vol. 8, Part 2,** 239; zoology studies, **Supp. 5,** 536

Harvard University Press, **Vol. 3, Part 2,** 493

Harvesting machinery, **Vol. 3, Part 1,** 195; **Vol. 3, Part 2,** 188; **Vol. 6, Part 2,** 296; **Vol. 8, Part 1,** 505

Harvey, A. McGehee, reference to, **Supp. 7,** 59

Harvey, C. B. H., reference to, **Supp. 6,** 632

Harvey, Sir John, deposed as governor of Virginia, **Vol. 8, Part 1,** 123 f.

Harvey, William H., reference to, **Supp. 3,** 564

Harvey, **Supp. 4,** 649, 653; **Supp. 6,** 311; **Supp. 7,** 238

Harvey Cushing, **Supp. 6,** 224

Harvey Society of New York, founding of, **Supp. 1,** 518

Hasheesh Eater, **Vol. 6, Part 1,** 491

Hastings, Sue, reference to, **Supp. 3,** 685

HastyPudding Club (Harvard), **Vol. 7, Part 2,** 247; **Vol. 10, Part 1,** 480 f.; **Supp. 5,** 629

Hatch Act (1887), **Vol. 2, Part 2,** 314; **Vol. 4, Part 2,** 394

Hatch Acts (1939 and 1940), **Supp. 3,** 707; **Supp. 6,** 602; **Supp. 7,** 326–27

Hatcher, Robert A., reference to, **Supp. 3,** 805

Hatcher's Run, Va., battle of, **Vol. 4, Part 1,** 237

Hat manufacture, **Vol. 3, Part 2,** 59; **Vol. 4, Part 1,** 209; **Vol. 9, Part 1,** 599. *See also* Clothing manufacture

Hats, **Supp. 5,** 501

Hatteras, and *Alabama,* naval battle, **Vol. 1, Part 2,** 342

Hatteras Inlet, N.C., operation at, **Vol. 2, Part 1,** 310; **Vol. 4, Part 1,** 366

Hauer, Joseph Mathias, reference to, **Supp. 5,** 609

Haugen, Gilbert N., reference to, **Supp. 3,** 496

Hauptmann, Bruno, reference to, **Supp. 3,** 142

Hauser, Gayelord, reference to, **Supp. 8,** 13

Hauss, Rosetta V., reference to, **Supp. 4,** 294, 298

Havana Conference (1947), **Supp. 8,** 90

Havemeyer, Henry O., reference to, **Supp. 6,** 26

Haverford College, **Vol. 4, Part 2,** 48; **Vol. 9, Part 1,** 27; philosophy studies, **Supp. 4,** 441–42; sociology studies, **Supp. 8,** 522

Haverford School, **Vol. 4, Part 2,** 49

Haverhill, Mass., Indian attack on, **Vol. 3, Part 1,** 554 f.

Havoc, June, reference to, **Supp. 8,** 363

Hawaii: annexation of (1896), **Vol. 1, Part 2,** 329, 389; **Vol. 2, Part 2,** 211; **Vol. 3, Part 1,** 109, 358; **Vol. 3, Part 2,** 551; **Vol. 4, Part 1,** 609; **Vol. 4, Part 2,** 333; **Vol. 5, Part 1,** 81; **Vol. 6, Part 2,** 108, 312; **Vol. 8, Part 1,** 458; **Vol. 9, Part 1,** 618 f.; **Vol. 10, Part 2,** 305; Bible translated into Hawaiian, **Vol. 1, Part 1,** 296; **Vol. 8, Part 1,** 561; diplomatic relations with, **Vol. 1, Part 1,** 187; **Vol. 1, Part 2,** 329, 388 f.; **Vol. 2, Part 1,** 535; **Vol. 3, Part 1,** 592 f.; **Vol. 4, Part 1,** 609; **Vol. 7, Part 2,** 405; economic and political system in, **Vol. 8, Part 1,** 560; education, **Vol. 1, Part 1,** 295; flight to, **Vol. 8, Part 2,** 79; governors, **Supp. 1,** 295; "Hawaii for the Hawaiians," **Vol. 4, Part 1,** 258; historical writings on, **Vol. 1, Part 1,** 176 f.; **Supp. 7,** 445–46; Home Rule party, **Vol. 5, Part 2,** 252; Homes Commission Act (1921), **Vol. 5, Part 2,** 252; missions, **Vol. 1, Part 1,** 295; **Vol. 2, Part 2,** 236 f.; **Vol. 3, Part 1,** 357; **Vol. 5, Part 2,** 229 f.; **Vol. 8, Part 1,** 560; newspaper, first in, **Vol. 1, Part 1,** 295; **Vol. 5, Part 1,** 618; pineapple industry, **Supp. 6,** 168; public service, **Vol. 3, Part 1,** 358; **Vol. 4, Part 1,** 258; **Vol. 5, Part 2,** 229 f., 252; **Vol. 6, Part 1,** 135; **Vol. 8, Part 1,** 560; **Vol. 8, Part 2,** 607; **Vol. 9, Part 2,** 517; revolution in, **Vol. 2, Part 2,** 398 f.; songs, **Vol. 1, Part 1,** 296; statehood, **Supp. 5,** 216–17; **Supp. 7,** 590; **Supp. 8,** 104; sugar industry, **Vol. 2, Part 1,** 535; **Vol. 9, Part 1,** 478 f.; sugar plantation, **Supp. 1,** 48; trade with, **Vol. 3, Part 2,** 400; **Vol. 5, Part 1,** 381; volcanoes, study of, **Vol. 5, Part 1,** 70; **Supp. 5,** 361; warship, first American, to visit, **Vol. 7, Part 2,** 461

Hawaiian Dredging and Construction Co., founding of, **Supp. 7,** 184–85

Hawaiian Pineapple Co., **Supp. 6,** 168–69

Hawaiian Volcano Observatory, **Supp. 5,** 361

Hawikuh Pueblo, N.Mex., excavation of, **Supp. 6,** 290

"Hawkeyes," origin of term, **Vol. 8, Part 2,** 153

Hawkins, Norval A., reference to, **Supp. 4,** 300

Hawkins Zouaves, **Vol. 4, Part 2,** 415

Hawks, Howard, **Supp. 7,** 234, 235

Hawley, Joseph R., reference to, **Vol. 10, Part 1,** 462 f.

Hawthorne, Nathaniel, **Vol. 5, Part 1,** 50, 242, 580; literary studies on, **Supp. 1,** 386; relations with Bacon, **Vol. 1, Part 1,** 475; relations with Longfellow, **Vol. 6, Part 1,** 383 f.; relations with Ticknor, **Vol.**

9, **Part 2,** 529; satirical portrait of, **Vol. 10, Part 1,** 122; witchcraft trial, **Vol. 4, Part 2,** 424; writings on, **Supp. 7,** 18

Hay, John, references to, **Vol. 1, Part 1,** 106; **Vol. 4, Part 2,** 432; **Vol. 7, Part 1,** 511; **Supp. 6,** 254

Hayden, Carl, reference to, **Supp. 7,** 105

Hayden, Ferdinand V., reference to, **Supp. 3,** 380

Hayden, Horace H., reference to, **Vol. 1, Part 2,** 61

Hayden Planetarium (New York City): building design for, **Supp. 6,** 234; establishment of, **Supp. 2,** 293

Hayden's Forge, first ironworks, **Vol. 7, Part 1,** 505

Hayes, Helen, references to, **Supp. 4,** 104; **Supp. 5,** 525; **Supp. 6,** 401

Hayes, Max, reference to, **Supp. 3,** 347

Hayes, Roland, reference to, **Supp. 7,** 549

Hayes, Rutherford B., **Vol. 9, Part 1,** 365; "bargain" of, **Vol. 4, Part 2,** 450; election, *see* Hayes-Tilden election; nomination of, **Vol. 7, Part 1,** 587; relations with Blaine, **Vol. 1, Part 2,** 325; relations with Blair, **Vol. 1, Part 2,** 340

Hayes, Samuel P., reference to, **Supp. 4,** 11

Hayes, William C., reference to, **Supp. 4,** 901

Hayes-Binet Intelligence Tests, **Supp. 4,** 11

Hayes-Tilden election, **Vol. 3, Part 2,** 218, 344, 361; **Vol. 4, Part 2,** 29; **Vol. 5, Part 1,** 87; **Vol. 9, Part 2,** 112 f., 540

Hay fever, first desensitizing treatment of, **Supp. 6,** 123; study of, **Vol. 8, Part 2,** 411

Haygood, Atticus Green, reference to, **Supp. 3,** 129

Hay-Herrán Treaty (1903), **Vol. 1, Part 2,** 110; **Vol. 4, Part 2,** 4; **Vol. 8, Part 2,** 138

Hayman, Al, reference to, **Supp. 3,** 276

Haymarket Riot (Chicago, 1886), **Vol. 1, Part 1,** 231; **Supp. 2,** 142

Haymes, Joe, reference to, **Supp. 6,** 172

Hayne, Paul Hamilton, reference to, **Vol. 9, Part 2,** 558 f.

Hayne, Robert Y., reference to, **Vol. 10, Part 1,** 585 f.

Hay-Pauncefote Treaty (1900), **Vol. 1, Part 2,** 110; **Vol. 4, Part 2,** 435; **Vol. 6, Part 1,** 348; **Vol. 8, Part 2,** 138; **Vol. 10, Part 2,** 102; **Supp. 4,** 599

Hays, Arthur Garfield, reference to, **Supp. 8,** 853

Hays, Will, reference to, **Supp. 7,** 71

Hayward, John, reference to, **Supp. 7,** 221

Haywood, William D. ("Big Bill"): references to, **Supp. 3,** 298, 438; **Supp. 5,** 699; **Supp. 7,** 118; trial of, **Vol. 7, Part 1,** 593; **Supp. 2,** 50, 142

Hazeltine Corporation, **Supp. 4,** 452

Head's Spring Temperance Society, **Vol. 7, Part 2,** 43

Health, Clark W., reference to, **Supp. 4,** 582

Health. *See* Diet and nutrition; Hospitals; International Board of Health; Medicine; Occupational health and safety; Physical fitness; Public health; *specific medical disciplines*

Health, public, **Vol. 1, Part 2,** 493; **Vol. 4, Part 2,** 45; **Vol. 8, Part 1,** 390 f.; **Vol. 8, Part 2,** 356; appointment of national secretary of, urged, **Vol. 8, Part 1,** 575; code of laws, **Vol. 9, Part 1,** 403; conservation of, **Vol. 3, Part 2,** 419; writings on, **Vol. 4, Part 2,** 147 f.; **Vol. 5, Part 1,** 443; **Vol. 7, Part 1,** 277 f., 495 f.

Health, Education, and Welfare, Department of (HEW), **Supp. 6,** 130

Health food, **Supp. 5,** 378–79, 452–53. *See also* Diet and nutrition

Health insurance: national advocates, **Supp. 3,** 18; **Supp. 6,** 703; prepayment plans, **Supp. 3,** 122, 313; private, **Supp. 4,** 747; retired people, **Supp. 8,** 10. *See also* Blue Cross and Blue Shield; Insurance

Health-maintenance organizations (HMOs), Kaiser Permanente founding, **Supp. 8,** 309

Health Services, Inc., **Supp. 3,** 122

Healthy Babies Are Happy Babies, **Supp. 7,** 428

Hearing. *See* Audiology; Deaf and deafness

Hearing aids, **Supp. 8,** 209

Hearst, Phoebe Apperson, references to, **Supp. 3,** 144, 626; **Supp. 5,** 283, 284, 287; **Supp. 6,** 353, 438, 463

Hearst, William Randolph: Annenberg relationship, **Supp. 3,** 19–20; Block association, **Supp. 3,** 80; building commissions by, **Supp. 6,** 463, 464; Chandler relationship, **Supp. 3,** 156; circulation war, **Supp. 3,** 19, 144; **Supp. 6,** 686; *Citizen Kane,* **Supp. 3,** 80; **Supp. 5,** 464; critical writings on, **Supp. 4,** 481–82; Davies relationship, **Supp. 7,** 165–66; foreign policy, **Supp. 3,** 397; Fowler relationship, **Supp. 6,** 214; motion picture industry, **Supp. 6,** 440 –41; newspaper interests, **Supp. 3,** 425, 427–28; **Supp. 5,** 456, 657, 658; political interests, **Supp. 8,** 207, 320; Pulitzer rivalry, **Supp. 5,** 551; references to, **Supp. 3,** 718; **Supp. 4,** 62, 404, 644, 872; **Supp. 5,** 244, 323; von Wiegand relationship, **Supp. 7,** 758–59

Heart: electrocardiography, **Supp. 6,** 117; first surgery on valve, **Supp. 4,** 209; inorganic salts to maintain beat of, **Supp. 3,** 369; research on, **Supp. 3,** 806; studies of the, **Vol. 5, Part 2,** 366; **Vol. 7, Part 1,** 120; surgery, **Supp. 7,** 59; ventricular fibrillation, **Supp. 4,** 390

Heart disease: diagnosis of, **Supp. 2,** 84; **Supp. 4,** 494; smoking link, **Supp. 7,** 192

Hearth and Home, **Vol. 8, Part 2,** 352

Heart Is a Lonely Hunter, The, **Supp. 8,** 400, 401

Heat: body studies, **Supp. 3,** 32; cramps, **Supp. 3,** 243; hot-air, **Vol. 3, Part 1,** 549; steam, **Vol. 7, Part 1,** 581; **Vol. 8, Part 1,** 115 f.

"Heathen Chinee," **Vol. 4, Part 2,** 363

Heavenly Discourse, **Supp. 3,** 837

Heavy water, **Supp. 4,** 488–89

Hebras Zion, founding of, **Supp. 3,** 756

Hebrew: Bible, translated into English, **Vol. 5, Part 2,** 2; *Cyclopedia of Biblical Literature,* , **Vol. 8, Part 2,** 165; dictionary, **Vol. 4, Part 1,** 247; language, grammar of, **Vol. 4, Part 1,** 247; **Vol. 7, Part 1,** 87, 547 f.; literature, dictionary of, **Vol. 5, Part 2,** 2; **Vol. 8, Part 2,** 574; literature and language, revival as a spoken language, **Supp. 1,** 407; literature and language, studies in, **Supp. 2,** 145; printing in Philadelphia, **Vol. 6, Part 1,** 137; study of, **Vol. 3, Part 1,** 459 f.; **Vol. 4, Part 2,** 262, 287; **Vol. 7, Part 1,** 118; **Vol. 8, Part 2,** 422, 612; teaching of, **Vol. 4, Part 1,** 560; **Vol. 6, Part 2,** 282; **Vol. 7, Part 1,** 48, 86, 547, 584; technical institute established, **Vol. 6, Part 1,** 155

Hebrew Immigrant Aid Society, founding of, **Supp. 4,** 262

Hebrew Union College (Cincinnati, Ohio), **Vol. 3, Part 1,** 259; **Vol. 5, Part 2,** 488; **Vol. 10, Part 2,** 426; **Supp. 4,** 659, 905

Hebrew University of Jerusalem, first president, **Supp. 4,** 539

Hecht, Ben: MacArthur collaboration, **Supp. 6,** 400–1; references to, **Supp. 5,** 73, 74, 323; **Supp. 6,** 628; **Supp. 7,** 148, 413; **Supp. 8,** 547

Hecla Architectural Iron Works, **Vol. 8, Part 1,** 138 f.

Hedding, Elijah, reference to, **Vol. 9, Part 2,** 321

Heflin, Thomas, reference to, **Supp. 4,** 50

Heidelberg College, founding of, **Vol. 4, Part 1,** 376

Heifetz, Jascha, references to, **Supp. 6,** 352; **Supp. 7,** 124

Heins, George Lewis, reference to, **Supp. 3,** 197

Heins, John, reference to, **Supp. 6,** 397

Heinz Memorial Chapel (Pittsburgh, Pa.), stained glass windows, **Supp. 3,** 183

Heinze, F. A., reference to, **Vol. 9, Part 2,** 589 f.

Heinze-Morse banks, **Vol. 7, Part 1,** 240

Heisenberg, Werner, reference to, **Supp. 7,** 133, 784

Heisman Trophy, first black awarded, **Supp. 7,** 167–68

Helburn, Theresa, reference to, **Supp. 3,** 811

HELCO. *See* Hartford Electric Co.

Helena, Ark., battle of (1863), **Vol. 5, Part 1,** 176; **Vol. 6, Part 2,** 291; **Vol. 8, Part 1,** 188, 216; **Vol. 9, Part 1,** 63

Helena, Mont., state capitol at, **Vol. 9, Part 2,** 589

Helen's Babies, **Vol. 4, Part 2,** 67 f.

Helft, Jacques, reference to, **Supp. 6,** 552

Helical measuring instrument, invention of, **Supp. 1,** 120

Helicon Hall (Englewood, N.J.), **Supp. 6,** 328; **Supp. 8,** 594

Helicopter: development of, **Supp. 5,** 377, 378; first commercial license, **Supp. 6,** 50; invention of, **Vol. 2, Part 2,** 553; **Supp. 1,** 76

Helium, **Supp. 4,** 184; production of, **Vol. 7, Part 1,** 136

Hell Gate, **Vol. 6, Part 1,** 442, 473 f.

Hell Gate Bridge (New York City), **Supp. 6,** 594; **Supp. 7,** 11

Heller, Louis B., reference to, **Supp. 6,** 344

Hellman, Lillian, references to, **Supp. 3,** 315; **Supp. 7,** 314; **Supp. 8,** 704

Hell's Canyon (Idaho), **Supp. 7,** 213, 562

Hellzapoppin, **Supp. 7,** 588–89

Helmle, Frank J., reference to, **Supp. 5,** 133

Helmle and Corbett, **Supp. 5,** 133–34

Helsinki railroad station (Finland), **Supp. 4,** 714

Hematology. *See* Blood

Hemingway, Ernest: first story published, **Supp. 6,** 571; references to, **Supp. 4,** 769; **Supp. 6,** 21; **Supp. 7,** 560

Hemoglobin, **Supp. 4,** 643

Hempstead, Charles S., reference to, **Vol. 10, Part 1,** 504 f.

Henderson, Joseph L., reference to, **Supp. 6,** 512

Henderson, Lawrence J., references to, **Supp. 3,** 137; **Supp. 4,** 565; **Supp. 5,** 122; **Supp. 8,** 50

Henderson, Leon, references to, **Supp. 3,** 660; **Supp. 4,** 458; **Supp. 5,** 558, 559

Henderson, Lightner, reference to, **Supp. 3,** 611–12

Henderson, Richard, reference to, **Vol. 6, Part 1,** 357

Henderson, Yandell, reference to, **Supp. 3,** 163

Heney, Francis J., references to, **Supp. 3,** 394; **Supp. 6,** 590

Henley Royal Regatta (Great Britain), **Supp. 6,** 331

Henri, Robert, references to, **Supp. 2,** 238; **Supp. 3,** 818; **Supp. 5,** 472, 625; **Supp. 7,** 170; **Supp. 8,** 279

Henry, Alexander, reference to, **Vol. 8, Part 1,** 61

Henry, Arthur, reference to, **Supp. 3,** 233–34

Henry, Joseph, references to, **Vol. 1, Part 2,** 150; **Vol. 7, Part 1,** 248 f., 452 f.; **Vol. 10, Part 1,** 618 f.

Henry, O., references to, **Vol. 9, Part 1,** 245; **Supp. 6,** 5

Henry, Patrick, references to, **Vol. 2, Part 2,** 96; **Vol. 5, Part 1,** 118, 537, 597; **Vol. 7, Part 1,** 369, 424, 483; **Vol. 7, Part 2,** 417 f.; **Vol. 9, Part 2,** 332; **Vol. 10, Part 1,** 87 f.

Henry J (automobile), **Supp. 8,** 309

Henry Street Settlement House (New York City), **Supp. 2,** 687; **Supp. 6,** 499; **Supp. 7,** 466; visiting nurse service, **Supp. 6,** 167

Henson, Matthew, reference to, **Supp. 5,** 539

Heparin, **Supp. 3,** 370

Hepburn, Katharine, references to, **Supp. 4,** 55; **Supp. 5,** 296; **Supp. 7,** 682; **Supp. 8,** 659, 660

Hepburn, Katharine Houghton (actress's mother), reference to, **Supp. 5,** 742

Hepburn Act, **Vol. 2, Part 2,** 145, 154; **Vol. 4, Part 2,** 566; **Vol. 8, Part 1,** 248 f.;

Hepburn Rate Act (1906), passage of, **Supp. 1,** 42

Herald of Gospel Liberty, earliest religious newspaper, **Vol. 9, Part 1,** 38, 259

Herbariums, **Vol. 1, Part 2,** 546; **Vol. 3, Part 1,** 538 f., 606 f.; **Vol. 7, Part 1,** 17; **Vol. 8, Part 1,** 104 f.; **Vol. 9, Part 1,** 127; **Supp. 1,** 632; **Supp. 3,** 23, 815; **Supp. 4,** 16–17, 266

Herbart, Johann Friedrich, references to, **Supp. 2,** 424

Herbert, Victor, references to, **Supp. 1,** 222; **Supp. 3,** 553

Herbicides. *See* Pesticides and herbicides

Her Cardboard Lover, **Supp. 3,** 368

Hercules mine, **Vol. 5, Part 1,** 446

Heredity. *See* Genetics

Heresy, **Vol. 8, Part 1,** 127 f., 292 f.; Congregational church, **Vol. 2, Part 1,** 351; Episcopal church, **Vol. 9, Part 2,** 34

Herman Melville, **Supp. 7,** 18

Hermaphroditism, **Supp. 3,** 854

Herndon, Hugh, references to, **Supp. 6,** 52, 493

Herndon, William H., reference to, **Vol. 6, Part 1,** 246 f.

Herne, James A., reference to, **Supp. 4,** 369

Hernia, strangulated, first operation in U.S., **Vol. 10, Part 1,** 480 f.

Heroin, **Supp. 7,** 485

Herold, David E., reference to, **Vol. 1, Part 2,** 449

Herpetology. *See* Reptiles

Herreshoff Motor Co., **Supp. 7,** 245

Herrick, Clarence L., reference to, **Supp. 3,** 172

Herrmann, John, reference to, **Supp. 8,** 255

Herron, George D., reference to, **Vol. 7, Part 1,** 2

Hersey, John, reference to, **Supp. 7,** 114

Hershey, Pa., founding of, **Supp. 3,** 358

Hershfield, Harry, reference to, **Supp. 5,** 18

Herter, Christian, reference to, **Supp. 6,** 350

Hertig, Arthur T., reference to, **Supp. 4,** 802

Hertz, Gustav, reference to, **Supp. 7,** 258

Hertzfeld, Karl, reference to, **Supp. 4,** 337

Hertzsprung, Ejnar, reference to, **Supp. 6,** 561

Herzl, Theodor, references to, **Supp. 2,** 265; **Supp. 4,** 905

Hess, Thomas B., reference to, **Supp. 7,** 260

Hess, V. F., reference to, **Supp. 7,** 134

Hetch Hetchy Valley dam project, **Supp. 4,** 522, 664; **Supp. 5,** 395

Heuer, George J., reference to, **Supp. 3,** 625

HEW. *See* Health, Education, and Welfare, Department of

Hexaphenylethane, **Supp. 4,** 336

Hey, D. H., reference to, **Supp. 6,** 334

Heye Foundation, **Supp. 6,** 289–90

Heyl, Paul, reference to, **Supp. 7,** 76

Heyward, DuBose, reference to, **Supp. 4,** 13

Hiawatha, **Vol. 6, Part 1,** 385; **Vol. 8, Part 1,** 104 f.

Hi-Bred Corn Co., founding of, **Supp. 7,** 760

Hickman, Clarence N., reference to, **Supp. 3,** 306

Hickok, Lorena, references to, **Supp. 7,** 660, 664

Hicks, Elias, reference to, **Vol. 7, Part 1,** 288 f.

Hicks, Sue K., reference to, **Supp. 6,** 528

Hicksite movement, **Vol. 7, Part 1,** 288 f.

Hidatsa Indians, **Supp. 5,** 430

Hieroglyphics, Mayan, **Vol. 1, Part 2,** 492

Higgins, Aldus C., reference to, **Supp. 6,** 27

Higgins, Andrew Jackson, reference to, **Supp. 8,** 603

Higgins, Marguerite, reference to, **Supp. 8,** 520
Higgins Industries, **Supp. 5,** 299
Higginson, T. W., references to, **Vol. 5, Part 1,** 606; **Vol. 8, Part 2,** 522; **Vol. 9, Part 1,** 464
Higher education. *See* Education; Universities and colleges; *specific institutions*
High-fidelity sound, **Supp. 5,** 324. *See also* Audio systems
High-frequency transmission, **Supp. 3,** 748, 768–69
High Noon, **Supp. 7,** 143–44
High Voltage Engineering Corporation, **Supp. 8,** 000
Highways. *See* Road building
Hildebrand, George, reference to, **Supp. 6,** 663
Hilgard, J. E., reference to, **Vol. 7, Part 1,** 452 f.
Hill, A. P., reference to, **Vol. 6, Part 1,** 125 f.
Hill, Archibald V., reference to, **Supp. 5,** 489
Hill, Adams Sherman, reference to, **Vol. 10, Part 1,** 649 f.
Hill, B. H., reference to, **Supp. 4,** 144
Hill, Cumorah, reference to, **Vol. 9, Part 1,** 310
Hill, D. H., reference to, **Vol. 6, Part 1,** 124
Hill, David B., reference to, **Vol. 7, Part 2,** 213
Hill, James J., references to, **Vol. 2, Part 2,** 233; **Vol. 7, Part 1,** 177, 299; **Vol. 9, Part 1,** 52; **Supp. 3,** 381, 735, 736, 823; **Supp. 7,** 89
Hill, Joe, reference to, **Supp. 7,** 248
Hill, John Alexander, reference to, **Supp. 4,** 523
Hill, Percival, reference to, **Supp. 4,** 370, 371
Hill and Knowlton, **Supp. 5,** 271
Hillman, Sidney, references to, **Supp. 4,** 75, 356, 458; **Supp. 6,** 378; **Supp. 7,** 172
Hillsborough, battle of, **Vol. 4, Part 1,** 571
Hillsboro Mob (N.C.), **Vol. 10, Part 1,** 26
Hill School, history of, **Vol. 6, Part 2,** 505
Hillsdale College, presidency of, **Vol. 3, Part 2,** 257
Himes, Norman E., reference to, **Supp. 6,** 602
Hines, Duncan, Foundation, **Supp. 6,** 292
Hines, James J., reference to, **Supp. 5,** 665
Hinks, Arthur Robert, reference to, **Supp. 6,** 560
Hiram College, **Vol. 5, Part 1,** 66; **Vol. 4, Part 2,** 438
Hiroshima and Nagasaki, atomic bombing of, **Supp. 8,** 230, 231
Hispanic American Historical Review, founding of, **Supp. 5,** 577
Hispanic-Americans, historical writings on, **Supp. 5,** 77, 577
Hispanic Review, founding of, **Supp. 2,** 132
Hiss, Alger, references to, **Supp. 5,** 19, 665; **Supp. 7,** 114
Histology, **Vol. 3, Part 2,** 201; research in, **Supp. 6,** 295–96
Historical fiction, **Supp. 3,** 93; **Supp. 4,** 13–14, 163–65, 583; **Supp. 5,** 266–67, 297–98, 620, 747–48; **Supp. 6,** 544, 544–46; **Supp. 7,** 148; **Supp. 8,** 180–82
Historical Geography in the United States, **Supp. 4,** 113
Historical materials, collections of, **Vol. 3, Part 2,** 559; **Vol. 7, Part 1,** 351; **Vol. 9, Part 1,** 538
Historical Outlook, founding of, **Supp. 2,** 419
Historical Records Survey, **Supp. 2,** 40
Historical societies: Georgia, **Supp. 1,** 472; Jewish, **Supp. 1,** 473
Historical Society of Pennsylvania, **Vol. 8, Part 1,** 401; **Vol. 10, Part 1,** 546
Historic sites and buildings: Alabama, **Supp. 1,** 591; California missions, **Supp. 3,** 88; Dearborn, Mich., museums, **Supp. 4,** 302; Death Valley, **Supp. 5,** 613; Fossil Cycad National Monument, **Supp. 5,** 743–44; Japanese preservation, **Supp. 5,** 730; Jefferson Memorial, **Supp. 4,** 448; La Villita (San Antonio, Tex.) restoration, **Supp. 5,** 481; Lincoln Memorial, **Supp. 1,** 322; New England preservations and resto-

rations, **Supp. 3,** 567; **Supp. 4,** 24; photography of, **Supp. 5,** 373; Rockefeller endowments, **Supp. 6,** 549; Roosevelt, Theodore, homes, **Supp. 7,** 311; Washington, D.C., restorations, **Supp. 7,** 425; Washington Monument, **Supp. 1,** 157; Williamsburg restoration, **Supp. 1,** 165; **Supp. 4,** 696; **Supp. 5,** 388
Historiography, **Supp. 5,** 557
History *(see also specific subjects):* American, ancient, **Supp. 6,** 612; American, colonial, **Supp. 3,** 15–16; American, writings on, **Supp. 1,** 166, 673, **Supp. 2,** 495; **Supp. 4,** 3–4; **Supp. 5,** 234–35; **Supp. 8,** 552, 580; American banking and politics study, **Supp. 8,** 243; American bibliography, **Supp. 8,** 663–64; American cultural, **Supp. 3,** 672–73; American diplomatic studies, **Supp. 7,** 683–84; American frontier, writings on, **Supp. 7,** 771–72; **Supp. 8,** 60; American intellectual, writings on, **Supp. 8,** 271–74; American political and constitutional, **Supp. 3,** 336–37; American regional, **Supp. 5,** 320–21; American social, **Supp. 3,** 287; **Supp. 6,** 696–97; American social, writings on, **Supp. 7,** 79–80, 741–42; **Supp. 8,** 692, 693; American studies, **Supp. 5,** 5–10, 667; American West, writings on, **Supp. 5,** 169; ancient civilizations studies, **Supp. 5,** 595–96; ancient slave systems, **Supp. 5,** 736; black, **Supp. 4,** 911; **Supp. 5,** 642; **Supp. 6,** 490; British, writings on, **Supp. 8,** 472–73, 580; Civil War and Reconstruction era, writings on, **Supp. 5,** 498; comparative, **Supp. 4,** 824; constitutional, **Supp. 4,** 530–31; cycles in, **Supp. 7,** 677; economic, teaching of, **Supp. 4,** 322; economic interpretation of, **Supp. 4,** 61–64; editing of, **Supp. 3,** 262, 285–86, 287, 337; **Supp. 7,** 253; Elizabethan English, **Supp. 6,** 531–32; European, **Supp. 4,** 162; European, writings on, **Supp. 2,** 564; **Supp. 7,** 517–18; **Supp. 8,** 50; geographic interpretation of, **Supp. 1,** 119; "great man" theory of, **Supp. 6,** 279; Hawaiian studies, **Supp. 7,** 445–46; intellectual, **Supp. 3,** 47; **Supp. 7,** 482; **Supp. 8,** 51; interdisciplinary studies, **Supp. 8,** 271–73; Latin American studies, **Supp. 5,** 577; **Supp. 6,** 277–78; medieval studies, **Supp. 1,** 285, 705; **Supp. 3,** 765–66; **Supp. 7,** 741–42; modern nationalism studies, **Supp. 7,** 329–30; multiple causation of human progress theory, **Supp. 4,** 413; new approach to, **Vol. 10, Part 1,** 63 f.; new social sciences approach to, **Supp. 2,** 564–66; **Supp. 4,** 62, 152, 162, 824; **Supp. 8,** 50; original documents, **Supp. 2,** 40; **Supp. 4,** 1–2; pageants about, **Supp. 3,** 427; popular writings on, **Supp. 3,** 790; **Supp. 4,** 116, 368; pre-Islamic civilization, **Supp. 3,** 572–73; Quaker, **Supp. 4,** 441–42; quantitative approach to, **Supp. 5,** 429–30; relativism in, **Supp. 3,** 47–48; research in field of, **Vol. 2, Part 1,** 63; **Vol. 6, Part 1,** 68; **Vol. 8, Part 2,** 137 f., 276; **Vol. 10, Part 1,** 603 f.; revisionism, **Supp. 3,** 555; revisionist Civil War, **Supp. 5,** 557–58; revisionist World War I, **Supp. 7,** 735; **Supp. 8,** 169; socialist interpretation of, **Supp. 4,** 746–47; source material, early use of, **Vol. 10, Part 1,** 603 f.; source standards, **Supp. 3,** 285–86; South (U.S.), **Supp. 3,** 31–32; **Supp. 5,** 671–72; **Supp. 6,** 491–92; Spanish-American, **Supp. 5,** 77, 570; Spanish influence on American, **Supp. 2,** 561; state commissions, **Supp. 4,** 176; teaching of, **Vol. 1, Part 1,** 70, 314; **Vol. 4, Part 1,** 568 f.; **Vol. 4, Part 2,** 18, 57, 116,; **Vol. 5, Part 1,** 178, 244, 277; **Vol. 5, Part 2,** 241; **Vol. 7, Part 1,** 239, 274 f., 330 f.; **Vol. 8, Part 2,** 486; **Vol. 9, Part 1,** 214, 221, 314, 316, 430, 578; **Vol. 10, Part 1,** 92 f.; **Vol. 10, Part 2,** 2; **Supp. 2,** 563; **Supp. 3,** 287; **Supp. 6,** 491; **Supp. 7,** 329–30, 684–85, 770; textbooks, **Supp. 1,** 484; **Supp. 2,** 564; **Supp. 6,** 278; **Supp. 7,** 568; women's studies programs, **Supp. 6,**

2, 256; Greenbank, **Vol. 8, Part 1,** 84; Green Bottom, **Vol. 5, Part 2,** 43; Greenfield, **Vol. 8, Part 1,** 237; Green Hill, **Vol. 8, Part 1,** 604; Greenway, **Vol. 6, Part 1,** 88; Greenwich House, **Vol. 10, Part 1,** 485 f.; Greystone, **Vol. 9, Part 2,** 541; Grove, The (N.C.), **Vol. 5, Part 2,** 210; Grove, The (N.Y.), **Vol. 10, Part 1,** 421 f.; Gunston Hall, **Vol. 5, Part 2,** 360; Habrede-Venture, **Vol. 9, Part 2,** 84; Hampden Place, **Vol. 8, Part 1,** 644; Hampton Plantation, **Vol. 8, Part 1,** 395; Hare Forest, **Vol. 9, Part 2,** 349; Hayes, **Vol. 5, Part 2,** 150; Hayfield, **Vol. 5, Part 2,** 203; **Vol. 9, Part 1,** 127; Hazelfield, **Vol. 10, Part 1,** 37; Hazelwood, **Vol. 9, Part 2,** 331; Hermitage, **Vol. 5, Part 1,** 527 f.; **Vol. 8, Part 1,** 36; **Vol. 9, Part 2,** 366, 564; **Vol. 10, Part 1,** 156; Highland Grove, **Vol. 5, Part 2,** 282; Hill Crest, **Vol. 9, Part 2,** 395; Hill of the Painted Men, **Vol. 8, Part 1,** 120; Hobcaw, **Vol. 8, Part 1,** 425; Homus, **Vol. 8, Part 1,** 202; Hope, **Vol. 9, Part 2,** 72; Indian Hill Farm, **Vol. 8, Part 1,** 73; Jessamine Hill, **Vol. 10, Part 1,** 641 f.; Johnson Hall, **Vol. 5, Part 2,** 104, 127; Kalorama, **Vol. 1, Part 2,** 427; Kenmore, **Vol. 6, Part 1,** 214; King's Bend, **Vol. 5, Part 2,** 407; La Belle Knoll, **Vol. 10, Part 1,** 414; Lang Syne, **Vol. 6, Part 1,** 605; Landsdowne, **Vol. 5, Part 2,** 68; Laudamus Farm, **Vol. 8, Part 1,** 614; Leesylvania, **Vol. 6, Part 1,** 107, 117; Levinworth Manor, **Vol. 8, Part 1,** 149; Liberty Hall, **Vol. 5, Part 2,** 11, 326; Liendo, **Vol. 7, Part 1,** 95, 479; Lindenhurst, **Vol. 10, Part 1,** 407 f.; Lindenshade, **Vol. 5, Part 2,** 13; Lindenwald, **Vol. 10, Part 1,** 156; Lipona, **Vol. 7, Part 1,** 339; Little Versailles, **Vol. 1, Part 1,** 130; Longwood, **Vol. 8, Part 1,** 192; Low Foxton, **Vol. 8, Part 1,** 247; Magnolia Plantation, **Vol. 10, Part 1,** 457 f.; Malmaison, **Vol. 6, Part 1,** 144; Mansfield, **Vol. 10, Part 1,** 552 f.; Mansion House, **Vol. 8, Part 2,** 186; Maplewood, **Vol. 3, Part 1,** 522; Marshes Seat, **Vol. 10, Part 1,** 604 f.; Matoax, **Vol. 8, Part 1,** 363; **Vol. 10, Part 1,** 32, 36, 38; Mattaponi, **Vol. 1, Part 2,** 511; Meadow Farm, **Vol. 9, Part 2,** 349; Meadow Garden, **Vol. 10, Part 1,** 403 f.; Menokin, **Vol. 6, Part 1,** 105; Meridian Hill, **Vol. 8, Part 1,** 84; Millwood, **Vol. 4, Part 2,** 213; Monmouth Plantation, **Vol. 8, Part 1,** 316; Montgomery Place, **Vol. 6, Part 1,** 312; Monticello, **Vol. 5, Part 2,** 18, 26, 34, 222; **Vol. 6, Part 1,** 52, 204; **Vol. 7, Part 1,** 10, 88, 487; **Vol. 8, Part 1,** 358, 369, 371; **Vol. 9, Part 2,** 526; Montpelier, **Vol. 9, Part 2,** 393; Morven, **Vol. 9, Part 2,** 46 f.; Morven Park, **Vol. 9, Part 2,** 238; Mount Airy, **Vol. 9, Part 1,** 171; Mount Lowe, **Vol. 6, Part 1,** 453; Mount Pitt, **Vol. 5, Part 2,** 200; Mount Radnor, **Vol. 9, Part 2,** 442; Mount Vernon, **Vol. 2, Part 2,** 601; **Vol. 3, Part 2,** 225; **Vol. 7, Part 1,** 297; **Vol. 8, Part 1,** 604; **Vol. 8, Part 2,** 292; **Vol. 10, Part 1,** 508 f.; Mount Welcome, **Vol. 5, Part 2,** 146; Needham, **Vol. 9, Part 2,** 320; Needwood, **Vol. 6, Part 1,** 132; New Hope, **Vol. 10, Part 1,** 641 f.; Oak Grove, **Vol. 5, Part 2,** 148; Oak Lawn, **Vol. 8, Part 1,** 82; Ogontz, **Vol. 7, Part 1,** 432; Old Ironsides, **Vol. 9, Part 2,** 7; Old Place, **Vol. 8, Part 1,** 256; Ophir Farm, **Vol. 8, Part 1,** 484; Ophir Place, **Vol. 5, Part 1,** 142; Pembroke, **Vol. 7, Part 1,** 384; Pine Grove, **Vol. 10, Part 1,** 406 f.; Pines, The, **Vol. 9, Part 2,** 514; Plantation, **Vol. 5, Part 2,** 421; Polk Place, **Vol. 8, Part 1,** 38; Pontine, **Vol. 5, Part 2,** 163; Pooshee, **Vol. 8, Part 1,** 396; Poplar Grove, **Vol. 9, Part 2,** 584; Poplar Mount, **Vol. 3, Part 2,** 45; Popodickon, **Vol. 8, Part 1,** 137; Port Tobago, **Vol. 6, Part 1,** 369; Poynton Manor, **Vol. 9, Part 2,** 84; Ravenhill, **Vol. 10, Part 1,** 607 f.; Retreat, **Vol. 5, Part 2,** 403; **Vol. 9, Part 2,** 138; Rion Hall, **Vol. 6, Part 1,** 483; Rippon Lodge, **Vol. 10, Part 1,** 508 f.; Roanoke, **Vol. 8, Part**

1, 366; Rock Castle, **Vol. 9, Part 1,** 254; Rosemount, **Vol. 5, Part 2,** 348; **Vol. 9, Part 2,** 395; Rosewell, **Vol. 7, Part 2,** 138 f.; Rosmont, **Vol. 9, Part 2,** 651; Runnymede, **Vol. 8, Part 1,** 238; Sabot Hill, **Vol. 8, Part 2,** 545; Sevenels, **Vol. 6, Part 1,** 453; Shad, The, **Vol. 7, Part 1,** 629; Shadwell, **Vol. 7, Part 1,** 10; Shady Hill, **Vol. 7, Part 1,** 569; Sherwood Forest, **Vol. 10, Part 1,** 91; Sidney, **Vol. 9, Part 1,** 344; Silk Hope, **Vol. 5, Part 2,** 111; Slate-roof House, **Vol. 7, Part 1,** 554 f.; Smithfield, **Vol. 8, Part 1,** 206 f.; Soldier's Retreat, **Vol. 1, Part 1,** 271; Springfields, **Vol. 9, Part 2,** 340; Spring Garden, **Vol. 8, Part 1,** 643; Spring Hill, **Vol. 10, Part 1,** 552 f.; Stenton, **Vol. 6, Part 1,** 359, 362; Stepney, **Vol. 5, Part 2,** 42; Stratford, **Vol. 6, Part 1,** 96, 105, 108 f., 116 f., 120, 132; Summerton Plantation, **Vol. 8, Part 1,** 395; Sunnyside, **Vol. 5, Part 1,** 504, 511; Tazewell Hall, **Vol. 8, Part 1,** 353, 362, 367, 372; Terra Rubra, **Vol. 5, Part 2,** 362; Torch Hill, **Vol. 9, Part 2,** 525; Town Head, **Vol. 9, Part 2,** 361; Trotwood, **Vol. 7, Part 1,** 132; Tuckahoe, **Vol. 8, Part 1,** 370, 372; Turkey Island, **Vol. 8, Part 1,** 361, 371 f.; Turrets, **Vol. 8, Part 1,** 210 f.; Turtle Bay, **Vol. 8, Part 1,** 19 f.; Vernon House, **Vol. 1, Part 2,** 512; Wakefield, **Vol. 9, Part 2,** 139; **Vol. 10, Part 1,** 509 f.; Waln-Grove, **Vol. 10, Part 1,** 387 f.; Walnut Grove, **Vol. 6, Part 1,** 607, 610 f.; Wantoot, **Vol. 8, Part 1,** 394; Warner Hall, **Vol. 6, Part 1,** 214; Wayside, **Vol. 6, Part 1,** 425; Wehaw, **Vol. 5, Part 2,** 414; Wellston, **Vol. 10, Part 1,** 638 f.; Westover, **Vol. 6, Part 1,** 558; Whitehall, **Vol. 9, Part 1,** 26; White House (Boston), **Vol. 1, Part 1,** 73; White House of Confederacy, **Vol. 7, Part 1,** 11; Willington, **Vol. 8, Part 1,** 542; Willowbrook, **Vol. 9, Part 2,** 511; Wilson Park, **Vol. 10, Part 1,** 470 f.; Windsor Forest, **Vol. 10, Part 1,** 528 f.; Wood End, **Vol. 8, Part 1,** 247; Wormsloe, **Vol. 5, Part 2,** 197; Wye House, **Vol. 6, Part 1,** 331; **Vol. 7, Part 1,** 505 f.

Homestead strike (1892), **Vol. 4, Part 2,** 27; **Supp. 3,** 94

"Home, Sweet Home," writing of, **Vol. 7, Part 2,** 328

Homiletics, **Vol. 8, Part 1,** 89 f.; teaching of, **Vol. 9, Part 1,** 201; writings on, **Vol. 6, Part 1,** 552; **Vol. 8, Part 1,** 13 f., 89 f., 374

Homosexuality, psychiatric view of, **Supp. 4,** 808

Honduras, **Vol. 1, Part 2,** 62; "interoceanic railway," survey for, **Vol. 5, Part 2,** 14

Hone, Philip, **Vol. 5, Part 1,** 503; diary of, **Vol. 5, Part 2,** 393

Honolulu, education in, **Vol. 7, Part 1,** 5

Honolulu Advertiser, **Vol. 9, Part 2,** 517

Honolulu Star Bulletin, **Supp. 5,** 216

"Honor system," in education, **Vol. 5, Part 2,** 148; **Vol. 10, Part 1,** 32

Hook, Charles R., reference to, **Supp. 3,** 781

Hooker, Joseph, references to, **Vol. 5, Part 1,** 559; **Vol. 6, Part 1,** 125; **Vol. 9, Part 1,** 217

Hooker Electrochemical Co., **Supp. 3,** 26

Hookworm, **Supp. 3,** 738; **Supp. 5,** 232, 605; eradication of, **Supp. 1,** 639; pathogenicity of, **Supp. 1,** 33; study of, **Vol. 4, Part 2,** 45

Hooper, Ben W., reference to, **Supp. 3,** 449

Hooperating, **Supp. 5,** 310–11

Hoor, G. F., reference to, **Vol. 7, Part 1,** 571

Hoosac Tunnel (Mass.), **Vol. 3, Part 1,** 251, 334; **Vol. 4, Part 2,** 400; **Vol. 6, Part 1,** 37; **Vol. 7, Part 1,** 297; **Vol. 7, Part 2,** 329; **Vol. 8, Part 2,** 592; **Vol. 9, Part 2,** 99

Hoosiers, The, **Supp. 4,** 629

"Hootchy Kootchy" dance, **Supp. 4,** 88

Hoover, Herbert C., **Vol. 5, Part 1,** 609; **Vol. 9, Part 2,** 372; Barnes, J. H., relationship, **Supp. 6,** 36–37;

Belgian relief, **Vol. 9, Part 2,** 477; bonus marchers, **Supp. 6,** 240; family, **Supp. 8,** 275; food relief administration, **Supp. 3,** 622; **Supp. 4,** 699; foreign relations, **Supp. 6,** 187; **Supp. 7,** 112; German reparations moratorium, **Supp. 6,** 188; Haiti, commission on, **Supp. 6,** 211; Herter relationship, **Supp. 8,** 257; Hinshaw relationship, **Supp. 5,** 304; presidential candidacy, **Supp. 3,** 720; **Supp. 5,** 442; **Supp. 7,** 86; presidential policies, **Supp. 3,** 646–47; references to, **Supp. 7,** 85, 488; Sullivan, M., relationship, **Supp. 5,** 667; Wilbur relationship, **Supp. 4,** 892, 893, 894; writings on, **Supp. 6,** 601

Hoover, J. Edgar, references to, **Supp. 4,** 794; **Supp. 5,** 590; **Supp. 8,** 322, 323, 335

Hoover Commissions on the Organization of the Executive Branch of the Government, **Supp. 6,** 692

Hoover Dam (Boulder Dam), **Supp. 3,** 397, 814; **Supp. 4,** 198; **Supp. 6,** 182, 507; **Supp. 7,** 360; construction, **Supp. 8,** 308; design and engineering, **Supp. 8,** 573

Hoover International Corporation, predecessor, **Supp. 5,** 313–14

Hoover Library, development of, **Supp. 2,** 40

Hoover's Gap, Tenn., operations at (June 1863), **Vol. 8, Part 1,** 521

Hoover War Library, **Supp. 1,** 9

Hope-Aiken Watershed Act (1953), **Supp. 8,** 278

Hopedale Community, Mass., **Vol. 1, Part 1,** 556 f.; **Vol. 3, Part 1,** 435

Hope Institute, **Vol. 3, Part 2,** 269

Hopewell, Hudson's ship, **Vol. 5, Part 1,** 338

Hopi Indians, **Supp. 6,** 720; linguistic studies of, **Supp. 3,** 820

Hopkins, Arthur, references to, **Supp. 5,** 375; **Supp. 6,** 65

Hopkins, Harry: references to, **Supp. 3,** 646, 652, 653, 654; **Supp. 4,** 578; **Supp. 5,** 515, 642; **Supp. 6,** 601, 660, 661; **Supp. 7,** 787; **Supp. 8,** 176, 301; writings on, **Supp. 5,** 624

Hopkins, Johns, references to, **Vol. 1, Part 2,** 267; **Vol. 7, Part 1,** 24

Hopkins, Lemuel, reference to, **Vol. 7, Part 1,** 559

Hopkins, Mark, references to, **Vol. 3, Part 2,** 372; **Vol. 7, Part 1,** 5

"Hopkinsianism," **Vol. 5, Part 1,** 217

Hopkinson, Joseph, reference to, **Vol. 8, Part 2,** 588

Hopper, DeWolf, reference to, **Supp. 6,** 305

Hopper, Edward, references to, **Supp. 5,** 493, 636; **Supp. 8,** 339

Hopper, Hedda, reference to, **Supp. 7,** 143

Hopson, Howard, reference to, **Supp. 3,** 138

Hopwood, Avery, reference to, **Supp. 6,** 543

Horgan, Paul, reference to, **Supp. 3,** 848

"Horizontal Bill," **Vol. 7, Part 1,** 233

Hormel, Jay Catherwood, reference to, **Supp. 4,** 396

Hormel and Co., **Supp. 4,** 395–96; **Supp. 5,** 314–15

Hormones: adrenalin synthesis, **Supp. 5,** 149; discovery of, in pure form, **Vol. 9, Part 2,** 275; oral contraceptives, **Supp. 8,** 503; ovarian, **Supp. 2,** 51; sex-related, **Supp. 4,** 460, 498; steroid, **Supp. 5,** 28. *See also* Endocrine glands; *specific hormones*

Hornaday, William Temple, reference to, **Supp. 3,** 229

Hornbeck, Stanley K., references to, **Supp. 6,** 269, 270; **Supp. 7,** 112, 303

"Hornblower, Horatio" (fictional character), **Supp. 8,** 182

Horne, F. J., reference to, **Supp. 6,** 339

Horne, Herbert P., reference to, **Supp. 3,** 785

Horner, Henry, reference to, **Supp. 4,** 451

Hornet, **Vol. 9, Part 2,** 7

Horney, Karen, reference to, **Supp. 7,** 6

Horney, Karen, Clinic (New York City), founding of, **Supp. 5,** 317

Horowitz, David, reference to, **Supp. 3,** 143

Horse-car lines, New York City, **Vol. 6, Part 1,** 40

Horse racing: gambling circuits, **Supp. 3,** 20; horse breeding and training, **Supp. 5,** 567, 569, 757; **Supp. 7,** 399–401, 695–96; **Supp. 8,** 174–75, 263–64, 299, 367, 566; jockeys, **Supp. 8,** 565, 566; modernization, **Supp. 8,** 76; officials, **Supp. 8,** 75–76; pari-mutuel betting, **Supp. 1,** 114; radio broadcasts, **Supp. 7,** 494–95; stable ownership, **Supp. 8,** 13. *See also* Harness racing

Horses: blankets, manufacture of, **Vol. 4, Part 1,** 380; breeding of, **Vol. 3, Part 2,** 459, **Vol. 4, Part 2,** 84, 454; **Vol. 5, Part 1,** 562; **Vol. 5, Part 2,** 441; **Vol. 7, Part 1,** 145, 182 f., 425 f.; **Vol. 8, Part 1,** 456; **Vol. 8, Part 2,** 335 f.; **Vol. 9, Part 1,** 200; **Vol. 10, Part 1,** 373 f.; paintings of, **Vol. 7, Part 1,** 373; **Vol. 8, Part 1,** 497; **Vol. 10, Part 1,** 1 f.; Percheron, introduction of, **Vol. 10, Part 1,** 400 f.; railroads, early use of as motive power, **Vol. 3, Part 1,** 258; statues of, **Vol. 8, Part 2,** 222; trotting, **Vol. 10, Part 1,** 373 f.; wild, taming of, **Vol. 8, Part 1,** 385; writings on, **Vol. 7, Part 1,** 132; **Vol. 8, Part 1,** 385; **Vol. 10, Part 1,** 2, 373 f.

Horses, race, **Vol. 3, Part 1,** 213; **Vol. 3, Part 2,** 545; **Vol. 4, Part 1,** 206; **Vol. 5, Part 1,** 20; **Vol. 5, Part 2,** 130 f., 283; **Vol. 8, Part 1,** 107 f.; **Vol. 8, Part 2,** 505; **Vol. 9, Part 1,** 211 f.; **Vol. 9, Part 2,** 365 f.; **Vol. 10, Part 1,** 373 f.; American horses in English and French races, **Vol. 3, Part 1,** 552 f.; antibetting legislation, **Vol. 3, Part 1,** 552 f.; breeding for racing in Kentucky, **Vol. 6, Part 1,** 411 f.; **Vol. 6, Part 2,** 180; importation from England, drug-detection tests for, **Supp. 8,** 76; evolutionary studies of, **Supp. 1,** 340; **Vol. 3, Part 1,** 213; **Vol. 9, Part 2,** 641; training of, **Supp. 8,** 174–75. *See also* Horse racing

Horse Shoe Bend, battle of. *See* Creek war in Alabama, 1813

Horseshoe nails, manufacture of, **Vol. 3, Part 1,** 547 f.

Horsley, Victor, reference to, **Supp. 3,** 201

Horticulture (general), **Vol. 1, Part 1,** 56, 246, 655; **Vol. 2, Part 1,** 237, 251, 327, 453; **Vol. 2, Part 2,** 184, 380; **Vol. 3, Part 1,** 177, 417 f., 419; **Vol. 4, Part 1,** 53 f., 98, 144, 359, 398, 557; **Vol. 4, Part 2,** 229, 236, 312, 356, 530; **Vol. 5, Part 1,** 24, 272, 305, 380 f.; **Vol. 5, Part 2,** 341; **Vol. 6, Part 1,** 287, 363, 393 f.; **Vol. 6, Part 2,** 137, 492, 637; **Vol. 7, Part 1,** 315, 335 f., 405 f.; **Vol. 7, Part 2,** 248, 464; **Vol. 8, Part 1,** 145 f., 229 f., 233 f.; **Vol. 8, Part 2,** 64, 90, 92, 144, 160, 354, 355, 361, 383 f., 401; **Vol. 9, Part 2,** 147, 514, 596, 597; **Vol. 10, Part 1,** 68, 444 f.; **Vol. 10, Part 2,** 123; blackberry raising, **Vol. 6, Part 1,** 363; chemical solutions, **Supp. 3,** 247; citrus fruits, **Vol. 4, Part 2,** 356; commercial nurseries, **Supp. 1,** 594; desert plants, study of, **Vol. 9, Part 1,** 427; development as science, **Supp. 5,** 30–31; ferns, **Vol. 3, Part 1,** 606 f.; **Vol. 10, Part 1,** 116; fig growing, **Vol. 8, Part 2,** 91; fruit-growing, Oregon, **Vol. 6, Part 1,** 498; grape culture, **Vol. 3, Part 1,** 491; **Vol. 8, Part 2,** 93; home-gardening promotion, **Supp. 4,** 564; hybridization, **Vol. 1, Part 2,** 26; **Vol. 8, Part 2,** 93; **Supp. 4,** 357; **Supp. 5,** 629; jalap plant, introduction of, **Vol. 2, Part 2,** 487; landscape gardening, **Supp. 6,** 196; lemon, **Vol. 4, Part 1,** 145; medicinal plants, **Supp. 3,** 433; nurseries, **Vol. 1, Part 2,** 192; **Vol. 5, Part 2,** 341; **Vol. 8, Part 1,** 233; **Vol. 9, Part 1,** 146; orchids, **Vol. 4, Part 2,** 229; organizations, **Supp. 1,** 541; pathology studies, **Supp. 3,** 400–1; plant breeding, **Supp. 4,** 862–63; plant diseases, **Supp. 1,** 462; **Supp. 2,** 215; plant growth measurement, **Supp. 6**, 69; plant illustrations, **Supp. 1**, 121; plant introduction gardens, **Supp. 5**, 214; plant physiology, **Supp. 4**, 192, 500–1; **Supp. 6**, 176; plants, scientific study of, **Vol. 7, Part 1**, 606 f.; **Vol. 7, Part 1**, 266 f.; **Vol. 7, Part 2**, 480 f.; **Vol. 8, Part 1**, 154 f., 233, 236 f., 239 f.; **Vol. 8, Part 2**, 309; **Vol. 9, Part 1**, 263, 458; **Vol. 9, Part 2**, 477, 596; **Vol. 10, Part 2**, 321; poinsettia, **Vol. 8, Part 1**, 30 f.; pomology, **Vol. 2, Part 1**, 48; **Vol. 2, Part 2**, 489; **Vol. 3, Part 1**, 418 f.; **Vol. 4, Part 1**, 261; **Vol. 6, Part 1**, 535; **Vol. 6, Part 2**, 252; **Vol. 8, Part 1**, 145; **Vol. 9, Part 2**, 439; rose growing, **Supp. 4**, 194–95; **Supp. 5**, 555; strawberry cultivation, **Vol. 5, Part 1**, 272; **Vol. 6, Part 1**, 394; tomatoes disease resistant, **Vol. 8, Part 1**, 239 f.; water culture, **Supp. 4**, 382; writings on, **Vol. 2, Part 1**, 49, 236, 266 f.; **Vol. 2, Part 2**, 489; **Vol. 3, Part 1**, 177, 418. 419; **Vol. 4, Part 1**, 53, 144, 398, 557; **Vol. 4, Part 2**, 530; **Vol. 5, Part 1**, 272; **Vol. 5, Part 2**, 341, 572; **Vol. 8, Part 1**, 233 f.; **Vol. 8, Part 2**, 84; **Vol. 10, Part 1**, 36, 444 f.; **Vol. 10, Part 2**, 123. *See also* Botanic gardens; Herbariums; *specific garden names*

Horticulture (by state): California, **Vol. 1, Part 2**, 599; **Vol. 4, Part 2**, 229; **Vol. 5, Part 2**, 300; **Vol. 6, Part 1**, 162, 481, 498; **Vol. 8, Part 1**, 145; **Vol. 8, Part 2**, 90, **Vol. 9, Part 1**, 548; **Vol. 10, Part 2**, 184; Connecticut, **Vol. 1, Part 2**, 599; Florida, **Vol. 4, Part 2**, 356; Louisiana, **Vol. 8, Part 1**, 589; Massachusetts, **Vol. 1, Part 2**, 319; **Vol. 10, Part 2**, 210; Michigan, **Vol. 6, Part 1**, 535 f.; New Mexico, **Vol. 8, Part 1**, 229 f.; New York, **Vol. 9, Part 2**, 439; Pennsylvania, **Vol. 7, Part 2**, 452; Texas, **Vol. 6, Part 2**, 482; **Vol. 7, Part 1**, 335 f.

Horton, George Plant, reference to, **Supp. 6**, 262
Horton, Henry H., reference to, **Supp. 3**, 449
Hospital for the Ruptured and Crippled (New York City), **Supp. 4**, 887
Hospital for the Women of Maryland, founding of, **Supp. 1**, 437
Hospitals, **Vol. 4, Part 1**, 301; **Vol. 8, Part 1**, 213 f.; **Vol. 9, Part 2**, 85; blacks', **Supp. 5**, 104; building architecture, **Supp. 5**, 301; children's wards, **Vol. 8, Part 1**, 317 f.; design and services, **Supp. 3**, 312; in Thailand, **Supp. 3**, 486; medically trained administrators, **Supp. 3**, 312; mental, **Supp. 1**, 243; **Supp. 2**, 711–12; **Supp. 3**, 50–51, 102; **Supp. 4**, 571; military, **Vol. 2, Part 2**, 251 f.; **Vol. 5, Part 1**, 109; **Vol. 7, Part 1**, 409; **Vol. 9, Part 2**, 550, 584; nurses aides, **Supp. 4**, 93; patients' records, **Supp. 5**, 111; pediatric, **Supp. 3**, 74–75; **Supp. 5**, 1–2; philanthropy, **Supp. 3**, 435; social work, **Supp. 6**, 97–98; tuberculosis, **Supp. 7**, 251; women's, **Supp. 1**, 437. *See also specific hospital names*
Hospital ship, for fishermen at sea, **Vol. 8, Part 2**, 313
Hotchkiss School, **Vol. 2, Part 1**, 237
Hot dog, baseball concession fare, **Supp. 7**, 719
Hotel management, **Vol. 1, Part 1**, 102, 639; **Vol. 1, Part 2**, 418; **Vol. 3, Part 1**, 431; **Vol. 3, Part 2**, 452; **Vol. 4, Part 1**, 318, 331; **Vol. 5, Part 2**, 169, 528; **Vol. 6, Part 2**, 279; **Vol. 7, Part 1**, 7, 482; **Vol. 7, Part 2**, 191; **Vol. 8, Part 1**, 115 f.; **Vol. 8, Part 2**, 98; **Vol. 9, Part 1**, 537, 596 f.; Chicago, **Vol. 3, Part 1**, 431; New York, **Vol. 1, Part 1**, 400 f.; **Vol. 1, Part 2**, 149
Hotels: architecture, **Vol. 8, Part 2**, 99; building of, **Vol. 4, Part 2**, 240; **Vol. 8, Part 2**, 98; development of, **Supp. 1**, 272; labor movement, **Supp. 6**, 598; modern, **Vol. 1, Part 2**, 419; nature resorts, **Supp. 1**, 554; Wright design, **Supp. 6**, 713
Hot Springs, Ark., first scientific analysis of water, **Vol. 3, Part 1**, 507 f.

"Hot Water War," **Vol. 4, Part 1**, 34
Houdini, Harry, reference to, **Supp. 8**, 314
Houdry Process Corporation, founding of, **Supp. 7**, 368
Hough, Will M., reference to, **Supp. 7**, 1
Houghton, Arthur Amory, Jr., reference to, **Supp. 5**, 756
Houghton, Henry O., reference to, **Vol. 8, Part 2**, 522
Houghton Library (Cambridge, Mass.), **Supp. 7**, 387
Houghton Mifflin Co., **Supp. 5**, 542; growth of, **Supp. 6**, 251; Riverside textbooks, **Supp. 3**, 206
Hound and Horn, **Supp. 7**, 55
Houqua, clipper ship, **Vol. 6, Part 1**, 444
Hours of work. *See* Wages and hours
House, Edward M.: Page, Walter Hines, and, **Vol. 7, Part 2**, 144; references to, **Supp. 3**, 532; **Supp. 4**, 171, 725; **Supp. 5**, 79, 697; **Supp. 6**, 207; **Supp. 7**, 536, 683–84, 796; Wilson, Woodrow, and, **Vol. 10, Part 2**, 355 f.
House and Garden, **Supp. 3**, 547
House and Home, **Supp. 7**, 384
House Divided, **Supp. 5**, 747–48
Houseman, John, reference to, **Supp. 5**, 464; **Supp. 7**, 61
House of David (cult), founding of, **Supp. 1**, 615–16
House of Governors, **Vol. 5, Part 2**, 217
House of Mirth, The, **Supp. 2**, 704, 705
House of Morgan. *See* Morgan and Co.
House of Representatives, United States: agricultural interests, **Supp. 4**, 480; **Supp. 6**, 86–87; Agriculture Committee, **Supp. 8**, 277–78; Appropriations Committee, **Supp. 7**, 105, 110–11, 733–34; **Supp. 8**, 2, 300; Armed Services Committee, **Supp. 7**, 78; assassination attempt in, **Supp. 8**, 300; Banking and Currency Committee, **Supp. 3**, 178, 730; **Supp. 4**, 331; **Supp. 5**, 248; **Supp. 8**, 615–16; conservatives, **Supp. 5**, 715–16; **Supp. 6**, 588; **Supp. 7**, 84–85; **Supp. 7**, 212, 639, 733–34; **Supp. 8**, 268–69, 703; dean of, **Supp. 5**, 598; Democratic Committee on Committees, **Supp. 8**, 206; Democratic leadership in, **Supp. 5**, 318–19; Democratic Steering Committee, **Supp. 6**, 132; ethics issues, **Supp. 6**, 437; **Supp. 8**, 649; first black member from North, **Supp. 5**, 166; first black standing committee head, **Supp. 8**, 121; first congresswoman from Deep South, **Supp. 5**, 582; first compact set of rules, **Vol. 8, Part 1**, 350 f.; fist fights in, **Supp. 5**, 139; Foreign Affairs Committee, **Supp. 4**, 88; **Supp. 5**, 198; Foreign Aid Committee, **Supp. 8**, 257; Government Operations Committee, **Supp. 8**, 269; Hawaiian representation, **Supp. 5**, 217; Immigration and Naturalization Committee, **Supp. 5**, 598; **Supp. 6**, 320; Indian concerns, **Supp. 5**, 662; insurgents, **Supp. 3**, 558; **Supp. 4**, 481, 669; **Supp. 5**, 666; Interstate and Foreign Commerce Committee, **Supp. 3**, 256–57; **Supp. 6**, 132; isolationists, **Supp. 5**, 396–97; **Supp. 6**, 613–14, 636; Judiciary Committee, **Supp. 7**, 730; Labor Committee, **Supp. 6**, 480; labor interests, **Supp. 7**, 302; labor legislation, **Supp. 8**, 245–46; liberals, **Supp. 4**, 465; majority rule, **Vol. 8, Part 1**, 457 f.; Maverick bloc, **Supp. 5**, 480–81; Military Affairs Committee, **Supp. 4**, 446; **Supp. 6**, 436–37; military interests, **Supp. 8**, 538; minority leaders, **Supp. 6**, 636; Mother's Day resolution, **Supp. 5**, 290; New Deal opposition, **Supp. 5**, 715; **Supp. 8**, 27, 532; oldest member, **Supp. 8**, 615; Old Guard, **Supp. 4**, 861; oratory, **Supp. 7**, 459; party responsibility, principle of, established, **Vol. 8, Part 1**, 457 f.; personal encounters, **Vol. 6, Part 1**, 533; **Supp. 6**, 614; procedure of, **Vol. 5, Part 1**, 63; prohibitionism, **Supp. 4**, 853; **Supp. 5**, 701; proportional representation, **Supp. 1**, 461; public flogging of members, **Supp. 1**, 667; radi-

calism, **Supp. 5,** 466–67; reform of rules, **Vol. 8, Part 1,** 456 f.; regional interests, **Supp. 7,** 31, 224; Republican leadership, **Supp. 8,** 128, 420–21, 422; Rules Committee, **Supp. 3,** 544, 558; **Supp. 4,** 481; **Supp. 5,** 139, 598–99; **Supp. 6,** 588; **Supp. 7,** 636, 637; "Southern Manifesto" on school desegregation, **Supp. 8,** 25; space program, **Supp. 7,** 79; speakership, **Vol. 2, Part 1,** 477, 495; **Vol. 2, Part 2,** 121; **Vol. 6, Part 1,** 394 f.; **Vol. 7, Part 1,** 307; **Supp. 1,** 344, 617; **Supp. 2,** 19, 82; **Supp. 7,** 634–37; **Supp. 8,** 207, 421; taxation measures, **Supp. 5,** 712; trade measures, **Supp. 6,** 280; Un-American Activities Committee, **Supp. 5,** 139; **Supp. 6,** 219, 392, 526; **Supp. 7,** 52, 244–45, 397, 597, 609, 766–67; **Supp. 8,** 162, 425–26, 492, 506–7, 511, 551, 648, 703–4; Un-American Activities Committee, founding, **Supp. 5,** 599; Vietnam War policies, **Supp. 8,** 507; Ways and Means Committee, **Supp. 3,** 345; **Supp. 5,** 180–81; **Supp. 6,** 125–26, 535; **Supp. 8,** 206; women elected to, **Supp. 4,** 446–47; **Supp. 6,** 479–81. *See also* Congress, United States; Lobbying; Senate, United States

House of the Holy Family, **Vol. 8, Part 1,** 205
House of Truth, **Supp. 7,** 261
Housewares, cooking utensils, **Supp. 6,** 624
Housing: apartment houses, **Vol. 3, Part 1,** 327; bungalow style, **Supp. 5,** 256–57; colonial, **Vol. 5, Part 1,** 91; comprehensive planning, **Supp. 2,** 738; cooperative, **Supp. 6,** 615; development, **Vol. 3, Part 2,** 419; low-income, design of, **Supp. 4,** 282; model, **Vol. 9, Part 1,** 301; prefabricated, **Supp. 6,** 26; **Supp. 7,** 308; public, **Supp. 3,** 656; **Supp. 5,** 631, 675, 719; public, federally subsidized, **Supp. 3,** 730, 838; public health relationship, **Supp. 6,** 702; reform, **Vol. 10, Part 2,** 86; **Supp. 3,** 52–53, 837–38; **Supp. 6,** 654–55; restrictive covenants, **Supp. 4,** 397; **Supp. 7,** 318, 319; suburban developments, **Supp. 7,** 469–70; tenement, **Supp. 3,** 743–44; **Supp. 6,** 23, 26, 522; urban, **Supp. 5,** 630, 631; Usonian designs, **Supp. 6,** 714. *See also* Architecture; Model communities

Housing Study Guild, founding of, **Supp. 2,** 739
Houston, David F., reference to, **Supp. 8,** 84
Houston, Sam: biography of, **Supp. 5,** 364; references to, **Vol. 5, Part 1,** 264; **Vol. 5, Part 2,** 161; **Vol. 8, Part 1,** 89; **Vol. 8, Part 2,** 237
Houston, Tex.: business ventures, **Supp. 6,** 324, 325; early history of, **Vol. 8, Part 1,** 546 f.; port development, **Supp. 6,** 135
Houston Chronicle, **Supp. 6,** 325
Houston Post, **Supp. 7,** 349, 350
Howard, Eugene, reference to, **Supp. 4,** 400–1
Howard, John Galen, reference to, **Supp. 6,** 463
Howard, Maxwell, reference to, **Supp. 8,** 566
Howard, O. O., reference to, **Supp. 3,** 836
Howard, Sidney, reference to, **Supp. 8,** 529
Howard University: administration, **Supp. 2,** 456; **Supp. 6,** 568; founding of, **Vol. 5, Part 1,** 280; history studies, **Supp. 4,** 911; law school, **Supp. 4,** 397, 398; patrons, **Supp. 5,** 343; Phi Beta Kappa chapter, **Supp. 5,** 437; philosophy studies, **Supp. 5,** 436; sociology studies, **Supp. 7,** 266; zoology studies, **Supp. 3,** 402–3
Howe, Elias, references to, **Vol. 5, Part 1,** 95; **Vol. 9, Part 1,** 189
Howe, Julia Ward, biography of, **Supp. 3,** 630
Howe, Louis: references to, **Supp. 5,** 682; **Supp. 7,** 659; Roosevelt, F. D., relationship, **Supp. 3,** 642, 644–47
Howe, Samuel Gridley, reference to, **Vol. 2, Part 1,** 38; **Supp. 8,** 316

Howe, Will, reference to, **Supp. 5,** 272
Howe, Sir William, reference to, **Vol. 5, Part 1,** 481
Howe, William F., reference to, **Vol. 5, Part 1,** 368
Howell, Harry, reference to, **Supp. 6,** 357
Howell, William H., reference to, **Vol. 10, Part 1,** 621 f.; **Supp. 6,** 671
Howells, John Mead, reference to, **Supp. 3,** 743
Howells, William Dean, references to, **Vol. 5, Part 1,** 579; **Vol. 5, Part 2,** 360; **Vol. 7, Part 2,** 556; **Supp. 4,** 816, 817; **Supp. 5,** 95–96
Howes, Wright, reference to, **Supp. 7,** 295
Howland, John, reference to, **Supp. 3,** 74, 243
Howland, Silas W., reference to, **Supp. 3,** 116–17
How to Win Friends and Influence People, **Supp. 5,** 102
Hoyle, Alexander E., reference to, **Supp. 3,** 196
Huancayo Magnetic Observatory (Lima, Peru), **Supp. 6,** 205
Hubbard, Gardiner H., reference to, **Vol. 1, Part 2,** 149, 151
Hubbard, Robert ("Cal"), reference to, **Supp. 5,** 458
Hubbert, Marion King, reference to, **Supp. 5,** 558
Hubble, Edwin, reference to, **Supp. 3,** 208; **Supp. 8,** 597
Huber, G. Carl, reference to, **Supp. 3,** 369
Hubert, Conrad, reference to, **Supp. 7,** 150
Hückel, Erich, reference to, **Supp. 8,** 123
Huckleberry Finn, **Vol. 2, Part 2,** 192, 195
Hudson, Henry, reference to, **Vol. 5, Part 1,** 338
Hudson Bay, early explorations near, **Vol. 8, Part 1,** 320 f.
Hudson County, N.J., political machine, **Supp. 6,** 265
Hudson Guild, **Supp. 3,** 175, 246
Hudson Motor Car Co., establishment of, **Supp. 2,** 102
Hudson River: blockade of, during Revolution, **Vol. 10, Part 2,** 432; boats (*see also* Hudson River Day Line), **Vol. 3, Part 2,** 164; **Vol. 7, Part 1,** 471; bridges, **Supp. 7,** 11; exploration, **Vol. 5, Part 1,** 338 f.; law granting Livingston and Fulton navigation rights, **Vol. 3, Part 1,** 488; paintings of, **Vol. 5, Part 2,** 72; tunnels under, **Vol. 1, Part 2,** 408; **Vol. 4, Part 2,** 446; **Vol. 5, Part 1,** 142; **Vol. 8, Part 1,** 406; **Supp. 2,** 146, 559; **Supp. 4,** 690, 757
Hudson River Day Line, **Vol. 7, Part 2,** 9 f.
Hudson River Railroad, **Vol. 1, Part 2,** 443; **Vol. 5, Part 1,** 313; **Vol. 5, Part 2,** 60
Hudson River school, **Vol. 5, Part 1,** 488
Hudson's Bay Co., **Vol. 1, Part 2,** 145; **Vol. 3, Part 1,** 336 f.; **Vol. 4, Part 2,** 17; **Vol. 5, Part 2,** 441; **Vol. 7, Part 1,** 640; **Vol. 8, Part 1,** 320 f.
Hudson Tunnel, for Pennsylvania Railroad, plans for, **Vol. 8, Part 1,** 406
Huebsch, Benjamin W., references to, **Supp. 3,** 13; **Supp. 7,** 306
Huggins, Miller, reference to, **Supp. 5,** 40–41
Hughes, Charles Evans: insurance investigation, **Vol. 6, Part 1,** 562; references to, **Supp. 3,** 99, 100, 396, 559, 668, 717; **Supp. 5,** 286, 342, 571, 572, 573, 574, 575; **Supp. 7,** 361
Hughes, Howard, references to, **Supp. 6,** 145, 146, 221, 308; **Supp. 7,** 71, 587
Hughes, John, reference to, **Vol. 6, Part 1,** 591
Hughes, Langston, reference to, **Supp. 6,** 314, 321
Hughes, Ted, reference to, **Supp. 7,** 621–22
Hughes Aircraft Co., **Supp. 7,** 73
Huguenots: settlements of, **Vol. 1, Part 1,** 509; **Vol. 3, Part 1,** 534 f.; **Vol. 4, Part 2,** 375 f.; **Vol. 6, Part 1,** 30; writings on, **Vol. 1, Part 1,** 510 f.
Hull, Cordell, references to, **Supp. 3,** 449, 647, 657; **Supp. 5,** 519, 537; **Supp. 6,** 230; **Supp. 7,** 303, 777
Hull, Susanna E., reference to, **Vol. 1, Part 2,** 149

Hydrogen: characteristics, **Supp. 5,** 413; discovery in atomic form, **Supp. 6,** 364; in solar atmosphere, **Supp. 6,** 561

Hydrogen bomb, **Supp. 5,** 455; **Supp. 7,** 565; **Supp. 8,** 200, 484; public opposition to, **Supp. 8,** 301. *See also* Atomic bomb

Hydrographic Office, United States, **Vol. 1, Part 2,** 397 f.

Hydrography, **Vol. 1, Part 2,** 397 f.; **Vol. 3, Part 2,** 157; **Vol. 4, Part 1,** 549 f.; **Vol. 6, Part 1,** 55–58; **Vol. 7, Part 1,** 47, 457; **Vol. 9, Part 1,** 156

Hydrology, **Supp. 4,** 567; writings on, **Vol. 8, Part 1,** 324 f.

Hydrolosis, studies in, **Vol. 9, Part 2,** 544

Hydrometallurgy, **Vol. 3, Part 1,** 27

Hydrometers, perfection of, **Vol. 9, Part 2,** 273

Hydrophobia, study of, **Vol. 6, Part 2,** 486; **Vol. 9, Part 2,** 388

Hydroplanes **Supp. 1,** 214; **Supp. 4,** 124. *See also* Aviation

Hydrotherapy, **Vol. 1, Part 2,** 29; **Vol. 5, Part 2,** 459

Hydrothermal theory, **Supp. 2,** 386

Hygeia, **Supp. 3,** 104

Hylan, John F., references to, **Supp. 3,** 718; **Supp. 5,** 286; **Supp. 6,** 88; **Supp. 7,** 779

Hyman, Stanley Edgar, reference to, **Supp. 7,** 385

Hymnal, Methodist, **Vol. 4, Part 1,** 405

Hymn books, editing of, **Vol. 4, Part 1,** 462; **Vol. 4, Part 2,** 387, 438; **Vol. 6, Part 1,** 38

Hymns, writing of, **Vol. 1, Part 2,** 142; **Vol. 2, Part 1,** 152; **Vol. 2, Part 2,** 531, 567; **Vol. 3, Part 1,** 333 f., 335, 337, 491; **Vol. 3, Part 2,** 481; **Vol. 4, Part 1,** 311; **Vol. 4, Part 2,** 203, 388, 395 f.; **Vol. 5, Part 1,** 138, 242; **Vol. 5, Part 2,** 119, 295 f.; **Vol. 6, Part 1,** 14, 479; **Vol. 7, Part 1,** 314, 569, 595, 605 f.; **Vol. 7, Part 2,** 192; **Vol. 8, Part 1,** 175, 374, 645; **Vol. 8, Part 2,** 37, 352 f., 539, 606; **Vol. 9, Part 1,** 343; **Vol. 9, Part 2,** 444, 475; **Vol. 10, Part 1,** 108, 651 f.; **Vol. 10, Part 2,** 239

Hyperinsulinism, **Supp. 6,** 698

Hypnosis, **Supp. 5,** 329, 330; for birth delivery, **Supp. 6,** 555

Hypodermic needle, **Supp. 7,** 678, 679

Hypoglycemia, insulin-produced, **Supp. 6,** 563–64

Hypoplastic anemia, **Supp. 3,** 75

Hypothalamus, **Supp. 3,** 620; rage and, **Supp. 3,** 135

I

IBM Corp. *See* International Business Machines Corporation

IBRD. *See* International Bank for Reconstruction and Development

Ibsen, first presentation of, in America, **Vol. 7, Part 1,** 73

ICAO. *See* International Civil Aviation Organization

Icarian colonies (Ill.), **Vol. 2, Part 1,** 391; **Vol. 6, Part 1,** 389

ICC. *See* Interstate Commerce Commission

Ice, artificial, first in U.S., **Vol. 6, Part 1,** 452; exportation, **Vol. 10, Part 1,** 47 f.; manufacture, **Vol. 10, Part 1,** 84; shipping, **Vol. 7, Part 1,** 240; **Vol. 10, Part 1,** 47 f.

Icelandic, first teaching of, in America, **Vol. 9, Part 1,** 252

Icelandic Literary Societies, **Vol. 3, Part 2,** 417

Iceman Cometh, The, **Supp. 7,** 34

Ice skating, **Supp. 7,** 528; **Supp. 8,** 253–54

Ichthyology, **Vol. 3, Part 1,** 169 f.; **Vol. 3, Part 2,** 63; **Vol. 5, Part 2,** 213; **Vol. 6, Part 1,** 191; writings on, **Vol. 5, Part 1,** 130; **Vol. 8, Part 1,** 322 f.

Ickes, Harold, L., references to, **Supp. 3,** 647, 651, 795, 796; **Supp. 4,** 392–93, 666; **Supp. 5,** 485; **Supp. 6,** 392, 451, 660, 661, 671, 692

I Confess: The Truth About American Communism, **Supp. 7,** 291

Iconoclast, **Supp. 1,** 109

Idaho: governorship, **Vol. 1, Part 2,** 611; **Vol. 4, Part 2,** 419 f.; labor riots, **Vol. 4, Part 2,** 419, 468; legal service, **Vol. 7, Part 2,** 592; mining, **Vol. 4, Part 2,** 419; **Vol. 8, Part 1,** 156; political service, **Vol. 1, Part 2,** 611; **Vol. 3, Part 1,** 210; **Vol. 4, Part 2,** 419; **Vol. 6, Part 1,** 528; **Vol. 9, Part 1,** 131; politics, **Supp. 6,** 681; **Supp. 7,** 212–13; **Supp. 8,** 508; public service, **Vol. 4, Part 2,** 419; **Vol. 9, Part 1,** 131; Sun Valley resort, **Supp. 5,** 270–71; territorial governorship, **Vol. 9, Part 1,** 131 f.; **Vol. 9, Part 2,** 456; woman suffrage, adoption of, **Vol. 3, Part 1,** 513 f.

Iddings, Joseph P., reference to, **Supp. 4,** 194

Idealism, absolute, **Supp. 6,** 505

Idlewild Airport (New York City). *See* Kennedy International Airport

Igneous rocks, **Supp. 4,** 194; **Supp. 6,** 145, 153

ILGWU. *See* International Ladies' Garment Workers' Union

Iliad, translation of, **Vol. 7, Part 1,** 326–27

Ilion, N.Y., history of **Vol. 8, Part 1,** 496

Illinois: agricultural libraries in schools, introduction of, **Vol. 1, Part 2,** 321; agricultural society, first in, **Vol. 1, Part 2,** 289; antislavery movement in, **Vol. 1, Part 2,** 128; **Vol. 6, Part 1,** 435; archaeology, **Vol. 9, Part 1,** 389; architecture, **Supp. 5,** 208; botany, **Vol. 2, Part 1,** 327; boundary disputes, **Vol. 8, Part 1,** 77 f.; canal building, **Vol. 6, Part 2,** 332; Civil War period, **Vol. 10, Part 2,** 600; coal survey in, **Vol. 6, Part 1,** 189; Congregational church, **Vol. 10, Part 1,** 58; Democratic party, **Vol. 3, Part 1,** 398 f.; education in, **Vol. 1, Part 2,** 439; **Vol. 3, Part 1,** 510 f.; **Vol. 5, Part 1,** 271; **Vol. 8, Part 1,** 77 f., 120 f., 152; **Vol. 10, Part 1,** 645 f., 657 f.; entomology, **Vol. 10, Part 1,** 388 f.; Episcopal church in, **Vol. 6, Part 2,** 116; **Vol. 9, Part 1,** 6; ethics issues, **Supp. 6,** 74; frontier church activities, **Vol. 2, Part 1,** 547; fur trading, **Vol. 2, Part 1,** 582; geology of, **Vol. 10, Part 2,** 538; "George Smith's money," **Vol. 9, Part 1,** 268; German immigration to, **Vol. 5, Part 2,** 496; gerrymandering in, **Vol. 3, Part 1,** 398; governors, **Vol. 1, Part 1,** 231; **Vol. 1, Part 2,** 302, 432 f.; **Vol. 2, Part 2,** 296 f.; **Vol. 3, Part 1,** 510 f.; **Vol. 3, Part 2,** 41 f., 520 f.; **Vol. 6, Part 2,** 410 f.; **Vol. 7, Part 1,** 648 f.; **Vol. 7, Part 2,** 187 f.; **Vol. 8, Part 1,** 519 f.; **Vol. 10, Part 2,** 599 f.; **Supp. 2,** 182, 318; **Supp. 3,** 467–68; **Supp. 7,** 721–22; history of, **Vol. 1, Part 2,** 236; **Vol. 8, Part 1,** 77 f.; **Vol. 10, Part 1,** 657 f.; Icarian colonies, **Vol. 2, Part 1,** 391; **Vol. 6, Part 1,** 389; Indian mounds, **Vol. 9, Part 1,** 389; Indians in, **Vol. 4, Part 1,** 510; industrial history of, **Vol. 8, Part 1,** 9 f., 263 f.; jurisprudence in, **Vol. 2, Part 1,** 575; land claims, **Vol. 1, Part 2,** 432; land speculation, **Vol. 4, Part 2,** 247; "Latin settlement," **Vol. 5, Part 2,** 496; laws, digest of, **Vol. 8, Part 1,** 77 f.; lead mining, **Vol. 6, Part 2,** 496; legal service, **Vol. 1, Part 2,** 313, 382, 439, 580, 611; **Vol. 3, Part 1,** 110, 282, 291, 397; **Vol. 4, Part 1,** 605; **Vol. 6, Part 1,** 267, 344; **Vol. 8, Part 1,** 77, 519; **Vol. 9, Part 1,** 534; **Vol. 9, Part 2,** 634–35; **Vol. 10, Part 1,** 2, 19; **Vol. 10, Part 2,** 347, 469 f.; library, first, **Vol. 3, Part 2,** 479; Lincoln's life in, **Vol. 6, Part 1,** 243 f.; liquor control, **Vol. 8, Part 1,** 992; Lutheran church, **Vol. 4, Part 2,** 394; market gardening in, **Vol. 7, Part 2,** 464; Medical Practice Act, importance of, **Vol. 8, Part 1,** 390; missionary work in, **Vol. 1, Part 1,** 547; **Vol. 4, Part 1,** 235, 510; **Vol. 6, Part 2,** 280; **Vol. 10,**

Part 1, 58; natural history of, **Vol. 5, Part 2,** 338; pioneer life in, **Vol. 1, Part 2,** 432; **Vol. 2, Part 1,** 198; **Vol. 3, Part 2,** 478; **Vol. 6, Part 2,** 280, 529, 610; **Vol. 7, Part 2,** 593; **Vol. 8, Part 1,** 519 f.; political parties, midcentury, **Vol. 4, Part 2** 247; political service, **Vol. 1, Part 1,** 231; **Vol. 1, Part 2,** 110, 302, 313, 382, 432, 439, 580; **Vol. 3, Part 1,** 111 f., 398, 510, 520; **Vol. 3, Part 2,** 41; **Vol. 5, Part 2,** 496; **Vol. 6, Part 2,** 181, 244, 410, 491; **Vol. 7, Part 1,** 648; **Vol. 7, Part 2,** 187; **Vol. 8, Part 1,** 392, 519; **Vol. 9, Part 1,** 106, 191, 629; **Vol. 10, Part 1,** 19, 504 f., 657 f.; **Vol. 10, Part 2,** 600; politics, **Supp. 3,** 710–11; **Supp. 4,** 180, 280, 751–52; **Supp. 5,** 450, 598; **Supp. 6,** 683–84; **Supp. 7,** 702; **Supp. 8,** 121, 127–29, 391–92; progressive movement in, **Supp. 5,** 579; public service, **Vol. 1, Part 2,** 44; **Vol. 3, Part 1,** 510 f.; **Vol. 4, Part 2** 134 f.; **Vol. 6, Part 2,** 379; **Vol. 7, Part 2,** 252; **Vol. 8, Part 1,** 263 f., 359 f.; **Vol. 9, Part 1,** 483 f.; **Vol. 10, Part 1,** 657 f.; public utilities in, **Vol. 8, Part 1,** 9 f.; railroad development in, **Vol. 4, Part 2** 247; **Vol. 8, Part 1,** 359 f., 392; Republican party in, **Vol. 1, Part 2,** 382; **Vol. 7, Part 2,** 187; **Vol. 8, Part 1,** 392; school system, organization of, **Vol. 10, Part 1,** 68; scientific services, **Vol. 10, Part 1,** 582; social reform, **Vol. 10, Part 2,** 386; statehood, admission to, **Vol. 8, Part 1,** 77 f.; Swedenborgian church in, **Vol. 6, Part 2,** 544; territory, organization of, **Vol. 8, Part 1,** 77 f.; Whigs in pre-Civil War politics, **Vol. 4, Part 2** 246; wool manufacture, **Vol. 8, Part 1,** 405. *See also city and institution names*

Illinois Agricultural Association, **Supp. 3,** 319
Illinois & Rock River Railroad, **Vol. 8, Part 1,** 9 f.
Illinois Association, organization of, at Yale, **Vol. 10, Part 1,** 58
Illinois Central Railroad Co., **Vol. 1, Part 2,** 182; **Vol. 3, Part 2,** 402; **Vol. 4, Part 2** 297; **Vol. 5, Part 2,** 35; **Vol. 6, Part 1,** 495; **Vol. 7, Part 2,** 72; **Supp. 4,** 193
Illinois College, **Vol. 1, Part 1,** 547; **Vol. 1, Part 2,** 128, 571; founding of, **Vol. 10, Part 1,** 58
Illinois Farmers' Institute, **Supp. 3,** 68, 216
Illinois Female College, **Vol. 5, Part 1,** 616
Illinois Industrial University. *See* University of Illinois
Illinois Institute of Technology: architecture, **Supp. 8,** 436; design institute, **Supp. 4,** 591
Illinois Miner, **Supp. 3,** 10
Illinois Miners and Mechanics' Institute, **Vol. 9, Part 2,** 65
Illinois Monthly Magazine, **Vol. 4, Part 2** 135
Illinois Municipal League, founding of, **Supp. 4,** 260
Illinois Natural History Society, **Vol. 9, Part 2,** 426; **Vol. 10, Part 1,** 68
Illinois Pipe-line Co., **Vol. 3, Part 1,** 367
Illinois Staats-Zeitung, **Vol. 8, Part 1,** 384
Illinois State Normal School, **Vol. 1, Part 2,** 44; **Vol. 2, Part 2,** 376; **Vol. 9, Part 2,** 581
Illinois Wesleyan University, **Vol. 3, Part 2,** 262
Illinois Women Suffrage Association, **Vol. 1, Part 2,** 581
Illuminism, **Vol. 7, Part 1,** 246
Illustrated Flora of the Northern United States, Canada, and the British Possessions, An, **Supp. 1,** 121
Illustrated Graphic News, **Vol. 10, Part 1,** 111
Illustrating, **Vol. 1, Part 1,** 465 f.; **Vol. 1, Part 2,** 93, 95, 168, 396; **Vol. 2, Part 1,** 17, 610; **Vol. 2, Part 2,** 480; **Vol. 3, Part 1,** 75 f.; **Vol. 3, Part 2,** 56; **Vol. 4, Part 1,** 41 f., 162, 193 263; **Vol. 4, Part 2** 542; **Vol. 5, Part 1,** 225; **Vol. 5, Part 2,** 294 f.; **Vol. 6, Part 1,** 284, 353; **Vol. 7, Part 1,** 53; **Vol. 7, Part 2,** 424 f., 438 f.; **Vol. 8, Part 1,** 287 f., 490 f., 497, 511 f.; **Vol. 8, Part 2,** 113, 202, 339, 371; **Vol. 9, Part 1,** 227, 575; **Vol. 9, Part 2,** 322, 346, 512

Illustration, **Supp. 1,** 298; **Supp. 6,** 204, 287; advertising, **Supp. 5,** 428–29; book, **Supp. 3,** 44, 69, 300, 848; **Supp. 5,** 580, 672–73; **Supp. 7,** 17, 48, 436; **Supp. 8,** 493, 494; botanic, **Supp. 1,** 121; **Supp. 4,** 17; brush drawing, **Supp. 5,** 473; children's books, **Supp. 3,** 69; **Supp. 4,** 310; **Supp. 5,** 93; **Supp. 6,** 372–73; Christy Girl, **Supp. 5,** 112, 113; decoration, **Supp. 1,** 514; Gibson Girl, **Supp. 3,** 300–1; **Supp. 4,** 826; magazine, **Supp. 3,** 573–74; **Supp. 5,** 625; **Supp. 8,** 493; magazine covers, **Supp. 5,** 428, 429, 594; medical, **Supp. 3,** 106–7, 412; military, **Supp. 5,** 112; natural history, **Supp. 4,** 736–37; Petty Girl, **Supp. 5,** 637; scientific subjects, **Supp. 1,** 428
Illustrations of Masonry, **Vol. 7, Part 1,** 189
Illustrative art, development of, **Vol. 3, Part 1,** 423 f.
Illustrators. For complete list *see* Occupations Index
ILO. *See* International Labor Office
Il Progresso, Italian daily, first in U.S., **Vol. 1, Part 2,** 1
ILWU. *See* International Longshoremen's and Warehousemen's Union
Imagists, French, influence on Amy Lowell, **Vol. 6, Part 1,** 454; **Supp. 4,** 285–86
Imago, **Supp. 4,** 716
I Married Adventure, **Supp. 5,** 371
IMF. *See* International Monetary Fund
Immigrants' Protective League, **Supp. 2,** 1; **Supp. 4,** 107
Immigration, **Vol. 1, Part 1,** 646; **Vol. 5, Part 1,** 257; **Vol. 6, Part 2,** 326 f., 467; **Vol. 7, Part 1,** 33; **Vol. 8, Part 1,** 142 f.; **Vol. 8, Part 2,** 35 f.; adult education programs, **Supp. 8,** 9; anthropological study, **Supp. 3,** 84; assimilation advocacy, **Supp. 5,** 380–81; Catholic, **Vol. 9, Part 1,** 113; Catholic immigrants' resettlement, **Supp. 4,** 335; Chinese, **Vol. 1, Part 1,** 308; **Vol. 5, Part 2,** 269; **Vol. 9, Part 2,** 640; deportation cases, **Supp. 5,** 389; Ellis Island, **Vol. 7, Part 1,** 432; **Vol. 8, Part 2,** 169, 313; **Vol. 9, Part 2,** 549; examination at point of emigration, **Vol. 8, Part 1,** 142 f.; first authentic novel about, **Supp. 5,** 96; German, **Vol. 8, Part 2,** 87; histories of, **Supp. 7,** 28; Irish, **Vol. 3, Part 2,** 440; **Vol. 9, Part 2,** 4; Jewish Americanization, **Supp. 3,** 513; Jewish writings on, **Supp. 5,** 95–96; labor, European, first attempt at importation, **Vol. 4, Part 2,** 279; legislation, **Supp. 1,** 472; **Supp. 2,** 46; liberalization efforts, **Supp. 6,** 472; Massachusetts Colony, exclusion of immigrants from, **Vol. 10, Part 2,** 410; "melting pot" concept, **Supp. 4,** 23; national-origin restrictions, **Supp. 3,** 215, 346, 389, 502, 632; **Supp. 5,** 444–45, 561; **Supp. 6,** 320; **Supp. 7,** 644, 766, 767; National Research Council studies, **Supp. 6,** 718; nonrestrictive advocacy, **Supp. 5,** 598; Norwegian, **Vol. 3, Part 2,** 478; **Vol. 5, Part 1,** 612; **Vol. 6, Part 1,** 9; **Vol. 7, Part 1,** 419; **Vol. 7, Part 2,** 390; **Vol. 8, Part 1,** 487 f.; **Vol. 8, Part 2,** 124, 274; personal writings on, **Supp. 5,** 4–5; quota principle, **Vol. 3, Part 1,** 310; **Vol. 8, Part 2,** 183; racially nonrestrictive quota system, **Supp. 3,** 322, 323; regulation of, **Vol. 8, Part 1,** 142 f.; restrictive, eugenic basis for, **Supp. 4,** 413; restrictive legislation, **Supp. 4,** 792; Roman Catholic aid, **Supp. 5,** 722; social work, **Vol. 8, Part 1,** 295; **Supp. 6,** 1–2; **Supp. 7,** 341–42; sociological study of, **Supp. 6,** 726; studies on, **Supp. 2,** 278–79; survey of, **Vol. 3, Part 1,** 310; textbook on, **Vol. 5, Part 2,** 52; United States Bureau of, **Vol. 7, Part 1,** 432; war brides, **Supp. 7,** 541–42; World War I aliens, **Supp. 3,** 65; Zionist organizations, **Supp. 3,** 756. *See also* Refugees; *specific national and racial groups*
Immigration and Nationality Act (1952), passage of, **Supp. 5,** 445; **Supp. 7,** 766
Immigration and Naturalization Service, United States, **Supp. 8,** 35

437; women, first academy for young, **Vol. 4, Part 2** 34; writers, **Supp. 4,** 816–17
"Indiana," land enterprise, **Vol. 9, Part 2,** 638
Indian Affairs, Bureau of, **Vol. 6, Part 2,** 89; **Supp. 3,** 846; **Supp. 7,** 43, 393–94, 505, 506
Indiana Asbury University. *See* De Pauw University
Indiana Christian Home Missionary Society, **Vol. 4, Part 1,** 407
Indiana Civil Service Reform Association, **Vol. 9, Part 2,** 248
Indiana Civil Service Reform Organization, **Supp. 1,** 315
Indiana Historical Society, **Vol. 7, Part 2,** 210
Indiana Hospital for the Insane, **Vol. 9, Part 2,** 249
Indiana Institution for the Education of the Blind, **Vol. 2, Part 2,** 107
Indiana Medical College, **Vol. 3, Part 2,** 469
Indiana Medical Society, **Vol. 7, Part 2,** 286
Indianapolis, Ind.: public service, **Vol. 6, Part 2,** 8, 563; Roman Catholic diocese, **Supp. 8,** 537
Indianapolis 500. *See* Automobile racing
Indianapolis News, **Vol. 5, Part 1,** 324
Indianapolis Repertory Company, **Supp. 3,** 797
Indiana Sentinel, **Vol. 9, Part 1,** 244
Indiana State Board of Charities, **Supp. 3,** 388
Indiana University, **Vol. 4, Part 2** 119; **Vol. 5, Part 1,** 158; **Vol. 5, Part 2,** 212; **Vol. 6, Part 2,** 440; **Vol. 7, Part 1,** 281; **Vol. 10, Part 2,** 578; football team, **Supp. 5,** 458; genetics studies, **Supp. 8,** 449, 450; history studies, **Supp. 8,** 60; human sexuality studies, **Supp. 6,** 342–44; sociology studies, **Supp. 4,** 808–9
Indian Reorganization Act (1934), **Supp. 5,** 119, 319; **Supp. 7,** 393; **Supp. 8,** 99
Indians, American (general): agents for, **Vol. 3, Part 2,** 443, 455, 536; **Vol. 4, Part 2** 215; **Vol. 5, Part 1,** 355 f.; **Vol. 6, Part 1,** 617; **Vol. 7, Part 1,** 379, 407; **Vol. 9, Part 1,** 144, 146; **Vol. 9, Part 2,** 31, 137; Albany Conference (1745), **Vol. 9, Part 2,** 431; alphabet, Dakota, **Vol. 8, Part 1,** 61 f.; anthropoligical studies, **Supp. 2,** 9, 176, 593; **Supp. 3,** 82–84; **Supp. 4,** 179; **Supp. 6,** 353; 612–13; archaeological studies, **Supp. 5,** 533–34; archaeological studies in Mexico, **Supp. 4,** 605–6; art, research in, **Vol. 1, Part 1,** 588; art exhibitions, **Supp. 8,** 126; artifact collection, **Supp. 6,** 289–90; autobiography of Indian chief, **Vol. 1, Part 2,** 314; Bacon's Rebellion, **Vol. 6, Part 2,** 361; Bering Strait migration theory, **Supp. 3,** 372; Bethlehem, Pa., raids on, **Vol. 8, Part 1,** 113 f.; Bible translations, **Vol. 1, Part 1,** 478; **Vol. 5, Part 2,** 110; **Vol. 8, Part 1,** 61 f.; bibliographies, **Supp. 2,** 163; books, translation of, **Vol. 4, Part 2** 144; books for, **Vol. 5, Part 1,** 576; boundary disputes with, **Vol. 5, Part 2,** 126; captives, **Vol. 4, Part 1,** 501; **Vol. 5, Part 2,** 39, 47; **Vol. 8, Part 2,** 201; **Vol. 9, Part 1,** 216, 285; Catholic mission schools for, **Supp. 5,** 185–86; chiefs, **Vol. 1, Part 2,** 314; **Vol. 4, Part 1,** 101; **Vol. 4, Part 2** 28; **Vol. 5, Part 2,** 115, 218 f., 255, 350, 367, 583; **Vol. 6, Part 1,** 182, 299 f., 362 f.; **Vol. 7, Part 1,** 560, 621; **Vol. 8, Part 1,** 294; **Vol. 8, Part 2,** 178, 375 f., 542; **Vol. 9, Part 1,** 13, 109, 192, 194, 469; **Vol. 9, Part 2,** 375 f., 474 f., 580; **Vol. 10, Part 1,** 409 f.; Cienequeilla, battle of, **Vol. 3, Part 1,** 93 f.; citizenship for, **Vol. 8, Part 1,** 175 f., 335 f.; civil government for, **Vol. 7, Part 2,** 225; Civil War, Cherokees' part in, **Vol. 10, Part 1,** 537 f.; contemporary, writings on, **Supp. 7,** 449; conversion of, **Vol. 4, Part 2** 611; **Vol. 8, Part 1,** 294; Court of Indian Offenses, **Vol. 4, Part 1,** 502; crafts, **Supp. 1,** 437; cultural anthropological studies, **Supp. 4,** 71–72; culture, **Supp. 1,** 651; Dawes, status of, under, **Vol.**

8, Part 1, 335 f.; dialects, **Vol. 4, Part 2** 94; Easton, Pa., Treaty of, **Vol. 9, Part 2,** 481; education, **Vol. 1, Part 1,** 216, 238; **Vol. 1, Part 2,** 478 f.; **Vol. 2, Part 1,** 4, 46; **Vol. 3, Part 1,** 376, 477 f.; **Vol. 4, Part 1,** 101; **Vol. 4, Part 2** 332, 380, 414; **Vol. 5, Part 2,** 115, 504; **Vol. 6, Part 1,** 176, 428 f.; **Vol. 6, Part 2,** 453, 471, 496; **Vol. 7, Part 2,** 336; **Vol. 8, Part 1,** 111, 175 f.; **Vol. 8, Part 2,** 30; **Vol. 10, Part 2,** 58; **Supp. 4,** 165–66; **Supp. 7,** 43; equestrian sculpture of, **Supp. 3,** 210–11; ethnographic studies, **Supp. 1,** 252; **Supp. 4,** 907–8; **Supp. 6,** 524–25; ethnological studies, **Vol. 3, Part 1,** 553 f.; **Vol. 3, Part 2,** 126; **Vol. 5, Part 2,** 205 f., 208; **Vol. 7, Part 1,** 183 f., 512; **Vol. 7, Part 2,** 603; **Vol. 8, Part 2,** 55, 278; **Supp. 3,** 582; **Supp. 4,** 761–62; **Supp. 6,** 392–93; **Supp. 7,** 710–11; evangelism, **Vol. 7, Part 1,** 529; folklore, **Vol. 5, Part 1,** 566; **Vol. 5, Part 2,** 206; **Vol. 7, Part 1,** 460 f.; **Vol. 8, Part 1,** 301 f.; **Supp. 3,** 582; **Supp. 6,** 612; French alliance, breakup of, **Vol. 8, Part 1,** 113 f.; French and Indian War, plight of Abnakis during, **Vol. 8, Part 1,** 330 f.; fur trappers, attack on, **Vol. 4, Part 2** 546; "ghost dance," **Vol. 10, Part 2,** 541; governmental supervision of, **Vol. 1, Part 1,** 33 f., 39; **Vol. 1, Part 2,** 390; **Vol. 3, Part 1,** 149 f., 243, 349; **Vol. 3, Part 2,** 41, 66, 483; **Vol. 4, Part 1,** 31, 171; **Vol. 4, Part 2** 186, 414; **Vol. 5, Part 1,** 263 f., 363, 449, 500, 523, 577; **Vol. 5, Part 2,** 100, 103, 124 f., 126, 247, 293, 573; **Vol. 6, Part 1,** 195, 260 f., 291 318, 362, 550, 587, 611; **Vol. 6, Part 2,** 89; **Vol. 7, Part 1,** 40, 126, 246, 379, 407, 437, 594; **Vol. 7, Part 2,** 225, 601; **Vol. 8, Part 1,** 99 f., 121 f., 146 f., 175 f., 335 f.; **Vol. 8, Part 2,** 475, 611; **Vol. 9, Part 1,** 109, 121, 145, 231, 468; **Vol. 9, Part 2,** 359 f., 375 f.; **Vol. 10, Part 2,** 69, 255, 391; government policies, **Supp. 2,** 291; **Supp. 5,** 319, 342, 662; **Supp. 7,** 122; government policy reforms, **Supp. 8,** 98–99; government relations, **Supp. 3,** 846; **Supp. 4,** 165–66; Great Britain, relations with, **Vol. 6, Part 1,** 300; **Vol. 8, Part 1,** 18 f.; **Vol. 9, Part 2,** 359 f.; **Vol. 10, Part 1,** 109; Greenville, Treaty of, **Vol. 3, Part 1,** 255; guiding immigrants through Indian lands, **Vol. 3, Part 1,** 34; historical writings on, **Supp. 5,** 430; history of, **Supp. 6,** 612; idealization of, **Supp. 4,** 737; Inca civilization, **Supp. 4,** 670; **Supp. 6,** 59; interpreting, **Vol. 4, Part 1,** 323; **Vol. 9, Part 1,** 487; **Supp. 4,** 237; inventions by, **Vol. 8, Part 2,** 586; King Philip's War, **Vol. 4, Part 1,** 360; **Vol. 8, Part 1,** 290 f.; land, matters relating to, **Vol. 3, Part 1,** 176; **Vol. 4, Part 1,** 502; **Vol. 4, Part 2** 531; **Vol. 5, Part 2,** 40; **Vol. 7, Part 1,** 642; **Vol. 8, Part 1,** 274, 341 f., 426, 595; **Vol. 10, Part 1,** 26; languages, study of, **Vol. 1, Part 1,** 585; **Vol. 3, Part 1,** 277, 385, 507; **Vol. 3, Part 2,** 460; **Vol. 4, Part 1,** 192; **Vol. 4, Part 2** 104; **Vol. 5, Part 2,** 33; **Vol. 6, Part 1,** 561 f.; **Vol. 7, Part 1,** 559; **Vol. 8, Part 1,** 61 f., 605; **Vol. 8, Part 2,** 586; **Vol. 9, Part 1,** 51; **Vol. 9, Part 2,** 389; **Vol. 10, Part 1,** 9 f.; law codification, **Supp. 8,** 99; leadership, **Supp. 8,** 647; linguistics studies, **Supp. 3,** 819–20; Logstown, Treaty of, **Vol. 4, Part 1,** 48; Lost Valley, battle of, **Vol. 5, Part 2,** 182; Loyalists, relations with, **Vol. 8, Part 2,** 100; Maine, writings, **Supp. 4,** 248–49; massacres, **Vol. 1, Part 1,** 145; **Vol. 1, Part 2,** 217; **Vol. 3, Part 1,** 554 f.; **Vol. 3, Part 2,** 350; **Vol. 4, Part 2** 362; **Vol. 5, Part 1,** 437; **Vol. 5, Part 2,** 47, 100, 371; medical practice among, **Vol. 6, Part 1,** 272; Medicine Lodge Treaty, **Vol. 8, Part 1,** 294; medicine men, **Vol. 9, Part 1,** 193, 371; missionary work among, *see* Missions, Indian; missions, **Supp. 1,** 134, 158–59, 218–19, 289–90; mixed marriages, **Vol. 1, Part 1,** 345, 521; **Vol. 4, Part 2** 276; **Vol. 6, Part 1,** 98; **Vol. 7, Part 1,** 458; **Vol. 8, Part 1,** 18 f.; **Vol. 8, Part 2,**

Institute for Advanced Study (Princeton), **Supp. 3**, 31; **Supp. 6**, 30, 208–9, 653–54, 656; administration, **Supp. 8**, 484; art history studies, **Supp. 8**, 490; mathematical physics studies, **Supp. 5**, 738; military and foreign policy seminar, **Supp. 5**, 195; physics studies, **Supp. 5**, 204

Institute for Government Research, founding of, **Supp. 6**, 250

Institute for International Social Research, **Supp. 8**, 69, 70

Institute for Jewish Studies, founding of, **Supp. 2**, 695

Institute for Religious and Social Studies, **Supp. 8**, 398, 408

Institute for Research in Land Economics, founding of, **Supp. 3**, 250

Institute for Sex Research, founding of, **Supp. 6**, 343

Institute for the Study of Law, founding of, **Supp. 2**, 501

Institute of American Meat Packers, **Vol. 3, Part 1**, 357

Institute of Child Welfare Research, founding of, **Supp. 3**, 677

Institute of Current World Affairs, establishment of, **Supp. 2**, 130

Institute of Design (Chicago), forerunner, **Supp. 4**, 591

Institute of Educational Research, founding of, **Supp. 3**, 677

Institute of Ethnic Affairs, founding of, **Supp. 8**, 99

Institute of Federal Taxation, founding of, **Supp. 5**, 412

Institute of Human Relations, **Supp. 5**, 330; founding of, **Supp. 2**, 562

Institute of Management, founding of, **Supp. 3**, 5

Institute of Medicine of Chicago, founding of, **Vol. 5, Part 1**, 465; **Supp. 1**, 616

Institute of Musical Art, **Vol. 5, Part 2**, 461; founding of, **Supp. 2**, 140

Institute of Pacific Relations, **Supp. 6**, 250, 350, 615

Institute of Phrenology, **Vol. 10, Part 1**, 643 f.

Institute of Public Administration, **Supp. 5**, 639

Institute of Radio Engineers, founding of, **Supp. 6**, 298

Institute of Scientific Research, founding of, **Supp. 2**, 598

Institute of the Missionary Sisters of the Sacred Heart, **Supp. 1**, 147

Institute of Tropical Medicine and Hygiene, **Supp. 1**, 33

Institutional Church, **Vol. 5, Part 2**, 237

Institut Pasteur, **Supp. 4**, 468

Insulation, research in, **Supp. 1**, 296

Insulin: crystallization of, **Supp. 2**, 4; first commercially produced in U.S., **Supp. 4**, 499; groundwork for discovery of, **Supp. 6**, 53; hyperinsulinism, **Supp. 6**, 698; overdose and hunger, **Supp. 6**, 100; shock treatment using, **Supp. 6**, 563–64

Insull, Martin, reference to, **Supp. 3**, 279

Insull, Samuel, reference to, **Supp. 5**, 270; **Supp. 6**, 684

Insurance, **Vol. 1, Part 1**, 599; **Vol. 2, Part 2**, 380; **Vol. 3, Part 1**, 209, 463 f.; **Vol. 3, Part 2**, 242; **Vol. 4, Part 2**, 168; **Vol. 6, Part 1**, 562, 577; **Vol. 7, Part 1**, 39; **Vol. 10, Part 1**, 119; accident, **Vol. 1, Part 2**, 54; employee groups, **Supp. 2**, 87; executives, **Supp. 6**, 497; fire, **Vol. 1, Part 1**, 216; **Vol. 6, Part 1**, 405; **Vol. 8, Part 1**, 139 f.; industrial, **Vol. 3, Part 1**, 463 f.; industrial accident, **Supp. 2**, 404; investigation, **Vol. 3, Part 1**, 246; **Vol. 5, Part 1**, 451; **Vol. 6, Part 1**, 60; laws, **Vol. 3, Part 1**, 485; **Vol. 6, Part 1**, 208; **Vol. 10, Part 2**, 549; life, **Vol. 3, Part 1**, 463 f.; **Vol. 3, Part 2**, 419; **Vol. 4, Part 2** 500; **Vol. 6, Part 1**, 588; **Vol. 6, Part 2**, 12; **Vol. 7, Part 1**, 323; **Vol. 7,**

Part 2, 313, 547; marine, **Vol. 3, Part 1**, 485 f.; **Vol. 9, Part 2**, 105; mutual system of, **Vol. 7, Part 2**, 529; premium system, **Supp. 2**, 586; savings-bank, for workers, **Supp. 3**, 95; social, **Supp. 2**, 586; teaching of, **Supp. 7**, 373; traveler's, **Vol. 1, Part 2**, 54; unemployment, **Supp. 7**, 543, 764; workmen's compensation, **Vol. 8, Part 2**, 531. *See also* Blue Cross and Blue Shield; Health insurance; Life insurance; Social Security

Insurance Co. of North America, **Vol. 7, Part 2**, 518

Intelligence, hereditary origins, **Supp. 2**, 406

Intelligence operations. *See* Central Intelligence Agency; Espionage; *names of specific wars*

Intelligence tests, **Supp. 5**, 59; **Supp. 6**, 240–41, 626–27, 718; Binet-Simon, **Supp. 4**, 439; children, **Supp. 2**, 269; for blind, **Supp. 4**, 11; for blind children, **Supp. 5**, 347; for World War I draftees, **Supp. 8**, 44; multiple correlation, **Supp. 5**, 685; Otis group measurement, **Supp. 7**, 594. *See also* Tests and measurements

Inter-American Bar Association, founding of, **Supp. 3**, 821

Inter-American Commission of Women, **Supp. 7**, 718

Interborough Co., **Vol. 9, Part 1**, 124

Inter-Catalog of Medical and Veterinary Zoology, **Supp. 3**, 738

Interchurch World Movement, **Vol. 7, Part 1**, 403; **Supp. 6**, 548

Intercollegiate Socialist Society, founding of, **Supp. 8**, 593–94

Interdenominational Christian Temperance Alliance of Ohio, **Vol. 5, Part 2**, 517

Interdenominational Conference of Woman's Boards of Foreign Missions, **Supp. 4**, 467

Interest rates, prices and, **Supp. 4**, 272–73

Interferometer, **Supp. 1**, 58

Interior, Department of the (U.S.), **Vol. 1, Part 1**, 555; **Vol. 3, Part 2**, 238; **Vol. 5, Part 1**, 74; **Vol. 5, Part 2**, 552, 573; **Vol. 6, Part 1**, 586–87; **Vol. 7, Part 1**, 539; **Vol. 8, Part 2**, 469; **Vol. 9, Part 1**, 281; **Vol. 9, Part 2**, 362, 459; administration, **Supp. 1**, 300; **Supp. 3**, 845–46; **Supp. 4**, 317–18, 893–94; **Supp. 5**, 342–43; **Supp. 6**, 684; **Supp. 8**, 2, 352; conservation policy controversy, **Supp. 1**, 300; **Supp. 4**, 664–65; **Supp. 6**, 416–17; Indian affairs, **Supp. 5**, 119; **Supp. 8**, 126; murals, **Supp. 3**, 380; Soil Erosion Service, **Supp. 6**, 53. *See also* Natural resources; Teapot Dome scandal

Interior decoration, **Vol. 2, Part 1**, 186; **Vol. 4, Part 2**, 596; first woman decorator, **Supp. 4**, 229; institutional, **Supp. 8**, 140–41; Victorian revival, **Supp. 4**, 290

Intermolecular forces, **Supp. 6**, 346

Internal-combustion engine, **Supp. 6**, 332

Internal Revenue Service (IRS): administration, **Supp. 4**, 356; counsel, **Supp. 5**, 357; organized crime and, **Supp. 6**, 264; Prohibition enforcement, **Supp. 7**, 805–6

Internal Security Act (1950). *See* McCarran Act (1950)

International Association of Chiefs of Police, **Supp. 5**, 639

International Association of Colored People of the World, **Supp. 5**, 755

International Association of Machinists, **Supp. 6**, 411

International Astronomical Union, founding of, **Supp. 2**, 271

International Bank for Reconstruction and Development (IBRD), **Supp. 8**, 616; first president, **Supp. 6**, 453; **Supp. 7**, 295–96; founding of, **Supp. 5**, 247, 713; **Supp. 8**, 446

International banking and finance, **Supp. 3**, 219; **Supp. 5**, 247; Dawes Plan, **Supp. 7**, 809–10; invest-

Iowa Improved Stock Breeders' Association, **Vol. 5, Part 2,** 453
Iowa Law School, **Vol. 2, Part 2,** 289
Iowa State Agricultural College, **Vol. 4, Part 2** 34; **Vol. 5, Part 2,** 453; **Vol. 10, Part 1,** 617 f.
Iowa State College of Agriculture and Mechanic Arts, **Vol. 1, Part 2,** 96; **Vol. 7, Part 2,** 197
Iowa State Teachers' Association, **Vol. 7, Part 2,** 285
Iowa State University: expansion, **Supp. 3,** 387; presidency, **Supp. 2,** 419
"Ioway Outfit," **Vol. 7, Part 1,** 41
IQ tests. *See* Intelligence tests
Iran: Anglo-Russian agreement, **Supp. 6,** 579; diplomacy with U.S., **Supp. 6,** 245; **Supp. 8,** 5–6, 275; oil dispute with Great Britain, **Supp. 8,** 276; scholarship on, **Supp. 2,** 338–39; Teheran Conference declaration on, **Supp. 7,** 377
Ireland, John, references to, **Vol. 5, Part 1,** 496 f.; **Supp. 3,** 568, 680
Ireland: diplomacy with, **Vol. 7, Part 2,** 557; emigration from, to United States, **Vol. 3, Part 2,** 440; **Vol. 5, Part 1,** 353; **Vol. 8, Part 2,** 57 f., 63, 248, 321; **Vol. 9, Part 2,** 4; **Vol. 10, Part 2,** 615; freedom, cause of, **Vol. 5, Part 1,** 405; **Vol. 7, Part 1,** 36; **Vol. 8, Part 1,** 156 f.
Irish-Americans: novels about, **Supp. 8,** 477; physical type survey, **Supp. 5,** 312; political activity, **Supp. 4,** 277–78, 858–59; **Supp. 6,** 139, 142, 661
Irish Citizen, **Vol. 7, Part 1,** 36
Irish Emigrant Society, **Vol. 8, Part 1,** 156 f.
Irish Free State, **Vol. 3, Part 1,** 265; **Vol. 4, Part 1,** 335; **Vol. 9, Part 2,** 242
Irish Land League, **Vol. 3, Part 2,** 518
Irish Republican Brotherhood, **Vol. 3, Part 1,** 265
"Irish Rescue Party," **Vol. 4, Part 1,** 359
Irish Societies of New York, **Vol. 8, Part 2,** 19
Irish World, **Vol. 3, Part 2,** 518
Iron (nutrient): anemia relationship, **Supp. 4,** 581–82, 276; average human requirement, **Supp. 5,** 623
Iron and Steel Magazine, founding of, **Supp. 2,** 595
"Iron Brigade," **Vol. 5, Part 2,** 400
"Ironclad oath," **Vol. 4, Part 1,** 150
Ironclad vessels, **Vol. 3, Part 1,** 211, 529 f.; **Vol. 8, Part 1,** 97; **Vol. 8, Part 2,** 78–85
Iron industry: Bessemer process, **Vol. 7, Part 2,** 356; brokerage, **Vol. 6, Part 1,** 155; building, early use, in, **Vol. 1, Part 2,** 407; **Vol. 3, Part 1,** 211, 529 f.; **Vol. 8, Part 1,** 138 f., 639 f.; conveyors in, **Vol. 2, Part 1,** 103; factory conditions, **Vol. 4, Part 2** 605; galvanizing process, **Vol. 6, Part 1,** 141; manufacturing, **Vol. 1, Part 1,** 219, 268 f.; **Vol. 1, Part 2,** 127, 217; **Vol. 2, Part 1,** 35, 114, 149, 272, 338; **Vol. 2, Part 2,** 327, 396, 409; **Vol. 3, Part 1,** 362, 395; **Vol. 3, Part 2,** 124, 243, 251, 405, 452, 573; **Vol. 4, Part 1,** 4, 38 f., 199, 593; **Vol. 4, Part 2** 9, 343, 379, 605; **Vol. 5, Part 1,** 48, 57, 433 f.; **Vol. 5, Part 2,** 40, 54, 156, 162, 426; **Vol. 6, Part 1,** 73, 139, 174, 395, 500, 551; **Vol. 6, Part 2,** 398; **Vol. 7, Part 1,** 79, 505, 540, 642 f.; **Vol. 7, Part 2,** 20 f., 206, 330, 550; **Vol. 8, Part 1,** 89, 115 f., 138 f., 149, 314 f.; **Vol. 8, Part 2,** 504 f., 513 f.; **Vol. 9, Part 1,** 25, 48, 125, 621; **Vol. 9, Part 2,** 17, 236 f., 258, 325, 427 f., 568; **Vol. 10, Part 1,** 400 f., 635; **Vol. 10, Part 2,** 399, 412; mining, **Vol. 2, Part 1,** 90; **Vol. 3, Part 1,** 90; **Vol. 3, Part 2,** 79, 118; **Vol. 4, Part 1,** 183; **Vol. 5, Part 1,** 505; **Vol. 6, Part 2,** 397, 487, 572; **Vol. 7, Part 1,** 20, 135; **Vol. 8, Part 1,** 264 f.; **Vol. 10, Part 2,** 375; pig iron, **Vol. 3, Part 1,** 548 f.; **Vol. 9, Part 1,** 219; smelting, first, **Vol. 1, Part 2,** 217; wages, sliding scale of, **Vol. 5, Part 2,** 162; woman, first, in, **Vol. 6, Part 1,** 500

Iroquois Confederacy, **Supp. 8,** 647
Irradiation. *See* Radiation
Irrigation, **Vol. 3, Part 1,** 606; **Vol. 4, Part 2** 84; **Vol. 6, Part 1,** 505; **Vol. 7, Part 1,** 433, 457; **Vol. 8, Part 1,** 121 f.; **Vol. 10, Part 2,** 212; Colorado, **Vol. 3, Part 1,** 605; **Vol. 7, Part 1,** 434; ditching machines, **Vol. 8, Part 1,** 369; electric powered, **Supp. 3,** 192; first Hawaiian, **Supp. 1,** 48; Florida Everglades, **Vol. 2, Part 1,** 96; laws relating to, **Vol. 6, Part 2,** 4; litigation, **Supp. 1,** 620; national program, **Supp. 4,** 563–64; project design, **Supp. 2,** 304; New Mexico, **Vol. 3, Part 1,** 606; Southern California, **Supp. 5,** 310; Western development, **Supp. 2,** 443; **Supp. 4,** 567. *See also* Dams; Drainage
IRS. *See* Internal Revenue Service
Irvin, Rea, reference to, **Supp. 5,** 594
Irving, Washington: biography of, **Vol. 5, Part 1,** 505; influence of, **Vol. 9, Part 1,** 70; printing of works, **Vol. 1, Part 1,** 526; references to, **Vol. 4, Part 1,** 505; **Vol. 5, Part 1,** 503 f., 512; **Vol. 5, Part 2,** 316 f.; **Vol. 7, Part 1,** 96, 643; **Vol. 7, Part 2,** 321, 328 f.
Irvingites, Catholic Apostolic church, **Vol. 1, Part 1,** 299
Irwin, Amelia, reference to, **Supp. 6,** 8
Irwin, Inez Hayes, reference to, **Supp. 5,** 532
Isaak Walton League, **Vol. 3, Part 1,** 299
Isbrandtsen Lines, founding of, **Supp. 5,** 348
Isis, **Supp. 6,** 564, 565
Island No. 10, capture of (1862), **Vol. 3, Part 1,** 107; **Vol. 3, Part 2,** 500; **Vol. 8, Part 1,** 76
Isle of Pines, ceding of, to Cuba, **Vol. 8, Part 1,** 333
Isles of Shoals, **Vol. 9, Part 2,** 397
Isolationism. *See* Foreign relations; World War I; World War II
Isomorphism, **Supp. 8,** 344
Isostasy: doctrine of, **Vol. 3, Part 1,** 555; **Vol. 4, Part 2,** 452; mathematical formulation of, **Supp. 2,** 56; writings on, **Vol. 1, Part 1,** 643
Isotopic tracers, **Supp. 3,** 693–94
Israel, Harold, reference to, **Supp. 6,** 137
Israel: American Zionist relations, **Supp. 7,** 690; diplomacy with U.S., **Supp. 7,** 498; Eichmann trial, **Supp. 8,** 456; independence, **Supp. 5,** 599; **Supp. 6,** 431; U.S. recognition of, **Supp. 5,** 515. *See also* Middle East; Palestine; Suez Crisis (1956); Zionism
Israel Philharmonic, predecessor, **Supp. 6,** 643–44
Israfel: The Life and Times of Edgar Allen Poe, **Supp. 4,** 13, 14
Isthmian Canal Commission, **Vol. 1, Part 1,** 258; **Vol. 7, Part 1,** 191, 347, 537; **Vol. 7, Part 2,** 288; **Vol. 8, Part 2,** 193. *See also* Panama Canal
Isthmian Canal project, early history of, **Vol. 1, Part 1,** 258; **Vol. 1, Part 2,** 327–28; **Vol. 2, Part 2,** 186; **Vol. 4, Part 1,** 16; **Vol. 4, Part 2** 439; **Vol. 6, Part 2,** 108, 201; **Vol. 7, Part 1,** 181, 191, 347, 537; **Vol. 7, Part 2,** 288; **Vol. 8, Part 2,** 193. *See also* Panama Canal
Isthmus of Tehuantepec, projected railway across, **Vol. 3, Part 1,** 587 f.
Italian-Americans: banks for, **Supp. 4,** 325–26; labor movement, **Supp. 3,** 777–78; **Supp. 6,** 238; political activity, **Supp. 4,** 464; writings on, **Supp. 8,** 457
Italian Villas and Their Gardens, **Supp. 8,** 494
Italy: anti-Fascism, **Supp. 6,** 237; art history, **Supp. 6,** 56–57; culture, spread of, **Vol. 3, Part 1,** 71 f.; diplomacy with U.S., **Supp. 6,** 254, 388–89; **Supp. 7,** 815; **Supp. 8,** 395; diplomatic service, **Vol. 5, Part 2,** 400; **Vol. 7, Part 2,** 141; **Vol. 9, Part 1,** 497; historical writings on, **Supp. 2,** 402; influence on Sargent, **Vol. 8, Part 2,** 363 f.; mannerism art studies, **Supp. 8,** 194; missions, **Vol. 9, Part 2,** 326; opera, Italian, introduction of, **Vol. 9, Part 1,** 177.

See also Vatican; World War I; World War II

I Tatti, **Supp. 6,** 57; **Supp. 7,** 673

ITT. *See* International Telephone and Telegraph Corporation

Iuka, Miss., battle of, **Vol. 5, Part 1,** 442; **Vol. 7, Part 2,** 48; **Vol. 8, Part 1,** 216; **Vol. 8, Part 2,** 163; **Vol. 10, Part 1,** 185

Ives, J. C., reference to, **Vol. 7, Part 1,** 445

Ives and Myrick Insurance Co., founding of, **Supp. 5,** 351

Ives Co., **Supp. 7,** 150

Ivory soap, **Supp. 1,** 610

Iwerks, Ub, references to, **Supp. 8,** 129–30, 131

Iwo Jima, World War II action, **Supp. 5,** 66; **Supp. 8,** 603

IWW. *See* Industrial Workers of the World

J

Jaboulay, Mathieu, reference to, **Supp. 3,** 140

Jackson, Andrew, bas-relief of, **Vol. 4, Part 1,** 152; biography of, **Vol. 6, Part 1,** 226; **Supp. 5,** 364; campaign of, **Vol. 6, Part 1,** 109; close friendship with, **Vol. 3, Part 1,** 363 f.; Creek Indians and, **Vol. 4, Part 2** 414; dissolution of cabinet as result of Peggy O'Neale stir, **Vol. 3, Part 1,** 610; Felix Grundy, and, **Vol. 4, Part 2** 33; Florida, **Vol. 7, Part 1,** 414; Hall case, **Vol. 4, Part 2** 124; opposition to policies of, **Vol. 3, Part 1,** 510 f.; references to, **Vol. 1, Part 1,** 87; **Vol. 1, Part 2,** 157, 211; **Vol. 2, Part 1,** 104; **Vol. 5, Part 1,** 263, 365, 474, 526 f.; **Vol. 5, Part 2,** 257, 264, 325 f.; **Vol. 6, Part 1,** 226, 310, 518; **Vol. 7, Part 1,** 91; **Vol. 7, Part 2,** 115 f.; **Vol. 8, Part 1,** 34 f.; **Vol. 8, Part 2,** 9 f., 507, 604; **Vol. 9, Part 1,** 319, 412; **Vol. 9, Part 2,** 645 f.; **Vol. 10, Part 1,** 89 f.; relations with Clay, **Vol. 2, Part 2,** 176 f.; re-formation of cabinet, **Vol. 10, Part 2,** 106; war against national bank, **Vol. 1, Part 2,** 157

Jackson, Charles T., reference to, **Vol. 7, Part 1,** 269

Jackson, Chevalier Lawrence, reference to, **Supp. 6,** 318

Jackson, F. J. Foakes, reference to, **Supp. 4,** 468

Jackson, James, reference to, **Vol. 10, Part 1,** 480 f.

Jackson, Joe, reference to, **Supp. 8,** 574, 575

Jackson, Robert H., references to, **Supp. 6,** 156, 662

Jackson, Robert Tracy, references to, **Supp. 4,** 205, 206

Jackson, "Stonewall": nickname, origin of, **Vol. 1, Part 2,** 124; **Vol. 9, Part 2,** 642; references to, **Vol. 5, Part 1,** 556; **Vol. 6, Part 1,** 123 f., 391, 420; **Vol. 8, Part 2,** 71 f.; statue of, **Vol. 7, Part 1,** 4

Jackson, Tony, reference to, **Supp. 3,** 541

Jackson Hole Wildlife Park (Wyo.), founding of, **Supp. 7,** 31; **Supp. 8,** 486

Jacksonians, The, **Supp. 6,** 693

"Jacksonis Americus," pseudonym for Tilden, **Vol. 9, Part 2,** 538

Jackson-Monroe correspondence, **Vol. 6, Part 1,** 26

Jacobi, Abraham, references to, **Vol. 7, Part 1,** 628; **Supp. 3,** 159

Jacobi, Leonard, reference to, **Supp. 3,** 26

Jacobin Club, Charleston, S.C., **Vol. 4, Part 2,** 285

"Jacobinism," **Vol. 1, Part 1,** 245

Jacobs, Randall, reference to, **Supp. 8,** 23

Jacobson, Paul, references to, **Supp. 4,** 336, 337

Jacob Tome Institute, founding of, **Vol. 9, Part 2,** 578

Jacoby, Oswald, reference to, **Supp. 6,** 380

Jadassohn, Salomon, reference to, **Supp. 1,** 161

Jails. *See* Prisons

James, Arthur H., references to, **Supp. 3,** 20; **Supp. 7,** 615–16

James, Edmund J., references to, **Vol. 7, Part 2,** 298 f. **Supp. 4,** 40, 227

James, Harry, reference to, **Supp. 8,** 163

James, Henry: references to, **Vol. 5, Part 1,** 310; **Supp. 6,** 174; **Supp. 7,** 55; Wharton relationship, **Supp. 2,** 703, 704, 705; writings on, **Supp. 4,** 560

James, Jesse, references to, **Vol. 6, Part 1,** 433; **Vol. 9, Part 2,** 634

James, Walter B., reference to, **Supp. 4,** 49

James, William, references to, **Vol. 5, Part 1,** 311; **Vol. 7, Part 2,** 400 f.; **Vol. 8, Part 2,** 152, 207 f.; **Vol. 9, Part 1,** 410; **Supp. 3,** 51, 577, 578, 608, 682; **Supp. 4,** 20, 21, 387, 766, 767, 832, 833; **Supp. 6,** 454, 504, 505; **Supp. 7,** 201, 481

James Foundation, founding of, **Supp. 3,** 381–82

Jameson, J. Franklin, references to, **Supp. 3,** 15–16; **Supp. 8,** 369, 370

James River Canal, **Vol. 2, Part 2,** 580; **Vol. 8, Part 2,** 30

Jamestown, Va., **Vol. 4, Part 1,** 190, 439; **Vol. 5, Part 1,** 391; **Vol. 7, Part 1,** 468; **Vol. 9, Part 1,** 295; first legislative assembly in America, **Vol. 8, Part 1,** 110; first printing-press south of Massachusetts, **Vol. 7, Part 1,** 596; removal of capital from, **Vol. 7, Part 1,** 500

Janet, Pierre, reference to, **Supp. 3,** 190–91

Japan: anthropological cultural study of, **Supp. 4,** 72; art, **Vol. 5, Part 1,** 450; art and culture studies, **Supp. 3,** 341, 465; **Supp. 5,** 729–30; atomic bombing of, **Supp. 8,** 230, 231; baseball in, **Supp. 8,** 479; Bible translated into Japanese, **Vol. 3, Part 2,** 80; **Vol. 4, Part 1,** 8, 564; diplomatic relations with U.S., **Vol. 1, Part 1,** 563; **Vol. 1, Part 2,** 277; **Vol. 3, Part 1,** 245; **Vol. 4, Part 2** 60, 324; **Vol. 6, Part 1,** 570, 573; **Vol. 6, Part 2,** 18; **Vol. 7, Part 2,** 488; **Vol. 8, Part 1,** 254 f.; **Vol. 9, Part 2,** 423; **Vol. 10, Part 2,** 561; **Supp. 2,** 580; **Supp. 3,** 323; **Supp. 5,** 333; **Supp. 6,** 211; **Supp. 7,** 112–13, 303; education in, **Vol. 7, Part 1,** 242, 358; English-language newspapers, **Supp. 4,** 284–85; General Le Gendre in, **Vol. 6, Part 1,** 146; geological surveys for, **Vol. 6, Part 1,** 515; historical writings on, **Supp. 8,** 360; Imperial College of Agriculture and Engineering, **Vol. 9, Part 2,** 38; Imperial Research Institute, **Vol. 9, Part 2,** 275; labor movement, **Supp. 6,** 648; medicine, **Vol. 9, Part 2,** 384; Methodist church in, **Supp. 1,** 208; missionary activities, **Vol. 1, Part 2,** 236; **Vol. 2, Part 1,** 154; **Vol. 3, Part 1,** 132, 177, 198; **Vol. 4, Part 1,** 563 f.; **Vol. 4, Part 2,** 317; **Vol. 5, Part 2,** 560 f.; **Vol. 6, Part 2,** 122; **Vol. 10, Part 2,** 250; missions in, **Supp. 3,** 322–23; **Supp. 5,** 681; **Supp. 6,** 649; peace treaty, **Supp. 6,** 178; Perry's mission to (1853), **Vol. 4, Part 1,** 334, 481; **Vol. 4, Part 2** 324; **Vol. 7, Part 2,** 488; **Vol. 8, Part 1,** 462; physical education, **Vol. 6, Part 1,** 160; postwar industrial rehabilitation, **Supp. 7,** 190; post-World War II occupation of, **Supp. 5,** 730; pre-World War II expansionism, **Supp. 3,** 657–59; **Supp. 4,** 171, 679, 786; **Supp. 5,** 333; **Supp. 6,** 269–70; **Supp. 7,** 362; **Supp. 8,** 617; publicity, **Vol. 5, Part 1,** 258; scientific school, first, **Vol. 1, Part 2,** 345; service to, **Vol. 4, Part 2,** 567; **Vol. 7, Part 1,** 358; students from, in U.S., **Vol. 7, Part 1,** 566; studies of, **Vol. 9, Part 1,** 533; surrender conditions, **Supp. 7,** 813; tea, first, from, **Vol. 4, Part 2** 68; trade relations with, **Vol. 2, Part 2,** 186; **Vol. 4, Part 2** 324; U.S. minister to, first, **Vol. 3, Part 1,** 245; U.S. occupation policies, **Supp. 7,** 490–92, 493; **Supp. 8,** 699; U.S. restrictions on immigration, **Supp. 3,** 323; **Supp. 6,** 320; war with China, **Supp. 4,** 750–51; **Supp. 6,** 230; Wright's architecture in, **Supp. 6,** 712, 713; writings on, **Vol. 1, Part 1,** 473; **Vol. 4, Part 1,** 623; **Vol. 4,**

Part 2, 486 f.; **Vol. 5, Part 2,** 475, 534, 606; **Vol. 6, Part 1,** 468 f., 573; **Vol. 8, Part 2,** 485. *See also* Pearl Harbor attack; World War II

Japan Advertiser, **Supp. 4,** 284

Japanese-Americans: immigration policies toward, **Supp. 3,** 323; **Supp. 6,** 230; internment during World War II, **Supp. 3,** 661; **Supp. 4,** 286, 787; **Supp. 5,** 43, 343, 358, 574–75; **Supp. 7,** 292, 457; **Supp. 8,** 650

Japanese current, first study of, **Vol. 3, Part 1,** 394

Japanese Exclusion Treaty (1905), **Vol. 4, Part 2** 434; **Vol. 8, Part 2,** 139

Japanese Sculpture of the Suiko Period, **Supp. 5,** 729

Japanning, **Vol. 5, Part 2,** 152

Japan Society, founding of, **Supp. 5,** 308

Jarvis, J. W., reference to, **Vol. 5, Part 1,** 481

Jaundice, **Supp. 7,** 340

Java, missions, **Supp. 8,** 425

Jay, John: Carmichael, William, relations with, **Vol. 2, Part 1,** 497; Gardoqui negotiations, **Vol. 7, Part 1,** 87 f.; probably first portrait engraved, **Vol. 9, Part 2,** 530; Spain, **Vol. 6, Part 1,** 302. *See also* Jay Treaty

Jay Treaty, **Vol. 1, Part 1,** 78; **Vol. 2, Part 2,** 135; **Vol. 4, Part 1,** 106; **Vol. 4, Part 2** 176; **Vol. 8, Part 2,** 7, 9, 12, 26, 398; **Vol. 6, Part 1,** 312; **Vol. 7, Part 1,** 88, 210; **Vol. 8, Part 1,** 355; **Vol. 8, Part 2,** 49; **Vol. 9, Part 2,** 651; **Vol. 10, Part 1,** 524, 565; Jefferson's opinion of, **Vol. 5, Part 2,** 26

Jayhawking, **Vol. 7, Part 1,** 97

Jazz: bands, **Supp. 2,** 502; **Supp. 4,** 510; **Supp. 5,** 106; **Supp. 8,** 163, 697–98; bebop style, **Supp. 5,** 534; blues trumpet, **Supp. 5,** 529–30; Chicago style, **Supp. 8,** 561; clarinet, **Supp. 6,** 42–43; "Condon mob," **Supp. 8,** 562; drummers, **Supp. 5,** 105–6; first composer, **Supp. 3,** 541–42; first in Soviet Union, **Supp. 3,** 690; "hot," **Supp. 5,** 293; influence on art, **Supp. 7,** 170, 171; introduced in Europe, **Supp. 3,** 187; King Creole band, **Supp. 2,** 502; "Krazy Kat" pantomime, **Supp. 3,** 357; modal scales in, **Supp. 8,** 100; novel about, **Supp. 8,** 20; orchestral compositions, **Supp. 5,** 103–4; organ, **Supp. 3,** 798; piano, **Supp. 3,** 797–99; **Supp. 6,** 619–20; **Supp. 7,** 131; saxophone, **Supp. 8,** 100; singing, **Supp. 5,** 32–33; **Supp. 6,** 299–300; swing, **Supp. 5,** 534–35; trombone, **Supp. 7,** 735–36

Jazz Age, **Supp. 6,** 287–88

Jazz Singer, The, **Supp. 4,** 440; **Supp. 5,** 121, 630; **Supp. 8,** 459

Jeanes Fund. *See* Negro Rural School Fund

Jeannette, Arctic voyage of the, **Vol. 1, Part 1,** 240; **Vol. 3, Part 1,** 228

Jeans, fashion of, **Supp. 5,** 386

Jeffers, Robinson, reference to, **Supp. 5,** 4

Jefferson, Blind Lemon, reference to, **Supp. 8,** 695, 696

Jefferson, Joseph, references to, **Vol. 5, Part 1,** 143 f., 255

Jefferson, Mark S. W., reference to, **Supp. 4,** 98

Jefferson, Thomas, **Vol. 1, Part 1,** 246; **Vol. 3, Part 1,** 512 f.; **Vol. 4, Part 2** 176; **Vol. 5, Part 1,** 206; **Vol. 5, Part 2,** 210; **Vol. 6, Part 1,** 360; **Vol. 7, Part 1,** 10, 88 f., 483, 484, 502, 505, 645; **Vol. 7, Part 2,** 137 f.; **Vol. 8, Part 2,** 395; **Vol. 9, Part 1,** 129, 343, 400; **Vol. 9, Part 2,** 309, 332, 526, 575, 645; **Vol. 10, Part 2,** 224; biographies of, **Vol. 8, Part 1,** 347; **Supp. 6,** 72, 73; critics, one of most outspoken, **Vol. 8, Part 1,** 363 f.; descendant of, **Supp. 6,** 124–25; election of, **Vol. 1, Part 2,** 64; **Vol. 7, Part 1,** 216; first published collection of the works of, **Vol. 8, Part 1,** 369 f.; guardian of, **Vol. 4, Part 2** 375; Jouett, famous ride of, **Vol. 5, Part 2,** 222; Lewis-Clark expedition, plan for, **Vol. 6, Part 1,** 221; Madison, James, rela-

tions with, **Vol. 6, Part 2,** 189 f.; Marshall, John, relations with, **Vol. 6, Part 2,** 320 f.; personal Bible, **Supp. 2,** 5; political pamphleteering, **Vol. 2, Part 1,** 425; private secretary to, **Vol. 6, Part 1,** 220; sculpture depicting, **Supp. 3,** 89; sourcebook on, **Vol. 8, Part 1,** 368 f.; writings of, **Supp. 3,** 285; **Supp. 5,** 388; writings on, **Supp. 3,** 555; **Supp. 5,** 681

Jefferson Barracks, Mo., **Vol. 1, Part 1,** 410; **Vol. 6, Part 1,** 80

Jefferson College, **Vol. 1, Part 2,** 366; **Vol. 3, Part 1,** 340; **Vol. 8, Part 2,** 125

Jeffersonians, The, **Supp. 6,** 693

Jefferson Medical College, **Vol. 1, Part 2,** 25; **Vol. 7, Part 2,** 198, 311; founding of, **Vol. 3, Part 1,** 615 f.; **Vol. 6, Part 1,** 579–80; **Vol. 9, Part 1,** 328

Jefferson Memorial (Washington, D.C.): architecture of, **Supp. 2,** 539; **Supp. 5,** 300; creation of, **Supp. 4,** 448; inscription selection, **Supp. 4,** 448; **Supp. 5,** 681

Jefferson School of Social Science, founding of, **Supp. 8,** 132

Jeffries, James J. ("Jim"), reference to, **Supp. 4,** 433

Jehovah's Witnesses: flag salute issue, **Supp. 3,** 451; **Supp. 4,** 796; **Supp. 5,** 358, 575; **Supp. 7,** 264; leadership, **Supp. 3,** 678–79

Jekyll, Gertrude, reference to, **Supp. 6,** 196

Jelliffe, Smith Ely, reference to, **Supp. 4,** 108

"Jelly Roll Blues," **Supp. 3,** 541

Jenkins' Ferry, battle of, **Vol. 1, Part 1,** 579; **Vol. 2, Part 2,** 105; **Vol. 5, Part 2,** 425; **Vol. 9, Part 1,** 556; **Vol. 9, Part 2,** 340

Jenner, William E., reference to, **Supp. 5,** 554

Jennings, Hughie, reference to, **Supp. 8,** 106

Jensen Industries, **Supp. 7,** 395

Jerome, Jerome K., reference to, **Vol. 6, Part 1,** 397

Jerome, William T., reference to, **Supp. 4,** 827

Jersey City, N.J.: founding of, **Vol. 8, Part 1,** 318 f.; politics, **Supp. 5,** 212–13; **Supp. 6,** 265–66, 479–80, 651

Jerseys, the, governorship of, **Vol. 4, Part 2,** 180

"Jersey Settlement," **Vol. 3, Part 2,** 106

Jervis, John B., reference to, **Vol. 6, Part 1,** 548

Jessel, George, references to, **Supp. 6,** 619; **Supp. 7,** 106

Jessup expedition, **Vol. 8, Part 1,** 276 f.

Jesuit Order, **Vol. 1, Part 2,** 141 f.; **Vol. 3, Part 2,** 392, 396; **Vol. 4, Part 1,** 458, 527; **Supp. 7,** 444–48; California, **Vol. 3, Part 1,** 422; **Vol. 5, Part 2,** 420; **Vol. 8, Part 1,** 109 f.; conversion of Iroquois chief by, **Vol. 4, Part 1,** 130–31; education, **Vol. 2, Part 2,** 432 f.; establishment, **Vol. 1, Part 1,** 222; Indian attacks on, **Vol. 5, Part 2,** 75; history of, **Vol. 2, Part 1,** 464; Maryland, **Vol. 4, Part 2** 250; missions, **Vol. 3, Part 2,** 276 f.; **Vol. 5, Part 2,** 419; **Vol. 6, Part 1,** 10 f.; **Supp. 1,** 158–59; **Supp. 7,** 447; publications, **Supp. 7,** 448; recollect priests, relations with, **Vol. 6, Part 1,** 231; seismological service, **Supp. 1,** 579–80; universities, **Supp. 1,** 159

Jesus Christ: black sculpture of, **Supp. 7,** 610; novels about, **Supp. 5,** 182; **Supp. 7,** 235; paintings of martyrdom, **Supp. 7,** 465; philosophical writings on, **Supp. 5,** 225; popular writings on, **Supp. 4,** 741; **Supp. 5,** 527–28; **Supp. 8,** 27; scholarship on, **Supp. 4,** 152; **Supp. 7,** 624; theological writings on, **Supp. 7,** 575. *See also* Christianity

Jet propulsion: development of, **Supp. 6,** 183; first academic course in, **Supp. 8,** 439–440

Jet Propulsion Laboratory, **Supp. 7,** 411

Jewell Ridge case, **Supp. 5,** 358

Jewelry, ancient, **Supp. 1,** 477

Jewelry trade, **Vol. 9, Part 2,** 533

Johnston, Douglas H., reference to, **Supp. 6,** 468
Johnston, Joseph, reference to, **Vol. 6, Part** 1, 576
Johnston, Joseph E., references to, **Vol. 6, Part** 1, 123 f.; **Vol. 8, Part 2,** 546
Johnston, Samuel, reference to, **Vol. 5, Part 2,** 210
Johnston, William M. reference to, **Supp. 6,** 538
Johnstone, Edward R., reference to, **Supp. 4,** 11
Johnstown flood, **Vol. 5, Part 2,** 123, 135, 209; **Vol. 7, Part 1,** 301
Joint Committee Against Communism, **Supp. 6,** 350
Joint Committee on Conduct of War (1862-64), **Vol. 2, Part 1,** 618; **Vol. 2, Part 2,** 470; **Vol. 5, Part 2,** 246; **Vol. 9, Part 1,** 623; **Vol. 10, Part 1,** 304
Joint Palestine Survey Commission, founding of, **Supp. 2,** 695
Jolson, Al, references to, **Supp. 4,** 225; **Supp. 5,** 121, 629, 630; **Supp. 6,** 536; **Supp. 8,** 251
Jones, Bassett, references to, **Supp. 5,** 558, 559
Jones, Ernest, references to, **Supp. 4,** 108, 109, 716, 717
Jones, Eugene Kinckle, reference to, **Supp. 6,** 285
Jones, Faith, reference to, **Supp. 6,** 103
Jones, George, refusal of bribe by, **Vol. 10, Part 1,** 81
Jones, Isham, reference to, **Supp. 3,** 406
Jones, Jacob, reference to, **Vol. 1, Part 2,** 241
Jones, Jennifer, reference to, **Supp. 7,** 682
Jones, Jesse H., references to, **Supp. 6,** 135, 136; **Supp. 7,** 761; **Supp. 8,** 89
Jones, John Paul, references to, **Vol. 3, Part 2,** 268; **Vol. 5, Part 1,** 210; **Vol. 8, Part 1,** 92 f.; **Vol. 9, Part 1,** 156
Jones, John Price, Corporation, **Supp. 7,** 401-2
Jones, Mary, reference to, **Supp. 6,** 196
Jones, Robert Edmond, reference to, **Supp. 3,** 35
Jones, Samuel ("Golden Rule"), references to, **Supp. 3,** 298; **Supp. 7,** 85
Jones, Spike, and His City Slickers, **Supp. 7,** 403-4
Jones, William Atkinson, reference to, **Supp. 3,** 614
Jonesborough, Ga., capture of, **Vol. 1, Part 1,** 266; **Vol. 5, Part 1,** 194; **Vol. 9, Part 1,** 95; **Vol. 8, Part 1,** 380
Jordan, Camille, reference to, **Supp. 5,** 491
Jordan, David Starr, references to, **Vol. 3, Part 2,** 62; **Vol. 5, Part 1,** 277; **Vol. 7, Part 1,** 598; **Supp. 3,** 205-6, 262, 602
Jordan, Sara Murray, reference to, **Supp. 5,** 405
Joseph, Chief, reference to, **Supp. 3,** 836
Joseph in Egypt, **Supp. 8,** 433
Joss, Addie, reference to, **Supp. 6,** 663
Jouett, Captain John, famous ride of, **Vol. 5, Part 2,** 222
Journal General of Physiology, founding of, **Supp. 7,** 592
Journalism (for complete list of journalists, *see* Occupations Index): agricultural, **Vol. 8, Part 1,** 40 f.; **Supp. 3,** 319; Asian affairs, **Supp. 4,** 679, 749-51; black, early, **Vol. 8, Part 2,** 253; black-related, **Supp. 7,** 767; Boston, **Vol. 2, Part 1,** 456; **Vol. 2, Part 2,** 118, 198; **Vol. 3, Part 2,** 374; **Vol. 4, Part 2** 41, 109; **Vol. 5, Part 2,** 361, 457, 458; **Vol. 6, Part 1,** 285, 508, 563; **Vol. 8, Part 2,** 239, 359; **Vol. 9, Part 2,** 319, 609; business forecasting, **Supp. 8,** 19; California, **Vol. 1, Part 1,** 443 f.; **Vol. 1, Part 2,** 602; **Vol. 2, Part 2,** 323; **Vol. 5, Part 2,** 408; **Vol. 9, Part 1,** 195; cartoons, *see* Cartoons and caricatures; Catholic, **Supp. 6,** 478-79, 448; Chicago, **Vol. 2, Part 1,** 94; **Vol. 2, Part 2,** 374; **Vol. 5, Part 2,** 109, 489; **Vol. 6, Part 1,** 60, 609 f.; **Vol. 8, Part 2,** 492; **Vol. 9, Part 2,** 82, 317; child-care advice, **Supp. 6,** 382; child-oriented, **Supp. 3,** 44-45; civic-minded, **Supp. 4,** 222, 738; Civil War, **Vol. 9, Part 1,** 409 f.; Cleveland election, **Vol. 6, Part 1,** 283; college, **Vol. 8, Part 2,** 57; colonial, **Vol. 3, Part 1,** 347 f.; columnist, one of

first in America, **Vol. 3, Part 2,** 364; **Vol. 5, Part 1,** 320; **Vol. 9, Part 2,** 317; columns, "About New York," **Supp. 6,** 58; columns, advice, **Supp. 5,** 244; columns, "As Pegler Sees It," **Supp. 8,** 498-99; columns, "Backstairs at the White House," **Supp. 8,** 607; columns, "Between You and Me," **Supp. 3,** 166; columns, black-oriented, **Supp. 8,** 287-88; columns, book, **Supp. 1,** 92; columns, "Broadway After Dark," **Supp. 8,** 444; columns, "Conning Tower," **Supp. 6,** 4, 5; columns, daily, **Supp. 2,** 431; columns, "Easy Chair," **Supp. 5,** 168, 169; columns, etiquette, **Supp. 6,** 514; columns, "Fair Enough," **Supp. 8,** 498; columns, gossip, **Supp. 7,** 433, 444; **Supp. 8,** 282; columns, "Letters from a Senator's Wife," **Supp. 8,** 328; columns, "lovelorn," **Supp. 3,** 504; columns, "My Day," **Supp. 7,** 660; columns, oldest continuous on sports, **Supp. 5,** 724; columns, "Pitching Horseshoes," **Supp. 8,** 547; columns, "Seeing Things," **Supp. 8,** 54; columns, show business, **Supp. 8,** 547; columns, "Stories of the Streets and of the Towns," **Supp. 3,** 3; columns, "Sun Dial," **Supp. 7,** 617-18; columns, syndicated, **Supp. 2,** 69; **Supp. 7,** 665; columns, "Washington Merry-Go-Round," **Supp. 8,** 496; Communist China affairs, **Supp. 8,** 635; Communist-oriented, **Supp. 7,** 268-69; Connecticut, **Vol. 10, Part 2,** 565; consumer protection, **Supp. 7,** 69; criticism, *see* Criticism; Democratic newspaper, first in West, **Vol. 3, Part 2,** 231; documentary, **Supp. 5,** 511; early attempt at unbiased presentation, **Vol. 8, Part 1,** 409 f.; editorials, *see* Newspapers, editorials; effect of *New York Sun's* style, **Vol. 3, Part 1,** 51; ethics issues, **Supp. 3,** 851; **Supp. 4,** 668; ethics of, **Vol. 7, Part 1,** 335; exposé, *see subhead* muckraking; "family type," **Vol. 1, Part 2,** 437; feature writing, **Supp. 2,** 415; financial, **Supp. 3,** 564-65; **Supp. 6,** 457-58; **Supp. 8,** 338; first American newspaper in Paris, **Vol. 3, Part 2,** 212; first astronomical magazine, **Vol. 7, Part 1,** 39; first "comic strips," **Vol. 7, Part 2,** 112; first daily in U.S., **Vol. 3, Part 1,** 514 f.; **Vol. 8, Part 1,** 139 f., 638; first "extra," **Vol. 8, Part 1,** 299 f.; first illustrated dailies in U.S., **Vol. 6, Part 1,** 186; **Vol. 8, Part 1,** 332 f., 440; first illustrated weekly, **Vol. 3, Part 1,** 155; first Italian paper, **Vol. 1, Part 2,** 1; first newspaper chain, **Vol. 8, Part 2,** 518; first newspaper in German, **Vol. 9, Part 2,** 557; first newspaper in Hawaii, **Vol. 1, Part 1,** 295; **Vol. 5, Part 1,** 618; first newspaper in Middle Colonies, **Vol. 1, Part 2,** 553; first newspaper in New Jersey, **Vol. 7, Part 2,** 227; first newspaper in New York, **Vol. 1, Part 2,** 564; first newspaper in Pennsylvania, **Vol. 1, Part 2,** 553; first newspaper in South Carolina, **Vol. 10, Part 1,** 644 f.; first newspaper in Utah, **Vol. 2, Part 2,** 353; first newspapers in U.S., **Vol. 2, Part 1,** 456; **Vol. 4, Part 2,** 304; **Vol. 8, Part 1,** 139 f.; first newspaper syndicate, **Vol. 8, Part 2,** 518; first newspaper to have literary supplement, **Vol. 1, Part 2,** 559; first paper devoted to woman's rights, **Vol. 3, Part 1,** 141; first papers published by a woman, **Vol. 1, Part 2,** 385, 581; first religious newspaper, **Vol. 7, Part 1,** 251; first successful penny paper, **Vol. 3, Part 1,** 155; first woman Pulitzer Prize winner, **Supp. 5,** 447; foreign correspondents, **Supp. 3,** 612-13; **Supp. 5,** 60, 78-79, 362-63, 446-47; **Supp. 6,** 183-84, 197-98, 366, 543; **Supp. 7,** 115-16, 643, 758-59; **Supp. 8,** 172, 232-33, 259-60, 498, 639, 675; freedom of the press, **Vol. 3, Part 2,** 560; **Vol. 10, Part 2,** 649; "Harding Bible, The," **Vol. 4, Part 2** 259; headlines, startling use of, **Vol. 9, Part 1,** 10; historical writings on, **Supp. 1,** 441; **Supp. 7,** 559; humorous, **Supp. 3,** 53-54; interviews, **Supp. 7,** 512 -13; investigative reporting, **Supp. 3,** 80, 91-92;

Supp. 6, 616–17; "journalist's creed," **Supp. 1,** 709; Kentucky, **Vol. 9, Part 2,** 607; labor issues, **Supp. 3,** 10, 347, 355–56; **Supp. 5,** 653–54, 663–64, 484; **Supp. 8,** 675; left-wing, **Supp. 8,** 216, 255–56; liberal, **Supp. 4,** 850–51; **Supp. 6,** 202; liberal southern, **Supp. 7,** 323–24; literary syndicalism, **Vol. 9, Part 2,** 125; livestock publication, **Vol. 4, Part 1,** 380; Louisiana, **Vol. 9, Part 2,** 509; Massachusetts, **Vol. 3, Part 1,** 437 f.; **Vol. 8, Part 1,** 73 f.; **Vol. 8, Part 2,** 461| medical, **Vol. 9, Part 1,** 190| Minnesota, **Vol. 2, Part 2,** 367; *Moon Hoax,* **Vol. 3, Part 1,** 155; muckraking, **Supp. 2,** 14, 626; **Supp. 3,** 675, 762; **Supp. 4,** 46–47, 518, 662, 707; **Supp. 5,** 141, 286, 406, 666–67, 698–99; **Supp. 6,** 6; **Supp. 8,** 496–97; **Supp. 8,** 498–99, 594–95; natural history, **Supp. 3,** 8–9; news agencies, **Supp. 4,** 630–31; newspaper editing, **Vol. 3, Part 2,** 476, 486 f., 515; **Vol. 4, Part 1,** 425; **Vol. 4, Part 2,** 11; **Vol. 5, Part 1,** 396; **Vol. 5, Part 2,** 45, 48, 160, 417 f., 444, 452; **Vol. 6, Part 2,** 159, 166, 267, 297, 568; **Vol. 7, Part 1,** 48, 204 f.; **Vol. 7, Part 2,** 475; **Vol. 8, Part 2,** 468, 491, 514; **Vol. 8, Part 2,** 526; **Vol. 9, Part 1,** 577; **Vol. 9, Part 2,** 98; **Vol. 10, Part 2,** 292, 617, 633; newspaper illustrating, **Vol. 8, Part 2,** 113; "newspaper of record" concept, **Supp. 3,** 787–88; newspaper publishing, **Vol. 1, Part 2,** 437, 565; **Vol. 5, Part 1,** 535; **Vol. 6, Part 2,** 130; **Vol. 7, Part 1,** 271; **Vol. 7, Part 2,** 376 f., 643; **Vol. 8, Part 2,** 517, 519 f.; **Vol. 10, Part 2,** 500; New York, **Vol. 6, Part 1,** 354 f.; North Carolina, **Vol. 9, Part 2,** 582; organizations, *see specific names;* Philadelphia, **Vol. 1, Part 2,** 417; **Vol. 5, Part 1,** 203; photography, **Vol. 9, Part 1,** 380; **Supp. 4,** 361; **Supp. 7,** 115–16, 535–36; pioneer women in field of, **Vol. 1, Part 2,** 513 f., 581; **Vol. 4, Part 2** 281 f., 303; **Vol. 6, Part 1,** 288; **Vol. 8, Part 2,** 518; political, **Supp. 3,** 702, 816; **Supp. 4,** 574–75; **Supp. 5,** 19, 152–53, 205, 497–98, 518–19, 626, 504–5; **Supp. 6,** 601–2; **Supp. 7,** 249–50, 320–21, 706, 739–40; **Supp. 8,** 149–50, 173–74, 394–95, 496–97; presidential relations, **Supp. 3,** 649–50; **Supp. 4,** 704; **Supp. 5,** 196–97; **Supp. 8,** 160, 607; press freedom landmark decision (1941), **Supp. 3,** 157; pro-German, **Supp. 7,** 756–57, 759; Quaker, **Vol. 6, Part 1,** 212; racing news, **Supp. 3,** 20; radio, *see* Radio, news commentary; reform criticism of, **Supp. 3,** 59–60; religious, **Vol. 3, Part 2,** 53; **Vol. 7, Part 1,** 439; **Vol. 8, Part 2,** 348; **Supp. 6,** 315–16; **Supp. 7,** 345–46; religious weekly, one of first in U.S., **Vol. 4, Part 2** 157; reprint periodicals, **Vol. 6, Part 1,** 295; San Francisco earthquake and fire coverage, **Supp. 4,** 417; satiric essays, **Supp. 4,** 804; science, **Supp. 5,** 65; **Supp. 6,** 327–28; **Supp. 8,** 119–20; scientific newspapers, first in U.S., **Vol. 8, Part 1,** 101 f.; second black weekly in U.S., **Vol. 8, Part 1,** 403; second newspaper in U.S., **Vol. 5, Part 2,** 458; sensationalism, *see subhead* yellow; social criticism by, **Supp. 6,** 330, 571–72; **Supp. 8,** 433, *see also subhead* muckraking; socialist-oriented, **Supp. 5,** 264; Soviet Union affairs, **Supp. 8,** 635; sports, **Supp. 1,** 527, 704; **Supp. 4,** 708–9; **Supp. 5,** 568, 724; **Supp. 6,** 366; **Supp. 8,** 498; Swedish newspapers, **Vol. 7, Part 1,** 550; syndicated columns, *see subhead* columns, syndicated; syndication, **Supp. 4,** 38; teaching of, **Vol. 5, Part 2,** 60, 391; **Vol. 6, Part 1,** 110; **Vol. 8, Part 1,** 260 f.; **Vol. 9, Part 1,** 578; **Vol. 10, Part 2,** 292; **Supp. 1,** 87, 391, 708; **Supp. 2,** 610; Tennessee, **Vol. 7, Part 1,** 601; tennis, **Supp. 6,** 538; theatrical, **Supp. 3,** 276–77; third newspaper in U.S., **Vol. 1, Part 2,** 553; war correspondence, **Vol. 7, Part 2,** 154; **Vol. 8, Part 1,** 451; war correspondents, *see subhead* foreign correspondents; "War of the News Giants," **Vol. 7, Part 2,** 545; Washington corre-

spondents, *see subheads* political; presidential relations; wire services, **Supp. 7,** 144–45; women's interests, **Supp. 1,** 91; **Supp. 8,** 471; women's rights, **Supp. 3,** 355–56; writings on, **Supp. 4,** 704; yellow, **Vol. 5, Part 2,** 156; **Vol. 10, Part 1,** 445; **Supp. 1,** 94; **Supp. 2,** 63, 242; **Supp. 3,** 427; **Supp. 5,** 284–85, 453; **Supp. 6,** 686. *See also* Magazines; Newspapers; Publishing *(for publication ownership and management)*

Journalists. For complete list, *see* Occupations Index

Journal of Agricultural Research, founding of, **Supp. 1,** 461–62

Journal of American Ethnology and Archaeology, **Vol. 4, Part 2,** 519

Journal of Applied Physics, predecessor, **Supp. 4,** 818

Journal of a Residence in America, **Vol. 5, Part 2,** 315

Journal of Biological Chemistry editing of, **Supp. 2,** 36; founding of, **Supp. 2,** 4

Journal of Cancer Research, **Vol. 10, Part 1,** 608

Journal of Chronic Diseases, predecessor, **Supp. 6,** 461

Journal of Clinical Investigation, founding of, **Supp. 6,** 547

Journal of Commerce, **Vol. 4, Part 2** 157 f.; **Vol. 9, Part 2,** 73 f.

Journal of Education, **Vol. 9, Part 1,** 67

Journal of Experimental Medicine: editing, **Supp. 8,** 556; founding of, **Supp. 2,** 4

Journal of Forestry, **Vol. 3, Part 2,** 336

Journal of Geology, **Vol. 8, Part 2,** 310

Journal of Geomorphology, founding of, **Supp. 3,** 390

Journal of Health, **Vol. 4, Part 2** 148

Journal of Home Economics, **Supp. 3,** 68

Journal of Humanistic Psychology, founding of, **Supp. 8,** 424

Journal of Negro History, founding of, **Supp. 4,** 911

Journal of Nervous and Mental Disease, **Supp. 3,** 386

Journal of Neurophysiology, editing, **Supp. 2,** 162

Journal of Parasitology, founding of, **Supp. 3,** 802

Journal of Pharmacology and Experimental Therapeutics, founding of, **Supp. 2,** 4

Journal of Philosophy, Psychology, and Scientific Method, founding of, **Supp. 2,** 734

Journal of Physical Chemistry, founding of, **Supp. 5,** 36

Journal of Political Economy: editing, **Supp. 8,** 668; founding of, **Supp. 1,** 487

Journal of Religion, **Vol. 9, Part 1,** 270

Journal of Social Forces, founding of, **Supp. 5,** 520

Journal of Speculative Philosophy, **Vol. 4, Part 2** 329

Journal of the American Chemical Society, **Supp. 5,** 407

Journal of the American Folklore Society, **Supp. 3,** 83

Journal of the American Institute of Architects, editing, **Supp. 2,** 709

Journal of the American Medical Association, socialized medicine article, **Supp. 6,** 664

Journal of the Franklin Institute, **Vol. 5, Part 2,** 203

Journal of the Outdoor Life, founding of, **Supp. 2,** 71

Journal of Transpersonal Psychology, founding of, **Supp. 8,** 424

Journal of Travels over the Rocky Mountains, **Vol. 7, Part 2,** 186

Journal of Urology, founding of, **Supp. 3,** 854

Journals, **Vol. 6, Part 1,** 221; **Vol. 8, Part 1,** 55, 61, 68 f., 307 f.; **Vol. 10, Part 1,** 20 f., 537; collection of, **Vol. 3, Part 2,** 512; Continental Congress, of, **Vol. 5, Part 1,** 385; De Long's ill-fated polar expedition, **Vol. 3, Part 1,** 228; fur trader, of a, **Vol. 6, Part 1,** 5; livestock, **Vol. 8, Part 2,** 335; Reeves, Arthur Middleton, **Vol. 8, Part 1,** 470; technical editing of, **Vol. 5, Part 2,** 426. *See also* Diaries and memoirs

Journeyman Tailors' Union of America, **Vol. 6, Part 1,** 170

Joyce, James, references to, **Supp. 3,** 844; **Supp. 5,** 270, 587; **Supp. 6,** 497; **Supp. 7,** 40, 306, 374

406; creation of, **Vol. 6, Part 1,** 52; criminal division, **Supp. 5,** 455; ethics issues, **Supp. 3,** 213–14; **Supp. 8,** 406; mural, **Supp. 6,** 597; Prohibition enforcement, **Supp. 7,** 786; prosecutors, **Supp. 6,** 3, 502; reforms, **Supp. 4,** 794; **Supp. 6,** 137–38, 156; U.S. attorneys, **Supp. 3,** 116–17; World War I legal issues, **Supp. 5,** 730

Juvenile books, first collection of, in U.S., **Vol. 8, Part 1,** 51 f.

Juvenile courts, **Supp. 1,** 485; **Supp. 3,** 279, 462–63; **Supp. 5,** 84, 746; **Supp. 7,** 251

Juvenile delinquency, **Vol. 1, Part 1,** 520; **Vol. 4, Part 1,** 217; **Vol. 7, Part 1,** 389; adult responsibility, **Supp. 3,** 462; prevention, **Supp. 4,** 870, **Supp. 5,** 137–38; reformatories, **Supp. 4,** 471–72; social work, **Supp. 7,** 28; **Supp. 8,** 40; Virginia Industrial School for Colored Girls, **Supp. 4,** 53–54

Juvenile Protective Association, **Supp. 8,** 40

Juvenile Psychopathic Institute, founding of, **Supp. 1,** 485

Juvenile Rambler, probably first magazine for children, **Vol. 1, Part 1,** 143

J. Walter Thompson Co., **Supp. 6,** 672; **Supp. 7,** 641–42

K

Kafka, Franz, first published work, **Supp. 7,** 798

Kahn, Otto, references to, **Supp. 1,** 4; **Supp. 6,** 233

Kahn, Roger, reference to, **Supp. 6,** 366

Kairos Circle, founding of, **Supp. 7,** 746

Kaiser, Georg, reference to, **Supp. 4,** 868

Kaiser Aluminum Corporation, **Supp. 8,** 309

Kaiser-Frazer Corporation, founding of, **Supp. 8,** 309

Kaiser Permanente organization, **Supp. 8,** 309

Kalamazoo College, **Vol. 4, Part 1,** 603

Kalich, Bertha, reference to, **Supp. 3,** 277

Kallen, Horace, reference to, **Supp. 6,** 96

Kallikak Family: A Study in the Heredity of Feeble-mindedness, The, **Supp. 6,** 241

Kallir, Otto, references to, **Supp. 7,** 566, 557

Kamen, M. C., reference to, **Supp. 5,** 273

Kane, Elias Kent, references to, **Vol. 1, Part 2,** 433; **Vol. 2, Part 1,** 14

Kanin, Garson, reference to, **Supp. 7,** 355

Kansas: admission to statehood, **Vol. 8, Part 2,** 618; Agricultural College, **Vol. 1, Part 1,** 267; **Vol. 3, Part 2,** 252; agriculture, **Vol. 1, Part 1,** 316; **Vol. 5, Part 2,** 504; Beecher Bible and Rifle Colony, **Vol. 8, Part 2,** 150; "border ruffians," **Vol. 5, Part 2,** 576–77; Brown, John, **Vol. 9, Part 1,** 544; **Vol. 9, Part 2,** 522; business service, **Vol. 6, Part 1,** 618–9; cattle breeding, **Vol. 4, Part 2** 326; cattle shipping, **Vol. 6, Part 1,** 618 f.; civil war in, **Vol. 7, Part 2,** 579; Emigrant Aid Assiciation, **Vol. 4, Part 2** 380; first constitutional prohibitory amendment, **Vol. 8, Part 2,** 304; first radio station, **Supp. 3,** 103–4; fraudulent elections in 1871, **Vol. 2, Part 1,** 405; Free-Soil movement, **Vol. 3, Part 1,** 570 f., **Vol. 4, Part 1,** 394; Free-State movement, **Vol. 3, Part 1,** 202; **Vol. 5, Part 2,** 576; **Vol. 8, Part 2,** 36, 175; Frontier Guard, **Vol. 5, Part 2,** 576; geological researches, **Vol. 8, Part 1,** 247; governors, **Vol. 1, Part 1,** 315 f.; **Vol. 2, Part 1,** 506; **Vol. 2, Part 2,** 523 f.; **Vol. 6, Part 1,** 204 f.; **Vol. 6, Part 2,** 341 f.; **Vol. 7, Part 1,** 197 f.; **Vol. 8, Part 2,** 303; **Supp. 4,** 12; **Supp. 5,** 101; **Supp. 7,** 677–78; **Supp. 8,** 706; growth of, **Vol. 6, Part 2,** 342; guerrillas, **Vol. 8, Part 1,** 294 f; history of, **Vol. 1, Part 2,** 482; **Vol. 2, Part 1,** 506; **Vol. 8, Part 1,** 54 f.; **Vol. 8, Part 1,** 294 f.; **Vol. 9, Part 1,** 480; **Vol. 9, Part 2,** 403–4; Indian schools, **Vol. 4, Part 2** 380; Lane's Army of the North, **Vol. 5, Part 2,** 576; "law

and order," **Vol. 9, Part 1,** 20; Lecompton Constitution, **Vol. 2, Part 1,** 411; **Vol. 3, Part 1,** 401; legal service, **Vol. 3, Part 1,** 410; Mennonite settlements, **Vol. 5, Part 2,** 504; Montgomery, James, **Vol. 7, Part 1,** 97; Mormon church in, **Vol. 4, Part 2** 380; newspapers, **Vol. 8, Part 1,** 10 f.; **Vol. 8, Part 2,** 146; **Supp. 3,** 816–17; **Supp. 4,** 12; paintings of, **Supp. 4,** 204; paleontology, **Vol. 10, Part 2,** 310; "Peace now reigns in Kansas," **Vol. 4, Part 1,** 203; political service, **Vol. 1, Part 1,** 315; **Vol. 2, Part 2,** 524; **Vol. 3, Part 1,** 202, 243; **Vol. 4, Part 1,** 203; **Vol. 4, Part 2** 380; **Vol. 6, Part 1,** 204; **Vol. 7, Part 2,** 70, 393, 549; **Vol. 8, Part 1,** 10, 54, 463; **Vol. 8, Part 2,** 35, 175, 303; **Vol. 9, Part 1,** 20, 524; politics, **Vol. 1, Part 2,** 399; **Vol. 8, Part 2,** 36; **Vol. 4, Part 2** 326; **Vol. 5, Part 2,** 576–77; **Vol. 8, Part 2,** 150; **Supp. 1,** 677; **Supp. 3,** 105–6, 544–45, **Supp. 5,** 101; **Supp. 8,** 277, 591–92; Populist party, **Vol. 6, Part 1,** 205; Prohibition, **Vol. 6, Part 2,** 342; public service, **Vol. 2, Part 2,** 250; **Vol. 5, Part 1,** 462; raids, **Vol. 1, Part 1,** 403; sanitation, **Vol. 6, Part 1,** 357–8; science, **Vol. 8, Part 1,** 247; separation of, from Colorado, **Vol. 3, Part 1,** 243; settlement of, **Vol. 7, Part 2,** 71; slavery, **Vol. 3, Part 1,** 202, 400 f.; **Vol. 3, Part 2,** 69; **Vol. 4, Part 1,** 204; **Vol. 5, Part 2,** 576; **Vol. 8, Part 2,** 35; "squatter sovereignty," **Vol. 4, Part 1,** 550; temperance, **Vol. 7, Part 1,** 394; Wakarusa War, **Vol. 3, Part 1,** 202

Kansas City, Mo., jazz style, **Supp. 5,** 534

Kansas City, Mo., first bureau of charities in, **Vol. 1, Part 2,** 220

Kansas City, Mo.: Jewish charities, **Supp. 4,** 79; Pendergast machine, **Supp. 3,** 596–97, 621

Kansas City Athletics (baseball), **Supp. 6,** 415

Kansas City Star (Mo.), **Vol. 7, Part 1,** 428; editorial page, **Supp. 5,** 279

Kansas Commoner, **Vol. 8, Part 2,** 105

Kansas Farmer, **Vol. 1, Part 1,** 316; **Vol. 7, Part 2,** 393

Kansas Industrial Act (1920), **Supp. 4,** 12

Kansas-Nebraska Act (1854), **Vol. 1, Part 1,** 403; **Vol. 1, Part 2,** 158; **Vol. 2, Part 1,** 88, 132, 211; **Vol. 2, Part 2,** 548; **Vol. 3, Part 1,** 344, 400–2; **Vol. 3, Part 2,** 224, 348 f.; **Vol. 4, Part 1,** 203, 607–8; **Vol. 5, Part 1,** 17, 187; **Vol. 5, Part 2,** 576–77; **Vol. 7, Part 2,** 187, 241, 578–79; **Vol. 8, Part 1,** 463, 570; **Vol. 8, Part 2,** 35, 617; **Vol. 9, Part 1,** 20, 331; **Vol. 9, Part 2,** 210, 214, 590, 601; **Vol. 10, Part 1,** 19 f., 122, 357, 599; Branch's speeches on, **Vol. 1, Part 2,** 598; events leading up to, **Vol. 3, Part 1,** 400; newspaper comment, **Vol. 1, Part 2,** 515; passage of, **Vol. 7, Part 2,** 578

Kansas News, **Vol. 8, Part 1,** 10 f.

Kansas State Agricultural College, **Vol. 4, Part 1,** 395; presidency, **Supp. 5,** 364–65

Kansas State University, football team, **Supp. 5,** 458

Kansas Tribune, **Vol. 3, Part 1,** 410

Kant, Immanuel, reference to, **Supp. 3,** 697

Karno, Fred, reference to, **Supp. 7,** 462

Károlyi, Count Michael, reference to, **Supp. 4,** 62

Kaskaskia, capture of, **Vol. 2, Part 2,** 128; **Vol. 8, Part 1,** 51

Kast, Ludwig, reference to, **Supp. 3,** 435

Katz, Milton, reference to, **Supp. 7,** 276

Katzenbach, Nicholas, reference to, **Supp. 8,** 322

Kauffmann, John, reference to, **Supp. 8,** 335

Kaufman, George S., references to, **Supp. 3,** 333, 842; **Supp. 6,** 311; **Supp. 7,** 325, 803; **Supp. 8,** 170–71

Kaufman, Irving R., reference to, **Supp. 5,** 589

KDKA (radio station), founding of, **Supp. 3,** 184–85

Kean, Charles, reference to, **Vol. 1, Part 2,** 453

Kearsarge, fight with *Alabama,* **Vol. 8, Part 2,** 581

"Kirby, Rip" (fictional character), **Supp. 6**, 530, 531
Kirby, Rollin, references to, **Supp. 7**, 369, 370
Kirchwey, Freda, reference to, **Supp. 3**, 420
Kirk-Holden War, **Vol. 7, Part 2**, 361; **Vol. 8, Part 1**, 379
Kirkland, James H., reference to, **Supp. 3**, 129
Kirstein, Lincoln, reference to, **Supp. 7**, 55
Kirtland Society of Natural Science, **Vol. 5, Part 2**, 439
"Kitchen Cabinet," **Vol. 3, Part 1**, 610; **Vol. 4, Part 1**, 540; **Vol. 5, Part 1**, 532; **Vol. 5, Part 2**, 326; **Vol. 6, Part 1**, 226; **Vol. 10, Part 1**, 154
Kites: aeronautical experiments with, **Vol. 8, Part 2**, 184; high-altitude exploration, **Supp. 3**, 479
Kittredge, George Lyman, references to, **Supp. 3**, 454; **Supp. 4**, 502
Kitty Foyle, **Supp. 6**, 465
Klauber, Adolph E., reference to, **Supp. 4**, 187
Kleiber, Erich, reference to, **Supp. 6**, 456
Klein, Arthur L., reference to, **Supp. 8**, 439
Klein, Felix, references to, **Supp. 3**, 574, 575, 791
Klingensmith, Frank L., reference to, **Supp. 4**, 300
Klondike, verse about, **Supp. 6**, 574
Klopfer, Donald, reference to, **Supp. 7**, 3
Klystron device, **Supp. 4**, 358
K-Mart stores, founding of, **Supp. 8**, 348
Knapp, Charles, reference to, **Supp. 8**, 236
Knapp, Joseph Palmer, reference to, **Supp. 3**, 442–43
Knappen Engineering, founding of, **Supp. 5**, 396
Knaths, Karl, reference to, **Supp. 6**, 552
Knauff, Ellen, reference to, **Supp. 7**, 542
Kneisel Quartet, **Vol. 5, Part 2**, 460 f.; **Vol. 9, Part 2**, 305
Knickerbocker Magazine, **Vol. 2, Part 2**, 137, 149
Knickerbocker School, **Vol. 7, Part 1**, 207
Knickerbocker Whist Club (New York City), **Supp. 6**, 134
Knight, Charles Y., reference to, **Supp. 5**, 654
Knight, Robert, reference to, **Supp. 6**, 527
Knight Errant, **Supp. 3**, 196
Knights of Columbus, founding of, **Vol. 6, Part 2**, 53
Knights of Labor, **Vol. 1, Part 1**, 231; **Vol. 4, Part 1**, 215, 240; **Vol. 5, Part 2**, 195; **Vol. 8, Part 1**, 142; **Vol. 9, Part 1**, 581; **Vol. 9, Part 2**, 640; **Supp. 3**, 249, 346, 516. *See also* Haymarket Riot
Knights of Pythias. *See* Order of the Knights of Pythias
Knights of Pythias Band, **Supp. 6**, 275
Knights of the Golden Circle, **Vol. 3, Part 2**, 168; **Vol. 5, Part 1**, 271; **Vol. 5, Part 2**, 378; **Vol. 7, Part 1**, 263
Knitting machinery, **Vol. 3, Part 2**, 132; **Vol. 5, Part 2**, 554; **Vol. 9, Part 1**, 190
Knoblauch (Knoblock), Edward, reference to, **Supp. 3**, 277
Knock on Any Door, **Supp. 7**, 558
Knoll Associates, **Supp. 4**, 715; **Supp. 7**, 670
Knopf, Alfred A., references to, **Supp. 6**, 445, 471; **Supp. 7**, 2; **Supp. 8**, 341–42
Knopf, Alfred A., Co., **Supp. 8**, 341–43; book design, **Supp. 6**, 186
Knowland, William F., reference to, **Supp. 8**, 341
Knowledge: philosophical theory of, **Supp. 2**, 639; **Supp. 7**, 471; vital symbolism concept, **Supp. 2**, 9–10. *See also* Learning
Know-Nothing party, **Vol. 1, Part 1**, 578, 605; **Vol. 1, Part 2**, 350, 515; **Vol. 3, Part 2**, 6, 381; **Vol. 4, Part 1**, 307, 142; **Vol. 5, Part 1**, 26; **Vol. 5, Part 2**, 238; **Vol. 6, Part 1**, 40, 240; **Vol. 7, Part 1**, 528; **Vol. 7, Part 2**, 59; **Vol. 8, Part 2**, 58, 248, 617; **Vol. 9, Part 2**, 379; **Vol. 10, Part 2**, 323
Knox, Frank, references to, **Supp. 3**, 543; **Supp. 6**, 339, 340; **Supp. 7**, 720

Knox, Seymour, reference to, **Supp. 6**, 689
Knox College, **Vol. 1, Part 2**, 351; **Vol. 4, Part 1**, 99
Knoxville, Tenn., public service to, **Vol. 6, Part 2**, 48
Knoxville campaign (1863), **Vol. 1, Part 2**, 586; **Vol. 2, Part 1**, 177, 236, 311; **Vol. 5, Part 1**, 392; **Vol. 5, Part 2**, 425; **Vol. 6, Part 2**, 121
Knoxville Gazette, **Vol. 8, Part 2**, 190
Knudsen, William S., references to, **Supp. 4**, 300, 301; **Supp. 7**, 794; **Supp. 8**, 610
Kobe College, founding of, **Vol. 3, Part 1**, 132
Koch, Robert, references to, **Vol. 7, Part 1**, 541; **Supp. 3**, 400; **Supp. 4**, 48, 684, 865; **Supp. 6**, 481
Kocourek, Albert, reference to, **Supp. 3**, 186
Kodachrome, invention of, **Supp. 7**, 511, 512
Kodak Co. *See* Eastman Kodak Co.
Koffka, Kurt, references to, **Supp. 3**, 808; **Supp. 8**, 343
Köhler, Wolfgang, references to, **Supp. 3**, 429, 808
Kohler Co. management, **Supp. 2**, 366
Kohut Foundation, establishment of, **Vol. 5, Part 2**, 491
Kolhörster, Werner, reference to, **Supp. 7**, 134
Kollmar, Richard Tompkins, reference to, **Supp. 7**, 433
Kolster Radio Corporation, **Supp. 6**, 591
Konoye, Fumumaro, reference to, **Supp. 7**, 303
Koppers Co., **Supp. 5**, 643
Korda, Alexander, reference to, **Supp. 7**, 461
Korea, **Vol. 1, Part 1**, 324; **Vol. 3, Part 1**, 579 f.; **Vol. 4, Part 1**, 526; **Vol. 6, Part 1**, 146, 468; **Vol. 8, Part 2**, 78; Bible translations into Korean, **Vol. 5, Part 2**, 172; **Vol. 10, Part 1**, 113; diplomatic relations with, **Vol. 3, Part 2**, 560; **Vol. 4, Part 1**, 526; **Vol. 9, Part 2**, 613; emigration from, to Hawaiian Islands, **Vol. 5, Part 2**, 172; laws, **Vol. 4, Part 1**, 526; missions, **Vol. 1, Part 1**, 224, 324; **Vol. 5, Part 2**, 171 f.; **Vol. 6, Part 2**, 122; newspapers, **Vol. 5, Part 2**, 172; writings on, **Vol. 5, Part 2**, 172
Korean Commission, **Vol. 9, Part 2**, 423
Korean War: American ground forces command, **Supp. 4**, 857; army engineers, **Supp. 6**, 509; aviation in, **Supp. 8**, 292, 633; cease-fire, **Supp. 6**, 326–27; congressional opposition to, **Supp. 5**, 467; defense production, **Supp. 5**, 482; **Supp. 7**, 587; expansion advocacy, **Supp. 5**, 478; foreign correspondents, **Supp. 8**, 259–60; MacArthur recall, **Supp. 5**, 676, 706; **Supp. 6**, 432; **Supp. 7**, 74, 492–93; **Supp. 8**, 421–22; military action, **Supp. 7**, 351–52; naval fleet, **Supp. 5**, 622; **Supp. 6**, 326; political issues over, **Supp. 5**, 676; support for, **Supp. 7**, 763; United Nations Command, **Supp. 8**, 699
Kornei, Otto, reference to, **Supp. 8**, 71
Kossel, Albrecht, reference to, **Supp. 5**, 149
Kossuth's cause, **Vol. 5, Part 2**, 418
Koszta affair, **Vol. 5, Part 1**, 477
Koussevitzky, Serge, references to, **Supp. 4**, 715; **Supp. 6**, 456; **Supp. 7**, 652; **Supp. 8**, 145
Koverman, Ida, references to, **Supp. 6**, 440; **Supp. 8**, 281–82
Kowal, Charles T., reference to, **Supp. 5**, 540
Kozelugh, Karel, reference to, **Supp. 6**, 539
Kozlowski, Anthony, reference to, **Supp. 5**, 305
Kraft Foods Co., founding of, **Supp. 5**, 399–400
"Kraft Music Hall" (radio program), **Supp. 5**, 188, 400; **Supp. 6**, 89; **Supp. 7**, 403
Kramer, Stanley, reference to, **Supp. 8**, 660
Kramers, H. A., reference to, **Supp. 7**, 134
Krasner, Lee, reference to, **Supp. 6**, 512, 513
Krause, Allen K., reference to, **Supp. 4**, 49
Krauth, Charles Porterfield, reference to, **Vol. 8, Part 2**, 441
Krazy Kat (jazz pantomime), **Supp. 5**, 103, 104

Kresge, S. S., Co., founding of, **Supp. 8,** 347–49
Kresge Foundation, founding of, **Supp. 8,** 348–49
Kress, S. H., Co., founding of, **Supp. 5,** 401
Kreuger, Ivar, references to, **Supp. 4,** 258; **Supp. 6,** 250, 287
Krey, Laura, reference to, **Supp. 6,** 251
Kroeber, A. L., reference to, **Supp. 6,** 524
Kroger Grocery and Baking Co., founding of, **Supp. 2,** 367–68
Kronprinzessin Cecilie, decision in case of, **Vol. 8, Part 1,** 285 f.
Krueger, Louise, reference to, **Supp. 6,** 557
Kuhn, Loeb & Co., **Supp. 1,** 457
Kühne, Wilhelm, reference to, **Supp. 3,** 163
Ku Klux Klan, **Vol. 1, Part 2,** 432; **Vol. 2, Part 1,** 595; **Vol. 2, Part 2,** 187; **Vol. 3, Part 2,** 533; **Vol. 4, Part 1,** 424; **Vol. 4, Part 2,** 215; **Vol. 5, Part 1,** 81; **Vol. 5, Part 2,** 114; **Vol. 8, Part 1,** 33 f., 64 f., 118 f.; **Vol. 8, Part 2,** 384, 499; **Vol. 10, Part 1,** 118; editorial opposition to, **Supp. 3,** 816–17; **Supp. 6,** 11; **Supp. 7,** 324; judicial opposition to, **Supp. 8,** 24; legislation against, **Supp. 3,** 718–19; membership exposé, **Supp. 3,** 80; political opposition to, **Supp. 3,** 267, 331; **Supp. 7,** 242; political support for, **Supp. 5,** 701; political support from, **Supp. 3,** 317–18; **Supp. 5,** 290; **Supp. 6,** 507; resurgence of, **Supp. 3,** 708–9; **Supp. 4,** 235; **Supp. 7,** 361; targets of, **Supp. 3,** 463; writings supporting, **Supp. 4,** 876
Kullback, Solomon, reference to, **Supp. 8,** 196
Kunsman, Charles H., reference to, **Supp. 6,** 151
Kwakiutl Indians, **Supp. 3,** 83

L

Labor, Department of (U.S.), **Vol. 6, Part 1,** 171; administration, **Supp. 2,** 122; **Supp. 4,** 219–20, 724; **Supp. 5,** 194–95, 692; **Supp. 7,** 543–44, 609–10; black issues, **Supp. 6,** 285; established, **Vol. 1, Part 2,** 335; **Vol. 10, Part 2,** 545; Industries and Immigration Bureau, **Supp. 5,** 381; Women's Bureau, **Supp. 2,** 408; **Supp. 7,** 12–13
Labor and Aid Society, **Vol. 4, Part 1,** 238
Labor and labor movement, **Vol. 4, Part 1,** 288; **Vol. 4, Part 2,** 38, 468; **Vol. 5, Part 2,** 82, 195 f., 268 f., 277 f.; **Vol. 6, Part 1,** 52, 133, 373, 511; **Vol. 6, Part 2,** 150, 154, 212; **Vol. 7, Part 1,** 51 f., 121 f., 276 f., 544 f.; **Vol. 8, Part 1,** 142 f.; **Vol. 8, Part 2,** 128, 358, 436 f.; **Vol. 9, Part 1,** 154, 399, 581; **Vol. 9, Part 2,** 257 f., 267, 640; **Vol. 10, Part 2,** 402, 487, 556; American Federation of Labor, **Vol. 2, Part 2,** 338, 612; **Vol. 3, Part 1,** 510; **Vol. 4, Part 1,** 370; **Vol. 5, Part 2,** 278; **Vol. 6, Part 1,** 170, 521; **Vol. 6, Part 2,** 150; **Vol. 7, Part 1,** 545; **Vol. 8, Part 1,** 142 f.; arbitration and mediation system, **Supp. 5,** 263, 651; **Supp. 6,** 74, 411, 706; Bedaux unit incentive system, opposition to, **Supp. 3,** 49–50; black leaders, **Supp. 6,** 648; bureaus, establishment of, by states, **Vol. 8, Part 1,** 142 f., 545; "business unionism," **Supp. 4,** 75; Catholic reform programs, **Supp. 2,** 135; **Supp. 3,** 680–81; **Supp. 4,** 232–33; **Supp. 8,** 589; collective bargaining, **Supp. 2,** 73, 166; company towns, **Supp. 2,** 366; conciliation, World War I period, **Vol. 7, Part 2,** 216; Department of Labor, creation of, **Vol. 1, Part 2,** 335; **Vol. 6, Part 1,** 171; **Vol. 7, Part 1,** 419, 591; economics, **Supp. 6,** 503–4; **Supp. 6,** 705–6; eight-hour day, **Vol. 6, Part 2,** 150; **Vol. 9, Part 2,** 1 f.; employer relations, **Supp. 2,** 66; employment benefits, **Supp. 8,** 348; equal employment opportunity, **Supp. 4,** 397; **Supp. 7,** 382, 425; fair employment practices, **Supp. 5,** 692; **Supp. 6,** 480; **Supp. 7,** 122, 382, 425, 459, 543; fatigue studies, **Supp. 8,** 684; federal policies, **Supp. 8,** 366;

Golden Rule reforms, **Supp. 1,** 453; grievances bill, **Supp. 2,** 213; group insurance, **Supp. 2,** 87; handicapped, employment of, **Supp. 6,** 414; history of, **Supp. 3,** 178–79; human needs in employment, **Supp. 8,** 424; importation of European, **Vol. 4, Part 2** 279; incentive system, **Supp. 3,** 49–50; industrial accident insurance, **Supp. 2,** 404; international, **Supp. 5,** 511; **Supp. 6,** 707; Italian-American workers, **Supp. 3,** 777–78; Italian Socialist Federation, **Supp. 6,** 238; journalism, **Supp. 3,** 347, 355–56; **Supp. 5,** 653–54, 663–64; **Supp. 6,** 484; Knights of Labor, **Vol. 5, Part 2,** 195; **Vol. 8, Part 1,** 142 f.; **Vol. 9, Part 1,** 581; **Vol. 9, Part 2,** 640; **Supp. 3,** 249, 946; Labor Day, first observance of, **Vol. 8, Part 1,** 118 f.; Labor Reform Convention (1872), **Vol. 3, Part 1,** 111; legal counsel, **Supp. 2,** 142, 691; **Supp. 6,** 541; legislation experts, **Supp. 1,** 294, 567; **Supp. 3,** 18; legislation protecting, **Supp. 2,** 50; **Supp. 3,** 654, 655–56, 717–18; **Supp. 4,** 407, 607, 614; **Supp. 5,** 718–19; **Supp. 6,** 480; **Supp. 7,** 543; legislation restricting, **Supp. 4,** 12, 724; **Supp. 7,** 110–11, 801; **Supp. 8,** 25, 245–46, 269; management relations, **Supp. 3,** 96; **Supp. 6,** 136, 548; Manly report on, **Supp. 4,** 543; migrant workers, **Supp. 8,** 301; New Unionism, **Supp. 4,** 375–76; NRA policies, **Supp. 3,** 651; party, opposition to formation of, **Vol. 8, Part 1,** 142 f.; pension systems, **Supp. 2,** 404, 542–43, 645; piecework system, introduction of, **Vol. 7, Part 2,** 263; productivity and working conditions, **Supp. 4,** 565–66; profit-sharing benefits, **Supp. 1,** 275, 370 –71; **Supp. 2,** 87; **Supp. 4,** 432; **Supp. 5,** 165; publications, **Vol. 4, Part 2,** 55; reform, **Supp. 7,** 360, 607–9; religious leaders' involvement with, **Supp. 3,** 733–34; **Supp. 4,** 111, 904; **Supp. 5,** 445–46; **Supp. 6,** 25; **Supp. 8,** 680–81; riots of 1877, **Vol. 4, Part 2** 419, 450; **Vol. 5, Part 2,** 196; savings-bank life insurance, **Supp. 3,** 95; schools, **Supp. 8,** 458; Socialist party, **Supp. 3,** 10, 297–98, 347, 373, 516–17, 532–33; "Solidarity Forever," **Supp. 7,** 118; stock purchase options, **Supp. 5,** 315; strike, Homestead, Pa. (1892), **Vol. 4, Part 1,** 30; Supreme Court decisions, **Supp. 4,** 407, 537; **Supp. 5,** 358, 714; ten-hour day, early experiment with, **Vol. 8, Part 1,** 465; unions, **Vol. 1, Part 1,** 376 f.; **Vol. 2, Part 1,** 216, 434, 545; **Vol. 3, Part 1,** 183; **Vol. 3, Part 2,** 323; **Vol. 4, Part 1,** 369 f.; **Vol. 4, Part 2** 228, 468; **Vol. 8, Part 1,** 112 f., 142; **Vol. 9, Part 2,** 1; **Vol. 10, Part 1,** 416 f.; **Vol. 10, Part 2,** 273, 349; wages and hours, *see* Wages and hours; "Wisconsin school" writings on, **Supp. 3,** 178; women's activism in, **Supp. 1,** 346, 463; **Supp. 2,** 408; **Supp. 3,** 355–56, 576–77, 639; **Supp. 5,** 69–70; women's working conditions, **Supp. 4,** 623–26; workers' benefits, **Supp. 6,** 381, 615; working conditions' improvement, **Supp. 1,** 610; **Supp. 2,** 184; World War II disputes, **Supp. 3,** 660; **Supp. 6,** 28; writings on, **Supp. 3,** 249; **Supp. 6,** 597. *See also* Child labor; Government employees; Management; Occupational health and safety; Strikes; Trade unions; Unemployment; Wages and hours
Labor Management Relations Act (1947). *See* Taft-Hartley Act
Labor Reform Act (1959), **Supp. 8,** 322
Labor's League for Political Education, founding of, **Supp. 5,** 255
Labor Temple, **Supp. 3,** 110; founding of, **Supp. 3,** 734
Labrador, first mission to, **Vol. 8, Part 1,** 113 f.
Lackawanna Coal & Iron Co. **Vol. 1, Part 2,** 338
Laconia State School, founding of, **Supp. 2,** 388
La Crosse and Milwaukee Railroad, **Vol. 1, Part 2,** 33
Lactic acid, **Supp. 5,** 489

Vol. **7, Part 1,** 642; **Vol. 8, Part 1,** 426; Western grazing interests, **Supp. 7,** 31

Land-Grant College Endowment Act, **Vol. 1, Part 1,** 238; **Vol. 7, Part 1,** 199

Land-grant colleges, **Supp. 3,** 209; **Supp. 5,** 49

Landis, James M., reference to, **Supp. 7,** 263

Landis, Kenesaw Mountain, references to, **Supp. 1,** 74; **Supp. 6,** 74, 589; **Supp. 7,** 118, 129, 646; **Supp. 8,** 85–86, 575

Landon, Alfred M., references to, **Supp. 3,** 429, 655, **Supp. 7,** 274; **Supp. 8,** 421

Landrum-Griffin Labor Management Act (1959), **Supp. 7,** 543; **Supp. 8,** 25, 366

Landscape architecture, **Vol. 2, Part 2,** 204; **Vol. 3, Part 2,** 70; **Vol. 4, Part 2** 230; **Vol. 6, Part 1,** 457; **Vol. 7, Part 2,** 24, 29, 30; **Vol. 8, Part 1,** 336 f.; **Vol. 10, Part 1,** 605; **Supp. 1,** 594; **Supp. 3,** 490–91; **Supp. 5,** 359–70; **Supp. 6,** 196, 485–86; gardening, **Vol. 3, Part 1,** 417; **Vol. 7, Part 2,** 26 f., 269, 417, 600; **Vol. 8, Part 1,** 1; **Vol. 8, Part 2,** 355, 361, 383 f.

Landscape painting, **Supp. 1,** 227, 458; **Supp. 3,** 112. *See also* Painting

Lane, Chester, references to, **Supp. 6,** 155, 186

Lane, Franklin K., references to, **Supp. 4,** 216; **Supp. 6,** 121

Lane, Harry, reference to, **Supp. 4,** 904

Lane College, founding of, **Vol. 5, Part 1,** 177

Lane Theological Seminary, **Vol. 1, Part 2,** 136; **Vol. 9, Part 2,** 299

Laney, Al, reference to, **Supp. 6,** 363

Lang, Fritz, reference to, **Supp. 7,** 478

Lang, Jennings, reference to, **Supp. 8,** 678

Langerhans, islets of, **Supp. 3,** 483; **Supp. 6,** 53

Langley, Samuel P., references to **Vol. 6, Part 2,** 239; **Vol. 9, Part 2,** 397

Langley (ship), **Supp. 4,** 685

Langmuir, Irving, references to, **Supp. 4,** 488; **Supp. 5,** 273; **Supp. 6,** 695

Langmuir isotherm and probe, **Supp. 6,** 365

Langner, Lawrence, references to, **Supp. 3,** 811, 812; **Supp. 6,** 285

Language, **Supp. 4,** 90

Language As Gesture, **Supp. 7,** 56

Language. *See* Dictionaries; Philology; Speech; *specific languages*

Lanham Defense Housing Act (1940), **Supp. 7,** 459

Lanier, Sidney, references to, **Vol. 9, Part 2,** 262, 559; **Vol. 10, Part 1,** 442 f.

Lanman, Charles R., reference to, **Vol. 10, Part 1,** 474 f.

Lansing, Robert, references to, **Supp. 3,** 139, 605, 606; **Supp. 5,** 137; **Supp. 6,** 177

Lansing-Ishii agreement, **Vol. 5, Part 2,** 610

Lanterns on the Levee: Recollections of a Planter's Son, **Supp. 3,** 598

Laos: medical relief work in, **Supp. 7,** 190–91; neutralization of, **Supp. 7,** 422

Lap robes, manufacture of, **Vol. 4, Part 1,** 380

Lard-burning lamp, invention, **Vol. 10, Part 1,** 483 f.

Lardner, David, reference to, **Supp. 6,** 366

Lardner, James, reference to, **Supp. 6,** 366

Lardner, Ring, references to, **Supp. 6,** 365, 366–67; **Supp. 7,** 413; **Supp. 8,** 649

Lark, The, founding of, **Supp. 5,** 94

Larkin, Jim, reference to, **Supp. 3,** 718

Larkin Building (Buffalo, N.Y.), **Supp. 6,** 712

Laryngectomy, first successful total, **Supp. 3,** 202

Laryngology, **Vol. 1, Part 1,** 191, 383; **Vol. 1, Part 2,** 467; **Vol. 3, Part 2,** 119; **Vol. 4, Part 1,** 547; **Vol. 5, Part 1,** 625; **Vol. 5, Part 2,** 465, 515; **Vol. 6, Part 1,** 140, 160, 268; **Vol. 6, Part 2,** 94, 450; **Vol. 8, Part 2,** 306, 411, 562; **Vol. 9, Part 1,** 185, 195; research

in, **Supp. 1,** 181; **Supp. 6,** 317–18

Laryngoscope, founding of, **Supp. 3,** 311

Laryngoscope, use of, **Vol. 2, Part 2,** 275

Larynx, cancer diagnosis and treatment, **Supp. 4,** 185–86

La Salle, Robert Cavelier, Sieur de, references to, **Vol. 5, Part 2,** 223; **Vol. 6, Part 2,** 526; **Vol. 9, Part 2,** 587

La Salle, Ill., public service to, **Vol. 6, Part 2,** 422

La Scala Opera Company (Milan, Italy): management of, **Supp. 2,** 222–23; Toscanini association, **Supp. 6,** 323, 642–43, 644; **Supp. 8,** 19

Lascher, Andrew, reference to, **Supp. 6,** 318

Las Guasimas, Cuba, battle of, **Vol. 8, Part 2,** 137; **Vol. 9, Part 1,** 16; **Vol. 10, Part 2,** 51, 467

Laski, Harold J., references to, **Supp. 3,** 471, 473; **Supp. 6,** 271; **Supp. 8,** 50

Lasky, Blanche, references to, **Supp. 6,** 368, 370

Lasky, Jesse L., references to, **Supp. 6,** 158–59, 439; **Supp. 8,** 677–78

Lassen Peak, eruption of, **Supp. 1,** 247

Lasser, J. K., and Co., founding of, **Supp. 5,** 412

La Starza, Roland, reference to, **Supp. 8,** 417

Lastex, **Supp. 7,** 169

Last Hurrah, The, **Supp. 8,** 477, 660

Last of the Mohicans, The, **Vol. 2, Part 2,** 402, f.

Las Vegas, Nev., organized crime in, **Supp. 6,** 264

Late George Apley, The, **Supp. 6,** 428

Lathe, flat-turret, invention of, **Supp. 1,** 378

Lathrop, Barbour, reference to, **Supp. 5,** 213–14

Lathrop, John E., reference to, **Supp. 5,** 699

Lathrop, Julia, biography of, **Supp. 1,** 12

Latin America: Alliance for Progress, **Supp. 7,** 421; archaeological expeditions, **Supp. 5,** 711; diplomacy during World War II, **Supp. 7,** 778; diplomacy with U.S., **Vol. 1, Part 2,** 327; **Vol. 2, Part 1,** 219, 420; **Vol. 10, Part 2,** 325, 357; **Supp. 2,** 25, 580; **Supp. 7,** 777–78; ethnology studies, **Supp. 1,** 648; exploration, **Supp. 6,** 59; Good Neighbor policy, **Supp. 4,** 171, 706; **Supp. 5,** 89, 332; Good Neighbor policy forerunner, **Supp. 4,** 406; historical studies of, **Supp. 1,** 655; **Supp. 5,** 77; **Supp. 6,** 277–78; longest suspension bridge, **Supp. 6,** 594; mammology expeditions, **Supp. 5,** 678; missions, **Supp. 2,** 500; **Supp. 8,** 537; paleobotany, **Supp. 3,** 62; retail stores, **Supp. 8,** 705; U.S. experts on, **Supp. 4,** 705–6; U.S. mutual security agreements, **Supp. 3,** 657. *See also specific countries*

Latin literature and language: classical studies, **Supp. 2,** 204; medieval, **Supp. 4,** 68; poetry, **Supp. 1,** 701; scholarship on, **Supp. 1,** 657; sixteenth-century poems and plays, **Supp. 4,** 110; teaching of, **Supp. 2,** 454; translations, **Supp. 7,** 742; **Supp. 8,** 236

Latitude, determination of the variation of, **Vol. 3, Part 1,** 373; **Vol. 8, Part 1,** 95 f., 465

La Tour, Charles de, reference to, **Vol. 8, Part 2,** 318

La Tour, Le Blond de, reference to, **Vol. 7, Part 2,** 318 f.

"La Tour, Marie" (fictional character), **Supp. 7,** 633

Latrobe, Benjamin Henry: biography of, **Supp. 6,** 272; references to, **Vol. 6, Part 1,** 24; **Vol. 7, Part 1,** 10; **Vol. 9, Part 2,** 505

"Latrobe's Folly," **Vol. 6, Part 1,** 26

Latter-Day Saints. *See* Mormon church

Lattimore, Owen, reference to, **Supp. 5,** 410; **Supp. 8,** 133

Laughing Boy, **Supp. 7,** 449

Laughing gas, use of, in dentistry, **Vol. 8, Part 1,** 604

Laughlin, Harry H., reference to, **Supp. 3,** 215

Laughlin, J. Laurence, reference to, **Supp. 4,** 584

Laundries, Civil War, **Vol. 1, Part 2,** 238

Laurel, Stan, reference to, **Supp. 6**, 276
Laurel and Hardy (comedy team), **Supp. 6**, 276; **Supp. 7**, 463–64
Laurel Falls Camp for Girls (Ga.), **Supp. 8**, 605, 606
Lauritsen, Charles C., reference to, **Supp. 8**, 483
Lausanne Conference on Near Eastern Affairs (1922–23), **Supp. 7**, 303
Lausche, Frank J., reference to, **Supp. 6**, 614
Lautner, John, references to, **Supp. 6**, 681; **Supp. 7**, 291
Lavender Mist (painting), **Supp. 6**, 513
La Victoire, ship which brought Lafayette to America, **Vol. 5, Part 2**, 536
L'Avvenire, **Supp. 3**, 777
Law (for complete list of lawyers jurists, etc., *see* Occupations Index), **Vol. 1, Part 1**, 94, 329, 342, 368, 386, 445, 617; **Vol. 2, Part 1**, 401; **Vol. 2, Part 2**, 83 f.; **Vol. 3, Part 1**, 311, 619; **Vol. 3, Part 2**, 486; **Vol. 4, Part 1**, 12, 15, 126, 175, 182, 306, 315, 369, 382, 487, 518, 578 f.; **Vol. 5, Part 1**, 211, **Vol. 5, Part 2**, 106, 114, 128, 180, 345 f.; **Vol. 6, Part 1**, 341; **Vol. 7, Part 1**, 69, 466, 638; **Vol. 7, Part 2**, 627; **Vol. 9, Part 2**, 79, 96, 239; **Vol. 10, Part 1**, 406; administrative, **Supp. 2**, 250; admiralty, **Vol. 1, Part 2**, 177, 231; **Vol. 2, Part 1**, 99, 370, 399; **Vol. 3, Part 1**, 60, 79 f., 592 f.; **Vol. 3, Part 2**, 454; **Vol. 5, Part 2**, 64; **Vol. 9, Part 2**, 28, 105; agricultural, **Supp. 4**, 50; American Indian, **Supp. 5**, 119–20; American Indian codification; **Supp. 8**, 99; antitrust, **Supp. 5**, 27, 174; **Supp. 7**, 547; appellate, **Supp. 5**, 155, 156; associations, **Supp. 8**, 662–63; attorneys general, U.S., **Vol. 7, Part 1**, 108; **Vol. 7, Part 2**, 587, 627; **Vol. 8, Part 1**, 353 f.; **Vol. 8, Part 2**, 347; **Vol. 9, Part 1**, 518; banking, **Vol. 3, Part 1**, 388 f.; **Supp. 4**, 325–26, 331, 332; bankruptcy, **Supp. 4**, 825; bar admission standards, **Supp. 2**, 685; bar associations, **Supp. 1**, 223; British common, historical writings collection, **Supp. 1**, 154; business, **Supp. 4**, 192–93; **Supp. 7**, 792; canon, **Vol. 3, Part 1**, 368; case method of teaching, **Supp. 3**, 820; **Supp. 4**, 77; cases, *see* Law cases; church, **Vol. 4, Part 1**, 194; **Vol. 7, Part 1**, 625; circuit riding, **Vol. 4, Part 2** 497; **Vol. 5, Part 2**, 169, 226; **Vol. 8, Part 2**, 15; **Vol. 9, Part 1**, 382; circumstantial evidence defined, **Vol. 10, Part 1**, 592 f.; civil, **Vol. 5, Part 2**, 569; civil liberties issues, **Supp. 5**, 280; **Supp. 6**, 104–6; civil rights issues, **Supp. 4**, 397–98; **Supp. 8**, 323, 333–34; codification, **Vol. 2, Part 2**, 587; **Vol. 8, Part 1**, 29 f., 33 f., 52 f., 426; colonial, **Vol. 1, Part 1**, 421; **Vol. 6, Part 1**, 525; **Vol. 8, Part 1**, 426; commercial, **Vol. 3, Part 1**, 388 f.; **Vol. 5, Part 2**, 460; **Vol. 9, Part 2**, 96 f.; **Supp. 2**, 93, 501; **Supp. 7**, 792; common, **Supp. 1**, 420–21; **Supp. 2**, 94; **Supp. 7**, 475; common, codification of, **Vol. 4, Part 1**, 385, 583; **Vol. 4, Part 2** 212; **Vol. 8, Part 2**, 321; comparative studies, **Supp. 3**, 821; compendium of, **Vol. 3, Part 1**, 64; conservation, **Supp. 4**, 481–82, 666; constitutional, **Vol. 4, Part 1**, 273; **Vol. 5, Part 2**, 572, 573; **Vol. 6, Part 2**, 318 f.; **Vol. 9, Part 2**, 406; **Supp. 1**, 367, 422–23; **Supp. 8**, 139; corporation, **Vol. 2, Part 2**, 131; **Vol. 2, Part 1**, 281; **Vol. 3, Part 1**, 47, 291, 309, 311, 341, 388 f.; **Vol. 5, Part 2**, 241; **Vol. 6, Part 1**, 269; **Vol. 7, Part 1**, 591; **Vol. 7, Part 2**, 30 f.; **Vol. 8, Part 1**, 449, 634; **Vol. 8, Part 2**, 29, 424; **Supp. 1**, 223; **Supp. 2**, 131, 470; **Supp. 3**, 117; courts, coercion of, by popular feeling, **Vol. 3, Part 1**, 160; criminal, **Vol. 2, Part 2**, 174; **Vol. 4, Part 1**, 66, 231, 360, 472; **Vol. 5, Part 1**, 116; **Supp. 2**, 142; **Supp. 3**, 65–66; **Supp. 6**, 665; criminal, deterrence theory of, **Supp. 3**, 822; debtors, for relief of, **Vol. 3, Part 1**, 599 f.; demurrage, **Vol. 5, Part 2**, 573; economics and, **Supp. 6**, 271; editorial work, **Vol. 6, Part 1**, 471;

Vol. 9, Part 1, 253; enforcement of, **Vol. 6, Part 2**, 643; **Supp. 2**, 535, 715; equal employment, **Supp. 7**, 382; equity, **Vol. 8, Part 1**, 440; **Vol. 9, Part 2**, 103 f.; ethical standards in, **Supp. 1**, 99, 204; ethics, **Vol. 6, Part 1**, 149; evidence, **Vol. 9, Part 2**, 406; federal v. state, **Supp. 3**, 99; fees, large, **Vol. 3, Part 1**, 309; habeas corpus, **Vol. 1, Part 2**, 422; **Vol. 5, Part 1**, 467; historical studies, **Supp. 2**, 133; homestead, **Vol. 5, Part 2**, 82; immigration, **Supp. 1**, 472; **Supp. 2**, 46; impeachment, **Vol. 4, Part 1**, 236; intemperance, statutes to prevent, **Vol. 5, Part 2**, 79; international, **Vol. 2, Part 1**, 494; **Vol. 2, Part 2**, 464; **Vol. 3, Part 1**, 61, 296, 592; **Vol. 5, Part 2**, 609; **Vol. 6, Part 1**, 53, 238; **Vol. 8, Part 2**, 241; **Vol. 9, Part 1**, 43, 392; **Vol. 9, Part 2**, 42; irrigation, **Vol. 6, Part 2**, 4; journals, **Vol. 9, Part 1**, 65; judges, popular election of, **Vol. 5, Part 1**, 77; judicial review, **Vol. 2, Part 2**, 536 f.; **Vol. 10, Part 2**, 588; jurisprudence, **Vol. 8, Part 1**, 440; Korean, **Vol. 4, Part 1**, 526; law, Indians, regarding, **Vol. 3, Part 1**, 149 f.; **Vol. 4, Part 1**, 502; law, insurance, **Vol. 3, Part 1**, 485 f.; **Vol. 6, Part 1**, 208; legislative power, **Vol. 4, Part 1**, 255; libraries, **Vol. 5, Part 2**, 445; maritime, **Vol. 1, Part 2**, 360; **Vol. 3, Part 1**, 60; **Vol. 3, Part 2**, 454; **Vol. 10, Part 1**, 446; martial, **Vol. 5, Part 2**, 569; "midnight judges," **Vol. 5, Part 2**, 28; **Vol. 6, Part 1**, 101; military, **Vol. 3, Part 1**, 111, 115; mining, **Vol. 3, Part 1**, 238; **Vol. 6, Part 1**, 275; **Vol. 8, Part 1**, 415; **Vol. 9, Part 2**, 13, 589; patent, **Vol. 1, Part 2**, 360; **Vol. 2, Part 2**, 481, 613; **Vol. 3, Part 1**, 288; **Vol. 4, Part 2** 249, 590; **Vol. 5, Part 2**, 41, 464 f.; **Vol. 6, Part 1**, 27; **Vol. 8, Part 1**, 75 f., 504 f.; **Vol. 8, Part 2**, 567; **Vol. 9, Part 1**, 614; **Vol. 9, Part 2**, 99; philosophies of, **Supp. 3**, 185–86; **Supp. 6**, 216; **Supp. 7**, 99–100; precedent, sanctity of, **Vol. 3, Part 1**, 355; Prohibition, **Supp. 3**, 706; **Supp. 4**, 853; Prohibition enforcement, **Supp. 7**, 786, 805–6; property, **Vol. 4, Part 1**, 255, 444, 456, 559; **Vol. 5, Part 2**, 195, 197 f.; public relief, **Supp. 4**, 810; railroad, **Vol. 3, Part 1**, 245 f.; **Vol. 4, Part 1**, 609; **Vol. 5, Part 2**, 450; **Vol. 7, Part 2**, 375; **Vol. 8, Part 1**, 440, 541; **Vol. 9, Part 2**, 28; **Supp. 3**, 167–68; railroad labor representation, **Supp. 6**, 542; reform, **Vol. 1, Part 1**, 431; **Vol. 3, Part 2**, 360, 373; **Vol. 4, Part 2** 81; **Vol. 6, Part 1**, 396; **Vol. 8, Part 1**, 211 f.; reporting, **Vol. 5, Part 2**, 128, 424; **Vol. 8, Part 1**, 10 f.; reports, first complete, **Vol. 5, Part 2**, 424; riots, **Vol. 4, Part 1**, 255; school, first in America, **Vol. 8, Part 1**, 496; securities, **Vol. 5, Part 2**, 195; slavery, **Vol. 4, Part 1**, 121, 315, 607; **Vol. 9, Part 2**, 37; social, **Supp. 1**, 323; social psychology of, **Supp. 2**, 562; special pleading, **Vol. 8, Part 1**, 426; state uniformity, **Supp. 3**, 737; **Supp. 7**, 792; statute improvement, **Supp. 5**, 107–8; strikes, **Vol. 3, Part 2**, 556; studies in, **Supp. 1**, 420; **Supp. 2**, 501; teaching of, **Vol. 1, Part 1**, 246, 247, 614; **Vol. 1, Part 2**, 375; **Vol. 2, Part 2**, 239, 289; **Vol. 3, Part 1**, 571; **Vol. 3, Part 2**, 75; **Vol. 4, Part 1**, 453, 456, 520 f.; **Vol. 4, Part 2** 212, 529; **Vol. 5, Part 1**, 111, 124, 134, 382; **Vol. 5, Part 2**, 285, 435, 585; **Vol. 6, Part 1**, 369; **Vol. 7, Part 1**, 26 f.; **Vol. 8, Part 1**, 52 f., 469; **Vol. 8, Part 2**, 57, 451, 459; **Vol. 9, Part 1**, 29, 35, 250, 292, 531; **Vol. 9, Part 2**, 141, 320, 402, 404, 405, 406; **Vol. 10, Part 1**, 363, 499; **Supp. 1**, 323, 358, 497; **Supp. 2**, 482; **Supp. 3**, 43, 185–86, 700; **Supp. 4**, 490–91, 680, 793–94; **Supp. 7**, 474–75, 627, 792; **Supp. 8**, 17, 138–39, 285; textbooks, **Vol. 2, Part 1**, 166; **Vol. 5, Part 1**, 53; trial, **Supp. 2**, 629, 674; veterans, **Supp. 3**, 661; voting rights, **Supp. 8**, 334, 335; women in, **Vol. 1, Part 2**, 581; writings on, **Vol. 1, Part 1**, 73, 81, 309, 329, 546, 593; **Vol. 1, Part 2**, 193, 260, 296, 491; **Vol. 2, Part 1**, 16, 20, 27,

L'Esaminatore, official Catholic organ, **Vol. 5, Part 2,** 589

Lescohier, Don D., reference to, **Supp. 3,** 178

Leslie, Frank, references to, **Vol. 7, Part 1,** 186, 392

Leslie, Miriam Florence Folline (Mrs. Frank), reference to, **Supp. 4,** 158; **Supp. 7,** 779

Letchworth Village (N.Y.), **Vol. 6, Part 1,** 194; administration, **Supp. 2,** 388

"Letheon," early name for ether, **Vol. 7, Part 1,** 269

"Letter from Birmingham Jail," **Supp. 8,** 994

Lettering. *See* Calligraphy; Typographical design

Let Us Now Praise Famous Men, **Supp. 5,** 511

Leuba, James, reference to, **Supp. 4,** 766, 767

Leukemia: "Auer bodies," **Supp. 4,** 34; X-ray treatment, **Supp. 4,** 581

Levant, Oscar, reference to, **Supp. 3,** 690

Levees, construction of, along Mississippi, **Vol. 3, Part 2,** 403; **Vol. 4, Part 2** 353

Levene, P. A. T., reference to, **Supp. 4,** 287

Lever House (New York City), design, **Supp. 7,** 691

Levi-Civita, Tullio, reference to, **Supp. 7,** 216

Levin, Hymie, reference to, **Supp. 6,** 263, 264

Levine, Charles A., reference to, **Supp. 6,** 51

Levine, Philip, reference to, **Supp. 3,** 441–42

Levitt, Alfred S., reference to, **Supp. 7,** 469–70

Levitt, William J., reference to, **Supp. 7,** 469–70

Levitt and Sons, **Supp. 7,** 469–70

Levittown, N.Y., **Supp. 7,** 470

Levy, Jules, reference to, **Supp. 6,** 241

Lew, Henri, references to, **Supp. 6,** 357, 358

Lewis, Gilbert N., reference to, **Supp. 4,** 839

Lewis, J. Hamilton, references to, **Supp. 3,** 710; **Supp. 6,** 636

Lewis, John L., references to, **Supp. 3,** 656, 660; **Supp. 4,** 75, 376; **Supp. 5,** 248–49; **Supp. 5,** 254, 282, 339–40, 509–10, 654, 691, 714; **Supp. 7,** 81–82, 172; **Supp. 8,** 207, 290, 510–11, 652

Lewis, Oscar, references to, **Supp. 3,** 373; **Supp. 6,** 533

Lewis, Paul A., references to, **Supp. 3,** 441; **Supp. 4,** 34, 287

Lewis, Robert, reference to, **Supp. 5,** 53

Lewis, Ruth Maslow, references to, **Supp. 8,** 377, 378

Lewis, Sinclair: Kelley relationship, **Supp. 6,** 328, 329; references to, **Supp. 5,** 85, 272; **Supp. 6,** 95; **Supp. 7,** 740

Lewis, Thomas, reference to, **Supp. 6,** 117

Lewis and Clark expedition, **Vol. 2, Part 2,** 143, 319, 435; **Vol. 4, Part 1,** 178; **Vol. 5, Part 2,** 29; **Vol. 6, Part 1,** 221, 291; **Vol. 7, Part 2,** 51; **Vol. 8, Part 1,** 255; **Vol. 8, Part 2,** 278; history of, **Vol. 1, Part 1,** 203

Lewisohn, Adolph, reference to, **Supp. 5,** 426–27

Lewisohn, Ludwig, reference to, **Supp. 5,** 673

Lewisohn, Margaret Seligman, reference to, **Supp. 5,** 427

Lewisohn Brothers, establishment of, **Supp. 2,** 383

Lexer, Erich, reference to, **Supp. 3,** 67

Lexicography, **Vol. 1, Part 1,** 218; **Vol. 3, Part 1,** 458, 464, 512, 567, 570, 597, 606; **Vol. 4, Part 1,** 399 f.; **Vol. 5, Part 2,** 2, 490 f.; **Vol. 8, Part 1,** 59 f., 95 f., 116 f., 122 f., 305, 330; **Vol. 9, Part 2,** 440; **Vol. 10, Part 1,** 594 f.; **Vol. 10, Part 2,** 56. *See also* Dictionaries; Words

Lexington, Mass., battle at, **Vol. 3, Part 1,** 150; **Vol. 7, Part 1,** 530; **Vol. 7, Part 2,** 233; **Vol. 8, Part 1,** 515; **Vol. 9, Part 1,** 531; **Vol. 10, Part 1,** 415; civic service, **Vol. 5, Part 1,** 337; normal school, first state, **Vol. 7, Part 2,** 404

Lexington, Mo., battle of, **Vol. 8, Part 1,** 216

Lexington, race horse, **Vol. 9, Part 2,** 366

Lexington Morning Herald, **Supp. 1,** 114

"Lexington of the Seas," **Vol. 7, Part 1,** 610

Lexow investigation, **Vol. 7, Part 1,** 280; **Vol. 7, Part 2,** 245

Leyte, World War II action, **Supp. 4,** 589; **Supp. 6,** 268

Lhévinne, Rosina, reference to, **Supp. 3,** 459

Liability, legal writings on, **Supp. 3,** 43

Libbey, Edward Drummond, references to, **Vol. 7, Part 2,** 100; **Vol. 9, Part 1,** 611

Libby Prison, **Vol. 1, Part 1,** 636; **Vol. 6, Part 1,** 557 f.; **Vol. 9, Part 2,** 636

Libel law and suits, **Vol. 3, Part 1,** 276; **Vol. 3, Part 2,** 167; **Vol. 4, Part 2** 182; **Vol. 8, Part 1,** 112, f., 118 t.; **Vol. 8, Part 2,** 282 f.; AP political cartoon suit, **Supp. 3,** 852; *Confidential* series suits, **Supp. 5,** 406; Ford-Hearst suit, **Supp. 4,** 288, 302; **Supp. 5,** 450; Hiss-Chambers suit, **Supp. 5,** 665; **Supp. 7,** 114; Reynolds-Pegler suit, **Supp. 7,** 643; **Supp. 8,** 498; suits against Pearson, **Supp. 8,** 497; Tinkham-Cannon suit, **Supp. 6,** 636; wartime, **Supp. 6,** 105

Liberal Christian League, **Vol. 2, Part 2,** 310

Liberalism: journalistic voice of, **Supp. 4,** 850–51; non-Communist left, **Supp. 3,** 777; theological, **Supp. 4,** 512–13, 525–26; writings on, **Supp. 3,** 731; **Supp. 4,** 804

Liberal party, founding of, **Supp. 7,** 156

Liberal Republican movement, **Vol. 2, Part 1,** 106; **Vol. 5, Part 2,** 421; **Vol. 8, Part 2,** 122, 473

Liberator: **Supp. 7,** 268; abolition paper, **Vol. 4, Part 1,** 169; **Vol. 5, Part 2,** 112; **Vol. 9, Part 2,** 299; **Supp. 7,** 268; founding of, **Supp. 3,** 852; **Supp. 4,** 528; **Supp. 8,** 149

Liberia, **Vol. 1, Part 1,** 394 f.; **Vol. 3, Part 2,** 104; **Vol. 4, Part 2** 56, 371; **Vol. 5, Part 2,** 97 f.; **Vol. 7, Part 1,** 16; **Vol. 8, Part 2,** 11, 212, 253; botany of, **Supp. 2,** 113; colonization of, **Vol. 6, Part 2,** 545; development of, **Supp. 2,** 188; diplomatic relations with U.S., **Vol. 8, Part 2,** 10; **Vol. 9, Part 1,** 155, 375; **Vol. 10, Part 1,** 66 f.; **Supp. 7,** 767–68; first president of, **Vol. 8, Part 2,** 10; missions, **Vol. 2, Part 1,** 555; **Vol. 3, Part 1,** 156; **Vol. 7, Part 2,** 428

Liberia College, founding of, **Vol. 9, Part 2,** 623

Liberia Co., founding of, **Supp. 4,** 778

Liberty, **Supp. 5,** 527; founding of, **Supp. 2,** 670; **Supp. 5,** 453

Liberty, Hancock's sloop, **Vol. 4, Part 2** 218

Liberty Bell, **Vol. 7, Part 1,** 554

"Liberty Boys," **Vol. 9, Part 2,** 361

Liberty Hall Academy, forerunner of Washington and Lee University, **Vol. 8, Part 1,** 222

Liberty League, **Supp. 6,** 679; founding of, **Vol. 4, Part 1,** 385; **Vol. 6, Part 1,** 368;

Liberty loans, **Vol. 4, Part 1,** 241; **Vol. 5, Part 1,** 56; **Supp. 3,** 480; **Supp. 4,** 469; **Supp. 6,** 376

Liberty Memorial (Kansas City, Mo.), **Supp. 1,** 537

Liberty party, **Vol. 1, Part 2,** 293; **Vol. 2, Part 2,** 28; **Vol. 5, Part 1,** 151; **Vol. 6, Part 1,** 116; **Vol. 9, Part 1,** 271

Libman-Sacks disease, **Supp. 4,** 494

Libraries and library work: administration, **Supp. 4,** 845–46; Americana, **Supp. 5,** 9, 10; as popular education tool, **Supp. 3,** 90–91, 416; bookstacks, fireproof, **Vol. 8, Part 1,** 138 f.; branch, early experiments in, **Vol. 8, Part 1,** 171 f.; branch for blacks, **Supp. 3,** 280–81; branch system, **Supp. 3,** 90–91; **Supp. 4,** 19; building and equipment of, **Vol. 3, Part 1,** 604; catalog cards, **Supp. 3,** 510; **Supp. 5,** 753; catalogs for, **Vol. 1, Part 1,** 218; **Vol. 3, Part 1,** 15 f.; **Vol. 5, Part 2,** 666; **Vol. 10, Part 1,** 107; catalog uniformity, **Supp. 3,** 326–27; circulating, **Vol. 1, Part 1,** 335; **Vol. 1, Part 2,** 162; **Vol. 3, Part**

2, 356; **Vol. 4, Part 2** 591; **Vol. 6, Part 1,** 427; **Vol. 7, Part 1,** 510; **Vol. 9, Part 2,** 445; classification systems, **Supp. 5,** 554; contributions to development of, **Vol. 1, Part 1,** 640; **Vol. 1, Part 2,** 557, 610; **Vol. 3, Part 1,** 121, 143, 192, 277, 550; **Vol. 3, Part 2,** 55, 206, 254 f., 475, 479, 487, 493, 519, 541; **Vol. 4, Part 1,** 21, 557, 617; **Vol. 4, Part 2** 42, 51, 321, 483; **Vol. 5, Part 1,** 137, 191, 244, 335, 516; **Vol. 5, Part 2,** 206, 215, 606; **Vol. 6, Part 1,** 148, 172, 231, 570; **Vol. 7, Part 1,** 127, 134, 172, 413 f., 447; **Vol. 8, Part 1,** 65, 229; **Vol. 8, Part 2,** 382, 525; **Vol. 9, Part 1,** 24, 49, 147, 198, 229, 303, 317, 463 f., 562; **Vol. 9, Part 2,** 135, 330, 521, 587; **Vol. 10, Part 1,** 558 f.; **Vol. 10, Part 2,** 403; decimal classification, **Supp. 1,** 242; first conference of librarians, **Vol. 4, Part 1,** 557; **Vol. 8, Part 1,** 66 f.; first in county jail, **Vol. 4, Part 1,** 271; first free in New York City, **Vol. 8, Part 1,** 168 f.; history research center, **Supp. 3,** 262; journals, **Supp. 1,** 101; **Supp. 5,** 753; mercantile, **Vol. 10, Part 2,** 471; microfilm and microfiche, **Supp. 8,** 120; naval, **Supp. 6,** 348; New York Conference of Librarians, **Vol. 5, Part 2,** 66; organization of, **Vol. 2, Part 1,** 20; **Vol. 3, Part 1,** 57, 143; **Vol. 6, Part 1,** 2; **Vol. 8, Part 1,** 66 f.; organizations, *see specific names;* physiology, **Supp. 6,** 223, 224; presidential, **Supp. 4,** 176; **Supp. 6,** 541; public libraries, **Vol. 1, Part 2,** 610; **Vol. 2, Part 2,** 583; **Vol. 5, Part 2,** 66, 445; **Vol. 8, Part 1,** 66 f.; **Vol. 9, Part 2,** 549; **Vol. 10, Part 1,** 558 f.; reference library, first official, **Vol. 6, Part 1,** 570; research and scholarly, **Supp. 6,** 398–99; schools for library work, **Vol. 6, Part 1,** 148; **Vol. 8, Part 1,** 17; standards, **Supp. 1,** 101; teaching of, **Supp. 1,** 242; **Supp. 3,** 280; **Supp. 4,** 19; **Supp. 5,** 47; traveling, establishment of, **Vol. 3, Part 1,** 192; women writers' collection, **Supp. 6,** 576; World's Congress of Librarians, **Vol. 4, Part 1,** 558; writings on, **Vol. 3, Part 1,** 604; **Vol. 4, Part 1,** 558; **Vol. 5, Part 2,** 66; **Vol. 7, Part 2,** 467; **Vol. 8, Part 1,** 17, 66. *See also* American Library Association; Archives; Bibliographies; Libraries (specific); *names of specific libraries*

Libraries (specific): Astor, *see* New York Public Library; Avery Architectural Library, **Supp. 6,** 272; Baltimore, **Vol. 8, Part 1,** 171 f.; Boston Medical, **Vol. 8, Part 1,** 275; **Vol. 9, Part 2,** 94; Boston Public, **Vol. 1, Part 2,** 24, 53; **Vol. 4, Part 1,** 617; **Vol. 6, Part 2,** 100; **Vol. 7, Part 2,** 241; **Vol. 9, Part 2,** 405, 528; **Vol. 10, Part 2,** 161, 403; Buffalo, N.Y., **Vol. 10, Part 1,** 426; California, **Vol. 3, Part 1,** 121; Chicago, **Vol. 1, Part 1,** 448; Galveston, Tex., **Vol. 8, Part 2,** 166; Harvard University, **Vol. 8, Part 1,** 308 f.; Lenox Library, New York City, **Vol. 6, Part 1,** 172; **Vol. 7, Part 1,** 126; New York Academy of Medicine, **Vol. 8, Part 1,** 269 f.; New York Public, **Vol. 1, Part 1,** 335, 445; **Vol. 1, Part 2,** 268; **Vol. 7, Part 2,** 107; **Vol. 8, Part 1,** 17, 125 f., 634 f.; **Vol. 8, Part 2,** 382; Tilden, New York City, **Vol. 9, Part 2,** 541; University of Pennsylvania, **Vol. 7, Part 2,** 441; University of Pennsylvania Law School, **Vol. 5, Part 2,** 445; Wisconsin State Historical Society, **Vol. 3, Part 1,** 551 f.; Yale University, **Vol. 3, Part 1,** 277; **Vol. 3, Part 2,** 79; **Vol. 8, Part 2,** 480

Library Journal, founding of, **Vol. 6, Part 1,** 231; **Supp. 1,** 101

Library of American Biography, **Vol. 7, Part 2,** 341, 343

Library of Congress, **Vol. 4, Part 1,** 285; **Vol. 5, Part 1,** 385; **Vol. 5, Part 2,** 31; **Vol. 9, Part 1,** 463; **Vol. 9, Part 2,** 587; administration, **Supp. 5,** 554–55; annex construction, **Supp. 5,** 554; Bibliography, Division of, **Vol. 4, Part 1,** 617; Bollingen Prize in Poetry, **Supp. 7,** 347; Catalog Division, **Supp. 3,** 326; chamber music auditorium, **Supp. 5,** 129, 554;

classification system, **Supp. 5,** 664; collections, **Supp. 5,** 586; designing of, **Vol. 7, Part 2,** 411; folk-song archives, **Supp. 4,** 502; foreign copying program, **Supp. 8,** 369; Manuscripts Division, **Supp. 1,** 343; **Supp. 2,** 191–92; **Supp. 3,** 285–86; **Supp. 3,** 534; mosaics in, **Supp. 1,** 247; murals in, **Vol. 7, Part 2,** 352; Music Division, **Supp. 3,** 252; **Vol. 9, Part 1,** 395; reclassification, **Supp. 3,** 510; statues in, **Vol. 1, Part 2,** 12

Library of Education, **Vol. 1, Part 1,** 624

Library of Southern Literature, **Vol. 9, Part 1,** 245

Lichenology, **Vol. 10, Part 1,** 43

Lick Observatory, **Vol. 3, Part 1,** 292; **Vol. 5, Part 1,** 136, 432; **Vol. 5, Part 2,** 279; **Vol. 6, Part 1,** 234; **Vol. 7, Part 1,** 6, 454; **Vol. 8, Part 2,** 412

Liebig, Justus von, reference to, **Vol. 8, Part 1,** 96

Liebler, Theodore A., reference to, **Supp. 4,** 842–43

Liebold, Ernest G., reference to, **Supp. 4,** 300

Lie-detector, introduction of, **Vol. 8, Part 2,** 445

Life (general-interest magazine), **Vol. 1, Part 1,** 573; **Vol. 7, Part 1,** 53; **Supp. 7,** 382, 383, 384, 436, 437; drama criticism, **Supp. 3,** 53–54; editorial writing, **Supp. 5,** 152–53; founding of, **Supp. 8,** 394–96; illustrations, **Supp. 3,** 300–1; **Supp. 7,** 17; movie reviews, **Supp. 5,** 623

Life (humor magazine), editing, **Supp. 1,** 544–45

Life Begins at Forty, **Supp. 5,** 546

Lifeboats, **Vol. 3, Part 2,** 582

Life Extension Institute, **Supp. 4,** 275

Life in a Mexican Village: Tepoztlán Restudied, **Supp. 8,** 378

Life insurance, **Vol. 1, Part 1,** 599; **Vol. 3, Part 1,** 463; **Vol. 3, Part 2,** 419; **Vol. 4, Part 2** 500; **Vol. 5, Part 1,** 450; **Vol. 6, Part 1,** 495, 562, 588; **Vol. 6, Part 2,** 12; **Vol. 7, Part 1,** 248, 265, 323; **Vol. 7, Part 2,** 56, 313, 381, 471, 547; **Vol. 8, Part 2,** 351; actuarial studies, **Supp. 4,** 384–85; investigations of, **Vol. 8, Part 2,** 96; mortality, first table of, **Vol. 6, Part 1,** 577 f.; organization of companies, **Vol. 6, Part 1,** 588; **Vol. 8, Part 2,** 267; pioneer work in, **Vol. 3, Part 1,** 463 f.; reform, **Vol. 3, Part 2,** 402; **Vol. 4, Part 2** 501; **Vol. 6, Part 2,** 12

Life masks, **Vol. 2, Part 1,** 97

Life of Michelangelo Buonarroti, The, **Supp. 3,** 785

Life of Reason: Of the Phases of Human Progress, The, **Supp. 5,** 602

Lifesaving service, **Vol. 2, Part 2,** 483; **Vol. 3, Part 2,** 582; **Vol. 5, Part 2,** 379 f.; **Vol. 7, Part 1,** 460; **Vol. 8, Part 1,** 214 f.

Life with Father, **Supp. 8,** 108–9, 383

Liggett, Hunter, reference to, **Supp. 6,** 429

Liggett and Myers Tobacco Co., **Supp. 5,** 567

Light: and visual acuity, **Supp. 3,** 269–70; arc lamp, **Supp. 2,** 658; earth's effect on circuit time, **Supp. 3,** 291; gas-filled incandescent lamp, **Supp. 6,** 365; growth-related studies, **Supp. 6,** 69; incandescent lamp, **Supp. 1,** 279, 373; **Supp. 2,** 702; infrared, **Supp. 4,** 658; refraction of, **Supp. 1,** 187; study of, **Vol. 4, Part 1,** 249; **Vol. 6, Part 2,** 594 f.; ultraviolet research, **Supp. 5,** 441, 496; **Supp. 6,** 69; vision stimulation studies, **Supp. 4,** 367. velocity of, **Vol. 6, Part 1,** 442–3; **Vol. 7, Part 1,** 453. *See also* Electricity and electrification

Light, The. *See* Brazilian Traction, Light and Power Co.

Light Horse of the City of Philadelphia, **Vol. 6, Part 1,** 75

Lighthouse Board: establishment of, **Vol. 9, Part 2,** 599; building, **Vol. 1, Part 1,** 163; **Vol. 3, Part 1,** 529 f.; **Vol. 4, Part 2** 353; **Vol. 5, Part 1,** 515; **Vol. 5, Part 2,** 110; **Vol. 6, Part 1,** 228; **Vol. 8, Part 1,** 28 f.; **Vol. 9, Part 1,** 265; **Vol. 9, Part 2,** 249, 397,

599; **Vol. 10, Part 1,** 616 f.; first skeleton iron tower, in U.S., **Vol. 9, Part 2,** 249; government contracts, **Vol. 6, Part 1,** 228; reflectors, **Vol. 6, Part 1,** 228; service, **Vol. 5, Part 2,** 50

Lighthouse for the Blind, **Supp. 3,** 364–65

Lighting: arc, **Vol. 3, Part 1,** 376; **Vol. 5, Part 1,** 261; **Vol. 10, Part 1,** 376 f.; electric lamps, **Vol. 6, Part 2,** 436; **Vol. 7, Part 2,** 128; **Vol. 8, Part 2,** 268; flood, **Vol. 8, Part 2,** 268; gas, **Vol. 6, Part 2,** 227; kerosene, **Vol. 3, Part 1,** 415; oil, **Vol. 3, Part 1,** 415; **Vol. 4, Part 2** 440

Lightner, Theodore, reference to, **Supp. 6,** 134

Lightnin' (play), **Vol. 1, Part 1,** 477

Lightning: investigation of, **Vol. 7, Part 2,** 388; protection from, **Supp. 2,** 199

Light quanta, **Supp. 5,** 202–3

Lilienthal, David E., references to, **Supp. 4,** 601; **Supp. 6,** 419, 437; **Supp. 7,** 18; **Supp. 8,** 179

Lilienthal, Gustav, reference to, **Vol. 2, Part 2,** 10

Lilienthal, Joseph L., reference to, **Supp. 7,** 59

Lilienthal, Otto, reference to, **Vol. 2, Part 2,** 10

Lilly, Eli, and Co., founding and growth of, **Supp. 4,** 499–500

Lily, possibly first paper published by a woman, **Vol. 1, Part 2,** 385

Lily-White movement, **Vol. 3, Part 1,** 585 f.; **Vol. 3, Part 2,** 554

Limnology, **Supp. 3,** 402; **Supp. 4,** 84

Límon, José, reference to, **Supp. 6,** 313

Lincoln, Abraham, **Vol. 1, Part 1,** 518; **Vol. 3, Part 1,** 110 f.; **Vol. 4, Part 1,** 310; **Vol. 5, Part 1,** 80, 182, 197, 283, 302, 307, 355, 401, 404; **Vol. 5, Part 2,** 224, 305, 390; **Vol. 6, Part 1,** 204, 306, 336, 435 f., 593; **Vol. 7, Part 1,** 352, 392, 425, 579, 586, 600; **Vol. 8, Part 2,** 368; **Vol. 9, Part 1,** 106 f., 191, 310, 440, 518, 572, 623; **Vol. 9, Part 2,** 60 f.; and his son, **Vol. 6, Part 1,** 267; assassination of, **Vol. 1, Part 2,** 449; **Vol. 3, Part 2,** 333; **Vol. 4, Part 2,** 194; **Vol. 5, Part 2,** 263 f., 284; **Vol. 8, Part 2,** 335; **Vol. 9, Part 2,** 298, 460, 616, 635; assassins, trial of, **Vol. 1, Part 2,** 277; **Vol. 5, Part 2,** 84; at Harrisburg, **Vol. 6, Part 1,** 572; biographies of, **Vol. 4, Part 2,** 433, 579; **Vol. 5, Part 2,** 563, **Vol. 7, Part 1,** 511; **Supp. 1,** 56; **Supp. 2,** 495; **Supp. 8,** 564; campaign of, **Vol. 2, Part 1,** 176; candidacy, one of first editors to propose, **Vol. 9, Part 2,** 60; collections of writings on, **Supp. 2,** 318; Cooper Institute speech, **Vol. 6, Part 1,** 248; **Vol. 7, Part 1,** 579; debates with Douglas, **Vol. 3, Part 1,** 402; **Vol. 6, Part 1,** 247 f.; election of, **Vol. 8, Part 2,** 618; father of, **Vol. 6, Part 1,** 242 f.; "Hardin County" cartoon on, **Supp. 5,** 732; inauguration, **Vol. 8, Part 2,** 196; in Black Hawk War, **Vol. 6, Part 1,** 244; Jaquess mission, failure of, **Vol. 4, Part 1,** 310; last days of, **Vol. 8, Part 2,** 613; law partner of, **Vol. 4, Part 2,** 579; marital relations, **Vol. 4, Part 2,** 268; **Vol. 6, Part 1,** 265 f.; Memorial, **Vol. 1, Part 1,** 478; **Vol. 2, Part 1,** 306; **Vol. 6, Part 1,** 563; mother of, **Vol. 6, Part 1,** 242 f.; nomination of, **Vol. 3, Part 1,** 110; **Vol. 3, Part 2,** 360; **Vol. 8, Part 2,** 447, 456; opposition to policies of, **Vol. 3, Part 1,** 120 f.; partnership with, **Vol. 6, Part 1,** 366; photographs of, **Supp. 7,** 529–30; political manager, **Vol. 5, Part 2,** 231; political rise, **Vol. 3, Part 1,** 402 f.; political rivals of, **Vol. 4, Part 2,** 246; relations with C. F. Adams, **Vol. 1, Part 1,** 42; relations with J. A. Andrew, **Vol. 1, Part 1,** 280; relations with Bancroft, **Vol. 1, Part 1,** 568; relations with J. Calhoun, **Vol. 2, Part 1,** 410; relations with S. P. Chase, **Vol. 2, Part 2,** 29; relations with S. Douglas, **Vol. 1, Part 1,** 394; relations with N. W. Edwards, **Vol. 3, Part 2,** 42; relations with W. P. Fessenden, **Vol. 3, Part 2,** 349; relations with H. Greeley, **Vol. 4, Part

1, 532; relations with H. Hamlin, **Vol. 4, Part 2,** 197 f.; relations with G. B. McClellan, **Vol. 6, Part 1,** 582 f.; relations with J. Medill, **Vol. 6, Part 2,** 491; relations with C. Schurz, **Vol. 8, Part 2,** 467; relations with E. D. Townsend, **Vol. 9, Part 2,** 615 f.; relations with S. H. Tree, **Vol. 9, Part 2,** 635 f.; sculpture of, **Supp. 1,** 322; **Supp. 3,** 88, 89; **Supp. 8,** 414; secretary of, **Vol. 4, Part 2,** 431; **Vol. 7, Part 1,** 510 f.; **Vol. 9, Part 2,** 60; statue of, **Vol. 5, Part 1,** 317; Washington, route to, **Vol. 8, Part 2,** 500; writings on, **Supp. 5,** 557

Lincoln, Mary Todd, reference to, **Vol. 6, Part 1,** 245 f.

Lincoln, Robert, reference to, **Vol. 7, Part 1,** 511

Lincoln, Nebr., development of, **Vol. 3, Part 2,** 51

Lincoln County War, **Vol. 2, Part 2,** 77

"Lincoln Guns," **Vol. 4, Part 2** 267

Lincoln League of America, founding of, **Supp. 5,** 633

Lincoln Memorial (Washington, D.C.), Anderson concert at, **Supp. 5,** 343; Lincoln statue, **Supp. 1,** 322

Lincoln Motor Co., executives, **Supp. 8,** 609–10

Lincoln-Roosevelt League, **Supp. 3,** 394; founding of, **Supp. 4,** 707

Lincoln School (Teachers College, New York City), **Supp. 3,** 552, 667; **Supp. 4,** 139; **Supp. 6,** 208

Lincoln Tunnel (N.Y.-N.J.), **Supp. 6,** 587

Lincoln University, **Vol. 10, Part 1,** 66

Lincoln-Zephyr automobile, **Supp. 3,** 284

Lind, Jenny, references to, **Vol. 1, Part 1,** 638; **Vol. 4, Part 1,** 209; **Vol. 5, Part 1,** 117

Lindbergh, Charles A.: Breckinridge relationship, **Supp. 6,** 75; kidnapping case, **Supp. 3,** 142; laboratory pump design, **Supp. 3,** 141; references to, **Supp. 4,** 303; **Supp. 5,** 547; **Supp. 6,** 51, 470; **Supp. 7,** 504, 779; **Supp. 8,** 373, 650, 679; rocket development, **Supp. 3,** 306–7

Lindenthal, Gustav, reference to, **Supp. 6,** 594

Lindgren, Carl C., reference to, **Supp. 3,** 540

Lindgren, Waldemar, reference to, **Supp. 4,** 765

Lindsay, Howard, reference to, **Supp. 8,** 108–9

"Line o' Type or Two, A," **Vol. 9, Part 2,** 317

Lingg, Claire, reference to, **Supp. 6,** 117

Ling-Temco-Vought, Inc., **Supp. 8,** 367

Linguistics. *See* Philology; *specific language*

Linguistic Society of America, **Vol. 1, Part 2,** 387

Linnaean Society of New York, founding of, **Supp. 3,** 518

Linotype machine, inventions relating to, **Vol. 6, Part 2,** 550; **Vol. 8, Part 1,** 484; **Vol. 8, Part 2,** 106

Lionel Corporation, **Supp. 7,** 150

Lipids, chemistry of, **Supp. 3,** 61

Lippincott's Magazine, **Vol. 5, Part 1,** 202; **Vol. 5, Part 2,** 429; **Vol. 9, Part 1,** 317

Lippmann, Walter, references to, **Supp. 3,** 852; **Supp. 4,** 510; **Supp. 5,** 85, 272; **Supp. 7,** 310, 316; **Supp. 8,** 520

Lip-reading, **Vol. 7, Part 1,** 528

Lipschultz, Louis, reference to, **Supp. 6,** 264

Liquor: control, local option, **Vol. 3, Part 2,** 166; **Vol. 6, Part 2,** 330; 1896 excise bill, **Vol. 8, Part 1,** 326 f.; legal distilleries in Illinois, **Vol. 8, Part 1,** 392; "legal suppressionism," **Vol. 3, Part 1,** 19; "Raines Law," **Vol. 8, Part 1,** 326 f.; writings on the question, **Vol. 3, Part 1,** 376; **Vol. 4, Part 1,** 449; **Vol. 5, Part 2,** 494 f. *See also* Alcohol; Prohibition

Lissák, Kalman, reference to, **Supp. 3,** 136

Lister, Joseph, reference to, **Supp. 1,** 240

Lister, antiseptic system of, **Vol. 4, Part 1,** 393

Litchfield, Conn., first law school in U.S., founded in, **Vol. 8, Part 1,** 469

Literacy test for citizenship, **Vol. 5, Part 2,** 32

Literary and Philosophical Society, **Vol. 2, Part 2,** 224
"Literary Confederacy," **Vol. 8, Part 2,** 344
Literary Digest, **Supp. 7,** 274, 649–50; founding of, **Vol. 4, Part 1,** 73; lexicography column, **Supp. 2,** 683; science editor, **Supp. 3,** 90
Literary Guild of America, **Supp. 4,** 239; **Supp. 6,** 628; founding of, **Supp. 7,** 306
Literary History of America, A, **Vol. 10, Part 1,** 649 f.
Literary Review, **Supp. 7,** 103; founding of, **Supp. 4,** 73; **Supp. 5,** 439
Literary World, **Vol. 3, Part 1,** 561 f.
Literati: Hartford, *see* Hartford Wits; New York City, nineteenth century, **Vol. 4, Part 1,** 276; **Vol. 5, Part 2,** 206; **Vol. 6, Part 1,** 56 f., 491; **Vol. 8, Part 2,** 344
Literature: classical works in translation courses, **Supp. 8,** 236; criticism, **Supp. 4,** 702, 847; **Supp. 5,** 89–90, 168–69, 356, 425, 542; **Supp. 7,** 18, 55–56, 79–81, 103–4, 219–22, 309–10, 638, 754; **Supp. 8,** 124, 353–54, 492, 493, 584–85, 667–68; Great Books courses, **Supp. 5,** 211–12; **Supp. 8,** 59; historical writings on, **Supp. 4,** 819–20; **Supp. 6,** 523–24; Little Masterpieces series, **Supp. 5,** 541–42; McClure's syndicate, **Supp. 4,** 517; Marxist criticism, **Supp. 7,** 268; neohumanism, **Supp. 1,** 36; Nobel Prize, **Supp. 5,** 423, 524; **Supp. 7,** 222, 234, 338; **Supp. 8,** 626; religious, **Supp. 8,** 431; teaching of, **Supp. 5,** 239. *See also* American literature; Black literature; Books; Children's literature; Classical literature; Criticism; English literature and language; Historical fiction; Poetry; Romance novels; Theater; *specific genres and languages*
Lithography, **Vol. 1, Part 1,** 166; **Vol. 1, Part 2,** 168; **Vol. 2, Part 2,** 69, 604; **Vol. 3, Part 1,** 170, 329; **Vol. 5, Part 1,** 107, 460, 520; **Vol. 5, Part 2,** 139; **Vol. 7, Part 1,** 469; **Vol. 7, Part 2,** 421, 439; **Vol. 8, Part 1,** 165 f.; **Vol. 8, Part 2,** 202, 470; **Supp. 7,** 15, 153; architectural, **Vol. 3, Part 1,** 103; chromolithography, **Vol. 8, Part 2,** 169; Civil War sketches, **Vol. 8, Part 2,** 169; colored, **Vol. 8, Part 1,** 165 f.; first in America, **Vol. 7, Part 2,** 92; inventions concerning, **Vol. 8, Part 1,** 165 f.; portraits of distinguished Americans, **Vol. 8, Part 2,** 169; "silver points," **Vol. 4, Part 2** 381
Lithotomy, **Vol. 5, Part 2,** 181; **Vol. 9, Part 1,** 451
Littauer Brothers, **Supp. 3,** 463–64
Little, Clarence Cook, reference to, **Supp. 3,** 121
Little and Browne, founding of, **Supp. 4,** 115
Little Bighorn, battle of, **Vol. 2, Part 2,** 530; **Vol. 3, Part 1,** 8; **Vol. 4, Part 1,** 101, 237; **Vol. 9, Part 2,** 379; **Supp. 5,** 430
Little Blue Books, **Supp. 5,** 264–65
Little, Brown and Co., growth of, **Supp. 4,** 526–27
"Little Cabinet," **Vol. 9, Part 2,** 599
"Little Church Around the Corner" (Church of the Transfiguration, New York City), **Vol. 5, Part 1,** 255
Little Citizens, **Vol. 5, Part 2,** 310
Little Colonel series, **Vol. 5, Part 2,** 138
"Little Giffen," **Vol. 9, Part 2,** 525
Little Galleries of the Photo-Secession ("291"), founding of, **Supp. 4,** 780, 781; **Supp. 5,** 471
Little House books, **Supp. 6,** 696
"Little Longfellow War," **Vol. 8, Part 1,** 19 f.
Little Orchestra Society of New York, **Supp. 8,** 578
"Little Orphan Annie" (comic strip), **Supp. 8,** 221–22
Little Red School House (New York City), **Supp. 3,** 376
Little Rock, Ark.: battle of (1863), **Vol. 2, Part 1,** 391; **Vol. 2, Part 2,** 105, 187; **Vol. 4, Part 1,** 237; **Vol. 5, Part 1,** 176; **Vol. 5, Part 2,** 425; **Vol. 6, Part 2,** 291; **Vol. 9, Part 1,** 556; school desegregation, **Supp. 8,** 57–58, 157

Little Theatre of St. Louis, founding of, **Supp. 1,** 519
Littleton, Jesse T., reference to, **Supp. 6,** 624
"Little Turtle," reference to, **Vol. 1, Part 1,** 34
Little Women, **Vol. 1, Part 1,** 141
Litton Industries, Inc., **Supp. 8,** 367
Liturgiology, **Vol. 5, Part 1,** 229
Liver: alcoholic cirrhosis, **Supp. 3,** 503; extract for anemia, **Supp. 4,** 581–82; **Supp. 5,** 122, 149
Liveright, Horace, reference to, **Supp. 3,** 14; **Supp. 7,** 335, 436
Livestock: bovine tuberculosis, **Supp. 4,** 684; breeding, **Vol. 1, Part 2,** 172; **Vol. 4, Part 2,** 483; **Supp. 2,** 416; cooperatives, **Supp. 1,** 644; disease control, **Supp. 1,** 444; **Supp. 3,** 737–38; feeding research, **Supp. 1,** 395; nutritional studies, **Supp. 5,** 276
Live Stock Journal, founding of, **Vol. 7, Part 1,** 100
Living Age, **Vol. 6, Part 1,** 295
Livingston, M. Stanley, cyclotron research, **Supp. 6,** 370
Livingston, Robert R., references to, **Vol. 5, Part 2,** 367; **Vol. 7, Part 1,** 88 f., 210; **Vol. 9, Part 1,** 614
Livingston College, administration, **Supp. 8,** 94
Livingstone, David, reference to, **Vol. 9, Part 1,** 510
Livingstons and De Lanceys, political quarrels of (N.Y.), **Vol. 6, Part 1,** 317
Livius, Peter, reference to, **Vol. 10, Part 1,** 656 f.
Llewellyn, Karl N., reference to, **Supp. 3,** 186
Lloyd, David, reference to, **Vol. 6, Part 1,** 361
Lloyd, Wray, reference to, **Supp. 5,** 605
Lloyd Library of Botany and Pharmacy (St. Louis), **Supp. 2,** 390
Lobbying: agricultural, **Supp. 8,** 468; American Indian Federation, **Supp. 7,** 393; conservationist, **Supp. 4,** 665–66; corporate, **Supp. 4,** 316; labor, **Supp. 4,** 376, 607; Prohibition, **Supp. 2,** 723; protective tariff, **Supp. 7,** 305; retired persons, **Supp. 8,** 10; trade unions, **Supp. 5,** 254; woman suffrage amendment, **Supp. 5,** 533; women's rights, **Supp. 5,** 532
Lobotomy, prefrontal, **Supp. 6,** 223
"Local option," **Vol. 3, Part 2,** 166; **Vol. 6, Part 2,** 330
Locke, Alain, references to, **Supp. 6,** 313, 314
Lockheed Aircraft Co.: founding of, **Supp. 8,** 385; predecessor, **Supp. 6,** 385
Locks, canal, **Vol. 3, Part 1,** 406; **Vol. 5, Part 2,** 97; **Vol. 6, Part 1,** 327; **Vol. 8, Part 1,** 28, 324; **Vol. 10, Part 1,** 616 f.
Locks, manufacture of, **Vol. 4, Part 1,** 582; **Vol. 5, Part 1,** 95; **Vol. 7, Part 2,** 493; **Vol. 8, Part 2,** 362; **Vol. 9, Part 2,** 613; **Vol. 10, Part 2,** 592
Lockwood, Charles D., reference to, **Supp. 6,** 137
"Locofoco," use of the term in politics, **Vol. 8, Part 1,** 94 f.
Locomotives, railroad: construction, **Vol. 1, Part 1,** 511, 541; **Vol. 1, Part 2,** 457, 529; **Vol. 2, Part 1,** 424; **Vol. 2, Part 2,** 361; **Vol. 3, Part 1,** 65, 458; **Vol. 3, Part 2,** 527, 579; **Vol. 4, Part 2,** 1, 345; **Vol. 5, Part 1,** 84, 148, 342; **Vol. 6, Part 2,** 378, 412; **Vol. 7, Part 1,** 556; **Vol. 7, Part 2,** 263, 361; **Vol. 8, Part 2,** 112; **Vol. 9, Part 1,** 620; **Vol. 9, Part 2,** 484; braking device, invention of, **Vol. 6, Part 2,** 303; "experiment," **Vol. 5, Part 2,** 59; first, **Vol. 2, Part 2,** 410; **Vol. 9, Part 1,** 616; inventions, concerning, **Vol. 5, Part 2,** 59, 97; "Star," **Vol. 7, Part 1,** 556; "Stourbridge Lion," **Vol. 5, Part 2,** 59
Locust Street Social Settlement (Hampton, Va.), **Supp. 4,** 53
Lodge, Henry Cabot: children of, **Supp. 3,** 464; Lawrence, W., relationship, **Supp. 3,** 448; League of Nations, **Supp. 3,** 472–73; references to, **Vol. 10, Part 1,** 494 f.; **Supp. 3,** 396
Loeb, Jacques, references to, **Supp. 3,** 236; **Supp. 4,** 287; **Supp. 6,** 671; **Supp. 7,** 592; **Supp. 8,** 502

5, 419; **Supp. 6,** 350; **Supp. 7,** 315, 367; **Supp. 8,** 492, 550–51; charges against government employees, **Supp. 5,** 479, 564, 676; **Supp. 7,** 751; charges against religious leaders, **Supp. 7,** 597; **Supp. 8,** 426; charges against teachers, **Supp. 7,** 132–33, 542; Civil Service Review Board, **Supp. 6,** 60; Communist China relations, **Supp. 4,** 750–51; Communist trials, **Supp. 5,** 389, 500, 564, 589–90, 714; **Supp. 7,** 52, 256, 389–90, 612; congressional investigations, **Supp. 8,** 648–49; deportation orders, **Supp. 5,** 136; ex-Communist witnesses, **Supp. 7,** 291; government appointments, **Supp. 6,** 143, 484–85; "guilt by association," **Supp. 8,** 426; Hiss case, **Supp. 5,** 19, 665; **Supp. 7,** 114–15; Idaho politics, **Supp. 6,** 681; Internal Security Act (1950), **Supp. 5,** 444–45; journalism on, **Supp. 5,** 19; labor movement, **Supp. 6,** 219, 598; **Supp. 8,** 511; left-wing front organizations, investigations of, **Supp. 8,** 425–42; legal defense, **Supp. 5,** 389; **Supp. 8,** 18; legislation, **Supp. 5,** 444–45; **Supp. 8,** 392; loyalty oaths, **Supp. 5,** 410, 480–81; McCarthyism, **Supp. 6,** 148, 404–6; **Supp. 6,** 432, 606, 645, 680; McCarthyism, writings on, **Supp. 8,** 272; motion picture industry, **Supp. 5,** 238; **Supp. 8,** 648–49, 704; passport issuance, **Supp. 8,** 590–91; "Red raids," **Supp. 3,** 65; **Supp. 4,** 670; Rosenberg case, **Supp. 5,** 588–90, 714; Subversive Activities Control Board, **Supp. 6,** 413; Supreme Court decisions, **Supp. 5,** 358, 714; **Supp. 7,** 96–97; Truman program, **Supp. 5,** 564; Un-American Activities Committee founding, **Supp. 5,** 599; Un-American Activities Committee hearings, **Supp. 5,** 139; **Supp. 6,** 526; **Supp. 7,** 244–45, 766–67; universities and colleges, **Supp. 6,** 640; World War I, **Supp. 7,** 506; **Supp. 8,** 488. *See also* Espionage

Lubitsch, Ernst, reference to, **Supp. 7,** 499

Lubrication, study of, **Vol. 3, Part 1,** 415; **Vol. 6, Part 1,** 617

Luce, Clare Boothe, reference to, **Supp. 8,** 394, 395–96

Luce, Harry Winters, reference to, **Supp. 7,** 727

Luce, Henry R., references to, **Supp. 5,** 734; **Supp. 7,** 114, 269–70, 383

Luciano, Charles ("Lucky"), references to, **Supp. 3,** 181; **Supp. 8,** 208

Luckhardt, Arno B., references to, **Supp. 3,** 458; **Supp. 6,** 100

Lucky Strike cigarettes, **Supp. 4,** 371; **Supp. 5,** 411

Lucy, Autherine, reference to, **Supp. 8,** 73

Lucy Cobb Institute, **Vol. 2, Part 2,** 247

Ludlow massacre (1914), **Vol. 5, Part 2,** 196; **Supp. 2,** 124; **Supp. 6,** 548

"Ludlow's Code," **Vol. 6, Part 1,** 494

Luft, Lorna, reference to, **Supp. 8,** 205

Luger, Paul, reference to, **Supp. 7,** 344

Luhan, Mabel Dodge, reference to, **Supp. 4,** 109; **Supp. 7,** 754

Lujan, Antonio, references to, **Supp. 7,** 486, 487

Luks, George, references to, **Supp. 5,** 624, 635, 636

Lumber, exchange of, for rum and sugar, **Vol. 3, Part 1,** 252

Lumber industry, **Vol. 3, Part 1,** 318 f.; **Vol. 3, Part 2,** 19, 343; **Vol. 4, Part 2,** 75, 94; **Vol. 7, Part 1,** 240; **Vol. 8, Part 2,** 272, 290, 396; **Vol. 9, Part 1,** 583; **Vol. 10, Part 1,** 361; cooperative forestry policies, **Supp. 3,** 7; development of, **Supp. 2,** 158; logging and milling, **Supp. 5,** 68–69; mill pooling, **Supp. 2,** 34; reforestation, **Supp. 2,** 264; sales and marketing, **Supp. 3,** 812–13; standard grading, **Supp. 2,** 264; strike, **Supp. 6,** 320; Texas, **Supp. 6,** 324; writings on, **Supp. 7,** 353. *See also* Trees

Luminescence, research in, **Supp. 2,** 487

Lummis, Charles F., reference to, **Supp. 3,** 88

Lunar studies. *See* Moon

Lunar theory, **Vol. 7, Part 1,** 453

Lunar tide, Great Lakes, **Vol. 4, Part 1,** 476

Lunceford, Jimmie, reference to, **Supp. 3,** 525

Lundin, Fred, reference to, **Supp. 3,** 771–72

Lundy's Lane, battle of, **Vol. 2, Part 1,** 125; **Vol. 5, Part 2,** 62; **Vol. 8, Part 1,** 100, 621; **Vol. 8, Part 2,** 506; **Vol. 10, Part 2,** 537

Lungs: cancer surgery, **Supp. 6,** 246; research on, **Supp. 2,** 458; smoking effects on, **Supp. 6,** 246; **Supp. 7,** 192

Lunt, Alfred, references to, **Supp. 5,** 525; **Supp. 6,** 286; **Supp. 8,** 444

Lusitania, **Vol. 4, Part 1,** 41; **Vol. 5, Part 1,** 324; **Vol. 5, Part 2,** 443; **Vol. 6, Part 1,** 278; **Supp. 5,** 241

Luther, Martin, writings on, **Supp. 3,** 726

Lutheran church, **Vol. 3, Part 1,** 29; **Vol. 3, Part 2,** 261; **Vol. 4, Part 1,** 38, 72; **Vol. 4, Part 2,** 429, 515; **Vol. 5, Part 2,** 503, 514; **Vol. 6, Part 1,** 270; **Vol. 7, Part 2,** 289; **Vol. 8, Part 2,** 441; **Vol. 9, Part 2,** 243 f.; **Vol. 10, Part 1,** 142, 402, 606 f., 653; activities of, **Vol. 4, Part 2** 22 f.; Augustana Synod, **Vol. 6, Part 1,** 270; biographies of clergymen, **Vol. 9, Part 2,** 65; Civil War, and, **Vol. 4, Part 2,** 429; clergy, **Vol. 1, Part 1,** 32, 466 f.; **Vol. 4, Part 1,** 461; **Vol. 4, Part 2,** 370, 538; **Vol. 5, Part 1,** 108, 118, 228, 268, 319, 422 f., 568; **Vol. 5, Part 2,** 373, 512; **Vol. 6, Part 1,** 335, 478 f.; **Vol. 7, Part 1,** 212 f., 306 f., 308 f., 549, 635; **Vol. 7, Part 2,** 289, 574; **Vol. 8, Part 2,** 284, 412 f., 439, 441 f., 449 f., 563; **Vol. 9, Part 1,** 418, 477; **Vol. 9, Part 2,** 40; colleges, **Vol. 8, Part 2,** 285; community, **Vol. 5, Part 2,** 313; dissension within, **Vol. 3, Part 1,** 201; **Vol. 4, Part 1,** 590 f., **Vol. 4, Part 2** 370, 429; English, use of, in, **Vol. 5, Part 2,** 512; funds of, **Vol. 6, Part 1,** 169; Illinois, **Vol. 4, Part 2,** 384; Iowa, **Vol. 3, Part 1,** 201; **Vol. 4, Part 2,** 23; liturgy, **Supp. 1,** 449; Maryland, **Vol. 5, Part 2,** 502, 514; middle colonies, **Vol. 7, Part 1,** 311; missionary work, **Vol. 2, Part 1,** 445; **Vol. 3, Part 1,** 29; **Vol. 4, Part 2** 292, 538, 608; **Vol. 5, Part 2,** 514; **Vol. 7, Part 1,** 78 f.; **Vol. 9, Part 2,** 599 f.; Missouri Synod, **Vol. 10, Part 1,** 402 f.; **Supp. 4,** 540–41; Moravian's and, **Vol. 4, Part 2,** 474; Norwegian branch of, **Vol. 3, Part 1,** 308; **Vol. 5, Part 1,** 269, 319; organization, **Vol. 3, Part 2,** 260; Palestine representative, **Supp. 3,** 272; Pennsylvania, **Vol. 3, Part 1,** 201, 232; **Vol. 4, Part 2,** 538; **Vol. 5, Part 2,** 502; **Vol. 6, Part 2,** 247, 452; **Vol. 7, Part 1,** 306 f.; publications, **Vol. 8, Part 2,** 439, 442; Swedish, **Vol. 3, Part 2,** 182; theology, **Vol. 5, Part 1,** 268–69, 423; **Vol. 7, Part 1,** 635; **Vol. 5, Part 2,** 77; **Vol. 8, Part 2,** 440 f.; writings on, **Vol. 4, Part 1,** 462, 591; **Vol. 4, Part 2,** 474; **Vol. 5, Part 2,** 77, 373; **Vol. 6, Part 1,** 170, 270; **Vol. 8, Part 1,** 551; **Vol. 8, Part 2,** 413, 441, 444, 450; **Vol. 9, Part 2,** 244; **Vol. 10, Part 1,** 606, 653

Lutheran Church Review, **Vol. 5, Part 2,** 503

Lutheran Historical Society, **Vol. 7, Part 1,** 213

"Lutheran Hour" (radio program), **Supp. 4,** 541

Lutheran Intelligencer, **Vol. 8, Part 2,** 414

Lutheran Observer, **Vol. 5, Part 2,** 503, 514

Lutheran Quarterly, **Vol. 10, Part 1,** 142

Lutheran Seminary (Milwaukee, Wis.), **Vol. 5, Part 1,** 108

Lutheran Standard, first issue of, **Vol. 4, Part 1,** 590

Luther College (Iowa), founding of, **Vol. 5, Part 2,** 495; **Vol. 8, Part 1,** 208 f.

"Lux Radio Theater, The" (radio program), **Supp. 6,** 159–60

Luzerne County Agricultural Society, **Vol. 2, Part 2,** 110

Luzon, World War II action, **Supp. 7,** 490

Lyceum movement, **Vol. 5, Part 1,** 130; **Vol. 5, Part 2,** 404; **Vol. 6, Part 1,** 164; **Vol. 8, Part 1,** 60 f.; **Vol. 8, Part 2,** 226; **Vol. 9, Part 2,** 101

Lyceum of Natural History (New York City), establishment of, **Vol. 9, Part 2,** 596

Lyceum Theatre (New York City), **Supp. 3,** 333; founding of, **Supp. 2,** 211

"Lyceum" Village, **Vol. 5, Part 1,** 131

Lycoming Gazette, **Vol. 7, Part 2,** 132

Lye, labeling as poison, **Supp. 6,** 317

Lymphocytes, **Supp. 4,** 616

Lymph system: embryological studies, **Supp. 5,** 600; writings on, **Supp. 4,** 866

Lynch, Edward, reference to, **Supp. 6,** 448

Lynch, Frederick, reference to, **Supp. 6,** 25

Lynch, John L., reference to, **Supp. 3,** 20

Lynchburg, Va., operation at (1864), **Vol. 5, Part 1,** 401; **Vol. 9, Part 1,** 361

Lynching: first law against, **Supp. 8,** 67; writings on, **Supp. 5,** 740

"Lynch law," **Vol. 1, Part 1,** 373; **Vol. 6, Part 1,** 519 f.

Lynd, Helen, references to, **Supp. 3,** 30; **Supp. 4,** 908; **Supp. 5,** 35; **Supp. 8,** 398–99

Lynd, Robert S., references to, **Supp. 3,** 30; **Supp. 4,** 908; **Supp. 5,** 35; **Supp. 8,** 407

Lynd, Staughton, reference to, **Supp. 8,** 398

Lyndon School of Agriculture, **Vol. 10, Part 1,** 139

Lyon, Mary, reference to, **Vol. 7, Part 1,** 16

Lyon, Matthew, references to, **Vol. 4, Part 2** 10; **Vol. 9, Part 2,** 386

Lyons Musical Academy, founding of, **Vol. 9, Part 1,** 103

Lysenko, Trofim D., reference to, **Supp. 8,** 449

Lythgoe, Albert M., reference to, **Supp. 3,** 627

M

M (movie), **Supp. 7,** 478

Macadam, use of in road construction, **Vol. 4, Part 2** 61; **Vol. 8, Part 1,** 74 f.

McAdoo, William Gibbs: presidential bid, **Supp. 3,** 644, 670, 719; **Supp. 5,** 497; references to, **Vol. 9, Part 2,** 144; **Supp. 3,** 114, 772; **Supp. 4,** 537; **Supp. 7,** 512, 537, 796; **Supp. 8,** 592; West relationship, **Supp. 6,** 682–83

Macalaster College, **Vol. 6, Part 1,** 543; **Vol. 7, Part 1,** 408

McAndrew, William, reference to, **Supp. 3,** 772

MacArthur, Charles, references to, **Supp. 5,** 323; **Supp. 7,** 148, 331, 413; **Supp. 8,** 547

MacArthur, Douglas: bonus marchers, **Supp. 6,** 240; Eisenhower relationship, **Supp. 8,** 154; journalism on, **Supp. 8,** 497; Korean War, **Supp. 5,** 676, 706; **Supp. 6,** 432; **Supp. 8,** 421–22; 633; Philippine command, **Supp. 8,** 637–38, 698; references to, **Supp. 7,** 74, 215, 363, 451; Whitney relationship, **Supp. 8,** 698–99; World War II, **Supp. 5,** 720; **Supp. 6,** 170, 268, 340; **Supp. 8,** 23–24, 48, 351

McCall's magazine, **Supp. 8,** 357

McCarran Act (1950), **Supp. 8,** 392, 590, 703; passage of, **Supp. 5,** 544

McCarran-Walter Act (1946), **Supp. 7,** 766

McCarran-Walter Act (1952). *See* Immigration and Nationality Act

McCarthy, Eugene, reference to, **Supp. 8,** 324

McCarthy, Joseph R.: anti-Tydings campaign, **Supp. 7,** 751; Army hearings, **Supp. 6,** 680; **Supp. 8,** 57; censure vote, **Supp. 6,** 681; **Supp. 7,** 31, 74, 213, 383, 419–20; **Supp. 8,** 178, 302, 322, 701; charges

against G. Marshall, **Supp. 6,** 432; condemnation of Carlson, **Supp. 4,** 147; congressional opposition to, **Supp. 5,** 690; **Supp. 8,** 654; Eisenhower relationship, **Supp. 8,** 156; journalism exposés of, **Supp. 8,** 497; Kohlberg relationship, **Supp. 6,** 350; Matthews relationship, **Supp. 8,** 426; media support, **Supp. 8,** 373, 498; Murrow TV program on, **Supp. 7,** 567; opposition to, **Supp. 7,** 468; **Supp. 8,** 272–73, 285, 392; references to, **Supp. 5,** 343, 404, 410, 676; **Supp. 7,** 315, 451, 510, 511; **Supp. 8,** 288, 406, 492, 701; support for, **Supp. 6,** 360, 441; **Supp. 7,** 212–13, 250; **Supp. 8,** 128, 150; survey of public reaction to, **Supp. 6,** 605–6. *See also* Loyalty issues, McCarthyism

McCarthy, Tommy, reference to, **Supp. 5,** 189

Macartney, Clarence E., reference to, **Supp. 6,** 195

Macbeth Gallery Show (1908), **Supp. 5,** 636

McClellan, G. B., references to, **Vol. 6, Part 1,** 123 f., 253 f.; **Vol. 9, Part 1,** 518 f., 613

McClellan, John L., reference to, **Supp. 8,** 208

McClennen, Edward F., reference to, **Supp. 3,** 98

McClintic, Guthrie, references to, **Supp. 6,** 517; **Supp. 7,** 283

McCloy, John J., reference to, **Supp. 7,** 276

McClure, S. S., references to, **Supp. 3,** 762, 816; **Supp. 4,** 662; **Supp. 5,** 698

McClure's Magazine, **Vol. 7, Part 1,** 551; **Supp. 3,** 761, 816; **Supp. 4,** 46–47, 368, 417–18, 841–42; **Supp. 5,** 530, 666, 698; **Supp. 6,** 6; editing of, **Supp. 4,** 662; founding of, **Supp. 4,** 517–18

McCollum, E. V., reference to, **Supp. 4,** 381–82

McComb, Samuel, reference to, **Supp. 3,** 191

McCord Zulu Hospital (South Africa), founding of, **Supp. 4,** 519–20

McCormack, John, reference to, **Supp. 6,** 69

McCormick, Cyrus, reference to, **Vol. 5, Part 1,** 432

McCormick, Joseph Medill, references to, **Supp. 3,** 772; **Supp. 5,** 448, 633

McCormick, Katharine Dexter, reference to, **Supp. 8,** 503

McCormick, Robert R., references to, **Supp. 4,** 644, 645; **Supp. 7,** 296, 473, 603

McCormick, Robert Sanderson, reference to, **Supp. 5,** 449

McCormick Hospital (Thailand), founding of, **Supp. 4,** 529–30

McCormick Theological Seminary, **Vol. 6, Part 1,** 608

McCosh, Isabella Guthrie, reference to, **Vol. 6, Part 1,** 617

McCosh, James, reference to, **Vol. 7, Part 1,** 359

McCoy, John, reference to, **Supp. 3,** 848

McCrory, J. G., reference to, **Supp. 8,** 347

McCullough, Paul, reference to, **Supp. 6,** 112

McCully, Newton, reference to, **Supp. 7,** 749

McCutcheon, John T., reference to, **Supp. 3,** 3

McDaniel, Hattie, reference to, **Supp. 7,** 44

McDonald, David, reference to, **Supp. 7,** 229

MacDonald, Dwight, reference to, **Supp. 7,** 80

MacDonald, Jeanette, reference to, **Supp. 8,** 151

McDonald Observatory, founding of, **Supp. 7,** 726

McDonough, John, reference to, **Vol. 6, Part 1,** 561

McDougall, Alexander, reference to, **Vol. 8, Part 2,** 539

McDougall, William, reference to, **Supp. 3,** 151

McDougall Shipbuilding Co., **Supp. 6,** 36

MacDowell, Edward, reference to, **Vol. 5, Part 1,** 367; **Supp. 4,** 135

McDowell, Ephraim, reference to, **Vol. 5, Part 1,** 549

MacDowell, Frances Knapp, reference to, **Supp. 4,** 125

McDowell, John R., reference to, **Supp. 6,** 500

Vol. 7, Part 2, 194, 450; Vol. 9, Part 1, 475, 621; Vol. 9, Part 2, 89, 454; Vol. 10, Part 1, 422 f., 598 f.; painting for, Vol. 4, Part 2, 591; Pennsylvania, history of, in, Vol. 8, Part 2, 282; revelations of, alleged, Vol. 7, Part 1, 189; ritual writings on, Vol. 10, Part 1, 577 f.; vigilante method, Vol. 5, Part 2, 592; women in, Vol. 2, Part 2, 554; writings on, Vol. 4, Part 1, 584; Vol. 6, Part 2, 98; Vol. 7, Part 1, 189

Masques, Supp. 6, 417–18

Massachusetts: agriculture, Vol. 4, Part 1, 383; Vol. 10, Part 1, 541 f.; banishment from, Vol. 5, Part 1, 436; Vol. 8, Part 2, 221; banking, Vol. 3, Part 1, 106; Vol. 10, Part 2, 482; bishop, first in, Vol. 1, Part 2, 35; blacks, legal rights of, Vol. 2, Part 2, 585; Blue Hill Observatory, Vol. 8, Part 2, 183 f.; "Body of Liberties," Vol. 10, Part 1, 433 f.; boundary disputes, Vol. 1, Part 2, 460; Vol. 5, Part 2, 41, 150, 608; Vol. 7, Part 2, 290 f.; Vol. 8, Part 1, 422, 426; Vol. 10, Part 1, 121; capital punishment, Vol. 8, Part 1, 381; Catholic church, Vol. 10, Part 2, 277; charities, state, first in America, Vol. 5, Part 1, 297; Vol. 8, Part 2, 326; charter, colonial, Vol. 1, Part 2, 579; Vol. 3, Part 1, 86; Vol. 8, Part 1, 356 f.; Vol. 10, Part 2, 408; Civil Service Commission, Supp. 5, 730; Civil War, supplying of troops for, Vol. 1, Part 1, 280; Vol. 10, Part 2, 324; colonial period, Vol. 1, Part 2, 319, 420, 436; Vol. 2, Part 2, 634 f.; Vol. 3, Part 1, 180, 484 f., 501 f.; Vol. 3, Part 2, 155; Vol. 4, Part 1, 611; Vol. 4, Part 2, 396, 420; Vol. 5, Part 1, 200, 333, 362; Vol. 6, Part 1, 97, 198, 262; Vol. 6, Part 2, 386, 391 f., 394, 433; Vol. 7, Part 2, 599; Vol. 8, Part 1, 161 f., 290 f., 292 f., 356 f.; Vol. 8, Part 2, 221, 318 f.; Vol. 9, Part 2, 113, 390; Vol. 10, Part 1, 627 f; Vol. 10, Part 2, 20, 194, 259, 284, 288, 336, 394 f., 409 f.; Supp. 1, 174; Constitution, federal, Vol. 1, Part 2, 501; Constitution, state, framing of, Vol. 1, Part 2, 499; Vol. 7, Part 2, 271; counterfeiting, colonial period, Vol. 3, Part 1, 273; Democratic party, Vol. 4, Part 2, 563; dominion movement in, Vol. 1, Part 1, 301; Vol. 10, Part 2, 31; Dorrellites in, Vol. 3, Part 1, 382 f.; education, Vol. 3, Part 1, 301, 369, 503 f., 563 f.; Vol. 5, Part 1, 29; Vol. 6, Part 1, 72; Vol. 6, Part 2, 241 f., 266; Vol. 7, Part 2, 404; Vol. 8, Part 1, 276 f., 307 f., 381, 646; Vol. 8, Part 2, 151; Vol. 9, Part 1, 33; Vol. 10, Part 1, 551, 645 f.; elections, Vol. 1, Part 2, 556; England, colonial relations with, Vol. 6, Part 2, 391 f.; Vol. 10, Part 2, 412; Episcopal church, Vol. 6, Part 1, 87; "equivalent lands," to Connecticut, Vol. 8, Part 1, 426; Federalist party, Vol. 9, Part 2, 144 f., 380, 395; Free Soil party, Vol. 2, Part 2, 111; Vol. 5, Part 1, 86, 89; fur trade, Vol. 10, Part 2, 240; geology of, Vol. 5, Part 1, 69 f.; government, transition from provincial to commonwealth, Vol. 1, Part 2, 499; governors, Vol. 1, Part 1, 279 f., 577 f.; Vol. 1, Part 2, 221, 500, 579; Vol. 2, Part 1, 357 f.; Vol. 2, Part 2, 110 f., 510 f.; Vol. 3, Part 1, 404 f., 484 f.; Vol. 3, Part 2, 155 f.; Vol. 4, Part 1, 142, 579 f.; Vol. 4, Part 2, 41 f.; Vol. 6, Part 1, 377 f., 562 f.; Vol. 7, Part 1, 259 f.; Vol. 8, Part 1, 534 f.; Vol. 8, Part 2, 250 f.; Vol. 9, Part 2, 145, 215 f.; Vol. 10, Part 1, 499 f.; Vol. 10, Part 2, 408; Supp. 1, 194; Supp. 4, 858–59; Supp. 5, 692; Supp. 6, 140; Supp. 8, 258; health, first state board of, Vol. 1, Part 2, 493; Hopedale Community, Vol. 3, Part 1, 435; Hutchinson, Anne, expulsion of, Vol. 5, Part 1, 436; immigrants, exclusion of, Vol. 10, Part 2, 410; Indians, relations with, Vol. 2, Part 1, 480; Vol. 3, Part 1, 176; Vol. 6, Part 2, 590; Vol. 10, Part 2, 287; Industrial Safety Division, Supp. 3, 577; industry, Vol. 3, Part 1, 435, 563 f.; Vol. 7, Part 2, 58; Vol. 8, Part 1, 344; Vol. 10, Part 1, 497 f., 501 f., 503;

Vol. 10, Part 2, 310, 412; insane, care of, Vol. 3, Part 1, 323 f.; Vol. 8, Part 1, 275 f., 404; "Ipswich Group," Vol. 8, Part 2, 318; jerrymandering in, Vol. 9, Part 2, 145; journalism in, Vol. 3, Part 1, 437 f.; Vol. 8, Part 1, 73 f.; Vol. 8, Part 2, 461; judiciary, Supp. 4, 269; lawyer, first professional in, Vol. 6, Part 1, 87; legal history of, Vol. 1, Part 1, 186; Vol. 7, Part 2, 272; Vol. 8, Part 1, 426, 577; Vol. 10, Part 1, 433 f.; legal service, Vol. 1, Part 2, 166, 174, 297, 549; Vol. 2, Part 2, 609, 634; Vol. 3, Part 1, 63, 132, 134, 251, 261, 276, 280, 483; Vol. 5, Part 1, 86, 89, 295, 535; Vol. 6, Part 1, 263, 464–5, 467; Vol. 6, Part 2, 557, 582; Vol. 7, Part 1, 260, 476; Vol. 7, Part 2, 22, 150, 156, 225, 546, 565, 576; Vol. 8, Part 1, 194, 381, 577; Vol. 8, Part 2, 380; Vol. 9, Part 1, 42, 65, 541; Vol. 9, Part 2, 51, 103, 110, 144 f., 386; Vol. 10, Part 1, 74, 415 f., 433 f., 494 f., 499 f.; Vol. 10, Part 2, 70, 235; libraries, free public, Vol. 3, Part 2, 206; Vol. 10, Part 1, 558 f.; Louisburg expedition, Vol. 1, Part 2, 420; Loyalists, Vol. 6, Part 1, 175 f.; Vol. 8, Part 2, 221; Maine and New Hampshire withdrawal of, from, Vol. 8, Part 1, 356 f.; Masons in, Vol. 4, Part 2, 321; militia, Vol. 4, Part 1, 611; Vol. 6, Part 1, 73; navy, Vol. 10, Part 1, 101; normal schools, Vol. 3, Part 1, 563 f.; Vol. 6, Part 2, 242; orchards, first in, Vol. 1, Part 2, 319; periodicals, Vol. 10, Part 2, 239; political history, Vol. 2, Part 1, 357, 396; Vol. 4, Part 2, 563; Vol. 6, Part 1, 108 f.; Vol. 10, Part 2, 416; political irregularities, Supp. 8, 219; political service, Vol. 1, Part 1, 254, 280, 578; Vol. 1, Part 2, 144, 160, 166, 205, 246, 297, 420, 498, 502, 549, 551, 556; Vol. 2, Part 2, 111, 310, 510, 577, 579, 623, 633; Vol. 3, Part 1, 4, 14, 52, 63, 66, 132, 134, 149, 176, 261, 276, 280, 405, 435, 481, 547, 563, 573, 613; Vol. 4, Part 1, 87, 142, 182, 579; Vol. 4, Part 2, 41, 219, 459; Vol. 5, Part 1, 439; Vol. 6, Part 1, 196, 264, 305, 347, 348, 377, 562; Vol. 7, Part 1, 259; Vol. 7, Part 2, 14, 98, 159, 254, 477, 531, 543, 548, 551, 567, 582; Vol. 8, Part 1, 161, 195, 308, 344, 281, 430, 534, 579, 621; Vol. 8, Part 2, 59, 251; Vol. 9, Part 1, 120, 143, 165; Vol. 9, Part 2, 104, 113, 144 f.; Vol. 10, Part 1, 40, 48, 53, 122, 130, 415 f., 478 f., 482 f., 497 f., 585 f., 607; Vol. 10, Part 2, 323, 416; politics, Supp. 3, 740; Supp. 4, 277–78; Supp. 6, 551–52, 636; Supp. 7, 419; Supp. 8, 257, 420–21; politics and Catholic church, Supp. 3, 569–70; Protestant Episcopal bishoprics, Supp. 3, 447–48; public service, Vol. 1, Part 2, 33, 551, 607; Vol. 2, Part 2, 380 f., 461 f., 473, 531, 624 f.; Vol. 3, Part 1, 58 f., 524; Vol. 4, Part 2, 3, 41 f., 97, 109, 307; Vol. 5, Part 1, 86, 185, 203, 336; Vol. 6, Part 1, 48, 228, 259, 263 f., 297, 417–18, 508; Vol. 7, Part 1, 7, 59; Vol. 7, Part 2, 477; Vol. 8, Part 1, 276, 290 f., 292 f., 307 f.; Vol. 8, Part 2, 239, 245, 277, 461, 556; Vol. 10, Part 1, 627 f.; Public Service Commission, Supp. 3, 240–41; punishment system of, Vol. 1, Part 2, 174; railroads, Vol. 5, Part 1, 561; reform movements in, Vol. 7, Part 2, 546 f.; Vol. 8, Part 1, 381 f.; Vol. 8, Part 2, 58; regicides in, Vol. 8, Part 2, 319; religious controversies, Vol. 3, Part 1, 584; Vol. 6, Part 1, 87; Vol. 7, Part 2, 541, 598; Vol. 10, Part 2, 62, 427, 481; representative government, beginnings of, Vol. 7, Part 2, 541; Republican party, Vol. 1, Part 2, 489; Vol. 2, Part 1, 289, 358 f., 542; Revolutionary War agitation, in, Vol. 4, Part 2, 420; Vol. 6, Part 2, 218; Vol. 7, Part 2, 565; Vol. 9, Part 2, 499; Vol. 10, Part 2, 540, 635; Sacco-Vanzetti trial, Vol. 8, Part 2, 279; seal, state, designing of, Vol. 8, Part 1, 515; shipbuilding, Vol. 10, Part 1, 548 f.; silversmith, Vol. 8, Part 2, 338; slavery, agitation against, Vol. 3, Part 1, 268; Vol. 5, Part 1, 86 f., 89; **Vol. 6, Part 1,** 263; **Vol. 8, Part 1,** 499 f.; **Vol. 8, Part 2,** 326; Sons of Liberty, **Vol. 4, Part 2,** 420; state employee unionization, **Supp. 6,** 586; State House, mural paintings in, **Vol. 8, Part 1,** 479; trade unions, **Vol. 2, Part 2,** 473; taxes, colonial resistance to, **Vol. 10, Part 2,** 427; temperance movement, **Vol. 1, Part 1,** 255; **Vol. 8, Part 1,** 381; Unitarianism, **Vol. 8, Part 1,** 622, 645; Whig party, **Vol. 2, Part 2,** 87; War of 1812, refusal of, to furnish troops, **Vol. 9, Part 2,** 145; water supply, **Vol. 9, Part 1,** 460 f.; **Vol. 8, Part 1,** 553

Massachusetts, battleship, **Vol. 4, Part 1,** 485

Massachusetts Abolitionist, **Vol. 9, Part 2,** 595

Massachusetts Agricultural College, **Vol. 2, Part 2,** 147; **Vol. 3, Part 2,** 473; **Vol. 4, Part 1,** 383; **Vol. 9, Part 2,** 39, 396

Massachusetts Anti-Slavery Society, **Vol. 2, Part 2,** 308; **Vol. 3, Part 1,** 407

Massachusetts Bay Colony "Remonstrance and Humble Petition," **Supp. 1,** 174

Massachusetts Bay Co., **Vol. 8, Part 1,** 292 f.

Massachusetts Bureau of Statistics and Labor, **Vol. 7, Part 2,** 19; **Vol. 10, Part 2,** 546

Massachusetts Civic League, **Vol. 8, Part 1,** 275 f.; founding of, **Supp. 2,** 374

Massachusetts Co., **Vol. 3, Part 1,** 612

Massachusetts Department of Mental Health, **Supp. 3,** 102

Massachusetts Fish and Game Protective Association, **Vol. 8, Part 2,** 323

Massachusetts General Hospital, **Vol. 5, Part 1,** 546; **Vol. 6, Part 1,** 465; **Vol. 8, Part 1,** 282 f.; genitourinary surgery, **Supp. 3,** 121; research, **Supp. 3,** 243–44; social service department, **Supp. 4,** 101; **Supp. 6,** 97–98

Massachusetts Highway Commission, **Vol. 8, Part 1,** 74 f.

Massachusetts Historical Society, **Vol. 1, Part 2,** 147; **Vol. 3, Part 1,** 133, 419 f.; **Vol. 4, Part 1,** 10, 556; **Vol. 5, Part 2,** 54; **Vol. 7, Part 1,** 31; **Vol. 8, Part 1,** 196 f.; **Supp. 3,** 286; **Supp. 6,** 125

Massachusetts Homeopathic Medical Society, **Vol. 9, Part 2,** 278

Massachusetts Horticultural Society, **Vol. 3, Part 1,** 177; **Vol. 5, Part 2,** 341; **Vol. 7, Part 2,** 248

Massachusetts Humane Society, **Vol. 10, Part 1,** 479 f.

Massachusetts Institute of Technology (MIT), **Vol. 4, Part 2,** 523; **Vol. 6, Part 2,** 120; **Vol. 7, Part 1,** 493; **Vol. 7, Part 2,** 562; **Vol. 8, Part 1,** 74 f.; **Vol. 9, Part 2,** 128; aeronautical engineering studies, **Supp. 6,** 665; atom-smasher invention, **Supp. 8,** 665–66; Brandeis business law lectures, **Supp. 3,** 94; chemistry studies, **Supp. 8,** 103; electrical engineering studies, **Supp. 3,** 745–47; **Supp. 5,** 354–55; engineering studies, **Supp. 1,** 680; first woman admitted to, **Supp. 3,** 631; founding of, **Vol. 3, Part 2,** 473; **Vol. 8, Part 2,** 115, 225; **Vol. 9, Part 1,** 99; **Vol. 9, Part 2,** 567; **Vol. 10, Part 1,** 551; gifts to, **Supp. 8,** 600; group dynamics studies, **Supp. 4,** 485; Harvard engineering school merger, **Supp. 3,** 471; mathematics studies, **Supp. 7,** 784–85; mechanical engineering studies, **Supp. 3,** 220; mining engineering studies, **Supp. 3,** 631; physical chemistry studies, **Supp. 2,** 494; presidency, **Supp. 5,** 126; radiation laboratory, **Supp. 4,** 358–59; **Supp. 7,** 275; sanitary biology, **Supp. 3,** 324; sewage experimental station, **Supp. 6,** 701

Massachusetts Law Quarterly, **Vol. 9, Part 1,** 65

Massachusetts Medical Society, **Vol. 1, Part 1,** 332; **Vol. 8, Part 1,** 194 f.; **Vol. 10, Part 1,** 50

Massachusetts Mental Hygiene Association, **Vol. 8, Part 1,** 275 f.

Massachusetts Naval Brigade, **Vol. 8, Part 1,** 276

Massachusetts Peace Society, **Vol. 8, Part 1,** 381

Massachusetts School of Art, **Vol. 7, Part 2,** 465

Massachusetts Society for the Prevention of Cruelty to Animals, **Vol. 1, Part 1,** 303

Massachusetts Society for the University Education of Women, **Vol. 9, Part 2,** 276

Massachusetts State Board of Education, **Vol. 8, Part 1,** 381

Massachusetts State College, presidency, **Supp. 4,** 44

Massachusetts State Society for Mental Hygiene, **Supp. 3,** 119

Massachusetts Teachers' Association, **Vol. 10, Part 1,** 645 f.

Massachusetts Tariff Reform League, **Vol. 7, Part 2,** 582

Massacres, **Vol. 1, Part 1,** 145; **Vol. 1, Part 2,** 217; **Vol. 4, Part 2,** 362; **Vol. 5, Part 1,** 437; **Vol. 5, Part 2,** 47, 100, 371; **Vol. 7, Part 1,** 401; Boston, **Vol. 1, Part 1,** 415; Deerfield, **Vol. 10, Part 2,** 270; Fetterman, **Vol. 8, Part 1,** 437; Fort Dearborn, **Vol. 5, Part 2,** 422; Fort Mimms, **Vol. 10, Part 1,** 135; Fort Pillow, **Vol. 3, Part 2,** 532; **Vol. 9, Part 1,** 237; **Vol. 9, Part 2,** 183; Haverhill, Mass., **Vol. 3, Part 1,** 554 f.; Meeker, **Vol. 7, Part 2,** 638; Mountain Meadows, **Vol. 6, Part 1,** 115; St. Francis, 1757; **Vol. 8, Part 2,** 108; Whitman, **Vol. 1, Part 1,** 30; **Vol. 10, Part 2,** 142; Wyoming, Pa., **Vol. 2, Part 1,** 372; Yellow Creek, **Vol. 2, Part 2,** 538

Massee, May, reference to, **Supp. 7,** 307

Masseria, Joe (The Boss), references to, **Supp. 7,** 632, 784; **Supp. 8,** 208

Masses, The, **Supp. 3,** 852; **Supp. 5,** 635; **Supp. 7,** 268; editorial policy, **Supp. 8,** 149; editors' trial, **Supp. 8,** 124–25

Masses Publishing Co. v. *Patten,* **Supp. 7,** 317

Mass production, moving, **Supp. 4,** 303–4

Mass transit. *See* Transit systems

Master Building (New York City), architecture of, **Supp. 5,** 133

Mastoid operation, first in Chicago, **Vol. 5, Part 1,** 248

Matabele rebellions (southern Africa), **Supp. 4,** 126–27

Matamoras, Mex., occupation of (1846), **Vol. 9, Part 2,** 350

Matches: manufacture of, **Vol. 1, Part 1,** 590; **Vol. 7, Part 1,** 143; **Vol. 9, Part 1,** 600; safety, **Supp. 4,** 257–58

Maternal health. *See* Motherhood; Obstetrics

Mathematical bibliography, **Vol. 9, Part 2,** 109; instruments, manufacture of, **Vol. 5, Part 1,** 130 f.; physics, **Vol. 7, Part 2,** 397; prodigies, **Vol. 2, Part 2,** 283; **Vol. 7, Part 1,** 514; **Vol. 8, Part 2,** 287; tables, **Vol. 8, Part 2,** 225

Mathematics (for complete list of mathematicians, *see* Occupations Index): application to economics, **Supp. 6,** 459, 656; application to sociology, **Supp. 6,** 482–83; Bateman functions and expansions, **Supp. 4,** 58; calculus of variations, **Supp. 3,** 86–87; **Supp. 5,** 67–68; colonial period, **Vol. 4, Part 1,** 591, 609; **Vol. 6, Part 1,** 136; demographic, **Supp. 4,** 505–6; elasticity, **Supp. 4,** 873–74; ergodic theorem, **Supp. 3,** 70–71; finite fields, **Supp. 5,** 175; functional analysis theory, **Supp. 3,** 761; functions theory, **Supp. 3,** 574–75; general analysis, **Supp. 1,** 562; geometry, **Supp. 2,** 473; **Supp. 6,** 653; geometry, new differential, **Supp. 7,** 216; geometry of numbers, **Supp. 3,** 79; groups theory, **Supp. 3,** 79; **Supp. 5,** 491; harmonic analysis, **Supp. 7,** 784; harmonic curves, **Vol. 8, Part 1,** 602; historical writings on, **Supp. 1,** 149; **Supp. 5,** 491; journals, **Supp. 1,** 562, 675; logical foundations of, **Supp. 5,** 338; logic of,

Vol. 3, Part 2, 386; musical composition, application to, Supp. 3, 690; number theory, Supp. 5, 175; Supp. 6, 49; Supp. 8, 514–15; partition function, Supp. 8, 514; physics application, Supp. 5, 528–29; probability and error in, Vol. 3, Part 1, 197; relativity theory framework, Supp. 5, 738; Riemann mapping theorem, Supp. 3, 575; spectral theory of unbounded self-adjoint operators in Hilbert space, Supp. 6, 655; teaching of, Supp. 1, 146; Supp. 3, 721–22, 760, 791; Supp. 5, 130–31, 338; textbooks, Supp. 1, 145–46; Weyl sum, Supp. 5, 738; writings on, Supp. 2, 27; Supp. 3, 722; Supp. 4, 421, 879–80. *See also* Statistics

Mather, Cotton, references to, Vol. 2, Part 1, 410; Vol. 6, Part 1, 198; Vol. 9, Part 2, 389; Vol. 10, Part 1, 122; Vol. 10, Part 2, 238

Mather, Increase, references to, Vol. 7, Part 2, 551 f.; Vol. 10, Part 2, 238, 427

Mather, Richard, reference to, Vol. 10, Part 1, 627 f.

Matheus, John Frederick, reference to, Supp. 6, 690

Mathews, Shailer, reference to, Supp. 3, 322; Supp. 4, 152

Mathewson, Christy, reference to, Supp. 1, 530

Matisse, Henri, references to, Supp. 4, 174, 175, 771, 780; Supp. 6, 552, 553; Supp. 7, 25

Matsu. *See* Quemoy and Matsu

Matthew, William Diller, reference to, Supp. 3, 316–17

Matthews, Francis, reference to, Supp. 8, 329

Mattresses, manufacture of, Vol. 6, Part 1, 334

Mature Mind, The, Supp. 8, 489

Mauerer, Alfred, reference to, Supp. 5, 471

Maulbetsch, Johnny, reference to, Supp. 7, 595

Mauna Loa, Supp. 5, 361

Maurer, James H., reference to, Supp. 3, 255

Maury, Antonia C., reference to, Supp. 3, 130

"Maverick," term coined, Supp. 5, 480

Maxim, Hiram, reference to, Vol. 7, Part 1, 298

Maxim gun, invention of, Vol. 6, Part 2, 437

Maximilian, effort to expel from Mexico, Vol. 2, Part 1, 461; Vol. 8, Part 2, 85

Max Planck Institute, naming of, Supp. 8, 122

Maxwell, James Clark, reference to, Supp. 4, 58

Maxwell Land Grant, Vol. 3, Part 1, 606

Maxwell Street Settlement (Chicago), Supp. 3, 488

May, Rollo, reference to, Supp. 7, 747

Mayan civilization: archaeological studies, Supp. 1, 685; Supp. 4, 606–7; Supp. 7, 432; hieroglyphic writings, Vol. 1, Part 2, 492; writings on, Vol. 9, Part 2, 426

Maybank, Burnett, reference to, Supp. 8, 682

May Department Stores Co., Supp. 8, 427–28

Mayer, Louis B., references to, Supp. 6, 657, 658; Supp. 8, 576–77, 646, 649, 659, 660

Mayfield, Earle B., reference to, Supp. 7, 137

Mayflower, Vol. 2, Part 1, 30; Vol. 7, Part 1, 525; Vol. 10, Part 2, 20; account of, Vol. 7, Part 1, 254; organizer of, Vol. 3, Part 1, 5

Maynard, Leonard A., reference to, Supp. 4, 37

Mayo, Frank, reference to, Supp. 6, 334

Mayo, George Elton, references to, Supp. 3, 351; Supp. 8, 684

Mayo, Henry T., reference to, Supp. 6, 338

Mayo, William James, reference to, Vol. 7, Part 1, 354; Supp. 3, 121

Mayo Clinic, Supp. 3, 121; Supp. 6, 130, 131, 697; founding of, Supp. 2, 438–440; laboratory research, Supp. 3, 832

Mayo Foundation for Medical Education and Research, founding of, Supp. 2, 440

Mayo Graduate School of Medicine, predecessor, Supp. 3, 832

Mayors. For complete list, *see* Occupations Index

Mayors, U.S. Conference of. *See* Conference of Mayors

Maytag Co., founding of, Supp. 2, 441

Mead, Elwood, reference to, Supp. 3, 846

Mead, George Herbert, references to, Supp. 3, 779; Supp. 6, 671; Supp. 8, 639

Mead, James M., reference to, Supp. 6, 437

Mead, Margaret, references to, Supp. 4, 71, 72; Supp. 8, 189

Mead, McKim and White, Supp. 5, 388

Meade, George G., references to, Vol. 6, Part 1, 126; Vol. 9, Part 1, 150 f.; Vol. 9, Part 2, 253, 255

Meadville Theological School, Vol. 6, Part 1, 303; Vol. 9, Part 1, 547, 551; founding of, Vol. 5, Part 1, 358 f.

Meaning and Truth of Religion, The, Supp. 4, 513

Meaning of Adult Education, The, Supp. 5, 431

Means, J. Howard, reference to, Supp. 3, 244

Means, Rice W., reference to, Supp. 6, 507

Meany, George, references to, Supp. 8, 528, 653

Measurements: electrical, Vol. 8, Part 2, 154; physical devices for, Vol. 8, Part 2, 199

Meat chopper, invention of, Vol. 9, Part 1, 535

Meat-packing industry, Vol. 1, Part 1, 111, 347 f.; Vol. 2, Part 2, 584 f.; Vol. 3, Part 1, 356, 603; Vol. 5, Part 1, 326, 437; Vol. 7, Part 1, 217 f.; Vol. 9, Part 2, 16, 245 f.; Vol. 10, Part 2, 343; canning and processing, Supp. 4, 395–96; Supp. 5, 314–15; Chicago investigation, Supp. 5, 70; financial reorganization, Supp. 5, 550–51; inspection of, Vol. 8, Part 2, 236; Supp. 1, 258; management, Supp. 2, 644–45; Supp. 8, 109–11; manufacturing, Supp. 7, 519–20; muckraking on, Supp. 3, 675; novel about, Supp. 8, 594; price-fixing charges, Supp. 8, 110, 111; refrigerator cars, Vol. 9, Part 2, 245; scandals, Vol. 1, Part 1, 348; unionization, Supp. 2, 408; Supp. 4, 279–80; Supp. 7, 254, 255; Supp. 8, 589

Meat products, hot dog, Supp. 7, 719

Mechanical engineering. *See* Engineering, mechanical

Mechanical Engineers' Pocket-Book, Vol. 5, Part 2, 349

Mechanical inventions, encyclopedia of, Vol. 5, Part 2, 464 f.

Mechanical laboratory, first in country, Vol. 9, Part 2, 518

Mechanical power, development of, Supp. 1, 670

Mechanics' Institute Library, Vol. 8, Part 1, 65 f.

Mechanics' Line, shipping, Vol. 5, Part 2, 372

Mechanicsville, Va., battle of, Vol. 6, Part 1, 123, 583. *See also* Seven-Days' Battles

Mechanism of Mendelian Heredity, The, Supp. 3, 540

Mecklenberg Resolution (1775), Vol. 2, Part 1, 571; Vol. 6, Part 2, 343; Vol. 8, Part 1, 42

Medallions, Vol. 1, Part 1, 503; Vol. 2, Part 1, 427; Vol. 4, Part 1, 336

Medford, Mass., early history of, Vol. 2, Part 1, 75; Vol. 8, Part 2, 331

"Medford Crackers," Vol. 3, Part 2, 577

Mediaeval Academy of America, founding of, Supp. 2, 291; Supp. 3, 618

Mediaeval Mind, The, Supp. 3, 765–66

Mediaeval Sinhalese Art, Supp. 4, 177

Medical and Chirurgical Faculty of Maryland, Vol. 1, Part 1, 340

Medical and Surgical History of the War of the Rebellion, Vol. 1, Part 1, 631

Medical Bibliography, Vol. 6, Part 2, 561

Medical College of Maryland, Vol. 8, Part 1, 131 f.; Vol. 9, Part 1, 42

Medical College of South Carolina, Vol. 3, Part 1, 305

Medical Institute of Philadelphia, Vol. 2, Part 2, 20

Medical Library and Journal Society, Vol. 7, Part 2, 505

Medico-Chirurgical College, Philadelphia, founding of, **Vol. 7, Part 2,** 16

Medico-Legal Journal, **Vol. 1, Part 2,** 154

Medico-Legal Society of New York, **Vol. 1, Part 2,** 154; **Vol. 8, Part 2,** 111

MEDICO (Medical International Corporation Organization), founding of, **Supp. 7,** 191

Medieval Academy of America, founding of, **Supp. 3,** 197

Medieval history. *See* Middle Ages

Medill, Joseph, references to, **Supp. 5,** 448, 449

Medina, Harold, references to, **Supp. 7,** 180, 390

Mediterranean anemia. *See* Cooley's anemia

Mediums, controversy concerning, **Vol. 3, Part 1,** 84; **Vol. 3, Part 2,** 570

Meek, Joseph L., reference to, **Vol. 7, Part 1,** 458

Meeker massacre, **Vol. 7, Part 2,** 638

Meeropol, Michael and Robert, reference to, **Supp. 5,** 589–90

Mees, Charles E., reference to, **Supp. 4,** 743, 744

Megiddo, excavation of, **Supp. 3,** 272

Meiklejohn, Alexander, reference to, **Supp. 6,** 271

Meilland, Francis, reference to, **Supp. 5,** 555

Mellon, Andrew, references to, **Supp. 5,** 357, 561; **Supp. 7,** 361

Mellon, Richard K., reference to, **Supp. 8,** 361

Mellon Institute of Industrial Research, founding of, **Supp. 2,** 447

Melodeons, making of, **Vol. 4, Part 2,** 196

Meltzer, Samuel J., references to, **Supp. 4,** 34, 287

Melville, Herman, reference to, **Vol. 1, Part 1,** 108; scholarship on, **Supp. 5,** 587

Memoirs, **Vol. 2, Part 1,** 227; **Vol. 3, Part 2,** 126, 212, 475; **Vol. 4, Part 2,** 31, 481; **Vol. 5, Part 1,** 117, 292, 467, 596, 611; **Vol. 5, Part 2,** 309; **Vol. 6, Part 1,** 359, 374, 378, 594; **Vol. 7, Part 1,** 273, 300, 372, 563, 634; **Vol. 8, Part 1,** 16, 73, 141 f., 208, 264, 284 f., 369 f.; **Vol. 8, Part 2,** 26 f., 241, 372, 411, 580 f., 596 f., 598; **Vol. 9, Part 1,** 81, 88, 97, 102, 162, 248, 304, 313, 367; **Vol. 10, Part 1,** 75, 168, 449 f., 504 f., 558 f. (*See also* Diaries; Journals

Memoirs of a Superfluous Man, **Supp. 3,** 555

Memorial Day, establishment of, **Vol. 6, Part 1,** 364

Memorial Hospital (New York City), cancer research and treatment, **Supp. 3,** 258

Memorial Movement, **Vol. 7, Part 1,** 314

Memphis, Tenn.: Crump machine, **Supp. 5,** 144–45; De Soto's discovery of Mississippi near, **Vol. 3, Part 1,** 257; founding of, **Vol. 7, Part 2,** 115; medical care, **Vol. 7, Part 2,** 626; sanitation, **Vol. 10, Part 1,** 456 f.

Memphis Institute, **Vol. 8, Part 1,** 152 f.

Menace, anti-Catholic magazine, **Vol. 3, Part 2,** 478

Men and Religion Forward Movement: administration, **Supp. 2,** 20; **Supp. 5,** 579; founding of, **Supp. 2,** 617–18

Men and Steel, **Supp. 8,** 675

Mencken, H. L.: Dreiser relationship, **Supp. 3,** 232, 235, 236; references to, **Vol. 9, Part 1,** 91; **Supp. 3,** 107, 413; **Supp. 5,** 4; **Supp. 6,** 471, 571, 616; **Supp. 7,** 3, 19–20, 331; **Supp. 8,** 341–42, 364

Mendel, Lafayette B., reference to, **Supp. 3,** 163

Mendel's laws of heredity, **Supp. 3,** 215, 539–40; **Supp. 4,** 252, 516

Mendelssohn, Louis, reference to, **Supp. 7,** 245

Mendelssohn Club, **Vol. 4, Part 1,** 274; **Vol. 5, Part 2,** 486

Mengelberg, Willem, reference to, **Supp. 7,** 549

Ménière's disease, **Supp. 4,** 214

Meningitis, **Vol. 7, Part 1,** 559; serum for, **Supp. 4,** 287

Menninger, Charles Frederick, reference to, **Supp. 8,** 428

Menninger, Karl, references to, **Supp. 5,** 484; **Supp. 8,** 429

Menninger, William C., reference to, **Supp. 5,** 484

Menninger Clinic, **Supp. 6,** 527; **Supp. 8,** 429–30; founding of, **Supp. 5,** 484

Menninger School of Psychiatry, **Supp. 8,** 429

Mennonite church, **Vol. 1, Part 2,** 405; **Vol. 4, Part 1,** 353; **Vol. 5, Part 2,** 491, 503; bishop of, first in America, **Vol. 8, Part 1,** 632, Charite, organized 1908, **Vol. 5, Part 2,** 504; Kansas settlement, **Vol. 5, Part 2,** 504

Menotti, Gian-Carlo, references to, **Supp. 7,** 61, 124

Menorah, founding of, **Vol. 7, Part 2,** 407

Men's League for Women Suffrage, **Vol. 1, Part 1,** 413

Mental: computations, prodigy, **Vol. 8, Part 2,** 287; cure, books on, **Vol. 3, Part 2,** 213; defectives, care of, **Vol. 6, Part 1,** 468; diseases, treatment of, **Vol. 1, Part 1,** 446; **Vol. 8, Part 1,** 404; **Vol. 10, Part 2,** 511; dissociation, **Vol. 8, Part 1,** 230 f.; healing, **Vol. 4, Part 1,** 631; **Vol. 8, Part 1,** 304 f.; hygiene, **Vol. 4, Part 2,** 412; **Vol. 8, Part 1,** 275 f., 404; **Vol. 8, Part 2,** 313

Mental health and illness: child development movement, **Supp. 2,** 119; clinics, **Supp. 2,** 388, 711–12; **Supp. 5,** 301, 484; community facilities, **Supp. 3,** 50–51, 128; **Supp. 6,** 17; counseling services, **Supp. 7,** 466; disease relationship, **Supp. 2,** 24; emotional adjustment, **Supp. 3,** 128; first children's clinic, **Supp. 1,** 485; heredity studies, **Supp. 4,** 618; hospitals, **Supp. 1,** 243–44; **Supp. 3,** 50–51, 320; insulin shock treatment, **Supp. 6,** 563–64; interpersonal relations, **Supp. 4,** 806–8; law and, **Supp. 3,** 102; **Supp. 6,** 403; legislation regarding, **Supp. 2,** 712; neurotic character structure origin, **Supp. 5,** 316–17; occupational therapy, **Supp. 1,** 131; personal development writings, **Supp. 8,** 488; physiologic basis, **Supp. 3,** 172; **Supp. 6,** 403–4; popular writings on, **Supp. 8,** 189; psychobiological concept of, **Supp. 4,** 570–72; psychotherapy, **Supp. 2,** 736; **Supp. 4,** 571; **Supp. 8,** 430; religion and, **Supp. 7,** 64–65; research in, **Supp. 2,** 665; self-help movement, **Supp. 5,** 434; state treatment of, **Supp. 3,** 102. *See also* Psychiatry; Psychoanalysis; *specific disorders*

Mental hygiene movement. *See* Mental health and illness

Mentally retarded: care of, **Vol. 6, Part 1,** 468; education of, **Vol. 2, Part 1,** 117; **Vol. 10, Part 2,** 199; **Supp. 4,** 438–39; **Supp. 7,** 284; genetic relationship, **Supp. 4,** 618; institutions for, **Supp. 2,** 388; **Supp. 3,** 388–89; research on, **Supp. 6,** 240–41

Mentor, first magazine for blind, **Vol. 9, Part 1,** 294

Mercantile Agency, **Vol. 3, Part 1,** 503; **Vol. 9, Part 2,** 303

Mercantile Library, founding of, **Vol. 10, Part 2,** 471

Mercer, Lucy, references to, **Supp. 3,** 643; **Supp. 7,** 659, 661

Mercersburg Academy, **Vol. 5, Part 1,** 501

Mercersburg College, **Vol. 1, Part 1,** 324

Mercersburg Seminary, **Vol. 8, Part 2,** 417–18

"Mercersburg theology," **Vol. 1, Part 1,** 324; **Vol. 8, Part 1,** 389

Mercer University, founding of, **Vol. 8, Part 2,** 330; **Vol. 9, Part 1,** 99; presidency of, **Vol. 10, Part 1,** 31; removal of, **Vol. 10, Part 1,** 31 f.

Merchandising, **Vol. 1, Part 1,** 332, 336, 341, 396, 464, 602; **Vol. 2, Part 1,** 102; **Vol. 2, Part 2,** 295 f., 491; **Vol. 4, Part 1,** 320; **Vol. 4, Part 2,** 218, 220; **Vol. 6, Part 1,** 132; **Vol. 7, Part 1,** 359 f.; **Vol. 7, Part 2,** 525, 630; **Vol. 8, Part 2,** 536; **Vol. 9, Part 1,**

Vol. 5, Part 1, 152; **Vol. 5, Part 2**, 50, 256; **Vol. 6, Part 1**, 129, 315, 524; **Vol. 6, Part 2**, 82, 576; **Vol. 7, Part 1**, 120 f., 426; **Vol. 7, Part 2**, 185, 260, 314, 487; **Vol. 8, Part 1**, 85 f., 183 f., 293 f., 298 f., 319 f., 529 f., 596; **Vol. 8, Part 2**, 72, 196, 244, 341, 343, 426 f., 579; **Vol. 9, Part 1**, 136, 215, 320; **Vol. 9, Part 2**, 48 f., 620; **Vol. 10, Part 1**, 34, 128, 425; naval vessels listed, **Vol. 6, Part 1**, 129, 315; territorial acquisitions, **Vol. 8, Part 1**, 34 f.; Texas, **Vol. 2, Part 1**, 491

Mexico: American frontier in 1844, **Vol. 8, Part 2**, 306; animal surveys, **Supp. 1**, 572; anthropological studies, **Supp. 8**, 378; archaeological excavations, pre-Columbian, **Supp. 3**, 786; botanical explorations, **Vol. 5, Part 2**, 425; **Vol. 8, Part 1**, 236 f.; **Vol. 8, Part 2**, 160; botanical studies, **Supp. 3**, 153; boundary survey of, **Vol. 1, Part 2**, 7; **Vol. 9, Part 2**, 260; California, acquisition from, by U.S., **Vol. 3, Part 2**, 263; **Vol. 5, Part 2**, 617; **Vol. 6, Part 2**, 373; **Vol. 8, Part 1**, 34 f.; diplomatic relations with, **Vol. 1, Part 2**, 225, 377; **Vol. 3, Part 2**, 108; **Vol. 4, Part 1**, 84, 538; **Vol. 6, Part 1**, 193, 269; **Vol. 7, Part 1**, 234 f.; **Vol. 8, Part 1**, 379; **Vol. 8, Part 2**, 85; **Vol. 9, Part 1**, 20, 210; **Vol. 9, Part 2**, 474; **Vol. 10, Part 2**, 643; **Supp. 1**, 589; **Supp. 3**, 156; **Supp. 4**, 217; **Supp. 5**, 332; **Supp. 6**, 207, 451, 452; folk art, **Supp. 8**, 126; French, retirement of, **Vol. 5, Part 2**, 88; maps, **Vol. 5, Part 1**, 348; Maximilian in, **Vol. 2, Part 1**, 461; **Vol. 8, Part 2**, 85; Maya civilization studies, **Supp. 4**, 605–6; medical work in, **Vol. 5, Part 1**, 429; Methodist church, **Vol. 2, Part 1**, 363; mineralogy, **Supp. 6**, 212, 213; mining promotion, **Supp. 3**, 259; minister to, first, **Vol. 8, Part 1**, 30 f.; missions in, **Vol. 2, Part 1**, 363, 369; **Vol. 6, Part 1**, 95; **Vol. 10, Part 1**, 54; national hymn, writing, **Vol. 7, Part 1**, 595; ornithology study, **Supp. 6**, 255; photography of, **Supp. 6**, 685; Pious Fund, claim against, **Vol. 7, Part 2**, 426; railroad building in, **Vol. 7, Part 2**, 195; **Vol. 8, Part 2**, 527; real estate development, **Supp. 3**, 154–55; social anthropological studies, **Supp. 6**, 532–34; Treaty of 1828, **Vol. 3, Part 2**, 108; Trist, activities of, **Vol. 9, Part 2**, 646; typhus fever, **Vol. 5, Part 1**, 429; U.S. oil claims, **Supp. 7**, 377; Water Treaty, **Supp. 6**, 455; Wood, Leonard, expedition led by, **Vol. 7, Part 2**, 296; writings on, **Vol. 8, Part 1**, 30 f., 503, 634; **Vol. 9, Part 1**, 316

Mexico City: capture of (1847), **Vol. 8, Part 2**, 509; **Vol. 9, Part 2**, 646; paving of, **Supp. 1**, 255

Meyer, Adolf, references to, **Supp. 3**, 51, 127–28; **Supp. 4**, 107; **Supp. 6**, 367, 672

Meyer, Eugene, references to, **Supp. 3**, 492; **Supp. 7**, 295–96; **Supp. 8**, 432, 433

MGM. *See* Metro-Goldwyn-Mayer

Miami, Fla., gambling in, **Supp. 3**, 20

Miami Beach, Fla., tourism promotion, **Supp. 5**, 270

Miami Indians: disastrous expedition against, **Vol. 8, Part 2**, 294; Little Turtle, relations with, **Vol. 6, Part 1**, 300

Miami Tribune, founding of, **Supp. 3**, 20

Miami University (Ohio), **Vol. 3, Part 1**, 615 f.; **Vol. 5, Part 2**, 249; **Vol. 8, Part 1**, 271 f.; Foundation for Population Research, **Supp. 3**, 635

Michael Reese Hospital (Chicago, Ill.), pediatrics service, **Supp. 5**, 1

Michelson, Albert A., references to, **Supp. 3**, 291; **Supp. 5**, 495

Michigan: boundary disputes, **Vol. 2, Part 2**, 185; Catholic church, **Vol. 1, Part 1**, 448 f.; **Vol. 6, Part 1**, 139; canal building, **Vol. 10, Part 1**, 616 f.; deaf, state school for, **Vol. 3, Part 2**, 151; education, **XIV.** 583, 637; **Vol. 10, Part 1**, 617 f., 652 f.; exploration,

Vol. 2, Part 1, 582; **Vol. 6, Part 1**, 395; forestry, **Vol. 1, Part 2**, 87; fruit growing in, **Vol. 6, Part 1**, 535 f.; fungi of, **Vol. 5, Part 2**, 263; geology, **Vol. 2, Part 1**, 90; **Vol. 5, Part 1**, 254; governors, **Vol. 1, Part 1**, 179 f., 534 f., 654 f.,; **Vol. 1, Part 2**, 329 f., 368 f.; **Vol. 3, Part 1**, 341 f.; **Vol. 6, Part 1**, 586 f.; **Vol. 6, Part 2**, 375 f.; **Vol. 7, Part 2**, 621 f.; **Vol. 10, Part 1**, 463 f.; **Vol. 10, Part 2**, 483 f.; **Supp. 4**, 640; **Supp. 8**, 57; iron, discovery of, **Vol. 2, Part 1**, 338; industrial development, **Vol. 3, Part 1**, 547 f.; jurisprudence in, **Vol. 2, Part 1**, 608; land surveys. **Vol. 2, Part 1**, 90; legal service, **Vol. 2, Part 1**, 456; **Vol. 2, Part 2**, 392; **Vol. 3, Part 1**, 390; **Vol. 3, Part 2**, 468; **Vol. 6, Part 1**, 424; **Vol. 10, Part 2**, 220, 507; library work, early, **Vol. 3, Part 1**, 143; missionary work, **Vol. 1, Part 1**, 585; **Vol. 7, Part 2**, 583; **Vol. 8, Part 1**, 550; mining, **Vol. 2, Part 1**, 338; **Vol. 8, Part 1**, 264 f.; **Vol. 10, Part 2**, 162; Mormonism, opposition to, **Vol. 9, Part 2**, 124; pioneer days in, **Vol. 2, Part 1**, 340, 563; **Vol. 10, Part 2**, 483; political service, **Vol. 1, Part 1**, 179, 534, 655; **Vol. 1, Part 2**, 291, 329, 368; **Vol. 2, Part 1**, 336; **Vol. 3, Part 1**, 109, 234, 296; **Vol. 3, Part 2**, 313, 341; **Vol. 5, Part 1**, 282, 363; **Vol. 6, Part 1**, 141, 327, 586; **Vol. 6, Part 2**, 144; **Vol. 7, Part 2**, 583, 621; **Vol. 9, Part 2**, 124; **Vol. 10, Part 1**, 463 f.; **Vol. 10, Part 2**, 247, 483; politics, **Supp. 3**, 550, 596; **Supp. 4**, 299, 612–13; **Supp. 5**, 505, 702–5; **Supp. 8**, 268–69; politics, Civil War period, **Vol. 2, Part 1**, 336; public service, **Vol. 1, Part 2**, 369; **Vol. 5, Part 1**, 278; reforms, **Vol. 1, Part 1**, 534; Republican party, **Vol. 2, Part 1**, 618; **Vol. 6, Part 1**, 327; Roman Catholic diocese, **Supp. 5**, 263–64; scientific services, **Vol. 8, Part 1**, 192 f.; shipping, **Vol. 2, Part 1**, 338; statehood, admission to, **Vol. 6, Part 2**, 376; **Vol. 10, Part 2**, 483; steel industry, **Vol. 3, Part 1**, 547 f.; Sunday school, first, **Vol. 9, Part 1**, 33; surgery, **Vol. 6, Part 1**, 537; territorial code, first, **Vol. 1, Part 2**, 50; territory, extent of, **Vol. 3, Part 1**, 349

Michigan Car Co., **Vol. 7, Part 1**, 445

Michigan Central Railroad, **Vol. 5, Part 2**, 224

Michigan Railroad Commission, **Supp. 3**, 188

Michigan Southern & Northern Indiana Railroad, **Vol. 5, Part 2**, 60

Michigan State Agricultural College, **Vol. 6, Part 2**, 613

Michigan State College, women, establishing courses for, **Vol. 6, Part 2**, 463

Michigan State Normal School: geography studies, **Supp. 4**, 423–24; at Ypsilanti, **Vol. 10, Part 1**, 617 f.

Michigan State Psychopathic Hospital, founding of, **Supp. 2**, 24

Michigan State Teachers' Association, **Vol. 10, Part 1**, 617 f.

Michigan State University: mechanical engineering studies, **Supp. 6**, 181; social research, **Supp. 8**, 685

Microbiology, **Supp. 2**, 225; **Supp. 3**, 354; **Supp. 6**, 481–82; soil, **Supp. 3**, 387; virus bacteria differentiation, **Supp. 7**, 648. *See also* Bacteriology

Microfilm: early work with, **Supp. 6**, 70; library use of, **Supp. 6**, 399; **Supp. 8**, 120; postal service use of, **Supp. 6**, 661

Micropaleontology, **Supp. 4**, 205–6

Microphone, invention of, **Vol. 5, Part 1**, 347; **Supp. 1**, 75

Microscopes, for diagnosis, **Supp. 4**, 790; writings on, **Supp. 4**, 516

Microscopy, **Vol. 1, Part 1**, 106; **Vol. 2, Part 2**, 132; **Vol. 5, Part 2**, 79; **Vol. 6, Part 1**, 151, 202; **Vol. 7, Part 2**, 370; **Vol. 8, Part 1**, 589; **Vol. 8, Part 2**, 562 f.; **Vol. 10, Part 1**, 435 f.; **Vol. 10, Part 2**, 650; **Supp. 3**, 40; **Supp. 6**, 704

Microtome, **Vol. 7, Part 1,** 30
Microwaves: radar development, **Supp. 4,** 358–59; radio relay, **Supp. 6,** 85
Middle Ages: architecture, **Supp. 1,** 600; armor collection, **Supp. 2,** 415; art collection, **Supp. 2,** 22; art studies, **Supp. 8,** 545; Chaucer chronology, **Supp. 4,** 819–20; church drama studies, **Supp. 3,** 855; Cloisters collection, **Supp. 4,** 902; Hebrew literature, **Supp. 2,** 145; Latin literature and language studies, **Supp. 4,** 68; manuscripts, **Supp. 3,** 109; religious sensibility studies, **Supp. 3,** 769 66, scholarship on, **Supp. 2,** 290; **Supp. 7,** 741–42; stained glass, **Supp. 3,** 183–84; textbooks on, **Supp. 1,** 285; towns, studies of, **Supp. 5,** 655–56; writings on, **Supp. 1,** 705; **Supp. 3,** 617–18
Middlebury, Vt., **Vol. 7, Part 2,** 167
Middlebury College, **Vol. 1, Part 2,** 593; **Vol. 4, Part 2,** 195; **Vol. 7, Part 2,** 167; **Vol. 8, Part 1,** 280 f.
Middle East: archaeology, **Supp. 3,** 37; Byzantine studies, **Supp. 5,** 708–9; education, **Supp. 2,** 517; Lebanon crisis (1958), **Supp. 8,** 158; missionary work in, **Supp. 4,** 860; pre-Islamic civilizations, studies on, **Supp. 3,** 572–73; scholarship on, **Supp. 7,** 709–10; Suez crisis (1956), **Supp. 6,** 179; **Supp. 8,** 147, 158, 276. *See also country and institution names*
Middle English studies, **Supp. 3,** 109
Middle States Oil Corporation, **Supp. 1,** 381
Middletown, Conn., **Vol. 3, Part 1,** 395
Middletown, **Supp. 4,** 908; **Supp. 5,** 35; **Supp. 8,** 398–99
Middletown in Transition, **Supp. 3,** 30
Middle West (U.S.): art reflecting, **Supp. 3,** 841, 204–5; fiction about, **Supp. 4,** 329; **Supp. 5,** 14–15, 422–24; literature associated with, **Supp. 4,** 629–30; progressive movement, **Supp. 6,** 578; sociological study, **Supp. 8,** 398–99; writings on, **Supp. 4,** 816–17. *See also specific states and city names*
Midget, **Vol. 9, Part 2,** 126 f.
"Midnight judges," **Vol. 1, Part 1,** 80; **Vol. 5, Part 2,** 28 f.; **Vol. 6, Part 1,** 101; **Vol. 6, Part 2,** 319 f.
"Midnight Order," **Vol. 3, Part 1,** 545 f.
Midway, World War II action, **Supp. 4,** 589; **Supp. 5,** 450; **Supp. 6,** 340; **Supp. 8,** 619
Midway Studios, **Supp. 2,** 647
Midwifery, **Vol. 1, Part 1,** 599; **Vol. 3, Part 1,** 267; **Vol. 6, Part 1,** 510; **Vol. 9, Part 1,** 117; first physician to practice, **Vol. 6, Part 1,** 333; School of, **Vol. 3, Part 2,** 160; training program, **Supp. 2,** 495; **Supp. 3,** 28
Migraine, cause of, **Vol. 8, Part 1,** 317 f.
Migrant labor, **Supp. 7,** 456; **Supp. 8,** 301, 625
Migratory Bird Law (1913), **Supp. 3,** 593
Milbank, Tweed, Hadley, and McCloy, **Supp. 8,** 662
Mildred series, **Vol. 3, Part 2,** 390
Miles, Robert E. J., reference to, **Supp. 4,** 551
Military: "Adventurers," colonizers in the West, **Vol. 6, Part 1,** 517; commission, trial of civilians, by, **Vol. 3, Part 1,** 111; education, **Vol. 4, Part 1,** 206; **Vol. 6, Part 1,** 39; **Vol. 7, Part 2,** 282; engineering, **Vol. 1, Part 1,** 163, 500, 626; **Vol. 2, Part 2,** 78; **Vol. 3, Part 1,** 210; **Vol. 3, Part 2,** 550; **Vol. 4, Part 1,** 52, 138, 343, 612; **Vol. 4, Part 2,** 151; **Vol. 5, Part 1,** 101 f.; **Vol. 6, Part 1,** 69, 182, 495 f.; **Vol. 6, Part 2,** 257; **Vol. 7, Part 1,** 100 f., 154; **Vol. 8, Part 1,** 406, 647; **Vol. 8, Part 2,** 592; **Vol. 9, Part 2,** 247, 260, 363; history, **Vol. 2, Part 2,** 109; **Vol. 3, Part 1,** 352, 394, 396 f.; hospitals, **Vol. 7, Part 1,** 409; law, **Vol. 3, Part 1,** 115; manuals, **Vol. 7, Part 1,** 510; monuments, **Vol. 8, Part 2,** 107; prisons, **Vol. 9, Part 2,** 616; Quaker attitude regarding service, **Vol. 6, Part 1,** 70; service, selective, **Vol. 5, Part 2,** 251; Student Army Training Corps, **Vol. 6, Part 2,** 120; surgery, **Vol. 3, Part 2,** 538; **Vol. 8, Part 2,** 585;

tactics, **Vol. 3, Part 1,** 579 f.; **Vol. 7, Part 1,** 229; **Vol. 8, Part 2,** 507; **Vol. 10, Part 1,** 130; writings, **Vol. 2, Part 1,** 50, 119; **Vol. 3, Part 1,** 210, 248, 467 f., 579 f.; **Vol. 4, Part 1,** 141, 144; **Vol. 5, Part 2,** 146, 150, 264, 315, 498; **Vol. 6, Part 2,** 210; **Vol. 7, Part 1,** 154; **Vol. 8, Part 1,** 514; **Vol. 8, Part 2,** 71, 152,; **Vol. 9, Part 2,** 530; **Vol. 10, Part 1,** 130. *See also* Armed forces and defense; *specific branches of the armed forces; specific war names*
Military Academy, U.S. *See* United States Military Academy
Military Historical Society of Massachusetts, **Vol. 8, Part 2,** 152
Militia of Christ for Social Service, founding of, **Supp. 4,** 232
Milk: child nourishment, **Supp. 3,** 159; condensed and evaporated, **Supp. 2,** 306; **Supp. 3,** 750; fat-test, **Supp. 1,** 37; infant diarrhea treatment, **Supp. 5,** 1; malted, **Supp. 2,** 316, 688; modifying of, **Vol. 6, Part 2,** 502; nutrients in, **Supp. 5,** 276; pasteurization and sanitation, **Vol. 8, Part 2,** 553; **Vol. 9, Part 2,** 130; **Supp. 2,** 353, 514; **Supp. 4,** 701; **Supp. 5,** 144; school programs, **Supp. 8,** 468
Milk chocolate, **Supp. 3,** 358
Milky Way, **Supp. 6,** 30
Millard's Review of the Far East, founding of, **Supp. 4,** 679
Millay, Edna St. Vincent, references to, **Supp. 8,** 124, 645
Millenarianism, **Supp. 1,** 615–16; **Supp. 3,** 678
Millenarian, The, **Vol. 8, Part 1,** 453
Millennial Dawn, tremendous sale of, **Vol. 8, Part 2,** 240
Millennial Harbinger, **Vol. 6, Part 1,** 401
Millennium, calculations on, **Vol. 1, Part 1,** 432; **Vol. 5, Part 2,** 313
Miller, Arthur, references to, **Supp. 7,** 546; **Supp. 8,** 31
Miller, Charles R., reference to, **Supp. 3,** 787
Miller, Dayton C., reference to, **Vol. 7, Part 1,** 192
Miller, Don, reference to, **Supp. 7,** 729
Miller, Earl, references to, **Supp. 7,** 660, 662, 664
Miller, Glenn, reference to, **Supp. 3,** 690
Miller, Henry, references to, **Supp. 7,** 292, 293
Miller, Joaquin, reference to, **Vol. 6, Part 1,** 433
Miller, Kenneth Hayes, reference to, **Supp. 5,** 472
Miller, Thomas W., prosecution of, **Supp. 3,** 117
Miller, William, reference to, **Vol. 5, Part 1,** 60
Millers' National Association, **Vol. 1, Part 1,** 504
Millet, Jean Francois, reference to, **Vol. 5, Part 1,** 397
Milligan, Lambdin P., reference to, **Vol. 5, Part 1,** 182
Milligan, Maurice M., reference to, **Supp. 3,** 597
Milligan case before Supreme Court, **Vol. 3, Part 2,** 360 f.
Millikan, Robert A., references to, **Supp. 2,** 494; **Supp. 3,** 291; **Supp. 5,** 202; **Supp. 6,** 150, 151; **Supp. 7,** 133, 134, 344, 619; **Supp. 8,** 439, 440
Millinery. *See* Hats
Milling: industry, **Vol. 1, Part 2,** 157; flour, **Vol. 1, Part 1,** 503; **Vol. 3, Part 1,** 524 f.; **Vol. 3, Part 2,** 90, 209, 525; **Vol. 7, Part 2,** 604 f., 607; **Vol. 10, Part 1,** 495 f.; grain, **Vol. 3, Part 2,** 51; machinery, **Vol. 5, Part 1,** 286
Millions of Cats, **Supp. 4,** 310
Millis, Harry A., reference to, **Supp. 6,** 379
Mills College, **Vol. 7, Part 1,** 6, 16 f.; building program, **Supp. 6,** 463; presidency, **Supp. 4,** 687–88
"Mills money," **Vol. 7, Part 1,** 14
Mill Spring, Ky., battle of. *See* Logan's Cross Roads
"Milquetoast, Caspar" (fictional character), **Supp. 5,** 732

Milton Academy (Pa.), **Vol. 5, Part 2,** 249
Milwaukee, Wis.: industrial development, **Vol. 1, Part 1,** 219; founding, **Vol. 5, Part 2,** 247 f.; German Catholicism, **Vol. 6, Part 2,** 580; library service, **Vol. 7, Part 2,** 384; Lutheran Seminary, **Vol. 5, Part 1,** 108; newspapers, **Supp. 3,** 19–20; public service, **Vol. 7, Part 2,** 326, 535; Roman Catholic diocese, **Supp. 6,** 607; **Supp. 7,** 533; Socialist politics in, **Supp. 4,** 733, 746; **Supp. 7,** 348
Milwaukee and St. Paul Railroad, **Vol. 7, Part 1,** 40
Milwaukee College, **Vol. 7, Part 1,** 252
Milwaukee-Downer College, **Vol. 5, Part 2,** 612
Milwaukee Journal, **Supp. 1,** 576; **Supp. 7,** 299
Milwaukee Leader, **Supp. 1,** 74; **Supp. 3,** 10; **Supp. 4,** 746; **Supp. 7,** 348
Milwaukee Sanitarium, **Supp. 1,** 244
Milwaukee Sentinel, **Vol. 5, Part 2,** 400
Milwaukee Töchter Institute, **Vol. 4, Part 1,** 262
Mind. *See* Intelligence tests; Learning; Psychology; Thinking
Mind and the World-Order, **Supp. 7,** 471–72
Mind in the Making, The, **Supp. 2,** 564
Mind of Primitive Man, The, **Supp. 3,** 84
Miner, Luella, reference to, **Supp. 3,** 288–89
Mineral Leasing Act (1920), **Supp. 4,** 481
Mineralogy, **Vol. 1, Part 2,** 570; **Vol. 2, Part 1,** 180, 184, 187; **Vol. 5, Part 1,** 50, 240; **Vol. 5, Part 2,** 276 f., 486 f.; **Vol. 6, Part 1,** 70; **Vol. 7, Part 2,** 114; **Vol. 9, Part 1,** 2 f., 71, 304; book on, first, **Vol. 2, Part 2,** 189; chemistry applied to, **Vol. 5, Part 2,** 276; classification studies, **Supp. 2,** 386; collections, **Vol. 1, Part 1,** 248; **Vol. 1, Part 2,** 173; **Vol. 4, Part 1,** 245; **Vol. 6, Part 1,** 71; **Vol. 8, Part 2,** 90; **Vol. 9, Part 1,** 262; **Vol. 9, Part 2,** 629; **Supp. 6,** 212; field studies, **Supp. 1,** 176; identification, **Supp. 1,** 177; silica particles causing tuberculosis, **Supp. 4,** 314; teaching of, **Vol. 5, Part 1,** 254; **Vol. 5, Part 2,** 486; **Vol. 10, Part 2,** 263; textbooks, **Supp. 1,** 221; writings on, **Vol. 3, Part 1,** 268; **Vol. 5, Part 2,** 487
Mineral water, first bottled in U.S., **Vol. 3, Part 1,** 538 f.
Minersville School District v. *Gobitis*, **Supp. 4,** 796
Mines, Bureau of, **Vol. 5, Part 1,** 167; **Vol. 6, Part 2,** 254; engineering, **Supp. 4,** 690
Mine-sweeping, origin of, **Vol. 10, Part 1,** 135
Mine Workers. *See* United Mine Workers
Minhag America, Jewish prayer book, **Vol. 5, Part 2,** 254
Miniatures, **Vol. 9, Part 2,** 649; engraving of, detail of process (1797), **Vol. 8, Part 2,** 305; ivory, **Vol. 7, Part 1,** 247; painting, **Vol. 3, Part 1,** 516 f.; **Vol. 3, Part 2,** 603; toy trains, **Supp. 7,** 150
Minimum wage, **Supp. 3,** 655–56; **Supp. 4,** 900
Minimum Wage Law for Women, District of Columbia, **Vol. 9, Part 2,** 271
Mining (general; for list of mining engineers, *see* Occupations Index): Alaskan conservation, **Supp. 3,** 96, 321; Alaskan copper, **Supp. 3,** 321; Alder Gulch, **Vol. 4, Part 2,** 402; "Apex Law," **Vol. 4, Part 2,** 507; **Vol. 9, Part 2,** 589; Assay Office, U.S., **Vol. 5, Part 2,** 135; **Vol. 9, Part 2,** 597; colonial period, **Vol. 4, Part 2,** 379; **Vol. 6, Part 1,** 4; Comstock lode, **Vol. 2, Part 2,** 333; **Vol. 3, Part 2,** 246; **Vol. 5, Part 2,** 283; **Vol. 7, Part 1,** 612; **Vol. 9, Part 2,** 146; development of, **Supp. 1,** 413; engineering, **Supp. 1,** 357; **Supp. 5,** 556; **Supp. 7,** 357–58; financing of, **Vol. 9, Part 1,** 27; Gardner Mine fraud, **Vol. 3, Part 1,** 391; geological, **Supp. 4,** 765–66; government supervision, **Vol. 8, Part 1,** 415; Hunt and Douglas process, **Vol. 3, Part 1,** 396; industrial development, **Supp. 6,** 606–7; inventions, **Vol. 1, Part 2,** 412; labor movement, **Supp. 6,** 548; labor unions, **Vol. 4, Part 2,** 468; laws relating to, **Vol. 3, Part 1,** 238; **Vol. 6,**

Part 1, 275; **Vol. 8, Part 1,** 415; **Vol. 9, Part 2,** 13 f., 423, 589; Leadville Mine, **Vol. 7, Part 1,** 461, 507; **Vol. 9, Part 2,** 263; leases, **Supp. 2,** 148; Little Pittsburgh Mine, **Vol. 9, Part 2,** 263; locomotives, first underground, **Vol. 8, Part 2,** 189; machinery, **Vol. 1, Part 1,** 551; **Vol. 2, Part 1,** 187; **Vol. 5, Part 2,** 36, 38; **Vol. 6, Part 1,** 82, 230; **Vol. 8, Part 1,** 518; **Supp. 1,** 544; **Supp. 2,** 101; mass-production process; **Supp. 6,** 316–17; Mexico, **Supp. 3,** 259; ores, testing of, **Vol. 3, Part 1,** 547 f.; prospecting, **Supp. 5,** 613; rock drills, **Vol. 5, Part 1,** 472; **Vol. 6, Part 1,** 230; **Vol. 8, Part 1,** 343; **Vol. 8, Part 2,** 587; Russell process in, **Vol. 3, Part 1,** 27; safety measures, **Supp. 2,** 200; **Supp. 4,** 690; sintering process, **Supp. 4,** 245–46; statistics, **Vol. 8, Part 1,** 415; teaching of, **Vol. 2, Part 1,** 612; **Vol. 3, Part 2,** 56; **Vol. 9, Part 2,** 64 f.; **Vol. 10, Part 1,** 619 f.; **Supp. 3,** 631; textbooks on, **Supp. 2,** 200; U.S. Bureau of Mines, **Vol. 5, Part 1,** 167; **Vol. 6, Part 2,** 254; water control, **Supp. 1,** 620; woman expert, **Vol. 4, Part 2,** 381; writings on, **Vol. 1, Part 1,** 643; **Vol. 2, Part 1,** 73, 186 f.; **Vol. 4, Part 1,** 199; **Vol. 8, Part 1,** 415; **Vol. 9, Part 1,** 460; **Vol. 9, Part 2,** 64 f.; **Supp. 1,** 714; **Supp. 7,** 358. *See also specific ores*
Mining (by location): Colorado, **Vol. 2, Part 1,** 186, 511; **Vol. 2, Part 1,** 590; **Vol. 3, Part 1,** 210; **Vol. 5, Part 1,** 43; **Vol. 10, Part 1,** 619 f.; Idaho, **Vol. 4, Part 2,** 419; **Vol. 8, Part 1,** 546; Iowa, **Vol. 3, Part 1,** 475; Kentucky, **Vol. 6, Part 1,** 189; Michigan, **Vol. 2, Part 1,** 338; Montana, **Vol. 3, Part 1,** 45; **Vol. 9, Part 2,** 589; Nevada, **Vol. 6, Part 2,** 76; **Vol. 9, Part 2,** 13 f., 146; Oregon, **Vol. 8, Part 1,** 456; Pennsylvania, **Vol. 1, Part 2,** 530; Peru, **Vol. 7, Part 2,** 9; Utah, **Vol. 4, Part 1,** 9; **Vol. 7, Part 2,** 209, 451; West, the, **Vol. 2, Part 1,** 187; **Vol. 2, Part 2,** 144 f.; **Vol. 8, Part 2,** 35
Mining (by product): coal, **Vol. 1, Part 2,** 338; **Vol. 2, Part 2,** 108, 110; **Vol. 4, Part 1,** 9; **Vol. 6, Part 1,** 189; **Vol. 8, Part 2,** 189; copper, **Vol. 1, Part 1,** 112; **Vol. 3, Part 1,** 45, 396 f.; **Vol. 4, Part 1,** 577; **Vol. 4, Part 2,** 37 f.; **Vol. 5, Part 1,** 289, 360, 431, 573; **Vol. 6, Part 1,** 4; **Vol. 7, Part 1,** 461; **Vol. 8, Part 1,** 264 f.; **Vol. 8, Part 2,** 263, 304; diamond, **Vol. 10, Part 2,** 261; gold, **Vol. 1, Part 1,** 396, 443, 446; **Vol. 1, Part 2,** 228; **Vol. 2, Part 1,** 62, 300; **Vol. 3, Part 1,** 210; **Vol. 3, Part 2,** 246; **Vol. 4, Part 1,** 22, 168, 316; **Vol. 4, Part 2,** 363, 387; **Vol. 5, Part 1,** 81; **Vol. 5, Part 2,** 55 f., 188, 407, 583; **Vol. 6, Part 1,** 516; **Vol. 6, Part 2,** 76, 314; **Vol. 7, Part 1,** 6, 612; **Vol. 8, Part 1,** 450; **Vol. 8, Part 2,** 11, 35, 205, 248; **Vol. 9, Part 1,** 273; **Vol. 9, Part 2,** 87, 315, 384; iron, **Vol. 2, Part 1,** 90; **Vol. 3, Part 1,** 90; **Vol. 3, Part 2,** 79, 118; **Vol. 4, Part 1,** 183; **Vol. 5, Part 1,** 505; **Vol. 6, Part 1,** 73; **Vol. 6, Part 2,** 397, 487, 572; **Vol. 7, Part 1,** 20, 135; **Vol. 8, Part 1,** 264 f., **Vol. 10, Part 2,** 375; lead, **Vol. 1, Part 1,** 435 f.; **Vol. 1, Part 2,** 392; **Vol. 3, Part 1,** 457, 475; **Vol. 4, Part 2,** 546; **Vol. 5, Part 2,** 600; **Vol. 6, Part 2,** 496 f.; niter, **Vol. 8, Part 1,** 329 f.; salt, **Vol. 3, Part 2,** 322; silver, **Vol. 4, Part 1,** 337; **Vol. 5, Part 1,** 137, 446, 609; **Vol. 7, Part 1,** 507, 612; **Vol. 8, Part 1,** 326; **Vol. 8, Part 2,** 336; **Vol. 9, Part 2,** 263
Mining Herald, founding of, **Supp. 2,** 200
Ministers' Institute (Unitarian), **Vol. 1, Part 2,** 169
Minkowski, Rudolph, reference to, **Supp. 6,** 31
Minneapolis, Minn.: art, **Vol. 5, Part 2,** 485; **Vol. 10, Part 1,** 361 f.; civic service, **Vol. 6, Part 1,** 414 f., 478; **Vol. 7, Part 1,** 636; milling industry, **Vol. 3, Part 1,** 524 f.; **Vol. 7, Part 2,** 605
Minneapolis Daily News, founding of, **Supp. 4,** 132
Minneapolis, St. Paul & Sault Ste. Marie Railway (Soo Line), **Supp. 3,** 783, 823

Mitchell, John Ames, reference to, **Supp. 3**, 300
Mitchell, John H., reference to, **Supp. 4**, 844
Mitchell, Joseph, reference to, **Supp. 7**, 473
Mitchell, Margaret, references to, **Supp. 7**, 682; **Supp. 8**, 368
Mitchell, S. Weir, references to, **Vol. 7, Part 1**, 321, 542; **Vol. 8, Part 2**, 560; **Supp. 3**, 435
Mitchell, Sidney Z., reference to, **Supp. 3**, 192
Mitchell, Wesley C., references to, **Supp. 3**, 177, 248; **Supp. 5**, 485; **Supp. 6**, 599; **Supp. 8**, 443
Mitchell, William D., reference to, **Supp. 7**, 361
Mitchell Motor Car Co., **Supp. 4**, 621
Mitochondria, **Supp. 6**, 53, 54, 295–96
Mix, Tom, reference to, **Supp. 4**, 734–35
Mixed Claims Commission, **Vol. 7, Part 2**, 217
Mob behavior, **Supp. 3**, 511
Mobile, Ala.: capture of, **Vol. 2, Part 1**, 207, 469; **Vol. 3, Part 2**, 289; **Vol. 9, Part 1**, 95, 556; Catholic church, **Vol. 8, Part 1**, 108 f.; envisioned as commercial center of South, **Vol. 3, Part 1**, 178; founding of, **Vol. 1, Part 2**, 251
Mobile Act, passage of, **Vol. 7, Part 2**, 613
Mobile Bay, battle of, **Vol. 3, Part 2**, 289; **Vol. 5, Part 2**, 221
Mobile Institute, **Vol. 7, Part 2**, 629
Mobsters. *See* Organized crime
Moby Dick, evaluation of, **Vol. 6, Part 2**, 523
Model A car, **Supp. 3**, 284; **Supp. 4**, 301, 302, 457; **Supp. 8**, 610
Model communities: Disney World, **Supp. 8**, 131; Forest Hills Gardens (New York City), **Supp. 6**, 26; Free Acres (Summit, N.J.), **Supp. 2**, 272; Goodyear Heights Allotment Co. (Akron, Ohio), **Supp. 5**, 618; Hershey, Pa., **Supp. 3**, 358; Kohler village (Sheboygan, Wis.), **Supp. 2**, 366; planning, **Supp. 2**, 738; Southern California, **Supp. 5**, 309. *See also* Utopian communities
Modeling, **Supp. 7**, 140–41
Modeling, wax, **Vol. 8, Part 1**, 158 f.; **Vol. 10, Part 2**, 562
Model T car, **Supp. 3**, 283, 284; **Supp. 4**, 295–97, 300–3, 456, 457; **Supp. 8**, 609–10
Modern dance, **Supp. 5**, 129; **Supp. 8**, 620–21, 643–44
Modern History, **Supp. 7**, 330
Modern History of Warships, **Supp. 4**, 399
Modern Language Association of America, **Vol. 3, Part 2**, 93; **Vol. 4, Part 2**, 357; **Vol. 9, Part 2**, 423; **Supp. 3**, 22, 109
Modern Language News, **Supp. 5**, 409
Modern Language Notes, **Vol. 9, Part 2**, 571
Modern Maturity, founding of, **Supp. 8**, 10
Modern Quarterly, founding of, **Supp. 2**, 89
Modigliani, Amadeo, reference to, **Supp. 6**, 194
Modjeska, Helena, references to, **Vol. 1, Part 1**, 659, 660; **Supp. 3**, 713
Modoc Indian campaign (1873), **Vol. 2, Part 1**, 469; **Vol. 4, Part 1**, 287
Modotti, Tina, reference to, **Supp. 6**, 685
Moe, Henry Allen, reference to, **Supp. 3**, 321–22
Mohawk & Hudson Railway, **Vol. 5, Part 2**, 59
Mohawk Drama Festival, **Supp. 3**, 287
Mohawk Indians, **Vol. 1, Part 2**, 604; **Vol. 4, Part 2**, 370; Bible translation for, **Vol. 4, Part 1**, 8; English affiliation with, **Vol. 4, Part 2**, 532; ministry to, **Vol. 7, Part 1**, 646 f.
Mohawk Valley: history of, **Vol. 1, Part 2**, 604; land developments, **Vol. 3, Part 1**, 465 f.
Mohr, Otto L., reference to, **Supp. 3**, 540
Moisseiff, Leon S., reference to, **Supp. 6**, 594
Molasses Act, **Vol. 7, Part 2**, 283
Molders' Union. *See* International Molders and Foundry Workers Union

Molecules: biology, **Supp. 6**, 283; **Supp. 8**, 450; diple moment measurement, **Supp. 8**, 122–23; Franck-Condon principle, **Supp. 7**, 259; interactions, **Supp. 6**, 346; macromolecules, **Supp. 6**, 346; physics, **Supp. 8**, 482, 627–28; valence and electronic structure of, **Supp. 4**, 488–89
Moley, Raymond, references to, **Supp. 3**, 647; **Supp. 6**, 23–24, 34, 161
Moline Plow Co., **Supp. 3**, 399
Molino Del Ray, battle of, **Vol. 8, Part 2**, 509
Mollusks: collecting of, **Vol. 6, Part 1**, 71; researches in, **Vol. 1, Part 2**, 357; **Vol. 1, Part 2**, 70; **Vol. 9, Part 1**, 585; **Supp. 1**, 661
Mondrian, Piet, reference to, **Supp. 7**, 183–84
Monel (alloy), **Supp. 5**, 652–53
Monetary system: circular flow, **Supp. 4**, 307; compensated dollar standard, **Supp. 4**, 274; easy-money policy, **Supp. 8**, 446; economic theory relationship to, **Supp. 4**, 585–88; federal regulation advocacy, **Supp. 4**, 748; free-silver movement, **Supp. 2**, 289; gold standard advocacy, **Supp. 5**, 651; greenback controversy, **Supp. 4**, 585; managed currency theory, **Supp. 2**, 696; non-metal-based advocacy, **Supp. 5**, 138–40; quantity theory, **Supp. 3**, 413–14; quantity theory, criticism of, **Supp. 1**, 487–88; removal from gold standard, **Supp. 3**, 649, 652, 839; supply and prices, **Supp. 8**, 79; writings on, **Supp. 2**, 577. *See also* Coinage; Gold standard; Silver
Money: books on, **Vol. 1, Part 1**, 510; "sound," **Vol. 3, Part 2**, 252; study of, **Vol. 3, Part 1**, 226; **Vol. 6, Part 1**, 273; **Vol. 9, Part 2**, 323
Money, **Supp. 8**, 79
Mongolia, paleontology in, **Supp. 3**, 316; **Supp. 6**, 18
Monism, **Vol. 7, Part 1**, 95–96
Monitor: battle with *Merrimac*, **Vol. 2, Part 1**, 207; **Vol. 3, Part 1**, 529 f.; **Vol. 3, Part 2**, 173, 532, 568; **Vol. 4, Part 1**, 366, 574; **Vol. 5, Part 1**, 343; **Vol. 5, Part 2**, 164, 278; **Vol. 6, Part 2**, 225; **Vol. 9, Part 2**, 554, 638; **Vol. 10, Part 1**, 630; **Vol. 10, Part 2**, 531; building of, **Vol. 1, Part 1**, 21; **Vol. 3, Part 1**, 211; **Vol. 4, Part 2**, 9; **Vol. 8, Part 2**, 200; **Vol. 9, Part 1**, 310; **Vol. 10, Part 2**, 400; report on, **Vol. 5, Part 2**, 14
"Monitor's letters" (1768), **Vol. 6, Part 1**, 96
Monkey trial. *See* Evolutionism; Scopes trial
Monmouth, battle of, **Vol. 1, Part 1**, 177; **Vol. 2, Part 1**, 315; **Vol. 2, Part 2**, 366; **Vol. 1, Part 2**, 570; **Vol. 5, Part 2**, 476, 537; **Vol. 6, Part 1**, 100; **Vol. 9, Part 1**, 603; **Vol. 10, Part 1**, 518, 564
Monmouth College, **Vol. 10, Part 1**, 372 f.
Monnier, Adrienne, reference to, **Supp. 7**, 40
Monocacy, battle of, **Vol. 3, Part 1**, 598; **Vol. 10, Part 1**, 375
Monologues, **Vol. 8, Part 2**, 249; **Supp. 6**, 174
Monometalism, **Vol. 9, Part 2**, 636
Monophone, invention of, **Vol. 9, Part 1**, 490
Monopolies, automobile industry suit, **Supp. 4**, 295–96; base pricing, **Supp. 4**, 268; economic theory, **Supp. 8**, 82; laws regulating, **Vol. 1, Part 2**, 428; telephone, **Supp. 8**, 211–12. *See also* Antitrust actions
Monotype, invention of, **Vol. 5, Part 2**, 611
Monroe, Harriet, reference to, **Supp. 8**, 563
Monroe, James, reference to, **Vol. 5, Part 1**, 529 f.; **Vol. 6, Part 2**, 192; **Vol. 7, Part 1**, 416, 534; **Vol. 9, Part 2**, 570
Monroe, Marilyn, reference to, **Supp. 7**, 668
Monroe, Paul, reference to, **Supp. 3**, 677
Monroe Doctrine, **Vol. 1, Part 1**, 86–87; **Vol. 3, Part 2**, 507; **Vol. 7, Part 1**, 90, 92; **Vol. 8, Part 1**, 37–38; **Vol. 8, Part 2**, 139, 232; Buchanan, J., and, **Vol. 2, Part 1**, 210, fundamental character, first change in,

Vol. 8, Part 1, 34 f.; origins, Vol. 6, Part 2, 192; Roosevelt, T.R., and, Vol. 8, Part 2, 139 f.

Monsky, Henry, reference to, Supp. 4, 283

Montallegro font, Supp. 3, 785

Montana: banditry, Vol. 8, Part 1, 15 f.; constitution of, Vol. 1, Part 2, 605; copper, effect of, on state history, Vol. 3, Part 1, 45; copper mining, Vol. 3, Part 1, 45; Vol. 4, Part 2, 403, 507; Vol. 8, Part 2, 263; governor of, Vol. 9, Part 2, 589 f.; history of, Vol. 1, Part 2, 538; Indians, Vol. 8, Part 1, 135 f., 394; irrigation, Vol. 4, Part 2, 403; legal service, Vol. 1, Part 2, 605; Vol. 5, Part 1, 243; Vol. 8, Part 2, 336; map of first, Vol. 3, Part 1, 207; mineral resources survey, Supp. 1, 176; mining laws, Vol. 9, Part 2, 589; missions, Vol. 2, Part 1, 67; Vol. 8, Part 1, 394; paleontology, Vol. 10, Part 2, 310; pioneering, Vol. 4, Part 1, 256; Vol. 4, Part 2, 193; Vol. 6, Part 2, 534; political parties, early, Vol. 8, Part 2, 337; political service, Vol. 1, Part 2, 605; Vol. 2, Part 2, 144; Vol. 4, Part 2, 403; Vol. 6, Part 2, 199; Vol. 8, Part 1, 135; Vol. 4, Part 2, 403; Vol. 9, Part 2, 589; Vol. 10, Part 1, 393 f.; politics, Supp. 7, 561–62; public service, Vol. 3, Part 2, 20; Vol. 4, Part 1, 256; Republican party, Vol. 8, Part 2, 337; rivers, exploration of, Vol. 6, Part 2, 299; silver mining, Vol. 4, Part 2, 403; statehood, admission to, Vol. 2, Part 1, 544; Vol. 2, Part 2, 145; Vol. 9, Part 2, 589; writings on, Supp. 5, 320–21

Montana Power Co., Vol. 8, Part 2, 263

Montana State University, Supp. 1, 176

Montclair Art Gallery and Museum, Vol. 3, Part 2, 214

Monterey, Calif., Vol. 8, Part 1, 109 f.

Monterey, Mexico, battle of, Vol. 8, Part 1, 316, 625; Vol. 9, Part 2, 351; Vol. 10, Part 1, 83; Vol. 10, Part 2, 537

Montessori, Maria, reference to, Supp. 6, 90, 202

Montessori methods, Vol. 9, Part 1, 349

Montgomerie Charter, Vol. 7, Part 1, 363

Montgomery, Alan, reference to, Supp. 3, 37

Montgomery, Bernard, reference to, Supp. 8, 155

Montgomery, Bob, reference to, Supp. 6, 301

Montgomery, Helen Barrett, references to, Supp. 4, 647, 648

Montgomery, Ala.: civil rights movement in, Supp. 8, 333–34; first public-library building, Vol. 7, Part 1, 348

Montgomery Advertiser, editorial leadership, Supp. 1, 347

Montgomery Ward and Co., Supp. 6, 27–28; Supp. 8, 35, 705

Monthly Anthology, Vol. 5, Part 2, 431

Monticello (Va.), restoration of, Supp. 5, 388

Montreal, expedition against, Vol. 5, Part 2, 126

Monumental City, (steamship), Vol. 4, Part 1, 164

Monuments: architecture of, Vol. 3, Part 1, 420; Vol. 4, Part 2, 389; historical, Vol. 8, Part 1, 368 f.; military, Vol. 8, Part 2, 107

Moody, Dan, reference to, Supp. 4, 776

Moody, Dwight L.: biography of, Supp. 6, 195; references to, Vol. 1, Part 2, 376; Vol. 8, Part 1, 512 f.; Vol. 8, Part 2, 352; Vol. 10, Part 1, 606 f.

Moody, Helen Wills, references to, Supp. 6, 425, 426

Moody, William Vaughn, references to, Supp. 6, 19, 391

Moody Memorial Church, Supp. 5, 346

Moody's Magazine, Supp. 6, 458

Moon, Parker T., reference to, Supp. 7, 330

Moon: motions of, Vol. 7, Part 1, 453 f.; Vol. 9, Part 2, 50; Supp. 2, 69; space program, Supp. 7, 424, 429; topography, writings on, Supp. 4, 766

Mooney, Edward, reference to, Supp. 8, 613

Mooney, Rena, reference to, Supp. 3, 532

Mooney, Thomas J. (Tom), references to, Supp. 5, 499; Supp. 7, 248, 455; Supp. 8, 586

"Moon Hoax," Vol. 3, Part 1, 155; Vol. 6, Part 1, 339

Moon Is Blue, The, Supp. 6, 288, 289; Supp. 7, 71

Moore, A. Harry, reference to, Supp. 6, 265

Moore, Aaron, reference to, Supp. 5, 647–48

Moore, Douglas, reference to, Supp. 3, 57

Moore, Eliakim, reference to, Supp. 3, 86

Moore, Gordon B., reference to, Supp. 6, 671

Moore, Marianne, reference to, Supp. 5, 660

Moore, Oscar, reference to, Supp. 7, 131

Moore, Underhill, reference to, Supp. 3, 186

Moore, William, trial of, Vol. 9, Part 1, 355

Moore's Creek, battle of, Vol. 2, Part 1, 571

Moos, Malcolm, reference to, Supp. 8, 159

Moose, Loyal Order of. *See* Loyal Order of Moose

Moot, founding of, Vol. 9, Part 1, 357

Moral Decision, The, Supp. 7, 99

Moral development, Supp. 4, 767

Moral optimism, Supp. 4, 525–26

Moral Re-Armament movement, Supp. 7, 89

Moran, James J., reference to, Supp. 7, 585

Moran Towing and Transportation Co., Supp. 7, 552–53

Moravian church, Vol. 1, Part 1, 312; Vol. 1, Part 2, 402; Vol. 2, Part 2, 214; Vol. 3, Part 2, 190; Vol. 4, Part 2, 31; Vol. 5, Part 1, 569; Vol. 6, Part 1, 198 f., 421; Vol. 8, Part 1, 473 f.; Vol. 8, Part 2, 130, 465, 482 f.; Vol. 9, Part 1, 109, 428; Vol. 10, Part 2, 658; formation of, Vol. 7, Part 1, 529; history of, Vol. 6, Part 1, 199; Vol. 8, Part 2, 482; missions, Vol. 2, Part 1, 441; Vol. 4, Part 2, 495 f.; Vol. 5, Part 2, 248; Vol. 8, Part 1, 113 f.; Vol. 10, Part 2, 646; writings on, Vol. 6, Part 1, 421; Vol. 8, Part 1, 474; Vol. 8, Part 2, 130

Moravian College, Vol. 5, Part 1, 569; Vol. 8, Part 2, 456

More, Paul Elmer, references to, Supp. 1, 36; Supp. 7, 624

Morehead, John M., reference to, Vol. 8, Part 2, 383

Morehead Foundation, Supp. 7, 554

Morehouse, D. W., reference to, Supp. 7, 572

Morehouse College, administration, Supp. 2, 315

Morelli, Giovanni, reference to, Supp. 6, 56

"Morey" letter, libel indictment based on, Vol. 8, Part 1, 118 f.

Morgan, Arthur E., references to, Supp. 4, 601, 602

Morgan, Dennis, reference to, Supp. 7, 107

Morgan, Edwin B., reference to, Vol. 10, Part 1, 639 f.

Morgan, Helen, reference to, Supp. 8, 546

Morgan, Henry S., reference to, Supp. 7, 715

Morgan, J. Pierpont, references to, Vol. 1, Part 1, 483; Vol. 5, Part 2, 38; Vol. 9, Part 1, 598 f.; Supp. 3, 321, 375, 783, 785; Supp. 4, 345; Supp. 5, 148, 505, 550; Supp. 6, 622

Morgan, Thomas Hunt, references to, Supp. 2, 60; Supp. 5, 367, 368; Supp. 8, 448, 499

Morgan, J. P., & Co., Vol. 4, Part 2, 372; Vol. 7, Part 1, 234; Vol. 9, Part 1, 453; Supp. 4, 320, 469–70, 682; Supp. 6, 376–77; Supp. 7, 715, 782–83; international loans, Supp. 3, 537–38; oil interests, Supp. 3, 505; utility holding companies, Supp. 3, 138

Morgan, Stanley, and Co., Supp. 7, 715

Morgan Guaranty Trust Co. of New York, Supp. 7, 783

"Morgan Horse," Vol. 7, Part 1, 183

Morgan Library (New York City), Supp. 3, 375; Supp. 4, 345

Morgan's raid (U.S. Civil War), Vol. 5, Part 1, 96; Vol. 9, Part 2, 594

Morgenstern, Oskar, reference to, **Supp. 6,** 656

Morgenthau, Henry, Jr., references to, **Supp. 2,** 501; **Supp. 3,** 647, 653, 656; **Supp. 4,** 604; **Supp. 6,** 124, 229, 230; **Supp. 8,** 445

Morgenthau, Henry, Co., founding of, **Supp. 4,** 603

Morgenthau Plan, **Supp. 5,** 335

Morison, George S., reference to, **Supp. 3,** 367

Morison, Samuel Eliot, reference to, **Supp. 6,** 268, 341

Morley, Christopher, reference to, **Supp. 5,** 439; **Supp. 7,** 103

Morley, Edward W., reference to, **Supp. 3,** 523–24

Mormon church, **Vol. 1, Part 1,** 446; **Vol. 1, Part 2,** 601, 611; **Vol. 3, Part 2,** 521; **Vol. 4, Part 1,** 258; **Vol. 5, Part 2,** 258, 377; **Vol. 6, Part 1,** 115; **Vol. 8, Part 2,** 3 f.; **Vol. 9, Part 1,** 311 f., 313, 384; **Vol. 9, Part 2,** 123 f., 333; **Vol. 10, Part 2,** 621; administration, **Supp. 5,** 640; *Book of Mormon,* **Vol. 8, Part 1,** 600 f.; **Vol. 9, Part 1,** 310 f.; **Vol. 9, Part 2,** 334; church-state separation issues, **Supp. 3,** 727; colonization, **Vol. 6, Part 1,** 115; **Vol. 8, Part 1,** 175; **Vol. 9, Part 1,** 23; **Vol. 10, Part 2,** 499, 621; disturbances of 1857, **Vol. 2, Part 1,** 33, 290; **Vol. 2, Part 2,** 593; **Vol. 3, Part 1,** 256; **Vol. 5, Part 2,** 136; **Vol. 6, Part 1,** 134, 258; **Vol. 6, Part 2,** 274; **Vol. 8, Part 1,** 90; **Vol. 8, Part 2,** 510; **Vol. 9, Part 1,** 247, 331; **Vol. 10, Part 2,** 560, 622; government, U.S., conflict with, **Vol. 10, Part 2,** 622, 644; history of, **Vol. 6, Part 1,** 283; **Vol. 8, Part 1,** 600 f; hymns, **Vol. 9, Part 1,** 385; Kansas, **Vol. 4, Part 2,** 380; leadership, **Supp. 1,** 448, 607; **Supp. 7,** 126; **Supp. 8,** 408–9; *Lectures on Faith,* authorship of, **Vol. 8, Part 1,** 601; Michigan, opposition of, **Vol. 9, Part 2,** 124; military organization of, **Vol. 6, Part 1,** 115; missionary work, **Vol. 4, Part 1,** 337; **Vol. 8, Part 2,** 4; **Supp. 1,** 607; **Supp. 5,** 681; Missouri, conflict with, **Vol. 1, Part 2,** 409; **Vol. 3, Part 1,** 365; **Vol. 8, Part 1,** 175; monuments, **Supp. 6,** 720; *Mormonism Unveiled,* **Vol. 6, Part 1,** 115; persecutions, **Vol. 2, Part 1,** 474; polygamy, **Vol. 4, Part 2,** 334; **Vol. 6, Part 1,** 115; **Vol. 8, Part 1,** 341 f., 601; **Vol. 9, Part 2,** 334; presidency of, **Vol. 9, Part 1,** 386; **Vol. 9, Part 2,** 333 f.; prophet, **Vol. 9, Part 1,** 310 f.; psychological aspects of, **Vol. 8, Part 1,** 610; publications, **Vol. 8, Part 2,** 4; Salt Lake City, building of, **Vol. 10, Part 2,** 621 f.; spread of, **Vol. 10, Part 2,** 152, 499; "Twelve Apostles," **Vol. 9, Part 2,** 333 f.; writings on, **Vol. 9, Part 2,** 124 f.; **Vol. 10, Part 1,** 68; **Vol. 10, Part 2,** 610; Young, Brigham, **Vol. 10, Part 2,** 620 f.

Morning Courier and New York Enquirer, first issue of, **Vol. 1, Part 2,** 196

Morocco, diplomatic relations with, **Vol. 4, Part 2,** 50

"Moron," term coined, **Supp. 6,** 240

Morphine, addiction studies, **Supp. 3,** 242

Morrill Tariff Act, **Vol. 7, Part 1,** 198; **Vol. 7, Part 2,** 206

Morris, George Pope, reference to, **Vol. 7, Part 1,** 608

Morris, George Sylvester, reference to, **Supp. 5,** 170

Morris, Newbold, reference to, **Supp. 8,** 406

Morris, Robert: biography of, **Supp. 2,** 495; reference to, **Vol. 7, Part 1,** 142, 430, 504

Morris, Robert Hunter, reference to, **Vol. 7, Part 1,** 637

Morris, William, references to, **Vol. 5, Part 1,** 323; **Supp. 4,** 177

Morrisania, **Vol. 7, Part 1,** 213 f., 218 f., 224 f.

Morris Brown College, **Vol. 4, Part 1,** 96

Morris Canal, **Vol. 8, Part 1,** 506

Morrison, Charles Clayton, references to, **Supp. 3,** 457; **Supp. 6,** 315

Morris Plan Co., **Vol. 9, Part 2,** 614

Morristown, N.J., **Vol. 8, Part 1,** 369

Morrow, Dwight W., references to, **Supp. 3,** 218; **Supp. 6,** 182, 187

Morrow, Edwin, reference to, **Supp. 6,** 591

Morse, Samuel F. B., references to, **Vol. 5, Part 1,** 412, 536; **Vol. 5, Part 2,** 326; **Vol. 7, Part 1,** 248 f.; **Vol. 8, Part 1,** 49 f.; **Vol. 9, Part 2,** 611

Morse, Wayne, references to, **Supp. 6,** 618; **Supp. 8,** 395–96, 590

Mortality, infant. *See* Infant mortality

Mortgages, farm, **Supp. 4,** 406, 480

Mortimer, Lee, reference to, **Supp. 5,** 406

Morton, Julius Sterling, reference to, **Supp. 3,** 209

Morton, Levi P., biography of, **Supp. 6,** 410

Morton, Oliver P., reference to, **Vol. 5, Part 1,** 241

Morton, Samuel George, reference to, **Vol. 7, Part 1,** 597

Morton, W. T. G., references to, **Vol. 5, Part 1,** 537; **Vol. 6, Part 1,** 375; **Vol. 10, Part 1,** 640 f.

Mosaics, **Supp. 1,** 247; **Supp. 4,** 890–91; **Supp. 7,** 522–23

Mosby, J. S., prosecution of, **Vol. 8, Part 2,** 29

Moscow Art Theatre, **Supp. 3,** 297

Moscow Daily News, founding of, **Supp. 8,** 635

Moscow purge trials (1930s), **Supp. 6,** 184

Moses, George, reference to, **Supp. 3,** 559

Moses, Robert, references to, **Supp. 3,** 718; **Supp. 7,** 586

Moses Brown School, **Vol. 2, Part 1,** 150; **Vol. 4, Part 2,** 49

Moskowitz, Belle, references to, **Supp. 3,** 645, 718, 719

Mosler, Thomas Bird, reference to, **Vol. 5, Part 1,** 162

"Mosquito fleet," Confederate navy, **Vol. 5, Part 1,** 152; **Vol. 9, Part 2,** 394

Mosquitos: study of, **Vol. 3, Part 1,** 413, 578 f.; **Vol. 3, Part 2,** 388; **Vol. 5, Part 2,** 381, 448; **Vol. 9, Part 1,** 298; **Supp. 4,** 400; as virus host, **Supp. 5,** 383; yellow fever and, **Supp. 3,** 736; **Supp. 6,** 434

Moss, use of, for surgical dressings, **Vol. 9, Part 1,** 276

Most Happy Fella, The, **Supp. 8,** 386

Mother Angela, reference to, **Vol. 9, Part 1,** 400

Mother Earth, founding of, **Supp. 2,** 247

Motherhood: maternal childbirth death prevention, **Supp. 3,** 222–23; unwed, services for, **Supp. 3,** 221. *See also* Obstetrics

"Mother Macree," **Vol. 7, Part 2,** 9

Mother's Day, **Supp. 5,** 290

Mother's Magazine, **Vol. 10, Part 2,** 171

Motherwell, Robert, reference to, **Supp. 6,** 512

Motion Picture Association of America, **Supp. 7,** 397

Motion Picture Magazine, **Supp. 3,** 76

Motion Picture Producers and Distributors of America, Inc., **Supp. 5,** 281–82

Motion pictures, **Vol. 3, Part 2,** 333; **Vol. 5, Part 1,** 78; **Vol. 6, Part 1,** 355 f.; **Vol. 7, Part 2,** 463; **Vol. 8, Part 2,** 16; **Vol. 9, Part 1,** 164; Academy of Motion Picture Arts and Sciences, **Supp. 7,** 32; **Supp. 8,** 678; African exploration, **Supp. 5,** 371; animated cartoons, **Supp. 8,** 129–30; anthropological study of, **Supp. 8,** 510; B-films, **Supp. 8,** 712; black films, **Supp. 5,** 490; blacklisting, **Supp. 5,** 238, 419; **Supp. 7,** 315, 397; **Supp. 8,** 492, 550–51, 704; black stereotypes in, **Supp. 4,** 695; **Supp. 5,** 451; **Supp. 7,** 163; censorship, **Supp. 4,** 535; **Supp. 5,** 281–82, 677; **Supp. 6,** 288–89; **Supp. 7,** 71; China, **Supp. 8,** 495; cinematography, **Supp. 3,** 73–74; Cinerama, **Supp. 5,** 721–22; close-up technique, **Supp. 3,** 73, 76; color, use of, **Vol. 9, Part 2,** 647; color film, **Supp. 2,** 338; **Supp. 7,** 406–8; comedy, **Supp. 1,** 636–37; **Supp. 4,** 270; **Supp. 6,** 13, 128, 276, 573, 609; **Supp. 7,** 107, 515–16; composers, **Supp. 6,** 352; costume design, **Supp. 5,** 386; **Supp. 6,** 9;

Supp. 7, 591–92; counterculture, Supp. 5, 162–63; criticism, Supp. 5, 12, 623; Supp. 8, 491, 584–85; Dead End Kids, Supp. 8, 220–21; dialogue writing, Supp. 5, 464; direction, Supp. 6, 76–77, 609–10, 657–58; Supp. 7, 65–66, 87, 160, 177–78, 240–41; Supp. 8, 671–72; directorial innovations, Supp. 4, 349–51; dissolve technique, Supp. 3, 607; distribution, Supp. 7, 692–93; *Dr. Kildare* series, Supp. 5, 44; documentaries, Supp. 5, 225–26; Supp. 7, 241; earliest talking, Supp. 7, 176–77; early developments in, Supp. 3, 75–76; early technology, Supp. 1, 121; Edison patents, Supp. 1, 280–81; first black Academy Award winner, Supp. 5, 451; first black star, Supp. 7, 44; first book contract movie rights clause, Supp. 4, 60; first fan magazine, Supp. 3, 76; first five-reel American film, Supp. 3, 607; first indoor lighted movie, Supp. 3, 73; first sound, Supp. 4, 440; Supp. 5, 121, 630; Supp. 8, 459–60; gangster films, Supp. 6, 668; German, psychological study of, Supp. 8, 346; gossip columns about, Supp. 8, 282; Hearst interests, Supp. 5, 286–87; historical studies of, Supp. 8, 346–47; horror films, Supp. 6, 395; Supp. 8, 312; industry leaders, Supp. 6, 118–19, 158–60, 368–69, 439–50, 667–68; industry standardization, Supp. 1, 279; "It" girl, Supp. 8, 678; loyalty investigation, Supp. 8, 648–49; makeup, Supp. 1, 165; music direction, Supp. 5, 630; Supp. 8, 465–66, 688–89; musicals, Supp. 4, 226; Supp. 6, 89, 273, 274, 663; Supp. 7, 178, 628–29; Supp. 8, 204–5; musical scores, Supp. 8, 251–52, 688–89; newsreels, Supp. 5, 230, 286; Supp. 6, 291; Supp. 8, 393–94; operettas, Supp. 7, 499; Supp. 8, 151; Oriental roles, Supp. 7, 802; "patent war," Supp. 4, 734; penny arcades, Supp. 5, 726; pioneers in, Supp. 4, 734–35; production, Supp. 2, 368, 657; Supp. 5, 229–30; Supp. 6, 431; Supp. 7, 681–82; Supp. 8, 677–78; production code, Supp. 6, 288–89; projection, Supp. 5, 321–22; rating system, Supp. 6, 479; Roaring Twenties, Supp. 7, 68; romances, Supp. 8, 66–67; science fiction, Supp. 6, 530; Supp. 8, 379; screen credits establishment, Supp. 5, 229; screenwriting, Supp. 3, 264; Supp. 5, 12, 120–21, 209–10, 624; Supp. 6, 11, 106, 133, 214, 288–89, 476, 609, 628; Supp. 7, 232–33, 234, 331–32, 583–84; Supp. 8, 45, 108–9; 492, 622; "screwball" comedies, Supp. 3, 466; serials, Supp. 2, 710; Supp. 3, 76; sex goddesses, Supp. 7, 546; Supp. 8, 412–13; *Sherlock Holmes* series, Supp. 8, 519; short subjects, Supp. 3, 54; silent era, Supp. 3, 443–44; Supp. 6, 76–77, 618–19; Supp. 7, 229–30, 462–63, 563; Supp. 8, 214; slapstick comedy, Supp. 5, 210–11; Supp. 7, 208, 238, 462–64; Supp. 7, 589; Supp. 8, 314–15; social-consciousness films, Supp. 8, 453, 456, 550; song lyrics, Supp. 3, 406; sophisticated comedy, Supp. 4, 509; sound development, Supp. 5, 230; special effects, Supp. 7, 579–80; star system, Supp. 7, 68, 142–44; studios, Supp. 6, 439–50, 667–68; Supp. 8, 576–77; "Tarzan" movies, Supp. 4, 129; Technicolor development, Supp. 7, 406–8; theater chains, Supp. 2, 584; Supp. 8, 320, 576–77; Todd-AO process, Supp. 6, 638; travelogues, Supp. 6, 302; unionization, Supp. 8, 459–60, 492; Westerns, Supp. 3, 462; Supp. 4, 363–64; Supp. 6, 466; Supp. 7, 229, 286–87; Supp. 8, 248, 712; wide-screen processes, Supp. 5, 721–22; Supp. 7, 692–93; wild-animal films, Supp. 4, 734; "women's movies," Supp. 8, 188; World War II films, Supp. 6, 668. *See also* Acting

Motivation. *See* Behaviorism

Motivation and Personality, Supp. 8, 423–24

Moton, Robert R., reference to, Supp. 6, 568

Motor, founding of, Supp. 5, 286

Motorcycles, manufacture of, Supp. 1, 213

Mott, John R., reference to, Supp. 7, 29

Mott, Lucretia, reference to, Vol. 9, Part 1, 521 f.

Mould, Adelaide Manola, reference to, Supp. 6, 309

Moulders' International Union, Vol. 9, Part 2, 258

Moulton, Elton J., reference to, Supp. 5, 508

Moulton, Harold G., references to, Supp. 5, 508, 537, 538; Supp. 6, 271

Mound-builders, Indian, Vol. 2, Part 1, 51; Vol. 3, Part 1, 113; Vol. 7, Part 2, 619; Vol. 9, Part 2, 406

Mountain climbing, Vol. 4, Part 2, 502; Vol. 8, Part 2, 184; Vol. 9, Part 2, 448

Mountain Meadows massacre, Vol. 6, Part 1, 115

Mount Auburn Cemetery, founding of, Vol. 1, Part 2, 258

Mount Berry School for Boys, Supp. 3, 63

Mount Carmel, Ill., Vol. 1, Part 2, 103

Mount Hermon School, Vol. 7, Part 1, 104

Mount Holyoke College: missionary work, Supp. 3, 288; presidency, Supp. 4, 912–13

Mount Holyoke Seminary, founding of, Vol. 6, Part 1, 532; Vol. 9, Part 2, 572

Mount McKinley, Supp. 4, 674

Mount Mitchell, Vol. 7, Part 1, 46

Mount Monadnock, Vol. 9, Part 2, 399

Mount Morris Park (N.Y.), Vol. 7, Part 2, 600

Mount Rainier, Supp. 4, 896

Mount Rushmore National Memorial (S.Dak.), carving of, Supp. 2, 492; Supp. 3, 89

Mount St. Mary's College, Vol. 6, Part 1, 559; Vol. 8, Part 1, 266 f.

Mount Sinai Hospital (New York City): electrocardiography, Supp. 6, 117; gynecology and obstetrics, Supp. 6, 554, 555; neurological bed service, Supp. 3, 682; pathology laboratory, Supp. 4, 493, 667–68; psychiatric outpatient clinic, Supp. 5, 517; social services and outpatient departments, Supp. 3, 312

Mount Vernon Ladies' Association of the Union, Vol. 2, Part 2, 601

Mount Washington, early exploration of, Vol. 3, Part 1, 13

Mount Wilson Observatory (California), Supp. 2, 271

"Mouse, Mickey" (fictional character), Supp. 8, 130, 131

"Movement Cure," Vol. 9, Part 2, 318

Movies. *See* Motion pictures

Movie stars. For complete list, *See* Occupations Index

Mowing machine, first use of, Vol. 3, Part 2, 110

Mozart, Wolfgang Amadeus, operas popularized, Supp. 6, 324

Muckraking, Vol. 6, Part 1, 332; Vol. 8, Part 2, 497. *See also* Journalism

Mudd, Samuel A., reference to, Vol. 1, Part 2, 450

Mugwump movement, Supp. 1, 101

Mugwumps (1884–89), Vol. 1, Part 2, 326; Vol. 2, Part 2, 207; Vol. 7, Part 2, 469; Vol. 9, Part 1, 97

Muhammad, Elijah, reference to, Supp. 7, 508

Muhammad Speaks, founding of, Supp. 7, 508

Muhlenberg College, presidency of, Vol. 7, Part 1, 306; Vol. 8, Part 2, 563

Muir, John, references to, Vol. 5, Part 2, 293; Supp. 2, 16; Supp. 4, 522

Mulberry, attempted cultivation of, Vol. 3, Part 1, 595

Muller, Hermann J., reference to, Supp. 3, 540

Muller, Richard, reference to, Supp. 6, 256

"Mulligan Letters" (1876), Vol. 1, Part 2, 324; Vol. 2, Part 2, 207; Vol. 5, Part 2, 422

Mulligan, P. B., and Co., Supp. 6, 618

"Mullins, Moon" (fictional character), Supp. 6, 699

Mullins, Paddy, reference to, Supp. 6, 700

Music Box Theatre (New York City), **Supp. 3,** 333

Music Lovers' Encyclopedia, **Supp. 6,** 309

Musicology: Bach works, **Supp. 6,** 357–58; teaching of, **Supp. 3,** 252–53

Music School Settlement (New York City), **Supp. 4,** 545; **Supp. 6,** 426, 427

Musket, manufacture for Revolution, **Vol. 7, Part 1,** 503

Muslim Mosque, Incorporated, founding of, **Supp. 7,** 508

Mussolini, Benito: biography of, **Supp. 1,** 173; references to, **Supp. 3,** 658, 659; **Supp. 4,** 518; **Supp. 5,** 447; **Supp. 6,** 140, 170, 237, 388–89; Toscanini opposition to, **Supp. 6,** 643

Muste, A. J., reference to, **Supp. 6,** 161

Mutiny of 1793, **Vol. 5, Part 2,** 568

"Mutt and Jeff" (fictional characters), **Supp. 5,** 223–24

Mutual Life Insurance Co., **Vol. 6, Part 1,** 588; **Vol. 6, Part 2,** 12; **Vol. 7, Part 1,** 323

Mutual Welfare League, **Vol. 7, Part 2,** 75

My America, **Supp. 5,** 4

Myasthenia gravis, **Supp. 7,** 59

Mycology: **Vol. 5, Part 2,** 262; **Vol. 7, Part 2,** 373; **Vol. 9, Part 2,** 398; plant pathology, **Supp. 3,** 400, 815; rust fungi studies, **Supp. 3,** 23

My Fair Lady, **Supp. 7,** 325

Myrdal, Gunnar, sociological studies, **Supp. 6,** 605

Myrick, Julian, reference to, **Supp. 5,** 351

Mystery fiction, **Supp. 6,** 543

Mystery of Hamlet, The, **Supp. 6,** 418

Mystery stories. *See* Detective stories

Mysticism, **Vol. 4, Part 1,** 615; **Vol. 4, Part 2,** 323; **Vol. 5, Part 2,** 312 f.; **Vol. 7, Part 1,** 577 f.; study of, **Supp. 4,** 441–42; **Supp. 7,** 380–81

Mythology, writings on, **Supp. 1,** 434

"My Wild Irish Rose," **Vol. 7, Part 2,** 9

N

NAACP. *See* National Association for the Advancement of Colored People

Nagasaki. *See* Hiroshima and Nagasaki

Nail manufacture: by hand, **Vol. 9, Part 2,** 491; by machinery, **Vol. 1, Part 1,** 254; **Vol. 8, Part 1,** 429, 522; **Vol. 9, Part 2,** 243

NAM. *See* National Association of Manufacturers

Nanking University, founding of, **Supp. 3,** 268

Nanook of the North, **Supp. 5,** 225–26

Nantucket, Mass., **Vol. 2, Part 2,** 267; Athenaeum, **Vol. 7, Part 1,** 67; colonial life in, **Vol. 3, Part 2,** 488; genealogy of, **Vol. 3, Part 2,** 489; history of, **Vol. 3, Part 2,** 488; **Vol. 6, Part 2,** 456; purchase of, **Vol. 7, Part 2,** 599; Revolutionary period, **Vol. 8, Part 2,** 186; topographical studies of, **Vol. 3, Part 2,** 489; War of 1812 period, **Vol. 6, Part 2,** 178; whaling, **Vol. 7, Part 1,** 67; **Vol. 8, Part 2,** 186; wives secured by labor purchase, **Vol. 3, Part 2,** 488

Napalm, **Supp. 7,** 617

Naphtha, separation of crude oil from, **Vol. 8, Part 2,** 95

Napoleonic wars, privateering, **Vol. 3, Part 1,** 250

Napoleon prints and cartoons, collection of, **Vol. 8, Part 1,** 489

Napoleon III and Confederacy, **Vol. 9, Part 1,** 210 f.

"Narcissus," music by Nevin, **Vol. 7, Part 1,** 441

Narcotics: abuse rehabilitation, **Supp. 8,** 424; alcohol as, **Supp. 3,** 354; consciousness-enhancing, **Supp. 7,** 381; detection in horse racing, **Supp. 8,** 76; government supervision of, **Vol. 8, Part 1,** 103 f.; heroin, **Supp. 7,** 485; juvenile use of, **Supp. 8,** 40; legislation, **Supp. 5,** 138; **Supp. 6,** 280; opium traffic control, **Supp. 1,** 116; safe use in medicine, **Supp. 3,**

242; traffic in, **Supp. 5,** 736–37; **Supp. 7,** 485

Narragansett, part played by, in battle of Manila Bay, **Vol. 3, Part 1,** 269 f.

NASA. *See* National Aeronautics and Space Administration

Nash car, **Supp. 4,** 621

Nash-Kelvinator Corporation, **Supp. 4,** 621

Nash Motors Co., founding of, **Supp. 4,** 620

Nash's Magazine, **Supp. 5,** 286

Nashville, battle of, **Vol. 2, Part 2,** 45, 464, 476; **Vol. 3, Part 2,** 533; **Vol. 5, Part 1,** 194; **Vol. 6, Part 1,** 131; **Vol. 8, Part 2,** 453; **Vol. 9, Part 1,** 237, 508; **Vol. 9, Part 2,** 434; **Vol. 10, Part 1,** 401; **Vol. 10, Part 2,** 335

Nashville, Tenn., **Vol. 1, Part 2,** 157; **Vol. 9, Part 1,** 494

Nashville Banner, **Vol. 5, Part 1,** 396; **Vol. 9, Part 1,** 495

Nashville Convention (1850), **Vol. 2, Part 1,** 457; **Vol. 2, Part 2,** 242; **Vol. 3, Part 1,** 363; **Vol. 5, Part 1,** 403; **Vol. 5, Part 2,** 102; **Vol. 9, Part 1,** 21

Nashville Tennessean, **Supp. 3,** 449

Nassau Hall, building of, **Vol. 9, Part 1,** 335

Nasser, Gamal Abdel, reference to, **Supp. 8,** 276

Nast, Condé, references to, **Supp. 4,** 199, 200; **Supp. 6,** 107–8

Nast, Thomas, campaign against Tweed, **Vol. 10, Part 1,** 81

Natchez, operation at. *See* Vicksburg campaign

Natchez Indians, **Vol. 1, Part 2,** 251; **Vol. 6, Part 1,** 226

Nathan, George Jean: relations with Mencken, **Supp. 6,** 444, 445; reference to, **Supp. 7,** 3

Nation, The, **Vol. 4, Part 1,** 347, 349; **Vol. 5, Part 1,** 307; **Vol. 5, Part 2,** 564; **Vol. 6, Part 1,** 195; **Vol. 7, Part 1,** 57; **Vol. 8, Part 2,** 546; **Vol. 10, Part 2,** 105; drama criticism, **Supp. 5,** 425; editing, **Supp. 2,** 498; **Supp. 4,** 487; foreign correspondent, **Supp. 8,** 172; movie reviews, **Supp. 5,** 12

National Academy of Design, **Vol. 1, Part 1,** 249, **Vol. 2, Part 2,** 596, **Vol. 7, Part 2,** 35; first exhibition by, **Vol. 3, Part 1,** 535 f.; founded, **Vol. 3, Part 1,** 516 f.; **Vol. 4, Part 1,** 2; **Vol. 9, Part 2,** 611; gifts to, **Vol. 1, Part 1,** 233

National Academy of Sciences, **Vol. 4, Part 1,** 252; **Vol. 7, Part 2,** 395; **Vol. 9, Part 1,** 163; first psychologist elected to, **Supp. 3,** 150; first woman Draper Medal recipient, **Supp. 3,** 131; first woman member, **Supp. 5,** 600; forest commission, **Supp. 4,** 663–66; gift to, **Supp. 6,** 154; Research Council, **Supp. 5,** 733; spiral nebulae debate (1920), **Supp. 3,** 208

National Advisory Committee for Aeronautics, **Supp. 3,** 12; **Supp. 4,** 486, 487; **Supp. 6,** 182, 183, 665–66; **Supp. 7,** 381–82

National Aeronautic Association, founding of, **Supp. 2,** 109

National Aeronautics and Space Administration, astronaut program, **Supp. 8,** 81, 225, 694

National Agricultural Convention, **Vol. 5, Part 2,** 446

National Air Transport, **Supp. 5,** 385; founding of, **Supp. 2,** 109; **Supp. 5,** 294

National American Woman Suffrage Association, **Supp. 5,** 532; founding of, **Supp. 4,** 156–58

National Anti-Slavery Standard, **Vol. 2, Part 2,** 68

National Archives, founding of, **Supp. 2,** 342; **Supp. 4,** 176; **Supp. 8,** 370

National Archives Building, **Supp. 2,** 342, 539

National Association for American Composers and Conductors, founding of, **Supp. 2,** 268

National Association for the Advancement of Colored People (NAACP), **Vol. 4, Part 1,** 633; **Supp. 3,** 828; **Supp. 5,** 548, 740, 741; **Supp. 6,** 494, 568; adminis-

National Farm School, **Vol. 5, Part 2,** 501

National Federation of Business and Professional Women's Clubs, founding of, **Supp. 5,** 543

National Federation of Settlements, **Supp. 6,** 499–500

National Florence Crittenton Missions, **Vol. 2, Part 2,** 550 f.

National Football League: commissioners, **Supp. 6,** 47–48; predecessor, **Supp. 5,** 684

National Foundry Association, **Vol. 7, Part 1,** 450

National Gallery of Art (Washington, D.C.): architecture of, **Supp. 5,** 300, 301; Dale Collection, **Supp. 7,** 161–62; design, **Supp. 2,** 539; founding of, **Supp. 2,** 451; French art collection, **Supp. 5,** 151; Gellatly Collection, **Supp. 1,** 337; Kress Collection, **Supp. 5,** 401

National Gazette and Literary Register, **Vol. 10, Part 1,** 391 f.

National Geographic Magazine, editing, **Supp. 8,** 228

National Geographic Society, **Vol. 1, Part 1,** 525; **Vol. 1, Part 2,** 152; **Vol. 8, Part 2,** 484; **Supp. 7,** 76; **Supp. 8,** 228; founding of, **Vol. 4, Part 1,** 124; **Vol. 5, Part 1,** 325; **Vol. 8, Part 1,** 152; **Supp. 1,** 355; **Supp. 3,** 518

National Grange. *See* Grange movement

National Guard, **Vol. 3, Part 2,** 576; **Vol. 4, Part 2,** 368; California, **Supp. 5,** 43; Fighting Sixty-ninth Regiment, **Supp. 1,** 268; New York, **Supp. 6,** 337; Pennsylvania, **Supp. 7,** 53; training requirement, **Supp. 7,** 78–79; writings on, **Supp. 6,** 309

National Health and Welfare Retirement Association, **Supp. 6,** 615

National Health Council, founding of, **Supp. 2,** 177

National Herbarium, **Vol. 1, Part 2,** 546; **Vol. 8, Part 2,** 160

National Herbart Society, founding of, **Supp. 2,** 424

National Historical Magazine, founding of, **Supp. 8,** 328

National Housing Association, **Supp. 6,** 26, 654

National Industrial Commission, **Vol. 5, Part 2,** 516

National Industrial Conference Board, **Supp. 7,** 404–5

National Industrial Recovery Act (1933), **Supp. 3,** 399 –400, 650; **Supp. 4,** 50, 432; **Supp. 5,** 54, 254, 510, 631; **Supp. 6,** 615; opposition to, **Supp. 7,** 249; unconstitutionality of, **Supp. 3,** 99, 839; **Supp. 4,** 406–7; **Supp. 6,** 679. *See also* National Recovery Administration

National Industrial Recovery Board, **Supp. 4,** 376

National Industries for the Blind, **Supp. 5,** 347–48

National Institute for the Promotion of Science and the Useful Arts, **Vol. 8, Part 1,** 30 f.

National Institute of Arts and Letters, **Vol. 7, Part 2,** 473 f.

National Institute of Science, founding of, **Supp. 1,** 3

National Institutes of Health: medical statistics, **Supp. 7,** 192; predecessor, **Supp. 4,** 701

National Intelligencer, **Vol. 8, Part 2,** 542

Nationalism, **Vol. 1, Part 2,** 164; **Vol. 8, Part 1,** 491; studies in, **Supp. 7,** 330

National Jeffersonian Democrats, founding of, **Supp. 3,** 623

National Junior Republic (Washington, D.C.), **Vol. 1, Part 2,** 471

National Kindergarten Association, founding of, **Supp. 5,** 437

National Labor College, founding of, **Supp. 4,** 233

National Labor Relations Act (1935), **Supp. 5,** 254; **Supp. 7,** 609; constitutionality upheld, **Supp. 4,** 407; legal status, **Supp. 6,** 679; passage of, **Supp. 3,** 654–55; **Supp. 5,** 718–19. *See also* Taft-Hartley Act

National Labor Relations Board (NLRB): chairman, **Supp. 8,** 34; factions on, **Supp. 6,** 379; founding of, **Supp. 3,** 651; **Supp. 5,** 718–19; McKinsey report on, **Supp. 8,** 366–67

National Labor Relations Boards, **Supp. 4,** 579–80

National Labor Relations Board v. Jones and Laughlin Steel Corp., **Supp. 4,** 407

National Labor Union, **Vol. 9, Part 2,** 258, 640; founding of, **Vol. 2, Part 1,** 434

National Lawyers Guild, formation of, **Supp. 3,** 227

National League (baseball), **Supp. 5,** 393; early years of, **Vol. 8, Part 1,** 418

National League for the Protection of the Family, **Vol. 3, Part 1,** 308

National League of Decency, founding of, **Supp. 4,** 535

National League of Women Voters. *See* League of Women Voters

National Legislative League, **Vol. 1, Part 2,** 344

National Longshoremen's Association, **Vol. 5, Part 2,** 278 f.

National Mediation Board, **Supp. 6,** 379

National Medical Convention, **Vol. 5, Part 2,** 468

National Merit Scholarship Corporation, **Supp. 7,** 276

National Monetary Commission, **Vol. 5, Part 2,** 189; **Vol. 9, Part 2,** 363

National Municipal League, **Vol. 1, Part 2,** 428; **Supp. 6,** 468; founding of, **Supp. 4,** 870

National Museum: founding and growth of, **Vol. 6, Part 2,** 373; mound collections, **Vol. 9, Part 2,** 426

National Museum of Engineering and Industry, **Vol. 8, Part 1,** 91 f.

National Music Teachers' Association, **Vol. 8, Part 1,** 200 f.

National Negro Business League, **Supp. 3,** 535; **Supp. 5,** 648; founding of, **Supp. 3,** 391; **Supp. 6,** 568

National Negro Congress, **Supp. 6,** 285

National Negro Insurance Association, founding of, **Supp. 5,** 648

National Observatory, **Vol. 1, Part 1,** 91; **Vol. 5, Part 2,** 403; **Vol. 10, Part 1,** 91

National Organization for Public Health Nursing, **Supp. 4,** 65; founding of, **Supp. 2,** 687

National parks. *See* Forestry; Parks

National Park Service, **Vol. 6, Part 2,** 399; founding of, **Supp. 4,** 522; **Supp. 6,** 486

National People's party, **Vol. 6, Part 1,** 332

National Popular Government League, **Supp. 4,** 641

National Portrait Gallery of Distinguished Americans, **Vol. 6, Part 1,** 381

National Prison Association of the United States **Vol. 7, Part 2,** 610

National Progressive League, founding of, **Supp. 2,** 691; **Supp. 4,** 544

National Progressive Republican League, **Vol. 5, Part 2,** 545; founding of, **Supp. 2,** 55, 237; **Supp. 3,** 558, 604, 816; **Supp. 4,** 665

National Progressives of America (1938), founding of, **Supp. 7,** 450–51

National Prohibition party, **Vol. 1, Part 2,** 310

National Psychological Association for Psychoanalysis, founding of, **Supp. 8,** 523

National Radio Astronomy Observatory, **Supp. 7,** 727; founding of, **Supp. 4,** 423

National Railway Co., **Vol. 7, Part 2,** 62

National Reclamation Association, predecessor, **Supp. 4,** 563

National Recovery Administration (NRA), **Supp. 3,** 670; **Supp. 5,** 515, 654; **Supp. 7,** 36, 171–72; activities, **Supp. 3,** 399–400; child labor, **Supp. 3,** 228; codes, **Supp. 4,** 457; **Supp. 6,** 378, 448, 622; Ford's relationship with, **Supp. 4,** 302; founding of, **Supp. 3,** 650–54; legal counsel, **Supp. 6,** 542; legal decisions on, **Supp. 4,** 406–7; New York, **Supp. 7,** 780

National Recreation Association, founding of, **Supp. 2,** 375

National Refugee Service, **Supp. 3**, 281

National Republican party, **Vol. 9, Part 2**, 641

National Research Council, **Supp. 3**, 150–51; **Supp. 5**, 64; drug addiction studies, **Supp. 3**, 242; food and nutrition subcommittee, **Supp. 3**, 68; founding of, **Supp. 1**, 156; human sexuality studies, **Supp. 6**, 343, 344, 718; postdoctoral fellowships, **Supp. 5**, 495–96

National Resources Planning Board, **Supp. 5**, 485; dismantling of, **Supp. 3**, 661

National Retired Teachers Association, founding of, **Supp. 8**, 9–10

National Review, **Supp. 7**, 115; **Supp. 8**, 150, 426

National Rifle Association, **Vol. 2, Part 2**, 105

National Road, extension of, **Vol. 5, Part 2**, 467

National Science Foundation: first director, **Supp. 8**, 687; founding of, **Supp. 6**, 335–36

National Sculpture Society, **Vol. 1, Part 2**, 301, 304; **Vol. 8, Part 1**, 125 f.; **Vol. 10, Part 1**, 427 f.; founding of, **Supp. 3**, 2, 673

National Security Act (1947), **Supp. 4**, 306; **Supp. 8**, 147

National Security League, **Supp. 6**, 410

National Self Government Committee, founding of, **Supp. 4**, 870

National Service Board for Religious Objectors, **Supp. 6**, 217

National Society for the Prevention of Blindness, **Supp. 3**, 364

National Society for the Study of Education, **Vol. 7, Part 2**, 238

National Society of Mural Painters, **Vol. 2, Part 2**, 578

National Society of Penal Information, **Vol. 7, Part 2**, 76

National Steel Corporation, **Vol. 7, Part 1**, 143; founding of, **Supp. 6**, 678–79; **Supp. 8**, 289

National Student Federation, **Supp. 7**, 566

National Television System Committee, **Supp. 6**, 32

National Temperance Advocate, **Vol. 9, Part 1**, 546

National Temperance Society, **Vol. 3, Part 1**, 19, 353

National Trades' and Workers' Association, **Vol. 8, Part 1**, 112 f.

National Trades Union, **Vol. 7, Part 1**, 121

National Tuberculosis Association, founding of, **Supp. 2**, 71, 197, 371

National Typographical Union, **Vol. 2, Part 2**, 364

National Union Convention, **Vol. 8, Part 1**, 410

National Union for Social Justice, **Supp. 6**, 613, 647

National Union Movement, **Vol. 8, Part 1**, 582

National University (Peking), paleontology studies, **Supp. 4**, 344

National Urban League. *See* Urban League

National Vocational Guidance Association, founding of, **Supp. 2**, 45

National War Labor Board, **Supp. 7**, 172

National Wildlife Federation, **Supp. 7**, 164

National Women's party, **Supp. 4**, 157, 576; **Supp. 5**, 474; founding of, **Supp. 7**, 717–18

National Women's Trade Union League, **Supp. 3**, 355; **Supp. 4**, 626; **Supp. 7**, 196; founding of, **Supp. 2**, 689; **Supp. 3**, 576

National Youth Administration, **Supp. 5**, 56; founding of, **Supp. 7**, 787

Nation of Islam. *See* Black Muslims

"Nations of the North," winning of, to Spanish rule, **Vol. 3, Part 1**, 229

Nationwide News Service, **Supp. 3**, 20, 21

Native-American movement, **Vol. 6, Part 1**, 200

Native Americans. *See* Indians, American; *specific groups*

Native Races, **Vol. 1, Part 1**, 570

Native Son, **Supp. 5**, 419; **Supp. 6**, 715, 716

Native's Return, The, **Supp. 5**, 4

Nativism. *See* Racism

"Nativism" riots of 1844 in Philadelphia, **Vol. 6, Part 1**, 200

NATO. *See* North Atlantic Treaty Organization

Natural gas, **Vol. 6, Part 1**, 233; development of, **Supp. 2**, 146; **Supp. 5**, 259–60; first pipeline in the U.S., **Vol. 7, Part 2**, 636; first use as fuel in manufacturing, **Vol. 7, Part 2**, 635 f.; pipelines, **Supp. 2**, 146, 334; production and distribution, **Supp. 7**, 97–98; regulation of, **Supp. 6**, 404

Natural Gas Act (1938), **Supp. 6**, 484

Natural history, **Vol. 1, Part 1**, 423 f., 466; **Vol. 1, Part 2**, 238; **Vol. 3, Part 2**, 127, 159, 307, 510; **Vol. 4, Part 1**, 132 f., 351, 375, 446; **Vol. 4, Part 2**, 94, 339, 564; **Vol. 5, Part 1**, 236; **Vol. 5, Part 2**, 211 f., 338 f., 438 f., 513; **Vol. 6, Part 1**, 71; **Vol. 6, Part 2**, 482; **Vol. 7, Part 1**, 265; **Vol. 8, Part 1**, 322 f.; **Vol. 8, Part 2**, 377; **Vol. 9, Part 1**, 22; **Vol. 9, Part 2**, 480, 596; **Vol. 10, Part 1**, 421 f.; biological survey, **Supp. 3**, 517–18; bird portraits, **Vol. 4, Part 1**, 53; cactus plantation, **Vol. 5, Part 2**, 513; crustacea, **Vol. 9, Part 2**, 32; deep-sea fish, **Vol. 4, Part 1**, 381; explorations, **Vol. 5, Part 2**, 338–9; first museum of, in U.S., **Vol. 3, Part 2**, 307; first nature trail, **Supp. 3**, 478; first summer camp for study of, **Vol. 3, Part 2**, 511; fishes, collection of, **Vol. 9, Part 2**, 94; in Illinois, **Vol. 5, Part 2**, 338; magazines, **Supp. 8**, 228; mollusks, **Vol. 9, Part 2**, 32; nature, study of, **Vol. 2, Part 1**, 572; **Vol. 5, Part 1**, 447; **Vol. 5, Part 2**, 62; **Vol. 7, Part 1**, 193, 242; **Vol. 7, Part 2**, 126; **Vol. 9, Part 2**, 400, 491 f.; paintings of, **Supp. 5**, 50; poisonous plants, **Vol. 5, Part 2**, 513; poisonous reptiles, **Vol. 5, Part 2**, 513; popular writings on, **Supp. 7**, 605–6; shells, collection of, **Vol. 9, Part 2**, 94; studies in, **Supp. 3**, 8–9; teaching of, **Vol. 1, Part 1**, 121; **Vol. 7, Part 1**, 45; **Vol. 8, Part 2**, 287, 402; tropical research, **Supp. 7**, 45, 46; writings on, **Vol. 1, Part 2**, 421; **Vol. 2, Part 1**, 331 f.; **Vol. 3, Part 1**, 392, 483; **Vol. 3, Part 2**, 450; **Vol. 4, Part 1**, 260, 360, 381, 382; **Vol. 4, Part 2**, 157; **Vol. 5, Part 1**, 250, 525; **Vol. 5, Part 2**, 438, 513; **Vol. 6, Part 1**, 70; **Vol. 6, Part 2**, 390; **Vol. 7, Part 2**, 193, 316; **Vol. 8, Part 1**, 144 f., 298, 394 f.; **Vol. 8, Part 2**, 391; **Vol. 9, Part 1**, 22; **Vol. 9, Part 2**, 94; **Vol. 10, Part 1**, 430 f., 580 f.; **Vol. 10, Part 2**, 44; **Supp. 3**, 636; **Supp. 4**, 167–68, 736–37; **Supp. 8**, 354; youth training in, **Supp. 3**, 44–45. *See also* Conservation; Wilderness and wildlife preserves

Natural History Museum (New York City). *See* American Museum of Natural History

Naturalists. For complete list, *See* Occupations Index

Natural resources: federal regulation of, **Supp. 4**, 481–82, 664; **Supp. 8**, 104. *See also* Conservation; *specific types*

Nature. *See* Natural History; *specific aspects*

Naughty Marietta, **Supp. 7**, 499; **Supp. 8**, 151

Nautical: devices, **Vol. 8, Part 1**, 321 f.; instruments, manufacture of, **Vol. 1, Part 2**, 398; **Vol. 5, Part 2**, 401; inventions, **Vol. 1, Part 2**, 407; publications, **Vol. 1, Part 2**, 398

Nautical Almanac, **Vol. 8, Part 2**, 225

Nautical Almanac Office, **Vol. 7, Part 1**, 452

Nautilus, a "diving boat," **Vol. 4, Part 1**, 70

Nauvoo, Ill., Mormons at, **Vol. 9, Part 1**, 311; **Vol. 9, Part 2**, 333

Navajo Indians, ceremonial art museum, **Supp. 6**, 688; education program, **Supp. 7**, 43; ethics system, **Supp. 5**, 644–45; sculptures depicting, **Supp. 6**, 720; tribal leadership, **Supp. 4**, 237–38; weaving trade, **Supp. 1**, 437–38

Naval Academy, U.S. (Annapolis). *See* United States Naval Academy

nursing, **Vol. 3, Part 1,** 217; operations office, **Supp. 1,** 70; **Supp. 6,** 373, 408; Orient, **Vol. 8, Part 1,** 424; Pacific Fleet, **Supp. 6,** 267–68; Pacific Plans Division, **Supp. 6,** 326; paintings, **Vol. 8, Part 1,** 511 f.; Pennsylvania, **Vol. 8, Part 1,** 430; periscope invented, **Vol. 8, Part 2,** 27; Portsmouth prison reform controversy, **Supp. 4,** 820; preparedness advocacy, **Supp. 8,** 41; *President* and *Little Belt*, **Vol. 3, Part 1,** 188; public works projects, **Supp. 5,** 343; *Randolph* and *True Briton*, **Vol. 1, Part 2,** 242; *Randolph* and *Yarmouth*, **Vol. 1, Part 2,** 242; reforms, **Vol. 4, Part 2,** 106; **Supp. 3,** 275; **Supp. 4,** 216–17; *Reindeer* and *Wasp*, **Vol. 1, Part 2,** 348; reorganization, **Supp. 2,** 614; **Supp. 8,** 152; research, **Vol. 7, Part 2,** 607; **Supp. 8,** 687; retired list of officers on half-pay created, **Vol. 3, Part 1,** 336; scientific progress of, **Vol. 3, Part 1,** 106 f.; Secretary of the Navy, **Vol. 1, Part 1,** 486; **Vol. 4, Part 1,** 481; **Vol. 5, Part 2,** 205; **Vol. 6, Part 1,** 377; **Vol. 7, Part 1,** 108, 264; **Vol. 8, Part 1,** 206 f.; **Vol. 9, Part 2,** 63, 601, 622 f.; **Vol. 10, Part 1,** 629 f.; *Serapis*, **Vol. 3, Part 2,** 268; Siberia, **Vol. 3, Part 2,** 559; smoke screens, developed, **Vol. 3, Part 1,** 614 f.; South Seas, **Vol. 4, Part 2,** 451; **Vol. 8, Part 2,** 77 f., 289; space program, **Supp. 8,** 81; Spanish-American War, preparation, **Vol. 3, Part 1,** 270 f.; strategy, **Supp. 6,** 629; submarine flotilla of the Atlantic Fleet, **Vol. 4, Part 1,** 485; tactics, **Vol. 3, Part 1,** 614 f.; **Vol. 5, Part 1,** 152; telescope sight, **Supp. 3,** 275; *Tigress*, **Vol. 4, Part 1,** 595; *Trent*, **Vol. 4, Part 1,** 594; *True Briton* and *Randolph*, **Vol. 1, Part 2,** 242; "turret vessels," **Vol. 3, Part 2,** 568; underway replenishment support force, **Supp. 8,** 30; War of 1812, **Vol. 2, Part 1,** 337; **Vol. 6, Part 1,** 50; **Vol. 8, Part 2,** 77; war rules, **Vol. 5, Part 2,** 147; *Wasp* and *Atlanta*, *Wasp* and *Avon*, *Wasp* and *Reindeer*, **Vol. 1, Part 2,** 348; West India squadron, **Vol. 7, Part 2,** 186; wireless used, **Vol. 3, Part 1,** 614 f.; women's naval reserve (WAVES), **Supp. 7,** 289; wood and steel, **Vol. 10, Part 2,** 347; world tour of, **Vol. 8, Part 2,** 139; writings on, **Vol. 1, Part 2,** 188; **Vol. 5, Part 2,** 14, 170, 298, 462; **Vol. 6, Part 1,** 489; **Vol. 6, Part 2,** 91, 121, 207; **Vol. 7, Part 2,** 243 f.; **Vol. 8, Part 2,** 86, 543; **Vol. 9, Part 1,** 178, 196; **Vol. 10, Part 1,** 21 f., 425; **Vol. 10, Part 2,** 585; **Supp. 3,** 275; **Supp. 4,** 821; *Yarmouth* and *Randolph*, **Vol. 1, Part 2,** 242. *See also* United States Naval Academy; *names of specific wars*

Navy Athletic Association, founding of, **Supp. 1,** 687

Navy Day, **Supp. 6,** 75

Nazareth, Pa., history of academy at, **Vol. 8, Part 1,** 473

Nazareth Unitarian Society, organization of, **Vol. 5, Part 1,** 612

Nazism: American party, **Supp. 8,** 540–41; art, **Supp. 6,** 552; diplomacy with, **Supp. 4,** 898; ethnological study of, **Supp. 6,** 394; *Kristallnacht*, **Supp. 7,** 740; movies opposing, **Supp. 6,** 668; opposition to, **Supp. 3,** 85; **Supp. 6,** 25, 201, 451, 643; **Supp. 7,** 498; post–World War II denazification program, **Supp. 3,** 590; **Supp. 6,** 407; study of, **Supp. 5,** 514; support for, **Supp. 4,** 792–93. *See also* Fascism; Holocaust; War crimes; World War II

NBC Symphony Orchestra: Rodzinski association, **Supp. 6,** 550; Toscanini association, **Supp. 6,** 643, 644; **Supp. 7,** 124

Neal, John Randolph, reference to, **Supp. 6,** 528; **Supp. 8,** 853

Neale, Leonard, reference to, **Vol. 9, Part 2,** 376

Near East: missions, **Vol. 1, Part 2,** 371; relief, **Vol. 8, Part 2,** 261; **Vol. 9, Part 2,** 513 f. *See also* Middle East

Near East Relief, Inc.: organization of, **Supp. 2,** 28; predecessor, **Supp. 4,** 604

Nearing, Scott, references to, **Supp. 4,** 32; **Supp. 7,** 268

Nebraska: botanical survey, **Supp. 7,** 625; Catholic service, **Vol. 7, Part 1,** 618; editorial service, **Vol. 8, Part 2,** 172; first resident of, **Vol. 8, Part 2,** 370; governors, **Vol. 2, Part 2,** 573 f.; **Vol. 4, Part 1,** 77 f.; **Vol. 7, Part 1,** 257; **Supp. 3,** 114; legal service, **Vol. 5, Part 1,** 132; "little TVA," **Supp. 3,** 560; national bank, first in, **Vol. 2, Part 2,** 535; novels about, **Supp. 4,** 154–55; political service, **Vol. 2, Part 2,** 573; **Vol. 4, Part 1,** 77; **Vol. 5, Part 1,** 78, 132; **Vol. 6, Part 2,** 230; **Vol. 7, Part 1,** 257; **Vol. 8, Part 2,** 380; politics, **Supp. 3,** 556–61; **Supp. 5,** 318–19, 479, 739; public service, **Vol. 7, Part 2,** 133; railroad incorporation law in, **Vol. 6, Part 2,** 293; Republican party, formation of, **Vol. 5, Part 1,** 78; state capitol architectural design, **Supp. 3,** 196; state fair, **Vol. 4, Part 1,** 77; statehood admission, **Vol. 6, Part 2,** 293; Territory, organization of, as, **Vol. 3, Part 1,** 399 f.

Nebraska state capitol, interior design, **Supp. 7,** 522

Nebulae, **Supp. 5,** 325–26; photographs of, **Vol. 5, Part 2,** 279

Neely, Matthew, reference to, **Supp. 6,** 335

Neff, John M., reference to, **Supp. 7,** 111

Negri, Pola, references to, **Supp. 4,** 508, 509

Negrín, Juan, reference to, **Supp. 3,** 137

Negro American League (baseball), **Supp. 3,** 378

Negroes. *See* Blacks

Negro Factories Corporation, founding of, **Supp. 2,** 221

Negro Family in the United States, The, **Supp. 7,** 266

Negro History Week, **Supp. 4,** 911

Negro in American Civilization, The, **Supp. 8,** 521

Negro in Chicago, The (report), **Supp. 6,** 321

Negro Labor Committee, **Supp. 7,** 156

Negro League (baseball), **Supp. 4,** 327–28

Negro Rural School Fund, **Vol. 5, Part 2,** 13; organization of, **Supp. 2,** 150

"Negro" school of literature, **Vol. 6, Part 1,** 276

Negro World, founding of, **Supp. 2,** 221

Neighborhood Guild, **Supp. 3,** 175

Neighborhood Playhouse (New York City), **Supp. 2,** 687; **Supp. 5,** 52–53; **Supp. 7,** 367

Neighborhoods: criteria, **Supp. 3,** 684; unit concept, **Supp. 3,** 601

Neilson, Francis, reference to, **Supp. 3,** 554

Nelson, Donald M., references to, **Supp. 3,** 660; **Supp. 4,** 458

Nelson, Gaylord, reference to, **Supp. 8,** 701

Nelson, Horatio, reference to, **Vol. 1, Part 2,** 242

Nematology, research in, **Supp. 1,** 182

Nemiroff, Robert, reference to, **Supp. 7,** 319

Nemours Foundation, **Supp. 1,** 271

Neohumanism, **Supp. 1,** 36

Neoprene, development of, **Supp. 2,** 97, 489

Nepera Chemical Co., **Supp. 3,** 26

Nephritis. *See* Kidneys

Nephrolithotomy, first in America, **Vol. 9, Part 2,** 535

Neptune, **Vol. 4, Part 2,** 162

Nernst, Walther, reference to, **Supp. 6,** 364

Nervous disorders. *See* Mental health and illness

Nervous system: behavior influenced by, **Supp. 3,** 172; convulsion, photographs of, **Supp. 1,** 241; development of, **Supp. 6,** 282–83; disease studies, **Supp. 4,** 249–50; **Supp. 8,** 429; fiber categorization, **Supp. 7,** 280; impulse conduction, **Supp. 6,** 100; **Supp. 7,** 226, 280; perception theory, **Supp. 8,** 344, 345; reflex actions, **Supp. 2,** 390; research on, **Supp. 3,** 805–6; research on origin of, **Supp. 5,** 536; synapse structure, **Supp. 6,** 296; transmitters, **Supp. 3,** 134–36. *See also* Neurology

Nesbitt, Evelyn, reference to, **Supp. 4**, 826–27

Ness, Eliot, reference to, **Supp. 7**, 806

Nestle-LeMur Co., founding of, **Supp. 5**, 512

Netherlands, **Vol. 7, Part 1**, 456; **Vol. 8, Part 1**, 285; diplomacy, **Vol. 3, Part 1**, 89; mission to, **Vol. 5, Part 1**, 346

Neuberger, Maurine Brown, reference to, **Supp. 6**, 475

Neuberger, Richard L., reference to, **Supp. 7**, 814

Neuralgia, facial, **Supp. 4**, 214

Neuroanatomy, studies in, **Supp. 1**, 439, 584; **Supp. 6**, 295–96

Neurological Institute of New York, founding of, **Supp. 4**, 249–50

Neurology, **Vol. 1, Part 2**, 93; **Vol. 3, Part 2**, 18, 469; **Vol. 4, Part 2**, 180, 210; **Vol. 5, Part 1**, 97; **Vol. 5, Part 2**, 451; **Vol. 7, Part 1**, 3, 267 f.; **Vol. 8, Part 1**, 136 f., 282 f.; **Vol. 8, Part 2**, 560; **Vol. 9, Part 1**, 461, 534; **Vol. 10, Part 1**, 613 f.; diagnostic procedures, **Supp. 4**, 214, 250; expert medical testimony, **Supp. 3**, 385; **Supp. 6**, 403; Kennedy syndrome, **Supp. 5**, 384; neuroanatomy, **Supp. 1**, 439, 584; **Supp. 6**, 295–96; neuropathology, **Supp. 1**, 241; **Supp. 2**, 24; organic, **Supp. 2**, 161; psychiatric relationship to, **Supp. 4**, 618; **Supp. 8**, 429–30; research in, **Supp. 1**, 220; **Supp. 2**, 516; sensory perception, **Supp. 2**, 156; shell-shock studies, **Supp. 5**, 383; strychnine studies, **Supp. 2**, 161; surgery, *see* Neurosurgery; teaching of, **Supp. 3**, 620; translation of writings on, **Supp. 3**, 386; writings on, **Vol. 5, Part 2**, 451; **Vol. 7, Part 1**, 62; **Vol. 9, Part 1**, 535; **Vol. 10, Part 1**, 613 f.; **Supp. 3**, 386, 682; **Supp. 4**, 250. *See also* Brain; Nervous system; Psychiatry; Psychoanalysis

Neuropathology, research in, **Supp. 1**, 241; **Supp. 2**, 24

Neurophysiology, **Supp. 7**, 226, 280–81, 476–77

Neuropsychiatry, **Vol. 9, Part 1**, 410; **Vol. 10, Part 1**, 613 f.

Neurosis, basis of, **Supp. 5**, 316–17

Neurosurgery, **Supp. 2**, 137, 209; **Supp. 6**, 130–31, 223–24

Neurotransmitters: early studies in, **Supp. 3**, 134–37; noradrenaline discovery, **Supp. 3**, 136

Neutra, Richard J., reference to, **Supp. 5**, 606

Neutral Ground Agreement (1806). *See* Sabine expedition, La. (1806)

Neutrality: "Freedom of the Seas," **Vol. 4, Part 1**, 70; legal aspects of, **Vol. 9, Part 2**, 105; Proclamation, 1793, **Vol. 5, Part 2**, 8

Neutrality Acts (1935, 1936, 1937), **Supp. 5**, 731; **Supp. 8**, 441

Neutrino, **Supp. 5**, 220

Neutrons: bombardment reactions, **Supp. 5**, 273; research in, **Supp. 5**, 220, 221; **Supp. 6**, 501

Nevada: botany in, **Vol. 6, Part 1**, 162; free-silver agitation, **Vol. 9, Part 2**, 14; frontier life, **Vol. 9, Part 2**, 247; gold rush, **Supp. 5**, 613; governors, **Vol. 1, Part 2**, 358 f.; legal service, **Vol. 1, Part 2**, 102; mining, **Vol. 6, Part 2**, 76; mining law in, **Vol. 9, Part 2**, 13 f.; political service, **Vol. 1, Part 2**, 358; **Vol. 7, Part 1**, 600; politics, **Supp. 5**, 443; public service, **Vol. 7, Part 1**, 462; woman suffrage, **Supp. 5**, 473–74, 742;

Nevins, Allan, reference to, **Supp. 3**, 32

Nevler, Leona, reference to, **Supp. 7**, 531–32

New America, **Supp. 8**, 681

New American Cyclopaedia, edition of, **Vol. 8, Part 1**, 624

New American Orchardist, The, **Vol. 5, Part 2**, 341

New Amsterdam, **Vol. 5, Part 2**, 371; **Vol. 6, Part 2**, 500, 591; **Vol. 7, Part 1**, 34; **Vol. 10, Part 1**, 162; commerce, **Vol. 4, Part 2**, 592; **Vol. 6, Part 1**, 156; first church edifice in, **Vol. 1, Part 2**, 406; surveying

work, **Vol. 5, Part 1**, 336

Newark, N.J.: development, **Vol. 2, Part 1**, 296; **Vol. 10, Part 2**, 571; first bishop of, **Vol. 1, Part 2**, 74; philanthropic services, **Vol. 10, Part 1**, 432 f.; public service, **Vol. 2, Part 2**, 328 f.; street paving fraud in, **Vol. 8, Part 1**, 588; water supply, **Supp. 1**, 663

Newark College, **Vol. 4, Part 1**, 268

Newark Library, development of, **Vol. 3, Part 1**, 57

Newark Museum, **Vol. 3, Part 1**, 318; **Supp. 3**, 30–31; **Supp. 6**, 96

New Bedford, Mass.: founding and naming of, **Vol. 8, Part 2**, 246; history of, **Vol. 4, Part 2**, 4; **Vol. 8, Part 1**, 586 f.; raided by British (1778), **Vol. 8, Part 2**, 246; shipping industry, **Vol. 8, Part 2**, 246; whaling industry, **Vol. 8, Part 2**, 41, 246

New Bern, N.C.: colonial architecture of, **Vol. 4, Part 2**, 417; German Palatines there, **Vol. 6, Part 1**, 58

Newberry, Truman H., references to, **Supp. 3**, 559; **Supp. 4**, 299

Newberry Library (Chicago), **Vol. 7, Part 1**, 447; **Vol. 9, Part 2**, 587; **Supp. 4**, 846; **Supp. 7**, 295

Newbery Medal, **Supp. 7**, 525

New Brunswick, N.J.: civic service, **Vol. 8, Part 2**, 486; legal service, **Vol. 1, Part 2**, 375; Presbytery of, **Vol. 1, Part 2**, 340

New Brunswick Theological Seminary, **Vol. 10, Part 2**, 482

Newburgh, N.Y., founding of, **Vol. 5, Part 2**, 484

Newburgh Letters (1783), **Vol. 1, Part 1**, 355; **Vol. 2, Part 1**, 80; **Vol. 4, Part 1**, 187; **Vol. 7, Part 1**, 510; **Vol. 8, Part 1**, 284 f.; **Vol. 10, Part 1**, 519

Newbury, Mass., **Vol. 7, Part 2**, 242

Newburyport, Mass., **Vol. 3, Part 1**, 282; **Vol. 8, Part 1**, 179; **Supp. 6**, 427, 428; anthropological study of, **Supp. 8**, 684; legal service, **Vol. 1, Part 2**, 549; public service, **Vol. 7, Part 2**, 280, 597

New Caledonia, **Supp. 3**, 583

New capitalism, **Supp. 7**, 809

New Cascade Tunnel (Wash.), **Supp. 7**, 90

New Challenge, founding of, **Supp. 6**, 715

New Choral Society of New York, conducting of, **Vol. 5, Part 2**, 486

New Church, **Vol. 1, Part 1**, 644; **Vol. 8, Part 1**, 448 f. *See also* Swedenborgian church,

New-Church Magazine for Children, **Vol. 8, Part 1**, 455

New Colophon, founding of, **Supp. 7**, azine for Children, **Vol. 8, Part 1**, 455

New Colophon, founding of, **Supp. 7**, 3

Newcomb, Simon, reference to, **Vol. 5, Part 1**, 136

Newcombe, Don, reference to, **Supp. 8**, 142

Newcomer, J. Sidney, reference to, **Supp. 7**, 280

New Criticism, **Supp. 7**, 55, 219, 347, 442; **Supp. 8**, 325–27

New Deal, **Vol. 10, Part 2**, 495; agricultural policies, **Supp. 3**, 319, 434; **Supp. 6**, 487, 559, 638–39; **Supp. 7**, 760–61; **Supp. 8**, 445, 700; American Indian organization opposing, **Supp. 7**, 393–94; antitrust actions, **Supp. 3**, 168; **Supp. 8**, 17; arts projects, **Supp. 8**, 176–77; black representation in, **Supp. 4**, 251; Brain Trust, **Supp. 3**, 399–400, 647; **Supp. 8**, 679; business relationship, **Supp. 5**, 165; **Supp. 6**, 520, 615, 675; child labor codes, **Supp. 3**, 228; congressional opposition, **Supp. 5**, 114, 139, 561–62, 674–75, 703, 715; **Supp. 7**, 312; **Supp. 8**, 27, 68, 247, 268–69, 532; congressional relations, **Supp. 5**, 180–81; congressional support, **Supp. 7**, 467–68, 541; **Supp. 8**, 508; construction projects, **Supp. 8**, 308–9; economic policies, **Supp. 3**, 649–51; **Supp. 8**, 79; Farm Security Administration, **Supp. 6**, 12; Federal Arts Project, **Supp. 3**, 112; **Supp. 6**, 96, 97; federal patronage in, **Supp. 6**, 260, 419, 601; "first hundred days," **Supp. 3**, 650; first steel code, **Supp. 6**, 622;

fiscal policies, **Supp. 6**, 33–34, 377; journalism criticizing, **Supp. 5**, 664; labor legislation, **Supp. 5**, 718–19; labor relations, **Supp. 3**, 347; **Supp. 4**, 376; **Supp. 5**, 263; **Supp. 8**, 375–76; legal defense of, **Supp. 2**, 501; **Supp. 5**, 174, 572; legislation, **Supp. 7**, 635; National Emergency Council, **Supp. 6**, 542, 660; organizations opposing, **Supp. 8**, 592–93; political activity against, **Supp. 4**, 42, 480; public utilities policies, **Supp. 3**, 138; relief legislation, **Supp. 4**, 810; "second," **Supp. 3**, 654–56; social welfare policies, **Supp. 7**, 488, 787; state programs, **Supp. 4**, 612–13; **Supp. 5**, 459; **Supp. 6**, 474–75; Supreme Court decisions on, **Supp. 3**, 99–100, 755, 789, 839; **Supp. 4**, 406–7, 537, 795–97; **Supp. 5**, 358, 572–75; **Supp. 6**, 137–38; **Supp. 7**, 263; **Supp. 8**, 35; *Survey*, **Supp. 6**, 330; tax legislation, **Supp. 5**, 180–81, 712; term coined, **Supp. 3**, 647; work-relief concept, **Supp. 4**, 391–92. *See also* Public works; *specific agencies and legislation*
"New Divinity," opposition to, **Vol. 10, Part 1**, 85
New Durham, N.H., birthplace of the Freewill Baptist denomination, **Vol. 8, Part 1**, 345 f.
New England: agriculture, **Vol. 3, Part 2**, 473; **Vol. 10, Part 2**, 210; "American System of Tariff," **Vol. 6, Part 1**, 45; architectural tradition, **Supp. 4**, 24, 115; birds of, **Vol. 8, Part 2**, 324; blacks imported to, **Vol. 7, Part 2**, 406; Cape Cod, writings on, **Supp. 3**, 461; Catholic church, **Supp. 3**, 568–71; coast survey, **Vol. 3, Part 1**, 106; composers, **Supp. 3**, 42; Confederacy of (1650), **Vol. 4, Part 2**, 396; discovery of, **Vol. 2, Part 1**, 39; Episcopal church, **Vol. 8, Part 2**, 529; exploration of, **Vol. 1, Part 2**, 378; **Vol. 10, Part 1**, 562 f.; federalism in, **Vol. 7, Part 2**, 566 f.; glaciers' effect on, **Vol. 10, Part 2**, 512; historic preservations and restorations, **Supp. 3**, 567; history and folklore studies, **Supp. 3**, 423–24; history of, **Vol. 2, Part 2**, 336; **Vol. 3, Part 1**, 612; **Vol. 5, Part 1**, 333; **Vol. 5, Part 2**, 370; **Vol. 7, Part 1**, 361, 476; **Vol. 8, Part 2**, 388; **Vol. 9, Part 1**, 142; **Vol. 9, Part 2**, 653; iron works in, **Vol. 6, Part 1**, 73; Indian wars in, **Vol. 10, Part 1**, 8; Loyalists, **Vol. 1, Part 2**, 54; **Vol. 6, Part 1**, 175; **Vol. 10, Part 2**, 266; map of, **Vol. 1, Part 2**, 378; Methodist church, **Vol. 6, Part 1**, 112; manufacturing in, **Vol. 3, Part 1**, 563 f.; piracy, **Vol. 3, Part 1**, 483; **Vol. 8, Part 1**, 140 f.; religious persecution, **Vol. 3, Part 2**, 488; tariff, **Vol. 6, Part 1**, 45, 108 f.; textile industry, **Vol. 1, Part 1**, 348; **Vol. 6, Part 1**, 45 f., 47, 51; War of 1812, opposed, **Vol. 9, Part 2**, 145; westward migration from, **Supp. 7**, 353–54; woolen manufacture, **Vol. 6, Part 1**, 51; **Vol. 8, Part 1**, 334; writers, **Supp. 6**, 252; writings on, **Vol. 1, Part 1**, 434; **Vol. 4, Part 1**, 12; **Vol. 5, Part 2**, 72. *See also specific state and city names*
New England Agricultural Society, **Vol. 6, Part 1**, 418
New England Almanack, The, **Vol. 3, Part 1**, 23; **Vol. 4, Part 2**, 390
New England Anti-Slavery Society, **Vol. 3, Part 1**, 407; **Vol. 4, Part 1**, 169; **Vol. 5, Part 2**, 112
New England Bureau of Education, **Vol. 7, Part 2**, 48
New England Club of Loyalists, **Vol. 1, Part 2**, 393
New England Confederation, **Vol. 1, Part 2**, 579
New England Conservatory of Music, **Vol. 3, Part 1**, 513; **Vol. 5, Part 2**, 214; **Vol. 9, Part 2**, 605; **Supp. 1**, 161, 162
New England Council, **Vol. 8, Part 2**, 183
New England Courant, **Vol. 3, Part 2**, 599
New England Divorce Reform League, **Vol. 3, Part 1**, 308
New England Emigrant Aid Co., **Vol. 3, Part 2**, 69; **Vol. 6, Part 1**, 48; **Vol. 8, Part 1**, 54 f.; **Vol. 8, Part 2**, 35; **Vol. 9, Part 2**, 402 f.

New England Farmer, **Vol. 3, Part 2**, 347
New England Female Medical College, **Vol. 4, Part 1**, 604
New England Galaxy, **Vol. 9, Part 2**, 592
New England Girlhood, A, **Vol. 5, Part 2**, 614
New England Historic Genealogical Society, **Vol. 5, Part 2**, 54; **Vol. 9, Part 2**, 503
New England Hospital for Women and Children, **Vol. 10, Part 2**, 619
New England Mutual Life Insurance Co., **Vol. 7, Part 2**, 547
New England Primer, **Vol. 4, Part 2**, 304
New England Review, **Vol. 8, Part 1**, 186 f.
New-Englands Plantation, **Vol. 5, Part 1**, 12
New England Tract Society, **Vol. 7, Part 1**, 245
New England Trust Co., **Vol. 2, Part 2**, 111
New England's Rarities Discovered, **Vol. 5, Part 2**, 219–20
New France: downfall of, **Vol. 3, Part 1**, 317; founding of, in Florida, **Vol. 8, Part 1**, 533; martyrdom, **Vol. 5, Part 2**, 75; missions, **Vol. 5, Part 2**, 74 f.
New Granada, **Vol. 5, Part 2**, 173
New Hampshire: agriculture, **Vol. 8, Part 2**, 120; boundary disputes with Connecticut, **Vol. 8, Part 1**, 426; codification of laws, **Vol. 8, Part 1**, 579 f.; education, **Vol. 4, Part 2**, 76; **Vol. 8, Part 1**, 12 f., 345 f.; exile of governor, **Vol. 10, Part 1**, 656 f.; federalists in, **Vol. 7, Part 2**, 575; geology of, **Vol. 5, Part 1**, 70; governors, **Vol. 1, Part 2**, 9 f., 162 f., 227 f.; **Vol. 2, Part 2**, 54 f.; **Vol. 4, Part 1**, 311; **Vol. 4, Part 2**, 300 f.; **Vol. 7, Part 1**, 195 f.; **Vol. 7, Part 2**, 575; **Vol. 8, Part 2**, 121; **Vol. 9, Part 1**, 291 f.; **Supp. 4**, 899–900; **Supp. 5**, 689; **Supp. 7**, 73; historian, state, **Vol. 1, Part 2**, 488; history of, **Vol. 1, Part 2**, 153; **Vol. 2, Part 2**, 603; **Vol. 3, Part 2**, 304 f.; **Vol. 6, Part 2**, 581; **Vol. 7, Part 1**, 127; **Vol. 10, Part 1**, 653 f., 656 f.; land grants, **Vol. 6, Part 1**, 307; legal service, **Vol. 1, Part 2**, 210, 380; **Vol. 2, Part 2**, 111; **Vol. 3, Part 1**, 354, 409; **Vol. 6, Part 1**, 304; **Vol. 6, Part 2**, 366; **Vol. 8, Part 1**, 230, 341, 427, 478, 564, 579; **Vol. 9, Part 1**, 291, 293; **Vol. 10, Part 1**, 566 f.; **Vol. 10, Part 2**, 388; maps of, **Vol. 5, Part 2**, 588; Massachusetts, withdrawal from, **Vol. 8, Part 1**, 356 f.; "Old Home Week," origin of, **Vol. 8, Part 2**, 121; political service, **Vol. 1, Part 2**, 11, 144, 153, 162, 227, 275, 334; **Vol. 2, Part 2**, 54; **Vol. 3, Part 1**, 600; **Vol. 3, Part 2**, 293; **Vol. 4, Part 1**, 304, 311, 409; **Vol. 4, Part 2**, 105, 300; **Vol. 5, Part 1**, 35; **Vol. 5, Part 2**, 587, 588; **Vol. 7, Part 1**, 196; **Vol. 7, Part 2**, 303, 575; **Vol. 8, Part 1**, 12; **Vol. 8, Part 2**, 121; **Vol. 9, Part 1**, 291; **Vol. 10, Part 1**, 28, 566 f., 585 f., 653 f., 656 f.; **Vol. 10, Part 2**, 388, 488; politics, **Supp. 3**, 425, 543; **Supp. 4**, 164–65, 899–900; **Supp. 5**, 689–90; printer, first in, **Vol. 3, Part 2**, 561; public service, **Vol. 1, Part 2**, 5 f.; **Vol. 3, Part 2**, 494 f.; **Vol. 4, Part 1**, 304 f; **Vol. 4, Part 2**, 105, 446; **Vol. 5, Part 1**, 34, 5; **Vol. 5, Part 2**, 404 f.; **Vol. 6, Part 1**, 81, 304, 308; **Vol. 6, Part 2**, 580; **Vol. 7, Part 2**, 340; **Vol. 8, Part 1**, 12 f.; reforestation in, **Vol. 8, Part 2**, 121; Republican party, **Vol. 8, Part 2**, 120; Revolutionary War period, **Vol. 10, Part 2**, 71
New Hampshire Historical Society, **Vol. 1, Part 2**, 6; **Vol. 7, Part 1**, 127
New Hampshire Journal, **Vol. 7, Part 1**, 127
New Hampshire Medical Society, **Vol. 1, Part 2**, 11; founding of, **Vol. 7, Part 2**, 340
New Harmony, Ind., **Vol. 3, Part 2**, 479; **Vol. 6, Part 1**, 190; **Vol. 7, Part 1**, 402; **Vol. 7, Part 2**, 119; **Vol. 8, Part 2**, 224, 402; **Vol. 9, Part 2**, 648
New Haven, Conn., **Vol. 3, Part 1**, 612, **Vol. 6, Part 1**, 138; business and civic service, **Vol. 9, Part 1**, 456; colonial architecture of, **Vol. 5, Part 1**, 83;

34, 500, 502, 579–80; **Vol. 2, Part 1,** 358; **Vol. 3, Part 2,** 288; **Vol. 6, Part 1,** 288, 442; **Vol. 8, Part 1,** 87; Catholic church, **Vol. 1, Part 1,** 321; charities, **Vol. 4, Part 2,** 398; **Vol. 5, Part 2,** 547; cholera epidemic, **Vol. 9, Part 2,** 85; city charter of, **Vol. 3, Part 1,** 545 f.; civic service, **Vol. 4, Part 2,** 353; **Vol. 5, Part 1,** 300; Creole families of, **Vol. 1, Part 2,** 479; Delgado Museum of Art, **Vol. 4, Part 2,** 353; draining of, **Vol. 1, Part 2,** 111; **Vol. 8, Part 2,** 125; early settlement, **Vol. 3, Part 1,** 534; educational service, **Vol. 3, Part 1,** 493 f.; **Vol. 9, Part 1,** 404; flood control, **Vol. 8, Part 1,** 589; founding, of, **Vol. 1, Part 2,** 251; **Vol. 7, Part 2,** 318 f.; French newspapers, **Vol. 9, Part 2,** 383; gambling licensed, **Vol. 8, Part 2,** 28; health service, **Vol. 8, Part 1,** 575; inner navigation canal, **Supp. 3,** 910; Jackson's defense of, in War of 1812, **Vol. 8, Part 1,** 480; jazz, **Supp. 2,** 502; **Supp. 3,** 541; **Supp. 5,** 106; **Supp. 6,** 41; legal service, **Vol. 5, Part 1,** 300; medical development in, **Vol. 9, Part 2,** 85; *Picayune,* **Vol. 5, Part 2,** 327; **Vol. 7, Part 1,** 499; **Supp. 5,** 244; political service, **Vol. 1, Part 2,** 140, 461; politics, **Supp. 7,** 555; reform, **Vol. 3, Part 2,** 292; religious services, **Vol. 3, Part 1,** 473 f.; riots in, **Vol. 1, Part 2,** 351; **Vol. 5, Part 2,** 305; **Vol. 6, Part 2,** 39; **Vol. 7, Part 1,** 487; **Vol. 7, Part 2,** 611; **Vol. 10, Part 1,** 458; Roman Catholic diocese, **Supp. 7,** 668–69; sanitation, **Vol. 5, Part 2,** 193; school desegregation, **Supp. 8,** 500; stones, **Vol. 5, Part 2,** 390; surgery in, **Vol. 9, Part 2,** 85; theater in, **Vol. 3, Part 1,** 133; **Vol. 6, Part 1,** 493; Vieux Carré, **Vol. 6, Part 1,** 19; White League, **Vol. 4, Part 2,** 353; yellow fever epidemic in, **Vol. 9, Part 2,** 85

New Orleans Canal Co., **Supp. 4,** 193

New Orleans Polyclinic, absorption by Tulane, **Vol. 3, Part 1,** 582

New Panama Canal Co., **Supp. 4,** 193

Newport, R.I., **Vol. 6, Part 1,** 547; Congregationalism, **Vol. 9, Part 2,** 18; founding of, **Vol. 2, Part 2,** 258; history of, **Vol. 6, Part 2,** 271; **Vol. 8, Part 1,** 445; influence of library at, **Vol. 8, Part 1,** 445; Naval Academy, removal to, during Civil War, **Vol. 8, Part 2,** 72; Philosophical Society of, **Vol. 8, Part 1,** 445; privateering from, **Vol. 1, Part 2,** 512; settlement of, **Vol. 2, Part 2,** 155; **Vol. 3, Part 1,** 604

New Purchase, The, **Vol. 4, Part 2,** 119

New Republic, The, **Vol. 9, Part 2,** 121; columns, **Supp. 7,** 249; correspondents, **Supp. 7,** 261, 320; editing, **Supp. 6,** 15, 392; **Supp. 7,** 762, 811–12; founding of, **Supp. 1,** 210; **Supp. 7,** 10, 316; poetry editor, **Supp. 4,** 841

New Scholasticism, The, founding of, **Supp. 2,** 506

New School Association, founding of, **Supp. 3,** 563

New School for Social Research, **Supp. 3,** 809; **Supp. 5,** 431; **Supp. 7,** 801; **Supp. 8,** 488; founding of, **Supp. 2,** 563; **Supp. 4,** 63, 586–87; **Supp. 5,** 172; German refugee scholars, **Supp. 4,** 80

New School Presbyterian Church, **Vol. 1, Part 2,** 595; **Vol. 4, Part 2,** 396

News collecting, early, **Vol. 9, Part 2,** 592

Newsday, founding of, **Supp. 7,** 603–4

"New Side," **Vol. 9, Part 2,** 370

"New South," **Vol. 5, Part 1,** 57; **Vol. 5, Part 2,** 552

Newspaper Enterprise Association, **Supp. 5,** 499

Newspaper Feature Service, **Supp. 3,** 428

"Newspaperman's newspaper," (*New York Sun*), **Vol. 3, Part 1,** 52

Newspapers: Asian correspondents, **Supp. 4,** 679; association, **Vol. 2, Part 1,** 37; black, **Supp. 2, 3;** **Supp. 3,** 535, 596, 632–33; **Supp. 7,** 203, 204; broadcasting interests, **Supp. 5,** 615; cartoons and caricatures, *see* Cartoons and caricatures; civic

improvement, **Supp. 4,** 222; color press, **Supp. 2,** 242; columnist work, **Vol. 3, Part 2,** 364; **Vol. 9, Part 2,** 317; comic strips, *see* Comic strips; comic strips, origin of, **Vol. 7, Part 2,** 112; dealers consolidated, **Vol. 3, Part 1,** 278 f.; Denver wars between, **Supp. 1,** 95; editing of, **Vol. 3, Part 2,** 476, 486 f., 515; **Vol. 4, Part 1,** 425; **Vol. 4, Part 2,** 11; **Vol. 6, Part 1,** 396; **Vol. 5, Part 2,** 45, 48, 160, 417, 444, 452; **Vol. 6, Part 2,** 159, 166, 267, 290, 568; **Vol. 7, Part 1,** 48, 204 f.; **Vol. 7, Part 2,** 475; **Vol. 8, Part 2,** 468, 491, 511, 526; **Vol. 9, Part 1,** 577; **Vol. 9, Part 2,** 98; **Vol. 10, Part 2,** 292, 617, 633; editorials, **Supp. 1,** 391; **Supp. 3,** 850–51; **Supp. 5,** 279, 391–92, 499; **Supp. 6,** 676–77; English-language in Europe, **Supp. 4,** 687; English-language in Japan, **Supp. 4,** 284–85; feature syndication, **Supp. 3,** 427–28; **Supp. 4,** 693; first in California, **Vol. 2, Part 2,** 323; first chain of, **Vol. 8, Part 2,** 518; first daily in U.S., **Vol. 3, Part 1,** 514 f.; **Vol. 8, Part 1,** 139 f., 638; first "extra," **Vol. 8, Part 1,** 299 f.; first in France, **Vol. 4, Part 1,** 91; first in Hawaii, **Vol. 1, Part 1,** 295; **Vol. 5, Part 1,** 618; first illustrated daily in U.S., **Vol. 8, Part 1,** 332 f.; first with literary supplement, **Vol. 1, Part 2,** 559; first in the middle colonies, **Vol. 1, Part 2,** 553; first in New Jersey, **Vol. 7, Part 2,** 227; first in Pennsylvania, **Vol. 1, Part 2,** 553; first penny, **Vol. 3, Part 1,** 155; **Vol. 6, Part 1,** 60; first penny, **Vol. 9, Part 2,** 82; first prize contests used, **Vol. 3, Part 2,** 572; first scientific, **Vol. 8, Part 1,** 101 f.; first in South Carolina, **Vol. 10, Part 1,** 644 f; first syndicate, **Vol. 8, Part 2,** 518; first in U.S., **Vol. 2, Part 1,** 456; **Vol. 4, Part 2,** 304; **Vol. 8, Part 1,** 139 f.; first in Utah, **Vol. 2, Part 2,** 353; German, **Vol. 4, Part 1,** 262; **Vol. 5, Part 2,** 259; **Supp. 1,** 72; Greek-American, **Supp. 7,** 102–3; Hearst chain, **Supp. 5,** 283–84, 448–49; Hearst-Pulitzer competition, **Supp. 3,** 144; **Supp. 5,** 284; illustrated methods, **Vol. 8, Part 2,** 113; Jewish, **Supp. 3,** 513, 711–12; letters-to-the-editor, **Supp. 5,** 488; management, **Supp. 3,** 144, 816–17; **Supp. 4,** 12, 189, 215–16, 217, 686–87; **Supp. 5,** 55–56; **Supp. 7,** 369–70; monopolies, **Supp. 4,** 180; New South, **Supp. 8,** 404–5; "newspaper of record" concept, **Supp. 3,** 787–88; **Supp. 5,** 362–63; period collection of, **Vol. 3, Part 1,** 553 f.; **Vol. 3, Part 2,** 519; political importance of in colonial period, **Vol. 3, Part 1,** 212; printing processes, **Supp. 2,** 733; publishing, **Vol. 1, Part 2,** 437, 565; **Vol. 5, Part 1,** 535; **Vol. 6, Part 2,** 130; **Vol. 7, Part 1,** 271; **Vol. 7, Part 2,** 376 f., 643; **Vol. 8, Part 2,** 517, 519 f.; **Vol. 10, Part 2,** 500; rapid service developed; **Vol. 10, Part 1,** 574 f.; rotogravure picture sections, **Supp. 5,** 394, 551; Scripps-Howard chain, **Supp. 2,** 606; second in colonies, **Vol. 3, Part 2,** 17; **Vol. 5, Part 2,** 458; sketch artists, **Supp. 2,** 238; Southern California boosting by, **Supp. 3,** 156; special sections, **Supp. 5,** 552; sports editing, **Vol. 5, Part 2,** 92; syndication, **Supp. 4,** 38; tabloids, **Supp. 4,** 645–46; **Supp. 5,** 205, 323, 449, 453; telegraph used by, **Vol. 1, Part 2,** 198; third in U.S., **Vol. 1, Part 2,** 553; wirephotos, **Supp. 5,** 323–24; wire services, **Supp. 1,** 510; **Supp. 5,** 286; women connected with, **Vol. 1, Part 2,** 581; **Vol. 8, Part 2,** 518; women's page, **Supp. 1,** 91; writings on, **Supp. 4,** 481–82; **Supp. 7,** 473; Yiddish-language, **Supp. 5,** 95, 96, 597. *See also* Journalism; Publishing; *specific publications*

News service, foreign, promotion of, **Vol. 6, Part 1,** 61

New Sweden: history of, **Vol. 8, Part 1,** 238 f., 627; immigration to, **Vol. 9, Part 2,** 447

Newsweek, **Supp. 6,** 23–24, 366–67; **Supp. 7,** 296

New Testament, scholarship, **Supp. 4,** 467–68

New Theatre (New York City), founding of, **Supp. 2,** 10

New thought, **Vol. 3, Part 2,** 464,; **Vol. 7, Part 1,** 318; **Vol. 8, Part 1,** 304 f.

Newton, Mass., **Vol. 7, Part 2,** 398, 495

Newton Theological Institution, **Vol. 5, Part 1,** 235, 270

Newtowne (Cambridge), Mass., founding of, **Vol. 8, Part 1,** 66 f.

New towns. _See_ Model communities

New Universal Atlas, A, **Vol. 7, Part 1,** 61

New World (journal), **Vol. 3, Part 2,** 222

New World: Problems in Political Geography, The, **Supp. 4,** 99

New York Academy of Medicine, **Vol. 8, Part 1,** 269 f.; **Vol. 9, Part 1,** 606; **Vol. 10, Part 2,** 282

New York Adult Education Council, founding of, **Supp. 2,** 186

New York Advocate, **Vol. 1, Part 1,** 575

New York Age, **Supp. 3,** 535; **Supp. 7,** 767

New York American, **Supp. 6,** 213–14; comic strips, **Supp. 5,** 456

New York & Erie Railroad, **Vol. 6, Part 1,** 405 f.

New York and New Jersey Telephone Co., **Supp. 3,** 299

New York & Ohio Co., **Vol. 7, Part 2,** 128

New York Anti-Slavery Society, **Vol. 5, Part 2,** 12; **Vol. 9, Part 2,** 5

New York Aquarium, **Supp. 8,** 485–86

New York Associated Press, **Vol. 1, Part 2,** 84; **Vol. 9, Part 2,** 74

New York Association for the Blind, **Supp. 3,** 364

New York Barge Canal, **Supp. 3,** 311

New York Bible Society, **Vol. 3, Part 1,** 345

New York Botanical Garden, **Vol. 2, Part 1,** 100; **Vol. 7, Part 2,** 480; **Vol. 8, Part 2,** 269; **Vol. 9, Part 2,** 597; administration, **Supp. 2,** 374; **Supp. 6,** 450; founding and development of, **Supp. 1,** 122; orchid collection, **Supp. 4,** 16–17

New York Bureau of Municipal Research, **Supp. 2,** 608

New York Canoe Club, **Vol. 1, Part 1,** 150

New York Celtics (basketball), **Supp. 8,** 358

New York Central Railroad, **Vol. 2, Part 1,** 158; **Vol. 2, Part 2,** 446; **Vol. 8, Part 1,** 253 f., 582; **Vol. 8, Part 2,** 424; **Vol. 9, Part 1,** 236; **Supp. 1,** 574; early history of, **Vol. 10, Part 1,** 172 f.; Richardson-Young takeover, **Supp. 6,** 540, 721–22

New York Central Railroad Station (Rochester), architecture, **Supp. 4,** 105

New York Charity Organization Society, **Vol. 6, Part 1,** 468; **Vol. 7, Part 2,** 410; **Supp. 4,** 227, 546–47

New York Citizen, **Vol. 8, Part 2,** 134

New York City: acting in, **Vol. 4, Part 1,** 314; adult education, **Supp. 3,** 511; American Labor party, **Supp. 5,** 466–67; **Supp. 8,** 512; antinoise movement, **Vol. 8, Part 1,** 541; architecture, **Vol. 1, Part 1,** 587; **Vol. 3, Part 1,** 104; **Vol. 4, Part 2,** 240; **Vol. 6, Part 1,** 599 f.; **Vol. 6, Part 2,** 232; **Vol. 8, Part 1,** 507 f.; **Vol. 8, Part 2,** 98; **Supp. 4,** 281–82; **Supp. 5,** 133–34, 408; **Supp. 6,** 26; assessment and taxation, **Supp. 6,** 522; Astor library, **Vol. 1, Part 1,** 39; Astor Place riots, **Vol. 3, Part 1,** 41, 553; banking, **Vol. 1, Part 2,** 443; **Vol. 2, Part 2,** 359, 613; **Vol. 3, Part 1,** 486 f.; **Vol. 6, Part 1,** 490; **Vol. 6, Part 2,** 22; **Vol. 7, Part 1,** 259, 360; **Vol. 9, Part 1,** 616; **Vol. 9, Part 2,** 132; **Vol. 10, Part 1,** 438; banking panics, **Vol. 2, Part 2,** 375; **Vol. 3, Part 1,** 484 f.; Bar Association, **Vol. 6, Part 2,** 327; Bedloe's Island, **Vol. 1, Part 1,** 592; Bellevue Hospital, **Vol. 6, Part 1,** 240; **Vol. 10, Part 1,** 150; **Vol. 10, Part 2,** 463; black leadership in, **Supp. 4,** 607–8; **Supp. 5,** 548; blizzard of 1888, **Vol. 8, Part 1,** 393; Booth's Theatre, **Vol. 1, Part 1,**

256; **Vol. 1, Part 2,** 446; Boston, first post road to, **Vol. 6, Part 1,** 437; Botanical Garden, _see_ New York Botanical Garden; Brick Church, **Vol. 9, Part 1,** 480; bridges, **Supp. 3,** 530–31; Broadway Tabernacle, **Vol. 9, Part 2,** 299, 303; Brooklyn consolidated with, **Vol. 9, Part 2,** 123; building construction, **Supp. 1,** 342, 430; **Supp. 6,** 337, 593; **Supp. 7,** 800; Cathedral of St. John the Divine, **Vol. 3, Part 2,** 354; **Vol. 4, Part 1,** 594; **Vol. 4, Part 2,** 389; **Vol. 5, Part 1,** 421; Catholic archbishop, first, **Vol. 3, Part 1,** 470 f.; Catholic church, **Vol. 1, Part 2,** 373; **Vol. 6, Part 2,** 226; Catholic mayor of, first, **Vol. 4, Part 1,** 463; Central Park, **Vol. 4, Part 1,** 471; **Vol. 4, Part 2,** 5; **Vol. 7, Part 2,** 25 f., 600; **Vol. 8, Part 2,** 200, 464; **Vol. 9, Part 1,** 151; Century Club, **Vol. 1, Part 2,** 169; **Vol. 3, Part 1,** 535 f.; Chamber of Commerce, **Vol. 2, Part 2,** 582; **Vol. 6, Part 1,** 445 f., 450; **Vol. 8, Part 1,** 348 f.; Charity Organization Society, _see_ New York Charity Organization Society; charter of 1873, **Vol. 1, Part 2,** 373; charter revision, **Supp. 2,** 250, 497; Child Hygiene Bureau, **Supp. 3,** 28; Children's Welfare Federation, **Supp. 3,** 159; cholera epidemic of 1830, **Vol. 8, Part 2,** 238; Choral Society, **Vol. 4, Part 2,** 505; Church of the Ascension, **Vol. 4, Part 1,** 491; City Club, **Vol. 5, Part 2,** 307; City Hall, **Vol. 6, Part 2,** 232; **Supp. 6,** 26; city seal of, **Vol. 6, Part 1,** 181; civic and philanthropic service, **Vol. 1, Part 1,** 549; **Vol. 1, Part 2,** 359; **Vol. 2, Part 2,** 166, 566; **Vol. 3, Part 1,** 279, 346 f., 378, 462 f., 493; **Vol. 4, Part 1,** 475, 535; **Vol. 4, Part 2,** 491 f.; **Vol. 5, Part 1,** 573 f.; **Vol. 5, Part 2,** 308, 334; **Vol. 6, Part 1,** 172, 181; **Vol. 6, Part 2,** 293; **Vol. 7, Part 1,** 37, 168 f., 615; **Vol. 7, Part 2,** 56, 72, 243, 410, 630; **Vol. 8, Part 1,** 106 f., 127 f., 278, 348 f.; **Vol. 8, Part 2,** 570, 572; **Vol. 9, Part 1,** 209; **Vol. 9, Part 2,** 129 f.; "Cleopatra's Needle," **Vol. 3, Part 1,** 277; **Vol. 3, Part 2,** 276; **Vol. 4, Part 1,** 437; clothing factory, early, **Vol. 7, Part 2,** 45; clothing industry in, **Vol. 7, Part 2,** 45; commerce commission, **Supp. 5,** 634; Committee on Safety, **Supp. 4,** 603; **Supp. 7,** 608; Communist party, **Supp. 5,** 500; community councils, **Supp. 6,** 484; Conference of Charities and Corrections, founded, **Vol. 9, Part 2,** 15; consolidation plan for, **Vol. 9, Part 2,** 123; Consumers' League, **Supp. 7,** 608; Cooper Union, **Vol. 2, Part 2,** 410; **Vol. 4, Part 2,** 605; **Vol. 8, Part 2,** 467; corruption investigations, **Supp. 4,** 856; **Supp. 6,** 570; **Supp. 7,** 4–5, 585–86; Cotton Exchange, **Vol. 5, Part 1,** 484; crime investigations, **Supp. 7,** 585–86; Crystal Palace, **Vol. 3, Part 1,** 258; defense, **Vol. 3, Part 1,** 210; **Vol. 9, Part 2,** 247, 599; directories of, **Vol. 9, Part 2,** 652; docks, **Vol. 7, Part 1,** 607 f.; **Vol. 9, Part 1,** 338; draft riots in, **Vol. 4, Part 1,** 47; **Vol. 10, Part 1,** 145; early history of, **Vol. 1, Part 2,** 68; education, **Vol. 3, Part 1,** 346 f., 458 f.; **Vol. 4, Part 2,** 47; **Vol. 5, Part 1,** 405; **Vol. 8, Part 1,** 44 f., 351 f.; **Vol. 9, Part 1,** 353; education board, **Supp. 8,** 135; Emergency Relief Bureau, **Supp. 6,** 102; engineering, **Vol. 7, Part 1,** 473; engraving, "historical," of 1806, **Vol. 6, Part 1,** 165; epidemics, **Supp. 4,** 287; Exhibition of the Industries of All Nations, **Vol. 3, Part 1,** 258; Federal Art Project, **Supp. 7,** 184; Federal Hall, **Vol. 6, Part 1,** 166; financial management of, **Vol. 4, Part 1,** 535; fire-alarm system, **Supp. 1,** 554; firehouses, architecture of, **Vol. 6, Part 1,** 86; fire prevention, early advocacy of, **Vol. 3, Part 1,** 248; first comprehensive zoning, **Supp. 6,** 522; first municipal art exhibit, **Supp. 8,** 240; first omnibus in, **Vol. 9, Part 1,** 583; first savings bank in, **Vol. 7, Part 2,** 630; free circulating library, **Vol. 3, Part 2,** 356; fusion movements, **Supp. 4,** 825–26; **Supp. 5,** 285–86; Fusion party in, **Vol. 7, Part 1,** 37 f.; garment industry, **Supp. 3,** 609–10; *Gazette,* New York's first newspaper, **Vol. 1, Part 2,** 564; "ghetto," **Vol. 8, Part 2,** 165; Gold Exchange, **Vol. 2, Part 2,** 298; Grace Church, **Vol. 5, Part 1,** 421; **Vol. 8, Part 1,** 127 f.; Gramercy Park, **Vol. 8, Part 2,** 220; Greenwich Village, **Vol. 10, Part 1,** 485 f.; *A Guide to the City of New York,* published 1836, **Vol. 3, Part 1,** 319; handicapped education, **Supp. 3,** 365; harbor, **Supp. 7,** 552–53; Harlem River Bridge, **Vol. 5, Part 2,** 201; health department, **Supp. 3,** 312; **Supp. 6,** 424; Hearst newspapers in, **Supp. 5,** 284–85; Hell Gate Bridge, construction of, **Vol. 8, Part 1,** 418; home-rule issue, **Supp. 3,** 717, 718; hospital, **Vol. 1, Part 1,** 598; hospital commissioner, **Supp. 3,** 313, 320; hotels, **Vol. 1, Part 1,** 400 f.; **Vol. 1, Part 2,** 419; housing and parks, **Supp. 3,** 744; **Supp. 5,** 630–31; **Supp. 6,** 615; Irish Societies of, **Vol. 8, Part 2,** 19; Jewish organizations, **Supp. 4,** 539; journalism, **Vol. 2, Part 2,** 455 f.; **Vol. 3, Part 2,** 576; **Vol. 5, Part 1,** 424, 483; **Vol. 6, Part 1,** 283; **Vol. 7, Part 1,** 534, **Vol. 7, Part 2,** 538 f.; **Vol. 8, Part 1,** 260 f., 409, 474 f.; **Vol. 8, Part 2,** 475; **Vol. 9, Part 2,** 551; judicial reform, **Supp. 6,** 87–88; Kips Bay, **Vol. 7, Part 1,** 367; laws, codification of, **Vol. 1, Part 2,** 374; lighting system, electric, **Vol. 5, Part 2,** 509; literati of, **Vol. 1, Part 2,** 469; **Vol. 3, Part 2,** 305; lithograph of, **Vol. 5, Part 1,** 460; Little Church Around the Corner, **Vol. 5, Part 1,** 255; **Vol. 7, Part 1,** 204; Lower East Side, **Supp. 3,** 329, 330; Lyceum of Natural History, **Vol. 3, Part 1,** 204; Madison Square Presbyterian Church, **Vol. 7, Part 2,** 245; Manhattan elevated railway, **Vol. 8, Part 1,** 221; Manhattan Island, purchase of, **Vol. 7, Part 1,** 34; mass meetings, Civil War, **Vol. 4, Part 2,** 405; mayor, first native-born, **Vol. 10, Part 1,** 164; mayors, **Supp. 2,** 330; **Supp. 4,** 465–66, 855–56; **Supp. 5,** 227; **Supp. 7,** 585–86; medical schools in, **Vol. 6, Part 2,** 268; medical services, **Supp. 6,** 81–82; Merchantile Agency, first of its kind, **Vol. 3, Part 1,** 503; **Vol. 9, Part 1,** 558 f; **Vol. 10, Part 2,** 409; Metropolitan Museum of Art, **Vol. 5, Part 2,** 144; Metropolitan Street Railway Co., **Vol. 7, Part 2,** 358 f.; Municipal Art Committee, **Supp. 7,** 70; Murray Hill, **Vol. 7, Part 1,** 367; National City Bank, **Vol. 9, Part 2,** 26; "Neutral Ground," around, during Revolution, **Vol. 3, Part 1,** 214; newspaper, first, **Vol. 1, Part 2,** 564; Pathological Society, **Vol. 7, Part 2,** 505; Peace Society, **Vol. 3, Part 1,** 345; Philharmonic Society, *see* New York Philharmonic; *New York Picayune,* **Vol. 9, Part 2,** 488; nightclubs, **Supp. 8,** 546, 547, 562; official greeters, **Supp. 7,** 779–80, 496; organized crime in, **Supp. 7,** 484–85, 632–33; **Supp. 8,** 396–97; parades, **Supp. 7,** 779, 780; Park Avenue Hotel, **Vol. 9, Part 2,** 4; park planning, **Vol. 1, Part 2,** 408; **Vol. 8, Part 2,** 220; parks, **Supp. 4,** 213; Pennsylvania Station, **Vol. 8, Part 1,** 406, 418; "People's University," **Vol. 6, Part 1,** 155; philanthropy, **Vol. 6, Part 1,** 172; **Supp. 6,** 24; piano manufacture, **Vol. 10, Part 1,** 581; pilotage system in harbor, **Vol. 1, Part 2,** 398; police, **Vol. 2, Part 1,** 386; **Vol. 6, Part 1,** 229; **Vol. 8, Part 2,** 136; **Supp. 3,** 116; **Supp. 7,** 779–80; political reform movements, **Supp. 3,** 605, 717–18; **Supp. 4,** 465–66, 547, 825–26, 870, 885–86, 904; **Supp. 8,** 467, *see also subhead:* fusion movements; politics, **Supp. 4,** 88, 464–66, 542–43; **Supp. 6,** 88, 141–42, 280, 294–95; **Supp. 8,** 27, 397; Polyclinic Hospital, **Vol. 10, Part 2,** 576; Port Authority, **Supp. 1,** 589; Post-Graduate Medical School, **Vol. 8, Part 2,** 132; Presbyterian church, **Supp. 5,** 116–17; printing in colonial period, **Vol. 1, Part 2,** 564; **Vol. 7, Part 2,** 226; **Vol. 8, Part 1,** 637 f.; Prison Association, **Vol. 3, Part 1,** 493; prisons,

Supp. 8, 495; progressive education, **Supp. 3,** 375–76; Prohibition enforcement, **Supp. 7,** 805; as prominent port, **Vol. 6, Part 2,** 306; prostitution reform efforts, **Supp. 5,** 698, 699; public health, **Vol. 1, Part 2,** 262 f.; **Vol. 3, Part 1,** 377; **Vol. 5, Part 1,** 607; **Vol. 8, Part 1,** 44 f.; **Vol. 9, Part 1,** 187, 348; **Supp. 2,** 121; **Supp. 6,** 192; public parks, **Vol. 7, Part 2,** 600; public schools, **Vol. 6, Part 1,** 155; **Vol. 6, Part 2,** 124, 445; **Vol. 9, Part 1,** 353; public utilities, **Supp. 3,** 138, 715–16; public welfare, **Vol. 6, Part 2,** 179; railroad development, **Vol. 2, Part 2,** 446 f.; Rapid Transit Commission, **Vol. 8, Part 1,** 634; real estate, **Vol. 1, Part 1,** 397; **Vol. 2, Part 2,** 136; **Vol. 5, Part 2,** 392; **Vol. 6, Part 1,** 448; **Vol. 9, Part 2,** 69 f., 132; **Supp. 2,** 64; **Supp. 6,** 23, 24; reform measures, **Vol. 4, Part 1,** 335; **Vol. 5, Part 1,** 523; **Vol. 6, Part 1,** 229; **Vol. 7, Part 2,** 56, 506; **Vol. 8, Part 1,** 607; **Vol. 9, Part 1,** 593; restaurant business, **Vol. 3, Part 1,** 227; **Vol. 9, Part 1,** 97 f.; Riverside Drive, construction of, **Vol. 6, Part 1,** 548; Roman Catholic diocese, **Supp. 8,** 613–15; St. Patrick's Cathedral, **Vol. 8, Part 1,** 507 f.; St. Thomas Church, **Vol. 4, Part 1,** 388; sanitation, **Vol. 8, Part 1,** 607; **Vol. 8, Part 2,** 404; **Vol. 10, Part 1,** 456 f.; **Supp. 4,** 855; savings bank, first, **Vol. 7, Part 2,** 630; school buildings, **Supp. 5,** 301; School of Philanthropy, **Vol. 6, Part 1,** 223; school system centralization, **Supp. 4,** 134; school system survey, **Supp. 3,** 328; Seabury corruption investigation, *see subhead:* corruption investigations; Seamen's Institute, **Vol. 7, Part 2,** 129; settlement work, **Supp. 3,** 175; shipbuilding, **Vol. 1, Part 2,** 156, 215; **Vol. 2, Part 2,** 46; **Vol. 8, Part 2,** 341 f.; shipyards, **Vol. 1, Part 2,** 156; silver-workers of, **Vol. 1, Part 2,** 406; **Vol. 6, Part 1,** 181; skyscrapers, **Supp. 3,** 611–12; slavery, **Vol. 1, Part 2,** 507; **Vol. 9, Part 2,** 583; slum clearance, **Vol. 8, Part 1,** 607; **Supp. 2,** 684; Socialist activity in, **Vol. 3, Part 1,** 223; **Vol. 8, Part 2,** 129; social leadership of McAllister, **Vol. 4, Part 2,** 357; **Vol. 6, Part 1,** 547 f.; Social Reform Club, **Vol. 2, Part 2,** 566; **Supp. 3,** 297–98, 545; social register, **Supp. 5,** 707–8; social work, **Supp. 4,** 391–92; **Supp. 6,** 102–3; Sons of Liberty, **Vol. 8, Part 2,** 495; "Stalwart" supremacy in, **Vol. 8, Part 1,** 484; steamship, launching of first oceanic, **Vol. 1, Part 2,** 156; Stock Exchange, **Vol. 2, Part 2,** 76, 133; **Vol. 4, Part 2,** 393 f.; **Vol. 5, Part 1,** 247; streetcar strike, **Vol. 5, Part 2,** 196; street railways, **Vol. 1, Part 2,** 408; **Vol. 2, Part 2,** 544; **Vol. 4, Part 2,** 605; **Vol. 6, Part 1,** 478; **Vol. 7, Part 2,** 56, 277; **Vol. 8, Part 2,** 265 f.; **Vol. 9, Part 1,** 124; **Vol. 9, Part 2,** 232, 241; subway system, **Vol. 1, Part 2,** 408; **Vol. 2, Part 2,** 544; **Vol. 4, Part 1,** 8; **Vol. 4, Part 2,** 605; **Vol. 7, Part 2,** 56, 277, 602; **Vol. 9, Part 1,** 124; **Supp. 2,** 559, 675; **Supp. 4,** 855; **Supp. 5,** 228; teachers' issues, **Supp. 8,** 132; teachers' training in, **Vol. 3, Part 1,** 347; temperance reform in, **Vol. 3, Part 1,** 221; tenements, supervision of, **Vol. 1, Part 2,** 373; **Vol. 8, Part 2,** 551; **Vol. 8, Part 1,** 607; theater, only one in 1796, **Vol. 3, Part 1,** 516 f.; theaters in, **Vol. 1, Part 1,** 256; **Vol. 1, Part 2,** 446; **Vol. 5, Part 2,** 284; **Vol. 8, Part 1,** 221; Tilden Library, **Vol. 9, Part 2,** 541; Tompkins Square labor demonstration, **Vol. 9, Part 2,** 252; traffic congestion in, **Vol. 8, Part 1,** 138 f.; traffic regulation, **Supp. 3,** 253–54; transit strike, **Supp. 8,** 513; transportation in, **Vol. 2, Part 2,** 544; **Vol. 5, Part 1,** 483; **Vol. 6, Part 2,** 17; **Vol. 7, Part 2,** 277, 602; **Vol. 8, Part 1,** 418; **Vol. 9, Part 1,** 529, 568, 583; **Vol. 9, Part 2,** 241; Trinity Church, **Vol. 2, Part 1,** 86; **Vol. 3, Part 1,** 327 f.; **Vol. 5, Part 1,** 93; tunnel engineering, **Supp. 4,** 690, 757; Union League Club, **Vol. 1, Part 2,** 169; **Vol. 7, Part 2,** 26;

Vol. 8, Part 2, 134; universities and colleges, **Supp. 5,** 488; University Club, **Vol. 5, Part 1,** 180; Washington Square, **Vol. 3, Part 2,** 56; **Vol. 5, Part 1,** 615; **Vol. 5, Part 2,** 530; **Vol. 9, Part 2,** 15; water supply, **Vol. 3, Part 1,** 406; **Vol. 5, Part 2,** 59; **Vol. 6, Part 1,** 39; **Vol. 8, Part 1,** 324 f., 607; **Vol. 9, Part 1,** 307 f., **Vol. 10, Part 2,** 21; **Supp. 1,** 663, 700; **Supp. 2,** 558; Welfare Council, **Supp. 3,** 362; WPA construction projects, **Supp. 5,** 642–43; writings on, **Vol. 1, Part 1,** 188; **Vol. 3, Part 1,** 319; **Vol. 4, Part 1,** 629; **Vol. 5, Part 1,** 308, 615; **Vol. 5, Part 2,** 310, 383, 556; **Vol. 9, Part 1,** 338; yellow fever epidemic, **Vol. 1, Part 1,** 275; **Vol. 6, Part 1,** 309; YMCA building, **Vol. 6, Part 1,** 556; zoning law, **Supp. 4,** 56. *See also specific sections, buildings, and attractions*
New York City Opera, *Die tote Stadt* production, **Supp. 6,** 351–52
New York Clearing House, **Vol. 2, Part 1,** 476; **Vol. 2, Part 2,** 261, 613; **Vol. 3, Part 2,** 22, 524; **Vol. 9, Part 2,** 304, 542
New York College of Dentistry, **Vol. 7, Part 2,** 252
New York College for the Training of Teachers, **Vol. 3, Part 1,** 347
New York Commercial Advertiser. See New York Globe
New York Commission of Charities, **Vol. 8, Part 1,** 253 f.
New York Committee of One Hundred, **Vol. 5, Part 2,** 197; **Vol. 7, Part 2,** 631
New York Committee of Safety, **Vol. 7, Part 2,** 340, 417 f.; **Vol. 8, Part 2,** 341 f.; **Vol. 9, Part 2,** 365; Committee of Sixty, **Vol. 6, Part 1,** 316 f.
New York Conference of Librarians (1853), **Vol. 5, Part 2,** 66
New York Confidential, **Supp. 5,** 406
New York Consolidated Gas Co. *See* Consolidated Edison Co.
New York Courier, **Vol. 1, Part 2,** 196
New York Court of Common Pleas, **Vol. 3, Part 1,** 41 f.
New York Cricket Club, **Vol. 8, Part 1,** 107 f.
New York Curb Exchange. *See* American Stock Exchange
New York Daily News: comic strip, **Supp. 6,** 699; drama criticism, **Supp. 4,** 548–49; founding of, **Supp. 4,** 646; **Supp. 5,** 449
New York Daily Times, **Vol. 8, Part 1,** 409
New York Drama Critics' Circle Award, **Supp. 6,** 11, 15, 471
New York Dramatic Mirror, **Vol. 3, Part 2,** 423
New York Edison Co., **Vol. 6, Part 1,** 235; **Vol. 7, Part 1,** 368
New York Employment Club, founding of, **Vol. 3, Part 1,** 272
New York Enquirer, **Vol. 1, Part 2,** 196
New Yorker: articles and profiles, **Supp. 6,** 236–37, 422, 423; **Supp. 7,** 38, 473–74; **Supp. 8,** 447; book-review column, **Supp. 8,** 492; cartoons, **Supp. 4,** 386; **Supp. 8,** 15–16; drama criticism, **Supp. 5,** 464; fiction, **Supp. 8,** 480, 481; first cover, **Supp. 5,** 594; founding of, **Supp. 5,** 593–94; humor, **Supp. 7,** 743; illustrations, **Supp. 6,** 287; Mencken autobiography, **Supp. 6,** 446; poetry reviews, **Supp. 8,** 42, 43; television column, **Supp. 6,** 366; typography, **Supp. 7,** 2; "Wayward Press" column, **Supp. 3,** 54
New Yorker-Staats-Zeitung, **Vol. 7, Part 2,** 106 f.
New York Etching Club, **Vol. 9, Part 1,** 233
New York Evening Graphic, **Supp. 5,** 453
New York Evening Journal, drama criticism, **Supp. 5,** 658; yellow journalism, **Supp. 5,** 284, 285
New York Evening Mail, **Supp. 6,** 4
New York Evening Post, **Vol. 2, Part 1,** 202; **Vol. 3, Part 1,** 203; **Vol. 4, Part 1,** 347; **Vol. 4, Part 2,** 178; **Vol.**

6, Part 1, 147, 195, 208, 283; **Vol. 7, Part 1,** 378, 548; **Vol. 8, Part 2,** 469; **Vol. 10, Part 2,** 105; **Supp. 4,** 322, 850; **Supp. 7,** 103; book reviews, **Supp. 5,** 439; drama criticism, **Supp. 8,** 54; editing, **Supp. 2,** 498; editorial writing, **Supp. 4,** 804–5; music criticism, **Supp. 7,** 124
New York Evening World, **Vol. 6, Part 1,** 354 f.; **Vol. 8, Part 1,** 260 f.; **Supp. 3,** 144; **Supp. 5,** 552
New York Eye Infirmary, founding of, **Vol. 3, Part 1,** 207
New York Free Circulating Library. *See* New York Public Library
New York Gazeteer, **Vol. 8, Part 1,** 638
New York Giants (baseball), **Supp. 1,** 530; **Supp. 6,** 488–89; **Supp. 8,** 713
New York Giants (football), **Supp. 7,** 595–96; **Supp. 8,** 389
New York Globe, **Supp. 3,** 329; **Supp. 8,** 108
New York Gold Exchange, **Vol. 2, Part 2,** 298
New York Heart Association, **Supp. 6,** 117; founding of, **Supp. 2,** 742
New York Herald, **Vol. 1, Part 2,** 199; **Vol. 5, Part 1,** 106; **Vol. 7, Part 1,** 548; **Vol. 8, Part 1,** 409, 474; **Supp. 3,** 841–42; **Supp. 5,** 78–79; Civil War coverage, **Supp. 1,** 441; foreign correspondents, **Supp. 8,** 639–40
New York Herald Tribune, **Vol. 4, Part 2,** 432 f.; **Vol. 8, Part 2,** 282; **Vol. 9, Part 1,** 92; cartoons, **Supp. 5,** 732; "Conning Tower" column, **Supp. 6,** 4, 5, 113; editorial policies, **Supp. 8,** 441, 520–21; foreign correspondents, **Supp. 8,** 259–60; formation of, **Supp. 4,** 686–87; literary editor, **Supp. 8,** 667–68; "On the Record" column, **Supp. 7,** 740; reporting, **Supp. 5,** 18–19
New-York Historical Society, **Vol. 1, Part 2,** 70, 204, 568; **Vol. 2, Part 2,** 224; **Vol. 3, Part 1,** 279; **Vol. 3, Part 2,** 356; **Vol. 4, Part 2,** 417; **Vol. 5, Part 1,** 240; **Vol. 7, Part 1,** 125; **Vol. 7, Part 2,** 630; **Supp. 8,** 664
New York Home for Incurables, founding of, **Vol. 3, Part 2,** 356
New York Hospital, **Supp. 6,** 123, 546–47
New York Humane Society, **Vol. 7, Part 1,** 360
New York Institution for the Blind, **Vol. 2, Part 2,** 107; **Vol. 8, Part 2,** 238
New York Institution for the Instruction of the Deaf and Dumb, **Vol. 7, Part 2,** 391
New York Intercollegiate Bureau of Occupations, **Vol. 9, Part 2,** 534
New York Journal, **Vol. 8, Part 1,** 332 f.; editing, **Supp. 2,** 63
New York Journal American, founding of, **Supp. 5,** 285
New York Journal of Commerce, **Vol. 4, Part 2,** 98; **Vol. 8, Part 1,** 228 f.; **Vol. 9, Part 2,** 73 f., 299, 303
New York Juvenile Asylum, **Vol. 8, Part 2,** 238
New York Kindergarten Society, **Supp. 5,** 437
New York Knickerbockers (basketball), **Supp. 8,** 358
New York Laryngological Society, **Vol. 1, Part 2,** 467
New York Law Institute, founding of, **Vol. 1, Part 1,** 314
New York Law Journal, **Vol. 6, Part 1,** 602; **Vol. 9, Part 2,** 636
New York Law School, **Vol. 2, Part 2,** 25; **Vol. 3, Part 1,** 571 f.
New York Law Society, founding of, **Supp. 2,** 501
New York Ledger, **Vol. 1, Part 2,** 437; **Vol. 7, Part 2,** 281
New York Life Insurance Co., **Vol. 1, Part 1,** 599; **Vol. 6, Part 1,** 495, 562; **Vol. 7, Part 2,** 56, 381, 471; **Supp. 1,** 470
New York Life Insurance Co. Building, **Supp. 6,** 593
New York Mail, cartoons and caricatures, **Supp. 8,** 217
New York Medical College, **Vol. 1, Part 1,** 601; **Vol. 3, Part 1,** 376

1, 11; National Guard, **Vol. 7, Part 2,** 553; nursing education, **Supp. 5,** 251; penal reform, **Supp. 3,** 420–21; planning, **Supp. 2,** 739; political service, **Vol. 1, Part 2,** 170, 204, 231, 259, 308, 369, 476, 568, 584; **Vol. 2, Part 2,** 99, 138, 225, 253, 558; **Vol. 3, Part 1,** 138, 212, 214, 245, 247, 294 f., 322, 325, 378, 387, 465, 480, 519, 602; **Vol. 3, Part 2,** 326, 397, 480, 486; **Vol. 4, Part 1,** 335; **Vol. 4, Part 2,** 405; **Vol. 5, Part 1,** 10, 28, 113, 395, 401; **Vol. 6, Part 1,** 227, 316, 319, 449, 528; **Vol. 6, Part 2,** 78, 124, 275, 641; **Vol. 7, Part 1,** 83, 126, 514 f., 622; **Vol. 7, Part 2,** 46, 82, 107, 215, 331, 474; **Vol. 8, Part 1,** 4 f., 132, 179, 229, 253, 283, 302, 318, 326, 347, 409, 442, 582; **Vol. 8, Part 2,** 6, 28, 137, 255, 615; **Vol. 9, Part 1,** 6, 444; **Vol. 9, Part 2,** 129, 427, 510 f., 537, 583; **Vol. 10, Part 1,** 80, 151, 154, 163, 166, 390, 406 f., 598 f.;; **Vol. 10, Part 2,** 245, 257, 456, 490, 566, 598, 628; politics, **Supp. 3,** 641–46, 717–21, 751; **Supp. 4,** 511–12, 855–56; **Supp. 5,** 285–86, 493–94, 715–16, 717–19; **Supp. 6,** 535, 588, 660; **Supp. 7,** 382–83, 467, 468, 521, 659–60, 733–34; **Supp. 8,** 323; Power Authority, **Supp. 6,** 484; prison reform, **Vol. 3, Part 1,** 378; **Vol. 7, Part 2,** 75; **Supp. 4,** 471–72; **Supp. 5,** 427; Prohibition (1854), **Vol. 3, Part 1,** 353; public health, **Supp. 6,** 701; **Supp. 7,** 251–52; public service, **Vol. 1, Part 2,** 239; **Vol. 2, Part 2,** 410, 443, 618; **Vol. 3, Part 1,** 486, 488; **Vol. 3, Part 2,** 447, 484; **Vol. 4, Part 2,** 173 f., 205; **Vol. 5, Part 1,** 28; **Vol. 5, Part 2,** 399; **Vol. 6, Part 1,** 32, 215, 232, 313 f.; **Vol. 7, Part 1,** 422; **Vol. 7, Part 2,** 293, 472; **Vol. 8, Part 1,** 99 f., 138, 243, 253 f., 324, 634; **Vol. 8, Part 2,** 134, 220, 255, 292, 342, 349, 478 f.; **Vol. 9, Part 1,** 460; **Vol. 9, Part 2,** 130 f.; **Vol. 10, Part 1,** 598 f.; "Quids" political party, **Vol. 6, Part 1,** 222; railroad development in, **Vol. 2, Part 2,** 446 f.; Republican party, organization of, **Vol. 2, Part 2,** 138; Revolution period; **Vol. 3, Part 1,** 214 f., 404; **Vol. 8, Part 1,** 452; Revolution of 1689, **Vol. 6, Part 1,** 156; Roman Catholic diocese, **Supp. 8,** 613–15; sanitation, **Vol. 4, Part 2,** 308; settlement of, **Vol. 6, Part 2,** 265; **Vol. 10, Part 2,** 227, 297; Socialist party, **Supp. 3,** 853; **Supp. 5,** 635; **Supp. 8,** 649–50; Social Welfare Board, **Supp. 3,** 4; society, colonial, **Vol. 8, Part 2,** 475, 477; "Stalwarts," **Vol. 4, Part 2,** 450; **Vol. 5, Part 2,** 543 f.; **Vol. 8, Part 1,** 4 f.; **Vol. 8, Part 2,** 28 f.; statutes, revision of, **Vol. 9, Part 2,** 511; Supreme Court, youngest justice, **Supp. 2,** 496; Supreme Court of, **Vol. 4, Part 1,** 360; surveying, **Vol. 3, Part 1,** 274; unemployment insurance pooled-fund plan, **Supp. 3,** 19; Uniform Commercial Code, **Supp. 7,** 474; U.S. attorneys, **Supp. 3,** 117, 181; **Supp. 4,** 785; **Supp. 6,** 141; welfare, **Supp. 4,** 391–92; *Westchester County During the American Revolution,* **Vol. 3, Part 1,** 152; White Charter Commission, **Vol. 3, Part 1,** 11; woman suffrage, **Supp. 4,** 157; **Supp. 6,** 79; **Supp. 7,** 778–79; workmen's compensation law, **Vol. 4, Part 1,** 335

New York State Agricultural College. *See* Cornell University

New York State Agricultural Society, **Vol. 3, Part 1,** 210; **Vol. 5, Part 2,** 90; **Vol. 7, Part 2,** 297

New York State Charities Aid Association, **Vol. 8, Part 2,** 474

New York State Conference of Charities and Corrections, organized, **Vol. 9, Part 2,** 15

New York State Farm Bureau Federation, predecessors, **Supp. 4,** 37

New York State Historical Society, **Supp. 3,** 287

New York State Institute for the Study of Malignant Diseases (Buffalo), **Vol. 7, Part 2,** 208; **Supp. 6,** 126

New York State Library, director, **Supp. 8,** 664

New York State Ranger School, founding of, **Supp. 4,** 44

New York State Temperance Society, **Vol. 3, Part 1,** 221

New York State Woman's Suffrage Association, **Vol. 1, Part 2,** 344

New York Stock Exchange, **Vol. 2, Part 2,** 76, 133; **Vol. 4, Part 2,** 393 f.; **Vol. 5, Part 1,** 247

New York Sun, **Vol. 1, Part 2,** 80; **Vol. 3, Part 1,** 51 f., 155; **Vol. 4, Part 2,** 475; **Vol. 5, Part 1,** 65; **Vol. 5, Part 2,** 539; **Vol. 6, Part 1,** 339; **Vol. 6, Part 2,** 413; **Vol. 7, Part 1,** 44; **Vol. 9, Part 2,** 252; **Supp. 6,** 6, 290–91; art criticism, **Supp. 7,** 494; columns, **Supp. 8,** 444; editorship, **Supp. 1,** 510; political cartoons, **Supp. 8,** 218; "Sun Dial" column, **Supp. 7,** 617–18

New York Sunday School Union, **Vol. 6, Part 1,** 406

New York Symphony Orchestra, predecessor of New York Philharmonic, **Supp. 3,** 33, 64–65; **Supp. 6,** 426

New York Symphony Society, predecessor of New York Philharmonic, **Supp. 4,** 210, 211, 212

New York Tax Reform Association, founding of, **Supp. 2,** 272

New York Teacher, **Vol. 9, Part 1,** 64

New York Telegram, **Supp. 7,** 369

New York Telephone Co., **Supp. 3,** 299

New York Theological Seminary, **Vol. 6, Part 1,** 554

New York Times, **Vol. 4, Part 1,** 7; **Vol. 5, Part 1,** 148, 424; **Vol. 5, Part 2,** 171, 231; **Vol. 6, Part 1,** 455; **Vol. 6, Part 2,** 620; **Vol. 7, Part 1,** 601; **Vol. 8, Part 1,** 408, 409; **Vol. 9, Part 1,** 175; **Vol. 9, Part 2,** 252, 539; authorized biographies, **Supp. 6,** 58, 148; *Current History,* **Vol. 7, Part 1,** 601; *Dictionary of American Biography* funding, **Supp. 2,** 186, 342; drama criticism, **Supp. 3,** 842; **Supp. 7,** 412, 811; editorial policies in 1870–1920, **Vol. 2, Part 1,** 554; financial column, **Supp. 3,** 564–65; first bridge column, **Supp. 6,** 380; first woman editorial board member, **Supp. 5,** 447; foreign correspondents, **Supp. 5,** 60; founding of, **Vol. 8, Part 1,** 408 f.; **Vol. 9, Part 1,** 175; labor correspondent, **Supp. 5,** 653–54; legal counsel, **Supp. 8,** 224; medical reporting, **Supp. 4,** 667–68; music criticism, **Supp. 2,** 8; **Supp. 5,** 183; "newspaper of record," **Supp. 5,** 787–88; **Supp. 5,** 362–63; Paris bureau, **Supp. 6,** 183–84; political caricatures, **Supp. 4,** 159–60; publishing, **Supp. 7,** 199–200; **Supp. 8,** 636; science articles, **Supp. 6,** 327, 328; "Topics of the Times," **Supp. 4,** 804; Tweed, attack on, **Vol. 10, Part 1,** 81; typography, **Supp. 7,** 2

New York Times Building, construction of, **Supp. 3,** 612

New York Times Index, **Supp. 3,** 788

New York Times Magazine, The: double-crostic puzzle, **Supp. 6,** 342; illustrated interviews in, **Supp. 4,** 160

New York Tract Society, **Vol. 3, Part 1,** 345

New York Trade School, **Vol. 1, Part 1,** 421

New York Tribune, **Vol. 3, Part 1,** 50 f.; **Vol. 4, Part 1,** 529 f., 533; **Vol. 4, Part 2,** 383, 480; **Vol. 5, Part 1,** 104; **Vol. 5, Part 2,** 135; **Vol. 7, Part 2,** 188; **Vol. 8, Part 1,** 483, f., 624; **Vol. 8, Part 2,** 51, 57; **Vol. 9, Part 1,** 223, 261; **Vol. 9, Part 2,** 403, 487; art criticism, **Supp. 4,** 182–83; founding of, **Vol. 8, Part 1,** 408 f.; Fresh Air Fund, **Vol. 7, Part 2,** 209; Platt, T. C., attacks on, **Vol. 8, Part 1,** 485; "scoops" of Smalley, **Vol. 9, Part 1,** 224; sports column, **Supp. 5,** 568; syndicated column, **Supp. 5,** 667; under Horace Greeley, **Vol. 6, Part 2,** 36; union boycott of, **Vol. 8, Part 1,** 484

New York University, **Vol. 6, Part 1,** 619 f.; **Vol. 7, Part 2,** 311; **Vol. 9, Part 1,** 37, 471; administration,

Supp. 1, 125; **Supp. 5**, 109; anesthesia program, **Supp. 6**, 553, 554; building architecture, **Supp. 5**, 388; English studies, **Supp. 3**, 109; founding of, **Vol. 2, Part 2**, 481; Hall of Fame, **Vol. 6, Part 1**, 619–20; Institute of Fine Arts, **Supp. 8**, 195; law school, **Supp. 6**, 651; Medical College, promotion of, **Vol. 7, Part 2**, 153; physiology studies, **Supp. 7**, 699; poetry center, **Supp. 7**, 442; psychology studies, **Supp. 6**, 222; State Museum, **Vol. 2, Part 2**, 156; tax studies, **Supp. 5**, 412

New York Woman Suffrage party, founding of, **Supp. 4**, 157

New York Women's Press Club, **Vol. 2, Part 2**, 561

New York World, **Vol. 2, Part 2**, 241, 256 f.; **Vol. 5, Part 1**, 106, 424; **Vol. 6, Part 2**, 267, 568; **Vol. 8, Part 1**, 253 f., 260 f.; **Vol. 8, Part 2**, 533; **Vol. 9, Part 2**, 616; **Supp. 3**, 170, 702, 842; **Supp. 4**, 885; **Supp. 6**, 5, 11, 15, 299, 536, 616–17; **Supp. 7**, 369, 370, 758, 767; comic strips, **Supp. 5**, 262; editorial cartoons, **Supp. 5**, 391–92, 499; editorship, **Supp. 1**, 653; Hearst competition, **Supp. 5**, 284; music criticism, **Supp. 7**, 124; Washington correspondent, **Supp. 4**, 574–75

New York World's Fair (1939-40): aquacade, **Supp. 8**, 547; American Artists Today exhibit, **Supp. 6**, 97; Birth Series exhibit, **Supp. 4**, 230; design of, **Supp. 7**, 691; GM Futurama exhibit, **Supp. 6**, 234; music director, **Supp. 5**, 183; organization of, **Supp. 7**, 780; sculpture, **Supp. 8**, 415; Todd attractions, **Supp. 6**, 637

New York World Telegram, **Supp. 6**, 601–2; **Supp. 7**, 368, 370, 472

New York World Telegram and Sun, **Supp. 7**, 369; "Broadway After Dark" column, **Supp. 8**, 444

New York Yankees (baseball), **Vol. 5, Part 1**, 346; **Supp. 2**, 589; **Supp. 4**, 710–11; **Supp. 7**, 27; **Supp. 8**, 542; development of, **Supp. 5**, 40–41

New York Zoological Park, administration, **Supp. 2**, 317; **Supp. 8**, 485–86; architecture, **Supp. 2**, 369; gateway sculpture, **Supp. 8**, 414–15; reptile collection, **Supp. 3**, 228–29; specimen contributions, **Supp. 6**, 23

New York Zoological Society, **Supp. 7**, 45–46; administration, **Supp. 8**, 485–86

Neylan, John Francis, reference to, **Supp. 5**, 287

Nez Percé Indians, surrender of, **Vol. 4, Part 1**, 237; **Vol. 5, Part 1**, 280; **Vol. 5, Part 2**, 219; **Vol. 6, Part 2**, 614

NFL. *See* National Football League

Niacin, **Supp. 7**, 233

Niagara Falls, N.Y., **Vol. 4, Part 1**, 136; bridge, **Vol. 8, Part 2**, 592; electric power, source of, **Vol. 8, Part 1**, 375 f.; obelisk dam above, construction of, **Vol. 8, Part 1**, 359 f.; power canal utilized, **Vol. 3, Part 1**, 159; power project, **Supp. 3**, 251, 769; waterpower development, **Vol. 8, Part 1**, 99 f.; **Vol. 8, Part 2**, 575

Niagara Falls Power Co., **Vol. 4, Part 2**, 283; **Vol. 8, Part 1**, 375 f.; **Vol. 8, Part 2**, 199

Niagara frontier, **Vol. 6, Part 1**, 595

Niagara Hudson Power Co., **Supp. 3**, 138

Niagara Movement, founding of, **Supp. 7**, 202

Niblo's Gardens, **Vol. 7, Part 1**, 542

Nicaragua: American retaliation against (1854), **Vol. 5, Part 1**, 152; canal proposal, **Supp. 4**, 193; diplomacy with U.S., **Vol. 1, Part 2**, 465; **Vol. 3, Part 1**, 314; **Vol. 5, Part 2**, 554; **Vol. 10, Part 1**, 363 f.; **Supp. 6**, 359; exploring expedition, **Vol. 6, Part 1**, 500; filibustering in, **Vol. 8, Part 2**, 343; inauguration of an American president, **Vol. 10, Part 1**, 363 f.; invasion of, by William Walker, **Vol. 7, Part 2**, 572; **Vol. 8, Part 1**, 356, 503; ornithology study, **Supp. 6**, 255

Nicaragua Canal Co., **Vol. 5, Part 1**, 247

Nicaragua canal project, **Vol. 1, Part 2**, 266; **Vol. 3, Part 1**, 116, 421 f.; **Vol. 5, Part 1**, 69; **Vol. 6, Part 2**, 537, 575

Nichols, Edward, reference to, **Vol. 7, Part 1**, 412

Nicholson, Alma Stotts, reference to, **Supp. 7**, 573

Nicholson, Francis, reference to, **Vol. 1, Part 2**, 336

Nicholson, Seth B., reference to, **Supp. 5**, 540

Nick Carter dime novels, **Vol. 5, Part 2**, 51

Nickel: mining, **Supp. 1**, 687; new uses for, **Supp. 5**, 652–53

Nickel and dime stores. *See* Five and dime stores

Nickelodeon, **Supp. 2**, 368

Nicknames and epithets: "Abe Martin," **Vol. 5, Part 1**, 324; "Admiral of the Lakes," **Vol. 7, Part 1**, 446; "Ambassador of Heaven," **Vol. 3, Part 1**, 256; "American Addison," **Vol. 3, Part 1**, 236; "American Cicero," **Vol. 3, Part 2**, 534; "American Cruikshank," **Vol. 5, Part 2**, 139; "American Erskine," **Vol. 5, Part 1**, 115; "American Hogarth," **Vol. 5, Part 2**, 506; "American Joan of Arc," **Vol. 1, Part 2**, 415; "American Newman," **Vol. 5, Part 2**, 558; "American Tragedian," **Vol. 3, Part 1**, 81; "Angel of the Battlefield," **Vol. 1, Part 1**, 318; "Angel of the Stockyards," **Supp. 2**, 408; "Annalist of Yale," **Vol. 3, Part 1**, 276; "Antiquarian of Nassau Street," **Vol. 4, Part 1**, 460; "Apostle of Peace," **Vol. 5, Part 2**, 527; "Apostle to the Illinois Indians," **Vol. 4, Part 1**, 510; "Apostle to the Lost," **Vol. 6, Part 1**, 553; "Apostle to the Sioux," **Vol. 4, Part 2**, 264; "Apostle to the Slavs," **Vol. 8, Part 2**, 420; "archbishop of fundamentalism," **Supp. 5**, 345–46; "Art Jockey," **Vol. 1, Part 1**, 166; "Atomic General," **Supp. 8**, 230; "Aunt Fanny," **Vol. 4, Part 1**, 84 f.; "B," **Supp. 7**, 315; "Babe," **Supp. 4**, 710–11; "Barley Jim," **Vol. 9, Part 2**, 312; "Baskerville of America," **Vol. 9, Part 2**, 436; "Beau James," **Supp. 4**, 855; "Beau Jonathan," **Vol. 4, Part 2**, 470; "Beloved Man of the Four Nations," **Vol. 4, Part 2**, 414; "Beloved Woman," **Vol. 10, Part 1**, 433; "Bengal Tiger," **Vol. 10, Part 1**, 83; "Benicia Boy," **Vol. 4, Part 2**, 500; "Bet-You-a-Million Gates," **Vol. 4, Part 1**, 189; "Big Ban," **Vol. 5, Part 2**, 92; "Big Bill," **Supp. 5**, 340, 686; "Bigfoot," **Vol. 10, Part 1**, 377 f.; "Big Guts," **Vol. 8, Part 1**, 238 f.; "Big Poison," **Supp. 7**, 768; "Big Sid," **Supp. 5**, 105; "Billy Sunday of the South," **Supp. 8**, 304; "Billy, the Flower-Hunter," **Vol. 1, Part 2**, 28; "Billy the Kid," **Vol. 9, Part 1**, 192; "Bird," **Supp. 5**, 534; "Birdie," **Supp. 8**, 261; "Bishop Dan," **Vol. 10, Part 1**, 75; "Bishop of Hampshire County," **Vol. 10, Part 1**, 99; "Bismarck of Western Politics," **Vol. 5, Part 2**, 365; "Black Ben," **Vol. 3, Part 2**, 509; "Black Dan," **Vol. 10, Part 1**, 585 f.; "Black Daniel Webster," **Vol. 10, Part 1**, 440; "Black Hawk," **Vol. 8, Part 2**, 41 f.; "Black Jack," **Supp. 4**, 655; "Black Mike," **Supp. 7**, 130; "Blackrobe," **Vol. 3, Part 1**, 256; "Black Sam," **Vol. 4, Part 1**, 1; "Bloody Shirt," **Vol. 3, Part 2**, 503; "Bo," **Supp. 5**, 458; "Bobbin Boy of Massachusetts," **Vol. 1, Part 1**, 577; "Bojangles," **Supp. 4**, 695; "Bold Man of Bean Hill," **Vol. 3, Part 1**, 550; "Bonanza King," **Vol. 9, Part 2**, 263; "Boston Rebel," **Vol. 6, Part 1**, 453, 465; "Boy Major," **Vol. 7, Part 2**, 408; "Boy Preacher," **Vol. 3, Part 2**, 554; "Brazilian Bombshell," **Supp. 5**, 500; "Brick," **Vol. 8, Part 1**, 53 f.; "Brother Pourquoi," **Vol. 10, Part 1**, 405; "Brutal Friend," **Vol. 5, Part 2**, 490; "Buckskin Joe," **Supp. 2**, 133; "Buffalo Bill," **Vol. 2, Part 2**, 260 f., 522 f.; **Vol. 5, Part 1**, 480, 483; **Vol. 5, Part 2**, 238; **Vol. 7, Part 1**, 603 f.; "Bula Matari," **Vol. 9, Part 1**, 512; "Bull," **Vol. 10, Part 1**, 655 f.; "Bulldog," **Supp. 4**, 857; "Buncombe Bob," **Supp. 7**,

644; "Burbank of the Range," **Vol. 4, Part 1,** 394; "Calico Charlie," **Vol. 3, Part 2,** 544; "California Humorist," **Vol. 10, Part 1,** 572 f.; "Camp-Meeting John," **Vol. 7, Part 1,** 548; "Captain Nat," **Supp. 2,** 299; "Cast-Iron Charlie," **Supp. 8,** 609; "Cattle King," **Vol. 9, Part 2,** 134; "Champion Crank," **Vol. 9, Part 2,** 626; "Chep," **Supp. 7,** 555; "Chesterdale," **Supp. 7,** 161; "Chesterfield of the House," **Vol. 8, Part 1,** 538; "Chesterfield of the Navy," **Vol. 10, Part 1,** 128; "Chief," **Supp. 5,** 287; "Children's Statesman," **Supp. 7,** 483; "Chinese," **Vol. 10, Part 1,** 419 f.; "Christian Statesman," **Vol. 4, Part 1,** 17; "Clem," **Supp. 7,** 494; "Clown Prince," **Supp. 7,** 49; "Cocky," **Supp. 5,** 125; "Coin," **Supp. 2,** 288; "Coke King," **Vol. 4, Part 1,** 30; "Colonel," **Supp. 2,** 319; **Supp. 5,** 449; "Colonel Bill," **Vol. 4, Part 1,** 577; "Colorado," **Vol. 5, Part 2,** 73; "Confederate Von Lückner," **Vol. 8, Part 1,** 420; "conscience of Chicago," **Supp. 8,** 40; "Cool Philosopher," **Vol. 9, Part 2,** 124; "Copey," **Supp. 5,** 131; "Copperhead," **Vol. 9, Part 1,** 8; "Corporal Tanner," **Vol. 9, Part 2,** 297; "Cotton King," **Vol. 8, Part 1,** 566; "Cotton Tom," **Supp. 5,** 290; "Count of the Holy Roman Empire," **Vol. 4, Part 1,** 378; "Cracker," **Supp. 8,** 574; "creator of American characters," **Vol. 8, Part 1,** 413; "Dark Horse," **Vol. 8, Part 1,** 34 f.; "D'Artagnan of the AEF," **Supp. 7,** 488; "Daughter of the Confederacy," **Vol. 3, Part 1,** 146; "Dazzy," **Supp. 7,** 751; "Deacon Bill," **Supp. 7,** 501; "deaf and dumb poet," **Vol. 7, Part 1,** 377; "dean of American poets," **Supp. 2,** 430; "dean of inconsistency," **Supp. 7,** 21; "dean of Negro publishers," **Supp. 2,** 3; "dean of the mining and metallurgical professions," **Vol. 3, Part 1,** 396; "Death Valley Scotty," **Supp. 5,** 613; "Defender of the Constitution," **Vol. 10, Part 1,** 585 f.; "Detroit's Edison," **Vol. 10, Part 1,** 168; "Ding," **Supp. 7,** 163; "Diplomatic Corps," **Vol. 4, Part 1,** 135; "Diplomat of the Church," **Vol. 4, Part 2,** 371; "Doctor's Boys," **Vol. 3, Part 1,** 513; "Don Juan Largo," **Vol. 10, Part 1,** 466; "Duchess of Bubbly Creek," **Supp. 2,** 408; "Dude," **Supp. 5,** 475; "Electric Charlie," **Supp. 7,** 794; "Elevator King," **Vol. 7, Part 2,** 371; "Elizabeth Fry of America," **Vol. 4, Part 1,** 238; "Emperor," **Vol. 9, Part 1,** 328; "Empress of the Blues," **Supp. 2,** 616; "Engine Charlie," **Supp. 7,** 794; "Farmer Smith," **Vol. 9, Part 1,** 269; "Father Murrow," **Vol. 7, Part 1,** 371; "father of the American anthracite-iron industry," **Vol. 9, Part 2,** 428; "father of American anthropology," **Vol. 7, Part 1,** 183; "father of American drama," **Vol. 3, Part 1,** 516 f.; "father of American history," **Vol. 1, Part 1,** 569; "father of American mapmaking," **Vol. 4, Part 1,** 124; "father of the American Medical Assocation," **Vol. 3, Part 1,** 139; "father of American playgrounds," **Supp. 2,** 374; "father of American radio," **Vol. 2, Part 1,** 255; "father of American surgery," **Vol. 7, Part 2,** 555; "father of American watchmaking," **Vol. 3, Part 1,** 240; "father of architects," **Vol. 1, Part 1,** 433; "father of baseball," **Vol. 2, Part 1,** 587; "father of the cheap land system," **Vol. 1, Part 2,** 211; "father of Chinese geology," **Supp. 4,** 344; "father of Congregationalism in Dakota," **Vol. 10, Part 1,** 429 f.; "father of cotton manufacturing in the South," **Vol. 4, Part 1,** 600; "father of entomology in America," **Vol. 8, Part 2,** 40; "father of Greater New York," **Vol. 4, Part 1,** 535; "father of greenbacks," **Vol. 9, Part 1,** 436; "father of iron shipbuilding in America," **Vol. 8, Part 1,** 640; "father of the Maine law," **Vol. 3, Part 1,** 411; "father of the Marshall Plan," **Supp. 8,** 90; "father of the Minnesota railroad system," **Vol. 8, Part 1,** 538; "father of missions," **Vol.**

7, **Part 1,** 15; "father of modern American blast furnace practice," **Vol. 4, Part 1,** 199; "father of modern American journalism," **Supp. 1,** 441; "father of modern photography," **Supp. 4,** 779, 781; "father of New York State Barge Canal," **Vol. 9, Part 2,** 260; "father of the New York turf," **Vol. 3, Part 1,** 213; "father of Niagara power," **Vol. 8, Part 1,** 376; "father of our national architecture," **Vol. 5, Part 2,** 34; "father of the nuclear submarine," **Supp. 8,** 231–32; "father of Presbyterianism in Kentucky," **Vol. 8, Part 1,** 537; "father of radio," **Supp. 7,** 177; "father of reclamation," **Vol. 10, Part 1,** 472 f.; "father of secession," **Vol. 8, Part 1,** 527; "father of the Senate," **Vol. 1, Part 1,** 317; "father of the skyscraper," **Vol. 5, Part 2,** 55; "father of tree surgery in America," **Vol. 3, Part 1,** 88; "father of trusts," **Supp. 1,** 306; "father of the United Nations," **Supp. 5,** 334; "father of the University of Georgia," **Vol. 1, Part 1,** 531; "father of Wisconsin," **Vol. 3, Part 1,** 216; "Father Ritchie," **Vol. 8, Part 1,** 628; "Father Welles," **Vol. 10, Part 1,** 629 f.; "Fatty," **Vol. 10, Part 1,** 389; "Fiery Star," **Vol. 1, Part 2,** 445; "Fighting Bob," **Vol. 3, Part 2,** 210; "Fighting Dick," **Vol. 8, Part 1,** 570; "Fighting Engineer," **Vol. 1, Part 1,** 496; "Fighting Joe," **Vol. 5, Part 1,** 196; "Fighting Parson," **Vol. 5, Part 2,** 191; **Vol. 9, Part 2,** 234; "Fighting Quaker," **Vol. 10, Part 1,** 539; **Supp. 2,** 511; "Fighting Surgeon of the Revolution," **Vol. 3, Part 1,** 414; "Fire Alarm," **Vol. 3, Part 2,** 503; "first citizen of Atlanta," **Vol. 5, Part 1,** 485; "first citizen of Connecticut," **Vol. 1, Part 1,** 547; "first citizen of Minnesota," **Vol. 9, Part 1,** 618; "first citizen of Newark," **Vol. 3, Part 1,** 57; "first citizen of Richmond, Va." **Vol. 5, Part 1,** 121; "first jester in California," **Vol. 3, Part 1,** 452; "Fitznoodle," **Vol. 10, Part 1,** 147; "Florence Nightingale of America," **Vol. 1, Part 1,** 318; "Flying Dutchman," **Vol. 10, Part 1,** 154; **Supp. 5,** 716; "Forty-Eight Hours," **Vol. 1, Part 1,** 392; "Forty Thieves," **Vol. 10, Part 1,** 80; "founder of American architectural education," **Vol. 10, Part 1,** 452 f.; "Four Horsemen" (Notre Dame), **Supp. 7,** 729; "Free Trapper," **Vol. 8, Part 1,** 250 f.; "Fritz," **Supp. 7,** 459; "Fuss and Feathers," **Vol. 8, Part 2,** 511; "Garbage Lady," **Supp. 2,** 408; "Gashouse Gang," **Supp. 7,** 514; "Generous John," **Supp. 7,** 734; "Gentleman George," **Vol. 1, Part 1,** 645; "geographer to the United States," **Vol. 5, Part 1,** 435; "Georgia Peach," **Supp. 7,** 128; "Girl with the Bee-Stung Lips," **Supp. 7,** 563; "Goddess in the Cloud," **Vol. 8, Part 1,** 472; "Godless Anne," **Vol. 8, Part 2,** 204; "Golden Rule Jones," **Supp. 1,** 454; "Golden Rule Nash," **Vol. 7, Part 1,** 384 f.; "Gold-Plated Hart," **Supp. 7,** 325; "Good Gray Governor," **Vol. 3, Part 2,** 342; "Goody," **Supp. 8,** 502; "Grandma," **Supp. 7,** 556; "grandmother of American sentimental novel," **Supp. 8,** 471; "Gray Eagle," **Vol. 7, Part 1,** 20, 600; "gray eminence of the Republican party," **Supp. 7,** 73; "Great Agnostic," **Vol. 5, Part 1,** 469; "Great Commoner of medicine," **Vol. 9, Part 2,** 85; "Great Pacificator," **Vol. 8, Part 2,** 508 f.; "Great Renegade," **Vol. 4, Part 1,** 323; "Grecian," **Vol. 3, Part 1,** 79; "Gum-Shoe Bill," **Vol. 9, Part 2,** 88; "Hammering Hank," **Supp. 7,** 351; "Handsome Jack," **Vol. 10, Part 1,** 33; "hero of Fort McHenry," **Vol. 1, Part 1,** 347; "Hell 'n Maria," **Supp. 5,** 160; "He-Who-Sees-in-the-Dark," **Supp. 4,** 128; "Hoboken Bill," **Supp. 7,** 437; "Home Run," **Supp. 7,** 27; "Honest Harold," **Supp. 5,** 342–43; "Honest John," **Vol. 3, Part 1,** 134; "Honest lawyer," **Vol. 8, Part 1,** 422; "Honus," **Supp. 5,** 716; "Hoosier poet," **Vol. 8, Part 1,** 611; "Hoot," **Supp. 7,** 286;

"Horace Mann of the South," **Vol. 8, Part 2,** 219; "Horse, The," **Vol. 10, Part 1,** 83; "Horse-Head," **Vol. 4, Part 1,** 253; "Hot Dog King," **Supp. 7,** 719; "Howlin' Mad," **Supp. 8,** 602; "Hurry-up," **Supp. 4,** 917; "Ice King," **Vol. 7, Part 1,** 240; "I-Don't-Care Girl," **Supp. 4,** 815; "Ike," **Supp. 8,** 159; "Indian Man," **Supp. 7,** 450; "Inspired Declaimer," **Vol. 8, Part 1,** 207 f.; "Jack Dempsey of the Navy," **Supp. 8,** 41; "Jack Downing, Major," **Vol. 9, Part 1,** 345; "Jack the Liar," **Vol. 8, Part 1,** 451; "Jersey cow candidate," **Vol. 5, Part 1,** 90; "Jersey Slick," **Vol. 9, Part 2,** 599; "Johnny Appleseed," **Vol. 2, Part 2,** 17; "John Taylor of Caroline," **Vol. 9, Part 2,** 331; "Jonker," **Vol. 10, Part 1,** 178; "Josiah Allen's wife," **Vol. 5, Part 1,** 150; "Judge Wick," **Vol. 8, Part 1,** 611; "Julia of Julias," **Vol. 3, Part 1,** 170; "King," **Supp. 7,** 131; "King of the Cherokees," **Vol. 2, Part 2,** 592; "King of Clowns," **Supp. 8,** 356; "Kingfisher," **Supp. 5,** 707; "King Hendrick," **Vol. 4, Part 2,** 532; "King of Jazz," **Supp. 8,** 697, 698; "King Kelly," **Vol. 5, Part 2,** 310; "King Lincoln," **Vol. 10, Part 1,** 145; "King of the Lobby," **Vol. 10, Part 1,** 439; "King Rolette," **Vol. 8, Part 2,** 117; "King of the Slab," **Supp. 5,** 759; "King of the Southern Iron Word" **Vol. 3, Part 1,** 179; "King's Botanist," **Vol. 8, Part 2,** 126; "Lame Lion," **Vol. 3, Part 1,** 68; "Landlord of New York," **Vol. 1, Part 1,** 401; "Last Literary Cavalier," **Vol. 4, Part 2,** 456; "Leadbelly," **Supp. 4,** 475–77, 502; "Lean Jimmy," **Vol. 5, Part 2,** 177; "Leaping Parson," **Supp. 8,** 418; "Learned Blacksmith," **Vol. 2, Part 1,** 328; "Lefty," **Supp. 8,** 478–79; "Light-Horse Harry," **Vol. 10, Part 1,** 509 f.; "Lips," **Supp. 5,** 529; "Little Ellick," **Vol. 9, Part 1,** 569; "Little Flower," **Supp. 4,** 464; "Little General," **Vol. 5, Part 2,** 578; "Little Giant from Connecicut," **Vol. 10, Part 1,** 384 f.; "Little Magician," **Vol. 10, Part 1,** 154; "Little Mo," **Supp. 8,** 101; "Little Mother of the Prisons," **Supp. 2,** 49; "Little Napoleon of Baseball," **Supp. 1,** 530; "Little Poison," **Supp. 7,** 768; "Little Van," **Vol. 10, Part 1,** 155; "Little Villain," **Vol. 8, Part 1,** 409; "Logician of the West," **Vol. 3, Part 2,** 237; "Lonesome Charley," **Vol. 8, Part 1,** 516; "Long John," **Vol. 10, Part 1,** 657 f.; "Lucky," **Supp. 7,** 484; "Ma," **Supp. 7,** 242; "Machine Gun," **Supp. 5,** 381; "Madam Knight," **Vol. 5, Part 2,** 468; "Mad Jack," **Vol. 8, Part 1,** 397; "Mad Poet," **Vol. 2, Part 2,** 160; "Maker of Champions," **Supp. 7,** 152; "Maker of Painters," **Vol. 1, Part 1,** 310; "Man on Horseback," **Vol. 10, Part 1,** 552 f.; "Man with the Iron Hand," **Vol. 9, Part 1,** 587; "Man Mountain Dean," **Supp. 5,** 417; "Martyr Abolitionist," **Vol. 6, Part 1,** 434; "Martyr Spy," **Vol. 4, Part 2,** 107; "Master of Corn," **Vol. 8, Part 1,** 477; "Mayor Von O'Hall," **Vol. 4, Part 2,** 115; "Merry Mortician," **Supp. 5,** 739; "Miracle Worker," **Supp. 8,** 316; "Missionary to the Armenians," **Vol. 3, Part 1,** 565 f.; "Moses," **Vol. 10, Part 1,** 27; "Moses and Aaron," **Vol. 3, Part 1,** 85; "Moses of the Mormons," **Vol. 9, Part 2,** 123; "Mother Bailey," **Vol. 1, Part 1,** 494; "Mother Bloor," **Supp. 5,** 70; "Mother of the Confederacy," **Vol. 6, Part 1,** 42; "Mother Jones," **Vol. 5, Part 2,** 195; "Mother Margaret," **Vol. 4, Part 2,** 398; "mother of Methodism in America," **Vol. 4, Part 2,** 493; "Mother Stewart," **Vol. 9, Part 2,** 8; "mother of the FBI," **Supp. 4,** 446; "Mr. and Mrs. Swing," **Supp. 5,** 32; "Mr. Capitalist," **Supp. 5,** 551; "Mr. Moneybags of Morristown," **Vol. 8, Part 1,** 369; "Mr. National Defense," **Supp. 5,** 715; "Mr. Republican," **Supp. 5,** 676; "Mr. Reserve," **Supp. 7,** 78; "Mr. Sam," **Supp. 7,** 636; "Mr. Willie," **Vol. 1, Part 1,** 334; "Muley Bob," **Supp. 5,** 181; "Nap," **Supp.**

8, 558–59; "Napoleon of the Drama," **Vol. 4, Part 1,** 40; "Napoleon of the Turf," **Vol. 5, Part 2,** 130; **Vol. 9, Part 2,** 365; "Napoleon of the West," **Vol. 8, Part 2,** 252; "Negro Debs," **Supp. 7,** 155; "Nestor of American literature," **Vol. 9, Part 2,** 58; "Nestor of the German-American journalists," **Vol. 8, Part 1,** 185; "Number-Two Wood," **Supp. 8,** 702; "Ohio Mower," **Vol. 1, Part 1,** 551; "Old Boy in Specs," **Vol. 3, Part 1,** 138; "Old Brains," **Vol. 4, Part 2,** 151; "Old Bullion," **Vol. 1, Part 2,** 211; "Old Captain Harris," **Vol. 9, Part 2,** 360; "Old Dander," **Vol. 9, Part 2,** 489; "Old Davy," **Vol. 10, Part 1,** 63; "Old Duck," **Vol. 3, Part 2,** 229; "Old Duckboard," **Supp. 2,** 81; "Old Duke," **Vol. 9, Part 2,** 47; "Old Dutch Cleanser," **Vol. 1, Part 2,** 358; "Old Figers," **Vol. 4, Part 2,** 24; "Old Flintlock," **Vol. 4, Part 2,** 232 f.; "Old Gimlet Eye," **Supp. 2,** 81; "Old Hero," **Vol. 8, Part 1,** 34 f.; "Old Hickory," **Vol. 5, Part 1,** 531; **Vol. 8, Part 1,** 34 f.; "Old Ranger," **Vol. 8, Part 1,** 519; "Old Roman," **Vol. 9, Part 1,** 202; **Vol. 9, Part 2,** 515; "Old Rosy," **Vol. 8, Part 2,** 164; "Old Rough and Ready," **Vol. 9, Part 2,** 353; "Old Sachem," **Vol. 5, Part 2,** 33; "Old Slackwater," **Vol. 7, Part 1,** 148; "Old Tom," **Vol. 9, Part 2,** 434; "Old War Horse," **Vol. 3, Part 1,** 263; "Old Whitey," **Vol. 8, Part 1,** 576; "Old Zach," **Vol. 6, Part 1,** 47; "Oliver Oldschool," **Vol. 8, Part 2,** 368; "Oliver Optic," **Vol. 1, Part 1,** 102; "Orphans' Friend," **Vol. 3, Part 1,** 562 f.; "our most delightful old lady," **Vol. 8, Part 2,** 332; "Our Patrick Henry," **Vol. 5, Part 2,** 492; "Outlaw of the Bronx," **Vol. 3, Part 1,** 214; "Owl," **Vol. 8, Part 2,** 252; "Pap," **Vol. 9, Part 2,** 434; "Papa," **Supp. 5,** 106; "Pappy," **Supp. 8,** 477; "Pathfinder of the Pacific," **Vol. 3, Part 2,** 266; "Patrick Henry of the West," **Vol. 7, Part 1,** 356; "Patriot Printer," **Vol. 10, Part 1,** 374 f.; "Patton of the Pacific," **Supp. 7,** 351; "Peace-Maker," **Vol. 5, Part 2,** 147; "Pee Wee," **Supp. 8,** 561; "Pepper," **Supp. 7,** 513; "Percy Bysshe Shelley Pinchback," **Vol. 7, Part 2,** 611; "Perfect Fool," **Supp. 8,** 710; "Peter of the Mills," **Vol. 3, Part 1,** 214; "physician of Wall Street," **Supp. 4,** 193; "physician's physician," **Vol. 3, Part 1,** 25; "Pirate of Peru," **Vol. 4, Part 1,** 463; "Pitchfork Ben," **Vol. 9, Part 2,** 548; **Supp. 3,** 78; "Plumed Knight," **Vol. 5, Part 1,** 470; **Vol. 9, Part 2,** 147; "poet of the American Revolution," **Vol. 4, Part 1,** 27 f.; "poet of Charleston," **Vol. 4, Part 2,** 455; "poet of the Confederacy," **Vol. 8, Part 2,** 260; "poet of the Italian theatre," **Vol. 3, Part 1,** 71; "poet laureate of the Confederacy," **Vol. 9, Part 2,** 558; "poet laureate of Freemasonry," **Vol. 7, Part 1,** 225; "poet laureate of the Revolution," **Vol. 3, Part 1,** 508 f.; "poet of the Shenandoah Valley," **Vol. 6, Part 1,** 483; "Pop," **Supp. 5,** 727; "Pope," **Vol. 9, Part 2,** 60; "Pope Dwight," **Vol. 3, Part 1,** 576 f.; "Pops," **Supp. 8,** 697; "Poughkeepsie Seer," **Vol. 3, Part 1,** 105; "Praying Student," **Vol. 8, Part 1,** 232 f.; "Priest of the Poor," **Vol. 3, Part 2,** 311; "Prince John," **Vol. 10, Part 1,** 151; "Prince of the Oyster Pirates," **Vol. 6, Part 1,** 370; "Prince of Schaghticoke," **Vol. 5, Part 2,** 461; "Pudge," **Supp. 5,** 289; "purple cow man," **Supp. 5,** 94; "Queen of the Blues," **Supp. 7,** 769; "Rabbit," **Supp. 5,** 465; "Railroad Bishop," **Vol. 9, Part 1,** 23; "Rajah," **Supp. 7,** 365; "Red Fox of Kinderhook," **Vol. 10, Part 1,** 154; "Rico," **Supp. 7,** 464; "Rock of the Marne," **Supp. 2,** 397; "rowboat secretary," **Supp. 8,** 329; "Roxy," **Supp. 2,** 584; "Rube," **Supp. 8,** 217; "Run Forever," **Vol. 5, Part 2,** 492; "Russian Columbus," **Vol. 8, Part 1,** 523; "Rustic Bard," **Vol. 3, Part 1,** 315; "Sage of Nininger," **Vol. 3, Part 1,** 369; "Sage of Pittsfield," **Vol. 3, Part 1,** 149; "St.

Thomas of Cantingbury," **Vol. 8, Part 1,** 363 f.; "Sam Slick," **Vol. 7, Part 1,** 201; "Samson," **Vol. 3, Part 1,** 255; "Savior of Georgia," **Vol. 10, Part 1,** 83; "Sawney," **Vol. 10, Part 1,** 579 f.; "Schoolboy," **Supp. 7,** 663; "Scotch Tom," **Vol. 7, Part 1,** 425; "Shag," **Supp. 8,** 587; "Silent Man from Tennessee," **Vol. 4, Part 1,** 207; "Silver Dick," **Vol. 1, Part 2,** 355; "Silver-Masked Tenor," **Supp. 6,** 691; "Silver-Tongued Orator of the House of Bishops," **Vol. 8, Part 1,** 352 f.; "Silver-Tongued Spell-Binder of the Pacific Coast," **Vol. 3, Part 1,** 226; "Simon Suggs," **Vol. 5, Part 1,** 202; "Single-Speech," **Vol. 4, Part 2,** 521; "Sitting Bull," **Supp. 5,** 669; "Slow Trot," **Vol. 9, Part 2,** 434; "Smiling Statesman," **Vol. 10, Part 1,** 601 f.; "Sockless Jerry," **Vol. 9, Part 1,** 180; "Spike," **Supp. 5,** 65; **Supp. 7,** 300, 403; "Spy of the Cumberland," **Vol. 3, Part 1,** 4; "Star-Giver General to the United States," **Vol. 8, Part 1,** 215 f.; "Star of the West," **Vol. 3, Part 1,** 428; "Steamboat," **Vol. 4, Part 1,** 338; "Stonewall," **Vol. 8, Part 1,** 44 f.; "Stonewall Jackson of the West," **Vol. 8, Part 1,** 41 f.; "Storm King," **Vol. 3, Part 2,** 185; "Stout Steve," **Supp. 7,** 596; "Strangler," **Supp. 8,** 371; "Sugartail," **Vol. 4, Part 2,** 309; "Sunny Jim," **Supp. 2,** 493; "Sunny Sol," **Supp. 7,** 373; "Swamp Fox of the Tennessee Valley," **Vol. 8, Part 2,** 70; "Tardy George," **Vol. 9, Part 2,** 255; "Tarheel Führer," **Supp. 7,** 644; "Tariff Andy," **Vol. 9, Part 2,** 6; "Ten Thousand Dollar Beauty," **Vol. 5, Part 2,** 310; "Three-Finger," **Supp. 8,** 396; "Tommy," **Supp. 5,** 682; "Tom-Tom," **Supp. 5,** 290; "Tory Hunter," **Vol. 3, Part 2,** 314; "Tragedy Queen of the American Stage," **Vol. 3, Part 1,** 428; "Trumpet King of the West," **Supp. 5,** 529; "Tune Detective," **Supp. 7,** 707; "Uncle Ben," **Vol. 1, Part 1,** 516; "Uncle Billy," **Vol. 4, Part 1,** 418; "Uncle Frank," **Supp. 4,** 661; "Uncle Henry," **Vol. 9, Part 1,** 269; "Uncle of the Human Race," **Vol. 10, Part 1,** 439; "Uncle Jerry," **Vol. 8, Part 2,** 236; "Uncle John," **Vol. 8, Part 2,** 548; "Uncle Mike," **Supp. 5,** 360; "Van Am," **Vol. 10, Part 1,** 149; "Verbose Annie," **Supp. 5,** 447; "Vinegar Joe," **Supp. 4,** 782; "Virginian Saint Michael," **Vol. 8, Part 1,** 363 f.; "Wahoo Sam," **Supp. 8,** 105; "Warwick of Massachusets Politics," **Vol. 8, Part 2,** 59; "Watchdog of the Treasury," **Vol. 5, Part 1,** 158; **Vol. 10, Part 1,** 504 f.; "Wee Charlie," **Vol. 1, Part 1,** 642; "Whirlwind," **Vol. 3, Part 2,** 562; "White Woman of the Genesee," **Vol. 5, Part 2,** 39; "Whitefield of Nova Scotia," **Vol. 1, Part 1,** 219; "Wild Horse of the Osage," **Supp. 7,** 513; "William the Silent," **Vol. 5, Part 2,** 286; "Wizard of Ooze," **Supp. 8,** 128; "Woman Who Always Prays," **Vol. 3, Part 1,** 477 f.; "Yellowstone," **Vol. 5, Part 2,** 309; "York's Tall Son," **Vol. 8, Part 1,** 107 f.; "Young Fox," **Vol. 10, Part 1,** 151; "Zeus," **Vol. 8, Part 2,** 332; "Ziggy," **Supp. 8,** 163

Niebuhr, Reinhold, reference to, **Supp. 7,** 574, 576
Nielsen, A. C., Co., **Supp. 5,** 310–11
Nieman, Lucius W., reference to, **Supp. 7,** 299
Nier, Alfred O., references to, **Supp. 4,** 818; **Supp. 6,** 371
Nightclubs, **Supp. 3,** 536; **Supp. 5,** 501; **Supp. 8,** 38–39, 546, 547, 562
Nighthawks, **Supp. 8,** 280
Night vision, studies in, **Supp. 4,** 357
Nimitz, Chester W., references to, **Supp. 5,** 621, 695; **Supp. 6,** 268, 339, 340, 629; **Supp. 7,** 490; **Supp. 8,** 42
"999" racing car, **Supp. 4,** 637
"Ninety-nine-Year Case," **Vol. 8, Part 1,** 9 f.

Ninety-six, battle of, **Vol. 4, Part 1,** 572
Niter, mining of, **Vol. 8, Part 1,** 329 f.
Nitric oxide, isolation of, **Vol. 8, Part 1,** 223 f.
Nitrogen, **Supp. 4,** 838; cyanamide process, **Supp. 3,** 439–40; discovery of, **Vol. 5, Part 1,** 50
Nitrogen-15 isotope, **Supp. 3,** 693
Nitrogen peroxide, isolation of, **Vol. 8, Part 1,** 223 f.
Nitroglycerin, early use of, **Vol. 7, Part 1,** 297
Nitrous oxide: anesthetic, use of, **Vol. 2, Part 2,** 322; dentistry use of, **Vol. 10, Part 1,** 640 f.; isolation of, **Vol. 8, Part 1,** 223 f.;
Nitti, Frank, references to, **Supp. 6,** 263, 264
Nivison, Josephine Verstille, reference to, **Supp. 8,** 279–80
Nixon, Richard M., references to, **Supp. 5,** 19, 343; **Supp. 7,** 73, 115, 420, 723; **Supp. 8,** 6, 282, 341
Nixon, Samuel, reference to, **Supp. 3,** 276
"Nize Baby" (comic strip), **Supp. 5,** 262
Nizer, Louis, reference to, **Supp. 7,** 643
Nkrumah, Kwame, reference to, **Supp. 7,** 205
NLRB. *See* National Labor Relations Board
Nobel Prizes: chemistry, **Supp. 5,** 670; **Supp. 6,** 365; **Supp. 8,** 123; literature, **Supp. 5,** 423, 524; **Supp. 7,** 222, 234, 338; **Supp. 8,** 626; peace, **Supp. 1,** 12; **Supp. 2,** 357, 580; **Supp. 4,** 137, 442; **Supp. 5,** 160, 335, 508; **Supp. 6,** 428; **Supp. 7,** 29; **Supp. 8,** 335; physics, **Supp. 3,** 769; **Supp. 5,** 202, 220, 494, 496; **Supp. 6,** 151, 372; **Supp. 7,** 75, 133, 258, 344; **Supp. 8,** 628; physiology or medicine, **Supp. 3,** 136, 140–41, 440, 540; **Supp. 4,** 581; **Supp. 5,** 489; **Supp. 6,** 127, 223; **Supp. 7,** 226, 281, 341, 476; **Supp. 8,** 450, 556
Noble, Ray, reference to, **Supp. 3,** 524
Noel, Miriam, references to, **Supp. 6,** 713, 714
Noeldeke, Theodor, reference to, **Supp. 6,** 641
Noguchi, Hideyo, reference to, **Supp. 4,** 287
Noise, **Supp. 3,** 254
Noisy Book, **Supp. 5,** 92–93
Noland, Kenneth, reference to, **Supp. 7,** 479–80
Nolde, Emil, reference to, **Supp. 6,** 552
Nonimportation Act (1806), **Vol. 5, Part 2,** 30
Nonintercourse Act (1809), **Vol. 5, Part 2,** 30 f.
Nonpartisan Direct Legislation League (1897), founding of, **Supp. 4,** 844–45
Nonpartisan League (agricultural) (1915), **Vol. 6, Part 1,** 271; **Supp. 4,** 308–9, 479, 480; **Supp. 5,** 430; **Supp. 6,** 86–87, 360–61, 645; **Supp. 8,** 1
Nonpartisan League (labor) (1936), founding of, **Supp. 4,** 75, 376; **Supp. 8,** 376
Non-Resistance Society, formed, **Vol. 8, Part 1,** 306 f.
Non-Sectarian Anti-Nazi League, **Supp. 6,** 25
Nook Farm, **Vol. 5, Part 1,** 195
Noonan, Gregory, reference to, **Supp. 5,** 564
Noradrenaline, **Supp. 3,** 136
Norden Laboratories Corporation, **Supp. 7,** 577
Norfolk, Conn., musical festivals, at, **Vol. 9, Part 2,** 64
Norfolk (ship), **Vol. 1, Part 1,** 505
Norfolk, Va., **Vol. 6, Part 2,** 445; **Vol. 7, Part 2,** 139 f.; as naval base, **Vol. 3, Part 1,** 189; **Vol. 6, Part 1,** 572; **Vol. 7, Part 2,** 576
Normal schools, **Vol. 8, Part 2,** 250; Alabama, **Vol. 7, Part 2,** 41; California, **Vol. 7, Part 1,** 578; first state, **Vol. 7, Part 2,** 404; Illinois, **Vol. 1, Part 2,** 44; **Vol. 2, Part 2,** 376, 418; **Vol. 9, Part 2,** 581; Kentucky, **Vol. 8, Part 1,** 643; Massachusetts, **Vol. 2, Part 1,** 420; **Vol. 3, Part 1,** 563 f.; Michigan, **Vol. 10, Part 1,** 617 f.; Missouri, **Vol. 1, Part 1,** 538; modern type of, **Vol. 5, Part 1,** 128; New Jersey, **Vol. 4, Part 2,** 360; Wisconsin, **Vol. 8, Part 2,** 307
Normal Training Kindergarten (New York City), organized, **Vol. 5, Part 2,** 500

O'Connor, Basil, reference to, **Supp. 3,** 643
O'Connor, Edwin, reference to, **Supp. 6,** 141
O'Connor, Jack, reference to, **Supp. 6,** 357
O'Connor, Leslie M., reference to, **Supp. 3,** 438
O'Connor, Richard, reference to, **Supp. 7,** 394
Odd Fellows, Order of, **Vol. 7, Part 1,** 503
Oden, Melita, reference to, **Supp. 6,** 626
Odets, Clifford, reference to, **Supp. 5,** 237
O'Dwyer, William, references to, **Supp. 5,** 227; **Supp. 8,** 397, 512
Office of Naval Records and Library, **Supp. 6,** 348
Office of Naval Research, **Supp. 8,** 687
Office of Price Administration. *See under* World War II
Office of Public Opinion Research, founding of, **Supp. 8,** 69
Office of Strategic Services (OSS). *See under* World War II
Office of War Information (OWI). *See under* World War II
Officers' Training Corps. *See* Reserve Officers' Training Corps
Of Thee I Sing, **Supp. 7,** 551
Ogburn, William F., references to, **Supp. 5,** 520; **Supp. 6,** 604
Ogden, Marguerite, reference to, **Supp. 6,** 3
Ogden, Robert C, reference to, **Vol. 10, Part 1,** 407 f.
Ogden, Utah, founding of, **Vol. 7, Part 1,** 641
"Ogden movement," **Vol. 7, Part 1,** 642
Ogdensburg, founding of, **Vol. 7, Part 1,** 643
Oglethorpe, J. E., treaties with Indians, **Vol. 9, Part 1,** 580
Ogontz School for Young Ladies, **Vol. 8, Part 1,** 335 f.
O'Gorman, James A., references to, **Supp. 3,** 642, 643
O'Hara, John, references to, **Supp. 3,** 339; **Supp. 6,** 236
Ohio: admission to statehood, **Vol. 2, Part 1,** 294; **Vol. 8, Part 2,** 295; **Vol. 10, Part 2,** 540; agriculture, **Vol. 2, Part 1,** 600; **Vol. 5, Part 2,** 445 f.; **Vol. 7, Part 2,** 62 f.; **Vol. 9, Part 2,** 641; **Vol. 10, Part 1,** 444 f.; antislavery movement, **Vol. 6, Part 1,** 224; archaeology in, **Supp. 1,** 316; "black laws," repeal of, **Vol. 3, Part 1,** 241; boundary disputes, **Vol. 2, Part 2,** 185; canal building, **Vol. 2, Part 1,** 113; **Vol. 5, Part 2,** 296, 521; **Vol. 6, Part 2,** 569; Catholic church, **Vol. 8, Part 1,** 266 f.; **Vol. 10, Part 2,** 632; cattle importation, **Vol. 8, Part 1,** 503; city planning boards, **Supp. 3,** 66; Civil War period, **Vol. 2, Part 1,** 95; **Vol. 8, Part 1,** 483; **Vol. 10, Part 2,** 505; common law crimes, **Vol. 4, Part 1,** 385; constitution of 1845, **Vol. 5, Part 1,** 77; Episcopal church, **Vol. 3, Part 1,** 343; **Vol. 6, Part 1,** 179; expedition into, Burr's association with, **Vol. 3, Part 1,** 166; Franklin County Agricultural Society, **Vol. 3, Part 1,** 242; Free Soil party, **Vol. 8, Part 1,** 591; French claims in, **Vol. 3, Part 1,** 317; **Vol. 8, Part 2,** 293; geological researches, **Vol. 7, Part 2,** 62; **Vol. 8, Part 1,** 247; governors, **Vol. 1, Part 1,** 210 f.; **Vol. 1, Part 2,** 16 f.; **Vol. 2, Part 1,** 94 f., 347 f.; **Vol. 2, Part 2,** 457 f., 476 f.; **Vol. 3, Part 1,** 241 f.; **Vol. 3, Part 2,** 502, 504, 544; **Vol. 4, Part 2,** 276, 278; **Vol. 1, Part 1,** 84 f., 419 f.; **Vol. 6, Part 1,** 487, 549; **Vol. 6, Part 2,** 509; **Vol. 7, Part 1,** 235, 287; **Vol. 7, Part 2,** 312; **Vol. 9, Part 2,** 535, 567, 641; **Vol. 10, Part 2,** 470, 540; **Supp. 6,** 129; historical writings on, **Supp. 1,** 330; history of, **Vol. 5, Part 1,** 21, 288; **Vol. 8, Part 1,** 258 f.; **Vol. 9, Part 2,** 330,; Indians, fights with, **Vol. 1, Part 2,** 481; **Vol. 3, Part 1,** 75; industrial service, **Vol. 6, Part 2,** 397; **Vol. 10, Part 1,** 635; judges, popular election of, **Vol. 5, Part 1,** 77; judicial review, **Vol. 2, Part 2,** 536 f.; judiciary, **Supp. 8,** 4; legal service, **Vol. 1, Part 2,** 375; **Vol. 2, Part 1,** 460; **Vol. 3, Part 1,** 162, 164; **Vol. 4, Part 1,** 234; **Vol. 4, Part 2,** 202; **Vol. 5, Part 1,** 77, 84, 544; **Vol. 6, Part 1,** 52, 84, 146; **Vol. 7, Part 1,** 388; **Vol. 7, Part 2,** 8; **Vol. 8, Part 1,** 258, 377, 544; **Vol. 9, Part 1,** 34, 440; **Vol. 9, Part 2,** 264–265, 300, 515; **Vol. 10, Part 1,** 363, 410, 444, 620; **Vol. 10, Part 2,** 283; library service, **Vol. 9, Part 2,** 330; manufacturing enterprises, **Vol. 3, Part 1,** 244; Methodism, **Vol. 9, Part 2,** 482; missions, **Vol. 1, Part 1,** 487; **Vol. 3, Part 1,** 343; **Vol. 5, Part 2,** 166; opening-up of territory, **Vol. 3, Part 1,** 13 f.; paleontology, **Vol. 10, Part 2,** 597; Peace Democrats, **Vol. 10, Part 1,** 144 f.; pioneer days, **Vol. 2, Part 1,** 294; **Vol. 3, Part 2,** 390; **Vol. 6, Part 2,** 509; **Vol. 8, Part 1,** 284 f.; **Vol. 10, Part 2,** 470, 644, 646; politics, **Vol. 2, Part 1,** 348, 521; **Vol. 2, Part 2,** 473 f.; **Vol. 4, Part 2,** 448; **Vol. 5, Part 1,** 85; **Vol. 6, Part 2,** 105; **Supp. 3,** 213; **Supp. 4,** 317–18; **Supp. 5,** 674; **Supp. 6,** 132, 613–14; **Supp. 7,** 49–50, 84–86, 95–96; pre–Civil War agitation, **Vol. 6, Part 2,** 491; Presbyterianism, **Vol. 10, Part 2,** 340; progressive wave in 1910, **Vol. 4, Part 2,** 277; public schools, **Vol. 4, Part 2,** 43; **Vol. 5, Part 1,** 21; **Vol. 5, Part 2,** 70; **Vol. 6, Part 1,** 146, 224, 233 f.; **Vol. 6, Part 2,** 58; **Vol. 7, Part 2,** 569; **Vol. 9, Part 2,** 115, 641; **Vol. 10, Part 2,** 99; public service, **Vol. 1, Part 2,** 16, 102, 156, 277, 375; **Vol. 2, Part 2,** 476; **Vol. 3, Part 1,** 217, 241; **Vol. 3, Part 2,** 384, 544; **Vol. 4, Part 2,** 14, 24, 169, 277, 351, 448, 587; **Vol. 5, Part 1,** 419; **Vol. 5, Part 2,** 336; **Vol. 6, Part 1,** 84, 223, 233, 487, 549; **Vol. 6, Part 2,** 127, 490, 510; **Vol. 7, Part 1,** 227, 235, 356, 587; **Vol. 7, Part 2,** 313, 368, 420, 556; **Vol. 8, Part 1,** 135, 258, 271, 377, 554, 591; **Vol. 9, Part 1,** 20, 84, 87, 100, 554; **Vol. 9, Part 2,** 93, 265, 535, 641; **Vol. 10, Part 1,** 143, 459, 620, 628; **Vol. 10, Part 2,** 470, 505, 540; Republican party, **Vol. 2, Part 1,** 376; Roman Catholic dioceses, **Supp. 3,** 694–95; school legislation, **Vol. 9, Part 2,** 301; social reform, **Vol. 10, Part 2,** 541; surveys of, **Vol. 5, Part 2,** 372; transportation, **Vol. 5, Part 2,** 296 f.; Washington's expedition into, **Vol. 3, Part 1,** 317; waterpower, early, **Vol. 6, Part 1,** 139; woman suffrage, **Supp. 8,** 4; Women's Temperance Crusade, **Vol. 1, Part 2,** 423
Ohio Archaeological Association, founding of, **Vol. 2, Part 1,** 50; **Vol. 7, Part 2,** 392
Ohio Automobile Co., **Vol. 7, Part 2,** 128
Ohio Co., **Vol. 3, Part 1,** 13, 316 f., 367; **Vol. 5, Part 2,** 127; **Vol. 7, Part 2,** 271, 293; **Vol. 8, Part 1,** 284 f.; **Vol. 10, Part 2,** 53
Ohio Fuel Corporation, predecessor, **Supp. 5,** 260
Ohio Medical College, **Vol. 3, Part 1,** 426 f.
Ohio Press (Columbus), **Vol. 9, Part 2,** 301
Ohio River: exploration, **Vol. 2, Part 1,** 582; flood control, **Supp. 4,** 564; flooding (1937), **Supp. 4,** 247
Ohio School Journal, **Vol. 6, Part 1,** 404
Ohio Society of New York, **Vol. 3, Part 2,** 239
Ohio Wesleyan University, **Vol. 1, Part 2,** 34; **Vol. 6, Part 2,** 556; **Vol. 9, Part 2,** 482
Oil: Acme Oil Co., **Vol. 1, Part 1,** 337; by-product research, **Supp. 4,** 661; California, **Vol. 7, Part 2,** 386; companies, **Supp. 3,** 260–61; **Supp. 4,** 568–69, 660–61; **Supp. 6,** 584–85; company mergers, **Supp. 4,** 775–76; cone-type drills, **Vol. 5, Part 1,** 351; conservation advocacy, **Supp. 2,** 155, 553; **Supp. 7,** 771–72, 804; corporate executives, **Supp. 5,** 236; cotton seed used for, **Vol. 3, Part 1,** 507 f.; crude, separation of naphtha from, **Vol. 8, Part 2,** 95; discovery-depletion allowance, **Supp. 4,** 338; documentary film on drilling, **Supp. 5,** 226; drilling, first driving of pipe to bedrock, **Vol. 3, Part 1,** 428; drilling methods, **Supp. 7,** 615; exporting of, **Supp. 2,** 572; first successful well, **Vol. 3, Part 1,** 427 f.; **Vol. 7,**

Part 1, 297; geological studies, **Vol. 4, Part 2,** 444; geology of, **Supp. 2,** 681; **Supp. 7,** 803–5; industry, **Vol. 1, Part 2,** 301; **Vol. 3, Part 2,** 602; **Vol. 6, Part 1,** 540; **Vol. 8, Part 1,** 168 f.; **Vol. 8, Part 2,** 56, 65; industry reversionary interest concept, **Supp. 8,** 454; Iran's nationalization of, **Supp. 8,** 276; leases, Teapot Dome, **Vol. 3, Part 1,** 234 f.; **Vol. 4, Part 2,** 255; **Vol. 8, Part 2,** 86, 194; **Vol. 10, Part 1,** 393 f.; lighting, **Vol. 3, Part 1,** 415; **Vol. 4, Part 2,** 440; Mexican fields, **Supp. 6,** 451; **Supp. 7,** 377; monopoly, **Supp. 9,** 571–79; multinational companies, **Supp. 8,** 455; NRA code, **Supp. 2,** 30; Oklahoma fields, **Supp. 3,** 505; **Supp. 6,** 469; paleontological research application to, **Supp. 4,** 205, 206; Pennsylvania, **Vol. 1, Part 1,** 26; **Vol. 2, Part 1,** 496; **Vol. 3, Part 1,** 427 f.; **Vol. 3, Part 2,** 85; **Vol. 6, Part 1,** 340; **Vol. 8, Part 1,** 168 f.; **Vol. 8, Part 2,** 95; **Vol. 10, Part 1,** 179; **Vol. 10, Part 2,** 107; pipelines, **Vol. 3, Part 1,** 367; **Vol. 3, Part 2,** 452; **Vol. 4, Part 2,** 401; **Vol. 8, Part 2,** 95; **Supp. 2,** 133; **Supp. 4,** 568–69, 661; production, **Vol. 3, Part 1,** 367; **Vol. 4, Part 2,** 36; **Vol. 5, Part 2,** 262; **Vol. 6, Part 1,** 339 f.; **Vol. 7, Part 2,** 544; **Vol. 8, Part 2,** 65; products, extension of uses for, **Vol. 3, Part 1,** 415; quotas in commerce, **Supp. 2,** 30; refineries, **Supp. 2,** 133, 568–69, 679; **Supp. 4,** 568–69; refining, **Vol. 3, Part 1,** 415, 367; **Vol. 5, Part 2,** 371 f.; **Vol. 6, Part 2,** 562; **Vol. 7, Part 1,** 297 f., 443; **Vol. 7, Part 2,** 330; **Vol. 9, Part 1,** 148; reserves, leasing of, **Vol. 3, Part 1,** 156, 234 f.; shale industry, **Vol. 1, Part 2,** 34; **Vol. 3, Part 1,** 156 f.; sperm oil, efforts to find substitutes for, as lubricant, **Vol. 3, Part 1,** 415; **Vol. 3, Part 2,** 401; Standard Oil Co., **Vol. 1, Part 1,** 337; **Vol. 3, Part 1,** 341 f.; **Vol. 3, Part 2,** 85, 451, 487; **Vol. 4, Part 2,** 21, 81, 401; **Vol. 6, Part 1,** 60, 332, 340; **Vol. 8, Part 2,** 65, 95; studies in, **Vol. 6, Part 1,** 540; **Vol. 9, Part 1,** 163 f.; system of railroad rebates, **Vol. 9, Part 2,** 70; technology advances, **Supp. 6,** 332–33; Texas, **Vol. 6, Part 1,** 483; **Supp. 4,** 775; **Supp. 6,** 135–36, 540–41; tidelands bill, **Supp. 8,** 104; transportation of by water, **Vol. 8, Part 1,** 464; tube and tank process for crude, **Supp. 3,** 247; well machinery, **Supp. 1,** 453; writings on, **Supp. 3,** 762. *See also* Gasoline; Natural gas; Petrochemistry; Petrology; Teapot Dome scandal

Oils and fats, margarine development, **Supp. 3,** 247; **Supp. 5,** 400

Okakura, Kakuzo, reference to, **Supp. 3,** 465

Okeechobee Lake, battle of, **Vol. 9, Part 2,** 350

O'Keeffe, Georgia, reference to, **Supp. 4,** 781

Okinawa, World War II action, **Supp. 3,** 118; **Supp. 4,** 323, 589; **Supp. 5,** 66; **Supp. 6,** 268; **Supp. 7,** 352

Oklahoma: banditry in early days, **Vol. 3, Part 1,** 40 f.; civil government for Indians, **Vol. 7, Part 2,** 225; early state history, **Vol. 9, Part 2,** 546; governors, **Supp. 1,** 380; **Supp. 3,** 506; **Supp. 6,** 468–70; **Supp. 7,** 429; oil wells, **Supp. 3,** 505; pioneering, **Vol. 10, Part 2,** 530; politics, **Supp. 3,** 10; **Supp. 4,** 338; **Supp. 5,** 662; **Supp. 7,** 738–39; public service, **Vol. 8, Part 1,** 111; **Vol. 8, Part 2,** 20 f.; statehood, **Supp. 4,** 641

Oklahoma!, **Supp. 6,** 273–74, 286, 638; **Supp. 7,** 497, 692, 693

Oklahoma Agricultural and Mechanical College, presidency, **Supp. 5,** 49

Oklahoma Leader, **Supp. 3,** 10

Oland, Warner, reference to, **Supp. 1,** 80

O'Laughlin, Michael, reference to, **Vol. 1, Part 2,** 449

Olcott, Henry Steel, reference to, **Vol. 1, Part 2,** 362

Old Age Revolving Pension Plan. *See* Townsend Plan

Old American Co., sole theatrical concern in New York City in 1796, **Vol. 3, Part 1,** 516 f.

"Old Cattleman" stories, **Vol. 6, Part 1,** 205

Old Colony Building (Chicago), steel framing, **Supp. 3,** 611

Old English, syntax studies in, **Supp. 2,** 88

Older, Fremont, references to, **Supp. 3,** 394, 532; **Supp. 6,** 590

Oldfield, Barney, references to, **Supp. 4,** 293; **Supp. 6,** 163

"Old Folks' Concerts," **Vol. 5, Part 2,** 320

"Old Home Week," origin of, **Vol. 8, Part 2,** 121

Old Ironsides. See Constitution

Old Jules, **Supp. 8,** 566–67

Old Maid and the Thief, The, **Supp. 7,** 125

Old Man and the Sea, The, **Supp. 7,** 339

Old Northwest. *See* Northwest Territory

Old Northwest: Pioneer Period (1815–1840), The, **Supp. 8,** 60

Olds, Ransom E., reference to, **Supp. 4,** 243

Oldsmobile car, **Supp. 4,** 638

Old South Church (Boston), **Vol. 5, Part 1,** 88, **Vol. 9, Part 2,** 390, 392

Old Swamp Church, **Vol. 7, Part 1,** 307

Old Testament. *See* Bible

O'Leary, Irwin, reference to, **Supp. 7,** 4

Oleomargarine, early use of, **Vol. 9, Part 2,** 245. *See also* Margarine

Oliphant, Herman, reference to, **Supp. 3,** 186

Oliphant, Lawrence, reference to, **Vol. 10, Part 1,** 421

Olive Branch Petition, **Vol. 7, Part 2,** 156

Oliver, Sy, reference to, **Supp. 4,** 510

"Oliver Optic," **Vol. 1, Part 1,** 103

Olivet College, founding of, **Vol. 7, Part 1,** 230; **Vol. 9, Part 1,** 112

Olivier, Laurence, reference to, **Supp. 8,** 368–69

Olmsted, Frederick Law, references to, **Vol. 10, Part 1,** 605 f.; **Supp. 3,** 533; **Supp. 6,** 26

Olmstead, John C., reference to, **Supp. 6,** 485

Olsen and Johnson (comedy team), **Supp. 7,** 588–89

Olson, Culbert L., references to, **Supp. 3,** 156, 533

Olson, Floyd B., reference to, **Supp. 3,** 226

Olustee, battle of, **Vol. 2, Part 2,** 315; **Vol. 4, Part 2,** 421; **Vol. 9, Part 1,** 12

Olvany, George W., reference to, **Supp. 6,** 141–42

Olympia, construction of, for Navy, **Vol. 3, Part 1,** 292

Olympic games, **Vol. 7, Part 1,** 356; rowing, **Supp. 6,** 331; swimming, **Supp. 8,** 336–37; track and field, **Supp. 3,** 487; **Supp. 5,** 683–84, 722; **Supp. 7,** 152

Olympic National Park, **Supp. 7,** 764

Omaha, Nebr., **Vol. 2, Part 2,** 536; **Vol. 7, Part 1,** 618; starting point of the Union Pacific Railroad, **Vol. 3, Part 1,** 542 f.; Trans-Mississippi Exposition, **Vol. 4, Part 1,** 221; **Vol. 8, Part 2,** 172

Omaha Daily Bee, **Vol. 8, Part 2,** 172

Omaha Indians, **Vol. 9, Part 2,** 522

Omaha World-Herald, **Vol. 9, Part 2,** 522

O'Mahoney, Joseph C., reference to, **Supp. 7,** 31

Omnibus: first in New York, **Vol. 9, Part 1,** 583; first west of Mississippi, **Vol. 10, Part 1,** 638 f.

"Omnibus" (television program), **Supp. 6,** 680

Oncology, **Supp. 3,** 258. *See also* Cancer

Onderdonk, Henry U., reference to, **Vol. 8, Part 2,** 530

O'Neal, Edward A., reference to, **Supp. 6,** 12

O'Neale, Margaret ("Peggy") references to, **Vol. 3, Part 1,** 610; **Vol. 5, Part 1,** 474, 532; **Vol. 7, Part 2,** 42; **Vol. 9, Part 1,** 319

Oneida Community, **Vol. 4, Part 1,** 99; **Vol. 4, Part 2,** 589; **Vol. 7, Part 1,** 590; **Supp. 5,** 492

Oneida Indians, **Vol. 2, Part 2,** 432 f.

O'Neill, Eugene: Bennett relationship, **Supp. 3,** 58, 59; references to, **Supp. 4,** 330, 355, 503, 504, 843; **Supp. 5,** 375; **Supp. 6,** 471

Pancreas: function, **Supp. 6,** 189, 190; research on, **Supp. 6,** 598, 697; structure of, **Supp. 6,** 53, 100

Paneth, Friedrich ("Fritz"), references to, **Supp. 4,** 337; **Supp. 6,** 334

Pangborn, Clyde, reference to, **Supp. 6,** 52

Panhandle Stockman's Association, **Vol. 4, Part 1,** 394

Panics, **Vol. 2, Part 1,** 471; **Vol. 2, Part 2,** 375; **Vol. 3, Part 1,** 486 f.; **Vol. 4, Part 2,** 393; **Vol. 5, Part 2,** 115, 601; of 1765, **Vol. 8, Part 2,** 46; of 1837, **Vol. 1, Part 1,** 268; **Vol. 9, Part 2,** 19; **Vol. 10, Part 1,** 155; of 1857, **Vol. 2, Part 1,** 212; **Vol. 2, Part 2,** 243; **Vol. 4, Part 2,** 393; **Vol. 5, Part 2,** 69; of 1873, **Vol. 4, Part 1,** 499; **Vol. 4, Part 2,** 450; **Vol. 5, Part 2,** 68; **Vol. 8, Part 1,** 578; **Vol. 9, Part 1,** 86–87; of 1893, **Vol. 2, Part 1,** 495; **Vol. 2, Part 2,** 210; **Vol. 3, Part 2,** 3; **Vol. 9, Part 2,** 88, 425; of 1913, **Vol. 10, Part 2,** 357; "Black Friday," **Vol. 4, Part 1,** 454; "Lawson panic," **Vol. 4, Part 1,** 578

Pankhurst, Emmeline, references to, **Supp. 6,** 40, 41

"Pansy" books, **Supp. 1,** 20

Pantarchy, **Vol. 1, Part 1,** 298

Pantepec Oil Co., **Supp. 8,** 455

Pantheism, **Vol. 5, Part 2,** 457

Pantheon Books, founding of, **Supp. 7,** 799

Pantomimes, **Vol. 3, Part 2,** 566 f.

Pantzer, Katharine F., reference to, **Supp. 7,** 387

Paoli, battle of, **Vol. 10, Part 1,** 563

Papanicolaou, George N., reference to, **Supp. 2,** 632

Paper and paper products: bags, making of, **Vol. 2, Part 2,** 575; **Vol. 7, Part 1,** 165; disposable drinking cup, **Supp. 5,** 144; dress patterns, **Vol. 2, Part 1,** 375; manufacture, **Vol. 2, Part 2,** 54, 74 f., 510, 551; **Vol. 3, Part 2,** 250, 357; **Vol. 4, Part 1,** 49; **Vol. 4, Part 2,** 250; **Vol. 5, Part 2,** 281 f.; **Vol. 6, Part 2,** 641; **Vol. 7, Part 2,** 643; **Vol. 8, Part 1,** 534; **Vol. 9, Part 2,** 544; **Vol. 10, Part 2,** 10; manufacturing technology, **Supp. 1,** 500; mill, first in colonies, **Vol. 8, Part 1,** 632; mill, first in New England, **Supp. 1,** 392; newspaper manufacture, **Supp. 2,** 301; wood, early experiments with, **Vol. 4, Part 2,** 259

Paperback books: Little Blue Books, **Supp. 5,** 264–65; Pocket Books, **Supp. 6,** 583; **Supp. 8,** 579; Viking Portable Library, **Supp. 7,** 307

Papist-Protestant controversy, colonial New York, **Vol. 6, Part 1,** 181

Pap test, development of, **Supp. 2,** 632; **Supp. 7,** 598–99

Parachutes, **Supp. 7,** 679

Paracutin volcano, **Supp. 6,** 213

Parade, **Supp. 7,** 243

Parades (New York City), **Supp. 7,** 779, 780

Paraguay: diplomatic relations with, **Vol. 7, Part 1,** 608; **Vol. 7, Part 2,** 422; **Vol. 9, Part 1,** 136 f.; naval expedition to, **Vol. 8, Part 1,** 596

Paralysis, rehabilitation methods, **Supp. 1,** 317

Paramecium, **Supp. 4,** 910

Paramount Pictures, **Supp. 4,** 350; **Supp. 6,** 76–77, 159, 369; **Supp. 8,** 677–78

Paramount Theater (New York City), stage-band policy, **Supp. 7,** 301

Parapsychology. *See* Psychic phenomena

Parasitology, **Vol. 6, Part 1,** 151; **Vol. 7, Part 1,** 542; intestinal disease research, **Supp. 4,** 462; research in, **Supp. 1,** 666; syphilis research, **Supp. 4,** 288; writings on, **Supp. 3,** 802–3

Parathyroid gland, **Supp. 3,** 483

"Parchesi," invention of, **Vol. 6, Part 1,** 479

Parc National Albert (Congo), **Supp. 8,** 3

Parents' Magazine, **Supp. 6,** 382

Parent-Teacher Associations, early, **Vol. 2, Part 1,** 345

Parepa-Rosa Opera Company, **Vol. 8, Part 2,** 92

Paresthesia, early description of, **Vol. 8, Part 1,** 282 f.

Pareto, Vilfredo, reference to, **Supp. 3,** 351

Pari-mutuel betting law, **Supp. 1,** 114

Paris: American chapel, **Vol. 5, Part 2,** 428; American Embassy, purchase of, **Vol. 4, Part 2,** 588; art scene, **Supp. 6,** 552; expatriates in, **Supp. 4,** 768–70; 771; **Supp. 6,** 497–98, 716; **Supp. 7,** 40–41, 334–36, 560; **Supp. 8,** 656; international exposition at, **Vol. 1, Part 1,** 445; newspaper, first American, **Vol. 3, Part 2,** 212; traffic regulation, **Supp. 3,** 254; World War II liberation, **Supp. 7,** 350

Paris, Treaty of (1783), **Vol. 1, Part 1,** 77; **Vol. 3, Part 2,** 594–95; **Vol. 5, Part 2,** 7, 21; **Vol. 6, Part 1,** 35; **Vol. 8, Part 1,** 355

Paris, Treaty of (1898), **Vol. 3, Part 1,** 110, 164; **Vol. 4, Part 1,** 52, 516; **Vol. 6, Part 2,** 108; **Vol. 8, Part 1,** 485

Paris Herald, **Supp. 4,** 686

Paris Peace Conference (1919), **Vol. 1, Part 2,** 138; **Supp. 7,** 262, 683, 687–88, 782; **Supp. 8,** 146, 495; financial adviser, **Supp. 3,** 219; German reparations, **Supp. 4,** 470; Jewish delegations committee, **Supp. 3,** 489

Park, Edwards A., reference to, **Supp. 3,** 775

Park, Robert E., references to, **Supp. 4,** 831; **Supp. 6,** 321, 532, 533

Park, Roy H., reference to, **Supp. 6,** 292

Park, amusement, first in U.S., **Vol. 10, Part 1,** 48

Park College, founding of, **Vol. 6, Part 1,** 542

Parker, Dorothy, references to, **Supp. 3,** 53; **Supp. 6,** 259; **Supp. 7,** 413; **Supp. 8,** 529

Parker, Francis Wayland, reference to, **Supp. 5,** 60–61

Parker, George H., reference to, **Supp. 3,** 133

Parker, James Reid, reference to, **Supp. 4,** 386

Parker, John J., reference to, **Supp. 3,** 559

Parker, Theodore: references to, **Vol. 5, Part 2,** 404; **Vol. 6, Part 1,** 387; **Vol. 7, Part 1,** 587; **Supp. 5,** 138; biography of, **Vol. 10, Part 1,** 615 f.;

Parkes, Alexander, reference to, **Vol. 5, Part 1,** 448

Parkes process, **Vol. 1, Part 1,** 528

Parkhurst, Charles H., references to, **Vol. 5, Part 1,** 573; **Vol. 7, Part 1,** 280; **Vol. 8, Part 2,** 521

Parkman, Francis, references to, **Vol. 7, Part 1,** 569; **Vol. 9, Part 1,** 47; **Vol. 9, Part 2,** 405; **Supp. 5,** 430

Parkman, George, reference to, **Vol. 10, Part 1,** 592 f.

Parks, William, reference to, **Vol. 7, Part 1,** 596

Parks: landscape architecture, **Supp. 3,** 490–91; **Supp. 5,** 369–70; **Supp. 6,** 485–86; municipal facilities, **Supp. 3,** 217; national, **Vol. 2, Part 2,** 78; **Vol. 4, Part 2,** 86, 439 f.; **Vol. 5, Part 1,** 492 f.; **Vol. 5, Part 2,** 492 f.; **Vol. 6, Part 1,** 495; **Vol. 6, Part 2,** 399; **Vol. 8, Part 2,** 355; **Supp. 2,** 348; **Supp. 4,** 896; national, development of, **Supp. 2,** 265; **Supp. 4,** 522; national, in Hawaii, **Supp. 5,** 361; national, legislation, **Supp. 7,** 764; national, maps of, **Supp. 4,** 558; national, Rocky Mountain, **Supp. 1,** 555; national, wilderness system, **Supp. 7,** 814; National Park Service, **Supp. 6,** 486; New York City, **Supp. 4,** 213; playgrounds, **Supp. 1,** 595; public, **Vol. 1, Part 1,** 50 f.; **Vol. 1, Part 2,** 408; **Vol. 3, Part 2,** 56, 70; **Vol. 4, Part 2,** 5; **Vol. 5, Part 1,** 250; **Vol. 6, Part 2,** 492; **Vol. 7, Part 1,** 315; **Vol. 7, Part 2,** 25 f., 30, 117, 197, 472, 482, 600; **Vol. 8, Part 1,** 157 f., 405; **Vol. 8, Part 2,** 37, 220, 355, 464; **Vol. 9, Part 1,** 151, 545; **Vol. 9, Part 2,** 123; **Vol. 10, Part 1,** 647; public, Baltimore, **Vol. 6, Part 1,** 27; public, Boston, **Vol. 7, Part 2,** 26 f.; public, Brooklyn, **Vol. 9, Part 2,** 123; public, Chicago, **Vol. 2, Part 1,** 306; public, District of Columbia, **Vol. 8, Part 1,** 379; public, New York City, **Supp. 4,** 213; public, Philadelphia, **Vol. 10, Part 1,** 647; urban, **Supp. 5,** 630; wilderness and wildlife preserves, **Supp. 4,** 483; **Supp. 8,** 486

Parkway Community House (Chicago), **Supp. 8,** 80
Parliamentary procedure, **Vol. 5, Part 2,** 26; **Supp. 1,** 631
Parmly, Eleazer, reference to, **Vol. 2, Part 1,** 155
Parochial schools, **Vol. 3, Part 1,** 562 f.; **Vol. 4, Part 2,** 415; **Vol. 8, Part 2,** 596; busing, **Supp. 5,** 358; desegregation, **Supp. 8,** 537; development of, **Supp. 3,** 393; **Supp. 4,** 334–35; **Supp. 7,** 533; federal aid issue, **Supp. 8,** 25, 115–16; free high schools, **Supp. 5,** 179
Parole system, **Supp. 1,** 228; beginnings of, **Vol. 10, Part 2,** 385
Parran, Thomas, reference to, **Supp. 6,** 460
Parrington, Vernon L., reference to, **Supp. 4,** 63
Parsons, Elsie Clews, reference to, **Supp. 4,** 71
Parsons, Frank, reference to, **Supp. 2,** 45
Parsons, Lucy A., reference to, **Vol. 7, Part 1,** 252
Parsons, Louella, reference to, **Supp. 8,** 281, 282
Parsons, Thomas William, reference to, **Vol. 5, Part 1,** 273
Parthenon (Athens), reconstruction financing, **Supp. 2,** 185
Parties. *See* Entertaining
Partisan Review, **Supp. 7,** 80, 239; founding of, **Supp. 7,** 269
Pascin, Jules, reference to, **Supp. 3,** 292
Passavant Memorial Hospital, **Supp. 3,** 302
Passionist Order, establishment of, **Vol. 7, Part 1,** 619
Pasteur effect and reaction (glucose metabolization), **Supp. 6,** 595
Pasteurization: beer, **Supp. 1,** 142; milk, **Vol. 8, Part 2,** 553; **Supp. 2,** 315, 514; **Supp. 5,** 144
Pastor, Tony, references to, **Vol. 7, Part 2,** 290; **Supp. 2,** 661
Pastorius Colony (Pa.), **Vol. 5, Part 1,** 80
Patch, Alexander, III, reference to, **Supp. 3,** 583
Patent for Prospective Emigrants to America, **Vol. 3, Part 1,** 5
"Patent leather," first factory for, in America, **Vol. 1, Part 2,** 529
Patent medicine, **Vol. 1, Part 1,** 413, 450; **Vol. 3, Part 1,** 586 f.; **Supp. 5,** 143; advertisements for, **Vol. 8, Part 2,** 197; manufacture of, **Vol. 7, Part 2,** 624 f.
Patent Office, United States, **Vol. 5, Part 2,** 203; **Vol. 7, Part 2,** 136, 351
Patents: cheese processing litigation, **Supp. 5,** 400; copying machine development, **Supp. 8,** 71; Edison litigation, **Supp. 1,** 280; Ford infringement suit, **Supp. 4,** 295–96; government supervision, **Vol. 3, Part 2,** 110, 228; **Vol. 5, Part 2,** 33, 203; **Vol. 6, Part 1,** 146 f.; **Vol. 7, Part 2,** 136, 149, 351; **Vol. 8, Part 1,** 2 f.; law, **Vol. 1, Part 2,** 360; **Vol. 2, Part 2,** 481, 613 f.; **Vol. 3, Part 1,** 288; **Vol. 4, Part 2,** 249, 590; **Vol. 5, Part 2,** 41, 464 f.; **Vol. 6, Part 1,** 27; **Vol. 8, Part 1,** 75 f., 504 f.; **Vol. 8, Part 2,** 106, 567; **Vol. 9, Part 1,** 614; **Vol. 9, Part 2,** 99; **Supp. 1,** 703; movie industry suit, **Supp. 4,** 734; radio and wireless transmission suits, **Supp. 4,** 452; **Supp. 5,** 21; **Supp. 7,** 177. *See also* fields of patents
Patents, Bureau of, **Vol. 7, Part 2,** 149
Paterson, N.J., early history of, **Vol. 3, Part 1,** 290
Paterson, **Supp. 7,** 790–91
"Paterson's Practice Laws," **Vol. 7, Part 2,** 294
Paterson Strike Pageant (1913), **Supp. 7,** 486
Path, theosophical monthly, **Vol. 5, Part 2,** 233
Pathfinder, **Supp. 7,** 615
Pathological Institute (New York City), **Supp. 4,** 571
Pathology, **Vol. 2, Part 1,** 260; **Vol. 3, Part 1,** 77 f., 208; **Vol. 3, Part 2,** 320 f., 433; **Vol. 4, Part 2,** 44 f.; **Vol. 5, Part 2,** 306; **Vol. 7, Part 2,** 208, 354 f.; **Vol. 8, Part 1,** 252 f., 391, 404; **Vol. 9, Part 2,** 23; **Vol. 10, Part 1,** 493 f., 621 f.; blood culture studies,

Supp. 4, 494; cancer, **Supp. 3,** 257–58; chemical aspects of, **Supp. 3,** 806–7; early books on, **Vol. 5, Part 1,** 233; **Vol. 9, Part 2,** 23; etiological disease classification, **Supp. 3,** 483; frozen-tissue diagnostic method, **Supp. 3,** 832; histologic, **Supp. 3,** 502–3; hospital teaching, **Supp. 1,** 206; **Supp. 3,** 502–3; immunology research, **Supp. 4,** 287–88; plant, **Supp. 3,** 814–15; surgical, **Supp. 1,** 91; **Supp. 6,** 664; tuberculosis and silicosis studies, **Supp. 4,** 314; typhus research, **Supp. 4,** 667–68; writings on, **Vol. 3, Part 1,** 306; **Vol. 8, Part 1,** 252 f.
Pathological Society: New York, **Vol. 7, Part 2,** 505; Philadelphia, **Vol. 3, Part 1,** 24; **Vol. 7, Part 2,** 129
Patman, Wright, reference to, **Supp. 6,** 90
Paton, Alan, reference to, **Supp. 5,** 419
Paton, R. Townley, reference to, **Supp. 7,** 70
Patowmack Co., **Vol. 5, Part 2,** 122
Patri, Angelo, reference to, **Supp. 5,** 237
Patrick, Mason M., references to, **Supp. 3,** 17; **Supp. 8,** 47, 185
"Patriot-printer of 1776," **Vol. 1, Part 2,** 564
Patriots, The, **Vol. 3, Part 2,** 17; **Vol. 7, Part 1,** 326
Patriot War (1838–39). *See* Aroostock War
Patten, Simon Nelson, reference to, **Vol. 8, Part 2,** 531; **Supp. 4,** 227
"Patten Men," **Vol. 7, Part 2,** 299
Patterns of Culture, **Supp. 4,** 71–72, 73
Patterson, Eleanor Medill ("Cissy"), references to, **Supp. 4,** 645; **Supp. 7,** 603; **Supp. 8,** 282, 496
Patterson, Ellen, reference to, **Supp. 6,** 318
Patterson, John H., references to, **Supp. 6,** 332, 674
Patterson, Joseph Medill, references to, **Supp. 4,** 644; **Supp. 5,** 449; **Supp. 6,** 699; **Supp. 7,** 603
Patterson, Malcolm R., references to, **Supp. 1,** 656; **Supp. 3,** 449
Patterson, Robert P., reference to, **Supp. 6,** 437
Patterson, Robert W., reference to, **Supp. 5,** 449
Patton, Charley, reference to, **Supp. 6,** 274–75
Patton, George S., references to, **Supp. 3,** 583; **Supp. 4,** 857; **Supp. 8,** 497
Paul, Alice, references to, **Supp. 4,** 157; **Supp. 6,** 41; **Supp. 7,** 717, 718
Paul, John R., reference to, **Supp. 3,** 775
Paul, Maury, reference to, **Supp. 7,** 752
Pauley, Edwin W., reference to, **Supp. 5,** 343
Pauli, Wolfgang, reference to, **Supp. 5,** 219–20
"Pauline system," **Vol. 9, Part 2,** 345
Pauling, Linus, reference to, **Supp. 8,** 590
Paulist Order, **Vol. 4, Part 2,** 604; **Vol. 6, Part 1,** 15; **Supp. 6,** 237–38
Paulist Press, founding of, **Supp. 2,** 72
Paul Revere and the World He Lived In, **Supp. 8,** 181
Paulus Hook, battle of, **Vol. 1, Part 1,** 176; **Vol. 1, Part 2,** 356; **Vol. 6, Part 1,** 107; **Vol. 10, Part 1,** 518
Paving, **Vol. 8, Part 1,** 442
Pavlov, I. P., reference to, **Supp. 5,** 329
Pavlova, Anna, references to, **Supp. 3,** 282; **Supp. 5,** 74–75; **Supp. 8,** 670
Pawnee Indians, **Vol. 7, Part 1,** 560; **Supp. 2,** 265; **Supp. 3,** 460
Pawnee (ship), **Vol. 1, Part 1,** 528
Pawtucket, R.I., founding of, **Vol. 5, Part 2,** 40, **Vol. 9, Part 1,** 206; **Vol. 10, Part 2,** 222
Paxon, Frederic Logan, references to, **Supp. 6,** 6; **Supp. 8,** 59
Payne, Oliver H., reference to, **Supp. 2,** 570
Payne, William H., reference to, **Supp. 3,** 328
Payne-Aldrich Tariff Act (1909), **Vol. 1, Part 2,** 232; **Vol. 7, Part 2,** 331; **Vol. 9, Part 2,** 269; **Supp. 3,** 464
Payola scandal, **Supp. 7,** 267
Peabody, George, references to, **Vol. 5, Part 1,** 214; **Vol. 8, Part 2,** 537

2, 368; Sunday, operation of streetcars on, **Vol. 8, Part 1,** 428; supreme court, **Supp. 3,** 415; Tories in, **Vol. 7, Part 1,** 131; **Vol. 8, Part 2,** 177; Union Canal, **Vol. 1, Part 1,** 540; "Warhawks" among the Quakers, **Vol. 8, Part 2,** 9; Whigs in, **Vol. 7, Part 1,** 131; **Vol. 8, Part 2,** 177; Whiskey Rebellion, **Vol. 8, Part 1,** 401; writings on, **Vol. 5, Part 2,** 45 f.; Wyoming Valley region, **Vol. 7, Part 2,** 258. *See also city and institution names*

Pennsylvania Academy of the Fine Arts, oldest art school in America, **Vol. 3, Part 1,** 590 f.; **Vol. 7, Part 2,** 346, 349; **Vol. 8, Part 1,** 401; **Vol. 8, Part 2,** 7, 187, 235, 372

Pennsylvania Agricultural Society, **Vol. 8, Part 1,** 143 f.

Pennsylvania Archives, documentary index, **Vol. 4, Part 2,** 472

Pennsylvania Association of Public Accountants, **Supp. 6,** 397

Pennsylvania Central Airlines, founding of, **Supp. 7,** 16

Pennsylvania College. *See* Gettysburg College

Pennsylvania Commission on Old-Age Pensions, **Supp. 3,** 255

Pennsylvania Evening Post, **Vol. 9, Part 2,** 611–12

Pennsylvania Farmer, **Vol. 8, Part 2,** 9

Pennsylvania German Dialect, The, **Vol. 6, Part 1,** 78

Pennsylvania-German Society, **Vol. 8, Part 2,** 282

Pennsylvania Historical Society, **Vol. 7, Part 2,** 448

Pennsylvania Horticultural Society, **Vol. 7, Part 2,** 452

Pennsylvania Hospital, **Vol. 1, Part 2,** 433; **Vol. 2, Part 2,** 239; **Vol. 5, Part 2,** 274; **Vol. 7, Part 2,** 129, 413

Pennsylvania Institution, **Supp. 4,** 11

Pennsylvania Journal and Weekly Advertiser, **Vol. 1, Part 2,** 558; **Vol. 7, Part 1,** 550

Pennsylvania Magazine of History, **Vol. 5, Part 2,** 215

Pennsylvania Manufacturers' Association, **Supp. 7,** 305, 306

Pennsylvania Military College, **Vol. 8, Part 1,** 49 f.

Pennsylvania Motor Truck Association, **Supp. 6,** 91

Pennsylvania Packet, first daily in U.S., **Vol. 3, Part 1,** 514 f.; **Vol. 8, Part 1,** 139 f.

Pennsylvania Pharmaceutical Association, **Vol. 8, Part 1,** 498

Pennsylvania Railroad, **Vol. 2, Part 1,** 160, 565; **Vol. 3, Part 1,** 18; **Vol. 4, Part 1,** 450; **Vol. 5, Part 1,** 262, 392; **Vol. 5, Part 2,** 455 f.; **Vol. 7, Part 1,** 176; **Vol. 7, Part 2,** 305; **Vol. 8, Part 1,** 417 f.; **Vol. 8, Part 2,** 7, 500 f.; **Vol. 9, Part 1,** 616; **Vol. 9, Part 2,** 396, 484, 486; **Vol. 10, Part 2,** 350; electrification of, **Supp. 1,** 34; **Supp. 4,** 370; **Supp. 8,** 93; management, **Supp. 8,** 92–94; strike against, **Supp. 8,** 513

Pennsylvania Society for Promoting the Abolition of Slavery, **Vol. 7, Part 2,** 413

Pennsylvania State University, **Vol. 1, Part 1,** 404; **Vol. 8, Part 1,** 257 f.; **Vol. 9, Part 1,** 430; **Vol. 10, Part 1,** 556 f.; forestry studies, **Supp. 4,** 43–44; medical school, **Supp. 3,** 358; organic chemistry studies, **Supp. 4,** 888

Pennsylvania Tuberculosis and Health Society, **Supp. 2,** 196

Pennsylvania Working Home for Blind Men, **Vol. 7, Part 2,** 305

Penny arcades, **Supp. 5,** 726

"Penny's Society," **Vol. 4, Part 1,** 475

Penobscot expedition (1779), **Vol. 8, Part 2,** 316

Penobscot Indians, **Supp. 4,** 248, 761–62

Penology, **Vol. 2, Part 1,** 50, 61, 614; **Vol. 7, Part 1,** 319; National Society of Penal Information, **Vol. 7, Part 2,** 76; parole system, **Vol. 10, Part 2,** 385; penal codes, **Vol. 6, Part 1,** 311; **Vol. 9, Part 2,** 75; peni-

tentiary system, **Vol. 5, Part 2,** 432; writings on, **Vol. 3, Part 1,** 571 f. **Vol. 6, Part 1,** 237

Penrod, **Supp. 4,** 816, 817

Penrose, Spencer and Richard, reference to, **Supp. 6,** 316

Pens: fountain, **Vol. 10, Part 1,** 533 f.; steel, **Vol. 3, Part 2,** 187

Pensacola lands, speculation in, **Vol. 3, Part 1,** 609 f.

Pensions: Act of 1879, **Vol. 2, Part 2,** 208; Act of 1890, **Vol. 7, Part 1,** 539; advocacy organizations, **Supp. 8,** 9–10; early employment plans, **Supp. 2,** 404, 645; Mothers' Pension Act, **Vol. 6, Part 1,** 354 f.; Pennsylvania state commission, **Supp. 3,** 517; Pension Office, **Vol. 7, Part 1,** 347; **Vol. 9, Part 2,** 297 f.; reorganization of system, **Vol. 3, Part 2,** 159; soldiers', **Vol. 4, Part 2,** 526; studies in, **Supp. 2,** 542–43; teachers, **Supp. 1,** 328; **Supp. 2,** 542; **Supp. 8,** 9–10; Townsend Plan, **Supp. 6,** 646–47; **Supp. 7,** 195; trade union, **Vol. 9, Part 2,** 86. *See also* Social security

Pentagon Building (Washington, D.C.), construction of, **Supp. 5,** 643

Pentecostalism, **Supp. 4,** 876

Peonage, **Vol. 3, Part 2,** 488; **Vol. 8, Part 2,** 241

People's Choral Union, founding of, **Supp. 2,** 140

People's Council of America, founding of, **Supp. 4,** 539

People's Institute (New York City), **Supp. 3,** 511, 563; **Supp. 8,** 58, 98

People's Legislative Service, **Supp. 4,** 544

People's Singing Classes, founding of, **Supp. 2,** 140

People's party. *See* Populist movement

People, Yes, The, **Supp. 8,** 564

Peoria, Ill., **Vol. 1, Part 2,** 574

Pepper, George Hubbard, reference to, **Supp. 6,** 289

Pepper, George Wharton, reference to, **Supp. 7,** 305

Pepper, importation of, **Vol. 3, Part 2,** 157

Pepperell, William, reference to, **Vol. 1, Part 2,** 578

Pepperidge Farm, founding of, **Supp. 8,** 559–61

Pepper Laboratory for Clinical Research, **Supp. 3,** 243

"Pepper Young's Family" (radio serial), **Supp. 6,** 104

Peptides, **Supp. 3,** 61; **Supp. 5,** 122

Pequot War, **Vol. 3, Part 2,** 156; **Vol. 4, Part 1,** 138; **Vol. 6, Part 2,** 367; **Vol. 9, Part 2,** 83; episode leading to, **Vol. 7, Part 2,** 12; writings on, **Vol. 10, Part 1,** 110

Perception, theory of, **Supp. 8,** 344, 345

"Percussion pill," invention of, **Vol. 4, Part 2,** 62

Percy, LeRoy, reference to, **Supp. 4,** 78

Percy Jones Hospital (Battle Creek, Mich.), **Supp. 6,** 345

Pere Marquette Railroad, **Supp. 5,** 550

"Perfectionists," **Vol. 7, Part 1,** 589

Periscope, invention of, **Vol. 4, Part 1,** 27

Peristalsis, **Supp. 3,** 133–34

Peritonitis, **Vol. 7, Part 1,** 353; **Supp. 6,** 215

Perkins, Charles A., reference to, **Supp. 3,** 773

Perkins, Frances, references to, **Supp. 3,** 400, 645, 647, 718; **Supp. 5,** 631; **Supp. 8,** 648

Perkins, George W., references to, **Supp. 3,** 604; **Supp. 4,** 665

Perkins, Maxwell, references to, **Supp. 2,** 731, 732; **Supp. 3,** 383, 686; **Supp. 5,** 559; **Supp. 7,** 336

Perkins, S. Albert, reference to, **Supp. 6,** 319–20

Perkins Institution for the Blind, **Supp. 4,** 11; **Supp. 8,** 316

Perlman, Alfred, reference to, **Supp. 6,** 721

Perlman, Selig, reference to, **Supp. 3,** 179

Permanent Court of International Justice. *See* World Court

Pernicious anemia. *See* Anemia

Perón, Juan, reference to, **Supp. 6,** 451

Perrot, Henri, reference to, **Supp. 3,** 55

Perry, Antoinette, reference to, **Supp. 4,** 649

Perry, Matthew C., references to, **Vol. 6, Part 1,** 574; **Vol. 7, Part 1,** 503; **Vol. 9, Part 2,** 310, 315

Perry, Norman, reference to, **Supp. 6,** 301

Perry, O. H., references to, **Vol. 9, Part 1,** 625; **Vol. 9, Part 2,** 348 f.

Perry, Ralph Barton, reference to, **Supp. 5,** 503

Perry-Mansfield School of Theatre, **Supp. 7,** 367

Perryville, battle of, **Vol. 1, Part 2,** 586; **Vol. 2, Part 1,** 241; **Vol. 4, Part 2,** 240; **Vol. 5, Part 2,** 425; **Vol. 8, Part 1,** 40; **Vol. 9, Part 2,** 433

Perseus A (galaxy), **Supp. 6,** 31

Pershing, John J., references to, **Supp. 3,** 398–99, 584, 588, 606; **Supp. 4,** 123, 359, 360; **Supp. 5,** 69, 159, 160, 186, 468, 530–31; **Supp. 6,** 254, 429; **Supp. 8,** 262, 498

Persia: authority on, **Vol. 9, Part 1,** 55; diplomatic relations with, **Vol. 1, Part 2,** 38, 189, 506; **Vol. 8, Part 2,** 241; missions in, **Vol. 1, Part 2,** 37; **Vol. 3, Part 1,** 565 f.; **Vol. 3, Part 2,** 418; **Vol. 4, Part 1,** 486; **Vol. 7, Part 2,** 475; **Vol. 9, Part 2,** 53; **Vol. 10, Part 2,** 344; writings on, **Vol. 1, Part 2,** 189; **Vol. 10, Part 2,** 344. *See also* Iran

Person, Harlow S., reference to, **Supp. 5,** 558

Personality: development theories, **Supp. 8,** 424; psychological multistudy approaches, **Supp. 8,** 7–9; public v. private, **Supp. 4,** 830–31; studies in, **Supp. 1,** 264

Personal Narrative, plagiarizing of, **Vol. 7, Part 2,** 310

Personnel management, **Supp. 2,** 45; **Supp. 4,** 747; **Supp. 6,** 520; psychological tests, **Supp. 5,** 612

Personnel Research Foundation, founding of, **Supp. 5,** 59

Peru, **Vol. 4, Part 1,** 463; diplomatic relations with, **Vol. 7, Part 2,** 571; **Vol. 8, Part 2,** 38; **Vol. 10, Part 1,** 49; **Supp. 4,** 670; Grace-Donoughmore Contract of 1890, **Vol. 4, Part 1,** 463; mining, **Vol. 7, Part 2,** 9; writings on, **Vol. 10, Part 1,** 107; Yale expedition, **Supp. 6,** 59

Peruvian bark, discovery of substitute for, **Vol. 2, Part 2,** 187

Pestalozzi, influence of, **Vol. 5, Part 2,** 266; **Vol. 7, Part 1,** 402

Pesticides and herbicides: anti–boll weevil campaign, **Supp. 4,** 601; environmental impact of, **Supp. 7,** 109–10; labeling and control, **Supp. 3,** 683. *See also* Insects

"Pet crime," U.S. coinage, **Vol. 8, Part 2,** 301

Peter, Hugh, references to, **Vol. 7, Part 1,** 552; **Vol. 9, Part 1,** 627 f.

Peter Bent Brigham Hospital (Boston), **Supp. 3,** 806; **Supp. 4,** 208–9; **Supp. 5,** 111

Peterboro Colony, establishment of, **Vol. 6, Part 2,** 27

Peterkin Papers, **Vol. 4, Part 2,** 107

Peter Pan, **Supp. 5,** 8

Peter Parley books, **Vol. 4, Part 1,** 403; **Vol. 6, Part 1,** 455

Petersburg, Va., siege of, **Vol. 1, Part 2,** 112, **Vol. 4, Part 1,** 497; **Vol. 6, Part 1,** 127; **Vol. 9, Part 1,** 363

Peterson, Frederick, references to, **Supp. 4,** 107, 108

Peterson, Roger Tory, reference to, **Supp. 6,** 255

Peterson's Magazine, **Vol. 7, Part 2,** 513

Petition, right of, **Vol. 1, Part 1,** 92

Petition to the King, drafting of, **Vol. 3, Part 1,** 299 f.

Petri, Egon, reference to, **Supp. 6,** 456

Petri Wine Co., **Supp. 7,** 613–14

Petrochemistry, development of, **Supp. 3,** 239, 247; **Supp. 6,** 334

Petroff, S. A., reference to, **Supp. 4,** 49

Petroleum industry, **Vol. 1, Part 2,** 301; **Vol. 3, Part 2,** 602; **Vol. 6, Part 1,** 540; **Vol. 8, Part 2,** 56, 65; beginnings of, **Vol. 8, Part 1,** 168 f.; products, extension of uses for, **Vol. 3, Part 1,** 415. *See also* Oil

Petrology, **Vol. 5, Part 1,** 457; **Vol. 10, Part 1,** 527 f.; magmatic school development in, **Supp. 6,** 70–71; mapping and classification, **Supp. 4,** 194; theory development, **Supp. 6,** 144; writings on, **Vol. 10, Part 1,** 527 f.

Petty, George, reference to, **Supp. 5,** 637

Pew, Joseph N., references to, **Supp. 3,** 20; **Supp. 7,** 305; **Supp. 8,** 143

Pewter, craftsmanship in, **Vol. 1, Part 2,** 400; **Vol. 3, Part 1,** 67

Peyser, Jay, reference to, **Supp. 3,** 833

Peyser, Julius, reference to, **Supp. 3,** 833

Peyton Place, **Supp. 7,** 531–32

Pfister Chemical Co., **Supp. 7,** 617

Pforzheimer, Carl H., references to, **Supp. 5,** 387, 586

Pharmaceuticals. *See* Drugs

Pharmacies. *See* Drug stores

Pharmacognosy, **Vol. 5, Part 2,** 499

Pharmacology: chemical synthesis studies, **Supp. 8,** 102; education standards, **Supp. 2,** 591; medicinal plants, **Supp. 3,** 432–33; pioneer work in, **Vol. 5, Part 1,** 236; **Vol. 5, Part 2,** 393, 513; research in, **Supp. 3,** 805–6; **Supp. 4,** 410–11; teaching of, **Supp. 2,** 4; **Supp. 3,** 342–43; writings on, **Supp. 2,** 389. *See also* Drugs; *specific types of drugs*

Pharmacopeia, **Vol. 8, Part 1,** 498; **Vol. 9, Part 1,** 424, 488; first in U.S., **Vol. 2, Part 1,** 157; revisions of, **Vol. 2, Part 1,** 35; **Vol. 8, Part 1,** 154 f., 192 f., 242 f., 535

Pharmacopeia of the United States of America, The, revision of, **Supp. 4,** 411

Pharmacy, **Vol. 4, Part 1,** 63; **Vol. 6, Part 1,** 49; **Vol. 8, Part 1,** 192 f., 242, 390, 497 f., 535; **Vol. 8, Part 2,** 285 f., 528; **Vol. 9, Part 1,** 255, 487; Pharmacy Act of 1872, **Vol. 7, Part 2,** 259; teaching of, **Vol. 6, Part 1,** 278; **Vol. 6, Part 2,** 213; **Vol. 7, Part 2,** 258; **Vol. 8, Part 1,** 154 f., 192 f.; writings on, **Vol. 6, Part 2,** 213; **Vol. 8, Part 1,** 242 f., 498, 535

Phase Rule, The, **Supp. 5,** 36

Phelan, Frank M., reference to, **Vol. 9, Part 2,** 267

Phelps and Gorham Purchase (1791), **Vol. 3, Part 2,** 601; **Vol. 4, Part 1,** 434; **Vol. 7, Part 1,** 222; **Vol. 7, Part 2,** 531; **Vol. 10, Part 2,** 297

Phelps, Dodge & Co., **Supp. 3,** 381

Phelps-Stokes Foundation, first black director, **Supp. 7,** 748

Phenix Cheese Co., **Supp. 5,** 400

Phenolic resins, **Supp. 3,** 26

Phi Beta Kappa Society, **Vol. 1, Part 1,** 520, 544; **Vol. 3, Part 2,** 235, 304, 326, 487; **Vol. 4, Part 2,** 150, 260, 360; **Vol. 5, Part 1,** 52 f., 132, 206, 260, 300; **Vol. 5, Part 2,** 304, 343, 379; **Vol. 6, Part 1,** 224, 388, 405, 416, 429; **Vol. 7, Part 1,** 245, 283, 300, 528, 562; **Vol. 8, Part 2,** 135; **Vol. 9, Part 1,** 239, 470; **Vol. 9, Part 2,** 135, 306, 398; Amherst Chapter, founding of, **Vol. 10, Part 1,** 99; first chapter at black institution, **Supp. 5,** 437; first Kentucky chapter, **Supp. 5,** 461; founding of, **Vol. 9, Part 1,** 128; Harvard Chapter, founding of, **Vol. 1, Part 2,** 8; orations, **Vol. 3, Part 2,** 223; **Vol. 5, Part 1,** 45, 49, 53, 128

"Phi Chi," Bowdoin song, **Vol. 7, Part 1,** 43

Philadelphia, Pa.: Academy of Music, **Vol. 3, Part 2,** 437; architectural sculpture, **Supp. 3,** 123–24; architecture, **Vol. 5, Part 2,** 274; **Vol. 6, Part 1,** 21, 168, 551; **Vol. 9, Part 1,** 336 f.; art service, **Vol. 4, Part 2,** 378; **Vol. 8, Part 2,** 470; **Vol. 9, Part 1,** 635; banking development, **Vol. 3, Part 1,** 455 f.; baseball, professional, **Vol. 8, Part 1,** 418; Beef Steak Club, **Vol. 5, Part 2,** 456; black-owned banks, **Supp. 4,** 916; Building Association League of Philadelphia, **Vol. 8, Part 2,** 104; business in, **Vol. 5, Part 1,** 377; **Vol. 6, Part 1,** 543; **Vol. 9, Part 1,** 190, 599; **Vol. 10, Part 1,** 407 f.; Catholic Club of, **Vol. 8, Part 2,** 104; Centennial Exposition (1876), **Vol. 6, Part 1,** 187; **Vol. 7, Part 1,** 413; **Vol. 8, Part 2,** 7, 197, 577; **Vol. 9, Part 2,** 424; Chemical Society of Philadelphia, **Vol. 10, Part 2,** 491; Chestnut Street Female Seminary, **Vol. 8, Part 1,** 335 f.; Consolidation Act, **Vol. 8, Part 1,** 211 f., 335 f.; drainage system for, **Vol. 5, Part 2,** 456; economic life in early, **Vol. 10, Part 2,** 23; education, **Vol. 3, Part 1,** 408 f., 459 f.; **Vol. 4, Part 2,** 359 f.; **Vol. 5, Part 1,** 261; **Vol. 6, Part 1,** 544; **Vol. 8, Part 1,** 71; **Vol. 9, Part 1,** 635; Episcopal church, **Vol. 6, Part 2,** 173; Episcopal Hospital, **Vol. 8, Part 1,** 124 f.; ferry over Schuylkill, colonial, **Vol. 8, Part 2,** 156; financial center, as a, **Vol. 10, Part 2,** 610; fire insurance company, first in America, **Vol. 8, Part 1,** 139 f.; first woman on education board, **Supp. 5,** 432; foreign trade, **Vol. 1, Part 2,** 464; "gas fight" of 1905, **Vol. 3, Part 1,** 355 f.; glassworks, **Vol. 3, Part 1,** 586 f.; harbor for, **Vol. 8, Part 1,** 406; Haseltine Art Galleries, **Vol. 4, Part 2,** 378; history of, **Vol. 3, Part 1,** 514 f.; **Vol. 10, Part 2,** 14; hospital, **Vol. 7, Part 2,** 263; House of Industry, **Vol. 7, Part 2,** 257; Kelly family, **Supp. 6,** 331; labor movement in, **Vol. 10, Part 2,** 556; laying out city, **Vol. 5, Part 1,** 159; **Vol. 7, Part 2,** 435; legal service, **Vol. 1, Part 2,** 281; **Vol. 4, Part 2,** 355; **Vol. 5, Part 1,** 469; **Vol. 9, Part 2,** 543; library work, **Vol. 4, Part 1,** 557; **Vol. 7, Part 2,** 452, 455; **Vol. 8, Part 2,** 231; **Vol. 9, Part 1,** 317; Light Horse of the City of, **Vol. 6, Part 1,** 75; Lutheran church, **Vol. 6, Part 2,** 247; magazine publications, **Vol. 1, Part 2,** 417; mass meeting in 1776, **Vol. 8, Part 1,** 646; medical service, **Vol. 2, Part 1,** 400; **Vol. 3, Part 1,** 494 f.; **Vol. 5, Part 1,** 553; **Vol. 6, Part 1,** 143, 149 f.; **Vol. 7, Part 1,** 202, 379, 553; **Vol. 7, Part 2,** 259, 554; **Vol. 10, Part 1,** 103; **Vol. 10, Part 2,** 109; Methodist preacher, first, in, **Vol. 7, Part 2,** 609; military maps of, for use during Civil War, **Vol. 5, Part 2,** 456; "Morris's Folly," **Vol. 6, Part 1,** 168; municipal government, **Supp. 4,** 262; museums, **Vol. 7, Part 2,** 345 f., 351; **Supp. 4,** 452; **Supp. 5,** 388; music, **Vol. 4, Part 1,** 274; **Vol. 8, Part 2,** 423; **Vol. 9, Part 2,** 339 f.; "nativism riots," **Vol. 6, Part 1,** 200; newspapers, politics of (1829), **Vol. 4, Part 2,** 250; Orphan Society, **Vol. 4, Part 1,** 505; park system, **Vol. 6, Part 2,** 492; **Vol. 10, Part 1,** 647; politics, **Supp. 7,** 302; politics (1866–81), **Vol. 6, Part 2,** 138; *Press, The,* **Vol. 9, Part 1,** 246; printing in, **Vol. 1, Part 1,** 501; **Vol. 10, Part 2,** 649; public service, **Vol. 1, Part 1,** 503, 542; **Vol. 1, Part 2,** 358; **Vol. 3, Part 1,** 455 f., 459 f.; **Vol. 4, Part 1,** 321; **Vol. 4, Part 2,** 250, 294, 337, 344; **Vol. 5, Part 1,** 263, 439; **Vol. 6, Part 1,** 149 f., 168, 329, 495, 497 f., 543 f.; **Vol. 6, Part 2,** 130, 143, 173, 474, 486, 558, 634; **Vol. 7, Part 1,** 142, 200 f.; **Vol. 7, Part 2,** 429, 451 f., 508; **Vol. 8, Part 1,** 203 f., 400, 427 f.; **Vol. 8, Part 2,** 228, 235; **Vol. 9, Part 1,** 3, 115, 255; **Vol. 9, Part 2,** 487, 614, 620; **Vol. 10, Part 1,** 103 f., 647; **Vol. 10, Part 2,** 2, 30 f., 185, 303; publishing in, **Vol. 4, Part 2,** 355; real estate development, **Vol. 2, Part 1,** 234; records, public, **Vol. 8, Part 1,** 296 f.; reform movements, **Vol. 3, Part 2,** 432, 437; **Vol. 6, Part 1,** 68; "Republican Court," **Vol. 1, Part 2,** 273; Revolutionary War period, **Vol. 2, Part 1,** 400; **Vol. 6, Part 2,** 287, 306; Roman Catholic bishopric, **Supp. 5,** 179; St. Augustine's Rectory, **Vol. 2, Part 1,** 518; scientific services to, **Vol. 3, Part 1,** 538 f.;

shipping (1753), **Vol. 4, Part 2,** 476; social life, **Vol. 6, Part 1,** 359 f.; **Vol. 8, Part 2,** 231; social reform, **Supp. 6,** 515; state hospital for women and infants, **Vol. 7, Part 2,** 264; street railways in, **Vol. 3, Part 1,** 459 f.; theater in, **Vol. 3, Part 1,** 37; **Vol. 7, Part 1,** 206 f.; *Times, The,* **Vol. 6, Part 1,** 593–94; Tuesday Club, organization of, **Vol. 3, Part 1,** 236; Union League of, **Vol. 1, Part 2,** 417, 464; war relief work in, during Revolution, **Vol. 8, Part 1,** 452; water supply for, **Vol. 6, Part 1,** 21; Wharton School, **Vol. 5, Part 1,** 574; Whitfield, preaching of, **Vol. 8, Part 2,** 75, 227; Woman's Hospital, **Vol. 8, Part 1,** 301; yellow fever epidemic, **Vol. 4, Part 1,** 466; **Vol. 8, Part 1,** 427, 443

Philadelphia (frigate), **Vol. 1, Part 1,** 506; **Vol. 3, Part 1,** 187

Philadelphia Academy of Surgery, **Vol. 7, Part 2,** 129

Philadelphia & Reading Railroad **Vol. 4, Part 1,** 461; **Vol. 5, Part 2,** 277

Philadelphia Athletics (baseball), **Supp. 5,** 48, 124–25; **Supp. 6,** 357, 358, 415, 581–82; **Supp. 7,** 27, 128, 129, 130; **Supp. 8,** 186, 543, 544

Philadelphia Daily News, **Supp. 5,** 205

Philadelphia Dental College, **Vol. 6, Part 2,** 164

Philadelphia Divinity School, **Supp. 4,** 595

Philadelphia Eagles (football), **Supp. 6,** 47

Philadelphia Evening Ledger, **Supp. 7,** 615

Philadelphia Evening Telegraph, **Vol. 5, Part 1,** 203

Philadelphia Inquirer, **Supp. 3,** 20; **Supp. 6,** 232

Philadelphia Museum of Art, construction of, **Supp. 1,** 609

Philadelphia Music Teachers' Association, **Vol. 8, Part 1,** 200 f.

Philadelphia Neurological Society, founding of, **Supp. 1,** 241

Philadelphia Orchestra, conductors, **Supp. 6,** 550

Philadelphia Phillies (baseball), **Supp. 6,** 347, 356

Philadelphia *Public Ledger,* **Supp. 1,** 212–13

Philadelphia Rapid Transit Co., **Vol. 7, Part 1,** 71

Philadelphia Record, **Vol. 9, Part 1,** 189

Philadelphia School of Design for Women, **Vol. 7, Part 2,** 500

Philadelphia Society for Ameliorating the Miseries of Public Prisons, **Vol. 8, Part 1,** 139 f.

Philadelphia Story, The, **Supp. 4,** 55

Philadelphia Zeitung, first German-language newspaper in America, **Vol. 9, Part 2,** 557

Philanthropy: Astor projects, **Supp. 6,** 23, 24; Ball projects, **Supp. 3,** 29–30; **Supp. 5,** 34; Bamberger projects, **Supp. 3,** 30–31; Blaine projects, **Supp. 5,** 61; Cabot projects, **Supp. 7,** 98; Cullen projects, **Supp. 6,** 136; cultural, **Supp. 4,** 87; Falk projects, **Supp. 4,** 261–62; Fels projects, **Supp. 4,** 262–63; Ford projects, **Supp. 4,** 303; fund-raising, **Supp. 7,** 401–2; Guggenheim projects, **Supp. 3,** 321–22; Harkness projects, **Supp. 2,** 284; Hayden projects, **Supp. 2,** 293; Heckscher projects, **Supp. 3,** 348–49; Hershey projects, **Supp. 3,** 358; James projects, **Supp. 3,** 381–82; Kahn projects, **Supp. 1,** 457–58; Kent projects, **Supp. 4,** 452; Kresge projects, **Supp. 8,** 348–49; Lehman projects, **Supp. 7,** 466; Lewisohn projects, **Supp. 5,** 427; Littauer projects, **Supp. 3,** 464; Loeb projects, **Supp. 1,** 503–4; McKinley projects, **Supp. 1,** 532; Mallinckrodt projects, **Supp. 8,** 412; medical, **Supp. 3,** 435; music, **Supp. 5,** 128–29; philosophical basis of foundations, **Supp. 3,** 416–17; Reynolds projects, **Supp. 5,** 567; Richardson projects, **Supp. 6,** 541; Rockefeller projects, **Supp. 2,** 574–75; **Supp. 4,** 696–97; **Supp. 6,** 548–49; Roman Catholic church, **Supp. 6,** 608; Rose projects, **Supp. 8,** 548; Sloan projects, **Supp. 8,** 600; Speyer projects, **Supp. 3,** 729; Straus projects, **Supp. 6,** 607; Wade projects, **Supp. 1,** 695; writings on, **Supp. 2,** 374; youth programs, **Supp. 5,** 324. *See also* Charitable organizations

Philbrick, Herbert, references to, **Supp. 6,** 681; **Supp. 7,** 390

Philco Corporation, **Supp. 3,** 143

Philharmonic Society of New York, **Vol. 3, Part 1,** 377; **Vol. 4, Part 2,** 504; **Vol. 10, Part 1,** 543. *See also* New York Philharmonic

Philharmonic-Symphony of New York, founding of, **Supp. 4,** 212. *See also* New York Philharmonic

Philippi, battle of, **Vol. 6, Part 1,** 582; **Vol. 7, Part 1,** 228

Philippine Journal of Science, **Supp. 6,** 450

Philippines, **Vol. 3, Part 1,** 110; **Vol. 5, Part 1,** 458; **Vol. 9, Part 2,** 363; **Vol. 10, Part 2,** 561; acquisition of, **Vol. 1, Part 1,** 154; **Vol. 3, Part 1,** 110, 164; **Vol. 3, Part 2,** 503; **Vol. 4, Part 1,** 52, 516; **Vol. 6, Part 2,** 108; agriculture, **Vol. 7, Part 2,** 632; botany, **Supp. 6,** 450; Catholic church, **Vol. 4, Part 1,** 241; Commission, **Vol. 3, Part 1,** 234; **Vol. 7, Part 1,** 275; **Vol. 9, Part 2,** 268; education, **Vol. 8, Part 1,** 152; first president of, **Supp. 3,** 613–15; "hitching post," as a, **Vol. 3, Part 1,** 164; imperialistic policy toward, **Vol. 2, Part 1,** 193; independence movement, **Supp. 3,** 699; **Supp. 6,** 227, 280, 280–81; **Supp. 7,** 377; insurrection, **Vol. 4, Part 1,** 94; **Vol. 6, Part 2,** 573; **Vol. 7, Part 2,** 95; **Vol. 9, Part 1,** 287; Manila Bay, battle of, **Supp. 3,** 275; medical research and education, **Supp. 4,** 803; military governorship of, **Vol. 7, Part 2,** 95; missions, **Supp. 1,** 115–16; **Supp. 5,** 178–79; monetary system, **Supp. 3,** 414; nursing in, **Supp. 7,** 247; protectorate, establishing of, **Vol. 6, Part 2,** 108; U.S. presence in, **Supp. 1,** 284; **Supp. 2,** 579; **Supp. 3,** 218, 669; **Supp. 4,** 612, 655–56; **Supp. 5,** 42, 459, 460, 468; **Supp. 5,** 530; **Supp. 6,** 190–91, 210–11, 429, 579; **Supp. 7,** 488–89, 786; **Supp. 8,** 154, 638; Wood, Leonard, administration of, **Vol. 10, Part 2,** 468 f.; World War II action, **Supp. 5,** 719–20; **Supp. 6,** 268; **Supp. 7,** 215, 352, 489, 490; **Supp. 8,** 48, 351, 619, 638, 698

Philippine Sea, battle of the, **Supp. 8,** 619

Philistine, **Vol. 5, Part 1,** 323

Phillips, Duncan, reference to, **Supp. 4,** 241

Phillips, John S., reference to, **Supp. 3,** 762; **Supp. 4,** 517, 518

Phillips, William, reference to, **Supp. 5,** 332

Phillips Academy, Andover, **Vol. 1, Part 1,** 82, 561 f.; **Vol. 7, Part 2,** 548; **Vol. 9, Part 2,** 343; architectural planning of, **Vol. 8, Part 1,** 1 f.; founding of, **Vol. 7, Part 2,** 543; principal of, first, **Vol. 7, Part 2,** 358; reorganization of, **Vol. 8, Part 2,** 151

Phillips Brooks House, founding of, **Vol. 7, Part 2,** 159

Phillips Exeter Academy, **Vol. 1, Part 2,** 153; **Vol. 8, Part 1,** 80; **Vol. 9, Part 2,** 290; founding of, **Vol. 7, Part 2,** 542

Phillips Petroleum Co., **Supp. 7,** 428; founding of, **Supp. 4,** 660–61

Phillips University, founding of, **Vol. 7, Part 2,** 544

Philology, **Vol. 1, Part 1,** 148; **Vol. 2, Part 1,** 45, 53, 110; **Vol. 3, Part 1,** 108; **Vol. 3, Part 2,** 131, 484; **Vol. 4, Part 1,** 157, 281, 588; **Vol. 4, Part 2,** 48, 81, 95, 124 f., 132, 357, 401, 603; **Vol. 5, Part 2,** 446 f.; **Vol. 6, Part 1,** 78, 262, 429; **Vol. 8, Part 1,** 470, 535; **Vol. 8, Part 2,** 39 f., 55, 212, 423 f., 432 f., 561; **Vol. 9, Part 1,** 64, 126, 244, 248; **Vol. 10, Part 1,** 31; **Vol. 10, Part 2,** 342; *Dictionary of the German and English Languages,* **Vol. 1, Part 1,** 108; educational values of, **Vol. 8, Part 1,** 219 f.; English historical grammar, **Vol. 2, Part 1,** 45; **Vol. 4, Part 2,** 343; **Vol. 6, Part 2,** 269; English literature and language

studies, **Supp. 3,** 422–24; Esperanto promotion, **Supp. 4,** 185; foreign language, education in, **Supp. 2,** 132; human language capacity, **Supp. 4,** 90–91; Indian, **Vol. 3, Part 1,** 525; **Vol. 7, Part 2,** 565; **Vol. 10, Part 1,** 9 f.; linguistic relativity theory, **Supp. 3,** 84, 819–20; Middle English studies, **Supp. 3,** 109; Old English studies, **Supp. 2,** 88; Romance language studies, **Supp. 3,** 21–22; Sanskrit studies, **Supp. 3,** 444–45; Semitic studies, **Supp. 3,** 37, 374–75; **Supp. 6,** 641; Spanish and Latin American speech, **Vol. 6, Part 2,** 278; writings on, **Vol. 3, Part 1,** 525 f., 563; **Vol. 5, Part 2,** 3, 446; **Vol. 8, Part 1,** 219 f., 321 f.; **Vol. 8, Part 2,** 39 f., 433; **Vol. 9, Part 1,** 65; **Vol. 9, Part 2,** 572; **Vol. 10, Part 1,** 31; **Supp. 2,** 683

Philosopher's Holiday, **Supp. 5,** 199

Philosophical Review, **Vol. 8, Part 2,** 595; founding of, **Supp. 3,** 698

Philosophy, **Vol. 1, Part 2,** 503; **Vol. 3, Part 2,** 420; **Vol. 4, Part 1,** 153, 631; **Vol. 4, Part 2,** 15, 471, 498; **Vol. 5, Part 1,** 590 f.; **Vol. 5, Part 2,** 525, 526, 547; **Vol. 6, Part 1,** 328; **Vol. 7, Part 2,** 399 f.; **Vol. 8, Part 2,** 595; aesthetic, **Vol. 8, Part 1,** 408; American, **Vol. 8, Part 1,** 611; **Vol. 9, Part 1,** 344; Aristotelian, **Supp. 2,** 735; of biology, **Supp. 4,** 427; body/mind relationship, **Supp. 2,** 639; book collecitons, **Supp. 1,** 619; Chicago school (functionalism), **Supp. 1,** 548, **Supp. 3,** 780; critical realism, **Supp. 2,** 639; **Supp. 3,** 608; epistemological dualism, **Supp. 7,** 482; first attempt to unite German and American method, **Vol. 8, Part 1,** 389 f.; first scholarly journal, **Supp. 3,** 698; fruitlands, **Vol. 1, Part 1,** 140; Hegel, introduction to America, **Vol. 2, Part 1,** 65; historical writings on, **Supp. 2,** 671; idealistic, **Vol. 9, Part 1,** 593; **Supp. 1,** 332, 683; individualism, **Supp. 5,** 224–25; in India, **Supp. 1,** 713–14; influence on study of, in U.S., **Vol. 2, Part 2,** 535; instrumentalism (experimentalism), **Supp. 5,** 170–72; Jewish, history of, **Vol. 7, Part 1,** 436–37; Kierkegaardian, **Supp. 2,** 643–44; of law, **Supp. 6,** 216; **Supp. 7,** 99–100; lectures on, **Vol. 5, Part 2,** 525; logic, **Supp. 4,** 168–70, 879–80; logical positivism, **Supp. 5,** 562–63; **Supp. 8,** 74–75; metaphysics, **Supp. 4,** 881–83; mystical, **Vol. 1, Part 2,** 307; naive realism, **Supp. 2,** 735; natural, **Vol. 3, Part 2,** 30 f., 236; **Vol. 6, Part 1,** 442 f.; **Vol. 8, Part 1,** 506; of Navaho Indians, **Supp. 5,** 644–45; neorealism, **Supp. 2,** 622; **Supp. 5,** 503–4; **Supp. 6,** 505; Nietzsche, books on pagan, **Vol. 8, Part 2,** 316; objective idealism, **Supp. 3,** 697; **Supp. 8,** 265–66; personalism, **Vol. 1, Part 2,** 523; personalistic idealism and theism, **Supp. 5,** 90–92; of physics, **Supp. 7,** 74–75, 134–35; physiological, **Vol. 2, Part 1,** 215; pluralism, **Supp. 5,** 436; process of becoming theory, **Supp. 4,** 879–84; realism, **Supp. 4,** 387; reason and interpretation studies, **Supp. 5,** 602–3; relating to religion, **Vol. 5, Part 1,** 5; **Vol. 6, Part 1,** 616; **Supp. 4,** 525–26; **Supp. 6,** 13–14, 45–46; **Supp. 7,** 745–47; of science, **Supp. 8,** 191; scientific humanism, **Supp. 6,** 83; social, **Supp. 1,** 547–48; space-time relativity, **Supp. 5,** 563; systems of, in nineteenth century, **Vol. 2, Part 1,** 548; teaching of, **Vol. 4, Part 1,** 66; **Vol. 4, Part 2,** 185; **Vol. 5, Part 1,** 216, 311, 455; **Vol. 5, Part 2,** 525; **Vol. 7, Part 1,** 111, 209, 317, 448, 526; **Vol. 8, Part 2,** 206 f., 556; **Vol. 9, Part 1,** 494; **Vol. 9, Part 2,** 302, 537; **Vol. 10, Part 2,** 349; **Supp. 2,** 540; **Supp. 4,** 883–84; **Supp. 7,** 701–2; **Supp. 8,** 58–59; textbooks on, **Vol. 4, Part 2,** 409 f.; utilitarianism, **Vol. 1, Part 1,** 136; validity of knowledge, **Supp. 7,** 471–72; writings on, **Vol. 1, Part 2,** 33, 383, 504, 523; **Vol. 2, Part 1,** 65, 548; **Vol. 2, Part 2,** 535; **Vol. 3, Part 1,** 96 f., 108, 141, 162, 169, 180, 225, 339, 472

infrared radiation, **Supp. 4,** 658; ionization of gases, **Supp. 5,** 126; light, study of, **Vol. 6, Part 2,** 594 f.; magnetization, **Vol. 3, Part 1,** 87 f.; **Vol. 8, Part 2,** 198; mathematical, **Supp. 4,** 839; **Supp. 5,** 528–29; Michelson-Morley ether-drift experiments, **Supp. 3,** 523–24; microwave electronics, **Supp. 4,** 358–59; molecular, **Supp. 8,** 627–28; molecular-beam laboratories, **Supp. 8,** 628; Nobel Prize, **Supp. 5,** 202, 220, 495, 496; **Supp. 7,** 75, 258, 344; **Supp. 8,** 628; nuclear, **Supp. 6,** 370; **Supp. 7,** 10–11, 300, 731–32; philosophy of, **Supp. 7,** 74–75, 134–35; quantum mechanics, **Supp. 6,** 655; quantum theory, **Supp. 4,** 488, 818, 838–39; **Supp. 5,** 203–4, 219–21, 495–96, 529, 563; **Supp. 6,** 655; **Supp. 7,** 133, 258– 59, 517; **Supp. 8,** 628; radioactive alpha decay theory, **Supp. 8,** 199; relativity theory, **Supp. 5,** 202–3; **Supp. 6,** 653; research in, **Supp. 6,** 500–1; shock waves, **Supp. 6,** 656; soil, **Supp. 7,** 76; sound reproducing machine, **Vol. 3, Part 1,** 221; spectrum, research in, **Vol. 6, Part 1,** 213; teaching of, **Vol. 4, Part 2,** 58; **Vol. 6, Part 1,** 399; **Vol. 6, Part 2,** 448; **Vol. 7, Part 1,** 491 f., 525; **Vol. 8, Part 2,** 114, 277; **Vol. 9, Part 1,** 37; **Vol. 9, Part 2,** 652, 654; **Supp. 3,** 523; **Supp. 4,** 818; technical experiments, **Vol. 8, Part 2,** 198; terrestrial magnetism, **Vol. 1, Part 1,** 461 f.; textbooks, **Supp. 5,** 154; theoretical, **Vol. 2, Part 1,** 261; **Supp. 8,** 122–23, 190–91, 482–85; theoretical, annual conferences on, **Supp. 8,** 199; thermal, **Supp. 1,** 57; ultraviolet spectroscopy, **Supp. 5,** 441; vortex streets theory, **Supp. 7,** 410– 11; writings on, **Vol. 9, Part 2,** 655; **Vol. 10, Part 1,** 584 f.; **Supp. 3,** 11, 291. *See also* Biophysics; Geophysics; Nuclear physics; Quantum theory

Physiography, **Vol. 4, Part 2,** 444; **Vol. 8, Part 2,** 243; **Vol. 10, Part 1,** 124; fieldwork, **Supp. 4,** 32–33; teaching of, **Supp. 4,** 119

Physiological Zoology, **Supp. 5,** 110

Physiology, **Vol. 1, Part 2,** 106; **Vol. 3, Part 2,** 472; **Vol. 4, Part 2,** 465; **Vol. 5, Part 1,** 205; **Vol. 5, Part 2,** 366 f., 459; **Vol. 6, Part 1,** 349 f.; **Vol. 6, Part 2,** 520; **Vol. 8, Part 1,** 317 f.; adrenal glands, **Vol. 9, Part 2,** 9; behaviorism, **Supp. 3,** 172; **Supp. 6,** 367– 68; biochemical, **Supp. 3,** 163–64, 350–51; blood, **Supp. 3,** 369–70; body heat, **Supp. 3,** 32; body temperature, **Supp. 4,** 58–59; cerebral ape and human studies, **Supp. 6,** 223; circulatory system, **Supp. 4,** 390; cocaine, **Supp. 3,** 430; digestion, **Supp. 3,** 133– 34; effect of drugs, **Vol. 3, Part 1,** 6; **Vol. 8, Part 1,** 317 f.; emotions, **Supp. 3,** 134–37; endocrinology, **Vol. 8, Part 2,** 306; experiments in connection with meteorology, **Vol. 6, Part 1,** 280; fatigue, **Supp. 3,** 351; laboratory, first in America, **Vol. 1, Part 2,** 494 f.; laboratory equipment, production of, **Supp. 4,** 676; laboratory instruction in, **Supp. 2,** 373; library on, **Supp. 6,** 223, 224; nerve impulse conduction, **Supp. 7,** 226, 280; Nobel Prize, **Supp. 4,** 581; **Supp. 5,** 489; **Supp. 7,** 226, 281, 341, 476; **Supp. 8,** 450; optical, **Supp. 3,** 269–70; perceptual theory, **Supp. 8,** 344, 345; pioneer work, **Vol. 6, Part 2,** 338; plant, **Supp. 4,** 191–92, 381–82, 500–501, 862–63; **Supp. 6,** 176; plant-sodium studies, **Supp. 7,** 592; public health studies, **Supp. 6,** 175; renal, **Supp. 7,** 699– 700; research in, **Supp. 2,** 391; **Supp. 4,** 34; **Supp. 6,** 100; reproductive system, **Supp. 3,** 6; systematic teaching, pioneer, **Vol. 3, Part 1,** 512 f.; teaching of, **Vol. 2, Part 2,** 616 f.; **Vol. 5, Part 1,** 252; **Vol. 9, Part 1,** 298; **Vol. 9, Part 2,** 478; **Supp. 4,** 676; vision, study of, **Vol. 9, Part 2,** 647; writings on, **Vol. 9, Part 2,** 9 f. *See also* Anatomy

Physiology of Man, **Vol. 3, Part 2,** 473

Piaget, Jean, reference to, **Supp. 6,** 527

Piano: manufacture, **Vol. 1, Part 2,** 550; **Vol. 2, Part 2,** 65; **Vol. 5, Part 2,** 448; **Vol. 6, Part 2,** 364; **Vol. 9, Part 1,** 551, 567 f.; **Vol. 9, Part 2,** 637; **Vol. 10, Part 1,** 581; player piano, **Vol. 6, Part 2,** 168; **Vol. 9, Part 2,** 637; playing, **Vol. 1, Part 1,** 491; **Vol. 3, Part 1,** 205; **Vol. 4, Part 1,** 442, 614, 616; **Vol. 5, Part 1,** 117, 621; **Vol. 5, Part 2,** 217 f., 442; **Vol. 6, Part 1,** 238; **Vol. 6, Part 2,** 378; **Vol. 7, Part 2,** 265; **Vol. 9, Part 1,** 103, 590; **Vol. 9, Part 2,** 305 f., 421, 556; **Vol. 10, Part 1,** 581; **Vol. 10, Part 2,** 453; studies, **Vol. 8, Part 1,** 200 f.; teaching, **Vol. 7, Part 2,** 458; **Vol. 9, Part 2,** 305 f.

Picasso, Pablo, references to, **Supp. 4,** 174, 175, 619, 768, 771, 780; **Supp. 6,** 194, 512, 552, 553

Piccard, Auguste, references to, **Supp. 7,** 618, 619

Pichel, Irving, reference to, **Supp. 7,** 412

Pick, E. P., reference to, **Supp. 3,** 441

Pickering, Edward Charles, reference to, **Supp. 6,** 561

Pickering, John, impeachment of, **Vol. 7, Part 1,** 505

Pickering, Timothy, reference to, **Vol. 6, Part 1,** 465

Pickett's charge, **Vol. 5, Part 1,** 387; **Vol. 6, Part 1,** 126; **Vol. 9, Part 2,** 642

Pickford, Mary, references to, **Supp. 2,** 368; **Supp. 4,** 350; **Supp. 5,** 443; **Supp. 8,** 214

Pictorial Field Book of the Revolution, **Vol. 6, Part 1,** 422

Pierce, Franklin, references to, **Vol. 3, Part 1,** 335; **Vol. 4, Part 2,** 426, 428 f.

Pierian Sodality, **Vol. 3, Part 1,** 567 f.

Pierpont Morgan Library. *See* Morgan Library

Pietism, **Vol. 7, Part 1,** 310; **Vol. 9, Part 1,** 428

Pigeon Creek, Ind., Lincoln's home, **Vol. 6, Part 1,** 243 f.

Piggly Wiggly grocery chain, **Supp. 5,** 604; **Supp. 7,** 141

"Pigs in Clover," invention of, **Vol. 6, Part 1,** 479

Pike County Ballads, **Vol. 4, Part 2,** 432; **Vol. 7, Part 1,** 511

Pikes Peak: auto race, **Supp. 2,** 525; exploration of, **Vol. 5, Part 1,** 576; **Vol. 7, Part 2,** 599; gold rush, **Vol. 9, Part 2,** 263

Pilcher, Lewis Stephen, reference to, **Supp. 6,** 664

Pilgrims, **Vol. 1, Part 1,** 146, 216; **Vol. 2, Part 1,** 30; **Vol. 3, Part 2,** 156 f.; **Vol. 7, Part 1,** 254, 261; **Vol. 10, Part 2,** 20; church, **Vol. 10, Part 2,** 400; organization, **Vol. 3, Part 1,** 5, 319; Plymouth Colony, early days in, **Vol. 1, Part 2,** 560 f.; **Vol. 2, Part 1,** 551; **Vol. 9, Part 1,** 500; relations with Indians, **Vol. 6, Part 2,** 380. *See also* Plymouth Colony

Pilgrim Trust, founding of, **Supp. 2,** 284

Pillar of Fire Church, founding of, **Supp. 4,** 875–76

Pilot, **Vol. 3, Part 1,** 361; **Vol. 7, Part 2,** 53

Pilot-boat service, improvement in, **Vol. 8, Part 1,** 481

Pim, Richard, reference to, **Supp. 6,** 131

Pima Indians, **Supp. 4,** 71–72

Pinchot, Gifford, references to, **Supp. 1,** 300; **Supp. 3,** 7, 96, 321, 603, 604, 724–25; **Supp. 4,** 43, 481, 522; **Supp. 5,** 666, 699; **Supp. 6,** 509–10, 515; **Supp. 7,** 305, 606, 607

Pinckney, Thomas, reference to, **Vol. 9, Part 1,** 129

Pinckney draft of Constitution, **Vol. 7, Part 2,** 612

Pinckney's Treaty (1795), **Vol. 7, Part 2,** 619; **Vol. 8, Part 1,** 355; **Vol. 9, Part 1,** 129; **Vol. 10, Part 1,** 509 f., 524

Pineapple industry, **Supp. 6,** 168–69

Pine Ridge Agency, troubles at, **Vol. 2, Part 1,** 519; **Vol. 6, Part 2,** 615; **Vol. 8, Part 1,** 437; **Vol. 9, Part 1,** 193

Pingree, Hazen S., references to, **Supp. 3,** 188, 231

Pink, Louis, reference to, **Supp. 5,** 631

Pinkerton, Allan, references to, **Vol. 6, Part 1,** 584; **Vol. 9, Part 1,** 193

Pink eye. *See* Conjunctivitis

Pinkham, Lydia E., fraud case, **Supp. 5,** 666

Pinkney, William, reference to, **Vol. 7, Part 1, 88 f.**

Pin manufacture, **Vol. 5, Part 1,** 291; **Vol. 8, Part 1,** 522; **Vol. 9, Part 2,** 218

Pintard, John, reference to, **Vol. 8, Part 2,** 593

Pioneer, **Vol. 6, Part 1,** 459

"Pioneer," first Pullman car, **Vol. 8, Part 1,** 263 f.

Pioneering, **Vol. 1, Part 1,** 475, 554; **Vol. 2, Part 1,** 256, **Vol. 3, Part 1,** 349, **Vol. 4, Part 1,** 93, 178, 250; **Vol. 4, Part 2,** 314; **Vol. 5, Part 2,** 47; **Vol. 6, Part 1,** 4, 357, 365, 533; **Vol. 6, Part 2,** 50; **Vol. 7, Part 1,** 483; **Vol. 8, Part 2,** 25, 251, 274; **Vol. 9, Part 1,** 61, 284; historical writings on, **Supp. 8,** 60; novels about, **Supp. 4,** 38–39, 154, 877–78; **Supp. 5,** 14–15; **Supp. 8,** 533, 567. *See also* Frontier

"Pious Fund of the Californias," **Vol. 3, Part 1,** 422; **Vol. 7, Part 2,** 426

Piper Aircraft Corporation, founding of, **Supp. 8,** 504

Piper case, **Vol. 5, Part 1,** 455

Piracy, **Vol. 3, Part 1,** 483; **Vol. 3, Part 2,** 128; **Vol. 4, Part 2,** 161 f.; **Vol. 5, Part 1,** 474; **Vol. 5, Part 2,** 116 f.; **Vol. 8, Part 1,** 140 f., 287, 299 f.; **Vol. 8, Part 2,** 85; Barbary pirates, **Vol. 1, Part 1,** 504; **Vol. 5, Part 2,** 7, 22, 30; **Vol. 6, Part 1,** 77; bibliographer and writer on, **Vol. 8, Part 1,** 287 f.; Captain Kidd, **Vol. 5, Part 2,** 367; **Vol. 6, Part 1,** 319; Charleston, S.C., **Vol. 5, Part 2,** 116 f.; hanging of pirates, in Boston, **Vol. 8, Part 1,** 299 f.; Jones, John Paul, as pirate, **Vol. 5, Part 2,** 184 f.; Mississippi River, **Vol. 6, Part 2,** 374; suppression of, in the West Indies, **Vol. 4, Part 2,** 382; **Vol. 8, Part 1,** 83 f.

Pirenne, Henri, reference to, **Supp. 5,** 655

Pirson, Louis V., reference to, **Supp. 4,** 194

Pisan Cantos, **Supp. 7,** 347

Pissarro, Camille, reference to, **Supp. 6,** 552

Pistols, manufacturing of, **Vol. 7, Part 1,** 561; **Vol. 8, Part 1,** 498 f.

Pi-Suñer, Jaime, reference to, **Supp. 6,** 223

"Pitcher, Molly," references to, **Vol. 5, Part 1,** 574; **Vol. 6, Part 1,** 500

Pitch-pipe, introduction of, **Vol. 1, Part 2,** 270

Pitkin, Horace T., reference to, **Supp. 3,** 476

Pitkin, Walter B., reference to, **Supp. 5,** 503

Pittsburgh, Pa.: Carnegie libraries, **Supp. 4,** 19; cholera epidemic in, **Vol. 3, Part 1,** 220; Croghan Hall, **Vol. 2, Part 2,** 556; education, **Vol. 3, Part 1,** 511 f.; Fort Dunmore built at original site of, **Vol. 3, Part 1,** 317, 519 f.; glassworks, **Vol. 7, Part 2,** 4, 638; KDKA radio station, **Supp. 3,** 184–85; Kingsley House, **Vol. 5, Part 1,** 101; museum, **Vol. 5, Part 2,** 557; philanthropy, **Vol. 9, Part 2,** 397; politics, **Supp. 8,** 360–61; public service, **Vol. 1, Part 2,** 545; **Vol. 4, Part 2,** 60; **Vol. 6, Part 1,** 590; **Vol. 6, Part 2,** 197; **Vol. 7, Part 2,** 20; **Vol. 8, Part 2,** 526; steel center, as a, **Vol. 6, Part 2,** 583; synod, founding of, **Vol. 7, Part 2,** 289; water supply, **Vol. 7, Part 2,** 540; writings about, **Vol. 5, Part 2,** 559

Pittsburgh Academy, establishment of, **Vol. 1, Part 2,** 545

Pittsburgh Coal Co., organization of, **Vol. 7, Part 2,** 20

Pittsburgh Federation of Jewish Philanthropies, founding of, **Supp. 4,** 261–62

Pittsburgh Gazette, first issue, **Vol. 8, Part 2,** 526

Pittsburgh Landing, Tenn., battle of. *See* Shiloh, battle of

Pittsburgh Pirates (baseball), **Supp. 5,** 716–17; **Supp. 7,** 501, 502, 768–69

Pittsburgh Post Gazette, **Supp. 3,** 80

Pittsburgh Safety Glass Corporation, founding of, **Supp. 7,** 169

Pittsburgh Skin and Cancer Foundation, establishment of, **Vol. 8, Part 1,** 449

Pittsburgh Steelers (football), **Supp. 6,** 47

Pittsburgh Survey (urban survey), **Supp. 6,** 329–30

Pittsburgh Symphony, **Supp. 7,** 640

Pittsburgh Times, founding of, **Vol. 7, Part 1,** 443

Pituitary gland: blood flow to, **Supp. 6,** 704; function, **Supp. 6,** 386; separate functions of, **Supp. 3,** 370

Placenta, **Supp. 6,** 704

Plagiarism, **Vol. 7, Part 1,** 49; **Vol. 8, Part 1,** 47 f.

Plagioclase solid solution, **Supp. 6,** 71

Plaindealer, radical paper of 1837, **Vol. 6, Part 1,** 148

Plains Indians, culture, **Supp. 1,** 651

Plain Talk, **Supp. 6,** 350

Planck, Max, references to, **Supp. 5,** 202, 495; **Supp. 8,** 122

Planetariums, **Supp. 2,** 293

Plankton, **Supp. 4,** 461, 462

Planned communities. *See* Model communities

Planned Parenthood Association of Baltimore, founding of, **Supp. 4,** 391

Planned Parenthood Federation of America, founding of, **Supp. 8,** 569

Planned Parenthood Federations, **Supp. 6,** 602

Planning boards. *See* City planning; Zoning

"Plan of Union," Congregationalists and Presbyterians, **Vol. 1, Part 1,** 480, 628

Plantations (for specific names, *see* Homesteads), **Vol. 4, Part 1,** 489; **Vol. 4, Part 2,** 65, 188, 213, 214; **Vol. 5, Part 1,** 206, 348; **Vol. 6, Part 1,** 524; **Vol. 7, Part 1,** 14; cotton and sugarcane, **Vol. 9, Part 1,** 427; development of, **Vol. 3, Part 2,** 439; historical studies, **Supp. 1,** 597; life in South Carolina, **Vol. 6, Part 1,** 33; of the South, **Vol. 6, Part 1,** 88, 90

Planter, famous dispatch boat, **Vol. 9, Part 1,** 224 f.

Plant Industry, Bureau of, **Vol. 4, Part 2,** 312

Plants: breeding of, **Vol. 2, Part 1,** 266 f.; **Vol. 8, Part 1,** 233, 236 f., 239, 589; **Vol. 9, Part 1,** 458; collections of, **Vol. 8, Part 2,** 484; introduction of, into U.S., **Vol. 7, Part 2,** 481; **Vol. 10, Part 2,** 321; pathology of, **Vol. 8, Part 1,** 239 f.; **Vol. 8, Part 2,** 309; **Vol. 9, Part 1,** 263; scientific study of, **Vol. 3, Part 1,** 606 f.; **Vol. 8, Part 1,** 154 f.; **Vol. 9, Part 2,** 477, 596. *See also* Botany; Horticulture

"Plasma," term coined, **Supp. 6,** 364–65

Plastics: Bakelite, **Supp. 3,** 26–27; development of, **Supp. 6,** 334; from petroleum wastes, **Supp. 3,** 239; urea-formaldehyde, **Supp. 3,** 247

Plastic surgery: flap technique, **Supp. 4,** 220–21; for leprosy, **Supp. 4,** 530; reconstructive, **Supp. 2,** 706–7; **Supp. 6,** 632

Plate, William J., reference to, **Supp. 8,** 113–14

Plate-glass manufacture, **Vol. 3, Part 2,** 517; **Vol. 5, Part 1,** 74; **Vol. 7, Part 2,** 636

Platinum, pioneer use of, **Vol. 4, Part 2,** 344

Plato, writings on, **Supp. 5,** 224–25

Platt, Thomas C., references to, **Vol. 7, Part 1,** 623; **Vol. 8, Part 1,** 302 f., 326 f., 485; **Supp. 3,** 464

Platt Amendment, **Vol. 1, Part 1,** 154; **Vol. 6, Part 2,** 108 f.; **Vol. 8, Part 1,** 2 f.; **Vol. 8, Part 2,** 137.

Plattsburgh, battle of, **Vol. 4, Part 1,** 523; **Vol. 6, Part 2,** 20, 156

Play, first written in U.S., **Vol. 5, Part 1,** 402

Playboy, **Supp. 8,** 412

Players' Club, founder of, **Vol. 1, Part 2,** 447; **Vol. 5, Part 2,** 16

Playground Association of America, founding of, **Supp. 2,** 375

Playgrounds, **Supp. 1,** 595; **Supp. 2,** 374–75

Playwrights. For complete list, *see* Occupations Index

Playwrights' Company, **Supp. 5,** 624; **Supp. 6,** 15; founding of, **Supp. 2,** 325; **Supp. 8,** 529

Playwriting, first school of, **Vol. 8, Part** 1, 221

Pleasant Hill, battle of, **Vol. 1, Part** 1, 579; **Vol. 2, Part** 1, 469; **Vol. 2, Part 2,** 105; **Vol. 5, Part 2,** 425

Plebiscites, **Supp. 5,** 723–24

Pleistocene era, classification of glacial drift, **Supp. 3,** 456

Pleurisy, treatment of, **Vol. 10, Part 2,** 585

Pleyel harpsichord, **Supp. 6,** 357, 358

Plimpton, George A., reference to, **Supp. 3,** 722

Plows: cast-iron, **Vol. 6, Part** 1, 614; improved drill, devised, **Vol. 4, Part** 1, 98; inventions, **Vol. 6, Part** 1, 607 f., 614; manufacture, **Vol. 3, Part** 1, 193 f.; **Vol. 3, Part 2,** 251; **Vol. 6, Part** 1, 614; perfection of steam, **Vol. 8, Part** 1, 522

Plumber and Sanitary Engineer, founding of, **Supp. 1,** 552

Plumbing, improvements in, **Supp. 1,** 552

Plumb Plan, **Supp. 2,** 351; **Supp. 3,** 241

Plummer, Henry S., reference to, **Supp. 3,** 832

Plums, development of American varieties of, **Vol. 8, Part** 1, 233

Plutonium, manufacture of, **Supp. 6,** 371; **Supp. 8,** 230, 231

Plymouth, Mass., history of, **Vol. 3, Part** 1, 147 f.

Plymouth Brethren, **Vol. 7, Part** 1, 558; **Vol. 9, Part** 1, 274; **Supp. 5,** 346

Plymouth car, **Supp. 4,** 301, 302

Plymouth Colony, **Vol. 1, Part 2,** 560 ff.; **Vol. 2, Part** 1, 167, 551; **Vol. 3, Part** 1, 5 f., 172; **Vol. 7, Part** 1, 261; **Vol. 9, Part** 1, 500; **Vol. 10, Part 2,** 393, 400

Plymouth County Academy, **Vol. 7, Part** 1, 59

PM, **Supp. 8,** 379; founding of, **Supp. 6,** 202

Pneumatic: drill, invention of, **Vol. 4, Part 2,** 401; hoisting, **Vol. 7, Part** 1, 547; tools, **Supp. 1,** 446; tunnels, **Vol. 1, Part 2,** 81

Pneumatics, in construction, **Supp. 2,** 469

Pneumatic Steel Association, organized, **Vol. 3, Part** 1, 548 f.

Pneumoencephalography, **Supp. 4,** 214

Pneumonia: epidemic, **Supp. 3,** 483; research on, **Vol. 7, Part** 1, 628; **Supp. 5,** 63

Pocahontas, **Vol. 9, Part** 1, 295; biography of, **Vol. 8, Part 2,** 31; capture of, **Vol. 1, Part** 1, 345; descendants of, in Virginia, **Vol. 8, Part 2,** 26; husband of, **Vol. 1, Part** 1, 345; **Vol. 8, Part 2,** 118

Pocket Books, Inc., **Supp. 7,** 243; founding of, **Supp. 6,** 583; **Supp. 8,** 579

Pocket Magazine, The, founding of, **Supp. 2,** 633

"Pocket veto," **Vol. 8, Part 2,** 347

Poe, Edgar Allan, **Vol. 2, Part** 1, 41; **Vol. 2, Part 2,** 81 f.; **Vol. 3, Part 2,** 305; **Vol. 4, Part 2,** 339; **Vol. 5, Part** 1, 68, 73, 110, 483, **Vol. 6, Part** 1, 212, 339, 558; **Vol. 7, Part** 1, 25, 399; **Vol. 9, Part** 1, 245, 576; **Vol. 10, Part** 1, 378 f.; "Bells, The," published, **Vol. 8, Part 2,** 372; biographies of, **Vol. 4, Part 2,** 344; **Supp. 4,** 13, 14; **Supp. 6,** 523; psychological analysis of, **Supp. 8,** 353; publishing of works of, **Vol. 8, Part** 1, 440 f.; **Vol. 9, Part** 1, 497, 553; "Raven, The," manuscript, **Vol. 9, Part 2,** 357; relations with Chivers, **Vol. 2, Part 2,** 81 f.; relations with Griswold, **Vol. 4, Part 2,** 11 f.; relations with Osgood, **Vol. 7, Part 2,** 77; relations with Thomas Willis White, **Vol. 10, Part 2,** 121; relations with Helen Whitman, **Vol. 10, Part 2,** 143; study of, **Supp. 7,** 797

Poet in the Desert, The, **Supp. 3,** 837

Poet Lore **Vol. 2, Part 2,** 152

Poetry, **Vol. 1, Part** 1, 158, 373, 583, 609 f.; **Vol. 1, Part 2,** 46, 139 f., 345, 365, 383, 416, 423 f., 435, 470, 542, 558, 577, 590; **Vol. 2, Part** 1, 69, 75, 79, 81 f., 111, 155, 171, 183, 190, 199 f., 264, 273, 285 f., 322, 370 f., 381, 473, 530, 553, 556, 579, 613; **Vol. 2, Part 2,** 7 f., 53, 149, 158 f., 160, 218 f., 220, 237, 344, 356, 388, 390 f., 396, 452 f., 501, 503, 513, 562 f., 578; **Vol. 3, Part** 1, 20, 71 f., 94 f., 199, 248, 281, 294, 297 f., 366, 369, 381, 383, 384, 431 f., 476 f., 484 f., 491 f., 505 f., 513 f., 516 f., 546 f., 550 f., 569 f., 573 f., 595 f., 600 f.; **Vol. 3, Part 2,** 125, 208, 258 f., 347, 450 f., 541; **Vol. 4, Part** 1, 27 f., 103, 277, 298, 305, 346, 452 f., 561, 573; **Vol. 4, Part 2,** 111, 130, 149 f., 237, 363, 455, 525, 606; **Vol. 5, Part** 1, 52 f., 60, 68, 110, 144, 162, 170 f., 205 f., 215, 245, 273, 291 f., 310, 335, 375, 417, 459, 542, 612; **Vol. 5, Part 2,** 13, 37, 101, 154, 160, 373, 417, 466, 505 f., 522, 523, 526, 602, 604 f., 614; **Vol. 6, Part** 1, 14 f., 16, 17, 65, 212, 276, 278, 281, 284, 346, 382 f., 387 f., 411, 433, 454, 460 f., 470, 483 f., 508, 538; **Vol. 6, Part 2,** 63, 84, 104, 131, 139, 227, 287, 517, 566, 606; **Vol. 7, Part** 1, 78, 207 f., 266, 291, 378, 459, 499, 520, 607, 608 f.; **Vol. 7, Part 2,** 47, 53, 68, 70, 77, 157 f., 211, 275, 339, 460, 489, 513 f., 556 f., 586, 595, 625; **Vol. 8, Part** 1, 16 f., 19 f., 46 f., 61 f., 65 f., 92 f., 104 f., 111, 121 f., 133 f., 151 f., 163 f., 171, 181 f., 186 f., 188 f., 201 f., 204, 223 f., 226 f., 247 f., 285, 298, 301 f., 311 f., 322 f., 331 f., 348, 374, 388, 408, 431, 434 f., 450, 481 f., 493 f., 509, 587, 611 f.; **Vol. 8, Part 2,** 63, 119, 156, 167 f., 192, 241, 242, 345, 352, 390, 399, 485, 534, 555, 608; **Vol. 9, Part** 1, 42, 82, 158, 171, 470 f., 523, 552, 561, 586 f.; **Vol. 9, Part 2,** 50, 54, 58, 75, 102, 109 f., 134 f., 256, 263, 315 f., 357 f., 397, 428 f., 430, 444, 460, 483, 558–59; **Vol. 10, Part** 1, 44 f., 45, 54, 124, 168, 378 f., 392 f., 426, 432, 440 f., 454, 457, 484, 572 f., 617; **Vol. 10, Part 2,** 37, 84, 139, 145 f., 173 f., 203, 252, 306, 343, 348, 446, 479, 513, 518, 578; **Supp. 2,** 428–30; **Supp. 3,** 598; **Supp. 4,** 840–41; **Supp. 5,** 73–74, 658–61; **Supp. 7,** 390–91, 653–55; **Supp. 8,** 291, 582; abandonment of neoclassical rules in, **Vol. 10, Part** 1, 10; American commemorative, **Supp. 6,** 417–18; black, **Supp. 4,** 200–201, 528; **Supp. 7,** 236–37; **Supp. 8,** 286–88; blank verse, **Supp. 1,** 633–34; Buddhist influence, **Supp. 8,** 327; Civil War, **Vol. 9, Part 2,** 525; colonial, **Vol. 7, Part** 1, 602 f.; confessional, **Supp. 7,** 621–22; criticism, **Supp. 4,** 694, 812; **Supp. 7,** 390–91; **Supp. 8,** 42, 43; "Croaker Papers," **Vol. 3, Part** 1, 431; cubism relationship, **Supp. 7,** 789; development of American, **Vol. 4, Part 2,** 419 f.; epic, in America, **Vol. 3, Part** 1, 573 f.; **Supp. 3,** 57–58; epigrammatic, **Supp. 8,** 492, 493; free verse, **Supp. 8,** 563–64; free-verse drama, **Supp. 3,** 341; French imagists, **Vol. 6, Part** 1, 454; fugitive school, **Supp. 6,** 461; Harlem Renaissance, **Supp. 4,** 200–1; Harris Collection of American, **Vol. 4, Part** 1, 561; **Vol. 4, Part 2,** 305; historical writings on, **Supp. 8,** 350; household, **Vol. 1, Part** 1, 135; imagists, **Supp. 4,** 285–86; innovative, **Supp. 7,** 218–22; lecturing on, **Supp. 4,** 13; little magazines, **Supp. 8,** 349–50; lyric, **Supp. 1,** 623; **Supp. 4,** 576–77; **Supp. 8,** 42–43; mock epic, **Supp. 5,** 30; New Criticism, **Supp. 7,** 55–56, 347, 442; nonsense, **Supp. 3,** 629; **Supp. 5,** 94; old French, **Supp. 3,** 22; philosophical inhumanism, **Supp. 7,** 392; popular verse, **Supp. 6,** 258–59, 574–75; prison experiences, **Supp. 6,** 238; proletarian, **Supp. 2,** 239–40; publications, **Supp. 2,** 466; readings, technique of Vachel Lindsay, **Vol. 6, Part** 1, 276; regional, **Supp. 5,** 118–19; romantic, **Supp. 3,** 454–55; **Supp. 4,** 73; satirical, **Vol. 10, Part** 1, 11; "sentence-sound" blank verse narrative, **Supp. 7,** 270–73; social reform themes, **Supp. 4,** 811–12; **Supp. 6,** 113; sonnets, **Supp. 6,** 462; *Spoon River Anthology,* **Supp. 4,** 555; symbolism, **Supp. 1,** 206; teaching of, **Supp. 7,** 653–55; traditional, **Supp. 7,** 346–47; typographical experimentation, **Supp. 7,** 158, 159; "variable foot," **Supp. 7,** 790; writings on, **Supp. 3,** 72–73, 475–76; Yiddish, **Vol. 10, Part 2,**

Polls. *See* Public opinion

Poll tax, **Supp. 6,** 526; **Supp. 7,** 416; opposition to, **Vol. 7, Part 2,** 123

Pollution: control legislation, **Supp. 8,** 616; industrial fumes reduction, **Supp. 4,** 184–85; **Supp. 5,** 273; sewage, **Supp. 2,** 169–70, 353. *See also* Air pollution; Ecology

Polo, **Vol. 8, Part 2,** 222; **Vol. 10, Part 2,** 160; **Supp. 3,** 360–61; **Supp. 6,** 210; popularized in U.S., **Vol. 4, Part 1,** 450

Polychromatic printing, **Vol. 1, Part 1,** 457

Polygamy: Edmunds bill to suppress, in Utah, **Vol. 8, Part 1,** 341 f.; Mormon church, **Vol. 3, Part 2,** 25; **Vol. 4, Part 2,** 334; **Vol. 6, Part 1,** 115; **Vol. 8, Part 1,** 601; **Vol. 9, Part 1,** 312 f.

Polygraph, **Vol. 5, Part 2,** 33

Polymerization, **Supp. 6,** 334

Polymers: processing of, **Supp. 2,** 97; research in, **Supp. 2,** 505; solutions, electrical characteristics of, **Supp. 6,** 346

"Polyphonic prose," **Vol. 6, Part 1,** 453 f.

Polytechnic Institute of Brooklyn, biochemistry studies, **Supp. 6,** 595

Pomeroy, Wardell B., reference to, **Supp. 6,** 343

Pomeroy Circular, **Vol. 2, Part 2,** 30; **Vol. 4, Part 1,** 532; **Vol. 8, Part 1,** 54; **Vol. 9, Part 1,** 473; **Vol. 10, Part 1,** 304

Pomology, **Vol. 2, Part 1,** 48; **Vol. 2, Part 2,** 489; **Vol. 3, Part 1,** 418, 419; **Vol. 4, Part 1,** 261; **Vol. 6, Part 1,** 535; **Vol. 6, Part 2,** 252; **Vol. 8, Part 1,** 145 f.; **Vol. 9, Part 2,** 439; writings on, **Vol. 4, Part 1,** 261; **Vol. 8, Part 1,** 233 f; **Vol. 10, Part 1,** 444 f.

Pomona Hall, **Vol. 5, Part 1,** 359

Pond, Adeline Valentine, reference to, **Supp. 3,** 1

Pontiac's conspiracy. *See* Conspiracy, Pontiac

Pony express, **Vol. 1, Part 1,** 28; **Vol. 4, Part 1,** 168; **Vol. 5, Part 2,** 353; **Vol. 6, Part 2,** 215; **Vol. 8, Part 2,** 252

Poole, Ernest, reference to, **Supp. 7,** 320

Poole, William Frederick, reference to, **Supp. 3,** 326

"Pooled" credit, **Vol. 9, Part 2,** 305

Poole's Index to Periodical Literature, forerunner of, **Vol. 8, Part 1,** 66 f.

Poor, Henry Varnum, reference to, **Supp. 3,** 278; **Supp. 6,** 457–58

Poor People's Campaign, founding of, **Supp. 8,** 335

Poor Richard's Almanack. See Almanacs

Pope, Arthur Upham, reference to, **Supp. 6,** 557

Pope, John, Union general, **Vol. 6, Part 1,** 123

Pope, John Russell, reference to, **Supp. 5,** 300

Pope, William J., reference to, **Supp. 6,** 71

Pope John XXIII, references to, **Supp. 8,** 115, 614–15

Pope Leo XIII: conference of, with Taft, **Vol. 9, Part 2,** 268; social encyclicals, **Supp. 3,** 680, 681

Pope Paul VI, references to, **Supp. 8,** 116, 615

Pope Pius XI, Kellogg-Briand Pact support, **Supp. 4,** 137

Pope Pius XII, references to, **Supp. 5,** 589; **Supp. 6,** 608, 623; **Supp. 8,** 613

Popular Democratic Party (Puerto Rico), founding of, **Supp. 5,** 545

Popular fiction, **Supp. 4,** 372

Popular Science, origin of, **Vol. 4, Part 2,** 148; **Vol. 10, Part 2,** 616, 617

Popular Science Monthly, **Supp. 6,** 327

"Popular sovereignty": coining of phrase, **Vol. 3, Part 1,** 400; effect of Dred Scott decision on, **Vol. 3, Part 1,** 402

Population: as a basis for representation, **Vol. 5, Part 2,** 94; birthrate drop, **Supp. 4,** 45; black demographics, **Supp. 6,** 605; colonial, **Vol. 3, Part 1,** 277; growth and economic welfare studies, **Supp. 4,** 267–68; rural to urban shift of, **Supp. 4,** 366; stable theory of, **Supp. 4,** 505–7; statistical studies on growth of, **Supp. 7,** 192

Populism, **Supp. 4,** 338; **Supp. 8,** 272

Populist movement, **Vol. 1, Part 1,** 214; **Vol. 3, Part 1,** 370, 382; **Vol. 5, Part 1,** 132; **Vol. 5, Part 2,** 516; **Vol. 6, Part 1,** 205, 332, 426; **Vol. 7, Part 1,** 197 f.; **Vol. 7, Part 2,** 393; **Vol. 8, Part 1,** 40 f., 142 f.; **Vol. 8, Part 2,** 105; **Vol. 9, Part 1,** 180, 199; **Vol. 10, Part 1,** 549, 568

Populist party, in Oregon, **Supp. 4,** 844–45

Porcelain, collecting of, **Vol. 3, Part 2,** 435; **Vol. 6, Part 1,** 210; **Vol. 8, Part 1,** 228 f.

Porgy and Bess, **Supp. 2,** 230, 303

Pork, **Supp. 3,** 737–38

"Pork-barrel" legislation, **Vol. 8, Part 1,** 34 f.

Pornography: *American Mercury* case, **Supp. 7,** 19–20; book censorship, **Supp. 7,** 292, 293; court decisions, **Supp. 7,** 149; postal service code, **Supp. 6,** 661. *See also* Censorship

Porter, Cole, references to, **Supp. 6,** 637; **Supp. 7,** 803; **Supp. 8,** 108, 383

Porter, Commodore David, references to, **Vol. 3, Part 2,** 286; **Vol. 9, Part 2,** 378, 394

Porter, Fitz-John, reference to, **Vol. 8, Part 2,** 454

Porter, Katherine Anne, reference to, **Supp. 8,** 256

Porter, William Sydney, reference to, **Supp. 1,** 109

Porter, Fitz-John, case (1862–85), **Vol. 5, Part 1,** 401; **Vol. 8, Part 1,** 91, 188

"Porter Mortar Fleet," Civil War, **Vol. 8, Part 2,** 200

Porter's School, Miss, Farmington, Conn., founding of, **Vol. 5, Part 2,** 287; **Vol. 8, Part 1,** 103

Port Folio, leading literary periodical in America in 1812, **Vol. 1, Part 2,** 243; **Vol. 3, Part 1,** 236; **Vol. 4, Part 2,** 143

Port Gibson, Miss., battle of. *See* Vicksburg campaign

Port Hudson, siege of, **Vol. 1, Part 1,** 428, 579; **Vol. 3, Part 1,** 412; **Vol. 4, Part 1,** 495, 614; **Vol. 4, Part 2,** 28; **Vol. 7, Part 2,** 415; **Vol. 9, Part 1,** 92

Portland, Maine, **Vol. 3, Part 1,** 172, 411; **Vol. 5, Part 1,** 517; **Vol. 8, Part 1,** 71 f.; construction and repair of harbor fortifications, **Vol. 7, Part 2,** 169; harbor construction, **Supp. 1,** 157

Portland, Oreg., founding of, **Vol. 6, Part 1,** 434; municipal reform, **Supp. 4,** 904; public service, **Vol. 7, Part 2,** 445; **Vol. 8, Part 1,** 456

Portland Courier, the first daily in Maine, **Vol. 9, Part 1,** 345

Portland Oregonian, The, **Vol. 7, Part 1,** 54; **Vol. 8, Part 2,** 491

Portland Transcript, influence of the, **Vol. 7, Part 2,** 558

Portmanteau Theatre, **Supp. 3,** 796–99

Port of New York, development of, **Vol. 9, Part 1,** 338

Port of New York Authority, **Supp. 6,** 187, 587; **Supp. 7,** 11–12, 553; collector, **Supp. 4,** 542; founding of, **Supp. 1,** 589

Portrait painting. *See* Painting, portrait

Portrait photography, **Supp. 7,** 455–56

Portraits: bas-reliefs, **Vol. 8, Part 1,** 166 f.; busts, **Vol. 4, Part 2,** 366; **Vol. 8, Part 1,** 158 f., 166 f.; **Vol. 8, Part 2,** 298; engraving of, **Vol. 3, Part 1,** 535 f.; **Vol. 5, Part 2,** 509; **Vol. 6, Part 1,** 165; **Vol. 6, Part 2,** 331; **Vol. 10, Part 2,** 603; of George Washington, **Vol. 7, Part 1,** 550; **Vol. 7, Part 2,** 346; **Vol. 8, Part 2,** 21, 122, 182, 386; masks, collecting of, **Vol. 5, Part 1,** 445; of presidents, **Vol. 8, Part 1,** 453; series of, of men prominent in the American Revolution, **Vol. 3, Part 1,** 553 f.

Portrait sculpture, **Supp. 8,** 414, 415

Port Republic, Va., battle of, **Vol. 1, Part 1,** 578; **Vol. 3, Part 2,** 230; **Vol. 5, Part 1,** 557; **Vol. 9, Part 1,** 107

Port Royal, S.C., capture of, **Vol. 3, Part 1,** 529 f.; founding of French colony on present site of, **Vol. 8, Part 1,** 533

Portsmouth, designed by Josiah Barker, **Vol. 1, Part 1,** 606

Portsmouth, N.H.: construction and repair of the fortifications of, **Vol. 7, Part 2,** 169; mayor of, **Vol. 5, Part 2,** 169; peace parley for Russo-Japanese War (August 1905), **Vol. 4, Part 2,** 435; **Vol. 9, Part 2,** 82; trade from, **Vol. 5, Part 2,** 590

Portugal: claims of, resulting from War of 1812, **Vol. 8, Part 1,** 400; diplomacy, **Vol. 1, Part 2,** 41; **Vol. 3, Part 1,** 176; **Vol. 7, Part 2,** 582

Portuguese literature and language, studies in old, **Supp. 1,** 481

Positron, discovery of, **Supp. 5,** 496

Post, Charles William, references to, **Supp. 3,** 411; **Supp. 5,** 379

Post, Wiley, reference to, **Supp. 6,** 493

Postage: canceling machine, **Vol. 3, Part 1,** 237; reduced from three to two cents, **Vol. 4, Part 1,** 608

Postage stamps: engravings of, **Vol. 5, Part 2,** 159; first authorized issue of, **Vol. 1, Part 2,** 47; first five-cent, **Vol. 10, Part 1,** 639 f.; printing of first penny, **Vol. 7, Part 2,** 472

Postal savings system, creation of, **Vol. 6, Part 1,** 61; **Vol. 9, Part 2,** 269

Postal Service, United States, **Vol. 2, Part 1,** 454; **Vol. 2, Part 2,** 91, 185, 300, 541; **Vol. 3, Part 1,** 147, 364, 387; **Vol. 4, Part 1,** 342; **Vol. 4, Part 2,** 181, 397; **Vol. 7, Part 2,** 313, 368, 566; **Vol. 8, Part 1,** 344 f.; **Vol. 10, Part 1,** 407; **Vol. 10, Part 2,** 352; administration, **Supp. 6,** 660–61; airmail, **Supp. 2,** 487; **Supp. 3,** 157; **Supp. 5,** 86, 294, 385; **Supp. 6,** 64, 221; **Supp. 8,** 185, 707–8; censorship by, **Supp. 5,** 453, 638; **Supp. 6,** 661; **Supp. 7,** 20; **Supp. 8,** 605; delivery cutbacks, **Supp. 8,** 134; early, **Vol. 3, Part 2,** 589; **Vol. 4, Part 2,** 70; ethics issues, **Supp. 6,** 64; fast mail service between New York and Chicago, initiated, **Vol. 5, Part 2,** 65; first career postmaster general, **Supp. 8,** 133–34; legislation, **Supp. 7,** 521; motor service, **Supp. 2,** 486; pony express, **Vol. 5, Part 2,** 353; postmaster generals, **Vol. 2, Part 2,** 300; **Vol. 4, Part 2,** 397, 469; **Vol. 5, Part 1,** 182, 297, 589; **Vol. 5, Part 2,** 93, 325, 362, 391 f.; **Vol. 7, Part 1,** 522; **Vol. 7, Part 2,** 327, 566; **Vol. 9, Part 1,** 246; **Supp. 1,** 409; **Supp. 2,** 74, 122; **Supp. 4,** 356; **Supp. 5,** 281; **Supp. 7,** 86; rural free delivery, **Vol. 2, Part 1,** 482; **Vol. 4, Part 2,** 440; **Vol. 7, Part 2,** 313; **Vol. 9, Part 1,** 456; **Vol. 10, Part 1,** 549 f.; star route, **Vol. 2, Part 1,** 26; **Vol. 3, Part 1,** 387; **Vol. 4, Part 1,** 148 f.; **Vol. 5, Part 1,** 589; street letter boxes, **Vol. 2, Part 1,** 482; World War II, **Supp. 6,** 661

Postal Telegraph Co., formation of, **Vol. 6, Part 2,** 76

Postcards, collections, **Supp. 2,** 112

Poster art, **Vol. 7, Part 2,** 424; **Supp. 8,** 493, 494

Posters, war, **Supp. 6,** 204

Post Office. *See* Postal Service, United States

Post-trader system in War Department, critic of, **Vol. 4, Part 2,** 478

Postum, first production of, as coffee substitute, **Vol. 8, Part 1,** 112 f.

Postum Cereal Co., **Supp. 6,** 61; **Supp. 7,** 379

Potash, manufacture of, **Supp. 1,** 682

Potawatomi language, **Vol. 5, Part 1,** 107

Potomac Aqueduct, construction of, **Vol. 10, Part 1,** 57

Potomac Navigation Co., George Washington, president of, **Vol. 5, Part 2,** 122; **Vol. 8, Part 2,** 223

Potsdam Conference (1945), **Supp. 5,** 335; **Supp. 6,** 147; **Supp. 7,** 91; **Supp. 8,** 89

Pottery: archaeological significance, **Supp. 3,** 272; collecting of, **Vol. 3, Part 2,** 161, 435; **Vol. 6, Part 1,** 210, 447

Potts' disease, studies of, **Vol. 9, Part 2,** 318

Poulenc, Francis, reference to, **Supp. 6,** 358

Poulsen, Valdemar, reference to, **Supp. 7,** 394

Poulter, Thomas C., reference to, **Supp. 6,** 92

Poultry, inventions on incubators and brooders, **Vol. 8, Part 1,** 505

Pound, Ezra, references to, **Supp. 4,** 285; **Supp. 7,** 318, 372, 399, 947, 789, 790, 791

Pound, Roscoe: legal philosophy of, **Supp. 6,** 104, 216; references to, **Supp. 3,** 116; **Supp. 7,** 475

Poverty: Poor People's Campaign, **Supp. 8,** 335; statistical study of, **Supp. 3,** 373; theory of culture of, **Supp. 8,** 378. *See also* Homeless; Welfare

Powderly, Terence V., reference to, **Supp. 3,** 346

Powder mill, first in Connecticut, **Vol. 7, Part 2,** 641

Powell, Adam Clayton, Jr., references to, **Supp. 5,** 548; **Supp. 6,** 142, 489; **Supp. 8,** 497

Powell, John Wesley, reference to, **Supp. 3,** 724

Powell, Lewis Thornton, relations with John Wilkes Booth, **Vol. 1, Part 2,** 450

Powell, William, reference to, **Supp. 8,** 187

Powell Musical Institute, Brooklyn, N. Y., established, **Vol. 8, Part 1,** 144

Power of Sympathy, The, first American novel, **Vol. 7, Part 1,** 266

Power plants, **Vol. 3, Part 2,** 457; **Vol. 5, Part 2,** 509; development of hydroelectric, **Vol. 3, Part 2,** 2; **Vol. 8, Part 1,** 375 f.; electric, **Vol. 7, Part 1,** 367 f.; generation and transmission devices, **Vol. 6, Part 2,** 239; loom machinery, **Vol. 6, Part 2,** 377; stoking inventions, **Vol. 5, Part 2,** 168

Powers, Francis Gary, references to, **Supp. 8,** 135, 147, 159

Powers, Grover F., reference to, **Supp. 3,** 775

Power supply. *See* Power plants; Public utilities; *specific types of power*

Powhatan, references to, **Vol. 3, Part 2,** 108; **Vol. 7, Part 1,** 468

Powhatan federation, influence of, in Virginia, **Vol. 8, Part 1,** 160 f.

Practical Christianity, **Supp. 4,** 271–72

Practical System of Rhetoric, **Vol. 7, Part 1,** 466 f.

Pragmatism, **Vol. 5, Part 1,** 597 f.; **Vol. 7, Part 1,** 112; **Vol. 7, Part 2,** 400; **Supp. 1,** 548; **Supp. 3,** 363; **Supp. 6,** 505; **Supp. 7,** 471–72, 481, 482; representational, **Supp. 4,** 525–26

Prairie Club, founding of, **Supp. 3,** 599

Prairie Farmer, **Supp. 4,** 132; founding of, **Vol. 10, Part 2,** 557

Prairie school of architecture, **Supp. 3,** 599; **Supp. 6,** 712

Pratt, Charles, **Vol. 7, Part 1,** 566; reference to, **Supp. 1,** 596–97

Pratt, Frederic B., reference to, **Supp. 4,** 56

Pratt, Parley P., reference to, **Vol. 9, Part 2,** 333

Pratt, William V., references to, **Supp. 5,** 6; **Supp. 6,** 348

Pratt bridge and roof truss, **Vol. 8, Part 1,** 179

Pratt Consolidated Coal Co., **Supp. 5,** 556

Pratt Institute (Brooklyn, N.Y.): administration, **Supp. 1,** 597; **Supp. 8,** 135; founded, **Vol. 8, Part 1,** 17, 168 f.

Pratt Institute Free Library, first free public library in New York City or Brooklyn, **Vol. 8, Part 1,** 17, 168 f.

Pratt Institute of Music and Art (Pittsburgh, Pa.), founded, **Vol. 8, Part 1,** 177 f.

"Pratt's Astral Oil," trade name for first high-quality illuminating oil, **Vol. 8, Part 1,** 168 f.

Supp. 7, 761; Willkie candidacy, **Supp. 3,** 400, 497, 829; **Supp. 5,** 152; **Supp. 8,** 394, 421, 617

Presidential election (1944): Republican nomination contest, **Supp. 3,** 830; **Supp. 7,** 616; Roosevelt, F. D., campaign, **Supp. 3,** 664; "Stop Willkie" movement, **Supp. 7,** 616; Truman vice-presidential candidacy, **Supp. 4,** 356, 376; **Supp. 7,** 762; **Supp. 8,** 361; Wallace vice-presidency, opposition to, **Supp. 4,** 51

Presidential election (1948): civil rights issues, **Supp. 5,** 741; Dixiecrats, **Supp. 6,** 710–11; Taft bid, **Supp. 5,** 675; **Supp. 7,** 49, 84; Truman candidacy, **Supp. 8,** 36–37, 405; Wallace third-party candidacy, **Supp. 7,** 763; **Supp. 8,** 511, 512

Presidential election (1952): Eisenhower candidacy, **Supp. 7,** 384; **Supp. 8,** 144, 156; Kefauver bid, **Supp. 7,** 416; labor role in, **Supp. 5,** 255; Stevenson candidacy, **Supp. 7,** 722; Taft bid, **Supp. 5,** 676; **Supp. 7,** 49, 84

Presidential election (1956): Democratic keynote address, **Supp. 8,** 91–92; Kefauver bid, **Supp. 8,** 406; Kefauver vice-presidential candidacy, **Supp. 7,** 416; Stevenson candidacy, **Supp. 7,** 723

Presidential election (1960): cold war issues, **Supp. 8,** 6–7; Kennedy candidacy, **Supp. 7,** 420; **Supp. 8,** 322; Kennedy-Johnson nomination, **Supp. 7,** 636; **Supp. 8,** 361; press endorsements, **Supp. 8,** 396

Presidential election (1968), Kennedy, Robert F., bid, **Supp. 8,** 324

"President making" at Lotos Club, New York, and Blackstone Hotel, Chicago, **Vol. 4, Part 2,** 372

President, naval exploits of, **Vol. 3, Part 1,** 188

President: Office and Powers, The, **Supp. 7,** 146

Presley, Elvis, reference to, **Supp. 6,** 301

Press: cipher system, devised, **Vol. 5, Part 2,** 158; clipping service, originator of, **Vol. 8, Part 2,** 129; "Gordon," **Vol. 4, Part 1,** 422; liberty of, **Vol. 3, Part 1,** 212; **Vol. 3, Part 2,** 560; **Vol. 4, Part 1,** 201; service, practical cooperative, organized, **Vol. 5, Part 2,** 158; screwpower, **Vol. 5, Part 2,** 97. *See also* Journalism; Newspapers; Publishing

Press, freedom of the. *See* Civil liberties

Press agents. *See* Public relations

Presser Foundation, established, for music philanthropies, **Vol. 8, Part 1,** 200 f.

Press of the Crippled Turtle, founding of, **Supp. 7,** 559

"Press on Wheels," **Vol. 4, Part 1,** 9

Pressure gauge, **Supp. 1,** 121

Press Wireless, founding, **Supp. 3,** 155

Preston Retreat, the incorporation of, **Vol. 8, Part 1,** 203 f.

Preventive medicine, **Vol. 3, Part 2,** 301; **Supp. 3,** 158, 409–10; **Supp. 4,** 684, 700–1; **Supp. 5,** 632

Price, Thomas Randolph, relations with Walter Hines Page, **Vol. 7, Part 2,** 142

Price-fixing: base pricing, **Supp. 4,** 268; legislation, **Supp. 6,** 260

Prices: base pricing, **Supp. 4,** 268; consumer index, **Supp. 7,** 794; economic cost analysis, **Supp. 8,** 668–69; fixing charges, **Supp. 8,** 11, 110; fluctuation and gold supply, **Supp. 2,** 696; historical study of U.S., **Supp. 2,** 175; interest-rate relationship, **Supp. 4,** 272–73; Model T, **Supp. 4,** 300–1; money supply relationship, **Supp. 8,** 79; wartime control of, **Supp. 4,** 587

Price supports. *See* Agriculture; *commodity name*

Pridham, Edwin, reference to, **Supp. 7,** 394

Priestley, Joseph: Andrews, John, relationship, **Vol. 1, Part 1,** 245, 294; name as scientific term, **Vol. 8, Part 1,** 223

"Primacy of the Pacific" foreign policy, **Vol. 4, Part 1,** 258

Primaries: constitutional right to, **Supp. 5,** 575; Oregon system, **Supp. 4,** 844

"Prime Street," **Vol. 7, Part 1,** 223

Primogeniture, repeal of law of, in Massachusetts, **Vol. 4, Part 1,** 137; abolition of, in Virginia, **Vol. 5, Part 2,** 20

Primrose, George H., partnership with, **Vol. 3, Part 1,** 338

Prince, Morton, reference to, **Supp. 3,** 190

Prince, Wesley, reference to, **Supp. 7,** 131

Prince, William Wood, reference to, **Supp. 5,** 551

Prince Albert (pipe tobacco), **Supp. 5,** 565, 566

Prince of the House of David, The, **Vol. 5, Part 1,** 479

"Prince of Platform Orators," applied to Tyng, Stephen Higgins on, **Vol. 10, Part 1,** 101

Princes (boat), **Vol. 5, Part 2,** 371

Prince Society: founding of, **Vol. 9, Part 2,** 503; publications of, **Vol. 3, Part 1,** 172; **Vol. 9, Part 1,** 204

Princeton, battle of, **Vol. 6, Part 2,** 541; **Vol. 7, Part 1,** 87; **Vol. 8, Part 2,** 294; **Vol. 9, Part 2,** 192; **Vol. 10, Part 1,** 516–17

Princeton Research Park, founding of, **Supp. 7,** 650

Princeton Theological Seminary: founders of, **Vol. 1, Part 2,** 70; president of first, **Vol. 7, Part 2,** 316

Princeton *Tiger,* **Vol. 2, Part 2,** 162

Princeton University: astronomy studies, **Supp. 6,** 560; biology studies, **Supp. 5,** 127; Blair Hall, **Vol. 1, Part 2,** 339; botany and genetics studies, **Supp. 5,** 629; chapel, stained glass windows, **Supp. 3,** 183; Cliosophic Society, **Vol. 7, Part 2,** 293; constitutional law studies, **Supp. 7,** 146; economic studies, **Supp. 3,** 211, 414; **Supp. 4,** 267–68; English literature and language studies, **Supp. 5,** 645–46; **Supp. 7,** 56; fellowship, **Vol. 1, Part 2,** 477; first professor of the history of art at, **Vol. 8, Part 1,** 228 f.; founding of, **Vol. 1, Part 1,** 126; **Vol. 1, Part 2,** 144; **Vol. 2, Part 1,** 313; **Vol. 3, Part 1,** 302; **Vol. 10, Part 2,** 436; four-course plan of study, **Supp. 7,** 216; French language studies, **Supp. 3,** 22; geology studies, **Supp. 4,** 730; graduate school, founding of, **Supp. 3,** 810; graphic arts studies, **Supp. 7,** 3; Greek language and literature studies, **Supp. 4,** 143–44; history of, **Vol. 2, Part 1,** 498; **Vol. 3, Part 1,** 102; **Vol. 6, Part 2,** 128, 629; history studies, **Supp. 6,** 409–10; **Supp. 8,** 692; incorporation, one of first, **Vol. 9, Part 1,** 353; mathematics studies, **Supp. 6,** 653–54; modern-language studies, **Supp. 5,** 239; Nassau Hall, **Vol. 9, Part 1,** 335; physics studies, **Supp. 5,** 126; preceptorial system, **Vol. 10, Part 2,** 354; presidents, **Vol. 3, Part 1,** 301; **Vol. 3, Part 2,** 37, 391; **Vol. 6, Part 1,** 615, 616; **Vol. 7, Part 1,** 359; **Vol. 7, Part 2,** 315 f.; **Vol. 9, Part 1,** 344; **Vol. 9, Part 2,** 11, 653; **Vol. 10, Part 2,** 354; **Supp. 1,** 399–400; psychology studies, **Supp. 8,** 69; public and international affairs school, **Supp. 4,** 224; science studies, **Supp. 1,** 399; Theological Seminary, **Supp. 6,** 195. *See also* Institute for Advanced Study

Princeton University Press, **Vol. 8, Part 2,** 517; **Supp. 5,** 614

Principal Pictures Corporation, **Supp. 3,** 443–44

Principles of Economics (Taylor), **Vol. 9, Part 2,** 323

Principles of Judicial Proof, **Supp. 3,** 821

Principles of Mathematics, **Supp. 4,** 879–80

Principles of Mining, **Supp. 7,** 358

Principles of Psychology, **Vol. 5, Part 1,** 592 f.

Principles of Sociology, The, **Supp. 1,** 339–40

Prinkipo Conference, Wilson's appointees to, **Vol. 4, Part 2,** 595

Printers' Ink, advertising trade journal, **Vol. 8, Part 2,** 198

Produce Exchange, reorganization of, Vol. 7, Part 2, 56

Producers. For complete list, *see* Occupations Index

Producers' Coöperatives, advocated as method of abolishing the wage system, **Vol. 8, Part 1,** 142 f.

Producing Managers' Association, Actors' Equity strike, **Supp. 3,** 174, 333

Productivity, studies in, **Supp. 4,** 565–66

Professional Lawn Tennis Association of the United States, **Supp. 6,** 539

Profile engravings of distinguished Americans, Saint Mémin, **Vol. 8, Part 2,** 305

Profiles in Courage, **Supp. 7,** 420

Profit-sharing, **Vol. 7, Part 1,** 419

Progress and Poverty, **Supp. 6,** 570

Progressive education. *See* Education, progressive

Progressive Education Association, **Supp. 7,** 43

Progressive movement, **Supp. 4,** 641; Brandeis on investor and consumer protection, **Supp. 3,** 95; California, **Supp. 3,** 395–96; Chicago, **Supp. 5,** 579; conservation efforts, **Supp. 4,** 663–66; economics, **Supp. 6,** 705; goals, **Supp. 6,** 522; journalism, **Supp. 1,** 210; **Supp. 4,** 707; **Supp. 5,** 141, 666–67; lawyers in, **Supp. 3,** 167–68; **Supp. 6,** 541–42; Pennsylvania, **Supp. 4,** 491; Philadelphia social reform, **Supp. 6,** 515; reforms, **Supp. 4,** 522; Senate, **Supp. 3,** 105–6, 108; **Supp. 6,** 578; Socialist mayors, **Supp. 4,** 511–12; sociology of, **Supp. 5,** 591, 592–93; urban leaders, **Supp. 5,** 485; Wisconsin, **Supp. 3,** 178, 249–50; writers associated with, **Supp. 4,** 164–65; writings on, **Supp. 8,** 272, 593–95. *See also* Social reform

Progressive party (1912): founding of, **Vol. 5, Part 2,** 544; **Vol. 8, Part 2,** 86, 142; **Supp. 4,** 170, 665; Illinois, **Supp. 5,** 579; journalistic support, **Supp. 3,** 816; Kansas, **Supp. 3,** 544–45; New Hampshire, **Supp. 5,** 689; Ohio, **Supp. 7,** 85–86; platform, **Supp. 4,** 107; presidential elections, **Supp. 3,** 105–6, 395, 397; radical nucleus, **Supp. 3,** 604; Republican connections, **Supp. 3,** 710–11; Senate, **Supp. 4,** 669 –70; Wisconsin, **Supp. 5,** 403–4

Progressive party (1948), **Supp. 4,** 147; **Supp. 7,** 763; **Supp. 8,** 511; alleged Communist links, **Supp. 6,** 681

Progressive party of Wisconsin (1934), **Supp. 7,** 450

Prohibition, **Vol. 1, Part 1,** 512, 628; **Vol. 1, Part 2,** 310, 319, 334; **Vol. 2, Part 1,** 497, 591; **Vol. 3, Part 1,** 353; **Vol. 3, Part 2,** 6, 109, 227, 334, 335, 342, 413, 542; **Vol. 4, Part 1,** 73, 115, 171; **Vol. 4, Part 2,** 376, 436; **Vol. 5, Part 2,** 519; **Vol. 6, Part 2,** 342; **Vol. 8, Part 1,** 212; **Vol. 8, Part 2,** 303; **Vol. 9, Part 1,** 7, 74, 148, 546; **Vol. 10, Part 2,** 516; activities of W. J. Bryan, **Vol. 1, Part 1,** 197; advocacy of, **Supp. 1,** 251–52, 360; **Supp. 2,** 723; **Supp. 3,** 132, 449; **Supp. 5,** 80, 442; **Supp. 6,** 548, 682–83; Anti-Saloon League, **Vol. 5, Part 2,** 517; **Vol. 6, Part 1,** 171, 276; **Vol. 6, Part 2,** 483; **Vol. 10, Part 2,** 55; associations to repeal, **Supp. 5,** 194; bootlegging, **Supp. 4,** 140–42; **Supp. 5,** 737; **Supp. 6,** 263; cartoons ridiculing, **Supp. 5,** 391; Catholic support, **Supp. 2,** 135; congressional opposition to, **Supp. 4,** 446; federal legislation, **Supp. 4,** 853; historical writings on, **Supp. 7,** 20; Kansas, **Supp. 7,** 678; law enforcement, **Supp. 2,** 715; **Supp. 3,** 117; **Supp. 6,** 360; **Supp. 7,** 786, 805–6; lecturing to promote, **Supp. 4,** 741; **Supp. 5,** 701, 702; **Supp. 8,** 505; legality of, **Supp. 6,** 3; legislation authorship, **Supp. 3,** 706; "local option" question, **Vol. 6, Part 2,** 330; moderate voices for, **Supp. 7,** 345; opposition to, **Supp. 6,** 591–92, 636; political issue, **Supp. 2,** 723; **Supp. 3,** 720; **Supp. 4,** 136; **Supp. 7,** 786; political use of, **Supp. 3,** 318; press opposition to, **Supp. 5,** 449–50; Prohibition National Convention, **Vol. 9, Part 2,** 234; Prohibition

party, **Vol. 1, Part 2,** 310; **Vol. 3, Part 1,** 412; **Vol. 4, Part 2,** 387; **Vol. 8, Part 2,** 304; **Supp. 5,** 702; publications promoting, **Supp. 4,** 161; repeal movement, **Supp. 2,** 207; **Supp. 3,** 181; **Supp. 6,** 480; repeal of, **Supp. 1,** 86; **Supp. 3,** 649; Salvation Army support of, **Supp. 4,** 96; speakeasy, **Supp. 6,** 382; **Supp. 8,** 38; Virginia Anti-Saloon League, **Supp. 3,** 132; Women's Christian Temperance Union, **Vol. 3, Part 2,** 553; **Vol. 4, Part 2,** 436; **Vol. 6, Part 1,** 85, 86; women's organizations opposing, **Supp. 5,** 157; writings on, **Supp. 3,** 794. *See also* Alcohol; Temperance

Projectiles, machinery for the manufacture of, **Vol. 3, Part 1,** 580 f.; **Vol. 6, Part 1,** 82

"Project method," **Vol. 7, Part 1,** 558

Prokofiev, Sergei, references to, **Supp. 6,** 456, 550

Proletarian literature, **Supp. 7,** 239–40, 269, 583–84; **Supp. 8,** 137, 216–17

Prometheus Fountain (sculpture), **Supp. 8,** 414

"Promiscuous sitting" in Methodist church, **Vol. 5, Part 1,** 490

Promised Land, The, **Supp. 4,** 23

Promise of American Life, The, **Supp. 1,** 201, 210

Pronunciation, studies in, **Vol. 6, Part 1,** 430

Proofreading, **Vol. 9, Part 2,** 357

Propaganda, **Vol. 5, Part 2,** 297. *See also* Public relations; World War I; World War II

Property. *See* Real estate

Property cases, **Vol. 4, Part 1,** 255, 444, 456, 559. *See also* Law

Property tax, **Supp. 1,** 385; **Supp. 2,** 272; **Supp. 6,** 522

Proskauer, Joseph, reference to, **Supp. 3,** 718

Prospect Park (Brooklyn), landscaping of, **Vol. 6, Part 1,** 294; **Vol. 7, Part 2,** 26 f.

Prostate gland, surgery of, **Supp. 3,** 854

Prostitution: bordellos, **Supp. 4,** 255–56; **Supp. 7,** 4–5; Chicago, **Supp. 5,** 274–75; journalistic exposé, **Supp. 5,** 698; organized crime link, **Supp. 7,** 485; reform movements against, **Supp. 4,** 759; **Supp. 5,** 296–97; study of problem, **Vol. 4, Part 1,** 171

Proteases, **Supp. 6,** 595

Protection or Free Trade, **Vol. 4, Part 1,** 215

Protective tariff, **Vol. 2, Part 1,** 12, 491, 544; **Vol. 2, Part 2,** 176; **Vol. 3, Part 1,** 289; **Vol. 4, Part 2,** 457; **Vol. 5, Part 2,** 163, 300; **Vol. 6, Part 2,** 106; **Vol. 8, Part 1,** 457; **Vol. 9, Part 1,** 44, 204, 622; **Vol. 9, Part 2,** 237. *See also* Tariff

Protein: amino acid chain, **Supp. 3,** 441–42; **Supp. 4,** 720; chemistry, **Supp. 3,** 60–61; **Supp. 5,** 122–23, 149; **Supp. 6,** 346; chromosomal nucleoproteins, **Supp. 6,** 596; colloidal systems, **Supp. 3,** 315; enzyme identification as, **Supp. 5,** 622, 623, 670; human requirement studies, **Supp. 3,** 163; investigation, **Vol. 7, Part 2,** 74; metabolism of, **Supp. 1,** 307; research in, **Supp. 1,** 560; **Supp. 2,** 379; for surgery patients, **Supp. 6,** 190

Protestant Charities Aid Association of New York, founding of, **Supp. 1,** 541

Protestant Episcopal church (for complete list of clergymen, bishops etc., *see* Occupations Index): adaptation of Book of Common Prayer, **Vol. 8, Part 1,** 249 f.; as agency to bring about new social order, advocacy of, **Vol. 10, Part 2,** 251; altar and Book of Common Prayer design, **Supp. 3,** 784, 785; Anglo-Catholicism, **Supp. 3,** 195; **Supp. 6,** 45–46; bishops, **Supp. 1,** 115–17, 169–70, 329, 678; black leadership, **Supp. 1,** 645; broad churchmanship, advocacy of, **Vol. 10, Part 1,** 498; cathedrals, **Vol. 5, Part 2,** 422; **Vol. 6, Part 1,** 301; Christian Social Union, **Supp. 3,** 249; church organization, **Vol. 3, Part 1,** 216; Church Pension Fund, **Supp. 3,** 448; colonial history of, **Vol. 4, Part 2,** 417; Council of Bishops,

Supp. 1, 329; "Cowley Fathers," **Vol. 4, Part 1,** 470; drafting of constitution for American, **Vol. 8, Part 1,** 294 f.; divinity school faculty, **Supp. 3,** 37; divorce, attitude toward, **Vol. 4, Part 1,** 491; Emmanuel Movement, **Supp. 3,** 190–91; episcopacy question, **Vol. 5, Part 1,** 235; executive offices, **Vol. 4, Part 2,** 360; first missionary bishop, **Vol. 5, Part 2,** 321; first trial of a bishop, **Vol. 7, Part 2,** 39; formation of, in America, **Vol. 10, Part 2,** 121; General Convention of 1895, **Vol. 5, Part 2,** 590; girls' school, **Supp. 1,** 170; in Hawaii, **Supp. 1,** 624; institutional church, **Supp. 1,** 618; leadership, **Supp. 2,** 258; legislation, advancement of, **Vol. 3, Part 1,** 335; **Vol. 5, Part 1,** 112; liturgy, **Vol. 7, Part 1,** 137; Massachusetts bishopric, **Supp. 3,** 447–48; missions, **Vol. 3, Part 1,** 333; **Vol. 4, Part 2,** 264; **Vol. 5, Part 2,** 321; **Vol. 6, Part 1,** 64, 95; **Supp. 1,** 115–16, 134; **Supp. 2,** 258; **Supp. 4,** 677–78; New York City diocese, **Supp. 4,** 546–48; Oxford Movement, **Supp. 1,** 668; presiding bishop, **Supp. 6,** 649; publications and societies, **Vol. 5, Part 1,** 93; **Vol. 6, Part 1,** 296; reunification with Rome issue, **Supp. 2,** 201; reunion of northern and southern branches, **Vol. 8, Part 1,** 313 f.; service to, **Vol. 1, Part 1,** 18, 204; **Vol. 1, Part 2,** 35, 335; **Vol. 2, Part 2,** 51, 599; **Vol. 3, Part 2,** 98, 155, 203; **Vol. 4, Part 2,** 60, 490; **Vol. 4, Part 2,** 416, 491; **Vol. 5, Part 1,** 222; **Vol. 6, Part 2,** 258; **Vol. 7, Part 1,** 643; **Vol. 9, Part 1,** 301, 356; slave ownership, attitude toward, **Vol. 1, Part 1,** 277 f.; social reform, **Supp. 6,** 600, 649; Training School (Philadelphia), **Vol. 4, Part 2,** 262; writings on, **Vol. 3, Part 2,** 412; **Vol. 4, Part 1,** 471, 594; **Vol. 4, Part 2,** 417; **Vol. 5, Part 2,** 410, 423; **Vol. 6, Part 1,** 302

Protestant Episcopal church (by locality): Alabama, **Vol. 10, Part 2,** 315; California, **Vol. 5, Part 2,** 422 f.; Connecticut, **Vol. 6, Part 1,** 75; **Vol. 10, Part 2,** 42; Delaware, first bishop of, **Vol. 6, Part 1,** 95; Illinois, **Vol. 2, Part 1,** 274; **Vol. 6, Part 2,** 116; **Vol. 9, Part 1,** 6; Maine, expansion in, **Vol. 2, Part 1,** 276; Massachusetts Bay Colony, antiepiscopal views in, **Vol. 6, Part 1,** 87; New England, **Vol. 8, Part 2,** 529; New Jersey, first confirmation in, **Vol. 8, Part 1,** 249 f.; New York, **Vol. 3, Part 1,** 216, 334 f.; North Carolina, beginnings in, **Vol. 8, Part 1,** 398; Ohio, **Vol. 3, Part 1,** 343; **Vol. 6, Part 1,** 179; Oregon, first bishop of, **Vol. 8, Part 2,** 501; Pennsylvania, **Vol. 8, Part 1,** 124 f., 249 f.; Rhode Island, **Vol. 9, Part 1,** 359; South, spread of through the, **Vol. 2, Part 1,** 172; **Vol. 6, Part 1,** 64; **Vol. 7, Part 2,** 629; South Carolina, first bishop of, **Vol. 9, Part 1,** 336; Vermont, first bishop of, **Vol. 5, Part 1,** 212; Virginia, **Vol. 5, Part 2,** 75; **Vol. 6, Part 1,** 160; **Vol. 6, Part 2,** 183, 480; **Vol. 10, Part 2,** 316

Protestants and Other Americans United for the Separation of Church and State, **Supp. 7,** 597

Protocols of the Wise Men of Zion, **Supp. 1,** 78

Protoplasm: crystalline changes in, **Supp. 6,** 282; study of, **Vol. 7, Part 1,** 95

Protozoa: life-cycle studies, **Supp. 3,** 126–27; research on, **Supp. 4,** 461–62

Provence, writings of, **Vol. 5, Part 1,** 614 f.; **Vol. 8, Part 1,** 202

Providence, R.I., Butler Hospital, history of, **Vol. 8, Part 1,** 404; civic service to, **Vol. 6, Part 1,** 289; **Vol. 8, Part 1,** 584; **Vol. 9, Part 1,** 54, 290; early Catholicism in, **Vol. 10, Part 1,** 98 f.; public health, **Supp. 3,** 158

Providence Hospital (Washington), founding of, **Vol. 9, Part 2,** 586

Provident Hospital (Baltimore), founding of, **Supp. 3,** 271

Provident Loan Society, **Supp. 3,** 729

Provincetown, Mass., writers' colony, **Supp. 8,** 674, 675

Provincetown Players, **Vol. 2, Part 2,** 372 f.; **Supp. 3,** 329; **Supp. 4,** 576; **Supp. 8,** 350; founding of, **Supp. 4,** 330; **Supp. 5,** 523; **Supp. 8,** 675

Provincial Congress of Massachusetts (colonial), **Vol. 5, Part 1,** 345; **Vol. 6, Part 1,** 260

Provisional Executive Committee for Central Zionist Affairs, founding of, **Supp. 4,** 905

Prudden, T. Mitchell, reference to, **Supp. 3,** 257

Prudential Friendly Society, first policy written in, **Vol. 3, Part 1,** 463 f.

Prudential Insurance Co., **Supp. 4,** 384; **Supp. 5,** 177–78; early development of, **Vol. 3, Part 1,** 463 f.

Pryor's Band, **Supp. 3,** 610–11

Psallonian Society, founding of, **Vol. 9, Part 1,** 46

Psalmody, **Vol. 3, Part 2,** 449; **Vol. 6, Part 1,** 530

Psalm-singing, **Vol. 9, Part 2,** 390

Psalm tunes, compiled, **Vol. 9, Part 2,** 236

Psittacosis ("parrot fever"), **Supp. 7,** 648

Psychiatric Institute (New York City): administration, **Supp. 1,** 471; predecessor, **Supp. 4,** 571

Psychiatrists. For complete list, *see* Occupations Index

Psychiatry: **Vol. 1, Part 1,** 458; **Vol. 1, Part 2,** 160; **Vol. 2, Part 2,** 213; **Vol. 3, Part 1,** 595 f.; **Vol. 3, Part 2,** 412; **Vol. 4, Part 2,** 411, 412; **Vol. 5, Part 1,** 97; **Vol. 5, Part 2,** 207, 324, 325, 354; **Vol. 7, Part 1,** 489; **Vol. 8, Part 1,** 404; **Vol. 8, Part 2,** 116, 313, 559; **Vol. 9, Part 1,** 462; **Vol. 10, Part 1,** 613; alcoholism and suicide, **Supp. 6,** 461; clinical education in, **Supp. 4,** 572; community mental health movement, **Supp. 6,** 17; editing, **Supp. 3,** 385–86; emotional conflict and maladjustment, **Supp. 3,** 128; foundation grants, **Supp. 6,** 252–53; history of, **Supp. 6,** 724–25; interpersonal relations theory, **Supp. 4,** 805–8; neuropsychiatry, **Supp. 6,** 403–4; nomenclature of disorders, **Supp. 8,** 429–30; physiological approach to, **Supp. 4,** 618; popularization of, **Supp. 8,** 429–30; psychobiological, **Supp. 6,** 181; psychosis treatment, **Supp. 6,** 220; research and training centers, **Supp. 5,** 484; social work, criticism of, **Supp. 4,** 811; training in, **Supp. 1,** 131, 471; **Supp. 2,** 24; **Supp. 3,** 128; treatment and rehabilitation, **Supp. 3,** 320. *See also* Mental health and illness; Psychoanalysis

Psychiatry (journal), founding of, **Supp. 4,** 806, 807

Psychical research, **Vol. 3, Part 2,** 478; **Vol. 5, Part 1,** 341, 455; **Vol. 7, Part 1,** 338; **Vol. 9, Part 1,** 3; **Vol. 10, Part 1,** 417 f.

Psychic phenomena: extrasensory perception, **Supp. 6,** 612; philosophical opposition to, **Supp. 5,** 561; psychological investigation of, **Supp. 8,** 44; research in, **Supp. 2,** 407; writings on, **Supp. 4,** 878

Psychoanalysis: anthropological application, **Supp. 5,** 583–84; behaviorism and, **Supp. 4,** 387; diverging views in, **Supp. 7,** 6–7; early advocacy, **Supp. 2,** 711; early U.S. practitioners, **Supp. 3,** 383; first American-born analyst, **Supp. 4,** 130–31; first analyst in U.S., **Supp. 4,** 107–8; Freud collaboration, **Supp. 4,** 117–18; humanism in, **Supp. 6,** 724–25; juvenile paresis analogy with, **Supp. 8,** 429; lay analysis, **Supp. 3,** 385; orthodox Freudian, **Supp. 3,** 190–91; popularization of, **Supp. 3,** 191, 320; psychology and, **Supp. 4,** 572; for psychosis, **Supp. 6,** 220; self-development emphasis, **Supp. 5,** 302, 315–17; theory systemization, **Supp. 6,** 527–28; training analysis, **Supp. 5,** 517–18; training in, **Supp. 4,** 263, 716–17; writings on, **Supp. 3,** 386; **Supp. 8,** 523–24. *See also* Mental health and illness

Psychoanalytic Review, founding of, **Supp. 2,** 712; **Supp. 4,** 108

738; Sanitary Commission, U.S., **Vol. 8, Part 2,** 600; sanitary engineering, **Supp. 1,** 326; school programs, **Supp. 5,** 553; state departments, **Supp. 5,** 601; statistical studies, **Supp. 2,** 646; **Supp. 4,** 384–85; **Supp. 7,** 192; teaching of, **Supp. 3,** 244; **Supp. 5,** 233; tuberculosis crusade, **Vol. 5, Part 2,** 483; **Vol. 8, Part 2,** 188, 281; typhoid crusade, **Vol. 5, Part 2,** 483; venereal disease education and prevention, **Supp. 4,** 758–59; writings on, **Supp. 4,** 474–75, 684; **Supp. 6,** 117; Yellow Fever Commission, **Vol. 8, Part 1,** 460; **Vol. 9, Part 1,** 117, 592. *See also* Epidemics; Epidemiology; Occupational health and safety; Social hygiene

Public Health Association of America, **Vol. 1, Part 2,** 268; **Vol. 4, Part 2,** 369; **Vol. 8, Part 1,** 390

Public Health Council, first state, **Supp. 7,** 252

Public Health Service, United States, **Vol. 8, Part 2,** 313; **Vol. 9, Part 2,** 513; international relations, **Supp. 7,** 195; statistical studies, **Supp. 7,** 192; venereal disease, **Supp. 6,** 423–24, 460

Public housing, **Supp. 3,** 730; **Supp. 5,** 631; federally subsidized, **Supp. 3,** 838

Public Housing Act (1949), **Supp. 5,** 719

Publicity, use of, **Vol. 1, Part 1,** 606 f.; **Vol. 5, Part 2,** 73; **Vol. 6, Part 1,** 571

Publicity work. *See* Advertising and marketing; Public Relations

Public land. *See* Land and land use; Parks

Public Ledger (Philadelphia), **Vol. 2, Part 2,** 70; **Vol. 3, Part 1,** 455 f., 514 f.; **Vol. 5, Part 1,** 104

Public opinion: broadcast audience measurement, **Supp. 5,** 310–11; Gallup poll inception, **Supp. 4,** 189; government policy relationship, **Supp. 8,** 69, 70; presidential election (1936), **Supp. 7,** 274, 649; psychological research in, **Supp. 8,** 69–70; research poll technique development, **Supp. 7,** 649–50; social distance scale, **Supp. 3,** 578; survey testing methodology, **Supp. 6,** 604–5; tests and measurements, **Supp. 5,** 434, 685, 686

Public Opinion Index for Industry, founding of, **Supp. 7,** 650

Public parks, **Vol. 2, Part 1,** 306; **Vol. 6, Part 1,** 27; **Vol. 6, Part 2,** 492; **Vol. 7, Part 2,** 26 f., 482; **Vol. 8, Part 1,** 405; **Vol. 8, Part 2,** 355; **Vol. 9, Part 2,** 123; **Vol. 10, Part 1,** 647. *See also* Parks

Public Parks Protective Association, **Vol. 3, Part 2,** 56

Public relations: corporate, **Supp. 1,** 489–90; **Supp. 5,** 303; development of, **Supp. 6,** 90–91; political parties, **Supp. 4,** 575; press agents, **Supp. 5,** 270–71; **Supp. 6,** 536

Public school education. *See* Education

Public School Society (1805), organization of, **Vol. 2, Part 2,** 222 f.

Public speaking. *See* Lecturing; Oratory

Public utilities, **Vol. 1, Part 2,** 582; **Vol. 3, Part 1,** 356 f.; **Vol. 4, Part 2,** 372; **Vol. 6, Part 1,** 79; **Vol. 8, Part 1,** 9; **Vol. 9, Part 2,** 449, 644; **Vol. 10, Part 2,** 202, 203, 429, 455 f.; California legislation, **Supp. 3,** 395; central stations, **Supp. 2,** 333; Con Edison founding, **Supp. 3,** 138; development of, **Supp. 1,** 531, 630; **Supp. 2,** 154; entrepreneurs, **Supp. 3,** 192–93; ethics issues, **Supp. 6,** 590–96, 684; executive management of, **Supp. 3,** 746–47; **Supp. 4,** 180, 264–65; federal preference clause, **Supp. 8,** 2; first research department, **Supp. 3,** 231; holding companies, **Supp. 3,** 138, 526–27; **Supp. 4,** 394–95; **Supp. 5,** 260, 750–51; holding company legislation, **Supp. 3,** 654; **Supp. 4,** 544; legal counsel, **Supp. 3,** 829; municipal ownership, **Supp. 2,** 583, 691; New York City, **Supp. 4,** 404; public v. private ownership, **Supp. 3,** 250; **Supp. 6,** 216, 437, 484; **Supp. 8,** 179; rate-setting, **Supp. 2,** 560, 584; **Supp. 3,** 95, 231,

241; standardized evaluation, **Supp. 3,** 188; valuation and depreciation of properties, **Supp. 3,** 98; World War II measures, **Supp. 8,** 352. *See also* Electricity and electrification; Gas; Water

Public Utility Holding Company Act (1935), **Supp. 5,** 480; **Supp. 7,** 635; consitutionality of, **Supp. 5,** 358; groundwork for, **Supp. 6,** 122; opposition to, **Supp. 3,** 829; passage of, **Supp. 4,** 544

Public welfare, **Vol. 4, Part 1,** 160; **Vol. 6, Part 2,** 179; **Vol. 9, Part 2,** 567

Public works: art, **Supp. 3,** 112; Boston politics and, **Supp. 6,** 139–40; Civilian Conservation Corps, **Supp. 6,** 411–12; concept development, **Supp. 3,** 653, 654; **Supp. 6,** 378; countering unemployment, **Supp. 5,** 139–40, 403; New Deal construction projects, **Supp. 8,** 308; New Deal relief policy, **Supp. 4,** 391–92; New York City, **Supp. 4,** 466

Public Works Administration, **Supp. 2,** 170; **Supp. 3,** 795; **Supp. 4,** 392; building projects, **Supp. 5,** 342–43; founding of, **Supp. 3,** 650–51, 656; Mississippi Valley Committee, **Supp. 6,** 122

Publishers. For complete list, *see* Occupations Index

Publishers' Trade List Annual, first publication of, **Vol. 6, Part 1,** 231

Publisher's Weekly, **Vol. 6, Part 1,** 231

Publishing, **Vol. 1, Part 1,** 131, 360, 509, 570, 600; **Vol. 1, Part 2,** 162, 249; **Vol. 2, Part 1,** 29, 367, 487; **Vol. 2, Part 2,** 70, 304, 554; **Vol. 4, Part 1,** 72, 398, 460; **Vol. 4, Part 2,** 54, 355; **Vol. 5, Part 1,** 255 f., 384; **Vol. 5, Part 2,** 444, 447, 458, 591; **Vol. 6, Part 1,** 69, 70, 285, 423 f.; **Vol. 6, Part 2,** 444; **Vol. 7, Part 1,** 278, 331, 334, 352; **Vol. 7, Part 2,** 143; **Vol. 8, Part 1,** 440 f.; **Vol. 8, Part 2,** 371, 541; **Vol. 9, Part 2,** 21, 62, 435 f.; **Vol. 10, Part 2,** 294, 348, 471; agriculture, **Vol. 5, Part 2,** 231; Annenberg interests, **Supp. 3,** 19–21; Bibles and prayer books, **Vol. 6, Part 1,** 287; Block group, **Supp. 3,** 80–81; book, **Supp. 5,** 85, 272, 614; book clubs, **Supp. 8,** 577–78; book editing, **Supp. 3,** 686; Borzoi imprint, **Supp. 8,** 341–43; children's books, **Vol. 9, Part 2,** 436, **Vol. 10, Part 2,** 603; **Supp. 2,** 59; *Christian News*, **Vol. 10, Part 1,** 113; Covici-Friede, **Supp. 7,** 148–49; Cowles interests, **Supp. 4,** 189; Doubleday, Doran, **Supp. 4,** 239–40; **Supp. 6,** 171–72; E. P. Dutton & Co., **Supp. 3,** 498–99; farm-oriented, **Supp. 4,** 132; Gannett chain development, **Supp. 6,** 226–27; *Godey's Lady's Book*, **Vol. 4, Part 1,** 344; Grosset & Dunlap, **Supp. 1,** 362; Huebsch-Viking, **Supp. 7,** 374; Joyce's works, **Supp. 7,** 40; Kipling, first, **Vol. 1, Part 1,** 550; Knoxville *Sentinel*, **Vol. 10, Part 1,** 104; litigation, **Supp. 8,** 224; Little Blue Books, **Supp. 5,** 264–65; Little, Brown and Co., growth, **Supp. 4,** 526–27; Little Masterpieces series, **Supp. 5,** 541–42; *Los Angeles Times* growth, **Supp. 3,** 155–56; McClure syndicate, **Supp. 4,** 662; McGraw-Hill company founding, **Supp. 4,** 523–24; magazines, **Vol. 1, Part 1,** 573; **Vol. 3, Part 2,** 47, 54, 477; **Vol. 6, Part 1,** 110; **Vol. 7, Part 1,** 353; **Vol. 10, Part 2,** 80; **Supp. 1,** 212–13; **Supp. 3,** 547; **Supp. 5,** 394, 637–38, 760–61; **Supp. 7,** 527–28; mass-market books, **Supp. 4,** 239–40; music (*see also subhead:* sheet music), **Vol. 1, Part 1,** 202; **Vol. 2, Part 2,** 146; **Vol. 3, Part 1,** 321 f.; **Vol. 4, Part 1,** 363; **Vol. 6, Part 1,** 38; **Vol. 7, Part 1,** 133; **Vol. 7, Part 2,** 512; **Vol. 8, Part 2,** 434 f., 440; **Vol. 9, Part 1,** 589; **Supp. 4,** 486; **Supp. 5,** 218; **Supp. 6,** 275; **Supp. 7,** 198–99; music editing, **Supp. 4,** 276–77; newspaper, **Vol. 1, Part 2,** 171, 437, 565; **Vol. 5, Part 1,** 535; **Vol. 5, Part 2,** 458; **Vol. 6, Part 2,** 36, 38, 130; **Vol. 7, Part 1,** 271; **Vol. 7, Part 2,** 18, 250, 376, 643; **Vol. 8, Part 2,** 517, 519 f.; **Vol. 10, Part 2,** 500, 576; **Supp. 1,** 212–13; **Supp. 4,** 644, 645–46, 686–87; **Supp. 5,** 283–84, 615; **Supp. 7,**

199–200, 243–44, 295–96, 299, 603–4; **Supp. 8,** 636 –37; W. W. Norton founding, **Supp. 3,** 563–64; organizations, **Supp. 2,** 59, 72; Pantheon Books, **Supp. 7,** 799; printing processes, **Supp. 2,** 733; promotion and distribution, **Supp. 6,** 583; Random House, **Supp. 7,** 3; reference works, **Supp. 5,** 752– 53; religious, **Vol. 8, Part 1,** 512 f.; **Supp. 6,** 171; Rinehart and Co., **Supp. 8,** 536; scholarly presses, **Supp. 6,** 154–55; school books, **Vol. 4, Part 2,** 43; **Vol. 6, Part 1,** 230; second-run editions, **Supp. 1,** 369; sheet music, **Supp. 3,** 833–34; **Supp. 4,** 88; Simon and Schuster, **Supp. 8,** 579; song, **Supp. 4,** 836; syndicates, **Supp. 3,** 427–28; teaching materials, **Supp. 2,** 419; technical books and magazines, **Supp. 4,** 523–24; Time Inc., **Supp. 8,** 393–96; *Uncle Tom's Cabin,* **Vol. 5, Part 2,** 69; Viking Press, **Supp. 7,** 306–7. *See also* Books; Censorship; Copyright; Magazines; Newspapers; Typographical design

Publishing houses: Catholic, **Vol. 5, Part 2,** 329 f.; Clarke Co., Robert, **Vol. 2, Part 2,** 162; D. Appleton & Co., **Vol. 1, Part 1,** 326, 334 f.; **Vol. 2, Part 1,** 262; Dodd Mead & Co., **Vol. 3, Part 1,** 340 f.; Ginn and Co., **Vol. 4, Part 1,** 317; Holt & Co., Henry, **Vol. 5, Part 1,** 180; Lippincott, J. B., **Vol. 6, Part 1,** 287; Little, Brown and Co., **Vol. 2, Part 1,** 127; **Vol. 6, Part 1,** 297; McClurg, A. C., **Vol. 6, Part 1,** 595 f.; Merriam & Co., **Vol. 6, Part 2,** 552; Putnam and Sons, G. P., **Vol. 8, Part 1,** 279, 285; Scribner's Sons, Charles, **Vol. 2, Part 1,** 291; **Vol. 8, Part 2,** 515 f.

Pucinski, Roman, reference to, **Supp. 8,** 366
Puck: cartoons, **Supp. 2,** 504; founding of, **Vol. 5, Part 2,** 264, 352–53
Puebla, siege of, **Vol. 8, Part 2,** 509
Pueblo, houses, **Vol. 7, Part 1,** 185
Pueblo Indians, **Vol. 6, Part 1,** 501; **Supp. 3,** 582; **Supp. 7,** 486–87, 570; first reports of, **Vol. 7, Part 1,** 594; researches among, **Vol. 3, Part 2,** 353; uprisings of, **Vol. 3, Part 1,** 260
Puerperal fever, **Supp. 3,** 223
Puerto Rican Telephone Co., **Supp. 6,** 43
Puerto Rico: botany of, **Supp. 2,** 113; conquest of, by Ponce de León, Juan, **Vol. 8, Part 1,** 56 f.; first native-born governor, **Supp. 5,** 545; governors, **Vol. 2, Part 2,** 322; **Supp. 3,** 669; **Supp. 4,** 903; **Supp. 5,** 545; labor movement in, **Supp. 2,** 331; leadership in, **Vol. 7, Part 1,** 329; military governor of portion of, **Vol. 10, Part 1,** 104; political career of Commissioner Larrinaga, **Vol. 6, Part 1,** 8; politics, **Vol. 7, Part 1,** 329–30; public finances, **Supp. 2,** 311; public school system, **Vol. 3, Part 1,** 608 f.; terrorist attempts, **Supp. 8,** 300; U.S. administration of, **Supp. 2,** 332, 579
Puget Sound controversy, **Vol. 4, Part 2,** 280; **Vol. 8, Part 2,** 510; **Vol. 7, Part 2,** 570. *See* Yakima Indian War
Pugilism, **Vol. 3, Part 2,** 443; **Vol. 4, Part 2,** 500; **Vol. 7, Part 1,** 233; **Vol. 8, Part 1,** 585
Pujo Committee, **Vol. 7, Part 1,** 177, 178
Pulaski, Casimir, reference to, **Vol. 1, Part 1,** 270
Pulitzer, Herbert, reference to, **Supp. 6,** 616
Pulitzer, Joseph, references to, **Supp. 3,** 91, 144; **Supp. 5,** 284, 551; **Supp. 6,** 686
Pulitzer, Ralph, reference to, **Supp. 6,** 616
Pulitzer Prizes, establishment of, **Vol. 8, Part 1,** 260 f.
Pulitzer Publishing Co., **Supp. 5,** 551–52
Pulley, iron, **Vol. 10, Part 1,** 503 f.
Pullman Co., **Vol. 6, Part 1,** 267; **Vol. 8, Part 1,** 263 f.; **Vol. 8, Part 2,** 594; boycott of cars of, **Vol. 3, Part 1,** 183; first car, **Vol. 8, Part 1,** 263 f.
Pullman strike (1894), **Vol. 1, Part 1,** 231; **Vol. 2, Part 2,** 211; **Vol. 3, Part 1,** 183; **Vol. 4, Part 2,** 21; **Vol.**

6, Part 2, 615; **Vol. 8, Part 1,** 263; **Vol. 9, Part 2,** 267; **Vol. 10, Part 2,** 505
Pulp fiction, **Supp. 3,** 264
Pulp manufacturing, **Vol. 3, Part 2,** 250
Pulte Medical College, founded, **Vol. 8, Part 1,** 264
Pulteney Purchase, **Vol. 3, Part 2,** 601; **Vol. 9, Part 2,** 651; **Vol. 10, Part 2,** 297
Pumping engines for waterworks and sewers, **Vol. 6, Part 1,** 81
Pumping machinery, **Vol. 7, Part 1,** 450
Pumps, revolving cistern stand, invention of, **Vol. 3, Part 1,** 395
Pumps, water, manufacturing of, **Vol. 4, Part 1,** 178; **Vol. 7, Part 2,** 172; **Vol. 10, Part 2,** 539
Pupin, Michael I., references to, **Supp. 3,** 299; **Supp. 5,** 494
Puppetry, **Supp. 3,** 684–85; **Supp. 6,** 186
Purcell, William Gray, reference to, **Supp. 5,** 208
Purdue University: botany studies, **Supp. 3,** 23; founded, **Vol. 8, Part 1,** 268
Pure Food and Drug Act (1906), preservatives and additives, **Supp. 3,** 164
Pure food movement, **Vol. 1, Part 2,** 116; **Vol. 4, Part 2,** 506, 568; **Vol. 5, Part 2,** 524; **Vol. 6, Part 1,** 567; **Vol. 9, Part 1,** 74; **Vol. 10, Part 1,** 582 f.; **Vol. 10, Part 2,** 215
Puritan in Babylon, A, **Supp. 3,** 817
Puritans, **Vol. 3, Part 2,** 155; **Vol. 5, Part 1,** 88; clergy, **Vol. 2, Part 2,** 460 f.; **Vol. 7, Part 1,** 572–73; **Vol. 9, Part 1,** 83; example of, **Vol. 9, Part 1,** 90; first to be converted to Catholicism, **Vol. 10, Part 1,** 98; historical research on, **Supp. 7,** 538; Maryland, controversies, battle of the Severn, **Vol. 9, Part 2,** 88; Massachusetts, **Vol. 10, Part 2,** 194; Papists and, **Vol. 4, Part 1,** 135; religious outlook, **Vol. 8, Part 2,** 202; social freedom under, **Vol. 10, Part 1,** 104. *See also* Pilgrims
Purity Clubs, **Supp. 8,** 434
"Purkey, Private Oscar" (fictional character), **Supp. 7,** 618
"Purple Cow" poem, **Supp. 5,** 94
Purrysburg, S.C., settlement of, **Vol. 5, Part 2,** 117; **Vol. 8, Part 1,** 270 f.
Putnam, Frederick W., references to, **Supp. 3,** 83, 372; **Supp. 5,** 533
Putnam, Herbert, reference to, **Supp. 3,** 285, 326–27
Putnam, Israel, **Vol. 6, Part 1,** 333
Putnam, James J., references to, **Supp. 3,** 191; **Supp. 6,** 98
Putnam & Sons, G. P., **Supp. 3,** 285; founding of, **Vol. 8, Part 1,** 279 f., 285
Putnam's Monthly Magazine, pioneer use of American material rather than foreign reprints, **Vol. 2, Part 1,** 41; **Vol. 8, Part 1,** 279 f.
Putney community, **Vol. 7, Part 1,** 590
"Puts and calls," stock market about 1872, **Vol. 8, Part 2,** 292
Puzzles: crossword, **Supp. 6,** 583; double-crostic, **Supp. 6,** 341–42
Pyle, Howard, reference to, **Supp. 3,** 847; **Supp. 6,** 94; **Supp. 8,** 493
Pyloroplasty, **Supp. 3,** 271
Pynson Printers, founding of, **Supp. 7,** 2–3
Pyrex ovenware, **Supp. 3,** 365; **Supp. 6,** 624
Pyrography, **Vol. 5, Part 2,** 413
Pyrometallurgy, **Vol. 1, Part 1,** 343
Pyrometer, **Vol. 1, Part 2,** 407; invention of, **Supp. 1,** 120

Q

Qavam, Ahmad, reference to, **Supp. 8,** 6
Quackery, opposition to, **Vol. 4, Part 2,** 554
Quacks, medical, **Supp. 3,** 103–4
Quadrant, inventions concerning, **Vol. 4, Part 1,** 345
Quakers (Society of Friends), **Vol. 1, Part 2,** 523; **Vol. 2, Part 2,** 266, 331 f; **Vol. 3, Part 2,** 186, 210 f., 352; **Vol. 4, Part 1,** 237 f., 244, 605, 634; **Vol. 4, Part 2,** 159; **Vol. 5, Part 1,** 6, 86, 141, 334, 389, 610 f.; **Vol. 5, Part 2,** 4, 13, 46, 199, 463, 519; **Vol. 6, Part 1,** 136, 330, 334 f., 431; **Vol. 7, Part 1,** 200 f., 289, 508, 554; **Vol. 7, Part 2,** 413 f.; **Vol. 8, Part 2,** 342, 393, 410 f., 493; **Vol. 9, Part 1,** 28, 115 f.; **Vol. 9, Part 2,** 336, 441 f., 444; **Vol. 10, Part 1,** 386; American Friends' Peace Association, **Vol. 5, Part 2,** 4; Baltimore Association, **Vol. 5, Part 2,** 4; Baptist radicals and, **Vol. 8, Part 2,** 101; "Birthright," **Vol. 8, Part 2,** 50; "Christian Quakers," **Vol. 5, Part 2,** 289 f.; conscientious objectors, **Supp. 6,** 217; doctrines, interpretation of, **Vol. 8, Part 2,** 246; **Vol. 10, Part 2,** 461; education, **Vol. 1, Part 2,** 178; "fighting," **Vol. 10, Part 2,** 23; Five Years' Meeting, **Vol. 5, Part 2,** 4; Friends' Boarding Home, **Vol. 5, Part 2,** 13; *Friends' Journal* and *Friends' Intelligencer*, merger of, **Vol. 5, Part 2,** 46; Gwynedd meeting, **Vol. 8, Part 2,** 9; Haverford Collection of Quakeriana, **Supp. 1,** 463; historical writings on, **Supp. 4,** 441–42; history of, **Vol. 4, Part 2,** 160; **Vol. 5, Part 1,** 140; **Vol. 7, Part 1,** 280 f.; **Vol. 9, Part 1,** 28; itinerant preaching, **Vol. 8, Part 2,** 342; Kansas and Missouri politics, effect on, **Vol. 6, Part 1,** 204; marriage with Indians, **Vol. 8, Part 2,** 179; "marrying out of meeting," **Vol. 8, Part 2,** 174; missionary preaching to Indians, **Vol. 2, Part 1,** 592; opposition to, **Vol. 3, Part 2,** 204; persecution, **Vol. 3, Part 1,** 584; **Vol. 3, Part 2,** 156; **Vol. 7, Part 1,** 573; **Vol. 8, Part 1,** 399; press, first in America, **Vol. 5, Part 1,** 611; promotion of, **Vol. 4, Part 2,** 473; public relations, **Supp. 5,** 303; Quietism, **Vol. 8, Part 2,** 343; radical group, in, **Vol. 6, Part 1,** 63; Schism of 1827 (Orthodox v. Hicksite), **Vol. 3, Part 2,** 232 f.; **Vol. 5, Part 1,** 86, 224; settlements, **Vol. 3, Part 2,** 330; "Shakers," first colony of, **Vol. 6, Part 1,** 95; slavery, attitude toward, **Vol. 4, Part 1,** 606; **Vol. 6, Part 1,** 63; **Vol. 10, Part 2,** 517; societies, **Vol. 4, Part 2,** 369; theology of, **Supp. 4,** 442–43; "transformed," **Vol. 10, Part 1,** 120; "War Hawks," **Vol. 8, Part 2,** 9; writings, **Vol. 3, Part 2,** 211; **Vol. 4, Part 1,** 244; **Vol. 5, Part 1,** 86; **Vol. 6, Part 1,** 63, 212, 287; **Vol. 7, Part 2,** 429; **Vol. 8, Part 1,** 273 f., 399; **Vol. 10, Part 1,** 387
Quantum theory, **Supp. 4,** 488, 818, 838–39; **Supp. 5,** 203–4, 219–21, 495–96, 529, 563; **Supp. 6,** 655; **Supp. 7,** 133, 517; **Supp. 8,** 190; causality studies, **Supp. 8,** 190; decisive proof of, **Supp. 7,** 258–59; molecular, **Supp. 8,** 122, 482; nuclear physics application, **Supp. 8,** 199, 628
Quarantine Service, establishment of, **Vol. 2, Part 1,** 536
Quarrie Publications, **Supp. 7,** 243
Quarries, **Vol. 6, Part 1,** 154; **Vol. 8, Part 1,** 245 f.; **Vol. 8, Part 2,** 98
Quarterly Journal of Economics, first periodical of its kind, **Vol. 3, Part 1,** 503 f.
Quarterly Review of Biology, founding of, **Supp. 2,** 522
Quay, Matthew S., references to, **Vol. 2, Part 1,** 436; **Vol. 6, Part 1,** 590
Quebec: founding of, **Vol. 2, Part 1,** 606; siege of (1756), **Vol. 6, Part 2,** 84; siege of (1775), *see* Canada, invasion of, 1775
Quebec Conference (1944), **Supp. 5,** 334

Quedagh Merchant (ship), **Vol. 5, Part 2,** 369
Queed, **Vol. 4, Part 2,** 342
Queen's College (N.J.). *See* Rutgers University
Queens College (N.Y.), sociology and anthropology studies, **Supp. 8,** 509
"Queen's Head," R.I. tavern, **Vol. 1, Part 2,** 512
Queenston Heights, Canada, battle of, **Vol. 3, Part 1,** 175; **Vol. 10, Part 1,** 210
Quemoy and Matsu islands, **Supp. 8,** 158, 223
Quezon, Manuel, references to, **Supp. 4,** 612; **Supp. 6,** 211, 280–81; **Supp. 7,** 488
Quids, N.Y. political party, **Vol. 6, Part 1,** 222
Quigley, Martin, reference to, **Supp. 7,** 71
Quincy, Josiah, references to, **Vol. 6, Part 1,** 533; **Vol. 8, Part 1,** 29 f.
Quincy, Mass.: education, **Vol. 7, Part 2,** 221; origin of the name, **Vol. 8, Part 1,** 308 f.
Quincy Journal, **Vol. 10, Part 1,** 111
Quinine, use of, **Vol. 8, Part 2,** 353
Quinine sulphate, manufacture of, **Vol. 10, Part 1,** 607 f.
Quitman, John A., reference to, **Vol. 9, Part 2,** 510
"Quit-rent" controversy, **Vol. 5, Part 2,** 140
Quiz shows, radio, **Supp. 6,** 5

R

Rabbi, first to be ordained in U.S., **Vol. 1, Part 2,** 219
Rabi, Isidor I., reference to, **Supp. 8,** 628
Race relations: Boys Town opposition to racism, **Supp. 4,** 283; study of, **Supp. 3,** 577–79; traditional southern view of, **Supp. 3,** 598; writings on, **Supp. 4,** 251. *See also* Blacks; Civil rights movement; Racism; Segregation
Race Traits and Tendencies of the American Negro, **Supp. 4,** 384, 385
Rachmaninoff, Sergei, reference to, **Supp. 3,** 707
Racial segregation. *See* Segregation
Racine College, **Vol. 5, Part 2,** 322; **Vol. 7, Part 2,** 207
Racism: American Nazi party activities, **Supp. 8,** 541; *Birth of a Nation*, charges against, **Supp. 4,** 350; in education theory, **Supp. 3,** 206; eugenic basis, **Supp. 3,** 84, 177, 215–16, 445–46; **Supp. 6,** 354; in fiction, **Supp. 6,** 354; immigration restrictions, **Supp. 5,** 561; in Louisiana, **Supp. 6,** 391; "100 percent Americanism" advocacy, **Supp. 3,** 709; political, **Supp. 3,** 78; **Supp. 6,** 525–26; in sociological thought, **Supp. 5,** 592; southern political, **Supp. 4,** 78; **Supp. 8,** 499–500; in Texas politics, **Supp. 3,** 267; "white supremacy" advocacy, **Supp. 5,** 177, 290; writings on, **Supp. 8,** 605–6; writings promoting, **Supp. 4,** 235, 384–85, 792. *See also* Eugenics; Holocaust; Ku Klux Klan; Segregation
Racketeering. *See* Organized crime
Rackham, Horace H., reference to, **Supp. 4,** 294
Radar: development and application, **Supp. 4,** 358; **Supp. 8,** 686; pulse-echo, **Supp. 7,** 58
Radcliffe-Brown, Alfred, references to, **Supp. 8,** 683, 684
Radcliffe College, **Vol. 3, Part 2,** 73; **Vol. 4, Part 1,** 297; **Vol. 5, Part 1,** 13; **Vol. 6, Part 1,** 72; **Vol. 7, Part 2,** 174; development of, **Supp. 1,** 146; history studies, **Supp. 8,** 169–70
Radial velocities, **Supp. 6,** 8
Radiation: cancer therapy, **Supp. 3,** 258; effects on plants, **Supp. 6,** 176; fallout research, **Supp. 7,** 344; food, **Supp. 1,** 398; health hazards, **Supp. 4,** 112; **Supp. 8,** 449, 450; infrared, **Supp. 4,** 658; photon theory of, **Supp. 7,** 10; quantum theory of, **Supp. 5,** 495; secondary X-radiation, **Supp. 1,** 614; (*See also* X rays); studies in, **Vol. 7, Part 1,** 491–92; **Vol. 9, Part 2,** 653. **Supp.** *See also* X rays

Ray, James Earl, reference to, **Supp. 8,** 335
Ray, Man, reference to, **Supp. 5,** 184
Rayburn, Sam, reference to, **Supp. 8,** 630
Raymond, Gene, reference to, **Supp. 7,** 499
Rayon, manufacture of, **Supp. 5,** 366
Razors, disposable blades, **Supp. 1,** 345
RCA. *See* Radio Corporation of America
RDX (cyclonite), **Supp. 5,** 28
REA. *See* Rural Electrification Administration
Reader's Digest, **Supp. 5,** 528; **Supp. 7,** 321, 346, 643;
    Supp. 8, 150
Reader's Guide to Periodical Literature, **Supp. 5,** 753–54
Reading: braille, **Supp. 3,** 365; "Dick and Jane" text-
    books, **Supp. 6,** 248; frequently used words, **Supp.
    4,** 833; tachistoscope, **Supp. 3,** 229–30; teaching
    methods, **Supp. 4,** 89–90; **Supp. 6,** 248. *See also*
    Books; Learning
Readinger Adler, publication of, **Vol. 6, Part 1,** 292
Readjuster movement in Virginia (1872-76), **Vol. 1,
    Part 1,** 592; **Vol. 4, Part 1,** 422; **Vol. 5, Part 1,** 358;
    Vol. 5, Part 2, 322; **Vol. 6, Part 2,** 212
Reagan, Ronald, references to, **Supp. 8,** 220, 649
Real estate, **Vol. 1, Part 1,** 397 f.; **Vol. 8, Part 2,** 386;
    bonds, first issue of, for building projects, **Vol. 9,
    Part 2,** 132; Boston, **Vol. 2, Part 2,** 136; Cincinnati,
    Vol. 6, Part 1, 394; Houston, **Supp. 6,** 135, 136;
    New York City, **Supp. 6,** 23, 24; Oregon land law,
    Supp. 6, 682; restrictive covenants, **Supp. 6,** 502;
    Southern California development, **Supp. 3,** 154–56;
    Supp. 5, 309–10; tax assessment, **Supp. 1,** 385;
    Supp. 6, 522. *See also* Land and land use; Zoning
Reality: A Journal of Artists' Opinion, **Supp. 8,** 280
Reams Station, Va., battle of. *See* Richmond campaign
Reaping machine, **Vol. 3, Part 2,** 132; **Vol. 6, Part 1,**
    610 f.; invention of, **Vol. 5, Part 1,** 431; **Vol. 6, Part
    1,** 607
Rebates, railroad, **Vol. 9, Part 2,** 70
Rebel Without a Cause, **Supp. 5,** 162, 163
Recent Social Trends in the United States, **Supp. 5,** 485
Reciprocal Trade Program, **Supp. 6,** 126
Reclamation Act (1902), **Vol. 4, Part 2,** 483; **Supp. 4,**
    563
Reclamation projects, **Vol. 3, Part 2,** 403; **Vol. 7, Part
    1,** 457
Reclamation Service, United States, **Supp. 3,** 814, 845
    –46; dam building, **Supp. 1,** 225; **Supp. 8,** 572–73
Recollect Friars, **Vol. 4, Part 2,** 540; **Vol. 6, Part 1,**
    231
Recollections. *See* Memoirs
Reconstruction, **Vol. 1, Part 1,** 24, 138; **Vol. 1, Part
    2,** 334; **Vol. 2, Part 1,** 512; **Vol. 2, Part 2,** 28; **Vol.
    3, Part 1,** 120; **Vol. 3, Part 2,** 25, 439, 564; **Vol. 4,
    Part 1,** 233, 391, 532, 539, 541; **Vol. 4, Part 2,** 83,
    261, 449, 462; **Vol. 5, Part 1,** 357, 373, 423; **Vol. 5,
    Part 2,** 103; **Vol. 6, Part 2,** 159; **Vol. 7, Part 1,** 263,
    352, 487; **Vol. 8, Part 1,** 33 f., 410; **Vol. 8, Part 2,**
    195; **Vol. 9, Part 1,** 21, 81, 624; **Vol. 9, Part 2,** 604;
    Vol. 10, Part 1, 6, 19; Act of Congress, **Vol. 7, Part
    2,** 447; Alabama, **Vol. 2, Part 1,** 33; Arkansas, **Vol.
    1, Part 2,** 61; **Vol. 2, Part 1,** 408; **Vol. 2, Part 2,** 187;
    Vol. 4, Part 1, 150; **Vol. 8, Part 1,** 33, 436; "Central
    Directory," **Vol. 5, Part 2,** 85; Committee of Fif-
    teen, **Vol. 5, Part 2,** 115; Georgia, **Vol. 1, Part 1,**
    133, 430; **Vol. 2, Part 1,** 143, 258; **Vol. 4, Part 1,**
    424; **Vol. 5, Part 2,** 44; **Vol. 6, Part 2,** 13; **Vol. 10,
    Part 2,** 411, 441; historical writings on, **Supp. 1,**
    303; **Supp. 5,** 498; investigation of, first scholarly,
    Vol. 3, Part 1, 523 f.; Kentucky, **Vol. 2, Part 1,** 55;
    Vol. 3, Part 1, 114; Louisiana, **Vol. 1, Part 1,** 192
    f.; **Vol. 2, Part 1,** 218, 402, 459; **Vol. 3, Part 1,** 545;
    Vol. 6, Part 2, 555; Mississippi, **Vol. 2, Part 1,** 593;
    Vol. 4, Part 1, 233; **Vol. 4, Part 2,** 327; **Vol. 5, Part

2, 352; **Vol. 9, Part 2,** 78; **Vol. 10, Part 2,** 609; North
    Carolina, **Vol. 2, Part 1,** 77; **Vol. 3, Part 1,** 287; **Vol.
    6, Part 2,** 570; **Vol. 7, Part 1,** 115; **Vol. 8, Part 1,**
    64; **Vol. 10, Part 1,** 69; **Vol. 10, Part 2,** 536; novels
    based on, **Vol. 9, Part 2,** 604; policy of the North,
    Vol. 2, Part 1, 512; South Carolina, **Vol. 2, Part 1,**
    364, 404, 595; **Vol. 2, Part 2,** 58; **Vol. 6, Part 2,** 1
    f.; **Vol. 7, Part 2,** 59, 483; **Vol. 8, Part 1,** 118 f.; **Vol.
    8, Part 2,** 332; **Vol. 10, Part 2,** 558; Tennessee, **Vol.
    2, Part 1,** 136; **Vol. 3, Part 2,** 311; **Vol. 5, Part 2,**
    83; Texas, **Vol. 2, Part 1,** 443; **Vol. 3, Part 1,** 112;
    Vol. 7, Part 2, 369; **Vol. 8, Part 1,** 433 f.; Union
    offices in South, **Vol. 4, Part 2,** 594; Virginia, **Vol.
    2, Part 1,** 439; **Vol. 6, Part 2,** 382; **Vol. 10, Part 2,**
    429; Wade-Davis Manifesto, **Vol. 3, Part 1,** 120;
    West Virginia, Vol. 6, Part 2, 404;
Reconstruction Finance Corporation (RFC), **Supp. 5,**
    160; **Supp. 6,** 33, 325, 453; **Supp. 8,** 89, 308, 309;
    founding of, **Supp. 7,** 362; **Supp. 8,** 207; scandal,
    Supp. 7, 562
Recordings: binaural sound research, **Supp. 6,** 365;
    bird songs, **Supp. 7,** 8; country and western, **Supp.
    5,** 749; duplicating system, **Supp. 1,** 76; early black
    jazz, **Supp. 2,** 502; harpsichord, **Supp. 6,** 358; high-
    fidelity sound equipment, **Supp. 5,** 324; Ives' com-
    positions, **Supp. 5,** 353; jazz, **Supp. 6,** 299–300;
    Supp. 7, 131; popularizing concert singers, **Supp. 3,**
    484–85; rock and roll, **Supp. 6,** 301; **Supp. 7,** 267;
    sound and action synchronization, **Supp. 1,** 121;
    talking books for blind, **Supp. 5,** 347. *See also* Audio
    systems; Phonograph
Record-keeping supplies, **Supp. 3,** 618–19
Records of the New York Stage, **Vol. 5, Part 1,** 498
Recreation, constructive aspects of, **Supp. 2,** 375
Red Badge of Courage, The, **Supp. 4,** 38
Red Caps. *See* International Brotherhood of Red Caps
Red Cross. *See* American Red Cross; International Red
    Cross
Redemptorist Order in U.S., **Vol. 4, Part 2,** 515; **Vol.
    8, Part 2,** 286
Redfield, Robert, reference to, **Supp. 8,** 378
Red Hot Peppers (jazz group), **Supp. 3,** 542
Rediscount rates, **Supp. 3,** 730
Re-discovery of America, The, **Supp. 8,** 192
Redman, Don, references to, **Supp. 5,** 292, 293
Redpath, James, reference to, **Vol. 8, Part 1,** 60 f.
Red River campaign (1864), **Vol. 1, Part 1,** 579; **Vol.
    2, Part 1,** 469; **Vol. 2, Part 2,** 105; **Vol. 5, Part 2,**
    425, 441
Red River Transportation Co., **Vol. 5, Part 2,** 441
Red Star Line, establishment of, **Vol. 9, Part 2,** 397
Redwoods, conservation, **Supp. 3,** 520; **Supp. 4,** 429;
    Supp. 6, 486
Redwoods, Sequoyah, naming of, **Vol. 8, Part 2,** 586
Reece, Carroll, reference to, **Supp. 7,** 276
Reed, Daniel, reference to, **Supp. 8,** 422
Reed, David A., reference to, **Supp. 6,** 320
Reed, James, reference to, **Supp. 6,** 388
Reed, John, reference to, **Supp. 5,** 580; **Supp. 7,** 486
Reed, Thomas B., references to, **Vol. 5, Part 1,** 63;
    Vol. 9, Part 1, 526
Reed, Walter, references to, **Vol. 2, Part 1,** 525; **Vol.
    4, Part 2,** 45; **Vol. 7, Part 1,** 582; **Vol. 9, Part 1,** 592
Reed College, first president, **Supp. 4,** 307; founding
    of, **Vol. 8, Part 1,** 456
Reed-Johnson Immigration Act (1924), **Supp. 5,** 561
Reed organ, invention of, **Vol. 4, Part 1,** 336
Reedy, William Marion, references to, **Supp. 3,** 851;
    Supp. 6, 10
Reedy's Mirror, importance of, **Vol. 8, Part 1,** 464
Reese, Eleanor, reference to, **Supp. 6,** 162

Rhode Island Woman's Club, **Vol. 3, Part 1,** 423

Rhodes, James E., reference to, **Vol. 9, Part 2,** 337

Rhodes, J. F., reference to, **Vol. 1, Part 2,** 484

Rhodes Scholarship, **Supp. 6,** 29, 30; American secretary, **Supp. 8,** 601; first black recipient, **Supp. 5,** 436

Rhythm of the Ages, The, **Supp. 4,** 344

Riboflavin, **Supp. 6,** 595

Ricci-Curbastro, Gregorio, reference to, **Supp. 7,** 216

Rice, **Vol. 2, Part 1,** 326; **Vol. 2, Part 2,** 307, 317, 512; **Vol. 3, Part 1,** 275, 381, 546, 604; **Vol. 3, Part 2,** 322, 324, 580, 559; **Vol. 4, Part 1,** 174, 575; **Vol. 5, Part 1,** 219, 227; **Vol. 5, Part 2,** 40, 204, 402; **Vol. 6, Part 1,** 53, 289; **Vol. 8, Part 1,** 126; **Vol. 9, Part 1,** 289, 475; **Vol. 10, Part 1,** 121, 412, 434 f., 437; mills, **Vol. 6, Part 1,** 486 f.; plantations, **Vol. 1, Part 1,** 224; **Vol. 2, Part 2,** 180; **Vol. 5, Part 2,** 414; seeds, smuggling of, by Jefferson, **Vol. 5, Part 2,** 22

Rice, David, memoirs, **Supp. 1,** 83

Rice, Elmer, reference to, **Supp. 4,** 104

Rice, Francis O., reference to, **Supp. 4,** 337

Rice, Grantland, reference to, **Supp. 7,** 729

Rice Institute: architecture, **Supp. 3,** 196; genetics studies, **Supp. 8,** 449

Rich, Isaac, reference to, **Vol. 10, Part 1,** 490 f.

Rich, Obadiah, reference to, **Vol. 5, Part 1,** 509

Richards, Alfred Newton, reference to, **Supp. 6,** 175

Richards, Ellen H., reference to, **Vol. 7, Part 1,** 575

Richards, Theodore W., reference to, **Supp. 3,** 349–50

Richardson, Helen Patges, reference to, **Supp. 3,** 237–38

Richardson, H. H., reference to, **Vol. 5, Part 2,** 533; **Vol. 7, Part 1,** 545

Richardson, J. P. ("Big Bopper"), reference to, **Supp. 6,** 301

Richardson, Owen W., references to, **Supp. 5,** 126; **Supp. 6,** 150–51, 653–54

Richardson, Bellows, Henry and Co., founding, **Supp. 6,** 222

Richardson Foundation, **Supp. 6,** 541

Richfield Oil Co., **Supp. 6,** 585

Richman, Julia, reference to, **Supp. 8,** 442–43

Richmond, Ky., battle of, **Vol. 1, Part 2,** 586; **Vol. 2, Part 1,** 241; **Vol. 3, Part 1,** 131; **Vol. 4, Part 2,** 240; **Vol. 5, Part 2,** 245; **Vol. 7, Part 1,** 426; **Vol. 8, Part 1,** 40; **Vol. 9, Part 2,** 433

Richmond, Va., campaign (1864–65), **Vol. 2, Part 2,** 463; **Vol. 3, Part 1,** 598; **Vol. 3, Part 2,** 602; **Vol. 4, Part 1,** 25, 27, 343, 366, 371, 558; **Vol. 4, Part 2,** 505; **Vol. 6, Part 1,** 123, 391, 583; **Vol. 6, Part 2,** 205; **Vol. 8, Part 2,** 90; **Vol. 9, Part 2,** 170, 215

Richmond and Danville Railroad, **Vol. 1, Part 1,** 282

Richmond College, establishment of, **Vol. 9, Part 2,** 326, 328

Richmond Enquirer, **Vol. 8, Part 1,** 628

Richmond Examiner, **Vol. 3, Part 1,** 67; **Vol. 5, Part 1,** 357

Richmond Female Institute, **Vol. 9, Part 2,** 328

"Richmond Junto," **Vol. 8, Part 1,** 628; **Vol. 7, Part 2,** 484

Richmond News Leader, **Supp. 3,** 115; **Supp. 5,** 233–34

Richmond Terminal (railroad holding company), **Supp. 3,** 125

Rich Mountain, battle of, **Vol. 4, Part 1,** 159; **Vol. 6, Part 1,** 582; **Vol. 8, Part 2,** 163; **Vol. 9, Part 2,** 183

Richter, Paul, reference to, **Supp. 6,** 221

Rickard, Tex, references to, **Supp. 5,** 359–60; **Supp. 6,** 700

Rickenbacker, Edward V., reference to, **Supp. 7,** 16

Rickets: prevention and cure, **Supp. 1,** 398; studies in, **Vol. 5, Part 1,** 314; vitamin D for, **Supp. 5,** 623

Ricketts, Edward F., references to, **Supp. 8,** 625, 626

Ricketts, Howard Taylor, references to, **Supp. 3,** 832; **Supp. 6,** 697

Ridgway, Erman J., reference to, **Supp. 7,** 320

Ridgway, Matthew B., references to, **Supp. 7,** 53, 492; **Supp. 8,** 157

Riehl, Alois, reference to, **Supp. 8,** 435

Riemann, Georg Friedrich Bernhard, reference to, **Supp. 7,** 216

Riemann mapping theorem, **Supp. 3,** 575

Rifle, invention and manufacture, **Vol. 1, Part 1,** 325, 550; **Vol. 1, Part 2,** 209; **Vol. 5, Part 1,** 247, 286; **Vol. 5, Part 2,** 460; **Vol. 6, Part 1,** 51; **Vol. 7, Part 1,** 561; **Vol. 8, Part 1,** 101, 496; **Vol. 8, Part 2,** 2; **Vol. 9, Part 1,** 447; **Vol. 10, Part 2,** 379

Rigdon, Sidney, reference to, **Vol. 9, Part 1,** 311; **Vol. 4, Part 2,** 334

Riggs, John Mankey, reference to, **Vol. 10, Part 1,** 640 f.

Rights of Man, **Vol. 5, Part 2,** 24; **Vol. 7, Part 2,** 162 f.

Rigney, Dorothy Comiskey, reference to, **Supp. 6,** 121

Rigney, John, reference to, **Supp. 6,** 121

Rig-Veda Repetitions, **Vol. 1, Part 2,** 387

Riis, Jacob, reference to, **Supp. 8,** 534

Riley, Charles V., reference to, **Vol. 10, Part 1,** 388 f.

Riley, James Whitcomb, reference to, **Vol. 7, Part 1,** 599 f.

Rinehart, Frederick, references to, **Supp. 8,** 535, 536

Rinehart, Mary Roberts, references to, **Supp. 6,** 171–72, 309; **Supp. 8,** 535

Rinehart, Stanley, reference to, **Supp. 6,** 172

Rinehart and Co., **Supp. 6,** 543; founding of, **Supp. 8,** 536

Ringgold Gap, Ga., action at. *See* Chattanooga-Ringgold campaign (1863)

Ring of Freedom, founding of, **Supp. 7,** 740

Ringling Brothers–Barnum and Bailey Circus, **Supp. 6,** 8, 112; **Supp. 7,** 41, 42

Riordan, Patrick, reference to, **Supp. 3,** 325

Riots: antiabolitionist, **Vol. 3, Part 2,** 311; draft (1863), **Vol. 4, Part 1,** 47, 238; **Vol. 10, Part 1,** 145; military suppression of, **Vol. 8, Part 2,** 219; New Orleans (1872–74), **Vol. 4, Part 2,** 450; Stamp Act, **Vol. 3, Part 1,** 465 f.; **Vol. 5, Part 2,** 138; theater, **Vol. 3, Part 2,** 530; *See also* Riots, labor

Riots, labor: Coeur d'Alene (1892–99), **Vol. 2, Part 2,** 145; **Vol. 3, Part 1,** 45; **Vol. 4, Part 2,** 419; **Vol. 5, Part 1,** 507; **Vol. 8, Part 2,** 263; Haymarket (1886), **Vol. 1, Part 1,** 231; Homestead (1892), **Vol. 2, Part 1,** 502; **Vol. 4, Part 1,** 30; Pullman (1894), **Vol. 1, Part 1,** 231; **Vol. 2, Part 2,** 211; **Vol. 3, Part 1,** 183; **Vol. 6, Part 2,** 615; **Vol. 7, Part 2,** 32, 264 f.; railroad (1877), **Vol. 4, Part 2,** 368, 450

Ripley, William Z., reference to, **Supp. 6,** 572

"Ripley's Believe It or Not!", **Supp. 4,** 693

Rise of American Civilization, The, **Supp. 4,** 62, 63; **Supp. 6,** 41

Rise of David Levinsky, The, **Supp. 5,** 96

Rise of the City, The, **Supp. 7,** 676

Rise of the Dutch Republic, The, **Vol. 7, Part 1,** 284

Ritchey, George W., reference to, **Supp. 3,** 208

Ritchie, Albert C., reference to, **Supp. 3,** 12

Ritchie, Thomas, reference to, **Vol. 8, Part 1,** 7 f.

Rittenberg, David, reference to, **Supp. 3,** 693

Ritter, William Emerson, references to, **Supp. 3,** 752; **Supp. 4,** 460; **Supp. 8,** 119

Ritz-Carlton Hotel (New York City), **Supp. 6,** 164–65; **Supp. 7,** 48

Riva-Rocci sphygmomanometer, **Supp. 3,** 201

Rivera, Diego, reference to, **Supp. 8,** 586

Riverboats. *See* Ships

River Rouge Ford Plant (Dearborn, Mich.), **Supp. 4,** 300

Rivers: control of, **Vol. 3, Part 1,** 587 f.; **Vol. 3, Part 2,** 87, 179, 192; **Vol. 7, Part 1,** 617; navigation of, **Supp. 1,** 658. *See also* Mississippi River; Dams

Riverside Church (New York City): endowment, **Supp. 6,** 548; founding of, **Supp. 8,** 183–84

Riverside Press, **Vol. 5, Part 1,** 256; **Vol. 8, Part 2,** 522

Rives, Hallie Erminie, references to, **Supp. 6,** 686, 687

Rives, William C., reference to, **Vol. 10, Part 1,** 90

RKO Pictures, founding of, **Supp. 8,** 320

Roach, Hal, references to, **Supp. 6,** 276; **Supp. 7,** 463

"Road agents" of Far West, **Vol. 8, Part 2,** 337

Road building, **Vol. 1, Part 1,** 577; **Vol. 4, Part 1,** 59; **Vol. 5, Part 2,** 467; **Vol. 6, Part 2,** 485; **Vol. 8, Part 1,** 74 f., 641; **Vol. 8, Part 2,** 567; **Vol. 9, Part 1,** 485; **Vol. 10, Part 2,** 260; asphalt, use of, **Vol. 1, Part 1,** 586; **Vol. 10, Part 1,** 471 f.; **Supp. 1,** 255; Connecticut highway system, **Supp. 4,** 197; Delaware, **Supp. 1,** 272; gasoline tax for, **Supp. 1,** 671; interstate highway proponents, **Supp. 6,** 507; Ledo and Burma roads, **Supp. 6,** 508; macadam, use of, **Vol. 4, Part 2,** 61; **Vol. 8, Part 1,** 74 f., 442; New Mexico, **Supp. 1,** 671; New York City, **Supp. 1,** 136; rural areas, **Supp. 4,** 665; urban expressways, **Supp. 6,** 115

Road to Xanadu, The, **Supp. 3,** 475

Roan, Henry, reference to, **Supp. 5,** 566

Roanoke, Va., settlement, **Vol. 3, Part 1,** 73 f.; **Vol. 5, Part 2,** 581

Roanoke Island affair, **Vol. 1, Part 2,** 183

Robards, Jason, Jr., reference to, **Supp. 5,** 525

Robards, Rachel, reference to, **Vol. 5, Part 1,** 526 f.

Robb, Russell, reference to, **Supp. 3,** 746

Robe, The, **Supp. 5,** 182

Robert College (Turkey), **Vol. 4, Part 2,** 195; **Vol. 8, Part 2,** 1; **Vol. 10, Part 1,** 500 f.; **Supp. 4,** 319

Roberts, George Brooke, reference to, **Vol. 7, Part 1,** 355

Roberts, James M. ("Red"), reference to, **Supp. 5,** 458

Roberts, Kenneth, reference to, **Supp. 3,** 848

Roberts, Owen J., references to, **Supp. 4,** 407, 537; **Supp. 8,** 331

Robertson, Frederick, reference to, **Vol. 7, Part 1,** 328

Robert's Rules of Order Revised, **Supp. 1,** 631

Robeson, Paul, references to, **Supp. 3,** 418; **Supp. 5,** 490, 525; **Supp. 7,** 204, 319; **Supp. 8,** 696

Robin Hood (operetta), **Supp. 2,** 619

Robins, Elizabeth, reference to, **Supp. 5,** 578

Robins, Margaret Dreier, references to, **Supp. 3,** 355; **Supp. 4,** 106

Robins, Raymond, references to, **Supp. 3,** 457; **Supp. 7,** 320

Robinson, Bill ("Bojangles"), reference to, **Supp. 6,** 637

Robinson, Boardman, reference to, **Supp. 8,** 173

Robinson, Edward, reference to, **Vol. 7, Part 1,** 547; **Supp. 4,** 290

Robinson, Edwin Arlington, references to, **Supp. 4,** 840, 841; **Supp. 5,** 231

Robinson, Frances, reference to, **Supp. 3,** 399

Robinson, Holton D., reference to, **Supp. 6,** 594

Robinson, James Harvey, references to, **Supp. 4,** 62, 63, 587; **Supp. 8,** 50

Robinson, Joan, reference to, **Supp. 8,** 82

Robinson, John, reference to, **Vol. 7, Part 2,** 104 f.

Robinson, Joseph, references to, **Supp. 3,** 720; **Supp. 4,** 145; **Supp. 6,** 35; **Supp. 7,** 787; **Supp. 8,** 36

Robinson, Stuart, reference to, **Vol. 8, Part 2,** 60

Robinson-Patman Act (1936), **Supp. 5,** 27

Robischon, Ernest, reference to, **Supp. 8,** 440

Robison, Samuel, reference to, **Supp. 8,** 469

Roche, Kevin, reference to, **Supp. 7,** 671

Rochester, Minn., Mayo Clinic, **Vol. 6, Part 2,** 467

Rochester, N.Y.: architecture, **Supp. 4,** 105; founding of, **Vol. 8, Part 2,** 64; Gannett in, **Supp. 6,** 226–27; history of, **Vol. 3, Part 1,** 48; park system, **Vol. 8, Part 1,** 157 f.; public service, **Vol. 7, Part 2,** 473; **Vol. 8, Part 1,** 393; as station for Underground Railroad, **Vol. 3, Part 1,** 117; water supply for, **Vol. 8, Part 1,** 324 f.; **Vol. 8, Part 2,** 13

Rochester Academy of Science, **Supp. 3,** 40–41

Rochester Daily Advertiser, **Vol. 7, Part 2,** 52

Rochester Museum of Arts and Sciences, founding of, **Supp. 3,** 41

Rochester Theological Seminary, **Vol. 8, Part 2,** 43

Rock, John, references to, **Supp. 4,** 802; **Supp. 8,** 503

Rock, William T. ("Pop"), reference to, **Supp. 3,** 76

Rock and roll, **Supp. 7,** 267; heavy metal, **Supp. 8,** 252–53; singers, **Supp. 6,** 301–2; **Supp. 8,** 305–6

Rock drill, invention of, **Vol. 5, Part 1,** 472; **Vol. 6, Part 1,** 230; **Vol. 8, Part 1,** 343; **Vol. 8, Part 2,** 587

Rockefeller, Abby Aldrich, reference to, **Supp. 8,** 240

Rockefeller, John D., references to, **Vol. 3, Part 1,** 341 f.; **Vol. 3, Part 2,** 451; **Vol. 4, Part 2,** 287; **Vol. 5, Part 1,** 184; **Vol. 6, Part 2,** 572; **Vol. 8, Part 2,** 65; photograph of, **Supp. 3,** 296; reference to, **Supp. 7,** 173; writings on, **Supp. 3,** 762

Rockefeller, John D., Jr.: Metropolitan Museum concerts, **Supp. 6,** 426; oil interests, **Supp. 6,** 585; references to, **Supp. 6,** 208, 249, 562; **Supp. 8,** 183, 545

Rockefeller, John D., III, China Medical Board, **Supp. 4,** 346

Rockefeller, Laura Spelman, Memorial, **Supp. 6,** 559

Rockefeller, Nelson, reference to, **Supp. 8,** 126

Rockefeller Center (New York City): architecture of, **Supp. 1,** 430; **Supp. 5,** 134; chandelier, **Supp. 7,** 308; endowment, **Supp. 6,** 549; Rivera murals, **Supp. 8,** 586

Rockefeller Foundation, **Vol. 2, Part 1,** 378; **Vol. 4, Part 1,** 183; **Vol. 7, Part 2,** 355; **Vol. 10, Part 1,** 621 f.; administration, **Supp. 4,** 251; **Supp. 5,** 161; **Supp. 7,** 516; Chinese medical problems, **Supp. 4,** 346–47; Fatigue Laboratory, **Supp. 3,** 351; founding of, **Supp. 2,** 575; hookworm eradication, **Supp. 1,** 639; **Supp. 5,** 232; human sexual behavior research grants, **Supp. 6,** 252–53, 343, 344; International Health Division, **Supp. 3,** 324, **Supp. 5,** 605; **Supp. 6,** 249–50; **Supp. 7,** 247; Medical Education Division, **Supp. 3,** 244; **Supp. 6,** 252–53, 343; medical philanthropy, **Supp. 6,** 549; Natural Sciences Division, **Supp. 7,** 516; nursing program, **Supp. 4,** 65; postdoctoral fellowships, **Supp. 5,** 495–96; presidency, **Supp. 3,** 794; public opinion research, **Supp. 8,** 69; rural life study, **Supp. 5,** 320–21; war relief, **Supp. 1,** 640

Rockefeller Institute for Medical Research, **Supp. 3,** 61, 140–41, 774; **Supp. 4,** 34, 573–74, 615–16, 643; **Supp. 6,** 117, 249; **Supp. 7,** 281, 591; cancer studies, **Supp. 8,** 555–56; directors, **Supp. 4,** 287; first woman member, **Supp. 5,** 600; founding of, **Supp. 2,** 574; immunology studies, **Supp. 3,** 441–42; **Supp. 4,** 380–81; typhus epidemic, **Supp. 4,** 803; viral disease research, **Supp. 7,** 648, 649. *See also* Rockefeller University

Rockefeller Plaza (New York City), sculpture, **Supp. 8,** 414

Rockefeller Sanitary Commission, hookworm disease control, **Supp. 3,** 738

Rockefeller University, founding of, **Supp. 6,** 549

Rockets: jet-assisted airplane takeoff, **Supp. 7,** 411; liquid-fuel, **Supp. 3,** 306–8; propulsion theory, **Supp. 3,** 305–8; writings on, **Supp. 8,** 379–80. *See also* Aerodynamics; Jet propulsion; Missiles; Space exploration

Roosevelt, Theodore, **Vol. 4, Part 2,** 334; **Vol. 5, Part 1,** 75; **Vol. 6, Part 1,** 347, 348, 609 f.; **Vol. 6, Part 2,** 587; **Vol. 7, Part 1,** 179; **Vol. 8, Part 1,** 2, 4; **Vol. 9, Part 1,** 44, 466; **Vol. 9, Part 2,** 268, 363, 548; Aldrich, Allison and Platt, relations with, **Vol. 1, Part 1,** 155, 221; bibliography of, **Supp. 8,** 664; "big stick," **Vol. 8, Part 2,** 139; biography of, **Supp. 4,** 491; **Supp. 6,** 521; Bonaparte, Charles Joseph, relations with, **Vol. 1, Part 2,** 427; Butler relationship, **Supp. 4,** 135; cartoons depicting, **Supp. 7,** 164; conservation policies, **Vol. 2, Part 2,** 145; **Vol. 7, Part 1,** 316; **Supp. 2,** 265; **Supp. 4,** 664–66; family, **Supp. 3,** 199, 667–69; **Supp. 7,** 658; Garfield, J. R., relationship, **Supp. 4,** 317; Gilson relationship, **Supp. 1,** 333; Hart relationship, **Supp. 3,** 336, 337; Hay, John, relationship, **Vol. 4, Part 2,** 435 f.; Hill, E. C., relationship, **Supp. 6,** 291; idealization of, **Supp. 7,** 311; influence of, **Supp. 6,** 85; Johnson, H. W., relationship, **Supp. 3,** 395; Library of Congress archives, **Supp. 3,** 285; muckraking statement, **Supp. 4,** 46–47; political opposition to, **Vol. 8, Part 1,** 416; presidential candidacy, **Supp. 5,** 303; presidential library, **Supp. 7,** 311; Robins relationship, **Supp. 5,** 579; Robinson, E. A., poetry, **Supp. 1,** 633; Roosevelt, F. D., relationship, **Supp. 3,** 641, 642; Root relationship, **Supp. 2,** 578–81; "Rough Riders," organization of, **Vol. 8, Part 2,** 137; **Supp. 6,** 206; St. Gaudens, Augustus, relationship, **Vol. 8, Part 2,** 301; sculpture of, **Supp. 3,** 89; Taft, W. H., relationship, **Vol. 8, Part 2,** 141 f.; **Vol. 9, Part 2,** 270; **Supp. 2,** 581, 582; **Supp. 5,** 707–8; "Teddy Bear" inception, **Supp. 4,** 76; western policy, **Vol. 8, Part 2,** 141; White, W. A., relationship, **Supp. 3,** 816; Wood, Leonard, relationship, **Vol. 10, Part 2,** 467 f.; writings on, **Supp. 7,** 311
Roosevelt, Theodore, Jr., reference to, **Supp. 3,** 667
Roosevelt Business and Professional League, founding of, **Supp. 2,** 636
Roosevelt Dam, **Supp. 2,** 304
Roosevelt Hospital (New York City), allergy clinic, **Supp. 6,** 123
Roosevelt Memorial Association, **Vol. 9, Part 2,** 477
Roosevelt University (Chicago), founding of, **Supp. 6,** 202
Root, Elihu: mission to Russia, **Vol. 3, Part 1,** 510; references to, **Vol. 8, Part 1,** 2 f.; **Supp. 3,** 98, 700; **Supp. 4,** 784, 785; **Supp. 5,** 286
Root beer, **Supp. 2,** 306
Root, Clark, Howland and Ballantine (law firm), **Supp. 6,** 33
Rope making, **Vol. 4, Part 1,** 377; **Vol. 9, Part 1,** 62; **Vol. 9, Part 2,** 632
Roraback, J. Henry, reference to, **Supp. 6,** 59
"Rosary, The," **Vol. 7, Part 1,** 441
Rose, Billy, reference to, **Supp. 5,** 87
Rose, Billy, Foundation, founding of, **Supp. 8,** 548
Rose, Fred, reference to, **Supp. 5,** 748
Rose, Margo, reference to, **Supp. 3,** 685
Rose, Mary Swartz, reference to, **Supp. 3,** 677
Rose, Rufus, reference to, **Supp. 3,** 685
Rosecrans, Gen. William, reference to, **Vol. 9, Part 1,** 363
Roseland Ballroom (New York City), **Supp. 5,** 292, 293
Rosenbach Co., **Supp. 5,** 586–87
Rosenberg, Ethel, references to, **Supp. 7,** 52, 204
Rosenberg, Julius, references to, **Supp. 7,** 52, 204
Rosenblatt, Gertrude Goldsmith, reference to, **Supp. 8,** 549
Rosenblueth, Arturo, references to, **Supp. 3,** 136, 137
Rosenbusch, Harry, reference to, **Supp. 6,** 70

Rosenfeld, Paul, reference to, **Supp. 3,** 14
Rosenman, Samuel I., reference to, **Supp. 3,** 645
Rosenthal, Herman, reference to, **Supp. 4,** 885–86
Rosenwald, Julius, references to, **Vol. 8, Part 2,** 540; **Supp. 3,** 403; **Supp. 8,** 705
Rosenwald, Julius, Fund, **Supp. 4,** 251; **Supp. 6,** 11, 12, 321
Rosenwald, Lessing J., reference to, **Supp. 5,** 586
Roses, growing of, **Supp. 4,** 194–95, 523; **Supp. 5,** 555
Rosetta Stone, translation of, **Vol. 7, Part 1,** 254–55
Rosine Association, founding of, **Vol. 9, Part 2,** 620
Rosminian Order, **Vol. 3, Part 1,** 96
Ross, Charles G., reference to, **Supp. 3,** 92
Ross, Edward A., references to, **Vol. 5, Part 1,** 277; **Supp. 3,** 248
Ross, Harold, references to, **Supp. 5,** 464; **Supp. 6,** 236, 287; **Supp. 7,** 2, 473–74, 743; **Supp. 8,** 447, 491
Ross, Robert, reference to, **Supp. 6,** 194
Ross election bill, **Vol. 3, Part 1,** 467 f.
Rossville, Ga., operation at. *See* Chickamaugua campaign
Rostovtzeff, Michael, reference to, **Supp. 5,** 736
Rotary International, founding of, **Supp. 4,** 362
Rotch, Arthur, reference to, **Supp. 3,** 195
Roth, Rose, reference to, **Supp. 6,** 100–1
Roth, Rudolf, reference to, **Supp. 3,** 444
Rothacker, Watterson, reference to, **Supp. 7,** 579–80
Rothko, Mark, reference to, **Supp. 8,** 467
Rothschild, L. F., brokerage house, **Supp. 6,** 305
"Rough Riders," organization of, **Vol. 8, Part 2,** 137
Round Hill School, **Vol. 1, Part 1,** 565
Rous, Peyton, references to, **Supp. 4,** 615, 616
Rousseau, Jean-Jacques, writings on, **Supp. 3,** 691
Rover Boy's Series, **Vol. 9, Part 2,** 125
Rowing, **Vol. 2, Part 2,** 377 f., 469; **Vol. 7, Part 2,** 602; **Supp. 6,** 331
Rowland, Clarence ("Pants"), **Supp. 8,** 713
Rowland, Henry A., references to, **Supp. 3,** 11, 291
Rowlett, Frank, reference to, **Supp. 8,** 196
Rowohlt, Ernst, Publishing House, **Supp. 7,** 798
Roxas, Manuel, reference to, **Supp. 3,** 614
Roxbury, Mass.: early history of, **Vol. 3, Part 1,** 430; first factory-made watches produced in, **Vol. 3, Part 1,** 239
Roxbury Tammany Club (Boston), **Supp. 6,** 139
Royal American Regiment, **Vol. 1, Part 2,** 480
Royal and Ancient Golf Club of St. Andrews, first American captain, **Supp. 8,** 487
Royal Commission on London Traffic, **Vol. 7, Part 2,** 277
Royal Geographical Society of London, **Vol. 5, Part 2,** 561
Royalist gazettes, Revolutionary period, **Vol. 8, Part 2,** 24
Royal Society, one of few Americans elected to, **Vol. 3, Part 1,** 483
Royce, Josiah, references to, **Vol. 5, Part 1,** 311, 594; **Vol. 9, Part 1,** 410; **Supp. 1,** 150; **Supp. 3,** 608; **Supp. 6,** 504, 505; **Supp. 7,** 471, 481; **Supp. 8,** 265, 266
Roycroft Shop, **Vol. 5, Part 1,** 323
Royle, Selena, reference to, **Supp. 4,** 187
Ruark, Robert, reference to, **Supp. 5,** 439
Rubber: importation of, **Supp. 1,** 305; synthetic, **Supp. 2,** 97, 489, 505; **Supp. 3,** 239, 522; **Supp. 5,** 191, 273, 366; **Supp. 6,** 334; **Supp. 7,** 169; **Supp. 8,** 123; litigation over patents, **Vol. 3, Part 1,** 159, 288; manufacture, **Vol. 2, Part 1,** 470; **Vol. 4, Part 2,** 396, 413; **Vol. 4, Part 2,** 465, 466; **Vol. 5, Part 1,** 290; tire production, **Supp. 5,** 617–18, 380; vulcanization, **Vol. 3, Part 1,** 25, 288; **Vol. 4, Part 1,** 413 f.; **Supp. 2,** 505; **Supp. 3,** 522; World War II mea-

Supp. 5, 287; **Supp. 7,** 609; Theological Seminary, founding of, **Vol. 8, Part 2,** 504; vigilantes, **Vol. 5, Part 2,** 408; water supply, **Supp. 4,** 664

San Francisco Bulletin, editorship, **Supp. 1,** 580

San Francisco Call, **Vol. 9, Part 1,** 479

San Francisco Chronicle, **Vol. 3, Part 1,** 283 f.; **Vol. 7, Part 1,** 551; **Supp. 5,** 356

San Francisco Conference (1945), **Supp. 5,** 537–38

San Francisco Examiner: campaign against Southern Pacific Railroad, **Supp. 5,** 283; drama criticism, **Supp. 5,** 657, 658

San Francisco–Oakland Bay Bridge, **Supp. 2,** 470; **Supp. 3,** 531

San Francisco Opera Company, **Supp. 6,** 670; ballet choreography, **Supp. 5,** 76

San Francisco Symphony, **Supp. 3,** 359; **Supp. 7,** 549

San Francisco World's Fairs. *See* Golden Gate International Exposition (1939); Panama-Pacific International Exposition (1915)

Sanger, Margaret, references to, **Supp. 4,** 231; **Supp. 6,** 602; **Supp. 8,** 503

Sanitarium, first for tuberculosis, **Vol. 10, Part 1,** 3

Sanitation, **Vol. 1, Part 1,** 597; **Vol. 3, Part 1,** 78; **Vol. 3, Part 2,** 275; **Vol. 4, Part 1,** 433; **Vol. 4, Part 2,** 100, 576 f.; **Vol. 5, Part 2,** 193, 265, 275, 277, 418; **Vol. 6, Part 1,** 606; **Vol. 8, Part 1,** 324 f., 390 f., 475, 553 f.; **Vol. 8, Part 2,** 553; **Vol. 9, Part 1,** 102, 495; **Vol. 10, Part 1,** 456 f.; Baltimore, **Vol. 8, Part 1,** 502; Boston, **Vol. 8, Part 1,** 308 f.; Chicago, **Vol. 8, Part 1,** 390; engineering studies, **Supp. 1,** 326; home, **Supp. 5,** 553; household plumbing, **Supp. 1,** 552; Massachusetts, **Vol. 5, Part 2,** 419; Memphis, **Vol. 10, Part 1,** 456 f.; milk, **Supp. 4,** 701; New Orleans, **Vol. 5, Part 2,** 193; New York, **Vol. 4, Part 2,** 308; **Vol. 8, Part 1,** 607; **Vol. 8, Part 2,** 404; **Vol. 10, Part 1,** 456 f.; Panama Canal Zone, **Vol. 3, Part 1,** 78; **Vol. 4, Part 1,** 431; public education in, **Supp. 5,** 143–44; Sanitary Commission, U.S., **Vol. 2, Part 2,** 136; **Vol. 3, Part 2,** 212; **Vol. 4, Part 2,** 308; **Vol. 5, Part 1,** 251, 297; **Vol. 5, Part 2,** 355, 404; **Vol. 7, Part 1,** 446; **Vol. 7, Part 2,** 26; **Vol. 8, Part 2,** 474, 600; **Vol. 9, Part 1,** 563; **Vol. 9, Part 2,** 24; Washington, D.C., **Vol. 6, Part 2,** 204; writings on, **Vol. 4, Part 1,** 432; **Vol. 5, Part 2,** 419; **Vol. 8, Part 1,** 554; **Vol. 10, Part 1,** 456 f. *See also* Public health; Sewerage

San Jacinto, battle of, **Vol. 2, Part 1,** 417, 293; **Vol. 5, Part 1,** 265; **Vol. 5, Part 2,** 553; **Vol. 6, Part 2,** 5

San Jose, Calif., first mayor of, **Vol. 1, Part 2,** 146

San Juan Hill, Cuba, battle of, **Vol. 6, Part 1,** 62; **Vol. 8, Part 2,** 137; **Vol. 9, Part 1,** 16; **Vol. 10, Part 2,** 51, 467

Sankey, Ira D., reference to, **Vol. 7, Part 1,** 103

San Lorenzo, treaty of, **Vol. 7, Part 2,** 619; **Vol. 8, Part 1,** 353 f.

San Simeon (Hearst estate), **Supp. 3,** 156; **Supp. 5,** 287, 288; **Supp. 6,** 464; **Supp. 7,** 166

Sanskrit: literature, **Supp. 2,** 339; **Supp. 3,** 444–45; study of, **Vol. 4, Part 1,** 588; **Vol. 4, Part 2,** 125; **Vol. 9, Part 2,** 441; **Vol. 10, Part 2,** 168

Santa Catalina Island (Calif.), development of, **Supp. 1,** 715

Santayana, George, references to, **Supp. 5,** 658, 659, 661; **Supp. 6,** 504, 505

Santa Fe, N.Mex., **Vol. 1, Part 2,** 161; Catholic missionary service, **Vol. 5, Part 2,** 567; engagement at (1846), **Vol. 3, Part 1,** 365; **Vol. 5, Part 2,** 273; expedition, **Vol. 4, Part 1,** 329; **Vol. 6, Part 2,** 132; founding of, **Vol. 7, Part 2,** 548; Tertio Millennial Pageant, **Vol. 8, Part 1,** 229 f.; traders of, **Vol. 4, Part 1,** 597; **Vol. 5, Part 2,** 554; **Vol. 6, Part 2,** 111; **Vol. 8, Part 2,** 306;

Santa Fe Railroad, **Vol. 8, Part 1,** 620 f.; **Vol. 8, Part 2,** 33

Santa Fe Trail, **Vol. 1, Part 2,** 120; **Vol. 5, Part 1,** 151, 483; **Vol. 9, Part 1,** 144; **Vol. 10, Part 2,** 525

Santiago, Cuba: Schley-Sampson controversy, **Vol. 3, Part 2,** 503; **Vol. 8, Part 1,** 416, 419; siege of, **Vol. 3, Part 1,** 416; **Vol. 6, Part 1,** 62; **Vol. 6, Part 2,** 646; **Vol. 8, Part 2,** 137, 322 f., 438; **Vol. 9, Part 1,** 16; **Vol. 10, Part 2,** 51, 467

Santo Domingo: black rebellion, **Vol. 8, Part 2,** 305; diplomatic relations, **Vol. 5, Part 2,** 598; **Vol. 6, Part 1,** 76; **Vol. 9, Part 1,** 388; proposed annexation of (1873), **Vol. 1, Part 1,** 460; **Vol. 3, Part 2,** 398; **Vol. 4, Part 1,** 499; **Vol. 7, Part 1,** 287; **Vol. 8, Part 2,** 468; **Vol. 9, Part 2,** 212

Sao Paulo, Brazil, **Supp. 4,** 81–82

Sapir, Edward, references to, **Supp. 3,** 820; **Supp. 4,** 71, 806, 807; **Supp. 8,** 509

Sapir, Jacob, reference to, **Supp. 4,** 762

Sapiro, Aaron, reference to, **Supp. 4,** 299

Sarah Morris Children's Hospital (Chicago), founding of, **Supp. 5,** 2

Saranac Lake, N.Y., Trudeau tuberculosis sanatorium, **Supp. 2,** 71; **Supp. 3,** 431; **Supp. 4,** 48–49, 314, 577

Saratoga, N.Y., battle of (1777), **Vol. 1, Part 1,** 364–65; **Vol. 4, Part 1,** 185–86; **Vol. 6, Part 1,** 260; **Vol. 7, Part 2,** 575; **Vol. 8, Part 2,** 478; **Vol. 9, Part 1,** 531; **Vol. 10, Part 1,** 517; **Vol. 10, Part 2,** 223

Saratoga Springs, N.Y., **Vol. 1, Part 2,** 29; **Vol. 7, Part 1,** 234; **Vol. 8, Part 1,** 280 f.; **Vol. 8, Part 2,** 478

Sardinia, diplomatic relations, **Vol. 5, Part 2,** 418; **Vol. 7, Part 1,** 524 f.

Sardi's restaurant (New York City), **Supp. 8,** 571–72

Sargent, Charles Sprague, reference to, **Supp. 6,** 196

Sargent, John Singer, references to, **Vol. 1, Part 2,** 120; **Vol. 2, Part 2,** 39; *Four Doctors,* **Supp. 3,** 413

Satire: cabaret, **Supp. 4,** 867–68; "fables in slang," **Supp. 3,** 3, 4; musical, **Supp. 5,** 351; **Supp. 7,** 403–4, 737; *New Yorker* cartoons, **Supp. 4,** 386; **Supp. 8,** 15–16; novels, **Supp. 5,** 422–23; poetic, **Supp. 7,** 158; political journalism, **Supp. 4,** 804; television, **Supp. 7,** 442–43; verse, **Supp. 8,** 492; writings, **Vol. 1, Part 2,** 545; **Vol. 3, Part 1,** 573 f.; **Vol. 3, Part 2,** 347, 450 f.; **Vol. 5, Part 1,** 215, 387; **Vol. 5, Part 2,** 605; **Vol. 6, Part 1,** 336; **Vol. 8, Part 1,** 65 f., 111; **Vol. 9, Part 1,** 517; **Vol. 10, Part 1,** 146 f.

Saturday Evening Gazette, **Vol. 2, Part 2,** 118

Saturday Evening Post **Vol. 7, Part 2,** 513; **Supp. 1,** 212, 213; **Supp. 7,** 512–13; cover illustration, **Supp. 5,** 428, 429; editing, **Supp. 2,** 393; fiction in, **Supp. 3,** 171; **Supp. 6,** 116, 354, 543

Saturday Night Club (Baltimore), founding of, **Supp. 3,** 107

Saturday Review of Literature, **Supp. 7,** 638; **Supp. 8,** 393; columns, **Supp. 6,** 465; double-crostic puzzle, **Supp. 6,** 342; editing, **Supp. 5,** 168; founding and growth of, **Supp. 4,** 73, 470; **Supp. 5,** 439; **Supp. 7,** 103–4; predecessor, **Supp. 4,** 322; "Seeing Things" column, **Supp. 8,** 54

Sauk Indians, **Vol. 5, Part 2,** 350

Sault Ste. Marie, first ship canal, **Vol. 2, Part 1,** 338; **Vol. 5, Part 2,** 225

Saunders, Clarence, reference to, **Supp. 7,** 141

Savage Station, battle of. *See* Seven Days' Battles

Savannah, first transatlantic steamship voyage, **Vol. 8, Part 2,** 106, 410

Savannah, Ga., **Vol. 4, Part 1,** 427 f.; **Vol. 5, Part 2,** 165; **Vol. 6, Part 1,** 448; Indians, fortifying against, **Vol. 3, Part 1,** 182; Loyalists, **Vol. 4, Part 1,** 476 f.; secession, plea for, **Vol. 5, Part 2,** 165; operation at (1779–82), **Vol. 4, Part 2,** 240; **Vol. 6, Part 1,** 260; **Vol. 8, Part 1,** 260; **Vol. 9, Part 1,** 96

Science, **Supp. 3,** 150; founding of, **Vol. 1, Part 2,** 152; **Vol. 5, Part 1,** 325; **Vol. 7, Part 1,** 328

Science and Health, **Vol. 3, Part 2,** 9 f.; **Vol. 10, Part 2,** 190

Science and the Modern World, **Supp. 4,** 881–83

Science fiction: comic strips, **Supp. 6,** 166, 530; magazines, **Supp. 8,** 209–10; movies, **Supp. 8,** 379; novels, **Supp. 6,** 49; writing of, **Supp. 4,** 128–29

Science News Letter, founding of, **Supp. 8,** 119, 120

Science Service, founding of, **Supp. 3,** 635–36; **Supp. 8,** 119–20

Science Talent Search, **Supp. 8,** 119–20

Scientific American, **Vol. 7, Part 1,** 329; **Vol. 8, Part 1,** 101 f.

Scientific humanism, **Supp. 6,** 83

Scientific management, **Vol. 8, Part 1,** 91 f.

Scientists. For complete list, *see* Occupations Index

Scopes, John T., references to, **Supp. 4,** 692; **Supp. 6,** 528–29

Scopes trial: academic freedom issues, **Supp. 8,** 582–84; Bible expert for defense, **Supp. 7,** 624; defense, **Supp. 2,** 143; **Supp. 4,** 542; judge, **Supp. 6,** 528–29; play about, **Supp. 8,** 31–32; prosecution, **Supp. 4,** 692; **Supp. 7,** 631

Scott, Dred: counsel for, **Vol. 1, Part 2,** 339; owner of, **Vol. 8, Part 2,** 488 f.; decision, **Vol. 1, Part 2,** 133, 339, 392; **Vol. 2, Part 1,** 212, 457; **Vol. 2, Part 2,** 610; **Vol. 3, Part 1,** 402; **Vol. 4, Part 1,** 121, 181, 231; **Vol. 4, Part 2,** 311; **Vol. 6, Part 1,** 248; **Vol. 6, Part 2,** 128; **Vol. 7, Part 1,** 432; **Vol. 7, Part 2,** 241; **Vol. 8, Part 2,** 488, 503, 617; **Vol. 9, Part 1,** 571; **Vol. 9, Part 2,** 293

Scott, Howard, references to, **Supp. 5,** 558, 559;

Scott, Walter, references to, **Vol. 4, Part 1,** 505; **Vol. 5, Part 1,** 507

Scott, William R., reference to, **Supp. 5,** 92

Scott, Winfield, references to, **Vol. 5, Part 1,** 73 f.; **Vol. 6, Part 1,** 121; **Vol. 9, Part 2,** 350 f., 363; **Vol. 9, Part 2,** 646

Scottsboro cases, **Supp. 3,** 755; **Supp. 4,** 397, 537

Scotty's Castle (Death Valley, Calif.), **Supp. 5,** 613

Scouting, **Vol. 1, Part 1,** 493; **Vol. 3, Part 1,** 331; **Vol. 4, Part 2,** 27 f.; **Vol. 5, Part 1,** 230; **Vol. 5, Part 2,** 1, 309; **Vol. 6, Part 1,** 586; **Vol. 7, Part 1,** 395 f., 560; **Vol. 8, Part 1,** 517; **Vol. 9, Part 2,** 31; **Supp. 4,** 126–27

Scranton, William, reference to, **Supp. 8,** 361

Scranton, Pa., **Vol. 1, Part 2,** 412 f.; founding of, **Vol. 3, Part 1,** 306; **Vol. 8, Part 2,** 514; Polish National Catholic Church founding, **Supp. 5,** 304

Screen Actors' Guild: founding of, **Supp. 8,** 492; residual payments boycott by, **Supp. 8,** 712

Screens, window, **Vol. 2, Part 1,** 334

Screen Writers' Guild, founding of, **Supp. 6,** 476

Screws: manufacture of, **Vol. 1, Part 1,** 310; **Vol. 4, Part 1,** 374; **Vol. 9, Part 1,** 446; **Vol. 9, Part 2,** 632; standard threads for, **Vol. 8, Part 2,** 577

Scriabin, Alexander, reference to, **Supp. 3,** 690

Scribner's, Charles, Sons, **Supp. 4,** 651–52; **Supp. 5,** 615; **Supp. 7,** 336; Brownell, association with, **Vol. 2, Part 1,** 173; Burlingame, association with, **Vol. 2, Part 1,** 291

Scribner's Monthly, **Vol. 2, Part 1,** 291, 297; **Vol. 4, Part 1,** 276; **Vol. 5, Part 1,** 147, 542, 564, 589, 614; **Vol. 5, Part 2,** 388; **Vol. 9, Part 2,** 322; **Supp. 5,** 559, 614; founding of, **Vol. 8, Part 2,** 516; illustrations, **Vol. 1, Part 1,** 4; first issue of, **Vol. 9, Part 1,** 340; *Putnam's Magazine* merged into, **Vol. 8, Part 1,** 279 f.

Scrip, founding of, **Supp. 2,** 100

Scripps, E. W., reference to, **Supp. 7,** 369; **Supp. 8,** 119

Scripps College: curriculum development, **Supp. 2,** 9; founding of, **Vol. 8, Part 2,** 519

Scripps-Howard newspaper, **Vol. 2, Part 2,** 325; **Vol. 6, Part 2,** 166

Scripps-Howard Publishing, **Supp. 2,** 606; **Supp. 7,** 369–70

Scripps Institution of Oceanography, **Supp. 5,** 710; founding of, **Supp. 3,** 635–36; **Supp. 4,** 461; predecessor, **Supp. 3,** 752–53

Scripps-MacRae Press Association, **Vol. 6, Part 2,** 166; **Vol. 8, Part 2,** 518

Scripture, Edward Wheeler, reference to, **Supp. 4,** 731

Scroll, The, **Supp. 6,** 14

Sculling. *See* Rowing

Sculptors. For complete list, *See* Occupations Index

Sculpture, **Vol. 1, Part 1,** 134, 239 f., 428, 462, 503, 552; **Vol. 1, Part 2,** 2, 12, 300, 304, 305, 533, 547; **Vol. 2, Part 1,** 18, 89; **Vol. 2, Part 2,** 162, 212 f., 270 f., 348 f., 524 f.; **Vol. 3, Part 1,** 278, 371 f., 420 f., 558 f.; **Vol. 3, Part 2,** 120 f., 240 f.; **Vol. 4, Part 1,** 1 f., 456, 457, 469, 470, 586 f., 589; **Vol. 4, Part 2,** 358, 365, 378; **Vol. 5, Part 1,** 242, 317, 356, 518, 548; **Vol. 5, Part 2,** 317 f., 412, 413; **Vol. 6, Part 1,** 31; **Vol. 6, Part 2,** 16, 350, 472, 484; **Vol. 7, Part 1,** 4 f., 18, 303, 321 f., 478, 626; **Vol. 7, Part 2,** 179 f., 284; **Vol. 8, Part 1,** 158 f., 166, 274 f., 312 f., 497, 613 f.; **Vol. 8, Part 2,** 7, 102, 107, 222, 234, 296 f.; **Vol. 9, Part 1,** 133, 169; **Vol. 9, Part 2,** 75 f., 109f.; **Vol. 10, Part 1,** 427 f., 467 f.; **Vol. 10, Part 2,** 155; **Supp. 1,** 477–78; **Supp. 3,** 818; American Indian depiction, **Supp. 4,** 533–34; animal, **Vol. 1, Part 2,** 11; **Vol. 5, Part 2,** 317 f.; **Vol. 8, Part 1,** 125 f.; architectural, **Supp. 3,** 2, 123–25; avant-garde, **Supp. 7,** 696–98; black themes, **Supp. 7,** 610–11; bronzes, **Supp. 8,** 414–15; casting methods (1872), **Vol. 8, Part 2,** 103; "Checkers up at the Farm," **Vol. 8, Part 2,** 102; collections, **Supp. 2,** 22; color in, **Supp. 7,** 14; direct carving, **Supp. 8,** 715; equestrian, **Vol. 1, Part 2,** 304; **Vol. 2, Part 1,** 123; **Vol. 8, Part 1,** 125 f.; **Supp. 5,** 231–32; frontier life, **Vol. 1, Part 2,** 463; "gelatine mould," **Vol. 8, Part 2,** 103; generalized forms, **Supp. 3,** 278; Gettysburg, **Vol. 8, Part 1,** 125 f.; Gothic, **Supp. 2,** 22; Indian equestrian themes, **Supp. 3,** 210–11; life masks, **Vol. 2, Part 1,** 97; limestone, **Supp. 5,** 200; marble, **Supp. 2,** 21, 647; masks, **Supp. 2,** 418; medallions, **Vol. 2, Part 1,** 427; monuments, **Supp. 3,** 88–89, 123–25, 673–74; **Supp. 6,** 597, 720; Mount Rushmore heads, **Supp. 3,** 89; multiple materials used in, **Supp. 7,** 15; National Sculpture Society, **Vol. 8, Part 1,** 125 f.; **Vol. 10, Part 1,** 427 f.; neoclassic, **Vol. 8, Part 1,** 615 f.; neoclassic, twentieth-century, **Supp. 4,** 619; New York Public Library, **Vol. 1, Part 2,** 12; Old Testament figures, **Vol. 7, Part 1,** 304; portrait, **Supp. 3,** 1, 124; **Supp. 4,** 533–34; portrait busts, **Supp. 5,** 231; **Supp. 8,** 414, 415; public, **Supp. 1,** 143, 321–22, 515–16, 575–76; public figures, **Supp. 5,** 153; realism, **Supp. 6,** 720; religious, **Supp. 7,** 530–31; Romanesque, **Supp. 1,** 601; symbolism, **Vol. 4, Part 1,** 469; teaching of, **Supp. 2,** 647; vorticist group, **Supp. 6,** 194; war memorial, **Supp. 4,** 534; Washington, D.C., **Vol. 1, Part 1,** 240; Wilde's tomb, **Supp. 6,** 193

Scurvy, prevention and cure, **Supp. 1,** 398

Sea Adventure, ship of Virginia colonists, **Vol. 8, Part 2,** 117

Sea Around Us, The, **Supp. 7,** 108–9

Seaboard Air Line Railway, **Vol. 10, Part 1,** 455 f.

Seabury, Samuel (clergyman), reference to, **Vol. 5, Part 1,** 620

Seabury, Samuel (jurist), references to, **Supp. 3,** 646; **Supp. 4,** 465, 856; **Supp. 5,** 285; **Supp. 6,** 88, 141, 142; **Supp. 7,** 4

Seafarers' International Union, **Supp. 6,** 396

Seafaring life, **Vol. 1, Part 1,** 524; **Vol. 3, Part 1,** 217; **Vol. 3, Part 2,** 157; **Vol. 7, Part 1,** 467 f., 611 f.; **Vol. 9, Part 1,** 19, 97 f.;

Sea Horse, Ogelen's steamboat, **Vol. 7, Part 1,** 637

Seal fishing, **Vol. 1, Part 2,** 328; **Vol. 4, Part 1,** 229; **Vol. 4, Part 2,** 408; **Vol. 7, Part 1,** 195; **Vol. 8, Part 1,** 285 f.; **Vol. 8, Part 2,** 74

Seals, studies on, **Supp. 1,** 291

Seaman's Friend, **Vol. 3, Part 1,** 60

Seaman's Institute (New York City), **Vol. 7, Part 2,** 129

Seamen, first organization for betterment of conditions, **Vol. 10, Part 1,** 46

Seamen's Bethel (Boston), **Vol. 9, Part 2,** 321

Seamen's Friend Society, **Vol. 6, Part 1,** 84

Searle, Charles E., reference to, **Supp. 3,** 685

Searle, G. D., and Co., **Supp. 8,** 503

Sears, Frederick R., Jr., reference to, **Supp. 3,** 701

Sears, Roebuck, and Co., **Supp. 6,** 473; **Supp. 8,** 705

Seascapes. *See* Painting, marine

"Seaside Library," **Vol. 7, Part 1,** 331–2

Sea stories, **Supp. 8,** 182

SEATO. *See* Southeast Asia Treaty Organization

Seatrain Lines, Inc., founding of, **Supp. 3,** 502

Seattle, Wash.: history and growth of, **Vol. 2, Part 1,** 284; Indian attack upon, **Vol. 6, Part 1,** 182; municipal power plant, **Supp. 2,** 583; public service, **Vol. 1, Part 2,** 592; **Vol. 6, Part 1,** 79; **Vol. 6, Part 2,** 56

Seattle-Tacoma Shipbuilding Corporation, founding of, **Supp. 8,** 308

Seaver, John W., reference to, **Vol. 10, Part 1,** 635

Sea Witch, (clipper ship), **Vol. 4, Part 1,** 626

Sebastian, Benjamin, reference to, **Vol. 5, Part 1,** 486

Seceders, religious sect, **Vol. 5, Part 1,** 55

Secession movements, **Vol. 1, Part 1,** 207, 648; **Vol. 1, Part 2,** 312, 571; **Vol. 2, Part 1,** 9, 104, 177 f., 415–16; **Vol. 2, Part 2,** 22, 242; **Vol. 3, Part 2,** 46, 168; **Vol. 4, Part 1,** 598; **Vol. 4, Part 2,** 207, 214, 225; **Vol. 5, Part 1,** 135, 139, 517, 604 f.; **Vol. 5, Part 2,** 83, 102, 129, 552; **Vol. 6, Part 2,** 323; **Vol. 7, Part 2,** 560; **Vol. 8, Part 1,** 216 f., 410; **Vol. 8, Part 2,** 105; **Vol. 9, Part 2,** 591; **Vol. 10, Part 1,** 72; Alabama, **Vol. 10, Part 2,** 593; Davis, Jefferson, **Vol. 3, Part 1,** 125 f.; Democratic viewpoint, **Vol. 1, Part 1,** 388; Florida, **Vol. 10, Part 2,** 638; foreseeing of, in 1835, **Vol. 10, Part 1,** 37; Georgia, **Vol. 2, Part 2,** 248 f.; **Vol. 5, Part 2,** 165; **Vol. 6, Part 1,** 61; Kentucky, **Vol. 8, Part 1,** 148 f., 186 f.; Louisiana, **Vol. 1, Part 2,** 182; **Vol. 8, Part 1,** 251; Maryland, **Vol. 3, Part 1,** 119 f.; **Vol. 7, Part 1,** 602; Mississippi, **Vol. 10, Part 1,** 547; Missouri, **Vol. 3, Part 1,** 365, 495 f.; **Vol. 4, Part 1,** 121; **Vol. 5, Part 2,** 470; **Vol. 8, Part 1,** 185; **Vol. 9, Part 2,** 13; North Carolina, **Vol. 3, Part 1,** 287; novel dealing with, **Vol. 3, Part 1,** 199; open letters on, **Vol. 8, Part 1,** 410; planter, views of, **Vol. 3, Part 1,** 21 f.; Presbyterian church, attitude toward, **Vol. 10, Part 2,** 345; reestablishment of state governments following, **Vol. 5, Part 2,** 84 f.; Rhode Island colony, **Vol. 3, Part 1,** 605; South Carolina, **Vol. 2, Part 1,** 213; **Vol. 4, Part 1,** 325; **Vol. 7, Part 2,** 560; **Vol. 8, Part 1,** 395, 526 f.; **Vol. 10, Part 1,** 56 f.; Southern Whigs, opposition to, **Vol. 4, Part 2,** 561; Tennessee, **Vol. 2, Part 1,** 577; **Vol. 6, Part 2,** 461; **Vol. 8, Part 1,** 93 f.; Texas, **Vol. 8, Part 1,** 433; **Vol. 10, Part 2,** 188; treason, as, **Vol. 5, Part 2,** 113; Virginia, **Vol. 1, Part 2,** 462, 473; **Vol. 6, Part 1,** 217; **Vol. 8, Part 1,** 206 f., 255 f., 637; **Vol. 8, Part 2,** 30 f.

Secret Service, United States, **Vol. 1, Part 1,** 523; **Vol. 3, Part 2,** 165; **Vol. 4, Part 2,** 550; **Vol. 10, Part 1,** 135

Secret societies, agitation concerning, **Vol. 8, Part 2,** 3

Securities. *See* Stock market

Securities and Exchange Commission (SEC), **Supp. 6,** 216; **Supp. 7,** 453; **Supp. 8,** 112, 219–20; establishment of, **Supp. 2,** 195; first chairman, **Supp. 8,** 320

Securities Exchange Act (1934), **Supp. 1,** 84; **Supp. 7,** 635; passage of, **Supp. 3,** 654

Sedgwick, Ellery, reference to, **Supp. 5,** 16

Sedgwick, John, reference to, **Vol. 6, Part 1,** 125 f.

Sedition, **Supp. 6,** 105

Sedition laws: constitutionality of, **Vol. 5, Part 2,** 29; opposition to, **Vol. 3, Part 1,** 184; victim of, early, **Vol. 4, Part 2,** 390

Sedwick, William Thompson, reference to, **Supp. 6,** 701

"See It Now," **Supp. 7,** 566–67

Seeds, germination of, **Supp. 4,** 192

Seeger, Pete, references to, **Supp. 8,** 234, 235

Seeing Eye, The, founding of, **Supp. 4,** 253–55

Segregation: armed forces, **Supp. 3,** 661; **Supp. 5,** 741; **Supp. 8,** 118–19; black blood plasma, **Supp. 4,** 243; boxing, **Supp. 4,** 432–33; eugenics argument, **Supp. 3,** 215; hospitals, **Supp. 3,** 271; interstate transportation ban on, **Supp. 8,** 322, 333; Jim Crow laws, **Supp. 3,** 391; major league baseball teams, **Supp. 4,** 327–28; New Deal policies against, **Supp. 5,** 343; religious opposition to, **Supp. 4,** 547, 837; **Supp. 8,** 537; "separate but equal" ruling, **Supp. 4,** 397; South Carolina judicial opinions against, **Supp. 8,** 682; writings on, **Supp. 6,** 321; **Supp. 8,** 605–6. *See also* Civil rights movement; School desegregation

Seidel, Emil, references to, **Supp. 7,** 348; **Supp. 8,** 563

Seismograph, use of, **Vol. 10, Part 1,** 106

Seismological observatory, **Vol. 9, Part 2,** 585 f.

Seismological Society of the Pacific, **Supp. 3,** 479

Seismology. *See* Earthquakes

Selden, George B., references to, **Supp. 4,** 292, 295, 296

Seldes, Marian, reference to, **Supp. 8,** 584

Selective Service. *See* Draft

Selective Service Act (1917), **Vol. 4, Part 2,** 253; **Vol. 5, Part 2,** 251; **Vol. 10, Part 2,** 361; **Supp. 3,** 399

Selective Service Act (1940), **Supp. 5,** 531, 715

Selective Service System, first director, **Supp. 4,** 247

Self-actualization, **Supp. 8,** 424

Self-help and improvement: marital advice, **Supp. 8,** 11–12; public speaking guide, **Supp. 5,** 102; writings on, **Supp. 5,** 102, 434, 546; **Supp. 8,** 489

Self-incrimination law, **Supp. 1,** 451

Seligman, Edwin R. A., reference to, **Supp. 4,** 62; **Supp. 6,** 459

Selma, Ala.: capture of, **Vol. 2, Part 1,** 469; **Vol. 3, Part 2,** 533; **Vol. 10, Part 2,** 335; civil rights demonstrations, **Supp. 8,** 334

Selznick, David O., reference to, **Supp. 6,** 441

Selznick International Studios, founding of, **Supp. 7,** 682

Semaphore telegraph systems, railroads, **Vol. 5, Part 2,** 498; **Vol. 8, Part 2,** 97

Semenenko, Serge, reference to, **Supp. 6,** 668

Seminole campaigns: of 1812, **Vol. 1, Part 2,** 520; **Vol. 5, Part 2,** 403; **Vol. 7, Part 1,** 90; **Vol. 7, Part 2,** 76; of 1818, **Vol. 1, Part 1,** 86; **Vol. 3, Part 2,** 264; **Vol. 4, Part 1,** 83, 93; **Vol. 5, Part 1,** 529; **Vol. 5, Part 2,** 521; **Vol. 6, Part 2,** 70; **Vol. 7, Part 1,** 91; of 1835–42, **Vol. 2, Part 1,** 423; **Vol. 4, Part 1,** 93, 316; **Vol. 5, Part 2,** 63; **Vol. 8, Part 2,** 507; **Vol. 9, Part**

1, 331; **Vol. 9, Part 2,** 350, 441, 474

Semitic literature and language: education in, **Supp. 2,** 252; studies on, **Vol. 5, Part 1,** 513; **Vol. 5, Part 2,** 3; **Vol. 8, Part 2,** 333; **Vol. 9, Part 2,** 262; **Supp. 2,** 5; **Supp. 3,** 37, 374–75; **Supp. 4,** 595–96; **Supp. 6,** 641

Senate, United States (for complete list of congressmen and senators, *see* Occupations Index), **Supp. 4,** 220, 723–24; Aeronautical and Space Sciences Committee, **Supp. 7,** 429; agricultural interests, *see subhead:* farm bloc; antitrust advocacy, **Supp. 7,** 590; Appropriations Committee, **Supp. 7,** 74; Atomic Energy Committee, **Supp. 5,** 455; Banking and Currency Committee, **Supp. 4,** 641; **Supp. 5,** 382; bipartisan conservative coalition, **Supp. 5,** 443–45, 674–77; bipartisan foreign policy, **Supp. 5,** 704–5; censure votes, **Supp. 4,** 78; **Supp. 6,** 405; **Supp. 7,** 213, 317, 383, 419; **Supp. 8,** 178, 302, 322, 701; civil rights legislation opposition, **Supp. 7,** 398–99; conservative-liberal Republican split, **Supp. 8,** 144; conservatives in, **Supp. 3,** 754; **Supp. 4,** 43; **Supp. 6,** 234–35, 507; **Supp. 7,** 31, 73–74, 212, 644, 678, 750; **Supp. 8,** 478; contested seats, **Supp. 5,** 290–91; Crime Committee, **Supp. 6,** 264; defense contracts investigation, **Supp. 7,** 72–73, 95, 521, 764; demagoguery in, **Supp. 3,** 78; direct election of members, **Supp. 2,** 54; **Supp. 3,** 105; District of Columbia Committee, **Supp. 6,** 472; Eisenhower support, **Supp. 7,** 50; election to, first regulation of, **Vol. 9, Part 2,** 45; environmental protection advocacy in, **Supp. 6,** 475; ethics issues, **Supp. 3,** 550; **Supp. 4,** 752; **Supp. 6,** 59–60, 361; **Supp. 7,** 607; farm bloc, **Supp. 3,** 496–97, 559, 723–24; **Supp. 5,** 290; **Supp. 7,** 738–39; federal patronage, **Supp. 6,** 419; filibusters, **Supp. 4,** 78; Finance Committee, **Supp. 3,** 334–35, 727; **Supp. 6,** 234, 235, 455; first anti–Vietnam War members, **Supp. 8,** 26; first blind member, **Supp. 4,** 338; first member from New Mexico, **Supp. 3,** 259; first members from Alaska, **Supp. 8,** 26; first members from Arizona, **Supp. 7,** 21–22; first woman candidate, **Supp. 5,** 474; first woman elected to, **Vol. 3, Part 2,** 318; **Supp. 4,** 144–45; first working reporter member, **Supp. 5,** 505; fistfights in, **Vol. 3, Part 2,** 501; Foreign Relations Committee, **Supp. 2,** 51–52; **Supp. 3,** 543; **Supp. 6,** 235, 578; **Supp. 7,** 137–38; **Supp. 8,** 223, 701; Foreign Relations Committee of Eight, **Supp. 5,** 334; Guggenheim interests in, **Supp. 3,** 321; Indian Affairs Committee, **Supp. 4,** 641; influence peddling investigation, **Supp. 5,** 307; Internal Security Committee, **Supp. 5,** 444; **Supp. 6,** 681; **Supp. 8,** 133; internationalism, **Supp. 4,** 331–32; **Supp. 7,** 23; investigations, **Vol. 8, Part 2,** 86; Investigations Committee, **Supp. 3,** 622; **Supp. 8,** 322; isolationism in, **Supp. 3,** 396–97, 558–59; **Supp. 5,** 703–5, 739; Johnson, L. B., opposition to, **Supp. 8,** 323–24; Judiciary Committee, **Supp. 5,** 444; **Supp. 6,** 336, 362; **Supp. 7,** 21–22; La Follette civil liberties committee, **Supp. 5,** 403–4; labor legislation, **Supp. 5,** 718–19; Labor or Management Improper Activities Committee, **Supp. 7,** 383; last senator chosen by Missouri legislature, **Supp. 3,** 621; League of Nations, opposition to, **Supp. 4,** 858; liberal Republicanism, **Supp. 7,** 382–83; **Supp. 8,** 653–56; liberals in, **Supp. 6,** 260, 472, 569; **Supp. 7,** 122, 225; **Supp. 8,** 405; McCarthyism in, **Supp. 6,** 405, 432; **Supp. 7,** 751; **Supp. 8,** 128, 426; majority leaders, **Supp. 4,** 862; **Supp. 5,** 676; **Supp. 6,** 35–36; **Supp. 8,** 391–92; mavericks, **Supp. 8,** 301; medical-related bills, **Supp. 5,** 337; Military Affairs Committee, **Supp. 5,** 715; **Supp. 6,** 335; Naval Affairs Committee, **Supp. 7,** 312; New Deal opposition, **Supp. 5,** 114, 561–62,

703; **Supp. 7,** 312; **Supp. 8,** 247; New Deal support, **Supp. 3,** 334–35; **Supp. 5,** 718–19; **Supp. 7,** 467–68, 541; **Supp. 8,** 508; Old Guard, **Supp. 4,** 861–62; organized-crime investigation, **Supp. 7,** 416, 586; **Supp. 8,** 208, 322; Park Commission, **Supp. 3,** 533–34; **Supp. 6,** 485; pension bills, **Supp. 7,** 195; political idealism, **Supp. 5,** 681; president pro tempore, **Supp. 3,** 335; Progressive movement in, **Supp. 3,** 105–6, 108, 558–59; **Supp. 4,** 641–42, 669–70; **Supp. 6,** 578; public land policy, **Supp. 8,** 104, 105; regional interests, **Supp. 7,** 111, 429; "renegades" in, **Supp. 4,** 309; Republican leadership, **Supp. 8,** 128–29; salary of, **Vol. 1, Part 2,** 236; secretary, **Supp. 8,** 36; social legislation, **Supp. 7,** 562; "Sons of the Wild Jackass," **Supp. 3,** 108; **Supp. 6,** 578; southern agricultural interests, **Supp. 4,** 50–51; southern conservatives, **Supp. 8,** 68; southern progressives, **Supp. 3,** 449; of states, equal representation, **Vol. 9, Part 2,** 144; Teapot Dome investigation, **Supp. 4,** 482; Truman, support for, **Supp. 7,** 326–27, 764; Wilson, opposition to, **Supp. 3,** 330–31, 622; **Supp. 4,** 669–70; Wilson, support for, **Supp. 3,** 706; World War I neutrality resolution, **Supp. 4,** 338. *See also* Congress, United States; House of Representatives, United States; Lobbying

Seneca Indians, **Supp. 7,** 392–94; history of, **Vol. 8, Part 1,** 437 f.

Sennett, Mack, references to, **Supp. 2,** 672; **Supp. 3,** 443; **Supp. 6,** 619; **Supp. 7,** 177, 238

Sensory perception, heat and cold, **Supp. 2,** 156

Sentence and Theme, **Supp. 1,** 687; founding of, **Supp. 1,** 697

"Sentinel register," first thermostat, **Vol. 4, Part 2,** 561

Separatist Society of Zoar, Ohio, founding of, **Vol. 1, Part 2,** 271

Separatism, colonial controversy concerning, **Vol. 3, Part 2,** 156

Sequoyah: name given to redwood trees, **Vol. 8, Part 2,** 586; proposed Indian state of, **Vol. 8, Part 1,** 111

Sequoyah Constitution (1905), **Supp. 6,** 469

Serapis, naval battle with, **Vol. 3, Part 2,** 268; **Vol. 5, Part 2,** 185

Serbia, typhus epidemic, **Supp. 4,** 468, 803; **Supp. 5,** 336

Serigraphy, **Supp. 7,** 15

Sermons, collection of, **Vol. 1, Part 1,** 501

Serra, Junipero, reference to, **Vol. 7, Part 2,** 196 f.

Serro do Mar (Brazil), hydroelectric power, **Supp. 4,** 81–82

Servants of Relief for Incurable Cancer, **Vol. 1, Part 1,** 227

Service, John, referencs to, **Supp. 6,** 60, 230, 231

Servicemen's Readjustment Act (1944). *See* GI Bill of Rights

Servites, **Vol. 7, Part 1,** 190

Set designers. For a complete list, *see* Occupations Index

Seth, Andrew, reference to, **Supp. 3,** 696

Seton, Anya, reference to, **Supp. 4,** 737

Seton, Ernest Thompson, reference to, **Supp. 4,** 872

Settlement house movement, **Supp. 1,** 11; **Supp. 2,** 408, 655; **Supp. 3,** 246; **Supp. 4,** 603; **Supp. 5,** 616, 630–31; **Supp. 6,** 499–500; **Supp. 7,** 320, 481; **Supp. 8,** 534–35; Boston, **Vol. 10, Part 1,** 41; Chicago, **Supp. 5,** 579; financing, **Supp. 2,** 608; first for blacks, **Supp. 4,** 53; music instruction, **Supp. 4,** 545; philanthropic gifts for, **Supp. 3,** 729. *See also specific names*

Seven Arts, **Supp. 7,** 79

Seven-Days' Battles, **Vol. 2, Part 1,** 360; **Vol. 2, Part 2,** 463; **Vol. 3, Part 1,** 598; **Vol. 3, Part 2,** 602; **Vol.**

4, **Part 2**, 505; **Vol. 5, Part 1**, 27, 343, 558; **Vol. 6, Part 1**, 123, 391, 583; **Vol. 6, Part 2**, 475, 205; **Vol. 8, Part 1**, 90; **Vol. 9, Part 2**, 215, 170; **Vol. 10, Part 1**, 473; **Vol. 10, Part 2**, 137. *See also* Peninsular Campaign

Seven Lively Arts, The, **Supp. 8**, 585

Seven Pines, Va., battle of (1862), **Vol. 2, Part 1**, 560; **Vol. 2, Part 2**, 463; **Vol. 5, Part 1**, 27, 343; **Vol. 5, Part 2**, 145, 272, 366; **Vol. 6, Part 1**, 123, 391, 583; **Vol. 8, Part 1**, 90; **Vol. 9, Part 1**, 272–73; **Vol. 10, Part 2**, 137

Seven Storey Mountain, The, **Supp. 8**, 431

Seventh-Day Adventists, **Supp. 5**, 378–79; **Supp. 7**, 631; health principals, **Supp. 3**, 409–10

Seventh Day Baptists of Ephrata, historical study of, **Vol. 8, Part 2**, 282

Seventh Heaven, **Supp. 7**, 65

Sevier, John, reference to, **Vol. 1, Part 1**, 268; **Vol. 5, Part 1**, 528; **Vol. 9, Part 2**, 563

Sewall, May Wright, reference to **Vol. 5, Part 2**, 208

Sewanee Review, The, founding of, **Supp. 2**, 666

Seward, William H., references to, **Vol. 6, Part 1**, 249 f.; **Vol. 7, Part 1**, 158; **Vol. 8, Part 1**, 409; **Vol. 10, Part 1**, 598 f.; **Supp. 1**, 366

Sewell, E. G., reference to, **Supp. 3**, 20

Sewerage: disposal systems, **Supp. 2**, 408; pollution, **Supp. 2**, 353; studies, **Supp. 6**, 701; systems, development of, **Supp. 1**, 351; treatment of, **Supp. 1**, 389; **Supp. 2**, 169–70. *See also* Public health; Sanitation

Sewing machine: inventions concerning, **Vol. 1, Part 1**, 465; **Vol. 1, Part 2**, 265; **Vol. 3, Part 2**, 43; **Vol. 4, Part 1**, 246, 457, 606; **Vol. 5, Part 1**, 259, 284 f.; **Vol. 9, Part 1**, 189; **Vol. 10, Part 2**, 320; manufacture of, **Vol. 1, Part 1**, 248; **Vol. 5, Part 1**, 286; **Vol. 5, Part 2**, 509; **Vol. 8, Part 1**, 74 f., 499 f.; **Vol. 10, Part 2**, 52

Sex differences. *See* Gender

Sex education, **Supp. 3**, 463; **Supp. 4**, 231, 759; **Supp. 7**, 427, 708; pioneer work in, **Vol. 7, Part 1**, 193, 236 f.

Sex hormones: embryonic, **Supp. 4**, 498; first synthesis of, **Supp. 5**, 28. *See also* Endocrine glands

Sex-linked traits. *See* Genetics

Sexuality: fraudulent rejuvenation claims, **Supp. 3**, 103–4; free expression advocacy, **Supp. 3**, 454, 463; journalism exploiting, **Supp. 5**, 453; Kinsey studies, **Supp. 6**, 252, 343–44, 718; National Committee on Maternal Health research, **Supp. 6**, 81–82; National Research Council studies, **Supp. 6**, 718; psychoanalytic deemphasis, **Supp. 3**, 191; psychological theories on, **Supp. 4**, 805; social hygiene movement, **Supp. 4**, 758–59. *See also* Gender

Sexually transmitted diseases. *See* Venereal disease

Seymour, Charles, reference to, **Supp. 4**, 22

Seymour, Horatio, reference to, **Vol. 9, Part 2**, 540

Shades, window, invention of, **Vol. 2, Part 1**, 334

Shahan, Thomas J., reference to, **Supp. 4**, 353

Shaker colonies, **Vol. 3, Part 2**, 198 f.; **Vol. 6, Part 1**, 95 f.; **Vol. 9, Part 1**, 285

Shakespeare, William: acting of, **Vol. 1, Part 1**, 647; **Vol. 4, Part 2**, 73, 75; **Vol. 5, Part 1**, 285; **Vol. 7, Part 1**, 73; **Vol. 9, Part 1**, 402; acting of, by blacks, **Vol. 1, Part 1**, 160; Baconian theory, **Vol. 1, Part 1**, 475; **Vol. 3, Part 1**, 370; **Vol. 5, Part 1**, 169, 244; **Vol. 7, Part 1**, 620; **Supp. 5**, 20; editing of works of, **Vol. 4, Part 1**, 78 f.; **Vol. 8, Part 2**, 119; **Supp. 4**, 624; folio collections, **Supp. 5**, 586–87; masque for, **Supp. 6**, 481; musical comedy adaptation, **Supp. 3**, 339; paintings of plays of, **Vol. 1, Part 1**, 7; productions of works of, **Supp. 4**, 477–79, 552–54; **Supp. 5**, 268–69; **Supp. 7**, 496; readings from, **Vol. 5, Part 2**, 316, 570; scholarship on, **Supp. 3**, 423–24; **Supp.**

4, 4–5, 110, 634; sculpture of characters, **Vol. 4, Part 1**, 457; studies in, **Vol. 5, Part 1**, 340 f.; **Vol. 5, Part 2**, 523; **Vol. 9, Part 1**, 472; **Vol. 10, Part 1**, 367 f.; writings on, **Vol. 1, Part 1**, 148; **Vol. 5, Part 2**, 154; **Vol. 7, Part 1**, 292; **Vol. 9, Part 1**, 190; **Vol. 10, Part 1**, 367 f.; **Vol. 10, Part 2**, 114

Shakespeare and Company (Paris bookstore), **Supp. 7**, 40, 41

Shakespeariana, collecting of, **Vol. 3, Part 2**, 487; **Vol. 9, Part 1**, 372; **Vol. 9, Part 2**, 432

Shaler, Nathanial S., reference to, **Vol. 9, Part 2**, 308

Shanghai American School, founding of, **Supp. 2**, 549

Shanghai Anglo-Chinese College, **Vol. 1, Part 1**, 215, 263

Shankar, Ravi, reference to, **Supp. 8**, 100

Shannon, Joseph B., reference to, **Supp. 3**, 596

Shapley, Harlow, references to, **Supp. 3**, 208; **Supp. 5**, 326; **Supp. 6**, 56

Shapp, Milton, reference to, **Supp. 8**, 361

Sharecropping. *See* Tenant farming

Share-Our-Wealth Society, founding of, **Supp. 1**, 508

Sharkey, Jack, reference to, **Supp. 6**, 700

Sharon, William, divorce case, **Vol. 9, Part 2**, 380

Sharp, Lester W., reference to, **Supp. 4**, 253

Sharp, William, reference to, **Vol. 5, Part 1**, 614

Sharp and Dohme, Merck merger, **Supp. 6**, 448

"Sharps and Flats," **Vol. 3, Part 2**, 363; **Vol. 9, Part 2**, 317

Sharpsburg, Md., battle of. *See* Antietam, battle of

Shasta Dam, **Supp. 4**, 198–99

Shaw, Anna H., reference to, **Vol. 5, Part 1**, 312

Shaw, George Bernard, references to, **Supp. 4**, 369, 528; **Supp. 7**, 283, 322, 325, 496

Shaw, Lemuel, murder trial, charges of, **Vol. 10, Part 1**, 592 f.

Shaw, Samuel, reference to, **Vol. 8, Part 2**, 539

Shawn, Edwin Myers ("Ted"), references to, **Supp. 7**, 366; **Supp. 8**, 620–21

Shawn, William, reference to, **Supp. 5**, 594

Shawnee Indians, **Vol. 9, Part 2**, 358 f., 375; war with, *see* Northwestern Indians

Shaw University, founding of, **Vol. 3, Part 2**, 189

Shays' Rebellion (1786–87), **Vol. 1, Part 1**, 100; **Vol. 6, Part 1**, 77, 260–61; **Vol. 8, Part 1**, 196; **Vol. 9, Part 1**, 50, 77; **Vol. 9, Part 2**, 51; **Vol. 10, Part 1**, 96, 521

Shear, T. Leslie, reference to, **Supp. 4**, 144

Shearn, Clarence, reference to, **Supp. 5**, 287–88

Sheehan, William F., reference to, **Supp. 3**, 642

Sheeler, Charles: reference to, **Supp. 3**, 284; writings on, **Supp. 3**, 673

Sheen, Fulton J., reference to, **Supp. 7**, 52

Sheep-raising and importing, **Vol. 1, Part 1**, 599; **Vol. 3, Part 1**, 251; **Vol. 3, Part 2**, 478 f.; **Vol. 4, Part 1**, 256; **Vol. 4, Part 2**, 162, 204; **Vol. 5, Part 1**, 374, 624 f.; **Vol. 8, Part 1**, 143 f.; **Vol. 9, Part 2**, 525; writings on, **Vol. 8, Part 1**, 324 f.

Sheet metal, **Vol. 1, Part 2**, 73; **Vol. 5, Part 1**, 57; **Vol. 6, Part 1**, 82

Sheet music, **Supp. 3**, 833–34; **Supp. 4**, 88

Shelby, Isaac, reference to, **Vol. 6, Part 1**, 357

Shelby Musical College, founding of, **Vol. 5, Part 2**, 207

Sheldon, Edward, references to, **Supp. 3**, 34; **Supp. 6**, 400

Sheldon Jackson College, **Vol. 3, Part 1**, 608 f.

Shelford, Victor E., reference to, **Supp. 3**, 169

Shells, collecting of, **Vol. 3, Part 2**, 269; **Vol. 4, Part 1**, 446; **Vol. 6, Part 1**, 67, 70 f.; **Vol. 8, Part 1**, 192, 395 f.; **Vol. 8, Part 2**, 401 f.; **Vol. 9, Part 1**, 548, 585; **Vol. 9, Part 2**, 599

Vol. **8, Part 2**, 569; *Margaret*, **Vol. 5, Part 1**, 152; *Mary Pierce*, **Vol. 5, Part 1**, 152; *Monticello*, **Vol. 5, Part 1**, 152; *Neptune*, **Vol. 6, Part 2**, 271; *North Heath*, **Vol. 9, Part 1**, 486; *Nutfield*, **Vol. 8, Part 2**, 85; *Owl*, **Vol. 6, Part 2**, 196; *Pioneer*, **Vol. 2, Part 2**, 635; *Planter*, **Vol. 6, Part 2**, 271; *Princess Royal*, **Vol. 8, Part 1**, 293; **Vol. 9, Part 2**, 518; *Quaker City*, **Vol. 2, Part 2**, 259; *Robert E. Lee*, **Vol. 7, Part 2**, 308; **Vol. 9, Part 2**, 262; **Vol. 10, Part 2**, 228; *St. Nicholas*, **Vol. 5, Part 1**, 152; *Susan Beirne*, **Vol. 9, Part 1**, 486; *Theodora*, **Vol. 6, Part 2**, 196; *Wild Dagrell*, **Vol. 8, Part 2**, 85

Built in America, sold to foreign countries: *Dunderberg*, **Vol. 10, Part 1**, 579; *General Admiral*, **Vol. 10, Part 1**, 579; *Re di Portogallo*, **Vol. 10, Part 1**, 579; *Re d'Italia*, **Vol. 10, Part 1**, 579; *Rochambeau*, **Vol. 10, Part 1**, 579; *Saratoga*, **Vol. 10, Part 1**, 424; *United States*, **Vol. 6, Part 2**, 306

California "gold rush": *Brooklyn*, **Vol. 1, Part 2**, 602; *Brutus*, **Vol. 8, Part 1**, 322; *Eliza*, **Vol. 1, Part 2**, 228; *Mount Vernon*, **Vol. 10, Part 1**, 384; *Panama*, **Vol. 6, Part 1**, 445; **Vol. 6, Part 2**, 110; *Tarolinta*, **Vol. 7, Part 1**, 612; *Thomas Perkins*, **Vol. 8, Part 2**, 116

Clipper: *Amphitrite*, **Vol. 4, Part 2**, 142; *Andrew Jackson*, **Vol. 2, Part 2**, 534; *Ann McKim*, **Vol. 4, Part 1**, 626; **Vol. 6, Part 2**, 102; *Aramingo*, **Vol. 10, Part 2**, 16; *Australia*, **Vol. 10, Part 1**, 578; *Bald Eagle*, **Vol. 6, Part 2**, 72; *Black Hawk*, **Vol. 10, Part 1**, 578; *Black Prince*, **Vol. 2, Part 2**, 120; *Celestial*, **Vol. 10, Part 1**, 578; *Challenge*, **Vol. 10, Part 1**, 535–78; *Chariot of Fame*, **Vol. 6, Part 2**, 72; *Comet*, **Vol. 10, Part 1**, 578; *Contest*, **Vol. 6, Part 1**, 444; **Vol. 10, Part 2**, 16; *Dashing Wave*, **Vol. 5, Part 1**, 3; *Dreadnought*, **Vol. 9, Part 2**, 67; *Empress of the Seas*, **Vol. 6, Part 2**, 72; *Eureka*, **Vol. 10, Part 2**, 16; *Express*, **Vol. 4, Part 2**, 142; *Flyaway*, **Vol. 10, Part 1**, 578; *Flying Childers*, **Vol. 4, Part 2**, 142; *Flying Cloud*, **Vol. 2, Part 2**, 533; **Vol. 6, Part 2**, 72; **Vol. 7, Part 1**, 33; **Vol. 9, Part 2**, 52, 625–26; *Flying Dutchman*, **Vol. 10, Part 1**, 578; *Flying Fish*, **Vol. 4, Part 2**, 142; *Game Cock*, **Vol. 4, Part 2**, 142; *Gazelle*, **Vol. 10, Part 1**, 578; *Glory of the Seas*, **Vol. 6, Part 2**, 73; *Golden City*, **Vol. 10, Part 2**, 16; *Golden Gate*, **Vol. 10, Part 2**, 16; *Golden State*, **Vol. 10, Part 2**, 16; *Great Republic*, **Vol. 6, Part 2**, 72; **Vol. 7, Part 2**, 190; *Hoogly*, **Vol. 4, Part 2**, 142; *Hornet*, **Vol. 10, Part 2**, 16; *Houqua*, **Vol. 6, Part 1**, 44; **Vol. 7, Part 2**, 190; *Intrepid*, **Vol. 10, Part 1**, 578; *Invincible*, **Vol. 10, Part 1**, 578; *Jacob Bell*, **Vol. 6, Part 1**, 444; *James Baines*, **Vol. 6, Part 2**, 72; *John Gilpin*, **Vol. 4, Part 2**, 142; *Kathay*, **Vol. 10, Part 2**, 16; *Levere*, **Vol. 2, Part 1**, 308; *Lightning*, **Vol. 6, Part 2**, 72; *Messenger*, **Vol. 1, Part 2**, 156; *Mystery*, **Vol. 4, Part 2**, 142; *Natchez*, **Vol. 10, Part 1**, 534; *N. B. Palmer*, **Vol. 10, Part 2**, 16; *North Wind*, **Vol. 7, Part 1**, 33; *Northern Light*, **Vol. 2, Part 2**, 120; *Oneida*, **Vol. 2, Part 2**, 533; *Oriental*, **Vol. 1, Part 2**, 156; **Vol. 4, Part 2**, 142; **Vol. 7, Part 2**, 190; *Polynesia*, **Vol. 4, Part 2**, 142; *Race Horse*, **Vol. 4, Part 2**, 142; *Rainbow*, **Vol. 4, Part 1**, 626; *R. B. Forbes*, **Vol. 4, Part 2**, 142; *Resolute*, **Vol. 10, Part 2**, 16; *Romance of the Seas*, **Vol. 6, Part 2**, 72; *Samuel Russell*, **Vol. 6, Part 1**, 444; **Vol. 7, Part 2**, 190; *Sea Serpent*, **Vol. 7, Part 1**, 33; *Sea Witch*, **Vol. 4, Part 1**, 626; **Vol. 10, Part 1**, 534; *Snapdragon*, **Vol. 10, Part 1**, 578; *Sovereign of the Seas*, **Vol. 6, Part 2**, 72; *Staffordshire*, **Vol. 9, Part 2**, 625; *Stag Hound*, **Vol. 6, Part 2**, 72; *Star of Empire*, **Vol. 6, Part 2**, 72; *Surprise*, **Vol. 4, Part 2**, 142; *Sweepstakes*, **Vol. 10, Part 2**, 16; *Sword Fish*, **Vol. 10, Part 1**, 578; *Telegraph*, **Vol. 4, Part 2**, 142; *Trade Wind*, **Vol. 1, Part 2**, 156; *Uncowah*, **Vol. 10, Part 1**, 578; *Westward Ho*, **Vol. 6, Part 2**, 72; *White Squall*, **Vol. 1, Part 2**,

156; *Witchcraft*, **Vol. 8, Part 2**, 116; *Wizard*, **Vol. 4, Part 2**, 142; **Vol. 7, Part 1**, 317; *Young America*, **Vol. 10, Part 1**, 578

Colonial: *Ann*, **Vol. 6, Part 2**, 617; *Anne*, **Vol. 7, Part 1**, 43, 59, 254, 261; **Vol. 7, Part 2**, 12, 406; **Vol. 9, Part 1**, 500; *Arbella*, **Vol. 7, Part 2**, 546; **Vol. 8, Part 1**, 290; **Vol. 10, Part 1**, 479; **Vol. 10, Part 2**, 409, 567; *Archangel*, **Vol. 10, Part 1**, 562; *Canterbury*, **Vol. 6, Part 1**, 361; *Confidence*, **Vol. 10, Part 2**, 209; *Defence*, **Vol. 5, Part 1**, 329; **Vol. 7, Part 2**, 204; *Desire*, **Vol. 7, Part 2**, 406; *Discoverer*, **Vol. 8, Part 1**, 235; *Discovery*, **Vol. 7, Part 1**, 468; **Vol. 8, Part 1**, 110; *Eendracht*, **Vol. 7, Part 1**, 34; *Elizabeth*, **Vol. 3, Part 1**, 34; **Vol. 6, Part 1**, 531; **Vol. 7, Part 1**, 72; *Elizabeth and Mary*, **Vol. 9, Part 2**, 542, 543; *Fama*, **Vol. 8, Part 1**, 239; *Fellowship*, **Vol. 4, Part 1**, 139; *Fortune*, **Vol. 3, Part 1**, 5, 334; **Vol. 5, Part 1**, 515; **Vol. 7, Part 1**, 254; **Vol. 7, Part 2**, 184; **Vol. 10, Part 2**, 393–94; *Friendship*, **Vol. 2, Part 2**, 72; **Vol. 5, Part 1**, 80; *Gift of God*, **Vol. 8, Part 1**, 78; *Godspeed*, **Vol. 4, Part 1**, 439; **Vol. 7, Part 1**, 468; *Griffin*, **Vol. 4, Part 2**, 459; **Vol. 5, Part 1**, 425–36; **Vol. 7, Part 1**, 34; *Gyllene Haj*, **Vol. 8, Part 1**, 627; *Harinchk*, **Vol. 5, Part 2**, 370; *Harle*, **Vol. 9, Part 2**, 180; *Het Meemotze* (The Little Gull), **Vol. 7, Part 1**, 34; *Het Vliegende Hert* (The Flying Stag), **Vol. 7, Part 1**, 34; *Hoop*, **Vol. 10, Part 2**, 15; *James*, **Vol. 3, Part 2**, 151; *John*, **Vol. 3, Part 1**, 163; *Jollif Galley*, **Vol. 3, Part 1**, 272; *Kent*, **Vol. 7, Part 2**, 434; *Key of Colmar*, **Vol. 7, Part 1**, 34; *Lion*, **Vol. 6, Part 1**, 514; **Vol. 10, Part 2**, 409; *Little James*, **Vol. 7, Part 1**, 254; *Lyon*, **Vol. 7, Part 2**, 406; *Mary and John*, **Vol. 3, Part 1**, 605; **Vol. 4, Part 1**, 488; **Vol. 6, Part 1**, 493; **Vol. 7, Part 1**, 72; **Vol. 8, Part 1**, 78; **Vol. 9, Part 2**, 149–53; *Mayflower*, **Vol. 1, Part 1**, 129, 145, 146, 524; **Vol. 1, Part 2**, 237, 430, 559; **Vol. 2, Part 1**, 30, 551; **Vol. 2, Part 2**, 136, 146, 119; **Vol. 3, Part 1**, 5; **Vol. 4, Part 1**, 57, 557, 622; **Vol. 5, Part 1**, 312, 313, 420, 606; **Vol. 5, Part 2**, 556; **Vol. 6, Part 2**, 564, 622; **Vol. 7, Part 1**, 254, 334, 577; **Vol. 7, Part 2**, 406; **Vol. 8, Part 1**, 187, 188, 230, 456, 495; **Vol. 8, Part 2**, 600; **Vol. 9, Part 1**, 289, 500, 524; **Vol. 10, Part 1**, 363, 478, 485, 487, 488, 537; **Vol. 10, Part 2**, 20, 393, 394; *Neptune*, **Vol. 7, Part 2**, 108; *Olive Branch*, **Vol. 8, Part 1**, 235; *Orangenboom*, **Vol. 5, Part 2**, 508; *Orn*, **Vol. 8, Part 1**, 627; *Paragon*, **Vol. 7, Part 2**, 406; *Prosperous*, **Vol. 3, Part 1**, 34; *Restaurationen*, **Vol. 7, Part 2**, 390; *Rose*, **Vol. 7, Part 2**, 551; *San Carlos*, **Vol. 3, Part 2**, 244; *Sea Adventure*, **Vol. 4, Part 1**, 190; **Vol. 8, Part 2**, 117; **Vol. 9, Part 2**, 120; *Speedwell*, **Vol. 2, Part 1**, 551; **Vol. 3, Part 1**, 5; **Vol. 7, Part 1**, 261; **Vol. 8, Part 1**, 235; **Vol. 10, Part 2**, 393; *Starr*, **Vol. 3, Part 1**, 34; *Susan and Ellen*, **Vol. 5, Part 1**, 70; *Susan Constant*, **Vol. 7, Part 1**, 468; *Swan*, **Vol. 8, Part 1**, 239; *Swift*, **Vol. 5, Part 1**, 80; *Thistle*, **Vol. 6, Part 2**, 632; *Three Saints*, **Vol. 9, Part 1**, 68; *Treasurer*, **Vol. 8, Part 1**, 19; *Trial*, **Vol. 1, Part 2**, 485; *Vine*, **Vol. 7, Part 2**, 118; *Welcome*, **Vol. 10, Part 1**, 386; **Vol. 5, Part 2**, 181, 265, 463; *William*, **Vol. 10, Part 1**, 216

Experimental and scientific: *Albatross*, **Vol. 1, Part 1**, 113; **Vol. 3, Part 1**, 614; **Vol. 7, Part 1**, 598; **Vol. 8, Part 2**, 464; *Aunt Sally*, **Vol. 7, Part 1**, 161; *Babcock*, **Vol. 9, Part 2**, 520; *Balloon*, **Vol. 7, Part 1**, 471; *Burnside*, **Vol. 9, Part 1**, 480; *Clermont*, **Vol. 2, Part 2**, 46; **Vol. 4, Part 1**, 71; **Vol. 6, Part 1**, 324; **Vol. 7, Part 1**, 471; **Vol. 8, Part 2**, 106; **Vol. 9, Part 1**, 615; *Columbia Maid*, **Vol. 8, Part 2**, 223; *Condor*, **Vol. 5, Part 1**, 238; *Eagle*, **Vol. 8, Part 2**, 106; *Francis B. Ogden*, **Vol. 7, Part 1**, 639; *Fulton or Robert Fulton*, **Vol. 3, Part 2**, 5; **Vol. 4, Part 1**, 71, 245; **Vol. 6, Part 2**, 593; *Geographe*, **Vol. 6, Part 1**, 190; *Great Eastern*,

Vol. 5, Part 2, 566; *Hassler,* Vol. 8, Part 1, 141; Vol. 10, Part 2, 109; *J. Y. Mason,* Vol. 10, Part 1, 318; *Juliana,* Vol. 9, Part 1, 615–19; *Le Hardi,* Vol. 6, Part 1, 190; *Little Juliana,* Vol. 9, Part 1, 615–19; *Nautilus,* Vol. 4, Part 1, 70; *New Era,* Vol. 4, Part 1, 627; *New Orleans,* Vol. 8, Part 2, 134; *North America,* Vol. 9, Part 1, 608; *Peedee,* Vol. 8, Part 2, 107; *Phoenix,* Vol. 8, Part 2, 106; Vol. 9, Part 1, 615–19; *Polacca,* Vol. 5, Part 1, 232; Vol. 8, Part 2, 134; Vol. 9, Part 1, 615; *Robert F. Stockton,* Vol. 7, Part 1, 639; *Rushlight,* Vol. 9, Part 2, 520; *Savannah,* Vol. 2, Part 1, 257; Vol. 3, Part 1, 339; Vol. 8, Part 2, 106, 107, 410; Vol. 9, Part 1, 315; *Sea Horse,* Vol. 7, Part 1, 637–39; *Stoudinger,* Vol. 4, Part 1, 243; *Walker,* Vol. 10, Part 1, 568

Exploration: *Advance,* Vol. 4, Part 2, 120; Vol. 5, Part 2, 256; Vol. 7, Part 2, 337; *Adventure,* Vol. 4, Part 1, 523; *Albatross,* Vol. 1, Part 1, 113; Vol. 3, Part 1, 614; Vol. 7, Part 1, 598; Vol. 8, Part 2, 464; *Alert,* Vol. 10, Part 1, 135; *America,* Vol. 6, Part 2, 575; *Annawan,* Vol. 7, Part 2, 190; *Antelope,* Vol. 7, Part 1, 514; *Archangel,* Vol. 10, Part 1, 562; *Beaver,* Vol. 5, Part 1, 399; *Betsey,* Vol. 3, Part 2, 266; *Columbia,* Vol. 4, Part 1, 523; *Concord,* Vol. 4, Part 1, 439; *Discoverer,* Vol. 8, Part 1, 235; *Discovery,* Vol. 5, Part 1, 339; *Eaglet,* Vol. 4, Part 2, 17; *Florence,* Vol. 10, Part 1, 102; *Fram,* Vol. 7, Part 2, 364; *George Law,* Vol. 6, Part 2, 575; *Griffon,* Vol. 4, Part 2, 540; Vol. 6, Part 1, 11; Vol. 6, Part 2, 526; Vol. 9, Part 2, 587; *Gulnare,* Vol. 7, Part 2, 323; *Halve Moen (Half Moon),* Vol. 5, Part 1, 339; *Herd,* Vol. 7, Part 2, 190; *Hersilia,* Vol. 7, Part 2, 190; *Hope,* Vol. 5, Part 1, 478; *Hopewell,* Vol. 5, Part 1, 338; *James Monroe,* Vol. 7, Part 2, 190; *Jeannette,* Vol. 1, Part 1, 240; *Kite,* Vol. 7, Part 2, 363; *La Concepción,* Vol. 7, Part 1, 273; *Lady Washington,* Vol. 4, Part 1, 523; *Le Don de Dieu,* Vol. 2, Part 1, 606; *Nonsuch,* Vol. 4, Part 2, 17; *Olive Branch,* Vol. 8, Part 1, 235; *Pandora,* Vol. 6, Part 2, 46; *Pelican,* Vol. 5, Part 1, 456; *Polaris,* Vol. 4, Part 2, 120; Vol. 10, Part 1, 102; *Prometheus,* Vol. 2, Part 1, 309; *Roosevelt,* Vol. 7, Part 2, 365; *St. Julien,* Vol. 2, Part 1, 605; *San Antonio,* Vol. 8, Part 1, 109; *San Carlos,* Vol. 1, Part 1, 447; Vol. 8, Part 1, 109; Vol. 3, Part 2, 244; *San Salvador,* Vol. 2, Part 1, 396; *Seraph,* Vol. 7, Part 2, 190; *Three Saints,* Vol. 9, Part 1, 67; *Tigress,* Vol. 10, Part 1, 102; *Tonquin,* Vol. 3, Part 2, 282; Vol. 8, Part 2, 173; *Victoria;* Vol. 2, Part 1, 396; *Warrior,* Vol. 2, Part 1, 309; *Washington,* Vol. 5, Part 2, 329; *White Falcon,* Vol. 7, Part 2, 364; *Windward,* Vol. 7, Part 2, 364;

Filibuster: *Akbar,* Vol. 4, Part 2, 142; *Cadet,* Vol. 7, Part 2, 190; *Caroline,* Vol. 10, Part 1, 135; *Enterprise,* Vol. 7, Part 1, 195; *Houston,* Vol. 8, Part 2, 324; *Restormel,* Vol. 9, Part 1, 156; *Tampico;* Vol. 7, Part 2, 190

Foreign, in naval engagements: *Admiral Duff,* Vol. 8, Part 1, 182; *Alert,* Vol. 3, Part 1, 414; *Almirante Oquendo,* Vol. 10, Part 1, 319; *America,* Vol. 6, Part 2, 577; *Amphion,* Vol. 3, Part 2, 536; *Arancand,* Vol. 10, Part 2, 524; *Arundel,* Vol. 8, Part 1, 518; *Austin,* Vol. 7, Part 1, 120; *Belvidera,* Vol. 3, Part 2, 85; Vol. 7, Part 1, 97; Vol. 7, Part 2, 486; Vol. 8, Part 2, 76, 77; Vol. 9, Part 2, 139; *Bonne Citoyenne,* Vol. 6, Part 1, 50; *Boxer,* Vol. 6, Part 1, 561; *Brandzen,* Vol. 3, Part 1, 202; *Burford,* Vol. 10, Part 2, 180; *Cacique,* Vol. 3, Part 1, 202; *Carleton,* Vol. 4, Part 1, 543; *Carnation,* Vol. 8, Part 1, 480; *Castilla,* Vol. 3, Part 1, 271; *Chen Yuen,* Vol. 6, Part 2, 49; *Cherub,* Vol. 3, Part 1, 416; Vol. 3, Part 2, 286; Vol. 8, Part 1, 84; *Chester,* Vol. 10, Part 1, 486; *Colon,* Vol. 2, Part 2, 123; *Columbus,* Vol. 10, Part 2, 524; *Concord,* Vol. 7,

Part 2, 484; *Cristobal Colon,* Vol. 6, Part 2, 647; *Cuba,* Vol. 6, Part 2, 196; *Culloden,* Vol. 9, Part 2, 280; *Detroit,* Vol. 7, Part 2, 490; *Don Antonio de Ulloa,* Vol. 3, Part 1, 271; *Don Jorge Juan,* Vol. 10, Part 1, 633; *Dover Prize,* Vol. 8, Part 1, 141; *Duc de Bourgogne,* Vol. 4, Part 1, 140; *Duras* (renamed *Bonhomme Richard*), Vol. 5, Part 2, 185; *Endymion,* Vol. 3, Part 1, 188; *Esmeralda,* Vol. 8, Part 1, 85; *Falcon,* Vol. 8, Part 1, 196; *Firm,* Vol. 8, Part 1, 518; *Flamand,* Vol. 5, Part 2, 567; *Flora,* Vol. 6, Part 2, 151; *Fox,* Vol. 6, Part 2, 236; *Friend's Adventure,* Vol. 9, Part 1, 408; *Frolic,* Vol. 5, Part 2, 176; *Furor,* Vol. 10, Part 1, 319; *Galveztown,* Vol. 4, Part 1, 120; *Gaspée,* Vol. 10, Part 2, 66; *Glasgow,* Vol. 5, Part 1, 64, 209, 212; Vol. 5, Part 2, 184; Vol. 8, Part 2, 316; Vol. 10, Part 2, 66; *Granicus,* Vol. 2, Part 2, 271; *Guadalupe,* Vol. 7, Part 1, 121; *Guerrerd,* Vol. 8, Part 1, 85; *Guerrière,* Vol. 7, Part 1, 202; *Hazard,* Vol. 7, Part 1, 535; *Hebrus,* Vol. 5, Part 2, 270; *Hermione,* Vol. 5, Part 2, 537; *Heroína,* Vol. 5, Part 2, 67; *Hinchimbroke,* Vol. 4, Part 1, 554; *Hind,* Vol. 10, Part 1, 40; *Hyperion,* Vol. 6, Part 2, 195; *Infanta Maria Teresa,* Vol. 10, Part 1, 319; *Intrepid,* Vol. 1, Part 1, 633; *Invincible,* Vol. 5, Part 2, 67; *Iris,* Vol. 3, Part 1, 33; Vol. 7, Part 1, 358, 502; *Isabel,* Vol. 5, Part 2, 558; *Jersey,* Vol. 7, Part 2, 484, 631; Vol. 8, Part 1, 182; Vol. 9, Part 2, 280; *Junon,* Vol. 9, Part 2, 306; *La Nymphe,* Vol. 5, Part 2, 538; *Launceton,* Vol. 10, Part 1, 486; *Lautaro,* Vol. 10, Part 2, 524; *La Vengeance,* Vol. 4, Part 2, 539; Vol. 10, Part 1, 22; *La Victoire,* Vol. 5, Part 2, 536; *Lealtad,* Vol. 8, Part 1, 85; *Le Formidable,* Vol. 6, Part 2, 469; *L'Entreprenant,* Vol. 6, Part 2, 469; *Leopard,* Vol. 1, Part 1, 212, 650; Vol. 2, Part 1, 309; Vol. 3, Part 1, 188; Vol. 5, Part 2, 30; Vol. 7, Part 1, 358, 486; Vol. 7, Part 2, 627; Vol. 8, Part 2, 76, 505; Vol. 9, Part 1, 135; Vol. 9, Part 2, 307, 355; *Little Belt,* Vol. 1, Part 1, 507, Vol. 7, Part 2, 486; Vol. 8, Part 1, 188; Vol. 8, Part 2, 76; Vol. 9, Part 2, 139; *Liverpool,* Vol. 8, Part 1, 430; *Lord Sandwich,* Vol. 6, Part 1, 299; *Lowestoffe's Prize,* Vol. 7, Part 2, 28; *Maidstone,* Vol. 10, Part 1, 437; *Majestic,* Vol. 3, Part 1, 188; *Maria Isabel,* Vol. 10, Part 2, 524; *Mary,* Vol. 6, Part 2, 195; Vol. 9, Part 1, 408; *Massachusetts,* Vol. 10, Part 1, 101; *Medea,* Vol. 6, Part 1, 299; Vol. 10, Part 2, 276; *Mercury,* Vol. 6, Part 2, 151; *Mermaid,* Vol. 10, Part 1, 486; *Mindanao,* Vol. 10, Part 1, 340; *Monarch,* Vol. 9, Part 2, 518; *Montaga,* Vol. 6, Part 1, 50; *Montezuma,* Vol. 7, Part 1, 121; *Ostrich,* Vol. 7, Part 2, 28; *Otter,* Vol. 7, Part 1, 502; *Peacock,* Vol. 6, Part 1, 50; *Pelican,* Vol. 6, Part 1, 204; *Perry,* Vol. 4, Part 2, 493; *Phoebe,* Vol. 3, Part 1, 416; Vol. 3, Part 2, 286; Vol. 8, Part 1, 84; *Plantagenet,* Vol. 8, Part 1, 480; *Pluton,* Vol. 10, Part 1, 319; *Poictiers,* Vol. 5, Part 2, 176; *Pomona,* Vol. 8, Part 2, 76; Vol. 3, Part 1, 188; Vol. 6, Part 2, 236; *Porcupine,* Vol. 9, Part 2, 408; *Portland,* Vol. 1, Part 2, 242; *Prince of Orange,* Vol. 10, Part 1, 101; *Prudent,* Vol. 10, Part 1, 21; *Queen Charlotte,* Vol. 7, Part 2, 491; *Rachel,* Vol. 10, Part 2, 524; *Rainbow,* Vol. 6, Part 2, 151; *Recruit,* Vol. 7, Part 1, 413; *Reina Cristina,* Vol. 3, Part 1, 271; *Restoration,* Vol. 4, Part 1, 543; *Robert Fulton,* Vol. 8, Part 2, 5; *Roebuck,* Vol. 6, Part 1, 299; Vol. 8, Part 1, 430; Vol. 10, Part 2, 276; *Rose,* Vol. 10, Part 1, 486; Vol. 10, Part 2, 66; *Rota,* Vol. 8, Part 1, 480; *Royal George,* Vol. 8, Part 2, 343; *Royalist,* Vol. 5, Part 1, 460; *St. Albans,* Vol. 1, Part 1, 633; *Sally Rose,* Vol. 8, Part 1, 141; *Scarborough,* Vol. 9, Part 2, 450; *Scorpion,* Vol. 4, Part 1, 27; *Seaflower,* Vol. 9, Part 1, 408; *Serapis,* Vol. 3, Part 1, 33; Vol. 3, Part 2, 268; Vol. 5, Part 2, 185; *Shannon,* Vol. 5, Part 1, 623; Vol. 6, Part 1, 50, 308; *Shark,* Vol. 10, Part 2, 180; *Solebay,* Vol. 10, Part 1, 486; *Somerset,* Vol. 6, Part 2, 151; *Squirrel,*

3, **Part 2**, 255; **Vol. 7, Part 2**, 470; **Vol. 8, Part 2**, 85; *Charleston,* **Vol. 5, Part 1**, 153; **Vol. 8, Part 1**, 495; **Vol. 8, Part 2**, 22, 492; **Vol. 10, Part 2**, 393; *Charleston,* **Vol. 8, Part 1**, 97; *Chattahoochee,* **Vol. 5, Part 2**, 164; *Chattanooga,* **Vol. 9, Part 2**, 42; *Chenango,* **Vol. 8, Part 1**, 314; *Chesapeake,* **Vol. 1, Part 1**, 212, 650; **Vol. 2, Part 1**, 337; **Vol. 2, Part 2**, 40, 510; **Vol. 3, Part 1**, 188; **Vol. 3, Part 2**, 96; **Vol. 5, Part 1**, 376, 623; **Vol. 5, Part 2**, 30; **Vol. 6, Part 1**, 50, 308; **Vol. 7, Part 1**, 358, 486; **Vol. 7, Part 2**, 627; **Vol. 8, Part 2**, 76, 232, 505; **Vol. 9, Part 1**, 135, 309; **Vol. 9, Part 2**, 7, 307, 355; **Vol. 10, Part 1**, 22, 492; *Cheyenne,* **Vol. 2, Part 2**, 468; *Chicago,* **Vol. 2, Part 1**, 468; **Vol. 6, Part 2**, 207; **Vol. 8, Part 1**, 640; *Chickasaw,* **Vol. 7, Part 2**, 470; *Chicora,* **Vol. 5, Part 1**, 477; **Vol. 8, Part 1**, 97; **Vol. 9, Part 2**, 348; **Vol. 10, Part 1**, 34; *Chippewa,* **Vol. 4, Part 1**, 232; **Vol. 7, Part 2**, 534; **Vol. 8, Part 1**, 314, 424; **Vol. 9, Part 2**, 518; **Vol. 10, Part 1**, 568; *Choctaw,* **Vol. 8, Part 1**, 339; *Chocura,* **Vol. 4, Part 1**, 232; **Vol. 6, Part 2**, 479; **Vol. 7, Part 2**, 308; **Vol. 10, Part 1**, 23; *Cimarron,* **Vol. 9, Part 2**, 457; *Clara Dolson,* **Vol. 7, Part 2**, 314; *Clarence,* **Vol. 8, Part 1**, 420; *Cohoes,* **Vol. 8, Part 2**, 200; *Colonel Harney,* **Vol. 8, Part 2**, 74; *Colorado,* **Vol. 1, Part 1**, 502; **Vol. 3, Part 1**, 107, 269; **Vol. 4, Part 1**, 232; **Vol. 6, Part 1**, 173, 500; *Colorado,* **Vol. 6, Part 2**, 576; **Vol. 7, Part 2**, 606; **Vol. 8, Part 2**, 78, 244, 322; **Vol. 9, Part 1**, 554, 626; **Vol. 9, Part 2**, 394; **Vol. 10, Part 1**, 319; **Vol. 10, Part 2**, 585; *Colorado,* **Vol. 2, Part 1**, 468; **Vol. 2, Part 2**, 500; **Vol. 8, Part 2**, 22; *Columbia,* **Vol. 5, Part 2**, 164; **Vol. 6, Part 1**, 315; **Vol. 7, Part 1**, 320; **Vol. 7, Part 2**, 185, 444; **Vol. 8, Part 2**, 79, 341; **Vol. 10, Part 1**, 317, 318; **Vol. 10, Part 2**, 645; *Columbia,* **Vol. 1, Part 1**, 495, **Vol. 2, Part 1**, 255; **Vol. 2, Part 2**, 500; **Vol. 6, Part 2**, 522; **Vol. 8, Part 1**, 237; **Vol. 8, Part 2**, 79; *Columbia,* **Vol. 8, Part 1**, 97; *Columbia and John Adams,* **Vol. 8, Part 1**, 424; *Columbus,* **Vol. 1, Part 1**, 507; **Vol. 3, Part 1**, 380; **Vol. 5, Part 2**, 170; **Vol. 7, Part 2**, 140, 243; **Vol. 8, Part 1**, 596; **Vol. 10, Part 2**, 66; *Commodore Barney,* **Vol. 2, Part 2**, 636; *Commodore Hull,* **Vol. 7, Part 1**, 640; *Commodore McDonough,* **Vol. 9, Part 2**, 457; *Commodore Perry,* **Vol. 2, Part 2**, 635; *Concord,* **Vol. 1, Part 1**, 145, 226; **Vol. 3, Part 1**, 270; **Vol. 7, Part 2**, 487; **Vol. 8, Part 1**, 315; **Vol. 8, Part 2**, 77; **Vol. 10, Part 1**, 339, 340; *Confederacy,* **Vol. 4, Part 2**, 251; *Conemaugh,* **Vol. 6, Part 2**, 479; **Vol. 8, Part 1**, 293; **Vol. 9, Part 1**, 139; **Vol. 10, Part 2**, 1; *Conestoga,* **Vol. 8, Part 2**, 569; *Congress,* **Vol. 1, Part 2**, 348; **Vol. 3, Part 1**, 188; **Vol. 5, Part 1**, 377, 477; **Vol. 6, Part 1**, 524; **Vol. 7, Part 1**, 202, 203; **Vol. 8, Part 1**, 182; **Vol. 9, Part 1**, 215; **Vol. 10, Part 1**, 492; *Congress,* **Vol. 1, Part 2**, 88; **Vol. 2, Part 1**, 207; **Vol. 3, Part 1**, 530; **Vol. 5, Part 2**, 14, 164; **Vol. 6, Part 1**, 315, 500; **Vol. 6, Part 2**, 207, 465; **Vol. 7, Part 2**, 243, 260; **Vol. 8, Part 1**, 68, 86, 293, 319; **Vol. 8, Part 2**, 72, 343, 427; **Vol. 9, Part 1**, 178, 310; **Vol. 9, Part 2**, 42, 48; **Vol. 10, Part 1**, 128, 292, 568; **Vol. 10, Part 2**, 645; *Connecticut,* **Vol. 1, Part 1**, 226; **Vol. 1, Part 2**, 409; **Vol. 4, Part 1**, 485; **Vol. 5, Part 2**, 324; **Vol. 10, Part 1**, 349; *Consort,* **Vol. 3, Part 2**, 149; **Vol. 6, Part 1**, 553; **Vol. 8, Part 2**, 579; *Constellation,* **Vol. 1, Part 2**, 104, 241, 342; **Vol. 2, Part 1**, 206; **Vol. 3, Part 1**, 65, 380; **Vol. 3, Part 2**, 85; **Vol. 4, Part 2**, 539; **Vol. 5, Part 1**, 377; **Vol. 6, Part 1**, 315, 572; **Vol. 6, Part 2**, 20; **Vol. 7, Part 2**, 301, 320, 490, 625; **Vol. 8, Part 1**, 83, 85, 319, 424; **Vol. 8, Part 2**, 74, 76, 77, 234, 579; **Vol. 9, Part 1**, 136, 156, 310, 584, 626; **Vol. 9, Part 2**, 7, 307, 310, 364, 394; **Vol. 10, Part 1**, 22; **Vol. 10, Part 2**, 518; *Constitution,* **Vol. 1, Part 1**, 146, 452, 506, 507, 606, 650; **Vol. 1, Part 2**, 241; **Vol. 2, Part**

1, 206, 337; **Vol. 2, Part 2**, 40, 123; **Vol. 3, Part 1**, 188, 415, 530; **Vol. 3, Part 2**, 174; **Vol. 4, Part 1**, 523; **Vol. 5, Part 1**, 360, 361, 364, 376; **Vol. 5, Part 2**, 164, 170; **Vol. 6, Part 1**, 50, 315, 500, 573; **Vol. 6, Part 2**, 195; **Vol. 7, Part 1**, 98, 172, 202, 506, 507; **Vol. 7, Part 2**, 302, 461, 531; **Vol. 8, Part 1**, 182, 319, 424, 596; **Vol. 8, Part 2**, 72, 74, 246; **Vol. 9, Part 1**, 135, 136, 321, 553; **Vol. 9, Part 2**, 7, 122, 280, 306; **Vol. 10, Part 1**, 59, 60, 228, 425; **Vol. 10, Part 2**, 517; *Contoocook,* **Vol. 1, Part 1**, 529; *Convention,* **Vol. 4, Part 2**, 476; **Vol. 7, Part 2**, 28; *Coquette,* **Vol. 10, Part 2**, 466; *Corwin,* **Vol. 7, Part 2**, 532; **Vol. 10, Part 2**, 228; *Craven,* **Vol. 2, Part 2**, 519; *Cricket,* **Vol. 4, Part 1**, 437; *Crusader,* **Vol. 2, Part 2**, 518; **Vol. 6, Part 2**, 196; **Vol. 8, Part 1**, 529; *Culgoa,* **Vol. 8, Part 1**, 18; *Cumberland,* **Vol. 1, Part 1**, 606; **Vol. 2, Part 1**, 207; **Vol. 3, Part 1**, 30; **Vol. 3, Part 2**, 499, 531; **Vol. 5, Part 2**, 164; **Vol. 6, Part 1**, 315; **Vol. 7, Part 1**, 152, 203; **Vol. 7, Part 2**, 314; **Vol. 8, Part 1**, 68, 299, 319; **Vol. 8, Part 2**, 72, 568, 579; **Vol. 9, Part 1**, 310, 487; **Vol. 9, Part 2**, 139, 638; **Vol. 10, Part 1**, 128, 425; **Vol. 10, Part 2**, 1, 465, 425; *Cushing,* **Vol. 10, Part 2**, 392; *Cuyler,* **Vol. 8, Part 2**, 437; *Cyane,* **Vol. 1, Part 1**, 502, 528; **Vol. 2, Part 1**, 70; **Vol. 3, Part 1**, 530, 584; **Vol. 3, Part 2**, 85, 97; **Vol. 5, Part 1**, 152, 362; **Vol. 6, Part 2**, 465, 576; **Vol. 7, Part 2**, 461, 470, 486; **Vol. 8, Part 1**, 214; **Vol. 8, Part 2**, 196, 244; **Vol. 9, Part 2**, 139; *Docatah,* **Vol. 3, Part 1**, 584; **Vol. 6, Part 2**, 479; **Vol. 8, Part 1**, 319; **Vol. 8, Part 2**, 341; **Vol. 9, Part 2**, 42, 457; *Dale,* **Vol. 2, Part 1**, 543; **Vol. 2, Part 2**, 518; **Vol. 3, Part 1**, 380; **Vol. 6, Part 2**, 82; **Vol. 9, Part 1**, 156; **Vol. 10, Part 1**, 23; *Dauntless,* **Vol. 4, Part 1**, 74; *Deane,* **Vol. 4, Part 2**, 154; **Vol. 7, Part 1**, 506; **Vol. 10, Part 1**, 40; *Decatur,* **Vol. 2, Part 1**, 257; **Vol. 2, Part 2**, 308, 569; **Vol. 3, Part 2**, 287; **Vol. 5, Part 2**, 221; **Vol. 7, Part 2**, 444, 531; **Vol. 9, Part 2**, 394, 457; *Defence,* **Vol. 4, Part 2**, 251; **Vol. 7, Part 1**, 502; **Vol. 10, Part 2**, 524; *De Kalb,* **Vol. 8, Part 1**, 339; *Delaware,* **Vol. 1, Part 2**, 408; **Vol. 2, Part 1**, 70, 206, 257; **Vol. 3, Part 1**, 186; **Vol. 3, Part 2**, 287; **Vol. 5, Part 2**, 170, 615; **Vol. 6, Part 1**, 129, 315, 572; **Vol. 7, Part 2**, 301, 461; **Vol. 8, Part 1**, 67, 293; **Vol. 8, Part 2**, 196; *Denver,* **Vol. 7, Part 1**, 343; **Vol. 8, Part 2**, 22; **Vol. 10, Part 2**, 653; *De Soto,* **Vol. 1, Part 2**, 409; **Vol. 5, Part 1**, 303; **Vol. 8, Part 1**, 495; *Despatch,* **Vol. 4, Part 1**, 574; **Vol. 5, Part 2**, 250; *Destroyer,* **Vol. 3, Part 2**, 174, 175; *Dewey,* **Vol. 3, Part 2**, 158; *Dictator,* **Vol. 8, Part 1**, 314; **Vol. 8, Part 2**, 78; **Vol. 9, Part 2**, 518; *Dixie,* **Vol. 2, Part 2**, 123; **Vol. 3, Part 1**, 108; **Vol. 8, Part 2**, 554; *Dixie,* **Vol. 8, Part 1**, 237; *Dolphin,* **Vol. 3, Part 1**, 414; **Vol. 7, Part 1**, 506; **Vol. 10, Part 2**, 180; *Dolphin,* **Vol. 3, Part 1**, 106; **Vol. 4, Part 1**, 265; **Vol. 5, Part 2**, 615; **Vol. 6, Part 1**, 129, 315; **Vol. 6, Part 2**, 91, 196; **Vol. 7, Part 1**, 320; **Vol. 7, Part 2**, 140, 320, 461; **Vol. 8, Part 2**, 77; **Vol. 9, Part 1**, 553; **Vol. 10, Part 1**, 22, 23; *Dolphin,* **Vol. 7, Part 1**, 342; **Vol. 8, Part 1**, 640; **Vol. 9, Part 1**, 387; **Vol. 10, Part 2**, 206; *Draper,* **Vol. 2, Part 2**, 46; *Drayton,* **Vol. 3, Part 1**, 446; *Du Pont,* **Vol. 5, Part 2**, 380; *Dyer,* **Vol. 3, Part 1**, 585; *Eagle,* **Vol. 4, Part 2**, 539; **Vol. 9, Part 1**, 309; *Effingham,* **Vol. 1, Part 1**, 654; **Vol. 8, Part 1**, 82, 430; *Electra,* **Vol. 7, Part 2**, 314; **Vol. 8, Part 2**, 580; *Ellis,* **Vol. 2, Part 2**, 635; *Enrica,* **Vol. 8, Part 2**, 581; *Enterprise (or Enterprize),* **Vol. 1, Part 1**, 600; **Vol. 1, Part 2**, 348, 408; **Vol. 2, Part 1**, 337; **Vol. 3, Part 1**, 187; **Vol. 3, Part 2**, 85, 170; **Vol. 5, Part 1**, 361; **Vol. 5, Part 2**, 110, 270, 541; **Vol. 6, Part 1**, 49, 561, 564; **Vol. 6, Part 2**, 20; **Vol. 8, Part 1**, 83, 183; **Vol. 9, Part 1**, 41, 584; **Vol. 9, Part 2**, 645; **Vol. 10, Part 1**, 492; *Epervier,* **Vol. 3, Part 1**, 416; **Vol. 9, Part 1**, 136; **Vol. 9, Part 2**, 310;

203; Vol. 7, Part 2, 139, 275; Vol. 8, Part 1, 67, 319, 529; Vol. 8, Part 2, 74; Vol. 9, Part 1, 41, 625; Vol. 9, Part 2, 307; Vol. 10, Part 1, 292, 317; Vol. 10, Part 2, 584; *John Hancock,* Vol. 4, Part 2, 68; Vol. 8, Part 2, 77; *John Rice,* Vol. 8, Part 2, 325; *J. P. Kennedy,* Vol. 4, Part 2, 68; *Judah,* Vol. 6, Part 2, 576; *Juniata,* Vol. 2, Part 1, 586; Vol. 2, Part 2, 637; Vol. 3, Part 1, 64; 228, 269; Vol. 4, Part 1, 574; Vol. 6, Part 2, 149, 422; Vol. 7, Part 2, 532; Vol. 9, Part 2, 348; Vol. 10, Part 1, 135; *Kanawha,* Vol. 6, Part 2, 465; *Kansas,* Vol. 1, Part 1, 240; *Katahdin,* Vol. 1, Part 1, 259; Vol. 3, Part 2, 170; Vol. 8, Part 1, 183, 314; Vol. 8, Part 2, 85, 605; Vol. 10, Part 2, 206; *Katy,* Vol. 10, Part 2, 66; *Kearsarge,* Vol. 4, Part 1, 610; Vol. 5, Part 1, 311; Vol. 5, Part 2, 249, 462; Vol. 7, Part 1, 438; Vol. 8, Part 1, 167; Vol. 8, Part 2, 581; Vol. 10, Part 2, 392, 398; *Kennebec,* Vol. 6, Part 1, 568; Vol. 8, Part 2, 244; *Kentucky,* Vol. 2, Part 1, 468; Vol. 9, Part 2, 42; *Keokuk,* Vol. 8, Part 1, 529; *Keystone State,* Vol. 2, Part 2, 569; Vol. 5, Part 1, 477; Vol. 9, Part 2, 638; *Kineo,* Vol. 8, Part 1, 314; *Lackawanna,* Vol. 3, Part 2, 150; Vol. 4, Part 1, 595; Vol. 6, Part 1, 568, 574; Vol. 6, Part 2, 271; *Lafayette,* Vol. 10, Part 1, 337; *Lake Michigan,* Vol. 8, Part 1, 464; *Lancaster,* Vol. 2, Part 2, 637; Vol. 4, Part 1, 232; Vol. 5, Part 2, 462, 607; Vol. 6, Part 2, 521; Vol. 7, Part 1, 98, 504; Vol. 8, Part 1, 339, 597; Vol. 9, Part 2, 8; *Lawrence,* Vol. 3, Part 2, 96; Vol. 7, Part 2, 275, 308, 490, 491; Vol. 8, Part 1, 154, 596; *Layona,* Vol. 2, Part 2, 369; *Lee,* Vol. 6, Part 2, 236; *Lehigh,* Vol. 9, Part 2, 614; *Levant,* Vol. 2, Part 2, 326; Vol. 7, Part 1, 503; *Lexington,* Vol. 1, Part 1, 654; Vol. 3, Part 1, 33, 414; Vol. 10, Part 2, 180; *Lexington,* Vol. 1, Part 1, 502; Vol. 3, Part 1, 200; Vol. 5, Part 2, 221; Vol. 7, Part 2, 48, 492; Vol. 8, Part 1, 67, 319; Vol. 8, Part 2, 74, 579; Vol. 9, Part 1, 136; Vol. 9, Part 2, 122, 148; Vol. 10, Part 1, 337; *L'Indien,* Vol. 4, Part 1, 296; Vol. 5, Part 2, 184; *Little David,* Vol. 8, Part 1, 397; *Louisiana,* Vol. 3, Part 1, 614; Vol. 5, Part 2, 14; Vol. 7, Part 2, 302; Vol. 8, Part 1, 529; Vol. 10, Part 1, 319; *Louisiana,* Vol. 5, Part 1, 152; Vol. 10, Part 2, 228; *Louisville,* Vol. 6, Part 2, 479; *Loyall,* Vol. 7, Part 2, 185; *Macedonian,* Vol. 1, Part 1, 14, 212; Vol. 1, Part 2, 241; Vol. 2, Part 1, 14; Vol. 3, Part 1, 29 203, 416; Vol. 4, Part 1, 334; Vol. 5, Part 1, 303; Vol. 5, Part 2, 164, 170, 176, 607; Vol. 6, Part 1, 337; Vol. 6, Part 2, 91, 195, 207; Vol. 7, Part 2, 185, 320; Vol. 8, Part 1, 183, 299; Vol. 8, Part 2, 73; Vol. 9, Part 1, 215; Vol. 9, Part 2, 42, 310; Vol. 10, Part 1, 217, 339, 492; *Machias,* Vol. 3, Part 2, 170; Vol. 4, Part 1, 485; Vol. 8, Part 2, 605; *Machias Liberty,* Vol. 7, Part 1, 610; *Mackinaw,* Vol. 1, Part 2, 104; Vol. 6, Part 2, 646; *McRae,* Vol. 7, Part 1, 172; Vol. 8, Part 1, 420; *Madawaska,* Vol. 3, Part 2, 175; *Madison,* Vol. 2, Part 2, 510; Vol. 3, Part 2, 4; Vol. 5, Part 1, 477; Vol. 7, Part 1, 97; *Mahaska,* Vol. 7, Part 2, 220; Vol. 8, Part 1, 314; *Mahopac,* Vol. 10, Part 1, 568; *Maine,* Vol. 2, Part 1, 255, 468, 586; Vol. 2, Part 2, 500; Vol. 3, Part 1, 269; Vol. 4, Part 2, 41; Vol. 6, Part 2, 422; Vol. 8, Part 1, 3, 315; Vol. 8, Part 2, 241, 322, 512; Vol. 9, Part 1, 156; Vol. 10, Part 1, 135, 319; *Malvern,* Vol. 2, Part 2, 636; Vol. 8, Part 1, 88; *Manassas,* Vol. 3, Part 1, 136, 269; Vol. 3, Part 2, 288; Vol. 9, Part 1, 321; *Manhattan,* Vol. 7, Part 1, 504; *Maratanza,* Vol. 6, Part 1, 568; Vol. 9, Part 1, 626; *Marblehead,* Vol. 2, Part 1, 586; Vol. 6, Part 1, 564; Vol. 6, Part 2, 479; Vol. 8, Part 1, 495; *Marietta,* Vol. 5, Part 1, 318; Vol. 8, Part 1, 316; *Marion,* Vol. 3, Part 1, 584; Vol. 4, Part 1, 610; Vol. 7, Part 2, 444, 534, 606; Vol. 8, Part 1, 299; Vol. 10, Part 1, 568; *Mary Summers,* Vol. 5, Part 2, 549; *Maryland,*

Vol. 8, Part 2, 76; *Maryland,* Vol. 2, Part 1, 468; Vol. 5, Part 1, 472; Vol. 8, Part 1, 317; *Massachusetts,* Vol. 3, Part 2, 420; Vol. 4, Part 2, 234; Vol. 10, Part 2, 276; *Massachusetts,* Vol. 6, Part 2, 478; Vol. 9, Part 1, 321; *Massachusetts,* Vol. 2, Part 2, 123, 500; Vol. 3, Part 1, 269; Vol. 4, Part 1, 485; Vol. 8, Part 1, 167; Vol. 8, Part 2, 465; *Maumee,* Vol. 2, Part 2, 637; Vol. 9, Part 2, 518; *Mayflower,* Vol. 1, Part 1, 240; *Melville,* Vol. 8, Part 1, 237; *Memphis,* Vol. 6, Part 2, 271; *Mercedita,* Vol. 5, Part 1, 477; *Merrimac,* Vol. 2, Part 1, 70, 207; Vol. 3, Part 1, 532; Vol. 3, Part 2, 173, 532; Vol. 4, Part 1, 366, 574; Vol. 5, Part 1, 343; Vol. 5, Part 2, 14, 164, 278; Vol. 6, Part 1, 173, 315; Vol. 7, Part 1, 152; Vol. 7, Part 2, 243; Vol. 8, Part 1, 68, 97, 319, 339; Vol. 8, Part 2, 568; Vol. 9, Part 1, 310; Vol. 10, Part 2, 217, 400, 465, 531, 658; *Merrimac,* Vol. 6, Part 2, 225; Vol. 8, Part 1, 97; Vol. 9, Part 2, 311; Vol. 10, Part 1, 630; *Merrimack,* Vol. 10, Part 1, 318; *Metacomet,* Vol. 2, Part 2, 569; Vol. 3, Part 1, 584; Vol. 5, Part 2, 221; *Miami,* Vol. 4, Part 2, 71; Vol. 9, Part 2, 620; *Miantonomah,* Vol. 1, Part 2, 104; Vol. 3, Part 2, 569; Vol. 6, Part 2, 422; Vol. 8, Part 1, 640; Vol. 9, Part 1, 139, 149; *Michigan,* Vol. 2, Part 1, 543, 609; Vol. 3, Part 2, 170; Vol. 4, Part 1, 610; Vol. 5, Part 2, 607; Vol. 6, Part 2, 480; Vol. 7, Part 2, 220; Vol. 8, Part 1, 299; Vol. 9, Part 1, 626; Vol. 9, Part 2, 8, 457; *Michigan,* Vol. 2, Part 2, 423; Vol. 4, Part 2, 391; Vol. 5, Part 1, 515, 516; Vol. 7, Part 1, 481; Vol. 10, Part 1, 135; *Mingoe,* Vol. 8, Part 1, 293; *Minneapolis,* Vol. 1, Part 1, 495; Vol. 6, Part 2, 522; Vol. 7, Part 1, 343; *Minnesota,* Vol. 1, Part 1, 240; Vol. 2, Part 2, 635; Vol. 3, Part 1, 531; Vol. 5, Part 2, 170, 607; Vol. 6, Part 1, 173; Vol. 6, Part 2, 149, 465; Vol. 10, Part 1, 128, 318; Vol. 10, Part 2, 1; *Minnesota,* Vol. 4, Part 1, 485, 574; Vol. 8, Part 1, 512; *Mississippi,* Vol. 1, Part 1, 488; Vol. 1, Part 1, 600; Vol. 1, Part 2, 206; Vol. 2, Part 1, 14, 206; Vol. 2, Part 2, 423; Vol. 3, Part 1, 200; Vol. 3, Part 1, 269; Vol. 4, Part 2, 391; Vol. 6, Part 2, 21, 91, 557; Vol. 7, Part 2, 186, 314; Vol. 7, Part 2, 487; Vol. 9, Part 1, 321; Vol. 9, Part 2, 620; Vol. 10, Part 2, 645; *Mississippi,* Vol. 6, Part 2, 225; Vol. 8, Part 1, 97; *Missouri,* Vol. 2, Part 2, 423; Vol. 3, Part 2, 255; Vol. 4, Part 2, 391; Vol. 6, Part 2, 91; Vol. 7, Part 1, 320; Vol. 8, Part 1, 214; Vol. 10, Part 2, 397; *Missouri,* Vol. 2, Part 1, 468; Vol. 8, Part 1, 18, 317; *Mohawk,* Vol. 2, Part 2, 518; Vol. 5, Part 2, 176; Vol. 8, Part 2, 73; Vol. 9, Part 2, 149; *Mohican,* Vol. 1, Part 1, 258; Vol. 4, Part 1, 232; Vol. 5, Part 2, 324; Vol. 7, Part 2, 308; Vol. 9, Part 1, 178; Vol. 9, Part 2, 42; *Mohongo,* Vol. 3, Part 2, 170; Vol. 7, Part 1, 504; Vol. 9, Part 1, 178; *Monadnock,* Vol. 4, Part 2, 266; Vol. 7, Part 2, 260; Vol. 9, Part 2, 613, 614; *Monitor,* Vol. 2, Part 1, 207; Vol. 3, Part 1, 532; Vol. 3, Part 2, 170, 173, 174, 175, 176, 568; Vol. 4, Part 1, 366, 574; Vol. 5, Part 2, 14, 164, 278; Vol. 7, Part 2, 243, 321; Vol. 8, Part 1, 68, 314; Vol. 8, Part 2, 200; Vol. 9, Part 1, 310, 626; Vol. 9, Part 2, 311, 614, 638; Vol. 10, Part 1, 630; Vol. 10, Part 2, 400, 466, 531; *Monocacy,* Vol. 2, Part 1, 544; Vol. 5, Part 2, 324; Vol. 6, Part 2, 129; *Monongahela,* Vol. 1, Part 1, 600; Vol. 3, Part 1, 269; Vol. 4, Part 1, 574, 610; Vol. 4, Part 2, 3; Vol. 5, Part 2, 50; Vol. 6, Part 1, 568; Vol. 8, Part 2, 437; Vol. 9, Part 1, 156, 321; Vol. 9, Part 2, 149; *Montauk,* Vol. 1, Part 1, 488; Vol. 3, Part 1, 136; Vol. 3, Part 2, 255; Vol. 7, Part 2, 534; Vol. 8, Part 2, 200; Vol. 10, Part 2, 531; *Monterey,* Vol. 5, Part 2, 324; *Montezuma,* Vol. 1, Part 1, 504; Vol. 7, Part 1, 358; Vol. 9, Part 1, 41; *Montgomery,* Vol. 5, Part 1, 303; Vol. 5, Part 2, 221; Vol. 8, Part 1, 430; *Monticello,* Vol. 2, Part 2, 636; *Morris,* Vol. 10, Part

2, 397; *Mount Vernon*, **Vol. 8, Part 2**, 22; *Mullany*, **Vol. 7, Part 1**, 320; *Muscoota*, **Vol. 8, Part 2**, 200; *Muscota*, **Vol. 7, Part 2**, 314; *M. W. Chapin*, **Vol. 5, Part 2**, 221; *Nahant*, **Vol. 3, Part 1**, 532; **Vol. 6, Part 2**, 465; *Nancy*, **Vol. 7, Part 2**, 631; *Nanshan*, **Vol. 9, Part 2**, 8; *Nantucket*, **Vol. 1, Part 2**, 104; **Vol. 3, Part 2**, 255; *Narragansett*, **Vol. 3, Part 1**, 269; **Vol. 6, Part 2**, 479; **Vol. 8, Part 1**, 183; *Nashville*, **Vol. 6, Part 2**, 271; **Vol. 10, Part 2**, 531; *Nashville*, **Vol. 10, Part 2**, 392; *Natchez*, **Vol. 3, Part 1**, 300; **Vol. 3, Part 2**, 287; **Vol. 4, Part 1**, 19; **Vol. 6, Part 2**, 21, 82, 576; **Vol. 7, Part 2**, 444; **Vol. 8, Part 1**, 596; **Vol. 9, Part 1**, 136; **Vol. 10, Part 1**, 336; *Nausett*, **Vol. 6, Part 2**, 73; *Nautilus*, brig of 1812, **Vol. 2, Part 2**, 510; *Nautilus*, schooner of 1802, **Vol. 8, Part 1**, 182, 596; **Vol. 9, Part 1**, 394; *Nebraska*, **Vol. 8, Part 1**, 237; *Neptune*, **Vol. 10, Part 1**, 318; *Newark*, **Vol. 1, Part 1**, 600; **Vol. 2, Part 2**, 123; **Vol. 6, Part 1**, 564; **Vol. 7, Part 1**, 438; **Vol. 10, Part 1**, 319; *New Hampshire*, **Vol. 8, Part 1**, 293, 523; **Vol. 10, Part 2**, 393; *New Ironsides*, **Vol. 1, Part 2**, 146; **Vol. 2, Part 2**, 501; **Vol. 3, Part 1**, 532; **Vol. 6, Part 2**, 557; **Vol. 7, Part 2**, 321; **Vol. 8, Part 1**, 319; **Vol. 8, Part 2**, 73, 196; *New Jersey*, **Vol. 5, Part 2**, 380; *New Mexico*, **Vol. 8, Part 2**, 22; *New Orleans*, **Vol. 5, Part 1**, 471; *New York*, **Vol. 3, Part 1**, 187; *New York*, **Vol. 2, Part 1**, 586; **Vol. 2, Part 2**, 40, 500; **Vol. 3, Part 2**, 210; **Vol. 6, Part 2**, 480; **Vol. 7, Part 1**, 343; **Vol. 7, Part 2**, 535; **Vol. 8, Part 2**, 323, 438; **Vol. 10, Part 2**, 393; *Niagara*, **Vol. 3, Part 2**, 96 97; **Vol. 7, Part 1**, 97, 98; **Vol. 7, Part 2**, 490, 491; **Vol. 8, Part 1**, 154; **Vol. 9, Part 1**, 625; **Vol. 10, Part 1**, 59; *Niagara*, **Vol. 1, Part 1**, 600; **Vol. 2, Part 2**, 518; **Vol. 6, Part 1**, 173, 574; **Vol. 7, Part 1**, 426; **Vol. 7, Part 2**, 140, 185; **Vol. 8, Part 2**, 437; *Niagara* (cable-laying ship of 1850), **Vol. 9, Part 1**, 560; *Niagara* (finest ship in the Navy in 1860), **Vol. 6, Part 2**, 82; *Nicholson*, **Vol. 7, Part 1**, 507; *Niphon*, **Vol. 2, Part 2**, 636; *Nipsic*, **Vol. 3, Part 2**, 170; *Nonsuch*, **Vol. 5, Part 2**, 270; **Vol. 10, Part 1**, 60; *Norfolk*, **Vol. 1, Part 1**, 504, 505; **Vol. 3, Part 1**, 187; *North Carolina*, **Vol. 1, Part 2**, 395, 408; **Vol. 3, Part 1**, 530; **Vol. 6, Part 2**, 478; **Vol. 7, Part 2**, 487; **Vol. 8, Part 2**, 77, 196, 427; **Vol. 10, Part 1**, 292; *North Carolina*, **Vol. 8, Part 1**, 97; *North Dakota*, **Vol. 8, Part 1**, 18; *Ocean Queen*, **Vol. 1, Part 1**, 258; *Octorara*, **Vol. 2, Part 2**, 308; *Ohio*, **Vol. 1, Part 1**, 226; **Vol. 1, Part 2**, 104; **Vol. 2, Part 1**, 543; **Vol. 3, Part 1**, 530; **Vol. 3, Part 2**, 4, 149; **Vol. 4, Part 1**, 232, 366; **Vol. 5, Part 1**, 362; **Vol. 5, Part 2**, 164; **Vol. 6, Part 2**, 21, 271, 479; **Vol. 8, Part 1**, 299; **Vol. 9, Part 1**, 310; **Vol. 9, Part 2**, 48, 122, 139, 394, 620; **Vol. 10, Part 2**, 465; *Ohio*, **Vol. 8, Part 2**, 427; *Ohio*, **Vol. 2, Part 1**, 468; **Vol. 8, Part 2**, 492; *Old Ironsides*, **Vol. 8, Part 1**, 397, 515; **Vol. 10, Part 2**, 658; *Oliver Cromwell*, **Vol. 4, Part 2**, 251; *Olympia*, **Vol. 3, Part 1**, 270, 271, 292; **Vol. 3, Part 2**, 170; **Vol. 4, Part 1**, 610; **Vol. 5, Part 2**, 559; **Vol. 8, Part 2**, 129; **Vol. 8, Part 2**, 492; **Vol. 10, Part 1**, 339; *Omaha*, **Vol. 6, Part 2**, 149, 465; **Vol. 9, Part 1**, 178; *Oneida*, **Vol. 4, Part 1**, 610; **Vol. 5, Part 2**, 50; **Vol. 6, Part 1**, 129; **Vol. 7, Part 1**, 320; *Oneida*, **Vol. 8, Part 1**, 183; **Vol. 9, Part 1**, 149; **Vol. 9, Part 1**, 626; **Vol. 10, Part 2**, 518; *Onondaga*, **Vol. 8, Part 1**, 314, 315; **Vol. 8, Part 2**, 200; **Vol. 9, Part 1**, 321; *Ontario*, **Vol. 1, Part 2**, 241; **Vol. 2, Part 2**, 46, 349; **Vol. 3, Part 1**, 29, 106, 530; **Vol. 3, Part 2**, 97; **Vol. 6, Part 1**, 315, 561; **Vol. 7, Part 1**, 98; **Vol. 8, Part 1**, 319, 596; **Vol. 9, Part 1**, 626; **Vol. 10, Part 1**, 336; *Oregon*, **Vol. 5, Part 2**, 164; **Vol. 6, Part 1**, 553; *Oregon*, **Vol. 5, Part 1**, 318; **Vol. 6, Part 1**, 545; **Vol. 8, Part 1**, 316; **Vol. 8, Part 2**, 492; **Vol. 9, Part 1**, 218; **Vol. 10, Part 2**, 206; *Oregon*, **Vol. 1, Part 1**, 601; **Vol. 2, Part 2**, 123; **Vol. 3, Part 1**, 292, 614; **Vol. 4, Part 1**, 485;

Vol. 6, Part 2, 646; *Oreto (Florida)*, **Vol. 2, Part 1**, 258; **Vol. 8, Part 1**, 183; *Osage*, **Vol. 8, Part 2**, 569; *Ossifee*, **Vol. 2, Part 2**, 123; **Vol. 3, Part 1**, 584; **Vol. 3, Part 2**, 150; **Vol. 5, Part 1**, 303; **Vol. 8, Part 1**, 339; *Ottawa*, **Vol. 9, Part 1**, 626; *Owasco*, **Vol. 9, Part 2**, 149; *Ozark*, **Vol. 2, Part 1**, 468; *Pallas*, **Vol. 5, Part 2**, 185; *Palmetto State*, **Vol. 5, Part 1**, 477; **Vol. 7, Part 2**, 243; **Vol. 8, Part 1**, 97; **Vol. 9, Part 2**, 348; *Palos*, **Vol. 5, Part 2**, 462; *Pampero*, **Vol. 5, Part 2**, 593; *Pandora*, **Vol. 3, Part 1**, 228; *Panther*, **Vol. 1, Part 2**, 567; **Vol. 7, Part 1**, 343; *Passaic*, **Vol. 3, Part 1**, 446; **Vol. 8, Part 2**, 200; **Vol. 9, Part 1**, 178; **Vol. 10, Part 2**, 347; *Patapsco*, **Vol. 1, Part 1**, 258, 488; **Vol. 8, Part 1**, 293; **Vol. 8, Part 2**, 322; **Vol. 9, Part 1**, 626; *Patrick Henry*, **Vol. 7, Part 1**, 172; **Vol. 7, Part 2**, 243; **Vol. 10, Part 1**, 34; *Paul Jones*, **Vol. 8, Part 1**, 529; **Vol. 9, Part 1**, 554; *Pawnee*, **Vol. 1, Part 1**, 528; **Vol. 4, Part 1**, 626; **Vol. 5, Part 2**, 164; **Vol. 7, Part 2**, 534; **Vol. 8, Part 1**, 420; **Vol. 8, Part 2**, 196; **Vol. 10, Part 2**, 585; *Peacock*, **Vol. 1, Part 2**, 241; **Vol. 3, Part 1**, 200, 380; **Vol. 3, Part 2**, 149; **Vol. 5, Part 1**, 152; **Vol. 5, Part 2**, 201; **Vol. 6, Part 2**, 270; **Vol. 7, Part 1**, 98; **Vol. 7, Part 2**, 185, 461, 625; **Vol. 8, Part 2**, 5, 73; **Vol. 9, Part 2**, 348; **Vol. 10, Part 1**, 292, 492; *Pembina*, **Vol. 9, Part 2**, 7, 364; *Penguin*, **Vol. 6, Part 1**, 315; *Pennsylvania*, **Vol. 2, Part 1**, 468; **Vol. 2, Part 2**, 500; **Vol. 6, Part 1**, 545; **Vol. 8, Part 1**, 522; *Pensacola*, **Vol. 2, Part 1**, 14; **Vol. 3, Part 1**, 269; **Vol. 4, Part 1**, 232; **Vol. 6, Part 2**, 149; **Vol. 8, Part 1**, 97; **Vol. 8, Part 2**, 85, 464; **Vol. 9, Part 2**, 394; **Vol. 10, Part 1**, 128; *Pequot*, **Vol. 8, Part 1**, 293; *Perkins*, **Vol. 8, Part 1**, 237; *Perry*, **Vol. 3, Part 1**, 530; **Vol. 3, Part 2**, 500; **Vol. 5, Part 2**, 164; **Vol. 7, Part 2**, 139, 260, 314; **Vol. 8, Part 1**, 293, 299; **Vol. 9, Part 1**, 487; *Petrel*, **Vol. 2, Part 2**, 569; **Vol. 3, Part 1**, 270, 271; **Vol. 5, Part 2**, 559; **Vol. 8, Part 1**, 17, 86, 183; *Philadelphia*, **Vol. 1, Part 1**, 506; **Vol. 1, Part 2**, 241; **Vol. 3, Part 1**, 186, 187; **Vol. 5, Part 1**, 176; **Vol. 6, Part 1**, 49, 77; **Vol. 6, Part 2**, 20, 113; **Vol. 7, Part 1**, 152, 202; **Vol. 7, Part 2**, 301; **Vol. 8, Part 1**, 84, 182; **Vol. 9, Part 2**, 7; *Philadelphia*, **Vol. 5, Part 2**, 14; **Vol. 7, Part 2**, 314, 531; *Philadelphia*, **Vol. 1, Part 1**, 600; **Vol. 5, Part 1**, 471; **Vol. 8, Part 2**, 554; *Phoenix*, **Vol. 8, Part 2**, 72; *Pickering*, **Vol. 5, Part 1**, 479; **Vol. 8, Part 1**, 182; *Pinola*, **Vol. 2, Part 1**, 406; **Vol. 2, Part 2**, 569; *Pioneer*, **Vol. 8, Part 1**, 596; **Vol. 9, Part 2**, 310; *Pittsburg*, **Vol. 3, Part 2**, 500; **Vol. 9, Part 2**, 457; **Vol. 10, Part 1**, 337, 633; *Planter*, **Vol. 1, Part 2**, 224, 225; *Plunger*, **Vol. 5, Part 1**, 145; *Plymouth*, **Vol. 1, Part 1**, 528; **Vol. 2, Part 1**, 14; **Vol. 3, Part 1**, 30, 64; **Vol. 5, Part 2**, 164; **Vol. 9, Part 2**, 42; *Pocahontas*, **Vol. 1, Part 1**, 528; **Vol. 3, Part 1**, 445; **Vol. 6, Part 2**, 207; **Vol. 7, Part 1**, 504; **Vol. 10, Part 2**, 585; *Poinsett*, **Vol. 8, Part 2**, 579; *Polaris*, **Vol. 3, Part 1**, 228; **Vol. 4, Part 1**, 595; **Vol. 6, Part 2**, 521; *Polk*, **Vol. 7, Part 2**, 531; *Pontiac*, **Vol. 8, Part 2**, 244; *Pontoosuc*, **Vol. 9, Part 2**, 364, 518; *Porcupine*, **Vol. 2, Part 1**, 609; **Vol. 9, Part 1**, 625; *Porpoise*, **Vol. 1, Part 2**, 146; **Vol. 1, Part 2**, 408; **Vol. 2, Part 2**, 517; **Vol. 5, Part 2**, 615; **Vol. 6, Part 2**, 270; **Vol. 7, Part 2**, 308, 461, 625; **Vol. 8, Part 1**, 617; **Vol. 8, Part 2**, 85, 341, 579; **Vol. 9, Part 2**, 620; **Vol. 10, Part 1**, 317; **Vol. 10, Part 2**, 217; *Port Royal*, **Vol. 4, Part 1**, 232; *Portsmouth*, **Vol. 2, Part 1**, 337; **Vol. 6, Part 2**, 149; *Portsmouth*, **Vol. 1, Part 1**, 606; **Vol. 1, Part 2**, 146; **Vol. 2, Part 1**, 14; **Vol. 3, Part 1**, 380; **Vol. 3, Part 2**, 500; **Vol. 4, Part 1**, 21, 437; **Vol. 4, Part 1**, 610; **Vol. 5, Part 2**, 324; **Vol. 7, Part 1**, 98; **Vol. 7, Part 2**, 314; **Vol. 8, Part 1**, 514; **Vol. 9, Part 1**, 178; **Vol. 10, Part 2**, 228; *Potomac*, **Vol. 2, Part 1**, 543; **Vol. 3, Part 1**, 416; **Vol. 3, Part 2**, 157; **Vol. 6, Part 2**, 270, 478; **Vol. 7, Part 2**, 243, 338, 444; **Vol. 8, Part 1**,

7, Part 1, 610; *Tracy,* **Vol. 5, Part 1,** 212; *Tyger,* **Vol. 6, Part 2,** 21; *Tyrannicide,* **Vol. 9, Part 2,** 498; *Ulysses,* **Vol. 6, Part 2,** 149; *Virginia,* **Vol. 7, Part 2,** 29; *Volant,* **Vol. 6, Part 2,** 296; *Warren,* **Vol. 9, Part 2,** 498; *Wasp,* **Vol. 6, Part 2,** 149; *Weir,* **Vol. 7, Part 2,** 28; *Wilkes,* **Vol. 10, Part 2,** 276; *Yankee,* **Vol. 3, Part 1,** 275, 414; **Vol. 7, Part 2,** 461

Prizes, taken as: *Active,* **Vol. 7, Part 2,** 28; **Vol. 10, Part 2,** 276; *Alert,* **Vol. 8, Part 1,** 84; *Alexander Barclay,* **Vol. 3, Part 2,** 286; *Annabella,* **Vol. 10, Part 1,** 536; *Atalanta,* **Vol. 1, Part 1,** 654; **Vol. 1, Part 2,** 348; *Atlantic,* **Vol. 3, Part 1,** 416; *Avon,* **Vol. 1, Part 2,** 348; *Baille,* **Vol. 6, Part 2,** 236; *Birceau,* **Vol. 6, Part 1,** 299; *Caledonia,* **Vol. 9, Part 2,** 96; *Charleston,* **Vol. 10, Part 1,** 40; *Confiance,* **Vol. 6, Part 2,** 20; *Countess of Scarborough,* **Vol. 5, Part 2,** 185; *Cristobal Colon,* **Vol. 8, Part 2,** 438; *Cyane,* **Vol. 9, Part 2,** 7; *Detroit,* **Vol. 2, Part 1,** 609; **Vol. 3, Part 2,** 96; *Deux Amis,* **Vol. 8, Part 1,** 83; *Deux Anges,* **Vol. 6, Part 1,** 299; *Diligent,* **Vol. 7, Part 1,** 610; *Drake,* **Vol. 5, Part 2,** 184; *Eagle,* **Vol. 7, Part 2,** 461; *Edward,* **Vol. 1, Part 1,** 654; *Elizabeth,* **Vol. 10, Part 1,** 536; *Epervier,* **Vol. 7, Part 2,** 461; **Vol. 10, Part 1,** 292, 492; *Fly,* **Vol. 1, Part 2,** 348; *Flying Fish,* **Vol. 6, Part 1,** 299; *Fox,* **Vol. 6, Part 2,** 151; *Frolic,* **Vol. 1, Part 2,** 241; **Vol. 8, Part 2,** 73; *General Monk,* **Vol. 1, Part 1,** 633–34; *Georgiana,* **Vol. 3, Part 1,** 416; *Governor Tryon,* **Vol. 10, Part 1,** 536; *Guerrière,* **Vol. 1, Part 1,** 452; **Vol. 5, Part 1,** 361; **Vol. 8, Part 1,** 424; *Hampshire,* **Vol. 5, Part 1,** 456; *Hibernia,* **Vol. 5, Part 1,** 212; *High Flyer,* **Vol. 8, Part 2,** 77; *Hichenbrooke,* **Vol. 3, Part 2,** 66; *Hector,* **Vol. 3, Part 1,** 416; *Howe,* **Vol. 10, Part 1,** 536; *Independence,* **Vol. 10, Part 1,** 23; *Insurgente,* **Vol. 8, Part 1,** 83; **Vol. 8, Part 2,** 76; **Vol. 9, Part 1,** 584; **Vol. 10, Part 1,** 22; *Intrepid,* **Vol. 8, Part 1,** 182; **Vol. 8, Part 1,** 182; *Isabella II,* **Vol. 9, Part 1,** 156; *Jackal,* **Vol. 7, Part 1,** 506; *Jason,* **Vol. 5, Part 1,** 212; *Java,* **Vol. 1, Part 1,** 452; **Vol. 9, Part 1,** 135; *Joseph,* **Vol. 2, Part 2,** 368; *L'Amour de la Patrie,* **Vol. 9, Part 1,** 584; *La Vengeance,* **Vol. 9, Part 1,** 584; *Le Croyable,* **Vol. 3, Part 1,** 186; *Lord Hyde,* **Vol. 10, Part 1,** 40; *Macedonian,* **Vol. 1, Part 1,** 212; **Vol. 3, Part 1,** 188; **Vol. 8, Part 1,** 424; **Vol. 10, Part 1,** 292; *Madre de Dios,* **Vol. 7, Part 1,** 467; *Malek Adhel,* **Vol. 8, Part 1,** 470; *Margaretta,* **Vol. 7, Part 1,** 610; *Mariana Flora,* **Vol. 9, Part 2,** 48; *Martha,* **Vol. 3, Part 1,** 39; *Mashuda,* **Vol. 3, Part 1,** 189, 416; **Vol. 3, Part 2,** 85; **Vol. 9, Part 1,** 136; *Mastico,* **Vol. 3, Part 1,** 187; *Mellish,* **Vol. 5, Part 2,** 184; *Mirboka,* **Vol. 6, Part 2,** 20; *Mont Blanc,* **Vol. 2, Part 2,** 308; *Nancy,* **Vol. 6, Part 2,** 236; *Nautilus,* **Vol. 10, Part 1,** 492; *Ormigo,* **Vol. 9, Part 2,** 620; *Peacock,* **Vol. 2, Part 2,** 349; **Vol. 3, Part 2,** 531; *Penguin,* **Vol. 1, Part 2,** 214; **Vol. 2, Part 2,** 349; *Pigot,* **Vol. 9, Part 2,** 280; *Planter,* **Vol. 6, Part 2,** 195; *Prince of Orange,* **Vol. 2, Part 2,** 368; *Prosper,* **Vol. 7, Part 2,** 484; *Pursuit,* **Vol. 6, Part 2,** 195; *Queen Charlotte,* **Vol. 2, Part 1,** 609; *Rebecca,* **Vol. 3, Part 2,** 66; *Reindeer,* **Vol. 1, Part 2,** 348; *Resolution,* **Vol. 6, Part 1,** 50; *Sandwich,* **Vol. 7, Part 1,** 506; *St. Lawrence,* **Vol. 1, Part 2,** 534; *Scarborough,* **Vol. 7, Part 1,** 610; *Scourge,* **Vol. 8, Part 1,** 182; *Serapis,* **Vol. 5, Part 1,** 477; *Sir William Erskine,* **Vol. 10, Part 1,** 536; *Sparlin,* **Vol. 10, Part 1,** 536; *Spencer,* **Vol. 7, Part 1,** 507; *Tartar,* **Vol. 7, Part 2,** 484; *Tapnaquish,* **Vol. 7, Part 1,** 610; *Terror,* **Vol. 9, Part 2,** 156; *Thorn,* **Vol. 7, Part 1,** 506; **Vol. 10, Part 1,** 40; *Trepassy,* **Vol. 1, Part 1,** 654; *Tripoli,* **Vol. 9, Part 1,** 584; *True Briton,* **Vol. 1, Part 2,** 242; *Tulip,* **Vol. 6, Part 2,** 195; *Vainqueur,* **Vol. 9, Part 2,** 561; *Vigilante,* **Vol. 10, Part 1,** 101; *Viper,* **Vol. 7, Part 1,** 506

Riverboats: *A. B. Chambers;* **Vol. 6, Part 2,** 229; *Aleck Scott,* **Vol. 8, Part 2,** 575; *Antelope,* **Vol. 7, Part 1,** 514; *Armenia,* **Vol. 9, Part 2,** 57; *Balloon,* **Vol. 7, Part 1,** 471; *Bridgwater,* **Vol. 10, Part 1,** 179; *C. E. Hillman,* **Vol. 8, Part 1,** 188; *City of Baton Rouge,* **Vol. 1, Part 2,** 306; *Conestoga,* **Vol. 10, Part 1,** 179; *Enterprise,* **Vol. 9, Part 1,** 134; *Far West,* **Vol. 6, Part 2,** 299; *General Abner Lacock,* **Vol. 5, Part 2,** 521; *General Carroll,* **Vol. 8, Part 2,** 575; *Hail Columbia,* **Vol. 10, Part 1,** 179; *Heliopolis,* **Vol. 9, Part 1,** 134; *Hendrick Hudson,* **Vol. 9, Part 2,** 104; **Vol. 7, Part 1,** 471; *Henry von Phul,* **Vol. 8, Part 2,** 576; *Isaac Newton,* **Vol. 7, Part 1,** 471; *Islander,* **Vol. 5, Part 2,** 464; *J. M. White,* **Vol. 1, Part 2,** **Vol. 8, Part 2,** 575; *John D. Perry,* **Vol. 8, Part 1,** 188; *John J. Roe,* **Vol. 6, Part 2,** 299; *Jubilee,* **Vol. 8, Part 2,** 575; *Lioness,* **Vol. 5, Part 2,** 147; *Luella,* **Vol. 6, Part 2,** 299; *New Orleans,* **Vol. 9, Part 1,** 134; *New World,* **Vol. 7, Part 1,** 471; *North America,* **Vol. 7, Part 1,** 471; *Omega,* **Vol. 5, Part 2,** 517; *Paragon,* **Vol. 6, Part 2,** 305; *Pinta,* **Vol. 10, Part 1,** 179; *Pioneer,* **Vol. 10, Part 1,** 646; *Post Boy,* **Vol. 9, Part 1,** 134; *Prairie,* **Vol. 8, Part 2,** 575; *President,* **Vol. 8, Part 2,** 575; *Rambler,* **Vol. 8, Part 2,** 575; *Red Fox,* **Vol. 10, Part 1,** 179; *St. Clair,* **Vol. 10, Part 1,** 66; *South America,* **Vol. 7, Part 1,** 471; *Uncle Toby,* **Vol. 4, Part 1,** 630; *Washington,* **Vol. 9, Part 1,** 134; *Yellowstone,* **Vol. 5, Part 2,** 517

Schooners, traders, and pirate ships involved in incidents in American history: *Adieu,* **Vol. 9, Part 2,** 637; *America,* **Vol. 2, Part 2,** 579; **Vol. 5, Part 2,** 337; **Vol. 6, Part 2,** 501; *Ancona,* **Vol. 7, Part 2,** 425; *Arabic,* **Vol. 5, Part 2,** 610; *Arctic,* **Vol. 2, Part 2,** 306; **Vol. 8, Part 1,** 447; *Arrow,* **Vol. 5, Part 1,** 74; *Atahualpa,* **Vol. 9, Part 2,** 183; *Balmar,* **Vol. 10, Part 1,** 55; *Barracouta,* **Vol. 10, Part 1,** 303; *Bedford,* **Vol. 8, Part 2,** 186; *Bella,* **Vol. 2, Part 2,** 518; *Benjamin,* **Vol. 9, Part 1,** 165; *Betsey,* **Vol. 5, Part 2,** 184; *Beulah,* **Vol. 7, Part 1,** 360–67; *Black Warrior,* **Vol. 6, Part 2,** 277; **Vol. 7, Part 2,** 578; *Bombay,* **Vol. 7, Part 2,** 53; *Bonne Citoyenne,* **Vol. 6, Part 1,** 50; *Bounty,* **Vol. 9, Part 2,** 592; *Cato,* **Vol. 10, Part 1,** 40; *Central America,* **Vol. 4, Part 2,** 580; *Challenge,* **Vol. 10, Part 1,** 535; *Charles,* **Vol. 8, Part 1,** 299, 300; *Charming Peggy,* **Vol. 2, Part 2,** 368; *Chen Yuen,* **Vol. 6, Part 2,** 49; *Cincinnatus,* **Vol. 1, Part 1,** 634; *Commerce,* **Vol. 8, Part 2,** 391; *Continental,* **Vol. 8, Part 2,** 259; *Cotopaxi,* **Vol. 2, Part 2,** 244; *Courier,* **Vol. 9, Part 1,** 290; *Courrier,* **Vol. 7, Part 1,** 535; *Crescent City,* **Vol. 6, Part 1,** 40; *Dauphin,* **Vol. 7, Part 1,** 611; *Desperate,* **Vol. 9, Part 1,** 626; *Dessong,* **Vol. 4, Part 1,** 437; *Diana,* **Vol. 7, Part 2,** 490; *Dublin,* **Vol. 5, Part 2,** 201; *Echo,* **Vol. 7, Part 1,** 426; **Vol. 6, Part 2,** 196, 203; *Eclipse,* **Vol. 8, Part 1,** 424; *Eleanor,* **Vol. 5, Part 1,** 474; *Ella M. Doughty,* **Vol. 8, Part 1,** 286; *Empire,* **Vol. 8, Part 1,** 11–12; *Essex,* **Vol. 4, Part 2,** 162; *Fern,* **Vol. 10, Part 1,** 319; *Flying Fish,* **Vol. 6, Part 1,** 299; *Fox,* **Vol. 4, Part 2,** 120; *Friendship,* **Vol. 3, Part 1,** 416; **Vol. 3, Part 2,** 157; **Vol. 7, Part 2,** 338; *Galatea,* **Vol. 2, Part 2,** 368; *Gaspée,* **Vol. 2, Part 1,** 128; **Vol. 2, Part 2,** 267; **Vol. 5, Part 1,** 211, 220, 238; **Vol. 9, Part 1,** 529; **Vol. 10, Part 2,** 66; *Gazelle,* **Vol. 7, Part 2,** 53; *General Sherman,* **Vol. 2, Part 2,** 637; *George Law,* **Vol. 4, Part 2,** 580; *George Washington,* **Vol. 6, Part 1,** 204; *Gladiator,* **Vol. 9, Part 1,** 626; *Globe,* **Vol. 7, Part 2,** 320, 461; *Golden Rule,* **Vol. 8, Part 1,** 184; *Goodspeed,* **Vol. 8, Part 1,** 140; *Gorgon,* **Vol. 10, Part 1,** 292; *Greyhound,* **Vol. 4, Part 2,** 162; **Vol. 5, Part 1,** 304; *Hazard,* **Vol. 7, Part 1,** 535; *Henry,* **Vol. 6, Part 1,** 135; *Herbert Fuller,* **Vol. 10, Part 1,** 495; *Heroina,* **Vol. 5, Part 2,** 67; *Himaleh,* **Vol. 7, Part 2,** 34; *Home;* **Vol. 7, Part 1,** 582; *Hope,* **Vol. 5, Part 1,** 312; *Hougomont,* **Vol. 7, Part 2,** 53; *Hussar,* **Vol. 5, Part 1,** 477; *Illinois,* **Vol. 8, Part 2,** 11, 12; *Itata,* **Vol. 5, Part 1,** 153; *Jackal,*

Siberia, naval expeditions to, **Vol. 3, Part 2,** 559
Siberia and the Exile System, **Vol. 5, Part 2,** 331
Sibley College, **Vol. 9, Part 2,** 519
Sibyl, reform magazine, **Vol. 4, Part 2,** 376
Sicily, World War II action, **Supp. 8,** 155
Sickle-cell anemia, **Supp. 3,** 190
Sidereal Messenger, first astronomical magazine, **Vol. 7, Part 1,** 39
Siegel, Don, reference to, **Supp. 8,** 678
Siemens, A. G., **Supp. 6,** 44
Sierra Club, **Supp. 7,** 814
Sierra Nevada, geologic study of, **Supp. 4,** 558
"Sight method" of reading instruction, **Supp. 6,** 248
Signals and signaling devices, **Vol. 4, Part 2,** 477; **Vol. 7, Part 1,** 374; **Vol. 8, Part 2,** 56, 96; **Vol. 10, Part 1,** 618 f.
Signal Service, United States, **Vol. 4, Part 2,** 477
Sikorsky, Igor, references to, **Supp. 5,** 377, 378
Silent Spring, **Supp. 7,** 109–10
Silicon, reduction process, **Supp. 3,** 48–49
Silicon carbide, **Supp. 1,** 5
Silicosis, research in, **Supp. 2,** 371; **Supp. 4,** 314
Silk: culture, **Vol. 3, Part 1,** 540; **Vol. 3, Part 2,** 79; **Vol. 5, Part 2,** 111, 341; **Vol. 7, Part 1,** 23, 205; **Vol. 8, Part 1,** 234 f.; **Vol. 9, Part 2,** 298–99, 320; manufacture, **Vol. 2, Part 2,** 56, 244; **Vol. 3, Part 1,** 540; **Vol. 9, Part 1,** 202, 446
Sill, Edward Rowland, reference to, **Vol. 8, Part 2,** 206
Silliman, Benjamin, reference to, **Vol. 6, Part 1,** 394; **Vol. 7, Part 1,** 575
Sills, Beverly, reference to, **Supp. 8,** 381
Silsbee, J. L., reference to, **Supp. 6,** 711
Silva, Luigi, reference to, **Supp. 7,** 511
Silver: amorphous forms of, **Vol. 6, Part 1,** 71; coinage, pine tree shillings, **Vol. 5, Part 1,** 363; collecting of old, **Vol. 6, Part 1,** 210; free-silver movement, **Supp. 2,** 289; **Supp. 5,** 381; pricing, **Supp. 2,** 531; processing, **Supp. 2,** 147
Silver, Abba Hillel, reference to, **Supp. 4,** 906
Silver-lead bullion: "gumdrop" method of sampling, **Vol. 8, Part 1,** 326; mining, *see* Mining, silver
Silver nitrate, **Supp. 3,** 364; to prevent blindness, **Supp. 2,** 381
Silver party in politics, **Vol. 2, Part 1,** 192; **Vol. 7, Part 1,** 626 f.; **Vol. 9, Part 1,** 15
Silver Purchase Act (1890). *See* Sherman Silver Purchase Act (1890)
Silver Purchase Act (1934), **Supp. 3,** 730
"Silver question," **Vol. 1, Part 1,** 288 f., **Vol. 4, Part 1,** 391; **Vol. 4, Part 1,** 391; **Vol. 5, Part 1,** 238; **Vol. 9, Part 1,** 132; **Vol. 9, Part 2,** 362
Silver smelting, **Vol. 4, Part 2,** 403
Silversmiths, **Vol. 1, Part 1,** 456; **Vol. 1, Part 2,** 406; **Vol. 3, Part 1,** 501 f.; **Vol. 3, Part 2,** 29, 164, 425; **Vol. 4, Part 2,** 275; **Vol. 5, Part 1,** 424; **Vol. 6, Part 1,** 180 f.; **Vol. 8, Part 1,** 515, 571 f.; **Vol. 8, Part 2,** 338; **Vol. 9, Part 2,** 261; **Vol. 10, Part 2,** 395, "trade dollar" of 1873–87, **Vol. 6, Part 1,** 273
Silverware, manufacture of, **Vol. 4, Part 1,** 432
Silviculture, early activities in, **Vol. 6, Part 2,** 592
Simmons, Etolia Moore, reference to, **Supp. 7,** 38
Simmons, Furnifold M., reference to, **Supp. 4,** 42–43
Simmons College: founding of, **Vol. 5, Part 2,** 288; social work studies, **Supp. 4,** 101
Simms, Florence, reference to, **Supp. 7,** 185
Simon, A. W., reference to, **Supp. 7,** 134
Simon, Klara, reference to, **Supp. 6,** 219
Simon, Richard L, reference to, **Supp. 8,** 578
Simon, Theodore, reference to, **Supp. 6,** 240
Simon and Schuster, **Supp. 7,** 243; **Supp. 8,** 579; founding of, **Supp. 6,** 583–84

"Simple" ("Jesse B. Semple") (fictional character), **Supp. 8,** 288
Simpson, Jerry, reference to, **Supp. 3,** 544
Simpson, Wallis Warfield. *See* Windsor, Duke and Duchess of
Simpson, William, reference to, **Supp. 3,** 792
Simpson, Thatcher and Bartlett, **Supp. 4,** 825
Sims, William S., references to, **Supp. 6,** 348, 518
Sinai, founding of, **Vol. 3, Part 2,** 65
Sinai Temple (Mt. Vernon, N.Y.), **Supp. 8,** 307
Sinclair, Harry F., reference to, **Supp. 3,** 259, 260
Sinclair, Upton, references to, **Supp. 3,** 156, 471, 533; **Supp. 5,** 499; **Supp. 6,** 328
Sinclair Oil Co., **Supp. 3,** 669; founding of, **Supp. 6,** 584–85; Mexican oil claims, **Supp. 7,** 377
Singapore, World War II evacuation, **Supp. 8,** 30
Singer, E. A., reference to, **Supp. 6,** 261
Singer, I. J., reference to, **Supp. 6,** 567
Singer, Isaac Bashevis, reference to, **Supp. 3,** 712
Singers. For complete list, *see* Occupations Index
Singer Sewing Machine Co., building architecture, **Supp. 4,** 281
Singewald, Joseph T., reference to, **Supp. 5,** 206
Singewald, Quentin, reference to, **Supp. 5,** 206
Singing, **Vol. 1, Part 1,** 615; **Vol. 6, Part 1,** 74; **Vol. 8, Part 2,** 146 f., 339; **Vol. 10, Part 2,** 164; bel canto, **Supp. 4,** 223; blackface, **Supp. 4,** 440; blues, **Supp. 5,** 529–30; **Supp. 8,** 239, 305–6; "boop-boop-a-doop," **Supp. 8,** 310–11; choral, **Supp. 1,** 650; **Supp. 8,** 238; church solo, **Supp. 4,** 125; colonial period, **Vol. 10, Part 1,** 395 f.; concert, **Vol. 1, Part 1,** 638; **Vol. 1, Part 2,** 299; **Vol. 4, Part 1,** 209; **Vol. 5, Part 1,** 117; **Vol. 8, Part 2,** 167; **Vol. 10, Part 2,** 100; **Supp. 3,** 553–54; **Supp. 8,** 151, 380–81; country and western, **Supp. 5,** 748–49; educational books on, **Vol. 8, Part 2,** 92; gospel, **Supp. 7,** 769; "Irish tenor," **Supp. 3,** 484–85; jazz, **Supp. 5,** 32–33; Latin American style, **Supp. 5,** 500–1; motion pictures, **Supp. 8,** 204–5; nationwide auditions, **Supp. 4,** 452; opera, **Vol. 1, Part 2,** 299; **Vol. 2, Part 1,** 553; **Vol. 7, Part 1,** 549; **Vol. 8, Part 1,** 144; operettas, **Supp. 7,** 499; **Supp. 8,** 151; popular classical, **Supp. 4,** 596–97; popular recordings of, **Supp. 4,** 388–89; rhythm and blues, **Supp. 7,** 769–70; rock, **Supp. 8,** 305–6; rote, **Vol. 9, Part 2,** 405; sheet music, **Vol. 3, Part 1,** 833–34; **Supp. 4,** 88; "Silver-masked Tenor," **Supp. 6,** 691; *Sprechstimme* style, **Supp. 5,** 609; teaching of, **Vol. 8, Part 2,** 146 f.; **Vol. 9, Part 2,** 516 f.; **Supp. 1,** 655, 712; torch, **Supp. 3,** 536; vaudeville, **Supp. 4,** 814–15; **Supp. 8,** 661. *See also* Music; Opera, singing; Songs and songwriting; Theater, musicals
Single-tax, **Vol. 3, Part 2,** 314 f.; **Vol. 4, Part 1,** 174, 215; **Vol. 6, Part 2,** 53; **Supp. 4,** 844, 845; name, suggestion of, **Vol. 9, Part 1,** 52; protagonist, leading, **Vol. 8, Part 1,** 118 f.
Sing Sing Prison (Ossining, N.Y.): **Supp. 3,** 420; **Supp. 4,** 472; Mutual Welfare League, **Vol. 7, Part 2,** 75
Sinkov, Abraham, reference to, **Supp. 8,** 196
Sino-Japanese War (1937), **Supp. 4,** 750–51; **Supp. 6,** 230
Sinology. *See* China
Sinus, surgery on, **Vol. 6, Part 1,** 523
Sioux Indians, **Supp. 4,** 907; **Supp. 6,** 162; **Supp. 7,** 393; language, **Vol. 8, Part 1,** 605; powerful leader of, **Vol. 8, Part 1,** 438 f.; Sioux Confederacy, **Vol. 2, Part 2,** 530 f.; Sitting Bull, **Vol. 9, Part 1,** 192; treaty with Chippewa, **Vol. 3, Part 1,** 500 f.; uprising of 1862, **Vol. 8, Part 1,** 605; war (1875–76), **Vol. 2, Part 1,** 519; **Vol. 2, Part 2,** 260. *See also* Little Bighorn, battle of

Vol. 5, Part 1, 224, 576; Vol. 5, Part 2, 258; Vol. 6, Part 1, 163, 368; Vol. 8, Part 1, 117, 403; Vol. 8, Part 2, 84, 117, 315; Vol. 9, Part 1, 288, 379; Vol. 9, Part 2, 23, 304; Vol. 10, Part 1, 27; Van Buren's attitude toward, Vol. 10, Part 1, 155 f.; Virginia, Vol. 2, Part 1, 383; Vol. 8, Part 2, 216; Vol. 10, Part 1, 70; Wilmot Proviso, Vol. 2, Part 1, 49, 417; Vol. 5, Part 1, 604; Vol. 5, Part 2, 397; Vol. 6, Part 1, 586; Vol. 8, Part 1, 34 f.; Vol. 9, Part 2, 590; Vol. 10, Part 2, 317; Wisconsin, Vol. 3, Part 1, 375; World's Antislavery Convention in London, Vol. 8, Part 1, 499; writings on, Vol. 1, Part 1, 94, 352; Vol. 2, Part 1, 156, 161; Vol. 3, Part 1, 266; Vol. 3, Part 2, 411; Vol. 4, Part 1, 85, 217, 308, 391, 530 f.; Vol. 4, Part 2, 565 f.; Vol. 5, Part 2, 12; Vol. 8, Part 1, 407, 410, 444, 537; Vol. 9, Part 2, 100, 250, 253; Vol. 10, Part 1, 55 f.; Vol. 10, Part 1, 138; Supp. 3, 32, 337. See also Abolition movement

Slaves: ad valorem tax on, Vol. 3, Part 2, 107; Vol. 8, Part 1, 417; codes, Vol. 7, Part 1, 115; Vol. 10, Part 1, 70; owning, responsibilities of, Vol. 3, Part 1, 21 f.; rise of, to commanding position in abolitionist movement, Vol. 3, Part 1, 406 f.; ships, capture of, Vol. 9, Part 2, 48; trade, Vol. 1, Part 1, 90, 292; Vol. 3, Part 1, 275, 599 f.; Vol. 4, Part 1, 150; Vol. 4, Part 2, 446, 521; Vol. 6, Part 1, 32; Vol. 8, Part 2, 85

Slaves as soldiers: Confederate, Vol. 2, Part 2, 190 f.; Union, Vol. 2, Part 1, 358

Slave Systems of Greek and Roman Antiquity, Supp. 5, 736

Slavic literature and languages, teaching of, Supp. 4, 195–96

Sleeper, Jacob, reference to, Vol. 10, Part 1, 409 f

Sleeping Car Porters. See Brotherhood of Sleeping Car Porters

Sleeping cars: inventions relating to, Vol. 5, Part 2, 464; Vol. 10, Part 2, 497; manufacture of, Vol. 10, Part 2, 497

"Sleeping sickness," study of, Vol. 6, Part 2, 401

"Slide, Kelly, Slide," Vol. 5, Part 2, 310

Slide rule, invention of, Supp. 2, 27

Sloan, Alfred P., Jr.: cancer research endowment, Supp. 6, 333, 537; references to, Supp. 4, 244, 301, 682; Supp. 5, 193–94; Supp. 7, 794

Sloan, John, reference to, Supp. 5, 624

Sloan, W. Glenn, reference to, Supp. 6, 508

Sloan, Alfred P., Jr., Foundation, Supp. 8, 600

Sloan-Kettering Institute for Cancer Research (New York City), Supp. 6, 333, 537, 538; Supp. 8, 600

Slogans and phrases: "Gung Ho!", Supp. 4, 147; "Tin Pan Alley" coined, Supp. 4, 836

Slonimsky, Nicolas, reference to, Supp. 8, 145

Slosson, Edwin E., references to, Supp. 8, 119, 120

Slums, "great emancipator" of, in New York, Vol. 8, Part 1, 607

Slye, Maude, reference to, Supp. 3, 807

Small, Albion W., references to, Supp. 3, 514, 515, 793; Supp. 4, 828

Small, Len, reference to, Supp. 5, 450; Supp. 6, 74

Small Business Administration, founding of, Supp. 8, 616

Smallpox inoculation, Vol. 1, Part 1, 395; Vol. 4, Part 1, 97, 331; Vol. 5, Part 1, 158, 541, 546; Vol. 5, Part 2, 163; Vol. 8, Part 1, 391; Vol. 8, Part 2, 377; Vol. 10, Part 1, 150, 529 f.; early doubts as to advisability of, Vol. 3, Part 1, 408; first to introduce practice into America, Vol. 1, Part 2, 535; vaccine, first shipment of, Vol. 9, Part 1, 424

Smart, David A., Publishing Co., Supp. 5, 637

Smart Set, Supp. 4, 841; Supp. 6, 444, 445, 470, 471

Smedley, Agnes, reference to, Supp. 4, 147

Smellie, William, reference to, Vol. 6, Part 1, 333

Smelting: industrial development, Supp. 2, 383; ores, Vol. 2, Part 1, 511; Vol. 2, Part 2, 472; Vol. 4, Part 2, 37 f., 379, 403; Vol. 5, Part 1, 43; Vol. 7, Part 2, 504; Vol. 8, Part 1, 326; Vol. 9, Part 1, 57

Smith, Adam, study of, Supp. 8, 669

Smith, Albert E., reference to, Supp. 3, 75–76

Smith, Alfred E.: biography of, Supp. 6, 521; "Catholic and Patriot," Supp. 6, 572; Hearst relationship, Supp. 5, 286; New York governorship, Supp. 3, 668 –69; Supp. 4, 886; Supp. 5, 286, 493–94; Perkins relationship, Supp. 7, 608; presidential campaigns, Supp. 3, 114, 481, 681, 817; Supp. 7, 361; Prohibition stance, Supp. 3, 132; Supp. 7, 786; Raskob relationship, Supp. 4, 682–83; references to, Vol. 7, Part 1, 346; Vol. 9, Part 2, 126; Roosevelt, F. D., relationship, Supp. 3, 644–46, 653; Swope relationship, Supp. 6, 616; Tammany Hall, Supp. 6, 295; Walker relationship, Supp. 4, 855

Smith, Benjamin Eli, reference to, Vol. 9, Part 2, 357

Smith, Captain John, references to, Vol. 5, Part 1, 339; Vol. 7, Part 1, 468; Vol. 8, Part 1, 18 f.

Smith, Charles Shaler, reference to, Supp. 2, 29

Smith, David Eugene, reference to, Supp. 3, 677

Smith, Donald P., reference to, Supp. 3, 220

Smith, Ed ("Cotton"), reference to, Supp. 8, 682

Smith, Edgar Fahs, reference to, Supp. 4, 114

Smith, Erwin F., reference to, Supp. 3, 400

Smith, Frank L., reference to, Supp. 3, 559, 622

Smith, Gerald L. K., references to, Supp. 4, 480; Supp. 6, 614, 647

Smith, Gerrit, psychobiography of, Supp. 6, 279

Smith, Harrison, reference to, Supp. 7, 232

Smith, Holland, reference to, Supp. 7, 352

Smith, James Allen, reference to, Supp. 4, 62

Smith, Joseph, references to, Vol. 9, Part 1, 386; Vol. 9, Part 2, 124, 333 f.

Smith, Lowell H., reference to, Supp. 7, 16

Smith, Marcus A., reference to, Supp. 7, 21

Smith, Margaret Chase, reference to, Supp. 8, 654

Smith, Mary Logan. See Berenson, Mary Smith Costelloe

Smith, Ralph, reference to, Supp. 7, 352

Smith, S. F., reference to, Vol. 5, Part 1, 170

Smith, Sol, reference to, Vol. 6, Part 1, 493

Smith, Sophia, reference to, Vol. 8, Part 2, 557

Smith, Stevenson, reference to, Supp. 6, 261

Smith, Theobald, reference to, Vol. 7, Part 1, 542

Smith, Willie, references to, Supp. 4, 510, 511

Smith, Zilpha D., reference to, Supp. 2, 375

Smith Act (1940), Supp. 5, 500; Supp. 7, 96, 264

Smith College, Vol. 1, Part 2, 39; Vol. 8, Part 2, 557; Vol. 9, Part 2, 56; drama studies, Supp. 8, 177; English literature and language studies, Supp. 7, 18–19; expansion of, Supp. 4, 624–25; founding of, Vol. 8, Part 2, 557; Vol. 9, Part 1, 347; French studies, Supp. 3, 691; history studies, Supp. 8, 169; presidency, Supp. 4, 624–25; psychology studies, Supp. 3, 429

Smith's Magazine, Supp. 3, 235

Smithsonian Institution, Vol. 1, Part 1, 91, 514; Vol. 1, Part 2, 152; Vol. 5, Part 2, 66, 338 f., 595; Vol. 7, Part 2, 119; Vol. 8, Part 1, 525; Vol. 8, Part 2, 542; Vol. 10, Part 1, 5; Bureau of American Ethnology, Supp. 6, 611; founding of, Vol. 1, Part 1, 91; Vol. 4, Part 2, 552 f.; Vol. 8, Part 2, 233; geology collection, Supp. 6, 212; National Museum collection, Supp. 3, 732–33; petrographic collection, Supp. 4, 194; physical anthropology, Supp. 3, 372; rocket propulsion, Supp. 3, 306. See also Freer Gallery of Art

175; New Jersey, **Supp. 6,** 515–16; New York City, **Supp. 4,** 391–92; Pennsylvania, **Supp. 6,** 515; professional education in, **Supp. 1,** 237, 340, 485; **Supp. 2,** 2, 360, 376, 656, 694; **Supp. 3,** 4, 625; **Supp. 4,** 101, 106–7, 227, 232, 333, 810–11; **Supp. 5,** 520; **Supp. 6,** 1–2; psychiatric, criticism of, **Supp. 4,** 811; rescue missions, **Vol. 9, Part 1,** 176; settlement houses, establishing of, **Vol. 10, Part 2,** 504, 515; theory of, **Supp. 4,** 227–28; unwed mothers, **Supp. 3,** 221; Volunteers of America, **Supp. 2,** 48–49; Wisconsin reforms, **Supp. 7,** 787. *See also* Settlement house movement; Sociology; Welfare
Société Anonyme, Inc., founding of, **Supp. 5,** 184, 185
Société des Artistes Français, **Vol. 5, Part 2,** 463
Société Financière de Transports et d'Enterprise Industrielle (SOFINA), **Supp. 7,** 333
Society: café society, **Supp. 4,** 199; **Supp. 7,** 803; **Supp. 8,** 38–39; Duchin Orchestra's popularity with, **Supp. 5,** 188; etiquette books, **Supp. 6,** 514; Gibson illustrations, **Supp. 3,** 300; hostesses, **Supp. 7,** 519, 527; international, **Supp. 4,** 229–30; **Supp. 7,** 753; New York aristocratic, **Supp. 5,** 707–8; novels about aristocratic, **Supp. 2,** 703–5; playboys, **Supp. 8,** 416; socialites, **Supp. 4,** 797–98; Vanderbilt ball (1883), **Supp. 1,** 68; Washington, D.C., **Supp. 8,** 244, 328; women's clubs, **Supp. 5,** 505
Society for Advancement of Management. *See* Taylor Society
Society for Establishing Useful Manufactures, **Vol. 7, Part 2,** 294
Society for Ethical Culture. *See* Ethical Culture movement
Society for Experimental Biology and Medicine, founding of, **Supp. 1,** 518
Society for Pharmacology and Experimental Therapeutics, founding of, **Supp. 2,** 4
Society for Political Education, founding of, **Supp. 1,** 101
Society for Promoting Christian Knowledge,, **Vol. 7, Part 1,** 463
Society for Pure English, founding of, **Supp. 4,** 756
Society for the Advancement of Christianity in Pennsylvania, **Vol. 7, Part 2,** 592
Society for the Preservation of New England Antiquities, **Supp. 4,** 115–16; founding of, **Supp. 4,** 24
Society for the Preservation of Spanish Antiquities, **Vol. 8, Part 1,** 229 f.
Society for the Prevention of Crime, **Vol. 2, Part 2,** 568
Society for the Prevention of Pauperism, **Vol. 4, Part 1,** 217
Society for the Promotion of Engineering Education, **Vol. 5, Part 2,** 106
Society for the Promotion of Legal Knowledge and Forensic Eloquence, founding of, **Vol. 8, Part 1,** 401
Society for the Propagation of the Gospel, **Vol. 4, Part 2,** 418; **Vol. 5, Part 2,** 110; **Vol. 6, Part 1,** 74; **Vol. 8, Part 2,** 81
Society for the Protection of German Emigrants, **Vol. 8, Part 2,** 91
Society for the Publication of American Music, **Vol. 10, Part 1,** 73 f.; founding of, **Supp. 2,** 250
Society for the Reformation of Juvenile Delinquents, **Vol. 4, Part 1,** 217
Society of American Archivists, predecessor, **Supp. 8,** 369, 370
Society of American Artists, **Vol. 1, Part 2,** 120; **Vol. 3, Part 1,** 613 f.; **Vol. 4, Part 1,** 276; **Vol. 8, Part 1,** 296; **Vol. 8, Part 2,** 54; **Vol. 9, Part 1,** 119; founding of, **Supp. 1,** 514

Society of American Bacteriologists, founding of, **Supp. 2,** 353
Society of American Foresters, founding of, **Supp. 4,** 666
Society of American Wood-Engravers, **Vol. 5, Part 2,** 411; 509
Society of California Pioneers, **Vol. 5, Part 1,** 82; **Vol. 6, Part 1,** 234; **Vol. 9, Part 2,** 448
Society of Economic Geologists, **Vol. 7, Part 2,** 451; founding of, **Supp. 4,** 766
Society of Free Thinkers, founding of, **Supp. 2,** 182
Society of Friends. *See* Quakers
Society of Hebrew Education, **Vol. 3, Part 1,** 459 f.
Society of Iconophiles, **Vol. 1, Part 1,** 299
Society of Independent Artists, founding of, **Supp. 2,** 239
Society of Jesus (Jesuits), **Vol. 3, Part 2,** 327; **Vol. 6, Part 1,** 539; **Vol. 7, Part 1,** 82
Society of Mural Painters, founding of, **Supp. 2,** 42
Society of Naval Architects and Marine Engineers, founding of, **Supp. 1,** 151
Society of Painters in Pastel, **Vol. 1, Part 2,** 397
Society of Progressive Oral Advocates, founding of, **Supp. 3,** 311
Society of St. Sulpice, **Vol. 3, Part 1,** 470 f.
Society of the Atonement, founding of, **Supp. 2,** 201
Society of the Cincinnati, **Vol. 3, Part 1,** 430; **Vol. 3, Part 2,** 116, 194, 307, 323, 400 f.; **Vol. 4, Part 1,** 187; **Vol. 5, Part 1,** 417; **Vol. 5, Part 2,** 376, 423, 476, 498, 538; **Vol. 6, Part 1,** 166, 223; **Vol. 7, Part 1,** 510; **Vol. 7, Part 2,** 293; **Vol. 8, Part 2,** 62, 487; **Vol. 9, Part 1,** 369, 604; **Vol. 9, Part 2,** 596, 606, 616; founding of, **Vol. 3, Part 2,** 116, 323; **Vol. 5, Part 2,** 376, 498; **Vol. 8, Part 2,** 487
Society of the Holy Child Jesus, **Vol. 2, Part 2,** 347 f.
Society of the Sacred Heart, **Vol. 3, Part 1,** 477 f.; **Vol. 4, Part 2,** 242
Society of Surgeon Dentists of the City and State of New York, **Vol. 7, Part 2,** 251
Society of Women Geographers, founding of, **Supp. 6,** 576
Sociological jurisprudence, **Supp. 3,** 185–86; **Supp. 7,** 625–26, 627, 628
Sociology: American community studies, **Supp. 3,** 50; **Supp. 5,** 35; **Supp. 8,** 398–99, 684–85; black studies, **Supp. 7,** 266; **Supp. 8,** 81, 521–22; Chicago school of, **Supp. 6,** 321; Christian, **Supp. 2,** 655; **Supp. 3,** 514; class and change theories, **Supp. 8,** 407; collective behavior, **Supp. 3,** 511, 578–80; contemporary American issues, **Supp. 7,** 539–40; criminology theory, **Supp. 4,** 808–9; culture studies, **Supp. 4,** 908; **Supp. 6,** 727; first professorship in, **Supp. 1,** 340; history of, **Supp. 6,** 726; history studies and, **Supp. 2,** 563–66; homeostasis, **Supp. 3,** 137; human ecology system, **Supp. 3,** 578–79; legal philosophy and, **Supp. 6,** 216; **Supp. 8,** 17; marriage and family studies, **Supp. 3,** 799–800; of medicine, **Supp. 6,** 664–65; *Pittsburgh Survey* as investigative model, **Supp. 6,** 329–30; popularization of, **Supp. 5,** 591–92; regionalism studies, **Supp. 5,** 520–21; of religion, **Supp. 7,** 574–76; research, theoretical and empirical linkage, **Supp. 4,** 829, 830; role of women, writings on, **Supp. 3,** 581; rural life, **Supp. 2,** 727; **Supp. 3,** 683–84; **Supp. 4,** 312; sample survey, **Supp. 6,** 604–5; scientific approach to, **Supp. 3,** 351; statistical techniques, **Supp. 6,** 482–83, 604; teaching of, **Supp. 1,** 547; **Supp. 3,** 579–80, 793, 799; **Supp. 4,** 831; values and attitudes distinction, **Supp. 4,** 829; writings on, **Supp. 1,** 339–40, 388–89; **Supp. 4,** 828–31; **Supp. 6,** 54–55
Soda, manufacture of, **Vol. 2, Part 2,** 274; **Vol. 6, Part 2,** 417; **Vol. 9, Part 1,** 455

649; fundamentalism, **Supp. 3**, 129; historical writings on, **Supp. 1**, 303, 597; **Supp. 2**, 153; **Supp. 3**, 31–32; **Supp. 5**, 671–72; **Supp. 6**, 491–92; hookworm control, **Supp. 3**, 738; industrial development, **Vol. 3, Part 1**, 496 f.; **Vol. 3, Part 2**, 169; **Vol. 9, Part 2**, 581; labor movement in, **Supp. 6**, 433–34; liberal journalism, **Supp. 7**, 323–24; Loyalists' "Snow Campaign," **Vol. 8, Part 1**, 42; Methodism, spread of, **Vol. 2, Part 1**, 483; **Vol. 5, Part 2**, 579; New South journalism, **Supp. 8**, 404–5; novels about, **Vol. 7, Part 1**, 132; **Vol. 8, Part 1**, 395; photography of early architecture, **Supp. 5**, 373; race relations, **Supp. 6**, 11–12, 322; race relations, writings on, **Supp. 8**, 605–6; railroads, building, **Vol. 7, Part 2**, 647; rural vocational guidance, **Supp. 4**, 365–66; senatorial archetype, **Supp. 6**, 234; social and economic view of, **Vol. 9, Part 2**, 639; tenant farming, **Supp. 7**, 781; textile industry in, **Supp. 5**, 252; writings on, **Supp. 3**, 147–48

South Africa: African Methodist Episcopal Church diocese, **Supp. 5**, 259; medical missions, **Supp. 4**, 519–20; mining, **Supp. 2**, 701

South America: diamond mining, **Vol. 10, Part 2**, 261; diplomatic relations with, **Vol. 1, Part 1**, 271; **Vol. 3, Part 2**, 507; **Vol. 4, Part 2**, 162; **Vol. 7, Part 1**, 139; **Vol. 8, Part 2**, 83; explorations, **Vol. 2, Part 2**, 103; **Vol. 3, Part 2**, 465 f.; **Vol. 7, Part 1**,, 594; Indians, study of, **Vol. 3, Part 2**, 269; missionary work in, **Vol. 10, Part 2**, 474; promoter in, **Vol. 4, Part 2**, 517; **Vol. 5, Part 1**, 208–9; railroad building, **Vol. 2, Part 2**, 103; **Vol. 6, Part 2**, 501; **Vol. 10, Part 2**, 63; researches in, **Vol. 1, Part 1**, 571; Roosevelt, T. R., trip to, **Vol. 8, Part 2**, 143; shipping, American, **Vol. 1, Part 2**, 241; writings on, **Vol. 5, Part 2**, 565 f. *See also* Latin America; *specific country names*

Southampton, Long Island, founding of, **Vol. 7, Part 2**, 588

South Atlantic Quarterly, **Vol. 1, Part 2**, 39

South Bend, Ind., public service, **Vol. 7, Part 2**, 21

Southborough, Mass., history of, **Vol. 2, Part 1**, 299

South Carolina: Acadians, **Vol. 6, Part 1**, 538 f.; Act of 1828, opposition to, **Vol. 8, Part 1**, 30 f.; agriculture, **Vol. 4, Part 2**, 85, 609; **Vol. 8, Part 1**, 397; antebellum development, **Vol. 2, Part 1**, 365; architecture, **Vol. 7, Part 1**, 11 f.; banking, **Vol. 6, Part 1**, 131; Baptist State Convention, **Vol. 5, Part 2**, 130; Bluffton tariff movement, **Vol. 7, Part 2**, 59; **Vol. 8, Part 1**, 526; botany, **Vol. 10, Part 1**, 396 f.; boundary disputes, **Vol. 5, Part 2**, 140; **Vol. 8, Part 1**, 42; carpetbagging, **Vol. 1, Part 1**, 127; Civil War period, **Vol. 6, Part 2**, 203; **Vol. 10, Part 2**, 602; colonial administration, **Vol. 6, Part 2**, 234 f., 598; **Vol. 7, Part 1**, 379; **Vol. 8, Part 1**, 509; **Vol. 9, Part 2**, 649; **Vol. 10, Part 2**, 542, 604; colonization, **Vol. 2, Part 1**, 252; **Vol. 10, Part 2**, 11; Constitution, ratification of federal, **Vol. 2, Part 1**, 280; **Vol. 8, Part 1**, 237 f.; constitution, state, **Vol. 8, Part 2**, 258; cotton industry, **Vol. 4, Part 2**, 200; **Vol. 10, Part 1**, 570; Democratic party, **Vol. 7, Part 2**, 59; duelling, laws against, **Vol. 3, Part 1**, 152; education, **Vol. 4, Part 2**, 85; **Vol. 5, Part 2**, 130; **Vol. 6, Part 2**, 238; **Vol. 8, Part 1**, 444; **Vol. 9, Part 2**, 459; Episcopal bishop, first, **Vol. 9, Part 1**, 336; exploration of interior, **Vol. 10, Part 2**, 509; Federalists, **Vol. 4, Part 2**, 286; Female Institute (first women's school in South), **Vol. 6, Part 2**, 289; Fort King George, built 1721, **Vol. 1, Part 1**, 640; Georgia, help of, in founding, **Vol. 5, Part 2**, 117; governors, **Vol. 1, Part 1**, 71 f., 223 f.; **Vol. 1, Part 2**, 436; **Vol. 2, Part 1**, 252, 365 f., 595; **Vol. 3, Part 1**, 444 f.; **Vol. 4, Part 1**, 325; **Vol. 4, Part 2**, 85, 187 f., 189 f., 207 f., 213, 456; **Vol. 5, Part 2**, 117; **Vol. 6, Part 2**, 203 f., 251

f., 404 f.; **Vol. 7, Part 1**, 275 f., 293 f.; **Vol. 7, Part 2**, 59 f., 483 f., 559 f., 611 f., 617 f.; **Vol. 8, Part 2**, 257 f., 498 f.; **Vol. 9, Part 1**, 184 f.; **Vol. 9, Part 2**, 458 f., 547 f.; **Vol. 10, Part 2**, 253 f.; **Supp. 3**, 77–78; **Supp. 5**, 482; **Supp. 7**, 398; history of, **Vol. 2, Part 1**, 253; **Vol. 3, Part 1**, 182; **Vol. 5, Part 1**, 287; **Vol. 8, Part 1**, 30 f., 118 f., 270 f., 338, 395, 633 f.; **Vol. 9, Part 1**, 172, 277; ichthyology, **Vol. 5, Part 1**, 130; immigrants, social work among, **Vol. 8, Part 1**, 295; indigo culture, **Vol. 7, Part 2**, 616; industrial development, **Vol. 6, Part 2**, 235; **Vol. 10, Part 1**, 570; **Vol. 10, Part 2**, 254; insane, care of, **Vol. 2, Part 2**, 415; judiciary, **Supp. 8**, 682; judiciary prior to Civil War, **Vol. 2, Part 1**, 355; laws, codification of, **Vol. 8, Part 1**, 118 f.; legal service, **Vol. 1, Part 2**, 436, 609; **Vol. 3, Part 1**, 254; **Vol. 4, Part 1**, 634; **Vol. 5, Part 2**, 155; **Vol. 6, Part 1**, 131; **Vol. 7, Part 2**, 42; **Vol. 8, Part 1**, 118, 237, 425, 526; **Vol. 9, Part 1**, 172, 184, 360; limestone works in, **Vol. 8, Part 1**, 397; Loyalists, **Vol. 9, Part 2**, 489; **Vol. 10, Part 1**, 644 f.; **Vol. 10, Part 2**, 542; map of, first, **Vol. 3, Part 1**, 182; medical service, **Vol. 2, Part 2**, 415; **Vol. 6, Part 2**, 593; newspaper, first weekly, **Vol. 10, Part 1**, 644 f.; nullification movement, **Vol. 2, Part 1**, 414; **Vol. 3, Part 2**, 101, 115; **Vol. 4, Part 2**, 458; **Vol. 6, Part 2**, 35, 251, 601, 640; **Vol. 10, Part 1**, 56 f.; ornithology, **Vol. 10, Part 1**, 565; plantations, **Vol. 6, Part 1**, 33; political service, **Vol. 1, Part 1**, 71, 223, 229, 338; **Vol. 1, Part 2**, 436, 608, 609; **Vol. 2, Part 2**, 57; **Vol. 4, Part 1**, 325, 598; **Vol. 4, Part 2**, 85, 187, 189, 207, 215, 285, 458; **Vol. 5, Part 2**, 117; **Vol. 6, Part 1**, 33, 145, 472 f., 538; **Vol. 6, Part 2**, 34, 203, 251, 617, 640; **Vol. 7, Part 1**, 128, 275, 293; **Vol. 7, Part 2**, 59, 483, 514, 516, 559, 612; **Vol. 8, Part 1**, 30, 202, 207, 237, 327, 338, 425, 501, 526; **Vol. 8, Part 2**, 258, 498; **Vol. 9, Part 1**, 172, 184; **Vol. 9, Part 2**, 547; **Vol. 10, Part 2**, 254, 390; politics, **Supp. 3**, 78, 723–24; **Supp. 5**, 481–82; **Supp. 8**, 538; post-Revolution politics, **Vol. 2, Part 1**, 365, 368; pre-Civil War politics, **Vol. 6, Part 1**, 145; **Vol. 9, Part 2**, 474; pre-Revolutionary agitation, **Vol. 6, Part 2**, 599; printing, introducion of, **Vol. 8, Part 1**, 634; public service, **Vol. 3, Part 2**, 418; **Vol. 4, Part 1**, 475; **Vol. 4, Part 2**, 187, 190 f., 207, 212 f., 214, 457, 609; **Vol. 5, Part 1**, 165; **Vol. 5, Part 2**, 333, 360, 395; **Vol. 6, Part 1**, 35 f., 158, 473; **Vol. 6, Part 2**, 527; **Vol. 7, Part 1**, 579; **Vol. 7, Part 2**, 614 f.; **Vol. 8, Part 1**, 30 f.; **Vol. 9, Part 2**, 639; "Rangers," **Vol. 9, Part 2**, 489; Reconstruction, **Vol. 2, Part 1**, 364, 404, 595; **Vol. 2, Part 2**, 58; **Vol. 4, Part 1**, 373; **Vol. 6, Part 2**, 1; **Vol. 7, Part 2**, 59, 483; **Vol. 8, Part 1**, 118 f.; **Vol. 8, Part 2**, 332; **Vol. 10, Part 2**, 558; "Regulators," **Vol. 9, Part 2**, 489; representation in, reapportionment of, **Vol. 3, Part 1**, 254; Republican party, **Vol. 7, Part 2**, 613 f.; **Vol. 8, Part 1**, 327 f.; Revolutionary War period, **Vol. 2, Part 1**, 253, 465; **Vol. 4, Part 1**, 82 f., 134; **Vol. 8, Part 2**, 259; **Vol. 10, Part 2**, 299; rice seeds, smuggling of, **Vol. 5, Part 2**, 22; secession, **Vol. 2, Part 1**, 213; **Vol. 4, Part 1**, 325; **Vol. 7, Part 2**, 560; **Vol. 8, Part 1**, 395, 526 f.; **Vol. 10, Part 1**, 56 f., separation from North Carolina, **Vol. 5, Part 2**, 117; settler, first English in, **Vol. 10, Part 2**, 508; slavery, **Vol. 2, Part 1**, 416; slave trade, **Vol. 6, Part 1**, 32; **Vol. 3, Part 1**, 275; Swiss colonists, **Vol. 8, Part 1**, 270 f.; temperance reform, **Vol. 7, Part 2**, 43; trade, **Vol. 4, Part 1**, 296; Unionist party, **Vol. 5, Part 1**, 343; **Vol. 7, Part 2**, 483; **Vol. 8, Part 1**, 30 f.; Unitarian church, **Vol. 6, Part 1**, 131

South Carolina College, **Vol. 4, Part 2**, 560; founding of, **Vol. 7, Part 2**, 616; **Vol. 9, Part 2**, 507; history of, **Vol. 5, Part 2**, 518; reorganization of, **Vol. 7**,

Spies, service as, **Vol. 1, Part 1,** 563; **Vol. 4, Part 2,** 108; **Vol. 7, Part 1,** 106; **Vol. 8, Part 2,** 109; **Vol. 9, Part 2,** 138 f.; **Vol. 10, Part 1,** 659. *See also* Espionage

Spiller, William G., reference to, **Supp. 3,** 386

Spillman, William J., reference to, **Supp. 4,** 45

Spinach, nutritional value, **Supp. 5,** 623

Spinal cord: analgesia, **Supp. 6,** 435; surgery, **Supp. 6,** 130–31. *See also* Nervous system

Spinden, Herbert J., reference to, **Supp. 3,** 819

Spingarn, Joel E., reference to, **Supp. 4,** 135

Spink, Charles, reference to, **Supp. 7,** 711

Spinning machinery, **Vol. 2, Part 1,** 156; **Vol. 3, Part 1,** 600; **Vol. 6, Part 1,** 456; **Vol. 9, Part 2,** 508

Spiral nebulae, **Supp. 3,** 208

Spirit of St. Louis (airplane), **Supp. 4,** 473

Spirit of the Pilgrims (periodical), founding of, to controvert Unitarianism, **Vol. 8, Part 1,** 58

Spiritualism, **Vol. 2, Part 2,** 285; **Vol. 3, Part 1,** 84, 105, 353; **Vol. 3, Part 2,** 9, 571; **Vol. 4, Part 1,** 542, 631; **Vol. 4, Part 2,** 264, 322, 408, 473; **Vol. 5, Part 1,** 196, 249; **Vol. 5, Part 2,** 406; **Vol. 6, Part 1,** 103; **Vol. 7, Part 1,** 449, 470; **Vol. 8, Part 2,** 356; **Vol. 9, Part 1,** 439, 470; **Vol. 9, Part 2,** 510; Fox sisters, **Vol. 3, Part 1,** 540; investigations of, first public, **Vol. 8, Part 1,** 117; lectures delivered while in a state of trance, **Vol. 3, Part 1,** 105; prophecy, **Vol. 5, Part 2,** 160; satire on, **Vol. 7, Part 1,** 63; writings on, **Vol. 2, Part 1,** 179; **Vol. 3, Part 1,** 105, 354; **Vol. 4, Part 1,** 162; **Vol. 8, Part 1,** 117

Spirituals, **Supp. 3,** 225–26; **Supp. 4,** 126

Spofford, Daniel H., reference to, **Vol. 3, Part 2,** 10

Spoils system, **Vol. 1, Part 1,** 374; **Vol. 5, Part 2,** 29; **Vol. 8, Part 1,** 34 f.; **Vol. 8, Part 2,** 10; introduction of, **Vol. 6, Part 2,** 275; **Supp. 2,** 399

Spokane, Wash., early history of, **Vol. 3, Part 1,** 237 f.

Spoliation claims, French, **Vol. 1, Part 2,** 23

Sponges, studies of, **Vol. 5, Part 1,** 447

Spooner, John C., reference to, **Vol. 8, Part 2,** 396

Spoon River Anthology, **Supp. 4,** 555

Sporophyte, **Supp. 5,** 98

Sporting goods, manufacturing of, **Vol. 8, Part 1,** 418 f.; **Vol. 9, Part 1,** 420 f.

Sporting manual, first published in U.S., **Vol. 8, Part 1,** 107 f.

Sporting News, founding of, **Supp. 7,** 711–12

Sports: celebrities, **Supp. 5,** 686–88; collegiate policies, **Supp. 4,** 320; journalism, **Supp. 1,** 527; **Supp. 4,** 708–9; **Supp. 5,** 568; **Supp. 6,** 366; **Supp. 8,** 498; Madison Square Garden, **Supp. 6,** 337; municipal facilities, **Supp. 3,** 217; publicity and promotion, **Supp. 5,** 270, 724–25; radio coverage, **Supp. 7,** 378, 494–95, 707; women athletes, **Supp. 6,** 722–23; women's physical education, **Supp. 5,** 52. *See also* Olympic games; *specific sports:* Baseball; Football, *etc.*

Sports Illustrated, founding of, **Supp. 8,** 395

Spotswood, Alexander, reference to, **Vol. 1, Part 2,** 336

Spotsylvania Court House, battle of, **Vol. 1, Part 1,** 273; **Vol. 3, Part 2,** 230; **Vol. 4, Part 1,** 424, 496; **Vol. 4, Part 2,** 222; **Vol. 5, Part 1,** 25; **Vol. 6, Part 1,** 104, 126, 134, 392; **Vol. 6, Part 2,** 476; **Vol. 8, Part 2,** 548; **Vol. 9, Part 1,** 80; **Vol. 9, Part 2,** 172; **Vol. 10, Part 2,** 334

Spotted fever, treatment of, **Vol. 7, Part 1,** 559

Sprague, Frank J., reference to, **Supp. 3,** 251

Sprague, Otho S. A., Memorial Institute, **Supp. 3,** 807

Spratling, William, reference to, **Supp. 7,** 231

Spray, sloop of Slocum, **Vol. 9, Part 1,** 218

Spreckles, Claus Augustus ("Gus"), reference to, **Supp. 6,** 590

Sprigle, Raymond, reference to, **Supp. 3,** 80

Springfield, Ill., political life in days of Lincoln, **Vol. 4, Part 2,** 430

Springfield, Mass.: founding of, **Vol. 8, Part 1,** 292 f.; history of, early, **Vol. 10, Part 2,** 540; public service, **Vol. 1, Part 2,** 519; separation from the Connecticut government, **Vol. 8, Part 1,** 292 f.

Springfield, Mo., **Vol. 9, Part 1,** 62

Springfield *Daily News,* founding of, **Vol. 1, Part 2,** 163

"Springfield Junto," **Vol. 6, Part 1,** 366

Springfield Republican, **Vol. 1, Part 2,** 513–19; **Vol. 4, Part 1,** 622, **Vol. 5, Part 1,** 147, **Vol. 10, Part 2,** 135

Springfield rifle, **Vol. 1, Part 2,** 209

Spring Hill, Tenn., battle of, **Vol. 2, Part 2,** 45, 190, 476; **Vol. 3, Part 2,** 532; **Vol. 5, Part 1,** 194; **Vol. 8, Part 2,** 453; **Vol. 9, Part 1,** 508

Spring Hill College, founding of, **Vol. 8, Part 1,** 108 f.

Spruance, R. A., references to, **Supp. 6,** 267, 268

Sputnik, **Supp. 8,** 159

Spying. *See* Espionage; Spies

Squatter sovereignty, **Vol. 1, Part 1,** 403; **Vol. 3, Part 1,** 400; **Vol. 4, Part 1,** 550; **Vol. 6, Part 1,** 247; **Vol. 8, Part 2,** 617; **Vol. 10, Part 1,** 599. *See also* Kansas-Nebraska Act

Squier, Raymond Roscoe, reference to, **Supp. 6,** 181

Staël, Nicolas de, reference to, **Supp. 6,** 552

Stadium, first in U.S., **Vol. 5, Part 1,** 153

Stafford, Jean, reference to, **Supp. 7,** 474

Stagecoach lines, **Vol. 2, Part 1,** 374 f.; **Vol. 4, Part 1,** 549; **Vol. 5, Part 1,** 141; **Vol. 6, Part 1,** 163; **Vol. 6, Part 2,** 215; **Vol. 8, Part 2,** 146, 235, 252; robberies, **Vol. 1, Part 2,** 35

Stage design, **Vol. 9, Part 1,** 341; **Vol. 10, Part 1,** 133

Stage Door Canteen, founding of, **Supp. 4,** 187; **Supp. 5,** 415

Stage management, **Vol. 2, Part 2,** 156 f., 356 f.; **Vol. 4, Part 2,** 73; **Vol. 7, Part 2,** 172 f., 290; **Vol. 9, Part 1,** 370

Stained glass, **Vol. 4, Part 2,** 423, 438; **Vol. 5, Part 2,** 533 f.; **Vol. 6, Part 1,** 153; **Vol. 10, Part 2,** 244; **Supp. 3,** 183–84

Stainless steel, **Supp. 4,** 121–22

Stalin, Josef, references to, **Supp. 3,** 663; **Supp. 4,** 393; **Supp. 5,** 334; **Supp. 6,** 147, 184–85; **Supp. 7,** 204, 244, 255, 291; **Supp. 8,** 149–50, 172

Stallings, Laurence, reference to, **Supp. 6,** 15

Stamford, Conn., mayors, **Supp. 6,** 137

"Stalwarts," **Vol. 1, Part 2,** 324 f.; **Vol. 4, Part 2,** 450; **Vol. 5, Part 2,** 543 f.; **Vol. 8, Part 1,** 4 f.; **Vol. 8, Part 2,** 5, 28 f.

Stammering: A Psychoanalytic Interpretation, **Supp. 3,** 191

Stamp Act, **Vol. 1, Part 1,** 73, 385; **Vol. 2, Part 2,** 135, 287; **Vol. 3, Part 1,** 299; **Vol. 3, Part 2,** 428; **Vol. 5, Part 1,** 220, 416, 468; **Vol. 7, Part 1,** 133, 220, 637; **Vol. 8, Part 2,** 342; **Vol. 9, Part 2,** 504; **Vol. 10, Part 1,** 25 f.; Congress, **Vol. 8, Part 2,** 81, 320; enforcement of, **Vol. 3, Part 1,** 59; printing, effect of, on, **Vol. 4, Part 1,** 92; repeal of, **Vol. 3, Part 1,** 180; riots, **Vol. 3, Part 1,** 465 f.; **Vol. 5, Part 2,** 138; suggested, **Vol. 9, Part 1,** 26

Stamps: first authorized issue of, **Vol. 1, Part 2,** 47; first five-cent, **Vol. 10, Part 1,** 639 f.; introduction of, **Vol. 5, Part 1,** 589; **Vol. 5, Part 2,** 93; revenue, **Vol. 10, Part 1,** 637 f.

Standard, religious weekly, **Vol. 4, Part 1,** 215 f.; **Vol. 7, Part 1,** 439

Standard and Poor's, **Supp. 6,** 458

Standard Oil Co. *See* Oil, Standard Oil Co.

Standard Oil Co. of New Jersey, **Supp. 3,** 260–61; **Supp. 5,** 226, 236, 570; antiknock gasoline, **Supp. 3,** 522; mergers, **Supp. 4,** 775–76; writings on, **Supp. 3,** 762

Standard Oil Co. of Ohio, **Supp. 5**, 286; antitrust action, **Supp. 2**, 355, 573, 714; establishment of, **Supp. 2**, 569–75

Standards, Bureau of, creation of, **Vol. 9, Part 2**, 127 f.; first chief chemist, **Supp. 3**, 565–66; publication of, **Vol. 8, Part 2**, 154

Standing Order, religious sect, **Vol. 8, Part 2**, 32

Standish, Miles, reference to, **Vol. 1, Part 2**, 560

Stanford, Leland, references to, **Vol. 5, Part 1**, 409, 411; **Vol. 8, Part 2**, 354

Stanford-Binet test, **Supp. 6**, 626, 627

Stanford University: academic freedom issues, **Supp. 7**, 481; education studies, **Supp. 3**, 205–6; **Supp. 4**, 449; football team, **Supp. 4**, 896–97; **Supp. 5**, 728; **Supp. 8**, 588; geological studies, **Supp. 4**, 896–97; history studies, **Supp. 3**, 262; mathematics studies, **Supp. 3**, 79; mechanical engineering studies, **Supp. 6**, 182; microwave laboratory, **Supp. 4**, 358; presidency, **Supp. 4**, 892–93; psychology studies, **Supp. 6**, 626

Stanhope-Wheatcroft School of Acting (New York City), **Supp. 6**, 133

Stanislavski, Konstantin, reference to, **Supp. 3**, 297

Stanley, Henry M., reference to, **Vol. 1, Part 2**, 200

Stanley-Warner Co., **Supp. 7**, 692

Stanton, E. McM., reference to, **Vol. 6, Part 1**, 252 f.

Stanton, Elizabeth Cady, references to, **Vol. 7, Part 1**, 289; **Supp. 4**, 85, 86

Stanwyck, Barbara, references to, **Supp. 7**, 237; **Supp. 8**, 646

"Star," locomotive, **Vol. 7, Part 1**, 556

Star (Washington, D.C.), **Vol. 7, Part 1**, 586

Star Is Born, A, **Supp. 8**, 205

Stark, Harold R., references to, **Supp. 4**, 305; **Supp. 6**, 339

Stark, Lloyd C., reference to, **Supp. 3**, 597

Star of the West (steamer), **Vol. 1, Part 1**, 275; **Vol. 1, Part 2**, 111, 312; **Vol. 2, Part 1**, 213; **Vol. 3, Part 2**, 568; **Vol. 6, Part 1**, 250; **Vol. 8, Part 1**, 560; **Vol. 10, Part 1**, 630

Starrett Brothers, **Supp. 6**, 593

Star Route frauds (1882), **Vol. 1, Part 1**, 376; **Vol. 2, Part 1**, 26; **Vol. 3, Part 1**, 387; **Vol. 4, Part 1**, 149; **Vol. 5, Part 1**, 589

Stars: catalogues of, **Supp. 3**, 131; **Supp. 4**, 600; classification, **Supp. 3**, 130–31; **Supp. 6**, 7; distance measurements, **Supp. 1**, 283; double, **Supp. 1**, 674; **Supp. 5**, 13–14; galaxies, discovery of, **Supp. 5**, 540 –41; Hertzsprung-Russell diagram, **Supp. 6**, 561; movement of, **Supp. 1**, 324; parallax, **Supp. 3**, 692; **Supp. 6**, 560–61; population studies, **Supp. 6**, 31; position in southern hemisphere sky, **Supp. 5**, 541; positions and motions, **Supp. 3**, 692; radical velocities of, **Supp. 4**, 600; spectroscopic measurement of, **Supp. 4**, 600; T Coronae Borealis, discovery of, **Supp. 1**, 229; variable, **Supp. 3**, 130–31. *See also* Astronomy

Stars and Stripes, **Supp. 6**, 5

"Star-Spangled Banner, The," **Vol. 1, Part 1**, 347; **Vol. 5, Part 2**, 362 f.; **Vol. 7, Part 1**, 506; **Vol. 9, Part 1**, 200

Starch, manufacture of, **Vol. 5, Part 2**, 409 f.; **Vol. 7, Part 2**, 49

State, Department of (U.S.), **Vol. 1, Part 1**, 85 f.; **Vol. 1, Part 2**, 311; **Vol. 4, Part 1**, 15, 609; **Vol. 5, Part 2**, 23 f.; **Vol. 8, Part 1**, 353 f.; **Vol. 8, Part 2**, 618–19; **Vol. 10, Part 1**, 154; administration, **Supp. 1**, 582–83; **Supp. 3**, 219; **Supp. 4**, 170–71, 405–6, 777–78; 786; **Supp. 5**, 49, 331–35; **Supp. 6**, 387–88; **Supp. 7**, 777–78; **Supp. 8**, 6, 258, 275, 276; Clark Memorandum, **Supp. 7**, 126; cold war policies, **Supp. 6**, 179, 431, 432; Committee of Eight, **Supp. 7**, 23;

Consular Service, **Supp. 3**, 138–39, 467; consultants, **Supp. 5**, 731; early U.S. history archives, **Supp. 3**, 285; Far Eastern affairs, **Supp. 3**, 826; first foreign service exam, **Supp. 6**, 686; first woman to head major division, **Supp. 8**, 590; foreign aid policy, **Supp. 8**, 89–90; German research section, **Supp. 5**, 514; growth, **Supp. 5**, 331; Japanese policy, **Supp. 7**, 112–13; Latin American Division, **Supp. 4**, 706; **Supp. 7**, 777; loyalty issues, **Supp. 5**, 19, 665, 676; **Supp. 6**, 60, 405; **Supp. 7**, 114, 751; Marshall Plan, **Supp. 6**, 431; Mexican crisis (1915-16), **Supp. 3**, 606; Monroe Doctrine, **Supp. 7**, 126; Near Eastern Division, **Supp. 8**, 5; reorganization, **Supp. 4**, 777; **Supp. 6**, 451; trade policy, **Supp. 6**, 244; U.S. participation in World War II, **Supp. 3**, 528

State (newspaper), **Vol. 4, Part 1**, 373

State and the Church, The, **Supp. 3**, 681

State Historical Society of Missouri, founding of, **Supp. 1**, 709

State Historical Society of Wisconsin, **Vol. 3, Part 1**, 551 f.

State naval militia, first to be organized, **Vol. 8, Part 1**, 276

"State of the Union," Rhode Island committee of thirty-three on, **Vol. 8, Part 2**, 38

State teachers' association (N.Y.), formation of, **Vol. 2, Part 1**, 250

State universities, first federal grant, **Vol. 6, Part 1**, 275

State University of Iowa, psychology studies, **Supp. 4**, 731

State University of New York, **Vol. 6, Part 1**, 232; **Vol. 8, Part 2**, 127

Staten Island, N.Y.: actors' home on, **Vol. 1, Part 1**, 151; colonization, early, **Vol. 3, Part 1**, 265; Revolutionary military activity on, **Vol. 3, Part 1**, 303; Seamen's Asylum and Hospital, **Vol. 8, Part 1**, 348 f.

States (U.S.): Fourteenth Amendment due process clause, **Supp. 3**, 415; rights, Supreme Court decisions on, **Supp. 3**, 99. *See also specific state names*

States' rights, **Vol. 1, Part 1**, 591, 594; **Vol. 2, Part 2**, 134; **Vol. 3, Part 2**, 94, 117, 374, 482, 501; **Vol. 4, Part 1**, 427; **Vol. 4, Part 2**, 187, 527; **Vol. 5, Part 1**, 134, 403; **Vol. 5, Part 2**, 28, 155; **Vol. 6, Part 1**, 210; **Vol. 8, Part 1**, 363 f., 643; **Vol. 8, Part 2**, 290; **Vol. 9, Part 1**, 284, 360; **Vol. 10, Part 1**, 37; convention, **Vol. 9, Part 2**, 651; debate on, **Vol. 10, Part 1**, 585 f.; interpretation of, **Vol. 6, Part 2**, 323; legal cases concerning, **Vol. 4, Part 2**, 271

States' Rights party. *See* Dixiecrats

Static, source studies, **Supp. 4**, 422–23

Station for Experimental Evolution. *See* Cold Spring Harbor

Statistics, **Vol. 3, Part 2**, 68; **Vol. 5, Part 1**, 81, 257, 621 f.; **Vol. 5, Part 2**, 335, 494 f.; **Vol. 7, Part 1**, 562; **Vol. 8, Part 2**, 220, 425; **Vol. 9, Part 1**, 33 f.; American Statistical Association, **Vol. 5, Part 2**, 495; **Vol. 9, Part 1**, 33; biology, **Supp. 2**, 521; **Supp. 3**, 214–15, 477–78; business analysis, **Supp. 2**, 529; chemistry and physics, **Supp. 4**, 838–39; coal, **Vol. 9, Part 2**, 341; crime, **Supp. 5**, 639; criminal, **Vol. 5, Part 2**, 495; economics, **Supp. 4**, 35–36, 274–75; **Supp. 6**, 459; epidemiology, **Supp. 3**, 158; **Supp. 7**, 192; Federal Bureau of Statistics and Commerce, **Vol. 3, Part 1**, 225; **Vol. 8, Part 1**, 179 f.; **Vol. 10, Part 1**, 594 f., 637 f.; Fermi-Dirac, **Supp. 5**, 219, 221; first survey of U.S. poor, **Supp. 3**, 373; insurance industry, **Supp. 4**, 384–85; mining, **Vol. 8, Part 1**, 415; psychology, **Supp. 3**, 149–50; religious, **Vol. 3, Part 1**, 375 f.; scientific nature of, **Vol. 6, Part 2**, 467; sociology, **Supp. 6**, 483, 604–5; tabulation, mechanical, **Vol. 7, Part 2**, 573; teaching of, **Supp. 2**,

Steichen, Edward, references to, **Supp. 4**, 779, 780; **Supp. 5**, 470, 471; **Supp. 7**, 457; **Supp. 8**, 563, 564

Stein, Gertrude, references to, **Supp. 3**, 14; **Supp. 4**, 174–75, 770, 771; **Supp. 6**, 497–98, 625; **Supp. 7**, 754; **Supp. 8**, 432, 655–56

Stein, Leo, references to, **Supp. 4**, 767, 768

Stein, Michael, reference to, **Supp. 4**, 768

Stein, Sarah, reference to, **Supp. 4**, 768

Steinbeck, John, references to, **Supp. 7**, 149, 307; **Supp. 8**, 117

Steiner, Rudolf, philosophy of, **Vol. 7, Part 1**, 520

Steinman, David B., reference to, **Supp. 3**, 531

Steinway Hall (Chicago), **Supp. 3**, 598

Stelze, Charles, reference to, **Supp. 4**, 232

Stenography, **Vol. 5, Part 1**, 80 f.; shorthand method, **Supp. 4**, 347–48; **Supp. 8**, 546

Stephens, Alexander H., references to, **Vol. 5, Part 1**, 245 f., 404; **Vol. 9, Part 2**, 353, 590 f.

Stephens, James, reference to, **Vol. 7, Part 2**, 36

Stephens College (Mo.), founding of, **Vol. 9, Part 2**, 254

Stephenson, David C., reference to, **Supp. 3**, 709

Stephenson, N. W., reference to, **Supp. 6**, 310

Stereograph, **Vol. 9, Part 2**, 295

Stereotyping, invention of, **Vol. 2, Part 2**, 286

Sterilization, eugenic basis for, **Supp. 3**, 446

Sterling Oil and Refining Co., predecessors, **Supp. 4**, 776

Sterling Products, **Supp. 4**, 497

Stern, Curt, reference to, **Supp. 3**, 540

Stern, J. David, references to, **Supp. 3**, 20, 21

Sterne, Laurence, scholarship on, **Supp. 4**, 197

Sterne, Maurice, references to, **Supp. 3**, 112; **Supp. 6**, 257; **Supp. 7**, 486

Steroids, **Supp. 5**, 28

Stethoscope, use of, **Vol. 5, Part 1**, 240

Stettinius, Edward R., Jr., references to, **Supp. 4**, 458; **Supp. 5**, 332, 335, 537; **Supp. 7**, 721

Stettinius, Edward R., Sr., **Supp. 7**, 782–83

Steubenville, Ohio, steel strike, **Supp. 6**, 678

Steunenberg, Gov. Frank R.: assassination of, **Vol. 4, Part 2**, 468; reference to, **Supp. 5**, 699

Stevens, Elsie Kachel, references to, **Supp. 5**, 659, 660

Stevens, Harry M., Inc., **Supp. 7**, 719

Stevens, John F., reference to, **Supp. 7**, 89

Stevens, J. P., Co., **Supp. 8**, 367

Stevens, Nettie, reference to, **Supp. 4**, 516

Stevens, Raymond B., reference to, **Supp. 6**, 556

Stevens, Robert T., references to, **Supp. 6**, 540, 680; **Supp. 8**, 57

Stevens, Thaddeus, reference to, **Vol. 6, Part 1**, 436, 597; **Vol. 8, Part 1**, 410

Stevens-Duryea Motor Car Co., founding of, **Supp. 8**, 148–49

Stevens Institute of Technology, **Vol. 9, Part 2**, 27, 518 f.; first president, **Vol. 7, Part 1**, 254; founding of, **Vol. 9, Part 1**, 609;; presidency, **Supp. 5**, 154

Stevenson, Adlai E.: presidential candidacies, **Supp. 7**, 416; **Supp. 8**, 361; references to, **Supp. 5**, 255, 481; **Supp. 7**, 420, 421, 662

Stevenson, J. Ross, reference to, **Supp. 6**, 195

Stevenson, Robert Louis, reference to, **Supp. 4**, 517

Steward, Lavinia, reference to, **Supp. 7**, 193

Stewart, Anita, reference to, **Supp. 6**, 440

Stewart, Arthur Thomas, reference to, **Supp. 6**, 528

Stewart, Donald Ogden, reference to, **Supp. 7**, 335

Stewart, Fred, reference to, **Supp. 6**, 537

Stewart, George N., reference to, **Supp. 3**, 134–35

Stewart, Virgil A., reference to, **Vol. 7, Part 1**, 369

Stewart, W. K., Co., **Supp. 7**, 524

Stickney, Dorothy, reference to, **Supp. 8**, 382

Stieglitz, Alfred, references to, **Supp. 3**, 340; **Supp. 4**, 240–41; **Supp. 5**, 470, 471

Stiles, Ezra, references to, **Vol. 6, Part 1**, 402; **Vol. 7, Part 1**, 361

Stillwater, battle of, **Vol. 2, Part 2**, 107

Stillwell, Joseph W., references to, **Supp. 5**, 486–87; **Supp. 6**, 109–10, 231, 508; **Supp. 7**, 377, 680

Stimson, Henry L., references to, **Supp. 3**, 116, 425, 648; **Supp. 4**, 458, 459, 898; **Supp. 5**, 7, 187, 333, 334, 335; **Supp. 7**, 91, 112, 113, 261, 361; **Supp. 8**, 230

Stockard, Charles R., reference to, **Supp. 7**, 598

Stockbreeding, **Vol. 1, Part 1**, 599; **Vol. 1, Part 2**, 172; **Vol. 3, Part 2**, 478 f.; **Vol. 4, Part 1**, 256; **Vol. 4, Part 2**, 162, 204, 315, 483; **Vol. 5, Part 1**, 624 f.; **Vol. 5, Part 2**, 153; **Vol. 6, Part 1**, 92; **Vol. 6, Part 2**, 412; **Vol. 7, Part 1**, 72, 217 f., 243; **Vol. 8, Part 1**, 456; **Vol. 8, Part 2**, 311, 335; **Vol. 9, Part 1**, 30, 148; **Vol. 10, Part 1**, 617 f.

Stockbridge, early locomotive, **Vol. 8, Part 2**, 112

Stock market: branch brokerage firms, **Supp. 3**, 24; brokerage firms, **Supp. 7**, 379, 604; **Supp. 8**, 112–14; brokers, **Supp. 3**, 239; **Supp. 6**, 448–49; brokers, women, **Supp. 8**, 534; copper trading, **Supp. 2**, 292; crash (1929), **Supp. 4**, 470; **Supp. 7**, 361–62; credit purchases, **Supp. 1**, 84; employee stock-options, **Supp. 5**, 315; federal oversight legislation, **Supp. 7**, 635; illegal practices, **Supp. 8**, 113–14; investment publications, **Supp. 6**, 457–58; legislation, **Supp. 3**, 654; **Supp. 4**, 470; Morgan & Co., **Supp. 3**, 538; writings on, **Supp. 3**, 633; **Supp. 8**, 18–19. *See also* Investment banking; New York Stock Exchange

Stock speculations, **Vol. 5, Part 1**, 437; **Vol. 5, Part 2**, 283; **Vol. 6, Part 1**, 60, 157; **Vol. 8, Part 2**, 267

Stock ticker, **Vol. 5, Part 1**, 55, 247; **Vol. 6, Part 1**, 55; **Vol. 8, Part 1**, 75 f.

Stockyards. *See* Meat-packing industry

Stock Yards Labor Council, organizing of, **Supp. 4**, 279–80

Stoddard, John L., reference to, **Supp. 6**, 302

"Stoddardeanism," **Vol. 9, Part 2**, 59

Stoessel, Albert, reference to, **Supp. 3**, 65

Stokes, Anson Phelps, Jr., reference to, **Supp. 6**, 600

Stokes, Caroline Phelps, reference to, **Supp. 3**, 744

Stokes, Richard L., reference to, **Supp. 3**, 92

Stokowski, Leopold, references to, **Supp. 4**, 718; **Supp. 6**, 358, 365, 550

Stone, Hannah Mayer, reference to, **Supp. 6**, 602

Stone, Harlan Fiske, references to, **Supp. 5**, 359, 571, 572, 573, 574, 576; **Supp. 7**, 361; **Supp. 8**, 139

Stone, Lucy: daughter's biography of, **Supp. 4**, 86; references to, **Vol. 9, Part 1**, 36

Stone, Melville E., reference to, **Supp. 7**, 145

Stone, Phil, reference to, **Supp. 7**, 230

Stone, sculpture, **Supp. 3**, 278–79

Stone & Webster, **Supp. 3**, 744–47; **Supp. 4**, 453–54

Stone Mountain (Ga.) memorial, **Supp. 3**, 88–89

Stone's River, Tenn., battle of, **Vol. 1, Part 2**, 586; **Vol. 2, Part 1**, 9; **Vol. 4, Part 2**, 240; **Vol. 5, Part 2**, 145; **Vol. 8, Part 1**, 40; **Vol. 8, Part 2**, 163

Stone Telegraph and Telephone Co., founding of, **Supp. 3**, 748

Stony Point, N.Y., battle of, **Vol. 10, Part 1**, 564, 518

Stopes, Marie C., reference to, **Supp. 3**, 844

Stores, department, **Vol. 9, Part 2**, 129 f.; **Vol. 10, Part 1**, 407 f.

Stork Club, founding of, **Supp. 8**, 38–39

Storrs, Richard S., reference to, **Vol. 9, Part 2**, 347

Storrs Agricultural Experiment Station, **Vol. 5, Part 2**, 45

Storrow, T.W., reference to, **Vol. 5, Part 1**, 508

Story, Joseph B., references to, **Vol. 6, Part 2,** 321; **Supp. 7,** 792
Story, mystery, development of, **Vol. 8, Part 1,** 19 f.
Story of a Bad Boy, **Vol. 4, Part 2,** 71
Story of a Pioneer, **Vol. 9, Part 1,** 35
Story of My Life, The, **Supp. 8,** 317
Story of Philosophy, The, **Supp. 8,** 579
Story of the Great March, **Vol. 7, Part 1,** 494
Storyville (Boston nightclub), **Supp. 8,** 562
Stoughton Musical Society, founding of, **Vol. 1, Part 2,** 270
Stourbridge Lion (locomotive), **Vol. 5, Part 1,** 99
Stove-polish, invention of, **Vol. 3, Part 1,** 329
Stover, Charles B., reference to, **Supp. 3,** 175
"Stover, Dink" (fictional character), **Supp. 5,** 372
Stover at Yale, **Supp. 5,** 372
Stoves: base-burning, first, **Vol. 7, Part 1,** 581; coal-burning, invention of, **Vol. 2, Part 2,** 110; Latrobe, **Vol. 6, Part 1,** 28; Oberlin, **Vol. 9, Part 2,** 12
Stowe, Harriet Beecher: reference to, **Vol. 7, Part 1,** 252; writings on, **Supp. 3,** 672
Stowe, Lyman Beecher, references to, **Supp. 4,** 870; **Supp. 6,** 568
Straight Line Engine Co., **Vol. 9, Part 2,** 243
Strang, James J., reference to, **Vol. 9, Part 2,** 334
Strange, Michael, reference to, **Supp. 6,** 517
Strange Fruit, **Supp. 8,** 605
Stratemeyer, Edward, reference to, **Supp. 7,** 279
Straton, John Roach, reference to, **Supp. 7,** 624
Stratosphere, early writings on, **Vol. 8, Part 2,** 184
Stratton, Samuel W., reference to, **Supp. 3,** 473
Straus, Isidor, reference to, **Supp. 6,** 606
Straus, Nathan, references to, **Supp. 3,** 451; **Supp. 6,** 606
Straus, Oscar, references to, **Supp. 6,** 253, 606
Strauss, Lewis L., reference to, **Supp. 7,** 565, 590
Strauss, Richard, references to, **Supp. 8,** 641, 642
Stravinsky, Igor, reference to, **Supp. 7,** 548
Strawberries, cultivation of, **Vol. 5, Part 1,** 272; **Vol. 6, Part 1,** 394
Strayer, George D., references to, **Supp. 3,** 677; **Supp. 4,** 833
Street paving, graft in, **Vol. 8, Part 1,** 588
Street railways, **Vol. 3, Part 2,** 85, 459; **Vol. 4, Part 2,** 167, 226; **Vol. 5, Part 2,** 123; **Vol. 6, Part 1,** 478; **Vol. 7, Part 1,** 71; **Vol. 8, Part 2,** 527; **Vol. 9, Part 2,** 232; cable cars, **Vol. 4, Part 2,** 156; electric, early, **Vol. 9, Part 1,** 128; electrification, **Supp. 1,** 531; equipment development, **Supp. 1,** 669; streetcar, one of first in U.S., **Vol. 5, Part 1,** 325; streetcar building, pioneer, **Vol. 9, Part 1,** 583; strike, New York, **Vol. 5, Part 2,** 196; tramway of 1809, **Vol. 6, Part 1,** 154; trolley cars, early experiments with, **Vol. 3, Part 1,** 88
Street railways (by city): Brooklyn, N.Y., **Vol. 3, Part 2,** 480; **Vol. 6, Part 1,** 294; **Vol. 7, Part 1,** 71; **Vol. 7, Part 2,** 358; Chicago, **Vol. 10, Part 2,** 610; Louisville, Ky., **Vol. 1, Part 2,** 532; New York, N.Y., **Vol. 5, Part 2,** 196; **Vol. 7, Part 2,** 358 f.; **Vol. 8, Part 1,** 634; **Vol. 8, Part 2,** 265 f.; **Vol. 9, Part 1,** 124; **Vol. 9, Part 2,** 241; Philadelphia, Pa., **Vol. 3, Part 1,** 459 f.; **Vol. 7, Part 1,** 71; **Vol. 8, Part 1,** 428; St. Louis, Mo., **Vol. 10, Part 1,** 638 f.; San Francisco, Calif., **Vol. 3, Part 1,** 394; Washington, D.C., **Vol. 2, Part 2,** 383
Street Railways Advertising Co., establishment of, **Supp. 2,** 112
Street Railways Employees' Benevolent Association, **Supp. 1,** 511
Street Scene, **Supp. 4,** 104; **Supp. 8,** 288, 529
Streets of Paris, The (revue), **Supp. 5,** 500

Strelow, Albert, reference to, **Supp. 4,** 294
Streptococcus enteritis, **Supp. 4,** 494
Streptomycin, **Supp. 6,** 447; discovery of, **Supp. 2,** 387
Strickland, William, **Vol. 9, Part 2,** 628
Stricklett, Elmer, reference to, **Supp. 6,** 663
Strikes, **Vol. 4, Part 1,** 175, 288, 370; **Vol. 5, Part 2,** 46, 196; Actors' Equity Association, **Supp. 3,** 174, 333; automobile industry, **Supp. 4,** 612–13; **Supp. 8,** 419, 600, 652; Boston police (1919), **Supp. 1,** 194–95; **Supp. 3,** 471; coal industry, **Vol. 1, Part 1,** 260; **Vol. 5, Part 2,** 196; **Supp. 5,** 248–49; **Supp. 8,** 374, 375, 376, Consumers' Research, **Supp. 8,** 425; garment industry, New York, **Vol. 5, Part 2,** 196; **Supp. 3,** 96; **Supp. 4,** 374; government intervention, **Vol. 10, Part 1,** 119; Homestead steel, **Supp. 3,** 94; journalism on, **Supp. 8,** 675; "Little Steel," **Supp. 6,** 597; Ludlow massacres (1914), **Supp. 6,** 548; lumber industry, **Supp. 6,** 320; *New York Times,* **Supp. 7,** 200; opposition to, as industrial weapon, **Vol. 8, Part 1,** 142 f.; Pennsylvania, armed suppression of, **Vol. 4, Part 2,** 368; printing trade, **Vol. 1, Part 1,** 237; railroad, **Vol. 1, Part 1,** 490; **Vol. 2, Part 2,** 211; **Vol. 3, Part 1,** 183; **Vol. 5, Part 2,** 68; **Vol. 6, Part 1,** 133 f.; **Vol. 8, Part 1,** 142 f.; **Vol. 9, Part 2,** 86, 267; **Supp. 8,** 513; railroad injunction (1922), **Supp. 3,** 214; restrictive legislation, **Supp. 8,** 269; right-to-strike legislation, **Supp. 6,** 586; San Francisco electrical workers, **Supp. 3,** 532; San Francisco general (1934), **Supp. 5,** 287; **Supp. 7,** 609; sit-down, **Supp. 3,** 656; **Supp. 4,** 612–13; steel (1919), **Vol. 5, Part 2,** 196; steel industry, **Supp. 4,** 280; **Supp. 5,** 156, 445–46; **Supp. 5,** 510, 714; **Supp. 6,** 597, 678; **Supp. 7,** 228–29, 254–55, 290, 587; steel mill seizure, **Supp. 8,** 517; street car, New York, **Vol. 5, Part 2,** 196; Supreme Court on presidential seizure power, **Supp. 5,** 156, 714; textile industry, **Supp. 3,** 576–77; **Supp. 5,** 616; **Supp. 6,** 238; **Supp. 8,** 457; Toledo Auto-Lite (1934), **Supp. 8,** 458; transit system, **Supp. 8,** 513; treason, regarding of, as, **Vol. 3, Part 2,** 556; World War II, **Supp. 7,** 172
String galvanometer, first made in U.S., **Supp. 6,** 117
Striptease, **Supp. 8,** 363–65
Stritch, Samuel, reference to, **Supp. 8,** 613, 614
Strong, Benjamin, reference to, **Supp. 3,** 203
Structural engineering, **Supp. 1,** 680
"Structuralist" school, **Vol. 9, Part 2,** 564
Strychnine, studies of, **Supp. 2,** 161
Stuart, Charles, reference to, **Vol. 10, Part 1,** 625 f.
Stuart, Gilbert, references to, **Vol. 5, Part 2,** 223; **Vol. 9, Part 2,** 649
Stuart, J. E. B., reference to, **Vol. 6, Part 1,** 125, 585
Stuart, John Leighton, reference to, **Supp. 3,** 288
Stubble digger, introduction of, **Vol. 3, Part 1,** 585 f.
Studebaker Corporation, **Supp. 6,** 650
Student Army Training Corps, organization of, **Vol. 6, Part 2,** 120
Student government, **Supp. 1,** 100; **Supp. 4,** 870
Student Nonviolent Coordinating Committee, **Supp. 8,** 388; founding of, **Supp. 8,** 333, 539–40
Student Prince, The, **Supp. 5,** 585, 627
Student Volunteer Movement, **Supp. 3,** 476; **Supp. 5,** 506–8
Student Volunteer Movement for Foreign Missions, **Vol. 7, Part 1,** 105; **Vol. 7, Part 2,** 590
Study and Criticism of Italian Art, The, **Supp. 6,** 56
Study of Man, **Supp. 5,** 435
Sturtevant, Alfred H., references to, **Supp. 3,** 539–40; **Supp. 8,** 448
Stuttering, **Supp. 7,** 395–96
Stuyvesant, Peter, reference to, **Vol. 7, Part 1,** 516

Stutz Motor Car Co., **Supp. 3,** 314
Subject of the Artist (New York City art school), founding of, **Supp. 7,** 39
Submarines: aircraft, use of, against, **Vol. 3, Part 1,** 614 f.; building, **Vol. 2, Part 2,** 319; **Vol. 4, Part 1,** 485; **Vol. 5, Part 2,** 380; design and construction, **Supp. 5,** 725; detection, **Vol. 3, Part 1,** 221; **Supp. 4,** 818; **Supp. 5,** 188, 495; **Supp. 6,** 365, 501; **Supp. 7,** 516, 517; development of, **Supp. 3,** 120, 436–37; "diving boat," **Vol. 4, Part 1,** 70; experimentation, early, **Vol. 4, Part 1,** 70; first in Navy, **Supp. 3,** 120; invention of, **Vol. 5, Part 1,** 145; mines and torpedoes, **Vol. 2, Part 1,** 349; New London, Conn., base, **Supp. 6,** 338; nuclear, **Supp. 8,** 232; patents, **Vol. 8, Part 1,** 541; telegraphy, **Vol. 3, Part 1,** 336; **Vol. 10, Part 1,** 421; torpedo-boat, first successful, **Vol. 3, Part 1,** 211
Submarine Warfare, pamphlet of 1867, **Vol. 6, Part 1,** 65
Subtreasury, origin of, **Vol. 2, Part 2,** 177; **Vol. 10, Part 1,** 155, 355
Suburbs: "homecroft" advocacy, **Supp. 4,** 564; housing developments, **Supp. 7,** 469–70; planned garden, **Supp. 6,** 26; zoning restrictions, **Supp. 4,** 57
Subversives. *See* Espionage; Loyalty issues
Subways: building, **Vol. 1, Part 2,** 408; **Vol. 2, Part 2,** 544; **Vol. 4, Part 1,** 8; **Vol. 4, Part 2,** 605; **Vol. 7, Part 2,** 56, 277, 602; **Vol. 9, Part 1,** 124; **Vol. 10, Part 2,** 339; development of, **Supp. 2,** 559; **Supp. 4,** 56; engineering, **Supp. 4,** 757; speed control, **Supp. 5,** 228; unification of, **Supp. 2,** 675; **Supp. 4,** 466, 855
Success, magazine, founding of, **Vol. 6, Part 2,** 279
Successful Farming, founding of, **Supp. 7,** 527, 528
Sudan grass, discovery of, **Vol. 7, Part 2,** 632
Suez crisis (1956), **Supp. 6,** 179; **Supp. 8,** 147, 158, 276
Suffolk, Va., campaign, **Vol. 6, Part 1,** 124, 392; **Vol. 7, Part 2,** 381, 570
Suffolk Bank System, **Vol. 6, Part 1,** 51
Suffolk Resolves, carrying of, to Philadelphia, **Vol. 8, Part 1,** 515
Suffrage: property qualifications, **Vol. 8, Part 2,** 349; universal white male, establishment of, **Vol. 7, Part 2,** 613. *See also* Voting rights; Woman suffrage
Suffrage Study Club, **Supp. 6,** 79
Sugar Creek War, **Vol. 8, Part 1,** 42
Sugar industry: barter, sugar and rum for lumber, **Vol. 3, Part 1,** 252; beet sugar technology, **Supp. 1,** 431; cane studies, **Supp. 1,** 183; chemistry of, **Supp. 4,** 114; **Supp. 5,** 327–28; Hawaiian plantation, **Supp. 1,** 48; planting, **Vol. 2, Part 1,** 535; **Vol. 3, Part 1,** 585 f.; **Vol. 4, Part 1,** 256; **Vol. 9, Part 1,** 427, 478 f.; **Vol. 9, Part 2,** 338; importation of, **Vol. 7, Part 2,** 631; refining, **Vol. 1, Part 2,** 461; **Vol. 3, Part 1,** 585 f.; **Vol. 4, Part 2,** 336, 404 f.; **Vol. 5, Part 1,** 448; **Vol. 5, Part 2,** 464; **Vol. 7, Part 2,** 267; **Vol. 8, Part 2,** 512; **Vol. 9, Part 1,** 428; **Vol. 10, Part 1,** 457 f.; **Vol. 10, Part 2,** 187; refining, first time in U.S., **Vol. 1, Part 1,** 130; sugar-beet seed experimentation, **Vol. 8, Part 1,** 239 f.; tariffs, **Vol. 2, Part 2,** 459; **Vol. 4, Part 2,** 404; **Vol. 7, Part 2,** 101 f.; trust, **Vol. 4, Part 2,** 404. *See also* Glucose
Sulfa drugs, **Supp. 3,** 854; **Supp. 6,** 447
Sulfonamide drugs, **Supp. 7,** 477
Sulfuric acid, **Supp. 5,** 319–20
Sullivan, Anne, reference to, **Supp. 8,** 316–18
Sullivan, Eugene C., reference to, **Supp. 6,** 624
Sullivan, Harry Stack, reference to, **Supp. 4,** 131; **Supp. 6,** 220
Sullivan, Louis H., references to, **Supp. 2,** 537, 709; **Supp. 4,** 105, 106; **Supp. 5,** 207, 208; **Supp. 6,** 711, 713; **Supp. 8,** 463

Sullivan, Nikki, reference to, **Supp. 6,** 301
Sullivan and Cromwell, **Supp. 4,** 192–93; **Supp. 6,** 177, 178; **Supp. 8,** 147
Sullivan Island, S.C. *See* Charleston, S.C.
Sullivan's Rhode Island expedition (1778), **Vol. 4, Part 1,** 186; **Vol. 5, Part 2,** 537; **Vol. 9, Part 2,** 193; **Vol. 10, Part 1,** 518
Sulphur: dioxide, isolation of, **Vol. 8, Part 1,** 223 f.; production, **Vol. 3, Part 2,** 603; researches in, **Vol. 9, Part 1,** 235
Sulzberger, Arthur Hays, reference to, **Supp. 7,** 199–200
Sumeria, language studies, **Supp. 1,** 172
Summer school, first, **Vol. 9, Part 1,** 472
Summer School of the South, **Supp. 3,** 209
Sumner, Charles, references to, **Vol. 2, Part 1,** 88, 289; **Vol. 3, Part 2,** 398 f.; **Vol. 6, Part 1,** 436; **Vol. 7, Part 2,** 576; **Vol. 9, Part 1,** 516, 624; **Vol. 9, Part 2,** 210
Sun, eclipses of, **Vol. 3, Part 1,** 602 f.; spots, **Vol. 10, Part 2,** 415. *See also* Solar *headings*
Sun Also Rises, The, **Supp. 7,** 335, 336
Sunday, Billy, reference to, **Supp. 5,** 649
Sunday, observance of, **Vol. 8, Part 1,** 428; **Vol. 8, Part 2,** 114; **Vol. 9, Part 2,** 299
Sunday-school movement, **Vol. 1, Part 1,** 392, 628; **Vol. 2, Part 2,** 108; **Vol. 3, Part 1,** 522 f.; **Vol. 3, Part 2,** 492; **Vol. 4, Part 1,** 625; **Vol. 5, Part 1,** 425; **Vol. 5, Part 2,** 409, 589; **Vol. 7, Part 2,** 410; **Vol. 8, Part 1,** 539; **Vol. 9, Part 1,** 33, 43 f., 270; **Vol. 10, Part 1,** 8 f.; American Sunday-School Union, **Vol. 1, Part 1,** 392; **Vol. 4, Part 1,** 624 f.; **Vol. 5, Part 1,** 56, 132; **Vol. 6, Part 1,** 406; **Vol. 7, Part 2,** 127 f.; **Vol. 8, Part 1,** 539; associations, **Vol. 6, Part 1,** 44; first Sunday school in U.S., **Vol. 8, Part 1,** 381; lessons, uniform, **Vol. 4, Part 2,** 409; **Vol. 10, Part 1,** 9; publications, **Vol. 4, Part 2,** 360; **Vol. 5, Part 2,** 240, 369; **Vol. 6, Part 1,** 430–24; **Vol. 7, Part 1,** 451; writings on, **Vol. 6, Part 1,** 44; **Vol. 7, Part 2,** 411; **Vol. 8, Part 1,** 539; **Vol. 9, Part 2,** 307
Sun Oil Co., **Supp. 7,** 615
Sunset Boulevard, **Supp. 6,** 160, 658–59
Sunshine Society, founding of, **Supp. 1,** 19
Sunspots, magnetic fields, **Supp. 2,** 271
Sun Valley, Idaho, naming of, **Supp. 5,** 270–71
Superheterodyne circuit, **Supp. 5,** 21
Superior Oil Co. of Los Angeles, **Supp. 7,** 111
Supermarkets, **Supp. 7,** 141; A&P switch to, **Supp. 5,** 278; introduction of, **Supp. 5,** 604
Supernaturalism. *See* Psychic phenomena
Supreme Court, United States, **Vol. 1, Part 1,** 533 f., 595; **Vol. 1, Part 2,** 338, 360, 572; **Vol. 2, Part 1,** 23; **Vol. 2, Part 2,** 36, 634 f.; **Vol. 4, Part 1,** 61, 627 f.; **Vol. 4, Part 2,** 25; **Vol. 5, Part 1,** 183, 233, 394, 492; **Vol. 5, Part 2,** 122, 553; **Vol. 6, Part 1,** 313, 510; **Vol. 6, Part 2,** 88, 128, 319 f., 419; **Vol. 7, Part 1,** 108, 113, 422 f.; **Vol. 8, Part 1,** 285 f.; **Vol. 8, Part 2,** 347; **Vol. 9, Part 1,** 103 f.; **Vol. 9, Part 2,** 104, 239 f., 332, 472, 643; **Vol. 10, Part 1,** 393 f., 494 f., 508 f.; **Vol. 10, Part 2,** 96, 489, 506; antitrust decisions, **Supp. 3,** 168; **Supp. 7,** 96; appellate cases before, **Supp. 5,** 155, 156; building, new, Taft's advocacy of, **Vol. 9, Part 2,** 272; chief justices, **Supp. 5,** 713; church-state separation decisions, **Supp. 4,** 713; **Supp. 5,** 358; citizenship decisions, **Supp. 4,** 727; civil liberties decisions, **Supp. 3,** 168; **Supp. 4,** 407, 537, 614, 713, 796; **Supp. 5,** 358, 389, 574–75, 714; **Supp. 7,** 96, 263–64, 291, 541–42; civil rights decisions, **Supp. 4,** 397, 407, 796; **Supp. 5,** 713–14; **Supp. 6,** 502; **Supp. 7,** 96; **Supp. 8,** 406; Civil War period, **Vol. 4, Part 1,** 613; "clear and present danger" test, **Supp. 7,** 317; Congress, acts invalidated

by, Jefferson's views on, **Vol. 5, Part 2**, 29; conservative "Four Horsemen," **Supp. 4**, 537–38; court-packing move, **Supp. 3**, 100, 168, 227, 655; **Supp. 4**, 42, 407, 491, 537; **Supp. 5**, 357, 443, 481; **Supp. 6**, 138, 227, 234; **Supp. 7**, 263, 541, 730; decisions of, 1862–90, **Vol. 6, Part 2**, 638 f.; dissent record, **Supp. 4**, 538; formative period, **Vol. 5, Part 2**, 8; historical writings on, **Supp. 5**, 731; interstate commerce decisions, **Supp. 3**, 241; **Supp. 4**, 404–5; judges' bill, **Vol. 9, Part 2**, 271; judicial activism, **Supp. 4**, 796, 797; judicial disagreement on functions of, **Supp. 5**, 571; judicial self-restraint, **Supp. 3**, 94; **Supp. 4**, 795, 797; **Supp. 5**, 357–58; **Supp. 7**, 96, 264; justices, **Supp. 1**, 272, 417, 422–27; **Supp. 2**, 79, 93; **Supp. 3**, 97–100; **Supp. 4**, 613–14, 712–13, 794–97; **Supp. 5**, 357–59, 571–76; **Supp. 7**, 96–97, 263–85, 541–42; justices' positions on New Deal legislation, **Supp. 5**, 572–75; labor-related decisions, **Supp. 5**, 156, 249, 572, 574, 714; loyalty-security decisions, **Supp. 5**, 358, 589, 714; **Supp. 7**, 96–97, 317; Mooney case, **Supp. 3**, 533; New Deal legislation decisions, **Supp. 3**, 755, 789, 839; **Supp. 4**, 406–7, 537, 795–97; **Supp. 5**, 358, 572–75; **Supp. 7**, 263; **Supp. 8**, 35; nominations to (unconfirmed), **Supp. 6**, 494; organization of, **Vol. 3, Part 2**, 114; preferred freedoms concept, **Supp. 4**, 796–97; press freedom decisions, **Supp. 3**, 157; school desegregation decisions, **Supp. 5**, 156; **Supp. 7**, 501; **Supp. 8**, 25, 157; state courts, jurisdiction of, over, **Vol. 9, Part 2**, 105; state v. federal power decisions, **Supp. 3**, 754–55; steel industry seizure decision, **Supp. 5**, 156, 714; TVA decisions, **Supp. 8**, 179; Webster's theory about power of, **Vol. 10, Part 1**, 585 f.; woman, first, to practice before, **Vol. 6, Part 1**, 341; woman justices, issue of, **Supp. 8**, 5; writings on, **Supp. 5**, 549; **Supp. 6**, 143; **Supp. 7**, 146–47, 261; zoning decision, **Supp. 4**, 56–57. *See also* Judicial systems; Judiciary

Supreme Court Building, construction of, **Supp. 3**, 99

Supreme Court in United States History, The, **Supp. 5**, 731

Supreme Court justices. For complete list, *See* Occupations Index

Surface chemistry, **Supp. 6**, 365

Surgeon general, United States, **Supp. 4**, 791; smoking and health reports, **Supp. 7**, 192

Surgery, **Vol. 1, Part 1**, 636; **Vol. 1, Part 2**, 80; **Vol. 2, Part 1**, 507; **Vol. 2, Part 2**, 95, 339; **Vol. 3, Part 1**, 91, 385 f., 412 f., 478 f.; **Vol. 3, Part 2**, 219, 321, 331, 406 f.; **Vol. 4, Part 1**, 180, 221, 229, 259; **Vol. 4, Part 2**, 19 f., 32, 164 f., 185, 365; **Vol. 5, Part 1**, 239, 284, 364; **Vol. 5, Part 2**, 140 f., 181, 235, 376, 414 f., 580; **Vol. 6, Part 1**, 375, 523, 615; **Vol. 6, Part 2**, 428, 585; **Vol. 7, Part 1**, 72, 130; **Vol. 7, Part 2**, 198, 243, 276, 554 f., 602, 637; **Vol. 8, Part 1**, 121, 209 f., 360 f., 378, 486 f., 575 f.; **Vol. 8, Part 2**, 111, 358, 404; **Vol. 9, Part 1**, 132, 186 f., 195, 324, 348, 451; **Vol. 9, Part 2**, 33, 85, 575; **Vol. 10, Part 1**, 84, 395, 479 f., 611 f.; **Vol. 10, Part 2**, 473, 576; **Supp. 2**, 438; **Supp. 5**, 104; abdominal, **Vol. 1, Part 2**, 55; **Vol. 2, Part 1**, 254; **Vol. 3, Part 2**, 563; **Vol. 5, Part 1**, 549; **Vol. 6, Part 2**, 28; **Vol. 8, Part 1**, 213 f., 572; **Supp. 3**, 410; American Surgical Association, **Vol. 5, Part 1**, 100; **Vol. 7, Part 2**, 208; **Vol. 8, Part 1**, 575; animal ligature, **Vol. 5, Part 1**, 601; antiseptic methods, **Supp. 1**, 240; appendectomy, **Vol. 3, Part 2**, 434, 563 f.; **Vol. 5, Part 1**, 546; **Vol. 6, Part 1**, 555 f., 615; **Vol. 7, Part 1**, 380; **Supp. 1**, 236; appendectomy, first successful, in U.S., **Vol. 7, Part 2**, 243; asceptic, **Vol. 1, Part 2**, 224; **Vol. 5, Part 2**, 141, 580; **Vol. 8, Part 1**, 391; aural, **Vol. 2, Part 1**, 221; blood vessel, **Supp. 3**, 140; bone, **Vol. 7, Part 1**, 120, 409; **Vol. 10, Part 2**, 463; brain,

Supp. 2, 137; **Supp. 6**, 70, 131; breast cancer, **Supp. 6**, 70; cardiac, **Supp. 7**, 59; cataract removal, **Vol. 3, Part 1**, 478 f.; **Vol. 5, Part 1**, 541; certification in, **Supp. 6**, 246; cesarian section, first successful, in U.S., **Vol. 8, Part 1**, 583; Dieffenbach operation, **Vol. 3, Part 1**, 327; dissection of human body for instruction, first, **Vol. 1, Part 1**, 597; duct ligation, **Supp. 3**, 483; electricity, early use of, in, **Vol. 2, Part 1**, 385; electrosurgical knife (Bovie unit), **Supp. 6**, 69–70; endoaneurysmorrhaphy, **Supp. 6**, 494; ether charts, **Supp. 2**, 137; eye, **Supp. 3**, 301–2, 430–31; fee-splitting, **Supp. 6**, 245; first bacteriology lab, **Supp. 6**, 664; first heart valve, **Supp. 4**, 209; fistula operations, **Vol. 1, Part 1**, 186; Fowler position, **Supp. 6**, 214–15; frozen tissue sections, **Supp. 3**, 503; gallbladder, **Vol. 1, Part 2**, 433; **Vol. 8, Part 1**, 360 f., 378; **Supp. 6**, 632; gastric, **Supp. 3**, 271; gastro-intestinal, **Vol. 7, Part 2**, 374; genitourinary, **Vol. 2, Part 1**, 116, 393; **Vol. 5, Part 2**, 364; **Vol. 6, Part 2**, 384; **Supp. 3**, 121; **Supp. 4**, 507, 508; gynecological, **Vol. 6, Part 2**, 273; **Supp. 1**, 542; instruments, surgical, improvements in, **Vol. 7, Part 2**, 554 f.; intranasal, **Vol. 6, Part 1**, 268; journals, **Supp. 1**, 542, 599; limbs, artificial, **Vol. 1, Part 1**, 428; **Vol. 6, Part 2**, 288; mastoid operation, **Vol. 5, Part 1**, 248; military, **Vol. 1, Part 2**, 25, 105; **Vol. 2, Part 1**, 52; **Vol. 3, Part 2**, 307, 538; **Vol. 4, Part 1**, 272; **Vol. 4, Part 2**, 481; **Vol. 5, Part 2**, 375 f; **Vol. 6, Part 1**, 58 f., 440 f.; **Vol. 6, Part 2**, 243; **Vol. 7, Part 2**, 96 f., 109; **Vol. 8, Part 2**, 376, 585; **Vol. 9, Part 2**, 550; **Vol. 10, Part 2**, 492; neurological, **Supp. 2**, 209; **Supp. 4**, 213, 214, 249–50; obstetrics, **Vol. 10, Part 2**, 326; ophthalmic, **Vol. 5, Part 2**, 37 f.; **Vol. 6, Part 1**, 296; orthopedic, **Vol. 1, Part 2**, 22, 556 f.; **Vol. 3, Part 1**, 118 f.; **Vol. 5, Part 2**, 235 f.; **Vol. 6, Part 1**, 443; **Vol. 8, Part 2**, 404; **Vol. 9, Part 2**, 318, 343; **Vol. 10, Part 2**, 231; **Supp. 1**, 25–26, 40–41; **Supp. 4**, 887; **Supp. 6**, 344–45; osteotomy, **Vol. 10, Part 1**, 158; osteosarcoma, **Vol. 8, Part 1**, 360 f.; pathology of, **Supp. 1**, 91; plastic, **Vol. 2, Part 1**, 224; **Vol. 5, Part 2**, 492 f.; **Supp. 2**, 707; **Supp. 4**, 220–21, 530; **Supp. 6**, 632; postoperative care, **Supp. 6**, 190; procedures development, **Supp. 3**, 67; prostate gland, **Supp. 3**, 854; radical dissection, **Supp. 3**, 202; reproductive system, **Supp. 6**, 631–32; rubber gloves, use of, **Supp. 1**, 90; shock prevention, **Supp. 3**, 201; **Supp. 7**, 59; sinus, **Vol. 6, Part 1**, 523; skull tumors, **Vol. 1, Part 2**, 2; specialist teams, **Supp. 5**, 404–5; spinal cord, **Supp. 6**, 131; supplies, surgical, **Vol. 8, Part 2**, 528; surgeon-generalship, **Vol. 1, Part 1**, 631; **Vol. 1, Part 2**, 267; teaching of, **Vol. 2, Part 2**, 76; **Vol. 4, Part 2**, 465; **Vol. 5, Part 1**, 100, 161; **Vol. 6, Part 1**, 555 f.; **Vol. 7, Part 1**, 120, 290, 353 f., 372, 380, 409, 553, 616; **Vol. 7, Part 2**, 129; **Vol. 8, Part 2**, 404 f., 584; **Vol. 9, Part 1**, 324, 327, 606; **Vol. 9, Part 2**, 535; **Supp. 3**, 121–22, 458; textbook, first in colonies, **Vol. 5, Part 2**, 181; thoracic, **Supp. 6**, 246; tonsil operation, **Vol. 7, Part 1**, 616; training in, **Supp. 3**, 626; **Supp. 4**, 208–9; transplant studies, **Supp. 3**, 140–41; vascular, **Supp. 6**, 434–35; venereal disease, first specialist in U.S., **Vol. 2, Part 1**, 260; water, boiled, early faith in, **Vol. 3, Part 1**, 478 f.; women in field of, **Vol. 6, Part 1**, 340; writings on, **Vol. 2, Part 1**, 52, 93, 116, 199, 224, 254, 394; **Vol. 4, Part 2**, 19; **Vol. 5, Part 2**, 141, 181, 415, 580; **Vol. 6, Part 1**, 615; **Vol. 7, Part 1**, 324 f., 354, 380, 616; **Vol. 8, Part 1**, 213 f., 376, 378, 572; **Vol. 8, Part 2**, 44, 111; **Vol. 9, Part 1**, 403; **Vol. 9, Part 2**, 33, 318, 343; **Vol. 10, Part 1**, 84, 158, 395, 480 f., 581 f.; **Vol. 10, Part 2**, 576; **Supp. 1**, 218, 599. *See also* Anesthesia

Vol. 10, Part 1, 117 f.; Walker Act of 1846, **Vol. 3, Part 1,** 39; **Vol. 6, Part 1,** 210; **Vol. 8, Part 1,** 34 f.; **Vol. 10, Part 1,** 585 f.; Wilson bill, **Vol. 5, Part 2,** 178; **Vol. 7, Part 2,** 331; wool, **Vol. 4, Part 2,** 446; writings against protective, **Supp. 3,** 762; writings on, **Vol. 6, Part 1,** 293. *See also* Trade

Tariff Board, first chairmanship of, **Vol. 3, Part 2,** 144

Tariff Commission, **Vol. 4, Part 2,** 446

Tariff reform (1893), **Vol. 2, Part 1,** 495; **Vol. 2, Part 2,** 210; **Vol. 5, Part 1,** 335; **Vol. 7, Part 1,** 15

Tarkington, Booth, references to, **Supp. 2,** 726; **Supp. 6,** 545; **Supp. 7,** 656

Tarno, Fritz, reference to, **Supp. 6,** 708–9

Tarolinta, ship to California in gold rush, **Vol. 7, Part 1,** 612

"Tarzan" (fictional character), **Supp. 4,** 129

Tass, **Supp. 7,** 268, 269

Tate, Allen, references to, **Supp. 7,** 55, 56

Taussing, Helen B., reference to, **Supp. 7,** 59

Tavern signs, historical consequence of, **Vol. 8, Part 1,** 174 f.

Taxation, **Vol. 3, Part 1,** 299 f., 316, 499; **Vol. 3, Part 2,** 169; **Vol. 9, Part 1,** 234; **Vol. 10, Part 1,** 637 f.; capital gains, **Supp. 8,** 160; churches exempted from, **Vol. 8, Part 1,** 619; cuts advocates, **Supp. 6,** 455, 535; excess-profits, **Supp. 8,** 422; Excise Act, **Vol. 3, Part 2,** 560; gasoline tax for road building, **Supp. 1,** 671; Impressment Act, **Vol. 3, Part 1,** 128; income distribution goal, **Supp. 8,** 446; income tax, **Vol. 2, Part 1,** 120; **Supp. 1,** 533; **Supp. 2,** 148, 607; income tax exemptions, **Supp. 8,** 166; income tax in Wisconsin, **Supp. 1,** 385; income tax legislation, **Supp. 3,** 654; income tax preparation guide, **Supp. 5,** 412; income theory, **Supp. 4,** 748; Mellon plan, **Supp. 2,** 449–50; Minnesota, **Vol. 3, Part 2,** 42; Massachusetts Colony opposition, **Vol. 10, Part 2,** 427; New Deal policies, **Supp. 5,** 180–81, 712; oil-discovery depletion allowance, **Supp. 4,** 339; pay-as-you-go plan, **Supp. 6,** 559; poll tax, **Vol. 7, Part 2,** 123; **Supp. 6,** 526; **Supp. 7,** 416; progressive, **Supp. 2,** 607; property, **Supp. 1,** 385; **Supp. 2,** 272; **Supp. 6,** 522; "Sanborn Contracts," **Vol. 8, Part 1,** 578; school, **Vol. 3, Part 1,** 521 f.; **Vol. 8, Part 2,** 105; single tax, **Vol. 4, Part 1,** 174, 215; **Supp. 4,** 844, 845; slaves, **Vol. 3, Part 2,** 107; **Vol. 8, Part 1,** 417; stamp tax, **Vol. 5, Part 1,** 468; studies on, **Supp. 2,** 326; Virginia, **Vol. 3, Part 1,** 316; war, **Supp. 1,** 10; writings on, **Supp. 8,** 166. *See also* Tariff

Taxicabs, **Supp. 7,** 343

Taxidermy, **Vol. 1, Part 1,** 425; **Vol. 6, Part 2,** 457; Akeley method, **Vol. 1, Part 1,** 132

Taxonomy, **Vol. 3, Part 1,** 578 f.; **Vol. 4, Part 1,** 286; ornithological, **Supp. 3,** 161

Tax Payment Act (1943), **Supp. 6,** 559

Taylor, Al, reference to, **Supp. 6,** 303

Taylor, Charles Alonzo, **Supp. 4,** 821–22

Taylor, C. G., reference to, **Supp. 8,** 504

Taylor, Deems, references to, **Supp. 4,** 576; **Supp. 6,** 309

Taylor, E. B., reference to, **Supp. 3,** 83

Taylor, Elizabeth, references to, **Supp. 6,** 638; **Supp. 8,** 678

Taylor, Francis H. L., reference to, **Supp. 4,** 582

Taylor, Frederick W., references to, **Supp. 2,** 26; **Supp. 3,** 204, 224, 762; **Supp. 6,** 121

Taylor, Glen H., reference to, **Supp. 6,** 681

Taylor, Henry Osborn, references to, **Supp. 4,** 880–81, 883

Taylor, Laurette, references to, **Supp. 3,** 765; **Supp. 8,** 444

Taylor, Maxwell, reference to, **Supp. 8,** 157

Taylor, Myron C., references to, **Supp. 3,** 263; **Supp. 5,** 510; **Supp. 8,** 375

Taylor, Paul Schuster, reference to, **Supp. 7,** 456

Taylor, Zachary, relations with Henry Clay **Vol. 7, Part 2,** 178 f.

Taylor Society, **Supp. 2,** 27; **Supp. 5,** 164–65, 558

Taylor system of scientific management. *See* Taylor Society

Taylor-White process, **Vol. 9, Part 2,** 324

Tay-Sachs disease, **Supp. 3,** 682

Tchaikovsky, Peter Ilyich, reference to, **Supp. 4,** 211

Tea: first from Japan, **Vol. 4, Part 2,** 68; growing of, in South, **Vol. 9, Part 1,** 315; shipment of, to colonies, **Vol. 3, Part 1,** 430; toxic effects of, **Vol. 7, Part 1,** 267; trade in, **Vol. 4, Part 2,** 68

Teach, Edward, reference to, **Vol. 3, Part 2,** 16

Teachers: curriculum determination, **Supp. 3,** 552; kindergarten, **Supp. 4,** 874–75; **Supp. 5,** 437; loyalty oath issue, **Supp. 5,** 410, 480–81; **Supp. 7,** 542; **Supp. 8,** 133–34; materials for, **Supp. 2,** 419; organizations, **Supp. 1,** 328, 683, 712; **Supp. 2,** 419; pensions, **Supp. 1,** 328; **Supp. 2,** 542; **Supp. 8,** 9–10; training of, **Supp. 3,** 677; **Supp. 4,** 40; training in progressive methods, **Supp. 8,** 443; unionization, **Supp. 8,** 132. *See also* Education; *specific fields*

Teachers College. *See* Columbia University

Teachers' Institute, **Vol. 4, Part 2,** 415; **Vol. 8, Part 2,** 307

Teachers Insurance and Annuity Association, **Supp. 1,** 328; founding of, **Supp. 2,** 543

Teachers' Mutual Benefit Association, promotion of, **Vol. 4, Part 2,** 518

Teacher's Work Book, **Supp. 4,** 833

Teacher training, **Vol. 2, Part 2,** 418; **Vol. 3, Part 1,** 347; **Vol. 5, Part 1,** 128; **Vol. 7, Part 1,** 467; **Vol. 7, Part 2,** 404, 532; **Vol. 8, Part 1,** 222, 643; **Vol. 8, Part 2,** 250; **Vol. 9, Part 2,** 581; California, **Vol. 7, Part 1,** 578; Illinois, **Vol. 1, Part 2,** 44; **Vol. 2, Part 2,** 376; **Vol. 9, Part 2,** 581; Massachusetts, **Vol. 2, Part 1,** 420; **Vol. 3, Part 1,** 563 f.; Michigan, **Vol. 10, Part 1,** 617 f.; Missouri, **Vol. 1, Part 1,** 538; New Jersey, **Vol. 4, Part 2,** 360; New York, **Vol. 5, Part 2,** 500; Wisconsin, **Vol. 8, Part 2,** 307. *See also* Normal schools

Teagarden, Jack, reference to, **Supp. 8,** 561

Teamsters Union: AFL-CIO expulsion of, **Supp. 8,** 513, 528; CIO relations, **Supp. 7,** 119; corruption investigation, **Supp. 7,** 50; founding of, **Supp. 5,** 690–91; organized crime links, **Supp. 8,** 322

Teapot Dome scandal, **Vol. 3, Part 1,** 156, 234 f.; **Vol. 4, Part 2,** 255; **Vol. 5, Part 2,** 546; **Vol. 8, Part 2,** 194; **Vol. 10, Part 1,** 393 f. **Supp. 1,** 95, 196, 465; **Supp. 3,** 259–60, 481, 491, 669, 715, 845, 851; **Supp. 4,** 216, 482; **Supp. 6,** 455, 584; **Supp. 8,** 594; newspaper reporting, **Supp. 2,** 14; prosecution, **Supp. 2,** 536

Technicolor, **Supp. 7,** 406–7

Technicolor Corporation, **Vol. 9, Part 2,** 647

"Technological unemployment," **Vol. 10, Part 1,** 637 f.

Technology, **Vol. 3, Part 1,** 318 f.; **Vol. 10, Part 1,** 498 f.; origin of the term, **Vol. 1, Part 2,** 258; in South, **Vol. 5, Part 1,** 210–11; unemployment related to, **Supp. 5,** 558–59. *See also* Industrial research; *specific kinds*

Tecumseh, references to, **Vol. 5, Part 2,** 115, 583; **Vol. 8, Part 2,** 376 f.; **Vol. 9, Part 1,** 13; **Vol. 9, Part 2,** 375 f.

Teheran Conference (1943), **Supp. 3,** 663; **Supp. 5,** 334; **Supp. 7,** 377

Telautograph, invention of, **Vol. 6, Part 1,** 368

Texas: Amnesty Oath, **Vol. 1, Part 1,** 111; annexation of, **Vol. 1, Part 1,** 88 f., 566; **Vol. 1, Part 2,** 212, 225; **Vol. 2, Part 1,** 42, 49, 209, 287, 293, 417, 563; **Vol. 2, Part 2,** 178; **Vol. 3, Part 1,** 363, 543 f.; **Vol. 3, Part 2,** 298; **Vol. 4, Part 1,** 308; **Vol. 5, Part 1,** 266, 533; **Vol. 5, Part 2,** 162, 407, 553 f.; **Vol. 8, Part 1,** 37 f., 315, 576 f.; **Vol. 9, Part 1,** 240, 570; **Vol. 9, Part 2,** 48, 351; **Vol. 10, Part 1,** 91, 127, 156, 355 f., 590; **Vol. 10, Part 2,** 567; antislavery, **Vol. 1, Part 1,** 298; banking, **Vol. 2, Part 2,** 148; bird life studies, **Supp. 7,** 578, 579; botany, **Vol. 6, Part 1,** 274; **Vol. 6, Part 2,** 482; **Vol. 10, Part 2,** 546; boundary disputes, **Vol. 1, Part 2,** 125; **Vol. 8, Part 2,** 237; British protectorate, question of, **Vol. 5, Part 2,** 161; Catholic church, **Vol. 7, Part 1,** 625 f.; circuit courts, **Vol. 8, Part 2,** 13; colleges, establishment of, **Vol. 2, Part 1,** 288; commercial agreements with, **Vol. 4, Part 2,** 526; constitution of, **Vol. 8, Part 1,** 434; debts, **Vol. 8, Part 2,** 237; dictatorship in, **Vol. 3, Part 1,** 112; education, **Vol. 1, Part 1,** 538; **Vol. 5, Part 1,** 453; **Vol. 9, Part 1,** 240; "fencibles" in, **Vol. 8, Part 1,** 315 f.; Fourierism, **Vol. 2, Part 2,** 357 f.; **Vol. 4, Part 1,** 529; **Vol. 5, Part 1,** 578; French settlements, **Vol. 6, Part 2,** 527; frontier, **Vol. 2, Part 1,** 287; geology, **Vol. 1, Part 2,** 419; **Vol. 8, Part 2,** 91 f.; German colonies, **Vol. 8, Part 2,** 91 f.; governors, **Vol. 1, Part 2,** 160 f.; **Vol. 2, Part 2,** 278 f.; **Vol. 3, Part 1,** 112 f.; **Vol. 4, Part 2,** 526; **Vol. 5, Part 1,** 122 f., 331, 493 f.; **Vol. 6, Part 1,** 480 f.; **Vol. 7, Part 2,** 368 f.; **Vol. 8, Part 2,** 179 f.; **Supp. 3,** 266–67; **Supp. 4,** 776; **Supp. 7,** 242, 349–50; **Supp. 8,** 478; horticulture, **Vol. 7, Part 1,** 335 f.; immigration to, **Vol. 1, Part 1,** 438; independence, struggle for, **Vol. 1, Part 1,** 339; **Vol. 2, Part 1,** 287, 293; **Vol. 3, Part 2,** 263; **Vol. 4, Part 2,** 188, 526; **Vol. 6, Part 1,** 274; **Vol. 8, Part 1,** 577; **Vol. 8, Part 2,** 25 f.; **Vol. 10, Part 2,** 35; Indians, relations with, **Vol. 5, Part 2,** 582; **Vol. 8, Part 1,** 294; journalism, **Vol. 8, Part 1,** 576 f.; legal service, **Vol. 4, Part 1,** 95 f.; **Vol. 4, Part 2,** 315, 520; **Vol. 6, Part 1,** 520; **Vol. 7, Part 1,** 124; **Vol. 7, Part 2,** 287; **Vol. 8, Part 1,** 433; **Vol. 8, Part 2,** 13, 237, 403; **Vol. 10, Part 2,** 53, 302; medical service, **Vol. 8, Part 2,** 26; Methodist church, **Vol. 1, Part 2,** 234; Mexican War, activities during, **Vol. 2, Part 1,** 491; Mexico, relations with, **Vol. 5, Part 2,** 553; military expeditions, **Vol. 6, Part 1,** 376; newspapers, **Supp. 4,** 222; Norwegian settlements in, **Vol. 8, Part 1,** 488; oil industry, **Supp. 3,** 260–61; **Supp. 4,** 775; **Supp. 6,** 135–36, 540–41; **Supp. 8,** 454; oil wells, **Vol. 6, Part 1,** 483; Polish settlements, **Vol. 1, Part 2,** 30; political service, **Vol. 1, Part 2,** 77; **Vol. 2, Part 2,** 279, 586; **Vol. 3, Part 1,** 112; **Vol. 4, Part 1,** 183; **Vol. 5, Part 1,** 122, 265, 331, 493; **Vol. 5, Part 2,** 182; **Vol. 6, Part 1,** 12, 480 f.; **Vol. 7, Part 2,** 13; **Vol. 8, Part 1,** 133; **Vol. 8, Part 2,** 180, 237; **Vol. 10, Part 2,** 188; politics, **Supp. 3,** 706; **Supp. 5,** 480–81; **Supp. 7,** 137–38, 242–43, 459–60, 634–36, 730–31; **Supp. 8,** 205–6, 478, 506–7; provisional government, **Vol. 8, Part 2,** 236; public service, **Vol. 1, Part 1,** 437 f.; **Vol. 1, Part 2,** 171; **Vol. 3, Part 1,** 229; **Vol. 4, Part 1,** 183, 220; **Vol. 5, Part 1,** 493; **Vol. 5, Part 2,** 135 f.; **Vol. 6, Part 1,** 301; **Vol. 6, Part 2,** 5 f., 132, 201; **Vol. 7, Part 1,** 356, 407 f.; **Vol. 7, Part 2,** 216, 369; **Vol. 8, Part 1,** 294 f.; **Vol. 8, Part 2,** 26, 166; **Vol. 9, Part 1,** 74; **Vol. 10, Part 1,** 377 f.; **Vol. 10, Part 2,** 35, 289; railroads, **Vol. 8, Part 1,** 433 f., 546 f.; Rangers, **Vol. 5, Part 2,** 182, 582 f.; **Vol. 6, Part 1,** 301; Reconstruction, **Vol. 2, Part 1,** 443; **Vol. 3, Part 1,** 112; **Vol. 7, Part 2,** 369; **Vol. 8, Part 1,** 433 f.; reforms in, **Vol. 5, Part 1,** 122 f.; religious service, **Vol. 1, Part 1,** 517; **Vol. 9, Part 2,** 556; Republican

party, **Vol. 3, Part 2,** 453; Republic of, **Vol. 1, Part 1,** 338 f.; **Vol. 2, Part 1,** 293; **Vol. 5, Part 2,** 161 f., 553; **Vol. 6, Part 1,** 290; **Vol. 6, Part 2,** 528; **Vol. 7, Part 2,** 369; **Vol. 9, Part 1,** 240; **Vol. 10, Part 2,** 290; Secession Convention, **Vol. 8, Part 1,** 433; **Vol. 10, Part 2,** 188; Spanish-American legal procedure in, **Vol. 4, Part 2,** 520; statehood, admission to, **Vol. 1, Part 1,** 439 f.; "Strong Court," **Vol. 4, Part 1,** 96; survey, **Vol. 4, Part 2,** 369; "War Party," **Vol. 9, Part 2,** 630; writings on, **Vol. 1, Part 1,** 527; **Vol. 4, Part 2,** 201; **Vol. 8, Part 1,** 14, **Vol. 9, Part 1,** 334; **Vol. 10, Part 2,** 613; **Supp. 7,** 188–89

Texas Co. *See* Texaco

Texas Folklore Society, **Supp. 7,** 188

Texas Freeman, **Supp. 6,** 567

Texas Medical Center, **Supp. 6,** 136

Texas Rangers, **Supp. 7,** 770–71

Texas Republican, first Texas newspaper, **Vol. 6, Part 1,** 376

Texas Trust Co., **Supp. 6,** 324

Textbooks, **Vol. 1, Part 2,** 191, 274, 279; **Vol. 2, Part 1,** 119; **Vol. 2, Part 2,** 281 f., 283, 326, 431; **Vol. 3, Part 1,** 458 f., 464 f., 570 f.; **Vol. 3, Part 2,** 561; **Vol. 4, Part 1,** 433, 575, 581, 588; **Vol. 4, Part 2,** 603; **Vol. 5, Part 1,** 444, 475, 541; **Vol. 5, Part 2,** 227; **Vol. 6, Part 1,** 73, 81, 177, 212, 408, 589; **Vol. 6, Part 2,** 141, 210, 269; **Vol. 7, Part 1,** 94, 565; **Vol. 7, Part 2,** 31 f., 83, 236 f., 238, 332, 336, 394, 405 f., 441, 482, 525, 532, 568, 597 f., 629; **Vol. 8, Part 1,** 96 f., 221; **Vol. 8, Part 2,** 226; **Vol. 9, Part 2,** 54; **Vol. 10, Part 1,** 544 f., 594 f., 645 f., 655 f.; **Vol. 10, Part 2,** 99; American history, **Supp. 7,** 568; anatomy, **Supp. 2,** 423; black history, **Supp. 5,** 642; censorship, **Supp. 6,** 528, 558; **Supp. 7,** 330; chemistry, **Vol. 9, Part 1,** 235; **Supp. 1,** 376; civil engineering, **Supp. 1,** 148; commercial, **Vol. 9, Part 1,** 404; "Dick and Jane" reading, **Supp. 6,** 248; differential geometry, **Supp. 7,** 216; early, **Vol. 8, Part 2,** 330; economics, **Supp. 8,** 165; education, **Supp. 4,** 592; for educators, **Supp. 3,** 206; embryology, **Supp. 4,** 573; engineering, **Vol. 9, Part 1,** 429; European history, **Supp. 2,** 564; **Supp. 7,** 330; evolution, **Supp. 1,** 697; first advertising, **Supp. 7,** 101; first civics, **Supp. 3,** 285; first on plastic surgery, **Supp. 4,** 221; first social psychology, **Supp. 5,** 592; foreign language, **Supp. 1,** 406; general science, **Supp. 4,** 139, 140; geography, **Vol. 1, Part 2,** 343; **Supp. 1,** 7; **Supp. 4,** 33, 412–13, 423–24; geology, **Supp. 4,** 730; grammar, **Supp. 1,** 697; Greek, **Vol. 9, Part 1,** 398; gynecology, **Supp. 1,** 352; history, **Vol. 9, Part 1,** 556 f.; **Supp. 1,** 484; **Supp. 3,** 336; **Supp. 6,** 278–79; Latin, **Vol. 5, Part 1,** 475; law, **Vol. 2, Part 1,** 166; **Vol. 3, Part 1,** 571 f.; **Vol. 5, Part 1,** 53; **Vol. 9, Part 2,** 250; mathematics, **Supp. 1,** 145–46; medieval history, **Supp. 1,** 285; **Supp. 7,** 741; mineralogy, **Supp. 1,** 221; mining, **Supp. 7,** 358; music, **Vol. 8, Part 1,** 200 f.; music theory, **Supp. 3,** 309; neurology, **Supp. 3,** 386; nutrition, **Supp. 5,** 623; pathology, **Supp. 3,** 483; physics, **Supp. 5,** 154; physiology, **Supp. 3,** 370, 371; plant physiology, **Supp. 7,** 592; publishing of, **Supp. 5,** 272; scientific, **Vol. 4, Part 2,** 143; **Vol. 6, Part 1,** 398 f.; **Vol. 9, Part 1,** 556 f.; social studies, **Supp. 6,** 557–58; Spanish, **Vol. 5, Part 2,** 454, 496; surgery, **Supp. 3,** 67; tropical disease, **Supp. 4,** 803

Textile industry: "American System" in New England, **Vol. 6, Part 1,** 45; cotton, **Supp. 5,** 252; dyeing of, **Vol. 1, Part 1,** 563; **Vol. 6, Part 2,** 43, 417; **Vol. 7, Part 1,** 404; dyestuffs, **Supp. 7,** 616; inventions, **Vol. 2, Part 2,** 561; **Vol. 9, Part 2,** 508; knitting machine, **Vol. 5, Part 2,** 554; Lawrence, Mass., strike, **Supp. 3,** 576–77, 616; **Supp. 6,** 238; **Supp. 8,** 457; looms,

5, Part 2, 113

Treasure, Capt. Kidd's search for, **Vol. 3, Part 1,** 501 f.

Treasurer, The, early colonial trading ship, **Vol. 1, Part 1,** 346

Treasury, Department of the (U.S.), **Vol. 3, Part 2,** 486; **Vol. 4, Part 2,** 84; **Vol. 8, Part 1,** 220; **Vol. 8, Part 2,** 6; **Vol. 9, Part 1,** 460; administration, **Supp. 1,** 535; **Supp. 2,** 448; **Supp. 3,** 480–81, 331; **Supp. 5,** 712; **Supp. 6,** 124, 229, 376, 659–60; **Supp. 8,** 290, 445–46, 592; comptroller under Continental Congress, **Vol. 10, Part 1,** 17 f.; first comptroller of, **Vol. 3, Part 2,** 538; **Vol. 6, Part 1,** 52; **Vol. 8, Part 1,** 80 f.; first treasurer of, **Vol. 5, Part 1,** 51; Great Depression policies, **Supp. 6,** 33–34; secretaryship, **Vol. 2, Part 2,** 458; **Vol. 3, Part 2,** 237, 486; **Vol. 4, Part 2,** 61, 174 f.; **Vol. 5, Part 1,** 473; **Vol. 6, Part 2,** 249; **Vol. 7, Part 1,** 199 f.; **Vol. 8, Part 1,** 578; **Vol. 8, Part 2,** 233; **Vol. 10, Part 2,** 383, 444, 485, 495

Treasury Bill of 1846, **Vol. 8, Part 1,** 34 f.

Treatise on the System of Evidence in Trials at Common Law, A, **Supp. 3,** 821

Tree of Culture, The, **Supp. 5,** 435

Tree of Laughing Bells, The, **Vol. 6, Part 1,** 276

Trees, **Vol. 7, Part 1,** 559; diseases and care of, **Supp. 7,** 33; of the Pacific Coast, popular booklets on, **Vol. 6, Part 1,** 162; redwoods, preservation of, **Vol. 3, Part 1,** 485; ring studies, **Supp. 7,** 193–94; surgery, **Vol. 3, Part 1,** 88 f.; wood identification, **Supp. 3,** 621. *See also* Forestry; Lumber industry; Wilderness and wildlife preserves

Trelease, William, reference to, **Supp. 3,** 802

Trent affair (1861), **Vol. 1, Part 1,** 44; **Vol. 2, Part 1,** 564; **Vol. 3, Part 2,** 192, 255; **Vol. 4, Part 1,** 594; **Vol. 6, Part 1,** 250; **Vol. 6, Part 2,** 365; **Vol. 8, Part 2,** 619; **Vol. 9, Part 1,** 210–11, 619; **Vol. 10, Part 1,** 630; **Vol. 10, Part 2,** 217

Trenton, N.J., battle of (Dec. 26, 1776), **Vol. 1, Part 1,** 176; **Vol. 4, Part 1,** 569; **Vol. 6, Part 2,** 541; **Vol. 7, Part 1,** 87; **Vol. 7, Part 2,** 234; **Vol. 8, Part 2,** 294; **Vol. 9, Part 2,** 192; **Vol. 10, Part 1,** 516; early history of, **Vol. 2, Part 1,** 400

Trevilian Station, battle of, **Vol. 4, Part 2,** 214; **Vol. 9, Part 1,** 80; **Vol. 9, Part 2,** 172

"Triangle," Pennsylvania tract of land, **Vol. 5, Part 1,** 500

Triangle Film Corporation, **Supp. 6,** 573, 619

Triangle Publications, **Supp. 3,** 21

Triangle Shirtwaist Co. fire (1911), **Supp. 3,** 355–56, 717–18; **Supp. 5,** 718; **Supp. 7,** 608

Triangulation, **Vol. 3, Part 1,** 29 f.

Triborough Bridge (New York City), **Supp. 3,** 531; **Supp. 6,** 594; **Supp. 7,** 12

Tribune Co., **Supp. 5,** 449

Trichinosis, **Supp. 3,** 737–38

Trigeminal neuralgia, **Supp. 4,** 214

Trigg, H. L., reference to, **Supp. 6,** 569

Trilby, **Vol. 8, Part 1,** 132

Trinidad Asphalt Co., **Vol. 1, Part 1,** 586

Trinity Church (Boston). *See* Boston

Trinity Church (New York City), **Supp. 4,** 546–47. *See also* New York

Trinity College (Hartford, Conn.), **Vol. 3, Part 2,** 81; **Vol. 4, Part 1,** 406; **Vol. 5, Part 2,** 354; **Vol. 8, Part 1,** 127 f., 291 f.; **Vol. 10, Part 2,** 42; charter for, **Vol. 9, Part 1,** 327; founding of, **Vol. 2, Part 1,** 172

Trinity College (N.C.), forerunner of Duke University, **Vol. 3, Part 1,** 496 f.

Trinity College (Washington, D.C.), founding of, **Vol. 5, Part 2,** 245

Triode Audion, **Supp. 7,** 175–76

Tripoli, diplomacy, **Vol. 1, Part 2,** 241; **Vol. 3, Part 1,** 613

Tripolitan War (1801–05), **Vol. 1, Part 1,** 650; **Vol. 1, Part 2,** 241; **Vol. 2, Part 1,** 572; **Vol. 2, Part 2,** 40; **Vol. 3, Part 1,** 33, 188, 613; **Vol. 5, Part 1,** 361; **Vol. 5, Part 2,** 27, 30, 176; **Vol. 6, Part 1,** 49, 76; **Vol. 7, Part 1,** 219, 358, 612; **Vol. 7, Part 2,** 491; **Vol. 8, Part 1,** 83, 182, 424, 596; **Vol. 8, Part 2,** 76; **Vol. 9, Part 1,** 394 f., 584; **Vol. 9, Part 2,** 7, 48, 645; **Vol. 10, Part 1,** 22, 492 f.

Trippe, Juan, reference to, **Supp. 6,** 145

Tristram, **Supp. 1,** 633–34

Trolley car, experiments leading to, **Vol. 3, Part 1,** 88

Trombone playing, **Vol. 9, Part 2,** 556

Tropic of Cancer, **Supp. 7,** 292

Tropic of Capricorn, **Supp. 7,** 292, 293

Tropical diseases, research and control of, **Supp. 1,** 14, 32, 543; **Supp. 3,** 791, 803; **Supp. 5,** 605, 710. *See also specific diseases*

Tropical Woods, founding of, **Supp. 3,** 621

Tropism theory, **Vol. 6, Part 1,** 349 f.

Trotsky, Leon: references to, **Supp. 5,** 135, 173, 579, 664; **Supp. 7,** 244, 269; **Supp. 8,** 172; translator and literary agent of, **Supp. 8,** 149–50

Trout Lake Limnological Laboratory, founding of, **Supp. 3,** 402; **Supp. 4,** 85

Trowbridge, Alexander, reference to, **Supp. 3,** 199

Troy, N.Y., **Vol. 4, Part 2,** 9; early history, **Vol. 6, Part 2,** 275; medicine, **Vol. 10, Part 1,** 435 f.; public service to, **Vol. 6, Part 2,** 305

Trucks and trucking, four-wheel drive, **Supp. 3,** 165

Trudeau, Edward L., references to, **Supp. 3,** 431; **Supp. 4,** 48–49, 314, 577

Trudeau Sanitorium (N.Y.), **Vol. 10, Part 1,** 3. *See also* Saranac Lake, N.Y.

True Briton and *Randolph,* **Vol. 1, Part 2,** 242

True Relation, A, **Vol. 9, Part 1,** 295

True Story, founding of, **Supp. 5,** 453

Truman, Harry S., atomic bomb development, **Supp. 4,** 787–88; atomic bomb policy, **Supp. 7,** 732; Barkley relationship, **Supp. 6,** 36; Baruch relationship, **Supp. 7,** 37; Biddle relationship, **Supp. 8,** 35; Biffle relationship, **Supp. 8,** 36; civil rights measures, **Supp. 5,** 479, 515, 741; **Supp. 7,** 748; congressional relations, **Supp. 5,** 715–16; defense policy, **Supp. 8,** 303; Dixiecrat revolt against, **Supp. 6,** 710–11; Dulles, J. F., relationship, **Supp. 6,** 178; federal budget, **Supp. 7,** 734; Forrestal relationship, **Supp. 4,** 306; Hannegan relationship, **Supp. 4,** 355–56; Korean War policy, **Supp. 8,** 633; labor relations, **Supp. 4,** 724, 890; **Supp. 5,** 511; Leahy relationship, **Supp. 6,** 375; loyalty program, **Supp. 5,** 564; MacArthur recall, **Supp. 7,** 492–93; **Supp. 8,** 421–22, 633; McCarthyism and, **Supp. 6,** 405, 406; Marshall, G. C., relationship, **Supp. 6,** 431–32; pardons, **Supp. 6,** 437; Pendergast machine, **Supp. 3,** 596, 597; Potsdam Conference, **Supp. 6,** 147; presidential candidacy, **Supp. 8,** 405; press relations, **Supp. 5,** 626; **Supp. 8,** 395; Ross relationship, **Supp. 4,** 703–5; in Senate, **Supp. 7,** 764; steel seizure, **Supp. 5,** 156, 714; **Supp. 6,** 502, 679; **Supp. 7,** 96, 229, 587; **Supp. 8,** 517; vice-presidency, **Supp. 3,** 664; **Supp. 4,** 51, 356, 376; **Supp. 7,** 762; vice-presidential candidacy, **Supp. 8,** 361; White House balcony, **Supp. 6,** 158

Truman Doctrine, **Supp. 5,** 397, 704; **Supp. 6,** 431; **Supp. 8,** 90, 680; budget cuts, **Supp. 7,** 734; criticism of, **Supp. 7,** 49, 762; **Supp. 8,** 680; support for, **Supp. 7,** 326, 419

Trumbull, John, reference to, **Vol. 8, Part 2,** 360

Trumbull, United States frigate, **Vol. 9, Part 1,** 502

Trumbull Gallery (Yale), first art museum connected with a college in America, **Vol. 9, Part 2,** 136

Trumbull Papers, **Vol. 10, Part 1,** 16

Trumbull's "Declaration of Independence," **Vol. 3, Part 1,** 535 f.

Trump, John G., references to, **Supp. 8,** 665, 666

Trunk Line Association, **Vol. 3, Part 2,** 388; **Vol. 8, Part 2,** 7

Trust Co. of Cuba, **Supp. 3,** 218

Trusts: **Vol. 7, Part 1,** 108; **Vol. 7, Part 2,** 544; **Vol. 8, Part 2,** 651; beginnings of, **Vol. 3, Part 1,** 341 f., *see also* Antitrust actions; development of, **Supp. 2,** 571–73; fight with Guggenheim, **Vol. 4, Part 2,** 39; legal measures to restrict, **Vol. 4, Part 2,** 25; motion picture companies, **Supp. 5,** 229; Roosevelt, T. R., and, **Vol. 8, Part 2,** 140; writings on, **Vol. 3, Part 1,** 389. *See also* Antitrust actions

Truthseeker, **Vol. 1, Part 2,** 192

Truth Teller, **Vol. 8, Part 1,** 157

"Tryon's Palace," **Vol. 10, Part 1,** 26

Tryptophan, **Supp. 7,** 223

Tsiolkovskii, Konstantin E., references to, **Supp. 3,** 306, 308

Tuberculosis, **Vol. 1, Part 2,** 493; **Vol. 2, Part 1,** 231, 349 f.; **Vol. 3, Part 2,** 201, 301 f., 472, 550; **Vol. 4, Part 2,** 165; **Vol. 5, Part 1,** 215; **Vol. 7, Part 2,** 550 f.; **Vol. 10, Part 1,** 2 f.; American Congress on, **Vol. 1, Part 2,** 154; bacillus, **Supp. 4,** 435; biochemistry and pathology of, **Supp. 5,** 600; bovine, **Supp. 4,** 683; Christmas seal project, **Supp. 4,** 92; first clinic in Chicago, **Vol. 8, Part 2,** 281; French prevention commission, **Supp. 3,** 324; hospitals, **Supp. 7,** 251; housing reform and, **Supp. 3,** 837; organizations, **Supp. 2,** 176, 197; prevention campaign, **Supp. 7,** 251; preventorium for children, **Vol. 9, Part 2,** 130; prize essay on, **Vol. 3, Part 2,** 102; research, **Supp. 4,** 48–49, 314; **Supp. 6,** 357; research laboratory, **Vol. 4, Part 2,** 501; resistance and immunity studies, **Supp. 3,** 431–32; sanitarium, first in U.S., **Vol. 10, Part 1,** 3; treatment, **Supp. 2,** 70–71, 196, 370; **Supp. 4,** 577–78; tuberculin, **Supp. 1,** 258; writings on, **Vol. 6, Part 1,** 58; **Vol. 10, Part 1,** 3 f.; **Supp. 6,** 409

Tuberculosis Institute, **Vol. 7, Part 2,** 298

Tubing, invention of, **Vol. 2, Part 2,** 359

Tucker, Frederick St. George de Lautour, **Vol. 1, Part 2,** 456

Tudor Drama, The, **Supp. 4,** 110

Tuesday Club, **Vol. 3, Part 1,** 236; **Vol. 4, Part 2,** 170

Tufts, James H., reference to, **Supp. 6,** 671

Tufts University, **Vol. 1, Part 1,** 559; **Vol. 7, Part 1,** 22; **Vol. 10, Part 1,** 49; Fletcher School of Law and Diplomacy, **Supp. 5,** 751; neurology studies, **Supp. 4,** 617

Tugboats, **Supp. 7,** 552–53

Tugwell, Rexford G., references to, **Supp. 3,** 647; **Supp. 6,** 12

Tulane University, **Vol. 1, Part 2,** 525; **Vol. 2, Part 2,** 497; **Vol. 3, Part 1,** 582; **Vol. 3, Part 2,** 324; **Vol. 4, Part 1,** 257; **Vol. 5, Part 2,** 154; **Vol. 8, Part 1,** 575; **Vol. 8, Part 2,** 165; **Vol. 10, Part 1,** 51; medical school, **Supp. 6,** 434, 435; presidency, **Supp. 1,** 21, 250

Tulley's Almanack, **Vol. 4, Part 2,** 304

Tumors, **Vol. 1, Part 2,** 2; cerebral, writings on, **Supp. 2,** 139; "scent detector" for brain, **Supp. 4,** 250; surgical procedures for, **Supp. 4,** 214

Tuna fishing, **Vol. 5, Part 1,** 140

Tungsten filaments, **Supp. 6,** 695

Tun-huang caves, **Supp. 5,** 729

Tunis, diplomacy, **Vol. 3, Part 1,** 613; **Vol. 4, Part 2,** 481 f.; **Vol. 3, Part 1,** 251

Tunneling shield, **Vol. 1, Part 2,** 81

Tunnels, **Vol. 3, Part 1,** 334; contruction of, **Supp. 4,** 690; pneumatic, **Vol. 1, Part 2,** 81; railroad, **Vol. 8, Part 2,** 48; **Supp. 3,** 735, 737; **Supp. 7,** 90; subaqueous, **Supp. 2,** 145, 559; **Supp. 3,** 353, 479; **Supp. 4,** 757; **Supp. 6,** 187, 587; vehicular, **Vol. 7, Part 2,** 278; ventilation standards, **Supp. 3,** 353. *See also* Bridges; *specific tunnel names*

Tunney, James Joseph ("Gene"), reference to, **Supp. 3,** 602

Tupelo, operations about (1863–65), **Vol. 2, Part 1,** 293; **Vol. 6, Part 1,** 130; **Vol. 9, Part 1,** 237

Turandot, world premiere, **Supp. 6,** 643

Turbines, steam, development of, **Vol. 8, Part 1,** 544; **Vol. 8, Part 2,** 359; **Supp. 1,** 65; **Supp. 4,** 383–84

Turbo-blower, invention of, **Vol. 8, Part 1,** 544

Turbosupercharger engine, **Supp. 4,** 609

Turk, Robert, reference to, **Supp. 6,** 402

Turkey: Armenian massacre, **Supp. 4,** 604; **Supp. 6,** 253–54; diplomacy, **Vol. 1, Part 1,** 309; **Vol. 1, Part 2,** 417, 567; **Vol. 2, Part 1,** 139 f.; **Vol. 3, Part 1,** 294; **Vol. 7, Part 1,** 206; **Vol. 8, Part 1,** 529 f.; **Vol. 8, Part 2,** 77; **Vol. 9, Part 2,** 131; **Supp. 2,** 65; **Supp. 4,** 603–4, 772; **Supp. 7,** 303, 384; missions in, **Vol. 3, Part 1,** 565 f.; **Vol. 5, Part 1,** 191; **Vol. 8, Part 2,** 261, 421, 446; **Vol. 9, Part 1,** 73, 241; **Vol. 10, Part 1,** 500; **Vol. 10, Part 2,** 11; railway construction, **Supp. 1,** 171; Russia and war with, **Vol. 5, Part 2,** 187; trade relations with, **Vol. 7, Part 1,** 634 f.; Truman Doctrine, **Supp. 6,** 431; writings on, **Vol. 3, Part 1,** 204, 566 f. *See also* Greco-Turkish War

Turkish, Bible translation into, **Vol. 4, Part 1,** 384

Turkus, Burton B., reference to, **Supp. 7,** 585

Turner, Florence, reference to, **Supp. 6,** 619

Turner, Frederick Jackson, references to, **Vol. 9, Part 2,** 521; **Supp. 3,** 262, 336, 810; **Supp. 4,** 746, 747; **Supp. 5,** 429, 577

Turner, Roscoe, reference to, **Supp. 6,** 493

Turner Zeitung, **Vol. 8, Part 1,** 384

Turners Falls, Mass., **Vol. 2, Part 2,** 551

Turnure, Arthur, reference to, **Supp. 6,** 107

Turpentine, collection methods, **Supp. 2,** 301

Turpin, Ben, reference to, **Supp. 7,** 177

"Turret" vessels, **Vol. 3, Part 2,** 568

Tuscarora, diplomacy, **Vol. 3, Part 1,** 99

Tusculum College, founding of, **Vol. 3, Part 1,** 333

Tuskegee Houses, **Supp. 3,** 744

Tuskegee Institute, **Vol. 10, Part 1,** 506 f.; administration, **Supp. 2,** 476–77; agricultural studies, **Supp. 3,** 145–46; race relations conference, **Supp. 3,** 577; trustees, **Supp. 6,** 600

"Tutt, Emphraim" (fictional character), **Supp. 3,** 773–74

Tuve, Merle A., references to, **Supp. 6,** 370; **Supp. 8,** 199

Tuxedo Brass Band, **Supp. 5,** 106

Tuxedo Park, N.Y., **Vol. 6, Part 1,** 412; **Vol. 8, Part 1,** 210 f.

TVA. *See* Tennessee Valley Authority

TWA. *See* Transcontinental and Western Airlines; Trans World Airlines

Twain, Mark, **Vol. 1, Part 1,** 241; **Vol. 1, Part 2,** 306; **Vol. 2, Part 2,** 192 f.; **Vol. 3, Part 1,** 252; **Vol. 5, Part 1,** 580; **Vol. 6, Part 1,** 2, 433; **Vol. 8, Part 2,** 96, 575; **Vol. 9, Part 2,** 52; **Vol. 10, Part 1,** 82; illustrator for, **Supp. 3,** 44; reference to, **Supp. 8,** 316; writings on, **Supp. 2,** 509; **Supp. 5,** 168; **Supp. 7,** 80

Tweed, William M. ("Boss"), **Vol. 9, Part 1,** 9; escape and capture of, **Vol. 1, Part 1,** 105; Nast cartoons,

sacre, **Supp. 2,** 124; union-shop issue, **Supp. 7,** 172
United Mine Workers of America v. *Red Jacket Consolidated Coal and Coke Co.,* **Supp. 6,** 494
United Motors, **Supp. 8,** 598
United Nations (UN): African division, **Supp. 5,** 164; agricultural programs, **Supp. 6,** 639; Atomic Energy Commission, **Supp. 7,** 37; aviation, **Supp. 6,** 666; charter, **Supp. 5,** 198, 334, 537–38, 704; **Supp. 7,** 138, 289, 688; charter revision proposals, **Supp. 8,** 88; Cuban missile crisis, **Supp. 7,** 724; establishment of, **Supp. 4,** 777–78; Fulbright resolution (1943), **Supp. 4,** 89; International Law Commission, **Supp. 6,** 308; opponents, **Supp. 6,** 87, 361, 578; plebiscites, **Supp. 5,** 723–24; supporters, **Supp. 3,** 660, 663, 496, 504; U.S. ambassadors, **Supp. 7,** 23–24, 723–24; U.S. delegation, **Supp. 7,** 661–62, 721, 748; **Supp. 8,** 701; women's participation, **Supp. 6,** 413; writings on, **Supp. 8,** 408
United Nations Building, Rockefeller site gift for, **Supp. 6,** 549
United Nations Educational, Scientific, and Cultural Organization (UNESCO), founding of, **Supp. 4,** 449–50
United Nations Food and Agricultural Organization, **Supp. 4,** 341
United Nations International Children's Emergency Fund (UNICEF), founding of, **Supp. 7,** 599–600
United Nations Relief and Rehabilitation Administration, **Supp. 5,** 605, 704; directorship, **Supp. 7,** 467; founding of, **Supp. 4,** 89; medical consultants, **Supp. 7,** 195
United Neighborhood Houses, predecessor, **Supp. 5,** 631
United Norwegian Lutheran Church, **Vol. 2, Part 2,** 167
United Press (UP), **Supp. 3,** 166; **Supp. 6,** 601; **Supp. 7,** 369
United Press Association, **Vol. 8, Part 2,** 518; founded, **Vol. 6, Part 2,** 166; New York Associated Press, absorbed by, **Vol. 7, Part 2,** 545
United Press International (UPI), **Supp. 8,** 607
United Railroad Workers Union, **Supp. 8,** 513
United Railroads of San Francisco, **Supp. 3,** 126
United Service Organizations (USO), **Supp. 7,** 30; **Supp. 8,** 52
United States. For government agencies and departments, *see* inverted entries, e.g. Agriculture, Department of (U.S.); Court of Claims, United States; etc.
United States (frigate), **Vol. 3, Part 1,** 188; **Vol. 5, Part 1,** 361
United States (ship), **Supp. 5,** 725–26
United States Agricultural Society, **Vol. 4, Part 1,** 156; **Vol. 8, Part 2,** 51
United States Air Force Academy (Colorado Springs), design, **Supp. 7,** 691
United States attorneys. *See* Justice, Department of (U.S.)
United States Centennial Commission, **Vol. 4, Part 2,** 422
United States Christian Commission, **Vol. 4, Part 1,** 625; **Vol. 6, Part 1,** 557, 573; **Vol. 7, Part 1,** 103, 281
United States Commercial and Statistical Registers, **Vol. 4, Part 2,** 472
United States Committee for the Care of European Children, **Supp. 6,** 202
United States Customs House, architecture, **Supp. 1,** 341
United States Entomological Commission, **Vol. 8, Part 1,** 610
United States Express Co., **Vol. 7, Part 1,** 167

United States Golf Association, founding of, **Supp. 2,** 404
United States Grain Corporation, **Vol. 6, Part 1,** 275
United States Grain Marketing Corporation, founding of, **Supp. 1,** 661
United States Gypsum Co., founding of, **Supp. 6,** 27
United States Life-Saving Service, **Vol. 3, Part 2,** 582
United States mail. *See* Postal Service, United States
United States Mail Steamship Co., **Vol. 2, Part 2,** 306; **Vol. 8, Part 2,** 11
United States Magazine and Democratic Review, **Vol. 7, Part 2,** 89
United States Military Academy (West Point), **Vol. 2, Part 1,** 412; **Vol. 2, Part 2,** 590; **Vol. 3, Part 1,** 201; **Vol. 4, Part 1,** 504; **Vol. 5, Part 1,** 73; **Vol. 6, Part 2,** 209; **Vol. 7, Part 2,** 281; **Vol. 8, Part 2,** 507; **Vol. 9, Part 2,** 247; architecture, **Supp. 3,** 196; betrayed to English, **Vol. 1, Part 1,** 366 f.; competitive examinations initiated, **Vol. 5, Part 2,** 42; establishment of, **Vol. 9, Part 2,** 247, 410, 598; **Vol. 10, Part 2,** 281; famous class of, **Vol. 4, Part 2,** 221; football team, **Supp. 8,** 389; fortifications at, **Vol. 9, Part 2,** 606; improvement of courses, **Vol. 6, Part 2,** 209; instructors, **Supp. 4,** 655; superintendency of, **Vol. 3, Part 1,** 210; **Vol. 6, Part 1,** 121 f.; **Vol. 8, Part 2,** 454; **Supp. 7,** 488
United States National Museum, **Vol. 5, Part 2,** 485; **Supp. 6,** 453, 454
United States Naval Academy (Annapolis), **Vol. 1, Part 1,** 566; **Vol. 2, Part 1,** 206; **Vol. 2, Part 2,** 44; **Vol. 3, Part 1,** 614 f.; **Vol. 5, Part 2,** 170; **Vol. 7, Part 2,** 185, 320; **Vol. 8, Part 1,** 66 f., 83, 339, 424; **Vol. 8, Part 2,** 72 f., 322; **Vol. 10, Part 1,** 425; campus building architecture, **Supp. 4,** 281; Civil War period, **Vol. 8, Part 2,** 72, 74; commandants, **Supp. 1,** 39, 199; establishment of, **Vol. 1, Part 1,** 566; **Vol. 2, Part 2,** 44; **Vol. 10, Part 1,** 425; first chaplain, **Vol. 5, Part 2,** 170; first graduate to be made superintendent of, **Vol. 8, Part 1,** 339; first superintendent of, **Vol. 3, Part 1,** 529 f.; library organized at, **Vol. 8, Part 1,** 66 f.; organization of, **Vol. 3, Part 1,** 529 f.; removal of, to Newport, **Vol. 8, Part 2,** 72; systematized instruction, **Vol. 8, Part 1,** 339
United States Naval Institute, **Vol. 7, Part 2,** 220; **Vol. 9, Part 1,** 178
United States Naval Lyceum, **Vol. 7, Part 2,** 487
United States Naval Observatory, **Vol. 4, Part 2,** 266; **Vol. 6, Part 1,** 337; **Vol. 7, Part 1,** 39, 452 f.; **Vol. 7, Part 2,** 319; **Vol. 8, Part 2,** 78, 341; **Vol. 9, Part 1,** 196
United States Pacific Railway Commission, **Vol. 7, Part 2,** 313 f.
United States Reclamation Act, **Vol. 4, Part 2,** 483
United States Reduction and Refining Co., **Supp. 6,** 316
United States Rubber Co., **Supp. 1,** 306; **Supp. 7,** 169
United States Sanitary Commission, **Vol. 2, Part 2,** 136; **Vol. 3, Part 2,** 212; **Vol. 4, Part 2,** 308; **Vol. 5, Part 1,** 251, 297; **Vol. 5, Part 2,** 355, 404; **Vol. 7, Part 1,** 446; **Vol. 7, Part 2,** 26; **Vol. 8, Part 2,** 474; **Vol. 9, Part 1,** 563; **Vol. 9, Part 2,** 24
United States Shipping Co., **Vol. 7, Part 1,** 241
United States Soldiers' Home (Washington, D.C.), **Vol. 5, Part 2,** 315
United States Speaker, The, **Vol. 6, Part 1,** 440
United States Steel Corporation, **Vol. 4, Part 1,** 30; **Vol. 5, Part 1,** 57; **Vol. 7, Part 1,** 144, 177, 301; **Vol. 7, Part 2,** 471; **Vol. 8, Part 1,** 449; **Vol. 9, Part 1,** 598; antitrust actions against, **Supp. 4,** 317; **Supp. 6,** 591; base pricing, **Supp. 4,** 268; establishment of, **Supp. 2,** 600; executives, **Supp. 4,** 777; expansion,

Supp. 7, 228–29; finances, Supp. 6, 622; founding of, Supp. 6, 507; presidency, Supp. 3, 263; subsidiary, Supp. 7, 308; unionization, Supp. 5, 510; Supp. 8, 375; war production, Supp. 7, 587
United States Trust Co., created, Vol. 9, Part 2, 11
United States v. Carolene Products Co., Supp. 4, 796, 797
United States v. Roth, Supp. 6, 216
United States Women's Pure Food Vacuum Preserving Co., Vol. 5, Part 2, 160
United Steel Workers, Supp. 7, 228, 290, 587
United Synagogue of America, founding of, Supp. 2, 6
United Transport Service Employees, founding of, Supp. 6, 648
United Typothetae of America, Vol. 3, Part 1, 264
United Textile Workers, Vol. 2, Part 2, 338
United Vintners, Supp. 7, 614
United World Day of Prayer, Supp. 4, 648
United World Federalists, founding of, Supp. 8, 680
Unity, religious weekly, Vol. 5, Part 2, 180
"Unity of God, The," famous sermon, Vol. 9, Part 2, 391
Unity School of Christianity, Supp. 4, 271–72
Unity Temple (Oak Park, Ill.), Supp. 6, 712
UNIVAC computer, Supp. 6, 675
Universal Christian Conference on Life and Work, Supp. 3, 111; Supp. 6, 25
Universalist church, Vol. 1, Part 1, 83; Vol. 3, Part 2, 406; Vol. 4, Part 2, 216; Vol. 5, Part 2, 457 f.; Vol. 8, Part 2, 398; clergy, Vol. 1, Part 1, 559; Vol. 5, Part 2, 245; Vol. 5, Part 1, 336; Vol. 5, Part 2, 457; Vol. 8, Part 2, 397; Vol. 9, Part 1, 438 f.; doctrines of, Vol. 1, Part 1, 557; early days of, Vol. 10, Part 2, 377; first woman ordained, Vol. 2, Part 1, 151; founding of, in America, Vol. 7, Part 1, 360–61; influence of, Vol. 1, Part 1, 556; opposition to, Vol. 5, Part 2, 112; theological school, first of, Vol. 3, Part 2, 406; writings on, Vol. 10, Part 2, 172
Universal military training. *See* Armed forces and defense; Draft
Universal Negro Improvement and Conservation Association, organization of, Supp. 2, 221; Supp. 5, 554
Universal Peace Union, Vol. 6, Part 1, 431
Universal Pictures, Supp. 6, 610, 657; founding of, Supp. 2, 368
Universe and Life, The, Supp. 4, 427
Universities and colleges, academic freedom issues, Supp. 3, 151, 249, 471; Supp. 5, 410, 461; Supp. 8, 272; administration politics, Supp. 3, 387; Supp. 6, 98–99; architecture of, Supp. 2, 118, 362, 539; Supp. 4, 697–98; Asian studies programs, Supp. 8, 360; athletic policies, Supp. 4, 320; black, Supp. 2, 315, 456, 477; Supp. 4, 742, 916; Supp. 5, 56, 436; Supp. 6, 11–12; Supp. 8, 86–87, 94–95; black scholarships, Supp. 5, 56; China, Supp. 4, 677–78; China, first women's college, Supp. 3, 288; Chinese missionary, Supp. 3, 477; desegregation of, Supp. 8, 73, 322; entrance standards, Supp. 2, 361; Supp. 4, 134; evangelistic, Supp. 8, 304; experimental, Supp. 5, 308–9; Supp. 8, 530–31; faculty v. presidency, Supp. 3, 150–51; federal policies, Supp. 5, 761; first black Phi Beta Kappa chapter, Supp. 5, 437; first contemporary drama course, Supp. 4, 354; first ecology courses, Supp. 5, 374–75; football, Supp. 2, 302; Supp. 4, 236–37, 893, 917; Supp. 5, 289, 458, 727–28; Supp. 6, 48; Supp. 7, 167–68, 571–72, 712–13, 729; Supp. 8, 587–88; German model, Supp. 6, 207–8; gifted students, Supp. 2, 110; graduate education policy, Supp. 8, 73; Great Books curriculum, Supp. 5, 211–12; Supp. 8, 59; interdisciplinary history emphasis, Supp. 8, 273;

land-grant, Supp. 2, 365; Supp. 3, 209; Supp. 5, 49; liberal arts study, Supp. 6, 412; loyalty oath issue, Supp. 6, 640; presses, Supp. 6, 154–55; research institutes, Supp. 2, 60; sit-ins, Supp. 8, 333; social function of, Supp. 1, 21; Supp. 8, 73; student government, Supp. 1, 100; tutorial system, Supp. 6, 99; woman suffrage movement in, Supp. 5, 532; women's, Supp. 2, 79; Supp. 4, 625, 912–13; Supp. 6, 488; women's studies programs, Supp. 6, 41. *See also* Education; *specific institution names*
Universities, state: first federal grant to, Vol. 6, Part 1, 275; financial responsibilities for, Vol. 4, Part 2, 407
University Club (New York), founding, Vol. 5, Part 1, 180
University Elementary School (Chicago, Ill.), Supp. 5, 171
University extension, Vol. 7, Part 1, 292
University Museum (Philadelphia, Pa.), archaeology, Supp. 3, 272
University of Akron: founding of, Vol. 2, Part 1, 221; presidency, Supp. 5, 761
University of Alabama, Vol. 2, Part 1, 184; Vol. 4, Part 1, 151; Vol. 9, Part 1, 367; controversy over coal lands, Vol. 5, Part 2, 147; history studies, Supp. 6, 491; incorporation of, Vol. 7, Part 2, 561; integration, Supp. 8, 73; presidency, Supp. 8, 72–73
University of Arizona: Steward Observatory, Supp. 7, 193; tree-ring research, Supp. 7, 194
University of Arkansas, Vol. 5, Part 1, 27
University of Berlin, Supp. 5, 562
University of Buffalo: curriculum reform, Supp. 6, 99; first chancellor, Vol. 3, Part 2, 381; founding of, Vol. 8, Part 1, 283; medical department, founding of, Vol. 4, Part 2, 185; social work studies, Supp. 3, 4
University of California (Berkeley), Vol. 5, Part 2, 591; Vol. 8, Part 1, 276 f.; Vol. 8, Part 2, 432; Vol. 9, Part 1, 579; Vol. 10, Part 2, 45; agricultural chemistry studies, Supp. 4, 382; agricultural economics studies, Supp. 6, 638; anthropology studies, Supp. 6, 353, 393; architectural design, Supp. 6, 438, 463; astronomy studies, Supp. 4, 600; Bancroft Library, Supp. 5, 77; biochemistry studies, Supp. 4, 720; first dean of women, Supp. 8, 442; founding of, Vol. 2, Part 1, 351; Vol. 4, Part 2, 90; Vol. 9, Part 1, 550; Vol. 10, Part 2, 246; geology studies, Supp. 5, 416; gifts to, Vol. 4, Part 2, 488 f.; grounds, designing of, Vol. 7, Part 2, 26; history studies, Supp. 4, 824; law school, Supp. 4, 680; Supp. 7, 181–82; loyalty oath issue, Supp. 6, 640; paleontology studies, Supp. 3, 519; physics studies, Supp. 6, 370; Supp. 8, 482, 484; presidency, Vol. 4, Part 2, 156; Vol. 5, Part 1, 136; Vol. 5, Part 2, 303 f.; Vol. 6, Part 1, 88; Supp. 2, 92; Supp. 5, 43; psychology studies, Supp. 6, 639–40; Spanish literature and language studies, Supp. 4, 719; theoretical physics studies, Supp. 8, 482, 484; zoology studies, Supp. 4, 461
University of California (Los Angeles), philosophy studies, Supp. 5, 563; Supp. 8, 75; psychology studies, Supp. 1, 316
University of California (Riverside), agricultural studies, Supp. 4, 863
University of Chicago, Vol. 3, Part 2, 367; Vol. 4, Part 1, 183; Vol. 5, Part 1, 438; Vol. 7, Part 1, 160; Vol. 7, Part 2, 174, 238; Vol. 8, Part 2, 272, 408; Vol. 9, Part 1, 125; administration, Supp. 3, 793; anthropology studies, Supp. 6, 532–34; astronomical observatories, Supp. 6, 7; astronomy studies, Supp. 2, 270–71; Supp. 3, 634; Supp. 5, 508, 509; atomic bomb development, Supp. 7, 10–11, 259, 300, 732; Supp. 8, 229–30, 411; bacteriology studies, Supp. 2,

of, **Vol. 1, Part 1,** 207; **Vol. 6, Part 1,** 17; history of, **Vol. 9, Part 2,** 254; journalism school, **Vol. 5, Part 2,** 391; **Vol. 9, Part 1,** 578; **Supp. 1,** 708; **Supp. 4,** 704; law department, **Vol. 1, Part 2,** 375; military training, **Supp. 1,** 211; presidency of, **Vol. 5, Part 2,** 60; **Vol. 7, Part 1,** 25; **Vol. 8, Part 1,** 421

University of Montana, rural life study, **Supp. 5,** 320–21

University of Nashville, **Vol. 5, Part 2,** 91 f., 426; **Vol. 6, Part 1,** 278 f.; **Vol. 9, Part 1,** 542; Western Military Institute, absorption of, by, **Vol. 5, Part 2,** 91

University of Nebraska, **Vol. 2, Part 1,** 179; **Vol. 9, Part 2,** 257; botany studies, **Supp. 3,** 168–69

University of New Mexico, **Vol. 8, Part 1,** 229 f.

University of North Carolina, **Vol. 1, Part 2,** 57; **Vol. 4, Part 1,** 472 f.; **Vol. 8, Part 1,** 43 f.; **Vol. 8, Part 2,** 384, 212; **Vol. 9, Part 1,** 447; **Vol. 9, Part 2,** 231; drama studies, **Supp. 3,** 426–27; founding of, **Vol. 3, Part 1,** 98; **Vol. 7, Part 2,** 516; **Vol. 8, Part 1,** 39 f.; Morehead Foundation, **Supp. 7,** 554; predecessors, **Supp. 4,** 215; presidency, **Supp. 1,** 21; **Supp. 5,** 109; public health school, **Supp. 4,** 701; race relations promotion, **Supp. 6,** 12; reopening of, **Vol. 1, Part 2,** 57; social sciences studies, **Supp. 5,** 520

University of North Carolina Magazine, **Vol. 9, Part 2,** 231

University of North Dakota, **Vol. 9, Part 1,** 472; presidency, **Supp. 5,** 461

University of Northern Pennsylvania, reopening of, **Vol. 9, Part 2,** 55

University of Notre Dame, fottball "Four Horsemen," **Supp. 7,** 729; football team, **Supp. 5,** 568; gifts to, **Supp. 6,** 661; sculpture studies, **Supp. 7,** 531

University of Ohio, **Vol. 6, Part 1,** 275

University of Oklahoma, history studies, **Supp. 5,** 570

University of Oregon, **Vol. 2, Part 1,** 462

University of Orleans (La.), **Vol. 3, Part 1,** 249

University of Pennsylvania, **Vol. 3, Part 2,** 236, 270; **Vol. 4, Part 2,** 337; **Vol. 5, Part 1,** 579 f.; **Vol. 7, Part 1,** 3; **Vol. 7, Part 2,** 305 f., 454 f.; **Vol. 9, Part 1,** 255, 357, 429; dental school, **Vol. 3, Part 2,** 212; development of, **Vol. 3, Part 1,** 215; **Vol. 9, Part 2,** 24 f.; English literature studies, **Supp. 3,** 688–89; explorations of, **Vol. 5, Part 1,** 58 f.; first computer (ENIAC), **Supp. 6,** 675; football team, **Supp. 6,** 47; history studies, **Supp. 6,** 531; hospital, founding of, **Vol. 7, Part 1,** 557; law school, **Vol. 5, Part 2,** 445; **Vol. 9, Part 1,** 29; **Supp. 4,** 490–91; **Supp. 5,** 571, 576; mathematics studies, **Supp. 8,** 514–15; medical school, **Vol. 5, Part 1,** 234, 539; **Vol. 7, Part 1,** 172 f.; **Vol. 7, Part 2,** 453 f.; **Vol. 8, Part 1,** 136 f.; **Vol. 10, Part 2,** 458; **Supp. 2,** 209; **Supp. 3,** 243; **Supp. 4,** 650; **Supp. 5,** 438, 489; merger (1791), **Vol. 8, Part 1,** 137; **Vol. 8, Part 2,** 229; libraries, **Vol. 5, Part 2,** 445; **Vol. 7, Part 2,** 441; physiology studies, **Supp. 4,** 59; political science studies, **Supp. 4,** 705; presidency, **Supp. 4,** 320; psychology studies, **Supp. 3,** 149; School of Biology, **Vol. 5, Part 2,** 13; Semitic studies, **Supp. 3,** 37; **Supp. 4,** 595; University Museum, **Supp. 4,** 761–62; Veterinary School, **Vol. 7, Part 2,** 360; Wharton School of Finance, **Supp. 7,** 373; X-ray department, **Supp. 2,** 512; zoology studies, **Supp. 4,** 516

University of Pittsburgh, **Vol. 2, Part 1,** 182; **Vol. 5, Part 1,** 431; **Vol. 6, Part 1,** 613 f.; **Vol. 7, Part 2,** 540; astronomy studies, **Supp. 3,** 208, 692; Falk Medical Clinic, **Supp. 4,** 261–62; football team, **Supp. 5,** 728; Heinz Memorial Chapel, **Supp. 3,** 183

University of Rochester, **Vol. 1, Part 1,** 270; **Vol. 3, Part 1,** 268; **Vol. 5, Part 2,** 328; Eastman School of Music, **Supp. 1,** 276; medical and dental schools, **Supp. 1,** 276; presidency, **Supp. 1,** 401; **Supp. 2,** 556

University of St. Mary's of the Lake (Chicago), **Vol. 8, Part 1,** 295

University of South Carolina, **Vol. 1, Part 1,** 640; **Vol. 5, Part 2,** 518; **Vol. 6, Part 1,** 391, 555, 577; **Vol. 6, Part 2,** 434; founding of, **Vol. 3, Part 1,** 254

University of South Dakota, **Vol. 9, Part 2,** 643

University of Southern California, first baseball coach, **Supp. 8,** 107; founding of, **Supp. 2,** 716; library, **Supp. 1,** 255; track and field, **Supp. 7,** 152–53

University of Tennessee, **Vol. 1, Part 1,** 453; **Vol. 3, Part 2,** 186; agricultural studies, **Supp. 3,** 909; football team, **Supp. 7,** 571; founding of, **Vol. 2, Part 1,** 520; **Vol. 5, Part 1,** 367; **Vol. 5, Part 2,** 227; medical department, **Vol. 5, Part 2,** 207; presidency, **Supp. 3,** 209; **Supp. 4,** 601

University of Texas, **Vol. 6, Part 1,** 301; **Vol. 6, Part 2,** 589; **Vol. 8, Part 1,** 105 f.; **Vol. 9, Part 1,** 240; founding of, **Vol. 5, Part 1,** 377; **Vol. 8, Part 2,** 14; genetics studies, **Supp. 8,** 449; history studies, **Supp. 7,** 770–71

University of the City of New York. *See* New York University

University of the South, **Vol. 1, Part 1,** 411; administration, **Supp. 1,** 329; founding of, **Vol. 8, Part 1,** 39 f.; second founding of, **Vol. 8, Part 1,** 313 f.

University of Tokyo, **Vol. 7, Part 2,** 319

University of Toronto, graduate studies, **Supp. 2,** 422

University of Tulsa, **Vol. 8, Part 2,** 20

University of Utah, Asian studies, **Supp. 5,** 681

University of Vermont, **Vol. 1, Part 1,** 306, 436; **Vol. 1, Part 2,** 266; **Vol. 6, Part 2,** 300; founding of, **Vol. 1, Part 1,** 195; **Vol. 8, Part 2,** 331; gifts to, **Vol. 2, Part 2,** 361; medical department, **Vol. 9, Part 1,** 327; War of 1812, **Vol. 8, Part 2,** 331

University of Virginia, **Vol. 4, Part 1,** 306; **Vol. 5, Part 1,** 550; **Vol. 5, Part 2,** 32 f.; **Vol. 7, Part 1,** 28; **Vol. 9, Part 1,** 630; astronomy studies, **Supp. 1,** 674–75; early years of, **Vol. 10, Part 1,** 76; English literature and language studies, **Supp. 7,** 797; founding of, **Vol. 1, Part 1,** 195; **Vol. 2, Part 1,** 387; **Vol. 2, Part 2,** 254; **Vol. 5, Part 2,** 32; **Vol. 7, Part 1,** 486; **Vol. 9, Part 2,** 320; growth of, **Supp. 1,** 21–22; Jefferson rotunda, **Vol. 8, Part 1,** 336 f.; law school, **Vol. 6, Part 1,** 369; **Vol. 7, Part 1,** 26; **Supp. 1,** 497; medical school, **Vol. 2, Part 1,** 387; **Vol. 5, Part 1,** 253; presidency, **Supp. 1,** 21–22

University of Washington, **Vol. 10, Part 2,** 178; poetry studies, **Supp. 7,** 654–55

University of Wichita, presidency, **Vol. 5,** 365

University of Wisconsin, **Vol. 1, Part 1,** 53; **Vol. 1, Part 2,** 32; **Vol. 2, Part 1,** 514; **Vol. 8, Part 2,** 213; **Vol. 9, Part 1,** 588; agricultural chemistry studies, **Supp. 5,** 275; anesthesia studies, **Supp. 6,** 553; biochemistry studies, **Supp. 7,** 223; chemistry studies, **Supp. 4,** 5–6; dairy school, first in U.S., **Vol. 9, Part 1,** 280; economics studies, **Supp. 3,** 177–79, 249–50; **Supp. 6,** 585, 705; electrical engineering studies, **Supp. 5,** 354–55; English literature studies, **Supp. 3,** 454–55; experimental college, **Supp. 2,** 203; **Supp. 7,** 523–24; first premedical course at, **Supp. 4,** 84; graduate school, founding of, **Supp. 1,** 187; history studies, **Supp. 5,** 429; home economics studies, **Supp. 3,** 507; labor economics studies, **Supp. 6,** 503–4; library, **Supp. 3,** 326; library catalogue, **Supp. 3,** 326; limnology studies, **Supp. 3,** 402; mathematics studies, **Supp. 3,** 791; pharmacology studies, **Vol. 8, Part 1,** 154 f.; **Supp. 3,** 432–33; plant pathology studies, **Supp. 3,** 401; political sciences studies, **Supp. 5,** 521–22; presidency, **Supp. 2,** 203; **Supp. 4,** 84–85, 247; **Supp. 7,** 224, 450; psychology studies, **Supp. 3,** 383

University of Wooster, **Vol. 4, Part 1,** 602; **Vol. 9, Part 2,** 314

University of Wyoming, **Vol. 5, Part 1,** 321

University Players Guild (Falmouth, Mass.), **Supp. 6,** 610

University Press Association, **Supp. 6,** 155

University School (Petersburg, Va.), **Vol. 6, Part 1,** 559

University Settlement Society, **Supp. 3,** 175, 729

"Universology," **Vol. 1, Part 1,** 298

UNRRA. *See* United Nations Relief and Rehabilitation Administration

Unruh, Howard, reference to, **Supp. 6,** 58

Untermeyer, Louis, reference to, **Supp. 3,** 69

UP. *See* United Press

Updegraff, Allan, reference to, **Supp. 6,** 328

Updike, Daniel Berkeley, reference to, **Supp. 6,** 185

Upper Canada Rebellion, **Vol. 1, Part 2,** 248

Urania, collection of hymns, **Vol. 6, Part 1,** 530

Uranian Academy, **Vol. 1, Part 1,** 107

Uranium, **Supp. 6,** 370, 501; chain reaction research, **Supp. 5,** 220–21; fission, **Supp. 7,** 731–32; isotope separation, **Supp. 4,** 453–54; **Supp. 8,** 232; purification, **Supp. 8,** 411

Uranus, planet discovered, **Vol. 7, Part 1,** 32

Urban, Joseph, reference to, **Supp. 7,** 504

Urban areas. *See* Cities; City planning; Suburbs

Urban League: founding of, **Supp. 5,** 548; **Supp. 6,** 284–85; research surveys, **Supp. 6,** 321; **Supp. 8,** 521

Urease, biochemical isolation of, **Supp. 5,** 670

Urey, Harold C., references to, **Supp. 3,** 694; **Supp. 5,** 589

Urology, **Vol. 5, Part 1,** 239; **Vol. 7, Part 2,** 602; development of modern, **Supp. 3,** 853–54; research in, **Supp. 1,** 455; **Supp. 5,** 688

Urschel, Charles F., reference to, **Supp. 5,** 381–82

Ursinus College: first president, **Vol. 1, Part 2,** 426; founding of, **Vol. 1, Part 2,** 426

Uruguay: diplomacy with, **Vol. 7, Part 1,** 608; events leading to independence of, **Vol. 3, Part 1,** 202

U.S.A., **Supp. 8,** 137, 138

"Use" cult of mystics, **Vol. 4, Part 2,** 323

USIA. *See* Information Agency, United States

USO. *See* United Service Organizations

Usonian homes, **Supp. 6,** 714

USSR. *See* Soviet Union

U.S. Steel Corporation. *See* United States Steel Corporation

Utah: colonizing of, **Vol. 9, Part 1,** 386; constitutional convention, **Supp. 1,** 448; expedition to (1857–58), *see* Mormon disturbances; governors, **Supp. 2,** 147; legal service, **Vol. 10, Part 2,** 644; mining, **Vol. 3, Part 1,** 27; **Vol. 4, Part 1,** 9; **Vol. 7, Part 2,** 209, 451; missionary work in, **Vol. 9, Part 1,** 422; Mormon migration to, **Vol. 2, Part 2,** 592 f.; **Vol. 8, Part 1,** 175; newspaper, first daily in, **Vol. 2, Part 2,** 353; political service, **Vol. 1, Part 1,** 446; **Vol. 8, Part 2,** 4; politics, **Supp. 3,** 727, 753–54; **Supp. 5,** 681; polygamy, bill to suppress, in, **Vol. 8, Part 1,** 341 f.; public service, **Vol. 2, Part 2,** 353; surveys in, **Vol. 4, Part 2,** 52; territorial government set up for, **Vol. 3, Part 1,** 399

Utah Copper Co., **Supp. 6,** 316

Utilities. *See* Public utilities; *specific types*

Utopian communities, **Vol. 4, Part 2,** 323; **Supp. 1,** 345, 454; Oneida Community, **Supp. 5,** 492

Utopian theories, **Supp. 2,** 272

V

Vaccination, **Vol. 1, Part 1,** 395; **Vol. 3, Part 2,** 229; **Vol. 4, Part 1,** 361; **Vol. 4, Part 2,** 308; **Vol. 5, Part 2,** 163; **Vol. 6, Part 1,** 333; **Vol. 7, Part 1,** 559; **Vol. 9, Part 1,** 325; **Vol. 10, Part 1,** 479 f.

Vaccines, **Vol. 3, Part 2,** 547; diphtheria, **Supp. 5,** 1; poliomyelitis, **Supp. 5,** 512; **Supp. 7,** 649; typhus, **Supp. 4,** 667–68

Vacuum cleaner, **Supp. 5,** 313–14

Vagabond King, The, **Supp. 7,** 389

Vagnozzi, Egidio, reference to, **Supp. 8,** 614

Vagrants, most widely known of, **Vol. 8, Part 1,** 170 f.

Vail, Alfred, reference to, **Vol. 7, Part 1,** 249 f.

Vail, T. N., reference to, **Vol. 5, Part 1,** 325

Valachi, Joseph, reference to, **Supp. 8,** 209

Valens, Ritchie, reference to, **Supp. 6,** 301

Valentino, Rudolph, reference to, **Supp. 7,** 563

Val-Kill, N.Y., **Supp. 7,** 660, 664

Vallandigham, C. L., **Vol. 5, Part 1,** 183; **Vol. 6, Part 1,** 251; **Vol. 9, Part 2,** 568

Valley Forge (Pa.), **Vol. 5, Part 2,** 253; **Vol. 7, Part 1,** 141

Valley Hill Farm (Pa.), **Supp. 7,** 127

Valleys, term "superimposed" applied to, **Vol. 8, Part 1,** 146 f.

Valparaiso affair (1891), **Vol. 3, Part 2,** 551 f.; **Vol. 8, Part 2,** 438

Value, marginal utility principle of, **Supp. 2,** 106–7

Value, theory of, **Supp. 4,** 267–68, 272–73; **Supp. 6,** 505

Valves: electric, **Vol. 8, Part 2,** 133; Jenkins, **Vol. 5, Part 2,** 50; manufacturing of, **Vol. 5, Part 2,** 50

Valverde, battle of, **Vol. 2, Part 1,** 468, 531

Van Brunt, Henry, reference to, **Vol. 10, Part 1,** 452 f.

Van Buren, Martin, **Vol. 4, Part 2,** 189; **Vol. 5, Part 1,** 531; **Vol. 8, Part 1,** 30 f.; **Vol. 9, Part 2,** 511; anti-Texas letter of, **Vol. 8, Part 1,** 34 f.; relations with Benjamin Franklin Butler, **Vol. 2, Part 1,** 356; relations with Silas Wright, **Vol. 10, Part 2,** 565

Vancouver, Wash., founding of, **Vol. 6, Part 2,** 134

Vandalia scheme, **Vol. 5, Part 2,** 127; **Vol. 9, Part 2,** 638 f.; **Vol. 10, Part 2,** 32

Vandegrift, Margaret, reference to, **Vol. 5, Part 1,** 614

Vandenberg, Arthur H., references to, **Supp. 4,** 42; **Supp. 5,** 334, 505, 705; **Supp. 6,** 455; **Supp. 7,** 138; **Supp. 8,** 701

Vanderbilt, Commodore Cornelius: first philanthropy of, **Vol. 3, Part 1,** 192; references to, **Vol. 7, Part 1,** 234; **Vol. 10, Part 1,** 364

Vanderbilt, Cornelius, III, reference to, **Supp. 5,** 707

Vanderbilt, Gloria, reference to, **Supp. 7,** 752–53

Vanderbilt, Reginald Claypoole, reference to, **Supp. 7,** 752

Vanderbilt, William H., **Vol. 7, Part 1,** 176 f.; House of, work of Hunt, **Vol. 5, Part 1,** 390

Vanderbilt, William Kissam, reference to, **Supp. 1,** 68

Vanderbilt interests attacked, **Vol. 4, Part 2,** 393

Vanderbilt University, **Vol. 3, Part 1,** 192 f.; **Vol. 6, Part 2,** 170; **Vol. 8, Part 2,** 287; **Vol. 10, Part 1,** 173; **Vol. 10, Part 2,** 438; administration, **Supp. 8,** 72; history studies, **Supp. 6,** 491; medical school, **Supp. 6,** 546; presidency, **Supp. 2,** 361–62; secularization of, **Supp. 3,** 129

Van Devanter, Willis, references to, **Supp. 3,** 100; **Supp. 4,** 537; **Supp. 5,** 571; **Supp. 7,** 730

Van Dincklagen, Lubbert, relations with Everardus Bogardus, **Vol. 1, Part 2,** 406

Vandiver, Harry S., reference to, **Supp. 3,** 70

Van Doren, Carl, references to, **Supp. 7,** 306; **Supp. 8,** 667

Van Doren, Irita, reference to, **Supp. 8,** 520
Van Druten, John, reference to, **Supp. 6,** 610
Vanessa, opera, world premiere, **Supp. 6,** 457
Van Hise, Charles R., reference to, **Supp. 3,** 38, 265
Vanity Fair, **Vol. 2, Part 1,** 763; **Supp. 3,** 53, 547; development of, **Supp. 4,** 199–200; drama criticism, **Supp. 8,** 491, 492
Van Maanen, Adriaan, reference to, **Supp. 8,** 587–88
Vann, Robert L., reference to, **Supp. 6,** 260
Van Rensselaer, Stephen, reference to, **Vol. 3, Part 1,** 605
Van Rensselaer, as patrons, **Vol. 4, Part 2,** 370
Van Slyke, Donald D., reference to, **Supp. 3,** 351
Van Sweringen, O. P. and M. J., reference to, **Supp. 5,** 34–35
Van Vechten, Carl, reference to, **Supp. 5,** 659
Van Voorhis, Daniel, reference to, **Supp. 3,** 152
Vanzetti, Bartolomeo. *See* Sacco-Vanzetti case
Vardaman, James K., reference to, **Supp. 4,** 78
Vare, William S., references to, **Supp. 3,** 559, 622; **Supp. 5,** 204–5; **Supp. 6,** 509–10; **Supp. 7,** 305, 607
Vargas, Alberto, reference to, **Supp. 5,** 637
Varian, Russell H., reference to, **Supp. 4,** 358
Varieties of Religious Experience, The, **Vol. 5, Part 1,** 597
Variety, founding of, **Vol. 9, Part 1,** 167
Variety stores, **Supp. 8,** 347–49. *See also* Five and dime stores
Varuna, **Vol. 1, Part 2,** 409
Varnish, manufacturing of, **Vol. 7, Part 1,** 350
Vaschalde, Arthur Adolphe, reference to, **Supp. 3,** 375
Vascular surgery. *See* Blood vessels
Vassar, John G., reference to **Vol. 9, Part 2,** 329
Vassar, Matthew, reference to, **Vol. 1, Part 1,** 13
Vassar College, **Vol. 1, Part 1,** 472; **Vol. 5, Part 2,** 208; **Vol. 7, Part 1,** 58, 250, 329; charter of, **Vol. 5, Part 2,** 70; early history of, **Vol. 7, Part 1,** 555; **Vol. 8, Part 1,** 412 f.; experimental theater, **Supp. 8,** 175; psychology studies, **Supp. 2,** 698–99
Vassar Observatory, **Vol. 10, Part 2,** 164
Vatican, **Vol. 1, Part 2,** 359; diplomacy with U.S., **Supp. 6,** 623; **Supp. 8,** 613, 614; diplomatic service, **Supp. 8,** 294–95; first American to head Curia, **Supp. 6,** 608; Library, reorganization of, **Supp. 3,** 327; Sacra Rota, **Supp. 8,** 46; Second Council, **Supp. 7,** 534, 776; **Supp. 8,** 46, 115, 307, 537, 614–15. *See also* Catholic church
Vaudeville, **Vol. 5, Part 2,** 289; **Vol. 7, Part 2,** 290; **Vol. 8, Part 1,** 242 f.; **Vol. 8, Part 2,** 249; **Supp. 6,** 13, 112, 128, 368; **Supp. 8,** 64; black performers, **Supp. 4,** 695; blackface roles, **Supp. 7,** 106; child acts, **Supp. 8,** 314, 354–55, 363; comedy teams, **Supp. 4,** 400–1, 739; **Supp. 7,** 9; dance teams, **Supp. 7,** 657–58; Four Cohans, **Supp. 3,** 173; "Johnny's New Car" act, **Supp. 3,** 443; Keller-Sullivan routine, **Supp. 8,** 317; largest circuit, **Supp. 8,** 367; "Last of the Red Hot Mamas," **Supp. 8,** 661; magic acts, **Supp. 2,** 378, 661–62; **Supp. 7,** 57; management, **Supp. 2,** 32; master of ceremonies, **Supp. 7,** 237; miniature revues, **Supp. 8,** 695; risqué songs in, **Supp. 4,** 814–15; Shubert-Keith competition, **Supp. 5,** 627; slapstick routines, **Supp. 7,** 462; songwriting for, **Supp. 4,** 835–36; theater circuits, **Supp. 1,** 18; Williams and Walker cakewalk, **Supp. 3,** 187; writings on, **Supp. 8,** 584–85
Vaughan, Victor C., references to, **Supp. 3,** 121; **Supp. 6,** 481
Vaux, Calvert, relations with Frederick Law Olmsted, **Vol. 7, Part 2,** 25 f.
Veblen, Thorstein, references to, **Supp. 3,** 177, 248; **Supp. 4,** 584–87; **Supp. 6,** 96, 271, 598, 653

Veda. *See* Sanskrit
Vedic Concordance, **Vol. 1, Part 2,** 387
Vee, Bobby, reference to, **Supp. 6,** 302
Veeck, Bill, reference to, **Supp. 6,** 121
Vega (airplane), **Supp. 8,** 385
Vegetables: hybrid corn, **Supp. 5,** 629; nutritional value, **Supp. 5,** 623
Vegetarianism, **Vol. 7, Part 1,** 495–96; **Supp. 3,** 409; **Supp. 5,** 378, 452; **Supp. 6,** 113
Venereal disease, **Vol. 2, Part 1,** 260; **Vol. 4, Part 2,** 553; **Vol. 8, Part 1,** 588 f.; control of, **Supp. 5,** 604–5; inherited syphilis studies, **Supp. 8,** 429; prevention of, **Supp. 5,** 144; public education in, **Supp. 4,** 758–59; **Supp. 6,** 249; research on, **Supp. 4,** 288; treatment of, **Supp. 3,** 851; **Supp. 6,** 423–24, 460–61. *See also* Syphilis
Venereal Disease Control Act (1938), **Supp. 4,** 759
Venezuela: boundary dispute (1895), **Vol. 1, Part 2,** 71; **Vol. 2, Part 2,** 211; **Vol. 4, Part 2,** 335; **Vol. 5, Part 1,** 81; **Vol. 7, Part 2,** 33; **Vol. 8, Part 1,** 485; **Vol. 9, Part 2,** 100; oil development, **Supp. 8,** 455; relations with, **Vol. 1, Part 1,** 235; **Vol. 1, Part 2,** 392, 506; **Vol. 7, Part 2,** 283; **Vol. 8, Part 1,** 14 f.; **Vol. 8, Part 2,** 520; **Vol. 9, Part 2,** 608, 623
Ventilation, **Supp. 3,** 353; **Supp. 4,** 690; first systematic plan of, in any public building, **Vol. 8, Part 1,** 475
Ventriculography, **Supp. 4,** 214
Venturi, Lionello, reference to, **Supp. 6,** 552
Venus, observations of, **Vol. 3, Part 1,** 602 f.; **Vol. 6, Part 1,** 516; **Vol. 7, Part 1,** 454; **Vol. 8, Part 1,** 630; **Vol. 9, Part 2,** 18
Vera Cruz, Mexico, siege of (1847), **Vol. 6, Part 1,** 121; **Vol. 7, Part 2,** 306, 487, 604; **Vol. 8, Part 2,** 509; **Vol. 9, Part 1,** 331; **Vol. 9, Part 2,** 599; **Vol. 10, Part 1,** 83; **Vol. 10, Part 2,** 537
Verklärte Nacht (musical composition), **Supp. 5,** 608
Verlag Ullstein, reference to, **Supp. 6,** 39
Vermont: admission to Union, **Vol. 1, Part 2,** 575; **Vol. 2, Part 1,** 222; **Vol. 2, Part 2,** 80; **Vol. 9, Part 2,** 523; "Apostle of Vermont," **Vol. 7, Part 1,** 614; Articles of Confederation, **Vol. 8, Part 2,** 49; boundary disputes, **Vol. 5, Part 2,** 608; farming, early, **Vol. 7, Part 2,** 148; first Episcopal bishop in, **Vol. 5, Part 1,** 212; Fish Commission, **Vol. 9, Part 2,** 565; flora of, **Vol. 1, Part 2,** 593; geology of, **Vol. 5, Part 1,** 71; **Vol. 7, Part 2,** 471; governors, **Vol. 2, Part 1,** 360 f.; **Vol. 2, Part 2,** 78 f., 80 f.; **Vol. 3, Part 2,** 249; **Vol. 4, Part 1,** 59; **Vol. 4, Part 2,** 131 f.; **Vol. 5, Part 1,** 128 f.; **Vol. 6, Part 2,** 10 f., 423 f.; **Vol. 7, Part 2,** 146; **Vol. 8, Part 1,** 245 f.; **Vol. 9, Part 1,** 302 f.; Great Britain and, **Vol. 1, Part 1,** 194 f.; history of, **Vol. 2, Part 1,** 360; **Vol. 3, Part 2,** 305; **Vol. 4, Part 2,** 132, 391; **Vol. 6, Part 1,** 532; **Vol. 9, Part 1,** 204; land controversies, **Vol. 3, Part 1,** 465 f.; **Vol. 10, Part 1,** 653 f.; legal service, **Vol. 1, Part 2,** 575, 576; **Vol. 2, Part 2,** 73; **Vol. 3, Part 1,** 310; **Vol. 4, Part 2,** 379; **Vol. 6, Part 2,** 424, 528; **Vol. 8, Part 1,** 14, 190, 439; **Vol. 8, Part 2,** 49, 132; **Vol. 10, Part 1,** 97; natural history of, **Vol. 9, Part 1,** 480; name, origin of the, **Vol. 10, Part 2,** 635; pioneer founding of republic, **Vol. 8, Part 2,** 49; political service, **Vol. 1, Part 2,** 575, 576, 594; **Vol. 2, Part 2,** 78; **Vol. 3, Part 1,** 310, 600; **Vol. 3, Part 2,** 249; **Vol. 4, Part 1,** 59; **Vol. 4, Part 2,** 131; **Vol. 5, Part 1,** 129; **Vol. 6, Part 2,** 11, 222, 424; **Vol. 7, Part 2,** 146, 148, 193, 209, 528; **Vol. 8, Part 1,** 14, 33, 190, 245, 620; **Vol. 9, Part 1,** 203, 303; **Vol. 9, Part 2,** 523; politics, **Supp. 7,** 23; **Supp. 8,** 177–78; printing, early, **Vol. 4, Part 2,** 390; public service, **Vol. 3, Part 2,** 498; **Vol. 4, Part 2,** 378; **Vol. 7, Part 1,** 198, 216, 523; **Vol. 7, Part 2,** 209, 471; **Vol. 8, Part 1,** 245 f.; **Vol. 9, Part 1,** 283; railroad building in, **Vol. 9, Part 1,** 302; road

Virginia Literary Fund, established, **Vol. 10, Part 1,** 88
Virginia Medical and Surgical Journal, **Vol. 7, Part 2,** 97
Virginia Medical Journal, **Vol. 6, Part 1,** 575
Virginia Military Institute, **Vol. 2, Part 2,** 581; **Vol. 9, Part 1,** 115, 264; superintendents, **Supp. 3,** 453
Virginian, The, **Supp. 2,** 729–30;
Virginia Normal and Collegiate Institute (Petersburg), **Vol. 5, Part 2,** 598
Virginia Plan. *See* Constitutional Convention
Virginia Polytechnic Institute, **Vol. 6, Part 1,** 370
Virginia Quarterly Review, founding of, **Supp. 7,** 797
Virginia State Bar Association, **Vol. 1, Part 2,** 319
Virginia State Federation of Colored Women's Clubs, founding of, **Supp. 4,** 53–54
Virginia Theological Seminary, **Vol. 7, Part 1,** 137; **Vol. 7, Part 2,** 130
Virginius affair (1873), **Vol. 2, Part 2,** 628; **Vol. 3, Part 1,** 269; **Vol. 3, Part 2,** 399; **Vol. 9, Part 1,** 151
Virgo A (galaxy), **Supp. 6,** 31
Virology, **Supp. 7,** 648–49
Virus: cancer, **Supp. 4,** 615–16; **Supp. 8,** 556; chemical structure studies, **Supp. 4,** 381; early studies of, **Supp. 6,** 482; immunology studies, **Supp. 3,** 441; infection's pathological effects, **Supp. 7,** 648; measles, **Supp. 3,** 774; **Supp. 5,** 63–64; poliomyelitis, **Supp. 4,** 287–88; **Supp. 5,** 604; research on, **Supp. 5,** 382–83; yellow fever, **Supp. 5,** 605
Visible speech, **Vol. 1, Part 2,** 149, 152
Vision: corneal transplants, **Supp. 7,** 70; night vision, **Supp. 4,** 357; photoreception studies, **Supp. 4,** 367; physiology, **Vol. 9, Part 2,** 647; psychophysics of, **Supp. 2,** 406. *See also* Blind and blindness; Ophthalmology
Visitation Order, **Vol. 7, Part 1,** 401; **Vol. 9, Part 2,** 376
Visiting Nurse Service, **Supp. 2,** 687–88
Vitagraph Studios, founding of, **Supp. 3,** 76; **Supp. 6,** 618–19, 667–68
Vital statistics, **Vol. 6, Part 1,** 59, 577 f.; **Vol. 6, Part 2,** 467; **Vol. 8, Part 2,** 183; **Vol. 10, Part 2,** 198; first registration of birth, deaths, etc., **Vol. 9, Part 1,** 33
Vitamin B-12: and anemia, **Supp. 4,** 581; isolation of, **Supp. 5,** 122
Vitamin D, rickets relationship, **Supp. 1,** 398; **Supp. 5,** 623
Vitamins: B complex, **Supp. 6,** 595; biochemical studies of, **Supp. 8,** 197–98; deficiency and cardiovascular disturbances, **Supp. 3,** 806; deficiency research, **Supp. 7,** 223; development of, **Supp. 6,** 447; nutritional role research, **Supp. 5,** 276; quantitative bioassay of, **Supp. 5,** 623; research in, **Supp. 1,** 560; riboflavin, **Supp. 6,** 595
Viticulture, **Vol. 1, Part 1,** 109; **Vol. 3, Part 1,** 491 f.; **Vol. 4, Part 2,** 494; **Vol. 5, Part 1,** 430; **Vol. 7, Part 1,** 335 f.; **Vol. 8, Part 1,** 233 f.
Vivisection, **Vol. 3, Part 1,** 40; **Vol. 7, Part 1,** 53
Vocation Bureau of Boston, **Supp. 2,** 45
Vocational education, **Vol. 5, Part 1,** 348; **Vol. 9, Part 1,** 388; Federal Board of, **Vol. 6, Part 1,** 178; **Vol. 8, Part 2,** 113. *See also* Vocational guidance and training
Vocational Education Act (1946), **Supp. 8,** 24
Vocational guidance and training, counseling, **Supp. 2,** 45, 398, 728; Massachusetts, **Supp. 3,** 328; McHale Test for College Women, **Supp. 6,** 412; pioneer work in, **Supp. 4,** 364–66; work-study program, **Supp. 3,** 63
Vocational Rehabilitation Act (1946), **Supp. 8,** 24
Voegtlin, Carl, reference to, **Supp. 3,** 483
Vogt, J. H. L., reference to, **Supp. 6,** 70
Vogue, **Supp. 3,** 547; **Supp. 6,** 107–8; first number, **Vol. 4, Part 1,** 293; illustration, **Supp. 7,** 66; *Vanity Fair*

merger, **Supp. 4,** 200
Voice of America, **Supp. 8,** 640
Voice of Labor, **Vol. 8, Part 1,** 451
Voice of the Turtle, The, **Supp. 6,** 610, 652
Volcanoes: Hawaii, **Vol. 5, Part 1,** 70; Lassen Peak eruption, **Supp. 1,** 247; study of, **Supp. 5,** 361–62, **Supp. 6,** 153, 213; study of, during eruptions, **Vol. 4, Part 2,** 502
Volstead Act (1919), **Vol. 4, Part 2,** 253; legality of, **Supp. 6,** 3; passage of, **Supp. 4,** 853
Volunteers of America, founding of, **Supp. 2,** 48
Volunteer work: organized, advocacy of, **Supp. 4,** 228; Red Cross-sponsored, **Supp. 4,** 93
V-1 and V-2 rockets, **Supp. 3,** 307–8
Von Euler, Ulf, reference to, **Supp. 3,** 136
Von Humboldt, Alexander, reference to, **Vol. 1, Part 1,** 466
Von Kármán, Theodore, references to, **Supp. 8,** 439, 440
Von Neumann, John, **Supp. 3,** 70–71
Von Neumann, Marina, reference to, **Supp. 6,** 656
Von Steuben, Baron, reference to, **Vol. 7, Part 1,** 563
Von Stroheim, Erich, reference to, **Supp. 7,** 563
Von Tilzer, Albert, reference to, **Supp. 4,** 836
Von Zedwitz, Waldemar, reference to, **Supp. 6,** 134, 135
Voorhees Resolution, vote on, **Vol. 8, Part 1,** 410
Voronoff, Serge, reference to, **Supp. 6,** 632
Voting: Australian ballot system, **Vol. 4, Part 1,** 215; first Indian, **Vol. 9, Part 1,** 228. *See also* Elections; Voting rights; Woman suffrage
Voting rights: armed forces' absentee ballots, **Supp. 8,** 223; blacks in South, **Supp. 4,** 331, 384–85; **Supp. 8,** 334, 335, 682; federal enforcement policies, **Supp. 8,** 322–23; poll tax, **Supp. 6,** 526; **Supp. 7,** 416; poll tax abolishment, **Supp. 7,** 416; poll tax support, **Supp. 6,** 526; primaries, **Supp. 5,** 575; Supreme Court decisions, **Supp. 7,** 264. *See also* Woman suffrage
Voting Rights Act (1965), **Supp. 8,** 334, 500
Vox Humana, method of manufacture of, **Vol. 3, Part 1,** 221
Voyages, description of, during period 1790-1810, **Vol. 3, Part 1,** 217
Voyageurs, **Vol. 5, Part 1,** 326
VTOL (vertical takeoff and landing) aircraft, **Supp. 6,** 50
Vulcanism, early advocate of the possibilities of radioactivity in promoting, **Vol. 3, Part 1,** 555. *See also* Volcanoes
Vulval cancer, **Supp. 3,** 763

W

Wa-Wan Press, founding of, **Supp. 5,** 218
Wabash College, **Vol. 1, Part 1,** 532; **Vol. 3, Part 1,** 522
Waco University, **Vol. 2, Part 1,** 288
Waddell, John Alexander Low, reference to, **Supp. 3,** 331–32
Wade, James F., reference to, **Supp. 6,** 253
Wade-Davis bill (1864), **Vol. 5, Part 2,** 84
Wade-Davis Manifesto, **Vol. 3, Part 1,** 120; **Vol. 5, Part 2,** 113
Wadena (Minn.) *Pioneer Journal,* **Supp. 5,** 396
Wadsworth, James S., reference to, **Vol. 10, Part 1,** 421 f.
Wadsworth, James W., reference to, **Supp. 6,** 227
Wadsworth Atheneum (Hartford, Conn.), **Supp. 3,** 567
Wage and Hour Act (1941), constitutionality of, **Supp. 8,** 35

Wage Earner and His Problems, The, **Vol. 7, Part** 1, 52
Wages and hours: cost-of-living index, **Supp. 7,** 794; eight-hour day, **Supp. 1,** 269, 334; five-day week, **Supp. 4,** 455; five-dollar day, **Supp. 4,** 296–97, 304; forty-eight-hour week, **Supp. 4,** 432; government control measures, **Supp. 4,** 890; legislation, **Supp. 7,** 262; **Supp. 8,** 35; maximum-hours law for women, **Supp. 4,** 626; minimum-wage standards, **Supp. 3,** 655–56; **Supp. 4,** 900; portal-to-portal pay issue, **Supp. 5,** 358; profit-sharing, **Supp. 1,** 370–71; Saturday half-day, **Supp. 1,** 610; straight-time pay plan, **Supp. 4,** 996; **Supp. 5,** 315; Supreme Court decisions, **Supp. 4,** 537; **Supp. 5,** 572, 574; women and children, **Supp. 2,** 408. *See also* Labor and labor movement
Wagner, Richard: authority on, **Vol. 5, Part** 1, 368, production, **Vol. 7, Part** 1, 549; promotion of, **Vol. 8, Part** 2, 562; references to, **Supp. 3,** 359; **Supp. 4,** 210–11; **Supp. 6,** 643; rise in popularity of, **Vol. 3, Part** 1, 48 f.
Wagner, Robert F., references to, **Supp. 3,** 717, 838; **Supp. 5,** 227; **Supp. 8,** 616
Wagner, Robert F., Jr., reference to, **Supp. 5,** 718
Wagner Act. *See* National Labor Relations Act
Wagner Society, founding of, **Supp. 4,** 210–11
Wagner-Steagall National Housing Act (1937), **Supp. 3,** 656, 730, 838; **Supp. 5,** 631
Wagon, manufacture, **Vol. 3, Part** 2, 251; **Vol. 8, Part** 2, 471
Wagon Box fight, leader in, **Vol. 8, Part** 1, 437
Wagon train, **Vol. 1, Part** 2, 145; to California, **Vol. 8, Part** 2, 251
Wagon wheel, manufacture, **Vol. 8, Part** 2, 586
Wahoo Swamp, battle of, **Vol. 2, Part** 1, 423; **Vol. 5, Part** 2, 63; **Vol. 8, Part** 2, 507
Wainwright, Jonathan M., reference to, **Supp. 7,** 489
Waiting for Lefty, **Supp. 7,** 583
Wakarusa War (Kans.), **Vol. 3, Part** 1, 202
Wake Forest College (N.C.), endowment, **Supp. 5,** 567
Waksman, Selman, reference to, **Supp. 6,** 447
Walcott, Charles D., reference to, **Supp. 4,** 765–66
Walcott, "Jersey Joe," reference to, **Supp. 8,** 417
Wald, Lillian, references to, **Supp. 4,** 603; **Supp. 6,** 167, 664
Waldensians, **Vol. 5, Part** 2, 418
Waldie's Select Circulating Library, **Vol. 9, Part** 1, 303
Waldorf-Astoria Hotel (New York City), **Vol. 1, Part** 1, 400, 402; **Vol. 1, Part** 2, 418 f.; **Vol. 4, Part** 2, 241
Waldorf Hotel. *See* Waldorf-Astoria Hotel
Walgreen Co., development of, **Supp. 2,** 688
Walker, Alice, reference to, **Supp. 8,** 540
Walker, Edwin, reference to, **Supp. 8,** 57–58
Walker, Elisha, reference to, **Supp. 4,** 326
Walker, Frank C., reference to, **Supp. 5,** 638
Walker, James J. ("Jimmy"): Block relationship, **Supp. 3,** 80; investigation of, **Supp. 3,** 181, 646; **Supp. 6,** 88, 141, 142, 570; references to, **Supp. 4,** 465, 904; **Supp. 5,** 227; **Supp. 7,** 4
Walker, John Brisben, reference to, **Supp. 4,** 38
Walker, Ralph, reference to, **Supp. 5,** 721–22
Walker Act (1846) tariff, **Vol. 3, Part** 1, 39; **Vol. 6, Part** 1, 210; **Vol. 8, Part** 1, 34 f.; **Vol. 10, Part** 1, 585 f.
Walking, long-distance, **Vol. 10, Part** 2, 19; **Supp. 1,** 583
"Walking Purchase" (1737), **Vol. 7, Part** 2, 433
Walks and Talks on the Farm, **Vol. 4, Part** 2, 315
Walküre, Die, first U.S. performance, **Vol. 7, Part** 1, 434
Walla Walla, Wash., political service, **Vol. 1, Part** 2, 349

Wallace, George C., references to, **Supp. 7,** 425; **Supp. 8,** 676–77
Wallace, Henry A.: agricultural policy, **Supp. 3,** 594; **Supp. 6,** 459, 487, 638–39; **Supp. 8,** 699–700; Jones, J., relationship, **Supp. 6,** 325; presidential candidacy, **Supp. 8,** 511, 512; press relations, **Supp. 8,** 498; references to, **Supp. 4,** 356; **Supp. 7,** 661; vice-presidency, **Supp. 3,** 659, 664; **Supp. 6,** 260; vice-presidential candidacy, **Supp. 8,** 361
Wallace, Henry Cantwell, references to, **Supp. 3,** 134; **Supp. 6,** 638; **Supp. 7,** 759, 760
Wallace, Lew, reference to, **Vol. 3, Part** 1, 598; **Vol. 5, Part** 1, 241
Wallace, Mike, references to, **Supp. 8,** 387, 388
Wallace's Farmer, **Supp. 7,** 759
Wallach, Lester, reference to, **Vol. 7, Part** 1, 93
Waller, D. W., relations with Edwin Thomas Booth, **Vol. 1, Part** 2, 445
Waller, Fats, reference to, **Supp. 6,** 620
Walling, William English, reference to, **Supp. 3,** 576
Wallis, Hal B., reference to, **Supp. 7,** 239
Wall Street, **Vol. 4, Part** 2, 394; **Vol. 7, Part** 1, 143 f., 240, 258; **Vol. 8, Part** 2, 266 f., 292; **Vol. 10, Part** 2, 120; "Ryan Crowd," **Vol. 8, Part** 2, 266; Wilson, Woodrow, relations with, **Vol. 4, Part** 2, 372; writings on, **Vol. 8, Part** 1, 176 f. *See also* Banking; Finance
Walnut growing, **Vol. 9, Part** 2, 147
Walsh, Ernest, reference to, **Supp. 7,** 335
Walsh, Frank P., references to, **Supp. 3,** 532; **Supp. 4,** 543, 544; **Supp. 6,** 483, 484
Walsh, John Anthony, reference to, **Supp. 3,** 569
Walsh, Thomas J., reference to, **Supp. 3,** 259
Walt Disney World (Orlando, Fla.), founding of, **Supp. 8,** 131
Walter, Bruno, references to, **Supp. 6,** 324, 351; **Supp. 7,** 549
Walter Reed Hospital (Washington, D.C.), orthopedic section, **Supp. 6,** 344–45
Waltham, Mass.: cotton mills, first, **Vol. 6, Part** 1, 456 f.; watchmaking in, **Vol. 3, Part** 1, 239
Waltham (Mass.) Watch Co., **Supp. 5,** 190
Walther League, founding of, **Supp. 4,** 540–41
Walton, E. T. S., reference to, **Supp. 8,** 199
Walton, Isaak. *See Complete Angler*
Wanamaker, John, references to, **Vol. 4, Part** 2, 335; **Vol. 7, Part** 1, 641
Wanamaker Department Store (New York City), **Vol. 10, Part** 1, 408 f.; **Supp. 7,** 779
Waner, Lloyd, reference to, **Supp. 7,** 768
War: Association to Abolish, **Vol. 3, Part** 1, 357; cabinet, **Vol. 3, Part** 2, 568; chemical warfare, **Vol. 10, Part** 1, 109 f.; commerce in, **Vol. 10, Part** 1, 130 f.; correspondence, **Vol. 1, Part** 2, 90; **Vol. 3, Part** 2, 570; **Vol. 5, Part** 2, 328, 331 f.; **Vol. 6, Part** 1, 610 f.; **Vol. 6, Part** 2, 45; **Vol. 7, Part** 2, 154; **Vol. 8, Part** 1, 451, 482; **Vol. 8, Part** 2, 511; **Vol. 9, Part** 1, 396; **Vol. 9, Part** 2, 253, 316; efforts against, **Vol. 7, Part** 1, 28; executive power during, **Vol. 10, Part** 1, 19 f.; paintings of scenes of, **Vol. 3, Part** 2, 504; **Vol. 9, Part** 1, 371; **Vol. 9, Part** 2, 512 f.; **Vol. 10, Part** 2, 111, 651; prizes, **Vol. 8, Part** 2, 153; secretaryship, **Vol. 5, Part** 2, 563; **Vol. 8, Part** 1, 245 f., 403; **Vol. 10, Part** 1, 601 f.; telegraph used in, **Vol. 5, Part** 2, 482; writings, **Vol. 3, Part** 1, 345. *See also* Arms control and disarmament; Biological and chemical warfare; Peace, international; *names of specific wars*
War, Department of (U.S.), **Vol. 3, Part** 2, 194; **Vol. 4, Part** 2, 479; **Vol. 8, Part** 1, 30 f.; administration, **Supp. 1,** 336; **Supp. 4,** 785, 787–88; **Supp. 5,** 468–69, 538–39; **Supp. 7,** 377; **Supp. 8,** 706–7; aerial

Wertheimer, Max, references to, **Supp. 3,** 429; **Supp. 8,** 344; **Supp. 8,** 345

"We Shall Overcome" (song), **Supp. 8,** 334

Wesley, Charles, references to, **Vol. 1, Part 2,** 403; **Vol. 9, Part 2,** 133

Wesley, John, references to, **Vol. 1, Part 2,** 403; **Vol. 7, Part 1,** 360; **Vol. 9, Part 2,** 133

Wesleyan University (Conn.), **Vol. 1, Part 1,** 575; **Vol. 3, Part 2,** 416; **Vol. 5, Part 2,** 232; **Vol. 9, Part 1,** 605; **Vol. 10, Part 2,** 376; admission of women to, **Vol. 2, Part 2,** 596; psychology studies, **Supp. 3,** 229–30; as Wesleyan College, **Vol. 7, Part 2,** 580

Wesley Theological Institute, founding of, **Vol. 3, Part 1,** 233;

Wesson, Daniel Baird, reference to, **Vol. 9, Part 1,** 282

West, Andrew Fleming, reference to, **Supp. 4,** 143

West, Benjamin, **Vol. 9, Part 1,** 355; **Vol. 10, Part 1,** 12 f.; relations with John Singleton Copley, **Vol. 2, Part 2,** 425

West, James E., reference to, **Supp. 3,** 44

West, Walter, reference to, **Supp. 4,** 810

West (U.S.): art depicting, **Supp. 3,** 380, 382–83; **Supp. 5,** 420; books and movies about, **Supp. 1,** 6, 626; **Supp. 3,** 382–83; **Supp. 6,** 466; cowboy folk song collection, **Supp. 4,** 502; cowboy movies, **Supp. 4,** 734–35, 877–78; cowboy philosopher, **Supp. 1,** 637; development of, **Vol. 2, Part 2,** 189; **Supp. 1,** 414; explorations in, **Vol. 2, Part 2,** 234; **Vol. 6, Part 1,** 180, 380; **Vol. 6, Part 2,** 332; **Vol. 7, Part 2,** 481; **Vol. 7, Part 1,** 641; **Vol. 9, Part 1,** 631 f.; frontier life, **Vol. 2, Part 1,** 421, 531; **Vol. 8, Part 2,** 153; historical writings on, **Supp. 1,** 443; **Supp. 5,** 169; immigration to, **Vol. 2, Part 1,** 13, 33; **Vol. 5, Part 1,** 495; land use, **Supp. 3,** 169; missions in, **Vol. 1, Part 2,** 583; **Vol. 6, Part 1,** 93; New Englanders' migrations to, **Supp. 7,** 353–54; novels about, **Supp. 2,** 262–63, 729; **Supp. 3,** 382–83; **Supp. 4,** 877–78; photography of, **Supp. 3,** 380; topographic maps, **Supp. 1,** 3; **Supp. 4,** 557–58; trade in, **Vol. 5, Part 1,** 141; Wild West shows, **Supp. 3,** 460; writings on, **Vol. 4, Part 1,** 19; **Vol. 6, Part 2,** 622; **Supp. 3,** 382–83; **Supp. 8,** 567. *See also* state names

Westbrook, Frank, reference to, **Supp. 3,** 832

Westchester County, N.Y., development of, **Vol. 4, Part 2,** 491

West Coast Reporter, **Vol. 8, Part 1,** 52 f.

Western Academy of Art, **Vol. 2, Part 2,** 334, 443

Western Air Express, **Supp. 5,** 385

Western Air Lines, founding of, **Supp. 3,** 157

Western Association of Railway Executives, founding of, **Supp. 2,** 260

Western Christian Advocate, **Vol. 5, Part 2,** 410; **Vol. 7, Part 1,** 393; **Vol. 8, Part 1,** 478; **Vol. 9, Part 1,** 181

Western College (later Leander Clark College, Iowa), **Vol. 1, Part 2,** 96; **Vol. 5, Part 2,** 350

Western Consumers Union, founding of, **Supp. 7,** 69

Western Electric Co., **Supp. 6,** 84, 151–52, 614

Western Engineering Co., founding of, **Supp. 5,** 354

Western Forestry and Conservation Association, founding of, **Supp. 3,** 7

Western Federation of Miners, **Vol. 4, Part 2,** 419, 468

"Western" humor, **Vol. 6, Part 1,** 208; **Vol. 9, Part 2,** 509

Western Intelligencer, early Ohio newspaper, **Vol. 5, Part 2,** 373

Western Lancet, medical journal, **Vol. 6, Part 1,** 58

Western Law Journal, **Vol. 10, Part 1,** 363

Western Medical Review, founding of, **Supp. 2,** 612

Western Military Institute. *See* University of Nashville

Western Newspaper Union, **Vol. 1, Part 1,** 129 f.

Western New York Horticultural Society, **Vol. 9, Part 2,** 439

Western Pacific Railway, **Vol. 1, Part 2,** 410; **Vol. 5, Part 2,** 36; **Supp. 3,** 381–82

Western Pennsylvania Medical College, laryngology, **Supp. 6,** 318

Western Philosophical Association, founding of, **Supp. 1,** 683

Western Protestant, **Vol. 8, Part 1,** 544

Western Reserve: pioneering in, **Vol. 1, Part 1,** 475; influence of Yale on, **Vol. 3, Part 1,** 158

Western Reserve University: administration, **Supp. 2,** 663; applied social science studies, **Supp. 7,** 151; history of, **Vol. 3, Part 1,** 11; **Vol. 10, Part 1,** 581 f.; hygiene and public health studies, **Supp. 7,** 194; medical school, **Supp. 6,** 295, 296; pharmacology studies, **Supp. 3,** 342

Western Review and Miscellaneous Magazine, **Vol. 5, Part 1,** 396

Western Society of Engineers, **Vol. 10, Part 1,** 372 f.

Western Stock Journal and Farmer, **Vol. 5, Part 2,** 453

Western Union Telegraph Co., **Vol. 2, Part 2,** 445; **Vol. 3, Part 2,** 4; **Vol. 4, Part 1,** 555; **Vol. 7, Part 1,** 148; **Vol. 9, Part 1,** 176, 492; AT&T sale of, **Supp. 8,** 211; formed, **Vol. 8, Part 1,** 193 f.; **Vol. 9, Part 1,** 145 f.; mergers, **Vol. 7, Part 2,** 65; patent system of, **Vol. 8, Part 1,** 75 f.

Western Unitarian Conference, **Vol. 5, Part 2,** 179

Western United Corporation, formation of, **Supp. 4,** 180

Western Watchman, **Vol. 7, Part 2,** 521

Western World, publishing of Federalist sheet, **Vol. 9, Part 2,** 136 f.

Westervelt, Conrad, reference to, **Supp. 6,** 63

Westfield, Mass., service to, **Vol. 9, Part 1,** 76 f.

West Florida, annexation of, **Vol. 6, Part 2,** 191, 403; **Vol. 7, Part 1,** 90; **Vol. 10, Part 2,** 225

West India Co., **Vol. 3, Part 1,** 265

West India squadron, command of, **Vol. 7, Part 2,** 186

West Indies: birds of, **Vol. 6, Part 1,** 49; diplomacy, **Vol. 4, Part 1,** 538; law in, **Vol. 4, Part 1,** 136; missions in, **Vol. 6, Part 1,** 158; piracy, suppression of, **Vol. 4, Part 2,** 382; **Vol. 8, Part 1,** 83 f.; trade, **Vol. 2, Part 1,** 592; **Vol. 3, Part 2,** 444; **Vol. 4, Part 2,** 382; **Vol. 8, Part 2,** 341 f.

Westinghouse, George, reference to, **Supp. 3,** 456

Westinghouse Electric and Manufacturing Co., **Vol. 5, Part 2,** 358; **Vol. 9, Part 1,** 275, 514; **Vol. 9, Part 2,** 644; **Supp. 7,** 793; first shop committee with employee representation, **Vol. 8, Part 1,** 91 f.; formation of, **Vol. 10, Part 2,** 17; radio research, **Supp. 3,** 184–85; turbine engineering, **Supp. 4,** 383

West Jersey Society, **Vol. 1, Part 2,** 36

Westminster College (Mo.), president of, **Vol. 8, Part 1,** 544

Westminster Confession of Faith, **Vol. 3, Part 2,** 406

Westminster Theological Seminary, founding of, **Supp. 2,** 412

Westmoreland Association, **Vol. 6, Part 1,** 118

Weston, John C., reference to, **Supp. 7,** 4

Weston-Mott Axle Co., **Supp. 4,** 244

Westover, Russ, reference to, **Supp. 6,** 530

West Point. *See* United States Military Academy

West Point, N.Y., defenses of, **Vol. 9, Part 2,** 583

Westport Country Playhouse, **Supp. 7,** 458

West Virginia: constitution of, **Vol. 3, Part 2,** 298; creation of state, **Vol. 2, Part 1,** 493; **Vol. 3, Part 1,** 343; **Vol. 6, Part 1,** 239; **Vol. 7, Part 2,** 585; **Vol. 8, Part 2,** 163; **Vol. 10, Part 2,** 246; governors, **Vol. 1, Part 2,** 461 f.; **Vol. 3, Part 2,** 459; **Vol. 6, Part 2,** 404; **Supp. 6,** 472; legal service, **Vol. 1, Part 2,** 462; 603; **Vol. 7, Part 2,** 585; navigation in, **Vol. 5, Part 2,** 330; pioneering in, **Vol. 10, Part 2,** 644; political service, **Vol. 1, Part 1,** 409; **Vol. 1, Part 2,** 461, 603;

Williams College (Mass.), **Vol. 2, Part 1,** 534, 585; **Vol. 4, Part 1,** 620; **Vol. 5, Part 1,** 215 f.; **Vol. 7, Part 1,** 146; **Vol. 7, Part 2,** 482; **Vol. 8, Part 2,** 550; **Vol. 9, Part 1,** 481; college song, *The Mountains, The Mountains,* **Vol. 4, Part 1,** 326; founding of, **Vol. 10, Part 2,** 259; museum at, **Vol. 3, Part 1,** 268; presidency, **Supp. 3,** 293; **Supp. 4,** 224

Willis, Henry Stuart, reference to, **Supp. 3,** 431

Williston Seminary, **Vol. 10, Part 2,** 310

Willkie, Wendell L.: characterization of, **Supp. 5,** 343; presidential candidacy, **Supp. 3,** 400, 497, 659; **Supp. 5,** 152; **Supp. 6,** 618; **Supp. 7,** 414, 615–16, **Supp. 8,** 376, 394, 421, 617; Schneiderman defense by, **Supp. 5,** 389; Van Doren, Irita, relationship, **Supp. 8,** 667

Wills, C. Harold, references to, **Supp. 4,** 293, 295, 300

Wills, Helen. *See* Moody, Helen Wills

Willstätter, Richard, reference to, **Supp. 5,** 669–70

Willys-Overland Co., **Supp. 8,** 610

Wilmer, William Holland, reference to, **Supp. 7,** 70

Wilmer Ophthalmological Institute, founding of, **Supp. 2,** 722; **Supp. 7,** 70

Wilmington, Del., church building in, **Vol. 2, Part 2,** 609

Wilmington, N.C.: capture of, *see* Fort Fisher, N.C.; economic development, **Vol. 3, Part 1,** 480 f.

Wilmington & Northern Railroad, **Vol. 3, Part 1,** 528 f.

Wilmington & Weldon Railroad, **Vol. 1, Part 1,** 388,

Wilmington Chemical Corporation, founding of, **Supp. 3,** 239

Wilmot Proviso, **Vol. 2, Part 1,** 49, 417, 419, 564; **Vol. 5, Part 1,** 604; **Vol. 5, Part 2,** 397; **Vol. 6, Part 1,** 586; **Vol. 8, Part 1,** 34 f.; **Vol. 9, Part 2,** 352, 590; **Vol. 10, Part 2,** 317

Wilson, Alexander: Audubon and, **Vol. 1, Part 1,** 425; Backman, John, and, **Vol. 1, Part 1,** 466; Ord, George, and, **Vol. 7, Part 2,** 49

Wilson, Charles E., references to, **Supp. 6,** 618; **Supp. 7,** 794

Wilson, E. B., reference to, **Supp. 4,** 516

Wilson, E. D., reference to, **Supp. 5,** 273

Wilson, Edith Galt, reference to, **Supp. 5,** 697

Wilson, Edmund, references to, **Supp. 3,** 72, 539; **Supp. 8,** 136, 150

Wilson, Eleanor Randolph, reference to, **Supp. 3,** 480

Wilson, H. W., Co., founding of, **Supp. 5,** 752–53

Wilson, James, reference to, **Supp. 3,** 145

Wilson, Louis B., reference to, **Supp. 3,** 503

Wilson, Paul Caldwell, reference to, **Supp. 7,** 608

Wilson, Woodrow, **Vol. 4, Part 2,** 113; **Vol. 5, Part 1,** 393; **Vol. 9, Part 1,** 286; admirers of, **Supp. 6,** 75, 137, 228; Baker relationship, **Supp. 2,** 19; Barkley relationship, **Supp. 6,** 34; Baruch relationship, **Supp. 7,** 35–36; biography of, **Supp. 4,** 47; **Supp. 6,** 521; Brandeis relationship, **Supp. 3,** 97; campaign financing, **Supp. 2,** 129; civil rights record, **Supp. 4,** 581; Colby relationship, **Supp. 4,** 170–71; congressional supporters, **Supp. 3,** 706; Corwin relationship, **Supp. 7,** 146; Daniels relationship, **Supp. 4,** 216; Davies, J. E., relationship, **Supp. 6,** 146, 147; Dulles, J. F., relationship, **Supp. 6,** 177; economic policy, **Supp. 3,** 211–12; foreign policy, **Supp. 3,** 396; Fourteen Points, **Supp. 2,** 320; **Supp. 7,** 536; Hardwick opposition to, **Supp. 3,** 330–31; House relationship, **Supp. 2,** 319–20; League of Nations, **Supp. 3,** 472–74; **Supp. 6,** 388; Lowell, A. L., relationship, **Supp. 3,** 469; Morgenthau relationship, **Supp. 4,** 603; press relations, **Supp. 1,** 210; **Supp. 3,** 702; Princeton University policies, **Vol. 3, Part 2,** 386; **Supp. 1,** 399; **Supp. 3,** 810; **Supp. 4,** 143; psychobiography of, **Supp. 8,** 61; Reed relationship,

Supp. 3, 622; references to, **Supp. 1,** 210, 465; Senate opposition to, **Supp. 4,** 669–70; Senate support for, **Supp. 4,** 641–42; studies on, **Supp. 2,** 153; Thomas Riley Marshall and, **Vol. 6, Part 2,** 331; Tumulty relationship, **Supp. 5,** 696–97; Walter Hines Page and, **Vol. 7, Part 2,** 143 f.; and Wall Street, **Vol. 4, Part 2,** 372; wife, **Supp. 7,** 796; woman suffrage stance, **Supp. 4,** 157–58; **Supp. 7,** 717; **Supp. 8,** 244; World War I neutrality actions, **Supp. 4,** 725; writings on, **Supp. 7,** 683–84

Wilson, W. T. R., reference to, **Supp. 7,** 199

Wilson-Audubon controversy, **Vol. 7, Part 2,** 49

Wilson bill, **Vol. 2, Part 2,** 210; **Vol. 5, Part 2,** 178; exponent of, **Vol. 7, Part 2,** 331

Wilson Bulletin, founding of, **Supp. 5,** 374

Wilson Dam, **Supp. 2,** 119

Wilson-Gorman Tariff Act, **Vol. 7, Part 2,** 33

Wilson's Creek, battle of, **Vol. 6, Part 1,** 535; **Vol. 8, Part 1,** 216; **Vol. 8, Part 2,** 453; **Vol. 9, Part 1,** 153; **Vol. 9, Part 2,** 183

Winant, John G., reference to, **Supp. 3,** 543

Winchell, Newton H., reference to, **Supp. 3,** 695

Winchell, Walter, references to, **Supp. 6,** 232; **Supp. 8,** 39

Winchester, Va., battle of, **Vol. 1, Part 1,** 578; **Vol. 5, Part 1,** 557; **Vol. 9, Part 1,** 80, 107. *See also* Opequon Creek

Winchester Arms Co., **Vol. 5, Part 1,** 247; **Vol. 10, Part 2,** 379

Winchester rifle, invention and manufacturing of, **Vol. 5, Part 1,** 247; **Vol. 10, Part 2,** 379

Wind, measurement of, **Vol. 5, Part 1,** 252; **Vol. 7, Part 1,** 526

Windmills, manufacture of, **Vol. 7, Part 1,** 590–1

Windsor, Duke and Duchess of (Great Britain), **Supp. 3,** 50

Windsor, Conn.: genealogy, **Vol. 9, Part 2,** 21; early history of, **Vol. 9, Part 2,** 21

Wind tunnels, **Supp. 4,** 486; **Supp. 8,** 439, 440

Wine: importation of, **Vol. 7, Part 2,** 631; making, **Vol. 1, Part 1,** 109; **Vol. 2, Part 2,** 374 f.; **Vol. 4, Part 2,** 494; **Vol. 5, Part 1,** 430; **Vol. 7, Part 1,** 335 f.; trade, **Vol. 5, Part 2,** 246 f.

Wineries, **Supp. 7,** 614

Winesburg, Ohio, **Supp. 3,** 13

Wing, Shoudy and Putnam, **Supp. 6,** 87–88

Winnebago Indians, **Supp. 6,** 524–25

Winnebago War (1827), **Vol. 3, Part 1,** 349

Winnetka, Ill., individualized education in, **Supp. 7,** 42

Winning of Barbara Worth, The, **Supp. 3,** 846

Winnsboro Female Institute, **Vol. 5, Part 2,** 524

Winslow, Mary, reference to, **Supp. 7,** 718

Winslow Covenant, **Vol. 3, Part 1,** 3

Winter Garden (New York City), **Vol. 1, Part 2,** 446

Wintergreen Club (Boston), **Vol. 8, Part 2,** 45

Winters, Yvor, reference to, **Supp. 8,** 20

Winthrop, Bronson, reference to, **Supp. 4,** 785

Winthrop, John, **Vol. 5, Part 1,** 436; *History of New England, Vol. III,* discovery of, **Vol. 1, Part 1,** 361

Winthrop College (S.C.), **Vol. 5, Part 2,** 227; **Vol. 9, Part 2,** 548

Winthrop-Hoover controversy, **Vol. 5, Part 1,** 200

Wire: barbed, **Vol. 4, Part 1,** 331; **Vol. 4, Part 2,** 94; cables, first use of, for, **Vol. 8, Part 2,** 88; manufacture, **Vol. 3, Part 2,** 489; **Vol. 4, Part 1,** 188; **Vol. 4, Part 2,** 156; **Vol. 5, Part 2,** 53; **Vol. 6, Part 1,** 334; **Vol. 7, Part 1,** 165 f.; **Vol. 8, Part 2,** 189; **Vol. 10, Part 1,** 376 f., 501 f.; rope, first manufacture of, in America, **Vol. 8, Part 2,** 88; suspension bridges, **Vol. 4, Part 2,** 156

ship command, **Supp. 3**, 450; bazooka manufacture, **Supp. 4**, 122; biological warfare research, **Supp. 6**, 448; black market, **Supp. 5**, 737; black troops, **Supp. 8**, 118–19; blood plasma supplies, **Supp. 4**, 242–43; Brenner Pass battle, **Supp. 3**, 583; Carlson's Raiders, **Supp. 4**, 147; Catholic church, **Supp. 8**, 613; Central Pacific offensive, **Supp. 8**, 470; Chaplain Corps, **Supp. 8**, 505–6; China-Burma-India theater, **Supp. 4**, 782–83; **Supp. 5**, 486–87; **Supp. 6**, 109–10, 508; **Supp. 7**, 680; **Supp. 8**, 632; civil liberties issues, **Supp. 3**, 93; **Supp. 4**, 614; Civilian Conservation Corps, **Supp. 6**, 419; civilian defense, **Supp. 4**, 466; **Supp. 7**, 453, 661; Coast Guard, **Supp. 4**, 854; Combined Chiefs of Staff, **Supp. 7**, 703; CO-MINCH, **Supp. 6**, 339–40; Committee of American Defense, **Supp. 6**, 504; Committee to Defend America by Aiding the Allies, **Supp. 4**, 347, 470; **Supp. 5**, 481, 624; **Supp. 7**, 197, 289; **Supp. 8**, 244, 679; Communist party (U.S.) positions in, **Supp. 5**, 500; Conference of Allied Ministers of Education, **Supp. 4**, 449; conscientious objection, **Supp. 6**, 217; D-day invasion and follow-up, **Supp. 3**, 589–90; **Supp. 8**, 155; "Darlan deal," **Supp. 8**, 274; de-Nazification program, **Supp. 3**, 590; defense communications, **Supp. 8**, 179–80; defense contract scandal, **Supp. 6**, 437; Defense Mediation Board, **Supp. 7**, 172; defense production, **Supp. 4**, 303, 458–59; **Supp. 6**, 520; **Supp. 7**, 794; **Supp. 8**, 527; defense program, **Supp. 6**, 335; Defense Research Committee, **Supp. 4**, 430; defense transportation, **Supp. 3**, 241; diplomacy during, **Supp. 7**, 53, 377, 437–38, 778; **Supp. 8**, 495, 501; diplomacy, pre-U.S. entry, **Supp. 3**, 528–29; **Supp. 5**, 333; draft, **Supp. 4**, 247; **Supp. 5**, 715; economic impact, **Supp. 6**, 586; Economic Warfare Board, **Supp. 7**, 761; ethnic issues in U.S., **Supp. 3**, 661; **Supp. 4**, 286; **Supp. 5**, 43, 343, 574–75; **Supp. 7**, 292; **Supp. 8**, 650; "Europe First" strategy, **Supp. 6**, 430–31; **Supp. 8**, 154; European Theater, **Supp. 6**, 375; **Supp. 7**, 213; **Supp. 8**, 267–68; financing of, **Supp. 5**, 712–13; **Supp. 8**, 446; First Fleet command, **Supp. 6**, 375; food aid, **Supp. 6**, 217–18; foreign correspondents, **Supp. 3**, 612–13; **Supp. 5**, 60; **Supp. 6**, 148, 366; **Supp. 7**, 473, 566, 643, 759; **Supp. 8**, 259, 261; France, invasion of southern, *see subhead:* D-day; Free French forces, **Supp. 8**, 62; Greenland Patrol, **Supp. 7**, 698–99; ground combat forces mobilization, **Supp. 3**, 494; heroism in, **Supp. 7**, 419, 581; IBM role in, **Supp. 6**, 675; intelligence activities, **Supp. 6**, 170, 531; **Supp. 8**, 51, 147, 196; Italian campaign, **Supp. 8**, 147, 155; ITT role in, **Supp. 6**, 44; Japan, atomic bombing of, **Supp. 7**, 732; Japan, bombing of Tokyo, **Supp. 4**, 589; Japan, occupation of, **Supp. 8**, 699; Japan, peace treaty with, **Supp. 6**, 270; Japanese surrender, **Supp. 6**, 268; journalism, **Supp. 5**, 450; labor issues, **Supp. 5**, 248–49; **Supp. 6**, 28–29, 709; landing craft, **Supp. 5**, 299, 361; Latin American involvement, **Supp. 7**, 778; lend-lease program, **Supp. 3**, 659–60, 829; **Supp. 4**, 393, 458, 480; **Supp. 8**, 446; Library War Service Committee, **Supp. 4**, 846; Mark XV bombsight, **Supp. 7**, 577; medicine in, **Supp. 4**, 208–9, 468; **Supp. 5**, 64, 122–23, 336, 632, 733; **Supp. 7**, 328, 477, 649; **Supp. 8**, 608, 609; military command, **Supp. 3**, 662; military production, **Supp. 5**, 538–39; military research, **Supp. 5**, 28, 497; military segregation during, **Supp. 4**, 243; mobilization, **Supp. 3**, 494; **Supp. 8**, 706; Morgenthau Plan for postwar Germany, **Supp. 5**, 334–35; naval procurement, **Supp. 4**, 305; naval service, **Supp. 6**, 23, 188, 326, 408; Neutrality Acts, **Supp. 5**, 731; New Caledonia defense, **Supp. 3**, 583; Ninth Infantry Division, **Supp. 7**, 213–14; North

African campaign, **Supp. 3**, 589; **Supp. 8**, 154–55, 274; nursing, **Supp. 6**, 283–84; occupied territories administration, **Supp. 8**, 275; Office of Civilian Defense, **Supp. 7**, 661; Office of Economic Stabilization, **Supp. 3**, 660; **Supp. 5**, 72, 713; Office of Price Administration, **Supp. 3**, 660; **Supp. 6**, 80; Office of Production Management, **Supp. 4**, 458; Office of Scientific Research and Development, **Supp. 8**, 686; Office of Strategic Services, **Supp. 6**, 170–71, 531; **Supp. 8**, 51, 147; Office of War Information, **Supp. 4**, 72; **Supp. 5**, 624; **Supp. 6**, 148; **Supp. 7**, 307, 384; **Supp. 8**, 679–80, 696; Office of War Mobilization and Reconversion, **Supp. 5**, 712; **Supp. 6**, 335; Okinawa campaign, **Supp. 3**, 118; Pacific Fleet, **Supp. 5**, 66, 621; **Supp. 6**, 267–68; **Supp. 7**, 490; **Supp. 8**, 331, 619; Pacific Theater, **Supp. 3**, 450; **Supp. 4**, 147, 323–24, 589, 895; **Supp. 6**, 326, 577; **Supp. 7**, 352, 645, 749–50; **Supp. 8**, 603; pacifism, **Supp. 7**, 356; Paris liberation, **Supp. 7**, 350; passport policies, **Supp. 8**, 590; photojournalism, **Supp. 7**, 115–16; physical anthropology application in, **Supp. 5**, 312; Ploesti bombing, **Supp. 8**, 48; political analysis, **Supp. 5**, 514; political cartoons, **Supp. 5**, 672; posters, **Supp. 6**, 204; postwar planning, **Supp. 6**, 80, 178, 431; **Supp. 8**, 446; "Private Purkey," **Supp. 7**, 618; pro-German propaganda, **Supp. 7**, 757–58; propaganda, **Supp. 3**, 57, 368–69; **Supp. 6**, 170, 668; *see also subhead:* Office of War Information; psychiatry, **Supp. 8**, 429–30; psychological study of troops, **Supp. 6**, 605; psychological warfare, **Supp. 5**, 646–47, 406–7; **Supp. 7**, 384, 812; radio correspondents, **Supp. 6**, 148; **Supp. 7**, 566; RDX (cyclonite) explosive, **Supp. 5**, 28; refugees and refugee resettlement, *see* Refugees; relief efforts, **Supp. 7**, 599; reparations policy, **Supp. 8**, 89; rockets, **Supp. 3**, 307–8; Roosevelt administration bipartisanship, **Supp. 3**, 425–26; Roosevelt, F. D., as commander-in-chief, **Supp. 3**, 661–64; Rubber Survey Committee, **Supp. 7**, 36; science and technology, **Supp. 8**, 686; shipbuilding, **Supp. 4**, 848–49, 308; Sicily invasion, **Supp. 3**, 589; **Supp. 5**, 336; Singapore evacuation, **Supp. 8**, 30; Smaller War Plants Corporation, **Supp. 5**, 481; songs, **Supp. 8**, 386; Southwest Pacific Theater, **Supp. 5**, 720; **Supp. 7**, 215, 489–90; **Supp. 8**, 23–24, 351, 638; Soviet-U.S. relations during, **Supp. 6**, 147; Special Services Division, **Supp. 6**, 637; Stage Door Canteens, **Supp. 4**, 187; **Supp. 5**, 415; **Supp. 6**, 133; strategic bombing survey, **Supp. 5**, 178; submarine detection and defenses, **Supp. 4**, 818; **Supp. 6**, 501; supplies, **Supp. 5**, 643; Supply Priorities and Allocation Board, **Supp. 4**, 458; surplus property administration, **Supp. 8**, 89; synthetics development during, **Supp. 6**, 334; Third Army, XX Corps, **Supp. 4**, 857; Third Fleet command, **Supp. 6**, 268–69; troop demobilization, **Supp. 8**, 156; U.S. government preparation for, **Supp. 3**, 660–61; **Supp. 4**, 787; U.S. intervention advocacy, **Supp. 7**, 740; U.S. official neutrality policy, **Supp. 3**, 658–60; **Supp. 5**, 731; U-boat menace, **Supp. 5**, 344–45; unconditional surrender doctrine, **Supp. 3**, 662; **Supp. 5**, 334; **Supp. 7**, 812–13; USO activities, **Supp. 6**, 644; **Supp. 7**, 30; **Supp. 8**, 52; war bonds, **Supp. 5**, 712–13; War Labor Board, **Supp. 6**, 28; **Supp. 7**, 172; **Supp. 8**, 35; War Manpower Commission, **Supp. 5**, 460; War Production Board, **Supp. 3**, 660; **Supp. 5**, 481; **Supp. 6**, 473–74; **Supp. 7**, 92; **Supp. 8**, 352; War Relocation Authority, **Supp. 7**, 505; War Resources Board, **Supp. 7**, 36. *See also* Nazism; Pearl Harbor attack; War crimes

World Zionist Congress, **Supp. 4**, 906

World Zionist Organization, **Supp. 3**, 96; **Supp. 7**, 689

Worms, studies of, **Supp. 1,** 182

Worship, founding of, **Supp. 2,** 455

Worth, Patience, reference to, **Supp. 3,** 851

Wortman, Jacob L., reference to, **Supp. 3,** 316

Wounded Knee Creek, engagement at, **Vol. 5, Part 2,** 615; **Vol. 9, Part 1,** 193. *See also* Pine Ridge Agency, S.D.

Woytinsky, Emma Shadkan, reference to, **Supp. 6,** 708, 709, 710

WPA. *See* Works Progress Administration

WQXR (radio station), high-fidelity frequency modulation, **Supp. 6,** 299

Wray, Fay, reference to, **Supp. 6,** 658

Wrestling, **Supp. 5,** 417–18; **Supp. 8,** 371–72; Roman style, **Supp. 1,** 569

Wright, Edward, reference to, **Supp. 3,** 378

Wright, Frances, relations with Robert Dale Owen, **Vol. 7, Part 2,** 119

Wright, Frank Lloyd, references to, **Supp. 4,** 352; **Supp. 5,** 207, 208, 606; **Supp. 8,** 435, 463. *See also* Taliesin

Wright, J. Homer, reference to, **Supp. 4,** 580

Wright, Judge John C., reference to, **Vol. 10, Part 1,** 363

Wright, Richard, references to, **Supp. 5,** 419; **Supp. 6,** 314; **Supp. 8,** 81

Wright, Warren, reference to, **Supp. 7,** 399, 400

Wright, Wilbur, reference to, **Supp. 4,** 913–14

Wright Aeronautical Corporation, **Supp. 4,** 473–74; **Supp. 5,** 384; **Supp. 6,** 51

Wright brothers, relations with Octave Chanute, **Vol. 7, Part 2,** 11

Wright-Martin Corporation, founding of, **Supp. 5,** 475

Writers. For complete list, *see* Occupations Index

Writers' Club, founding of, **Supp. 1,** 649

Writing. *See* Literature

Writs of Assistance, **Vol. 4, Part 1,** 611

Wrought-iron, design, **Supp. 2,** 742

WTOP and WTOP-TV (radio-TV stations), **Supp. 6,** 452, 453; **Supp. 7,** 296

Wu Lei-ch'uan, reference to, **Supp. 3,** 289

Wundt, Wilhelm: influence of, **Vol. 7, Part 1,** 337; **Vol. 9, Part 2,** 564; references to, **Supp. 3,** 148, 149; **Supp. 4,** 90, 444; **Supp. 5,** 611

Wyandotte, Mich., **Vol. 3, Part 1,** 547 f.

Wyandotte Iron Works, **Vol. 5, Part 2,** 312

Wyeth, Andrew, references to, **Supp. 3,** 848, 849

Wyler, William, reference to, **Supp. 6,** 610

Wylie, Elinor, reference to, **Supp. 4,** 74

Wylie, Philip, reference to, **Supp. 6,** 530

Wyman, Isaac C., reference to, **Supp. 3,** 810

Wynn, Keenan, reference to, **Supp. 8,** 710

Wyoming: cattle raising, **Vol. 10, Part 1,** 472 f.; governor, first, **Vol. 10, Part 1,** 472 f.; governors, **Supp. 1,** 464; **Supp. 5,** 337; **Supp. 7,** 31; land, reclamation of, **Vol. 10, Part 1,** 472 f.; political service, **Vol. 5, Part 1,** 321; **Vol. 10, Part 1,** 472; politics, **Supp. 3,** 788; **Supp. 7,** 590; Territory, history as, **Vol. 2, Part 1,** 489

Wyoming Valley, Pa., colonization of, **Vol. 5, Part 2,** 47; conflicting claims by Pennsylvania and Connecticut to, **Vol. 3, Part 1,** 581 f.; massacre, **Vol. 1, Part 2,** 604; **Vol. 2, Part 1,** 362, 372; settlement of, **Vol. 3, Part 1,** 550

Wyoming Seminary (Pa.), **Vol. 7, Part 1,** 421

Wythe, George, reference to, **Vol. 6, Part 1,** 119

X

Xavier Union, **Vol. 4, Part 2,** 383

Xenia Theological Seminary, **Vol. 7, Part 1,** 147

Xenia News, **Vol. 8, Part 1,** 482

XERA (radio station), **Supp. 3,** 104

Xerox Co., founding of, **Supp. 8,** 72

X rays, **Vol. 1, Part 2,** 113; **Vol. 2, Part 1,** 407; **Vol. 5, Part 2,** 493; **Vol. 6, Part 1,** 173 f.; **Vol. 7, Part 1,** 268; barium, **Supp. 3,** 133; Bellevue Hospital department, **Supp. 3,** 360; cancer therapy, **Supp. 3,** 258; cancer treatment with, **Supp. 2,** 546; Compton effect experiments, **Supp. 7,** 10; development of, **Supp. 2,** 718; diagnostic and therapeutic uses of, **Supp. 1,** 41; **Supp. 2,** 546; **Supp. 3,** 523; **Supp. 4,** 112, 185–86, 214, 865; **Supp. 6,** 506; diffraction studies, **Supp. 2,** 595; **Supp. 8,** 123; Duane-Hunt law, **Supp. 1,** 267; dynamical theory of refraction, **Supp. 7,** 10; effects on blood-cell production, **Supp. 4,** 581; first photo in U.S., **Supp. 1,** 614; first U.S. experiments, **Supp. 3,** 130; health hazards from, **Supp. 4,** 112; medical machines, **Supp. 8,** 666; mutation induction, **Supp. 8,** 449; particle characteristics, **Supp. 7,** 133–34; research in, **Supp. 2,** 557. *See also* Radiation; Radiology

XYZ affair (1798), **Vol. 1, Part 1,** 78; **Vol. 3, Part 1,** 467 f.; **Vol. 4, Part 1,** 226; **Vol. 4, Part 2,** 177; **Vol. 5, Part 2,** 27; **Vol. 6, Part 2,** 318; **Vol. 7, Part 1,** 369; **Vol. 7, Part 2,** 615

Y

Y Cyfaill, influential Welsh religious paper, **Vol. 8, Part 2,** 201

Yachting, founding of, **Supp. 4,** 852

Yachts and yachting (for complete list of yachts, *see* Ships): designing and building, **Vol. 2, Part 1,** 275; **Vol. 4, Part 2,** 585; **Vol. 6, Part 1,** 43; **Vol. 9, Part 1,** 237, 559 f.; **Supp. 2,** 298; first American, **Vol. 2, Part 2,** 578; races, **Vol. 1, Part 1,** 641; **Vol. 3, Part 1,** 552 f.; **Vol. 3, Part 2,** 452; **Vol. 6, Part 1,** 43, 60; **Vol. 7, Part 2,** 147; **Vol. 8, Part 2,** 325; **Vol. 9, Part 2,** 33; **Vol. 10, Part 1,** 177; **Supp. 5,** 6–7

Yaddo (Saratoga Springs, N.Y.), **Supp. 7,** 18

Yagua Indians, **Supp. 7,** 241

Yakima Indian War, **Vol. 2, Part 1,** 560; **Vol. 3, Part 1,** 256; **Vol. 4, Part 2,** 280; **Vol. 5, Part 2,** 568; **Vol. 8, Part 2,** 242, 613; **Vol. 9, Part 1,** 79; **Vol. 10, Part 2,** 514

Yale Corporation, **Supp. 3,** :11

Yale Literary Magazine, **Vol. 3, Part 2,** 215, 383; **Vol. 7, Part 1,** 42

Yale Lock Co., **Vol. 9, Part 2,** 613

Yale Medical Library, collections of, **Supp. 2,** 139

Yale Publishing Association, **Supp. 6,** 154

Yale Review, **Supp. 1,** 294; **Supp. 4,** 197; founding of, **Supp. 7,** 103

Yale Scroll and Key, The, **Vol. 8, Part 1,** 96 f.

Yale University, **Vol. 1, Part 1,** 530, 535; **Vol. 3, Part 1,** 28, 276 f., 573 f.; **Vol. 4, Part 2,** 586; **Vol. 5, Part 1,** 52; **Vol. 5, Part 2,** 80; **Vol. 7, Part 2,** 223, 479,, 633; **Vol. 8, Part 1,** 96 f., 547; **Vol. 9, Part 1,** 10 f.; **Vol. 9, Part 2,** 160; **Vol. 10, Part 2,** 417; administration, **Supp. 6,** 600; admission, early, **Vol. 10, Part 1,** 10; anatomy studies, **Supp. 3,** 6; anthropology studies, **Supp. 5,** 435; archaeological collections, **Vol. 2, Part 2,** 168; archaeology studies, **Supp. 5,** 595; astronomy studies, **Supp. 3,** 692; band, **Vol. 1, Part 1,** 547; biological studies, **Supp. 6,** 282–83, 719; Boswell manuscript collection, **Supp. 5,** 350; botany studies, **Supp. 8,** 595–96; building architecture, **Supp. 4,** 698; change of, from college to university, **Vol. 3, Part 1,** 577 f.; chemistry studies, **Supp. 4,** 434; child development studies, **Supp. 7,** 284; divinity school, **Vol. 2, Part 1,** 86; **Vol. 3, Part 1,** 577

452

YMCA. *See* Young Men's Christian Association

YMHA. *See* Young Men's Hebrew Association

"Yoknapatawpha County" (fictional locale), **Supp. 7,** 232, 234

Yon, S. Constantino, reference to, **Supp. 3,** 849

Yonkers, N.Y., founding of, **Vol. 10, Part 1,** 178

York, Alvin C., Industrial Institute, **Supp. 7,** 808

York, Canada, capture of, **Vol. 1, Part 2,** 105; **Vol. 2, Part 2,** 41; **Vol. 3, Part 1,** 175; **Vol. 7, Part 2,** 600

Yorktown, siege of, **Vol. 4, Part 1,** 572; **Vol. 5, Part 2,** 538; **Vol. 6, Part 1,** 107; **Vol. 7, Part 1,** 424; **Vol. 8, Part 2,** 62; **Vol. 10, Part 1,** 519

Yosemite National Park, **Supp. 4,** 522, 664; **Supp. 5,** 395; **Supp. 6,** 486; establishment of, **Supp. 2,** 348

Yosemite Valley, **Vol. 7, Part 1,** 315; discovery of, **Vol. 6, Part 1,** 180; geologic study of, **Supp. 4,** 558; paintings of, **Supp. 8,** 714–15; as a state reservation, **Vol. 7, Part 1,** 315; **Vol. 7, Part 2,** 26

Young, Brigham, references to, **Vol. 1, Part 1,** 102; **Vol. 5, Part 2,** 258, 377; **Vol. 9, Part 1,** 24 f., 311 f.; **Vol. 9, Part 2,** 33 f.

Young, John Russell, reference to, **Supp. 3,** 326–27

Young, Lester ("Pres"), reference to, **Supp. 6,** 300

Young, Lyman, reference to, **Supp. 6,** 530

Young, Milton R., references to, **Supp. 7,** 73; **Supp. 8,** 1–2

Young, Owen D., references to, **Supp. 6,** 615; **Supp. 7,** 308; writings on, **Supp. 3,** 763

Young, Robert R., reference to, **Supp. 6,** 540

Young, Trummy, references to, **Supp. 4,** 510, 511

Young America movement, **Vol. 8, Part 2,** 334

Young Ireland movement, **Vol. 3, Part 1,** 264 f.; **Vol. 8, Part 2,** 388

Young Ladies' Academy, Philadelphia, first state charter for girls' education, **Vol. 8, Part 1,** 71

Young Men's Christian Association (YMCA), **Vol. 3, Part 1,** 347, 353; **Vol. 3, Part 2,** 296; **Vol. 4, Part 1,** 157, 625; **Vol. 4, Part 2,** 47; **Vol. 5, Part 2,** 589; **Vol. 6, Part 1,** 82, 556; **Vol. 7, Part 1,** 105; **Vol. 8, Part 2,** 7; **Vol. 9, Part 1,** 138; **Vol. 9, Part 2,** 23; **Vol. 10, Part 1,** 407 f.; **Supp. 5,** 324, 506; adult education, **Supp. 5,** 431; black constituency, **Supp. 7,** 748; China, **Supp. 4,** 514–15; World War I work, **Supp. 8,** 673

Young Men's Hebrew Association (YMHA), **Vol. 5, Part 2,** 2; English for immigrants classes, **Supp. 5,** 95

Young Men's Mutual Improvement Assocation, **Supp. 5,** 640

Young Men's Republican Club, **Vol. 7, Part 2,** 326

Young Plan (1929), **Supp. 7,** 810

Young Scratchers, **Supp. 1,** 101

Youngstown Sheet and Tube Plant, **Supp. 6,** 597

Youngstown Sheet and Tube v. *Sawyer*, **Supp. 7,** 96

Young Women's Christian Association (YWCA), **Vol. 8, Part 2,** 12; **Supp. 4,** 207; **Supp. 7,** 185–86, 427; building progam, **Supp. 6,** 463; National Board, **Supp. 7,** 708

Young Women's Hebrew Association (YWHA), founding of, **Supp. 2,** 453

Your Income Tax, **Supp. 5,** 412

Youth. *See* Adolescents; Children; Counterculture; Jazz Age;

Youth Aliya Bureau, **Supp. 3,** 757

Youth Corrections Act (1950), **Supp. 6,** 336

Youth Migration Institutes, founding of, **Supp. 4,** 366

Youth's Casket, **Supp. 1,** 63

Youth's Companion, **Vol. 2, Part 1,** 377; **Vol. 3, Part 2,** 513; **Vol. 4, Part 2,** 413; **Vol. 6, Part 1,** 526; **Vol. 9, Part 1,** 22, 527, 577; **Vol. 9, Part 2,** 483, 595; **Supp. 6,** 306; founding of, **Vol. 10, Part 2,** 306

Yowell, E. I., reference to, **Vol. 8, Part 1,** 95 f.

Yucatán, social anthropological study in, **Supp. 6,** 533

Yugoslavia: Catholic church, **Supp. 8,** 295; diplomacy with U.S., **Supp. 6,** 358; **Supp. 8,** 6, 495; sculpture, **Supp. 7,** 530–31; writings on, **Supp. 5,** 4–5

Yukon, first steamboat to go up, **Vol. 8, Part 1,** 406

Yukon Territory, verse about, **Supp. 6,** 574

YWCA. *See* Young Women's Christian Association

YWHA. *See* Young Women's Hebrew Association

Z

Zangara, Joseph, reference to, **Supp. 3,** 648

Zangwill, Israel, reference to, **Vol. 5, Part 1,** 459

Zanuck, Darryl F., reference to, **Supp. 8,** 465

Zeiss Optical Co., **Supp. 3,** 41

Zeitkunst movement, **Supp. 4,** 868

Zemlinsky, Alexander von, **Supp. 5,** 608

Zen, **Supp. 8,** 431

Zenatello, Giovanni, reference to, **Supp. 6,** 642

Zenger, John Peter, trial of, **Vol. 4, Part 2,** 182; **Vol. 9, Part 1,** 353

Zeppelin, first round-the-world flight, **Supp. 7,** 759

Zervas, Leonid, reference to, **Supp. 3,** 61

Zeta Beta Tau, founding of, **Supp. 2,** 252

Ziegfeld, Florenz, references to, **Supp. 5,** 87, 88, 210; **Supp. 7,** 106; **Supp. 8,** 65

Ziegfeld Follies, **Supp. 4,** 739; **Supp. 5,** 210; **Supp. 6,** 247; stage design, **Vol. 10, Part 1,** 133

Ziff-Davis Publishing Co., founding of, **Supp. 5,** 760–61

Zimbalist, Efrem, reference to, **Supp. 7,** 123

Zimmerman, J. F., reference to, **Supp. 3,** 276

Zimmermann, I. J., reference to, **Vol. 5, Part 2,** 313

Zimrath Yah, collection of synogogic music, **Vol. 5, Part 2,** 251

Zinc industry, **Vol. 4, Part 1,** 502; **Vol. 6, Part 1,** 141; **Vol. 6, Part 2,** 421; mining of, **Supp. 3,** 348

Zinn, Walter, reference to, **Supp. 7,** 732

Zinsser, Hans, references to, **Supp. 3,** 244; **Supp. 4,** 468, 668

Zinzendorf, Count, reference to, **Vol. 6, Part 1,** 421

Zion City, description of, **Vol. 3, Part 1,** 413

Zionism, **Vol. 3, Part 2,** 315; **Vol. 4, Part 1,** 441; **Vol. 4, Part 2,** 316, 512; **Vol. 8, Part 2,** 240; **Vol. 9, Part 1,** 166 f.; **Vol. 9, Part 2,** 130; American leadership, **Supp. 1,** 408; **Supp. 2,** 266–67; **Supp. 4,** 593–94, 905–6; American militancy, **Supp. 7,** 689–90; American opposition, **Supp. 7,** 289, 740; American organizations, **Supp. 8,** 549–50; Anglo-American Committee on Palestine, **Supp. 8,** 501–2; Brandeis program, **Supp. 3,** 96–97; **Supp. 7,** 262; Brandeis-Weizmann conflict, **Supp. 3,** 279–80; church support for, **Supp. 7,** 356; as cultural force, **Supp. 4,** 538–39; folk preaching, **Supp. 3,** 513; Israel independence advocacy, **Supp. 5,** 515; Jewish commonwealth concept, **Supp. 8,** 549–50; Jewish opposition to, **Supp. 4,** 659–60; Morrison-Grady plan, **Supp. 6,** 245; non-Jewish advocates of, **Supp. 6,** 25, 35; organizations, **Supp. 2,** 252, 453, 666; **Supp. 3,** 279–80, 756–57, 757; **Supp. 4,** 905; Paris Peace Conference (1919) on, **Supp. 3,** 489; precursor of, **Vol. 9, Part 2,** 262; writings on, **Supp. 5,** 425, 426

Zionist Organization of America, **Supp. 3,** 279–80, 757; founding of, **Supp. 4,** 905

Zion Research Foundation, **Vol. 6, Part 1,** 396

Zion's Herald, **Vol. 7, Part 2,** 244

Zion's Watch Tower, **Vol. 8, Part 2,** 240

Znaniecki, Florian, reference to, **Supp. 4,** 830

Zodiacal signs, **Vol. 9, Part 2,** 444 f.

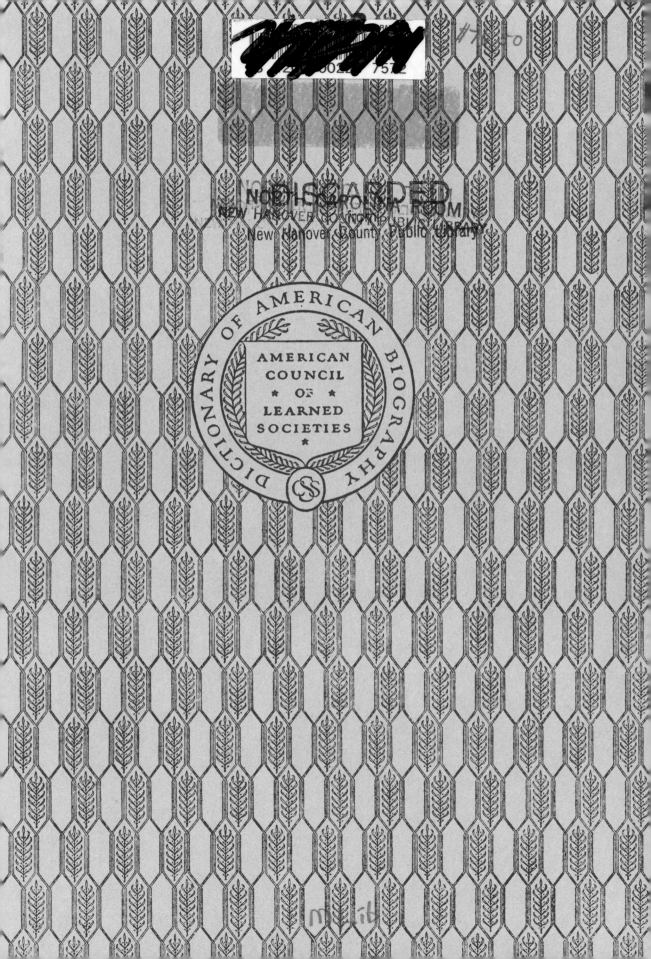

DICTIONARY OF AMERICAN BIOGRAPHY

AMERICAN
COUNCIL
* OF *
LEARNED
SOCIETIES
*